AMERICAN SONG

The Complete
Musical Theatre Companion

AMERICAN SONG

The Complete
Musical Theatre Companion

SECOND EDITION, 1877–1995

VOLUME 1: A-S

KEN BLOOM

SCHIRMER BOOKS
An Imprint of Simon & Schuster Macmillan
New York

PRENTICE HALL INTERNATIONAL
London Mexico City New Delhi Singapore Sydney Toronto

Schirmer Books
An Imprint of Simon & Schuster Macmillan
1633 Broadway
New York, NY 10019

Library of Congress Catalog Card Number: 95–49840

Set ISBN: 0–02–870484–3
Volume 1: 0–02–864573–1
Volume 2: 0–02–864572–3

Printed in the United States of America

Printing Number
1   2   3   4   5   6   7   8   9   10

Library of Congress Cataloging-in-Publication Data

Bloom, Ken, 1949–
    American song : the complete musical theatre companion / Ken
Bloom. —2nd ed.
        p.   cm.
    ISBN 0–02–864573–1 (v. 1). — ISBN 0–02–864572–3 (v. 2)
    1. Musicals—United States—Bibliography. 2. Songs, English–
–United States—Indexes.   I. Title.
ML128.M78B6   1996
782.1'4'0973—dc20   95–49840
                                                       CIP
                                                       MN

This paper meets the requirements of ANSI/NISO Z39.48–1992
(Permanence of Paper).

This edition is dedicated to
the memory of Arthur Siegel,
a composer, performer, educator,
and valued friend.

Acknowledgments

No book of this scope and magnitude could have been completed without the help of many dedicated people. I take the responsibility for any errors, but I would like to share any success with the many friends and coworkers who helped me with this book. Updating and expanding the book has taken almost as long as writing it.

Most of the research of the initial edition was undertaken at the Billy Rose Theatre Collection of the New York Public Library at Lincoln Center. Dorothy Swerdlove and her staff—Richard Lynch, Donald W. Fowle, Roderick Bladel, Daniel Patri, Vanessa Piala, David Bartholomew, Heidi Stock, Christine Karatnytsky, and Edward J. Sager—were exceptionally helpful in locating the tens of thousands of programs and clippings used as the basis of this book. I want to especially thank Louis Paul who supervised the retrieval of the research material. His staff—George Befanis, Guy Colas, Patricia Darby, Yewhallashet Hailemariam, Elizabeth Heyward, Peter Rodriquez and Mark Steve—made countless trips into the stacks to find materials. For this new edition I returned to the Billy Rose Theatre Collection where everyone was helpful, and dare I say it, caring. I want to acknowledge Louis Paul again and also his current staff—Clinton Manley, Raquel Romain, Shalisa Bland, Sherry Coleman, and Renita Harrell.

Weeks of research were spent at the small but remarkable Goodspeed Opera House Library of the Musical Theatre, an underused but impressive resource in East Haddam, Connecticut. Thanks to Michael Price, John Pike, Kristen A. Johnson, and Wade Russo. The library's collection of sheet music, programs, and recordings gave me invaluable information on interpolated songs, confirmed or revealed composer and lyricist credits on early songs, and helped me to discover many previously undocumented shows.

When I was compiling information a decade ago, many composers and lyricists made my job much easier through their interest and help. Several proof-read their own entries, offered their files for inspection, and/or allowed access to their ASCAP or BMI records. They are Lee Adams, Sammy Cahn, Sheldon Harnick, Burton Lane, Claibe Richardson, Mary Rodgers, Arthur Siegel, Stephen Sondheim, and Charles Strouse. Also of help were the estates of E.Y. Harburg (Ernie Harburg), Moose Charlap (Sandy Stewart), Bob Russell (Molly Hyman), and Arthur Schwartz (Paul Schwartz). My gratitude also to Kay Swift, Ron Simon of the Museum of Television and Radio, and Sally Gavin in Jule Styne's office. Theodore Chapin, managing director of the Rodgers and Hammerstein office, helped greatly with Rodgers, Hammerstein, and Hart material. Special thanks also to Edward Jablonski for his initial enthusiasm and support and his subsequent endurance when called upon repeatedly to verify facts. In addition, he selflessly offered his great knowledge of Harold Arlen's and George and Ira Gershwin's careers. Stanley Green loved to debate and discuss musical theatre and taught me some valuable lessons along the way. I miss him and his enthusiasm. Peter Filichia became a good friend in the years between the two editions of this book. Peter's fervor, kindness, and sense of humor has helped me as much as his intellectual contributions to my life and this book.

A special thanks is due to Michael Kerker of ASCAP. Michael was an early and vociferous supporter of this undertaking. Right before working on this second edition I finished work on a Tin Pan Alley book. For that book, Michael allowed me access to the records of over 125 composers and lyricists. From these lists (over 4,000 pages) I ascertained song credits and hundreds of songs cut from shows, as well as many shows that were unproduced or closed out of town.

Adrian Bryan-Brown of Boneau/Bryan-Brown, in addition to being a valuable friend, helped track down many facts and sources. While I worked on the first edition, Carl Earl Weaver put up with many interruptions to answer questions as well as provide moral support; it's a tragedy that he's not here to see this edition. Ellen Zeisler of the Zeisler Group helped greatly with the generous use of her office and research materials.

Collectors are often the most knowledgeable about the history of musical theatre. Some of their collections rival those of major libraries. These individuals invest time, money, space, and, most important, emotion. Among those who opened their homes to me when I researched the first edition were Dan Dietz and my friend Max Woodward. Mainerd Baker took the time to write me many pages of corrections and suggestions. His generosity is greatly appreciated. Michael Lavine opened his collection of vocal selections (including the Arthur Siegel collection). For this edition two individuals who are also good friends helped me greatly. Richard Norton made it his personal mission to supply me with information on hundreds of rare shows. He also helped clarify and correct information from the first edition. Robert Sixsmith provided me with many rare demos of produced and unproduced shows and helped me track down information on many songs and songwriters. Richard and Robert's devotion to this project was selfless and meant more to me than they might imagine.

Several individuals helped on specific shows. Marty Erskin diligently recorded information on songs with which he was associated. Ben Bagley provided valuable information on his productions. Paul Lazarus helped with the Stephen Sondheim musicals. Ezio Petersen, another good friend, provided information on the shows of Hugh Martin, Ralph Blane, and others. Karl Michael Emyrs cleared up information on the many incarnations of PETER PAN. John McGlinn helped with information on various orchestrators and on the unused songs from SHOW BOAT. My friend Michael Zande helped with credits for the songs in MOLLY. Finally, collector/author David Hummel allowed me access to his prodigious research on the many shows presented at the Cotton Club.

For the first edition Kevin Patterson and Millie Schoenbaum of Solters, Roskin, and Freedman and Jimmy Sapp of Hunt/Pucci answered questions on shows they represented. Also helpful were Joan Marlowe and Betty Blake of Proscenium Publications, publishers of "Theatre Information Bulletin."

Many people worked long, hard hours helping to do research and to proofread, correct, and organize the material in the first edition. I especially want to note the contributions of John Akamine, Susan Cohn, Susan Groberg, Scott Sedar, and Berthe Schuchat. Thanks too, to Bari Biern Sedar, Tom Dunlap, Ron Jewell, Elaine Joselovitz, Kathleen Masterson, Robbie McEwen, Karen McLaughlin, LuAnne Origer, Carol Raskind, Daniel Schuchat, Bob Schulte, Michael Shoop, and Bijou Spialek, all of whom helped in the research, proofreading, and generation of the book. My good friend Berthe Schuchat was again called to the front for this edition and helped me with research at the Billy Rose Theatre Collection.

My friends Barry Kleinbort and Joseph Weiss helped check the first edition. Once this update and expansion was completed, Barry Kleinbort (again), Roger Sturtevant and the afore mentioned Richard Norton read every page, every name, every song. They found hundreds of omissions, mistakes, and misinterpretations. Their enthusiasm, love for musical theatre, and integrity is only matched by their brilliant minds. These two gentlemen know their facts and, perhaps more important, know the theories and concepts of musical theatre. Their passion for the subject is unbounded. Without their help, this book and my life would be poorer.

I owe a debt of gratitude to Lucy Stille and my current agent Heide Lange of Sanford J. Greenburger Associates. Heide, especially, has supported me both professionally and personally. The remarkable John Thornton, friend, mentor, and publisher of the first edition, has been an inspiration throughout my adventures in publishing. And special thanks to the professionals at Schirmer Books who, believe it or not, cared as much for the quality of this book as I did. Despite tight deadlines and harrowing battles with the mysteries of computer science, they always supported me and the project with unfailing insight and humanity. So thanks to Phil Friedman, Jonathan Wiener, Richard Carlin, and Andrew Ambraziejus.

When I first compiled this book, back in the days when a computer was as big as a file cabinet and had to be kept in an air-conditioned safe house, Andrew Weiman wrestled the facts from the machinery. Now, in the nineties, a computer fits into a briefcase and yet is still just as maddening (to me). So special credit is due to Gus Horowitz of Two Rivers Computing who developed the program that made this book possible.

My friends have earned their place in these acknowledgments. In addition to those who helped directly and are credited above, I would like to recognize the support of Eric Abrahamson, Ken Benson, David Bishop, Helene Blue, Deborah Brody, Barbara Brown, Susan de Christofaro, Hap Erstein, Barbara Flinn, Denny Martin Flinn, Paul Ford, Sheila Formoy, Will Friedwald, Kit Grover, Richard L. Haight, Karen Hopkins, Craig Jacobs, Ken Kantor, Allan Knee, Ron Lasko, Dixie Morse,

Jay Morse, Paul Newman, Ken Olfson, Denis Peshkov, Vitali Podrez, Guy Riddick, David Rose, Arthur Siegel, David Simone, Karma Urso, Laurence Zwisohn, and always, Russell Metheny. My partners in recordings and theatre, Bill Rudman and Harry Bagdasian, showed remarkable patience, bearing with me during my absences in the depths of the world of musical comedy.

For patience, love, and laughs I want to especially thank Patricia Plowman, Justin, Travis, and Cory.

I am sure I may have slighted many other people who have helped on this project. I want to apologize herewith. Again, thanks to all those who made this gigantic task easier, not once but twice (!), by their help and support. If I have forgotten to list your name, I know you'll write me care of Schirmer and let me know.

KEN BLOOM
New York City
October 1995

Introduction

American Song includes data on over 4,800 American musicals. All Broadway, off-Broadway, and off-off-Broadway productions from 1877 to the fall of 1995 are included, together with all resident theatre productions of shows by major artists (and some minor), shows that closed out of town prior to Broadway, shows that toured and never intended to come to New York, selected nightclub shows, straight plays with original songs, vaudeville and burlesque shows, and English and French productions of shows by major American songwriters.

This book is basically the same as the previous edition with some exceptions. Most obvious is the inclusion of over 1,600 additional shows. I have also included, for the first time, original television musicals. There is a new entry for each show, with the name of the theatre in which the show opened.

The first part of this work lists all shows alphabetically. The second part consists of complete indexes to more than 70,000 songs and more than 27,000 personnel, as well as a chronological listing of titles.

This book was compiled for two reasons, first, to pay tribute to all the performers, artists, shows, and songs that have entertained us throughout the years; second, because there is no book of this scope available to the historian, theatre buff, or casual audience member. I hope as you browse through the book you will think of the songs as symbols of collaborative efforts by talented artists with one goal in mind, entertainment!

Many old songs and shows are lost, existing only as titles, but every year new discoveries make us hope that another rare script or piece of music will turn up in a theatrical archive or someone's yellowing scrapbook.

Musical comedy performers and theatre designers of the past have not been well remembered. We can see the black-and-white photos of sets and costumes but we forget that the originals had depth and color and movement. Performers, if preserved at all, were recorded or filmed on primitive equipment in media foreign to the artists' performing style. Between the stage actor and the audience are the footlights and orchestra pit. But between a stage actor and the audience watching his performance on a movie screen are hundreds of people and technical processes, each of which adds a barrier to the direct communication between actor and audience. No wonder performers of early musical theatre look so bad in old movies!

So, for the most part these people are forgotten. Pick up any contemporary history of the American musical and you will find Bob Fosse's name and Jerome Robbins's and maybe George Abbott's. But who remembers Carl Randall or Julian Mitchell? Aside from some reviews and clippings, it is as if these people never existed. We tend to forget that there would not have been a Fosse or an Abbott without the artistic precedent of a Randall or a Mitchell.

Lyricists fare even more poorly than directors. Programs list credits such as "Book by" or "Words by" without indicating who wrote the lyrics. If the information is not verified by sheet music, ASCAP records, copyright or recorded credit, no one is credited with lyrics.

Composers are easier to evaluate, as much of their music lives on. We tend, however, to denigrate composers whose work does not fit current ideas of what makes a good musical comedy song. It is a shame that some of us do not have the imagination or tolerance to appreciate Herbert or Friml or Romberg. But then those who revere Herbert and Romberg may not appreciate Sondheim. Perhaps the unfamiliar names on these pages will enable readers to appreciate their American musical theatre heritage, or at least to realize that others have paved the way for the present creative teams.

A word about procedures may be in order:

No information has been included unless it has been verified by programs, sheet music, clippings, ASCAP records, demo discs, copyright records, publishers, or by the composers or lyricists themselves. Print materials were consulted for information, but I have attempted in every case to get as close to the original work as possible. I always give the programs the benefit of the doubt unless copyright records, ASCAP records, or the sheet music prove the programs wrong.

The programs of shows prior to 1950, and especially shows prior to 1925, are notoriously incomplete—if they exist at all. In fact, when doing research, one quickly comes to the conclusion that there are very few facts in the world of musical theatre. Songs may have one title on the sheet music, another in the Broadway program, another for the out-of-town tryout, and yet another for the post-Broadway tour. I usually treated the New York opening-night program, the sheet music, and/or the ASCAP or BMI listings as the final authorities, but not always. For many shows, programs simply do not exist. Similarly, many old and crumbling programs have few songs listed, with no composers or lyricists credited. And frequently, interpolated songs were not credited at all. I suggest you check the index for duplicate song titles to see whether songs appeared in other shows attributed to other authors.

Most early shows contained many interpolations of popular songs of the day for stars to perform as vaudeville turns. (Look at the entry for BOMBO as an example.) In the song listings I did not use the word "specialty" unless I could identify the actual songs interpolated. Sometimes songs are listed as "A Bit of Nonsense" or other terms to that effect. I listed these titles in case the song was actually named "A Bit of Nonsense." Sometimes touring shows, especially in the early years, interpolated popular songs of the day. But I couldn't always determine if these songs were parodies, songs using the same titles, or the popular songs themselves.

One additional problem came with revues. Often song and sketch titles are not differentiated in programs. Sometimes I had to list all entries and note that some are sketches and some are songs.

I have attempted to identify songs cut prior or subsequent to openings and/or national tours. This is very problematic since songs were added to or cut from productions haphazardly.

"Opening Chorus" and "Finale" are listed only when I have reason to believe they were individual numbers and not simply medleys or reprises of songs in the show. I include dance numbers and ballets when I think I can identify the composer, or when the numbers were not simply variations on melodies from songs in the show.

Likewise, scene underscorings are listed only if

they were original compositions. See the ZIEGFELD FOLLIES for examples of this.

The indication that a show closed out of town simply means that the show did not play in a Broadway or off-Broadway theatre. Do not always assume that such a show was ever intended for a New York audience.

Whether the show played Broadway or off-Broadway is indicated below the title line. Shows that moved from off-Broadway to Broadway have their various opening dates and theatres listed in the notes section. The number of performances usually accounts for the entire run. The notes section should clarify how many performances took place at each venue. Please remember that the number of performances listed for a show is the one I felt to be most complete, taking into account benefit performances and other special events. Remember, too, that Best Plays averaged the number of performances in the first decades of this century. I used these numbers though they are often suspect.

Due to the suggestion of many readers, this edition of *American Song* lists the theatre in which the show played. But remember that theatres change names. And sometimes one name might be used over the years by more than one building. For example, the current Majestic Theatre, which opened in 1927, is not the same as the Majestic that stood at 5 Columbus Circle and opened in 1903 with THE WIZARD OF OZ. For the record, that first Majestic Theatre changed to the Park, Park Music Hall, Cosmopolitan, and Columbus Circle.

The terminology used in the programs of early shows presented other problems. For example, programs sometimes read "Directed by" or "Dialogue staged by" or "Entire production staged by" or "Production supervised by." Any person credited with staging the show or dialogue I list as the "Director." Sometimes a show will have two people listed under "staging" and no choreographer named. Almost certainly one of them choreographed the musical numbers; however, I list both under "Director" unless the division of duties is known.

Programs almost always list a person under "Music by." If the program reads "Music and lyrics by" and lists two people, I listed both individuals under composer and lyricist unless I knew that one only was the composer and the other the lyricist. I consulted the ASCAP biographical dictionary for this information. Please note that in some instances composers did write an occasional lyric and likewise lyricists did write an occasional tune. So do not assume I have made an error when you see a name in an unlikely category. Composers of interpolations were almost never credited.

Often rumors circulate about the actual composer or lyricist of a song. For example, musical theatre buffs have speculated on the role of Frank Loesser in the scores of THE PAJAMA GAME ("A New Town Is a Blue Town" and "Hernando's Hideaway") and WHOOP-UP ("Flattery"). Unless I could positively ascertain the authorship of ghost-written songs through sheet music, copyright, ASCAP or BMI records, I did not credit other songwriters.

Of the major contributors to the musical theatre, the ones who make it "theatrical" and not just "musical" are the designers. They fare most poorly in the programs. Lighting designers are almost never identified. If an individual's name is included under "Electrical Effects," I have assumed the person was the lighting designer. If companies like Kliegl Brothers are credited, I have not included them. Likewise, if a company like Bonwit Teller or a scenic studio receives credit for costumes or sets, I have omitted the credit. Also, if individuals are credited under "Scenery painted by," I have not included them, since early programs seemed to differentiate between scenic designers and painters, although the same names often appear in both categories.

For shows that closed out-of-town, songs are listed without indication of which were cut or added during tryout. Do not assume that all songs listed in these cases appeared in all performances.

Only shows that have at least one original song are listed here. However, revues like SOPHISTICATED LADIES do have all their songs listed although none were specifically written for that production.

Songs within a show that share the same title but are verifiably different are differentiated as "(1)" or "(2)" for your convenience. Please understand that these numbers are not part of the actual song titles.

The "Cast" section lists major performers only, although performers who later achieved fame are included even if they played smaller roles or were members of the ensemble. I thought this information was interesting.

Shows with identical titles are differentiated by the inclusion of the year in parentheses after the title. See the many versions of PHANTOM OF THE OPERA for examples. Sometimes productions sharing the same name were first produced in the same year. In those cases I listed an "(a)" and "(b)" following the title. Please note that these addenda are not part of the title.

Lyricists and composers of individual songs who are different from the lyricists and composers credited for the show at the beginning of an entry are listed in parentheses after the titles of their songs (L: Lyricist; C: Composer).

When known, original sources are identified by title. The type of work is noted in parentheses after the title along with the writers, when known.

Songs that were cut out-of-town or that were added after openings are noted in the footnotes. A footnote that reads, for example, "Out Scranton 11/28/49" indicates that the program used was an out-of-town program from Scranton for the date indicated; this was not necessarily the show's opening date in Scranton. Since all programs for every production could not be consulted, I am not implying that the song was either cut or added in Scranton, but rather that the song was included in Scranton and not New York. A comparison of this date with the opening date on Broadway will tell the reader whether the program is from the pre- or post-Broadway tour. Remember too that songs that were cut out-of-town were sometimes only included for one performance. Songs were often misnamed in early out-of-town programs. If the title was close to a title that appeared in New York, I ignored the out-of-town title. However, I couldn't catch all instances of mistakes in the out-of-town programs.

The footnote "Cut prior to New York" means that the song was either written for the show but not used, or included in a performance prior to the opening on Broadway. If I was able to ascertain that the song never was performed I have noted it as "unused" or "not used." If I found reference to songs not in programs or authors' listings (perhaps from an unidentifiable source), I noted the song as "Not in programs."

I have attempted to indicate in the footnotes if songs also appeared in other productions; however, because of the sheer volume of titles this was not always possible. Please use the index for this information. In the index you will find examples of songs that are obviously the same in two different shows with two different authors listed. This points up the lack of control and the rampant plagiarism of songs and ideas before copyright laws and the establishment of ASCAP, as well as the sloppy record keeping of early programs.

The footnote "ASCAP/Library of Congress only" indicates the song is not in programs but only registered with ASCAP or copyrighted.

American Song is an ambitious undertaking. I have taken every step possible to avoid errors; however, I can guarantee that some exist. If you find any inconsistencies or errors, please write to me care of Schirmer Books so that future editions can be more accurate. I guarantee that your comments and corrections will be considered and corrected in future editions.

I hope you enjoy this book and do a little research of your own into our musical theatre.

A

1 • A LA BROADWAY

OPENED: 09/22/1911   Theatre: Folies Bergere
Revue   Broadway: 8

Composer: Harold Orlob
Lyricist: Mabel H. Hollins; William Le Baron
Producer: Henry B. Harris; Jesse Lasky

Songs: In Loving Time; Philadelphia Drag; Rue Broadway; They Were Irish; You Have to Hand It to Them; You May Kiss Me Good-Night, Dear

Notes: An afterpiece to HELLO PARIS. *See HELLO PARIS.*

2 • A LA CARTE (1927)

OPENED: 08/17/1927   Theatre: Martin Beck
Revue   Broadway: 46

Composer: Herman Hupfeld
Lyricist: Herman Hupfeld
Librettist: George Kelly
Producer: Rosalie Stewart
Director: George Kelly

Choreographer: Sam Rose; **Costumes:** Maria Willenz; **Musical Director:** Milton Schwarzwald; **Orchestrations:** Hilding Anderson; Maurice DePackh; Charles Grant; Stephen Jones; Louis Katzman; Hans Spialek; **Set Design:** Livingston Platt; **Vocal Arranger:** Arthur Johnstone

Songs: Are You in Love? (C: Louis Alter); Baby's Blue; Calinda, The; Give Trouble the Air (C: Louis Alter; L: Leo Robin); Hors d'Oeuvres; Italy (C/L: Herman Hupfeld; Paul Lannin); Kangaroo (C: James P. Johnson; L: Henry Creamer); Never Again (C/L: Norma Gregg); Palm Beach Baby; Sort O' Lonesome; Stepping Out with Lulu (C: James C. Johnson; L: Henry Creamer); Sunny Spain (C/L: Norma Gregg); Swanee Melody (C: Louis Alter); Two Gat Gertie; Whiskers (C: James P. Johnson; L: Henry Creamer); Who Is This One? (C/L: Norma Gregg); Will We Meet Again? (C/L: Karl Kreck)

Cast: Bobbe Arnst; Harriet Hoctor; William Holbrook; Charles Irwin; Rose King; Little Billy; Jay Velie; Chick York

3 • A LA CARTE (1949)

OPENED: 11/16/1949   Theatre: El Capitan
Revue   Los Angeles

Composer: Victor Young
Lyricist: Edward Heyman
Librettist: Hal Fimberg; Ernst Matray; Henry Piffi
Producer: Edward Heyman; Ernst Matray; Maria Matray
Director: Ernst Matray; Maria Matray

Choreographer: Ernst Matray; Maria Matray; **Musical Director:** Harry Sukman

Songs: Bella Signora; Clara the Divine; Face in the Crowd, The [1]; Flower Song, The [1]; Folk Song 1950; Half of Me; I Ought to Know More About You [1]; I'm Gonna Make a Fool Out of April [1]; Opening; Poker Polka, The [1]; Sweetheart Semicolon [2]; There's No Man Like a Snowman [1]; Until Tonight; Venezia and Her Three Lovers (ballet) [1]

Cast: Dolores Boucher;Patricia Denise; Erika Lund; Gale Robbins; Bill Shirley; Joseph Warfield; George Zoritch

Notes: This show was reworked and became PARDON OUR FRENCH. *See PARDON OUR FRENCH.* [1] Used in PARDON OUR FRENCH. [2] Sheet music only.

4 • A . . . MY NAME IS ALICE

OPENED: 02/24/1984   Theatre: American Place
Revue   Off-Broadway: 353

Librettist: David Crane; Carol Hall; Marta Kauffman; Anne Meara; Cassandra Medley; Art Murray
Producer: Douglas F. Goodman; Rosita Sarnoff; Anne Wilder
Director: Julianne Boyd; Joan Micklin Silver

Choreographer: Edward Love; **Costumes:** Ruth Morley; **Lighting Designer:** Ann Wrightson; Musical Director: Michael Skloff; **Orchestrations:** Doug Katsaros; **Set Design:** Ray Recht

Songs: All Girl Band (C: Doug Katsaros; L: David Zippel); At My Age (C: Glen Roven; L: June Siegel); Bluer Than You (C: David Evans; L: Winnie Holzman); Educated Feet (C/L: Carol Hall); Emily, the M.B.A. (C: Stephen Lawrence; L: Mark Saltzman); French Song, The (C/L: Don Tucker); Good Thing I Learned to Dance (C: Stephen Lawrence; L: Mark Saltzman); Honeypot (C: Stephen Lawrence; L: Mark Saltzman); I Sure Like the Boys (C: Lucy Simon; L: Steve Teisch); Pay Them No Mind (C/L: Calvin Alexander; James Shorter); Portrait, The (C/L: Amanda McBroom); Pretty Young Men (C: Lucy Simon; L: Susan Birkenhead); Sisters (C: Cheryl Hardwick; L: Maggie Bloomfield); Trash (C: Michael Skloff; L: David Crane; Marta Kauffman); Welcome to Kindergarten (C: Michael Skloff; L: David Crane; Marta Kauffman)

Cast: Roo Brown; Randy Graff; Mary Gordon Murray; Alaina Reed; Charlaine Woodard

5 • ABE
Musical   Unproduced

Composer: Harold Rome
Lyricist: Harold Rome

Songs: That's the Law

Notes: No other information available.

6 • ABOUT FACE (0000)
Musical

Composer: Donald C. Beere; Frederick H. Foerster; John Miller; Francis E. Resta
Lyricist: Henry R. Brewerton; Karl F. Ockerhauser
Librettist: Henry R. Brewerton; Karl F. Ockerhauser

Notes: No other information available.

7 • ABOUT FACE! (1944)
OPENED: 05/26/1944
Revue

Composer: Frank Loesser
Lyricist: Frank Loesser
Librettist: Arnold Auerbach
Director: Robert H. Gordon

Songs: Dog Face; First Class Private Mary Brown [1]; Gee But It's Good to Be in the Army!; Lass with the Delicate Air (C: Lou Singer; L: Hy Zaret); One Little WAC (C: Eddie Dunstedter); PX Parade [3]; When He Comes Home [2]; Why Do They Call a Private a Private? (L: Peter Lind Hayes)

Cast: Vincente Gomez; Jules Munshin

Notes: Produced at Camp Shanks, New York and around the country in different productions. No program available. Music also by Jerry Livingston and others. [1] Also in PFC MARY BROWN, an Army show. [2] Also used in OK, U.S.A.! [3] May not be by Loesser.

8 • ABOUT TOWN
OPENED: 08/30/1906   Theatre: Herald Square
Musical   Broadway: 138

Composer: Raymond Hubbell
Lyricist: Joseph W. Herbert
Librettist: Joseph W. Herbert
Producer: Lew Fields; J.J. Shubert; Sam S. Shubert
Director: Julian Mitchell

Costumes: Caroline Siedle; **Musical Director:** William E. MacQuinn

Songs: Baby in the House (C: Unknown); Deutschland [1] (C/L: James Kendis; C: Herman Paley); Dinner Time (C/L: Addison Burkhardt); Duet (C: Melville Ellis); Gibson Girl, The (C: Raymond Hubbell); Girl with the Baby-Blue Tights, The (C: Melville Ellis; L: Addison Burkhardt); I'm a Fickle Maid (C: Melville Ellis); I'm Sorry (C: Albert Von Tilzer; L: Jack Norworth); In Amsterdam [2] (C: Unknown); Legend of the Mojaves, The (C: Gustave Kerker); Little Houston Street (C: Hans S. Linne); Opening Chorus [3] (C: Raymond Hubbell); Piccadilly Crawl, The (C: Melville Ellis); Same Old Girl, The; Seeing the Town in a Yap Wagon (C: Melville Ellis); Tipperary Nora (C/L: Ren Shields); When Tommy Atkins Marries Dolly Gray (C: Gus Edwards; L: Will D. Cobb)

Cast: George Beban; Vernon Castle; Louise Dresser; Lew Fields; Harry Fisher; Joseph W. Herbert; Edna Wallace Hopper; May Irwin; Jack Norworth; Blanche Ring

Notes: Second half was a burlesque of THE MUSIC MASTER. Later in the run a burlesque of THE GREAT DIVIDE titled THE GREAT DECIDE was substituted. [1] In Boston 2/11/07 this was credited to Melville Ellis. [2] This song was probably written by Melville Ellis. [3] In Boston 2/11/07 the opening chorus was credited to A. Baldwin Sloane.

9 • ABYSSINIA (1906)

OPENED: 02/20/1906   Theatre: Majestic
Musical   Broadway: 31

Composer: Will Marion Cook; Bert Williams
Lyricist: Alex Rogers; J.A. Shipp
Librettist: Alex Rogers; J.A. Shipp
Producer: Melville Raymond
Director: Alex Rogers; J.A. Shipp

Choreographer: Aida Overton Walker; **Musical Director:** James J. Vaughn; **Orchestrations:** Will Marion Cook

Songs: Answers That You Don't Expect to Get (L: Earle C. Jones); Build a Nest for Birdie [1] (C: J. Tim Brymn; L: R.C. McPherson); Capture of the Yaraboo, The; Dance of the Amhara Maids (inst.); Dance of the Falasha Maids (inst.); Dixie Ballet, The; Good-Bye Ethiopia; Here It Comes Again [2] (C: Bert Williams); Holiday in the Market; I'll Keep a Warm Spot in My Heart for You [3] (C: J. Rosamond Johnson; L: James Weldon Johnson); I'm a R-U-L-E-R [1]; Island of By-and-By (C: Bert Williams; L: Alex Rogers); It's Hard to Find a King Like Me (C: James J. Vaughn); Janho [4] (C: Will Marion Cook); Jolly Jungle Boys (C: Bert Williams; L: Earle C. Jones); Let It Alone (C: Bert Williams; L: Alex Rogers); Lion and the Monk, The (Die Trying) [2] (C: Bert Williams); Menelik's Tribute to Queen Tai Tu [2]; Ode to Menelik; Ode to the Sun (L: Earle C. Jones); Rastus Johnson, U.S.A. (C: Bert Williams); Sweetie Dear [1]; Twilight at Home Sweet Home [4]; Where My Forefathers Died (C: Bert Williams)

Cast: J.E. Lightfoot; Charles H. Moore; Alex Rogers; J.A. Shipp; Aida Overton Walker; George W. Walker; Bert Williams; Lotte Williams

Notes: [1] Out Wilkes-Barre 4/10/07. [2] Out Chicago 6/17/06. [3] Sheet music only. Not in program. [4] Cut prior to opening.

10 • ABYSSINIA (1987)

OPENED: 1987   Theatre: CSC
Musical   Off-Broadway

Composer: Ted Kociolek
Lyricist: James Racheff
Librettist: Ted Kociolek; James Racheff
Producer: Musical Theater Works
Director: Tazewell Thompson

Source: MARKED BY FIRE (Novel: Joyce Carol Thomas); **Choreographer:** Julie Arenal; Costumes: Amanda Klein; **Lighting Designer:** Clarke W. Thornton; **Set Design:** Evelyn Sakash; **Vocal Arranger:** Daryl Waters

Songs: Abby's Lament; Abyssinia; Blackberry Wine; Cry; Get Thee Behind Me, Satan!; Honey and Lemon; I Have Seen the Wind; Let Us Sing Praise [1]; Lift Up Your Voice!; Lightnin' Bug; Pickin' Up the Pieces; Ragtime Promenade [1]; Recipe; Rise and Fly; Sisters of Healing; Song of Mother Samuels; Song of the Field; Sound of a Ragtime Band, The; Ten Little Children [1]; There Has to Be a Reason

Cast: Lehman Beneby; Jennifer Leigh Warren

Notes: [1] In Goodspeed Opera House production (6/8/88).

11 • ACCIDENTAL DISCOVERY OF THE NORTH POLE, AN

OPENED: 1908
Musical   Closed out of town

Lyricist: George C. Johnson
Librettist: George C. Johnson

Orchestrations: Charles Keubler

Songs: Change Your Living; Hustle Back to Old New York; I Want to Fight for Uncle Sam; If Ever We Discover the North Pole; I'm an Actor; Little Log Cabin; Mummified Giant; My Town Is Just As Good As Your Town; Pork, Pork, Pork; Throw Your Arms Around Me Honey

Notes: Program from Boston 2/16/08.

12 • ACCIDENTALLY YOURS
OPENED: 1931
Musical

Composer: Jay Gorney
Lyricist: E.Y. Harburg
Librettist: McElbert Moore
Producer: J.F. Lebret

Source: DORINE UND DER ZUFALL (Musical: Jean Gilbert; Fritz Gruenbaum; Wilhelm Sterk)

Songs: Five Minutes of Spring [1]; My Little Prayer; You Started Something

Notes: No other information available. [1] Later in score of AMERICANA (1932).

13 • ACE OF DIAMONDS
OPENED: 1984
Musical   Unproduced

Composer: Melanie
Lyricist: Melanie
Librettist: Ed Kellaher
Producer: Seymour Vall
Director: Thommie Walsh

Choreographer: Tod Jackson; **Musical Director:** Joel Silberman

Notes: Based on the letters of Calamity Jane to her daughter Jane.

14 • ACES AND QUEENS
OPENED: 1925
Musical

Composer: Porter Granger; Freddie Johnson
Lyricist: Porter Granger; Freddie Johnson
Librettist: Porter Granger; Freddie Johnson
Producer: Foster & Marino
Director: Freddie Johnson

Songs: Anybody's Men Has Been My Man; Aunt Jemima (I'm Going Home); Black Bottom (dance); Coal Oil; Dancing; Dandy Dan; Don't Forget Bandanna Days; Dreary, Dreary, Rainy Days; Happy; Havin' a Wonderful Time; June; Keep a Diggin'; Midnight Cabaret; Not So Long Ago; Runnin'; Stop; Strolling; Take Me Back to Dixie Blues; Will You Love Me While You're Gone

Cast: Billy Andrews; Joe Byrd; Rudolf Gray; Henrietta Lovelass; E.E. Pugh; Grace Smith

Notes: No other information available.

15 • ACROSS THE CONTINENT IN THE STATIONARY EXPRESS
OPENED: 1907
Musical

Composer: Karl Hoschna
Lyricist: Charles Noel Douglas
Librettist: Charles Noel Douglas

Songs: All Aboard; All Aboard for Kankakee; All Aboard for Omaha!; All Aboard, Step Lively Do; Conductor of the Stationary Express, The; Finale; Get on to the Bride and Groom; Historical Spots; I've Seen No Indians Yet

Notes: A one-act musical written for the amateur market.

16 • ACT, THE
OPENED: 10/29/1977   Theatre: Majestic
Musical   Broadway: 233

Composer: John Kander
Lyricist: Fred Ebb
Librettist: George Furth
Producer: Cy Feuer; Ernest H. Martin; Shubert Organization

Choreographer: Ron Lewis; **Costumes:** Halston; **Dance Arranger:** Ron Melrose; **Lighting Designer:** Tharon Musser; **Musical Director:** Stanley Lebowsky; **Orchestrations:** Ralph Burns; **Set Design:** Tony Walton; **Vocal Arranger:** Earl Brown

Songs: Arthur in the Afternoon [1]; Bobo's; City Lights; Good Thing Going [2]; Hollywood, California [6]; Hot Enough for You?; Isn't This Better [5]; It's the Strangest Thing; Just When You Least Expect It [2]; Little Do They Know; Love Songs [2]; Money Tree, The; My Own Space; Only Game in Town, The [2]; Please, Sir [2]; Princess, The [2]; Shine It On; There Goes the Ball Game [3]; There When I Need Him; Turning (Shaker Hymn); Walking Papers [4]

Cast: Christopher Barrett; Gayle Crofoot; Mark

Goddard; Roger Minami; Liza Minnelli; Barry Nelson; Arnold Soboloff

Notes: Titled SHINE IT ON out of town. [1] Same music as "Mamie in the Afternoon" in A FAMILY AFFAIR. [2] Cut prior to opening. [3] Cut prior to opening. From movie NEW YORK, NEW YORK. [4] Added after opening. [5] Cut prior to opening. From movie FUNNY LADY. [6] Cut after opening.

17 • ACTORS' EQUITY BENEFIT
OPENED: 05/09/1920   Theatre: Metropolitan
                     Opera House
Revue   New York: 1

Director: Hassard Short

Choreographer: Carl Randall; **Costumes:** Hassard Short

Songs: Memories (C/L: Roy Webb)

Cast: Adele Astaire; Fred Astaire; Ethel Barrymore; Irene Bordoni; Charles Dale; Dorothy Dickson; John Drew; Louise Drew; Louise Groody; Jobyna Howland; Carl Hyson; Tessa Kosta; Florence Moore; Nance O'Neil; Carl Randall; Blanche Ring; Adele Rowland; Vivienne Segal; Hal Skelly; Joe Smith; Fred Stone; John Charles Thomas; Genevieve Tobin; Ernest Truex; Charles Winninger; Peggy Wood; Ed Wynn; Blanche Yurka; Flora Zabelle

Notes: The cast list is incomplete.

18 • ADAMANT EVE
OPENED: 11/17/1949
Musical

Composer: Clay Boland
Lyricist: S. Bickley Reichner
Librettist: Frederick R. Griffiths; Raimond D. Senior
Director: Frederick R. Griffiths; Raimond D. Senior

Choreographer: Walter Keenan; **Costumes:** Hugh MacMiller Jr.; Raimond D. Senior; **Musical Director:** Joseph F. Follmann Jr.; **Orchestrations:** Clay Boland; Al Boss; **Set Design:** Hugh MacMiller Jr.; Raimond D. Senior; **Vocal Arranger:** Clay Boland; Al Boss

Songs: Adamant Eve (L: Clay Boland; Darrell H. Smith); Before We Leave (L: Moe Jaffe); Bring Back Those Good Old Days (C: Clay Boland); Got You Right Where I Want You; I Didn't Know It Was That Good (L: Unknown); I Nominate You to Dominate Me (L: Daniel G. Foley Jr.); I'm Repressed (L: Clay Boland); Kissing Me (L: Moe Jaffe); Love Is (L: Clay Boland Jr.); Missouri Polka (L: Moe Jaffe); Never Underestimate the Power of a Woman (L: Darrell H. Smith); Paper Picker's Polka (L: Darrell H. Smith); Watch That First Step (C: Moe Jaffe); We Lobby for a Hobby (L: Darrell H. Smith); Your Life Is My Life; Zambaloo (L: Moe Jaffe)

Notes: Amateur show. Mask & Wig Club, University of Pennsylvania.

19 • ADAMSES, THE
OPENED: 1951
Play   Closed out of town

Composer: Mark Bucci
Lyricist: Mark Bucci
Author: Paula Jacobi

Notes: Couldn't find any information on this show except sheet music, which subtitled the play an "All Negro Play."

20 • ADELE
OPENED: 08/28/1913   Theatre: Longacre
Musical   Broadway: 196

Composer: Jean Briquet; Adolf Philipp
Lyricist: Edward Paulton
Librettist: Edward Paulton; Adolf Philipp
Producer: New Era Productions
Director: Ben Teal

Musical Director: Arthur Weld

Songs: Adele; Animals Are Better Off Than Humans to Day [1] (L: Edward Paulton); Clock Is Striking Ten, The; Close Your Eyes; Finale Act II; Gay Soldier Boy; Honeymoon with You, A; I Did Not Intend To [1]; Is It Worth While?; It's Love!; Like Swallow Flying; Matter of Opinion; My Last Farewell [1]; My Long Lost Love Lenore; Paris, Goodbye!; Somehow It's Not the Same [1] L: Edward Paulton); Strawberries and Cream; Tell Me That You Miss Me [1] (L: Edward Paulton); Waste of Time to Plan, A; Wedding

Bells; When the Little Birds Are Sleeping; Yesterday; You and Only You [1] (L: Edward Paulton); Yours for Me, and Mine for You

Cast: Georgia Caine; William Danforth; Hal Forde; Grace Walton; Alice Yorke

Notes: Adolf Philipp claimed that ADELE was based on a French operetta by Paul Herve. However, this was an original production. Philipp also claimed that composer Jean Briquet collaborated on the music. Briquet probably never existed. Paulton served to help Philipp with the English language. Note that footnotes claim that certain songs are from the original production with lyrics by Herve. This credit is probably false. [1] From original production with lyrics by Herve.

21 • ADRIENNE

OPENED: 05/28/1923   Theatre: George M. Cohan
Musical   Broadway: 235

Composer: Albert Von Tilzer
Lyricist: A. Seymour Brown
Librettist: A. Seymour Brown
Producer: Louis F. Werba
Director: Edgar MacGregor

Source: UNKNOWN (Story: Francis Bryant; William Stone); **Choreographer:** David Bennett; **Lighting Designer:** Tony Greshoff; **Musical Director:** Max Steiner; **Set Design:** Herbert Ward

Songs: As Long As the Wife Don't Know; Cheer Up; Dance with Me; Down Through the Ages [1]; Hindoo-Hop; I'd Be a Wild Man [1]; I'm Simply Wild About You [1]; Just a Pretty Little Home; King Solomon; Live While You're Here; Love Is All; Opening Chorus; Oriental Divertissement; Sing Sing; Sweetheart of Mystery; Where the Ganges Flows

Cast: Richard Carle; Vivienne Segal; Billy B. Van

Notes: [1] Out Philadelphia 5/14/23.

22 • ADVENTURES OF BELINDA FAIR, THE

Notes: *See BELINDA FAIR.*

23 • ADVENTURES OF MARCO POLO, THE

OPENED: 04/14/1956   Theatre: NBC
TV Musical

Music Based On: Rimsky-Korsakov
Composer: Mel Pahl; Clay Warnick
Lyricist: Edward Eager
Librettist: William Friedberg; Neil Simon
Producer: Max Liebman
Director: Max Liebman

Choreographer: James Starbuck; **Costumes:** Paul Dupont; **Musical Director:** Charles Sanford; Paul Ukena; **Orchestrations:** Irwin Kostal; **Set Design:** Frederick Fox

Songs: Beyond the Sunset; Epilogue; Garden of Imagining, The; Is It You; Market Day; Population; Silver Bells; Tartar Song, The; Uneasy Lies the Head; Who, Me?; Worlds; Xanadu; You'll Be Seeing Me

Cast: Alfred Drake; Ray Drakeley; Doretta Morrow; Arnold Moss; Paul Ukena; Margaret Wright

24 • AFFAIRS OF VANITY FAIR

OPENED: 1947   Theatre: Vanity Fair Cafe
Musical   Nightclub

Producer: Joe Howard

Songs: My Young and Foolish Heart (C: Ted Murry; L: Al Lewis; Charles Tobias); Pineapples (C: Ted Murry; L: Charles Tobias)

Notes: No other information available.

25 • AFGAR

OPENED: 11/08/1920   Theatre: Central
Musical   Broadway: 168

Composer: Charles Cuvillier
Lyricist: Douglas Furber
Librettist: Worton David; Fred Thompson
Producer: F. Ray Comstock; Morris Gest
Director: Frank Collins

Source: AFGAR, OU LES LOISIRS ANDALOUS (Musical: Andre Barde; Michel Carre fils); **Costumes:** Paul Poiret; **Musical Director:** Victor Baravalle; **Set Design:** Paul Poiret

Songs: Antiques [2]; Caresses (C/L: James V. Monaco); Ceremony of Veils; Dardanella [1] (C: Felix Bernard; Johnny S. Black; L: Fred Fisher); Dear Lonely Lover; Eyes of Blue [2]; Garden of Make Believe; Give the Devil His Due; I Give My Soul Into Your Keeping [2]; I Hate the Lovely Women (C: Harry Tierney; L: Joseph McCarthy); I Want Love [2] (C: Maurice Yvain; L: Irving Bibo; Cyrus D. Wood); Julie [2] (C: Maurice Yvain; L: Irving Bibo; Cyrus D. Wood); Live for Love; Make Believe [2]; Man from Mexico; 'Neath Thy Casement; Night Was Made for Love; No Man's Land [2]; Rose of Seville; Sunshine Valley; We're the Gentlemen of the Harem; Where Art Thou, Romeo? (C: Harry Tierney; L: Joseph McCarthy); Why Don't You? (C: Harry Tierney; L: Joseph McCarthy); You'd Be Surprised [1] (C/L: Irving Berlin)

Cast: Irving Beebe; Alice Delysia; Lupino Lane; W.H. Rawlins

Notes: [1] Added to London production for Delysia to sing. [2] Out Boston 12/26/21.

26 • AFRICANA (1927)
OPENED: 07/11/1927   Theatre: Daly's
Revue   Broadway: 77

Composer: Donald Heywood
Lyricist: Donald Heywood
Librettist: Donald Heywood
Producer: Earl Dancer
Director: Earl Dancer

Choreographer: Louis Douglas; **Costumes:** Charles LeMaire; **Musical Director:** Allie Ross; **Orchestrations:** William Still; **Set Design:** Walter Lewis; James Tichenor

Songs: Africana Stomp; Black Cargo; Bugle Blues (dance); Cake Walk Strut, The [2]; Clorinda; Dinah [1] (C: Harry Akst; L: Sam M. Lewis; Joe Young); Here Comes My Show Boat [2]; I'm Coming Virginia [3] (L: Will Marion Cook; Donald Heywood); My Special Friend Is Back in Town [1] (C: James C. Johnson; L: Andy Razaf); Shake That Thing [1] (C/L: Papa Charlie Jackson); Shine 'Em Up! [2]; Smile; Time Ain't Very Long; Weary Feet; You Can't Do What My Last Man Did [1] (C/L: James C. Johnson)

Cast: Snow Fisher; Billy Mills; Ed Pugh; Taylor & Johnson; Ethel Waters

Notes: [1] Added after opening. [2] Not in program. [3] Added after opening. Previously sung by Ethel Waters in MISS CALICO.

27 • AFRICANA (1934)
OPENED: 11/26/1934   Theatre: Venice
Musical   Broadway: 3

Composer: Donald Heywood
Lyricist: Donald Heywood
Additional Lyrics: Abe Tuvim
Librettist: Donald Heywood
Producer: Perry/Wood Company
Director: Peter Morell

Musical Director: Donald Heywood; **Orchestrations:** Philip Ellis; Fredda Feranda; **Set Design:** Anthony Continer

Songs: Just a Promise; No Peace in My Soul; Stop Beating Those Drums; Yamboo

Cast: Gretchen Branch; Joseph Byrd; Jack Carr; Nita Gale; Howard Gould; Walter Richardson; Hesla Tamanya

28 • AFTER HOURS
Notes: *See LEND AN EAR.*

29 • AFTER OFFICE HOURS
OPENED: 12/24/1900   Theatre: New York
Musical   Broadway

Composer: A. Baldwin Sloane
Lyricist: George V. Hobart
Librettist: George V. Hobart

Cast: Dan MacAvoy

Notes: A one-act musical. This proceeded THE GIDDY THRONG. *See THE GIDDY THRONG.*

30 • AFTER THE GIRL
OPENED: 1914
Revue   London: 105

Composer: Paul Rubens
Lyricist: Percy Greenbank; Paul Rubens
Producer: J.A.E. Malone

Musical Director: Gustav Wanda

Songs: 'Amstead 'Eath and Amsterdam (L: Paul Rubens); Bit of the Band, A; Dancing Duet (C: Percy Greenbank); Danube, The (L: Paul Rubens); Dear Old London Town; Finale Act I (L: Percy Greenbank); Finale Act II; Keep On Walking (L: Paul Rubens); Lovely Budapest; Lucky Dog!; Market Day (L: Percy Greenbank); Missis and the Guv'nor; Money; Oh! What a Pity! (L: Paul Rubens); Opening Chorus (L: Percy Greenbank); Say! Have You Seen a Daughter?; Student's Serenade, The (L: Percy Greenbank); Time of Night, The; Very Little Thing, A; Waiting for the Moon to Shine; Whoopsy Daisy; Wonderful Eyes (L: Paul Rubens)

Cast: Bonita; Mlle. Caumont; Clifton Crawford; Isobel Elsom; Lew Hearn; Guy Le Fevre; Mabel Sealby; Willie Stephens; Frederick Volpe

Notes: No other information available.

31 • AFTER YOU, MR. HYDE
OPENED: 06/24/1968
Musical   Closed out of town

Composer: Norman Sachs
Lyricist: Mel Mandel
Librettist: Lee Thuna
Producer: Albert W. Selden
Director: Howard Da Silva

Source: DOCTOR JEKYLL AND MR. HYDE (Novel: Robert Louis Stevenson); **Costumes:** David Toser; **Dance Arranger:** William Stegmeyer; **Lighting Designer:** Michael J. Hotopp; **Musical Director:** Pembroke Davenport; **Set Design:** Michael J. Hotopp; **Vocal Arranger:** William Stegmeyer

Songs: Better Man, A; Epilogue; Experiment, The; Home Away from Home; I Bought a Bicycle [1]; I'll Never Be a Lady; I'll Not Marry [2]; In a Far Off Corner of My Mind; Know What I Mean?; Life I Wanted, The; My World; No Ordinary Day; Nothing Like a Spot of Tea; Our Time Together [1]; Quite Like Him; Something Very, Very Good; What's the Matter with Me?

Cast: Jack Bittner; Alice Cannon; Alfred Drake; Nancy Dussault; Christopher Hewett; Keith Jochim

Notes: Some of the Mandel and Sachs songs were interpolated into a TV special DR. JEKYLL AND MR. HYDE (3/7/73) with a score by Lionel Bart. See under that name also. This musical was later reworked as JEKYLL AND HYDE. See under that title also. [1] Also in MY OLD FRIENDS. [2] Not in program.

32 • AGATHA SUE I LOVE YOU
OPENED: 12/14/1966   Theatre: Henry Miller's
Play   Broadway: 5

Author: Abe Einhorn
Producer: Judith Abbott; Edwin Wilson
Director: George Abbott

Costumes: Patton Campbell; **Lighting Designer:** Jean Eckart; William Eckart; **Set Design:** Jean Eckart; William Eckart

Songs: Agatha Sue (C/L: Sid Ramin)

Cast: Betty Garde; Lee Lawson; Corbett Monica; Renee Taylor; Ray Walston

33 • AH, MEN
OPENED: 05/11/1981   Theatre: South Street
Revue   Off-Broadway: 28

Composer: Will Holt
Lyricist: Will Holt
Librettist: Paul Shyre
Producer: Larry Carpenter; Jay Garon
Director: Paul Shyre

Costumes: Eldon Elder; **Dance Arranger:** Christopher Denny; **Lighting Designer:** John Gisondi; **Set Design:** Eldon Elder

Songs: Ah, Men; Daddy Blues; Illusions; It's Time; Last Minute Waltz, The [1]; Life We Led, The; Man Is for the Woman Made; My First; Truck Stop; We're Back; When After You Pass My Door

Cast: Jack Betts; Curt Dawson; Stephen Lang; Jane White

Notes: [1] Added after opening.

34 • AH! WILDERNESS
OPENED: 1956
Musical

Composer: Coleman Dowell

Lyricist: John Latouche
Producer: David Merrick

Source: AH! WILDERNESS (Play: Eugene O'Neill)

Notes: The songwriting team were writing what eventually became TAKE ME ALONG when Latouche's sudden death at the age of 40 stopped the project. Eight songs were completed.

35 • AIMEE
OPENED: 12/02/1973
Musical   Closed out of town

Composer: Worth Gardner
Lyricist: William Goyen
Librettist: William Goyen
Producer: Trinity Square Repertory
Director: Adrian Hall

Choreographer: Sharon Jenkins; **Costumes:** James Berton Harris; **Lighting Designer:** Richard Devin; **Musical Director:** Richard Cumming; **Set Design:** Eugene Lee

Songs: Aimee Is No Angel; Car of Love; Concrete and Steel; Joy, Joy, Joy; Lullaby of Sister Asleep in the Sea; One of Yours; Part of Jesus; Precious Lady; Welcome Home; Woman in a Prison

Cast: Marguerite Lenert; Pamela Payton-Wright

36 • AIN'T BROADWAY GRAND
OPENED: 04/18/1993   Theatre: Lunt-Fontanne
Musical   Broadway: 25

Composer: Mitch Leigh
Lyricist: Lee Adams
Librettist: Lee Adams; Thomas Meehan
Producer: Arthur Rubin
Director: Scott Harris

Choreographer: Randy Skinner; **Costumes:** Suzy Benzinger; **Dance Arranger:** Scot Woolley; **Lighting Designer:** Ken Billington; **Musical Director:** Nicholas Archer; **Orchestrations:** Chris Bankey; **Set Design:** David Mitchell; **Vocal Arranger:** Neil Warner

Songs: Ain't Broadway Grand; Big Job, A; Class; Girls Ahoy!; He's My Guy; It's Time to Go; Lindy's; Man I Married, The; Maybe, Maybe Not;

On the Street; Tall Dames and Low Comedy; Theater, the Theater, The; They'll Never Take Us Alive; Waiting in the Wings; You're My Star

Cast: Mike Burstyn; Scott Fowler; Merwin Goldsmith; Debbie Shapiro Gravitte; Alix Korey; Maureen McNamara; Bill Nabel; Luis Perez; Richard B. Shull

Notes: Titled MIKE when out of town.

37 • AIN'T IT THE TRUTH
OPENED: 12/19/1921   Theatre: Manhattan
                                          Opera House
Revue   Broadway: 17

Composer: Harry B. Olsen
Lyricist: Jude Brayton
Librettist: Jude Brayton
Director: Paul Blaufoix

Musical Director: Harry B. Olsen

Songs: Tally Ho; When You Come Back

Cast: Edith Thayer

Notes: No program available.

38 • AIN'T LOVE GRAND?
Notes: *See LOVELY LADY.*

39 • AIN'T MISBEHAVIN'
OPENED: 02/08/1978   Theatre: Longacre
Revue   Broadway: 1604

Composer: Thomas "Fats" Waller
Lyricist: Andy Razaf
Producer: Emanuel Azenberg; Ron Dante; Dasha Epstein; Jane Gaynor; Manhattan Theater Club; Shubert Organization

Songs: Ain't Misbehavin' [3] (C: Harry Brooks; Thomas "Fats" Waller); Black and Blue [3] (C: Harry Brooks; Thomas "Fats" Waller); Cash for Your Trash (L: Ed Kirkeby); Fat and Greasy (C/L: Porter Grainger; Charlie Johnson); Find Out What They Like; Handful of Keys [2] (L: Murray Horwitz; Richard Maltby Jr.); Honeysuckle Rose; How Ya' Baby (L: James C. Johnson); I Can't Give You Anything But Love [5] (C: Jimmy McHugh; L: Dorothy Fields); I'm

Gonna Sit Right Down and Write Myself a Letter (C: Fred E. Ahlert; L: Joe Young); It's a Sin to Tell a Lie (C/L: Billy Mayhew); I've Got a Feeling I'm Falling (C: Harry Link; Thomas "Fats" Waller; L: Billy Rose); I've Got My Fingers Crossed (C: Jimmy McHugh; L: Ted Koehler); Jitterbug Waltz [2] (L: Richard Maltby Jr.); Joint Is Jumpin', The (L: James C. Johnson; Andy Razaf); Keepin' Out of Mischief Now; Ladies Who Sing with the Band, The [4] (L: George Marion Jr.); Lookin' Good but Feelin' Bad (L: Lester A. Santly); Lounging at the Waldorf [2] (L: Richard Maltby Jr.); Mean to Me (C: Fred E. Ahlert; L: Roy Turk); Off-Time [3] (C: Harry Brooks; Thomas "Fats" Waller); Spreadin' Rhythm Around [2] (C: Jimmy McHugh; L: Ted Koehler; Richard Maltby Jr.); Squeeze Me (L: Clarence Williams); 'Tain't Nobody's Bizness If I Do [1] (C: Porter Grainger; L: Murray Horwitz; Richard Maltby Jr.; Everett Robbins); That Ain't Right [2] (C/L: Nat "King" Cole; L: Murray Horwitz; Richard Maltby Jr.); This Is So Nice [4] (L: George Marion Jr.); Two Sleepy People (C: Hoagy Carmichael; L: Frank Loesser); Viper's Drag, The (The Reefer Song) (C/L: Traditional); When the Nylons Bloom Again [4] (L: George Marion Jr.); Yacht Club Swing (C: Herman Autry; Thomas "Fats" Waller; L: James C. Johnson); Your Feet's Too Big (C/L: Ada Benson; Fred Fisher)

Cast: Nell Carter; Andre De Shields; Armelia McQueen; Ken Page; Charlaine Woodard

Notes: Based on an idea by Murray Horwitz and Richard Maltby, Jr. Transferred to Broadway from the Manhattan Theatre Club on 5/9/78. [1] Everett Robbins is a pseudonym. Additional lyrics written for this production. [2] Additional lyrics written for this production. [3] Brooks wrote the music for the verse. [4] From EARLY TO BED. [5] From BLACKBIRDS OF 1928. Some claim the song was written by Waller and Razaf.

40 • AIN'T SUPPOSED TO DIE A NATURAL DEATH
OPENED: 10/20/1971   Theatre: Ethel Barrymore
Musical   Broadway: 325

Composer: Melvin Van Peebles
Lyricist: Melvin Van Peebles
Librettist: Melvin Van Peebles
Producer: Emanuel Azenberg; Charles Blackwell; Robert Malina; Eugene V. Wolsk
Director: Gilbert Moses

Costumes: Bernard Johnson; **Lighting Designer:** Martin Aronstein; **Musical Director:** Harold Wheeler; **Set Design:** Kert Lundell

Songs: Catch That on the Corner; Come on Feet, Do Your Thing; Come Raising Your Leg on Me; Coolest Place in Town; Dozens, The; Funky Girl on Motherless Broadway; Heh Heh (Chuckle) Good Mornin' Sunshine; I Got the Blood; Just Don't Make No Sense; Lily Has Done the Zampoughi Every Time I Pulled Her Coattail; Mirror, Mirror on the Wall; Put a Curse on You; Salamaggis Birthday; Sera Sera Jim; Tenth and Greenwich; Three Boxes of Longs, Please; You Ain't No Astronaut; You Can't Get Up Before Noon without Being a Square; You Gotta Be Holdin' Out Five Dollars on Me

Cast: Barbara Alston; Marilyn B. Coleman; Bill Duke; Joe Fields; Arthur French; Minnie Gentry; Lauren Jones; Garrett Morris; Ralph Wilcox; Dick Anthony Williams

41 • AIR KING, THE
OPENED: 12/1909
Musical   Closed out of town

Composer: Raymond Hubbell
Lyricist: Harry B. Smith
Librettist: Harry B. Smith

Songs: Art with a Capital "A"; Farewell Prosperity; Girl I Used to Know, The; I Want to Be Kissed By a Matinee Idol; I'd Like to Go Up in an Airship; Newport Is Waiting for Me

Cast: Josephine Hall; Thomas Meighan; John Slavin

Notes: Closed in Chicago.

42 • AL CHEMIST SHOW, THE
OPENED: 04/05/1980
Musical   Closed out of town

Composer: Steve Allen
Lyricist: Steve Allen; James Booth
Librettist: James Booth

Musical Director: Mark Hoder

Songs: Al the Chemist; Be Rich; Carne Asada; Dream Girl; Feet, Get Movin'; Filthy Rich; Greed; Helluva Hullabaloo; Holy Smoke;

I Depend on Myself; I'm a Fairy; I'm Subtle, I'm Doll and I'm Ace; It's Twelve O'Clock; Legal Writ a Day, A; My Lucky Fly; No Sir, Yes Sir; Pals; Spanish; Spic and Span (1); Spic and Span (2); Things Are Very, Very Bad; Things Are Very, Very Good; We Are the Boys in Blue; We've Got Five Legs Among Us; You Want to Ruin Everything; You've Got to Have a Sense of Humor

Cast: James Booth; Georgia Brown; James Gleason; Scott Hylands; Al Mancini

43 • ALABAMA BOUND
OPENED: 1921
Musical

Librettist: Irvin C. Miller
Producer: Irvin C. Miller

Songs: Alabama Bound Blues; Answer; Baby Blues; Ballet Girl; Beautiful Girl; Come Back to Me Daddy; Day By Day; Dog, The; Dreamy Eyes Girl; Gingham Girl; Good Night My Dear; Home Again; Love Is a Fable; Love's Funny Propsition; McGory Girl; Musical Rass; Sundown; When Honey Sings an Old Time Song; Yodle Song

Cast: Emmett Anthony; Ida Brown; Irvin C. Miller; Anita Wilkins

Notes: No other information available. This may not have had original songs.

44 • ALADDIN (1958)
OPENED. 02/21/1958   Theatre: CBS
TV Musical

Composer: Cole Porter
Lyricist: Cole Porter
Librettist: S.J. Perelman
Producer: Richard Lewine
Director: Ralph Nelson

Musical Director: Robert Emmett Dolan; **Orchestrations:** Robert Russell Bennett

Songs: Aladdin; Come to the Supermarket in Old Peking; I Adore You; Make Way; No Wonder Taxes Are High; Opportunity Knocks but Once; Trust Your Destiny to a Star; Wouldn't It Be Fun [1]

Cast: Anna Maria Alberghetti; George Hall; Dennis King; Sal Mineo; Howard Morris; Basil Rathbone; Cyril Ritchard

Notes: [1] Not used because of time restraints in broadcast though recorded on cast album. This is the last songs written by Cole Porter.

45 • ALADDIN, JR.
OPENED: 04/08/1895   Theatre: Broadway
Musical   Broadway: 48

Composer: W.H. Batchelor; Jesse Williams
Librettist: J. Cheever Goodwin
Producer: David Henderson
Director: Richard Barker

Arrangements: W.F. Gloves; **Choreographer:** Carlo Coppe; **Costumes:** Howell Russell; **Dance Arranger:** Georgio Jacobi; **Lighting Designer:** Martin Krueger; James Pennyfeather; **Set Design:** Frederick Dangerfield

Songs: Alabama Coon; Beauteous Widow Bohea; Bow Down; Dorothy Flop; Emperor's Lot, An; Farewell, Fondest and Dearest; Fill High! Drink Deep!; Ha Ha Family, The; I Didn't Think She'd Do It; I Don't Suppose You Have; I Must Away; Infelice; I've Booked the Date; Laundry Trio; Love Among the Freabs; Magician of High Degree, A; Message of the Rose; Rackety Boys, The; Stars Alone Can Tell, The; To and Fro; Way He Arranges His Face, The; Women, Wine and Song

Cast: John E. Cain; Allene Crater; Ada Deaves; Joseph W. Herbert

46 • ALARM CLOCK, THE
OPENED: 1932
Musical

Composer: Martin Broones
Lyricist: Raymond B. Egan
Producer: Henry Duffy

Songs: I Don't Know How I Can Do Without You; Let's Be Dreamers in Love [1]; Sparrows in the Rain [1]

Notes: No other information available. [1] May not be in this show.

47 • ALASKAN, THE

OPENED: 08/12/1907   Theatre: Knickerbocker
Musical   Broadway: 29

Composer: Harry Girard
Lyricist: Joseph Blethen
Librettist: Joseph Blethen; Max Figman
Producer: John Cort

Songs: Arlee; Bah, Bah Black Sheep; Eskimo [1];
Face of the Girl I Love [2] (C: Jean Schwartz;
L: Richard Carroll); Finale Act I [3]; For I Dream
of You [2] (C: Theodore Northrup); Fossil Man,
The; Glittering Gold; Good, Better, Best; Good
Night [2]; Heart of My Heart, I'm Here
(C: Theodore Northrop; L: Arrington Prewitt);
Hi! Hi! Hi! [2] (C: Nat D. Mann; L: Richard
Carroll); I'd Give the Whole Show By Myself [3]
(L: Richard Carroll); Laughing Powders [2] (L:
Gus C. Weinberg); Legend of La La Lu, The [2];
Let's Rub Noses [2] (L: Richard Carroll); Moth
and the Bumble Bee, The [2] (C: Theodore
Northrop; L: Richard Carroll); Mother Did; My
Totem Pole; Naughty Little Lady, O; Opening
Chorus [2]; Party of the Second Part; Rainbow
and Thistle; Snowballing [2] (C: Louis F.
Gottschalk; L: Richard Carroll; Gus C. Weinberg);
Song of the Riffles [4]; There Is Gold Along the
River; Trouble Tree, The; Veasy Drew; We're the
Merry, Merry Chorus O [2] (L: Richard Carroll);
You for Me [2] (C: Theodore Northrop;
L: Richard Carroll); Yup and Away [4]

Cast: Richard Carroll; Gus Weinberg

Notes: [1] Sheet music only. [2] Out Kansas City
4/22/10. [3] Out Chicago 5/9/09. [4] Out Kansas
City 10/25/08.

48 • ALGERIA

OPENED: 08/31/1908   Theatre: Broadway
Musical   Broadway: 48

Composer: Victor Herbert
Lyricist: Glen MacDonough
Librettist: Glen MacDonough
Producer: Frank McKee
Director: George Marion

Musical Director: John McGhie

Songs: Ask Her While the Band Is Playing [1]
(L: Vincent Bryan); Bohemia, Good Bye [1]; Boule
Miche, The [1]; Foolish Gardener, The [1]; Great

White Easiest Way, The [1]; He Was a Soldier
Too [3] (L: Vincent Bryan); I'll Dream of Thee [3]
(L: Vincent Bryan); In Jail [1]; I've Been
Decorated [1]; Little Bird of Paradise [1]; Love Is
Like a Cigarette [2]; Only One of Anything [1];
Rose of the World [1]; Same Old Two, The [1];
Thanksgiving Day [3] (L: Vincent Bryan);
Twilight in Barakeesh [1]; You'll Feel Better
Then [1]

Cast: Helen Broderick; William Cameron;
Katherine Howland; Ida Brooks Hunt; Ernest
Lambert; George Marion; Florence Nash;
William Pruette

Notes: *See also ROSE OF ALGERIA.* [1] Later in
ROSE OF ALGERIA. [2] Later in ROSE OF
ALGERIA. Previously added to IT HAPPENED
IN NORDLAND. [3] Sheet music only.

49 • ALGERIAN, THE

OPENED: 10/23/1893   Theatre: Garden
Musical   Broadway

Composer: Reginald De Koven
Lyricist: Harry B. Smith
Librettist: Harry B. Smith

Songs: Algerian Serenade; Breton Boat Song;
Castles in Spain; Chanson; Couplets; Finale Act I;
Finale Act II; Finale Act III; Fire-Fly Dance; In
Old Villanelle; Love's Nest; March of the Watch;
Nubian Dance (inst.); Oh Rash Muezzin;
Opening Act II; Opening Chorus; Quintet;
Reveille, The; Sing Ho!; Sitting the Lute
A-Striking; Tambourine Song; Tartarin Now
Comes This Day; Tartarin the Terrible;
Weather-Vane, The

50 • ALI BABA AND THE FORTY THIEVES (1955)

OPENED: 12/26/1955   Theatre: Phoenix
Musical   Off-Broadway

Composer: George Kleinsinger
Lyricist: Joe Darion

Songs: Dance of the Jewels (inst.); Dance of the
Whirling Dervishes (inst.); Entrance of the Forty
Thieves (inst.); Morgiana's Dagger Dance (inst.);
Open Sesame; Song of Ali Baba and Zsa Zsa

Cast: Bil Baird

51 • ALI BABA AND THE FORTY THIEVES (1957)

OPENED: 1957   Theatre: Golden Records Record

Composer: Mary Rodgers
Lyricist: Sammy Cahn

Songs: 40 Thieves; I Love You Whoever You Are; My Own Individual Star; One of Us Is a Thief; One Rich Brother; Open Sesame!; They All Lived Happily Ever After; Year In, Year Out

Cast: Bing Crosby

Notes: An original musical produced for records.

52 • ALICE

OPENED: 05/31/1978
Musical   Closed out of town

Composer: Micki Grant
Lyricist: Micki Grant
Librettist: Vinnette Carroll
Producer: Lewis Allen; Mike Nichols
Director: Vinnette Carroll

Source: ALICE'S ADVENTURES IN WONDERLAND (Novel: Lewis Carroll); **Choreographer:** Talley Beatty; **Costumes:** Nancy Potts; **Lighting Designer:** Jennifer Tipton; **Musical Director:** Joyce Brown; **Orchestrations:** H.B. Barnum; **Set Design:** Douglas W. Schmidt; **Vocal Arranger:** H.B. Barnum

Songs: Alice [1]; Chess; Children Are; Consider; Disco; Everybody's Mad; Father William; Fun and Games; Hall of Mirrors Ballet; I Am Real; It's Lonely; Lobster Rock; Workin' for the Man

Cast: Debbie Allen; Hamilton Camp; Cleavant Derricks; Clinton Derricks-Carroll; Ronald Dunham; Alice Ghostley; Paula Kelly; Jane White

Notes: Formerly titled BUT NEVER JAM TODAY. Closed in Philadelphia 6/11/78. [1] Also in IT'S SO NICE TO BE CIVILIZED.

53 • ALICE AND THE EIGHT PRINCESSES

Notes: *See WONDERLAND.*

54 • ALICE IN CONCERT

OPENED: 12/09/1980   Theatre: New York Shakespeare Festival
Musical   Off-Broadway: 32

Composer: Elizabeth Swados
Lyricist: Elizabeth Swados
Producer: NY Shakespeare Fest.; Joseph Papp
Director: Joseph Papp

Source: ALICE'S ADVENTURES IN WONDERLAND (Novel: Lewis Carroll); **Source:** THROUGH THE LOOKING GLASS (Novel: Lewis Carroll); **Choreographer:** Graciela Daniele; **Costumes:** Theoni V. Aldredge; **Lighting Designer:** Arden Fingerhut; **Musical Director:** Elizabeth Swados; **Set Design:** Michael H. Yeargan; **Vocal Arranger:** Carolyn Dutton

Songs: Aged Aged Man, An; Alphabet; Beautiful Soup; Bill's Lament; Bird Song, The; Caterpillar's Advice; Cheshire Puss; Child of Pure Unclouded Brow; Down Down Down; Drink Me; Eating Mushrooms; Examination, The; Goodbye Feet; Humpty Dumpty; If You Knew Time; Jabberwocky; Lion and the Unicorn, The; Lobster Quadrille; Mock Turtle Lament; Never Play Croquet; No Room No Room; Pretty Piggy; Queen Alice; Rabbit's Excuse, The; Rabbit's House, The; Red Queen; Starting Out Again; Tweedledum and Tweedledee; Walrus and the Carpenter, The; What Is a Letter [1]; What There Is; White Knight, The; White Queen, The; White Roses Red; Wow Wow Wow

Cast: Betty Aberlin; Stuart Baker-Bergen; Richard Cox; Sheila Dabney; Rodney Hudson; Michael Jeter; Charles Lanyer; Mark Linn-Baker; Kathryn Morath; Amanda Plummer; Deborah Rush; Meryl Streep

Notes: *See also WONDERLAND IN CONCERT.* [1] Based on poem by Kenneth Patchen.

55 • ALICE IN WONDERLAND (1932)

OPENED: 12/12/1932   Theatre: Civic Repertory
Musical   Broadway: 127

Composer: Richard Addinsell
Lyricist: Lewis Carroll
Librettist: Florida Friebus; Eva Le Galliene
Director: Eva Le Galliene

Source: ALICE IN WONDERLAND (Novel: Lewis Carroll); **Source:** THROUGH THE LOOKING GLASS (Novel: Lewis Carroll); **Choreographer:** Ruth Wilson; **Set Design:** Irene Sharaff

Cast: Whitney Bissell; Sayre Crawley; Florida Friebus; Josephine Hutchinson; Burgess Meredith; Harold Moulton; Joseph Schildkraut; Richard Waring; Howard da Silva; Puppeteer: A. Spolidoro

Notes: No songs listed in program.

56 • ALICE IN WONDERLAND (1975)

OPENED: 02/19/1975   Theatre: Bil Baird
Musical   Off-Broadway: 51

Composer: Joe Raposo
Lyricist: Sheldon Harnick
Librettist: A.J. Russell
Producer: Amer. Pup. Arts Coun; Bil Baird
Director: Paul Leaf

Source: ALICE'S ADVENTURES IN WONDERLAND (Novel: Lewis Carroll); **Lighting Designer:** Peggy Clark; **Set Design:** Bil Baird

Songs: Chant; Flutter and Sway; I Like Nonsense; I Want to Go Home; Lobster Quadrille, The; So Small; Speak Roughly to Your Little Boy; Unbirthday Song; Walrus and the Carpenter, The; Welcome to Wonderland

Voice: Ivy Austin; Bil Baird; Margery Gray; Sheldon Harnick; George S. Irving; Rose Marie Jun; Bill Tost; Puppeteer: Peter Baird; Rebecca Bondor; Mary Case; Tim Dobbins; Olga Felgemacher; Steve Hansen; Steven Widerman

Notes: This show was followed by BIL BAIRD'S VARIETY. No program available.

57 • ALICE IN WONDERLAND OR WHAT'S A NICE KID LIKE YOU DOING IN A PLACE LIKE THIS?

OPENED: 03/30/1966   Theatre: ABC
TV Musical

Composer: Charles Strouse
Lyricist: Lee Adams

Source: ALICE'S ADVENTURES IN WONDERLAND (Novel: Lewis Carroll); **Musical Director:** Al Capps

Songs: I'm Home; Life's a Game; They'll Never Split Us Apart; Today's a Wonderful Day; What's a Nice Kid Like You Doing in a Place Like This

Voice: Mel Blanc; Henry Corden; Scatman Crothers; Bill Dana; Sammy Davis Jr.; Doris Drew; Don Messick

Notes: An original musical for television.

58 • ALICE THROUGH THE LOOKING GLASS (1966)

OPENED: 11/06/1966   Theatre: NBC
TV Musical

Composer: Moose Charlap
Lyricist: Moose Charlap; Elsie Simmons
Librettist: Albert Simmons; Elsie Simmons
Producer: Alan Handley; Bob Wynn
Director: Alan Handley

Source: ALICE THROUGH THE LOOKING GLASS (Story: Lewis Carroll); **Choreographer:** Tony Charmoli

Songs: Alice Is Coming to Tea; Backwards Alphabet, The; Come Out, Come Out, Wherever You Are; I Wasn't Meant to Be a Queen; Jabberwock Song; Keep on the Grass; Some Summer Day; There Are Two Sides to Everything; Through the Looking Glass; 'Twas Brillig; Who Are You?

Cast: Roy Castle; Robert Coote; Jimmy Durante; Nanette Fabray; Ricardo Montalban; Agnes Moorehead; Jack Palance; Judi Rolin; Smothers Brothers

Notes: An original musical for television.

59 • ALIVE AND KICKING

OPENED: 01/17/1950   Theatre: Winter Garden
Musical   Broadway: 46

Composer: Harold Rome
Lyricist: Harold Rome
Librettist: Jerome Chodorov; I.A.L. Diamond; Will Glickman; Henry Morgan; Joseph Stein; Mike Stuart

Producer: Ray Golden; William R. Katzell
Director: Robert H. Gordon

Choreographer: Jack Cole; **Costumes:** Raoul Pene du Bois; **Lighting Designer:** Mason Arvold; **Musical Director:** Lehman Engel; **Orchestrations:** George Bassman; **Set Design:** Raoul Pene du Bois, **Vocal Arranger:** Lehman Engel

Songs: Abou Ben Adhem (C/L: Ray Golden); Alive and Kicking (C: Hal Borne; L: Ray Golden; Sid Kuller); Cry, Baby, Cry [1]; French with Tears; If You Don't Love Me [2] (C: Hoagy Carmichael; L: Ray Golden; Paul Francis Webster); I'm All Yours (C: Leo Schumer; L: Mike Stuart); Love, It Hurts So Good; One! Two! Three! (C: Sonny Burke; L: Ray Golden; Paul Francis Webster); One Word Led to Another (C: Hal Borne; L: Ray Golden); Pals of the Pentagon; Propinquity (C: Sonny Burke; L: Ray Golden; Paul Francis Webster); There's a Building Going Up (C: Sammy Fain; L: Ray Golden; Paul Francis Webster); What a Delightful Day (C: Sammy Fain; L: Ray Golden; Paul Francis Webster); World of Strangers, A [3] (C: Sammy Fain; L: Ray Golden; Paul Francis Webster)

Cast. David Burns; Jack Cassidy; Jack Cole; Mickey Deems; Jack Gilford; Lenore Lonergan; Carl Reiner; Bobby Van; Gwen Verdon

Notes: [1] Originally in THAT'S THE TICKET. [2] Not used. [3] ASCAP/Library of Congress only.

60 • ALL ABOARD (1913)

OPENED: 06/05/1913   Theatre: 44th Street Roof
                                    Garden
Musical   Broadway: 108

Composer: Malvin F. Franklin; E. Ray Goetz
Lyricist: E. Ray Goetz
Librettist: Mark Swan
Producer: Lew Fields
Director: W.H. Post; William J. Wilson

Choreographer: William J. Wilson; **Costumes:** Melville Ellis; **Lighting Designer:** David Atchison; **Musical Director:** DeWitt Coolman; **Set Design:** H. Robert Law

Songs: All Aboard; Asia [2] (C: John Lindsay); Capt. Kidd; Goodbye Poor Old Manhattan; Honey You Were Made for Me [4] (C: Jack Glogau; L: Earl Carroll); In My Garden of Eden for Two (C: E. Ray Goetz); International Rag, The (C/L: Irving Berlin); Love Is Just the Same Old Game in Every Land; Monkey Doodle Doo [1] (C/L: Irving Berlin); Mr. Broadway U.S.A.; My Cubist Girl; Over the Ocean; Ragtime Yodeling Man; Rainy Day, A; Serafina (C: Joaquin Valverde); Somebody's Coming to My House (C/L: Irving Berlin); Take Me Back (C/L: Irving Berlin); Tokio Rag; Tulip Time; Under the Eastern Moon [3] (C: E. Ray Goetz); Wriggly Rag

Cast: Zoe Barnett; Lawrence D'Orsay; Carter De Haven; Lew Fields; George Monroe; Flora Parker; Will Philbrick

Notes: [1] Not same song as that in THE COCOANUTS. [2] Not in program. [3] Also known as "Under the China Moon." [4] Sheet music only.

61 • ALL ABOARD (1918)

OPENED: 1918
Musical   Closed out of town

Composer: Joe Wilton
Lyricist: Joe Wilton
Librettist: Joe Wilton
Producer: Joe Wilton
Director: Joe Wilton

Songs: Aunt Dinah; Cheer Up Father, Cheer Up Mother; Coffee Coolers Tea; Derby Day in Dixie; Everybody Else's Girl but Mine; God Bless the Ladies; How'd You Like to Be My Daddy?; I Think You're Wonderful; Lonesome Valley; Mississippi Miss; Naughty; Smiles; Soothing Serenade; They'll Know We're Over; When Alexander Takes His Ragtime Band

Cast: Monte Carlo Girls, The

Notes: The second half of this show was the REVUE DE LUXE. Closed in Chicago. Most of these songs were probably popular songs of the day.

62 • ALL ABOUT LIFE

OPENED: 1963
Industrial Show

Composer: Jerry Powell
Lyricist: Michael McWhinney

Librettist: Nat Greenblatt; Ed Nayor
Producer: Nat Greenblatt
Director: Ed Nayor

Choreographer: Bill McDonald; **Musical Director:** Rod Warren

Songs: As Advertised in Life; Big Parade, The; Big Walk, The; Do You Remember; Guantanamo; Opener; People You Like to Talk To; Personal Touch, The; Productivity; Rocky on the Rocks; Top Stories; 26 Market Mix; Typical People; Which Did You Say Was Number One?

Cast: Michael Allinson; Gloria Bleezarde; Bill Linton; Eliza Ross; Jay Stuart; Ronny Whyte

Notes: An industrial show produced for Life Magazine.

63 • ALL ABOUT LOVE
OPENED: 10/17/1951
Musical   Nightclub

Composer: Irvin Graham
Lyricist: Irvin Graham
Librettist: George Axelrod; Max Wilk
Director: George Hale

Choreographer: Diane Marsh; **Costumes:** Billy Livingston; **Musical Director:** Emile Petti; **Orchestrations:** Alfred Reed; **Set Design:** John Wisner

Cast: Arthur Maxwell; Gena Rowlands; Carmen Torres; Constance Towers

Notes: No songs listed in program of this nightclub musical.

64 • ALL AMERICAN
OPENED: 02/19/1962   Theatre: Winter Garden
Musical   Broadway: 80

Composer: Charles Strouse
Lyricist: Lee Adams
Librettist: Mel Brooks
Producer: L. Slade Brown; Edward Padula
Director: Joshua Logan

Choreographer: Danny Daniels; **Costumes:** Patton Campbell; **Dance Arranger:** John Morris; **Lighting Designer:** Jo Mielziner; **Musical**

Director: John Morris; **Orchestrations:** Robert Ginzler; **Set Design:** Jo Mielziner

Songs: Animal Attraction [2]; Back to School Again [3]; Fight Song, The; Have a Dream; I Can Teach Them [2]; I Couldn't Have Done It Alone; If I Were You; I'm Fascinating; I'm Not in Philadelphia [2]; It's Fun to Think; It's Up to Me [4]; I've Just Seen Her; I've Never Seen Anything Like It in My Life [2]; Living Alone [6]; Melt Us! (Old Immigration and Naturalization Rag, The); Nightlife; Once Upon a Time; Our Children; Physical Fitness; Pripoz Diva Se [2]; Real Me, The; Search Your Heart [1]; We Speak the Same Language; What a Country!; Which Way? [5]

Cast: Ray Bolger; Anita Gillette; Eileen Herlie; Ron Husmann; Fritz Weaver

Notes: [1] Sheet music only. [2] Not used. [3] Out Philadelphia prior to New York. [4] Dropped after opening. [5] Added after opening. [6] ASCAP/Library of Congress only.

65 • ALL AROUND CHICAGO
OPENED: 1905   Theatre: McVickers
Revue   Chicago

Producer: William Brady

Notes: A topical revue.

66 • ALL CLEAR
OPENED: 12/20/1939
Revue   London: 162

Producer: H.M. Tennent

Songs: Have You Met Miss Jones? [1] (C: Richard Rodgers; L: Lorenz Hart)

Cast: Bobby Howes

Notes: [1] Originally in I'D RATHER BE RIGHT.

67 • ALL FOR LOVE
OPENED: 01/22/1949   Theatre: Mark Hellinger
Revue   Broadway: 121

Composer: Lester Lee; Allan Roberts
Lyricist: Lester Lee; Allan Roberts
Librettist: Jane Bishir; Grace Hartman; Paul

Hartman; Ted Luce; Max Shulman; William K. Wells

Producer: Anthony B. Farrell; Sammy Lambert
Director: Edward Reveaux

Choreographer: Eric Victor; **Costumes:** Billy Livingston; **Musical Director:** Clay Warnick; **Set Design:** Edward Gilbert

Songs: All for Love; Benjamin B. O'Dell; Big Four, The (C/L: Peter Howard Weiss); Dreamer with a Penny; Farrell Girl, The; Humphrey Bogart Rhumba, The [1]; It's a Living; My Baby's Bored; My Heart's in the Middle of July; No Time for Nothin' but Love; Oh, How Unfortunate You Mortals Be; Prodigal Daughter (C: Peter Howard Weiss); Run to Me, My Love; Why Can't It Happen Again? (C: Michael Emer; L: Sammy Gallup)

Cast: Grace Hartman; Paul Hartman; Bert Wheeler; Patricia Wymore

Notes: [1] Not in program.

68 • ALL FOR THE LADIES

OPENED: 12/30/1912   Theatre: Lyric
Musical   Broadway: 112

Composer: Alfred G. Robyn
Lyricist: Henry Blossom
Librettist: Henry Blossom
Producer: Edwin T. Emery

Source: CRIME DES FEMMES (Play: Maurice Hennequin); **Choreographer:** Joseph C. Smith; **Costumes:** Melville Ellis; **Musical Director:** John Lund

Songs: A La Parisienne [1]; Don't Breathe a Word [1]; Everybody Knows It but Her Husband [1]; How Shall I E'er Forget [1] (C: John Lund; L: Henry Blossom); I'd Like to Have a Little Girl Like You Like Me; I'd Like to Have You Around [1]; If a Bee Can't Behave in a Beehive when Can a Bee Behave?; If I Were Only a Man; If You Love Me, Marry Me; I'll Marry Him for Love; (I Live But) In Dreams Alone; In Sunny Spain [1]; It's Permissible; Join Our Jubilee; My Zingara Maid [1]; Paris, Paris; Sunday Dress Parade, The; Sunshine Returns Again (Tell Me You Love Me) [1]; What a Change; Women, Women!

Cast: Sam Bernard; Adele Ritchie

Notes: This show was later boiled down to make the one-act musical THE MODISTE'S SHOP, which appeared in A GLIMPSE OF THE GREAT WHITE WAY. [1] Sheet music only.

69 • ALL FOR YOU

OPENED: 09/24/1925
Musical   Closed out of town

Composer: Arthur Freed
Lyricist: Arthur Freed
Librettist: Charles Grapewin; George V. Hobart
Producer: Thomas Wilkes
Director: Frank Smithson

Source: UP THE LINE JOHN HENRY (Play: George V. Hobart)

Songs: All for You; At the Hotel; Capering Coopers; Church Around the Corner; Cover Me with Kisses; Dance It Again with Me (C: Oliver Wallace); Egypt's No Place for a Lady; Fidgety Feet; Fu-Ji; (In a) Happy Home for Two; Hold Me in Your Arms Again; Housekeeping; If You Love Her (Tell Her So); In My Little Blue Bonnet; Keep That Schoolgirl Complexion; Keeping Out of Trouble; Little Raindrop; Mr. Cosy Corner Man (C: Byron Gay); My Oriental Symphony; Naughty Little Raindrop; Osculation; Remember Me; Stay at Home; There's a Little Bit of Spain in California; They Don't Look the Same in the Morning; When the Day Is Ended; You've Got to Dance to Win the Prince of Wales

Cast: William Gaxton

70 • ALL IN FUN

OPENED: 12/27/1940   Theatre: Majestic
Revue   Broadway: 3

Composer: Baldwin Bergersen
Librettist: Virginia Faulkner; Everett Marcy; Charles Sherman
Producer: Stella Holt; Leonard Sillman
Director: John Murray Anderson; Leonard Sillman

Costumes: Irene Sharaff; **Dance Arranger:** Glen Bacon; **Musical Director:** Ray Kavanaugh; **Orchestrations:** Hilding Anderson; Charles L. Cooke; **Set Design:** Edward Gilbert; **Vocal Arranger:** Pembroke Davenport

Songs: April in Harrisburg (1) (L: Virginia Faulkner); April in Harrisburg (2) [1] (L: Blanche Merrill); Back to My Shack [1] (L: June Sillman); Brunnhilde Steps Out [1]; But No [1] (L: Irvin Graham); Hokus Pokus [1] (C: Pembroke Davenport; L: Bob Russell); How Did It Get So Late So Early (C: Will Irwin; L: June Sillman); It's a Big, Wide, Wonderful World (C/L: John Rox); It's All in Fun (L: Bob Russell); I've Been Here Before with Love [1] (L: Virginia Faulkner); I've Grown Up (Reprise) [1] (C: Irvin Graham; L: June Sillman); I've Grown Up [1] (C/L: Irvin Graham); Just Strollin' (C: Glen Bacon); Lady Can Love, The [2] (C/L: Irvin Graham); Lazy Boy [1] (L: Virginia Faulkner); Lion Tamer [1] (L: Blanche Merrill); Love and I (L: Irvin Graham; June Sillman); Machine Age; Macumba (L: June Sillman); Man in the White House [1] (L: June Sillman); My Memories Started with You (L: June Sillman); Prettiest Place in Greece [1] (C: Irvin Graham; L: Virginia Faulkner); Quittin' Time (C/L: John Rox); That Man and Woman Thing (C/L: John Rox); Trailing Along in a Trailer [1] (L: Blanche Merrill); Where Can I Go from You? (L: Virginia Faulkner); Where's the Boy I Saved for a Rainy Day? (L: John Rox); Young Man with a Reefer

Cast: Imogene Coca; Red Marshall; Wynn Murray; Bill Robinson

Notes: [1] Cut 11/21/40. [2] Cut 11/21/40. Also in CALLING ALL STARS.

71 • ALL IN LOVE
OPENED: 11/10/1961   Theatre: Martinique
Musical   Off-Broadway: 141

Composer: Jacques Urbont
Lyricist: Bruce Geller
Librettist: Bruce Geller
Producer: J. Terry Brown Jr.; Stella Holt; Jacques Urbont
Director: Tom Brennan

Source: RIVALS, THE (Play: Richard Brinsley Sheridan); **Choreographer:** Jack Beaber; Costumes: Charles Lisanby; **Dance Arranger:** Ann Sternberg; **Lighting Designer:** Jules Fisher; **Musical Director:** Jacques Urbont; **Orchestrations:** Jonathan Tunick; **Set Design:** Charles Lisanby; **Vocal Arranger:** Jacques Urbont

Songs: All in Love; Day Dreams; Don't Ask Me; Good Old Ways, The; Honour; I Found Him [1];

I Love a Fool; Lady Was Made to Be Loved, The; More Than Ordinary Glorious Vocabulary, A; Odds; Poor; Quickly; To Bath Derry-O; What Can It Be?; Why Wives; Women Simple

Cast: David Atkinson; Gaylea Byrne; Lee Cass; Dom De Luise; Christina Gillespie; Mimi Randolph

Notes: [1] Later in SEVEN COMES ELEVEN.

72 • ALL IN ONE
OPENED: 04/19/1955   Theatre: Playhouse
Revue   Broadway: 47

Composer: Leonard Bernstein; Patton Campbell; Molly Parnis; Sylvan Rich
Lyricist: Leonard Bernstein
Producer: Richard Barr; Charles Bowden
Director: David Brooks

Lighting Designer: Eldon Elder; **Set Design:** Eldon Elder

Cast: Constance Brigham; Alice Ghostley; John Taliaferro; James Tushar; John Tyers

Notes: TROUBLE IN TAHITI was one act of this evening. The others were Tennessee Williams' 27 WAGONS FULL OF COTTON and a dance concert by Paul Draper. No songs listed in program.

73 • ALL KINDS OF GIANTS
OPENED: 12/18/1961   Theatre: Cricket
Musical   Off-Broadway: 16

Composer: Sam Pottle
Lyricist: Tom Whedon
Librettist: Tom Whedon
Producer: Noel Weiss
Director: Peter Conlow

Costumes: Merrill Sindler; **Lighting Designer:** Pat Simmons; **Musical Director:** Milton Seltzer; **Orchestrations:** Gordon Emerson; **Set Design:** Merrill Sindler

Songs: All Kinds of Giants; Be Yourself; Duel; Friends; Here We Are; If I Were Only Someone; Logic!; My Prince; My Star; Paint Me a Rainbow; State of the Kingdom; Suddenly Stop and Think; To Be a King

Cast: Claiborne Cary; Bill Hinnant; Richard Morse; Ralph Purdom; Tom Rummler

74 • ALL NIGHT STRUT!, THE
OPENED: 10/04/1979   Theatre: Theatre Four
Revue   Off-Broadway: 6

Librettist: Fran Charnas
Producer: Stanley A. Glickman; Karen Kantor; Ashton Springer; Philip Swaebe
Director: Fran Charnas

Choreographer: Fran Charnas; **Costumes:** Celia Eller; **Lighting Designer:** Glenn Heinmiller; **Musical Director:** Michael Dansicker; **Orchestrations:** Michael Dansicker; **Vocal Arranger:** Tom Fitt; Gil Lieb; Jess Richards; Jana Robbins; Dick Schermasser

Cast: Andrea Danford; Tony Rich

Notes: No songs written for this production.

75 • ALL OVER TOWN
OPENED: 05/1915
Musical   Closed out of town

Composer: Silvio Hein
Lyricist: Harry B. Smith
Librettist: Joseph Santley
Producer: Messrs. Shubert
Director: J.C. Huffman

Choreographer: Jack Mason; **Costumes:** Melville Ellis; **Musical Director:** Robert Hood Bowers

Songs: Athletic Girl, The [2]; Don't Tempt Me; I Can't Forget Your Eyes; I Cannot Take a Step Too Far; I Love My Movie Picture Man [2]; I'll Do What the Rest Do [1]; I'm Here Again [1]; It's An Awful Thing to Not Know Where You Are [2] (C: Benj. Hapgood Burt; L: Roy Atwell); Life's a Game of Polo; Little World of Two [2]; Modern Duel, The [1]; My Moving Picture Man; No One's to Blame but You; Not that She Was Prettier [1]; Opening Chorus; Opening Chorus Act II; Parisian Rag [1]; Some Little Bug Is Going to Find You [2] (L: Roy Atwell; Benjamin Hapgood Burt); Starlight [1]; Talk, Talk, Talk; That Parisian Trot [3]; Them Was Happy Days [1]; Toddle All Over Town

Cast: Marie Callahan; Blanche Deyo; Walter Jones; Lillian Lee; Joseph Santley; Richard Tabor

Notes: [1] Out Washington, D.C. 4/15. [2] Sheet music only. [3] Sheet music only. May be same as "Parisian Rag."

76 • ALL ROUND CHICAGO
OPENED: 1905   Theatre: McVickers
Revue   Chicago

Composer: A. Baldwin Sloane

Notes: No other information available.

77 • ALL STAR GAMBOLS
OPENED: 03/10/1913
Revue   Broadway: 8

Librettist: Marie Dressler
Director: Marie Dressler

Choreographer: Lester Swerd; **Costumes:** Marie Dressler; **Musical Director:** Frederick Schwartz

Songs: Come Back to Erin [1] (C/L: Claribol); Great Big Girl Like Me, A (C: A. Baldwin Sloane; L: Edgar Smith); My Heart Is Weary [1] (C/L: Goring; Thomas); Silver Ring, The [1] (C/L: Chaminade)

Cast: Jefferson De Angelis; Mary Desmond; Marie Dressler; Ethel Fairbanks; Frederick Hastings; May Hopkins; Eddie Rowley; Madge Voe; Harry Weber; Ethel Wilson

Notes: [1] Not written for this production.

78 • ALL STAR IDLERS OF 1921
OPENED: 07/14/1921   Theatre: Shubert
Revue   Broadway: 1

Composer: Will Morrissey
Lyricist: Will Morrissey
Librettist: Will Morrissey
Director: Frederick Manatt

Choreographer: Leon Errol; **Musical Director:** Victor Baravalle

Songs: Prizen Ivy, The; Quintette; Spirit of the Manager, The

Cast: Herbert Corthell; Jed Prouty; Ned Sparks; Robert Woolsey; Ed Wynn

Notes: From a program of 7/22/21, Stamford, CT.

79 • ALL STAR JAMBOREE

OPENED: 07/13/1921   Theatre: Cort
Revue   Broadway: 13

Producer: Edward Dowling; William Halligan
Director: William Halligan

Songs: Finale (C/L: Irving Berlin); Opening Chorus (C: Louis Silvers; L: Jack Yellen)

Cast: Edward Dowling; Bert Kalmar; Harry Ruby

80 • ALL THAT GLITTERS (1949)

OPENED:: 03/19/1949
Musical

Composer: Stephen Sondheim
Lyricist: Stephen Sondheim
Librettist: Stephen Sondheim
Producer: Cap and Bells, Inc.
Director: David C. Bryant

Source: BEGGAR ON HORSEBACK (Play: Marc Connolly; George S. Kaufman)

Songs: I Love You Etcetera; I Must Be Dreaming; I Need Love; Let's Not Fall in Love; When I See You

Cast: Betty Dissell; Jeanette Forsey; Ronald Moir; Donald Rackerby

Notes: Student show produced at Adams Memorial Theatre, Williamstown, Mass. No program available.

81 • ALL THAT GLITTERS (1980)

OPENED: 10/28/1980
Musical   Closed out of town

Composer: Robert Johanson
Lyricist: Robert Johanson
Librettist: Earl McCarroll
Director: Robert Johanson

Arrangements: David Evans; **Costumes:** Mary Thomasine Harkins; **Musical Director:** David Evans; **Set Design:** Michael Anania

Songs: I Am Frosine!; If You Only Knew Love; Light the Candles; Money Minuet, The; My Money; Revenge!; Separate Thoughts; When a Man Loves a Woman; Youth Remembers

Cast: Paul Jackel; Geraldine Librandi; Earl McCarroll; Maryann Plunkett; Peter Tamm; Lanie Zera

Notes: Next Move Theatre, Boston.

82 • ALL THE KING'S HORSES

OPENED: 01/30/1934   Theatre: Shubert
Musical   Broadway: 120

Composer: Edward A. Horan
Lyricist: Frederick Herendeen
Librettist: Frederickien
Producer: Charles H. AbramsHarry L. Cort
Director: Jose Ruben

Source: CARLO ROCCO (Play: Lawrence Clarke; Max Giersberg); **Choreographer:** Theodore Adolphus; **Costumes:** John N. Booth Jr.; **Musical Director:** Oscar Bradley; **Orchestrations:** Robert Russell Bennett; Hans Spialek; **Set Design:** Ward & Harvey

Songs: Charming; Evening Star; Fame Is a Phony [1]; Hair of the Heir, The; I Found a Song; Langenstein in Spring; Mamzelle Papazelle [1]; (I've Gone) Nuts Over You; Ouch; Romance Is Calling; Tamboree; You're Asking Me [1]

Cast: Russell Hicks; Nancy McCord; Guy Robertson; Betty Starbuck; Andrew Tombes

Notes: [1] Not in program.

83 • ALL TOGETHER NOW

OPENED: 06/08/1973
Musical   Closed out of town

Composer: G. Wood
Lyricist: G. Wood
Librettist: Nagle Jackson
Producer: Milwaukee Rep. Th.
Director: Nagle Jackson

Choreographer: William Reilly; **Costumes:** James Edmund Brady; **Musical Director:** Edmund Assaly; **Set Design:** Christopher M. Idoine

Songs: All Together Now; Franchise, A; Games; I'm My Own Encounter Groupñ Holy Divorce; Just Give Me the World; Longing to Be Elsewhere; Look at Me; Lullaby to Grow On; Mercy!; Okay, I'll Marry You; Only You;

Thirteen-Passenger Airport Limousine; This Too Shall Pass; What Gets Into Me?; Who Am I?

Cast: Charles Kimbrough; Mary Jane Kimbrough; G. Wood

Notes: No songs listed in program.

84 • ALLAH BE PRAISED!
OPENED: 04/20/1944   Theatre: Adelphi
Musical   Broadway: 20

Composer: Baldwin Bergersen
Lyricist: George Marion Jr.
Librettist: George Marion Jr.
Producer: Alfred Bloomingdale
Director: Robert H. Gordon; Jack Small

Choreographer: Jack Cole; **Costumes:** Miles White; **Lighting Designer:** George Jenkins; **Musical Director:** Ving Merlin; **Orchestrations:** Don Walker; **Set Design:** George Jenkins; **Vocal Arranger:** Don Walker

Songs: Allah Be Praised (C: Don Walker); Getting Oriental Over You (C: Don Walker); Katinka to Eva to Francis (C: Don Walker); Leaf in the Wind; Let's Go Too Far (C: Don Walker); Persian Way of Life, The (C: Don Walker); Secret Song; Sunrise on Sunset; What's New in New York?

Cast: Jack Albertson; Sheila Bond; Joey Faye; Patricia Morison; Sid Stone; Mary Jane Walsh

85 • ALLEGRO
OPENED: 10/10/1947   Theatre: Majestic
Musical   Broadway: 315

Composer: Richard Rodgers
Lyricist: Oscar Hammerstein II
Librettist: Oscar Hammerstein II
Producer: Theatre Guild, The
Director: Agnes de Mille

Choreographer: Agnes de Mille; **Costumes:** Lucinda Ballard; **Dance Arranger:** Trude Rittman; **Musical Director:** Salvatore Dell'Isola; **Orchestrations:** Robert Russell Bennett; **Set Design:** Jo Mielziner

Songs: Allegro; Come Home; Darn Nice Campus, A; Fellow Needs a Girl, A; Gentleman Is a Dope, The; I Know It Can Happen Again;May Be a

Good Idea for Joe; Joseph Taylor- Jr.; Money Isn't Ev'rything; Mountain Greenery [1] (L: Lorenz Hart); My Wife [2]; One Foot, Other Foot; Poor Joe; Sitting on the Porch in the Moonlight [3]; So Far; To Have and to Hold; Two Short Years [3]; What a Lovely Day for a Wedding; Wildcats; Winters Go By; Wish Them Well; Yatata, Yatata, Yatata; You Are Never Away

Cast: John Battles; Patricia Bybell; William Ching; John Conte; Annamary Dickey; Roberta Jonay; Sylvia Karlton; Lisa Kirk; Kathryn Lee; Muriel O'Malley; Evelyn Taylor

Notes: Choral Director: Crane Calder. Director of choral speech: Josephine Callan. [1] Originally in THE GARRICK GAIETIES (1926), in this show the song was played as dance music. [2] Cut. Music later used in SOUTH PACIFIC as "Younger Than Springtime." [3] Cut.

86 • ALLEZ-OOP
OPENED: 08/02/1927   Theatre: Earl Carroll
Revue   Broadway: 119

Composer: Philip Charig; Richard Myers
Lyricist: Leo Robin
Librettist: .P. McEvoy
Director: Carl Hemmer; Andy Rice

Choreographer: Carl Hemmer; **Musical Director:** Nicholas Kempner; **Set Design:** Karle O. Amend

Songs: Blow Hot and Heavy; Doin' the Gorilla; Hoof, Hoof; In the Heart of Spain; Kiss with a Kick, A; Pull Yourself Together; Star of Stars; What Did William Tell?; What Does It Mean?; Where Have You Been All My Life?

Cast: Charles Butterworth; Madeleine Fairbanks; Charles Haskell; Cecil Lean; Cleo Mayfield; Victor Moore; Bobby Watson

87 • ALL'S FAIR
Notes: *See BY JUPITER.*

88 • ALMA, WHERE DO YOU LIVE?
OPENED: 09/26/1910   Theatre: Weber
Musical   Broadway: 232

Composer: Adolf Philipp
Lyricist: George V. Hobart

Librettist: George V. Hobart
Producer: Joseph Weber
Director: Joseph Weber

Source: ALMA, WO WOHNST DU? (Musical: Adolf Philipp); **Musical Director:** Hugo Frey

Songs: Alma; Boo-Hoo-Who; Boogie Boo [1]; Childhood Days; Don't Let the Girlies Get You; Girlies; Kiss Me, My Love; Land of Beautiful Dreams, The; Love Me (The Tom Cat Song); Never More; Sail Home; Show Me Round and Around [1]

Cast: Charles A. Bigelow; Ethel Dovey; Kitty Gordon

Notes: [1] Out Washington, D.C. 11/12/11.

89 • ALMA'S RETURN
OPENED: 1914
Play   Closed out of town

Author: Jack Lait

Songs: There's a Little Spark of Love Still Burning (C: Fred Fisher; L: Joseph McCarthy)

Notes: No other information available on this playlet.

90 • ALMOST CRAZY
OPENED: 06/20/1955   Theatre: Longacre
Revue   Broadway: 15

Librettist: Robert A. Bernstein; Hal Hackady; James Shelton
Producer: John S. Cobb
Director: Christopher Hewett; Lew Kesler

Choreographer: William Skipper; **Costumes:** Stanley Simmons; **Lighting Designer:** John Robert Lloyd; **Musical Director:** Al Rickey; **Orchestrations:** Ted Royal; **Set Design:** John Robert Lloyd

Songs: Always Tell the Truth (C/L: Portia Nelson); As We Told You [1] (C: Lew Kesler; L: James Shelton); Burlesque (C: Bill Russell; L: Stan Hagler); But It's Love (C: Ray Taylor; L: Hal Hackady); Chat Noire (C: Ray Taylor; L: Jim Kaye); Come and Get Cozy with Me [2] (C: Lew Kesler; L: Carley Mills); Don't Bait for Fish You

Can't Find (C/L: Portia Nelson); Down to Eartha (C/L: Ray Taylor); Easy (C/L: James Shelton); Everything's Gonna Be Much Worse Next Year (C: Lew Kessler; L: James Shelton); Goin' to the Moon (C: Ed Scott; L: Leonard Adelson); Here Come the Blues (C: Gene DePaul; L: Don Raye); I Can Live Without It (C/L: Ray Taylor); Love in the Barnyard (C/L: Ray Taylor); More Fish (C/L: Unknown); Mother's Day (C: Portia Nelson; L: Joyce Geary); Vertigo (C: Ray Taylor; L: Helen Bragdon); Where Is the Girl? (C/L: James Shelton); Why Not Me? (C: Ed Scott; L: Sam Rosen)

Cast: Karen Anders; Vincent Beck; Babe Hines; Kay Medford; James Shelton

Notes: [1] Also in THE SHAPE OF THINGS though with music credited to James Shelton. [2] Also in THE SHAPE OF THINGS though with music credited to Carly Mills.

91 • ALOHA
Notes: *See HEATHEN!*

92 • ALOHA HAWAII
Musical   Closed out of town

Composer: R. Alex Anderson; Peter Lee; Fred T. Smith
Lyricist: R. Alex Anderson; Peter Lee; Fred T. Smith
Librettist: R. Alex Anderson; Peter Lee; Fred T. Smith
Producer: Peter Lee Zoellner
Director: Marvin Kline

Choreographer: Peggy Ryan; **Costumes:** Barbara Thurston; **Lighting Designer:** Jock Purinton; **Musical Director:** Virgil Davis; **Orchestrations:** Virgil Davis; John Powers; Donald Yap; **Set Design:** Jock Purinton

Cast: David Anderson; Jimmy Caesar; Diana Hale; Willa Knight

Notes: Produced in Hawaii in the 1960's. No program available.

93 • ALONE AT LAST
OPENED: 10/14/1915   Theatre: Shubert
Musical   Broadway: 180

Composer: Franz Lehar
Lyricist: Joseph W. Herbert; Matthew C. Woodward
Librettist: Edgar Smith
Producer: Messrs. Shubert
Director: Benrimo

Source: ENDUCH ALLEIN (Musical: Robert Bodanzky; A.M. Willner)

Songs: Bright Morning Star; Finale Act I; Lullaby [1]; Nature Divine (L: Matthew Woodward); Not Now but By the Moon (L: Matthew Woodward); Oh My Darling Tillie (L: Joseph W. Herbert); One in the Game of Love; Peasant Wedding Party, The; Picnic in the Sky (C: Gaetano Merola); Pretty Edelweiss (L: Matthew C. Woodward); Return to Warm My Heart Again (C: Gaetano Merola); Scandals in the Air; Some Little Bug Is Going to Find You Some Day [2] (C: Silvio Hein; L: Roy Atwell; Benj. Hapgood Burt); Sport [1]; Thy Heart Is My Prize (L: Matthew Woodward); Victory to the Bold; Waltz Entrancing (L: Joseph W. Herbert); We Don't Know Why We Love (C: Gaetano Merola; L: Darl MacBoyle)

Cast: Roy Atwell; Jose Collins; Elizabeth Goodhall; Madame Namara; John Charles Thomas

Notes: [1] Sheet music only. [2] Sheet music credits this song as also being in ALL OVER TOWN but it isn't in the program.

94 • ALONG CAME RUTH

OPENED: 02/23/1914   Theatre: Gaiety
Play   Broadway: 56

Author: Holman Day
Producer: Henry Savage
Director: George Marion

Source: UNKNOWN (Play: Fonson; Wicheler)

Songs: Along Came Ruth (C/L: Irving Berlin)

Cast: James Bradbury; Irene Fenwick; Mary Turner Gordon; Joseph Kilgour; Edgar Nelson; Vivian Wessell

95 • ALONG FIFTH AVENUE

OPENED: 01/13/1949   Theatre: Broadhurst
Revue   Broadway: 180

Composer: Gordon Jenkins
Lyricist: Tom Adair
Librettist: Nat Hiken; Charles Sherman
Producer: Arthur Lesser

Choreographer: Robert Sidney; **Costumes:** David Ffolkes; **Lighting Designer:** Peggy Clark; **Musical Director:** Irving Actman; **Orchestrations:** Gordon Jenkins; **Set Design:** Oliver Smith; **Vocal Arranger:** Gordon Jenkins

Songs: Best Time of Day, The; Call It Applefritters (C: Richard Stutz; L: Milton Pascal); Chant d'Amour (L: Nat Hiken); Creme de la Creme [1] (C: Robert Stolz; L: Milton Pascal); Fifth Avenue; Fugitive from Fifth Avenue, The (C: Richard Stutz; L: Nat Hiken); I Love Love in New York; If [1]; If This Is Glamour! (C: Richard Stutz; L: Rick French); In the Lobby; Maybe It's Because (C: Johnnie Scott; L: Harry Ruby); Santo Dinero (C: Richard Stutz; L: Milton Pascal); Skyscraper Blues; Trip Doesn't Care at All, A (C: Philip Kadison; L: Thomas Howell); Vacation in the Store; Weep No More; Window on the Avenue, A; With You So Far Away [2]

Cast: Carol Bruce; Jackie Gleason; Hank Ladd; Donald Richards; Nancy Walker

Notes: [1] Cut. [2] Added out of town after Broadway run.

96 • ALPSBURG

OPENED: 04/08/1910
Musical

Composer: Herbert Stothart
Librettist: Theo. Stempfel
Producer: Haresfoot Club
Director: Herbert Stothart

Songs: Apples! Oranges! Crackerjack! (L: Horatio G. Winslow); Battle of Roses, The (L: Walter Buchen); Bitter Twitter (L: Theo. Stempfel); Busy, Busy, Business Man, The (L: Theo. Stempfel); Finale Act I (L: George B. Hill; Theo. Stempfel); Love Game, The (L: Ralph Birchard; George B. Hill); Lovelight in Your Eyes, The (L: Walter Buchen); Mary (L: Ralph Birchard); Militant Suffragette, The (L: Ralph Birchard); My Edelweiss (L: Walter Buchen); Opening Chorus (L: George B. Hill); Opening Chorus Act II (L: Walter Buchen); Post Cards (L: Milton J. Blair); Sailing (L: Walter Buchen); Spooks of

Reichtenstein, The (L: George B. Hill); Spring Theme, The (inst.); Student Days (L: Ralph Birchard); Tale of the Chamois, The (L: Ralph Birchard); Tourists (L: Ralph Birchard)

Cast: Milton Blair; Walter Buchen; George B. Hill; Theo. Stempfel

Notes: Amateur show — University of Wisconsin.

97 • ALWAYS YOU
OPENED: 01/05/1920   Theatre: Central
Musical   Broadway: 66

Composer: Herbert Stothart
Lyricist: Oscar Hammerstein II
Librettist: Oscar Hammerstein II
Producer: Arthur Hammerstein
Director: Arthur Hammerstein

Choreographer: Robert Marks; **Costumes:** Paul Arlington; **Musical Director:** Herbert Stothart; **Set Design:** Julius Dove

Songs: Always You; Don't You Remember? [1]; Drifting On; Hayward's Harlem Hellions; I Never Miss; I'll Say So [2]; Let's Marry [3]; Misterioso [1]; My Pousse-Cafe; Passing Through; Same Old Places; Some Big Something; String of Girls, A [1]; Syncopated Heart; Tired Business Man; Voice of Bagdad, The; Woman; Wonderful War, A

Cast: Eduardo Ciannelli; Helen Ford; Bernard Gorcey; Ralph Herz; Julia Kelety; Russell Mack; Walter Scanlon; Anne Seymour

Notes: Titled 'TOINETTE and JOAN OF ARKANSAW out Washington, D.C. 12/29/19 - 1/3/20. No New York program available. [1] Cut. [2] Cut during New York run. [3] Out Harrisburg 8/31/20. This song was added during the run in New York instead of "I'll Say So."

98 • AMAZING ADELE, THE
OPENED: 12/26/1956
Musical   Closed out of town

Composer: Albert Selden
Lyricist: Albert Selden
Additional Lyrics: Sheldon Harnick
Librettist: Anita Loos

Producer: Morton Gottlieb; Albert Selden
Director: Jack Landau

Source: AMAZING ADELE, THE (Play: Pierre Barrillet; Pierre Gredy); **Choreographer:** Herbert Ross; **Costumes:** Thomas Becher; **Dance Arranger:** Peter Matz; **Lighting Designer:** Peggy Clark; **Musical Director:** Saul Schechtman; **Orchestrations:** Joe Glover; **Set Design:** Oliver Smith; **Vocal Arranger:** Peter Matz

Songs: A.P.I.S. Parade, The; Adele's Soliloquy [1]; Amazing Adele, The; Atlantic City Welcomes You; Blame It on the Depression; Count on Me; Go and Get Yourself a Yo-Yo; Go Away Devil; I Wonder; I'll Tell You to Your Face; Little Flapjack [1]; Midnight Swim Ballet, The; My Luck Has Changed; Never Again; Now Is the Time; Saturday Night; Something for a Rainy Day; Tango, The (dance); Treat 'Em Rough; Under the Boardwalk Ballet (dance); What Kind of a Grandma Are You?; Who Needs It; Ya Got the Time; You Belong

Cast: Cris Alexander; Peggy Cass; Dagmar; Grover Dale; Johnny Desmond; Joey Faye; Tammy Grimes; Babe Hines; Ken Le Roy; Enid Markey; Joe Ross; Charles Rule

Notes: Donald F. Duncan yo-yos used exclusively! [1] Not in program.

99 • AMAZING BONE, THE
OPENED: 11/25/1979
Musical   Off-Broadway

Composer: David Bishop
Lyricist: David Bishop; Kathleen Masterson
Librettist: Kathleen Masterson
Producer: MSO Productions; Theatre Collective

Source: AMAZING BONE, THE (Story: William Steig); **Choreographer:** Paul Thompson; **Costumes:** Linda Margosian; **Musical Director:** David Bishop; **Set Design:** Judy Juracek

Songs: Amazing Bone, The; Chase, The; Fox's Song; Grownups Song; I Didn't Make the World; Lullabye; Oh I Love Everything Dream Ballet; Pearl's Walking Song

Cast: Jonathan Bustle; Eileen FitzPatrick; Karen Jablons; Naomi Nissen; Eileen O'Brien; Daniel Sklar; Alexander Wolff

100 • AMAZONS, THE

OPENED: 04/28/1913   Theatre: Empire
Play   Broadway: 48

Author: Arthur Wing Pinero
Producer: Charles Frohman

Songs: My Otaheitee Lady (C: Jerome Kern;
   L: Charles H. Taylor)

Cast: Billie Burke; Shelley Hull

101 • AMBASSADOR

OPENED: 11/19/1972   Theatre: Lunt-Fontanne
Musical   Broadway: 9

Composer: Don Gohman
Lyricist: Hal Hackady
Librettist: Anna Marie Barlow; Don Ettlinger
Producer: Gene Dingenary; Nancy Levering;
   Miranda d'Ancona
Director: Stone Widney

Source: AMBASSADORS, THE (Novel: Henry
   James); **Choreographer:** Joyce Trisler; **Costumes:**
   Peter Rice; **Dance Arranger:** Trude Rittman;
   Lighting Designer: Martin Aronstein; **Musical
   Director:** Herbert Grossman; **Orchestrations:**
   Philip J. Lang; **Set Design:** Peter Rice; **Vocal
   Arranger:** Herbert Grossman

Songs: All of My Life; Boy Like That, A; Charming
   [1]; Gossip; Happy Man; I Know the Man;
   I Thought I Knew You [1]; It's a Woman [1];
   Kyrie Eleison; La Femme [1]; La Nuit d'Amour
   [1]; Lambert's Quandary; Lilas; Love Finds the
   Lonely; Mama; Man You Can Set Your Watch
   By, A [1]; Maxixe-Habanera; Not Tomorrow;
   Right Time, the Right Place, The; She Passed My
   Way; Something More; Surprise; Tell Her [1];
   Thank You, No; That's What I Need Tonight;
   This Utterly Ridiculous Affair [1]; Too Much to
   Forgive; Unveiled Threat, The [1]; Valse; What
   Can You Do with a Nude? [1]; What Happened
   to Paris?; Why Do Women Have to Call It Love;
   You Can Tell a Lady By Her Hat [1]; Young
   with Him

Cast: Danielle Darrieux; Howard Keel; Carmen
   Mathews

Notes: [1] Cut from London production before
   Broadway debut.

102 • AMBER EMPRESS, THE

OPENED: 09/19/1916   Theatre: Globe
Musical   Broadway: 15

Composer: Zoel Parenteau; Robert Planquette
Lyricist: Marc Connelly
Librettist: Marc Connelly
Producer: Madison Corey; Joseph Riter
Director: George Marion

Choreographer: Max Bendix; **Costumes:** Raymond
   Newton Hyde; Mrs. O'Kane

Songs: 'Appy 'Oliday, A [1]; Arrival of the Amber
   Express, The; Cannonading Eyes; Chinese Fox
   Trot, The; Divertissement; Don't Lose Your Way,
   Little Boy; Gossip; It's the Only One for Me; King
   Carnival; Kiss Affects Me Most of All, A;
   L'Amour- Toujours-L'Amour (Love Everlasting)
   [2] (C: Rudolf Friml; L: Catherine Chisolm
   Cushing); Love Flies Everywhere; Melody Will
   Keep You Young; Modest Man, The [1]; Open
   Your Heart to Love; Palace or Cot; Serenade,
   The; There's Always One You Can't Forget;
   There's Nothing So Uncertain As a Dead Sure
   Thing; They Can't Run Off the Reels Too Fast for
   Me; With Militant Stride; You're a Hero

Cast: Louise Allen; Lew Christy; Emma Janvier;
   Frank Lawlor; Donald Macdonald; George
   Schiller

Notes: [1] Out Boston 6/14/16. [2] Sheet music
   only. Also in BIBI OF THE BOULEVARDS.

103 • AMBER FLUID, THE

OPENED: 1924
Musical

Songs: If All My Thoughts Were Stars (C: Con
   Conrad; L: Arthur J. Lamb)

Notes: No other information available.

104 • AMEER, THE

OPENED: 12/04/1899   Theatre: Wallack's
Musical   Broadway: 51

Composer: Victor Herbert
Librettist: Kirke La Shelle; Frederick M. Ranken
Producer: Frank Daniels
Director: John Stapleton

Musical Director: Louis F. Gottschalk

Songs: Ah! Woe Is Me; Ameer, The; Another Shout; Armoured Knight, The; Away with Him; Continuous Performances; Cupid Will Guide; Fancies, Only Fancies; Finale Act III; Fond Love, True Love; Highwayman; I Am a Piratical Brigand; I'd Like It; If There's Any Kind of Crime; In Old Ben Franklin's Days; Lanciers; Let Others Boast; Let Those Who'd Wed; Little Poster Maid, The; Oh! What Is the Matter?; Old Maids Are Willing to Please; On Thy Lattice; Rubber Man, The; Soft to Sensuous Music Swaying; Soldier Needs No Truer Friend, A; Soldiers All; Surprise, Surprise, Astounding; Surrender, Surrender; Sweet Clarissa (Darky Love Song); Tell Me Pray; With Stealthy Footsteps Falling

Cast: William Corliss; William Danforth; Frank Daniels; Sadie Emmons; Helen Redmond; W.F. Rochester

105 • AMEN CORNER

OPENED: 11/10/1983   Theatre: Nederlander
Musical   Broadway: 28

Composer: Garry Sherman
Lyricist: Peter Udell
Librettist: Philip Rose; Peter Udell
Producer: Gil Gerard; Joel Goldstein; Judith Henry; Edward Mann; Prudhomme Prod. Ltd.
Director: Philip Rose

Source: AMEN CORNER, THE (Play: James Baldwin); **Choreographer:** Al Perryman; **Costumes:** Felix E. Cochren; **Dance Arranger:** George Butcher; **Lighting Designer:** Shirley Prendergast; **Musical Director:** Margaret Harris; **Orchestrations:** Dunn Pearson; Garry Sherman; **Set Design:** Karl Eigsti; **Vocal Arranger:** Garry Sherman

Songs: Amen Corner; Everytime We Call It Quits; Heat Sensation; I'm Already Gone; In the Real World; It Ain't No Fault of His [1]; Leanin' on the Lord; Love Dies Hard; Rise Up and Stand Again; Somewhere Close By; That Woman Can't Play No Piano; We Got a Good Thing Goin'; You Ain't Gonna Pick Up Where You Left Off

Cast: Keith Lorenzo Amos; Ruth Brown; Jean Cheek; Chuck Cooper; Rhetta Hughes; Roger Robinson; Helena-Joyce Wright

Notes: [1] Cut prior to opening

106 • AMERICA (1913)

OPENED: 08/30/1913   Theatre: Hippodrome
Revue   Broadway: 360

Composer: Manuel Klein
Lyricist: Manuel Klein
Librettist: John P. Wilson
Producer: Messrs. Shubert
Director: William J. Wilson

Set Design: Arthur Voegtlin

Songs: Dark Eyes; Ev'rybody Loves a Soldier [1]; Flower Ball (on a Summer Afternoon) [1]; Gay Excursion, A; Girl in the Gingham Gown, The; Goodbye, Hiram; Hippodrome Tango [1]; Lola; Mandy; Merry Little Chop! Chop! Chop!; Mister Soldier Man; My Wife's Gone; Ragtime in the Air; Though Hearts We May Secure; U.S.A. Limited, The

Notes: [1] Sheet music only.

107 • AMERICA (1981)

OPENED: 03/06/1981   Theatre: Radio City
                                      Music Hall
Revue   Broadway: 284

Composer: Tom Bahler; Mark Vieha
Lyricist: Tom Bahler; Mark Vieha
Librettist: Harvey Jacobs
Producer: Robert F. Jani; Radio City Mu. Hall
Director: Frank Wagner

Choreographer: Violet Holmes; Linda Lemac; Frank Wagner; **Costumes:** Michael Casey; **Lighting Designer:** Ken Billington; **Musical Director:** Mark Bahler; **Set Design:** Robert Guerra

Songs: Fifty Great Places All in One Place; Spirit of America, The

Cast: Wendy Edmead; Jeff Johnson; Reed Jones; Mark Morales; Iris Revson

108 • AMERICA, BE SEATED!

OPENED: 04/22/1964
Revue   N.Y. World's Fair

Composer: Sam Pottle
Lyricist: David Axelrod
Librettist: David Axelrod

Musical Director: Sy Oliver

Songs: America, Be Seated; Auckland, New Zealand; Blues, The; Carolin'; Fashion Plates, The; Feeling in the Air; Gonna Take My Time; High and Low; Hummingbird; My Dog; Please Mr. Banjo; Sailor's Life for Me, A; Sugar Cane; That's How a Woman Gets Her Man; Things Are Getting Better Every Day [1]; Travellin' Man; United Nation's Rag, The

Cast: Mae Barnes; Suzanne Charney; Peter Conlow; Jack De Lon; Lola Falana; Rico Froehlich; Louis Gossett; Ronny Graham; Brandon Maggart; Bibi Osterwald

Notes: This was performed at the Louisiana State Pavilion. [1] Cut prior to New York.

109 • AMERICA KICKS UP ITS HEELS

OPENED: 1983   Theatre: Playwrights Horizons
Musical   Off-Broadway

Composer: William Finn
Lyricist: William Finn
Librettist: Charles Rubin
Producer: Playwrights Horizons
Director: Mary Kyte; Ben Levit

Choreographer: Mary Kyte; **Costumes:** Santo Loquasto; **Lighting Designer:** Frances Aronson; **Musical Director:** Michael Starobin; **Orchestrations:** Michael Starobin; **Set Design:** Santo Loquasto

Songs: All Fall Down; All of Us Are Brothers; All of Us Are Niggers; America, Kick Up Your Heels; Ask Me No Question; Better World, A; Cutting Hair; Daddy and Me; Depression Is Over, The; Eleanor Roosevelt (A Discussion of Soup); Happiest Moment of My Life; I Don't Want to Be Fired Again; It Was Fun; Lullaby; My Day Has Come; Nobody's Ever Gonna Step on Me; Papa Says; Papa, You Won; Pull It Together; Push and Pull; Put It Together; Red Faces at the Kremlin; Why

Cast: Robin Boudreau; Robert Dorfman; Petty Hewett; I.M. Hobson; Rodney Hudson; Alexandra Korey; Dick Latessa; Patti LuPone; Lenora Nemetz

Notes: No official opening night. Later reworked into ROMANCE IN HARD TIMES. See under that title for further information.

110 • AMERICA SINGS

OPENED: 10/09/1934
Musical   Closed out of town

Music Based On: Stephen Foster
Composer: Karl Hajos
Lyricist: Stephen Foster
Librettist: Kay Kenney
Producer: Messrs. Shubert
Director: Frank McCormack

Choreographer: Sara Mildred Strauss; **Costumes:** Ernest Schrapps; **Music Adaptation:** Karl Hajos; **Orchestrations:** Karl Hajos; **Set Design:** Watson Barratt

Cast: Jules Bledsoe; Herbert Corthell; Marjorie Dille; Truman Gaige; Tom Heath; Allan Jones; Robert Emmett Keane; James McIntyre

111 • AMERICA'S SWEETHEART (1931)

OPENED: 02/10/1931   Theatre: Broadhurst
Musical   Broadway: 135

Composer: Richard Rodgers
Lyricist: Lorenz Hart
Librettist: Herbert Fields
Producer: Frank Mandel; Laurence Schwab
Director: Monty Woolley

Choreographer: Bobby Connolly; **Costumes:** Charles LeMaire; **Musical Director:** Alfred Newman; **Orchestrations:** Robert Russell Bennett; **Set Design:** Donald Oenslager

Songs: Cat Can Look at a Queen, A [4]; God Gave Me Eyes [1]; How About It?; I Want a Man; I'll Be a Star [4]; In Califor-n-i-a; Innocent Chorus Girls of Yesterday; I've Got Five Dollars; Lady Must Live, A; Mr. Dolan Is Passing Through; My Sweet; Now I Believe [4]; Opening, Act II; Sweet Geraldine; Tennessee Dan; There's So Much More [2]; Tonight or Never [4]; Two Unfortunate Orphans; We'll Be the Same; You Ain't Got No Savoir-Faire

Cast: Jeanne Aubert; Virginia Bruce; Inez Courtney; Dorothy Dare; Harriette Lake[3]; Vera Marsh; John Sheehan; Gus Shy; Jack Whiting

Notes: [1] Cut out of town. [2] Same music as "Someone Should Tell Them" which was cut from A CONNECTICUT YANKEE. [3] Later known as Ann Sothern. [4] Not used.

112 • AMERICA'S SWEETHEART (1985)

OPENED: 03/08/1985
Musical   Closed out of town

Composer: Robert Waldman
Lyricist: Alfred Uhry
Librettist: Alfred Uhry; John Weidman
Director: Gerald Freedman

Source: CAPONE (Book: John Kobler);
  Choreographer: Graciela Daniele; **Costumes:**
  Jeanne Button; **Lighting Designer:** Pat Collins;
  Musical Director: Liza Redfield; **Set Design:**
  Kevin Rupnik

Songs: All Fwoo; America's Sweetheart; Better
  Off Bad; Buddy Buddy; Call in the Tax
  Collector; Capone's Day in Court; Chicago
  Style; Crime Doesn't Pay; Florida; Flower of
  Their Days; Getting to Wilson; Happy Time Al;
  He Gets Away with Murder; Here's to a Lady;
  Last Ten Years, The; Love-Time; You'll Get
  Yours

Cast: Wayne Bryan; Donna English; Trevor Keeth;
  K.T. Sullivan; Stephen Vinovich

Notes: Hartford Stage Company.

113 • AMERICAN BEAUTY, AN

OPENED: 12/28/1898   Theatre: Casino
Musical   Broadway: 72

Composer: Gustave Kerker
Librettist: Hugh Morton
Producer: Thomas Canary; George W. Lederer
Director: George W. Lederer

Costumes: Mme. Siedle; **Set Design:** Ernest Albert;
  D. Frank Dodge; Ernest Gros

Cast: Harold Blake; William Cameron; Susanne
  Leonard; Lillian Russell; Jerome Sykes

Notes: No songs listed in program.

114 • AMERICAN ENTERPRISE

OPENED: 04/13/1994   Theatre: St. Clements
                                Church
Play   Off-Broadway: 15

Composer: Jeffrey Sweet
Lyricist: Jeffrey Sweet
Author: Jeffrey Sweet
Producer: N.Y. State Theatre Inst.
Director: Patricia Birch

Arrangements: Michael Vitali; **Costumes:** Brent
  Griffin; **Incidental Music:** Michael Vitali;
  Lighting Designer: John McLain; **Musical
  Director:** Betsy Riley; **Set Design:** Richard
  Finkelstein

Songs: Columbian Exposition, The; It's a Trust;
  Leave a Light; Maggie Murphy [2] (C/L: Dave
  Braham; Edward Harrigan); Porters on a
  Pullman Train [1] (C: Michael Vitali; L: Charles
  D. Crandall); Pullman Strike, The [4] (C: Lewis
  Hall; L: William M. Delaney); Shall We Plant a
  Tree?; Step by Step [3] (C/L: Traditional)

Cast: Joel Aroeste; David Brunce; Gerard Curran;
  Marshall Factora; Erol K.C. Landis; Erika Newell;
  John Romeo; Bernard J. Tarver; Paul Villani

Notes: [1] Lyrics written circa 1890. [2] Song
  written circa 1890. [3] Written in late 1800's. [4]
  Written circa 1894.

115 • AMERICAN IDEA, THE

OPENED: 10/05/1908   Theatre: New York
Musical   Broadway: 64

Composer: George M. Cohan
Lyricist: George M. Cohan
Librettist: George M. Cohan
Producer: George M. Cohan; Sam Harris
Director: George M. Cohan

Costumes: F. Richard Anderson; **Musical Director:**
  August Kleinecke; **Orchestrations:** Charles J.
  Gebest

Songs: American Ragtime Tune, The; Bold
  Gendarmes, The; Brothers and Sisters; Cohan's
  Pet Names (That's the Pet Name for Me);
  F-A-M-E; French Militaire; Gendarme's Dance,
  The; In Gay Paree; Isn't It Exasperating, Sadie?
  [2]; Meet Me in Rose Time Rosie [1]; My Garden
  That Blooms for You (C: Milton W. Lusk;
  L: William Kendall Evans); My Little
  Madamoiselle [2]; Order Wedding Bells for Two
  [2] (C: Jean Schwartz; L: William Jerome);
  Sullivan; That's Some Love; They Always Follow
  Me (C: Jean Schwartz; L: William Jerome); Too

Long from Longacre Square; We're Supposed to Be; Whoop-La-La

Cast: George Beban; Robert Daly; Trixie Friganza; Gertrude Vanderbilt

Notes: [1] Played between Acts II and III. Also in COHAN AND HARRIS MINSTRELS (1908). [2] Sheet music only.

116 • AMERICAN IN PARIS, THE
OPENED: 01/10/1910
Musical

Composer: Joe Hollander
Lyricist: Joe Hollander
Librettist: Fred Irwin
Producer: Fred Irwin

Songs: Best of Friends Must Part, The; Bixley Girl, The; Dinah Lee; Fatty; Favorite at Maxim's, A; Float Me; La Sorella Dance; Latest Fad, The; Sh-Sh Is the Word; Wearing of the Green

Cast: Florence Bennett; Mabel Cooper; Margaret Demarest; Gus Fay

Notes: A one-act vaudeville musical.

117 • AMERICAN JUBILEE
OPENED: 05/12/1940
Revue   N.Y. World's Fair

Composer: Arthur Schwartz
Lyricist: Oscar Hammerstein II
Producer: Albert Johnson; N.Y. World's Fair Co
Director: Leon Leonidoff

Choreographer: Catherine Littlefield; **Costumes:** Lucinda Ballard; **Musical Director:** Don Vorhees; **Orchestrations:** Hans Spialek; **Set Design:** Albert Johnson; **Vocal Arranger:** Ken Christie

Songs: Another New Day; By the People; For the People; How Can I Ever Be Alone?; Jenny Lind; My Bicycle Girl; Of the People; One in a Million; Star Spangled Banner, The (C: Unknown; L: Francis Scott Key); Tennessee Fish Fry; We Like It Over Here

Cast: Margaret Adams; Fred Ardath; Tony Blair; Irene Christie; Lee Frederick; Paul Haakon; Jack Howard; Joe Jackson; Gene Marvey; Harry

Meehan; Ray Middleton; Lucy Monroe; Wynn Murray; George L. Spaulding

Notes: Presented at the New York World's Fair May 12 to October 2, 1940.

118 • AMERICAN MAID, THE
OPENED: 03/13/1913   Theatre: Broadway
Musical   Broadway: 16

Composer: John Philip Sousa
Lyricist: Leonard Liebling
Librettist: Leonard Liebling
Producer: John Cort
Director: George Marion

Musical Director: Herbert Kerr

Songs: American Girl, The; Annabel; Bivouac, The; Cheer Up; Cleopatra's a Strawb'ry Blonde; Crystal Lute, The; Dinner Pail, The; From Maine to Oregon; I Can't Get 'Em Up; Matrimonial Mart, The; Most Omniscient Maid; My Love Is a Blower; Nevermore; Sweetheart; This Is My Busy Day; We Chant a Song of Labor; When You Change Your Name to Mine; With Pleasure

Cast: Louise Gunning; John Park; John G. Sparks

Notes: Features songs from THE GLASS BLOWERS also.

119 • AMERICAN PASSION
OPENED: 07/10/1983   Theatre: Joyce
Musical   Off-Broadway: 1

Composer: Willie Fong Young
Lyricist: Fred Burch; Willie Fong Young
Librettist: Fred Burch
Producer: Stuart Ostrow
Director: Patricia Birch

Choreographer: Patricia Birch; **Costumes:** William Ivey Long; **Dance Arranger:** Timothy Graphenreed; **Lighting Designer:** Richard Winkler; **Musical Director:** Timothy Graphenreed; **Orchestrations:** Timothy Graphenreed; **Set Design:** Heidi Landesman; **Vocal Arranger:** Timothy Graphenreed

Songs: Air Guitar; Anticipation; Backstage Girls; Balcony of the Faithful; Baseball Cards; Concert Tonight; Hi; I Light a Light; I Like His Ass;

I Think I Like His Eyes; In the Hallway; Limo to the Plaza; Loud Enough; One of Us Lucky Listeners Out Here; Shirts; There Ain't No Virgins in Queens; Tickets; We'll Sleep with the Radio On

Cast: Anne Marie Bobby; Erica Gimpel; Todd Graff; Lisa Ann Grant; Don Kehr; Liza Lauber; William Morrison; Martha Plimpton; Rosko; Sam Slovick

120 • AMERICAN SONG

Notes: *See WOODY GUTHRIE'S AMERICAN SONG.*

121 • AMERICAN WAY, THE

OPENED: 01/21/1939   Theatre: Center
Play   Broadway: 164

Author: Moss Hart; George S. Kaufman
Producer: Max Gordon; Sam Harris

Costumes: Irene Sharaff; **Lighting Designer:** Hassard Short; **Musical Director:** Oscar Levant; **Set Design:** Donald Oenslager

Songs: Lemon in the Garden of Love, A [1] (C: Richard Carle; L: M.E. Rourke)

Cast: Florence Eldridge; Fredric March; McKay Morris; Ruth Weston

Notes: [1] Also in THE SPRING CHICKEN.

122 • AMERICAN WIDOW, AN

Notes: *See BETSY (1911).*

123 • AMERICANA (1926)

OPENED: 07/26/1926   Theatre: Belmont
Revue   Broadway: 224

Lyricist: J.P. McEvoy
Librettist: J.P. McEvoy
Producer: Richard Herndon
Director: Allan Dinehart

Choreographer: Larry Ceballos; **Musical Director:** Gene Salzer; **Orchestrations:** Hans Spialek; **Set Design:** John Held Jr.

Songs: American Opera in Three Acts: Cavalier Americana, An [1] (C: Henry Souvaine);

American Revue Girls (C: Con Conrad); Blowing the Blues Away (C: Philip Charig; L: Ira Gershwin); Chiropractic Papa [1] (C: Con Conrad); Dreaming (C: Con Conrad; Henry Souvaine); For My Sweetheart [1] (C: Walter Donaldson; L: Gus Kahn); Just Lovin' (C: Henry Souvaine); Kosher Kleagle [2] (C: Philip Charig); My Love Works in a Greenhouse [1] (C: William F. Kirs; L: C.T.A.); Nobody Wants Me [2] (C: Henry Souvaine; L: Morrie Ryskind; Joe Young); Promise in Your Eyes [1] (C: James F. Hanley; L: B.G. DeSylva); Riverside Bus (C: Con Conrad); Scrubwoman's Ballet (inst.) (C: Henry Souvaine); Sunny Disposish (C: Philip Charig; L: Ira Gershwin); Swanee River Melody [3] (C: Charles Weinberg; L: Al Wilson); Tabloid Papers (C: Con Conrad); Thanks Awful (C: Sam M. Lewis; L: Joe Young); That Lost Barbershop Chord (C: George Gershwin; L: Ira Gershwin); Why Do Ya Roll Those Eyes? (C: Philip Charig; L: Morrie Ryskind); Without You [1] (C: Con Conrad; L: Benny Davis)

Cast: Roy Atwell; Lew Brice; Charles Butterworth; Betty Compton; Helen Morgan

Notes: [1] Out Long Branch, New Jersey 7/12/26. [2] Added after opening. [3] Added for tour.

124 • AMERICANA (1928)

OPENED: 10/30/1928   Theatre: Lew Fields
Revue   Broadway: 12

Composer: Roger Wolfe Kahn
Lyricist: Irving Caesar
Director: Allan Dinehart

Choreographer: Larry Ceballos; **Costumes:** John Held Jr.; **Musical Director:** Gene Salzer; **Orchestrations:** Hans Spialek; **Set Design:** John Held Jr.

Songs: American Revue Girls (C: Con Conrad; L: J.P. McEvoy); Ameri-can-can, The; He's Mine; Hot Pants; If I Love Again (C: Ben Oakland; L: John Murray); Jazz City (C: Henry Souvaine; L: J.P. McEvoy); Life As a Twosome [1] (C: Joseph Meyer); My Kinda Love (C: Louis Alter; L: Jo Trent); No Place Like Home; Sunny Disposish; Wild Oat Joe; Young Black Joe

Cast: Roy Atwell; Lew Brice

Notes: May have originally titled ONE WAY TO PARADISE. [1] Also in HERE'S HOWE (1928).

125 • AMERICANA (1932)

OPENED: 10/05/1932   Theatre: Shubert
Revue   Broadway: 77

Lyricist: E.Y. Harburg
Librettist: J.P. McEvoy
Producer: Lee Shubert
Director: Harold Johnsrud

Choreographer: John Boyle; Charles Weidman;
  Costumes: Constance Ripley; **Lighting
  Designer:** Albert Johnson; **Musical Director:**
  Jay Gorney; **Orchestrations:** Conrad Salinger;
  Set Design: Albert Johnson

Songs: Amour a la Militaire (inst.) (C: Bernard
  Herrmann); Brother Can You Spare a Dime?
  (C: Jay Gorney); Five Minutes of Spring [1] (C: Jay
  Gorney); Get That Sun Into You (C: Richard
  Myers); Let Me Match My Private Life with Yours
  (C: Vernon Duke); Ringside Madison Square
  Garden (inst.) (C: Winthrop Sargent); Satan's Li'l
  Lamb (C: Harold Arlen; L: E.Y. Harburg; Johnny
  Mercer); Uncle Sam Needs a "Man Who Can Take
  It" [2] (C: Unknown); Whistling for a Kiss
  (C: Richard Myers; L: E.Y. Harburg; Johnny
  Mercer); Would'ja for a Big Red Apple? (C: Henry
  Souvaine; L: Johnny Mercer); You're Not Pretty
  but You're Mine (C: Burton Lane)

Cast: Don Barclay; Albert Carroll; Peggy Cartwright;
  Lillian Fitzgerald; George Givot; Sue Hastings'
  Marionettes; Doris Humphrey Group; Letitia Ide;
  Jose Limon; Ralph Locke; Francetta Malloy; Lloyd
  Nolan; Alfred Rode; Gordon Smith; George
  Tapps; Tzigane Orchestra; Rex Weber

Notes: Also titled NEW AMERICANA. [1] Also in
  score of ACCIDENTALLY YOURS. [2]
  ASCAP/Library of Congress only.

126 • AMONG THE GIRLS

OPENED: 11/1919
Musical   Closed out of town

Composer: Raymond Hubbell
Lyricist: Henry Blossom; Glen MacDonough
Librettist: Henry Blossom; Roi Cooper Megrue
Producer: Selwyn and Co.
Director: R.H. Burnside; Percival Knight

Source: SEVEN CHANCES (Play: Roi Cooper
  Megrue); **Musical Director:** Victor Baravalle;
  Orchestrations: Frank Saddler

Songs: Camouflage Clutch, The; Come On, Jim
  (L: Henry Blossom); I Want to Go Back to the War
  (L: Henry Blossom; Percival Knight); I'm a
  Human Pousse Cafe (Cocktail Song) (L: Harry B.
  Smith); I'm Married, I'm Single, I'm Divorced, I'm
  in Love; In Dreams Alone; King Solomon; Ladies'
  Day; M-O-N-E-Y (L: Henry Blossom); Night Has
  a Thousand Eyes, The; Overseas Girl; Sayonara
  (L: Henry Blossom; George V. Hobart); Tell Me
  Tonight (L: Henry Blossom); We Head for Little
  Old New York Tomorrow (L: Glen MacDonough);
  Your Cigarette (L: Glen MacDonough)

Cast: Percival Knight

127 • AMOROUS FLEA, THE

OPENED: 02/17/1964   Theatre: East 78th St.
    Playhouse
Musical   Off-Broadway: 32

Composer: Bruce Montgomery
Lyricist: Bruce Montgomery
Librettist: Jerry Devine
Producer: Jerry Devine; Charles Hollerith Jr.
Director: Jack Sydow

Source: SCHOOL FOR WIVES, THE (Play:
  Moliere); **Costumes:** Donald Brooks; **Lighting
  Designer:** Jane Reisman; **Musical Director:** Ted
  Simons; **Orchestrations:** Lou Busch; **Set Design:**
  Bill Hargate

Songs: All About He; All About Him; All About
  Me; Amorous Flea, The; Closeness Begets
  Closeness; Dialogue on Dalliance; It's a Stretchy
  Day; Learning Love; Lessons on Life; Man Is a
  Man's Best Friend; March of the Vigilant Vassals;
  Other Side of the Wall; There Goes a Mad Old
  Man; Too Soon the Day [1]; When Time Takes
  Your Hand

Cast: Imelda De Martin; Jack Fletcher; Lew Parker;
  Philip Proctor; Ted Tiller

Notes: [1] Added to 1974 revival.

128 • . . . AND IN THIS CORNER

OPENED: 1964
Revue   Nightclub: 210

Composer: Rod Warren
Lyricist: Rod Warren
Librettist: Treva Silverman

Producer: Michael McWhinney; Rod Warren
Director: Jonathan Lucas

Choreographer: Jonathan Lucas; **Costumes:** Baba;
Musical Director: Dan Strickland

Songs: Ads Infinitum (L: Michael McWhinney);
. . . And In This Corner; Angel Recordings Is
Offering a Job (C/L: Unknown); Dear Abbey
(C: Jay Foote; L: Allison Roulston); Dying
Schwann, The; Elephant Joke (L: Michael
McWhinney); Happiness Is . . .; Judy Garland
National Anthem, The (C: Jerry Powell;
L: Michael McWhinney); Love's Labor's Lost [2]
(C: Jerry Powell; L: Michael McWhinney);
Monsignor Prom, The (C/L: Unknown); Mr.
Wanamaker's Home (L: Michael McWhinney;
Rod Warren); Our New Best Friends (C: Jerry
Powell; L: Michael McWhinney); Prince Edward
Skool (C: Jerry Powell; L: Michael McWhinney);
Subways Are for Skiing (L: Michael McWhinney);
Tokyo, Mon Amour; Tristan and Isolated; When
I Was Learning to Read; Where the Bulls Are
(C: Jay Foote; L: Allison Roulston)

Cast: Bill Brown; Virgil Curry; Marian Mercer;
Carol Morley

Notes: [1] No program available. [2] Also in
BELOW THE BELT.

129 • AND SO TO BED

OPENED: 10/17/1951   Theatre: New
Musical   London: 323

Composer: Vivian Ellis
Lyricist: Vivian Ellis
Librettist: J.B. Fagan
Producer: Jack de Leon
Director: Wendy Toye

Choreographer: Wendy Toye; **Costumes:** Elizabeth
Agombar; **Musical Director:** Mantovani; **Set
Design:** Stanley Moore

Songs: Amo, Amas [3]; And So to Bed; Ayre and
Fa-La; Bartholomew Fair; Beauty Retire [1];
Catch; Chine of Beef, A; Gaze Not on Swans [2];
Love Me Little, Love Me Long; Mopperty Mo;
Rigauden; Sarabande

Cast: Stella Chapman; Leslie Henson; Jesse Royce
Landis; Keith Michell; Dennis Quilley

Notes: [1] Lyrics based on poetry by William
Davaneut. [2] Lyrics based on poetry by Henry
Noel. [3] Lyrics based on poetry by John O'Keefe.

130 • AND THE VILLAIN STILL PURSUED HER

OPENED: 05/10/1912
Musical

Composer: Cole Porter
Lyricist: Cole Porter
Librettist: T. Gaillard Thomas II
Producer: Yale Univ. Dramatic Assn.
Director: Cole Porter; T. Gaillard Thomas II

Songs: Anytime; Barcelona; Charity; Come to
Bohemia; Dancing; Dear Doctor; Fare Thee Well;
I'm the Villain; Leaders of Society; Llewellyn;
Lovely Heroine, The; Queens of Terpsichore;
Silver Moon; Strolling; Submarine; That Zip
Cornwall Cooch; Twilight; We Are the Chorus
of the Show

Cast: Irving Beebe; Monty Woolley

Notes: Two shows: New Haven Lawn Club and
5/10/12 at Yale Club of NYC. New Haven
performances on 4/24/12.

131 • AND THE WORLD GOES 'ROUND

OPENED: 03/18/1991   Theatre: Westside
Revue   Off-Broadway: 408

Composer: John Kander
Lyricist: Fred Ebb
Producer: R. Tyler Gatchell Jr.; Gene R. Korf;
Peter Neufeld; Patrick J. Patek
Director: Scott Ellis

Choreographer: Susan Stroman; **Costumes:**
Lindsay W. Davis; **Dance Arranger:** David Loud;
Lighting Designer: Phil Monat; **Musical
Director:** David Loud; **Orchestrations:** David
Krane; **Set Design:** Bill Hoffman

Songs: All That Jazz [7]; And the World Goes
'Round [1]; Arthur in the Afternoon [5]; Cabaret
[12]; Class [7]; Coffee in a Cardboard Cup [2];
Colored Lights [4]; Grass Is Always Greener, The
[6]; Happy Time, The [3]; How Lucky Can You
Get [8]; I Don't Remember You [3]; Isn't This
Better? [8]; Kiss of the Spider Woman [9]; Marry

Me [4]; Maybe This Time [13]; Me and My Baby [7]; Money, Money [13]; Mr. Cellophane [7]; My Coloring Book; Only Love [10]; Pain [14]; Quiet Thing [11]; Ring Them Bells [15]; Rink, The [4]; Sara Lee [16]; Sometimes a Day Goes By [6]; There Goes the Ball Game [1]; We Can Make It [4]; Yes [2]

Cast: Robert Cuccioli; Karen Mason; Brenda Pressley; Jim Walton; Karen Ziemba

Notes: No original songs in this revue based on the works of Kander and Ebb. [1] From film NEW YORK, NEW YORK. [2] From show 70, GIRLS, 70. [3] From show THE HAPPY TIME. [4] From show THE RINK. [5] From show THE ACT. [6] From show WOMAN OF THE YEAR. [7] From show CHICAGO. [8] From film FUNNY LADY. [9] From show KISS OF THE SPIDER WOMAN. [10] From show ZORBA. [11] From show FLORA, THE RED MENACE. [12] From show CABARET. [13] From film CABARET. [14] Written for Chita Rivera's nightclub act. [15] From TV special LIZA WITH A Z. [16] Written for Kaye Ballard's nightclub act.

132 • AND VERY NICE TOO

OPENED: 05/09/1922
Musical   Closed out of town

Composer: Percy Wenrich
Lyricist: Raymond W. Peck
Librettist: Raymond W. Peck
Director: Walter Lawrence

Source: WOMAN HATERS, THE (Play: Carl Lindsay; Leo Stein); **Arrangements:** David Bennett; **Musical Director:** Clarence West

Songs: And Very Nice Too; Baby; Dance with Me; Hello, Hello; Letter Song, The; Love Will Do the Rest; Oh, John; Opening Chorus; Polka Duet; Rustic Anna; Wedding Anvils; When I Hear a Syncopated Strain; When You Come Back to Me; When Your Sweet Lips Meet Mine; Woman Always Pays, The

Cast: Alexander Clark; Danny Dare; Marguerite Denys; Francis Kennedy; Walter Lawrence; Norma Leslie; John B. Park; May Pollard; Amelia Stone

Notes: His Majesty's Theatre, Montreal.

133 • ANDRE CHARLOT REVUE OF 1924

OPENED: 01/09/1924   Theatre: Times Square
Revue   Broadway: 298

Librettist: Norah Blaney; Bert Lee; Dion Titheridge; R.P. Weston
Producer: Arch Selwyn; Edgar Selwyn
Director: Andre Charlot

Choreographer: David Bennett; **Costumes:** G.K. Benda; Guy De Gerald; **Musical Director:** Philip Braham; **Set Design:** Guy De Gerald; Marc-Henri

Songs: Cigarette Land (C: Bert Lee; L: R.P. Weston); How D'You Do [1] (C: Philip Braham; L: Eric Blore; Ronald Jeans); I Don't Know (C: Philip Braham; L: Ronald Jeans); I Might (C: Philip Braham; L: Ronald Jeans); It's a Far Far Better Thing (C: Philip Braham; L: Douglas Furber); Limehouse Blues (C: Philip Braham; L: Douglas Furber); March with Me [2] (C: Ivor Novello; L: Douglas Furber); Night May Have Its Sadness (C: Ivor Novello; L: Collie Knox); Parisian Pierrot (C/L: Noel Coward); Specially for You [1] (C/L: Noel Coward); There Are Times (C: Philip Braham; L: Ronald Jeans); There's Life in the Old Girl Yet (C/L: Noel Coward); You Were Meant for Me [2] (C: Eubie Blake; L: Noble Sissle)

Cast: Marjorie Brooks; Jack Buchanan; Constance Carpenter; Douglas Furber; Robert Hobbs; Gertrude Lawrence; Fred Leslie; Beatrice Lillie; Jessie Matthews; Herbert Mundin

Notes: [1] Not in program. [2] Also used in LONDON CALLING and CHARLOT REVUE OF 1926.

134 • ANDROCLES AND THE LION

OPENED: 11/15/1967   Theatre: NBC
TV Musical

Composer: Richard Rodgers
Lyricist: Richard Rodgers
Librettist: Peter Stone
Producer: Marc Merson
Director: Joe Layton

Source: ANDROCLES AND THE LION (Play: Bernard Shaw); **Dance Arranger:** David Baker;

Musical Director: Jay Blackton; **Orchestrations:** Robert Russell Bennett

Songs: Arena Pantomime, The (inst.); Don't Be Afraid of an Animal; Emperor's Thumb, The; Fine Young Man, A; Follow in Our Footsteps; Gladiators' Ballet; No More Waiting; Strangers; Strength Is My Weakness; Velvet Paws

Cast: Ed Ames; Brian Bedford; Noel Coward; John Cullum; Clifford David; Bill Hickey; Geoffrey Holder; Kurt Kasznar; George Mathews; William Redfield; George Reeder; Patricia Routledge; Bill Starr; Inga Swenson; Norman Wisdom

Notes: An original musical for television.

135 • ANGEL

OPENED: 05/10/1978   Theatre: Minskoff
Musical   Broadway: 5

Composer: Gary Geld
Lyricist: Peter Udell
Librettist: Ketti Frings; Peter Udell
Producer: Ellen Madison; Philip Rose
Director: Philip Rose

Source: LOOK HOMEWARD ANGEL (Play: Ketti Frings); **Source:** LOOK HOMEWARD, ANGEL (Novel: Thomas Wolfe); **Choreographer:** Robert Tucker; **Costumes:** Pearl Somner; **Dance Arranger:** William Cox; **Lighting Designer:** John Gleason; **Musical Director:** William Cox; **Orchestrations:** Don Walker; **Set Design:** Ming Cho Lee

Songs: All the Comforts of Home; Angel Theme; Astoria Gloria; Dime Ain't Worth a Nickle, A; Drifting; Fatty; Feelin' Loved; Fingers and Toes; Gant's Waltz; How Do You Say Goodbye; I Can't Believe It's You; I Got a Dream to Sleep On; If Ever I Loved Him; Like the Eagles Fly; Make a Little Sunshine; Railbird; Tomorrow I'm Gonna Be Old

Cast: Patti Allison; Grace Carney; Fred Gwynne; Joel Higgens; Justine Johnston; Leslie Ann Ray; Don Scardino; Frances Sternhagen

Notes: Titled LOOK HOMEWARD ANGEL originally, but title changed out of town.

136 • ANGEL FACE

OPENED: 12/29/1919   Theatre: Knickerbocker
Musical   Broadway: 57

Composer: Victor Herbert
Lyricist: Robert B. Smith
Librettist: Harry B. Smith; Robert B. Smith
Producer: George W. Lederer
Director: George W. Lederer

Choreographer: Julian Alfred; **Costumes:** O'Kane Conwell; **Lighting Designer:** Tony Greshoff; **Musical Director:** Harold Vicars; **Set Design:** Herbert Moore

Songs: Angel Face [2]; Call It a Day; Dance Excentrique (inst.) [2]; Elixir Motive (inst.) [2]; Everybody's Crazy Half of the Time [1]; Finale Act I; Finale Act II; Finale Act III; How Do You Get That Way?; I Don't Want to Go Home; I Might Be Your Once-in-a-While; If You Can Love Like You Can Dance; Lullaby (Bye Bye Baby); Man Should Have a Double When He's Single, A; Melodrama (inst.) [2]; My Idea of Something to Go Home To; One Step (inst.) [2]; Opening Chorus Act III [2]; Say When; Someone Like You; Sow Your Wild Oats Early; Those Since-I-Met-You Days; Tip Your Hat to Hattie; Why Do They Make Them So Beautiful (L: Melville Alexander; Robert B. Smith)

Cast: Tyler Brooks; Jack Donahue; Howard Johnson; John E. Young; Marguerite Zender

Notes: [1] Sometimes referred to as "Everybody's Crazy Part of the Time." [2] Sheet music only.

137 • ANGEL IN THE WINGS

OPENED: 12/11/1947   Theatre: Coronet
Revue   Broadway: 308

Composer: Carl Sigman
Lyricist: Bob Hilliard
Librettist: Paul Hartman; Hank Ladd; Ted Luce
Producer: Marjorie Ewing; Sherman Ewing
Director: John Kennedy

Choreographer: Edward Noll; **Costumes:** Julia Sze; **Lighting Designer:** Donald Oenslager; **Musical Director:** Phil Ingalls; **Orchestrations:** Fred Barovick; David Mann; **Set Design:** Donald Oenslager

Songs: Big Brass Band from Brazil; Breezy; Civilization (Bongo, Bongo, Bongo); Funny Papers [1]; Holler Blue Murder; If It Were Easy to Do; Long Green Blues; Tambourine; Thousand Islands Song, The; Wanderlust [1]

Cast: Grace Hartman; Paul Hartman; Elaine Stritch

Notes: [1] Out Philadelphia.

138 • ANGELA
OPENED: 12/03/1928   Theatre: Ambassador
Musical   Broadway: 40

Composer: Alberta Nichols
Lyricist: Mann Holiner
Librettist: Fanny Todd Mitchell
Producer: Messrs. Shubert
Director: George Marion

Source: ROYAL FAMILY, A (Play: Capt. Robert Marshall); **Choreographer:** Chester Dale; **Musical Director:** Joseph Benavente; **Orchestrations:** Emil Gerstenberger; **Set Design:** Watson Barratt

Songs: Baron, the Duchess, and the Count, The; Bearing Silver Platters; Bundle of Love; Don't Forget Your Etiquette; I Can't Believe It's True, Love Is Like That; Maybe So; Oui-Oui!!; Regal Romp, The; Scene Dansant; Tally-Ho; Weaker Sex, The

Cast: Florenz Ames; Eric Blore; Roy Hoyer; Gattison Jones; Jeanette MacDonald; Alison Skipworth; Pianist: Adam Carroll; Ralph Rainger

139 • ANGELINA
OPENED: 10/25/1989
Musical

Composer: Barry Kleinbort
Lyricist: Barry Kleinbort
Librettist: Barry Kleinbort
Director: David Holdgrive

Source: THAT SUMMER — THAT FALL (Play: Frank Gilroy); **Choreographer:** David Holdgrive; **Costumes:** Edmund Felix; **Lighting Designer:** Tom Sturge; **Musical Director:** Caryl Ginsburg Gershman; **Orchestrations:** Larry Moore; **Set Design:** James Wolk

Songs: Angelina; Bedroom Scene; Cat and Mouse; Coffee on the Stove; Do a Little Favor; End of Summer; Felicita; Fortunate Woman; Gelato Song; Grazie Dio; He Would Smile; Heat, The; I Can't Explain (1); I Can't Explain (2); I'll Never Want for More; Just Like That; Lezione; My Son; New York Women; Same, The; Summer Is Over, The; To Be Wanted; Victor's Announcement; Vidi Na Croce; Voices; What Would You Say?; When Summer Goes

Cast: Denise Ashlynd; Michael Curran; Robert Montano; Loria Parker; Michael G. Rotondi; Gayton Scott; David Serko; Alfred Toigo

Notes: Presented at the Cohoes Music Hall, Cohoes, N.Y.

140 • ANGRY HOUSEWIVES
OPENED: 09/07/1986   Theatre: Minetta Lane
Musical   Off-Broadway: 137

Composer: Chad Henry
Lyricist: Chad Henry
Librettist: A.M. Collins
Producer: Alice Field; M Square Productions; Mitchell Maxwell; Marvin R. Meit; Alan J. Schuster
Director: Mitchell Maxwell

Choreographer: Wayne Cilento; **Costumes:** Martha Hally; **Lighting Designer:** Allen Lee Hughes; **Musical Director:** Jonny Bowden; **Orchestrations:** Dave Brown; **Set Design:** David Jenkins

Songs: Betsy Moberly; Cold Cruel Dark; Eat Your @*!#&*!@#! Cornflakes; First Kid on the Block; Generic Woman; It's Gonna Be Fun; Love-O-Meter; Not at Home; Stalling for Time; Think Positive; Trouble with Me

Cast: Carolyn Casanave; Michael Lembeck; Vicki Lewis; Michael Manasseri; Lorna Patterson; Camille Saviola; Lee Wilkof; Nicholas Wyman

141 • ANHEUSER PUSH, THE
OPENED: 1904
Musical

Composer: Lee Johnson
Lyricist: Will Carleton
Librettist: Will Carleton

Songs: Flow'r of Kildaire, The; Kitty Malone; Mam'selle Frappe; Mama's China Twins; Marguerite; Moana, I Love You So; My Gondolier Queen Good Night; Old Rhineland, The; Toreador

Notes: Sheet music only.

142 • ANIMAL CRACKERS

OPENED: 10/23/1928   Theatre: 44th Street
Musical   Broadway: 213

Composer: Harry Ruby
Lyricist: Bert Kalmar
Librettist: George S. Kaufman; Morrie Ryskind
Producer: Sam H. Harris
Director: Oscar Eagle

Choreographer: Russell Markert; **Costumes:** Mabel Johnston; **Lighting Designer:** Otto F. Diehl; **Musical Director:** Anton Heindl; **Set Design:** Raymond Sovey

Songs: Cool Off; Go Places and Do Things; Hooray for Captain Spaulding!; Long Island Low Down, The; News; Opening Chorus; Waiting [1]; Watching the Clouds Roll By; We're Three of the Four Musketeers; When Things Are Bright and Rosy; Who's Been List'ning to My Heart?

Cast: Margaret Dumont; Chico Marx; Groucho Marx; Harpo Marx; Zeppo Marx

Notes: Kalmar and Ruby were masters of the humorous song. In fact, unlike many songwritesr they excelled at the specialty number while with only a few exceptions their ballads were undistinguished. "Hooray for Captain Spaulding" served as Groucho Marx's signature tune throughout his long career. [1] ASCAP/Library of Congress only.

143 • ANIMAL FAIR

OPENED: 04/18/1990
Musical   Closed out of town

Composer: Clark Gesner
Lyricist: Clark Gesner
Librettist: Clark Gesner
Director: Steve Stettler

Choreographer: Virginia Freeman; **Costumes:** Janet S. Morris; **Lighting Designer:** Charles MacLeod; **Musical Director:** Henry Aronson; **Orchestrations:** Michael Starobin; **Set Design:** Richard L. Hay

Songs: Bears in the Mud; Bird in a Cage, A; Cubs; Dawn Chorus; Discussions; Elephant Walk, He's Gone; Heron, The; I Am Me; I Went to the Animal Fair (C/L: Traditional); Make It Nice; Migration; Mouse and the Trap, The; Not Right; Pack My Bag; Polar Bear in a Zoo; There's Another Seed; Too Fast; Vase of Flowers, A; Waterhole, The

Cast: Aron Accurso; P.J. Benjamin; Michael Kelly Boone; Louisa Flaningam

Notes: Program of the Denver Center Theatre Company

144 • ANITA THE SINGING GIRL

Musical   Closed out of town

Composer: Harold Orlob

Notes: No other information available.

145 • ANKLES AWEIGH

OPENED: 04/18/1955   Theatre: Mark Hellinger
Musical   Broadway: 176

Composer: Sammy Fain
Lyricist: Dan Shapiro
Librettist: Guy Bolton
Producer: Anthony Brady Farrell; Fred F. Finklehoffe; Reginald Hammerstein; Howard Hoyt
Director: Fred F. Finklehoffe; Edward Clarke Lilley

Choreographer: Tony Charmoli; **Costumes:** Miles White; **Dance Arranger:** Roger Adams; Donald Pippin; **Lighting Designer:** George Jenkins; **Musical Director:** Salvatore Dell'Isola; **Orchestrations:** Don Walker; **Set Design:** George Jenkins; **Vocal Arranger:** Don Walker

Songs: Code, The; Dance Finale [1]; Eleven O'Clock Song; Headin' for the Bottom; Here's to Dear Old Us; His and Hers; Honeymoon; Italy; Kiss Me and Kill Me with Love; La Festa; Nothing at All [1]; Nothing Can Replace a Man; Old Fashioned Mothers; Ready Cash; Skip the Build-Up; Villain Always Gets It, The; Walk Like a Sailor

Cast: Thelma Carpenter; Mark Dawson; Gabriel Dell; Betty George; Betty Kean; Jane Kean; Lew Parker

Notes: [1] ASCAP/Library of Congress only.

146 • ANN REINKING . . . MUSIC MOVES ME

OPENED: 12/23/1984   Theatre: Joyce
Revue   Off-Broadway: 16

Additional Lyrics: Ellen Fitzhugh
Producer: Lee Gross Associates
Director: Alan Johnson

Choreographer: Alan Johnson; Costumes: Albert Wolsky; Dance Arranger: Ronald Melrose; Lighting Designer: Ken Billington; Musical Director: Ronald Melrose; Orchestrations: Joseph Gianono; Michael Gibson; Harold Wheeler; Set Design: Thomas Lynch; Vocal Arranger: Larry Grossman

Songs: Another Mr. Right (C: Jonathan Sheffer; L: David Zippel); Anything Goes (C/L: Cole Porter); Ballin' the Jack (C/L: Jim Burris; Chris Smith); Higher and Higher (C/L: Gary Jackson; Raynard Miner; Carl Smith); Hit Me with a Hot Note (C: Duke Ellington; L: Don George); I Can't Turn You Loose (C/L: Otis Redding); If Love Were All (C/L: Noel Coward); Isn't It Romantic (C: Richard Rodgers; L: Lorenz Hart); Just Once (C: Barry Manilow; L: Cynthia Weil); Nowhere to Run (C/L: Lamont Dozier; Brian Holland; Eddie Holland); Oh Baby, Won't You Please Come Home (C: Clarence Williams; L: Charles Warfield); Rescue Me (C/L: Raynard Miner; Carl Smith); Satin Doll (C: Duke Ellington; Billy Strayhorn; L: Johnny Mercer); Sing, Sing, Sing (C: Louis Prima); Stompin' at the Savoy (C: Benny Goodman; Edgar Sampson; Chick Webb; L: Andy Razaf); Tea for Two (C: Vincent Youmans; L: Irving Caesar); Unchained Melody (C: Alex North; L: Hy Zaret); Why Not? (Manhattan Carnival) (C/L: Michael Camilo; Julie Eigenberg; Hilary Koski); Wild Women (C/L: Ida Cox); You and Me (C: Peter Allen; L: Carole Bayer Sager)

Cast: Gary Chryst; Reed Jones; Michael Kubala; Rob Marshall; Sara Miles; Ann Reinking; Christina Saffran

147 • ANNA KARENINA

OPENED: 05/26/1992   Theatre: Circle in the Square
Musical   Broadway: 46

Composer: David Levine
Lyricist: Peter Kellogg
Librettist: Peter Kellogg
Producer: Circle in the Square
Director: Theodore Mann

Source: ANNA KARENINA (Novel: Leo Tolstoy); Choreographer: Patricia Birch; Costumes: Carrie Robbins; Dance Arranger: Nicholas Archer; Lighting Designer: Mary Jo Dondlinger; Musical Director: Nicholas Archer; Orchestrations: Peter Matz; Set Design: James Morgan

Songs: Everything's Fine; How Awful; How Many Men?; I'm Lost; In a Room; Karenin's List; Lowlands; Mazurka; Nothing Has Changed; On a Train; Only at Night; Peasants' Idyll; Rumors; That Will Serve Her Right; There's More to Life Than Love; This Can't Go On; Waiting for You; We Were Dancing; Would You?

Cast: Gabriel Barre; Ann Crumb; John Cunningham; Gregg Edelman; Melissa Errico; Jerry Lanning; Scott Wentworth

148 • ANNE OF GREEN GABLES

OPENED: 12/21/1971   Theatre: City Center
Musical   Off-Broadway: 16

Composer: Norman Campbell
Lyricist: Norman Campbell; Donald Harron
Librettist: Donald Harron
Producer: Canadian National Music Theatre; City Center, The
Director: Alan Lund

Source: ANNE OF GREEN GABLES (Novel: I.M. Montgomery); Choreographer: Alan Lund; Costumes: Marie Day; Lighting Designer: Ronald Montgomery; Musical Director: John Fenwick; Orchestrations: John Fenwick; Set Design: Murray Laufer

Songs: Anne of Green Gables; Avonlea, We Love You; Back to School Ballet; Did You Hear?; Facts, The; Gee, I'm Glad I'm No One Else but Me; General Store; Great Workers for the Cause; Humble Pie; Ice Cream; If It Hadn't Been for Me; I'll Show Him; Kindred Spirits; Learn Everything; Nature Hunt Ballet; Oh, Mrs. Lynde!; Pageant

Song; Picnic, The; Prince Edward Island [1]; We Clearly Requested; When I Say My Say; Where Did the Summer Go To?; Where Is Matthew Going? [2]; Where'd Marilla Come From? [2]; Wondrin'; Words, The

Cast: Grace Finley; Jeff Hyslop; Maude Whitmore

Notes: [1] Cut. [2] Same music.

149 • ANNETTE KELLERMAN'S BIG SHOW

OPENED: 1918
Revue

Director: Annette Kellerman

Musical Director: Carl C. Gray

Songs: Let Me Teach You How to Swim (C/L: Bert Grant); Over the Sea, Boys (C/L: Irving Berlin); Peacock Dance (inst.) (C: Carl C. Gray); Rose of Roses, A (C/L: Bert Grant); Walk Into My Heart (C/L: Ted Snyder)

Cast: Estelle House; Annette Kellerman; Kellerman Girls, The; Edmund Makalif

Notes: A vaudeville act. Information from Philadelphia program.

150 • ANNIE

OPENED: 04/21/1977   Theatre: Alvin
Musical   Broadway: 2377

Composer: Charles Strouse
Lyricist: Martin Charnin
Librettist: Thomas Meehan
Producer: Lewis Allen; Stephen R. Friedman; Irwin Meyer; Mike Nichols
Director: Martin Charnin

Source: LITTLE ORPHAN ANNIE (Comic Strip: Harold Gray); **Choreographer:** Peter Gennaro; **Costumes:** Theoni V. Aldredge; **Dance Arranger:** Peter Howard; **Lighting Designer:** Judy Rasmuson; **Musical Director:** Peter Howard; **Orchestrations:** Philip J. Lang; **Set Design:** David Mitchell

Songs: Annie; Apples [1]; Easy Street; He Doesn't Know [1]; I Don't Need Anything but You; I Think I'm Gonna Like It Here; It's Christmas [4]; It's the Hard-Knock Life; I've Never Been So Happy [1]; Just Wait [1]; Little Girls; Maybe; N.Y.C.; New Deal for Christmas, A; Prologue [1]; Something Was Missing [2]; That's Our Annie [1]; That's the Way It Goes [1]; Tomorrow; We Got Annie [3]; We'd Like to Thank You; You Won't Be an Orphan for Long; You're Never Fully Dressed Without a Smile

Cast: Laurie Beechman; Danielle Brisebois; Shelley Bruce; Sandy Faison; Robert Fitch; Dorothy Loudon; Andrea McArdle; Reid Shelton; Raymond Thorne

Notes: [1] Out prior to Broadway. [2] Music from "You Rat You" from the film THE NIGHT THEY RAIDED MINSKY'S. [3] Out prior to Broadway. Added to film version. [4] ASCAP/Library of Congress only.

151 • ANNIE 2

Notes: *See ANNIE TWO: MISS HANNIGAN'S REVENGE.*

152 • ANNIE DEAR

OPENED: 11/04/1924   Theatre: Times Square
Musical   Broadway: 103

Composer: Sigmund Romberg
Lyricist: Clifford Grey
Librettist: Clare Kummer
Producer: Florenz Ziegfeld
Director: Edward Royce

Costumes: Mme. Francis; **Musical Director:** Gus Salzer; **Set Design:** Karl Koeck

Songs: Annie (C/L: Clare Kummer); Bertie; Come to My Party [1] (C/L: Clare Kummer); Comedy Fantasie, A (C/L: Clare Kummer); Dance Eccentric (inst.); Etiquette (C/L: Clare Kummer); Finale; Gypsy Bride (C/L: Clare Kummer); Help, Help, Help (C/L: Clare Kummer); I Want to Be Loved [2] (C/L: Clare Kummer); In Love Again (C/L: Clare Kummer); Louisiana; Louwanna [3] (C: Sigmund Romberg; Jean Schwartz); Off to Wimblemere (C/L: Clare Kummer); One Man Is Like Another; Only Girl, The (L: Arthur Wimperis); Opening Chorus (C/L: Unknown); Radio Voices; Slither; Someone, Someday, Somewhere [4] (C: Rudolf Friml; L: Gene Buck); Twilly of Fifth Avenue; Whisper to Me; Wooing [4] (C/L: Clare Kummer)

Cast: Billie Burke; Marion Green; Ernest Truex; Bobby Watson; Jack Whiting

Notes: [1] Credited to Romberg in sheet music. [2] Credited to Romberg in his biography. Credit listed is that of the program. [3] Music credited to Clare Kummer in program. However, sheet music and ASCAP credit Romberg. [4] Sheet music only.

153 • ANNIE GET YOUR GUN

OPENED: 05/16/1946   Theatre: Imperial
Musical   Broadway: 1147

Composer: Irving Berlin
Lyricist: Irving Berlin
Librettist: Dorothy Fields; Herbert Fields
Producer: Oscar Hammerstein II; Richard Rodgers
Director: Joshua Logan

Choreographer: Helen Tamaris; **Costumes:** Lucinda Ballard; **Lighting Designer:** Jo Mielziner; **Musical Director:** Jay Blackton; **Orchestrations:** Robert Russell Bennett; Philip J. Lang; Ted Royal; **Set Design:** Jo Mielziner

Songs: Anything You Can Do; Ballyhoo; Colonel Buffalo Bill; Doin' What Comes Natur'lly; Girl That I Marry, The; I Got Lost in His Arms; I Got the Sun in the Morning; I'll Share It All with You; I'm a Bad, Bad Man; I'm an Indian Too; Moonshine Lullaby; My Defenses Are Down; Old Fashioned Wedding [1]; Take It in Your Stride [2]; There's No Business Like Show Business; They Say It's Wonderful; Who Do You Love, I Hope; Who Needs the Birds and Bees [3]; With Music [2]; You Can't Get a Man with a Gun

Cast: Harry Bellaver; Kenny Bowers; Kathleen Carnes; Ellen Hanley; Robert Lenn; Christina Lind; George Lipton; Marty May; Ethel Merman; Ray Middleton; Daniel Nagrin; Betty Anne Nyman; William O'Neal; Lea Penman; Lubov Roudenko

Notes: [1] Added to 1966 revival though written years before. [2] Cut prior to Broadway. [3] Written for 1966 revival but not used.

154 • ANNIE 2: MISS HANNIGAN'S REVENGE

OPENED: 01/04/1990
Musical   Closed out of town

Composer: Charles Strouse
Lyricist: Martin Charnin
Librettist: Thomas Meehan
Producer: Lewis Allen; Roger Berlind; Fifth Avenue Productions; Martin Heinfling
Director: Martin Charnin

Source: LITTLE ORPHAN ANNIE (Comic Strip: Harold Gray); **Choreographer:** Danny Daniels; **Costumes:** Theoni V. Aldredge; **Dance Arranger:** Peter Howard; **Lighting Designer:** Ken Billington; **Musical Director:** Peter Howard; **Orchestrations:** Michael Starobin; Larry Wilcox; **Set Design:** David Mitchell

Songs: All Dolled Up; All I've Got Is Me [1]; Annie 2; Beautiful; But You Go On; Changes; Coney Island; Cortez (C: Joseph Nohl; L: Dieter Dorfmunder); He Doesn't Know I'm Alive; He'll Be Here; How Could I Ever Say No; I Can Do No Wrong; I Could Get Used to This; If I Wasn't Around; Isn't This the Way to Go?; Just Let Me Get Away with This One; Lady of the House, The; Live a Long, Long Time; My Daddy; 1934; Perfect Kid, The; Rich Girls; Tenement Lullaby, The [1]; That's the Kind of Woman; When You Smile [1]; You Ain't Seen the Last of Me; You! You! You!; Younger Man, A [1]

Cast: Beau; Danielle Findley; Ronny Graham; Dorothy Loudon; Lauren Mitchell; Harve Presnell; Marian Seldes; Raymond Thorne

Notes: *See also* ANNIE WARBUCKS. [1] Later in ANNIE WARBUCKS.

155 • ANNIE WARBUCKS

OPENED: 08/09/1993   Theatre: Variety Arts
Musical   Off-Broadway: 200

Composer: Charles Strouse
Lyricist: Martin Charnin
Librettist: Thomas Meehan
Producer: Dennis Grimaldi; William P. Miller; Ben Sprecher
Director: Martin Charnin

Source: LITTLE ORPHAN ANNIE (Comic Strip: Harold Gray); **Choreographer:** Peter Gennaro; **Costumes:** Theoni V. Aldredge; **Lighting Designer:** Ken Billington; **Musical Director:** Keith Levenson; **Orchestrations:** Keith Levenson; **Set Design:** Ming Cho Lee

Songs: Above the Law; All Dolled Up; Annie Ain't Just Annie Anymore; Beginning [3]; But You Go On; Changes; I Always Knew; I Got Me [2]; It Would Have Been Wonderful; Leave It to the Girls; Love; Love Can Sometimes Make You Cry [3]; New Deal for Christmas, A [1]; Other Woman, The; Somebody's Gotta Do Somethin'; Tenement Lullaby, The [2]; That's the Kind of Woman; Wedding, Wedding; When You Smile [2]; Younger Man, A [2]

Cast: J.B. Adams; Cindy Lou; Harvey Evans; Joel Hatch; Marguerite Macintyre; Donna McKechnie; Kip Niven; Harve Presnell; Alene Robertson; Molly Scott; Raymond Thorne; Kathryn Zaremba

Notes: *See also ANNIE 2: MISS HANNIGAN'S REVENGE.* [1] From ANNIE. [2] From ANNIE 2: MISS HANNIGAN'S REVENGE. [3] ASCAP/Library of Congress only.

156 • ANNINA
Notes: *See MUSIC HATH CHARMS.*

157 • ANOTHER EVENING WITH HARRY STOONES
OPENED: 10/21/1961   Theatre: Gramercy Arts
Revue   Off-Broadway: 1

Composer: Jeff Harris
Lyricist: Jeff Harris
Librettist: Jeff Harris
Producer: Stenod Prods. Inc.
Director: G. Adam Jordan

Choreographer: Joe Milan; **Costumes:** Ruth Wagner; **Lighting Designer:** Robert E. Darling; **Musical Director:** Abba Bogin; **Orchestrations:** Abba Bogin; **Set Design:** Robert E. Darling; **Vocal Arranger:** Abba Bogin

Songs: Ballad of the Tree; Ballad to the International Business Machines Building; Ballet; Bang!; Betty Simpson; Butter Fingers; Carnival in Capri; Dancin' Free and Easy; Don't Laugh at Me; Dr. Rosalyn Green; Dream House; Indian Nuts; Invitation to the Basketball; Jersey; Love Is a Shovel [1]; Minnesota; Miss Greenwich Village; Miss Heinshlinger; Museum Piece (Naked Lady); Rage, The; Ragtime (inst.); Serena; Stephanie; Strangers on a Train; To Belong; Uh-Oh!; Upstairs at the Downstairs; Value;

Verrazano Narrows Bridge; Water on the Brain; Wrong Plan, The; You Won't Believe Me

Cast: Virgil Curry; Dom De Luise; Diana Sands; Barbra Streisand

Notes: [1] Not in program.

158 • ANOTHER MIDSUMMER NIGHT
OPENED: 06/26/1995   Theatre: Goodman
Musical   Chicago

Composer: Jeffrey Lunden
Lyricist: Arthur Perlman
Librettist: Arthur Perlman
Producer: Goodman Theater
Director: Michael Maggio

Choreographer: Danny Herman; **Costumes:** Catherine Zuber; **Lighting Designer:** Robert Christen; **Musical Director:** Bradley Vieth; **Orchestrations:** Bruce Coughlin; **Set Design:** Linda Buchanan

Songs: Aching; Another Midsummer Night; Everything's Changed; Fairyland; Follow Me; How Sweet Is the Taste of Revenge; I Never Guessed; It's Love — I Think; Lullaby; Midsummer Dream, A; Music of Love, The; This Is Wrong; Transform-ed; Wake Up; We Call on the Fairies; What a Mess; What Fools They Be

Cast: Jim Corti; Mary Ernster; Kathleen Rowe McAllen; Jessica Molaskey; Holly Resnik; Michael Rupert; Jim Walton; Nick Wyman

159 • ANTIQUES
OPENED: 06/19/1973   Theatre: Mercer-O'Casey
Musical   Off-Broadway: 8

Composer: Alan Greene; Laura Manning
Lyricist: Alan Greene; Laura Manning
Librettist: Dore Schary
Producer: Dore Schary Productions; Video Techniques Inc
Director: Marco Martone

Choreographer: Jeffrey K. Neill; **Costumes:** William Christians; **Lighting Designer:** R.H. Rizzio; **Set Design:** Bruno C. Scordino

Songs: Antiques; Bridges; Conversations; Don't Grow Old Gracefully; Grandma's Diary; 'Hey

Ma, You Were Right' Cantata, The; Look Underneath; Love Is Everything; Oh, What a Time We Had; Papa Bird; Pill, The; Red Kimono, The; Rent-a-Grandma; Solutions; They Don't Write Songs Like That Anymore; To Love Again; Victims of the Past; We Got Married

Cast: Charles Hudson; Laura Manning; Richard Marr; Betty Oakes; Eugene Smith; Ward Smith; Molly Stark

Notes: Previously produced on cable TV.

160 • ANY WEDNESDAY
OPENED: 02/18/1964   Theatre: Music Box
Play   Broadway: 982

Author: Muriel Resnik
Producer: Howard Erskine; George W. George; Frank Granat; Peter S. Katz; Edward Specter Prods.
Director: Henry Kaplin

Costumes: Theoni V. Aldredge; **Lighting Designer:** Tharon Musser; **Set Design:** Robert Randolph

Songs: Any Wednesday (C: Jerry Bock; L: Sheldon Harnick)

Cast: Sandy Dennis; Gene Hackman; Rosemary Murphy; Don Porter

161 • ANYA
OPENED: 11/29/1965   Theatre: Ziegfeld
Musical   Broadway: 16

Music Based On: Sergei Rachmaninoff
Composer: George Forrest; Robert Wright
Lyricist: George Forrest; Robert Wright
Librettist: George Abbott; Guy Bolton
Producer: Fred R. Fehlhaber
Director: George Abbott

Source: ANASTASIA (Play: Guy Bolton; Marcelle Maurette); **Choreographer:** Hanya Holm; **Costumes:** Patricia Zipprodt; **Lighting Designer:** Richard Casler; **Musical Director:** Harold Hastings; **Orchestrations:** Don Walker; **Set Design:** Robert Randolph

Songs: All Hail the Empress; Anya; Drawn to You [1]; Hand in Hand; Here Tonight, Tomorrow Where?; Homeward; If This Is Goodbye; Leben Sie Wohl;

Love and a Legacy [1]; Now Is My Moment [1]; On That Day; Quiet Land, A; Sense of Love and Humor, A [1]; Six Palaces; Snowflakes and Sweethearts (The Snowbird Song); So Proud; Song from Somewhere, A; That Prelude!; This Is My Kind of Love; Vodka, Vodka!

Cast: Lillian Gish; George S. Irving; Michael Kermoyan; John Michael King; Irra Petina; Constance Towers

Notes: [1] Cut prior to opening.

162 • ANYONE CAN WHISTLE
OPENED: 04/04/1964   Theatre: Majestic
Musical   Broadway: 9

Composer: Stephen Sondheim
Lyricist: Stephen Sondheim
Librettist: Arthur Laurents
Producer: Kermit Bloomgarden; Diana Krasny
Director: Arthur Laurents

Choreographer: Herbert Ross; **Costumes:** Theoni V. Aldredge; **Dance Arranger:** Betty Walberg; **Lighting Designer:** Jules Fisher; **Musical Director:** Herbert Greene; **Orchestrations:** Don Walker; **Set Design:** Jean Eckart; William Eckart; **Vocal Arranger:** Herbert Greene

Songs: A-1 March; Anyone Can Whistle; Come Play Wiz Me; Cookie Chase (waltzes), The; Everybody Says Don't; Hero Is Coming, A [1]; I'm Like the Bluebird; I've Got You to Lean On; Lame, the Halt and the Blind, The [1]; Me and My Town; Miracle Song; Natives Are Restless, The [1]; Parade Is Town, A; See What It Gets You; Simple [2]; There Won't Be Trumpets [1]; There's Always a Woman [1]; With So Little to Be Sure Of (1); With So Little to Be Sure Of (2) [1]

Cast: Gabriel Dell; Harvey Evans; James Frawley; Harry Guardino; Barbara Lang; Angela Lansbury; Peg Murray; Lee Remick; Tucker Smith; Arnold Soboloff; Lester Wilson

Notes: [1] Cut while out of town prior to Broadway. [2] Waltz section originally private birthday song for Mary Rodgers.

163 • ANYTHING GOES
OPENED: 11/21/1934   Theatre: Alvin
Musical   Broadway: 415

Composer: Cole Porter
Lyricist: Cole Porter
Librettist: Guy Bolton; Russel Crouse; Howard Lindsay; P.G. Wodehouse
Producer: Vinton Freedley
Director: Howard Lindsay

Choreographer: Robert Alton; **Costumes:** Jenkins; **Musical Director:** Earl Busby; **Orchestrations:** Robert Russell Bennett; Hans Spialek; **Set Design:** Donald Oenslager

Songs: All Through the Night; Anything Goes; Be Like the Bluebird; Blow, Gabriel, Blow; Bon Voyage; Buddy Beware [2]; Easy to Love [1]; Gypsy in Me, The; I Get a Kick Out of You [3]; Kate the Great [1]; Public Enemy Number One; There'll Always Be a Lady Fair (Sailor's Chanty); There's No Cure Like Travel [1]; Waltz Down the Aisle [1]; What a Joy to Be Young [1]; Where Are the Men?; You're the Top

Cast: Leslie Barrie; Vera Dunn; William Gaxton; Bettina Hall; George E. Mack; Ethel Merman; Victor Moore; Helen Raymond; Houston Richards; Vivian Vance

Notes: The original book was revised by Howard Lindsay and Russel Crouse. [1] Cut prior to opening. [2] Cut after opening. [3] Originally written for STAR DUST.

164 • APE OVER BROADWAY

OPENED: 03/12/1975   Theatre: Bert Wheeler
Musical   Off-Broadway: 11

Composer: Stephen Rose
Lyricist: Bill Vitale
Librettist: Bart Andrews; Mary McCartney
Producer: Allan Brown; Renee Semes Herz; Bill Vitale
Director: Jeffrey K. Neill

Choreographer: Jeffrey K. Neill; **Costumes:** Brent J. Porter; **Dance Arranger:** Frederick Roffman; **Lighting Designer:** Dan Leigh; Gail Van Voorhis; **Musical Director:** Frederick Roffman; **Set Design:** Dan Leigh; Gail Van Voorhis; **Vocal Arranger:** Frederick Roffman

Songs: Ape Can Save the World, An; Ape Over Broadway; Broadway; Flamingo Fuss; I'm in Like with You; I've Had Everything but a Man; Just a Whistle; Man Eating Ape Waltz, The; Mixed-Up

Media; My Friend; Nude-Lewd; Saga of Men and Marriage; Star Number, The; Triangle Song

Cast: Robert Calvert; Barbara Coggin; Jim Cyrus; Robert Lydiard; Curt Ralston; Jacqueline Reilly; Freyda-Ann Thomas; Phylis Ward

Notes: Limited engagement.

165 • APHRODITE

OPENED: 11/24/1919   Theatre: Century
Play   Broadway: 148

Lyricist: Arthur A. Penn
Librettist: Pierre Frondale; George C. Hazelton
Producer: F. Ray Comstock; Morris Gest
Director: E. Lyall Swete

Source: UNKNOWN (Novel: Pierre Louys); **Choreographer:** Michel Fokine; **Costumes:** Percy Anderson; Leon Bakst; **Set Design:** Joseph Harker; Phil Harker

Songs: Alexandria (C: Anselm Goetzl); Aphrodite Waltz (C: Unknown); Berenike Motif (C: Henri Fevrier); Demetrios Motif (C: Henri Fevrier); Dream of Demetrios, The (C: Unknown); Entrance of Queen Berenike (C: Anselm Goetzl); Eros, Eros (C: Anselm Goetzl); Opening Ensemble (C: Anselm Goetzl; L: E. Lyall Swete)

Cast: Hazel Alden; Dorothy Dalton; Richard Hale; McKay Morris; Mildred Walker

166 • APOLLO . . . IT WAS JUST LIKE MAGIC, THE

OPENED: 02/19/1981
Musical   Unproduced

Composer: Timothy Graphenreed
Lyricist: George Faison; Timothy Graphenreed; David Langston Smyrl
Librettist: George Faison; Timothy Graphenreed; David Langston Smyrl
Producer: Dann Byck; Jay Cohen; Doug Goodman; Richard Press; Ashton Springer
Director: George Faison

Choreographer: George Faison; **Costumes:** Bernard Johnson; **Lighting Designer:** William Mintzer; **Musical Director:** David Bishop; **Set Design:** Tom Schwinn; **Vocal Arranger:** David Bishop

Songs: All the Way to Here; Amateur Night; Baby's Eyes; Change Is Gonna Come, A; Didn't It Rain (C/L: Traditional); Everything Is Alright, Uptight (C/L: Unknown); Get Ready (C/L: William Robinson); Goodbye (Crossover); He'll Understand; Heard It Through the Grapevine (C/L: Barrett Strong; Norman Whitfield); It Was Just Like Magic; I've Got What It Takes and It Breaks My Heart to Give It Away (C/L: Unknown); J'ai Deux Amours (C/L: Unknown); La Vie en Rose (C: Edith Piaf; L: Mack David); Let the Good Times Roll (C/L: Unknown); Looks Like They Need Old Mame Again; Love Is Like an Itching in My Heart; Old Landmark, The; Phoey, Phoey; Program Your Return; What a Difference a Day Makes (C: Maria Grever; L: Stanley Adams); Why Do Fools Fall in Love (C/L: George Goldner; Frankie Lymon); Yesterdays; Your Place in the Sunshine

Cast: Shirley Black-Brown; Peggie Blue; Keith Davis; Morgan Freeman; Esther Marrow; S. Epatha Merkerson; Eleanor Mills; Marsha Perry; Herbert Rawlings; Kiki Shepard; Jai Oscar St. John; Ronald "Smokey" Stevens; Danny Strayhorn; Clarice Taylor; Carl Earl Weaver

Notes: Workshop performance only.

167 • APPLAUSE

OPENED: 03/30/1970   Theatre: Palace
Musical   Broadway: 896

Composer: Charles Strouse
Lyricist: Lee Adams
Librettist: Betty Comden; Adolph Green
Producer: Lawrence Kasha; Joseph Kipness
Director: Ron Field

Source: ALL ABOUT EVE (Film: Joseph Mankiewicz);

Source: WISDOM OF EVE, THE (Story: Mary Orr); **Choreographer:** Ron Field; **Costumes:** Ray Aghayan; **Dance Arranger:** Mel Marvin; **Lighting Designer:** Tharon Musser; **Musical Director:** Donald Pippin; **Orchestrations:** Philip J. Lang; **Set Design:** Robert Randolph; **Vocal Arranger:** Donald Pippin

Songs: Applause; Backstage Babble; Best Night of My Life, The; But Alive; Disco for Margo [7]; Fairfield Country [2]; Fasten Your Seat Belts; Get Her Away from Me [3]; God Bless! [3]; Good

Friends; Hurray Back; I'm Still Me [3]; Inner Thoughts; It Was Always You [1]; It'll Be Good for Me [3]; It's a Hit, It's a Flop [6]; Loneliest Man in Town [3]; Love Comes First [2]; Margo's Theme [1]; Nothing Can Get to Me Now [3]; One Hallowe'en [4]; One of a Kind; She's No Longer a Gypsy; Smashing New York Times [5]; Something Greater; Tell Your Friends [3]; Think How It's Gonna Be; Welcome to the Theatre; Well Wishers, The [1]; Who's That Girl?

Cast: Lauren Bacall; Len Cariou; Bonnie Franklin; Penny Fuller; Brandon Maggart; Robert Mandan; Lee Roy Reams; Ann Williams

Notes: [1] Cut. [2] Cut Baltimore prior to Broadway. [3] Cut prior to opening. From early demo tape. [4] Originally titled "Remember That Halloween." [5] Cut Baltimore prior to Broadway. Later used in A BROADWAY MUSICAL. [6] Cut Baltimore prior to Broadway. Music same as "I Don't Know" in DANCE A LITTLE CLOSER. [7] Cut Broadway prior to Broadway. Probably just a dance extension of "But Alive."

168 • APPLE BLOSSOMS

OPENED: 10/07/1919   Theatre: Globe
Musical   Broadway: 256

Composer: Victor Jacobi; Fritz Kreisler
Lyricist: William Le Baron
Librettist: William Le Baron
Producer: Charles Dillingham
Director: Fred G. Latham; Edward Royce

Source: UN MARIAGE SOUS LOUIS XV (Novel: Alexandre Dumas); **Musical Director:** William Daly; **Set Design:** Joseph Urban

Songs: Brothers (C: Victor Jacobi); Ensemble (1) (C: Victor Jacobi; Fritz Kreisler); Ensemble (2) (C: Fritz Kreisler); Girl, a Man, a Night, a Dance, A (C: Fritz Kreisler); I'll Be True to You (C: Victor Jacobi); I'm in Love (C: Fritz Kreisler); Letter Song [1] (C: Fritz Kreisler); Little Girls, Goodbye (C: Victor Jacobi); Marriage Knot, The (C: Fritz Kreisler); Nancy's Farewell (C: Fritz Kreisler); On the Banks of the Bronx (C: Victor Jacobi); Opening (C: Fritz Kreisler); Quintette and Phillip's Story (C: Unknown); Second Violin, The (C: Fritz Kreisler); Star of Love (C: Fritz Kreisler); Tambourin Chinois [1] (C: Fritz Kreisler); When the Wedding Bells Are Ringing (C: Victor Jacobi); When You Are Mine [1] (C: Victor

Jacobi); Who Can Tell? (C: Fritz Kreisler); You Are Free (C: Victor Jacobi)

Cast: Adele Astaire; Fred Astaire; Roy Atwell; Wilda Bennett; John Charles Thomas

Notes: [1] Not in program.

169 • APPLE PIE

OPENED: 02/13/1976   Theatre: Public
Musical   Off-Broadway: 72

Composer: Nicholas Meyers
Lyricist: Myrna Lamb
Librettist: Myrna Lamb
Producer: N.Y. Shakespeare Festival
Director: Joseph Papp

Costumes: Timothy Miller; **Lighting Designer:** Pat Collins; **Musical Director:** Liza Redfield; **Set Design:** David Mitchell

Songs: America, We're in New York; Break-up Rag; Counterman, The; Doctor, The; Father's Waltz; Final Judgement; Freedom Anthem; Gun Scene; Harry's Rag; Hundavieh; I'm Lise; Lise Dear; Love Scene; Marshall's Blues; Marshall's Reply; Mating Dance, The; Men Come with Guns; Mother's March; Reified Expression; Stockboy Blues, The; Survival Song; Too Much Motet, The; Trial, The; Victim Dream; Waltz of Lise's Childhood; Wedding, The; Yesterday Is Over

Cast: Lee Allen; Stephanie Cotsirilos; Robert Guillaume; Spain Logue; Joseph Neal; Lucille Patton; Robert Polenz; Ilsebet Anna Tebesli; John Watson

170 • APPLE TREE, THE

OPENED: 10/18/1966   Theatre: Shubert
Musical   Broadway: 463

Composer: Jerry Bock
Lyricist: Sheldon Harnick
Librettist: Jerry Bock; Jerome Coopersmith; Sheldon Harnick
Producer: Stuart Ostrow
Director: Mike Nichols

Source: DIARY OF ADAM AND EVE, THE (Story: Mark Twain); **Source:** LADY OR THE TIGER, THE (Story: Frank Stockton); **Source:** PASSIONELLA (Story: Jules Feiffer);

Choreographer: Herbert Ross; Lee Theodore; **Costumes:** Tony Walton; **Lighting Designer:** Jean Rosenthal; **Musical Director:** Elliot Lawrence; **Orchestrations:** Eddie Sauter; **Set Design:** Tony Walton; **Vocal Arranger:** Elliot Lawrence

Songs: Apple Tree (Forbidden Fruit), The; Beautiful, Beautiful World; Eden, Eden [4]; Eve (1); Eve (2)[6]; Feelings; Forbidden Love (In Gaul); Friends; George L. [1]; Go to Sleep Whatever You Are [1]; Godmother's Song [5]; Gorgeous; Here in Eden; I Am a Happy Man [2]; I Know; I'll Tell You a Truth; I'm Lost [3]; It's a Fish; I've Got What You Want; Make Way; Man [5]; Oh, to Be a Movie Star; One Third Princess [3]; Pasionella [3]; Peek-a-boo [4]; Rain Song [5]; Tiger, Tiger; Useful [3]; Wealth; What Makes Me Love Him; What Was That [3]; Which Door; (Who, Who, Who, Who) Who Is She?; Wow [5]; You Are Not Real

Cast: Alan Alda; Carmen Alvarez; Larry Blyden; Barbara Harris; Marc Jordan; Robert Klein

Notes: [1] Same music. [2] Cut in previews. [3] Cut. [4] Cut. Same music as "Go To Sleep." [5] Cut. May not be title [6] Cut. Same music as "Feelings."

171 • APPRENTICESHIP OF DUDDY KRAVITZ

OPENED: 09/30/1987
Musical   Closed out of town

Composer: Alan Menken
Lyricist: David Spencer
Librettist: Austin Pendleton; Mordecai Richler
Producer: Amer. Music Theatre Fest.
Director: Austin Pendleton

Source: APPRENTICESHIP OF DUDDY KRAVITZ, THE (Novel: Mordecai Richler); **Choreographer:** D.J. Giagni; **Costumes:** Ruth Morley; **Musical Director:** Eric Stern; **Orchestrations:** Steven Margoshes; Danny Troob; **Set Design:** Clarke Dunham

Cast: Anne Marie Bobby; Marty Brill; Michael Callan; Merwin Goldsmith; Harry Goz; John Horton; James Judy; Bob Morrisey; Stephen Pearlman; Lonny Price

Notes: Closed at American Music Theatre Festival. Originally titled DUDDY. No songs listed in program.

172 • APRIL SONG, AN

OPENED: 08/25/1980
Musical   Closed out of town

Composer: Mitch Leigh
Lyricist: Sammy Cahn

Source: LEOCADIA (Play: Jean Anouilh); **Costumes:** Miles White; **Lighting Designer:** Rick Belzer; **Musical Director:** David Friedman; **Orchestrations:** Gilbert Marre; **Set Design:** Robert D. Mitchell

Songs: April Song, An; Love Is Hate; On the Boulevard; She; Sing Me No April Songs; Try to Forget Me; You're Probably in Love

Cast: Julie Boyd; Glynis Johns

Notes: No songs listed in program.

173 • AQUACADE REVUE

OPENED: 1939
Revue   N.Y. World's Fair

Composer: Dana Suesse
Lyricist: Ted Fetter; Billy Rose
Producer: Billy Rose
Director: John Murray Anderson

Choreographer: Robert Alton; **Costumes:** Raoul Pene du Bois; **Lighting Designer:** John Murray Anderson; **Orchestrations:** Hans Spialek; **Set Design:** Albert Johnson

Songs: Camera Doesn't Lie, Neither Do I, The [1] (C: Joseph Burke; L: Edgar Leslie); It Happened in Miami; Roller Skating on a Rainbow (C: Harry Warren; L: Irving Kahal; Billy Rose); Yankee Doodle's Gonna Go to Town Again; You're Too Good to Be True; Yours for a Song

Cast: Morton Downey; Gertrude Ederle; Eleanor Holm; Fred Waring's W.F.G.C.; Johnny Weissmuller

Notes: *See also BILLY ROSE'S AQUACADE REVUE and NEW AQUACADE REVUE.* [1] ASCAP/Library of Congress only.

174 • ARABESQUE

OPENED: 10/10/1925
Musical   Closed out of town

Composer: Ruth White Warfield
Lyricist: Cloyd Head; Eunice Tietjens

Librettist: Cloyd Head; Eunice Tietjens

Notes: No other information available.

175 • ARABIAN GIRL AND 40 THIEVES, AN

OPENED: 04/29/1899   Theatre: Herald Square
Musical   Broadway: 33

Composer: W.H. Batchelor; John J. Braham; Meyer Lutz; Jesse Williams
Librettist: J. Cheever Goodwin
Director: Julian Mitchell

Choreographer: Filiberto Marchetti; **Costumes:** Will R. Barnes; Howell Russell; **Musical Director:** John J. Braham; **Set Design:** Fred Dangerfield; D. Frank Dodge; Henry E. Hoyt; Frank Rafter

Songs: Cobblers We; Combat Chorus; Dashing Militaire; Detectives Bold; Forty Gallant Thieves Are We; Hail to the Caliph; Honest Man, An; Hoo-doo-doo-doo-man; I'm a Little Lady; Let's Away; Open Sesame; Operatic Mountebanks; Orb Divine; Pictures; Song of the Forty Thieves; Sunshine of Love; Sweet William; To the Cave Away; Virginia Skedaddle; We Are the Band; Wedding Bells, The

Cast: Eddie Foy Sr.; Maud Gilbert; Clara Lane; Harry McDonough; Dorothy Morton; J.K. Murray

176 • ARABIAN NIGHTS (1922)

OPENED: 1923
Musical   Chicago

Composer: Harry Ruby
Lyricist: Bert Kalmar

Notes: No other information available.

177 • ARABIAN NIGHTS (1954)

OPENED: 06/25/1954   Theatre: Jones Beach
                       Marine
Musical   New York

Composer: Carmen Lombardo
Lyricist: John Jacob Loeb
Librettist: George Marion Jr.
Producer: Guy Lombardo
Director: Leon Leonidoff

Choreographer: Rod Alexander; **Costumes:** Richard Rychtarik; **Lighting Designer:** Gene Baum; **Musical Director:** Pembroke Davenport; **Orchestrations:** Joe Glover; **Set Design:** Richard Rychtarik; **Vocal Arranger:** Pembroke Davenport

Songs: Bridal Fete; Bring on the Bride to Be; Chase, The; Grand Vizier's Lament; Hail to the Sultan; Hero of All My Dreams; How Long Has It Been; It's Great to Be Alive; Long Ago Love, A; Marry the One You Love; Teeny Weeny Genie; Thousand and One Nights, A; Valley of Jewels; Whale of a Story, A; What a Pity; What's His Name

Cast: William Chapman; Jack Dabdoub; Hope Holiday; Lauritz Melchior; Buzz Miller; Helena Scott

Notes: This show was brought back the next summer also.

178 • ARCADIANS, THE
OPENED: 01/17/1910   Theatre: Liberty
Musical   Broadway: 136

Composer: Lionel Monckton; Howard Talbot
Lyricist: Arthur Wimperis
Librettist: Mark Ambient; Alexander M. Thompson
Producer: Charles Frohman
Director: Thomas Reynolds

Costumes: Wilhelm; **Musical Director:** Watty Hydes; **Set Design:** Homer Emens

Songs: All a Lie! (C: Howard Talbot); All Down Piccadilly (Willie from Piccadilly) (C/L: Lionel Monckton; L: Arthur Wimperis); Arcadya Is Ever Young (C/L: Lionel Monckton; L: Arthur Wimperis); Back Your Fancy (C: Lionel Monckton); Bring Me a Rose (C/L: Lionel Monckton; L: Arthur Wimperis); Charming Weather (C/L: Lionel Monckton; L: Arthur Wimperis); Cheer for Simplicitas! (C: Lionel Monckton); Come to Arcady [4] (C: Unknown); Fickle Fortune (L: Lionel Monckton); Finale Act I (C: Howard Talbot); Finale Act II (C: Howard Talbot); Finale Act III (L: Lionel Monckton); Girl with a Brogue, The (C: Lionel Monckton); Half Past Two [1] (C: Howard Talbot; L: Percy Greenbank; Arthur Wimperis); Have a Little Bit on Me [5]; I Like London (C: Howard Talbot);

I Quite Forgot Arcadia (C: Lionel Monckton); I'll Be a Sister to You [5]; Joy of Life, The (C: Howard Talbot); Ladies, The [2]; Light Is My Heart [3] (C: Howard Talbot); Little George Washington [5]; Look What Hovers There (Chorus of Fear) [1] (C: Howard Talbot); Love Will Win [5]; My Heart Flies Homing [1] (C: Howard Talbot); My Motter (C: Howard Talbot); Only Girl Alive (C: Howard Talbot); Opening Chorus (C: Howard Talbot); Opening Chorus Act II (C: Lionel Monckton); Opening Chorus Act III (C: Howard Talbot); Pipes of Pan Are Calling, The (C: Lionel Monckton); Shower Chorus [1] (C: Howard Talbot); Somewhere (C: Lionel Monckton); Sweet Simplicatas (C: Howard Talbot); Truth Is So Beautiful (C: Lionel Monckton); What Every Woman Knows [4]; Whoppers [5] (C: Lionel Monckton)

Cast: Ethel Cadman; Connie Ediss; Percival Knight; Marion Mosby; Frank Moulan; Alan Mudie; Julia Sanderson; Grace Studdiford

Notes: [1] Not in program. [2] Not in British vocal score. [3] Cut after opening. Replaced by "Come Back to Arcady." [4] Added after opening. [5] Added after London opening.

179 • ARE YOU A MASON?
Play   Closed out of town

Author: Leo Ditrichstein

Songs: I'm Going on a Long Vacation (C: Ted Snyder; L: Irving Berlin)

Cast: Leo Ditrichstein; Beth Tate

Notes: No other information available.

180 • ARE YOU WITH IT?
OPENED: 11/10/1945   Theatre: Century
Musical   Broadway: 266

Composer: Harry Revel
Lyricist: Arnold B. Horwitt
Librettist: George Balzar; Sam Perrin
Producer: James W. Gardiner; Richard Kollmar
Director: Edward Reveaux

Source: SLIGHTLY PERFECT (Novel: George Malcolm Smith); **Choreographer:** Jack Donahue; **Costumes:** Willa Kim; Raoul Pene du Bois;

Lighting Designer: George Jenkins; **Musical Director:** Will Irwin; **Orchestrations:** Joe Glover; Walter Paul; Ted Royal; Hans Spialek; Don Walker; **Set Design:** George Jenkins; **Vocal Arranger:** Clay Warnick

Songs: Are You With It?; Five More Minutes in Bed; Here I Go Again; In Our Cozy Little Cottage of Tomorrow; Just Beyond the Rainbow; Nutmeg Insurance; Poor Little Me; Send Us Back to the Kitchen; Slightly Perfect; Slightly Slightly; This Is My Beloved; Vivian's Reverie [1]; When a Good Man Takes to Drink (Music Based On: Harry Revel); You Gotta Keep Saying 'No'

Cast: Johnny Downs; Jane Dulo; Dolores Gray; Lew Parker; June Richmond; Joan Roberts

Notes: [1] From themes by Harry Revel, adapted by Will Irwin.

181 • ARI
OPENED: 01/15/1971   Theatre: Mark Hellinger
Musical   Broadway: 19

Composer: Walt Smith
Lyricist: Leon Uris
Librettist: Leon Uris
Producer: Ken Gaston; Leonard Goldberg

Source: EXODUS (Novel: Leon Uris);
Choreographer: Talley Beatty; **Costumes:** Sara Brook; **Dance Arranger:** Peter Howard; **Lighting Designer:** Nananne Porcher; **Musical Director:** Stanley Lebowsky; **Orchestrations:** Philip J. Lang; **Set Design:** Robert Randolph; **Vocal Arranger:** Stanley Lebowsky

Songs: Alphabet Song, The; Aphrodite; Ari's Promise; Ari's Soliloquy [2]; Ballet of the Warsaw Ghetto (dance) [2]; Children's Lament; Come and Spend Your Life with Me [2]; Don't Be Afraid to Love [2]; Don't I Know You From Somewhere [2]; Dov's Nightmare; Exodus, The; Falling Too Far [1]; Give Me One Good Reason; He'll Never Be Mine; HMJFC [1]; Hora-Galilee; I See What I Choose to See; I'm Alone [2]; Karen's Lullaby; Learning Hebrew [1]; Let the Good Book Lead the Way [1]; Lord Helps Those Who Help Themselves, The; Love Is for the Birds [2]; My Brother's Keeper; My Galilee; One Flag; Saga of the Haganah, The; Time to Love, A [1]; When He Is Broken [1]; Yerushaliam

Cast: C.K. Alexander; Ron Crofoot; David Cryer; Carol Estey; Jack Gwillim; Karen Jablons; Jacqueline Mayro; Casper Roos; Jamie Ross; John Savage; Constance Towers; Mark Zeller

Notes: Lyn Duddy and Jerry Bresler wrote at least two of these songs but they weren't credited in program. [1] Cut in Washington, D.C. prior to Broadway. [2] Cut prior to opening.

182 • ARIZONA
OPENED: 10/18/1900   Theatre: Weber and Fields
                                      Music Hall
Musical   Broadway

Composer: John Stromberg
Lyricist: Edgar Smith
Librettist: Edgar Smith
Producer: Lew Fields; Joseph Weber

Cast: Lew Fields; Joseph Weber

Notes: A burlesque on the play ARIZONA. No other information available.

183 • ARMS AND THE GIRL
OPENED: 02/02/1950   Theatre: 46th Street
Musical   Broadway: 134

Composer: Morton Gould
Lyricist: Dorothy Fields
Librettist: Dorothy Fields; Herbert Fields; Rouben Mamoulian
Producer: Anthony Brady Farrell; Theatre Guild, The
Director: Rouben Mamoulian

Source: PUSUIT OF HAPPINESS, THE (Play: Lawrence Langner; Armina Marshall);
Choreographer: Michael Kidd; **Costumes:** Audre; **Musical Director:** Frederick Dvonch; **Orchestrations:** Morton Gould; Philip J. Lang; **Set Design:** Horace Armistead

Songs: Cow and a Plough and a Frau, A; Don't Talk; Girl with a Flame, A; He Will Tonight; I Like It Here; I'll Never Learn; I'll Never See You Again [1]; I'm Scared [1]; Johnny Cake [1]; Little Old Cabin Door [2]; Mister Washington!; Nothin' for Nothin'; Plantation in Philadelphia; She's Exciting; That's My Fella; That's What I Told Him Last Night; There Must Be Something Better than Love; Uncle George; You Kissed Me

Cast: Florenz Ames; Seth Arnold; Pearl Bailey;
Lulu Belle Clarke; Nanette Fabray; Peter
Gennaro; Georges Guetary; Eda Heinemann;
Onna White

Notes: [1] Cut prior to Broadway. [2]
ASCAP/Library of Congress only.

184 • ARMS AND THE MAID

OPENED: 11/1930
Musical   Closed out of town

Composer: Jean Gilbert
Lyricist: Harry B. Smith
Librettist: Harry Clarke; Harry B. Smith
Producer: Messrs. Shubert
Director: Marcel Varnel

Source: HOTEL STADT-LEMBERG (Musical: Ernst
Neubach); Musical Director: Leonard Hornsey;
Set Design: Watson Barratt

Songs: All's Fair in Love and War; Forward March
into My Arms; I Gotta Keep My Eye on You;
I Like You; In My Heart, on My Mind; In Youth's
Fair Springtime; Leave It to Love; One Loves at
Sight; To Have, to Hold, to Love

Cast: Emma Kosary; Joseph Toner; Solly Ward;
Halfred Young

Notes: From program of 11/25/30 Philadelphia.
See also MARCHING BY.

185 • AROUND THE CLOCK

OPENED: 10/1906
Musical   Closed out of town

Composer: Lee Orean Smith
Lyricist: J.S. Hiller
Librettist: S.B. Cassin
Director: M.L. Heckert

Choreographer: Dan Dody; Costumes: Will R.
Barnes; Set Design: Ernest Albert; Frank Gates;
E.A. Morange

Songs: Around the Clock; Father Penn; Football
Girls at Vassar, The; Gay and Merry Play, The;
Hark to the Chimes; Idaho; Military Maid, The;
Playland; Rag Bag Man; Sarah of Sahara;
Spooning; Topical Song; Waiter Girl, The

Cast: Jack Lloyd; Bill Ritchie; Nina Vernon

Notes: Program of 10/08/06 Wilkes-Barre.

186 • AROUND THE MAP

OPENED: 11/01/1915   Theatre: New Amsterdam
Revue   Broadway: 104

Composer: Herman Finck
Lyricist: C.M.S. McLellan
Librettist: C.M.S. McLellan
Producer: Klaw & Erlanger
Director: Herbert Gresham

Choreographer: Julian Mitchell; Musical Director:
Charles Previn; Set Design: Joseph Urban

Songs: Billy the Bubbler (C/L: Louis A. Hirsch);
Chorus of Constant Lunchers, Constant Diners,
Constant Dancers and Constant Kissers
(C/L: Louis A. Hirsch); Chorus of Nurses; Dear
Old Fighting Boys, The; Dolly Dear; Goodness,
Ain't You Glad?; Here Comes Tootsi; I Don't
Know Her Name Yet; I'm Madame Kapinski; I'm
the Boom Boom Boomer; It's a Very Fine World;
Katie Clancy (C/L: Louis A. Hirsch); Lazy Lulu;
Let Us Stay Where the Crowd Is; Little Maud
Isn't Meant for You; My Waltz Queen [1];
Opening Chorus; Some Girl Has Got to Darn His
Socks (C/L: Louis A. Hirsch); Take Me on a Ride
of Joy; There's Only One Thing a Coon Can Do
(C/L: Louis A. Hirsch); Waltz Song; When the
Right Girl Comes Along

Cast: Bob Adams; Jacqueline Bonheur; Louise
Groody; William Norris; Georgia O'Ramey

Notes: [1] Sheet music only.

187 • AROUND THE TOWN

OPENED: 1906
Musical   Closed out of town

Librettist: George H. Emerick
Director: Ollie Mack

Musical Director: Herbert Dillea

Songs: Around the Town; At the Music Hall; Chair
Dance; College Life; Don't Count Your Chickens;
Girl That Leads the Band, The; Happy Tramp,
The; How'd You Like to Flirt with Me; Looks
Like Candy to Me; Love, Love, Love; Mooney

Time; Opening Chorus; Opening Chorus Act I; Opening Chorus Act II; Two Souls without a Single Thought; Walked Right Out Again; When We Strike Broadway

Cast: Bobby Harrington; Ollie Mack; Chas. A. Murray; Gus Pixley; Gertrude Rutledge

Notes: Program of Cedar Rapids.

188 • AROUND THE WORLD

OPENED: 09/02/1911   Theatre: Hippodrome
Revue   Broadway: 445

Composer: Manuel Klein
Lyricist: Manuel Klein
Librettist: Carroll Fleming
Producer: Messrs. Shubert
Director: Carroll Fleming

Choreographer: William J. Wilson; **Costumes:** Cora MacGeachy; **Set Design:** Arthur Voegtlin

Songs: 'Arry and 'Arriet; Auf Den Berg Es Is Schon; Ballet of the Butterflies; Blarney of Killarney; Die Vogelein Singen In Dem Wald; It's a Long Lane That Has No Turning [1]; Merry Month of May, The; Muezzin Call; Music of Forest Fires; My Old Town; Pretty Little Sunshade; Salute to the Toreador; See the Royal Parade; Sweet Senorita; Venetian Serenade

Cast: Sabry Dorsell; Felix Haney; Rose La Harte; Marceline

Notes: Part of this evening was THE BALLET OF THE BUTTERFLIES and THE FAIRIES GLEN AND THE GOLDEN BARGE. [1] There was a popular song of the same name copyrighted in 1917 which was written by Manuel Klein with lyrics by Arthur A. Penn. However the sheet music for this show doesn't credit Penn.

189 • AROUND THE WORLD IN EIGHTY DAYS (1946)

OPENED: 05/31/1946   Theatre: Adelphi
Musical   Broadway: 75

Composer: Cole Porter
Lyricist: Cole Porter
Librettist: Orson Welles
Producer: Mercury Theatre; Orson Welles
Director: Orson Welles

Source: AROUND THE WORLD IN EIGHTY DAYS (Novel: Jules Verne); **Choreographer:** Nelson Barclift; **Costumes:** Alvin Colt; **Lighting Designer:** Peggy Clark; **Musical Director:** Harry Levant; **Orchestrations:** Robert Russell Bennett; Ted Royal; **Set Design:** Robert Davison; **Vocal Arranger:** Mitchell Ayres

Songs: California Dance Scene; If You Smile at Me; Look What I Found; Love You [2]; Marine's Hymn, The; Mee-rah-lah; Missus Aouda [1]; Oka Saka Circus; Pipe Dreaming; Sea Chanty; Should I Tell You [1]; Slave Auction [1]; Snagtooth Gertie [1]; Suez Dance; Suttee Procession; There He Goes, Mr. Phileas Fogg; Wherever They Fly the Flag of Old England

Cast: Jack Cassidy; Victoria Cordova; Mary Healy; Larry Laurence[3]; Arthur Margetson; Julie Warren; Orson Welles

Notes: [1] Unused. [2] Same music as "If I Hadn't a Husband" which was unused in SEVEN LIVELY ARTS. [3] Later known as Enzo Stuarti.

190 • AROUND THE WORLD IN EIGHTY DAYS (1963)

OPENED: 06/22/1963   Theatre: Jones Beach
                                           Marine
Musical   Off-Broadway: 73

Composer: Sammy Fain
Lyricist: Harold Adamson
Librettist: Sig Herzig
Producer: Guy Lombardo
Director: Arnold Spector

Source: AROUND THE WORLD IN EIGHTY DAYS (Novel: Jules Verne); **Choreographer:** June Taylor; **Costumes:** Winn Morton; **Musical Director:** Mitchell Ayres; **Orchestrations:** Philip J. Lang; **Set Design:** George Jenkins

Songs: Are We Talking About the Same Thing?; Around the World [1] (C: Victor Young); Balloon Underplay (inst.); Barbary Coast [2] (C: Victor Young); Burning of the Henrietta (inst.); Carry On; Dance of Sacrifice (inst.); Fiesta in Spain [2] (C: Victor Young); Have You Heard About Philias Fogg? [2] (C: Victor Young); Hide Your Sister; Hindu Dance Tag (inst.); His Little World; Hong Kong [2] (C: Victor Young); I Hate to Travel; I'm a Sleuth; Indian Raid (inst.); Indian Scene (inst.); Lloyd's of London [2] (C: Victor

Young); Long Live the English Scene [2] (C: Victor Young); March of the Grenadiers (inst.); Once I Wondered; One-Woman Man; Sidewalks of Paris; Sky Symphony [2] (C: Victor Young); Spanish Villa (inst.); Way Out West [2] (C: Victor Young)

Cast: David Atkinson; Robert Clary; Dom De Luise; Peter Gladke; Jane Laughlin; Edmund Lyndeck; Barney Martin; Jan McArt; Leon Shaw

Notes: A summer production. [1] Music and lyrics written for the Mike Todd film. [2] Music from the Mike Todd film.

191 • ARRAH-NA-POGUE

OPENED: 09/07/1903   Theatre: 14th St.
Play   Broadway: 65

Composer: Andrew Mack
Lyricist: Andrew Mack
Author: Dion Boucicault
Producer: Rich and Harris
Director: William Seymour

Set Design: Joseph Physioc

Songs: Finnegan and His Flute [1]; Goodnight, My Love, Good Night; Heart of the Rose, The (C/L: Unknown); Joys of an Irish Dance (C/L: Barney Fagan); Somewhere [1]; Wearing of the Green, The [1]

Cast: Edith Barker; Andrew Mack

Notes: Revival of play which first opened 7/12/1865. [1] Sheet music only.

192 • ART CARNEY MEETS PETER AND THE WOLF

OPENED: 05/03/1959   Theatre: NBC
TV Musical

Composer: Serge Prokofiev
Lyricist: Sheldon Harnick; Ogden Nash
Librettist: A.J. Russell
Producer: Burt Shevelove
Director: Dick Feldman

Musical Director: Paul Weston

Cast: Bil and Cora Baird Marionettes; Art Carney;
Puppeteer: Bil Baird; Cora Baird

Notes: No other information available. See also the stage version of this show PETER AND THE WOLF.

193 • ART CARNEY MEETS THE SORCERER'S APPRENTICE

OPENED: 04/05/1959   Theatre: NBC
TV Musical

Composer: Paul Dukas
Lyricist: Ogden Nash
Librettist: A.J. Russell
Producer: Bert Shevelove
Director: Seymour Robbie

Musical Director: Paul Weston

Cast: Bil and Cora Baird Marionettes; Art Carney;
Puppeteer: Bil Baird; Cora Baird

Notes: No other information available.

194 • ART OF LIVING, THE

OPENED: 07/25/1960
Revue

Composer: David Heneker; Monty Norman
Lyricist: David Heneker; Julian More; Monty Norman
Librettist: Julian More
Producer: New Theatre Oxford
Director: Laurie Lister

Choreographer: Eleanor Fazan; **Musical Director:** Burt Rhodes; **Orchestrations:** Johnny Gregory; **Set Design:** Voytek

Songs: Adam & Yvette; Anything to Declare; Awkward Questions; Ballhouse Krazy Bar; Beyond the Horizon; Brainwash; Calling Your Loved Ones; D.F.C. and Bar; Dearest Mary; Diet of Wein; Drug Addicts; En Locacion; Fulfilling Requests; Go Home; Havana; Hot Water; It's a List; Lovelost; Mona Lisa Crouch; Monopoly; National Italian Sport; Neapolitan Nostalgia; Nubian of Lemon, The; Oh Lars!; Only Thing I Missed, The; Pappagalli; Pub Pianist; Shoom-Shi-Baasha; Sight Seeing; Story Teller, The; Strange Amusing People, A; Tailors of Hong Kong, The; Tobacco Road; Travel Now; Umbrella Man, The; Wisherman's Song, The

Cast: Judy Bruce; Stella Claire; Barbara Evans;

Carole Shelley; Hiram Sherman; Graham Stark; Edward Woodward

Notes: New Theatre, Oxford. Songs and sketches listed because they are not differentiated in program.

195 • ART OF MARYLAND, THE

Composer: John Stromberg
Lyricist: Joseph W. Herbert

Songs: Appearances Were Against Her; I Love You Dear; My Young Man

Cast: Lillian Swain

Notes: No other information available.

196 • ARTHUR FREED'S ORANGE GROVE THEATRE REVUE

OPENED: 1927
Revue   Los Angeles

Composer: Arthur Freed
Lyricist: Arthur Freed

Songs: In Our Orange Grove

Notes: No other information available.

197 • ARTHUR GODFREY'S TV CALENDAR SHOW

OPENED: 01/28/1953   Theatre: CBS
TV Musical

Composer: Lyn Duddy; Joan Edwards
Lyricist: Lyn Duddy; Joan Edwards

Musical Director: Archie Bleyer

Songs: Appreciation; Easter in Waikiki; Everything That's Yours Is Mine; First Snow of Winter, The; Give a Cheer; If It Wasn't for Your Father; I'm in Love Again; It's Autumn Again; It's the Irish in Me; Look Ahead; Rockaway Beach; Summer's Symphony

Cast: Cordettes, The; Janette Davis; Arthur Godfrey; Haleloke; Julius La Rosa; Mariners, The; Marion Marlowe; Frank Parker; Lu Ann Simms

198 • ARTHUR, THE MUSICAL

OPENED: 11/01/1990
Musical   Closed out of town

Composer: Michael Skloff
Lyricist: David Crane; Marta Kauffman
Librettist: David Crane; Marta Kauffman
Producer: Goodspeed Opera House
Director: Joseph Billone

Source: ARTHUR (Film: Steve Gordon); **Arrangements:** Jeffrey Saver; Michael Skloff; **Choreographer:** Daniel Pelzig; **Costumes:** Emily L. Ockenfels; **Dance Arranger:** Jeffrey Saver; Michael Skloff; **Lighting Designer:** John Hastings; **Musical Director:** Jeffrey Saver; **Set Design:** Linda Hacker; **Vocal Arranger:** John McKinney

Songs: Alone; Can I Live Without the Man; Carried Away; Champagne; Child Is Born, A; Coney Island; Family; Fun; Hold That Thought; I Love a Romance; Job I Highly Recommend, A; Love in Bergdorf Goodman; Magical Night; Memory of Tonight; One More Day; Really Great Mood; Try to Remember It All; We'll Get Through This; What Am I Doing Here; What I Never Knew; You Can't Have Everything

Cast: Deborah Carlson; Carolee Carmello; Claiborne Cary; Barry Finkel; Merwin Goldsmith; William Hardy; Jan Neuberger; Tara Tyrrell; Christopher Wells

Notes: Program from Goodspeed Opera House.

199 • ARTISTS AND MODELS (1923)

OPENED: 08/20/1923   Theatre: Shubert
Revue   Broadway: 312

Composer: Jean Schwartz
Lyricist: Harold Atteridge; Cyrus Wood
Librettist: Harold Atteridge; Watson Barratt; Clare Briggs; Helena Smith Dayton; James Montgomery Flagg; Fontaine Fox; Rube Goldberg; Harry Wagstaff Gribble; Harry Hershfield; George Rosener; H.T. Webster; Cyrus Wood
Producer: Messrs. Shubert
Director: Harry Wagstaff Gribble; M. Francis Weldon

Costumes: Ernest Schrapps; **Orchestrations:** Alfred Goodman; **Set Design:** Watson Barratt; Rea Irvin

Songs: Carmencita; Flower of the Woodland; Golfing Blues [1]; Jackie Coogan (L: Harold Atteridge); Johnnie; Music of Love [2] (C: Alfred Goodman; L: Cyrus D. Wood); One in a Million to Me [1] (L: Cyrus D. Wood); Say It with a Ukelele; Some How (L: Cyrus Wood); Take Me Back to Samoa Some More (L: Cyrus D. Wood)

Cast: Frank Fay; Grace Hamilton; Harry Kelly; Bob Nelson

Notes: [1] Sheet music only. [2] Credited to Goodman in program and Schwartz in sheet music.

200 • ARTISTS AND MODELS (1924)

OPENED: 10/15/1924   Theatre: Astor
Revue   Broadway: 258

Composer: Sigmund Romberg
Lyricist: Sam Coslow; Clifford Grey
Producer: Messrs. Shubert
Director: Harry Wagstaff Gribble

Choreographer: Seymour Felix; **Costumes:** Charles LeMaire; Ernest Schrapps; **Musical Director:** Harold Neiman; **Orchestrations:** Emil Gerstenberger; **Set Design:** Watson Barratt; Rollo Wayne

Songs: Always the Same; Artists and Models; Behind My Lady's Fan (C: Unknown); Charm [1]; Dancing Colors (C: Unknown); Follow Your Star [2]; Gold Digger's Blues, The [1] (C: Unknown); Good Night [3] (C: Con Conrad; L: Irving Bibo; Leo Wood); Grass Widows [1] (C: Unknown); Hula Lou [5] (C: Milton Charles; Wayne King); I Love to Dance When I Hear a March (C: J. Fred Coots); Je Vous Aime [1] (C: Unknown); Lily Pool, The [1]; Manners and Motions [1]; Mediterranean Nights (C: Unknown); Mirage, The [1]; Model Toddle (C: Unknown); Models, The [1] (C: Unknown); My Riviera Rose (C: Horatio Nicholls; L: Jean Frederick); Off to Greenwich Village (C: Unknown); Old Fashioned Tin Types [4]; Oo La La; Pull Your String; Sirens of the Sea [4]; Spanish Juanita [2] (C: Unknown); There Is Somebody for Everybody but Me [1] (C: Unknown); Titina [1] (C: Unknown); Tomorrow; Tomorrow's Another Day (1) (C: J. Fred Coots; L: Sam Coslow); Tomorrow's

Another Day (2) [1] (L: Clifford Grey); Under a Parasol [1]; What a Beautiful Face Will Do; What a Village Girl Should Know (C: Unknown); Which Do You Prefer? [1] (C: Unknown); Who's the Lucky Fellow? (C: J. Fred Coots)

Cast: Frank Gaby; Trini; Mabel Withee

Notes: In Atlantic City the music was also credited to Sam Coslow. In Baltimore the music was also credited to Maurie Rubens and Al Goodman. [1] Cut Atlantic City 9/15/25. [2] Out Baltimore 12/28/25. [3] Credited to Romberg in sheet only. [4] Sheet music only. [5] ASCAP/Library of Congress only.

201 • ARTISTS AND MODELS (1925)

OPENED: 06/24/1925   Theatre: Winter Garden
Revue   Broadway: 416

Composer: J. Fred Coots; Al Goodman; Maurie Rubens
Lyricist: Clifford Grey
Librettist: Harold Atteridge; Henry Wagstaff Gribble
Producer: Messrs. Shubert
Director: Alexander Leftwich; J.J. Shubert

Choreographer: Jack Haskell; Gertrude Hoffman; **Costumes:** Barbier; Erte; **Musical Director:** Harry Nieman; **Orchestrations:** Emil Gerstenberger; **Set Design:** Watson Barratt

Songs: Cellini's Dream (C: Unknown); Charleston (C: Unknown); Flex-a-tone (C: Unknown); Follow Your Star (C: J. Fred Coots); Let Me Dance (C: Unknown); Lucita (C: Unknown); Magic Garden of Love, The (C: Unknown); Maid of the Milky Way (C: Unknown); Mothers of the World (C: Sigmund Romberg); Oriental Memories (C: Unknown); Rotisserie, The (C: Unknown); Take a Little Baby Home with You (C: J. Fred Coots); Washington Square [1] (C: Cole Porter; L: Melville Gideon; E. Ray Goetz)

Cast: Phil Baker; Jay Brennan; Herbert Corthell; Billy B. Van; Frances Williams; Walter Wolf

Notes: Program credits J. Fred Coots, Alfred Goodman and Maurie Rubens with music. However, they did not collaborate. Composer credits listed only when verifiable. [1] In THE ECLIPSE as "In Chelsea Somewhere."

202 • ARTISTS AND MODELS (1927)

OPENED: 11/15/1927 Theatre: Winter Garden
Revue Broadway: 151

Composer: Harry Akst; Maurie Rubens
Lyricist: J. Keirn Brennan; Benny Davis; Jack Osterman
Producer: Messrs. Shubert
Director: J.C. Huffman; Charles Judels

Choreographer: Earl Lindsay; Jan Oyra; Ralph Reader; **Costumes:** Ernest Schrapps; Max Weldy; **Musical Director:** Max Meth; **Set Design:** Watson Barratt

Songs: Bangaway Isle; Bracelets [1] (C: Maurie Rubens; L: J. Keirn Brennan); Call of Broadway, The (C: Maurie Rubens; L: Ted Lewis, Jack Osterman); Chair Bottom Dance, The [2]; Chinchilla [3]; Clowns [3]; Do That Thing [3]; Here Am I-Broken Hearted (C: Ray Henderson; L: Lew Brown; B.G. DeSylva); How They Changed the Day [3]; I'll Be Your Artist and You Be My Model; Is Everybody Happy Now? (C: Maurie Rubens; L: Ted Lewis; Jack Osterman); Lobster Crawl, The (C: Ted Lewis; L: Benny Davis); Mirror Finale, The [3]; Oh, Lady; Oh, Peggy [3] (C: Harry Akst; L: Benny Davis); One Two Three Four [3]; Only One for Me, The (C: Harry Akst; L: Benny Davis); Organ, The [3]; Rheims Cathedral, The; Snap Out of It [4] (C: Harry Akst; L: Benny Davis); Start the Band; There's Nothing New in Old New York (C: Harry Akst; L: Benny Davis); Voice of the World, The [3]; What Women and Men Will Wear; You Dear

Cast: Lucille Arnold; Eddie Chester; Margie Evans; Catherine Gallimore; Walter Johnson; Jscherey & Hully; King & King; Ted Lewis; John McDowell; Florence Moore; Marietta O'Brien; Harry O'Neal; Jack Osterman; Jan Oyra; Chauncey Parsons; Nayan Pearce; Jack Pearl; Manila Powers; Kay Simmons; Jack Squires; Jo Storage; Gladys Wheaton

Notes: Program credits Harry Akst and Maurie Rubens as composers. They did not collaborate. Credits as lyricists are Benny Davis, Jack Osterman and J. Keirn Brennan. They did not collaborate. [1] Also in GAY PAREE (1929). [2] Out Brooklyn 9/26/27. [3] Out Atlantic City 8/27. [4] Out Brooklyn 9/26/27. Out Atlantic City 8/27.

203 • ARTISTS AND MODELS (1930)

OPENED: 06/10/1930 Theatre: Majestic
Revue Broadway: 55

Composer: Ernie Golden; Harold Stern
Lyricist: Ernie Golden; Harold Stern
Producer: Messrs. Shubert
Director: Frank Smithson

Source: DEAR LOVE (Musical: Herbert Clayton; Dion Titheradge; Joseph Tunbridge; Jack Waller; Haydn Wood; Laurie Wylie); **Choreographer::** Pal'mere Brandeaux; **Costumes:** Ernest Schrapps; **Musical Director:** Max Meth; **Set Design:** Watson Barratt

Songs: Budapest; Coeds [1]; Dance, Dance, Dance; Donna Clara [1]; I Want You to Love Me; In Old Havana Town; Jimmy and Me; L-O-V-E; Make It Hot [1]; Milk and Crackers [1]; My Real Ideal (C: Burton Lane; L: Sammy Lerner); Nargileh; Old Lady in the Shoe; Parisian Tango; Perfect Models; Phantoms of the Night [1]; Ro-Ro-Rollin' Along; Rumba, The; Sex Appeal; Sing Something Simple [1] (C/L: Herman Hupfeld); Tree, The; Two Perfect Lovers (C: Burton Lane; L: Sammy Lerner); Ups and Downs; Where You Are; Without a Shadow of a Doubt (C/L: Ord Hamilton)

Cast: Mary Adams; Phil Baker; Dolores DeMonde; Hazel Harris; Stanley Harrison; George Hassell; Naomi Johnson; Kay McKay; Vera Pearce; Wesley Pierce; Aileen Stanley; Harry Welsh; Halfred Young

Notes: [1] Out Newark 12/8/30.

204 • ARTISTS AND MODELS (1943)

OPENED: 11/05/1943 Theatre: Broadway
Revue Broadway: 27

Composer: Philip Charig
Lyricist: Milton Pascal; Dan Shapiro
Librettist: Frank Luther; Don Ross; Lou Walters
Producer: Don Ross; Lou Walters
Director: John Kennedy

Choreographer: Natalie Kamarova; **Costumes:** Katherine Kuhn; **Musical Director:** Max Meth; **Set Design:** Watson Barratt; **Vocal Arranger:** Clay Warnick

Songs: Afternoon Tea [1]; Blowing the Top; How'ja Like to Take Me Home; Isle of Meinisooris [1]; Let's Keep It That Way [2] (C/L: Ervin Drake); My Heart Is On a Binge; Sears Roebuck [1]; Swing Low, Sweet Harriet; Two a Day [1]; Way Up North in Dixie [1]; What Does the Public Want [1]; You Are Romance; You'll Know that It's Me

Cast: Sheila Bond; Francis Faye; Jane Froman; Jackie Gleason; Gloria Le Roy

Notes: [1] Out Boston 10/11/43. [2] ASCAP/Library of Congress only.

205 • ARTISTS' MODEL, AN
OPENED: 12/17/1895   Theatre: Broadway
Musical   Broadway: 56

Composer: Sidney Jones
Lyricist: Harry Greenbank
Librettist: Owen Hall
Producer: Charles Frohman; Al Neyman
Director: Sidney Ellison

Choreographer: John D'Auban; LeFranc, Mr.;
   Musical Director: Leopold Wenzel; **Set Design:**
   E.G. Unitt

Songs: Farewell Waltz [1] (C: Ludwig Held;
   L: Moritz West); Umpty Umpty Aye

Cast: Minnie Cathcart; Lawrence D'Orsay; Nellie Stewart

Notes: No songs listed in program. [1] From DER OBERSTEIGER.

206 • AS THE GIRLS GO
OPENED: 11/13/1948   Theatre: Winter Garden
Musical   Broadway: 414

Composer: Jimmy McHugh
Lyricist: Harold Adamson
Librettist: William Roos
Producer: Michael Todd
Director: Howard Bay

Choreographer: Hermes Pan; **Costumes:** Oleg
   Cassini; **Musical Director:** Max Meth;
   Orchestrations: Ted Royal; **Set Design:** Howard
   Bay; **Vocal Arranger:** Hugh Martin

Songs: American Cannes; As the Girls Go; Brighten Up and Be a Little Sunbeam; Father's Day; Holiday in the Country; It Takes a Woman to Get a Man; It's More Fun Than a Picnic; I've Got the President's Ear; Lucky in the Rain; Nobody's Heart but Mine; Rock, Rock, Rock; There Are Other Things a Girl Can Do [1]; There's No Getting Away from You; You Say the Nicest Things, Baby

Cast: Betty Lou Barto; Bill Callahan; Bobby Clark; Donny Harris; Cavada Humphrey; Kathryn Lee; Irene Rich; Betty Jane Watson

Notes: [1] Not in programs.

207 • AS THOUSANDS CHEER
OPENED: 09/30/1933   Theatre: Music Box
Revue   Broadway: 390

Composer: Irving Berlin
Lyricist: Irving Berlin
Librettist: Moss Hart
Producer: Sam H. Harris
Director: Hassard Short

Choreographer: Charles Weidman; **Costumes:**
   Irene Sharaff; Varady; **Lighting Designer:**
   Hassard Short; **Musical Director:** Frank Tours;
   Orchestrations: Adolph Deutsch; Helmy Kress;
   Eddie Powell; Frank Tours; Russell Wooding;
   Set Design: Albert Johnson

Songs: Easter Parade; Funnies, The; Harlem on My Mind; Heat Wave; How's Chances?; Lonely Heart; Majestic Sails at Midnight; Not for All the Rice in China; Our Wedding Day; Revolt in Cuba; Suppertime; To Be or Not to Be; We'll All Be in Heaven When the Dollar Goes to Hell [1]

Cast: Leslie Adams; Helen Broderick; Jerome Cowan; Hal Forde; Thomas Hamilton; Hamtree Harrington; Jose Limon; Marilyn Miller; Harry Stockwell; Ethel Waters; Clifton Webb

Notes: [1] Unused. [2] Not in programs.

208 • AS YOU WERE
OPENED: 01/27/1920   Theatre: Central
Revue   Broadway: 143

Composer: Herman Darewski
Lyricist: Arthur Wimperis
Librettist: Glen MacDonough
Producer: E. Ray Goetz
Director: George Marion

Source: PLUS CA CHANGE (Play: Pip);
  Choreographer:: Julian Mitchell; **Costumes:**
  Dorothy Armstrong; Homer Conant; Pieter
  Meyer; Mme. Pascaud; Paul Poiret; **Musical
  Director:** Louis Silvers; **Set Design:** Withald
  Gordon; Herbert Ward

Songs: Broadway Strut [1] (C: J. Fred Coots);
  Follow Mr. Watteau (L: Arthur Wimperis);
  Good Bye Helen of Troy [1] (C: Gitz Rice); Helen
  of Troy [4]; I Am Cleopatra (C/L: E. Ray Goetz);
  If You Could Care for Me; If You'll Only Say It
  with Flowers [2] (C/L: E. Ray Goetz); Live for
  All You're Worth (L: E. Ray Goetz; Arthur
  Wimperis); Make Hay, Hay, Hay [1]; 'Neath
  Egyptian Skies [1] (C: Gitz Rice); Ninon Was a
  Naughty Girl; On the Bosom of the Sleepy Nile
  (C/L: E. Ray Goetz; L: Howard Smith); Saturday
  Afternoon Till Monday Morning (C/L: E. Ray
  Goetz); Two (Little) Bits of Greece; Under
  Grecian Skies (C/L: E. Ray Goetz); Washington
  Square [3] (C: Melville Gideon; L: E. Ray Goetz;
  Cole Porter); When You're Dancing in a Nightie
  on the Lawn (C/L: E. Ray Goetz); Who Ate
  Napoleons with Josephine When Napoleon Was
  Away? (C: E. Ray Goetz; L: Alfred Bryan)

Cast: Sam Bernard; Irene Bordoni; Hugh Cameron;
  Ruth Donnelly; Clifton Webb

Notes: [1] Out Wilkes Barre 11/13/?? [2] Sheet
  music only. [3] Name changed to "In Chelsea
  Somewhere" when presented in the London
  show BUDDIES. [4] British sheet music only.

209 • ASINAMALI! (WE HAVE NO MONEY)

OPENED: 04/23/1987   Theatre: Jack Lawrence
Play   Broadway: 29

Author: Mbongeni Ngema
Producer: Robert A. Buckley; Jane Harmon; Nina
  Kenneally; Edward L. Schuman; Kenneth
  Waissman
Director: Mbongeni Ngema

Lighting Designer: Wesley France

Cast: Solomzi Bisholo; Thomas Cele; Bongani
  Hlophe; Bheki Mqadi; Bhoyi Ngema

Notes: No songs listed in program.

210 • ASK DAD

Notes: *See OH, MY DEAR.*

211 • ASPECTS OF LOVE

OPENED: 04/08/1990   Theatre: Broadhurst
Musical   Broadway: 377

Composer: Andrew Lloyd Webber
Lyricist: Don Black; Charles Hart
Librettist: Andrew Lloyd Webber
Director: Trevor Nunn

Source: ASPECTS OF LOVE (Novel: David
  Garnett); **Choreographer::** Gillian Lynne;
  Costumes: Maria Bjornson; **Lighting Designer:**
  Andrew Bridge; **Musical Director:** Paul Bogaev;
  Orchestrations: David Cullen; Andrew Lloyd
  Webber; **Set Design:** Maria Bjornson

Songs: Anything but Lonely; Chanson d'Enfance;
  Everybody Loves a Hero; Falling; First Man You
  Remember, The; Hand Me the Wine and the
  Dice; Journey of a Lifetime, The; Leading Lady;
  Love Changes Everything; Memory of a Happy
  Moment, A; Mermaid Song; Other Pleasures;
  Parlez-Vous Francais?; Seeing Is Believing; She'd
  Be Far Better Off with You; Stop, Wait, Please;
  There Is More to Love

Cast: Michael Ball; Walter Charles; Kevin Colson;
  Ann Crumb; Danielle Du Clos; Deanna Du Clos

212 • ASSASSINS

OPENED: 01/27/1991   Theatre: Playwrights
                         Horizons
Musical   Off-Broadway: 25

Composer: Stephen Sondheim
Lyricist: Stephen Sondheim
Librettist: John Weidman
Producer: Playwrights Horizons
Director: Jerry Zaks

Choreographer: D.J. Giagni; **Costumes:** William
  Ivey Long; **Lighting Designer:** Paul Gallo;

Musical Director: Paul Gemignani; **Set Design:** Loren Sherman

Songs: Another National Anthem; Ballad of Booth, The; Ballad of Czolgosz, The; Ballad of Guiteau, The; Everybody's Got the Right; Gun Song; How I Saved Roosevelt; Something Just Broke (November 22, 1963) [1]; Unworthy of Your Love

Cast: Jace Alexander; Patrick Cassidy; Joy Franz; Victor Garber; Greg Germann; Annie Golden; Lyn Greene; Jonathan Hadary; John Jellison; Eddie Korbich; Terrence Mann; Debra Monk; Marcus Olson; William Parry; Michael Shulman; Lee Wilkof

Notes: [1] Added to London production.

213 • AT EASE (1)

Revue

Composer: Arthur Schwartz
Lyricist: Howard Dietz

Songs: Break It Now, Buck Private [11] (C: Hoagy Carmichael; L: Johnny Mercer); Come Along to the Show [1]; Fancy, Fancy [8] (C: Vernon Duke; L: Ira Gershwin); Finale Marches On, The [9]; Hooray for Us! [5] (C: Harold Arlen; L: E.Y. Harburg); New War Situation [6] (C: Vernon Duke; L: Ira Gershwin); Sailor with the Tap-Tap-Tap, The [2]; Shakespearean Opening [3]; She Hasn't a Thing Except Me [8] (C: Vernon Duke; L: Ira Gershwin); Time Marches On [8] (C: Vernon Duke; L: Ira Gershwin); Uniform, The [4]; Wait Till You See Me in the Morning [10] (C: Hoagy Carmichael; L: Johnny Mercer); We Somehow Feel That You Enjoyed Our Show [7] (C: Vernon Duke; L: Ira Gershwin)

Notes: A USO/Camp show. [1] Same music as "Get Away from It All" from AT HOME ABROAD. [2] Revision of song "The Lady with the Tap" from AT HOME ABROAD. [3] From THE SHOW IS ON. [4] Revision of song "The Uniform Dance" from BETWEEN THE DEVIL. [5] Revised lyric from title song of HOORAY FOR WHAT! [6] Revision of "Economic Situation" from ZIEGFELD FOLLIES OF 1936. [7] Revision of "We Hope You'll Soon Be Dancing to Our Score" from ZIEGFELD FOLLIES OF 1936. [8] From ZIEGFELD FOLLIES OF 1936. [9] From THE SHOW IS ON. [10] From

WALK WITH MUSIC but with revised lyric here. [11] Revision of song "Break It Up, Cinderella" from WALK WITH MUSIC.

214 • AT EASE (2)

OPENED: 12/11/1942
Revue

Composer: Billy Robbins
Librettist: Robert Healy; Larry Pearl
Producer: Members of the 385th Inf.
Director: Larry Pearl

Songs: How Do You Like the Army; I'm Looking for a Lonely Soldier; Love Made a Fool of Me; Manhattan; Same As Love, The; Why Do I Dream?; You Are My Hope, Dear

Cast: Johann Adamski; Carl Carden; Tommy Hart; Manny Kann; Manny Kussack; Jess Lopez; Pat Murray; Harold Pearsall; Miles Riffle; Demetrius Sabbar; Pianist: Fred Peter; Billy Robbins

Notes: An Army musical revue. Program of Washington, D.C. Capitol Theatre used.

215 • AT GAY CONEY ISLAND

OPENED: 02/01/1897   Theatre: Columbus
Musical   Broadway: 8

Composer: Harry Bulger; J. Sherrie Mathews
Additional Music: Maurice Levi
Lyricist: Harry Bulger; J. Sherrie Mathews
Librettist: Levin C. Tees
Producer: Harry Bulger; Julian Matthews
Director: Julian Mitchell

Choreographer: H. Fletcher Rivers; **Set Design:** John H. Young

Cast: Harry Bulger; Josie De Witt; James Harrigan; J. Sherrie Mathews; Jessie Ralph

Notes: No program available.

216 • AT HOME ABROAD

OPENED: 09/19/1935   Theatre: Winter Garden
Revue   Broadway: 198

Composer: Arthur Schwartz
Lyricist: Howard Dietz
Librettist: Marc Connelly; Howard Dietz;

Reginald Gardiner; Raymond Knight; Dion
Titheradge
Producer: Messrs. Shubert
Director: Vincente Minnelli; Thomas Mitchell

Choreographer: Harry Losee; Gene Snyder;
Costumes: Vincente Minnelli; **Musical Director:**
Al Goodman; **Orchestrations:** Robert Russell
Bennett; David Raksin; Hans Spialek; Don
Walker; Phil Walsh; Russell Wooding; **Set
Design:** Vincente Minnelli

Songs: Alt Wein [2]; Death in the Afternoon;
Farewell, My Lovely; Get Away from It All [1];
Get Yourself a Geisha; Got a Bran' New Suit;
Hottentot Potentate; Lady with the Tap, The [3];
Loadin' Time; Love Is a Dancing Thing; O, Leo!;
O What a Wonderful World; Parec; Steamboat
Whistle, The [4]; That's Not Cricket; Thief in the
Night; Up the Creek [2]; When You're Away [5];
You May Be Far Away from Me [2]

Cast: 6 Spirits of Rhythm; Vera Allen; Continentals,
The; Eddie Foy Jr.; Reginald Gardiner; Paul
Haakon; Sue Hastings' Marionettes; Beatrice
Lillie; James MacColl; Woods Miller; Eleanor
Powell; Ethel Waters; Nina Whitney; Herb
Williams

Notes: [1] Music later used for "Come to Our
Show" from AT EASE. [2] Cut out of town. [3]
Revised with new lyric for "The Soldier with the
Tap-Tap-Tap" from AT EASE. [4] Also in
FOLLOW THE SUN. [5] ASCAP/Library of
Congress only.

217 • AT JOLLY 'COON'-EY ISLAND
OPENED: 1896

Composer: Billy Johnson
Lyricist: Bob Cole

Songs: At Jolly Coon-ey Island; Black Four Hundred
Ball; Down to Cooney Island; 4-11-44; Red Hots;
Song of the Bathers; Song of the Bloomers

Notes: Information from program from
Wilkes-Barre 11/20/1896.

218 • AT THE BALL
Notes: *See MISS DAISY.*

219 • AT THE BARRACKS
OPENED: 10/09/1912
Musical   Closed out of town

Composer: Robert Hood Bowers
Lyricist: Grant Stewart
Librettist: Cecil B. DeMille

Notes: No other information available.

220 • AT THE DROP OF A HAT
OPENED: 10/08/1959   Theatre: John Golden
Revue   Broadway: 215

Composer: Donald Swann
Lyricist: Michael Flanders
Producer: Alexander H. Cohen

Lighting Designer: Ralph Alswang

Songs: Bed [1]; Built Up Area [1]; Commonwealth
Fair [1]; Eine Kleine Nachtmusic Cha Cha Cha
[1]; Gnu, A; Happy Song, A; Hippopotamus;
Hog Beneath the Skin, The; Hundred Song, The
[1]; In the Bath; Je Suis le Tenebreux (L: Gerard
de Nerval); Judgement of Paris; Kokoraki;
Madeira, M'Dear?; Misalliance; Paris [1];
Philological Waltz; Reluctant Cannibal, The;
Satellite Moon; Sea Fever; Song of Reproduction;
Song of the Weather, A; Too Many Cookers [1];
Transport of Delight, A; Vanessa [1]; Wompom,
The; Youth of the Heart, The (L: Sidney Carter)

Cast: Michael Flanders; Donald Swann

Notes: Curtain by Hirschfeld. [1] Added to the
show and also included in some performances of
its sequel, AT THE DROP OF ANOTHER HAT.

221 • AT THE DROP OF ANOTHER HAT
OPENED: 12/27/1966   Theatre: Booth
Revue   Broadway: 105

Composer: Donald Swann
Lyricist: Michael Flanders
Producer: Alexander H. Cohen

Lighting Designer: Ralph Alswang

Songs: All Gall; Armadillo Idyll; Bilbo's Song
(L: J.R.R. Tolkien); By Air; Food for Thought; Gas

Man Cometh, The; Horoscope; Ill Wind
(C: Wolfgang Amadeus Mozart); In the Desert
(L: Donald Swann); Motor Perpetuo; P** P* B****
B** D******; Prehistoric Complaint; Sloth; Slow
Train; Song of Patriotic Prejudice, A; Thermo-
dynamic Duo; Twenty Tons of TNT; Twice Shy

Cast: Michael Flanders; Donald Swann

Notes: *See also AT THE DROP OF A HAT* for songs
that appeared in both shows. The show also
contained some of Flanders and Swann's animal
songs under the heading "From Our Bestiary."

222 • AT THE FRENCH BALL
OPENED: 04/26/1897   Theatre: Bijou
Musical   Broadway: 32

Librettist: Frederick E. Schrader

Musical Director: Edward Trantman

Cast: Reba Haight; Fanny Rice; John S. Terry

Notes: No program available.

223 • AT THE GRAND
OPENED: 07/07/1958
Musical   Closed out of town

Composer: George Forrest; Robert Wright
Lyricist: George Forrest; Robert Wright
Librettist: Luther Davis
Producer: L.A. Civic Light Opera; Edwin Lester
Director: Albert Marre

Source: GRAND HOTEL (Novel: Vicki Baum);
  Choreographer:: Ernest Flatt; **Costumes:**
  Adrian; **Dance Arranger:** Trude Rittman;
  Lighting Designer: Feder; **Musical Director:**
  Jay Blackton; **Orchestrations:** Arthur Kay;
  Albert Sendry; Al Woodbury; **Set Design:**
  Rouben Ter-Arutunian

Songs: Always Alone [1]; At the Grand; Bare
  Necessities, The; Blest?; Crescendo; End of Aria
  (from LA SARACENA); Feeding Time; Grand
  Tango, The; I Waltz Alone [3]; Isola [2]; It's Italy
  [1]; La Sarancena; Maria [1]; Press Conference
  (Blest!); See Rome and Live; Sophia; Table with a
  View, A [3]; Up [1]; Va Bene; We'll Take a Glass
  Together [3]; What You Need [3]

Cast: Neile Adams; David Atkinson; Joan Diener;
  Rico Froehlich; George Givot; Paul Muni; David
  Opatoshu; Vladimir Sokoloff

Notes: *See also GRAND HOTEL. LA SARECENA*
  was an old Italian opera invented and composed
  by Wright and Forrest. [1] On demo only. [2]
  Same music as "Elena" in KEAN. [3] Also in
  GRAND HOTEL.

224 • AT YALE
OPENED: 1906
Play   Closed out of town

Author: Owen Davis
Director: Jules Murry

Songs: Beulah (C/L: Unknown); Love's Young
  Dream (C/L: Daniel Dore); Sons of Eli (C/L:
  Unknown); You, My You (C/L: Edward Laska)

Cast: Paul Gilmore

Notes: From a Wilkes-Barre program 10/06/06.
  No other information available.

225 • AT YOUR SERVICE (1940)
OPENED: 1940
Play   Closed out of town

Music Based On: Giochino Rossini
Composer: Erich Wolfgang Korngold
Lyricist: William Okie
Author: Karla Martell; William Okie
Producer: Ben Stein
Director: Max Reinhardt

Source: SERVANT OF TWO MASTERS, A (Play:
  Carlo Goldoni)

Cast: John Bainbridge; Walter Brooke; Nanette
  Fabray; Jim Richardson; Ruth Sendholm

Notes: Program from San Francisco 1/40.

226 • AT YOUR SERVICE (1943)
OPENED: 1943
Revue

Lyricist: Edward Heyman
Author: Edward Heyman
Producer: Sac. Air Svc. Comm.

Songs: I Got the Bird on the Canary Island
(C: Paul Baker); I Wonder How She Is Tonight
(C: Cliff Fishback); Isn't Love a Rainbow?
(C: Pat Abernathy); It's Hot in Chile (C: Herbert
Sorkin)

Notes: An Army show. No other information
available.

227 • ATHENIAN TOUCH, THE
OPENED: 01/14/1964   Theatre: Jan Hus House
Musical   Off-Broadway: 1

Composer: Willard Straight
Lyricist: David Eddy
Librettist: J. Albert Fracht; Arthur Goodman
Producer: David Brown; Ronald Taylor
Director: Alex Palermo

Choreographer: Alex Palermo; **Costumes:** Don
Foote; **Lighting Designer:** Robert T. Williams;
Musical Director: Glen Clugston;
Orchestrations: Glen Clugston; Willard Straight;
Set Design: Robert T. Williams

Songs: Agent's Blood; All We Need to Know;
Awkward Little Boy; Eleleu!; Harmony, Sweet
Harmony; Have a Little Sooth on Me; Lady of
Leisure, A; Look Away; Love, You Are So
Difficult; Lysistrata; No Garlic Tonight; Singer
and the Song, The; There Goes Time; Today's the
Day; What Is a Woman; When You Write a
Greek Comedy

Cast: John Baylis; Marlon Marlowe; William
Martel; Butterfly McQueen; Will Richter

228 • ATHLETIC GIRL, THE
OPENED: 02/15/1905   Theatre: Colonial Music
                       Hall
Musical   New York

Composer: Jean Schwartz
Lyricist: George V. Hobart
Librettist: George V. Hobart
Director: Edward P. Temple

Set Design: Arthur Voegtlin

Songs: Back to Sioux Sioux City; Dumb Bell, The;
Good Night, Mr. Organ Grinder Man; Guess I'm
Seasick; Luna Park; Mr. Lawson, the Man from
Boston; My Indiana Anna; Opening Chorus Act

I; There's Only One Little Old New York; Topsy
Turvy Oskaloosa Lou

Cast: Edward J. Connolly; Billy Kent; William
Kent; Frank Lalor; Junie McCree

Notes: A one-act musical.

229 • ATLANTIC CITY
Musical   Unproduced

Composer: Cy Coleman
Lyricist: Christopher Gore
Producer: Producers Circle

Songs: Alderberan; Atlantic City; Cold in the
Morning; Day You Leave Me, The

Notes: No other information available.

230 • ATTA BABY
OPENED: 1923

Songs: You and I Atta Baby [1] (C: Carle Carlton;
L: Howard Johnson)

Notes: No other information available. [1] Howard
Johnson wrote a song of the same title for
TANGERINE the preceeding year.

231 • ATTA BOY
OPENED: 12/23/1918   Theatre: Lexington
Musical   Broadway: 24

Composer: Unknown
Lyricist: Unknown
Librettist: Ballard Macdonald; Nat Osborne;
Andre Sherri
Director: Jack Mason

Costumes: Andre Sherri; **Set Design:** Charles
LeMaire

Songs: Angel Child; Another Good Man Gone
Wrong (C: Nat Osborne; L: Ballard Macdonald);
Elephant Skid; Father Will Be with Us Soon
(C: Nat Osborne; L: H.H. Skerrett Jr.); Hold Me
In Your Arms; I Love Her and She Loves Me;
Just to Be a Little Boy Again; M'sieur Jimmy,
Come and Shake Z Shimmy (C: Nat Osborne;
L: Ballard Macdonald); Magic in Your Big Blue
Eyes, The (C: Nat Osborne; L: Ballard

Macdonald); On a Little Farm in Normandie; Opening Act II; Opening Ensemble; Ragtime Wedding, The; She's Like a Big Bouquet (C: Nat Osborne; L: Ballard Macdonald); Stars in the Service Flag, The; Strolling 'Round the Camp with Mary (C: Nat Osborne; L: Ballard Macdonald); Victory Song; With the Rose (I Send This Heart of Mine) (C: Nat Osborne; L: Ballard Macdonald); Worst Is Yet to Come, The

Cast: Frank Tinney

Notes: Produced by the soldiers of the Aberdeen Proving Grounds in Maryland.

232 • AUCASSIN AND NICOLETTE

Notes: *See FESTIVAL.*

233 • AUCTION PINOCHLE

OPENED: 1912   Theatre: 57th St.
Musical   Broadway: 150

Composer: Adolf Philipp
Lyricist: Edward A. Paulton
Librettist: Edward A. Paulton; Adolf Philipp
Producer: Oliver Morosco

Songs: Auction Pinochle Song; Blond Louise; Drawing the Line; I Ask You Why Dear; Louise; Nice Little Home Is What I Sigh For, A; Only Her Ankles; That's Right, Dear

Cast: Adolf Philipp

Notes: Philipp credits the source as being by Paul Herve and co-composition by Jean Briquet. Actually, Herve and Briquet probably did not exist. Paulton was hired to write the English version.

234 • AUF JAPAN

OPENED: 06/07/1903
Musical

Composer: Rudolf Friml

Notes: Presented at the Dresden Hoftheater.

235 • AUNT HANNAH

OPENED: 02/22/1900   Theatre: Bijou
Musical   Off-Broadway: 21

Composer: A. Baldwin Sloane
Lyricist: Clay M. Greene
Librettist: Mathew J. Royal
Producer: William A. Brady; Joseph R. Grismer
Director: oseph R. Grismer

Songs: Little Bo-Peep; Ma Tiger Lily; What's the Matter with Hannah; When the Cat's Away the Mice Will Play

Cast: John Bunny; Agnes Findlay

Notes: Songs not listed in program.

236 • AUTO RACE, THE

OPENED: 11/25/1907   Theatre: Hippodrome
Revue   Broadway: 312

Composer: Manuel Klein
Lyricist: Manuel Klein
Librettist: Manuel Klein; Edward Temple
Producer: G.M. Anderson; Messrs. Shubert
Director: Edward Temple

Songs: Four Seasons, The; Riding in a Motor Car; Starlight Maid; Sweet Is the Perfume of Summer Flowers; Those Days Gone By

Cast: J. Parker Coombs; William R. Hawley; Marceline; Margaret Townsend

Notes: Second half of show THE BATTLE OF PORT ARTHUR. Included also was CIRCUS EVENTS.

237 • AUTOMOBILE GRAVEYARD, THE

OPENED: 11/13/1961   Theatre: 41st St.
Play   Off-Broadway: 8

Composer: Mordecai Sheinkman
Lyricist: Kenward Elmslie
Author: Fernando Arrabal
Translator: Richard Howard
Producer: Gian Sciandra
Director: Herbert Machiz

Songs: Bang-Bang Tango

Cast: Gabriel Dell; Leila Martin; Estelle Parsons

Notes: There were two songs used. No program available.

238 • AUTUMN MANOEVRES

Notes: *See THE GAY HUSSARS.*

239 • AUTUMN'S HERE

OPENED: 10/25/1966   Theatre: Bert Wheeler
Musical   Off-Broadway: 80

Composer: Norman Dean
Lyricist: Norman Dean
Librettist: Norman Dean
Producer: Bob Hadley
Director: Hal LeRoy

Source: LEGEND OF SLEEPY HOLLOW (Story: Washington Irving); **Choreographer::** Hal LeRoy; **Costumes:** Eve Henrikson; **Lighting Designer:** Arthur Terjeson; **Musical Director:** Gordon Munford; **Orchestrations:** Norman Dean; **Set Design:** Robert Conley; Arthur Terjeson

Songs: Any Day Now; Autumn's Here; Beware As You Ride Through the Hollow; Boy, Do I Hate Horse Races; Brom and Katrina; Chase, The; Dark New England Night; Do You Think I'm Pretty?; Dutch Country Table; Fine Words and Fancy Phrases; For the Harvest Safely Gathered; It's a Long Road Home; Me and My Horse; Patience; Private Hunting Ground; Sleepy Hollow; Song of the Thirteen Colonies; This Is the Girl for Me; Who Walks Like a Scarecrow; You May Be the Someone; You Never Miss the Water

Cast: Fred Gockel; Zona Kennedy; Alan Lobos; Joyce Lynn; Bob Riehl; Karin Wolfe

240 • AVENUE X

OPENED: 02/21/1994   Theatre: Playwrights
                              Horizons
Musical   Off-Broadway: 48

Composer: Ray Leslee
Lyricist: John Jiler; Ray Leslee
Librettist: John Jiler
Director: Mark Brokaw

Choreographer: Ken Roberson; **Costumes:** Ellen McCartney; **Lighting Designer:** Donald Holder; **Musical Director:** Chapman Roberts; **Set Design:** Loy Arcenas; **Vocal Arranger:** Chapman Roberts

Songs: Africa; Big Lucy; Command Me; Follow Me; Gloria; Go There; Io Sono Cosi Stanco; Moonlight in Old Sicily; Palermo; Rap; Scat; Serves You Right; She's Fifteen; Thousand Summer Nights, A; 'Tis the End of Time; Waitin'; Where Are You Tonight?; Where Is Love?; Why; Woman of the World

Cast: Ted Brunetti; Chuck Cooper; Alvaleta Guess; Colette Hawley; Keith Johnston; John Leone; Roger Mazzeo; Harold Perrineau

Notes: No songs listed in program

241 • AWAY WE GO!

Notes: *See OKLAHOMA!*

242 • AWF'LLY NICE

OPENED: 09/07/1964
Revue   Closed out of town

Composer: Frank Stuart
Lyricist: Tom McKee
Librettist: Frank Orefice
Producer: Pal'mere Brandeaux; Frank Stuart
Director: Pal'mere Brandeaux

Lighting Designer: Peter Xantho; **Orchestrations:** Edward Barefield; **Set Design:** Charles Teichner

Songs: Awf'lly Nice; Elect Me President; My Song; Preview of Heaven

Cast: Al Bernie; Julie Gibson; Marie Wilson

Notes: Programs from New Haven 9/12/64 and Boston 9/7/64. No songs listed in program.

B

243 • B-R-A
OPENED: 1919
Musical

Composer: Milton Thomas [1]
Lyricist: Lorenz Hart

Songs: Green and Gray; He Lights Another Mecca; Horicon Hop; I Used to Love Them All; Our Cheerleader; Tee Ta Tee

Notes: A camp show written for Brant Lake Camp. [1] Pseudonym for Mickie Thomashefsky.

244 • B.S. MOSS VARIETIES
OPENED: 1931
Revue

Songs: If I Could Live My Life All Over Again (C: Harry Revel; L: Mack Gordon)

Notes: No other information available.

245 • BABE
Musical   Unproduced

Composer: Alan Menken
Lyricist: Howard Ashman
Librettist: Howard Ashman

Songs: Growin' Boy

Notes: This musical was abandoned by its writers.

246 • BABES AND THE BARON, THE
OPENED: 12/25/1905   Theatre: Lyric
Musical   Broadway: 45

Composer: H.E. Haines
Lyricist: Robert B. Smith; Charles M. Taylor
Librettist: Robert Courtneidge; A.M. Thompson
Producer: John C. Fisher
Director: R.H. Burnside

Songs: By the Light of the Honeymoon or Kiss Me and Say You'll Be Mine (C: Anne Caldwell; L: James O'Dea); English Bow, The; Farewell, Dear Toys (March of the Toys) (inst.) (C: Jerome Kern); Firefly and the Rose, The (C/L: Nat D. Mann); Gee, But This Is a Lonesome Town (C/L: Billy Gaston); How D'Ye Do? (C/L: F.R. Babcock); I Didn't Mean No Harm (C: J. Fred Helf); I Would Like to Be Your Pal [2] (L: Junie McCree); I Would Like to Marry You (C/L: Edward Laska); If I But Dared (C/L: Nat D. Mann); I'm Fond of You [1] (C: Harold Orlob); Is a Kiss [1] (C: Harry O. Sutton); It's a Jolly Good Thing to Be Alive; Knock Wood (C: Raymond Hubbell); Leader of the German Band, The [1] (C: Theodore Morse); Message of the Moonbeam [1] (C: Billie Taylor); Milo (You're Just My Style-O) (C: Alfred Solman; L: Benj. Hapgood Burt); Music of the Band, The (C/L: Browne; Lipton); My Little Laplander [1] (C: C.W. Murphy); Opening Chorus (1) (C: Raymond Hubbell); Opening Chorus (2) [1]; Opening Chorus Act II [2] (C: Raymond Hubbell); Outlaw Bold, An (C/L: Arthur Weld); Robin Hood's Arrest; Sweet Seventeen [1] (C: I. Tate); Tailor's Dummy; Think It Over (C/L: Alex A. Aarons); Two Little Applekins [1] (C: H.E. Haines)

Cast: La Petite Adelaide; Lillian Coleman; Maude Lambert; James C. Marlowe; Junie McCree

Notes: This show was at one time titled BABES IN THE WOOD. [1] Cut out of town. [2] Out Boston 2/6/06.

247 • BABES IN ARMS
OPENED: 04/14/1937   Theatre: Shubert
Musical   Broadway: 289

Composer: Richard Rodgers
Lyricist: Lorenz Hart
Librettist: Lorenz Hart; Richard Rodgers
Producer: Dwight Deere Wiman
Director: Robert Sinclair

Choreographer: George Balanchine; **Costumes:** Helene Pons; **Musical Director:** Gene Salzer;

Orchestrations: Hans Spialek; **Set Design:** Raymond Sovey

Songs: All at Once; All Dark People; Babes in Arms; I Wish I Were in Love Again; Imagine; Johnny One Note; Lady Is a Tramp, The; My Funny Valentine; Peter's Journey Ballet (inst.); Way Out West; Where or When; You Are So Fair

Cast: Alex Courtney; Clifton Darling; Alfred Drake; Mitzi Green; Ray Heatherton; Ray McDonald; Duke McHale; Wynn Murray; Fayard Nicholas; Harold Nicholas; Robert Rounseville

248 • BABES IN THE WOOD (1903)
OPENED: 1903
Musical   Closed out of town

Librettist: J.C. Huffman
Producer: John C. Fisher; New Stock Company

Songs: Are You Engaged (C: Harold Orlob; L: Addison Burkhardt); Art of Knowing How, The (C: C.N. Schneider; L: F.T. Cardoze); Farewell, Dear Toys (inst.) (C: Jerome Kern); Girlie with the Winsome Smile, The (C: Edward Jolly; L: R.H. Burnside); In the Land of Romance; Keep on A'Shining, Silv'ry Moon (C: Ben M. Jerome; L: Arthur J. Lamb); Ki-Yo (C: Andy Lewis; L: Aaron S. Hoffman); My Little Laplander; Now I Lay Me Down to Sleep (C/L: J. Fred Helf); Red, Red, Beautiful Red; Sequel to a Tale from Mother Goose; Star Babies, The (The "Boogie Boo" Man); Sweet Seventeen (C: James W. Tate; L: George Arthurs); Take Me on the Merry-Go-Round

Notes: Pittsburgh. Sheet music only.

249 • BABES IN THE WOOD (1964)
OPENED: 12/28/1964   Theatre: Orpheum
Musical   Off-Broadway: 45

Composer: Rick Besoyan
Lyricist: Rick Besoyan
Librettist: Rick Besoyan
Producer: Sandy Farber; Aaron Schroeder
Director: Rick Besoyan

Source: MIDSUMMER NIGHT'S DREAM, A (Play: William Shakespeare); **Choreographer:** Ralph Beaumont; **Costumes:** Howard Barker; **Dance**

Arranger: Arnold Goland; **Lighting Designer:** Paul Morrison; **Musical Director:** Natalie Charlson; **Orchestrations:** Arnold Goland; **Set Design:** Paul Morrison; **Vocal Arranger:** Arnold Goland

Songs: Alphabet Song, The; Anyone Can Make a Mistake; Babes in the Wood; Cavorting; Gossip Song, The; Helena; Helena's Solution; I'm Not for You; Little Tear; Love Is Lovely; Lover Waits, A; Midsummer Night; Moon Madness; Mother; Old Fashioned Girl; There's a Girl; This State of Affairs; Titania's Philosophy

Cast: Ruth Buzzi; Danny Carroll; Joleen Fodor; Carol Glade; Richard Charles Hoh; Kenneth McMillan; Edward Miller; Don Stewart; Elmarie Wendel

250 • BABES IN TOYLAND (1903)
OPENED: 10/13/1903   Theatre: Majestic
Musical   Broadway: 192

Composer: Victor Herbert
Lyricist: Glen MacDonough
Librettist: Glen MacDonough
Producer: Fred R. Hamlin; Julian Mitchell
Director: Julian Mitchell

Costumes: Caroline Siedle; **Musical Director:** Max Hirschfeld; **Set Design:** Homer Emens; John Young

Songs: Angel Over the Fields [3]; Babes in Toyland [3]; Barney O'Flynn; Beatrice Barefacts; Before and After; Birth of the Butterfly (inst.) [2]; Christmas Fair Waltz; Country Dance (inst.) [3]; Dance Eccentrique; Entrance of Contrary Mary (inst.); Floretta; From Heavens on High [3]; Gavotte (inst.); Go to Sleep Slumber Deep!; Hail to Christmas; Hang March (inst.); He Won't Be Happy Till He Gets It (L: Charles Noel Douglas); Health Food Man, The [2]; I Can't Do the Sum; If I Were a Man Like That [2]; In the Toymaker's Workshop (inst.); Jane; John Johnson [3]; Lancers [3]; Legend of the Castle; March of the Toys (inst.); Mary, Mary; Maybe; Melodramatic Music (inst.); Men, The [2]; Mignonette [3]; Military Ball, The (inst.); Moon Will Help You Out Maybe, The; My Castle in Spain; My Rag Doll Girl; Never Mind Bo-Peep We Will Find Your Sheep [1]; Old Fashioned Rose, An; Rock-a-Bye Baby; Song of the Poet [3]; Spanish Basque Carol [3]; Spider's Den, The (inst.);

Toyland; Toymakers Shop, The; Winter Song [3]; With Downcast Eye [2]

Cast: Mabel Barrison; George W. Denham; William Norris; Gus Pixley; Amy Ricard; Bessie Wynn

Notes: This Majestic theatre is not the current one built in 1927, but rather an earlier one which was on Columbus Circle. [1] Titled "Don't Cry Bo-Peep" in program. [2] Sheet music only. [3] ASCAP/Library of Congress only.

251 • BABES IN TOYLAND (1979)
OPENED: 12/21/1979   Theatre: Felt Forum
Musical   Off-Broadway: 16

Composer: Shelly Markham
Lyricist: Annette Leisten
Librettist: Ellis Weiner
Producer: American Ent. Enterprises
Director: Munson Hicks

Source: BABES IN TOYLAND (Musical: Victor Herbert; Glen MacDonough)

Choreographer:: Tony Stevens; **Costumes:** Michael J. Hotopp; Paul dePass; **Dance Arranger:** Bob Stecko; **Lighting Designer:** Associated Theatre Design; **Musical Director:** Bob Christianson; **Orchestrations:** Bob Christianson; **Set Design:** Michael J. Hotopp; Paul dePass; **Vocal Arranger:** Kirk Nurock

Songs: Bare Facts; Big Baby; Disco Toyland [4] (C: Victor Herbert); Don't Cry Bo-Peep (C: Victor Herbert; L: Glen MacDonough); Dream Toyland [2] (C: Victor Herbert); March of the Wooden Soldiers (inst.) [3] (C: Victor Herbert); Something Must Be Done [1] (C: Victor Herbert); Step Out in Front; Sweet Life; Two of Us, The

Cast: Lynn Hippen; C.A. Hutton; Roger Lawson; Debbie McLeod; S. Barkley Murray

Notes: [1] Same music as "I Can't Do the Sum." [2] Based on the song "Toyland." [3] From original production. [4] Same music as "Toyland."

252 • BABETTE
OPENED: 11/16/1903   Theatre: Broadway
Musical   Broadway: 59

Composer: Victor Herbert
Lyricist: Harry B. Smith

Librettist: Harry B. Smith
Producer: Charles Dillingham
Director: Al Holbrook; Fred G. Latham

Costumes: F. Richard Anderson; **Musical Director:** John Lund; **Set Design:** Homer Emens; John Young

Songs: Be Kind to Poor Pierrot; Butterfly Waltz [4]; Clockmaker's Song; Entrance of Babette; Finale Act I; Finale Act II; Finale Act III; He Who'd Thrive Must Rise at Five [3]; Hear the Coachman Crack His Whip [2]; Here in Pleasure's Favorite Court [4]; I'll Bribe the Stars; In the Land of Spain [1]; It's a Way We Have in Spain; Kermess Day [1]; Let's Hope of Thee My Guardian Be [4]; Letters I Write All the Day; Life of a Bold Free Lance, The; My Honor and My Sword (Borrow Trouble); My Lady 'Tis for Thee [2]; My Lady of the Manor; On the Other Side of the Wall; On the Stage; Opening Chorus; Opening Chorus Act II; Opening Chorus Act III; Pavanne; Peddler's Song [1]; Story of Babette [4]; There Once Was an Owl; To the Sound of the Pipe and the Roll of the Drum; Tony the Peddler; Vivianne the Vivandiere; We Are Very Highly Polished at the Court Don't You Know [1]; What Is Love? (Canzonetta) [3]; Where the Fairest Flow'rs Are Blooming (Butterfly Waltz Song)

Cast: Edward Connelly; Eugene Cowles; Louis B. Harrison; Richie Ling; Fritzi Scheff

Notes: [1] Added to revival St. Louis 8/7/39. [2] Not in program. [3] Sheet music only. [4] ASCAP/Library of Congress only.

253 • BABY
OPENED: 12/04/1983   Theatre: Ethel Barrymore
Musical   Broadway: 241

Composer: David Shire
Lyricist: Richard Maltby Jr.
Librettist: Sybille Pearson
Producer: Ivan Bloch; James B. Freydberg; Kenneth-John Productions; Manuscript Prods.; Suzanne J. Schwartz
Director: Richard Maltby Jr.

Source: UNKNOWN (Story: Susan Yankowitz)

Choreographer: Wayne Cilento; **Costumes:** Jennifer von Mayrhauser; **Lighting Designer:** Pat Collins; **Musical Director:** Peter Howard;

Orchestrations: Jonathan Tunick; **Set Design:** John Lee Beatty

Songs: And What If We Had Loved Like That; At Night She Comes Home to Me; Baby, Baby, Baby; Busy, Busy [2]; Easier to Love; Fatherhood Blues; I Chose Right [1]; I Want It All; I Wouldn't Go Back [2]; In One Cell [2]; Ladies Singin' Their Song, The; Patterns [2]; Plaza Song, The; Romance; Story Goes On, The; Two People in Love; We Start Today; What Could Be Better?; With You

Cast: Liz Callaway; James Congdon; Catherine Cox; Beth Fowler; Todd Graff; Martin Vidnovic

Notes: [1] Music same as instrumental theme for film ONLY WHEN I LAUGH. [2] Cut prior to opening.

254 • BABY BLUES

OPENED: 1919
Musical

Composer: C. Luckeyth Roberts
Lyricist: Alex Rogers
Librettist: Alex Rogers
Producer: Quality Amusement Company

Songs: Baby Blues; Daddy Moon; Jewel of the Nile; Rain Song, The; Rock-a-By-Baby Blues; Wedding, The

Cast: Ida Brown; Jim Burris; Estelle Cash; Alex Rogers; Lavinia Rogers; "Dink" Stewart

Notes: No other information available.

255 • BABY FACE O'FLYNN

OPENED: 08/13/1952   Theatre: Gallery Stage
Musical   Los Angeles

Lyricist: William C. Barnes
Librettist: Philip Pearce
Director: Allen Fletcher

Choreographer: Carol Eller; Mary Pat Sawyer; **Lighting Designer:** William Kibby; **Musical Director:** Donald Sheffrey; **Orchestrations:** Jack Kolarik; Donald Sheffrey; **Set Design:** Richard Hay

Songs: Alarm; Baby Face O'Flynn; Bashful Boy, A; Church Box Social; Clock, The; Don't Call Me;

Don't Say I Didn't Give You Anything; Foolish the Heart; Heaven's Blessed Me; I Am the Luckiest Boy; I Smile and That's All Right; I'm Luckier than Dorian Gray; It's Love, I Think; Master of His Fate; Musical Chairs; Sweetheart; Too Late for Yesterday; Very Nice Sermon, Parson Potter, A; Welcome the Boys Back to Meadowbridge, Cal.; Wonderful Sunday; You Make It Seem Like Halloween

Cast: William C. Barnes; William Bond; Ann Guilbert

256 • BACHELOR BELLES, THE

OPENED: 11/07/1910   Theatre: Globe
Musical   Broadway: 32

Composer: Raymond Hubbell
Lyricist: Harry B. Smith
Librettist: Harry B. Smith
Producer: Klaw & Erlanger
Director: Julian Mitchell

Costumes: F. Richard Anderson; Wilhelm; **Musical Director:** Albert Krause; **Orchestrations:** Frank Saddler

Songs: Bachelor Belles, The; Carmenita; Give Us a Ragtime Tune; If I Just Think of Her; I'm Dying for You; In Vanity Fair; Initiation of Daphne, The; It's Style That Makes the Girl; Kisses at Auction; My Toreador [1]; Popular Girl, A; Roses and Butterflies; Seven Ages of Society [1]; She Trimmed Them All So Nicely; Song of the Fashions; Summer Girl, The; Those Good Old Days Can Never Come Again (They Were the Happy Days); Trying It On; We May Be Happy Yet [2]; What Has Become of the Girl I Used to Know; When You Meet Her in the Summertime [1]; Why Don't You Be Nice to Some Nice Fellow?; You've Been Kissing the Blarney Stone

Cast: Eva Fallon; Adeline Genee; Frank Lalor; Mae Murray

Notes: [1] Sheet music only. [2] ASCAP/Library of Congress.

257 • BACHELOR'S DINNER

OPENED: 1913
Musical   Closed out of town

Composer: A. Seymour Brown
Lyricist: A. Seymour Brown

Songs: Adam and Eve Had a Wonderful Time (C: Albert Gumble); I Don't Want To (Oh, Come On); She's the Girl (C: Bert Grant); Somebody Loves You; That Tinkling Tango Tune (C: Albert Gumble); When Love Comes Knocking at Your Heart (C: Bert Grant)

Notes: No other information available.

258 • BACK AGAIN
OPENED: 04/29/1918
Musical   Closed out of town

Composer: Louis A. Hirsch
Lyricist: George V. Hobart; Frank Stammers
Librettist: George V. Hobart; Frank Stammers

Songs: Back Again; I Don't Know Which One to CHoose; I Love All the Boys; Somewhere a Girl Is Waiting; Steal Away; There She Goes; Upside Down; Wonderful Girl (L: Frank Stammers)

Cast: Lew Fields; Joseph Weber

Notes: Chestnut Street Theatre, Philadelphia.

259 • BACK COUNTRY
OPENED: 08/15/1978
Musical   Closed out of town

Composer: Stanley Walden
Lyricist: Jacques Levy
Librettist: Jacques Levy
Producer: Eugene V. Wolsk
Director: Jacques Levy

Source: PLAYBOY OF THE WESTERN WORLD (Play: John Millington Synge)

Choreographer:: Margo Sappington; **Costumes:** Pearl Somner; **Lighting Designer:** Neil Peter Jampolis; **Musical Director:** Stanley Walden; **Set Design:** Peter Larkin; **Vocal Arranger:** Stanley Walden

Songs: All the Men in My Life; As a Boy; As a Girl; Child of the Devil; Diamond Jim Brady; Fiddler's Tune, The; Hay Pitchin'; Heaven on My Mind; If You Will Spend Your Life with Me; Little Girl Again; Mother of Spring; Mr. Moon and Lady Fire; Old Man; Through the Shadows; Too Much Pain; Western Slope, The

Cast: Barbara Andres; Rex Everhart; Stuart Germain; Suzanne Lederer; Ken Marshall

Notes: Closed 9/24/78 Boston. Opened in Cohoes, N.Y.

260 • BACK HOME
Musical   Unproduced

Composer: Christopher Berg
Lyricist: Frank Evans
Librettist: Ron Sproat

Songs: As Much to Me; At Your Age; Christmas Stockings; Chummy; Did It Really Happen?; I'm Home; Lana Turner; Queer Fish; That was Jerry; What Are They Trying to Tell Us?

Notes: This show was workshopped various times.

261 • BACK TO BACHARACH AND DAVID
OPENED: 03/25/1993   Theatre: Club 53
Revue   Off-Broadway: 69

Composer: Burt Bacharach
Lyricist: Hal David
Producer: Jim David; Hal Luftig; Kathy Najimy; Alan D. Perry; Daryl Roth
Director: Kathy Najimy

Choreographer:: Javier Velasco; **Costumes:** David Loveless; **Lighting Designer:** Maura Sheridan; **Musical Director:** Steve Gunderson; **Orchestrations:** Steve Gunderson; **Set Design:** Peter Rogness; **Vocal Arranger:** Steve Gunderson

Songs: Alfie; Always Something There to Remind Me; Another Night; Any Old Time of the Day; Anyone Who Had a Heart; April Fools, The; Are You There with Another Girl; Close to You; Do You Know the Way to San Jose; Don't Make Me Over; House Is Not a Home, A; I Just Have to Breathe; I Say a Little Prayer for You; I'll Never Fall in Love Again; Just Don't Know What to Do with Myself; Knowing When to Leave; Let Me Be Lonely; Let Me Go to Him; Look of Love, The; Message to Michael; My Little Red Book; Nikki; One Less Bell to Answer; Promises, Promises; Reach Out for Me; This Empty Place; This Guy's in Love with You; Trains and Boats and Planes; 24 Hours from Tulsa; Walk on By; What the World Needs Now; Whoever You Are, I Love You; You'll Never Get to Heaven

Cast: Melinda Gilb; Steve Gunderson; Sue Mosher; Lillias White

Notes: No original songs in this show.

262 • BACKERS' AUDITION, A

OPENED: 12/20/1983   Theatre: Manhattan Theatre Club
Musical   Off-Broadway: 45

Composer: Douglas Bernstein; Denis Markell
Lyricist: Douglas Bernstein; Denis Markell
Librettist: Douglas Bernstein; Denis Markell
Producer: Manhattan Theater Club
Director: Martin Charnin

Choreographer: Janie Sell; **Costumes:** Linda Fisher; **Lighting Designer:** Marc B. Weiss; **Musical Director:** William Roy; **Set Design:** Ray Recht

Songs: Another Backers' Audition; Another New York Day; Better; Blue Manhattan Nights; Collaboration; Herman; Ick; Kalodner and Marks Revisited; Love Duet; Noah and Jeff; Over the Top; Regular Guy, A; Story of Lou, A; What Do They Want

Cast: Barbara Barrie; Douglas Bernstein; Mary D'Arcy; Bill Fagerbakke; Scott Robertson; William Roy; Dana Vance; Nicholas Woodeson

263 • BAD BOY AND HIS TEDDY BEARS, THE

OPENED: 12/30/1907   Theatre: Lincoln Square
Musical   New York

Composer: Ted Coleman
Lyricist: Frank Dupree
Librettist: Charles E. Blaney
Producer: Charles E. Blaney
Director: James R. Garey

Songs: Fairy Tales; I'm a Real Carnegie Hero; Man Who's Got a Mortgage on the Mist, The; Only a Story from Fairy Tales; Opening Act I; Opening Act II; Opening Act III; Teddy Bear and the Bee, The; Tell Me Again; When the Minstrels Come to Town; When the Teddy Bears Come to Life;

You Are Not the One for Me; You've Made a Hit with Me

Cast: William Barrows; Lew Engel; Harry Pilcer; William Platt; William Rhodes; E.T. Scott; Eileen Sheridan

264 • BAD GIRLS UPSET BY THE TRUTH

OPENED: 06/04/1995
Musical   Closed out of town

Lyricist: Jo Carol Pierce
Librettist: Jo Carol Pierce
Additional Dialogue: Guy Juke
Director: Ben Levit

Choreographer: David H. Milch, **Costumes:** Larisa Ratnikoff; **Incidental Music:** J.D. Foster; **Lighting Designer:** Jerold R. Forsyth; **Musical Director:** J.D. Foster; **Set Design:** David P. Gordon

Songs: Across the Great Divide; Apocalyptic Horses; Blue Norther; Borderline Tango; Burning Question; Cracked Her Shell; Does God Have Us By the Twat or What?; Good Folks of Lubbock, The; Harmony on High; I Blame God; In the Garden; Loose Diamond; My Boyfriend; Secret Dan; This Diamond Is Real; Vaginal Angel; What You Told Me to Do

Cast: Lisbeth Bartlett; Jennifer Childs; Mollie Hall; Tom McCarthy

Notes: American Musical Theatre Festival, Philadelphia.

265 • BAD HABITS OF 1925

OPENED: 02/08/1925
Revue

Composer: Richard Rodgers
Lyricist: Lorenz Hart
Director: Lorenz Hart; Irving Strouse

Choreographer: Sydney Oberfelder; Gene Richard; **Musical Director:** Richard Rodgers

Songs: Across the Garden Wall; College Baby (L: Robert A. Simon); Darling Will Not Grow Older [2]; I'd Like to Take You Home to Meet

My Mother; If I Were King [1]; In Gingham;
Mah-Jongg Maid; Merrie Merrie, The

Notes: Amateur production. [1] From score of
WINKLE TOWN. Also in A DANISH YANKEE
IN KING TUT'S COURT. [2] From score of
WINKLE TOWN.

266 • BAD HABITS OF 1926
OPENED: 04/30/1926   Theatre: Greenwich
                                          Village
Revue   Off-Broadway: 19

Composer: Manning Sherwin
Lyricist: Arthur Herzog Jr.
Director: Perry Ivins

Choreographer: Ralph Reader; **Costumes:** Joseph
Mullen; **Musical Director:** Bela Loblov;
Orchestrations: John Klenner; **Set Design:**
Joseph Mullen

Songs: Are We Downhearted?; Chorus Girl
Blues; Cinderella of Our Block; Funeral of
Charleston; Geisha Girl; Gone Away Blues;
Keep Your Shirt On; Lady Godiva (Go Bob
Your Hair); Let Me Be Myself [1]; Lifeguards,
The; Manhattan Transfer; Over the Garden
Wall; Station L-O-V-E; Student Robin Hood
of Pilsen, The (C: Randall Thompson; L:
Perry Ivins); When; Would-ja?

Cast: Molly Burnside; Harriet Hamill; Robert
Montgomery

Notes: [1] Added after opening.

267 • BAGEL SCANDALS
Notes: *See BAGELS AND YOX OF 1951.*

268 • BAGELS AND YOX OF 1951
(BAGEL SCANDALS)
OPENED: 03/30/1951   Theatre: Holiday
Revue   Broadway: 204

Composer: Sholom Secunda
Lyricist: Hy Jacobson
Producer: Irving Beckman; John Pransky

Dance Arranger: Jerome Goldstein; **Musical
Director:** Irving Carroll; **Vocal Arranger:** Jerome
Goldstein

Songs: Bagels and Yox; Chi-Ri-Bin; East Indian
Mambo; Let's Dance a Frailichs

Cast: Larry Alpert

269 • BAJOUR
OPENED: 11/23/1964   Theatre: Shubert
Musical   Broadway: 218

Composer: Walter Marks
Lyricist: Walter Marks
Librettist: Ernest Kinoy
Producer: Carroll Masterson; Harris Masterson;
Edward Padula; Norman Twain
Director: Lawrence Kasha

Source: UNKNOWN (Story: Joseph Mitchell);
Choreographer:: Peter Gennaro; **Costumes:**
Freddy Wittop; **Dance Arranger:** Richard de
Benedictis; **Lighting Designer:** Peggy Clark;
Musical Director: Lehman Engel;
Orchestrations: Mort Lindsey; **Set Design:**
Oliver Smith; **Vocal Arranger:** Lehman Engel

Songs: Bajour; Guarantees; Haggle, The; Honest
Man; I Can; Living Simply; Love Is a Chance;
Love-Line; Mean; Move Over, New York; Must
It Be Love?; Sew-Up, The (dance); Soon;
Variations on a Theme By Bird [1]; Was Always
[1]; Whatever I Say [1]; Where Is the Tribe for
Me?; Words, Words, Words

Cast: Michael Bennett; Herschel Bernardi; Robert
Burr; Nancy Dussault; Herbert Edelman; Lucie
Lancaster; Mae Questel; Chita Rivera; Gus
Trikonis

Notes: [1] Cut prior to opening.

270 • BAKER STREET
OPENED: 02/16/1965   Theatre: Broadway
Musical   Broadway: 313

Composer: Marian Grudeff; Raymond Jessel
Lyricist: Marian Grudeff; Raymond Jessel
Producer: Alexander H. Cohen
Director: Harold Prince

Source: VARIOUS SHERLOCK HOLMES STORIES
(Story: Arthur Conan Doyle)

Choreographer:: Lee Theodore; **Costumes:** Motley;
Dance Arranger: John Morris; **Lighting**

Designer: Jean Rosenthal; **Musical Director:** Hal Hastings; **Orchestrations:** Don Walker; **Set Design:** Oliver Smith

Songs: Buffalo Belle [1] (C: Jerry Bock; L: Sheldon Harnick); Cold Clear World of the Intellect (C: Jerry Bock; L: Sheldon Harnick); Cold, Cold World [2] (C: Jerry Bock; L: Sheldon Harnick); Dreary [2]; Finding Words for Spring; Five Senses, The [2]; I Know [2]; I Shall Miss You, Holmes (C: Jerry Bock; L: Sheldon Harnick); I'd Do It Again; I'm in London Again [3] (C: Jerry Bock; L: Sheldon Harnick); Isn't She Marvelous! [2]; It's So Simple; Jewelry; Leave It to Us, Gov; Letters; London Underworld (Baker Street Mystery) (dance); Married Man, A; Pursuit; Roof Space; Veritable Work of Art, A [2]; What a Night This Is Going to Be; Words [2]

Cast: Martin Gabel; Inga Swenson; Tommy Tune; Christopher Walken; Fritz Weaver

Notes: [1] Added after opening. [2] Not used. [3] Cut after opening.

271 • BAKER'S BROADWAY

Notes: *See 13 DAYS TO BROADWAY.*

272 • BAKER'S DOZEN

OPENED: 01/09/1964   Theatre: PLaza 9-
Revue   Nightclub: 469

Librettist: William F. Brown; Dee Caruso; Robert Elliott; Bill Levine; Treva Silverman
Producer: Julius Monk
Director: Julius Monk; Frank Wagner

Choreographer: Frank Wagner; **Costumes:** Bill Belew; **Lighting Designer:** Don Lamb; **Musical Director:** William Roy; **Vocal Arranger:** William Roy

Songs: Avon Garde (C/L: Rod Warren); Bag with Which You Shop, The (C/L: Lesley Davison); Baker's Dozen (C/L: William Roy); Barry's Boys [1] (C/L: June Reizner); Cries in the Common Marketplace (C/L: Lesley Davison); Fourteen Hours and Thirty-Seven Minutes (C/L: Clark Gesner); Gripe of the Group, The (C: William Dyer; L: Don Parks); Megalopolis (C/L: Lesley Davison); Merry-Go-Round (C/L: G. Wood); Mescaline Hat Dance (C: John Simon; L: Louis Botto); National Service Corps (C/L: Bud McCreery); New Italian Folk Song, A (C: Stan

Lebowsky; L: Fred Tobias); Old Eight Ten, The (C/L: G. Wood); Water Pollution (C: William Roy; L: Rod Warren); Wherefore Art Thou, Romeo (C: Margaret Perrin; L: George Ploner); Wonderful World-Wide Fair (C/L: Michael Brown)

Cast: Richard Blair; Ruth Buzzi; Barbara Cason; Robert Colston; Delphi Harrington; Nagle Jackson; Jamie Ross; William Roy; Jan Templeton; Paul Trueblood

Notes: [1] Also in DIME A DOZEN.

273 • BAKER'S WIFE, THE
OPENED: 05/11/1976
Musical   Closed out of town

Composer: Stephen Schwartz
Lyricist: Stephen Schwartz
Librettist: Joseph Stein
Producer: David Merrick
Director: John Berry

Source: LA FEMME DU BOULANGER (Novel: Jean Giono; Marcel Pagnol)

Choreographer:: Robert Tucker; **Costumes:** Theoni V. Aldredge; **Dance Arranger:** Daniel Troob; **Lighting Designer:** Jennifer Tipton; **Musical Director:** Robert Billig; **Orchestrations:** Don Walker; **Set Design:** Jo Mielziner

Songs: Any Day-Now Day; Baking, The; Bread; Buzz-A-Buzz [1]; Chanson; Endless Delights; Feminine Companionship [3]; For You [2]; Gifts of Love [2]; I Could Never Get Enough [2]; If I Have to Live Alone; If It Wasn't for You [1]; Little Taste of Heaven, A; Look for the Woman; Luckiest Man in the World, The; Meadowlark; Merci, Madame; New Musketeers [3]; Not in the Market; Pan for le Pain, A; Perfect Every Time; Plain and Simple [1]; Proud Lady; Romance; Serenade; Something's Got to Be Done; Voila [3]; Welcome to Concorde; What's a Man to Do?; When She Gets Home Tomorrow; Where Is the Warmth?

Cast: Keene Curtis; Patti LuPone; Portia Nelson; Kurt Peterson; Teri Ralston; David Rounds; Charles Rule; Paul Sorvino

Notes: [1] Added to British production in 1989. [2] Added to West Coast revival. [3] Added to Off-Off-Broadway production 1985.

274 • BAL-TABARIN, THE
OPENED: 1923
Musical   Closed out of town

Composer: J. Fred Coots; Jean Schwartz
Lyricist: McElbert Moore
Producer: J.J. Shubert; Lee Shubert
Director: Frank Smithson

Choreographer: Sammy Lee

Songs: Chiquette; Innocent Eyes; Lady [1]; My Rose

Notes: The sets and some of the songs from this show were used later in INNOCENT EYES. [1] Also in DEW DROP INN.

275 • BALANCING ACT
OPENED: 06/15/1992   Theatre: Westside
Musical   Off-Broadway: 56

Composer: Dan Goggin
Lyricist: Dan Goggin
Librettist: Dan Goggin
Producer: N.N.N. Company
Director: Dan Goggin; Tony Parise

Choreographer: Dan Goggin; Tony Parise; **Costumes:** Mary Peterson; **Lighting Designer:** Paul Miller; **Musical Director:** Michael Rice; **Orchestrations:** David Nyberg; Michael Rice; **Set Design:** Barry Axtell

Songs: California Suite; Casting Call, A; Chew Chewy Chow; Fifth from the Right, The; Hollywood 'n' Vinyl; Home Sweet Home; I Am Yours; I Knew the Music; I Left You There; Kid's Gonna Make It, The; Life Is a Balancing Act; Long, Long War, A; My Bio Is a Blank; Next Stop, New York City; Play Away the Blues; Tough Town, A; Twist of Fate, A; Welcome, Bienvenue; Where Is the Rainbow; Woman of the Century, The; You Heard It Here First

Cast: J.B. Adams; Diane Fratantoni; Suzanne Hevner; Christine Toy; Craig Wells

276 • BALKAN PRINCESS, THE
OPENED: 02/09/1911   Theatre: Herald Square
Musical   Broadway: 108

Composer: Paul Rubens
Lyricist: Paul Rubens; Arthur Wimperis
Librettist: Frank Curzon; Frederick Lonsdale
Producer: Lee Shubert; Sam S. Shubert
Director: William J. Wilson

Costumes: Melville Ellis; **Musical Director:** John McGhie

Songs: Angelina [1]; Dear Delightful Women; Don't Let's Meet Again; Dreaming; Entrance of Grand Duke [1]; Hard Life, A; Holidays; I Char; I Like You All; Lady and Gentleman; Man's a Man, A; Opera Ball, The; Prince's Chorus [1]; Stealing [1]; Sunshine of Springtime, The; Wonderful World

Cast: Alice Brady; Herbert Corthell; Louise Gunning; Christing Nielson; Robert Warwick

Notes: [1] Out Providence 1/19/11.

277 • BALL AT THE SAVOY
OPENED: 09/08/1933   Theatre: Theatre Royal, Drury Lane
Musical   London: 148

Composer: Paul Abraham
Lyricist: Oscar Hammerstein II
Librettist: Oscar Hammerstein II
Director: Reginald Hammerstein; Oscar Hammerstein II

Source: BALL IM SAVOY (Musical: Pal Abraham; Alfred Grunwald; Fritz Lohner-Beda)

Choreographer:: Jack Donahue; **Musical Director:** Charles Prentice; **Set Design:** Joseph Harker; Phil Harker

Songs: All I Want Is a Home; Baby, Wait till It Happens to You; Girl Like Nina, A; I Always Keep My Girl Out Late; I Live for Love; I Think I'm in Love with My Wife; If It's Good Enough for Gentlemen; I'll Show You Off; Le Marquis de Faublas; Moon Will Ride Away, The; Night Is Young, The; Oh Why, Oh Why, Oh Why; On the Bosphorus; Soliloquy; There Is a Ball at the Savoy; This Lovely Night; Up and Down

Cast: Rosy Barsony; Oskar Denes; Maurice Evans; Dick Francis; Natalie Hall

278 • BALLAD FOR A FIRING SQUAD

OPENED: 12/11/1968   Theatre: Theatre de Lys
Musical   Off-Broadway: 7

Composer: Edward Thomas
Lyricist: Martin Charnin
Librettist: Jerome Coopersmith
Producer: Edward Thomas
Director: Martin Charnin

Choreographer:: Alan Johnson; **Costumes:** Theoni V. Aldredge; **Lighting Designer:** James Tilton; **Musical Director:** Joyce Brown; **Orchestrations:** Larry Wilcox; **Set Design:** James Tilton

Songs: Ballad for a Firing Squad; Choice Is Yours, The [1]; Dance at the Salon [1]; Everyone Has Something to Hide [1]; Fritzie; Hello Yank [1]; How Young You Were Tonight [1]; I Did Not Sleep Last Night; I Don't See Him Very Much Anymore [1]; I'm Saving Myself for a Soldier [1]; Is This Fact? [1]; Maman [1]; Not Now, Not Here [1]; Sextette [1]; There Is Only One Thing to Be Sure Of; What Might Have Been; What Then?

Cast: Stanley Church; James Hurst; Adelle Rasey; Bruce Scott; Liz Sheridan; Neva Small; Renata Vaselle

Notes: *See also MATA HARI* of which this was a revision. [1] Originally in MATA HARI.

279 • BALLAD FOR BIMSHIRE

OPENED: 10/15/1963   Theatre: Mayfair
Musical   Broadway: 74

Composer: Irving Burgie
Lyricist: Irving Burgie
Librettist: Irving Burgie
Producer: Ossie Davis; Bernard Waltzer
Director: Ed Cambridge

Choreographer:: Talley Beatty; **Costumes:** Mozelle Forte; **Musical Director:** Sammy Benskin; **Orchestrations:** Sammy Benskin; Dick Vance; **Set Design:** Donald Ryder

Songs: Ballad for Bimshire; Belle Plain; Chant; Chicken's a Popular Bird; Deep in My Heart; Fore Day Noon in the Mornin'; Hail Britannia; Have You Got Charm?; I'm a Dandy; Lately I've Been Feeling So Strange; My Love Will Come By; My Master Plan; Pardon Me, Sir; Silver Earring; Street Cries; Vendor's Song; We Gon' Jump Up; Welcome Song; Yesterday Was Such a Lovely Day

Cast: Joe Callaway; Ossie Davis; Frederick O'Neal; Jimmy Randolph; Christine Spencer

280 • BALLAD OF JOHNNY POT, THE

OPENED: 04/26/1971   Theatre: Theatre Four
Musical   Off-Broadway: 16

Composer: Clinton Ballard
Lyricist: Carolyn Richter
Librettist: Carolyn Richter
Producer: Bob McDevitt; Wyler Productions
Director: Joshua Shelley

Choreographer:: Jay Norman; **Costumes:** Alvin Colt; **Dance Arranger:** Harrison Fisher; **Lighting Designer:** Lloyd Burlingame; **Musical Director:** Harrison Fisher

Songs: Ballad of Johnny Pot, The; Carol, A; Crazy; Dance of Distraction; Discarded Blues; Find My Way Alone; Hard Hat Stetsons; Have Some Pot; Head Down the Road; How Wonderful It Is; Johnny's Creed; Letter, The; Like It; Little Sparrows; Lonely Is the Life; Saskatchewan; Scared; Whaddaya Say, Kid; What About Me

Cast: Ben Bryant; Betty Buckley; John Bennett Perry; Jim Weston

281 • BALLAD OF SMOKEY THE BEAR

OPENED: 1966
TV Musical

Composer: Johnny Marks
Lyricist: Johnny Marks

Songs: All Together; Anyone Can Move a Mountain; Ballad of Smokey the Bear; Curiosity; Deliliah; Don't Wait; Serenade of the Trees; Tell It to a Turtle

Voice: James Cagney

282 • BALLAD OF SOAPY SMITH, THE

OPENED: 11/12/1984   Theatre: New York
Shakespeare Festival
Play   Off-Broadway: 25

Composer: Michael Weller
Lyricist: Michael Weller
Author: Michael Weller
Producer: N.Y. Shakespeare Festival; Joseph
Papp
Director: Robert Egan

Costumes: Robert Blackman; **Incidental Music:**
Norman Durkee; **Lighting Designer:** Jennifer
Tipton; **Set Design:** Eugene Lee

Cast: Dennis Arndt; Lori Tan Chinn; Christopher
Cooper; Jon DeVries; Pierre Epstein; James
Hillbrandt; Cherry Jones; Jimmy Smits

Notes: No songs listed in program.

283 • BALLET BALLADS

OPENED: 05/09/1948   Theatre: Maxine Elliott's
Revue   Broadway: 69

Composer: Jerome Moross
Lyricist: John Latouche
Producer: Nat Karson
Director: Mary Hunter

Choreographer: Paul Godkin; Hanya Holm;
Katherine Litz; **Musical Director:** Hugh Ross

Songs: I've Got Me; My Yellow Flower; Oh, Oh,
Baby; Ridin' on the Breeze

Cast: William Ambler; Barbara Ashley; John
Costello; Beau Cunningham; Barbara Downie;
Arthur Friedman; Paul Godkin; Arlouine
Goodjohn; Richard Harvey; Ted Lawrie; Robert
Lenn; Katherine Litz; Gertrude Lockway; Sono
Osato; Frank Seabolt; Sharry Traver; Eddie
Varrato; Sheila Vogelle

Notes: No program available. The evening
consisted of three ballets: SUSANNA AND THE
ELDERS, choreographed by Katherine Litz;
WILLIE THE WEEPER, choreographed by Paul
Godkin and THE ECCENTRICITIES OF DAVY
CROCKETT (AS TOLD BY HIMSELF),
choreographed by Hanya Holm.

284 • BALLET GIRL, THE (1897)

OPENED: 12/21/1897   Theatre: Manhattan
Musical   Broadway: 31

Composer: Carl Kiefert
Lyricist: Adrian Ross
Librettist: James T. Tanner
Producer: Edward E. Rice
Director: Frederic A. Leon; James T. Tanner

Choreographer: Augustus Sohlke; **Set Design:**
Frank Rafter; Hugh L. Reid; Alfred Williams

Songs: Bal Bullier; Ballet Girl, The; Beside the
Zuyder Zee; Boom, A; Clear! Clear!; Dancing;
Elopement, The; I Never Saw a Girl Like That; In
America; In the Ballet; Infant Marriage; Is It So?;
Janken and Meken; Little Bird, A; My Dickey Say
Nodings at All; My Home; Romance; She's the
Girl I Love; Stitch in Time, A; This Is a Serious
Matter; Vanity of Human Wishes; Wedding
Bells; What Occurence!

Cast: Charles Deagrave; David Lythgow; Marjorie
Relyea; Irene Vera

285 • BALLET GIRL, THE (1915)
Notes: *See THE PEASANT GIRL.*

286 • BALLET OF NIAGARA, THE

OPENED: 09/03/1910   Theatre: Hippodrome
Musical   Broadway: 333

Librettist: R.H. Burnside
Producer: R.H. Burnside
Director: Vincenzo Romeo

Costumes: Alfredo Edel

Cast: Nanette Flack; Slivers Oakley; Albertina
Rasch; Vincenzo Romeo

Notes: *See THE INTERNATIONAL CUP.*

287 • BALLROOM

OPENED: 12/14/1978   Theatre: Majestic
Musical   Broadway: 116

Composer: Billy Goldenberg
Lyricist: Alan Bergman; Marilyn Bergman
Librettist: Jerome Kass

Producer: Michael Bennett
Director: Michael Bennett

Source: QUEEN OF THE STARDUST BALLROOM
(Television Program: Jerome Kass)

Choreographer:: Bob Avian; Michael Bennett;
Costumes: Theoni V. Aldredge; **Lighting
Designer:** Tharon Musser; **Musical Director:**
Don Jennings; **Orchestrations:** Jonathan Tunick;
Set Design: Robin Wagner

Songs: Dance Montage, The; Dreams; Fifty Percent;
Goodnight Is Not Goodbye; How Can I Tell Her
[1]; I Love to Dance [2]; I Wish You a Waltz;
If Anyone Had Told Me [1]; I've Been Waiting
All My Life; Job Application, The [1]; Like Her
[1]; More of the Same; One By One; Somebody
Did All Right By Herself; Song for Dancing, A;
Stardust Waltz, The [2]; Tango Contest, The;
Terrific Band and a Real Nice Crowd, A; Who
Gave You Permission? [1]

Cast: Danny Carroll; Marilyn Cooper; Vincent
Gardenia; Sally-Jane Heit; Gene Kelton; Dorothy
Loudon; Rudy Tronto

Notes: [1] Cut out of town 9/78. [2] Same melody.

288 • BALLYHOO (1930)

OPENED: 12/22/1930   Theatre: Hammerstein
Musical   Broadway: 68

Composer: Louis Alter
Lyricist: Leighton K. Brill; Harry Ruskin
Librettist: Leighton K. Brill; Harry Ruskin
Producer: Arthur Hammerstein
Director: Reginald Hammerstein

Choreographer:: Earl Lindsay; **Costumes:** Charles
LeMaire; **Musical Director:** Oscar Bradley; **Set
Design:** Cirker & Robbins

Songs: Blow Hot-Blow Cold; How I Could
Go for You; If I Were You; I'm One of
God's Children (Who Hasn't Got Wings)
(L: Oscar Hammerstein II; Harry Ruskin);
No Wonder I'm Blue (L: Oscar Hammerstein II);
(Try This for) That Tired Feeling (C: Rudolf
Friml; L: Oscar Hammerstein II; Otto Harbach);
Throw It Out the Window

Cast: Chaz Chase; Jack Colby; W.C. Fields; Grace
Hayes; Max Hoffmann Jr.; Jeanie Lang; Janet

Reade; Andy Rice Jr.; Don Tomkins; Floria
Vestoff

289 • BALLYHOO OF 1932

OPENED: 09/06/1932   Theatre: 44th Street
Musical   Broadway: 94

Composer: Lewis E. Gensler
Lyricist: E.Y. Harburg
Librettist: Norman Anthony; Sig Herzig
Producer: Norman Anthony; Bobby Connolly;
Lewis E. Gensler; Russell Patterson

Choreographer: Bobby Connolly; **Costumes:**
Russell Patterson; **Musical Director:** Max Meth;
Orchestrations: Hans Spialek; **Set Design:**
Russell Patterson

Songs: As Long As We Have Bromo Seltzer in Our
Love Nest Baby, We're Through [1]; Ballyhooey
Lassies (Opening Act II) [1]; Ballyhujah; 'Cause
You Won't Do Right By Me [1]; Falling Off the
Wagon; How About a Little Date for Breakfast?
[1]; How Do You Do It?; I Lerve You [1]; I'm Off
You [1]; I'm One of God's Children [1]; Love,
Nuts and Noodles (Bring 'Em Back Alive); Man
About Yonkers; Old Fashioned Wedding; Riddle
Me This; She'll Be Coming 'Round the Catskill
Mountains [1]; Thank My Stars [1]; Thrill Me;
What Have You Got to Have?; You Satisfy [1]

Cast: Jeanne Aubert; Hugh Cameron; Gloria
Gilbert; Grace Hartman; Paul Hartman; Tom
Harty; Bob Hope; Eugene Howard; Willie
Howard; Vera Marshe; Lulu McConnell; Nina
Mae McKinney; Dorissa Nelova; Sunnie O'Dea;
Ralph Stanford; Donald Stewart

Notes: [1] ASCAP/Library of Congress only.

290 • BAMBOOLA (1929)

OPENED: 06/26/1929   Theatre: Royale
Revue   Broadway: 27

Composer: Bernard Maltin; D. Frank Marcus
Lyricist: Bernard Maltin; D. Frank Marcus
Librettist: D. Frank Marcus
Producer: Irving Cooper

Choreographer: Sam Rose

Songs: Ace of Spades; African Whoopie; Anna;
Dixie Vagabond; Evenin'; Hot Patootie Wedding

Night; Rub-a-Dub Your Rabbit's Foot; Shoutin' Sinners; Somebody Likes Me; Song of Harlem; Tailor Made Babies; Tampico Tune; Way to Do Bamboola, The

Cast: Dusty Andrews; Brevard Burnette; Billy Cortez; Revella Hughes; Isabell Washington

291 • BAMBOULA (1921)
OPENED: 1921
Musical

Composer: Edgar Powell; James Vaughn
Lyricist: Edgar Powell; James Vaughn
Librettist: J. Homer Tutt; Salem Tutt Whitney
Producer: J. Homer Tutt; Salem Tutt Whitney

Cast: Alonzo Fenderson; Emma Jackson; J. Homer Tutt; Alexander White; Salem Tutt Whitney

Notes: No other information available.

292 • BAMBOULA, THE (1925)
OPENED: 03/24/1925   Theatre: His Majesty's
Musical   London: 77

Lyricist: Irving Caesar; Douglas Furber
Librettist: Guy Bolton; H.M. Vernon
Producer: L. Morgan

Choreographer: J.W. Jackson; **Costumes:** Morris Angel; Debenham & Freebody; Mary Fisher; Maison Ross; B.J. Simmons; **Musical Director:** Percy Fletcher; **Set Design:** Joseph Harker; Phil Harker; Ernest J. Humphries; E.H. Ryan

Songs: Anything (C: Harry Rosenthal); On Such a Beautiful Night (C: Joseph Meyer); Rio Grande (C: Harry Rosenthal); Sing a Song in the Rain (C: Harry Rosenthal); Spring (C: Albert Sirmay); Your Kiss Told Me (C: Albert Sirmay)

Cast: James B. Carson; Vincent Clive; Frank Lalor; Billie Leonard; Dorothy Shale

Notes: No program available.

293 • BAND BOX FOLLIES, THE
OPENED: 09/05/1927   Theatre: Daly's
Revue   Broadway: 8

Composer: John Milton Hagen

Lyricist: Marion Gillespie; John Milton Hagen; Menlo Mayfield
Librettist: Ballard Macdonald; Menlo Mayfield
Producer: Greenwich Villagers,
Director: Jack Garn; Maxwell Platt

Choreographer: Jack Garn; **Musical Director:** George Kruger

Songs: Bluestep; Eyes of Love; Girlie with a Bustle; Greenwich Village Violet; I Follow the Ponies; Love Me Some Mo; Mimi; Moon and You and I, The; Ola in Her Little Gondola; Romance in a Dance, The; Rosemary; Samoa Sam; Sh! Sh! Shirley!; You Can't Stop the Sun from Shining

Cast: Wilda Ganeau; Margaret Speaks

Notes: Additional numbers by Lillian R. Devine and Louis Katzman but not identified in program.

294 • BAND WAGON, THE
OPENED: 06/03/1931   Theatre: New Amsterdam
Revue   Broadway: 262

Composer: Arthur Schwartz
Lyricist: Howard Dietz
Librettist: Howard Dietz; George S. Kaufman
Producer: Max Gordon
Director: Hassard Short

Choreographer: Albertina Rasch; **Costumes:** Kiviette; Constance Ripley; **Musical Director:** Al Goodman; **Orchestrations:** Robert Russell Bennett; **Set Design:** Albert Johnson

Songs: Ballet Music (inst.); Beggar Waltz, The (inst.) [1]; Confession; Dancing in the Dark; Flag, The (dance); High and Low [2]; Hoops; I Love Louisa; It Better Be Good; Miserable with You; Nanette; New Sun in the Sky; Sweet Music; When the Rain Goes Pitter Patter (inst.); Where Can He Be?; White Heat

Cast: Adele Astaire; Fred Astaire; John Barker; Helen Broderick; Peter Chamber; Philip Loeb; Tilly Losch; Frank Morgan; Francis Pierlot; Roberta Robinson; Jay Wilson

Notes: [1] Lyric later added for pop song "Is It All a Dream?" [2] First in HERE COMES THE BRIDE in London with lyric also credited to Desmond Carter.

295 • BANDANNA LAND

OPENED: 02/03/1908   Theatre: Majestic
Musical   Broadway: 89

Composer: Will Marion Cook
Lyricist: Alex Rogers
Librettist: Alex Rogers; J.A. Shipp
Producer: F. Ray Comstock

Choreographer: Aida Overton Walker; **Musical Director:** Will Marion Cook; James J. Vaughn

Songs: Any Old Place in Yankee Land Is Good Enough for Me; At Peace Wid de World [1] (C: Bert Williams; L: Mord Allen); Bon-Bon-Buddie; Corn Song; Dinah [2]; Ethiopia Ballet (inst.) (C: Al Johns); Exhortation; Fas' Fas' World [2]; Harlem Prince [3] (C/L: Unknown); I'd Rather Have Nothin' All de Time than Somethin' fo' a Little While (C: Bert Williams; L: John Lowitz); I'm Very Fond of Jokes [2]; In My Old Home [1] (C: Tom Lemonier; L: Mord Allen); It's Hard to Love Somebody When Your Somebody Don't Love You; Just the Same; Kinky (L: Mord Allen); Late Hours; Man from Conjure Land, The; Maori (C: William H. Tyers); Minuet; My Bandana Land (L: Mord Allen); Red, Red Rose; (You're in) The Right Church but the Wrong Pew [1] (C: Chris Smith; L: R.C. McPherson); Saucy Little Sadie [1]; Sheath Gown in Darktown, The [1] (C: J. Leubrie Hill; L: Mord Allen); Somebody Lied [2] (C/L: Jeff T. Branen; Evans Lloyd; Bert Williams); Somewhere (C/L: Joe Jordan; F.H. Williams; C: Bert Williams; L: Dave Kemper); Southland [1]; 'Tain't Gwine to Be No Rain; Until Then [2]; When I Was Sweet Sixteen (C: J. Leubrie Hill; Chris Smith; L: Mord Allen; R.C. McPherson)

Cast: J. Leubrie Hill; Abbie Mitchell; Alex Rogers; Lavinia Rogers; J.A. Shipp; Aida Overton Walker; George W. Walker; Bert Williams; Lottie Williams

Notes: In 1915 this show was revised as A BLACKVILLE CORPORATION. [1] Out of town 8/28/08. [2] Sheet music only. [3] Added when show became A BLACKVILLE CORPORATION.

296 • BANDIT PRINCE

Musical

Songs: Let Us Romance Together (C/L: Jeff Coldrey)

Cast: Freda Northcote

Notes: No other information available.

297 • BANJO EYES

OPENED: 12/25/1941   Theatre: Hollywood
Musical   Broadway: 126

Composer: Vernon Duke
Lyricist: John Latouche
Librettist: Izzy Elinson; Joe Quillan
Producer: Albert Lewis
Director: Albert Lewis; Hassard Short

Source: THREE MEN ON A HORSE (Play: George Abbott; John Cecil Holm)

Choreographer:: Charles Walters; **Costumes:** Irene Sharaff; **Lighting Designer:** Hassard Short; **Musical Director:** Raymond Sinatra; **Orchestrations:** Domenico Savino; **Set Design:** Harry Horner; **Vocal Arranger:** Clay Warnick

Songs: Banjo Eyes; Don't Let It Happen Again [1]; Greeting Cards, The; Hush-a-Bye Land [4]; I Always Think of Sally [4]; I'll Take the City; It Could Only Happen in the Movies (L: Harold Adamson); I've Got to Hand It to You; Leave My Women Alone [4] (L: Harold Adamson); Make with the Feet (L: Harold Adamson); My Song Without Words [4]; Nickel to My Name, A; Not a Care in the World [2]; Toast of the Boys at the Post, The [3] (L: George Sumner); We Did It Before, We'll Do It Again [3] (C: Cliff Friend; L: Charles Tobias); We're Having a Baby, My Baby and Me (L: Harold Adamson); What Every Young Man Should Know [4]; Who Started the Rhumba (Who Made the Rhumba); Yanks Are On the March Again, The [4] (C: Peter De Rose; L: Harold Adamson)

Cast: Eddie Cantor; Audrey Christie; June Clyde; Bill Johnson; Ray Mayer; Lionel Stander; Jacqueline Susann

Notes: [1] Out Philadelphia 12/2/41. [2] Added to CABIN IN THE SKY 1964. [3] Added after opening. [4] Not used.

298 • BANKER'S DAUGHTER, THE

OPENED: 01/22/1962   Theatre: Jan Hus House
Musical   Off-Broadway: 64

Composer: Peter Joseph; Sol Kaplan
Lyricist: Edward Eliscu
Librettist: Edward Eliscu
Producer: Paul Libin; Claire Nichtern
Director: David Brooks

Source: STREETS OF NEW YORK, THE (Play: Dion Boucicault); Lighting Designer: Jules Fisher; Musical Director: Arthur Lief; Orchestrations: Sol Kaplan; Set Design: Kim Swados

Songs: Both Ends Against the Middle; Carriage for Alida, A; Father's Daughter; Genteel; Gentlemen's Understanding; Head in the Stars; In a Brownstone Mansion; In Time; It's So Heartwarming; More Than One More Day; Nero, Caesar, Napoleon; One More Day; Say No More; Sleep, O Sleep; Such a Beautiful World; Sun Rises, The; Unexpectedly

Cast: David Daniels; Joelle Jons; Phil Leeds; Karen Morley; Helena Scott

299 • BAR MITZVAH BOY

OPENED: 10/31/1978   Theatre: Her Majesty's
Musical   London: 78

Composer: Jule Styne
Lyricist: Don Black
Librettist: Jack Rosenthal
Producer: Wolviston Ltd.
Director: Martin Charnin

Source: BAR MITZVAH BOY (Television Program: Jack Rosenthal)

Choreographer:: Peter Gennaro; Costumes: Gaelle Allen; Dance Arranger: Ray Holder; Lighting Designer: David Hersey; Musical Director: Alexander Faris; Orchestrations: Irwin Kostal; Set Design: Robin Don; Vocal Arranger: Alexander Faris

Songs: Always Me [2]; Bar Mitzvah, The; Bar Mitzvah of Eliot Green; Blessings Before Reading Torah [3]; Carriages at Midnight [3]; Cohens Are Coming, The [2]; Great News [3]; Hamakom [2]; Harolds of This World, The; If Only a Little Bit Sticks; I'm Grown Up [2]; It's Nothing [3]; I've Just Begun; Kill Him [3]; Morris Kaplan of Hampstead Gardens [1]; Only Myself to Blame [2]; Rita's Request (Kill Me); Simchas (Joyous Occasions); Sun Shines Out of Your Eyes; That's

Grown Up [2]; This Is Caplan's [3]; This Time Tomorrow; Thou Shalt Not; Trust Me; Victor's Request; We've Done All Right; What Harm Can It Do? [1]; Where's the Music Coming From?; Why; Why Can't He Like Me? [3]; Why Did I Do It? [2]; You Wouldn't Be You

Cast: Barry Angel; Joyce Blair; Ray C. Davis; Harry Towb

Notes: Titled SONG FOR A SATURDAY when Off-Broadway. [1] Cut prior to opening. [2] Added to American Jewish Theatre production 4/9/87. [3] ASCAP/Library of Congress only.

300 • BAR THAT NEVER CLOSES, THE

OPENED: 12/03/1972   Theatre: Astor Place
Musical   Off-Broadway: 33

Composer: Tom Mandel
Lyricist: John Braswell
Librettist: Louisa Rose
Producer: Bruce Mailman; Albert Poland
Director: John Braswell

Musical Director: Cathy MacDonald; Tom Mandel; Vocal Arranger: Cathy MacDonald; Tom Mandel

Songs: Circus of Jade; Dear Dear (L: Tom Mandel); Do It; I Don't Think I'll Ever Love You; Kaleidoscope (L: Louisa Rose); Precious Little Darkness (L: Louisa Rose); Recipe for Love; Tears of Ice (L: Louisa Rose); Two By Two (L: Louisa Rose); Walking with You

Cast: Mary Jo Kaplan; Jeannie Mortimer

301 • BARBARA FIDGETY

OPENED: 12/07/1899   Theatre: Weber and Fields
                                         Music Hall
Musical   Broadway

Composer: John Stromberg
Lyricist: Edgar Smith
Librettist: Edgar Smith
Producer: Lew Fields; Joseph Weber

Cast: Lew Fields; Joseph Weber

Notes: A one-act burlesque of BARBARA FRITCHIE.

302 • BARBARY COAST

OPENED: 02/28/1978
Musical   Closed out of town

Composer: William Penzer
Lyricist: William Penzer
Librettist: William Penzer
Producer: Barbary Coast Prod.
Director: Jack Bunch

Choreographer: Ed Nolfi; **Costumes:** Madeline Ann Graneto; **Dance Arranger::** Jack Quigley; **Lighting Designer:** Martin Aronstein; **Musical Director:** Joseph Stecko; **Orchestrations:** Philip J. Lang; **Set Design:** William Morris; **Vocal Arranger:** Jack Quigley

Songs: Barbary Coast; Count of Ten, The; Everybody Loves a Winner; Fight, The; Gentleman Jim; Go, Don't Want to Love You No More; Happy Time Rag; How Long Can a Heart Go on Loving; I Can See It All; Is It Love or Fascination; Love Is Everything; Love, Love, Love; Monkey Dance; Pink Police Gazette, The; Ride, Ride, Ride; Searching; There's Nothing Stranger Than Love; They Struck Her Name from the Blue Book Set 'Cause She Made Headlines in the Pink Police Gazette; Tong War, The; When Miss Park Avenue Does the Bumps; When You Dance with the One You Love; Without You There Is No Me; You're on the Barbary Coast

Cast: Denny Martin Flinn; Jerry Lanning; Alyson Reed; Marcia Rodd; Sab Shimono; Ben Wrigley

303 • BARE FACTS OF 1926

OPENED: 07/16/1926   Theatre: Triangle
Revue   Broadway: 107

Composer: Charles M. Schwab
Lyricist: Henry Myers
Librettist: Stuart Hamill
Producer: Kathleen Kirkwood
Director: Kathleen Kirkwood

Lighting Designer: Kathleen Kirkwood

Songs: Beautiful Shubert Poses of My Dreams; Cradle Song; Nice Girl; Orientale (C: Irenee Berge); Skyscrapers; Stand Up on Your Feet and Dance; Tea Time; Third from the End, The; Treat 'Em Rough; Triangle Blues; Won't You Tell Me?

Cast: Joseph Battle; Mary Doerr

304 • BAREFOOT BOY WITH CHEEK

OPENED: 04/03/1947   Theatre: Martin Beck
Musical   Broadway: 108

Composer: Sidney Lippman
Lyricist: Sylvia Dee
Librettist: Max Shulman
Producer: George Abbott
Director: George Abbott

Source: BAREFOOT BOY WITH CHEEK (Novel: Max Shulman); **Choreographer:** Richard Barstow; **Costumes:** Alvin Colt; **Lighting Designer:** Jo Mielziner; **Musical Director:** Milton Rosenstock; **Orchestrations:** Philip J. Lang; **Set Design:** Jo Mielziner; **Vocal Arranger:** Hugh Martin

Songs: After Graduation Day; Alice in Boogyland; Everything Leads Right Back to Love; I Knew I'd Know; I'll Turn a Little Cog; Legendary Eino Fflliikkiinneenn, The; Little Yetta's Gonna Get a Man; Star of the North Star State; Story of Carrot, The; There's Lots of Things You Can Do with Two (But Not with Three); Toast to Alpha Cholera, A; Too Nice a Day to Go to School; We Feel Our Man Is Definitely You; When You Are Eighteen; Who Do You Think You Are?

Cast: Red Buttons; Tommy Farwell; Ellen Hanley; William Redfield; Nancy Walker

305 • BARNUM

OPENED: 04/30/1980   Theatre: St. James
Musical   Broadway: 854

Composer: Cy Coleman
Lyricist: Michael Stewart
Librettist:
Producer: Cy Coleman; Judy Gordon; Lois F. Rosenfeld; Maurice Rosenfeld
Director: Joe Layton

Choreographer: Joe Layton; **Costumes:** Theoni V. Aldredge; **Lighting Designer:** Craig Miller; **Musical Director:** Peter Howard; **Orchestrations:** Hershy Kay; **Set Design:** David Mitchell; **Vocal Arranger:** Cy Coleman; Jeremy Stone

Songs: As Good As a Man [1]; At Least I Tried [1]; Bigger Isn't Better; Black and White; Colors of

My Life, The; Come Follow the Band; I Like Your Style; Join the Circus; Love Makes Such Fools of Us All [2]; Museum Song; Now You See It Now You Don't [1]; One Brick at a Time; Out There; Prince of Humbug, The; Thank God I'm Old; That's What the Poor Woman Is [1]; There's a Sucker Born Every Minute

Cast: Glenn Close; Leonard John Crofoot; Jim Dale; Terrence V. Mann; Sophie Schwab; Marianne Tatum; Terri White

Notes: [1] Cut prior to opening. [2] Music originally written for SWEET CHARITY but not used.

306 • BARON HUMBUG
OPENED: 1903
Musical

Composer: Lewis S. Thompson
Lyricist: R.A. Barnet; D.K. Stevens
Librettist: R.A. Barnet

Songs: Arethusa and the Snoozer (C: D.K. Stevens); Climb a Rose (C: Traditional); Cure for the Blues, A; Dear Waters of the Danube Blue (C: M.W. Daniels); Finale (C: Edward W. Corliss; L.S. Thompson); Finest Ever Is the Military Beau, The (C: Edward W. Corliss); In Bohemia; Jack-in-the-Box, The; Land of the Whisp'ring Sea; Legends of the Munkacs; Let's Forget We Ever Had a Care; Me Go Soldier! No, No, No!; Meet Me, Dear, on Saturday, a Little After Two (C: D.K. Stevens); No One Ever Died of Love (C: Traditional); Not Like Other Girls; Opening Chorus; P'r'aps a Puss (C: M.W. Daniels); Pretty Phrosia of the Sparkling Spa; Pull Me Up, O'Reilly; Put It in the Scrap Book; Quack! Said the Duck; Sylvia (C: M.W. Daniels); Tell Me Why You Love Me! (C: M.W. Daniels); That's a Clue; Water Sprite, A (C: M.W. Daniels); When I Lead the Band (C: B.C. Henry); When the Circus Comes to Town (C: D.K. Stevens); Where It's Day (C: Edward W. Corliss); Willing to Try (C: B.C. Henry)

Notes: Information from vocal selection only.

307 • BARON TRENCK, THE
OPENED: 03/11/1912   Theatre: Casino
Musical   Broadway: 40

Composer: Felix Albini
Lyricist: Frederick F. Schrader
Librettist: Henry Blossom
Producer: Whitney Opera Company

Source: BARON TRENCK (Musical: Felix Albini; Robert Bodanzky; A.M. Willner);
Choreographer: Al Holbrook; **Musical Director:** A. DeNovellis

Songs: Angel!; At Last I Find You; Baron Trenck [2]; Bold, Bad, Bandits [2] (C: Alfred G. Robyn; L: Henry Blossom); Cupid Is a Cruel Master (C: Alfred G. Robyn; L: Henry Blossom); Finale Act I [2]; I'd Like to Be a Soldier Gay; I'm from the Court of the Empress Queen; In Merry, Merry May (C: Felix Albini; Alfred Robyn); Incognito; Introduction Act II [2]; Introduction, Chorus and Melodrama; Just Like You [2]; Lottery Drawing, The [1]; Lydia Waltz Song, The [2]; Lydia's Entrance Song [2]; Maritza Darling [2]; My Heart's Mine Own (C: Alfred G. Robyn; L: Henry Blossom); My Lady Moon [1]; Once Upon a Time [2]; Opening Chorus Act I; Opening Chorus Act II; Pandour Does His Duty, A [2]; This Handsome Soldier Is Too Bold; Trenck Is My Name; Trenck March Song [2]; Trenck's Entrance [2]; We're Bold, Bad Bandits All; When a Pretty Girls Gets Married [2] (C: Felix Albini); When I Get Married (C: Alfred G. Robyn; L: Henry Blossom); When the Elves Hold Masquerade; With Song and Cheer

Cast: Blanche Duffield; Ethel Dufre Houston; John Slavin

Notes: [1] Out Boston 2/05/12. [2] Sheet music only.

308 • BARONESS FIDDLESTICKS, THE
OPENED: 11/21/1904   Theatre: Casino
Musical   Broadway: 25

Composer: Emil Brugiere
Lyricist: George DeLong
Librettist: George DeLong
Producer: MacDonald & Sullivan
Director: A.M. Holbrook

Cast: Anna Fitziu; John E. Henshaw; Richie Ling; Edna McClure

Notes: No program available.

309 • BARRIER, THE
OPENED: 11/02/1950   Theatre: Broadhurst
Musical   Broadway: 4

Composer: Jan Meyerowitz
Lyricist: Langston Hughes
Librettist: Langston Hughes
Producer: Michael Myerberg; Joel Spector
Director: Doris Humphrey

Choreographer: Charles Weidman; **Musical Director:** Herbert Zipper; **Set Design:** H.A. Condell

Cast: Marc Breaux; Wilton Clary; Reri Grist; Muriel Rahn; Laurence Tibbett

Notes: No songs listed in program.

310 • BARRY OF BALLYMORE
OPENED: 01/30/1910   Theatre: Academy of
                                              Music
Play   Broadway: 56

Composer: Ernest R. Ball; Chauncey Olcott
Lyricist: Rida Johnson Young
Librettist: Rida Johnson Young

Songs: Barry of Ballymore [2] (L: Chauncey Olcott); I Love the Name of Mary (L: George Graff Jr.); In the Sunshine of Your Love (L: Dave Reed Jr.); Mother Machree [1] (L: Rida Johnson Young); My Land (L: Bartley C. Costello); That Little Thatched Cottage All Covered with Vine [2]; Wild Rose (C: Ernest R. Ball; L: Louise Heald)

Cast: Howard Chambers; Nesta DeBecker; Chauncey Olcott; George Sydenham

Notes: No program available. [1] Also in ISLE O' DREAMS. [2] ASCAP/Library of Congress only.

311 • BATHING GIRL, THE
OPENED: 09/02/1895   Theatre: Fifth Avenue
Musical   Broadway: 1

Composer: Robert Coverly
Librettist: Rupert Hughes

Cast: William Blaisdell; Grace Golden; William Stephens

Notes: No program available.

312 • BATTLE IN THE SKIES
Notes: *See SPORTING DAYS.*

313 • BATTLE OF PORT ARTHUR
Notes: *See THE AUTO RACE.* This was the second half of the bill.

314 • BE KIND TO PEOPLE WEEK
OPENED: 03/23/1975   Theatre: Belmont
Musical   Off-Broadway: 100

Composer: Jack Bussins; Olin Ellsworth
Lyricist: Jack Bussins; Olin Ellsworth
Librettist: Jack Bussins; Olin Ellsworth
Producer: J. Arthur Elliot
Director: Quinton Raines

Choreographer: Bobby Lee; **Lighting Designer:** Anguss Moss; **Musical Director:** Jeremy Stone; **Orchestrations:** Jack Gale; **Set Design:** Bruce Monroe; **Vocal Arranger:** John Franceschina

Songs: All I Got Is You; Be Kind to People Week; Black Is Beautiful; Ecology; Freud Is a Fraud; I Have a Friend at the Chase Manhattan Bank; I Need You; I Will Give Him Love; I'm in Like with You; Mad About You, Manhattan; Smile Is Up, A; To Love Is to Live; What Ever Happened to the Good Old Days; When We See a Pretty Girl We Whistle; You're Divine

Cast: Daniel Brown; Nell Carter; Kenneth Cory; Naura Hayden; Alan Kass; Maureen Moore

315 • BE MY GUEST (0000)
Musical

Composer: Duke Ellington
Lyricist: John Latouche
Librettist: Doris Julian
Producer: Doris Julian; Perry Watkins

Choreographer: Ron Fletcher; **Set Design:** Perry Watkins

Notes: This show may not have ever been written let alone produced.

316 • BE MY GUEST (1957)
OPENED: 06/1957   Theatre: Mocambo
Revue   Los Angeles

Composer: Billy Barnes
Lyricist: Billy Barnes

Notes: Nightclub show. No other information available.

317 • BE YOURSELF (1924)
OPENED: 09/03/1924   Theatre: Sam H. Harris
Musical   Broadway: 93

Composer: Lewis E. Gensler; Milton Schwarzwald
Lyricist: Marc Connelly; George S. Kaufman
Librettist: Marc Connelly; George S. Kaufman
Producer: Wilmer & Vincent
Director: William Collier

Source: MISS MOONSHINE (Play: Marc Connolly; George S. Kaufman); **Choreographer:** Sammy Lee; **Costumes:** Charles LeMaire; Mark Mooring; **Musical Director:** Milton Schwarzwald; **Orchestrations:** Maurice DePackh; Stephen Jones

Songs: All of Them Was Friends of Mine [1] (C: Lewis E. Gensler); Banga Boo (C: Jay Gorney; Milton Schwarzwald; L: Owen Murphy); Can't You See I'm in Love [2] (L: Owen Murphy); Decent Thing to Do, The; Do It Now; Good Hand Organ and a Sidewalk's All We Need; Grandma's a Flapper Too; High in the Hills; I Came Here [3] (C: Lewis E. Gensler; L: Marc Connelly; Ira Gershwin; George S. Kaufman); Life in Town [3]; Little Bit of This, A; Money Doesn't Mean a Thing (C: Lewis Gensler; L: Ira Gershwin); My Road; Rain; Tennessee [3]; They Don't Make 'Em Like That Any More (C: Lewis E. Gensler; L: Ira Gershwin); Uh-Uh! (C: Milton Schwarzwald; L: Marc Connelly; Ira Gershwin; George S. Kaufman); What Of It? [5] (C: Lewis E. Gensler; L: Ira Gershwin); Wrong Thing at the Right Time (C: Milton Schwarzwald; L: Marc Connelly; Ira Gershwin; George S. Kaufman); You Must Come Over Blues [4] (C: Lewis E. Gensler; L: Ira Gershwin)

Cast: Georgia Caine; Jack Donahue; Queenie Smith; Norma Terris

Notes: [1] Not in program. [2] Added after opening. [3] Cut after opening. [4] Not used. Later in CAPTAIN JINKS. [5] Cut prior to opening.

318 • BE YOURSELF (1951)
OPENED: 1951

Composer: Eubie Blake
Lyricist: Grace Bouret

Songs: Be Yourself; Calling Romance; Deep End; Kiss in a Cab, A; Utterly Lovely; What Is Wrong with Me; You Spoke, I Never Heard a Word; You're My Silvery Symphony

Notes: No other information available.

319 • BEA'S PLACE
OPENED: 05/09/1979   Theatre: Westbeth
Musical   Off-Broadway: 16

Composer: John Goodwin
Lyricist: John Goodwin
Librettist: John Goodwin; Daniel O'Connor
Producer: Public Players, Inc.
Director: Daniel O'Connor

Costumes: Jack McGroder; **Lighting Designer:** Gail Dahl; **Musical Director:** Michael Holmes; **Orchestrations:** Michael Holmes; **Set Design:** Jack McGroder

Cast: Jonathan Bricklin; Al Franz; Howard Hagan; Janey Kelley; Shryl Rynharrt; Scott Stevensen; Gail Titunik; Barbara Trunz

320 • BEACHCOMBER CLUB REVUE OF 1946
OPENED: 1946   Theatre: Beachcomber
                                                    Club
Revue   Nightclub

Composer: J. Fred Coots
Lyricist: Edward Eager

Songs: Farewell My Lovely; Girl in the Front Porch Swing, The; Let's Go South; Little Washerwoman (Down in Rio), The; Sugar Cane

Notes: ASCAP/Library of Congress only.

321 • BEACHCOMBER NITES REVUE
OPENED: 1941   Theatre: Beachcomber
                                                    Club
Revue   Nightclub

Composer: Sam H. Stept
Lyricist: Benny Davis

Songs: Gaucho with the Black Mustache, The; When

Notes: No other information. Information from ASCAP/Library of Congress.

322 • BEAST IN ME, THE
OPENED: 05/16/1963   Theatre: Plymouth
Musical   Broadway: 4

Composer: Don Elliott
Lyricist: James Costigan
Librettist: James Costigan
Producer: Bonard Prods.
Director: John Lehue

Source: FABLES FOR OUR TIME (Story: James Thurber); **Choreographer:** James Butler; **Conductor:** Don Elliott; **Costumes:** Leo Van Witsen; Andy Warhol; **Lighting Designer:** Jean Rosenthal; **Musical Director:** Lehman Engel; **Orchestrations:** Bill Byers; **Set Design:** Jean Rosenthal

Songs: Bacchanale; Breakfast; Calypso Kitty; Eat Your Nice Lily, Unicorn; Glorious Cheese; Go, Go, Go; Hallelujah; I Owe Ohio; J'Ai; Percussion; So Beautiful; What Do You Say?; When I'm Alone; Why?; You're Delicious

Cast: Kaye Ballard; Bert Convy; James Costigan; Richard Hayes; Nancy Haywood; Allyn Ann McLerie; Judd Woldin

323 • BEAT THE BAND
OPENED: 10/14/1942   Theatre: 46th Street
Musical   Broadway: 67

Composer: John Green
Lyricist: George Marion Jr.
Librettist: George Abbott; George Marion Jr.
Producer: George Abbott
Director: George Abbott

Choreographer: David Lichine; **Costumes:** Freddy Wittop; **Musical Director:** Archie Bleyer; **Orchestrations:** Don Walker; **Set Design:** Samuel Leve

Songs: Afternoon of a Phony, The; America Loves a Band; Break It Up; Down Through the Agents; Ev'ry Other Heartbeat; Four Freedoms; Free, Cute and Size Fourteen; I'm Physical, You're

Cultured; Keep It Casual; Let's Comb Beaches; Men; Proud of You; Song of Two Islands; Steam Is on the Beam, The; Swimmers (dance), The [1]; Trumpet Solo [1]

Cast: Joan Caulfield; Stanley Donen; Doris Dowling; Jerry Lester; Susan Miller; Marc Platt; Jack Whiting

Notes: [1] Out of town only.

324 • BEAU BRUMMEL (1)
OPENED: 08/07/1933
Musical   Closed out of town

Composer: Harry Tierney
Lyricist: Raymond B. Egan; Edward Eliscu
Librettist: Gladys Unger
Producer: J.J. Shubert
Director: Jose Ruben

Source: BEAU BRUMMEL (Play: Clyde Fitch); **Choreographer:** William R. Holbrook; **Costumes:** Ernest R. Schrapps; **Musical Director:** Oscar Bradley; **Set Design:** Watson Barratt

Songs: I Give You the Ladies; I'll Suffer with You; Let Me Look Deep into Your Eyes; Locket in My Heart; London Cries; M'Lord and M'Lady; Nothing Happens Anymore; Our Rendezvous; Our Secret; Passe; Quadrille; Rendezvous; Rubadub Dub; Sunshine of Berkeley Square; There Must Be a First Time; Waltz Away the Night; We're Gentlemen; What a Privilege

Cast: Leonard Creeley; Berna Deane; George Hassell; Allan Jones; Nick Long Jr.; Nancy McCord; Doris Patston; Jack Sheehan

Notes: Program of MUNY Opera, St. Louis.

325 • BEAU BRUMMELL (2)
OPENED: 12/22/1933   Theatre: Saville
Play   London: 23

Composer: B.C. Hilliam
Lyricist: B.C. Hilliam
Author: B.C. Hilliam; Harold Simpson
Producer: Nigel Playfair

Source: BEAU BRUMMEL (Play: Clyde Fitch); **Choreographer:** Andree Howard; **Musical Director:** N.D. Blindt

Songs: At Such a Time as This; Beloved Mine; Birds' Nests; Confusion to the Perruquiers; Elopement in Elsinore, An (ballet); Love's Tale Is Told; Plea to the Duchess; So Very, Very Dry; We Shall See What We Shall See

Cast: Charles Hayes; Doris Hilditch; Noel Hood; Evelyn Neilson; Bruce Seton; Harry Welchman

326 • BEAUTIES, THE
Musical

Producer: Jesse Lasky

Songs: Boulevard (C/L: Unknown); Girls (C: Robert Hood Bowers; L: William Le Baron); I Could Say Goodnight to a Thousand Girls (But Only Dream of One) (C: Leo Edwards; L: Will D. Cobb); I'm Glad that I Came Home (C: Robert Hood Bowers; L: William Le Baron); I'm Longing for You (C/L: Alice Terhune); In Spain; Tango

Cast: Stewart Baird; Lora Lieb

Notes: A vaudeville musical. Information from sheet music.

327 • BEAUTIFUL PEOPLE (1)
Musical   Unproduced

Composer: Cy Coleman
Lyricist: James Lipton

Songs: Beautiful People; Come to Me; I'm Tall; It Was You; Magic Moments; Maybe There's More; Oh, Lady; Sacred Bodies; This Is What I Want; Too Many People; Would You Believe

Notes: No other information available.

328 • BEAUTIFUL PEOPLE (2)
Musical   Unproduced

Composer: Robert Kreis
Lyricist: Robert Kreis; Linda Marcus
Librettist: E. Howard Hunt

Songs: Self Made Man

Cast: Bruce Vernon Bradley; Christina Pierro

Notes: Workshop presentation. No program available.

329 • BEAUTIFUL UNKNOWN, THE
Notes: *See MY LADY'S GLOVE.*

330 • BEAUTY AND THE BEAST
OPENED: 04/18/1994   Theatre: Palace
Musical   Broadway

Composer: Alan Menken
Lyricist: Howard Ashman
Librettist: Linda Woolverton
Producer: Walt Disney Theatrical Pr.
Director: Robert Jess Roth

Source: BEAUTY AND THE BEAST (Story); **Choreographer:** Matt West; **Costumes:** Anne Hould-Ward; **Dance Arranger:** Glen Kelly; **Lighting Designer:** Natasha Katz; **Musical Director:** Michael Kosarin; **Orchestrations:** Danny Troob; **Set Design:** Stan Meyer; **Vocal Arranger:** David Friedman

Songs: Battle, The; Be Our Guest [1]; Beauty and the Beast [1]; Belle [1]; Gaston [1]; Home (L: Tim Rice); How Long Must This Go On? (L: Tim Rice); Human Again; If I Can't Love Her (L: Tim Rice); Maison des Lunes (L: Tim Rice); Me (L: Tim Rice); Mob Song, The [1]; No Matter What (L: Tim Rice); Something There [1]; Transformation (L: Tim Rice)

Narrator: David Ogden Stiers; **Cast:** Gary Beach; Tom Bosley; Susan Egan; Beth Fowler; Heath Lamberts; Stacey Logan; Terrence Mann; Burke Moses; Brian Press; Kenny Raskin; Gordon Stanley

Notes: Still playing as of press time. [1] From the Disney film.

331 • BEAUTY DOCTOR, THE (1907)
OPENED: 02/21/1907
Musical   Closed out of town

Composer: Fred Hylands; C.H. Kerr
Lyricist: Phil M. Hacker; Thomas W. Prior
Librettist: Howard M. Shelly
Producer: Fred E. Wright
Director: Will Philbrick

Costumes: Wolff Fordin; Madame Smith; **Musical Director:** Fred Hylands; **Set Design:** Arthur Voegtlin

335 • BEAUTY SHOP, THE

Songs: Angel Voices; Chorus Girl's Longing; College Days; Come Down, Mr. Man in the Moon; Culture Drill; Flirtation Sextette; Hail to the Queen of Beauty; I Never Would Believe It; Loved One, So Pure and Tender; My Flower of the South; My Little Mimi San; Myron Brown, Farewell; Nobody; On a Paper and a Comb; Opening Chorus; Queen of Beauty Am I, The; Stop, Thief; Will You Have a Gin Rickey?

Cast: Henrietta Tedro

Notes: From program Wilkes-Barre 2/21/07.

332 • BEAUTY DOCTORS, THE (1915)
OPENED: 1915
Musical   Closed out of town

Composer: Joe Hollander
Lyricist: Abe Leavitt
Librettist: Abe Leavitt

Songs: Arverne Rose; Beauty Doctors; Mississippi Cabaret; Rag with Me

Cast: Gus Fay; Harry K. Morton

Notes: A burlesque musical. Program from Toledo, Ohio.

333 • BEAUTY OF BATH, THE
OPENED: 03/19/1906   Theatre: Aldwych
Musical   London: 287

Composer: Herbert E. Haines
Lyricist: Charles H. Taylor
Librettist: Cosmo Hamilton; Seymour Hicks
Director: Seymour Hicks

Choreographer: Edward Royce; **Costumes:** Wilhelm; **Set Design:** Walter Hann

Songs: Beauty of Bath, The; Bridge; By Gentle Means (C/L: Frederick Norton); 'Earts in Bloomsbury; Entrance of the Bath Buns; Fair Women of England; Flying Machine, The; Frolic of a Breeze, The [1] (C: Jerome Kern; L: Clifford Harris; P.G. Wodehouse); George's Love Affair (C/L: Frederick Norton); Good Night, and Au Revoir; Hail! Mr. Beverly; Look In Her Heart and See; Looks Are No Matter If — (C/L: Frederick Norton); Mr. Chamberlain [1] (C/L: Jerome Kern; L: P.G. Wodehouse); Opening Chorus; Ready Maids, The; Smart Girls Day, A; Social Drum, The; Things You Never Learn at School, The; When a Little Girl's in Love; Where Do You Come From, My Pretty Maid

Cast: Sydney Fairbrother; Seymour Hicks; Ellaline Terriss; Master Valchera

Notes: [1] Lyric revised from CATCH OF THE SEASON.

334 • BEAUTY PRIZE, THE
OPENED: 09/05/1923   Theatre: Winter Garden
Musical   London: 213

Composer: Jerome Kern
Lyricist: P.G. Wodehouse
Librettist: George Grossmith; P.G. Wodehouse
Producer: George Grossmith

Choreographer: Fred Leslie; **Costumes:** Comelli; **Musical Director:** John Ansell; **Set Design:** Joseph Harker; Phil Harker

Songs: Concerted Number [1]; Cottage in Kent, A (L: George Grossmith; P.G. Wodehouse); Entrance Scene (L: George Grossmith; P.G. Wodehouse); Finale Act I (L: George Grossmith; P.G. Wodehouse); Finale Act II (L: George Grossmith; P.G. Wodehouse); For the Man I Love (L: George Grossmith; P.G. Wodehouse); Honeymoon Isle; I'm a Prize; It's a Long, Long, Day (L: George Grossmith; P.G. Wodehouse); Joy Bells; (You'll Find Me Playing) Mah-Jong (L: P.G. Wodehouse); Meet Me Down on Main Street (L: George Grossmith; P.G. Wodehouse); Melodrama; Moon Love; Non-Stop Dancing; Opening Act II; Opening Act III; Opening Chorus (L: George Grossmith; P.G. Wodehouse); We Will Take the Road Together (Finale Act III); When You Take the Road with Me (Opening Number) (L: P.G. Wodehouse); You Can't Make Love By Wireless [2] (L: George Grossmith; P.G. Wodehouse)

Cast: Dorothy Dickson; George Grossmith; Leslie Henson; Jack Hobbs; Heather Thatcher

Notes: [1] Sheet music only. [2] Music later used for "Bow Bells" in BLUE EYES.

335 • BEAUTY SHOP, THE
OPENED: 04/13/1914   Theatre: Astor
Musical   Broadway: 88

Composer: Charles J. Gebest
Lyricist: Rennold Wolf
Librettist: Channing Pollock
Producer: George M. Cohan; Sam H. Harris
Director: R.H. Burnside

Costumes: Max & Mahieu; **Musical Director:** Charles J. Gebest; **Set Design:** Unitt & Wickes

Songs: American Tourists — We'll Go to the Cabaret; Come Along, Little Girl, Come Along; Fishing Fleet Is Homeward Bound; Fishing Yarns; Give Us Your Kind Applause; I Love All the Boys in the World; I Love You Just the Same [2] (C: Dave Stamper; L: Gene Buck); I Want to Look Like Lillian Russell; I'm Longing My Dearie for You; In a Beauty Shop; In Corsica; Love's Hesitation (L: Maurice E. Marks); My Lady Fair; My Tango Queen; Old Doctor Budd; Poor Uncle Gasazus; Ring Out Glad Bells; Saturday Afternoon on Broadway; Sunshine Maxixe, The; Tale of a Mermaid, The; That's the Way a Woman Wants to Love a Man; There's a Maid; This Land We Now Forsake [1]; 'Twas in September (C: Silvio Hein; L: Benj. Hapgood Burt); Way a Woman Wants to Love a Man, The [3]; We Will Sail Back Home; When the Creditor Comes to Call; When You Hear the Umpah-Umpah in the Band; When You're All Dressed Up and No Place to Go (C: Silvio Hein; L: Benj. Hapgood Burt)

Cast: Joseph W. Herbert; Raymond Hitchcock; George Romaine; Marion Sunshine

Notes: This information from a program of 2/2/14 Washington, D.C. [1] Out Cleveland 10/6/13. [2] Not in program. [3] Sheet music only.

336 • BEAUTY SPOT, THE

OPENED: 04/10/1909   Theatre: Herald Square
Musical   Broadway: 137

Composer: Reginald De Koven
Lyricist: Joseph W. Herbert
Librettist: Joseph W. Herbert
Producer: F. Ray Comstock; Morris Gest
Director: Frank Smithson

Choreographer: Julian Alfred

Songs: Ballerina, The; Barcarolla; Boulevard Guide, The (C: Melville Gideon; L: E. Ray Goetz); Boys Will Be Boys; Change of Climate, A; Chariot [1];

Chick, Chick, Chick [1]; Choose Her in the Morning (C/L: Will R. Barnes; R.P. Weston); Cinematograph, The; Coo-ee; Coronet Dance; Creole Days; Dance of the Aboriginies [1]; Entrance of Flower Girls; Foolish Questions (C: A. Baldwin Sloane; L: William Lee); Garden of Girls, The; Goo-Goo; Haute Ecole; He Loved Her Tender; In a Hammock (Hammock Love Song) (Swinging the Summer Night Long); Jungle Man, The; Ode to Aphrodite; Pas Seul; Pretty Punchinello; Prince from Borneo, A; Salaam; She Sells Sea Shells (C: Harry Gifford; L: Terry Sullivan); Song of the Sea, A; Toujours La Politesse; Valse; Wading; We Give Him Time

Cast: Marguerite Clark; Jefferson DeAngelis; George MacFarlane; Grace Walton

Notes: [1] Sheet music only.

337 • BECOMING

OPENED: 06/15/1976   Theatre: Circle in the
Square
Revue   Off-Broadway: 2

Composer: Gail Edwards; Sam Harris
Lyricist: Gail Edwards; Sam Harris
Librettist: Gail Edwards; Sam Harris
Producer: Heartstrong Prod.
Director: John Mineo

Choreographer: John Mineo; **Costumes:** Nolan Drummond; Dee Dee Fote; **Dance Arranger:** Lawrence J. Blank; **Lighting Designer:** Martin Tudor; **Musical Director:** Lawrence J. Blank; **Set Design:** Dan Leigh

Songs: Believe in You; Birthday Song; Choices; Freer Love; From Now On; Goin' Back to That Feelin'; It Feels So Good to Be Alive Today; It's Not Easy to Change Your Life; Let It Be Today; Let's Get Started; Lonely Times; Look Inside; Lordy; Love Me Lightly; Mama; Valentine Song

Cast: Gail Edwards; Norman Meister; Anne Sward

338 • BEEHIVE

OPENED: 03/30/1986   Theatre: Top of the Gate
Revue   Off-Broadway: 600

Librettist: Larry Gallagher
Producer: Charles Allen; Betmar
Director: Larry Gallagher

Choreographer: Leslie Dockery; **Costumes:** David Dille; **Dance Arranger:** Skip Brevis; **Lighting Designer:** John Hickey; **Musical Director:** Skip Brevis; **Set Design:** John Hickey; **Vocal Arranger:** Skip Brevis

Songs: Academy Award; Ball and Chain; Beat Goes On, The; Beehive Dance, The; Come See About Me; Do Right Woman; Don't Sleep in the Subway; Downtown; Fool in Love, A; Give Him a Great Big Kiss; I Can Never Go Home Again; I Dream About Frankie; I Hear a Symphony; I Sold My Heart to the Junkman; I'm Sorry; It's My Party; Judy's Turn to Cry; Make Your Own Kind of Music; Me and Bobby McGee; My Boyfriend's Back; Name Game, The; Natural Woman, A; One Fine Day; Piece of My Heart; Proud Mary; Remember (Walking in the Sand); Respect; River Deep Mountain High; Rockin' Around the Christmas Tree; She's a Fool; Society's Child; Sweet Talkin' Guy; To Sir with Love; Try (Just a Little Bit Harder); Where Did Our Love Go?; Will You Still Love Me Tomorrow; Wishin' and Hopin'; You Don't Have to Say You Love Me; You Don't Own Me

Cast: Pattie Darcy; Alison Fraser; Jasmine Guy; Adriane Lenox; Gina Taylor; Laura Theodore

339 • BEG, BORROW OR STEAL

OPENED: 02/10/1960   Theatre: Martin Beck
Musical   Broadway: 5

Composer: Leon Pober
Lyricist: Bud Freeman
Librettist: Bud Freeman
Producer: Eddie Bracken; Carroll Masterson; Harris Masterson
Director: David Doyle; Billy Matthews

Source: UNKNOWN (Story: Bud Freeman; Marvin Seiger); **Choreographer:** Peter Hamilton; **Costumes:** Carter Morningstar; **Lighting Designer:** Carter Morningstar; **Musical Director:** Hal Hidey; **Orchestrations:** Hal Hidey; Peter Matz; **Set Design:** Carter Morningstar

Songs: Avalon Ballroom, The [1]; Beg, Borrow or Steal; Clara; Don't Stand Too Close to the Picture; Goin' Home Blues [1]; I Can't Stop Talking in Time; It Ain't Gonna Be Easy [1]; It's All in Your Mind; It's Never Been Done Before [1]; Let's Be Strangers Again; Little People; Love Is No Laughing Matter [1]; No One Knows Me;

Poetry and All That Jazz; Presenting Clara Spencer; Rafesville, U.S.A.; Rootless; Some Little People; Think; What Are We Gonna Do Tonight?; You Would Like Him [1]; You've Got Something to Say; Zen Is When

Cast: Eddie Bracken; Claiborne Cary; Betty Garrett; Bernice Massi; Biff McGuire; Larry Parks; Estelle Parsons; Betty Rhodes

Notes: This show's cast album, recorded before the show was produced, was named CLARA. [1] Cut prior to opening.

340 • BEGGAR STUDENT, THE

OPENED: 03/22/1913   Theatre: Casino
Musical   Broadway: 33

Composer: Carl Millocker
Librettist: A.F. Szilasi; Don Wilson
Producer: William A. Brady; Messrs. Shubert
Director: William J. Wilson

Musical Director: Robert Stolz

Songs: Bravo! Bravo!; But I Kissed Her on the Shoulder; I Tied the Knot; Legislature Sat in Poland, The; Man She Has Found, A; Our Country Is Free; To Go Shopping; When I Walked in the Land of Oaks; While Drinking and Eating

Cast: Louise Berthel; Arthur Cunnningham; Leo Frankel; DeWolf Hopper; Olin Howland; Parker Leonard; George MacFarlane; Adelaide Robinson; Harry Smith; Anna Wheaton

Notes: No other information available. This show was first performed in New York in 1883.

341 • BEGGAR'S HOLIDAY

OPENED: 12/26/1946   Theatre: Broadway
Musical   Broadway: 111

Composer: Duke Ellington
Lyricist: John Latouche
Librettist: John Latouche
Producer: John R. Sheppard Jr.; Perry Watkins
Director: Nicholas Ray

Source: BEGGAR'S OPERA, THE (Opera: John Gay); **Choreographer:** Valerie Bettis; **Costumes:** Walter Florell; **Lighting Designer:** Peggy Clark;

Musical Director: Max Meth; **Orchestrations:** Toots Camarata; Charles L. Cooke; Luther Henderson; Charles Huffine; Hershy Kay; Billy Strayhorn; Fred Van Epps; **Set Design:** Oliver Smith; **Vocal Arranger:** Crane Calder

Songs: Brown Penny [2]; Chase, The; Chorus of Citizens; Fol- de-rol-rol; Girls Want a Hero; Hunted, The; I Wanna Be Bad; In Between [3]; I've Got Me [1]; Lullaby for Junior; Maybe I Should Change My Ways; Ore from a Gold Mine; Quarrel for Three; Rooster Man; Scrimmage of Life, The; Take Love Easy; TNT; Tomorrow Mountain; Tooth and Claw; Wedding Ballet (dance); When I Walk with You; When You Go Down By Miss Jenny's; Women, Women, Women; Wrong Side of the Railroad Tracks, The

Cast: Marie Bryant; Alfred Drake; Avon Long; Jet MacDonald; Zero Mostel; Bernice Parks; Herbert Ross; Mildred Smith

Notes: [1] Same lyric as "I've Got Me" in BALLET BALLADS. [2] Lyric based on poem by W.B. Yeats. [3] Cut prior to opening.

342 • BEHIND THE FRIDGE
Notes: *See GOOD EVENING.*

343 • BEI MIR BISTU SCHOEN
OPENED: 10/21/1961   Theatre: Phyllis Anderson
Musical   Off-Broadway: 115

Composer: Sholom Secunda
Lyricist: Jacob Jacobs
Librettist: Louis Freedman
Producer: Jacob Jacobs

Musical Director: Sholom Secunda

Songs: Bei Mir Bistu Schoen; Blessings of the Havdoloh; Hora; Itsche; Joys from Children; Love Me; My Heart Told Me; Obeying Father; Social Security; Tain't Kosher; You Make Me Feel Younger

Cast: Leo Fuchs; Jacob Jacobs; Miriam Kressyn

344 • BELIEVERS, THE
OPENED: 05/09/1968   Theatre: Garrick
Revue   Off-Broadway: 295

Composer: Voices Inc.
Lyricist: Voices Inc.
Librettist: Jo Jackson; Joseph A. Walker
Producer: Jesse DeVore; Harold L. Oram
Director: Barbara Ann Teer

Costumes: Robert Pusilo; **Lighting Designer:** R. Robert Lussier; J.D. Regan; **Musical Director:** Brooks Alexander; **Set Design:** Joseph A. Walker; **Vocal Arranger:** Brooks Alexander

Songs: African Sequence; Believer's Chant; Believers' Laments; Burn This Town; Children's Games; City Blues; Daily Buzz; Early One Morning Blues; Field Hollers and Work Songs; He's Got the Whole World in His Hands; I Just Got in the City; I Turn to Jesus; I'm Gonna Do My Things; I'm So Glad; Jesus the Light of the World; Learn to Love; Naked Foot; School Don't Mean a Damn Thing; Sermon: The Life of Peter; This Old Ship; What Shall I Believe in Now?; Where Do I Go from Here?; Where Shall I Go?; You Never Know

Cast: Benjamin Carter; Jesse DeVore; Dorothy Dinroe; Barry Hemphill; Jo Jackson; Shirley Jackson; Shirley McKie; Don Oliver; Anje Ray; Veronica Redd; Ron Steward; Joseph A. Walker

Notes: Some of the songs are traditional spirituals.

345 • BELINDA!
OPENED: 05/03/1957
Musical   Closed out of town

Composer: Jack Olsson
Lyricist: Jack Olsson
Librettist: Jack Carr
Director: Robert Moore

Source: ENGAGED (Musical: W.S. Gilbert); **Choreographer:** Marcia Lee Merrill; Fran Nonziato; Diane Ross; **Conductor:** Frank Albright; **Costumes:** Joseph Lewis; **Dance Arranger:** Edward Cashman; **Musical Director:** Edward Cashman; **Set Design:** J.D. Waring

Songs: Belinda!; Fruit of My Heart; I'm Not Mercenary; Jack the Ripper; Make Your Mate Miserable; Money Is Better Than Men; My Affection Knows No Bounds; Oh, For That Country Air; Search for Roger Evans, The; Stygian Shore, The; That Happy Face; Two Can Live As Cheaply As One; Wedding Waltz, The;

What Is My Status; Where Is the Bride?; You and Only You; You Won't Find Any Gold in Scotland

Cast: Philip Bosco; Robert Gormley; Mary Grant; Mary Harrigan; James D. Rogers

Notes: Amateur show. Catholic University.

346 • BELINDA FAIR

OPENED: 03/25/1949   Theatre: Saville
Musical   London: 131

Composer: Jack Strachey
Lyricist: Eric Maschwitz
Librettist: Gilbert Lennox; Eric Maschwitz
Producer: John Buckley; Leslie Henson
Director: Charles Goldner

Choreographer: Pauline Grant; **Costumes:** Jeannetta Cochrane; **Musical Director:** Walter Stiasny; **Set Design:** Leon Davey

Songs: Ballad of Nellie Gwynne, The; English Are Barbarians, The; Finale Act I; Finale Act II; Finale Act III; Fool There Was, A; Gay Dragoon; Gay Little Ladies of Drury Lane; Golden Days of Good Queen Anne; Good Madam Geneva; Heigho! That I Should Fall in Love; I Dreamed I Was at Home Again; Let's Be Merry [2]; Lilac Tree, The; Love! Love! Love!; No Love, No Heartbreak; Off to the Low Countree; Oh! Marie; Still Dreaming; Travelling Englishman [1]; Women and Men

Cast: Adele Dixon; Geoffrey Hibbert; Stella Moray; Peter Yardley

Notes: [1] Cut. [2] Added.

347 • BELL FOR ADANO, A

OPENED: 06/02/1956   Theatre: CBS
TV Musical

Composer: Arthur Schwartz
Lyricist: Howard Dietz

Source: BELL FOR ADANO, A (Novel: John Patrick)

Songs: Bell for Adano, A; Fish; I'm Part of You; Okay, Mister Major; Why Not Surrender [1]

Cast: Anna Maria Alberghetti; Edwin Steffi; Barry Sullivan; Frank Yanconelli

Notes: Original TV musical. [1] Not used.

348 • BELLA

OPENED: 11/16/1961   Theatre: Gramercy Arts
Musical   Off-Broadway: 6

Composer: Jane Douglass
Lyricist: Tom O'Malley
Librettist: Lance Barklie; Tom O'Malley
Producer: Lance Barklie; Ned Hendrickson
Director: Richard C. Shank

Choreographer: Don Sky; **Costumes:** Dorine Ackerman; **Dance Arranger:** Jane Douglass; **Lighting Designer:** Richard B. Hughes; **Musical Director:** Jane Douglass; **Set Design:** Richard B. Hughes; **Vocal Arranger:** Jane Douglass

Songs: All About Evelyn; Big, Big; Could Be; For Love or Money; Hand in Hand; I'm Happy; It Isn't the Same; Kiss Me; Love Doesn't Grow on Trees; Madame from Paree; My Card; On the Seashore By the Sea; Seven Seas, The; Take a Chance; Time; Way Down in Lil' Old Texas

Cast: Will B. Able; Dodo Denny; Gloria Le Roy

349 • BELLE OF AVENUE A, THE

OPENED: 03/05/1906   Theatre: Majestic
Musical   Closed out of town

Composer: Egbert Van Alstyne
Lyricist: Harry Williams
Librettist: Aaron Hoffman
Producer: A.H. Woods
Director: Edward Rose

Choreographer: Hymes; **Costumes:** Bloodgood; **Musical Director:** Edward Walker

Songs: Belle of Avenue A, The; Cobweb Man, The; Good-a-Bye John [1]; Happy Days; Hurdy Gurdy Man, The; I Would Like to Have a Phonograph of You; In College; Indiana Anna; Parodies; Society; There's a Little Fighting Blood in Me; When the Band of Reubenville Turns Out; Why Don't You Try?; You're the Candy

Cast: Hal Clements; Marie Dumont; Maude Earl; Elfie Fay; Billy Kent

Notes: Program of Brooklyn, New York. [1] Later in THE RED MILL.

350 • BELLE OF BOHEMIA, THE

OPENED: 09/24/1900   Theatre: Casino
Musical   Broadway: 55

Composer: Ludwig Englander
Lyricist: Harry B. Smith
Librettist: Harry B. Smith
Producer: George W. Lederer
Director: George W. Lederer

Choreographer: Aurelia Coccia; **Costumes:** Mme. Siedle; **Musical Director:** Arthur Weld; **Set Design:** Ernest Albert; D. Frank Dodge; Joseph Physioc

Songs: Always Make Allowances for Love; Amateur Entertainer, The; Be Clever; Beer, Beautiful Beer; Belle of Bohemia, The; Blue Ribbon Girls, The; Champagne Waltz; Fairies' Lullaby; Girl Who Is Up-To-Date; He Was a Married Man; It's What Eve Said to Adam; Lady in the Moon, The; Matinee Girls; My Mobile Gal (C: Harry T. MacConnell; L: Robert B. Smith); Never Again; She Never Loved a Man as Much as That (C: Harry T. MacConnell; L: Robert B. Smith); Strolling Thru the River; Tell Me When I Shall Find Him; Wishing Cup, The

Cast: Irene Bentley; Sam Bernard; Marguerite Clark; Virginia Earle; Trixie Friganza; John Hyams; Anna Laughlin

351 • BELLE OF BOND STREET, THE

OPENED: 03/30/1914   Theatre: Shubert
Musical   Broadway: 48

Composer: Ivan Caryll; Lionel Monckton
Lyricist: Claude Aveling; Adrian Ross
Librettist: Harold Atteridge; Owen Hall
Producer: Messrs. Shubert
Director: Edwin T. Emery

Source: GIRL FROM KAY'S, THE (Musical: Ivan Caryll; Owen Hall); **Choreographer:** Jack Mason; **Costumes:** Melville Ellis; **Musical Director:** Leonard Hornsey

Songs: As I Came Up the Aisle; Bridal Bevy, The; Do the Funny Fox Trot [3] (C: Harry Carroll; L: Earl Carroll); Flacton-On-The-Sea; Gypsy Land [1]; Here's to the Bride [1]; Hoggenheimer of Park Lane; Honeymoon Trip All Alone, A; It's the Hat and Not the Girl; Little Tango Maid, A (C: Harry Carroll; L: Harold Atteridge); My Idea About the Boys [1]; Pierrotland; Prunella (C: Harry Carroll; L: Harold Atteridge); Tango Dip (C: Harry Carroll; L: Harold Atteridge); They Say I'm Frivolous; Tip Top Tipperary Mary (C: Harry Carroll; L: Ballard Macdonald); Too Many Cooks; Turkey Trotting Boy (Oh! You Turkey Trotter), The (C: Harry Carroll; L: Harold Atteridge); We've Come to Woo the Ladies; Who Paid the Rent for Mrs. Rip Van Winkle When Rip Van Winkle Was Away [2] (C: Fred Fisher; L: Alfred Bryan)

Cast: Sam Bernard; Lawrence D'Orsay; Gaby Deslys; Forrest Huff; Harry Pilcer; Fritzi Von Busing

Notes: [1] Out New York, 1915. [2] Also in DANCING AROUND. [3] ASCAP only.

352 • BELLE OF BRIDGEPORT, THE

OPENED: 10/29/1900   Theatre: Bijou
Musical   Broadway: 45

Composer: J. Rosamond Johnson
Lyricist: Bob Cole; James Weldon Johnson
Librettist: Glen MacDonough

Songs: Ain't Gwine to Work No More; Angeline (C/L: Cissie Loftus); Bullfrog Ben (C/L: Cissie Loftus); Dance on Friday Night (C/L: William Jefferson); Dandy Soldier Coon (C/L: Will Accooe); Mabel Moore (C/L: Will Accooe); Southern Queen; Troubles of My Own; Why Don't the Band Play?

Cast: Raymond Hitchcock; May Irwin

353 • BELLE OF BRITTANY, THE

OPENED: 11/08/1909   Theatre: Daly's
Musical   Broadway: 72

Composer: Howard Talbot
Lyricist: Percy Greenbank
Librettist: Leedham Bantock; P.J. Barron
Producer: Lee Shubert; Sam S. Shubert
Director: Frank Smithson

Costumes: Melville Ellis; **Musical Director:** Clarence Rogerson

Songs: All Roads Lead to Church [1]; Best Brittany, The; Bois D'Amour, The (Opening Chorus); Chorus and Entrance of Marquis [1]; Chorus of Daffodil Girls [1] (L: P.J. Barrow); Country Dance (inst.) [1]; Daffodil Time; Dawn of Love, The (L: P.J. Barrow; Percy Greenbank); Doggies and the Bone, The; Finacle Act I [1]; Finale Act II [1]; Girl with the Clocking on Her Stocking, The; Hero Proudly Comes, The (Chorus of Welcome) [1]; I'm Not a Lady's Maid; I'm Not a Marrying Man [1]; I'm Not That Sort of Picture [1]; In the Chest; In the Oven; Ingle Nook, The [1] (C: Marie Horne); It's Too Late Now; King of the Kitchen, The [1]; Kingdom of a Woman's Heart, The [1]; Little Cafe, A; Little Country Mice; Message of the Bells, The (Ding-Dong Bell) [1] (C: Marie Horne); My Wedding Morning [1]; Oh! I Must Go Home Tonight (C/L: William Hargreaves); Old Chateau, The; Sing to Your Dear One; Stepping Stones, The (C: Marie Horne); Trysting Tree, The (C: Marie Horne); Two Giddy Goats; Wreath the Golden Flower (Opening Act II) (L: P.J. Barrow)

Cast: Frank Daniels; Francis Kennedy

Notes: [1] From vocal score only.

354 • BELLE OF BROADWAY, THE
OPENED: 03/17/1902   Theatre: Winter Garden
Musical   Broadway: 24

Composer: A. Baldwin Sloane
Lyricist: George V. Hobart
Librettist: William H. Post
Producer: Sire Bros.
Director: Ned Wayburn

Cast: Donald Brian; Alexander Clark; Charles Prince; Thomas Q. Seabrooke; Amelia Summerville

Notes: No other information available.

355 • BELLE OF LONDON TOWN, THE
OPENED: 01/28/1907   Theatre: Lincoln Square
Musical   Broadway: 16

Composer: Julian Edwards

Lyricist: Stanislaus Stange
Librettist: Stanislaus Stange
Producer: Messrs. Shubert
Director: R.H. Burnside

Musical Director: Herman Perlet

Songs: As I Love You [1]; Balinda's Triumph [1]; Drink with Me the Night Away; Fairy Beauty's Queen; Guardians of the House; Hindoo Paradise; I Cannot Wait Till Monday; I Should Have Been Offended If My Waist You Hadn't Squeezed; I Was Born to Rule [2]; Lady of Society, The; Let Us Gossip of the Latest Court Flirtation; Light That Lies in Women's Eyes, The; Little Weather Vane, The; Love Her All the Time [1]; Love's Secret; Magician Love; My Heart Is True [1]; Next Sunday [1]; Spirit, Not the Letter [1]; Still the World Rolls On; They Pictured Me Like This; 'Tis a Merry, Merry World [1]; To Drink We Have No Fear; When Fortune Smiles; Wondrous Spell of Love [1]

Cast: Kathleen Clifford; Camille D'Arville; Orville Harrold; Giorgio Majeroni

Notes: [1] Sheet music only. [2] Sometimes referred to as "Men Are Born to Rule."

356 • BELLE OF MAYFAIR, THE
OPENED: 12/03/1906   Theatre: Daly's
Musical   Broadway: 140

Composer: Leslie Stuart
Librettist: Charles H.E. Brookfield; Cosmo Hamilton
Producer: Thomas W. Riley

Songs: And the Weeping Willow Wept (L: George Arthurs); Bells in the Morning (L: William Caine); Come to St. George's (L: Leslie Stuart); Eight Little Debutantes Are We (L: William Caine); Finale Act I (L: Basil Hood); Hello! Come Along, Girls! (L: Leslie Stuart); I Am a Military Man (L: William Caine); I Know a Girl (L: Leslie Stuart); I'll Wait for You, Little Girlie (Round at the Sweet Shop) [3] (L: George Arthurs); I'm a Duchess (L: Basil Hood); In Gay Mayfair (L: William Caine); In Montezuma [1]; Little Girl at the Sweet Shop, The; Matron and the Maid, The [1]; My Lady Fair; My Little Girl Is a Shy Little Girl (L: Basil Hood); Opening Chorus (L: Basil Hood); Opening Chorus Act II (L: Basil Hood); Pierrot [2]; Play the Game [1];

Said I to Myself (L: Basil Hood); We've Come from Court (L: Basil Hood); Welcome to Princess (L: Basil Hood); What Makes You the Woman? (L: George Arthurs); What Will the World Say [1]; Where You Go, Will I Go (L: Basil Hood); Why Do They Call Me a Gibson Girl? (L: Leslie Stiles)

Cast: Irene Bentley; Bessie Clayton; Jack Gardner; Christie MacDonald; Ignacio Martinetti; Valeska Suratt; Van Rensselaer Wheeler

Notes: [1] Sheet music only. [2] Out Kansas City 10/31/07. [3] London vocal score only.

357 • BELLE OF NEW YORK, THE
OPENED: 09/28/1897   Theatre: Casino
Musical   Broadway: 56

Composer: Gustave Kerker
Lyricist: Hugh Morton
Librettist: Hugh Morton
Producer: George W. Lederer
Director: George W. Lederer

Choreographer: Signor Francioli; **Costumes:** Mme. Siedle; **Set Design:** Ernest Albert; D. Frank Dodge; Ernest M. Gros

Songs: Anti-Cigarette Society, The; At Ze Naughty Folies Bergere; Belle of New York, The; Bom Bouche; Conumdrums [1]; Cora Angelique [1]; Cotton Moon; Don't Blame It All on Broadway; Follow On; For in the Fields [1]; For the Twentieth Time We'll Drink [1]; From Far Kohoes [1]; Good Bye Boys; Good Old Glory; Hello Little Miss U.S.A.; I Do, So There [1]; I Want to Go To-Morrow [2]; I've Got a Smile; La Belle Parisienne; Little Sister Kissie; Lucky Jim [2]; My Little Baby; Nice Young Man, A; Now That I Have Got Them, I Don't Want Them; Oh Sonny [1]; Oh! Teach Me How to Kiss, Dear; On the Beach at Narragansett [1]; Pretty Little China Girl [1]; Purity Brigade, The; Queen of Comic Opera; Simple Little Girl, A [1]; Take Me Down to Coney Island [1]; Teach Me How to Love; They All Follow Me; They Call Me the Belle of New York; Villain Still Pursued Her, The; We Come This Way [1]; We'll Dance in the Moonlight [1]; Wedding Glide; When a Man Is Twenty-One [1]; When I Was Born the Stars Stood Still [1]; When We Are Married; Wine Women and Song [1]; You and I; Young Man's Rescue League

Cast: William Cameron; Dan Daly; Ada Dare; Harry Davenport; Edna May; William Sloan; David Warfield

Notes: [1] From London vocal score. [2] Added after London opening.

358 • BELLE OF QUAKER TOWN, THE
OPENED: 07/1924
Musical

Composer: Harry Ruby
Lyricist: Bert Kalmar
Librettist: Aaron Hoffman

Notes: Stamford Connecticut. This is a revised version of THE TOWN CLOWN, it was revised again into NO OTHER GIRL. No program available.

359 • BELLE OF THE BALKINS
Notes: See PARANOIA.

360 • BELLE OF THE BARBER'S BALL, THE
Notes: See COHAN AND HARRIS MINSTRELS.

361 • BELLE OF THE WEST, THE
OPENED: 10/29/1905
Musical   Closed out of town

Composer: Karl Hoschna
Lyricist: Harry B. Smith
Librettist: Harry B. Smith
Producer: B.E. Forrester
Director: Edward Rose

Songs: Down By the Blue Rio Grande; Frog and the Owl, The; Holding Hands; It's So Different in London; Land of Romance; Ma Little Sioux Sue; My Little Lassoo; There Are Lots of Things Teacher Does Not Know; Those Were Happy Days; Waltz, The; Where the Flag Is Waving

Cast: Florence Bindley; Joseph Green; Arthur Otto; Ernest Otto; Jack Randolph

Notes: Played the Great Northern Theatre in Chicago. No program available. A clipping of 11/05 states there were 19 songs in the show.

362 • BELLE STARR

OPENED: 04/30/1969   Theatre: Palace
Musical   London: 16

Composer: Steve Allen
Lyricist: Steve Allen; Warren Douglas; Jerry Schafer
Librettist: Warren Douglas
Producer: Rory Calhoun; Clarke Reynolds; Jerry Shafer

Choreographer: Jack Card; **Lighting Designer:** Michael Northen; **Musical Director:** Maurice Arnold; **Set Design:** Peter Proud; **Vocal Arranger:** Maurice Arnold

Songs: Belle; Biggest Pair of 38's in Town; Dance Polka; Dirty, Rotten, Vicious, Nasty Guys; Gee, You're Pretty; Gunfighter's Ballad, The; Happy Birthday to Vegas; I'm a Lady; It Takes One to Know One; Lady Don't Do, A; Ladylike Lady Like Me; Never Had This Feeling Before; Story Song; We're Gonna Make History

Cast: Jack Card; Betty Grable

Notes: Also known as THE PIECEFUL PALACE and GO FOR YOUR GUN.

363 • BELLS ARE RINGING

OPENED: 11/29/1956   Theatre: Shubert
Musical   Broadway: 924

Composer: Jule Styne
Lyricist: Betty Comden; Adolph Green
Librettist: Betty Comden; Adolph Green
Producer: Theatre Guild, The
Director: Jerome Robbins

Choreographer: Bob Fosse; Jerome Robbins; **Costumes:** Raoul Pene du Bois; **Dance Arranger::** John Morris; **Lighting Designer:** Peggy Clark; **Musical Director:** Milton Rosenstock; **Orchestrations:** Robert Russell Bennett; **Set Design:** Raoul Pene du Bois; **Vocal Arranger:** Buster Davis; Herbert Greene

Songs: Bells Are Ringing; Better Than a Dream [3]; But I'm Always Sensitive to You (Hot and Cold); Don't Thank Me [5]; Drop That Name [1]; Hello, Hello There; I Love Your Sunny Teeth; I Met a Girl; I'm Going Back; Independent; Inspector Barnes [2]; Intuition [2]; Is It a Crime?; It's a Perfect Relationship; It's a Simple Little System; Just in Time; Long Before I Knew You; Marlon Mood, The [2]; Midas Touch, The; Mississippi Steamboat; Mom [2]; Mu-Cha-Cha; My Guiding Star [2]; On My Own; Oogie-Woogie-Shoogie [4]; Party's Over, The; Salzburg; Santa's Lullaby [2]; Sue! Sue! [2]; You Don't See Anything but It Hurts (Oh How It Hurts); You've Got to Do It

Cast: Frank Aletter; Sydney Chaplin; Dort Clark; Peter Gennaro; Judy Holliday; Eddie Lawrence; Jean Stapleton; Bernie West

Notes: [1] Called "The Name Dropping Gavotte" in previews. [2] Cut prior to New York opening. [3] Written for film (1958) then added to show after opening. [4] Cut during previews. [5] ASCAP/Library of Congress only. [6] Cut as a complete song. Fragment remains as intro to "Independent."

364 • BELMONT VARIETIES

OPENED: 09/26/1932   Theatre: Belmont
Revue   Broadway: 4

Librettist: Sam Bernard; Helen Leary; Nolan Leary
Producer: Richard G. Herndon
Director: Sam Bernard; Max Scheck

Orchestrations: Bernabe Roxas Solis

Songs: Autographs of You (C: Alvin Kaufman; L: Mildred Kaufman); Automotivation (C: Henry Lloyd; L: Sam Bernard Jr.; Bobby Burk); Back Seat of a Taxi (C: Serge Walter; L: Charles Kenny); Blind Alleys (C: Serge Walter; L: Charles Kenny); Bonbonera (C: Serge Walter; L: Charles Kenny); Dance (His Invitation to Love) (C: Alvin Kaufman; L: Mildred Kaufman); Degas Ballet (inst.) (C: Charles Godard); Etiquette (C: Henry Lloyd; L: Sam Bernard Jr.; Bobby Burk); Goona-Goona (C: Serge Walter; L: Charles Kenny); Hitting the New High (C: Henry Lloyd; L: Sam Bernard Jr.; Bobby Burk); I Paused, I Looked, I Fell (C: Henry Lloyd; L: Sam Bernard Jr.; Bobby Burk); Lament Mauricette (C: Henry Lloyd; L: Sam Bernard Jr.; Bobby Burk); Lontananza (C: Angelo Bettinelli); Lover, Where Are You Now? (C: Serge Walter); No Thank You (C: Alvin Kaufman; L: Mildred Kaufman); Park Avenue (C: Serge Walter; L: Charles Kenny); Primitive Ebony, The (C: Anna Bacon Dodge); River Will Sweep You Away, The (C: Henry Lloyd; L: Sam Bernard Jr.; Bobby Burk); Something New and It's You (C: Alvin Kaufman;

L: Mildred Kaufman); Sparkling Champagne (C: Victor Jacobi); That's You (C: Serge Walter; L: Charles Kenny); Tu Sais (C: Serge Walter; L: Charles Kenny); When Greek Meets Greek of Liza-Strata (C: Charles Posnak); Yes and No (C: Von Egen; L: Lucien La Reviere); You Took My Breath Away (C: Henry Lloyd; L: Sam Bernard Jr.; Bobby Burk)

Cast: Maryon Dale; Eddie Leslie

Notes: This show later reopened as MANHATTAN VANITIES and COSMO VANITIES but failed both times.

365 • BELOVED ROGUE
Notes: *See also VENUS IN SILK.*

366 • BELOW THE BELT
OPENED: 06/21/1966   Theatre: Downstairs at the Upstairs
Revue   Nightclub: 186

Composer: Rod Warren
Lyricist: Rod Warren
Producer: Rod Warren
Director: Sandra Devlin

Musical Director: Michael Cohen

Songs: Camp; Great Society Waltz, The; International Monopoly; Love's Labour Lost [1] (C: Jerry Powell; L: Michael McWhinney); Suburbia Square Dance (L: Michael McWhinney)

Cast: Richard Blair; Genna Carter; Madeline Kahn; Robert Rovin; Lily Tomlin; **Pianist:** Michael Cohen; Edward Morris

Notes: No program available. [1] Also in AND IN THIS CORNER.

367 • BEN FRANKLIN IN PARIS
OPENED: 10/27/1964   Theatre: Lunt-Fontanne
Musical   Broadway: 215

Composer: Mark Sandrich Jr.
Lyricist: Sidney Michaels
Librettist: Sidney Michaels
Producer: George W. George; Frank Granat
Director: Michael Kidd

Costumes: Motley; **Dance Arranger::** Roger Adams; **Lighting Designer:** Jack Brown; **Musical Director:** Donald Pippin; **Orchestrations:** Philip J. Lang; **Set Design:** Oliver Smith; **Vocal Arranger:** Donald Pippin

Songs: Balloon Is Ascending, A; Benjamin Did It [1]; Damn the Woman [1]; Diane Is; French Wench [1]; God Bless the Human Elbow; Half the Battle; Hic Haec Hoc; Hot Chocolate Days [1]; How Laughable It Is; I Invented Myself; I Love the Ladies; Lightning Rod Interlude [1]; Look for Small Pleasures; Minute Minuet [1]; Rocking Chair Interlude [1]; Since Last We Talked Alone [2]; Take Up with an Older Woman [1]; Tis Incredible As Love [2]; To Be Alone with You (C/L: Jerry Herman); Too Charming (C/L: Jerry Herman); Until You're Recognized [1]; We Sail the Seas; We've Got the British Lion By the Tail [2]; Whatever Became of Old Temple; When I Dance with the Person I Love; Won't They Be Surprised [1]; You're in Paris

Cast: Jack Fletcher; Bob Kaliban; Robert Preston; Ulla Sallert; Susan Watson; Byron Webster

Notes: [1] Not used. [2] Out Philadelphia.

368 • BEN MARDEN'S RIVIERA FOLLIES
Notes: *See RIVIERA FOLLIES OF 1937.*

369 • BERLIN TO BROADWAY WITH KURT WEILL
OPENED: 10/01/1972   Theatre: Theatre de Lys
Revue   Off-Broadway: 152

Composer: Kurt Weill
Librettist: Gene Lerner
Producer: Michael Arthur Film Prods.; Hank Kaufman; Gene Lerner
Director: Donald Saddler

Costumes: Frank Thompson; **Lighting Designer:** Thomas Skelton; **Musical Director:** Newton Wayland; **Orchestrations:** Newton Wayland; **Set Design:** Helen Pond; Herbert Senn

Songs: Ain't It Awful the Heat? [10] (L: Langston Hughes); Alabama Song [3] (L: Bertolt Brecht); As You Make Your Bed [3] (L: Bertolt Brecht; Arnold Weinstein); Barbara Song [1] (L: Marc Blitzstein; Bertolt Brecht); Bilbao Song [2]

(L: Bertolt Brecht; Michael Feingold); Cry the Beloved Country [11] (L: Maxwell Anderson); Deep in Alaska [3] (L: Bertolt Brecht; Arnold Weinstein); Happy Ending [1] (L: Marc Blitzstein; Bertolt Brecht); How Can You Tell an American? [6] (L: Maxwell Anderson); How to Survive [1] (L: Marc Blitzstein; Bertolt Brecht); Hymn to Peace [5] (L: Paul Green); I Wait for a Ship [4] (L: Alice Baker; Jacques Deval; Gene Lerner); Jealousy Duet [1] (L: Marc Blitzstein; Bertolt Brecht); Johnny's Song [5] (L: Paul Green); Lonely House [10] (L: Langston Hughes); Lost in the Stars [11] (L: Maxwell Anderson); Love Duet [1] (L: Marc Blitzstein; Bertolt Brecht); Love Song [12] (L: Alan Jay Lerner); Lullaby [10] (L: Langston Hughes); Mack the Knife [1] (L: Marc Blitzstein; Bertolt Brecht); Moon-Faced, Starry-Eyed [10] (L: Langston Hughes); Morning Anthem [1] (L: Marc Blitzstein; Bertolt Brecht); My Ship [7] (L: Ira Gershwin); Oh, Heavenly Salvation [3] (L: Bertolt Brecht; Arnold Weinstein); Pirate Jenny [1] (L: Marc Blitzstein; Bertolt Brecht); Progress [9] (L: Alan Jay Lerner); Sailor Tango [2] (L: Bertolt Brecht); September Song [6] (L: Maxwell Anderson); Song of the Guns [5] (L: Paul Green); Songs of Peace and War [5] (L: Paul Green); Speak Low [8] (L: Ogden Nash); Surabaya Johnny [2] (L: Bertolt Brecht; George Tabori); Tango Ballad [1] (L: Marc Blitzstein; Bertolt Brecht); That's Him [8] (L: Ogden Nash); Train to Johannesburg [11] (L: Maxwell Anderson); Trouble Man [11] (L: Maxwell Anderson); Useless Song [1] (L: Marc Blitzstein; Bertolt Brecht)

Cast: Margery Cohen; Ken Kercheval; Judy Lander; Jerry Lanning; Hal Watters

Notes: [1] From THE THREEPENNY OPERA. [2] From HAPPY END. [3] From THE RISE AND FALL OF THE CITY OF MAHAGONNY. [4] From MARIE GALANTE. [5] From JOHNNY JOHNSON. [6] From KNICKERBOCKER HOLIDAY. [7] From LADY IN THE DARK. [8] From ONE TOUCH OF VENUS. [9] From LOVE LIFE [10] From STREET SCENE. [11] From LOST IN THE STARS. [12] From LOVE LIFE.

370 • BESSIE CLAYTON VAUDEVILLE ACT

OPENED: 1919

Composer: Charles A. McCarron
Lyricist: Charles A. McCarron

Musical Director: Ernest G. Grooney

Cast: Cansinos, The; Bessie Clayton

Notes: No other information available. From a Philadelphia program.

371 • BESSIE MCCOY DAVIS' PERIOD DANCE REVIEW

OPENED: 1918

Composer: Percy Wenrich
Lyricist: Edward Madden

Musical Director: Hal Dyson

Songs: Ducky Daddies; Moon Men; My Friend Yama; Trench Girl; War Doll, The; We'll March to Victory Under the Stars and Stripes

Cast: Thomas Conkey; Henry Coote; Bessie McCoy Davis

Notes: From a Chicago program vaudeville show.

372 • BEST FOOT FORWARD

OPENED: 10/01/1941 Theatre: Ethel Barrymore
Musical Broadway: 326

Composer: Ralph Blane; Hugh Martin
Lyricist: Ralph Blane; Hugh Martin
Librettist: John Cecil Holm
Producer: George Abbott; Richard Rodgers
Director: George Abbott

Choreographer: Gene Kelly; **Costumes:** Miles White; **Musical Director:** Archie Bleyer; **Orchestrations:** Hans Spialek; Don Walker; **Set Design:** Jo Mielziner

Songs: Buckle Down Winsocki (C/L: Ralph Blane); Don't Sell the Night Short; Ev'ry Time (C/L: Hugh Martin); Guy Who Brought Me, The (C/L: Richard Rodgers; L: Hugh Martin); He Put the "Uh" in Mambo [4]; Hollywood Story [1]; I Know You By Heart; I'd Gladly Trade; Just a Little Joint with a Juke Box; My First Promise; Overture (C: Robert Russell Bennett); Raving Beauty, A [2]; Shady Lady Bird (C/L: Ralph Blane); That's How I Love the Blues (C/L: Hugh Martin); Three B's, The; Three Men on a Date; Wham [3]; What Do You Think I Am? (C/L: Hugh Martin); Where Do You Travel?; Wish I May [5]; You Are for Loving [2]

Cast: June Allyson; Kenneth Bowers; Maureen Cannon; Danny Daniels; Tommy Dix; Stanley Donen; Rosemary Lane; Marty May; Gil Stratton; Nancy Walker; Lou Wills Jr.

Notes: Martin and Blane wrote separately and then polished the numbers together. When the individual writers are known they are identified. The other songs, although written separately are grouped together. [1] Added to the 1963 revival. [2] Written for 1960 stage version of MEET ME IN ST. LOUIS and added to the 1963 revival of BEST FOOT FORWARD. [3] Written for 1951 production. [4] Written for 1954 TV version. [5] Written for the film version. Added to 1963 revvial.

373 • BEST LITTLE WHOREHOUSE GOES PUBLIC, THE

OPENED: 05/10/1994   Theatre: Lunt-Fontanne
Musical   Broadway: 15

Composer: Carol Hall
Lyricist: Carol Hall
Librettist: Larry L. King; Peter Masterson
Producer: MCA/Universal; Steve Phillips
  Director: Peter Masterson; Tommy Tune

Choreographer: Jeff Calhoun; Tommy Tune; **Conductor:** Robert Billig; **Costumes:** Bob Mackie; **Dance Arranger::** Wally Harper; **Lighting Designer:** Peggy Eisenhauer; Jules Fisher; **Musical Director:** Karl Jurman; **Orchestrations:** Peter Matz; **Set Design:** John Arnone; **Vocal Arranger:** Wally Harper

Songs: Brand New Start; Call Me; Change in Me; Here for the Hearing; If We Open Our Eyes; I'm Leavin' Texas; It's Been a While; Let the Devil Take Us; Nothin' Like a Picture Show; Piece of the Pie; Smut Song, The

Cast: Ronn Carroll; Kevin Cooney; Jim David; David Doty; Dee Hoty; Gina Torres

Notes: A sequel of sorts to THE BEST LITTLE WHOREHOUSE IN TEXAS.

374 • BEST LITTLE WHOREHOUSE IN TEXAS, THE

OPENED: 04/17/1978   Theatre: 46th Street
Musical   Broadway: 1669

Composer: Carol Hall
Lyricist: Carol Hall
Librettist: Larry L. King; Peter Masterson
Producer: Universal Pictures
Director: Peter Masterson; Tommy Tune

Source: UNKNOWN (Story: Larry L. King); **Choreographer:** Tommy Tune; **Costumes:** Ann Roth; **Lighting Designer:** Dennis Parichy; **Musical Director:** Robert Billig; **Set Design:** Marjorie Kellogg; **Vocal Arranger:** Robert Billig

Songs: Aggie Song (1); Aggie Song (2) [1]; Angelette March; Bus from Amarillo; Doatsey Mae; Doin' It and Sayin' It Are Two Different Things [1]; Girl You're a Woman; God Damn Everythang [2]; Good Old Girl; Hard Candy Christmas; Have a Memory on Me [1]; Keepin' Books [1]; Lil Old Bitty Pissant Country Place, A; Little Bit of Fixin', A [2]; Memory Song [2]; No Lies; Prologue; Pussy [1]; Sidestep, The; Sissy Wishing Well [1]; Texas Has a Whorehouse in It; 20 Fans; 24 Hours of Lovin'; Two Blocks from the Capitol Building [2]; Watch Dog Theme

Cast: Pamela Blair; Don Crabtree; Henderson Forsythe; Jay Garner; Carlin Glynn; Delores Hall; Marta Sanders

Notes: This show played 12 performances at the Actors Studio beginning October 20, 1977. It opened at the Entermedia Theatre on April 17, 1978 where it played for 85 performances. It then moved to Broadway on June 19, 1978 for 1584 performances. [1] Cut prior to opening. [2] Cut while off-off-Broadway.

375 • BETSY (1911)

OPENED: 12/11/1911   Theatre: Herald Square
Musical   Broadway: 32

Composer: Alexander Johnstone
Lyricist: Will B. Johnstone
Librettist: H. Kellett Chambers
Producer: Byron Chandler
Director: Edward Elsner

Musical Director: Charles E. Candee Jr.

Songs: Aristocracy; Composing; Day Before the Morning After, The; Dream Love; First Gray Hair; Laughter and Love; Love's Conquests; Only a Voice; Opening Ensemble; Snoop Snoop; There Came a Vision

Cast: Grace LaRue; Hassard Short

Notes: Originally titled AN AMERICAN WIDOW.

376 • BETSY (1926)

OPENED: 12/28/1926   Theatre: New Amsterdam
Musical   Broadway: 39

Composer: Richard Rodgers
Lyricist: Lorenz Hart
Librettist: Irving Caesar; David Freedman; William Anthony McGuire
Producer: Florenz Ziegfeld
Director: William Anthony McGuire

Choreographer: Sammy Lee; **Costumes:** Charles LeMaire; **Musical Director:** Victor Baravalle; **Set Design:** Bergman Studios; Frank Gates; E.A. Morange; Joseph Urban

Songs: At the Saskatchewan [1]; Birds on High (Birds Up High); Blue Skies (C/L: Irving Berlin); Bugle Blow; Burn Up [4]; Come and Tell Me [1]; Cradle of the Deep; Don't Believe [2] (C: M. Siegel; L: Irving Caesar); First We Throw Moe Out (Finaletto Act II) [5]; Follow On; I Guess We Should Be Satisfied (Finale Act I); If I Were You; In Our Parlor on the Third Floor Back; In Variety [1]; Is My Girl Refined? [1]; Kitzel Engagement, The; Ladies' Home Companion [3]; Leave It to Levy (L: Irving Caesar); Melican Man, A [4]; My Missus; One of Us Should Be Two; Push Around; Show Me How to Make Love [1]; Shuffle; Sing [6]; Six Little Kitzels [1]; Social Work [4]; Stonewall Moskowitz March (L: Irving Caesar; Lorenz Hart); Tales of Hoffman, The [1] (C: Al Segal; L: Irving Caesar); This Funny World; Transformation [1]; Viva Italia [4]; You're the Mother Type [1]

Cast: Belle Baker; Madeline Cameron; Dan Healy; Ed Hickey; Pauline Hoffman; Jimmy Hussey; Allen Kearns; Evelyn Law; Barbara Newberry; Bobbie Perkins; Al Shean; Ralph Whitehead

Notes: Libretto revised by William Anthony McGuire. [1] Cut prior to New York. [2] Cut and then added again after the show opened in New York. [3] Cut prior to New York. Later in A CONNECTICUT YANKEE. [4] Not used. [5] Same music as "Sing." [6] Same music as "First We Throw Moe Out." Also in the English production LADY LUCK and LADY FINGERS.

377 • BETTER 'OLE OR THE ROMANCE OF OLD BILL, THE

OPENED: 12/19/1918   Theatre: Greenwich Village
Musical   Broadway: 353

Composer: Herman Darewski
Librettist: Bruce Brainsfather; Arthur Elliot
Director: Percival Knight

Choreographer: Lily Leonora; **Costumes:** Madame Broich; **Musical Director:** Eliot Schenck; **Set Design:** Ernest Albert

Songs: Have a Little Regiment of Your Own (C/L: Percival Knight); I Wish I Was in Blighty (L: W.R. Titterton); Je Sais Que Vous Etes Gentil (It's Our Wedding Day) [1] (C: P.H. Christine; Percival Knight; L: Grant Stewart); My Word! Ain't We Carrying On [2] (L: Melville Gideon; James Heard; Percival Knight); She's Venus De Milo to Me (C/L: Peter Bernard; Oliver DeGerde); Tommy (L: James Heard); When You Look in the Heart of a Rose (C: Florence Methven; L: Marion Gillespie); When You Take That Trip Across the Rhine (C/L: Percival Knight)

Cast: Charles Coburn; Mrs. Charles Coburn; Charles McNaughton

Notes: [1] English version by Stewart and Knight. [2] Additional verses by Knight.

378 • BETTER TIMES

OPENED: 09/02/1922   Theatre: Hippodrome
Revue   Broadway: 405

Composer: Raymond Hubbell
Lyricist: R.H. Burnside
Librettist: R.H. Burnside
Producer: Charles Dillingham
Director: R.H. Burnside

Costumes: Will R. Barnes; Cora MacGeachy; William H. Matthews; Robert McQuinn; Gladys Monkhouse; **Lighting Designer:** Edward Demmher; **Musical Director:** A.J. Garing; **Orchestrations:** Hilding Anderson; Charles Miller; Frank Saddler; **Set Design:** Mark Lawson; Edward Roelker

Songs: Better Times; Blowing Bubbles All Day Long; Gloom and Joy; I Dreamt that I Went to the Grand Opera Ball; Just a Fan; My Golden Dream Ship; Peach Blossom Time; Summertime; Tale of a Fan; Up-To-Date Tune, An

Cast: Nanette Flack; Virginia Futrelle; Marceline; Robert McLellan; Long Tack Sam

379 • BETTY

OPENED: 10/03/1916   Theatre: Globe
Musical   Broadway: 63

Composer: Paul Rubens
Lyricist: Adrian Ross; Paul Rubens
Librettist: Frederick Lonsdale; Gladys Unger
Producer: Charles Dillingham
Director: Edward Royce

Costumes: Mme. Freisinger; **Musical Director:** William J. Daly; **Set Design:** Homer Emens

Songs: Cinderella; Dance with Me; Duchess of Dreams, The; Eyes Have a Language of Their Own (C: Silvio Hein; L: Benjamin Hapgood Burt); Here Comes the Groom (C/L: Benj. Hapgood Burt); High Life Down Stairs; I Feel So Happy; I Love the Girls; If It Were True (C: Ernest Steffan; L: Merlin Morgan); I'm Jotte, the Dressmaker; Little Harlequin, The; On a Saturday Afternoon; Opposite the Ducks [1]; Some Time (C: Harry Tierney; L: William Jerome); We Men Ought to Combine [1]; When You Grow to Be Twenty-One (When I Was Twenty-One) [2] (C: Jean Schwartz; L: Edgar Leslie)

Cast: Marion Davies; Joseph W. Herbert; Raymond Hitchcock; Joseph Santley; Ivy Sawyer

Notes: [1] Sheet music only. [2] Titled "When I Am Twenty-One" out of town.

380 • BETTY BE GOOD

OPENED: 05/04/1920   Theatre: Casino
Musical   Broadway: 31

Composer: Hugo Reisenfeld
Lyricist: Harry B. Smith
Librettist: Harry B. Smith
Producer: Stewart & Morrison
Director: David Bennett

Musical Director: Ross Mobley

Songs: Betty Behave; By Pango Pang Bay; I'd Like to Take You Away (Sam and Marion); Keep the

Love Lamps Burning in the Windows of Your Eyes; Listen to My Heart Beat; Same Old Stars, Same Old Moon (but Which Is the Girl?); Tell Me, Daisy; You Must Be Good Girls

Cast: Frank Crumit; Josephine Whittell

Notes: No songs listed in program.

381 • BETTY LEE

OPENED: 12/25/1924   Theatre: 44th Street
Musical   Broadway: 98

Composer: Con Conrad; Louis A. Hirsch
Lyricist: Irving Caesar; Otto Harbach
Librettist: Otto Harbach
Producer: Rufus LeMaire
Director: Bertram Harrison

Source: GOING SOME (Play: Paul Armstrong; Rex Beach); **Choreographer:** David Bennett; **Costumes:** Charles LeMaire; **Set Design:** P. Dodd Ackerman

Songs: Along the Rio Grande; Apache Argentine; Athletic Boy; Baby Be Good; Betty Lee (C: Con Conrad); Cheer, Girls, Cheer; Cowboy Songs; Daily Dozen, The; Give Him Your Sympathy; I Am Thinking of You [1] (C: Louis A. Hirsch; L: Irving Caesar); I'm Going to Dance at Your Wedding (C: Con Conrad; L: Irving Caesar); Just Lean on Me; Let's Kiss Goodbye [1] (C: Louis A. Hirsch; L: Otto Harbach); Little Pony of Mine; Monterey; Sweet Arabian Dreams (C: Louis A. Hirsch); Sweet Cactus Rose; They Always Run a Little Faster

Cast: Joe E. Brown; Gloria Foy; Hal Skelly

Notes: [1] Sheet music only.

382 • BETWEEN FRIENDS

OPENED: 05/01/1954
Revue   Closed out of town

Composer: Charles Gaynor
Lyricist: Charles Gaynor
Librettist: Charles Gaynor
Producer: Frederick Burleigh

Arrangements: George Bauer; **Choreographer:** Frank Wagner; **Costumes:** Elizabeth Birbari; **Musical Director:** George Bauer; **Set Design:** William J. Ryan

Songs: Angelina; Every Time I'm with You; Hand in Hand; Lark in the Park; Love Can Be; Man in the Moon; Somebody Should Have Told Me; Spider Woman; Survey, The; Susie Had a Song; Where the East Meets the West; You Make Me Dance

Cast: Ruth Kindl; Jenny Lou Law; William Patch; Doug Robinson; Malcolm Toy; Donna Jean Young

Notes: Played the Playhouse Theatre, Pittsburgh.

383 • BETWEEN THE DEVIL

OPENED: 12/23/1937   Theatre: Imperial
Musical   Broadway: 93

Composer: Arthur Schwartz
Lyricist: Howard Dietz
Librettist: Howard Dietz
Producer: Messrs. Shubert
Director: Edward Duryea Dowling; John Hayden; Hassard Short; Fred deCordova

Choreographer: Robert Alton; **Costumes:** Kiviette; **Musical Director:** Don Vorhees; **Set Design:** Albert Johnson

Songs: By Myself; Bye-Bye Butterfly Lover; Celina Couldn't Say 'No'; Cocktail, The; Don't Go Away Monsieur; Double Trouble; Experience; Five O'Clock; Fly By Night; Front Page News; Gendarme, The; How Do You Do? [2]; I Believe in You; I See Your Face Before Me; I'm Against Rhythm; I've Made Up My Mind; Night Before the Morning After, The; Triplets [3]; Uniform, The (dance) [1]; Wand'ring Lover [2]; Why Did You Do It?; You Have Everything

Cast: Eric Brotherson; Jack Buchanan; Debonairs, The; Adele Dixon; Vilma Ebsen; William Kendall; Evelyn Laye; Tune Twisters, The; Charles Walters

Notes: [1] In AT EASE with revised lyric. [2] Out New Haven 10/14/37. [3] Cut from FLYING COLORS.

384 • BEYOND THE FRINGE

OPENED: 10/27/1962   Theatre: John Golden
Revue   Broadway: 703

Composer: Dudley Moore
Lyricist: Dudley Moore

Librettist: Alan Bennett; Peter Cook; Jonathan Miller; Dudley Moore

Cast: Alan Bennett; Peter Cook; Jonathan Miller; Dudley Moore

Notes: Songs not listed in program.

385 • BIBI OF THE BOULEVARDS

OPENED: 02/06/1922
Musical   Closed out of town

Composer: Rudolf Friml
Lyricist: Catherine Chisholm Cushing
Librettist: Catherine Chisholm Cushing
Producer: Carl Hunt
Director: Carl Hunt

Choreographer: Bert French; **Musical Director:** Fred Fleming

Songs: Cherchez la Femme; Finale Act III; Have a Little Dance with Me; L'Amour-Toujours-L'Amour [1]; Merci Beaucoup; Opening Song and Dance; Perhaps; Read Between the Lines; Rozita; You, You, You

Cast: Albert Derbil; Dorothy Maynard

Notes: Program of 2/6/22 Springfield, Mass. used. [1] Also in THE AMBER EXPRESS.

386 • BIBLE SALESMAN, THE

Notes: *See DOUBLE ENTRY.*

387 • BIFF! BANG!

OPENED: 05/30/1919   Theatre: Century
Revue   Broadway: 19

Composer: William Schroeder
Lyricist: Robert Cohen; Philip Dunning; William Israel
Librettist: Philip Dunning
Director: Philip Dunning

Songs: Come Along with Me; (I've a) Corner in My Heart (For You); I Like Them Wild; Love in a Persian Garden; Love, Love, Love; Opening Chorus; Persian Love Song; Rendezvous Waltz, The; Sailor's Fox Trot Wedding; Skating Dance; Sport, The; That Gypsy Rag; Things We Pay Money to See; Waltz Specialty; We're Going Across

Notes: Acted by sailors from the Naval Training Station.

388 • BIFF! BING! BANG!

OPENED: 05/09/1921   Theatre: Ambassador
Revue   Broadway

Librettist: Jack McLaren
Producer: M.W. Plunkett

Choreographer: Alan Murray

Cast: Dumbells, The

Notes: No original songs in this show.

389 • BIFF-BOOM-BANG

OPENED: 1930
Revue   Nightclub

Composer: Harold Arlen
Lyricist: Ted Koehler

Songs: I Was Born with Blues in My Heart; I'll Call It Love; Old Fashioned; On the Beat; Shakin' the African; Steps

Notes: No other information available.

390 • BIG AS LIFE

OPENED: 1948
Musical

Composer: Jerry Bock
Lyricist: Jack Royce
Librettist: Dave Pollard
Producer: Haresfoot Club, The

Songs: Everybody Loves; Forest in the Sky; Great Wisconsin; Stairway Lullaby; Today; Why Sing a Love Song

Notes: A student show produced at the University of Wisconsin. No program available.

391 • BIG BOY

OPENED: 01/07/1925   Theatre: Winter Garden
Musical   Broadway: 48

Composer: James F. Hanley; Joseph Meyer
Lyricist: B.G. DeSylva
Librettist: Harold Atteridge

Producer: J.J. Shubert; Lee Shubert
Director: J.C. Huffman; Alexander Leftwich

Source: IN OLD KENTUCKY (Play: Charles T. Dazey); **Choreographer:** Larry Ceballos; Seymour Felix; **Musical Director:** Alfred Goodman; **Set Design:** Watson Barratt

Songs: As Long As I've Got My Mammy; Born and Bred in Old Kentucky; California, Here I Come (C: Joseph Meyer; L: B.G. DeSylva; Al Jolson); Come On and Play; Cookies and Bookies; Dance from Down Yonder, The; Day I Rode Half Fare; Hello 'Tucky; How I Love You [4] (C/L: Lew Brown; Cliff Friend); I Was Meant for Someone [6] (L: Ballard Macdonald); If You Knew Susie [1] (C: B.G. DeSylva); It All Depends on You [5] (C: Ray Henderson; L: Lew Brown; B.G. DeSylva); Keep Smiling at Trouble (Trouble's a Bubble) [2] (C: Lewis E. Gensler; L: B.G. DeSylva; Al Jolson); Lackawanna; Lead 'Em On; (Lead 'Em On) Miami (C: Con Conrad; L: B.G. DeSylva; Al Jolson); Nobody but Fanny [3] (C: Con Conrad; L: B.G. DeSylva; Al Jolson); On the Z-R-3 [6] (C: Walter Donaldson; L: Sam M. Lewis; Joe Young); Race Is Over, The; Something for Nothing; Tap the Toe; True Love; Welcome Home; Who Was Chasing Paul Revere? (C: Lewis E. Gensler; Joseph Meyer)

Cast: Edythe Baker; Franklyn Batie; Nancy Carroll; Al Jolson; Flo Lewis; Ralph Whitehead

Notes: Al Goodman created Jolson's orchestrations. [1] Publisher credits Joseph Meyer also. [2] Copyright records do not credit Jolson. [3] Sheet music only. [4] Not in programs. [5] ASCAP list only. In LIDO LADY (London). Added to GEORGE WHITE'S SCANDALS (1926). [6] ASCAP/Library of Congress only.

392 • BIG BROADCAST OF 1963

OPENED: 12/1962   Theatre: Charles
                              Playhouse
Revue   Closed out of town

Composer: Ronald Cass
Lyricist: Peter Myers
Librettist: Herb Hartig; Jack Holmes
Producer: Ben Bagley
Director: Vernon Lusby

Choreographer: Vernon Lusby; **Musical Director:** Vernon Holmes

Songs: Auf Wiedersehen (C/L: Stan Daniels; Raymond Jessel); Ballad of Beauregard Green, The; Balloons (C/L: Jack Holmes); Beauty Part, The (C: Claibe Richardson; L: Kenward Elmslie); Dark Lady of the Senates (C: John Pritchett; L: Peter Myers); Don't Let Me Down (C: Lionel Harris; L: Peter Myers; John Pritchett); Elsie in Her Pride (L: Peter Myers; Dick Vosburgh); Festivals (C/L: Jack Holmes); Goodbye Ike; It's a Great Little World; Lac-Des-Scenes (L: Peter Myers; Stanley Myers); Lest We Forget; Letter to J.D. Salinger, A (C/L: Michael McWhinney); Love Song (C/L: Peter Myers); Names (C/L: Jack Holmes); Sally, Irene and Mary (C: Norman L. Martin; L: Fred Ebb); Taken at Her Word (C/L: Peter Myers); Three Disguises; Three to the Bar (C/L: Herb Hartig); Time to Say Goodnight (C/L: Peter Myers; L: Francis Essex; Richard Waring); Two Miss Browns, The (C: Richard Addinsell; L: Arthur Macrae)

Cast: James C. Kenney; Amber Lynn; Elmarie Wendel; G. Wood; **Pianist:** Jack Holmes

Notes: Boston show.

393 • BIG DEAL

OPENED: 04/10/1986   Theatre: Broadway
Musical   Broadway: 70

Librettist: Bob Fosse
Producer: Roger Berlind; Jerome Minskoff; Shubert Organization
Director: Bob Fosse

Source: BIG DEAL ON MADONNA STREET (Film); **Choreographer:** Bob Fosse; **Costumes:** Patricia Zipprodt; **Dance Arranger::** Gordon Lowry Harrell; **Lighting Designer:** Jules Fisher; **Orchestrations:** Ralph Burns; **Set Design:** Peter Larkin; **Vocal Arranger:** Gordon Lowry Harrell

Songs: Ain't She Sweet (C: Milton Ager; L: Jack Yellen); Ain't We Got Fun (C: Richard A. Whiting; L: Raymond B. Egan; Gus Kahn); Beat Me Daddy Eight to the Bar (C/L: Al Lewis; Al Sherman); Button Up Your Overcoat (C: Ray Henderson; L: Lew Brown; B.G. DeSylva); Charley My Boy (C: Ted Fiorito; L: Gus Kahn); Chicago (C/L: Fred Fisher); Daddy, You've Been a Mother to Me (C/L: Fred Fisher); Everybody Loves My Baby (C/L: Jack Palmer; Spencer Williams); For No Good Reason at All (C: Abel Baer; L: Sam M. Lewis; Joseph Young); Hold Tight, Hold Tight (C: Milton Ager; L: Jack Yellen); I'm Just Wild About Harry (C: Eubie Blake; L: Noble Sissle); I'm Sitting on Top of the World; I've Got a Feelin' You're Foolin' (C: Nacio Herb Brown; L: Arthur Freed); Just a Gigolo (C: Leonello Casucci; L: Julius Brammer; Irving Caesar); Life Is Just a Bowl of Cherries (C: Ray Henderson; L: Lew Brown); Love Is Just Around the Corner (C: Lewis E. Gensler; L: Leo Robin); Me and My Shadow (C: Dave Dreyer; Al Jolson; L: Billy Rose); Music Goes 'Round and 'Round, The (C/L: Edward Farley; Red Hodgson; Michael Riley); Now's the Time to Fall in Love (C/L: Al Lewis; Al Sherman); Pick Yourself Up (C: Jerome Kern; L: Dorothy Fields); Who's Your Little Who-zis? (C: Ben Bernie; Hal Goering; L: Walter Hirsch); Yes Sir, That's My Baby (C: Walter Donaldson; L: Gus Kahn)

Cast: Gary Chapman; Wayne Cilento; Bruce Anthony Davis; Cleavant Derricks; Loretta Devine; Cady Huffman; Mel Johnson Jr.; Alde Lewis Jr.; Larry Marshall; Valerie Pettiford; Alan Weeks

394 • BIG RIVER: THE ADVENTURES OF HUCKLEBERRY FINN

OPENED: 04/25/1985   Theatre: Eugene O'Neill
Musical   Broadway: 1005

Composer: Roger Miller
Lyricist: Roger Miller
Librettist: William Hauptman
Producer: Dodger Productions; M. Anthony Fisher; Heidi Landesman; Rocco Landesman; Rick Steiner
Director: Des McAnuff

Source: ADVENTURES OF HUCKLEBERRY FINN, THE (Novel: Mark Twain); **Choreographer:** Janet Watson; **Costumes:** Patricia McGourty; **Lighting Designer:** Richard Riddell; **Musical Director:** Linda Twine; **Orchestrations:** Steven Margoshes; Danny Troob; **Set Design:** Heidi Landesman; **Vocal Arranger:** Linda Twine

Songs: Arkansas; Boys, The; Crossing Over; Do You Want to Go to Heaven; Free at Last; Guv'ment; Hand for the Hog; How Blest We Are; I, Huckleberry, Me; Leaving's Not the Only Way to Go; Muddy Water; River in the Rain; Royal Nonesuch, The; Waiting for the Light to

Shine; When the Sun Goes Down in the South; Worlds Apart; You Ought to Be Here with Me

Cast: Rene Auberjonois; Evalyn Baron; Reathel Bean; Susan Browning; Patti Cohenour; Gordon Connell; John Goodman; Bob Gunton; Daniel H. Jenkins; Ron Richardson; John Short; Jennifer Leigh Warren; William Youmans

395 • BIG SENSATION, THE
OPENED: 1919
Musical   Closed out of town

Composer: Joe Wilton
Lyricist: Joe Wilton
Librettist: Joe Wilton

Choreographer: Joe Wilton

Songs: All Aboard [1]; Chocolate Soldier; Dixie Is Dixie Now; Everybody Shimmies Now; Ja-Da; Jealous of Me; Johnny's Back in Town; Land of Jass; Oh La La; Rip Van Winkle; Rock a Bye Ma Baby; Sweet and Pretty; You Cannot Shake That Shimmie

Cast: Henry Lang; Flo Owens; Joe Wilton

Notes: Burlesque show. These may the popular songs or burlesques on them or new songs with the same titles as the popular songs. [1] Also in ALL ABOARD (1918).

396 • BIG SHOW, THE (1916)
OPENED: 08/31/1916   Theatre: Hippodrome
Revue   Broadway: 425

Composer: Raymond Hubbell
Lyricist: John Golden
Librettist: R.H. Burnside
Producer: Charles B. Dillingham
Director: R.H. Burnside

Choreographer: Leo Barruschee; Mariette Lorette; **Costumes:** Mme. Francis; Robert McQuinn; Frances Zeibarth; **Lighting Designer:** Joseph Ellsner; **Musical Director:** Raymond Hubbell; **Set Design:** Ernest Albert; Leon Bakst; Mark Dawson

Songs: Come On Down to Ragtime Town; Good Ship Honeymoon, The; Hello, I've Been Looking for You; Hippodrome Street Parade, The; Little

World of Our Own, A [5]; Merry Doll, The (inst.) [1] (C: Jules Einedshofer); My Skating Girl (1) (inst.) [2] (C: Jules Einedshofer); My Skating Girl (2) [3] (C: Max Darewski; Raymond Hubbell; L: C.H. Bovill; John L. Golden); On the Mountain; Poor Butterfly; Queen of the Land of Snow (inst.) [4] (C: Jules Einedshofer); Queen of the Mermaids (L: Anne Caldwell); We'll Stand By Our Country (L: R.H. Burnside; John Golden)

Cast: Charlotte; Johnny Davis; Dixie Girard; Fred Gregory; Bobby Hale; Haru Onuki; Anna Pavlowa; Robert Rosaire; Eddie Russell; Henry Taylor; Toto

Notes: Ice choreography by Leo Barruschee. [1] An ice ballet choreographed by Leo Barruschee. [2] This had dance music composed by Einedshofer and a song by the others. It too was choreographed by Leo Barruschee for the skaters. [3] This was the song which accompanied the ice ballet. [4] Ice choreography by Leo Barruschee. [5] Sheet music only.

397 • BIG SHOW, THE (1939) (1)
OPENED: 04/09/1939
Revue   Closed out of town

Composer: Dana Suesse
Lyricist: Ted Fetter; Billy Rose
Producer: Billy Rose
Director: John Murray Anderson

Choreographer: Robert Alton; **Costumes:** Raoul Pene du Bois; **Lighting Designer:** John Murray Anderson; **Set Design:** Albert Johnson

Songs: Greatest Show on Earth, The; I Wanna Go Back to Bali [1] (C: Harry Warren; L: Al Dubin); Lady of Tomorrow; Yours for a Song

Cast: James Barton; Jack Cole and His Dancers; Charles King; Ozzie Nelson and His Orch.

Notes: Sheet music only. No program available. [1] From film GOLD DIGGERS IN PARIS.

398 • BIG SHOW (1939) (2)
OPENED: 1939
Revue   Closed out of town

Composer: Irving Actman
Lyricist: George R. Brown

Producer: Will Morrissey; Paul M. Trebitsch
Director: Pal'mere Brandeaux

Songs: Hello, Mr. Love; I Still Can Hear Your Sighs!; So Close to Heaven; Tahiti; We May Not Get Another Chance; You're an Eyeful

399 • BIG STICK, THE
OPENED: 03/16/1908
Play   Closed out of town

Author: George V. Hobart
Director: Charley Grapewin

Musical Director: Leon Polachek

Songs: Christine Swanson; I Still Love You; I'm Afraid to Come Home in the Dark; Since Arrawana Married Barney Carney; Too a Roi-oor a Loi-a

Cast: Tony Hart; Clara Morton; Kate Morton; Paul Morton; Sam Morton; Edyth Warner

Notes: Program of Metropolis Theatre, N.Y. Also played the West End Theatre in New York 2/24/09. Neither program credits music or lyrics.

400 • BIG WINNER, THE
OPENED: 12/20/1974   Theatre: Eden
Musical   Off-Broadway: 119

Composer: Sol Kaplin
Lyricist: Wolf Younin
Librettist: David Opatoshu
Producer: Jewish Nostalgic Prod.; Harry Rothpearl
Director: David Opatoshu

Source: BIG WINNER, THE (Story: Sholom Aleichem); **Choreographer:** Sophie Maslow; **Costumes:** Jeffrey B. Moss; **Lighting Designer:** Tom Meleck; **Musical Director:** Jack Easton; **Set Design:** Jeffrey B. Moss

Songs: How Can I Tell Him She Loves Me; I Am a Tailor's Daughter; In-Laws; It's Delicious; Lottery Celebration; Love Song; Money, Wealth, Gold; Movie Montage; Tango, The; Tango Rehearsal; We're the People; Wedding Dance; Winners, Losers

Cast: Bruce Adler; Diane Cypkin; Miriam Kressyn; David Opatoshu; Stan Porter

401 • BIL BAIRD'S VARIETY
Notes: *See PETER AND THE WOLF.*

402 • BILLEE TAYLOR
OPENED: 02/19/1881   Theatre: Standard
Musical   Broadway

Composer: Edward Solomon
Lyricist: Henry Pottinger Stephens
Librettist: Henry Pottinger Stephens

Songs: All on Account of Eliza; Back Again, Back Again; Ballad of the Billow, The; Benny, Dear [1]; By Rule of Three [1]; Don't Go for to Leave Us, Richard Carr; Faithful Crew, The; Gallant Thunderbomb, The; Guileless Orphan, A; Hark the Merry Marriage Bells; Ifs and Ans; In Days Gone By; Poor Wicked Man, The; Revenge! Revenge!! and Retribution; See Here, My Lads, What Would You Do?; Self-Made Knight, The; Stay, Stay for I Am No Man; This Is a Statement Most Untoward; 'Tis Hard By Fate Thus to Be Parted; Today, Today, Is Holiday; Trim Little Phoebe [1]; Two Rivers, The (Yesterday and Tomorrow); Virtuous Gardener, The; We Stick to Our Letters; Wilful Girl, A [1]; With Fife and Drum

Cast: William Hamilton; A.W.F. McCollin; Nellie Mortimer; J.H. Ryley; W.H. Seymour

Notes: No program available. Songs listed from English version. [1] Added to 1893 English revival.

403 • BILLIE
OPENED: 10/01/1928   Theatre: Erlanger
Musical   Broadway: 112

Composer: George M. Cohan
Lyricist: George M. Cohan
Librettist: George M. Cohan
Producer: George M. Cohan

Source: BROADWAY JONES (Play: George M. Cohan)

Songs: Billie [1]; Bluff; Cause of the Situation, The; Come to St. Thomas's; Ev'ry Boy in Town's My Sweetheart; Friends; Go Home Ev'ry Once in a While (Ev'rybody Ought to Take a Day Back Home); Happy; I'm a One Girl Man; Jones' Family Friends, The; Personality [1]; They Fall in

Love, Those Wonderful Friends; Two of Us, The;
Where Were You-Where Was I?

Cast: June O'Dea; Joseph Wagstaff; Polly Walker

Notes: [1] Later placed in GEORGE M!

404 • BILLION DOLLAR BABY

OPENED: 12/21/1945   Theatre: Alvin
Musical   Broadway: 220

Composer: Morton Gould
Lyricist: Betty Comden; Adolph Green
Librettist: Betty Comden; Adolph Green
Producer: Paul Feigay; Oliver Smith
Director: George Abbott

Choreographer: Jerome Robbins; **Costumes:** Irene
Sharaff; **Musical Director:** Max Goberman; **Set
Design:** Oliver Smith

Songs: Bad Timing; Broadway Blossom;
Charleston (inst.); Dreams Come True; Faithless;
Havin' a Time; I'm Sure of Your Love; Life with
Rocky, A; Lovely Girl, A; Marathon Dance, The
(dance); Million Dollar Smile; One Track Mind;
Speaking of Pals; There I'd Be; Who's Gonna Be
the Winner?

Cast: David Burns; Danny Daniels; Don De Leo;
Helen Gallagher; Mitzi Green; Joan McCracken;
James Mitchell; William Tabbert; Richard
Thomas

405 • BILLIONAIRE, THE

OPENED: 12/29/1902   Theatre: Daly's
Musical   Broadway: 104

Composer: Gustave Kerker
Lyricist: Harry B. Smith
Librettist: Harry B. Smith
Producer: Klaw & Erlanger
Director: Herbert Gresham

Choreographer: Ned Wayburn; **Costumes:**
F. Richard Anderson; **Musical Director:**
A. DeNovellis

Songs: Glory (Glory and Liberty) [1] (C/L:
William Beck; Edward F. Cogley); If Yankee
Doodle Hadn't Come to Town [1] (C: Silvio
Hein; L: Alfred Bryan); Incidents in the Lives
of Famous Men; Just Cause the Moon Was

Shinin'; Money Burner [1]; Morality's a Matter
of Geography; My Little Pansy; There Are
Tricks in All Trades; To Be Truly Refined [1];
Toast Song [1]

Cast: Marie Doro; Sallie Fisher; Harry Kelly; Harry
MacDonough; May Robson; Julius Steger;
Jerome Sykes

Notes: [1] Sheet music only.

406 • BILLY

OPENED: 03/22/1969   Theatre: Billy Rose
Musical   Broadway: 1

Composer: Gene Allen; Ron Dante
Lyricist: Gene Allen; Ron Dante
Librettist: Stephen Glassman
Producer: Joseph Shoctor; Bruce W. Stark
Director: Arthur A. Seidelman

Source: BILLY BUDD (Novel: Herman Melville);
Choreographer: Grover Dale; **Costumes:** Theoni
V. Aldredge; **Dance Arranger:** Coleridge-Taylor
Perkinson; **Lighting Designer:** Martin Aronstein;
Musical Director: Jack Lee; **Orchestrations:**
Ronald Frangipane; **Set Design:** Ming Cho Lee

Songs: Billy; Bridge to Nowhere, The; Chanty;
Fiddlers' Green, The; In the Arms of a Stranger;
It Ain't Us Who Makes the Wars; Molly; My
Captain; Night and the Sea, The; Requiem;
Shaking Hands with the Wind; Watch Out for
Claggart/Work; Whiskers' Dance

Cast: John Beal; John Devlin; George Marcy;
Barbara Monte; Laurence Naismith; Michael
Peters; Robert Salvio; Dolph Sweet; Alan Weeks

407 • BILLY BARNES'
HOLLYWOOD

OPENED: 05/26/1964   Theatre: Las Palmas
Revue   Los Angeles

Composer: Billy Barnes
Lyricist: Billy Barnes
Librettist: Bob Rodgers
Producer: Allan Kramer; Al Morley; Bill Watters
Director: Bob Rodgers

Costumes: Bob Mackie; **Musical Director:** Hal
Hidey; **Set Design:** Spencer Davies

Songs: Academy Award Highlights; Cary: Who?; Dodo; Elizabeth; Freeway Song, The; Game, The; Hollywood Money Makers; Hollywood Museum; How Many Daddies; Joan; Job Interview; Movies in Flight; Nervous; Old Movies; She; Silent Screen, The; Small Town Girl; Stay with Me; TV Quiz Show; Unemployment Line; Where Is the Magic?; Wm. Desmond Taylor Murder Mystery

Cast: Ken Berry; Jeannine Burnier; Jack Grinnage; Joyce Jameson; Bob Rodgers; Caryl Rowe

Notes: Songs and sketches listed because they weren't differentiated in program.

408 • BILLY BARNES' L.A.

OPENED: 10/10/1962 Theatre: Coronet
Revue Los Angeles

Composer: Billy Barnes
Lyricist: Billy Barnes
Librettist: Bob Rodgers
Producer: George Eckstein; Bill Watters
Director: Bob Rodgers

Choreographer: Sylvia Lewis; **Costumes:** Max Berman and Sons; **Lighting Designer:** Arvid Nelson; **Musical Director:** Ray Henderson

Songs: Alcron; Art Film Premiere; Captain Schumaker; Chamber of Commerce Convention; Covina; Does Anybody Here Love Me?; Forties, The; Hollywood West; I've Never Attended at All; Job Hunter; Keep Away; L.A. Is; Lady and Bird; Little Leaguers; Los Angeles Is Just Like Any Other Town; Numbers; Pageant of Los Angeles, The; Pink Pussycat School; Senior Citizens; Sister Aimee; Theatre Comes to L.A.; Weather Report; Where Was the Music

Cast: Ken Berry; Steve Franken; Ann Guilbert; Tom Hatten; Joyce Jameson; Marlyn Mason

Notes: Songs and sketches listed because they weren't differentiated in program.

409 • BILLY BARNES PARTY

OPENED: 09/1961 Theatre: Cabaret Concert
Revue Los Angeles

Notes: No other information available.

410 • BILLY BARNES PEOPLE, THE

OPENED: 06/13/1961 Theatre: Royale
Revue Broadway: 7

Composer: Billy Barnes
Lyricist: Billy Barnes
Librettist: Bob Rodgers
Producer: John Pool
Director: Bob Rodgers

Costumes: Grady Hunt; **Dance Arranger:** Ray Henderson; **Musical Director:** Ray Henderson; **Set Design:** Spencer Davies; **Vocal Arranger:** Ray Henderson

Songs: Before and After; Damn-Alot; Dolls; Don't Bother; I Like You; If It Makes You Happy (The Syndicate Song); If It Wasn't for People; It's Not Easy; Let's Get Drunk; Marital Infidelity; Matinee, The; Second Best; The End?; There's Nothing Wrong with Our Values; What Do We Have to Hold on To?; Where Is the Clown?

Cast: Ken Berry; Jack Grinnage; Joyce Jameson; Jackie Joseph; Dave Ketchum; Dick Patterson; Patti Regan; Jo Anne Worley

411 • BILLY BARNES REVUE, THE

OPENED: 06/09/1959 Theatre: York Playhouse
Revue Broadway: 199

Composer: Billy Barnes
Lyricist: Billy Barnes
Librettist: Bob Rodgers
Producer: George Eckstein; Bob Reese
Director: Bob Rodgers

Lighting Designer: Peggy Clark; **Musical Director:** Billy Barnes; **Set Design:** Glenn Holse

Songs: Blocks; City of the Angels; Do a Revue; Fights, The [1]; Foolin' Ourselves [1]; Las Vegas [1]; Listen to the Beat!; One of Those Days; Too Long at the Fair [1]; Tyler My Boy [1]; What Ever Happened to #'s 1, 2, 3; Where Are Your Children [1]

Cast: Ken Berry; Bert Convy; Ann Guilbert; Joyce Jameson; Jackie Joseph; Bob Rodgers; Len Weinrib

Notes: Moved to Broadway on 8/5/59. [1] Previously in FOOLIN' OURSELVES.

412 • BILLY BARNES SHOW

Revue

Theatre: Cabaret
Los Angeles

Composer: Billy Barnes
Lyricist: Billy Barnes
Librettist: Bob Rodgers
Director: Bob Rodgers

Songs: Brave's Lament, The; City of the Angels, The; Confidentially; Ding Dong School; Fights, The; Foolin' Ourselves; Hamlet Comes Home; Hellahahana; Ivy League, The; Marry Me; Me Man — You Mansfield; Medicine Marches On; People; Rich People of Texas, The; Thirties, The; This Is the Love; Too Long at the Fair; Where Are Your Children

Cast: Doug Andrews; Billy Barnes; Joyce Jameson; Jackie Joseph; Patti Regan; Bob Rodgers; **Pianist:** Armin Hoffman

Notes: Some of these titles might be sketches.

413 • BILLY BARNES SUMMER REVUE

OPENED: 05/28/1962
Revue

Closed out of town

Composer: Billy Barnes
Lyricist: Billy Barnes
Librettist: Bob Rodgers
Producer: Billy Barnes; Al Morley; Ethelyn R. Thrasher
Director: Bob Rodgers

Musical Director: Billy Barnes; **Set Design:** Charles Evans

Songs: Blocks; City of the Angels; Classic Ingredients; Dissertation on Transportation, A; Doctors, The; Dolls; End, The; Fairly Fresh; Fights, The; Hellahahana; I Like You; I'm a Butterfly; Interview, The; Liberated Woman; Little Italy; Rich People of Texas; Something to Do; Tennessee Williams Note, A; Thirties, The; Too Long at the Fair; What Am I?; What Ever?; What Ever Happened?; Whatever Happened To?; Where Is the Clown?

Cast: Ken Berry; Jack Grinnage; Joyce Jameson; Marlyn Mason; Patti Regan; Bob Rodgers

Notes: Played the Playhouse-in-the-Park,
Philadelphia. Revived there on 06/07/63. Songs and sketches not differentiated in program so both are listed here.

414 • BILLY BISHOP GOES TO WAR

OPENED: 05/29/1980   Theatre: Morosco
Musical   Broadway: 90

Composer: John Gray; Eric Peterson
Lyricist: John Gray; Eric Peterson
Librettist: John Gray
Producer: Lewis Allen; Mike Nichols
Director: John Gray

Lighting Designer: Jennifer Tipton; **Set Design:** David Gropman

Songs: As Calm As the Ocean; Buried Alive in the Mud; Canada at War; December Nights; Empire Soiree, The; Friends Ain't S'posed to Die; General Sir Hugh M. Trenchard; Good Ship Caledonia, The; In the Sky; Lady St. Heller; My First Solo Flight; Nobody Shoots No-One in Canada; Off to Fight the Hun; Re-7, The

Cast: John Gray; Eric Peterson

Notes: Twelve performances on Broadway then moved to the Theatre de Lys Off-Broadway where it palyed an additional 78 performances. No songs listed in program.

415 • BILLY NONAME

OPENED: 03/02/1970   Theatre: Truck and
                                         Warehouse
Musical   Off-Broadway: 48

Composer: Johnny Brandon
Lyricist: Johnny Brandon
Librettist: Wm. Wellington Mackay
Producer: Joe Davis; Robert E. Richardson
Director: Lucia Victor

Choreographer: Talley Beatty; **Costumes:** Pearl Somner; **Dance Arranger:** Sammy Benskin; **Lighting Designer:** David F. Segal; **Musical Director:** Sammy Benskin; **Orchestrations:** Clark McClellan; **Set Design:** Jack Brown; **Vocal Arranger:** Sammy Benskin; Clark McClellan

Songs: At the End of the Day; Billy Noname; Black Boy; Boychild; Burn, Baby, Burn; Color

Me White; Different Drummer, A; Dream, The; Get Your Slice of Cake; Hello World; I Want to Live; It's Our Time Now; King Joe; Look Through the Window; Manchild; Mother Earth; Movin'; Roulette; Seduction; Sit In-Wade In; We Made a Promise; We're Gonna Turn On Freedom

Cast: Donnie Burks; Urylee Leonardos; Glory Van Scott; Alan Weeks; Hattie Winston

416 • BILLY ROSE'S AQUACADE

Notes: *See AQUACADE REVUE and NEW AQUACADE REVUE.*

417 • BILLY ROSE'S AQUACADE REVUE (TOUR)

OPENED: 1940
Revue

Composer: Dana Suesse
Lyricist: Stanley Joseloff; Billy Rose
Producer: Billy Rose
Director: John Murray Anderson

Choreographer: Robert Alton; **Costumes:** Raoul Pene du Bois; **Set Design:** Albert Johnson

Songs: Camera Doesn't Lie, The (C: Joe Burke; L: Edgar Leslie); Half and Half; Happy Birthday to Love; It Can't Happen Here; It Happened in Miami (L: Billy Rose); Strangers in the Dark C: Belle Fenstock; L: Stanley Adams; Billy Rose); We Rule the Waves

Cast: Frazee Sisters, The; Eleanor Holm; Bob Lawrence; Johnny Weissmuller

Notes: *See AQUACADE REVUE and NEW AQUACADE REVUE.* This is the touring version from a Cleveland program.

418 • BILLY ROSE'S CRAZY QUILT

OPENED: 05/19/1931   Theatre: 44th Street
Revue   Broadway: 67

Composer: Harry Warren
Lyricist: Mort Dixon; Billy Rose
Librettist: David Freedman; Herman Timberg
Producer: Billy Rose
Director: Billy Rose

Choreographer: Sammy Lee; **Costumes:** Fanny Brice; **Lighting Designer:** Clark Robinson; **Musical Director:** Charles Drury

Songs: Crazy Quilt (L: Mort Dixon; Bud Green); Crazy Quilt Sextette, The (L: E.Y. Harburg; Billy Rose); Have a Little Drinkee (C: Ned Lehac; L: Edward Eliscu); I Found a Million Dollar Baby; I Wanna Be Loved [4] (C: Johnny Green; L: Edward Heyman; Billy Rose); I Want to Do a Number with the Boys (C: Rowland Wilson; (L: Ned Wever); In the Merry Month of Maybe (L: Ira Gershwin; Billy Rose); It's in the Air (C: Louis Alter; L: E.Y. Harburg; Billy Rose); Kept in Suspense (C: Carroll Gibbons; L: James Dyrenforth; Billy Rose); Ladies of the Evening [4] (C/L: E.Y. Harburg; Billy Rose); Oh, It Looks Like Rain [3] (C: Milton Ager; L: E.Y. Harburg); Peter Pan (C: Carroll Gibbons; L: James Dyrenforth; Billy Rose); Rest Room Rose [1] (C: Richard Rodgers; L: Lorenz Hart); Sing a Little Jingle (L: Mort Dixon); To Think That Once We Were Sweethearts (And Now We're Not Even Friends) (C: James V. Monaco; L: Edgar Leslie; Billy Rose); Under the Clock at the Astor (C: Manning Sherwin; L: Ned Wever); Would You Like to Take a Walk? [2]

Cast: Phil Baker; Fanny Brice; Lew Brice; Rodger Davis; Ted Healy; Ethel Norris; Tamara

Notes: [1] Added after opening. [2] Also in SWEET AND LOW. [3] Not in programs. [4] ASCAP/Library of Congress only.

419 • BILLY ROSE'S MUSIC HALL REVUE

OPENED: 1934
Revue

Songs: Beautiful Face — Have a Heart (C: Leo Edwards; L: Billy Macdonald; Billy Rose)

Notes: No other information available.

420 • BILLY ROSE'S SHOW OF SHOWS

OPENED: 06/08/1936
Revue

Composer: Dana Suesse
Lyricist: Billy Rose
Director: John Murray Anderson

Choreographer: Robert Alton; Lauretta Jefferson; **Costumes:** Thomas Becher; Raoul Pene du Bois; **Musical Director:** Ray Steck; **Set Design:** Albert Johnson

Songs: Camera Doesn't Lie, The; Circus Is on Parade, The [1] (C: Richard Rodgers; L: Lorenz Hart); Lady Known As Lulu, The; Oriental Yogi; Shangri La (C: Rube Bloom)

Cast: Lulu Bates; Bob Cooper; Frazee Sisters, The; Bob Shelton; Hinda Wassau; Everett West; Willie West and McGinty

Notes: Produced at the Fort Worth Frontier Centennial. This revue was a tribute to Billy Rose's career. [1] From JUMBO.

421 • BILLY THE KID

OPENED: 01/11/1908
Play   Closed out of town

Composer: Joseph Santley
Lyricist: Joseph Santley
Author: Joseph Santley; Walter Woods
Director: Charles N. Wuerz

Songs: I Guess I'll Go Back to Home and Mother; When You Find the Girl Who Loves but You

Cast: Lorena Ferguson; John E. Kelly; James Light; Joseph Santley; Silverheels[1]

Notes: Program from Cedar Rapids. "Sixth Annual Starring Tour." [1] Note from program —"Known as the 'Bandit Horse' once owned by Tracy, the outlaw, was purchased from Deputy Sheriff Haynes, the capturer of Tracy, by Joseph Santley, for use with 'Billy the Kid.' Tracey and Haynes were real life characters depicted in this play.

422 • BIRD OF PARADISE (1912), THE

OPENED: 01/08/1912   Theatre: Daly's
Play   Broadway: 112

Music Based On: Traditional
Author: Richard Walton
Producer: Oliver Morosco

Songs: Burning Love (Ahi Wela); Farewell (Aloha Oe); Forget Me Not (Mai Poina Oe); Luana Waltz (C: Kapule Kanoa)

423 • BIRDIE

OPENED: 1933
Musical   Closed out of town

Composer: Abe Ellstein
Lyricist: Kenneth Webb
Producer: Jacob Kalich
Director: Monty Woolley

Source: UNKNOWN (Play: Claiborne Foster); **Costumes:** Verady; **Musical Director:** Abe Ellstein; **Orchestrations:** Abe Ellstein; **Set Design:** Cirker & Robbins

Songs: Atta-Boy, Atta-Girl; Didn't Your Mother Tell You?; How Long?; I Won't Give You the Bucket; I'm Looking for a Man; It's All in the Game; Love Came to Me; Mrs. Kraus's Boarding House; Song of the Tenement; You Go with Me

Cast: Roscoe Ails; Raymond Hackett; Lee Patrick; Molly Picon; Charlotte Reynolds

Notes: From a program of 12/11/33 Majestic Theatre, Brooklyn.

424 • BIRDS OF PARADISE

OPENED: 10/26/1987   Theatre: Promenade
Musical   Off-Broadway: 24

Composer: David Evans
Lyricist: Winnie Holzman
Librettist: David Evans; Winnie Holzman
Producer: John A. McQuiggan
Director: Arthur Laurents

Choreographer: Linda Haberman; **Costumes:** David Murin; **Lighting Designer:** Jules Fisher; **Musical Director:** Frederick Weldy; **Orchestrations:** Michael Starobin; **Set Design:** Philipp Jung

Songs: After Opening Night; Birds of Paradise; Checkhov; Coming True; Diva; Every Day Is Night; Imagining You; It's Only a Play; Penguins Must Sing; She's Out There; So Many Nights; Somebody; Something New; Things I Can't Forget; You're Mine

425 • BIRDS OF THE EVENING

OPENED: 04/26/1925
Revue

Composer: Silvio Hein
Lyricist: Benjamin H. Burt
Librettist: Benjamin Hapgood Burt
Director: Julian Mitchell

Musical Director: Silvio Hein

Cast: R.H. Burnside; Leon Errol; Wilton Lackaye; Thomas Meighan; Stanley Ridges; Oscar Shaw

Notes: Part of THE LAMBS ANNUAL PUBLIC SPRING GAMBOL. See that show for more information. A one-act musical. No songs listed in program.

426 • BISTRO CAR ON THE CNR, A

OPENED: 04/23/1978   Theatre: Playhouse
Revue   Off-Broadway: 82

Composer: Patrick Rose
Lyricist: Marv Campone; Richard Ouzounian
Librettist: D.R. Andersen
Producer: Bob Bisaccia; Jeff Britton
Director: Richard Ouzounian

Choreographer: Lynne Gannaway; **Costumes:** John Falabella; **Lighting Designer:** Ned Hallick; **Musical Director:** John Clifton; **Set Design:** John Falabella

Songs: Anarchist, The; At the Movies [1]; Bring Back Swing; CNR; Craftsmen [2]; Dewey and Sal; Eleven O'Clock Number [1]; Ensemble; Find Me [2]; Four Part Invention; Genuine Grade A Canadian Superstar; Guitarist; Here I Am Again; His Name Is Love [2]; I Don't Live Anywhere Anymore; Jubalay [2]; La Belle Province; Lady Lady; Lady Who Loved to Sing, The; Lullabye [2]; Madame La Chanson; Nocturne; Oh God, I'm Thirty; Other People's Houses; Passing By; Ready or Not; Sailor [2]; Share with You; Somebody Write Me a Love Song; Street Music; Sudden Death Overtime; Through Glass; 25 Miles; Wailing Wall [2]; Who Done It? [1]; Yesterday's Lover; You're Going Somewhere, We're Going Nowhere [2]

Cast: Marcia McClain; Patrick Rose; Henrietta Valor; Tom Wopat

Notes: Prior to Broadway titled JUBALAY. [1] Cut during previews. [2] Cut prior to New York.

427 • BITS & PIECES XIV

OPENED: 10/07/1964   Theatre: PLaza 9-
Revue   Nightclub

Librettist: Ronald Axe; William F. Brown; Dee Caruso; Richard Craven; Bill Levine; Sol Weinstein
Producer: Julius Monk
Director: Frank Wagner

Choreographer: Frank Wagner; **Costumes:** Bill Belew; **Musical Director:** William Roy

Songs: Alexander's Discount Rag (C: Stan Lebowsky; L: Fred Tobias); Ballad for a Park (C/L: Clark Gesner); Bits & Pieces XIV Finale (C/L: Michael Brown); Bits & Pieces XIV Opening (C: William Roy; L: William F. Brown); Don't Let Them Take the Paramount Away (C/L: Michael Brown); Feathered Friends (C: Marvin Hamlisch; L: Howard Liebling); Game Is Over!, The (C: Stan Lebowsky; L: Fred Tobias); Gathering of the Clan, The (C: George W. Linsenmann; L: Ernest A. Chambers); Love Letters Written to My Mother (C/L: Michael Brown); New York for Five Dollars a Day (C: Sam Pottle; L: David Axelrod; Tom Whedon); Peanut Butter Affair, The (C/L: Clark Gesner); Stand Up and Flex (C/L: Lesley Davison); Sticks and Stones [1] (C: Marvin Hamlisch; L: Howard Liebling); Won't You Come Home Judge Crater (C/L: Michael Brown); Wonderful, Wonderful, Wonderful (C/L: Lesley Davison); You're Something More Than I Bargained For (C: Sam Pottle; L: David Axelrod; Tom Whedon)

Cast: Barbara Cason; Roy Harrity; Nagle Jackson; Gerry Matthews; Barbara Minkus; Nancy Myers; Jamie Ross; **Pianist:** Robert Colston; Carl Norman

Notes: [1] Either cut after opening or added after opening.

428 • BITS AND PIECES

OPENED: 1920
Revue

Songs: Some Pretty Day (C: Fred E. Ahlert; L: Sam M. Lewis; Joe Young)

Notes: No other information available.

429 • BITTER SWEET
OPENED: 11/05/1929   Theatre: Ziegfeld
Musical   Broadway: 159

Composer: Noel Coward
Lyricist: Noel Coward
Librettist: Noel Coward
Producer: Arch Selwyn; Florenz Ziegfeld
Director: Noel Coward

Choreographer: Tilly Losch; **Costumes:** Ernest
    Stern; **Musical Director:** Arthur Jones; **Set
    Design:** G.E. Calthrop

Songs: Alas, the Time Is Past; Bonne Nuit, Merci;
    Call of Life, The; Dear Little Cafe; Evermore and
    a Day; Green Carnations; If Love Were All; If
    You Could Only Come with Me; I'll See You
    Again; Kiss Me; Ladies of the Town; Last Dance,
    The; Life in the Morning; Ta Ra Ra Boom De Ay;
    Tell Me, What Is Love?; That Wonderful Melody;
    Tokay; Ziegeuner

Cast: John Evelyn; Evelyn Laye; Patrick Ludlow;
    Gerald Nodin; Audrey Pointing

430 • BITTERSUITE
OPENED: 10/05/1987   Theatre: Palsson's Supper
                                      Club
Revue   Off-Broadway: 211

Composer: Elliot Weiss
Lyricist: Michael Champagne
Producer: M & P Enterprises; Palsson's Supper
    Club
Director: Michael Champagne

Lighting Designer: Eric Cornwell; **Musical
    Director:** Elliot Weiss

Songs: Apology, The; Bittersuite, The; Cliche
    Waltz, The; Dungeons and Dragons; Fathers and
    Sons; Flight of the Phoenix; How Little We've
    Learned; Ice Cream; I'll Be There; I'll Make a
    Space [1]; I'm Going to Live Forever [1]; I've Got
    to Be Famous [1]; John's Song; Life That Jack
    Built, The; Lonely Man, Lonely Woman [1];
    Mama Don't Cry; Money Is Honey [1];
    Narcissism Rag; One More Time; Our Favorite
    Restaurant; Rank & File [1]; Recipe, The; Snap
    Back; Soap Opera; Try a Little Harder [1];
    Twentieth Reunion; Win and Lose; You're Not
    Getting Older

Cast: Suzanne Blakeslee; David Edwards; Barbara
    Marineau; Byron Nease

Notes: A revised version titled BITTERSUITE —
    ONE MORE TIME opened at Palsson's on May
    16, 1988 and ran 16 performances. [1] From
    second edition.

431 • BIZARRITIES
OPENED: 1934   Theatre: Casino de Paris
Revue   Nightclub

Composer: Gerald Marks
Lyricist: Sammy Lerner
Producer: Continental Music Halls

Choreographer: Charles Mosconi

Songs: I Can Sew a Button (C: Gerald Marks;
    L: Sammy Lerner); Moody and Blue; My
    International Girl; Once in a While; 'Till
    Doomsday

Cast: George Jessel

Notes: No other information available.

432 • BLACK AND BLUE
OPENED: 01/26/1989   Theatre: Minskoff
Revue   Broadway: 824

Producer: Donald K. Donald; Mel Howard
Director: Hector Qrezzoli; Claudio Segovia

Choreographer: Cholly Atkins; Henry LeTang;
    Frankie Manning; Fayard Nicholas; **Costumes:**
    Hector Orezzoli; Claudio Segovia; **Dance
    Arranger:** Luther Henderson; Sy Johnson;
    Lighting Designer: Neil Peter Jampolis; Jane
    Reisman; **Orchestrations:** Luther Henderson;
    Sy Johnson; **Set Design:** Hector Orezzoli;
    Claudio Segovia; **Vocal Arranger:** Luther
    Henderson; Sy Johnson

Songs: After You've Gone (C/L: Henry Creamer;
    Turner Layton); Am I Blue (C: Harry Akst;
    L: Grant Clarke); Black and Blue (C: Harry
    Brooks; Thomas "Fats" Waller; L: Andy Razaf);
    Black and Tan Fantasy (inst.) (C: Duke Ellington;
    Bubber Miley); Body and Soul (C: Johnny Green;
    L: Howard Dietz; Frank Eyton; Edward Heyman;
    Robert Sour); Come Sunday (C/L: Duke
    Ellington); Confessin' (That I Love You) (C: Doc
    Daugherty; Ellis Reynolds; L: Al Nieburg); Cry

Like a Baby (C/L: Kirkland; Maybelle Smith); Daybreak Express (inst.) (C: Duke Ellington); East St. Louis Toodle-oo (inst.) (C: Duke Ellington); Everybody Loves My Baby (C/L: Jack Palmer; Spencer Williams); I Can't Give You Anything but Love (C: Jimmy McHugh; L: Dorothy Fields); I Gotta Right to Sing the Blues (C: Harold Arlen; L: Ted Koehler); I Want a Big Butter and Egg Man (C: Louis Armstrong; L: Percy Venable); If I Can't Sell It, I'll Keep Sittin' on It (C: Alexander Hill; L: Andy Razaf); I'm a Woman (C/L: McDaniel; Taylor); In a Sentimental Mood (inst.) (C: Duke Ellington); Memories of You (C: Eubie Blake; L: Andy Razaf); Mystery Song (C: Duke Ellington); Rhythm Is Our Business (C: Saul Chaplin; Jimmy Lunceford; L: Sammy Cahn); Royal Garden Blues (inst.) (C/L: Clarence Williams; Spencer Williams); St. Louis Blues (C/L: W.C. Handy); Stompin' at the Savoy (C: Benny Goodman; Edgar Sampson; Chick Webb; L: Andy Razaf); T'Ain't Nobody's Bizness If I Do (C/L: Porter Grainger; Graham Prince; Clarence Williams); That Rhythm Man (C: Harry Brooks; Thomas "Fats" Waller; L: Andy Razaf); Wednesday Night Hop (inst.) (C: Leslie Johnakins; Andy Kirk)

Cast: Bunny Briggs; Ralph Brown; Ruth Brown; Lon Chaney; Tanya Gibson; Cyd Glover; Savion Glover; Linda Hopkins; Ted Levy; Kevin Ramsey; Jimmy Slyde; Carrie Smith; Dormeshia Sumbay; Dianne Walker

Notes: No original songs in this revue.

433 • BLACK CREPE AND DIAMONDS

OPENED: 1914
Play   Closed out of town

Librettist: George Baldwin
Director: Jack Mason

Musical Director: Leon Polechek

Songs: Tea Time Tango Tune (C: Lewis F. Muir; L: L. Wolfe Gilbert)

Cast: George Baldwin; Alfred Gerard; Valeska Suratt

Notes: No other information available. Play with one song. From a Milwaukee program of January 1914.

434 • BLACK POLITICIAN

OPENED: 09/14/1907
Musical   Closed out of town

Composer: J. Tim Brymn
Lyricist: S.B. Cassin
Librettist: S.B. Cassin; Sherman H. Dudley
Producer: Sherman H. Dudley
Director: M. Heckert

Choreographer: H. Fletcher Rivers; **Costumes:** Hayden

Songs: Crow (C: James Reese Europe; L: R.C. McPherson); Darktown Band, The (C: James Reese Europe; L: R.C. McPherson); Don't Take Him Away (C: James Reese Europe; L: R.C. McPherson); Down Manila Bay (C: James Reese Europe; L: R.C. McPherson); Election Time (C: James Reese Europe; L: R.C. McPherson); Help Yourself (C: James Reese Europe; L: R.C. McPherson); Hezekiah Doo (C: James Reese Europe; L: R.C. McPherson); I Don't Like School (School Days) (C: James Reese Europe; L: R.C. McPherson); If I Ever Get Back to Cincinnati (C: Chris Smith; L: S.H. Dudley); Lady Lindy; Likin' Ain't Like Lovin' (C/L: James Reese Europe); Lolita (C: James Reese Europe; L: R.C. McPherson); My Hindoo Love; My Mexican Rose; Races, Races (C: James Reese Europe; L: R.C. McPherson); Smart Set Carbineers, The (C: James Reese Europe; L: R.C. McPherson); Society (C: James Reese Europe; L: R.C. McPherson); Spooney Sam (C: James Reese Europe; L: R.C. McPherson); Suwanee River (C: James Reese Europe; L: R.C. McPherson); Take Him Away, the Law Commands It (C: James Reese Europe; L: R.C. McPherson); Thinking of Home Sweet Home; When I Rule the Town (C: James Reese Europe; L: R.C. McPherson); When the Moon Plays Peek a Boo (C: James Reese Europe; L: R.C. McPherson)

Cast: Irvin Allen; James Burris; Will Carrington; Sherman H. Dudley; Tom Logan; Will Ramsey; John Smith

435 • BLACK RHYTHM

OPENED: 12/19/1936   Theatre: Comedy
Revue   Broadway: 6

Composer: Donald Heywood
Lyricist: Donald Heywood
Librettist: Donald Heywood

Producer: Earl Dancer; J.H. Levy
Director: Earl Dancer; Donald Heywood

Musical Director: Donald Heywood

Songs: Back in Circulation; Black Rhythm; Bow Down Sinners; Doin' the Toledo; Emaline; Here 'Tis; Orchids; Truckers Ball

Cast: Joe Byrd; Jeni LeGon; Avon Long; Babe Matthews; Walter Richardson; Maude Russell; Savoy Lindy Hoppers; Wen Talbott Choir; Geneva Washington; Speedy Wilson

436 • BLACK SHEEP AND HOW IT CAME TO WASHINGTON, A

OPENED: 01/06/1896   Theatre: Hoyt's
Musical   Broadway: 144

Composer: Harry Conor; William Devere; Otis Harlan; Charles H. Hoyt; Kelly; Richard Stahl
Lyricist: Harry Conor; William Devere; Otis Harlan; Charles H. Hoyt; Kelly; Richard Stahl
Librettist: Charles H. Hoyt
Producer: Charles H. Hoyt

Set Design: Arthur Voegtlin

Cast: Frankie Bailey; Bessie Clayton; Snitz Edwards; Otis Harlan

Notes: No program available.

437 • BLACKBERRIES OF 1930

OPENED: 1930   Theatre: Cotton Club
Revue   Nightclub

Director: Dan Healy

Songs: Bumpty-Bump (C: Duke Ellington; L: Irving Mills); Come Along Mandy (C/L: Unknown); Cotton Club Stomp (C: Duke Ellington; Irving Mills); Doin' the Crazy Walk (C: Duke Ellington; L: Irving Mills); Mystery Song, The (inst.) (C: Duke Ellington; Irving Mills); Swanee River Rhapsody (C: Duke Ellington; L: Clarence Gaskill; Irving Mills); You're the Reason I Fell in Love (C/L: Unknown)

Cast: Duke Ellington and His Orchestra

Notes: Information from sheet music. No other information available.

438 • BLACKBERRIES OF 1931

Notes: *See BROWN SUGAR.*

439 • BLACKBERRIES OF 1932

OPENED: 04/04/1932   Theatre: Liberty
Revue   Broadway: 24

Composer: Donald Heywood
Lyricist: Donald Heywood
Librettist: Eddie Green; Lee Posner
Producer: Ben Bernard; Max Rudnick
Director: Ben Bernard

Choreographer: Lew Crawford; Sidney Sprague; **Musical Director:** Sam Wooding; **Set Design:** Myer Kanin

Songs: Answer Is No, The; Blackberries; Brown Sugar; First Thing in the Morning; Harlem Mania; Love Me More-Love Me Less (C: Tom Peluso; L: Ben Bernard)

Cast: Eddie Green; Georgette Harvey; Johnny Lee Long; Jackie "Moms" Mabley; Dewey "Pigmeat" Markham; Tim Moore; Mantan Moreland

440 • BLACKBIRDS (1926)

Notes: *See LEW LESLIE'S BLACKBIRDS (1926).*

441 • BLACKBIRDS OF 1928

OPENED: 05/09/1928   Theatre: Liberty
Revue   Broadway: 519

Composer: Jimmy McHugh
Lyricist: Dorothy Fields
Producer: Lew Leslie
Director: Lew Leslie

Costumes: Kiviette; **Musical Director:** Allie Ross; **Orchestrations:** Alfred Goodman; Ken Macomber; Will Vodery

Songs: Baby! [1]; Bandanna Babies; Diga Diga Doo; Dixie; Doin' the New Low Down; Here Comes My Blackbird; I Can't Give You Anything But Love [2]; I Must Have That Man; Magnolia's Wedding Day; Porgy (Blues for Porgy); Shuffle Your Feet (And Just Roll Along); St. Louis Blues [3] (C/L: W.C. Handy)

Cast: Joseph Attles; Adelaide Hall; Johnny

Hudgins; Tim Moore; Mantan Moreland; Bill Robinson; Eloise Uggams; Aida Ward; Elisabeth Welch

Notes: [1] Cut after opening. [2] Dropped from HARRY DELMAR'S REVELS. For years there has been speculation that Fats Waller and Andy Razaf actually wrote this song. [3] Not written for this production.

442 • BLACKBIRDS OF 1929

OPENED: 1929   Theatre: Cotton Club
Revue   Nightclub

Composer: Jimmy McHugh
Lyricist: Dorothy Fields

Cast: Duke Ellington and His Orchestra

Notes: No other information available.

443 • BLACKBIRDS OF 1930

OPENED: 10/22/1930   Theatre: Royale
Revue   Broadway: 61

Composer: Eubie Blake
Lyricist: Andy Razaf
Librettist: Flournoy Miller
Producer: Lew Leslie
Director: Lew Leslie

Choreographer: Al Richards; **Costumes:** Vincente Minnelli; **Musical Director:** Eubie Blake; **Orchestrations:** Ken Macomber; **Set Design:** Ward & Harvey; **Vocal Arranger:** J. Rosamond Johnson

Songs: Baby Mine; Blackbirds on Parade; (Down at the Ole) Cabin Door; Dianna Lee; Dissatisfied Blues; Doin' the Mozambique; Green Pastures (L: Will Morrissey; Andy Razaf); Ham and Eggs; Harlem; How to Play an Ole Banjo; In Slumberland; Key to My Heart, The; Mammy's Jubilee; Memories of You; My Handy Man Ain't Handy No More; Papa-De-Da-Da (C/L: Clarence Todd; Clarence Williams; Spencer Williams); Roll, Jordan, Roll; Take a Trip to Harlem; That Lindy Hop; Under the Jungle Moon; Wakin' Up the Folks Down Stairs; We're the Berries; Who Said Blackbirds Are Blue; You're Lucky to Me

Cast: Jimmie Baskette; Berry Brothers, The; Buck & Bubbles; Minto Cato; Broadway Jones; Cecil Mack Choir, The; Flournoy Miller; Mantan

Moreland; Al Richards; Jazzlips Richardson; Neeka Shaw; Ethel Waters

444 • BLACKBIRDS OF 1934 (FIRST EDITION)

OPENED: 12/02/1933   Theatre: Apollo
Revue   Broadway: 25

Composer: Alberta Nichols
Lyricist: Mann Holiner
Librettist: Nat Dorfman; Mann Holiner; Lew Leslie
Producer: Sepia Guild Players
Director: Lew Leslie

Choreographer: Al Richards; **Costumes:** Charles LeMaire; **Musical Director:** Ken Macomber; **Orchestrations:** Ferde Grofe; Joe Jordan; Ken Macomber; Will Vodery; **Set Design:** Mabel A. Buell

Songs: Concentrate a Little on Love; Doin' the Shim Sham; Gentlemen of Japan; Great Gettin' Up Mornin' (C/L: Unknown); Hundred Years from Today, A (C: Victor Young; L: Ned Washington; Joe Young); I Just Couldn't Take It, Baby; I'm Walkin' the Chalk Line; Just a Song and Dance [1] (C: Victor Young; L: Ned Washington; Joe Young); Let Me Be Born Again (C: Victor Young; L: Ned Washington; Joe Young); Minstrel Man; Prologue; Tappin' the Barrel (C: Victor Young; L: Ned Washington; Joe Young); Victims of Voodoo Drums (C: Victor Young; L: Ned Washington; Joe Young); Voo Doo Pageant (inst.) (C: Victor Young); What-No Dixie? (C: Victor Young; L: Ned Washington; Joe Young); Your Mother's Son-in-Law

Cast: James Boxwill; Gretchen Branch; Pike Davis Orchestra, The; Toni Ellis; Eddie Hunter; Brady Jackson; Cecil Mack Choir, The; Jason Mason; Blue McAllister; Katheryn Perry; Bill Robinson; Phil Scott; Speedy Smith; Martha Thomas; Eloise Uggams; Slappy Wallace; Edith Wilson; Worthy & Thompson

Notes: Titled BLACKBIRDS of 1933. Out of town. See also BLACKBIRDS OF 1934, (Second Edition) which was a continuation of this show. [1] ASCAP/Library of Congress only.

445 • BLACKBIRDS OF 1934 (SECOND EDITION)

OPENED: 09/1934   Theatre: Apollo
Revue   Broadway

Producer: Lew Leslie

Vocal Arranger: Lew Leslie

Songs: Christmas Night in Harlem (C: Raymond Scott; L: Mitchell Parish); Moonglow [1] (C: Will Hudson; L: Eddie De Lange; Irving Mills); Rhapsody in Blue (inst.) [1] (C: George Gershwin); St. James Infirmary [1] (C/L: Joe Primrose)

Cast: Peg Leg Bates; Tim Moore; Bill Robinson; Valaida Snow; Edith Wilson

Notes: A revised edition of BLACKBIRDS OF 1933. Added songs listed here. [1] Not written for this show.

446 • BLACKBIRDS OF 1936

OPENED: 07/09/1936 Theatre: Gaiety
Revue London: 124

Composer: Rube Bloom
Lyricist: Johnny Mercer

Songs: Dixie Isn't Dixie Any More [1]; I Knew; Jo-Jo the Cannible Kid; Keep a Twinkle in Your Eye; South Wind; Swing Is the Thing, The; Why Can't It Be Me?; Your Heart and Mine

Cast: Nicholas Brothers

Notes: No other information available. [1] Later in RHAPSODY IN BLACK.

447 • BLACKBIRDS OF 1939

OPENED: 02/11/1939 Theatre: Hudson
Revue Broadway: 9

Composer: Unknown
Lyricist: Unknown
Librettist: Nat Dorfman; Fred F. Finklehoffe; Lew Leslie; John Monks Jr.
Producer: Lew Leslie
Director: Lew Leslie

Choreographer: Eugene Van Grona; **Costumes:** Frances Feist; **Orchestrations:** Ferde Grofe; Ken Macomber; **Set Design:** Mabel Buell; **Vocal Arranger:** J. Rosamond Johnson

Songs: Dixie Isn't Dixie Anymore [1]; Father Divine (C: Louis Haber; L: Dorothy Sachs);

I Did It for the Red, White and Blue (C: Rube Bloom; L: Johnny Mercer); Jojo the Cannibal Kid [1]; Name It and It's Yours (C: Sammy Fain; Abner Silver; L: Mitchell Parish); Rhapsody in Blue (inst.) (C: George Gershwin); Shake Your Bluesies with Dancing Shoesies (C: Louis Haber; L: Dorothy Sachs); Swing Struck (C: Vic Mizzy; L. Irving Taylor); Thursday (C: Louis Haber; L: Dorothy Sachs); You're So Indifferent (C: Sammy Fain; L: Mitchell Parish)

Cast: Bobby Evans; Sammy Fain; Kate Hall; Hamtree Harrington; Lena Horne; Dewey "Pigmeat" Markham; Taps Miller; Tim Moore

Notes: [1] From BLACKBIRDS OF 1936.

448 • BLACKOUTS OF 1942

OPENED: 1942
Revue

Songs: Say When (C/L: Harry Carroll; Pauline Carroll)

Notes: No other information available.

449 • BLACKVILLE STROLLERS

OPENED: 1908
Musical

Composer: J. Homer Tutt; Salem Tutt Whitney
Lyricist: J. Homer Tutt; Salem Tutt Whitney
Librettist: J. Homer Tutt; Salem Tutt Whitney

Cast: Marie Bell; Charles Bougla; W.A. Cook; George Day; Sarah Green; Gus Hall; Jeanette Murphy; J. Homer Tutt; Sara Venable; Salem Tutt Whitney

Notes: No other information available.

450 • BLAME IT ON THE MOVIES!

OPENED: 05/16/1989 Theatre: Criterion Center Stage Left
Revue Off-Broadway: 3

Composer: Billy Barnes
Lyricist: Billy Barnes
Producer: Roger Berlind; Gregory Harrison; Franklin R. Levy
Director: David Galligan

Choreographer: Larry Hyman; **Costumes:** Bonnie

Stauch; **Dance Arranger:** Ron Abel; **Lighting Designer:** Michael Gilliam; **Musical Director:** Ron Abel; **Set Design:** Fred Duer; **Vocal Arranger:** Ron Abel

Cast: Sandy Edgerton; Kathy Garrick; Bill Hutton; Christine Kellogg; Peter Marc; Dan O'Grady; Barbara Sharma; Patty Tiffany

Notes: Compiled and conceived by Ron Abel, Billy Barnes and David Galligan from an original idea by Franklin R. Levy.

451 • BLANCO
OPENED: 05/11/1984
Musical   Closed out of town

Composer: Skip Kennon
Lyricist: Michael Korie
Librettist: Vincent Dowling
Producer: Music Theater Workshop
Director: Susan H. Schulman

Source: SHEWING UP OF BLANCO POSNET, THE (Story: George Bernard Shaw); **Lighting Designer:** Jeffrey Schissler; **Musical Director:** Skip Kennon; **Set Design:** James Morgan

Songs: Across the Border; And That's Nice (L: Willy Holtzman); Ballad of Progress, The (1) (L: Skip Kennon); Ballad of Progress, The (2); Dancin' in the Middle (L: Skip Kennon); Dangerous; Enemy of the West; Fair Men, Square Men; Fountain of Forgiveness; Great Game; Hoedown Hanging; Hymn of Temperance (L: Willy Holtzman); I Done Good (1) (L: Willy Holtzman); I Done Good (2) (L: Skip Kennon); I Know a Town (1) (L: Willy Holtzman); I Know a Town (2) (L: Skip Kennon); I Know What You Need (L: Willy Holtzman); I Shut the Door; In the Eyes of a Child (1) (L: Willy Holtzman); In the Eyes of a Child (2); It's a Bad, Bad World (1) (L: Willy Holtzman); It's a Bad, Bad World (2) (L: Skip Kennon); It's Only Business (1) (L: Willy Holtzman); It's Only Business (2) (L: Skip Kennon); Let It Be Him (1) (L: Willy Holtzman); Let It Be Him (2) (L: Skip Kennon); Loose Ends (1) (L: Willy Holtzman); Loose Ends (2) (L: Skip Kennon); Lord, Keep Me Wicked; My Stagecoach Is A-Comin' in Real Soon (L: Skip Kennon); 'N That's Nice (L: Skip Kennon); No Good at Bein' Bad (L: Skip Kennon); Noble (L: Michael Korie); Our Town; P. Stone's Prayer (L: Willy Holtzman); Place of Your Own, A (L: Skip Kennon); Poor Horse; Prayer of Guidence (L: Skip Kennon); Pure America; Rainbow Woman; Round by Red Mountain; Rub-A-Dub-Dub (1) (L: Willy Holtzman); Rub-A-Dub-Dub (2) (L: Skip Kennon); Straight and Narrow Trail, The (1) (L: Willy Holtzman); Straight and Narrow Trail, The (2) (L: Skip Kennon); Verdict, The; We're Talkin' About Bout Blanco (L: Willy Holtzman); What's Possible (L: Willy Holtzman); When You Lose a Friend (L: Willy Holtzman)

Cast: David Barron; Stephen Costing; Sharon Daniels; Joseph Kolinksi; Alexandra Korey; Audrey Lavine; Stephen Lehew; Ron Raines; Mary Saunders

Notes: The credits are from a concert version of this show which workshopped at the Great Lakes Theatre Festival in Cleveland, Ohio. There were three sets of book and lyrics for this show. The songs are interspersed with appropriate lyricists credited. Michael Korie wrote the lyrics and Vincent Dowling the libretto of the first version. Willy Holtzman wrote book and lyrics to the second. Skip Kennon wrote the lyrics to the third version. [1] This entry is from a concert of the songs.

452 • BLARNEY STONE
Play   Closed out of town

Composer: Unknown
Lyricist: Unknown
Author: Edward Rose
Producer: George M. Gatts

Costumes: S.K. Viele; **Set Design:** S.K. Viele

Songs: Bit o' Pink and White, A; Kitty; Minstrel's Prayer, The; Mother in Ireland (C/L: Gerald Griffin; Herman Kahn; Tommy Lyman); Shamrock Flirtation; Top o' the Mornin'; When You Kiss the Blarney Stone

Cast: Walter Scanlon

453 • BLESS THE BRIDE
OPENED: 04/26/1947   Theatre: Adelphi
Musical   London: 886

Composer: Vivian Ellis
Lyricist: A.P. Herbert
Librettist: A.P. Herbert

Producer: C.B. Cochran
Director: Wendy Toye

Choreographer: Wendy Toye; **Costumes:** Tanya
Moiseiwitsch; **Musical Director:** Michael Collins;
Set Design: Tanya Moiseiwitsch

Songs: Any Man but Thomas T; Bless the Bride;
Bless the Sea; Bobbing-Bobbing; Come, Dance, My
Dear; Croquet, Croquet; Ducky; En Angleterre,
Les Demoiselles; Englishman, The; Fable for Two,
A; Fish, The; God Bless the Family; Here's a Kiss
for One and Twenty; I Was Never Kissed Before;
Ma Belle Marguerite; Mon Pauvre Petit Pierre; My
Big Moment; Oh, What Will Mother Say?; Silent
Heart, The; Summer; This Is My Lovely Day; This
Man Could Never Be a Spy; To France; Too Good
to Be True; Twenty-One Candles; Un Consomme;
Where Is the Times?

Cast: Diana Beall; Georges Guetary; Lizbeth Webb

454 • BLESS YOU ALL
OPENED: 12/14/1950   Theatre: Mark Hellinger
Revue   Broadway: 84

Composer: Harold Rome
Lyricist: Harold Rome
Librettist: Arnold Auerbach
Producer: Herman Levin; Oliver Smith
Director: John C. Wilson

Choreographer: Helen Tamiris; **Costumes:** Miles
White; **Dance Arranger:** Mischa Portnoff; Wesley
Portnoff; Don Walker; **Musical Director:**
Lehman Engel; **Orchestrations:** Don Walker;
Set Design: Oliver Smith; **Vocal Arranger:**
Lehman Engel

Songs: Bless You All; Desert Flame, The (C: Don
Walker); Do You Know a Better Way to Make a
Living; Don't Wanna Write about the South;
I Can Hear It Now; Just a Little White House;
Little Things Meant So Much to Me; Love Letter
to Manhattan; Love that Man; Roaring Twenties
Strike Back, The; Rose Is a Rose, A; Summer
Dresses; Take Off the Coat [1]; Voting Blues;
When; You Never Know What Hit You When
It's Love [1]

Cast: Pearl Bailey; Gene Barry; Valerie Bettis; Mary
McCarty; Jules Munshin; Donald Saddler; Swen
Swenson

Notes: [1] Originally in THAT'S THE TICKET.

455 • BLITZ!
OPENED: 05/08/1962   Theatre: Adelphi
Musical   London: 568

Composer: Lionel Bart
Lyricist: Lionel Bart
Librettist: Lionel Bart; Joan Maitland
Producer: Donald Albery
Director: Lionel Bart

Choreographer: Peter Wright; **Costumes:** Bernard
Sarron; **Musical Director:** Marcus Dods; **Set
Design:** Sean Kenny

Songs: Another Morning; As Long As This Is
England; Bake a Cake; Be What You Wanna Be;
Day After Tomorrow, The; Down the Lane; Duty
Calls!; Far Away; I Want to Whisper Something;
Is This Gonna Be a Wedding?; Leave It to the
Ladies; Mums and Dads; Opposites; Our Hotel;
Petticoat Lane (On a Saturday Ain't So Nice); So
Tell Me; Tell Him-Tell Her!; We're Going to the
Country; Who Wants to Settle Down?; Who's
This Geezer Hitler

Cast: Amelia Bayntun; Edward Caddick; Julie
Cohen; Deborah Cranston; Grazina Frame; Bob
Grant; Rose Hiller; Graham James; Kaplan Kaye;
Thomas Kempinski; Ann Taylor

456 • BLOCKHEADS
OPENED: 10/17/1984   Theatre: Mermaid
Musical   London

Composer: Hal Hackady; Alexander Peskanov
Lyricist: Hal Hackady
Librettist: Kay Cole; Michael Landwehr; Arthur
Whitelaw
Director: Arthur Whitelaw

Choreographer: Kay Cole; **Costumes:** David
Graden; **Set Design:** Tim Goodchild

Songs: Blockheads; G.A.; Goodbye, Mae; Have We
Still Got It?; Is This Where the Rainbow Ends?;
Laughs; Makin' Movies; Nothin' Personal; One
Cuff Link; Playin' the Halls; Rumors from Rome;
Sad Happy, Peek a Boo; Silence Is Golden; Star
Quality; Starting from Now; That Man Up There;
Timing; Whose Baby Blues

Cast: Simon Browne; Larry Dann; Susan Denaker; Richard Drabble; Mark Hatfield; Megg Nicol; Kenneth H. Waller

Notes: Based on the lives of Laurel and Hardy.

457 • BLONDE IN BLACK, THE
OPENED: 06/08/1903   Theatre: Knickerbocker
Musical   Broadway: 35

Composer: Gustave Kerker
Lyricist: Harry B. Smith
Librettist: Harry B. Smith
Producer: George W. Lederer
Director: Max Freeman

Choreographer: Carl Marwig; **Costumes:** Archie Gunn; **Lighting Designer:** Joseph George; **Musical Director:** Gustave Kerker; **Set Design:** D. Frank Dodge

Songs: Although I'm So Demure; Any Old Thing; Awake, Ma Chile; Come Home My Little Honeycomb [1] (C/L: Melville S. Collins); Country Belles; Cynthia Jones; Don't Overdo It; Eva Tanguay's Love Song [1] (C/L: Melville S. Collins); I Love Ze American Ragtime; I'm for You [1] (C/L: Melville S. Collins); Men Are Ambitious; My Ideal; She Walks Like This; Song of the Dawn; Stage Door Johnnies; They Are Angels Without Wings; T'was Love All the Day (Artist and Model); What's the Use of Love; Yankee Girl, The

Cast: Charles H. Bowers; Harry Conor; Albert Hart; Blanche Ring

Notes: [1] From version titled LITTLE SAMBO.

458 • BLONDE SINNER, THE
OPENED: 07/14/1926   Theatre: Cort
Musical   Broadway: 179

Composer: Leon De Costa
Lyricist: Leon De Costa
Librettist: Leon De Costa
Set Design: Walter Sherwood

Songs: Bye-Bye Babe; Don't You Cheat; If You Said What I Thought; Lips; Man Is a Mistake; Oh, What a Playmate You Could Make; Whispering Song, The

Cast: Marjorie Gateson; Edwin H. Kasper; Enid Markey; Howard St. John

459 • BLOOD
OPENED: 03/07/1971   Theatre: New York Shakespeare Festival
Musical   Off-Broadway: 14

Lyricist: Doug Dyer
Librettist: Doug Dyer
Producer: N.Y. Shakespeare Festival; Joseph Papp

Choreographer: Cora Cohan; **Costumes:** Theoni V. Aldredge; **Lighting Designer:** Keith Nelson; **Musical Director:** Patrick Fox; **Set Design:** Doug Dyer

Songs: Baby Rue (C: Patrick Fox; L: Avra Petrides); Before You Knew I Loved You (C: Maggie Hyatt); Cold Steel (C: Horald Griffiths); Destruction (C: Jim Turner); Don't Call Us (C: Jim Turner; L: Mary Boylan); Every Father (C: Patrick Fox; Linda Swenson; L: Doug Dyer; Horald Griffiths); Father, Father (C/L: Patrick Fox); Four Thousand Years (C: Patrick Fox); Gas Can (C: Patrick Fox); Hail to the Blood (C/L: Horald Griffiths); Hard Time War Time (C/L: Blood Company); Hear the Guns (C: Margaret Dorn; Elizabeth Howard; Tom Willis); Heebie-Jeebie Furies (C: Jim Turner); High Lonesome (C: Horald Griffiths); I Dreamt about My Home (C: Linda Swenson); I Had a Son (C/L: Mary Boylan); I Woke Up Today (C/L: Christopher Cox); Just a Little Bit (C/L: Horald Griffiths); Love Came to Me (C: Blood Company; Doug Dyer; Patrick Fox); Lullaby (C/L: Patrick Fox); Madness Murder (C: Margaret Dorn); Minute By Minute (C: Patrick Fox); Monkey in a Tree (C: David Cohen; L: Horald Griffiths); New Snow (C: Margaret Dorn); Nobody's Fault (C/L: Alex Ander); There You Go Again (C/L: Alex Ander); Walk On Home (C: Jim Turner); Whistles (C: Joyce Stanton; L: Patrick Fox)

Cast: Alexandra Barrie; Mary Boylan; Doug Dyer; Patrick Fox; Horald Griffiths

460 • BLOOD BROTHERS
OPENED: 04/25/1993   Theatre: Music Box
Musical   Broadway: 839

Composer: Willy Russell
Lyricist: Willy Russell

Librettist: Willy Russell
Producer: Bill Kenwright
Director: Bill Kenwright; Bob Tomson

Arrangements: Del Newman; **Costumes:** Andy Walmsley; **Lighting Designer:** Joe Atkins; **Musical Director:** Rick Fox; **Set Design:** Andy Walmsley

Songs: Bright New Day; Easy Terms; I'm Not Saying a Word; Kids Game; Light Romance; Long Sunday Afternoon; Madman; Marilyn Monroe; My Child; My Friend; Shoes Upon the Table; Tell Me It's Not True; That Guy

Cast: James Clow; Warwick Evans; Mark Michael Hutchinson; Stephanie Lawrence; Con O'Neill; Barbara Walsh

461 • BLOOD RED ROSES

OPENED: 03/22/1970 Theatre: John Golden
Musical Broadway: 1

Composer: Michael Valenti
Lyricist: John Lewin
Librettist: John Lewin
Producer: Louis S. Goldman; Seymour Vall
Director: Alan Schneider

Choreographer: Larry Fuller; **Costumes:** Deidre Cartier; **Lighting Designer:** Tharon Musser; **Musical Director:** Milton Seltzer; **Orchestrations:** Abba Bogin; Julian Stein; **Set Design:** Ed Wittstein

Songs: Black Dog Rum; Blood Red Roses [1]; Cream of English Youth, The; English Rose, The; Fourth Light Dragoons; Garden in the Sun, A; How Fucked Up Things Are; In the Country Where I Come From; Prelude; Soldier's Prayer (O Rock Eternal); Song of Greater Britain; Song of the Fair Dissenter Lass [1]

Cast: Philip Bruns; Jeannie Carson; Ronald Drake; Sydney Walker

Notes: [1] Also in LOVESONG.

462 • BLOOMER GIRL

OPENED: 10/05/1944 Theatre: Shubert
Musical Broadway: 657

Composer: Harold Arlen
Lyricist: E.Y. Harburg

Librettist: Sig Herzig; Fred Saidy
Producer: Nat Goldstone; John C. Wilson
Director: E.Y. Harburg; William Schorr

Source: LILITH (Play: Dan James); **Choreographer:** Agnes de Mille; **Costumes:** Miles White; **Lighting Designer:** Lemuel Ayers; **Musical Director:** Leon Leonardi; **Orchestrations:** Robert Russell Bennett; **Set Design:** Lemuel Ayers

Songs: Civil War Ballet (inst.); Eagle and Me, The; Evelina; Farmer's Daughter; I Got a Song [1]; I Never Was Born; It Was Good Enough for Grandma; Little Big Man [2]; Liza Crossing the Ice; Lullaby (Satin Gown and Silver Shoe); Man for Sale; Pretty As a Picture; Promise Me Not to Love Me [2]; Rakish Young Man with the Whiskers; Right As the Rain; Simon Legree; Style Show Ballet (inst.); Sunday in Cicero Falls; T'morra', T'morra'; 'Till We All Belong [2]; Welcome Hinges; When the Boys Come Home

Cast: Matt Briggs; David Brooks; Celeste Holm; Richard Huey; Joe E. Marks; Joan McCracken; Mabel Taliaferro; Dooley Wilson

Notes: [1] Originally written for the film version of CABIN IN THE SKY. [2] Registered by ASCAP in 1976.

463 • BLOSSOM TIME

OPENED: 09/28/1921 Theatre: Ambassador
Musical Broadway: 516

Music Based On: Heinrich Berte; Franz Schubert
Composer: Sigmund Romberg
Lyricist: Dorothy Donnelly
Librettist: Dorothy Donnelly
Producer: Messrs. Shubert
Director: J.C. Huffman

Source: DAS DREI MAEDELHAUS (Musical: Heinz Reichert; A.M. Willner); **Choreographer:** Frank M. Gillespie; **Musical Director:** Oscar Radin; **Set Design:** Watson Barratt

Songs: Finale Act I; Finale Act II; Keep It Dark; Let Me Awake; Lonely Hearts; Love Is a Riddle; Melody Triste; Moment Musical; My Springtime Thou Art; Only One Love Ever Fills the Heart; Opening; Opening Act III; Peace to My Lonely Heart [1]; Serenade; Song of Love; Tell Me Daisy; There Is Old Vienna Town [1]; Three Little Maids

Cast: Olga Cook; Howard Marsh; Bertram Peacock

Notes: [1] Sheet music only.

464 • BLUE BIRD REVUE, THE
OPENED: 1931
Revue   Closed out of town

Composer: N. Gogotsky
Lyricist: Leo Robin

Songs: Huntsman's Song of Love, The; 'Nichevo' Means Yes; On a Little Journey in Springtime with You (C: Walter Jurmann)

Notes: German lyrics by Fritz Rotter. No other information available.

465 • BLUE EYES (1921)
OPENED: 02/21/1921   Theatre: Casino
Musical   Broadway: 48

Composer: I.B. Kornblum
Lyricist: Zeke Meyers
Librettist: LeRoy Clemons; Leon Gordon
Producer: Morris Rose
Director: Clifford Brooke

Choreographer: Bert French; **Musical Director:** Eugene Salzer

Songs: Baby Walk; Blue Eyes [1] (C: Silvio Hein; L: George V. Hobart; Edward Paulton); Danger Ahead; Honeysuckle [1] (C: Silvio Hein; L: George V. Hobart; Edward Paulton); In ze Park; Just Suppose; So Long Jazz; Take Me to Heaven [1]; Wanting You (C: George Gershwin; L: Irving Caesar); When Gentlemen Disagree; When Gramercy Square Was Uptown; Without a Girl Like You; Woman [1] (C: Frank Tours; L: Clifford Grey)

Cast: Delyle Alda; Lew Fields; Mollie King; Ray Raymond; Andrew Tombes

Notes: [1] Sheet music only.

466 • BLUE EYES (1928)
OPENED: 04/27/1928   Theatre: Piccadilly
Musical   London: 276

Composer: Jerome Kern
Lyricist: Graham John

Librettist: Guy Bolton; Graham John
Producer: Lee Ephraim
Director: John Harwood

Choreographer: Fred Leslie; **Musical Director:** Kennedy Russell; **Orchestrations:** Robert Russell Bennett; **Set Design:** Joseph Harker; Phil Harker

Songs: Back to the Heather; Blue Eyes [1]; Bow Belles [10]; Charlie Is the Darling of My Heart; Curtsey, The; Do I Do Wrong? [2]; Do It Now (L: Harry Graham); Entrance of Orange and Flower Girls; Fair Lady; Finale Act I; Finaletto Act II; Finaletto-Scene 1; Good King James, The [3]; Henry [4]; His Majesty's Dragoons; If I Were King [5]; In Love [6]; In Voodoo [3]; Little Feet that Lightly Beat [3]; Long Live Nancy [11]; No One Else But You; Only Love [5] (C: Louis Ganne); Opening Number Act II; Praise the Day; Prince Do and Dare [3]; Romeo and Juliet; Scottish Medley (C/L: Traditional); Some Day [7]; Someone [8]; Trouble About the Drama, The; What Can I Say [4]; When I Marry Mr. Pilbeam [3]; Women [9] (C: Frank Tours; L: Clifford Grey); You Are There [4]

Cast: Kitty Attfield; Ethel Baird; Geoffrey Gwyther; Evelyn Laye; Mark Lester; Bertram Wallis

Notes: [1] Same music as "All Lanes Must Reach a Turning" in DEAR SIR. [2] Same music as "You're Devastating" in ROBERTA. Cut after opening. [3] Cut after opening. [4] Cut before opening. [5] Added out of town after London. [6] Similar music to "Alone at Last" in OH, I SAY! [7] Cut before opening. Same music. [8] Same music. Added after opening. [9] Added after opening. [10] Same music as "You Can't Make Love By Wireless" in THE BEAUTY PRIZE. [11] Not in program.

467 • BLUE HOLIDAY
OPENED: 05/21/1945   Theatre: Belasco
Revue   Broadway: 8

Composer: Al Moritz
Lyricist: Al Moritz
Producer: Doris Cole; Irwin Shapiro
Director: Monroe B. Hack

Choreographer: Katherine Dunham; **Costumes:** Kasia; **Musical Director:** Billy Butler; **Set Design:** Perry Watkins

Songs: Blue Holiday; Fiji Island Ballet (inst.)
(C: Herbert Kinsley); Free and Equal Blues
(C: Earl Robinson; L: E.Y. Harburg); Hard Time
Blues (C: Josh White; L: Warren Cooney); House
I Live In, The (C: Earl Robinson; L: Lewis Allan);
Sleep Time Lullaby; That's Where My Heart
Will Be

Cast: Willie Bryant; Chocolateers, The; Katherine
Dunham Dancers; Evelyn Ellis; Lillian
Fitzgerald; Muriel Gaines; Hall Johnson Choir;
Three Poms, The; Ethel Waters; Josh White; Mary
Lou Williams

Notes: Songs also credited to Duke Ellington and
Morey Amsterdam but not identified in
program.

468 • BLUE KITTEN, THE
OPENED: 01/13/1922 Theatre: Selwyn
Musical Broadway: 140

Composer: Rudolf Friml
Lyricist: William Cary Duncan; Otto Harbach
Librettist: William Cary Duncan; Otto Harbach
Producer: Arthur Hammerstein
Director: Leon Errol; Julian Mitchell; Edgar
Selwyn

Source: LE CHASSEUR DE CHEZ MAXIM'S (Play:
Yves Mirande; Gustave Quinson); **Musical
Director:** Herbert Stothart; **Set Design:** Clifford
Pember

Songs: Best I Ever Get Is the Worst of It, The
(L: William Cary Duncan); Blue Kitten Blues [1]
(L: Otto Harbach); Cutie (L: Otto Harbach);
Daddy [1] (L: Otto Harbach); Her Love Is Always
the Same; I Could Do a Lot for You; I Found a
Bud Among the Roses (L: Otto Harbach); Le
Minet Bleu (The Blue Kitten) (Meow) (L: Otto
Harbach); Madeleine [1] (L: Otto Harbach);
Smoke Rings (L: Otto Harbach); Sweet As You
Can Be; Tact; Twelve O'Clock Girl in a Nine
O'Clock Town, A (L: William Cary Duncan);
When I Waltz with You (L: Otto Harbach); Where
the Honeymoon Alone Can See (L: William Cary
Duncan)

Cast: Joseph Cawthorn; Lillian Lorraine; Marion
Sunshine; Robert Woolsey

Notes: [1] Sheet music only.

469 • BLUE MONDAY
Notes: *See GEORGE WHITE'S SCANDALS OF
1922.*

470 • BLUE MOON, THE (1906)
OPENED: 01/03/1906 Theatre: Casino
Musical Broadway: 76

Composer: Paul Rubens; Howard Talbot
Lyricist: Percy Greenbank; Paul Rubens
Librettist: Harold Ellis
Producer: Messrs. Shubert
Director: Frank Smithson

Costumes: Susie Kerwin

Songs: All My Girls; Burmah Girl; Chandra Nil
My Lotus Lily [2] (C/L: George A. Spink);
(Oh, Be Careful of the) Crocodile (C/L: Paul
Rubens); Don't Go Into the Lion's Cage Tonight
(C: E. Ray Goetz; L: John Gilroy); Don't You
Think It's Time to Marry? [1] (C: Gus Edwards;
L: Addison Burkhardt); Fairest of the Fair;
I Told a Friend of Mine; I Will Marry Him to
Make a Home for Mother [1] (C/L: Herbert
Ingraham); If You Only Knew How Much
I Loved You; Jugglar; La Koquette; Little Blue
Moon (C: Howard Talbot; L: Percy Greenbank);
Major's Song; Moon Dear [1]; Opening Chorus;
Pit-a-Pat; Poplar and the Rainbow, The [2]
(C/L: Paul Rubens); Put Me Among the Girls
[1]; She Didn't Know [2] (C/L: Paul Rubens);
Sometimes [2] (C/L: Paul Rubens); When Love
Comes Knocking at the Door [2] (C: Evelyn
Baker; L: Maud Shields); Why Don't You Take
One, Little Boy? (C/L: Will R. Anderson)

Cast: Petite Adelaide; Ethel Jackson; Grace LaRue;
Clara Palmer; James T. Powers; Templar Saxe

Notes: [1] Out Cedar Rapids 11/25/07. [2] Sheet
music only.

471 • BLUE MOON (1926)
OPENED: 1926
Musical

Composer: Donald Heywood
Lyricist: Donald Heywood; Irvin C. Miller
Librettist: Irvin C. Miller
Producer: Irvin C. Miller

Cast: Stewart Hampton; Lorenzo McLane; Princess Mysteria; Rinal

Notes: No other information available on this one-act musical.

472 • BLUE MOUSE, THE
OPENED: 11/30/1908   Theatre: Lyric
Play   Broadway: 232

Author: Clyde Fitch
Director: Clyde Fitch

Set Design: H. Robert Law

Songs: Love Me All the Time (C/L: Joseph E. Howard)

Cast: Mabel Barrison; Harry Conor; Rose Cooke; John Emerson

473 • BLUE PARADISE, THE
OPENED: 08/05/1915   Theatre: Casino
Musical   Broadway: 356

Composer: Edmund Eysler; Sigmund Romberg
Lyricist: Herbert Reynolds
Librettist: Edgar Smith
Producer: Messrs. Shubert
Director: Benrimo

Source: EIN TAG IM PARADIES (Musical: Edmund Eysler; Bela Jenbach; Leo Stein); **Choreographer:** Ed Hutchinson; **Musical Director:** Fred Walz

Songs: Auf Wiedersehen! (C: Sigmund Romberg); Duet and Dance [1] (C: Edmund Eysler); Finale [1] (C: Edmund Eysler); Folk Song and Yodle [1] (C: Leo Edwards); Here's to You My Sparkling Wine (C: Leo Edwards; L: Blanche Merrill); I Had a Dog (C: Leo Edwards); I'm Dreaming of a Wonderful Night (C: Edmund Eysler); I'm from Chicago (C: Sigmund Romberg); Just Win a Pretty Widow (C: Edmund Eysler); My Model Girl (C: Sigmund Romberg; L: Harold Atteridge); Old Blue Paradise; One Step Into Love (C: Sigmund Romberg); Tell the Town, Hello, Tonite (C: Sigmund Romberg; L: Harold Atteridge); There's Only One Who Rules My House; To Paradise We'll Gaily Trip (C: Edmund Eysler); Toast to Women's Eyes, A (C: Sigmund Romberg); Tune They Croon in the U.S.A., The (C/L: Cecil Lean); Vienna, How D'Ye Do? (C: Edmund Eysler); Vienna, Vienna (C: Edmund Eysler); Waltz of the Season (C: Edmund Eysler); We Wish You a Pleasant Journey [1] (C: Sigmund Romberg); Why Are We Invited Here? (C: Sigmund Romberg)

Cast: Frances Demarest; Cecil Lean; Ted Lorraine; Cleo Mayfield; Vivienne Segal

Notes: [1] Vocal score only.

474 • BLUE PLATE SPECIAL
OPENED: 10/18/1983   Theatre: Manhattan
                         Theatre Club
Musical   Off-Broadway: 48

Composer: Harris Wheeler
Lyricist: Mary L. Fisher
Librettist: Tom Edwards
Director: Art Wolff

Choreographer: Douglas Norwick; **Costumes:** David Murin; **Lighting Designer:** Arden Fingerhut; **Musical Director:** Jimmy Roberts; **Orchestrations:** Robby Merkin; **Set Design:** David Jenkins; **Vocal Arranger:** Robby Merkin

Songs: All American Male; At the Bottom Lookin' Up; Blue Plate Special; Halfway to Heaven; Honky Tonk Queen; I Ain't Looking Back; I'm Gonna Miss Those Tennessee Nights; Morning Glory Mountain; Never Say Never; Ramona's Lament; Satisfaction Guaranteed; Side of Fries; Twice as Nice

Cast: Gretchen Cryer; Ron Holgate; Tina Johnson; Mary Gordon Murray; Gordon Paddison; David Strathairn

475 • BLUE TRAIN, THE
OPENED: 10/05/1927   Theatre: Prince of Wales
Musical   London: 116

Composer: Robert Stolz
Lyricist: Reginald Arkell
Librettist: Reginald Arkell; Dion Titheridge
Producer: Jack Hulburt

Source: MADI (Musical: Alfred Grunwald; Walter Stein; Robert Stolz); **Musical Director:** Charles Prentice; **Set Design:** F.L. Lyndhurst

Songs: Blue Train, The (C: Jay Gorney; L: Dion Titheradge)

Cast: Eric Coxon; Lily Elsie; Henry Ford; Bobby Howes

Notes: No program available. Additional numbers by Ivy St. Helier.

476 • BLUEBEARD JR. OR FATIMA AND THE FAIRY

OPENED: 01/13/1889
Musical   Broadway

Composer: Unknown
Lyricist: Unknown
Librettist: Clay M. Greene
Producer: Ideal Extravaganza Company
Director: Richard Barker

Costumes: Arthur Chasemore; **Set Design:** Ernest Albert; Henry E. Hoyt; William Voegtlin

Songs: Angie Blossom's Party (C: G. Coes); Army So Grand, The; Grasshoppers Chorus (C: William Slaughter); He's on the Police Force Now (C: Richard Maddern); I Am the Author of Divorce (C/L: John Braham); If They Must Tear Me from Thy Heart (C: Fred J. Eustis; L: Clay M. Greene); Like June Skies (C: John Braham; L: John F. Harley); Little Lord Fauntleroy (C: Fred J. Eustis); Little Pie, The; Oriental Swell, An; Put a Nickel in the Slot (C: Richard Maddern; L: Clay M. Greene); When the Cat's Away the Mice Will Play

Cast: Frank Blair; Eddie Foy Sr.; Alice Johnston

477 • BLUES FOR MR. CHARLIE

OPENED: 04/23/1964   Theatre: ANTA
Play   Broadway: 148

Author: James Baldwin
Producer: Actors Studio, Inc.
Director: Burgess Meredith

Lighting Designer: Feder; **Set Design:** Feder

Songs: Blues for Mr. Charlie (C: Wrena Ford; L: Bobby Sharp)

Cast: Joe Don Baker; Pat Corley; Al Freeman Jr.; Pat Hingle; Rosetta Le Noire; Patricia Quinn; Diana Sands; Rip Torn; Ralph Waite; Ann Wedgeworth

478 • BLUES IN THE NIGHT

OPENED: 06/02/1982   Theatre: Rialto
Musical   Broadway: 53

Librettist: Sheldon Epps
Producer: Fred R. Krones; M2 Entertainment Inc; Mitchell Maxwell; Alan J. Schuster
Director: Sheldon Epps

Costumes: David Murin; **Lighting Designer:** Ken Billington; **Musical Director:** Chapman Roberts; **Orchestrations:** Sy Johnson; **Set Design:** John Falabella; **Vocal Arranger:** Chapman Roberts

Songs: Am I Blue (C: Harry Akst; L: Grant Clarke); Baby Doll (C/L: Bessie Smith); Blues Blues (C/L: Bessie Smith); Blues in the Night [1] (C: Harold Arlen; L: Johnny Mercer); Copenhagen (C/L: Charlie Darvis; Walter Melrose); Dirty No Gooder Blues (C/L: Bessie Smith); Four Walls (and One Dirty Window) Blues (C/L: Willard Robison); I Gotta Right to Sing the Blues (C: Harold Arlen; L: Ted Koehler); It Makes My Love Come Down (C/L: Bessie Smith); I've Got a Date with a Dream (C: Harry Revel; L: Mack Gordon); Kitchen Man (C: Alex Bellenda; L: Andy Razaf); Lover Man (C/L: Jimmy Davis; Roger Ramirez; Jimmy Sherman); Low (C/L: Milton Drake; Vernon Duke; Ben Oakland); New Orleans Hop-Scop Blues (C/L: George W. Thomas); Nobody Knows You When You're Down and Out (C/L: Jimmy Cox); Reckless Blues (C/L: Bessie Smith); Rough and Ready Man (C/L: Alberta Hunter); Take It Right Back (C/L: H. Grey); Take Me for a Buggy Ride (C/L: Leola Wilson; Wesley Wilson); These Foolish Things Remind Me of You (C/L: Harry Link; Holt Marvell; Jack Strachey); Wasted Life Blues (C/L: Bessie Smith); When a Woman Loves a Man (C: Bernard Hanighen; Gordon Jenkins; L: Johnny Mercer); Wild Women Don't Have the Blues (C/L: Ida Cox); Willow Weep for Me (C/L: Ann Ronell)

Cast: Charles Coleman; Jean Du Shon; Debbie Shapiro; Leslie Uggams

Notes: No songs written for this show. [1] From the film BLUES IN THE NIGHT.

479 • BLUES OPERA

Notes: *See FREE AND EASY.*

480 • BLUSHING BRIDE, THE
OPENED: 02/06/1922　Theatre: Astor
Musical　　　　　　　Broadway: 144

Composer: Sigmund Romberg
Lyricist: Cyrus Wood
Librettist: Cyrus Wood
Producer: J.J. Shubert; Lee Shubert

Songs: Bad Little Boy and Good Little Girl; Blushing Bride, The; Cazzaza; Different Days; Good Bye; I'll Bet on Anything but Girls; Just a Regular Girl; Love's Highway; Mr. and Mrs. Patter; Rosy, Posy; Silver Wedding, The; Springtime Is the Time for Loving; That's the Way It Goes; The Tick, Tick, Tick of the Ticker

Cast: Cecil Lean; Cleo Mayfield

481 • BOARDWARK, THE
OPENED: 1922

Composer: J. Russel Robinson
Lyricist: Roy Turk

Songs: Boardwalk Blues; Broadway Strut, The; If You Don't Think So You're Crazy

Notes: No other information available.

482 • BOCCACCIO
OPENED: 11/24/1975　Theatre: Edison
Musical　　　　　　　Broadway: 7

Composer: Richard Peaslee
Lyricist: Kenneth Cavander
Librettist: Kenneth Cavander
Producer: Rita Fredericks; Norman Kean; Theatre Now
Director: Warren Enters

Source: DECAMERON, THE (Story: Giovanni Boccaccio); **Choreographer:** Julie Arenal; **Costumes:** Linda Fisher; **Dance Arranger:** Walt Levinsky; **Lighting Designer:** Patrika Brown; **Musical Director:** Ken Bichel; **Orchestrations:** Walt Levinsky; Richard Peaslee; **Set Design:** Robert U. Taylor; **Vocal Arranger:** Walt Levinsky; Richard Peaslee

Songs: Apples in the Garden; Beatrice [1]; Best of Times, The; Egano D'Galluzzi; Game I Lost, A; God Is Good; Hold Me Gently; If You Had Seen; Let Your Body Have Its Way; Love Her Like a Blind Man; Love Was Just a Game; Lucky Anichino; Madonna Isabella; Masetto's Song; Men Who Have Loved Me, The; My Holy Prayer; Now My Season's Here; Nuns Song; Only in My Song; Pretend You're Living; Put the Devil in Hell; She Doctor; Time to Go

Cast: Armand Assante; D'Jamin Bartlett; Jill Choder; Munson Hicks; Caroline McWilliams; Virginia Vestoff; Michael Zaslow

Notes: [1] Cut prior to opening.

483 • BODY BEAUTIFUL, THE
OPENED: 01/23/1958　Theatre: Plymouth
Musical　　　　　　　Broadway: 60

Composer: Jerry Bock
Lyricist: Sheldon Harnick
Librettist: Will Glickman; Joseph Stein
Producer: Richard Kollmar; Albert Selden
Director: George Schaefer

Choreographer: Herbert Ross; **Costumes:** Noel Taylor; **Dance Arranger:** Genevieve Pitot; **Lighting Designer:** Jean Eckart; William Eckart; **Musical Director:** Milton Greene; **Orchestrations:** Ted Royal; **Set Design:** Jean Eckart; William Eckart; **Vocal Arranger:** Milton Green

Songs: All of These and More; Art of Conversation, The; Blonde Blues; Body Beautiful, The; Every Man for Himself [1]; Fair Warning; Gloria; He's Our Boy [1]; Hidden in My Heart [1]; Honeymoon Is Over, The; Just My Luck; Leave Well Enough Alone; Manly Art or Self Defense, The [1]; Mother Come and Fight with Me [1]; Nobility; Ooh, Merci Beaucoup [1]; Pffft!; Relatively Simple Affair, A; Summer Is; Uh-huh, Oh, Yeah!; Where Are They?

Cast: Mindy Carson; Steve Forrest; Mary Louise; Mara Lynn; Barbara McNair; Brock Peters; Jane Romano; Joe Ross; Lonnie Sattin; Jack Warden

Notes: [1] Cut prior to opening.

484 • BODY SHOP
OPENED: 1995　　　　Theatre: Westbeth
Musical　　　　　　　Off-Off-Broadway

Composer: Walter Marks
Lyricist: Walter Marks
Librettist: Walter Marks
Director: Sue Lawless

Choreographer: Tony Stevens; **Costumes:** Franne Lee; **Dance Arranger:** Deborah Hurwitz; **Lighting Designer:** Don Coleman; **Musical Director:** Deborah Hurwitz; **Orchestrations:** Deborah Hurwitz; **Set Design:** Tim Goodmanson

Songs: Angeline; Class Act; Desire; Doris' Nightmare; Find a Way; Matter of Time, A; Maybe It's Not Too Late; Mr. Maybe; My Turn; Suffer; Virtual Sexuality; Woman in Me, The; You Like Me

Cast: Donna Drake; Susan Flynn; Beth Glover; Russell Goldberg; Marine Jahan; Jodi Stevens; Pasean Wilson

Notes: "The Stripsational New Musical."

485 • BOJANGLES (1976)

OPENED: 1976
Musical   Closed out of town

Composer: Bruce Schwartz
Lyricist: Norman Mitgang

Songs: Bo's Theme (inst.) (C: Bill Brohn); Poor Johnny Brown; Vaudeville

486 • BOJANGLES (1980)

OPENED: 1980
Musical   Closed out of town

Composer: Charles Strouse
Lyricist: Sammy Cahn
Librettist: Norman Mitgang

Songs: Bojangles; (I Always Wanted to Be a) Dancin' Man; Follow the Way of the Lord; (All I Need Is a) Handshake; Hey, Boy!; Hey, Granny [1]; I Need Music; (Soon You'll See Me) In the Movies; It Hasn't Got a Chance; Makin' It (Seeing a Chance and Taking It); (There's) No Greater Sound (Than Da, Da, Da, Da)   ; Nobody Else But You; Sweetheart of the Nation [1]; (Tell Me) What Does He See in Me?

Notes: Later Doug Jones took over the libretto. [1] Cut.

487 • BOMBO

OPENED: 10/06/1921   Theatre: Jolson's 59th
                                          Street
Revue   Broadway: 218

Composer: Sigmund Romberg
Lyricist: Harold Atteridge
Librettist: Harold Atteridge
Producer: J.J. Shubert; Lee Shubert
Director: J.C. Huffman

Choreographer: Allan K. Foster; **Musical Director:** Alfred Goodman; **Set Design:** Watson Barratt

Songs: Ain't Love Grand [8] (C: Walter Donaldson; L: Con Conrad; B.G. DeSylva); Any Place Will Do with You [1]; April Showers [2] (C: Louis Silvers; L: B.G. DeSylva); Arcady (C/L: B.G. DeSylva; Al Jolson); Avalon (C: Vincent Rose; L: B.G. DeSylva; Al Jolson); Bebe [4] (C: Abner Silver; L: Sam Coslow); Bombo (C/L: B.G. DeSylva; Al Jolson); Bundle of Love, A [4] (C/L: B.G. DeSylva; Al Jolson); Bylo Bay, The; California Here I Come (C: Joseph Meyer; L: B.G. DeSylva; Al Jolson); Carolina Mammy (C/L: Billy Janus); Coo-Coo Song (C/L: B.G. DeSylva; Al Jolson); Daffodil, The; Dirty Hands, Dirty Face [10] (C: James V. Monaco; L: Grant Clarke; Edgar Leslie); Don't Cry Swanee [2] (C/L: Con Conrad; B.G. DeSylva; Al Jolson); Don't Send Your Wife to the Country (Keep Her Home and Love Her Yourself) (C: Con Conrad; L: Harold Atteridge; B.G. DeSylva); Down South (C: Walter Donaldson; L: B.G. DeSylva); Ginny Ginny Shore [1]; Girl Has a Sailor in Every Port, A; Give Me My Mammy (C: Walter Donaldson; L: B.G. DeSylva); Glide DeLuxe; Globe Trot, The; Horse Trot, The; How'd You Like to Be a Kid? (C: Jimmy McHugh; L: Bennett Sisters; Billy Colligan); I Call You Sunshine [8] (C: Louis Silvers; L: Irving Caesar; B.G. DeSylva); I'm Glad I'm Spanish; I'm Goin' South (C/L: Abner Silver; Harry Woods); In a Curio Shop [2]; In Old Granada [11]; In the Way Off There [4]; It's You (C: Con Conrad; L: Benny Davis); Jazza-Da- Dadda (Jazzadadadoo); Jimmy Valentine and Sherlock Holmes [1]; Kee-Kee-Koo (C: Nacio Herb Brown; L: King Zany); Last Dance, That's Out, The; Let the Little Joy Bells Ring [5] (C/L: Cliff Friend); Life Is a Gamble; Morning Will Come [2] (C/L: Con Conrad; B.G. DeSylva; Al Jolson); 'Neath Italian Skies; Nita [3]; No One Loves a Clown; Oh Boy! What Joy We Had in Barefoot Days [3] (C/L: James A. Brennan; Al Wilson); Oh, How She Can Dance (C/L: Cliff Friend); Oh, Oh Columbus; Old Fashioned Girl

(C/L: Al Jolson); Paradise Alley [6]; Rose of Spain; Sitting in a Corner [3]; Sleepy Village; Some Beautiful Morning I'll Find You in My Arms (C/L: Cliff Friend; Al Jolson); Swanee Rose [8] (C: George Gershwin; L: Irving Caesar; B.G. DeSylva); Sweet One; Tallahassee (C: C. Luckeyth Roberts; L: B.G. DeSylva); Tell Me with Smiles [9] (C/L: Cliff Friend; Walter Hirsch); That Barber in Seville [2] (C: Con Conrad); Three Little Vampires [3]; Through the Mist; Toot, Toot, Tootsie (Goodbye) (C/L: Ernie Erdman; Dan Russo; C: Gus Kahn; L: Ted Fiorito); Very Next Girl I See, The; Wait Until My Ship Comes In; Wetona; Who Cares? (C: Milton Ager; L: Jack Yellen); Yoo-Hoo (C: Al Jolson; L: B.G. DeSylva); You're in Kentucky [7]

Cast: Janet Adair; Forrest Huff; Al Jolson

Notes: Returned to Broadway 5/14/23 for 32 performances. Songs not by Romberg were interpolated by Jolson during run and tour. [1] Out Atlantic City 9/28/21. [2] Not in program. [3] Out 12/9/23. [4] Sheet music only. [5] Added during tour. [6] Out Washington, D.C. 4/8/23. [7] Out Oakland 5/18. [8] ASCAP/Library of Congress only. [9] ASCAP/Library of Congress only. Written in 1923 so might have been in tour after Broadway. [10] Jolson added his name as colyricist though probably did not contribute. [11] Published with Jolson's name added to Romberg's as cocomposer and with Romberg alone.

488 • BOMBOLLA

Notes: *See BAMBOOLA (1929).*

489 • BON BON BUDDY, JR.

OPENED: 1922
Musical

Composer: Maceo Pinkard
Librettist: Irvin C. Miller
Producer: Irvin C. Miller
Director: B. Eugene Field; Irvin C. Miller

Songs: Bandana Girls; Bon Bon Buddy, Jr.; Bound Me in My Mammy's Arms; Creole Girls from the Follies; Dance; Day Bert Williams Said Goodbye, The; Dixie Girls; Dog, The; For a Girl Like You; Forget All Your Troubles (and Smile); Give Me Plenty; Just Another Barber Shop Chord; Liza; Love Me (While Loving is Good); My Old Man;

Raggedy Blues; Struttin' Town; Ticklin' Tune; Walk You Baby Doll; Who's Tendin' the Fireman's Fire

Cast: Lydia Brown; William DuMont; Irvin C. Miller; Gertrude Saunders; George Wright

Notes: No other information available.

490 • BONANZA BOUND

OPENED: 12/26/1947
Musical   Closed out of town

Composer: Saul Chaplin
Lyricist: Betty Comden; Adolph Green
Librettist: Betty Comden; Adolph Green
Producer: Paul Feigay; Herman Levin; Oliver Smith
Director: Charles Sherman

Songs: Bonanza; Cruikshank March; Dance in the Snow; Dreams Come True; Fill 'Er Up; Inspiration; Little Fish; Misunderstood; No Man of Your Own; Spring; Summer in the Snow; Tell Me Why; This Was Meant to Be; Totem Dance; Up in Smoke; Vein of Gold, The; Versatile DaVincis, The; Wind (dance)

Cast: George Coulouris; Adolph Green; Hal Hackett; Allyn Ann McLerie; Carol Raye; Gwen Verdon

Notes: Closed in Philadelphia.

491 • BONE ROOM, THE

OPENED: 02/28/1975   Theatre: Portfolio
Revue   Off-Off-Broadway: 12

Composer: Harvey Schmidt
Lyricist: Tom Jones
Producer: Drew Katzman; John Schak
Director: John Schak

Choreographer: Janet Kerr; **Costumes:** Charles Blackburn; **Musical Director:** Ken Collins

Songs: Isn't That a Wonderful Way to Die? [1]

Cast: John Cunningham; Ray Stewart; Susan Watson

Notes: A workshop. [1] Later in PORTFOLIO REVUE.

492 • BONITA
Notes: *See THE LOVE CALL.*

493 • BONJOUR PARIS
Musical   Closed out of town

Songs: Love's Own Flower

Notes: No other information available.

494 • BOOK OF THE NIGHT
OPENED: 06/24/1991   Theatre: Goodman
Musical   Chicago

Composer: Thom Bishop; Louis Rosen
Lyricist: Thom Bishop; Louis Rosen
Librettist: Thom Bishop; Louis Rosen
Producer: Goodman Theatre
Director: Robert Falls

Choreographer: Marcia Milgrom Dodge;
Costumes: Gabriel Berry; **Lighting Designer:**
James F. Ingalls; **Musical Director:** Mark
Mitchell; **Set Design:** Michael Philipi

Songs: Alone Tonight; Changing Channels;
Closing: The Dark Before the Dawn; Covered
By the Night; Dreams; Empty Arms Hotel, The;
Half the Bed; In the Morning; Interlude:
Rhythms of a Summer Night; Just Say Yes;
Kill the Beast; Lullabye; Midnight Bar and Grill,
The; Never Is Now; North of the Border; Peace
Is in the Night; Rhythms of a Summer Night;
Saturday Night; Saturday Night's Our Night
to Be Alone; See You in the Dark; Seventeen on
Mars; Someone Else's Dream; Straight Soda
with a Lemon Twist; Things That Go Bump in
the Night; Two Wishes; Watching Her Sleep;
Where It Goes When It's Gone; Who's This
Stranger; Women in Their Summer Dresses;
You All Remember Jack

Cast: Keith Byron-Kirk; Vicki Lewis; Hollis Resnik;
David Studwell

495 • BOOM-BOOM
OPENED: 01/28/1929   Theatre: Casino
Musical   Broadway: 72

Composer: Werner Janssen
Lyricist: J. Keirn Brennan; Mann Holiner
Librettist: Fanny Todd Mitchell

Producer: Messrs. Shubert
Director: George Marion

Source: MLLE. MA MERE (Play: Louis Verneuil);
Choreographer: John Boyle; **Set Design:** Watson
Barratt

Songs: Be That Way; Best I Ever Get Is the Worst
of It, The [1]; Blow the Blues Away; Consoler of
Women [1]; He's Just My Ideal; I Wish I Were
Back in My Cradle [1]; Just a Big-Hearted Man;
Messin' Round; Nina; Oh How He Plays His
Ukulele [1]; On Top; Pick 'Em Up and Lay 'Em
Down; Psychological Moment [1]; Shake High,
Shake Low; We're Going to Make Boom-Boom;
What a Girl!; What Could I Do?

Cast: Jeanette MacDonald; Frank McIntyre; Stanley
Riggs

Notes: [1] Out Newark 1/21/29.

496 • BOOTH IS BACK IN TOWN
OPENED: 07/07/1983
Musical   Closed out of town

Composer: Arthur B. Rubenstein
Lyricist: Gretchen Cryer
Librettist: Austin Pendleton
Producer: PepsiCo Summerfare
Director: Word Baker

Choreographer: Louis Johnson; **Costumes:** Jeanne
Button; **Lighting Designer:** John McLain;
Musical Director: Joel Rainey; **Orchestrations:**
William D. Brohn; **Set Design:** Santo Loquasto

Songs: After the Rain; And a Little Child Shall Lead
Them to the Promised Land; Arcadia; Banjo,
Banjo; Bashful Bill; Baxter & Company; Booth! Is
Back in Town; California (Follow the Setting
Sun); California Cousins; Day I Left Her Last,
The; Don't Let the World Go By; 1845; Eye of the
Storm; Goodbye, Once Again; He'll Follow in His
Father's Footsteps; Late Bloomers; Life Begins
Today; Morning Will Break; Movin' On; No More
to Roam; Old King Lear; Old Men Should Say
Goodbye; On the Road Together; Player, The;
Shower of Stars, A; Sing a New Song; Sing to
Andy Jackson; Slipping By; Somewhere Between
a Laugh and a Cry; Stay and Rest Awhile in
California; We Gotta Have More; Welcome to the
Fold; When You're Home Again; Will You Marry
Me; You Gotta Have Light Entertainment; You
Will Never Be at Home

Cast: Leigh Beery; Philip Casnoff; Charles Cioffi; Grace Keagy; David Sabin; Swen Swenson

497 • BORN HAPPY
OPENED: 1943
Revue   Los Angeles

Producer: Sid Grauman

Choreographer: Addison Cary; **Orchestrations:** Lou Katzman; Charles Koff

Songs: Born Happy (C: Lew Pollack; L: Charles Newman); Chee Chee Girl, The; Delightful, Delicious, Delovely [1]; I Can't Do Without Love (C/L: Duke Mofletti); Is There a Latin in the House? (C: Lew Pollack; L: Charles Newman); Smoke Gets in Your Eyes (C: Jerome Kern; L: Otto Harbach); You Can't Hear a Pin Drop (C: Lew Pollack; L: Charles Newman)

Cast: Delta Rhythm Boys; John Mason; Velma Middleton; Bill Robinson; Mabel Scott; Emmett "Babe" Wallace; Whitey's Jitterbugs

Notes: No other information available. [1] Possibly "It's Delovely" by Cole Porter.

498 • BORN TO SWING
Revue   Closed out of town

Composer: Donald Heywood
Lyricist: Andy Razaf
Librettist: Eubie Blake; Andy Razaf
Producer: Irvin C. Miller

Choreographer: Addison Carey

Songs: Born to Swing; Buy a Bond for Baby; Isle of Zanzibar; Nicol in the Picolo; Rector Rhythm; Send Me a Man; Star Spangled Susan Brown (C: Irene Higginbotham); Sunday Dress

Cast: Eddie Rector; Margaret Simms

Notes: Presented in the 40's at the Lincoln Theatre, Philadelphia. No other information available.

499 • BORROWERS, THE
OPENED: 12/14/1973   Theatre: NBC
TV Musical

Composer: Rod McKuen
Lyricist: Rod McKuen

Librettist: Jay Presson Allen
Producer: Walt DeFaria; Warren L. Lockhart
Director: Walter C. Miller

Source: BORROWERS, THE (Novel: Mary Norton);
Musical Director: Bill Byers

Songs: Aunt Sophie (inst.); Borrowers, The (inst.); Come Dancing, John (inst.); Isn't It Something; Keep Running (inst.); Now You See Him, Now You Don't (inst.); Nursery, The (inst.); Off on the Great Adventure (inst.); Quiet, Pod's Thinking (inst.); This Is Our House; World Outside, The (inst.)

Cast: Eddie Albert; Judith Anderson; Shelby Flint; Tammy Grimes; Barnard Hughes; Dennis Larson; Rod McKuen; Beatrice Straight

500 • BOTTOMLAND
OPENED: 06/27/1927   Theatre: Princess
Musical   Broadway: 21

Composer: Clarence Williams
Librettist: Clarence Williams
Producer: Clarence Williams

Songs: Any Time (L: Joe Jordan); Bottomland (L: Jo Trent); Come On Home (C/L: Donald Heywood); Dancing Girl (L: Spencer Williams); Shootin' the Pistol (L: Chris Smith); Steamboat Days (L: Clarence Williams); When I March with April in May (L: Spencer Williams); You're the Only One (L: Len Gray)

Cast: Louis Cole; Craddock & Shandney; Katherine Henderson; Slim Henderson; James A. Lilliard; Sara Martin; Eva Taylor; Clarence Williams

501 • BOUFFES VARIETIES
Revue   Closed out of town

Songs: When Broadway Was a Pasture (C: Al Piantadosi; L: Joseph McCarthy)

Cast: Valeska Suratt

Notes: No other information available. From sheet music.

502 • BOW SING
Notes: *See LA BELLE PAREE.*

503 • BOW-WOWS

OPENED: 10/12/1927   Theatre: Prince of Wales
Revue   London: 124

Producer: Laddie Cliff
Director: Laddie Cliff

Songs: For Goodness' Sake (C: Vernon Duke; L: James Dyrenforth)

Cast: Elsie Gregory; Georges Metaxa

Notes: No program available.

504 • BOX OF TRICKS

OPENED: 07/13/1931
Revue   Closed out of town

Composer: George Jessel
Lyricist: George Jessel
Librettist: George Jessel

Costumes: George Jessel; **Set Design:** George Jessel

Cast: George Jessel

Notes: New Brighton Theatre, Brooklyn. No other information available.

505 • BOX PARTY

OPENED: 1923
Musical   Closed out of town

Songs: Just a Little Love Song (Mais le Son de Ta Voix) (C: Joe Cooper; L: Sam M. Lewis; Joe Young)

Notes: From sheet music. No other information available.

506 • BOY AND THE GIRL, THE

OPENED: 05/31/1909   Theatre: Aerial
                                          Gardens
Musical   Broadway: 24

Composer: Richard Carle; H.L. Heartz
Lyricist: Richard Carle; M.E. Rourke
Librettist: Richard Carle; M.E. Rourke

Choreographer: Gus Sohlke

Songs: I'm in a Position to Know; In Yucatan; Katie Come and Kiss Me; Poor Working Girl ; Seductive; Y-La

Cast: Barney Bernard; Marie Dressler

Notes: No program available.

507 • BOY FRIEND, THE

OPENED: 09/30/1954   Theatre: Royale
Musical   Broadway: 485

Composer: Sandy Wilson
Lyricist: Sandy Wilson
Librettist: Sandy Wilson
Producer: Cy Feuer; Ernest Martin
Director: Vida Hope

Choreographer: John Heawood; Conductor: Paul McGrane; **Costumes:** Robert Mackintosh; Reginald Wooley; **Lighting Designer:** Feder; **Musical Director:** Anton Coppola; **Orchestrations:** Charles L. Cooke; Ted Royal; **Set Design:** Feder

Songs: Boy Friend, The; Carnival Tango; Fancy Forgetting; I Could Be Happy with You; It's Never Too Late to Fall in Love; It's Nicer in Nice [2]; Perfect Young Ladies; Poor Little Pierette; Riviera, The (2); Riviera, The (1) [1]; Room in Bloomsbury, A; Safety in Numbers; Sur La Plage; Won't You Charleston with Me?; You-Don't-Want-To-Play-With-Me Blues

Cast: Ruth Altman; Julie Andrews; Eric Berry; John Herver; Geoffrey Hibbert; Dilys Lay; Moyna MacGill; Millicent Martin; Bob Scheerer; Ann Wakefield

Notes: [1] Cut. [2] Not in original Broadway production. In London prior to Broadway. Also in revival of 1970 which starred Judy Carne.

508 • BOY MEETS BOY

OPENED: 09/17/1975   Theatre: Actors'
                                          Playhouse
Musical   Off-Broadway: 463

Composer: Bill Solly
Lyricist: Bill Solly
Librettist: Bill Solly; Donald Ward
Producer: Edith O'Hara
Director: Ron Troutman

Lighting Designer: David Sackeroff; **Musical Director:** David Friedman; **Set Design:** David Sackeroff; **Vocal Arranger:** David Friedman

Songs: Boy Meets Boy; Clarence's Turn; Does Anybody Love You?; English Rose, The; Giving It Up for Love; It's a Boy's Life; It's a Dolly; Just My Luck; Let's; Marry an American; Me; Party in Room 203; What Do I Care?; You're Beautiful

Cast: Joe Barrett; Bobby Bowers; David Gallegly; Rita Gordon; Bobby Reed

509 • BOY WANTED, A
OPENED: 01/18/1897   Theatre: Star
Musical   Broadway: 16

Composer: Harry James
Librettist: Charles E. Blaney

Choreographer: Lillie Sutherland

Songs: Girl with the Naughty Wink, The; Handicap, The; Hot Tamale Alley; Ideal Girls, The; I'm the Boy; Julienne; Modern Century Girls, The; My Polly Is a Peach; Oriental March; Same Thing Over Again, The; Sweet Little Rosey Posey; Up-to-Date Policeman, The

Cast: Harry Clay Blaney; Claude Gillingwater; Nellie O'Neil; Knox G. Wilson

510 • BOY WITH THE BOODLE, THE
OPENED: 09/16/1907
Musical   Closed out of town

Composer: Antone
Lyricist: Howard Hall

Cast: Louise Horner; Joseph Weber

Notes: No program available.

511 • BOYS AND BETTY, THE
OPENED: 11/02/1908   Theatre: Wallack
Musical   Broadway: 112

Composer: Silvio Hein
Lyricist: George V. Hobart
Librettist: George V. Hobart
Producer: Daniel V. Arthur
Director: George Marion

Source LA PAPILION (Play: Robert Danceny; Rene Peter); **Musical Director:** Silvio Hein

Songs: At the Folies Bergere; Auf Wiedersehen; Gee! But You Look Awful Good to Me (L: Will D. Cobb); Girls! Girls! Girls!; I Love to Go Shopping; I Want to Go to Paris; Just the Same Old Situation [1]; Little Further, A; Marie Cahill's Arab Love Song; Opening Act I; Opening Act II; She Was a Dear Girl (C: Ted Snyder; L: Irving Berlin); Take Plenty of Shoes (C: Melville Gideon; L: Will D. Cobb); Tetrazzini Family, The; That's the Doctor Bill [1] (L: Henry S. Creamer); Whoop Her Up with a Whoop-La-La! (C/L: Will Marion Cook)

Cast: Edgar Atchinson-Ely; Marie Cahill; Eugene Cowles; Edgar Norton; Clara Palmer

Notes: [1] Sheet music only.

512 • BOYS AND GIRLS TOGETHER
OPENED: 10/01/1940   Theatre: Broadhurst
Revue   Broadway: 191

Composer: Sammy Fain
Lyricist: Irving Kahal; Jack Yellen
Librettist: Pat C. Flick; Ed Wynn
Producer: Ed Wynn
Director: Ed Wynn

Choreographer: Albertina Rasch; **Costumes:** Irene Sharaff; **Musical Director:** John McManus; **Orchestrations:** Robert Russell Bennett; Hans Spialek; Don Walker; **Set Design:** William Oden-Waller

Songs: I Want to Live (As Long As You Love Me) (L: Jack Yellen); Jitterbugging with the Young Folks [1] (L: Unknown); Latin in Me, The (L: Jack Yellen); Leading Girl, The (L: Jack Yellen); Liable to Catch On (L: Unknown); Such Stuff as Dreams Are Made Of (L: Irving Kahal); Sun'll Be Up in the Morning, The (L: Jack Yellen); Tchaikowsky [1] (L: Unknown); Times Square Dance (L: Jack Yellen); You Can't Put Catsup on the Moon (L: Irving Kahal)

Cast: Diane Apollon; Walter Long; Iris Marshall; Dell Parker; Kay Paulson; Ed Wynn

Notes: [1] Out Boston.

513 • BOYS FROM HOME, THE

OPENED: 1913
Musical   Closed out of town

Composer: Leon Berg
Lyricist: Albert Bagley
Librettist: Thomas Railey
Director: Dan Doty

Songs: Beautiful Isle of Love; Finale (C: Will Vodery; L: Henry Creamer); Ghost of the Violin [1]; Girls, Girls, Girls; He Was a Sailor; I Am a Pirate; I'd Rather Paint Than Fight; Opening (C: Will Vodery; L: Henry Creamer); Some Girls Pick Their Sweethearts from the Infantry; Tease, Tease, Tease; That Girl of Mine; We've Had a Lovely Time, So Long, Good-Bye

Cast: George Stone

Notes: Burlesque musical. [1] The popular song of the same name by Ted Snyder and Bert Kalmar was written in 1912.

514 • BOYS FROM SYRACUSE, THE

OPENED: 11/23/1938   Theatre: Alvin
Musical   Broadway: 235

Composer: Richard Rodgers
Lyricist: Lorenz Hart
Librettist: George Abbott
Producer: George Abbott
Director: George Abbott

Source COMEDY OF ERRORS, THE (Play: William Shakespeare); **Source:** MENAECHMI (Play: Plautus); **Choreographer:** George Balanchine; **Costumes:** Irene Sharaff; **Lighting Designer:** Jo Mielziner; **Musical Director:** Harry Levant; **Orchestrations:** Hans Spialek; **Set Design:** Jo Mielziner

Songs: Big Brother; Come with Me; Dear Old Syracuse; Falling in Love with Love; He and She; I Had Twins (He Had Twins); Ladies of the Evening; Let Antipholus In; Oh, Diogenes; Shortest Day of the Year, The; Sing for Your Supper; This Can't Be Love; What Can You Do with a Man?; You Have Cast Your Shadow on the Sea

Cast: Eddie Albert; Muriel Angelus; Carroll Ashburn; Ronald Graham; Teddy Hart; Burl

Ives; Wynn Murray; Jimmy Savo; Marcy Wescott

Notes: Ronald Graham (1913-1950) should not be confused with Ronny Graham, the comedian of New Faces of 1952, etc.

515 • BOYS OF COMPANY 'B', THE

OPENED: 04/08/1907   Theatre: Lyceum
Play   Broadway: 96

Author: Rida Johnson Young
Producer: Daniel Frohman
Director: Arnold Daly

Songs: Eileen (C/L: Percival Moore); Give Me a Good Cigar (C: Edward Laska; L: Kelly); So Long, So Long (No More Sunshine, Nothing but Rain) (C/L: Sadie Clarke)

Cast: John Barrymore; Arnold Daly; Paul Gilmore; Mack Sennett

Notes: No other information available. Songs also by Sadie Clark and Percival T. Moore.

516 • BOYS OF KILKENNY, THE

OPENED: 03/15/1897   Theatre: Star
Play   Broadway: 8

Composer: Joseph Healy; Charles Sullivan
Lyricist: Joseph Healy; Charles Sullivan
Librettist: Townsend Walsh
Author: Townsend Walsh
Director: William McGonigal

Set Design: Townsend Walsh

Songs: Dad's Old Violin [1]; Fly Song [1] (C/L: Chauncey Olcott); My Own Dear Sue; Only a Tear (C/L: George F. Braham; Edward Harrigan); Pretty Little Rose, A (C/L: Joseph Healy); Real Old Mountain Dew, The; Vagrants of Erin, The

Cast: Tessie Deagle; Joseph H. Hewaley; Charles Sullivan; Townsend Walsh

Notes: Healey and Sullivan probably did not collaborate. [1] Added out of town.

517 • BOYS WILL BE BOYS

OPENED: 1917
Musical   Closed out of town

Composer: Oscar Straus
Lyricist: Edward Paulton; Ferdinand Stolberg
Librettist: Edward Paulton; Ferdinand Stolberg

Source MEIN JUNGER HERR (Musical: Oscar Straus)

Notes: Wilmington, Del. No other information available.

518 • BRAINCHILD

OPENED: 03/25/1974
Musical   Closed out of town

Composer: Michel Legrand
Lyricist: Hal David
Librettist: Maxine Klein
Producer: Adela Holzer
Director: Maxine Klein

Choreographer: Leigh Abdallah; **Costumes:** Joseph G. Aulisi; **Lighting Designer:** Thomas Skelton; **Musical Director:** Thomas Pierson; **Orchestrations:** Michel Legrand; **Set Design:** Kert Lundell

Songs: But You Do It; Don't Pull Up the Flowers; Don't Talk, Don't Think; Easy Does It; Everything that Happens to You; First Time I Heard a Bluebird, The; I Know You Are There; I Never Met a Russian I Didn't Like; I'm Tired of Me; I've Been Starting Tomorrow; Just a Little Space Can Be a Growing Place; Let Me Be Your Mirror; Let Me Think for You; Low Bottom Woman; Many People Live Inside My Mind; No Faceless People; Sally Ensalada; What Is It?

Cast: Nancy Ann Denning; Tovah Feldshuh; Dorian Harewood; Ben Harney; Louise Hoven; Signa Joy; Gene Lindsey; Barbara Niles; Marilyn Pasekoff; Mark Siegel

Notes: Closed in Philadelphia 4/16/74.

519 • BRAVO GIOVANNI

OPENED: 05/19/1962   Theatre: Broadhurst
Musical   Broadway: 76

Composer: Milton Schafer
Lyricist: Ronny Graham

Librettist: A.J. Russell
Producer: Philip Rose
Director: Stanley Prager

Source CRIME OF GIOVANNI VENTURI, THE (Novel: Howard Shaw); **Choreographer:** Carol Haney; **Costumes:** Ed Wittstein; **Dance Arranger:** Luther Henderson; **Lighting Designer:** Robert Randolph; **Musical Director:** Anton Coppola; **Orchestrations:** Robert Ginzler; **Set Design:** Robert Randolph; **Vocal Arranger:** Anton Coppola

Songs: Ah! Camminare; Argument, The; Baloon, Baloona [1]; Beside a Bridge (Along the River Tiber) [1]; Bravo, Giovanni; Breachy's Law; Give All Your Love Away [1]; Here I Am [1]; If I Were the Man; I'm All I've Got; It's Love [1]; Jump In! (Connubiality); Kangaroo, The; Miranda; One Little World Apart; Rome; Signora Pandolfi; Steady, Steady; Time (Love Must Have Time) [1]; Uriti; Uriti Kitchen (dance); Virtue, Arrivederci; We Won't Discuss It

Cast: Rico Froehlich; George S. Irving; Maria Karnilova; Michele Lee; Lu Leonard; Buzz Miller; David Opatoshu; Cesare Siepi; Gene Varrone

Notes: [1] Cut prior to Broadway opening.

520 • BREAK IT UP

OPENED: 1950
Musical   Closed out of town

Composer: Mel Torme; Robert Wells
Lyricist: Mel Torme; Robert Wells
Librettist: Charles K. Peck Jr.
Producer: A.L. Jones
Director: William Eythe

Choreographer: Rod Alexander; **Orchestrations:** Jimmy Leyden; **Set Design:** Danny Johnson; **Vocal Arranger:** Jimmy Leyden

Songs: Back to American Furniture; Beauty, the Brawn and the Brain, The; Drinking Song; Flattery Will Get You Everywhere (C: David Saxon; L: Nancy Andrews); I Wouldn't Have It Any Other Way; Love You That Is; Mr. and Mrs. Ordinary People; Once in a Lifetime; One Finger, Keep Moving; That Kind of Guy; There's Another Auction Today; They'll Do It Everytime; We Owe Our Life to Duncan Phyfe; Why Must the Show Go On; You Rule the Kingdom of My Heart

Cast: Nancy Andrews; David Burns

521 • BREAKFAST AT TIFFANY'S

OPENED: 12/14/1966   Theatre: Majestic
Musical   Broadway

Composer: Bob Merrill
Lyricist: Bob Merrill
Librettist: Edward Albee
Producer: David Merrick
Director: Joseph Anthony

Source BREAKFAST AT TIFFANY'S (Novel: Truman Capote); **Choreographer:** Michael Kidd; **Costumes:** Freddy Wittop; **Dance Arranger:** Marvin Laird; **Lighting Designer:** Tharon Musser; **Musical Director:** Stanley Lebowsky; **Orchestrations:** Ralph Burns; **Set Design:** Oliver Smith; **Vocal Arranger:** Stanley Lebowsky

Songs: Bachelor, The [1]; Bessie's Blues [1]; Better Together; Breakfast at Tiffany's; Ciao, Compare; Freddy Chant; Grade 'A' Treatment; Holly Golightly; Holly Gollucci [1]; Home for Wayward Girls; I'm Not the Girl; I've Got a Penny [1]; Lament for Ten Men; Lulamae; My Nice Ways [1]; Nothing Is New in New York [1]; Rose, The [1]; Same Mistakes; Scum-Dee-Dum [1]; So Here We Are Again [1]; Stay with Me; Traveling [1]; When Daddy Came Home; Who Needs Her?; You've Never Kissed Her

Cast: Richard Chamberlain; Sally Kellerman; Larry Kert; Priscilla Lopez; Art Lund; Mary Tyler Moore

Notes: Originally titled HOLLY GOLIGHTLY and adapted and directed by Abe Burrows. Opened 10/10/66 and closed 12/14/66 during previews in New York. [1] From HOLLY GOLIGHTLY version.

522 • BREAKING INTO SOCIETY

OPENED: 10/02/1905   Theatre: West End
Musical   New York

Composer: Gus Edwards
Lyricist: Robert B. Smith
Librettist: Lee Arthur; Robert B. Smith

Director: Percy G. Williams

Songs: Bashful Chappie, The; Columbia's Colleen; Daughter of the Regiment, The (C: Gus Edwards; Leo Edwards); If Women Had Their Way; I'm the Boy; Jolly Yourself Along; Marriage Game; My Senorita; Ping Pong (C: Gus Edwards; Leo Edwards); Standing Pat (C: Gus Edwards; Leo Edwards); That's What the Papers Say; Ting-a-Ling-a-Ling Ping Pong; Up and Down the Boardwalk

Cast: Clara Morton; Kate Morton; Paul Morton; Sam Morton; Ford Sterling

523 • BRIAN BORU

OPENED: 10/19/1896   Theatre: Broadway
Musical   Broadway: 88

Composer: Julian Edwards
Lyricist: Stanislaus Stange
Librettist: Stanislaus Stange
Director: John Nash

Set Design: D. Frank Dodge

Cast: Richard F. Carroll; Max Figman; John C. Slavin; Amelia Summerville

Notes: No songs listed in program.

524 • BRIC-A-BRAC

OPENED: 10/20/1937
Play

Author: Syd Porcelain
Producer: Little Theatre Playes
Director: Paul Stewart

Songs: We're Identical (C: Vic Mizzy; L: Irving Taylor)

Cast: Helen Francis; Ethel Kinkin; Miriam Peyer

Notes: An N.Y.U. varsity show. Part of three one-acts, the others being COURT OF SEX APPPEALS and THE LORD'S PRAYER.

525 • BRIDAL NOT, THE

OPENED: 1918
Musical

Composer: Charles Gilpin
Lyricist: Charles Gilpin
Librettist: Edwin M. Lavino

Songs: Be My War Bride; Gee, But It's Great to Be Free; Hm, Hm, I Love Harmony; I Am Going to Be One of the Boys; If I Had a Sweetie Like You; May the Bride to Be Live Happily; Modern Wedding Day, The; War-Time Railroad Ride, A; When They Play Your Favorite Melody; Why Don't Some Baby Pick Me; Witches and Jack O'Lanterns (inst.)

Notes: Mask and Wig Club show at the University of Pennsylvania.

526 • BRIDAL TRAP, THE
OPENED: 05/31/1886   Theatre: Bijou Opera House
Musical

Composer: Edmond Audran
Lyricist: Sydney Rosenfeld
Librettist: Sydney Rosenfeld
Director: James Scanlan

Musical Director: S. Simonson

Songs: Bridal Chorus; Duet; Duet of the Robin and the Nightingale; Exit; Finale; Finale Act II; Finale Act III; How Proud Indeed I Ought to Feel; I Seek not for Rank; Idylle; Introduction; Love's Vow; Merrily! Verily! Oh!; No! Indeed You Are Not the Wife; Now Gaily Gather for Good Cheer; Once, Fickle Boy, You Wooed Me; Pleasure of Doubt, The; Romance and Rondeau; See There the Hostess of This Place; Soldiers' Chorus; Tavern Chorus; Tear Out Your Heart; Toilet Chorus; Trio; We Have a Way of Cooking Things; We've Come for Recreation; Who Shall Be Bold When Love Arrives?

Cast: Laura Clement; Francis Gaillard; E.S. Grant; Harry Mills; Roland Reed; Paul Vernon

Notes: Information from vocal score only.

527 • BRIDE ELECT, THE
OPENED: 04/11/1898   Theatre: Knickerbocker
Musical   Broadway: 64

Composer: John Philip Sousa
Librettist: John Philip Sousa

Producer: A.L. Erlanger; Marc Klaw; B.D. Stevens

Costumes: F. Richard Anderson; **Set Design:** Ernest M. Gros; Ben Teal

Cast: Mabella Baker; Nella Bergen; Albert Hart; Frank Pollock

Notes: No program available.

528 • BRIDE OF SIROCCO, THE
OPENED: 12/31/1976
Musical

Composer: Tim Grundmann
Lyricist: Tim Grundmann
Librettist: Tim Grundmann
Producer: Harry M. Bagdasian; Ken Bloom; New Playwrights' Theatre
Director: Ken Bloom

Choreographer: Martin Buckner; **Costumes:** Mary Kay MacGregor; **Dance Arranger:** Tim Grundmann; **Lighting Designer:** William J. Turnbull Jr.; **Musical Director:** Tim Grundmann; **Orchestrations:** Tim Grundmann; **Set Design:** Russell Metheny; **Vocal Arranger:** Tim Grundmann

Songs: Actor's Purgatory; All I Want to Do; Bella Stella New York; Bride of Sirocco; Brownie's Picnic, The; Cheeta's Aria; Comme Blonde Dumbellina; Dallas Last Night [1]; Grin-Tin-Tugger [1]; In This Heaven; MacSavage MacSpleen [1]; Naomi the Salesrat [1]; Tame Me; Taxi to Dreamland; Theme from the Bad Seed; There He Is (Our Elected Holy See); 3/4 Moon

Cast: A. David Johnson; Tanis Roach; Jan Frederick Shiffman; Dana Vance; **Pianist:** Tim Grundmann

Notes: [1] Added to revival.

529 • BRIDE TAMER, THE
OPENED: 06/12/1916   Theatre: Colonial
Musical

Composer: Percy Wenrich
Lyricist: Edgar Allen Woolf
Librettist: Edgar Allen Woolf

Notes: One-act musical.

530 • BRIGADOON
OPENED: 03/13/1947   Theatre: Ziegfeld
Musical   Broadway: 581

Composer: Frederick Loewe
Lyricist: Alan Jay Lerner
Librettist: Alan Jay Lerner
Producer: Cheryl Crawford
Director: Robert Lewis

Choreographer: Agnes de Mille; **Costumes:** David Ffolkes; **Musical Director:** Franz Allers; **Orchestrations:** Ted Royal; **Set Design:** Oliver Smith

Songs: Almost Like Being in Love; Brigadoon; Chase, The; Come to Me, Bend to Me; Down on MacConnachy Square; Farewell Music; From This Day On; Go Back to the Hills [1]; Heather on the Hill, The; I'll Go Home with Bonnie Jean; Jeannie's Packin' Up; Love of My Life, The; My Mother's Wedding Day; Once in the Highlands; There But for You Go I; Vendors' Calls; Waitin' for My Dearie

Cast: Marion Bell; Pamela Britton; David Brooks; Helen Gallagher; George Keane; James Mitchell; Lee Sullivan

Notes: [1] Added to revival (1980). Music is same as part of "McConnaghy Square."

531 • BRIGHT EYES
OPENED: 02/28/1910   Theatre: New York
Musical   Broadway: 40

Composer: Karl Hoschna
Lyricist: Otto Harbach
Librettist: Charles Dickson
Producer: Joseph M. Gaites
Director: Frederick Bishop

Source MISTAKES WILL HAPPEN (Play: Charles Dickson; Grant Stewart); **Choreographer:** Frederick A. Bishop; **Musical Director:** Gustave Salzer

Songs: Angelus, The; Arrival of Guests; Bumble Bee, The; Cheer Up, My Honey; Finale Act III; For You Bright Eyes; Gallop, Gallop; Good Old Days of Yore, The; Harem Scarem [3]; He's a Fan, Fan, Fan! (C: Florence Holbrook; L: Cecil Lean); If Only You Would Take a Tip from Me; I'll Be Your Chanticleer [1]; I'll Build for You a Little

Nest [2]; Lines in Mollie's Hands, The; Lots of Little Things Can Happen (In a Very Little While) [3]; Man on the Box, The; Mood You Are In, The; Mrs. Casey (C: Florence Holbrook; L: Collin Davis; Cecil Lean); My Old Fashioned Garden Flower [3]; On with the Rehearsal; Opening Chorus Act I; Opening Chorus Act II; Opening Chorus Act III; That's the Life of a Stable Boy; Tom Boy, Tom Boy; We Are Only Poor Weak Mortals After All [3]; What's the Use [3]

Cast: Florence Holbrook; Cecil Lean; Percy Lyndal; Reggie Murphy; Pauline Winters

Notes: [1] Out Minneapolis 9/3/11. [2] Not used. Sometimes referred to as "I'll Make for You a Little Nest." [3] Not used.

532 • BRIGHT LIGHTS OF 1944
OPENED: 09/16/1943   Theatre: Forrest
Revue   Broadway: 4

Composer: Jerry Livingston
Lyricist: Mack David
Producer: Alexander H. Cohen

Songs: Back Bay Beat; Damned Old Jeeter (C: Dick Liebert; L: George Blake); Don't Forget the Girl from Punxsutawney; Haven't We Met Before?; Lick, and a Riff, and a Slow Bounce, A (C: Al Scofield; L: Norman Zeno); That's Broadway (C/L: Teddy Hall; Gene Herbert); Thoughtless; We're Having Our Fling; Yes, I Love You Honey (C: James P. Johnson); You'd Better Dance; Your Face Is Your Fortune

Cast: James Barton; Buddy Clark; Charles Dale; Jayne Manners; Joe Smith; Frances Williams

533 • BRIMSTONE
OPENED: 06/29/1994
Musical   Closed out of town

Composer: Patrick Meegan
Lyricist: Mary Bracken Phillips
Librettist: Mary Bracken Phillips
Director: Julianne Boyd

Arrangements Keith Levenson; **Choreographer:** Daniel Levans; **Costumes:** David Murin; **Lighting Designer:** Victor En Yu Tan; **Musical Director:** Christine Caderette; Aaron Hague;

Orchestrations: Aaron Hague; **Set Design:** Ken Foy

Songs: Alba; Anthem; Blaze of Glory; Cautionary Tale, A; Child of My Heart; Diatribe; Eight Years; Fool That I Am; Hello, My Old Friend; I Remember Love; I Want My Country Back; If Not for the Ale; On the Edge; Ourselves Alone (Tiocfaedh Ar La); Paramilitary Dance; Skylark; Stand Your Ground; Verbal Abuse; Welcome Home; Wrenboy

Cast: Mark Honan; John Leone; Jeff McCarthy; Colleen Quinn; Scott Wichmann; Nick Wyman

Notes: Produced at the Berkshire Theatre Festival.

534 • BRING BACK BIRDIE

OPENED: 03/05/1981   Theatre: Martin Beck
Musical   Broadway: 4

Composer: Charles Strouse
Lyricist: Lee Adams
Librettist: Michael Stewart
Producer: L. Slade Brown; Shelly Gross; Lee Guber; Jim Milford
Director: Joe Layton

Costumes: Fred Voelpel; **Dance Arranger:** Daniel Troob; **Lighting Designer:** David Hays; **Musical Director:** Mark Hummel; **Orchestrations:** Gerald Alters; Gary Anderson; Stanley Applebaum; Ralph Burns; Scott Kuney; Philip J. Lang; Coleridge-Taylor Perkinson; Charles Strouse; Daniel Troob; Jim Tyler; **Set Design:** David Mitchell; **Vocal Arranger:** Mark Hummel

Songs: Baby, You Can Count on Me; Back in Show Biz Again; Bring Back Birdie; Don't Say F-A-T in Front of Conrad [1]; Filth; Half of a Couple; I Like What I Do; I Love 'Em All; Inner Peace; Man Worth Fightin' For, A; Middle Age Blues; Movin' Out; Shape Up [1]; Show Girls [1]; There's a Brand New Beat in Heaven; Twenty Happy Years; Well I'm Not!; When Will Grown-Ups Grow Up?; You Can Never Go Back [2]; Young

Cast: Marcel Forestieri; Maurice Hines; Maria Karnilova; Robin Morse; Donald O'Connor; Chita Rivera; Evan Seplow

Notes: [1] Cut prior to opening. [2] Same melody as "His Royal Highness" from I AND ALBERT.

535 • BRING IN THE MORNING

OPENED: 04/23/1994   Theatre: Variety Arts
Musical   Off-Broadway: 51

Composer: Gary William Friedman
Lyricist: Herb Schapiro
Librettist: Herb Schapiro
Producer: Jeff Britton; Edgar M. Bronfman
Director: Bertin Rowser

Choreographer: Michele Asaf; **Dance Arranger:** Louis St. Louis; **Musical Director:** Louis St. Louis; **Orchestrations:** Michael Gibson; **Set Design:** Ken Foy; **Vocal Arranger:** Gary William Friedman; Louis St. Louis

Songs: Another Cry; Awake and a Dream [1] (C/L: Bertin Rowser); Best Kept Secret [1] (C/L: Bertin Rowser); Bring in the Morning; Come Into My Jungle; Deliver My Soul; Funky Eyes; Ghetto of My Mind; Glory of Each Morning, The; Hector's Dream; I Want to Walk in a Garden; I'm on My Way; Let It Rain; Light of Your Love (La Luz de Tu Amor), The; Missing Person; Never Stop Believing; Not Your Cup of Tea; Something Is Wrong with Everyone Today; Trip; You (Tu)

Cast: Yassmin Alers; Roy Chicas; Sean Grant; Nicole Leach; Shannon Keyshard Peters; Imelda de los Reyes

Notes: Poems, stories and writings based on the writing of kids in the "Poets in Public Service, Inc." program. [1] "Inspired by students of Boys Harbor Performing Arts in East Harlem, N.Y.

536 • BRING ON THE GIRLS

OPENED: 10/22/1934
Play   Closed out of town

Author: George S. Kaufman; Morrie Ryskind
Producer: Sam H. Harris
Director: George S. Kaufman

Songs: Down on the Old-Time Farm (C: Arthur Schwartz; L: Morrie Ryskind)

Cast: Jack Benny; Muriel Campbell; Claire Carleton; Ralph W. Chambers; Porter Hall; Victor Killian; Oscar Polk; Loring Smith

Notes: Closed National Theatre, Washington, D.C.

537 • BRINGING UP FATHER (1914)

OPENED: 1914
Musical   Broadway

Composer: Frank H. Grey
Lyricist: Elven E. Hedges
Librettist: John P. Mulgrew; Thomas Swift
Producer: Gus Hill
Director: Frank Tannehill Jr.

Source BRINGING UP FATHER (Comic Strip: George McManus); **Choreographer:** Edward Hutchinson

Songs: Adam and Eve; All the Girls Are Lovely at the Seaside; Beautiful Girl; I'm Proud to Be a Yankee; Irish Suffragette, The; Love Is a Gift; Love, Love, Love; Moving Picture Mary; Tango Moon, The; Way Back in Old Dubuque; When I Was Twenty-One; Wild Irish Rose

Cast: John E. Cain; Grace Hanson; Lyda Kane; Tom Meade; Blanche Newcombe; Harry Truax

Notes: *See also BRINGING UP FATHER (1915)* Some of the same song titles are listed although the lyricists appear to be different.

538 • BRINGING UP FATHER (1915)

OPENED: 1915
Musical   Closed out of town

Composer: Frank Grey
Lyricist: Thomas Swift
Librettist: J.P. Mulgrew; Thomas Swift
Producer: Gus Hill
Director: George Gorman

Source BRINGING UP FATHER (Comic Strip: George McManus); **Choreographer:** Edward Hutchinson

Songs: America I Love You [1]; Back in Old Dubuque; Bandit Raffles I, A [3]; By the Susquehanna [2] (C: Louis Silver; L: Jean Havez); I Want You; I'd Like to Rent a Flat for You [3]; I'm a Lonesome Melody; Little Bit of Heaven, A [1]; Love Is a Gift; Love Is King; Love, Love, Love; Moving Picture Mary; One Summer's Day [3]; Roll On, Silvery Moon [1]; Same Old Sweethearts, The; Sweet Kentucky Lady [1];

Tango Moon; When I Was Twenty One [1]; Wild Irish Rose [1]

Cast: J.W. Bean; George Bradbury; Bert Byron; Louise Earl; Lotta Edwards; Dolly Gray; Elaine Grey; Walter Vernon

Notes: See also BRINGING UP FATHER (1914) and BRINGING UP FATHER IN NEW YORK. Note that some of the same song titles appear as in the 1914 version but with a different lyricist listed. Note also some songs appear to be standards but they may be original to this show but with familiar titles. [1] May be the well-known standard. [2] Called "Susquehanna Shore" in program. [3] Sheet music only.

539 • BRINGING UP FATHER (1925)

OPENED: 03/30/1925   Theatre: Lyric
Musical   Broadway: 24

Composer: Leo Edwards; Seymour Furth
Lyricist: R.F. Carroll
Librettist: Nat Leroy
Producer: Gus Hill

Source BRINGING UP FATHER (Comic Strip: George McManus)

Songs: Angel Without Wings, An; Gainesboro Glide, The; Girls of New York, The; Lady Bred in the Purple, A; Merry Go Round, The; Moonlight; My Lady's Fan; On Our Way to Spain; Play Me a Bagpipe Tune; Poppy the Dream Girl; That's the Irish in Her; We Hope to Make a Hit; Wedding Chimes; When Dad Was Twenty-One; When It Gets Dark

Cast: James Collins; Beatrice Harlowe; Leo Henning; Gertrude Lavella; Danny Simmons

540 • BRINGING UP FATHER ABROAD

OPENED: 1917
Musical   Closed out of town

Composer: Frank H. Grey
Lyricist: Edward Hutchinson
Librettist: John P. Mulgrew
Producer: Gus Hill
Director: Edward Hutchinson

Source BRINGING UP FATHER (Comic Strip:
George McManus); **Costumes:** Frank Hayden

Cast: Marion J. Benson; Ben B. Byron; John E. Cain;
Madeline Grey; Eddie Leamon; Kathleen Neal

Notes: No songs listed in this Chicago program.

541 • BRINGING UP FATHER AT THE SEASHORE (1920)

OPENED: 04/21/1921   Theatre: Manhattan
                                          Opera House
Musical   Broadway: 18

Composer: Tom Grady
Lyricist: Unknown
Librettist: Nat Leroy
Producer: Gus Hill
Director: Richard Carroll

Source BRINGING UP FATHER (Comic Strip:
George McManus); **Costumes:** Frank Hayden

Songs: Cat Duet; Forever Is a Long, Long Time; He
Went in Like a Lion; Hen and the Cow, The;
Moving Picture Mary [1]; Nobody Knows; On a
Moonlight Night; Opera and Rag Time; Tippery

Notes: Program of 1920 Ottawa, Canada. [1]
Same title in BRINGING UP FATHER (1915)
but credited to Frank Grey and Thomas Swift.
Is 'Tom Grady' a pseudonym for Grey and
Swift?

542 • BRINGING UP FATHER AT THE SEASHORE (1928)

OPENED: 1928   Theatre: Manhattan
                                          Opera House
Musical   New York

Composer: Unknown
Lyricist: Unknown
Producer: Gus Hill

Source BRINGING UP FATHER (Comic Strip:
George McManus)

Songs: Bathing Girl; Broken Blossoms; Grieving for
You; I Miss My Mammy's Kissin'; I Used to Love
You, but It's All Over Now; I Want a Daddy;
Jiggs and His Pipe; Just Like a Gypsy; Kewpie
Dolly; Margie; Opening Chorus; Orient, The

Cast: Frank M. Christie; Louise Earl; Nellie
Randall; Walter Vernon

543 • BROADWAY AND BUTTERMILK

OPENED: 08/15/1916   Theatre: Maxine Elliott's
Play   Broadway: 23

Composer: Charles N. Grant
Lyricist: Schuyler Greene
Author: Willard Mack
Producer: Frederic McKay
Director: Ben Teal

Musical Director: John R. Britz

Songs: Girls, If I Ever Get Married; I've Always
Been the Patsy (C: Dave Stamper); My
Grandfather's Girl (C/L: Will Dillon); Pickin'
'Em Up and Layin' 'Em Down; 'Twas Only an
Irishman's Dream (C: Rennie Cormack; L: Al
Dubin; John J. O'Brien)

Cast: Tommy Meade; Blanche Ring; Charles
Withers

Notes: Charles Millgram listed in program as
composer but program doesn't list any songs.
These songs are from sheet music and ascribed
to Charles N. Grant.

544 • BROADWAY BABY, A

OPENED: 12/04/1984
Musical   Closed out of town

Composer: Nacio Herb Brown
Lyricist: Arthur Freed
Librettist: Carl Kleinschmitt
Producer: Goodspeed Opera House
Director: Thommie Walsh

Arrangements Wally Harper; **Choreographer:**
Thommie Walsh; **Costumes:** William Ivey Long;
Lighting Designer: Marilyn Rennagel;
Orchestrations: Wally Harper; **Set Design:**
Nicky Nadeau

Songs: All I Do Is Dream of You [1]; Alone [2];
Beautiful Girl [3]; Broadway Melody [4]; Fit As a
Fiddle [5] (C: Al Goodhart; Al Hoffman); Good
Morning [6]; I Cried for You [6] (C/L: Gus
Arnheim; Arthur Freed; Abe Lyman); I'm Feelin'

Like a Million [7]; Love Is Where You Find It [13] (L: Earl Brent); Make 'Em Laugh [8]; Should I [9]; Sun Showers [7]; Temptation [10]; We'll Make Hay While the Sun Shines [10]; You Are My Lucky Star [11]; You Stepped Out of a Dream [12] (L: Gus Kahn); You Were Meant for Me [4]; Your Broadway and My Broadway [7]

Cast: Richard Blake; Heather Hope Gryning; Kim Hauser; Frank Charles Lutkus III; Kent Zbornak

Notes: Goodspeed Opera House — Norma Terris Theatre. No original songs in this show. [1] From film SADIE MCKEE. [2] From film A NIGHT AT THE OPERA. [3] From film STAGE MOTHER. [4] From film BROADWAY MELODY. [5] From film COLLEGE COACH. [6] From film BABES IN ARMS. [7] From film BROADWAY MELODY OF 1938. [8] From film SINGIN' IN THE RAIN. [9] From film OUR MODERN MAIDENS. [10] From film GOING HOLLYWOOD. [11] From film BROADWAY MELODY OF 1936. [12] From film ZIEGFELD GIRL. [13] From films A DATE WITH JUDY and THE KISSING BANDIT.

545 • BROADWAY BREVITIES OF 1920

OPENED: 09/29/1920   Theatre: Winter Garden
Revue   Broadway: 105

Librettist: George LeMaire
Producer: Rufus LeMaire
Director: J.C. Huffman

Choreographer: Jack Mason; **Costumes:** Charles LeMaire; **Musical Director:** Louis Gress; **Orchestrations:** Stephen Jones; Will Vodery; **Set Design:** Herbert Ward

Songs: Beautiful Faces (Need Beautiful Clothes) (C/L: Irving Berlin); Blow, Blow, Blow [1] (C/L: Con Conrad); Bright Eyes [1] (C/L: Con Conrad); Broadway Walk, The [2] (C: Archie Gottler; L: Blair Traynor); But Where [3] (C: Will Vodery; L: W. Russell); Cruel and Brutal [3] (C: Walter De Leon; L: W. Russell); Daddy [3] (C/L: Unknown); Dance of the Nymphs (C/L: Unknown); Drigo's Polka (C: Unknown); Eve Cost Adam Just One Bone [3] (C/L: Charles Bayha); I Love to Dance [4] (C: George Gershwin; L: Arthur Jackson); I Makes Mine Myself [3] (C: Robert Hood Bowers; L: Francis DeWitt); I Want to Know Where Tosti Went [3] (C/L: Chris Smith); I'm a Dancing Fool C: George Gershwin; L: Arthur Jackson; In a Doll's House [3] (C: Archie Gottler; L: Blair Traynor); In Cherry Blossom Time with You [2] (C/L: Dorothy Jardon; C: Joseph M. Daly); In the Canoe [2] (C: Archie Gottler; L: Blair Traynor); In the Snow-Covered Mountains of Switzerland [2] (C: Archie Gottler; L: Blair Traynor); Love, Honor and O Baby [4] (C: George Gershwin; L: Arthur Jackson); Love Me While the Snowflakes Fall [5] (C: George Gershwin; L: Arthur Jackson); Lu-Lu (C: George Gershwin; L: Arthur Jackson); Moon Shines on the Moonshine, The (C: Robert Hood Bowers; L: Francis DeWitt); My Broadway Chorus Girl [1] (C/L: Con Conrad); My Only One [2] (C: Joseph M. Daly; Dorothy Jardon; L: George Moriarty); New Amsterdam [2] (C: Archie Gottler; L: Blair Traynor); Rainy Afternoon [1] (C/L: Con Conrad); Rose of Old Seville [1] (C/L: Con Conrad); Smart Bootery Scene, The (C: Joseph M. Daly; Maurie Rubens; L: Dorothy Jardon); So This Is Broadway [2] (C: Archie Gottler; L: Blair Traynor); Somebody Else, Not Me [6] (C: James F. Hanley; L: Ballard Macdonald); Spanish Love (C: George Gershwin; L: Irving Caesar); Spring Dance (C: Unknown); Stolen Sweets [2] (C: Archie Gottler; L: Blair Traynor); Usual Opening Chorus, The (C/L: Unknown); We've Got the Stage Door Blues (C: Harry Ruby; L: Bert Kalmar); What Happened to the Original Six Floradora Boys [2] (C: Harry Ruby; L: Bert Kalmar); What Means Home to Me [2] (C: Archie Gottler; L: Blair Traynor); Won't You Let Me Take a Picture of You? (C/L: Unknown); You Must Have a Kick and Punch [2] (C: Archie Gottler; L: Blair Traynor)

Cast: Eddie Cantor; George LeMaire; Hal Van Rensellaer; Bert Williams

Notes: [1] Out Detroit 3/20/21. [2] Out 9/13/20. [3] Sheet music only. [4] Gershwin's authorship of these songs is in doubt but this is how they were credited in program. [5] Sometimes referred to as "Snowflakes." [6] ASCAP/Library of Congress only.

546 • BROADWAY, BROADWAY

OPENED: 07/31/1978
Play   Closed out of town

Author: Terrence McNally
Producer: Edgar Bronfman Jr.; Sagittarius Ent.
Director: Robert Drivas

Costumes: Florence Klotz; **Lighting Designer:** Ian Calderon; **Set Design:** Peter Larkin

Songs: Broadway, Broadway (C: Dan Goggin; L: Robert Lorick)

Cast: Richard Backus; James Coco; Geraldine Page

Notes: Also titled BYE, BYE, BROADWAY. Revised as IT'S ONLY A PLAY and produced at Manhattan Theatre Club.

547 • BROADWAY FOLLIES

OPENED: 03/15/1981   Theatre: Nederlander
Revue   Broadway: 1

Composer: Walter Marks
Lyricist: Walter Marks
Producer: Joseph Beruh; Edgar Lansbury; James M. Nederlander
Director: Donald Driver

Choreographer: Arthur Faria; **Costumes:** Alvin Colt; **Dance Arranger:** Marvin Laird; **Lighting Designer:** Robert Morgan; **Musical Director:** Marvin Laird; **Orchestrations:** Bill Byers; **Set Design:** Peter Larkin; **Vocal Arranger:** Marvin Laird

Songs: Barnyard, The; Broadway Follies; Paper Bag Rag, The; Piccadilly

Cast: Michael Davis; Travis Hudson; Tessie O'Shea; Robert Shields; Lorene Yarnell

548 • BROADWAY HONEYMOON, A

OPENED: 10/03/1913
Revue   Chicago

Composer: Joseph E. Howard; Herbert Stothart
Lyricist: Collin Davis
Librettist: Collin Davis

Songs: Broadway Honeymoon, A; Cotton Pickin Time in Tennessee (L: Mabel McCane); He's Mah Dancing Man; Oh You Wedding Belle; Salvation Glide, The; When the Love You Love Loves You

Notes: No program available. Produced at Joe Howard's Theatre.

549 • BROADWAY JUKEBOX

OPENED: 07/19/1990   Theatre: John Houseman
Revue   Off-Broadway: 50

Producer: Eric Krebs
Director: Bill Guske

Choreographer: Bill Guske; **Costumes:** Barbara Forbes; **Lighting Designer:** Stuart Duke; **Set Design:** James Morgan

Cast: Robert Michael Baker; Susan Flynn; Beth Leavel; Ed Linderman; Gerry McIntyre; Amelia Prentice; Sal Viviano

Notes: A revue featuring audience voting on which songs from obscure musicals should be performed. Ninety songs were available per show. Conceived by Ed Lindermann.

550 • BROADWAY MUSICAL, A

OPENED: 12/21/1978   Theatre: Lunt-Fontanne
Musical   Broadway: 1

Composer: Charles Strouse
Lyricist: Lee Adams
Librettist: William F. Brown
Producer: Garth H. Drabinsky; Norman Kean
Director: Gower Champion

Choreographer: Gower Champion; **Costumes:** Randy Barcelo; **Dance Arranger:** Donald Johnston; **Lighting Designer:** John DeSantis; Peter Wexler; **Musical Director:** Kevin Farrell; **Orchestrations:** Robert M. Freedman; **Set Design:** Peter Wexler; **Vocal Arranger:** Donald Pippin

Songs: Be Like a Basketball and Bounce Right Back [1]; Broadway, Broadway; Broadway Musical, A; Dancing [4]; Don't Tell Me; Goin' to Broadway [1]; Here in the Playbill [1]; I Hurry Home to You; It's Time for a Cheer-Up Song; I've Been in Those Shoes [1]; Jokes [1]; Just Tell Me What You Want [4]; Lawyers; Let Me Sing My Song; Love Song [2]; 1934 Hot Chocolate Jazz Babies Revue, The; Older and Wiser [4]; Opening Night [1]; Out-a-Town [1]; Smashing, New York Times [3]; Smoke and Fire; Together; What You Go Through; Who Am I? [1]; Who Says You Always Have to Be Happy? [1]; Why Does It Have to Be Funny? [4]; Wrong Song, A [1]; Yenta Power; You Gotta Have Dancing; You Only Get One Chance [1]

Cast: Warren Berlinger; Loretta Devine; Gwyda DonHowe; Anne Francine; Tiger Haynes; Patti Karr; Larry Marshall; Lary Riley; Alan Weeks

Notes: [1] Cut Riverside Church prior to Broadway. [2] Cut Riverside Church prior to Broadway. Also in MEDIUM RARE. [3] Cut from APPLAUSE. [4] Not used.

551 • BROADWAY NIGHTS

OPENED: 07/15/1929   Theatre: 44th Street
Revue   Broadway: 40

Composer: Maurie Rubens
Lyricist: Moe Jaffe; Sam Timberg
Librettist: Edgar Smith

Songs: Arabian Nights; Baby-Doll Dance (C: Maurie Rubens; Phil Svigals; L: J. Keirn Brennan; Moe Jaffe); Come Hit Your Baby; Heart of a Rose [1] (C: J. Fred Coots; Maurie Rubens; L: Harold Atteridge); Hotsy Totsy Hats; Right Man, The; White Lights Were Coming; Why Don't We?; Your Broadway and Mine (C: Maurie Rubens)

Cast: Frank Gaby; Odette Myrtil

Notes: [1] Also in GAY PAREE (1925).

552 • BROADWAY RASTUS (1915)

OPENED: 1915
Musical

Composer: Domer C. Brown
Additional Music: W.C. Handy; Bob Ticketts
Lyricist: Leigh Whipper
Librettist: Irvin C. Miller
Producer: Irvin C. Miller

Songs: Bye and Bye; Every Goodbye Ain't Gone; Every Shut Eye, Ain't Asleep; Every Woman's Got a Man but Me; I Was Mad for You; Some Day; Whip-o-Will; You Go Your Way and I'll Go Mine; You'd Too

Cast: Mae Boyd; James Hicks; Juanita Hicks; Henry Jines; Irvin C. Miller; Carrie Purnell; Leigh Whipper; Billie Young

Notes: No other information available.

553 • BROADWAY RASTUS OF 1923

OPENED: 1923
Musical

Composer: W. Aston Morgan
Lyricist: Pousseau Simmons
Librettist: Irvin C. Miller
Producer: Irvin C. Miller
Director: Quintard Miller

Cast: Irvin C. Miller; Quintard Miller; Jimmie Parker; Trixie Smith

Notes: No other information available.

554 • BROADWAY RASTUS (1925)

OPENED: 1925
Musical

Composer: Maceo Pinkard
Librettist: Irvin C. Miller
Producer: Irvin C. Miller
Director: Irvin C. Miller

Musical Director: Clarence Marks

Songs: Black Bottom Dance (dance); Closing Chorus; Dance, Let's Waltz; Dandy; Going South; Hello; Levee Moon; Levee Nights; Old-Fashioned Rose; Orange Grove; Planning; Plantation Follies; Runnin' Wild Blues; Savannah; Too Tired

Cast: Flo Brown; Gallie DeGaston; Aurora Greeley; John Henderson; Irvin C. Miller; Cecil Rivers; Blanche Thompson

Notes: No other information available.

555 • BROADWAY RHYTHM

OPENED: 1944
Musical   Unproduced

Composer: Jerome Kern
Lyricist: Oscar Hammerstein II

Songs: Contrary Mary; Good Girl; Oh, My Dear

Notes: From ASCAP/Library of Congress records only.

556 • BROADWAY SCANDALS OF 1928

OPENED: 07/07/1982   Theatre: O'Neal's 43rd
Revue   Off-Broadway: 39

Composer: Jeffrey Silverman
Lyricist: Walter Willison
Librettist: Walter Willison
Producer: Jeffrey Silverman; Ted Van Antwerp; Walter Willison
Director: Walter Willison

Choreographer: Jo Anna Lehmann; Gwen Hiller Lowe; Douglas Norwick; **Costumes:** Robert Turturice; **Lighting Designer:** Malcolm Sturchio; **Set Design:** Ron Placzek

Songs: Better Bein' Loved; Blowing Bubbles in the Bathtub; Broadway Wedding; Charleston Under the Moon; Give a Girl a Break!; Good Ol' Mammy Song, A; Happy Jest Bein' with Me; I Couldn't Say; I Gotta Hear a Song; Let's Go Boating; Man at the Piano, The; Mazie; Nobody Needs a Man As Bad As That!; Picture Me with You; Scandals!; Scandals Finale; Sodomanager; Tango; Things Have Never Been Better; When You Come to the End of Your Rainbow

Cast: Shelley Bruce; Kenny D'Aquuila; Jessica James; Jo Anna Lehmann; Gwen Hiller Lowe; Rose Scudder; Jeffrey Silverman; Walter Willison

557 • BROADWAY SHO-WINDOW

OPENED: 04/12/1936   Theatre: Broadway
Revue   Broadway: 24

Composer: Gus Edwards
Lyricist: Eugene Conrad
Librettist: Eugene Conrad
Producer: Gus Edwards
Director: Guthrie McConrad

Orchestrations: Arthur Gutman; **Set Design:** Clark Robinson

Songs: Hitch Your Wagon to a Star (C: Richard Lewine; L: Ted Fetter); Kiss Me Like This; Poverty Row or Luxury Lane (L: Howard Johnson); Spring Is In the Air; That Little Spanish Hacienda

Cast: Armida; Joe Cook Jr.; Thelma Lee

Notes: [1] Not in program.

558 • BROADWAY TO PARIS

OPENED: 11/20/1912   Theatre: Winter Garden
Revue   Broadway: 77

Composer: Anatole Friedland; Max Hoffmann
Lyricist: Harold Atteridge
Librettist: George Bronson Howard
Producer: Messrs. Shubert
Director: Morris Gest

Choreographer: Ned Wayburn; **Costumes:** Melville Ellis; Robert Jones; **Musical Director:** Max Hoffmann

Songs: Bird of Paradise [1] (C: Max Hoffmann); Come to Me Chimpanzee (C: Max Hoffmann); Everybody Loves a Chicken (C: Max Hoffmann); Eye That Never Sleeps, The (C: Max Hoffmann); Eyes, Eyes [2]; Garden of Girls, The; Gertrude Hoffman Glide, The (C/L: Max Hoffmann); Gertrude Hoffman March, The [1] (C: Max Hoffmann); Girl from Home Sweet Home, The [1] (C: Max Hoffmann); Hello Cupid, Send Me a Fellow; I'll Find a Boy (Girl); Let Me Show You Paris [2]; Loveland Express, The [2] (C: Max Hoffmann); Merry Merry Maids of the Old Front Row, The; Moulin Rouge Roulette [1] (C: Max Hoffmann); Mr. Yankee Doodle; Paree's a Branch of Broadway (C: Max Hoffmann); Ragtime Boxing Match, The; Ride Me Around with You, Dearie; Roller Rinkers; Take Me to That Swanee Shore (C: Lewis F. Muir; L: L. Wolfe Gilbert); You're the Girl [1] (C: Jean Schwartz; L: Grant Clarke; Edgar Leslie)

Cast: George Bickel; Irene Bordoni; Doyle & Dixon; Louise Dresser; Gertrude Hoffman; George Austin Moore; James C. Morton; Marion Sunshine; Florence Walton; Maurice Walton

Notes: I don't believe Friedland and Hoffmann collaborated on these songs. Also known as FROM BROADWAY TO PARIS. [1] Sheet music only. [2] Out Washington, D.C. 2/3/13.

559 • BROADWAY TO TOKIO

OPENED: 01/23/1900   Theatre: New York
Revue   Broadway: 88

Composer: A. Baldwin Sloane
Lyricist: Louis Harrison; George V. Hobart
Librettist: Louis Harrison; George V. Hobart
Director: Max Freeman

Choreographer: Carl Marwig; **Costumes:** Caroline Siedle; **Musical Director:** A. DeNovellis; **Orchestrations:** Karl Hoschna; Frank Saddler; **Set Design:** Ernest Albert; D. Frank Dodge; Henry E. Hoyt

Songs: Alive Again; Ballet (inst.) (C: Reginald De Koven); Ballet Eccentrique; Barcarole; Dig Ye Dagos Dig; Firefly Ballet (inst.) (C: Reginald De Koven); For Love of Cleopatra; Hunting for a Happy Little Home in Harlem; Incantation; Johnnies of Long Acre Square, The; Lovelorn Lily, The; Now I'se Got Some Money I'm Comin' 'Round (L: Frank Sloane); Opening Chorus; Salvation Hymn; Serpent of the Nile; Story of the Dance; Susie Mah Sue; Warrior's Song, The; We're a Comic Opera Company; When I'm Traveling on the Road; When O'Donahue Presided at the Grip

Cast: Otis Harlan; Alice Judson; Ignacio Martinetti; Joseph Ott; Josie Sadler; Joseph Sparks; Fay Templeton

560 • BROADWAY WHIRL, THE

OPENED: 06/08/1921   Theatre: Times Square
Revue   Broadway: 85

Composer: Harry Tierney
Lyricist: Richard Carle; Joseph McCarthy
Librettist: Thomas J. Gray
Producer: Artists Prod. Corp.
Director: Bert French

Songs: All Girls Are Like a Rainbow; Baby Dolls [1] (C: George Gershwin; L: B.G. DeSylva; John Henry Mears); Broadway Whirl, The; Button Me Up the Back; Carefree Cairo Town (C: Wyman; L: Thomas); From the Plaza to Madison Square; Let Cutie Cut Your Cuticle [1] (C: George Gershwin; L: B.G. DeSylva; John Henry Mears); Lime House Nights [1] (C: George Gershwin; L: B.G. DeSylva; John Henry Mears); Oh Babe (C: F. Henri; L: Jack Frost); Oh Dearie; Poppy Land [1] (C: George Gershwin; L: B.G. DeSylva; John Henry Mears); Stand Up and Sing for Your Father (C/L: Henry Burr; Ray Perkins); Stars of Broadway; Three Little Maids; Wood Alcohol Blues (C: E.S. Hutchinson; L: J. Hershkowitz)

Cast: Richard Carle; Jay Gould; Janet Sisters, The; Blanche Ring; Charles Winninger; Winona Winter

Notes: [1] Also in MORRIS GEST'S MIDNIGHT WHIRL.

561 • BROKEN IDOL, A

OPENED: 08/16/1909   Theatre: Herald Square
Musical   Broadway: 40

Composer: Egbert Van Alstyne
Lyricist: Harry Williams
Librettist: Hal Stephens
Producer: B.C. Whitney
Director: Gus Sohlke

Musical Director: Fred Eustis; **Set Design:** D. Frank Dodge

Songs: Alabam'; Am I Right [3]; Art of Making Up, The [2]; Broken Idol, A [1]; Cured; Finale Act I [3]; Go Back [1] (C: Charles Grapewin; Egbert Van Alstyne); Happy Days (C: Jean Schwartz); It Looks Like a Big Night To-Night [3]; Little China Doll, A; Marie; Opening Chorus; Poor Old Dad in New York for the Summer; Song of the Waiters [1]; That's Politics [3]; That's the Sign of a Honeymoon; Up in a Balloon; What Makes the World Go Round; Yankee Land

Cast: Otis Harlan; Forrest Huff; Madge Voe; Alice Yorke

Notes: [1] Sheet music only. [2] ASCAP/Library of Congress only. [3] Vocal score only.

562 • BROKEN TOYS

OPENED: 07/16/1982   Theatre: Actors'
                                 Playhouse
Musical   Off-Broadway: 29

Composer: Keith Berger
Lyricist: Keith Berger
Librettist: Keith Berger
Producer: Dani Ruska; Marina Spinola
Director: Carl Haber

Costumes: Karen Dusenbury; Mara Lonner; **Lighting Designer:** Kevin Jones; **Orchestrations:** Lou Forestieri; **Set Design:** Lisa Beck

Songs: Ain't Worth a Dime; Broken & Bent; Choo Choo Rap; Funny Wind-Up Toy; I Don't Play with Humans; I Don't Think I Like This Game; I Got That Other Lady's with My Baby Feeling;

Johnny Space; Kangaroo Court; Lady Ride with Me; Left Alone to Be; Let's Play Let's Say; Not of Her World; Play with Me; Prayer Song; Rag Doll Rag; So Ya Wanna Be a Toy; Temperance Song, The; This Life's the Right One for Me; We're on a Shelf in Your Attic; Weird Fun; Wind-Up in New York City

Cast: Keith Berger; Debra Greenfield; Oona Lind; Johnny Zeitz

563 • BRONX EXPRESS, THE
Play   Broadway

Composer: Turner Layton
Lyricist: Henry Creamer
Librettist: Owen Davis; Samuel R. Golding
Producer: Smicoeve Prod.
Director: Ossip Dymow

Source UNKNOWN (Unknown: Ossip Dymow); **Dance Arranger:** Don Walker; **Set Design:** Mabel A. Buell

Songs: Bronx Express; Dream Street Station; Where the Millionaires Live

Cast: Charles Coburn; Mrs. Charles Coburn

564 • BROOKLYN BRIDGE, THE
OPENED: 08/17/1983   Theatre: Quaigh
Musical   Off-Broadway: 28

Composer: Scott MacLarty
Lyricist: Dorothy Chansky
Librettist: Dorothy Chansky
Producer: Bridge Theatre Prod. Co.; Dorothy Chansky
Director: Marjorie Melnick

Choreographer: Missy Whitechurch; **Costumes:** Karen Gerson; **Lighting Designer:** Leslie Spohn; **Musical Director:** Harrison Fisher; **Set Design:** Terry Bennett

Songs: Ain't No Women There; All That I Know; Bridge to the Future; Brooklyn; Can I Do It All; Cash Politics; Every Day for Four Years; Finale; Keep Me Out of the Caisson; Love Means; Man in the Window, The; Roebling Plan, The; When You're the Only One

Cast: Bijou Clinger; Anne Gartlan; David Higlen;

Nick Jolley; Paul Merrill; Jack Sevier; John Leslie Wolfe

565 • BROTHERHOOD AND BILLYGOATS
Musical

Songs: O-K-M-N-X (C: Phil Baker; J. Russel Robinson; L: Billy Beck; Sid Silvers); We're Twenty Million Strong (C: Phil Baker; J. Russel Robinson; L: Billy Beck; Sid Silvers)

Notes: No other information available.

566 • BROTHERS
Notes: *See NEFERTITI.*

567 • BROWN BUDDIES
OPENED: 10/07/1930   Theatre: Liberty
Musical   Broadway: 113

Composer: Joe Jordan
Lyricist: Millard Thomas
Librettist: Carl Rickman
Producer: Marty Forkins
Director: Ralph Rose

Choreographer: Addison Carey; Charles Davis; **Costumes:** Ida Bell; Brooks; **Musical Director:** Charles L. Cooke; **Orchestrations:** Charles L. Cooke; Joe Jordan; **Set Design:** Theodore Kahn; Edward Sundquist

Songs: Betty Lou (C: Joe Jordan; L: J. Rosamond Johnson); Brown Buddies; Carry On; Dancin' 'Way Your Sin (C/L: James C. Johnson); Darky Rhythm (C: Peter Tinturin; L: Joe Young); Don't Leave Your Little Blackbird Blue (C/L: Porter Grainger; Joe Jordan); Excuse My Dust (C: Jesse Greer; L: Raymond Klages); Gettin' Off; Give Me a Man Like That (C: Art Sizemore; L: George A. Little); Happy (C: Nat Reed; L: Bob Joffe); I Hate Myself (For Falling in Love with You) (C: Abner Silver; L: Dave Oppenheim); I Lost Everything Losing You [1]; In Missouria; Missouri (C/L: Nat Reed); My Blue Melody; Sugar Cane; Sweety Mine; Taps; When a Black Man's Blue (C/L: Ed G. Nelson; C: Art Sizemore; L: George A. Little)

Cast: Shelton Brooks; Ada Brown; Pike Davis; William Fountaine; Adelaide Hall; Bill Robinson; Alma Smith

Notes: [1] Cut after opening.

568 • BROWN DERBY, THE

OPENED: 05/18/1925
Musical   Closed out of town

Composer: Paul Lannin; Ray Perkins
Lyricist: Clifford Grey
Librettist: Brian Marlow; F.S. Merlin
Producer: Fanny Brice; Charles Gordon
Director: Willard Mack

Choreographer: Jack Haskell; **Costumes:** Charles LeMaire; **Musical Director:** August Kleinecke; **Set Design:** Clark Robinson

Songs: Bert, Betty & Co.; Dirty Up the Alley; Going to Work; Land I Love; Meaning Me, Meaning You; One Little Smile; One Wonderful Day; Sari; Snap in My Heart; Trainers and Pugilists; Tripping Your Troubles Away; Up-Town Down-Town; When I'm with You; Woofus Bird

Cast: June Day; Elsa Ersi; Donald Kerr; John Sheehan; Bert Wheeler; Betty Wheeler

Notes: Program of New Haven used.

569 • BROWN SKIN MODELS

Notes: *See IRVIN C. MILLER'S BROWN SKIN MODELS.*

570 • BROWN SUGAR

OPENED: 1930   Theatre: Cotton Club
Revue   Nightclub

Composer: Harold Arlen
Lyricist: Ted Koehler
Producer: Ted Healy

Songs: Chase the Cat; Harlem's Hot As Hades; Heap o' Misery; La Rhumba; Linda; Misbehavin' Hips; My Man Must Dance; Song of the Gigolo; Toothache Blues

Notes: No other information available.

571 • BROWNIES, THE

OPENED: 11/12/1894   Theatre: 14th St.
Musical   Broadway: 96

Composer: Malcolm Douglas
Librettist: Palmer Cox

Producer: A.L. Erlanger; C.B. Jefferson; Marc Klaw
Director: Ben Teal

Choreographer: Carl Marwig; **Costumes:** Reginald Birch; Palmer Cox; **Set Design:** Charles Getz; J.W. Sommer

Cast: Mary Louise Day; Sydney Grant; Ida Mulle; Willis Pickert; Maudie Thompson

Notes: No songs listed in program.

572 • BROWNSTONE

OPENED: 10/08/1986   Theatre: Roundabout
Musical   Off-Broadway: 69

Composer: Peter Larson; Josh Rubins
Lyricist: Peter Larson; Josh Rubins
Librettist: Andrew Cadiff; Josh Rubins
Producer: Roundabout Theater Company
Director: Andrew Cadiff

Costumes: Ann Emonts; **Lighting Designer:** Richard Nelson; **Musical Director:** Don Jones; **Orchestrations:** Harold Wheeler; **Set Design:** Loren Sherman

Songs: Almost There; Babies on the Brain; Camouflage; Don't Tell Me Everything; Fiction Writer; Fiction Writer Duet; He Didn't Leave It Here; Hi There, Joan; I Just Want to Know; I Wasn't Home for Christmas; It Isn't the End of the World; It's a Funny Thing; Neighbors Above, Neighbors Below; Nevertheless; Not Today; One of Them; See That Lady There; Someone's Moving In; Someone's Moving Out; Spring Cleaning; Thanks a Lot; There She Goes; Water Through the Trees, The; We Came Along Too Late; We Should Talk; What Do People Do?; You Still Don't Know

Cast: Liz Callaway; Kimberly Farr; Ben Harney; Ernestine Jackson; Rex Smith

573 • BUBBE MEISES BUBBE STORIES

OPENED: 10/29/1992   Theatre: Cherry Lane
Play   Off-Broadway: 186

Librettist: Ellen Gould
Producer: Renee Blau; Richard Frankel; Paragon Park Prods.
Director: Gloria Muzio

Arrangements: Bob Goldstone; **Costumes:** Elsa Ward; **Lighting Designer:** Peter Kaczorowski; **Musical Director:** Bob Goldstone; **Set Design:** David Jenkins

Songs: Bridge Song (The Bubbe Rag), The (C: Scott Joplin; L: Holly Gewandter; Ellen Gould); Bubbe Meises Bubbe Stories; Chocolate Covered Cherries (C/L: Holly Gewandter); Fifty-Fifty (C: Joseph Romshinsky; L: Bruce Adler; Louis Gilrod; Jacques Levy; Zalmen Mlotek; Moishe Rosenfeld); Goldstein, Swank & Gordon; It's a Bubbe Meise (C/L: Holly Gewandter; Ellen Gould); Oy, How I Hate That Fellow Nathan (C: Albert Von Tilzer; L: Lew Brown); Oy, I Like Him [1] (C/L: Aaron Lebedeff; Alexander Olshanetsky; L: Jacques Levy); Road I'm Taking, The; Take More Out of Life (C/L: Ellen Gould); You're Dancing Inside Me

Notes: [1] Based on "Oh, I Like She."

574 • BUBBLES
OPENED: 09/09/1907
Musical   Closed out of town

Composer: Robin Bond
Lyricist: Genevieve Farrell; George Hanlon Jr.
Librettist: George Hanlon Jr.

Cast: Norma Seymoure; Florence Trevillion; Evelyn Westbrooke

Notes: Vaudeville musical. Program from Philadelphia.

575 • BUBBLES OR FASHION
Play   Closed out of town

Author: John Patton Russell; Anita Stewart

Songs: Bubbles (C: Mabelina Corby; L: Marjo Lewis)

Cast: Anita Stewart

Notes: No other information available.

576 • BUBBLING BROWN SUGAR
OPENED: 03/02/1976   Theatre: ANTA
Revue   Broadway: 766

Composer: Danny Holgate
Librettist: Loften Mitchell
Producer: Richard Bell; Robert M. Cooper; J. Lloyd Grant; Moe Septee; Ashton Springer
Director: Robert M. Cooper

Choreographer: Billy Wilson; **Costumes:** Bernard Johnson; **Lighting Designer:** Barry Arnold; **Musical Director:** Danny Holgate; **Set Design:** Clarke Dunham; **Vocal Arranger:** Chapman Roberts

Songs: Bubbling Brown Sugar (L: Emme Kemp; Lilian Lopez); C'mon Up to Jive Time (L: Unknown); Dutch's Song (L: Emme Kemp); Goin' Back in Time (L: Unknown); Harlem Makes Me Feel! (L: Ethel Kemp); Harlem '70 (L: Loften Mitchell); Harlem, Sweet Harlem (L: Loften Mitchell); Harlem Time (L: Unknown); I'm Alive [1] (L: Emme Kemp); Moving Uptown (L: Emme Kemp; Loften Mitchell); Patter Song — Through the Years [1] (L: Loften Mitchell); Strollin' (L: Unknown)

Cast: Joseph Attles; Ethel Beatty; Murphy Cross; Avon Long; Lonnie McNeil; Josephine Premice; Barry Preston; Stanley Ramsey; Vivian Reed; Barbara Rubenstein

Notes: [1] Cut prior to Broadway.

577 • BUBBLING OVER
OPENED: 1926
Musical   Closed out of town

Composer: Richard Myers
Lyricist: Leo Robin
Librettist: Clifford Grey
Producer: Edward Royce

Source BREWSTER'S MILLIONS (Play: Byron Ongley; Winchell Smith); **Musical Director:** Hilding Anderson; **Orchestrations:** Maurice DePackh; Emil Gerstenberger; Charles Miller; **Set Design:** Frank Gates; E.A. Morange

Songs: Breezin' Along [3]; Bubbling Over; Dreams Never Die; Everyone Celebrate; House that Monty's 'Jack' Built, The; I'm a One-Man Girl [2]; I'm a Red Hot Cradle Snatcher; It's All Right with Me If It's All Right with You; Montezuma; On the Riviera; Say It with a Uke; Shake Me and Wake Me; Snap Out of the Blues; Stepping All the Way Home; True to Two [1]; What Good Is Money?; What's Happened?

Cast: Cecil Lean; Jeanette MacDonald; Cleo Mayfield

Notes: [1] Later in MR. CINDERS. [2] Sheet music only. Later in MR. CINDERS. [3] Sheet music only.

578 • BUCK WHITE

OPENED: 12/02/1969   Theatre: George Abbott
Musical   Broadway: 7

Composer: Oscar Brown Jr.
Lyricist: Oscar Brown Jr.
Librettist: Oscar Brown Jr.
Producer: Zev Bufman; High John Prods.
Director: Oscar Brown Jr.; Jean Pace

Source BIG TIME BUCK WHITE (Play: Joseph Dolan Tuotti); **Costumes:** Jean Pace; **Dance Arranger:** Merl Saunders; Mike Terry; **Lighting Designer:** Martin Aronstein; **Musical Director:** Merl Saunders; **Orchestrations:** Mike Terry; **Set Design:** Edward Burbridge; **Vocal Arranger:** Merl Saunders; Mike Terry

Songs: Beautiful Allelujah Days; Better Far; Big Time Buck White Chant; Black Balloons; Get Down; H.N.I.C.; Honey Man Song; Look at Them; Mighty Whitey; Money, Money, Money; Nobody Does My Thing; Step Across That Line; Tap the Plate; We Came in Chains

Cast: Cassius Clay; David Moody; Ron Rich; Ted Ross

579 • BUDDIES

OPENED: 10/27/1919   Theatre: Selwyn
Musical   Broadway: 259

Composer: B.C. Hilliam
Lyricist: B.C. Hilliam
Librettist: George V. Hobart
Producer: Arch Selwyn; Edgar Selwyn

Musical Director: B.C. Hilliam

Songs: Altogether Too Fond of You; Antidote [1]; Buddies; Buddies Ensemble; Darling [2]; Fairy Tales (Cinderella Tale); Homes They Hold So Dear [3]; Hullo Home!; I Never Realized [4] (C/L: Cole Porter); Italie [1]; My Indispensable Girl; Please Learn to Love; To Be Together Is the Thing; Twilight Song; Wail of the Tale of the

Long, Long Trail, The [1]; We'll Settle Down in Washington Square [2]; Weaver of Dreams [1]

Cast: Donald Brian; Peggy Wood; Roland Young

Notes: Out of town program lists Melville Gideon as composer. Those out of town songs that credit Hilliam are noted above. [1] Out Stamford 8/5/19. [2] Out New York 8/29/19. [3] Sheet music only. [4] Also in THE ECLIPSE.

580 • BUDDY: THE BUDDY HOLLY STORY

OPENED: 11/04/1990   Theatre: Shubert
Musical   Broadway: 225

Librettist: Alan Janes
Producer: Paul Elliott; Laurie Mansfield; David Mirvish; Greg Smith
Director: Rob Bettinson

Costumes: Bill Butler; Carolyn Smith; **Lighting Designer:** Graham McLusky; **Musical Director:** Paul Jury; **Set Design:** Andy Walmsley

Songs: Blue Days, Black Nights; Changing All These Changes; Chantilly Lace; Everyday; Flower of My Heart; Heatbeat; It Doesn't Matter Anymore; It's So Easy to Fall in Love; Johnny B. Goode; La Bamba; Listen to Me; Looking for Someone to Love; Mailman Bring Me No More Blues; Maybe Baby; Not Fade Away; Oh Boy; Peggy Sue; Peggy Sue Got Married; Raining in My Heart; Rave On; Ready Teddy; Sweet Love; Texas Rose; That'll Be the Day; That's All Right; Think It Over; True Love Ways; Well All Right; Why Do Fools Fall in Love; Words of Love; You Send Me

Cast: Philip Anthony; Melanie Doane; Paul Hipp; Russ Jolly; David Mucci; Bobby Prochaska; Fred Sanders

Notes: No original songs in this show.

581 • BUGLAND

OPENED: 1919

Composer: Albert Von Tilzer
Lyricist: Bert Kalmar

Cast: Jessie Brown; Bert Kalmar

Notes: No other information available.

582 • BUNCH AND JUDY, THE

OPENED: 11/28/1922   Theatre: Globe
Musical   Broadway: 65

Composer: Jerome Kern
Lyricist: Anne Caldwell
Librettist: Anne Caldwell
Producer: Charles B. Dillingham
Director: Fred G. Latham

Costumes: Paul Poiret; **Musical Director:** Victor Baravalle; **Orchestrations:** Stephen Jones; **Set Design:** Paul Poiret

Songs: And Her Mother Came Too [3] (C: Ivor Novello; L: Dion Titheradge); Clansman March and Fling; Dance a la Russe; Entrance of Duke; Every Day in Every Way [1]; 'Have You Forgotten Me' Blues, The [2]; Hot Dog [3]; How Do You Do, Katinka?; Lovely Lassie; Minuet; Morning Glory; Naughty Nobleman; Pale Venetian Moon; Peach Girl; Silenzio; Times Square

Cast: Adele Astaire; Fred Astaire; Roberta Beatty; Ray Doolcy

Notes: [1] Chorus same as "Katy Did" from OH I SAY. [2] Titled "Why-Don't-You-Write-to-Me Blues" out of town. [3] Cut prior to opening.

583 • BUNDLE OF NERVES, A

OPENED: 03/13/1983   Theatre: Top of the Gate
Revue   Off-Broadway: 33

Composer: Brian Lasser
Lyricist: Edward Dunn; Geoff Leon
Producer: Howard J. Burnett; Leonard Finger; Terry Spiegel
Director: Arthur Faria

Choreographer: Arthur Faria; **Costumes:** David Toser; **Lighting Designer:** Barry Arnold; **Musical Director:** Clay Fullum; **Orchestrations:** Steven Margoshes; **Set Design:** Barry Arnold; **Vocal Arranger:** Steven Margoshes

Songs: After Dinner Drinks; Boogey Man; Bundle of Nerves; Connie; Fatality Hop, The; Flying; I Don't Know How to Have Sex; I Eat; I'm Afraid; News, The; Old Enough to Know Better; She Smiled at Me; Slice of Life; Studs; That Sound; Waiting; What Do You Do?; What's That?

Cast: Gary Beach; Carolyn Casanave; Ray Gill; Vicki Lewis; Karen Mason

584 • BUNK OF 1926

OPENED: 02/16/1926   Theatre: Heckscher
Revue   Broadway: 104

Composer: Gene Lockhart
Lyricist: Gene Lockhart
Librettist: Gene Lockhart; Percy Waxman
Producer: Talbot Productions
Director: Gene Lockhart

Choreographer: Adrian S. Perrin; **Musical Director:** Robert Armbruster; **Orchestrations:** Robert Armbruster; C.S. Copping; **Set Design:** William A. Hanna

Songs: Bunk; Chatter; Cuddle Up (C: Robert Armbruster); Do You Do the Charleston?; How Very Long Ago It Seems (L: Percy Waxman); In Washington Square (L: Percy Waxman); Milky Way, The (L: Percy Waxman); Modest Little Thing, A; Monte, the Model; Movie Melodrama, A (inst.) (C: Deems Taylor); Noches Espanolas; Opening Chorus (L: Percy Waxman); Those Mammy Boys (C: Robert Armbruster; L: Percy Waxman); Way to Your Heart, The; We're Going Away; You Told Me That You Loved Me But You Never Told Me Why (L: Percy Waxman)

Cast: Carol Joyce; Gene Lockhart

Notes: [1] Sheet music only.

585 • BUNTY BULLS AND STRINGS

Notes: *See HOKEY-POKEY.*

586 • BURGOMASTER, THE

OPENED: 12/31/1900   Theatre: Manhattan
Musical   Broadway: 33

Composer: Gustav Luders
Lyricist: Frank Pixley
Librettist: Frank Pixley

Songs: Aristocracy, The; Bathing Girls, The; Cupid Does Not Marry [1]; Dear Old College Days; Drinking Song [1]; Dutch Cadets, The; Finale [2]; Finale Act II [2]; Finale Act III [2]; Good-Bye New Amsterdam; I Drink from My Heart to You; I Love You Dear and Only You; If I Were a Hypnotist [1]; In Gay Paris; Just Keep Cool; Land of the Midnight Sun; Liberty Girl, The; Little Soubrette, The; Love Can't Say No; Merely a

Matter of Form; Modern Gladiator, The; Painting Chicago Red; Prologue of Dutch Girls [2]; Rainy Daisies, The; Reaching for the Cake; Summer Girl, The; Tale of the Kangaroo, The; We Always Work the Public; We're Civilized; We've Never Discovered Him Yet; Yo Ho! For a Jolly Good Sail

Cast: Henry E. Dixey; Raymond Hitchcock; Ruth White; Knox Wilson

Notes: [1] Sheet music only. [2] Vocal score only. [3] Vocal score titles this "Goodbye Mr. Amsterdam," a lyric which never appears in the song.

587 • BURLESQUE

OPENED: 09/12/1927   Theatre: Plymouth
Play   Broadway: 372

Composer: Peter De Rose; Albert Von Tilzer
Author: Arthur Hopkins; George Manker Watters
Producer: Arthur Hopkins
Director: Arthur Hopkins

Choreographer: Mary Jennings; **Musical Director:** Paul F. Van Loan; **Set Design:** Cleon Throckmorton

Songs: Either You Do or You Don't (L: Edward Grant; Jo Trent); I'm Wonderin' Who (L: Edward Grant; Jo Trent); Just an Hour of Love (L: Jo Trent)

Cast: Charles D. Brown; Oscar Levant; Paul Porter; Hal Skelly; Barbara Stanwyck; Eileen Wilson

588 • BURNING TO SING OR SINGING TO BURN

OPENED: 10/07/1904
Musical

Composer: Gustave Kerker
Librettist: R.H. Burnside

Notes: One-act vaudeville musical. Incomplete program.

589 • BUSKER ALLEY

OPENED: 1995
Musical   Closed out of town

Composer: Richard M. Sherman; Robert B. Sherman
Lyricist: Richard M. Sherman; Robert B. Sherman
Librettist: A.J. Carothers
Producer: Jujamcyn Theatres; TV Asahi; Barry Weissler; Fran Weissler
Director: Jeff Calhoun

Source ST. MARTIN'S LANE (SIDEWALKS OF LONDON) (Film: Clemence Dane); **Choreographer:** Jeff Calhoun; **Costumes:** Willa Kim; **Dance Arranger:** John McDaniel; **Lighting Designer:** Richard Pilbrow; **Musical Director:** John McDaniel; **Orchestrations:** William David Brohn; **Set Design:** Tony Walton; **Vocal Arranger:** John McDaniel

Songs: All Around the Town; Baby Me; Blow Us a Kiss [2]; Busker Alley; Charley the Busker; Crazy 'Appy Tears; Funnybone [1]; God Bless the Buskers [1]; He Has a Way; How Long Have I Loved Libby? [1]; Hula Love Song; I'm on the Inside; Libby [1]; Mates; Memory Ballet (inst.) [2]; Million Miles from You, A; Ordinary Couples; Plain Jane [2]; She Has a Way; Strays; Tap 'Appy Feet; Tin Whistle Tune; Waitin' for Ann; What to Do with 'Er; When Do I Get Mine?; When the Moonlight's Bright in Brighton; Where Are the Faces? [1]; Where the 'Ell Is 'Ome? [1]; World of Beautiful Girls, The

Cast: Brent Barrett; Drew Eliot; Laurie Gamache; Huber Marionettes, The; Marcia Lewis; Lee Mark Nelson; Darcie Roberts; Tommy Tune

Notes: [1] Cut prior to rehearsals. [2] Cut prior to opening.

590 • BUSKERS

Notes: *See BUSKER ALLEY.*

591 • BUSTER BROWN

OPENED: 01/24/1905   Theatre: Majestic
Musical   Broadway: 95

Composer: John W. Bratton
Lyricist: Paul West
Librettist: Charles Newman; Melville Raymond; George Totten Smith
Director: James Gorman; Melville Raymond

Source BUSTER BROWN (Comic Strip: R.E. Outcault); **Costumes:** A. Wilbur Crane; **Set Design:** Ernest Albert

Songs: Bo-Peep; Boy, the Woodshed and the Strap, The [1]; Buster Brown [1]; Buster Brown's Bobby Burns Brigade [1]; Buster's Chums; Come Down Susie [1]; Come Out Sue [6]; Cooks, The [1]; Cupid Is the Captain of the Army [2]; Dago [1]; French Maids, The; German Philosophy [1]; Gladys O'Flynn; Good Bye My Sailor Boy [2]; I Couldn't Make a Hit with Susie [1]; I'll Be Your Honey; Independence Day [1]; Katrina [3]; Laces and Graces [4]; Look Out for Her [3]; Love Me and the World Is Mine [5] (C: Ernest R. Ball; L: Dave Reed Jr.); Mary Jane and Her Little Playmates [1]; Mollie from Mayo [1]; Moon Dear [2]; Musical Cooks [3]; Old Board Walk, The [1]; Opening Chorus; Resolved (C: John W. Bratton; L: Paul West); Rock, Rock, Rock [1]; Rosebuds, The [1]; Sue, Sue I Love You; Sweetheart Sue; That's the Girl [6]; Try It on the Day [3]; Vacation Days [1]

Cast: George Ali; Master Gabriel

Notes: [1] Out Cedar Rapids 11/28/07. [2] Out Wilkes-Barre 1906. [3] Out Buffalo 3/28/04. [4] Out Washington, D.C. 12/20/04. [5] Out Wilkes-Barre 1906. Also in SIMPLE SIMON SIMPLE. Not written for this show. [6] Sheet music only.

592 • BUSY IZZY'S BOODLE

OPENED: 04/06/1908
Musical   Closed out of town

Composer: William J. McKenna
Lyricist: Frank Kennedy

Cast: George Sidney

Notes: No program available. A subway circuit show.

593 • BUT NEVER JAM TODAY

OPENED: 07/31/1979   Theatre: Longacre
Musical   Broadway: 7

Composer: Bert Keyes; Bob Larimer
Lyricist: Bob Larimer
Librettist: Vinnette Carroll; Bob Larimer
Producer: Anita MacShane; Arch Nadler; Urban Arts Th.

Source ALICE'S ADVENTURES IN WONDERLAND (Novel: Lewis Carroll); **Choreographer:** Talley Beatty; **Costumes:** William Schroder; **Dance Arranger:** H.B. Barnum; **Incidental Music:** Donald Johnston; **Lighting Designer:** Ken Billington; **Musical Director:** Donald Johnston; **Orchestrations:** H.B. Barnum; Larry Blank; Bert Keyes; **Set Design:** William Schroder; **Vocal Arranger:** Cleavant Derricks

Songs: All the Same for Me; And They All Call the Hatter Mad; But Never Jam Today; Curiouser and Curiouser; God Could Give Me Anything; I Like to Win; I've Got My Orders; Join the Dance [1]; Jumping from Rock to Rock; Long Live the Queen; Lullaby [1]; More I See People, The; My Little Room; Real Life Lullaby, A; Riddle of Life [1]; Riding for a Fall; Six Impossible Things [1]; Tell Some Pretty Lies to Me [1]; They; Twinkle Twinkle Little Star

Cast: Lynne Clifton-Allen; Cleavant Derricks; Charlene Harris; Jai Oscar St. John; Lynne Thigpen

Notes: This is a rewriting of ALICE. [1] Cut prior to opening.

594 • BUTTERFLIES ARE FREE

OPENED: 10/21/1969   Theatre: Booth
Play   Broadway: 1128

Author: Leonard Gershe
Producer: Max J. Brown; Byron Goldman; Arthur Whitelaw
Director: Milton Katselas

Costumes: Robert Mackintosh; **Lighting Designer:** Jules Fisher; **Set Design:** Richard Seger

Songs: Butterflies Are Free (C/L: Stephen Schwartz)

Cast: Blythe Danner; Keir Dullea; Michael Glaser; Eileen Heckart

595 • BUTTERFLY

OPENED: 10/10/1987
Musical   Closed out of town

Composer: Craig Safan
Lyricist: Mark Mueller

Librettist: Mark Mueller; Craig Safan
Producer: Sue Frost; Goodspeed Opera House
Director: Jack Hofsiss

Source MADAME BUTTERFLY (Opera: Giacomo Puccini); **Choreographer:** Patrice Soriero; **Costumes:** Jess Goldstein; **Lighting Designer:** Allen Lee Hughes; **Musical Director:** Jeanine Levenson; **Orchestrations:** Keith Levenson; **Set Design:** Loy Arcenas

Songs: Backstage; Citizen of the World; Different Worlds; Don't Tell Me; Everything I Said Was True; Favorite Song; Floating Away; Honor; I Stand Outside Myself; Magic Fan; Meet-Su- No; Middle Ground, The; Moshi, Moshi; My Japanese World; Next Dream, The; Nobody Looks at the Moon; Open the Windows; Paint My Dreams; Sister; Two Lands, Two Ladies; Waiting in a Garden; We Gave It a Shot

Cast: Michelle Artigas; Joseph Fong; Kevin John Gee; Peter Slutsker; Jack Wagner

Notes: Goodspeed Opera House.

596 • BUTTRIO SQUARE

OPENED: 10/14/1952   Theatre: New Century
Musical   Broadway: 7

Composer: Fred Stamer
Lyricist: Gen Genovese
Librettist: Gen Genovese; Billy Gilbert
Producer: Gen Genovese; Edward Woods
Director: Eugene Loring

Source UNKNOWN (Play: Hal Cranton; Gen Genovese); **Choreographer:** Eugene Loring; **Dance Arranger:** Roger Adams; **Lighting Designer:** Samuel Leve; **Musical Director:** Maurice Levine; **Orchestrations:** Don Walker; **Set Design:** Samuel Leve

Songs: Every Day Is a Holiday; Fraternization Ballet; Get Me Out; I Keep Telling Myself (C: Arthur Jones); I'll Tell the World; I'm Gonna Be a Pop; Let's Make It Forever; Love Swept Like a Storm; More and More; No Place Like the Country (C: Arthur Jones); One Is a Lonely Number; Take It Away (C: Roger Adams); Tarantula; You're Mine, All Mine

Cast: Lawrence Brooks; Billy Gilbert; Lois Hunt; Susan Johnson; Joan McCracken

597 • BUY BONDS, BUSTER

OPENED: 06/04/1972   Theatre: Theatre de Lys
Revue   Off-Broadway: 1

Composer: Jack Holmes
Lyricist: Bill Conklin; Bob Miller
Librettist: Jack Holmes
Producer: Wits' End
Director: John Bishop

Choreographer: Bick Goss; **Costumes:** William Pitkin; **Lighting Designer:** William Strom; **Musical Director:** Shelly Markham; **Set Design:** William Pitkin

Songs: Buy Bonds, Buster [1]; Canteen Serenade [1]; Chico Chico [1]; Donuts for Defense [1]; Dreamboat from Dreamland [1]; Flim Flam Floosie [1]; Freedom Choo-Choo, The [1]; Hat Crossover; Master Race Polka; My G.I. Joey [1]; Now and Then; O Say Can You See [1]; Pearl; So Long for Now; Tan 'n' Hot; These Are Worth Fighting For [1]; Us Two [1]; When the Bluebirds Fly All Over the World [1]; Woogie Boogie, The

Cast: Suellen Estey; Winston De Witt Hemsley; Virginia Martin; Rick Podell; Rowena Rollins

Notes: See also O SAY CAN YOU SEE!, an earlier version of this show. [1] Also in O SAY CAN YOU SEE!

598 • BUZZIN' AROUND

OPENED: 07/06/1920   Theatre: Casino
Revue   Broadway: 23

Composer: Will Morrissey
Lyricist: Edward Madden; Will Morrissey
Librettist: Edward Madden; Will Morrissey
Producer: Will Morrissey
Director: Will Morrissey

Choreographer: Ernest F. Young; **Musical Director:** Ivan Rudisill

Songs: Buzzin' Around; Ching-A-Ling Fling; Every Nation Has a Broadway of Its Own; Good Night Dear; How Could She Love Me Like That?; I'll Be Just the Same; O-I-L Spells Oil; Opening Ensemble; Pip Pip?; Poor Winter Garden Girl; Toot Toot; Voulez-Vous; Will You Forgive Us?

Cast: Elizabeth Brice; Will Morrissey; Ernest F. Young

599 • BY BERNSTEIN

OPENED: 11/23/1975   Theatre: Chelsea Theatre
                                            Center
Revue   Off-Broadway: 17

Composer: Leonard Bernstein
Lyricist: Betty Comden; Adolph Green
Librettist: Betty Comden; Adolph Green
Producer: Chelsea Theatre Center
Director: Michael Bawtree; Robert Kalfin

Costumes: Lawrence King; Michael H. Yeargan;
Lighting Designer: Marc B. Weiss; **Musical
Director:** Clay Fullum; **Orchestrations:** Thomas
Pierson; **Set Design:** Lawrence King; Michael H.
Yeargan; **Vocal Arranger:** Clay Fullum

Songs: Ain't Got No Tears Left [5] (L: Leonard
Bernstein); Another Love [4]; Captain Hook's
Soliloquy [8] (L: Leonard Bernstein); Coolie's
Dilemma, The [10] (L: Jerry Leiber); Dream
with Me [6]; Gabey's Comin' [4]; Here Comes
the Sun [12]; I Know a Fella [1] (L: Leonard
Bernstein); I'm Afraid It's Love [3]; In There [11]
(L: Stephen Sondheim); Intermission's Great,
The [3]; It's Got to Be Bad to Be Good [3] (L:
Leonard Bernstein); Kids Ain't (Like Everybody
Else) [4] (L: Stephen Sondheim); Lonely Me [3];
Ringaroundarosy [7] (L: John Latouche); Rio
Bamba, The [2] (L: Leonard Bernstein); Say
When [3]; Spring Will Come Again [12]; Story of
My Life, The [9]; Welcome [1]

Cast: Jack Bittner; Margery Cohen; Jim Corti; Ed
Dixon; Patricia Elliot; Kurt Peterson; Janie Sell

Notes: [1] Written for this show. [2] Music
originally FANCY FREE (ballet). [3] Cut from
ON THE TOWN. [4] Cut from WEST SIDE
STORY. [5] Cut from ON THE TOWN. Music
later in AGE OF ANXIETY SYMPHONY. [6] Cut
from PETER PAN. [7] Cut from CANDIDE. [8]
From PETER PAN. [9] Cut from WONDERFUL
TOWN. [10] Written for THE EXCEPTION AND
THE RULE. [11] Written for THE EXCEPTION
AND THE RULE. [12] Written for THE SKIN OF
OUR TEETH. Music later used for
CHICHESTER PSALMS.

600 • BY HEX

OPENED: 06/18/1956   Theatre: Tempo
Musical   Off-Broadway: 40

Composer: Howard Blankman

Lyricist: Howard Blankman; Richard Gehman;
John Rengier
Librettist: John Rengier
Producer: George Artman; Lester Hackett
Director: Bill Penn

Choreographer: Edmund Balin; **Costumes:** Rennie
Porocopio; **Lighting Designer:** John Moffat; **Set
Design:** Ed Flesh

Songs: Amishman, An; Antiques; Ferhuddled and
Ferhexed; I Can Learn; I Have Lived; I Know
My Love; It Takes Time; Market Day; Only a
Man; Shunned; Something New; Trouble with
Me; What Is Love?; Wonderful Bad, Wonderful
Good

Cast: Robert Caesar; Ken Cantril; Wynne Miller;
Tom Mixon; Rita Shay

601 • BY JUPITER

OPENED: 06/03/1942   Theatre: Shubert
Musical   Broadway: 427

Composer: Richard Rodgers
Lyricist: Lorenz Hart
Librettist: Lorenz Hart; Richard Rodgers
Producer: Richard Rodgers; Dwight Deere Wiman
Director: Joshua Logan

Source WARRIOR'S HUSBAND, THE (Play: Julian
F. Thompson); **Choreographer:** Robert Alton;
Costumes: Irene Sharaff; **Musical Director:**
Johnny Green; **Orchestrations:** Don Walker; **Set
Design:** Jo Mielziner; **Vocal Arranger:** Johnny
Green; Clay Warnick

Songs: Bottoms Up; Boy I Left Behind Me, The;
Careless Rhapsody; Ev'rything I've Got; Fool
Meets Fool [1]; For Jupiter and Greece; Gateway
of the Temple of Minerva, The; Greeks Have Got
the Girdle, The (Finaletto); Here's a Hand;
Jupiter Forbid; Life Was Monotonous [2]; Life
with Father; No, Mother, No; Nobody's Heart;
Nothing to Do But Relax [2]; Now That I've Got
My Strength; Wait Till You See Her [1]

Cast: Bertha Belmore; Ray Bolger; Irene Corlett;
Mark Dawson; Bob Douglas; Ronald Graham;
Robert Hightower; Jayne Manners; Constance
Moore; Monica Moore; Benay Venuta; Vera-Ellen

Notes: Titled ALL'S FAIR during tryouts. [1]
Dropped during run. [2] Cut prior to opening.

602 • BY STROUSE

OPENED: 02/01/1978   Theatre: Manhattan
Theatre Club
Revue   Off-Broadway: 156

Composer: Charles Strouse
Lyricist: Lee Adams
Producer: Norman Kean

Choreographer: Mary Kyte; **Musical Director:** Randy Barnett; **Set Design:** Connie Wexler; Peter Wexler

Songs: Applause [12]; Born Too Late [1] (L: Fred Tobias); Broadway Musical, A [15]; But Alive [12]; Bye Bye Birdie [9]; Colorful [3]; Don't Forget 127th Street [3]; Everything's Great [3]; Good Friends [12]; Half of Life [8]; How Lovely to Be a Woman [4]; Hunky Dory [13] (L: Charles Strouse); I Don't Want to Grow Old [2] (L: Charles Strouse); I'm Not in Philadelphia [7]; Living Alone (C: Charles Strouse); Lot of Livin' to Do, A [4]; Marjorie Morningstar [11]; Melt Us (Immigration Rag) [5]; N.Y.C. [6] (L: Martin Charnin); Night Song [3]; Once Upon a Time [5]; One Boy [4]; One Last Kiss [4]; One of a Kind [12]; Put on a Happy Face [4]; Some Bright Morning [10] (L: David Rogers); Stick Around [3]; This Is the Life [3]; Those Were the Days [14]; Tomorrow [6]; Welcome to the Theatre [12]; What a Country [5]; You're Never Fully Dressed Without a Smile [6] (L: Martin Charnin)

Cast: Gary Beach; Donna Marshall; Maureen Moore; Gail Nelson

Notes: No original songs in this show. [1] Pop song. [2] From unproduced show PALM BEACH. [3] From GOLDEN BOY. [4] From BYE BYE BIRDIE. [5] From ALL AMERICAN. [6] From ANNIE. [7] Cut from ALL AMERICAN. [8] From the unproduced film THE BORROWERS. [9] From the film BYE BYE BIRDIE. [10] From CHARLIE AND ALGERNON. [11] From unproduced musical MARJORIE MORNINGSTAR. [12] From APPLAUSE. [13] From HUNKY DORY. [14] From the TV series ALL IN THE FAMILY. [15] From A BROADWAY MUSICAL.

603 • BY THE BEAUTIFUL SEA

OPENED: 04/08/1954   Theatre: Majestic
Musical   Broadway: 268

Composer: Arthur Schwartz
Lyricist: Dorothy Fields
Librettist: Dorothy Fields; Herbert Fields
Producer: Lawrence Carr; Robert Fryer
Director: Marshall Jamison

Choreographer: Helen Tamiris; **Costumes:** Irene Sharaff; **Musical Director:** Jay Blackton; **Orchestrations:** Robert Russell Bennett; **Set Design:** Jo Mielziner; **Vocal Arranger:** Jay Blackton

Songs: Alone Too Long; Come to Blackpool [1] (L: Arthur Schwartz); Coney Island Boat; Good Time Charlie; Hang Up!; Happy Habit; Hooray for George the Third; I'd Rather Wake Up by Myself; It's All Mine [4]; It's Not Where You Start [5]; It's Up to You [4]; Lottie Gibson Specialty (Please Send Me Down a Baby Brother); Me and Pollyanna [4]; Moments from Shakespeare [2]; Mona from Arizona; More Love than Your Love; Old Enough to Love [3]; Sea Song (By the Beautiful Sea), The; Thirty Weeks of Heaven [2]; Throw the Anchor Away; Tuscaloosa [6]

Cast: Mae Barnes; Shirley Booth; Wilbur Evans; Richard France; Anne Francine; Thomas Gleason; Carol Leigh; Cameron Prud'homme; Libi Staiger

Notes: [1] Written for proposed English production (with English setting) in early 80's. [2] Cut during previews. [3] Same music as "Tuscaloosa." [4] Not used. [5] Not used. Notice this is the same title as another Dorothy Fields song in SEESAW. [6] Not used. Same music as "Old Enough to Love."

604 • BY THE SAD SEA WAVES

OPENED: 03/05/1900   Theatre: Grand Opera
House
Musical   Broadway

Composer: Gustav Luders
Lyricist: Harry Bulger; J. Sherrie Mathews
Librettist: Harry Bulger; J. Sherrie Mathews
Director: Ned Wayburn

Costumes: Ned Wayburn; **Musical Director:** Gustav Luders; **Set Design:** Lamphier & Buhler

Songs: Bell Chorus (C: DeWitt); Buttercups and Daisies (C: Harry Bulger; J. Sherrie Mathews); Calisthenic Song (C: Barney Fagan); Fiddle and I

(C: Harry Bulger; J. Sherrie Mathews); Finale [1] (C: Charles Gebest); Honolulu Lady (C: Harry Bulger; J. Sherrie Mathews); In Dear Old London; I'se Found Yo', Honey, Found Yo', Now Be Mine [1]; Japanese Baby [1]; La-Par Micado (Rag- Time Opera) (C: Harry Bulger; J. Sherrie Mathews); Man Who Invented Ragtime, The [1]; Military Model (C: Harry Bulger; J. Sherrie Mathews); Operatic Ensemble [1]; Operatic, Most Emphatic; Ragtime Mixes My Brain [1]; Soldiers in Love's War [1]; This Dear Little Fellow Was Cupid [1]; Told Me Yo' Had Money in the Bank [1]; Under-Takers' Frolic, The [1]; Willow Pattern Plate, The (C: Leslie Stuart); Yankee Banners (C: Harry Bulger; J. Sherrie Mathews); You Told Me Yo' Had Money in the Bank

Cast: Harry Bulger; Jane Lennox; J. Sherrie Mathews; Rose Melville; Ned Wayburn

Notes: [1] From program of 1900.

605 • BY THE WAY
OPENED: 12/28/1925   Theatre: Gaiety
Musical   Broadway: 177

Composer: Vivian Ellis
Lyricist: Graham John
Librettist: Ronald Jeans; Harold Simpson
Producer: A.L. Erlanger

Songs: Beauty of Bath, The; By the Way; Gather Roses While You May; High Street, Africa (C/L: Cumberland Clark; Everett Lynton; Huntley Trevor); Hum a Little Tune; I Know Someone Loves Me; In the Same Way I Love You (C: H.M. Tennant; L: Eric Little); I've Found the Bluebird [1] (C: Richard Myers; L: Leo Robin); London Bank Clerk Blues, The; My Castle in Spain (C/L: Isham Jones); Nippy; No One's Ever Kissed Me (C: Ronald Jeans; L: Philip Braham); Oh, How I've Waited for You (C: Nat D. Ayer; L: Harry Carlton); Shall We Join the Ladies; There's Nothing New Under the Sun; What Can They See in Dancing?

Cast: Jack Hurlburt

Notes: [1] Sheet music only.

606 • BYE, BYE, BARBARA
OPENED: 08/25/1924   Theatre: National
Musical   Broadway: 16

Composer: Monte Carlo; Alma Sanders
Lyricist: Monte Carlo; Alma Sanders
Librettist: Alonzo Price; Sidney Toler
Producer: Theodore Hammerstein; Adolf Meyer
Director: Alonzo Price

Costumes: William Weaver; **Musical Director:** Antonio Bafunno; **Orchestrations:** William M. Redfield; **Set Design:** Walter Shaffner

Songs: Amusing Myself; As Kipling Says: 'I Learned About Women from Her' (L: Benj. Hapgood Burt); Bo-Peep; Bye, Bye Barbara [1]; China; Curiosity; Gee, You Must Be in Love; Harmony; Kiss Invention; Let's Pretend [1]; Live for Today; One in the World for Me [1]; Pas Seul; Quaint Little House for Two; Sittin' in Clover; Why Don't They Leave the Sheik Alone?

Cast: John E. Hazzard; Janet Velie

Notes: [1] Sheet music only.

607 • BYE BYE BIRDIE
OPENED: 04/14/1960   Theatre: Martin Beck
Musical   Broadway: 607

Composer: Charles Strouse
Lyricist: Lee Adams
Librettist: Michael Stewart
Producer: L. Slade Brown; Edward Padula
Director: Gower Champion

Choreographer: Gower Champion; **Costumes:** Miles White; **Dance Arranger:** John Morris; **Lighting Designer:** Peggy Clark; **Musical Director:** Elliot Lawrence; **Orchestrations:** Robert Ginzler; **Set Design:** Robert Randolph

Songs: All Woman [1]; Baby, Talk to Me; English Teacher, An; He's Mine [2]; Healthy, Normal, American Boy, A; Honestly Sincere; How Lovely to Be a Woman; How to Kill a Man 100 Ways Ballet (inst.); Hymn for a Sunday Evening; Kids; Lot of Livin' to Do, A; Older and Wiser [1]; One Boy (One Girl); One Giant Step [2]; One Last Kiss; Put on a Happy Face; Rosie; Shriner's Ballet (inst.); So Long [2]; Spanish Rose; Telephone Hour, The; There Comes a Time [1]; We Love You, Conrad!; What Did I Ever See in Him?; World at Large, The [1]

Cast: Dick Gautier; Paul Lynde; Marijane Maricle;

Kay Medford; Michael J. Pollard; Chita Rivera; Dick Van Dyke; Susan Watson

Notes: [1] Cut prior to opening. [2] Written for 1991 revival.

608 • BYE BYE, BONNIE

OPENED: 01/13/1927   Theatre: Ritz
Musical   Broadway: 125

Composer: Albert Von Tilzer
Lyricist: Neville Fleeson
Librettist: Bide Dudley; Louis Simon
Director: Edgar MacGregor

Songs: Across the River from Queens; Anyone! Who Does That Can't Be So Dumb [1] (L: A. Seymour Brown); Bye, Bye, Bonnie; Have You Used Soft Soap?; I Like to Make It Cozy; Look in Your Engagement Book; Love Is Like a Blushing Rose [1]; Lovin' Off My Mind; Out of Town Buyers; Promise Not to Stand Me Up Again; September Night [1] (L: A. Seymour Brown); Tampico Tap; Toodle-oo; When You Get to Congress; You and I Love You and Me

Cast: Laine Blaire; Dorothy Burgess; William Frawley; Georgie Hale; Ruby Keeler

Notes: [1] Sheet music only.

609 • BYE, BYE, BROADWAY
Notes: *See BROADWAY, BROADWAY.*

C

610 • CABARET

OPENED: 11/20/1966   Theatre: Broadhurst
Musical   Broadway: 1166

Composer: John Kander
Lyricist: Fred Ebb
Librettist: Joe Masteroff
Producer: Harold Prince
Director: Harold Prince

Source: BERLIN STORIES, THE (Novel: Christopher Isherwood); **Source:** I AM A CAMERA (Play: John van Druten); **Choreographer:** Ron Field; **Costumes:** Patricia Zipprodt; **Lighting Designer:** Jean Rosenthal; **Musical Director:** Hal Hastings; **Orchestrations:** Don Walker; **Set Design:** Boris Aronson

Songs: Angel of Love [1]; Cabaret; Don't Go Sally [3]; Don't Tell Mama; Down-Down-Down [1]; Goodtime Charley [1]; Guten Abend [1]; Herman, My German [1]; I Don't Care Much [2]; If You Could See Her; It Couldn't Please Me More; It'll All Blow Over [1]; It's the End of the Party [1]; Man in the Mirror, The [1]; Married; Meeskite; Money Song, The; Never in Paris [1]; Perfectly Marvelous; Room-Mates [1]; So What?; Telephone Song; Tomorrow Belongs to Me; Two Ladies; What Would You Do?; Why Should I Wake Up?; Wilkommen

Cast: Bert Convy; Jack Gilford; Joel Grey; Jill Haworth; Lotte Lenya; Peg Murray; Edward Winter

Notes: [1] Cut prior to opening. [2] Cut in previews. Added to 1987 Broadway revival. [3] Added to 1987 Broadway revival.

611 • CABARET GIRL, THE

OPENED: 09/14/1922   Theatre: Winter Garden
Musical   London: 361

Composer: Jerome Kern
Lyricist: P.G. Wodehouse
Librettist: George Grossmith; P.G. Wodehouse

Producer: George Grossmith; J.A.E. Malone
Director: George Grossmith

Choreographer: Jack Haskell; **Costumes:** Dolly Tree; **Musical Director:** John Ansell

Songs: At the Ball (L: George Grossmith); Chopin Ad-Lib (Opening Chorus) [1]; Dancing Time (L: George Grossmith); Entrance Scena; Finale Act I (Vicar Song); Finale Act II; Finaletto Act I; First Rose of Summer [2] (L: Anne Caldwell; P.G. Wodehouse); Journey's End [4]; Ka-lu-a [3] (L: Anne Caldwell); London, Dear Old London; Looking All Over for You; Mr. Gravvins- Mr. Gripps (L: George Grossmith; P.G. Wodehouse); Nerves; Oriental Dreams (L: George Grossmith); Pergola Patrol, The [5]; Shimmy with Me; Those Days Are Gone Forever; Whoop-de-oodle-do!; You Want the Best Seats, We Have 'Em

Cast: Dorothy Dickson; Leigh Ellis; Norman Griffin; George Grossmith

Notes: [1] Same music as "Faith, Hope and Charity" in SHE'S A GOOD FELLOW. [2] With new Wodehouse lyric in SHE'S A GOOD FELLOW. [3] Previously in GOOD MORNING DEARIE. [4] Also in THE CITY CHAP. [5] Music used for "Is This Not a Lovely Spot" in SITTNG PRETTY.

612 • CABIN IN THE SKY

OPENED: 10/25/1940   Theatre: Martin Beck
Musical   Broadway: 156

Composer: Vernon Duke
Lyricist: John Latouche
Librettist: Lynn Root
Producer: Vinton Freedley; Albert Lewis
Director: George Balanchine; Albert Lewis

Choreographer: George Balanchine; **Costumes:** Boris Aronson; **Musical Director:** Max Meth; **Orchestrations:** Charles L. Cooke; Fudd Livingston; Domenico Savino; Nathan Van Cleve; **Set Design:** Boris Aronson; **Vocal Arranger:** Ralph Blane; Hugh Martin

Songs: Boogy-Woogy; Cabin in the Sky; Do What You Wanna Do; Egyptian Ballet; Flatfoot's Theme (inst.); Fugue; General's Song, The; Gospel; Great Day [1]; Honey in the Honeycomb; It's Not So Bad to Be Good; Jazz Fugue (inst.); Lazy Step; Little Poppa Satan [4]; Living It Up [1] (L: Vernon Duke); Love Me Tomorrow (But Leave Me Alone To-Day); Love Turned the Light Out; Make Way [1]; Man Upstairs, The [2]; My Old Virginia Home (On the River Nile); Not a Care in the World [3]; Pay Heed; Savannah; Taking a Chance on Love (L: Ted Fetter; John Latouche); Vision Ballet (inst.); Wade in the Water [1]; We'll Live All Over Again [2]

Cast: Todd Duncan; Katherine Dunham; Rex Ingram; Ethel Waters; Dooley Wilson

Notes: Originally titled LITTLE JOE. [1] Added to 1964 revival. [2] Not used. Added to 1964 revival. [3] Added to 1964 revival. Originally in BANJO EYES. [4] Not used.

613 • CADET GIRL, THE

OPENED: 07/25/1900   Theatre: Herald Square
Musical   Broadway: 48

Composer: Ludwig Englander
Lyricist: Harry B. Smith
Librettist: Harry B. Smith
Producer: A.H. Chamberlyn
Director: George Marion

Source LES DEMOISELLES DE SAINT-CYRIENS (Musical: DeCottons; Paul Gavault; Louis Varney)

Songs: Battalion of France; Cadets of St. Cry, The; Cantineer of the Regiment; Come, Gentle Stanger; Demon of the Deep, The; Gottet Got (L: J. Cheever Goodwin); I Annex It (L: J. Cheever Goodwin); In My Museum Now; Opening Chorus; Pavilion of Love, The; Special Train, The; They Are Nothing but Girls; Ve Vas Germans; We Are the Heiresses; We Cannot Let You Go; When a Girl Doesn't Know Where She Is

Cast: Dan Daly; Christie MacDonald; Adele Richie; Bessie Wynn

614 • CAESAR'S WIFE

OPENED: 1973
Musical   Unproduced

Composer: Lee Pockriss
Lyricist: Carolyn Leigh

Songs: All Woman; Am I in Love Again?; Caesar Comes; Cat's Away, The; Hurry on Home; Progress Report; Seen One, You've Seen 'Em All; Take My Place; That's Her (That's Him); Walk on Air; What Am I Doing Wrong?; You've Married a Man (Who's Been Married Before)

615 • CAFE CROWN

OPENED: 04/17/1964   Theatre: Martin Beck
Musical   Broadway: 3

Composer: Albert Hague
Lyricist: Marty Brill
Librettist: Hy Kraft; Sam Leve
Producer: Philip Rose; Swanlee
Director: Jerome Eskow

Source CAFE CROWN (Play: Hy Kraft); **Choreographer:** Ron Field; **Costumes:** Ruth Morley; **Musical Director:** Gershon Kingsley; **Orchestrations:** Hershy Kay; **Set Design:** Sam Leve; **Vocal Arranger:** Gershon Kingsley

Songs: All Those Years; Au Revoir Poland — Hello New York!; Do You Know What This Could Do to Me? [1]; Don't Make Me Nervous [1]; I'm Gonna Move; King Lear Ballet; Lifetime of Love, A; Magical Things in Life; Make the Most of Spring; Man Must Have Something to Live For, A; Mother's Heart, A; On a Day Such As This [1]; On This Wedding Day; Rhapsody for Pinochle Players [1]; So Long As It Isn't Shakespeare; Someone's Waiting [1]; That's the Life for Me; What's Gonna Be Tomorrow; What's the Matter with Buffalo?; You're a Stranger in This Neighborhood

Cast: Alan Alda; Monte Amundsen; Theodore Bikel; Sam Levene; Brenda Lewis; Tommy Rall

Notes: [1] Not in programs.

616 • CALAMITY JANE

OPENED: 06/05/1961
Musical   Closed out of town

Composer: Sammy Fain
Lyricist: Paul Francis Webster
Librettist: Charles K. Freeman
Producer: John Kennedy
Director: James Vincent Russo

Source CALAMITY JANE (Film: Sammy Fain; James O'Hanlon; Paul Francis Webster); **Choreographer:** Frank Westbrook; **Musical Director:** Edwin McArthur; **Orchestrations:** Philip J. Lang; **Vocal Arranger:** Philip J. Lang

Songs: Adelaid; Black Hills of Dakota; Careless with the Truth; Deadwood Stage, The; Everyone Complains About the Weather; Higher than a Hawk; Hive Full of Honey; Love You Dearly [1]; Men [1]; Secret Love; Weather Dance (inst.); Woman's Touch, A

Cast: Edith Adams; Lila Gage; George Gaynes; Allyn Ann McLerie; April Shawhan; Nolan Van Way; Lou Wills Jr.

Notes: Muni Opera, St. Louis. [1] From movie LUCKY ME.

617 • CALIFORNIA
OPENED: 11/20/1911
Musical   Closed out of town

Composer: Robert Hood Bowers
Lyricist: Grant Stewart
Librettist: Cecil DeMille
Producer: Jesse L. Lasky

Musical Director: E. Grooney

Songs: Finale; Goodbye California; I Love You, My Own; My Blood Is Blue; Save the Mission; Tape and Chain, The

Cast: William Gordon; Harry L. Griffith; P. O'Malley Jennings; Leslie Leigh; Francis K. Lieb

Notes: Vocal score only. Poli's Theatre, Springfield, Mass.

618 • CALIPH, THE
OPENED: 09/03/1896   Theatre: Broadway
Musical   Broadway: 48

Composer: Ludwig Englander
Lyricist: Harry B. Smith
Librettist: Harry B. Smith
Producer: Nat Roth
Director: Richard Barker

Costumes: Mme. Siedel; **Set Design:** Homer F. Emens; Ernest Gros

Cast: Ada Bernard; Jefferson De Angelis; Irene Perry; Melville Stewart; Alf C. Whelan

Notes: No songs listed in program.

619 • CALL ME MADAM
OPENED: 10/12/1950   Theatre: Imperial
Musical   Broadway: 644

Composer: Irving Berlin
Lyricist: Irving Berlin
Librettist: Russel Crouse; Howard Lindsay
Producer: Leland Hayward
Director: George Abbott

Choreographer: Jerome Robbins; **Costumes:** Raoul Pene du Bois; **Dance Arranger:** Jesse Meeker; Genevieve Pitot; **Musical Director:** Jay Blackton; **Orchestrations:** Don Walker; **Set Design:** Raoul Pene du Bois

Songs: Anthem for Presentation [3]; Best Thing for You, The; Call Me Madam [1]; Can You Use Any Money Today?; Free [2]; Hostess with the Mostes' on the Ball; It's a Lovely Day Today; (Welcome to) Lichtenburg; Marrying for Love; Mr. Monotony [4]; Mrs. Sally Adams; Ocarina, The; Once Upon a Time Today; Our Day of Independence [3]; Something to Dance About; They Like Ike; Washington Square Dance; We Still Like Ike [1]; You're Just in Love [5]; You've Got to Be Way Out to Be In [1]

Cast: Ralph Chambers; Pat Harrington; Alan Hewitt; Paul Lukas; Ethel Merman; Russell Nype; Tommy Rall; Lilia Skala; Galina Talva; Jay Velie

Notes: [1] Written for unproduced TV production in 1967. [2] Cut New Haven prior to New York. Music used for "Free" from film WHITE CHRISTMAS. [3] Not used. [4] Cut New Haven prior to New York. Also cut from film EASTER PARADE and show MISS LIBERTY. Finally in JEROME ROBBINS' BROADWAY. [5] Titled "You're Not Sick You're Just in Love" out of town.

620 • CALL ME MISTER
OPENED: 04/18/1946   Theatre: National
Revue   Broadway: 734

Composer: Harold Rome
Lyricist: Harold Rome

Librettist: Arnold Auerbach; Arnold B. Horwitt
Producer: Melvyn Douglas; Herman Levin
Director: Robert H. Gordon

Choreographer: John Wray; **Costumes:** Grace Houston; **Lighting Designer:** Carlton Winkler; **Musical Director:** Lehman Engel; **Orchestrations:** Charles Huffine; Ben Ludlow; Julian Work; **Set Design:** Lester Polakov

Songs: Along with Me; Call Me Mister; Drug Store Song, The; Face on the Dime, The; Goin' Home Train; His Old Man; Home of Our Own, A; Love Remains the Same [1]; Military Life; Red Ball Express, The; Senators' Song, The; South America, Take It Away; Surplus Blues (Little Surplus Me); When We Meet Again; Yuletide, Park Avenue

Cast: Paula Bane; Bill Callahan; Chandler Cowles; Betty Garrett; George Hall; Maria Karnilova; Alan Manson; Jules Munshin; Danny Scholl; Lawrence Winters

Notes: [1] ASCAP/Library of Congress only.

621 • CALLING ALL MEN
OPENED: 1937
Revue   Closed out of town

Composer: Baldwin Bergersen
Lyricist: June Sillman
Librettist: Albert Carroll; Robert Garland; Leonard Sillman
Producer: Raymond Moore
Director: Leonard Sillman

Set Design: Mercedes

Songs: Calling All Men; Charming Young Man (C: Irvin Graham); Definitely Not for Debs (L: Irvin Graham; June Sillman); Down to the Sea in Other People's Ships (C/L: Irvin Graham); First Act Finale (C: Irvin Graham; L: Victor Priscilla); I Must Waltz; Lady Can Love, The [1] (C/L: Irvin Graham); Let Your Hair Down; Little Things About You; Lombardy Hunting Breakfast (C: Irvin Graham; L: Everett Marcy); Marcel Mousse; Olly, Cholly, Wally (I'm Dolly); Purity Is Power (C: Irvin Graham); Rather Stay Home with You; Secretary Opening; Sixty Second Romance (C: Bud Harris; L: Lawrence Harris); So You Want to Go into the Theatre, Baby (C/L: Irvin Graham); Speak for Yourself, John; Will She or Won't She?

Cast: Richard Carlson; Imogene Coca; June Sillman

Notes: Irvin Graham is listed in program as Irving Graham. From a program of 7/5/37 Cape Cod, Mass. [1] Cut from ALL IN FUN.

622 • CALLING ALL STARS
OPENED: 12/13/1934   Theatre: Hollywood
Revue   Broadway: 35

Composer: Harry Akst
Lyricist: Lew Brown
Librettist: Alan Baxter; Lew Brown; A. Dorian Otvos
Producer: Lew Brown
Director: Lew Brown; Thomas Mitchell

Choreographer: Maurice L. Kussel; Sara Mildred Strauss; **Costumes:** Billy Livingston; **Lighting Designer:** Feder; **Musical Director:** Al Goodman; Tom Jones; **Orchestrations:** Conrad Salinger; Hans Spialek; **Set Design:** Nat Karson

Songs: Calling All Stars; He Just Beats a Tom-Tom; I Don't Want to Be President (If It Means Losing You); I'd Like to Dunk You in My Coffee; If It's Love; I'm Stepping Out of the Picture; I've Nothing to Offer; Just Mention Joe; My Old Hoss; Stepping Out of the Picture [2]; Straw Hat in the Rain; Thinking Out Loud; Wanna Buy a Duke? [1]

Cast: Phil Baker; Al Bernie; Patricia Bowman; Judy Canova; Edgar Fairchild; Patsy Flick; Lou Holtz; Robert Lindholm; Ella Logan; Everett Marshall; Mitzi Mayfair; Harry McNaughton; Gertrude Niesen; Martha Raye; Jack Whiting

Notes: [1] Out 12/19/34 Boston. [2] ASCAP list only.

623 • CAMELOT
OPENED: 12/03/1960   Theatre: Majestic
Musical   Broadway: 873

Composer: Frederick Loewe
Lyricist: Alan Jay Lerner
Librettist: Alan Jay Lerner
Producer: Moss Hart; Alan Jay Lerner; Frederick Loewe
Director: Moss Hart

Source ONCE AND FUTURE KING, THE (Novel: T.H. White); **Choreographer:** Hanya Holm;

Costumes: Adrian; Tony Duquette; **Dance Arranger:** Trude Rittman; **Lighting Designer:** Feder; **Musical Director:** Franz Allers; **Orchestrations:** Robert Russell Bennett; Philip J. Lang; **Set Design:** Oliver Smith; **Vocal Arranger:** Trude Rittman

Songs: Before I Gaze at You Again; C'est Moi; Camelot; Face to Face [1]; Fie On Goodness [2]; Follow Me; Guenevere; How to Handle a Woman; I Loved You Once in Silence; I Wonder What the King Is Doing Tonight; If Ever I Would Leave You; Jousts, The [3]; Lusty Month of May, The; Parade (inst.) [3]; Persuasion, The; Seven Deadly Virtues, The; Simple Joys of Maidenhood, The; Then You May Take Me to the Fair [2]; What Do the Simple Folk Do?

Cast: Julie Andrews; Mary Sue Berry; Richard Burton; John Cullum; M'el Dowd; Robert Goulet; David Hurst; Roddy McDowall; Bruce Yarnell

Notes: [1] Cut Boston prior to New York. [2] Cut after opening. [3] Same music.

624 • CAMP MEETING 1840
OPENED: 05/1976   Theatre: Judson Poets'
Revue   Off-Off-Broadway

Composer: Al Carmines
Lyricist: Al Carmines
Librettist: Al Carmines

Choreographer: Bob Herget; **Costumes:** Michele Edwards; **Set Design:** Ted Goldstein

Songs: Atheism; Binnie; Day of the People Is Coming, The; Does God Ever Make Mistakes?; Forgiveness; He Comes Home in the Evening; Healing; I Want to Go Home to God; Joy in the Earth; Knowledge; Open Your Heart; Satan; Seduction; Threnody

Cast: Reathel Bean; Essie Borden; Lou Bullock; Lee Guilliatt

625 • CAMPAIGNERS
Musical

Composer: Frederick J. Eustis
Lyricist: Willis Maxwell Goodhue
Librettist: Willis Maxwell Goodhue

Songs: I Want a Boy; It's Nice to Be a Widow; Mary Smith; My Yankee Rose; Spooning on Sunday Night; Take Me Down to Luna

Notes: Sheet music only. No program available.

626 • CAN YOU SMELL GAS?
OPENED: 04/29/1976   Theatre: Cherry Lane
Play   Off-Broadway

Composer: Tony Hatch; Rick Jones
Lyricist: Tony Hatch; Rick Jones
Librettist: Andrew Davies
Producer: Michael Maxwell

Lighting Designer: Michael Krones; **Musical Director:** Uel Wade; **Set Design:** Michael Krones

Songs: One and One

Cast: Linda Polen

Notes: No program available of this one-woman show.

627 • CANARY, THE
OPENED: 11/04/1918   Theatre: Globe
Musical   Broadway: 152

Composer: Ivan Caryll
Lyricist: Anne Caldwell; P.G. Wodehouse
Librettist: George Barr; Louis Verneuil
Producer: Charles B. Dillingham
Director: Fred G. Latham; Edward Royce

Set Design: Joseph Urban

Songs: Burglar Dance (inst.) (C: Vickers); Ding Dong [3] (C/L: Irving Berlin); Haunting Honeymoon, The [1] (L: Anne Caldwell); Hunting Song (L: Anne Caldwell); I Have Just One Heart for Just One Boy (C/L: Irving Berlin); I Wouldn't Give That for the Man Who Couldn't Dance [4] (C/L: Irving Berlin); It's the Little Bit of Irish [5] (C/L: Irving Berlin); Jazz Marimba (C: Harry Tierney; L: Anne Caldwell); Julie and Her Johnnies (L: P.G. Wodehouse); Love Me in the Spring (C: William B. Kernell; L: Richard Fechheimer); Oh, Doctor (C: Harry Tierney; L: Anne Caldwell); Oh Promise Me You'll Write to Him Today [2] (C: Jerome Kern; L: Harry Clarke); Only in Dreams (L: Harry B. Smith); Take a Chance (Little Girl and Learn to Dance)

(C: Jerome Kern; L: Harry B. Smith); That Little German Band (L: Benj. Hapgood Burt); That's What Men Are For; They're Getting Away with Murder (C: William B. Kernell; L: Richard Fechheimer); This Is the Time (C/L: Clifton Crawford); Thousands of Years Ago (L: P.G. Wodehouse); You're So Beautiful (C/L: Irving Berlin)

Cast: Joseph Cawthorn; Harland Dixon; James Doyle; Sam Hardy; Louis Harrison; Julia Sanderson

Notes: [1] Sheet music only. [2] Cut after opening. Same music as "I've Been Waiting for You All the Time" in SHE'S A GOOD FELLOW. [3] May have been cut after opening. Also in YIP YIP YAPHANK. [4] Credited to Benjamin Hapgood Burt in programs. [5] May have been cut.

628 • CANARY COTTAGE

OPENED: 02/05/1917   Theatre: Morosco
Musical   Broadway: 112

Composer: Earl Carroll
Lyricist: Earl Carroll
Librettist: Oliver Morosco
Producer: Oliver Morosco
Director: Oliver Morosco

Choreographer: Frank Rainger; Frank Stammers; **Set Design:** Robert McQuinn

Songs: As Long As I Have You; But in the Morning; Canary Cottage; Follow the Cook; I Never Knew; I'll Marry No Explorer [1]; It Ruined Marc Antony; It's Always Orange Day in California; More I See of Men the More I Love My Dog, The; Old Man Methuselah; Such a Chauffeur; That Syncopated Harp

Cast: Hugh Cameron; Herbert Corthell; Trixie Friganza; Carl McCullough; Charles Ruggles; Dorothy Webb

Notes: [1] Sheet music only.

629 • CAN-CAN

OPENED: 05/07/1953   Theatre: Shubert
Musical   Broadway: 892

Composer: Cole Porter
Lyricist: Cole Porter

Librettist: Abe Burrows
Producer: Cy Feuer; Ernest Martin
Director: Abe Burrows

Choreographer: Michael Kidd; **Costumes:** Motley; **Dance Arranger:** Genevieve Pitot; **Lighting Designer:** Jo Mielziner; **Musical Director:** Milton Rosenstock; **Orchestrations:** Philip J. Lang; **Set Design:** Jo Mielziner

Songs: Allez-Vous-En (Go Away); Am I in Love? [1]; Apaches, The (dance); C'est Magnifique; Can-Can; Come Along with Me; Every Man Is a Stupid Man; Garden of Eden Ballet, The (dance) [2]; Her Heart Was in Her Work [1]; I Am in Love; I Do [1]; I Like the Ladies [1]; I Love Paris; I Shall Positively Pay You Next Monday [1]; If Only You Could Love Me [1]; If You Loved Me Truly; It's All Right with Me; Laundry Scene [1]; Law, The [1]; Live and Let Live; Maidens Typical of France; Man Must His Honor Defend, A [1]; Montmart'; Never Give Anything Away; Never, Never Be an Artist; Nothing to Do but Work [1]; Quadrille (dance); To Think That This Could Happen to Me [1]; What a Fair Thing Is a Woman [1]; When Love Comes to Call [1]; Who Said Gay Paree [1]

Cast: Ralph Beaumont; Hans Conried; Peter Cookson; Dania Krupska; Phil Leeds; Lilo; Richard Purdy; Erik Rhodes; Gwen Verdon

Notes: [1] Unused. [2] Included "Snake Dance" and "The Inch Worm."

630 • CANDIDE

OPENED: 12/01/1956   Theatre: Martin Beck
Musical   Broadway: 73

Composer: Leonard Bernstein
Lyricist: Richard Wilbur
Librettist: Lillian Hellman
Producer: Lester Osterman; Ethel Linder Reiner
Director: Tyrone Guthrie

Source CANDIDE (Novel: Voltaire); **Costumes:** Irene Sharaff; **Lighting Designer:** Paul Morrison; **Musical Director:** Samuel Krachmalnick; **Orchestrations:** Leonard Bernstein; Hershy Kay; **Set Design:** Oliver Smith

Songs: Alleluia [16]; Auto Da Fe (What a Day) [12] (L: John Latouche; Stephen Sondheim); Best of All Possible Worlds, The (1); Best of All Possible

Worlds, The (2) [3] (L: John Latouche); Bon Voyage; Dear Boy [4]; Eldorado (L: Lillian Hellman); Gavotte [5] (L: Dorothy Parker); Glitter and Be Gay; I Am So Easily Assimilated (L: Leonard Bernstein); It Must Be So; King's Baracarolle, The [15]; Life Is Happiness Indeed [1] (L: Stephen Sondheim); Lisbon Sequence [6] (L: Leonard Bernstein); Make Our Garden Grow; Mazurka (inst.); Money, Money, Money [15]; My Love (L: John Latouche; Richard Wilbur); Nothing More Than This [15] (L: Leonard Bernstein); O Miserere [3]; Oh, Happy We; Pass the Soap [7] (L: Unknown); Pilgrim's Procession [8]; Quartet Finale; Quiet; Ringaroundarosy [9] (L: John Latouche); Sheep's Song [3] (L: Stephen Sondheim); Sweet to See Two Hearts So True [7] (L: Dorothy Parker); This World (2) [10] (L: Stephen Sondheim); This World (1) (L: John Latouche); Universal Good [15] (L: Leonard Bernstein); We Are Women [11] (L: Leonard Bernstein); Westphalia Chorale (L: Leonard Bernstein); What's the Use?; Words, Words, Words [13] (L: Leonard Bernstein); You Were Dead, You Know (L: John Latouche)

Cast: Max Adrian; Conrad Bain; William Chapman; Barbara Cook; Louis Edmonds; Irra Petina; Robert Rounseville

Notes: Songs that do not credit lyricists means writer is unknown. [1] Added revival 3/10/74. Same music as "Gavotte." [2] Added revival 3/10/74. Same song with the exception of lyric addition or change by the respective lyricists. [3] Added revival 3/10/74. [4] Out Boston prior to New York. Added to 1982 revival. [5] Same music as "Life Is Happiness Indeed." [6] Same music as "Auto de Fe" and "Ringaroundarosy" [7] Out Boston prior to New York. [8] Same music as "Alleluia." [9] Written for original production but not used. Same music as "Auto de Fe" and "Lisbon Sequence." [10] Added to revival 3/10/74. [11] Added to 1959 London revival. [12] Out Boston prior to New York. Same music as "Lisbon Sequence" and "Ringaroundarosy." Added to revival 3/10/74 with additional lyrics by Stephen Sondheim which were not used (but are on the recording). [13] Added to 1971 revival. [14] Added revival 3/10/74. Same music as "Gavotte." [15] Not used. [16] Added revival 3/10/74. Same music as "Pilgrim's Procession."

631 • CANDY KID, THE
OPENED: 1907
Musical   Closed out of town

Composer: W.R. William
Lyricist: Ray Raymond
Librettist: Lem B. Parker

Songs: Bye, Bye, Drowsy Eyes; Hark to the Scream of the Eagle; Past, the Present and Future, The

Cast: Ray Raymond

Notes: Closed in a New York suburb.

632 • CANDY SHOP, THE
OPENED: 04/27/1909   Theatre: Knickerbocker
Musical   Broadway: 56

Composer: John Golden
Lyricist: John Golden
Librettist: George V. Hobart
Producer: Charles B. Dillingham
Director: Fred G. Latham

Choreographer: William Rock

Songs: Back to the U.S.A. [2]; By Wireless; Bye and Bye [3]; Candy Shop, The [3]; Chinese Number [2]; Dan [1]; Evolution [3]; Fie, Fie, Fie [1]; Fishing [3]; Googy Oo; Help!! And the Villain Goes to Jail [2]; Home Again [3]; Honey Bunch [1]; Husband and Wife [3]; I'll Follow You; I'm Going to Follow the Boys [3]; In Vaudeville; India [3]; I've Been Married Once; Just Sisters; Just We Two [3]; Let's Go [3]; Mannequin's Ball [3]; Meet Me Down on the Corner [1]; Mister Othello [1]; Moonbeams [3]; My Dusky Baby [3]; Night at Luna, A [3]; Now That I've Got It, I Don't Want It; On Sunday Morning [3]; One I'm Looking For, The; Silvery Moon, The; Some Ragtime Opera [3]; Some Times You Get a Good One [3]; Sunshine of Your Smile [3] (C: Lillian Roy; L: Leonard Cooke); That Haunting Melody [3]; Toy Town [3]; When I Marry My Mary in Maryland; Whitewash Man, The; You're My Girl [1]

Cast: Louise Dresser; Maude Fulton; Frank Lalor; William Rock

Notes: [1] Sheet music only. [2] Out Lincoln, Nebraska 9/22/13. [3] Out Washington, D.C. 12/25/17.

633 • CANNIBAL KING, THE
OPENED: 1901
Musical

Composer: Will Marion Cook
Lyricist: Bob Cole; J. Rosamond Johnson
Librettist: Paul Laurence Dunbar; J. Rosamond Johnson
Producer: Bob Cole

Cast: Bob Cole; Coley Grant; Ernest Hogan; J. Rosamond Johnson; Aida Overton Walker; Ben Wise

Notes: No other information available.

634 • CANTERBURY TALES

OPENED: 02/03/1969   Theatre: Eugene O'Neill
Musical   Broadway: 121

Composer: John Hawkins; Richard Hill
Lyricist: Nevill Coghill
Librettist: Nevill Coghill; Martin Starkie
Producer: Frank Productions; Mgt. III Prods.
Director: Martin Starkie

Source CANTERBURY TALES, THE (Story: Geoffrey Chaucer); **Choreographer:** Sammy Bayes; **Costumes:** Loudon Sainthill; **Lighting Designer:** Jules Fisher; **Musical Director:** Oscar Kosarin; **Orchestrations:** John Hawkins; Richard Hill; **Set Design:** Derek Cousins

Songs: April Song; Beer Is Best (Beer, Beer, Beer); Canterbury Day; Chanticleer and Pertelote Duet [1]; Chanticleer, Pertelote, Fox Trio [1]; Come On and Marry Me Honey; Darling, Let Me Teach You How to Kiss; Good Night Hymn; Hymen, Hymen; I Am All A-Blaze; I Have a Noble Cock; If She Has Never Loved Before; I'll Give My Love a Ring; It Depends on What You're At; Love Will Conquer All; Mug Dance [2]; Pear Tree Quintet; Pilgrim Riding Music; Some Call It Love [1]; Song of Welcome; There's the Moon; What Do Women Want; When I Was a Boy [1]; Where Are the Girls of Yesterday

Cast: Hermione Baddeley; Roy Cooper; Sandy Duncan; Ed Evanko; Ann Gardner; Martyn Green; Bruce Hyde; George Rose; Reid Shelton

Notes: [1] In original London version only. [2] Out St. Louis 12/9/68.

635 • CANTERVILLE GHOST, THE

OPENED: 11/02/1966   Theatre: ABC
TV Musical

Composer: Jerry Bock
Lyricist: Sheldon Harnick
Librettist: Burt Shevelove
Producer: Joe Wishy
Director: Burt Shevelove

Source CANTERVILLE GHOST, THE (Film); **Arrangements** John Morris; **Musical Director:** John Morris

Songs: Canterville Hall; I Worry; If You Never Try; Overhead; Peace; Rattletrap; Undertow; Vengeance; You're Super

Cast: Madge Brindley; David Charkham; Mark Colesano; George Curzon; Douglas Fairbanks Jr.; Frankie Howerd; Peter Noone; Michael Redgrave; Natalie Schafer; Tippy Walker

636 • CAP OF FORTUNE, THE
Notes: *See SHOW GIRL (1902).*

637 • CAPE COD FOLLIES

OPENED: 09/18/1929   Theatre: Bijou
Revue   Broadway: 29

Composer: Alexander Fogarty
Lyricist: Stewart Baird
Librettist: Stewart Baird
Producer: Cape Playhouse, The
Director: Stewart Baird

Choreographer: John Lonergan; **Musical Director:** Martin Fried; **Orchestrations:** Hans Spialek

Songs: Boxing at Shadows; Cape Cod Chanty; Clutching at Shadows (L: Seymour Morris); Cranberry Pickin'; In a Cape Cod Garden; In the Swim; Looking at Life Through a Rainbow (C: Kenneth Burton; L: Walter Craig); Lure of the Cape, The; That Old Hooked Rug; That's the Time When I Miss You (L: Seymour Morris); That's Why We Misbehave (L: Urana Clarke; Edith Lois); Wonderful Cape Cod Girl; Wondering Who (L: George Fitch)

Cast: Dorothy Jones; Dorothy Llewellyn

638 • CAPITOL REVUE ('DEMI-TASSE')

OPENED: 10/24/1919   Theatre: Capitol
Revue   Broadway

Composer: Unknown
Lyricist: Unknown
Producer: Major Edward Bowes; Capitol Theatre
Director: Ned Wayburn

Songs: Come to the Moon (C: George Gershwin; L: Lou Paley; Ned Wayburn); Evening Star; How Can You Tell? (C: Harold Orlob; L: Ned Wayburn); In Arizona; Indian Summer (inst.) (C: Victor Herbert); Just for Me and Mary; Laughing Waters; Oh What a Moanin' Man; Story Book Ball, The; Swanee (C: George Gershwin; L: Irving Caesar); Underneath the Honey Moon (C: James F. Hanley; Robert A. King; L: Ballard Macdonald); You're the Finest of Them All

Cast: Paul Frawley; Jeanette MacDonald[1]; Pearl Regay; Mae West

Notes: No other information available. [1] In chorus — stage debut.

639 • CAPTAIN CARELESS
OPENED: 1906
Musical   Closed out of town

Composer: Clifton Crawford
Lyricist: Robert M. Baker; Clifton Crawford
Librettist: Robert M. Baker
Producer: B.C. Whitney
Director: Max Freeman

Choreographer: Gus Sohlke; **Costumes:** Caroline Siedle; **Musical Director:** Alexander Spencer

Songs: Blue Bell & the Hyacinth, The; Chocolates and Chiclets; Customary; Diplomacee; Gamester, The; Girl That You Leave Behind, The (L: R. Melville Baker); Information Bureau, The; Interrupted Tete-a-Tete, The; Little Boy Blue; Love O' Mine; Military Irresistibles, The; Military Wedding March; Mixing of the Ads, The; Old Waltz, The; Red, White & Blue; Santa Fe (L: R. Melville Baker); What Is Your Love to Me?; What's the Answer; Yesterday

Cast: Elfreda Busling; John E. Henshaw

Notes: Program Wilkes-Barre 10/4/06.

640 • CAPTAIN CUPID
OPENED: 05/15/1917
Musical   Closed out of town

Composer: William Schroeder
Librettist: William Cary Duncan; Rida Johnson Young

Notes: Shubert Theatre, Minneapolis.

641 • CAPTAIN JASPER
OPENED: 1907
Musical

Songs: Belle of New York, The; Nightingale, The; Sugar Babe; Sun-Blessed Are You

Cast: Charles Bougla; Will A. Cook; "Happy" Julius Glenn; Sarah Green; Sissieretta Jones; Johnny Livingston

Notes: No other information available.

642 • CAPTAIN JINKS
OPENED: 09/08/1925   Theatre: Martin Beck
Musical   Broadway: 167

Composer: Lewis E. Gensler
Lyricist: B.G. DeSylva; Stephen Jones
Librettist: Frank Mandel; Laurence Schwab
Producer: Frank Mandel; Laurence Schwab
Director: Edgar MacGregor

Source CAPTAIN JINKS OF THE HORSE MARINES (Play: Clyde Fitch); **Choreographer:** Sammy Lee; **Costumes:** Kiviette; **Musical Director:** Ivan Rudisill; **Set Design:** Frederick Jones

Songs: Ain't Love Wonderful (C: Stephen Jones); At the Party (C: Unknown); Fond of You (C: Lewis E. Gensler); I Do (C: Lewis E. Gensler); Kiki (C: Lewis E. Gensler); New Game, The (C: Unknown); New Love (C: Unknown); Oh! How I Hate Women (C: Unknown); Only One for Me, The (C: Lewis E. Gensler); Pals (C: Unknown); Prast Chi-Prast Chi [1] (C/L: Traditional); Sea Legs (C: Lewis E. Gensler); So This Is the States (C: Unknown); Strictly Business (C: Unknown); Wanna Lotta Love (C: Lewis E. Gensler); You Must Come Over Blues [2] (C: Lewis E. Gensler; L: Ira Gershwin); You Need a Man, Suzanne (C: Unknown)

Cast: Joe E. Brown; Louise Brown; J. Harold Murray; Marion Sunshine

Notes: [1] A Gypsy folk song. [2] Not used in BE YOURSELF.

643 • CAPTAIN JINKS OF THE HORSE MARINES

OPENED: 09/20/1975
Opera

Composer: Jack Beeson
Lyricist: Sheldon Harnick
Librettist: Sheldon Harnick

Source CAPTAIN JINKS OF THE HORSE MARINES (Play: Clyde Fitch); **Musical Director:** Russell Patterson

Cast: James Ditsch; Eugene Green; Keith Harmon; Ronald Highley; Carolyne James; Robert Owen Jones; Ralph Klapis; William Latimer; George Livings; Brian Steele; Carol Wilcox

Notes: No songs listed in the program of this opera. Premiered at the Kansas City Lyric Theater.

644 • CAPTAIN MISHLER

Musical

Composer: Gus Williams
Lyricist: Gus Williams
Librettist: Fred G. Maeder

Songs: Knock at the Window; Pretty Dark Blue Eyes; Tonight, Love; When I'm on Duty

Cast: Gus Williams

Notes: Sheet music only. No other information available.

645 • CAPTAIN RUFUS (1907)

OPENED: 08/12/1907   Theatre: Harlem Music
                                       Hall
Musical   New York

Composer: H. Lawrence Freeman
Librettist: Alfred Anderson; J. Ed Green
Producer: J. Ed Green
Director: J. Ed Green

Choreographer: Bill Johnson

Songs: Great Am I with a Capital I, The; I've Got Good Common Sense; Lilly, The; Morning Is

Dawning; Song of the Witches; Tale of the Monkey and the Snake, The

Cast: Charles Gilpin; Lotte Grady; J. Ed Green; Harrison Stewart; George White; Dan Wromley

646 • CAPTAIN RUFUS (1914)

OPENED: 1914
Musical

Librettist: Telford Anderson
Producer: Pekin Stock Company
Director: Jerry Mills

Songs: Amazon Land; Back to the U.S.A.; Chief of the Aggrivation; Just for a Night; My Mandiline; Sword and the Flag, The; Tail of the Monkey and the Snake [1]; You Ain't Nothin' Yet

Cast: Sidney Kirkpatrick; Charles Liverpool; Bessie Tribble; Lizzie Wallace

Notes: No other information available. [1] Probably same song as "Tale of the Monkey and the Snake" from CAPTAIN RUFUS (1907).

647 • CAPTAINS COURAGEOUS

OPENED: 05/12/1994
Musical

Composer: Frederick Freyer
Lyricist: Patrick Cook
Librettist: Patrick Cook
Producer: Goodspeed Opera House
Director: David Warren

Source CAPTAINS COURAGEOUS (Novel: Rudyard Kipling); **Source** CAPTAINS COURAGEOUS (Film: Marc Connelly; John Lee Mahin; Dale Van Every); **Choreographer:** John Carrafa; **Costumes:** Teresa Snider-Stein; **Lighting Designer:** Don Holder; **Musical Director:** Bob Goldstone; **Set Design:** James Youmans; **Vocal Arranger:** Frederick Freyer

Songs: Alone; Grand Banks Sequence; Heed the Signs; I Make Up This Song; I'm Harvey Ellesworth Cheyne; I'm Home; Jonah; Little Fish; Not So Bad; Oh, Lord Could She Go; One More Year; Out on the Sea; Regular Fellas; Song of the Sea; Ten Seconds; That's Where I'm Bound; They'll Be Here; You Never Saw

Cast: Terrance Flynn; Walter Hudson; Ramzi Khalaf; Charles Pistone

Notes: Goodspeed Opera House production.

648 • CARAVAN
OPENED: 1926
Revue

Librettist: Ralph Cullinan; Clifford Pember
Producer: Richard Herndon

Set Design: P. Dodd Ackerman

Songs: My Caravan (C/L: Jay Gorney)

Notes: No other information available. Information from sheet music.

649 • CAREFREE HEART, THE
OPENED: 09/30/1957
Musical   Closed out of town

Composer: George Forrest; Robert Wright
Lyricist: George Forrest; Robert Wright
Librettist: George Forrest; Robert Wright
Producer: Shamus Locke; Lynn Loesser
Director: H.C. Potter

Source DOCTOR IN SPITE OF HIMSELF, THE (Play: Moliere); **Source** SGANARELLE (Play: Moliere); **Choreographer:** Dania Krupska; **Costumes:** Miles White; **Lighting Designer:** Peggy Clark; **Musical Director:** Samuel Krachmalnick; **Orchestrations:** Don Walker; **Set Design:** Oliver Smith

Songs: Anatomy; Aristotle; At the Bottom of It — Love!; Bane of My Life; Be-Angeled [3]; Be-Deviled [3]; Bleed and Purge; Carefree Heart, The; Formula, Formulae, Formulorum; His Father's Son [1]; I Am Your Man; I Would Love You Still; Light in the Heart [1]; Loose in the Foot; Madam Is Mad [1]; Moliere; Odds and Ends [3]; Other Than That [3]; Promised [3]; Rich Man, Poor Man; Seventh Daughter [3]; She's Appealing, She's Alluring; Sunflower Seed [3]; To Cook My Gander's Goose; To the Clinic; 'Toinette [2]; Unpromised [3]; Who Is? You Are!; Woman Talk [3]; Would I Were

Cast: Jack Carter; Allen Case; Melville Cooper; Susan Johnson; Michael Kermoyan; Virginia Martin; Jacquelyn McKeever; William Olvis; Jayne Turner; Billie Worth

Notes: Titled THE LOVE DOCTOR in London 10/12/59. [1] Not in program. [2] Not in programs. Same music as 'Amsterdam' cut from KEAN. [3] From THE LOVE DOCTOR.

650 CARELESS RAPTURE
OPENED: 09/11/1936   Theatre: Theatre Royal, Drury Lane
Musical   London: 295

Composer: Ivor Novello
Lyricist: Ivor Novello
Librettist: Christopher Hassall
Director: Leontine Sagan

Choreographer: Joan Davis; Anthony Tudor; **Costumes:** Rene Hubert; **Musical Director:** Charles Prentice; **Set Design:** Alick Johnstone

Songs: Bridge of Lovers, The; Love Made the Song; Music in May; Opening Chorus; Opening Chorus Act II; Singing Lesson; Slow Rhythms of Long Ago; Wait for Me; Why Is There Ever Good-Bye?

Cast: Zena Dare; Dorothy Dickson; Olive Gilbert; Peter Graves; Ivor Novello; Minnie Rayner

651 • CARIB SONG
OPENED: 09/27/1945   Theatre: Adelphi
Musical   Broadway: 36

Composer: Baldwin Bergersen
Lyricist: William Archibald
Librettist: William Archibald
Producer: George Stanton
Director: Mary Hunter

Choreographer: Katherine Dunham; **Costumes:** Motley; **Lighting Designer:** Jo Mielziner; **Musical Director:** Pembroke Davenport; **Set Design:** Jo Mielziner

Songs: Basket — Make a Basket; Can't Stop the Sea; Girl She Can't Remain, A; Go Down to the River (Washer Woman Song); Go Sit By the Body; Go to Church on Sunday; Market Song; Oh, Lonely One; Shango Ritual; Sleep, Baby, Don't Cry; This Woman; Today I Is So Happy; Water Movin' Slow; Woman Is a Rascal; You Know, Oh Lord

Cast: Katherine Dunham; William Franklin; Avon Long

652 • CARMELINA

OPENED: 04/08/1979   Theatre: St. James
Musical   Broadway: 17

Composer: Burton Lane
Lyricist: Alan Jay Lerner
Librettist: Alan Jay Lerner; Joseph Stein
Producer: Joan Cullman; J.W. Fisher; Jujamcyn Productions; Roger L. Stevens
Director: Jose Ferrer

Source BUONA SERA, MRS. CAMPBELL (Film: Melvin Frank; Sheldon Keller; Dennis Norden); Choreographer: Peter Gennaro; Costumes: Donald Brooks; Dance Arranger: David Krane; Lighting Designer: Feder; Musical Director: Don Jennings; Orchestrations: Hershy Kay; Set Design: Oliver Smith; Vocal Arranger: Maurice Levine

Songs: All That He'd Want Me to Be; Carmelina; Church [1]; Come with Me to San Torino; I Must Have Her; I'm a Woman; Image of Me, The; It's Time for a Love Song; Love Before Breakfast; One More Walk Around the Garden; Signora Campbell; Someone in April [2]; Why Him?; Yankee Doodles Are Coming to Town

Cast: Georgia Brown; Marc Jordan; Grace Keagy; John Michael King; Virginia Martin; Gordon Ramsey; Howard Ross; Cesare Siepi; Jossie deGuzman

Notes: [1] Not in show. [2] Written for ON A CLEAR DAY YOU CAN SEE FOREVER.

653 • CARMEN JONES

OPENED: 12/02/1943   Theatre: Broadway
Musical   Broadway: 502

Composer: Georges Bizet
Lyricist: Oscar Hammerstein II
Librettist: Oscar Hammerstein II
Producer: Billy Rose
Director: Charles Friedman; Hassard Short

Source CARMEN (Opera: Georges Bizet; Ludovic Halevy; Henri Meilhac); Source CARMEN (Story: Prosper Merimee); Choreographer: Eugene Loring; Costumes: Raoul Pene du Bois; Lighting Designer: Hassard Short; Musical Director: Joseph Littau; Orchestrations: Robert Russell Bennett; Set Design: Howard Bay; Vocal Arranger: Robert Shaw

Songs: Beat Out Dat Rhythm on a Drum; Carmen Jones Is Goin' to Jail; Dat Ol' Boy; Dat's Love; Dat's Our Man; De Cards Don't Lie; Dere's a Cafe on de Corner; Dis Flower; Get Your Program for de Big Fight; Good Luck, Mr. Flyin' Man; Honey Gal O' Mine; If You Would Only Come Away; Lift 'Em Up and Put 'Em Down; My Joe; Pancho de Panther from Brazil; Stan' Up and Fight; Whizzin' Away Along de Track; You Talk Just Like My Maw

Cast: Glenn Bryant; Sibol Cain; Jack Carr; Cosy Cole; Carlotta Franzell; June Hawkins; Dick Montgomery; Napoleon Reed; Jessica Russell; Luther Saxon; Muriel Smith; Edward Lee Tyler

654 • CARMILLA

OPENED: 01/16/1972   Theatre: La Mama ETC.
Musical   Off-Broadway: 15

Composer: Ben Johnston
Librettist: Wilford Leach
Producer: La Mama
Director: John Braswell; Wilford Leach

Musical Director: Zizi Mueller

Songs: About the Ompire; By Moonlight, on the Odyllic Influence of the Moon; Conclusion; Descending; Funeral Passed By, A; Invitation, Carmilla Stays, An; Mesmerized; Mountbank, the Amulet, A; Our Household, a Dream; Passing Days; Saunter, Twilight, A; Strange Agony, A; We Compare Notes

Notes: No other information available.

655 • CARNAGE, A COMEDY

OPENED: 09/17/1989   Theatre: Public
Play   Off-Broadway: 25

Author: Tim Robbins; Adam Simon
Producer: N.Y. Shakespeare Festival
Director: Tim Robbins

Costumes: Neil Spisak; Lighting Designer: Robert Wierzel; Musical Director: David Robbins; Set Design: Catherine Hardwicke

Songs: After the End (C/L: Tim Robbins; C: Kyle Gass; David Robbins); Battle of Armageddon (C/L: Roy Acuff; McCloud); Land of God (C: Kyle Gass; L: Tim Robbins); Lost Highway (C/L: Leon Payne)

Cast: Anarchestra; Lee Arenberg; Ned Bellamy; Brett Hinkley; Shannon Holt

656 • CARNIVAL!
OPENED: 04/13/1961   Theatre: Imperial
Musical   Broadway: 719

Composer: Bob Merrill
Lyricist: Bob Merrill
Librettist: Michael Stewart
Producer: David Merrick
Director: Gower Champion

Source LILI (Film: Helen Deutsch); **Source** SEVEN SOULS OF CLEMENT O'REILLY, THE (Story: Paul Gallico); **Choreographer:** Gower Champion; **Costumes:** Freddy Wittop; **Dance Arranger:** Peter Howard; **Lighting Designer:** Will Steven Armstrong; **Musical Director:** Saul Schechtman; **Orchestrations:** Philip J. Lang; **Set Design:** Will Steven Armstrong; **Vocal Arranger:** Saul Schechtman

Songs: Always, Always You (It Was Always You); Beautiful Candy; Carnival Theme (Love Makes the World Go Round); Direct from Vienna; Ev'rybody Likes You; Fairyland; Golden, Delicious Fish [1]; Grand Imperial Cirque de Paris; Her Face; Humming; I Hate Him; I've Got to Find a Reason; Looking for Myself [2]; Magic, Magic; Mira (Can You Imagine That); Rich, The; Schlissel's Retort [2]; She's My Love; Sword, Rose and Cape; Tanz Mit Mir (Blue Bird Girls); Very Nice Man, A; Yes, My Heart; Yum Ticky-Ticky

Cast: Anna Maria Alberghetti; Kaye Ballard; Anita Gillette; Henry Lascoe; Luba Lisa; James Mitchell; Pierre Olaf; Jerry Orbach

Notes: Puppets designed by Tom Tichenor. [1] This is the introduction to "Beautiful Candy." [2] ASCAP/Library of Congress.

657 • CARNIVAL IN FLANDERS
OPENED: 09/08/1953   Theatre: New Century
Musical   Broadway: 6

Composer: Jimmy Van Heusen
Lyricist: Johnny Burke
Librettist: Preston Sturges
Producer: Mike Sloane; Paula Stone
Director: Preston Sturges

Source LA KERMESSE HEROIQUE (Film: Jacques Feyder; Charles Spaak; Bernard Zimmer); **Choreographer:** Jack Cole; Helen Tamiris; **Costumes:** Lucinda Ballard; **Dance Arranger:** Elie Siegmeister; **Lighting Designer:** Peggy Clark; **Musical Director:** Harold Hastings; **Orchestrations:** Don Walker; **Set Design:** Oliver Smith; **Vocal Arranger:** Elie Siegmeister

Songs: Battle Song [2]; Carnival Ballet (inst.); For a Moment of Your Love; Here's That Rainy Day; How Far Can a Lady Go?; I Feel Like They Feel in Castile [1]; I'm One of Your Admirers; In the Clear Light of Dawn [2]; It's a Fine Old Institution; It's a Matter of Military Tactics [1]; It's an Old Spanish Custom; Plundering of the Town (inst.), The; Ring the Bell; Seventeen Gun Salute, A; Small Things, The [2]; Something Better Than Being in Love [2]; Stronger Sex, The; Sudden Thrill, The; Take the Word of a Gentleman; That Man Is Doing His Worst to Make Good [2]; Unaccustomed As I Am [2]; Very Necessary You, The; You're Dead!

Cast: Lee Goodman; Dolores Gray; Paul Lipson; John Raitt; Paul Reed; Roy Roberts; Pat Stanley

Notes: In Los Angeles the book was by George Oppenheimer and Herbert Fields and the direction by Bretaigne Windust. Burke and Van Heusen were uncredited producers. [1] Out L.A. 7/6/53. [2] Cut.

658 • CAROL CHANNING WITH TEN STOUTHEARTED MEN
OPENED: 1970
Revue   Closed out of town

Librettist: Robert Emmett
Producer: Joe Layton
Director: Joe Layton

Choreographer: Joe Layton; **Costumes:** Fred Voelpel; **Dance Arranger:** Lee Norris; **Lighting Designer:** Danny Franks; **Musical Director:** Robert Hunter; **Set Design:** Fred Voelpel

Cast: Patrick Adiarte; Carol Channing; Leonard John Crofoot; Eddie Phillips; Denny Shearer; Tucker Smith

Notes: No original music in this production. No songs listed in program.

659 • CAROLINE

OPENED: 01/31/1923   Theatre: Ambassador
Musical   Broadway: 151

Composer: Edward Kunneke
Lyricist: Edward Delaney Dunn; Harry B. Smith
Librettist: Edward Delaney Dunn; Harry B. Smith
Producer: Messrs. Shubert
Director: Fred G. Latham

Source DER VETTER AUS DINGSDA (Musical: Herman Haller; Edward Kunneke; Edward Rideamus); **Choreographer:** Frank M. Gillespie; **Musical Director:** Fred Hoff; **Set Design:** Watson Barratt

Songs: Argentine (C: Al Goodman; Edward Kunneke); Hello, Hello [1] (C: Edward Kunneke); I'm Only a Pilgrim [2] (C: Edward Kunneke); It's a Thrill! [3]; Land of Enchantment (Land of Romance) [4] (C: Al Goodman; Edward Kunneke); Love's Last Day [4]; Man in the Moon, The [4]; Old Virginia Reel, The; Piper You Must Pay, The (Pay the Piper) (C: Edward Kunneke; L: Harry B. Smith); Rainbow Gold [1] (C: Al Goodman); Shoulder Arms [4] (C: Edward Kunneke; L: Harry B. Smith); Some Day [2] (C: Ralph Benatzky; L: Adrian Ross; Harry B. Smith); Sweetheart [4] (C: Edward Kunneke; L: Harry B. Smith); Telling Fortunes (Your Fortune) [4] (C: Edward Kunneke; L: Harry B. Smith); Till Dreams Come True [1] (C: Alfred Goodman); Tis a Glorious Day [3]; Way Down South (C: Alfred Goodman; L: Harry B. Smith); When I Say It's So, It's So; Who Cares for a Name; Will-O-the-Wisp [4] (C: Edward Kunneke; L: Harry B. Smith)

Cast: Tessa Kosta; J. Harold Murray

Notes: Titled VIRGINIA out of town where numbers were also credited to Al Goodman. Al songs credited to Eduard Kunneke are credited to Charles Kunneke in program. Although program lists Edward Rideamus as collaborator with Edward Delaney Dunn, no reference can be found on any sheet music or other programs to

Rideamus. The sheet music credits the book to Herman Haller and Edward Rideamus. Rideamus (real name Fritz Oliven) was a German lyricist and librettist who wrote the source with Herman Haller. [1] Out 12/22/22. Credited to Goodman according to program. [2] Sheet music only. [3] Out 12/22/22. [4] Claimed in Romberg's biography to have been written by him and published by Harms. No records at ASCAP refer to this.

660 • CAROUSEL

OPENED: 04/19/1945   Theatre: Majestic
Musical   Broadway: 890

Composer: Richard Rodgers
Lyricist: Oscar Hammerstein II
Librettist: Oscar Hammerstein II
Producer: Theatre Guild, The
Director: Rouben Mamoulian

Source LILIOM (Play: Ferenc Molnar); **Choreographer:** Agnes de Mille; **Costumes:** Miles White; **Dance Arranger:** Trude Rittman; **Musical Director:** Joseph Littau; **Orchestrations:** Don Walker; **Set Design:** Jo Mielziner

Songs: Blow High, Blow Low; Carousel Waltz (inst.); Geraniums in the Winder; Highest Judge of All, The; If I Loved You; June Is Bustin' Out All Over; Mister Snow; Real Nice Clambake, A; Soliloquy; There's Nothin' So Bad for a Woman (Stonecutters Cut It on Stone); What's the Use of Wond'rin'; When the Children Are Asleep; You'll Never Walk Alone; You're a Queer One, Julie Jordan

Cast: Jean Casto; Jan Clayton; Jean Darling; Lew Foldes; Christine Johnson; Pearl Lang; Bambi Linn; Ralph Linn; Eric Mattson; Robert Pagent; John Raitt; Murvyn Vye

Notes: Source adapted by Benjamin F. Glazer.

661 • CARRIE

OPENED: 05/12/1988   Theatre: Virginia
Musical   Broadway: 5

Composer: Michael Gore
Lyricist: Dean Pitchford
Librettist: Lawrence D. Cohen
Producer: Fredrich Kurz
Director: Terry Hands

Source CARRIE (Novel: Stephen King);
Choreographer: Debbie Allen; **Costumes:**
Alexander Reid; **Lighting Designer:** Terry
Hands; **Musical Director:** Paul Schwartz;
Orchestrations: Anders Eljas; Michael Starobin;
Harold Wheeler; **Set Design:** Ralph Kotai

Songs: Alma Mater; And Eve Was Weak; Carrie;
Destruction, The; Do Me a Favor; Don't Waste
the Moon; Dream On; Evening Prayers; Heaven;
I Remember How Those Boys Could Dance;
I'm Not Alone; In; It Hurts to Be Strong; Open
Your Heart; Out for Blood; Unsuspecting Hearts;
When There's No One; Wotta Night!

Cast: Betty Buckley; Charlotte D'Amboise; Paul
Gyngell; Linzi Hateley; Darlene Love; Gene
Anthony Ray; Sally Ann Triplett

662 • CASA MANANA
OPENED: 06/08/1936
Revue

Composer: Dana Suesse
Lyricist: Irving Kahal; Billy Rose
Producer: Fort Worth Frontier Cent.; Billy Rose
Director: John Murray Anderson

Costumes: Raoul Pene du Bois; **Set Design:** Albert
Johnson

Songs: Another Mile; Daisy, Daisy [1] (C/L: Harry
Dacre); Egyptianna (inst.) (C: Howard Godwin);
Frankie and Johnnie [1] (C/L: Traditional);
Gone with the Dawn [2] (L: Stanley Joseloff;
Billy Rose); Hot Time in the Old Town [1]
(C: Theodore M. Metz; L: Joe Hayden); In the
Good Old Summer Time, The [1] (C: George
Evans; L: Ren Shields); It Happened in Chicago;
Lone Star [3]; Meet Me in St. Louis, Louis [1]
(C: Kerry Mills; L: Andrew B. Sterling); Night Is
Young and You're So Beautiful, The; Oh! You
Beautiful Doll [1] (C: Nat D. Ayer; L: A. Seymour
Brown); St. Louis Blues, The [1] (C/L: W.C.
Handy); Why Do They Call Me a Gibson Girl [1]
(C/L: Unknown); You're in Paree; You're Like a
Toy Balloon

Cast: Californians, The; Gomez and Winona; Lime
Trio, The; Everett Marshall; Ann Pennington;
Sally Rand; Joe Venuti and His Orcheatra;
Walter Dare Wahl; Paul Whiteman and His
Orchestra

Notes: Presented at the Fort Worth Frontier
Centennial from 6/8/36 to either 11/30/36 or
12/1/36. [1] Not written for this show. [2] Sheet
music only. [3] ASCAP/Library of Congress only.

663 • CASABLANCA
Musical

Composer: Arthur Schwartz
Lyricist: Leo Robin

Source CASABLANCA (Film: Julius J. Epstein;
Philip G. Epstein; Howard W. Koch)

Songs: Lucky to Be Alive; To Love and to Lose [2];
Why Should I Care [1]

Notes: I don't know if this was completed or not.
[1] Later in NICHOLAS NICKLEBY. [2] Same
music as "Where Do I Go from You" which had
lyrics by Dorothy Fields.

664 • CASEY JONES
Musical   Unproduced

Composer: Vernon Duke
Lyricist: Sammy Cahn

Songs: Big Towns and the Small Towns, The;
Extenuatin' Circumstances; Fight Over Me; Girl
with the Prettiest Legs in Town, The; He Said;
Honor Me with This Dance; I Can Take It or Leave
It; I May Say Maybe; I'm Goin' Places; Ladies Like
Us; Man My Mother Married, The; Mister Harvey
Pruitt; Once I Fall; Parties; Railroad Woman, A;
Same As a Man; Step Up and Shake; There Comes
a Time; Wait Till You See New York; We're Alone
in the World; With a Man on First

665 • CASINO DE PARIS REVUE
OPENED: 1935   Theatre: Casino de Paris
Revue   Nightclub

Composer: Harry Akst; Elsa Maxwell
Lyricist: Lew Brown

Songs: I Don't Love You — Not Much; I'd Rather
Be with You; Lost My Rhythm, Lost My Music,
Lost My Man; Then You Walked in the Room;
You're Waltzing on My Heart

Notes: No other information available.

666 • CASINO GIRL, THE
OPENED: 03/19/1900   Theatre: Casino
Musical   Broadway: 91

Composer: Harry T. MacConnell
Lyricist: Harry B. Smith
Librettist: Harry B. Smith
Producer: George W. Lederer

Costumes: Caroline Siedle; **Musical Director:** A. DeNovellis; **Set Design:** Ernest Albert

Songs: Casino Girl, The; Chink! Chink!; Descriptive Song; Down De Lover's Lane (C: Ludwig Englander); Entrance Chorus of the Khedive; From Africa; How Actresses Are Made; I'll Put a Tax; Life Is a Toy Shop [2]; Mam'selle (C: Arthur Nevin); My New York (C: Ludwig Englander); Naughty Little Clock [1]; Opening Chorus (C: Ludwig Englander); Slave Dealers' Song; Song of the Drum Major; Sweet Annie Moore [2] (C/L: John H. Moore); Variety

Cast: Irene Bentley; Sam Bernard; Virginia Earle; Lotta Faust; Mayme Gehrue; Mabelle Gilman; Albert Hart

Notes: [1] Not in program. [2] Sheet music only.

667 • CASINO VARIETIES
OPENED: 1934
Revue   Nightclub

Lyricist: Arthur Swanstrom

Songs: Cuh-Razy for Love (C: J. Fred Coots); I'm All In (C: Louis Alter); My Carolina Hide-Away (C: J. Fred Coots)

Notes: No other information avaliable.

668 • CASPER THE YODLER
Musical

Composer: Charles T. Ellis
Lyricist: Charles T. Ellis
Librettist: William Carleton; Charles T. Ellis
Producer: Charles A. Wing

Songs: Buttonhole Bouquet, A; Hush a Baby Bye; Ireland's Native Green; Love's Lucky Emblem; Morning Lark; Piggy Back; Santa Claus; Sunshine Will Come Again

Cast: Charles T. Ellis

Notes: Sheet music only. No other information available.

669 • CASTAWAYS, THE
OPENED: 02/07/1977   Theatre: Promenade
Musical   Off-Broadway: 1

Composer: Don Pippin
Lyricist: Steve Brown
Librettist: Anthony Stimac
Producer: Jeff Britton
Director: Tony Tanner

Source SHE WOULD BE A SOLDIER (Play: Dennis Anderson; Mordecai Noah; Ron Whyte); **Costumes:** Patricia McGourty; **Lighting Designer:** Richard Winkler; **Musical Director:** Dorothy Opalach; **Orchestrations:** Bill Brohn; **Set Design:** Scott Johnson

Songs: All the World's a Hold [1]; Call Back the Times; Chase, The; Could Such a Face Be False; Dumplings; Exits and Entrances; I Won't Love a Soldier Boy; If I Had Wings [1]; Isn't She; Kind Sir (C: Gary William Friedman); Let's Mop Up These Yankees and Go Home [1]; My Love; Old Glory; She Can't Resist Me; She Would Be a Soldier; This Dawn; Whippoorwill

Cast: Gibby Brand; Joel Kramer; Rick Larson; Maureen Maloney; June Squibb; Kathleen Widdoes

Notes: [1] Unused.

670 • CASTLES IN THE AIR
OPENED: 09/06/1926   Theatre: Selwyn
Musical   Broadway: 162

Composer: Percy Wenrich
Lyricist: Raymond W. Peck
Librettist: Raymond W. Peck
Producer: James W. Elliott
Director: Frank S. Merlin

Choreographer: John Boyle; **Costumes:** John N. Booth Jr.; Hugh Willoughby; **Musical Director:** Max Bendix; **Orchestrations:** Frank Barry; **Set Design:** P. Dodd Ackerman; Hugh Willoughby

Songs: Baby; First Kiss of Love, The [2]; Girls and the Gimmies; I Don't Blame 'Em; I Would Like to

Fondle You; If You Are in Love with a Girl; Land of Romance; Lanterns of Love (L: R. Locke; Raymond W. Peck); Latavia; Latavian Chant, The; Love Rules the World; Love's Refrain; My Lips, My Love, My Soul; Opening; Other Fellow's Girl, The; Queen of Queens [1]; Rainbow of Your Smile, The; Singer's Career, Ha! Ha!, The; Sweetheart of Your Dreams, The

Cast: Bernard Granville; Thais Lawton; J. Harold Murray; Vivienne Segal

Notes: [1] Out Wilkes-Barre 3/21/27. [2] Sheet music only.

671 • CAT AND THE FIDDLE, THE (1910)

OPENED: 1910
Musical   Closed out of town

Composer: Unknown
Lyricist: Unknown

Songs: Dance of the Lunatics, The; Dance of the Rose, The; If I Were a Sailor; I've Never Been Introduced to You; Mother Goose and Baby Dolls; My Maid in the Moon; Oh, What a Lovely Dream; Old Oak Tree, The; Opening Chorus; Rosy Dreams; Under the Sea; Witches' Incantation, The; You'll Find It in the Almanac

Cast: Arthur Boylan; Rose Boylan; Harry B. Watson

Notes: Program from Wilkes-Barre 12/14/10.

672 • CAT AND THE FIDDLE, THE (1931)

OPENED: 10/15/1931   Theatre: Globe
Musical   Broadway: 395

Composer: Jerome Kern
Lyricist: Otto Harbach
Librettist: Otto Harbach
Producer: Max Gordon
Director: Jose Ruben

Choreographer: Albertina Rasch; **Costumes:** Kiviette; Constance Ripley; **Musical Director:** Victor Baravalle; **Orchestrations:** Robert Russell Bennett; **Set Design:** Henry Dreyfuss

Songs: Breeze Kissed Your Hair, The; Cafe Scene; Crystal Candelabra [2]; Don't Ask Me Not to

Sing [1]; Episode in Victor's Play 'The Passionate Pilgrim'; Finaletto; Ha! Cha! Cha!; I Watch the Love Parade (Crystal Candalabra); New Love Is Old, A; Night Was Made for Love, The; One Moment Alone; Opening Act One (Street Vendors) [3]; Poor Pierrot; She Didn't Say 'Yes'; Try to Forget

Cast: Doris Carson; Peter Chambers; Eddie Foy Jr.; Lawrence Grossmith; Bettina Hall; Flora Le Breton; George Meader; Georges Metaxa; Odette Myrtil; Jose Ruben; Lucette Valsy

Notes: [1] Cut out of town. Used in ROBERTA. [2] Not used. [3] Not in program.

673 • CATCH A STAR!

OPENED: 09/06/1955   Theatre: Plymouth
Revue   Broadway: 23

Librettist: Danny Simon; Neil Simon
Producer: Sy Kleinman
Director: Danny Simon

Choreographer: Lee Sherman; **Costumes:** Thomas Becher; **Dance Arranger:** Herb Schutz; **Musical Director:** Milton Greene; **Set Design:** Ralph Alswang

Songs: Bachelor Hoedown (C: Jerry Bock; L: Larry Holofcener); Boffola (C: Philip Charig; L: Ray Golden; Milton Pascal; Dan Shapiro); Carnival in Court (C: Jay Navarre; L: I.A.L. Diamond; Ray Golden); Catch a Star! (C: Sammy Fain; L: Paul Francis Webster); Everybody Wants to Be in Show Business (C: Philip Charig; L: Bud Burtson; Ray Golden); Fly, Little Heart (C: Jerry Bock; L: Larry Holofcener); Foreign Cars (C/L: Norman L. Martin); Gruntled (C/L: Sy Kleinman; C: Philip Charig; L: Ray Golden); Las Vegas (C: Sy Kleinman; L: Lee Adams; Ray Golden); Little Traveling Music, A (C: Hal Borne; L: Ray Golden; Paul Francis Webster); New Hollywood Plots (C: Sammy Fain; L: Paul Francis Webster); One Hour Ahead of the Posse (C: Philip Charig; L: Ray Golden; Dave Ormont); Story of Alice, The (C: Jerry Bock; L: Larry Holofcener); To Be or Not to Be in Love (C: Philip Charig; L: Ray Golden; Milton Pascal; Dan Shapiro); Twist My Arm (C: Sammy Fain; L: Paul Francis Webster); What a Song Can Do (C/L: Lee Norris; Bernie Wayne)

Cast: David Burns; Pat Carroll; Denny Desmond; Elaine Dunn; Jack Dunn; Helen Halpin; Calvin Holt

674 • CATCH ME IF I FALL

OPENED: 11/12/1990   Theatre: Promenade
Musical   Off-Broadway: 16

Composer: Barbara Schottenfeld
Lyricist: Barbara Schottenfeld
Librettist: Barbara Schottenfeld
Producer: Never or Now Company, The
Director: Susan Einhorn

Choreographer: Stuart Ross; **Costumes:** G.W. Mercier; **Lighting Designer:** Richard Nelson; **Musical Director:** Joseph Church; **Orchestrations:** Joe Gianono; **Set Design:** G.W. Mercier

Songs: Beach House, The; Business Is an Art; Catch Me If I Fall; Chaperone; Home Never Leaves You; I Know the Feeling; I Want You to Be; Isn't It Strange; It's Not a Real Wedding; Liberate; Love That Came Before, The; Never or Now; Opening Number; Sometimes at Night; Timing and Lightning; Veterinarian; When You Live in New York

Cast: David Burdick; A.D. Cover; Laura Dean; Ronnie Farer; James Judy; Jeanine Morick; Sal Viviano

675 • CATCH OF THE SEASON, THE

OPENED: 08/28/1905   Theatre: Daly's
Musical   Broadway: 104

Composer: William T. Francis
Lyricist: Charles H. Taylor
Librettist: Cosmo Hamilton; Seymour Hicks
Producer: Charles Frohman
Director: Ben Teal

Source CATCH OF THE SEASON, THE (Musical: Cosmo Hamilton; Seymour Hicks); **Costumes:** Ward; **Musical Director:** William T. Francis; **Set Design:** Ernest Gros

Songs: Any Other Day Will Do [2]; Auf Wiedersehen [4] (L: Vernon Roy); Back to Harrow [4] (L: J. Montague); Church Parade, The [2] (C: Herbert E. Haines); Cinderella! You Have Won; Cupid Is the Captain of the Army (C/L: Dave Reed Jr.); Entrance of Gibson Girls [4] (C: Evelyn Baker); Finale Act I (C: Herbert E. Haines); Finale Act II (C: Herbert E. Haines); Frolic of a Breeze [3] (C: Jerome Kern; L: Clifford Harris); Hail! Miss O'Halloran [4] (C: Evelyn Baker); If I Were King of Babylon [2] (C: Evelyn Baker); I'll Be a Good Little Girl [2] (C: Herbert E. Haines); It's All Done By Kindness; Little Bit of Dinner with a Friend (C: W.T. Francis); Little Girl You'll Do (C: Alfred Solman; L: Benj. Hapgood Burt); Molly O'Hallerhan (Edna May's Irish Song) [1] (C/L: Jerome Kern); Molly O'Halloran (C: Evelyn Baker); My Little Buttercup [2] (C: Luke Forwood); Oh, Mr. Chamberlain [3] (C: Jerome Kern; L: Charles H. Taylor); Opening Chorus (C: Herbert E. Haines); Opening Chorus Act II (C: Evelyn Baker; Herbert E. Haines); Quaint Old Bird (C: Theodore Morse; L: Edward Madden); Rainbow [2] (C: Henry E. Pether; L: Fred W. Leigh); Raining (C: Jerome Kern; L: Clifford Harris); Rosie Petals [2] (C: W.T. Francis); Seaweed (C/L: Fred Earle); Suppose [2] (C: Herbert E. Haines); Sylvia the Gibson Girl [2] (C: Hugh Rumbold; L: Frank Compton); Take Me on the Merry-Go-Round [2] (C/L: Jerome Kern); Tulips (Two Lips) [2] (C/L: Jerome Kern); Won't You Kiss Me Once Before I Go? [2] (C: Jerome Kern; L: Fred W. Leigh)

Cast: Fred Kaye; Edna May; Jane May; Farren Soutar; Fred Wright Jr.

Notes: Music for London production by Herbert E. Haines and Evelyn Baker. [1] Sheet music only. Also titled 'Edna May's Irish Song.' [2] Sheet music only. [3] Sheet music only. Lyric later revised for THE BEAUTY OF BATH. [4] Vocal score only.

676 • CATCHING THE BURGLAR

OPENED: 1918
Musical

Producer: Billy King

Songs: Before the World Began; I Miss the Mississippi Miss; I Wish You Good Luck; My Place of Business; Our Own Broadway

Cast: Leon Brooks; Bessie Brown; Blaine Brown; Billy King; James Thomas

Notes: No other information available.

677 • CATHERINE

OPENED: 01/19/1899   Theatre: Weber & Fields
                                    Bway Music Hall
Musical   Broadway

Composer: John Stromberg
Lyricist: Harry B. Smith
Librettist: Edgar Smith
Producer: Lew Fields; Joseph Weber

Cast: Josephine Allen; Nellie Beaumont; Rose Beaumont; Bessie Clayton; Peter F. Dailey; Lew Fields; John T. Kelly; Charles J. Rose; Fay Templeton; Joseph Weber

Notes: No songs listed in program.

678 • CATS

OPENED: 10/07/1982   Theatre: Winter Garden
Musical   Broadway

Composer: Andrew Lloyd Webber
Lyricist: T.S. Eliot
Producer: David Geffen; Cameron Mackintosh; Really Useful Company, The; Shubert Organization
Director: Trevor Nunn

Source OLD POSSUM'S BOOK OF PRACTICAL CATS (Poetry: T.S. Eliot); **Choreographer:** Gillian Lynne; **Costumes:** John Napier; **Lighting Designer:** David Hersey; **Musical Director:** Stanley Lebowsky; Rene Weigert; **Orchestrations:** David Cullen; Andrew Lloyd Webber; **Set Design:** John Napier

Songs: Ad-dressing of Cats, The; Awefull Battle of the Pekes and Pollicles, The; Ballad of Billy McCaw, The [1]; Bustopher Jones; Grizabella, the Glamour Cat; Growltiger's Last Stand; Gus: The Theatre Cat; Invitation to the Jellicle Ball, The; Jellicle Ball, The; Jellicle Songs for Jellicle Cats (L: T.S. Eliot; Trevor Nunn; Richard Stilgoe); Journey to the Heaviside Layer, The; Macavity; Marching Songs of the Pollicle Dogs, The; Memory (L: Trevor Nunn); Moments of Happiness, The; Mr. Mistoffelees; Mungojerrie and Rumpleteaser; Naming of Cats, The; Old Deuteronomy; Old Gumbie Cat, The; Rum Tum Tugger; Skimbleshanks

Cast: Kenneth Ard; Betty Buckley; Rene Ceballos; Rene Clemente; Wendy Edmead; Steven Gelfer; Harry Groener; Stephen Hanan; Janet L. Hubert; Reed Jones; Donna King; Christine Langner; Terrence V. Mann; Anna McNeely; Hector Jaime Mercado; Cynthia Onrubia; Ken Page; Timothy Scott; Bonnie Simmons

Notes: Still running as of this writing. [1] Cut for American version and subsequently cut in London run.

679 • CAT'S PAJAMAS, THE

OPENED: 05/31/1962   Theatre: Sheridan Square
Revue   Off-Broadway: 34

Producer: P.G.J. Productions
Director: Herb Suffin

Lighting Designer: Gigi Cascio; **Musical Director:** Monte Aubrey; Arthur Siegel; **Set Design:** James A. Taylor

Songs: In the Morning (C/L: Ronny Graham); It Depends on How You Look at Things (C: Arthur Siegel; L: June Carroll); Love Is Good for You (C: Arthur Siegel; L: June Carroll); Over the River and Into the Woods (C/L: Jack Holmes)

Cast: MacIntyre Dixon; Richard Libertini; Sylvia Lord

Notes: All songs previously in NEW FACES OF 1962.

680 • CAVIAR

OPENED: 06/07/1934   Theatre: Forrest
Musical   Broadway: 20

Composer: Harden Church
Lyricist: Edward Heyman
Librettist: Leo Randole
Producer: Patrick A. Leonard
Director: Clifford Brooke

Choreographer: John E. Lonergan; **Costumes:** Steele Savage; **Musical Director:** Ivan Rudisill; **Orchestrations:** Edward Powell; Hans Spialek; Don Walker; **Set Design:** Steele Savage

Songs: Apassionette; Cavachok; Dream Kingdom; Gypsy; Haywire (C: Edward Heyman); Here's to You; I Feel Sorta—; My Heart's an Open Book; Night Wind; Nothing Was Ever Like This [1]; Ocean Will Never Run Dry, The [1]; One in a Million; Prince Charming; Silver Sails; Tarts and Flowers; When Madame Reaches Her High C; You're One in a Million [1]; Your Prince Was Not So Charming

Cast: Walter Armin; Hugh Cameron; Dudley Clements; Jack Cole; Don Connolly; Alice

Dudley; Nanette Guilford; George Houston; Billie Leonard; Tesore Mio

Notes: [1] ASCAP/Library of Congress only.

681 • CELEBRATION
OPENED: 01/22/1969   Theatre: Ambassador
Musical   Broadway: 109

Composer: Harvey Schmidt
Lyricist: Tom Jones
Librettist: Tom Jones
Producer: Richard Chandler; Cheryl Crawford
Director: Tom Jones

Choreographer: Vernon Lusby; **Costumes:** Ed Wittstein; **Lighting Designer:** Ed Wittstein; **Musical Director:** Rod Derefinko; **Orchestrations:** Jim Tyler; **Set Design:** Ed Wittstein

Songs: Bored; Celebration; Fifty Million Years Ago; I'm Glad to See You've Got What You Want; It's You Who Makes Me Young; Love Song; My Garden; Not My Problem; Orphan in the Storm; Saturnalia; Somebody; Survive; Under the Tree; Where Did It Go?; Winter and Summer

Cast: Keith Charles; Michael Glenn-Smith; David Sabin; Ted Thurston; Susan Watson

682 • CENSORED SCENES FROM KING KONG
OPENED: 03/06/1980   Theatre: Princess
Musical   Off-Broadway: 5

Composer: Andy Roberts
Lyricist: Andy Roberts
Librettist: Howard Schuman
Producer: Eddie Kulukundis; Michael White
Director: Colin Bucksey

Choreographer: David Toguri; **Costumes:** Jennifer von Mayrhauser; **Lighting Designer:** Richard Nelson; **Musical Director:** Keith Herrmann; **Set Design:** Mike Porter

Songs: Banana Oil; He Ain't Scared of Nothing; Hot-Cha; Number One; Other Side of the Wall, The; Soft Shoe Freak

Cast: Stephen Collins; Alma Cuervo; Carrie Fisher; Edward Love; Peter Reigert; Christopher Sarandon

683 • CENTURY GIRL, THE
OPENED: 11/06/1916   Theatre: Century
Revue   Broadway: 200

Composer: Irving Berlin
Lyricist: Irving Berlin
Producer: Charles B. Dillingham; Florenz Ziegfeld
Director: Leon Errol; Ned Wayburn

Choreographer: Edward Royce; **Costumes:** Marie Cook; Raphael Kirchner; Cora MacGeachy; William Henry Matthews; **Musical Director:** Max Hoffmann; **Set Design:** Joseph Urban

Songs: Alice in Wonderland [1]; Birth of the Century Girl, The (C: Victor Herbert; L: Henry Blossom); Century Girl, The (C: Victor Herbert; L: Henry Blossom); Humpty Dumpty [2] (C: Victor Herbert; L: Henry Blossom); It Takes an Irishman to Make Love (L: Irving Berlin; Elsie Janis); Music Lesson, The; On the Trail of Her Wedding Gown [2]; Romping Red Heads, The [2] (C: Victor Herbert; L: Henry Blossom); Rosemary (C: Victor Herbert; L: Henry Blossom); Stone Age, The (scene) [3] (C: Victor Herbert); That Broadway Chicken Walk; They've Got Me Doing It Too; Toy Soldiers, The (inst.) (C: Victor Herbert); Uncle Sam's Children (inst.) (C: Victor Herbert); Under the Sea (C: Victor Herbert; L: Henry Blossom); When Uncle Sam Rules the Wave (C: Victor Herbert; L: Henry Blossom); You Belong to Me (C: Victor Herbert; L: Henry Blossom)

Cast: Sam Bernard; Hazel Dawn; Doyle & Dixon; Marie Dressler; Leon Errol; Irving Fisher; Elsie Janis; Joe Schenck; John Slavin; Lilyan Tashman; Frank Tinney; Gus Van

Notes: [1] Not the same song as in THE MUSIC BOX REVUE (1924). [2] Sheet music only. [3] Also titled 'The Ballet Loose.'

684 • CENTURY GROVE REVUE
OPENED: 07/12/1920   Theatre: Century
                       Promenade
Revue   Broadway: 150

Composer: Jean Schwartz
Lyricist: Alfred Bryan
Librettist: Howard Emmett Rogers
Producer: F. Ray Comstock; William Elliot; Morris Gest; Messrs. Shubert
Director: Lew Morton; Edward Royce

Choreographer: Jack Mason; **Musical Director:**
Oscar Radin

Songs: Bolsheviki Glide (C: Harry Tierney; L: Carl
Randall); Bottle Up a Pretty Girl; Campanile; Fig
Leaf Number; Hold Me; Inebriated Acrobation;
Keep Your Weight Down; Let Me Whisper in
Your Ear [1] (C/L: Unknown); Love Me in the
Candlelight; Marcelle; Millions of Tunes; My
Lady of the Cameo [1] (C/L: Unknown);
Shimmy Nods [1] (C/L: Unknown); Shimmy
Valentine; Shine On, Little Son; Some Nonsense;
Sphinx, The; Symphony in Dress (inst.);
Wouldn't You Like to Have Me Tell Your
Fortune; You Don't Know What I Know About
You (L: Alfred Bryan)

Cast: Green & Blyer; Hal Hixon; Madelon La Varre;
Lorraine and Walton; Vivian Oakland; Tot
Qualters; Walter Woolf

Notes: The sheet music for this show was
copyrighted in 1918. [1] May not be in show.

685 • CENTURY MIDNIGHT WHIRL

OPENED: 1918
Revue   Broadway

Composer: Harry Tierney
Lyricist: Joseph McCarthy; John Henry Mears
Director: Edward Royce

Costumes: Schneider-Anderson; **Musical Director:**
Frank Tours; **Orchestrations:** Maurice dePackh;
Set Design: Norman Bel Geddes

Songs: Button Me Up the Back; Flowers and Bees;
Good Morning; If They Ever Take the Sun Out
of Sunday (C: Harry Von Tilzer; L: William
Jerome); Milady's Perfume; (There's a) Million
Girls Around Me; Peggy (C: Neil Moret;
L: Harry Williams); Society's Shimmying Now;
Strolling Down the Avenue; Throw 'Em In;
Witches

Cast: Jay Gould; Carl Hyson; Charles King;
Ed Wynn

686 • CENTURY REVUE
Notes: *See CENTURY GROVE REVUE.*

687 • CERTAIN PARTY, A
OPENED: 04/24/1911   Theatre: Wallack
Musical   Broadway: 24

Composer: Robert Hood Bowers
Lyricist: Edgar Smith
Librettist: Edgar Smith
Director: William Collier

Choreographer: Joseph C. Smith; **Musical
Director:** Harry Braham

Songs: Emerald Isle; Fogarty; Get the Hook
(C: Tom Kelly); I Want a Boy (C: Tom Kelly);
I Want Another Situation Just Like That; If [1]
(L: Clay M. Greene); Love's Wireless Telephone;
Turkey Trot (C: Tom Kelly); Walking Delegate,
The; You Can Always Find Someone to Love
You [1] (L: Harry B. Smith); You're Going to Lose
Your Husband If You Do (C/L: Mabel Hite)

Cast: Mike Donlin; Mabel Hite; John T. Kelly

Notes: [1] Sheet music only.

688 • CHAMPAGNE CHARLIE
OPENED: 1901
Musical

Librettist: Augustus Thomas

Songs: Captain Reginald D'Arcy of the Guards
(C/L: George F. Spink); Champagne Charlie
March (inst.) (C: Joseph Nathan); Charlie the
Wineman (C: Jean Schwartz; L: William Jerome);
Flirtation (C: Harry Von Tilzer; L: George T.
Smith); Pretty Little China Maid (C/L: Maude
Nugent); Vaudeville Pets from the West, The (C:
Jean Schwartz; L: William Jerome)

Cast: Peter F. Dailey

Notes: No other information available.

689 • CHAMPAGNE, SEC
OPENED: 10/14/1933   Theatre: Morosco
Musical   Broadway: 113

Composer: Johann Strauss Jr.
Lyricist: Robert A. Simon
Librettist: Alan Child
Producer: Westport County Playhouse; Dwight
Deere Wiman
Director: Monty Woolley

Source DIE FLEDERMAUS (Opera: Richard Genee; Karl Haffner); **Costumes:** Brooks; **Musical Director:** Rudolph Thomas; **Set Design:** Jo Mielziner

Songs: Any Woman Except His Wife; Brother Dear; Csardas; Just for To-Night; Never Fear (Drinking Song); Oh My Dear Marquis

Cast: John Barclay; Kitty Carlisle; Paul Haakon; John E. Hazzard; Olive Jones; Joseph Macaulay; William McCarthy; George Talbert; Eleanor Tennis

Notes: No songs listed in program.

690 • CHANGE IN THE HEIR, A

OPENED: 04/29/1990   Theatre: Edison
Musical   Broadway: 17

Composer: Dan Sticco
Lyricist: George H. Gorham
Librettist: George H. Gorham; Dan Sticco
Producer: Stewart F. Lane
Director: David H. Bell

Choreographer: David H. Bell; **Costumes:** David Murin; **Dance Arranger:** Rob Bowman; **Lighting Designer:** Jeff Davis; **Musical Director:** Rob Bowman; **Orchestrations:** Robby Merkin; **Set Design:** Michael Anania

Songs: By Myself; Can I?; Duet; Exactly the Same as It Was; Fairy Tale, A; Family; Happily Ever After, After All; Here I Am; Hold That Crown; I Tried and I Tried and I Tried; Look at Me; Ordinary Family, An; Prologue; Shut Up and Dance; Take a Look at That; Weekend, The; When

Cast: Brooks Almy; Judy Blazer; Jeffrey Herbst; Jan Neuberger; Jennifer Smith

691 • CHANGE YOUR LUCK

OPENED: 06/06/1930   Theatre: George M. Cohan
Musical   Broadway: 16

Composer: James C. Johnson
Lyricist: James C. Johnson
Librettist: Garland Howard
Producer: Cleon Throckmorton
Director: Cleon Throckmorton

Choreographer: Lawrence Deas; Speedy Smith; **Costumes:** Hilda Farnham; **Musical Director:** Stanley Bennett; **Set Design:** Cleon Throckmorton; **Vocal Arranger:** Stanley Bennett

Songs: Ain't Puttin' Out Nothin'; Can't Be Bothered Now; Change Your Luck; Honesty; I'm Honest; Low Down Dance; Mr. Mammy Man; My Regular Man; Open That Door; Percolatin'; Religion in My Feet; Rhythm Feet; St. Louis Blues [1] (C/L: W.C. Handy); Sweet Little Baby O' Mine; Travellin'; Walk Together, Children; Wasting Away; We're Here; What Have I Done?; You Should Know

Cast: Sam Cross; Sterling Grant; Hamtree Harrington; Garland Howard; Alberta Hunter; Cora La Redd; Alberta Perkins; Neeka Shaw; Speedy Smith; Sammy Van; Leigh Whipper

Notes: [1] Not written for show.

692 • CHANGES

OPENED: 02/19/1980   Theatre: Theatre de Lys
Musical   Off-Broadway: 7

Composer: Addy Fieger
Lyricist: Danny Apolinar
Librettist: Dorothy Love
Producer: John Britton; Dorothy Love
Director: Dorothy Love

Choreographer: Ronn Forella; **Costumes:** Miles White; **Dance Arranger:** Larry Fallon; **Lighting Designer:** Richard Nelson; **Musical Director:** Hal Serra; **Orchestrations:** Larry Fallon; **Set Design:** Don Jensen; **Vocal Arranger:** Larry Fallon

Songs: All Because of You; All Of a Sudden It's Spring; Changes; Do You Want to Go; Happy New Year; Have I Got a Girl for You; Have I Got a Guy for You; Ideal Deal, The; Is This the Way; Isn't This Fun; Keep Love Away; Love Is a Whole Other Scene; Love Like Ours; Man About Town, The; Merry Christmas to Me; Running Out of Time; So Much for Me; Summer Ain't So Hot; Sunday; Three Beats Too Late

Cast: Irving Allen; Kelly Bishop; Larry Kert; Allen Lee; Trina Parks

Notes: Original dance music: Larry Fallon.

693 • CHAPEAU

OPENED: 07/24/1977
Musical   Closed out of town

Composer: Robert Waldman
Lyricist: Alfred Uhry
Librettist: Alfred Uhry
Producer: Acting Company, The
Director: Gerald Freedman

Source ITALIAN STRAW HAT, THE (Play: Eugene Labiche); **Choreographer:** Ethel Martin; **Costumes:** Santo Loquasto; **Lighting Designer:** David F. Segal; **Musical Director:** Henry Stram; **Orchestrations:** Hershy Kay; Eddie Sauter; **Set Design:** Santo Loquasto

Songs: Angel Angelica; Chapeau; Consider Yourself Unmarried; Cousins; Even for a Horse; Hello!; Here's to Surprises; Honor Code, The; Mango Tango, The; Song Cycle; Take What You Will; Wedding Bed Lies Waiting, The; Wedding Dance, The; Where Is My Wife?; Wouldn't You Think?

Cast: Brooks Baldwin; Mary Lou Rosato

694 • CHAPERONS, THE

OPENED: 06/05/1902   Theatre: New York
Musical   Broadway: 49

Composer: Isadore Witmark
Lyricist: Frederick Ranken
Librettist: Frederick Ranken
Producer: Frank L. Perley
Director: George W. Lederer

Musical Director: Max Hirschfeld

Songs: Billy's Very Good to Me [1] (L: C.N. Douglas); Bois D'Boulogne, The; Chaperon, The; Comic Opera Bandits; Egypt Land; Finale Act I; Finale Act II; Finale Act III; Flowers; Girlie Girl [1] (L: Bartley Costello); Hands Up; Happy When We Eat; He Winked at Me; In My Official Capacity; It Seems Like Yesterday; Just a Gentle Touch; Little Maid Who Couldn't Say No, The; Love in a Palace Is Better; Man Behind the Scenes, The; Millinery Mary; My Sambo; Noah's Ark; Oh, Love, Airy Like, Fairy Like; Opening Chorus; Opening Chorus Act II; Opening Chorus Act III; Somehow It Made Me Think of Home; Talk, Talk, Talk; To Stop a Marriage; Vive La Bohemia; We're All Good Fellows; When I Sang My Low C; Won't You Go with Us to Monte Carlo; You Musn't Blame the Copper Blame the Cook

Cast: Digby Bell; May Boley; Harry Conor; Trixie Friganza; Louise Gunning; Walter Jones; Joseph C. Miron; Eva Tanguay; Francis Wheeler; May de Sousa

Notes: [1] Sheet music only.

695 • CHAPLIN

OPENED: 08/12/1983
Musical   Closed out of town

Composer: Anthony Newley; Stanley Stephen Ross
Lyricist: Anthony Newley; Stanley Stephen Ross
Librettist: Anthony Newley; Stanley Stephen Ross
Producer: Sandy Gallin; Raymond Katz; James M. Nederlander; Arthur Rubin; David Susskind
Director: Michael Smuin

Choreographer: Claudia Asbury; Michael Smuin; **Costumes:** Willa Kim; **Musical Director:** Ian Fraser; **Orchestrations:** Chris Boardman; Bill Byers; Angela Morley; **Set Design:** Douglas W. Schmidt

Songs: American Dream, The; Bon Nuit, Papa; Dinner with W.R.; Doing the Charlie Chaplin; Funny Man; Going Places [1]; Heel Toe and Away We Go; I Belong Here [1]; If Only You Were Here; It Was Always You [1]; Joyeux Noel; Little Bit of Power and Powder and Paint, A; Love; Madame Butterfingers; Me and You; My Private Life; One Man Band; Read All About It [1]; Remember Me; Show Business Is My Life [1]; Sydney's Hymn; Thank You, Mr. Chaplin [1]; Thanks for Nothing; Wine, Women and Song [1]

Cast: Kathy Andrini; Marsha Bagwell; Sheri Cowart; Scott Grimes; Marc Jordan; Andrea Marcovicci; Anthony Newley; Mary Leigh Stahl; Ric Stonebeck

Notes: [1] Cut. In 1/83 script.

696 • CHARGE IT, PLEASE!

OPENED: 05/23/1991
Musical   Off-Broadway

Composer: Carlos Gorbea
Lyricist: Carlos Gorbea
Librettist: Carlos Gorbea
Producer: Puerto Rican Travelling Th.
Director: William Martin

Choreographer: Dennis Dennehy; Costumes: Mary Marsicano; Lighting Designer: Rick Butler; Musical Director: David Wolfson; Set Design: Rick Butler

Songs: Dance a Bomba at Funeral Time; Dear Love; Entr'acte; Listen to My Little Song; Loco Finale, A; Love and No Dinero; Love's in Full Bloom; Manhattan Shines; Shall We Take a Cruise; Show That Card

Cast: Fred Barrows; Mel Gorham; Joan Jaffe; Iraida Polanco; Jeannette Toro

697 • CHARITY GIRL, THE
OPENED: 10/02/1912   Theatre: Globe
Musical   Broadway: 21

Composer: Victor Hollander
Lyricist: Melville Alexander; Edward Peple
Librettist: Edward Peple
Producer: George W. Lederer
Director: George W. Lederer

Songs: Belle of the Beach, The; Champagne Song; Charity [1]; Come! Come!; Every Fellow Loves a Pretty Girl; Ghetto Glide; I'd Rather Be a Chippie Than a Charity Bum; Just We Two Dear; Magic Kiss, The; Things Unfeminine; Those Ragtime Melodies (C/L: Gene Hodgkins); When Texas Tommy Did the Turkey Trot (C/L: Billy Gaston; Edgar Selden); Yum Yum Time

Cast: Henry Finck; Marie Flynn; Ralph Herz; Aubrey L. Lyles; Flournoy Miller; Blossom Seeley

Notes: [1] Sheet music only.

698 • CHARLATAN, THE
OPENED: 09/05/1898   Theatre: Knickerbocker
Musical   Broadway: 40

Composer: John Philip Sousa
Lyricist: Charles Klein
Librettist: Charles Klein
Producer: E.R. Reynolds
Director: H.A. Cripps

Musical Director: Paul Steindorff

Songs: After Due Consideration; As the Agent; Before the Twilight Shadows; College Man, The; Day of Joy; Friends, Dear Friends; Good Morning; I Am the Seventh Son of a Seventh Son; Legend of the Frogs, The; Lilies of Your Love May Die, The; Love's the Pleasure, Love's the Pain; Matrimonial Guards, The; Mountebanks, Come Waken from Your Dreaming; Oh, Sunlit Sea Beyond the West; Opening Act II; Philosophic Tale Is Told, The; Pluto's Partner I; She Was a Maid of Sweet Simplicitee; Social Laws; Venus, Goddess of Love; When the Wintry Moon Is Bright

Cast: Nella Bergen; DeWolf Hopper; Alice Judson; Edmund Stanley

Notes: No program available.

699 • CHARLIE AND ALGERNON
OPENED: 09/14/1980   Theatre: Helen Hayes
Musical   Broadway: 17

Composer: Charles Strouse
Lyricist: David Rogers
Librettist: David Rogers
Producer: Fisher Theatre Foundation; Folger Theatre Group; John F. Kennedy Center; Isobel Robins Konecky
Director: Louis W. Scheeder

Source FLOWERS FOR ALGERNON (Novel: Daniel Keyes); Choreographer: Virginia Freeman; Costumes: Jess Goldstein; Lighting Designer: Hugh Lester; Musical Director: Liza Redfield; Orchestrations: Philip J. Lang; Set Design: Kate Edmunds

Songs: Charlie; Charlie and Algernon; Dream Safe with Me; Everything Was Perfect; Have I the Right; Hey Look at Me; His Name Is Charlie Gordon [1]; I Can't Tell You; I Got a Friend; I Really Loved You; Jelly Donuts and Chocolate Cake; Maze, The; Midnight Riding; No Surprises; Not Another Day Like This; Now; One Step at a Time [2]; Our Boy Charlie [1]; Reading; Some Bright Morning; Somebody New; Whatever Time There Is

Cast: P.J. Benjamin; Edward Earle; Sandy Faison; Patrick Jude; Julienne Marie

Notes: Titled FLOWERS FOR ALGERNON in London prior to New York. [1] In London prior to New York. [2] Cut Washington, D.C. prior to New York.

700 • CHARLOT 1928

OPENED: 1928   Theatre: Vaudeville
Revue   London

Librettist: Reginald Hargreaves; Austin Melford; Quentin Tod
Producer: Charles B. Cochran
Director: Quentin Tod

Choreographer: Barrie Oliver; **Costumes:** Peter Judge; **Set Design:** Laverdet; Marc-Henri

Songs: F.U.N.E.X. (C/L: Davy Burnaby; William Stephens); I'd Rather Cry Over You (C: Dan Dougherty; L: Phil Ponce); In the Swim (inst.) (C: Edward Cooper); Old Fashioned Boy (C: Rex Evans; L: Rowland Leigh); One-Way Walk, The (C: Vivian Ellis; L: Desmond Carter); Opening Chorus (C: Edward Cooper; L: Rowland Leigh); Pendulum of Time, The (C: Philip Braham; L: Donovan Parsons); Take a Little Walk (inst.) (C: Philip Braham); You've Got to Be in Love to Do That (C: Vivian Ellis; L: Donovan Parsons)

Cast: Betty Bolton; Davy Burnaby; Rex Evans; George Howe; Barrie Oliver; Quentin Tod; Sybil Wise

701 • CHARLOT REVUE OF 1924

Notes: *See ANDRE CHARLOT REVUE OF 1924.*

702 • CHARLOT REVUE OF 1926

OPENED: 11/10/1925   Theatre: Selwyn
Revue   Broadway: 140

Composer: Noel Coward
Lyricist: Noel Coward
Librettist: Norah Blaney; Bert Lee; Dion Titheradge; R.P. Weston
Producer: Arch Selwyn
Director: Jack Buchanan

Choreographer: Jack Buchanan; **Costumes:** G.K. Benda; Lucien Lelong

Songs: Animals Came in Two By Two [1] (C/L: Philip Braham); Baby Blues [1] (C/L: Ivor Novello; L: Ronald Jeans); Ballad Singer, The [1] (C: Leonard Henry; L: H.B. Headley); Be Careful What You Do [1] (C: Reginald Arkell; L: Geoffrey Gwyther); Carrie; Cup of Coffee, a Sandwich and You, A (C: Joseph Meyer; L: Al Dubin; Billy Rose); Follow Mister Cook (C: Philip Braham; L: Douglas Furber); Fox Has Left His Lair, The (C: Peggy Connor; L: Douglas Furber); Friendly Ghosts [2] (C: Richard Addinsell; L: Rowland Leigh); Gigolette (C: Franz Lehar; L: Irving Caesar); Girls I Am Leaving in England Today, The [1]; He's Reliable [1] (C: Leonard Henry; L: Laddie Cliff; H.B. Headley); How D'You Do (C: Philip Braham; L: Eric Blore; Dion Titheradge); I Don't Know [2]; Let's All Go Raving Mad (C: Philip Braham; L: Hugh E. Wright); Little Slut of Six, A [1]; Love's Lottery [1] (C: Billy Mayerl; L: Gene Paul); March with Me [3] (C: Ivor Novello; L: Douglas Furber); Mender of Broken Dreams, The (C/L: John W. Bratton); Mona When She Taps on Her Corona [1] (C: Jara Benes; L: Clifford Seyler); Mouse! Mouse! (C: Muriel Lillie; L: Hilda Brighton); Oxford Bags (C: Philip Braham; L: Arthur Wimperis); Poor Little Rich Girl; Roses Have Made Me Remember, The [1]; Russian Blues; Sealed Feet (C: Charles Prentice); Silly Little Hill [2] (C: Richard Addinsell; L: Rowland Leigh); Susannah's Squeaking Shoes (C: Muriel Lillie; L: Arthur Weigall); Take Them All Away (C/L: Jack Strachey); Those Were the Days [1] (C: Philip Braham; L: Ronald Jeans); Whimsical Peddler, The [2] (C: Pat Thayer; L: Donovan Parsons)

Cast: Jack Buchanan; Constance Carpenter; Douglas Furber; Gertrude Lawrence; Beatrice Lillie; Herbert Mundin; Hugh Sinclair

Notes: [1] Not in program. [2] Sheet music only. [3] Also in ANDRE CHARLOT REVUE OF 1924 and LONDON CALLING.

703 • CHARLOT'S MASQUERADE

OPENED: 09/04/1930
Revue   London

Lyricist: Rowland Leigh
Librettist: Ronald Jeans
Producer: Andre Charlot
Director: Ronald Jeans; Auriol Lee

Choreographer: Eric Coates; Harland Dixon; Cyril Scott; Quentin Tod; **Costumes:** S. Chermayeff;

Gordon Conway; Charles Judd; **Orchestrations:** Pierre de Caillaux; **Set Design:** A.E. Barrosa; S. Chermayeff; Philip Gough; Laverdet; Marc-Henri

Songs: Chic Technique (C: Reginald Casson); I Fell for You (C: William Walker); La, Lil, In Two International Cameos (C: Ivor Novello); Lady Clara (C: Kenneth Tod); Love Like That (C: Jack Strachey); Lullaby [1] (C: Richard Rodgers; L: Lorenz Hart); Manhattan Serenade (inst.) (C: Louis Alter); Night School for Revue, The (C: Reginald Casson); Party's Getting Wild, The (C: Harry Revel); Skating Shoes (C: Pierre de Caillaux); Sweet Temptation (C: Arthur Young); To Be or Not to Be Blues (C: Reginald Casson); Who Cares? (C: Norman Hackforth); Woman Porters (C: Reginald Casson)

Cast: Constance Carpenter; Florence Desmond; Anton Dolin; Henry Kendall; Beatrice Lillie; J.H. Roberts; Reginald Smith; Quentin Tod; Dora Vadimova; Patrick Waddington

Notes: No London program available. [1] Originally in SHE'S MY BABY, titled "A Baby's Best Friend."

704 • CHARLOT'S REVUE

OPENED: 09/23/1924　　Theatre: Prince of Wales
Revue　　London: 518

Librettist: Ronald Jeans
Producer: Dion Titheradge

Choreographer: Laddie Cliff; **Costumes:** G.K. Benda; **Musical Director:** Philip Braham; **Set Design:** Marc-Henri

Songs: That Forgotten Melody (C: Vincent Youmans; L: Douglas Furber)

Cast: Effie Atherton; Maisie Gay; Peter Haddon; Morris Harvey; Henry Kendall; Phyllis Monkman; Queenie Thomas; Sybil Wise

Notes: No program available. A new edition opened on 3/2/25. The original edition ran 216 performances. There were also songs by Noel Coward, Reginald Arkell, Donovan Parsons, Gordon McConnell, Jack Strachey, Irving Caesar, Percy Waxman, Philip Braham, Joseph Meyer, Jack Arnold, Arthur Samuels and Dave Stamper.

705 • CHARLOTTE SWEET

OPENED: 08/22/1982　　Theatre: Westside Arts
Musical　　Off-Broadway: 102

Composer: Gerald Jay Markoe
Lyricist: Michael Colby
Librettist: Michael Colby
Producer: Power Productions; Stan Raiff
Director: Edward Stone

Choreographer: Dennis Dennehy; **Costumes:** Michele Reisch; **Lighting Designer:** Jason Kantrowitz; **Musical Director:** Jan Rosenberg; **Orchestrations:** John McKinney; **Set Design:** Holmes Easley

Songs: A-Weaving; At the Music Hall; Bubbles in Me Bonnet; Charlotte Sweet; Christmas Buche, A; Circus of Voices, The; Darkness; Daughter of Valentine's Day, A; Dover; Farewell to Auld Lang Syne; Forever; Good Things Come; It Could Only Happen in the Theatre; Katinka; Keep It Low; Layers of Underwear; Letter (Me Charlotte Dear), The; Liverpool Sunset; Lonely Canary; My Baby and Me; On It Goes; Quartet Agonistes; Queenly Comments; Reckoning, The; Surprise! Surprise!; Vegetable Reggie; You See in Me a Bobby; Your High Note!

Cast: Mara Beckerman; Merle Louise; Michael McCormick; Christopher Seppe; Sandra Wheeler

706 • CHARM SCHOOL, THE

OPENED: 08/21/1920　　Theatre: Bijou
Play　　Broadway: 87

Author: Alice Duer Miller; Robert Milton
Producer: Robert Milton

Costumes: Gordon Conway

Songs: When I Discover My Man (C: Jerome Kern; L: Alice Duer Miller)

707 • CHARMER, THE

Notes: *See WHITE LILACS.*

708 • CHASE A RAINBOW

OPENED: 06/12/1980　　Theatre: Theatre Four
Musical　　Off-Broadway: 6

Composer: Harry Stone
Lyricist: Harry Stone
Librettist: Harry Stone
Producer: Joan Dunham; Segue Productions
Director: Sue Lawless

Choreographer: Bick Goss; **Costumes:** Rita Watson; **Lighting Designer:** Jeff Davis; **Musical Director:** John Franceschina; **Set Design:** Michael Rizzo

Songs: All the Years; Big City, The; Everything Happens for the Best; Happiest People, The; Have a Good Day; I Just Want to Know That You're All Right; I'm in Showbiz; I've Been Around the Horn; Let's Hear It for Me; Life on the Rocks; Listen Little Boy; Listen World; Mack Sennett Where Are You; Masquerade; My Meadow; Out of Love; People You Know, The; Segue; To Be or Not to Be; We're #1; Whenever You Want Me; You've Gotta Have a Passion

Cast: Suzanne Dawson; Chuck Karel; Stephen McNaughton; Jan Neuberger; Ted Pugh; Virginia Sandifur

709 • CHATTER BOX REVUE

OPENED: 1925
Revue

Composer: Richard A. Whiting
Lyricist: Raymond B. Egan
Librettist: Howard Emmett Rodgers
Producer: Jack Welsh
Director: Richard W. Krakeur

Choreographer: Max Scheck

Songs: Chatterbox Girl; Cinderella's Dreams; Keep Sakes; My Empty Arms; My Treasure Island; Rose of Tenement Row; Susan; Wanda

Notes: No program available. Sheet music only.

710 • CHAUVE SOURIS

OPENED: 02/01/1922   Theatre: 49th Street
Revue   Broadway: 544

Composer: Aliabieff; Gretchaninoff
Producer: F. Ray Comstock; Morris Gest

Costumes: Granier; **Set Design:** Sergei Soudeikine

Songs: Alluring Gypsy Girl, The; Anuska (C/L: Oscar Steiner; Oscar Virag); Chauve Souris (C/L: Eugene Platzman); Chinese Billikens (C: Alexei Archangelsky; L: Dailey Paskman); Clown, The; Dark Eyes (C/L: A. Salami); Dear Nightingale (C: Aliabeck; L: Dailey Paskman); Grief (C/L: Dailey Paskman); I Miss My Swiss, My Swiss Miss Misses Me (C: Abel Baer; L: L. Wolfe Gilbert); In a Little French Cafe (C: Sammy Fain; L: Mitchell Parish); Japanese Box, The; Katinka (C/L: Alexei Archangelsky; Czaroulch); Knife- Grinder's Daughter, The; Love in the Ranks; Minuet, The; Night Idyll (C: Alexei Archangelsky; L: Dailey Paskman); O, Katharina! [1] (C: Richard Fall; L: L. Wolfe Gilbert); Olaf, You Ought-a-Hear Olaf Laff (C: Abel Baer; L: L. Wolfe Gilbert); Parade of the Wooden Soldiers (C: Leon Jessel; L: Ballard Macdonald); Passing Regiment (C/L: Leigh; Strauss); Pierrot's Moonlight Serenade (C/L: Dailey Paskman); Porcelaine De Saxe (C/L: Frank Waller); Rendezvous of Love, The; Round the Ray Wain; Russian Barcarolle, A; Russian Toys, The; Siciliana; Song of the Black Hussars; Stenka Razin; Three Huntsmen (C/L: Dailey Paskman); 'Twas in the Month of May (C: Walter Kollo; L: Brian Hooker); Two Guitars; Volga Boat Song (C: Alexei Archangelsky; L: Dailey Paskman)

Cast: Nikita Balieff; Birse; Mesdames Deykarhanova; Ershova; Dianina Fechner; Gorodetsky; Karabanova; Komisarjevskaia; Lomakina; Vassilkova

Notes: Some of these song titles may be sketches. [1] Not in programs.

711 • CHEE-CHEE

OPENED: 09/25/1928   Theatre: Mansfield
Musical   Broadway: 32

Composer: Richard Rodgers
Lyricist: Lorenz Hart
Librettist: Herbert Fields
Producer: Lew Fields
Director: Alexander Leftwich

Source SON OF THE GRAND EUNUCH, THE (Novel: Charles Petit); **Choreographer:** Jack Haskell; **Costumes:** John Booth; **Musical Director:** Roy Webb; **Orchestrations:** Roy Webb; **Set Design:** John Hawkins

Songs: Await Your Love (Concubine's Song) [3]; Better Be Good to Me; Chee Chee's Second Entrance; Dear, Oh Dear; Farewell, O Life (Finale Act II) [4]; Finale Act I; Her Hair Is Black As Licorice [3]; Holy of Holies (Prayer) [3]; I Am a Prince [3]; I Bow a Glad Good Day (Tavern Opening) [3]; I Grovel to the Earth (Chee-Chee's First Entrance) [3]; I Grovel to Your Cloth (Chee-Chee's Third Entrance) [4]; I Must Love You [1]; I Wake at Morning [3]; I'll Never Share You (If You Were My Concubine) [5]; In a Great Big Way [3]; Joy Is Mine [6]; Just a Little Thing [3]; Khonghouse Song; Living Buddha (Impassive Buddha) [4]; Monastary Opening; Moon of My Delight; Most Majestic Domestic Officials, The [3]; Oh, Gala Day, Red-Letter Day [4]; Owl Song (Song of the Owl) [3]; Singing a Love Song [2]; Sleep, Weary Head [4]; Tartar Song, The [3]; Thank You in Advance [7]; We Are the Horrors of Deadliest Woe (Chorus of Torments) [4]; We're Men of Brains [3]; You Are Both Agreed (Finaletto, Scene 1) [3]

Cast: Helen Ford; Ralph Glover; William Griffith; George Hassell; George Houston; Philip Loeb; Stark Patterson; Dorothy Roye; Betty Starbuck; William Williams

Notes: [1] Same music as "Send for Me" from SIMPLE SIMON. [2] Same music as "I Still Believe in You" from SIMPLE SIMON. [3] Part of Act I sequence. [4] Part of Act II sequence. [5] Cut prior to opening. [6] Part of Act I sequence. May have been cut prior to opening. [7] Part of Act II sequence. Same music as "Moon of My Delight."

712 • CHEER UP

OPENED: 08/23/1917   Theatre: Harris
Musical   Broadway: 456

Composer: Raymond Hubbell
Lyricist: John Golden
Librettist: R.H. Burnside
Director: R.H. Burnside

Costumes: Will R. Barnes; Katherine H. Lovell; William H. Matthews; Robert McQuinn; Gladys Monkhouse; **Musical Director:** Raymond Hubbell; **Set Design:** H. Robert Law; Mark Lawson

Songs: Beautiful Queen of the Nile; Blushing Bride and Groom, The (C: Milton Ager; L: William

Jerome); Cheer Up, Liza!; Gee! What a Wonderful Mate You'll Be; Joy Town; Melody Land; My Bridal Rose; One, Two, Three; Opening Chorus; Patrol Mysterioso [1]; When Old New York Goes Dry (C/L: Benjamin Hapgood Burt); Won't You Follow Me There?

Cast: Harry Houdini; Nat Wills

Notes: [1] Sheet music only.

713 • CHEERIO

Notes: *See OH, KAY!*

714 • CHEERIO BOYS

Revue

Song: Cheerio Boys (C: Shoop, Cody; L: Morse, Dixie)

Notes: No other information available.

715 • CHERRIES ARE RIPE

OPENED: 09/21/1931
Musical   Closed out of town

Author: John Emerson; Anita Loos
Producer: Arch Selwyn
Director: John Emerson

Set Design: Henry Dreyfuss

Songs: Cherries Are Ripe (C: Lou Herscher; L: Ben Gordon; Allen Taub)

Cast: Mary Ellis; Emmett Joyce; Gavin Muir; Natalie Schafer; Richard Sterling; Basil Sydney; Herman Tapps

Notes: Information from National Theatre, Washington, D.C. The tour started with Vilma Banky and Rod La Roque starring and Constance Collier directing.

716 • CHERRY

Musical   Unproduced

Composer: Tom Baird
Lyricist: Ron Miller
Director: Joshua Logan

Source BUS STOP (Play: William Inge)

Songs: Cherry's Soliloquy; City Girls; Cooperatin' Nature; Green Grow the Lilacs; Grouchy; Hey, Butterfly; I Feel Love; If I Was a Man; I've Never Been a Woman Before; Je T'Aime Vous Paris; Little Lipstick Line, A; Men; Montana; Rainbows; Something to Believe In; Take a Look at Life; This Is Where the Bus Stops (C/L: Ilona Simon); Would I Lie to You; Ya' Won 'Em All for Cherry; Yesterday I Was You

717 • CHERRY BLOSSOM (1926)

OPENED: 01/18/1926
Musical   Closed out of town

Composer: Bernard Hamblen
Lyricist: Edward A. Paulton
Librettist: Edward A. Paulton
Producer: Anhalt & Bachelder; Eddie Dowling
Director: Eddie Dowling

Choreographer: M. Francis Weldon; **Costumes:** M. Francis Weldon; **Set Design:** P. Dodd Ackerman

Songs: Ask Me Beauty; China Loo; Family Fan, The; High Tide, Low Tide; If It Were Mine; I'm in Love; Investigate; Love Is a Bubble; Motor Boat, The; Pink Cherry Blossoms; Proud Pelican and the Priceless Gem, The; Strike for the Rent; Temple Bells; There Is No One Quite So Gifted; Things Which Are Equal to the Same Thing; When Love Is True Love

Notes: No program available. Closed in Syracuse, NY.

718 • CHERRY BLOSSOMS (1927)

OPENED: 03/28/1927   Theatre: 44th Street
Musical   Broadway: 56

Composer: Sigmund Romberg
Additional Music: Will Ortmann
Lyricist: Harry B. Smith
Additional Lyrics: J. Keirn Brennan
Librettist: Harry B. Smith
Producer: Messrs. Shubert
Director: Lew Morton

Source WILLOW TREE, THE (Play: Benrimo; Harrison Rhodes); **Choreographer:** Michio Ito; Ralph Reader; **Costumes:** Ernest Schrapps;

Musical Director: Alfred Goodman; **Set Design:** Watson Barratt

Songs: Feast of the Lanterns; Finale Act I; Finaletto; Happy Rickshaw Man (Jinrikisha Song) [2]; I Want to Be There; If You Know What I Think; I'll Peek-a-boo You; I've Waited for You [1]; Japanese Serenade; Legend Song; My Own Willow Tree [1]; 'Neath the Cherry Blossom Moon (C: Will Ortmann; L: J. Keirn Brennan); Opening; Opening Act III; Pit Solo; Romance; Some Day [1]; Tell Me Cigarette (Cigarette Song); Wait and See; Within the Land of Geishas; Woolworth of Japan, The

Cast: Desiree Ellinger; Bernard Gorcey; Howard Marsh

Notes: [1] Not in program. [2] ASCAP/Library of Congress.

719 • CHERRY GIRL, THE

OPENED: 12/21/1903   Theatre: Vaudeville
Musical   London: 215

Composer Ivan Caryll
Lyricist: Avery Hopwood
Librettist: Seymour Hicks
Producer: Charles Frohman; A. & S. Gatti

Choreographer: Willie Warde; **Costumes:** Wilhelm; **Musical Director:** Seymour Hicks; **Set Design:** W. Harford; R.C. McCleary

Songs: Bogeys; Bubble-Land; Coming of Dawn, The; Dat's de Way to Spell Chicken (C/L: Sidney L. Perrin; Bob Slater); Did He?; Entrance Picture Buyers; Finale Act I; Hail! Her Majesty; In the Studio; Just to Please You, Sue (C/L: Sydney L. Perrin); Miss Innocent (C/L: Bernard Rolt); My Little Hong Kong Baby (C: John W. Bratton; L: Paul West); Naughty Just for Once; Opening Chorus; Opening Chorus Act II; Over the Tiles; Painting; Pansy; Pussy Cats Three (C: Harold Samuel; L: George M. Slater); Telephone to the Moon; Those Loving Eyes (C: Manuel Klein; L: Rida Johnson Young); Watchmens' Chorus; What a Very Pretty Picture That Would Make

Cast: Seymour Hicks; Courtice Pounds; Ellaline Terriss; Master Valchera

Notes: No program available.

720 • CHERRY PIE REVUE

OPENED: 04/14/1926   Theatre: Cherry Lane
Revue   Off-Broadway: 37

Composer: Eugene L. Berton
Lyricist: Carroll Carroll
Producer: Inter-Theatre Arts, Inc.
Director: Harry Wagstaff Gribble

Choreographer: Jeannette Collett; George Sargent; Edwin S. Strawbridge; **Costumes:** Rhea Wells; **Set Design:** Rhea Wells

Songs: Barcometer Love; Charleston (South Carolina) (L: Spaulding Halt); Conventional Opening, A; Maybe It's Love (L: Edward L. Wever); Mirror Graphic News, The; Reykjavik (L: Carroll Carroll; Edward L. Wever); Some Baby; Twelve Miles Out from the Coast; Venetian Glass; Why Do You Love Me? (L: Edward L. Wever); Wicked Little Pair of Eyes (L: Carroll Carroll; Edward L. Wever)

Notes: No program available.

721 • CHESS

OPENED: 04/28/1988   Theatre: Imperial
Musical   Broadway: 68

Composer: Benny Andersson; Bjorn Ulvaeus
Lyricist: Tim Rice
Librettist: Richard Nelson
Producer: 3 Knights, Ltd.; Robert Fox, Ltd.; Shubert Organization, The
Director: Trevor Nunn

Choreographer: Lynne Taylor-Corbett; **Costumes:** Theoni V. Aldredge; **Dance Arranger:** Anders Eljas; **Lighting Designer:** David Hersey; **Musical Director:** Paul Bogaev; **Orchestrations:** Anders Eljas; **Set Design:** Robin Wagner; **Vocal Arranger:** Anders Eljas

Songs: Anthem; Arbiter's Song; Argument; Chess Hymn; Confrontation, The; Deal, The; Endgame; Florence Quits; Heaven Help My Heart; How Many Women; Hungarian Folk Song [1]; I Know Him So Well; Let's Work Together [1]; Lullaby (Apukad Eros Kezen) [1]; Merano; Merchandisers' Song; Model of Decorum & Tranquility, A; Mountain Top Duet; No Contest; Nobody's on Nobody's Side; One Night in Bangkok; Pity the Child; Press Conference [1]; So You Got What You Want [1]; Someone Else's Story; Story of Chess,

The [1]; Terrace Duet [1]; U.S. Versus U.S.S.R.; Where I Want to Be; Who'd Ever Guess It?; Whole New Board Game, A [1]; You and I; You Want to Lose Your Only Friend? [1]

Cast: Neal Ben-Ari; David Carroll; Philip Casnoff; Harry Goz; Kurt Johns; Judy Kuhn; Marcia Mitzman; Richard Muenz

Notes: [1] In London version only.

722 • CHIC

OPENED: 05/19/1959   Theatre: Orpheum
Musical   Off-Broadway: 6

Composer: Julian Stein
Lyricist: Lester Judson
Librettist: Lester Judson
Producer: Peter Pell
Director: Richard Altman

Choreographer: Jim Russell; **Costumes:** Theoni V. Aldredge; **Lighting Designer:** F.J. McAliece; **Musical Director:** Dorothea Freitag; **Orchestrations:** Dorothea Freitag; **Set Design:** Robert Soule

Songs: Angry Young Man, The; Basic [1] (C: Murray Grand; L: Lester Judson; Robin Miller); Charity (C: Murray Grand; L: Lester Judson; Robin Miller); Chic; East Side Story, The; Flattery (C: Edward C. Redding); Goal in My Life, The (C: Murray Grand); Happy Years, The (C: Raymond Taylor); Julie Is Mine (C: Raymond Taylor); Later (C: Dorothea Freitag); Man Up My Sleeve, A [1] (C: Lester Judson); Mediocrity (C: Murray Grand); Moscow Blues, The [1] (C: Murray Grand); Mouse, The (C/L: Edward C. Redding; L: Lester Judson); Summer Romance, A (C/L: Raymond Taylor; L: Lester Judson); Talk to Me; Tallahassee Lassie (C/L: Bob Crewe; Frederick A. Piscariello; Frank C. Slay); Teenage Love [1] (C: Murray Grand); There's No Room for People Any More; Thief (dance), The (C: Perry N. Lopez); We're Dying to Die [1]

Cast: Kelly Brown; Dale Monroe; Eileen Rodgers; Virginia de Luce

Notes: [1] Cut prior to opening.

723 • CHICAGO

OPENED: 06/01/1975   Theatre: 46th Street
Musical   Broadway: 947

Composer: John Kander
Lyricist: Fred Ebb
Librettist: Fred Ebb; Bob Fosse
Producer: James Cresson; Robert Fryer
Director: Bob Fosse

Source CHICAGO (Play: Maurine Dallas Watkins);
Choreographer: Bob Fosse; **Costumes:** Patricia
Zipprodt; **Dance Arranger:** Peter Howard;
Lighting Designer: Jules Fisher; **Musical
Director:** Stanley Lebowsky; **Orchestrations:**
Ralph Burns; **Set Design:** Tony Walton

Songs: All I Care About; All That Jazz; Cell Block
Tango; Chicago After Midnight (inst.); Class;
Curtain [1]; Funny Honey; I Can't Do It Alone;
I Know a Girl; It [1]; Keep It Hot (dance); Little
Bit of Good, A; Loopin' the Loop [2]; Me and My
Baby; Mister Cellophane; My Own Best Friend;
No [1]; Nowadays; Pansy Eyes [1]; R.S.V.P.
(dance); Razzle Dazzle; Rose Colored Glasses [1];
Roxie; Tap Dance (dance); Ten Percent [1]; We
Both Reached for the Gun; When Velma Takes
the Stand; When You're Good to Mama

Cast: Candy Brown; Christopher Chadman; Cheryl
Clark; Graciela Daniele; Gene Foote; Richard
Korthaze; Barney Martin; Mary McCarty; Jerry
Orbach; Chita Rivera; Ron Schwinn; Paul Solen;
Pamela Sousa; Gwen Verdon

Notes: [1] Cut prior to opening. [2] Cut prior to
opening. Music retained as overture.

724 • CHICAGO LOOP
OPENED: 1926
Musical   Unproduced

Composer: James P. Johnson
Lyricist: Henry Creamer; Ted Wing

Notes: No other information available.

725 • CHICAGO RHYTHM
OPENED: 1934   Theatre: Grand Terrace
                              Cafe
Revue   Chicago

Composer: Paul Denniker
Lyricist: Andy Razaf
Producer: Leonard Harper

Songs: Disappointed in Love; Ev'rybody Gets Hot;
Guess We're Gonna Get Along (C: Paul

Denniker; Cecelia Reeker); Rhythm Lullaby;
Snake in the Grass, A; That Grand Terrace Trot;
Twilight; Where Can I Find a Cherry; Who Made
Bluebeard Blue?

Cast: Pearl Baines; Earl Hines Orchestra; Alma
Smith

Notes: Also known as SOUTH SIDE RHYTHM.
No program available.

726 • CHICKEN CHOW MEIN
Musical

Songs: Gloaming (C/L: Herman Timberg)

Notes: Sheet music only. No other information
available.

727 • CHIEFTAIN, THE
OPENED: 09/09/1895   Theatre: Abbey's
Musical   Broadway: 54

Composer: Arthur Sullivan
Librettist: Francis C. Burnand
Director: Richard Barker

Costumes: Percy Anderson; **Musical Director:** A.
DeNovellis; **Set Design:** Henry E. Hoyt

Cast: John E. Brand; Lulu Glaser; Alice Holbrook;
W.A. Laverty; Christie MacDonald; Joseph C.
Miron; Edward P. Temple; Rhys Thomas; Francis
Wilson

Notes: No songs listed in program

728 • CHIFFON GIRL, THE
OPENED: 02/19/1924   Theatre: Lyric
Musical   Broadway: 103

Composer: Monte Carlo; Alma Sanders
Lyricist: Monte Carlo; Alma Sanders
Librettist: George Murray
Producer: Charles Capehart
Director: Everett Butterfield

Choreographer: Bert French; **Musical Director:**
Fred Hoff; **Orchestrations:** Charles Kreffert; **Set
Design:** William Weaver

Songs: Back in My Tumble Down Shack [1]; Bring
Back Your Heart to Me; Cafe Boheme, The;

Cuddle Me Up; Did You Come Back?; Dust Chasers; Flirtation [1]; Just One Rose; Little Devils; Maybe Yes or No; Mia Cara; My Chiffon Girl; My Tonita; New York Life; 1908; Rain Drops and the Rose [2]; Till the End of Time; We're Sweethearts; When the Sun Goes Down

Cast: Joseph Letora; Eleanor Painter

Notes: [1] Out Stamford. [2] Sheet music only.

729 • CHILDREN OF ADAM

OPENED: 08/17/1977   Theatre: Chelsea Westside Cabaret

Revue   Off-Broadway: 62

Composer: Stan Satlin
Lyricist: Stan Satlin
Librettist: John Driver
Producer: John A. Vaccaro; James J. Wisner
Director: John Driver

Choreographer: Ruella Frank; **Costumes:** Polly P. Smith; **Lighting Designer:** Robert F. Strohmeier; **Musical Director:** James J. Wisner; **Set Design:** Ernest Allen Smith; **Vocal Arranger:** James J. Wisner

Songs: Brides in Love; Cacophony; Children of Adam; Dreams; Equilib; Flowers and the Rainbow, The; I Can Feel; I Can Make It; I Must Go Now; It Ain't Easy; It's Really You; Just a Feeling; Life; Like a Park on Sunday; Maybe You Can See Yourself; Move Along; Mr. & Mrs. Myth; No More Games; Part of the Plan; Rise 'n' Love; Sex Is Animal; Sleep My Child; Sleepin' Around; Song Song; Sweetest Songs Remain to Be Sung, The; Walkin'; Wedding, The; What's Your Name?; Wooden People, The; You've Got to Die to Be Born Again

Cast: Gene Bua; Elizabeth Lathram; Karen Philipp; Robert Polenz; Roger Rathburn; Carole Schweid

Notes: Conceived by John Driver.

730 • CHILDREN OF EDEN

OPENED: 01/08/1991   Theatre: Prince Edward
Musical   London: 103

Composer: Stephen Schwartz
Lyricist: Stephen Schwartz
Librettist: John Caird

Producer: Atlantic Overtures; Children of Eden, Ltd.
Director: John Caird

Choreographer: Matthew Bourne; **Costumes:** Richard Sharples; **Lighting Designer:** David Hersey; **Orchestrations:** David Cullen; **Set Design:** John Napier

Songs: Ain't It Good; Children of Eden; Civilized Society; Close to Home; Degenerations; Dove Song, The; Expulsion, The; Generations; Hardest Part of Love, The; In the Beginning; In Whatever Time We Have; Let There Be; Lost in the Wilderness; Naming, The; Pursuit of Excellence, The; Return of the Animals, The (inst.); Shipshape; Spark of Creation, The; Stranger in the Rain; Wasteland; World Without You

Cast: Shion Abdillah; Adrian Beaumont; Earlene Bentley; Kevin Colson; Ramilles Corbin; Richard Lloyd-King; Ken Page; Shezwae Powell; Frances Ruffelle; Ray Shell; Martin Smith; Ashley Walters

731 • CHILDREN OF THE SUN, THE

OPENED: 1919
Musical

Librettist: J. Homer Tutt; Salem Tutt Whitney
Producer: J. Homer Tutt; Salem Tutt Whitney

Songs: Come and Dance with Me; Dear Old Dixie Home; Something About You I Like; Travelin'; We're Trarvelin'; Women All Go for Mine

Cast: Carrie King; Edward Tolliver; J. Homer Tutt; Virginia Wheeler; Salem Tutt Whitney

Notes: No other informatin available.

732 • CHILDREN'S CRUSADE, THE

OPENED: 04/29/1971
Musical   Closed out of town: 6

Composer: Jeff Alexander; Henry Myers; Larry Orenstein
Lyricist: E.Y. Harburg
Librettist: Henry Myers
Director: Anthony Wiles

Source OUR LIVES HAVE JUST BEGUN (Novel: Henry Myers)

Songs: Children's Play Song; Demon in the Compass; Good King Phillip [1]; Grown Ups; He Will Walk with Thee; Jerusalem; La Tra Ma La (Latramalay); Little Ships; Little World, Good Morning; Lost Sheep; Sermon, the Sword, and the Song, The; Song of Assisi, The; Wake Up; What a Day for a Miracle; When You Have Forgotten My Kisses (and I Have Forgotten Your Name); Who Will Walk with Me?; Wolf of Gubbio, The; Word Is Love, The

Cast: Wayne Grace; Scott Jacoby

Notes: Opened at the University of Vermont, Burlington. Also known as WHAT A DAY FOR A MIRACLE. [1] ASCAP/Library of Congress only.

733 • CHIN TOY
OPENED: 1920
Musical

Composer: Joseph E. Howard
Lyricist: I.B. Kornblum

Songs: Garden of Memory; Kiss from You, A (C: Joseph E. Howard; I.B. Kornblum; L: Zeke Meyers); My Chin Toy; Sweet Little Mary Ann (C: Joseph E. Howard; Jack King; L: Garfield Kilgour); Whistle a Song (C: Joseph E. Howard; I.B. Kornblum; L: Zeke Meyers); World Is Mine, The

Notes: Sheet music only. No other information available.

734 • CHINA DOLL, A
OPENED: 11/19/1904   Theatre: Majestic
Musical   Broadway: 18

Composer: Alfred E. Aarons
Lyricist: Harry B. Smith; Robert B. Smith
Librettist: Harry B. Smith; Robert B. Smith
Director: Max Freeman

Songs: Apple Mary Maguire (L: Harry B. Smith); Butterfly and the Clover, The; Cafe Chantant (L: Harry B. Smith); Dew on the Heather, The; Finale Act I (L: Harry B. Smith; Robert B. Smith); Finale Act II (L: Harry B. Smith; Robert B. Smith); Hist! Hist! Hist! (L: Harry B. Smith); How to Be Happy Though Married (L: Robert B. Smith); I Never Took a Lesson in My Life (L: Robert B. Smith); I Want to See the Happy Man (L: Robert B. Smith); If I Only Had a Theatre on Broadway (L: Harry B. Smith); If You Only Knew the Ways to Pull the Wires (L: Robert B. Smith); Lady with Money, A (L: Harry B. Smith); Mistakes Are Apt to Happen; My Little China Doll (L: Robert B. Smith); My Lucky Star; One Umbrella Would Be Big Enough for Two (L: Harry B. Smith); Opening Chorus (L: Harry B. Smith); Opening Chorus Act II (L: Harry B. Smith); Tale of the Wedding Bell, The (L: Robert B. Smith); That Man (L: Robert B. Smith); What Will China Do? (L: Robert B. Smith)

Cast: George Boniface Jr.; Corrine; Arthur Cunningham; Josephine Hall; Albert Hart; W.H. MacDonald; Helen Roynton

735 • CHINA ROSE
OPENED: 01/19/1925   Theatre: Martin Beck
Musical   Broadway: 126

Composer: A. Baldwin Sloane
Lyricist: Harry L. Cort; George E. Stoddard
Librettist: Harry L. Cort; George E. Stoddard
Producer: John Cort
Director: R.H. Burnside

Musical Director: Hilding Anderson

Songs: Calling You My Own; China Bogie Man; China Rose; Chinese Lantern Man; Chinese Potentate; Finale Act I; Great White Way in China; Hail the Bridegroom; Happy Bride; Home; I Like the Girls; I'm All Alone; I'm Hi, I'm Lo; I'm No Butterfly [1]; Just a Kiss; Legend of the Rose; Maiden Fair; Soldiers True; Sun Worship; Through the Bamboo; Tomorrow; We'll Build a Brand New Bamboo Bungalow; Who Am I Thinking Of?; Why Do They Make 'Em So Beautiful?

Cast: Harry Clarke; George Mack; J. Harold Murray; Olga Steck

Notes: Titled THE MOON MAIDEN out of town. See also under that title. [1] Cut Boston 12/24/24.

736 • CHIN-CHIN
OPENED: 10/20/1914   Theatre: Globe
Musical   Broadway: 295

Composer: Ivan Caryll
Lyricist: Anne Caldwell
Librettist: R.H. Burnside; Anne Caldwell

Producer: Charles Dillingham
Director: R.H. Burnside

Source UNKNOWN (Unknown: Anne Caldwell);
  Costumes: Wilhelm; **Set Design:** Homer Emens

Songs: Ballymooney and Biddy McGee [2] (C/L: Terence Lowry); Chin-Chin (Open Your Heart and Let Me In) (C/L: A. Seymour Brown); Chinese Honeymoon, A (L: Bryan; Williams); Chipper China Chaps; Danse Poetique; Finale Act I; Go Gar Sig Gong-Jue; Goodbye Girls, I'm Through [1] (L: John Golden); Grey Dove, The; In an Oriental Way; In January You May Love Mary; It's a Long Way to Tipperary (C: Jack Judge; L: Harry Williams); Love Moon; Mulberry Tree, The; Opening Chorus; Quaint Toys; Ragtime Temple Bells (L: James O'Dea); Shopping in the Orient; Strollers, The; Violet; Wedding Gifts of Silver; Will O' the Wisp (inst.)

Cast: Charles T. Aldrich; Helen Falconer; Dave Montgomery; Tot Qualters; Six Brown Brothers; Douglas Stevenson; Fred Stone; Belle Story

Notes: [1] Golden subconciously based on the tune on Caryll's song "Love Moon." [2] Sheet music only. The cover of this sheet credits the song to John Golden. The inside credits to "Trooper Terence Lowry." [3] Also in HIP-HIP-HOORAY.

737 • CHINESE HONEYMOON, A
OPENED: 06/02/1902 Theatre: Casino
Musical Broadway: 376

Composer: Howard Talbot
Lyricist: George Dance
Librettist: George Dance
Producer: Nixon & Zimmerman; Sam S. Shubert
Director: Gerald Coventry

Costumes: Caroline Siedle; **Lighting Designer:** Joseph C. Menchen; **Musical Director:** Herman Perlet; **Orchestrations:** Gustave Kerker; **Set Design:** D. Frank Dodge

Songs: A La Girl, The; But Yesterday [3]; Chinese Honeymoon, A; Chow-Chow's Honeymoon [4]; Click, Click [3]; Could I But Tell You; Dolly with a Dimple on Her Chin (Daisy with a Dimple on Her Chin); Egypt [4] (C/L: Clare Kummer); Emperor Hang Chow, The; Follow Your Leader [4] (C/L: Dance; Ernest Vousden); He Is the Bridegroom; I Hear They Want Some More [3];

I Knew at First Sight That I Loved Her; I Want to Be a Laidy; In Ylang-Ylang; Laughter Is Queen Tonight; Leader of Frocks and Frills, The (C: Melville Ellis; L: Robert B. Smith); Little Street in Heaven They Call Broadway, A (C: A. Baldwin Sloane); Maid of Pekin, The [4]; Mandie from Ohio [3]; Martha Spanks the Grand Pianner; Mr. Dooley [2] (C: Jean Schwartz; L: William Jerome); My Little Hong Kong Baby (C: John W. Bratton; L: Paul West); Nursery Rhymes (C: Jean Schwartz; L: William Jerome); Paper Fan, A; Penelope [3]; Perhaps (C/L: Melville Ellis); Roly Poly; Roses Red and White [1]; Royal Honeymoon, A; That Happy Land [3]; Tid Bits from the Plays; Twiddley Bits, The; Welcome, Official Mother-in-Law; When the Dreamer Awakes; With Weary Hearts; You Pat Me [3]

Cast: Aimee Angeles; William Pruette; Adele Richie; Thomas Q. Seabrooke; Mack Sennett; Van Rensselaer Wheeler; Annie Yeamans

Notes: Interpolated numbers by William Jerome and Robert B. Smith were credited in program but the songs were not identified. Note Mack Sennett's inclusion in the cast. [1] Cut 1/25/04 Newark. [2] Later in THE TOREADOR (London). [3] In original London production only. [4] Added after opening of London production.

738 • CHINESE LANTERN, THE
OPENED: 04/07/1922
Play Closed out of town

Composer: Richard Rodgers
Lyricist: Unknown
Author: Laurence Housman
Producer: Benjamin School for Girls

Songs: Anywhere; I Want to Be a Grocer; Partners; Wee China Rose

Cast: Dorothy Fields

Notes: Amateur show.

739 • CHOCOLATE BROWN
OPENED: 1921
Musical Chicago

Composer: Spencer Williams
Lyricist: Spencer Williams
Producer: Irvin C. Miller

Cast: William Fountain; Mildred Smallwood; Andrew Tribble; PeeWee Williams

Notes: No other information available.

740 • CHOCOLATE DANDIES, THE

OPENED: 09/01/1924　Theatre: Colonial
Revue　　　　　　　Broadway: 96

Composer: Eubie Blake
Lyricist: Noble Sissle
Librettist: Lew Payton; Noble Sissle
Producer: B.C. Whitney
Director: Eubie Blake; Julian Mitchell; Noble Sissle

Choreographer: Charles Davis; Julian Mitchell;
Costumes: John Newton Booth; Kiviette; Hugh Willoughby; **Lighting Designer:** Tony Greshoff;
Musical Director: Eubie Blake; **Orchestrations:** Lorenzo Calduel; **Vocal Arranger:** Lorenzo Calduel

Songs: Ain't Got No Worry Long As Your're My Baby [3] (C/L: Spencer Williams); All the Wrongs You Done to Me; Breakin' 'Em Down; Chocolate Dandies; Dixie Moon; Dumb Luck; Have a Good Time Everybody; I Lost My Head All Over You [3] (C/L: Spencer Williams); I'll Find My Love in D-I-X-I-E; In Bamville [4]; Jassamine Lane; Jazztime Baby [1]; Jockey's Life for Mine; Jump Steady; (Down in the) Land of Dancing Pickaninnies; Mammy's Lit'l Choc'late Cullud Chile; Manda; Run on the Bank; Slave of Love, The; Sons of Old Black Joe, The; Tahiti [5]; Take Down Dis Letter; That Charleston Dance; There's a Million Little Cupids in the Sky [2]; There's No Place as Grand as Bandana Land; Thinking of Me; You Ought to Know! [1] (C: Eubie Blake; Noble Sissle)

Cast: Josephine Baker; Eubie Blake; Ivan Harold Browning; Lottie Gee; Lew Payton; Noble Sissle; Valaida Snow; Elisabeth Welch

Notes: [1] Added after opening. [2] Cut before opening. [3] Not listed in program. [4] In show when titled IN BAMVILLE. [5] Cut before opening. In COCHRAN'S REVUE OF 1926.

741 • CHOCOLATE KIDDIES

OPENED: 1925
Revue　　　　　　　Nightclub

Composer: Duke Ellington
Lyricist: Jo Trent

Songs: Jig Walk; Jim Dandy; With You

742 • CHOCOLATE SOLDIER, THE (1909)

OPENED: 09/13/1909　Theatre: Lyric
Musical　　　　　　　Broadway: 296

Composer: Oscar Straus
Lyricist: Stanislaus Stange
Librettist: Stanislaus Stange
Producer: Fred C. Whitney
Director: Stanislaus Stange

Source ARMS AND THE GIRL (Play: George Bernard Shaw); **Source** DER TAPFERE SOLDAT (Musical: Rudolph Bernauer; Leopold Jacobson); **Choreographer:** Al Holbrook; **Costumes:** Hugo Baruch; **Musical Director:** A. DeNovellis; **Set Design:** Unitt and Wickes

Songs: After Today; Alexius the Heroic; Bulgaria Victorious; Chocolate Soldier, The; Falling in Love; Fatherland Is Free, The; Finale Act I; Finale Act II; Just a Commission; Letter Song, The; Melodrame; My Hero; Never Was There Such a Lover; Opening Chorus Act II; Our Heroes Come (inst.); Say Goodnight; Seek the Spy; Sweetheart [1]; Sympathy; Tale of a Coat, The; Thank the Lord the War Is Over; That Would Be Lovely; Then Shout Hurrah [1] (C: Max Bendix); Tiralala (Romance); We Are Marching Through the Night; We Are Searching for the Foe; We Too, Are Lonely; What Can We Do without a Man; Why Is It Love Makes Us Feel Queer?

Cast: Flavia Acaro; Jack Gardner; Ida Brooks Hunt; William Pruette

Notes: [1] Out New York 2/22. [2] Sheet music only.

743 • CHOCOLATE SOLDIER, THE (1955)

OPENED: 06/04/1955　Theatre: NBC
TV Musical

Composer: Oscar Straus
Lyricist: Carolyn Leigh
Librettist: William Friedberg; Will Glickman; Neil Simon
Producer: Max Liebman

Source CHOCOLATE SOLDIER, THE (Musical: Stanislaus Stange; Oscar Straus); **Musical Director:** Charles Sanford

Songs: Chocolate Soldier; Forgive; Letter Song; Marching to the Flight; Pick Your Hero; Quiet Voice, A; Seek the Spy; Such a Noble Lover; Tira, La La; War Is Over, The

Cast: Nelson Albert; David Atkinson; Rise Stevens; Akim Tamiroff

744 • CHOIR REHEARSAL, THE
OPENED: 1914

Songs: Wonderful Thing, A (C/L: Clare Kummer)

Cast: Sallie Fisher

Notes: No other information available.

745 • CHOPIN PROJECT
OPENED: 1923
Musical   Unproduced

Music Based On: Frederic Chopin
Composer: William Daly
Lyricist: Ira Gershwin[1]

Songs: Man, the Master; My All [3]; On the Wings of Romance; Someday You'll Realize [2]

Notes: [1] Used pseudonym Arthur Francis. [2] Verse music based on "Mazurka in A-flat, Op. 50, No. 2." Chorus music from 'Waltz in A-flat, Op. 34, No. 1 (Valse Brilliante)." [3] Chorus music based on "Etude in E Major, Op. 10, No. 3."

746 • CHORUS LINE, A
OPENED: 10/19/1975   Theatre: Shubert
Musical   Broadway: 6137

Composer: Marvin Hamlisch
Lyricist: Edward Kleban
Librettist: Nicholas Dante; James Kirkwood
Producer: N.Y. Shakespeare Festival; Joseph Papp
Director: Michael Bennett

Choreographer: Michael Bennett; **Costumes:** Theoni V. Aldredge; **Lighting Designer:** Tharon Musser; **Musical Director:** Donald Pippin;

Orchestrations: Bill Byers; Hershy Kay; Jonathan Tunick; **Set Design:** Robin Wagner; **Vocal Arranger:** Donald Pippin

Songs: And . . . ; At the Ballet; Dance: Ten, Looks: Three; Hello Twelve, Hello Thirteen, Hello Love; I Can Do That; I Hope I Get It; Joanne [1]; Music and the Mirror, The; Nothing; One; Sing!; Tap Combination, The; What I Did for Love

Cast: Scott Allen; Renee Baughman; Carole Bishop[2]; Pamela Blair; Wayne Cilento; Chuck Cissel; Clive Clerk; Kay Cole; Ronald Dennis; Donna Drake; Brandt Edwards; Patricia Garland; Carolyn Kirsch; Ron Kuhlman; Nancy Lane; Baayork Lee; Priscilla Lopez; Robert LuPone; Carmeron Mason; Donna McKechnie; Don Percassi; Carole Schweid; Michael Serrecchia; Michel Stuart; Thommie Walsh; Sammy Williams; Crissy Wilzak

Notes: Moved from Off-Broadway, where it opened 4/15/75. [1] Cut prior to opening. [2] Changed name to Kelly Bishop.

747 • CHOSEN, THE
OPENED: 01/06/1988   Theatre: Second Avenue
Musical   Off-Broadway: 6

Composer: Philip Springer
Lyricist: Mitchell Bernard
Producer: M Square Entertainment; Mitchell Maxwell; Marvin R. Meit; Alan J. Schuster; Robert de Rothschild
Director: Mitchell Maxwell

Source CHOSEN, THE (Novel: Chaim Potok); **Choreographer:** Richard Levi; **Costumes:** Ruth Morley; **Lighting Designer:** Thomas R. Skelton; **Musical Director:** Eric Stern; **Orchestrations:** Samuel Matlovsky; **Set Design:** Ben Edwards

Songs: Chosen, The; Danny's Plea; Greetings to You, Sabbath Angels; Holy Little World; Ladder to the Lord; My World; Our New Jerusalem; Play to Win; Prince and Me, The; Processional; Silence; Tear Down the Wall; Tune in My Heart; Wake Us with Your Song; Woman of Valor, A; Words

Cast: Richard Cray; George Hearn; Gerald Hiken; Rob Morrow; Lynnette Perry

748 • CHOW CHOW

Notes: *See THE RUNAWAYS.*

749 • CHRIS AND THE WONDERFUL LAMP

OPENED: 01/01/1900   Theatre: Victoria
Musical   Broadway: 58

Composer: John Philip Sousa
Lyricist: Glen MacDonough
Librettist: Glen MacDonough
Producer: Klaw & Erlanger; B.D. Stevens
Director: Ben Teal

Choreographer: Madame Malvina; **Costumes:** F. Richard Anderson; **Set Design:** Homer Emens; Frank Gates; Ernest Gros; E.A. Morange

Cast: Edna Wallace Hopper; May Norton; Jerome Sykes

Notes: No songs listed in program.

750 • CHRIS CROSSES

OPENED: 11/22/1946
Musical

Composer: Clay Boland
Lyricist: Moe Jaffe; Darrel H. Smith
Librettist: Robert F. Brown
Director: Benjamin F. Ricker

Choreographer: Walter Keenan; **Costumes:** Helen Stevenson West; **Musical Director:** Joseph F. Follmann Jr.; **Orchestrations:** Clay Boland; Al Boss; **Set Design:** Helen Stevenson West; **Vocal Arranger:** Clay Boland

Songs: As Ye Sow — Shall Ye Reap; Change of Watch; Chris Crosses; Christmas Eve; Holiday; I'll Take You All Over the World; Indian Dance; Interlude; It's the Same the Whole World Over; Little Grand Opera; Nina, the Pinta, and the Santa Maria, The; She Told Him Emphatically NO; That's What Made Those Happy Old Indians Dance; Wine Song, The; World Is Round-O, The

Cast: William Murphy; Henry Sullivan; Edward Wertimer

Notes: University of Pennsylvania Mask & Wig Club 59th annual production. Amateur show.

751 • CHRISTINE

OPENED: 05/07/1960   Theatre: 46th Street
Musical   Broadway: 12

Composer: Sammy Fain
Lyricist: Paul Francis Webster
Librettist: Pearl S. Buck; Charles K. Peck Jr.
Producer: Martin B. Cohen; Oscar S. Lerman
Director: Jerome Chodorov

Source MY INDIAN FAMILY (Book: Hilda Wernher); **Choreographer:** Hanya Holm; **Costumes:** Alvin Colt; **Dance Arranger:** Trude Rittman; **Lighting Designer:** Jo Mielziner; **Musical Director:** Jay Blackton; **Orchestrations:** Philip J. Lang; **Set Design:** Jo Mielziner; **Vocal Arranger:** Trude Rittman

Songs: Bharatha Natyan; Christine; Cobra Ritual Dance (inst.); Divali Festival, The; Doctor's Soliloquy, A; Freedom Can Be a Most Uncomfortable Thing; Happy Is the Word [1]; He Loves Her [2]; How to Pick a Man a Wife; I Love Him [2]; I Never Meant to Fall in Love; I'm Just a Little Sparrow; Ireland Was Never Like This; Kathakali; Lovely Girls of Akbarabad, The; My Indian Family; My Little Lost Girl; Room in My Heart; UNICEF Marching Song; We're Just a Pair of Sparrows [3]; Welcome Song (You're Indian Family); Woman I Was Before, The

Cast: Nancy Andrews; Daniel Keyes; Phil Leeds; Morley Meredith; Maureen O'Hara

Notes: [1] Cut prior to New York. [2] Same music. [3] ASCAP/Library of Congress only.

752 • CHRISTMAS CAROL, A (1954)

OPENED: 12/23/1954   Theatre: CBS
TV Musical

Composer: Bernard Herrmann
Lyricist: Maxwell Anderson
Librettist: Maxwell Anderson
Producer: Ralph Levy
Director: Ralph Levy

Source CHRISTMAS CAROL, A (Story: Charles Dickens); **Musical Director:** Bernard Herrmann

Songs: Bless Us Everyone; Dream Ends, The (inst.); Happy Ending, A (inst.); Holly Pine and Mistletoe; Humbug!; Journey into Christmas Past, The (inst.); Marley's Ghost; Santa Claus; Scrooge Rejoins the Human Race; Very Merry Christmas, A; What Shall I Give My Lad for Christmas?

Cast: Christopher Cook; Bonnie Franklin; Judy Franklin; Sally Fraser; Craig Hill; Queenie Leonard; Fredric March; Ray Middleton; Basil Rathbone; Bob Sweeney

Notes: Original television musical.

753 • CHRISTMAS CAROL, A (1981)

OPENED: 10/30/1981
Musical   Closed out of town

Composer: Michel Legrand
Lyricist: Sheldon Harnick
Producer: Barry Weissler; Fran Weissler
Director: Kenneth Frankel

Source CHRISTMAS CAROL, A (Story: Charles Dickens); **Choreographer:** Bick Goss; **Costumes:** Clifford Capone; **Dance Arranger:** Don York; **Lighting Designer:** Judy Rasmuson; **Orchestrations:** Steven Margoshes; **Set Design:** Jim Tilton; **Vocal Arranger:** Steven Margoshes

Songs: Bah! Humbug!; Balancing the Books; Bells of Christmas Day, The; Chained; Christmas Eve; Close Were We; Icy Ebenezer; Jig; Let There Be Time; My Two Feet Polka; One Family; One More Chance; Partners; Penny By Penny; Spirit of Christmas; Thank Heaven for Christmas; Twenty Questions

Cast: Gary Beach; Jack Dabdoub; Mary Gaebler; Richard Kiley; Dan Strickler

Notes: Also titled PENNY BY PENNY.

754 • CHRISTMAS CAROL, A (1994)

OPENED: 12/01/1994   Theatre: Paramount
Musical   Broadway: 85

Composer: Alan Menken
Lyricist: Lynn Ahrens
Librettist: Lynn Ahrens; Mike Ockrent

Producer: Madison Square Garden; Nickelodeon Family Classics
Director: Mike Ockrent

Source CHRISTMAS CAROL, A (Story: Charles Dickens); **Choreographer:** Susan Stroman; **Costumes:** William Ivey Long; **Dance Arranger:** Glen Kelly; **Incidental Music:** Glen Kelly; **Lighting Designer:** Peggy Eisenhauer; Jules Fisher; **Musical Director:** Paul Gemignani; **Orchestrations:** Michael Starobin; **Set Design:** Tony Walton

Songs: Abundance and Charity; Christmas Together; Dancing on Your Grave; God Bless Us Everyone; Jolly, Rich and Fat; Lights of Long Ago, The; Link By Link; Mr. Fezziwig's Annual Christmas Ball; Nothing to Do with Me; Place Called Home, A; Years Are Passing By, The; Yesterday, Tomorrow and Today

Cast: Walter Charles; Nick Corley; Ken Jennings; Jeff Keller; Joseph Kolinski; Michael Mandell; Mary Stout; Theara J. Ward; Robert Westenberg

Notes: The Paramount is a concert hall (formerly the Felt Forum space) in the Madison Square Garden complex.

755 • CHRISTMAS RAPPINGS

OPENED: 12/1975   Theatre: Judson Poets'
Revue   Off-Off-Broadway: 1

Composer: Al Carmines
Lyricist: Al Carmines
Librettist: Al Carmines

Choreographer: David Vaughan; Dan Wagoner; **Costumes:** Theo Barnes

Songs: Alleluia; And In That Region There Were Shepherds; And They Came with Haste; Blessed Art Man Among Women; But Mary Kept All Those Things in Her Heart; For Your Child Will Be Called the Prophet; Geneology; Go and Search Diligently for the Child; Hail Mary!; Holy Mary, Mother of God; How Can Those Things Be; I Am the Angel Gabriel; In the Beginning Was the Word; In Those Days a Decree Went Out; Joseph, Son of David, Do Not Fear to Take Mary for Your Wife; Lord, Now Let Thy Servant Depart in Peace; My Soul Magnifies the Lord; No Room in the Inn; Nova; Prayer; She Wrapped Him in Swaddling Clothes; Voice Was Heard

Wailing, A; Waiting; When They Saw the Star; Wise Men, The

Cast: Theo Barnes; Essie Borden; Al Carmines; Lee Guilliatt; Ira Siff; David Vaughan; Beverly Wideman; Margaret Wright

Notes: This was an annual event at the theatre which is part of the historic Judson Church in Greenwich Village.

756 • CHRONICLE OF A DEATH FORETOLD

OPENED: 06/15/1995   Theatre: Plymouth
Play   Broadway: 37

Composer: Michael John LaChiusa; Bob Telson
Lyricist: Michael John LaChiusa; Bob Telson
Librettist: Graciela Daniele; Jim Lewis
Producer: Lincoln Center Theater
Director: Graciela Daniele

Source CHRONICLE OF A DEATH FORETOLD (Novel: Gabriel Garcia Marquez);
Choreographer: Graciela Daniele; **Costumes:** Toni-Leslie James; **Dance Arranger:** Steve Sandberg; **Lighting Designer:** Beverly Emmons; Jules Fisher; **Musical Director:** Steve Sandberg

Cast: Yolanda Bavan; Lisa Loguillon; Luis Perez; Alexandre Proia; Saundra Santiago; George de la Pena

Notes: No songs listed in program.

757 • CHU CHEM

OPENED: 03/17/1989   Theatre: Ritz
Musical   Broadway: 44

Composer: Mitch Leigh
Lyricist: Jim Haines; Jack Wohl
Librettist: Ted Allen
Producer: Mitch Leigh Company, The; William D. Rollnick
Director: Albert Marre

Costumes: Kenneth M. Yount; **Lighting Designer:** Jason Sturm; **Musical Director:** Don James; **Orchestrations:** Michael Gibson; **Set Design:** Robert Mitchell

Songs: Be My Only Love; Boom!; Chu Chem; Empty Yourself; I Now Believe in Love; I Once

Believed; I'll Talk to Her; It Must Be Good for Me; It's Not the Truth; It's Possible; Love Is; Nothing at All; One at a Time; Orient Yourself; Our Kind of War; Re-Orient Yourself; River, The; Shame on You; This Coat; This Lovely Place; We Dwell in Our Hearts; Welcome; What Happened, What?; You'll Have to Change

Cast: Irving Burton; Kevin Gray; Alvin Lum; Chev Rodgers; Emily Zacharias; Mark Zeller

Notes: CHU CHEM's original production closed out of town in Philadelphia in 1966. This version premiered Off-Off-Broadway at the Jewish Repertory Theatre.

758 • CHU CHIN CHOW

OPENED: 10/22/1917   Theatre: Manhattan
     Opera House
Musical   Broadway: 208

Composer: Frederick Norton
Lyricist: Oscar Asche
Librettist: Oscar Asche
Producer: F. Ray Comstock; William Elliot; Morris Gest
Director: E. Lyall Swete

Choreographer: Mlle. Guida; Alexis Kosloff; **Costumes:** Percy Anderson; **Musical Director:** Gustave Ferrari; **Orchestrations:** Percy Fletcher; **Set Design:** Joseph Harker; Phil Harker

Songs: All My Days Till End of Life; Any Time's Kissing Time (C/L: Frederick Norton); At Siesta Time [2] (C: Grace Torrens; L: Arthur Anderson); Beans, Beans, Beans; Behold; Cleopatra's Dance; Cleopatra's Nile [3]; Cobbler's Song, The; Corraline; From Cairo, Bagdad, Khorasan; Hail the Grand Wazir [5]; Here Be Oysters Stewed in Honey (Opening Chorus); How Dear Is Our Day; I Am Chu Chin Chow of China; I Built a Fairy Palace in the Sky [3] (C: Frederick Norton); I Long for the Sun [1]; I Love You So (L: Hartley Carrick); I Shiver and Shake with Fear; If I Liken Thy Shape; I'll Sing and Dance; Javanese Dance; Lady, the Lover and the Jealous Husband, The [4]; Mahbuba [3]; My Desert Flower [5] (C: Frederick Norton); My Furry Castle in the Air [2]; My Head, My Head [5]; Olive Oil; Only a Slave [1]; Pale Hands I Loved [1]; Prayer in the Desert, The [5] (C: Frederick Norton); Serenade [3]; Song of the Scimitar, The; We Are the Robbers of the Woods; We Bring Ye Fruits; When a Man Is

Middle Aged [5] (C/L: Courtice Pound); When a
Pullet Is Plump It's Tender

Cast: Lucy Beaumont; Henry E. Dixey; Tessa Kosta;
Tyrone Power Sr.; Florence Reed

Notes: [1] Out St. Louis 8/16/43. [2] From the
revival of 1919. Revival produced by F. Ray
Comstock and Morris Gest and directed by
E. Lyall Swete. The choreography was by
A. Kosloff and Mlle. Guida. [3] London program.
[4] Sheet music only. [5] Added after London
opening.

759 • CINDERELLA (1957)

OPENED: 03/31/1957   Theatre: CBS
TV Musical

Composer: Richard Rodgers
Lyricist: Oscar Hammerstein II
Librettist: Oscar Hammerstein II
Producer: Richard Lewine
Director: Ralph Nelson

Source CENDRILLON, OU LA PETITE
PANTOUFLE DE VAIR (Fairy Tale: Charles
Perrault); **Choreographer:** Jonathan Lucas;
Costumes: Jean Eckart; William Eckart; **Lighting
Designer:** Robert Barry; **Musical Director:**
Alfredo Antonini; **Orchestrations:** Robert Russell
Bennett; **Set Design:** Jean Eckart; William Eckart

Songs: Do I Love You Because You're Beautiful?;
Gavotte (inst.); If I Weren't King [1]; Impossible;
In My Own Little Corner; It's Possible;
Loneliness of Evening; Lovely Night, A; Prince Is
Giving a Ball, The; Royal Dressing Room Scene;
Search, The (inst.); Stepsisters' Lament; Ten
Minutes Ago; Waltz for a Ball (inst.); When
You're Driving Through the Moonlight; Where
Is Cinderella? (inst.)

Cast: Edith Adams; Julie Andrews; Kaye Ballard;
Ilka Chase; Jon Cypher; Alice Ghostley; George
Hall; Howard Lindsay; Robert Penn; Dorothy
Stickney; Iggie Wolfington

Notes: [1] Cut before rehearsals. [2] Written for
SOUTH PACIFIC. Added to 1965 revival.

760 • CINDERELLA (1991)

OPENED: 12/19/1991   Theatre: Playhouse 91
Musical   Off-Broadway: 70

Composer: Dan Levy
Lyricist: Dan Levy; Amy Powers
Librettist: Norman Robbins
Producer: Riverside Shakespeare Co.
Director: Laura Fine

Source CINDERELLA (Fairy Tale); **Arrangements**
Dan Levy; **Costumes:** Gail Baldoni; **Lighting
Designer:** Stephen Petrillo; **Set Design:** Harry
Feiner

Songs: Bright Spring Morn; Dance at the Ball
Tonight; Delighted You Invited Me; Getting
Ready for the Ball; Happy Ending; His Highness;
I Am a Prince; It's What You Do (That Makes
Your Wishes Come True); Keep the Castle
Warm; La Petite Oiseau; Waitin' on the Women;
Your Sticks, Your Hat, Your Hand

Cast: John Keene Bolton; Diane Ciesla; Lora Lee
Cliff; Jim Fitzpatrick; Pat Flick; Mark Honan;
Robert Mooney; Anthony Stanton; Melanie
Wingert

761 • CINDERELLA AND THE PRINCE OR CASTLE OF HEART'S DESIRE

OPENED: 02/01/1904
Musical   Closed out of town

Composer: Edward W. Corliss; Louis Gottschalk
Additional Music: J.S. Chapman; D.K. Stevens;
D.J. Sullivan
Lyricist: R.A. Barnet; D.K. Stevens
Librettist: R.A. Barnet
Director: R.A. Barnet

Choreographer: Melvin B. Gilbert; **Musical
Director:** George Lowell Tracy

Cast: Reginald F. Bolles; F.A. Henderson

Notes: Boston program.

762 • CINDERELLA AT SCHOOL

OPENED: 1881   Theatre: Daly's
Musical   Broadway

Librettist: Woolson Morse

Choreographer: Fred Williams; **Costumes:**
Lanouette; **Musical Director:** E.R. Mollenhauer;
Set Design: James Roberts

Songs: Cause of Civilization, The; Columbia Won the Race Today; Come My Pretty Maiden; Cotton Cloth Ghost, A; Courting in the Moonlight; Did You Ever Hear Such Topics?; Fairest Maiden; Farewell; Green Are the Waving Branches; Hurrah! They Come; I Kiss My Hand to Thee; I'm Sure to Astonish You All; I've Got a Letter from My Jack; Linnet in the Tree, The; Lord Lawntennys and Pupils; Morning Mist Spread O'er the Mead, The; My Dear Young Ladies; Oh! No Regular Wits; Oh, Please My Dear Miss Tropics; Poor Cinderella; Pretty Little Shoe; Steeple; 'Tis Love Has Caused All Trouble; To Educate These Young Ladies; What Is Love?; Why Am I So Sad Today?; You Are an Orphan

Cast: John Brand; May Fielding; Harry Lacy; Charles LeClercq; Ada Rehan

Notes: Composer and lyricist not credited in program.

763 • CINDERELLA MAN, THE

OPENED: 01/17/1916   Theatre: Hudson
Play   Broadway: 192

Composer: Victor Herbert
Author: Edward Childs Carpenter
Producer: Oliver Morosco
Director: Robert Milton

Songs: Out of His Heart He Builds a Home (L: Edward Childs Carpenter); Punchinello (inst.); Yesterthoughts (inst.)

Cast: Frank Bacon; Phoebe Foster; Shelley Hull

764 • CINDERELLA ON BROADWAY

OPENED: 06/24/1920   Theatre: Winter Garden
Musical   Broadway: 126

Composer: Bert Grant
Lyricist: Harold Atteridge
Librettist: Harold Atteridge
Producer: J.J. Shubert; Lee Shubert
Director: J.C. Huffman

Choreographer: Allan K. Foster; **Costumes:** Homer Conant; Madame Haverstick; Cora MacGeachy; S. Zalud; **Musical Director:** Oscar Radin; **Set Design:** Watson Barratt; Homer Conant

Songs: All the Little Glooms Start Dancing; Any Little Melody; Bull and Bear [2]; Chair Ballet; Cinderella on Broadway; Cindy; Fairy Dance; Girl Belongs to You; Glorias, The; Hold Me [1]; House That Jack Built, The; I Have Somebody's Heart; Jazzing the Alphabet; Joy Dance; Labor Agitator, The [1]; Lady of Mars; Land Beyond the Candle Light, The; Last Waltz I Had with You, The; Lullaby, A; Miniatures; Minuet; Naughty Eyes; Old King Cole; Old Music Masters [3]; One Little Boy Had Money [2]; Patchland [2]; Phantom Loves; Pierrot Land [2]; Precious Jewels; Primrose Way; Rock Me in Your Loving Arms [1]; Rolling Up the Barcarolle [1]; Romantic Blues [1]; Roulette Dance; Silk Stocking Trail, The [2]; Stars We Know; That Girl Belongs to Me [2]; Theda Bara [1]; Three Musketeers of Broadway [1]; Topics of the Day [2]; Toy Dance; Wheel of Fate; Whistle and I'll Come to Meet You; Why Don't You Get a Sweetie?

Cast: Flo Burt; John T. Murray; George Price; Shirley Royce; Al Sexton

Notes: Additional music by Al Goodman but not identified in program. [1] Out Boston 10/18/20. [2] Out New Haven 6/14/30. [3] Not in programs.

765 • CINDERS

OPENED: 04/03/1923   Theatre: Dresden
Musical   Broadway: 31

Composer: Rudolf Friml
Lyricist: Edward Clark
Librettist: Edward Clark
Producer: Edward Royce
Director: Edward Royce

Set Design: P. Dodd Ackerman

Songs: Argentine Arango, The; Belles of the Bronx, The; Cinders (L: Anne Caldwell; Edward Clark); Fashion Parade, The; Flame of Love; Get Together; Grandma's Day; I'm Simply Mad About the Men; La Favorite; Modern Bride [1]; Moonlight on the Waters; On Hawaiian Shores; One Good Time; Rags Is Royal Raiments; Things That Cannot Be Explained [1]; Three Thousand Years Ago; Wedding Bells [1]; You and I [2]; You Got What Gets 'Em; You Remind Me of Someone

Cast: George Bancroft; Walter Regan; Queenie Smith

Notes: [1] Out Washington D.C. 3/25/23. [2] ASCAP/Library of Congress only.

766 • CINDY

OPENED: 03/19/1964   Theatre: Gate
Musical   Off-Broadway: 428

Composer: Johnny Brandon
Lyricist: Johnny Brandon
Librettist: Joe Sauter; Mike Sawyer
Producer: Stuart Wiener
Director: Marvin Gordon

Choreographer: Marvin Gordon; **Conductor:** Sammy Benskin; **Costumes:** Patricia Quinn Stuart; **Lighting Designer:** Martin Aronstein; **Musical Director:** Clark McClellan; **Orchestrations:** Clark McClellan; **Set Design:** Robert T. Williams

Songs: Call Me Lucky; Cindy; Genuine Feminine Girl, A; Got the World in the Palm of My Hand; If It's Love; If You've Got It, You've Got It; Is There Something to What He Said?; Laugh It Up; Let's Pretend; Life That I Planned for Him, The; Once Upon a Time; Papa, Let's Do It Again; Think Mink; Tonight's the Night; What a Wedding; Who Am I?

Cast: Johnny Harmon; Tommy Karaty; Sylvia Mann; Joe Masiell; Jacqueline Mayro; Thelma Oliver; Mark Stone

767 • CINGALEE, THE

OPENED: 10/24/1904   Theatre: Daly's
Musical   Broadway: 33

Composer: Lionel Monckton
Lyricist: Percy Greenbank; Adrian Ross
Librettist: James T. Tanner
Producer: J.C. Duff

Musical Director: Louis F. Gottschalk; **Set Design:** John Young

Songs: Bear Away the Bride; Course of True Love, The; Crocodile, The; I'm a Merry Maiden; In Gay Ceylon; Make a Fuss of Me; Monkeys, The; My Cinnamon Tree; My Heart Is At Your Feet; On the Lake (The New Year Festival); Opening Chorus; Parahara, The; Pearl of Sweet Ceylon; Peggy; Reading, Writing, Arithmetic; She's All Right; Something Devilish Wrong; Tea, Tea, Tea; There's Nothing Much More to Say; Wedding March; White and Brown Girl; With a Boo; You and I

Cast: Martha Carine; Blanche Deyo; William Norris; Melville Stewart

Notes: Additional numbers by Paul Rubens, but not identified in program.

768 • CIRCUS DAY

OPENED: 09/30/1901
Musical

Composer: George A. Nichols
Lyricist: George A. Nichols
Librettist: Owen Davis

Notes: Metropolis Theatre.

769 • CIRCUS EVENTS

Notes: *See THE AUTO RACE* and *see PIONEER DAYS.*

770 • CIRCUS GIRL, THE

OPENED: 04/23/1897   Theatre: Daly's
Musical   Broadway: 75

Composer: Ivan Caryll; Lionel Monckton
Lyricist: Harry Greenbank; Adrian Ross
Librettist: W. Palings; James T. Tanner
Producer: Augustin Daly

Set Design: Ernest M. Gros; Henry E. Hoyt; J.A.E. Malone

Songs: Not a Proper Way to Treat a Lady

Cast: Blanche Astley; Virginia Earle; Herbert Gresham; James T. Powers; Cyril Scott

Notes: No songs listed in program. [1] Later in SISTER MARY.

771 • CIRCUS PRINCESS, THE

OPENED: 04/25/1927   Theatre: Winter Garden
Musical   Broadway: 192

Composer: Emmerich Kalman
Lyricist: Harry B. Smith

Librettist: Harry B. Smith
Producer: J.J. Shubert; Lee Shubert
Director: J.C. Huffman; M.H. Varnell

Source DIE ZIRKUSPRINZESSIN (Musical: Julius Brammer; Alfred Grunwald; Emmerich Kalman); **Choreographer:** Allan K. Foster; **Musical Director:** Al Goodman; **Set Design:** Watson Barratt

Songs: Bravo, Bravo; Dear Eyes That Haunt Me; Girls, I Am True to You All (I'm True to Everyone); Guarded; Hussars' Song, The; I Dare to Speak of Love to You; I Dream of Your Eyes [1]; I Like the Boys; Joy Bells; Like You; Love Is an Idle Dream [1]; Lovely Vienna [2]; Same Old Love Songs; Silhouette; There's Something About You; Waiters; We Two Shall Meet Again [1]; What D'Ya Say? (C: Jesse Greer; L: Raymond Klages); (But) Who Cares?; You Are Mine Evermore [1]

Cast: George Bickel; Ted Doner; Gloria Foy; Poodles Hanneford; Guy Robertson; Desiree Tabor

Notes: [1] Sheet music only. [2] ASCAP/Library of Congress only.

772 • CITY CHAP, THE (1910)
OPENED: 1910
Musical

Composer: Benjamin Hapgood Burt
Librettist: George Ade

Notes: Produced at Purdue University.

773 • CITY CHAP, THE (1925)
OPENED: 10/26/1925   Theatre: Liberty
Musical   Broadway: 72

Composer: Jerome Kern
Lyricist: Anne Caldwell
Librettist: James Montgomery
Producer: Charles B. Dillingham
Director: R.H. Burnside

Source FORTUNE HUNTER, THE (Play: Winchell Smith); **Musical Director:** Victor Baravalle; **Orchestrations:** Robert Russell Bennett; **Set Design:** James Reynolds

Songs: Bubbles of Bliss; City Chap, The; Fountain of Youth, The; Go-Getter, The; He Is the Type [5];

If You Are As Good As You Look; I'm Head and Heels in Love [4] (C: Leo Edwards; L: Irving Caesar); Journey's End (L: P.G. Wodehouse); June Bells [1]; Like the Nymphs of Spring; No One Knows (How Much I'm in Love); Pill a Day, A; Sympathetic Someone; Walking Home with Josie; When I Fell in Love with You [2]; Why [3]

Cast: Phyllis Cleveland; Irene Dunne; Skeets Gallagher; George Raft

Notes: [1] Same music as "Joy Bells" from THE BEAUTY PRIZE. Out Philadelphia 9/28/25. [2] Cut after opening. [3] Out Philadelphia 9/28/25. [4] Sheet music only. [5] Also in THE CABARET GIRL.

774 • CITY JUNKET
OPENED: 1979
Musical   Unproduced

Composer: William Elliott
Lyricist: Kenward Elmslie

Source CITY JUNKET (Play: Kenward Elmslie)

Songs: Who'll Prop Me Up in the Rain

Notes: Five songs were written for this unproduced show.

775 • CITY OF ANGELS
OPENED: 12/11/1989   Theatre: Virginia
Musical   Broadway: 878

Composer: Cy Coleman
Lyricist: David Zippel
Librettist: Larry Gelbart
Producer: Roger Berlind; Jujamcyn Theaters; Shubert Organization, The; Suntory International Corp.; Nick Vanoff
Director: Michael Blakemore

Choreographer: Walter Painter; **Costumes:** Florence Klotz; **Lighting Designer:** Paul Gallo; **Musical Director:** Gordon Lowry Harrell; **Orchestrations:** Billy Byers; **Set Design:** Robin Wagner; **Vocal Arranger:** Cy Coleman; Yaron Gershovsky

Songs: Alaura's Theme [1]; All Ya Have to Do Is Wait; Ball Is in Your Court, The [3]; Buddy

System, The; City of Angels Theme (inst.) [2]; Double Talk; Ev'rybody's Gotta Be Somewhere; Funny; It Needs Work; L.A. Blues [1]; Lost and Found; Stay with Me; Tennis Song; What You Don't Know About Women; With Every Breath I Take; Ya Gotta Look Out for Yourself; You Can Always Count on Me; You're Nothing Without Me

Cast: Rene Auberjonois; James Cahill; Gregg Edelman; Shawn Elliott; Randy Graff; Dee Hoty; Alvin Lum; Kay McClelland; James Naughton; Evan Thompson; Scott Waara; Rachel York

Notes: [1] Used instrumentally only in show. [2] Used instrumentally only in show. Lyric cut in previews. [3] Not used.

776 • CITY SCENE

Notes: *See PARADISE ISLAND EAST.*

777 • CLARA

Notes: *See BEG, BORROW OR STEAL.*

778 • CLEAVAGE

OPENED: 06/23/1981   Theatre: Playhouse
Musical   Broadway: 1

Composer: Buddy Sheffield
Lyricist: Buddy Sheffield
Librettist: Buddy Sheffield; David Sheffield
Producer: Up Front Productions
Director: Rita Baker

Choreographer: Alton Geno; **Costumes:** James M. Miller; **Lighting Designer:** Michael J. Hotopp; Paul dePass; **Musical Director:** Keith Thompson; **Orchestrations:** Keith Thompson; **Set Design:** Morris Taylor

Songs: All the Lovely; Believe in Me, or I'll Be Leavin' You; Boys Will Be Girls; Bringing Up Badger; Cleavage; Give Me an And; Just Another Song; Lead 'Em Around By the Nose; Living in Sin; Only Love; Puberty; Reprise Me; Sawing a Couple in Half; Surprise Me; Thrill of the Chase, The; Voices of the Children

Cast: Daniel David; Tom Elias; Mark Fite; Sharon Scruggs; Dick Sheffield; Pattie Tierce

779 • CLIMB HIGH

Composer: Stephen Sondheim
Lyricist: Stephen Sondheim

Songs: All Year Long; Climb High; Cristobel; Nice Town; Rodgers and Hammerstein; School of Hard Knocks; Yoo Hoo, Hi There!

Notes: No other information available.

780 • CLINGING VINE, THE

OPENED: 12/25/1922   Theatre: Knickerbocker
Musical   Broadway: 188

Composer: Harold A. Levey
Lyricist: Zelda Sears
Librettist: Zelda Sears
Producer: Henry W. Savage
Director: Ira Hards

Choreographer: Julian Alfred; **Costumes:** Peggy Hoyt; **Musical Director:** Harold A. Levey

Songs: Age of Innocence; Clinging Vine, The; Cupid; Grandma; Homemade Happiness; Lady Luck; Little Bit of Paint, A; Love Needs No Single Words [1]; Omar Khayyam Was Right [1]; Once Upon a Time; Pathway to Paradise, The [1]; Roumania; Serenade; Song Without Words; Spring Fever

Cast: Irene Dunne; Nathaniel Wagner; Peggy Wood

Notes: [1] Sheet music only.

781 • CLIPPITY CLOP AND CLEMENTINE

OPENED: 1973
Musical   Unproduced

Composer: Harold Arlen
Lyricist: Harold Arlen
Librettist: Leonard Melfi

Songs: Clippity Clop and Clementine; Dreamin' Suits Me Just Fine; Happy Recipe, A; I Had a Love Once; Is What's It's All About; Organic Food; Ridin' Through the Park in a Hansom Cab; This Way or No Way at All

Notes: One-act musical.

782 • CLOCK SHOP, THE
OPENED: 1915
Musical

Composer: John Golden
Lyricist: John Golden
Librettist: John Golden
Producer: John W. Dunne

Musical Director: Byrd Dougherty

Songs: All the World's a Clock Shop; Gretchen Maedchen Mine; Key to Your Heart, The

Cast: Paul McGail; Charles Uffer

Notes: A one-act vaudeville musical.

783 • CLORINDY, THE ORIGIN OF THE CAKEWALK
OPENED: 07/05/1898　Theatre: Casino Roof
　　　　　　　　　　　Garden
Musical　　　　　　　　Broadway

Composer: Will Marion Cook
Lyricist: Paul Laurence Dunbar
Librettist: Paul Laurence Dunbar
Producer: Edward E. Rice

Musical Director: Will Marion Cook

Songs: Darktown Is Out Tonight; Jump Back, Honey; Who Dat Say Chicken in Dis Crowd?

Cast: Ernest Hogan

Notes: A one-act musical. This show was to open on June 28, 1898 but a sudden thunderstorm just prior to curtain drenched the proceedings and the opening was put off.

784 • CLOSER THAN EVER
OPENED: 11/06/1989　Theatre: Cherry Lane
Revue　　　　　　　　Off-Broadway: 288

Composer: David Shire
Lyricist: Richard Maltby Jr.
Producer: Janet Brenner; Michael Gill; Daryl Roth
Director: Richard Maltby Jr.; Steven Scott Smith

Choreographer: Marcia Milgrom Dodge; **Costumes:** Jess Goldstein; **Lighting Designer:** Natasha Katz; **Musical Director:** Patrick Scott

Brady; **Set Design:** Philipp Jung; **Vocal Arranger:** Patrick Scott Brady

Songs: Another Wedding Song (L: David Shire); Back on Base (L: David Shire); Bear, the Tiger, the Hamster and the Mole, The; Cause I'm Happy (L: David Shire); Closer Than Ever; Doors; Fandango; Father of Fathers; I Wouldn't Go Back; If I Sing; It's Never That Easy; I've Been Here Before; Life Story; March of Time, The; Miss Byrd; Next Time; One of the Good Guys; Patterns [1]; She Loves Me Not; Sound of Muzak, The; There; There's Nothing Like It; Three Friends; Wedding Song; What Am I Doing?; You Wanna Be My Friend

Cast: Brent Barrett; Patrick Scott Brady; Sally Mayes; Richard Muenz; Lynne Wintersteller

Notes: [1] Cut from BABY.

785 • CLOUD NINE
OPENED: 05/18/1981　Theatre: Theatre de Lys
Play　　　　　　　　　Off-Broadway: 971

Author: Caryl Churchill
Producer: Harvey J. Klaris; Michel Stuart
Director: Tommy Tune

Costumes: Gene London; Michel Stuart; **Lighting Designer:** Marcia Madeira; **Set Design:** Lawrence Miller

Songs: Cloud Nine (C/L: Maury Yeston)

Cast: Don Amendolia; Veronica Castang; Zeljko Ivanek; Jeffrey Jones; E. Katherine Kerr; Nicolas Surovy; Concetta Tomei

786 • CLOWNAROUND
OPENED: 04/27/1972
Musical　　　　　　　Closed out of town

Composer: Moose Charlap
Lyricist: Alvin Cooperman
Librettist: Alvin Cooperman
Producer: Theatre Now
Director: Gene Kelly

Choreographer: Howard Jeffrey; **Lighting Designer:** Sean Kenny; **Orchestrations:** Jack Elliott; Allyn Ferguson; **Set Design:** Sean Kenny

Songs: Animal Band; Balloon; Clown Alley; Clowns; Clowns Say Goodnight; Here Are Your Children; I Need a Ship; Laugh Song; Silhouette; Sunny Day; Thingamajig; You're a Clown

Notes: There was a television special of the same name on CBS on 5/26/72 which used the some of these songs.

787 • CLOWNS IN CLOVER
OPENED: 1933
Revue   Closed out of town

Composer: Jimmy McHugh
Lyricist: Dorothy Fields
Librettist: Nat Dorfman; Lew Leslie
Producer: Lew Leslie
Director: Lew Leslie

Choreographer: Merriel Abbott; Lew Leslie; **Costumes:** Lester Ltd.; **Musical Director:** Ray Kavanaugh; **Orchestrations:** William Harrigan Daly; Maurice DePackh; Ferde Grofe; Ken Macomber; **Set Design:** Rollo Wayne

Songs: At Sea; Clowns in Clover; Don't Blame Me; Hey Young Fella Close Your Old Umbrella; I'm Full of the Devil; Make Up Your Mind [1]; Margineers [1]; My Favorite Person; Night in Paris, A (C/L: Eddie Lambert); Play a Half a Chorus; Positively Love You; Prologue

Cast: Larry Adler; Dorothy Dare; Hal Forde; Lew Hearn; Walter Woolf

Notes: [1] Also in THE INTERNATIONAL REVUE.

788 • CLUB, THE
OPENED: 10/14/1976   Theatre: Circle in the
                        Square Downtown
Revue   Off-Broadway: 667

Librettist: Eve Merriam
Producer: Circle in the Square
Director: Tommy Tune

Costumes: Kate Carmel; **Dance Arranger:** Alexandra Ivanoff; **Lighting Designer:** Cheryl Thacker; **Musical Director:** Alexandra Ivanoff; **Set Design:** Kate Carmel; **Vocal Arranger:** Alexandra Ivanoff

Cast: Joanne Beretta; Marlene Dell; Julia J. Hafner; Gloria Hodes; Memrie Innerarity; Carole Monferdini; Terri White

Notes: All songs are from the period 1894-1905. There were no original songs in this show.

789 • C'MON & HEAR
OPENED: 03/22/1994   Theatre: McCarter
Musical   Closed out of town

Composer: Irving Berlin
Lyricist: Irving Berlin
Librettist: David Bishop; George Faison
Director: George Faison

Arrangements: David Bishop; **Choreographer:** George Faison; **Conductor:** Linda Twine; **Costumes:** Toni-Leslie James; **Dance Arranger:** Timothy Graphenreed; **Lighting Designer:** Richard Nelson; **Musical Director:** Linda Twine; **Set Design:** Chris Barreca

Songs: Alexander's Ragtime Band; All of My Life; Always; Be Careful, It's My Heart; Better Luck Next Time; Blue Skies; Cheek to Cheek; Cohen Owes Me Ninety-Seven Dollars; Empty Pockets Filled with Love; Everybody Step; For Your Country and My Country; Free; God Bless America; How About Me?; How Deep Is the Ocean; I Left My Door Open and My Daddy Walked Out; I Love a Piano; I'll Capture Her Heart; It's a Walk-In with Walker; Let Me Sing and I'm Happy; Let Yourself Go; Let's Face the Music and Dance; Let's Have Another Cup of Coffee; Lonely Heart; Manhattan Madness; Marching Along with Time; Oh! How I Hate to Get Up in the Morning; Pretty Girl Is Like a Melody, A; Puttin' on the Ritz; Remember; Russian Lullaby; Say It Isn't So; Shaking the Blues Away; Snookey Ookums; Song of Freedom; Steppin' Out with My Baby; Supper Time; That International Rag; This Is the Army, Mister Jones; Top Hat, White Tie and Tails; What'll I Do?; Yiddisha Nightingale; You Can Have Him; You Keep Coming Back Like a Song; You're Just in Love

Cast: Laurie Beechman; John Hickok; James Hindman; Rodney Scott Hudson; Ted L. Levy; Stephanie Pope; Karyn Quackenbush; Mary Testa; Alton Fitzgerald White; Carol Woods

Notes: No original songs in this show.

790 • COACH WITH THE SIX INSIDES, THE

OPENED: 11/26/1962   Theatre: Village South
Musical   Off-Broadway: 114

Composer: Teiji Ito
Librettist: Jean Erdman
Director: Jean Erdman

Source FINNEGAN'S WAKE (Novel: James Joyce);
   Costumes: Robert de Mora; **Lighting Designer:**
   Dan Butt; **Set Design:** Robert de Mora

Cast: Anita Dangler; Van Dexter; Jean Erdman;
   Leonard Frey; Sheila Roy

Notes: No songs listed in program.

791 • COCHRAN'S 1930 REVUE

OPENED: 03/27/1930   Theatre: London Pavilion
Revue   London

Composer: Vivian Ellis
Lyricist: Beverely Nichols
Librettist: Beverely Nichols
Director: Frank Collins

Choreographer: George Balanchine; Boris Kochno;
   Ralph Reader; **Costumes:** Oliver Messel; Doris
   Zinkeisen; **Musical Director:** Charles Prentice;
   Set Design: Marc-Henri; Oliver Messel; Rex
   Whistler; Doris Zinkeisen

Songs: Bakerloo, The; Chasing the Talkies Away;
   Dancing Alone; Heaven (C: Ivor Novello); In a
   Venetian Theatre (L: Vivian Ellis); Kid Brother
   (C/L: Unknown); Mary; Piccadilly (L: Rowland
   Leigh); Piccadilly, 1830 (inst.) (C: Ivor Novello);
   Since Eros Went Away (C: Beverely Nichols);
   Still a Debutante (L: Rowland Leigh); Wind in
   the Willows, The (C: Vivian Ellis; L: Desmond
   Carter); With a Song in My Heart [1] (C: Richard
   Rodgers; L: Lorenz Hart)

Cast: Ada-May; Douglas Byng; Joan Clarkson;
   Maisie Gay; Eric Marshall; Ada May; Molly
   Molloy; Gunda Mordhorst; Roy Royston;
   Pianist: Leslie Hutchinson

Notes: [1] Originally in SPRING IS HERE.

792 • COCHRAN'S REVUE OF 1926

OPENED: 04/29/1926   Theatre: London Pavilion
Revue   London

Librettist: Ronald Jeans
Director: Frank Collins

Choreographer: Leonide Massine; Max Rivers;
   Costumes: Andre Derain; Madame Marcus;
   Doris Zinkeisen; **Musical Director:** Ernest Irving;
   Set Design: Andre Derain

Songs: All the Little Birds in Nests Agree (C: Pat
   Thayer; L: Donovan Parsons); Birdcage Walk
   (C: Pat Thayer; L: Donovan Parsons); Botany
   Babies (C: Con West; L: Donovan Parsons); Come
   On, Feets, Let's Go (C: Pat Thayer; Donovan
   Parsons); Fair Senorita of the Argentine (C: Pat
   Thayer; L: Donovan Parsons); Head Over Heels
   (C: Pat Thayer; L: Donovan Parsons); I Travel the
   Road (C: Pat Thayer; L: Donovan Parsons);
   I'm Crazy About the Charleston [2] (C: Richard
   Rodgers; L: Donovan Parsons); Let's Get Married
   Right Away (C: Eubie Blake; L: Noble Sissle);
   (Just) a Little Thing Called Rhythm (C/L: Chick
   Endor; Ward); Southend-on-Sea (C/L: Con West);
   Tahiti [1] (C: Eubie Blake; L: Noble Sissle);
   Wedding Day (C: Eubie Blake; L: Noble Sissle)

Cast: Hermione Baddeley; Billy Bradford; Douglas
   Byng; Joan Clarkson; Annie Croft; Florence
   Desmond; Marion Hamilton; Basil Howes;
   Leonide Massine; Will Rogers[3]; Kate
   Strudwick; Ernest Thesiger

Notes: [1] Originally written for CHOCOLATE
   DANDIES. [2] Same music as "Maybe It's Me" in
   THE FIFTH AVENUE FOLLIES and dropped
   after opening. [3] Joined cast after opening.

793 • COCKEYED TIGER, THE

OPENED: 01/13/1977   Theatre: Astor Place
                              Theater
Revue   Off-Broadway: 5

Composer: Nicholas Meyers
Lyricist: Eric Blau
Librettist: Eric Blau
Producer: James J. Wisner
Director: Eric Blau

Arrangements: Nicholas Archer; Nicholas Meyers;
   Jimmy Wisner; **Choreographer:** Buzz Miller;
   Gemze de Lapp; **Costumes:** Donald Jensen;
   Lighting Designer: Crimmins & Smith; **Set
   Design:** Donald Jensen

Songs: Daddy Oh!; Good Times; It's a Long, Long
   March to Kansas City; Littleflea Hop, The; Tyger,

Tyger; We're Together; You Were a Hell of a Crowd Tonight; You've Got to Be a Tiger, Tiger

Cast: Chris Campbell; James Nisbet Clark; Robert Matthews; Janet McCall; Leon Morenzie; Joseph Neal; Jack Scalici; Elly Stone; Wendy Wolfe

Notes: There were also songs by Bert Kalmar and Harry Ruby in this score.

794 • COCKLES AND CHAMPAGNE

OPENED: 1953

Songs: Darling They're Playing Our Song (C/L: Sam Coslow)

Notes: No other information available.
Information from ASCAP/Library of Congress.

795 • COCKTAIL

Musical   Closed out of town

Composer: Ralph Benatzky

Source COCKTAIL (Musical: Ralph Benatzky; Karl Vollmoeller)

Notes: No other information available.

796 • COCKTAIL BAR

OPENED: 01/13/1937
Musical   Closed out of town

Composer: Lloyd Chase
Lyricist: Lloyd Chase
Librettist: Lloyd Chase
Producer: Boris Charsky
Director: Alexander Leftwich

Choreographer: Bunny Weldon; **Costumes:** Geraldine Beckwith; **Musical Director:** Mario Silva; **Orchestrations:** George Crozier; **Set Design:** George Ormston

Songs: At the Cocktail Bar; Broken Romance; Everyone Starts to Dance; Falling in Love; I'll Stay There; I'm the Captain of the Ship; Just to You; Little Continental, A; Little Dash of Love, A; Lovely Lady; Play, Play, Play; Rhumba, The; Some Day I'll Wander; When True Love Is True

Cast: Sam Ash; Jack Good; Ethelind Terry

797 • COCKTAILS 5 TO 7

OPENED: 1935

Composer: Jean Schwartz
Lyricist: Rowland Leigh

Songs: And I'm So Glad; As Long As There's Love; Charm; My Gink; Paris in Spring; Paris Police; Take Love While You May; Times May Change; Twilight Rhythms; Whoops My Dear

Notes: No other information available.

798 • COCO

OPENED: 12/18/1969   Theatre: Mark Hellinger
Musical   Broadway: 332

Composer: Andre Previn
Lyricist: Alan Jay Lerner
Librettist: Alan Jay Lerner
Producer: Frederick Brisson
Director: Michael Benthall

Choreographer: Michael Bennett; **Costumes:** Cecil Beaton; **Dance Arranger:** Harold Wheeler; **Lighting Designer:** Thomas Skelton; **Musical Director:** Robert Emmett Dolan; **Orchestrations:** Hershy Kay; **Set Design:** Cecil Beaton

Songs: Always Mademoiselle; Brand New Dress, A; But That's the Way You Are; Coco; Fiasco; Gabrielle; Let's Go Home; Mademoiselle Cliche de Paris; Money Rings Out Like Freedom, The; Ohrbach's, Bloomingdale's, Best and Saks; On the Corner of the Rue Cambon; Preparation, The; Someone on Your Side [1]; Turn on the Lights [1]; When Your Lover Says Goodbye; Woman Is How She Loves, A; World Belongs to the Young, The

Cast: Will B. Able; Jeanne Arnold; Rene Auberjonois; Jon Cypher; Gale Dixon; Robert Fitch; Katharine Hepburn; David Holliday; George Rose; Dan Siretta

Notes: [1] Cut prior to opening.

799 • COCOANUTS, THE

OPENED: 12/08/1925   Theatre: Lyric
Musical   Broadway: 375

Composer: Irving Berlin
Lyricist: Irving Berlin

Librettist: George S. Kaufman
Director: Oscar Eagle

Choreographer: Sammy Lee; **Costumes:** Charles LeMaire; **Musical Director:** George Hirst; **Orchestrations:** Frank Tours; **Set Design:** Woodman Thompson; **Vocal Arranger:** Arthur Johnstone

Songs: Bellhops, The; Can't You Tell? [3]; Everyone in the World Is Doing the Charleston [4]; Five O'Clock Tea; Florida By the Sea; Gentlemen Prefer Blondes [4]; Guests, The; Little Bungalow, A; Lucky Boy; Minstrel Days; Monkey Doodle-Doo [5]; Take 'Em Away (He's Breakin' My Heart) [3]; Tale of a Shirt, The; Tango Melody; Ting-a-Ling (The Bells'll Ring) [4]; Too Many Sweethearts [2]; We Should Care (Let the Lazy Sun Refuse to Care) [6]; We Should Care (Let the Sky Start to Cry); What's There About Me (Why Am I a Hit with the Ladies?); When We're Running a Little Hotel of Our Own [3]; Why Do You Want to Know Why? [4]; With a Family Reputation

Cast: Jack Barker; Brox Sisters, The; Phyllis Cleveland; Margaret Dumont; Marx Brothers, The; Janet Velie; Frances Williams

Notes: [1] Not in program. [2] Sheet music only. Title also used in MARX BROTHERS REVUE OF 1923 but are they the same song? In MUSIC BOX REVUE. [3] Sheet music only. [4] According to sheet music "Added to 'New Summer Edition.'" [5] Not same song as in ALL ABOARD. [6] Not used.

800 • COHAN AND HARRIS MINSTRELS (1908)

OPENED: 08/03/1908   Theatre: New York
Revue   Broadway: 24

Composer: George M. Cohan
Lyricist: George M. Cohan
Librettist: George M. Cohan
Producer: George M. Cohan; Sam H. Harris
Director: George M. Cohan

Choreographer: James Gorman; **Musical Director:** Carl Schilling

Songs: Answer; At the Barber's Ball [1]; Big Brown Boo Loo Eyes; Gibson Coon, The [1]; Good Bye, Mr. Ragtime; I'll Be True to My Honey Boy; Kiss

Your Minstrel Boy Goodbye (C: Jean Schwartz; L: William Jerome); Love Days; Meet Me in Rose Time Rosie [2]; Oh! You Coon [1]; Rag Time Quadrille (dance) [1]; When the Minstrels Come to Town [3]

Cast: Julian Eltinge; George Evans; Eddie Leonard; Harry M. Morse; Rice and Prevost

Notes: When touring in 1909 THE BELLE OF THE BARBER'S BALL was replaced by the one-act musical THE FIREMAN'S PICNIC. [1] Appeared as part of the one-act musical THE BELLE OF THE BARBER'S BALL [2] Also in THE AMERICAN IDEA. [3] In COHAN AND HARRIS MINSTREL'S (1909). [4] Lyrics ascribed to Harry Williams in some sources.

801 • COHAN AND HARRIS MINSTRELS (1909)

OPENED: 08/16/1909   Theatre: Lincoln Square
                      New York

Composer: George M. Cohan
Lyricist: George M. Cohan
Librettist: George M. Cohan
Producer: George M. Cohan; Sam H. Harris

Songs: Any Old Port in a Storm; Down Where the Watermelons Grow; Hat My Father Wore, The; I'm Going Home; Rose of Killarney, The; Wedding Bells, The; When the Minstrels Come to Town

Cast: Earl Benham; Vaughn Comfort; George Evans; John King; Sam Lee; John P. Rogers; Harry Van Fossen

Notes: This show contained a one-act musical THE FIREMAN'S PICNIC. However its songs were not listed in the program.

802 • COHAN AND HARRIS MINSTRELS (1912)

OPENED: 1912
Revue

Producer: George M. Cohan; Sam Harris

Songs: Lead Me to That Beautiful Band (L: E. Ray Goetz)

Cast: Happy Lambert

803 • COHAN AND HARRIS MINSTRELS (1909)

OPENED: 08/16/1919   Theatre: New York
Revue   Broadway: 16

Composer: George M. Cohan
Lyricist: George M. Cohan
Librettist: George M. Cohan
Producer: George M. Cohan; Sam H. Harris
Director: George M. Cohan

Cast: Arthur Alexander; Earl Benham; Vaughn Comfort; George "Honey Boy" Evans; John King; Stan Lee; Clarence Marks; Will Oakland; John P. Rogers; Thomas Scott; Harry Von Fossen

Notes: No program available.

804 • COHAN REVUE OF 1916, THE

OPENED: 02/09/1916   Theatre: Astor
Revue   Broadway: 165

Composer: George M. Cohan
Lyricist: George M. Cohan
Librettist: George M. Cohan
Producer: George M. Cohan; Sam H. Harris
Director: George M. Cohan

Costumes: Cora MacGeachy; **Musical Director:** Charles J. Gebest

Songs: Alone at Last; Balloon Girls, The; Busy, Busy, Busy; Crying Jane; Dancing Pirates, The; Fair and Warmer Cocktail, The; Gaby; He Can Cure You of Love; It's a Long Way from Broadway to Edinboro Town; Julia, Donald and Joe; My Musical Comedy Maiden; Opening Chorus; Running Around with Chorus Girls; That Frisco Melody; 'Under Fire' Dance, The; You Can Tell That I'm Irish; Young America; Ziegfeld Rag

Cast: John Boles; Harry Bulger; Richard Carle; Harry Delf; Little Billie; Elizabeth Murray; Fred Santley; Valli Valli; Charles Winninger

805 • COHAN REVUE OF 1918, THE

OPENED: 12/31/1917   Theatre: New Amsterdam
Revue   Broadway: 96

Composer: George M. Cohan
Lyricist: George M. Cohan
Librettist: George M. Cohan
Producer: George M. Cohan; Sam H. Harris
Director: George M. Cohan

Choreographer: George M. Cohan; James Gorman; Jack Mason; **Musical Director:** Charles J. Gebest; **Orchestrations:** Frank Saddler

Songs: All Dressed Up in a Tailor Made; Bad Chinaman from Shanghai, A (C/L: Irving Berlin); Down Where the Jack O' Lanterns Grow (C/L: Irving Berlin; George M. Cohan); Ensemble; Eyes of Youth See the Truth, The (C: Irving Berlin; George M. Cohan); Gathering of the Slaves, The (inst.) (C: Unknown); King of Broadway (C/L: Irving Berlin); Man Is Only a Man, A (C/L: Irving Berlin); Old Maid Blues [2] (C: David W. Guion; L: Web Maddox); Our Acrobatic Melodramatic Home; Pipers of Pan Dance (dance) (C: Unknown); Polly, Pretty Polly (Polly with a Past) (C: Irving Berlin); Potash and Perlmutter Ball, The; Regretful Blues (C: Cliff Hess; L: Grant Clarke); Show Me the Way (C/L: Irving Berlin); Spanish (C: Irving Berlin; L: George M. Cohan); Their Hearts Are Over Here; Wedding of Words and Music, The (C/L: Irving Berlin); When Ziegfeld's Follies Hit the Town; Who Do You Love? [1] (C: James Brockman; L: Ed Moran)

Cast: Nora Bayes; Irving Fisher; Fred Santley; Charles Winninger

Notes: [1] ASCAP credits to James F. Hanley and Gene Buck. [2] Sheet music only.

806 • COHEN ON THE EAST SIDE

OPENED: 1915
Musical

Composer: J.B. Earley
Librettist: Harry Steppe
Director: Dan Doda

Songs: Blinky Winky Chinatown; Girls from the Follies; He's My Kiddo; I'm the Broadway Kid; Joyous Love; Let's Sing, Sing, Sing; Love Me or Leave Me Alone; My Southern Queen; Sweethearts; Tennessee; There Ain't No Fun in That; They Blame It All on Me; Yiddisher Wedding

Cast: Girls from the Follies, The; Harry Steppe

Notes: Burlesque musical.

807 • COLETTE (1970)

OPENED: 05/06/1970 Theatre: Ellen Stewart
Play Off-Broadway: 101

Composer: Harvey Schmidt
Lyricist: Tom Jones
Librettist: Elinor Jones
Producer: Cheryl Crawford
Director: Gerald Freedman

Source EARTHLY PARADISE (Book: Colette);
Costumes: Theoni V. Aldredge; **Lighting
Designer:** Roger Morgan; **Musical Director:**
Harvey Schmidt; **Set Design:** David Mitchell

Songs: Autumn Afternoon [1]; Bouilloux Girls,
The; Earthly Paradise; Femme du Monde;
Growing Older [2]; His Love [1]; Love Is Not
a Sentiment [2]; Music Hall; Willy Will Grow
Cold [3]

Cast: Barry Bostwick; Zoe Caldwell; Keene Curtis;
Mildred Dunnock; Charles Siebert

Notes: *See COLETTE (1970). Also see COLETTE
COLLAGE.* EARTHLY PARADISE is a collection
of Colette's autobiographical writings compiled
by Robert Phelps. [1] Added to later production.
[2] Added to later production and to
pre-Broadway tryout of COLETTE (1982). [3]
Used instrumentally only.

808 • COLETTE (1982)

OPENED: 02/09/1982
Musical Closed out of town

Composer: Harvey Schmidt
Lyricist: Tom Jones
Librettist: Tom Jones
Producer: John F. Kennedy Center; Harry Rigby
Director: Dennis Rosa

Choreographer: Carl Jablonski; **Costumes:** Raoul
Pene du Bois; **Dance Arranger:** David Krane;
Lighting Designer: Gilbert V. Hemsley Jr.;
Musical Director: Larry Blank; **Orchestrations:**
Larry Wilcox; **Set Design:** John Conklin; **Vocal
Arranger:** Larry Blank

Songs: Act Two Opening; Autumn Afternoon,
The [2]; Be My Lady; Claudine; Come to Life;
Curiosity; Do It for Willy; Do Not Hold On;
Dreams of Egypt; Father of Claudine, The;
Growing Older [1]; I Miss You; Joy; La
Vagabonde; Love Is Not a Sentiment Worthy of
Respect [1]; Madame Colette; Music Hall [1];
Music Hall Scandal; Oo-La-La; Riviera Nights;
Room Is Filled with You, The; Semiramis;
Something for the Summer (Something for the
Winter); There's Another World; Two Claudines;
Victory; Why Can't I Walk Through That Door?;
Woman of the World; You Could Hurt Me

Cast: Rhoda Butler; Marta Eggerth; Robert
Helpmann; Ron Raines; John Reardon; Diana
Rigg; Marti Stevens; Martin Vidnovic

Notes: *See COLETTE (1970). See also COLETTE
COLLAGE.* [1] Also in 1974 production. [2] Only
in 1974 production in Stockbridge,
Massachusetts.

809 • COLETTE COLLAGE

OPENED: 03/31/1983 Theatre: York Playhouse
Musical Off-Broadway: 17

Composer: Harvey Schmidt
Lyricist: Tom Jones
Librettist: Tom Jones
Producer: York Players
Director: Fran Soeder

Source EARTHLY PARADISE (Book: Colette);
Choreographer: Janet Watson; **Costumes:** Sigrid
Insull; **Lighting Designer:** Mary Jo Dondlinger;
Musical Director: Eric Stern; **Set Design:** James
Morgan

Songs: Autumn Love; Be My Lady; Claudine;
Come to Life; Do It for Willy; Dreams of Egypt;
Father of Claudine, The; Growing Older; I Miss
You; Joy; Love Is Not a Sentiment Worthy of
Respect; Madame Colette; Music Hall, The;
Oo-La-La; Opening; Riviera Nights; Simple
Country Wedding, A; Something for the
Summer; Somewhere; There's Another World;
Two Claudines; Why Can't I Walk Through That
Door?; Willy Will Grow Cold; Woman of the
World; You Could Hurt Me

Cast: Terry Baughan; Joanne Beretta; George Hall;
Steven F. Hall; Timothy Jerome; Jana Robbins

Notes: *See COLETTE (1982).* EARTHLY PARADISE is a collection of Colette's autobiographical writings compiled by Robert Phelps.

810 • COLLECTING THE PLAID
Play

Author: Pat Plowman
Director: James Luther Humphrey

Songs: Moldova, Country of My Birth (C: Alexander Leanca; L: Miron Leanca)

Cast: Cory Plowman; Justin Plowman; Travis Plowman

Notes: No other information available

811 • COLLEGE DAYS
OPENED: 1906
Musical

Composer: Frederick V. Bowers
Lyricist: Harry Hoyt

Songs: Darling (L: Lamb); I'd Be Happy If That Was Mine; You're the One Best Bet

Cast: Frederick V. Bowers

Notes: No other information available. A one-act musical.

812 • COLLEGE WIDOWER
Notes: *See HIGGLEDY-PIGGLEDY.*

813 • COLORED ARISTOCRATS, THE
OPENED: 1909
Musical

Composer: Aubrey L. Lyles; Sidney Perrin
Lyricist: Aubrey L. Lyles; Flournoy E. Miller
Librettist: Aubrey L. Lyles; Flournoy E. Miller
Producer: Aubrey L. Lyles; Flournoy E. Miller; Irvin C. Miller

Songs: Caroline; Chocolate Mandy; Dreamy Day; Fare Thee Well; For the Last Time, Call Me Sweeheart; Meet Me By the Candy Pole; Pleading Eyes; Why Moses Never Saw the Promised Land

Cast: Cassie Burch; Cliff Green; Georgia Hutchinson; Flournoy E. Miller; Irvin C. Miller

Notes: No other information available.

814 • COME ACROSS
OPENED: 09/14/1938
Musical   Closed out of town

Librettist: Guy Beauchamp; Michael Pertwee
Producer: William A. Brady; George Bushar; John Tuerk
Director: Edward Clarke Lilley

Set Design: Watson Barratt

Songs: Somebody (C: Cammann Newberry; L: Arnett McKennan); There's No Wolf Around My Door (C/L: Gaspar Bacon)

Cast: Cameron Hall; A.P. Kaye; Helen Trenholme; Arthur Vinton; Richard Waring

Notes: The Playhouse, N.Y. No songs listed in program.

815 • COME ALONG
OPENED: 04/08/1919   Theatre: Nora Bayes
Musical   Broadway: 47

Composer: John L. Nelson
Lyricist: John L. Nelson
Librettist: Bide Dudley
Producer: Mame Productions
Director: Frank Jackson; Edward Royce

Choreographer: Jack Mason; **Musical Director:** Milan Roder; **Set Design:** Homer Emens; Frank Gates; E.A. Morange

Songs: At the Prohibition Ball (C: Abner Silver; L: Alex Gerber); Big Drum, Little Drum; Big Offense; But You Can't Believe Them (C/L: Blanche Merrill); Cuckoo; Doughnuts for Doughboys; Gas; In Her Little Blue Bonnet with the Red Ribbon on It; K.P.; Long, Long Time; Mother Dear; Rollin' de Bones a Coblenz on de Rhine; She's Salvations Sal (C: Frederic Watson; L: Bide Dudley); Thoughts; When They're Beautiful; When You Are Happy; Yankee Land

Cast: Paul Frawley; Allen Kearns; Marjorie Pringle;
Harry Tighe

816 • COME ALONG MANDY
OPENED: 1924
Musical

Composer: Donald Heywood
Lyricist: J. Homer Tutt; Salem Tutt Whitney
Librettist: J. Homer Tutt; Salem Tutt Whitney
Producer: J. Homer Tutt; Salem Tutt Whitney

Cast: J. Homer Tutt; Salem Tutt Whitney

Notes: No other information available.

817 • COME AS YOU ARE
OPENED: 03/1955   Theatre: Versailles
     Restaurant
Revue   Nightclub

Composer: Arthur Siegel
Lyricist: June Carroll
Producer: Nick and Arnold; Leonard Sillman
Director: David Thimar

Costumes: Thomas Becker; Musical Director:
Salvatore Gioe; Orchestrations: Buddy Dufault;
Set Design: Robert Galster

Songs: April Fool; Believe It or Not; Boy Most
Likely to Succeed [1]; Come As You Are;
Co-Operation; I Thought They'd Never Go
Home; Lola (White Witch of Jamaica) [1]; Not a
Dull Moment; Sophisticated Songs; Things They
Told Us Not to Do, The; Wish You Were Fanny;
You're Bad for Me

Cast: June Carroll; Johnny Laverty; Paul Lynde;
Connie Sawyer; Dick Smart; Inga Swenson

Notes: [1] Later in NEW FACES OF 1956.

818 • COME OF AGE
OPENED: 01/12/1935   Theatre: Maxine Elliott's
Musical   Broadway: 35

Composer: Richard Addinsell
Lyricist: Clemence Dane
Librettist: Clemence Dane
Producer: Delos Chappell
Director: Clemence Dane

Costumes: Valentina; Musical Director: Macklin
Morrow; Set Design: James Reynolds

Songs: Golden Perbanou, The; I Came to Your
Room; I Come Out of a Dream; I'm Afraid of the
Dark; River Song, The; Too Much Work

Cast: Judith Anderson; John W. Austin; Stephen
Haggard; Frederick G. Lewis; Muriel Rahn;
Pianist: Morton Gould

819 • COME ON AND PLAY
OPENED: 02/15/1954   Theatre: Harout's Ivar
Revue   Los Angeles

Composer: Danny Jackson; Raisa
Additional Music: Charles Nicholas Vedder
Lyricist: Danny Jackson; Raisa
Librettist: Danny Jackson; Raisa

Notes: No other information available.

820 • COME ON STRONG
OPENED: 10/04/1962   Theatre: Morosco
Play   Broadway: 36

Author: Garson Kanin
Producer: Hillard Elkins; Al Goldin
Director: Garson Kanin

Costumes: Oleg Cassini; J. Michael Travis;
Lighting Designer: John Harvey; Set Design:
Oliver Smith

Songs: Come On Strong (C: Jimmy Van Heusen;
L: Sammy Cahn)

Cast: Carroll Baker; Van Johnson

Notes: Lena Horne sang on the recording used in
the show.

821 • COME OUT SWINGING
OPENED: 04/27/1951
Musical

Composer: Edward Cashman
Lyricist: Leo Brady; Edward Cashman
Librettist: Leo Brady
Director: Rev. Gilbert V. Hartke

Choreographer: Mary Day; Costumes: Joseph Lewis; Musical Director: Sidney Seidenman Jr.; Set Design: James D. Waring

Songs: Don't Be Like Your Old Man; Follow the Fiddler; I Wonder What It's Like; I'm in Love; I'm in Love; Just Be Available; Keep in Shape; Nobody Holds My Hand; Once Is Enough; Roundhouse O'Leary; She's a Queen; Small-Time Crook, The; Take a Trip; We Learned a Trade; What's This? A Kiss; You Can Stay

Cast: Robert Conforti; Ted Doyle; Joan Marie Nelson; H. Joseph Plummer; Gil Rathbun; Rickie Rudel; Diana Shane

Notes: Amateur show. Catholic University.

822 • COME OVER HERE

OPENED: 04/19/1913   Theatre: London Opera
House
Revue   London

Composer: Louis A. Hirsch; J. Rosamond Johnson
Lyricist: Frank Sturgis; Harry Williams
Librettist: Wilson Mizner; Max Pemberton
Producer: Clifford C. Fischer
Director: Gus Sohlke

Musical Director: Phil Saxe

Songs: Alabam; Be My Guiding Star of Love; Cake Walk Parade; Come Over Here; El Choclo Tango; Everybody Loves a Chicken; He Did; If a Table at Romano's Could Talk [2]; Mandy [1]; Midnight Masquerade; Military March; My Sumurun Girl (C: Louis A. Hirsch; L: Al Jolson); Oh! You Sweet Sweet Day; Peg of My Heart (C: Fred Fisher; L: Alfred Bryan); Picture Show, The; Roll The Cotton Bales; Sporting Times; Take Me in Your Arms; When I Reach Old London Town

Cast: Franklyn Bellamy; Maidie Burker; Ethel Cadman; Chas. Hart; Oscar Schwary; May Yohe

Notes: Hirsch and Johnson did not collaborate but I couldn't determine who wrote what. [1] The Irving Berlin "Mandy" was written in 1918 for YIP, YIP, YAPHANK. [2] Probably a British version of the American song "If a Table at Rector's Could Talk" by Raymond Hubbell and Will D. Cobb.

823 • COME SUMMER

OPENED: 02/18/1969   Theatre: Lunt-Fontanne
Musical   Broadway: 7

Composer: David Baker
Lyricist: Will Holt
Librettist: Will Holt
Producer: Hal James; Albert W. Selden
Director: Agnes de Mille

Source RAINBOW ON THE ROAD (Novel: Esther Forbes); Choreographer: Agnes de Mille; Costumes: Stanley Simmons; Dance Arranger: David Baker; John Berkman; Lighting Designer: Thomas Skelton; Musical Director: Milton Rosenstock; Orchestrations: Carlyle Hall; Set Design: Oliver Smith; Vocal Arranger: Trude Rittman

Songs: Birch Bark Boat [1]; Come Summer; Faucett Falls Fancy; Feather in My Shoe; Fine; Fine, Thank You, Fine; Golden Love [1]; Good Time Charlie; Goodbye, My Bachelor; How Far Away Is Far Away? [1]; Hymn [1]; Jude's Holler; Let Me Be; Loggers' Song, The; Moonglade; No; Road to Hampton; Rockin'; Skin and Bones; So Much World; Think Spring; Wild Birds Calling; Women

Cast: Ray Bolger; David Cryer; Cathryn Damon; John Gerstad; Margaret Hamilton; Dorothy Sands; Barbara Sharma

Notes: [1] Cut prior to New York opening.

824 • COME TO BOHEMIA

OPENED: 04/27/1916   Theatre: Maxine Elliott's
Musical   Broadway: 20

Composer: Kenneth M. Muchison
Lyricist: George S. Chappell
Librettist: George S. Chappell
Director: Jacques Coini

Songs: In Poster Land (C: Raymond Hubbell; L: Glen MacDonough); On the Shimmering Glimmering Nile (C: Raymond Hubbell; L: Glen MacDonough); She Doesn't Exist at All (C: Raymond Hubbell; L: Glen MacDonough); When Somebody Isn't There (C: Raymond Hubbell; L: Glen MacDonough)

Cast: Natalie Ault; William Danforth; Walter Percival; Ada Mae Weeks; Fritz Williams

Notes: No program available.

825 • COMEDY
OPENED: 11/06/1972
Musical   Closed out of town

Composer: Luigi Creatore; Hugo Peretti; George David Weiss
Librettist: Lawrence Carra; Luigi Creatore; Hugo Peretti; George David Weiss
Producer: Joseph Beruh; Stuart Duncan; Edgar Lansbury
Director: Lawrence Carra

Source GREAT MAGICIAN, THE (Play: Basillio Locatelli); **Choreographer:** Stephen Reinhardt; **Costumes:** William Pitkin; **Dance Arranger:** Mel Marvin; **Lighting Designer:** Roger Morgan; **Musical Director:** Joseph Stecko; **Orchestrations:** Jack Andrews; **Set Design:** William Pitkin; **Vocal Arranger:** Mel Marvin

Songs: Breakin' the Spell; Buttercup; Comedy; Friend Is a Friend, A; God Bless the Fig Tree; Gotta Hang My Wash Out to Dry; I'm the Cockalorum; Love Is Such a Fragile Thing; Magnetic; Open Your Heart; Sacrifice; Smile, Smile, Smile; Tarantella; Where Is My Love; Whirlwind Circle

Cast: George Lee Andrews; Joseph Bova; Suellen Estey; Diane Findlay; George S. Irving; Marc Jordan; Bill McCutcheon; Marilyn Saunders; Joseph R. Sicari; Frank Voha

Notes: Closed 11/18/72 in Boston. *See SMILE, SMILE, SMILE.*

826 • COMEDY TONIGHT
OPENED: 12/18/1994   Theatre: Lunt-Fontanne
Revue   Broadway: 8

Producer: Alexander H. Cohen; Max Cooper
Director: Alexander H. Cohen

Choreographer: Albert Stephenson; **Costumes:** Alvin Colt; **Lighting Designer:** Richard Nelson; **Musical Director:** Peter Howard; **Set Design:** Ray Klausen

Songs: Three [1] (C: John Kander; L: Fred Ebb)

Cast: Joy Behar; Michael Davis; Dorothy Loudon; Mort Sahl

Notes: Only original song listed. [1] Cut prior to Broadway.

827 • COMIC SUPPLEMENT (OF AMERICAN LIFE), THE
OPENED: 01/09/1925
Musical   Closed out of town

Composer: Con Conrad
Lyricist: J.P. McEvoy
Librettist: J.P. McEvoy
Producer: Florenz Ziegfeld
Director: Augustin Duncan

Choreographer: Julian Mitchell; **Costumes:** John Held Jr.; **Musical Director:** Victor Baravalle; **Set Design:** Norman Bel Geddes

Songs: American Prelude (C: Henry Souvaine); By the Side of the Road (C: Henry Souvaine); Cafeteria Chow; Cafeteria March (C: Henry Souvaine); City Street Scene (C: Henry Souvaine); Cop and the Nurse, The (C: Henry Souvaine); Dreaming [1] (C: Con Conrad; Henry Souvaine); Goo Goo Goo; Jungle Joy (C: Henry Souvaine; L: Con Conrad); Kissing (L: Harold Atteridge); Little Two By Four; Lovin' You (C: Henry Souvaine); Marriage License (C: Henry Souvaine); On the Beaches; On the Radio; Opening Chorus; Scrubwoman's Ballet (Dance) (C: Unknown); Sunday Poipers

Cast: Betty Compton; Ray Dooley; W.C. Fields; Brooke Johns; Clarence Nordstrom

Notes: [1] Sheet music only.

828 • COMIN' UPTOWN
OPENED: 12/20/1979   Theatre: Winter Garden
Musical   Broadway: 45

Composer: Garry Sherman
Lyricist: Peter Udell
Librettist: Philip Rose; Peter Udell
Producer: Ridgely Bullock; Albert W. Selden
Director: Philip Rose

Source CHRISTMAS CAROL, A (Story: Charles Dickens); **Choreographer:** Michael Peters; **Costumes:** Ann Emonts; **Dance Arranger:** Timothy Graphenreed; **Lighting Designer:** Gilbert V. Hemsley Jr.; **Musical Director:** Howard Roberts; **Orchestrations:** Garry

Sherman; **Set Design:** Robin Wagner; **Vocal Arranger:** Garry Sherman

Songs: Born Again; Christmas Is Comin' Uptown; Get Down Brother Get Down; Get Your Act Together; Goin' Gone; Have I Finally Found My Heart?; It Won't Be Long; Lifeline; Nobody Really Do; Now I Lay Me Down to Sleep; One Way Ticket to Hell; Sing a Christmas Song; What Better Time for Love

Cast: Kevin Babb; Loretta Devine; Tiger Haynes; Gregory Hines; Robert Jackson; Larry Marshall; Saundra McClain; John Russell

829 • COMING ATTRACTIONS
OPENED: 11/22/1981   Theatre: Playwrights Horizons
Play   Off-Broadway: 176

Composer: Jack Feldman
Lyricist: Jack Feldman; Bruce Sussman
Author: Ted Tally
Producer: Playwrights Horizons
Director: Andre Ernotte

Choreographer: Theodore Pappas; **Costumes:** Ann Emonts; **Lighting Designer:** Paul Gallo; **Orchestrations:** Arnold Gross; **Set Design:** Andrew Jackness

Songs: Just Look at Me Now; Magic of Me, The; Miss America Now (The Fairest of the Fair); You Gotta Go Out with a Bang!

Cast: Christine Baranski; Larry Block; Griffin Dunn; June Gable; Jonathan Hadary; Dan Strickler; Allan Wasserman

Notes: No songs listed in program.

830 • COMING THRO' THE RYE
OPENED: 01/09/1906   Theatre: Herald Square
Musical   Broadway: 34

Composer: J. Sebastian Hiller; A. Baldwin Sloane
Lyricist: George V. Hobart
Librettist: George V. Hobart
Producer: Will J. Block Amusement Co.
Director: Lewis Hooper

Musical Director: Paul Schindle

Songs: Any Time, Any Place, Any Way [3];

Because of You (C: A. Baldwin Sloane); Camp Meeting Time [2]; Clancy; Come My Love to Araby [4] (C: A. Baldwin Sloane); Dolly Dear; Everything Seems Funny to Me [3]; Fiji (C: A. Baldwin Sloane); Finale Act I; Get Busy [1] (C: Albert Von Tilzer); Goodbye Little Too Too San [4] (C: John Sebastian Hiller); Googy-Oogy-Oo [1] (C: E.E. Rice); I Don't Want to Be a Sailor [2]; I Guess I'll Take the Train Back Home [2] (C: Billie Taylor; L: Jeff T. Branen); I Know a Girl Like You [2] (C/L: Billie Taylor); I Love You Because You Are You [4] (C: A. Baldwin Sloane); I Wonder If That's the Answer [1] (C: J. Sebastian Hiller); In My Canoe (C: Ted Snyder; L: Ed Rose); It Must Be Love [3]; Mary My Prairie Fairy [3] (C: George Lederer); Military Man, The; Moolbari [1]; Mother Pin a Rose on Me [3] (C/L: Bob Adams; C: Paul Schindler; L: Sam M. Lewis); My Broncho Boy (C: A. Baldwin Sloane); Nicest Man I Ever Saw, The [1] (C: A. Baldwin Sloane); On Chestnut Street [1] (C: A. Baldwin Sloane); Opening Chorus; Sand Man, The; Spoofing [2]; Spoon Time (C: Albert Von Tilzer; L: Addison Burkhardt); Spy on Time [1] (C: Albert Von Tilzer); Squaw Man Travesty (C: Theodore Bendix); That's What the Rose Said to Me [3]; They Are Waiting for Me (C/L: Dave Lewis); Turn Over [4] (C: Taylor); Whoa, Bill (C: A. Baldwin Sloane); Woman of Importance, A [2]; Won't You Let Me Put My Arms Around You [2]; Work, Work, Work [1] (C: J. Sebastian Hiller); You're an Indian (C: Evans Lloyd; L: Jeff T. Branen)

Cast: Frank Doane; Alice Fisher; Riley Hatch; Stella Mayhew; Dan McAvoy; John Park; Amelia Stone

Notes: Sloane and Hiller did not collaborate. Their songs are identified when known. [1] Out Louisville 11/20/05. [2] Out New Bedford. [3] Out Kansas City 1/27/08. [4] Sheet music only.

831 • COMMON FLESH
OPENED: 08/12/1935   Theatre: Hollytown
Play   Los Angeles

Author: Bob Forteppe; Arthur Jatim
Producer: Boris Petroff; Jim Timony
Director: Boris Petroff

Source UNKNOWN (Story: Fred Stanley)

Songs: We're Identical (C: Phil Boutelje; L: Harry Tobias)

Cast: Mary Arden; Gloria Gordon; Paul Hammond; Maidel Turner; Michael Whalen; Guy Wilkerson

Notes: No song listed in program.

832 • COMPANY
OPENED: 04/26/1970   Theatre: Alvin
Musical   Broadway: 690

Composer: Stephen Sondheim
Lyricist: Stephen Sondheim
Librettist: George Furth
Producer: Harold Prince
Director: Harold Prince

Choreographer: Michael Bennett; Costumes: D.D. Ryan; Dance Arranger: Wally Harper; David Shire; Lighting Designer: Robert Ornbo; Musical Director: Harold Hastings; Orchestrations: Jonathan Tunick; Set Design: Boris Aronson

Songs: Another Hundred People; Barcelona; Being Alive; Company; Getting Married Today; Happily Ever After [1]; Have I Got a Girl for You; Ladies Who Lunch, The; Little Things You Do Together, The; Marry Me a Little [1]; Multitudes of Amys [1]; Poor Baby; Side By Side By Side; Someone Is Waiting; Sorry- Grateful; Tick, Tock (Dance); Wedding Is Off, The [1]; What Would We Do Without You?; You Could Drive a Person Crazy

Cast: Barbara Barrie; Charles Braswell; Susan Browning; George Coe; Cathy Corkill; John Cunningham; Steve Elmore; Carol Gelfand; Beth Howland; Dean Jones; Charles Kimbrough; Merle Louise; Donna McKechnie; Pamela Myers; Teri Ralston; Marilyn Saunders; Elaine Stritch; Dona D. Vaughn

Notes: Larry Kert took over for Dean Jones shortly after opening. [1] Cut prior to opening.

833 • CON-CURERS, THE
OPENED: 05/17/1898   Theatre: Weber & Fields
                               Broadway Mus. Hall
Musical   Broadway

Composer: John Stromberg
Librettist: Edgar Smith; Louis de Lange

Notes: No program available.

834 • CONNECTICUT YANKEE, A
OPENED: 11/03/1927   Theatre: Vanderbilt
Musical   Broadway: 421

Composer: Richard Rodgers
Lyricist: Lorenz Hart
Librettist: Herbert Fields
Producer: Lyle D. Andrews; Lew Fields
Director: Alexander Leftwich

Source CONNECTICUT YANKEE IN KING ARTHUR'S COURT, A (Novel: Mark Twain); Choreographer: Busby Berkeley; Costumes: John Hawkins Jr.; Musical Director: Roy Webb; Orchestrations: Roy Webb; Set Design: John Hawkins Jr.; Vocal Arranger: Clay Warnick

Songs: At the Round Table (Knight's Opening); Britain's Own Ambassadors [1]; Camelot Samba, The [4]; Can't You Do a Friend a Favor? [4]; Evelyn, What Do You Say?; Home Companion, A; I Blush [1]; I Don't Know How [5] (C: Vivian Ellis; L: Desmond Carter); I Feel at Home with You; I Never Thought of That [5] (C: Vivian Ellis; L: Desmond Carter); Ibbidi Bibbidi Sibbidi Sab (Finale Act I); Morgan Le Fay [6]; My Heart Stood Still [3]; Nothing's Wrong; On a Desert Island with Thee; Sandwich Men, The; Someone Should Tell Them [2]; This Is My Night to Howl [4]; Thou Swell; To Keep My Love Alive [4]; Ye Lunchtime Follies [4]; You Always Love the Same Girl [4]; You're What I Need [1]

Cast: Nana Bryant; Constance Carpenter; June Cochrane; Celeste Deuth; G. Douglas Evans; Paul Everton; William Gaxton; William Norris; William Roselle; Jack Thompson

Notes: Art Director: Herbert Ward. [1] Cut prior to New York [2] Cut prior to New York. Same music as "There's So Much More" from AMERICA'S SWEETHEART. [3] In ONE DAMN THING AFTER ANOTHER in London. [4] Added for 1943 revival. [5] Added for London production (1929) when show was titled A YANKEE AT THE COURT OF KING ARTHUR. [6] Cut prior to New York. Same song as "Evelyn, What Do You Say?, with only title line changed.

835 • CONNIE'S HOT CHOCOLATES (1929)
Notes: See HOT CHOCOLATES (1929).

836 • CONNIE'S HOT CHOCOLATES (1935)

Notes: *See HOT CHOCOLATES (1935).*

837 • CONQUERING HERO, THE

OPENED: 01/16/1961   Theatre: ANTA
Musical   Broadway: 8

Composer: Moose Charlap
Lyricist: Norman Gimbel
Librettist: Larry Gelbart
Producer: Roger L. Stevens; Robert Whitehead
Director: Bob Fosse

Source HAIL THE CONQUERING HERO (Film: Preston Sturges); **Choreographer:** Bob Fosse; **Costumes:** Patton Campbell; **Dance Arranger:** Fred Werner; **Lighting Designer:** Jean Rosenthal; **Musical Director:** Sherman Frank; **Orchestrations:** Robert Ginzler; Sid Ramin; **Set Design:** William Pitkin; Jean Rosenthal; **Vocal Arranger:** Robert Ginzler; Sid Ramin

Songs: Campaign, The; Eight Weight Lifters [1]; Five Shots of Whiskey; Girls! Girls!; Hail, the Conquering Hero!; I Had Big Plans [1]; I'm Beautiful; Must Be Given to You; One Mother Each; Only Rainbows; Past the Age of Innocence [1]; River Bank, The; Rough Times; Truth; Won't You Marry Me?; Wonderful, Marvelous You; Yours, All Yours

Cast: Kay Brown; Bob Kaliban; Kenny Kealy; Elizabeth Kerr; Jane Mason; John McMartin; Tom Poston; Lionel Stander; Fred Stewart

Notes: Bob Fosse's contributions were uncredited. [1] Cut.

838 • CONRACK

OPENED: 11/07/1991
Musical   Closed out of town

Composer: Lee Pockriss
Lyricist: Anne Croswell
Librettist: Granville Burgess
Producer: Goodspeed Opera House
Director: Lonny Price

Source WATER IS WIDE, THE (Novel: Pat Conroy); **Choreographer:** Gregg Burge; **Costumes:** Charlotte M. Yetman; **Lighting Designer:** Stuart Duke; **Musical Director:** Tim Weil; **Set Design:** Ann Sheffield

Songs: Bye, Bye, Conrack!; City Lights; Find Me a Body; He Gon' Stay; Hey, I'm Talkin' to You, Beethoven!; Hopes An' Dreams; Letting Go; Lookin' Good!; Regular Family, A; This Is Your Life!; Tune in Tomorrow; Water Is Wide, The; White Liberal to the Rescue; Your Night to Howl

Cast: John D. Anthony; Matthew Bennett; Joran Corneal; Cory King; Denise Morgan

Notes: Goodspeed Opera House.

839 • CONTINENTAL VARIETIES

OPENED: 10/03/1934   Theatre: Little
Revue   Broadway: 78

Composer: Jean Delettre
Producer: Harold B. Franklin; Arch Selwyn
Director: Henry Dreyfuss

Musical Director: Iza Volpin; **Orchestrations:** Vicente Escudero

Songs: Attends! [1]; D'Amour en Amour [1]; Dancing with My Darling (L: Mitchell Parish); Hands Across the Table (L: Mitchell Parish); I Found a Bit of Paris in Old New York [1] (L: Gladys Unger); I Need New Words [1] (L: E.Y. Harburg); Is It the Singer Or Is It the Song? [1]; It's a Thrill All Over Again [1] (L: Gladys Unger); Je Ne Savais Pas [1]; Let Me Draw You a Picture [1] (L: Irving Taylor); Moi, Je Crache Dans l'Eau [1]; Parlez Moi d'Amour (C/L: Jean Lenoir); Prenez Mes Roses [1]; Si Petite (C: Gaston Claret; L: Pierre Boyle); Speak to Me with Your Eyes (L: Mitchell Parish); This Is the Kiss of Romance (L: Mitchell Parish)

Cast: Nikita Balieff; Lucienne Boyer; Lydia Chaliapine; Vicente Esudero; Emma Runitch; Sacre Monte Gypsies; Iza Volpin Orchestra

Notes: Maurice Aubert may have written other music but isn't identified in programs or sheet music. [1] Not in program.

840 • CONTRAST, THE

OPENED: 11/27/1972   Theatre: Eastside
                                     Playhouse
Musical   Off-Broadway: 24

Composer: Don Pippin
Lyricist: Steve Brown

Librettist: Anthony Stimac
Producer: Peter Cookson
Director: Anthony Stimac

Source CONTRAST, THE (Play: Royall Tyler);
Choreographer: Bill Guske; **Costumes:** Robert
Pusilo; **Lighting Designer:** C. Murawski;
Musical Director: Dorothea Freitag; **Set Design:**
David Chapman; **Vocal Arranger:** Don Pippin

Songs: Dear Lord Chesterfield; For Men [2]; House
Full of People, A; Hundred Thousand Ways, A;
I Never [2]; I Was in the Closet; It's Too Much;
Keep Your Little Eye Upon the Main Chance,
Mary; Life Without Him, A [1]; Prologue; She
Can't Really Be; So Far; So They Call It New
York; Sort of Courting Song, A; That Little
Monosyllable; Were You Saying Something? [2];
Woman Rarely Ever, A; Wouldn't I

Cast: Pamela Adams; Grady Clarkson; Robert G.
Denison; Philip MacKenzie; Ty McConnell; Patti
Perkins

Notes: [1] Cut prior to opening and put in
FASHION as "A Life Without Her." [2] Cut prior
to opening.

841 • CONVERSATION PIECE

OPENED: 10/23/1934   Theatre: 44th Street
Musical   Broadway: 55

Composer: Noel Coward
Lyricist: Noel Coward
Librettist: Noel Coward
Producer: Charles B. Cochran; Harold B. Franklin;
Arch Selwyn
Director: Noel Coward

Costumes: G.E. Calthrop; **Musical Director:** Victor
Baravalle; **Orchestrations:** Charles Prentice; **Set
Design:** G.E. Calthrop

Songs: Charming, Charming; Dear Little Soldiers;
English Lesson; I'll Follow My Secret Heart;
Melanie's Aria; Mothers and Sons [1];
Nevermore; Regency Rakes; There's Always
Something Fishy About the French

Cast: Maidie Andrews; Antony Brian; Irene
Browne; Pierre Fresnay; Sidney Grammer; Carl
Harbord; Sylvia Leslie; Moya Nugent; Yvonne
Printemps; George Sanders; Betty Shale; Athole
Stewart; Pat Worsley

Notes: [1] In published text only.

842 • COOL OFF!

OPENED: 03/31/1964
Musical   Closed out of town

Composer: Howard Blankman
Lyricist: Howard Blankman
Librettist: Jerome Weidman
Director: Herbert Machiz

Choreographer: Bob Herget; **Dance Arranger:**
Genevieve Pitot; **Lighting Designer:** Klaus
Holm; **Musical Director:** John Lesko;
Orchestrations: Larry Wilcox; **Set Design:**
Stewart Chaney

Songs: At My Age; Ballad of the Dauntless
Courier; Ballet; Bessie's Bossa Nova; Can This Be
Why We Came Here?; Cool Off; Dream Ago, A;
For the Life of Me; Only Wonderful; Plenty of
Zip; Suburbia; Take Care; Warm Up; Where Do
We Go From Here?; Witch Hazel

Cast: Hermione Baddeley; Stuart Damon; Stanley
Holloway; Sheila Sullivan

Notes: Closed Philadelphia 4/4/64.

843 • COOLEST CAT IN TOWN, THE

OPENED: 06/22/1978   Theatre: City Center Little
                                         Theater
Musical   Off-Broadway: 21

Composer: Diane Leslie
Lyricist: William Gleason
Librettist: William Gleason
Producer: A. Arthur Altman; Jean Altman;
Joseph H. Lillis Jr.
Director: Frank Carucci

Choreographer: Mary Lou Crivello; **Costumes:**
Faded Glory; **Musical Director:** Bob Goldstone

Songs: Bop Will Never Die, The; Born to Rock and
Roll; Coolest Cat in Town, The; Disco Rag; Don't
Bite the Hand That Feeds You [1]; Don't Say
Shoo-Be-Do-Bop; Hula Hoop; Let's Live It Over
Again; Lost My Cool; Melinda Schecker; Mr.
Know It All; One Kiss; Rock Back the Clock; So
What?; Superstar; Suspended Animation; You're
My Last Chance

Cast: Christopher Callan; Joey Faye; Michael Hayward-Jones; William Perry; Rowena Rollins; Jerry Sroka

Notes: [1] Cut prior to opening.

844 • CO-OPTIMISTS OF 1930, THE

OPENED: 04/04/1930   Theatre: Hippodrome
Revue   London

Composer: Arthur Schwartz
Lyricist: Greatrex Newman
Librettist: Greatrex Newman
Director: Leslie Henson

Songs: Dancing Town (L: Howard Dietz; Greatrex Newman); Moment I Saw You, The [1] (L: Howard Dietz; Greatrex Newman); Nothing Up Our Sleeve; Steeplejack; Stuff to Give the Troops, The; Sunday Afternoon

Cast: Stanley Holloway; Elsie Randolph; Cyril Ritchard

Notes: No program available. [1] Used in THREE'S A CROWD without Newman credited.

845 • COPACABANA (1985)

OPENED: 12/03/1985   Theatre: CBS
TV Musical

Composer: Barry Manilow
Lyricist: Bruce Sussman

Musical Director: Artie Butler

Songs: Aye-Caramba; Big City Blues; Blue (inst.); Call Me Mr. Lucky; Changing My Tune; Copacabana (At the Copa); El Bravo; Let's Go Steppin'; Lola; Man Wanted; Sweet Heaven (I'm in Love Again); Who Needs to Dream

Cast: Barry Manilow; Annette O'Toole

Notes: *See also COPACABANA (1994).*

846 • COPACABANA (1994)

OPENED: 06/23/1994   Theatre: Prince of Wales
Musical   London

Composer: Barry Manilow

Lyricist: Jack Feldman; Bruce Sussman
Librettist: Jack Feldman; Barry Manilow; Bruce Sussman
Producer: Apollo Leisure Group; Barry Clayton Concerts Ltd.
Director: Roger Redfarn

Arrangements Barry Manilow; Andy Rumble; Choreographer: Dorian Sanchez; Costumes: Hugh Durrant; Lighting Designer: Hugh Vanstone; Musical Director: Andy Rumble; Orchestrations: Barry Manilow; Andy Rumble; Set Design: Martin Grant

Songs: Ay Caramba; Bolero de Amor; Changing My Tune; Copacabana; Dancin' Fool; El Bravo!; Jingle, The; Jump, Shout, Boogie; Just Arrived; Man Wanted; Mermaid's Tale, The; Night on the Town; Sweet Heaven; Thank You; This Can't Be Real; Welcome to Havana!; Who Am I Kidding?; Who Needs to Dream?

Cast: Howard Attfield; Nicola Dawn; Jenny Logan; Richard Lyndon; Anna Nicholas; Duncan Smith; Gary Wilmot

Notes: *See also COPACABANA (1985).*

847 • COPACABANA REVUE (1942)

OPENED: 10/17/1942   Theatre: Copacabana
Revue   Nightclub

Composer: Ted Murray
Lyricist: Benny Davis
Director: Don Loper

Costumes: Don Loper

Songs: Are You Kiddin' Bud?; Brazilian Boogie Woogie; Let It Be Gay; No Hard Feelings; This Is New York; You Just Can't Copa with a Copacabana Baby

Cast: Berry Brothers; Joe E. Lewis; Frank Marti Orchestra; Connie Russell; Olga San Juan; Ted Straeter's Orchestra

Notes: Complete song list not available.

848 • COPACABANA REVUE (1943)

OPENED: 03/10/1943   Theatre: Copacabana
Revue   Nightclub

Composer: George Forrest; Robert Wright
Lyricist: George Forrest; Robert Wright
Producer: Larry Ceballos
Director: Walter Florell

Arrangements: Ted Straeter; **Choreographer:** Larry Ceballos; **Musical Director:** Ted Straeter

Songs: Let's Make a Night of It

Cast: Martha Burnett; Capella & Patricia; Jimmy Durante; Eddie Jackson

Notes: No program available. No song list available.

849 • COPACABANA REVUE (1943)
OPENED: 06/02/1943   Theatre: Copacabana
Revue   Nightclub

Composer: George Forrest; Robert Wright
Lyricist: George Forrest; Robert Wright
Producer: Pal'mere Brandeaux

Costumes: Joe Lewis

Songs: I'm Going Moroccan for Jimmy [1]

Cast: Nat Brandywine Orchestra; Diane Davis; Chandra Kaly Dancers; Frank Marti Orchestra; Betty Jane Smith; Mary Jane Walsh

Notes: Complete song list not available. [1] Music used for "Rahadlakum" in KISMET.

850 • COPACABANA REVUE (1944)
OPENED: 1944   Theatre: Copacabana
Revue   Nightclub

Composer: Irving Actman
Lyricist: Eddie De Lange
Producer: Monte Proser

Songs: April Can't Do This to Me; Bahia (C: Sam Stept); I Can Still Remember (C: Sam Stept); La Pintada; Loveliness of You, The (C: Sam Stept); Poco Loco (C: Sam Stept); Sky Ran Out of Stars, The; We're Off to the Races (C: Sam Stept); Who's Got a Match?; You Gotta Go East to Go West (C: Sam Stept)

Notes: Sheet music only. No other information available.

851 • COPACABANA REVUE (1944)
OPENED: 09/20/1944   Theatre: Copacabana
Revue   Nightclub

Composer: Josef Myrow
Lyricist: Eddie De Lange
Producer: Al Siegal
Director: Douglas Coudy

Costumes: Ted Shaw

Songs: La Orchidea (Orchid Lady); Touch of You, A; Way That I Want You, The; You Just You

Cast: Rose Blaine; Frankie Connors; Johnny Johnstone; Joe E. Lewis; Abe Lyman Orchestra; Betty Anne Nyman

Notes: No complete song list available.

852 • COPACABANA REVUE (1946)
Notes: *See A NIGHT AT THE COPA.*

853 • COPACABANA REVUE (1948)
OPENED: 04/14/1948   Theatre: Copacabana
Revue   Nightclub

Composer: Bob Russell
Lyricist: Bob Russell
Director: Douglas Coudy

Costumes: Billy Livingston

Songs: Chu Cha Chacha Olay; It's Oh So Nice in Your Arms

Cast: Vivian Blaine; Warde Donovan; Jerry Lewis; Ray Malone; Dean Martin

Notes: No complete song list available.

854 • COPACABANA REVUE (1950)
OPENED: 01/11/1950   Theatre: Copacabana
Revue   Nightclub

Composer: Bob Hilliard
Lyricist: Bob Hilliard
Director: Doug Coudy

Costumes: Billy Livingston

Songs: Fly; Salt Water Pirate from Sugar Loaf Hill Brazil; Who Loves to Ride on a Slide Trombone?

Cast: Patricia Adair; Fernando Alvarez Orchestra; Michael Durso Orchestra; Lena Horne; Michael Shaughnessy

Notes: No complete song list available.

855 • COPACABANA REVUE (1950)

OPENED: 02/12/1950   Theatre: Copacabana
Revue   Nightclub

Composer: Michael Durso; Marvin Kahn
Lyricist: Mel Mitchell
Director: Doug Coudy

Costumes: Sal Anthony; Orchestrations: Deac Eberhard

Songs: Pick a Partner

Cast: Al Bernie; Michael Durso Orchestra; Four Esquires; Peggy Lee; Frank Marti Orchestra

Notes: No complete song list available.

856 • COPACABANA REVUE (1950)

OPENED: 02/22/1950   Theatre: Broadway
Revue   Nightclub

Composer: Dave Mann
Lyricist: Bob Hilliard
Director: Douglas Coudy

Costumes: Billy Livingston

Songs: Dearie

Cast: Patricia Adair; Fernando Alvarez Orchestra; Geraldine DuBois; Michael Durso Orchestra; Ted Lewis; Paul White

Notes: Complete song list not available.

857 • COPACABANA REVUE (1950)

OPENED: 05/10/1950   Theatre: Copacabana
Revue   Nightclub

Composer: Dave Mann; Carl Sigman
Lyricist: Bob Hilliard
Producer: Jack Entratter; Jules Podell
Director: Doug Coudy

Costumes: Billy Livingston; Orchestrations: Eliot G. "Deac" Eberhard

Songs: Arm with a Bow in Its Hand; Beautiful Sunshine Makes a Beautiful Day; Sour Apple Serenade

Cast: Fernando Alvarez Orchestra; Toni Arden; Betty Bruce; Michael Durso Orchestra; Jerry Lewis; Dean Martin

Notes: No complete song list available.

858 • COPACABANA REVUE (1951)

OPENED: 04/04/1951   Theatre: Copacabana
Revue   Nightclub

Composer: Lyn Duddy; Joan Edwards
Lyricist: Lyn Duddy; Joan Edwards
Producer: Jack Entratter; Jules Podell
Director: Douglas Coudy

Costumes: James Carroll; Billy Livingston;
Orchestrations: Eliot G. Eberhard

Songs: Farmer's Daughter; First Snow of Winter; Variety Is the Spice of Life, Life, Life

Cast: Fernando Alvarez Band; Toni Arden; Jimmy Durante; Mike Durso Band; Maria Gambarelli; Eddie Jackson

Notes: No other information available.

859 • COPACABANA REVUE (1952)

OPENED: 10/08/1952   Theatre: Copacabana
Revue   Nightclub

Composer: Joan Edwards
Lyricist: Lyn Duddy
Director:

Costumes: Billy Livingston

Songs: Carnival in Rio; Widow from Amarillo

Cast: Michael Durso Orchestra; Betty Kean; Jane Kean; Joe E. Lewis; Frank Marti Orchestra; Nicholas Brothers; Jack Purcell

Notes: No complete song list available.

860 • COPACABANA REVUE (1953)

OPENED: 04/22/1953   Theatre: Copacabana
Revue   Nightclub

Composer: Harold Karr
Lyricist: Matt Dubey
Director: Doug Coudy

Costumes: Billy Livingston; **Orchestrations:** Eliot G. Everhard

Songs: For Love or Money; We've Got an Evening with Jimmy

Cast: Jules Buffano; Jimmy Durante; Michael Durso Orchestra; Eddie Jackson; Frank Marti Orchestra; Jack Roth

Notes: No complete song list available.

861 • COPACABANA REVUE (1954)

OPENED: 04/07/1954   Theatre: Copacabana
Revue   Nightclub

Composer: Dave Mann
Lyricist: Bob Hilliard
Director: Douglas Coudy

Costumes: Michi; **Orchestrations:** Philip J. Lang

Songs: I'm in Favor of Friendship

Cast: Sammy Davis Jr.; Michael Durso Orchestra; Sandy Evans; Betty Lorraine; Frank Marti Orchestra; Will Mastin Trio; Mary Small

Notes: Complete song list unavailable.

862 • COPACABANA REVUE (1954)

OPENED: 05/26/1954   Theatre: Copacabana
Revue   Nightclub

Composer: Dave Mann
Lyricist: Bob Hilliard
Director: Douglas Coudy

Costumes: Michi; **Orchestrations:** Philip J. Lang

Songs: Somebody Stole de Wedding Bell; Wallflower

Cast: Barry Sisters; Jules Buffano; Jimmy Durante; Michael Durso Band; Frank Marti Band; Jack Roth

Notes: No complete song list available

863 • COPACABANA REVUE (1954)

OPENED: 06/10/1954   Theatre: Copacabana
Revue   Nightclub

Composer: Norman Gimbel
Lyricist: Norman Gimbel
Producer: Jules Podell

Songs: Absurd As a Chuck-a-Walla Bird; Affair of the Heart, An; Cocoanut Tree, The; Summer Love

Cast: Michael Durso Orchestra; Sonny Howard; Sam Levinson; Frank Marti Orchestra; Bob Warren; Joanne Wheatley

Notes: No complete song list available.

864 • COPACABANA REVUE (1958)

OPENED: 09/17/1958   Theatre: Copacabana
Revue   Nightclub

Composer: Marvin Kahn
Lyricist: Mel Mitchell
Director: Doug Coudy

Costumes: Billy Livingston; **Orchestrations:** Deac Eberhard

Songs: Wholesome Honeys Here at Home

Cast: Toni Arden; Joe E. Lewis; Lois Ray; Bob Warren

Notes: No complete song list available.

865 • COPACABANA REVUE (1960)

OPENED: 03/02/1960   Theatre: Copacabana
Revue   Nightclub

Composer: Marvin Kahn
Lyricist: Mel Mandel
Director: Doug Coudy

Arrangements: Paul Shelley; **Costumes:** Billy Livingston

Songs: Acapulco Polka; Cocktails at the Copa

Cast: Sue Carson; Earl Grant; Frank Martos Orchestra; Paul Shelley

Notes: No complete song list available.

866 • COPACABANA REVUES

Revue	Theatre: Copacabana Nightclub

Notes: There were many Copa revues for which I could identify no songs. Instead of taking up too much space listing full credits and no songs, here is a list of writers and the dates of the Variety reviews — Robert Wright and George Forrest: 5/5/43. Tom Adiar: 1/10/49. Bob Hilliard and Dave Mann: 3/29/50; 5/9/51; 6/20/51; 11/25/53. Lyn Duddy and Joan Edwards: 11/22/50; 1/10/51; 11/14/51; 4/2/52; 4/16/52; 12/3/52. Matt Dubey and Harold Karr: 3/11/53; 5/10/53; 6/17/53; 8/10/53. Norman Gimbel: 7/7/54. George Campbell and Marvin Moore: 3/30/55. Marvin Kahn and Mel Mitchell: 10/23/57; 12/17/58; 2/1/59; 3/18/59; 7/15/59; 10/29/59. Michael Durso, Mel Mitchell and Marvin Kahn: 5/23/56; 8/14/57; 2/26/58; 4/23/58. Marvin Kahn and Mel Mandel: 4/00/59; 1/27/60; 3/30/60; 4/27/60. Paul Anka: 9/14/60; 11/16/60; 7/12/61; 1/23/63; 2/27/63; 4/10/63; 2/23/67. Bob Hilliard and Milton De Lugg: 6/39/50; 6/8/60; 8/3/60; 5/22/63; 8/13/63; 9/18/63; 11/30/63. Jerry Seelen and Mort Lindsay: 9/13/61; 12/13/61. George Harwell and Al Foster: 4/11/62. Joe and Noel Sherman: 9/19/62; 10/21/62; 10/24/62; 12/12/62. Ivan Lane and Jay Sarnoff: 1/22/64. Al Foster: 5/28/58; 7/9/58; 7/30/58; 9/16/59; 10/28/59. Al Foster and Keefe Braselle: 7/1/59; 7/15/59; 8/5/59; 8/26/59; 9/23/64.

867 • COPACABANA SHOW IN MIAMI

OPENED: 1946

Revue	Nightclub

Composer: Ted Murry
Lyricist: Benny Davis

Songs: Make Mine Latin; Overture to Love; Pay Attention to the Girls; 10th Avenue Waltz; This Is Miami; Winter in California

Notes: No other information available. Information from ASCAP/Library of Congress.

868 • COPPER AND BRASS

OPENED: 10/17/1957   Theatre: Martin Beck
Musical   Broadway: 36

Composer: David Baker
Lyricist: David Craig
Librettist: David Craig; Ellen Violett
Producer: Lyn Austin; Thomas Noyes
Director: Marc Daniels

Choreographer: Anna Sokolow; **Costumes:** Alvin Colt; **Dance Arranger:** John Morris; **Lighting Designer:** Jean Eckart; William Eckart; **Musical Director:** Maurice Levine; **Orchestrations:** Ralph Burns; **Set Design:** Jean Eckart; William Eckart; **Vocal Arranger:** Maurice Levine

Songs: Argentine Tango; Baby's Baby; Bringing Up Daughter; Call the Police; Career Guidance; Cool Combo Mambo; Cool Credo; Don't Look Now; Hong Kong; I Need All the Help I Can Get; La Vie Boheme [1]; Little Woman; Me and Love; Remember the Dancing; Sweet William; Unmistakable Sign; Wearing of the Blue; Why Her?; You Walked Out

Cast: Alan Bunce; Alice Pearce; Benay Venuta; Nancy Walker; Dick Williams

Notes: [1] Cut prior to opening.

869 • COPPERFIELD

OPENED: 04/13/1981   Theatre: ANTA
Musical   Broadway: 13

Composer: Joel Hirschhorn; Al Kasha
Lyricist: Joel Hirschhorn; Al Kasha
Librettist: Joel Hirschhorn; Al Kasha
Producer: Don Gregory; Mike Merrick
Director: Rob Iscove

Source DAVID COPPERFIELD (Novel: Charles Dickens); **Choreographer:** Rob Iscove; **Costumes:** John David Ridge; **Dance Arranger:** Donald Johnston; **Incidental Music:** Donald Johnston; **Lighting Designer:** Ken Billington; **Musical Director:** Larry Blank; **Orchestrations:** Irwin Kostal; **Set Design:** Tony Straiges; **Vocal Arranger:** Larry Blank

Songs: Anyone; Bottle Song; Circle Waltz, The; Copperfield; Here's a Book; I Don't Want a Boy; I Wish He Knew; Lights of London, The; Mama Don't Get Married; Something Will Turn Up; Umble; Up the Ladder; Villainy Is the Matter; With the One I Love

Cast: Leslie Denniston; Beulah Garrick; Barrie Ingham; George S. Irving; Carmen Mathews;

Brian Matthews; Linda Poser; Evan Richards; Lenny Wolpe

870 • CORA
OPENED: 11/28/1911
Musical

Composer: Cole Porter
Lyricist: Cole Porter
Librettist: T. Gaillard Thomas II
Producer: Phi Opera Company
Director: Peter C. Bryce; T. Gaillard Thomas II

Songs: Cablegram; Concentration; Cora, the Fair Chorine; Fair One; Far, Far Away; Goodbye Boys; Hello, Miss Chapel Street; Le Reve d'Absinthe; Ma Petite Ninette; Mother Phi; My Home Town Girl; Old Rat Mort, The; Poker; Queen of the Yale Dramat; Rolling, Rolling; Rosebud; Saturday Night; We're Off

Cast: Cole Porter; T. Gaillard Thomas II

Notes: Produced as fall initiation play of Delta Kappa Epislon fraternity.

871 • CORKSCREWS
OPENED: 10/06/1982
Revue   Off-Broadway: 15

Composer: Arthur Siegel
Lyricist: Tony Lang
Librettist: Tony Lang
Producer: Theater Opera Music Inst.
Director: Miriam Fond

Choreographer: Miriam Fond. **Costumes:** Van Broughton Ramsey; **Lighting Designer:** Margit Allen

Songs: Ballad of Norman, The; Betamax Blues, The; Child Within, The [3]; Chutzpah [3]; Collector's Item (Moose Murders) [1]; Confession; Creative Block; Died & Died & Died; Evelyn Woods Hoedown [1]; Family Affair, A [3]; Forever Fantasticks [1]; 4001 [1]; Getting Around [3]; Guilt [3]; Handkerchief Song [3]; Healthy Relationship [3]; I Like Me; I'm Into Music; I'm Not Queer; Let It All Hang Out (C: Paul Trueblood); Looking for Love; Made for Each Other [1]; Maiden's Prayer (Anorexia); Make It Another; New Soft Shoe, The [3]; Not Getting Murdered Today; Opening Number [3]; People; Performance Art [2]; Secret Love [3]; Send Out

for Food (Take-Out); She Is Making Norman Antsy; Slight Case of Murder [3]; Tina and Nina; Too!; Up the Hill There; What I Need the Most

Cast: Tony Aylward; Barbara Barsky; James Hosbein; Gail Oscar

Notes: [1] Not in program. [2] Added to 3/12/92 revival. [3] Not used. Unknown date.

872 • CORNED BEEF AND ROSES
Notes: *See SWEET AND LOW.*

873 • COSMO VANITIES
Notes: *See BELMONT VARIETIES.*

874 • COSTA PACKET
OPENED: 10/05/1972   Theatre: Theatre Royal
Musical   London

Composer: Lionel Bart; Alan Klein
Lyricist: Lionel Bart; Alan Klein
Librettist: Frank Norman
Producer: Theatre Workshop
Director: Joan Littlewood

Choreographer: Judith Paris; **Costumes:** Willie Burt; **Musical Director:** David Gold; **Set Design:** Guy Hodgkinson; Mark Pritchard

Cast: J. Aitken; Gaye Brown; Avis Bunnage; Suzan Cameron; Larry Dann; Griffith Davies; Philip Davis; Ken Hill; Valerie Walsh

Notes: No program available.

875 • COTTON CLUB EXPRESS
OPENED: 1937   Theatre: Cotton Club
Revue   Nightclub

Composer: Duke Ellington
Lyricist: Irving Mills
Producer: Cotton Club, The
Director: Clarence Robinson

Musical Director: Will Vodery

Songs: Black and Tan Fantasy (inst.) (C: Duke Ellington; Bubber Miley); Chile; Cotton Club Express (inst.); Don't Know If I'm Comin' or Goin' (C: Lupin Fein; L: Lee Wainer); Miss Otis Regrets (C/L: Cole Porter); Old Plantation

(C/L: Lee David; John Redmond); Peckin';
Rockin' in Rhythm (C: Harry Carney; Duke
Ellington); Tap Mathematician (C/L: Unknown);
Taps Is Tops (C/L: Unknown); Where Is the
Sun? (C/L: Lee David; John Redmond)

Cast: Ivy Anderson; Duke Ellington and His
Orchestra; Nicholas Brothers, The; George
Dewey Washington; Ethel Waters

876 • COTTON CLUB PARADE (1932) (TWENTIETH EDITION)

OPENED: 10/23/1932   Theatre: Cotton Club
Revue   Nightclub

Composer: Harold Arlen
Lyricist: Ted Koehler
Producer: Ted Healy
Director: Ted Healy

Choreographer: Elida Webb; **Costumes:** Gene

Songs: A La Lenox Avenue; All Aboard; Deep Sea
Divin' Papa; High Flyin' Man; In the Silence of
the Night; I've Got the World on a String; Let's
Put on the Ritz; Minnie the Moocher's Wedding
Day; My Military Man; New Kind of Rhythm;
Pool Room Papa; That's What I Hate About
Love; Wail of the Reefer Man; You Gave Me
Ev'rything But Love

Cast: Roy Atkins; Cab Calloway and His Orchestra;
Leitha Hill; Nicholas Brothers, The; Carolynne
Snowden; Swan & Lee; Aida Ward; Lucille
Wilson

Notes: Songs from various sources. These songs
may not have been in the show at the same
time.

877 • COTTON CLUB PARADE (1932) (TWENTY-FIRST EDITION)

OPENED: 10/23/1932   Theatre: Cotton Club
Revue   Nightclub

Composer: Harold Arlen
Lyricist: Ted Koehler

Songs: Bill Robinson Stomp; Calloway for
President [1] (C: George Gershwin; L: Cab
Calloway; Ira Gershwin); Flat Tire Papa; Harlem

Holiday; I've Got the World on a String; Jungle
in Manhattan; Raisin' Hades in Green Pastures;
That's How Darkies Keep Warm; That's What I
Hate About Love; Trial of Minnie the Moocher,
The; Wail of the Reefer Man, The

Cast: Roy Atkins; Cab Calloway and His Orchestra;
Leitha Hill; Nicholas Brothers; Alma Smith;
Carolyn Snowden; Swan & Lee; Elmer Turner;
Aida Ward; Henri Wessels

Notes: [1] Based on "Wintergreen for President"
from OF THEE I SING.

878 • COTTON CLUB PARADE (1933) (TWENTY-SECOND EDITION)

OPENED: 04/06/1933   Theatre: Cotton Club
Revue   Nightclub

Composer: Harold Arlen
Lyricist: Ted Koehler
Producer: Dan Healy

Songs: Calico Days; Get Yourself a New Broom;
Happy As the Day Is Long; I'm Looking for
Another Handy Man; Love Is the Thing
(C: Victor Young; L: Ned Washington); Muggin'
Lightly; Raisin' the Rent; Stormy Weather

Cast: Duke Ellington and His Orchestra; Sally
Goodings; Cora La Redd; George Dewey
Washington; Ethel Waters; Henry "Rubber Legs"
Williams

879 • COTTON CLUB PARADE (1933) (TWENTY-THIRD EDITION)

OPENED: 1933   Theatre: Cotton Club
Revue   Nightclub

Composer: Harold Arlen
Lyricist: Ted Koehler

Songs: Got a Need for You (C/L: Unknown);
Harlem Fan Tan (C/L: Unknown); Harlem
Hospitality (C: Jerry Arlen; L: James Van
Heusen); Keep Tempo (C/L: George A. Little;
Jack Stanley); Lady with the Fan, The; Little
Town Gal (C/L: Jeanne Burns); On a Steamer
Coming Over (C: Lou Handman; L: Joe
Goodwin; Nat Schwartz); There's a House in
Harlem for Sale (C/L: Jerry Arlen; James Van

Heusen); Way Up North in Southland (C: James C. Johnson; L: Nat Schwartz; George Whiting)

Cast: Cab Calloway and His Orchestra; Aida Ward

880 • COTTON CLUB PARADE (1934) (TWENTY-FOURTH EDITION)

OPENED: 03/23/1934   Theatre: Cotton Club
Revue   Nightclub

Composer: Harold Arlen
Lyricist: Ted Koehler
Producer: Dan Healy
Director: Dan Healy

Songs: As Long As I Live; Breakfast Ball; Here Goes; Ill Wind; Primitive Prima Donna; Those Who Dance; Twice a Year; You Sure Don't Know How to Shake That Thing

Cast: Adelaide Hall; Juan Hernandez; Leitha Hill; Lena Horne; Avon Long; Jimmy Lunceford and His Orchestra; Pops and Louie

881 • COTTON CLUB PARADE (1934) (TWENTY-FIFTH EDITION)

OPENED: 1934   Theatre: Cotton Club
Revue   Nightclub

Composer: Ben Oakland
Lyricist: Irving Mills; Mitchell Parish

Songs: Dixie After Dark; I'm a Hundred Percent for You; Jingle of the Jungle; Like a Bolt from the Blue; Ridin' High; Sidewalks of Cuba

882 • COTTON CLUB PARADE (1935) (TWENTY-SIXTH EDITION)

OPENED: 1935   Theatre: Cotton Club
Revue   Nightclub

Composer: Rube Bloom
Lyricist: Ted Koehler

Songs: Cotton; Dinah Lou; Good for Nothin' Joe; Rhythm River; Truckin'; Waiting in the Garden

Cast: Lena Horne; Jimmy Lunceford and His Orchestra; Nina Mae McKinney; Miller & Mantan

Notes: This was the final show at the uptown Cotton Club.

883 • COTTON CLUB PARADE (1936) (TWENTY-SEVENTH EDITION)

OPENED: 09/24/1936   Theatre: Cotton Club
Revue   Nightclub

Composer: Benny Davis
Lyricist: J. Fred Coots
Director: Clarence Robinson

Choreographer: Clarence Robinson;
Orchestrations: Will Vodery

Songs: Alabama Barbecue; Black Magic; Class; Copper Colored Gal, Cotton Blossom Lane; Doin' the Susi-Q; Frisco Flo; Hi-De-Ho Miracle Man, The; I'm at the Mercy of Love; Jungle Jingle; Minnie the Moocher (C/L: Cab Calloway; Clarence Gaskill; Irving Mills); Swingtime on the Swanee; That's What You Mean to Me; There's Love in My Heart for You; Wedding of Mr. and Mrs. Swing, The

Cast: Avis Andrews; Berry Brothers, The; Cab Calloway and His Orchestra; Bill Robinson; Henri Wessels

Notes: This is the first revue at the new downtown Cotton Club.

884 • COTTON CLUB PARADE (1937) (THIRD EDITION)

OPENED: 1937   Theatre: Cotton Club
Revue   Nightclub

Composer: Benny Davis
Lyricist: J. Fred Coots

Songs: Bill Robinson Walk, The [1]; Go South, Young Man; Harlem Bolero; Hi-De-Ho Romeo; I'm a Lady; I'm Always in the Mood for You; Nightfall in Louisiana; Parade of the Chocolate Dolls; Savage Rhythm; She's Tall, She's Tan, She's Terrific (Tall, Tan and Terrific); So I'll Never Be a Millionaire; Spades Is Trumps

Cast: Avis Andrews; Cab Calloway and His Orchestra; Mae Johnson; Nicholas Brothers, The; Tramp Band, The

Notes: [1] Added after opening. [2] Not in program.

885 • COTTON CLUB PARADE (1937)

OPENED: 1937
Revue
Theatre: Cotton Club
Nightclub

Composer: John Redmond
Lyricist: Lee David

Songs: Black and Tan Fantasy (inst.) (C: Duke Ellington; Bubber Miley); Cantcha Kinda Go for Me; Chile (C: Reginald Foresythe; L: Andy Razaf); Cotton Club Express (C: Duke Ellington; L: Irving Mills); Don't Know If I'm Comin' or Goin' (C/L: Lupin Fein; Lee Weiner); Headin' for Heaven (Down South); Miss Otis Regrets (C/L: Cole Porter); Music Makin' Man, The (C: J. Fred Coots; L: Haven Gillespie); Old Plantation; Peckin' (inst.) (C: Duke Ellington); Rockin' in Rhythm (inst.) (C: Harry Carney; Duke Ellington; Irving Mills); Stormy Weather [1] (C: Harold Arlen; L: Ted Koehler); Tap Is Tops (C: Reginald Foresythe; L: Andy Razaf); Tap Mathematician [2] (C/L: Unknown); Where Is the Sun?

Cast: Ivy Anderson; Bill Bailey; Duke Ellington and His Orchestra; Nicholas Brothers, The; George Dewey Washington; Ethel Waters

Notes: [1] From COTTON CLUB PARADE (1933). [2] May not have been a song.

886 • COTTON CLUB PARADE (1938)

OPENED: 03/09/1938
Revue
Theatre: Cotton Club
Nightclub

Composer: Duke Ellington
Lyricist: Irving Mills; Henry Nemo

Songs: Black Magic [2] (C: J. Fred Coots; L: Benny Davis); Braggin' in Brass (inst.); Carnival in Caroline; Clowns in Color; Dinah's in a Jam (inst.); Gal from Joe's, A (inst.) (L: Irving Mills); Hi-De-Ho Romeo [3] (C: J. Fred Coots; L: Benny Davis); Hip Chick (inst.); I Let a Song Go Out of My Heart [1] (C: Duke Ellington; John Redmond; L: Irving Mills; Henry Nemo); If You Were in My Place; I'm a Lady [3] (C: J. Fred Coots; L: Lee David); I'm Slappin' Seventh Avenue (with the

Sole of My Shoe) (inst.); Lesson in C, A (inst.); Posin' (inst.); Rainy Day Sadie; Rhythm in Waltztime (inst.); Skrontch (Doin' the Skrontch); Swingtime in Honolulu

Cast: 4 Step Brothers, The; Ivy Anderson; Peg Leg Bates; Chocolateers, The; Duke Ellington and His Orchestra; Mae Johnson; Aida Ward

Notes: [1] Cut prior to opening. [2] From COTTON CLUB PARADE (1936). [3] From COTTON CLUB PARADE (1937).

887 • COTTON CLUB PARADE (1938) (FOURTH EDITION)

OPENED: 09/28/1938
Revue
Theatre: Cotton Club
Nightclub

Composer: J. Fred Coots
Lyricist: Benny Davis

Songs: A-Tisket A-Tasket (C/L: Al Feldman; Ella Fitzgerald); Boogie-Woogie, The; Congo-Conga; Highland Swing, The; I'm Madly in Love with You; I've Got a Heart Full of Rhythm; Jive (A Lesson in Jive) (C/L: Chu Berry; Cab Calloway; Benny Payne); Miss Hallelujah Brown; Picketing the Old Plantation; Preacher, The; Rock Me; Scarlett O'Hara from Seventh Avenue; Style; Swing Low Sweet Chariot (C/L: Traditional); Thanks to You Mr. Handy; There's a Sunny Side to Everything

Cast: Berry Brothers, The; Cab Calloway and His Orchestra; Dandridge Sisters, The; W.C. Handy; Mae Johnson; Nicholas Brothers, The; June Richmond

888 • COTTON CLUB PARADE (1939) (WORLD'S FAIR EDITION)

OPENED: 03/24/1939
Revue
Theatre: Cotton Club
Nightclub

Composer: Rube Bloom
Lyricist: Ted Koehler

Songs: Don't Worry 'Bout Me; Easy Ridin' Papa; Floogie Walk; Ghost of Smokie Joe, The; Glorified at Last; Got No Time; If I Were Sure of You; Jitterbug Jamboree; Mayor of Harlem, The (Meet the Mayor); Somewhere in Africa; Sunday Morning in Harlem; Sweepin' Up; Voodoo; What

Goes Up, Must Come Down (and Baby, You've Been Flyin' too High)

Cast: Cab Calloway and His Orchestra; Katheryn Perry; Bill "Bojangles" Robinson; Sister Rosetta Tharpe

Notes: [1] May be from a different 1939 edition.

889 • COTTON CLUB PARADE (1939) (SIXTH EDITION)

OPENED: 11/01/1939   Theatre: Cotton Club
Revue   Nightclub

Composer: Saul Chaplin
Lyricist: Sammy Cahn

Songs: It's My Turn Now; Love's Got Me Down Again; Shorty George; You're a Lucky Guy; You're Just a No Account

Cast: Louis Amstrong and His Orchestra; Stump and Stumpy; Maxine Sullivan; Midge Williams

Notes: No program available.

890 • COTTON CLUB PARADE (1940) (SEVENTH EDITION)

OPENED: 1940   Theatre: Cotton Club
Revue   Nightclub

Songs: My Moment Supreme (C/L: Henry Armstrong; Clarence Kelley; Andy Kirk; Lorenzo Pack)

Cast: Andy Kirk and His Clouds of Joy; Pha Tyrell

891 • COTTON CLUB REVIEW OF 1956

Notes: *See COTTON CLUB REVUE (1957).*

892 • COTTON CLUB REVUE (1927) (ELEVENTH EDITION)

OPENED: 12/04/1927   Theatre: Cotton Club
Revue   Nightclub

Composer: Jimmy McHugh
Lyricist: Dorothy Fields
Producer: Dan Healy

Songs: Dancemania; Doin' the Frog; Harlem River

Quiver (Brown Berries); Jazzmania; Red Hot Band

Cast: Mildred Dixon; Duke Ellington Orchestra; Earl "Snakehips" Tucker; Henri Wessels; Edith Wilson

Notes: The title is not exact. Dan Healy was also credited along with Fields and McHugh, although he probably did not contribute to the songs.

893 • COTTON CLUB REVUE (1928) (TWELFTH EDITION)

OPENED: 1928   Theatre: Cotton Club
Revue   Nightclub

Composer: Duke Ellington

Songs: I'm a Broken Hearted Blackbird (C: Jimmy McHugh; L: Dorothy Fields); Mooche, The (inst.)

Cast: Duke Ellington and His Orchestra

Notes: No other information available.

894 • COTTON CLUB REVUE (1928) (THIRTEENTH EDITION)

OPENED: 1928   Theatre: Cotton Club
Revue   Nightclub

Composer: Jimmy McHugh
Lyricist: Dorothy Fields

Songs: Harlemania; Japanese Dream

Cast: Duke Ellington and His Orchestra

Notes: No other information available.

895 • COTTON CLUB REVUE (1929) (FOURTEENTH EDITION)

OPENED: 1929   Theatre: Cotton Club
Revue   Nightclub

Composer: Jimmy McHugh
Lyricist: Dorothy Fields

Songs: Arabian Lover; Cotton Club Stomp (inst.)

(C: Harry Carney; Duke Ellington; Johnny Hodges); Freeze and Melt; Goin' to Town (inst.) (C: Duke Ellington; Bubber Miley); Hot Feet; Misty Mornin' (inst.) (C: Duke Ellington; Arthur Whetsol)

Cast: Duke Ellington and His Orchestra

Notes: No other information available.

896 • COTTON CLUB REVUE (FALL 1931) (NINETEENTH EDITION)

OPENED: 1931   Theatre: Cotton Club
Revue   Nightclub

Songs: Minnie the Moocher (C/L: Cab Calloway; Clarence Gaskill; Irving Mills)

Cast: Cab Calloway and His Orchestra; Cora La Redd; Swan & Lee; Aida Ward

Notes: This may not be the exact title. Probably a continuation of RHYTHMANIA.

897 • COTTON CLUB REVUE, THE

OPENED: 1937   Theatre: London
                      Palladium
Revue   London

Composer: Benny Davis
Lyricist: J. Fred Coots

Choreographer: Clarence Robinson; **Musical Director:** Teddy Hill

Songs: Barbeque; Class; Copper Colored Gal; Jungle; Wedding of Mr. and Mrs. Jazz!, The

Cast: Bill Bailey; Alberta Hunter; Harold Norton and Margot; Jessye Scott; Rollin Smith; Three Berry Brothers

Notes: Featured songs from the COTTON CLUB PARADE (1936) (TWENTY-SEVENTH EDITION).

898 • COTTON CLUB REVUE (1957)

OPENED: 07/09/1957   Theatre: Theatre Under
                      the Stars
Revue   Nightclub

Composer: Benny Davis
Lyricist: Clay Boland

Musical Director: Eddie Barefield

Songs: Beginnin' of Sinnin'; Big Town Blues; Born to Be Happy; Doin' the Town (C: Howard Steiner); Never Had It So Good; Sinful; Sweeter Than Sweet; Tzotskele (My Darling)

Cast: Cab Calloway; Malcolm Dodds and the Tunedrops; Mauri Leighton

Notes: Listed in ASCAP as COTTON CLUB REVIEW OF 1956.

899 • COTTON LAND

OPENED: 1924
Revue

Composer: James P. Johnson

Cast: Billy Higgins; James P. Johnson; Gertrude Saunders; Dickie Wells

Notes: No other information available.

900 • COTTON PATCH GOSPEL

OPENED: 10/10/1981   Theatre: Lamb's
Musical   Off-Broadway: 193

Composer: Harry Chapin
Lyricist: Harry Chapin
Librettist: Tom Key; Russell Treyz
Producer: Philip M. Getter
Director: Russell Treyz

Source: COTTON PATCH VERSION OF MATTHEW AND JOHN (Novel: Clarence Jordan); **Costumes:** John Falabella; **Lighting Designer:** Roger Morgan; **Musical Director:** Tom Chapin; **Set Design:** John Falabella

Songs: Agony Round; Are We Ready?; I Did It; It Isn't Easy; Jubilation; Mama Is Here; Sho' Nuff; Somethin's Brewin'; Spitball; There Ain't No Busy Signals; Turn It Around; We Got to Get Organized; We're Going to Atlanta; We're Gonna Love It; What Does Atlanta Mean to Me; When I Look Up; You Are Still My Boy

Cast: Scott Ainslie; Tom Key; Jim Lauderdale; Michael Mark

901 • COUNT ME IN

OPENED: 10/08/1942   Theatre: Ethel Barrymore
Musical   Broadway: 61

Composer: Ann Ronell
Lyricist: Ann Ronell
Librettist: Leo Brady; Walter Kerr
Producer: Chic Johnson; Ole Olsen; Messrs.
  Shubert
Director: Robert Ross

Choreographer: Robert Alton; **Costumes:** Irene
  Sharaff; **Musical Director:** John McManus;
  Orchestrations: Robert Russell Bennett; Hans
  Spialek; Don Walker; **Set Design:** Howard Bay;
  Vocal Arranger: Clay Warnick

Songs: All Out Bugle Call; On Leave for Love;
  Papa's Return; Someone in the Know;
  Ticketyboo; Way My Ancestors Went, The;
  We're Still on the Map; Who Is General Staff?;
  Why Do They Say They're the Fair Sex?; Woman
  of the Year, The; You've Got It All

Cast: Jean Arthur; Charles Butterworth; Luella
  Gear; Mary Healy; Hal LeRoy; June Preisser

902 • COUNT OF LUXEMBOURG, THE

OPENED: 09/16/1912   Theatre: New Amsterdam
Musical   Broadway: 120

Composer: Franz Lehar
Lyricist: Basil Hood; Glen MacDonough; Adrian
  Ross
Librettist: Glen MacDonough
Producer: Klaw & Erlanger
Director: Herbert Gresham

Source: DER GRAF VON LUXEMBURG (Musical:
  Robert Bodanzky; Franz Lehar; A.M. Willner);
  Choreographer: Julian Mitchell; **Costumes:**
  Comelli; **Lighting Designer:** Frank Detering;
  Musical Director: Anton Heindl

Songs: Are You Going to Dance (L: Basil Hood);
  Bohemia [3] (L: Basil Hood); Boys [3] (L: Adrian
  Ross); Carnival! (L: Basil Hood); Carnival for
  Life, A (L: Adrian Ross); Count of Luxembourg,
  The (L: Adrian Ross); Cousins of the Czar
  (L: Basil Hood); Day Dreams; Finale Act I
  (L: Adrian Ross); Hail Angele, Our Nightingale
  (L: Adrian Ross); Her Glove [3] (L: Adrian Ross);
  I Am in Love (L: Basil Hood); In Society

(L: Adrian Ross); Kukuska (dance) (inst.) [3];
Land of Make Believe; Love Breaks Every Bond
(L: Basil Hood); Love, Good-Bye [1]; Love Spats;
Luxembourg Valse; Make the Most of Carnival!;
Pierrette and Pierrot [3] (L: Basil Hood); Pretty
Butterfly [3] (L: Basil Hood); Remind Me [2];
Rootsie-Pootsie (L: Basil Hood; Adrian Ross);
Say Not Love Is a Dream (Valse-Song) (L: Basil
Hood); Twenty Thousand Pounds [2] (L: Adrian
Ross); Wedding March, The

Cast: George Monroe; Frank Moulan; Ann
  Swinburne; Fred Walton

Notes: Lyricists are credited from London vocal
  score, before MacDonough Americanized the
  lyrics. [1] Out Boston 8/26/12. [2] Sheet music.
  [3] London vocal score only.

903 • COUNTER MELODY

OPENED: 1948
Musical   Unproduced

Composer: Peter De Rose
Lyricist: Otto Harbach

Songs: Hands Off; It's So Easy to Sing (About
  Things in the Southland); Let Us Dance Till the
  Dawn; No Used Actin' Coy with a Boy from
  Illinois

Notes: Information from ASCAP/Library of
  Congress.

904 • COUNTESS COQUETTE

OPENED: 02/28/1913
Musical   Closed out of town

Composer: Anatole Friedland
Lyricist: Melville Alexander
Producer: Charles Sinclair

Source: UNKNOWN (Musical: Marcel Janvier)

Songs: And It Rained, Rained, Rained; Do Not
  Wed at All; Hello, Cupid Send me a Fellow; Let's
  Be Happy; Off to Maxim's; Oh Pity Poor Old
  Solomon; On Parade; Opening Chorus Act I;
  Parisian Flip, The; Picture of Real Life, The; Pink
  Poodle, The; Pity Poor Old Solomon; Saxophone,
  The; Spring Time; Vacation Days; Way to Kiss,
  The; We Want Our Wages; Wonderful Land of
  Romance

Cast: Vera Allen; Harry Paull; Templar Saxe; Maude Williams

Notes: Program of Lincoln, Nebraska.

905 • COUNTESS MARITZA
OPENED: 09/18/1926   Theatre: Shubert
Musical   Broadway: 321

Composer: Emmerich Kalman
Lyricist: Harry B. Smith
Librettist: Harry B. Smith
Producer: J.J. Shubert; Lee Shubert
Director: J.C. Huffman

Source: GRAFIN MARIZA (Musical: Julius Brammer; Alfred Grunwald); **Choreographer:** Jack Mason; Carl Randall; **Musical Director:** Leon Leonardi; **Set Design:** Watson Barratt

Songs: Brown-Eyed Girl; (Come at the) Call of Love (C: Al Goodman); Dear Home of Mine, Goodbye; Don't Tempt Me; Flirtation Dance; Golden Dreams (C: Harry K. Morton); Gypsy Passion [3]; Hola, Follow, Follow Me (Song of Greeting); I'll Keep on Dreaming; In the Days Gone By; Love Has Found My Heart [1] (C: Al Goodman); Make Up Your Mind; Music Thrills Me, The; One I'm Looking For, The; Play Gypsies, Dance Gypsies; Say Yes, Sweetheart, Say Yes [2]; Sister Mine [2]; Who Am I?; Why Is the World So Changed Today?; Why Work and Slave All Day [3]

Cast: Yvonne D'Arle; Harry K. Morton; Carl Randall; Walter Woolf

Notes: [1] Melody revised by Alfred Goodman. [2] Sheet music only. [3] ASCAP/Library of Congress only.

906 • COUNTRY GIRL, A (1902)
OPENED: 09/22/1902   Theatre: Daly's
Musical   Broadway: 112

Composer: Lionel Monckton
Lyricist: Adrian Ross
Librettist: James T. Tanner
Producer: Augustin Daly
Director: J.C. Duff

Costumes: Percy Anderson; **Set Design:** Walter Burridge; Henry E. Hoyt

Songs: Arcadians, The; Beware; Boy and Girl; Come Down to Devonshire [3]; Coo! (C: Paul Rubens; L: Percy Greenbank); Coronation, The; Dance for Jack, A [2]; Dear Little Maid; Finale Act I; Finale Act II; Hail to the King!; I Can Laugh, I Can Love (C: Paul Rubens; L: Percy Greenbank); In the King's Name — Stand!; It Will All Come Right [2] (L: Rutland Barrington; Adrian Ross); Language of Love, The [2]; Molly the Marchioness; Mr. & Mrs. Brown (C: Paul Rubens; L: Percy Greenbank); Mrs. Quinton Raikes; My Crinoline [3]; My Little Girlie [2] (C: Leedham Bantock; L: Frank Tours); My Own Little Girl; My Partners (C: Arthur Bruhns; L: Adrian Ross); Not the Little Boy She Knew [2] (C: Paul Rubens; L: Percy Greenbank); Peace! Peace!; Pink Hungarian Band, The; Pixies [3]; Quarreling (C: Paul Rubens; L: Percy Greenbank); Rajah of Bhong, The; Real Smart Set, The [2]; Sailor Man, The [3]; Sailor's Life, The (C/L: Traditional); Season, The [2]; She's Acting [2] (C: Paul Rubens; L: Percy Greenbank); Shooting; Take Your Pretty Partner; There's Plenty of Love in the World [3]; Try Again, Johnny; Two Little Chicks (C: Paul Rubens; L: Percy Greenbank); Under the Deodar; When I Was a Country Girl [2] (C/L: Richard Temple); When I Was a Girl [2] (C: Paul Rubens; L: Percy Greenbank); When the Birds Begin to Sing; Worst Woman in London, The [2]; Yo Ho, Little Girls, Yo Ho!

Cast: Minnie Ashley; Adine Bouvier; Grace Freeman; William Norris; Melville Stewart

Notes: No songs listed in New York program. Songs listed from London vocal score. [1] From sheet music only. [2] Added after London opening. [3] Added to London revival in 1914.

907 • COUNTRY GIRL, THE (1911)
OPENED: 1911   Theatre: Peoples
Musical   New York

Composer: Perlmutter; Wohl
Lyricist: H. Altman

Songs: As du Kenst Nit un Weist Nit, Nemt Man Sich Nit Unter; Bist Mein Krein, Mein Welt; Das Bissele Erd; Frauen-Rechte

Cast: B. Bernstein

Notes: A Yiddish show. No other information available.

908 • COUPLA WHITE CHICKS SITTING AROUND TALKING, A

OPENED: 04/20/1980 Theatre: Astor Place
Play Off-Broadway: 440

Composer: Loudon Wainwright III
Lyricist: Loudon Wainwright III
Author: John Ford Noonan
Producer: Maryellen Flynn; Sweet Olive, Inc.; Bonnie Weeks
Director: Dorothy Lyman

Costumes: Gary Lisz; **Lighting Designer:** F. Mitchell Dana; **Set Design:** Charles Cosler

Cast: Eileen Brennan; Susan Sarandon

Notes: No songs listed in program.

909 • COURT BY GIRLS

OPENED: 1913
Musical Closed out of town

Composer: Max S. Witt
Lyricist: Thomas J. Gray
Producer: Max S. Witt
Director: Lester Brown

Songs: Come and Take Me Out of Lonely Land

Cast: Joe Enico; Lena Pinaud; Estelle Thebaud; Helene Violette

Notes: No other information available. A vaudeville musical.

910 • COURTESAN, THE

OPENED: 1923
Musical Closed out of town

Composer: Jean Schwartz
Lyricist: Harold Atteridge
Librettist: Harold Atteridge; Harry Wagstaff Gribble
Producer: Messrs. Shubert
Director: J.C. Huffman

Choreographer: Alexander Demidoff; M. Francis Weldon; **Costumes:** Travis Banton; Erte; **Musical Director:** Al Goodman

Songs: After You Feed the Little Chickens They Want a Little Chicken Feed; At the Stage Door; Dancing; Doing the Apache (C: Sigmund Romberg); First Lesson, The [1] (L: E. Ray Goetz; William Jerome); Follow the Midnight Sun [1] (L: E. Ray Goetz; William Jerome); In the Cottage of My Heart; Love in a Haystack; Madame Pompadour [1] (C: Sigmund Romberg; Jean Schwartz); Radiant Diamonds (C: Sigmund Romberg); Welcome America; When I Look at You; When the Sandman's on His Way (C: Sigmund Romberg); When You Love; Why Should I Let You? [1] (C: Sigmund Romberg; Jean Schwartz); Yankee Doodle Oo-La-La, The

Cast: Donald Brian; Nancy Carroll; Herbert Corthell; Alice Delysia; Dolores; Fay Marbe; Harry McNaughton; Barnett Parker

Notes: Program 10/23 New Haven. [1] Sheet music only.

911 • COURTIN' TIME

OPENED: 06/13/1951 Theatre: National
Musical Broadway: 37

Composer: Don Walker
Lyricist: Jack Lawrence
Librettist: William Roos
Producer: Michael Ellis; James Russo
Director: Alfred Drake

Source: FARMER'S WIFE, THE (Play: Eden Phillpotts);**Choreographer:** George Balanchine; **Costumes:** Saul Bolasni; **Dance Arranger:** Bill Jonson; **Lighting Designer:** Ralph Alswang; **Musical Director:** Robert Zeller; **Orchestrations:** Don Walker; **Set Design:** Ralph Alswang; **Vocal Arranger:** Don Walker

Songs: Araminta to Herself; Choose Your Partner; Fixin' for a Long Cold Winter; Golden Moment; Goodbye, Dear Friend, Goodbye; Heart in Hand; I Do! He Doesn't!; Johnny Ride the Sky; Maine Will Remember the Maine; Man Never Marries a Wife, A [1]; Masculinity; Old-Fashioned Glimmer in Your Eye, An; Sensible Thing to Do, The; Smile Awhile; Today at Your House, Tomorrow at Mine; Too Much Trouble; Wishbone Song, The

Cast: Joe E. Brown; Carmen Mathews; Billie Worth

Notes: [1] ASCAP/Library of Congress only.

912 • COURTSHIP OF MILES STANDISH, THE

OPENED: 1957
Musical   Unproduced

Composer: Mary Rodgers
Lyricist: Mary Rodgers; Leslie Stevens
Librettist: Mary Rodgers; Leslie Stevens

Songs: Another Find Day; Clap Your Hands All Ye People; Fair Plymouth Maiden; If You Ask; Mayflower Will Sail, The; Mistress Mullen and Master Alden; On My Wedding Day; So Near and Yet So Far; What a Lovely Wife; Where's the Funeral

913 • COUSIN LUCY

OPENED: 08/27/1915   Theatre: Cohan
Musical   Broadway: 43

Composer: Jerome Kern
Lyricist: Schuyler Greene
Librettist: Charles Klein
Producer: A.H. Woods
Director: Robert Milton

Songs: Cheer Up, Eat and Grow Thin [3] (C/L: E. Ray Goetz); I'm at Your Service Girls (C: Ted D. Ward; L: Edward Grossmith); I've Loved Only Once (C/L: Unknown); Keep Going; Society; Sweetheart (C: Percy Wenrich; L: Edward Madden); Those Come Hither Eyes [2]; Two Heads Are Better Than One [1] (L: Schuyler Greene; Jerome Kern); When You Skate with a Wonderful Girl (C/L: Unknown)

Cast: Leo Donnelly; Julian Eltinge; Jane Oaker; Olive Tell

Notes: [1] Later the music was adapted to "There's No Better Use for Time That Kissing" in ROCK-A-BYE BABY. [2] Same music as "That 'Come Hither' Look in THEODORE AND CO. [3] ASCAP/Library of Congress only.

914 • COW PATTYS, THE

OPENED: 1995
Revue

Composer: Donna Stevens
Lyricist: Donna Stevens
Librettist: Adrienne Braswell; Joy Cunningham; C.K. McFarland; Donna Stevens

Arrangements: Tom Hale; Thomas Hart; Gary Powell; Mary Reynolds; **Lighting Designer:** Root Choyce; David Rose; **Set Design:** Reina

Songs: Bobbi McGee [1] (C/L: Kris Kristofferson); Cow Patty (C/L: Jim Stafford); If Jesus Was a Cowboy; M Word (C/L: Emily Kaitz; Chuck Rich); Picture (C/L: Vivian Thompson); She-Ro (C/L: Adrienne Braswell; Donna Stevens); Texas Lullabye; Tumblin Down; Why Don't Ya Waltz with Me?; Wrangler

Cast: Adrienne Braswell; Joy Cunningham; C.K. McFarland; Donna Stevens

Notes: Produced at Casa Manana in Fort Worth, Texas. Credits were difficult to ascertain since they were listed in a cutsy fashion, i.e. Safecracker, Pony Express, Trail Boss, etc. [1] Not written for show.

915 • COWBOY

OPENED: 08/19/1975

Composer: Richard Riddle
Lyricist: Richard Riddle
Librettist: Jess Gregg
Producer: Goodspeed Opera House
Director: Robert Tucker

Choreographer: Robert Tucker; **Costumes:** David Toser; **Lighting Designer:** Peter M. Ehrhardt; **Musical Director:** Lynn Crigler; **Set Design:** Fred Voelpel

Songs: Charlie; Cowboy; Dutchman's Pants, The; Goin' East; Hey, Kid!; Horse; Hunker Down Cowboy; I'll Dream Your Dream; Loud and Tacky; Montana; Pass the Bread and Butter; Seems to Me; Singin' to 'Em; Waste of Rice, A; You Look Like My Valley

Cast: David Canary; Zan Charisse; Travis Hudson; Gary Sandy; Nicholas Wyman

Notes: Goodspeed Opera House.

916 • COWBOY AND THE LEGEND, THE

OPENED: 09/16/1980
Musical   Closed out of town

Composer: Hal Hester

Lyricist: Benjamin Bradford; Hal Hester; Chandler Warren
Librettist: Benjamin Bradford
Producer: Cecil Gorey; N.E.T.W.O.R.K.
Director: William Martin

Choreographer: Bick Goss; Costumes: Frank J. Boros; Lighting Designer: Paul Lindsay Butler; Musical Director: Hal Hester; Set Design: Frank J. Boros

Songs: Ain't Never Gonna Find Another Love Song; Blues; Boy, Do I Need You Now; Cowboy; Do I Take Him Back?; Don't Make Me Cry; I Am Small; I Belong to the World; Loner, The; Lookin' for Me; Morning Star; No Substitute for a Man; One Day at a Time; Romper Room; Secrets; Time to Get Movin'; Wasn't I Loved By You; Welcome to a Small Town; Where in the World; You Make Me Oh, So Glad to Be Me

Cast: Eartha Kitt; Tuck Milligan

917 • COWBOY GIRL, THE

OPENED: 1906
Musical   Closed out of town

Composer: W.R. Williams
Lyricist: Lem B. Parker
Librettist: Lem B. Parker
Producer: Kilroy & Britton

Musical Director: H.E. Sigman

Songs: All the World's in Love; Boston Tourist Girls; Cowboy Girl, The; Four Bad Men from Arizona; He Treated Me White; If the Man in the Moon Were a Coon [1] (C/L: Fred Fisher); Little Girlie You Have Caught My Eye [1] (C: Charles E. Mullen; L: Harold Atteridge); Opening Chorus; Song of the Saved, The; There's a Room to Rent in My Heart for You; There's No Fool Like an Old Fool; We're Woolly Westerners; Whittling [3]; Wouldn't You Like to Flirt with Me? [2]

Cast: Billy Denere; Ray Raymond; Julia Rowland

Notes: Program 10/11/1906 Toledo. [1] Sheet music only. [2] Out Wilkes-Barre 1/20/07. [3] Titled "Whistling" in Wilkes-Barre program although sheet calls it "Whittling."

918 • CRADLE SONG

Notes: *See KALEIDOSCOPE (1987).*

919 • CRADLE WILL ROCK, THE

OPENED: 01/03/1938   Theatre: Windsor
Musical   Broadway: 104

Composer: Marc Blitzstein
Lyricist: Marc Blitzstein
Librettist: Marc Blitzstein
Producer: Sam H. Grisman; John Houseman; Mercury Theatre
Director: Orson Welles

Musical Director: Marc Blitzstein; Orchestrations: Marc Blitzstein

Songs: Ah, There You Are; Art for Art's Sake; Cradle Will Rock, The; Croon-Spoon; Do I Have to Say?; Doctor and Ella; Drugstore Scene; Ex-Foreman; Freedom of the Press, The; Gus and Sadie Love Song; Hard Times; Honolulu; Hotel Lobby Scene; Hurry Up and Telephone; I'm Checkin' Home Now; Joe Worker; Leaflets; Let's Do Something; Listen, Fellas!; Lovely Morning; Moll's Song; Mrs. Mister and Reverend Salvation; Nickel Under the Foot; Oh, What a Filthy Night Court; Polyphonic; Rich, The; So That's the Way; Stuck Like a Sandwich; Summer Weather; Triple Flank Maneuver; War! War!

Cast: John Adair; Marc Blitzstein; Peggy Condray; Howard Da Silva; Will Geer; Le Roi Operti; Hiram Sherman; Olive Stanton

Notes: This show's first performance was at the Venice Theater on 6/16/137. It played the Venice for two weeks in defiance of the WPA. The show later toured the country and played a few weekend performances. The production listed herein was the first commerical production.

920 • CRANKS

OPENED: 11/26/1956   Theatre: Bijou
Revue   Broadway: 40

Composer: John Addison
Lyricist: John Addison; John Cranko
Producer: Richard Charlton; John Krimsky
Director: John Cranko

Lighting Designer: Paul Morrison; Musical Director: Anthony Bowles; Set Design: John Piper

Songs: Adrift; Arthur, Son of Martha; Blue; Chiromancy; Cold Comfort; Dirge; Don't Let

Him Know You; Goodnight; I'm the Boy (You Should Say 'Yes' To); Metamorphosis; Sea Song; Telephone Tango; Valse Anglaise; Where Has Tom Gone?; Who Is It Always There?; Who's Who; Would You Let Me Know?

Cast: Hugh Bryant; Anthony Newley; Annie Ross; Gilbert Vernon

921 • CRAZY FOR YOU
OPENED: 02/19/1992　　Theatre: Shubert
Musical　　　　　　　Broadway

Composer: George Gershwin
Lyricist: Ira Gershwin
Librettist: Ken Ludwig
Producer: Roger Horchow; Elizabeth Williams
Director: Michael Ockrent

Source: GIRL CRAZY (Musical: Guy Bolton; George Gershwin; Ira Gershwin; John McGowan); **Choreographer:** Susan Stroman; **Costumes:** William Ivey Long; **Dance Arranger:** Peter Howard; **Lighting Designer:** Paul Gallo; **Musical Director:** Paul Gemignani; **Orchestrations:** William D. Brohn; **Set Design:** Robin Wagner

Songs: Bidin' My Time; But Not for Me; Could You Use Me; Embraceable You; I Can't Be Bothered Now; I Got Rhythm; K-ra-zy for You; Naughty Baby (L: Desmond Carter; Ira Gershwin); Nice Work If You Can Get It; Real American Folk Song Is a Rag, The; Shall We Dance?; Slap That Bass; Someone to Watch Over Me; Stiff Upper Lip; They Can't Take That Away from Me; Things Are Looking Up; Tonight's the Night (L: Ira Gershwin; Gus Kahn); What Causes That?

Cast: Bruce Adler; Jodi Benson; Gerry Burkhardt; Ronn Carroll; Jane Connell; Harry Groener; Michael Kubala; Manhattan Rhythm Kings

Notes: Still running as of this writing. No original songs in this production.

922 • CRAZY NOW
OPENED: 09/10/1972　　Theatre: Eden
Revue　　　　　　　　Off-Broadway: 1

Composer: Norman Sachs
Lyricist: Maura Cavanagh; Richard Smithies
Librettist: Richard Smithies

Producer: B.F. Concerts
Director: Voigt Kempson

Choreographer: Voigt Kempson; **Costumes:** Margaret Tobin; **Lighting Designer:** Wilson King; **Musical Director:** Jim Litt

Songs: Algae; Beautiful; Crazy Now; Dirty Mind; Get Naked; Great Connection; Hard Times; Highway Narrows; Marginal People; Regulation Purple; Shaftway Danger; Sherman's Mom; Something to Do with My Hands; Tears; Toll Basket

Cast: Carla Benjamin; William Buell; Glenn Mure; Rosalie; John Scoullar

923 • CRAZY QUILT
Notes: *See BILLY ROSE'S CRAZY QUILT.*

924 • CRAZY WITH THE HEAT
OPENED: 01/14/1941　　Theatre: 44th Street
Revue　　　　　　　　Broadway: 99

Composer: Dana Suesse
Lyricist: Dana Suesse
Librettist: Lew Brown; Arthur Stander; Sidney Zelinka
Producer: Kurt Kasznar
Director: Kurt Kasznar

Choreographer: Catherine Littlefield; Carl Randall; **Costumes:** Maria Humans; Lester Polakov; **Dance Arranger:** Jacques Dallin; **Lighting Designer:** Albert Johnson; **Musical Director:** Harold Levey; **Orchestrations:** Jacques Dallin; **Set Design:** Albert Johnson; **Vocal Arranger:** Jacques Dallin

Songs: Afternoon of a Black Faun [3]; Air Conditioning [3] (C/L: John Latouche); But Where Is Love [3] (C/L: Charlotte Kent); Crazy with the Heat (1) [3] (C: Rudi Revil; L: Carl Kent; Walter Nones); Crazy with the Heat (2) (C: Rudi Revil; L: Irvin Graham); Day Before Yesterday (1) [3] (C: Rudi Revil; L: Luther Cleveland; John Latouche); Day Before Yesterday (2) (C: Rudi Revil; L: John Latouche); Dying to Meet You [3] (C: Frederick Ney; L: Gus Schirmer Jr.); Going Up [3] (C: Carl Kent; L: Kurt Kasznar); Great American Roof, The (C/L: Carl Kent; L: Walter Nones); Hour for

Lunch [3] (C: Rudi Revil; L: Luther Cleveland; John Latouche); How Far Is It to Broadway? [3]; I Don't Need the Moonlight [3]; I Guess I'll Have to Count Some Sheep [3]; I Put It Right Back Where I Found It [3]; Il Pleurait [1] (C: Rudi Revil; L: Maurice Vandair); I'm a Bundle from Britain [2] (C/L: Lois Long; Don Thorburn); It Should Happen to Me [1] (C: Elsie Thompson; L: Richard Kollmar); Life with Father [3] (C/L: Milton Berle; Jack Rose); Male Animal, The (C/L: Milton Berle; Jack Rose); Old Ghosts for Ancient Castles, Extended Ltd. [3] (C: Rudi Revil; L: John Latouche); Oyster [3] (C/L: Walter Nones); Really Quite Armless [3] (C: Luther Davis; L: John Cleveland); Sascha's Got a Girl (C/L: Irvin Graham); Some Day (C: Rudi Revil; L: Kurt Kasznar; Carl Kent); Sweetie Pie [3] (C: Rudi Revil; L: Kurt Kasznar; Carl Kent); This Way Out [1] (C/L: Unknown); Three Blind Mice [3]; Three Little Maids [3]; Three Smart Girls [3]; Three Smarter Girls [3]; Time of Your Life (C: William Provost; L: Pete Kite Smith); Twist of the Wrist (C/L: Irvin Graham); Walking with Miss Harkness [3] (C: Rudi Revil; L: Kurt Kasznar; John Latouche); Who's to Blame (C/L: Vernon Duke); Yacht Song [1] (C/L: Walter Nones); Yes My Darling Daughter (C/L: Jack Lawrence); You Should Be Set to Music (C/L: Irvin Graham)

Cast: Luella Gear; Willie Howard; Marie Nash; Carl Randall

Notes: After seven performances the show moved to the 46th Street Theater for an additiional 92 performances. [1] Cut after opening. [2] Added after opening. [3] Cut 7/29/40.

925 • CREOLE FOLLIES, THE (FIRST EDITION)

OPENED: 01/1924
Revue

Theatre: Club Alabam
Nightclub

Musical Director: Fletcher Henderson

Cast: Arthur Bryson; Fletcher Henderson and His Orchestra; Maude Mills; Edith Wilson

Notes: No program available. The Club Alabam was in the basement of the 44th Street Theatre Building at 216 W. 44th Street. The space was previously titled the Little Club and then the Club Balagan.

926 • CREOLE FOLLIES, THE (SECOND EDITION)

OPENED: 03/1924
Revue

Theatre: Club Alabam
Nightclub

Producer: Harry Goldberg

Musical Director: Fletcher Henderson

Cast: Andy Razaf; Doc Straine; Edith Wilson

Notes: No program available.

927 • CREOLE FOLLIES, THE (THIRD EDITION)

OPENED: 1924
Revue

Theatre: Club Alabam
Nightclub

Producer: Harry Goldberg

Songs: Honeysuckle Rose [1] (C/L: Andy Razaf)

Cast: Andy Razaf; Sam Wooding and His Orchestra

Notes: No other information available. [1] Not the same song as Razaf, Waller and Brooks' standard. Only the title is shared.

928 • CRICKET ON THE HEARTH

OPENED: 12/18/1967   Theatre: NBC
TV Musical

Composer: Maury Laws
Lyricist: Jules Bass
Librettist: Romeo Muller; Arthur Rankin Jr.
Producer: Jules Bass; Arthur Rankin Jr.
Director: Jules Bass; Arthur Rankin Jr.

Arrangements: Perry Botkin Jr.; Norman Luboff; Wayne Robinson; **Musical Director:** Perry Botkin Jr.; Sid Feller; Norman Luboff

Songs: Cricket on the Hearth; Don't Give Your Love Away; First Christmas, The; Fish 'n' Chips; Parade of the Toys (inst.); Smiles Go with Tears; That Was Yesterday; Through My Eyes; Waltz for Christmas, A (inst.)

Cast: Ed Ames; Hans Conried; Paul Frees; Abbe Lane; Norman Luboff Choir; Roddy McDowall; Danny Thomas; Marlo Thomas

Notes: Original TV musical.

929 • CRINOLINE GIRL

OPENED: 03/16/1914   Theatre: Knickerbocker
Musical   Broadway: 88

Composer: Percy Wenrich
Lyricist: Julian Eltinge
Librettist: Otto Harbach
Producer: A.H. Woods
Director: John Emerson

Costumes: Julian Eltinge; **Musical Director:**
J. Albert Browne

Songs: Game of Eyes; In My Dream of You; That
Tempting Tango; When Martha Was a Girl

Cast: Herbert Corthell; Julian Eltinge; Helen
Luttrell; Joseph S. Marba; Herbert McKenzie;
James C. Spottswood; Edna Whistler

930 • CRISS CROSS

OPENED: 10/12/1926   Theatre: Globe
Musical   Broadway: 210

Composer: Jerome Kern
Lyricist: Anne Caldwell; Otto Harbach
Librettist: Anne Caldwell; Otto Harbach
Producer: Charles Dillingham
Director: R.H. Burnside

Choreographer: David Bennett; **Musical Director:**
Alfred Newman; **Orchestrations:** Robert Russell
Bennett; Maurice DePackh; **Set Design:** James
Reynolds

Songs: Ali Baba Babies, The; Bread and Butter [1];
Cinderella Girl; Cinderella's Ride; Criss Cross
[1]; Dance of the Camel Boys; Dance of the
Four Leaf Clovers; Dance of the Golden Sprite;
Dear Algerian Land; Dreaming of Allah;
Flap-a-Doodle; Hydrophobia Blues; I Love My
Little Susie (Camel Song) (L: Anne Caldwell); In
Araby with You [3] (L: Oscar Hammerstein II;
Otto Harbach); Indignation Meeting; Kiss a Four
Leaf Clover [1]; Leaders of the Modern Regime;
Portrait Parade, The; Rose of Delight; She's on
Her Way; (I Love My Little) Susie (L: Anne
Caldwell); That Little Something [4] (L: Bert
Kalmar; Harry Ruby); Travelogue; You
Will-Won't You? [2]

Cast: Dorothy Francis; George Herman; Oscar
"Rags" Ragland; Dorothy Stone; Fred Stone

Notes: [1] Cut out of town. [2] Same music as
"Bought and Paid For" in THE LAUGHING
HUSBAND and "I've Looked for Trouble" in
London version of SUNNY. [3] Same music as
"I Can't Forget Your Eyes" in OH, I SAY! and as
"Sunshine" in SUNNY. [4] Added to tour after
New York. Later in LUCKY.

931 • CROSS MY HEART

OPENED: 09/17/1928   Theatre: Knickerbocker
Musical   Broadway: 64

Composer Harry Tierney
Lyricist: Joseph McCarthy
Librettist: Daniel Kussell
Producer: Sammy Lee
Director: John Harwood

Costumes: Mabel E. Johnston; **Musical Director:**
Louis Gress; **Orchestrations:** Maurice DePackh;
Set Design: P. Dodd Ackerman

Songs: Arrival of Guests; Come Along, Sunshine;
Dream Sweetheart; Good Days and Bad Days;
Hot Sands [1]; In the Gardens of Noor-Ed-Deen;
Lady Whippoorwill; Reception; Right Out of
Heaven Into My Arms; Salaaming the Rajah;
Scheherazade Serenade; Sold; Step Up and Pep
Up the Party; Such Is Fame; Thanks for a Darn
Nice Time; We'll Have Our Good Days [2]

Cast: Edgar Fairchild; Mary Lawlor; Lulu
McConnell; Clarence Nordstrom; Ralph Rainger;
Bobby Watson

Notes: [1] Out Bronx 11/19/28. [2] Sheet music
only.

932 • CROSS YOUR FINGERS

OPENED: 05/04/1956
Revue

Librettist: Joe Coogan; Mary Pat Daley;
Rev. Gilbert V. Hartke; Dan Rodden
Director: Rev. Gilbert V. Hartke

Choreographer: Carole Macho; **Musical Director:**
Danny Ruslander; **Orchestrations:** Norman
Katz; **Set Design:** J. Waring

Songs: BBIWY Blues (C/L: Jim Radomski);
Calypso (C/L: James Radomski); Country Girl
(C: Danny Ruslander; L: Eithne Tabor); Cross

Your Fingers (C: Danny Ruslander; L: James Elward); Dream (C/L: Dorothy Sennett); Here I Go Again (C/L: Jim Radomski); Hot Rod (C: Danny Ruslander; L: James Bateman); I Almost Asked You to Marry Me (C/L: Jim Radomski); Madly for Adlai (C/L: Jim Radomski); Mr. Bluebeard (C/L: Jim Radomski); My Billy Boy (C: Danny Ruslander; L: Eithne Tabor); Nancy (C: Danny Ruslander; L: Eithne Tabor); People Are No Damn Good (C/L: James Radomski); Professor Hossenpfeffer's Saucer-Sighters (C: Danny Ruslander; L: Barbara Birmingham); Spring (C: Danny Ruslander; L: James Bateman); Trinket Vendor (C: Danny Ruslander; L: Paul DiGiovanni); West Is Best (C: Roberta Beckman; L: Barbara Birmingham)

Cast: Philip Bosco; Wilma Burke; Mart Crowley[2]; Paul Di Giovanni; Nancy Dunkle; Molly Holden; Jim Radomski[1]

Notes: Amateur show. Catholic University. [1] Later known as James Rado, coauthor of HAIR. [2] Author of BOYS IN THE BAND.

933 • CRUCIBLE, THE
OPENED: 01/22/1953   Theatre: Martin Beck
Play   Broadway: 197

Author: Arthur Miller
Producer: Kermit Bloomgarden
Director: Jed Harris

Costumes: Edith Lutyens; **Set Design:** Boris Aronson

Songs: Hymn (C/L: Alex Miller); Lullaby (C/L: Ann Ronell)

Cast: Jean Adair; Janet Alexander; Arthur Kennedy; E.G. Marshall; Madeleine Sherwood; Fred Stewart; Beatrice Straight

934 • CRUISE OF THE 'SUMMER GIRL', THE
Musical

Composer: Victor Beigel; Reginald De Koven; Melville Ellis; Aime Lauchaume; William F. Peters; B. Sherman-Fowler; Richard Henry Warren; Safford Waters
Lyricist: J. Cheever Goodwin; Harry B. Smith; Safford Waters

Librettist: Louis Fitzgerald Jr.
Producer: Strollers, The
Director: Frank Smithson

Musical Director: Richard Henry Warren

Songs: Actors in Society; Butterflies of Fashion; Chaparone Song; Dusky Dream; Hotel Clerk's Song; Manana (C: Aime Lauchaume; L: J. Cheever Goodwin); Mandy; Mary Ann McManus; Mermaid Song; Merry Mummers; Opening Chorus; Polo Song; Summer Girl; There'll Be Trouble Sure; Yachting Song; You and I Love

Cast: Louis Fitzgerald Jr.; Grace Hoyt; May Irwin; Margaret Wheeler

Notes: Songs not listed in program — just described! A Christmas presentation of The Strollers at the Grand Ballroom of the Waldorf-Astoria.

935 • CRY FOR US ALL
OPENED: 04/08/1970   Theatre: Broadhurst
Musical   Broadway: 9

Composer: Mitch Leigh
Lyricist: William Alfred; Phyllis Robinson
Librettist: William Alfred
Producer: C. Gerald Goldsmith; Mitch Leigh
Director: Albert Marre

Source: HOGAN'S GOAT (Play: William Alfred); **Choreographer:** Todd Bolender; **Costumes:** Robert Fletcher; **Lighting Designer:** Howard Bay; **Musical Director:** Herbert Grossman; **Orchestrations:** Carlyle Hall, **Set Design:** Howard Bay

Songs: Aggie, Oh Aggie; Broken Heart, or the Wages of Sin, The; Call in to Her; Confessional, The; Cruelty Man, The; Cry for Us All; End of My Race, The; Home Free All; How Are You Since?; I Lost It; I Was the Slave [2]; I'm My Own Woman [2]; Leg of the Duck, The; Macula Non Est In Te [2]; Mayor's Chair, The; Search Your Heart [1]; See No Evil; Splendor of Her Gaze, The [2]; Swing Your Bag; Take My Hand [2]; That Slavery Is Love; This Cornucopian Land; Verandah Waltz, The; Where Are All the Good Times Gone [2]; Who to Love If Not a Stranger

Cast: Steve Arlen; Joan Diener; Helen Gallagher; William Griffis; Tommy Rall; Robert Weede; Dolores Wilson

Notes: [1] Added after opening. [2] Out New Haven 1/29/70.

936 • CRYRIS
Notes: *See FAD AND FANCY.*

937 • CRYSTAL HEART, THE
OPENED: 02/15/1960   Theatre: East 74th Street
Musical   Broadway: 9

Composer: Baldwin Bergersen
Lyricist: William Archibald
Librettist: William Archibald
Producer: Charles Kasher
Director: William Archibald

Choreographer: William Archibald; Costumes: Ted Van Griethuysen; Lighting Designer: Richard Casler; Musical Director: Baldwin Bergersen; Set Design: Richard Casler

Songs: Agnes and Me; Bluebird; D-O-G; Desperate; Fireflies; Girl with a Ribbon, A; Handsome Husbands; How Strange the Silence; I Must Paint; I Wanted to See the World; It Took Them; Lovely Bridesmaids; Lovely Island; Madam, I Beg You!; Monkey When He Loves, A; My Heart Won't Learn; Tea Party; When I Drank with My Love; Year Is a Day, A; Yes, Aunt

Cast: John Baylis; Mildred Dunnock; Bob Fitch; Bryon Mitchell; Joe Ross; Jeanne Shea; John Stewart; Virginia Vestoff

938 • CUPID AND CO
OPENED: 11/14/1904
Musical   Closed out of town

Composer: A. Baldwin Sloane
Lyricist: E. Tracy Sweet
Librettist: James A. Waldron
Director: Julien Barton

Musical Director: Leo O'Rourke

Songs: Be a Jolly Molly; Monkey Doodle Dandy; Moon Bird (C/L: Dempsey; Schmid); New Ideas (C/L: D.W. Reeves); Sing Us a Good Ragtime Song; You'll Come Back

Cast: Jessie Mae Hall; Jack Marvin; Robert Vaughn; Augusta West

Notes: Wilkes-Barre. Sloane and Sweet may have written a different CUPID AND COMPANY around the same time. The credits, songs, are for the Waldron version which came from a Patchogue, Long Island program. That program offered the following: "Suggestions to Patrons: Peanut eating positively forbidden."

939 • CUPID AT VASSAR
OPENED: 08/23/1907
Musical   Closed out of town

Composer: A. Baldwin Sloane
Lyricist: George Totten Smith
Librettist: Owen Davis
Producer: Jules Murry
Director: Herbert Hirschman

Costumes: Dorothy Neumann; Set Design: Alvin Colt

Songs: Christmas Tidings; College Glees [1]; Dear Daisy Chain; Fudge, Fudge, Fudge; Game of Basket Ball, The; I Only Want the Band to Play a Waltz for Me; I Won't Go Way Back Home Again; I'm Scared; In the Days When Grandma Dear Was Young; Poppy and the Pink, The; That's How I Love You

Cast: Florence Gear; Lillian Stephens

Notes: Waterbury, Conn. [1] Out 11/27/07 Cedar Rapids. This may not be a song per se, but rather college songs.

940 • CURL AND THE JUDGE, THE
OPENED: 1901   Theatre: Weber and Fields
                                  Music Hall
Musical   Broadway

Composer: John Stromberg
Lyricist: Edgar Smith
Librettist: Edgar Smith
Producer: Lew Fields; Joseph Weber

Cast: Lew Fields; Joseph Weber

Notes: No program available. A one-act burlesque on THE GIRL AND THE JUDGE.

941 • CURLEY MCDIMPLE
OPENED: 11/22/1967   Theatre: Bert Wheeler
Musical   Off-Broadway: 931

Composer: Robert Dahdah
Lyricist: Robert Dahdah
Librettist: Mary Boylan; Robert Dahdah
Producer: Curley Company, The
Director: Robert Dahdah

Costumes: John Hirsch; **Dance Arranger:** Bob Atwood; **Lighting Designer:** Barry Arnold; **Musical Director:** Bob Atwood; **Orchestrations:** Keith McClelland; **Set Design:** Richard Jackson

Songs: Are There Any More Rosie O'Grady's?; At the Playland Jamboree; Be Grateful for What You've Got; Cup of Coffee, A; Curley McDimple; Curley's the Girlie for Me [1]; Dancing in the Rain; Dwarf's Song; Hi De Hi De Hi, Hi De Hi De Ho; I Try; I've Got a Little Secret; Love Is the Loveliest Love Song; Meanest Man in Town, The; Something Nice Is Going to Happen; Stars and Lovers; Swing-a-Ding-a-Ling; You Little Monkey, You [1]

Cast: Norma Bigtree; Helon Blount; Paul Cahill; George Hillman; Bayn Johnson; Bernadette Peters

Notes: Butterfly McQueen was added to the cast on 5/9/68. [1] Cut after opening.

942 • CURSE OF AN ACHING HEART, THE

OPENED: 01/25/1982   Theatre: Little
Play   Broadway: 32

Composer: Claibe Richardson
Lyricist: William Alfred
Author: William Alfred
Producer: William Alfred; Margot Harley; John Houseman; Everett King; Sidney Shlenker; David Weil
Director: Gerald Gutierrez

Costumes: Nancy Potts; **Lighting Designer:** Dennis Parichy; **Orchestrations:** Bruce Pomahac; **Set Design:** John Lee Beatty

Songs: Ain't Love Grand; Give Us a Kiss [1]; I'm in Love with the Girl on the Car [2]; Love to Your Heart's Desire; Make It New; Spring, Spring, Spring [2]; Thorsping; Time Drags

Cast: Francine Beers; Faye Dunaway; Dale Helward; Bernie McInerney; Audrie Neenan

Notes: [1] Cut in previews. [2] Cut prior to New York.

943 • CURTAIN GOING UP

OPENED: 02/15/1952
Revue   Closed out of town

Librettist: George Axelrod; Mel Brooks; Charles Scheuer; Max Wilk
Producer: Mervyn Nelson

Choreographer: Paul Steffen; **Costumes:** Frank Thompson; **Lighting Designer:** Peggy Clark; **Musical Director:** Milton Rosenstock; **Orchestrations:** Don Walker; **Set Design:** Peggy Clark

Songs: Christmas Shopping (C/L: Bert Kalmar Jr.); Curtain Going Up (C/L: Michael Brown); Dance Hall (C/L: Michael Brown); Doctor Scholl (C/L: Charlotte Kent); Fall River Folly [1] (C/L: Michael Brown); Give Me Four Beats (C: Arthur Siegel; L: Charlotte Kent); I Gotta Make My Own Music (C: Arthur Siegel; L: Charlotte Kent); I Love You, I Love You, I Love You (C/L: Michael Brown); Indian Giver (C/L: Irvin Graham); Leave Them Wanting More (C: Dean Fuller; L: David Craig); Let Me Love You (C/L: Bart Howard); Lonely for My New York (C/L: Charlotte Kent); Lot of Lovin' (C/L: Charlotte Kent); Miss Rhinestone (C/L: Irvin Graham); Money (C/L: Ed Hein); Rich Woman (C/L: Irvin Graham); Swamp Boy (C/L: Michael Brown); Take Care of Yourself (C/L: Bart Howard); This Is the Day (C/L: Bart Howard); We Come to the Theatre (C/L: Charlotte Kent)

Cast: Phil Leeds; Alan Ross; Larry Storch

Notes: [1] Later in NEW FACES OF 1952 as "Lizzie Borden."

944 • CUT THE RIBBONS

OPENED: 09/20/1992   Theatre: Westside
Revue   Off-Broadway: 25

Composer: Nancy Ford
Lyricist: Mae Richard
Producer: George Elmer; Phase Three Productions
Director: Sue Lawless

Arrangements: Sande Campbell; Patti Wyss; Ron Zito; **Choreographer:** Sam Viverito; **Costumes:** Terrence O'Neill; **Lighting Designer:** Michael Hotopp; **Musical Director:** Sande Campbell; **Orchestrations:** Sande Campbell; Patti Wyss; Ron Zito; **Set Design:** Michael Hotopp

Songs: Am I Ready for This (C: Cheryl Hardwick); Balancing (C: Cheryl Hardwick); Because of Her (C: Mildred Kayden); Bed (C: Cheryl Hardwick); Cut the Ribbons; Door Is Closed, The; Four-Two-Two (C: Mildred Kayden); Her Career; I Dare You Not to Dance (C: Cheryl Hardwick); I Just Can't Move in Her Shadow; Instinct (C: Cheryl Hardwick); Isabel (C: Cheryl Hardwick); It's a Party (C: Cheryl Hardwick); Kick Me Again; Let Her Go; Lookin' Good (C: Cheryl Hardwick); Mom Will Be There (C: Mildred Kayden); Mommy Number Four (C: Mildred Kayden); Period Piece, A (C: Mildred Kayden); She Loves You (C: Mildred Kayden); T'ai Chi (C: Cheryl Hardwick); That Woman in the Mirror (C: Cheryl Hardwick); Try Not to Need Her (C: Mildred Kayden); Two-Two-Four (C: Mildred Kayden); Where's My Picture? (C: Mildred Kayden)

Cast: Georgia Engel; Barbara Feldon; Donna McKechnie

945 • CYRANO (1971)

OPENED: 05/02/1971
Musical   Yale University

Composer: David L. Shire
Lyricist: Richard Maltby Jr.
Librettist: Richard Maltby Jr.
Producer: Yale Univ. Dramatic Assn.
Director: Nikos Psacharopoulos

Source: CYRANO DE BERGERAC (Play: Edmond Rostand); **Choreographer:** Geoffrey Waddell; **Costumes:** Joy; **Lighting Designer:** Stephen Hamlin; **Musical Director:** Jay Brower; **Orchestrations:** Jay Brower; **Set Design:** John Conklin

Songs: As If for the First Time; Autumn; Balcony Trio; Cadet's March; Had You But Wit; I Love Someone; Let the Play Begin; Letter Comes, A; Lise Loves Everybody; My Love Is Like a Butterfly; Not Long Ago; Only Beautiful; Silly Little Dance of Life; Speak to Me of Love; Stargazer; Touch of Sweetness, A

Cast: David Adnopoz; Dick Cavett; John Cunningham; Bartlett Giamatti[1]; Bill Hinnant; John Jenkins; J. Jewett Langdon; Carrie Nye; Austin Pendleton; Tom Rummler; Toni Smith

Notes: An amateur musical. [1] This chorus member later grew up to become the commissioner of baseball.

946 • CYRANO (1973)

OPENED: 05/13/1973   Theatre: Palace
Musical   Broadway: 49

Composer: Michael J. Lewis
Lyricist: Anthony Burgess
Librettist: Anthony Burgess
Producer: APJAC International; Richard Gregson
Director: Michael Kidd

Source: CYRANO DE BERGERAC (Play: Edmond Rostand); **Costumes:** Desmond Heeley; **Lighting Designer:** Gilbert V. Hemsley Jr.; **Musical Director:** Thomas Pierson; **Orchestrations:** Philip J. Lang; **Set Design:** John Jensen

Songs: Almond Tarts [1]; Amorous Morons [1]; Autumn Carol; Bergerac; Capdedious [1]; Cyrano's Nose; From Now Till Forever; Gascon Flute Song [1]; Gascon Marching Song [1]; I Never Loved You; It's She and It's Me; La France, La France; Love Is Not Love; Man Without Words, A [1]; No, Thank You; Panache [1]; Panouche [1]; Paris Cuisine; Pocapdedious; Roxana; Tell Her; Thither, Thother, Thide of the The; You Have Made Me Love

Cast: Leigh Berry; Tovah Feldshuh; Patrick Hines; Mark Lamos; Christopher Plummer; Patricia Roos; Arnold Soboloff

Notes: [1] Out Guthrie Theatre, Minneapolis 1973.

947 • CYRANO DE BERGERAC (1899)

OPENED: 09/18/1899   Theatre: Knickerbocker

Composer: Victor Herbert
Lyricist: Harry B. Smith
Librettist: Stuart Reed
Director: A.M. Holbrook

Source: CYRANO DE BERGERAC (Play: Edmond Rostand)

Songs: Cadets of Gascony; Chorus of Poets; Come the Gallants of the Court; Diplomacy; Finale Act I; Finale Act II; Finale Act III; I Am a Court

Coquette; I Come from Gascony; I Must Marry a Handsome Man; I Wonder; King's Musketeers, The; Let the Sun of Thine Eyes; 'Neath Thy Window; Opening Chorus; Opening Chorus Act II; Over the Mountain; Ragueneau's Cafe; Since I Am Not for Thee; Song of the Nose; Those Were the Good Old Times

Cast: Charles H. Bowers; Lulu Glaser; A.M. Holbrook; Josephine Intropidi; Peter Lang; Frances Wilson; Laura Wise

948 • CYRANO DE BERGERAC (1932)

OPENED: 11/04/1932
Musical   Closed out of town

Composer: Samuel Pokrass
Lyricist: Charles O. Locke
Librettist: Charles O. Locke
Producer: Messrs. Shubert
Director: Edward Clarke Lilley

Source: CYRANO DE BERGERAC (Play: Edmond Rostand); **Choreographer:** Raymond Midgley; **Costumes:** Ernest Schrapps; **Set Design:** Watson Barratt

Songs: Cyrano; Lisette; Little Musketeer; Mamselle; My Nose; Pavanne; Shadow of a Kiss; Song of the Balcony; Song of the Gaston Cadets; Sweets to the Sweet; Tell Me of Love; True Love Is a Star; What My Lips Can Never Say; Woo Me

Cast: Gladys Baxter; Truman Gaige; George Hassell; George Houston; Allan Jones

Notes: Later titled ROXANNE. *See also THE WHITE PLUME*, a later production of this musical.

949 • CYRANO THE MUSICAL (1993)

OPENED: 11/21/1993   Theatre: Neil Simon
Musical   Broadway: 137

Composer: Ad Van Dijk
Lyricist: Peter Reeves; Koen Van Dijk
Additional Lyrics: Sheldon Harnick
Librettist: Koen Van Dijk
Producer: Peter T. Kulok; Joop Van Den Ende
Director: Eddy Habbema

Source: CYRANO DE BERGERAC (Play: Edmond Rostand); **Arrangements:** Tony Cox; **Costumes:** Yan Tax; **Lighting Designer:** Reiner Tweebeke; **Musical Director:** Constantine Kitsopoulos; **Set Design:** Paul Gallis

Songs: Aria; Balcony Scene; Battle, The; Confrontation; Courage Makes a Man; Cyrano's Story; Duel, The; Even Then; Evening Made for Lovers, An; Evening, The; Every Day, Every Night; Everything You Wrote; Hate Me; He Loves to Make Us Laugh; I Have No Words; Letter, The, Letter for Roxane, A; Loving Her; Message from Roxanne, A; Moonsong; Moonsong; Old Wound, An; One Fragment of a Moment; Opera, Opera; Poetry; Ragueneau's Patisserie; Rhyming Menu; Roxane's Confession; Stay with Me!; Tell Her Now; Two Musketeers; Visit from De Guiche; What a Reward; When I Write; Where's All This Anger Coming From; White Sash, A

Cast: Elizabeth Acosta; Jordan Bennett; Ed Dixon; Timothy Nolen; Anne Runolfsson; Paul Schoeffler; Paul Anthony Stewart; Bill Van Dijk

Notes: First produced in Amsterdam. Jordan Bennett appeared as Cyrano at certain performances. Peter Reeves wrote the English lyrics. Harnick supplied additional lyrics.

950 • CYRANOSE DE BRICABRAC

OPENED: 11/03/1898   Theatre: Weber & Fields
                       Broadway Mus. Hall
Musical   Broadway

Composer: John Stromberg
Librettist: Smith; Edgar Smith

Notes: No program available. Also included THE HEATHEN, a parody of THE CHRISTIAN.

D

951 • DAARLIN' JUNO

OPENED: 05/14/1976   Theatre: Long Wharf
Musical   Closed out of town: 28

Composer: Marc Blitzstein
Lyricist: Richard Maltby Jr.
Librettist: Geraldine Fitzgerald; Richard Maltby Jr.; Joseph Stein
Director: Arvin Brown

Source: JUNO (Musical: Marc Blitzstein; Joseph Stein); **Arrangements:** Thomas Fay; **Costumes:** Bill Walker; **Lighting Designer:** Ronald Wallace; **Musical Director:** Thomas Fay; **Set Design:** David Jenkins

Cast: Emery Battis; Joyce Ebert; Geraldine Fitzgerald; Sean Griffin; Suzanne Lederer; Milo O'Shea

Notes: *See JUNO.* This was a revial with new lyrics by Richard Maltby, Jr., and new songs by Thomas Fay and Richard Maltby, Jr. The book was rewritten by Geraldine Fitzgerald and Richard Maltby, Jr.

952 • DADDY GOODNESS

OPENED: 08/19/1979
Musical   Closed out of town

Composer: Ken Hirsch
Lyricist: Ron Miller
Librettist: Ron Miller; Shauneille Perry
Producer: Motown; Ashton Springer
Director: Phil Oesterman

Source: DADDY GOODNESS (Play: Louis Sapin; Richard Wright); **Choreographer:** Mike Malone; **Costumes:** Bernard Johnson; **Dance Arranger:** Danny Holgate; **Lighting Designer:** Jennifer Tipton; **Musical Director:** Lea Richardson; **Orchestrations:** Robert M. Freedman; **Set Design:** Santo Loquasto; **Vocal Arranger:** Danny Holgate

Songs: Big Business; Daddy's Decision; Don't Touch That Dial; Goodness Don't Come Easy When You're Bad; Hungry; I Don't Wanna Do It Alone No More; I Got Religion; Lottie's Purification; One More Step; Outside O' That You're Doin' Fine; People Make Me Cry; Spread Joy; True Love Is the Mother of Us All; We'll Let the People Decide; You're Home

Cast: Clifton Davis; Freda Payne; Rod Perry; Ted Ross; Dan Strayhorn

Notes: Closed 9/30/79 Washington D.C. Choral Arrangements: Chapman Roberts.

953 • DAFFY DILL

OPENED: 08/22/1922   Theatre: Apollo
Musical   Broadway: 69

Composer: Herbert Stothart
Lyricist: Oscar Hammerstein II
Librettist: Guy Bolton; Oscar Hammerstein II
Producer: Arthur Hammerstein
Director: Julian Mitchell

Costumes: Charles LeMaire; **Musical Director:** Herbert Stothart; **Set Design:** Clifford Pember

Songs: Captain Kidd's Kids; Chinky Chink; Cinderella Meets the Prince; Coachman's Heart, A; Doctor (L: Kenneth Keith); Fair Enough; I'll Build a Bungalow; I'm Fresh from the Country; Kindergarten Blues; Let's Play Hookey; My Boy Friend; My Little Redskin; One Flower That Blooms for You [1]; Pirate's Gold; Prince Charming; Tartar [1]; Two Little Ruby Rings; You Can't Lose Me [1]

Cast: Rollin Grimes; Genevieve Markam; Harry Mayo; Ben Mulvey; Georgia O'Ramey; Irene Olsen; Guy Robertson; Marion Sunshine; Frank Tinney

Notes: [1] Out Atlantic City 10/19/22.

954 • DAIRYMAIDS, THE

OPENED: 08/26/1907   Theatre: Criterion
Musical   Broadway: 86

Composer: Paul Rubens; Frank Tours

Lyricist: Arthur Wimperis
Librettist: Robert Courtneidge; A.M. Thompson
Producer: Charles Frohman

Songs: Beside the Country Stile (C: W.T. Francis; L: J.B. Loughrey); Cheer Up! Girls (C: Jerome Kern; L: M.E. Rourke); Dat Friend of Mine [2] (C: Egbert Van Alstyne; L: Harry Williams); Doctor Byrne (C: W.T. Francis; L: J.B. Loughrey); Down the Strand [2] (C/L: E.G. McLellan; Bernard Rolt); Dreamland; Good Night [2] (C: Paul Rubens; L: Unknown); Gymnasium Chorus [2] (C: Paul Rubens; L: Unknown); Hay Ride, The (C: Jerome Kern; L: M.E. Rourke); Home Again [2] (C/L: Frank Tours); How the Winds Blow [2] (C: Frank Tours; L: Unknown); Hullo! Little Stranger! (C/L: Paul Rubens; Arthur Wimperis); I Must Have a Lot of Little Girls All Around Me (C: Frank E. Tours; L: Paul Rubens); I'd Like to Meet Your Father (C: Jerome Kern; L: M.E. Rourke); In Barcelona [2] (C: James W. Tate; L: Eustace Baynes; Vernon Roy); It's Naughty to Be Kissed (C: W.T. Francis; L: J.B. Loughrey); I've a Million Reasons Why I Love You (C: Jerome Kern; L: M.E. Rourke); Lazy Land [2] (C: Paul Rubens; L: Unknown); Little Eva [1] (C: Jerome Kern; L: M.E. Rourke); Little Wild Rose; Love Among the Daisies (C: Frank E. Tours); Man Who Wrote the 'Merry Widow Waltz', The (C: E. Ray Goetz; L: Vincent Bryan); Mary in the Dairy; Mary McGee (C: Jerome Kern; L: M.E. Rourke); Never Marry a Girl with Cold Feet! (C: Jerome Kern; L: M.E. Rourke); Oh, Mr. Brown [2] (C: Harry Von Tilzer; L: Unknown); Poaching [2] (C: Paul Rubens; L: Unknown); Quarrel Duet [2] (C/L: J.J. Montague; Paul Rubens); Sandow Girl, The (C/L: Paul Rubens); Thrush, The; Tinker, Tailor (C: Paul Rubens)

Cast: Donald Hall; Julia Sanderson

Notes: Songs not listed in program. During the run of this show songs came and went. The composers did not collaborate. They are credited as known. [1] Sheet music and ASCAP credit as written. Some other sources credit W.T. Francis and J.B. Loughrey. [2] Out Park Theatre, Boston 01/06/08.

955 • DALY DREAMS

OPENED: 06/08/1919

New York

Librettist: Edward Paulton

Notes: One performance at the Metropolitan Opera House. A one-act in the annual Lambs Gambol.

956 • DAMES AT SEA

OPENED: 12/20/1968 Theatre: Bouwerie Lane
Musical Off-Broadway: 575

Composer: Jim Wise
Lyricist: Robin Miller
Librettist: George Haimsohn; Robin Miller
Producer: Jordan Hott; Jack Millstein
Director: Neal Kenyon

Choreographer: Neal Kenyon; **Costumes:** Peter Harvey; **Lighting Designer:** Martin Aronstein; **Musical Director:** Richard J. Leonard; **Set Design:** Peter Harvey; **Vocal Arranger:** Richard J. Leonard

Songs: Beguine, The; Broadway Baby [2]; Choo-Choo Honeymoon; Dames at Sea; Echo Waltz, The (L: George Haimsohn); Good Times Are Here to Stay (L: George Haimsohn); I'll Show You the Ropes [1]; It's You; Let's Have a Simple Wedding; Raining in My Heart; Sailor of My Dreams, The (L: George Haimsohn); Singapore Sue (L: George Haimsohn); Star Tar; That Mister Man of Mine; There's Something About You; Wall Street

Cast: David Christmas; Steve Elmore; Tamara Long; Bernadette Peters; Joseph R. Sicari; Sally Stark

Notes: [1] Cut after opening. [2] Added after opening.

957 • DAMN YANKEES

OPENED: 05/05/1955 Theatre: 46th Street
Musical Broadway: 1019

Composer: Richard Adler; Jerry Ross
Lyricist: Richard Adler; Jerry Ross
Librettist: George Abbott; Douglass Wallop
Producer: Frederick Brisson; Robert E. Griffith; Harold Prince
Director: George Abbott

Source: YEAR THE YANKEES LOST THE PENNANT, THE (Novel: Douglass Wallop); **Choreographer:** Bob Fosse; **Costumes:** Jean

Eckart; William Eckart; **Dance Arranger:** Roger Adams; **Musical Director:** Harold Hastings; **Orchestrations:** Don Walker; **Set Design:** Jean Eckart; William Eckart

Songs: For an Autograph [1]; Game, The; Goodbye, Old Girl; Little Brains-a Little Talent, A; Man Doesn't Know, A; Musical Chairs [3]; Near to You; Never Feel Sorry for Anybody [3]; Not Meg [2]; One Would Have to Be Blind [3]; Shoeless Joe from Hannibal Mo.; Six Months Out of Every Year; Those Were the Good Old Days; Two Lost Souls; We've Got to Win [3]; Whatever Lola Wants (Lola Gets); Who Needs Baseball [3]; Who's Got the Pain?; You've Got to Have Heart

Cast: Rae Allen; Shannon Bolin; Russ Brown; Stephen Douglass; Nathaniel Frey; Jimmy Komack; Eddie Phillips; Robert Shafer; Jean Stapleton; Gwen Verdon; Ray Walston

Notes: [1] Cut prior to opening. [2] Cut after opening. [3] Out Boston 4/11/55.

958 • DANCE A LITTLE CLOSER

OPENED: 05/11/1983   Theatre: Minskoff
Musical   Broadway: 1

Composer: Charles Strouse
Lyricist: Alan Jay Lerner
Librettist: Alan Jay Lerner
Producer: Frederick Brisson; John F. Kennedy Center; Jerome Minskoff; James M. Nederlander
Director: Alan Jay Lerner

Source: IDIOT'S DELIGHT (Play: Robert E. Sherwood); **Choreographer:** Billy Wilson; **Costumes:** Donald Brooks; **Lighting Designer:** Thomas Skelton; **Musical Director:** Peter Howard; **Orchestrations:** Jonathan Tunick; **Set Design:** David Mitchell

Songs: Another Life; Anyone Who Loves [2]; Auf Wiedersehen; Dance a Little Closer [3]; Happy, Happy New Year; He Always Comes Home to Me; Homesick; I Don't Know [1]; I Got a New Girl; I Never Want to See You Again; It Never Would Have Worked; Mad; No Man Is Worth It; On Top of the World; There's Always One You Can't Forget; There's Never Been Anything Like Us; What Are You Going to Do About It?; Why Can't the World Go and Leave Us Alone?; Woman Who Thinks I'm Wonderful, A

Cast: Colleen Ashton; Len Cariou; I.M. Hobson; Alyson Reed; Liz Robertson; George Rose

Notes: [1] Same music as "It's a Hit, It's a Flop" cut from APPLAUSE. [2] Sheet music only. [3] Music same as "What Became of Me" written for London production of GOLDEN BOY.

959 • DANCE AND GROW THIN

OPENED: 1917
Revue

Composer: Irving Berlin
Lyricist: Irving Berlin

Songs: Birdie; Cinderella Lost Her Slipper; Dance and Grow Thin (C: George W. Meyer); Letter Boxes; Mary Brown; There's Something Nice About the South [1]; Way Down South

Cast: Leon Errol; Irving Fisher; Gertrude Hoffman; Joe Jackson; Joe Schenck; Gus Van

Notes: No program available. The Cocoanut Grove was on the roof of the Century Theatre. [1] Sheet music only.

960 • DANCE DREAM

OPENED: 03/17/1913
Musical

Composer: John Golden
Lyricist: E. Ray Goetz
Director: Hassard Short

Costumes: Hassard Short

Cast: Coit Albertson

Notes: A one-act vaudeville musical that was originally produced as part of a Lambs' Gambol. Milwaukee program.

961 • DANCE ME A SONG

OPENED: 01/20/1950   Theatre: Royale
Revue   Broadway: 35

Composer: James Shelton
Lyricist: James Shelton
Librettist: Robert Anderson; Wally Cox; Lee Goodman; James Kirkwood; Marya Mannes; Vincente Minnelli; George S. Oppenheimer; James Shelton

Producer: Dwight Deere Wiman
Director: James Shelton

Choreographer: Robert Sidney; **Costumes:** Irene Sharaff; **Lighting Designer:** Jo Mielziner; **Musical Director:** Tony Cabot; **Orchestrations:** Robert Russell Bennett; **Set Design:** Jo Mielziner

Songs: Dance Me a Song; I'm the Girl; It's the Weather; Lilac Wine; Love; Matilda; My Little Dog Has Ego (C/L: Herman Hupfeld); One Is a Lonely Number (C: Albert Hague; L: Maurice Valency); Paper Ballet; Strange New Look [1]

Cast: Wally Cox; Bob Fosse; Lee Goodman; Babe Hines; James Kirkwood; Heidi Krall; Marion Lorne; Joan McCracken; Biff McGuire; Mary Ann Niles; Erik Rhodes; Donald Saddler; Bob Scheerer

Notes: In Boston songs credited to Leonard Bernstein, Richard Myers, Langston Hughes, Dean Fuller, David Craig, Alec Wilder, Edward Eager, Herman Hupfeld and Bud Gregg but individual songs were not listed. Sketches were also be Nancy Hamilton, Samuel Taylor and Russell Beggs in Boston. [1] Cut.

962 • DANCE ON A COUNTRY GRAVE

OPENED: 04/21/1977   Theatre: Hudson Guild
Musical   Off-Broadway

Composer: Kelly Hamilton
Lyricist: Kelly Hamilton
Librettist: Kelly Hamilton
Producer: Hudson Guild Theatre
Director: Robert Brewer

Source: RETURN OF THE NATIVE (Novel: Thomas Hardy); **Choreographer:** Bill Grossman; **Costumes:** Donna Meyer; **Lighting Designer:** Curt Ostermann; **Set Design:** Tom Warren

Songs: Can Ye Fancy That?; Cities of Light; Country Spell; Dance on a Country Grave; Dark Side of My Love, The; Egon Edgon Band, The; Gamblin' Hand, The; Green Gravel; Lonely Sparrows of Essex, The; Old Mister Fate; Self-Sacrificing Woman; Sunday Morning Social Call; Tout le Monde; Unexpected Love; Who Would Have Thought?

Cast: Kevin Kline; Donna Theodore

Notes: Later revised and published under the name SAGA.

963 • DANCE WITH ME

OPENED: 01/23/1975   Theatre: Mayfair
Musical   Broadway: 396

Composer: Greg Antonacci
Lyricist: Greg Antonacci
Librettist: Greg Antonacci
Producer: Ted Ravinett; Steve Rubenstein
Director: Joel Zwick

Choreographer: Joel Zwick; **Costumes:** Susan Hum Buck; **Lighting Designer:** Scott Johnson; **Set Design:** Scott Johnson

Cast: Greg Antonacci; John Bottoms; Deborah Rush; Joel Zwick

Notes: No songs listed in program.

964 • DANCIN'

OPENED: 03/27/1978   Theatre: Broadhurst
Revue   Broadway: 1774

Producer: Jules Fisher
Director: Bob Fosse

Choreographer: Bob Fosse; **Costumes:** Willa Kim; **Dance Arranger:** Gordon Lowry Harrell; **Lighting Designer:** Jules Fisher; **Musical Director:** Gordon Lowry Harrell; **Orchestrations:** Ralph Burns; **Set Design:** Peter Larkin; **Vocal Arranger:** Gordon Lowry Harrell

Songs: American Women (C/L: Traditional); Big Noise from Winnetka (inst.) (C: Ray Bauduc; Bob Crosby; Bob Haggart; Gil Robin); Chaconne (inst.) (C: Johann Sebastian Bach); Crunch Granola Suite (C/L: Neil Diamond); Dancin' (inst.) (C: Ralph Burns); Dixie (C/L: Traditional); Easy (C/L: Melissa Manchester); Gary Owen (C/L: Traditional); Here You Come Again (C/L: Barry Mann; Cynthia Weil); Hot August Night (C/L: Neil Diamond); I Wanna Be a Dancin' Man (C: Harry Warren; L: Johnny Mercer); If It Feels Good, Let It Ride (C/L: Melissa Manchester; Carole Bayer Sager); Ionisation (inst.) (C: Edgard Varese); I've Got Them Feelin' Too Good Today Blues (C/L: Jerry Leiber; Mike Stoller); Mr. Bojangles (C/L: Jerry Jeff Walker); Pack Up Your Troubles in Your Old Kit Bag and Smile, Smile, Smile (C: Felix Powell; L: George Asaf); Rally Round the Flag (C/L: Traditional); Sing, Sing, Sing (inst.) (C: Louis Prima); Stars and Stripes Forever, The (C: John Philip Sousa); Under the

Double Eagle (C/L: Traditional); Was Dog a Doughnut (C/L: Cat Stevens); When Johnny Comes Marching Home (C/L: Traditional); Yankee Doodle Dandy (C/L: George M. Cohan)

Cast: Sandahl Bergman; Rene Ceballos; Christopher Chadman; Wayne Cilento; Jill Cook; Richard Korthaze; John Mineo; Ann Reinking; Blane Savage; Charles Ward

Notes: No original songs in this show.

965 • DANCING AROUND

OPENED: 10/10/1914   Theatre: Winter Garden
Musical   Broadway: 145

Composer: Harry Carroll; Sigmund Romberg
Lyricist: Harold Atteridge
Librettist: Harold Atteridge
Producer: Winter Garden Company
Director: J.C. Huffman

Choreographer: Jack Mason; **Costumes:** Melville Ellis; **Dance Arranger:** Melville Ellis; **Lighting Designer:** Nick Kronyack; **Orchestrations:** Oscar Radin; Frank Saddler

Songs: Afternoon Tea, An; Army Club, The [1]; Bring Along Your Dancing Shoes [2] (C: Grace LeRoy; L: Gus Kahn); Buying Little Things for Me [1]; Call to the Colors, The; Dance Conceptions [1]; Dance Eccentrique [1]; Dancing the Blues Away [3] (C/L: Fred Fisher; L: Howard Johnson; Joseph McCarthy); Down in Waterloo [3] (C: Albert Gumble; Jack Wells; L: Alfred Bryan); Everybody Rag with Me [3] (C: Grace LeRoy; L: Gus Kahn); Fading Girl [1]; Fashion's Slave, A; Garden of Girls [2]; Grand Canal [1]; He Is Sweet, He Is Good; Honeymoon Express [4] (C/L: Fred Fisher); I Was Born on the Isle of Man; I'll Make a Man of You [3] (C/L: Unknown); I'm Glad My Wife's in Europe (C: Archie Gottler; L: Coleman Goetz; Howard Johnson); I'm Seeking for Siegfried [2]; Irish and Proud of It, Too; It's a Long Way to Tipperary (C: Jack Judge; L: Harry Williams); Maybe Land [1]; My Lady of the Telephone (C: Jean Gilbert); My Rainbow Beau; Never Trust a Soldier Man; Oh, You John [1]; She Used to Be the Slowest Girl in Town [3] (C: Raymond Walker; L: Charles McCarron); Shepherd Gavotte, The; Shuffling Shiveree, The; Silhouette Ballet [1]; Somebody's Dancing with My Girl; Someone's Calling Me [3] (C/L: Unknown); Tennessee, I Hear You Calling (C: Harry Robe; L: Jeff

Godfrey); There's Something About You; Trini; Venetia [1]; Venetian Carnival, The; What Are You Gonig to Do with Me? [1]; When an Englishman Marries a Parisian; When I Leave the World Behind [3]; When the Grown Up Ladies Act Like Babies [3] (C: Maurice Abrahams; L: Edgar Leslie; Joe Young); When Tommy Atkins Smiles at All the Girls; Who Paid the Rent for Mrs. Rip Van Winkle (When Rip Van Winkle Went Away) [5] (C: Fred Fisher; L: Al Bryan); World's a Stage for Every Girl, The [1]

Cast: Harland Dixon; James Doyle; Melville Ellis; Bernard Granville; Al Jolson; Georgia O'Ramey; Lucy Weston

Notes: [1] Not in program, just in Romberg's biography. [2] Out Washington D.C. 11/29/16. [3] Sheet music only. [4] Not in programs. [5] Not in programs. Also in THE BELLE OF BOND STREET.

966 • DANCING COED, THE

OPENED: 12/29/1936
Musical   Closed out of town

Composer: Gerald Dolan
Lyricist: Edward J. Lambert
Librettist: Edward J. Lambert
Producer: Louis F. Werba
Director: Bernard Steele

Choreographer: John Pierce; **Set Design:** Harry Gordon Bennett

Songs: Jibin'

Cast: Ralph Blane; Vicki Cummings; Mary Healy; Lew Hearn

Notes: Clipping from Werba's Brighton Theatre. No program available.

967 • DANCING DUCHESS, THE (0000)

Musical   Closed out of town

Composer: Robert Stolz

Source: DIE TANZGRAFIN (Musical: Robert Bodanzky; Jacobson; Robert Stolz)

Notes: No other information available. This show premiered in 1921 in Berlin.

968 • DANCING DUCHESS (1914)

OPENED: 08/19/1914   Theatre: Casino
Musical   Broadway: 13

Composer: Milton Lusk
Lyricist: R.H. Burnside; C.H. Kerr
Librettist: R.H. Burnside; C.H. Kerr
Producer: Dancing Duchess Company
Director: R.H. Burnside

Choreographer: Vera Maxwell; Wallace McCutcheon; **Costumes:** Will R. Barnes; Arthur D. Brooks; **Musical Director:** John McGhie; **Orchestrations:** Otto C.A. Meorz; Frank Saddler; **Set Design:** H. Robert Law

Songs: Bumble Bee and the Butterfly, The; Celestine; Danube So Blue; Do You Like Me [1]; Everybody's Happy in Vienna; Fol-De-Rol-Lol; I Like You; I'm Looking for a Girl Like Venus [1] (L: R.H. Burnside); I've Been Looking for You (L: R.H. Burnside); Love Is a Summer's Morning; Nay, Nay Pauline; Never Whirl; Nothing Like Ragtime After All [1]; Oh How I Love Her Family [1]; On with the Dance; Ragtime Whirl, The; Song of Songs, The; Tango Breakfast, The; That's the Kind of a Man You Ought to Marry; That's the Way to Win a Girl

Cast: Harry Davenport; Otis Harlan; John Hyams; Dorothy Jardon; Ada Lewis; Leila McIntyre

Notes: [1] Sheet music only.

969 • DANCING GIRL, THE

OPENED: 01/24/1923   Theatre: Winter Garden
Musical   Broadway: 142

Composer: Sigmund Romberg
Lyricist: Harold Atteridge; Irving Caesar
Librettist: Harold Atteridge; Irving Caesar
Producer: J.J. Shubert; Lee Shubert
Director: J.C. Huffman

Musical Director: Al Goodman; **Set Design:** Watson Barratt

Songs: Any Little Girl Will Fall; Bowery of Today, The; Cuddle Me As We Dance [1] (L: Harold Atteridge); Cuddle Up [1] (C: George Gershwin); Hail U.S.A.; I'm a Devil with the Ladies; I've Been Waiting for You [7] (C: Jay Gorney; L: Harold Atteridge); I've Been Wanting You (C: A.J. Carey; Al Goodman; L: Harold Atteridge); Lucky in

Love; My Love Bouquet; On the Boulevard [3]; Pango Pango (C: George Gershwin); Play Me a Tune [6] (C/L: Cole Porter); Romance (L: Harold Atteridge); Spanish Dance [2]; Story of a Butterfly, The [3]; Story of Fung Toy [3]; That American Boy of Mine [4] (C: George Gershwin; L: Irving Caesar); That Romance of Mine; There Was the Punch [5] (C/L: Cole Porter); Trini [2]; Venetian; Versailles; Way Down in Pago Pago (L: Harold Atteridge; Carley Mills); What Have You to Declare?; Why? [1] (L: Harold Atteridge); Why Am I So Sad? (C: George Gershwin)

Cast: Kitty Doner; Ted Doner; Marie Dressler; Nat Nazzarro Jr.; Jack Pearl; Cyril Scott; Trini

Notes: [1] Sheet music only. [2] Only in Romberg biography [3] Out New Haven 1/5/23. [4] Same music as "No One Else but that Girl of Mine" in THE PERFECT FOOL. [5] Originally in HITCHY-KOO OF 1922 as "The American Punch" and "It's the Punches." [6] Also in HITCHY-KOO OF 1922 and ONE DAMN THING AFTER ANOTHER. [7] Not in programs.

970 • DANCING HONEYMOON, THE

Notes: *See BATTLING BUTTLER.*

971 • DANCING IN THE STREETS

OPENED: 1943
Musical   Closed out of town

Composer: Vernon Duke
Lyricist: Howard Dietz
Librettist: Howard Dietz; John Cecil Holm; Matt Taylor
Producer: Vinton Freedley
Director: Edgar MacGregor

Choreographer: Robert Alton; **Costumes:** Kiviette; **Lighting Designer:** Robert Edmond Jones; **Musical Director:** Max Meth; **Orchestrations:** Ray Sinatra; Hans Spialek; **Set Design:** Robert Edmond Jones; **Vocal Arranger:** Clay Warnick

Songs: Bay of Botany; Boys, Boys, Boys [1]; (Got a) Bran' New Daddy; Can Can; Comforts of Home, The; Dancing in the Streets; Ella the Elephant [1]; Farewell for a While [1]; Friendly Bar, A; Hip; I Have Grown to Love New York [1]; I'm in Love with a Dame [1]; In My Dreams; Indefinable Charm; Irresistible You; Keep Your Amateur

Standing; Kiss Your Baby Goodbye; Swattin' the Fly; Tallahassee; This Particular Party [1]; Under My Umbrella [2]; We've Been Through the Mill Together

Cast: Ernest Cossart; Dudley Diggs; Mary Martin

Notes: From a program of Boston 3/23/1943. [1] Not used. [2] Not used. Also not used in ZIEGFELD FOLLIES OF 1943.

972 • DANCING YEARS

OPENED: 03/23/1939   Theatre: Theatre Royal, Drury Lane
Musical   London: 187

Composer: Ivor Novello
Lyricist: Christopher Hassall
Librettist: Ivor Novello
Director: Leontine Sagan
Producer: Theatre Royal Drury Lane; Tom Arnold

Arrangements: Suria Magito; **Choreographer:** Freddie Carpenter; **Costumes:** Morris Angel; M. Berman; Louis Brooks; Frederick Dawson; L & H. Nathan; **Musical Director:** Charles Prentice; **Orchestrations:** Charles Prentice; **Set Design:** Joseph Carl; Edward Delaney; Alick Johnstone

Songs: I Can Give You the Starlight; In Praise of Love; Life Belongs to You; Lorelei; My Dearest Dear; Primrose; Uniform; Waltz of My Heart; When It's Spring in Vienna; Wings of Sleep, The

Cast: Mary Ellis; Olive Gilbert; Peter Graves; Ivor Novello; Minnie Raynor

Notes: The blitz interrupted the run. The show reopened 3/14/42 at the Adelphi for 969 more performances.

973 • DANDELION WINE

OPENED: 03/10/1972
Musical   Closed out of town

Composer: Billy Goldenberg
Lyricist: Larry Alexander
Librettist: Ray Bradbury
Producer: California State College at Fullerton
Director: Kirk Mee

Source: DANDELION WINE (Novel: Ray Bradbury); **Costumes:** Dwight Richard Odle; **Lighting Designer:** Darrell F. Winn; **Musical**

Director: Bill Beck; **Set Design:** S. Todd Muffatti

Songs: Boy with Magic in His Eyes, A; Dandelion Wine; Drummerboy at Shiloh, The; Fireflies (L: Ray Bradbury); Happiness Machine, The (L: Ray Bradbury); Hey Listen, Johnny Johnny; Hey Nonny No; I Got Statistics; Immortality (L: Ray Bradbury); Long Time Coming, A; 1999; Paira Litefoot Tennis Sneakers; Special Summer; Tomorrow All Day; Walk Through the Night; Wizards of Wizards

Cast: Michael Strong

974 • DANGEROUS CHRISTMAS OF RED RIDING HOOD, THE

OPENED: 11/28/1965   Theatre: ABC
TV Musical

Composer: Jule Styne
Lyricist: Bob Merrill
Librettist: Robert Emmett
Producer: Dorothy Dicker; Richard Lewine; Jim Stanley
Director: Sid Smith

Source: LITTLE RED RIDING HOOD (Fairy Tale); **Arrangements:** Walter Scharf; **Choreographer:** Lee Theodore; **Costumes:** Raoul Pene du Bois; **Musical Director:** Walter Scharf; **Set Design:** Raoul Pene du Bois

Songs: Along the Way; Ding-a-ling, Ding-a-ling; Granny; Granny's Gulch; I'm Naive; My Red Riding Hood; Poor Mouse; Red Riding Hood Improvisation (inst.); Snubbed; We Wish the World a Happy Yule; We're Gonna Howl Tonight; Woodsman's Serenade

Cast: Animals, The; Vic Damone; Liza Minnelli; Cyril Ritchard

975 • DANGEROUS GAMES

OPENED: 10/19/1989   Theatre: Nederlander
Musical   Broadway: 4

Composer: Astor Pizzolla
Lyricist: William Finn
Librettist: Graciela Daniele; Jim Lewis
Producer: Jules Fisher; James M. Nederlander; Arthur Rubin
Director: Graciela Daniele

Choreographer: Graciela Daniele; Tina Paul; **Costumes:** Patricia Zipprodt; **Dance Arranger:** Rodolfo Alchourron; James Kowal; **Lighting Designer:** Peggy Eisenhauer; **Musical Director:** James Kowal; **Set Design:** Tony Straiges; **Vocal Arranger:** Rodolfo Alchourron; James Kowal

Cast: Richard Amaro; Rene Ceballos; Philip Jerry; John Mineo; Dana Moore; Tina Paul; Luis Perez

Notes: No songs listed in program.

976 • DANGEROUS MAID, A (1898)
OPENED: 11/12/1898 Theatre: Casino
Musical Broadway: 65

Composer: Frederick J. Eustis; Leopold Schenck
Librettist: Sydney Rosenfeld
Producer: George W. Lederer; George B. McClellan
Director: George W. Lederer

Source: HEISSES BLUT (Musical); **Costumes:** Mme. Siedle; **Musical Director:** Frederick J. Eustis; **Set Design:** Ernest Albert; D. Frank Dodge

Songs: Kiss Me, Honey, Do (C: John Stromberg); Song of the Mormon (L: Louis Harrison)

Cast: Sam Bernard; Laura Burt; Richard Carroll; Madge Lessing; Charles Plunkett

Notes: No songs listed in program. Louis Harrison wrote the lyrics to three songs.

977 • DANGEROUS MAID, A (1921)
OPENED: 03/21/1921
Musical Closed out of town

Composer: George Gershwin
Lyricist: Ira Gershwin [1]
Librettist: Charles W. Bell
Producer: Eddie Leonard; Edgar MacGregor
Director: Eddie Leonard

Musical Director: Al Lassar

Songs: Anything for You; Boy Wanted [2]; Dancing Shoes; Every Girl Has a Way (Every Girl Has a Method of Her Own); Just to Know You Are Mine; Pidgee Woo; Simple Life, The; Sirens, The [3]; Some Rain Must Fall; True Love

Cast: Amelia Bingham; Juliette Day; Juanita Fletcher; Vinton Freedley; Creighton Hale

Notes: Ira Gershwin used the pseudonym Arthur Francis. Closed Nixon Apollo Theatre, Pittsburgh 04/30/21. Juliette Day replaced by Vivienne Segal during run. A vaudeville musical. Program from Philadelphia used. [1] Used pseudonym Arthur Francis. [2] With revised lyric by Gershwin and Desmond Carter, used in PRIMROSE. [3] Later revised and put in PRIMROSE as "Four Little Sirens."

978 • DANISH YANKEE IN KING TUT'S COURT, A
OPENED: 05/31/1923
Musical

Composer: Richard Rodgers
Lyricist: Dorothy Crowthers; Herbert Fields; Richard Rodgers
Librettist: Dorothy Crowthers; Herbert Fields; Richard Rodgers
Producer: Institute of Musical Art
Director: Herbert Fields

Musical Director: Richard Rodgers

Songs: Bob-o-Link; College Baby (L: Robert A. Simon); Egyptian Night (C: Sigmund Krumgold); Hermits, The [1] (L: Lorenz Hart); If I Were King [2] (L: Lorenz Hart); If You're Single (L: Lorenz Hart); King Tut's Birthday; My Cleopatra; Send for Nielsen; Song of the Moon; Wake Up Miss Aida; Will You Forgive Me? (L: Lorenz Hart)

Notes: Amateur production. [1] Written for the score of the unproduced WINKLE TOWN. Later in TEMPLE BELLES and DEAREST ENEMY. [2] Written for the score of the unproduced WINKLE TOWN. Also used in BAD HABITS OF 1925.

979 • DANTON'S DEATH
OPENED: 11/02/1938 Theatre: Mercury
Play Broadway: 21

Composer: Marc Blitzstein
Lyricist: Marc Blitzstein
Author: Georg Buchner
Translator: Geoffrey Dunlop
Producer: John Houseman; Orson Welles
Director: Orson Welles

Incidental Music: Marc Blitzstein; **Set Design:** Jan Tichacek

Songs: Ca Ira (C: Traditional); Ho Christina [1]; La Carmagnole [2] (C: Traditional); Ode to Reason

Cast: Joseph Cotten; Ruth Ford; Arlene Francis; Martin Gabel; Vladimir Sokoloff; Orson Welles; Mary Wickes

Notes: No program available. [1] French revolutionary song with new lyrics by Blitzstein. [2] French revolutionary song with new lyrics by Blitzstein. Kurt Weill used the song in a 1927 Berlin production of Strindberg's GUSTAV III.

980 • DARKEST AMERICANS
OPENED: 1918
Musical

Composer: C. Luckeyth Roberts
Lyricist: J. Homer Tutt; Salem Tutt Whitney
Librettist: J. Homer Tutt; Salem Tutt Whitney
Producer: J. Homer Tutt; Salem Tutt Whitne

Musical Director: C. Luckeyth Roberts

Songs: Blue Fever; Jolly Jazz Joy Man; Sambos Will Get You If You Don't Watch Out, The; That Creole Flower Garden of Mine

Cast: Alonzo Fenderson; William Fountain; Emma Jackson; Carrie King; J. Homer Tutt; Al F. Watts; Virginia Wheeler; Salem Tutt Whitney

Notes: No other information available.

981 • DARKTOWN AFFAIRS
OPENED: 04/22/1929
Revue   Closed out of town

Composer: Mae Brown; Garland Howard; J.A. Shipp; Speedy Smith
Lyricist: Mae Brown; Garland Howard; J.A. Shipp; Speedy Smith
Librettist: Mae Brown; Garland Howard; J.A. Shipp; Speedy Smith
Producer: Jake Stouse

Choreographer: Mae Brown; Garland Howard; Speedy Smith; **Musical Director:** Stanley Bennett

Songs: Chicken Bone; Dance Porto Rico; Foolishness; Function Bound; Going to Miss Me; Home Brew; Hot Foot Dance; How About Me?; Kicking the Mule; Liza; Loving Friends; Milindy; Milindy Blues; Page Mr. Jackson; Sally Ann; Sally Ann Revival; Social Function Stomp; Under the Moon; Walk Together; Wedding Day; Your Sins Will Find You Out

Cast: Kitty Brown; Mae Brown; Robert Davis; Zudora De Gaston; Garland Howard; Joe Loomis; Hatty Noles; Speedy Smith

Notes: Werba's Brooklyn Theatre.

982 • DARKTOWN CIRCUS DAY
OPENED: 1903
Musical

Composer: Bob Cole; J. Rosamond Johnson; Gustave Kerker
Lyricist: Bob Cole; J. Rosamond Johnson
Producer: Black Patti Troubadours

Musical Director: Anton Goeckner

Songs: Ain't Going to Stay Here Any Longer; Behold the Queen; Castle on the Nile; In Lovers Lane; Mandy; Strolling Around the Circus Tent; Under the Bamboo Tree; Waltz Song [1] (C: Gustav Kerker; L: Hugh Morton); What Became of the Monk; When the Circus Comes to Town

Cast: Charles Bougla; Anthony D. Byrd; Will A. Cook; James Crosby; Ida Forcen; J. Ed Green; John Green; Sissieretta Jones; Bobby Kemp

Notes: No other information available. Sissieretta Jones (the Black Patti) also sang "Miserere" from TROVATORE and "Quintette" from MARTHA. [1] From BELLE OF NEW YORK.

983 • DARKTOWN FOLLIES (1913)
OPENED: 1913   Theatre: Lafayette
Revue   Harlem

Producer: J. Leubrie Hill

Songs: At the Ball, That's All (C/L: J. Leubrie Hill)

Cast: James P. Johnson

Notes: No other information available.

984 • DARKTOWN FOLLIES (1916)
OPENED: 1916
Revue

Composer: J. Leubrie Hill
Lyricist: J. Leubrie Hill
Librettist: Alex Rogers
Producer: J. Leubrie Hill
Director: J. Leubrie Hill

Costumes: Mahieu

Songs: Cabaret Shows; Chink, Chink, Chink; Darktown Follies Dance (dance); Do Re Mi Ragtime; Goodby Forever; Goodby Ragtime; Here, There and Everywhere; Hoola-Boola Love Song; It's a Long Way from Here to Dixie; Keep a Little Love Light Burning; Lou My Lou; Milo; Musical Pleasure; Ragtime; Sure Cure for the Blues; Syncopation; Trombone Man; Tuskegee; When the Right Boy Comes Along

Cast: Jim Burris; Opal Cooper; Alonzo Fenderson; J. Leubrie Hill; Alex Rogers; Dink Stewart; Charles Woody

Notes: No other information available.

985 • DARKTOWN FOLLIES (1940'S)
Musical   Closed out of town

Producer: Local 840, U.A.W.
Director: William King

Conductor: George Madden; **Costumes:** Marguerite Govatos; **Set Design:** Marguerite Govatos; Ernie Hinds; Walter Stan

Cast: Betty Boyle; Helen Brady; Rip D'Onofrio; Bucky Edwards; Vesta Ford; Ernie Hinds; Walter Stan

Notes: No songs listed. No program available. Produced in the 1940's.

986 • DARKTOWN FROLICS OF 1921
OPENED: 10/11/1921
Revue   Closed out of town

Producer: S.H. Dudley

Songs: Home Again Blue; I Am a Little Jazz; Japanese Sandman, The; Jazz Band Man, The; My Bumble Bee; My Mammy

Cast: Berrington & Berrington; Ebbie Burton; Corine Gibson; Edward Langford; Gonzell White's Jazz Rabbits

Notes: Orpheum Theatre, Harrisburg, Pa. These songs may be the popular songs of the day or they might be sketches.

987 • DARKTOWN POLITICIAN, THE
OPENED: 1913
Musical

Composer: T.L. Carwell; J. Homer Tutt; Salem Tutt Whitney
Lyricist: J. Homer Tutt; Salem Tutt Whitney
Librettist: J. Homer Tutt; Salem Tutt Whitney
Producer: Salem Tutt Whitney

Cast: Blanche Thompson; J. Homer Tutt; Salem Tutt Whitney

Notes: No other information available. One review claimed there were 25 songs in this show.

988 • DARKYDOM
OPENED: 10/23/1915   Theatre: Lafayette
Musical   New York

Composer: Will Marion Cook
Librettist: Aubrey L. Lyles; Flournoy Miller

Cast: Aubrey L. Lyles; Flournoy Miller

989 • DARLING OF THE DAY
OPENED: 01/27/1968   Theatre: George Abbott
Musical   Broadway: 32

Composer: Jule Styne
Lyricist: E.Y. Harburg
Producer: Joel Schenker; Theatre Guild, The
Director: Noel Willman

Source: BURIED ALIVE (Play: Arnold Bennett); **Choreographer:** Lee Theodore; **Costumes:** Raoul Pene du Bois; **Dance Arranger:** Trude Rittman; **Lighting Designer:** Peggy Clark; **Musical Director:** Buster Davis; **Orchestrations:** Ralph

Burns; **Set Design:** Oliver Smith; **Vocal Arranger:** Buster Davis

Songs: Blushing Bride, A [1]; Butler in the Abbey; Come Back to God (Me) [3]; Darling of the Day [3]; Don't Pour the Thames Into the Rhine [3]; Double Soliloquy; Gentleman's Gentleman, A; He's a Genius; Henry Leek [3]; I'm Simply Mad for Bones [3]; Isn't This a Day [3]; It's Enough to Make a Lady Fall in Love; I've Got a Rainbow Working for Me Now; Lady Alice [3]; Let's See What Happens; Lying in State [3]; Mad for Art; Money, Money, Money; Not on Your Nellie; Panache; Priam Faril [3]; Putney on the Thames [2]; That Something Extra Special; That Stranger in Your Eyes [3]; To Get Out of This World Alive; Under the Sunset Tree; Westminster Funeral [3]; What Makes a Marriage Merry; When I Marry Alice [3]

Cast: Brenda Forbes; Teddy Green; Marc Jordan; Vincent Price; Patricia Routledge; Peter Woodthorpe

Notes: Nunnally Johnson was credited with the libretto out of town. [1] Cut prior to opening. [2] Cut prior to opening. Contains music from "Strange Duet" from SUBWAYS ARE FOR SLEEPING. [3] ASCAP/Library of Congress only.

990 • DARLING OF THE GALLERY GODS, THE

Notes: *See MID SUMMER NIGHT'S FANCIES.*

991 • DARWIN'S THEORIES

OPENED: 10/18/1960   Theatre: Madison
                                        Avenue
Musical   Off-Broadway: 3

Composer: Darwin Venneri
Lyricist: Darwin Venneri
Librettist: Alan Alda
Producer: Arthur Grasso
Director: Stanley Phillips

Choreographer: Louis Johnson; **Lighting Designer:** Warren Crave; **Musical Director:** Nino Silva; **Set Design:** Robert Paine Grose

Songs: Carried Away; I Know How You Wonder; I'm Living in the Past with a Love That Cannot Last; Love Is Strange; Love Me a Little; Stars

Seem So Low Tonight, The; Strange Weather; We'll Always Stay in Love; What's in a Name?

Cast: Alan Alda; James Coco; Patricia Fay

992 • DAS BARBECU

OPENED: 10/10/1994   Theatre: Minetta Lane
Musical   Off-Broadway

Composer: Scott Warrender
Lyricist: Jim Luigs
Librettist: Jim Luigs
Producer: Steven Baruch; Dasha Epstein; Richard Frankel; Margery Klain; Leavitt/Fox/Mages; Daryl Roth; Jack Viertel; Thomas Viertel
Director: Christopher Ashley

Source: DER RING DES NIBELUNGEN (Operas: Richard Wagner); **Choreographer:** Stephen Terrell; **Costumes:** Eduardo Sicangco; **Dance Arranger:** Michael Kosarin; **Lighting Designer:** Frances Aronson; **Musical Director:** Jeff Halpern; **Orchestrations:** Bruce Coughlin; **Set Design:** Eduardo Sicangco

Songs: After the Gold Is Gone; Bang! [1]; Barbecue for Two; Country Fair; Hog-Tie Your Man; If Not Fer You; Little House for Me, A; Makin' Guacamole; Public Enemy Number 1; Ring of Gold in Texas, A; River of Fire; Rodeo Romeo; Siegfried! [1]; Slide a Little Closer; Texas Aristocracy [1]; Tumbleweed Square Dance, The [1]; Turn the Tide; Wanderin' Man; What I Had in Mind

Cast: Carolee Carmello; Julie Johnson; Sally Mayes; Jerry McGarity; J.K. Simmons

Notes: Commissioned and premiered by the Seattle Opera in 1991. [1] Out Goodspeed Opera House prior to New York.

993 • DASHING BELLES OF YESTERDAY AND THE DUMBBELLES OF TODAY, THE

OPENED: 04/26/1925
Musical

Composer: Raymond Hubbell
Lyricist: Gene Buck
Director: Julian Mitchell

Songs: Beautiful Bicycle Belle; Dumb-Dumb-Dumb-Dumbbell

Cast: Horace Braham; Frank McHugh; Stanley Ridges; Oscar Shaw; Hal Skelly

Notes: Part of THE LAMBS ANNUAL PUBLIC SPRING GAMBOL. See under that name for additional information.

994 • DAUGHTER OF ROSIE O'GRADY, THE

OPENED: 1925
Musical   Closed out of town

Composer: Joseph Santley
Lyricist: Cliff Hess
Librettist: Edgar Allen Woolf
Director: Pat Rooney

Choreographer: David Bennett

Songs: Bit O' Dancin', A; Give Me the Girls; Goodbye, Good Luck; Homeward Bound; I'll Follow You; Irish Moon; Raisin' the Dust; Rosie O'Grady's a Charleston Lady Now; Two Best Girls I Love You [1]; When Mother Was a Girl; Wherever You Go [1]

Cast: Marion Bent; Frank Corbet; Helen O'Shea; Pat Rooney; Pat Rooney III

Notes: Baltimore program [1] Sheet music only.

995 • DAUGHTER OF THE REVOLUTION, THE

OPENED: 05/27/1895   Theatre: Broadway
Musical   Broadway: 40

Composer: Ludwig Englander
Librettist: J. Cheever Goodwin
Director: Richard Barker

Source: 1776 (Musical: Ludwig Englander; Leo Goldmark)

Cast: Camille D'Arville; Harry MacDonough; Hadden Mostyn; Harry Stanley

Notes: No program available. A revised version of 1776 (1884), a musical that premiered at the Thalia Theatre on 2/26/1884.

996 • DAVY CROCKETT

OPENED: 1938
Musical   Unproduced

Composer: Kurt Weill
Lyricist: H.R. Hayes

Source: DAVY CROCKETT (Play: H.R. Hayes)

Songs: All Goes Badly; Battle of the Alamo (inst.); Hand Is Quicker Than the Eye, The; I'm a Rolling Stone; Letter Song; Look Your Partner Straight in the Eye; Politics; Song of the Trees; Time Is Standing Still; Watch Out for Me; When I'm in Congress; Where the Green Pines Shadow the Ground

997 • DAVY JONES' LOCKER

OPENED: 12/24/1972   Theatre: Bil Baird
Musical   Off-Broadway: 79

Composer: Mary Rodgers
Lyricist: Mary Rodgers
Librettist: Arthur Birnkrant; Waldo Salt
Producer: American Puppet Arts Council
Director: Lee Theodore

Puppeteer: Bil Baird; Peter Baird; Pady Blackwood; Olga Felgemacher; Carl Harms; Simon Sisters, The; Frank Sullivan; William Tost; Byron Whiting

998 • DAY AND A NIGHT IN NEW YORK, A

OPENED: 08/30/1895   Theatre: Garrick
Musical   Broadway: 63

Composer: Mrs. Christine; Edmund Vance Cooke; William Devere; Charles H. Hoyt; Richard Stahl; Mr. Waters; Charles Zimmerman
Librettist: Charles H. Hoyt
Producer: Charles H. Hoyt; McKee
Director: Charles H. Hoyt

Choreographer: Thomas Evans; **Costumes:** Barnes; Jackson; **Set Design:** Arthur Voegtlin

Songs: Bird, a Bottle and a Cigarette, A; Can You Forget?; Dutch Comedians; Jolly Old Tar; Languid Man; Lucie; New Belle of New York, The; '98; Perfect Gentlemen, A; Please the Ladies; Rabbit's Foot; Susie; They All Know Better Now

Cast: William Devere; Lillian Dix; Louise Gunning; Otis Harlan; Nellie O'Neil; Charles Zimmerman

999 • DAY BEFORE SPRING, THE

OPENED: 11/22/1945   Theatre: National
Musical   Broadway: 165

Composer: Frederick Loewe
Lyricist: Alan Jay Lerner
Librettist: Alan Jay Lerner
Producer: John C. Wilson
Director: Edward Padula; John C. Wilson

Choreographer: Anthony Tudor; **Costumes:** Miles White; **Orchestrations:** Harold Byrns; **Set Design:** Robert Davison

Songs: Ballet of the Book According to Gerald; Day Before Spring, The; Friends to the End; God's Green World; I Love You This Morning; Invitation, The; Jug of Wine, A; Katherine Receives Advice; My Love Is a Married Man; This Is My Holiday; Where's My Wife?; You Haven't Changed at All

Cast: John Archer; Bill Johnson; Irene Manning; Patricia Marshall

1000 • DAY IN HOLLYWOOD/ A NIGHT IN THE UKRAINE, A

OPENED: 05/01/1980   Theatre: Royale
Revue   Broadway: 588

Composer: Frank Lazarus
Lyricist: Dick Vosburgh
Librettist: Dick Vosburgh
Producer: Alexander H. Cohen; Hildy Parks
Director: Tommy Tune

Choreographer: Tommy Tune; Thommie Walsh; **Costumes:** Michel Stuart; **Dance Arranger:** Wally Harper; **Lighting Designer:** Beverly Emmons; **Musical Director:** Wally Harper; **Set Design:** Tony Walton; **Vocal Arranger:** Wally Harper

Songs: Again; All God's Chillun Got Movie Shows [2]; Best in the World, The (C/L: Jerry Herman); Doin' the Production Code; Duel! A Duel!, A; Famous Feet; Goldwyn & Warner & May'r & Zanuck & Cohn [2]; I Love a Film Cliche (C: Trevor Lylleton); It All Comes Out of the Piano; Just Go to the Movies (C/L: Jerry Herman); Just Like That; Movie Fan's Love Song [2]; Movies Are Your Best Entertainment [2]; Natasha; Nelson [1] (C/L: Jerry Herman); Night in the Ukraine, A; Samovar the Lawyer; Sing Me a Sensible Song [2]

Cast: Kate Draper; David Garrison; Niki Harris; Peggy Hewett; Stephen James; Frank Lazarus; Priscilla Lopez; Albert Stephenson

Notes: [1] Same music as "Song of Advice" in THE GRAND TOUR. [2] Songs from London production not in New York.

1001 • DAY IN PARIS, A

Notes: Also known as A DAY IN PARIS.

1002 • DAY IN THE LIFE OF JUST ABOUT EVERYONE, A

OPENED: 03/09/1971   Theatre: Bijou
Musical   Off-Broadway: 8

Composer: Earl Wilson Jr.
Lyricist: Earl Wilson Jr.
Librettist: Michael Sawyer; Earl Wilson Jr.
Producer: Robert Shelly
Director: Tom Panko

Costumes: Miles White; **Lighting Designer:** Andrew Greenhut; **Musical Director:** Elman Anderson; Bill Cunningham; **Orchestrations:** Donald Pippin; **Set Design:** Andrew Greenhut; **Vocal Arranger:** Donald Pippin

Songs: Brief Dissertation on the Relevancy of a Liberal Education in a Contemporary Society, A; Everybody Loves a Single Girl; Faces Without Names; Fare Thee Well; Give Us This Day; Goin' Home; Got to Be a Woman Now; He's Beginning to Look a Lot Like Me; If I Could Live My Life Again; Isn't That What Makes Life Worthwhile; Merrill, Lynch, Pierce, Fenner and Clyde; Out of Town; Paper Tiger; People in the Street, The; Safe; Two Grown-Up People at Play; View from My Window, The; Visiting Hours; Waltz for Two Balloons, A; What Do I Do Now?; When I Was a Child; Woman Is Just a Female, A

Cast: Dickie Evans; Daniel Fortus; June Gable; Bennett Kinsey; Earl Wilson Jr.

Notes: Additional Dialogue: Michael Sawyer.

1003 • DEACON AND THE LADY, THE

OPENED: 10/04/1910   Theatre: New York
Musical   Broadway: 16

Composer: Alfred E. Aarons
Lyricist: George Totten Smith
Librettist: George Totten Smith
Producer: Alfred E. Aarons; Louis F. Werba

Choreographer: Eddie Clark

Songs: Dreams; I Love a Yankee Girl; It's Queer What a Little Love Will Do; Mr. Tannhauser; Tiger Love

Cast: Eva Fallon; Harry Kelly; Fletcher Norton; Clara Palmer; Ed Wynn

Notes: No New York program available.

1004 • DEAR DESPERATE
OPENED: 01/23/1981   Theatre: New Playwrights
Musical   Washington

Composer: Tim Grundmann
Lyricist: Tim Grundmann
Librettist: Tim Grundmann
Producer: Harry M. Bagdasian; New Playwrights' Theatre
Director: Harry M. Bagdasian

Choreographer: Robert Sachelli; **Costumes:** Peter J. Zakutansky; **Lighting Designer:** Allen Lee Hughes; **Musical Director:** Tim Grundmann; **Orchestrations:** Tim Grundmann; **Set Design:** Russell Metheny; **Vocal Arranger:** Tim Grundmann

Songs: After the Flickers; Boy What a Perfect Waste of Time Is Love; Dear Desperate; Dear Mrs. Brown; Don't You Hate It?; I Was Thinking of You; I'll Never Get Over the Guy; In the Park; It's Charming; Luna Park; Myrtle Gets an Idea; Myrtle Is a Sensation; Questions; What If She's Awfully Pretty?; Yrs. Truly

Cast: Wayne Anderson; Frank Edwards; Amelia Estin; James Festa; Tonette Hartmann; Porter Koontz; Nick Olcott; Barbara Rappaport; Tanis Roach; Steve Skardon; Valerie Stanislawczyk; Michael Willis

1005 • DEAR DOROTHY
OPENED: 1916
Musical   Closed out of town

Composer: A. Baldwin Sloane

Notes: Presented by the Paint and Powder Club, Baltimore.

1006 • DEAR ENEMY
Notes: *See DEAREST ENEMY.*

1007 • DEAR LIAR
OPENED: 03/17/1960   Theatre: Billy Rose
Play   Broadway: 52

Composer: Sol Kaplan
Lyricist: Edward Eliscu
Author: Jerome Kilty
Producer: Guthrie McClintic
Director: Jerome Kilty

Costumes: Cecil Beaton; **Incidental Music:** Sol Kaplan; **Lighting Designer:** Jean Rosenthal; **Set Design:** Donald Oenslager

Songs: Dear Liar; Mon Ami

Cast: Brian Aherne; Katharine Cornell

Notes: No songs listed in program.

1008 • DEAR LOVE
Notes: *See ARTISTS AND MODELS (1930).*

1009 • DEAR ME
OPENED: 01/17/1921   Theatre: Republic
Play   Broadway: 144

Author: Hale Hamilton; Luther Reed
Producer: John Golden
Director: Winchell Smith

Set Design: Wade Douglas

Songs: Dear Me (C: John Golden; L: Grace LaRue); Flowers, Who'll Buy? (C/L: Lucille De Mert); Only a Little Moss Rose (C: Ward-Stephens; L: Ethel Watts Mumford)

Cast: Hale Hamilton; Grace LaRue

1010 • DEAR OSCAR
OPENED: 11/16/1972   Theatre: Playhouse
Musical   Off-Broadway: 5

Composer: Addy Fieger
Lyricist: Caryl Gabrielle
Librettist: Caryl Gabrielle
Producer: Mary W. John

Costumes: Mary McKinley; **Dance Arranger:** Harold Hastings; **Lighting Designer:** David F. Segal; **Musical Director:** Arnold Gross; **Set Design:** William Pitkin; **Vocal Arranger:** Harold Hastings

Songs: Actor, The; Good, Good Times; How Dare He; If I Could; Oscar Wilde Has Said It; Perfect Understanding, The; Poor Bosie; Swan and Edgar's; There Where the Young Men Go; Tit Street; We Like Things the Way They Are; We'll Have a Party; We're Only Lovers; When Did You Leave Me; Wot's 'Is Name

Cast: Tommy Breslin; Nancy Cushman; Tinker Gillespie; Len Gochman; Richard Kneeland; Roger Leonard; Sylvia O'Brien; Russ Thacker

1011 • DEAR SIR

OPENED: 09/23/1924   Theatre: Times Square
Musical   Broadway: 15

Composer: Jerome Kern
Lyricist: Howard Dietz
Librettist: Edgar Selwyn
Producer: Philip Goodman
Director: Clifford Brooke

Choreographer: David Bennett; **Costumes:** Kiviette; James Reynolds; **Musical Director:** Gus Salzer; **Orchestrations:** Allen Foster; **Set Design:** Raymond Sovey

Songs: All Lanes Much Reach a Turning [2]; Dancing Time; Follow Handy Andy [1]; Grab a Girl; Gypsy Caravan [1]; I Want to Be There; If You Think It's Love, You're Right; Mormon Life, A; My Houseboat on the Harlem; Opening Chorus; Seven Days; There's Lots of Room for You [1]; To the Fair; Weeping Willow Tree [3]; What's the Use

Cast: Walter Catlett; Claire Luce; Oscar Shaw; Genevieve Tobin

Notes: [1] Out Newark 9/15/24. [2] Music later used for title song of BLUE EYES. [3] Same music as "The Curtsey" in BLUE EYES.

1012 • DEAR WORLD

OPENED: 02/06/1969   Theatre: Mark Hellinger
Musical   Broadway: 132

Composer: Jerry Herman
Lyricist: Jerry Herman
Librettist: Jerome Lawrence; Robert E. Lee
Producer: Alexander H. Cohen
Director: Joe Layton

Source: MADWOMAN OF CHAILLOT, THE (Play: Jean Giraudoux); **Choreographer:** Joe Layton; **Costumes:** Freddy Wittop; **Dance Arranger:** Dorothea Freitag; **Lighting Designer:** Jean Rosenthal; **Musical Director:** Donald Pippin; **Orchestrations:** Philip J. Lang; **Set Design:** Oliver Smith; **Vocal Arranger:** Donald Pippin

Songs: And I Was Beautiful; Dear World; Dickie; Each Tomorrow Morning; Garbage; Have a Little Pity [1]; I Don't Want to Know; I Like Me [1]; I've Never Said I Love You; Kiss Her Now; Memory; Money Song, The [1]; One Person; Pearls; Sensible Woman, A [1]; Spring of Next Year, The; Thoughts; Through the Bottom of the Glass [1]; Voices

Cast: Jane Connell; Michael Davis; Miguel Godreau; Pamela Hall; Angela Lansbury; William Larsen; Joe Maisell; Carmen Mathews; Ty McConnell; Milo O'Shea; Kurt Peterson; Gene Varrone

Notes: The source was adapted by Maurice Valency. [1] Cut prior to opening.

1013 • DEAREST ENEMY

OPENED: 09/18/1925   Theatre: Knickerbocker
Musical   Broadway: 286

Composer: Richard Rodgers
Lyricist: Lorenz Hart
Librettist: Herbert Fields
Producer: George Ford
Director: John Murray Anderson; Harry Ford; Charles Sinclair

Choreographer: Carl Hemmer; **Costumes:** Hubert Davis; Mark Mooring; James Reynolds; **Musical Director:** Richard Rodgers; **Orchestrations:** Emil Gerstenberger; **Set Design:** Clark Robinson

Songs: Ale, Ale, Ale [1]; Bye and Bye; Cheerio; Dear Me [1]; Dearest Enemy; Full-Blown Roses; Gavotte; Girls Do Not Tempt Me [1]; Heigh-Ho, Lackaday; Here in My Arms [2]; Here's a Kiss; Hermits, The (What Do All the Hermits Do in Springtime) [3]; How Can We Help But Miss You; I Beg Your Pardon; I'd Like to Hide It; Old Enough to Love; Pipes of Pansy, The [5]; Sweet Peter; Tho We've No Authentic Reason (Finale Act I); War Is War; Where the Hudson River Flows

Cast: Flavia Arcaro; Helen Ford; Percy French; Alden Gay; Andrew Lawlor Jr.; Jane Overton; Charles Purcell; John Seymour; Helen Spring; Marian Williams

Notes: Titled DEAR ENEMY while out of town. Titled SWEET REBEL in pre-production. [1] Cut before New York. [2] In LIDO LADY in London. [3] From score of WINKLE TOWN. Also in A DANISH YANKEE IN KING TUT'S COURT and TEMPLE BELLES. [4] From score of WINKLE TOWN. [5] Cut prior to New York. Also cut from the scores of THE GIRL FRIEND, PEGGY-ANN and SHE'S MY BABY.

1014 • DEARIE

OPENED: 09/05/1920
Musical   Closed out of town

Composer: Malvin Franklin
Lyricist: Malvin Franklin; John P. Wilson
Librettist: John P. Wilson
Producer: Lee Morrison
Director: Lee Morrison

Source: WILDFIRE (Play: George Broadhurst; George V. Hobart); **Choreographer:** Max Scheck; **Costumes:** Mme. Helene Price; **Musical Director:** Malvin Franklin

Songs: African Golf; After You're Married a While; Breakfast Ball, The; Days of Long Ago, The; Dearie, My Dearie; Derby Day; Following the Hounds; I Think So Much of All the Boys; Johnny from London Town; My Easy Ridin' Man; My New Kentucky Home; Southern Nights; Take a Little Tip from Me; That Linger Longer Look

Cast: Cosmo Bellew; Georgiana Hewitt; Joseph McCallion; John Merkyl; Edwin Walter; Letty Yorke

Notes: Closed in Detroit.

1015 • DEATH OF BARON VON RICHTHOFEN AS WITNESSED FROM EARTH, THE

OPENED: 07/29/1982   Theatre: New York Shakespeare Festival
Musical   Off-Broadway: 45

Composer: Des McAnuff
Lyricist: Des McAnuff
Librettist: Des McAnuff
Producer: N.Y. Shakespeare Festival; Joseph Papp
Director: Des McAnuff

Choreographer: Jennifer Muller; **Costumes:** Patricia McGourty; **Lighting Designer:** Richard Nelson; **Musical Director:** Michael Roth; **Orchestrations:** Michael Starobin; **Set Design:** Douglas W. Schmidt; **Vocal Arranger:** Des McAnuff; Michael Roth; Michael Starobin

Songs: All I Wanted Was a Cup of Tea; April Twenty One; Congratulations; Dear Icarus; England-The U.K.; Four White Horses; Good Luck; Here We Are; I Don't Ask About Tomorrow; If I Have the Will; It's All Right for God; I've Got a Girl; 1918; Our Red Knight; Sarah; Save the Last Dance; Sitting in the Garden; Skies Have Gone Dry, The; Speed; Stand Up the Fatherland; Sweet Eternity; Take What You Can

Cast: Bob Gunton; Mark Linn-Baker; John Vickery; Robert Westenberg

1016 • DEBUTANTE, THE

OPENED: 12/07/1914   Theatre: Knickerbocker
Musical   Broadway: 48

Composer: Victor Herbert
Lyricist: Robert B. Smith
Librettist: Harry B. Smith; Robert B. Smith
Producer: John C. Fisher
Director: George Marion

Choreographer: Allan K. Foster; **Costumes:** Cora MacGeachy; William Henry Matthews; **Musical Director:** Carlo Edward; **Orchestrations:** Victor Herbert

Songs: All for the Sake of a Girl; Baker's Boy and the Chimney Sweep, The; Call Around Again; Cubist Opera, The; Dancing Lesson, The; Debutante One-Step [2]; Face Behind the Mask, The; Fate; Gay Life, The [1]; Golden Age, The; Love Is a Battle; Love of the Lorelei, The; Married Life; Never Mention Love When We're Alone; On a Sunny Afternoon [2]; Opening Chorus; Peggy's a Creature of Moods; Professor Cupid; Sextette; Springtime of Love Is Fairest [2]; Take Me Home with You [2]; When I Played Carmen; Will-O-the Wisp, The

Cast: William Danforth; Hazel Dawn

Notes: [1] Sheet music only. [2] ASCAP/Library of Congress.

1017 • DECAMERON, THE

OPENED: 04/12/1961   Theatre: East 74th Street
Musical   Off-Broadway: 39

Composer: Edward Earle
Lyricist: William Tarr; Yvonne Tarr
Librettist: Yvonne Tarr
Producer: Selma Tamber
Director: Burry Fredrik

Source: LOVE TALES, THE (Story: Giovanni Boccaccio); **Choreographer:** Edward Earle; **Costumes:** Frank Thompson; **Lighting Designer:** Ian Cadenhead; **Set Design:** John Conklin

Songs: Ballad of Tancred; Barnabo; Come, Sweet Love; Cuckold's Delight; Deceive Me; Golden Goblet; I Know, I Know; Love Is Paradise; Nightingale; Pirate's Song, The; Talk; 1348; What's Wrong with Me?; Women!

Cast: Louis Edmonds; DeAnn Mears; Jan Miner; Bob Roman

1018 • DECLINE AND FALL OF THE ENTIRE WORLD AS SEEN THROUGH THE EYES OF COLE PORTER, THE

OPENED: 03/30/1965   Theatre: Square East
Revue   Off-Broadway: 273

Composer: Cole Porter
Lyricist: Cole Porter
Producer: Ben Bagley
Director: Ben Bagley

Choreographer: Vernon Lusby; **Costumes:** Charles Fatone; **Dance Arranger:** Skip Redwine; **Lighting Designer:** Jules Fisher; **Musical Director:** Skip Redwine; **Vocal Arranger:** Skip Redwine

Songs: But in the Morning, No; By the Mississinewah; Come on In; Don't Look at Me That Way; Down in the Depths; Farming; Find Me a Primitive Man; Gigolo; Girls; How's Your Romance; I Happen to Like New York; I Introduced; I Loved Him But He Didn't Love Me; I Worship You; I'm in Love with a Soldier Boy; I've Got You on My Mind; I've Still Got My Health; Leader of a Big Time Band; Let's Do It; Let's Fly Away; Make It Another Old Fashioned; Most Gentlemen Don't Like Love; Ooh-La-La; Red Hot and Blue; Ridin' High; Tale of the Oyster; Throwin' a Ball Tonight; Tomorrow; Wake Up and Dream; What Shall I Do?; When I Was a Little Cuckoo

Cast: Carmen Alvarez; Kaye Ballard; William Hickey; Harold Lang; Elmarie Wendel

Notes: No original songs in this show.

1019 • DEEP HARLEM

OPENED: 01/07/1929   Theatre: Biltmore
Musical   Broadway: 8

Composer: Joe Jordan
Lyricist: Henry Creamer; J. Homer Tutt
Librettist: J. Homer Tutt; Salem Whitney
Producer: Samuel Gusman
Director: Henry Creamer

Songs: Deep Harlem; Deliver; I Shall Love You; Kentucky; Mexican Blues

Cast: Chappie Chappelle; John Mason; Neeka Shaw; J. Homer Tutt; Salem Whitney

Notes: No program available.

1020 • DEEP RIVER

OPENED: 10/04/1926   Theatre: Imperial
Musical   Broadway: 32

Composer: W. Frank Harling
Lyricist: Laurence Stallings
Producer: Arthur Hopkins
Director: Arthur Hopkins

Musical Director: Sepp Morscher; **Set Design:** Woodman Thompson

Songs: Ashes and Fire; Cherokee Rose; De Old Clay Road; Dis Is de Day; Love Lasts a Day; Po' Li'l Black Chile; Serenade Creole; Soft in de Moonlight; Two Little Stars

Cast: Luis Alberni; Bessie Allison; Roberto Ardelli; Jules Bledsoe; Frederick Burton; Arthur Campbell; Lottice Howell; Rue McClendon

Notes: No songs listed in program.

1021 • DEFENDER, THE
OPENED: 07/03/1902   Theatre: Herald Square
Musical   Broadway: 60

Composer: Charles Denee
Lyricist: Allen Lowe
Librettist: Allen Lowe; Frank Mandel
Producer: A.H. Chamberlyn
Director: Frank Smithson

Musical Director: George P. Towle; **Set Design:** D. Frank Dodge

Songs: Anglo-Saxons of Today; Boys Before the Mast, The; Gavotte; Good Night; Hail to the Baronet; Houp-La; I'll Be Your Rainbow; In the Good Old Summertime (C: George Evans; L: Ren Shields); Jack O'Lantern Man; Lift the Cup; Lighthouse and the Boat; Little Fly; Love Is Queen of the Sea; Man Who Hypnotized McCarthy, The; Pinky Panky Poo; Queens of Society; Vesper Bells; Welcome, Jellie Canvas

Cast: Emma Carus; Alexander Clark; Harry Davenport; Paula Edwardes; Blanche Ring

1022 • DELILAH
Notes: *See THE VAMP.*

1023 • DEMI-DOZEN
OPENED: 10/11/1958   Theatre: Upstairs at the
                                       Downstairs
Revue   Nightclub

Librettist: Bill Dana
Producer: Julius Monk
Director: John Heawood

Vocal Arranger: Stan Keen

Songs: Grand Opening (C: Harvey Schmidt; L: Tom Jones); Guess Who Was There [1] (C/L: Bud McCreery); Holy Man and the New Yorker, The [2] (C: Harvey Schmidt; L: Tom Jones); Intellectual's Rag, The (C/L: Jay Thompson); Mister Off-Broadway (C: Harvey Schmidt; L: Tom Jones); Monks Merrie Minstrel Show (C/L: Bud McCreery); One and All (C/L: Harvey Schmidt); Race of the Lexington Avenue Express, The (C: Harvey Schmidt; L: Tom Jones); Seasonal Sonata, A (C: Harvey Schmidt; L: Tom Jones); Statehood Hula (C: Harvey Schmidt; L: Tom Jones); Sunday in New York (C/L: Portia Nelson); 3rd Avenue El (C/L: Michael Brown); Yes Sirree (C: Michael Hughes; L: Joan Wile); You Fascinate Me So (C: Cy Coleman; L: Carolyn Leigh)

Cast: Jean Arnold; Ceil Cabot; Jane Connell; Jack Fletcher; George Hall; Gerry Matthews

Pianist: Gordon Connell; Stan Keen

Notes: This show ran over 500 performances. [1] Also in MEDIUM RARE. [2] Also in PIECES OF EIGHT.

1024 • DEMI-TASSE
Notes: *See THE CAPITOL REVUE.*

1025 • DENNING
Notes: *See MURDER ON BROADWAY.*

1026 • DERE MABLE
OPENED: 1920
Musical   Closed out of town

Composer: Raymond Hodges
Lyricist: John Hodges; Edward Streeter
Librettist: Edward Streeter
Producer: Marcus Klaw
Director: George Marion

Choreographer: Joseph C. Smith; **Costumes:** Schneider & Anderson; **Set Design:** Homer Emens

Songs: Back Home [2] (C: George Gershwin; L: Ira Gershwin); Before Me Lies the World [1] (C: Rosamond Hughes; L: John Hodges; Edward Streeter); (Madammuzzelle) Bon Nuit; Canteen Girl (L: Louis Harrison); I Don't Know Why (When I Dance with You) (C: George Gershwin; L: Irving Caesar); I Want to Be Wanted by You

(C: George Gershwin; L: Irving Caesar); In Gay Philopolis (L: Louis Harrison); Island of Do As You Please; One Little Girl I Prize, The (C/L: Sam Ash; J. Keirn Brennan; Bert Rule); Rube Jazz Dance (inst).; That's What They Like About Me; We're Pals (C: George Gershwin; L: Irving Caesar); When a Band That Is Jazz (L: Louis Harrison); When Love Comes Knocking at Your Heart [1] (C/L: Sam Ash; J. Keirn Brennan; Bert Rule); Why Must We Say Good-Bye [1] (C/L: Sam Ash; J. Keirn Brennan; Bert Rule); Your Eyes Have Told Me So (C: Egbert Van Alstyne; L: Gus Kahn)

Cast: Sam Ash; Louis Bennison; Hattie Burks; George Cukor; Robert Woolsey

Notes: Note George Cukor's inclusion in the cast. [1] Sheet music only. [2] Program erroneously credits Irving Caesar with lyrics.

1027 • DESERT SONG, THE

OPENED: 11/30/1926   Theatre: Casino
Musical   Broadway: 465

Composer: Sigmund Romberg
Lyricist: Oscar Hammerstein II; Otto Harbach
Librettist: Oscar Hammerstein II; Otto Harbach; Frank Mandel
Producer: Frank Mandel; Laurence Schwab
Director: Arthur Hurley

Choreographer: Bobby Connolly; **Costumes:** Vyvyan Donner; Mark Mooring; **Musical Director:** Oscar Bradley; **Set Design:** Woodman Thompson

Songs: Ali-Up [1]; All Hail to the General; Azuri's Dance of Triumph (inst.); Banishment, The; Desert Song, The; Dreaming in Paradise (Love's Dear Yearning); Eastern and Western Love; Farewell; French Military Marching Song; Has Anybody Seen My Bennie [4] (L: Oscar Hammerstein II; Otto Harbach; Harry B. Smith); High on a Hill; Ho! (The Riff Song); I Want a Kiss; I'll Be a Buoyant Girl; Let Love Go; Let's Have a Love Affair [2]; Love Is a Two-Edged Sword [1]; Margot; Morocco Dance of Marriage (inst.); My Little Castagnette; Not for Him [1]; O Pretty Maids of France [3]; One Alone; One Flower Grows Alone in Your Garden; One Good Man Gone Wrong; Romance; Sabre Song, The (L: Oscar Hammerstein II; Otto Harbach; Frank Mandel); Song of the Brass Key; Then You Will

Know (L: Oscar Hammerstein II; Otto Harbach; Frank Mandel); Tropics [3]; Why Did We Marry Soldiers?

Cast: Nellie Breen; Eddie Buzzell; Glen Dale; Robert Halliday; Margaret Irving; William O'Neal; Pearl Regay; Vivienne Segal

Notes: Titled LADY FAIR prior to New York. [1] Cut prior to Broadway. [2] Cut after opening. [3] Not in program. [4] ASCAP/Library of Congress only.

1028 • DESIRES OF 1927

OPENED: 10/1926
Revue   Closed out of town

Composer: James C. Johnson
Lyricist: Andy Razaf
Producer: Irvin C. Miller

Songs: Desire; My Texas Man; Sweet Virginia Blues; When; Wondering When

Cast: Adelaide Hall; J. Homer Tutt

Notes: No program available. "Sweet Virginia Blues" is the only song definitely from the score.

1029 • DESTRY RIDES AGAIN

OPENED: 04/23/1959   Theatre: Imperial
Musical   Broadway: 472

Composer: Harold Rome
Lyricist: Harold Rome
Librettist: Leonard Gershe
Producer: Max Brown; David Merrick
Director: Michael Kidd

Source: DESTRY RIDES AGAIN (Novel: Max Brand); **Choreographer:** Michael Kidd; **Costumes:** Alvin Colt; **Dance Arranger:** Genevieve Pitot; **Lighting Designer:** Jean Rosenthal; **Musical Director:** Lehman Engel; **Orchestrations:** Philip J. Lang; **Set Design:** Oliver Smith; **Vocal Arranger:** Lehman Engel

Songs: Anyone Would Love You; Are You Ready, Gyp Watson?; Ballad of the Gun; Bottleneck; Every Once in a While; Fair Warning; Good Good Thing, A [3]; (You're a) Handy Thing to Have Around the House [1]; Hoop-de-Dingle; I Hate Him; I Know Your Kind; I Say Hello; (We're) Ladies; Let's Talk About a Woman [2];

Not Guilty; Once Knew a Fella; Only Time Will Tell; Respectability; Ring on the Finger; Rose Lovejoy of Paradise Alley; Social, The; Sunshine Song, The [3]; Swap Her for a Mule [1]; Tomorrow Morning

Cast: Scott Brady; Marc Breaux; Don Crabtree; Dolores Gray; Andy Griffith; Rosetta LeNoire; Oran Osburne; Jack Prince; Libi Staiger; Elizabeth Watts

Notes: [1] Cut prior to New York. [2] Cut. Originally written for FANNY. [3] ASCAP/Library of Congress only.

1030 • DEVIL'S DEPUTY, THE
OPENED: 09/10/1894 Theatre: Abbey's
Musical Broadway: 72

Composer: Edward Jakobowski
Librettist: J. Cheever Goodwin
Director: Richard Barker

Costumes: Percy Anderson; **Musical Director:** Ernest Catenhusen; **Set Design:** Homer Emens; Richard Marston

Cast: Homer Emens; Lulu Glaser; Christie MacDonald; J.C. Miron; Adele Ritchie; Rhys Thomas; Francis Wilson

Notes: No songs listed in program.

1031 • DEW DROP INN (1917)
OPENED: 1917
Musical Closed out of town

Composer: A. Baldwin Sloane
Lyricist: John E. Hazzard; Percival Knight
Librettist: John E. Hazzard; Percival Knight
Director: Frank Smithson

Musical Director: Manuel Klein

Songs: Have You Anything On for Tonight; Husking Bee; I'll Be Coming Home to You; It's the Jay Town; Mandala; Other Days and Now; Road House Rag; Some Day; Sweetest Little Prison in the World, The; That Wonderful Girl; Through Twilight Lane; Travel On; You Kind O' Look Good to Me

Cast: Percival Knight

Notes: From a program of Detroit 10/14/17.

1032 • DEW DROP INN (1920)
OPENED: 1920
Musical Closed out of town

Composer: Dan Dody
Lyricist: Dan Dody
Librettist: Billy Watson
Producer: I.H. Herk
Director: I.H. Herk; Billy Watson

Choreographer: Dan Dody

Songs: Bye Lo; Carolina Sunshine; Chop Sticks and Room 202; Everybody's Crazy Over Dixie; If You'll Only Say My Honey You'll Be Mine; Mary [1]; Number 10; Oo-La-La, Wee Wee; Opening Act II; Opening Chorus; Over the River; Sahara; Wedding of Minnie Chimmie and Mr. Jazz, The; When My Baby Smiles at Me [1]; You Don't Need the Wine to Have a Wonderful Time [1]; You Ought to See the Women Swimming

Cast: Billy Watson

Notes: From a program of Wilkes-Barre 4/12/20. Some of these songs were probably the famous popular songs of the day. [1] May be popular song of the day.

1033 • DEW DROP INN (1923)
OPENED: 05/17/1923 Theatre: Astor
Musical Broadway: 52

Composer: Alfred Goodman
Lyricist: Cyrus Wood
Librettist: Walter De Leon; Edward Delaney Dunn
Producer: Messrs. Shubert
Director: Fred G. Latham

Choreographer: M. Francis Weldon; **Musical Director:** Alfred Newman; **Set Design:** Watson Barratt

Songs: Girl May As Well Marry Well, A; Goodbye Forever (C: Rudolf Friml; Alfred Goodman); I'm a Flapper Lady (C: J. Fred Coots; Jean Schwartz; L: McElbert Moore); Lady [1] (C: J. Fred Coots; Jean Schwartz; L: McElbert Moore); (If There Were Not Any) Men; Moonlight Waltz; Opening Ensemble; Porter! Porter!; Pretty Ankle; Primrose Path, The; Struttinest Strutter, The; Travesty; We

Two (C: Rudolf Friml; Al Goodman); You Can't Experiment on Me

Cast: James Barton; Harry Clarke; Jack Squire; Mabel Withee

Notes: The show reopened on 7/30/23 for an additional 31 performances. [1] From score of BAL-TABARIN. ASCAP credits this song to Friml and Goodman.

1034 • DIAMOND FOR CARLA, A
OPENED: 1959
TV Musical

Composer: Sammy Fain
Lyricist: Paul Francis Webster

Songs: Amigos; Diamond for Carla, A; For the Love of You; Fountain of Dreams; Trousseau Song

Notes: No other information available.

1035 • DIAMOND IN THE ROUGH
OPENED: 1968
Musical   Unproduced

Composer: Vernon Duke
Lyricist: John Everest

Songs: Afternoon Delight; Ban the Book!; Censorship; Diamond in the Rough; Ev'ry One of Us; Grand Manner, The; I May Never Get Well Again; I'm Not His Sister Anymore; Jumpin' Frog; Live and Love a Lot; Man You Are, The; New Pilgrim's Prayer, The; New Year Filled with Love, A; Perfect Chaperone, The; Please Be Patient with Me; Quadrille, The; Safe Little World; She Has to Be the Right Girl; We're All Going on a Honeymoon; What Do You Wanna Get Married For?; When I Was a Little Boy; You Are Youth

1036 • DIAMOND LIL
OPENED: 04/09/1928   Theatre: Royale
Play   Broadway: 323

Author: Mae West
Producer: Jack Linder
Director: Mae West

Songs: Diamond Lil [1] (C/L: Robert Sterling); Heart of the Bowery [2] (C/L: Unknown)

Cast: Curtis Cooksey; Herbert Duffy; J. Merrill Holmes; Jack La Rue; Mae West

Notes: [1] Dropped after opening. [2] Added after opening.

1037 • DIAMOND STUDS
OPENED: 01/14/1975   Theatre: Westside
Musical   Off-Broadway: 232

Composer: Bland Simpson; Jim Wann
Lyricist: Bland Simpson; Jim Wann
Librettist: Jim Wann
Producer: Chelsea Theatre Center
Director: John L. Haber

Choreographer: Patricia Birch

Songs: Abiding with You [2]; Bright Morning Star [1]; Cakewalk into Kansas City; I Don't Need a Man to Know I'm Good; Jesse James Robbed This Train; K.C. Line [1]; King Cole [1]; Mama Fantastic; New Prisoner's Song [1]; Northfield, Minnesota; Pancho Villa; Put It Where the Moon Don't Shine; Saloon Piano; Sleepy Time Down South; These Southern States That I Love; Unreconstructed Rebel, The (C/L: Jan Davidson); When I Get the Call [1]; When I Was a Cowboy; Year of Jubilo, The [1]

Cast: Joyce Cohen; Bill Hicks; Mike Sheehan; Bland Simpson; Rick Simpson; Tommy Thompson; Jim Wann; Jim Watson

Notes: [1] Based on traditional song. [2] Not in program.

1038 • DIAMONDS
OPENED: 12/16/1984   Theatre: Circle in the Square Downtown
Revue   Off-Broadway: 122

Librettist: Bud Abbott; Ralph G. Allen; Roy Blount Jr.; Richard Camp; Lou Costello; Lee Eisenberg; Sean Kelly; John Lahr; Arthur Masella; Harry Stein; John Weidman; Alan Zweibel
Producer: Harold DeFelice; Kenneth-John Productions; Stephen G. Martin; Louis W. Scheeder
Director: Harold Prince

Choreographer: Theodore Pappas; **Costumes:** Judith Dolan; **Lighting Designer:** Ken Billington; **Musical Director:** Paul Gemignani; **Orchestrations:** Paul Gemignani; **Set Design:** Tony Straiges

Songs: Boys of Summer, The (C/L: Larry Grossman); Diamonds Are Forever (C: John Kander; L: Fred Ebb); Escorte-Moi (Take Me Out to the Ball Game) (C: Albert von Tilzer; L: Jack Norworth); Favorite Sons (C: Larry Grossman; L: Ellen Fitzhugh); He Threw Out the Ball (C: Larry Grossman; L: Ellen Fitzhugh); Hundreds of Hats (C: Jonathan Sheffer; L: Howard Ashman); In the Cards (C: Alan Menken; L: David Zippel); Ka-razy (C: Doug Katsaros; L: David Zippel); Let's Play Ball (C/L: Gerard Alessandrini); 1919 (C/L: Jim Wann); Song for a Hunter College Graduate (C: Jonathan Sheffer; L: Howard Ashman); Song for a Pinch Hitter (C: Larry Grossman; L: Ellen Fitzhugh); Stay in Your Own Backyard (C: Lyn Udall; L: Karl Kennett); Vendors (C: Cy Coleman; L: Betty Comden; Adolph Green); What You'd Call a Dream (C/L: Craig Carnelia); Winter in New York (C: John Kander; L: Fred Ebb)

Cast: Loni Ackerman; Susan Bigelow; Jackee Harry; Scott Holmes; Dick Latessa; Larry Riley; Nestor Serrano; Chip Zien

1039 • DICK BUTTON'S ICE-TRAVAGANZA

Notes: *See ICE-TRAVAGANZA.*

1040 • DICK VAN DYKE SHOW, THE

OPENED: 1962   Theatre: CBS
TV Show

Director: John Rich

Songs: This Nearly Was Mine [1] (C: Richard Rodgers; L: Oscar Hammerstein II); Twizzle, The (C/L: Mack David; Jerry Livingston)

Cast: Jack Albertson; Morey Amsterdam; Richard Deacon; Jerry Lanning; Mary Tyler Moore; Rose Marie; Dick Van Dyke

Notes: [1] From SOUTH PACIFIC.

1041 • DICK WHITTINGTON

OPENED: 1909
Musical

Composer: Manuel Klein
Lyricist: Edward A. Paulton
Producer: Lee Shubert; Sam S. Shubert

Songs: After Dark; I Think Such a Lot of You; If I Had You in My Canoe; March Along to the Sound of the Band; McCoy; Proposal Duet; Yodeling Yan

Notes: No other information available.

1042 • DID YOU EVER?

OPENED: 1915   Theatre: Winter Garden
                      Broadway

Producer: Messrs. Shubert

Songs: My Bird of Paradise (My Honolulu Girl) (C/L: Irving Berlin)

Cast: Blossom Seeley

Notes: A vaudeville show.

1043 • DIE BALLKONIGIN

OPENED: 1913
Musical

Composer: Evelyn Baker; Herbert E. Haines
Lyricist: Fritz Luner; Karl Tuschl
Librettist: Fritz Luner; Karl Tuschl

Source: CATCH OF THE SEASON, THE (Musical: Evelyn Baker; Herbert E. Haines; Cosmo Hamilton; Seymour Hicks; Charles H. Taylor)

Songs: Die Susse Pariserin (C: Jerome Kern; L: Fritz Luner)

Notes: Opened in Vienna. The Kern song might have been written for THE CATCH OF THE SEASON of which this is an adaptation.

1044 • DIE LINDENWIRTIN

OPENED: 03/30/1933
Musical

Composer: Michael Krausz
Lyricist: Rudolf Schanzer; Ernst Welisch; Joe Young
Librettist: Rudolf Schanzer; Ernst Welisch

Songs: Blame It on the Wine (Zu Jeder Liebe Gehort ein Glaschen Wein); Sweetheart on the Rhine (Du Blonde Lindenwirtin Vom Rhein); When our Hearts Go Waltzing Along (Mein Herz Hat Leise Dein Herz Gegrusst); You're the First Thing I Pray for Each Morning (Du Bist Mein Morgen — Und Mein Nachtgebetchen)

Notes: Performed at the Metropole Theatre, Berlin. The Young songs were registered with ASCAP in 1931.

1045 • DIFFERENT TIMES

OPENED: 05/01/1972   Theatre: ANTA
Musical   Broadway: 24

Composer: Michael Brown
Lyricist: Michael Brown
Librettist: Michael Brown
Producer: Bowman Productions
Director: Michael Brown

Choreographer: Tod Jackson; **Costumes:** David Guthrie; **Lighting Designer:** Martin Aronstein; **Musical Director:** Rene Wiegert; **Orchestrations:** Arthur Harris; Norman Paris; Ted Royal; **Set Design:** David Guthrie; **Vocal Arranger:** Rene Wiegert

Songs: Daddy, Daddy; Different Times; Everything in the World Has a Place; Forward into Tomorrow; Genuine Plastic; He Smiles; Here's Momma; I Dreamed About Roses; I Feel Grand; I Like You; I Miss Him; I Wish I Didn't Love Him; I'm Not Through; Life of a Woman, The; Marianne; One More Time; Seeing the Sights; Sock Life in the Eye; Spirit Is Moving, The; Thanks a Lot; When They Start Again; Words I Never Said, The; You're Perfect

Cast: Mary Jo Catlett; Patti Karr; Joe Masiell; Mary Bracken Phillips; Jamie Ross

1046 • DIFFICULT WOMAN, THE

OPENED: 04/25/1962   Theatre: Barbizon-Plaza
Musical   Off-Broadway: 1

Composer: Richard Freitas
Lyricist: George Mysels; Morty Neff

Librettist: Maurice Alevy; Malcolm Boylan
Producer: Donald C. Fetzko; Nikardi Productions
Director: Maurice Alevy

Source: UNKNOWN (Play: Conrado N. Roxolo); **Costumes:** Louis Kennel; **Lighting Designer:** Louis Kennel; **Musical Director:** Richard Freitas; **Orchestrations:** Richard Freitas; **Set Design:** Louis Kennel

Songs: Bull Blood and Brandy; Dream Ballet; 'El Cuando'; Grandioso; Hangman's Plea, The; I Won't Take No for an Answer; Malumbo; Milonga; Minuet; One in My Position; Patience and Gentleness; Poor Isabel; Siesta; Taking Inventory; This Is the Day; Throw the House Out of the Window; Tormented; Ulterior Motive; Ungrateful; What a Life

Cast: Odetta McEwen; Warren Robertston; Jack Russell

1047 • DIG WE MUST

OPENED: 07/04/1959
Revue   Closed out of town

Composer: David Baker
Lyricist: Ira Wallach
Librettist: Ira Wallach
Producer: David Baker; Ronald Rawson
Director: Ruth Rawson

Choreographer: Edmund Balin; **Costumes:** William Hargate; **Lighting Designer:** Dan Butt; **Set Design:** William Ritman

Songs: Camp Headstrong; Doin' the Consumer; Downstream; Duet for 5 People; Fellowship; Jag; Just Us; Lou; Putnams of Westport, The; Silent Heart; Take Us to Our Leader; Think, Inc.; Thrown Together; You and I

Cast: John Bartes; Bob Dishy; Alice Ghostley; Gerald Hiken; Paul Lynde; Eileen Rodgers; Evelyn Russell; Pianist: John Morris

Notes: A show in East Hampton.

1048 • DILLY

OPENED: 1955
Musical   Unproduced

Composer: Vernon Duke
Lyricist: Jerome Lawrence; Robert E. Lee

Songs: Another Day, Another Buck; Bachelorhood; Backlot Blues, The; Dilly; Don'tcha Hate It; Farewell to New York; He's Back in Town; Holiday in Hollywood; I Sure Have Been in Love; I'm About to Become a Lover; In Our Chateau in Brooklyn; It's Been Done; Just Lucky, I Guess; Kissing Song, The; Lad for Ev'ry Lass, A; Look at Me; Love Me Now; Lucre, Love or Liquor; Mocambo Mambo; Now Is the Time for All Good Men; Roses in the Rain; Since Yesterday; Small Talk; Small World; Story Conference, The; Take the Money; There's Nothing Like This Old Fasioned; Though I Said No to You Yesterday; Village Called Hollywood, A; What If You're Not; Who's Excited

1049 • DIME A DOZEN

OPENED: 10/18/1962   Theatre: PLaza 9-
Revue   Nightclub: 728

Librettist: William F. Brown; Dee Caruso; Bill Levine; Bruce Williamson
Producer: Julius Monk
Director: Julius Monk; Frank Wagner

Costumes: Donald Brooks; **Lighting Designer:** Don Lamb; **Orchestrations:** William Roy; **Set Design:** Robert Miller; Ed Wittstein; **Vocal Arranger:** William Roy

Songs: Alumnae Report (C: Jay Foote; L: Allison Roulston); Barry's Boys (C/L: June Reizner); Battle Hymn of the Rialto (C: Jay Foote; L: Allison Roulston); Bless This School (C: William Roy; L: Maxwell Edward Siegel); Cholesterol Love Song (C/L: June Reizner); Collecting of the Plaid (C/L: Lesley Davison); Dime a Dozen (C: William Roy; L: William Brown); Johnny Come Lately (C: Claibe Richardson; L: Seymour Zogott); Le Hot Spot [2] (C: Jay Foote; L: Allison Roulston); Lincoln Center [1] (C/L: Rod Warren); Making of a Man, The (C: Alec Wilder; L: William Engvick); Marching for Peace (C/L: Lesley Davison); Minnows and the Sharks, The (C: Jay Foote; L: Allison Roulston); Ode to an Eminent Daily (C: William Roy; L: Bruce Williamson); Plaza Waltz Waltz, The (C/L: Michael Brown); Requiem for Everyone (C/L: Bud McCreery); Slow Down Moses (C/L: Michael Brown); Something Good Like You (C: Sam Pottle; L: Tom Whedon); Ten Percent Banlon (C/L: Lesley Davison); Thor (C/L: Jack Holmes)

Cast: Susan Browning; Jack Fletcher; Gerry Matthews; Rex Robbins; Fredricka Weber; Mary Louise Wilson

Pianist: Robert Colston; Carl Norman; William Roy

Notes: [1] Added after opening. From DRESSED TO THE NINES. [2] Cut after opening.

1050 • DINAH

OPENED: 1923
Musical

Composer: Tim Brymn
Lyricist: Tim Brymn
Librettist: Irvin C. Miller
Producer: Irvin C. Miller

Cast: May Barnes; Will A. Cook; Alonzo Fenderson; Lemuel Jackson; Irvin C. Miller; Cecil Rivers; Gertrude Saunders; Margaret Simms

Notes: No other information available.

1051 • DION O'DARE

OPENED: 1907
Play   Closed out of town

Composer: Frank Herson; Fiske O'Hara
Lyricist: Frank Herson; Fiske O'Hara
Producer: Charles E. Blaney

Songs: If It Wasn't for the Fairies; My Little Irish Rose; Norah McNamara; O'Hara See Saw; Sprig of Shamrock, A

Cast: Frank Herson; Fiske O'Hara

Notes: Information from sheet music.

1052 • DIRI

OPENED: 1919

Songs: Gee I'm Glad that I'm from Dixie So I Can Get a Dixie Welcome Home (C: Eubie Blake; L: Noble Sissle)

Notes: No other information available.

1053 • DISPATCHES

OPENED: 04/19/1979   Theatre: Public
Revue   Off-Broadway: 77

Composer: Elizabeth Swados
Lyricist: Elizabeth Swados

Librettist: Elizabeth Swados
Producer: N.Y. Shakespeare Festival; Joseph Papp
Director: Elizabeth Swados

Source: DISPATCHES (Book: Michael Herr);
Costumes: Hilary Rosenfeld; **Lighting Designer:** Jennifer Tipton; **Set Design:** Patricia Woodbridge

Songs: Back in the World Now; Beautiful for Once; Bougainvillea (L: Dan San; Trich Watanabe); Breathing In; Crazy; Flip Religion; Freezing and Burning; Ground Was Always in Play, The; Helicopter, Helicopter; I See a Road; Mix, The; Prayers in the Delta; Quakin' and Shakin'; Six Fucking Shades of Green; Song of the LURP; Stoned in Saigon; Take the Glamour Out of War; These Were the Faces; This War Gets Old; Thou Shalt Not Be Afraid; Tiger Lady

Cast: Penelope Bodry; Ray Contreras; Karen Evans; Tony Franklin; Rodney Hudson; Roger Lawson; Joan MacIntosh; Paul McCrane; William Parry; David Schecter; Gedde Watanabe

1054 • DISTRICT LEADER, THE
OPENED: 04/30/1906   Theatre: Wallack
Musical   Broadway: 8

Composer: Joseph E. Howard
Lyricist: Joseph E. Howard
Librettist: Joseph E. Howard

Songs: Heart to Let, A; Home Is Home; Make Your Own Sunshine (L: Collin Davis); Same Old Story (L: Arthur Gillespie); Sing Sing Sammy Sen; So (L: Collin Davis); Something Doing Around My Heart; Union Square [1]; Way Down in Jersey; What's the Use of Dreaming?; When You Go Out to Dine; Won't You Be My Girlie?; You're the Sweetest Girl I Know (L: Arthur Gillespie)

Cast: Mabel Barrison; Joseph E. Howard; Dave Lewis

Notes: Program from Toledo 10/04/08. No New York program available. Later revised as LOVE AND POLITICS. See under that show for additional songs. [1] Out 12/14/06 Cedar Rapids.

1055 • DIVA IS DISMISSED, THE
OPENED: 10/30/1994   Theatre: Public
One-Person Show   Off-Broadway

Composer: Jenifer Lewis
Lyricist: Jenifer Lewis
Librettist: Jenifer Lewis; Charles Randolph-Wright
Producer: N.Y. Shakespeare Festival
Director: Charles Randolph-Wright

Lighting Designer: David Castaneda; **Musical Director:** Michael Skloff

Songs: And I Was Fired (C/L: Jenifer Lewis; C: Michael Skloff; L: Mark A. Brown; Charles Randolph-Wright); Climb; Grandma Small; I Wanna Come Home (C/L: Jenifer Lewis; Charles Randolph-Wright; Michael Skloff); Killer Cheer (L: Jenifer Lewis; Charles Randolph-Wright); Staring at the Moon

Cast: Jenifer Lewis

1056 • DIVERSIONS
OPENED: 11/07/1958   Theatre: Downtown
Revue   Off-Broadway: 85

Composer: Buster Davis
Lyricist: Steven Vinaver
Librettist: Steven Vinaver
Producer: New Princess Company
Director: Steven Vinaver

Costumes: Charles Hanford; **Lighting Designer:** A. William Strom; **Musical Director:** Buster Davis; **Set Design:** A. William Strom

Songs: Bolero [1]; Boots [1]; Detective Story [1]; Fill the Cup [1]; Five Plus One [1]; Goodnight [1]; He Follows Me Around; Hello [1]; Here Comes the Ballad; Listening [1]; Musicians [1]; Prayer; Production Number [1]; Subway Rag; Three Cans of Film [1]; Touch and Go; White Is the Dove; You're Nothing; You're Wonderful

Cast: Aline Brown; Nancy Dussault; Peter Feldman; Gabi Mann; Thom Molinaro; Cy Young

Notes: [1] These are songs from the preview.

1057 • DIXIE BREVITIES
OPENED: 1925
Revue

Composer: Inez Dennis; Marcus Slayter
Librettist: Quintard Miller
Producer: Quintard Miller; Marcus Slayter

Cast: Covan and Florence; Inez Dennis; George Wilshire

Notes: No other information available.

1058 • DIXIE TO BROADWAY
OPENED: 10/29/1924   Theatre: Broadhurst
Revue   Broadway: 77

Composer: Arthur Johnston; George W. Meyer
Lyricist: Grant Clarke; Roy Turk
Librettist: Walter De Leon; Tom Howard; Sidney Lazarus; Lew Leslie
Producer: Lew Leslie
Director: Lew Leslie

Musical Director: Will Vodery

Songs: Blues Have Got Me, The [1]; Dixie Dreams (C: Arthur Johnston; L: Grant Clark); Dixie Wildflowers; He Only Comes to See Me Once in a While [3]; Heebie Jeebie Blues [2]; If My Dreams Come True; I'm a Little Blackbird Looking for a Bluebird [3]; Jazz Time Came from the South; Jungle Nights in Dixieland (Jungle Town Has Moved to Dixieland) [3]; Mandy Make Up Your Mind [3] (C: George W. Meyer); Prisoners Up to Date; Put Your Old Bandana On; Trottin' to the Land of Cotton Melodies

Cast: Shelton Brooks; Hamtree Harrington; Florence Mills

Notes: [1] Out Philadelphia 2/23/25. [2] Out Atlantic City 8/4/24. [3] Also in LEW LESLIE'S BLACKBIRDS (1926).

1059 • DO BLACK PATENT LEATHER SHOES REALLY REFLECT UP?
OPENED: 05/27/1982   Theatre: Alvin
Musical   Broadway: 5

Composer: Alaric Jens; James Quinn
Lyricist: Alaric Jens; James Quinn
Librettist: John R. Powers
Producer: Daniel A. Golman; Libby Adler Mages; Mavin Productions
Director: Mike Nussbaum

Source: DO BLACK PATENT LEATHER SHOES REALLY REFLECT UP? (Book: John R. Powers); **Choreographer:** Thommie Walsh; **Costumes:**

Nancy Potts; **Dance Arranger:** Peter Larson; **Lighting Designer:** Marilyn Rennagel; **Musical Director:** Larry Hochman; **Orchestrations:** Jerome Jay Dryer; **Set Design:** James Maronek; **Vocal Arranger:** Jerome Jay Dryer; Larry Hochman

Songs: Cookie Cutters; Doo-Waa, Doo-Wee; Friends, the Best Of; Get Ready, Eddie; Greatest Gift, The; How Far Is Too Far; I Must Be in Love; It's the Nuns; Late Bloomer and Prom Montage; Little Fat Girls; Mad Bombers and Prom Queens; Patron Saints; Private Parts [1]; Thank God; We're Saving Ourselves for Marriage [1]

Cast: Ellen Crawford; Robert Fitch; Catherine Fries; Amy Miller; Maureen Moore; Russ Thacker

Notes: [1] Out prior to Broadway.

1060 • DO I HEAR A WALTZ?
OPENED: 03/18/1965   Theatre: 46th Street
Musical   Broadway: 220

Composer: Richard Rodgers
Lyricist: Stephen Sondheim
Librettist: Arthur Laurents
Producer: Richard Rodgers
Director: John Dexter

Source: TIME OF THE CUCKOO, THE (Play: Arthur Laurents); **Choreographer:** Herbert Ross; **Costumes:** Beni Montresor; **Dance Arranger:** Richard de Benedictis; **Lighting Designer:** Jules Fisher; **Musical Director:** Frederick Dvonch; **Orchestrations:** Ralph Burns; **Set Design:** Beni Montresor

Songs: Bargaining; Do I Hear a Waltz? (1) [2] (C: Stephen Sondheim); Do I Hear a Waltz? (2); Everybody Loves Leona [1]; Here We Are Again; Moon in My Window; No Understand; Perfectly Lovely Couple; Perhaps [1]; Philadelphia [1]; Someone Like You; Someone Woke Up; Stay; Take the Moment; Thank You So Much; Thinking; This Week Americans; Two By Two [1]; We're Gonna Be All Right (2); We're Gonna Be All Right (1) [1]; What Do We Do? We Fly!

Cast: Elizabeth Allen; Helon Blount; Carol Bruce; Fleury D'Antonakis; Stuart Damon; James Dybas; Sergio Franchi; Michael Lamont; James

Luisi; Jack Manning; Julienne Marie; Casper Roos; Madeleine Sherwood; Christopher Votos

Notes: [1] Cut during tryout. [2] Not used.

1061 • DO RE MI

OPENED: 01/26/1960   Theatre: St. James
Musical   Broadway: 400

Composer: Jule Styne
Lyricist: Betty Comden; Adolph Green
Librettist: Garson Kanin
Producer: David Merrick
Director: Garson Kanin

Source: DO RE MI (Novel: Garson Kanin);
   Choreographer: Marc Breaux; Deedee Wood;
   Costumes: Irene Sharaff; **Dance Arranger:** David
   Baker; **Musical Director:** Lehman Engel;
   Orchestrations: Luther Henderson; **Set Design:**
   Boris Aronson; **Vocal Arranger:** Buster Davis

Songs: Adventure; All of My Life; All You Need Is a Quarter; Ambition; Asking for You; Come On Down to Venezuala; Cry Like the Wind; Don't Be Ashamed of a Teardrop [1]; Fireworks; I Know about Love; It's Legitimate; Juke Box Hop, The; Late, Late Show, The; Life's Not That Simple [1]; Love in Outer Space; Make Someone Happy; She Doesn't Understand Me [2]; Success; Take a Job; V.I.P.; Waiting, Waiting; What's New at the Zoo?

Cast: David Burns; Nancy Dussault; George Givot; Al Lewis; George Mathews; John Reardon; Phil Silvers; Nancy Walker

Notes: [1] Cut after opening. [2] Cut prior to opening.

1062 • DO YOU KNOW THE MILKY WAY?

OPENED: 10/16/1961   Theatre: Billy Rose
Play   Broadway: 16

Composer: Alex Fry
Lyricist: Lyon Phelps
Librettist: Karl Wittlinger
Producer: Dick Button; Paul Feigay; Ninon Tallon
Director: Herbert Berghof

Costumes: Edith Lutyens Bel Geddes; **Lighting Designer:** Lee Watson; **Set Design:** Colin Low

Songs: Child's Song, The; Do You Know the Milky Way?; Vagabond Song, The

Cast: Hal Holbrook; George Voskovec

1063 • DOCTOR JAZZ

OPENED: 03/19/1975   Theatre: Winter Garden
Musical   Broadway: 5

Composer: Buster Davis
Lyricist: Buster Davis
Librettist: Buster Davis
Producer: Cyma Rubin
Director: Donald McKayle

Choreographer: Donald McKayle; **Costumes:** Raoul Pene du Bois; **Incidental Music:** Luther Henderson; **Lighting Designer:** Feder; **Musical Director:** Buster Davis; **Orchestrations:** Luther Henderson; **Set Design:** Raoul Pene du Bois; **Vocal Arranger:** Buster Davis

Songs: All I Want Is My Black Baby Back; Anywhere the Wind Blows; Blues My Naughty Sweetie Gve to Me (C/L: Arthur Swanstrom; C: Carey Morgan; L: Charles McCarron); Charleston Rag (inst.) (C: Eubie Blake); Cleopatra Had a Jazz Band (C: J.L. Morgan; L: Jack Coogan); Dr. Jazz (C: Joseph "King" Oliver; L: Walter Melrose); Everybody Leaves You; Evolution Papa; Free and Easy; Georgia Shows 'Em How; Good-Time Flat Blues (C/L: A.J. Piron); I Love It (C: Harry Von Tilzer; L: E. Ray Goetz); I've Got Elgin Watch Movements in My Hips; Juba Dance; Look Out for Lil; Rehearsal Tap; Swannee Strut; Those Sheik-of-Araby Blues; We've Got Connections

Cast: Paul Eichel; Lola Falana; Quitman D. Fludd III; Lillian Hayman; Hector Jaime Mercado; Dan Strayhorn; Bobby Van

Notes: Associate orchestrators: Dick Hyman and Sy Oliver.

1064 • DOCTOR SELAVY'S MAGIC THEATRE

OPENED: 11/23/1972   Theatre: Mercer-O'Casey
Musical   Off-Broadway: 144

Composer: Stanley Silverman
Lyricist: Tom Hendry
Producer: Lyn Austin; Oliver Smith
Director: Richard Foreman

Musical Director: Stanley Silverman;
  Orchestrations: Stanley Silverman; **Set Design:**
Richard Foreman

Songs: Bankrupt Blues; Dearest Man; Doesn't It Bug
You; Dusky Shadows; Every New Beginning [1];
Fireman's Song; Future for Sale; I Live By My
Wits; Let's Hear It for Daddy Moola; Life on the
Inside; Long Live Free Enterprise; Money in the
Bank; More You Get, The; Party's Gonna End;
Poor Boy (L: Stanley Silverman); Requiem
(L: Richard Foreman; John Hirsch); Strawberry-
Blueberry; Three Menu Songs; What Are You
Proposing; Where You Been Hiding Till Now

Cast: Ron Faber; Jessica Harper; George McGrath;
Barry Primus

Notes: Lenox Arts Center production. [1] Not in
program.

1065 • DOING OUR BIT

OPENED: 10/18/1917   Theatre: Winter Garden
Revue   Broadway: 130

Composer: Sigmund Romberg; Herman Timberg
Lyricist: Harold Atteridge
Librettist: Harold Atteridge
Producer: J.J. Shubert; Lee Shubert
Director: J.C. Huffman

Choreographer: Allan K. Foster; **Costumes:** Homer
Conant; **Musical Director:** Oscar Radin; **Set
Design:** Joseph Physioc; John Young

Songs: Adopt a Pretty Baby; Colonial Ballet;
Dance, Dance, Dance; Doing My Bit; Egyptian
Rag; Fashion Show, The; Fiesta; Fine Feathers
(C: Sigmund Romberg); For the Sake of
Humanity (C: Sigmund Romberg); Gimme This
— Gimme This — Gimme That [3] (C: Nat
Vincent; L: L. Wolfe Gilbert; Alex Sullivan);
Gypsy Man, The; Hello, Miss Tango!; I May Be
Small, But I Have Big Ideas; I'd Like to See the
Kaiser With a Lily in His Hand [2] (C/L: Billy
Frisch; Howard Johnson; Henry Leslie); I'm the
Brother of the Lily of the Valley [2] (C: Anatole
Friedland; L: L. Wolfe Gilbert; Henry Lewis); Let
Her Go; Loving Daddy, A [1]; Mister Rag and I;
Nothing On To-Day; Oh, You Sweeties;
Old-Fashioned Girls; Orange Blossoms; Perfect
Jewels; Phantom of Your Smile, The; Roses; Sally
Down Our Alley [1]; Wild, Wild Women, The [2]
(C: Al Piantadosi; L: Henry Lewis; Al Wilson);

You Make Me Feel So Foolish, When I'm Making
Love to You [2] (C: Fred Fisher; L: Alfred Bryan;
Henry Lewis; Joseph McCarthy)

Cast: Sam Ash; James J. Corbett; Rosetta Duncan;
Vivian Duncan; Ada Lewis; Henry Lewis;
Herman Timberg; Frank Tinney; Ed Wynn

Notes: [1] Cut after opening. [2] Sheet music only.
[3] ASCAP/Library of Congress only.

1066 • DOLL GIRL, THE

OPENED: 08/25/1913   Theatre: Globe
Musical   Broadway: 88

Composer: Leo Fall
Lyricist: Harry B. Smith
Librettist: Harry B. Smith
Producer: Charles Frohman

Source: RIQUETTE ET SA MERE (Musical: Leo
Stein; A.M. Willner); **Source:** UNKNOWN (Play:
A. de Caillavet; de Fleurs); **Choreographer:**
Edward Royce; **Musical Director:** Gustave
Salzer

Songs: Brittany; Come On Over Here [1] (C: Walter
Kollo; L: Jerome Kern; Harry B. Smith);
Foolishness [2]; Hola! Hola! [2]; If We Were on
Our Honeymoon (Railway Duet) (C: Jerome
Kern); I'm Going Away (C: Jerome Kern); In the
Movies; It Is I; Julia Dear [2]; Little Thing Like a
Kiss, A [4] (C: Jerome Kern); Now and Then;
Opening Act II [6]; Papa; Rosalilla of Sevilla;
Russian Dance (Opening Act Two) [3] (C: Jerome
Kern); Serenade; That Ragtime Dinner Band
(C: Will E. Haines; L: Wilfred Chandler); That's
Love with a Capital L (C: P.H. Christine); What
Do You Say, Dolly Dear?; When Three Is
Company (Cupid Song) [5] (C: Jerome Kern;
L: M.E. Rourke); When You're on the Stage; Will
It All End in Smoke? (C: Jerome Kern); You're So
Fascinating

Cast: Richard Carle; Charles McNaughton; Hattie
Williams

Notes: [1] Originally in THE WOMAN HATERS.
[2] In out of town program of 11/10/13. [3] Sheet
music. [4] Later revised as "Greenwich Village"
in OH LADY! LADY!! [5] Music later used for
"Just Because You're You" in ZIEGFELD
FOLLIES OF 1917. [6] ASCAP/Library of
Congress only.

1067 • DOLLAR PRINCESS, THE

OPENED: 09/06/1909   Theatre: Knickerbocker
Musical   Broadway: 288

Composer: Leo Fall
Lyricist: George Grossmith
Librettist: George Grossmith
Producer: Charles Frohman
Director: J.A.E. Malone

Source: DIE DOLLARPRINZESSIN (Musical: Leo Fall; Fritz Grunbaum; A.M. Willner); **Musical Director:** W.T. Francis; **Set Design:** Ernest Gros

Songs: America, Look Out [2]; Boat Sails on Wednesday, A [4] (C: Jerome Kern; L: George Grossmith; Adrian Ross); Chewska; Dollar Princess, The [2]; Dollar Princesses, The; Finale Act I; Finale Act II; Follow Me Around [1]; Hip, Hip, Hurrah!; I Can Say Truly Rural (C/L: George Arthurs; Worton David); Inspection; Lady Fortune; Lion's Queen [2] (C: Richard Fall); Love! Love! Love! (C: Frank Tours; L: Adrian Ross); Love's a Race; Marquis of Jolifontaine, The; My Dream of Love; Not Here! Not Here! (C: Jerome Kern; L: M.E. Rourke); Opening Act III (C: W.T. Francis); Opening Chorus; Paragraphs; Red, White and Blue [4] (C: Jerome Kern; L: Adrian Ross); Reminiscence; Riding Lesson, The; Ring of Roses (Hansel and Gretel) [2]; Self Made Maiden, A; Tennis; Then You Go?; Typewriting

Cast: Donald Brian; Percival Knight; Valli Valli

Notes: [1] Out Philadelphia 1/13/11. [2] Sheet music only. [3] Sheet music only. Revised later as "The Land of 'Let's Pretend'" from THE GIRL FROM UTAH. [4] Written for London production.

1068 • DOLL'S LIFE, A

OPENED: 09/23/1982   Theatre: Mark Hellinger
Musical   Broadway: 5

Composer: Larry Grossman
Lyricist: Betty Comden; Adolph Green
Librettist: Betty Comden; Adolph Green
Producer: Robert Fryer; Joseph Harris; Mary Lea Johnson; James M. Nederlander; Martin Richards; Sidney L. Shlenker; Warner Theatre Productions
Director: Harold Prince

Choreographer: Larry Fuller; **Costumes:** Florence Klotz; **Lighting Designer:** Ken Billington;

Musical Director: Paul Gemignani; **Orchestrations:** Bill Byers; **Set Design:** Tazeena Firth; Timothy O'Brien

Songs: Arrival; Arrival in Christiana [2]; At Last; Can't You Hear I'm Making Love to You [2]; Departure; Finale (Can You Hear Me Now?); Grand Cafe, The; Jailer, Jailer; Learn to Be Lonely; Letter from Klemnacht; Letter to the Children; Loki and Baldur; New Year's Eve; No More Mornings; Power; Prologue; Rare Wines; Rats and Mice and Fish; Stay With Me, Nora; There She Is; Toy Store [1]; Two People Who Love [1]; What Now? [2]; Woman Alone, A; You Interest Me; You Puzzle Me [2]

Cast: Patti Cohenour; Peter Gallagher; George Hearn; Betsy Joslyn; Barbara Lang; Carol Lurie; Edmund Lyndeck; Penny Orloff; Larry Small; David Vosburgh

Notes: A sequel to A DOLL'S HOUSE. [1] Not used. [2] Added to 1994 Off-Off-Broadway revival.

1069 • DOLLY

OPENED: 04/20/1954
Musical   Closed out of town

Composer: Richard Valente
Lyricist: Richard Valente
Librettist: Richard Valente

Notes: Produced at the Tower Theater, Atlanta.

1070 • DOLLY DIMPLES

Notes: *See LITTLE DOLLY DIMPLES.*

1071 • DOLLY VARDEN

OPENED: 01/27/1902   Theatre: Herald Square
Musical   Broadway: 154

Composer: Julian Edwards
Lyricist: Stanislaus Stange
Librettist: Stanislaus Stange
Producer: F.C. Whitney
Director: Al Holbrook

Source: COUNTRY GIRL, THE (Play: David Garrick); **Choreographer:** Cervallo; **Costumes:** Caroline Siedle; **Musical Director:** Enrico Morreale; **Set Design:** Homer Emens; John H. Young

Songs: Aural Misunderstanding (I'm Whirling, Twirling), An; Brides and Grooms; Cannibal Maid, The; Country Girl, The; Dolly Varden; Finale Act II; For the Benefit of Man; For the Knot There's No Untying; Girl You Love, The; He Must Be Punished; Lay of the Jay, The; Le Savoir Faire; Loveable Love; My Ship's the Girl for Me; Navy, The; Our Captain Is Sarcastic; Song of Expense, A; Song of the Sword, The; Swing, My Pretty One, Swing; 'Tis Love That Most Enriches; To Be with Thee; We Met in Lover's Lane; What Love Means; When Lovers Are Alone

Cast: Lulu Glaser; Van Rensselaer Wheeler

Notes: [1] Sheet music only.

1072 • DON'T BOTHER ME, I CAN'T COPE

OPENED: 04/19/1972   Theatre: Playhouse
Musical   Broadway: 1065

Composer: Micki Grant
Lyricist: Micki Grant
Producer: Arch Lustberg; Edward Padula
Director: Vinnette Carroll

Choreographer: George Faison; **Costumes:** Edna Watson; **Lighting Designer:** B.J. Sammler; **Musical Director:** Danny Holgate; **Set Design:** Richard A. Miller; **Vocal Arranger:** Danny Holgate

Songs: All I Need; Don't Bother Me, I Can't Cope; Fighting for Pharoah; Good Vibrations; Help; I Gotta Keep Movin'; It Takes a Whole Lot of Human Feeling; Lookin' Over from Your Side; Love Power; My Name Is Man; Questions; So Little Time; So Long Sammy; Thank Heaven for You; They Keep Coming; Time Brings About a Change; When I Feel Like Moving; You Think I Got Rhythm?

Cast: Alberta Bradford; Alex Bradford; Charles Campbell; Hope Clarke; Micki Grant; Bobby Hill; Marie Thomas; Arnold Wilkerson

1073 • DON'T GET GOD STARTED

OPENED: 10/29/1987   Theatre: Longacre
Revue   Broadway: 86

Composer: Marvin Winans
Lyricist: Marvin Winans
Librettist: Ron Milner
Producer: Barry Hankerson; Jeffrey Day Sharp
Director: Ron Milner

Costumes: Victoria Shaffer; **Lighting Designer:** Shirley Prendergast; **Musical Director:** Steven Ford; **Set Design:** Llewellyn Harrison; **Vocal Arranger:** Ronald Winans

Songs: Abide with Me (C/L: Traditional); After Looking for Love; Always; Bring Back the Days of Yea and Nay; Can I Build My Home in You; Change Your Nature; Cry Loud (Lift Your Voice Like a Trumpet); Denied Stone; Don't Turn Your Back; He'll Make It Alright; I Made It; It's Alright Now; Let the Healing Begin; Millions; Renew My Mind; Slipping Away from You; Still in Love with You; Turn Us Again; What's Wrong with Our Love

Cast: Vanessa Bell Armstrong; Ernie Banks; Giancarlo Esposito; Chip Fields

1074 • DON'T PLAY US CHEAP!

OPENED: 05/16/1972   Theatre: Ethel Barrymore
Musical   Broadway: 164

Composer: Melvin Van Peebles
Lyricist: Melvin Van Peebles
Librettist: Melvin Van Peebles
Producer: Melvin Van Peebles
Director: Melvin Van Peebles

Costumes: Bernard Johnson; **Lighting Designer:** Martin Aronstein; **Musical Director:** Harold Wheeler; **Set Design:** Kert Lundell

Songs: Ain't Love Grand; Big Future; Book of Life, The; Break That Party; 8 Days a Week; Feast on Me; I'm a Bad Character; It Makes No Difference; Know Your Business; Phony Game, The; Quittin' Time; Saturday Night; Smash Him; Some Days It Seems That It Just Don't Even Pay to Get Out of Bed; You Cut Up the Clothes in the Closet of My Dreams

Cast: Mabel King; Avon Long; Esther Rolle

1075 • DON'T STEP ON MY OLIVE BRANCH

OPENED: 11/01/1976   Theatre: Playhouse
Musical   Broadway: 16

Composer: Ron Eliran
Lyricist: Ron Eliran
Librettist: Harvey Jacobs
Producer: Norman Kean
Director: Jonathan Karmon

Source: UNKNOWN (Unknown: Harvey Jacobs); **Choreographer:** Jonathan Karmon; **Costumes:** Pierre D'Alby; **Lighting Designer:** William H. Batchelder; **Musical Director:** David Krivoshei; **Set Design:** James Tilton

Songs: Come with Me [2]; Have a Little Fun [2]; I Believe [2]; I Hear a Song [2]; I Live My Life in Color; It Was Worth It [2]; Jerusalem; Moonlight; My Land [2]; Nothing Like Home [1]; Only Love; Somebody's Stepping on My Olive Branch; Tired Heroes; We Love a Conference; World's Greatest Magical Act, The; Young Days [2]

Cast: Gail Benedict; Darleen Boudreaux; Ron Eliran; Riki Gal; Hanan Goldblatt; Ruthi Navon; Rivka Raz

Notes: [1] Also in NIGHTSONG. [2] Cut prior to New York.

1076 • DONNYBROOK!

OPENED: 05/18/1961   Theatre: 46th Street
Musical   Broadway: 68

Composer: Johnny Burke
Lyricist: Johnny Burke
Librettist: Robert E. McEnroe
Producer: Fred Herbert; David Kapp
Director: Jack Cole

Source: QUIET MAN, THE (Film: Frank Nugent); **Choreographer:** Jack Cole; **Costumes:** Rouben Ter-Arutunian; **Dance Arranger:** Laurence Rosenthal; **Lighting Designer:** Klaus Holm; **Musical Director:** Clay Warnick; **Orchestrations:** Robert Ginzler; **Set Design:** Rouben Ter-Arutunian; **Vocal Arranger:** Clay Warnick

Songs: Courting (dance), The; Day the Snow Is Meltin', The; Dee-lightful Is the Word; Donnybrook; Dowdling [1]; Ellen Roe; For My Own; He Makes Me Feel I'm Lovely; I Have My Own Way; I Wouldn't Bet One Penny; If It Isn't Everything [2]; Loveable Irish, The; Mr. Flynn; Quiet Life, A; Sad Was the Day; Sez I; Sunday Morning; Toast to the Bride, A; When It's

Summer [3] (C: Cole); Wisha Wurra

Cast: Philip Bosco; Grace Carney; Joan Fagan; Eddie Foy Jr.; Susan Johnson; Art Lund; Clarence Nordstrom

Notes: [1] Out Washington D.C. 5/2/61. [2] Cut. [3] ASCAP only.

1077 • DOONESBURY

OPENED: 11/21/1983   Theatre: Biltmore
Musical   Broadway: 104

Composer: Elizabeth Swados
Lyricist: Garry Trudeau
Librettist: Garry Trudeau
Producer: Universal Pictures; James Walsh
Director: Jacques Levy

Source: DOONESBURY (Comic Strip: Garry Trudeau); **Choreographer:** Margo Sappington; **Costumes:** Patricia McGourty; **Lighting Designer:** Beverly Emmons; **Musical Director:** Jeff Waxman; **Orchestrations:** Elizabeth Swados; **Set Design:** Peter Larkin; **Vocal Arranger:** Jeff Waxman

Songs: Another Memorable Meal; Baby Boom Boogie Boy; Chairman's Song, The [1]; Complicated Man; Get Together; Graduation; Guilty; I Came to Tan; I Can Have It All; It's the Right Time to Be Rich; Just a House; Just One Night; Mother; Muffy and the Topsiders; Real Estate

Cast: Barbara Andres; Gary Beach; Ralph Bruneau; Kate Burton; Laura Dean; Mark Linn-Baker; Albert Macklin; Keith Szarabajka; Lauren Tom

Notes: [1] Cut prior to opening

1078 • DORCAS

OPENED: 12/21/1896   Theatre: Lyric
Musical   Broadway: 80

Composer: Watty Hydes; Clement Locknay
Librettist: Edward Paulton; Harry Paulton
Director: Edward Paulton

Cast: Eva Davenport; Marie Davenport; Charles Earle; Charles Meyer

Notes: No songs listed in program.

1079 • DORI

OPENED: 10/17/1985
Musical   Closed out of town

Composer: Elliot Weiss
Lyricist: Eric Blau
Librettist: Eric Blau
Producer: Reuben Hoppenstein; Leah Posluns;
Reva Stern
Director: John Going

Choreographer: David Holdgrive; **Lighting
Designer:** Ron Montgomery; **Musical Director:**
Rick Fox; **Set Design:** Iaian Aitken

Songs: Abdullah; Appearances; Baksheesh; Book of
Dori, The; Dancing in the Temple; Diaspora; Do
You Know What the Children Are Doing
Today?; I Am Moving; I Won't Be Home for a
Long, Long Time; Intrigue; Let's Play at Love;
Let's Play the Game; Papa Is a Traveler; Promise,
The; Prophecy; Wasn't That a Miracle?; What
Happened Here?; Why Do You Betray Me;
Wildest Dream, The; World Without Us, A

Cast: Marie Baron; David Brammel; Sean Hewitt;
Gary Krawford

Notes: Leah Posluns Theatre, Toronto

1080 • DOROTHY

OPENED: 11/05/1887   Theatre: Standard
Musical   Broadway

Composer: Alfred Cellier
Librettist: B.C. Stephenson

Choreographer: Rose Bracket; **Costumes:** Mme
Martens; **Musical Director:** A. DeNovellis

Songs: Are You Sure That They Are All in Bed?; Be
Wise in Time; Contentment I Give You; Dancing
Is not What It Used to Be; Dorcas; Duke of
Berkshire; Father's Pride and Joy, A; Hark
For'ard! (Away); I Am the Sherrif's Faithful Man;
I Hear the Quarter Chime; Lads and Lasses; No
Time Has Come When I Must Yield; Now Take
Your Seats; Queen of My Heart [1]; Though Born
a Man of High Degree; Time Has Come, The; To
Bed; Under the Pump; We're Sorry to Delay You;
What Joy Untold; What Noise Was That?; Who
Swore to Be Good and True? (You Swear to Be
Good and True); With Such a Dainty Dame

Cast: William Hamilton; Rose Leighton; Eugene
Oudin; Harry Paulton; Lillian Russell; Agnes
Stone

Notes: No songs listed in program. Songs from
British production. [1] Added after opening in
London.

1081 • DOUBLE ENTRY

OPENED: 02/20/1961   Theatre: Martinique
Musical   Off-Broadway: 56

Composer: Jay Thompson
Lyricist: Jay Thompson
Librettist: Jay Thompson
Producer: Happy Medium Theatre; Albert C.
Lasher; Paul Lehman
Director: Bill Penn

Lighting Designer: Howard Becknell; **Musical
Director:** Jay Thompson; **Orchestrations:** Jay
Thompson; **Set Design:** Howard Becknell

Songs: All the Young Men; Dear Madame
Scarlatina; Fortune, The; Kinda Sorta Doin'
Nothing; Miss Lucy Long [1]; Oldest Trick in the
World, The; Real Rich Ladies; Same Old Summer
[1]; Sweep; White Slavery Fandango, The

Cast: Jane Connell; Ted Lambrinos; Rosetta
LeNoire; Garrett Morris

Notes: This show was composed of two one-act
musicals: THE BIBLE SALESMAN and THE
OLDEST TRICK IN THE WORLD. [1] These two
songs were in THE BIBLE SALESMAN.

1082 • DOUBLE FEATURE

OPENED: 10/08/1981   Theatre: Common, The
Musical   Off-Broadway: 7

Composer: Jeffrey Moss
Lyricist: Jeffrey Moss
Librettist: Jeffrey Moss
Producer: Karl Allison; Allen Grossman; Nan
Pearlman
Director: Sheldon Larry

Choreographer: Adam Grammis; **Costumes:** Rizis
Von Brandenstein; **Dance Arranger:** Glen Roven;
Michael Starobin; **Lighting Designer:** Marilyn
Rennagel; **Musical Director:** Michael Lee

Stockler; **Orchestrations:** Michael Starobin; **Set Design:** Stuart Wurtzel; **Vocal Arranger:** Michael Starobin

Songs: Double Feature [1]; First Touch of Autumn, The; How's It Gonna End?; Just As It Should Be; Little Bit of This Morning, A; Old Movies; One Step at a Time; Our Last Dance Together; Wallpaper; We Saw a Movie Together; What If I Asked You for a Dance?; When I Met Her

Cast: Pamela Blair; Don Scardino; Carole Shelley; Stephen Vinovich

Notes: Originally titled PARTNERS. [1] Out New Haven 11/29/79.

1083 • DOVE OF PEACE, THE

OPENED: 11/14/1912   Theatre: Broadway
Musical   Broadway: 16

Composer: Walter Damrosch
Lyricist: Wallace Irwin
Librettist: Wallace Irwin

Songs: As Long As Man Loves Woman; Brag and Bluster Song, The; Caveman and the Cavewoman, The; Dove of Peace; Far, Oh Far Is the Mango Island; March of the Militant Suffragettes, Ochone!; Oh, the World of Peace; Pre-Historic Man; Prisoners Stand Up!; Promise Me Tomorrow You Will Again Love Me; Sailors 'Fake' Walk, The; Song of the Crowing Hens; Two Little Cannibal Ladies; What Lips Are Made For; Woman, How Dare You!

Cast: Arthur Deagon; Frank Pollock; Ernest Torrence; Alice Yorke

Notes: No program available.

1084 • DOWN IN BOM-BOM BAY

OPENED: 1915

Songs: On the Good Ship Whipoorwill (C: Walter Donaldson; L: Coleman Goetz)

Notes: No other information available.

1085 • DOWN IN THE VALLEY

OPENED: 01/14/1950   Theatre: NBC
TV Musical

Composer: Kurt Weill
Lyricist: Arnold Sundgaard
Librettist: Arnold Sundgaard
Director: Charles Polacheck

Musical Director: Peter Herman Adler

Songs: Brack Weaver, My True Love; Down in the Valley [1]; Hoe-Down; Hop Up, My Ladies [1]; Little Black Train, The [1]; Lonesome Dove, The [1]; Sourwood Mountain [2]; Where Is the One Who Will Mourn Me When I'm Gone?

Cast: Richard Barrows; Marion Bell; Robert Holland; Ray Jacquemot; Roy Johnston; William McGraw; Kenneth Smith

Notes: This opera was premiered on July 15, 1948 at the University of Indiana performed by students and guest artists Marion Bell (of the original cast of Brigadoon). That production was broadcast on NBC radio on August 7, 1948. [1] Based on the folk song. [2] ASCAP/Library of Congress only.

1086 • DOWNRIVER

OPENED: 01/10/1975
Musical   Off-Broadway

Composer: John Braden
Lyricist: John Braden
Librettist: Jeff Tambornino

Source: ADVENTURES OF HUCKLEBERRY FINN, THE (Novel: Mark Twain)

Songs: Auction Sell (What a Grand Day for an Auction Sell), The; Bound Away; Come Home, Runaway; Downriver; Every Other Saturday Night; Fare-Thee-Well, The; Hallelujah, He's on His Way; Introduction, The; It's a Hard Life Bein' a Bum; Just Like Love; Musicale, The; Plan (Tom and Huck's Argument), The; Possibilities; River Rats; Shine Down Lord; 'Til Our Good Luck Comes Along; Tom and Huck's Argument; Waiting; Waltz of the Cameleopard, The; You've Brightened Up My Day

Cast: John Bottoms; James Greene; David Patrick Kelly; Marcia McClain; Samuel E. Wright

Notes: St. Clements program with additional songs from Musical Theatre Works. The date above is from the Musical Theatre Works program.

1087 • DR. BEANS FROM BOSTON

OPENED: 1912
Musical

Composer: Will Vodery
Lyricist: Henry S. Creamer
Producer: S.H. Dudley

Songs: Bathing; Dearest Memories; Drinking; Eternity; Grand Finale; Idle Dream; Let's Make Love; Messenger Boy; Opening Chorus; Rain; Sunshine; Virginia; What Did I Say That For?

Cast: James Burris; S.H. Dudley; Daisy Martin; Arthur Talbot; Henry Troy

Notes: No other information available.

1088 • DR. DELUXE

OPENED: 04/17/1911   Theatre: Knickerbocker
Musical   Broadway: 32

Composer: Karl Hoschna
Lyricist: Otto Harbach
Librettist: Otto Harbach
Producer: Joseph M. Gaites
Director: Frank Smithson

Musical Director: Gus Salzer; **Set Design:** P. Dodd Ackerman

Songs: Accent Makes No Difference in the Language of Love, The; Begging [1]; Family Brawl, The; Finale Act III; For Every Boy That's Lonely, There's a Girl Who's Lonely Too; Harum Scarem, The; Hide and Seek; I Question Not [1]; (War Is Hell But Oh You) Jealousy; Jealousy (War Is Hell, But Oh, You Green-Eyed Monster, Jealousy!); Just Keep the Dear Boys Guessing [1]; Love Is a Race; Mamma's Little Pet; Man of the World, A; No One but You!; Opening Chorus Act II; Opening Chorus Act III; Opening Number; Skeltons in the Closet; That Will Keep Him True to You; That's the Way to Treat a Little Doggie; What We Want and What We Get (C/L: Edward Laska); What's the Use of Saying No; When Tender Love You Are Confessing [1] (C: Frank Tours); When the Old Top Hummed (The Humming Top)

Cast: Lillian Berry; Ralph Herz; William Pruette; Ernest Truex; Taylor Williams

Notes: [1] Sheet music only.

1089 • DR. JEKYLL AND MR. HYDE

OPENED: 03/07/1973   Theatre: NBC
TV Show

Composer: Lionel Bart; Norman Sachs
Lyricist: Lionel Bart; Mel Mandel
Librettist: Sherman Yellen
Producer: Burt Rosen
Director: David Winters

Source: STRANGE CASE OF DR. JEKYLL AND MR. HYDE, THE (Novel: Robert Louis Stevenson)

Cast: Kirk Douglas; Susan George; Susan Hampshire; Stanley Holloway; Donald Pleasence; Michael Redgrave

Notes: Some of the Sachs/Mandel songs were interpolated into Bart's score having originally been used in the stage show AFTER YOU, MR. HYDE. See under that show also. Bart wrote the majority of songs on his own. No other information available.

1090 • DR. SYNTAX

OPENED: 06/23/1894   Theatre: Broadway
Musical   Broadway: 169

Composer: Woolson Morse
Lyricist: J. Cheever Goodwin
Librettist: J. Cheever Goodwin
Director: H.A. Cripps; Joseph Humphreys

Set Design: Ernest Gros

Songs: By Jove, It Is a Pretty Slipper [1]; By the Old Oak Tree; Cinderella Song [1]; Could'st Thou But Know [1]; Don't Be So Cruel, Ducky Dear! [1]; Hammock Built for Two; How Strangely Sweet [1]; No Peach Hangs Too High for Him; So Long, Mary; When Two Hearts Are One; You and

Cast: DeWolf Hopper; Edna Wallace Hopper

Notes: A rewriting of the 1881-82 show CINDERELLA AT SCHOOL. [1] Sheet music only.

1091 • DR. WILLY NILLY
OPENED: 06/04/1959   Theatre: Barbizon-Plaza
Musical   Off-Broadway: 12

Composer: Pembroke Davenport
Lyricist: Edward Eager
Librettist: Alfred Drake; Edward Eager
Producer: Knickerbocker Productions
Director: Alfred Drake

Source: DOCTOR IN SPITE OF HIMSELF, THE
(Play: Moliere); **Orchestrations:** Pembroke
Davenport; Joe Glover; **Set Design:** Ed Wittstein

Songs: Doctor Will Fix You, The; Dr. Willy Nilly;
It's Wonderful Being a Genius; Jacqueline; Punch
and Judy

Cast: Richard Blair; Howard Da Silva; Paul Dooley;
Nancy Dussault

Notes: No songs listed in program.

1092 • DRAGONS
OPENED: 05/12/1984
Musical   Off-Broadway: 6

Composer: Sheldon Harnick
Lyricist: Sheldon Harnick
Librettist: Sheldon Harnick
Producer: Music Theater Workshop
Director: Robert Brink

Source: DRAGONS (Play: Yevgeny Schwartz);
Choreographer: Helen Butleroff; **Costumes:**
Karen Gerson; **Dance Arranger:** Manford
Abrahamson; Bob Goldstone; **Lighting
Designer:** Jeffrey Schissler; **Musical Director:**
Bob Goldstone; **Orchestrations:** Bob Goldstone;
Set Design: James Morgan; **Vocal Arranger:**
Bob Goldstone

Songs: Battle, The; Book in the Cave, The; Brave
Girl; Dragon's Challenge; Glory to the Dragon;
Glory to the Dragon Slayer; I Can't Stand
Dragons; I Love Power; If I Die Young; It Isn't
Fair; It Would Have Been Something [1];
Mayor's Invocation; Mighty Race, A; No Profit in
That; Pain and Sorrow; Passacaglia for Three
Severed Heads; Prelude with Fanfares (inst.); Set
Us Free; Suddenly; Take Care of One Another;
Tiptoe March; Wars' Child; We're a Family;
Wedding, The; What a Pretty Girl; You Could
Say I Miss Him

Cast: John Beal; Jack Dabdoub; Jack Eddleman;
Vicki Lewis; Danny Masterson; Mark McGrath;
Tom McKinney; Ted Pritchard; Carole-Ann
Scott; Christopher Wells

Notes: A workshop performance. [1] Cut.

1093 • DRAT!
OPENED: 10/18/1971   Theatre: McAlpin Rooftop
Musical   Off-Broadway: 1

Composer: Steven Metcalf
Lyricist: Fred Bluth
Librettist: Fred Bluth
Producer: Theatre 1972
Director: Bluth

Lighting Designer: Richard Nelson; **Musical
Director:** Steven Metcalf; **Orchestrations:**
Donald Pippin

Songs: Bye and Bye; Chase, The; Desperation
Quintet!; Drat!; Early Bird Eddy; Friday, Friday;
Frightened of the Dark; Has Anyone Here Seen
My Daddy; Kick It Around; Lean on Me; Little
Fairies; My Geranium; Sally; Walkin' in the Rain;
Where Is the Man for Me?; You and I

Cast: Walter Bobbie; Jane Connell; Bonnie Franklin;
Gary Gage; Donna Sands; Carol Swarbrick;
James "Red" Wilcher

1094 • DRAT! THE CAT!
OPENED: 10/10/1965   Theatre: Martin Beck
Musical   Broadway: 8

Composer: Milton Schafer
Lyricist: Ira Levin
Librettist: Ira Levin
Producer: Jerry Adler; Norman Rosemont
Director: Joe Layton

Choreographer: Joe Layton; **Costumes:** Fred
Voelpel; **Dance Arranger:** Genevieve Pitot;
Lighting Designer: David Hays; **Musical
Director:** Herbert Grossman; **Orchestrations:**
Clare Grundman; Hershy Kay; **Set Design:**
David Hays; **Vocal Arranger:** Herbert Grossman

Songs: Being a Parent [3]; Dancing with Alice;
Deep in Your Heart; Drat! The Cat!; Holmes and
Watson; I Like Him; I Will Capture the Cat [2];
Ignoble Theft of the Idol's Eyes [1]; It's Terrible [3];
It's Your Fault; Justice Triumphant; Let's Go;

Money [2]; My Son, Uphold the Law; Pox Upon the Traitor's Brow, A; Purefoy's Lament; She Touched Me; She's Roses; Today Is a Day for a Band to Play; 2% Income Tax, The [2]; Upside Down Thief, The [1]; Wild and Reckless

Cast: Jane Connell; Charles Durning; Sandy Ellen; Jack Fletcher; David Gold; Elliott Gould; Lu Leonard; Dan Siretta; Gene Varrone; Lesley Ann Warren

Notes: [1] Ballet. [2] Cut prior to opening. [3] Not used.

1095 • DREAM CITY
OPENED: 12/25/1906　Theatre: Weber
Musical　　　　　　Broadway: 102

Composer: Victor Herbert
Lyricist: Edgar Smith
Librettist: Edgar Smith
Producer: Joseph Weber
Director: Al Holbrook

Costumes: Will R. Barnes; Mme. Castel-Bert; **Musical Director:** Louis F. Gottschalk; **Set Design:** Ernest Albert

Songs: Beautiful Dreamtown; Bound for the Opera; Down a Shady Lane; Fairy Boat, A [3]; Farmer's Life, A; Hannah; I Don't Believe I'll Ever Be a Lady; I Have to Laugh; I Love You [2]; Improvements; In a Strenuous Grand Opera Moment [3]; In Vaudeville; Intermezzo; Knight of Noble Mien [3]; Lancers' Waltz [2]; Love By Telephone; March; Nancy, I Fancy You; Oh, the Heat and the Skeet!; On the Phone; Opening Chorus [3]; Operatic Maiden, An [3]; Pas de Nuit, Ravenous Rooster, The; Rustic Patrol; Shy Suburban Maid, A; Ta, Ta, My Dainty Little Darling [1]; Volunteer Fireman, The

Cast: Lillian Blauvelt; Maurice Farkoa; Otis Harlan; William T. Hodge; Cecilia Loftus; Joseph Weber

Notes: Second half of bill was THE MAGIC KNIGHT. [1] Sheet music only. [2] ASCAP/Library of Congress only. [3] In THE MAGIC KNIGHT.

1096 • DREAM GIRL, THE (1924)
OPENED: 08/20/1924　Theatre: Ambassador
Musical　　　　　　Broadway: 118

Composer: Victor Herbert
Lyricist: Rida Johnson Young
Librettist: Harold Atteridge; Rida Johnson Young
Producer: J.J. Shubert; Lee Shubert
Director: J.C. Huffman

Source: ROAD TO YESTERDAY, THE (Play: Beulah Marie Dix; Evelyn Greenleaf Southerland); **Choreographer:** David Bennett; **Musical Director:** Al Goodman; **Set Design:** Eleanor Abbott; Watson Barratt

Songs: All Year 'Round (C: Sigmund Romberg); At the Rainbow's End [1]; Beware of Me [3]; Broad Highway [2] (C: Sigmund Romberg); Bubbles [4] (C: Sigmund Romberg; L: Harold Atteridge); Cling Cling [3]; Dancing 'Round; Finale Act I; Gypsy Girl [5]; Gypsy Life [5]; I Want to Go Home [6] (C: Sigmund Romberg; L: Harold Atteridge); If Somebody Only Would Find Me [2]; Maiden Let Me In; Make Love in the Morning [1]; Making a Venus; My Dream Girl (I Loved You Long Ago); My Hero; Old Songs; Saxophone Man [6] (C: Sigmund Romberg; L: Harold Atteridge); Sights of London [3]; Stop, Look and Listen

Notes: [1] Cut after opening. [2] Not in program. [3] Out New Haven 4/21/??. [4] ASCAP credits this song to Herbert and Rida Johnson Young on Herbert's carriage card. ASCAP also credits the song to Romberg, Schwartz and William Jerome. [5] ASCAP/Library of Congress only. [6] ASCAP also credits this song to Romberg, Schwartz and William Jerome.

1097 • DREAM GIRL (1960)
OPENED: 1960
Musical　　　　　　Unproduced

Composer: Cy Coleman
Lyricist: Carolyn Leigh

Source: DREAM GIRL (Play: Elmer Rice)

Songs: Gemutlichkeit; In My Own Irresistible Way; Spare Me Your Kindness

1098 • DREAM SONG, THE
OPENED: 10/23/1919
Play　　　　　　Closed out of town

Composer: Victor Herbert
Lyricist: Edward Locke

Author: Edward Locke
Director: G. Delamater; Priestley Morrison

Musical Director: Hayden Owen

Songs: Farewell; Lovelight

Cast: Ferike Boros; George Stuart Christie; Margaret Owen; Walter Wilson

Notes: Central Music Hall Theatre of Chicago.

1099 • DREAM TEAM, THE
OPENED: 04/23/1985
Musical   Closed out of town

Composer: Thomas Tierney
Lyricist: John Forster
Librettist: Richard Wesley
Director: Dan Siretta

Arrangements: William Foster McDaniel; **Choreographer:** Dan Siretta; **Costumes:** Judy Dearing; **Lighting Designer:** Beverly Emmons; **Musical Director:** William Foster McDaniel; **Orchestrations:** J. "Billy" Ver Planck; **Set Design:** James Leonard Joy

Songs: Cloud of Joy; Dancing On and On; Don't Let a Good Thing Go; Doncha Feel Proud?; Dream Team; Green; Hey Star; On the Road with the Roadrunners; Seems Like a Good Idea; These Sorry Men; We Belong Up There; Whole New Ballgame, A; Wonderful Game, The; You Ain't Seen Ball; You're My Family Now

Cast: Lynne Clifton Allen; Edwin Battle; Stanley Wayne Mathis; S. Epatha Merkerson; Larry Riley; James Stovall; Reginald Veljohnson

Notes: Goodspeed Opera House — Norma Terris Theatre.

1100 • DREAM TIME
Notes: *See SWING.*

1101 • DREAM WITH MUSIC
OPENED: 05/18/1944   Theatre: Majestic
Musical   Broadway: 28

Composer: Clay Warnick
Lyricist: Edward Eager

Librettist: Dorothy Kilgallen; Ben Roberts; Sidney Sheldon
Producer: Richard Kollmar
Director: Richard Kollmar

Choreographer: George Balanchine; **Costumes:** Miles White; **Musical Director:** Max Meth; **Set Design:** Stewart Chaney

Songs: Baby, Don't You Count on Me; Battle of the Genie; Be Glad You're Alive; Come with Me; Give, Sinbad, Give; I'll Take the Solo; I'm Afraid I'm in Love; Lion and the Lamb, The; Love at Second Sight; Moon Song, The; Mouse Meets Girl; Mr. and Mrs. Wrong; Relax and Enjoy It; Women Against the World

Cast: Ronald Graham; Joy Hodges; Jerry Ross; Vera Zorina

Notes: Music based on classical themes.

1102 • DREAMER AND THE RUNNER, THE
Notes: *See AN UNFINISHED SONG.*

1103 • DREAMGIRLS
OPENED: 12/20/1981   Theatre: Imperial
Musical   Broadway: 1522

Composer: Henry Krieger
Lyricist: Tom Eyen
Librettist: Tom Eyen
Producer: Bob Avian; Michael Bennett; Geffen Records; Shubert Organization
Director: Michael Bennett

Choreographer: Michael Bennett; Michael Peters; **Costumes:** Theoni V. Aldredge; **Lighting Designer:** Tharon Musser; **Musical Director:** Yolanda Segovia; **Orchestrations:** Harold Wheeler; **Set Design:** Robin Wagner; **Vocal Arranger:** Cleavant Derrick

Songs: Ain't No Party; And I Am Telling You I'm Not Going; Cadillac Car; Dream Girls; 'Dreams' Melody; Faith in Myself; Fake Your Way to the Top; Family; Goin' Downtown; Got to Be Good Times; Hard to Say Goodbye, My Love; Heavy; I Meant You No Harm; I Miss You Old Friend; I Want You Baby; I'm Looking for Something; I'm Somebody; Love Love You Baby; Move (You're Steppin' on My Heart); One More

Picture Please; One Night Only; Only the Beginning; Party, Party; Press Conference; Quintette; Rap, The; Steppin' to the Bad Side; Takin' the Long Way Home; This Is Gonna Be My Time [1]; When I First Saw You

Cast: Obba Babatunde; Deborah Burrell; Vondie Curtis-Hall; Cleavant Derricks; Loretta Devine; Sheila Ellis; Tony Franklin; Ben Harney; Jennifer Holliday; Sheryl Lee Ralph; David Thome

Notes: [1] Cut prior to opening.

1104 • DREAMSTUFF
OPENED: 04/02/1976   Theatre: WPA
Musical   Off-Off-Broadway

Composer: Marsha Malamet
Lyricist: Howard Ashman
Librettist: Dennis Green
Director: James Nicola

Source: TEMPEST, THE (Play: William Shakespeare)

Songs: Curse, The; Full Fathom Five; Get Down; Goodbye Magic; It's Beautiful; My Own Way; No More Enchantment; One More Lullabye; Tempest; Where the Bee Sucks; You Love a Child

Cast: Thomas Callaway; Dick Latessa; Pat Lavalle; Betty Maul; Barbara Niles; Kitty Rea

1105 • DREAMY KID, THE
OPENED: 1942
Opera   Unproduced

Composer: James P. Johnson

Source: UNKNOWN (Play: Eugene O'Neill)

Notes: No other information available for this one-act opera.

1106 • DRESS PARADE, THE
Notes: *See MID SUMMER NIGHTS FANCIES.*

1107 • DRESSED TO THE NINES
OPENED: 09/22/1960   Theatre: Upstairs at the
                                 Downstairs
Revue   Nightclub

Librettist: Linda Ashton; Ernest Chambers; Marian Grudeff; Michael McWhinney
Producer: Julius Monk
Director: Julius Monk

Choreographer: Frank Wagner; **Costumes:** Nilo; **Vocal Arranger:** William Roy

Songs: Billy's Blues (C/L: William Roy); Bring Back the Roxy to Me (C/L: Michael Brown); Come In and Browse (C/L: G. Wood); Con Edison (C/L: Unknown); Cook's Tour (C/L: Lesley Davison); Dressed to the Nines (C/L: William Roy); Four Seasons (C: William Roy; L: Louis Botto); Ft. Lauderdale (C: William Roy; L: Michael McWhinney); Hate Song, The (C: Michael Barr; L: Dion McGregor); Lincoln Center [1] (C/L: Rod Warren); Names (C/L: Jack Holmes); Nanny (C/L: Raymond Jessel); Sociable Amoeba (C/L: Jack Urbont); Thanks to You (I'm a Brand New Woman) (C/L: Bart Howard); Theatre's in the Dining Room, The (C: William Roy; L: Michael McWhinney); Tiny Town (C/L: Jack Holmes)

Cast: Ceil Cabot; Gordon Connell; Bill Hinnant; Gerry Matthews; Pat Ruhl; Mary Louise Wilson

Pianist: Carl Norman; William Roy

Notes: [1] Later added to DIME A DOZEN.

1108 • DRIFTER, THE GRIFTER AND HEATHER MCBRIDE, A
OPENED: 06/17/1982   Theatre: 47th Street
Musical   Off-Broadway: 9

Composer: Bruce Petsche
Lyricist: John Gallegher
Librettist: John Gallegher
Producer: Popcorn Productions
Director: Dick Sasso

Choreographer: George Bunt; **Costumes:** Michael Sharp; **Lighting Designer:** Richard Winkler; **Musical Director:** Jeremy Harris; **Set Design:** Michael Sharp; **Vocal Arranger:** Jeremy Harris

Songs: Fat Luigi; Find a Way; Fly with Me; Getaway; Hair Pulling Ballet; Hey Kiddo, You Through Again; Holding the Bag; Honesty; I Dream; Just Our Way of Doing Business; Little Little; Love Song; Remember the Dream; Skidaddle; Tiny International Empire; Tippity Top

Cast: Mary Ellen Ashley; Elizabeth Austin; Dennis Bailey; William Chuck Karel; Ronald Young

1109 • DU BARRY WAS A LADY

OPENED: 12/06/1939   Theatre: 46th Street
Musical   Broadway: 408

Composer: Cole Porter
Lyricist: Cole Porter
Librettist: B.G. DeSylva; Herbert Fields
Producer: B.G. DeSylva
Director: Edgar MacGregor

Choreographer: Robert Alton; **Costumes:** Raoul Pene du Bois; **Musical Director:** Gene Salzer; **Orchestrations:** Robert Russell Bennett; Ted Royal; Hans Spialek; **Set Design:** Raoul Pene du Bois; **Vocal Arranger:** Ralph Blane; Hugh Martin

Songs: But in the Morning, No; Come On In; Danse Erotique; Danse Tzigane; Danse Victoire; Do I Love You?; Dream Song; Du Barry Was a Lady; Ev'ry Day a Holiday; Friendship; Gavotte; Give Him the Oo-La-La; In the Big Money [2]; It Ain't Etiquette; It Was Written in the Stars; Katie Went to Haiti; L'Apres Midi d'un Boeuf; Mesdames and Messieurs; Well, Did You Evah! [1]; What Have I? [2]; When Love Beckoned; Where's Louis?

Cast: Betty Allen; Walter Armin; Bonnie Baker; Johnny Barnes; Hugh Cameron; Janis Carter; Harold Cromer; Betty Grable; Ronald Graham; Adele Jergens; Bert Lahr; Ethel Merman; Audrey Palmer; Roy Ross; Geraldine Spreckels; Jack Stanton; Kay Sutton; Charles Walters

Notes: [1] Also in film HIGH SOCIETY. [2] Not used.

1110 • DUBARRY, THE

OPENED: 11/22/1932   Theatre: George M. Cohan
Musical   Broadway: 87

Composer: Carl Millocker
Lyricist: Rowland Leigh
Librettist: Desmond Carter; Rowland Leigh
Producer: Morris Green; Tillie Leblang
Director: Morris Green; Rowland Leigh

Source: DIE DUBARRY (Operette: Paul Knepler; Ignaz M. Willeminsky); **Choreographer:** Dorothea Burke; **Costumes:** Vincente Minnelli; **Musical Director:** Gustave Salzer; **Orchestrations:** Theo Mackeben; **Set Design:** Vincente Minnelli

Songs: Beauty; Dance for the Gentlemen; Dubarry, The; Forlane (Music Based On: Maurice Ravel); Ga-Ga; Gustave; Happy Little Jeanne; I Give My Heart; If I Am Dreaming; In the Bois; On the Stage; Opening Chorus; Pantalettes; Road to Happiness, The; Royal March; Today; Without Your Love

Cast: Nana Bryant; Max Figman; Consuelo Flowerton; Marion Green; William Hain; Pert Kelton; Grace Moore; Robinson Newbold; Helen Raymond; Percy Waram

Notes: Music revised by Theo Mackeben. The British version's book was by Leigh and Desmond Carter.

1111 • DUCHESS, THE

OPENED: 10/16/1911   Theatre: Lyric
Musical   Broadway: 24

Composer: Victor Herbert
Lyricist: Joseph W. Herbert; Harry B. Smith
Librettist: Joseph W. Herbert
Producer: Lee Shubert; Sam S. Shubert
Director: J.C. Huffman

Musical Director: John McGhie; Oscar Radin; **Orchestrations:** Victor Herbert

Songs: Coryphee, The; Cupid Tell Me Why (Love That's Sincere); Duchess, The [2]; Entrance of Rose (Auction Song); Finale Act I; Finale Act II; Finale Ultimo; Girlie-Land, A; Hunt, The (Opening Act II); Hunting Song (The Chase); If I Should Dream of You (When Out on the Desert); I'm Such a Romantic Girl; Isn't It Nasty of Papa?; It's the Bump; Land of Maidens [2]; Land of Sultan's Dreams, The; Latest Society Pet, The; Let Me Be Free; Life Is a Riddle; Old Noblesse, The; Opening Chorus Act II; Play the Game; Sally; Sham [1]; Teach Me to Forget; There Is a Soul Mate; Upsi-Daisy; What's the Use of Moonlight?

Cast: May Boley; John E. Hazzard; Fritzi Scheff; Lillian Spencer

Notes: Titled MLLE. ROSITA out of town. [1] Not in programs. [2] ASCAP/Library of Congress only.

1112 • DUCHESS MISBEHAVES, THE

OPENED: 02/13/1946   Theatre: Adelphi
Musical   Broadway: 5

Composer: Frank Black
Lyricist: Gladys Shelley
Librettist: Joe Bigelow; Gladys Shelley
Producer: A.P. Waxman
Director: Martin Manulis

Choreographer: George Tapps; **Costumes:** Willa Kim; **Lighting Designer:** Carlton Winkler; **Musical Director:** Charles Sanford; **Orchestrations:** Don Walker; **Set Design:** A.A. Ostranger; **Vocal Arranger:** Clay Warnick

Songs: Art; Broadminded; Couldn't Be More in Love; Dance of the Matador (dance) [1] (C: Manuel De Falla); Fair Weather Friends; Honeymoon Is Over, The; I Hate Myself in the Morning; Katie Did in Madrid; Lost; Men; Morning in Madrid; My Only Romance; Nightmare, The; Nuts; Ole Ole

Cast: Audrey Christie; Joey Faye; Paula Laurence; George Tapps

Notes: [1] Music based on De Falla's "Ritual Fired Dance."

1113 • DUCHESS OF CHICAGO, THE

OPENED: 1929
Musical   Closed out of town

Composer: Emmerich Kalman
Lyricist: Edward Eliscu
Librettist: Julius Brammer; Alfred Gruenwald
Producer: Messrs. Shubert
Director: Busby Berkeley; Stanley Logan

Source: DIE HERZOGIN VON CHICAGO (Musical: Julius Brammer; Alfred Gruenwald; Emmerich Kalman); **Choreographer:** Busby Berkeley; **Musical Director:** John McManus

Songs: Hands Across the Sea; Having My Own Sweet Way; In Chicago (C: Maurie Rubens; Sammy Timberg); Look in My Eyes (C: Maurie Rubens); My Rosemarie; On the Up and Up (C: Maurie Rubens); Song of Vienna

Cast: Eric Blore; Margaret Breen; Lillian Taiz; Tiller Girls, The; Arthur Treacher; Walter Woolf

Notes: Additional songs by Maurie Rubens and Herman Timberg but not identified in program.

1114 • DUCHESS OF DANTZIC, THE

OPENED: 01/16/1905   Theatre: Daly's
Musical   Broadway: 93

Composer: Ivan Caryll
Lyricist: Henry Hamilton
Librettist: Henry Hamilton
Producer: George Edwardes
Director: Holbrook Blinn

Source: MADAME SANS GENE (Play: Sardou); **Musical Director:** Ivan Caryll; **Set Design:** Thomas Mangan

Songs: Buy, Buy, Buy [1]; Chorus of Assistants; Chorus of Courtiers [1]; Chorus of Laundresses; Chorus of Soldiers; Dear Francois [1]; Do You Remember?; Entrance of Napoleon; Finale Act I; Finale Act II; First Right Then Left [1]; His Majesty Orders [1]; I'm Milliner Monarch of Paris [1]; La Petit Caporal (L: Adrian Ross); Legend Olden, The; Letter Song; Love and Ever Love; Mirror Song, The; My Sabots (L: Adrian Ross); Opening Chorus Act II; Real Good Cry Together, A; Sans-Gene; Though Many a Happy Year Hath Flown [1]; Wine of France

Cast: Adrienne Augarde; Holbrook Blinn; Cecil Cameron; May Francis; Evie Greene

Notes: No songs listed in program. [1] May not be actual title.

1115 • DUDDY

Notes: *See THE APPRENTICESHIP OF DUDDY KRAVITZ.*

1116 • DUDE (THE HIGHWAY LIFE)

OPENED: 10/09/1972   Theatre: Broadway
Musical   Broadway: 16

Composer: Galt MacDermot
Lyricist: Gerome Ragni

Librettist: Gerome Ragni
Producer: Adela Holzer; Peter Holzer
Director: Tom O'Horgan

Costumes: Randy Barcelo; **Dance Arranger:** Horace Ott; **Musical Director:** Thomas Pierson; **Orchestrations:** Horace Ott; **Set Design:** Eugene Lee; Franne Lee; Roger Morgan; **Vocal Arranger:** Horace Ott

Songs: A-Stage; Air Male; Baby Breath; Dawn, A; Days of This Life, The; Dude All Dude; Earth, The; Eat It; Electric Prophet; Garden for Two, A [1]; Go Holy Ghost; Goodbyes; Handsomest Man, The; Hum Drum Life; I Love My Boo Boo; I Never Knew; I'm Small; Jesus Hi; Mountains, The; My Darling I Love You March; No-One; Pears and Peaches; Say What You Want to Say [1]; So Long Dude; Song to Sing, A; Suzie Moon; Sweet Dreams; Talk to Me About Love; Theatre/Theatre; Undo; Wah Wah Wah; Weeping [1]; Who Will Be the Children; Who's It?; Y.O.U.; You Can Do Nothing About It

Cast: Rae Allen; Salome Bey; Nell Carter; Ralph Carter; Carol Estey; Delores Hall; Nat Morris; William Redfield

Notes: [1] Not in program.

1117 • DUGAN THE DEPUTY

Closed out of town

Composer: Leon Errol
Lyricist: Leon Errol
Librettist: Leon Errol
Producer: Halfdau Jebe

Notes: No other information available.

1118 • DUKE OF DULUTH, THE

OPENED: 09/11/1908   Theatre: Majestic
Musical   Broadway: 24

Composer: Max S. Witt
Lyricist: George Broadhurst
Librettist: George Broadhurst
Producer: George Broadhurst; Currie
Director: Max Witt

Choreographer: Sam Marion; Jack Mason; **Costumes:** Will R. Barnes; **Musical Director:** Max Witt

Songs: Death or Victory; Dream, The; G.O.P.; I Like Your Way (L: James J. Walker); If My Man Could Do It for Me; Land of Wot, The; My Dainty Dresden Shepherdess; My Sweet Wild Rose; Nicodemus; No Peach Hangs too High for Him; Percy (C: Max Hoffmann; L: Vincent Bryan); Poor Old Man (L: Vincent Bryan); Rosita; Strenuous; Sweetest Part of Loving Is to Dream, The; Take a Trip in My Auto; There's One Sweetheart I'll Never Forget; Through All Eternity; Trolley Line, The; While in My Submarine; Zenedee

Cast: Eleanor Brooks; Georgia Brooks; Stanley Hawkins; Henry Norman; Nat M. Wills

1119 • DUMAS AND SON

OPENED: 08/01/1967
Musical   Closed out of town

Music Based On: Camille Saint-Saens
Composer: George Forrest; Robert Wright
Lyricist: George Forrest; Robert Wright
Librettist: Jerome Chodorov
Producer: L.A. Civic Light Opera; Edwin Lester
Director: Joseph Anthony

Choreographer: Tony Charmoli; **Costumes:** Freddy Wittop; **Lighting Designer:** Peggy Clark; **Musical Director:** Robert La Marchina; **Orchestrations:** Harper MacKay; **Set Design:** Oliver Smith; **Vocal Arranger:** Harper MacKay

Songs: Action in the Auction; Another April; Bowl of Gold, A; Cold of Nichette, The; Cruel One; Grand Panjandrum; Is It Too Late?; King of Fools; Monkey on a String; Night of St. Leandre; On the Rue Macabre; Portrait of Marie, A; Prodigal Papa; Proud Inside; Sale Is On, The; Show Is On!, The; So Will I Love My Love; Ssh! Dumas at Work!; Stay in My Arms; Theatre!; Young Man About Paris; Younger with the Years

Cast: Truman Gaige; Hermione Gingold; Edward Everett Horton; Gregory Morton; Frank Poretta; Gilbert Price; Inia TeWiata; Constance Towers

1120 • DURANTE

OPENED: 08/12/1989
Musical   Closed out of town

Composer: Jimmy Durante
Lyricist: Jimmy Durante

Librettist: John Aylesworth; Charles Peppiatt; Frank Peppiatt
Producer: First Durante Tour Company
Director: Ernest O. Flatt

Choreographer: Toni Kaye; **Costumes:** Christina Poddubiuk; **Dance Arranger:** David Krane; Grant Sturiale; **Lighting Designer:** Sholem Dolgoy; **Musical Director:** Grant Sturiale; **Orchestrations:** James E. Dale; **Set Design:** Cameron Porteous; **Vocal Arranger:** David Krane; Grant Sturiale

Songs: A Razz a Ma Tazz (C/L: David Coleman; Irving Taylor); Bill Bailey (C/L: Unknown); Courtship Ballet (inst.) (C: David Krane); Did You Ever Get the Feeling; Don't Lose Your Sense of Humor; Goodnight, Goodnight (C/L: Jackie Barnett; Jimmy Durante); Grandpa's Spells (C/L: Fred Morton); Hello, Hello, Hello (C: David Krane; L: John Aylesworth; Frank Peppiatt); I Can Do Without Broadway; I Love Ya, Love Ya, Love Ya (C/L: Jack Barnett; Jules Buffano; Jimmy Durante); I'll Do the Strutaway (C/L: Harry Donnelly; Jimmy Durante; L: Irving Caesar); Inka Dinka Doo (C/L: Jimmy Durante; Ben Ryan); Jimmy the Well-Dressed Man; One Room Home; People Would Laugh (C: Grant Sturiale; L: Lonny Price); Put Your Arms Around Me Honey (C: Albert Von Tilzer; L: Junie McCree); September Song (C: Kurt Weill; L: Maxwell Anderson); We're the Men (C/L: Unknown); What a Day; What Do I Have to Say (C/L: Jerry Powell); Whispering (C/L: Richard Coburn; Vincent Rose; John Schonberger); Who Will Be with You When I'm Far Away (C/L: William H. Farrell; C: Jimmy Durante; L: Jimmy Durante)

Cast: Joel Blum; Jane Johanson; Evan Pappas; Lonny Price; Ralph Small

1121 • DUTCH GIRL, THE

OPENED: 1925
Musical   Closed out of town

Composer: Emmerich Kalman
Lyricist: Joe Burrows
Librettist: Guy Bragdon
Producer: Raymond O. Brackett
Director: Guy Bragdon

Source: DAS HOLLANDWEIBECHEN (Musical: Bela Jenbach; Emmerich Kalman; Leo Stein); **Choreographer:** Carl Hemmer

Songs: Be Happy; Boat Song, The; Bridal Hour, The [1]; Brighter Days Are Coming; By the Silver Sea (L: Harry Graham); Dreamland Lover, The [1]; Gypsy Dance; Hail to the Bride; Huzzar March; Little Dutch Girl, The; Love in a Cottage; Love Is a Tingling Tune; Prince of My Maiden Fancies (L: Harry Graham); Tired; Voice I Can't Forget, The; Waltz; When Tu-lips Are True; Women Always Get Their Way

Cast: Phoebe Crosby; Irene Dunne; Frank Gardiner; John E. Hennings; Walter McNally

Notes: Program from New Haven 1/12/25. [1] Sheet music only.

1122 • DYNAMITE TONIGHT!

OPENED: 03/15/1964   Theatre: York Playhouse
Musical   Off-Broadway: 1

Composer: William Bolcom
Lyricist: Arnold Weinstein
Librettist: Arnold Weinstein
Director: Paul Sills; Arnold Weinstein

Choreographer: Sylvill Fort; **Lighting Designer:** Peter Hunt; **Set Design:** Willa Kim

Cast: George Gaynes; Lou Gilbert; Barbara Harris; Gene Wilder

Notes: No songs listed in program.

E

1123 • EARL AND THE GIRL, THE

OPENED: 11/04/1905   Theatre: Casino
Musical   Broadway: 148

Composer: Ivan Caryll
Lyricist: Percy Greenbank
Librettist: Seymour Hicks
Producer: Sam S. Shubert

Songs: Animal Trainer, The [2]; Come Along with Me [2]; Cupid's Mistakes [2]; Daisy [2]; Daphne Sue [2]; Earl of Stole; Grenadiers; How'd You Like to Spoon with Me (C: Jerome Kern; L: Edward Laska); I Would Like to Marry You [1] (C/L: Edward Laska); If It's Good Enough for Rector It's Good Enough for Me [2]; Ladies Maid [2]; Little Lady in Distress; Mediterranean Blue; My Southern Belle [1] (C: Max C. Eugene [3]; L: Jerome Kern); Nicolini; One Night Only; Shopping; Sporting Song

Cast: Georgia Caine; Eddie Foy Sr.; Victor Morley; Zelma Rawlston; Templar Saxe; Amelia Summerville

Notes: [1] Sheet music only. [2] Out Chicago 4/9/05. [3] Pseudonym for Max Dreyfus.

1124 • EARL AND THE GIRLS, THE

OPENED: 1913
Musical

Composer: Dave Stamper
Lyricist: Gene Buck
Producer: Jesse Lasky

Songs: Chic, Chic, Chic, Chic, Chicken; If the Moon Was a Great Big Banjo; I'm Really Disappointed with America; Jockey Song

Cast: Courtney Sisters

Notes: A one-act vaudeville musical.

1125 • EARL CARROLL'S PALM ISLAND REVUE

OPENED: 1936
Revue

Composer: Josef Myrow
Lyricist: Irving Mills
Producer: Earl Carroll

Songs: Beautiful Charms; By the Candlelight; Hot Spell; I'm in Love; Juba; Ringside Table for Two

Notes: No other information available.

1126 • EARL CARROLL'S SKETCH BOOK (1929)

OPENED: 07/01/1929   Theatre: Earl Carroll
Revue   Broadway: 392

Librettist: Eddie Cantor; Eddie Welch
Producer: Earl Carroll
Director: Earl Carroll; Edgar MacGregor

Choreographer: LeRoy Prinz; **Costumes:** Florence Weber; **Lighting Designer:** Max Teuber; **Musical Director:** Ray Kavanaugh; **Orchestrations:** Domenico Savino; **Set Design:** Bernard Lohmuller

Songs: Crashing the Golden Gate (C: Phil Cohen; Jay Gorney; L: E.Y. Harburg); Don't Hang Your Dreams on a Rainbow (C: Arnold Johnson; L: Irving Kahal); Fascinating You (C/L: Benee Russell; Charles Tobias; C: Vincent Rose; L: Harry Tobias); For Someone I Love (C: Ted Snyder; L: Benny Davis); Kinda Cute (C: Jay Gorney; L: E.Y. Harburg); Legs, Legs, Legs (C: Jay Gorney; L: E.Y. Harburg); Like Me Less-Love Me More (C: Jay Gorney; L: E.Y. Harburg); Lilly [1] (C/L: Unknown); My Sunny South (C/L: Abner Silver); Papa Likes a Hot Papoose (C: Jay Gorney; L: E.Y. Harburg); Rhythm of the Waves (C: Vincent Rose; L: Charles Tobias; Harry Tobias); Sketch Book [2] (C/L: Unknown); Song of Symbols (C/L: Unknown); Song of the Moonbeams

(C: Vincent Rose; L: Charles Tobias; Harry Tobias); Tip-Toe Tap-Tap (C: Irving Actman; L: Jean Herbert); You Beautiful So and So (C: Ted Snyder; L: Billy Rose)

Cast: William Demarest; George Givot; Don Howard; Frances Joyce; Patsy Kelly; Will Mahoney; Phelps Twins; Three Sailors

Notes: [1] Cut after opening. [2] Added for tour.

1127 • EARL CARROLL'S SKETCH BOOK (1935)

OPENED: 06/04/1935   Theatre: Winter Garden
Revue   Broadway: 207

Librettist: Eugene Conrad
Producer: Earl Carroll
Director: Earl Carroll; Edward Clarke Lilley

Choreographer: Boots McKenna; **Musical Director:** Ray Kavanaugh; **Set Design:** Clark Robinson

Songs: Anna Louise of Louisiana (C: Will Irwin; L: Norman Zeno); At Last (C: Henry Tobias; L: Sam M. Lewis; Charles Tobias); Doll Dance, The (C: Murray Mencher; L: Charles Newman; Charles Tobias); Gringola (C: Murray Mencher; L: Charles Newman; Charles Tobias); Let the Man Who Makes the Gun (C: Gerald Marks; L: Raymond B. Egan); Let's Swing It (C: Murray Mencher; L: Charles Newman; Charles Tobias); Mardi Gras Day in New Orleans (C: Will Irwin; L: Norman Zeno); Rustle of Your Bustle, The (C: Will Irwin; L: Norman Zeno); Silhouettes Under the Stars (C: Murray Mencher; L: Charles Newman; Charles Tobias); Sunday Night in New York (C: Murray Mencher; L: Charles Newman; Charles Tobias); There's Music in a Kiss (C/L: Al Lewis; Al Sherman; Abner Silver); Through These Portals Pass the Most Beautiful Girls in the World (C: Murray Mencher; L: Charles Newman; Charles Tobias); Twenty-Four Hours a Day [2]; Young Ideas [1] (C: Murray Mencher; L: Charles Newman; Charles Tobias)

Cast: Sybil Bowan; Ken Murray; Sunnie O'Dea; Billy Revel; Beryl Wallace

Notes: [1] Not in program. [2] ASCAP/Library of Congress only.

1128 • EARL CARROLL'S VANITIES FEATURING THE NEW CHARLOT REVUE

OPENED: 01/03/1927   Theatre: Earl Carroll
Revue   Broadway: 151

Composer: Morris Hamilton
Lyricist: Grace Henry
Librettist: Ronald Jeans
Producer: Earl Carroll
Director: Earl Carroll

Choreographer: David Bennett; Anton Dolin

Songs: Alabama Stomp (C: James P. Johnson; L: Henry Creamer); All Is Vanity; Climbing Up the Ladder of Love [4] (C: Jesse Greer; L: Raymond Klages); Cool 'Em Off [2]; Hugs and Kisses [1] (C: Louis Alter; L: Raymond Klages); In the Twilight; Open the Gates of Madrid [2]; Pepita; We Are the Show Girls; When the Hansom Cabs Were Lined Up on the Ranks; Who Do You Love [3] (C: Jesse Greer; L: Raymond Klages)

Cast: Henry Lytton Jr.; Charles Mack; Jessie Matthews; George Moran; Herbert Mundin

Notes: Extension of EARL CARROLL'S VANITIES OF 1926 with additional cast and songs mainly from the CHARLOT REVUE OF 1926. As of 2/21/27 it was billed as EARL CARROLL'S VANITIES OF 1927. *See also CHARLOT REVUE OF 1926, EARL CARROLL'S VANITIES OF 1927* and *EARL CARROLL'S VANITITES OF 1926.* [1] Added 2/21/27. [2] Added 10/31/27. [3] Later credited in program to Raymond Klages and Hugo Frey. [4] Also in EARL CARROLL'S VANITIES OF 1926.

1129 • EARL CARROLL'S VANITIES OF 1923

OPENED: 07/05/1923   Theatre: Earl Carroll
Revue   Broadway: 204

Composer: Earl Carroll
Lyricist: Earl Carroll
Librettist: William Collier
Producer: Earl Carroll
Director: William Collier

Choreographer: Sammy Lee; **Costumes:** Paul Arlington; **Musical Director:** William Daly; **Set Design:** R. Reid Macguire

Songs: Band Plays Home Sweet Home, The; Birth of a New Revue, The; Chasing Little Rainbows; Cretonne Girl; Fine Feathers; Get in a Bathing Suit; Girl Is Like Sunshine, A (C: William Daly; J. Russel Robinson; L: Roy Turk); Girls Were Made for Dancing; Jazzmania; Mr. Wagner's Wedding March; Pretty Peggy; Soul of a Harp, The [1]; Two Time Dan [2] (C: J. Russel Robinson; L: Roy Turk); When the Snowflakes Fall [1]; Whoa Pagliacci

Cast: Joe Cook; Bernard Granville; Peggy Hopkins Joyce; Dorothy Knapp

Notes: [1] Added after opening. [2] ASCAP/Library of Congress only.

1130 • EARL CARROLL'S VANITIES OF 1924

OPENED: 09/10/1924   Theatre: Music Box
Revue   Broadway: 134

Composer: Earl Carroll
Lyricist: Earl Carroll
Librettist: Earl Carroll
Producer: Earl Carroll
Director: Earl Carroll

Choreographer: Sammy Lee; **Musical Director:** Ira Jacobs; **Set Design:** Max Lee

Songs: Counting the Hours; Get Them All Over at Once; In the South of France; On a Christmas Night; Over the Radio; Perfume; Shadowland; Tiddelee Tot; Tondelayo; Twelve Little Heels

Cast: Joe Cook; Desiree Tabor; Sophie Tucker

1131 • EARL CARROLL'S VANITIES OF 1925

OPENED: 07/06/1925   Theatre: Earl Carroll
Revue   Broadway: 440

Composer: Clarence Gaskill
Lyricist: Clarence Gaskill
Librettist: William A. Grew
Producer: Earl Carroll
Director: Earl Carroll

Choreographer: David Bennett; M. Senia Gluck; **Costumes:** Charles LeMaire; **Musical Director:** Don Vorhees; **Set Design:** Karle O. Amend

Songs: Adorable [3] (C/L: Tom Ford; Ray Wynburn); Advancement; At the Gate of Roses [2]; Beautiful Ladies of the Night [1]; Bird Ballet, The; Bottle of Canada Dry, A; C-H-A-R-L-E-S-T-O-N; Chow Mein Girls [1]; Coffee Pot; Color Ballet, The; Dorothy [1]; Drill, The; Hippity Hop, The [1]; Hot Off the Oven; I'm a Stew; I'm the Major Bozo; Kiss in the Moonlight, A [1]; Lonesome; Love in the Shadows [1]; Northwest Mounted Police, The; One, Two, Three, Four; Pango Pango Maid (C: Irving Bibo; L: Fred Phillips); Ponies on Parade; Pot Pourri; Rhythm of the Day [1] (C: Owen Murphy; L: Donald Lindley); Sentimental Sally; Shake Yourself Out of Here; Somebody's Crazy About You (C: Jay Gorney; L: Owen Murphy); Thinking of You; This Is a Night Club; Venetian Nights; We Are the Waiters [1]; Yes or No; Yvonne [1]

Cast: Pearl Eaton; Bobby Folsom; Vivian Hart; Betty Healy; Ted Healy; Wallace McCutcheon; Jack Norton; Margorie Peterson; Kathryn Ray; Julius Tannen; M. de Jari

Notes: [1] Added after opening. [2] Added for tour. [3] Added for tour. Later in EARL CARROLL'S VANITIES OF 1926.

1132 • EARL CARROLL'S VANITIES OF 1926

OPENED: 08/24/1926   Theatre: Earl Carroll
Revue   Broadway: 154

Composer: Morris Hamilton
Lyricist: Grace Henry
Librettist: William A. Grew; Stanley E. Rauh
Producer: Earl Carroll
Director: Earl Carroll; William A. Grew

Choreographer: David Bennett; **Musical Director:** Don Vorhees; **Set Design:** August Vimnera

Songs: Adorable [3] (C/L: Tom Ford; Ray Wynburn); Alabama Stomp (C: James P. Johnson; L: Henry Creamer); All Is Vanity; Broadway to Madrid; Chinese Idol, The (C/L: Berton Braley; Alex James; M. de Jari); Climbing Up the Ladder of Love [2] (C: Jesse Greer; L: Raymond Klages); Cool 'Em Off [1]; Excuse My Dust (C: Spencer; L: Wells); Hanging

Gardens of Babylon, The (C/L: Monte Carlo; C: Alma Sanders); Here Am I [1]; Hugs and Kisses [1] (C: Louis Alter; L: Raymond Klages); Lady of the Veil [1]; Lament of Shakespeare [1]; Legionnaires [1]; Melody Makers [1]; More Than Enough [1]; Natacha (C/L: Berton Braley; Alex James; M. de Jari); Open the Gates of Madrid [1]; Pepita; Twilight; Very, Very, Very [1]; We Are the Show Girls

Cast: Charles Dale; Harry Delf; Dorothy Knapp; Charles Mack; George Moran; Joe Smith; Julius Tannen

Notes: The program consulted for this entry was of 8/24/26, the opening week of the show. Since the show underwent so many incarnations the notes below may help to explain seeming discrepancies in the song lists. *See also EARL CARROLL'S VANITIES FEATURING THE NEW CHARLOT REVUE* which was an extension of this show. After that title the show became known as EARL CARROLL'S VANITIES OF 1927 with no break in the run. To make matters even more confusing *see CHARLOT REVUE OF 1926*. Because of this problem of titles vs. song lists, most songs are not cross-referenced to other shows. [1] Not in program. Some of these songs may have been in the later editions of this show. These songs were from sheet music and under the above title. [2] Also in EARL CARROLL'S VANITIES FEATURING THE NEW CHARLOT REVUE. [3] Previously added to tour of EARL CARROLL'S VANITIES OF 1925.

1133 • EARL CARROLL'S VANITIES OF 1927

Notes: *See EARL CARROLL'S VANITIES FEATURING THE NEW CHARLOT REVUE.*

1134 • EARL CARROLL'S VANITIES OF 1928

OPENED: 08/06/1928   Theatre: Earl Carroll
Revue   Broadway: 200

Composer: Morris Hamilton
Lyricist: Grace Henry
Librettist: W.C. Fields; Joe Frisco; Paul Gerard Smith; Robert T. Tarrent
Producer: Earl Carroll
Director: Earl Carroll; Edgar MacGregor

Choreographer: Busby Berkeley; **Costumes:** Mabel Johnston; William H. Matthews; **Musical Director:** Ray Kavanaugh; **Orchestrations:** Elman Anderson; Arthur Lange; Suszon; **Set Design:** Hugh Willoughby

Songs: Blue Shadows (C: Louis Alter; L: Raymond Klages); Flutterby Baby; Getting the Beautiful Girls (C: Joe Burke; Michael McCleary; L: Ned Washington; George Whiting); I'm Flyin' High (C/L: Roy Doll; Jack Le Soir; Abner Silver); My Arms Are Open (C: Michael Cleary; L: Ned Washington); Oh, How That Man Can Love (C/L: Herb Magidson; Lillian Roth); Once in a Lifetime (C: Jesse Greer; L: Raymond Klages); Opening Chorus; Painting a Vanities Girl (C/L: Ernie Golden); Pretty Girl; Raquel (C: Joseph Burke; L: George Whiting); Rose of the World; Say It with Girls; Vaniteaser (C: Michael Cleary; L: Paul James); Watch My Baby Walk (C: Peter De Rose; L: Jo Trent); Wheels; You Alone [1] (C: Bernard Maltin; L: Jean Fraser)

Cast: Richard Bold; Gordon Dooley; Ray Dooley; W.C. Fields; Joe Frisco; Dorothy Knapp; Martha Morton; Joey Ray; Lillian Roth; Jean Tennyson

Notes: [1] Not in program.

1135 • EARL CARROLL'S VANITIES OF 1930

OPENED: 07/01/1930   Theatre: New Amsterdam
Revue   Broadway: 215

Composer: Harold Arlen; Ted Koehler
Librettist: Eugene Conrad; Eddie Welch
Producer: Earl Carroll
Director: Earl Carroll; Priestly Morrison

Choreographer: LeRoy Prinz; **Costumes:** Charles LeMaire; Vincente Minnelli; **Musical Director:** Ray Kavanaugh; **Orchestrations:** Domenico Savino; **Set Design:** Hugh Willoughby

Songs: Contagious Rhythm; Going Up (C: Jay Gorney; L: E.Y. Harburg); Goodnight Sweetheart [1] (C: Ray Noble; L: James Campbell; Reg Connelly); Hittin' the Bottle; I Came to Life When I Found You (C: Jay Gorney; L: E.Y. Harburg); Knee Deep in June (C: Jay Gorney; L: E.Y. Harburg); Love Boats (C: Jay Gorney; L: E.Y. Harburg); March of Time, The; One Love; Out of a Clear Blue Sky; Ring Out the Blues [2]

(C: Jay Gorney; L: E.Y. Harburg); Rumba Rhythm (C: James P. Johnson; L: Stella Unger)

Cast: Irene Ahlberg; Faith Bacon; Jack Benny; Dorothy Britton; Collette Sisters, The; Frank Condos; Harry Condos; John Hale; Patsy Kelly; Jimmy Savo; Harry Stockwell; Betty Veronica; Thelma White; Herb Williams

Notes: 8th Edition. [1] Not in program. [2] ASCAP/Library of Congress only.

1136 • EARL CARROLL'S VANITIES OF 1931

OPENED: 08/27/1931   Theatre: Earl Carroll
Revue   Broadway: 300

Composer: Burton Lane
Lyricist: Harold Adamson
Librettist: Ralph Spence; Eddie Welch
Producer: Earl Carroll
Director: Earl Carroll; Edgar MacGregor

Choreographer: Georgie Hale; Gluck Sandor; **Costumes:** Charles LeMaire; Vincente Minnelli; **Musical Director:** Ray Kavanaugh; **Orchestrations:** Domenico Savino; **Set Design:** Vincente Minnelli; Hugh Willoughby

Songs: Cute Peekin' Knees [1]; Dance of the Dinosaur (inst.) (C: Herbert Grossman); Going to Town with Me; Goodnight Sweetheart [2] (C: Ray Noble; L: James Campbell; Reg Connelly); Have a Heart; Heigh Ho, the Gang's All Here; I'm Back in Circulation Again (C: Michael Cleary; L: Max Lief; Nathaniel Lief); It's Great to Be in Love (C/L: Cliff Friend); I've Got Ants in My Pants [3] (C/L: Cliff Friend); Let's Talk About the Weather [1] (C/L: Charlotte Kent); Love Came Into My Heart [4]; Mahoneyphone, The; Oh, My Yes [4]; Parasols on Parade (C: Larry Beeson; L: Clifford Adams); Sandy Mahatma Gandy (C: Bob Gereghty; L: Will Mahoney); Tonight or Never (C/L: Jack Meskill; Vincent Rose; Raymond Klages)

Cast: Irene Ahlberg; Dan Carthay; William Demarest; Jack Durant; Helen Lynd; Will Mahoney; Woods Miller; Frank Mitchell; Olive Olsen; Lucille Page; Lillian Roth; Slate Brothers; Beryl Wallace; Milton Watson

Notes: [1] Not in programs. [2] Also in EARL CARROLL'S VANITIES OF 1930. [3] Also called "Bugology." [4] Cut after opening.

1137 • EARL CARROLL'S VANITIES OF 1932

OPENED: 09/27/1932   Theatre: Broadway
Revue   Broadway: 87

Librettist: Jack McGowan
Producer: Earl Carroll
Director: Earl Carroll; Edgar MacGregor

Choreographer: Ned McGurn; Gluck Sandor; **Costumes:** Vincente Minnelli; **Musical Director:** Ray Kavanaugh; **Orchestrations:** Edward B. Powell; **Set Design:** Vincente Minnelli

Songs: Along Came Love (C: Henry Tobias; L: Haven Gillespie; Charles Tobias); Forsaken Again (C: Richard Myers; L: Edward Heyman); I Gotta Right to Sing the Blues (C: Harold Arlen; L: Ted Koehler); Love You Are My Inspiration (C: Andre Renaud; L: Ted Koehler); Most Beautiful Girls in the World, The [1] (C: Harold Arlen; L: Ted Koehler); My Darling (C: Richard Myers; L: Edward Heyman); Rockin' in Rhythm (C: Harold Arlen; L: Ted Koehler); Swingin' Along [1] (C: Harold Arlen; L: Ted Koehler); Take Me Away (C: Peter Tinturin; L: Sidney Clare; Charles Tobias)

Cast: Milton Berle; Helen Broderick; Keith Clark; Robert Cummings; Marcelle Edwards; Will Fyffe; John Hale; Helen Jackson Girls, The; Harriet Hoctor; Josephine Huston; Patsy Kelly; Andre Randall; Andre Renaud; Lillian Shade; Edwin Styles; Max Wall; Beryl Wallace

Notes: [1] Not in programs. Probably not used.

1138 • EARL CARROLL'S VANITIES OF 1940

OPENED: 01/13/1940   Theatre: St. James
Revue   Broadway: 25

Composer: Charles Rosoff
Lyricist: Dorcas Cochran
Librettist: Earl Carroll
Producer: Earl Carroll
Director: Earl Carroll

Choreographer: Eddie Prinz; **Costumes:** Jean Le Seyeux; **Musical Director:** Lionel Newman; **Set Design:** Jean Le Seyeux

Songs: American Bolero (inst.) (C: Nacio Herb Brown); Angel (C: Peter De Rose; L: Mitchell

Parish); Bagpipes on Parade [1] (C: Harry Von Tilzer; L: Earl Carroll; Jack F. Mahoney); Can the Can-Can; Charming; I Want My Mama (C: Jararaca Paiva; Vincente Paiva; L: Al Stillman); Lady Has Oomph, The; Song of the Sarong, The; Starlit Hour, The (C: Peter De Rose; L: Mitchell Parish); Westward Ho!

Cast: Jerry Lester; Susan Miller; Beryl Wallace; Johnny Woods

Notes: [1] ASCAP/Library of Congress only.

1139 • EARL OF RUSTON
OPENED: 05/05/1971   Theatre: Billy Rose
Musical   Broadway: 5

Composer: Peter Link
Lyricist: C.C. Courtney; Ragan Courtney
Librettist: C.C. Courtney; Ragan Courtney
Producer: David Black
Director: C.C. Courtney

Set Design: Neil Peter Jampolis

Songs: Earl Is Crazy; Earl Was Ahead; Easy to Be Lonely; Guitar Song; Insane Poontang (C: C.C. Courtney; Ragan Courtney); I've Been Sent Back to the First Grade (C: C.C. Courtney); Just Your Old Friend; Mama, Earl Done Ate the Tooth Paste Again (C: C.C. Courtney; Ragan Courtney); Mama, Mama, Mama; My Name Is Leda Pearl (C: C.C. Courtney); Probably (C: C.C. Courtney; Ragan Courtney); Revival, The; Silvers Theme; Standing; You Still Love Me (C: C.C. Courtney)

Cast: Jean Waldo Beck; C.C. Courtney; Ragan Courtney

1140 • EARLY TO BED
OPENED: 06/17/1943   Theatre: Broadhurst
Musical   Broadway: 380

Composer: Thomas "Fats" Waller
Lyricist: George Marion Jr.
Librettist: George Marion Jr.
Producer: Richard Kollmar

Choreographer: Robert Alton; **Costumes:** Miles White; **Musical Director:** Archie Bleyer; **Orchestrations:** Don Walker; **Set Design:** George Jenkins

Songs: Early to Bed; Get Away, Young Man; Girl Who Doesn't Ripple When She Bends; Hi-De-Ho-High; Ladies Who Sing with the Band, The; Long Time No Song; Me and My Old World Charm; On Your Mark [1]; Slightly Less than Wonderful; Supple Couple; There's a Man in My Life; There's 'Yes' in the Air (Martinique); This Is So Nice; When the Nylons Bloom Again

Cast: Muriel Angelus; Jane Deering; Choo Choo Johnson; Jane Kean; Richard Kollmar; John Lund; George Zoritch

Notes: [1] May be a cut song. It was copyrighted unpublished at the same time as the rest of the score.

1141 • EARTHQUAKE, THE
Notes: *See THE INTERNATIONAL CUP.*

1142 • EAST IS WEST (1918)
OPENED: 12/25/1918   Theatre: Astor
Play   Broadway: 680

Composer: Robert Hood Bowers
Author: John B. Hymer; Samuel Shipman
Producer: William Harris
Director: Clifford Brooke

Songs: Chinese Lullaby; East Is West (C: Silvio Hein; L: Hassard Short); Overture

Cast: Fay Bainter; Hassard Short

Notes: Original Chinese songs by Robin Hood Bowers. No songs listed in program.

1143 • EAST IS WEST (1929)
Notes: *See MING TOY.*

1144 • EAST OF SUEZ
OPENED: 09/21/1922   Theatre: Eltinge
Play   Broadway: 102

Author: Somerset Maugham
Producer: A.H. Woods
Director: Lester Lonergan

Set Design: Clifford Pember

Songs: Chinese Flower (C: Robert Hood Bowers; L: Francis DeWitt)

Cast: John Halliday; Howard Lang; Leonard Mudie; Gypsy O'Brien; Catherine Proctor; Florence Reed

Notes: Lyrics from the Chinese of Su Tong Po.

1145 • EAST WIND

OPENED: 10/27/1931   Theatre: Manhattan
Musical   Broadway: 23

Composer: Sigmund Romberg
Lyricist: Oscar Hammerstein II
Librettist: Oscar Hammerstein II; Frank Mandel
Producer: Frank Mandel; Laurence Schwab
Director: Oscar Hammerstein II

Choreographer: Bobby Connolly; **Costumes:** Charles LeMaire; **Musical Director:** Oscar Bradley; **Orchestrations:** Hans Spialek; **Set Design:** Donald Oenslager

Songs: Americans Are Coming, The; Are You Love?; Bearded Stranger [2]; Congai; East Wind; Embrace Me; I Saw Your Eyes; I'd Be a Fool; It's a Wonderful World; Minnie; Regardez-Moi; These Tropics; Wedding Scene; When You Are Young; You Are My Woman; Young Man in Love [1]

Cast: Gus Howard; Charlotte Lansing; Vera Marsh; Dennie Moore; J. Harold Murray; Joe Penner; William Williams

Notes: [1] Cut. [2] Out Pittsburgh 10/6/31.

1146 • EASTER SHOW

OPENED: 04/02/1993   Theatre: Radio City Music
                         Hall
Revue   Broadway: 28

Composer: Larry Grossman
Lyricist: Hal Hackady
Producer: Radio City Music Hall Prods
Director: Scott Salmon

Choreographer: Scott Salmon; **Costumes:** Erte; Jose Lengson; Eduardo Sicangco; **Dance Arranger:** Gordon Lowry Harrell; Mark Hummel; Marvin Laird; Ethyl Will; **Lighting Designer:** Ken Billington; Jason Kantrowitz; Billy B. Walker;

Musical Director: Don Pippin; **Orchestrations:** Michael Gibson; Dick Lieb; Glenn Osser; Jim Tyler; **Set Design:** Erte; Eduardo Sicangco; **Vocal Arranger:** Don Pippin

Songs: How About Me; I Know; Put a Little Spring in Your Step (C/L: Jeffrey Ernstoff); Think About That

Cast: Joel Blum; James Darrah; Rockettes, The

Notes: There were also several traditional songs used in this annual show. Part of this production was THE GLORY OF EASTER pageant. Only original songs listed.

1147 • EASY ANGEL, AN

OPENED: 10/17/1904
Musical

Composer: Rose De Haven
Lyricist: Morris S. Silver
Librettist: Morris S. Silver

Cast: Carter De Haven; Rose De Haven

Notes: One-act vaudeville musical. No songs listed in program.

1148 • EASY DAWSON

OPENED: 08/22/1905   Theatre: Wallack
Play   Broadway: 56

Composer: Harry Braham
Author: Edward E. Kidder
Producer: Henry W. Savage
Director: George Marion

Musical Director: Harry Braham

Songs: Adelaide Caprice; And the World Goes On (C: Harry O. Sutton; L: Jean Lenox); Auto Galop; Comedy; Easy Dawson March; Entre Act; Fireman's Parade, The (C: Harry O. Sutton; L: Jean Lenox); It's a Waste of Time to Worry (C/L: Raymond Brown); Let Her Drown (C/L: Phil Ray); Little Yellow Bird [1] (C/L: William Hargreeves; C.W. Murphy); Zabelle Waltz

Cast: John Bunny; Julie Herne; Raymond Hitchcock

Notes: [1] This was a popular British song of the 1890's, indicating that the other songs may not have been written for this production.

1149 • EATING RAOUL

OPENED: 05/13/1992   Theatre: Union Square
Musical   Off-Broadway: 47

Composer: Jed Feuer
Lyricist: Boyd Graham
Librettist: Paul Bartel
Producer: Joan Cullman; Stewart F. Lane; Richard Norton; Max Weitzenhoffer
Director: Tony Kotite

Source: EATING RAOUL (Film: Paul Bartel);
Choreographer: Lynne Taylor-Corbett;
Costumes: Franne Lee; **Lighting Designer:**
Peggy Eisenhauer; **Musical Director:** Albert Ahronheim; **Orchestrations:** Joseph Gianono;
Set Design: Loren Sherman; **Vocal Arranger:**
Albert Ahronheim; Jed Feuer

Songs: Basketball; Eating Raoul; Empty Bed;
Happy Birthday Harry; Hot Monkey Love; La La Land; Lovers in Love; Mary; Meet the Blands;
Momma Said; Mucho Macho Trip; One Last Bop;
Opening; Sexperts; Small Restaurant, A; Swing, Swing, Swing; Think About Tomorrow; Thought Occurs, A; Tool for You; You Gotta Take Pains

Cast: Cindy Benson; Courtenay Collins; Eddie Korbich; M.W. Reid; Susan Wood; Adrian Zmed

1150 • ECCENTRICITIES OF DAVY CROCKETT (AS TOLD BY HIMSELF), THE

Notes: *See BALLET BALLADS.*

1151 • ECHO, THE

OPENED: 08/17/1910   Theatre: Globe
Musical   Broadway: 53

Composer: Deems Taylor
Lyricist: William Le Baron; Deems Taylor
Librettist: William Le Baron; Deems Taylor
Producer: Charles Dillingham
Director: Fred G. Latham

Choreographer: Al Holbrook; William Rock;
Musical Director: DeWitt C. Coolman

Songs: I Don't Want to Be a Soldier (C: Karl Hoschna; L: George V. Hobart); Newport Glide, The (C: Jean Schwartz; L: William Jerome);
Whistle While You're Lonely (C: Jerome Kern;
L: M.E. Rourke); Yankee Doodle Guards, The

(C/L: DeWitt Coolman; John Golden); You're Just the Girlie that I Adore (C: Nat D. Ayer;
L: A. Seymour Brown)

Cast: Roszika Dolly; Yancsi Dolly; Eva Fallon; John E. Hazzard; Bessie McCoy; George White

Notes: No songs listed in program.

1152 • ECHOES OF BROADWAY

Producer: Edward L. Butler

Songs: Whispering Pines (C: Jerome Kern; L: M.E. Rourke)

Cast: Eddie Nelson; Henry Stremel

Notes: No other information available.

1153 • ECLIPSE, THE

OPENED: 11/12/1919   Theatre: Garrick
Musical   London: 117

Composer: Herman Darewski; Melville Gideon
Lyricist: Adrian Ross
Librettist: E. Phillips Oppenheim; Fred Thompson
Producer: C.B. Cochran
Director: Charles Hawtrey

Choreographer: A.H. Majilton; **Costumes:** Adrian Samoiloff; **Musical Director:** J.B. Hastings; **Set Design:** Adrian Samoiloff

Songs: I Never Realized [1] (C/L: Cole Porter); In Chelsea Somewhere [2] (C: Melville Gideon;
L: E. Ray Goetz; Cole Porter)

Cast: Teddy Girard; Dorothy Hanson; Alfred Lester; Farren Soutar

Notes: No other information available. [1] Also in BUDDIES. [2] In AS YOU WERE as "Washington Square."

1154 • ED WYNN CARNIVAL

OPENED: 04/05/1920   Theatre: New Amsterdam
Revue   Broadway: 150

Composer: Ed Wynn
Lyricist: Ed Wynn
Librettist: Ed Wynn

Producer: B.C. Whitney
Director: Ned Wayburn

Musical Director: Antonio Bafunno;
  Orchestrations: Stephen Jones; Frank Saddler;
  Set Design: Joseph Physioc

Songs: And They Held High Carnival [1]; C'est
  Toi [1]; Can You Tell (C: Lou Handman; Ray
  Miller; L: Alex Sullivan); Come Along to the
  Carnival; Egyptian Dance; Gladiators; Goodbye
  Sunshine, Hello Moon (C: William Eckstein; L:
  Gene Buck); Hero Song [1]; I Love the Land of
  Old Black Joe (C: Walter Donaldson; L: Grant
  Clarke); In Old Japan (L: Alfred Bryan); Irish
  Were Egyptians Long Ago, The [1]; It Must Be
  You [1] (C: Con Conrad; L: Bobby Jones); March
  of the Gladiators [1]; My Log Fire Girl; My
  Sahara Rose (C: Walter Donaldson; L: Grant
  Clarke); Oo, How I Love to Be Loved By You [3]
  (C: George Gershwin; L: Lou Paley); Palmy
  Days, The; Rather Than See You Once in a While
  (C: Walter Donaldson; L: Grant Clarke); Rose of
  Spain [2] (C: Tom Brown; Billy Fazioli; Ray
  Miller; L: Fred Fisher); Sphinx of the Desert;
  Springtime [1] (C/L: Jack Malroy); Thumbs
  Down [1]; When I Was Small

Cast: Earl Benham; Marion Davies; Richie Ling;
  Henry Regal; Herbert Russell; Fay West; Lillian
  Wood; Ed Wynn

Notes: [1] Out Toledo 1/18/20. [2]
  ASCAP/Library of Congress only. [3] Also in
  score of LA-LA-LUCILLE!.

1155 • EDDIE'S CATCHY TUNES

OPENED: 04/25/1979   Theatre: New Playwrights'
Musical   Closed out of town

Composer: Tim Grundmann
Lyricist: Tim Grundmann
Librettist: Tim Grundmann
Producer: Harry M. Bagdasian; Ken Bloom; New
  Playwrights' Theatre
Director: Ken Bloom

Choreographer: Anne Reynolds Day; **Costumes:**
  Peter J. Zakutansky; **Dance Arranger:** Tim
  Grundmann; **Lighting Designer:** Tomm
  Tomlinson; **Musical Director:** Tim Grundmann;
  Orchestrations: Tim Grundmann; **Set Design:**
  Russell Metheny; **Vocal Arranger:** Tim
  Grundmann

Songs: Eddie's Catchy Tunes; How to Be a Muse;
  I Am a Tiny Mermaid in the Sea; I Got Plans for
  You Baby; Is It Love?; Isn't This a Fine Kettle of
  Fish; It Stinks; It's a Fact It's Easy; I've Had It
  with Men [1]; March for Brotherhood; Mosquito
  Queen; My Big Break; Nautical Domesticity;
  Nobody Does That to Me; Oh What a Happy
  Fisherman Am I; Opening Night; Pagan Death
  March; Tear It Up; Telegram; There's a Song Up
  There; Velvoota Cheese Jingle; What Happened?;
  Work It Girl!

Cast: Donald F. Campbell; Agnes Cummings;
  T.G. Finkbinder; Tonette Hartmann; A. David
  Johnson; Barbara Rappaport; Holly Reich; Tanis
  Roach; Jan Frederick Shiffman; Dana Vance;
  Richard White; Bill Whitman; Jim Wilder

Notes: [1] Cut prior to opening.

1156 • EDGAR LEE MASTERS' SPOON RIVER ANTHOLOGY

Notes: *See SPOON RIVER ANTHOLOGY.*

1157 • EDMUND BURKE

OPENED: 10/02/1905   Theatre: Majestic
Play   Broadway: 28

Composer: Chauncey Olcott
Lyricist: Chauncey Olcott
Author: Theodore Burt Sayre
Producer: Augustus Pitou
Director: Edgar Selwyn

Costumes: H.A. Ogden; **Incidental Music:** Frank A.
  Mandeville

Songs: Little Bird's Story; Miss Mary (C/L:
  Theodore H. Northrup; Chauncey Olcott);
  You Can Sail in My Boat; Your Heart Alone
  Must Tell

Cast: Mace Greenleaf; Daniel Jarrett; Chauncey
  Olcott; Edna Phillips; Edith Smith[1]; Ethel Smith
  (Jack Pickford)[1]; Lotte Smith (Lotte Pickford);
  Gladys Smith (Mary Pickford)

Notes: [1] This may be the same person. The
  program reads "Edith" and Mack Sennett's
  autobiography says Jack Pickford used the name
  Ethel.

1158 • EDUCATION OF H*Y*M*A*N K*A*P*L*A*N, THE

OPENED: 04/04/1968   Theatre: Alvin
Musical   Broadway: 28

Composer: Oscar Brand; Paul Nassau
Lyricist: Oscar Brand; Paul Nassau
Librettist: Benjamin Bernard Zavin
Producer: Andre Goulston
Director: George Abbott

Source: EDUCATION OF H*Y*M*A*N
K*A*P*L*A*N, THE (Novel: Leo Rosten);
Choreographer: Jaime Rogers; **Costumes:** Winn
Morton; **Dance Arranger:** Lee Holdridge;
Lighting Designer: Martin Aronstein; **Musical
Director:** Julian Stein; **Orchestrations:** Larry
Wilcox; **Set Design:** Jean Eckart; William Eckart;
Vocal Arranger: Julian Stein

Songs: All American; Anything Is Possible; Best of
Friends, The [1]; Day I Met Your Father, The;
Dedicated Teacher, A; Homework [1]; I Never
Felt Better in My Life; Julius Caesar; Lieben Dich
[2]; Loving You [2]; Old Fashioned Husband;
OOOO-EEEE; Spring in the City; Strange New
World; When Will I Learn

Cast: Tom Bosley; Nathaniel Frey; Gary Krawford;
Hal Linden; Donna McKechnie; Barbara Minkus;
Honey Sanders; Mimi Sloan

Notes: [1] Out prior to New York. [2] Same song.

1159 • EFX

OPENED: 03/22/1995
Revue

Composer: Tony Christopher; Gary Goddard; Don
Grady; Ed King; Jeff Krushin
Additional Music: Michael Crawford
Lyricist: Andy Belling; Doug Brayfield; Tony
Christopher; Gary Goddard; R.A. Robertson
Librettist: Tony Christopher; Gary Crawford;
Bruce Vilanch
Producer: Jeremiah Harris; MGM Grand
Director: Scott Faria; Anthony van Laast

Choreographer: Anthony van Laast; **Costumes:**
Theoni V. Aldredge; **Lighting Designer:** Natasha
Katz; **Musical Director:** Don Grady; **Set Design:**
David Mitchell

Songs: Arrival; Battle with the Morlocks; EFX;
Escape; Flying Kaganovich, The; Greatest
Showman in the Universe, The; H.G. Wells'
Laboratory; Intergalactic Circus of Wonders,
The; Intergalatic Circus Finale; Magic That
Surrounds You, The; Morgana's Entrance;
Morlock Exterior; Nexus; Seance, The; Slave
Dance; Sprite Dance, The; 3-D Adventure; To
the Future; Tonight; Wizard's Dual, The

Cast: Michael Crawford; Stewart Daylida; Lisa
Geist; Kevin Koehbi; Jeffrey Polk; Rick Stockwell;
Tim Walsh

Notes: MGM Grand Hotel, Las Vegas.

1160 • EIGHT PRINCESSES, THE
Notes: *See WONDERLAND.*

1161 • 80 DAYS

OPENED: 1988
Musical   Closed out of town

Composer: Ray Davies
Lyricist: Ray Davies
Librettist: Snoo Wilson

Source: AROUND THE WORLD IN EIGHTY
DAYS (Novel: Jules Verne); **Choreographer:**
Dianne McIntyre; **Costumes:** Susan Hilferty;
Lighting Designer: David F. Segal; **Musical
Director:** Jonny Bowden; **Orchestrations:** Robby
Merkin; **Set Design:** Douglas W. Schmidt; **Vocal
Arranger:** Jonny Bowden; Danny Troob

Songs: Against the Tide; Be Rational; 80 Days;
Empire Song, The; Finale; Here!; It Could Have
Been Him; Just Passing Through; Ladies of the
Night; Let It Be Written; Members of the Club;
Mongolia Song; No Surprises; On the Map; Place
in Your Heart, A; Tell Him, Tell Her; Welcome to
India; Well-Bred Englishman; Who Is This Man

Cast: Brooks Almy; Don Amendolia; Stephen
Bogardus; Jay Garner; Randy Graff; Scott Harlan;
Timothy Landfield; Lannyl Stephens

Notes: Program from La Jolla Playhouse,
California.

1162 • EILEEN

OPENED: 03/19/1917   Theatre: Shubert
Play   Broadway: 64

Composer: Victor Herbert
Lyricist: Henry Blossom
Librettist: Henry Blossom
Producer: Joseph Weber
Director: Fred G. Latham

Choreographer: George Marion; **Costumes:** R.N. Hyde; **Musical Director:** Arthur Kautzenbach

Songs: Blamen Is Our Birthright [1]; Come Tom [2]; Cupid, the Cunnin' Pandeen; Die, Die, Die Like a Soldier [2]; Dinny's Serenade; Eileen, Allana Asthore; Entrance of Humpy Grogan; Erin Slanthogal Go Bragh [3]; Finale Act I; Finale Act II; Finale Ultimo; Free Trade and a Misty Moon; General Dance [3]; Glad, Triumphant Hour; I'd Love to Be a Lady; If Eve Had Left the Apple on the Bough; In Erin's Isle; In the Name of the King [3]; Ireland My Sireland; Irish Have a Great Day Tonight, The; Irish Reel [3]; Jig (inst.); Life's a Game at Best; Man That Can Die Like a Soldier [3]; My Good Friends of Erin's Isle [2]; My Little Irish Rose; Opening Chorus Act II; Reveries; Round, A; Song of Acolytes; Stars and Rosebuds; Thine Alone; Too-Re-Loo-Re (A French Pavanne); When Ireland Stands Among the Nations of the World; When Love Awakes (Love's Awakening); When Shall I Again See Ireland [2]; Withdraw

Cast: Grace Breen; Edward Martindel; Walter Scanlon

Notes: Originally titled HEARTS OF ERIN. [1] Out Cleveland 1/1/17. [2] Not listed in program. [3] ASCAP/Library of Congress.

1163 • EILEEN ASTHORE

OPENED: 10/22/1906   Theatre: New York
Play   Broadway: 16

Composer: Chauncey Olcott
Lyricist: Chauncey Olcott
Author: Theodore Burt Sayre
Producer: Augustus Pitou

Musical Director: Gus Salzer

Songs: Day Dreams; Eileen Asthore; Eyes that Come from Ireland [1] (L: Richard Le Gallienne); For Love of Thee (Olcott's Love Song); Wearers of the Green

Cast: Richard Dillon; Florence Lester; Chauncey Olcott; Gertrude Stanley

Notes: [1] Sheet music only.

1164 • EL BRAVO!

OPENED: 06/16/1981   Theatre: Entermedia
Musical   Off-Broadway: 47

Composer: John Clifton
Lyricist: John Clifton
Librettist: Jose Fernandez; Thom Schiera
Producer: Edward Merzvinsky; Sidney Shlinker; Kenneth Waissman
Director: Patricia Birch

Choreographer: Patricia Birch; **Costumes:** Carrie F. Robbins; **Dance Arranger:** Louis St. Louis; **Lighting Designer:** Neil Peter Jampolis; **Musical Director:** Herbert Kaplan; **Orchestrations:** Gary Anderson; Michael Gibson; **Set Design:** Tom Lynch; **Vocal Arranger:** Herbert Kaplan; Louis St. Louis

Songs: Adios Barrio; And Furthermore; Bailar; Chiquita Bonita; El Bravo; Fairy Tales; Gotta Get Out; Gray [1]; He Says; Hey Chico; Honest John's Game; Que Pasa, My Love; Shoes; That Latin Lure; Torture

Cast: Quitman Fludd III; Michael Jeter; Keith Jochim; Aurelio Padron; Ray de Mattis

Notes: [1] Cut prior to opening.

1165 • EL CAPITAN

OPENED: 04/20/1896   Theatre: Broadway
Musical   Broadway: 112

Composer: John Philip Sousa
Lyricist: Charles Klein
Librettist: Charles Klein
Director: H.A. Cripps

Costumes: C.F. Siedle; **Musical Director:** John S. Hiller; **Set Design:** Ernest Gros

Songs: Bah! Bah!; Behold El Capitan; Bowed with Tribulation; Ditty of the Drill; Don Medigua, All for Thy Coming Wait; Don Medigua, Here's Your Wife; Finale Act I; Finale Act II; From Peru's Majestic Mountains; He Cannot, Must Not, Shall Not, Dare Not Wed You; If You Examine Human Kind; I've a Most Decided Notion; Lo, the Awful Man Approaches; Nobles of Castilian Birth; O, Spare a Daughter's Aching

Heart; O, Warrior Grim; Oh, Beautiful Land of Spain; Semper Fidelis; Sweetheart, I'm Waiting; Typical Tune of Zanzibar, A; We Beg Your Kind Consideration; When Some Serious Affliction; When We Hear the Call for Battle; You See in Me

Cast: Louise Carlisle; DeWolf Hopper; Alfred Klein; Edna Wallace

Notes: No program available.

1166 • EL COCA-COLA GRANDE

OPENED: 02/13/1973   Theatre: Mercer Arts Center
Revue   Off-Broadway: 1114

Composer: Cast, The
Lyricist: Cast, The
Producer: Gil Adler; Jack Temchin; John A. Vaccaro

Choreographer: Anna Nygh; **Set Design:** Mischa Petrow; **Vocal Arranger:** John Neville-Andrews; Alan Shearman

Cast: Ron House; John Neville-Andrews; Alan Shearman; Diz White; Sally Willis

Notes: Title changed to EL GRANDE DE COCA-COLA after opening. No songs listed in program.

1167 • EL GRANDE DE COCA-COLA

Notes: *See EL COCA-COLA GRANDE.*

1168 • ELEANOR (1969)

OPENED: 1969
Musical   Unproduced

Composer: Cy Coleman
Lyricist: Dorothy Fields
Librettist: Jerome Coopersmith

Songs: After Forty It's Patch, Patch, Patch; Charge; Good Impression, A; I Can't Let You Go; I Struck Out; Keep It in the Family; Love and Logic; Meat and Potatoes; Old Kitchen Sink, The; Red Hot Tomatoes; Sixty Percent of the Accidents; So What Now?; What Do I Do?; When Did You Know; Whisper on the Wind

Notes: Based on the life of Eleanor Roosevelt.

1169 • ELEANOR (DON'T FRIGHTEN THE HORSES!) (1986)

OPENED: 08/15/1986
Musical   Closed out of town

Composer: Nancy Ford
Lyricist: Gretchen Cryer
Librettist: Gretchen Cryer; Rhonda Lerman
Director: Gretchen Cryer

Source: ELEANOR (Book: Rhonda Lerman); **Arrangements:** Nancy Ford; **Choreographer:** Ann Reinking; **Costumes:** Claudia Brown; **Lighting Designer:** Dale Jordan; **Musical Director:** Michael O'Flaherty; **Set Design:** James Youmans

Songs: Feeling in My Chest, A; I Could Teach Her; If I Could Make a Difference; Isn't She Lovely; It Was Love; Menu, The; Miss Hickok Was in Love; No Regret; One Helluva Party; Picnic, The; Sensible Decisions; She Would Rather Light a Candle; Things We Leave Unspoken, The; War Is Bully; Washington Summers; We'll See the World Together; What a Team; When One Marries an Exceptional Woman

Cast: Allison Janney; Caroline Kava; Michael O'Flaherty; Mary Bracken Phillips; Howard Platt; Nancy Ringham; Dana Zeller-Alexis

Notes: Williamstown Theatre Festival.

1170 • ELEANOR SLEEPS HERE

Notes: *See FIRST LADY SUITE.*

1171 • ELIZABETH AND ESSEX

OPENED: 01/31/1980   Theatre: South Street
Musical   Off-Broadway: 24

Composer: Doug Katsaros
Lyricist: Richard Engquist
Librettist: Mark Bramble; Michael Stewart
Producer: Encompass the Music Theatre
Director: Nancy Rhodes

Source: ELIZABETH THE QUEEN (Play: Maxwell Anderson); **Choreographer:** Sharon Halley; **Costumes:** A. Christina Giannini; **Lighting Designer:** Carol B. Sealey; **Musical Director:** Jack Gaughan; **Orchestrations:** Doug Katsaros;

Set Design: Michael C. Smith; **Vocal Arranger:** Doug Katsaros

Songs: All I Remember Is You; As You Are; Cheers; Fa La; First to Know Ireland, The; Gloriana; Gossip; I'll Be Different; It Takes a Man; Lady Lies, The; Love Knots; Not Now; She's a Woman

Cast: Florence Lacey; Estelle Parsons; Gordon Stanley; Richard White

1172 • ELMER GANTRY

OPENED: 1988
Musical

Composer: Mel Marvin
Lyricist: John Bishop; Robert Satuloff
Librettist: John Bishop
Director: David H. Bell

Source: ELMER GANTRY (Novel: Sinclair Lewis); **Costumes:** David Murin; **Lighting Designer:** Pat Collins; **Musical Director:** Rob Bowman; **Orchestrations:** Michael Gibson; **Set Design:** Marjorie Bradley Kellogg

Cast: John Almberg; Joe Barrett; Casey Briggs; Ray de Mattis; Laura Kenyon; Queen Esther Marrow; Sharon Scruggs; J.K. Simmons

Notes: Ford's Theatre, Washington, D.C.

1173 • ELOPERS, THE

OPENED: 1904
Musical

Composer: Hugo Frey
Lyricist: Frederick Herendeen
Librettist: Arthur Gillespie; George E. Stoddard
Producer: Harry Cort
Director: Charles Mast

Songs: Casey; Chaperon, The; Cuckoo Clock; Ev'ry Road Is the Right Road; My Cupie Doll; System of My Own; Tango Band, The; Twilight; Whistle It; You-Just-You

Notes: No other information available.

1174 • ELSIE

OPENED: 04/02/1923   Theatre: Vanderbilt
Musical   Broadway: 40

Composer: Eubie Blake
Lyricist: Noble Sissle
Librettist: Charles W. Bell
Producer: John Jay Scholl
Director: Edgar MacGregor

Choreographer: Walter Brooks; Bert French; **Musical Director:** Eugene Salzer

Songs: Baby Buntin'; Clouds of Love (C: Alma Sanders; L: Monte Carlo); Elsie (1) [2]; Elsie (2) (C: Alma Sanders; L: Monte Carlo); Everybody's Struttin' Now; Firefly, The (C: Alma Sanders; L: Monte Carlo); Glow Worm [1] (C: Alma Sanders; L: Monte Carlo); Hearts in Tune; Honeymoon Home (C: Monte Carlo; Alma Sanders; L: Alfred Bryan); I Like to Walk with a Pal Like You; I'll Find the Key to Your Heart [1] (C: Alma Sanders; L: Monte Carlo); Jazzing Thunder Storming Dance (Thunderstorm Dance); Jingle Step [1]; Lovin' Chile [2]; My Crinoline Girl; One Day in May (C: Alma Sanders; L: Monte Carlo); Regular Guy, A; Sand Flowers; Symphonic Poem (inst.) (C: Eugene Salzer); Two Hearts in Tune [3]; Two Lips Are Roses (C: Monte Carlo; Alma Sanders; L: Alfred Bryan); With You [1]

Cast: Vinton Freedley; Stanley Ridges; Marguerite Zender

Notes: [1] Cut Columbus, Ohio 12/21/22. [2] Not used. [3] Sheet music only.

1175 • ELSIE JANIS AND HER GANG (1919)

OPENED: 12/01/1919   Theatre: George M. Cohan
Revue   Broadway: 55

Composer: B.C. Hilliam; William B. Kernell
Lyricist: Richard Fechheimer; Elsie Janis
Librettist: Elsie Janis
Producer: Charles Dillingham; Florenz Ziegfeld
Director: Elsie Janis

Costumes: Charles LeMaire; **Musical Director:** William Schroeder

Songs: Ah Oui; Apres la Guerre; Gee But It's Great to Meet a Girl from Home (C: William B. Kernell; L: Richard Fechheimer); I Love Them Just a Little Bit; In the Latin Quarter (C: William B. Kernell; L: Richard Fechheimer); It's My Temperament

(My Artistic Temperament) (C: William B. Kernell; L: Richard Fechheimer); Just a Little After Taps (C: William B. Kernell; L: Richard Fechheimer); Just a Little Touch of Paris (C: William B. Kernell; L: Richard Fechheimer); Let's Go (C: William B. Kernell; L: Richard Fechheimer); M.P., The (C: William B. Kernell; L: Richard Fechheimer); Somewhere in America (C: William B. Kernell; L: Richard Fechheimer); Songs We Sang; When I Took My Jazz Band to The Fatherland

Cast: Elsie Janis; Eva Le Gallienne

1176 • ELSIE JANIS AND HER GANG (1922)

OPENED: 01/16/1922   Theatre: Gaiety
Revue   Broadway: 56

Composer: Elsie Janis
Lyricist: Elsie Janis

Costumes: Will R. Barnes; Charles LeMaire;
  Musical Director: John McManus;
  Orchestrations: Maurice DePackh

Songs: All the World Is Wonderful [3] (C: Seymour Simons); Bonus Blues, The (C: Carey Morgan; Arthur Swanstrom); Broadway; Come, the Night Descends; Discontent (C: Herman Finck); Goodbye Girls I'm Through; I Met a Girl on Monday [1]; I've Been Waiting; I've Got the Red White and Blues [2]; Love in the Springtime Is Not What It Used to Be (C: George Hirst); Memories; Mon Homme (C: Maurice Yvain; L: Jacques Charles; Albert Willemetz); Montmartre; Nuthin' (C/L: Seymour Simons); Property Man; Too Young to Love; Why All This Fuss About Spain; Will You Remember

Cast: Florence Courtney; Elsie Janis; Lane McLeod; Elizabeth Morgan; Gus Shy

Notes: [1] Cut Salt Lake City 4/18/22. [2] Sheet music only. [3] Sheet music credits the music to William Kernell.

1177 • ELUSIVE LADY, THE

OPENED: 1922
Musical

Composer: Raymond Hubbell
Lyricist: Glen MacDonough

Librettist: Glen MacDonough
Producer: Jacques Pierre
Director: Priestly Morrison

Choreographer: Earl Lindsay

Songs: Cute Little Beaut from Butte, Montana; Desert Love; Detectives, The; Fascination; Heart o' Me; I'll Break the Bank at Monte Carlo; National Anthem of Zoolakia; Opening; Tune Like You, A; Violin and Cello; Vivandiere, The; When You're Asleep in Your Bed at Night

Cast: Julian Eltinge

Notes: No other information available.

1178 • EMERALD ISLE, THE (1902)

OPENED: 09/01/1902   Theatre: Herald Square
Musical   Broadway: 56

Composer: Kate Condon; Arthur Sullivan
Lyricist: Edward German
Librettist: Basil Hood
Producer: Sam S. Shubert
Director: R.H. Burnside

Songs: At an Early Stage of Life; Have You Heard the Brave News; I Am the Lord Lieutenant; If You Wish To Appear As an Irish Type; I'm Descended from Brian Boru; It Is Past My Comprehension; Many Years Ago; Of Viceroys Tho' We've Had; Oh Setting Sun; On the Heights of Glentann; Saxon Stranger, A; Song of the Devonshire Man; That We're Soldiers; Their Fathers Fought; They've Courage High; Two's Company — Three's None

Cast: W.T. Carleton; Jefferson DeAngelis

1179 • EMERALD ISLE, THE (1920)

OPENED: 1920
Play

Songs: Gone Is the Smile (C: I.M. Greene; L: Irving Caesar)

Notes: No other information available.

1180 • EMPEROR OF SAN FRANCISCO, THE

Notes: *See GOLDEN GATE.*

1181 • ENCHANTED CAP, THE

Songs: Colonial Days (C/L: Bob Winter)

Cast: Hilder; Hosmer

Notes: No other information available.

1182 • ENCHANTED ISLE
OPENED: 09/19/1927   Theatre: Lyric
Musical   Broadway: 32

Composer: Ida Hoyt Chamberlin
Lyricist: Ida Hoyt Chamberlin
Librettist: Ida Hoyt Chamberlin
Producer: American Allied Arts
Director: Oscar Eagle

Choreographer: Jack Connors; **Musical Director:** Charles Berton; **Orchestrations:** Charles Berton; **Set Design:** Ida Hoyt Chamberlin

Songs: Abandon; Business Is Business; California; Close in Your Arms; Could I Forget; Cowboy Girl; Enchanted Castle; Enchanted Isle; Hacienda Garden; Harmonica Dance; Jazz; Julianne; Love Thought Garden; Roulette; Voice of the High Sierras; What a Jamboree; Who, Gal

Cast: Greek Evans; Kathryn Reece; Basil Ruysdael; Hansford Wilson

1183 • ENCHANTRESS, THE
OPENED: 10/19/1911   Theatre: New York
Musical   Broadway: 72

Composer: Victor Herbert
Lyricist: Harry B. Smith
Librettist: Fred De Gresac
Producer: Joseph M. Gaites
Director: Fred G. Latham

Choreographer: Frederick A. Bishop; **Costumes:** Ralph Riggs; **Musical Director:** Gus Salzer; **Orchestrations:** Victor Herbert

Songs: All Your Own Am I; And That Little Girl Is You; Art Is Calling Me (I Want to Be a Prima Donna); Ballet [2]; Champagne Song; Chorus and Entrance of Regent; Come Little Fishes (Gold Fish Song); Come to Sunny Spain; Dreaming Princess, The; Entrance of Herr Bangkeyski and the Piano King [1]; Entrance of Prince Ivan; Entrance of Vivien; Every Girl's a Soldier in the Army of Love [1]; Finale Act I [2]; Finale Act II [2]; How to Tell a Fairy Tale [3]; If You Can't Be Happy as You Want to Be (Just Be as Happy as You Can); I've Been Looking for a Perfect Man; Last Little Girl Is You, The [3]; Lover Come Back; Madrigal [2]; March Chorus and Entrance of the Regent [4]; March of the Prince's Regiment [1]; One Word from You; Opening Chorus Act II; Opening Number; Or Know the Reason Why [1]; Polla [3]; Rose, Lucky Rose; That Pretty Little Song; They All Look Good when They're Far Away; To the Land of My Own Romance; When the Right Man Sings Tra-La-La; When You Look in Her Eyes [4]

Cast: Nina Barbour; Ida Fitzhugh; Kitty Gordon; Ralph Riggs

Notes: [1] Cut prior to New York. [2] Not in program. [3] Sheet music only. [4] ASCAP/Library of Congress only.

1184 • ENCLAVE, THE
OPENED: 11/15/1973   Theatre: Theatre Four
Play   Off-Broadway: 22

Author: Arthur Laurents
Producer: Joseph Beruh; Edgar Lansbury; Clinton Wilder
Director: Arthur Laurents

Costumes: Robert Mackintosh; **Incidental Music:** Stephen Sondheim; **Lighting Designer:** Robert Randolph; **Musical Director:** Paul Gemignani; **Set Design:** Robert Randolph

Cast: Steve Elmore; Don Gantry; Barton Heyman; Peg Murray; Rochelle Oliver

Notes: No songs in this show.

1185 • END OF THE TRAIL, THE
OPENED: 11/05/1907
Musical   Closed out of town

Composer: William Jossey
Lyricist: William Jossey
Librettist: William Jossey
Producer: Lincoln J. Carter
Director: William Jossey

Songs: Cow Boy; I'm the Sheriff; Mexico; Red Man

Cast: Julia Gray; Robert Harland; William Jossey; Frederick Loomis; Will H. Stevens

Notes: Program of Cedar Rapids.

1186 • END OF THE WORLD
OPENED: 05/06/1984   Theatre: Music Box
Play   Broadway: 33

Author: Arthur Kopit
Producer: Michael Frazier; John F. Kennedy Center
Director: Harold Prince

Costumes: William Ivey Long; **Lighting Designer:** Ken Billington; **Set Design:** Clarke Dunham

Songs: What Can One Man Do? (C: Larry Grossman; L: Ellen Fitzhugh)

Cast: Barnard Hughes; Linda Hunt; John Shea

1187 • ENEMY, THE
OPENED: 10/20/1925   Theatre: Times Square
Play   Broadway: 202

Author: Channing Pollock
Producer: Crosby Gaige; Robert Milton

Musical Director: George Martens

Songs: Enemy Overture, The (C: Reynell Wreford); We're Going to Rush the Russians (C: Reynell Wreford)

Cast: Walter Abel; Fay Bainter; Jane Seymour; Russ Whytal

1188 • ENGLISH DAISY, AN
OPENED: 01/18/1904   Theatre: Casino
Musical   Broadway: 41

Composer: Alfred Muller-Norden
Lyricist: Edgar Smith
Librettist: Edgar Smith
Producer: Lew Fields; Joseph Weber
Director: Ben Teal

Source: ENGLISH DAISY, AN (Musical: Seymour Hicks; Walter Slaughter); **Set Design:** John H. Young

Songs: At the Music Hall (C: Jean Schwartz); Big Indian Chief (C: J. Rosamond Johnson; L: Bob Cole); Charlie [1] (L: Alfred Muller-Norden); Coon, the Moon and the Octaroon, The; Downcast Eye, The [2] (C: Jerome Kern; L: Edgar Smith); He'll Be There! [3] (C: Jerome Kern; L: J. Cheever Goodwin); I Adore a Certain Party; I Am the English Daisy (L: Alfred Muller-Norden); I Love You, Mon Cherie [1] (C/L: Paul Rubens); Military Man, The; Moon, the Coon, and the Octoroon, The [1] (C: Maude Nugent; L: Will A. Heelan); Prepossessing Maid; Saturday Till Monday [3] (C: Jerome Kern; L: John H. Wagner); Spanish Dance; To the End of the World Together (C: Jerome Kern; L: Edgar A. Smith); Under Thy Rose Wreathed Window [1] (L: Alfred Muller-Norden); Who-Who-Who- Hoolahan [1] (C: Jean Schwartz; L: William Jerome); Wine, Wine! (Champagne Song) (C: Jerome Kern; L: Edgar Smith); You Couldn't Get On without Me, Girls

Cast: Charles A. Bigelow; Frank Lalor; Christie MacDonald; Templar Saxe; Truly Shattuck

Notes: [1] Sheet music only. [2] Added to tour after Broadway. [3] ASCAP/Library of Congress.

1189 • ENTER JULIET
OPENED: 1977
Musical   Unproduced

Composer: Morton Gould
Lyricist: Carolyn Leigh

Source: JULIET OF THE SPIRITS (Film: Federico Fellini)

Songs: Anniversary Song (Rememberance); Enter Juliet; He's a Guy; I Get Married; Loozeyana; Nothing Is Forever; Remembrance; Today's the Day; What Beautiful Is; Who Needed You; Wind in the Night, The; Without Him

1190 • ENTER LAUGHING
OPENED: 03/13/1963   Theatre: Henry Miller's
Play   Broadway: 419

Author: Joseph Stein
Producer: Morton Gottlieb
Director: Gene Saks

Source: ENTER LAUGHING (Book: Carl Reiner); **Costumes:** Ed Wittstein; **Lighting Designer:** Ed Wittstein; **Set Design:** Ed Wittstein

Songs: Enter Laughing (C: Jerry Bock; L: Sheldon Harnick)

Cast: Alan Arkin; Vivian Blaine; Barbara Dana; Pierre Epstein; Irving Jacobson; Alan Mowbray; Michael J. Pollard; Sylvia Sidney; Walt Wandersman

Notes: The song may not have appeared in the show.

1191 • ENTRE-NOUS

OPENED: 12/30/1935   Theatre: Cherry Lane
Musical   Off-Broadway: 47

Composer: Richard Lewine
Lyricist: Will B. Johnstone

Songs: A.J. (C: Harry Archer); Am I? (C: Harry Archer); Entre-Nous; High Hat; I'll See You Home (C: Harry Archer); Kick in the Pants (C: Harry Archer); Let's Get Married or Something (L: Ted Fetter); Let's Go; Sunday Morning Churchman (L: Norman Zeno); Under My Skin (C: Harry Archer); What Can I Give You? (C: Philip Broughton); When Opportunity Knocks (L: Ted Fetter); With You, With Me (L: Richard Lewine)

Notes: No program available.

1192 • EPHRAHAM JOHNSON FROM NORFOLK

OPENED: 1908
Musical

Librettist: Marion Brooks; Flournoy E. Miller
Director: Marion Brooks

Songs: Darktown Grenadiers; Hard to Love Somebody When Somebody Don't Love You; Here Today but When Tomorrow Comes, I'll Be Gone; I Want You; I'd Like to Know Your Address; Napinee; Nuf Sed; On One Summer Night; Since You Called Me Dear; Society; What Will Your Answer Be?

Cast: Marion Brooks; Master Dozzel; Flournoy E. Miller; James Moore

Notes: No other information available.

1193 • ERMINIE

OPENED: 05/10/1886   Theatre: Casino
Musical   Broadway

Composer: Edward Jakobowski
Lyricist: Claxson Bellamy; Edward Paulton
Librettist: Claxson Bellamy; Edward Paulton
Director: Harry Paulton

Source: L'AUBERGE DES ADRETS (Play: Benjamin Antier; Saint-Amand; Paul Yanthe); **Source:** UNKNOWN (Play: Robert Macaire); **Costumes:** Dazian; **Musical Director:** Jesse Williams; **Set Design:** Henry E. Hoyt; T.S. Plaisted

Songs: Around in a Whirl; At Midnight on My Pillow Lying (The Dream Song); Blissful Pleasure, I Profess, The; Darkest the Hour; Dear Mother, in Dreams I See Her (The Lullaby); Downy Jailbirds of a Feather; Finale Act I; Good Night; Here on Lord and Lady Waiting; Jail-Birds of a Feather; Join in Pleasure; Joy Attend on Erminie; Lullaby; Opening Chorus; Opening Chorus Act II; Past and Future; Sighing Swain, The; Soldier's Life [1] (L: Irving Caesar); Soldier's Life, A; Supper Chorus; Vive le Marquis; What the Dicky Birds Say; When Love Is Young; Woman's Dress

Cast: W.S. Daboll; Max Freeman; Pauline Hall; Jennie Weathersby; Francis Wilson

Notes: No songs listed in program. Songs are from English version. [1] Added to revival of 1/3/21 which had a revised book by Marc Connelly.

1194 • ERNEST IN LOVE

OPENED: 05/04/1960   Theatre: Gramercy Arts
Musical   Off-Broadway: 111

Composer: Lee Pockriss
Lyricist: Anne Croswell
Librettist: Anne Croswell
Producer: Noel Behn; Robert Kamlot
Director: Harold Stone

Source: IMPORTANCE OF BEING EARNEST, THE (Play: Oscar Wilde); **Choreographer:** Frank Derbas; **Costumes:** Ann Roth; **Dance Arranger:** Gershon Kingsley; **Lighting Designer:** Peter Dohanos; **Musical Director:** Liza Redfield; **Orchestrations:** Gershon Kingsley; **Set Design:** Peter Dohanos; **Vocal Arranger:** Gershon Kingsley

Songs: Come Raise Your Cup; Ernest in Love; Handbag Is Not a Proper Mother, A; Hat, The; How Do You Find the Words?; Lost [1]; Metaphorically Speaking [1]; Mr. Bunbury [1]; Muffin Song, The; My Eternal Devotion [1]; My Very First Impression [1]; Perfection [1]; Wicked Man, A [1]; You Can't Make Love

Cast: Louis Edmonds; Christina Gillespie; George Hall; Margot Harley; John Irving; Lucy Landau; Leila Martin; Gerrianne Raphael; Sara Seegar; Alan Shayne

Notes: [1] From the original 1957 TV version of this show titled WHO'S ERNEST?

1195 • ESTABLISHMENT, THE
OPENED: 01/23/1963   Theatre: Strollers Theatre Club
Revue   Off-Broadway: 118

Composer: John Bird; Patrick Gowers; Tony Kinsey; Christopher Logue; Stanley Myers
Lyricist: John Bird; Patrick Gowers; Tony Kinsey; Christopher Logue; Stanley Myers
Producer: Peter Cook; John Krimsley; Nicholas Luard
Director: Nicholas Garland

Lighting Designer: Jules Fisher

Songs: Asses Song, The; Go to the Wall; Johnny; Sitting Around; Water and the Flame, The

Cast: John Bird; Eleanor Bron; John Fortune; Jeremy Geidt; Carole Simpson

Notes: No songs listed in program.

1196 • ETERNAL ROAD, THE
OPENED: 01/07/1937   Theatre: Manhattan Opera House
Play   Broadway: 153

Composer: Kurt Weill
Author: Franz Werfel [1]
Producer: Crosby Gaige; Meyer W. Weisgal
Director: Max Reinhardt

Choreographer: Benjamin Zemach; **Costumes:** Norman Bel Geddes; **Lighting Designer:** Norman Bel Geddes; **Set Design:** Norman Bel Geddes

Songs: Dance of the Golden Calf; David's Psalm; March to Zion, The; Promise; Song of Miriam; Song of Ruth

Cast: Katherine Carrington; Thomas Chalmers; Roger De Koven; Olive Deering; Charles Hale; Sam Jaffe; Kurt Kasznar; Lotte Lenya; Baruch Lumet; Sidney Lumet; Joseph Macaulay; Rosamond Pinchot; Dick Van Patten

Notes: No program available. [1] Translation by Ludwig Lewisohn. Adapted by William A. Drake.

1197 • ETERNAL WALTZ, THE
OPENED: 1913   Theatre: Palace
Musical

Composer: Leo Fall
Lyricist: Austen Hurgon
Librettist: Austen Hurgon
Producer: Martin Beck
Director: Joseph Hart

Songs: Hush, and I'll Sing You a Waltz-Song; I Am the "Dernier Cri"; Man Who Feels the Dart, A; Thanks for Kindness Condescending; Toast We'll Give You To-Night, A; Two-Step (inst.); Waltz, the Waltz, The

Cast: Mabel Berra; Cyril Chadwick; Jules Epailly

Notes: A one-act vaudeville operetta that appeared at the Palace Theater, N.Y. 3/25/13.

1198 • EUBIE!
OPENED: 09/20/1978   Theatre: Ambassador
Revue   Broadway: 439

Composer: Eubie Blake
Lyricist: Noble Sissle
Producer: Ashton Springer
Director: Julianne Boyd

Choreographer: Henry LeTang; Billy Wilson; **Costumes:** Bernard Johnson; **Dance Arranger:** Danny Holgate; **Lighting Designer:** William Mintzer; **Musical Director:** Vicki Carter; **Orchestrations:** Neal Tate; **Set Design:** Karl Eigsti; **Vocal Arranger:** Chapman Roberts

Songs: Baltimore Buzz; Charleston Rag; Daddy; Dixie Moon; Gee, I Wish I Had Someone to Rock

Me in the Cradle of Love; Goodnight Angeline (L: James Reese Europe; Noble Sissle); High Steppin' Days (L: Johnny Brandon); Hot Feet; If You've Never Been Vamped by a Brownskin; I'm a Great Big Baby (L: Andy Razaf); I'm Craving for that Kind of Love; I'm Just Simply Full of Jazz; I'm Just Wild About Harry; In Honeysuckle Time; Low Down Blues; Memories of You (L: Andy Razaf); My Handy Man Ain't Handy Any More (L: Andy Razaf); Oriental Blues; Roll Jordan (L: Andy Razaf); Shuffle Along; There's a Million Little Cupids in the Sky; Weary (L: Andy Razaf); You Got to Get the Gittin While the Gittin's Good (L: Flournoy E. Miller)

Cast: Ethel Beatty; Lynnie Godfrey; Gregory Hines; Maurice Hines; Lonnie McNeil; Marion Ramsey; Alaina Reed

Notes: No songs original to this production. Originated as a revival of SHUFFLE ALONG at The Theatre Off Park.

1199 • EVA

OPENED: 12/30/1912　　Theatre: New Amsterdam
Musical　　Broadway: 24

Composer: Franz Lehar
Lyricist: Glen MacDonough
Librettist: Glen MacDonough
Producer: Klaw & Erlanger
Director: Herbert Gresham

Source: EVA (DAS FABRIKSMADEL) (Operetta: Robert Bodanzky; Franz Lehar; A.M. Willner); **Choreographer:** Julian Mitchell; **Costumes:** F. Richard Anderson; **Lighting Designer:** Frank Detering; **Musical Director:** Hugo Reisenfeld

Songs: Cinderella; Finale Act I; Imp of Montmartre, The; Joy and Glass; Let Us Whirl, Swirl, Twirl; Life Is a Masquerade; On the Day I Marry; Quarrel, The; So Unreal Does This Seem; Starlight Guards, The; To What I Say, Attention Pay; Unrepentant Butterfly, The; Up-To-Date Troubador, The; Vision Song, The (Love Is a Pilgrim); Voice of Paris, The; We'll the New Master Greet; When the Parisian Goes for a Ride [2]; Zwanzinette [2]

Cast: Sallie Fisher; Wallace McCutcheon; Walter Percival

Notes: [1] Out 11/27/??. [2] Sheet music only.

1200 • EVENING PRIMROSE

OPENED: 11/16/1966　　Theatre: ABC
TV Musical

Composer: Stephen Sondheim
Lyricist: Stephen Sondheim
Librettist: James Goldman
Producer: Willard Levitas
Director: Paul Bogart

Source: EVENING PRIMROSE (Story: John Collier)

Songs: I Remember; I'm Here; Take Me to the World; When?

Cast: Charmian Carr; Larry Gates; Anthony Perkins; Dorothy Stickney

Notes: Presented as an ABC STAGE 67 production.

1201 • EVENING WITH JOAN CRAWFORD, AN

OPENED: 01/20/1981　　Theatre: Orpheum
Musical　　Off-Broadway: 15

Composer: Nick Branch; Joseph Church
Lyricist: Malcolm Arnold; Joe Bianco
Director: Julian Neil

Choreographer: Sydney Smith; **Costumes:** Barbara Gerard; **Lighting Designer:** Paul Everett; **Musical Director:** Joseph Church; **Set Design:** J. Patrick Mann

Songs: Ain't No Place Like Home; Blame It All on Me; Except of Course Men; Give 'Em Hell; Hollywood Lullaby; Take a Vacation; Too Much Money Blues; What's It to Be a Legend; You're One of a Kind

Cast: Joyce Fullerton; Michael J. Hume; Fracaswell Hyman; Michael Kemmerling; Lee Speaks

1202 • EVER GREEN

OPENED: 12/03/1930　　Theatre: Adelphi
Musical　　London: 254

Composer: Richard Rodgers
Lyricist: Lorenz Hart
Librettist: Benn W. Levy
Producer: Charles B. Cochran
Director: Frank Collins

Choreographer: Buddy Bradley; Billy Pierce; **Costumes:** Reville Ltd.; **Musical Director:** Richard Crean; **Orchestrations:** Robert Russell Bennett; **Set Design:** Ernest Stern

Songs: Beauty Contest (Miss Hampstead Heath) (Opening the Beauty Contest) (Opening Act I) [1]; Colour of Her Eyes, The [2]; Dancing on the Ceiling [3]; Dear! Dear!; Doing a Little Clog Dance (Doing a Little Waltz Clog); Harlemania; Hot Blues (inst.); If I Give in to You; Impromptu Song (Talking Song); In the Cool of the Evening; Je M'em Fiche du Sex Appeal!; La Femme a Toujours Vingt Ans! (Lovely Woman's Ever Young) [4]; Lion King, The; No Place but Home (If We're in China); Nobody Looks at the Man; Quand Notre Vieux Etait Tout Neuf (When the Old World Was New) [4]; Waiting for the Leaves to Fall (She Was Poor)

Cast: Joyce Barbour; Albert Burdon; Sonnie Hale; W.E.C. Jenkins; Jessie Matthews

Notes: [1] Cut prior to opening. [2] Cut from HEADS UP! [3] Cut from SIMPLE SIMON when titled "He Dances On My Ceiling." [4] French lyrics by J. Lenoir.

1203 • EVER YOURS

OPENED: 1933
Musical   Unproduced

Composer: Cole Porter
Lyricist: Cole Porter
Librettist: Guy Bolton
Producer: Gilbert Miller

Songs: Coffee; Gypsy Song; Ilsa's Song; It All Seems So Long Ago; It's Probably Just As Well; Night of the Ball, The; Once Upon a Time; Polka Mazurka, The; When Love Comes Your Way [1]; When We Waltz Down the Aisle [3]; Yours [2]

Notes: Sometimes titled ONCE UPON A TIME and YOURS, EVER YOURS. [1] Cut from NYMPH ERRANT. In JUBILEE. [2] Not used. From JUBILEE. [3] Cut from JUBILEE and ANYTHING GOES.

1204 • EVERYBODY LOVES ME

OPENED: 11/08/1956
Play   Closed out of town

Author: Mannie Manheim; Arthur Marx
Producer: Max Gordon
Director: Robert B. Sinclair

Costumes: Guy Kent; **Lighting Designer:** Edward Gilbert; **Set Design:** Edward Gilbert

Songs: When the Wind Is Still (C/L: Martha Manheim; Irene Marx)

Cast: Jack Carson; Pat Harrington; Conrad Janis; Temple Texas

1205 • EVERYBODY OUT THE CASTLE IS SINKING

OPENED: 12/26/1964
Play   Closed out of town

Author: Henry Ephron; Phoebe Ephron
Producer: Lester Braunstein; Fred F. Finklehoffe
Director: Henry Ephron

Costumes: Florence Klotz; **Lighting Designer:** George Jenkins; **Set Design:** George Jenkins

Songs: Everybody Out the Castle Is Sinking (C: Elliot Lawrence; L: Henry Ephron; Phoebe Ephron)

Cast: Marge Champion; Elizabeth Hartman; Richard Mulligan; Nigel Patrick; Hiram Sherman

Notes: Closed in Philadelphia.

1206 • EVERYBODY WORKS BUT FATHER

OPENED: 11/30/1906
Musical   Closed out of town

Composer: Howard Webster
Lyricist: Howard Webster
Producer: A.S. Webster

Musical Director: Howard Webster

Songs: Finale Act I; Friends; Just One Country, Just One Flag; Just You and I; Opening Chorus Act II; Pansy; Please Be a Poppa to Us; Ship Ahoy; Silver Bells; Slumber; Spooning; Such a Lonesome Place

Cast: Clare Atkinson; Arthur Carleton; Harrison Greene; Kathryn B. Roberts; Frances Vaughn

Notes: Program of Cedar Rapids.

1207 • EVERYBODY'S WELCOME

OPENED: 10/13/1931   Theatre: Shubert
Musical   Broadway: 127

Composer: Sammy Fain
Lyricist: Irving Kahal
Librettist: Lambert Carroll
Producer: Messrs. Shubert
Director: William Mollison

Source: UP POPS THE DEVIL (Play: Frances Goodrich; Albert Hackett); **Choreographer:** William Holbrook; Albertina Rasch; **Costumes:** Alison McLellan Hunter; **Musical Director:** Tom Jones; **Set Design:** Watson Barratt

Songs: (I'm) All Wrapped Up in You (C: Harry Revel; L: Harold Adamson; Mack Gordon); As Time Goes By [1] (C/L: Herman Hupfeld); Blue Danube Ballet [3]; Dance of the Mirrors [3]; Even As You and I; Feather in a Breeze; He Looked at Her, She Looked at Him [2] (C: Manning Sherwin; L: Arthur Lippmann); I Shot the Works (C: Manning Sherwin; L: Arthur Lippmann; Milton Pascal); Is Rhythm Necessary?; Lease on My Heart; Lover's Luck [2]; Nature Played a Dirty Trick on You (C: Manning Sherwin; L: Arthur Lippmann; Milton Pascal); Nocturne [4]; One in a Million (C: Harry Revel; L: Mack Gordon); Pie Eyed Piper; Ta Ta, Old Bean (C: Manning Sherwin; L: Edward Eliscu); That's Good, That's Bad [2]

Cast: Jimmy Dorsey; Tommy Dorsey; Cecil Lean; Ann Pennington; Oscar Shaw; Jack Sheehan; Ann Sothern; Frances Williams

Notes: [1] Also in CASABLANCA (1943), a film, in case you didn't know. [2] Out Newark 9/14/31. [3] Dropped after opening and replaced by "Nocturne." [4] Added after opening.

1208 • EVERYTHING

OPENED: 08/22/1918   Theatre: Hippodrome
Musical   Broadway: 461

Additional Music: John Philip Sousa
Librettist: R.H. Burnside

Producer: Charles Dillingham
Director: R.H. Burnside

Costumes: Will R. Barnes; William H. Matthews; Robert McQueen; Gladys Monkhouse; **Incidental Music:** John Philip Sousa; **Lighting Designer:** Joseph Elsner; **Musical Director:** A.J. Garing

Songs: Circus Is Coming to Town, The (C/L: Irving Berlin); Come Along to Toy Town (Come Along to Toyland) [1] (C/L: Irving Berlin); Every Girl Is Doing Her Bit Today [2] (C: James W. Tate; L: Clifford Harris; P.H. Valentine); Everything Is Hunky Dory Down in Honky Tonk Town (C: Harry Tierney; L: Joseph McCarthy); Follow the Flag (C: Raymond Hubbell; L: R.H. Burnside); I Like New York (C/L: Harry Redford; R.P. Weston); (Come to) The Land of Romance (C: William Daly; L: John Golden); Liberty (C: J.M. Rumshinsky; L: Darl MacBoyle); On Atlantic Beach (C: Harry Tierney; L: Joseph McCarthy); Rainbow from the U.S.A., A (C: Percy Wenrich; L: William Jerome; Jack F. Mahoney); Roll Along (C: Max Darewski; L: R.H. Burnside; John Golden); Sunshine Alley (C/L: Bert Lee; R.P. Weston; L: R.H. Burnside; John Golden); You're the Very Girl I've Looked For (C: William Daly; L: R.H. Burnside; John Golden)

Cast: Charles T. Aldrich; Tom Brown; DeWolf Hopper; Harry Houdini; Bert Levy; Belle Story

Notes: [1] From GOING UP. [2] Sheet music only.

1209 • EVERYTHING WILL BE ALL RIGHT

OPENED: 1924

Composer: Harry Carroll
Lyricist: Harry Carroll

Songs: Elsie, There Isn't Anybody Else-Y but You; Faded Rose; Mamie McGee

Notes: No other information available.

1210 • EVERYWOMAN

OPENED: 02/27/1911   Theatre: Herald Square
Play   Broadway: 144

Composer: George Whitefield Chadwick
Author: Walter Browne
Producer: Henry W. Savage
Director: George Marion

Costumes: Hy Mayer

Songs: Conscience's Song No. 1; Conscience's Song No. 2; Passion's Song

Cast: Wilda Bennett; Patricia Collinge; Laura Nelson Hall; Stella Hammerstein; Edward Mackay; James Stevens

Notes: Songs not listed in program. Sheet music only.

1211 • EVITA
OPENED: 09/25/1979   Theatre: Broadway
Musical   Broadway: 1568

Composer: Andrew Lloyd Webber
Lyricist: Tim Rice
Producer: Robert Stigwood
Director: Harold Prince

Choreographer: Larry Fuller; **Costumes:** Tazeena Firth; Timothy O'Brien; **Lighting Designer:** David Hersey; **Musical Director:** Rene Wiegert; **Orchestrations:** Hershy Kay; Andrew Lloyd Webber; **Set Design:** Tazeena Firth; Timothy O'Brien

Songs: Actress Hasn't Learned, The; And the Money Kept Rolling In; Another Suitcase in Another Hall; Art of the Possible, The; Buenos Aires; Dice Are Rolling; Don't Cry for Me Argentina [2]; Eva Beware of the City; Eva's Final Broadcast; Goodnight and Thank You; High Flying Adored; I'd Be Surprisingly Good for You; Lady's Got Potential, The [1]; Lament; Montage; New Argentina, A; Oh What a Circus [2]; On the Balcony of the Casa Rosada; On This Night of a Thousand Stars; Peron's Latest Flame; Rainbow High; Rainbow Tour; Requiem for Evita; Santa Evita; She Is a Diamond; Waltz for Eva and Che

Cast: Bob Gunton; Patti LuPone; Jane Ohringer; Mandy Patinkin; Mark Syers

Notes: A Bio-Musical of Eva Peron. [1] Cut prior to opening. [2] Same music.

1212 • EXCEEDING THE SPEED LIMIT
OPENED: 12/23/1912   Theatre: Cohan's Grand
                                    Opera House
Musical   Chicago

Composer: Arthur H. Gutman
Lyricist: Carter De Haven; Arthur Gillespie
Librettist: Antony Mars

Songs: Darling; Hang Together; Home to You; I Want a Little Lovin'; I'd Like to Marry them All; It's a Secret; My Turkish Opal (C: Edna Williams); Opening Chorus Act II; Story Medley; That Champagne Glide; When Love Calls You

Cast: Carter De Haven; Elizabeth Murray; Flora Parker

Notes: May be based on a French musical with music by Antony Mars.

1213 • EXCELSIOR, JR.
OPENED: 11/25/1895   Theatre: Hammerstein's
                                    Olympia
Musical   Broadway: 144

Composer: George Lowell Tracy
Librettist: R.A. Barnet

Set Design: Henry E. Hoyt; Frank Rafter

Songs: Alpine Horn, The (C: A. Baldwin Sloane; George Lowell Tracy); Ballet Music (C: A. Baldwin Sloane); Continuous Show (C: Unknown); Excelsior; Friar's Life, A; Gavotte and Solo Dance (C: A. Baldwin Sloane); Grandpa's Hat (C: A. Baldwin Sloane); Gussie Giles (C: Courier Gyde; George Lowell Tracy); Hush, Silence (C: A. Baldwin Sloane); I Love You, Evaline; I'm a Very Fly Conductor (C: A. Baldwin Sloane); I'm Excelsior; Long Ago; Men, Men, You Are Foolish Men; Morning Breaking; My Little Sunday Girl (C: A. Baldwin Sloane); My Love Is Fair (C: Edward E. Rice); Paraphrase on Upidee; Solo Dance (C: A. Baldwin Sloane); Take Him to Evaline (C: A. Baldwin Sloane; George Lowell Tracy); 20th Century Girl, The; Waltz Serenade (C: Unknown); What Do You Think She'll Do (C: Edward E. Rice); When a Youth and a Maid Pine and Love (C: A. Baldwin Sloane); Yodel Song (C: Unknown)

Cast: Charles A. Bigelow; Marie Cahill; Richard Carle; Arthur Dunn; Harry Earle; Matthew Ott; Clara Palmer; Charles A. Pusey; Fay Templeton; Theresa Vaughn

1214 • EXCEPTION AND THE RULE, THE
OPENED: 1968
Musical   Unproduced

Composer: Leonard Bernstein
Lyricist: Stephen Sondheim
Librettist: John Guare
Producer: Stuart Ostrow
Director: Jerome Robbins

Source: EXCEPTION AND THE RULE, THE (Play: Bertolt Brecht)

Songs: Coolie's Dilemma, The [2] (L: Jerry Leiber); Coolie's Prayer; Folk Dance; Give Me the Open Air; Greek Dance; Han; In There [2]; Merchant's March (1); Merchant's March (2); Prologue March [1]; Race Through the Desert (I Have Got to Get There in Seven Days Flat); Suspicion Song; Take Break Blues; They Got This Little Secret; Trial, The; Urga

Notes: Once was to be titled THE RACE TO URGA and A PRAY BY BLECHT. [1] Music used in MASS. [2] Also in BY BERNSTEIN.

1215 • EXCESS BAGGAGE
OPENED: 12/26/1927   Theatre: Ritz
Play   Broadway: 216

Author: John McGowan
Producer: Crimmens and Bryant Barbour
Director: Melville Burke

Choreographer: John Boyle; **Musical Director:** Morris Zentner; **Set Design:** P. Dodd Ackerman

Songs: All My Life (C: Philip Charig); Best Things in Life Are Free, The (C: Ray Henderson; L: Lew Brown; B.G. DeSylva); Everybody Loves My Girl (C: Lewis); For Old Times' Sake (C: Ray Henderson; L: Lew Brown; B.G. DeSylva); Hours I Spent with You, The (C: Joseph Young); Maybe I'll Baby You (C: Dave Stamper); Rickety- Rackety- Shack (C: Harry Tobias); That Funny Fellow; Those Two Girls and That Boy

Cast: Morton Downey; Eric Dressler; Doris Eaton; Miriam Hopkins; Frank McHugh

Notes: Some interpolations added to the score.

1216 • EXCHANGE
OPENED: 02/08/1970   Theatre: Mercer-O'Casey
Musical   Off-Broadway: 1

Composer: Mike Brandt; Michael Knight; Robert J. Lowery
Lyricist: Mike Brandt; Michael Knight; Robert J. Lowery
Librettist: Eric Levy
Producer: Parallel Productions; Stephanie Sills
Director: Sondra Lee

Costumes: Stanley Simmons; **Lighting Designer:** William Mintzer; **Musical Director:** Tom Janusz; **Orchestrations:** Tom Janusz; **Set Design:** Peter Harvey

Songs: All Over My Mind; Anthem; Balnesmoor Lane [1] (C/L: Susan Kay); Carrion Train; Come on Train; Coonskin Cap; Dancing Through Life-time; Flower Song, The; Flying Somehow; I Can Make It; If I Had the Answers; If You Listen to My Song; King; L.A. Incident; Madrigal, A; Maybe Tomorrow; Mumble Nothing; Never Ever Land; Pied Piper; Puddles; Santa Barbara; Understand It; Why Don't You Believe Me?; Wish [1]; Wondering; World [1]

Cast: Penelope Bodry; Igors Gavon; Megan Kay

Notes: Originally titled TAMALPAIS EXCHANGE. [1] Cut prior to opening.

1217 • EXHIBIT II
OPENED: 03/10/1901   Theatre: Weber and Fields Music Hall
Musical   Broadway

Composer: John Stromberg
Lyricist: Edgar Smith
Librettist: Edgar Smith
Producer: Lew Fields; Joseph Weber

Cast: Lew Fields; Joseph Weber

Notes: A one-act musical.

1218 • EXPERIENCE
OPENED: 10/27/1914   Theatre: Booth
Play   Broadway: 255

1221 • EXPRESSING WILLIE

Composer: Silvio Hein
Author: George V. Hobart
Producer: William Elliot
Director: George V. Hobart; J.C. Huffman

Costumes: Melville Ellis; Incidental Music: Walter Woolf; **Musical Director:** Carlo Edwards; **Set Design:** Theodore Reisig

Songs: Experience Fox-Trot, The; Experience One-Step, The; Modern Song, The

Cast: William Elliot; Madeline Howard; Ben Johnson; May McManus; Dorothy Parker

Notes: Songs and cabaret music: Silvio Hein.

1219 • EXPERIENCE UNNECESSARY

OPENED: 12/30/1931   Theatre: Longacre
Play   Broadway: 70

Author: Gladys Unger
Director: H.C. Potter

Source: UNKNOWN (Play: Wilhelm Sterck); **Costumes:** Alison McLellan Hunter; Ernest Schrapps; **Set Design:** Watson Barratt

Songs: We Were Waltzing (C/L: Herman Hupfeld)

Cast: Rex O'Malley; Verree Teasdale; Walter Woolf

1220 • EXPLORERS, THE

OPENED: 1902
Musical   Closed out of town

Composer: Walter H. Lewis
Lyricist: Bert Leston Taylor
Librettist: Bert Leston Taylor

Songs: Cupid Might Have Been a Little Coon; Finale Act II; French Marine Ashore, A; Funny Bone of a Mastodon, The; German Mannerchoer, The; Happy Hotel Cleaners; Hush! Little Lion; Is There a Maid?; It Simply Happened So; Knight of the Chafing Dish, A; Lion Tamers, The; Love's Highway; Mayonnaise Marines, The; Merry Kindergarteners, The; My Lady Champagne; Northward Ho!; Out on the Sea; Pretty Girl in Gray; Son of the Hill and Plain, The; Things I Didn't See, The; Tropic Night Is Past, The

Cast: Richard Carle; John Hynes; Josie Intropodi; Carlton King; Agnes Paul; Ruth White; Knox Wilson

Notes: Sheet music only.

1221 • EXPRESSING WILLIE

OPENED: 10/16/1924   Theatre: 48th Street
Play   Broadway: 293

Author: Rachael Crothers
Producer: Equity Players
Director: Rachael Crothers

Musical Director: Oscar Lifshey

Songs: Express Yo-self (C: John Egan; L: Rachael Crothers)

Cast: Louise Closser Hale; Merle Maddern; Molly McIntyre; Richard Sterling; Warren William

F

1222 • F. JASMINE ADDAMS
OPENED: 10/27/1971   Theatre: Circle in the Square

Musical   Off-Broadway: 6

Composer: G. Wood
Lyricist: G. Wood
Librettist: Carson McCullers; G. Wood
Producer: Circle in the Square
Director: Theodore Mann

Source: MEMBER OF THE WEDDING, THE (Novel: Carson McCullers); **Choreographer:** Patricia Birch; **Costumes:** Joseph G. Aulisi; **Dance Arranger:** Luther Henderson; **Lighting Designer:** Roger Morgan; **Musical Director:** Liza Redfield; **Orchestrations:** Luther Henderson; **Set Design:** Marsha Louis Eck; **Vocal Arranger:** Luther Henderson

Songs: Another Day; Baby, That's Love; Did I Make a Good Impression?; Do Me a Favor; F. Jasmine Addams; Good As Anybody; Grey Eyes [1]; How About You and Me; How Sweet Is Peach Ice Cream; If I Had a ...; Miss Pinhead; Quite Suddenly; Sunshine Tomorrow; Travelin' On; We of Me, The

Cast: Bill Bishop; Johnny Doran; William LeMassena; Theresa Merritt; Erika Peterson; Neva Small

Notes: [1] Cut before opening.

1223 • FABLES OF 1924
Musical

Producer: George Choos

Songs: Alabam' Banjo Man (C/L: Art Conrad; Frank Gillen)

Notes: No other information available.

1224 • FACE THAT WINS, THE
OPENED: 1910

Musical   Closed out of town

Composer: Unknown
Lyricist: Unknown

Songs: Athletic; Billiken Man; How We Miss You Georgie Cohan; Loving Eyes; Marathon, The; Octette; Paree; Pony Ballet; That's the Reason; Yakiana Rag

Cast: Alice Maizee; Frank Pierce; Edna Roberts

Notes: Billed as "Fred Irwin's Big Show." What Fred Irwin did is unknown. Note that several song titles seem to be popular songs of the day.

1225 • FACE THE MUSIC
OPENED: 02/17/1932   Theatre: New Amsterdam
Musical   Broadway: 166

Composer: Irving Berlin
Lyricist: Irving Berlin
Librettist: Irving Berlin; Moss Hart
Producer: Sam H. Harris
Director: George S. Kaufman; Hassard Short

Choreographer: Albertina Rasch; **Costumes:** Kiviette; Weld; **Lighting Designer:** Hassard Short; **Musical Director:** Frank Tours; **Orchestrations:** Robert Russell Bennett; Maurice DePackh; Frank Tours; **Set Design:** Albert Johnson

Songs: City Hall; Dear Old Crinoline Days; Drinking Song; I Don't Want to Be Married (I Just Wanna Be Friends); I Say It's Spinach (— and the Hell with It); Let's Have Another Cup of Coffee; Lunching at the Automat; Manhattan Madness; My Beautiful Rhinestone Girl; On a Roof in Manhattan; Soft Lights and Sweet Music; Torch Song; You Must Be Born with It

Cast: Mary Boland; David Burns; Katherine Carrington; Clyde Fillmore; Edward Gargan; Jack Good; Margaret Lee; Joseph Macaulay; J. Harold Murray; Hugh O'Connell; Oscar Polk; Jean Sargent; Andrew Tombes

1226 • FAD AND FOLLY

OPENED: 11/27/1902   Theatre: Mrs. Osborn's
Playhouse
Musical   Broadway: 34

Composer: Henry Waller
Lyricist: Paul West
Librettist: Rupert Hughes; Safford Waters

Songs: Belle of Avenue A, The (C/L: Safford
Waters); Lovers' Roost (C/L: George "Honey
Boy" Evans); Microbes; There's a Strange
Fascination About the Stage; Try, Try Again

Cast: Kathleen Clifford; Harry Conor; Richard
Lambert; Blanche Ring

Notes: No program available. This was a revised
version of TOMMY ROT. Songs also by
F. Chandler, Henry Blossom Jr., Jackson
Gowraud, John W. Barton and W.F. Peters. One
act of this show was titled CRYRIS, a parody of
IRIS (a popular play that opened at the Criterion
Theater on 9/23/02. CRYRIS had a book by
Joseph W. Herbert and music by Henry Waller.

1227 • FADE OUT-FADE IN

OPENED: 05/26/1964   Theatre: Mark Hellinger
Musical   Broadway: 271

Composer: Jule Styne
Lyricist: Betty Comden; Adolph Green
Librettist: Betty Comden; Adolph Green
Producer: Lester Osterman; Jule Styne
Director: George Abbott

Choreographer: Ernest Flatt; **Costumes:** Donald
Brooks; **Dance Arranger:** Richard de Benedictis;
Lighting Designer: Jean Eckart; William Eckart;
Musical Director: Colin Romoff; **Orchestrations:**
Ralph Burns; Ray Ellis; Robert Prince; **Set
Design:** Jean Eckart; William Eckart; **Vocal
Arranger:** Buster Davis

Songs: Call Me Savage [2]; Close Harmony;
Dangerous Age, The; Everybody Loves a
Winner [6]; F.F. (Forbidden Fruit) [4]; Fade Out-
Fade In; Fear; Fiddler and the Fighter, The; Girl to
Remember, A [5]; Go Home Train [3]; I'm with
You; It's Good to Be Back Home; It's Great [6]; L.Z.
in Quest of His Youth (ballet); Lila Tremaine [3];
Menu Song [6]; My Fortune Is My Face; My
Heart Is Like a Violin; Notice Me [1]; Oh Those
Thirties [3]; Take the Time to Fall in Love [6]; Tea

Time in Timbuctoo [6]; They're at the Post [6];
Usher from the Mezzanine, The; What Is This
Thing I've Got [6]; You Mustn't Be Discouraged

Cast: Carol Burnett; Jack Cassidy; Don Crichton;
Tiger Haynes; Lou Jacobi; Mitchell Jason; Tina
Louise; Dick Patterson; Virginia Payne; Aileen
Poe; Reuben Singer

Notes: [1] Added after show reopened on
Broadway. [2] Same music as "Witches Brew" in
HALLELUJAH, BABY! [3] Dropped after show
reopened on 2/15/65. [4] Cut. Used in TV
musical GETTING MARRIED. [5] Added after
show reopened on Broadway. Same music as
"Hey, What's Your Name" in film THE KID
FROM BROOKLYN. [6] Not used.

1228 • FADS AND FANCIES

OPENED: 03/08/1915   Theatre: Knickerbocker
Musical   Broadway: 48

Composer: Raymond Hubbell
Lyricist: Glen MacDonough
Librettist: Glen MacDonough
Producer: Klaw & Erlanger
Director: Herbert Gresham

Choreographer: Julian Mitchell; **Musical Director:**
Raymond Hubbell

Songs: Alimony Alley; Automobilla; I'm Lonely
for Only One; I'm Still Your Single; In Search of
a Thrill [1]; It's Heaven to Boheme; Love on the
American Plan; Mary Ann O'San; Music with
Meals; Never Again; Take It from Me; They Do
You Much Better at Home; Three Little Words;
We'll Take Care of You All (Refugee Song) [2]
(C: Jerome Kern; L: Harry B. Smith); Yuca
Tango, The

Cast: Leo Carrillo; Laura Hamilton; Madge
Lessing; Tom MacNaughton; Frank Moulan

Notes: No program available. One review stated
there were 20 songs. [1] Sheet music titled "I'm
Seeking a Thrill." [2] Cut from THE GIRL FROM
UTAH.

1229 • FAGGOT, THE

OPENED: 06/18/1973   Theatre: Judson Memorial
Church
Musical   Off-Broadway: 182

Composer: Al Carmines
Lyricist: Al Carmines
Librettist: Al Carmines
Producer: Richard Lipton; Bruce Mailman
Director: Al Carmines

Choreographer: David Vaughn; **Costumes:** T.E.
Mason; **Lighting Designer:** Gary Weathersbee;
Musical Director: John R. Williams; **Set Design:**
T.E. Mason

Songs: Art Song; Desperation; Five-Minute
Opera, The; Gay Bar Cantata, The; Hari
Krishna; Hustler, The; I'll Take My Fantasy;
Nookie Time; Ordinary Things; What Is a
Queen; Women with Women- Men with Men;
Your Way of Loving

Cast: Peggy Atkinson; Essie Borden; Al Carmines;
Marilyn Child; Tony Clark; Lee Guilliatt;
Julie Kurnitz; Philip Owens; David Pursley;
Ira Siff

1230 • FAIR CO-ED, THE

OPENED: 02/01/1909   Theatre: Knickerbocker
Musical   Broadway: 136

Composer: Gustav Luders
Lyricist: George Ade
Librettist: George Ade
Producer: Charles Dillingham
Director: Fred G. Latham

Choreographer: William Rock; **Costumes:**
F. DeWalbe; **Musical Director:** Robert Hood
Bowers; **Set Design:** Homer Emens

Songs: Almost; Barn Dance Schottische; College
Medley [1]; Dans des Hottentots; Day of the
Game, The; Finale Act III; Finale I; Girl I Knew,
The; Here in the Starlight; I'll Dream of That
Sweet Co-ed; Isle of the Philippines, An; Leave It
to the Boys in the Navy; Little Girl That's Wise,
A; Opening Chorus; Opening Chorus Act II;
Opening Chorus Act III; Please Don't Keep Me
Waiting; Real American Girl, The; Sing Hey for
the Chaperon; Valse (Billet Doux)

Cast: Harry Depp; Edgar Halstead; Elsie Janis;
James Reaney

Notes: Songs not listed in program. [1] Arranged
by Robert Hood Bowers.

1231 • FAIR ENOUGH

OPENED: 1939
Musical   Harvard University

Composer: Elliot Forbes; Francis Lawrence; Alan
Jay Lerner; Sherwood Rollins
Lyricist: Alan Jay Lerner
Librettist: Alan Jay Lerner; J. David Preston;
Morgan Preston
Producer: Hasty Pudding Club
Director: Edward Clarke Lilley

Choreographer: William Holbrook; **Conductor:**
Leroy Anderson; **Musical Director:** Richard
Lewine

Songs: Blame It on Chichita; From Me to You
(C/L: Alan Jay Lerner); Home Again; Home
Made Heaven (C/L: Alan Jay Lerner); I Dream
of You; I Just Gotta Make Love (C/L: Sherwood
Rollins); Lottery Blues

Notes: Amateur show.

1232 • FALLEN ANGEL

OPENED: 04/14/1994   Theatre: Circle in the
                                          Square Downtown
Musical   Off-Broadway: 32

Composer: Billy Boesky
Lyricist: Billy Boesky
Librettist: Billy Boesky
Producer: Roger Hess; Peter Holmes a Court
Director: Rob Greenberg

Costumes: Wendy A. Rolfe; **Lighting Designer:**
Christopher Akerlind; **Musical Director:** Steve
Postell; **Set Design:** David Birn

Songs: All Right; Coming and Going (C: Billy
Boesky; Steve Postell); Fallen Angel (C: Billy
Boesky; Steve Postell); Falling in Love; Hey
Lady (C: Billy Boesky; Michael McCoy); More
Than You Know (C/L: Billy Boesky; Deanna
Kirk; C: Kevin Bents); Silo (C/L: Billy Boesky;
Josh Klaussner); Southbound Train (C: Billy
Boesky; Steve Postell); Till I'm Gone (C: Billy
Boesky; Steve Postell); Unveil My Eyes

Cast: George Coe; Shannon Conley; Susan Gibney;
Corey Glover; Jonathan Goldstein

1233 • FALLOUT
OPENED: 05/20/1959   Theatre: Renata
Revue   Off-Broadway: 31

Composer: Robert Kessler
Lyricist: Martin Charnin
Librettist: Martin Charnin; Jerry Goldman; Abe Goldsmith; David Panich
Producer: Harvey Stuart; David Taynton
Director: Harvey Stuart

Choreographer: Buddy Schwab; **Costumes:** Fred Voelpel; **Dance Arranger:** Saul Schechtman; **Lighting Designer:** Fred Voelpel; **Musical Director:** Saul Schechtman; **Set Design:** Fred Voelpel; **Vocal Arranger:** Saul Schechtman

Songs: Bwee Dah [1] (C: David Hollister); Clandestine [2]; Dramatized Message, A (C/L: Paul Nassau); End, The; I Think I'd Like to Fall in Love (C: Martin Charnin); Individuals (C: Gerald Alters; L: Herb Hartig); Look; Love Is (C: Martin Charnin); Oh Say, Can You See?; Oriental [2]; Problem (C: Alan Friedman; L: Dennis Marks); Sixteenth Summer; Someone Waiting; String Quartet (C/L: Paul Nassau); Too Many Questions (C/L: Paul Nassau); Victoria Trio, The (C/L: Paul Nassau); We're Betting on You; You're My Man

Cast: Grover Dale; Paul Dooley; Charles Nelson Reilly; Joy Lynne Sica; Virginia Vestoff

Notes: [1] Based on a theme by Robert Kessler. [2] Later in PIECES OF EIGHT.

1234 • FALSETTOLAND
OPENED: 05/06/1990   Theatre: Playwright's Horizons
Musical   Off-Broadway: 215

Composer: William Finn
Lyricist: William Finn
Librettist: William Finn; James Lapine
Producer: Playwrights Horizons
Director: James Lapine

Arrangements: Michael Starobin; **Costumes:** Franne Lee; **Lighting Designer:** Nancy Schertler; **Musical Director:** Michael Starobin; **Set Design:** Douglas Stein

Songs: About Time; Another Miracle of Judaism; Baseball Game, The; Canceling the Bar Mitzvah; Day in Falsettoland, A; Days Like This; Everyone Hates His Parents; Falsettoland; Holding to the Ground; Jason's Bar Mitzvah; Miracle of Judaism; More Racquetball; Planning the Bar Mitzvah; Something Bad Is Happening; Unlikely Lovers; What More Can I Say?; What Would I Do?; Year of the Child; You Gotta Die Sometime

Cast: Stephen Bogardus; Danny Gerard; Heather MacRae; Janet Metz; Faith Prince; Michael Rupert; Chip Zien

Notes: Played 54 performances at Playwrights Horizons then moved to the Lortel for an additional 161 performances. The third musical in the "Marvin Trilogy." The first two shows were IN TROUSERS and MARCH OF THE FALSETTOS.

1235 • FALSTAFF
OPENED: 12/25/1928   Theatre: Coburn
Play   Broadway: 15

Composer: Porter Steele
Lyricist: Brian Hooker
Author: James Plaisted Webber
Producer: Charles Coburn
Director: Richard Boleslavsky; Henry Stillman

Choreographer: Richard Boleslavsky; Ted Shawn; **Costumes:** Millie Davenport; **Set Design:** Louis Kennel

Songs: Beside Your Window; Heart's Desire; Love Is a Torment; Memory, A; St. George for England

Cast: Lawrence Cecil; Charles Coburn; Mrs. Charles Coburn; Marjorie Marquis; Ethel Morrison; Kathryn Reece; John Seymour; Shepperd Strudwick

Notes: Songs not listed in program.

1236 • FAME
OPENED: 03/25/1989
Musical

Composer: Steven Margoshes
Lyricist: Jacques Levy
Librettist: Jose Fernandez
Producer: Walnut Street Theatre
Director: David Saint

Choreographer: Jennifer Muller; **Costumes:** Randy Barcelo; Incidental Music: Kevin Stites; **Lighting Designer:** Joshua Starbuck; **Musical Director:** Steven Margoshes; **Orchestrations:** Steven Margoshes; Harold Wheeler; **Set Design:** Alexander Okun

Songs: Bring on Tomorrow; Can't Keep It Down; Dance Class [1]; Dancin' on the Sidewalk; Fame (C: Michael Gore; L: Dean Pitchford); Hard Work; I Gotta Find a Way; I Want to Make Magic; In L.A.; Let's Play a Love Scene; Mabel's Prayer [1]; Pas de Deux, The (inst.); Pray I Make P.A.; Teacher's Argument, The; There She Goes; These Are My Children; Think of Meryl Streep; Tyrone's Rap

Cast: Christian Canciani; Ebony Jo-Ann; Allen Hidalgo; Michael O'Steen; Harold Perrineau Jr.; David Rogers

Notes: Walnut Street Theatre, Philadelphia program used. [1] In London production 6/27/95, Cambridge Theatre.

1237 • FAMILY AFFAIR, A
OPENED: 01/27/1962   Theatre: Billy Rose
Musical   Broadway: 65

Composer: John Kander
Lyricist: James Goldman; William Goldman
Librettist: James Goldman; William Goldman
Producer: Andrew Siff
Director: Harold Prince

Choreographer: John Butler; Bob Herget; **Costumes:** Robert Fletcher; **Dance Arranger:** Gerald Alters; **Lighting Designer:** David Hays; **Musical Director:** Stanley Lebowsky; **Orchestrations:** Robert Ginzler; **Set Design:** David Hays

Songs: Anything for You; Beautiful; Every Girl Wants to Get Married; Family Affair, A; Harmony; I'm Worse than Anybody; Kalua Bay; Mamie in the Afternoon [2]; Milwaukee [1]; My Son, the Lawyer; Now, Morris; Revenge; Right Girls; Siegal-Nathan's Marching Songs; Summer Is Over; There's a Room in My House; Wedding, The; What I Say Goes; Wonderful Party

Cast: Lulu Bates; Shelley Berman; Morris Carnovsky; Don Crabtree; Cathryn Damon; Jack De Lon; Rita Gardner; Eileen Heckart; Larry Kert; Linda Lavin; Bibi Osterwald; Paula Trueman

Notes: [1] Cut prior to opening. [2] Cut prior to opening. Rewritten as "Arthur in the Afternoon" in THE ACT.

1238 • FAMILY ALBUM
OPENED: 11/24/1936   Theatre: National
Play   Broadway: 113

Composer: Noel Coward
Lyricist: Noel Coward
Author: Noel Coward
Producer: John C. Wilson
Director: Noel Coward

Musical Director: John McManus; **Set Design:** G.E. Calthrop

Songs: Hearts and Flowers; Here's a Toast; Let's Play a Tune on the Music Box; Princes and Princesses

Cast: Joyce Carey; Noel Coward; Gertrude Lawrence; Moya Nugent; Edward Underdown; Alan Webb

Notes: Part of TONIGHT AT 8:30.

1239 • FANCHON AND MARCO SATIRES OF 1920, THE
Notes: *See SATIRES OF 1920.*

1240 • FANCY FREE
OPENED: 04/11/1918   Theatre: Astor
Musical   Broadway: 116

Composer: Augustus Barratt
Lyricist: Augustus Barratt
Librettist: Dorothy Donnelly; Edgar Smith
Producer: J.J. Shubert; Lee Shubert
Director: J.C. Huffman

Choreographer: Jack Mason

Songs: Cocktail of Flowers, A (C/L: Clifton Crawford); Girls Would Have Me Blushing, The [2]; Give Me the Moonlight [3]; Helen Manicure Girl, The; If You're Crazy About the Women [1]; Love Comes a Stealing; Make Up; Modern Girls; My Bibliophile; Pretty Baby Doll from Paree; Rat-Tat-A-Tat; Road to Anywhere, The [1]; Sister Sue; Someone Has Your Number; Sweet Seventeen [1]; Tinkle-Inkle-Inkle; Tiny

Flat, A; What Am I Going to Do [1]; When I Came to America [1]; When the Moon Shines Down

Cast: Harry Conor; Clifton Crawford; Marilyn Miller; Ed Wynn

Notes: [1] Out Stamford, Connecticut 4/8/18. [2] Sheet music only. [3] Out Stamford, Connecticut 4/8/18. The popular song "Give Me the Moonlight, Give Me the Girl" by Albert Von Tilzer and Lew Brown was written in 1917.

1241 • FANCY THAT
Musical

Director: Frank T. Davis

Songs: After You Say I Love You (C: Larry Conley; L: Billy Curtis)

Cast: Maurice Holland; Katherine Skidmore

Notes: No other information available.

1242 • FANNY
OPENED: 11/04/1954   Theatre: Majestic
Musical   Broadway: 888

Composer: Harold Rome
Lyricist: Harold Rome
Librettist: S.N. Behrman; Joshua Logan
Producer: Joshua Logan; David Merrick
Director: Joshua Logan

Source: CESAR (Play: Marcel Pagnol); **Source:** FANNY (Play: Marcel Pagnol); **Source:** MARIUS (Play: Marcel Pagnol); **Choreographer:** Helen Tamiris; **Costumes:** Alvin Colt; **Dance Arranger:** Trude Rittman; **Lighting Designer:** Jo Mielziner; **Musical Director:** Lehman Engel; **Orchestrations:** Philip J. Lang; **Set Design:** Jo Mielziner

Songs: Be Kind to Your Parents; Birthday Song; Cold Cream Jar Song; Does He Know [2]; Every Night [1]; Fanny; I Have to Tell You; I Like You; Let's Talk About a Woman [3]; Love Is a Very Light Thing; Never Too Late for Love; Octopus Song; Other Hands, Other Hearts; Oysters, Cockles and Mussels (Fish Market); Panisse and Son; Restless Heart; Shika Shika; Thought of You, The; To My Wife; Wedding Dance; Welcome Home; Why Be Afraid to Dance?

Cast: Nejla Ates; Alan Carney; Florence Henderson; Ezio Pinza; Gerald Price; Dran Seitz; Tani Seitz; Walter Slezak; William Tabbert

Notes: [1] Added 1957 for L.A. Civic Light Opera production. [2] Added after opening. [3] Cut. Later also cut from DESTRY RIDES AGAIN.

1243 • FANTANA
OPENED: 01/14/1905   Theatre: Lyric
Musical   Broadway: 298

Composer: Raymond Hubbell
Lyricist: Robert B. Smith
Librettist: Sam S. Shubert; Robert B. Smith
Producer: Sam S. Shubert
Director: R.H. Burnside

Set Design: D. Frank Dodge; Frank E. Gates; E.A. Morange; John Young

Songs: Because I Am Not Understood [1]; Can-Can vs. Cake-Walk; Darby and Joan; Drop In on Me at Luncheon; Drop In on Me, At Luncheon; Entrance of Fantana; Fantana Song [1]; Farewell Waltz, The; Finale Act II; Girl at the Helm, The; Hail Celestial Potentate; His Little Sister; Hold the Lanterns High; In My Riksha of Bamboo; It Is the Girl and Not the Horse That Wins the Prize; It's the Girl and Not the Horse That Wins the Prize; Japanese Citizens We; Just My Style; La Danse Parisienne et La Americaine [2]; Lantern Fete; Laughing Little Almond Eyes; Lesson in Etiquette, A; My Word; North, South, East or West; Oh! Silvery Moon [1]; Opening Chorus; Secret, The (Gossip Song); She Can Do Little Who Can't Do This; Song of the Pipe; Tammany (C: Gus Edwards; L: Vincent Bryan); That's Art; To Japan; Truculent Governor, I, A; Waltz Duet, The; What Would Mrs. Grundy Say

Cast: George Beban; Jefferson De Angelis; Douglas Fairbanks Jr.; Adele Ritchie; Julia Sanderson

Notes: [1] Sheet music only. [2] Called "The Can-Can Versus the Cake Walk" in sheet music.

1244 • FANTASTIC FRICASSEE, A
OPENED: 09/11/1922   Theatre: Greenwich Village
Revue   Off-Broadway: 111

Librettist: Maxwell Bodenheim; Ben Hecht; Leona Kahl
Producer: Marguerite Abbott Barker
Director: Edwin Strawbridge

Choreographer: Edwin Strawbridge; **Costumes:** Gilberg Rose; Pauline Wells; **Musical Director:** Roy Shields; **Set Design:** Andre Chotin; John Decker; Dorothy Hunt

Songs: Montmarte Fair and the Magic Dolls, The (C: W. Franke Harling); Prologue (C: A. Baldwin Sloane; L: Allen Abbott); Tahiti (C/L: Bobby Edwards); Virgins of the Sun (C: Julius Mattfeld); Waiting for You (C: W. Franke Harling)

Cast: Remo Bufano; Jeanette MacDonald; Marta Nova

Notes: Note Jeanette MacDonald's inclusion in the cast of this early off-Broadway show.

1245 • FANTASTICKS, THE

OPENED: 05/03/1960   Theatre: Sullivan St. Playhouse

Musical   Off-Broadway

Composer: Harvey Schmidt
Lyricist: Tom Jones
Librettist: Tom Jones
Producer: Lore Noto
Director: Word Baker

Source: LES ROMANESQUES (Play: Edmond Rostand); **Costumes:** Ed Wittstein; **Musical Director:** Julian Stein; **Orchestrations:** Julian Stein; **Set Design:** Ed Wittstein

Songs: Abduction Ballet [2]; Abductions, (and so forth) [4]; Follow Along with Me [1]; Happy Ending; Have You Ever Been to China? [1]; I Can See It; I Have Acted Like a Fool [1]; It Depends on What You Pay; Metaphor; Much More; Never Say No; Plant a Radish; Rape Ballet [3]; Round and Round; Soon It's Gonna Rain; There Is a Curious Paradox; They Were You; This Is the Perfect Time to Be in Love; This Plum Is Too Ripe; Try to Remember

Cast: George Curley; Rita Gardner; Tom Jones [5]; William Larsen; Kenneth Nelson; Jerry Orbach; Hugh Thomas

Notes: Still running as of press time. [1] Cut prior to New York. [2] New title of "Rape Ballet." Title changed in New York production. [3] Same music as "Abductions, (and so forth)." This ballet music was later titled "Abduction Ballet." [4] Written for 1990 national tour with Robert Goulet. Music based on "The Rape Ballet." [5] Used pseudonym Thomas Bruce.

1246 • FASCINATING FLORA

OPENED: 05/20/1907   Theatre: Casino
Musical   Broadway: 113

Composer: Gustave Kerker
Lyricist: R.H. Burnside
Librettist: R.H. Burnside; Joseph W. Herbert
Producer: R.H. Burnside; F. Ray Comstock
Director: F. Ray Comstock

Songs: Ballooning (C: Jerome Kern; L: Paul West); Bulls and Bears; Captain Willie Brown; Entrance of American Girls; Entrance of Fascinating Flora (L: Smith); I'd Rather Two-Step; I'm a Marvelous Musician; In Paris; It's Going to Be a Pretty Wedding; Katy Was a Business Girl [2] (C: Jerome Kern; L: Paul West); Little Church Around the Corner, The [2] (C: Jerome Kern; L: M.E. Rourke); Nice Little Girls and Boys; Off to New York; Old Yankee Land for Me (C: Harry O. Sutton; L: Jean Lenox); Oshkosh (C/L: Keith; John Kemble); Right Now [1] (C: Fred Fisher; L: Jerome Kern); Romance and Reality (C: A. Baldwin Sloane; L: Louis Harrison); Splash Me; Subway Express, The (C: Jerome Kern; L: James O'Dea); What Will Happen Then?; Zuyder Zee (C: Kerry Mills; L: Scott)

Cast: Fred Bond; Louis Harrison; Ada Lewis; Adele Ritchie

Notes: [1] Sheet music only. [2] Dropped before New York.

1247 • FASCINATING WIDOW, THE (1911)

OPENED: 09/11/1911   Theatre: Liberty
Musical   Broadway: 56

Composer: F.A. Mills; Jean Schwartz
Lyricist: Otto Harbach
Librettist: Otto Harbach
Producer: A.H. Woods
Director: George Marion

Choreographer: Jack Mason

Songs: Clinging Vine [1] (C: Karl Hoschna); Danny Cupid at the Bat [1] (C: Karl Hoschna); Don't Go in the Water Daughter [1] (C: Jean Schwartz; L: William Jerome); Don't Take Your Beau to the Seashore (C: Irving Berlin; L: E. Ray Goetz); Don't You Make a Noise (C: Kerry Mills; L: Sam M. Lewis); Everybody Likes a College Girl [4] (C: Kerry Mills; L: Sam M. Lewis); Fascinating Widow, The (C: Karl Hoschna); Girlies You've Kissed in Dreams, The [1] (C: Karl Hoschna); I Don't Think I Love You, I Know I Do [1] (C: Egbert Van Alstyne; L: Harry Williams); If Only Someone Would Teach Me [1] (C: Karl Hoschna); If You'll Only Lead the Way [1] (C: Karl Hoschna); I'm to Be a Blushing Bride (C: Kerry Mills; L: Sam M. Lewis); Lots of Little Things Can Happen [1] (C: Karl Hoschna); Merry Wedding Bells [1] (C: Jean Schwartz; L: Edward Madden); Nighty Girl [1] (C: Karl Hoschna); Put Your Arms Around Me Honey [5] (C: Kerry Mills; L: Sam M. Lewis); Ragtime College Girl, The (C: Kerry Mills; L: Sam M. Lewis); Something That I Can't Explain [1] (C: Jean Schwartz; L: William Jerome); To Take a Dip in the Ocean [4] (C: Kerry Mills; L: Sam M. Lewis); Valse Julian; With Downcast Eye (Wedding Song) [1] (C: Karl Hoschna); You've Built a Fire Down in My Heart [3] (C/L: Irving Berlin; Alfred Bryan)

Cast: Natalie Ault; Julian Eltinge; Eddie Garvie; Winona Winter

Notes: [1] Sheet music only. [2] Also in ZIEGFELD FOLLIES OF 1911 and THE NEVER HOMES. [3] ASCAP credits E. Ray Goetz along with Berlin. The sheet music only credits Berlin. [4] ASCAP/Library of Congress only. [5] The famous song of the same name was written a year earlier by Albert Von Tilzer and Junie McCree.

1248 • FASCINATING WIDOW, THE (1917)

OPENED: 1917
Musical   Closed out of town

Composer: Percy Wenrich
Lyricist: Otto Harbach
Librettist: Otto Harbach
Producer: Daresford Prod. Company
Director: J.W. Ashley

Musical Director: Clarence Love

Songs: College Trot, The; Don't Go in the Water; I Love You Sweetheart; Joan of Arc; Merry Wedding Bells; Nightie Parade; Spanish; Widow Fascinating, The

Cast: Eddie Garvie; Julia Gifford; Thomas Martelle; Mabelle Pierre

Notes: *See also Harbach's other THE FASCINATING WIDOW, a different show.*

1249 • FASHION

OPENED: 02/18/1974
Musical   Off-Broadway: 94

Composer: Donald Pippin
Lyricist: Steve Brown
Librettist: Anthony Stimac
Producer: R. Scott Lucas
Director: Anthony Stimac

Source: FASHION (Play: Anna Cora Mowatt); **Costumes:** Bieff-Herrera; **Dance Arranger:** Donald Pippin; **Lighting Designer:** Spencer Mosse; **Musical Director:** Susan Romann; **Set Design:** Robert U. Taylor; **Vocal Arranger:** Donald Pippin

Songs: Good Old American Way, The; I Must Devise a Plan; It Was for Fashion's Sake (1) [2]; It Was for Fashion's Sake (2) [3]; Life without Her, A [4]; Meet Me Tonight; My Daughter the Countess; My Title Song; Penitentiary Blues [1]; Rococo Rag; Take Me; What Kind of Man Is He?; Why Should They Know About Paris?; You See Before You What Fashions Can Do [2]; You're Out of Fashion [3]

Cast: Sydney Blake; Rhoda Butler; Jan Buttram; Mary Jo Catlett; Joanne Gibson; Ty McConnell; Susan Romann; Holland Taylor; Sandra Thornton; Henrietta Valor

Notes: [1] Cut prior to opening. [2] Cut after opening. [3] Added after opening. [4] Written but unused for THE CONTRAST as "A Life Without Him."

1250 • FASHIONS OF 1924

OPENED: 07/18/1923   Theatre: Lyceum
Revue   Broadway: 13

Composer: Ted Snyder
Lyricist: Harry B. Smith

Producer: Fashion Productions
Director: Alexander Leftwich

Choreographer: John V. Lowe; **Costumes:** Adrian; Travis Banton; Arnold Daly; Marie Nordstrom; Sophie Rosenburg; **Musical Director:** Milan Roder; **Orchestrations:** Arthur Lange; Milan Roder

Songs: Abie's Irish Rose [1] (C/L: James F. Hanley); Bride, The (C: Arthur Gutman; L: Frances Nordstrom); Bring on the Girls; Here Comes the Kid (C: Eric Nardo; L: Frances Nordstrom); In Days of Long Ago; Just a Little Bit of Love; Love Through the Ages; Miss Whoozis and Mr. Whatchaname; Oh, Joe!; One Last Waltz (One More Waltz); Passing Fancies; Stepping; Violet in Broadway's Garden, A

Cast: Ina Hayward; John V. Lowe; Carlotta Monterey; Edith Taliaferro

Notes: [1] ASCAP/Library of Congress only.

1251 • FAST AND FURIOUS

OPENED: 09/15/1931   Theatre: New Yorker
Revue   Broadway: 6

Composer: Harry Revel
Lyricist: Mack Gordon
Librettist: Forbes Randolph; John Wells
Producer: Forbes Randolph
Director: Howard Smith

Choreographer: Jack Donahue; Al Richards; **Costumes:** Blythe; Eaves; Schneider & Anderson; **Musical Director:** Joe Jordan; **Set Design:** Cirker & Robbins

Songs: Agaba-Saba Dance (inst.) [1] (C: Porter Grainger); Boomerang (C: Joe Jordan; L: J. Rosamond Johnson); Dance of the Moods (inst.) (C: Porter Grainger); Doing the Dumbbell; Fast and Furious; Frowns; Hot Feet; Hot, Hot Mama (C/L: Porter Grainger); Jacob's Ladder (C: Allie Wrubel; L: J. Rosamond Johnson); Let's Raise Hell (C/L: Porter Grainger); Modernistic (C: Porter Grainger; L: John Dallavo); Pansies on Parade (C/L: Porter Grainger); Rumbatism; Shadows on the Wall; So Lonesome (C: Joe Jordan; L: J. Rosamond Johnson); Three Dames Ziegfeld Failed to Glorify, The [1] (C: Porter Grainger; L: J. Rosamond Johnson); Walkin' on Air; Where's My Happy Ending? (L: Harold Adamson; Mack Gordon)

Cast: Lois Deppe; Ruby Elzy; Dusty Fletcher; Ruby Greene; Edna Guy; Juan Hernandez; Jackie "Moms" Mabley; Tim Moore; Etta Moten; Neeka Shaw

Notes: [1] Out Jackson Heights, N.Y. 8/?/31.

1252 • FAST COMPANY

Notes: *See IN GAY COMPANY.*

1253 • FAT PIG

OPENED: 11/20/1987
Musical

Composer: Henry Krieger
Lyricist: Henry Krieger
Librettist: Mark Bramble; Jenny Hakesworth
Director: Mark Bramble

Source: LE COCHON QUI VOULAIT MAIGRIR (Musical)

Notes: Opened at the Haymarket Theatre, Leicester.

1254 • FATAL BLONDE, THE

Notes: *See THUMBS UP!*

1255 • FAUNTLEROY

OPENED: 07/02/1981
Musical   Closed out of town

Composer: Johnny Burke
Lyricist: Johnny Burke; Mavor Moore
Librettist: Mavor Moore
Producer: Robert E. Dubberley; David L. March
Director: Alan Lund

Source: LITTLE LORD FAUNTLEROY (Novel: Francis Hodgson Burnett); **Choreographer:** Alan Lund; **Costumes:** Brian Jackson; **Dance Arranger:** John Fenwick; **Lighting Designer:** Robert Montgomery; Music Adaptation: John Fenwick; **Musical Director:** Fen Watkin; **Orchestrations:** John Fenwick; Doug Randie; **Set Design:** Brian Jackson; **Vocal Arranger:** John Fenwick

Songs: Dee-Lightful [1]; 4th of July Parade; God Bless You All the Day; He Made Me Feel I'm Lovely [1]; I Hate Little Boys; I Have My Own Way of Loving Him [1]; I Wish You Needed Me;

If the Girl Has Charm; I'm Myself; It's the Company; Refer them to Me; Worry Not a Whit Not I

Cast: Duane Woods

Notes: Only original songs listed. Johnny Burke was dead at the time of this production. [1] From score of DONNYBROOK.

1256 • FEARLESS FRANK

OPENED: 06/15/1980   Theatre: Princess
Musical   Broadway: 12

Composer: Dave Brown
Lyricist: Andrew Davies
Librettist: Andrew Davies
Producer: David Black; Robert Fabian
Director: Robert Gillespie

Source: MY LIFE AND LOVES (Book: Frank Harris); Choreographer: Michael Vernon; Costumes: Carrie F. Robbins; Lighting Designer: Ruth Roberts; Musical Director: Michael Rose; Orchestrations: Michael Reed; Set Design: Martin Tilley

Songs: Come Help Yourself to America, or Frank in the Melting Pot [1]; Dandy Night Clerk or How to Get On in the Hotel Trade; Evening News-A Song of Success; Examination Song, or Get Me on That Boat, The; Fearless Frank; Free Speech, Free Thought, Free Love; Great Men, Great Days, or the King of the Cafe Royal; Greatest Man of All, The; Halted at the Very Gates of Paradise-A Song of Frustration; Le Maitre de la Conte, or Maupassant Tells All; Man Who Made His Life into a Work of Art, The; Mr. Harris It's All Over Now!; My Own, or True Love at Last; My Poor Wee Lassie-A Scottish Lament; Nora the Nursemaid's Door; Oh, Catch Me Mr. Harris, 'Cause I'm Falling for You!; Oh Mr. Harris You're a Naughty, Naughty Man!; Riding the Range-A Song of the Old West

Cast: Evalyn Baron; Steve Burney; Ann Hodapp; Valerie Mahaffey; Kristen Meadows; Olivier Pierre; Niall Toibin; Alex Wipf

Notes: [1] Cut during previews.

1257 • FEATHERTOP (1961)

OPENED: 10/19/1961   Theatre: ABC
TV Musical

Composer: Mary Rodgers
Lyricist: Martin Charnin
Producer: Tony Charmoli
Director: Dean Whitmore

Source: FEATHERTOP (Novel: John Marsh); Musical Director: Richard Priborsky

Songs: Day I Say I Do, The; Easy Come, Easy Go; Family Tree; Gentlemen of Breeding; I'm a Man; Incantation Ballet (inst.); Intimate Friends; Perfect Strangers

Cast: Hans Conreid; Jackie Joseph; Pat Lloyd; Shirley Mills; Cathleen Nesbitt; Hugh O'Brian; Jane Powell; Anthony Teague

1258 • FEATHERTOP (1984)

OPENED: 10/17/1984   Theatre: WPA
Musical   Off-Off-Broadway: 33

Composer: Skip Kennon
Lyricist: Skip Kennon
Librettist: Bruce Peyton
Director: Susan H. Schulman

Source: FEATHERTOP (Story: Nathaniel Hawthorne); Choreographer: Michael Lichtefeld; Costumes: David Murin; Lighting Designer: Craig Evans; Musical Director: Sand Lawn; Set Design: Edward T. Gianfrancesco

Songs: Alleluia; As I'd Like to Be [1]; Better; Dreams to Do [1]; Eighteen Years Ago [1]; Happily the Days Are Running By; Here I Am; Hi-Ho [1]; Hidden Princess, The [1]; Home; Incantations, The; It's Only the Best Yet; Last Incantation, The; Marvelous, Curious and Strange; New World, The; One, Two, Three; Practically Speaking [1]; Sense of Motherly Pride, A [1]; Someday; Something Different; Spring Day; They Had to Change; Tomorrow and Tomorrow [1]

Cast: Charles Bari; David Barron; Stephen Bogardus; Laura Dean; Jason Graae; Alexandra Korey

Notes: [1] Out Pennsylvania Stage Company 11/23/80.

1259 • FEMALE DRUMMER, A

OPENED: 12/26/1898   Theatre: Star
Musical   Broadway: 72

Composer: Frank David
Lyricist: Charles E. Blaney
Producer: Charles E. Blaney; Vance

Songs: Annual Ball; Burlesque Trio [2]; Dandy Waiters of the Golden Light; Female Drummer, A; Golden Light, The; Green [2]; Ground and Lofty Dancing; Hannah Jackson Greene [2]; In the Department Store; I've Got Another Baby; Kitty More [2]; Maggie O'Connor; Monday and Tuesday; My Own Best Love; Pinkey, My Darling; Salesladies' Annual Ball, The; Singing Models, The; Swellest Thing, The; Terpsichorean Trifle, A; You Ain't One, Two, Three

Cast: Johnstone Bennett [1]; Eugene Canfield; Oscar Figman; Nellie O'Neil; George Richards; Willis P. Sweatnam

Notes: A drummer was a salesperson. [1] A famous male impersonator. [2] From program of 1/23/1899.

1260 • FENCING MASTER, THE

OPENED: 11/14/1892   Theatre: Casino
Musical   Broadway: 120

Composer: Reginald De Koven
Lyricist: Harry B. Smith
Librettist: Harry B. Smith

Songs: Ev'ry Knight Must Have a Star; Life of a Rover, The; Nightingale and the Rose, The; Opening Chorus; Serenade; Will O' the Wisp Song

Cast: William Broderick; Jerome Sykes; Marie Tempest; Hubert Wilke

Notes: No program available. Song titles not listed in vocal score.

1261 • FENWICK

OPENED: 12/08/1968   Theatre: NBC
TV Musical

Composer: Jack A. Boring
Lyricist: Patti Jacob

Musical Director: Don Elliott

Songs: Fenwick; In the Toyshop; Keep Thy Faith, Children; Santa Land

Cast: Anita Bryant; Walter Slezak

1262 • FESTIVAL

OPENED: 05/16/1979   Theatre: City Center
                                        Downstairs
Musical   Off-Broadway: 7

Composer: Stephen Downs
Lyricist: Stephen Downs; Randal Martin; Bruce Vilanch
Librettist: Stephen Downs; Randal Martin
Producer: Roger Berlind; Franklin R. Levy; Mike Wise
Director: Wayne Bryan

Source: AUCASSIN & NICOLETTE (Chantefable); **Choreographer:** Stan Mazin; **Costumes:** Madeline Ann Graneto; **Dance Arranger:** Tony Berg; **Lighting Designer:** George Gizienski; **Musical Director:** David Spear; **Set Design:** George Gizienski; **Vocal Arranger:** Tony Berg

Songs: Ballad of Oh and For the Love; Beata Biax; Ceremony, The; Escape, The; Fairlight Glen [1]; Father's Argument/Aucassin's Reply [1]; Gifts to You; I Can't Remember; Just Like You; Let Him Love You; Minstrel's Advice [1]; Oh, Dear! [1]; One Step Further; Our Song; Pirates Song; Prelude to War and War; Put the Ribbons On [1]; Recital [1]; Roger the Ox; Sewing Rainbows [1]; She [1]; Special Day; Time Is Come, The; Torelore [1]; Unfinished Song; When the Lady Passes; You Are Me, I Am Thee [1]

Cast: Bill Hutton; Tina Johnson; Michael Magnusen; Maureen McNamara; Lindy Nisbet; Roxann Parker; Michael Rupert; Leon Stewart; John Windsor

Notes: Additional book and special material by Bruce Vilanch. [1] Cut prior to New York.

1263 • FESTIVITIES OF 1927

OPENED: 1928

Songs: If I Can Take You from Someone (C/L: Joseph E. Howard)

Notes: No other information available.

1264 • FIDDLE-DEE-DEE

OPENED: 09/06/1900   Theatre: Weber & Fields'
                                        Music Hall
Musical   Broadway: 262

Composer: John Stromberg
Lyricist: Edgar Smith
Librettist: Edgar Smith
Producer: Lew Fields; Joseph Weber
Director: Julian Mitchell

Costumes: Will R. Barnes; **Musical Director:** C. Herbert Kerr

Songs: Andy Mack; Beautiful Arizona; Bobby; Come Back My Honey Boy to Me; Come One, Come All and See the Sights; Comic Opera, The; De Cakewalk Queen; Fads; Fetch Yo' Baby Home [1]; Fiddle-Dee-Dee March; I Sigh for a Change; I'm a Respectable Working Girl; Je Ne la Comprend Pas; Latest Cure for Ennui, The; Ma Blushing Rosie, My Posey Sweet; McSorley's Trip to Paris; Opening Chorus; Signor Gazanna [1]; Sweethearts in the Sky; Swiss Warble; Tell Us Pretty Ladies; That's About the Size of It; Tips of Gay Paree, The; Uncle Sam's Boys in Blue

Cast: Bessie Clayton; Lew Fields; DeWolf Hopper; Bonnie Maginn; Charles J. Ross; Lillian Russell; Fay Templeton; David Warfield; Joseph Weber

Notes: [1] Sheet music only.

1265 • FIDDLER ON THE ROOF

OPENED: 09/22/1964   Theatre: Imperial
Musical   Broadway: 3242

Composer: Jerry Bock
Lyricist: Sheldon Harnick
Librettist: Joseph Stein
Producer: Harold Prince
Director: Jerome Robbins

Source: TEVYE AND HIS DAUGHTERS (Story: Sholom Aleichem); **Choreographer:** Jerome Robbins; **Costumes:** Patricia Zipprodt; **Dance Arranger:** Betty Walberg; **Lighting Designer:** Jean Rosenthal; **Musical Director:** Milton Greene; **Orchestrations:** Don Walker; **Set Design:** Boris Aronson; **Vocal Arranger:** Milton Greene

Songs: Anatevka; As Much As That [3]; Bottle Dance, The; Chavaleh; Dear Sweet Sewing Machine [3]; Do You Love Me?; Epilogue; Far from the Home I Love; Fiddler on the Roof [5]; Get Thee Out [3]; Hora [3]; How Much Richer Could One Man Be [3]; I Just Heard; If I Were a Rich Man; If I Were a Woman [4]; Letters from America [3]; Little Bit of This, A [3]; Mama, Mama [2]; Matchmaker, Matchmaker; Miracle of Miracles; Never Say a Butcher Has No Soul [2]; New World [2]; Now I Have Everything; Poppa Help Me [2]; Sabbath Prayer; Sunrise, Sunset; Tailor, Motel Kamzoil, The; Tevye's Dream; To Life; To Marry for Love [3]; Tradition; We've Never Missed a Sabbath Yet [1]; Wedding Dance; What a Life [2]; When the Messiah Comes [4]; You Could Have the Richest Man in Town [3]

Cast: Beatrice Arthur; Bert Convy; Tanya Everett; Michael Granger; Maria Karnilova; Joanna Merlin; Julia Migenes; Zero Mostel; Austin Pendleton; Joe Ponazecki

Notes: [1] Not used. Part of melody made into "Matchmaker." [2] Not used. [3] Cut Detroit 8/64. [4] Out Washington, D.C. 9/64. [5] Based on the "Fiddler's Theme," this was a pop song.

1266 • FIDDLERS THREE

OPENED: 09/03/1918   Theatre: Cort
Musical   Broadway: 87

Composer: Alexander Johnstone
Lyricist: William Cary Duncan
Librettist: William Cary Duncan
Producer: John Cort
Director: J. Clifford Brooke

Choreographer: Carl Randall; **Costumes:** Mary Blackburn; **Orchestrations:** Domenic Sodero

Songs: As the Flitting Swallows Fly; Can It Be Love at Last?; Come to My Heart [3] (C: Otto Motzan; L: Darl MacBoyle); Don't You Think You'll Miss Me; Fiddlers Three [2]; For Love; It Was All on Account of Nipper [1]; Just a Slip of the Tongue [1]; Love of a Day; Love That's Gone [1]; One Hour Sweetheart, with You; Proud Little Pages; Rap, Rap, Rap [1]; Virtuosos Great Are We [1]; When the Fiddle Bows Begin to Fly

Cast: Louise Groody; Josie Intropodi; Hal Skelly

Notes: [1] Out Washington, D.C. 10/15/19. [2] Sheet music only. [3] ASCAP/Library of Congress.

1267 • FIFTH AVENUE FOLLIES, THE

OPENED: 01/1926
Musical   Nightclub

Composer: Richard Rodgers
Lyricist: Lorenz Hart
Librettist: Harold Atteridge; Ballard Macdonald
Producer: Billy Rose
Director: Seymour Felix

Costumes: Booth; **Lighting Designer:** L.A. Nestler; **Musical Director:** Reginald Childs; **Set Design:** Booth

Songs: City Flat, A; Do You Notice Anything?; Finale; High Hats; In the Name of Art; Lillie, Lawrence and Jack [3]; Mammy's Knee (C/L: Jack Donahue); Maybe It's Me [1]; Mike; Olive, An (C/L: Bert Hanlon); So Does You Old Mandarin (C/L: H. Adler; Oscar Herman; Harry Weill); Susie; Where's That Little Girl (with the Little Green Hat)? [2]

Cast: Harry Archer's Orchestra; Edith Babson; Richard Bennett; Albert Burke; Doris Canfield; Johnne Clare; Bobbie Cliff; Cecil Cunningham; Ednor Frilling; Bert Hanlon; Oscar Herman; Harry Weill

Notes: [1] Same music as "I'm Crazy 'Bout the Charleston" in COCHRAN'S REVUE OF 1926. Also in PEGGY ANN. [2] Same music as "What's the Use?" in LIDO LADY. [3] May have same music as "Tennis Champs" in THE GARRICK GAIETIES (1926).

1268 • 5TH OF JULY

OPENED: 04/27/1978   Theatre: Circle Repertory
Play   Off-Broadway: 669

Author: Lanford Wilson
Producer: Circle Repertory Company
Director: Marshall W. Mason

Costumes: Laura Crow; **Lighting Designer:** Marc B. Weiss; **Set Design:** John Lee Beatty

Songs: Your Loving Eyes (C/L: Jonathan Hogan)

Cast: Jeff Daniels; Jonathan Hogan; William Hurt; Joyce Reehling; Nancy Snyder; Helen Stenborg; Danton Stone; Amy Wright

Notes: This play transferred to Broadway's New Apollo Theater, opening on 11/5/80. The play ran 158 performances at Circle Rep. When on Broadway the title was spelled FIFTH OF JULY. The Broadway production ran 511 performances. The total above is the total of both runs.

1269 • 5TH SEASON, THE

OPENED: 10/12/1975   Theatre: Eden
Musical   Off-Broadway: 122

Composer: Dick Manning
Lyricist: Dick Manning
Librettist: Luba Kadison
Producer: Jewish Nostalgic Prods.; Harry Rothpearl
Director: Joseph Buloff

Source: FIFTH SEASON, THE (Play: Sylvia Regan); **Choreographer:** Sophie Maslow; **Costumes:** Jeffrey B. Moss; **Lighting Designer:** Bob McCarthy; **Musical Director:** Renee Solomon; **Set Design:** Jeffrey B. Moss

Songs: Believe in Yourself; Fifth Season, The; Friday Night (L: Luba Kadison); From Seventh Avenue to Seventh Heaven; Goodbye; How Did This Happen to Me; Mom! You Don't Understand; My Son, the Doctor

Cast: Gene Barrett; Joseph Buloff; David Carey; Gerri-Ann Frank; Evelyn Kingsley; Miriam Kressyn; Elias Patron; Stan Porter; Jack Rechzeit; Raquel Yossiffon

Notes: Yiddish adaptation of lyrics by Isaac Dogim.

1270 • FIFTY-FIFTY LTD.

OPENED: 10/27/1919   Theatre: Comedy
Musical   Broadway: 40

Composer: Leon De Costa
Lyricist: Leon De Costa
Librettist: William Lennox; Margaret Michael
Director: William H. Post

Source: ALL THE COMFORTS OF HOME (Play: William Gillette); **Choreographer:** Walter Brooks; **Set Design:** Mabel A. Buell

Songs: Entirely Surrounded By Girls [1] (C: Harry Carroll; L: Harold Atteridge); Every Little Girl Has a Way of Her Own; Honey Bunch; If It Wasn't for the Wife [1] (C: Harry Carroll; L: Harold Atteridge); Is It the Girl or Is It the Gown?; Little Bit of Jazz, A; Magic Place, The; Me and My Dog; Moonshine of Kentucky (Give Me the Moonshine of My Old Kentucky Home) [1] (C: Harry Carroll; L: Harold Atteridge); Move into My Heart [1] (C: Harry Carroll; L: Harold

Atteridge); My Might-Have-Been; Nanette; Nerves; Rose, a Child, a Butterfly, A [1] (C: Harry Carroll; L: Harold Atteridge); Silence of Love; So Long-Goodbye; Spooky Nights; That Was Wonderful; Wish for a Wish; Won't You Cuddle Up a Little Closer?

Cast: Herbert Corthell; John Slavin; Gertrude Vanderbilt

Notes: No other information available. [1] Sheet music only.

1271 • FIFTY MILES FROM BOSTON

OPENED: 02/03/1908   Theatre: Garrick
Play   Broadway: 32

Composer: George M. Cohan
Lyricist: George M. Cohan
Author: George M. Cohan
Producer: George M. Cohan; Sam H. Harris
Director: George M. Cohan

Costumes: F. Richard Anderson; **Musical Director:** Al E. Gaylord; **Orchestrations:** Charles J. Gebest

Songs: Ain't It Awful; Boys Who Fight the Flames, The; Brookfield Two-Step, The [1]; Harrigan; Jack and Jill; Small Town Girl, A; Waltz with Me

Cast: Edna Wallace Hopper; Emma Janvier; James C. Marlowe; George Parsons; Lawrence Wheat

Notes: [1] ASCAP/Library of Congress only.

1272 • FIFTY MILLION FRENCHMEN

OPENED: 11/27/1929   Theatre: Lyric
Musical   Broadway: 254

Composer: Cole Porter
Lyricist: Cole Porter
Librettist: Herbert Fields
Producer: E. Ray Goetz
Director: Monty Woolley

Choreographer: Larry Ceballos; **Costumes:** James Reynolds; **Musical Director:** Gene Salzer; **Set Design:** Norman Bel Geddes

Songs: American Express, The; At Longchamps Today; Boy Friend Back Home, The [2]; Do You Want to See Paris [4]; Down with Everybody but Us [1]; Emigrants, The [5]; Find Me a Primitive Man; Happy Heaven of Harlem, The; Heaven of Harlem, The [1]; I Worship You [1]; I'm in Love; I'm Unlucky at Gambling; It Isn't Done; Let's Step Out [2]; Let's Turn on the Love Interest [6]; My Harlem Wench [1]; Paree, What Did You Do to Me?; Please Don't Make Me Be Good [1]; Queen of Terre Haute, The [1]; Snake in the Grass Ballet, The (inst.) [1]; Somebody's Going to Throw a Big Party; Tale of an Oyster, The [3]; That's Why I Love You [1]; Toast of Volstead, A; Watching the World Go By [1]; Where Would You Get Your Coat?; Why Don't We Try Staying Home [1]; Why Shouldn't I Have You?; Yankee Doodle; You Do Something to Me; You Don't Know Paree; You've Got That Thing

Cast: Helen Broderick; Betty Compton; William Gaxton; Evelyn Hoey; Jack Thompson; Genevieve Tobin

Notes: [1] Cut before opening. [2] Added after opening. [3] Cut after opening. [4] Earlier version in LA REVUE DES AMERICAINES as "Omnibus." [5] Cut prior to opening. In WAKE UP AND DREAM as "Entrance of Emigrants. [6] Not used.

1273 • FIG LEAVES ARE FALLING, THE

OPENED: 01/02/1969   Theatre: Broadhurst
Musical   Broadway: 4

Composer: Albert Hague
Lyricist: Allen Sherman
Librettist: Allen Sherman
Producer: John Bowab; Lawrence Carr; Joseph Harris
Director: George Abbott

Choreographer: Eddie Gasper; **Conductor:** Jack Lee; **Costumes:** Robert Mackintosh; **Dance Arranger:** Jack Lee; **Lighting Designer:** Tharon Musser; **Musical Director:** Abba Bogin; **Orchestrations:** Manny Alban; **Set Design:** Jean Eckart; William Eckart

Songs: All Is Well in Larchmont; All of My Laughter; Did I Ever Really Live?; Down the Drain [1]; Fig Leaves Are Falling, The; For Our Sake; For the Rest of My Life; Give Me a Cause; I Like It; Juggling [1]; Light One Candle; Like Yours; Lillian; Lillian, Lillian, Lillian; My Aunt

Minnie [1]; Not Tonight [1]; Oh, Boy; Old Fashioned Song; Signs [1]; Today I Saw a Rose; We

Cast: David Cassidy; Kenneth Kimmins; Dorothy Loudon; Barry Nelson; Jenny O'Hara; Louise Quick

Notes: [1] Cut prior to opening.

1274 • FILIBUSTER, THE
OPENED: 1904
Musical   Closed out of town

Composer: William Lorraine
Lyricist: John P. Wilson
Librettist: John P. Wilson
Producer: George A. Kingsbury; Samuel E. Rork
Director: James Francis

Musical Director: George Lowell Tracy

Songs: At Least That Is My Supposition; Cruise of a Deep Sea-Going Hack, The; Dolce Far Niente Land; Ensemble; Entrance of Cortez and Pizzaro; Entrance of Female Chorus; Filibuster, The; Finale Act I; Finale Act II; Finale Act III; Graft; How I Put Down the War; Johny Wise; Opening Chorus; Opening Chorus Act II; Opening Chorus Act III; Rebellion Promoter, A; Revolutionary Song; School of Love, The; Shore of the Sun-Down Sea, The; Soldier of Fortune, A; Toreador, The; Way People Have from Italia, The; Welcome Chorus; When Pizzaro Struck These Parts; When You Shine on Me (Sunbeam, Oh, Sunbeam) (L: John P. Wilson; Rida Johnson Young)

Cast: Charles W. Cole; Edwin S. Drowne; Henry D. Gardner; Frank Lawlor

Notes: Tremont St. Theatre, Boston.

1275 • FINE AND DANDY
OPENED: 09/29/1930   Theatre: Erlanger
Musical   Broadway: 246

Composer: Kay Swift
Lyricist: Paul James
Librettist: Joe Cook; Donald Ogden Stewart
Producer: Lewis E. Gensler; Morris Green
Director: Morris Green; Frank McCoy

Choreographer: Merriel Abbott; Dave Gould; Tom Nip; Eugene Van Grona; **Costumes:** Charles

LeMaire; **Musical Director:** Gene Salzer; **Orchestrations:** Hans Spialek; **Set Design:** Henry Dreyfuss

Songs: Can This Be Love?; Chant; Finaletto; Fine and Dandy; Fordyce; I'll Hit a New High; Jig Hop, The; Let's Go Eat Worms in the Garden; Mechanical Ballet; Nobody Breaks My Heart [1]; Opening Act II; Rich or Poor; Starting at the Bottom; Thing I Can't Seem to Forget; Waltz Ballet; Wedding Bells; Wheels of Steel

Cast: Alice Boulden; Dave Chasen; Joe Cook; John Ehrle; Dora Maugham; David Morris; Nell O'Day; Eleanor Powell; Joe Wagstaff

Notes: [1] Not in program.

1276 • FINE AND PRIVATE PLACE, A
OPENED: 08/03/1989
Musical   Closed out of town

Composer: Richard Isen
Lyricist: Erik Haagensen
Librettist: Erik Haagensen
Producer: Goodspeed Opera House
Director: Robert Kalfin

Source: FINE AND PRIVATE PLACE, A (Novel: Peter S. Beagle); **Lighting Designer:** Fred Kolo; **Musical Director:** Henry Aronson; **Set Design:** Fred Kolo

Songs: Argument; Because of Them All; Close Your Eyes; Do Something; How Can I Leave Here?; I'm Not Going Gently; It's None of My Business; Let Me Explain; Much More Alive; No One Ever Knows; Prologue; Quartet; Stop Kidding Yourself; Telepathetique, The; What Did You Expect?; What Should I Do?; You Know What I Mean

Notes: Goodspeed Opera House.

1277 • FINGS AIN'T WOT THEY USED T'BE
OPENED: 12/17/1959   Theatre: Stratford East
Musical   London: 962

Composer: Lionel Bart
Lyricist: Lionel Bart
Librettist: Frank Norman

Producer: Donald Albery
Director: Joan Littlewood

Set Design: John Bury

Songs: Big Time; Carve Up!; Ceilin's Comin' Dahn, The; Cochran Will Return; Contempery; Cop a Bit of Pride; Fings Ain't Wot They Used T'Be; G'Night Dearie; Laying Abaht; Meatface; Polka Dots; Proceeding in a Westerly Direction; Prologue; Student Ponce, The; Where Do Little Birds Go?; Where It's Hot

Cast: James Booth; Edward Caddick; Tom Chatto; Glynn Edwards; Paddy Joyce; Miriam Karlin; Toni Palmer; Barbara Windsor

Notes: Transferred to The Garrick Theatre 2/11/60 for 897 performances.

1278 • FINIAN'S RAINBOW
OPENED: 01/10/1947   Theatre: 46th Street
Musical   Broadway: 725

Composer: Burton Lane
Lyricist: E.Y. Harburg
Librettist: E.Y. Harburg; Fred Saidy
Producer: William R. Katzell; Lee Sabinson
Director: Bretaigne Windust

Choreographer: Michael Kidd; **Costumes:** Eleanor Goldsmith; **Lighting Designer:** Jo Mielziner; **Musical Director:** Milton Rosenstock; **Orchestrations:** Robert Russell Bennett; Don Walker; **Set Design:** Jo Mielziner; **Vocal Arranger:** Lyn Murray

Songs: Begat, The; How Are Things in Glocca Morra?; If This Isn't Love; Look to the Rainbow; Look to the Rainbow Dance (inst.); Necessity; Old Devil Moon; Something Sort of Grandish; That Great Come and Get It Day; This Time of the Year; When I'm Not Near the Girl I Love; When the Idle Poor Become the Idle Rich

Cast: Anita Alvarez; Royal Dano; Lorenzo Fuller; Ella Logan; Dolores Martin; Lyn Murray Singers, The; Robert Pitkin; Donald Richards; Albert Sharpe; Sonny Terry; David Wayne

1279 • FINKEL'S FOLLIES
OPENED: 12/15/1991   Theatre: John Houseman
Revue   Off-Broadway: 65

Composer: Elliot Finkel
Lyricist: Phillip Namanworth
Librettist: Robert H. Livingston
Producer: Eric Krebs
Director: Robert H. Livingston

Choreographer: James J. Mellon; **Costumes:** Mimi Maxmen; **Lighting Designer:** Bob Bessoir; **Musical Director:** Mike Huffman; **Set Design:** Mimi Maxmen

Songs: Abi Tsu Zein Mit Dir (As Long As I'm with You); Belz (Wonderful Girl of Mine) (C: Alexander Olshanetsky); Di Greene Kuzeene (My Little Cousin) (C/L: Abe Schwartz); Ich Hob Dich Tzufil Lieb (I Love You Too Much) (C: Alexander Olshanetsky); Kleine Soft Shoe, A; Mi-Komash Melon (What Is the Meaning?) (C/L: A. Reisen; N.L. Saslavsky); Mom, I Want to Be in Yiddish Vaudeville; Not on the Top (C/L: Abe Ellstein); Odenemya; Oy Mama (C: Abe Ellstein; L: Molly Picon); Ringa Zinga; Rozinkes Mit Mandlen (Raisins and Olives) (C/L: Abraham Goldfaden); Tankhum (C/L: Solomon Golub); That Something Special; These Are the Jokes; Tzi Vus Darf Ich Zein Du? (Why Do I Have to Be Here?); Vaudeville, Kosher Style; Vee Zenen Meine Zibn Gute Yor (Where Are My Seven Good Years) (C/L: David Meyerowitz); Yiddish Vaudeville Tonight; Yossel, Yossel (Joseph, Joseph) (C/L: Nellie Casman); You Were Meant for Me

Cast: Mary Ellen Ashley; Fyvush Finkel; Avi Ber Hoffman; Laura Turnbull

1280 • FIORELLO!
OPENED: 11/23/1959   Theatre: Broadhurst
Musical   Broadway: 796

Composer: Jerry Bock
Lyricist: Sheldon Harnick
Librettist: George Abbott; Jerome Weidman
Producer: Robert E. Griffith; Harold Prince
Director: George Abbott

Choreographer: Peter Gennaro; **Costumes:** Jean Eckart; William Eckart; **Dance Arranger:** Jack Elliott; **Lighting Designer:** Jean Eckart; William Eckart; **Musical Director:** Harold Hastings; **Orchestrations:** Irwin Kostal; **Set Design:** Jean Eckart; William Eckart

Songs: Bum Won, The; Business Is Fundamentally Sound [2]; Gentleman Jimmy; Home Again;

I Love a Cop; Little Tin Box; Marie's Law; Name's LaGuardia, The; On the Side of the Angels; Politics and Poker; Temporarily Unemployed [2]; Till the Bootlegger Comes [2]; Till Tomorrow; Trieste [2]; Unfair; Very Next Man, The; When Did I Fall in Love?; Where Do I Go from Here? [1]

Cast: Tom Bosley; Howard Da Silva; Mark Dawson; Nathaniel Frey; Ellen Hanley; Bob Holiday; Ron Husmann; Eileen Rodgers; Pat Stanley; Patricia Wilson

Notes: A bio-musical of Fiorello LaGuardia. [1] Cut prior to opening. [2] Unused.

1281 • FIORETTA

OPENED: 02/05/1929   Theatre: Earl Carroll
Musical   Broadway: 111

Composer: G. Romilli
Lyricist: G. Romilli
Librettist: Charles Andrews; George Bagby
Producer: Earl Carroll
Director: Clifford Brooke

Choreographer: LeRoy Prinz; **Costumes:** Charles LeMaire; William H. Matthews; **Orchestrations:** Domenico Savino

Songs: Alone with You (C: George Bagby; L: Grace Henry; Jo Trent); Blade of Mine (C: George Bagby; L: Grace Henry); Carissima (L: Grace Henry); Carnival; Chant; Coronation; Doing a Dance [1]; Dream Boat (C: George Bagby; L: Grace Henry; Jo Trent); Duel, The [1]; Fioretta; Marietta [1]; My Heart Belongs to You; Pierrot and Pierrette; Roses of Red; Royal Barge [1]; Soliloquy [1]; Wedding; Wicked Old Willage of Wenice

Cast: Lionel Atwill; Jay Brennan; Fanny Brice; Leon Errol; George Houston; Dorothy Knapp

Notes: [1] Out Washington, D.C. 1/6/29.

1282 • FIRE OF FLOWERS

OPENED: 01/29/1976   Theatre: Provincetown
                                    Playhouse
Revue   Off-Broadway: 38

Composer: Peter Copani; David McHugh; Lawrence Pitilli; Christian Staudt; Bob Tuthill; Ed Vogel
Lyricist: Peter Copani

Librettist: Peter Copani
Producer: Peoples Performing Company
Director: Don Signore

Lighting Designer: Richard Harper; **Musical Director:** Ed Vogel; **Set Design:** Richard Harper

Songs: Blind Junkie; Down on Me [1] (C/L: Peter Copani; Chris Staudt); Drug Free; God Is in the People [1] (C/L: Peter Copani; Chris Staudt); I Love the Sun; I Need to Know; If Jesus Walked [1] (C/L: Peter Copani; Chris Staudt); I'm Afire; In the Name of Love [1] (C/L: Peter Copani; Chris Staudt); Instant Hate; Keep Hope Alive; L'America Ha Fato per Te [1] (C/L: Peter Copani; Chris Staudt); Love Comes and Goes; Lover's Dream, A; Make Them Hate [1] (C/L: Peter Copani; Chris Staudt); More Than Love; One of Us [1] (C/L: Peter Copani; Chris Staudt); Pairs of One; Poppy Fields; Riot; Special Man, A [1] (C/L: Peter Copani; Chris Staudt); Strawberries, Pickles and Ice Cream [1] (C/L: Peter Copani; Chris Staudt); Street Jesus [1] (C/L: Peter Copani; Chris Staudt); Today Will Be; Verily, Verily; Wait and See [1] (C/L: Peter Copani; Chris Staudt); When We Are Together; Who Can Say? [1] (C/L: Peter Copani; Chris Staudt)

Cast: Larry Campbell; Sylvia Miranda; Val Reiter; Gwen Sumter

Notes: [1] Also in STREET JESUS.

1283 • FIREBRAND, THE

OPENED: 10/15/1924   Theatre: Morosco
Play   Broadway: 287

Author: Edwin Justus Mayer
Producer: Liveright; Frank Mandel; Laurence Schwab
Director: Arthur Hurley

Costumes: Woodman Thompson; **Set Design:** Woodman Thompson

Songs: Voice of Love, The (Cellini's Love Song) (C: Robert Russell Bennett; Maurice Nitke; L: Ira Gershwin)

Cast: Eden Gray; Allyn Joslyn; Lillian Kingsburry; Charles McCarthy; Frank Morgan; Brandon Peters; Edward G. Robinson; Joseph Schildkraut

1284 • FIREBRAND OF FLORENCE, THE

OPENED: 03/22/1945　Theatre: Alvin
Musical　Broadway: 43

Composer: Kurt Weill
Lyricist: Ira Gershwin
Librettist: Ira Gershwin; John Haggott; Edwin Justus Mayer
Producer: Max Gordon
Director: John Murray Anderson; John Haggott

Source: THE FIREBRAND (Play: Edwin Justus Mayer); **Choreographer:** Catherine Littlefield; **Costumes:** Raoul Pene du Bois; **Dance Arranger:** Kurt Weill; **Lighting Designer:** Jo Mielziner; **Musical Director:** Maurice Abravanel; **Orchestrations:** Kurt Weill; **Set Design:** Jo Mielziner; **Vocal Arranger:** Kurt Weill

Songs: Alessandro the Wise; Bell of Doom Is Clanging, The (Song of the Hangman); Come to Florence (Civic Song); Come to Paris; Dizzily, Busily; Duchess's Entrance; Hear Ye! Hear Ye!; How Wonderfully Fortunate; I Am Happy Here; I Had Just Been Pardoned; I Know Where There's a Cozy Nook (The Nozy Cook); Just in Case (We're Soldiers of a Duchy); (There'll Be) Life, Love, and Laughter; Little Naked Boy, The; Love Is My Enemy; My Dear Benvenuto; My Lord and Ladies; My Lords and Ladies; Nighttime Is No Time for Thinking, The; One Man's Death Is Another Man's Living; Our Master Is Free Again; Rhyme for Angela, A; Sing Me Not a Ballad; Souvenirs; There'll Be Life, Love, and Laughter; This Night in Florence; When the Duchess Is Away; World Is Full of Villains, The; You Have to Do What You Do Do [2]; You're Far Too Near Me

Cast: Melville Cooper; Ferdi Hoffman; Lotte Lenya; Beverly Tyler; Earl Wrightson

Notes: Titled MUCH ADO ABOUT LOVE out of town. [1] Not used. [2] Based on "Song of the Zodiac" and "No Matter Under What Star You're Born" — both not used in LADY IN THE DARK.

1285 • FIREFLY, THE

OPENED: 12/02/1912　Theatre: Lyric
Musical　Broadway: 120

Composer: Rudolf Friml
Lyricist: Otto Harbach

Librettist: Otto Harbach
Director: Fred G. Latham

Choreographer: Signor Albertieri; Sammy Lee; **Costumes:** W. Matthews; **Musical Director:** Gaetano Merola; **Set Design:** P. Dodd Ackerman; Reisig-Dove

Songs: American Beauty Rose, An; Away for a Lovely Ocean Cruise [1]; Beautiful Ship from Toy-Land The; Call Me Uncle; Dawn of Love, The (Kiss Me and 'Tis Day) (L: L'Alba D'Amore); De Trop; Giannina Mia; Girl with the Come Hither Eyes [1]; He Says Yes, She Says No!; In Sapphire Seas; I've Found It at Last; Ladies Fair [1]; Latest Thing from Paris, The; Love Is Like a Firefly; Opening Waltz; See! My Cloak!; Something; Sympathy; Tommy Atkins on a Dress-Parade (I Want to Be a Jolly Soldier); Trip to Bermuda, A; We'll Barricade Her [1]; We're Going to Make a Man of You; When a Maid Comes Knocking at Your Heart; Woman's Smile, A

Cast: Roy Atwell; Craig Campbell; Sammy Lee; Audrey Maple; Ruby Norton; Emma Trentini

Notes: [1] Not in program or vocal score.

1286 • FIREMAN'S FLAME, THE

OPENED: 10/09/1937　Theatre: American Music Hall
Musical　Off-Broadway: 204

Composer: Richard Lewine
Lyricist: Ted Fetter
Librettist: John Van Antwerp
Producer: John Krimsky; John Van Antwerp
Director: Morgan Lewis

Costumes: Kermit Love; **Musical Director:** Al Evans; **Orchestrations:** Ben Ludlow; **Set Design:** Eugene Dunkel; **Vocal Arranger:** Leslie Litomy

Songs: Do My Eyes Deceive Me?; Doin' the Waltz; Fire Belles' Gallop; Fireman's Flame, The; Hose Boys; I Like the Nose of Your Face; It's a Lovely Night on the Hudson River; Moth and the Flame; Mother Isn't Getting Any Younger; We're Off

Cast: Philip Bourneuf; Grace Coppin; Ben Cutler; Alan Handley; Isham Keith; Rose Lieder; Harry Meehan; Cynthia Rogers

Notes: John Van Antwerp used the psedonym Jerrold Krimsky for this production.

1287 • FIREMAN'S PICNIC, THE

Notes: *See COHAN AND HARRIS MINSTRELS (1909).*

1288 • FIREWORKS OF 1930

OPENED: 06/26/1930   Theatre: Lafayette
Musical   New York

Producer: Emory Hutchins

Cast: Jimmy Johnson's Syncopaters; Mamie Smith; George Dewey Washington

Notes: No program available.

1289 • FIRST, THE

OPENED: 11/17/1981   Theatre: Martin Beck
Musical   Broadway: 37

Composer: Bob Brush
Lyricist: Martin Charnin
Librettist: Joel Siegel
Producer: Peter Bobley; Neil Bogart; Zev Bufman; Michael Harvey
Director: Martin Charnin

Choreographer: Alan Johnson; **Costumes:** Carrie F. Robbins; **Dance Arranger:** Luther Henderson; **Lighting Designer:** Marc B. Weiss; **Musical Director:** Mark Hummel; **Orchestrations:** Luther Henderson; **Set Design:** David Chapman; **Vocal Arranger:** Joyce Brown

Songs: Bloat (Fat Don't Finish First); Brooklyn Dodger Strike, The; Bums [1]; Dancin' Off Third (dance); First, The; He's Gonna Keep His Eye on Us [2]; Is This Year Next Year?; It Ain't Gonna Work!; It's a Beginning; Jack Roosevelt Robinson; National Pastime (This Year's Nigger), The; Opera Ain't Over, The; Playing Field, The; Southern Hospitality [1]; There Are Days and There Are Days; Will We Ever Know Each Other; You Do-Do-Do-It Good!

Cast: Clent Bowers; David Alan Grier; David Huddleston; Lonette McKee; Court Miller; Trey Wilson

Notes: A bio-musical of Jackie Robinson. [1] Cut. [2] Not used.

1290 • FIRST IMPRESSIONS

OPENED: 03/19/1959   Theatre: Alvin
Musical   Broadway: 92

Composer: Glenn Paxton
Lyricist: Robert Goldman; George David Weiss
Librettist: Abe Burrows
Producer: George Gilbert; Edward Specter; Jule Styne Organization
Director: Abe Burrows

Source: PRIDE AND PREJUDICE (Play: Helen Jerome); **Source:** PRIDE AND PREJUDICE (Novel: Jane Austen); **Choreographer:** Jonathan Lucas; **Costumes:** Alvin Colt; **Dance Arranger:** John Morris; **Lighting Designer:** Charles Elson; **Musical Director:** Frederick Dvonch; **Orchestrations:** Don Walker; **Set Design:** Peter Larkin; **Vocal Arranger:** Buster Davis

Songs: As Long As There's a Mother; Assembly Dance, The; Five Daughters; Fragrant Flower; Gentleman Never Falls Wildly in Love, A; Goodbye, Kind Sir, Goodbye [1]; Have You Heard the News?; Heart Has Won the Game, The; House in Town, A; I Feel Sorry for the Girl; I Suddenly Find It Agreeable; I'm Me; It's the Thing to Do [2]; Jane; Let's Fetch the Carriage; Love Will Find Out the Way; Not Like Me [3]; Perfect Evening, A; Silly Brats and Rum [1]; So This Is How It Is [2]; This Really Isn't Me; Wasn't It a Simply Lovely Wedding?

Cast: Polly Bergen; Mary Finney; Hermione Gingold; Farley Granger; Ellen Hanley; Christopher Hewett; Donald Madden; Phyllis Newman; Lauri Peters

Notes: [1] Cut out of town. [2] Added to Equity Library Theater production 11/10/72. [3] Cut prior to opening. Added to Equity Library Theater production 11/10/72.

1291 • FIRST LADY SUITE

OPENED: 12/15/1993   Theatre: Public
Musical   Off-Broadway: 15

Composer: Michael John LaChiusa
Lyricist: Michael John LaChiusa
Librettist: Michael John LaChiusa
Director: Kristen Sanderson

Choreographer: Janet Bogardus; **Costumes:** Tom Broecker; **Lighting Designer:** Brian MacDevitt; **Musical Director:** Alan Johnson; **Set Design:** Derek McLane

Cast: Priscilla Baskerville; Maureen Moore; Carolann Page; Alice Playten; Debra Stricklin; David Wasson; Carol Woods

1292 • FIRST LOVE
OPENED: 1912
Musical

Composer: Anatole Friedland
Lyricist: Melville Alexander
Librettist: Raymond W. Peck
Director: Lester Browne

Musical Director: M.S. Bentham

Songs: First Love (C: Anatole Friedland; Lulu Glaser); I Never Knew What Love Could Do; Way to Kiss, The

Cast: Lester Browne; Lulu Glaser; Thomas D. Richards

Notes: 1912 Playlet. Information from a Milwaukee vaudeville program of 1/13/13.

1293 • FIRST MANHATTAN MUSIC HALL REVUE
OPENED: 1935
Revue

Composer: Harry Akst
Lyricist: Lew Brown

Songs: I Feel It in My Bones; I'm Gonna Fall in Love; You Get a Lot of Help when You're in Love

Notes: No other information availble.

1294 • FIRSTBORN, THE
OPENED: 04/30/1958   Theatre: Coronet
Play   Broadway: 38

Composer: Leonard Bernstein
Lyricist: Leonard Bernstein
Author: Christopher Fry
Producer: Katharine Cornell; Roger L. Stevens
Director: Anthony Quayle

Costumes: Robert Fletcher; **Lighting Designer:** Tharon Musser; **Set Design:** Boris Aronson

Cast: Jack Betts; Katharine Cornell; Robert Drivas; Chris Gampel; Mildred Natwick; Anthony Quayle; Michael Strong; Torin Thatcher; Michael Wager; Kathleen Widdoes

Notes: This play was produced "under the auspices of the America-Israel Cultural Foundation, in tribute to Israel's 10th Anniversary."

1295 • FISHER MAIDEN, THE
OPENED: 10/05/1903   Theatre: Victoria
Musical   Broadway: 32

Composer: Harry Von Tilzer
Lyricist: Arthur J. Lamb
Librettist: Arthur J. Lamb
Producer: Harry Von Tilzer
Director: Harry Von Tilzer

Choreographer: Joseph C. Smith; **Costumes:** Dazian; **Musical Director:** Fred Perkins; **Set Design:** Ernest Albert

Songs: Coo-ee, Coo-ee; Daughter of the Moon Am I, A; Down on a South Sea Isle; He Dangled Me on His Knee; Highly Important Fly, The; I'm a Fisher Maiden [1]; I'm in Love with the Beautiful Bugs; Laughing Song; Let the Band Play; Maydee (Pretty Little South Sea Island Lady); Oh, Marjorie; On a Beautiful Distant Island [1]; Opening Chorus; Roses for the Girl I Love; Sail on the Tail of a Whale, A; Secret Society; Under the Mulberry Tree; We're Secret Society Members; When You Go Down to London Town

Cast: Edna Bronson; Frances Cameron; Dorothy Jardon; George A. MacFarlane; Al Shean; Bessie Tannehill

Notes: [1] ASCAP/Library of Congress only.

1296 • FIVE GUYS NAMED MOE
OPENED: 04/08/1992   Theatre: Eugene O'Neill
Musical   Broadway: 445

Librettist: Clarke Peters
Producer: Cameron Mackintosh
Director: Charles Augins

Choreographer: Charles Augins; **Costumes:** Noel Howard; **Lighting Designer:** Andrew Bridge; **Musical Director:** Reginald Royal;

Orchestrations: Neil McArthur; **Set Design:** Tim Goodchild; **Vocal Arranger:** Chapman Roberts

Songs: Ain't Nobody Here but Us Chickens (C/L: Alex Kramer; Joan Whitney); Azure Te (C/L: Bill Davis; Don Wolf); Beware, Brother, Beware (C/L: Dick Adams; Morry Lasco; Fleecie Moore); Caldonia (C/L: Fleecie Moore); Choo, Choo, Ch'boogie (C/L: Denver Darling; Milt Gabler; Vaughn Horton); Dad Gum Your Hide Boy (C/L: Browley Brit); Don't Let the Sun Catch You Crying (C/L: Jo Greene); Early in the Morning (C/L: Dallas Bartley; Leo Hickman; Louis Jordan); Five Guys Named Moe (C/L: Jerry Bresler; Larry Wynn); Hurry Home (C/L: Buddy Bernier; Robert Emmerich; Joseph Meyer); I Know What I've Got (C/L: Louis Jordan; Sid Robin); I Like 'Em Fat Like That (C/L: Claude Demetriou; Louis Jordan); If I Had Any Sense (C/L: R. McCoy; C. Singleton); Is You Is or Is You Ain't My Baby? (C/L: S. Austin; Louis Jordan); Let the Good Times Roll (C/L: Fleecie Moore; Sam Theard); Life Is So Peculiar (C: Jimmy Van Heusen; L: Johnny Burke); Look Out, Sister (C/L: Louis Jordan; Sid Robin); Messy Bessy (C/L: Jon Hendricks); Pettin' and Pokin' (C/L: Lora Lee); Push Ka Pi Shi Pi (C/L: Louis Jordan; Walt Merrick; Joe Willoughby); Root, Petite and Gone (C/L: Louis Jordan; Spencer Lee); Safe, Sane and Single (C/L: Hy Heath; Louis Jordan; Johnny Lange); Saturday Night Fish Fry (C/L: Louis Jordan; Ellis Walsh); What's the Use of Getting Sober (C/L: Bubsy Meyers)

Cast: Jerry Dixon; Doug Eskew; Milton Craig Nealy; Kevin Ramsey; Jeffrey D. Sams; Glenn Turner

Notes: No original songs in this show.

1297 • 5 O'CLOCK GIRL, THE

OPENED: 10/10/1927 Theatre: 44th Street
Musical Broadway: 278

Composer: Harry Ruby
Lyricist: Bert Kalmar
Librettist: Guy Bolton; Fred Thompson
Producer: Philip Goodman
Director: John Harwood

Choreographer: Jack Haskell; **Costumes:** Charles LeMaire; **Musical Director:** Gus Salzer; **Set Design:** Norman Bel Geddes

Songs: Any Little Thing; Following in Father's Footsteps; Happy Go Lucky; I'm One Little Party; Lonesome Romeos; Opening; Opening Act II; Society Ladder; Tea Time Tap; Tell the World I'm Through; Thinking of You; Up in the Clouds; We Want You [1]; Who Did? You Did; Why Am I So Wonderful [2]; Window Cleaners, The [3]

Cast: Louis John Bartels; Danny Dare; Mary Eaton; Pert Kelton; Sammy Lee; Al Shaw; Oscar Shaw

Notes: [1] Also in TOP SPEED (1929). [2] Added for London production. [3] Added for London production. Previously in THE GREENWICH VILLAGE FOLLIES (1925). Also in the HOLLYWOOD MUSIC BOX REVUE (1927).

1298 • 5, 6, 7, 8 . . . DANCE!

OPENED: 06/15/1983 Theatre: Radio City Music Hall
Revue New York: 149

Composer: Wally Harper
Lyricist: David Zippel
Librettist: Bruce Vilanch
Producer: Radio City Music Hall Prod.
Director: Ron Field

Choreographer: Ron Field; **Costumes:** Lindsay W. Davis; **Dance Arranger:** Mark Hummel; Donald York; **Lighting Designer:** Richard Nelson; **Musical Director:** Thomas Helm; **Orchestrations:** Bill Byers; **Set Design:** Tom H. John

Songs: Bad Habits (C/L: Billy Field; Tom Price); Body Language (C/L: Barry Fasman; Steve Sperry); Broadway Rhythm (C: Arthur Freed; L: Nacio Herb Brown); Dance (C/L: Paul Jabara); Dance with Me (C/L: R. Parker Jr.; David Robinson); Five, Six, Seven, Eight . . . DANCE!; I Go to Rio (C/L: Peter Allen; Adrienne Anderson); I Love to Dance (C: Billy Goldenberg; L: Alan Bergman; Marilyn Bergman); I'm Flying (C: Moose Charlap; L: Carolyn Leigh); It Only Happens when I Dance with You (C/L: Irving Berlin); It's Better with a Band; It's Not What You Weigh; Life Is a Dance (C/L: Gavin Christopher); Make Way for Tomorrow (C: Jerome Kern; L: Ira Gershwin; E.Y. Harburg); Neverland (C: Moose Charlap; L: Carolyn Leigh); One Step (C: David Shire; L: Richard Maltby Jr.); She Just Loves Las Vegas!; Singers Protest; Where Did You Learn to Dance (C: Josef

Myrow; L: Mack Gordon); You Mustn't Kick It Around (C: Richard Rodgers; L: Lorenz Hart)

Cast: Marge Champion; Don Correia; Sandy Duncan; Bill Irwin; Armelia McQueen; Rockettes, The; Ken Sacha

Notes: Harper/Zippel songs only ones written for this show.

1299 • FLAG IS BORN, A

OPENED: 09/05/1946   Theatre: Alvin
Play   Broadway: 120

Composer: Kurt Weill
Author: Ben Hecht
Producer: American League for a Free Palestine
Director: Luther Adler

Choreographer: Zamira Gon; **Costumes:** John Boyt; **Lighting Designer:** George Gabhardt; **Musical Director:** William Tarrasch; **Orchestrations:** Isaac Van Grove; **Set Design:** Robert Davison

Cast: Celia Adler; Luther Adler; Marlon Brando; Sidney Lumet; Quentin Reynolds

Notes: No songs in this production. This show was produced to raise money for the American League for a Free Palestine. The show raised over a million dollars in contributions with its tough anti-British stance. Some of the money raised went to buy a large yacht, christened the S.S. Ben Hecht. The Ship was used to carry refugees to Palestine. It was later captured by the British and afterwards became the flagship of the Israeli Navy. Note also the young Sidney Lumet in the cast of this show.

1300 • FLAHOOLEY

OPENED: 05/14/1951   Theatre: Broadhurst
Musical   Broadway: 40

Composer: Sammy Fain
Lyricist: E.Y. Harburg
Librettist: E.Y. Harburg; Fred Saidy
Producer: Cheryl Crawford
Director: E.Y. Harburg; Fred Saidy

Choreographer: Helen Tamiris; **Costumes:** David Ffolkes; **Lighting Designer:** Howard Bay; **Musical Director:** Maurice Levine;

Orchestrations: Ted Royal; **Set Design:** Howard Bay; **Vocal Arranger:** Maurice Levine

Songs: Arabian for 'Get Happy'; B.G. Bigelow, Inc.; Birds (C/L: Moises Vivanco); Christmas Song [3]; Come Back Little Genie; Consternation; Day Late and a Dollar Short [4]; Enchantment (C/L: Moises Vivanco); Finale; Flahooley; Happy Hunting; He's Only Wonderful; Here's to Your Illusions; I Whoever I Am [4]; In Times Like These; Inner Office Scene; Jump, Little Chillun; Lament; Little Bit of Magic [2] (C: Burton Lane); Najala's Lament (C/L: Moises Vivanco); Najala's Song of Joy (C/L: Moises Vivanco); No More Flahooleys!; Rock, Little Children [5]; Scheherazade Interlude [1]; Sing the Merry; Song of the Enchanted Rope [1]; Spirit of Capsulanti; Springtime Cometh, The; Stop the Flahooleys; Telephone Switchboard Scene; That Mysterious Lady Called Love [3] (C: J. Fred Coots); Where Has the Rainbow Gone? [6]; Who Said There Ain't No Santa Claus? (1); Who Said There Ain't No Santa Claus? (2) [2] (C: Burton Lane); World Is Your Balloon, The; You Need a Little Magic [3]; You Too Can Be a Puppet

Cast: Bil Baird's Marionettes; Lulu Bates; Barbara Cook; Irwin Corey; Jerome Courtland; Fay De Witt; Marilyn Ross; Yma Sumac; Ted Thurston; Rowan Tudor

Notes: *See also JOLLYANNA.* Lane was the original composer but left the project after completing three songs. Two are indicated in the song list. The third's music became "It Happens Every Time" from film GIVE A GIRL A BREAK. [1] Cut before opening. [2] Not used. Written for show by the original composer. When Harburg refused to work on the libretto, Lane withdrew. [3] ASCAP/Library of Congress. [4] Written in 1973. [5] Written in 1976. [6] Written in 1978.

1301 • FLAMS, THE

OPENED: 11/26/1894   Theatre: Bijou
Musical   Broadway: 32

Lyricist: Edward Paulton; Harry Paulton
Librettist: Edward Paulton; Harry Paulton
Director: W.D. Mann

Set Design: Homer F. Emens

Songs: Boating Song (C/L: William P. Brown); Dandy Colored Coon; Days of Long Ago; I

Don't Want to Play in Your Back Yard (C: H.W. Petrie; L: Phillip Wingate); Man That Broke the Bank at Monte Carlo, The (C/L: Fred Gilbert); Naughty Continong, The; Ours Is a Happy Little Home; Tommy Atkins

Cast: William F. Hoey; John C. Rice; Cheridah Simpson; Matt Woodward

Notes: There may not be any original songs in this show.

1302 • FLASHES OF THE GAY WHITE WAY

OPENED: 1925

Composer: George D. Weist [1]
Lyricist: Mack Gordon; Anton Scibilia

Songs: Hey, Hey, Fever; I'm a Little Jail Bird Looking for a Love Bird Like You; Snap Your Fingers

Notes: No other information available. [1] Later known as George David Weist.

1303 • FLATBUSH FOLLIES

OPENED: 1949
Revue

Songs: Brooklyn Belle (C/L: Zeke Manners)

Notes: No other information available.

1304 • FLATBUSH TOSCA

OPENED: 05/22/1975
Musical   Off-Off-Broadway

Composer: Don Crusar
Lyricist: Harvey Fierstein
Librettist: Harvey Fierstein
Director: Harvey Tavel

Source: TOSCA (Opera); **Arrangements:** Ned Levy; **Set Design:** Donald L. Brooks

Cast: Harvey Fierstein; Kevin Geer; Norman Jacob; Ned Levy; Luis Macia; Suzanne Smith; John Byron Thomas

Notes: No program available.

1305 • FLEUR-DE-LIS

OPENED: 08/29/1895   Theatre: Palmer's
Musical   Broadway: 65

Composer: William Furst
Lyricist: J. Cheever Goodwin
Librettist: J. Cheever Goodwin
Director: Richard Barker

Source: PERVENCHE (Musical: Henri Chivot; Alfred Duru); **Set Design:** Richard Marston

Cast: Jefferson De Angelis; Ida Fitzhugh; Della Fox; Melville Stewart; Alfred Wheelan

Notes: No songs listed in program.

1306 • FLIM-FLAM

OPENED: 1983
Musical

Composer: Albert Hague
Lyricist: Lee Adams
Librettist: Milburn Smith

Source: RANSOM OF RED CHIEF, THE (Story: O. Henry)

Songs: Big Day; Daughter of the Devil; Down on the Farm; Flim-Flam; Garden of Love, A; I Hope I Don't Love Him; I See . . .; Image of His Papa, The; La Cabeza . . .; Men!; Money Means Nothing to Me; Progress; Strictly Business; That's Me; What a Woman; What Is a Street Man; Without Me; You Go Your Way

Notes: Also known as SURPRISE! No program available.

1307 • FLIRTING PRINCESS, THE

OPENED: 11/01/1909   Theatre: La Salle
Musical   Chicago

Composer Joseph E. Howard
Lyricist: Frank Adams; Will M. Hough
Librettist: Frank Adams; Will M. Hough
Producer: Mort H. Singer
Director: Joseph C. Smith

Orchestrations: Hilding Anderson

Songs: Ask the Cabby; Cairo; He Loves My Dreamy Eyes (C/L: Harold Orlob); He's the

Champion of Them All, Little Maxie Rosenthal [2] (L: Vincent Bryan); I Fell in Love All By Myself [1]; I Would Rather Look at You Than Kiss Any Other Girl (C/L: Harold Orlob); It Looked Good to Me (C/L: Harold Orlob); I've Been Kissed in San Francisco (C/L: Harold Orlob); Les Deux Temps Parisienne (C/L: Harold Orlob); My Jack O'Lantern; Never Choose a Girl from Her Photograph (C/L: Harold Orlob); Oh, the Men (C/L: Harold Orlob); Opening Chorus; Pale Golden Star; Song of the Butterfly; Tell Her in the Golden Summer [1]; There Are Too Many Girls in the World; Vampire Dance; We Don't Believe It [1] (C/L: Harold Orlob)

Cast: Violet Dare; Harry Pilcer

Notes: Programs from Chicago 12/6/09 and Kansas City 8/20/10. [1] Sheet music only. [2] ASCAP/Library of Congress only.

1308 • FLO-FLO

OPENED: 12/20/1917   Theatre: Cort
Musical   Broadway: 220

Composer: Silvio Hein
Lyricist: Edward Paulton
Librettist: Fred De Gresac
Producer: John Cort
Director: Walter Brooks

Choreographer: David Bennett; **Costumes:** R. Kerner; **Musical Director:** Paul Schindler; Theodore Stearns

Songs: All I Want [3]; Any How, I'm Pleased to Meet You [1]; Behind the Fan [1]; Business Is Business; Don't Trust Them; Eccentric Dance; For the Sake of Auld Lang Syne [5] (C: Howard Whitney; L: Collin Davis); Girl of Pearl I Love You [5] (C: Howard Whitney; L: Collin Davis); Good-Bye Happy Days; Hon-o-lulu [1]; Hop Scotch [5] (C: Howard Whitney; L: Collin Davis); I Don't Know What You See in Me; If It Wasn't for My Wife and Family; In Spain; It Isn't Much [4]; Lingerie; Love's Paradise [2]; On the River Nile; Opening Act II; Pheira [5] (C: Howard Whitney; L: Collin Davis); Sarah from Sahara (C: Hugo Frey; L: George Edwards); That's the Kind of a Boy for Me; There's One Little Girl [5]; There's Only One Little Girl; When a Small Town Girl Meets a Small Town Boy (L: George Edwards); Wonderful Creature, A; Would You Love Me; Would You Say No?; Ziegfeld Girl, The

Cast: James B. Carson; Oscar Figman; Leon Leonard; Vera Michelena; Ruby Norton; Kate Stout; Frank Wilcox

Notes: [1] Out Wilkes-Barre 11/28/17. [2] Out Waterville 9/13/13. [3] Added New York City 1918. [4] From undated out of town program. [5] Sheet music only.

1309 • FLORA BELLA

OPENED: 09/11/1916   Theatre: Casino
Musical   Broadway: 112

Composer: Milton Schwarzwald
Lyricist: Percy Waxman
Librettist: Dorothy Donnelly; Cosmo Hamilton
Producer: John Cort
Director: Richard Ordynski

Source: FLORA BELLA (Musical: Andre Barde; Charles Cuvillier; Felix Doermann); **Choreographer:** Carl Randall; **Costumes:** Mme. Kerner; **Musical Director:** Gustave Salzer; **Set Design:** Joseph Urban

Songs: Adam (C: Charles Cuvillier); Blossom of My Own; Cat and Mice (C: Charles Cuvillier); Creep, Creep, the World's Asleep; Finale; Flora Bella (L: Earl Carroll); Flora Offering; Give Me All of You (L: Earl Carroll); Good Day, Good Night; Hail to the Golden Calf; Hypnotizing (C: Charles Cuvillier); It Is Very Hard to Bring Up Father (L: Percy Waxman); Love Is a Dance (C: Charles Cuvillier); On to Petrograd (C: Charles Cuvillier); Procession of Peasants (C: Charles Cuvillier); We'll Dance Till Dawn of Day; You're the Girl (L: Victor Schertzinger); Young Men Take a Tip from Me (C: Charles Cuvillier)

Cast: Lina Abarbanell; Charles Prucell

1310 • FLORA, THE RED MENACE

OPENED: 05/11/1965   Theatre: Alvin
Musical   Broadway: 87

Composer: John Kander
Lyricist: Fred Ebb
Librettist: George Abbott; Robert Russell
Producer: Harold Prince
Director: George Abbott

Source: LOVE IS JUST AROUND THE CORNER (Novel: Lester Atwell); **Choreographer:** Lee

Theodore; **Costumes:** Donald Brooks; **Dance Arranger:** David Baker; **Lighting Designer:** Tharon Musser; **Musical Director:** Harold Hastings; **Orchestrations:** Don Walker; **Set Design:** Jean Eckart; William Eckar

Songs: All I Need Is One Good Break; Dear Love; Express Yourself; Flame, The; Hello, Waves; I Believe You [1]; I Got a Right to Know [1]; Joke, The [2]; Keepin' It Hot [2]; Kid Herself, The [1]; Knock, Knock; Money in the Bank [1]; Not Every Day of the Week; Palomino Pal; Prologue; Quiet Thing, A; Sign Here; Sing Happy; Tree of Life Ballet, The; Unafraid; Where Did Everybody Go? [2]; You Are You; You Feel Too Much [1]

Cast: James Cresson; Cathryn Damon; Bob Dishy; Dortha Duckworth; Robert Kaye; Joe E. Marks; Liza Minnelli; Mary Louise Wilson

Notes: The music heard on the original cast album as the overture is really the exit music. [1] Cut prior to opening. [2] Written for 1987 Off-Broadway revival.

1311 • FLORENTINE GARDEN REVUE

OPENED: 1941   Theatre: Florentine Garden
Revue   Nightclub

Composer: Roy Ingraham
Lyricist: David Oppenheim
Librettist: Dave Gould

Songs: Golden Wedding Waltz, The; Swingin' with the Swing Shift

Cast: Jimmy Grier's Orchestra

Notes: Los Angeles club. No other information available.

1312 • FLORIDA GIRL

OPENED: 11/02/1925   Theatre: Lyric
Musical   Broadway: 40

Composer: Milton Susskind
Lyricist: Benjamin Hapgood Burt; Paul Potter
Librettist: Benjamin Hapgood Burt; William A. Grew; Paul Potter
Producer: Earl Carroll
Director: Earl Carroll

Songs: As a Troubador; Beautiful Sea; Chinky China Charleston; Collegians, The; Dance of the Porters; Daphne; Down to the Cellar [1]; Hysterical Ensemble [1]; Into Society; Lady of My Heart; Mr. and Mrs. [1]; Oh You!; Oranges; Skipper; Smile On; Take a Little Dip [1]; Travel, Travel, Travel; Treat 'Em Rough [1]; Trouble; Twice Told Tale, A [1]; Valse Ballet [1]; Venetian Skies; Wee Toy [1]

Cast: Lester Allen; Irving Bebee; Ritz Brothers, The; Vivienne Segal

Notes: Titled OH YOU out of town. [1] Out Washington, D.C. 10/5/25.

1313 • FLORODORA

OPENED: 11/10/1900   Theatre: Casino
Musical   Broadway: 505

Composer: Leslie Stuart
Lyricist: Ernest Boyd-Jones; Paul Rubens; Leslie Stuart
Librettist: Owen Hall; Frank Pixley
Producer: John C. Fisher; Thomas Ryley
Director: Willie Edouin; Lewis Hooper

Musical Director: Arthur Weld; **Set Design:** Moses & Hamilton

Songs: Beautiful Garden Girl [5]; Caramba [1] (C: Milan Roder; L: Harry B. Smith); Chorus of Welcome to Gilfain [1] (L: Ernest Boyd-Jones); Come and See Our Island; Come to St. Georges [10]; Credit's Due to Me, The (L: Ernest Boyd-Jones); Fellow Who Might Be Galloping, The (L: Ernest Boyd-Jones); Finale Act I [2] (L: Ernest Boyd-Jones); Flowers A-Blooming So Gay (L: Ernest Boyd-Jones); Have Your Bumps Read [8] (C: Cyril Ornadel; L: David Croft; Peter Croft); He Didn't Like the Look of It at All [4]; He Loves Me-He Loves Me Not; Hello People [11]; I Must Love Some One [2]; I Want to Be a Military Man (L: Frank Clement); I Want to Marry a Man, I Do (L: Paul Rubens); Island of Love, The [3] (C: Ivan Caryll; L: Aubrey Hopwood); I've an Inkling (C/L: Paul Rubens); Jack and Jill [5]; Land of Honor [7]; Love Will Find You [1]; Millionaire, The [1]; Opening Chorus Act II [2]; Phrenology (L: Ernest Boyd-Jones); Prapsis, The [6]; Queen of the Philippine Islands (C/L: Paul Rubens); Silver Star of Love [2] (L: Leslie Stuart); Somebody; Tact (L: Paul Rubens); Tell Me Pretty Maiden

(L: Leslie Stuart); Under the Shade of the Sheltering Palms (L: Leslie Stuart); We Are the Clerks [1]; We Get Up at 8 A.M. [1]; When an Interfering Person [2]; When I Leave Town (L: Paul Rubens); When We're on the Stage; When You're a Millionaire (L: Ernest Boyd-Jones); Willie Was a Gay Boy (L: Alfred Murray)

Cast: Sydney Deane; Willie Edouin; R.E. Graham; Daisy Green; Edna Wallace Hopper; Fannie Johnstone; Marjorie Relyea; Cyril Scott

Notes: [1] Added to revival of Broadway 1920. [2] Vocal selection only. [3] Sheet music only. [4] Added after London opening. [5] Added to 1915 London revival. [6] Added to 1931 London revival. [7] Added to score after 1931. [8] Added to 1950's English touring production. [10] Added to revival of Broadway 1920. From THE BELLE OF MAYFAIR. [11] Added to revival of Broadway 1920. From HAVANA

1314 • FLOSSIE

OPENED: 06/23/1924   Theatre: Lyric
Musical   Broadway: 23

Composer: Armand Robi
Lyricist: Ralph Murphy
Librettist: Armand Robi
Producer: Charles Mulligan
Director: Armand Robi

Choreographer: Jack Connors; **Lighting Designer:** Ben Leffler; **Musical Director:** Harold Lewis; **Set Design:** Nicholas Yellenti

Songs: Battle Cry of Freedom, The; Blind Man's Bluff; First Is Last, The; Flossie; 'Fraid Cat (C: Harold Lewis); I Want to Be a Santa Claus; I'm in Wonderland; Just Another New Step (C: Harold Lewis); Now Is the Time; Poogie-Woo; That's in My Line; Walla Walla; When Things Go Wrong You Will Be Mine [1]

Cast: Alice Cavanaugh; Doris Duncan; Sydney Grant

Notes: [1] Sheet music only.

1315 • FLOWER DRUM SONG

OPENED: 12/01/1958   Theatre: St. James
Musical   Broadway: 600

Composer: Richard Rodgers
Lyricist: Oscar Hammerstein II
Librettist: Joseph Fields; Oscar Hammerstein II
Producer: Joseph Fields; Oscar Hammerstein II; Richard Rodgers
Director: Gene Kelly

Source: FLOWER DRUM SONG, THE (Novel: C.Y. Lee); **Choreographer:** Carol Haney; **Costumes:** Irene Sharaff; **Dance Arranger:** Luther Henderson; **Lighting Designer:** Peggy Clark; **Musical Director:** Salvatore Dell'Isola; **Orchestrations:** Robert Russell Bennett; **Set Design:** Oliver Smith

Songs: Chop Suey; Don't Marry Me; Fan Tan Fannie; Gliding Through My Memoree; Grant Avenue; Hundred Million Miracles, A; I Am Going to Like It Here; I Enjoy Being a Girl; Like a God; Love Look Away; My Best Love [1]; Other Generation, The; Sunday; You Are Beautiful; You Be the Rock I'll Be the Roll

Cast: Patrick Adiarte; Larry Blyden; Anita Ellis; Juanita Hall; Arabella Hong; Ed Kenney; Keye Luke; Rose Quong; Jack Soo; Pat Suzuki; Miyoshi Umeki; Conrad Yama

Notes: [1] Cut prior to opening.

1316 • FLOWER OF THE RANCH, THE

OPENED: 04/20/1908   Theatre: Majestic
Musical   Broadway: 16

Composer: Joseph E. Howard
Lyricist: Joseph E. Howard
Librettist: Joseph E. Howard
Producer: Joseph E. Howard Amusement Co.

Songs: Baby Lou [4]; Big Banshee, The [5] (L: Frank R. Adams; Will M. Hough); Build a Little Fence Around Today [2] (L: Collin Davis); California, Claremont (L: Collin Davis); Christina Swanson [4]; Garrison Ball, The [1]; Gibson School Marm, The [2]; Girl Behind the Counter, The [2] (L: Bob Adams); I Need the Morning Air [4]; In the Days of '49; In the Shacks that Little Flower Built [1]; In Vaudeville; Just Say You Care; Light That Lies in Women's Eyes, The [1]; Love Up a Tree [1] (L: Collin Davis); Lu Lu Babe [3]; My Lolo Maid; My Old Town [4] (L: Frank R. Adams; Will M. Hough); Pajama and the Nightie, The; Round-Up, The [1];

Same Old Story, The [1] (L: Arthur Gillespie); Sweetheart Ties [3]; That's What a Fellow Does When He's in Love; Watching the Blue Smoke Curl (L: Collin Davis); What's the Use of Dreaming; Worried (L: Collin Davis)

Cast: La Petite Adelaide; Mabel Barrison; Joseph E. Howard; Edward Hume; A.A. Klein; Frederick Knight; J.P. McSweeney; Ike Oliver; Frederick Rogers

Notes: This show played the Majestic Theatre on Columbus Circle, not the current Majestic Theatre which was built in 1927. [1] Out Pittsburgh 2/30/08. [2] Out Kansas City 9/29/07. [3] Out Lincoln 10/4/10. [4] Sheet music only. [5] Out Pittsburgh 2/3/08. Also in THE UMPIRE.

1317 • FLOWERS FOR ALGERNON

Notes: *See CHARLIE AND ALGERNON.*

1318 • FLUFFY RUFFLES

OPENED: 09/07/1908   Theatre: Criterion
Musical   Broadway: 48

Composer: William T. Francis
Lyricist: Wallace Irwin
Librettist: John J. McNally
Producer: Charles Frohman
Director: Ben Teal

Source: FLUFFY RUFFLES (Comic Strip: Wallace Morgan); **Costumes:** Alfredo Edel; **Musical Director:** Gus Salzer

Songs: Aida McCluskie (C: Jerome Kern; L: C.H. Bovill); Dining Out (C: Jerome Kern; L: George Grossmith); Echo of My Heart; Evolution; Fluffy Ruffles; Get Your Partner for the Barn Dance (C: Joel P. Corin; L: Felix F. Feist); I Love to Sit and Look at You (C: Rooney; L: Edward Madden); I Wonder Why Jane Is a Suffragette; Look at You; Love's Bouquet (C/L: E.S. Brill); Meet Her with a Taximeter [2] (C: Jerome Kern; L: C.H. Bovill); Mrs. Cockatoo [4] (C: Jerome Kern; L: C.H. Bovill); O Rubber at the Swizzle Sisters [4]; Poor Old Fluff [1]; Salome [5] (L: John E. Hazzard); Screams [1]; Strolling [1]; Sweetest Girl, Silly Boy I Love You (Reckless Boy, I Love You) (C: Jerome Kern; L: Wallace Irwin); Take Care [4] (C: Jerome Kern; L: C.H.

Bovill); That's a Thing That's Really Wanted [3] (C: Jerome Kern; L: C.H. Bovill); There's Something Rather Odd About Augustus (C: Jerome Kern; L: C.H. Bovill); Willie's Got Another Girl Now (C: Leigh; L: Paul Potter); Won't You Harmonize with Me; Won't You Let Me Carry Your Parcel (C: Jerome Kern; L: C.H. Bovill)

Cast: John Bunny; Jack Gardner; George Grossmith; Violet Heming; Mabel Mercer; Adele Rowland

Notes: [1] Cut out of town. [2] Not in programs. [3] Not used. [4] Sheet music only. [5] Cut out of town. ASCAP credits Joseph E. Howard with music. Credits above from sheet music.

1319 • FLY BLACKBIRD

OPENED: 02/05/1962   Theatre: Mayfair
Musical   Off-Broadway: 127

Composer: James Hatch; C. Jackson
Lyricist: James Hatch; C. Jackson
Librettist: Jerome Eskow; James Hatch; C. Jackson
Producer: Helen Jacobson
Director: Jerome Eskow

Choreographer: Talley Beatty; **Costumes:** Robert Soule; **Lighting Designer:** Jules Fisher; **Musical Director:** Gershon Kingsley; **Orchestrations:** Gershon Kingsley; **Set Design:** Robert Soule; **Vocal Arranger:** Gershon Kingsley

Songs: Big Betty's Song; Couldn't We; Everything Comes to Those Who Wait; Fly Blackbird; Gong Song, The; I'm Sick of the Whole Damn Problem; Lilac Tree; Love Elixir, The; Mister Boy; Natchitoches, Louisiana; Now; Old White Tom; 'Ousing Cha-Cha, The; Right Way; Rivers to the South; Step on a Stone [1]; Think It Over [1]; Twilight Song; Wake Up; Who's the Fool? [1]

Cast: Helon Blount; Jack Crowther; Micki Grant; Robert Guillaume; Avon Long; Mary Louise; Thelma Oliver; Gilbert Price; Glory Van Scott

Notes: [1] Cut prior to opening.

1320 • FLY-BY-KNIGHTS, THE

Notes: *See THE RAMBLERS.*

1321 • FLY WITH ME

OPENED: 03/24/1920
Musical   Columbia University

Composer: Richard Rodgers
Lyricist: Lorenz Hart
Librettist: Lorenz Hart; Milton Kroopf; Philip Leavitt

Choreographer: Herbert Fields; **Musical Director:** Richard Rodgers

Songs: Another Melody in F; College on Broadway, A; Don't Love Me Like Othello [1]; Dreaming True; Gone Are the Days; Gunga Din; I Love You; If I Only Were a Boy; If You Were You; Inspiration; Moon and You, The (Moonlight and You) [1]; Peek-in Peking; Penny for Your Thoughts, A; There's Always Room for One More (L: Oscar Hammerstein II); Third Degree of Love, The; Twinkling Eyes (L: Richard Rodgers); Weaknesses (L: Oscar Hammerstein II); Working for the Government

Notes: Amateur production. [1] Also in SAY IT WITH JAZZ.

1322 • FLYING COLORS

OPENED: 09/15/1932   Theatre: Imperial
Musical   Broadway: 181

Composer: Arthur Schwartz
Lyricist: Howard Dietz
Librettist: Howard Dietz; Corey Ford; George S. Kaufman; Charles Sherman
Producer: Max Gordon
Director: Howard Dietz

Choreographer: Albertina Rasch; **Costumes:** Constance Ripley; **Lighting Designer:** Norman Bel Geddes; **Musical Director:** Al Goodman; **Orchestrations:** Robert Russell Bennett; Edward Powell; Arthur Schutt; Hans Spialek; **Set Design:** Norman Bel Geddes; **Vocal Arranger:** Robert Emmett Dolan; Andre Kostelanetz

Songs: All's Well; Alone Together; Celebration; Day After Day; Fatal Fascination [3]; It Was Never Like This; Just Around the Corner; Lost in the Crowd; Louisiana Hayride; Meine Kleine Akrobat [2]; Mother Told Me So; My Heart Is Part of You; Rainy Day, A; Riding Habit; Shine On Your Shoes, A; Smokin' Reefers; Triplets [1]; Two-Faced Woman

Cast: Larry Adler; Charles Butterworth; Imogene Coca; Buddy Ebsen; Vilma Ebsen; Tamara Geva; Patsy Kelly; George Kirk; Philip Loeb; Monette Moore; Jean Sargent; Clifton Webb; Jay Wilson

Notes: [1] Cut. Used in BETWEEN THE DEVIL. [2] Used later in British show FOLLOW THE SUN. [3] Added after opening.

1323 • FLYING HIGH

OPENED: 03/03/1930   Theatre: Apollo
Musical   Broadway: 355

Composer: Ray Henderson
Lyricist: Lew Brown; B.G. DeSylva
Librettist: Lew Brown; B.G. DeSylva; John McGowan
Producer: George White
Director: Edward Clarke Lilley; George White

Choreographer: Bobby Connolly; **Costumes:** Charles LeMaire; **Musical Director:** Al Goodman; **Set Design:** Joseph Urban

Songs: Air Minded; Good for You-Bad for Me; Happy Landing; I Could Love a Man Like That [1]; I'll Get My Man; I'll Know Him; I'm Flying High; Mrs. Krause's Blue-Eyed Baby Boy; Red Hot Chicago; Rusty's Up in the Air; Thank Your Father (Thank Your Mother); This Will Be The First Time for Me; Wasn't It Beautiful While It Lasted?; Without Love

Cast: Grace Brinkley; Russ Brown; Gale Quadruplets, The; Dorothy Hall; Bert Lahr; Pearl Osgood; Gus Schilling; Oscar Shaw; Kate Smith

Notes: [1] ASCAP/Library of Congress only.

1324 • FLYING ISLAND

OPENED: 1922
Musical   Unproduced

Composer: George Gershwin
Lyricist: Clifford Grey

Songs: Sweetheart [1]; When the Mites Go By [2]

Notes: No other information available. [1] Used in THE RAINBOW. Music later used for "Baby!" in TELL ME MORE. [2] Music later used for "When Cadets Parade," not used in ROSALIE.

1325 • FOGGY DAY, A

OPENED: 1987
Musical   Unproduced

Composer: George Gershwin
Lyricist: Ira Gershwin
Librettist: Neil Simon
Producer: Emanuel Azenberg

Songs: Do, Do, Do; Embraceable You; Foggy Day, A; Someone to Watch Over Me; They Can't Take That Away from Me

Notes: Following a workshop this musical was "postponed."

1326 • FOLIES BERGERE (1969)

OPENED: 1969
Revue

Composer: Henri Betti
Lyricist: Johnny Bradford
Librettist: Maynard Sloate
Producer: Michel Gyarmathy; Maynard Sloate

Arrangements: Jerry Fielding; **Choreographer:** Tony Charmoli; Anna Rudas; Tibor Rudas; **Costumes:** Michel Gyarmathy; **Set Design:** Michel Gyarmathy; **Vocal Arranger:** Randy Van Horne

Cast: Rita Agnese; George Carl; Fred Roby; Francois Szony; Bob Williams; Si Zentner & His Orchestra

Notes: Tropicana Hotel, Las Vegas. No songs listed in program.

1327 • FOLIES BERGERE COMPANY

OPENED: 04/27/1911   Theatre: Teller's
Revue   Broadway: 92

Composer: Robert Hood Bowers
Lyricist: Harry B. Smith; Robert B. Smith
Librettist: Channing Pollock [2]; Rennold Wolf [2]
Producer: Henry B. Harris; Jesse Lasky
Director: George Marion

Songs: Alexander's Ragtime Band [3] (C/L: Irving Berlin); Answer Me (C/L: Irving Berlin; Ted Snyder; C: Bryan; L: Vincent Bryan); Chic, Chic, Chic [1]; Dear Old Broadway [1] (C/L: Irving Berlin); Don't Stop Mr. Jenkinson [1] (C/L: Unknown); Down the Strand [1]; Down to the Folies Bergere (C/L: Irving Berlin; Vincent Bryan; Ted Snyder); Ensenanza [1]; He Reminds Me of Someone I Want to Forget [2] (C/L: Unknown); How Do You Do? [1] (C: Melville Gideon; L: Harold Atteridge); How'd You Like to Be the Shoe Store Man [2] (C: Maurice Levi); I Beg Your Pardon [1]; I'll Be a Sister to You [1]; Keep a Taxi Waiting, Dear [2] (C/L: Irving Berlin; Vincent Bryan; Ted Snyder); March of the Beauties of the Nation (inst.) [1]; March of the Delegations from All Parts of the World (inst.) [2]; March of the Infernal Guards [2]; March of the New York Clubs [2] (C: Maurice Levi); March of the Toreadors (inst.) [1]; Opening Chorus [1]; Piccadilly Band, The [1] (C: Melville Gideon; L: Harold Atteridge); Sarasa [1] (C/L: Unknown); Spanish Love [1] (C/L: Irving Berlin; Vincent Bryan; Ted Snyder)

Cast: Ina Claire; Laddie Cliff; Otis Harlan; Ada Lewis; Darl MacBoyle

Notes: This show contained three parts — HELL, TEMPTATIONS (a ballet) and GABY. [1] From GABY. [2] From HELL. [3] Cut out of town after one matinee performance in Atlantic City.

1328 • FOLIES BERGERE REVIEW, THE

OPENED: 04/15/1930
Revue

Composer: Eubie Blake
Lyricist: Will Morrissey; Jack Scholl
Producer: Will Morrissey

Choreographer: Nat Cash

Songs: Green Pastures [2] (L: Will Morrissey; Andy Razaf); Loving You the Way I Do [1]; Tropical Moon

Notes: No other information available. [1] Also in HOT RHYTHM. [2] Also in BLACKBIRDS OF 1930.

1329 • FOLLIES

OPENED: 04/04/1971   Theatre: Winter Garden
Musical   Broadway: 522

Composer: Stephen Sondheim
Lyricist: Stephen Sondheim
Librettist: James Goldman
Producer: Harold Prince
Director: Michael Bennett; Harold Prince

Choreographer: Michael Bennett; Costumes: Florence Klotz; Dance Arranger: John Berkman; Lighting Designer: Tharon Musser; Musical Director: Hal Hastings; Orchestrations: Jonathan Tunick; Set Design: Boris Aronson

Songs: Ah, but Underneath [6]; Ah, Paris!; All Things Bright and Beautiful [4]; Beautiful Girls; Bolero d'Amour (dance) (C: John Berkman); Bring on the Girls [2]; Broadway Baby; Can That Boy Fox Trot [1]; Could I Leave You?; Country House [6]; Don't Look at Me; God-Why-Don't- You-Love-Me Blues, The; I'm Still Here; In Buddy's Eyes; In Someone's Eyes [1]; It Wasn't Meant to Happen [1]; Little White House [1]; Live, Laugh, Love; Losing My Mind; Love Will See Us Through; Loveland; Make the Most of Your Music [6]; One More Kiss; Pleasant Little Kingdom [1]; Rain on the Roof; Right Girl, The; Road You Didn't Take, The; Social Dancing (inst.) [6]; Story of Lucy and Jessie, The; That Old Piano Roll [3]; Too Many Mornings; Uptown Downtown [1]; Waiting for the Girls Upstairs; Who Could Be Blue? [1]; Who's That Woman?; World's Full of Boys, The [5]; You're Gonna Love Tomorrow

Cast: Michael Bartlett; Helon Blount; Dorothy Collins; Ethel Barrymore Colt; Fifi D'Orsay; Graciela Daniele; Yvonne De Carlo; Harvey Evans; Victor Griffin; Mary Jane Houdina; Justine Johnston; Dick Latessa; Victoria Mallory; Mary McCarty; John McMartin; Michael Misita; Arnold Moss; Gene Nelson; Kurt Peterson; Marti Rolph; Virginia Sandifur; Ethel Shutta; Alexis Smith; Sheila Smith; Marcie Stringer; Jayne Turner

Notes: [1] Cut. [2] Cut. Added to the film STAVISKY as music "Auto Show." [3] Cut. Used as underscoring. [4] Cut. Music used as prologue. [5] Cut. Added to STAVISKY as incidental theme "Operette." [6] Added to 1987 London production.

1330 • FOLLIES OF 1909
Notes: See ZIEGFELD FOLLIES OF 1909.

1331 • FOLLIES OF 1910
Notes: See ZIEGFELD FOLLIES OF 1910.

1332 • FOLLIES OF THE DAY
OPENED: 1909   Theatre: Lincoln Square
Revue   New York

Composer: Albert Von Tilzer
Lyricist: Barney Gerard
Librettist: Barney Gerard
Producer: Milner & Gehard

Songs: Atlantic City; Finale; Give Me Old Broadway and I'll Be Satisfied; Honest, You're the Only One for Me; If Ever I Get in the White House Chair; I've Got No Use for Opera when There's Ragtime Around; My Banjo Girl; My Heart Goes Out to Dixieland; One Night Stand; Opening Chorus; Rigoletto; Roll Me Out on the Boardwalk; Rosa Rosetta; When I Hear My Country Calling; Would You Like to Learn to Like Me?; You're Just the Sort of Boy for a Girl Like Me

Cast: M. Clarke; Harry Fox; Gertrude Hayes; Florrie Millership; Lillian Millership; Ida Sturges; John West

1333 • FOLLOW A STAR
OPENED: 09/17/1930   Theatre: Winter Garden
Musical   London: 118

Composer: Vivian Ellis
Lyricist: Douglas Furber
Librettist: Douglas Furber; Dion Titheridge
Producer: Jack Hulbert; Paul Murray
Director: Jack Hulbert

Choreographer: Jack Hulbert; Costumes: Guy de Gerald; Musical Director: Sydney Baynes; Set Design: F.L. Lyndhurst

Songs: Don't Wear Your Heart on Your Sleeve; First Weekend in July, The; Follow a Star (L: Jack Yellen); I Never Can Think of the Words (L: Jack Yellen); If Your Kisses Can't Hold the Man You Love Your Tears Won't Bring Him Back (L: Jack Yellen); I'm an International Sweetheart (L: Jack Yellen); That's Where the South Begins (C: Ted Shapiro; L: Jack Yellen)

Cast: Phyl Arnold; Frederick Carpenter; Jack Clewes; Rosaline Corneille; Charles

Courtneidge; Jack Hulbert; Ted Shapiro; Sophie Tucker

1334 • FOLLOW ME

OPENED: 11/29/1916   Theatre: Casino
Musical   Broadway: 78

Composer: Sigmund Romberg
Lyricist: Robert B. Smith
Librettist: Leo Ascher; Felix Doermann
Producer: Messrs. Shubert

Source: WAS TUT MAN NICHT ALLES AUS LIEBE (Musical: Leo Ascher; Felix Doermann); **Choreographer:** Allan K. Foster; Jack Mason; **Musical Director:** Frank Tours

Songs: Adam Was the Only Lover; Bird of Gay Bohemia, The [2] (C: Harry Tierney; L: Anna Held); Bombo-Shay, The [2] (C: Turner Layton; L: Henry Creamer; Henry Lewis); Don't Play with Me (L: Unknown); Follow Me (C/L: Helen Trix); Fool Me [4] (C: Jack Wells; L: Alfred Bryan); Girls Are Getting Wiser (Every Day), The (C: Harry Tierney; L: Alfred Bryan; Anna Held); Happyland (C: Harry Tierney; L: Alfred Bryan); How Would You Like to Bounce a Baby on Your Knee (C: Harry Tierney; L: Alfred Bryan; Anna Held); I Always See Them Safely Home (C: Jack Gulon; L: Howard Johnson); I Am True to All; I Brought Red Roses in December to You [2] (C: Harry Tierney; L: Alfred Bryan; Anna Held); I Want to Be Good but My Eyes Won't Let Me (C: Harry Tierney; L: Alfred Bryan; Anna Held); It's a Cute Little Way of My Own [2] (C: Harry Tierney; L: Alfred Bryan; Anna Held); It's Making Me Love You All the More (C/L: Unknown); It's the Little Things That Count Most Ev'ry Way (C: Harry Tierney; L: Alfred Bryan); La Parisian Peacock [2] (C/L: Unknown); Little Bit of Nonsense, A; Love Is a Wonderful Thing [2] (C: Anatole Friedland; L: L. Wolfe Gilbert); Milady's Toilette Set (C: Harry Tierney; L: Alfred Bryan); My Bohemian Fashion Girl (C: Harry Tierney; L: Alfred Bryan); Oh I Want to Be Good but My Eyes Won't Let Me [6] (C: Harry Tierney; L: Alfred Bryan; Anna Held); Oh Johnny, Oh Johnny, Oh! (C: Abe Olman; L: Ed Rose); Sextette [3]; Stop Tickling Me; Tete-A-Tete with You, A; There's Just a Little Bit of Monkey Still Left in You and Me (C: James V. Monaco; L: Grant Clarke); There's Something About You Makes Me Love You [1] (C: Arthur Lange; L: Henry Lewis); Two Happy Tadpoles; Violin Song, The; What Did Eve Give Adam for Christmas (C/L: Henry Lewis); What Do You Want to Make Those Eyes at Me For (When They Don't Mean What They Say!) [3] (C: James V. Monaco; L: Howard Johnson; Joseph McCarthy); When a Man Is Single (C: Frank Tours); When the Girls Grow Older They Grow a Little Bolder [5] (C: George W. Meyer; L: Sam M. Lewis); Word of Love, A (C: Frank Tours)

Cast: Edith Day; Anna Held; Harry Tighe

Notes: [1] Out Standard Theatre, NYC 5/7/17. [2] Out Washington, D.C. 3/5/17. [3] Out Baltimore 2/26/17. [4] Not in program. [5] ASCAP credits as above and also to Jean Schwartz, Sam M. Lewis and Joe Young. [6] Sheet music only.

1335 • FOLLOW THE GIRL

OPENED: 03/02/1918   Theatre: 44th Street Roof
                               Garden
Musical   Broadway: 25

Composer: Zoel Parenteau; Sigmund Romberg
Lyricist: Harold Atteridge; Henry Blossom
Librettist: Henry Blossom
Producer: E. Ray Goetz; Raymond Hitchcock
Director: Edward Clark

Choreographer: Walter Brooks

Songs: Daddy Dear (C: Zoel Parenteau; L: Henry Blossom); Don't Lose Your Way [1] (C: Zoel Parenteau; L: Henry Blossom); Easy Come, Easy Go [2]; Ever By Your Side (C: Sigmund Romberg; L: Harold Atteridge); Everything Is Rosy Now [1] (C: B.G. DeSylva; L: Harold Atteridge); Honeymoon Land (C: Sigmund Romberg; L: Harold Atteridge); I Can't See You All [2]; I Like the Boys (C: Zoel Parenteau; L: Henry Blossom); I'm a Very Different Girl; I'm Married, I'm Single, I'm Divorced, I'm in Love [2]; It's the Only One for Me [2] (C: Zoel Parenteau; L: Henry Blossom); Life Is One Thing After Another [2]; Merry and Bright [2]; No Matter What or Where (C: Zoel Parenteau; L: Henry Blossom); On Our Little Merry-Go-Round (C: Zoel Parenteau; L: Henry Blossom); There's Always One You Can't Forget [1] (C: Zoel Parenteau; L: Henry Blossom); There's Something About You [2]; Under the Honeymoon [1] (C: Zoel Parenteau; L: Henry Blossom); Women, Wine and Jazz (C: Zoel Parenteau; L: Henry Blossom)

Cast: George Bickel; Walter Catlett; William Danforth; Jobyna Howland

Notes: In Stamford, Parenteau credited with book also. Parenteau also credited with lyricist in Stamford. Marc Connelly credited on sheet music. No New York program found. J.C. Huffman credited with direction in Best Plays. [1] Sheet music only. [2] Out Stamford 2/1/18. Zoel Parenteau also credited as a lyricist in Stamford.

1336 • FOLLOW THE GIRLS

OPENED: 04/08/1944   Theatre: 44th Street
Musical   Broadway: 882

Composer: Philip Charig
Lyricist: Milton Pascal; Dan Shapiro
Librettist: Guy Bolton; Eddie Davis; Fred Thompson
Producer: Albert Borde; David Wolper
Director: Harry Delmar; Fred Thompson

Choreographer: Catherine Littlefield; **Costumes:** Lou Eisele; **Lighting Designer:** Howard Bay; **Musical Director:** Will Irwin; **Orchestrations:** Charles L. Cooke; Joe Glover; Bobby Haggart; George Leeman; Walter Paul; Cornell Tannassy; Van Cleve; Ernie Watson; Julian Work; **Set Design:** Howard Bay; **Vocal Arranger:** Bobby Tucker

Songs: At the Spotlight Canteen; Follow the Girls; I Wanna Get Married; I'm Gonna Hang My Hat; John Paul Jones; Out for No Good; Thanks for a Lousy Evening; Today Will Be Yesterday Tomorrow; Twelve O'Clock and All Is Well; Where You Are; You Don't Dance; You're Perf

Cast: Irina Baranova; Jackie Gleason; Walter Long; Gertrude Niesen; Frank Parker; Buster West

1337 • FOLLOW THE PARADE

OPENED: 04/12/1936   Theatre: Mayan
Revue   Los Angeles

Composer: Jack Dale
Lyricist: Jack Dale
Librettist: Jack Robinson; Gene Stone
Producer: Federal Theatre Project
Director: Eda Edson; Jack Robinson; Gene Stone

Arrangements: Ross Maggio; **Costumes:** Edith McLaughlin; **Musical Director:** William Kranth; **Set Design:** Frederick Stover

Songs: Crazy House Suite; Dionne Quintuplets (C/L: Gene Stone); Falling Star (C/L: Gene Stone); Follow the Parade (L: Gene Stone); Magic Toy Shop [1]; On a Holiday; Paraphrase of St. Louis Blues; Pick Me Up; Watching the Parade Go By (C: Adrian Mack; L: Gene Stone)

Cast: Anna Chandler; Fern Dale; Richard Edwards; Rex Faulkner; Pat Kelly; Patsy King; Billy Mack; Carrie Snyder

Notes: Also produced on 5/16/36 at the Hollywood Playhouse. A Federal Theatre project production. [1] A one-act musical within this show.

1338 • FOLLOW THE SUN

OPENED: 02/04/1936   Theatre: Adelphi
Revue   London: 204

Composer: Arthur Schwartz
Lyricist: Desmond Carter; Howard Dietz
Librettist: Ronald Jeans; John Hastings Turner
Producer: Charles B. Cochran

Songs: Dangerous You [4] (L: Desmond Carter); Follow the Sun; How High Can a Little Bird Fly [1] (L: Howard Dietz); Meine Kleine Akrobat [2] (L: Howard Dietz); Nicotina (L: Desmond Carter); Sleigh Bells (L: Howard Dietz); Steamboat Whistle, The [3] (L: Howard Dietz)

Cast: Nick Long Jr.; Claire Luce

Notes: No program available. [1] From radio serial THE GIBSON FAMILY. [2] From FLYING COLORS. [3] From AT HOME ABROAD. [4] Melody same as "I'll Pay the Check" in STARS IN YOUR EYES.

1339 • FOLLOW THRU

OPENED: 01/09/1929   Theatre: 46th Street
Musical   Broadway: 401

Composer: Ray Henderson
Lyricist: Lew Brown; B.G. DeSylva
Librettist: B.G. DeSylva; Laurence Schwab
Producer: Frank Mandel; Laurence Schwab
Director: Edgar MacGregor

Choreographer: Bobby Connolly; **Costumes:** Kiviette; **Musical Director:** Al Goodman; **Set Design:** Donald Oenslager

Songs: Button Up Your Overcoat; Daring Gibson Girl, The; Follow Thru; He's a Man's Man; I Could Give Up Anything but You; I Want to Be Bad; It's a Great Sport; Married Men and Single Men; My Lucky Star; 1908 Life, The; (If There Were) No More You; Still I'd Love You; Then I'll Have Time for You; Wouldn't Fool Me, Would You?; You Wouldn't Fool Me

Cast: John Barker; Madeline Cameron; Irene Delroy; Jack Haley; Margaret Lee; Zelma O'Neal; Eleanor Powell

1340 • FOOL HOUSE, THE

OPENED: 1906
Musical   Closed out of town

Composer: George Fletcher
Lyricist: Harry Dull
Librettist: Lew Hastings
Producer: Harry Dull

Songs: Bit of Nonsense, A; Candy Kid (C: Searl Allen); Fool House, The; Forgetful Maid, A; Ghost of a Hoodoo Man; He Walked Right In; How'd You Like to Kiss a Girl Like Me; Jack Rose; Jolly Old Pirates; Jubilee; Look! Who's Here; Love, Love, Love; Ma Ma Ho Ne; Night Time; Nothing New Beneath the Sun; Rag Man, The; Tommy Robbins

Cast: John Hunting; Lew Hunting; Mollie Hunting; Tony Hunting

Notes: Program from Wilkes-Barre 12/13/06.

1341 • FOOLIN' OURSELVES

OPENED: 01/16/1957
Revue   Closed out of town

Composer: Billy Barnes
Lyricist: Bob Rodgers
Librettist: Bob Rodgers
Producer: Paul Gregory
Director: Gene Nelson; Bob Rodgers

Choreographer: Gene Nelson; **Costumes:** Roso Corbin; **Dance Arranger:** Walter Sheets; **Musical Director:** Richard Pribor;

Set Design: Joel Schiller; **Vocal Arranger:** Walter Sheets

Songs: Confidentially; Enterprising People; Extraordinary Girl; Fights, The [1]; Foolin' Ourselves [1]; Hellahahana; I Like Trains; Ivy League, The; Name of the State Is Texas!, The; Thirties, The; Too Long at the Fair [1]; Tyler M'Boy [1]; Vegas Revisited [1]; Where Are Your Children? [1]

Cast: Sue Carson; Joyce Jameson; Paul Jayson; Gene Nelson; Patti Regan

Notes: Songs and sketches listed, as program didn't differentiate. Produced in Santa Barbara, California. [1] Also in THE BILLY BARNES REVUE.

1342 • FOOLS RUSH IN

OPENED: 12/25/1934   Theatre: Playhouse
Revue   Broadway: 14

Composer: Will Irwin
Lyricist: Norman Zeno
Librettist: Viola Brothers Shore; Richard Whorf; Norman Zeno
Producer: William A. Brady; Marilyn Miller
Director: Leonard Sillman

Choreographer: Arthur Bradley; Chester O'Brien; Edwin Strawbridge; **Costumes:** Russell Patterson; **Musical Director:** Max Meth; **Orchestrations:** Robert Russell Bennett; Conrad Salinger; Hans Spialek; **Set Design:** Eugene Dunkel; Russell Patterson

Songs: After the Wedding [1]; Bacchanale [1] (C: Albeniz); Because You Might Say Yes [1] (C: Richard Lewine; L: June Sillman); Building Up to a Let-Down; Ca, C'est Sixth Avenue (C/L: Lee Brody; Richard Jones); Don't Be Like an Eskimo [1] (C/L: Bert Clarke; George Clarke); Ghost Town; Harlem Barcarolle [1] (C: Bascom Little Jr.; L: Lee Brody; June Sillman); I See Him Over There [1] (C/L: James Shelton); I Want to Dance; I'm Mad [1] (C: Alfred Simon); I'm So in Love; It's Not Their Mother [1] (C/L: Richard Lewine); Jazz Jubilee [1] (C: Goddard Lieberson); Jim Dandy; Ladies of Wealth [1]; Let's Hold Hands (C: Richard Lewine; L: June Sillman); Life of Sin; Love All; Love, Come Take Me; Napoleon; New Sensation; Not Me, Not Much [1]; Opening [1] (C/L: Richard Lewine); Opening Act II [1]; Party's Over, The; Personal

Appearance; Rhythm in My Hair; Shoes; Sitting Over There; Sixty Second Romance (C: Bud Harris; L: Lawrence Harris); Smiling at the Sea [1] (C: Warburton Guilbert; L: June Sillman); Song of Spring [1]; Story of Buster, The; They Mean It Baby [1]; Two Get Together; Waiting for Trolley Cars to Pass [1] (C/L: Ted Goldsmith; C: W. Post); We Have Thrown Our Dolls Away [1]; Wicked, Unwholesome, Expensive (C/L: John Rox); Willie's Little Whistle; Witch Woman [1] (C: Roy Krummer; L: Fred Cooper); Years Later [1]; Yesterday an Egg [1]

Cast: Cliff Allen; Miriam Battista; Betzi Beaton; Robert Burton; Vandy Cape; Imogene Coca; Elinor Flynn; Janet Fox; Billie Heywood; Peggy Hovenden; Dorothy Kennedy-Fox; Teddy Lynch; Billy Milton; Edward Potter; Leonard Sillman; Cyrena Smith; Roger Stearns; Karl Swenson; Miriam Todd; Olga Vernon; Charles Walters; O.Z. Whitehead; Richard Whorf

Notes: [1] Out of town summer 1934.

1343 • FOOTLIGHTS

OPENED: 08/19/1927   Theatre: Lyric
Revue   Broadway: 43

Composer: Harry Denny
Lyricist: Harry Denny
Librettist: Roland Oliver
Director: Bunny Weldon

Costumes: Mahieu; **Musical Director:** Oscar Radin; **Orchestrations:** Otto Drescher; **Set Design:** August Vimnera

Songs: Champagne; College Pals; Ducks Call It Luck, The; Footlight Walk; I Adore You (C: Rene Mercier; L: Sam Coslow; Ballard Macdonald); Just When I Thought I Had You All to Myself (C/L: Harry Denny; Joe Fletcher); Love-O-Love; Roam On, My Little Gypsy Sweetheart (C: Ted Snyder; L: Irving Kahal; Francis Wheeler); Sahara Moon (C/L: Harry Denny; Dave Ringle); Sure Sign You Really Love Me; You Can't Walk Back from an Aeroplane (C/L: Irving Bibo; William B. Friedlander)

Cast: Hazel Dean; Harry Denny; Jack Goyle; Le Roi Operti; Louis Sorin; J. Kent Thurber; Ruth Wheeler; Jack Wilson

Notes: Roland Oliver is Henry White. Title changed during run to BEYOND THE FOOTLIGHTS.

1344 • FOR COLORED GIRLS WHO HAVE CONSIDERED SUICIDE/WHEN THE RAINBOW IS ENUF

OPENED: 09/15/1976   Theatre: Booth
Revue   Broadway: 862

Author: Ntozake Shange
Producer: Woodie King Jr.; N.Y. Shakespeare Festival; Joseph Papp
Director: Oz Scott

Choreographer: Paula Moss; **Costumes:** Judy Dearing; **Lighting Designer:** Jennifer Tipton; **Set Design:** Ming Cho Lee

Songs: I Found God in Myself (C: Diana Wharton; L: Ntozake Shange)

Cast: Trazana Beverley; Laurie Carlos; Rise Collins; Aku Kadogo; Janet League; Paula Moss

Notes: Previously produced at the Henry Street Settlement's New Federal Theatre, then moved to the Public Theatre on 5/17/76 where it played 120 performances. The number of performances indicated above combines both the off-Broadway and Broadway runs.

1345 • FOR GOODNESS SAKE

OPENED: 02/20/1922   Theatre: Lyric
Musical   Broadway: 103

Composer: William Daly; Paul Lannin
Lyricist: Arthur Jackson
Librettist: Fred Jackson
Producer: Alex A. Aarons
Director: Priestly Morrison

Choreographer: Allan K. Foster; **Costumes:** Paul Arlington; **Musical Director:** William Daly; **Set Design:** P. Dodd Ackerman

Songs: All My Life [3] (C: Paul Lannin); All to Myself; Every Day (C: William Daly); French Pastry Walk, The (C: William Daly; Paul Lannin; L: Ira Gershwin; Arthur Jackson); Greatest Team of All; Hubby [2]; In the Days of Wild Romance; Oh Gee! Oh Gosh! (C: William Daly; L: Ira Gershwin); Opening Chorus; Someone (C: George Gershwin; L: Ira Gershwin); Tra-La-La [4] (C: George Gershwin; L: Ira Gershwin); Twilight; When Somebody Cares [1];

When You're in Rome; Whichness of the Whatness, The

Cast: Adele Astaire; Fred Astaire; Helen Ford; Vinton Freedley; Marjorie Gateson; John E. Hazzard; Charles Judels

Notes: Titled FOLLOW THROUGH in London. [1] Cut after opening. [2] Added after opening. [3] Sheet music only. [4] Cut after opening. Lyric later revised for film AN AMERICAN IN PARIS.

1346 • FOR LOVE OR MONEY

OPENED: 03/29/1977   Theatre: Circle Repertory
Revue   Off-Broadway: 9

Composer: Jason McAuliffe
Lyricist: Jay Jeffries
Producer: Circle Repertory Company
Director: Susan Lehman

Choreographer: Kathie Kallaghan; **Musical Director:** Daniel Glosser; **Set Design:** Michael Massee

Songs: Brief Encounter; Confessional; Counterpoint; Geography; Living Love; Mamma's Cooking; Other Alternatives; Snap Decision; Taboo or Not Taboo; That Happy Melody; Where Have I Been All My Life?

Cast: Kate Kelly; Ken Kimmins; Sharon Madden; Jason McAuliffe

1347 • FOR THE LOVE OF SUZANNE

OPENED: 10/29/1974   Theatre: Martinique
Musical   Off-Off-Broadway: 10

Composer: Deed Meyer
Lyricist: Deed Meyer
Librettist: Bill Galarno
Director: Robert Drean

Source: MASKED BALL, THE (Play: Alexandre Bisson; Albert Carre); **Choreographer:** Blair Hammond; **Costumes:** Trudy Barilum; **Lighting Designer:** Jeannean Babcock; **Musical Director:** Jerry DePuit; **Orchestrations:** Jerry DePuit; **Set Design:** Gregory Etchison

Songs: Dramatis Personnae; For the Love of Suzanne; God Fearing Wife; Greatest Show in

France, The; How It All Ends; Les Poulettes; Let's Not Say Goodbye; Meanwhile; Midnight Waltz, The; Nightmare; Remembering; Stranger & a Scandal, A; 'Til Then

Cast: Richard Flanders; Lucy Holmes; Jeanne Schlegel; Clifton Steere; Paul Thomas

1348 • FORBIDDEN BROADWAY

OPENED: 01/15/1982   Theatre: Palsson's
Revue   Nightclub: 2332

Lyricist: Gerard Alessandrini
Producer: Playkill Productions, Inc.
Director: Gerard Alessandrini; Michael Chapman; Jeff Martin

Costumes: Chet Ferris; **Musical Director:** Fred Barton

Songs: Forbidden Broadway (C/L: Gerard Alessandrini)

Cast: Gerard Alessandrini; Fred Barton; Bill Carmichael; Nora Mae Lyng; Chloe Webb

Notes: Only original song listed. The show changed during its long run. Parody lyrics were added to Broadway songs.

1349 • FORBIDDEN BROADWAY 1990

OPENED: 01/23/1990   Theatre: Theater East
Revue   Off-Broadway: 576

Composer: Gerard Alessandrini
Lyricist: Gerard Alessandrini
Producer: Jonathan Scharer
Director: Gerard Alessandrini; Phillip George

Costumes: Erika Dyson

Songs: Forbidden Broadway 90 Phantom of the Musical, The; Who Do They Know?

Cast: Suzanne Blakeslee; Philip Fortenberry; Jeff Lyons; Marilyn Pasekoff; Bob Rogerson

1350 • FORBIDDEN BROADWAY 1991 1/2

OPENED: 06/20/1991   Theatre: Theater East
Revue   Off-Broadway: 237

Composer: Gerard Alessandrini
Lyricist: Gerard Alessandrini
Producer: Jonathan Scharer
Director: Gerard Alessandrini

Costumes: Erika Dyson; **Musical Director:** Brad Ellis

Songs: Forbidden Broadway 1991 1/2; Phantom of the Musical, The; Who Do They Know?

Cast: Mary Denise Bentley; Suzanne Blakeslee; Brad Ellis; Herndon Lackey; Jeff Lyons

1351 • FORBIDDEN LAND, THE
OPENED: 01/16/1905
Musical   Closed out of town

Composer: Frederic Chapin
Lyricist: Guy F. Steeley
Librettist: Guy F. Steeley
Producer: Dearborn Theatre Management
Director: Joseph W. Herbert

Musical Director: Frank Palma

Songs: All Is Well; Almighty Dollar, The; Ay Vant to Go Back to Sveden; Hurrah for the Shassa Gail; I See My Picture in Your Eyes; I'm a Potentate; Love at First Sight; My Shassa Maid; My Venetian Maid [1]; Oh, Buddha!; Oh! Pity Me!; Three Maids and a Man; Tibetan Dance; Touring 'Round; We'll Put Him to Work [1]; We're the Jolly Chain Gang [1]; We're Tramps Upon Our Way; When My Brother Beats the Big Bass Drum; When My Name Is Writ in History

Cast: William Cameron; W.H. Clark; Ethel Johnson; Joseph A. Phillips; Mary Ryan; Gus Weinberg; Alma Youlin

Notes: [1] Sheet music only.

1352 • FORBIDDEN MELODY
OPENED: 11/02/1936   Theatre: New Amsterdam
Musical   Broadway: 32

Composer: Sigmund Romberg
Lyricist: Otto Harbach
Librettist: Otto Harbach
Producer: Sam H. Grisman; Jack Kirkland
Director: Macklin Megley; Jose Ruben

Costumes: Ten Eyck; **Musical Director:** Robert Emmett Dolan; **Orchestrations:** Don Walker; **Set Design:** Sergei Soudeikine

Songs: Blame It on the Night; Bucharest; Hear the Gypsies Playing; How Could a Fellow Want More; Just Hello; Lady in the Window; Moonlight and Violins; No Use Pretending; Opening; Shadows That Walk in the Night; Two Ladies and a Man; Waltz Fantasies; When a Girl Forgets to Scream; You Are All I've Wanted

Cast: Carl Brisson; Leo Chalzel; Lillion Clark; Joseph Greenwald; Daniel Harris; June Havoc; Ruby Mercer; Jack Sheehan; Arthur Vinton; Ruth Weston

1353 • FOREVER PLAID
OPENED: 05/20/1990   Theatre: Steve McGraw's
Musical   Off-Broadway

Librettist: Stuart Ross
Producer: Gene Wolsk
Director: Stuart Ross

Arrangements: James Raitt; **Choreographer:** Stuart Ross; **Costumes:** Debra Stein; **Lighting Designer:** Jane Reisman; **Musical Director:** James Raitt; **Set Design:** Neil Peter Jampolis

Cast: Gabriel Barre; Stan Chandler; Jason Graae; Guy Stroman

Notes: No original songs in this show.

1354 • FORTUNA
OPENED: 01/03/1962   Theatre: Maidman
Musical   Off-Broadway: 5

Composer: Francis Thorne
Lyricist: Arnold Weinstein
Librettist: Arnold Weinstein
Producer: Sam Cohn; John Wulp
Director: John Wulp

Source: FORTUNA CON 'F' MAISCULA (Play: Armando Curcio; Eduardo de Filippo); **Choreographer:** Glen Tetley; **Costumes:** Willa Kim; **Lighting Designer:** William Ritman; **Musical Director:** Jack Lee; **Orchestrations:** Jack Lee; Julian Stein; **Set Design:** William Ritman

Songs: Angelica; Call Him Papa; Checking the Facts; Fortuna with a Capital 'F' (L: Arnold Weinstein; John Wulp); Ice House Fire, The; In My Hat (L: Arnold Weinstein; John Wulp); Million Goes to Million; O Stomach of Mine, We Eat!; Police; Premeditated Luck; So What? Why Not!; Someone Such as Me; Speak in Silence; Speech; What a Lovely Dream (L: Arnold Weinstein; John Wulp)

Cast: Ted Beniades; Patricia Birch; Jane Connell; Gabriel Dell; Blaine Stauffer

1355 • FORTUNE TELLER, THE
OPENED: 09/26/1898 Theatre: Wallack's
Musical Broadway: 40

Composer: Victor Herbert
Lyricist: Harry B. Smith
Librettist: Harry B. Smith
Director: Julian Mitchell

Musical Director: Herman Perlet; **Set Design:** Joseph Physioc

Songs: Always Do As People Say You Should; Champagne Song; Chorus of Hussars; Entrance of the Count; Finale to Second Act; Guten Morgen, Buon Giorna, Bon Jour; Gypsy Jan; Here We Are, a Gypsy Troupe Quite Famous; Ho! Ye Townsmen; Hungaria's Hussars (Chorus of Huzzars); Lily and the Nightingale, The; Little Gypsy Sweetheart (Gypsy Love Song); March; Masstoso; Only in the Play; Opening Chorus of Schoolgirls; Power of the Human Eye, The; Romany Life (Czardas); Serenades of All Nations; She Said I Was So Lonely; Signor Monsieur Muldoni; Sing to Me Gypsy; Slumber On, My Little Gypsy Sweetheart (The Fortune Teller); Speak Irma, I Implore Thee; Thro' the Forest; Wher'er in the Thick of the Fight; With Lance in Rest

Cast: May Boley; Joseph Cawthorne; Richard Golden; Joseph Herbert; Alice Neilson; Marguerita Sylva

Notes: No songs listed in program.

1356 • FORTY-FIVE MINUTES FROM BROADWAY
OPENED: 01/01/1906 Theatre: New Amsterdam
Musical Broadway: 90

Composer: George M. Cohan
Lyricist: George M. Cohan
Librettist: George M. Cohan
Producer: Klaw & Erlanger
Director: George M. Cohan

Costumes: F. Richard Anderson; **Musical Director:** Frederic Solomon; **Set Design:** Ernest Albert; Frank Marsden; John Young

Songs: Forty-Five Minutes from Broadway; Gentlemen of the Press; I Want to Be a Popular Millionaire; Mary's a Grand Old Name; Retiring from the Stage [1]; So Long Mary; Stand Up and Fight Like Hell

Cast: Donald Brian; Victor Moore; Julia Ralph; Marion Singer; Fay Templeton

Notes: [1] Sheet music only.

1357 • '49ERS, THE
OPENED: 11/07/1922 Theatre: Punch and Judy
Revue Broadway: 15

Composer: Lewis E. Gensler; Arthur Samuels
Lyricist: Franklin P. Adams; Morrie Ryskind
Librettist: Robert Benchley; Marc Connelly; Howard Dietz; George S. Kaufman; Ring Lardner; Dorothy Parker; Morrie Ryskind
Director: Marc Connelly; George S. Kaufman; Howard Lindsay

Choreographer: Albert Carroll; **Costumes:** W.H. Matthews; **Set Design:** Sheldon K. Viele

Songs: Allegorical Blues, The (C: Lewis E. Gensler; L: Morrie Ryskind); Back Back Back to Akron (C: Lewis E. Gensler; L: Robert E. Sherwood); F.P.A. (C/L: Unknown); Power of Light (C: Morrie Ryskind; L: Howard Dietz)

Cast: Albert Carroll; Ruth Gillmore; Clyde Hunnewell; May Irwin; Howard Lindsay; Beryl Mercer; Margot Myers; Sidney Toler; Ira Uhr; Roland Young

Notes: No program available.

1358 • 41 IN A SACK
OPENED: 03/25/1960 Theatre: 41st St.
Musical Off-Broadway: 45

Composer: Martin Roman
Lyricist: Shai K. Ophir
Librettist: Shai K. Ophir
Director: Shai K. Ophir

Costumes: Brachah Klausner

Songs: American in Paris; Beggar and Poet; Between Me and Myself; Bistro; Cigarettes; Family Farewell; Flamenco Dancer; Gazelles; Gentlemen's Duel; Gladiators; Movie; Narcissus; Nightmare; Not My Day; Ode to Love; Prologue; Tiger; Voyeur As Conscience

Cast: Sol Backar; Barbara Loden; Shai K. Ophir; Nira Paaz

Notes: These may be dance numbers and not actual songs.

1359 • 42ND STREET

OPENED: 08/25/1980   Theatre: Winter Garden
Musical   Broadway: 3486

Composer: Harry Warren
Lyricist: Al Dubin
Librettist: Mark Bramble; Michael Stewart
Producer: David Merrick
Director: Gower Champion

Source: 42ND STREET (Novel: Bradford Ropes); 42ND STREET (Film: Rian James; James Seymour); **Choreographer:** Gower Champion; **Costumes:** Theoni V. Aldredge; **Dance Arranger:** Donald Johnston; **Lighting Designer:** Tharon Musser; **Musical Director:** John Lesko; **Orchestrations:** Philip J. Lang; **Set Design:** Robin Wagner; **Vocal Arranger:** John Lesko

Songs: About a Quarter to Nine [6]; Audition; Dames [3]; 42nd Street [1]; Getting Out of Town [8] (L: Mort Dixon); Go Into Your Dance [6]; I Know Now [5]; Lullaby of Broadway [4]; Shadow Waltz [2]; Shuffle Off to Buffalo [1]; Sunny Side to Every Situation [7] (L: Johnny Mercer); We're in the Money [2]; You're Getting to Be a Habit with Me [1]; Young and Healthy [1]

Cast: Joseph Bova; Danny Carroll; Robert Colston; Carole Cook; Don Crabtree; Tammy Grimes; Jerry Orbach; Stan Page; Karen Prunczik; Lee Roy Reams; Wanda Richert; Ron Schwinn

Notes: No songs original to this production. Book called "Lead-Ins and Crossovers" in program.

[1] From film 42ND STREET. [2] From film GOLD DIGGERS OF 1933. [3] From film DAMES. [4] From film GOLD DIGGERS OF 1935. [5] From film THE SINGING MARINE. [6] From film GO INTO YOUR DANCE. [7] From film HARD TO GET. [8] From song "Gotta Go to Town" originally in THE LAUGH PARADE.

1360 • FORWARD MARCH (1914)

OPENED: 04/13/1914
Musical   Closed out of town

Composer: John Golden
Lyricist: Frank Craven; John Golden
Librettist: John Golden
Producer: George M. Cohan; Sam H. Harris
Director: Sam Forrest; Julian Mitchell

Source: LOVE AMONG THE LIONS (Unknown: F. Anstey)

Songs: Circus Band, The; Clown and the Bareback Riders, The; Exactly Like a Man; I Ain't to Blame; I'll Do It for You; I'm Going to Be Married Today; Take Me Along; We Want Our Pay; Wedding March; You've Got to Pay for What You Get; You've Still Got a Lot to Learn; Zoological Rag

Cast: Charles Dow Clark; William Collier; Lenora Navasio; Clara Palmer

Notes: Program of Atlantic City 4/13/14.

1361 • FORWARD MARCH (1932)

OPENED: 1932
Musical

Notes: *See STRIKE ME PINK.*

1362 • FOUR BELOW

OPENED: 03/04/1956   Theatre: Upstairs at the
                                       Downstairs
Revue   Nightclub

Composer: Michael Brown; Murray Grand; Bud McCreery; Harvey Schmidt; William Sheidy
Lyricist: Michael Brown; Murray Grand; Tom Jones; Bud McCreery; William Sheidy
Producer: Julius Monk
Director: John Heawood

Musical Director: Murray Grand

Songs: Candygram Song, The (C: Claibe Richardson; L: Kenward Elmslie)

Cast: June Ericson; Jack Fletcher; Dody Goodman; Gerry Matthews; Pianist: Murray Grand; Stan Keen

Notes: No other information available.

1363 • FOUR BELOW STRIKES BACK

OPENED: 09/24/1969   Theatre: Upstairs at the Downstairs
Revue   Nightclub

Librettist: Herbert Hartig; Tom Jones; Lois Korey; John Meyer
Producer: Julius Monk
Director: Julius Monk

Vocal Arranger: William Roy

Songs: Castro Tango!, The (C/L: Bruce Williamson); Charlie Chan (C/L: William Roy); Family Fallout Shelter (C/L: Bruce Williamson); Four Seasons (C: William Roy; L: Louis Botto); It's a Wonderful Day to Be Seventeen (C: Ronny Graham; L: Tom Jones); Jefferson Davis Tyler's General Store [1] (C/L: Edward C. Redding); Leave Your Mind Alone (C/L: Ronny Graham); Lola Montez (C/L: Michael Brown); Love, Here I Am (C/L: Walter Marks); Man Tan (C/L: Ronny Graham); Merry-Go, Merry-Go-Round (C/L: G. Wood); Opening (C/L: Bud McCreery); Payola (C: William Roy; L: Bruce Williamson); Sitwells, The (C/L: Bud McCreery); Speak No Love (C/L: Edward C. Redding)

Cast: Nancy Dussault; George Furth; Jenny Lou Law; Cy Young; Pianist: Robert Colston; Paul Trueblood

Notes: [1] Also in TONGUE IN CHEEK (1958).

1364 • FOUR IN HAND

OPENED: 11/1967   Theatre: PLaza 9-
Revue   Nightclub

Producer: Julius Monk

Songs: Race of the Lexington Avenue Express, The [1] (C: Harvey Schmidt; L: Tom Jones); Take a Trippie with a Hippie; That New-Time Religion (C/L: June Reizner)

Cast: Terry O'Mara; Rex Robbins; Liz Sheridan; Mary Louise Wilson; Alex Wipf

Notes: [1] From DEMI-DOZEN.

1365 • FOUR JEWS IN A ROOM BITCHING
Notes: *See MARCH OF THE FALSETTOS.*

1366 • FOUR SAINTS IN THREE ACTS

OPENED: 02/20/1934   Theatre: 44th Street
Opera   Broadway: 48

Composer: Virgil Thompson
Lyricist: Gertrude Stein
Librettist: Maurice Grosser
Producer: Harry Moses
Director: John Houseman

Choreographer: Frederick Ashton; **Costumes:** Kate Drain Lawson; **Lighting Designer:** Feder; **Musical Director:** Alexander Smallens; **Set Design:** Florine Stettheimer; **Vocal Arranger:** Eva Jessye

Cast: Abner Dorsey; Altona Hines; Bruce Howard; Edward Matthews; Beatrice Robinson-Wayne

Notes: No musical numbers listed. Eva Jessye credited as Choral Director.

1367 • FOUR SEASONS, THE
Notes: *See THE AUTO RACE.*

1368 • FOURFLUSHER, THE

OPENED: 04/13/1925   Theatre: Apollo
Play   Broadway: 56

Author: Cesar Dunn
Producer: Mark Hilliard

Songs: Wondering (C: Harry Ruby; L: Bert Kalmar)

Cast: Louise Allen; Spencer Charters; Margaret Dumont; Russell Mack; John Daly Murphy; Edward Poynter; Nan Sunderland

Notes: No program available.

1369 • 1491

OPENED: 10/28/1969   Theatre: Dorothy
                           Chandler Pavilion
Musical   Los Angeles

Composer: Meredith Willson
Lyricist: Meredith Willson
Librettist: Ira Barmark; Richard Morris; Meredith Willson
Producer: Edwin Lester; San Francisco Civic Light Opera; Los Angeles Civic Light Opera
Director: Richard Morris

Choreographer: Danny Daniels; **Costumes:** Miles White; **Dance Arranger:** Julian Stein; **Lighting Designer:** Peggy Clark; **Musical Director:** Julian Stein; **Orchestrations:** Irwin Kostal; **Set Design:** Oliver Smith; **Vocal Arranger:** Julian Stein

Songs: Birthday . . .; But I Will Never Say [2]; Every Woman Is a Queen [2]; For My Glory Land; Genius; Get a Map; Glory-Land Intro [2]; I'll Never Say I Love You; Isabella Catholica [2]; Lady; Lash the Wheel [1]; Near but Never Too Near; One Does Not Smile [2]; Pretty Girl [2]; Queen and the Sailor, The; River Song, The; Sail On [1]; Siege at Loha [2]; Silken Song, The; Tio Paco; Trastmara Rose, The; What Does a Queen Have? [1]; Why Not; With Love [2]; Woman; Wonderful Plan, The

Cast: Steve Arlen; Gino Conforti; John Cullum; Jean Fenn; Kathryn Hays; Chita Rivera

Notes: [1] Dropped after opening. [2] Unused. [3] ASCAP/Library of Congress only.

1370 • FOURTH AVENUE NORTH

OPENED: 09/27/1961   Theatre: Madison Avenue
                            Playhouse
Revue   Off-Broadway: 2

Composer: Bill Borden
Producer: Michael Batterberry; Shippen Geer
Director: Michael Batterberry

Choreographer: Tilda Morse; **Costumes:** John Pratt; **Lighting Designer:** Joseph Stell; **Musical Director:** Leslie Harnley; **Set Design:** Joseph Stell

Songs: Beauty Treatment (C: Bob Kessler; L: Martin Charnin); Christmas Trees (C: Leslie Harnley; L: Richard Craven); Fourth Avenue North (C: Charles S. Marvin); Hold Me (L: Shippen Geer); Institute for Psychodrama (C: Robert Dennis); Jenny (C: Cy Walter; L: Chilton Ryan); Let's Not Go Away This Summer (C/L: Bill Borden); Lonely Heartache; Lonely Man (C: George Allen; L: Glen Mallin); Love at an Auction (C/L: Murray Grand); Mr. Corbett (L: Charles S. Marvin); So Long As He Loves You (C/L: Bart Howard); Troubador (C: G. Bertoncini; L: W. Dwyer; J. Harvey); White Russian New York (C: T. LeGrady)

Cast: Clint Anderson; Linda Lavin; Gerrianne Raphael

Notes: Songs and sketches not differentiated in program.

1371 • FOURTUNE

OPENED: 04/27/1980   Theatre: Actors'
                            Playhouse
Musical   Off-Broadway: 241

Composer: Ronald Melrose
Lyricist: Bill Russell
Librettist: Bill Russell
Producer: Jonathan Scharer
Director: Ron Troutman

Choreographer: Troy Garza; **Costumes:** Joan Culkin; **Dance Arranger:** Janet Hood; **Lighting Designer:** Michael Newton-Brown; **Musical Director:** Janet Hood; **Set Design:** Harry Silverglat; **Vocal Arranger:** Janet Hood

Songs: Complications; Fantasy; Four Part Harmony; Fourtune; Funky Love; I'd Rather Be a Fairy than a Troll; I'll Try It Your Way; Making It; No One Ever Told Me Love Would Be So Hard; On the Road; Rich and Famous; What Do I Do Now?; Women in Love

Cast: Ken Arthur; Gail Hebert; Barbara Richardson; Justin Ross

1372 • FOXFIRE

OPENED: 11/11/1982   Theatre: Ethel Barrymore
Play   Broadway: 213

Composer: Jonathan Holtzman

Lyricist: Susan Cooper; Hume Cronyn; Jonathan Holtzman
Author: Susan Cooper; Hume Cronyn

Source: FOXFIRE (Book: Eliot Wiggenton);
Costumes: Linda Fisher; **Lighting Designer:** Ken Billington; **Musical Director:** Jonathan Holtzman; **Orchestrations:** Jonathan Holtzman; **Set Design:** David Mitchell

Songs: Cornshucking; Dear Lord; I Don't Wanna Talk About Her [1]; I Wish I Knew Now [1]; My Feet Took T'Walkin'; Sweet Talker

Cast: Keith Carradine; Hume Cronyn; Jessica Tandy; Trey Wilson

Notes: [1] Out Stamford prior to Broadway.

1373 • FOXY

OPENED: 02/16/1964   Theatre: Ziegfeld
Musical   Broadway: 72

Composer: Robert Emmett Dolan
Lyricist: Johnny Mercer
Librettist: Ian McLellan Hunter; Ring Lardner Jr.
Producer: David Merrick
Director: Robert Lewis

Source: VOLPONE (Play: Ben Jonson);
Choreographer: Jack Cole; **Costumes:** Robert Fletcher; **Dance Arranger:** Hal Schaefer; **Lighting Designer:** Robert Randolph; **Musical Director:** Donald Pippin; **Orchestrations:** Eddie Sauter; Hal Schaefer; **Set Design:** Robert Randolph; **Vocal Arranger:** Donald Pippin

Songs: Bon Vivant; Case of Rape, A [1]; Celia's First Essay [1]; Child of the West, A [1]; Delta's Lament [2]; Foxy [2]; I'll Get Even [2]; I'm Way Ahead of the Game; In Loving Memory [1]; It's Easy When You Know How; Larceny and Love; Letter of the Law, The [1]; Life's Darkest Moment [1]; Many Ways to Skin a Cat; Money Isn't Everything; My Weight in Gold; Power of Love, The [1]; Prologue; Rabbit's Foot [2]; Respectability [1]; Rollin' in Gold; Run, Run, Run Cinderella; S.S. Commodore Ebenezer McAffee the Third; Share and Share Alike [1]; Shivaree [1]; Take It from a Lady [1]; Talk to Me Baby; This Is My Night to Howl; Till It Goes Outta Style [1]

Cast: Larry Blyden; Cathryn Damon; John

Davidson; Edward Greenhalgh; Robert H. Harris; Bert Lahr; Julienne Marie; David Rounds

Notes: [1] Cut prior to opening. [2] ASCAP/Library of Congress only.

1374 • FOXY GRANDPA

OPENED: 02/17/1902   Theatre: 14th St.
Musical   Broadway: 120

Composer: Joseph Hart
Lyricist: Joseph Hart
Librettist: R. Melville Baker

Source: FOXY GRANDPA (Comic Strip: Charles Schultze); **Musical Director:** William H. Batchelor

Songs: Banjo Dance; Barn Dance, The; Bathing Lesson, The; Before and After Taking; Country Club, The; Country Quadrille; Dancing Dollies; First Submarine Boat, The; Frisa Linda; Funny Family, The; La Parisienne; Military Charley; My Clementine; Neapoli; Polly; Story of Two Bad Boys, The; Tight Rope Walker, The

Cast: Clifton Crawford; Carrie DeMar; Joseph Hart

1375 • FOXY QUILLER

OPENED: 11/05/1900   Theatre: Broadway
Musical   Broadway: 50

Composer: Reginald De Koven
Lyricist: Harry B. Smith
Librettist: Harry B. Smith
Producer: Klaw & Erlanger Opera Co.
Director: Ben Teal

Costumes: F. Richard Anderson; **Musical Director:** A. DeNovellis

Songs: Cheating Peddler, The; Foxy Quiller's Entrance Chorus; Mandolin Serenade; Polly Wants a Cracker; Quiller Has the Brain; Shepherd's Duet; Song of the Sword, The [1]; Strollers, The; Swearing Skipper, The; Winding, Winding

Cast: Georgia Caine; Josie Intropodi; Harry MacDonough; Julius Steger; W.G. Stewart; Jerome Sykes; Adolph Zink

Notes: Sometimes titled FOXY QUILLER IN CORSICA. [1] Not in program.

1376 • FOXY QUILLER IN CORSICA

Notes: *See FOXY QUILLER.*

1377 • FRANCIS

OPENED: 12/15/1981   Theatre: St. Peter's Church
Musical   Off-Broadway: 30

Composer: Steven Jankowski
Lyricist: Kenny Morris
Librettist: Joseph Leonardo
Producer: Praxis Group
Director: Frank Martin

Costumes: Martha Kelly; **Lighting Designer:** Thomas Bowen; **Musical Director:** Larry Esposito; **Set Design:** Neil Bierbower; **Vocal Arranger:** Larry Esposito

Songs: All the Time in the World; Ballet San Damiano; Bidding the World Farewell; Canticle of Pleasure; Fire in My Heart, The; For the Good of Brotherhood; Francis; I'm Ready Now!; Legend of King Arthur, The; Legend of Old Rufino, The; Miracle Town; New Madness, The; Oh, Brother!; Praises to the Sun!; Road to Paradise, The; Serenade; Two Keys; Walking All the Way to Rome

Cast: Lloyd Battista; John Dossett; Kenny Morris; Donna Murphy; Tom Rolfing; K.C. Wilson

1378 • FRANK FAY'S FABLES

OPENED: 02/06/1922   Theatre: Park
Revue   Broadway: 32

Composer: Clarence Gaskill
Lyricist: Clarence Gaskill
Librettist: Frank Fay
Producer: Harry L. Cort
Director: Frank Fay

Choreographer: Kuy Kendall; **Costumes:** Ann Burrows; Helen A. Haas; William H. Matthews; **Musical Director:** Gus Salzer; **Set Design:** P. Dodd Ackerman

Songs: Arms of the China Wall; Baby Moon; Columbus Wouldn't Know Columbus Circle As It Is Today; Fables (Don't Believe Their Fables); It's a Pop, Pop, Popular Song; It's Up to a Cop to Cop a Pretty Maid; Merry Little Widows, The; My Land; Oh, What a Happy Day; That Swanee River Melody; Two Are One (You Need Two Souls but One Thought)

Cast: Frank Fay; Bernard Granville; Helen Groody; Olga Steck

1379 • FRANK GAGLIANO'S CITY SCENE

Notes: Title of two one-act plays, one with music. *See PARADISE GARDENS EAST.*

1380 • FRANK MERRIWELL, OR HONOR CHALLENGED

OPENED: 04/24/1971   Theatre: Longacre
Musical   Broadway: 1

Composer: Larry Frank; Skip Redwine
Lyricist: Larry Frank; Skip Redwine
Librettist: Larry Frank; Heywood Gould; Skip Redwine
Producer: Stanley Barnett; Sandy Farber
Director: Neal Kenyon

Source: FRANK MERRIWELL'S SCHOOL DAYS (Novel: Burt L. Standish); **Choreographer:** Neal Kenyon; Conductor: Jack Holmes; **Costumes:** Frank Thompson; **Dance Arranger:** Jack Holmes; **Lighting Designer:** John Gleason; **Musical Director:** Jack Lee; **Orchestrations:** Arnold Goland; **Set Design:** Tom H. John; **Vocal Arranger:** Jack Lee

Songs: Broadway of My Heart, The; Don't Turn His Picture to the Wall; Fallin'-Out-of-Love Rag, The; Frank, Frank, Frank; Howdy, Mr. Sunshine; I'd Be Crazy to Be Crazy Over You; In Real Life; Inza; Ladies Auxilliary Picnic Community, The [1]; Look for the Happiness Ahead; Manuel Your Friend; Now It's Fall; Only Our Love [1]; Only Yesterday [1]; Prim and Proper; Pure in Heart, The; There's No School Like Our School; Winter's Here

Cast: Walter Bobbie; Linda Donovan; Larry Ellis; Bill Hinnant; Neva Small; Gary Keith Stevens

Notes: [1] Cut prior to opening.

1381 • FRANK SILVERS REVUE
OPENED: 1925
Revue

Composer: Sam Coslow; Frank Silvers
Lyricist: Sam Coslow; Frank Silvers

Songs: Call of the Great White Way, The; Icky Wicky Woo

Notes: No other information available. ASCAP/Library of Congress only.

1382 • FRANKIE
OPENED: 10/06/1989   Theatre: York
Musical   Off-Off-Broadway

Composer: Joseph Turrin
Lyricist: Gloria Nissenson
Librettist: George Abbott
Director: George Abbott; Donald Saddler

Source: FRANKENSTEIN (Novel: Mary Shelley)

Notes: No songs listed in program.

1383 • FREAKING OUT OF STEPHANIE BLAKE, THE
OPENED: 10/30/1967   Theatre: Eugene O'Neill
Play   Broadway

Composer: Jeff Barry
Lyricist: Jeff Barry
Author: Richard Chandler
Producer: Cheryl Crawford; Carl Schaeffer
Director: Michael Kahn

Costumes: Jeanne Button; **Lighting Designer:** Ben Edwards; Jean Rosenthal; **Set Design:** Ben Edwards; Jean Rosenthal

Cast: Jean Arthur; Frankie Cover; William Devane; Joseph Hardy; Jan Miner

Notes: Closed in previews. No songs listed in program.

1384 • FREDERIKA
OPENED: 02/04/1937   Theatre: Imperial
Musical   Broadway: 94

Composer: Franz Lehar

Lyricist: Edward Eliscu
Librettist: Edward Eliscu
Producer: Messrs. Shubert
Director: Hassard Short

Source: FREDERICA (Musical: Harry Pepper; Adrian Ross); **Source:** FRIEDERIKE (Operetta: Ludwig Hezer; Fritz Lohner-Beda); **Choreographer:** Chester Hale; **Costumes:** William Weaver; **Musical Director:** Hilding Anderson; **Orchestrations:** William Challis; **Set Design:** Watson Barratt

Songs: Bane of Man, The; I Asked My Heart; Jealousy Begins at Home; Kiss to Remind You, A; One; Out in the Sun; Rising Star; Rose in the Heather; Shepherd Ballet, The; Stormy Love; Why Did He Kiss My Heart Awake?; Word to Remind You, A

Cast: Todd Bolender; Charles Columbus; Helen Gleason; Edith Gresham; Dennis King; Edith King; Doris Patston; George Trabert; Ernest Truex; Arthur Vinton

1385 • FREE AND EASY
OPENED: 12/17/1959
Musical

Composer: Harold Arlen
Lyricist: Johnny Mercer
Producer: Stanley Chase
Director: Robert Breen

Musical Director: Quincy Jones

Songs: Baby's Born, A [5]; Bees 'n' Flowers; Bettin' Calls; Black Magic [4]; Blind Man; Blow de Whistle; Blues Boogie; Blues in the Night [3]; Cake Song; Cakewalk Turns: Blues (inst.); Cakewalk Turns: Boogie (inst.); Cakewalk Turns: Dixieland (inst.); Cakewalk Turns: Genteel Bastard (inst.); Cakewalk Turns: Minuet (inst.) [10]; Cakewalk Turns: Pandemonium (inst.); Cakewalk Turns: Soft-Shoe, Sword Dance (inst.); Cakewalk Turns: Tambourine (inst.); Cakewalk Turns: Tangissimo (inst.); Cakewalk Turns: Waltz (inst.); Cakewalk Your Lady [1]; Champagne fo' de Lady; Come Rain or Come Shine [1]; Conjure Man; Curse; De Right Answer; Della's Entrance (Whatcha Sayin' Della?); Dis Is de Day; Dis Little While; Dissolves (inst.); Dressing Up Sequence (Riding on the Moon) (inst.) [1]; Easy Street; Elegy (inst.); First March (inst.); Fix Yo'self Up; Flower Vendor; Free and Easy (Any Place I Hang My Hat Is Home) [1]; High, Low, Jack and the Game [1]; Higher den de Moon; I Ain't Afraid; I Gotta Right to Sing the Blues [7] (L: Ted Koehler); I Had Myself a True Love [1]; I Wonder What Became of Me? [1]; Ill Wind [6] (L: Ted Koehler); Killing Sequence; Ladies 'n' Gentlemen; Least That's My Opinion [1]; Leavin' Time [1]; Legalize My Name [1]; Like Clouds Up in the Sky; Live Hard, Work Hard, Love Hard [8] (L: Ralph Blane); Look What a Hole You're In; Lookin' fo' Somebody; Lullaby [1]; Lumpin'; Many Kinds of Love; Natchul Man [2]; News Chant; One for the Road [9]; Race; Racin' Forms [1]; Rainbow [11]; Reap the Harvest; Second March (inst.); Second Wind; Sleep Peaceful Mr. Used-to-Be [1]; Snake Eyes; Somethin' Ya Gotta Find Out Yo'self [1]; Streak o' Lightnin'; Sweetnin' Water; Then Suddenly; Third March (inst.); Toastin' Sequence; Whatcha Sayin?; Wheel 'em and Deal 'em; Woman's Prerogative, A [1]; Won't Dat Be de Blessed Day; Ya Pushin' Ya Luck

Cast: Irving Barnes; Martha Flowers; Ruby Green; Paul Harris; Elijah Hodges; Moses LaMarr; Harold Nicholas; James Randolph; Irene Williams

Notes: Consisted of previously used songs, mostly from ST. LOUIS WOMAN. An operatic treatment of ST. LOUIS WOMAN with other Arlen standards incorporated. Produced in Amsterdam and Paris (1/15/60). [1] From show ST. LOUIS WOMAN. [2] May be "Li'l Augie Is a Natural Man" from ST. LOUIS WOMAN. [3] From BLUES IN THE NIGHT (film). [4] Same as "That Old Black Magic" from STAR SPANGLED RHYTHM (film). [5] May be same song as "Leavin' Time" from ST. LOUIS WOMAN. [6] From COTTON CLUB PARADE (1934). [7] From EARL CARROLL'S VANITIES OF 1932. [8] From MY BLUE HEAVEN (film). [9] May be same song as "One for My Baby" from SKY'S THE LIMIT (film). [10] Same music as "American Minuet," commissioned for Meredith Willson's radio show. [11] May be same song as "Somewhere Over the Rainbow" from the film THE WIZARD OF OZ.

1386 • FREE AS AIR

OPENED: 06/06/1957   Theatre: Savoy
Musical   London: 417

Composer: Julian Slade
Lyricist: Dorothy Reynolds; Julian Slade
Librettist: Dorothy Reynolds
Producer: Linnit & Dunfee
Director: Denis Carey

Choreographer: Mark Stuart; **Costumes:** Rosemary Carvill; Hilary Virgo; **Musical Director:** Philip Martell; **Set Design:** Patrick Robertson

Songs: Boat's In, The; Daily Echo; Festudo; Free to Sing; Geraldine; Girl from London, The; Her Mummy Doesn't Like Me Any More; Holiday Island; I'd Like to Be Like You; I'm Up Early; I've Got My Feet on the Ground; Let the Grass Grow; Man from the Mainland, A; Nothing but Sea and Sky; Terhou; We're Holding Hands

Cast: Patricia Bredin; Roy Godfrey; Gillian Lewis; Dorothy Reynolds; Len Rossiter

1387 • FREE FOR ALL

OPENED: 09/08/1931   Theatre: Manhattan
Musical   Broadway: 15

Composer: Richard A. Whiting
Lyricist: Oscar Hammerstein II
Librettist: Oscar Hammerstein II; Laurence Schwab
Producer: Frank Mandel; Laurence Schwab
Director: Oscar Hammerstein II

Choreographer: Bobby Connolly; **Costumes:** Kiviette; **Musical Director:** John McManus; **Set Design:** Donald Oenslager

Songs: Ain't Everything Grand! [1]; Carefree Miner, The [1]; Free for All; Girl Next Door, The; How I React to You [1]; I Love Him, the Rat; Just Eighteen; Living in Sin; Men and Women Are Awful; Nevada Moonlight; Not That I Care; Open Your Eyes [1]; Psychoanalyse Me [1]; Russian Song [1]; Slumber Song (Goodnight); Tonight; When Your Boy Becomes a Man

Cast: Edward Emery; Benny Goodman's Orchestra; Doris Groday; Jack Haley; Peter Higgins; David Hutcheson; Grace Johnson; Dorothy Knapp; Philip Lord; Vera Marsh; Tamara

Notes: [1] Cut prior to New York.

1388 • FREE LANCE, THE

OPENED: 04/16/1906   Theatre: New Amsterdam
Musical   Broadway: 35

Composer: John Philip Sousa
Lyricist: Harry B. Smith
Librettist: Harry B. Smith
Producer: Klaw & Erlanger
Director: Herbert Gresham

Costumes: F. Richard Anderson; **Musical Director:** Anton Heindl

Songs: Ah Lovely Art, We Worship at Thy Shrine; Assembling of the Two Courts [2]; At Last; By Proxy; Carrier Pigeon, The; Come, My Dear; Come Ye Heroes All (The Emperor's War Song); Conundrums; Dramatic Situation [1]; Ducal Cousin, Give You Greeting; Finale Act I; Finale Act II; Forever Delighting in Fighting [1]; Friendship's Sacred Touch; Goose Girl, The; Griselda, the Goose-Girl in Me You Behold; Hair; Hither Bring the Bold Intruder; I Am a Potentate [1]; I Do It All By Proxy; I Never Was Right in My Life [4]; I'm the Potentate; It Depends on the Hair; Legend of the Sons of Samson, The; Let Us Greet With Joy Pretended [1]; Little Bas Bleu [1]; Melodrama and Refrain; Mystery of History, The; On Parchment This with Grey Goose Quill [3]; On to Victory; Release That Man; Riddles [1]; Song of the Dice [1]; Song of the Free Lance (I Am a Salaried Warrior); Stop It [3]; Three Ideas of Love; Three Love Stories; With Apparent Ebullition; Women Are All Perfect Pearls; Youth's the Time of Fun and Folly (Youth Must Have Its Fling)

Cast: Nella Bergen; Joseph Cawthorn; Monte Elmo; Louis Haines; Felix Haney; Albert Hart; Jeannette Lowrie; Geraldine Malone; Fanny Midgley; Sim Pulen; Henry J. Santra; George Talman

Notes: [1] Out Philadelphia 4/2/06. [2] Added to a revival New York 1/7/?. [3] In revival 11/21/79. [4] Out Cedar Rapids 9/20/06.

1389 • FREE TO BE - YOU AND ME

OPENED: 03/11/1974   Theatre: ABC
TV Musical

Musical Director: Stephen Lawrence

Songs: Free to Be - You and Me (C: Stephen Lawrence; L: Bruce Hart); Girl Land (C: Mary Rodgers; L: Bruce Hart); Glad to Have a Friend Like You (C/L: Carol Hall); Helping (C/L: Shel Silverstein); It's All Right to Cry (C/L: Carol Hall); Parents Are People (C/L: Carol Hall); Sisters and Brothers (C: Stephen Lawrence; L: Bruce Hart); When We Grow Up (C: Stephen Lawrence; L: Shelley Miller); William's Doll (C: Mary Rodgers; L: Sheldon Harnick)

Cast: Alan Alda; Harry Belafonte; Mel Brooks; Jack Cassidy; Dick Cavett; Carol Channing; Billy De Wolfe; Rosey Grier; Shirley Jones; Robert Morse; New Seekers; Diana Ross; Diana Sands; Sisters and Brothers, The; Tom Smothers; Marlo Thomas

1390 • FREEDOMLAND

OPENED: 1960
Amusement Park

Composer: Jule Styne
Lyricist: George David Weiss

Songs: Chicago Fire, The; Danny the Dragon; Jalopy Song, The; Johnny Freedom; Little Old New York; On the Showboat; Pine Country; San Francisco Fran; Satellite City; So Long Ma (I'm Headin' for New Orleans)

Notes: This park was demolished and Co-op City (a high-rise development) was built on its site.

1391 • FRENCH DOLL, THE

OPENED: 02/20/1922   Theatre: Lyceum
Play   Broadway: 120

Author: A.E. Thomas
Producer: E. Ray Goetz
Director: W.H. Gilmore

Source: JEUNES FILLES DE PALACES (Play: Paul Armont; Marcel Gerbidon); **Set Design:** Herbert Ward

Songs: Do It Again! (C: George Gershwin; L: B.G. DeSylva); Gee! But I Hate to Go Home Alone [2] (C: James F. Hanley; L: Joe Goodwin); When Eyes Meet Eyes (When Lips Meet Lips) (C: Gus Edwards; L: Will D. Cobb); You Don't Love As Good As I Do [1] (C/L: E. Ray Goetz; Paul Rubens; Hugh Wright)

Cast: Eugene Borden; Irene Bordoni; Don Burroughs; Adrienne D'Ambricourt; Edouard Durand; Thurston Hall; James Hunter; Laura Lussier; William Williams

Notes: [1] Out Indianapolis 12/11/??. [2] ASCAP/Library of Congress only.

1392 • FRENCH MAID, THE
OPENED: 09/27/1897 Theatre: Herald Square
Musical Broadway: 160

Composer: Walter Slaughter
Librettist: Basil Hood
Producer: Edward E. Rice

Costumes: M.L. Dowling; **Set Design:** D. Frank Dodge; Frank Rafter

Songs: Admiral, The (C: Donald MacGregor; L: Augustus Powers); Bit Too Far, A [1]; Brave Gendarmes [1]; Britannia's Song [1]; Castles in the Air [1]; Chambermaids; Charity's Useful Disguise; Do Not Jump at Your Conclusions; Finale (C: Herman Perlet); Gay Gendarme, The (C: Herman Perlet; L: Henry Norman); I'll Read You Such a Dance; It Is Their Nature To; It's Even My Endeavor; It's Gone Eight Bells [1]; I've Her Portrait Nex' My Heart; Je ne le Comprends Pas; Jolly British Tar; La Femme de Chambre; Love That Is True; Maharajah, The; Pretty Suzette; Rhapsodie Table d'Hote (C: E.E. Rice; L: William Barton); Twas Twenty-Seven Bells by the Waterbury Watch (C: Donald MacGregor; L: Arthur Augustus Powers); You Can Read It in My Eyes (C: Herman Perlet; L: Henry Norman)

Cast: Charles A. Bigelow; Eva Davenport; John Gourlay; George Honey; Anna Robinson; Marguerita Sylva; Edward S. Wentworth

Notes: [1] London 10/9/1897.

1393 • FRESH AIRS
OPENED: 1950
Revue

Composer: Charles Strouse
Lyricist: Lee Adams

Songs: I Can't Sleep; Let's Fly Away; Tame Me; To Get Us All Together; (Let Me Walk) Under Your Umbrella

Notes: No other information available.

1394 • FRIAR'S FESTIVAL, THE
OPENED: 05/14/1908
Revue

Songs: Friar's Song, The (C: Victor Herbert; L: Charles Emerson Cook)

Notes: A show for the Friar's Club.

1395 • FRIARS FROLIC
OPENED: 05/08/1932 Theatre: Metropolitan
Opera House
Musical New York

Composer: Milton Ager; Phil Charig; Walter Donaldson; Newman Fier; Harry Revel; Louis Silvers
Lyricist: Walter Donaldson; Newman Fier; Mack Gordon
Producer: Max Gordon; Sam H. Harris
Director: R.H. Burnside; Danny Dare

Costumes: Charles Chrisdie; **Musical Director:** Louis Silvers; **Set Design:** John Henry Beaumont

Songs: It's About Time (C/L: Unknown); Lights Up (C: Harry Revel; L: Mack Gordon)

Cast: Phil Baker; Jack Benny; Eddie Foy Jr.; Joe Frisco; Bert Lahr; Hal LeRoy; Georgie Price; Harry Richman; Pat Rooney; Smith & Dale; Arthur Tracy

1396 • FRIARS FROLIC FOR MAYOR J.J. WALKER
OPENED: 05/19/1929
Revue

Librettist: Irving Caesar; Bert Kalmar; Harry Ruby; Morrie Ryskind
Director: Lou Holtz

Musical Director: Thomas McManus; Harry Rosenthal; **Orchestrations:** Leo Russotto; **Vocal Arranger:** Leo Russotto

Songs: La Tickero [1] (C/L: Irving Caesar)

Cast: Irving Caesar; Maurice Chevalier; Clayton, Jackson & Durante; Joe Cook; Jack Haley; Lou Holtz; Sam Jaffe; George Jessel; Bert Kalmar; Georgie Price; Harry Ruby; John Philip Sousa; Rudy Vallee and His Orchestra; Bert Wheeler

Notes: Metropolitan Opera House. This Revue contained the one-act opera LA TICKERO by Irving Caesar. There was also a playlet titled SOLD DOWN THE RIVER by Kalmar, Ruby, Caesar and Ryskind. I'm not sure if it had songs or not. [1] "A 15-18-20 Per Cent American Opera."

1397 • FRIARS FROLIC IN HONOR OF TED LEWIS

OPENED: 12/15/1946   Theatre: Imperial
Revue

Librettist: Goodman Ace; Matt Brooks; Sam Ward
Director: William Brandell

Musical Director: Samuel Fidler

Songs: Friar's Song [1] (C: Victor Herbert; L: Charles Emerson Cook); North Dakota, South Dakota, Minnesota Moon (C/L: Phil Charig; Milton Pascal; Dan Shapiro)

Cast: Milton Berle; Jesse Block; June Havoc; Lew Parker; Smith & Dale

Notes: [1] Not written for this production.

1398 • FRIAR'S FROLIC OF 1911

OPENED: 1911
Revue

Songs: Alexander's Ragtime Band (C/L: Irving Berlin)

Notes: No other information available.

1399 • FRIAR'S FROLIC OF 1916

OPENED: 05/28/1916   Theatre: New Amsterdam
Revue   Broadway: 1

Producer: A.L. Erlanger; Sam H. Harris
Director: George M. Cohan

Songs: Friars' Parade (C/L: Irving Berlin)

Cast: Irving Berlin; George M. Cohan; William Collier; Harrison Fisher; Frank Tinney

Notes: No program available.

1400 • FRIARS FROLIC OF 1949

OPENED: 1949
Revue

Songs: This Is My Night with Trixie (C: Joe Cooper; L: L. Wolfe Gilbert)

Notes: No program available.

1401 • FRIEND FRITZ

OPENED: 01/26/1893   Theatre: New Park
Musical   New York

Composer: Julian Edwards
Lyricist: Stanislaus Stange
Librettist: Stanislaus Stange

Source: L'AMI FRITZ (Play: Chatrian; Erckmann); **Set Design:** L.W. Shavel

Cast: Charles Harris; Marion Manola; John Mason; Edward P. Temple

Notes: Brooklyn program used. No songs listed in program. Ran for one month.

1402 • FRIMBO

OPENED: 11/09/1980   Theatre: Grand Central
                              Terminal
Revue   Off-Broadway: 1

Composer: Howard Harris
Lyricist: Jim Wann
Librettist: John L. Haber
Producer: Dodger Productions; John L. Haber; Louis Busch Hager
Director: John L. Haber

Source: ALL ABOARD WITH E.M. FRIMBO (Story: Anthony Hiss; Rodgers E.M. Whitaker); **Costumes:** Patricia McGourty; **Dance Arranger:** Howard Harris; **Lighting Designer:** Fred Buchholz; **Musical Director:** Howard Harris; **Set Design:** Fred Buchholz; Karl Eigsti; **Vocal Arranger:** Howard Harris

Songs: Ballad of Frimbo; Frimbo Special; Going

Home; Gone Everywhere but Home; I Hate Trains; Lady By Choice; Mama Frimbo; Mileage Millionaire, The; Names of Trains; Ode to Steam; On a Train at Night; Siberia; That's the Way to Make It Move; Train, The; Train Walking; Trains or Me

Cast: Pattie D'Arcy; Deborah May; Cass Morgan; Pauletta Pearson; Larry Riley; Richard B. Shull

1403 • FRITZ IN TAMMANY HALL

OPENED: 10/16/1905   Theatre: Herald Square
Musical   Broadway: 48

Composer: Jean Schwartz
Lyricist: William Jerome
Librettist: John J. McNally
Producer: Klaw & Erlanger
Director: Herbert Gresham; Ned Wayburn

Costumes: F. Richard Anderson; **Lighting Designer:** H. Bissing

Songs: Dear Little Wise Old Bowery, The; Dear Old Farm, The; East Side Lil; East Side Walk; I Don't Want a Little Canoe; I'm a Woman of Importance; In Bad Man's Land; In Old New York; In Tammany Hall; Man Behind the Club, The; My Irish Daisy; My Sweet; Tammany Ball, The; When You're in Love; Yankee Doodle Boodle

Cast: Joseph Cawthorn; Melville Ellis; Ada Lewis; Stella Mayhew; George Austin Moore; Julius Tannen

1404 • FRIVOLITIES OF 1920

OPENED: 01/08/1920   Theatre: 44th Street
Revue   Broadway: 61

Composer: William B. Friedlander
Lyricist: William B. Friedlander
Librettist: William Anthony McGuire
Producer: G.M. Anderson
Director: William Anthony McGuire

Choreographer: Edward Bower; Allan K. Foster; William B. Friedlander; **Musical Director:** Harry Auracher

Songs: Adam and Eve [1]; Araby; Cuddle-Uddle, The; Echo Song; Farmerettes, The; In Barcelona [1]; In Peacock Alley; Jazz Up Jasper

(C/L: Harry Auracher; Tom Johnstone); League of Nations, The; Military Marches [1]; Military Wedding of the Nations; Music; My Frivolity Girl (C/L: Harry Auracher; Tom Johnstone); Oh How I Love You [2] (C/L: Dave Dreyer; Henry Lewis; Andrew B. Sterling); On a Moonlight Night; Peachie (C: Albert Gumble; L: Jack Yellen); Pretty Little Cinderella [1] (C: Nathaniel Vincent; L: Blanche Franklyn); Pretty Polly (C/L: Harry Auracher; Tom Johnstone); Spanish Aria, A; Squidgulums; What Is Love?

Cast: Dolly Best; Colin Chase; Frank Davis; Irene Delroy; Edward Gallagher; Grace Lee; Henry Lewis; Moss and Fry

Notes: [1] Sheet music only. [2] ASCAP/Library of Congress only.

1405 • FRIVOLOUS GERALDINE

OPENED: 12/22/1912   Theatre: Olympic
Musical   Chicago

Composer: Joseph E. Howard; Herbert Stothart
Lyricist: Theodore Stempfel Jr.
Librettist: Theodore Stempfel Jr.

Songs: Bread and Cheese and Kisses (L: Horatio G. Winslow); Cello Fellow, The; Dancing Man; Dear Old Wisconsin Days; From You, For Me; Going Home to Lulu (C/L: Joseph E. Howard); Just Say That You Will Miss Me; Love for a Day; Those Wonderful Eyes (C: Joseph E. Howard); Underneath the Cotton Moon [1] (C: George W. Meyer; L: Sam M. Lewis); Waltz Me Around and Around in the Old Ball Room (C/L: Joseph E. Howard)

Notes: Closed out of town. [1] ASCAP/Library of Congress.

1406 • FROGS, THE

OPENED: 05/20/1974
Musical   Yale University: 8

Composer: Stephen Sondheim
Lyricist: Stephen Sondheim
Librettist: Burt Shevelove
Producer: Yale Repertory Theatre
Director: Burt Shevelove

Source: FROGS, THE (Play: Aristophanes); **Choreographer:** Carmen de Lavallade;

Costumes: Jeanne Button; **Lighting Designer:** Carol M. Waaser; **Musical Director:** Don Jennings; **Orchestrations:** Jonathan Tunick; **Set Design:** Michael H. Yeargan

Songs: Evoe! (Hymn to Dionysos); Evoe for the Dead; Fear No More; Frogs, The; Invocation and Instructions to the Audience [1]; It's Only a Play; Sound of Poets, The; Travel Music (chant)

Cast: Larry Blyden; Jerome Dempsey; Dan Desmond; Alvin Epstein; Jeremy Geidt; Anthony Holland; Stephen R. Lawson; Charles Levin; Ron Recasner; Michael Vale; Carmen de Lavallade

Notes: Presented in Yale's swimming pool. [1] Originally a cut song from A FUNNY THING HAPPENED ON THE WAY TO THE FORUM.

1407 • FROLICS OF THE NIGHT

OPENED: 1918
Revue

Composer: Nat Osborne
Lyricist: Will H. Smith

Songs: Atlantic City; Frolics of the Nite; Good-Bye Boys; Good Nite, Germany; Keep Out of the Water; Meet Me at the Front Door; Not the Back; Real American Girls; Real Live Man; Tweet, Tweet, Tweet; You Got Something I Want; You Must Whistle Like This

Notes: Burlesque revue.

1408 • FROM A TO Z

OPENED: 04/20/1960   Theatre: Plymouth
Revue   Broadway: 21

Librettist: Woody Allen
Producer: Carroll Masterson; Harris Masterson
Director: Christopher Hewett

Choreographer: Ray Harrison; **Costumes:** Fred Voelpel; **Dance Arranger:** Jack Holmes; **Lighting Designer:** Fred Voelpel; **Musical Director:** Milton Greene; **Orchestrations:** Jay Brower; Jonathan Tunick; **Set Design:** Fred Voelpel; **Vocal Arranger:** Milton Greene

Songs: Balloons (C/L: Jack Holmes); Best Gold (C/L: Jerry Herman); Charlie (C/L: Norman L.

Martin; L: Fred Ebb); Counter Melody [1] (C: Mary Rodgers; Jay Thompson; L: Marshall Barer); Four for the Road (C: Paul Klein; L: Fred Ebb; Lee Goldsmith); Grand Jury Jump (C: Paul Klein; L: Fred Ebb); Hire a Guy (C: Mary Rodgers; L: Marshall Barer); I Said to Love (C: Paul Klein; L: Fred Ebb); Interlude (inst.) (C: Jack Holmes); Pill Parade (C/L: Jay Thompson); Red Shoes (C: Jack Holmes); Sound of Schmaltz, The (C: William Dyer; L: Don Parks); South American Way (C/L: Norman Martin; L: Fred Ebb); Time Stop (C: Paul Klein; L: Fred Ebb); Togetherness (C/L: Dickson Hughes; Everett Sloane); What Next? (C: Charles Zwar; L: Alan Melville)

Cast: Stuart Damon; Bob Dishy; Alvin Epstein; Hermione Gingold; Louise Hoff; Elliott Reid; Paula Stewart; Virginia Vestoff

Notes: Sketches by others also. [1] Also in TIMOTHY GREY'S TABOO REVUE.

1409 • FROM ACROSS THE BIG POND

OPENED: 09/07/1907   Theatre: Circle
Musical   New York

Composer: Adolf Philipp
Lyricist: Adolf Philipp
Librettist: Adolf Philipp; Mortimer M. Theise

Source: UBER'N GROSSEN TEICH (Musical: Adolf Philipp)

Songs: Election Returns; Louis Is All Right; Marie from Paree; True Irish Girl, The

Cast: Adolf Philipp

Notes: No program available. Later titled ACROSS THE POND. Source also titled NEW YORK IN WORT UND BILD.

1410 • FROM BROADWAY TO PARIS (1912)

Notes: *See BROADWAY TO PARIS.*

1411 • FROM BROADWAY TO PARIS (????)

Revue

Producer: George Hale; Edmond Sayag
Director: William Morris Jr.

Songs: Country Cousin (C: Peter De Rose; L: Jo Trent); Seasick Blues; Sticky Feet (C: Peter De Rose; L: George Hale; Jo Trent)

Notes: No other information available.

1412 • FROM BROOKS WITH LOVE

OPENED: 04/06/1983   Theatre: Harold Clurman
Revue   Off-Broadway: 20

Composer: George Koch; Russ Taylor
Lyricist: Wayne Sheridan
Librettist: Wayne Sheridan
Producer: Joseph L. Runner
Director: William Michael Maher

Choreographer: Robin Reseen; **Costumes:** Carol H. Buele; **Lighting Designer:** Paul Sullivan; **Musical Director:** Jim Fradrich; **Orchestrations:** Jim Fradrich; **Set Design:** Tom Barnes; **Vocal Arranger:** Jim Fradrich

Songs: Brendan's Dream; Customer's Nightmare, The; Eggs; I'll Be Someone Today; It's Nice; Jerry's Dream; Let's Go; Love Is a Feeling; Lynn's Dream; Main Floor, The; Marjorie's Dream; Move Over You Guys; New Kind of Husband, A; Rocco's Dream; Security; Service, The; Shopping; Showbiz; Unemployment; We'd Like to Go Back; Will They Remember

Cast: Ralph Anthony; Gwen Arment; Fred Bishop; Gillian Walke

1413 • FROM VIENNA

OPENED: 06/20/1939   Theatre: Music Box
Revue   Broadway: 79

Composer: Otto Andreas; Walter Drix; Werner Michel
Librettist: David Greggory; Peter Hammerschlag; Lothar Metzl; Werner Michel; Jura Soyfer; Hans Welgel
Producer: Refugee Artists Group, The
Director: Herbert Berghof

Costumes: Irene Sharaff; **Lighting Designer:** Hassard Short; **Set Design:** Donald Oenslager

Cast: Otto Andreas; John Banner; Jimmy Berg; Fred Essler; Nelly Franck; Hans Herberth; Karl Mueller; Elizabeth Neumann; Maria Pichler; Illa Roden

Notes: No program available.

1414 • FULL SPEED AHEAD

OPENED: 12/25/1942
Musical   Closed out of town

Composer: Irving Actman; Jean Schwartz
Lyricist: Rowland Leigh
Librettist: Rowland Leigh
Producer: Producers Associates; J.J. Shubert
Director: Rowland Leigh; Barrie O'Daniels

Choreographer: Boots McKenna; **Musical Director:** George Hirst

Songs: Brazilian Samba; Dream Dance; Gorgeous to Gaze At; Got a New Boy Friend; Happiness Calling; I Don't Repent; If Only You (C: H. Leopold Spitalny; L: Rowland Leigh); I'm a Sailor; I'm on My Way to Paradise (C: H. Leopold Spitalny; L: Rowland Leigh); I'm So Glad; In Trinidad; Romp in the Hay; Ruisenor; Seniorita (C: H. Leopold Spitalny; L: Rowland Leigh); She Can't Make Coffee; Tropicana; You've Got to Be Fast; You've Got to Pay

Cast: Leonard Ceeley; Jack Good; Emma Otero

Notes: Philadelphia program.

1415 • FUN FOR THE MONEY

OPENED: 08/1941   Theatre: Hollywood
                              Playhouse
Revue   Los Angeles

Composer: Franz Steininger
Lyricist: Forman Brown
Librettist: Charles Sherman
Producer: George Shafer
Director: Dave Gould

Costumes: Georgia Anderson; **Musical Director:** Waldemar Guterson; **Orchestrations:** David Tambin

Songs: American Way, The; Boogie-Woogie- Katie (C: Eddie Scott; L: George R. Brown); Can't Stop Now (C: Irving Actman; Milton Berle; L: George R. Brown); Good Old Fashioned Way, The; It's Fun for the Money Tonight; I've Got a New Rhythm for Old Shoes (C: Irving Actman; L: George Brown); Keep It Under Your Sombrero; Last Words of Divine Devore, The (C/L: Chet Forrest; Robert Wright); Man Who Leads the Band, The; Millionaires Don't Whistle (C/L: Chet Forrest; Robert Wright); My Heart Is a Drum; Oh! Mr. Hays; On Account of Because; Paprika; Raah-Too-Tee- Too (C: Henry Bluestone; Bill Shaw; L: George R. Brown); Time to Say Good Night Again; We're Photogenic (C: Howard Godwin; L: Forman Brown); Word to Mr. Jones, A (C/L: Chet Forrest; Robert Wright)

Cast: Dolores Gray; Anne Jeffreys; Betty Kean; Jane Kean

Notes: Program from Los Angeles.

1416 • FUN TO BE FREE

OPENED: 10/05/1941   Theatre: Madison Square
                                     Garden
Revue   New York: 1

Librettist: Ben Hecht; Charles MacArthur
Director: Brett Warren

Incidental Music: Kurt Weill

Songs: Arms for the Love of America (C/L: Irving Berlin); I Hear America Singing (C: George Kleinsinger; L: Walt Whitman)

Cast: Tallulah Bankhead; Jack Benny; Ann Wiggins Brown; Eddie Cantor; Melvyn Douglas; Morton Downey; Paul Draper; Lynn Fontanne; Betty Grable; Helen Hayes; George Jessel; Jan Kiepura; Ella Logan; Burgess Meredith; Ethel Merman; George Raft; Harry Richman; Bill Robinson; Franchot Tone; Sophie Tucker

Notes: A benefit for Fight for Freedom, Inc. There were a lot more people in the cast. The credits (excepting cast and songs) were for a sketch titled FUN TO BE FREE. The rest of the evening consisted of the two songs listed and many speeches.

1417 • FUNABASHI

OPENED: 01/06/1908   Theatre: Casino
Musical   Broadway: 32

Composer: Safford Waters
Lyricist: Safford Waters
Librettist: Irvin Cobb
Producer: Thomas W. Ryley
Director: Al Holbrook

Musical Director: Frank Palma

Songs: Ambassador of Peace; Boo-Ra-Boo; Butterfly and the Rose, The; Dear Old Story, The; Diplomats; Entrance of Meorema; Finale Act I; Flirtation; For a Girl Can Love a Sailor (L: Wallace Irwin); Girl Behind the Man Behind the Gun, The; Girls of Every Land, The; Her Baggage Was Checked for Troy; Hi Yah; I Walked Around (L: Vincent Rose; Ted Snyder); I'd Guess You (L: Carolyn Wells); In Old Japan; Island of Love, The; It's Only a Piece of Advice (L: Unknown); I've Been Discharged by Them All (L: Paul West); Little Japan Lady, A; Love Is Victor; Miss Yankee Doodle (L: Carolyn Wells); My Matrimonial Bon Bon; One, Two, Three-Down and Out (L: Paul West); When I've Made Up My Mind to a Thing; When There Isn't a Girl About (L: Unknown)

Cast: Percy Ames; Alice Fisher; Maude Fulton; Vera Michelena; Joseph Miron; Walter Percival; William Rock

1418 • FUNERAL MARCH FOR A ONE MAN BAND

OPENED: 05/04/1974
Play   Off-Broadway: 12

Composer: Mel Marvin
Lyricist: Robert Satuloff
Author: Ron Whyte
Producer: Michael Shepley
Director: Leonard Peters

Costumes: Carol Oditz; **Lighting Designer:** Paul Gallo; **Musical Director:** John McKenney; **Set Design:** Salvatore Tagliarino

Songs: Christmas Prayer; Father and Son; Hallucination; I Am Not Afraid; Kill It Now; Mom and Dad; My Love Song; Oh Babe; School Spirit; Teenage Tenderness; When You Weren't Lookin'

Cast: Ellen Barber; Dennis Boutsikaris; Rob Derosa; Dwight Schultz; June Squibb; Thomas Toner

1419 • FUNNY FACE
OPENED: 11/22/1927   Theatre: Alvin
Musical   Broadway: 250

Composer: George Gershwin
Lyricist: Ira Gershwin
Librettist: Paul Gerard Smith; Fred Thompson
Producer: Alex A. Aarons; Vinton Freedley
Director: Edgar MacGregor

Choreographer: Bobby Connolly; **Costumes:** Kiviette; **Musical Director:** Alfred Newman; **Set Design:** John Wenger

Songs: Acrobats [3]; Aviator [12]; Babbitt and the Bromide, The; Birthday Party; Blue Hullaballoo [11]; Bluebeard [3]; Come Along, Let's Gamble (Finale Act I) [9]; Come! Come! Come Closer! [7]; Dance Alone with You (Why Does Everybody Have to Cut In) [1]; Finest of the Finest, The [12]; Funny Face; He Loves and She Loves; High Hat; How Long Has This Been Going On [2]; In the Swim (If You Will Take Our Tip) [10]; Invalid Entrance [3]; Let's Kiss and Make Up [8]; Look at the Damn Thing Now [5]; My One and Only (What Am I Gonna Do); Once [6]; 'S Wonderful; Tell the Doc; We're All A- Worry, All Agog [3]; When the Right One Comes Along [14]; When You're Single [12]; World Is Mine, The [4]; Your Eyes, Your Smile (Those Eyes) [13]

Cast: Adele Astaire; Fred Astaire; Betty Compton; Allen Kearns; William Kent; Gertrude McDonald; Victor Moore; Pianist: Victor Arden; Phil Ohman

Notes: [1] Cut prior to opening. Rewritten as "Ev'rybody Knows I Love Somebody." [2] Dropped, with revised lyric added to ROSALIE. [3] Not used. [4] Cut prior to opening and put in NINE-FIFTEEN REVUE (1930) under the title "Toddlin' Along." [5] Added to London production 11/8/28. [6] Same lyric as "Once" in TELL ME MORE. [7] Not used. Music later used for "Let's Kiss and Make Up." [8] Same music as for the unused "Come! Come! Come Closer!" [9] All but the last eight bars deleted prior to Broadway. [10] Some of the music and lyrics were from "The Moon Is on the Sea" from OH,

KAY! [11] Cut after opening. [12] Cut prior to opening. [13] Cut prior to opening. Music of verse later used for the verse of "You Started It" which was not used in GIRL CRAZY and the film DELICIOUS. [14] Music later used for "Say So" from ROSALIE.

1420 • FUNNY GIRL
OPENED: 03/26/1964   Theatre: Winter Garden
Musical   Broadway: 1348

Composer: Jule Styne
Lyricist: Bob Merrill
Librettist: Isobel Lennart
Producer: Ray Stark
Director: Garson Kanin; Jerome Robbins

Choreographer: Carol Haney; **Costumes:** Irene Sharaff; **Dance Arranger:** Luther Henderson; **Lighting Designer:** Robert Randolph; **Musical Director:** Milton Rosenstock; **Orchestrations:** Ralph Burns; **Set Design:** Robert Randolph; **Vocal Arranger:** Buster Davis

Songs: Absent Minded Me [3]; Baltimore Sun [1]; Cornet Man; Do Puppies Go to Heaven? [1]; Don't Rain on My Parade; Downtown Rag [2]; Eddie's Fifth Encore [2]; Find Yourself a Man; Funny Girl [5]; He [1]; He's Got Larceny in His Heart [1]; Helluva Group, A [2]; Henry Street; His Love Makes Me Beautiful; Home [2]; I Did It on Roller Skates [1]; I Tried [1]; I Want to Be Seen with You Tonight; If a Girl Isn't Pretty; I'm the Greatest Star; Individual Thing [4]; It's Home [2]; Music That Makes Me Dance, The; My Daughter Fanny the Star [1]; Nicky Arnstein [6]; People; Racing Form Lullaby [1]; Rat-Tat-Tat-Tat (Private Schwartz); Sadie, Sadie (Married Lady); Sleep Now, Baby Bunting [2]; Something About Me [2]; Temporary Arrangement, A [2]; Took Me a Little Time [2]; When I Talk about You [1]; Who Are You Now?; Who Taught Her Everything?; You Are Woman

Cast: Sydney Chaplin; Lainie Kazan; John Lankston; Kay Medford; Danny Meehan; Jean Stapleton; Barbra Streisand

Notes: A bio-musical of Fanny Brice. [1] Not used. [2] Cut out of town. [3] Cut prior to opening. [4] Cut. Put into score of PRETTYBELLE. [5] Not used. Not same as title song in film version. [6] ASCAP/Library of Congress only.

1421 • FUNNY MONEY

OPENED: 1930
Musical

Composer: George Gillins; F.B. Woods
Lyricist: Tim Owsley
Producer: Tim Owsley

Songs: Absence; All the Time in Dixie; Blue; Can't Help It; Dance of the Ghost; For Sale; In Love with You; it's All Over Now; Little Kiss, A; My Soul; Same Old Silas, The; Steppin'; Whoopee

Cast: Katie Bryant; Manzie Campbell; Bobby Gillins; Tim Green and Roberta; Kike Gresham; Marion Gresham; Allie Johnson; Princess White Durrah; Fred Wiggins

Notes: No other information available. This might also have been titled SILAS GREEN FROM NEW ORLEANS.

1422 • FUNNY THING HAPPENED ON THE WAY TO THE FORUM, A

OPENED: 05/08/1962   Theatre: Alvin
Musical   Broadway: 965

Composer: Stephen Sondheim
Lyricist: Stephen Sondheim
Librettist: Larry Gelbart; Burt Shevelove
Producer: Harold Prince
Director: George Abbott

Source: Plays (Plautus); **Choreographer:** Jack Cole; **Costumes:** Tony Walton; **Dance Arranger:** Hal Schaefer; **Lighting Designer:** Jean Rosenthal; **Musical Director:** Hal Hastings; **Orchestrations:** Irwin Kostal; Sid Ramin; **Set Design:** Tony Walton

Songs: Bring Me My Bride; Comedy Tonight; Echo Song, The [3]; Everybody Ought to Have a Maid; Farewell [2]; Free; Funeral Dirge; Gaggle of Geese, The [1]; House of Marcus Lycus, The (1); House of Marcus Lycus, The (2) [1]; I Do Like You [1]; I, Miles Gloriosus [1]; I'm Calm; Impossible; Invocation [4]; Love, I Hear; Love Is in the Air [5]; Lovely; Miles Gloriosus; Once Upon a Time (Your Eyes Are Blue) [1]; Pretty Little Picture; Something About a War [1]; That Dirty Old Man; That'll Show Him; Window Across the Way [1]

Cast: David Burns; John Carradine; Brian Davies; Jack Gilford; Ronald Holgate; Ruth Kobart; Preshy Marker; Zero Mostel; Raymond Walburn

Notes: Based on the plays of Plautus. [1] Cut prior to Broadway. [2] Added for 1972 revival. [3] Cut prior to Broadway and added to 1972 revival. [4] Cut prior to Broadway. Later used in THE FROGS. [5] Lyric cut and music retained as underscoring.

1423 • FUNZAPPOPPIN

OPENED: 06/30/1949   Theatre: Madison Square Garden
Revue

Composer: Chuck Gould; Chic Johnson; Ole Olsen
Lyricist: Chuck Gould; Chic Johnson; Ole Olsen
Producer: Arthur Wirtz
Director: Chic Johnson; Ole Olsen

Choreographer: Catherine Littlefield; **Musical Director:** Jack Pfeiffer; **Set Design:** Becker Bros. Studios

Songs: Funzapoppin; I'd Like to Be a Sitter for a Baby Like You (C/L: Chic Johnson; Perry Martin; Ole Olsen); Oh, What a Night for a Party; 6 Gun Joe from Cicero; Swing on the Corner

Cast: Choraleers, The; Clark Bros.; Gloria Gilbert; Bill Hayes; Chic Johnson; June Johnson; Marty May; Nirska; J.C. Olsen; Ole Olsen; Gloria Short

1424 • FURS AND FRILLS

OPENED: 10/09/1917   Theatre: Casino
Musical   Broadway: 32

Composer: Silvio Hein
Lyricist: Edward Clark
Librettist: Edward Clark
Producer: Arthur Hammerstein
Director: Edward Clark

Choreographer: Robert Marks; **Costumes:** Harry Collins; L. Wenzelberg; **Set Design:** P. Dodd Ackerman

Songs: Always Take Mother's Advice; Butterfly [1] (C: Claude E. MacArthur); Deception Is the Better Part of Valor [1] (C: Claude E. MacArthur); Do You Follow Me? [4]; Does Polly Want Wally?;

Furs and Frills; Heart of My Heart; Highland Kiltie Rag, The [3]; I'm So Happy [4]; It Must Be Now [1] (C: Claude E. MacArthur); It's Easy to Lie to Your Husband; Love's Menu [1]; (Gee! But This Sure Is My) Lucky Day (C: Claude E. MacArthur); Make Yourselves at Home (C: Silvio Hein; L: Oscar Hammerstein II); Opening Chorus; Pot Pourri [2]; Short Farewell Is Best, A; Spring [1] (C: Claude E. MacArthur); Tale of a Coat, The; We're So Happy [4]; When My Wife Returns; You Can't Take It with You When You Die; Yuletide Spirit, The

Cast: Frances Demarest; Ruby Norton; Ernest Torrence

Notes: [1] Out Washington, D.C. 8/18/18. [2] Out Wilkes-Barre 1/3/18. [3] Out Hartford 9/20/17. [4] Sheet music only.

1425 • FURTHER MO'

OPENED: 05/17/1990　　Theatre: Village Gate
　　　　　　　　　　　　　　　Downstairs
Musical　　　　　　　Off-Broadway: 174

Composer: Vernel Bagneris
Lyricist: Vernel Bagneris
Librettist: Vernel Bagneris
Producer: Michael Frazier; Nortzar Productions
Director: Vernel Bagneris

Arrangements: Lars Edegran; Orange Kellin; **Choreographer:** Pepsi Bethel; **Costumes:** Jo Ann Clevenger; **Lighting Designer:** John McKernon; **Musical Director:** Orange Kellin; **Set Design:** Charles McClennahan; **Vocal Arranger:** Topsy Chapman; Lars Edegran

Songs: Alabamy Bound (C: Ray Henderson; L: B.G. DeSylva; Bud Green); Baby, Won't You Please Come Home (C/L: Charles Warfield; Clarence Williams); Boogie Woogie; Boot-It Boy; Clarinet Marmalade; Come On In; Don't

Advertise Your Man; Funny Feathers; Had to Give Up Gym; Here Comes the Hot Tamale Man; Home Sweet Home (C: Sir Henry Rowley Bishop; L: John Howard Payne); Hot Time in the Old Town Tonight (C: Theodore M. Metz; L: Joe Hayden); Messing Around; Mississippi Mud (C/L: Harry Barris); My Man (C: Maurice Yvain; L: Channing Pollock); One Hour Mama; Positively No (Construction Gang); Pretty Doll; Sally Dog; Shake It and Bake It; Sweet Man; Sweetie Dear; Trouble in Mind; West Indies Blues; Wild Women

Cast: Vernel Bagneris; Topsy Chapman; Sandra Reaves- Phillips; Frozine Thomas; James "Red" Wilcher

Notes: A sequel to ONE MO' TIME.

1426 • FUTURE, THE

OPENED: 03/22/1974　　Theatre: Judson Poets'
Musical　　　　　　　　Off-Off-Broadway

Composer: Al Carmines
Lyricist: Al Carmines
Librettist: Al Carmines

Songs: Cold-Hearted Waltz; Don't Feed the Animals; Fair One; Finale; I Remember Efficiency Rag; It's a Monochrome World; Life Is Simple As Water; Little Girl; Love Aria; Mama Goddess; Mr. Used-To's Gone Forever; Mumblin' Fool; Old Fashioned Waltz; Once Upon a Time; Outcasts; Perfection's Palace; Pleasure Capsules; Rediscovery of the Eunuch, The; She's in Love with Death; Survey of Western Culture; Time Flies; We Are the Way We Are; We're Clowns; We're Still Here; When the Wind Blows

Cast: Reathel Bean; Essie Borden; Semina De Laurentis; Lee Guilliatt; Bruce Hopkins; Julie Kurnitz; Ira Siff

G

1427 • GABRIELLE

OPENED: 01/1975
Musical   Closed out of town

Composer: Gilbert Becaud
Lyricist: Jason Darrow
Librettist: Jose Quintero
Producer: Frankie Hewitt
Director: Jose Quintero

Choreographer: Dan Siretta; **Costumes:** Franne Lee; **Lighting Designer:** Jules Fisher; **Musical Director:** William Cox; **Orchestrations:** Garry Sherman; **Set Design:** Eugene Lee

Songs: Cheer Up, Madame; Cherry Trees Are Blue, The; Don Juan; Et Maintenant; Gabrielle; Gilbert Becaud; Home; If I Could Choose One Day; L'Important C'est La Rose; Little Girl, The; Masquerade, The; One Night; Rosy and John; Seul sur Son Etoile; Waiting

Cast: Marilyn Cooper; Tammy Grimes; Laurence Guittard; Robin Hoff; Danny Meehan; David Sabin

1428 • GABY

Notes: This show, under the title FOLIES BERGERE COMPANY, contained three parts — HELL, TEMPTATIONS (a ballet) and GABY. See FOLIES BERGERE COMPANY for information.

1429 • GAIETY GIRL, A

OPENED: 09/18/1894   Theatre: Daly's
Musical   Broadway: 79

Composer: Sidney Jones
Lyricist: Harry Greenbank
Librettist: Owen Hall
Producer: Augustin Daly
Director: George Edwardes

Set Design: Hugh Logan Reid

Songs: Beneath the Skies; Boys of the Household Brigade, The (L: Harry Hamilton); Carnival Chorus; Finale; Here on Sunlit Sands; High Class Chaperone; It Seems to Me; Jimmy on the Chute (C/L: Harry Greenbank); O Sing a Welcome; Oh, My Daughter; Poor Pierrot; Private Tommy Atkins (C: S. Potter; L: Henry Hamilton); Stiboo, Stibee; Sunshine Above; That Ladies Cannot Bathe; To My Judicial Mind; To the Barracks We Have Come; We're Awfully Anxious; When a Masculine Stranger Goes By; When in Town; When Once I Get Hold of a Good-Looking He?; When Your Pride Has Had a Tumble

Cast: Fred Kaye; Harry Monkhouse; Maud Robson; Charles Ryley

Notes: No songs listed in program.

1430 • GAIETY JUBILEE, THE

OPENED: 1909
Revue

Composer: John L. Golden
Lyricist: George V. Hobart
Librettist: George V. Hobart

Songs: Come to My Land of Love Dreams; I Used to Sigh for the Silvery Moon (C: Herman Darewski; L: Lester Barrett); In Bed; Le Vrai Tango Argentin (El Choclo) (inst.); Marry Me to the Music of a Big Brass Band; Naughty Widow Wise; Please Please Please; She Pushed Me Into the Parlour; When I Marry Mary in Maryland

Cast: Gene Luneska; Tom Waters

Notes: Produced at Anderson's Gaiety Theatre, San Francisco. No other information available.

1431 • GALILEO

Notes: *See STARCROSSED.*

1432 • GALLAGHER AND SHEAN VAUDEVILLE ACT

OPENED: 1924
Revue

Songs: In Dutch (C: William Cary Duncan;
L: Irving Caesar)

Cast: Ed Gallagher; Al Shean

Notes: A vaudeville act. No other information
available.

1433 • GALLOPER, THE
OPENED: 01/22/1906   Theatre: Garden
Play   Broadway: 76

Author: Richard Harding Davis
Producer: Henry W. Savage
Director: George Marion

Set Design: Walter Burridge

Songs: Land of Make Believe, The (C: Lester Keith;
L: John Kemble)

Cast: Herbert Corthell; Raymond Hitchcock;
Harry Stone

1434 • GAMBLERS, THE
OPENED: 10/31/1910   Theatre: Maxine Elliott's
Play   Broadway: 192

Author: Charles Klein
Producer: Authors Producing Co., The

Songs: If I Came Back to You and Said I'm Sorry
(C: Gus Edwards; L: Will D. Cobb)

Cast: Jane Cowl; William B. Mack; George Nash;
Charles Stevenson

Notes: ASCAP lists the song under 1913. No
program available.

1435 • GAMBLER'S PARADISE
OPENED: 1975
Musical   Closed out of town
Composer: Norman Sachs
Lyricist: Mel Mandel
Librettist: Ira Wallach
Producer: Robert K. Adams; William Patterson
College
Director: Christopher Hewett

Choreographer: Bob Herget; **Costumes:** Bambi
Stoll; **Dance Arranger:** Leon Odenz; **Lighting**

Designer: Rosemary Gant; H.E. Thrasher;
Musical Director: John Lesko; **Orchestrations:**
Harrison Fisher; **Set Design:** George Mayer;
H.E. Thrasher

Songs: Bathtub, the Lodge, and the Rafter, The;
Before the Miracle; But It's Wrong; Feel Like
Waltzing; Happy Ending; Island in the Sun;
Like Wow; Little Music in Your Life, A; Man
I Am with Her, The; One Way or Another;
Polyandry; Processional; Quite Like Him;
Ruthless; Something Like Someone; South Sea
Island Real Estate Association of Mariposa, The;
Ugga-Da-Bugga-Da-Boo

Cast: Alfred Drake; Suellen Estey; Laurie Franks

1436 • GAME IS UP, THE (FIRST EDITION)
OPENED: 09/29/1964   Theatre: Upstairs at the
                              Downstairs
Revue   Nightclub: 260

Librettist: R.G. Brown; Bill Kaufman; Paul
Koreto; Joan Rivers; Les Roberts; Hap Schlein;
Treva Silverman; Rod Warren
Producer: Rod Warren
Director: Jonathan Lucas

Songs: Adam Clayton Powell (C/L: Rod Warren);
Doll Song, The (C/L: James Rusk); Forgotten
Words (C/L: Rod Warren); Freedom (C/L:
Frank Underwood); Game Is Up, The (C/L: Rod
Warren); Hip Hooray (C/L: James Rusk); I'm
the Girl (C/L: Alan Friedman); Loves in My
Life, The (C: Julian Stein; L: Nino Banome);
76 Foolish Things (C/L: Les Roberts); Sunday
Television (C/L: Rod Warren); Tinsel (C/L:
John Meyer); Tokyo, Mon Amour (C/L: Rod
Warren); Trio Con Brio (C: Blair Weille;
L: Bruce Williamson); Uncle Sam Wants Who?
(C: Marvin Hamlisch; L: Howard Liebling);
What's in a Name? (C/L: Les Roberts)

Cast: Richard Blair; R.G. Brown; Virgil Curry;
Judy Knaiz; Marian Mercer; Carol Morley;
Pianist: Michael Cohen; Daniel Strickland

1437 • GAME IS UP, THE (SECOND EDITION)
OPENED: 03/11/1965   Theatre: Upstairs at the
                              Downstairs
Revue   Nightclub: 132

Songs: Doris (C: Marvin Hamlisch; L: Howard Liebling); Great Society Waltz, The (C/L: Rod Warren); Radio City Music Hall (C/L: Rod Warren)

Notes: Only songs new to this edition listed.

1438 • GAME IS UP, THE (THIRD EDITION)

OPENED: 06/15/1965   Theatre: Upstairs at the Downstairs
Revue   Nightclub: 228

Producer: Rod Warren
Director: Sandra Devlin

Songs: Camp (C/L: Rod Warren); Counterpoint (C/L: Alan Friedman); Day the Peace Action Broke Out, The (C/L: Rod Warren); I Like the Job (C: Michael Cohen; L: Linda Ashton); Lady Bird (C/L: Lesley Davison); Suburbia Square Dance (C: Rod Warren; L: Michael McWhinney)

Cast: Betty Aberlin; Richard Blair; R.G. Brown; Ruth Buzzi; Linda Lavin

1439 • GAME OF LOVE, THE

OPENED: 09/1985
Musical   Closed out of town

Composer: Jacques Offenbach
Additional Music: Nancy Ford
Lyricist: Tom Jones
Librettist: Tom Jones
Director: Gerald Freedman

Source: LAST AFFAIRS OF ANATOL, THE (Play: Arthur Schnitzler); **Arrangements:** Nancy Ford; **Choreographer:** Gerald Freedman; **Costumes:** Lewis D. Rampino; **Lighting Designer:** Spencer Mosse; **Musical Director:** Stuart W. Raleigh; **Set Design:** John Ezell

Songs: Anatol's Last Night; Come Buy a Trinket; Fill Up the Cup; Finishing with an Affair; Garden of Love, The; Hypnotism Song, The; I Love to Be in Love; Ilona's Rampage; In Vienna; It's for the Young; Listen to the Rain; Love Conquers All; Menage-a-Trois; Music of Bavaria, The; Oyster Waltz, The; Seasons; Take Me; There's a Room

Cast: Max Black; Robert Black; Jossie de Guzman; Donna English; John Reeger

Notes: Great Lakes Theatre Festival, Cleveland. This is a rewrite of Jones' show ANATOL which premiered in 1960 at the City Hall Theatre, Hamilton, Bermuda.

1440 • GANG'S ALL HERE, THE

OPENED: 02/18/1931   Theatre: Imperial
Musical   Broadway: 23

Composer: Lewis E. Gensler
Lyricist: Owen Murphy; Robert A. Simon
Librettist: Russel Crouse; Oscar Hammerstein II; Morrie Ryskind
Producer: Lewis E. Gensler; Morris Green
Director: Oscar Hammerstein II; Frank McCoy

Choreographer: Dave Gould; Tilly Losch; **Costumes:** Russell Patterson; **Musical Director:** Gene Salzer; **Orchestrations:** Hans Spialek; **Set Design:** Henry Dreyfuss

Songs: Adorable Julie; Baby Wanna Go Bye-Bye With You; By Special Permission of the Copyright Owners I Love You; Dumb Girl; Gang's All Here, The; Gypsy Rose; How Can I Get Rid of Those Blues?; Husband, Lover and Wife; In the Pink [1]; It Always Takes Two; Moon, Wind, and Sun; More Than Ever [2]; Speak-Easy; Speaking of You; What Have You Done to Me?; Yes Sir, Very Good Sir! [1]; You're Looking Very Good, Marie [1]

Cast: John Gallaudet; Ted Healy; Tom Howard; Hal LeRoy; Gina Malo; Jack McCauley; Zelma O'Neal

Notes: [1] Cut out of town. [2] Sheet music only.

1441 • GANTRY

OPENED: 02/14/1970   Theatre: George Abbott
Musical   Broadway: 1

Composer: Stanley Lebowsky
Lyricist: Fred Tobias
Librettist: Peter Bellwood
Producer: Joseph Cates; Jerry Schlossberg
Director: Onna White

Source: ELMER GANTRY (Novel: Sinclair Lewis); **Choreographer:** Onna White; **Costumes:** Ann

Roth; **Dance Arranger:** Dorothea Freitag; **Lighting Designer:** Jules Fisher; **Musical Director:** Arthur Rubinstein; **Orchestrations:** Jim Tyler; **Set Design:** Robin Wagner; **Vocal Arranger:** Stanley Lebowsky

Songs: Foresight; Gantry's Reaction; He Was There; He's Never Too Busy; Katie Jonas; Offer Yourself to Him [1]; Play Ball with the Lord; Promise of What I Could Be, The; She Was a Woman [1]; Show Him the Way; Someone I've Already Found; Thanks, Sweet Jesus!; These Four Walls; Wave a Hand; We Can All Give Love; We're Sharin' Sharon; You Have to Go with Me [1]

Cast: Bob Gorman; Zale Kessler; Rita Moreno; David Sabin; Robert Shaw; Ted Thurston

Notes: [1] Cut prior to opening.

1442 • GARDEN MATINEE
OPENED: 1906

Songs: Entr'acte (inst.) (C: Rudolf Friml)

Notes: No other information available.

1443 • GARDEN OF DREAMS
Musical

Composer: Harry J. Lincoln
Lyricist: Carl Loveland

Songs: I'm the Most Forgetful Man; Only a Dream of You

Notes: No other information available.

1444 • GARDEN OF EDEN, THE
OPENED: 1916
Musical

Lyricist: Harry B. Smith
Librettist: Harry B. Smith

Notes: Unfinished and unproduced.

1445 • GARRETT O'MAGH
OPENED: 01/07/1901   Theatre: 14th St.
Play   Broadway: 81

Composer: Chauncey Olcott
Lyricist: Chauncey Olcott
Author: Augustus Pitou
Director: Augustus Pitou

Songs: Gra Ma Chree; Ireland a Gra Ma Chree; Lass I Love, The; My Sweet Queen; Paddy's Cat

Cast: Charles Abbott; Edith Barker; Tottie Carr; Margaret Fitzpatrick; Daniel Gilfether; Chauncey Olcott

1446 • GARRICK GAIETIES, THE (1925)
OPENED: 05/17/1925   Theatre: Garrick
Revue   Broadway: 231

Composer Richard Rodgers
Lyricist: Lorenz Hart
Librettist: Howard J. Green; Sam Jaffe; Benjamin M. Kaye; Edith Meiser; Morrie Ryskind; Louis Sorin; Arthur Sullivan
Producer: Theatre Guild, The
Director: Philip Loeb

Choreographer: Herbert Fields; **Costumes:** Carolyn Hancock; **Musical Director:** Richard Rodgers; **Set Design:** Carolyn Hancock

Songs: And Thereby Hangs a Tail [2]; April Fool; Black and White [1]; Butcher, Baker, Candle-Stick Maker (C: Mana-Zucca; L: Benjamin M. Kaye); Do You Love Me?; Finale; Gilding the Guild; Guild Guilded, The [1]; Joy Spreader (A Jazz Opera), The [1]; Ladies of the Box Office; Manhattan [3]; Old-Fashioned Girl, An (L: Edith Meiser); On with the Dance [2]; Rancho Mexicano (C: Tatanacho); Sentimental Me [2]; Soliciting Subscriptions; Stage Managers' Chorus (Walk Upon Your Toes) [1] (L: Dudley Diggs; Lorenz Hart); Three Musketeers, The [3]; Working with a Scarf (inst.)

Cast: Romney Brent; June Cochrane; Hildegarde Halliday; Sterling Holloway; Libby Holman; Edith Meiser; Sanford Meisner; Betty Starbuck; Lee Strasberg

Notes: There were only special performances until the regular run began on 6/8/25. [1] Dropped after opening. [2] Added after opening. [3] From score of WINKLE TOWN.

1447 • GARRICK GAIETIES, THE (1926)

OPENED: 05/10/1926   Theatre: Garrick
Revue   Broadway: 174

Composer: Richard Rodgers
Lyricist: Lorenz Hart
Librettist: Herbert Fields; Chester D. Heywood; Edward Hope; Marion Page Johnson; Benjamin M. Kaye; Newman Levy; Philip Lord
Producer: Theatre Guild, The
Director: Philip Loeb

Choreographer: Herbert Fields; **Costumes:** Carolyn Hancock; **Musical Director:** Roy Webb; **Set Design:** Carolyn Hancock

Songs: Allez-Up [3]; American Beauty Rose [5]; Back to Nature [5]; David Crockett (Davy Crockett) (Who Kept the Wolves Away from the Door When Davy Crockett Went to War) [5]; Four Little Song Pluggers; Gigolo; I Call Upon You Gentlemen (Finale Act II) [1]; Idles of the King; It May Rain [5]; Keys to Heaven; L'Apres Midi d'un Papillon (inst.); Little Souvenir, A [2]; Mexico (To Hell with Mexico) [5]; Mountain Greenery [4]; Queen Elizabeth; Six Little Plays (Requiescat in Pace); Sleepyhead [8]; Somebody Said [6]; Tennis Champs (Helen! Susanne! and Bill!) [7]; We Can't Be As Good As Last Year; What's the Use of Talking?

Cast: Romney Brent; Jack Edwards; Blanche Fleming; William M. Griffith; Hildegarde Halliday; Sterling Holloway; Dorothy Jordan; Philip Loeb; Edith Meiser; Betty Starbuck

Notes: [1] Cut after opening. [2] Cut prior to New York. [3] Added after opening. [4] Later interpolated into ALLEGRO. [5] Part of "The Rose of Arizona," a mini-operetta. [6] Not used. [7] May have same music as "Lillie, Lawrence and Jack" in THE FIFTH AVENUE FOLLIES. [8] Cut after opening. Also cut prior to opening of THE GIRL FRIEND.

1448 • GARRICK GAIETIES, THE (1930)

OPENED: 06/04/1930   Theatre: Guild
Revue   Broadway: 155

Librettist: Carroll Carroll; Gretchen Finletter; Landon Herrick; Sterling Holloway; Sally Humason; Benjamin M. Kaye; Newman Levy; Leo Poldine; Louis Simon
Producer: Theatre Guild, The
Director: Philip Loeb

Choreographer: Olin Howland; **Costumes:** Kate Drain Lawson; Henri Pene du Bois; Louis Simon; **Musical Director:** Tom Jones; **Set Design:** Kate Drain Lawson

Songs: Ankle Up the Altar with Me (C: Richard Myers; L: Edward Eliscu); Beauty (C: Ned Lehac; L: Allen Boretz); Do Tell (C: Charles M. Schwab; L: Henry Myers); Four Infant Prodigies (C: Ned Lehac; L: Allen Boretz); George and Mary (C: Charles M. Schwab; L: Thomas McKnight); Got It Again (C: Ned Lehac; L: Allen Boretz); I Am Only Human After All (C: Vernon Duke; L: Ira Gershwin; E.Y. Harburg); I'm Grover (C: Vernon Duke; L: Newman Levy); In the Bathroom [4] (C: Jay Gorney; L: Howard Dietz); I've Got It Again (C: Ned Lehac; L: Allen Boretz); Johnny Wanamaker (C: Kay Swift; L: Paul James); Just a Sister (C/L: Thomas McKnight); Lazy Levee Loungers (C/L: Willard Robison); Little Privacy, A [4] (C: Vernon Duke; L: E.Y. Harburg); Love Is Like That (C: Ned Lehac; L: Allen Boretz); Mei Lan-Fang (C: Vernon Duke; L: E.Y. Harburg); Opening Number [1] (C: Richard Rodgers; L: E.Y. Harburg); Out of Breath (C: Everett Miller; L: Johnny Mercer); Put It Away Till Spring (C: Peter Nolan; L: Josiah Titzell); Rose of Arizona [3] (C: Richard Rodgers; L: Lorenz Hart); Scheherzade (C/L: Harold Goldman); Shavian Shivers [5] (C: Vernon Duke; L: E.Y. Harburg); There Ain't No Love [4] (C: Vernon Duke; L: E.Y. Harburg); Three Musketeers, The [2] (C: Richard Rodgers; L: Lorenz Hart); Too, Too Divine [6] (C: Vernon Duke; L: E.Y. Harburg); Triple Sec [7] (C: Marc Blitzstein; L: Ronald Jeans); Unaccustomed As I Am [4] (C: Vernon Duke; L: E.Y. Harburg); When the Sun Meets the Moon in Finale-Land (C: Charles M. Schwab; L: Henry Myers); You Lost Your Opportunity (C: Charles M. Schwab; L: Henry Myers)

Cast: Nan Blackstone; Neal Caldwell; Katherine Carrington; Albert Carroll; Ruth Chorpenning; Imogene Coca; Ted Fetter; Hildegarde Halliday; Ray Heatherton; William Holbrook; Sterling Holloway; Otto Hulett; Philip Loeb; Edith Meiser; James Norris; Cynthia Rogers; Rosalind Russell; Roger Stearns; Donald Stewart; William Tannen; Velma Vavra; Doris Vinton

Notes: Duke writes in his autobiography that he and Harburg added five songs to the tour. [1] Added for touring edition. Same music as "Six Little Plays" in THE GARRICK GAIETIES (1926). [2] Originally in THE GARRICK GAIETIES (1925). Added for touring edition. [3] Originally in THE GARRICK GAIETIES (1926). Added for touring edition. [4] Added for touring edition that played 12 performances in New York, 10/16/30, Guild Theatre, prior to tour. [5] Same music as "Too Too Divine" from British show OPEN YOUR EYES. [6] Not in program. [7] An original one-act opera.

1449 • GARRICK GAIETIES, THE (1930) (SECOND EDITION)

Notes: *See THE GARRICK GAIETIES (1930)* for songs in this edition.

1450 • GATES OF PARADISE, THE

OPENED: 11/25/1977
Musical   Off-Broadway: 12

Composer: Bill Vitale
Lyricist: Bill Vitale
Librettist: Ed Kuczewski
Producer: Fantasy Factory, The
Director: Bill Vitale

Choreographer: Jay Fox; **Costumes:** Milly Russell; **Lighting Designer:** Dan Abrahamsen; **Musical Director:** Richard Fiocca; **Orchestrations:** Richard Fiocca; **Set Design:** W.J. Giampa; **Vocal Arranger:** Richard Fiocca

Songs: Accompaniment; Bad Trip; Canticle Charon; Dying Is; Falling Star; It's Easy-Let-Go; Main Event, The; Montevideo; Passing Through Exotic Places; Poodle & Canary, also Tom & Jerry Menage a Culinary Croak, The; Seamy Side of Heaven; Seventh Sacrament, The; Treeless Leaflets of Times Square, The

Cast: Ed Kuczewski; Joan Neuman

Notes: Limited engagement.

1451 • GATSBY

Musical   Unproduced

Composer: Lee Pockriss
Lyricist: Carolyn Leigh

Source: GREAT GATSBY, THE (Novel: F. Scott Fitzgerald)

Songs: Bad News; Myrtle's March; Sooner or Later

Notes: An unfinished musical. No other information available.

1452 • GAY COMPANY

Notes: *See IN GAY COMPANY.*

1453 • GAY DIVORCE

OPENED: 11/29/1932   Theatre: Ethel Barrymore
Musical   Broadway: 248

Composer: Cole Porter
Lyricist: Cole Porter
Librettist: Samuel Hoffenstein; Kenneth Webb
Producer: Tom Weatherly; Dwight Deere Wiman
Director: Howard Lindsay

Choreographer: Barbara Newberry; Carl Randall; **Costumes:** Raymond Sovey; **Musical Director:** Gene Salzer; **Orchestrations:** Robert Russell Bennett; Hans Spialek; **Set Design:** Jo Mielziner

Songs: After You, Who?; Fate [1]; How's Your Romance?; I Love Only You [2]; I Still Love the Red, White and Blue; I've Got You on My Mind [3]; Mr. and Missus Fitch; Never Say No [2]; Night and Day; Salt Air [4]; Waiters V. Waitresses [2]; Weekend Affair, A [5]; What Will Become of Our England?; Why Marry Them?; You're in Love

Cast: Fred Astaire; Eric Blore; Roland Bottomley; Luella Gear; G.P. Huntley; Claire Luce; Erik Rhodes; Betty Starbuck

Notes: [1] Not used. Same music as "Salt Air." [2] Added to London production 11/2/33. [3] Not used in THE NEW YORKERS and STAR DUST. [4] Same music as "Fate." [5] Not used.

1454 • GAY GORDONS, THE

OPENED: 09/11/1907   Theatre: Aldwych
Musical   London: 229

Composer: Walter Davidson; Guy Jones; Frank E. Tours

Lyricist: C.H. Bovill; Walter Davidson; Henry Hamilton; Arthur Wimperis; P.G. Wodehouse
Librettist: Seymour Hicks
Producer: Charles Frohman
Director: Seymour Hicks

Choreographer: Edward Royce; **Costumes:** Wilhelm; **Musical Director:** Frank E. Tours; **Set Design:** Philip Howden; R.C. McCleary

Songs: Everybody Loves Me Up in London (C: Frank Tours; L: Unknown); Now that My Ship Has Come In (C: Guy Jones; L: P.G. Wodehouse); You, You, You (C: Guy Jones; L: P.G. Wodehouse)

Cast: A.W. Baskcomb; Barbara Deane; Fred Emney; Sydney Fairbrother; Seymour Hicks; William Lugg; Ellaline Terriss

Notes: No program available.

1455 • GAY HUSSARS, THE

OPENED: 07/29/1909   Theatre: Knickerbocker
Musical   Broadway: 44

Composer: Emmerich Kalman
Lyricist: Grant Stewart
Librettist: Maurice Brown Kirby
Producer: Henry W. Savage
Director: George Marion

Source: EIN HERBSTMANOEVER (Musical: Robert Bodanzky; Emmerich Kalman; Karl Von Bakony); **Lighting Designer:** Joseph Wilson; **Musical Director:** Gus Salzer

Songs: Army Directory, The; Dreaming of Love; Finale Act I; Finale Act II; Finale Act III; Gay Hussars, The; Heart to Heart; Hungarian Song and Dance; Hussar's Quadrille; Kitty Please Give Me a Kiss; Love Is a Traitor; Misfit Soldier, A (Orders but Confuse Me) [3] (L: Maurice Brown Kirby); My Friend Lebel; O, Silver Moon! (Forgive! Forgive!); Oh! You Bold Bad Men (L: Maurice B. Kirby); Particular Marguerite [2] (C/L: John L. Golden); Sex Delicious; Shine Out, All You Little Stars [1] (C: Jerome Kern; L: M.E. Rourke); Soldier's Life, A; Vagrant Fancies

Cast: Anna Bussert; Bobby North; Florence Reid; Muriel Terry

Notes: Titled AUTUMN MANOEVRES in London prior to New York. [1] Not in program. [2] Out Chicago 6/5/10. [3] Kirby not credited in vocal score.

1456 • GAY LIFE, THE

OPENED: 11/18/1961   Theatre: Shubert
Musical   Broadway: 113

Composer: Arthur Schwartz
Lyricist: Howard Dietz
Librettist: Fay Kanin; Michael Kanin
Producer: Kermit Bloomgarden
Director: Gerald Freedman

Source: ANATOL (Play: Arthur Schnitzler); **Choreographer:** Herbert Ross; **Costumes:** Lucinda Ballard; **Dance Arranger:** Robert Starer; **Lighting Designer:** Jean Rosenthal; **Musical Director:** Herbert Greene; **Orchestrations:** Don Walker; **Set Design:** Oliver Smith; **Vocal Arranger:** Herbert Greene

Songs: Bloom Is Off the Rose, The; Bring Your Darling Daughter; Come A-Wandering with Me; Come Away [1]; Drink the Waters [1]; For the First Time; Gay Life, The [1]; Girl Like That, A [1]; I Lost the Love of Anatol [1]; I Love a Wedding [1]; I Never Had a Chance; I Wouldn't Marry You; If It Hadn't Been for You [1]; I'm Glad I'm Single; Just What I Wanted [1]; Label on the Bottle, The; Magic Moment; Now I'm Ready for a Frau; Oh, Mein Liebchen; Something You Never Had Before; This Kind of a Girl; Vignettes [1]; What a Charming Couple [2]; Who Can? You Can!; Why Go Anywhere at All? [2]; You Will Never Be Lonely; You're Not the Type

Cast: Elizabeth Allen; Jeanne Bal; Walter Chiari; Barbara Cook; Lu Leonard; Jules Munshin; Loring Smith

Notes: [1] Cut out of town. [2] Cut after opening.

1457 • GAY MODISTE, THE

OPENED: 04/17/1914
Musical   Closed out of town

Composer: Hugh W. Hubert
Lyricist: Hugh W. Hubert
Librettist: Billy W. Watson
Producer: Joe Hurtig
Director: Joe Hurtig

Choreographer: Dan Dody

Songs: I'm on My Way to Mandalay; In Gay Paree; Never Too Old to Love; Parisian Glide; Smother Me with Kisses; This Is the Life; You're My Girl

Cast: Ida Bayton; Dolly Fields; Blanche Frey; Billy Watson

Notes: Part of TWO HOT KNIGHTS.

1458 • GAY MUSICIAN, THE
OPENED: 05/18/1908   Theatre: Wallack
Musical   Broadway: 21

Composer: Julian Edwards
Lyricist: Charles J. Campbell
Librettist: Edward Siedle
Producer: Amus Producing Company
Director: Julian Edwards

Choreographer: Roger Gray; **Costumes:** Mme. Castel-Bert; **Musical Director:** A. DeNovellis; **Set Design:** Ernest Albert; James Fox

Songs: At Last I Hold You; Box Office Tells the Story, The; Come Along (It's a Trifling Affair); Cup of Tea, A; Daintily and Lightly; Dance Hilda [2]; Danse D'Une Coquette (inst.); Dearest, Best, Divine; Disposition [1]; D'Une Coquette; Fishing [2]; Hail! To the Queen of Beauty; Hi! Allez! Hoopla! (Finale Act I); I Have My Doubts; I Want to Be Your Baby Boy; It's a Long, Long Time; It's the Unexpected Happens; Lesson in Dancing, A [2]; Lovelight Beaming from Your Eyes, The; My Soldier Boy; Not As Simple As I Look; Sad Bad Man [1]; Saucy Sparrow, The; Take That; That Melody; That's How I Get Treated; We Won't Do a Thing to His Opera; What a Dry World This Would Be

Cast: Joseph C. Miron; Walter Percival; Amelia Stone

Notes: [1] Cut out of town. [2] Sheet music only.

1459 • GAY NEW YORK
OPENED: 02/01/1906
Musical   Closed out of town

Composer: Harry Trappert
Librettist: Maurice Hageman
Director: M.L. Heckert

Choreographer: Edward B. Adams; **Costumes:** Will R. Barnes; Frank Hayden; J. Henry Rowley; **Lighting Designer:** Joseph Menchen; **Set Design:** Ernest Albert; C.W. Valentine

Songs: Dainty Mignon; Gay New York; Hinkee Dee; Julia; March; Message from Mars; Model's Complaint; Newport By the Sea; On the Links; Students on a Lark; Why So Late

Cast: Dan Mason; Louis Sanford

Notes: Program from Wilkes-Barre.

1460 • GAY PAREE (1925)
OPENED: 08/18/1925   Theatre: Shubert
Revue   Broadway: 181

Composer: J. Fred Coots; Al Goodman; Maurie Rubens
Lyricist: Clifford Grey
Librettist: Harold Atteridge
Producer: Messrs. Shubert
Director: Charles Judels

Choreographer: Alexis Kosloff; Earl Lindsay; **Musical Director:** Charles Drury; **Orchestrations:** Emil Gerstenberger; **Set Design:** Watson Barratt

Songs: Baby's Baby Grand (C: J. Fred Coots; Alfred Goodman); Bamboo Babies (C: James F. Hanley; Joseph Meyer; L: Ballard Macdonald; Al Sherman); Beautiful Girls [1]; Every Girl Must Have a Little Bull (C: J. Fred Coots; Alfred Goodman); Florida Mammy; Give Me the Rain (C: Lester Allen; L: Henry Creamer); Glory of the Morning Sunshine, The; Heart of a Rose [2] (C: J. Fred Coots; Maurie Rubens); Hocus Pocus [1] (C: James F. Hanley; L: Lew Brown); I Can't Believe That You're in Love with Me [1] (C: Jimmy McHugh; L: Clarence Gaskill); I Was Meant for Someone (C: James F. Hanley; L: Ballard Macdonald); Oh! Boy!, What a Girl [1] (C: Bessinger; Wright; L: Bud Green); Opera in 1860, The; Study in Legs, A; (My) Sugar Plum [4] (C: Joseph Meyer; L: B.G. DeSylva); Tillie of Longacre Square (C: James F. Hanley; L: Harold Atteridge; Ballard Macdonald); Toddle Trot; Venetian Nights; Venetian Wedding Moon; Vision of Hassan, A; Wedgewood Maid; Wide Pants Willie [3] (C: James F. Hanley; L: Harold Atteridge; Henry Creamer); Wonderful Girl (C: J. Fred Coots; Alfred Goodman)

Cast: Newton Alexander; Richard Bold; Chandler Christy; Eddie Conrad; Claudia Dell; Beth Elliott; Ruth Gillette; Viola Griffith; Jack Haley; George LeMaire; Winnie Lightner; Prosper and Maret; Chic Sale; Salt and Pepper; Wilfred Seagram; Bartlett Simmons; Billy B. Van; Margaret Wilson

Notes: [1] Sheet music only. [2] Also in BROADWAY NIGHTS. [3] Atteridge not credited by ASCAP. [4] J. Fred Coots also credited as cocompser in some sources. ASCAP lists James F. Hanley as the sole composer.

1461 • GAY PAREE (1926)

OPENED: 11/09/1926   Theatre: Winter Garden
Revue   Broadway: 175

Composer: J. Fred Coots; Alberta Nichols; Maurie Rubens
Lyricist: Clifford Grey; Mann Holiner
Librettist: Harold Atteridge
Producer: Messrs. Shubert
Director: J.C. Huffman; Charles Judels

Choreographer: Seymour Felix; **Musical Director:** Harry Nieman; **Set Design:** Watson Barratt

Songs: Bachanol; Bad Little Boy with Dancing Legs; Beautiful Fan, A; Broken Rhythm; College Days; Do That Doo-Da (C: Maurie Rubens; L: J. Keirn Brennan); Fine Feathers; 'Je T'Aime' Means I Love You (C/L: Powers Gouraud); Kandahar Isle; More We Dance, The; No More Dancing; Oriental Nights; Paris Is a Paradise for Coons; Shaking the Blues Away; There Never Was a Town Like Paris

Cast: Newton Alexander; Jane Aubert; Richard Bold; Chester Fredericks; Frank Gaby; Jack Haley; Max Hoffmann Jr.; Ben Holmes; Douglass Leavitt; Winnie Lightner; Mary Milburn; Chic Sale; Helen Wehrle

1462 • GAY PAREE (1929)

OPENED: 1929
Musical   Closed out of town

Composer: Maurie Rubens
Lyricist: J. Keirn Brennan
Librettist: Harold Atteridge
Producer: Franklyn Betie; Frank Gaby; Chic Sale; Messrs. Shubert
Director: Thomas A. Hart

Choreographer: LeRoy Prinz; **Costumes:** Ernest Schrapps; **Musical Director:** Albert Bertin; **Set Design:** Watson Barratt

Songs: Bracelets [1]; Chinese Love Boat, The; Cock-a-Doodle- Doo; Down on the Bangway Isle; Full of Pep; Hold 'Em Cowboy; Mothers of the World; Nodding Away; Rhythm of Joy; Start the Band; Tell Me You Are Happy; Tree of Love, The; Twilight Voices; What Men and Women Will Wear

Cast: Franklyn Batie; Margie Evans; Sylvia Froos; Frank Gaby; Lillian Herbert; Oliver Reese; Stanley Rogers; Chic Sale; Charlotte Terry

Notes: Curran Theatre, San Fancisco. [1] Also in ARTISTS AND MODELS (1927).

1463 • GAY RASCAL, THE

Notes: *See THE LIAR.*

1464 • GAY WHITE WAY, THE

OPENED: 10/07/1907   Theatre: Casino
Revue   Broadway: 105

Composer: Ludwig Englander
Lyricist: Sydney Rosenfeld
Librettist: . Clarence Harvey; Sydney Rosenfeld
Producer: R.H. Burnside; Lee Shubert; Sam S. Shubert

Set Design: Arthur Voegtlin

Songs: Aren't You the Girl I Met at Sherry's (C: Louis A. Hirsch; L: E. Ray Goetz); Brewster the Millionaire; Broadway Show, The; Climbing the Ladder of Love; Dixie Dan (C: Seymour Furth; L: Will D. Cobb); Duchess of Killarney, The [3] (C: Louis A. Hirsch; L: E. Ray Goetz); Great White Way; If You Must Make Eyes at Someone; Le Kic-King; Love's Merry-Go-Round (C/L: E. Ray Goetz); My Irish Gibson Girl; Parisianna Anna [3] (C: Louis A. Hirsch; L: E. Ray Goetz); Rag-Time Banjo Serenade, The [3] (C: Louis A. Hirsch; L: E. Ray Goetz); Rain-in-the-Face; School of Acting; Somebody's Been Around Here Since I've Been Gone (C: John W. Bratton; L: Paul West); Theodore; Tiddle Om Pom [2]; Without the Girl — Inside! [1] (C/L: Jerome Kern; L: M.E. Rourke); You've Got to Do That Salome Dance

Cast: Alexander Carr; Jefferson De Angelis; Melville Ellis; Maude Raymond; Blanche Ring

Notes: [1] Not in program. [2] An English song "Tiddley-Om-Pom" by Leigh and Powell was written in 1907. This might be that song. [3] Sheet music only.

1465 • GAYEST MANHATTAN OR AROUND NEW YORK IN NINETY MINUTES

OPENED: 03/22/1897   Theatre: Koster & Bial's
Musical   Broadway: 8

Composer: Ludwig Englander
Lyricist: Harry B. Smith
Librettist: Harry B. Smith

Cast: Henry E. Dixey; Flo Irwin; R.A. Roberts; June Stone

Notes: This show included two songs by Matt Woodward. No songs listed in program.

1466 • GAYEST MANHATTAN (1898)

OPENED: 1898
Musical   Closed out of town

Composer: W.H. Batchelor
Lyricist: John F. Harley
Librettist: W.H. Lytell
Producer: Koster & Bial
Director: John F. Harley

Songs: And Mrs. Grundy Winked; But Wasn't It an Odd Place to Do It; Dandy Sparrow Cops, The; Flirtation Duet; For Sweet Charity's Sake; For Thee, My Love; From Skowhegan, Maine, B'Gosh; Gayest Manhattan; Good Old Palmy Days, The; I'm a Practical Politician; Life Is What We Make It; March of the New York Dailies; My Husband Taught Me to Be One of the Boys; My Thoughts Would Still Be with Thee; Ring the Praises Merrily; Roses and Thorns; Ruler of Central Park, The; Susie Smith from Troy; Travesty; When Love Was Born; Will Somebody Tell Me Why?

Cast: George Carr; Jessica Duncan; Frank Gardiner; Jean McIlmoyle

Notes: In program of 3/10/1898 Lytell is credited with lyrics. In 10/24/1898 the lyrics were credited to Harley.

1467 • GAY'S THE WORD

OPENED: 02/16/1951   Theatre: Saville
Musical   London: 504

Composer: Ivor Novello
Lyricist: Alan Melville
Librettist: Ivor Novello
Producer: Tom Arnold
Director: Jack Hulbert

Choreographer: Eunice Crowther; Irving Davies; **Costumes:** Berkeley Sutcliffe; **Musical Director:** Robert Probst; **Set Design:** Edward Delaney

Songs: Bees Are Buzzin'; Englishman in Love, An; Everything Reminds Me of You; Father Thames; Finder Please Return; Gaiety Glad; Guards of the Parade; If Only He'd Looked My Way; It's Bound to Be Right on the Night; Matter of Minutes, A; On Such a Night As This; Ruritania; Sweet Thames; Vitality

Cast: Cicely Courtneidge; Thorley Walters; Lizbeth Webb; Josephine Wray; John Wynyard

1468 • GEECHIE

OPENED: 1926
Musical   Unproduced

Composer: James P. Johnson
Lyricist: Henry Creamer

Notes: No other information available.

1469 • GEEZER OF GECK, THE

OPENED: 07/24/1905
Musical   Closed out of town

Composer: Paul Schindler
Lyricist: Roger J. Adams
Librettist: Roger J. Adams
Producer: Will J. Block
Director: Frank Tannehill Jr.

Choreographer: Ad Neuburger; **Costumes:** Mme. Freisinger; **Lighting Designer:** Joseph George; **Musical Director:** Paul Schindler; **Set Design:** D. Frank Dodge

Songs: All Alone; Away to Jail; Boo-Gee-Boo, The; Dainty Cupid; Daisyland; Day We Longed For, The; Drink Drink, Drink; Fakir Man, The; Fourth of July, The; I Remember Nothing After That; Minstrels on Parade, The; Oh, Those Eyes; Pretty Eskimo; Same Old Sun, The; Stage, Stage; When in Love; When You Come to Town; Willie Off the Yacht

Cast: Louis Kelso; Maym Kelso; Dave Lewis; John Park; Amelia Stone; Florence Townsend

Notes: Titled LOVELAND in Washington, D.C.

1470 • GEISHA, THE

OPENED: 09/09/1896   Theatre: Daly's
Musical   Broadway: 161

Composer: Sidney Jones
Lyricist: Harry Greenbank
Librettist: Owen Hall
Producer: Augustin Daly
Director: Augustin Daly

Costumes: Percy Anderson; **Set Design:** Henry E. Hoyt; W. Telbin

Songs: Amorous Goldfish, The; Attention Pray!; Before Our Eyes; C'est Moi [1] (C: Percy Greenbank; L: Frank E. Tours); Chin-Chin-Chinaman; Ching-a-ring-a-ree; Chivalry; Chon Kina; Chorus of Lamentation; Day Born of Love; Dear Little Jappy-Jap-Jappy, The; Geisha Are We; Geisha's Life, A; Happy Japan; Here They Come; Hey-diddle-diddle! When Man Is in Love; I Can't Refrain from Laughing [1] (C/L: Napoleon Lambelet); If That's Not Love — What Is; If You Will Come to Tea; Interfering Parrot, The; It's Coming Off Today [1]; Jack's the Boy (C: Lionel Monckton); Japanese March; Jewel of Asia, The (C: James Philp); Jolly Young Jacks Are We; Kissing Duet; Love! Love!; Molly Mine [1] (C: Sidney Jones; L: Adrian Ross); Oh, Will They Sell Our Master Up; Star of My Soul; Though of Staying Too Long You're Accusing Us; Toy Duet; Toy Monkey, The (C: Lionel Monckton); We're Going to Call on the Marquis; Wedding, The [1] (C: Sidney Jones; L: Adrian Ross); What Will the Marquis Do? [1]; When I Was But a Tiny Tot; With Splendour Auspicious; You're a Charming Little Geisha

Cast: Bette D'Arcy; Isadora Duncan; Herbert Gresham; Mabel Strickland; Van Rensselaer Wheeler

Notes: No program available. Songs from English version. Additional songs were also by James Philp. [1] Added after opening in London.

1471 • GENERATION

OPENED: 10/06/1965   Theatre: Morosco
Play   Broadway: 299

Composer: Jerry Bock
Lyricist: William Goodhart
Author: William Goodhart
Producer: Frederick Brisson
Director: Gene Saks

Costumes: Albert Wolsky; **Incidental Music:** Jerry Bock; **Lighting Designer:** George Jenkins; **Set Design:** George Jenkins

Songs: Generation (C: Jerry Bock; L: William Goodhart)

Cast: Sandy Baron; Don Fellows; Henry Fonda; A. Larry Haines; Richard Jordan; Holly Turner

1472 • GENIUS, THE

OPENED: 10/03/1906   Theatre: Bijou
Musical   Broadway: 35

Composer: Paul Rubens
Lyricist: Vincent Bryan
Librettist: Cecil B. DeMille; Vincent DeMille
Producer: Mort H. Singer
Director: William H. Post

Choreographer: Harry Pilcer

Cast: Herman Hershberg; Madge Kennedy; Henry Woodruff

Notes: Program of Kansas City 11/3/1910. No New York program available. No songs listed in program. Note the DeMille's participation in this show.

1473 • GENTLEMAN JOE, THE HANSOM CABBY

OPENED: 01/06/1896   Theatre: Fifth Avenue
Musical   Broadway: 10

Composer: Walter Slaughter
Lyricist: Basil Hood

Librettist: Basil Hood
Director: Richard Barker

Musical Director: Herman Perlet

Songs: In Gay Paree; I've Always Been Brought Up Polite; Lalage Potts That's Me; My Dream of You; Only Fancy; Opening Chorus; Wink of His Eye, The; Won't You Come to Margate

Cast: Henry Hallem; Willard Lee; Laura Moore; Adelaide Worth

Notes: Songs are from Act I only. The program was incomplete.

1474 • GENTLEMEN BE SEATED!
OPENED: 10/10/1963 Theatre: City Center
Revue Off-Broadway: 3

Composer: Jerome Moross
Lyricist: Edward Eager
Librettist: Edward Eager; Jerome Moross
Producer: N.Y. City Center
Director: Robert Turoff

Choreographer: Paul Draper; **Costumes:** Henry Heymann; **Musical Director:** Emerson Buckley; **Set Design:** William Pitkin

Songs: Ballad of Belle Boyd, The; Ballad of Stonewall Jackson, The; Belle Boyd's Back in Town; Belle Boyd, Where Have You Been?; Contraband Ball, The; Fare You Well; Freedom Train, The; From Atlanta to the Sea; Grand March; Have You Seen Him, Did He Pass This Way?; I Can't Remember; I Spy; I'm a Pinkerton Man; I'm Mathew P. Brady, the Camera Man; In the Sunny Old South; It's Quiet on the Potomac Tonight; It's the Witching Hour By the Old Water Tower; Look Who I Am, Surprise! Surprise!; Miss Dorothea Dix; Mocking Bird; Mr. Brady Takes a Photograph; O, Miss Walkaround, Come Walking Out with Me; Oh, the Picnic at Manassas; Pardon, Ma'am; Shiloh; Tap Dance Drill; This Isn't a Gentlemen's War Anymore; This Was the War, What Did It Do for Me and You? . . . Didn't It, Did It?; Waltzing in the Shadow; What Has Become to Beauty?; Why Ain't We Got a Dome?

Cast: Charles Atkins; Carol Brice; Alice Ghostley; Avon Long; Dick Shawn

1475 • GENTLEMEN PREFER BLONDES
OPENED: 12/08/1949 Theatre: Ziegfeld
Musical Broadway: 740

Composer: Jule Styne
Lyricist: Leo Robin
Librettist: Joseph Fields; Anita Loos
Producer: Herman Levin; Oliver Smith
Director: John C. Wilson

Source: GENTLEMEN PREFER BLONDES (Novel: Anita Loos); **Choreographer:** Agnes de Mille; **Costumes:** Miles White; **Dance Arranger:** Trude Rittman; **Musical Director:** Milton Rosenstock; **Orchestrations:** Don Walker; **Set Design:** Oliver Smith; **Vocal Arranger:** Hugh Martin

Songs: Button Up with Esmond; Bye Bye Baby; Coquette; Could You Love a Dreamer [3]; Diamonds Are a Girl's Best Friend; Gentlemen Prefer Blondes; Homesick Blues; House on Rittenhouse Square, A [3]; I Feel So Jazzy [3]; I Love What I'm Doing; I'm A'Tingle, I'm A'Glow; In the Champs de Mars [2]; It's Delightful Down in Chile; It's High Time; Just a Kiss Apart; Keeping Cool with Coolidge; Little Girl from Little Rock, A; Look at Me [3]; Mamie Is Mimi; Practice Scherzo, The [4]; Sunshine; Talk to Me Tomorrow [3]; You Kill Me [1]; You Say You Care

Cast: Yvonne Adair; Anita Alvarez; Eric Brotherson; Carol Channing; Rex Evans; George S. Irving; Mort Marshall; Jack McCauley; Howard Morris; Alice Pearce; Reta Shaw

Notes: *See LORELEI*, a reworking of this show. [1] Added to London production. From film MACAO. [2] Part of "Sunshine." [3] Not used. [4] Music later used as main theme of titular ballet of THE RED SHOES.

1476 • GENTLEMEN UNAFRAID
OPENED: 06/03/1938
Musical Closed out of town

Composer: Jerome Kern
Lyricist: Oscar Hammerstein II; Otto Harbach
Librettist: Oscar Hammerstein II; Otto Harbach
Producer: Municipal Theatre Association of St. Louis; Richard Berger

Choreographer: Theodore Adolphus; Al White Jr.; **Costumes:** Billy Livingston; **Musical Director:** George Hirst; **Set Design:** Raymond Sovey

Songs: Abe Lincoln Has Just One Country; Army Blue [4]; Bonnie Blue Flag [4]; Boy with a Drum [3] (L: Otto Harbach); Cantible (A Song without Words) (inst.) [5]; De Land O' Good Times; Garden Scene [4]; Gentlemen Unafraid; How Would I Know? (I Wish Dat Dere Wasn't No War) (L: Oscar Hammerstein II); Interlude in the Dark (We Are a Band of Brothers) [4]; It's Gayer Whistling as You Go (Gaily I Whistle a Song) (L: Otto Harbach); Kissing Rock, The [3]; Little Wily Miss [3]; Little Zouave; Many a Lofty Mountain [1] (L: Oscar Hammerstein II); Mister Man; Opening (Greet Your Candidate); Our Last Dance; Sweet as a Rose [1]; Virginia Hoe Down; What Kind of Soldier Are You?; What's Become of the Night [3]; When a New Star [3] (L: Otto Harbach); When You Hear That Humming (L: Otto Harbach); Your Dream (Is the Same As My Dream) [2]

Cast: Minto Cato; Annamary Dickey; Ronald Graham; Avon Long; Hope Manning; Ralph Riggs; Richard "Red" Skelton; Barry Sullivan

Notes: Released in 1942 by National Theatre Conference as HAYFOOT, STRAWFOOT. Asst. Musical Director: Jacob Schwartzdorf (Jay Blackton). [1] Cut before opening. [2] Used later in ONE NIGHT IN THE TROPICS (film). [3] Added to score when retitled HAYFOOT, STRAWFOOT. [4] ASCAP/Library of Congress only. [5] Not in programs.

1477 • GEOGRAFOOF, THE

OPENED: 1958
Musical

Composer: Jay Gorney
Lyricist: Henry Myers

Songs: Congo Ivory; Cuckoo Clock; Don't Be a Geografoof; Foof to Old Geography; Have a Cup of Tea; Honduran Mahongany; Italianesque Scene; Mysterious Scene; Piano Talk; There's a Country; Viva Italia

Notes: No other information available.

1478 • GEORGE M!

OPENED: 04/10/1968   Theatre: Palace
Musical   Broadway: 435

Composer: George M. Cohan
Lyricist: George M. Cohan
Librettist: Fran Pascal; John Pascal; Michael Stewart
Producer: David Black; Konrad Matthai; Lorin Price
Director: Joe Layton

Choreographer: Joe Layton; **Costumes:** Freddy Wittop; **Lighting Designer:** Martin Aronstein; **Musical Director:** Jay Blackton; **Orchestrations:** Philip J. Lang; **Set Design:** Tom H. John; **Vocal Arranger:** Jay Blackton

Songs: All Aboard for Broadway [1]; All in the Wearing [2]; All Our Friends [3]; American Ragtime, The [4]; Barnum and Bailey Rag [5]; Belle of the Barber's Ball, The [6]; Billie [7]; City, The [17]; Dancing Our Worries Away [8]; Down By the Erie Canal [5]; Forty-five Minutes from Broadway [9]; Give My Regards to Broadway [10]; Great Easter Sunday Parade, The [17]; Hannah's a Hummer [11]; Harrigan [12]; I Want to Hear a Yankee Doodle Tune [13]; I Was Born in Virginia [1]; I'd Rather Be Right [14]; Mary [9]; Musical Comedy Man [15]; Musical Moon [16]; My Town [17]; Nellie Kelly I Love You [2]; Oh, You Wonderful Boy [18]; Over There [19]; Popularity [20]; Push Me Along in My Pushcart [21]; Ring to the Name of Rosie [22]; So Long, Mary [9]; Twentieth Century Love [23]; Yankee Doodle Boy [10]; You're a Grand Old Flag [1]

Cast: Loni Ackerman; Jonelle Allen; Jacqueline Alloway; Susan Belson; Danny Carroll; Gene Castle; Jerry Dodge; Jamie Donnelly; Harvey Evans; Joel Grey; Betty Ann Grove; Angela Martin; Jill O'Hara; Bernadette Peters

Notes: A bio-musical of George M. Cohan. Music and lyrics revised by Mary Cohan. Music supervisor: Laurence Rosenthal. [1] From GEORGE WASHINGTON, JR. (1906). [2] From LITTLE NELLIE KELLY (1922). [3] Revised from "They're All My Boys" from LITTLE NELLIE KELLY (1922). [4] From THE AMERICAN IDEA (1908). [5] From HELLO, BROADWAY! (1914). [6] 1912 pop song. [7] From BILLIE (1928). [8] From "Dancing My Worries Away" from LITTLE NELLIE KELLY (1922). [9] From FORTY-FIVE MINUTES FROM BROADWAY (1906). [10] From LITTLE JOHNNY

JONES (1904). [11] From THE WISE GUY (1899). [12] From FIFTY MILES FROM BOSTON (1908). [13] From MOTHER GOOSE (1903). [14] From I'D RATHER BE RIGHT (1937). [15] From "Musical Comedy Maid" from THE HONEYMOONERS. [16] From THE LITTLE MILLIONAIRE (1911). [17] Unknown source. [18] From "Oh, You Wonderful Girl" from THE LITTLE MILLIONAIRE (1911). [19] 1917 pop song. [20] 1906 pop song. [21] From THE GOVERNOR'S SON (1901). [22] From THE RISE OF ROSIE O'REILLY (1923). [23] From THE MERRY MALONES (1927).

1479 • GEORGE WASHINGTON BULLION ABROAD

OPENED: 1915
Musical

Composer: J. Homer Tutt; James Vaughn; Salem Tutt Whitney
Lyricist: J. Homer Tutt; Salem Tutt Whitney
Librettist: J. Homer Tutt; Salem Tutt Whitney
Producer: J. Homer Tutt; Salem Tutt Whitney

Musical Director: James Vaughn

Songs: Allah Oh! Allah!; Body Guards of the Prince; Dance of Death; Deep Blue Sea, The; Dinner Bells; Dog Gon I'm Young Again; Don't Do That to Me Dear; Gin, Gin, Gin; Going Back to Dixieland; Golden Days; Goodby My Old Kentucky Home; Help Cometh from Above; Italy and My Rose; Levee Pastimes; Love Me Anywhere; Maryanna; Moonlight Pace; No Matter How Good You Treat the World You Never Get Out Alive; Shine On Southern Moon; Strutting Sam; We're Sailing Along; When You Hear the Old Kentucky Blues

Cast: Hattie Akers; Will Dixon; Sam Gardner; Frank Jackson; Ethel Marshall; George McClain; Ethelyn Proctor; Luke Scott; Blanche Thompson; J. Homer Tutt; Salem Tutt Whitney

Notes: No other information available.

1480 • GEORGE WASHINGTON, JR.

OPENED: 12/12/1906   Theatre: Herald Square
Musical   Broadway: 81

Composer: George M. Cohan
Lyricist: George M. Cohan

Librettist: George M. Cohan
Producer: Sam Harris
Director: George M. Cohan

Songs: All Aboard for Broadway; Colonial Chorus [2]; Ethel Levey's Virginia Song; He Was a Wonderful Man; If Washington Should Come to Life; I'll Be There with Bells On; I've Never Been Over There; Wedding of the Blue and the Gray, The; You Can Have Broadway [1]; You're a Grand Old Flag

Cast: George M. Cohan; Helen Cohan; Jerry Cohan; Ethel Levey; Truly Shattuck; Willis Sweatnam

Notes: [1] Sheet music only. [2] Out of town 9/16/06.

1481 • GEORGE WHITE'S MUSIC HALL VARIETIES

OPENED: 11/22/1932   Theatre: Casino
Revue   Broadway: 71

Librettist: William K. Wells; George White
Producer: George White
Director: George White

Choreographer: Russell Markert; **Costumes:** Kiviette; Charles LeMaire; **Musical Director:** Alfred Goodman; **Orchestrations:** Maurice DePackh; **Set Design:** Dazian

Songs: Birds of a Feather (C: Carmen Lombardo; L: Irving Caesar); Bottle and a Bird, A (C/L: Irving Caesar); Cabin in the Cotton (C: Harold Arlen; L: Irving Caesar; George White); Hold Me Closer (C/L: Frank Littau; Max Rich; Jack Scholl); Hundred Years Ago, A (C: Cliff Friend; L: Herb Magidson); Let's Turn Out the Lights and Go to Bed (C/L: Herman Hupfeld); Oh, Lady (C: Sam H. Stept; L: Herbert Magidson); Rah, Rah, Rah (C: Sam Stept; L: Irving Caesar; Herb Magidson); (And) So I Married the Girl (C: Sam H. Stept; L: Herbert Magidson); Sweet Liar (C/L: Irving Caesar); There Never Was a Girl Like You (C: Cliff Friend; L: Herb Magidson); Two Feet in Two- Four Time (C: Harold Arlen; L: Irving Caesar); Waltz that Brought You Back to Me, The (C: Carmen Lombardo; L: Irving Caesar)

Cast: Helen Arnold; Lily Damita; Vivian Fay; Betty Kean; Hilda Knight; Bert Lahr; Loomis Sisters, The; Eleanor Powell; Harry Richman

1482 • GEORGE WHITE'S SCANDALS (1919)

OPENED: 06/02/1919　Theatre: Liberty
Revue　　　　　　　Broadway: 128

Composer: Herbert Spencer; Richard A. Whiting
Lyricist: Arthur Jackson; George White
Producer: George White
Director: Edgar MacGregor

Choreographer: George White; **Musical Director:** Julius Linzberg

Songs: Broadway Belles; Girls Are Like the Weather to Me; I Could Be Happy with One Little Boy If There Were No Others Around (C: Richard A. Whiting; L: Arthur Jackson); I'll Be There; Land of Heart's Desire (C: Richard A. Whiting; L: Arthur Jackson); My Little Address Book (C: Richard A. Whiting; L: Arthur Jackson); Peacock Parade, The [2] (C: Richard A. Whiting; L: Arthur Jackson); Step This Way (C: Richard A. Whiting; L: Arthur Jackson); Suwannee River; Those Beautiful Girls [1]; Three Mile Limit Cafe (C: Richard A. Whiting; L: Arthur Jackson); Up Above the Stars

Cast: George Bickel; Lou Holtz; Ona Munson; Ann Pennington; Yvette Rugel; George White

Notes: [1] Added after opening. [2] Also titled "Peacock Alley."

1483 • GEORGE WHITE'S SCANDALS (1920)

OPENED: 06/07/1920　Theatre: Liberty
Revue　　　　　　　Broadway: 134

Composer: George Gershwin
Lyricist: Arthur Jackson
Librettist: Andy Rice; George White
Producer: George White
Director: George White

Musical Director: Alfred Newman;
　Orchestrations: Frank Saddler

Songs: Everybody Swat the Profiteer; Idle Dreams; My Lady; My Old Love Is My New Love [1]; On My Mind the Whole Night Long; Queen Isabella [1]; Scandal Walk; Songs of Long Ago; Tum On and Tiss Me

Cast: Lester Allen; Sascha Beaumont; Lou Holtz;

Lester O'Keefe; Ann Pennington; George "Doc" Rockwell; George White

Notes: [1] Not used.

1484 • GEORGE WHITE'S SCANDALS (1921)

OPENED: 07/11/1921　Theatre: Liberty
Revue　　　　　　　Broadway: 97

Composer: George Gershwin
Lyricist: Arthur Jackson
Librettist: Bugs Baer; George White
Producer: George White
Director: John Meehan; George White

Costumes: Gilbert Adrian; Ada Fields; Alice O'Neil; Albertine Randall Wheelan; **Musical Director:** Alfred Newman; **Set Design:** Herbert Ward

Songs: Drifting Along with the Tide; I Love You; Mother Eve (C: James F. Hanley; L: Ballard Macdonald); She's Just a Baby; Sunny South Sea Isles; Where East Meets West

Cast: Lester Allen; Bert Bordon; Tess Gardella; Charles King; George LeMaire; Ann Pennington; Olive Vaughn; George White

1485 • GEORGE WHITE'S SCANDALS (1922)

OPENED: 08/28/1922　Theatre: Globe
Revue　　　　　　　Broadway: 89

Composer: George Gershwin
Lyricist: B.G. DeSylva; E. Ray Goetz
Librettist: W.C. Fields; Andy Rice; George White
Producer: George White
Director: George White

Costumes: Erte; **Musical Director:** Max Steiner; **Set Design:** Herbert Ward; John Wenger

Songs: Argentina (L: B.G. DeSylva); Blue Monday Blues [1] (L: B.G. DeSylva); (Little) Cinderelatives [2] (L: B.G. DeSylva); Grab Bag, The (L: E. Ray Goetz); Has Anyone Seen My Joe [1] (L: B.G. DeSylva); I Can't Tell Where They're From When They Dance; I Found a Four Leaf Clover (L: B.G. DeSylva); I'll Build a Stairway to Paradise (L: B.G. DeSylva; Ira Gershwin); I'm Gonna See My Mother [1] (L: B.G. DeSylva); Just a Tiny Cup of Tea (L: B.G. DeSylva); Moth For My Flame, The; My Heart Will Sail Across the Sea; Oh, What She Hangs Out She Hangs Out in Our Alley; Where Is the Man of My Dreams

Cast: Lester Allen; Richard Bold; Dolores Costello; W.C. Fields; Winnie Lightner; Jack McGowan; Pearl Regay; Coletta Ryan; George White; Paul Whiteman and His Orchestra

Notes: [1] From BLUE MONDAY, a brief opera that was cut after opening. [2] Cut after opening.

1486 • GEORGE WHITE'S SCANDALS (1923)

OPENED: 06/18/1923   Theatre: Globe
Revue   Broadway: 168

Composer: George Gershwin
Lyricist: B.G. DeSylva; E. Ray Goetz; Ballard Macdonald
Librettist: William K. Wells; George White
Producer: George White
Director: George White

Costumes: Erte; Cora MacGeachy; **Musical Director:** Charles Drury

Songs: Garden of Love [1] (L: B.G. DeSylva); Gold Digger, The [2] (C/L: James F. Hanley); Home Lights I Long to See [3] (C: Harry Carroll; L: Ballard Macdonald); How Ya Gonna Keep Your Mind on Dancing When You're Dancing with Someone You Love (C: James F. Hanley; L: Lew Brown); (On the Beach at) How've You Been? [2] (L: B.G. DeSylva); Katinka; Laugh Your Cares Away; Let's Be Lonesome Together (L: B.G. DeSylva; E. Ray Goetz); Life of a Rose, The (L: B.G. DeSylva); Little Scandal Dolls; Lo-La-Lo (L: B.G. DeSylva); Look in the Looking Glass; Stingo-Stungo [2] (C/L: James F. Hanley; L: Lew Brown); There Is Nothing Too Good for You (L: B.G. DeSylva; E. Ray Goetz); Throw 'Er in High! [2] (L: B.G. DeSylva; E. Ray Goetz); Where Is She? (L: B.G. DeSylva); You and I (In Old Versailles) (C: George Gershwin; Jack Green; L: B.G. DeSylva)

Cast: Lester Allen; Richard Bold; Johnny Dooley; Helen Hudson; Winnie Lightner; Tom Patricola; Olive Vaughn

Notes: [1] Added to road tour. [2] Not in program. [3] ASCAP/Library of Congress.

1487 • GEORGE WHITE'S SCANDALS (1924)

OPENED: 06/30/1924   Theatre: Apollo
Revue   Broadway: 198

Composer: George Gershwin
Lyricist: B.G. DeSylva
Librettist: William K. Wells; George White
Producer: George White
Director: George White

Costumes: Erte; **Musical Director:** William Daly; **Orchestrations:** Maurice DePackh

Songs: I Love You, My Darling [1]; I Need a Garden; I'm Going Back; Just Missed the Opening Chorus; Kongo Kate; Lovers of Art; Mah-Jongg [2]; Night Time in Araby; Rose of Madrid; Somebody Loves Me (L: B.G. DeSylva; Ballard Macdonald); Tune In (to Station J.O.Y.); Year After Year (We're Together)

Cast: Richard Bold; Dolores Costello; Helene Costello; Helen Hudson; Winnie Lightner; Will Mahoney; Tom Patricola; Williams Sisters, The

Notes: [1] Not in program. [2] Not in program. Not used in SWEET LITTLE DEVIL.

1488 • GEORGE WHITE'S SCANDALS (1925)

OPENED: 06/22/1925   Theatre: Apollo
Revue   Broadway: 169

Composer: Ray Henderson
Lyricist: Lew Brown; B.G. DeSylva
Librettist: William K. Wells; George White
Producer: George White
Director: George White

Costumes: Erte; **Musical Director:** William Daly; **Orchestrations:** Maurice DePackh

Songs: All Alone (C/L: Irving Berlin); Beware of the Girl with the Fan; Even As You and I; Fly, Butterfly (L: B.G. DeSylva); Girl of Tomorrow, The; I Want a Loveable Baby; Lovely Lady; Read What the Papers Say; Room Enough for Me; Rose-Time; Say It with a Sable (L: B.G. DeSylva); We Want the Charleston (Give Us the Charleston) (L: B.G. DeSylva); What a World This Would Be; Whosis-Whatsis, The

1489 • GEORGE WHITE'S SCANDALS (1926)

Cast: Gordon Dooley; Harry Fox; Aubrey L. Lyles; Flournoy Miller; Helen Morgan; Tom Patricola

1489 • GEORGE WHITE'S SCANDALS (1926)

OPENED: 06/14/1926   Theatre: Apollo
Revue   Broadway: 432

Composer: Ray Henderson
Lyricist: Lew Brown; B.G. DeSylva
Librettist: William K. Wells; George White
Producer: George White
Director: George White

Choreographer: George White; **Costumes:** Erte; **Musical Director:** William Daly; **Orchestrations:** Maurice DePackh; **Set Design:** William Oden-Waller; Gustave Weidhaus

Songs: Are You Satisfied; Birth of the Blues; Black Bottom, The [1]; David and Lenore; Girl Is You and the Boy Is Me, The; Here I Am [2]; It All Depends on You [3]; Lady Fair; (This Is My) Lucky Day; My Jewels; Rhapsody in Blue (inst.) (C: George Gershwin); Sevilla; Talent Is What the Public Wants; Tweet-Tweet; Twenty Years Ago; Walking Dogs Around

Cast: Fairbanks Twins, The; Eugene Howard; Willie Howard; McCarthy Sisters, The; Tom Patricola; Ann Pennington; Harry Richman; Frances Williams

Notes: [1] Also in GEORGE WHITE'S SCANDALS (1929). [2] Added after opening. [3] Added after opening. In LIDO LADY and, according to ASCAP records used in BIG BOY.

1490 • GEORGE WHITE'S SCANDALS (1928)

OPENED: 07/02/1928   Theatre: Apollo
Revue   Broadway: 230

Composer: Ray Henderson
Lyricist: Lew Brown; B.G. DeSylva
Librettist: William K. Wells; George White
Producer: George White
Director: George White

Choreographer: Russell Markert; **Costumes:** Erte; Charles LeMaire; Max Weldy; **Musical Director:** William Daly; **Orchestrations:** Maurice DePackh; **Set Design:** G.A. Weidhaus

Songs: (A Real) American Tune; Blue Grass; Bums; Fathers of the World [1]; I'm on the Crest of a Wave; Not As Good As Last Year; Old Fashioned Girl, An; Pickin' Cotton; Second Childhood; Stars, Stars Shining Bright You May See Future Stars Tonight; (Origin of the) Tap Dance; What D'Ya Say?; (I Love to Be 'Neath the Old Apple Tree) Where You r Name Is Carved with Mine

Cast: Eugene Howard; Willie Howard; Tom Patricola; Ann Pennington; Harry Richman; Frances Williams

Notes: [1] Not used.

1491 • GEORGE WHITE'S SCANDALS (1929)

OPENED: 09/23/1929   Theatre: Apollo
Revue   Broadway: 159

Composer: Cliff Friend; George White
Lyricist: Irving Caesar; Cliff Friend
Librettist: William K. Wells; George White
Producer: George White
Director: George White

Costumes: Erte; Orry Kelly; Charles LeMaire; Cora MacGeachy; Max Weldy; **Orchestrations:** Maurice DePackh; **Set Design:** William Oden-Waller; Ted Weidhaus

Songs: Bigger and Better Than Ever; Black Bottom, The [2] (C: Ray Henderson; L: Lew Brown; B.G. DeSylva); Bottoms Up; Drop Your Kerchief (L: Irving Caesar); 18 Days Ago (C: Ray Henderson; L: Lew Brown; B.G. DeSylva); I'm Marching Home to You [1] (C/L: Al Lewis; Al Sherman; Abner Silver); Is Izzy Azzy Woz? [1] (L: Irving Caesar); Love Birds (L: Irving Caesar); Sitting in the Sun (Just Wearing a Smile) (L: Unknown); There's Something Spanish in Your Eyes [1] (L: Irving Caesar); You Are My Day Dreams (L: Irving Caesar)

Cast: Abbott Dancers, The; Elm City Four, The; Eugene Howard; Willie Howard; Mitchell & Durant; Carolyn Nolte; Florence Robinson; Scott Sisters, The; George White; Jack White; Frances Williams

Notes: [1] Not in program. [2] Not in program. In GEORGE WHITE'S SCANDALS (1926).

1492 • GEORGE WHITE'S SCANDALS (1931)

OPENED: 09/14/1931   Theatre: Apollo
Revue   Broadway: 204

Composer: Ray Henderson
Lyricist: Lew Brown
Librettist: Lew Brown; Irving Caesar; Harry Conn; George White
Producer: George White
Director: George White

Costumes: Charles LeMaire; **Musical Director:** Alfred Goodman; **Orchestrations:** Howard Jackson; **Set Design:** Joseph Urban

Songs: Anvil Chorus [3]; Back from Hollywood; Beginning of Love, The; Empire State Opening [3]; Gigolos [1]; Here It Is; If I Thought I Could Live without You I'd Die [1]; I'm in That Mood [1]; Ladies and Gentlemen, That's Love; Life Is Just a Bowl of Cherries; My Name's Marie, Who Wants to Be My Peanut Vendor [2]; My Song; Only, Only, Only in My Dreams [2]; Song of the Foreign Legion (Foreign Legion Number); That's Why Darkies Were Born; This Is the Missus; Those Were the Good Old Days; Thrill Is Gone, The; You Didn't Live to Love [1]

Cast: Joan Abbott; Jane Alden; Barbara Blair; Ray Bolger; Ethel Barrymore Colt; Dorothy Dixon; Harry Dixon; Alice Faye; Gale Quadruplets, The; Eugene Howard; Willie Howard; Loomis Sisters, The; Everett Marshall; Ross McLean; Ethel Merman; Peggy Moseley; Rudy Vallee

Notes: [1] Out Atlantic City 8/10/31. [2] Cut. [3] ASCAP lists only.

1493 • GEORGE WHITE'S SCANDALS (1936)

OPENED: 12/25/1935   Theatre: New Amsterdam
Revue   Broadway: 110

Composer: Ray Henderson
Lyricist: Jack Yellen
Librettist: A. Dorian Otvos; Howard Shiebler; William K. Wells; George White
Producer: George White
Director: George White

Choreographer: Russell Markert; **Costumes:** Charles LeMaire; **Musical Director:** Tom Jones; **Orchestrations:** Robert Russell Bennett; Conrad Salinger; **Set Design:** Walter Jagermann; Russell Patterson

Songs: Anything Can Happen (L: Ballard Macdonald; Jack Yellen); Buxom Mrs. Bascom, The; Cigarette; I Like It with Music; I'm the Fellow Who Loves You; I've Got to Get Hot; Life Begins at Sweet Sixteen; May I Have My Gloves?; Models; Pied Piper of Harlem; Tell the Truth [1]; Truckin' in My Tails

Cast: Apollo Quartet, The; Gracie Barrie; Jane Cooper; Lois Eckhart; Cliff Edwards; Hal Forde; Eugene Howard; Willie Howard; Estelle Jayne; Bert Lahr; Peggy Moseley; Rudy Vallee; Harold Willard

Notes: [1] Not used.

1494 • GEORGE WHITE'S SCANDALS (1939)

OPENED: 08/28/1939   Theatre: Alvin
Revue   Broadway: 120

Composer: Sammy Fain
Lyricist: Jack Yellen
Librettist: Matt Brooks; Eddie Davis; George White
Producer: George White
Director: William K. Wells; George White

Choreographer: George White; **Musical Director:** Charles Drury; **Orchestrations:** Lew Harris; Ted Royal; Hans Spialek; Don Walker; **Set Design:** Albert Johnson

Songs: Are You Havin' Any Fun? [3]; Good Night, My Beautiful; Hat Like That, A [1]; In Waikiki; Mexiconga, The (L: Herb Magidson; Jack Yellen); Our First Kiss; Smart Little Girls; Something I Dreamed Last Night [2] (L: Herb Magidson; Jack Yellen); Song's for Free, The

Cast: Betty Allen; Lois Andrews; Ben Blue; Eugene Howard; Willie Howard; Kim Loo Sisters, The; Knight Sisters, The; Ella Logan; Colette Lyons; Fred Manatt; June Mann; Craig Mathues; Raymond Middleton; Ann Miller; Billy Rayes; Harry Stockwell; Three Stooges, The; Harold Whalen; Jack Williams; Ross Wyse Jr.; **Pianist:** Victor Arden; Phil Wall

Notes: [1] Cut after opening. [2] Added after opening. [3] Originally in second edition of ZIEGFELD FOLLIES OF 1936.

1495 • GEORGIA

OPENED: 1940
Musical

Songs: After I've Spent My Best Years on You (C: Joe Davis; L: Andy Razaf); Stop Pretending (C/L: Buddy Johnson)

Notes: No other information available.

1496 • GEORGIA AVENUE

OPENED: 07/30/1985
Musical   Closed out of town

Composer: Howard Marren
Lyricist: Joe Masteroff
Librettist: Joe Masteroff
Producer: Goodspeed Opera House
Director: Fran Soeder

Source: IMITATION OF LIFE (Novel: Fannie Hurst); **Arrangements:** Uel Wade; **Costumes:** Andrew B. Marlay; **Lighting Designer:** Curt Ostermann; **Musical Director:** Uel Wade; **Set Design:** James Leonard Joy

Songs: And Now It's Spring; Dancing on Saturday Night; Freight Train; Georgia Avenue; Girl with the Orange Hair, The; Hush You Now; 'I' Before 'E'; I Never Knew My Husband; I Wish Leola Here; I'm Just a Memory; Leola and Me; Let's Go to the Ritz; Lord Jesus; Maybe Leola Call Today; Me and Delilah; Oh, This Is a Happy Day; Otter Song, The; Pullman Dining Car; Someday Soon; Take Her Lord; Time Stand Still; Used to Me

Cast: Teresa Bowers; Kim Crosby; Louise Edeiken; Gregg Edelman; Beth Fowler; Jaime Leigh; Staci Sove

Notes: Norma Terris Theatre, Goodspeed Opera House.

1497 • GEORGY

OPENED: 02/26/1970   Theatre: Winter Garden
Musical   Broadway: 4

Composer: George Fischoff
Lyricist: Carole Bayer
Librettist: Tom Mankiewicz
Producer: Ira Bernstein; Fred Coe; Joseph P. Harris
Director: Peter Hunt

Source: GEORGY GIRL (Novel: Margaret Forster); **Source:** GEORGY GIRL (Film: Margaret Forster; Peter Nichols); **Choreographer:** Howard Jeffrey; **Costumes:** Patricia Zipprodt; **Dance Arranger:** Marvin Laird; **Lighting Designer:** Jo Mielziner; **Musical Director:** Elliot Lawrence; **Orchestrations:** Eddie Sauter; **Set Design:** Jo Mielziner; **Vocal Arranger:** Elliot Lawrence

Songs: And She Would Smile [2]; Baby, A; Birthdays [2]; Electric Windows [2]; For You I Will Live [2]; Frickered Fling [1]; Georgy; Gettin' Back to Me; Half of Me; Howdjadoo; Just for the Ride; Life's a Holiday; Make It Happen Now; Me Myself and I [2]; No One Has Gotten to Georgy [2]; Not with Me [2]; Ol Pease Puddin'; Party Dance [2]; Sign on the Dotted Line [2]; So What?; Sock- It-Rock-It to Your Heart [2]; Something Special; Sweet Memory; There's a Comin' Together; This Time Tomorrow [1]; Toy Balloon [2]; Yesterday Is Where I'll Stay [2]; You, Me and London Town [2]

Cast: Louis Beachner; John Castle; Pi Douglass; Stephen Elliot; Arthur Faria; Melissa Hart; Dilys Watling

Notes: [1] Cut New Haven 1/10/70. [2] Not used.

1498 • GERTRUDE STEIN'S FIRST READER

OPENED: 12/15/1969   Theatre: Astor Place
Revue   Off-Broadway: 40

Composer: Ann Sternberg
Lyricist: Gertrude Stein
Librettist: Gertrude Stein
Producer: Bob Cato; John Bernard Myers
Director: Herbert Machiz

Lighting Designer: Patrika Brown; **Music Adaptation:** Ann Sternberg; **Musical Director:** Ann Sternberg; **Set Design:** Kendall Shaw

Songs: Be Very Careful; Big Bird; Blackberry Vine, The; Dog, A; Genius; How They Do, Do; In a Garden; Jenny; New World; Riding Lesson; Sunshine; Three Sisters Who Are Not Sisters, The; Wild Pen; Wildflowers

Cast: Michael Anthony; Joy Garrett; Frank Giordano; Sandra Thornton

1499 • GET SET

OPENED: 1923
Musical

Composer: Porter Grainger; Donald Heywood
Additional Music: William Benton Overstreet; Bob Ricketts
Lyricist: Porter Grainger; Donald Heywood
Librettist: Joe Bright
Producer: Harlem Producing Company

Choreographer: John Dancy; Boots Marshall

Songs: Finale First Act; Georgia; Get Set; Hoo Che Ans; Jigi Hoo; Jimmie and Charlie; Let's Forget Bandana Days; Lindy Lee; Melody of Love; Old Kentucky Blues; Pay Day; Shake It; Strolling; Tee-dle-oo; They Won't; Trying; Two Eyes in Dixie

Cast: Joe Bright; Lawrence Chenault; Bessie Clark; Donald Heywood; Jennie Plate; Henry Rector; Walter Richardson; Hilda Thompson; Ethel Waters

Notes: No other information available.

1500 • GET THEE TO CANTERBURY

OPENED: 01/25/1969   Theatre: Sheridan Square Playhouse
Musical   Off-Broadway: 20

Composer: Paul Hoffert
Lyricist: David Secter
Librettist: David Secter; Jan Steen
Producer: David Secter
Director: Jan Steen

Source: CANTERBURY TALES (Story: Geoffrey Chaucer); **Choreographer:** Darwin Knight; **Costumes:** Jeanne Button; **Lighting Designer:** Michael Davidson; **Musical Director:** Jerald B. Stone; **Orchestrations:** Paul Hoffert; **Set Design:** James F. Gohl

Songs: Alison Dear; Ballad of Sir Topaz; Bottom's Up; Buy My Pardons; Canter Banter; Day of Judgement; Death Beware; Dreams; Everybody Gets It in the End; Get Thee to Canterbury; Journey, The; On the Relative Merits of Education and Experience; Prologue, The; Shadows; Simple Wife, A; Take a Pick; Where Are the Blossoms?

Cast: Walker Daniels; Travis Hudson; Paul Renault; Shev Rodgers; Shoshanna Rogers

1501 • GETTING A POLISH

OPENED: 11/07/1910   Theatre: Wallack
Play   Broadway: 48

Author: Booth Tarkington; Harry Leon Wilson
Producer: Liebler & Company
Director: Hugh Ford

Musical Director: Harry Braham; **Set Design:** Frank Gates; E.A. Morange

Songs: Baltimore Bombashay, The [1] (C/L: Stanley Murphy); He Sympathized with Me [2] (C: Ted Snyder; L: Irving Berlin); My Wife Bridget [2] (C/L: Irving Berlin); Teaching Me Fadder to Waltz (C/L: Michael Carey); That Opera Rag (C: Ted Snyder; L: Irving Berlin); That Toledo Tune [1] (C: Lou Piantadosi; L: Joseph McCarthy)

Cast: Frank Bixby; Rosalind Coghlan; George Fawcett; May Irwin; John Junior; John Daly Murphy

Notes: [1] Cut after opening. [2] Sheet music only.

1502 • GETTING TOGETHER

OPENED: 03/18/1918   Theatre: Lyric
Play   Broadway: 8

Composer: Gitz Rice
Lyricist: Gitz Rice
Librettist: Claude W. Bostock; Ian Hay; Percival Knight; J. Hartley Manners
Director: Holbrook Blinn; Frederick Stanhope

Musical Director: Howard Cook; **Set Design:** Clifford Pember

Songs: Come My Lad and Be a Soldier (C/L: Harrison Brockbank); I Want to Go Home; Keep Your Head Down Fritzi Boy [1]; Little Lad; Mary Lee [2] (L: Harold Robe); My Boy [1] (C/L: Bruno Huhn); Old Pal of Mine (L: Harold Robe); Road that Leads Back Home [1]; Till the Liberty Bells Ring Out [1]; Trench Fantasy, A (C: Roy Webb); We Stopped Them on the Marne; Who Carries the Gun (L: Rudyard Kipling); You've Got to Go In or Go Under (L: Percival Knight)

Cast: Leonard Barry; Blanche Bates; Holbrook Blinn; Dorothy Knight; Percival Knight; Gitz Rice; William Roselle; William Rowland; Edwin Taylor

Notes: This production, a wartime benefit show, closed after one week. But it reopened on June 3, 1918 for an additional 104 performances. [1] Out Washington, D.C. [2] Sheet music only.

1503 • GHOST GOES WEST, THE
OPENED: 1967
Musical   Unproduced

Composer: Jule Styne
Lyricist: Stanley Styne
Librettist: Ernest Kinoy

Songs: All a Dream; Anything That's Near to Where You Are; Call of the Clans, The; Keep Our Love on an Even Keel [1]; One Glourie; Spell Me a Riddle; You'll Be Returning Again

Notes: These are approximate song titles. [1] Same music as "Getting Married," in SUBWAYS ARE FOR SLEEPING.

1504 • GIBSON GIRL REVIEW, THE
Revue   Closed out of town

Composer: Alfred Solman
Lyricist: Paul West
Producer: Bissing; Alfred Solman

Songs: Gibson Bathing Girl, The; Gibson Sailor, The; Gibson Widow, The

1505 • GIDDY THRONG, THE
OPENED: 12/24/1900   Theatre: New York
Revue   Broadway: 164

Composer: A. Baldwin Sloane
Lyricist: Sydney Rosenfeld
Producer: Messrs. Sire
Director: Frank Smithson

Choreographer: Carl Marwig; **Set Design:** Lewis & MacCoughtry

Songs: Devil's Dream, The (ballet); March of Old Glory

Cast: Emma Carus; Mabel Fenton; Louis Harrison; Charles H. Prince; Pat Rooney; Amelia Summerville; May Yohe

Notes: No other songs listed in program. Preceded by AFTER OFFICE HOURS. *See AFTER OFFICE HOURS.*

1506 • GIFT FOR THE BRIDE, A
OPENED: 12/01/1945
Play   Closed out of town

Composer: Jean Schwartz
Lyricist: Rowland Leigh
Author: Rowland Leigh
Producer: Jules J. Leventhal; Messrs. Shubert
Director: Rowland Leigh; Andrew Solt

Source: UNKNOWN (Play: S. Bakeffi; Andrew Solt); **Costumes:** Watson Barratt; **Lighting Designer:** Watson Barratt; **Set Design:** Watson Barratt

Songs: All the Time; Charm; Home from Home; See You in the Morning (C/L: Jay Rogers)

Cast: Paul Kaye; Stapleton Kent; Louise Rainer

1507 • GIFT OF THE MAGI, THE (1958)
OPENED: 12/09/1958   Theatre: CBS
TV Musical

Composer: Richard Adler
Lyricist: Richard Adler
Librettist: Wilson Lehr
Producer: George Schaefer
Director: George Schaefer

Source: GIFT OF THE MAGI, THE (Story: O. Henry); **Musical Director:** Hal Hastings; **Orchestrations:** Don Walker

Songs: Better Word Than Love, A; Christmas in Your Heart; He's a Company Man; It's Much Too Nice to Cut; My Sugar Is the Salt of the Earth; Name's the Same, The; What to Do?

Cast: Tammy Grimes; Home Town Quartet, The; Sally Ann Howes; Gordon MacRae; Bibi Osterwald; Howard St. John

1508 • GIFT OF THE MAGI (1975)

OPENED: 12/01/1975   Theatre: Players
Musical   Off-Broadway: 48

Composer: Ronnie Britton
Lyricist: Ronnie Britton
Librettist: Ronnie Britton
Producer: Wayne Clark; Joseph Tiraco
Director: M.T. Knoblauh

Source: GIFT OF THE MAGI, THE (Story: O. Henry); **Costumes:** Neil Cooper; **Lighting Designer:** Jerryn Michaels; **Musical Director:** James Fradrich; **Set Design:** Michael Dulin; **Vocal Arranger:** James Fradrich

Songs: Beautiful Children, The; Brave You; Day After Day; Della's Desire; Finale; Gift, The; He Did It, She Did It!; I've Got Something Better; Kids Are Out; Magi Waltz, The; Make Him Think I'm Still Pretty; Mr. James Dillingham Young; Penny Saved, A; Pretty Lady; Quiet Morning; Sullivan Street Flat; There You Go Again; Till Tomorrow; Washington Square; You'd Better Tell Her!

Cast: William Brockmeier; Bill March; Paige O'Hara; Mary Saunders

1509 • GIFTS OF THE MAGI, THE (1990)

OPENED: 12/04/1990   Theatre: Lamb's
Musical   Off-Broadway: 32

Composer: Randy Courts
Lyricist: Randy Courts; Mark St. Germain
Librettist: Mark St. Germain
Producer: Lamb's Theater Company
Director: Carolyn Rossi Copeland

Source: GIFT OF THE MAGI, THE (Story: O. Henry); **Choreographer:** Richard O'Connor; **Costumes:** Hope Hanafin; **Incidental Music:** Steven M. Alper; **Lighting Designer:** Heather Carson; **Musical Director:** Steven M. Alper; **Orchestrations:** Douglas Besterman

Songs: Bum Luck; Christmas to Blame; Gift of Christmas, The; Gifts of the Magi, The; Greed; How Much to Buy My Dream; Jim and Della; Once More; Pockets; Restaurant, The; Same Girl, The; Star of the Night

Cast: Richard Blake; Paul Jackel; Sarah Knapp; Ron Lee Savin; Gordon Stanley; Lyn Vaux

Notes: This became an annual production at the Lamb's. Previous editions were all Off-Broadway presentations.

1510 • GIG, THE

OPENED: 08/10/1995
Musical

Composer: Douglas J. Cohen
Lyricist: Douglas J. Cohen
Librettist: Douglas J. Cohen
Director: Victoria Bussert

Source: GIG, THE (Film: Frank Gilroy); **Choreographer:** Daniel Stewart; **Costumes:** Tom Reiter; **Lighting Designer:** Mary Jo Dondlinger; **Musical Director:** David Evans; **Orchestrations:** Michael Gibson; **Set Design:** James Morgan; **Vocal Arranger:** Douglas J. Cohen; David Evans; Michael Gibson

Songs: Beautiful; Benny Goodman; Biff-Boom-Bang!; Choices; Departures; Drifting; Farewell Mere Existence, Hello Jazz; Four Hours Away from Paradise; I Can't Live Without Your Horn; Play Nice; Real Nice Trip, A; Ricki Is Back in Town!; Time Out; Time to Put the Toys Away

Cast: Stephen Berger; Alison Bevan; David Brummel; Donna English; James Judy; Ilene Kristen; Don Mayo; William Parry; Charles Pistone

Notes: Goodspeed at Chester.

1511 • GIGI

OPENED: 11/13/1973   Theatre: Uris
Musical   Broadway: 103

Composer: Frederick Loewe
Lyricist: Alan Jay Lerner
Librettist: Alan Jay Lerner
Producer: Edwin Lester; Saint-Subber
Director: Joseph Hardy

Source: GIGI (Film: Alan Jay Lerner); **Source:** GIGI (Story: Colette); **Choreographer:** Onna White; **Costumes:** Oliver Messel; **Dance Arranger:** Trude Rittman; **Lighting Designer:** Thomas

Skelton; **Musical Director:** Ross Riemueller; **Orchestrations:** Irwin Kostal; **Set Design:** Oliver Smith

Songs: Contract, The [1]; Da Da Da Da [2]; Earth and Other Minor Things, The; Gigi [3]; I Never Want to Go Home Again; I Remember It Well [5]; I'm Glad I'm Not Young Anymore [3]; In This Wide, Wide World; It's a Bore [3]; Night They Invented Champagne, The [3]; Paris Is Paris Again; Parisians, The [3]; Say a Prayer for Me Tonight [4]; She's Not Thinking of Me (Waltz at Maxim's) [3]; Telephone, The; Thank Heaven for Little Girls [3]

Cast: Sandahl Bergman; Leonard John Crofoot; Gordon De Vol; Alfred Drake; Truman Gaige; Maria Karnilova; Daniel Massey; Agnes Moorehead; Joe Ross; Karin Wolfe

Notes: [1] This number contains the music of "A Toujours" which was written for the film GIGI but only used as underscoring. [2] Cut. [3] From film score. [4] From film score. Written for the score of MY FAIR LADY. [5] From film score. Similar lyric to a song from LOVE LIFE.

1512 • GILDA RADNER, LIVE FROM NEW YORK

OPENED: 08/02/1979   Theatre: Winter Garden
Revue   Broadway: 51

Composer: Paul Shaffer
Lyricist: Gilda Radner
Librettist: Anne Beatts; Lorne Michaels; Marilyn Suzanne Miller; Don Novello; Michael O'Donoghue; Gilda Radner; Paul Shaffer; Rosie Shuster; Alan Zweibel
Producer: Ron Delsener; Lorne Michaels

Choreographer: Patricia Birch; **Costumes:** Franne Lee; Karen Roston; **Lighting Designer:** Roger Morgan; **Musical Director:** Howard Shore; **Set Design:** Eugene Lee; Akira Yoshimura

Songs: Gimme Mick; Goodbye Saccharine (C/L: Hardwick; Marilyn Suzanne Miller; Paul Shaffer); Honey (Touch Me with My Clothes On); I Love to Be Unhappy; If You Look Close; Let's Talk Dirty to the Animals (C/L: Michael O'Donoghue)

Cast: Don Novello; Gilda Radner; Paul Shaffer

Notes: Songwriter credits not listed in program.

1513 • GINGER

OPENED: 10/16/1923   Theatre: Daly's
Musical   Broadway: 30

Composer: Harold Orlob
Lyricist: H.I. Phillips
Librettist: H.I. Phillips
Producer: Harold Orlob
Director: Walter Brooks

Choreographer: John Hughes; **Costumes:** Max Cohn; **Musical Director:** Leon Rosebrook; **Set Design:** P. Dodd Ackerman

Songs: Before You Take a Man; Dance Divertissement [1]; Dance of the Dolls [1]; Don't Forget; Don't Judge a Girl by Her Name; Ginger; He Failed to Underwrite a Happy Home; I Know I Could [1]; If I Ever Get My Dander Up; In the Mountains [1]; In the Papers [1]; Kiss Ensemble [1]; Love's Art; Mating Time; Mountain Moon; Oh, Doctor Koo-ay [1]; Pretty Girl; Quarrel Duet; Quartette; Take a Chance; Teach Me How; Temptation [1]; That Ought to Count for Something; Those Were the Good Old Days [1]; What Will the Neighbors Say [1]

Cast: Nellie Breen; Leeta Corder; Walter Douglas; Chas. J. Stine; Norman Sweetser; Thos F. Swift

Notes: Titled TAKE A CHANCE out of town. [1] Cut Boston 9/3/23 and Wilmington 1/24/23 when titled TAKE A CHANCE.

1514 • GINGER SNAPS

OPENED: 12/31/1929   Theatre: Belmont
Revue   Broadway: 7

Composer: Donald Heywood
Lyricist: Donald Heywood; George Morris
Librettist: Donald Heywood; George Morris; J. Homer Tutt
Producer: J. Homer Tutt; Salem Tutt Whitney
Director: Donald Heywood; George Morris; J. Homer Tutt

Choreographer: George Stamper; **Set Design:** Ben Glick

Songs: Big Boy, I Gotta Belong to You; Birth of Dixie; Crazy Walk; I'll Do Anything for Love; Let's Make Hey, Hey, Hey (While the Sun Is Shinin'); My Jungle Home; Same Old Clown,

The; Spread Your Knees; Sweet Lips; You're
Something to Write Home About

Cast: Vivian Barber; Roscoe "Red" Simmons;
George Stamper; Boots Swan; J. Homer Tutt

Notes: Some titles may be sketch titles.

1515 • GINGERBREAD MAN, THE
OPENED: 12/25/1905   Theatre: Liberty
Musical   Broadway: 16

Composer: A. Baldwin Sloane
Lyricist: Frederick Ranken
Librettist: Frederick Ranken
Producer: Harry E. Converse; Mason Peters

Songs: Beautiful Land of Bon Bon; Do You Believe
in Santa Claus [1]; Every Little Something;
Evil Eye; Gingerbread Cadets, The [3]; I Must
Have Been Mistaken [1]; Incantation [1]; John
Dough; Kisses [1]; March On Oh Soldier [1];
Mazie; Moon, Moon, Moon; Nursery Rhymes;
Old Rameses; Queen of My Dreams [1];
Springtime [2]; That Awful Bogie Man; Toast
'To Sally' [3]; Wise Old Owl [3]

Cast: Frankie Bailey; Helen Bertram; Almyra
Forrest; Gilbert Gregory; Lillian Leon; Homer
Lind; J.P. MacSweeney; W.H. Mack; Ross Snow;
Gus Weinberg

Notes: The musical reopened, at the New York
Theatre, on May 21, 1906 for an additional 16
performances. [1] Out Wilkes-Barre 1/2/07. [2]
Out Kansas City 4/2/08. [3] Sheet music only.

1516 • GINGHAM GIRL, THE
OPENED: 08/28/1922   Theatre: Earl Carroll
Musical   Broadway: 322

Composer: Albert Von Tilzer
Lyricist: Neville Fleeson
Librettist: Daniel Kussel
Producer: Daniel Kussel; Lawrence Schwab
Director: Daniel Kussel; Edgar MacGregor

Choreographer: Sammy Lee

Songs: Business Is Bad [1]; Down East Flapper, The;
Finale Act I; Flapper Club, The [2]; 42nd Street
Strut [1]; Gingham Girl, The; Greenwich Village
(Down Greenwich Village Way); Just As Long As

You Have Me; Libby [1]; Love and Kisses [1];
Newlyweds; Plunk (Plunk, Plunk, Plunk); Sweet
Cookies; Tell Her While the Waltz Is Playing; That
Wonderful Thing Called Love; Them Song, The
[2]; Twinkle in Your Eye, The; When My Buddy
Steps with Me; You Must Learn the Latest Dances

Cast: Louise Allen; Eddie Buzzell; Helen Ford;
Walter Jones

Notes: No New York program available. Songs as
of 9/19/24, Erie, Pa. [1] Sheet music only. [2]
Vocal score only.

1517 • GIPSY TRAIL, THE
OPENED: 12/04/1917   Theatre: Plymouth
Play   Broadway: 111

Author: Robert Housam
Producer: Arthur Hopkins
Director: Arthur Hopkins

Songs: Down on the Gipsy Trail (C: Nat Osborne;
L: Sam Ehrlich)

Cast: Effie Ellsler; Phoebe Foster; Ernest
Glendinning; Roland Young

1518 • GIRL AND THE BANDIT, THE
OPENED: 01/09/1905
Musical   Closed out of town

Composer: Fredrick Coit-Wright
Lyricist: Cornelia Tyler
Librettist: J. Cheever Goodwin; Cornelia Tyler
Producer: Perley Opera Company
Director: Frank Smithson

Musical Director: Herman Perlet

Songs: Anxious; Bandit Am I, A; Berry and the
Brook; Captain Kidd (Was a Private Man) [1]
(C/L: Benjamin Hapgood Burt); Carnival, The;
Ceylon [1] (C: James Kendis; Herman Paley;
L: James O'Dea); Coroner Said Oh!, The; Court
Etiquette; Cuckoo Trio [2]; Dreamland;
Farewell, My Belle [1] (C: Florence McPherran;
L: W.I. Titus); Goblin Man; Half of the World
Laughs; Haste to Thy Window [2]; In a Garden
One Day [2]; In Beauty's Garden; In Timbuktu;
Little Eden; Maids of Forest [2]; Man Has Other

Things to Do [2]; Man In the Moon; Moonlight Legion [2]; My Head Is Like a Whirring Top [2]; My Venetian Rose (Sweet Venetian Rose, A); O Maid Divine; Opening Chorus and Tarantelle; Row, Row, Boatman [2]; Seven Little Crows [2]; Sextette; Soldier Song; Summer of Love [2]; Toast, The; Troubador; Trust Me, Love Me; Violetta Mia; Woods Are Full of Birds, The; You've Got to Give Them What They Want [2]

Cast: Henry Bergman; Viola Gillette; Mabel Hite; George MacFarlane

Notes: [1] Sheet music only. [2] Out Cedar Rapids 9/24/06.

1519 • GIRL AND THE DRUMMER, THE

OPENED: 1910
Musical   Closed out of town

Composer: Augustus Barratt
Lyricist: George Broadhurst
Librettist: George Broadhurst
Producer: William A. Brady

Source: WHAT HAPPENED TO JONES (Play: George Broadhurst)

Songs: Come Along, Pretty Girl [1] (C: Jerome Kern; L: M.E. Rourke); Herman, Let's Dance That Beautiful Waltz [2] (C: Irving Berlin; L: Ted Snyder); We'll Build a Bungalow

Cast: Herbert Corthell; Marie Flynn; Belle Gold; Vera Michelena; Hans Robert

Notes: No other information available. [1] Also in THE KING OF KADONIA. [2] Also in TWO MEN AND A GIRL.

1520 • GIRL AND THE GAMBLER, THE

OPENED: 11/05/1906
Musical   Closed out of town

Composer: Joseph S. Nathan
Lyricist: Felix F. Feist
Librettist: Hal Reid
Producer: B.E. Forrester
Director: Byron Ongley

Set Design: John Young

Songs: How'd You Like to Like a Girl Like Me [1]; Imitation [1] (C/L: Florence Bindley); Let's Get Acquainted [1] (C/L: Von Tilzer); Mooney Time; Sunflower [1] (L: Corin)

Cast: Florence Bindley; Darwin Kerr; John McKee; Inda Palmer

Notes: Program of the Grand Opera House, Brooklyn. [1] Sheet music only.

1521 • GIRL AND THE GOVERNOR, THE

OPENED: 02/04/1907   Theatre: Manhattan
Musical   Broadway: 26

Composer: Julian Edwards
Lyricist: S.M. Brenner
Librettist: S.M. Brenner
Producer: Jefferson De Angelis Opera Company; Frank McKee
Director: Jefferson De Angelis

Songs: Amorous Pigeon, The [1]; Bull Frog and the Governor, The [2]; Chords Like These [1]; Don Pasquale De Mesquita; Entrance of Governor; Farewell, Fond Dreams of Love; Finale Act I; Finale Act II; Finale Act III; First Kiss, The; Guess Who I Am; Have You Ever Heard It Told That Way Before?; Heart of a Sailor Is True, The; I Am So Fair; I Die for Love of You [2]; I Hope That My Hope Comes True [2]; I Would Like a Frank Opinion; It Is Wonderful; I've a Very Nasty Temper So Beware; Land of the Brave and Home of the Free, The; Laughing Ha Ha [1]; Let Gloomy Thoughts Go Hang; Moment to Scheme, A; Musical Bullfrogs, The; Musical Lover I'd Be, A; Opening Chorus; Opening Chorus Act III; Pigeon and the Weathercock, The; Pray What Would I Do [2]; Said the Governor; She Sighs in Vain; That's the Kind of Noble Savage That I Am; There's a Popular Impression [1]; We Dance at a Wedding [1]; When a Maiden Won't; Who Would a Bachelor Be?; Wouldn't It Puzzle You? [1]

Cast: Loraine Bernard; Andrew Bogart; Jefferson De Angelis; Ritchie Ling; Joseph C. Miron; Estelle Wentworth

Notes: [1] Out Wilkes-Barre 10/17/06. [2] Sheet music only.

1522 • GIRL AND THE KAISER, THE

OPENED: 11/22/1910   Theatre: Herald Square
Musical   Broadway: 64

Composer: Georges Jarno
Lyricist: Leonard Liebling
Librettist: Leonard Liebling
Producer: Lee Shubert; Sam S. Shubert
Director: Sidney Ellison

Source: DAS MUSIKANTENMADEL (Musical: Bernhard Buchbinder; Georges Jarno);
Costumes: Melville Ellis; **Musical Director:** Oscar Radin

Songs: At Court; Butterfly, Butterfly; Cradled in Thy Arms; Free Etiquette; Hungarian Rhythmic Air; Laughing and Happy Am I; Mine Forever More; Music of Viol; O, Kaiser, My Kaiser; Only a Gypsy; Tailor Man, A; With a Glance Demure

Cast: Flavia Arcaro; William Bonelli; Harry Conor; Lulu Glaser

1523 • GIRL AND THE WIZARD, THE

OPENED: 09/27/1909   Theatre: Casino
Musical   Broadway: 96

Composer: Julian Edwards
Lyricist: Robert B. Smith
Librettist: J. Hartley Manners
Producer: Lee Shubert; Sam S. Shubert
Director: Ned Wayburn

Songs: Black Butterfly, The; By the Blue Lagoon (C: Jerome Kern; L: Percival Knight); Frantzi Frankenstein (C: Jerome Kern; L: Percival Knight); How Can You Toot? (C: George Dougherty; Seymour Furth; L: Will Heelan; Ned Wayburn); I Wonder If You're Lonely (C: George Byrd Dougherty; L: Ned Wayburn); La Belle Parisienne (C: Louis A. Hirsch; L: Edward Madden); Land of Love, The; Love Me Dear [3] (C/L: Edward Madden); Military Mary Ann (C: Louis A. Hirsch; L: Edward Madden); Oh, How That German Could Love [2] (C: Ted Snyder; L: Irving Berlin); Opera Comique (C/L: Melville Gideon); Reveille; Song of the Heart; Suzette and Her Pet [1] (C: Jerome Kern; L: Percival Knight); Way to a Girlie's Heart, The [3]; Wedding Fete, The; What Wealth Is Here; When I Sang Toreador (C/L: Melville Gideon)

Cast: Sam Bernard; Corson Clarke; Kitty Gordon; Percy Hammond; Henry Holt; Flora Parker; William Roselle; Harriet Stanton; Oliver Sterling

Notes: Kern songs orchestrated by G.C.M. Snelling. George Daugherty is the same person as G. Byrd Dougherty. [1] Not in program. [2] Out of town program only. [3] Sheet music only.

1524 • GIRL AT THE GATE, THE

OPENED: 09/01/1912   Theatre: La Salle
Musical   Chicago

Composer: Ben Jerome
Librettist: Frederick Donaghey; Will M. Hough
Director: R.H. Burnside

Costumes: William Henry Matthews Jr.; **Musical Director:** R.H. Burnside

Songs: Come Along, Honey!; Gee! It's Great to Be a Sailor!; Her Eyes Kept Saying 'Kiss Me!' All the Time; I Can't Find a Girl Like You!; I Wish My Honeymoon Would Shine!; In Panama; Let's Get Married; Love's Wireless Telephone; My Raggedy Doll; Off for San Francisco Town; On Dreamy Bay; Song of the Southern Seas, The; Suzanne; Why Speak of Love When There's Work to Be Done?; World's All Wrong Again, The; You Can Flirt in All Kinds of Languages

Cast: Herbert Corthell; Cathryn Rowe Palmer; Lucy Weston; Olive Wyndham

1525 • GIRL AT THE HELM, A

OPENED: 09/05/1908
Musical   Closed out of town

Composer: Raymond Hubbell
Lyricist: Robert B. Smith
Librettist: Robert B. Smith
Producer: Mort H. Singer
Director: Al Holbrook

Costumes: Will R. Barnes; **Orchestrations:** Hilding Anderson

Songs: All I Want in the Wide, Wide World Is You; Christening of the Boat, The; Fishing Is an Art; I Don't Love You Well Enough for That; In My Little Runabout; In Walked Bill; Long, Long Green, The; Man I Marry Must Be a Man, The; Not All but Nearly; Opening Chorus; You Are All the World to Me

Cast: Florence Holbrook; Cecil Lean

1526 • GIRL BEHIND THE COUNTER, THE

OPENED: 10/01/1907   Theatre: Herald Square
Musical   Broadway: 260

Composer: Howard Talbot
Lyricist: Arthur Anderson
Librettist: Edgar Smith
Producer: Lew Fields; Lee Shubert; Sam S. Shubert
Director: J.C. Huffman; Julian Mitchell

Source: GIRL BEHIND THE COUNTER, THE (Musical: Arthur Anderson; Leedham Bantock; Howard Talbot); **Set Design:** Arthur Voegtlin

Songs: Ah! Eh! Oh!; Bandbox Girl, The; Cherry in the Glass, The (C: Paul Lincke; L: Will D. Cobb); Enid [4]; Enterprising Frenchman, The; Frivolity; Glow Worm, The [3] (C/L: Paul Lincke; L: Lilla Cayley Robinson); I Got to See de Minstrel Show (C: Harry Von Tilzer; L: Vincent Bryan); I Mean to Marry a Man [1]; I Want to Be Loved Like a Leading Lady (C: Herman Avery Wade; L: Paul West); If You'll Walk with Me (C: Paul Rubens; L: Edgar Selden); In Gay Paree [4]; Land Where the Best Man Wins, The [4]; Life Is Just What You Make It [4]; Mam'selle Ninette [4]; Mr. Moon [2]; Much Obliged to You [1]; Now I've Married a Millionaire; Passing By; Propose [2]; Shopping; Sir Walter Raleigh [4]; Under the Yum Yum Tree [2]; (C: Harry Von Tilzer; L: Andrew B. Sterling); Way of Trade, The; When I Was in the Chorus at the Gaiety [1] (C: Harry Von Tilzer); When You Steal a Kiss or Two (Making Love) (C/L: Kenneth S. Clarke); Won't You Buy?

Cast: George Beban; Vernon Castle; Louise Dresser; Connie Ediss; Lotta Faust; Lew Fields; Ignacio Martinetti; Edith Ethel McBride; May Naudain; William Rock; Topsy Siegrist; A. Van Sant

Notes: *See STEP THIS WAY.* [1] Added after opening. [2] Out Wilkes-Barre 9/27/10. [3] Lincke's original German language song was titled "Gluhwurmchen." [4] Sheet music only.

1527 • GIRL BEHIND THE GUN, THE

OPENED: 09/16/1918   Theatre: New Amsterdam
Musical   Broadway: 160

Composer: Ivan Caryll
Lyricist: P.G. Wodehouse
Librettist: Guy Bolton; P.G. Wodehouse
Producer: Klaw & Erlanger
Director: Edgar MacGregor

Source: MADAME ET SON FILLEUL (MADAME AND HER GODSON) (Play: Maurice Hennequin; Pierre Veber); **Choreographer:** Julian Mitchell; **Musical Director:** Charles Previn; **Set Design:** Clifford Pember

Songs: Back to the Dear Old Trenches; Flags of Allies; Girl Behind the Man Behind the Gun, The; Godsons and Godmothers; Happy Family; I Like It; I'm True to Them All and They're Just as True to Me [1] (C/L: George M. Cohan); Oh! How Warm It Is Today; Opening Chorus Act II; Opening Chorus Act III; Some Day Waiting Will End; There's a Light in Your Eyes; There's Life in the Old Dog Yet; True to Me; Women Haven't Any Mercy on a Man

Cast: Wilda Bennett; Donald Brian; John E. Hazzard; John E. Young

Notes: [1] Sheet music only.

1528 • GIRL CRAZY

OPENED: 10/14/1930   Theatre: Alvin
Musical   Broadway: 272

Composer: George Gershwin
Lyricist: Ira Gershwin
Librettist: Guy Bolton; John McGowan
Producer: Alex A. Aarons; Vinton Freedley
Director: Alexander Leftwich

Choreographer: George Hale; **Costumes:** Kiviette; **Musical Director:** Earl Busby; **Orchestrations:** Robert Russell Bennett; **Set Design:** Donald Oenslager

Songs: And I Have You [3]; Are You Dancing? [1]; Barbary Coast; Bidin' My Time; Boy! What Love Has Done to Me!; Bronco Busters; But Not for Me; Could You Use Me?; Dawn of a New Day [4]; Embraceable You [2]; Entr'acte (Stop Put That Stick Down); Gambler of the West, The [3]; Goldfarb! That's I'm!; I Got Rhythm; Land of the Gay Caballero; Lonesome Cowboy, The; Sam and Delilah; Something Peculiar [1] (L: Lou Paley); Treat Me Rough; When It's Cactus Time in Arizona; You Can't Unscramble Scrambled Eggs [1]

Cast: Antonio DeMarco; Renee DeMarco; Jimmy Dorsey; Roger Edens; Foursome, The; Benny Goodman; Eunice Healey; Willie Howard; Allen Kearns; William Kent; Gene Krupa; Ethel Merman; Glenn Miller; Red Nichols Orchestra; Lew Parker; Ginger Rogers; Jack Teagarden

Notes: The orchestra included Benny Goodman, Glenn Miller, Red Nichols, Jimmy Dorsey, Jack Teagarden and Gene Krupa. [1] Not used. [2] Written for the unproduced show MING TOY. [3] Cut prior to Broadway. [4] Written for the opening of the 1939 New York World's Fair, this number was revised by Ira Gershwin for the 1960 revival of GIRL CRAZY.

1529 • GIRL FRIEND, THE
OPENED: 03/17/1926   Theatre: Vanderbilt
Musical   Broadway: 301

Composer: Richard Rodgers
Lyricist: Lorenz Hart
Librettist: Herbert Fields
Producer: Lew Fields
Director: John Harwood

Choreographer: Jack Haskell; **Costumes:** Booth; **Musical Director:** Ernest Cutting; **Orchestrations:** Maurice DePackh; **Set Design:** P. Dodd Ackerman; Willoughby & Jones

Songs: Blue Room, The; Cabarets; Creole Crooning Song; Damsel Who Done All the Dirt, The; Girl Friend, The; Good Fellow, Mine; Goodbye, Lennie!; He's a Winner (Sporting Life) (Reporters' Opening); Hey! Hey!; Hum To [1]; I'd Like to Take You Home; In New Orleans [1]; Pipes of Pansy, The [1]; Simple Life, The; Sleepyhead [2]; Town Hall Tonight; Turkey in the Straw [1]; Two of a Kind [1]; What Is It?; Why Do I?

Cast: Evelyn Cavanaugh; June Cochrane; Frank Doane; Francis X. Donegan; Eva Puck; Sammy White

Notes: [1] Cut before opening. [2] Cut before opening. Also cut from THE GARRICK GAIETIES (1926).

1530 • GIRL FROM BRAZIL, THE
OPENED: 08/30/1916   Theatre: 44th Street
Musical   Broadway: 61

Composer: Sigmund Romberg; Robert Winterberg
Lyricist: Matthew Woodward
Librettist: Edgar Smith
Producer: Messrs. Shubert
Director: Benrimo

Source: DIE SCHONE SCHWEDIN (Musical: Julius Brammer; Alfred Grunwald); **Choreographer:** Allan K. Foster; **Musical Director:** Gaetano Merola

Songs: Bachelor Girl and Boy, A (C: Sigmund Romberg); Barcarole; Childhood Days (C: Sigmund Romberg); Come Back, Sweet Dream! (C: Sigmund Romberg); Darling, I Love You So! (C: Robert Winterberg); Financial Viking, The (C: Sigmund Romberg); Heart to Heart; How Like Her Papa! [1]; I May Believe Half-That's All [1]; I Want to Be a Romeo (C: Sigmund Romberg); I'm Such a Nervous Man [1]; Ivy and Oak (C: Sigmund Romberg); Like the Fjords of Scandinavia [2] (C: Sigmund Romberg); Lona, Partner, Lona [1]; My Senorita (C: Sigmund Romberg); Oh You Lovely Ladies; Opening; Pancho and Pepita [1]; Right Brazilian Girl, The (C: Sigmund Romberg); Ski-ing; Some Day [2]; Stolen Kisses (C: Sigmund Romberg); Then Love Will Come [2] (C: Sigmund Romberg)

Cast: Frances Demarest; Hal Forde; George Hassell; Maude Odell

Notes: Originally titled A BRIZILIAN HONEYMOON. [1] Sheet music only. [2] Listed in Romberg "biography" only.

1531 • GIRL FROM BRIGHTON, THE
OPENED: 08/31/1912   Theatre: Academy of
                                Music
Musical   Broadway: 49

Composer: William Becker
Lyricist: Jean C. Havez
Librettist: Aaron Hoffman
Producer: William Fox
Director: Jack Mason

Choreographer: Jack Mason; **Costumes:** Paul Arlington

Songs: Academy Rag, The; After Vespers (C/L: Neil Moret); Brand New Soldier Tune, A [1] (C: George Botsford); Brighton Beach Rag (L: William Becker); Get Rich Quick Wallingford [1] (C: Raymond Walker; L: William Tracey); Honeymoon Days [1] (C: Les Copeland); I Want to Go Back to New York [1]; I Wonder Where I Met You [1] (C: George Gotsford); Keep Away from the Fellow Who Owns an Automobile [1]; Melody Man (C: Les Copeland); Minstrel Tune [1]; Oh, You Silv'ry Bells (Jingle Bells) (C: George Botsford); Opening Chorus [1]; Since You Said You Loved Me; Turkey Trot, The [1]; Waiting for the Robert E. Lee [1] (C: Lewis F. Muir; L: L. Wolfe Gilbert)

Cast: Frank Caverly; Robert Dailey; Harry First; Kitty Flynn; Mark Hart; Henry Lewis; Ann Orr; Sophia Petrayer; Al Raymond; Maude Rockwell; Clay Smith

Notes: [1] Out Brooklyn 8/31/12.

1532 • GIRL FROM BROADWAY, THE

OPENED: 1906
Musical   Closed out of town

Composer: Ben Bergman; Joe Goodwin; Karl L. Hoschna
Lyricist: Charles Noel Douglas
Librettist: Rube Bernstein; Herbert Hall Winslow
Director: Charles Sinclair

Songs: Back in My Hometown; Bathing Girl, The; Colored Gentlemen's Ball; Cupid; Dat's de Way I Lubs You, Honey Mine; Eccentricities; Girl from Broadway, The; Goodbye Pal [1]; He Loves Me, He Loves Me Not; Hobo Man; Hoop La; I Cannot Marry You All; I Don't Want Any in Mine; I Would Like to Paint a Picture of You All; If War Is What Sherman Said It Was; It's Up to You to Do the Rest; Little Bit of Heaven, A; Little Red School; Love Me As You Used to Do; Love's Language; Millionaire's Daughters; Oh

Joe, with Your Fiddle and Bow; Opening Chorus; Opening Ensemble; Put Me to Sleep with an Old Fashioned Lullaby; Rocky Road to Dublin; Something Happened; Soothing Symphony; Tally-Ho; Teddy Bear and Dresden Doll; That's Easy for a Little Girl to Do; Want a Little More; We'll Never Make a Lady Out of You; When I Dream of Annie Laurie; You'll Always Be the Same Sweet Girl

Cast: Grace Edmond; Dot Leighton; Robert H. Wilson

Notes: A burlesque musical. In a program from Wilkes-Barre of 10/19/06 the show was billed as "A New York Success" but no New York information was available. Program of Toledo 4/3/16 also used. The show also played the 14th Street Theatre in Chicago, opening on 1/14/07. [1] Sheet music only.

1533 • GIRL FROM CHILD'S, THE

OPENED: 1924
Musical   Closed out of town

Composer: Tom Johnstone
Lyricist: Phil Cook
Librettist: Archie Colby; Al Jackson
Director: Alonzo Price

Choreographer: Raymond Midgley; **Costumes:** Orry Kelly

Songs: Charity Ball, The; High Hats; House that Jazz Built, The; I'll Do All My Dancing with One Girl; Little Miss Nobody; Love Set, The; Mary; Neckin' Time in Great Neck; Only a Paper Rose; Quiet Life at Child's, A; Society Snobs; Twitter; You're a Perfect Little Lady

Cast: Irving Fisher; Thomas Mann; Ann Milburn; Virginia Watson

1534 • GIRL FROM COOK'S, THE

OPENED: 11/01/1927   Theatre: Gaiety
Musical   London: 38

Composer: Jean Gilbert; Raymond Hubbell
Lyricist: R.H. Burnside; Greatrex Newman
Librettist: R.H. Burnside; Greatrex Newman
Producer: R.H. Burnside
Director: R.H. Burnside

Source: UNKNOWN (Musical: Franz Arnold; Ernest Bach); **Choreographer:** Larry Ceballos; **Musical Director:** Leonard Hornsey; **Orchestrations:** Robert Russell Bennett; Frank Tours

Songs: Glorious Land of Hope; I'm in Love, It's a Wonderful Feeling; I've Got You and You've Got Me; Land of Hope and Glory; Language of Cauli-Flowers, The; Life Is a Game of Chance; Love Is Not All That It Seems to Be; My Sweetheart; Road to Happiness, The; Springtime; Stella; Wine, Women and Song; Women; You Tell Him

Cast: W.H. Berry; Margaret Campbell; Edmund Gwenn; Billie Leonard; Eva Sternroyd

Notes: No program available

1535 • GIRL FROM DIXIE, THE

OPENED: 12/14/1903   Theatre: Madison Square
Musical   Broadway: 26

Lyricist: Harry B. Smith
Librettist: Harry B. Smith
Producer: Nixon & Zimmerman; Sam S. Shubert
Director: R.H. Burnside

Songs: American Heiress, An (C: Theo M. Tobani); Bubbles (C: Max Witt); Dissipated Kitten, The (C: A. Baldwin Sloane); Dixie Land (C/L: M.G. Watson); Finale Act I (C: Ludwig Englander); Glory (C: W.E. Bock); Happy Days in Dixie (C: Kerry Mills); Honey (C: H.J. Green); Johnny Strong (C: E.D. Prussian; L: Harry Raymond); Love in an Orchard (C: Ben Jerome); Lover's A-B-C, The (C: Max Witt); Mary from Maryland (C: George Norton); Sunflower and the Sun, The (C: Will Marion Cook); Way Down South (C: Unknown); When I Look Into Those Lovey Dovey Eyes [1] (C: Manuel Klein; L: Rida Johnson Young); When the Moon Comes Over the Hill (C: J. Rosamond Johnson; L: Bob Cole); You, You, You (C/L: E.H. Pendleton)

Cast: Irene Bentley; William H. Bentley; Charles H. Bowers; Arnold Daly; Ferdinand Gottschalk; Albert Hart; Rose Hart; Vernon H. Lee; Evelyn Nesbitt; Loraine Osborne

Notes: Kurt Ganzl in his magnificent ENCYCLOPEDIA OF THE MUSICAL THEATRE writes that Cole and Johnson interpolated six songs in the score. [1] Sheet music only.

536 • GIRL FROM HOME, THE

OPENED: 05/03/1920   Theatre: Globe
Musical   Broadway: 24

Composer: Silvio Hein
Lyricist: Frank Craven
Librettist: Frank Craven
Producer: Charles B. Dillingham
Director: R.H. Burnside

Source: DICTATOR, THE (Play: Richard Harding Davis); **Costumes:** O'Kane Conwell; **Musical Director:** Anton Heindl

Songs: All Ashore; Bit o' Breeze; By the Palmest Tree; El Presidente; I Miss a Place Called Home [1]; I'll Be Dictator [3]; It's a Wonderful Spot; I've Got a Great Idea [1]; Just Say Goodbye; Manana; Marimba; Miss Me [2]; Money Quartet [4]; Nine Little Missionaries; Ocean Blues; Our Presidents; Porto Banos; Somewhere Sometime; Spanish Jazz, The [1]; Try, Try, Try [2]; Vanity; We Are the Missionaries [1]; We're All at Sea [1]; Wireless Heart, The; You're the Nicest Girl I Ever Knew [1]

Cast: Gladys Caldwell; Frank Craven; Marion Sunshine; Flora Zabelle

Notes: Titled THE NEW DICTATOR in Washington, D.C. 3/8/20. [1] Out Washington, D.C. 3/8/20. [2] Out Philadelphia 4/26/20. [3] Out prior to New York. [4] Sheet music only.

1537 • GIRL FROM KAY'S, THE

OPENED: 11/02/1903   Theatre: Herald Square
Musical   Broadway: 223

Composer: Ivan Caryll
Librettist: Owen Hall
Producer: George Edwardes; Charles Frohman

Musical Director: Gus Salzer

Songs: Bob and Me (C: Howard Talbot; L: Claude Aveling); Bonnet Shop (L: Adrian Ross); Bride's Song (C/L: Bernard Rolt); Bridesmaids (C: Cecil Cook; L: Adrian Ross); Chorus of Guests (C: Cecil Cook; L: Adrian Ross); Customers at Kay's (L: Adrian Ross); Egypt (C/L: Clare

Kummer); Finale Act I (C: Meyer Lutz; L: Adrian Ross); Finale Act II (C: Cecil Cook; L: Adrian Ross); Girl from Kay's, The [1] (L: Unknown); Glass Glass (C: Paul A. Rubens; L: Aubrey Fitzgerald); Goody, Goody Girls [2] (L: Claude Aveling); High Old Time [1] (C: A.D. Cammeyer; L: Claude Aveling); I Don't Care (C/L: Paul Rubens); Love at the Door [2] (L: Adrian Ross); Lucy Lindy Lady (C/L: Dave Reed Jr.); Make It Up (L: Claude Aveling); Matilda and the Builder (C: Ernest Bucalossi; L: J. Hickory Wood); Mr. Hoggenheimer of Park Lane (L: Unknown); Mr. Mosenstein, Mrs. Hoggenheimer (L: Adrian Ross); My Birthday Party (C: Paul Rubens; L: Percy Greenbank); My Little Love Bird (C/L: Maurice J. Stonehill); Opening Chorus Act II [2] (C: Cecil Cook; L: Adrian Ross); Relations [2] (L: Claude Aveling); Semi- Detached [4] (L: Adrian Ross); Smiling Sambo (C: Howard Talbot; L: Percy Greenbank); Sufficiency (C/L: Clare Kummer); That's So Papa [3] (C: Meyer Lutz; L: Adrian Ross); Tips (C: Cecil Cook; L: Adrian Ross); Tips (L: Unknown); Under the Bamboo Tree (C: J. Rosamond Johnson; L: Bob Cole); Valse (C: Ivan Caryll).

Cast: Sam Bernard; Harry Davenport; Marie Doro; Grace Dudley; Willie Edouin; Elsie Ferguson; Maude Granger; Homer Granville; May Harding; Ernest Lambert; Winchell Smith; George R. Sprague; Hattie Williams.

Notes: [1] Out Charleston 1/14/05. [2] Sheet music only. [3] On sheet music Lionel Monckton credited with music. [4] Lyrics credited to Claude Aveling on score.

1538 • GIRL FROM MONTMARTRE, THE

OPENED: 08/05/1912   Theatre: Criterion
Musical   Broadway: 64

Composer: Henry Bereny
Lyricist: Harry B. Smith; Robert B. Smith
Librettist: Harry B. Smith; Robert B. Smith
Producer: Charles Frohman
Director: Thomas L. Reynolds

Source: DAS MADEL VON MONTMARTRE (Musical: Georges Feydeau; Rudolf Schanzer); **Musical Director:** Harold Vicars, **Set Design:** Homer Emens

Songs: Africa [2]; Bohemia (C: Jerome D. Kern; L: Robert B. Smith); Don't Turn My Picture to the Wall (C: Jerome Kern; L: Robert B. Smith); Ghost Quintette; Half-Past Two (C: Howard Talbot; L: Percy Greenbank; Arthur Wimperis); Hoop-La-La Papa! (Hoop-la Father Doesn't Care) (C: Jerome Kern; L: M.E. Rourke); I'll Be True to You; I'll Be Waiting 'Neath Your Window (C: Jerome Kern; L: James Duffy); In Spirit Land; It's Perfectly All Right [2]; I've Taken Such a Fancy to You (C: Jerome Kern; L: Clifford Harris); Love Will Win [1] (C: Lionel Monckton; L: Arthur Wimperis); Myrella [3]; Oh, Doctor; One of the Boys; Ooo, Ooo Lena (C: Jerome Kern; L: John Golden); Polly and the Polka [3] (C: Howard Talbot; L: Percy Greenbank); Popsey Wopsey; Serenade; Sleeping Chair, The [2]; Something Like This (C: F. Wagner; L: Harry B. Smith); Temperament [2]; Vienna Roll; When I Lost You (C/L: Paul Rubens)

Cast: Marion Abbott; Richard Carle; William Danforth; Mary Gilmore; George Lydecker; Lennox Pawle; Hattie Williams

Notes: [1] Originally in THE ARCADIANS. [2] Out Boston 4/22/12. [3] Out N.Y. 4/17/13.

1539 • GIRL FROM NANTUCKET, THE

OPENED: 11/08/1945   Theatre: Adelphi
Musical   Broadway: 12

Composer: Jacques Belasco
Lyricist: Kay Twomey
Librettist: Hy Cooper; Harold Herman; Paul Stanford
Producer: Henry Adrian
Director: Henry Adrian; Edward Clarke Lilley

Source: UNKNOWN (Story: Bernie Giler; Fred Thompson); **Choreographer:** Van Grona; Val Roset; **Costumes:** Lou Eisele; **Lighting Designer:** Albert Johnson; **Musical Director:** Harry Levant; **Orchestrations:** Jacques Belasco; Ted Royal; **Set Design:** Albert Johnson; **Vocal Arranger:** Jacques Belasco; Ted Royal

Songs: Boukra Fill Mish Mish; From Morning Till Night; Hammock in the Blue; Hooray for Nicoletti (L: Burt Milton; Kay Twomey); I Love That Boy; I Want to See More of You; Isn't It a

Lovely View?; Let's Do and Say We Didn't (C/L: Hughie Prince; Dick Rogers); Magnificent Failure (C/L: Hughie Prince; Dick Rogers); Morning in Manhattan [2] (L: Burt Milton); New Nantucket [2]; Nothing Matters; Painting a Mural of Muriel [2]; Saga of the Sea [2] (L: Burt Milton); Sons of the Sea; Take the Steamer to Nantucket; Tendin' to My Knittin' [1] (L: Burt Milton; Kay Twomey); That's How I Know that I'm in Love [2]; What's a Sailor Got?; What's He Like?; When a Hick Chick Meets a City Slicker (L: Burt Milton); Your Fatal Fascination

Cast: Adelaide Bishop; George L. Headley; Jane Kean; Bob Kennedy; Marion Niles; Helen Raymond

Notes: [1] Out Philadelphia 10/9/45. [2] Out Boston 10/22/45.

1540 • GIRL FROM PARIS, THE
OPENED: 12/08/1896   Theatre: Herald Square
Musical   Broadway: 248

Composer: Ivan Caryll
Librettist: George Dance
Producer: Edward E. Rice
Director: Frank Smithson

Choreographer: H. Fletcher Rivers; **Costumes:** M.L. Dowling; **Set Design:** D. Frank Dodge; Frank Rafter

Songs: Battersea Butterfly, The; Cock-a-doodle; Ding-Dong; Festive Continong, The; Girl from Paris, The; Hail, the Hero of the Day; He Took It in a Good-Natured Way; Hi! For the Thames on a Summer's Day; I'm All the Way from Gay Paree; Isn't It Wonderful; It's a Good Thing to Have; Just for a Kiss; Let's Have a Fling; Now, Darling, We Must Part [1] (C/L: Will P. Brown); Oh, Tender Remembrance; Proper Air, The [1]; Reste La [1]; Shooters; Sister Mary Jane's Top Note; So Take You a Warning; Somebody; Then Off We Go; Tootle, Tootle; Tweedledum and Tweedledee; Upon the Stage

Cast: Charles A. Bigelow; Josephine Hall; Joseph W. Herbert; Clara Lipman; John Savage; Frank Smithson

Notes: [1] Added after opening.

1541 • GIRL FROM SHANLEY'S, THE
OPENED: 1913
Musical

Composer: Eddie Adair
Lyricist: Eddie Adair
Librettist: H.C. Gant
Director: Eddie Adair

Songs: Floating with Your Summer Girl; Ragtime Goblin Man, The; Shanley Girl, The; Society Bells; Take Me with You, Mary; That's Why They Call Me the Shanley Girl; When the Right Girl Comes Along

Notes: Program of 1/13/13 Milwaukee. A vaudeville musical.

1542 • GIRL FROM THE STATES, THE
Notes: *See THE GOLDEN WIDOW.*

1543 • GIRL FROM UP THERE, THE
OPENED: 01/07/1901   Theatre: Herald Square
Musical   Broadway: 96

Composer: Gustave Kerker
Lyricist: Hugh Morton
Librettist: Hugh Morton
Producer: Charles Frohman
Director: Julian Mitchell

Costumes: Mme. Siedle; **Musical Director:** Max Hirschfeld; **Set Design:** Ernest Albert; Ernest Gros

Cast: Edna Aug; Grace Belmont; Harry Conor; Harry Davenport; Virginia Earle; Otis Harlan; Harry Kelly; Edna May; Dave Montgomery; Farren Souter; Fred Stone; Lawrence Wheat; Alf C. Whelan; Nat Wills

Notes: No songs listed in program.

1544 • GIRL FROM UTAH, THE
OPENED: 08/24/1914   Theatre: Knickerbocker
Musical   Broadway: 120

Composer: Sidney Jones; Paul Rubens
Lyricist: Percy Greenbank; Adrian Ross
Librettist: James T. Tanner
Producer: Charles Frohman
Director: James Darling; J.A.E. Malone

Musical Director: Gus Salzer

Songs: (I'd Like to Wander with) Alice in Wonderland (C: Jerome Kern; L: Harry B. Smith); At Our Tango Tea Last Week (C: Worton David; L: Bert Lee); At the Bottom of Brixton Hill [4]; Ballin' the Jack [4] (C: Chris Smith; L: James Henry Burris); Call Right Here [2]; Come Back Little Girl [3] (C/L: Augustus Barratt); Dance with Me [3]; Donald Brian Polka, The; D'Ye Folly Me; Ferban Waltz [3]; Florrie the Flapper (C: Herman Finck; L: Arthur Wimperis); Garden Gate [2]; Gilbert the Filbert [5] (C: Herman Finck; L: Arthur Wimperis); Girl from Utah; Girl in the Clogs and the Shawl (C/L: Harry Castling; C.W. Murphy); Grown Up Children [4] (C/L: Unknown); I Want to Be the Captain [3]; In the Movies [3]; Kissing Time [4] (L: Harry Castling; C.W. Murphy); Land of Let's Pretend, The [6] (C: Jerome Kern; L: Harry B. Smith); Molly Dear, It's You I'm After [3] (C: Henry E. Pether; L: Frank Wood); Mother Will Be Pleased [2]; Music of Love, The (C: Paul Rubens; L: Percy Greenbank); Nothing at All; Only to You; Phyllis Tango [1]; Same Sort of Girl [7] (C: Jerome Kern; L: Harry B. Smith); Step This Way; They Didn't Believe Me [8] (C: Jerome Kern; L: Herbert Reynolds); Una [1] (C: Paul Rubens; L: Percy Greenbank); We'll Take Care of You All (The Little Refugees) [4] (C: Jerome Kern; L: Harry B. Smith); We're Getting on Very Well; When We Meet the Mormon; Where Has Una Gone?; Why Don't They Dance the Polka Anymore (C: Jerome Kern; L: Harry B. Smith); You Never Can Tell [2] (C: Jerome Kern; L: Harry B. Smith)

Cast: George Bishop; Donald Brian; Joseph Cawthorn; Venita Fitzhugh; Julia Sanderson

Notes: [1] Sheet music only. [2] Cut after opening. [3] Added after opening. [4] Cut after opening. Used in FADS AND FANCIES. [5] Cut after opening. Also in THE PASSING SHOW OF 1914 and THE PASSING SHOW in London. [6] Sheet music only. Music same as "Not Here! Not Here!" from THE DOLLAR PRINCESS. [7] Music same as "Best Sort of Mother, Best Sort of Child" from ROSY RAPTURE. [8] Also used in TONIGHT'S THE NIGHT!

1545 • GIRL FROM VIENNA, THE

Notes: *See THE WHITE HEN.*

1546 • GIRL FROM WYOMING, THE

OPENED: 10/29/1938   Theatre: American Music Hall
Musical   Broadway: 86

Composer: Richard Lewine
Lyricist: Ted Fetter
Librettist: John Van Antwerp
Producer: John Krimsky; John Van Antwerp
Director: Robert Ross

Choreographer: John Pierce; **Costumes:** Peggy Clark; **Musical Director:** Al Evans; **Orchestrations:** Ben Ludlow; **Set Design:** Eugene Dunkel

Songs: Boston in the Spring; Dear Horse; Dying Cowboy, The; Hats Off; Kickin' the Corn Around; Life's a Circus; Lullaby of the Plain; Manuelo; Our Home; Ride, Cowboy, Ride; Stay East Young Man

Cast: Anne Hunter; Philip Huston; Tony Kraber; George Petrie; James Russo; Jackie Susann; June Walker

Notes: John Van Antwerp billed as Jerrold Krimsky for this show.

1547 • GIRL FROM YAMA, THE

OPENED: 11/04/1907
Musical   Closed out of town

Composer: Alfred E. Aarons
Lyricist: Robert B. Smith
Librettist: George Totten Smith
Producer: Alfred E. Aarons

Notes: Sometimes titled YAMA. No other information available.

1548 • GIRL IN PINK TIGHTS, THE

OPENED: 03/05/1954   Theatre: Mark Hellinger
Musical   Broadway: 115

Composer: Sigmund Romberg
Lyricist: Leo Robin
Librettist: Jerome Chodorov; Joseph Fields

Producer: Shepard Traube
Director: Shepard Traube

Choreographer: Agnes de Mille; **Costumes:** Miles White; **Dance Arranger:** Trude Rittman; **Lighting Designer:** Eldon Elder; Music Adaptation: Don Walker; **Musical Director:** Sylvan Levin; **Orchestrations:** Don Walker; **Set Design:** Eldon Elder

Songs: Cardinal's Guard Are We, The; Going to the Devil with Me; I Promised Their Mothers; In Paris and in Love; Lost in Loveliness; Love Is the Funniest Thing; My Heart Won't Say Goodbye; Out of the Way; Pas de Deux (inst.); Roll Out the Hose, Boys; That Naughty Show from Gay Paree; Up in the Elevated Railway; We're All in the Same Boat; When I Am Free to Love; You've Got to Be a Little Crazy

Cast: David Atkinson; Charles Goldner; Jeanmaire; Alexandre Kalioujny; Brenda Lewis

1549 • GIRL IN STATE ROOM "B"
OPENED: 02/27/1919
Musical   Closed out of town

Lyricist: William K. Wells
Librettist: William K. Wells

Musical Director: Hal Dyson

Songs: Bubbling Wine; Experience; Eyes; Friendship; Game of Love; I Think I'd Better Go Home; I'd Like to See More of You!; Jazz with Me; Mad-Cap Dance; Prohibition Song; Slacking; Wonderful Love; You Can't Stop Me from Loving You; You're a Clever Kid

Cast: Dan McNeil; Marjorie Pringle; George B. Thripp

Notes: Program of Atlantic City. No composer credit in program although it states "Numbers Arranged by Raymond B. Perez."

1550 • GIRL IN THE KIMONO, THE
OPENED: 11/11/1910
Musical   Closed out of town

Composer: Phil Schwartz
Lyricist: Harold Atteridge

Librettist: Helen Bagg
Producer: William Ziegfeld
Director: Virgil Bennett

Musical Director: Hampton Durand

Songs: Aviation; Boogey Boo Lady, The; C.Q.D. (Help! I'm in Love); Cafe 'Round the Corner, A; Chum Highball (C/L: Hampton Durand); Corner of My Heart, A; Diff'rence of Drink, The; Do You Believe in Flirting; Hello, Mr. Moon Man; I Love to Love a Mason (C: Hampton Durand; L: Swibard); Motor Girls; Oh, That Beautiful Rag (C: Ted Snyder; L: Irving Berlin); Only a Kiss; Sweetheart from the Emerald Isle; Tale of the Bachelor and the Maid, The; When Two Love Dearly (C: Franz Lehar)

Cast: Willie Dunlay; Frances Warren

1551 • GIRL IN THE PRIVATE ROOM, THE
OPENED: 1920
Musical   Closed out of town

Composer Gitz Rice
Lyricist: Edward Clark
Librettist: Edward Clark
Producer: Messrs. Shubert
Director: Edward Clark

Source: THIRD PARTY, THE (Play: Frederick Arthur; Joclyn Brandon); **Musical Director:** Victor Baravalle

Songs: All's Fair in Love and War; And Then Came a Carriage Filled with Flowers; Dancing the Razz-Ma-Tazz; Different Days- Different Ways; Good-Bye, Take Care of Yourself; Hat Check Dance; I Love My Art; Look for the Rainbow; My Old New Jersey Home; Silver Wedding Day; Some Things Cannot Be Explained; Table for Two, A

Cast: John Lowe; Vivian Oakland; Eugene Redding; Queenie Smith

Notes: Program 9/13/20 Atlantic City.

1552 • GIRL IN THE SPOTLIGHT
OPENED: 07/12/1920   Theatre: Knickerbocker
Musical   Broadway: 54

Composer: Victor Herbert
Lyricist: Robert B. Smith
Librettist: Robert B. Smith
Producer: George W. Lederer
Director: George W. Lederer

Choreographer: Julian Alfred; **Costumes:** William H. Matthews; **Lighting Designer:** Tony Greshoff

Songs: Catch 'em Young, Treat 'em Rough, Tell 'em Nothing; Come Across; Everything Has Stung Me But a Bee [1]; Girl in the Spotlight [5]; I Cannot Sleep Without Dreaming of You; I Have Waited for You [1]; I Knew Him When; I Know I Shall Meet Her Someday [1]; I Learned About Women (from Her) [1]; I Love the Ground You Walk On; I'll Be There; In My Looking Glass; It Would Happen Anyway; Let's Pretend [2]; Marry Me and See [4]; Night Time, The [3]; Only You [4]; Oo La La; Savage I Remain, A; Somewhere I Know There's a Girl for Me; Springtime Dance [1]; Tell 'Em Nothing [5]; There's a Tender Look in Your Eyes; Twas in the Month of June; Where Were You [2]

Cast: Johnny Dooley; Mary Milburn; Hal Skelly

Notes: Robert B. Smith credited as Richard Bruce in program. [1] Out Stamford 7/7/20. [2] Out 2/6/21. [3] Out 2/6/21. Also cut from OUI MADAME. [4] Sheet music only. [5] ASCAP/Library of Congress only.

1553 • GIRL IN THE TAXI (1910)

OPENED: 10/24/1910   Theatre: Astor
Musical   Broadway: 48

Librettist: Stanislaus Stange
Producer: A.H. Woods
Director: Carter De Haven

Source: FILS A PAPA (Play: Anthony Mars)

Songs: Mr. Pat O'Hare (C/L: Benjamin Hapgood Burt)

Cast: Fremont Benton; Fred Bond; Carter De Haven; Jeanette Eageard; Frank Farrington; Max Freeman; John Glendenning; Laura Guerite; Jessie Millward

Notes: No New York program available. The score was written by various writers.

1554 • GIRL IN THE TAXI, THE (1912)

OPENED: 09/05/1912   Theatre: Lyric
Musical   London: 385

Composer: Jean Gilbert
Librettist: Frederick Fenn; Arthur Wimperis
Producer: P. Michael Faraday
Director: P. Michael Faraday

Source: DIE KEUSCHE SUZANNE (Musical: Jean Gilbert; Georg Okonkowski); **Musical Director:** Jacques Heuvel

Songs: Lilt That's Lazy and Dreamy and Hazy (Waltz-Song); Suzanne, Suzanne, We Love You to a Man

Cast: Yvonne Arnaud; Robert Averell; Arthur Playfair

1555 • GIRL IN THE TRAIN, THE

OPENED: 10/03/1910   Theatre: Globe
Musical   Broadway: 40

Composer: Leo Fall
Lyricist: Harry B. Smith
Librettist: Harry B. Smith
Producer: Charles Dillingham
Director: Fred G. Latham

Source: DIE GESCHIEDENE FRAU (Musical: Leo Fall; Victor Leon); **Choreographer:** A.M. Holbrook; **Costumes:** Anna Conkwright; Wilhelm; **Musical Director:** Max Hirschfeld; **Set Design:** Homer Emens

Songs: Children, You Seem Rather Distant to Me; Eeny Meeny Miny Mo; Ensemble (1); Ensemble (2); Finale Act I; Finale Act II; Finale Act III; Follow Me; Girl in the Train, The; Gonda Waltzes; Goodbye [2] (C/L: Clare Kummer); I'm Fancy Free; In My Dreams of You [1]; Kermess Dance and Song; Let Us Be Married [1]; Oh Married Life; Opening Chorus Act II; That's Why Lots of People Marry; When Love Is Free [1]; Why Not, Why Not?; Women Get the Best of Us, The [1]; You Must Be Mine Dear

Cast: Claude Gillingwater; Vera Michelena; James Reaney

Notes: [1] Out 2/1/11. [2] Sheet music only.

1556 • GIRL OF MINE (1917)

OPENED: 1917
Musical   Closed out of town

Composer: Ray Peabody
Lyricist: David M. Wolff
Librettist: David M. Wolff
Producer: E.P. Churchill
Director: Virgil Bennett

Songs: College Days; Dance of Time; From Here to Shanghai [1]; Girl of Mine; Kid Days Again; Ku Klux Klan; Love's Young Dream; Morning Exercises; Nobody Loves a Fat Man; Scandal; Strutter's Ball, The; Very Good Friends of Mine; Washington D.C.; When a Fellow's Twenty-One; Yes

Cast: Sylvia "Cuddles" De Rankie; Russell Frost; Velma Hinkle; Iona Jacobs; John P. Morse; Frank Neville; Grace Rheams

Notes: From program Orpheum Theatre 3/29/17. [1] The popular song of the same name by Irving Berlin was written in 1916. This might be that song.

1557 • GIRL O' MINE (1918)

OPENED: 01/28/1918   Theatre: Bijou
Musical   Broadway: 48

Composer: Frank Tours
Lyricist: Philip Bartholomae
Librettist: Philip Bartholomae
Producer: Elisabeth Marbury; J.J. Shubert; Lee Shubert
Director: J. Clifford Brooke; Edward P. Temple

Choreographer: Allan K. Foster; Edward Hutchinson; **Musical Director:** Frank Tours; **Set Design:** Watson Barratt

Songs: Birdies in the Trees, The; Changing Styles; Could You Love a Man Like Me?; Every Cloud Is Silver-Lined; Fatal Step; Girl o' Mine; I Like to Play with the Boys; It's Only Been Done on the Stage; It's the Woman Who Pays; Love Is Just a Fairy Tale [1]; Meet Me Girlie; My Service Flag; Not So Fast; Omar Khayyam; Rag Time Wedding Bells; Rug, Snug [1]; Saturday Night [1]; Shrug Your Shoulders [1]; Sorority Girls; To-Day Is the Day; Toddler's Ball; Winning Race, The; You're Just the One I've Waited For [2] (C/L: Manuel Klein)

Cast: Dorothy Dickson; Frank Fay; Edna Wallace Hopper; Carl Hyson; Marie Nordstrom

Notes: Previously titled OH MAMA! Later revised into THE VICTORY GIRL. [1] Cut after opening. [2] Sheet music only.

1558 • GIRL OF MY DREAMS, THE

OPENED: 08/07/1911   Theatre: Criterion
Musical   Broadway: 40

Composer: Karl Hoschna
Lyricist: Otto Harbach
Librettist: Wilbur Nesbit
Producer: Joseph M. Gaites
Director: Frank Smithson

Musical Director: C.E. MacArthur

Songs: Autumn Moon [1]; Bachelor Days; Belles of the Tally-Ho Boarding School; Dear Little Games of Guessing; Doctor Tinkle Tinker; Every Girlie Loves Me but the Girl I Love; Girl of My Dreams, The; Girl Who Wouldn't Spoon, The; Harbor of Home [1]; I Wonder If You Care [4]; I'm Ready to Quit and Be Good; Letter You Shouldn't Have Sent, The; My Wife! My Wife!; On Sunday Morning [1]; Ooh! (Maybe It's a Robber); Pack Up Your Heart [1]; Quaker Talk; Sauce for the Gander Is Sauce for the Goose; Something Very Mysterious; Story of a Marionette; That Soul Inspiring Sneeze [3]; Tommy Rot [2]

Cast: Harry Clarke; John Hyams; Anna Laughlin; Leila McIntyre

Notes: [1] Out 6/6/??. [2] Out Chicago 8/6/10. [3] Out Boston 2/27/11. [4] Sheet music only.

1559 • GIRL OF TODAY, A

OPENED: 1913
Musical   Closed out of town

Librettist: Porter Emerson Browne
Producer: Charles Frohman

Songs: You Know and I Know (and We Both Understand) [1] (C: Jerome Kern; L: Schuyler Greene)

Notes: This show closed in Washington, D.C. No

program available. [1] Later in NOBODY HOME.

1560 • GIRL OF TOMORROW, THE

OPENED: 10/18/1915 Theatre: La Salle
Musical Chicago

Composer: Joseph E. Howard; Herbert Stothart
Lyricist: Joseph Neal
Librettist: Frederick Herendeen; Joseph Neal
Producer: Western Producing Co.
Director: Frank Smithson

Songs: Bachelor Bear; Cabareting in Pumpkinville; Cake Walk Promenade; Chicago Trot; Chilli Con-Can (Chili Glide); Eugenic Kiss; Everybody's Cabareting; Finale Act I; Finale Act II; First Call of Love [1]; Have a Little Sip with Me; Hello Chicago; Legend, The; Let's Go A-Roaming; My Heart's Achin' for Macon [1]; Opening Chorus; Opening Chorus Act II; Pass the Contribution Box; Same Old Girl, The [1]; Some of These Nights (L: Harry Breen; Joseph Neal); Somebody Told Me; Story of the Sea; Tea, Toast and Kisses; That Melodious Melody; That Strictly Neutral Jag; Things Are So Different Now-a-Days [1]

Cast: A.F. Butler; Regina Connelli; Frank Conroy; Joseph E. Howard; George LeMaire; Mabel McCane; Elsie Moore; Wayne Nunn; Fred Waelder

Notes: [1] ASCAP/Library of Congress only.

1561 • GIRL ON THE FILM, THE

OPENED: 12/29/1913 Theatre: 44th Street
Musical Broadway: 64

Composer: Willie Bredschneider; Walter Kollo; Albert Sirmay
Lyricist: Adrian Ross
Librettist: James T. Tanner
Producer: Messrs. Shubert

Source: FILMZAUBER (Musical: Rudolf Bernauer; Walter Kollo; Rudolf Schanzer); **Costumes:** Comelli; **Musical Director:** Leonard Hornsbee

Songs: Ah! Che Vedo; Correspondence; Diggywig Two-Step [1]; Down By the Countryside; Give Me Something in a Uniform [1] (C: Paul Rubens;

L: Percy Greenbank); Good Old Mill, The [1] (C: Albert Sirmay); I Heard That Tale Before; In Bond Street; Napoleon and the Miller's Daughter [1] (C: Walter Kollo); Oh! If You Were a Girl; Oh! Oh! Oh! [1]; Steady Freddy [1]; Tommy Won't You Teach Me How to Tango; Town and Country [1] (C: Albert Sirmay); Won't You Come and Waltz with Me? (C: Albert Sirmay); You Don't See It but It's There

Cast: Connie Ediss; George Grossmith; John McArdle; Paul Plunkett; Madeline Seymour; Vera Sinclair; Emmy Wehlen; Grafton Williams

Notes: [1] Sheet music only.

1562 • GIRL OVER THERE, THE

OPENED: 10/02/1907
Musical Closed out of town

Composer: P. Sweningston
Librettist: Harry Sheldon White
Producer: Walter C. Lindsay
Director: Arthur Sanders

Musical Director: Phil Walker

Songs: Finale Act III; Fishing; Garden of Love's Desire, The; Girl of the Golden West; Good Old Fashioned Western Smile, A (C: Hilding Anderson; L: Colin Davis); Habit As We Go Along, The; Love Bug Sting, The; My Little Kodak Girl (C: Hilding Anderson; L: Colin Davis); Next Morning Tells Another Tale; Old Glory; Seems to Me I've Heard of That Before; Something We Keep Q.T.

Cast: Elsie Crescy; Geo. A. Lemming; Mabel McCane; Cecil Summers; Ben Turbitt

Notes: Cedar Rapids program.

1563 • GIRL QUESTION, THE

OPENED: 08/03/1908 Theatre: Wallack
Musical Broadway: 32

Composer: Joseph E. Howard
Lyricist: Frank Adams; Will M. Hough
Librettist: Frank Adams; Will M. Hough
Producer: Askin-Singer Co.
Director: George F. Marion

Set Design: John H. Young

Songs: Be Sweet to Me Kid; College Days; Do Something; Girl You Dream About, The; I Hate to Work on Monday; I'd Like to Have You Call Me Honey; It's Good-Bye Pal; Old Buck and Wing, The (C: Hilding Anderson; L: Joseph E. Howard); She Has Trouble with Her Eyes [1]; There Is No Place Like Home; Waltz Me 'Till I'm Dreamy; When Eyes Like Yours Look Into Eyes Like Mine

Cast: Helen Broderick; Lester Brown; Dan Bruce; Isabel D'Armond; Harry Hanlon; Edwin Maynard; Junie McCree; Georgia Drew Mendum

Notes: [1] ASCAP/Library of Congress only.

1564 • GIRL WHO CAME TO SUPPER, THE

OPENED: 12/08/1963   Theatre: Broadway
Musical   Broadway: 112

Composer: Noel Coward
Lyricist: Noel Coward
Librettist: Harry Kurnitz
Producer: Herman Levin
Director: Joe Layton

Source: SLEEPING PRINCE, THE (Play: Terence Rattigan); **Costumes:** Irene Sharaff; **Dance Arranger:** Genevieve Pitot; **Lighting Designer:** Peggy Clark; **Musical Director:** Jay Blackton; **Orchestrations:** Robert Russell Bennett; **Set Design:** Oliver Smith; **Vocal Arranger:** Jay Blackton

Songs: Cocoanut Girl, The; Come Be My True Love [3]; Coronation Chorale (Westminster Abbey); Curt, Clear and Concise; Don't Take Our Charlie for the Army; Here and Now; How Do You Do, Middle Age; If Only Mrs. Applejohn Were Here [1]; I'll Remember Her; I'm a Lonely Man [1]; I've Been Invited to a Party; Just People [1]; London Is a Little Bit of All Right; Lonely; Long Live the King-If He Can [1]; My Family Tree [4]; Paddy MacNeil and His Automobile; Saturday Night at the Rose and Crown; Sir or Ma'am; Six Lilies of the Valley; Soliloquies; Stingaree, The (dance); Swing Song; This Time It's True Love [2]; Time Will Tell [1]; Walla Walla Boola, The; Welcome to Pootzie Van Doyle; What Ho, Mrs. Brisket; What's the Matter with a Nice Beef Stew [1]; When Foreign Princes Come to Visit Us; Yasni Kozkolai

Cast: Irene Browne; Roderick Cook; Jose Ferrer; Florence Henderson; Lucie Lancaster; Tessie O'Shea

Notes: [1] Cut prior to opening. [2] Same music as "Come Be My True Love." [3] Cut. Same music as "This Time It's True Love." [4] Half of the song is from the song "Countess Mitzi" from OPERETTE.

1565 • GIRL WHO SMILES, THE

OPENED: 08/09/1915   Theatre: Lyric
Musical   Broadway: 104

Composer: Jean Briquet
Lyricist: Edward A. Paulton; Adolf Philipp
Librettist: Edward A. Paulton; Adolf Philipp
Producer: Times Producing Co.
Director: Ben Teal

Source: UNKNOWN (Musical: Paul Herve; Adolf Philipp); **Musical Director:** Augustus Barratt

Songs: At Last United [2]; Baby Mine; Breath from Bohemia, A; Cozy Corner [1]; Dance Me Goodbye; Father Never Raised Any Foolish Children [1]; Girl from Paree, A; Have You Heard the Scandal [1]; Honeymoon in May, A; I Forgot the Number of the House [1]; I Whispered It to the Roses; I'm Built for Speed [1]; Join the Families [1]; Let Us Dance [2]; Life Has Just Begun; Little Difference at Breakfast, A [1]; Oh Pauline; Story of a Sparrow, The; Teach Me to Smile; We're Looking for Marie; When Labor Comes into Its Own; Wine, Wine, Wine [1]; You Are My Little Cupid; Your Picture

Cast: Natalie Ault; Ralph Bunker; William Danforth; Paul Decker; Jennie Dickerson; Marie Fanchonetti; Clara Lawrence; Marie McDonald; Lillian Spencer; Fred Walton

Notes: Jean Briquet and Paul Herve were almost certainly pseudonyms for Philipp. There probably was no source for this musical. [1] Out 2/4/16. [2] Sheet music only.

1566 • GIRLIES

OPENED: 06/03/1910   Theatre: New Amsterdam
Musical   Broadway: 88

Composer: Egbert Van Alstyne
Lyricist: Harry Williams

Librettist: George V. Hobart
Producer: Frederick W. Thompson

Choreographer: Jack Mason

Songs: Baby Talk; Bull Frog and the Dove, The; Going Up (in My Aeroplane); Honolulu Rag; Life Is a Merry-Go-Round (C: Benjamin Hapgood Burt; L: John Golden); Meet Me Down By the River [3]; My Irish Girl; Play That Wedding March Backwards [1]; Ring Me Up in the Morning; Rowing Song, The; Since Hiram Went to Yale [2]; Take Me to the Masquerade; That's Good; Who Are You with Tonight?; You Can Find It in the Papers Every Day

Cast: Joseph Cawthorn; Doris Mitchell; Jed Prouty; Maude Raymond; Ernest Truex

Notes: Related in some way to THE COMIC SUPPLEMENT. [1] Sheet music only. [2] Sheet music only. Written in 1906. [3] ASCAP/Library of Congress only.

1567 • GIRLS AGAINST THE BOYS, THE

OPENED: 11/02/1959   Theatre: Alvin
Musical   Broadway: 16

Composer: Richard Lewine
Lyricist: Arnold B. Horwitt
Librettist: Arnold B. Horwitt
Producer: Albert Selden
Director: Aaron Ruben

Choreographer: Boris Runanin; **Costumes:** Sal Anthony; **Dance Arranger:** John Morris; **Lighting Designer:** Ralph Alswang; **Musical Director:** Irving Actman; **Orchestrations:** Robert Ginzler; Sid Ramin; **Set Design:** Ralph Alswang

Songs: Girls Against the Boys, The; Girls and Boys; Here It Comes Again [1] (C: Albert Hague); I Gotta Have You; Light Travelin' Man (C: Albert Hague); Lolita [1]; Nobody Else but You (C: Albert Hague); Old Fashioned Girl; Overspend; Rich Butterfly; Thank You, Doctor; Too Young to Live; Where Did We Go? Out

Cast: Maureen Bailey; Mace Barrett; Shelley Berman; Martin Charnin; Imelda De Martin; Richard France; Buzz Halliday; Bert Lahr; Joy Nichols; Dick Van Dyke; June Walker; Nancy Walker; Cy Young

Notes: [1] Cut prior to opening.

1568 • GIRLS OF AMERICA

OPENED: 1907
Musical   Closed out of town

Composer: N. Harris Ware
Lyricist: John Saunders
Librettist: John Saunders
Director: John Saunders

Musical Director: D. Parsons Goodrich

Songs: Broad, Majestic Hudson, The; Conversation Song; Daughters of the Trusts; Dollar, The; Down on de Ole Yazoo; Etiquette; Goozy Woozy; Heroes Just the Same; My Idea of Love; Opening Chorus; Opening Chorus Act III; Persevere; Pink and the Butterfly, The; Proverbs Up-to- Date; Rita; Still the Heart Hopes On; Story of a Bird, The; Susie Blair; Vanity

Notes: Program of 6/5/07 Hartford.

1569 • GIRLS OF GOTTENBURG, THE

OPENED: 09/02/1908   Theatre: Knickerbocker
Musical   Broadway: 103

Composer: Ivan Caryll; Lionel Monckton
Lyricist: Basil Hood; Adrian Ross
Producer: Charles Frohman
Director: J.A.E. Malone

Musical Director: W.T. Francis

Songs: Always Come Back to You [2]; Beer Girl, The; Berlin on the Spree (C: Lionel Monckton; L: Basil Hood); Birds in the Trees, The [3] (C: Ivan Caryll; L: Adrian Ross); Clementine [4] (C: W.T. Francis; L: J.B. Loughrey); Common Little Girl, A [3] (C: Lionel Monckton; L: Ralph Roberts); Do You Know Mr. Schneider? (C/L: Lionel Monckton; L: George Grossmith Jr.); Finale Act II (C: Ivan Caryll; L: Adrian Ross); Fraulein Katrina (inst.) [1] (C: Jerome Kern; L: George Grossmith Jr.); Frieda (C: Jerome Kern; L: M.E. Rourke); Girls of Gottenburg, The (C: Ivan Caryll; L: Adrian Ross); Glass of Beer, A (C/L: Lionel Monckton); Here's to the Girl (C/L: Will R. Anderson); I Can't Say You're the Only One (C: Jerome Kern; L: C.H. Bovill); I Love My Love with an "A" (J'Aime Mon Amour) [3]

(C: Ivan Caryll; L: Adrian Ross); I Remember You [4] (C: Harry Von Tilzer; L: Vincent Bryan); I Will Be Waiting for You [4]; Kolossal [3] (C: Ivan Caryll; L: Adrian Ross); Madel Mine (C: Philip Braham; L: C.H. Bovill); Nothing at All [4] (C: Jerome Kern; L: M.E. Rourke); Off to Gottenburg (C: Lionel Monckton; L: Adrian Ross); Only Girl, The (C: Lionel Monckton; L: Basil Hood); Opening Chorus (C: Ivan Caryll; L: Adrian Ross); Opening Chorus Act I Scene 2 (C: Lionel Monckton; L: Adrian Ross); Opening Chorus Act II (C: Lionel Monckton; L: Basil Hood); Otto of Roses (C: Ivan Caryll; L: George Grossmith Jr.); Queenie with Her Hair in a Braid (C: W.T. Francis; L: John E. Hazzard); Remember You; Rhinegold [3] (C: Lionel Monckton; L: Adrian Ross); Sergeants [3] (C: Ivan Caryll; L: Adrian Ross); Special Envoy (C: Lionel Monckton; L: Basil Hood); Sprechen Sie Deutsch, Mein Herr? [2] (C: Lionel Monckton; L: Adrian Ross); Strolling and Patrolling [3] (C: Ivan Caryll; L: Adrian Ross); Titsy-Bitsy Girl (C: Lionel Monckton; L: Basil Hood); Two Little Sausages (C/L: Lionel Monckton); Two Step (Away Down Indiana) [3] (C: J.B. Boldi; Octave Cremieux; L: C.H. Bovill); What Is It? (C: Lionel Monckton; L: Basil Hood)

Cast: James Blakeley; Ernest Cossart; Louise Dresser; Eddie Garvie; John E. Hazzard; Wallace McCutcheon

Notes: [1] Out before New York. [2] Added after opening. [3] In London version. [4] Sheet music only.

1570 • GIRLS OF HOLLAND, THE
OPENED: 11/18/1907 Theatre: Lyric
Musical Broadway: 15

Composer: Reginald De Koven
Lyricist: Stanislaus Stange
Librettist: Stanislaus Stange
Producer: Lee Shubert; Sam S. Shubert
Director: Al Holbrook

Songs: Ariella; Captain Cupid; Could You Love Me?; Dainty Cavalier [1]; Gay Fusilier, The; I Want You for My All Time Girl; I'm the Doctor; In Paradise [1]; Joy of a Kiss, The; Love on a Summer's Day [1]; Men of Spain, The; Message of the Bells [1]; My Ladye Faire; Oh, Boy!; Our Doctor Comes; Pray Go Gently [1]; Rooster and the Lark, The; Sabot Dance;

Serenade D'Amour (Song of Love); Seven Reasons Why, The [1]; Snowman's Dream, The [1]; Spanish Grandee [1]; Unveiling of the Statue, The; We Sing a Jubilee; Wedding Day, The; Why Is It?; Wine, Women and Song [1]

Cast: Harry MacDonough; Vera Michelena; Mary Nash; Edward M. Tavor

Notes: Originally titled THE SNOWMAN. [1] From sheet music only when show was titled THE SNOWMAN.

1571 • GIRLS OF SUMMER
OPENED: 11/19/1956 Theatre: Longacre
Play Broadway: 56

Author: N. Richard Nash
Producer: Cheryl Crawford
Director: Jack Garfein

Costumes: Kenn Barr; **Lighting Designer:** Lee Watson; **Set Design:** Boris Aronson

Songs: Girls of Summer (C/L: Stephen Sondheim)

Cast: Pat Hingle; George Peppard; Arthur Storch; Shelley Winters

1572 • GIRLS UPSTAIRS, THE
Notes: See FOLLIES.

1573 • GIRLS WILL BE GIRLS (1906)
OPENED: 1906
Musical Closed out of town

Librettist: R. Melville Baker; Joseph Hart
Producer: William A. Brady

Musical Director: N. Harris Ware

Songs: Ah Bon Ben Ala; Arrival of Madeline (C/L: N. Harris Ware); Ask Dodge [1]; Boys in Blue (C/L: N. Harris Ware); Broadway Girls; Different Ways of Proposing; Dora Lane; Good Morning Teacher; He Walked Right In, Turned Around and Walked Right Out Again (C: Maxwell Silver; L: Ed Rose); How'dy Do; In Society [1]; Moon Eyes; Mr. Rubber Ball Professor; My Brown Eyed Daisy [1]; Off to Jail (C/L: N. Harris Ware); Sally (C/L: N. Harris

Ware); Shady Side of Broadway (C/L: Clifton Crawford); She Thinks Nothing of It Now [1]; Song of U.S.A. (C/L: N. Harris Ware); Swinging (C: A. Baldwin Sloane); That Little Girl Is You [1]; This Is the Day (C/L: N. Harris Ware); When the Girl You Love Says "Yes" [1]

Cast: Max Hoffmann; Al Leech; Jack Van Epps

Notes: Program 12/26/06 Wilkes-Barre. [1] Sheet music only.

1574 • GIRLS WILL BE GIRLS (1917)

Notes: *See LOVE O' MIKE.*

1575 • GIRLS, GIRLS, GIRLS

OPENED: 09/25/1980   Theatre: Public
Musical   Off-Broadway: 30

Composer: Cheryl Hardwick
Lyricist: Marilyn Suzanne Miller
Librettist: Marilyn Suzanne Miller
Producer: N.Y. Shakespeare Festival; Joseph Papp
Director: Bob Balaban

Songs: Betty Song, The; Credit Card; Divorce; Frances' Ballad; High School; Lovers; Man/Woman; Opening; Planet of No Thigh Bulge; Punk; Street Lady; Val's Ballad; Vicki Lawrence

Cast: Valri Bromfield; Frances Conroy; Anne DeSalvo; Judith Ivey; Jay Sanders

1576 • GIROFLE-GIROFLA

OPENED: 05/08/1893   Theatre: Academy of
                              Music
Musical   New York

Composer: Charles Lecocq
Librettist: J. Cheever Goodwin; Matt C. Woodward
Producer: T.R. French

Source: GIROFLE-GIROFLA (Musical: Charles Lecocq; Eugene Leterrier; Albert Vanloo); **Musical Director:** Charles Puerner; **Set Design:** Joseph Clare; Henry E. Hoyt; Richard Marsden

Cast: William T. Carleton; Ada Dare; Louis Harrison; Rose Leighton; Lillian Russell

Notes: Brooklyn program only. No songs listed in program. First produced in America at the Park Theatre, 02/02/1875 in French.

1577 • GLAD TO SEE YOU

OPENED: 1944
Musical   Closed out of town

Composer: Jule Styne
Lyricist: Sammy Cahn
Librettist: Eddie Davis; Fred Thompson
Producer: David Wolper
Director: Busby Berkeley

Choreographer: Valerie Bettis; **Costumes:** Travis Banton; **Lighting Designer:** Howard Bay; **Musical Director:** Max Meth; **Set Design:** Howard Bay; **Vocal Arranger:** Clay Warnick [2]

Songs: Any Fool Can Fall in Love; B Apostrophe, K Apostrophe, L-Y-N [1]; Can't You Read Between the Lines; Come On! Come On!; Don't Be Subtle, Don't Be Coy; Give Us Dames; Grown-Ups Are the Stupidest People; I Don't Love You No More, No More; I Guess I'll Hang My Tears Out to Dry; I Lost My Beat; I Murdered Them in Chicago; I'll Hate Myself in the Morning; I'm Laying Away a Buck; Innocent Stander-By [3]; Just for You; Ladies Don't Have Fun; Love and I Went Waltzing; Most Unusual Weather (For This Time of Year); So This Is Italy; What Did I Do?

Cast: Gene Barry; Kenny Bowers; Eddie Foy Jr.; June Knight; Joseph Macaulay; Sammy White; Jane Withers

Notes: [1] Later used in THE WEST POINT STORY (film). [2] Billed as Buck Warnick. [3] ASCAP/Library of Congress only.

1578 • GLIMPSE OF THE GREAT WHITE WAY, A

OPENED: 10/27/1913   Theatre: 44th Street
Musical   Broadway: 12

Composer: Alfred G. Robyn
Lyricist: Henry Blossom
Librettist: Henry Blossom
Producer: Lew Fields

Choreographer: Joseph C. Smith; **Costumes:** Melville Ellis

Songs: If I Were Only a Man; I'll Marry Him for Love; Permissible; What a Change

Cast: Sam Bernard; Frances Demarest; Forrest Huff

Notes: These songs were in the last part of the show, which was titled THE MODISTE'S SHOP. This was a smaller version of ALL FOR THE LADIES.

1579 • GLITTERING GLORIA

OPENED: 02/15/1904   Theatre: Daly's
Musical   Broadway: 22

Composer: Bernard Rolt
Lyricist: Hugh Morton
Librettist: Hugh Morton
Producer: John C. Fisher; Thomas W. Ryley

Songs: Cordelia Malone [1] (C: Jean Schwartz; L: William Jerome); Little Mary

Cast: Percy Ames; Eugene O'Rourke; Phyllis Rankin; Adele Ritchie; Cyril Scott

Notes: No program available. [1] Later in THE ORCHID in London.

1580 • GLORIANNA

OPENED: 10/28/1918   Theatre: Liberty
Musical   Broadway: 96

Composer: Rudolf Friml
Lyricist: Catherine Chisholm Cushing
Librettist: Catherine Chisholm Cushing
Producer: John Cort
Director: Clifford Brooke

Choreographer: Bert French; Costumes: Harry Collins; Mme. Kerner; Set Design: Joseph Urban

Songs: Best Man Never Gets the Worst of It, The; Caveman, The [1]; Chianti [2]; Dance of the Levants; Dance of the Porters; Dancing Lesson, The; Everyday Will Be Sunday When the Town Goes Dry; Frocks and Frills; Glorianna [3]; I Have My Fingers Crossed, Why Don't You [1]; I Love But You [1]; I Love You Dear [1]; Just a Little Laughter; Love! Love! Love! [2]; March On [1]; Nenette and Rin-Tin-Tin (Rintintin); Oriental Song [2]; So Undulating,

So Fascinating [2]; Speak for Yourself John; Tell Me, Crystal Ball; Toodle-Oo!; When a Girl

Cast: Alexander Clark; Eleanor Painter; Ralph Whitehead

Notes: [1] Out Washington, D.C. 9/16/18. [2] Sheet music only. [3] ASCAP/Library of Congress only.

1581 • GLORIOUS AGE, THE

OPENED: 05/11/1975   Theatre: Theatre Four
Musical   Off-Broadway: 9

Composer: Cy Young
Lyricist: Cy Young
Librettist: Mark Gordon; Cy Young
Producer: Jane Manning; Carol McGroder
Director: John-Michael Tebelak

Choreographer: Dick Stephens; Costumes: Jennifer von Mayrhauser; Dance Arranger: Stephen Reinhardt; Lighting Designer: Barry Arnold; Musical Director: Robert W. Preston; Orchestrations: Stephen Reinhardt; Set Design: Stuart Wurtzel; Vocal Arranger: Stephen Reinhardt

Songs: All about the Plum; Child of the Shade; Everyone Should Play a Musical Instrument; Future Looks Promising, The; Glorious Age; La, La, La; Maybe There's a Place; Mother Love; Must Be a Witch in Town; Ray, Ray; Relic Seller Theme; Stay on the Path; Teach the Children; Theologian Theme; Turn My Life Is Taking, The; Whoop De Doo

Cast: D'Jamin Bartlett; George Riddle; Don Scardino; Carol Swarbrick

1582 • GLORY

OPENED: 12/25/1922   Theatre: Vanderbilt
Musical   Broadway: 74

Composer: Harry Tierney
Lyricist: James Dyrenforth; Joseph McCarthy
Librettist: James Montgomery
Producer: Vanderbilt Producing Co.
Director: Bert French

Musical Director: Max Hirschfeld

Songs: Glory (C: Maurice DePackh; L: James Dyrenforth); Goodly Little Things We Do, The

(C: Maurice DePackh; L: James Dyrenforth); Little White House with Green Blinds, A (L: Joseph McCarthy); Moon Was Good Enough for Dad and Mother, The (C: Maurice DePackh; L: James Dyrenforth); Mother's Wedding Dress (L: Joseph McCarthy); Opening, The (L: Joseph McCarthy); Opening Act II (L: Joseph McCarthy); Popularity (L: Joseph McCarthy); Post Office; Same Old Story, The; Saw Mill River Road (L: Joseph McCarthy); Upper Crust, The (L: Joseph McCarthy); We've Got to Build (L: Joseph McCarthy); When the Curfew Rings at Nine (C/L: Al W. Brown); When the Tenor Married the Soprano (and the Alto Married the Bass) (C: Maurice DePackh; L: James Dyrenforth)

Cast: Jack Clifford; Helen Groody; Patti Harrold; Flo Irwin; Walter Ryan

1583 • GLORY OF EASTER, THE
Notes: *See EASTER SHOW.*

1584 • GO EASY MABEL
OPENED: 05/08/1922   Theatre: Longacre
Musical   Broadway: 16

Composer: Charles George
Lyricist: Charles George
Librettist: Charles George
Producer: Hudson Productions Co.
Director: Julian Alfred; Bertram Harrison

Musical Director: Ross Mobley; **Set Design:** P. Dodd Ackerman

Songs: Ethel Levey's Smile Song; Girls, Girls, Girls; Go Easy, Mabel; Honey, I Love You; I Want a Regular Man; Lapse of Time, A; Love Is King; Oh, Papa; Old Fashioned Man Is Hard to Find, An; Unveiling of a Broadway Girl, The; When You Dance with the Girl You Love

Cast: Will J. Deming; Margaret Dumont; Ethel Levey; Estelle Winwood

1585 • GO FLY A KITE
OPENED: 1966
Revue   Closed out of town

Composer: John Kander; Walter Marks
Lyricist: Fred Ebb; Walter Marks

Musical Director: Ted Simons; **Orchestrations:** Larry Wilcox

Cast: Valerie Harper; Dean Stolber; Ted Thurston; Mary Louise Wilson

Notes: No other information available.

1586 • GO FOR YOUR GUN
Notes: *See BELLE STARR.*

1587 • GO-GO
OPENED: 03/12/1923   Theatre: Daly's
Musical   Broadway: 138

Composer: C. Luckeyth Roberts
Lyricist: Alex Rogers
Librettist: Harry L. Cort; George E. Stoddard
Producer: John Cort
Director: Walter Brooks

Costumes: Shirley Barker; **Musical Director:** Hilding Anderson

Songs: Any Old Time at All; Doggone Whippoorwill; Go-Go Bug; Good Bye, Honey Falls; Have You Any Little Thing; Honey; I'm Scared of You; Indian Moon; Isabel; Lolly-Papa; Mailman Must Be Mad at Me, The; Mo'lasses; New York Town; Old Man's Darling, An; Pat Your Feet; Rosetime and You; Strut; Struttin' the Blues Away; Universal Lullaby [1]; Uno; When You Dance with a Wonderful Girl [2]; Wonderful Dance

Cast: Don Barclay; Bernard Granville; Josephine Stevens

Notes: [1] Out Atlantic City 3/5/23. [2] Sheet music only.

1588 • GO TO IT
OPENED: 12/24/1916   Theatre: Princess
Musical   Broadway: 23

Composer: John Golden
Lyricist: Anne Caldwell; John Golden; John E. Hazzard

Librettist: Anne Caldwell; John Golden; John E. Hazzard
Producer: F. Ray Comstock; William Elliot
Director: Frank Smithson

Choreographer: David Bennett; **Musical Director:** Max Hirschfeld

Songs: Come Along Little Girls; Doesn't Anybody Want Me?; Every Little While (1) [3] (C: Jerome Kern); Every Little While (2) [4] (C: James W. Tate; L: Clifford Harris); Extra!; Girls If You Ever Get Married; Go to It (C: Raymond Hubbell; L: Max Darewski); Keep Me from Falling Asleep; Kiss Your Soldier Boy Au Revoir; Ladies Day; Languanay; Lemon Peels [2]; Liking and Loving [1]; Little By Little and Bit By Bit (C: Worton David; L: Schuyler Greene); Little World of Our Own, A; London Taps (The Broken Doll); Love Me Just a Little Bit; Mr. Love [1]; O'Houlihan [1]; Pigeon Walk, The [1]; There's Something About You Dear That Appeals to Me (C: John Golden; Silvio Hein; L: Frank Craven); Toddle All Over the Town [1]; When You're in Love You'll Know (C/L: John Golden; Jerome Kern); Where's the Little Boy for Me? (C: Charles N. Grant; L: Schuyler Greene); You're the Girl (That Sets Me Stuttering) (C: Charles N. Grant; L: Schuyler Greene)

Cast: Helen Bond; Wellington Cross; Percival Knight; Gertrude Vanderbilt

Notes: [1] Out Buffalo 10/2/16. [2] Out Buffalo 9/21/16. [3] Sheet music only. [4] Credited to Joseph W. Tate and Ernie Golden on recording.

1589 • GOBLIN MARKET

OPENED: 04/13/1986   Theatre: Circle in the Square Downtown
Musical   Off-Broadway: 89

Composer: Polly Pen
Lyricist: Christina Rossetti
Producer: Pat Daily; Ken Marsolais; James Scott
Director: Andre Ernotte

Source: GOBLIN MARKET (Poetry: Christina Rossetti); **Choreographer:** Ara Fitzgerald; **Costumes:** Kitty Leech; Muriel Stockdale; **Lighting Designer:** Phil Monat; **Musical Director:** Lawrence Yurman; **Orchestrations:** James McElwaine; **Set Design:** William Barclay

Songs: Come Buy, Come Boy; Do You Not Remember Jeanie; Here They Come; Like a Lily; Lizzie, Lizzie, Have You Tasted; Mirage (C: Charles Ives); Mouth So Charmful (C: Antonio Lotti; L: Theodore Baker); Passing Away; Sisters, The (C: Johannes Brahms); Sleep, Laura, Sleep (L: Christopher Morgenstern); Some There Are Who Never Venture (L: John Gay; Peggy Harmon; Polly Pen); Two Doves; We Must Not Look

Cast: Terri Klausner; Ann Morrison

1590 • GOD BLESS CONEY

OPENED: 05/03/1972   Theatre: Orpheum
Musical   Off-Broadway: 3

Composer: John Glines
Lyricist: John Glines
Librettist: John Glines
Producer: Paul B. Reynolds
Director: Bob Schwartz

Arrangements: Robert Rogers; **Costumes:** Margaretta Maganini; **Lighting Designer:** William Mintzer; **Musical Director:** Robert Rogers; **Orchestrations:** Robert Rogers; **Set Design:** Don Tirrell

Songs: Coney Island, The; Eight-horse Parlay; God Bless All the Misfits; God Bless Coney; Goodbye Hives; He Looked at Me; Here Comes the Rabbi; Here We Are; Intermission Rag; Love Life; Man and Wife; Music Hall Medley; Seagulls; Subway to Coney; Throw Out the Lifeline

Cast: William Francis; Bill Hinnant; Ann Hodapp; Johnny La Motta; Marcia Lewis; Liz Sheridan

1591 • GOD BLESS YOU, MR. ROSEWATER

OPENED: 10/14/1979   Theatre: Entermedia
Musical   Off-Broadway: 61

Composer: Alan Menken
Lyricist: Howard Ashman
Librettist: Howard Ashman
Producer: Edith Vonnegut
Director: Howard Ashman

Source: GOD BLESS YOU, MR. ROSEWATER

(Novel: Kurt Vonnegut); **Choreographer:** Mary Kyte; **Costumes:** David Graden; **Dance Arranger:** Jimmy Roberts; **Lighting Designer:** Craig Evans; **Musical Director:** David Friedman; **Orchestrations:** Daniel Troob; **Set Design:** Edward T. Gianfrancesco; **Vocal Arranger:** David Friedman

Songs: Cheese Nips; Dear Ophelia (L: Dennis Green); Eliot Rosewater; Eliot, Sylvia; Firestorm Consuming Indianapolis, A [1]; I'll Build a Statue; Look Who's Here; Mushari's Waltz; Plain Clean Average Americans; Poem by William Blake, A; Rhode Island Tango (L: Dennis Green); Rosewater Foundation, The; Since You Came to This Town; Thank God for the Volunteer Fire Brigade (L: Dennis Green); 30 Miles from the Banks of the Ohio

Cast: David Christmas; Frederick Coffin; Anne DeSalvo; Pierre Epstein; Jonathan Hadary; Janie Sell

Notes: The play opened at the WPA Theatre where it played 12 performances. It then moved to the Entermedia for an additional 49 performances. [1] Cut prior to opening.

1592 • GOD IS A (GUESS WHAT?)

OPENED: 12/17/1968   Theatre: St. Marks Playhouse
Musical   Off-Broadway: 32

Composer: Coleridge-Taylor Perkinson
Lyricist: Ray McIver
Librettist: Ray McIver
Producer: Negro Ensemble Company
Director: Michael A. Schultz

Choreographer: Louis Johnson; **Costumes:** Bernard Johnson; **Lighting Designer:** Marshall Williams; **Set Design:** Edward Burbridge

Songs: Black-Black Song, The; Darkies Song, The; God Will Take Care; Golden Rule Song, The; Lynch-Him Song, The; Lyncher's Prayer, The; Mighty Fortress, A; Sit Down Song, The; Sonny-Boy Slave Song, The

Cast: Rosalind Cash; David Downing; Arthur French; Julian Harris; Esther Rolle; Clarice Taylor

1593 • GODDESS OF LIBERTY, THE

OPENED: 12/22/1909   Theatre: Weber
Musical   Broadway: 29

Composer: Joseph E. Howard
Lyricist: Frank Adams; Will M. Hough
Librettist: Frank Adams; Will M. Hough
Producer: Joseph E. Howard; Ned Wayburn
Director: John Cromwell; Joseph E. Howard

Musical Director: Hugo Frey

Songs: Blow the Smoke Away [3]; Boola Boola; Don't Choose a Gibson Girl [2]; Don't Forget the Number [4] (L: Addison Burkhardt; Collin Davis); Down Goes the Price of Eggs; Dreaming; Goddess of Liberty, The [3]; Haunted Pool, The; Here's to Your Last Girl; Honeymoon Trail [1]; Hush, I Think I Hear Him [1]; I Wonder Who's Kissing Her Now [1] (C: Joseph E. Howard; L: Harold Orlob); If All Moons Were Honey Moons; I'll Bet You; Laughing Song; Let's Pretend You Love Me [3]; Lonely; Oskee Wow Wow [3]; Please Keep Me Young in Your Heart [3]; Something; Taxi, Taxi [3]; Those Wonderful Eyes (C/L: Joseph E. Howard); Tummy-Tummy-Tum; Where Are They Now [3]

Cast: Edward Abeles; Charles Aveling; May DeSousa; Frances Demarest; Charles Fletcher; Bert Smith

Notes: [1] Out Boston 5/16/10. [2] Titled "Don't Choose a College Girl" in programs. [3] Sheet music only. [4] Also in THE SWEETEST GIRL IN PARIS.

1594 • GODDESS OF TRUTH, THE

OPENED: 02/26/1896   Theatre: Abbey's
Musical   Broadway: 45

Composer: Julian Edwards
Librettist: Stanislaus Stange
Director: Max Freeman

Musical Director: Paul Steindorff; **Set Design:** Henry E. Hoyt

Cast: Leo Ditrichstein; A.M. Holbrook; Richie Ling; Lillian Russell; Frederic Solomon; Herbert Florence Willis

Notes: No songs listed in program.

1595 • GODSPELL

OPENED: 05/17/1971   Theatre: Cherry Lane
Musical   Off-Broadway: 2651

Composer: Stephen Schwartz
Lyricist: Stephen Schwartz
Librettist: John-Michael Tebelak
Producer: Joseph Beruh; Stuart Duncan; Edgar
   Lansbury
Director: John-Michael Tebelak

Source: GOSPEL ACCORDING TO ST.
   MATTHEW, THE (Book: St. Matthew);
   Costumes: Susan Tsu; **Lighting Designer:**
   Lowell B. Aschziger; **Vocal Arranger:** Stephen
   Schwartz

Songs: Alas for You; All for the Best; All Good
   Gifts; Bless the Lord; By My Side (C: Peggy
   Gordon; L: Jay Hamburger); Day by Day; Learn
   Your Lessons Well; Light of the World; On the
   Willows; Prepare Ye the Way of the Lord; Save
   the People; Tower of Babble; Turn Back, O Man;
   We Beseech Thee

Cast: Lamar Alford; Peggy Gordon; David
   Haskell; Joanne Jonas; Robin Lamont; Sonia
   Manzano; Jeffrey Mylett; Stephen Nathan;
   Herb Simon

Notes: The show played 2118 performances
   off-Broadway at the Cherry Lane and then the
   Promenade Theatre. It moved to the Broadhurst
   Theatre on 6/22/76. After stops at the Plymouth
   and Ambassador theatres it closed after an
   additional 557 performances.

1596 • GOGO LOVES YOU

OPENED: 10/09/1964   Theatre: Theatre de Lys
Musical   Off-Broadway: 2

Composer: Claude Leveilee
Lyricist: Gladys Shelley
Librettist: Anita Loos
Producer: Fredena Productions
Director: Fred Weintraub

Choreographer: Marvin Gordon; **Costumes:**
   Alfred Lehman; **Lighting Designer:** Jules Fisher;
   Musical Director: Everett Gordon; **Set Design:**
   Kert Lundell

Songs: Bazoom; College of L'Amour; Gogo;
   Happy Love Affair; He Can, I Can; Keep in

Touch; Life Is Lovely; My Uncle's Mistress;
Parnasse; Prima Donna; Quelle Heure Est-il?;
Savoir Faire; Tell Me the Story of Your Life;
There Is No Difference; Woman Makes the Man

Cast: Dorothy Greener; Judy Henske; Gene
   Lindsey; Arnold Soboloff

1597 • GOING HOLLYWOOD

Musical   Closed out of town

Composer: Jonathan Sheffer
Lyricist: David Zippel
Librettist: Joseph Leonardo; David Zippel
Director: Joseph Leonardo

Source: ONCE IN A LIFETIME (Play: Moss Hart;
   George S. Kaufman)

Songs: Another Mr. Right; Gingham and Orchid;
   Give 'Em What They Want; Gotta Go West;
   Hollywood Rhythm; If I Could Dance with You;
   Made for the Movies; Motto; Open Your Mouth;
   Page Jingle #1, 2, 3, 4 and 5; Smiling Rainbows;
   This Darling Industry; Three Little Bears; Today
   I'm Smiling Rainbows Upside Down; Waiting in
   the Wings; We Don't Talk Anymore; You Know
   Who

Cast: Hy Anzell; David Garrison; Judy Kaye;
   Karen Morrow; Patrick Quinn; Alyson Reed;
   Virginia Seidel; Martin Vidnovic; Carol Wolfe

Notes: Credits for a workshop at Paper Mill
   Playhouse, Millburn, N.J.

1598 • GOING UP

OPENED: 12/25/1917   Theatre: Liberty
Musical   Broadway: 351

Composer: Louis A. Hirsch
Lyricist: Otto Harbach
Librettist: Otto Harbach
Producer: George M. Cohan; Sam Harris
Director: James Montgomery; Edward Royce

Source: AVIATOR, THE (Play: James
   Montgomery); **Musical Director:** Gus Salzer;
   Orchestrations: Frank Saddler

Songs: Come Along to Toy Town [1] (C/L: Irving
   Berlin); Do It for Me; Down! Up! Left! Right!;
   Everybody Ought to Know How to Do the Tickle

Toe; Going Up; Here's to the Two of You; I Want a Boy Who's Determined to Do As I Say; If You Look in Her Eyes; I'll Bet You; Kiss Me; Opening Number; There's a Brand New Hero; Touch of a Woman's Hand, The; When the Curtain Falls (C/L: Irving Berlin)

Cast: Frank Craven; Ruth Donnelly; Donald Meek; Marion Sunshine

Notes: [1] Sheet music only. Also used in EVERYTHING.

1599 • GOLD BUG, THE

OPENED: 09/14/1896   Theatre: Casino
Musical   Broadway: 28

Composer: Victor Herbert
Lyricist: Glen MacDonough
Librettist: Glen MacDonough
Producer: Thomas Canary; George W. Lederer

Musical Director: Gustave Kerker

Songs: Gold Bug March (inst.); One for Another; Owl and the Thrush, The

Cast: Marie Cahill; Ada Dare; Virginia Earle; Max Figman; Molly Fuller; John Slavin; George Walker; Bert Williams

Notes: No program available.

1600 • GOLDEN APPLE, THE

OPENED: 03/11/1954   Theatre: Phoenix
Musical   Broadway: 173

Composer: Jerome Moross
Lyricist: John Latouche
Librettist: John Latouche
Producer: Alfred DeLiagre; Phoenix Theatre; Roger L. Stevens
Director: Norman Lloyd

Choreographer: Hanya Holm; **Costumes:** Alvin Colt; **Lighting Designer:** Klaus Holm; **Musical Director:** Hugh Ross; **Orchestrations:** Hershy Kay; Jerome Moross; **Set Design:** Jean Eckart; William Eckart

Songs: Calypso; Church Social, The; Circe, Circe; Come Along, Boys; Departure for Rhododendron, The; Doomed, Doomed, Doomed; Goona-Goona [3]; Hector's Song; Helen Is Always Willing; Heroes Come Home, The; Introducin' Mr. Paris; It was a Glad Adventure; It's the Going Home Together; Judgement of Paris, The; Lazy Afternoon; Mother Hare's Seance; My Love Is on the Way; My Picture in the Papers; Nothing Ever Happens in Angels' Roost; Scylla and Charybdis; Sewing Bee, The; Storebought Suit; Tirade, The [2]; Ulysses Soliloquy; We've Just Begun [1]; Windflowers (When We Were Young)

Cast: Kaye Ballard; Shannon Bolin; Stephen Douglass; Priscilla Gillette; Martha Larrimore; Jonathan Lucas; Portia Nelson; Bibi Osterwald; Jerry Stiller; Jack Whiting

Notes: This musical transferred to the Alvin Theatre for 125 performances after 48 performances off-Broadway. [1] Cut prior to Broadway move. [2] Added for Broadway. [3] Originally titled "By Goona-Goona Lagoon."

1601 • GOLDEN BOY

OPENED: 10/20/1964   Theatre: Majestic
Musical   Broadway: 569

Composer: Charles Strouse
Lyricist: Lee Adams
Librettist: William Gibson; Clifford Odets
Producer: Hillard Elkins
Director: Arthur Penn

Source: GOLDEN BOY (Play: Clifford Odets); **Choreographer:** Donald McKayle; **Costumes:** Tony Walton; **Lighting Designer:** Tharon Musser; **Musical Director:** Elliot Lawrence; **Orchestrations:** Ralph Burns; **Set Design:** Tony Walton

Songs: Can't You See It? [4]; Colorful; Don't Forget 127th Street; Everything Is Lovely in the Morning [5] (L: Charles Strouse); Everything's Great; Fight, The; Finale; Gimme Some (Beer and Whiskey); Golden Boy; Hey, Joe [6]; Honey [2]; I Want to Be with You; Lorna's Here; Manly Art, The [2]; Night Song; No More; Playground Songs [2]; Poppa [2]; Road Tour, The; Stick Around; There Comes a Time [2]; There's a Party Going On [1]; There's Music in That Boy [2]; This Is the Life; Underneath the Marquee [2]; What Became of Me? [7]; While the City Sleeps; Winners [5]; Workout; Yes I Can [3]; You're No Brother, No Brother of Mine [1]

Cast: Johnny Brown; Billy Daniels; Sammy Davis Jr.; Jeannette DuBois; Louis Gossett; Jaime Rogers; Kenneth Tobey; Paula Wayne

Notes: [1] Added to London production (6/4/68). [2] Cut prior to New York. [3] Added after opening. Written for London production. [4] Cut after opening. [5] Added to 1984 revival. [6] Written for 1984 revival but not used. [7] Written for London production. Music used for title song of DANCE A LITTLE CLOSER. [8] Cut prior to New York then added to London production (6/4/68).

1602 • GOLDEN BUTTERFLY, THE
OPENED: 10/12/1908   Theatre: Broadway
Musical   Broadway: 48

Composer: Reginald De Koven
Lyricist: J. Hayden-Clarendon
Librettist: Harry B. Smith
Director: A.M. Holbrook

Musical Director: Anton Heindl

Songs: Away to Moscow; Belle of the Ring, The [1]; Bottle Imp, The; Butterfly and the Clover; Don't Forget Me; Elf King, The; Goblin's Bride, The; Golden Butterfly, The; Great Musicians; Haunted Cask, The; Heart of Mine; In Paris; Man About Town, The; Mem'ry's Garden; Military Review; Off to Russia; On the Boulevard; Opening Ensemble; Originality; Queen of the Ring, The; Recognized Man of the Hour; Singing Lessons; Stolen Opera, The; Tell Me Once Again; Vintage, The; Wandering Minstrel's Song

Cast: Gladys Coleman; Louis B. Harrison; Walter Percival; Charles Purcell; Grace Van Studdiford

Notes: [1] Sheet music only.

1603 • GOLDEN DAWN
OPENED: 11/30/1927   Theatre: Hammerstein
Musical   Broadway: 184

Composer: Emmerich Kalman; Herbert Stothart
Lyricist: Oscar Hammerstein II; Otto Harbach
Librettist: Oscar Hammerstein II; Otto Harbach
Producer: Arthur Hammerstein
Director: Reginald Hammerstein

Choreographer: David Bennett; **Costumes:** Mark Mooring; **Musical Director:** Herbert Stothart; **Set Design:** Joseph Urban

Songs: Africa; Consolation; Dawn (C: Robert Stolz; Herbert Stothart); Here in the Dark; It's Always the Way [1]; Jungle Shadows; Mulunghu Thabu; My Bwana; We Two; When I Crack My Whip

Cast: Jacques Cartier; Robert Chisholm; Hazel Drury; Kurnar Ghoshal; Paul Gregory; Louise Hunter; Archie Leach [2]; Gil Squires; Marguerita Sylva; Nydia d'Arnell

Notes: Musical numbers originally not listed as separate songs. [1] Sheet music only. [2] Cary Grant.

1604 • GOLDEN FLEECE, THE
OPENED: 11/18/1953
Musical

Composer: Allison Fleitas
Lyricist: Allison Fleitas
Librettist: Franklin C. Tramutola
Producer: Samuel S. Stroud
Director: Chester R. Cooper; Buddy Rogers

Choreographer: Walter F. Keenan; **Costumes:** Jenia Miller; **Incidental Music:** Al Boss; **Musical Director:** Frank Juele; **Orchestrations:** Al Boss; **Set Design:** Robert Patterson; **Vocal Arranger:** Al Boss; Clay Warnick

Songs: Butler Is a Butler, A; California; Fireman's Ball (C/L: Henning Ludlow); Free As a Breeze; Little Bit of Love Won't Hurt You; Minstrel Show (C: John C. Hackney; L: Daniel G. Foley Jr.); Money Runs Through My Fingers; San Francisco Waltz; Shooting Gallery; They Finished Me in the East (C/L: Daniel G. Foley Jr.); Welcome Home; What Do We Do About This (C/L: Henning Ludlow)

Cast: T. Gillespie; R. Green; N. Peters

Notes: Amateur show. Mask & Wig Club, University of Pennsylvania.

1605 • GOLDEN GATE
OPENED: 1964
Musical   Unproduced

Composer: John Kander
Lyricist: Fred Ebb
Librettist: Richard Morris

Songs: Anywhere You Are; Certain Girl, A [1]; Dear Lord; Emperor, The; Everybody's Favorite City; Golden Gate; Happy New Year; I'll Bet Two Dollars; I've Always Loved You; One of the Smart Ones; Royal Rounds, The; Simple Thing Like That, A; Start All Over Again; There Is Nothing Wrong with My Life; Yesterday Is Yesterday

Notes: This show was written as a demo for George Abbott to prove that Kander and Ebb were up to the task of writing FLORA, THE RED MENACE. They were. Sometimes titled THE EMPEROR OF SAN FRANCISCO. [1] Used in THE HAPPY TIME.

1606 • GOLDEN GIRL, THE

OPENED: 03/16/1909   Theatre: La Salle
Musical   Chicago

Composer: Joseph E. Howard
Lyricist: Frank R. Adams; Joseph E. Howard
Librettist: Frank R. Adams; Will M. Hough
Director: Ned Wayburn

Musical Director: Hugo Marks

Songs: Don't Forget the Girl You Left Behind [1]; Everybody Wonders Why They Married; Golden Girl, The; I Can't Love Everybody; I Hear a Woodpecker Knocking at My Family Tree; I Would Rather Fight Like Ma; I'll Sing of a Lady [2]; I'm Afraid to Be Alone; Indian Love Song; Land of Used-to-Be, The; My Ship of Dreams [2]; Sword for Mine, The [2]

Cast: Sydney Craven; Franklyn Farnum; Marie Flynn; Joseph Niemeyer; Harry Nilsen; Grace Sparks

Notes: [1] There is a sheet of a song titled "The Girl I Left Behind." Same song? [2] From 9/19/09 program.

1607 • GOLDEN GOOSE, THE

OPENED: 11/29/1917
Musical   Closed out of town

Composer: Silvio Hein

Lyricist: Schuyler Green; Herbert Reynolds
Librettist: Edgar Smith

Notes: Atlantic City.

1608 • GOLDEN HORSESHOE, THE

OPENED: 09/15/1898   Theatre: Irving Place
Musical   Broadway: 32

Composer: Carl Pleininger
Librettist: Robert Breitenbach
Producer: Carl Rosenfeld; Theodore Rosenfeld
Director: Carl Rosenfeld

Cast: Franz Ebert; Helen Linder; Max Walter

Notes: No songs listed in program.

1609 • GOLDEN LAND, THE

OPENED: 11/11/1985   Theatre: Second Avenue
Revue   Off-Broadway: 277

Producer: Sherwin M. Goldman; Moishe Rosenfeld; Westport Productions
Director: Jacques Levy

Choreographer: Donald Saddler; **Costumes:** Natasha Landau; **Dance Arranger:** Zalmen Mlotek; **Lighting Designer:** John McLain; **Musical Director:** Zalmen Mlotek; **Orchestrations:** Peter Sokolow; **Set Design:** Lindsey Decker; **Vocal Arranger:** Zalmen Mlotek

Songs: Am Yisroel Khay! (The Jewish People Live) (C: S. Beresovsky; Schlomo Carlbach; L: M. Knapheis; Jacques Levy; Zalmen Mlotek; Moishe Rosenfeld); Amerike, Hurrah for Onkl Sem (America, What a Name!) (C: Arnold Perlmutter; Herman Wohl); Ballad of the Triangle Fire (C/L: Ruth Rubin); Belz, Mayn Shtetle Belz (C: Alexander Olshanetsky; L: Jacob Jacobs); Bread and Roses (C: Caroline Kohlsaat; L: James Oppenheim); Briderlekh Tayere (Dear Brothers, Help) (C/L: Abe Schwartz); Brivele Der Mamen (A Letter to Mother), A (C/L: Solomon Shmulewitz); Brother, Can You Spare a Dime? (C: Jay Gorney; L: E.Y. Harburg); Dem Peddlers Brivele (The Peddler's Letter) (C: Ziske Feigenbaum; Jacob Leiserowitz; L: Yankl Brisker); Di Fon Fun Frayhayt (The Flag of Freedom) (C: Arnold Perlmutter; L: Louis Gilrod; Herman Wohl); Ellis Island (Ellis Island,

So Awesome and Cold!) (C/L: Solomon Shmulewitz; L: Jacques Levy); Fifty, Fifty (C: Joseph Rumshinsky; L: Bruce Adler; Louis Gilrod; Jacques Levy; Zalmen Mlotek; Moishe Rosenfeld); Fonye Ganev (Ivan the Czar, The Rogue) (C/L: Traditional); Fraytik Oyf Der Nakht (Friday Night) (C: Unknown; L: Jacques Levy; Moishe Rosenfeld); Fun Downtown-Uptown (From Downtown, We Move Uptown) (C: Joseph Rumshinsky; L: Jacques Levy; Chane Mlotek; Zalmen Mlotek; Moishe Rosenfeld; Boris Thomashefsky); Gebentsht Iz Amerike (C: Arnold Perlmutter; Herman Wohl; L: Jacques Levy; Zalmen Mlotek; Moishe Rosenfeld); Give Me Your Tired, Your Poor (The New Colossus) (C: Max Helfman; L: Emma Zazarus); Got Un Zayn Mishpet Iz Gerekht (God and His Judgment Are Right) (C: D. Meyerovitch; L: Louis Gilrod); Ikh Bin a Border Bay Mayn Vayb (I Am a Border at My Wife's House) (C/L: Rubin Doctor; L: Bruce Adler); Ikh Breng Aykh a Grus Fun Di Trenches (I Bring You Greetings from the Trenches) (C/L: Isodore Lillian); It Shouldn't Happen to a Dog (C/L: Menasha Skulnick; L: Jacques Levy); Joe and Paul's (C/L: Sholom Secunda); Khulem, A (C: Traditional; L: Jacques Levy); Lebn Zol Kolumbus (Long Live Columbus!) (C: Arnold Perlmutter; Herman Wohl; L: Louis Gilrod; Jacques Levy); Lekho Dodi, Ko Riboyn Olam, Sholem Aleykhem, Gut Vokh (C/L: Traditional); Lozt Arayan (Let Us In) (C/L: Unknown); Mamenyu, Elegy of the Triangle Fire Victims (C: Joseph Rumshinsky; L: Anschel Schorr); Mayn Yidishe Meydele (C: Sholom Secunda; L: Anschel Schorr); Mir Forn Kayn Amerike (We're Going to America, Goodbye Mother Russia) (C/L: Arnold Perlmutter; Herman Wohl); Motl Der Opereyter (Motl the Operator) (C/L: Chaim Tauber; L: Jacques Levy); Oy, I Like Him (Oy, I Like She) (C/L: Aaron Lebedeff; Alexander Olshanetsky; L: Jacques Levy); Papirosn (Buy Cigarettes) (C/L: Herman Yablokoff; L: Jacques Levy); Rebel Girl (C/L: Joe Hill); Rumania, Rumania (C/L: Aaron Lebedeff); Sabbath Queen (C: Minkovsky; L: C.N. Bialik); Shnel Loyfn Di Reder (The Wheels Turn Quickly) (C: Lazar Weiner; L: David Edelshtat); Show You Care (C: Traditional; L: Jacques Levy; Zalmen Mlotek; Moishe Rosenfeld); Troyerik Zayn Darf Men Nit (Why Be Sad . . . ?) (C: Arnold Perlmutter; Herman Wohl; L: Jacques Levy; Zalmen Mlotek; Moishe Rosenfeld); Vi Shver S'iz Tsu Sheydn (How Hard to Leave Old

Homes) (C: Arnold Perlmutter; Herman Wohl; L: Jacques Levy; Eleanor Reissa); Vu Nemt Men Parnose? (How Do I Make a Living?) (C/L: D. Meyerovitch; L: Jacques Levy); Watch Your Step (C: Unknown; L: Jacques Levy); We Go to Work (C/L: Traditional); When Rosie Lived on Essex Street (C/L: Addison Burkhardt); Yenki Doodl Fort Uptown (Yankee Doodle Rides Uptown) (C/L: Unknown); Yidl Mitn Fidl (Yiddle with His Fiddle) (C: Abraham Ellstein; Traditional; L: Jacques Levy; Itsik Manger)

Cast: Bruce Adler; Phyllis Berk; Joanne Borts; Avi Hoffman; Marc Krause; Neva Small

1610 • GOLDEN MOTH, THE
OPENED: 10/05/1921   Theatre: Adelphi
Musical   London: 281

Composer: Ivor Novello
Lyricist: P.G. Wodehouse
Librettist: Fred Thompson; P.G. Wodehouse
Producer: Austen Hurgon

Costumes: A. Dubens; Idare & Co.; Guyvers, Potterton, Pettit, Gemmel and Tocher; Adele de Paris; Musical Director: Ernest Longstaffe; R.C. McCleery; Set Design: Marc-Henri

Songs: Dartmoor Days; Dear Eyes that Shine; Fairy Prince; Finale Act I; Gathering Nuts in May; Give Me a Thought Now and Then; If I Lost You; Island of Never-Mind-Where, The; Lonely Soldier; My Girl; Romance Is Calling; We've Had a Busy Day

Cast: Thorpe Bates; W.H. Berry; Bobbie Comber; Herbert Fenwick; Marston Garsia; Mostyn Godfrey; Fred Maguire; Robert Michaelis; M. Noel

1611 • GOLDEN RAINBOW
OPENED: 02/04/1968   Theatre: Shubert
Musical   Broadway: 385

Composer: Walter Marks
Lyricist: Walter Marks
Librettist: Ernest Kinoy
Producer: Ira Bernstein; Joseph P. Harris
Director: Arthur Storch

Source: A HOLE IN THE HEAD (Play: Arnold Shulman); Choreographer: Tom Panko;

Costumes: Alvin Colt; **Dance Arranger:** Marvin Hamlisch; Luther Henderson; **Lighting Designer:** Robert Randolph; **Musical Director:** Elliot Lawrence; **Orchestrations:** Jack Andrews; Pat Williams; **Set Design:** Robert Randolph; **Vocal Arranger:** Elliot Lawrence

Songs: All in Fun; Desert Moon; Fall of Babylon, The; For Once in Your Life; Golden Rainbow; He Needs Me Now; How Could I Be So Wrong; It's You Again, Kid; I've Got to Be Me; Life's a Gamble [1]; Live It Up [1]; No Chance, No Dice, No Deal [1]; Suddenly You [1]; Taking Care of You; Taste; Time Is Now, The [1]; 24 Hours a Day; We Got Us

Cast: Eydie Gorme; Scott Jacoby; Steve Lawrence; Joseph Sirola

Notes: [1] Cut prior to opening.

1612 • GOLDEN SCREW, THE

OPENED: 01/27/1967   Theatre: Provincetown Playhouse
Musical   Off-Broadway: 40

Composer: Tom Sankey
Lyricist: Tom Sankey
Librettist: Tom Sankey
Director: Robert Siegler

Musical Director: David Lucas; **Set Design:** C. Murawski

Songs: Bad Girl [1]; Beautiful People; Bottom End of Bleecker Street; Can I Touch You; Hard Times-Good Times; I Can't Make It Anymore; I Can't Remember; I Heard My Mother Crying; Jesus Come Down; Little White Dog; New Evaline; That's Your Thing, Baby; Trip Tick Talking Blues [1]; 2000 Miles; You Won't Say No

Cast: Patrick Sullivan

Notes: [1] Not in program.

1613 • GOLDEN WIDOW, THE

OPENED: 1909
Musical   Closed out of town

Composer: Melville Gideon; Louis Hirsch
Lyricist: Edward Madden
Librettist: Joseph W. Herbert; Glen MacDonough

Producer: Lee Shubert; Sam S. Shubert
Director: J.C. Huffman

Choreographer: William J. Wilson; **Costumes:** Melville Ellis; **Musical Director:** Albert Krause

Songs: Bo Peep; Clocking in the Stocking; Coralee; Dance Coquette [2] (C: Melville Gideon; L: Edgar Leslie); Don't Put Out the Light; Have You Seen My Girl (C: Jerome Kern); Howdy! How D'Ye Do? (C: Jerome Kern; L: M.E. Rourke); I Got You; I Want You to See My Girl (C/L: Harry Castling; Fred Godfrey); Keep Your Foot on the Soft Pedal [3] (C: Harry Von Tilzer; L: Will Dillon); Loving Ways; Noisy Illinois; On and Off the Stage; Other Page Is Missing, The; Peek-a-boodle Man; Publicity; Rag Time Land (C: Melville Gideon; L: E. Ray Goetz); Round the World; Sheriffs; Taxi Cab; Tiddley Pom [1]; Under the Linden; Weenie and Widgee

Cast: Alfred Cahill; Alexander Clark; Louise Dresser; Connie Ediss; Jobyna Howland; Walter Lawrence

Notes: Closed after performances in Washington, Cincinnati and Cleveland. From program of 10/26/09 Washington, D.C. Originally titled THE GIRL FROM THE STATES. [1] There was an English song "Tiddley-Om-Pom" written by Leigh and Powell in 1907. Same song? [2] ASCAP/Library of Congress only. [3] Sheet music only.

1614 • GOLDILOCKS (1958)

OPENED: 10/11/1958   Theatre: Lunt-Fontanne
Musical   Broadway: 161

Composer: Leroy Anderson
Lyricist: Joan Ford; Jean Kerr; Walter Kerr
Librettist: Jean Kerr; Walter Kerr
Director: Walter Kerr

Choreographer: Agnes de Mille; **Costumes:** Castillo; **Dance Arranger:** Laurence Rosenthal; **Lighting Designer:** Feder; **Musical Director:** Lehman Engel; **Orchestrations:** Leroy Anderson; Philip J. Lang; **Set Design:** Peter Larkin

Songs: Are We Feeling Any Better; Bad Companions; Beast in You, The; Chance He'll Never Stray, A [1]; Come to Me [1]; Give the Little Lady a Great Big Hand; Guess Who [1];

Heart of Stone; Hello, My Love, Hello [1]; I Can't Be in Love; I Never Know When; If I Can't Take It with Me [1]; Lady in Waiting; Lazy Moon; Little Girls Should Be Seen [1]; No One'll Ever Love You; Pirate Dance (Huckleberry Island Ballet); Pussy Foot, The; Save a Kiss; Shall I Take My Heart and Go?; There Never Was a Woman; This Is My Last Spring [1]; Town House Maxixe Dance, The; Two Years in the Making; Who's Been Sitting in My Chair?

Cast: Don Ameche; Kelly Brown; Nathaniel Frey; Margaret Hamilton; Russell Nype; Pat Stanley; Elaine Stritch; Gene Varrone

Notes: [1] Cut prior to New York.

1615 • GOLDILOCKS (1969)

OPENED: 1969   Theatre: NBC
TV Musical

Composer: Richard M. Sherman; Robert B. Sherman
Lyricist: Richard M. Sherman; Robert B. Sherman

Musical Director: Doug Goodwin

Songs: Don't Settle for Less (Than the Best); Human Race, The; Take a Longer Look

Cast: Bing Crosby; Kathryn Crosby; Mary Frances Crosby; Paul Winchell

1616 • GONE WITH THE WIND

OPENED: 08/28/1973
Musical   Closed out of town

Composer: Harold Rome
Lyricist: Harold Rome
Librettist: Horton Foote
Producer: Harold Fielding
Director: Joe Layton

Source: GONE WITH THE WIND (Novel: Margaret Mitchell); **Choreographer:** Joe Layton; **Costumes:** Patton Campbell; **Dance Arranger:** Trude Rittman; **Lighting Designer:** H.R. Poindexter; **Musical Director:** Jay Blackton; **Orchestrations:** Keith Amos; **Set Design:** David Hays; **Vocal Arranger:** Trude Rittman

Songs: Ashley's Departure [2]; Atlanta Burning [3]; Bazaar Hymn [3]; Because There's You; Blissful Christmas [5]; Blueberry Eyes (Kokemomo No Hitomi) [3]; Bonnie Blue Flag [5]; Bonnie Gone (Boni No Shi) [3]; Brand New Friends [3]; Cakewalk [3]; Gambling Man [6]; Gone with the Wind [3]; Goodbye My Honey [6]; How Lucky [3]; How Often, How Often [3]; If Only [3]; It Doesn't Matter Now [3]; Johnny Is My Darling [3]; Little Wonders (Kawaii Odoroki) [2]; Lonely Stranger (Passing Through) (Sabishii Tabibito) [3]; Love You; Marrying for Fun [3]; Miss Fiddle-Dee-Dee [3]; My Soldier (Home Again) (Watashi No Heishi) [3]; Newlyweds' Song, The [6]; O'Hara [6]; Quadrille [3]; Scarlett (Skarettu) [4]; Sister, Brother; Soldier's Goodbye, A [2]; Southern Lady, A [3]; Strange and Wonderful (Fushigisa to Subarashisa de Ippai) [2]; Tara [1]; Time for Love, A (Imakoso Koi No Toki); Today's the Day (He Loves Me) [5]; Tomorrow Is Another Day [3]; Two of a Kind (Nitamono Doshi) [3]; Virginia Reel [3]; We Belong to You (Watashi Mo Kokoro Mo Anatano Monoyo) [3]; Wedding [2]; What Is Love [6] (L: William Shakespeare); Where Is My Soldier Boy? [3]; Which Way Is Home? (Ie Wa Doko) [2]; Why Did They Die? [3]

Cast: Theresa Merritt; Terence Monk; Udana Power; Pernell Roberts; Cheryl Robinson; Lesley Ann Warren

Notes: First produced in Japan (1/3/70) as SCARLETT. It then was produced in London (5/3/72) at the Drury Lane Theatre where it ran for 397 performances. This production opened in Los Angeles at the Dorothy Chandler Pavilion and then toured before closing. Songs in Japanese production can be identified by their Japanese transliteration following the English title or, if transliteration is unknown, by footnotes 5 and 6. Those songs without either Japanese transliteration or footnotes were never used in any production (I think). [1] Same music as "Scarlett." [2] In London production — not American. [3] In American production of GONE WITH THE WIND. [4] In American production of GONE WITH THE WIND. Same music as "Tara." [5] In American production and Japanese production but Japanese transliteration unknown. [6] In Japanese production only but Japanese transliteration unknown.

1617 • GOOD BOY

OPENED: 09/05/1928   Theatre: Hammerstein
Musical   Broadway: 253

Composer: Harry Ruby; Herbert Stothart
Lyricist: Bert Kalmar
Librettist: Oscar Hammerstein II; Otto Harbach;
Henry Myers
Producer: Arthur Hammerstein
Director: Reginald Hammerstein

Choreographer: Busby Berkeley; **Costumes:** Mark
Mooring; **Musical Director:** Herbert Stothart;
Set Design: John Wenger

Songs: Disappointed Suitors [1]; Don't Be Like
That [2]; Down in Arkansas; Good Boy; Good
Boy Wedding March; I Have My Moments;
I Wanna Be Loved by You; Let's Give a Cheer [2];
Manhattan Walk; Nina; Oh, What a Man [3];
Papa Got Hot [1]; Peacock Alley [1]; Some Sweet
Someone; Something to Call Our Own [1]; This
Little Doll [1]; Three Bears, The [3]; Twinkle
Little Stars [1]; Voice of the City; What Makes
You So Wonderful?; When I Hit Broadway [1];
You're the One [1] (C: Arthur Schwartz; L: Otto
Harbach)

Cast: Evelyn Bennett; Charles Butterworth; Eddie
Buzzell; Dan Healy; Sam Hearn; Helen Kane;
Borrah Minevitch; Barbara Newberry; Effie
Shannon

Notes: [1] Cut prior to opening. [2] Added after
opening. [3] Cut after opening.

1618 • GOOD COMPANIONS, THE (1931)

OPENED: 10/01/1931   Theatre: 44th Street
Play   Broadway: 68

Composer: Richard Addinsell
Lyricist: Frank Eyton; Harry Graham
Librettist: Edward Knoblock; J.B. Priestley
Producer: Lee Shubert; Julian Wylie

Source: GOOD COMPANIONS, THE (Novel:
J.B. Priestley); **Musical Director:** Harry Lee
Danziger; **Set Design:** Rollo Wayne

Songs: Going Home; Slipping Around the
Corner

Cast: George Carney; Vera Lennox; Hugh Sinclair;
Valerie Taylor

Notes: No songs listed in program.

1619 • GOOD COMPANIONS, THE (1974)

OPENED: 07/11/1974   Theatre: Her Majesty's
Musical   London: 252

Composer: Andre Previn
Lyricist: Johnny Mercer
Librettist: Ronald Harwood
Producer: Bernard Delfont; Richard M. Mills;
Richard Pilbrow
Director: Braham Murray

Choreographer: Jonathan Taylor; **Costumes:**
Malcolm Pride; **Lighting Designer:** John B. Read;
Musical Director: Denys Rawson;
Orchestrations: Angela Morley; Herbert W.
Spencer; **Set Design:** Malcolm Pride

Songs: All Mucked Up; And Points Beyond; Aye,
Lad; Camaraderie; Dance of Life; Darkest
Before the Dawn; Extravaganza [1]; Footloose [2];
Good Companions; Goodbye; Great North
Road [2]; I'll Tell the World; Little Lost Dream [1];
Little Travelling Music, A; On My Way [2];
Pleasure of Your Company; Pools, The; Slippin'
Around the Corner; Stage Door John; Stage
Struck; Susie for Everybody; Ta, Luv

Cast: Ray C. Davis; Judi Dench; Christopher Gable;
Jeannie Harris; Hope Jackman; John Mills;
Malcolm Rennie; Roy Sampson; Marti Webb

Notes: [1] Cut prior to opening. [2] Same music.

1620 • GOOD DOCTOR, THE

OPENED: 11/27/1973   Theatre: Eugene O'Neill
Play   Broadway: 208

Composer: Peter Link
Lyricist: Neil Simon
Author: Neil Simon
Producer: Emanuel Azenberg; Eugene V. Wolsk
Director: A.J. Antoon

Source: UNKNOWN (Story: Anton Chekhov);
Costumes: Tony Walton; **Lighting Designer:**
Tharon Musser; **Set Design:** Tony Walton

Songs: Kind Gentle Looking Person, A

Cast: Barnard Hughes; Marsha Mason;
Christopher Plummer; Frances Sternhagen

Notes: No songs listed in program.

1621 • GOOD EVENING

OPENED: 11/14/1973   Theatre: Plymouth
Revue   Broadway: 438

Composer: Dudley Moore
Lyricist: Peter Cook; Dudley Moore
Librettist: Peter Cook; Dudley Moore
Producer: Alexander H. Cohen; Bernard Delfont
Director: Jerry Adler

Set Design: Robert Randolph

Songs: Chanson; Die Flabbergast; Kwai Sonata, The; Madrigal

Cast: Peter Cook; Dudley Moore

1622 • GOOD GOOD FRIENDS

Musical   Unproduced

Composer: Murray Grand
Lyricist: Murray Grand
Librettist: Patrick Dennis

Costumes: Arnold Scaasi

Notes: No other information available.

1623 • GOOD GRACIOUS ANNABELLE

OPENED:10/31/1916   Theatre: Republic
Play   Broadway: 111

Author: Clare Kummer
Producer: Anthony Hopkins
Director: Anthony Hopkins

Set Design: Robert Edmond Jones

Songs: Other Eyes (C/L: Clare Kummer)

Cast: Lola Fisher; Walter Hampden; Helen Lee; Edwin Nicander; Roland Young

1624 • GOOD LUCK, SAM!

OPENED: 12/09/1918   Theatre: Lexington
Musical   New York

Composer: Louis G. Merrill
Lyricist: Edward Anthony
Librettist: Edward Anthony

Producer: Boys of Camp Merritt, The
Director: Frank Lea Short

Choreographer: Michael Ring; **Costumes:** Robert Edmond Jones; **Orchestrations:** Gene Rawtenburg; **Set Design:** Robert Edmond Jones

Songs: Duet; Fourflushers; Fred's Farewell; Good Luck Sam!; Into the Kitchen Boys; It's Nice to Get Money from Home; It's the Same Old Chow; Knitting Chorus; Love's Sextette, A; O Need I Speak; Opening Chorus; Prisoner, Prisoner, Run Along; Prisoners Chorus; Song of the Pictures; There Once Was a War [1]; There's a Trace of the War in Everyone's Home; Watermelon and a Pair O' Dice

Cast: Joseph LeGrange Abbott; N.D. Cohen; Lorenz Gilbert; Christopher Hayes; Leo Herrup

Notes: "A Picture of Soldier Life in a Musical Comedy Farce." "Big Brothered By George M. Cohan." [1] Sheet music only.

1625 • GOOD MORNING, DEARIE

OPENED: 11/01/1921   Theatre: Globe
Musical   Broadway: 347

Composer: Jerome Kern
Lyricist: Anne Caldwell
Librettist: Anne Caldwell
Producer: Charles Dillingham
Director: Edward Royce

Costumes: Herman Patrick Teppe; **Musical Director:** Victor Baravalle; **Orchestrations:** Stephen Jones; **Set Design:** Frank Gates, E.A. Morange

Songs: Blue Danube Blues; Coolie Dance (inst.); Dance du Fragonard; Dance Eccentrique (inst.); Didn't You Believe?; Easy Pickin's; Entrance of the Sailors (When the Guns Are Booming); Every Girl; Finale Act I; Finaletto Scene One; Good Morning Dearie; Green River Glide [1]; Ka-Lu-A [2]; Le Sport American; 'Melican Papa (Chink Song); My Lady's Dress [1]; Niagara Falls; Opening of Dance Hall Scene (Ring Those Bells) [3]; Pas de Deux; Rose Marie; Rose Ruby [1]; Sing-Song Girl; Teddy Toddle, The; Toddle Quartette; Way Down Town

Cast: Harland Dixon; Louise Groody; Ada Lewis; Leo Reisman's Orchestra; Oscar Shaw

Notes: [1] Cut in Atlantic City prior to opening. [2] Also in THE CABARET GIRL. [3] Not in programs.

1626 • GOOD MORNING, JUDGE

OPENED: 02/06/1919   Theatre: Shubert
Musical   Broadway: 140

Composer: Lionel Monckton; Howard Talbot
Lyricist: Percy Greenbank; Adrian Ross
Librettist: Frederick Thompson
Producer: Messrs. Shubert
Director: Wybert Stamford

Choreographer: Jack Mason; **Costumes:** S. Zalud; **Musical Director:** Frank Paret; **Set Design:** Dodge & Castle

Songs: Dinky Doodle Dicky (C: Howard Talbot; L: Percy Greenbank); Game that Ends with a Kiss, A; Here Comes the Bride (C: George W. Meyer; L: E. Ray Goetz); I Am the Boy (and I Am the Girl) (C: Louis Silvers; L: B.G. DeSylva); I Want to Go Bye-Bye; I Was So Young (and You Were So Beautiful) (C: George Gershwin; L: Alfred Bryan; Irving Caesar); I'm Not Jealous [2] (C: Fred Mayo; Ed G. Nelson; L: Harry Pease); I've Got a Pair of Swinging Doors that Lead Right Into My Heart (C: Bert Grant; L: Sam M. Lewis; Joe Young); Little Miss Melody [2] (C: Lionel Monckton; L: Percy Greenbank); Love Came First when I Saw You [2] (C/L: Harold Vicars); Make Hay Little Girl (C: Lionel Monckton; L: Percy Greenbank); Midnight Cabaret; Oh That We Two Were Maying; One Night, One Waltz, One Girl [1]; Opening Chorus; Pansy Day; Some Quiet Afternoon [3] (C: Egbert Van Alstyne; L: Gus Kahn); Sporty Boys; Take Me (Back Again) [2] (C/L: Edward F. Breier; Edward A. Weinstein); That Has Nothing to Do with You; There's More to the Kiss than the X X X (C: George Gershwin; L: Irving Caesar); Young Folks and Old Folks

Cast: George Hassell; Charles King; Mollie King; Nellie King; Edward Martindel; Jack Paulton

Notes: [1] Cut Pittsburgh 11/10/19. [2] Sheet music only. [3] Sheet music only. Sometimes listed as "Some Sweet Morning."

1627 • GOOD MR. BEST, THE

OPENED: 08/30/1897   Theatre: Garrick
Musical   Broadway: 16

Composer: Frederick Dana; Tom Le Mack; Henry J. Sayers
Librettist: John J. McNally
Producer: William Harris; Charles T. Rich
Director: R.A. Roberts

Set Design: Joseph Physioc; John A. Thompson

Songs: Beautiful, Gay Paree; Dancing Turk, The; Flowers of the Harem; If I Could Only Get a Decent Sleep; Mammy's Little Pumpkin-Colored Coons (C/L: Hillman; Perrin); O'Dooley's First Five O'Clock Tea; Puff-Puff; Sadie; Swellest Thing in Town, The; Waltz of the Mazy; Zim Boom Ta-ra

Cast: Joseph Coyne; Sam Marion; R.A. Roberts; Josie Sadler; John Sparks; Julius P. Witmark; Annie Yeamans

1628 • GOOD NEWS

OPENED: 09/06/1927   Theatre: Chanin's 46th St.
Musical   Broadway: 551

Composer: Ray Henderson
Lyricist: Lew Brown; B.G. DeSylva
Librettist: B.G. DeSylva; Laurence Schwab
Producer: Frank Mandel; Laurence Schwab
Director: Frank MacGregor

Choreographer: Bobby Connolly; **Costumes:** Kiviette; **Musical Director:** Alfred Goodman; **Set Design:** Donald Oenslager

Songs: After Commencement (inst.) [1] (C/L: Ralph Blane; Hugh Martin); Baby! What?; Best Things in Life Are Free, The; Flaming Youth; Girl of the Pi Beta Phi, A; Good News; Happy Days; He's a Ladies Man; In the Meantime; Just Imagine; Knothole Scene; Lucky in Love; On the Campus; Tait Song; Today's the Day; Together [2]; Varsity Drag, The

Cast: Inez Courtney; Mary Lawlor; Zelma O'Neal; George Olsen and His Orchestra; John Sheehan; Gus Shy

Notes: [1] Written for 1974 revival. [2] ASCAP/Library of Congress only.

1629 • GOOD NIGHT, PAUL

OPENED: 09/03/1917   Theatre: Hudson
Musical   Broadway: 40

Composer: Harry B. Olsen
Lyricist: Charles Dickson; Roland Oliver
Librettist: Charles Dickson; Roland Oliver
Producer: Ralph Herz
Director: Benrimo

Songs: Constancy; Eenie-Weenie, Lovey Dovey
  (L: Roland Oliver); Flattery; Gowns; I Like You;
  I've Given My Heart to You Dear; Lovey Dovey;
  Mary Ann O'Shea (C: Arthur E. Aerseth;
  L: George C. Mack); Nothing Seems Right, Oh!
  The World Is All Wrong; On Monday Wear a
  Blue One [1]; Poor Mary Ann O'Shea [1]; Purity;
  Sailin' Away on the Henry Clay (C: Egbert Van
  Alstyne; L: Gus Kahn); Serenade; Sleep My
  Darling [1]; You Have a Straight and Shapely
  Back [1]

Cast: Burrell Bardaretto; Ralph Herz; Frank Lalor;
  Audrey Maple; Elizabeth Murray

Notes: [1] Sheet music only.

1630 • GOOD SPORTS

OPENED: 11/05/1992
Musical

Composer: Carol Hall
Lyricist: Carol Hall
Librettist: Susan Rice
Producer: Goodspeed Opera House
Director: J. Randall Hugill

Choreographer: J. Randall Hugill; **Costumes:**
  Charlotte M. Vetman; **Dance Arranger:**
  Andrew Lippa; **Lighting Designer:** Mary Jo
  Dondlinger; **Orchestrations:** Brad Flickinger;
  Andrew Lippa; Michael O'Flaherty; **Set
  Design:** James Morgan

Songs: Don't Even Start; Educated Feet; Good
  Sports; If She Walked Home with Me; Old-
  Fashioned Lover; One Little Taste of Glory;
  Pals; Slow Dance; So Much Better; Too Bad;
  Twilight Double Header; Woman I Am, The;
  Workout; You Could Learn to Love Me, Rosie;
  Younger Men

Cast: Gregory Butler; William Parry; Karyn
  Quackenbush; Ray Xifo

Notes: Goodspeed at Chester.

1631 • GOOD TIMES

OPENED: 08/09/1920   Theatre: Hippodrome
Musical   Broadway: 455

Composer: Raymond Hubbell
Lyricist: R.H. Burnside
Librettist: R.H. Burnside
Producer: Charles B. Dillingham
Director: R.H. Burnside

Costumes: Will R. Barnes; **Set Design:** H. Robert
  Law; Mark Lawson

Songs: Cling! Cling!; Colorland; Down in the
  Valley of Dreams; Hands Up; Hello
  Imagination; Land I Love, The; Shadowland
  Ballet (inst.) [1] (C: Max Steiner); Wedding of the
  Dancing Doll, The; You Can't Beat the Luck of
  the Irish; You're Just Like a Rose

Cast: Abdallah's Arabs; Nanette Flack; Hanneford
  Family; Joe Jackson; Joseph Parsons; Belle Story

Notes: [1] Scored by Max Steiner.

1632 • GOOD-BYE BILL

OPENED: 04/22/1918   Theatre: 44th Street Roof
Musical   Broadway

Composer: William B. Kernell
Lyricist: Richard B. Fechheimer
Librettist: Richard B. Fechheimer
Producer: U.S. Ambulance Service
Director: Edwin R. Wolfe

Choreographer: Calvin King; **Musical Director:**
  Edward Mellon; **Vocal Arranger:** Edward
  Mellon

Songs: Boys, Be Proud that You're a USAAC;
  Bring Me a Blonde; Buy a Bond; Good-Bye Bill;
  I Didn't Hesitate 'Cause I Knew that I Was Lost [1];
  I'm the Guy; Jazz Band Am the Firstest Aid for
  Me, A [1] (C: Louis Duggan); Je Ne Parle Pas
  Anglais [1] (C: Louis Duggan); Just a Little After
  Taps; Ladies of London and Paris, The [1]; Old
  Camp Chef, The [1]; Patsy Bolivar; Till I Come
  Home to You [1]; We're Recrootin'; Whitewings
  Marimba, The

Cast: Milton E. Claypoole; Robert Covington;
  Richard B. Fechheimer; Charles Hamp; George
  W. Kowalski

Notes: A service musical. [1] Not in program.

1633 • GOODBYE GIRL, THE

OPENED: 03/04/1993   Theatre: Marquis
Musical   Broadway: 188

Composer: Marvin Hamlisch
Lyricist: David Zippel
Librettist: Neil Simon
Producer: Emanuel Azenberg; Richard Kagan; Stewart F. Lane; Gladys Nederlander; James M. Nederlander; Office Two-One Inc.
Director: Michael Kidd

Source: GOODBYE GIRL, THE (Film: Neil Simon); **Choreographer:** Graciela Daniele; **Costumes:** Santo Loquasto; **Dance Arranger:** Mark Hummel; **Lighting Designer:** Tharon Musser; **Musical Director:** Jack Everly; **Orchestrations:** Billy Byers; Torrie Zito; **Set Design:** Santo Loquasto

Songs: Beat Behind, A; Elliot Garfield Grant; Footsteps; Good News, Bad News; How Can I Win?; I Can Play This Part; I'm Outta Here [1]; Jump for Joy; My Rules; No More; Paula (An Improvised Love Song); Richard Interred; This Is As Good As It Gets; Too Good to Be Bad (2 Good 2 B Bad); 2 Good 2 B Bad; What a Guy; Who Would've Thought?

Cast: Susann Fletcher; Tammy Minoff; Bernadette Peters; Martin Short; Scott Wise; Carol Woods

Notes: [1] Out Chicago 12/29/92.

1634 • GOODTIME CHARLEY

OPENED: 03/03/1975   Theatre: Palace
Musical   Broadway: 104

Composer: Larry Grossman
Lyricist: Hal Hackady
Librettist: Sidney Michaels
Producer: Max Brown; Byron Goldman
Director: Peter Hunt

Choreographer: Onna White; **Costumes:** Willa Kim; **Dance Arranger:** Daniel Troob; **Incidental Music:** Arthur B. Rubinstein; **Lighting Designer:** Feder; **Musical Director:** Lawrence J. Blank; Arthur B. Rubinstein; **Orchestrations:** Jonathan Tunick; **Set Design:** Rouben Ter-Arutunian

Songs: All She Can Do Is Say No [1]; Bits and Pieces; Born Lover; Castles of the Loire, The (ballet) [2] (C: Arthur B. Rubenstein); Confessional; Coronation; Goodtime Charley; History; I Am Going to Love the Man You're Going to Be; I Leave the World; Merci, Bon Dieu; One Little Year; To Make the Boy a Man; Tomorrow's Good Old Days [1]; Visions and Voices; Why Can't We All Be Nice; You Still Have a Long Way to Go

Cast: Kenneth Bridges; Susan Browning; Jay Garner; Joel Grey; Grace Keagy; Ann Reinking; Charles Rule; Richard B. Shull; Louis Zorich

Notes: Peter Stone doctored the script. [1] Cut prior to opening. [2] Music based on songs from the score.

1635 • GOREY STORIES

OPENED: 10/30/1978   Theatre: Booth
Revue   Broadway: 1

Composer: David Aldrich
Lyricist: Edward Gorey
Author: Edward Gorey
Producer: Terry Allen Kramer; Hale Matthews; Harry Rigby; John Wulp
Director: Tony Tanner

Costumes: David Murin; **Lighting Designer:** Roger Morgan; **Musical Director:** Martin Silvestri; **Set Design:** Edward Gorey

Cast: Tobias Haller; Julie Kurnitz; Susan Marchand; Dennis McGovern; Leon Shaw; Gemze de Lappe

Notes: This play was originally produced at the WPA Theatre on December 1, 1977 where it played for seven performances. Stephen Currens adapted the lyrics and stories of Edward Gorey.

1636 • GOSPEL AT COLONUS, THE

OPENED: 03/24/1988   Theatre: Lunt-Fontanne
Musical   Broadway: 61

Composer: Bob Telson
Lyricist: Lee Breuer
Librettist: Lee Breuer
Producer: Dodger Productions; Fifth Avenue

Productions; Louis Busch Hager; Liza Lorwin; Playhouse Square Center
Director: Lee Breuer

Source: ANTIGONE (Play: Dudley Fitts; Robert Fitzgerald; Sophocles); **Source:** OEDIPUS AT COLONUS (Play: Robert Fitzgerald; Sophocles); **Source:** OEDIPUS REX (Play: Dudley Fitts; Robert Fitzgerald; Sophocles); **Costumes:** Ghrett Hynd; **Lighting Designer:** Julie Archer; **Set Design:** Alison Yerxa

Songs: Ah! Heaven's Height Has Cracked!; All My Heart's Desire; Eternal Sleep; Evil; Fair Colonus; How Shall I See You Through My Tears?; Lift Him Up; Lift Me Up; Live Where You Can; No Never; Now Let the Weeping Cease; Numberless Are the World's Wonders; Oh Sunlight of No Light; Stop, Do Not Go On; Voice Foretold, A; Who Is This Man?; You Break My Heart

Cast: Sam Butler Jr.; Kevin Davis; J.J. Farley; Five Blind Boys of Alabama; Clarence Fountain; Morgan Freeman; Institutional Radio Choir; J.D. Steele Singers, The; Martin Jaycox; Carolyn Johnson-White; Robert Earl Jones; Rev. Earl F. Miller; Isabell Monk; Soul Stirrers, The; Jevetta Steele

Notes: This show premiered at the Brooklyn Academy of Music on November 8, 1983 and ran for 28 performances.

1637 • GOT TU GO DISCO
OPENED: 06/25/1979   Theatre: Minskoff
Musical   Broadway: 8

Composer: Nat Adderley Jr.; Steve Boston; Ray Chew; John Davis; Thomas Jones; Kenny Lehman; Wayne Morrison; Eugene Narmore; Jerry Powell; Betty Rowland
Lyricist: Nat Adderley Jr.; Steve Boston; Ray Chew; John Davis; Thomas Jones; Kenny Lehman; Wayne Morrison; Eugene Narmore; Jerry Powell; Betty Rowland
Librettist: John Zodrow
Producer: Jerry Brandt
Director: Larry Forde

Choreographer: Troy Garza; Jo Jo Smith; **Costumes:** Joe Eula, **Lighting Designer:** S.A. Cohen; **Musical Director:** Kenny Lehman; **Set Design:** James Hamilton; **Vocal Arranger:** Mitch Kerper; Kenny Lehman

Songs: All I Need; Bad Glad Good and Had; Cassie; Chic to Cheap; Dance Fever [1]; Disco Shuffle; Gettin' to the Top; Got Tu Go Disco; Hanging Over and Out; If That Didn't Do It It Can't Be Done; In and Out; Inter-mish-un; It Won't Work; Pleasure Pusher; Puttin' It On; Takin' the Light; Trust Me

Cast: Irene Cara; Jane Holzer; Patrick Jude; Patti Karr; Joe Masiell; Lisa Raggio; Justin Ross; Laurie Dawn Skinner

Notes: [1] Cut prior to opening.

1638 • GOTTA GETAWAY!
OPENED: 06/16/1984   Theatre: Radio City Music Hall
Revue   Broadway: 151

Librettist: James Lecesne
Producer: Patricia Morinelli; Radio City Music Hall Prods
Director: Larry Fuller

Choreographer: Larry Fuller; Conductor: Robert Billig; **Costumes:** Michael Casey; **Dance Arranger:** Michael Rice; **Lighting Designer:** Clarke W. Thornton; **Musical Director:** Gene Palumbo; **Orchestrations:** Bill Brohn; Michael Gibson; **Set Design:** Eduardo Sicangco, **Vocal Arranger:** Robert Billig; Gene Palumbo

Songs: Bubble, Bubble (C: Gene Palumbo; L: Chip Orton); Come to the Supermarket in Old Peking (C/L: Cole Porter); Folies Bergere (C/L: Maury Yeston); Gotta Getaway (C/L: Glen Roven); Hello Beautiful (C/L: Walter Donaldson); Here in Minipoora (C/L: Marc Elliot; Marc Shaiman); Higher and Higher (C/L: Gary Jackson; Raynard Miner; Carl Smith); Hot Voo-Doo (C: Sam Coslow; L: Ralph Rainger); I'm Throwing a Ball Tonight (C/L: Cole Porter); La Cumparcita (C: G.H. Matos Rodriguez); Le Dernier Pierrot (C: Pierre Porte; L: Pascal Sevran); Manhattan (C/L: Marc Elliot; Marc Shaiman); Once You've Seen a Rainbow (C: Gene Palumbo; L: Chip Orton); Peking (ballet) (C: Eric Watson); Stairway to Paradise (C: George Gershwin; L: Ira Gershwin); Take Good Care of that Lady (C/L: Marc Elliot; Marc Shaiman); This Heart of Mine (C: Harry Warren; L: Arthur Freed); Too Marvelous for Words (C/L: Richard A. Whiting); Use Your Imagination (C/L: Cole Porter)

Cast: Tony Azito; Loretta Devine; Joy Holiday; Ron Holiday; Liliane Montevecchi; Alyson Reed; Rockettes, The

Notes: Not all songs written for this show.

1639 • GOTTS SCHTROFF

OPENED: 1910
Musical   New York

Composer: J.M. Rumshisky
Lyricist: J.M. Rumshisky

Songs: Die Novim; Gutte Nacht

Cast: Jacob Adler

Notes: No other information available on this Yiddish language show.

1640 • GOVERNOR'S SON, THE

OPENED: 02/25/1901   Theatre: Savoy
Musical   Broadway: 32

Composer: George M. Cohan
Lyricist: George M. Cohan
Librettist: George M. Cohan
Producer: L.C. Behman
Director: Ned Wayburn

Costumes: Thomas McIlvane; **Lighting Designer:** Julian C. Lavin; **Musical Director:** Charles J. Gebest; **Set Design:** C. Walsh Valentine

Songs: And the Manager Said . . .?; Behold the Governor; Governor of the State, The; Governor's Son, The; I Love Everyone in the Wide Wide World [3]; I Want My Ragtime [3]; If Bill Gillette Could Only See Me Now [4]; Jolly Good Fellow; Lucy; Ma Honey Babe; Mysterious Maid, The [3]; Never Breathe a Word of This to Mother; Night Time [3]; Nothing New Beneath the Sun [3]; Oh! Mr. Moon; Push Me Along in My Pushcart [3]; Quakertown Cadets, The; Real Girls, The; Regular William Gillette, A (Regular Mr. Gillette); Rosie; Soldiers of the Stage, The [1]; Story of the Wedding March, The; Then I'd Be Satisfied [2]; Too Many Miles from Broadway; We Love to Live; Weeping Widow, The; Widow's Wile, A; Wine Divine

Cast: George M. Cohan; Helen Cohan; Jerry Cohan; Josie Cohan; Katherine Gordon; William Keough; Ethel Levey; Minnie Sinn; Will H. Sloan; Georgie White

Notes: [1] Cut prior to opening. [2] Out Cleveland 12/15/02. [3] Added to revival of 1903 (Aerial Gardens, June, 4). [4] Sheet music only.

1641 • GOVERNORS, THE

OPENED: 01/03/1898   Theatre: Hoyt's
Musical   Broadway: 16

Composer: Harry Vokes; Happy Ward
Librettist: Harry Vokes; Happy Ward
Producer: E.D. Stair

Cast: Anna Chance; Harry Vokes; Margaret Daly Vokes; Happy Ward

Notes: No program available.

1642 • GOWNS BY ROBERTA

Notes: *See ROBERTA.*

1643 • GRAB BAG, THE

OPENED: 10/06/1924   Theatre: Globe
Revue   Broadway: 184

Composer: Ed Wynn
Lyricist: Ed Wynn
Librettist: Ed Wynn
Producer: A.L. Erlanger; Ed Wynn
Director: Julian Mitchell

Costumes: Mabel Johnston; Charles LeMaire; Alice O'Neil; **Musical Director:** Max Steiner; **Set Design:** John Wenger

Songs: Annie Laurie Rag; Ballet of the North Wind; Chorus Girl's Song, A; Flame of Love [1]; Grab Bag, The; Heart of My Rose, The; I Want a Home [1]; Moth for My Flame, The; When I Was the Dandy and You Were the Belle (C: Dave Dreyer; Lou Handman; L: Herman Ruby); When the One You Love Loves You (C: Abel Baer; Paul Whiteman; L: Cliff Friend)

Cast: Janet Adair; Marion Fairbanks; Shaw and Lee; Jay Velie; Ed Wynn

Notes: [1] Sheet music only.

1644 • GRAB ME A GONDOLA

OPENED: 11/27/1956   Theatre: Lyric
Musical   London: 695

Composer: James Gilbert
Lyricist: James Gilbert; Julian More
Librettist: Julian More
Producer: Donald Albery; Neil Crawford
Director: John Counsel; Eleanor Fazan

Choreographer: Eleanor Fazan; **Costumes:** Scott Gray; Herbert Sidon; **Musical Director:** Stanley Myers; **Set Design:** Hal Henshaw; Stanley Moore

Songs: Bid Him a Fond Goodbye; Chianti; Cravin' for the Avon; Grab Me a Gondola; Jimmy's Bar; Lonely in a Crowd; Man Not a Mouse; Motor Car Is Treacherous, The; My Biography; New to Me; Plain in Love; Rig O' the Day, The (Mink); Rockin' at the Cannon Ball; Star Quality; What Are the Facts; When I Find That Girl; Worst Thing That Happened to Me, The

Cast: Joan Heal; Johnny Ladd; Dennis Quilley

Notes: Opened at the Lyric Hammersmith Theatre and then moved on 12/26/56 to the Lyric Theatre in London for an additional 673 performances.

1645 • GRADUATE, THE
OPENED: 1987
Musical   Unproduced

Composer: Bob Merrill
Lyricist: Bob Merrill
Librettist: Bob Merrill
Producer: Nederlander Organization; Gladys Rackmil

Source: GRADUATE, THE (Novel: Charles Webb)

Notes: No other information available.

1646 • GRAFTER, THE
OPENED: 1905
Musical   Closed out of town

Composer: W.C. Polla
Lyricist: James O'Dea
Librettist: Guy F. Steeley
Director: James Gorman

Songs: Artists and Models [1]; Coachmen and Maids; Guess Again; Hear the Hunter's Horn; I Could Use Five; In Dear Old Grandma's Day; Independence Day; Little Mary Wise; My

Bungalow Babe [1]; My Indian Summer Moon; My Picture of You [1]; They Sent for Me [1]

Cast: Charles Bates; Lucy Daly; William Friend; William Maxwell; Hap Ward

Notes: Program from Cedar Rapids. [1] These songs may be interpolated. They were listed apart from the rest of the score in programs. Yet it was clear they were part of the show.

1647 • GRAFTERS, THE
OPENED: 02/02/1908
Musical   Closed out of town

Composer: Leon Errol
Lyricist: Leon Errol
Librettist: Leon Errol

Musical Director: George Glass

Songs: Coaching Chorus; Cute Little Dance, A; Deutschland; French Flirt; I Like You; Marintch at Coney Island; Miss New York; Much Obliged to You; Old Glory; Parisian Dance; Some Day; When the Moon Plays Peekaboo with You

Cast: Stella Chatelaine; Leon Errol; Nat Franklin; Joseph P. Ward; Pauline Westerly

Notes: Leon Errol's credits unsure.

1648 • GRAHAM CRACKERS
OPENED: 01/23/1963   Theatre: Upstairs at the
                         Downstairs
Revue   Off-Broadway: 286

Composer: David Shire
Lyricist: Richard Maltby Jr.
Librettist: Woody Allen; Ronald Axe; David Axelrod; Dee Caruso; Bruce Hart; Herbert Hartig; William Levine; Eliza Ross; Peter Salamando
Producer: Ronny Graham
Director: Ronny Graham

Choreographer: Lee Theodore; **Dance Arranger:** David Shire; **Musical Director:** David Shire; **Vocal Arranger:** David Shire

Songs: Always Autumn; Come Join the Party; Crossword Puzzle; Doodlin' Song, A (C: Cy Coleman; L: Carolyn Leigh); Facts and Figures;

Gelber Meets the Wolfgang (C: Sam Pottle; L: David Axelrod); Love Song, A; Lovely Light (L: Richard Maltby Jr.; Edna St. Vincent Millay); Memorabilia (C/L: John Meyer); Saturday Night (C: Sam Pottle; L: David Axelrod); Sound of Muzak, The; Summer in New York (C/L: James Rusk); Time of the Cuckold, The (C/L: Ronny Graham); Treble (C/L: James Rusk)

Cast: Mona Abboud; Anita Darian; Ann Fraser; Bob Kaliban; Bill McCutcheon; McLean Stevenson; **Pianist:** David Shire; Richard de Benedictis

1649 • GRAND HOTEL

OPENED: 11/12/1989   Theatre: Martin Beck
Musical   Broadway: 1077

Composer: George Forrest; Robert Wright
Additional Music: Wally Harper
Lyricist: George Forrest; Robert Wright; Maury Yeston
Librettist: Luther Davis
Producer: Sam Crothers; Kenneth D. Greenblatt; Sander Jacobs; Mary Lea Johnson; Jujamcyn Theaters; Paramount Pictures; Martin Richards
Director: Tommy Tune

Source: GRAND HOTEL (Novel: Vicki Baum); **Choreographer:** Tommy Tune; **Costumes:** Santo Loquasto; **Lighting Designer:** Jules Fisher; **Musical Director:** Jack Lee; **Orchestrations:** Peter Matz; **Set Design:** Tony Walton

Songs: As It Should Be; At the Grand Hotel (C/L: Maury Yeston); Bonjour Amour (C/L: Maury Yeston); Boston Merger, The; Crooked Path, The; Everybody's Doing It (C/L: Maury Yeston); Fire and Ice; Grand Parade, The (C/L: Maury Yeston); Grand Waltz, The (L: George Forrest; Robert Wright); Happy (L: George Forrest; Robert Wright); How Can I Tell Her; I Waltz Alone [1]; I Want to Go to Hollywood (C/L: Maury Yeston); Love Can't Happen (C/L: Maury Yeston); Maybe My Baby Loves Me (L: George Forrest; Robert Wright); No Encore (L: George Forrest; Robert Wright); Roses at the Station (C/L: Maury Yeston); Some Have, Some Have Not; Table with a View [1]; Twenty-Two Years (C/L: Maury Yeston); Villa on a Hill (L: George Forrest; Robert Wright); We'll Take a Glass Together [1]; What She Needs [1]; Who Couldn't Dance with You (L: George Forrest; Robert Wright)

Cast: Karen Akers; David Carroll; David Jackson; Mitchell Jason; Ken Jennings; Timothy Jerome; Michael Jeter; Jane Krakowski; Liliane Montevecchi; Lynnette Perry; Danny Strayhorn; Walter Willison; John Wylie

Notes: *See also AT THE GRAND*, an earlier version of this show. [1] From AT THE GRAND.

1650 • GRAND MOGUL, THE

OPENED: 03/25/1907   Theatre: New Amsterdam
Musical   Broadway: 40

Composer: Gustav Luders
Lyricist: Frank Pixley
Librettist: Frank Pixley
Producer: Klaw & Erlanger
Director: Herbert Gresham

Source: LE GRAND MOGUL (Musical: E. Audran; Chivot; Duru)

Songs: Aloha (I Love You); Annexation; By and By [1]; Bye and Bye; Cheer Up; Cupid's Private Code; Dreams [2]; Entrance of Governor; Finale Act I; Finale Act II; Finale Act III; Gently Through the Palms; Good Old-Fashioned Way, The; Help Yourself; Honolulu; I'm the Only One of My Kind; Land which My Heart Calls Home, The; Lotus, The; Marching with the Circus Band [1]; Military Man, The; My Hula-Hula Girl; Nestle By My Side; (Love Is) Not for a Day; Not for a Day; Only a Clover Blossom [2]; Opening Chorus Act II; Up in a Balloon [2]; What Do You Mean?

Cast: Maude Lillian Beri; John Dunsmore; George Austin Moore; Frank Moulan; Elsa Ryan

Notes: [1] Out Kansas City 12/8/07. [2] Sheet music only.

1651 • GRAND STREET FOLLIES, THE (1923)

OPENED: 06/16/1923   Theatre: Neighborhood
                                            Playhouse
Revue   Off-Broadway

Lyricist: Albert Carroll
Director: Agnes Morgan

Costumes: Alice Beer; **Dance Arranger:** Albert Carroll

Songs: As Far As Thought Can Reach; Color Organ, The; Green Ring, The; In the Beginning; Making Light of Day; Mattress House, The; Personality (C/L: Albert Carroll); Royal Damn Fango, The; Tragedy of an Elderly Gentleman, The

Cast: Albert Carroll; Whitford Kane; Lily Lubell; Aline MacMahon; Junius Matthews; Agnes Morgan; Paula Trueman

Notes: "Book by everybody. Music by great composers arranged by Lily Hyland." No way of distinguishing songs from sketches.

1652 • GRAND STREET FOLLIES, THE (1924)

OPENED: 05/20/1924   Theatre: Neighborhood
                          Playhouse
Revue   Off-Broadway: 172

Composer: Lily Hyland
Lyricist: Agnes Morgan
Librettist: Agnes Morgan

Choreographer: Albert Carroll; **Costumes:** Aline Bernstein; **Set Design:** Aline Bernstein

Songs: English Favorite, An (L: Agnes MacDonald); Epilogue; Midnight Show Trio, A (C: Max Ewing; L: Albert Carroll); South Sea Islands According to Broadway, The (L: Dan Walker); Verdict Finale, The (C: Max Ewing; L: Albert Carroll)

Cast: Albert Carroll; Aline MacMahon; Dorothy Sands

Notes: No songs identified in program.

1653 • GRAND STREET FOLLIES, THE (1925)

OPENED: 06/18/1925   Theatre: Neighborhood
                          Playhouse
Revue   Off-Broadway: 166

Composer: Lily Hyland
Lyricist: Agnes Morgan
Librettist: Agnes Morgan
Director: Agnes Morgan

Choreographer: Albert Carroll; **Costumes:** Aline Bernstein; Russell Wright; **Incidental Music:**

Lily Hyland; **Lighting Designer:** Russell Wright; **Set Design:** Russell Wright

Songs: Broadway Mammy Blues; Elizabeth's Song (C/L: Dan Walker); Glory, Glory, Glory (I Want to Be Glorified) (L: Dan Walker); L'Irlandesa Rosa Dell' Abie [1] (L: Marc Loebell)

Cast: Albert Carroll; Aline MacMahon; Agnes Morgan

Notes: [1] Also in THE GRAND STREET FOLLIES (1929).

1654 • GRAND STREET FOLLIES, THE (1926)

OPENED: 06/15/1926   Theatre: Neighborhood
                          Playhouse
Revue   Off-Broadway: 55

Lyricist: Agnes Morgan
Librettist: Agnes Morgan
Director: Agnes Morgan

Costumes: Aline Bernstein; **Lighting Designer:** Albert Hawkes; **Musical Director:** Howard Barlow; **Orchestrations:** Randall Thompson; **Set Design:** Aline Bernstein

Songs: Aurory Bory Alice (C: Lily Hyland); Beatrice Lillie Ballad (C: Randall Thompson); Boosters' Song of the Far North, The (C: Randall Thompson); Discontented Bandits, The (C: Lily Hyland); Eskimo Blues (C: Walter Gustave Haenschen; L: Robert A. Simon); Fixed for Life (C: Randall Thompson); Ice Mazurka (C: Randall Thompson); If You Know What I Mean (C: Arthur Schwartz; L: Albert Carroll; Theodore Goodwin); Little Igloo for Two [1] (C: Arthur Schwartz); My Icy Floe (C: Randall Thompson); Polar Bear Strut, The (C: Arthur Schwartz; L: Theodore Goodwin); Reindeer Dance (C: Lily Hyland); Skating Ballet (C: Lily Hyland); Taxi Drivers' Lament (C: Randall Thompson); Uncle Tom's Cabin (C: Arthur Schwartz; Randall Thompson)

Cast: Vera Allen; Helen Arthur; Albert Carroll; Irene Lewisohn; Paula Trueman; Dan Walker

Notes: [1] Also in THE GRAND STREET FOLLIES (1929).

1655 • GRAND STREET FOLLIES, THE (1927)

OPENED: 05/19/1927   Theatre: Neighborhood
                                  Playhouse
Revue   Off-Broadway: 148

Composer: Max Ewing
Lyricist: Agnes Morgan
Librettist: Agnes Morgan
Director: Agnes Morgan

Costumes: Aline Bernstein; **Musical Director:**
   Howard Barlow; **Set Design:** Aline Bernstein

Songs: Banquet, The; Bedtime Story, A; Don't Ask
   Her Mother; I Long to Be Simple (C: Max
   Ewing); If You Haven't Got 'It'; I'll Agree If
   You'll Agree (C: Arthur Brander); I'm Not Blue,
   I'm Mauve (C: Max Ewing; L: Albert Carroll);
   La Prisonniere (L: Albert Carroll); Naughty
   Nineties, The; Say It with Toes (C: Edward
   Richett); Silver Apron Strings; Stars with Stripes
   (L: Marc Loebell; Dorothy Sands); Three Little
   Maids; Unaccustomed As I Am; Where the
   Wild Thyme Grows [1]

Cast: Aline Bernstein; Albert Carroll; Marc
   Loebell; Agnes Morgan; Dorothy Sands; Lois
   Shore

Notes: [1] Sheet music only. Title reads "Where
   the Wild Time Grows."

1656 • GRAND STREET FOLLIES, THE (1928)

OPENED: 05/28/1928   Theatre: Booth
Revue   Broadway: 144

Lyricist: Agnes Morgan
Librettist: Agnes Morgan
Producer: Actor-Managers, The
Director: Agnes Morgan

Choreographer: James Cagney; Michel Fokine;
   Costumes: Aline Bernstein; **Musical Director:**
   Fred Fleming; **Set Design:** Aline Bernstein

Songs: Briny Blues, The (C: Serge Walter);
   Command to Love (C: Serge Walter); From
   Tango to Taps [1] (C: Serge Walter); Hey, Nonny,
   Hey (C: Max Ewing); Husky, Dusky Annabelle
   (C: Max Ewing); It's Just a Little Love Song
   (C/L: Max Ewing); Marked Millions (C: Lily

Hyland); My Southern Belle [1] (C: Lily Hyland;
   L: Marc Loebell); Someone to Admire, Someone
   to Adore [1] (C: Serge Walter); Spiritual (C/L:
   Max Ewing); Tu Sais (C: Serge Walter)

Cast: Vera Allen; James Cagney; Albert Carroll;
   Harold Hecht; Dorothy Sands

Notes: Note James Cagney's inclusion in the cast.
   [1] Also in THE GRAND STREET FOLLIES
   (1929).

1657 • GRAND STREET FOLLIES, THE (1929)

OPENED: 05/01/1929   Theatre: Booth
Revue   Broadway: 85

Lyricist: Agnes Morgan
Librettist: Agnes Morgan
Producer: Actors-Managers Inc., The; Paul Moss
Director: Agnes Morgan

Choreographer: Dave Gould; **Costumes:** Aline
   Bernstein; **Musical Director:** Fred Fleming; **Set
   Design:** Aline Bernstein

Songs: ABC of Traffic Sketch, The (inst.) (C: Arthur
   Schwartz); Age of Innocence Sketch, The (inst.)
   (C: Arthur Schwartz); Amoeba's Lament, The
   (inst.) (C: Arthur Schwartz); Awarding the Prize
   Sketch (C: Lily Hyland); British Maidens
   (C: Max Ewing); Don't Do It (C: Arthur
   Schwartz); Double Standard, The (C: Arthur
   Schwartz); From Tango to Taps [3]; Garden of
   Eden Sketch (C: Will Irwin); Girl I Might Have
   Been, The (C/L: Max Ewing); His Honor, the
   Mayor (C: Max Ewing; L: Albert Carroll); I Love
   You but I Like You Even More (I Love You and I
   Like You) [4] (C: Arthur Schwartz; L: Max Lief;
   Nathaniel Lief); I Need You So (C: Arthur
   Schwartz; L: Howard Dietz; David Goldberg);
   I'll Never Forget (C: Max Ewing; L: Albert
   Carroll); I've Got You On My Mind (C/L: Max
   Ewing); Jolly Troubador Sketch, The (inst.)
   (C: Arthur Schwartz); L'Irlandesa Rosa Dell'
   Abie [1] (L: Marc Loebell); Little Igloo for Two
   [2] (L: Marc Loebell); My Dynamo (C: Arthur
   Schwartz); My Southern Belle [3] (C: Lily
   Hyland; L: Marc Loebell); Pilgrim Fathers, The
   (C: Serge Walter); Priam's Little Congai (C: Will
   Irwin); Rome Is Burning; Room with a Bath, A
   (C: Max Ewing); Someone to Admire, Someone
   to Adore [3] (C: Serge Walter); South of the Rio
   Grande (C: Lily Hyland); Stepping Stones, The

(C: Serge Walter); Textile Troops, The (C: Max Ewing); Town & Country Suite (C: Lily Hyland); Vineyards of Manhattan, The (inst.) (C: Arthur Schwartz); What Did Della Wear (When Georgie Came Across)? (C: Arthur Schwartz; L: Albert Carroll; Agnes Morgan)

Cast: Michael Barry; James Cagney; Albert Carroll; Ella Franbau; Katherine Gauthier; George Heller; Kathleen Kidd; Marc Loebell; Lily Lubell; Junius Matthews; Agnes Morgan; Paula Trueman; Robert White

Notes: [1] Also in THE GRAND STREET FOLLIES (1925). [2] Also in THE GRAND STREET FOLLIES (1926). [3] Also in THE GRAND STREET FOLLIES (1928). [4] Also in HERE COMES THE BRIDE.

1658 • GRAND TERRACE REVUE, THE (1937)

OPENED: 1937   Theatre: Grand Terrace
Revue   Nightclub

Producer: Ed Fox

Songs: Baby, What Else Can I Do (C: Gerald Marks; L: Walter Hirsch); Bear Down (C/L: J. Edgar Dowell; Lou Fox); Everyone's Wrong but Me (C: Saul Chaplin; L: Sammy Cahn); If You Should Ever Leave (C: Saul Chaplin; L: Sammy Cahn); It's the Things You Do with Your Feet; Me and Columbus; Muddy Shoes; Posin' (C: Saul Chaplin; L: Sammy Cahn); Timbuctoo (C: Gerald Marks; L: Walter Hirsch); Waltz in Blue

Notes: Nightclub Revue. Information from sheet music. Sometimes referred to as the NEW GRAND TERRACE REVUE.

1659 • GRAND TERRACE REVUE, THE (1938)

OPENED: 1938   Theatre: Grand Terrace
Revue   Nightclub

Composer: Saul Chaplin
Lyricist: Sammy Cahn

Songs: Don't Let the Rhythm Go to Your Head; (I've Been) Saving Myself for You; They Say I Oughta Dance; What Do You Hear from the Mob in Scotland

Notes: No other information available.

1660 • GRAND TOUR, THE

OPENED: 01/11/1979   Theatre: Palace
Musical   Broadway: 61

Composer: Jerry Herman
Lyricist: Jerry Herman
Librettist: Mark Bramble; Michael Stewart
Producer: James M. Nederlander; Jack Schlissel
Director: Gerald Freedman

Source: JACOBOWSKY AND THE COLONEL (Play: S.N. Behrman; Franz Werfel); **Choreographer:** Donald Saddler; **Costumes:** Theoni V. Aldredge; **Dance Arranger:** Peter Howard; **Lighting Designer:** Martin Aronstein; **Musical Director:** Wally Harper; **Orchestrations:** Philip J. Lang; **Set Design:** Ming Cho Lee; **Vocal Arranger:** Donald Pippin

Songs: For Poland; Having Someone There [1]; I Belong Here; I Think I Think; I Want to Live Each Night [1]; I'll Be Here Tomorrow; Marianne; Mazeltov; More and More/Less and Less; Mrs. S.L. Jacobowsky; One Extraordinary Thing; Song of Advice [2]; Two Possibilities [1]; We're Almost There; Wedding Conversation; What Am I with You [1]; You I Like

Cast: Chevi Colton; Joel Grey; Ron Holgate; Travis Hudson; Ken Kantor; Grace Keagy; Florence Lacey; Stan Page; Theresa Rakov; Gene Varrone; Stephen Vinovich

Notes: Tommy Tune came in out of town to help with direction and mainly choreography. He was responsible for the choreography of "You I Like" and some other changes. [1] Cut before opening. [2] Cut before opening. Same music as "Nelson" in A DAY IN HOLLYWOOD/A NIGHT IN THE UKRAINE.

1661 • GRAND VIZIER, THE

OPENED: 03/04/1895   Theatre: Harlem Opera House
Musical   Broadway: 8

Composer: Frederick Gagel
Librettist: Edgar Smith

Cast: Walter Allen; Florence Nilley; Carrie Perkins; Thomas Q. Seabrooke

Notes: No songs listed in program.

1662 • GRASS HARP, THE

OPENED: 11/02/1971   Theatre: Martin Beck
Musical   Broadway: 7

Composer: Claibe Richardson
Lyricist: Kenward Elmslie
Librettist: Kenward Elmslie
Producer: Richard Barr; Michael Harvey; Charles Woodward
Director: Ellis Rabb

Source: GRASS HARP, THE (Novel: Truman Capote); **Source:** GRASS HARP, THE (Play: Truman Capote); **Choreographer:** Rhoda Levine; **Costumes:** Nancy Potts; **Dance Arranger:** John Berkman; **Lighting Designer:** James Tilton; **Orchestrations:** Robert Russell Bennett; Jonathan Tunick; J. "Billy" Ver Planck; **Set Design:** James Tilton

Songs: Brazil [1]; Call Me Babylove; Chain of Love; Cool Cool Elbow [1]; Dropsy Cure Weather; Floozies (1); Floozies (2) [1]; Gentle Sufficiency of Abundance, A [1]; Hang a Little Moolah on the Washline; I Believe in Babylove; I Trust the Wrong People [1]; If There's Love Enough; I'll Always Be in Love; Indian Blues; Marry with Me; Miss Got Rocks [1]; One and Only Person in the World, The; One Thing in Particular [1]; Pick Yourself a Flower; Reach Out; Something for Nothing; Spit 'n Whittle [1]; Take a Little Sip; Talkin' in Tongues; Them As Has Gets [1]; Think Big Rich; This One Day; Walk Into Heaven; What Do I Do Now?; Where's My Sister [1]; Whooshin' Through My Flesh; Yellow Drum; Yoofry [1]

Cast: Carol Brice; Barbara Cook; Ruth Ford; Karen Morrow; Max Showalter; Russ Thacker

Notes: [1] Cut before opening.

1663 • GRASS WIDOW, THE

OPENED: 12/03/1917   Theatre: Liberty
Musical   Broadway: 48

Composer: Louis A. Hirsch
Lyricist: Channing Pollock; Rennold Wolf
Librettist: Channing Pollock; Rennold Wolf
Producer: Madison Corey
Director: George Marion

Source: LE PERIL JAUNE (Play: Bisson St. Albin)

Songs: All the Girls Have Got a Friend in Me; B & O, The; C.D.Q.; Dance with Me; Farewell (Letter Song); Grass Widow, The; Just You and Me; Ladies of Portugal [1]; Love! Love! Love! [1]; Somewhere There's Someone for Me; Song of Love, The (C: Louis Hirsch); Soup; What's the Use of Loving Only One Girl; When the Saxophone Is Playing; Whirlwind Whirl, The; You Can't Be a Husband Today

Cast: Natalie Ault; George Marion; Howard Marsh; Victor Morley

Notes: [1] Sheet music only.

1664 • GREASE

OPENED: 02/14/1972   Theatre: Broadhurst
Musical   Broadway: 3388

Composer: Warren Casey; Jim Jacobs
Lyricist: Warren Casey; Jim Jacobs
Librettist: Warren Casey; Jim Jacobs
Producer: Maxine Fox; Kenneth Waissman
Director: Tom Moore

Choreographer: Patricia Birch; **Costumes:** Carrie F. Robbins; **Dance Arranger:** Louis St. Louis; **Lighting Designer:** Karl Eigsti; **Musical Director:** Louis St. Louis; **Orchestrations:** Michael Leonard; **Set Design:** Douglas W. Schmidt; **Vocal Arranger:** Louis St. Louis

Songs: All Choked Up; All Clear [1]; Alma Mater; Alone at a Drive-In Movie; Beauty School Dropout; Born to Hand-Jive; Comin' at Ya [1]; Foster Beach [1]; Freddy, My Love; Grease [1]; Greased Lightnin'; In My Day [1]; Inquest of Love [1]; It's Rainin' on Prom Night; Kiss It [1]; Look at Me, I'm Sandra Dee (1); Look at Me, I'm Sandra Dee (2) [2]; Mooning; Rock 'n' Roll Party Party Queen; Shakin' at the High School Hop; Summer Nights; Tattoo Song [1]; There Are Worse Things I Could Do; Think of All the Starving Orphans [1]; Those Magic Changes (Rock Progression); We Go Together; Yee-Eeuucchh [1]

Cast: Adrienne Barbeau; Meg Bennett; Barry Bostwick; James Canning; Carole Demas; Tom Harris; Timothy Meyers; Kathi Moss; Alan Paul; Marya Small; Garn Stephens

Notes: Moved from the Eden Theater Off-Broadway on June 7, 1972. [1] Cut. [2] Cut. Different music out of town.

1665 • GREAT AMERICAN BACKSTAGE MUSICAL, THE

OPENED: 09/15/1982
Musical   Closed out of town

Composer: Bill Solly
Lyricist: Bill Solly
Librettist: Bill Solly; Donald Ward
Producer: Goodspeed Opera House
Director: Michael Montel

Choreographer: Dan Siretta; **Costumes:** David Toser; **Dance Arranger:** Russell Warner; **Lighting Designer:** Craig Miller; **Musical Director:** Lynn Crigler; **Orchestrations:** David Krane; Russell Warner; **Set Design:** James Leonard Joy

Songs: Ba-Boom!; Being Made Love To; Crumbs in My Bed; End, The; Girl in Short Supply, The; Going Places; I Could Fall in Love; I Got the What?; I'll Wait for Joe; News of You; Nickel Worth of Dreams; On the Avenue; Opening Number; Pie and Coffee; Safe Home; Signature Tune; Star of the Show, The; When the Money Comes In; You Should Be Made Love To

Cast: Dennis Bailey; Jill Cook; Faith Prince

Notes: Goodspeed Opera House.

1666 • GREAT BEHMAN SHOW, THE

Musical

Songs: No Matter Who or What You Are It's Great to Be in Love (C: Paul Rubens; L: Crane Wilbur)

Cast: Florence Mills

Notes: No other information available.

1667 • GREAT DAY!

OPENED: 10/17/1929   Theatre: Cosmopolitan
Musical   Broadway: 37

Composer: Vincent Youmans
Lyricist: Edward Eliscu; Billy Rose
Librettist: William Anthony McGuire
Producer: Vincent Youmans
Director: R.H. Burnside; Frank M. Gillespie

Choreographer: LeRoy Prinz; **Costumes:** Mabel Johnston; **Musical Director:** Nicholas Kempner; Paul Lannin; **Orchestrations:** Stephen Jones; Frank Skinner; **Set Design:** Frank Gates; E.A. Morange

Songs: Before I Go [8]; Bismark Is a Herring, Napoleon Is a Cake [6]; Dancing in the Moonlight [6]; Do We Understand Each Other [6]; (I Ask You) Does It Pay to Be a Lady?; Doo, Dah, Deh [6]; Flood, The [5]; Great Day [4]; Happy Because I'm in Love; Help Us Tonight [1]; Homestead Must Be Sold, The [3]; I Ain't Afraid of Scarecrows (I Ain't Scared of Crows); I Can't Make My Heart Behave [10]; I Like What You Like; I Wish You'd Never Grow Up at All [6]; Mardi Gras [6]; Mean Man [6]; Meet the Boy Friend — Don't Laugh [3]; More Than You Know; One Love [7]; Open Up Your Heart; Play the Game; Poor Little Orphans (Sixteen of 'Em) [6]; Right Off the Board [6]; River Song [3]; Si, Si, Senor; Sweet As Sugar Cane [2]; Sweet Emmy Lou [5]; Sweet Sixteen [5]; Wedding Bells Ring On [9]; Without a Song [4]

Cast: Lois Deppe; Maude Eburne; Walter C. Kelly; Aubrey L. Lyles; Mayo Methot; Flournoy Miller; Ethel Norris; Allan Prior; Billy Taylor

Notes: [1] Same music as "I Love You, I Love You" in WILDFLOWER and "What's a Kiss Among Friends" in HIT THE DECK. [2] Same music as "Virginia" in RAINBOW and "If I Told You" in WILDFLOWER and "The Road Home" in THROUGH THE YEARS. [3] Cut prior to opening. [4] Orchestrations by Frank Skinner. [5] Out Boston 9/29. [6] Out Philadelphia prior to New York. [7] Cut after opening. [8] Not used. [9] Cut after opening. Same music as "We're on Our Way to India" in TWO LITTLE GIRLS IN BLUE. [10] ASCAP/Library of Congress only.

1668 • GREAT DAY IN N' ORLEANS

OPENED: 12/30/1929
Revue   Closed out of town

Composer: James P. Johnson
Producer: Flournoy Miller
Director: Flournoy Miller

Notes: Philadelphia, PA. No program available.

1669 • GREAT GRANDSON OF JEDEDIAH KOHLER, THE

OPENED: 03/22/1982   Theatre: Circle Repertory
Play   Off-Broadway: 15

Composer: Jonathan Holtzman
Lyricist: Jonathan Holtzman
Author: John Bishop
Director: John Bard Manulis; Marshall W. Mason

Costumes: Laura Crow; **Lighting Designer:**
Dennis Parichy; **Set Design:** Karl Eigsti

Cast: Michael Ayr; William Hurt; Edward Seamon

Notes: No songs listed in program.

1670 • GREAT LADY

OPENED: 12/01/1938   Theatre: Majestic
Musical   Broadway: 20

Composer: Frederick Loewe
Lyricist: Earle Crooker
Librettist: Lowell Brentano; Earle Crooker
Producer: J.H. Del Bondio; Dwight Deere Wiman
Director: Bretaigne Windust

Choreographer: William Dollar; **Costumes:**
Lucinda Ballard; Scott Wilson; **Musical
Director:** John Fredhoven; **Orchestrations:** Hans
Spialek; **Set Design:** Albert Johnson

Songs: And So Will You; I Have Room in My
Heart; I Never Saw a King Before; In the
Carefree Realm of Fancy; Keep Your Hand on
My Heart; Little Corporal, The; Madame Is at
Home; May I Suggest Romance; Promenade, A;
Sisters Under the Skin; Sweet William; There
Had to Be the Waltz; Though Tongues May Wag;
To Whom It May Concern; Why Can't This
Night Last Forever?

Cast: Alicia Alonzo; Leda Anchutina; Irene
Bordoni; Tullio Carminati; Walter Cassel;
Andre Eglevsky; Helen Ford; Paul Godkin;
Nora Kaye; Dorothy Kirsten; Annabelle Lyon;
Joseph Macaulay; Jerome Robbins; Robert
Shanley; Shepperd Strudwick; Norma Terris

1671 • GREAT MACDADDY, THE

OPENED: 02/12/1974   Theatre: St. Marks
                                        Playhouse
Musical   Off-Broadway: 72

Composer: Coleridge-Taylor Perkinson
Author: Paul Carter Harrison
Producer: Negro Ensemble Company
Director: Douglas Turner Ward

Choreographer: Dianne McIntyre; **Costumes:**
Mary Mease Warren; **Lighting Designer:** Ken
Billington

Cast: Marjorie Barnes; Adolph Caesar; David
Downing; Al Freeman Jr.; Sati Jamal; Alton
Lathrop; Howard Porter; Alvin Ronn Pratt;
Charles Weldon; Hattie Winston

1672 • GREAT MAGOO, THE

OPENED: 12/02/1932   Theatre: Selwyn
Play   Broadway: 11

Author: Gene Fowler; Ben Hecht
Producer: Billy Rose
Director: George Abbott

Costumes: Constance Ripley; **Orchestrations:**
Edward Powell; **Set Design:** Herman Rosse

Songs: It's Only a Paper Moon (If You Believed in
Me) [1] (C: Harold Arlen; L: E.Y. Harburg; Billy
Rose)

Cast: Joe Fields; Percy Kilbride; Dennie Moore

Notes: [1] Titled "If You Believe in Me" in
program. A current rumor circulating among
the upper echelon of American Popular Song
buffs is that Lorenz Hart actually wrote with
Gershwin while Rose took the credit.

1673 • GREAT MAN'S WHISKERS, THE

Notes: *See THE GREAT MAN'S WHISKUS.*

1674 • GREAT MAN'S WHISKUS, THE

OPENED: 02/13/1973   Theatre: NBC
TV Show

Composer: Earl Robinson
Lyricist: E.Y. Harburg

Librettist: John Paxton
Producer: Universal City Studios
Director: Philip Leacock

Source: GREAT MAN'S WHISKERS, THE (Play: Adrian Scott)

Songs: Things Go Bump in the Night; Wilderness Man

Cast: Beth Brickell; Dean Jones; John McGiver; Harve Presnell; Isabel Sanford; Ann Sothern; Dennis Weaver

Notes: Alternate title: THE GREAT MAN'S WHISKERS. Leonard Maltin lists this program as being aired in 1971. ASCAP registered this show in 1969.

1675 • GREAT MEN — PAST AND PRESENT

Theatre: Weber & Fields B'way Mus. Hall
Musical   Broadway

Composer: John Crook
Lyricist: Henry Tyrrel

Notes: Part of HURLY BURLY. No songs listed for this song cycle.

1676 • GREAT SCOT! (1965)

OPENED: 11/10/1965   Theatre: Theatre Four
Musical   Off-Broadway: 38

Composer: Don McAfee
Lyricist: Nancy Leeds
Librettist: Mark Conradt; Gregory Dawson
Producer: Edward H. Davis; Scotia Productions
Director: Charles Tate

Choreographer: Joyce Trisler; **Costumes:** Patton Campbell; **Lighting Designer:** Theda Taylor; **Musical Director:** Joe Raposo; **Orchestrations:** Gershon Kingsley; Stephen Lawrence; Joe Raposo; **Set Design:** Helen Pond; Herbert Senn

Songs: Brandy in Your Champagne; Great Scot!; Happy New Year; He Knows Where to Find Me; He's Not for Me; I Left a Dream Somewhere; I'll Find a Dream Somewhere; I'll Still Love Jean; I'm Gonna Have a Baby; Original Sin; Princes' Street; That Big-Bellied Bottle; That Special Day;

We're Gonna Have a Wedding; What a Shame; Where Does a Man Begin?; Where Is That Rainbow?; You're the Only One

Cast: Allan Bruce; Jack Eddleman; Joleen Fodor; Charles Hudson; Charlotte Jones

1677 • GREAT SCOTT (1954)

OPENED: 08/11/1953
Musical   Closed out of town

Composer: Bob Holter
Lyricist: Easter Yahya
Librettist: Easter Yahya

Notes: Produced at the Great Neck Summer Theater.

1678 • GREAT TEMPTATIONS, THE

OPENED: 05/18/1926   Theatre: Winter Garden
Musical   Broadway: 197

Composer: Maurie Rubens
Lyricist: Clifford Grey
Librettist: Harold Atteridge
Producer: Messrs. Shubert
Director: J.C. Huffman

Choreographer: Earl Lindsay; **Musical Director:** Harry N. Leman; **Set Design:** Watson Barratt

Songs: Any Step; Atlantic City Girl, The; Beauty Is Vanity; Chevalier of the Highway, The [2]; Dancing Town; Garden of Memories, A; Guards of Fantasy, The; Love Birds [1] (C: Kenneth Burton); Never Say the World Was Made to Cry; Pin Cushion, A; Querida; Sesquicentennial Baby, The; Spider's Web, The (C: Milton Schwarzwald); Temptation Strut, The (C: Earl Lindsay; Maurie Rubens); Valencia (C: Jose Padilla); White Rose, Red Rose [1] (C: C.R. Moretty)

Cast: Florenz Ames; Jack Benny; Hazel Dawn; Jay C. Flippen; Aubrey L. Lyles; Flournoy Miller

Notes: [1] Sheet music only. [2] Not in program.

1679 • GREAT TO BE ALIVE!

OPENED: 03/23/1950   Theatre: Winter Garden
Musical   Broadway: 52

Composer: Abraham Ellstein
Lyricist: Walter Bullock
Librettist: Walter Bullock; Sylvia Regan
Producer: Vinton Freedley; Anderson Lawler; Russell Markert
Director: Mary Hunter

Choreographer: Helen Tamiris; **Costumes:** Stewart Chaney; **Dance Arranger:** Genevieve Pitot; **Lighting Designer:** Stewart Chaney; **Musical Director:** Max Meth; **Orchestrations:** Robert Russell Bennett; Don Walker; **Set Design:** Stewart Chaney; **Vocal Arranger:** Crane Calder

Songs: Blue Day; Call It Love; Dreams Ago; From This Day On; Headin' for a Weddin'; It's a Long Time Till Tomorrow; Let's Have a Party; Redecorate; Riddle, The; Story of Kitty, The; Thank You, Mrs. Butterfield; That's a Man Everytime; There's Nothing Like It; Waltz; What a Day!; When the Sheets Come Back from the Laundry; Who Done It?; You Appeal to Me

Cast: Rod Alexander; Valerie Bettis; Mark Dawson; Stuart Erwin; Bambi Linn; Vivienne Segal

1680 • GREAT WALTZ, THE (1934)

OPENED: 09/22/1934   Theatre: Center
Musical   Broadway: 297

Composer: Johann Strauss Jr.; Johann Strauss Sr.
Lyricist: Desmond Carter
Librettist: Moss Hart
Producer: Max Gordon
Director: Hassard Short

Source: WALTZES FROM VIENNA (Operetta: Caswell Garth); **Source:** WALZER AUS WIEN (Operetta: Ernst Marischka; Heinz Reichert; A.M. Willner); **Choreographer:** Harold Belfer; Albertina Rasch; **Costumes:** Irene Sharaff; Doris Zinkeisen; **Lighting Designer:** Hassard Short; **Musical Director:** Frank Tours; **Orchestrations:** Julius Bittner; G.A. Clutsam; Herbert Griffith; Erich Wolfgang Korngold; Frank Tours; **Set Design:** Albert Johnson

Songs: At Dommayer's [1] (L: Chet Forrest; Robert Wright); Blue Danube Waltz (L: Chet Forrest; Robert Wright); Buzza Buzza Buzz [1]; Danube So Blue; Doings at Dommayer's, The; For We Love You Still; I'm in Love Vienna (1)

(L: Forman Brown); I'm in Love with Vienna (2) [2]; Like the Rose (Paris Song) (L: Forman Brown); Look Before You Leap; Love and Gingerbread (L: Forman Brown); Love and War; Love Will Find You; Love's Never Lost; Morning; Music (L: Chet Forrest; Robert Wright); Music [1]; Night; Of Men and Violins [1]; On Love Alone; People and Pastry [1]; Radetsky March [1]; Star in the Sky, A; When You Love Me with All My Heart; Without My Love [1]; You Are My Songs

Cast: Marie Burke; Jessie Busley; Marion Claire; Ernest Cossart; Alexandra Danilova; Robert Fischer; Meg Mundy; Dennis Noble; H. Reeves-Smith; Guy Robertson; Solly Ward

Notes: Returned to New York on 8/5/35 for 48 performances. *See also THE GREAT WALTZ (1953).* [1] Added for San Francisco revival 1949. [2] Added for San Francisco revival 1949. Song with same name in MGM 1938 film version with lyrics by Oscar Hammerstein II. This may or may not be the same song.

1681 GREAT WALTZ, THE (1953)

OPENED: 1953
Musical   Los Angeles

Music Based On: Johann Strauss Jr.; Johann Strauss Sr.
Lyricist: Desmond Carter
Librettist: Milton Lazarus
Producer: L.A. Civic Light Opera; Edwin Lester
Director: Vladimir Rosing

Source: GREAT WALTZ, THE (Musical: Moss Hart); **Choreographer:** Ernest Loring; **Costumes:** Adele Palmer; **Lighting Designer:** Laird Davis; Music Adaptation: Erich Wolfgang Korngold; **Musical Director:** Arthur Kay; **Set Design:** Furth Ullman

Songs: Better to Be Loved (L: Chet Forrest; Robert Wright); Doings at Dommayer's, The (L: Chet Forrest; Robert Wright); Of Men and Violins (L: Chet Forrest; Robert Wright); Stars in Your Wine (L: Forman Brown); State of the Dance, The (L: Chet Forrest; Robert Wright); Two By Two (L: Chet Forrest; Robert Wright); With All My Heart (L: Desmond Carter); Wonderful Sun in the Sky, A (L: Forman Brown); You Are My Songs (L: Forman Brown)

Cast: Sig Arno; John Banner; Virginia Gibson; Florence Henderson; Dorothy Kirsten; Bill Shirley; John Charles Thomas

Notes: See Broadway production for original sources. Edward Chodorov's version played London's Drury Lane, 07/06/1970, for 706 performances.

1682 • GREEK SLAVE, A
OPENED: 11/28/1899   Theatre: Herald Square
Musical   Broadway: 29

Composer: Sidney Jones; Lionel Monckton
Lyricist: Harry Greenbank; Adrian Ross
Librettist: Owen Hall
Producer: Fred C. Whitney

Songs: All Is Fair; Bear the God of Love Along; By Bacchus, Chorus of Saturnalia; Chorus of Welcome; Confidential; Far Above You Is My Throne; Forgive; Freedom; Frog He Lived in a Pond, A; Girl of My Heart, The; Golden Isle, The; Hail! Antonia, Hail!; Here at Baiae on the Bay; I Cannot Love; I Should Rather Like to Try; I Want to Be Popular [1]; I'm a Naughty Girl [1]; Lost Pleiad, The; Love in Mine Eyes [1]; Nothing but Nerves; Oh, What Will Be the End of It?; On the Dial; Processional March (inst.); Revels, The; Song of Love, A; Topsy Turvy; What Homage of Human Lovers; Whirligig

Cast: Minnie Ashley; Richard Carle; Hugh Chilvers; Kate Michelena; Dorothy Morton; Herbert Sparling

Notes: No program available. Songs listed are from London production. [1] Added after opening in London.

1683 • GREEK TO YOU
OPENED: 1937
Musical   Unproduced

Composer: Cole Porter
Lyricist: Cole Porter
Librettist: Russel Crouse; Howard Lindsay
Producer: Vinton Freedley

Songs: Greek to You; It Never Entered My Head; Melos, That Lovely Smiling Isle; Wild Wedding Bells

1684 • GREEN POND
OPENED: 11/22/1977   Theatre: Westside
Musical   Off-Broadway: 32

Composer: Mel Marvin
Lyricist: Robert Montgomery
Librettist: Robert Montgomery
Producer: Chelsea Theatre Center
Director: David Chambers

Costumes: Marjorie Kellogg; **Lighting Designer:** Arden Fingerhut; **Orchestrations:** Mel Marvin; **Set Design:** Marjorie Kellogg; **Vocal Arranger:** Mel Marvin

Songs: Alligator Meat; Brother to Brother; Daughter; Eyes of Egypt, The; Green Pond; Hard to Love; How We Get Down; Hurricane; I Live Alone; On the Ground at Last; Pleasant Company; Priceless Relics; Woman to Woman

Cast: Stephanie Cotsirilos; Christine Ebersole; Stephen James; Richard Ryder

1685 • GREENWICH VILLAGE FOLLIES, THE (1919)
OPENED: 07/15/1919   Theatre: Greenwich
                             Village
Revue   Off-Broadway: 232

Composer: A. Baldwin Sloane
Lyricist: ohn Murray Anderson; Arthur Swanstrom
Librettist: John Murray Anderson; Philip Bartholomae
Producer: Bohemians, The
Director: John Murray Anderson

Musical Director: Hilding Anderson; **Orchestrations:** Hilding Anderson; **Set Design:** Shirley Barker; Charles B. Falls

Songs: All That I Need is a Hallway [1] (C/L: Alex Gerber; Murry Roth; Abner Silver); Black Laugh, The [2]; Critics' Blues, The [1]; I Want a Daddy Who Will Rock Me to Sleep (L: John Murray Anderson; Philip Bartholomae); I'll See You in C-U-B-A [3] (C/L: Irving Berlin); I'll Sell You a Girl; I'm Ashamed to Look the Moon in the Face; I'm Just a Lone Vampire [2]; I'm the Hostess of a Bum Cabaret [1]; I'm the Mistress of a Bum Cabaret [1]; I've a Sweetheart in Each

Star; Message of the Cameo, The; My Little Javanese (L: John Murray Anderson; Philip Bartholomae); My Marionette; Passe-Pied [2]; Red, Red As the Rose (L: John Murray Anderson; Philip Bartholomae); Stolen Melody, The; Such a Little Queen [2]; When My Baby Smiles at Me [1] (C: BIll Munro; L: Ted Lewis; Andrew B. Sterling)

Cast: Bessie McCoy Davis; Harry Delf; Ted Lewis

Notes: Also titled GREENWICH VILLAGE NIGHTS. [1] Sheet music only. [2] Out Washington, D.C. 11/8/20. [3] Added after opening.

1686 • GREENWICH VILLAGE FOLLIES, THE (1920)

OPENED: 08/30/1920   Theatre: Greenwich Village
Revue   Off-Broadway: 217

Composer: A. Baldwin Sloane
Lyricist: John Murray Anderson; Arthur Swanstrom
Librettist: Thomas J. Gray
Producer: Bohemians, The
Director: John Murray Anderson

Costumes: Robert E. Locher; **Musical Director:** Charles Previn; **Orchestrations:** A.C. Columbo; Mornay D. Helm; **Set Design:** Robert E. Locher

Songs: At the Krazy Kat's Ball; Come to Bohemia; Down in Arkansas [1] (C/L: George "Honey Boy" Evans); I'll Be Your Valentine; I'll See You in C-U-B-A [3] (C/L: Irving Berlin); I'm a Lonesome Little Raindrop (C: James F. Hanley; L: Joe Goodwin; Murray Roth); Just Snap Your Fingers at Care [2] (C: Louis Silvers; L: B.G. DeSylva); Just Sweet Sixteen; Marimba [3] (C: Johnny Black; L: Cliff Hess; Howard Johnson); Murder in My Heart; Naked Truth, The; Parfum d'Amour; Sextette Number (C: Harry Ruby; L: Bert Kalmar); Song of the Samovar; Tam, Tam, Tam Tam Tam; Tsin; Wait Until You See My Madeline [1] (C: Von Tilzer)

Cast: Jay Brennan; Frank Crumit; Harriet Gimble; Howard Marsh; Bert Savoy

Notes: [1] Not in programs. [2] DeSylva not credited in sheet music. [3] Sheet music only.

1687 • GREENWICH VILLAGE FOLLIES, THE (1921)

OPENED: 08/31/1921   Theatre: Shubert
Revue   Broadway: 167

Composer: Carey Morgan
Lyricist: John Murray Anderson; Arthur Swanstrom
Librettist: John Murray Anderson; Arthur Swanstrom
Producer: John Murray Anderson
Director: John Murray Anderson

Songs: Bang! Bang! Bang!; Blue Beard [1]; Easin' Along (C: Thomas Morris; L: Irving Bibo); Fate (It Was Fate when I First Met You) (C/L: Byron Gay); Haunted Violin, The; I Want a Picture of You (C/L: Percy Wenrich); I'm Up in the Air Over You; Jekyll and Hyde [1]; Last Waltz, The; Mlle. Loose Heels [1]; Oh! Hugh Ho! [1]; Snow Flake; Sundown Brings Back Memories of You [2] (C: Charles Edmonds; L: Paul Cunningham; Al Dubin); Sweet Simplicity [1]; Three O'Clock in the Morning [1] (C: Julian Robledo; L: Dorothy Terris); Toddle-Dee-Doo [3] (C: Phil Baker; Ernie Golden; L: Sidney D. Mitchell); When Dreams Come True

Cast: Irene Franklin; Peggy Hope; Donald Kerr; Ted Lewis

Notes: [1] Sheet music only. [2] Not in program. [3] ASCAP/Library of Congress only.

1688 • GREENWICH VILLAGE FOLLIES, THE (1922)

OPENED: 09/12/1922   Theatre: Shubert
Revue   Broadway: 209

Composer: Louis A. Hirsch
Lyricist: John Murray Anderson; Irving Caesar
Librettist: George V. Hobart
Producer: Bohemians, The
Director: John Murray Anderson

Choreographer: Carl Randall; Alexander Yakovieff; **Costumes:** Howard Greer; **Set Design:** Howard Greer

Songs: Beautiful Girls (C: Harry Ruby; L: Bert Kalmar); Chauve-Souris of Our Own, A; Cinderella Blues; Gee, I Wish I Was a Caveman's Kid [1] (C/L: E. Golden; Ponce);

Georgette (C: Ray Henderson; L: Lew Brown);
Good-Bye to Dear Old Alaska; Greenwich
Village Nights; Havana Nights; Jenny Lind [1];
Kiss from a Red-Headed Miss, A; Manhattan
Nights; Nightingale, Bring Me a Rose [1];
Parisian Nights; Sixty Seconds Every Minute I
Think of You; Sweetheart Lane; When Songs
Were Sung [1]; You Are My Rain Beau

Cast: Lucille Chalfonte; John Hazzard; Carl
Randall; Savoy & Brennan

Notes: Ballets by Alexander Yakovieff. [1] Sheet
music only.

1689 • GREENWICH VILLAGE FOLLIES, THE (1923)

OPENED: 09/20/1923   Theatre: Winter Garden
Revue   Broadway: 131

Composer: Con Conrad; Louis A. Hirsch
Lyricist: John Murray Anderson
Librettist: John Murray Anderson
Producer: Bohemians, The
Director: John Murray Anderson; Lew Fields

Choreographer: Larry Ceballos; Michio Ito;
Costumes: Howard Greer; **Musical Director:**
Alfred Newman; **Orchestrations:** Robert Russell
Bennett

Songs: Annabelle Lee (C: Louis A. Hirsch);
Barcarole, The; Birthday of the Infantata, The
(C: Louis A. Hirsch; L: Josephine Adair);
Bustle; Cock-a-Doodle Doo (C: Con Conrad;
L: Cliff Friend); Conchita (C: Lewis E. Gensler);
Dancing Step Child (C: Con Conrad); Dream
Lovers, The [1] (L: John Murray Anderson;
Irving Caesar; Con Conrad); Everytime
(C: Con Conrad); Golden Trail (C: Louis A.
Hirsch); Hot Hindoo [6] (C: Lewis E. Gensler;
L: Ira Gershwin [3]); I Am Thinking of You [2]
(C: Louis A. Hirsch); Kama's Garden (C: Louis
A. Hirsch); Lovey (C: Con Conrad); Moonlight
Kisses (C: Con Conrad); My Cavalier [1];
My Isle of Sweethearts [1]; Old Folks at Home,
The [5] (C: Richard A. Whiting; L: Raymond B.
Egan; Gus Kahn); Raisin' the Roof (C: Con
Conrad); Seeing Stars; She's So Different
Now [5] (C: Sam H. Stept; L: George Chimola;
Thomas Malie); Spanish Love [4] (C: George
Gershwin; L: Irving Caesar); Where Is My
Boy [1]; Whiskers [1] (C: Lewis E. Gensler; L:
Rube Goldberg)

Cast: Irene Delroy; Tom Howard; Mandells, The;
Daphne Pollard; Eva Puck; Ruth Urban;
Sammy White

Notes: [1] Out Brooklyn 5/4/25. [2] Sheet music
only. [3] Gershwin used the pseudonym Arthur
Francis. [4] Out Brooklyn 5/4/25. Used in
BROADWAY BREVITIES (1920). [5]
ASCAP/Library of Congress only. [6] Probably
cut before opening.

1690 • GREENWICH VILLAGE FOLLIES, THE (1924)

OPENED: 09/16/1924   Theatre: Shubert
Revue   Broadway: 131

Composer: Cole Porter
Lyricist: Cole Porter
Librettist: Arthur Caesar; Irving Caesar; Lew
Fields; William K. Wells
Producer: Morris Green; A.L. Jones
Director: John Murray Anderson; Lew Fields

Choreographer: Larry Ceballos; **Costumes:** James
Reynolds; **Musical Director:** Alfred Newman;
Set Design: James Reynolds

Songs: Ain't Love Grand? [2] (C: Jay Gorney;
L: John Murray Anderson; Irving Caesar; Owen
Murphy); Bom-Bom-Beedle-Um-Bo (C: Jay
Gorney; L: Irving Caesar; Owen Murphy);
Bring Me a Radio [4]; Brittany [4]; Broadcast a
Jazz [4]; Could You Get Along with Me [2]
(C: Jay Gorney; L: John Murray Anderson;
Irving Caesar; Owen Murphy); Do a Little This,
Do a Little That (C: Lee David; L: Benton Ley);
Dollys and Their Collies, The [4]; Garden of
Used to Be, The (C: Jay Gorney; L: Owen
Murphy); Gibson Girls' Entrance [3]; Greenwich
Village Ladies Barber Shop [3]; Happy Melody
[9] (C: Phil Charig; L: John Murray Anderson;
Irving Caesar); I Love a Girl in a Shawl [3];
I Want Twins [4]; I'm in Love Again [8]; I've Got
Quelque Chose [5]; Let Every Day Be a Holiday
[1] (C/L: Unknown); Life of a Sailor, The [3];
Make Every Day a Holiday [4]; My Long Ago
Girl [4]; Syncopated Pipes of Pan [6]; Toy of
Destiny [4]; Two Little Babes in the Wood [7];
Understudies [3]; Untitled Waltz [3]; Wait for
the Moon [4]; When Evening Shadows Fall
(C: Jay Gorney; L: Irving Caesar; Owen
Murphy); Zulu Lou (C: Jay Gorney; L: Owen
Murphy)

Cast: Bobbe Arnst; Dolly Sisters, The; Georgie Hale; Vincent Lopez and His Orchestra; Moran & Mack

Notes: [1] Added after N.Y. opening. [2] Out New Haven 3/9/25. [3] Not used. [4] Dropped after opening. [5] Not used. Also not used in PARIS. [6] Later in PHI- PHI as "Ragtime Pipes of Pan." [7] Dropped after opening. Later in PARIS. [8] Added after N.Y. opening. Later in London show UP WITH THE LARK. [9] ASCAP/Library of Congress lists only.

1691 • GREENWICH VILLAGE FOLLIES, THE (1925)

OPENED: 12/24/1925   Theatre: Chanin's 46th St.
Revue   Broadway: 180

Composer: Harold Levey
Lyricist: Owen Murphy
Producer: Bohemians, The
Director: Hassard Short

Choreographer: Larry Ceballos; Alexander Gabrilov; **Costumes:** Gilbert Adrian; Charles LeMaire; Mark Mooring; **Musical Director:** Alfred Newman; **Set Design:** Clark Robinson

Songs: Curse of Cinderella, The; Dancing Doctor, The; Go South (C: Richard Myers; L: Owen Murphy); Happy Prince [3] (C: Willy Engelberger; L: John Murray Anderson; Irving Caesar); Lady of the Snow, The [2]; Life Is Like a Toy Balloon; Life of the Party, The (C: Richard Myers; L: Harry Ruskin); See Yourselves in the Mirror; Whistle Away Your Blues [1] (C: Richard Myers; L: Leo Robin); Window Cleaners, The [4] (C: Harry Ruby; L: Bert Kalmar); Wouldn't You?; You Have-Me-I-Have-You

Cast: Kendall Capps; Irene Delroy; Jane Green; Sam Hearn; Tom Howard; Joe Lyons; Frank McIntyre; Florence Moore; Clarence Nordstrom; Rene Riano; Della Vanna

Notes: Ballet by Alexander Gabrilov. Prologue by Norman Mitchell and Russell Medcraft. [1] Added after opening. [2] Also in THE GREENWICH VILLAGE FOLLIES (1925) (SPRING EDITION). [3] ASCAP/Library of Congress only. [4] Later in the London production of THE FIVE O'CLOCK GIRL and in the HOLLYWOOD MUSIC BOX REVUE.

1692 • GREENWICH VILLAGE FOLLIES, THE (1925) (SPRING EDITION)

OPENED: 03/15/1926   Theatre: Shubert
Revue   Broadway: 180

Composer: Harold Levey
Lyricist: Owen Murphy
Librettist: A. Seymour Brown; Tom Howard; Herman J. Mankiewicz; Norma Mitchell; A. Dorian Otvos; Arthur Raphael; Lewis Waller
Producer: Bohemians, The
Director: Hassard Short

Choreographer: Larry Ceballos; Jack Heisler; **Musical Director:** Alfred Newman; **Set Design:** Clark Robinson

Songs: Faded Flowers (L: Lew Brown; Sidney Clare); Follow Me; Greenwich Village Green, The; How Do You Do; Lady of the Snow [1]; Sincerest Form of Flattery (L: Lew Brown; Sidney Clare); Those Knowing Nurses (L: Lew Brown; Sidney Clare)

Notes: Revised spring edition for which these songs were added. [1] Also in THE GREENWICH VILLAGE FOLLIES (1925).

1693 • GREENWICH VILLAGE FOLLIES, THE (1928)

OPENED: 04/09/1928   Theatre: Winter Garden
Revue   Broadway: 158

Composer: Ray Perkins; Maurie Rubens
Lyricist: Max Lief; Nathaniel Lief
Librettist: Harold Atteridge
Producer: Bohemians, The
Director: J.C. Huffman

Choreographer: Chester Hale; Ralph Reader; **Costumes:** Ernest Schrapps; **Musical Director:** Max Meth; **Set Design:** Watson Barratt

Songs: All the World Loves a Lover [4] (C: Maurie Rubens; L: Harold Atteridge); Brooklyn Heights; Calypso Island [1] (C: Ray Perkins); Cinderella [1] (C: Ray Perkins); Colonial Days [1] (C: Ray Perkins); Dirty Dig (C: Maurie Rubens); Down at the Village (C: Maurie Rubens); Get Your Man; Golden Gate (C: Maurie Rubens); High, High Up in the Clouds (C: Maurie Rubens); Kickin' a Hole in the

Sky [1] (C: Ray Perkins); Little Boy's Blue [2] (C: Maurie Rubens); Padlock Your Blues; Pinky Panki [1] (C: Ray Perkins); Slaves of Broadway (C: Maurie Rubens); Subway Sun, The; What's the Reason (C: Maurie Rubens; L: Harold Atteridge); Who's the Boy?; Why Should We Be Wasting Time? [3] (C: J. Fred Coots; Maurie Rubens; L: Eddie Conrad)

Cast: Sheila Barrett; Grace Brinkley; Benny Fields; Jans & Whalen; Grace LaRue; Lola Raine; Doc Rockwell; Blossom Seeley; Jack Stanford; Bobby Watson

Notes: [1] Out Newark 1/17/28. [2] Added after opening. [3] Sheet music only. [4] Not in programs.

1694 • GREENWICH VILLAGE FOLLIES, THE (1934)

OPENED: 1934
Revue

Composer: Harry Carroll
Lyricist: George J. Bennett

Choreographer: Chester Hale

Songs: Beautiful You; Kiss the Bride Now; Shadows on the Wall; Walk the Plank; Washington Square; Wedding Waltz

Notes: No other information available.

1695 • GREENWICH VILLAGE FOLLIES, THE (1976)

OPENED: 06/10/1976   Theatre: New Follies
Revue   Off-Broadway

Composer: Ronnie Britton
Lyricist: Ronnie Britton
Librettist: Ronnie Britton
Producer: Donald Elliott; Joseph Triaco
Director: Ronnie Britton

Costumes: Kapton; **Lighting Designer:** Steve Loew; **Musical Director:** Max Lifshitz

Songs: Ballet Erotique; Bicentennial March; Expose, The; Garbage-Ella [1]; Girl with the Curls, The; Greenwich Village Follies; Hello, New York; Introduction; I've Been in Love; Le Grand Rape; Let Me Sing!; Long Ago, or Yesterday?; Look at Me; Melody of Manhattan; Merry-Go-Round;

Most Unusual Pair; Nude with Violin; Ole Soft Core; Pandora; Quartet for Losers; Rock 'n' Roll Star; We Wanna Star; You Show Me Yours

Cast: Jacqueline Carol; Gregory Cook; Linda David; Danny Freedman; Marisa Lyon; Lance Marcone; Philippe de Brugada

Notes: [1] Also in TWANGER.

1696 • GREENWICH VILLAGE NIGHTS

Notes: See THE GREENWICH VILLAGE FOLLIES (1919).

1697 • GREENWICH VILLAGE U.S.A.

OPENED: 09/28/1960   Theatre: One Sheridan
                      Square
Revue   Off-Broadway: 87

Composer: Jeanne Bargy
Lyricist: Jeanne Bargy; Herb Corey; Frank Gehrecke
Librettist: Frank Gehrecke
Producer: Allan Hodshire
Director: Frank Gehrecke; Allan Hodshire

Choreographer: Jim Russell; **Costumes:** Nilo; **Dance Arranger:** Jeanne Bargy; **Lighting Designer:** Jules Fisher; **Musical Director:** Bill Costa; **Orchestrations:** Bill Costa; **Set Design:** Robert Soule; **Vocal Arranger:** Jeanne Bargy

Songs: Birth of a Beatnik; BLT Baby, You Bore Me; Brownstone; Espresso House; Greenwich Village U.S.A.; Happy Guy; How About Us Last Nite; How Can Anyone So Sweet; It Pays to Advertise; It's a Nice Place to Visit; Ladies of the House; Love's Melody; Miss Hi-Fie; Mulhaney's Song; N.Y.U.; Off Broadway Broads; Save the Village; Shopkeepers Trio; Sunday Brunch; Tea Party; That's How You Get Your Kicks; Time to Call It Quits; We Got Love; Weekend Shopping; When the Village Goes to Sleep; Why Can't We Be Unhappy?

Cast: Jack Betts; Sara Lou Cooper; Pat Finley; Judy Guyll; Dawn Hampton; James Harwood; Jane A. Johnston; Burke McHugh; James Pompeii; Ken Urmston

Notes: Some of these are sketches and some are song titles.

1698 • GREENWILLOW

OPENED: 03/08/1960   Theatre: Alvin
Musical   Broadway: 97

Composer: Frank Loesser
Lyricist: Frank Loesser
Librettist: Frank Loesser; Lesser Samuels
Producer: Frank Productions; Robert A. Willey
Director: George Roy Hill

Source: GREENWILLOW (Novel: B.J. Chute);
Choreographer: Joe Layton; **Costumes:** Alvin
Colt; **Lighting Designer:** Feder; **Musical
Director:** Abba Bogin; **Orchestrations:** Don
Walker; **Set Design:** Peter Larkin

Songs: A-Tangle, A-Dangle; Andrews's Fantasy
('Yes' Ballet) (inst.); Autumn Courting,
The (inst.); Bless This Day [1]; Call, The [2];
Call to Wander, The [2]; Clang Dang the Bell;
Could've Been a Ring; Day Borrowed from
Heaven, A; Dorrie's Wish; Faraway Boy;
Gideon Briggs, I Love You; Gideon's Charm [3];
Greenwillow Christmas; Greenwillow Walk
(inst.); Hallow'eve (dance); He Died Good;
Head on Her Shoulders, A [3]; Music of Home,
The; My Beauty [1]; Never Will I Marry;
Riddleweed [1]; Sermon, The; Summertime
Love; Walking Away Whistling; What a
Blessing; Yes [1]

Cast: Lee Cass; William Chapman; Grover Dale;
Dortha Duckworth; Cecil Kellaway; Pert
Kelton; Ellen McCown; Anthony Perkins

Notes: [1] Cut prior to opening. [2] Same music. [3]
ASCAP/Library of Congress only.

1699 • GRIND

OPENED: 04/16/1985   Theatre: Mark Hellinger
Musical   Broadway: 79

Composer: Larry Grossman
Lyricist: Ellen Fitzhugh
Librettist: Fay Kanin
Producer: Michael Frazier; Kenneth D. Greenblatt;
Mary Lea Johnson; James M. Nederlander;
John J. Pomerantz; Harold Prince; Martin
Richards
Director: Harold Prince

Source: UNPRODUCED SCREENPLAY (Film: Fay
Kanin); **Choreographer:** Lester Wilson;

Costumes: Florence Klotz; **Dance Arranger:** Tom
Fay; **Lighting Designer:** Ken Billington;
Musical Director: Paul Gemignani;
Orchestrations: Bill Byers; Jim Tyler; Harold
Wheeler; **Set Design:** Clarke Dunham

Songs: All Things to One Man; Cadava; Century
of Progress, A; Crazy Place, The; Down; Finale;
From the Ankles Down; George [1]; Grind, The;
I Get Myself Out; I Talk, You Talk; Katie, My
Love; Line, The; My Daddy Always Taught Me
to Share; Never Put It in Writing; New Man;
Sweet Thing Like Me, A; This Must Be the Place;
Those Eyes of Mine; Timing; Who Is He?; Why,
Mama, Why; Yes, Ma'am

Cast: Hope Clarke; Leonard John Crofoot; Joey
Faye; Leilani Jones; Stubby Kaye; Timothy
Nolen; Valerie Pettiford; Marion Ramsey; Ben
Vereen; Lee Wallace; Carol Woods

Notes: Dance music arrangement for "New Man"
by Gordon Harrell. Additional choreography by
Bob Fosse. [1] Cut.

1700 • GROUNDHOG

OPENED: 04/14/1992   Theatre: Manhattan
                                      Theatre Club
Musical   Off-Broadway: 40

Composer: Elizabeth Swados
Lyricist: Elizabeth Swados
Librettist: Elizabeth Swados
Producer: Manhattan Theater Club
Director: Elizabeth Swados

Arrangements: Ann Marie Milazzo; Michael
Sottile; **Costumes:** G.W. Mercier; **Lighting
Designer:** Natasha Katz; **Musical Director:** Ann
Marie Milazzo; Michael Sottile; **Set Design:** G.W.
Mercier

Songs: Abduction; ACLU; Battle Hymn of Ground-
hog; Bellevue and the Judge; Bill and Willa;
Closing Arguments; Cooper Square; Danilo's
Rap; Doctor's Canon; Experts; Flight to Health;
Groundhog Has Won; Groundhog Is Becoming
Important; Groundhog Is Going to Trial;
Harmonica Man; Hearing Voices; Hey Ground-
hog; Hymn to Spring; If I Am Released; Judge
Decision, The; Just Trust Me; Lawyer's Lament;
My Movie Is Going to Trial; My Movie of the
Week; One More Day; Open the Door; Pay Phone;
Project Heal; Rewrite Your Own Story; Someone

Is Discovering Something; Street People; Sweet Bitter Candy; Testimony; Then Year Blues; This Isn't How I Imagined a Trial to Be; Weather Report #1; What Could I Have Done?; Who Will It Be?; Why Did I Forget?; Willard Scott; Yes/No

1701 • GROVER'S CORNERS

OPENED: 07/29/1987
Musical   Closed out of town

Composer: Harvey Schmidt
Lyricist: Tom Jones
Librettist: Tom Jones
Producer: Kary M. Walker
Director: Dominic Missimi

Source: OUR TOWN (Play: Thornton Wilder); **Choreographer:** Dominic Missimi; **Costumes:** Nancy Missimi; **Lighting Designer:** Diane Williams; John Williams; **Musical Director:** Kevin Stites; **Orchestrations:** David Siegel; **Set Design:** Diane Williams; John Williams; **Vocal Arranger:** Kevin Stites

Songs: Birthday Girl; Conclusion; Day After Day; Do Not Hold On; Evening; Goodbye, World; Hearty Breakfast, A; I Notice You; I Only Want Someone to Love Me; It Isn't Hard to Get Married; Maybe; Out Town; Snapshots, Photographs; Time Goes By

Cast: Michael Bartsch; Tom Jones; Harvey Schmidt; Deanna Wells

Notes: Produced at the Marriott Lincolnshire Resort & Theatre, Illinois.

1702 • GUNMETAL BLUES

OPENED: 04/04/1992   Theatre: AMAS
Musical   Off-Broadway: 45

Composer: Marion Adler; Craig Bohmler
Lyricist: Marion Adler; Craig Bohmler
Librettist: Scott Wentworth
Producer: AMAS Musical Theatre
Director: Davis Hall

Choreographer: Patricia L. Paige; **Costumes:** Eduardo Sicangco; **Lighting Designer:** Scott Zielinski; **Musical Director:** Craig Bohmler; **Orchestrations:** Craig Bohmler; **Set Design:** Eduardo Sicangco; **Vocal Arranger:** Craig Bohmler

Songs: Blonde Song, The; Childhood Days; Don't Know What I Expected; Facts; Finale; Gunmetal Blues; I'm the One That Got Away; Jenny; Mansion Hill; Not Available in Stores!; Put It on My Tab; Shadowplay; Skeletons; Spare Some Change; Take a Break; Virtuoso, The; Welcome to This Window; Well-to-Do Waltz, The

Cast: Marion Adler; Michael Knowles; Daniel Marcus; Scott Wentworth

1703 • GUS EDWARDS'S BANDBOX REVUE

OPENED: 1917
Revue   Closed out of town

Composer: Gus Edwards
Lyricist: Will D. Cobb; Jean Havez
Librettist: Gus Edwards
Producer: B.F. Keith
Director: Gus Edwards

Songs: Captain Kiddo; Kiss for Cinderella (L: Jean Havez); Laddie Boy (L: Will D. Cobb); Little Miss Vogue; My First Long Pants; Pagliacci; There's No More Regular Kids; Toys, Toys, Toys; When I Grow Up I'm Going to Be a Soldier (L: Jean Havez)

Cast: Cuddles Edwards; Marie Hall; Lucille Kent; Goldie Krusader; George Price

Notes: Vaudeville revue. Program from Philadelphia 7/28/17.

1704 • GUS EDWARDS'S NEW SONG REVUE OF 1914

OPENED: 1914
Revue

Composer: Gus Edwards
Lyricist: Will D. Cobb; Jean Havez; Edward Madden; Blanche Merrill; Frank L. Stanton
Librettist: Gus Edwards

Songs: Just Around the Corner from Broadway (L: Blanche Merrill); Shadowland (L: Blanche Merrill)

Notes: Vaudeville revue featuring The Fountain of Youth in Six Spouts. Songs from ASCAP list. No songs listed in program.

1705 • GUS THE BUS
Notes: *See MY BOY FRIEND.*

1706 • GUYS AND DOLLS
OPENED: 11/24/1950   Theatre: 46th Street
Musical   Broadway: 1194

Composer: Frank Loesser
Lyricist: Frank Loesser
Librettist: Abe Burrows; Jo Swerling[3]
Producer: Cy Feuer; Ernest Martin
Director: George S. Kaufman

Source: IDYLL OF MISS SARAH BROWN, THE (Story: Damon Runyon); **Choreographer:** Michael Kidd; **Costumes:** Alvin Colt; **Lighting Designer:** Jo Mielziner; **Musical Director:** Irving Actman; **Orchestrations:** George Bassman; Ted Royal; **Set Design:** Jo Mielziner; **Vocal Arranger:** Herbert Greene

Songs: Action [1]; Adelaide's Lament; Bushel and a Peck, A; Crap Game Dance, The (inst.); Follow the Fold; Fugue for Tinhorns [2]; Getting Dressed [1]; Guys and Dolls; Havana Dance (inst.); If I Were a Bell; I'll Know; It Feels Like Forever [1]; I've Never Been in Love Before; Luck Be a Lady; Marry the Man Today; More I Cannot Wish You; My Time of Day; Oldest Established, The; Shango [1]; Sit Down, You're Rockin' the Boat; Sue Me; Take Back Your Mink; Three Cornered Tune [4]; Travelin' Light [1]; Tune for Humming, A [1]

Cast: Robert Alda; Isabel Bigley; Vivian Blaine; Peter Gennaro; Stubby Kaye; Sam Levene; Nedda Packer; Tom Pedi; Eddie Phillips; B.S. Pully; Paul Reed; Pat Rooney Sr.; Buddy Schwab; Johnny Silver; Onna White

Notes: [1] Cut prior to opening. [2] Same melody as "Three Cornered Tune." [3] Swerling's contributions were minimal. [4] Cut prior to opening. Same music as "Fugue for Tinhorns."

1707 • GYPSY, THE (1912)
OPENED: 11/14/1912   Theatre: Park
Musical   Broadway: 12

Composer: Gustav Luders
Lyricist: Frank Pixley

Librettist: Frank Pixley
Producer: John Cort
Director: A.M. Holbrook

Songs: Ain't That Delicious; Bobolink, The; Every Year Is a Leap Year; Flirting; Friend of a Friend of Mine; Gems of the Night; Girls, Girls; Goodnight and Sweet Dreams; Gypsy Rover, The; I Love You As You Are; I Wish I Were Rich; If You Were a Rose; It Really Doesn't Pay to Be Too Good; My Daffodil; Push the Button; Tail of the Honey Bee, A; There's a Corner of My Heart That's Empty; We Know, Sweetheart, We Know

Cast: Ronald Hamilton Earle; John Hazzard; Eleanor Kent; Ernest Lambert; Francis Lieb; Josephine Morse; Violet Seaton; Blanche West; Anna Wilkes

Notes: No program available.

1708 • GYPSY (1959) (A)
OPENED: 1959
Musical

Composer: Cy Coleman
Lyricist: Carolyn Leigh

Songs: Firefly; To Be a Performer [1]

Notes: Coleman and Leigh wrote these songs on spec in order to get the job of writing GYPSY. They didn't. [1] Later used in LITTLE ME.

1709 • GYPSY (1959) (B)
OPENED: 05/21/1959   Theatre: Broadway
Musical   Broadway: 702

Composer: Jule Styne
Lyricist: Stephen Sondheim
Librettist: Arthur Laurents
Producer: Leland Hayward; David Merrick
Director: Jerome Robbins

Source: GYPSY (Book: Gypsy Rose Lee); **Choreographer:** Jerome Robbins; **Costumes:** Raoul Pene du Bois; **Dance Arranger:** John Kander; Betty Walberg; **Lighting Designer:** Jo Mielziner; **Musical Director:** Milton Rosenstock; **Orchestrations:** Robert Ginzler; Sid Ramin; **Set Design:** Jo Mielziner

Songs: All I Need Is the Girl; Baby June and Her Newsboys [3]; Cow Song [5]; Dainty June and Her Farmboys; Everything's Coming Up Roses; If Momma Was Married; Let Me Entertain You [4]; Let's Go to the Movies [1]; Little Lamb; Madame Rose's Toreadorables [3]; May We Entertain You [4]; Momma's Talkin' Soft [1]; Mr. Goldstone, I Love You; Nice She Ain't [1]; Rose's Turn; Small World; Smile, Girls [1]; Some People; (If I Had) Three Wishes for Christmas [1]; Together, Wherever We Go; Tomorrow's Mother's Day [1]; Who Needs Him? [1]; You Gotta Get a Gimmick; You'll Never Get Away from Me [2]

Cast: Lane Bradbury; Sandra Church; Marilyn Cooper; Imelda De Martin; Erv Harmon; Maria Karnilova; Jack Klugman; Mort Marshall; Jacqueline Mayro; Ethel Merman; Karen Moore; Peg Murray; Michael Parks; Joe Silver; Paul Wallace; David Winters

Notes: On the original cast recording, Stephen Sondheim speaks the "88 cents" line in the song "Some People." [1] Cut prior to opening. [2] Same music as "I'm in Pursuit of Happiness" from the television musical THE RUGGLES OF REDGAP. [3] Same music. [4] Same music. [5] Not in programs.

1710 • GYPSY BLONDE

OPENED: 06/25/1934　　Theatre: Lyric
Musical　　　　　　　Broadway: 24

Composer: Michael Balfe
Lyricist: Frank Gabrielson
Librettist: Kenneth Johns
Producer: Dmitri Ostrov
Director: Dmitri Ostrov

Source: BOHEMIAN GIRL, THE (Musical: Alfred Bunn); **Choreographer:** Vaughn Godfrey; **Costumes:** Eaves; **Musical Director:** Fred Hoff; **Set Design:** Karle O. Amend

Songs: Bliss Forever Past; Broad Highway, The; Come with the Gypsy Bride; Comrade Your Hand; Dance Gypsy (C: Paul J. Girlando); Heart Bow'd Down, The; Hunter's Dance; I Dreamt I Dwelt in Marble Halls; I'm a Gypsy Blonde; In the Gypsy's Life; Introductory Chorus; Is No Succor Near?; Malaguena; Ombo; Silence; 'Tis Sad to Leave; You'll Remember Me

Cast: Helene Arden; Belle Didjah; John Dunsmore; Isabel Henderson; Jon Hendricks; George Trabert; Evelyn Wyckoff

1711 • GYPSY LADY

OPENED: 09/17/1946　　Theatre: Century
Musical　　　　　　　Broadway: 49

Music Based On: Victor Herbert
Lyricist: George Forrest; Robert Wright
Librettist: Henry Myers
Producer: Edwin Lester
Director: George Forrest; Lew Kessler; Robert Wright

Choreographer: Aida Broadbent; **Costumes:** Miles White; **Lighting Designer:** Adrian Awan; **Musical Director:** Arthur Kay; **Orchestrations:** Arthur Kay; **Set Design:** Boris Aronson; **Vocal Arranger:** Arthur Kay

Songs: Andalusia Bolero; Ballet Divertissement (dance); Facts of Life Backstage, The; Gypsy Love Song [1] (C: Victor Herbert; L: Harry B. Smith); I Love You, I Adore You; Interlude; Keepsakes; Life Is a Dirty Business; My First Waltz; My Treasure; On a Wonderful Day Like Today; Pantomime; Piff Paff; Reality; Romany Life [1] (C: Victor Herbert; L: Harry B. Smith); Springtide; World and I, The; Young Lady a la Mode

Cast: Helena Bliss; Melville Cooper; Clarence Derwent; Billy Gilbert; Jack Goode; Joseph Macaulay

Notes: Based on previously written songs by Herbert. [1] From THE FORTUNE TELLER.

1712 • GYPSY LOVE

OPENED: 10/17/1911　　Theatre: Globe
Musical　　　　　　　Broadway: 31

Composer: Franz Lehar
Lyricist: Harry B. Smith; Robert B. Smith
Librettist: Harry B. Smith; Robert B. Smith
Producer: A.H. Woods
Director: George Marion

Source: ZEIGEUNERLIEBE (Musical: Robert Bodanzky; Franz Lehar; A.M. Willner); **Costumes:** Mueltzer; Paul Poiret; Mme. Sotager;

Musical Director: Louis F. Gottschalk; **Set Design:** Ernest Albert

Songs: Baby Duet; Come As a Carrier Dove [1]; Defying the Storm; Duett; Ensemble; Finale Act I; Gypsy Born and Bred Am I [1]; Gypsy Love; I Will Give You All for Love; Lessons in Love; Love for a Year, Love for a Day [1]; Love Is Like the Rose; Love's Sorcery; Matrimony; Melody of Love, The; Opening Chorus Act II; There Is a Land of Fancy; Wedding Guests; When I'm Waltzing with You

Cast: Arthur Albro; George Bickel; Frances Demarest; Carl Hayden; Marguerita Sylva

Notes: [1] Sheet music only.

Notes: From Washington, D.C. program 10/14/28.

H

1713 • HAARLEM NOCTURNE

OPENED: 11/18/1984 Theatre: Latin Quarter
Revue Broadway: 49

Librettist: Andre De Shields; Murray Horwitz
Producer: Barry Weissler; Fran Weissler
Director: Andre De Shields; Murray Horwitz

Costumes: Jean-Claude Robin; **Lighting Designer:**
Marc B. Weiss; **Musical Director:** Marc Shaiman;
Orchestrations: Marc Shaiman; **Set Design:**
David Chapman; **Vocal Arranger:** Marc Shaiman

Songs: B.Y.O.B. (C/L: Andre De Shields); Bad Boy
(C/L: Lil Armstrong); Harlem Nocturne (C: Earle
Hagen; L: Dick Rogers); Heads or Tails (C/L:
Dennis Andreopoulos); Hit the Road Jack (C/L:
Percy Mayfield); Jungle Hip Hop (C/L: Andre
De Shields); Louie [1] (C/L: Marc Shaiman);
Love in the Morning (C/L: Steve Lemberg);
Love's Sad Glance (C: Marc Shaiman; L: Ula
Hedwig); Lush Life (C/L: Billy Strayhorn); Mary
Mack (C/L: Traditional); New York Is a Party
(C: Marc Shaiman; L: Robert I); Now Is the Time
(C/L: Andre De Shields); Release Yourself
(C: Unknown; L: Larry Graham); Say It Again
(C/L: Dennis Andreopoulos); Secret Love
(C: Kenny Moore; L: Alex Brown); Sweet Dreams
(Are Made of This) (C: Annie Lennox; L: D.A.
Stewart); Symphony Rap (C/L: Andre De
Shields); Waterfaucet Blues (C/L: Unknown);
What Becomes of the Broken Hearted (C/L:
J. Dean; P. Riser; Marc Witherspoon); Wishful
Thinking (C/L: Marti McCall; Kenny Moore;
Zedrick Turnbough)

Cast: Debra Byrd; Andre De Shields; Ellia English;
Marc Shaiman; Freida Williams

Notes: There was also a medley of songs including
"The Way We Were" by Marilyn and Alan
Bergman and Marvin Hamlisch; "Locomotion"
by Carole King and Gerald Coffin, "My
Boyfriend's Back" by Bob Feldman, Gerald
Goldstein and Richard Gottehrer, "Chapel of
Love" by Jeff Barry, Ellie Greenwich and Phil
Spector, "Soldier Boy" by Florence Green and
Luther Dixon, "Come and Get These Memories"
by Eddie Holland, Lamont Dozier and Brian
Holland, "Da Doo Run Run" by Jeff Barry, Ellie
Greenwich and Phil Spector, "Wishing and
Hoping" by Burt Bacharach and Hal David,
"He's So Fine" by Ronald Mack, "My Sweet
Lord" by George Harrison, "Please Mr.
Postman" by Brian Holland, Robert Bateman and
Freddie Gorman, "Tell Him" by Burt Russell,
"Baby Love" by Eddie Holland, Brian Holland
and Lamont Dozier, "And Then He Kissed Me"
by Jeff Barry, Ellie Greenwich and Phil Spector,
"Leader of the Pack" by Jeff Barry, Ellie
Greenwich and Phil Spector, "The Shoop Shoop
Song" by Rudy Clark, "He's Sure the Boy I
Love" by Cynthia Weil and Barry Mann, " I Can
Never Go Home Anymore" by George Norton,
"He's a Rebel" by Gene Pitney, "The Girl I'm
Gonna Marry" by Ellie Greenwich, Tony Powers
and Phil Spector, "Not Too Young to Get
Married" by Jeff Barry, Ellie Greenwich, Phil
Spector and Thomas Elliott, and "Memory" by
Andrew Lloyd Webber and Trevor Nunn. [1]
Cut prior to opening.

1714 • HAGAR THE HORRIBLE

OPENED: 1987
Musical Unproduced

Composer: Gary William Friedman
Lyricist: Dennis Green
Librettist: Douglas Wyman

Source: HAGAR THE HORRIBLE (Comic Strip)

Songs: Banquet, The; Brunhilde's; Byzantine
Things; Civilization; Finale; Goodbye; Head
Over Heels; Holy Frygga; Opening; Your Turn

1715 • HAGGADAH, THE

OPENED: 03/31/1980 Theatre: Public
Musical Off-Broadway: 64

Composer: Elizabeth Swados
Lyricist: Elizabeth Swados
Librettist: Elizabeth Swados
Producer: N.Y. Shakespeare Festival; Joseph Papp
Director: Elizabeth Swados

Source: HAGGADAH, THE (Book); **Costumes:** Julie Taymor; **Lighting Designer:** Arden Fingerhut; **Set Design:** Julie Taymor

Songs: Blessing, A; Burning Bush; By the Waters of Babylon; Country that Is Missing; Crossing the Red Sea; Dayenu Chant; Death of Moses; Death of the Firstborn; Elijah; Four Questions; God of Faithful; God of Mercy; Golden Calf; Hebrew Benediction; Look at the Children; Pesach Has Come to the Ghetto; Pharoah's Chant; Plagues, The; Prelude; Puppet Rebbe; Shepherd Song; Slave Chant; Song of Songs; Ten Commandments; Three Midrash; We Are All Dead Men; Who Is Like Unto Thee; Why Hast Thou Done Evil to These People?

Cast: Roger Babb; Suzanne Baxtresser; Shami Chaikin; Patrick Jude; David Schechter; Svee Scooler; Ira Siff

Notes: Narration adapted from texts by Elie Wiesel.

1716 • HAIL MARY
OPENED: 1960
TV Musical

Composer: Jerry Livingston
Lyricist: Leonard Adelson

Songs: Child Is Born, A; Christ Is Alive; Go Forth; Hail Mary; Joseph; Lady of the Roses, The; Mary's Prayer; My Son

Notes: No other information available.

1717 • HAIR
OPENED: 10/17/1967 Theatre: Biltmore
Musical Broadway: 1836

Composer: Galt MacDermot
Lyricist: James Rado; Gerome Ragni
Librettist: James Rado; Gerome Ragni
Producer: Michael Butler
Director: Tom O'Horgan

Choreographer: Julie Arenel; **Costumes:** Nancy Potts; **Lighting Designer:** Jules Fisher; **Musical Director:** Galt MacDermot; **Set Design:** Robin Wagner

Songs: Abie Baby; Ain't Got No; Air; Aquarius; Bed, The; Black Boys/White Boys; Climax [1]; Colored Spade; Dead End [1]; Don't Put It Down [7]; Donna; Easy to Be Hard; Electric Blues; Exanaplanatooch [1]; Eyes Look Your Last [3]; Flesh Failures (Let the Sun Shine In); Frank Mills; Going Down; Good Morning Starshine; Hair; Hare Krishna; Hashish; Hello There [6]; I Believe in Love; I Dig [2]; I Got Life; I'm Hung; Initials; Manchester; Manhattan Beggar [2]; Mess o' Dirt [2]; Mr Berger [2]; My Conviction; Oh Great God of Power [4]; Om Mane Padme [4]; One Thousand Year Old Man [2]; Prisoners in Niggertown (Three Five Zero Zero); Rally, The [2]; Reading the Writing [2]; Red, Blue and White [5]; Sentimental Ending [2]; Sheila Franklin [8]; So Sing the Children on the Avenue [2]; Sodomy; Walking in Space; Washing the World [2]; What a Piece of Work Is Man; Where Do I Go?; You Are Standing on My Bed [2]

Cast: Steve Curry; Ronald Dyson; Sally Eaton; Paul Jabara; Diane Keaton; Lynn Kellogg; Melba Moore; Shelley Plimpton; James Rado; Gerome Ragni; Lamont Washington

Notes: HAIR opened at the Public's Anspacher Theatre where it ran for 49 performances. It then moved to the Cheetah nightclub on December 22, 1967 for an additional 45 performances. The show opened at the Biltmore on April 29, 1968. Best Plays says that the show ran 1750 performances on Broadway. The cast listed is that of the Broadway production. The Off-Broadway production was directed by Gerald Freedman with musical direction by John Morris, scenery by Ming Cho Lee, costumes by Theoni V. Aldredge and lighting by Martin Aronstein. The cast included Jonelle Allen, Ed Crowley, Walker Daniels, Steve Dean, Sally Eaton, Marijane Maricle, Jill O'Hara, Shelley Plimpton, Gerome Ragni, Paul Jabara, Arnold Wilkerson and Susan Batson. [1] Cut between Cheetah and Broadway. [2] Written for show but not used anywhere. [3] Song cut. Partially used as part of "Flesh Failures." [4] Partially used in show. [5] Title changed to "Don't Put It Down." [6] Incorporated into "Don't Put It Down." [7] Contains "Om Mane Padme." Titled "Don't Put It Down" at Cheetah. [8] Song cut. Partially used on Broadway.

1718 • HAIRPIN HARMONY
OPENED: 10/01/1943 Theatre: National
Musical Broadway: 3

Composer: Harold Orlob
Lyricist: Harold Orlob
Producer: Harold Orlob
Director: Carl Randall

Costumes: Mahieu; **Musical Director:** Arthur Norris; **Set Design:** Donald Oenslager

Songs: Hairpin Harmony [1]; I'm a Butter Hoarder; I'm Tickled Pink; Pickaninny Pie [1]; That's My Approach to Love; What-a-Ya-Say [1]; What Do the Neighbors Say?; Without a Sponsor; You Can Be Like Grandpa; You're the Reason

Cast: Carlyle Blackwell; Maureen Cannon; Lennie Kent

Notes: [1] Not in program.

1719 • HALALA!

OPENED: 03/09/1986   Theatre: Douglas
                                       Fairbanks
Musical   Off-Broadway: 31

Composer: Welcome Msomi
Lyricist: Welcome Msomi
Librettist: Welcome Msomi
Producer: Eric Krebs
Director: Welcome Msomi

Choreographer: Thuli Dumakude; **Lighting Designer:** Whitney Quesenbery; **Vocal Arranger:** Thuli Dumakude

Songs: Bayakhala (They Mourn); Halala Song, The; Koze Kubenini (Until When); Sonoba (We Shall Conquer)

Cast: Thuli Dumakude; Lorraine Mahlangu; Mandla Msomi; Seth Sibanda; Linda Tshabalala; Michael Xulu

1720 • HALF A KING

OPENED: 09/14/1896   Theatre: Knickerbocker
Musical   Broadway: 64

Composer: Ludwig Englander
Lyricist: Harry B. Smith
Librettist: Harry B. Smith
Director: Richard Barker

Source: LE ROI DE CARREAU (Musical: Eugene Leterrier)

Songs: Bold Pierre; Bon Jour; Convent Song; If I Were Really a King; Love Makes the World Go Round, Boys!; Lovely Lady; My Boy, You're in Society; Serenade; Would You Ask?

Cast: Lulu Glaser; Peter Lang; Christie MacDonald; J.C. Miron; Agnes Paul; Blanche Plunkett; Edward P. Temple; Francis Wilson

Notes: No songs listed in program.

1721 • HALF A SIXPENCE

OPENED: 04/25/1965   Theatre: Broadhurst
Musical   Broadway: 512

Composer: David Heneker
Lyricist: David Heneker
Librettist: Beverly Cross
Producer: Allen-Hodgdon; Harold Fielding; Harry Rigby; Stevens Productions
Director: Gene Saks

Source: KIPPS (Novel: H.G. Wells); **Choreographer:** Onna White; **Costumes:** Loudon Sainthill; **Dance Arranger:** Robert Prince; **Lighting Designer:** Jules Fisher; **Musical Director:** Stanley Lebowsky; **Orchestrations:** Jim Tyler; **Set Design:** Loudon Sainthill; **Vocal Arranger:** Buster Davis

Songs: All in the Cause of Economy; Flash, Bang, Wallop; Half a Sixpence; Hip, Hop, Hoorah! [2]; I Don't Believe a Word of It [1]; I Know What I Am; I Only Want a Little House [1]; If the Rain's Got to Fall; I'll Build a Palace for My Girl [1]; I'm Not Talking to You [1]; Long Ago; Money to Burn; Oak and the Ash, The [1]; Old Military Canal, The; One That's Run Away [1]; Party's on the House, The; Proper Gentleman, A; She's Too Far Above Me

Cast: Norman Allen; Grover Dale; James Grout; Polly James; Will Mackenzie; Carrie Nye; Ann Shoemaker; Tommy Steele

Notes: [1] Used in London but not Broadway. [2] Cut prior to original London opening.

1722 • HALF A WIDOW

OPENED: 09/12/1927   Theatre: Waldorf
Musical   Broadway: 16

Composer: Shep Camp
Lyricist: Frank Dupree; Harry B. Smith

Librettist: Frank Dupree; Harry B. Smith
Producer: Wally Gluck
Director: Edwin T. Emery; Lawrence Marston

Choreographer: Billy Pierce; Benny Rubin;
Costumes: Orry Kelly; **Musical Director:** Harry
C. Redfield; **Set Design:** P. Dodd Ackerman

Songs: America; Babette's Military Dance;
Babette's Wedding Day; France Will Not Forget
(C/L: Gordon Johnstone; Geoffrey O'Hara);
Hayfoot, Strawfoot (C/L: Harry Donaghy; H.
DeSilva Jockin; Henry Jockin; Edgar Welch);
I Don't Want to Be a Soldier; I Wonder If She
Cares; I Wonder If She Will Remember; I'm
Thru' with War; It's Great to Be a Doughboy
(L: Frank Dupree); I've Got the Man [1]; Let's
Laugh and Be Merry; Longing for You (L: Frank
Dupree); Look at Me Now [1]; Opening Chorus;
Soldier Boy; Song and Dance; Spanish Love;
Step, Step, Step (C/L: Joe Brandfon; Jack
Murray); Tell Me Again (L: Frank Dupree);
Thousand Times, A; Under the Midsummer
Moon (L: Harry B. Smith); You're a Wonderful
Girl

Cast: Julia Kelety; Gertrude Lang; Benny Rubin;
Halfred Young

Notes: [1] Cut New Haven 8/8/27.

1723 • HALF MOON, THE

OPENED: 11/01/1920   Theatre: Liberty
Musical   Broadway: 48

Composer: Victor Jacobi
Lyricist: William Le Baron
Librettist: William Le Baron
Producer: Charles Dillingham
Director: Fred G. Latham

Choreographer: Allan K. Foster; **Musical Director:**
Harold Vicars

Songs: Dancing Band, The; Days That Used to Be;
Deep in Your Eyes; Father and Son; Finale Act I;
Girls Along Fifth Avenue, The; Half Moon!;
Innocent Girls; Just Friends; Little Book, The;
Love Makes Us Gay; Serenade; Stay Awhile;
What's the Matter with Women?; When You
Smile; You're Just the Girl for Me

Cast: Joseph Cawthorn; Edna May Oliver; Joseph
Santley; Ivy Sawyer; Oscar Shaw

1724 • HALF MOON INN (1923)

OPENED: 03/19/1923
Musical

Producer: Players Club of Columbia U.

Songs: Jack and Jill [1] (C: Richard Rodgers;
L: Lorenz Hart)

Notes: Amateur show produced at the Grand Ballroom of the Hotel Astor. [1] From SAY MAMA.

1725 • HALF MOON INN (1925)

OPENED: 03/09/1925
Musical

Producer: Players Club of Columbia U.

Songs: Babbitts in Love (C: Richard Rodgers;
L: Lorenz Hart); Crossword Puzzle Song
(C/L: Richard Rodgers)

Notes: Amateur show produced at the Grand
Ballroom of the Waldorf-Astoria Hotel.

1726 • HALF PAST EIGHT

OPENED: 12/09/1918
Revue   Closed out of town

Composer: George Gershwin
Lyricist: Edward P. Perkins
Producer: Edward P. Perkins
Director: Edward P. Perkins

Songs: Cupid; Half Past Eight (C/L: Unknown);
Hong Kong; I'll Meet You (C/L: Unknown); In
Cinema Land (C/L: Unknown); It's Rather a
Lark (C/L: Unknown); Little Sunbeam (C/L:
Unknown); Mind Where You Are Going (C/L:
Unknown); My Middy (C/L: Unknown); Ten
Commandments of Love, The; There's Magic in
the Air (L: Ira Gershwin); They Won't Have Me
(C/L: Unknown); Won't You Buy a Little Flag
(C/L: Unknown)

Cast: Clef Club Orchestra; Joe Cook; Sybil Vane

Notes: Six performances in Syracuse, New York.

1727 • HALF-PAST WEDNESDAY

OPENED: 04/06/1962   Theatre: Orpheum
Musical   Off-Broadway: 2

Composer: Robert Colby
Lyricist: Robert Colby; Nita Jonas
Librettist: Anna Marie Barlow
Producer: Hal Raywin; Jerome Rudolph
Director: Hal Raywin

Source: RUMPELSTILTSKIN (Story: Brothers Grimm); Choreographer: Gene Bayliss; Costumes: Robert Fletcher; Dance Arranger: Natalie Charlson; Julian Stein; Lighting Designer: Jules Fisher; Musical Director: Julian Stein; Orchestrations: Julian Stein; Set Design: Lloyd Burlingame; Vocal Arranger: Julian Stein

Songs: Companionship; Give 'Em a Lollipop; Grandfathers; How Lovely, How Lovely; If-If-If-If; If You Did It Once; I've Got a Goose; Jumpin' Jehosephat; Ladies in Waiting; Spinning Song; To-Whit-To-Whoo; We Know a Secret; What's the Fun of Being King; What's the Name of What's-His-Name?; Who? Where? What?; You're the Sweet Beginning

Cast: Dom De Luise; Sean Garrison; Audre Johnston

Notes: Played two performances then reopened for four more on 4/28/62.

1728 • HALL OFF FAME, THE
OPENED: 01/30/1902   Theatre: New York
Musical   Broadway: 152

Composer: A. Baldwin Sloane; Mae Anwerda Sloane
Lyricist: George V. Hobart
Librettist: Sydney Rosenfeld
Producer: Sire Bros.
Director: Ned Wayburn

Set Design: St. John Lewis

Cast: Alexander Carr; Emma Carus; Marie Dressler; Louis Harrison; Ada Lewis; Junie McCree; Edythe Moyer; Charles Prince; Amelia Summerville

Notes: No program available. Bob Cole and Billy Johnson interpolated songs into this show.

1729 • HALLELUJAH, BABY!
OPENED: 04/26/1967   Theatre: Martin Beck
Musical   Broadway: 293

Composer: Jule Styne
Lyricist: Betty Comden; Adolph Green
Librettist: Arthur Laurents
Producer: Hal James; Jane C. Nusbaum; Harry Rigby; Albert W. Selden
Director: Burt Shevelove

Choreographer: Kevin Carlisle; Costumes: Irene Sharaff; Dance Arranger: Luther Henderson; Lighting Designer: Tharon Musser; Musical Director: Buster Davis; Orchestrations: Peter Matz; Set Design: Jean Eckart; William Eckart; Vocal Arranger: Buster Davis

Songs: Another Day; Back in the Kitchen; Being Good Isn't Good Enough; Big Talk [6]; Breadline Dance; Clem's Drill (Dance Drill); Farewell, Farewell; Feet Do Yo' Stuff; Freedom March (dance) [5]; Hallelujah, Baby!; Hey [2]; I Don't Know Where She Got It; I Want to Get Arrested [8]; I Wanted to Change Him [3]; Limbo Dance (Under the Ropes) [1]; My Own Morning; Not Mine; Now's the Time; Slice, The; Smile, Smile; Talking to Yourself; Ugly, Ugly Gal [7]; Watch My Dust [3]; When the Weather's Better [1]; Witches Brew [4]; You Ain't Gonna Shake Them Feathers No More [6]; You and Me [8]; You're Welcome [1]; Your Kind of Man [8]

Cast: Clifford Allen; Allen Case; Marilyn Cooper; Lillian Hayman; Winston De Witt Hemsley; Robert Hooks; Garrett Morris; Paul Reid Roman; Kenneth Scott; Barbara Sharma; Leslie Uggams; Alan Weeks

Notes: [1] Added for tour. [2] Added after opening. [3] Cut after opening. [4] Same music as "Call Me Savage" in FADE OUT-FADE IN. [5] Part of "Now's the Time." [6] Cut prior to opening. [7] Cut prior to opening. Same music as "Gettin' Some" from ONE NIGHT STAND. [8] Not used.

1730 • HALLOWEEN
OPENED: 09/20/1972
Musical   Closed out of town

Composer: Mitch Leigh
Lyricist: Sidney Michaels
Librettist: Sidney Michaels
Producer: Jerome Minskoff; Albert W. Selden
Director: Albert Marre

Source: SALTPETER IN THE RHUBARB (Play: Sidney Michaels); **Choreographer:** Bert Michaels; **Costumes:** Juliellen Weiss; **Lighting Designer:** Howard Bay; **Musical Director:** John Lesko; **Orchestrations:** Carlyle Hall; **Set Design:** Howard Bay

Songs: Bazoom! [1]; Come to These Holy Arms; Halloween; I Want to Be Your Mother; In the Autumn in the Night; Is It Madness, Is It? [1]; It'll Be Green Again; Love in a Barbershop; Lucky [1]; Nothing I've Ever Read [1]; Organized Sex; Run Away with Me; Saltpeter in the Rhubarb; Seduction Is a Holy Thing; Strange Variation of Love, A [1]; This Life Is Fantasy; Where Have I Been All My Life?; Would You Marry a Nut Like Me?

Cast: Billy Barty; Margo Moser; Dick Shawn; William Simington; David Wayne

Notes: Songs not listed in program. Played New Hope, Pennsylvania 9/20/72. [1] Not used or cut after opening.

1731 • HAM TREE, THE

OPENED: 08/28/1905   Theatre: New York
Musical   Broadway: 90

Composer: Jean Schwartz
Lyricist: William Jerome
Librettist: George V. Hobart
Producer: Klaw & Erlanger
Director: Herbert Gresham; Ned Wayburn

Songs: All the World Is Dancing Mad [1]; Desdie, My Desdemona; Good-Bye, Sweet Old Manhattan Isle; Ham Tree Barbecue, The; Honey, Love Me All the Time; In a Bungalo [1]; Jingle Feet [1]; Merry Minstrel Band, The; Minstrel Parade, The [1]; Mr. Lawson the Man from Boston [2]; Old Home Week in Alabama [1]; On an Automobile Honeymoon; Rajah Glide, The [1]; Sweethearts of Every Town (Drummer Song); Walking; When the Cat's Away

Cast: W.C. Fields; Thomas K. Heath; Jobyna Howland; Forrest Huff; James McIntyre; David Torrence

Notes: [1] Added to 1914 revival. [2] ASCAP/Library of Congress only.

1732 • HAMELIN: A MUSICAL TALE FROM RATS TO RICHES

OPENED: 11/10/1985   Theatre: Circle in the
                   Square Downtown
Musical   Off-Broadway: 33

Composer: Richard Jarboe; Harvey Shield
Lyricist: Richard Jarboe; Harvey Shield; Matthew Wells
Librettist: Richard Jarboe; Harvey Shield; Matthew Wells
Producer: Craig Anderson
Director: Ron Nash

Choreographer: Jerry Yoder; **Costumes:** Mark Bridges; **Lighting Designer:** Rick Belzer; **Set Design:** Steven Rubin

Songs: Better Keep Your Promise; Charismatic; Doing My Job; Easy for Me; Feel the Beat; Follow the Music Man; Gold; I'll Remember; Mayor Doesn't Care, The; Mother; Paradise; Rat Trap; Serving the People; We're Rats; What a Day; You've Outstayed Your Welcome

Cast: Scott Fless; Patrick Hamilton; G. Wayne Hoffman; Steven Jacob; Liz Larsen

1733 • HAMMERSTEIN'S NINE O'CLOCK REVUE

OPENED: 10/04/1923   Theatre: Century Roof
Revue   Broadway: 12

Librettist: Morris Harvey; Harold Simpson

Songs: Flannel Petticoat Gal, The [1] (C: Vincent Youmans; L: William Cary Duncan; Oscar Hammerstein II); I Wonder Why the Glow-worm Winks His Eye at Me (C: Herbert Stothart; L: Oscar Hammerstein II); Shadow Man (C: Max Darewski); Snow Ball Rolling (C: Max Darewski); Susannah's Squeaking Shoes (C: Muriel Lillie; L: Arthur Weigall); That's the Tune (C: Max Darewski; L: Graham John; Nelson Keys)

Cast: Eva Brick; Colin Campbell; Cicely Debenham; Morris Harvey; Frank Hector; Phyllis Joyce; Irene Olsen; Wynn Richmond; Ann Rogers; William Valentine

Notes: [1] Later in MARY JANE MCKANE.

1734 • HAND IN HAND

OPENED: 07/06/1948
Musical   Closed out of town

Composer: Dean Fuller
Lyricist: Leonard Gershe
Librettist: Leonard Gershe
Producer: Redge Allen; Evelyn Freyman; Richard Skinner
Director: Gus Schirmer Jr.

Choreographer: Douglas Coudy; **Set Design:** Sointu Syrjala; **Vocal Arranger:** David Craig; Dean Fuller

Songs: Come What May; Happiest Day of My Life, The; I've Got a Mind of My Own; Just Imagine; Let's Drink; Many, Many Men; Mind of My Own; South Grape High; What Must I Be to Be Yours; Yours and Mine

Cast: Lenore Lonergan; Viola Roache

Notes: Programs of Olney, Md. and Clinton, N.J. used.

1735 • HANDS UP

OPENED: 07/22/1915   Theatre: 44th Street
Musical   Broadway: 52

Composer: Sigmund Romberg
Lyricist: E. Ray Goetz
Librettist: Edgar Smith
Producer: Messrs. Shubert
Director: Benrimo

Choreographer: Jack Mason; **Set Design:** H. Robert Law

Songs: Best Little Sweetheart of All, The [1]; Cling a Little Closer; Cute Little Summery Time (C: Jean Schwartz; L: E. Ray Goetz; William Jerome); Esmeralda (C/L: Cole Porter); Evolution of a Rag; Ginger Girl; Howdy-Do, Goodbye (C: Harold Atteridge); I'm Simply Crazy Over You [1] (C: Jean Schwartz; L: E. Ray Goetz; William Jerome); It's a Clue; On the Levee Along Broadway; Opening of Atlantic City [1]; Orange Blossom Time in San Jose [2] (C: E. Ray Goetz; Sigmund Romberg); Orange Girl; Pirate's Rag (C: Bert Grant; Joe Young; L: Grant Clarke; E. Ray Goetz); Popular Rag [2] (C: Cliff Hess); Safety First Love [1] (L: Harold Atteridge); Sing Tango Tea (L: Harold Atteridge); Sing Sing Tango Tea [1] (L: Harold Atteridge); Tiffany Girl; Ting-A-Ling; Way Down on Honolulu Bay [1]; What's the Name of That Tune [1] (L: Harold Atteridge); When I Teach You How to Swim; You Can't Fool a New York Kid

Cast: Alice Dovey; Irene Franklin; Burton Green; George Hassell; Ralph Herz; Donald Macdonald; Bobby North; Will Rogers; Florence Walton; Maurice Walton

Notes: Specialty numbers composed by Schuyler Greene according to program but not identified. [1] Not in programs. [2] ASCAP/Library of Congress only.

1736 • HANG DOWN YOUR HEAD AND DIE

OPENED: 10/15/1964   Theatre: Mayfair
Musical   Off-Broadway: 1

Composer: David Wright
Lyricist: David Wright
Librettist: David Wright
Producer: Marion Javits
Director: Braham Murray

Choreographer: Braham Murray; **Costumes:** Fred Voelpel; **Lighting Designer:** Fred Voelpel; **Musical Director:** Jonathan Anderson; **Set Design:** Fred Voelpel

Songs: Alcatraz; Ballad for Christmas (C/L: Greg Stephens); Brother Men (C: Francois Villon; L: Ivan Williams); English Way to Die, The; Gallows Pole (C/L: Traditional); Gordie (C/L: Traditional); Hang Down Your Head and Die (C/L: Lanny Meyers); Hanging Johnny (C/L: Traditional); I Want Gas; Innocent Man Is Never Hanged, An; Jack Ketch (C/L: Greg Stephens); Long Way from Home, A (C/L: Greg Stephens); Magic Number, The; Sam Hill (C/L: Traditional); Show's the Thing, The; There's Gonna Be a Commission (C/L: Vashti Bunyan; Robert Hewison); Tin Cup (C/L: Jonathan Anderson); Tripe Seller's Lament (C/L: Ivan Williams; C: Traditional)

Cast: Michael Berskon; Ben Bryant; Jordan Charney; David Garfield; Jenny O'Hara; Jill O'Hara; James Rado; Gerome Ragni; Remak Ramsay

1737 • HANG ON TO THE GOOD TIMES

OPENED: 01/22/1985   Theatre: Manhattan
                                   Theatre Club
Revue   Off-Broadway: 40

Composer: Nancy Ford
Lyricist: Gretchen Cryer
Producer: Manhattan Theater Club
Director: Richard Maltby Jr.

Choreographer: Kay Cole; **Costumes:** Karen Gerson; **Dance Arranger:** Cheryl Hardwick; Steven Margoshes; **Lighting Designer:** Mary Jo Dondlinger; **Musical Director:** Cheryl Hardwick; **Orchestrations:** Cheryl Hardwick; Steven Margoshes; **Set Design:** James Morgan; **Vocal Arranger:** Cheryl Hardwick; Steven Margoshes

Songs: Big Bill Murphy (L: Gretchen Cryer; Nancy Ford); Blackberry Wine (C: Gretchen Cryer); Changing [1]; Dear Tom; Do Watcha Gotta Do (C: Gretchen Cryer); Goin' Home with My Children; Hang on to the Good Times; Happy Birthday; In a Simple Way I Love You; Last Day on the Job; Lonely Lady (C: Gretchen Cryer); Mary Margaret's House in the Country; News, The; Old Friend [2]; Put in a Package and Sold; She's My Girl; Strong Woman Number [2]; Too Many Women in My Life; White Trash Motel; You Can Kill Love; You Can Never Know My Mind

Cast: Terri Klausner; Cass Morgan; Don Scardino; Charlaine Woodard

Notes: [1] From SHELTER. [2] From I'M GETTING MY ACT TOGETHER AND TAKING IT ON THE ROAD.

1738 • HANKY-PANKY

OPENED: 08/05/1912   Theatre: Broadway
Musical   Broadway: 104

Composer: A. Baldwin Sloane
Lyricist: E. Ray Goetz
Librettist: Edgar Smith
Producer: Lew Fields
Director: Gus Sohlke

Costumes: Cora MacGeachy; **Musical Director:** Paul Schindler; **Orchestrations:** Hilding Anderson

Songs: Boola Boola; College Days; Dawn of Love, The; Dixie Love Song; Dollar Bill's the Flag That Rules the World, The; Hanky-Panky Glide, The (C: Harry Cooper; Joe Cooper; L: Ballard Macdonald); I'll Take a Ragtime Tune; Lyre Bird and the Jay, The; Meet Me at the Stage Door Tonight; Million Dollar Ball, The (C: Irving Berlin); My Hero (Parody); Oh, You Circus Days (C: James V. Monaco; L: Edith Maida Lessing); Old-Time Ball, The [1]; On the Mississippi [2] (C: Harry Carroll; Arthur Fields; L: Ballard Macdonald); Opening Chorus; Ragtime Opera (Ragtime Sextette) [3] (C/L: Irving Berlin); Roll on Missouri; Rose of Pyramid Land; Someone Is Coming from Dixie [1]; Tennis; That Baboon Baby Dance [4] (C: Joe Cooper; L: Dave Oppenheim); Under the Ragtime Flag; Where the Edelweiss Is Blooming

Cast: Harry Cooper; Carter De Haven; William Montgomery; Florence Moore; Christine Nielson; Bobby North; Max Rogers

Notes: [1] Out Lincoln, Nebraska 4/8/13. [2] Also in THE WHIRL OF SOCIETY. [3] Music based on "Sextette" from LUCIA DI LAMMERMOOR. Also used in THE WHIRL OF SOCIETY. [4] Sheet music only.

1739 • HANNAH . . . 1939

OPENED: 05/31/1990   Theatre: Vineyard
Musical   Off-Off-Broadway: 46

Composer: Bob Merrill
Lyricist: Bob Merrill
Librettist: Bob Merrill
Producer: Vineyard Theatre, The
Director: Douglas Aibel

Choreographer: Tina Paul; **Costumes:** James Scott; **Dance Arranger:** Stephen Milbank; **Incidental Music:** Stephen Milbank; **Lighting Designer:** Phil Monat; **Musical Director:** Stephen Milbank; **Orchestrations:** Bob Goldstone; **Set Design:** G.W. Mercier; **Vocal Arranger:** Stephen Milbank

Songs: Ah, Our Germans; Gentle Afternoon; Hannah Will Take Care of You; Hotsy Totsy Nazi [3]; Kissed on the Eyes; Learn About Life [2]; Martina; No Give, No Take; Opening; Pearl We Called Prague, The; Pretty Thing; Radio Dance (dance); Sew a Button [1]; So Good to See You; Someday; We Dance; Wear a Little Grin (inst.); Who Is Hannah?

Cast: Leigh Beery; Tony Carlin; Patti Perkins; Neva Small; Lori Wilner; Julie Wilson

Notes: No program available. [1] Cut during previews. Previously in THE PRINCE OF GRAND STREET. [2] Cut during previews. [3] Cut prior to New York.

1740 • HANNAH SENESH

OPENED: 04/10/1985   Theatre: Cherry Lane
Play   Off-Broadway: 161

Author: David Schechter
Producer: Perry Bruskin; William Ross
Director: David Schechter

Source: DIARIES AND POEMS (Poetry: Hannah Senesh); **Costumes:** David Woolard; Incidental Music: Steven Lutvak; **Lighting Designer:** Vivien Leone; **Set Design:** Jennifer Gallagher

Songs: Blessed Is the Match (C: Steven Lutvak; L: Hannah Senesh); Eli, Eli (C: D. Zehavi; L: Hannah Senesh); One, Two, Three (C: Elizabeth Swados; L: Hannah Senesh); Rainbow Song, The (C/L: Steven Lutvak); Shtil Di Nacht (C: Unknown; L: Hirsh Gilk); Soon (C/L: David Schechter); Zog Nit Keyn Mol (C: Dmitiri Pokrass; L: Hirsh Gilk)

Cast: John Fistos; David Schechter; Lori Wilner

Notes: Source English translation by Marta Cohn and Peter Hay.

1741 • HANS ANDERSEN

OPENED: 12/17/1974   Theatre: London
                                            Palladium
Musical   London

Composer: Frank Loesser
Lyricist: Frank Loesser
Librettist: Beverly Cross
Producer: Harold Fielding

Source: HANS CHRISTIAN ANDERSEN (Film: Moss Hart; Frank Loesser); **Musical Director:** Michael Reed; **Orchestrations:** Alyn Ainsworth; Peter Knight; Michael Reed; Alan Roger

Songs: Anywhere I Wander [3]; (You've Got to) Dare to Take a Chance (C/L: Marvin Laird); Don't Talk to Me About Those Happy Days (C/L: Marvin Laird); Ecclesiasticus I Can Spell (C/L: Marvin Laird); For Hans Tonight (C/L: Marvin Laird); Have I Stayed Away Too Long [4]; I'm Hans Christian Andersen [3]; In Your Eyes [2]; Inch Worm [3]; Jenny Kissed Me [1]; King's New Clothes, The [3]; No Two People [3]; This Town (C/L: Marvin Laird); Thumbelina [3]; Truly Loved [2]; Tune for Humming, A [5]; Ugly Duckling, The [3]; Wonderful Copenhagen [3]

Cast: Colette Gleeson; Lila Kaye; Milo O'Shea; Tommy Steele; Bob Todd

Notes: No program available. [1] Reworking of "Don't Introduce Me to That Angel, " cut from WHERE'S CHARLEY. [2] From PLEASURES AND PALACES. [3] From original film version. [4] Cut prior to opening. A Loesser trunk song. [5] Cut from WHERE'S CHARLEY?

1742 • HANS BRINKER OR THE SILVER SKATES

OPENED: 02/09/1958   Theatre: NBC
TV Musical

Composer: Hugh Martin
Lyricist: Hugh Martin
Librettist: Sally Benson
Director: Sidney Lamet; **Producer:** Mildred Freed Alberg; Paul Feigay
Musical Director: Franz Allers
Costumes: Noel Taylor; **Lighting:** William Knight

Source: HANS BRINKER AND THE SILVER SKATES (Story: Mary Maples Dodge); **Choreographer:** John Butler; **Vocal Arrangements:** Buster Davis; **Orchestrations:** Irwin Kostel; **Dance Arrangements:** John Morris;)

Songs: Clop, Clop, Clop; Hello Springtime; I Happen to Love You; Ice [1]; I'm a Very Lucky Boy; Job for Me, A [2]; More the Merrier, The (The More We Are the Merrier We Be); Silver Skates (inst.); Today Is Your Birthday [2]; Trinka Brinker

Cast: Dick Button; Vinny Corrod; Tab Hunter; Peggy King; Carmen Mathews; Jarmila Novotna; Basil Rathbone

Notes: [1] Later in Broadway version of MEET ME IN ST. LOUIS. [2] ASCAP/Library of Congress only.

1743 • HANS, THE FLUTE PLAYER

OPENED: 09/20/1910   Theatre: Manhattan
                                            Opera House
Musical   Broadway: 79

Composer: M. Louis Ganne
Lyricist: A. St. John Brennan
Librettist: Georges Mitchell; Maurice Vaucaire
Director: Jacques Coini

Source: HANS, LE JOUER DE FLUTE (Musical: Louis Ganne; Georges Mitchell; Maurice Vaucaire); **Choreographer:** Pauline Verhoeven; **Costumes:** Landolff of Paris; **Musical Director:** Josiah Zuro

Songs: Ah, I Laugh; Buy a Kiss; Entrance of Hans; Father Is a Business Man; I Come from Afar; I Love Him; Listen to My Prayer; National Hymn; Pray Excuse; Prepare the Dolls; Read My Sighs; Set the Table; Song of the Dolls; Song of the Flute; Time of Dolls Is Past, The; Triumphant Entry of Hans; You Do Not Understand

Cast: George W. Callahan; Georges Chadal; Frank Doane; Mr. Doran; Felice Lyne; Frank Pollock; Olive Ulrich

Notes: No songs listed in program.

1744 • HANSEL AND GRETEL

OPENED: 04/27/1958   Theatre: NBC
TV Musical

Composer: Alec Wilder
Lyricist: William Engvick
Librettist: Yasha Frank
Producer: Herbert M. Moss
Director: Paul Bogart; Yasha Frank

Arrangements: Glenn Osser; **Choreographer:** Onna White; **Musical Director:** Glenn Osser

Songs: Eenie Meenie Miney Moe (The Counting Song); Evening Song (Soft Through the Woodland); Market Today; Men Run the World; Morning Song; Much Too Happy Dancing (The Hansel and Gretel Song); What Are Little Girls Made Of

Cast: Red Buttons; Barbara Cook; Stubby Kaye; Paula Laurence; Rudy Vallee

1745 • HAPPIEST GIRL IN THE WORLD, THE

OPENED: 04/03/1961   Theatre: Martin Beck
Musical   Broadway: 96

Composer: Jacques Offenbach
Lyricist: E.Y. Harburg
Librettist: Henry Myers; Fred Saidy

Producer: Lee Guber
Director: Cyril Ritchard

Source: LYSISTRATA (Play: Aristophanes); **Choreographer:** Dania Krupska; **Costumes:** Robert Fletcher; **Dance Arranger:** Gerald Alters; **Lighting Designer:** Jean Eckart; William Eckart; **Musical Director:** Robert De Cormier; **Orchestrations:** Robert Russell Bennett; Hershy Kay; **Set Design:** Jean Eckart; William Eckart; **Vocal Arranger:** Robert De Cormier

Songs: Adrift on a Star; Cheers for the Hero; Chic, Chic, Chic [3]; Diana's Arrival in Athens (dance); Diana's Transformation (dance); Entrance of the Courtesans; Eureka; Excuse My Laughter [2]; Five Minutes of Spring; Glory That is Greece, The; Greek Marine Hymn, The; Happiest Girl in the World, The; Honestly [1]; How Soon, Oh Moon?; Hup-Two-Three [1]; Little Old Gehenna [2]; Lonesomest Girl in the World, The [4]; Love-Sick Serenade; Lysistrata's Serenade [3]; Magic Falute [3]; My Mind Says No [3]; Never Be-Devil the Devil; Never Trust a Virgin; Oath, The; Old Pied Piper, The [3]; Olympics, The (The Greeks Had a Word for It) (dance); Persian Women [3]; Pied Piper's Can-Can, The (dance); Politics [2]; Rhodopa's Tavern [3]; Sabre Song [3]; Scratch a Wife and Find a Doll [3]; Shall We Say Farewell?; Sick, Sick, Sick [3]; Simple Serenade [2]; Strategy [2]; That'll Be the Day; Vive la Virtue; We're Off to the Races [3]; Whatever That May Be; When Your Heart Is Too Young [2]; Where Have I Heard That Song Before? [3]; Who Needs a Woman? [3]

Cast: Lainie Kazan; Lu Leonard; Cyril Ritchard; Janice Rule; Dran Seitz; Bruce Yarnell

Notes: Source acknowledges Aristophanes and Bullfinch. [1] Cut before opening. [2] Not used. [3] ASCAP/Library of Congress only. [4] ASCAP/Library of Congress only. Same music as "The Happiest Girl in the World."

1746 • HAPPIEST NIGHT OF HIS LIFE, THE

OPENED: 02/20/1911   Theatre: Criterion
Musical   Broadway: 24

Composer: Albert Von Tilzer
Lyricist: Junie McCree; Sydney Rosenfeld
Librettist: Junie McCree; Sydney Rosenfeld
Producer: H.H. Frazee; George Lederer
Director: George Lederer

Musical Director: Rudolf Berliner; **Set Design:** Ernest Albert

Songs: Because It Can't Sit Down; Blind Man's Buff; Etiquette; Fiddler Must Be Paid, The; Happiest Night of His Life, The; Hurry, Boys; I'm Just One of My Teens; Jane; Joy Ride, A; Little Church Around the Corner, The; Nectar for the Gods; New York and Chicago; Oh, What a Beautiful Morning; There's One Born Every Minute; Things Left Unsaid; Tradesmen Ensemble; Twenty-Four Hours of Love; We Are Laughing Widows; What a Difference When You're Married

Cast: Emma Littlefield; Junie McCree; Victor Moore; Gertrude Vanderbilt

1747 • HAPPY

OPENED: 12/05/1927   Theatre: Earl Carroll
Musical   Broadway: 82

Composer: Frank Grey
Lyricist: Earle Crooker; McElbert Moore
Librettist: Vincent Lawrence; McElbert Moore
Producer: Murray Phillips
Director: Walter Brooks

Choreographer: Walter Brooks; Jack Heisler; **Musical Director:** Carlton Kelsey

Songs: Blacksheep; Check Your Troubles; Happy; Here's to You, Jack; Hitting on High; If You'll Put Up with Me; Lorelei; Mad About You; One Good Friend; Plastic Surgery; Serpentine, The; Sunny Side of You; Through the Night; What a Lovely Night; Which Shall It Be? (L: Ethelberta Hasbrook); Younger Generation, The

Cast: Madeleine Fairbanks; Hermes Pan [1]; Fred Santley

Notes: [1] Chorus member.

1748 • HAPPY AS LARRY

OPENED: 01/06/1950   Theatre: Coronet
Musical   Broadway: 3

Composer: Mischa Portnoff; Wesley Portnoff
Lyricist: Donagh MacDonagh
Librettist: Donagh MacDonagh
Producer: Leonard Sillman
Director: Burgess Meredith

Source: HAPPY AS LARRY (Play: Donald MacDonough); **Choreographer:** Anna Sokolow; **Costumes:** Motley; **Musical Director:** Franz Allers; **Orchestrations:** Charles L. Cooke; Rudolph Goehr; **Set Design:** Motley; **Vocal Arranger:** Herbert Greene

Songs: And So He Died; Cup of Tea, A; Dance of the Fates; Dirty Dog, The; Doctor's Dance, The; Double Death; Double Murder; Flatulent Ballad, The; Give the Doctor the Best in the House; He's a Bold Rogue; He's with My Johnny; I Remember Her; It's Pleasant and Delightful; Loyalist Wife, The; Mrs. Larry, Tell Me This; Three Old Ladies from Hades; Tobacco Blues, The; Without a Stitch

Cast: Gene Barry; Henry Calvin; Irwin Corey; Burgess Meredith; Barbara Perry; Marguerite Piazza

Notes: Mobiles by Alexander Calder.

1749 • HAPPY BIRTHDAY (1946)

OPENED: 10/31/1946   Theatre: Broadhurst
Play   Broadway: 564

Author: Anita Loos
Producer: Oscar Hammerstein II; Richard Rodgers
Director: Joshua Logan

Costumes: Lucinda Ballard; Incidental Music: Robert Russell Bennett; **Lighting Designer:** Jo Mielziner; **Set Design:** Jo Mielziner

Songs: I Haven't Got a Worry in the World (C: Richard Rodgers; L: Oscar Hammerstein II)

Cast: Dort Clark; Helen Hayes; Louis Jean Heydt; Enid Markey; Ralph Theodore; Grace Valentine; Musa Williams

1750 • HAPPY BIRTHDAY (1975)

OPENED: 1975
Musical   Closed out of town

Composer: Gerry Mulligan
Lyricist: Judy Holliday
Librettist: Anita Loos
Producer: James Hatcher
Director: James Hatcher

Source: HAPPY BIRTHDAY (Play: Anita Loos); **Lighting Designer:** Paul H. Bowen; **Set Design:** Paul H. Bowen

Songs: All My Life; Daughter, A; Fights and Assignations; Friendly Neighborhood Dump; Hold Me; House, The; I Can't Wait to Get Married; I Want Something Lovely; In This Superior Establishment; I've Got a Friend; Minor Prophets, The; Plain Girls; Soliloquy

Cast: Marilyn Bishop; Gary Conway; Fannie Flagg; Anne Randolph; Virginia Schmitt

Notes: Program of the Town and Gown Theatre at the University of Alabama, Birmingham.

1751 • HAPPY CAVALIER, THE
OPENED: 1921
Play   Closed out of town

Composer: Ernest R. Ball
Lyricist: George Graff
Librettist: Anne Nichols
Author: Anne Nichols

Songs: Happy Cavalier Overture, The (inst.); I'm Always in Love with Someone; Laddy Buck of Mine (L: J. Keirn Brennan); Let Me Remember; Little Man

Cast: Laurette Allen; Fiske O'Hara

Notes: Chicago program 8/14/21.

1752 • HAPPY DAYS (1907)
OPENED: 08/08/1907
Musical   Closed out of town

Composer: A. Baldwin Sloane
Lyricist: Al Leech
Librettist: H. Hilbert Chalmers

Notes: Atlantic City.

1753 • HAPPY DAYS (1919)
OPENED: 08/23/1919   Theatre: New York
                                       Hippodrome
Revue   Broadway: 452

Composer: Raymond Hubbell
Lyricist: R.H. Burnside
Librettist: R.H. Burnside
Producer: Charles Dillingham
Director: R.H. Burnside

Costumes: Will R. Barnes; **Lighting Designer:** Joseph Elsner; **Musical Director:** A.J. Garing

Songs: Be a Party at the Party Tonight; Beautiful Golden Land; Don't You Remember Those School Days [1]; Happy Days; I've Found the Girl I've Been Looking For; Jazz Time City; Let's Go to Fairyland; Life's a Race; Love Is (Very) Wonderful; Marriage of the Lily and the Rose, The; My Beautiful American Rose [2]; My Sing Song Girl [1]; Somewhere There's Some Girl [1]; Stately American Rose, The

Cast: Hanneford Family, The; Happy Jack Lambert; Belle Story

Notes: May also be referred to as HERE AND THERE. Clipping for HERE AND THERE indicates music by Sousa and Berlin, but doesn't identify the songs. Clipping credits cast as DeWolf Hopper, Joe Jackson, Tiller Girls, Albertina Rasch, Kathleen Pope and Willie Frick. [1] Also in HERE AND THERE (see note). [2] Sheet music only. May be same song as "The Stately American Rose."

1754 • HAPPY DOLLAR, THE
OPENED: 05/09/1954
Musical   Closed out of town

Composer: William Friml
Lyricist: John Latouche
Librettist: Lee Falk
Producer: James Coligan; James Dunn; Don Medford
Director: Johnny George

Choreographer: Vivien Altfeld; **Musical Director:** Bill Knight

Songs: Give the Devil His Dues; Hero Hill; I Don't Need No Wimmin'; Live for a Moment; Maybe You're My Man; Sal; Scratch

Cast: Dick Culver; Jay Froman; Jody Kirk; Carolyn Richter

Notes: Houston, Texas. No program available. Eddie Bracken was originally listed for the lead.

1755 • HAPPY END
OPENED: 03/08/1977   Theatre: Martin Beck
Musical   Broadway: 112

Composer: Kurt Weill
Lyricist: Bertolt Brecht
Librettist: Bertolt Brecht
Producer: Michael Harvey
Director: Robert Kalfin

Source: HAPPY END (Play: Elisabeth Hauptmann); **Choreographer:** Patricia Birch; **Costumes:** Carrie F. Robbins; **Lighting Designer:** Jennifer Tipton; **Musical Director:** Roland Gagnon; **Set Design:** Robert U. Taylor

Songs: Ballad of the Lily of Hell; Bilbao Song, The; Brother, Give Yourself a Shove; Don't Be Afraid; God Bless Rockefeller [1]; Happy End, The; In Our Childhood's Bright Endeavor; Lieutenants of the Lord; Liquor Dealer's Dream, The [2]; Mandalay Song, The; March Ahead; Sailor's Tango, The; Song of the Big Shot; Surabaya Johnny

Cast: Tony Azito; Grayson Hall; Christopher Lloyd; Benjamin Rayson; Liz Sheridan; Meryl Streep

Notes: Opened at the Brooklyn Academy of Music where it played 37 performances. The production moved to Broadway on May 7, 1977 for an additional 75 performances. Lyrics and book adapted by Michael Feingold from the Brecht original. [1] In original German production. [2] Music later used in JOHNNY JOHNSON as "Prologue."

1756 • HAPPY GO LUCKY

OPENED: 09/30/1926 Theatre: Liberty
Musical Broadway: 52

Composer: Lucien Denni
Lyricist: Gwynne Denni; Helena Evans
Librettist: Helena Evans
Producer: A.L. Erlanger

Songs: Choose Your Flowers; Cinderella [2] (C: James F. Hanley; L: Gwynne Denni; Clifford Grey); Free, Free, Free; Happy Go Lucky; Happy Melody; How Are You, Lady Love? (L: Gwynne Denni); In Vaudeville; It's In, It's Out; It's Wonderful; Love Thoughts; Sing a Little Song (L: Gwynne Denni); Tinker, Tailor [1] (C: James F. Hanley; L: Desmond Carter); Wall Street Zoo; When I Make a Million for You (I Want a Million for You, Dear); You're the Fellow the Fortune Teller Told Me All About; Zip

Cast: Lina Abarbanell; Nydia D'Arnell; Taylor Holmes; Jack Squires

Notes: [1] Sheet music only. [2] Sheet music only. Denni not credited by ASCAP.

1757 • HAPPY HAUNTING

OPENED: 11/07/1992
Musical

Composer: Gerald Markoe
Lyricist: Michael Colby
Librettist: Michael Colby

Choreographer: John Sannuto; **Costumes:** Laura Inga; **Lighting Designer:** Jonathan Rosenbloom; **Musical Director:** C. Colby Sachs; **Set Design:** Jonathan Rosenbloom

Songs: As Things Go Bump; Asp, An; Backstage at the Vic; Comeuppance; Confused; Eee!; Fugue Furioso; Good in Black; Halloween Party; I Can't Wait; Isn't It Creepy; Jack-o'-Lantern; Just for What You Are; Moody Moorland Moon; Nanny Fling, The; Nearsighted Gambler; Now Hush!; On to the Buffet; So Am I; Tarts; When I'm High; When You Lock a Weary Warlock from His Room; Wrong!

Cast: Sarah Downs; Jeff Elsass; Susan Fanale; Mim Goloboff; Brad Menendez; Chuck Sachs; Janet Turner

Notes: Opened at the Harry Warren Theatre, Brooklyn.

1758 • HAPPY HOOLIGAN'S TRIP AROUND THE WORLD (1906)

OPENED: 1906
Musical Closed out of town

Composer: James T. Brymn
Lyricist: Maurice Hagerman
Librettist: Maurice Hagerman
Director: M.L. Heckert

Source: HAPPY HOOLIGAN (Comic Strip: Frederick Burr Opper); **Costumes:** Will R. Barnes; **Musical Director:** Leo Merriman; **Set Design:** Ernest Albert

Songs: Auction Day; Away to the Dungeon Cell; Bullfrog & Coon; Cherry Blossoms; Easy Street; Molly O; Moonlight; Old Black Crow, The; Opening Number; Railroad; Russian Maidens, The; To Our Homes We'll Go; Why Don't You Try?; Yokohama

Cast: Al Lewis; W.J. McDermott; Joe J. Sullivan

Notes: Vocal Director: J. Fletcher Rivers. See *HAPPY HOOLIGAN'S TRIP (1907)* where Prof. Rivers is credited. This is probably the same person, but in the World of Musical Comedy, you never know. Program of 1/4/06 Wilkes-Barre.

1759 • HAPPY HOOLIGAN'S TRIP AROUND THE WORLD (1907)

OPENED: 1907
Musical   Closed out of town

Composer: Professor Rivers
Director: M.L. Heckert

Source: HAPPY HOOLIGAN (Comic Strip: Frederick Burr Opper); **Costumes:** Hayden

Songs: Choo Choo Cars; Do Re Mi Fa Sol La Si Do; Follow Me; Grand Old Rag; I Love Them All; I Said My Last Farewell; Ida Ho the Cowboy Girl; If the Man in the World Were a Coon [1]; My Only One; Why Can't a Girl Be a Soldier; Yokohama Little Charmer; You've Got to Be an American to Feel That Way

Cast: Jack Lyle; Joseph L. Sullivan

Notes: Program of Wilkes-Barre, Pa. 1/28/07. These seem to be popular songs of the day or songs using their names. Professor Rivers is probably the same as J. Fletcher Rivers, the Vocal Director of HAPPY HOOLIGAN'S TRIP AROUND THE WORLD (1906). [1] Probably actually the song "If the Man in the Moon Were a Coon."

1760 • HAPPY HUNTING

OPENED: 12/06/1956   Theatre: Majestic
Musical   Broadway: 412

Composer: Harold Karr
Lyricist: Matt Dubey

Librettist: Russel Crouse; Howard Lindsay
Producer: Jo Mielziner
Director: Abe Burrows

Choreographer: Alex Romero; **Costumes:** Irene Sharaff; **Dance Arranger:** Roger Adams; **Lighting Designer:** Jo Mielziner; **Musical Director:** Jay Blackton; **Orchestrations:** Ted Royal; **Set Design:** Jo Mielziner

Songs: Bikini Dance; Don't Tell Me; Everyone Who's 'Who's Who'; For Love or Money; Game of Love, The [1]; Gee, But It's Good to Be Here; Happy Hunting; If'n; I'm a Funny Dame; I'm Old Enough to Know Better (And Young Enough Not to Care) [2] (C/L: Kay Thompson); It's Like a Beautiful Woman; Just a Moment Ago [2] (C/L: Kay Thompson); Just Another Guy [3]; Mr. Livingstone; Mutual Admiration Society; New-Fangled Tango, A; Postage Stamp Principality; She's Just Another Girl [3]; This Is What I Call Love [1]; This Much I Know; Wedding-of-the-Year Blues

Cast: Leon Belasco; Mary Finney; Virginia Gibson; Fernando Lamas; Ethel Merman; Estelle Parsons; Gordon Polk; Olive Templeton

Notes: [1] Cut after opening. [2] Added after opening. [3] Same song.

1761 • HAPPY HYPOCRITE, THE

OPENED: 09/05/1968   Theatre: Bouwerie Lane
Musical   Broadway: 17

Composer: James Bredt
Lyricist: Edward Eager
Librettist: Edward Eager
Producer: Arete Spero
Director: Tony Tanner

Source: HAPPY HYPOCRITE, THE (Story: Max Beerbohm); **Costumes:** Deidre Cartier; **Lighting Designer:** Jules Fisher; **Musical Director:** Richard J. Leonard; **Orchestrations:** Richard J. Leonard; **Set Design:** Michael Horen

Songs: Almost Too Good to Be True; Amorous Arrow, The; Deep in Me; Don't Take Sides; Echo Song; Face of Love, The; Hell Hath No Fury; I Must Smile; Miss Mere; Mornings at Seven; Once, Only Once; Song of the Mask, The; Street Song; Wedding Pantomime

Cast: John Aman; Keith Cota; Rosemarie Heyer; Joan Kroschell

Notes: Additional material by Tony Tanner.

1762 • HAPPY NEW YEAR
OPENED: 05/10/1980   Theatre: Morosco
Musical   Broadway: 17

Composer: Cole Porter
Lyricist: Cole Porter
Librettist: Burt Shevelove
Producer: Allan Francis; Hale Matthews; Leonard Soloway
Director: Burt Shevelove

Source: HOLIDAY (Play: Philip Barry);
Choreographer: Donald Saddler; **Costumes:** Pierre Balmain; **Dance Arranger:** Charles H. Coleman; **Lighting Designer:** Ken Billington; **Musical Director:** Buster Davis; **Orchestrations:** Luther Henderson; Daniel Troob; **Set Design:** Michael Eagan; **Vocal Arranger:** Buster Davis

Songs: After You, Who? [7]; At Long Last Love [1]; Bless the Bride [11]; Boy, Oh, Boy (L: Burt Shevelove); Easy to Love [4]; Find Me a Primitive Man [5]; Good-bye, Little Dream, Good-bye [13]; I Am Loved [9]; I'm in Love at Last [11]; Let's Be Buddies [3]; Let's Make It a Night [8]; Night and Day [7]; Once Upon a Time [6]; Ours [2]; Red, Hot and Blue [2]; Ridin' High [2]; See for Yourself [11]; To Hell with Everybody but Us [12]; When Your Troubles Have Started [10]; You Do Something to Me [5]

Cast: Richard Bekins; Leslie Denniston; Kimberly Farr; John McMartin; William Roerick; Lara Teeter

Notes: A new show using Porter songs. [1] From YOU NEVER KNOW. [2] From RED, HOT AND BLUE. [3] From PANAMA HATTIE. [4] From BORN TO DANCE. [5] From FIFTY MILLION FRENCHMEN. [6] From unproduced musical ONCE UPON A TIME. [7] From GAY DIVORCE. [8] Cut from SILK STOCKINGS. [9] From OUT OF THIS WORLD. [10] Cut from RED, HOT AND BLUE. [11] Cut prior to opening. Lyrics probably by Buster Davis. [12] Cut prior to opening. Cut from OUT OF THIS WORLD. [13] Cut prior to opening. Also cut from RED, HOT AND BLUE. Written for film BORN TO DANCE but not used. In O MISTRESS MINE (London).

1763 • HAPPY RETURNS
OPENED: 04/19/1938
Revue   London

Composer: Arthur Johnston
Lyricist: Ian Grant
Producer: Charles B. Cochran
Director: Edward Duryea Dowling

Choreographer: Buddy Bradley; **Costumes:** Doris Zinkeisen; **Musical Director:** Frank Collinson; **Set Design:** Ernest Stern

Songs: Buy Yourself a Balloon (C/L: Herman Hupfeld); By Strauss [6] (C: George Gershwin; L: Ira Gershwin); Dancing on the Ceiling [5] (C: Richard Rodgers; L: Lorenz Hart); Dixie Dreams [8] (L: Grant Clarke); Down and Out Blues (C/L: Sam Mayo); Dream Duet, The (C: Jacques Offenbach; L: A.P. Herbert); Get Yourself a Geisha [7] (C: Arthur Schwartz; L: Howard Dietz); Highland Swing; If You Care for Me (C: Herman Darewski; L: Arthur Wimperis); I'm a Little Blackbird [9] (C: Arthur Johnston; George W. Meyer; L: Grant Clarke; Roy Turk); Mitzi (C: Arthur Schwartz; L: Howard Dietz); Must Have a Chorus; My Heart Stood Still [4] (C: Richard Rodgers; L: Lorenz Hart); Paris [1] (C: Arthur Schwartz; L: Howard Dietz); Piccadilly, The; Rhythm [3] (C: Richard Rodgers; L: Lorenz Hart); Sunday in the Park [2] (C/L: Harold Rome); Things [10] (C: Harold Arlen; L: Ira Gershwin; E.Y. Harburg); Weep and You Dance Alone; You Ain't Got Time for Love; You Are My Melody

Cast: Patricia Burke; Constance Carpenter; Bud Flanagan; Beatrice Lillie; Edward Matthews

Notes: [1] Same as "Paree" in AT HOME ABROAD. [2] In PINS AND NEEDLES. [3] Also in OH, PLEASE! and THE SHOW IS ON. [4] Also in ONE DAM THING AFTER ANOTHER and A CONNECTICUT YANKEE. [5] Originally in the show EVER GREEN. [6] Originally in THE SHOW IS ON. [7] Originally in AT HOME ABROAD. [8] Also in DIXIE TO BROADWAY (1924). [9] Also in LEW LESLIE'S BLACKBIRDS and DIXIE TO BROADWAY (1924). [10] Also in LIFE BEGINS AT 8:40.

1764 • HAPPY TIME, THE
OPENED: 01/19/1968   Theatre: Broadway
Musical   Broadway: 286

Composer: John Kander
Lyricist: Fred Ebb
Librettist: N. Richard Nash
Producer: David Merrick
Director: Gower Champion

Source: HAPPY TIME, THE (Play: Samuel Taylor); **Source:** HAPPY TIME, THE (Story: Robert L. Fontaine); **Choreographer:** Gower Champion; **Costumes:** Freddy Wittop; **Dance Arranger:** Marvin Laird; **Lighting Designer:** Jean Rosenthal; **Musical Director:** Oscar Kosarin; **Orchestrations:** Don Walker; **Set Design:** Peter Wexler; **Vocal Arranger:** Oscar Kosarin

Songs: Allez Oop [2]; Among My Yesterdays; Being Alive [1]; Catch My Garter; Certain Girl, A [3]; Getting Younger Every Day [2]; Happy Time, The; He's Back; I Don't Remember You; I Won't Go [2]; If You Leave Me Now [2]; I'm Sorry [2]; In His Own Good Time [2]; Jeanne — Marie [2]; Life of the Party, The; Please Stay; Running [2]; Seeing Things; St. Pierre; Tomorrow Morning; Without Me

Cast: Jeanne Arnold; Robert Goulet; Michael Rupert; David Wayne

Notes: [1] Cut after opening. [2] Cut prior to New York. [3] Previously in GOLDEN GATE, an unproduced show written for George Abbott as a demo for the job of composing FLORA, THE RED MENACE.

1765 • HAPPY TIMES

OPENED: 1958
Musical   Unproduced

Composer: Eubie Blake
Lyricist: Noble Sissle

Songs: Don't Make a Plaything Out of My Heart; They Had to Get the Rhythm Out of Their Souls

1766 • HAPPY TOWN

OPENED: 10/07/1959   Theatre: 54th St.
Musical   Broadway: 5

Composer: Gordon Duffy; Harry M. Haldane; Paul Nassau
Lyricist: Paul Nassau
Librettist: Max Hampton
Producer: B and M Productions
Director: Allan A. Buckhantz

Choreographer: Lee Scott; **Costumes:** J. Michael Travis; **Lighting Designer:** Paul Morrison; **Musical Director:** Samuel Krachmalnick; **Orchestrations:** Nicholas Carras; **Set Design:** Curt Nations; **Vocal Arranger:** Samuel Krachmalnick

Songs: As Busy As Anyone Can Be; Beat of a Heart, The; Celebration!; Heaven Protect Me!; Hoedown!; I Am What I Am!; I Feel Like a Brother to You; I'm Stuck with Love; It Isn't Easy; Legend of Black-Eyed Susan Grey, The; Mean; Nothing in Common; Opportunity!; Pick-Me-Up!; Something Special; Talkin' 'bout You; When the Time Is Right; Y' Can't Win

Cast: Biff McGuire; Liz Pritchett; Cindy Robbins; Edwin Steffe; Lee Venora; Tom Williams

1767 • HAPPY YOUNGSTERS

OPENED: 1908
Musical   Chicago

Composer: William F. Peters
Lyricist: Harold Atteridge
Librettist: Harold Atteridge

Notes: No other information available.

1768 • HAPPYLAND OR THE KING OF ELYSIA

OPENED: 10/02/1905   Theatre: Lyric
Musical   Broadway: 82

Composer: Reginald De Koven
Lyricist: Frederick Ranken
Librettist: Frederick Ranken
Producer: Lee Shubert; Sam S. Shubert
Director: R.H. Burnside

Musical Director: Herman Perlet

Songs: Behold the King; Black Sheep, The; Charge, Boys, Charge; Cupid's Grammar; Finale Act I; Finale Act II; Girls, Girls, Girls (What's a Maiden?); Give Me Thy Heart Love; Hail Gentle Eros; Happy Is the Summer's Day; How I Love Flowers; Just Eighteen Years Ago; Lily and the Moon, The; Mimette; Music; My Human Mermaid; My Wish [1]; Oh, Goddess; Oh, Joy! Oh, Bliss! (A Sickening Sadness Sits on Me); Opening Ensemble; Pretty Maiden; Robin Red Breast; Royal Hussars Are We; Shy Strephon; So Then Away; Soldier of Love, A; Surrender; Take Her, My Boy, She's Yours;

'Twas the Rose; Under Wicket; Victoria; What Is the Difference?

Cast: Marguerite Clark; Will Danforth; George B. Frothingham; DeWolf Hopper

Notes: [1] Sheet music only.

1769 • HARD JOB BEING GOD

OPENED: 05/15/1972   Theatre: Edison
Musical   Broadway: 6

Composer: Tom Martel
Lyricist: Tom Martel
Librettist: Bob Yde
Director: Bob Yde

Source: OLD TESTAMENT, THE (Book);
Choreographer: Lee Theodore; **Costumes:** Mary Whitehead; **Lighting Designer:** Patrika Brown; **Musical Director:** Roy Bittan; **Set Design:** Ray Wilke

Songs: Amos Gonna Give You Hell; Battle; Buy a Slave; Eleven Commandments, The; Famine; Festival; Hail David; Hard Job Being God; I'm Countin' on You; Moses' Song; Passover; Prayer; Psalm of Peace, A; Ruth; Shalom L'Chaim; Ten Plagues, The; Tribes; Very Lonely King, A; What Do I Have to Do?; Wherever You Go; You're on Your Own

Cast: Gini Eastwood; Stu Freeman; Tom Martel; Anne Sarofeen; John Twomey

1770 • HARK!

OPENED: 05/22/1972   Theatre: Mercer-O'Casey
Musical   Off-Broadway: 152

Composer: Dan Goggin
Lyricist: Robert Lorick
Librettist: Marvin Solley
Producer: Robert Lissauer
Director: Darwin Knight

Costumes: Danny Morgan; **Lighting Designer:** Chenault Spence; **Musical Director:** Sande Campbell; **Orchestrations:** John Lissauer; **Set Design:** Chenault Spence; **Vocal Arranger:** Sande Campbell

Songs: All Glory to the Young [2] (C/L: Charles Burr); All Good Things; Alma Mater [2]; Big Day Tomorrow; Coffee Morning; Conversation Piece; Different Stage, A [3]; Dying Business, A (C: Norman L. Martin; L: Fred Ebb); Early Sunday; Epilogue; Everybody's Gone to California [3]; George; Hark!; Here's to You, Mrs. Rodriguez; Hip Hooray for America (C/L: Jim Rusk); How Am I Doin', Dad?; Human Voice, A [3]; I See the People; Icarus; In a Hundred Years; It's Funny about Love; Lullaby; Man, Oh Man [2] (C/L: Bernardo Segall); Mis-Handel-ed Tribute (To the Nixon Administration), A [3]; Mister Producer [3]; Molly; Mr. Simpson?; Old Is Not in Years [2]; Outstanding Member, The; Pill, The [2] (C: Rod Warren; L: Michael McWhinney); Pretty Jack; Senior Citizen's Ball [2] (C/L: Tom Paisley); Six Little Kids; Small Circle of Friends [2]; Smart People; Star Song, The [3]; Suburbia Square Dance [1] (C: Rod Warren; L: Michael McWhinney); Sun Down; Take a Look; Too Bad [3]; Waltz with Me, Lady; Watching the Wildlife [2] (C/L: Tom Paisley); What D'Ya Wanna Be?; What's Your Sign; Which Hat Shall I Wear? [2]; Why Should the Young Men Fight the Wars? [2] (C/L: Charles Burr)

Cast: Jack Blackton; Dan Goggin; Danny Guerrero; Sharron Miller; Elaine Petricoff; Marvin Solley

Notes: [1] Also in BELOW THE BELT. [2] Cut prior to opening. [3] Added for tour.

1771 • HARLEM HEATWAVE

OPENED: 1960
Revue

Composer: Benny Davis
Lyricist: Benny Davis

Songs: Class; High-Hat, Low-Down; Life; Primitive Island; Rockin' and Rollin' in Loch Lomond; Time to Love Is Now, The

Notes: No other information available. Information from ASCAP/Library of Congress.

1772 • HARLEM HOTCHA

OPENED: 11/1932   Theatre: Connie's Inn
Revue   Nightclub

Composer: James P. Johnson
Lyricist: Andy Razaf
Producer: Ted Blackmon
Director: Teddy Blackman

Songs: Aintcha Got Music; Harlem Hotcha; I Was So Weak, Love Was So Strong; My Headache; Stop That Dog; Summer Was Made for Lovers; Yours All Yours

Cast: Louise Cook; Dixie Nightingales; Cora Green; Don Redman and His Orchestra; Earl "Snake Hips" Tucker

Notes: Cabaret show.

1773 • HARLEM UPROAR HOUSE

OPENED: 09/1937   Theatre: Harlem Uproar House

Revue   Nightclub

Composer: Doris Fisher; Fred Fisher
Lyricist: Doris Fisher; Fred Fisher

Choreographer: Miriam Schiller

Songs: Pineapple Swing; Whiffin' the Weed

Cast: Dewey Brown; Big Time Crip; Lillian Fitzgerald; Erskine Hawkins and His Band; Bobby Hayes

Notes: No program available. Information from reviews.

1774 • HARMONY HILL

OPENED: 1934
Musical

Composer: Geoffrey O'Hara
Lyricist: Harry B. Smith

Songs: Behold a Prima Donna; Color Music; Ding Dong; Harmony Hill; He Isn't My Style at All; I Want a Wife that Can Cook; I Was Waiting for You; I've Been Fooling Around; Musical Culture; Now the Wedding Day Is Here; Oompa, Oompa; Our Honeymoon; Papa, At Last I Met You; Prunes, Prisms, Potatoes; Ta Rah Ta Rah; Tell Me Why; They Follow Me Around; Wedding Chorus; You Love Me

Notes: No other information available.

1775 • HAROLD AND MAUDE

OPENED: 02/07/1980   Theatre: Martin Beck
Play   Broadway: 4

Composer: David Amram
Lyricist: David Amram
Author: Colin Higgins
Producer: Courtney Burr; Frank Milton; Nancy Rosenthal; Max Weitzenhoffer
Director: Robert Lewis

Source: HAROLD AND MAUDE (Film: Colin Higgins); **Costumes:** Florence Klotz; **Lighting Designer:** Neil Peter Jampolis; **Set Design:** Tony Straiges

Cast: Denny Dillon; Ruth Ford; Janet Gaynor; Marc Jordan; Berit Lagerwall; Keith McDermott; Nita Novy

Notes: No songs listed in program.

1776 • HARRIGAN 'N HART

OPENED: 01/31/1985   Theatre: Longacre
Musical   Broadway: 5

Composer: Dave Braham
Lyricist: Edward Harrigan
Librettist: Michael Stewart
Producer: Arnold Bernhard; Elliot Martin; Shubert Organization
Director: Joe Layton

Source: MERRY PARTNERS, THE (Book: E.J. Kahn Jr.); **Choreographer:** D.J. Giagni; **Costumes:** Ann Hould-Ward; **Dance Arranger:** John McKinney; **Lighting Designer:** Richard Nelson; **Musical Director:** Peter Howard; **Orchestrations:** John McKinney; **Set Design:** David Mitchell; **Vocal Arranger:** John McKinney

Songs: Ada with the Golden Hair; Clara Jenkins' Socialistic Tea [1]; Dip Me in the Golden Sea; Girl of the Mystic Star; I Love to Follow a Band; I Need This One Chance (C: Max Showalter; L: Peter Walker); If I Could Trust Me (C: Max Showalter; L: Peter Walker); I've Come Home to Stay (C: Max Showalter; L: Peter Walker); Knights of the Mystic Star; Love Put on Your Orange Blossoms [1]; Maggie Murphy's Home (C: Dave Braham; L: Edward Harrigan); McNally's Row of Flats (C: Dave Braham; L: Edward Harrigan); Mulligan Guards (C: Dave Braham; L: Edward Harrigan); Old Barn Floor, The; Put Me in My Little Bed; Sam Johnson's Colored Cakewalk; Savannah Sue [1]; She's Our Gretel; Silly Boy; Skidmore Fancy Ball; Something New, Something Different (C: Max Showalter; L: Peter Walker);

Such an Education Has My Mary Ann; Sweetest Love (C: Max Showalter; L: Peter Walker); That Old Feather Bed; That's My Partner (C: Max Showalter; L: Peter Walker); We'll Be There (C: Max Showalter; L: Peter Walker); What You Need Is A Woman (C: Max Showalter; L: Peter Walker); Wonderful Me

Cast: Cleve Asbury; Clent Bowers; Christine Ebersole; Harry Groener; Mark Hamill; Roxie Lucas; Amelia Marshall; Armelia McQueen

Notes: Sources also included "Material compiled by Nedda Harrigan Logan." [1] From Goodspeed Opera House tryout prior to Broadway.

1777 • HARRY CARROLL'S PICKINGS

OPENED: 02/02/1925
Revue   Los Angeles

Composer: Harry Carroll; Arthur Freed
Lyricist: Ballard Macdonald
Librettist: Ballard Macdonald

Songs: California, Here We Go; Charleston Time; Chop Sticks; Cuckoo Clock, The; Hay Foot, Straw Foot; He Had to Pay the Piper; Hollywood; Hot Steps; I'm a Pickford that Nobody Picked (L: Arthur Freed; Ballard Macdonald); In Our Own Orange Grove; It Happened in 1600; Mission Bells; Next Tuesday; Oriental Pearl; Portion of Caviar, A; Rosie Posies; Sing Me a Song; Sweet Pickings (C: Harry Carroll); Wedding Bells Were Ringing, The

Notes: No other information available. A Hollywood revue.

1778 • HARRY CARROLL'S REVUE

OPENED: 1929
Revue

Composer: Harry Carroll; Jesse Greer
Lyricist: Raymond Klages
Librettist: Andy Rice

Choreographer: Antonio DeMarco

Songs: Blue Step; Japanese Toyland; Out of a Clear Blue Sky; What Do I Care

Notes: No other information available.

1779 • HARRY DELMAR'S REVELS

OPENED: 11/28/1927   Theatre: Shubert
Revue   Broadway: 114

Composer: Jesse Greer
Lyricist: Ballard Macdonald; Billy Rose
Librettist: William K. Wells
Producer: Samuel Baerwitz; Harry Delmar

Choreographer: Chester Hale; **Costumes:** Jeanne Hackett; **Lighting Designer:** Clark Robinson; **Musical Director:** John L. McManus; **Set Design:** Clark Robinson

Songs: Golden Memories of Perfume; I Love a Man in a Uniform (C: James V. Monaco); If You Have Troubles Laugh Them Away (Laff 'em Away) (C/L: Lester Lee); Irresistible You (C: James V. Monaco); Jigaboo Jig, The (C: Lester Lee); My Rainbow (C: Lester Lee; L: Jeanne Hackett); Naga Saki; Say It with a Solitaire (C: James V. Monaco); Undersea Ballet

Cast: Frank Fay; Patsy Kelly; Bert Lahr; Winnie Lightner

1780 • HASSARD SHORT'S RITZ REVUE

OPENED: 09/17/1924   Theatre: Ritz
Revue   Broadway: 109

Producer: Hassard Short
Director: Clyde North

Choreographer: Seymour Felix; Chester Hale; **Costumes:** Charles LeMaire; **Musical Director:** Augustus Barratt; **Set Design:** Clark Robinson

Songs: Beedle-Um-Bee (C: Martin Broones; L: William Gaston; Eric Valentine); Broadway Boudoir (C: Frank Tours; L: Anne Caldwell); Crystal Wedding Day (C: Frank Tours; L: Anne Caldwell); Dancing Blues (C: W. Franke Harling); From Cottage to Subway (C: Roy Webb; L: Kenneth Webb); Hello Girl (C: Werner Janssen; L: Roger Gray); I Long to Belong (C: Jay Gorney; L: Owen Murphy); Little Black Cat, The (C: Raymond Hubbell; L: Anne Caldwell); Midsummer Night's Dream, A (C: Frank Tours; L: Anne Caldwell); Monsieur Beaucaire

(C: Frank Tours; L: Anne Caldwell); Perfect Day, A (C: Martin Broones; L: Harry Raskin; May Tally); Red Ladies, The (C: Roy Webb; L: Kenneth Webb); Scandal, and a Cup of Tea (C: Roy Webb; L: Kenneth Webb); Springtime (C: Roy Webb; L: Kenneth Webb); Sun Girl (C: Frank Tours; L: Anne Caldwell); Too Tall (C: Martin Broones; L: Harry Raskin; May Tally); Uking the Uke (C: W. Franke Harling); Wanderer, The (C: Tom Burke; Jay Gorney; L: Owen Murphy); What the Men Will Wear (C: Roy Webb; L: Kenneth Webb); When You and I Were Dancing (C: H.M. Tennant; L: Graham John)

Cast: Jay Brennan; Madeleine Fairbanks; Hal Forde; Charlotte Greenwood; Raymond Hitchcock

1781 • HATFIELDS & MCCOYS

OPENED: 06/20/1970
Musical

Composer: Ewel Cornett
Lyricist: Billy Edd Wheeler
Librettist: Billy Edd Wheeler
Director: Ewel Cornett

Choreographer: Jerry Rose; **Costumes:** Cynthia Krick; **Musical Director:** Robert Elkins; **Set Design:** Thomas P. Struthers

Cast: Bonnie Bray; David Bray; James Maddux; Allan Ross; Kathy Zeller

Notes: A summer historical drama presented by the West Virginia Historical Drama Association at Grandview State Park, Beckley, West Virginia. No songs listed in program.

1782 • HATS OFF TO ICE

OPENED: 06/22/1944   Theatre: Center
Revue   Broadway: 890

Composer: John Fortis
Lyricist: James Littlefield
Producer: Sonja Henie; Arthur M. Wirtz
Director: Catherine Littlefield

Songs: Hats Off to Ice; Headin' West; Here's to Luck; Isle of the Midnight Rainbow; Love Will Always Be the Same; With Every Star; You've Got What It Takes

Cast: Brandt Sisters; Carol Lynne; Pat Marshall; Lucille Page; Don Loring Rogers; Geoffe Stevens

1783 • HAVANA

OPENED: 02/11/1909   Theatre: Casino
Musical   Broadway: 272

Composer: Leslie Stuart
Lyricist: Adrian Ross
Librettist: James T. Powers
Producer: Lee Shubert; Sam S. Shubert
Director: Ned Wayburn

Source: HAVANA (Musical: George Goldsmith; Graham Hill); **Musical Director:** Clarence Rogerson; **Set Design:** Arthur Voegtlin

Songs: I'm a Cuban Girl; According How You Take 'Em [3]; And Then That Cigar Went Out [3]; Beware of the Bomb [3]; Cupid's Telephone (C: George Arthurs); Filibuster Brown [3]; Finale Act I; Finale Act II; Girl with the Yellow Roses, The; Hello, People! (L: George Arthurs); How Did the Bird Know That?; If I Was a Rular Despotical [3]; Little Miquette [3]; Little Supper Table for Two [3] (L: George Arthurs); Merry Widow, The [3]; My Husband; My Little Deutcher Girl [4] (C/L: Frank Leo; L: James T. Powers); On the Shores of Sheepshead Bay [2]; Opening Chorus Act III; Slopes of Denmark Hill, The [3]; Sun Is Down and Over the Town, The; Tis Noon of Tropic Day; Waiting for Me [3]; Way Down in Pensacola (L: Leslie Stuart); Welcome to the Lovely Bride to Be; What Shall I Do with the Rest?; Would You Like to Motor with Mater? (L: George Arthurs); Yacht, The; Zara

Cast: Eva Davenport; Edith Decker; Ernest Hare; Ernest Lambert; Clara Palmer; James T. Powers; William Pruette

Notes: [1] Not in program. [2] In London titled "On the Slopes of Denmark Hill." [3] In London vocal score. [4] American version by Powers.

1784 • HAVE A HEART

OPENED: 01/11/1917   Theatre: Liberty
Musical   Broadway: 76

Composer: Jerome Kern
Lyricist: P.G. Wodehouse
Librettist: Guy Bolton; P.G. Wodehouse

Producer: Henry W. Savage
Director: Edward Royce

Musical Director: Gus Salzer; **Orchestrations:** Frank Saddler; **Set Design:** Henry Ives Cobb Jr.

Songs: And I Am All Alone (L: Jerome Kern; P.G. Wodehouse); Bright Lights [1]; Come Out of the Kitchen; Daisy [4]; Finale Act I; Finale Act II; Have a Heart [7]; Honeymoon Inn; I'm Here Little Girls, I'm Here [6]; I'm So Busy (L: Schuyler Greene; P.G. Wodehouse); It's a Sure Sign [6] (L: R.P. Weston); Look in His Eyes [5] (L: Herbert Reynolds); My Wife-My Man; Napoleon [2]; Nightingale, The (Turk's Song) (Samarkand) [6]; Peter Pan [4]; Polly Believed in Prepardness [4]; Reminiscences (inst.) [6]; Road that Lies Before, The; Shop; That's the Life [4]; They All Look Alike [8]; What Would You Do for $50,000 [3] (C: Harry Tierney; L: Alfred Bryan); Whirlwind Trot [3]; Why Can't It Happen to Me? [4]; You Said Something (L: Jerome Kern; P.G. Wodehouse)

Cast: Flavia Arcaro; Louise Dresser; Peggy Fears; Marjorie Gateson; Thurston Hall; Donald Macdonald; Billy B. Van

Notes: [1] From 1916 tune "Toodle-oo" with lyrics by P.G. Wodehouse and Schuyler Greene. In vocal score only. [2] Originally written for MISS SPRINGTIME. [3] Added for tour. [4] Cut prior to opening. [5] From LIEBER AUGUSTIN and MISS CAPRICE as "Look in His Eyes." [6] In vocal score only. [7] Not the same song as in ZIEGFELD FOLLIES OF 1916. [8] Sheet music only.

1785 • HAVE I GOT A GIRL FOR YOU

OPENED: 10/29/1986   Theatre: Second Avenue
Musical   Off-Broadway: 78

Composer: Dick Gallagher
Lyricist: Dick Gallagher
Librettist: Joel Greenhouse; Penny Rockwell
Producer: George Grec; Frank Laraia; Helen Mintzer; David Singer
Director: Bruce Hopkins

Choreographer: Felton Smith; **Conductor:** Michael Rice; **Costumes:** Kenneth M. Yount; **Lighting Designer:** Jeffrey Schissler; **Musical Director:** Michael Rice; **Set Design:** Harry Darrow

Songs: Always for Science; Don't Open the Door; Gilfriends for Life; Have I Got a Girl for You; Hollywood; I Love Me; Mary's Lament; Monster's Song, The; Opera, The; Peasants' Song, The; Something

Cast: Semina De Laurentis; J.P. Dougherty; Angelina Fiordellsi; Walter Hudson; Gregory Jbara; Ritamarie Kelly; Dennis Parlato

1786 • HAVE I GOT ONE FOR YOU

OPENED: 01/07/1968   Theatre: Theatre Four
Musical   Off-Broadway: 1

Composer: Jerry Blatt
Lyricist: Jerry Blatt; Lonnie Burstein
Librettist: Jerry Blatt; Lonnie Burstein
Producer: Harlan P. Kleiman
Director: Roberta Sklar

Costumes: John Conklin; **Lighting Designer:** Peter Hunt; **Musical Director:** Alan Marlowe; **Orchestrations:** David Friedman; **Set Design:** John Conklin

Songs: Chapter One; Chicken Song, The; Fly Away; Getaway Quintet, The; Have I Got a Girl for You; I Should Stay; Imagine Me; It's Comin' True; Livin' in a Hole; My Dream Is Through; Nice Girl Like You, A; Ode to Marcello; Presentation, The; So It Goes; 3/4 Drag; Toad's Lament, The; What a Bore

Cast: Gloria De Haven; Anne Kaye; John Michael King; Ted Pugh

1787 • HAY FEVER

OPENED: 12/12/1985   Theatre: Music Box
Play   Broadway: 124

Author: Noel Coward
Producer: Roger Peters
Director: Brian Murray

Costumes: Jennifer von Mayrhauser; **Lighting Designer:** Arden Fingerhut; **Set Design:** Michael H. Yeargan

Songs: No, My Heart (C: John Kander; L: Fred Ebb)

Cast: Barbara Bryne; Mia Dillon; Roy Dotrice; Rosemary Harris; Robert Joy; Charles

Kimbrough; Deborah Rush; Campbell Scott; Caroline Seymour

1788 • HAYFOOT STRAWFOOT (1927)

OPENED: 1927
Musical   Unproduced

Songs: Kissing Eyes (C: Emmerich Kalman; Herbert Stothart; L: Oscar Hammerstein II; Otto Harbach)

Notes: No other information available.

1789 • HAYFOOT, STRAWFOOT (1938)

Notes: *See GENTLEMEN UNAFRAID.*

1790 • HAYSEED, THE

Notes: *See OUR NELL.*

1791 • HAZEL FLAGG

OPENED: 02/11/1953   Theatre: Mark Hellinger
Musical   Broadway: 190

Composer: Jule Styne
Lyricist: Bob Hilliard
Librettist: Ben Hecht
Producer: Anthony B. Farrell; Jule Styne
Director: David Alexander

Source: NOTHING SACRED (Film: Ben Hecht); **Choreographer:** Robert Alton; **Costumes:** Miles White; **Lighting Designer:** Harry Horner; **Musical Director:** Pembroke Davenport; **Orchestrations:** Don Walker; **Set Design:** Harry Horner; **Vocal Arranger:** Hugh Martin

Songs: Autograph Chant (An Autograph of Hazel Flagg); Every Street's a Boulevard in Old New York; Everybody Loves to Take a Bow; Hello, Hazel; How Do You Speak to an Angel?; I Feel Like I'm Gonna Live Forever; I'm Glad I'm Leaving; Laura De Maupassant; Little More Heart, A; Make the People Cry [1]; Money Burns a Hole in My Pocket [1]; My Wild Imagination [1]; Paris Gown (ballet); Rutland Bounce, The (Dance); Salomee (with Her Seven Veils); Something in the Wind [1]; Think How Many People Never Find Love [2]; Who Is the Bravest?; World Is Beautiful Today, The [3]; You're Gonna

Dance with Me, Willie

Cast: Helen Gallagher; John Howard; Thomas Mitchell; Sheree North; Benay Venuta; Jack Whiting

Notes: [1] Added after reopening. [2] Cut prior to opening. [3] Cut after reopening. Music later used in THE RED SONGS as "When It Happens to You."

1792 • HE AND SHE

OPENED: 1949
Musical   Unproduced

Composer: Vernon Duke
Lyricist: Ogden Nash

Songs: Darling, It's Been Fun, Hasn't It?; Here Comes the Spring; Little Love, a Little Money, A [1]; Nothing Ever Happens [2]; Welcome to My Heart; Woman and the Bottle, The; You Belong to the Night; You Bring Out the Worst in Me

Notes: [1] Used in THE LITTLEST REVUE. [2] Cut from THE LITTLEST REVUE.

1793 • HE CAME FROM MILWAUKEE

OPENED: 09/10/1910   Theatre: Casino
Musical   Broadway: 117

Composer: Louis A. Hirsch; Ben Jerome
Lyricist: Edward Madden
Librettist: Mark Swan
Producer: Lee Shubert; Sam S. Shubert

Costumes: Melville Ellis

Songs: Bring Back My Lena to Me (C/L: Irving Berlin; Ted Snyder); Come Back to Bohemia; Consequences; Coronation, The; If You Were There with Me [1]; In Gypsy Land; Love Is Like a Red, Red Rose; Man I Love, The; Merry Wedding Bells; Queen of the Jungle Show [1]; Sentimental Moon, The; There's an Aeroplane Air About You; There's Nothing on the Level Any More [1]; Tie a Red Ribbon on Me [1]; When We Are Married to You and Me; Zinga-Zula Man, The

Cast: Sam Bernard; Louis Harrison; Adele Rowland; Amelia Summerville; Winona Winter

Notes: Melville Ellis may have contributed numbers to this show. [1] Sheet music only.

1794 • HE DIDN'T WANT TO DO IT

OPENED: 08/20/1918   Theatre: Broadhurst
Musical   Broadway: 23

Composer: Silvio Hein
Lyricist: George Broadhurst
Librettist: George Broadhurst
Producer: George Broadhurst
Director: Clifford Brooke

Choreographer: Bert French; **Musical Director:** Theodore Stearns

Songs: Everyone He Swear at the Waiter; I'm Dying to Dance with Oscar; I'm Fond of the Girls; I'm Only a Girl from the City; It's the Scotch; Nothing Escapes Me; Song of the Trees, The; Song of the World, The; Spirit of the Carnival, The; What Mother Used to Say to Me; What Would You Do in a Case Like That?; You're the Only One for Me

Cast: Helen Shipman; Ned Sparks; Ernest Torrence

1795 • HE LOVED THE LADIES

OPENED: 05/10/1927   Theatre: Frolic
Play   Broadway: 7

Author: Herbert Hall Winslow
Producer: Lepane Amusement Co.
Director: Jack Roseleigh

Songs: Pretty Words (C: Harry R. Cohen; L: Harry D. Kerr)

Cast: Ada Lytton Barber; John Carmody; Isabel Dawn; Gertrude Fowler; Ernie Mack; Lyons Wickand

Notes: Play with song. No music mentioned in New York program.

1796 • HEAD OVER HEELS (1918)

OPENED: 08/29/1918   Theatre: Cohan
Musical   Broadway: 100

Composer: Jerome Kern
Lyricist: Edgar Allen Woolf

Librettist: Albert T. Viola; Edgar Allen Woolf
Producer: Henry W. Savage
Director: George Marion

Source: SHADOWS (Story: Nailbro Bartley);
Choreographer: Julian Mitchell; **Musical Director:** Harold Levey

Songs: All the World Is Swaying; Any Girl [2]; At the Dansant; Big Show, The; Butterflies of Fashion [1]; Charity Bazaar, The; Every Bee Has a Bud All His Own (C: Harold Levey); Funny Little Something; Girl for Each Day of the Week [1]; Head Over Heels; Houp-La; I Was Lonely; Ladies Have a Care; Let's Build a Little Nest [3] (L: Jerome Kern; Edgar Allen Woolf); Me; Mitzi's Lullaby; Moments of the Dance, The; (Today Is) Spring; Twenty-five Years Ago [1]; Vorderveele; With Type A-Ticking

Cast: Joe Keno; Boyd Marshall; Edward Sells

Notes: Titled HOUP-LA out of town. [1] Out Stamford 5/20/18. [2] Out Boston prior to opening. [3] Out Boston prior to opening. Same music as in same titled song in A POLISH WEDDING.

1797 • HEAD OVER HEELS (1981)

OPENED: 12/05/1981   Theatre: Harold Clurman
Musical   Off-Broadway: 22

Composer: Albert T. Viola
Lyricist: William S. Kolborne Jr.
Librettist: William S. Kolborne Jr.
Producer: Aristotle Productions
Director: Jay Binder

Source: WONDER HAT (Play: Kenneth Sawyer Goodman); **Choreographer:** Terry Rieser; **Costumes:** John Falabella; **Lighting Designer:** Jeff Davis; **Musical Director:** Herbert Kaplan; **Orchestrations:** John Clifton; **Set Design:** John Falabella; **Vocal Arranger:** Herbert Kaplan

Songs: Aqua Vitae; As If; Castles in the Sand; Could He Be You?; Finaletto; How Do You Keep Out of Love?; I'm in Love; Lullabye to Myself; New Loves for Old; Nowhere; Perfection

Cast: Elizabeth Austin; Dennis Bailey; John Cunningham; Gwyda DonHowe; Michael Wright

1798 • HEAD WAITERS (SECOND EDITION), THE

Musical

Producer: E.D. Stair

Songs: Art of Exercising, The; Conversational Dance; I Was Just Going to Ask You About That; Lenore; Martial Music of the Fife and Drum, The; Mary Jape; My Auto Girl; My Moonlight Lou; My Morning Glory; My Pony Pony Girl; New Pas; Perhaps Love's Dream Will Last Forever; Song of Summer Time, The; Susan Dear Sue; 'Tis You I Love; You're My Honey

Cast: Lucy Daly; Harry Vokes; Margaret Daly Vokes; Happy Ward

Notes: No other information available.

1799 • HEADIN' SOUTH

OPENED: 1928
Musical   Closed out of town

Composer: Jean Schwartz
Lyricist: Alfred Bryan
Librettist: Edgar Smith
Director: Cyrus D. Wood

Choreographer: LeRoy Prinz; **Costumes:** Ernest Schrapps; **Musical Director:** Max Meth; **Set Design:** Watson Barratt

Songs: Bit of Gingham, A; Dancing on the Levee; Draggin' the Chain; Fly Up to Heaven; Glorianna; Hot Choc'late; It's a Pleasure; June; Live and Love; Mammy Sue; Mister Mississippi; Pick a Pickaninny; Plantation Days; Sensational Stomp; Shining Shoes; Struttin' Hound

Cast: Mabel Elaine; Thomas K. Heath; Vivian Holt; James McIntyre; June Taylor

1800 • HEADS UP!

OPENED: 11/11/1929   Theatre: Alvin
Musical   Broadway: 144

Composer: Richard Rodgers
Lyricist: Lorenz Hart
Librettist: Jack McGowan; Paul Gerard Smith
Producer: Alex A. Aarons; Vinton Freedley
Director: Georgie Hale

Choreographer: Georgie Hale; **Costumes:** Kiviette; **Musical Director:** Alfred Newman; **Orchestrations:** Robert Russell Bennett; **Set Design:** Donald Oenslager

Songs: As Though You Were There [1]; Bootlegger's Chanty (We're an English Ship) [1]; Color of Her Eyes, The; Finaletto Scene 1 [1]; Harlem on the Sand [1]; Have You Been True to Me [5]; I Can Do Wonders with You [3]; It Must Be Heaven; It's a Man's World [1]; Jazz Reception (Kindly Nullify Your Fears) (Opening Act I — Me for You) [1]; Knees; Lass Who Loved a Sailor, The; Me for You; Mind Your P's and Q's [1]; Mother Grows Younger [6]; My Man Is on the Make; Now Go to Your Cabin (Finale Act I) [1]; Ongsay and Anceday; Playboy; Ship Without a Sail, A; Sky City [1]; Sweetheart, You Make Me Laugh [1]; They Sing! They Dance! They Speak! [5]; Three Bears, The [5]; Why Do You Suppose? [2]; You've Got to Surrender

Cast: Ray Bolger; Victor Moore; Barbara Newberry; Reynolds Sisters, The; Betty Starbuck; Janet Velie; Jack Whiting; **Pianist:** Phil Ohman

Notes: Titled ME FOR YOU out of town. When out of town the book was credited to Owen Davis. [1] Cut prior to opening. [2] Same music as "How Was I To Know?", which was cut from SHE'S MY BABY. [3] Cut prior to opening. Added to SIMPLE SIMON. [4] Cut prior to opening. Also cut from SPRING IS HERE. Used in EVER GREEN. [5] Cut prior to opening of ME FOR YOU. [6] Titled "Daughter Grows Older" in the London production.

1801 • HEART BREAKERS, THE

OPENED: 05/30/1911   Theatre: Princess
Musical   Chicago

Composer: Harold Orlob
Lyricist: Frank R. Adams; Will M. Hough
Librettist: Frank R. Adams; Will M. Hough
Director: Ned Wayburn

Choreographer: Ned Wayburn; **Musical Director:** Hilding Anderson; **Set Design:** J.C. Becher; Howard Tuttle

Songs: Antidotes (C: Melville Gideon); I'd Leave My Honeymoon for You; If I Had a Hundred Hearts; I've Never Had a Sweetheart (C: Melville Gideon); My Honolulu Honey Lou (C: Melville

Gideon); Never Lose Your Heart in the Bright Moonlight; Opening Chorus; Some Golden Day [1]; Somewhere She's Flirting with Someone; Songs You Used to Sing to the Girls You Used to Love, The; Two to Duluth (C: Melville Gideon)

Cast: George Damerel; Sallie Fisher; Harry Pilcer

Notes: Program of 05/30/11 used. [1] Sheet music only.

1802 • HEART O' MINE
Musical

Songs: Heart o' Mine (C: Herbert Spencer; L: Fleta Ian Brown)

Notes: No other information available.

1803 • HEART OF PADDY WHACK, THE
OPENED: 1914
Play   Closed out of town

Composer: Ernest R. Ball
Lyricist: J. Keirn Brennan
Author: Rachael Crothers
Producer: George M. Cohan; Sam Harris
Musical Director: George Lyding

Songs: Broth of a Boy, A; Heart of Paddy Whack, The; Irish Eyes of Blue (L: J. Edward Killalea); Little Bit of Heaven (Shure They Call It Ireland), A; Who Knows (L: Paul Laurence Dunbar)

Cast: Chauncey Olcott

1804 • HEARTBEATS
OPENED: 07/07/1993
Musical

Composer: Amanda McBroom
Lyricist: Amanda McBroom
Librettist: Amanda McBroom
Producer: Goodspeed Opera House
Director: Bill Castellino

Choreographer: Bill Castellino; **Costumes:** Charlotte M. Yetman; **Lighting Designer:** Richard Winkler; **Musical Director:** Ann-Carol Pence; **Orchestrations:** Bill Elliott; **Set Design:** Linda Hacker; **Vocal Arranger:** Gerald Sternbach

Songs: All This Time (C: Tom Snow); Anyone Can Do the Heartbreak (C: Tom Snow); Anything But the Truth (C: Gerald Sternbach); Dance; Hitch Hiker; Hurt Somebody Blues (C: Michele Brourman); I Like to Look (C: Gerald Sternbach); If This Is Love; I'm Fine; Jeff's Song (C: Gerald Sternbach); Jennifer's Song (C: Gerald Sternbach); Monday's Mail (Mail # 1) (C: Gerald Sternbach); Old Habits Die Hard (C: Michele Brourman); Putting Things Away; Reynosa; Rose, The; Serve 'Em Right; Ship in a Bottle; Shopper's Fugue (C: Gerald Sternbach); Somebody (C: Gerald Sternbach); Tell Me What You Want (C: Michele Brourman); Tuesday's Mail (Mail # 2) (C: Gerald Sternbach); Way of the Heart, The; When Love Grows Up

Cast: Gilles Chiasson; Nicholas Cokas; Hilary James; Julie Lea Johnson; Karen Mason; John Leslie Wolfe

Notes: Goodspeed Opera House.

1805 • HEARTS AND DIAMONDS
OPENED: 06/01/1926   Theatre: Strand
Musical   London: 46

Composer: Max Darewski; Bruno Granichstaedten
Lyricist: Graham John
Librettist: P.G. Wodehouse; Laurie Wylie
Producer: Arthur Bourchier
Director: Theodore Komisarjevsky

Source: DER ORLOV (Musical: Bruno Granichstaedten; Ernst Marischka); **Choreographer:** Edward Dolly; **Costumes:** Theodore Komisarjevsky; **Set Design:** Theodore Komisarjevsky

Cast: Louise Edvina; Anita Elson; Lupino Lane; Georges Metaxa

Notes: No other information available.

1806 • HEARTS ARE TRUMPS
OPENED: 02/21/1900   Theatre: Garden
Play   Broadway: 93

Author: Cecil Ralph
Producer: Charles Frohman

Songs: Hearts Are Trumps (C: Egbert Van Alstyne; L: Unknown)

Cast: Amelia Bingham; May Buckley; Cecil B. DeMille; Florence Howard; Wano Lamonthe; Sara Perry; Florence Robinson; Grant Stewart; Joseph A. Weber

Notes: Act III, Scene 4 featured a film made by William Paley and "reproduced by the famous Kalatechnoscope." This song may not have been used in the production, the sheet music says it is "dedicated to Charles Frohman's production." This was Cecil B. DeMille's debut as an actor.

1807 • HEARTS OF ERIN
Notes: *See EILEEN.*

1808 • HEARTS ON PARADE
OPENED: 1934
Musical

Songs: Haunting Me (C: Josef Myrow; L: Eddie De Lange)

Notes: No other information available.

1809 • HEATHEN!
OPENED: 05/21/1972   Theatre: Billy Rose
Musical   Broadway: 1

Composer: Eaton Magoon Jr.
Lyricist: Eaton Magoon Jr.
Librettist: Robert Helpmann; Eaton Magoon Jr.
Producer: Ken Gaston; Leonard J. Goldberg
Director: Lucia Victor

Choreographer: Sammy Bayes; **Costumes:** Bruce Harrow; **Dance Arranger:** Mel Marvin; **Lighting Designer:** Paul Sullivan; **Musical Director:** Clay Fullum; **Orchestrations:** Larry Fallon; **Set Design:** Jack Brown; **Vocal Arranger:** Mel Marvin

Songs: Aloha; Aloha Lord [2]; Aunties [1]; Battle Cry; Bring on the Heavenly Host [1]; Christianity; Church Ballet [1]; Comforts of Boston, The [2]; Eighth Day; Fire and Brimstone [2]; For You Brother [1]; Glory Be [2]; Heathen; House of Grass; I Hear Hawaii [2]; Important Things [1]; In English [1]; Kialalani; Kava Ceremony; Lei of Memories [3]; Man Among Men, A; More Better Go Easy; My Sweet Tomorrow; No Way in Hell; Paradise;

Rising Surf, The [1]; Sometimes It Rains [2]; Sounds of a World [1]; Spear Games; Suffer [2]; Surfing Ballet [2]; Tattoo Dance [1]; Thank Heaven for the Heathen [1]; This Is Someone I Could Love; Undressing Dance, The [1]; What Is Her Name?; Word of the Lord, The

Cast: Yolande Bavan; Edward Rambeau; Russ Thacker

Notes: Originally titled THANK HEAVEN FOR THE HEATHEN. Revised version titled ALOHA. [1] Cut prior to New York [2] From revised version ALOHA. [3] From revised version ALOHA. Also in 13 DAUGHTERS.

1810 • HEAVEN HELP THE ANGELS
Notes: *See ANGEL IN THE WINGS.*

1811 • HEAVEN ON EARTH (1948)
OPENED: 09/16/1948   Theatre: New Century
Musical   Broadway: 12

Composer: Jay Gorney
Lyricist: Barry Trivers
Librettist: Barry Trivers
Producer: Eddie Darling; Ned C. Litwack; Monte Proser
Director: John Murray Anderson

Choreographer: Nick Castle; **Costumes:** Raoul Pene du Bois; **Lighting Designer:** John Murray Anderson; **Musical Director:** Clay Warnick; **Orchestrations:** Robert Russell Bennett; **Set Design:** Raoul Pene du Bois; **Vocal Arranger:** Hugh Martin

Songs: Anything Can Happen; Apple Jack; Bench in the Park; Don't Forget to Dream; Gift Number; Heaven on Earth; Home Is Where the Heart Is; In the Back of a Hack; Letter, The; Musical Tour of the City; Push a Button in a Hutton; Wedding in the Park; What's the Matter with Our City?; You're So Near (So Near and Yet So Far); You're the First Cup of Coffee

Cast: David Burns; Irwin Corey; Peter Lind Hayes; Dorothy Jarnac

1812 • HEAVEN ON EARTH (1986)
Notes: *See OLYMPUS ON MY MIND.*

1813 • HEEBIE JEEBIES

OPENED: 06/03/1981   Theatre: Westside Arts
Revue   Off-Broadway: 37

Librettist: Mark Hampton; Stuart Ross
Producer: Peter Alsop; Joseph Butt; Spencer Tandy
Director: Stuart Ross

Choreographer: Stuart Ross; **Costumes:** Carol Oditz; **Lighting Designer:** Richard Winkler; **Musical Director:** Howard A. Roberts; **Orchestrations:** Christopher Bankey; **Set Design:** Michael Sharp; **Vocal Arranger:** Elise Bretton

Songs: Crazy People (C: James Monaco; L: Edgar Leslie); Darktown Strutter's Ball (C/L: Shelton Brooks); Dinah (C: Harry Akst; L: Sam M. Lewis; Joe Young); Everybody Loves My Baby (C/L: Jack Palmer; Spencer Williams); Goin' Home [3] (C/L: William Arms Fisher); Heebie Jeebies, The (C/L: Boyd Atkins); I'm Gonna Cry; Let Yourself Go [4] (C/L: Irving Berlin); Life Is Just a Bowl of Cherries [5] (C: Ray Henderson; L: Lew Brown); Minnie the Moocher's Wedding Day (C: Harold Arlen; L: Ted Koehler); Music Goes Round and Round, The (C: Edward Farley; Michael Riley; L: "Red" Hodgson); Nights When I Am Lonely; Nothing Is Sweeter Than You; Object of My Affection, The (C/L: Jimmy Grier; Coy Poe; Pinky Tomlin); Rock 'N' Roll; Sentimental Gentleman from Georgia (C: Frank Perkins; L: Mitchell Parish); Shout, Sister, Shout; Sing a Little Jingle [1] (C: Harry Warren; L: Mort Dixon); Spend an Evening in Caroline [2]; St. Louis Blues (C/L: W.C. Handy); That's How Rhythm Is Born; These Foolish Things [6] (C: Harry Link; Jack Strachey; L: Holt Marvell); Until the Real Thing Comes Along (C/L: Sammy Cahn; Saul Chaplin; L.E. Freeman); We Gotta Put the Sun Back in the Sky; We're on the Highway to Heaven; Whatja Do to Me; When I Take My Sugar to Tea (C: Sammy Fain; Pierre Norman; L: Irving Kahal); You Ought to Be in Pictures (C: Dana Suesse; L: Edward Heyman)

Cast: Memrie Innerarity; Audrey Lavine; Nancy McCall

Notes: No songs original to this production. [1] Part of a medley that included "The Best Things in Life Are Free," "Pennies from Heaven" and "I Can't Give You Anything but Love." Originally in the show CRAZY QUILT. [2] Cut prior to New York. [3] Music based on the Largo of the symphony "From the New World" by Anton Dvorak, op. 95. [4] From film FOLLOW THE FLEET. [5] From GEORGE WHITE'S SCANDALS. [6] From show SPREAD IT ABROAD.

1814 • HEELS TOGETHER

OPENED: 09/15/1942
Musical   Closed out of town

Composer: Harry Archer
Lyricist: Harlan Thompson
Librettist: Gladys Shelley; Harlan Thompson
Producer: Olneys, The
Director: Edgar MacGregor

Source: LITTLE JESSE JAMES (Musical: Harry Archer; Harlan Thompson); **Choreographer:** Dan Eckley; **Musical Director:** Alan Moras; **Set Design:** Elwell

Cast: Donald Burr; Lee Dixon; Joan Roberts

Notes: The score consisted of the songs included in the revival of LITTLE JESSE JAMES. *See LITTLE JESSE JAMES.*

1815 • HEIDI

OPENED: 10/01/1955   Theatre: NBC
TV Musical

Music Based On: Robert Schumann
Composer: Clay Warnick
Lyricist: Carolyn Leigh
Librettist: William Friedberg; Neil Simon
Producer: Max Liebman
Director: Max Liebman; Milton Lyon

Source: HEIDI (Novel: Johanna Spyri); **Arrangements:** Irwin Kostal; **Choreographer:** James Starbuck; **Costumes:** Paul du Pont; **Lighting Designer:** Fred McKinnon; **Musical Director:** Charles Sanford; **Set Design:** Frederick Fox; **Vocal Arranger:** Clay Warnick

Songs: At Such a Tender Age; Greener Pastures; Heidi; I Go My Way; I Love to Ramble; Out Comes Oom-Pa-Pa; Pick Yourself a Star; Table Manners; Yodel Song

Cast: Bil & Cora Baird Marionettes; Jeannie Carson; Robert Clary; Wally Cox; Richard Eastham; Bill Gibberson; Elsa Lanchester; Schmeed Trio; Jo Van Fleet; Natalie Wood

1816 • HELEN

OPENED: 11/22/1978   Theatre: AMAS
Musical   Off-Broadway: 12

Composer: Johnny Brandon
Lyricist: Johnny Brandon
Librettist: Lucia Victor
Producer: AMAS Repertory Theatre
Director: Lucia Victor

Source: ILIAD (Poetry: Homer); **Choreographer:** Bernard Johnson; **Costumes:** Bernard Johnson; **Dance Arranger:** Danny Holgate; **Lighting Designer:** Paul Sullivan; **Musical Director:** Danny Holgate; **Set Design:** Michael Meadows; **Vocal Arranger:** Carl Maultsby

Songs: Bite Your Tongue; Bring It on Home; Come on and Dance; Dance of the Golden Apple; Diplomacy; Do Us a Favor; Do What You Must; Good or Bad; Helen; Hold on Tight; Nothing Ever Happens in Greece; Somebody Touched Me; Somethin's Doin'; There Are Ways of Gettin' Things Done; You Never Know the Mind of a Woman; You've Got It

Cast: Pauletta Pearson; Fran Salisbury

1817 • HELEN GOES TO TROY

OPENED: 04/24/1944   Theatre: Alvin
Musical   Broadway: 96

Music Based On: Jacques Offenbach
Composer: Erich Wolfgang Korngold
Lyricist: Herbert Baker
Librettist: John Meehan Jr.; Gottfried Reinhardt
Producer: New Opera Company, The; Yolanda Mero-Irion
Director: Melville Cooper; Herbert Graf

Source: LA BELLE HELENE (Operetta: Jacques Offenbach); **Choreographer:** Leonide Massine; **Costumes:** Ladislas Czettel; **Lighting Designer:** Robert Edmond Jones; **Musical Director:** Erich Wolfgang Korngold; **Set Design:** Robert Edmond Jones

Songs: Advice to Husbands; Bring on the Concubines; Come to the Sacrifice; Come with Me; Dance of Procreation (dance); Dance of the Ladies in Waiting; Drinking Song and Dance; Entrance of the Kings; Extra! Extra!; Go to Naxos; Grecian Frieze; If Helen Only Knew; If Menelaus Only Knew It; Introduction of the Kings; Is It a

Dream?; Judgement of Paris, The; Little Chat, A; Love at Last; Opera Parody; Prologue to the Second Act; Shepherd Song, The; Sweet Helen; Take My Advice; Tsing-la-la; Waltz and Can-Can (dance); What Will the Future Say?; Where Is Love?

Cast: William Horne; Jarmila Novotna; Ernest Truex

1818 • HELEN OF TROY

Musical   Unproduced

Music Based On: Jacques Offenbach
Composer: Vernon Duke
Lyricist: Marshall Barer

Songs: I'm Called the King; Invocation to Venus; Judgement of Paris, The; No One Is Perfect; Queen Is Always on Display, A

1819 • HELEN OF TROY, NEW YORK

OPENED: 06/19/1923   Theatre: Selwyn
Musical   Broadway: 193

Composer: Harry Ruby
Lyricist: Bert Kalmar
Librettist: Marc Connelly; George S. Kaufman
Producer: George Jessel; Rufus LeMaire
Director: Bert French; Bertram Harrison

Musical Director: Fred Hoff; **Orchestrations:** Arthur Lange

Songs: Advertising; Cry Baby; Helen of Troy, New York; I Like a Big Town, I Like a Small Town; If I Never See You Again; It Was Meant to Be (1); It Was Meant to Be (2) [2] (C: W. Franke Harling; L: Lorenz Hart); Keep a Goin' (C/L: Byron Gay); Little Bit of Jazz, A; Look for the Happy Ending; My Ideal; Nijigo Novgo Glide; Somebody Like You Somebody Like Me [1] (C/L: Victor Arden; Phil Ohman); Up on Your Toes; What Makes a Business Man Tired?; What the Girls Will Wear

Cast: Roy Atwell; Helen Ford; Paul Frawley; Tom Lewis; Queenie Smith

Notes: [1] Out Baltimore 12/3/23. [2] Out Baltimore 12/3/23. Note song of same name in show.

1820 • HELL
Notes: *See FOLIES BERGERE COMPANY.*

1821 • HELLO 1921
OPENED: 1921
Revue

Composer: Marie Lucas; Frank Montgomery
Additional Music: Florence McClain; Jim
    Vaughn
Lyricist: Frank Montgomery
Additional Lyrics: Florence McClain; Jim
    Vaughn
Producer: Frank Montgomery

Arrangements: Marie Lucas; **Dance Arranger:**
    Frank Montgomery

Cast: Toots Hoy; Frank Montgomery; Blondie
    Robinson; Chinese Walker

Notes: No other information available.

1822 • HELLO AGAIN
OPENED: 01/30/1994   Theatre: Lincoln Center
Musical   Off-Broadway: 65

Composer: Michael John LaChiusa
Lyricist: Michael John LaChiusa
Librettist: Michael John LaChiusa
Director: Graciela Daniele

Source: LA RONDE (Play: Arthur Schnitzler);
    Choreographer: Graciela Daniele; **Costumes:**
    Toni-Leslie James; **Lighting Designer:** Peggy
    Eisenhauer; Jules Fisher; **Musical Director:**
    David Evans; **Orchestrations:** Michael Starobin;
    Set Design: Derek McLane

Songs: Ah, Maien Zeit!; Angel of Mercy; At the
    Prom; Bed Was Not My Own, The; Hello Again;
    I Gotta Little Time; In Some Other Life; Listen to
    the Music; Mistress of the Senator; Montage; One
    I Love, The; Rock with Rock; Safe; Silent Movie;
    Story of My Life; Tom; We Kiss; Zei Gezent

Cast: Judy Blazer; Carolee Carmello; John Dossett;
    Malcolm Gets; John Cameron Mitchell; Donna
    Murphy; Michael Park; Dennis Parlato; Michele
    Pawk; David A. White

Notes: No songs listed in program.

1823 • HELLO ALEXANDER
OPENED: 10/07/1919   Theatre: 44th Street
Musical   Broadway: 56

Composer: Jean Schwartz
Lyricist: Alfred Bryan
Librettist: Edgar Smith; Emily M. Young
Producer: J.J. Shubert; Lee Shubert

Choreographer: Allan K. Foster

Songs: Baseball; Beale Street Blues; Cleopatra [3]
    (C: Harry Tierney); Ghost of Old Black Joe; Give Me
    the South All the Time; Have a Smile (dance) [2];
    Hawaiian Moonlight; Hush-a-Bye My Baby; I'm
    Glad I'm from Dixie; Juno, My Honeymoon Girl [2];
    Mississippi Lullaby [4]; My Choc'late Soldier
    Sammy Boy [2]; My Curley Headed Baby; My Isle
    of Golden Dreams [1] (C: Walter Blaufuss; L: Gus
    Kahn); North and South [2]; Old Fashioned Rag;
    Old Oaken Bucket with Love [2]; On the Road to
    Calais [4]; Pantomime Baseball; (Pretty Up, Pretty
    Up) Pretty Baby; Rock-a-Bye- Baby; Roses of
    Picardy; Shimmying Everywhere [2]; Swanee
    Glide; Tampa Bay; Tell Me; Those Dixie Melodies;
    Two Lips from Georgia; Up in the Air; When
    Those Mason-Dixon Minstrels Hit Town; Why Are
    Chickens So High?; Yazoo Rag; Yip! Yip!; You're
    Living Right Next Door to Heaven When You Live
    in Dixieland

Cast: Johnny Burke; Lou Clayton; Gilda Gray;
    McIntyre & Heath; Eva Puck; Dan Quinlan;
    Sammy White

Notes: Some of these songs were probably well
    known songs interpolated into the score. [1]
    Sheet music only. Also in OH, LOOK! [2]
    Out-of-town program only. [3] Out-of-town
    program only. Also in SINBAD. Music may be
    by Jean Schwartz. [4] Sheet music only.

1824 • HELLO AMERICA
OPENED: 1918
Musical   Closed out of town

Composer: Nat Osborne
Lyricist: W.H. Smith
Librettist: Sam Dody; Sam M. Lewis; Frank L.
    Wakefield
Director: Joe Hurtig

Choreographer: Arthur Conrad

Songs: Allies Forever; Borneo; Clothing; Finale; Follow Me; Hello America; Hello America Minstrels; I'm a Real American Girl; I'm Lonesome, Dear; Mammie's Going to Kiss Your Tears Away; Mother, Dixie and You; Oh, For the Life of a Chorus Girl; Pickaninny's Paradise, The [1] (L: Sam Erlich); Rehearsal; Simple Little Ingenue; Sweet Emmaline, My Gal; Sweet Little Buttercup [2]; Ventriloquism; Washington; When the Young Men Are Away; Whiting; You Can't Do That to an Irishman

Cast: Arthur Conrad; Sam Dody; Kitty Giasco; Ina Hayward; Sam M. Lewis; Primrose Sisters; George White

Notes: Program of Atlantic City 4/29/18. [1] Sheet music only. [2] The popular song "Sweet Little Buttercup" by Herman Paley and Alfred Bryan was written in 1917. This might be that song interpolated into the score.

1825 • HELLO BEAUTIFUL

OPENED: 1939   Theatre: International Casino

Revue   Nightclub

Producer: Georgie Hale

Songs: To You (C/L: Benny Davis; Tommy Dorsey; Ted Shapiro)

Cast: Harry Richman

Notes: Sheet music only.

1826 • HELLO, BROADWAY!

OPENED: 12/25/1914   Theatre: Astor
Musical   Broadway: 123

Composer: George M. Cohan
Lyricist: George M. Cohan
Librettist: George M. Cohan
Producer: George M. Cohan; Sam Harris

Choreographer: James Gorman; Ned Wayburn; **Costumes:** Cora MacGeachy; **Musical Director:** Charles J. Gebest

Songs: Barnum & Bailey Rag; Broadway Tipperary; Chinese Celebration (C: Jean Schwartz); Down by the Erie Canal; Hello, Broadway; Hippodrome Folks; I Wanted to

Come to Broadway; It Pays to Advertise; Jesse James Glide, The; Look Out for Mr. Wu; My Flag; My Miracle Man; Pygmalion Roses; Sneaky Steps; That Old Fashioned Cake Walk; Those Irving Berlin Melodies; Two Dandy Darkies; Two Playhouses, The

Cast: George M. Cohan; William Collier; Tom Dingle; Louise Dresser; Florence Moore; Lawrence Wheat; Peggy Wood

1827 • HELLO DADDY!

OPENED: 12/26/1928   Theatre: Mansfield
Musical   Broadway: 196

Composer: Jimmy McHugh
Lyricist: Dorothy Fields
Librettist: Herbert Fields
Producer: Lew Fields
Director: John Murray Anderson; Alexander Leftwich

Source: THE HIGH COST OF LOVING (Play: Frank Mandel); **Choreographer:** Russell Markert; **Costumes:** Charles LeMaire; **Musical Director:** Max Steiner; **Orchestrations:** Maurice DePackh; Arthur Johnstone; Stephen Jones; Fudd Livingston; Hans Spialek; **Set Design:** Herman Rosse

Songs: As Long as We're in Love; Futuristic Rhythm; I Want Plenty of You; In a Great Big Way; Let's Sit and Talk about You; Maybe Means Yes; Out Where the Blues Begin; Party Line; Three Little Maids from School; Your Disposition Is Mine

Cast: Lew Fields; George Hassell; Allen Kearns; Mary Lawlor; Ben Pollack and His Orchestra; Betty Starbuck

1828 • HELLO, DOLLY!

OPENED: 01/16/1964   Theatre: St. James
Musical   Broadway: 2844

Composer: Jerry Herman
Lyricist: Jerry Herman
Librettist: Michael Stewart
Producer: David Merrick
Director: Gower Champion

Source: MATCHMAKER, THE (Play: Thornton Wilder); **Choreographer:** Gower Champion; **Costumes:** Freddy Wittop; **Dance Arranger:**

Peter Howard; **Lighting Designer:** Jean Rosenthal; **Musical Director:** Shepard Coleman; **Orchestrations:** Philip J. Lang, **Set Design:** Oliver Smith; **Vocal Arranger:** Shepard Coleman

Songs: Before the Parade Passes By (2) [5]; Before the Parade Passes By (1) [5] (C: Charles Strouse; L: Lee Adams); Before the Parade Passes By (3) [9]; Come and Be My Butterfly [1]; Dancing; Elegance [6] (C/L: Jerry Herman; Bob Merrill); Ernestina [2]; Goodbye Song, The [2]; Hello, Dolly!; I Put My Hand In; It Only Takes a Moment; It Takes a Woman; Love, Look in My Window [3]; Motherhood [7] (C/L: Jerry Herman; Bob Merrill); No, a Million Times, No! [2]; Penny in My Pocket [2]; Polka Contest, The [4]; Put on Your Sunday Clothes; Ribbons Down My Back; So Long, Dearie; We Only Remember [8]; World, Take Me Back [3]; You're a Damned Exasperating Woman [2]

Cast: Eileen Brennan; David Burns; Mary Jo Catlett; Carol Channing; Gordon Connell; Jerry Dodge; David Hartman; Charles Karel; Sondra Lee; Alice Playten; Charles Nelson Reilly

Notes: [1] Cut after opening. [2] Cut prior to New York. [3] Added in 1970, although originally written prior to actual production. [4] Added after opening. [5] Strouse and Adams came out of town to help with the score. They wrote a song titled "Before the Parade Passes By" but it wasn't used. Herman then took the title and wrote his own original song. [6] Written by Merrill for NEW GIRL IN TOWN. Song revised by Herman for HELLO, DOLLY! [7] Merrill's song revised by Herman. [8] Not used. Later put into HENRY, SWEET HENRY. [9] Not used.

1829 • HELLO EVERYBODY

OPENED: 1923
Revue   Closed out of town

Composer: J. Fred Coots
Lyricist: McElbert Moore
Librettist: Albert Klein

Choreographer: David Bennett; **Set Design:** H. Robert Law

Songs: Ali Baba; Dickey Birds; Etiquette; Hawaiian Night in Dixie; Hoffmann Belles (C/L: Max Hoffmann); I Want to Step; Japanese Willow [1];

On the Screen; Red Riding Hood on Broadway [1]; Star of Stars; While I'm Swinging

Cast: Gertrude Hoffman; Harry Lauder; Willie Lauder

Notes: Program from Newark 1/23/23. [1] ASCAP/Library of Congress only.

1830 • HELLO, LESTER!
Notes: *See JIM JAM JEMS.*

1831 • HELLO, LOLA

OPENED: 01/12/1926   Theatre: Eltinge
Musical   Broadway: 47

Composer: William B. Kernell
Lyricist: Dorothy Donnelly
Librettist: Dorothy Donnelly
Producer: Messrs. Shubert
Director: Seymour Felix

Source: SEVENTEEN (Novel: Booth Tarkington); **Source:** SEVENTEEN (Play: Stannard Mears; Stanislaus Stange); **Choreographer:** Seymour Felix; **Costumes:** Ernest Schrapps; **Musical Director:** Charles Sieger

Songs: Baxter's Party; Bread and Butter and Sugar; Don't Stop; Five Foot-Two; Grau Brae Nicht; Hello, Cousin Lola; High Toned Trot [1]; I Know Something; In the Dark; Keep It Up; Little Boy Blue; Lullaby; My Baby Talk Lady; My Brother Willie; She Never Spent a Cent on Me [1]; Shush Katy [2]; Sophie; Step on the Gasoline; Story Book Land [2]; Summertime, The; Swinging on the Gate; Take 'Em to the Door Blues [2]; That Certain Party; Water, Water, Wildflowers; While We Go Waltzing Around [1]

Cast: Edythe Baker; Elisha Cook Jr.; Nanette Flack; Jay C. Flippen; Richard Keene; Margaret Sullavan; Marjorie White

Notes: [1] Out Newark 11/16/25. [2] Out Washington, D.C. 11/29/25.

1832 • HELLO MUDDAH, HELLO FADDUH

OPENED: 12/05/1992   Theatre: Circle in the Square Downtown
Revue   Off-Broadway: 235

Lyricist: Allan Sherman
Librettist: Douglas Bernstein; Rob Krausz
Producer: David A. Blumberg; Diane F. Krausz; Jennifer R. Manocherian
Director: Michael Leeds

Choreographer: Michael Leeds; **Costumes:** Susan Branch; **Lighting Designer:** Howard Werner; **Musical Director:** David Evans; **Orchestrations:** David Lawrence; **Set Design:** Michael E. Downs; **Vocal Arranger:** David Evans

Songs: Ballad of Harry Lewis, The; Crazy Downtown; Did I Ever Really Live? [1] (C: Albert Hague); Disraeli; Down the Drain [1] (C: Albert Hague); Good Advice; Grow Mrs. Goldfarb; Harvey and Sheila; Harvey Bloom; Hello Muddah, Hello Fadduh; Here's to the Crabgrass; I Can't Dance; Jump Down, Spin Around; Kiss of Myer; Like Yours [1] (C: Albert Hague); Mexican Hat Dance; No One's Perfect; One Hippopotami; Opening Goulash; Phil's Medley; Sarah Jackman; Shake Hands with Your Uncle Max; Sir Greenbaum's Madrigal

Cast: Stephen Berger; Tovah Feldshuh; Jason Graae; Paul Kreppel; Mary Testa

Notes: No original songs in this show. The Sherman lyrics were parodies set to previously existing songs. [1] From THE FIG LEAVES ARE FALLING.

1833 • HELLO PAREE (1919)

OPENED: 1919
Musical   Closed out of town

Composer: John O. Grant
Lyricist: John O. Grant; Truehart
Producer: Hart Operating Co.

Songs: Belgian Rose; Ching Chong; Cotton Pickers Ball; Daddy Mine; Don't Be Cross with Me; Dreamy Egypt; I Want a Doll; In Love with All the Girls; Lump of Sugar; Mammy's Chocolate Soldier; Night Boat to Albany; Oui Oui Marie; Pray for Sunshine; Sis, Boom, Ah; Where Have You Been Hiding; Yanks Are at It Again, The

Cast: Elsie Donnelly; John O. Grant; Emily Nice; Nellie Nice; Ralph Rogers

Notes: Burlesque musical. Several of these songs are probably popular songs of the day.

1834 • HELLO, PAREE (1954)

OPENED: 11/24/1954
Revue   Closed out of town

Composer: Michael Emer
Lyricist: Alex Alstone; Mel Martin; Charles Trenet
Producer: William L. Taub
Director: Mervyn Nelson

Choreographer: Tommy Wonder; **Costumes:** Georgie Drew; **Musical Director:** Otto Frolich; **Orchestrations:** Bernie Thrall; **Set Design:** Nikki Eastman

Songs: Absinthe; Come with Me; Hello, Paree; La Chanteuse; La Seine; Montparnasse; Oh, No; Petite Mama

Cast: Michel Allard; Hope Hampton

1835 • HELLO PARIS (1911)

OPENED: 08/19/1911   Theatre: Folies Bergere
Musical   Broadway: 38

Composer: J. Rosamond Johnson
Lyricist: J. Leubrie Hill
Librettist: William Le Baron
Producer: Henry B. Harris; Jesse Lasky
Director: Ned Wayburn

Songs: Aeroplane Rag, That; Fascination Waltz; Frisco Frizz, The (C: Ned Wayburn; L: Collin Davis); Hello Paris; Look Me Over; Loving Moon; Sentimental Tommy (C: A. Baldwin Sloane; L: E. Ray Goetz); Siberian Whirl, The; You're the Nicest Little Girl I Ever Knew

Cast: Nita Allen; Zeke Colvan; Minerva Coverdale; James J. Morton; Harry Pilcer

Notes: *Also see A LA BROADWAY*, which was the second part of this show.

1836 • HELLO, PARIS (1930)

OPENED: 11/15/1930   Theatre: Shubert
Musical   Broadway: 33

Composer: Maurie Rubens; Russell Tarbox
Lyricist: Frank Bannister; Charles O. Locke
Librettist: Edgar Smith
Producer: Messrs. Shubert
Director: Ben Holmes

Source: THEY HAD TO SEE PARIS (Novel: Homer Croy); **Choreographer:** Pal'mere Brandeaux; George Cunningham; **Musical Director:** Tom Jones; **Set Design:** Watson Barratt

Songs: Dance Your Troubles Away; Deep Paradise (C: Russell Tarbox; L: Charles O. Locke); Every Bit of You [1] (C/L: Kenneth Fried; Adrian Samish); Free, White and Twenty-One; Give It; Gotta Have Hips Now (C: Russell Tarbox; L: Charles O. Locke); I Know I Ought to Say No; I Stumbled Over You [1] (C: Maurie Rubens; L: Henry Dagand); I'll Admit [1] (C: Maurie Rubens; L: Henry Dagand); Love Racketeer; Lucky Little Me and You; Mr. Hot Stuff; O-K-L-A-H-O-M-Λ; Paris; Prairie Blues (C: Russell Tarbox; L: Charles O. Locke); Roll Along, Covered Wagon; Rosie Road; Unaccustomed As I Am

Cast: Mary Adams; Charles Columbus; Lois Deppe; Jack Good; Georgia Hayes; Nat C. Hines; Claire Hooper; Jubilee Singers, The; Louis LaGranna; Maurice LePue; Olga Markoff; Stella Mayhew; Don Morrell; Riva Reyes; J. Clifford Rice; Chic Sale; Marie Starner; Polly Walker; Ethel Wilson

Notes: During tryouts lyrics attributed to Ned Washington and Charles O. Locke and the music to Tarbox and Michael Cleary. Also known as SO THIS IS PARIS. [1] Not in program.

1837 • HELLO, SUCKER

OPENED: 07/08/1969
Musical   Closed out of town

Composer: Wilson Stone
Lyricist: Wilson Stone
Librettist: Larry B. Marks; Robert Ennis Turoff
Producer: Shelly Gross; Lee Guber
Director: Larry Fuller

Choreographer: Larry Fuller; **Costumes:** Evelyn Norton Anderson; **Lighting Designer:** Lester Tapper; **Musical Director:** Herbert Hecht; **Set Design:** Gordon Micunis

Songs: Al Smith for President [1]; Approach the Lady Gently; Be My Guest; Beautiful Buddies; Finale, Act I [1]; Hello, Sucker; Hello to France; I Know a Lot About You; If Mama Could See Us; I'm the Little Girl; Nobody Nobody Knows; One Girl; Rally, The; Somewhere; Texas Guinan's Playground [1]; Too Hot for Paris; Top of the

Climb; We're Off to Guinan's; Where Is That Lucky Star?

Cast: Joseph Mascolo; Tom Mixon; Dennis Patrick; Ed Penn; Martha Raye

Notes: [1] Out Forth Worth, Texas. The show opened at Casa Manana with Ruta Lee in the lead. This was a bio-musical of Texas Guinan.

1838 • HELLO, SUE

OPENED: 1922
Musical   Chicago

Composer: William Overstreet
Librettist: Billy King
Producer: Billy King

Cast: Billy Gunn; Billy King; Rastus Lee

Notes: No other information available.

1839 • HELLO, YOURSELF!!!!

OPENED: 10/30/1928   Theatre: Casino
Musical   Broadway: 87

Composer: Richard Myers
Lyricist: Leo Robin
Librettist: Walter De Leon
Producer: George Choos
Director: Clarke Silvernail

Choreographer: Dave Gould; **Costumes:** Charles LeMaire; **Musical Director:** Paul Yartin; **Orchestrations:** Maurice DePackh; **Set Design:** P. Dodd Ackerman; **Vocal Arranger:** Fred C. Buck Jr.; Frank Hower; Paul Mertz

Songs: Bobby's Nightmare; Daily Dozen; Finale Act I; He Man; Hello, Yourself; I Want the World to Know; Jericho [1]; Say That You Love Me; Tired of It All; To the Dance [1]; True Blue; We Might Play Tiddle De Winks; You've Got a Way with You

Cast: Blaine Cordner; Lucy Monroe; Al Sexton; Fred Waring & His Pennsylvanians

Notes: [1] Out Philadelphia 10/15/1928.

1840 • HELLZAPOPPIN (1938)

OPENED: 09/22/1938   Theatre: 46th Street
Revue   Broadway: 1404

467

Composer: Sammy Fain
Lyricist: Charles Tobias
Librettist: Chic Johnson; Ole Olsen
Additional Dialogue: Tom McKnight
Producer: Chic Johnson; Ole Olsen; Messrs. Shubert
Director: Edward Duryea Dowling

Choreographer: Gae Foster; **Costumes:** Mahieu; Joan Personette; Veronica; **Musical Director:** Harold Stern; **Vocal Arranger:** Philip Ellis

Songs: Abe Lincoln (C/L: Alfred Hayes; Earl Robinson); Blow a Balloon Up to the Moon; Boomps-a-Daisy [1] (L: Annette Mills); Fuddle-Dee-Duddle (Funny Little Tune); Gay Nineties, The; Havana for a Night [1] (C: Gonzalo Curiel; L: Oscar Hammerstein II); Hellzapoppin'; It's Time to Say 'Aloha'; Mosquito [1]; Shaganola; Strolling Thru the Park; We Won't Let It Happen Here (C: Don George; L: Teddy Hall); When McGregor Sings Off Key; When You Look in Your Looking Glass (C: Paul Mann; Stephen Weiss; L: Sam M. Lewis)

Cast: Aloha Maids, The; Dewey Barton; Charioteers, The; Bettymae Crane; Beverly Crane; Theo Hardeen; Chic Johnson; Ray Kinney; George Mann; Walter Nilsson; Ole Olsen; Radio Rogues, The; Hal Sherman; Whitey Steppers; Shirley Wayne

Notes: [1] Added during run.

1841 • HELLZA-POPPIN (1967)

OPENED: 04/1967
Revue   Closed out of town

Composer: Marian Grudeff; Raymond Jessel
Lyricist: Marian Grudeff; Raymond Jessel
Producer: Alexander Cohen
Director: Jerry Adler

Choreographer: Buddy Schwab; **Costumes:** Raoul Pene du Bois; **Dance Arranger:** John Berkman; **Lighting Designer:** Jules Fisher; **Musical Director:** John Berkman; **Orchestrations:** Don Walker; **Set Design:** Raoul Pene du Bois

Songs: Air Strip; Central Park; Hellzapoppin'; Just Like an Old Time Movie; Montreal; Undeniably Mine

Cast: Will B. Able; Jackie Alloway; Jack Fletcher;

Luba Lisa; Brandon Maggart; Soupy Sales; Ted Thurston

Notes: No songs listed in program. A presentation at Expo 67, Montreal Canada.

1842 • HELLZAPOPPIN (1976)

OPENED: 11/22/1976
Revue   Closed out of town

Composer: Hank Beebe
Lyricist: Bill Heyer
Librettist: Hank Beebe; Abe Burrows; Bill Heyer
Producer: Alexander H. Cohen; Jerome Minskoff; Maggie Minskoff
Director: Jerry Adler

Choreographer: Donald Saddler; **Costumes:** Alvin Colt; **Dance Arranger:** Gordon Lowry Harrell; **Lighting Designer:** Robert Randolph; **Musical Director:** John Lesko; **Orchestrations:** Ralph Burns; **Set Design:** Robert Randolph

Songs: Back to Him; Bouncin' Back for More [1] (C: Cy Coleman; L: Carolyn Leigh); Dare to Do; Eighth Avenue (C: Jule Styne; L: Carolyn Leigh); Hello Mom; Hellzapoppin (C: Jule Styne; L: Carolyn Leigh); Husband, a Love, a Wife, A; Hymn to Her, A; I'm All Yours [3] (C: Jule Styne; L: Carolyn Leigh); Just Because We're Kids [2]; Let's Put a Man on the Sun; Make Way for a Star [3] (C: Jule Styne; L: Carolyn Leigh); Miracle Happened, A; My Jug [2]; Once I've Got My Cane; One to a Customer (C: Jule Styne; L: Carolyn Leigh); That Chaplin Man [3] (C: Jule Styne; L: Carolyn Leigh); Top That If You Can [3] (C: Jule Styne; L: Carolyn Leigh); What Did You Do? [2] (C: Jule Styne; L: Carolyn Leigh)

Cast: Jill Choder; Herbert Edelman; Mercedes Ellington; Joey Faye; Justine Johnston; Jerry Lewis; Brandon Maggart; Michael Mann; Lynn Redgrave; Bob Williams

Notes: Closed 1/22/77 at the Colonial Theatre in Boston. [1] Written for WILDCAT but not used. [2] Not in program. [3] ASCAP/Library of Congress only.

1843 • HELLZAPOPPIN OF 1949

OPENED: 1949
Revue

Director: Leon Leonidoff

Choreographer: Dave Gould; **Musical Director:** Dave Schooler; **Vocal Arranger:** Pembroke Davenport

Notes: No other information available.

1844 • HELTER SKELTER
OPENED: 04/06/1899   Theatre: Weber & Fields
                     Broadway Music Hall
Musical   Broadway

Composer: John Stromberg
Lyricist: Harry B. Smith
Librettist: Edgar Smith

Notes: No program available.

1845 • IIEN-PECKS, THE
OPENED: 02/04/1911   Theatre: Broadway
Musical   Broadway: 137

Composer: A. Baldwin Sloane
Lyricist: Vincent Bryan; E. Ray Goetz
Librettist: Glen MacDonough
Producer: Lew Fields

Songs: Don't Forget the Beau You Left at Home; Drifting (L: E. Ray Goetz); He's the Wonder of Them All; In the Shadows [1] (C: Herman Finck); It's Not the Trick Itself, but It's the Tricky Way It's Done; It's the Shirt; I've Had a Lovely Time, Good Night; June; Just Tell Me with Your Eyes; Little Italy; Manicure Girl, The (C: Jerome Kern; L: Frederick Day); Something Tells Me I Am Going to Love You; Toddling the Todalo; Try This on Your Pianna Anna (L: E. Ray Goetz); White Light Alley (L: E. Ray Goetz); Wine Maid Divine (L: E. Ray Goetz)

Cast: Vernon Castle; Lew Fields; Gertrude Quinlan; Blossom Seeley; Sam Watson

Notes: No program available. [1] Sheet music only.

1846 • HENRY, SWEET HENRY
OPENED: 10/23/1967   Theatre: Palace
Musical   Broadway: 80

Composer: Bob Merrill

Lyricist: Bob Merrill
Librettist: Nunnally Johnson
Producer: Edward Specter; Norman Twain
Director: George Roy Hill

Source: WORLD OF HENRY ORIENT, THE (Novel: Nora Johnson); **Choreographer:** Michael Bennett; **Costumes:** Alvin Colt; **Dance Arranger:** William Goldenberg; Marvin Hamlisch; **Lighting Designer:** Robert Randolph; **Musical Director:** Shepard Coleman; **Orchestrations:** Eddie Sauter; **Set Design:** Robert Randolph; **Vocal Arranger:** Shepard Coleman

Songs: Academic Fugue; Agreer, The [1]; Dearest Darling [1]; Do You Ever Go to Boston?; Forever; Frantically Romantic [2]; Guess What [2]; Henry, Sweet Henry; Here I Am; I Wonder How It Is (To Dance with a Boy); I'm Blue Too; In Some Little World; Knickerbocker Grey's March [3]; Life Oh Life [3]; Love of My Life [1]; Mommy Cat [2]; My Kind of Person [1]; Nobody Steps on Kafritz; One More Day of Sunshine [3]; People Watchers; Pillar to Post; Poor Little Person; Pretty Thing [2]; Reckless Rooster March [3]; Some Little World [3]; Somebody, Someplace [1]; To Be Artistic; Weary Near to Dyin'; Whereas; (You Look Like a) Woman in Love (to Me); You Might Get to Like Me [1]

Cast: Don Ameche; Milo Boulton; Carol Bruce; Louise Lasser; Alice Playten; Neva Small; Robin Wilson

Notes: [1] Cut prior to opening. [2] Out Detroit 8/18/67. [3] ASCAP/Library of Congress only.

1847 • HER FAMILY TREE
OPENED: 12/27/1920   Theatre: Lyric
Musical   Broadway: 90

Composer: Seymour Simons
Lyricist: Seymour Simons
Librettist: Bugs Baer; Al Weeks
Producer: Nora Bayes
Director: Hassard Short

Choreographer: Carl Randall; **Costumes:** Shirley Barker; **Musical Director:** Arthur Gutman; **Orchestrations:** Arthur Gutman; **Set Design:** P. Dodd Ackerman

Songs: As We Sow; Boom Whee!; Broadway Blues, The [2]; Gold- Diggers, The; I Love You;

Love Is Come to Me [1]; No Other Gal; Ouija Board; Remember the Rose [2] (L: Sidney D. Mitchell); Romantic Knight, A; When Cupid Flys Away [1]; Where Tomorrows Begin; Why Worry?

Cast: Nora Bayes; Frank Morgan; Randall Sisters, The; Donald Sawyer; Julius Tannen

Notes: [1] Sheet music only. [2] Added after opening.

1848 • HER FIRST ROMAN
OPENED: 10/20/1968   Theatre: Lunt-Fontanne
Musical   Broadway: 17

Composer: Ervin Drake
Lyricist: Ervin Drake
Librettist: Ervin Drake
Producer: Joseph Cates; Henry Fownes
Director: Derek Goldby

Source: CAESAR AND CLOEPATRA (Play: George Bernard Shaw); **Choreographer:** Dania Krupska; **Costumes:** Michael Annals; **Dance Arranger:** Peter Howard; **Lighting Designer:** Martin Aronstein; **Musical Director:** Peter Howard; **Orchestrations:** Don Walker; **Set Design:** Michael Annals; **Vocal Arranger:** Don Walker

Songs: Caesar Is Wrong (C: Jerry Bock; L: Sheldon Harnick); Dangerous Age, The; Hail Sphinx; He Pleasures Me [1]; Her First Roman; I Cannot Make Him Jealous; I Don't Know Where I'm Going [1]; I Fell In with Evil Companions [1]; In Vino Veritas; Just for Today; Kind Old Gentleman (C: Jerry Bock; L: Sheldon Harnick); Let Me Lead the Way [1]; Magic Carpet; Many Young Men from Now; Mummy That Was, The [1]; Parable of the Monkey, The [1]; Pleasure Him [2]; Ptolemy (C: Jerry Bock; L: Sheldon Harnick); Rome; Save Me from Caesar; Things We Think We Are, The; What Are We Doing in Egypt?; When My Back Is to the Wall [1]; Wrong Man, The [1]

Cast: Cal Bellini; Diana Corto; Richard Kiley; Bruce MacKay; Claudia McNeil; Brooks Morton; Barbara Sharma; Leslie Uggams

Notes: [1] Cut prior to opening. [2] ASCAP/Library of Congress only.

1849 • HER LITTLE HIGHNESS
OPENED: 10/13/1913   Theatre: Liberty
Musical   Broadway: 16

Composer: Reginald De Koven
Lyricist: Channing Pollock; Rennold Wolf
Librettist: Channing Pollock; Rennold Wolf
Producer: Werba & Luescher
Director: George Marion; Julian Mitchell

Source: SUCH A LITTLE QUEEN (Play: Channing Pollock)

Songs: Ancient Rules of Observing Etiquette; C.O.D.; Come Along and Tell Me; Czardas; Drink and Be Merry; Heimweh; Ladies, The; Mary Ann; My Fairy Prince; My King Can Do No Wrong [1]; One Little Girl; Philadelphia Press, The [2]; Practical Patriots; Romanza [2]; Self Made Man, A; When the Landlord Comes Knocking at the Door; When the Queen Wakes Up in the Morning [1]; When You're Sweet Sixteen

Cast: Mitzi Hajos; Wallace McCutcheon; Mae Murray

Notes: [1] Out Boston 9/6/13. [2] Sheet music only.

1850 • HER MASTER'S VOICE
OPENED: 10/23/1933   Theatre: Plymouth
Play   Broadway: 220

Author: Clare Kummer
Producer: Max Gordon
Director: Worthington Miner

Set Design: Raymond Sovey

Songs: Only with You (C/L: Clare Kummer)

Cast: Laura Hope Crews; Frances Fuller; Elizabeth Patterson; Roland Young

1851 • HER REGIMENT
OPENED: 11/12/1917   Theatre: Broadhurst
Musical   Broadway: 40

Composer: Victor Herbert
Lyricist: William Le Baron
Librettist: William Le Baron
Producer: Joseph Weber
Director: Fred G. Latham

Musical Director: Fritz Stahlberg

Songs: American Serenade, The; Art Song; As the Years Roll By; Devil and the Deep Blue Sea, The; Finale Act I; Finale Act II; Girl Behind the Gun, The [1]; If Things Were What They Seem [1]; Little Farm in Normandy, A; Nerves [1]; Oh, My!; Opening Ensemble; Soldier Men; Some Day; Superlative Love; 'Twixt Love and Duty; Vive la France!; You Never Can Tell How a Marriage Will Take

Cast: Donald Brian; Hugh Chilvers; Pauline French; Josie Intropodi; Sidney Jarvis; Audrey Maple; Frank Moulan

Notes: [1] ASCAP/Library of Congress only.

1852 • HER SOLDIER BOY
OPENED: 12/06/1916   Theatre: Astor
Musical   Broadway: 198

Composer: Emmerich Kalman; Sigmund Romberg
Lyricist: Rida Johnson Young
Librettist: Rida Johnson Young
Producer: Messrs. Shubert
Director: J.J. Shubert

Source: AZ OBSITOS (Musical: Emmerich Kalman; Victor Leon); **Choreographer:** Jack Mason; **Costumes:** Mme. Kahn; **Musical Director:** Augustus Barratt; **Set Design:** P. Dodd Ackerman; Edward Sundquist

Songs: All Alone in a City Full of Girls (C: Sigmund Romberg); Amsterdam (C/L: Augustus Barratt); Army, The [1]; Cuckoo [1] (C: Emmerich Kalman); Fairy Song; Golden Sunshine (C: Emmerich Kalman); He's Coming Home (C: Sigmund Romberg); History (C/L: Clifton Crawford); Home Again (C: Sigmund Romberg; L: Augustus Barratt); I'd Be Happy Anywhere with You (C: Sigmund Romberg); Kiss Waltz, The (C: Sigmund Romberg); Little Neutral Dog [1] (C: Emmerich Kalman); Lonely Princess, The (The Sleeping Princess) (C: Sigmund Romberg); Married Man Makes the Best Soldier [1]; Military Stamp (C/L: Clifton Crawford); Mother (1) [3] (C: Emmerich Kalman; L: Darl MacBoyle); Mother (2) [3] (C: Sigmund Romberg); Oh, Heart of Mine [1] (C: Emmerich Kalman); Opening; Our Native Land [1] (C: Emmerich Kalman); Pack Up Your Troubles in Your Old Kit Bag [2] (C: Felix Powell;

L: George Asaf); Ragtime Fight [1]; Slavery (C/L: Clifton Crawford); Song of Home (C: Emmerich Kalman); Ta-Ra- Ta [1] (C: Emmerich Kalman)

Cast: Clifton Crawford; Louise Galloway; Adele Rowland; John Charles Thomas

Notes: [1] Sheet music only. [2] Listed in program as "Smile, Smile, Smile." [3] Were there two songs titled "Mother?" There are two different sheets by two different publishers. Which is the song used in the show?

1853 • HERE AND THERE (1919)
Notes: See HAPPY DAYS.

1854 • HERE AND THERE (1920)
Notes: See PICCADILLY TO BROADWAY.

1855 • HERE COMES THE BRIDE
OPENED: 02/20/1930   Theatre: Piccadilly
Musical   London: 175

Composer: Arthur Schwartz
Lyricist: Desmond Carter
Librettist: Bert Lee; R.P. Weston
Producer: Julian Wylie
Director: Julian Wylie

Choreographer: Frederick Lord; **Costumes:** G.E. Calthrop; **Musical Director:** Leonard Hornsey

Songs: Bang! There Goes My Heart; Congratulations; Finale; High and Low [1] (L: Desmond Carter; Howard Dietz); Hot (L: Desmond Carter; Lew Levenson); I Love You and I Like You (Love You but I Like You Even More) [2] (L: Max Lief; Nathaniel Lief); I'll Always Remember (L: Desmond Carter; Max Lief; Nathaniel Lief); I'm Like a Sailor (Home from the Sea) (L: Desmond Carter; Howard Dietz); Impossible Men; No One to Blame but You; Opening; Rose in My Hair, A (A Rose in Your Hair); Why Not Have a Little Party?

Cast: Vera Bryer; Jean Colin; Richard Dolman; Edmund Gwenn; Clifford Mollison

Notes: [1] Not the same song as in THE BAND WAGON. [2] Also in THE GRAND STREET FOLLIES (1929).

1856 • HERE GOES THE BRIDE

OPENED: 11/03/1931 Theatre: Chanin's 46th St.
Musical Broadway: 7

Composer: John Green
Lyricist: Edward Heyman
Librettist: Peter Arno; Roger Pryor
Producer: Peter Arno
Director: Edward Clarke Lilley

Choreographer: Russell Markert; **Costumes:** Kiviette; **Musical Director:** Adolph Deutsch; **Orchestrations:** Conrad Salinger; **Set Design:** Peter Arno; Dale Stetson

Songs: Hello, My Lover, Goodbye; I Love a Parade [3] (C: Harold Arlen; L: Ted Koehler); Inside Story, The; It Means So Little to You [1] (C: Richard Myers); It's My Nature; Music in My Fingers (C: Richard Myers); My Sweetheart 'Tis of Thee; Ohhh! Ahhh!; One Second of Sex [2]; Remarkable People We (C: Richard Myers); Shake Well Before Using; We Know Reno; Well, You See; What's the Difference

Cast: Eric Blore; Grace Brinkley; Bobby Clark; Dudley Clements; Vicki Cummings; Dorothy Dare; Paul Frawley; John Gallaudet; Frances Langford; Philip Lord; Paul McCullough; Coletta Ryan

Notes: [1] Credited to Green in program, Myers on sheet music. [2] Credited to Myers in program, Green on sheet music. [3] Sheet music only.

1857 • HERE IS THE NEWS

OPENED: 08/15/1960
Revue

Composer: Patrick Gowers
Lyricist: John Bird
Librettist: John Bird
Additional Material: Ken Hoare; Eugene Ionesco; Howard Sackler; N.F. Simpson; Andrew Sinclair
Director: John Bird

Choreographer: Rhoda Levine; **Musical Director:** Donald Purchese

Songs: Always or More; Association Word Game; Busker, The; Country Dancing; Devotion; English Breakfast; Folk Lore; General Election; Good-bye World; Guilty Party; It Might Be Love; Lady, The; Last One, The; Lonely Woman; One Foot In; Opening; Over the Coals; Parable; Raptures of the Deep; Revival of the Fittest; Rubies for a Queen; Sandy's Bags; Screening the Cast; Silence; Sitting Around; Soldiers of the Queen; Take It Mr. Gladstone; Vacancy

Cast: Valentine Dyall; Richard Goolden; Sheila Hancock; Cleo Laine

Notes: New Theatre, Oxford, England. Songs and sketches listed because they are not differentiated in program.

1858 • HERE WE ARE AGAIN

OPENED: 12/06/1941
Musical

Composer: Arnold Johnson
Lyricist: John Hayden
Director: John Wray

Cast: Earle Crooker; A.J. Herbert; Bill Tallman

Notes: Part of the LAMBS ANNUAL DINNER, GAMBOL AND BALL at the Waldorf-Astoria Hotel. See under that name for other credits. No songs identified in program.

1859 • HERE'S HOWE!

OPENED: 05/01/1928 Theatre: Broadhurst
Musical Broadway: 71

Composer: Roger Wolfe Kahn; Joseph Meyer
Lyricist: Irving Caesar
Librettist: Paul Gerard Smith; Fred Thompson
Producer: Alex A. Aarons; Vinton Freedley

Choreographer: Sammy Lee; **Costumes:** Kiviette; **Musical Director:** Paul Lannin; **Set Design:** John Wenger

Songs: Beauty in the Movies; Boston Post Road; Crazy Rhythm; Dismissal Whistle; Here's Howe; I'd Rather Dance Here Than Hereafter; Imagination (C: Joseph Meyer); Life As a Twosome [1]; New Love, A; Opening Act II

Cast: Ben Bernie; Eric Blore; Irene Delroy; William Frawley; Allen Kearns; Fuzzy Knight; June O'Dea

Notes: [1] Also in AMERICANA (1928).

1860 • HERE'S LOVE

OPENED: 10/03/1963   Theatre: Shubert
Musical   Broadway: 334

Composer: Meredith Willson
Lyricist: Meredith Willson
Librettist: Meredith Willson
Producer: Stuart Ostrow
Director: Stuart Ostrow

Source: MIRACLE ON 34TH STREET (Film: George Seaton); **Source:** MIRACLE ON 34TH STREET (Story: Valentine Davies); **Choreographer:** Michael Kidd; **Costumes:** Alvin Colt; **Dance Arranger:** Peter Howard; **Lighting Designer:** Tharon Musser; **Musical Director:** Elliot Lawrence; **Orchestrations:** Don Walker; **Set Design:** Jean Eckart; William Eckart; **Vocal Arranger:** Elliot Lawrence

Songs: Arm in Arm; Big Ca-lown Balloons, The [1]; Bugle, The; Dear Mr. Santa Claus (If Santa Claus Were Crazy) [3]; Expect Things to Happen; Fa La La, Fa, Fa La La [3]; Here's Love; Look, Little Girl; Love, Come Take Me Again (ballet) [2]; Macy's Parade [4]; My State; My Wish; Nothing in Common; Parade (dance) [1]; Pine Cones and Holly Berries; Plastic Alligator, The; She Hadda Go Back; That Man Over There; We Live on Park [3]; You Don't Have to Prove It If You Sing It [3]; You Don't Know

Cast: Larry Douglas; David Doyle; William Griffis; Fred Gwynne; Cliff Hall; Valerie Lee; Laurence Naismith; Janis Paige; Paul Reed; Craig Stevens

Notes: [1] Same music. [2] No lyrics were used in this production although the complete song is now in the amateur production script. [3] Cut. [4] ASCAP/Library of Congress only.

1861 • HERE'S OUR GIRL

Musical

Composer: Skip Kennon
Lyricist: Ellen Fitzhugh

Source: BIG BLOND, THE (Story: Dorothy Parker)

Notes: No other information available.

1862 • HERE'S THE PITCH

OPENED: 12/09/1947
Musical

Composer: Courtney Crandall
Lyricist: William M. Scudder
Librettist: Craig P. Gilbert
Director: John F. Baird

Choreographer: John Pierce; **Costumes:** Patricia Havens; **Set Design:** Lawrence L. Goldwasser

Songs: All's Right with the World; Baby Ain't a Baby No More; Baseball; Believe; Extra-currickeler Girl; Great Guy; In a Town; In the Lobby of the Ritz; Just as Long as I Have You; Little Ladybird; Never Trust a Man; Rally Chant; So Well So Soon; When We Were Young

Cast: Theodore Alegretti; Frederick Lamont

Notes: A Hasty Pudding Club show. The 100th Annual production.

1863 • HERE'S TO THE GIRL

Musical

Composer: Vinton Freedley
Lyricist: John King Hodges
Librettist: Grace Henry; John King Hodges; Edward Streeter

Songs: Nicest Girl I Know, The; Romance; Rubenstein Rag, The

Cast: Helen Hoadley

Notes: No other information available.

1864 • HERE'S WHERE I BELONG

OPENED: 03/03/1968   Theatre: Billy Rose
Musical   Broadway: 1

Composer: Robert Waldman
Lyricist: Alfred Uhry
Librettist: Alex Gordon [3]
Producer: Mitch Miller
Director: Michael Kahn

Source: EAST OF EDEN (Novel: John Steinbeck); **Choreographer:** Tony Mordente; **Costumes:** Ruth Morley; **Dance Arranger:** Arnold Goland; **Lighting Designer:** Jules Fisher; **Musical Director:** Theodore Saidenberg; **Orchestrations:** Norman Leyden; Glenn Osser; Jonathan Tunick; **Set Design:** Ming Cho Lee; **Vocal Arranger:** Theodore Saidenberg

Songs: Act Like a Lady; Ballet; Cal Gets By; Don't Tell Momma [2]; Good Boy [1]; He's Out of His Mind [2]; Here's Where I Belong; Mr. Mouse [1]; No Time; Oh, It Used to Be [2]; Perfect [1]; Progress; Pulverize the Kaiser; Raising Cain; Send-Off, The; Soft Is the Sparrow; Sweeping Change [1]; Sweetheart [2]; Tell Me About Your Eden [1]; Top of the Train; Waking Up Sun; We Are What We Are; We're a Home; Where Have I Been?; You're Momma's

Cast: James Coco; Ken Kercheval; Walter McGinn; Heather McRae; Paul Rogers; Nancy Wickwire

Notes: [1] Cut before opening. [2] Not in program. [3] A pseudonym. Terrence McNally left the show prior to opening.

1865 • HERMAN VAN VEEN: ALL OF HIM

OPENED: 12/12/1982   Theatre: Ambassador
Revue   Broadway: 6

Composer: Herman van Veen
Lyricist: Christopher Adler; Willem Wilmink
Producer: Michael Frazier; Harlekyn U.S.A. Company; Joost Taverne; Ron van Eeden
Director: Michel LaFaille

Costumes: Ellen van der Horst; **Lighting Designer:** Rob Munnik; **Musical Director:** Erik van der Wurff; **Set Design:** Gerard Jongerius; Ed de Boer

Songs: Back of Life, The; Cranes; Do You Remember? (L: Christopher Adler; Hans Lodeizen); Fence, The (C: Erik van der Wurff); Girl, A (C: Herman van Veen; Erik van der Wurff); Hello (C: Herman van Veen; Erik van der Wurff); Heroes (C: Chris Pilgrim; L: Christopher Adler; Rob Chrispijn); Hole-in-One (C: Herman van Veen; Erik van der Wurff); I Don't Want Any Help (C/L: Herman van Veen; C: Erik van der Wurff; L: Christopher Adler); I Won't Let That Happen to Him (C: Georges Delerue); Interview, The (C: Herman van Veen; Erik van der Wurff); Jacob Is Dead (C: Herman van Veen); Kitchen Sink (C/L: Herman van Veen; C: Erik van der Wurff; L: Christopher Adler); Loose Woman, A; Ode to Suicide (C: Joop Stokkermans; L: Christopher Adler; Guus Vleugel); Parade of Clowns (C: Herman van Veen; Erik van der Wurff; L: Christopher Adler; Rob Chrispijn); Rules of Asylum (C: Herman van Veen; L: Rob Chrispijn); Sarabande (C: J.B. Senaille; Herman van Veen; Erik van der Wurff); Station (C: Herman van Veen; Erik van der Wurff); Tell Me Who I Was (C: Philippe-Gerard; L: Christopher Adler; W. Gebe Wilmink; Willem Wilmink); Time Passed Her By (C/L: Jean Ferrat; L: Christopher Adler); What a Day (C: Erik van der Wurff)

Cast: Herman van Veen

1866 • HERMITS AT HAPPY HOLLOW, THE

OPENED: 05/30/1910
Musical   Closed out of town

Composer: John S. Zamecnik
Librettist: Clarence Vincent Kerr
Producer: Hermit Club of Cleveland
Director: R.H. Burnside

Choreographer: Thomas Bennett; **Set Design:** Arthur Voegtlin

Songs: At Happy Hollow; Billy Phibbs Is Married; Chauffeur's Song, The (C: Henry L. Sanford); Did He? Yes, He Did!; Gentle Jane (C: Richard S. Spencer); Hark to the Sound of the Hunter's Horn; Hooray for the Bridgroom; I'm Looking for a Girl; It's Merely a Matter of Time (C: Henry L. Sanford); Life Is Like a Dance; M-O-N-E-Y; Mary (C: Henry L. Sanford); Mister Sun; Phoebe Snow (C: Henry L. Sanford); Society Circus, The; Ten Little Chorus Girls; What's the Use? (C: Henry L. Sanford); When You Love a Girl; You're the Girl (C: Henry L. Sanford)

Cast: Gardner Abbott; Walter S. Bowler; Horation N. Herriman; Felix Hughes; George B. Pettengill

Notes: Program of Cleveland.

1867 • HERMITS IN MEXICO, THE

OPENED: 05/28/1923   Theatre: B.F. Keith's 105th St.
Musical   New York

Composer: MacSlator Bethel; Milton W. Lusk
Lyricist: R.H. Burnside; Horation N. Herriman
Librettist: Horation N. Herriman
Producer: Hermit Club of Cleveland
Director: R.H. Burnside

Choreographer: Cissie Hayden; **Costumes:** Arthur D. Brooks; **Musical Director:** Homer Walters; **Set Design:** Arthur D. Brooks

Songs: Bootlegging Blues; Cactus Flower; Daughter of Senator Fish, The; Dreams; Drunken Sisters, The; Eccentric Dance; Egyptian Dance; Forsa del Destino; Friendship; How to Be a Bandit; I Want to Go Home; Jazz Band All My Own; Let's Paint the Town Red; Mexican Rose; Springtime; Strange Things Time Will Do; Taking Chances; We Always Get Our Man; You're the Girl; Youth

Cast: George T. Greenfield; Horation N. Herriman; William C. Keough; Jack Randall; Edgerton B. Williams

Notes: Amateur show.

1868 • HERMITS IN PARIS, THE
OPENED: 05/27/1912
Musical   Closed out of town

Composer: John S. Zamecnik
Lyricist: R.H. Burnside
Librettist: Clarence Vincent Kerr
Producer: Hermit Club of Cleveland
Director: R.H. Burnside

Costumes: Will R. Barnes; **Set Design:** H. Robert Law

Songs: Always Something Doing in Paris; At the Brookside Inn (C: Jean Schwartz; L: William Jerome); At the Hotel Amerique; Carnival of Dance, The; Dress! Dress! Dress!; Girls from the Folies Bergeres, The; He's Not the Prince; If I Met a Nice Little Girl; If You Could Learn to Love Me (C: Milton Lusk); It's Hard to Understand the Men; Matter We Can Easily Arrange, A; My Aeroplane Maid (C: Milton Lusk); There's Always Something Doing in Paree; Things I've Heard, The; Tips! Tips! Tips!; Toujour la Politesse; True Love Never Dies; We've Been Sent by the President; What Do You Think; What Is All This Excitement About; When You Visit Paris; When You're in Love; Woman, Delightful Woman

Cast: Gardner Abbott; Forrest J. Dresser; Horation N. Herriman; Carl F. Morse; James J. Pettit

Notes: Program of Cleveland, Ohio.

1869 • HERMITS IN VIENNA, THE
OPENED: 1914
Musical   Closed out of town

Composer: Milton Lusk; Meade; Royon
Librettist: R.H. Burnside

Costumes: Abbott; Landon; Meade; **Set Design:** Abbott; Landon; Meade

Notes: No other information available.

1870 • HERMITS ON MAIN STREET, THE
OPENED: 05/23/1921
Musical

Composer: Milton Lusk
Librettist: George Ade

Notes: Hermit's Club Frolic at Cleveland's Opera House.

1871 • HERO IS BORN, A
OPENED: 10/01/1937   Theatre: Adelphi
Musical   Broadway: 50

Composer: Lehman Engel
Lyricist: Agnes Morgan
Librettist: Theresa Helburn
Producer: WPA Federal Theatre
Director: Agnes Morgan
Source: UNKNOWN (Story: Andrew Lang); **Choreographer:** Sylvia Manning; **Costumes:** Alexander Jones; **Musical Director:** Alexander Saron; **Orchestrations:** Alexander Saron; **Set Design:** Tom Adrian Cracraft

Songs: Best Dance of All, The; Combat; Feline Wisdom; Fiddle Dee Dee; Hurray for Life; Keeping Prigio Company; Last Word, The; Love-Lorn Maid, A; Magic Gifts; Matters Culinary; Music in the Air; Off to Gluckstein; Prigio Didn't Know; Question of Gait, A (L: Thomas Burke); Royal March, The; Secret of Success, The; Song of Prigio, The; They Say; Tra La La; We Believe; Woe Is Me

Cast: Marjorie Brown; Edward Forbes; John Furman; Drue Leyton; Helen Morrow; William Phelps; Ben Starkie; Frederic Tozere; Margaret Wycherly

1872 • HERRINGBONE
OPENED: 06/16/1982   Theatre: Playwrights Horizons
Play   Off-Broadway: 50

Composer: Skip Kennon
Lyricist: Ellen Fitzhugh
Author: Tom Cone
Producer: Playwrights Horizons
Director: Ben Levit

Source: HERRINGBONE (Play: Tom Cone);
Choreographer: Theodore Pappas; **Costumes:**
Karen Matthews; **Lighting Designer:** Frances
Aronson; **Set Design:** Christopher Nowak

Songs: Cheap Exit, The; Chicken and the Frog,
The; George; God Said; Herringbone; Lily Pad
Tango; Little Mister Tippy Toes; Lullabye; Not
President, Please; Ten Year; 3/4 for Three; Tulip
Print Waltz; Uncle Billy; What's a Body to Do?

Cast: Skip Kennon; David Rounds

1873 • HEY, MA . . . KAYE BALLARD

OPENED: 02/27/1984   Theatre: Promenade
Revue   Off-Broadway: 63

Composer: Leslie Eberhard; David Levy
Lyricist: Leslie Eberhard; David Levy
Author: Kaye Ballard
Producer: Karl Allison; Bryan Bantry
Director: Susan H. Schulman

Costumes: William Ivey Long; **Lighting Designer:**
Ruth Roberts; **Musical Director:** Robert Billig;
Orchestrations: Robby Merkin; **Set Design:**
Linda Hacker

Songs: All the Magic Ladies; Always, Always
You [2] (C/L: Bob Merrill); Cookin' Breakfast for
the One I Love [7] (C: Henry Tobias; L: Billy
Rose); Down in the Depths [3] (C/L: Cole Porter);
Hey, Ma; Lazy Afternoon [1] (C: Jerome Moross;
L: John Latouche); Nana (C/L: Jerry Goldberg;
Danny Sachs); Nobody But You [8] (C: George
Gershwin; L: B.G. DeSylva; Arthur Jackson);
Old Tunes (C: Charles Strouse; L: Lee Adams);
Someone Special (C/L: Joseph Connolly; David
Schaefer); Supper Club; Teeny Tiny [4] (C: David
Walker; L: Kaye Ballard; Marshall Barer);
Thinking of You [5] (C: Harry Ruby; L: Bert
Kalmar); Up There; Without a Song [6]
(C: Vincent Youmans; L: Edward Eliscu; Billy
Rose); You Don't Need It; You Made Me Love
You (C: James V. Monaco; L: Joseph McCarthy)

Cast: Kaye Ballard; **Pianist:** Arthur Siegel

Notes: [1] From THE GOLDEN APPLE. [2] From
CARNIVAL! [3] From RED, HOT AND BLUE.
Sung by Ballard in THE DECLINE AND FALL
OF THE ENTIRE WORLD AS SEEN THROUGH
THE EYES OF COLE PORTER. [4] From Ballard's
nightclub act. [5] From THE 5 O'CLOCK GIRL.
[6] From GREAT DAY! [7] From film BE
YOURSELF. [8] From LA, LA LUCILLE.

1874 • HEY NONNY NONNY!

OPENED: 06/06/1932   Theatre: Shubert
Revue   Broadway: 38

Composer: Michael Cleary
Lyricist: Max Lief; Nathaniel Lief
Librettist: Florence Calkins; Richy Craig Jr.; Ogden
Nash; Harry Ruskin; Frank Sullivan; E.B. White
Producer: John H. Del Bondio; Forrest C. Haring
Director: Alexander Leftwich

Choreographer: Dave Gould; **Costumes:** Mme.
Berthe; Helene Pons; **Musical Director:** Sherry
Magee; **Set Design:** Jo Mielziner; Raymond
Sovey

Songs: Be a Little Lackadaisical (C/L: Herman
Hupfeld); For Better or for Worse; Hey Nonny
Nonny (C: Will Irwin; L: Ogden Nash); I Didn't
Know That It Was Loaded; I'm Really Not That
Way (C: Will Irwin; L: Malcolm McComb); In
Those Good Old Horsecar Days (C: Will Irwin;
L: Malcolm McComb); Lady in Waiting
(C: Alberta Nichols; L: Mann Holiner); Let's Go
Lovin' (C/L: Herman Hupfeld); Manhattan
Lullaby; Minsky's Metropolitan Grand Opera;
On My Nude Ranch with You; Orientale
Moderne (C: Will Irwin); Personally Yours;
Season Ended, The; Tell Me Something About
Yourself; This Is Different, Dear; Three Little
Columnists; Wouldn't That Be Wonderful (C/L:
Herman Hupfeld)

Cast: Joan Carter-Waddell; Richy Craig Jr.; Frances
Maddux; Jack McCauley; Frank Morgan; Jerry
Norris; Ralph Sanford; Anne Seymour; Ernest
Sharpe; Penny Singleton

1875 • HI AND DRI

OPENED: 1919
Musical   Closed out of town

Composer: Manuel Klein
Lyricist: Edward Paulton

Librettist: A. Douglas Leavitt; Augustin McHugh; Edward P aulton

Notes: Revised as IT'S UP TO YOU. See that show also.

1876 • HI-DE-HO
OPENED: 05/06/1933
Musical   Closed out of town

Composer: Edgar Dowell; Hughie Walker
Lyricist: Edgar Dowell; Hughie Walker
Librettist: Addison Carey; John Mason
Producer: Charles Holland
Director: Addison Carey; Charles Davis

Costumes: Hilda Farnum; **Dance Arranger:** Aaron Thompson; **Orchestrations:** Aaron Thompson; **Vocal Arranger:** Aaron Thompson

Songs: At the Block Party; At the Camp Meeting; Chillun, Be Yourself; Debil, The; Down Home; Dr. Jazz; Get Happy; Hi-De-Ho; I Can Take It; It Rains All the Time; One Way to Love; Shake Your Furnace

Cast: Jules Bledsoe; John Mason; Julian Jean McKinney; Slappy Wallace

1877 • HI DIDDLE DIDDLE
OPENED: 10/03/1934   Theatre: Savoy
Revue   London

Songs: Miss Otis Regrets (C/L: Cole Porter)

Cast: Douglas Byng; Greta Nissen; John Tilley

1878 • HI, PAISANO!
OPENED: 09/30/1961   Theatre: York Playhouse
Musical   Off-Broadway: 3

Composer: Robert Holton
Lyricist: June Carroll
Librettist: Ernest Chambers
Producer: Aaron Gardner
Director: Vassili Lambriuos

Costumes: James Bidgood; **Lighting Designer:** Dom Poleo; **Musical Director:** Joseph Stecko; **Set Design:** Mario Vanarelli; **Vocal Arranger:** Charles Gross

Songs: Ballet; Born in America; Carousel; Cubes and Abstracts; Dino Repetti; Dino's in Love; Dozen Husbands; Faith; Girl He Adores; Hi, Paisano; I Know What He's Up To; It Happens Every Day; Let Me Drown; Office Under the Sky; Over Forty; Reason to Marry; Sounds of Silence; Table Tango; Teresa; Time We Talked; What Is Your Name?

Cast: David Canary; Jorie Remus; Marie Santell

1879 • HI YA, GENTLEMEN
OPENED: 11/29/1940
Musical   Closed out of town

Composer: Johnny Green
Lyricist: Harold Adamson
Librettist: Fred Finklehoffe; John Monks Jr.; Sid Silvers
Producer: Alex A. Aarons; Robert G. Ritchie

Choreographer: Bobby Connolly; **Costumes:** Tom Lee; **Musical Director:** Johnny Green; **Orchestrations:** Robert Russell Bennett; Hans Spialek; Don Walker; **Set Design:** Tom Lee; **Vocal Arranger:** Gene DePaul; Pete King; Hugh Martin

Songs: Ad Astra; America Marches On; Down in Fraternity Row; Go 'Way Blues, Ya Bother Me!; Hi Ya, Gentlemen; I Heard You Were Lovely; I'll Take the High Note; Never a Dull Moment; See How They Run; Some Things You Can't Learn in College; Spinner Learned the Conga; Up in Jessica's Room; Whereas; You're a Character

Cast: Max Baer; Audrey Christie; Ella Logan; Erik Rhodes; Sid Silvers

Notes: Program of Hartford, Conn.

1880 • HI, YANK!
OPENED: 08/07/1944
Revue

Composer: Jesse Berkman; Frank Loesser; Alex North
Lyricist: Jesse Berkman; Jack Hill; Frank Loesser
Librettist: Arnold Auerbach; Bob Eastright; Jack Hill; Ed Milk; Martin Weldon
Producer: Hy Gardner
Director: David E. Fitzgibbon

Choreographer: Jose Limon; **Costumes:** Al Hamilton; Robert T. Stevenson; Edward E. Wolf; **Set Design:** Al Hamilton; Stevenson; Edward E. Wolf

Songs: Classification Blues (C/L: Frank Loesser); General Orders, The (C/L: Unknown); Little Red Roof Tops (C/L: Frank Loesser); Most Important Job, The (C/L: Frank Loesser); My Gal and I (C: Frank Loesser; L: Jack Hill); Report from the Caribbean (C/L: Unknown); Saga of the Sack (C: Frank Loesser; L: Hy Zaret); Yank, Yank, Yank (C/L: Frank Loesser)

Cast: David Brooks; Joshua Shelley

Notes: Produced at Theatre No. 5, Fort Dix, New Jersey. Music and lyrics not credited.

1881 • HIGGLEDY-PIGGLEDY

OPENED: 10/20/1904   Theatre: Weber Music Hall
Musical   Broadway: 185

Composer: Maurice Levi
Lyricist: Edgar Smith
Librettist: Edgar Smith
Producer: Joseph Weber; Florenz Ziegfeld
Director: Frank Hatch [2]; George Marion [1]; Joseph Weber [3]

Choreographer: Sam Marion; **Set Design:** Ernest Albert

Songs: Big Indian and Little Maid [5]; College Chaperone, The [4]; Days of Forty-Nine, The [5]; For You, Honey, for You [4]; Game of Love, A [7]; Grand Prix, The [7]; Great Big Girl Like Me, A [7]; Higher Education, The [6]; I'm So Lonesome [7]; In Gay Paree [4]; In the Chorus [7]; Mama's Boarding House [6]; Miss Watermelon Sweet [4]; Nancy Clancy [7]; Next Summer in Dear Old New York [7]; Poor Little Red Papoose [5]; Revels of the Jewels [7]; Socrates Jackson (An Educated Coon) [6]

Cast: Charles A. Bigelow; Sam Collins; Marie Dressler; Anna Held; Bonnie Maginn; Joseph Weber

Notes: The first act was directed by George Marion. The Second act was called THE COLLEGE WIDOWER and was directed by Frank Hatch and George Marion. The third act was titled THE SQUAW MAN'S GIRL OF THE GOLDEN WEST. [1] Directed first act and co-directed second act. [2] Co-directed second act. [3] Directed third act. [4] Sheet music only. [5] Part of Act Three. [6] Part of Act Two. [7] Part of Act One.

1882 • HIGH AND DRY (1926?)

OPENED: 05/10/1926
Musical   Closed out of town

Composer: Manuel Klein
Lyricist: Edward Paulton; Mason Wright
Librettist: Douglas Leavitt; Augustin McHugh
Producer: William Moore Patch
Director: Julian Alfred; William J. O'Neil

Musical Director: John McManus

Songs: Gertie; Her Jazz Drummer; I'll Always Believe in You; One Small Umbrella, Dear; Ouija, Ouija; Someone to Console Me

Cast: Franklyn Ardell; Harry Clarke; Juanita Fletcher; Eleanor Henry; Mason Wright

Notes: Atlantic City program. The question mark in the title is in the real title. Mason Wright contributed additional lyrics. Also John McManus might have written some of the songs.

1883 • HIGH AND DRY (1942)

OPENED: 12/05/1942
Musical

Composer: Rick Besoyan
Lyricist: Rick Besoyan
Librettist: Mary Johnson; Lois de Freitas

Arrangements: Verd McKean; **Musical Director:** Verd McKean

Songs: High and Dry; I Can't Make Up My Mind; I'll Keep Loving You; It's Love; Just Friends; Lovely; Since You Came My Way; You Appeal to Me; You Look Just Like Margie; You Should Oughta Be for Me

Cast: Rick Besoyan [1]; Carol Brumm; Bob Dreyer; Mary Johnson; Lois de Freitas

Notes: Amateur show. Alameda High School. [1] Billed as Dick Besoyan.

1884 • HIGH & DRY (1950)

OPENED: 09/11/1950   Theatre: Las Palmas
Musical   Los Angeles

Composer: Stan Keyava
Lyricist: Bernard Ide
Librettist: Gene Ellis; Scott Fransworth
Producer: Alvin B. Baranov; Paul P. Schreibman
Director: Harold J. Kennedy

Choreographer: Jack Baker; **Costumes:** Damar Myers; **Musical Director:** Stan Keyava; **Set Design:** Thomas O'Neill

Songs: Anytime of Day; Available Me; Ballet; Clear Day; Come on Over; Fable of the Cable Car, The; Gentlemen of the Leased Wire Press; High and Dry; How Do You Go About It; I Must Be Missing Something; I Sell Nothing but the Best; It Takes an Idea Man; Make Mine the Same; Next Time We Love; Shocking, Uncouth, Middleclass; What's Going on Around Here?; Your Most Exciting Set of Bones

Cast: Skeets Gallagher; Dave Le Grant; Sharon Randall; Norwood Smith; Julie Van Zandt

1885 • HIGH AS A KITE

OPENED: 11/25/1940
Revue

Composer: Clay Boland
Lyricist: Bickley Reichner
Director: Clay Boland

Choreographer: Walter F. Keenan; **Costumes:** John Edward Friend; **Musical Director:** Joseph F. Follmann Jr.; **Set Design:** John Edward Friend

Songs: Americadenya; Girl with the Major General, The; High As a Kite; I'll Sing Your Praises; I'll Take Down My Etchings; Isn't He a Terrific Guy; Jive Guy; Let's Get Back to Bach; Minuet; My Gal; Not So Long Ago; Pepperpot; She Loves Me; Wasn't He a Terrific Guy; Watching the Stars Go By; Where Do You Hang Your Heart?

Cast: Robert Fletcher Dawson; Frederick Richard Griffiths; Bobby Troup; Sidney Wertimer Jr.

Notes: Amateur show. 53rd annual production of the Mask and Wig show celbrating Bicentennial of University of Pennsylvania.

1886 • HIGH BUTTON SHOES

OPENED: 10/09/1947   Theatre: New Century
Musical   Broadway: 727

Composer: Jule Styne
Lyricist: Sammy Cahn
Librettist: George Abbott [5]; Stephen Longstreet; Phil Silvers [5]
Producer: Joseph Kipness; Monte Proser
Director: George Abbott

Source: SISTERS LIKED THEM HANDSOME, THE (Novel: Stephen Longstreet);
Choreographer: Jerome Robbins; **Costumes:** Miles White; **Lighting Designer:** Peggy Clark; **Musical Director:** Milton Rosenstock; **Orchestrations:** Philip J. Lang; **Set Design:** Oliver Smith; **Vocal Arranger:** Bob Martin

Songs: Bathing Beauty Ballet (inst.); Bird Watcher's Song (We're the Ladies' Walking Society); Bless Our Home [3]; Can't You Just See Yourself; Castle Walk, The (dance); Get Away for a Day in the Country; Gone Are the Days [4]; He Tried to Make a Dollar; I Owe You a Kiss [6]; I Still Get Jealous; If Someone Should Ask You [3]; I'll Give You One Guess [3]; I'm Betwixt and Between [1]; Innocent Stander-By, The [3]; It's a Wonderful Day for a Ball Game [6]; Little Pitchers Have Big Ears [3]; Million Dollar Pier [3]; Next to Texas, I Love You; Nobody Ever Died for Dear Old Rutgers; On a Sunday by the Sea; On the Banks of the Old Raritan [2]; Papa, Won't You Dance with Me?; Peanut Butter Sandwiches and Hard Boiled Eggs [3]; She's a Good Kid [3]; She's Right (Security); Summer Incident; Tango (dance); There's Nothing Like a Model T; Too Soon [3]; You're a Sweet Patootie [3]; You're My Girl (Boy)

Cast: Nanette Fabray; Joey Faye; Helen Gallagher; Paul Godkin; Jack McCauley; Phil Silvers

Notes: [1] Cut. Later the music for title phrase became the first lines of "Everything's Coming Up Roses" from GYPSY. [2] Added to 1982 revival at Goodspeed Opera House. [3] Either cut or not used. [4] Either cut or not used. Same music as "The Cow Song" from GYPSY. [5] Uncredited. [6] ASCAP/Library of Congress only.

1887 • HIGH DIPLOMACY

OPENED: 06/06/1969   Theatre: Westminster
Musical   London: 172

Composer: George Fraser; William L. Reed
Lyricist: Hugh Steadman; Alan Thornhill
Librettist: Hugh Steadman; Alan Thornhill
Producer: Westminster Productions
Director: Henry Carr

Choreographer: Virginia Mason; **Costumes:** Dorothy Phillips; **Musical Director:** John W. Daley; **Set Design:** Cameron Johnson

Songs: Children in the Dark; Efficiency; Everything That He Does; For Certain; For Everyone, Everywhere; Give 'Em What They Want; Hail to the Precarious Isles!; High Diplomacy; If I Don't, Nobody Else Will; Is She on Our Side?; It's Crazy, It's Mad; Just Between You and Me; No Stamp Attached; Oldest Au Pairs in the Business, The; Operator, The; Reading People; What They Say and What They're Meaning; Will There Be a Street in the Future; X Marks the Spot

Cast: Patricia Bredin; Donald Scott; Donald Simpson; Muriel Smith

1888 • HIGH JINKS

OPENED: 12/10/1913 Theatre: Lyric
Musical Broadway: 213

Composer: Rudolf Friml
Lyricist: Otto Harbach
Librettist: Otto Harbach
Producer: Arthur Hammerstein
Director: Frank Smithson

Songs: Afternoon [3]; All Aboard for Dixieland [3] (C: George L. Cobb; L: Jack Yellen); Bubbles, The; Chi-Chi; Come Hither Eyes; Dixiana Rise, The; Dr. Grouch Is Going Away; High Jinks; High Jinks Tangle; I Know Your Husband Very Well; I'm Through with Roaming Romeos; Is This Love at Last [2]; It Isn't Your Fault [1] (C: Jerome Kern; L: M.E. Rourke); Jim; Life without Love [2]; Love's Own Kiss; Not Now, but Later; Something Seems Tingle- Ingleing; When Sammy Sang the Marseillaise

Cast: Snitz Edwards; Elaine Hammerstein; Tom Lewis; Ignacio Martinetti; Elizabeth Murray; Robert Pitkin; Mana Zucca

Notes: Leo Dietrichstein also credited with book out of town. [1] Written for London version of this show. Later use d in 90 IN THE SHADE and music used for "It Wasn't My Fault" with a

Harry B. Smith lyric in LOVE O' MIKE. [2] Not in Wilmington program. [3] Out Wilmington 10/5/15.

1889 • HIGH KICKERS

OPENED: 10/31/1941 Theatre: Broadhurst
Musical Broadway: 171

Composer: Harry Ruby
Lyricist: Bert Kalmar
Librettist: George Jessel; Bert Kalmar; Harry Ruby
Producer: Alfred Bloomingdale; Nat Karson
Director: Edward Sobol

Choreographer: Carl Randall; **Musical Director:** Val Ernie; **Set Design:** Nat Karson

Songs: Cigarettes; Din't Cha Mother Tell You Nothin'?; Girls, The; I've Got Somethin'; Memories; My Sweetheart Mamie; Opening Chorus (George M. Krause's High Kickers); Panic in Panama; Time to Sing; Waltzing in the Moonlight; You're on My Mind

Cast: Betty Bruce; Chaz Chase; George Jessel; Rose King; Joe Marks; Mary Marlow; Dick Monahan; Stuart Morgan Dancers; Sophie Tucker; Billy Vine; Chick York; **Pianist:** Ted Shapiro

1890 • HIGH ROLLERS SOCIAL AND PLEASURE CLUB, THE

OPENED: 04/21/1992 Theatre: Helen Hayes
Revue Broadway: 12

Composer: Allen Toussaint
Lyricist: Allen Toussaint
Producer: Judy Gordon; Dennis Grimaldi; Martin Markinson; Allen M. Shore
Director: Alan Weeks

Arrangements: Allen Toussaint; **Choreographer:** Alan Weeks; **Costumes:** Theoni V. Aldredge; **Lighting Designer:** Beverly Emmons; **Musical Director:** Allen Toussaint; **Orchestrations:** Allen Toussaint; **Set Design:** David Mitchell

Songs: All These Things; Black Widow Spider; Bourbon Street Parade; Challenge Dance; Chicken Shack Boogie; Dance the Night; Don't You Feel Me Leg; Feet Don't Fail Me Now; Fiyou on the Bayou; Fun Time; Golden Crown; Heebie Jeebie Dance; Hey Mama; I Like It Like That; Injuns Here We Come; It Will Stand;

Jambalaya; Jelly Roll; Jockomo; Lady Marmalade; Let the Good Times Roll; Lipstick Traces; Marie Leveau; Mellow Sax; Mos Scoscious; Mother- in-Law; Mr. Mardi Gras; Ooh Poo Pa Doo; Open Up; Rockin' Pneumonia; Saints Go Marching In; Sea Cruise; Sittin' in Ya Ya; Such a Night; Tell It Like It Is; Tu Way Pocky Way; Walk on Gilded Splinters; We All Need Love; Working in a Coal Mine; You Can Have My Husband; You're the One

Cast: Keith Robert Bennett; Deborah Burrell-Cleveland; Lawrence Clayton; Eugene Fleming; Michael McElroy; Vivian Reed; Nikki Rene; Allen Toussaint; Tarik Winston

Notes: Some songs not written by Toussaint but not identified in program.

1891 • HIGH SPIRITS

OPENED: 04/07/1964   Theatre: Alvin
Musical   Broadway: 375

Composer: Timothy Gray; Hugh Martin
Lyricist: Timothy Gray; Hugh Martin
Librettist: Timothy Gray; Hugh Martin
Producer: Robert Fletcher; Lester Osterman
Director: Noel Coward

Source: BLITHE SPIRIT (Play: Noel Coward);
Choreographer: Danny Daniels; **Costumes:** Robert Fletcher; Valentina; **Dance Arranger:** William Goldenberg; **Lighting Designer:** Jules Fisher; **Musical Director:** Fred Werner; **Orchestrations:** Harry Zimmerman; **Set Design:** Robert Fletcher; **Vocal Arranger:** Timothy Gray; Hugh Martin

Songs: Bicycle Song, The; English Summer Day, An [2]; Exorcism, The (dance); Exorcism Revisited, The [5]; Faster Than Sound [1] (C/L: Hugh Martin); Flowers [2]; Forever and a Day; Forever Nearer to Me [3]; Go Into Your Trance; Have an Umbrella [2]; Home Sweet Heaven; I Know Your Heart; If I Gave You; Is There Anybody There Tango [5]; I've Never Had a Manifestation [2]; Nothing Ever Happens in London [2]; Sandwich Man, The; Season, The [4]; Society, The [2]; Something Is Coming to Tea; Something Tells Me [6]; Talking to You; They Don't Make 'Em Like That Anymore [7]; Was She Prettier Than I?; What in the World Did You Want?; Where Is the Man I Married?; Would You Let Me? [5]; You'd Better Love Me

Cast: Carol Arthur; Tammy Grimes; Margaret Hall; Beth Howland; Laurence Keith; Beatrice Lillie; Louise Troy; Edward Woodward

Notes: Martin and Gray wrote four additional songs for a planned revival in 1983. It never happened. [1] Written by Martin for film ATHENA and ZIEGFELD FOLLIES OF 1956. [2] Cut prior to opening. [3] Written for proposed Broadway revival. [4] Cut prior to opening. Same music as "Something Tells Me." [5] Not used. [6] Same music as "The Season." [7] ASCAP/Library of Congress only.

1892 • HIGH TIME

OPENED: 08/17/1953
Revue   Closed out of town

Librettist: Danny Simon; Neil Simon; Joseph Stein
Producer: Robert E. Perry
Director: Ray Golden; Dale Wasserman

Choreographer: Danny Daniels; **Costumes:** Ariel Baleff; **Dance Arranger:** Dorothea Freitag; **Lighting Designer:** Dale Wasserman; **Musical Director:** Gerald Alters; **Set Design:** Ariel Baleff

Songs: High Time (C: Milton Berle; L: Ray Golden); I'm All Yours (C: Leo Schumer; L: Ray Golden; Michael Stewart); It Takes a Lot of Do-Re-Mi (C: Philip Charig; L: Ray Golden); Jefferson Davis Tyler's General Store (C/L: Edward C. Redding); Little Quonset in Neponset, A (C: Irma Jurist; L: Danny Shapiro); One Hour Ahead of the Posse (C: Philip Charig; L: Ray Golden; David Ormont); Pie-Eyed Piper of Heidsieck, The (C: Hal Borne; L: Ray Golden); That's for Me (C: Gerald Marks; L: Milton Pascal); To Be or Not to Be in Love (C: Philip Charig; L: Ray Golden; Milton Pascal); Trial in Trinidad (C: Irma Jurist; L: I.A.L. Diamond; Ray Golden); Understudy, The (C: Gerald Marks; L: Milton Pascal); Vicious Circle (C/L: Ray Golden; Sheldon Harnick); What a Delightful Day (C: Philip Charig; L: Leonard Gershe; David Ormont)

Cast: Gabriel Dell; Hal Loman; **Pianist:** Gerald Alters; Dorothea Freitag

1893 • HIGH TOR

OPENED: 03/10/1956   Theatre: CBS
TV Musical

Composer: Arthur Schwartz
Lyricist: Maxwell Anderson
Librettist: Maxwell Anderson

Source: HIGH TOR (Play: Maxwell Anderson);
  Musical Director: Joseph J. Lilley

Songs: John Barleycorn; Little Love, a Little While,
  A; Living One Day at a Time; Once Upon a Long
  Ago; Sad Is the Life of the Sailor's Wife; When
  You're in Love

Cast: Julie Andrews; Bing Crosby; Everett Sloane

Notes: Original TV musical.

1894 • HIGHER AND HIGHER
OPENED: 04/04/1940   Theatre: Shubert
Musical   Broadway: 84

Composer: Richard Rodgers
Lyricist: Lorenz Hart
Librettist: Gladys Hurlbut; Joshua Logan
Producer: Dwight Deere Wiman
Director: Joshua Logan

Choreographer: Robert Alton; **Costumes:** Lucinda
  Ballard; **Musical Director:** Al Goodman;
  Orchestrations: Hans Spialek; **Set Design:** Jo
  Mielziner

Songs: Barking Baby Never Bites, A; Blue Monday;
  Disgustingly Rich; Ev'ry Sunday Afternoon;
  From Another World; How's Your Health?; I'm
  Afraid; It Never Entered My Mind; It's Pretty in
  the City [1]; Life! Liberty! (and the Pursuit of
  You) [1]; Lovely Day for a Murder; Morning's at
  Seven [2]; Nothing but You

Cast: Robert Chisholm; Eva Condon; Lee Dixon;
  Marta Eggerth; Leif Erickson; Janet Fox; Joseph
  Granville; Jack Haley; Shirley Ross; Robert
  Rounseville; Sharkey the Seal; Hilda Spong;
  Billie Worth

Notes: [1] Cut. [2] Title suggested by the play of
  same name.

1895 • HIGHWAY LIFE, THE
Notes: *See DUDE.*

1896 • HIGHWAYMAN, THE
OPENED: 12/13/1897   Theatre: Broadway
Musical   Broadway: 144

Composer: Reginald De Koven
Lyricist: Harry B. Smith
Librettist: Harry B. Smith
Producer: Andrew A. McCormick
Director: Max Freeman

Choreographer: Carl Marwig; **Costumes:** Mme.
  Siedle; **Set Design:** John H. Young

Songs: Beau of Georgian Days, The [1]; Bread,
  Cheese and Kisses; Chorus of Villagers; Do You
  Remember Love; Farewell to the King's
  Highway; Farmer and the Scarecrow, The; Finale
  Act I; Finale Act II; Gipsy Song; Gretna Green;
  Highwayman, The; In London Town; In the
  Morning [1]; Kitty O'Brien; Kleptomania [1];
  Marching Away; Moonlight Song, A; On the
  Track; Opening Chorus and Dance Act III;
  Sailor's Song, A [1]; Town and Country [1]; Vive
  la Bagatelle; While the Four Winds Blow

Cast: Nellie Braggins; Hilda Clark; Joseph O'Hara;
  Jerome Sykes

Notes: No program available. [1] Not in vocal
  score.

1897 • HIJINKS!
OPENED: 12/18/1980   Theatre: Cheryl Crawford
Musical   Off-Broadway: 37

Librettist: Steve Brown; Robert Kalfin; John
  McKinney
Producer: Chelsea Theatre Center; Fisher Theatre
  Foundation; Roger L. Stevens
Director: Robert Kalfin

Source: CAPTAIN JINKS OF THE HORSE
  MARINES (Play: Clyde Fitch); **Choreographer:**
  Larry Hayden; **Costumes:** Elizabeth P. Palmer;
  Lighting Designer: Paul Everett; **Musical
  Director:** Michael O'Flaherty; **Orchestrations:**
  John McKinney; **Set Design:** Sandro LaFerla

Songs: Auld Lang Syne (C/L: Traditional;
  L: Robert Burns); Beautiful Dreamer (C/L:
  Stephen Foster); Boy's Best Friend Is His
  Mother, A [1] (C/L: Harry Miller; J.P. Skelly;
  L: Steve Brown); Captain Jinks of the Horse
  Marines (C/L: William Lingard); Champagne
  Charlie [1] (C/L: Alfred Lee; George
  Leybourne; L: Steve Brown); Dad's a Millionaire
  [1] (C/L: Henry Clay Work; L: Steve Brown);
  Goodbye My Lady Love (C/L: Joseph E.

Howard); Home Sweet Home (C/L: John Howard Payne); Hour for Thee and Me, The (C/L: Stephen Foster); If You've Only Got a Moustache (C/L: George Cooper; Stephen Foster); La Traviata Waltzes (inst.) [4] (C: Giuseppe Verdi); Last Rose of Summer (C/L: Traditional); Love's Old Sweet Song (C/L: G. Clifton Bingham; J.L. Molloy); Mermaid's Evening Song, The (C/L: J.E. Carpenter; S. Glover); Mother's Smile, A (C/L: Mary E. Hewitt; W.V. Wallace); Poor Kitty Popcorn (The Soldier's Pet) (C/L: Henry Clay Work); Shew! Fly, Don't Bother Me (C/L: Frank Campbell); Silver Threads Among the Gold (C/L: H.P. Danks; Eben E. Rexford); Star Spangled Banner (C: Unknown; L: Francis Scott Key); Take Them Away They'll Drive Me Crazy (C/L: Henry Clay Work; L: Steve Brown); That Gal Is a High Born Lady [1] (C/L: Barney Fagan; L: Steve Brown); Then You'll Remember Me [3] (C: M.W. Balfe; L: Alfred Bunn); Those Tassels on Her Boots (C/L: Robert Cooms); Wait 'Till the Sun Shines Nellie (C: Harry Von Tilzer; L: Andrew B. Sterling); Walking Down Broadway (C/L: William Lingard; Charles E. Pratt); Whispering Hope (C/L: Septimus Winner); Will Thou Be Gone, Love? [2] (C/L: Stephen Foster; L: William Shakespeare); Will You Love Me in December As You Do in May? (C: Ernest R. Ball; L: James J. Walker)

Cast: Evalyn Baron; Bruce Conner; Elizabeth Devine; Scott Ellis; Joseph Kolinski; Sarah Lowman; Michael O'Flaherty; Marian Primont; Jeannine Taylor

Notes: No original songs in this show. [1] Additional lyrics by Steve Brown. [2] Lyrics based on lines from Shakespeare's ROMEO AND JULIET. [3] From THE BOHEMIAN GIRL. [4] Melodies from the opera LA TRAVIATA.

1898 • HILARITIES
OPENED: 09/09/1948   Theatre: Adelphi
Revue   Broadway: 14

Composer: Stanley Arnold; Buddy Kaye; Carl Lampl
Lyricist: Stanley Arnold; Buddy Kaye; Carl Lampl
Librettist: Morey Amsterdam; Howard Harris; Sidney Zelinka
Producer: Ken Robey; Stan Zucker
Director: Morey Amsterdam

Choreographer: George Tapps; **Musical Director:** Ruby Zwerling; **Orchestrations:** Elliot Jacoby; **Set Design:** Crayon

Cast: Morey Amsterdam; Nancy Andrews; Connie Stevens; Sid Stone; George Tapps

Notes: No songs listed in program.

1899 • HIMBERANA
OPENED: 11/13/1953   Theatre: Carnegie Hall
Revue   1

Producer: Richard Himber

Songs: Love Is Not for Children (C/L: Richard Himber)

Cast: Senator Claghorn; Richard Himber Orchestra; Ray Middleton; Jack Pearl; Orson Welles; Henry Youngman

Notes: A magic and comedy revue.

1900 • HIP! HIP! HOORAY! (1907)
OPENED: 10/10/1907   Theatre: Weber's
Revue   Broadway: 64

Composer: Gus Edwards
Lyricist: Edgar Smith
Librettist: Edgar Smith
Director: Julian Mitchell

Costumes: Mme. Castel-Bert; Mme. De Wolfe; Cora MacGeachy; William H. Matthews; J. Henry Rowley; **Lighting Designer:** Tom Smith; **Musical Director:** Anton Heindl

Songs: All I Want in the Wide, Wide, World Is You, Just You; College Boy's Dream [1]; Coon College; Fashion (L: Whitford Watson); Frolics of Pierrot, The [1]; Here in the Moonlight on the Fence; Here on the Fence at Doolittle College; How'd You Like to Take Me Home with You (L: Will D. Cobb); In Philadelphia (L: Whitford Watson); Leader of Fashion Am I; Let's Wander Off Nowhere; Mandy [1]; Old Friends (L: Sam Erlich); Put Me Among the Girls; Tootsie Tripper; Wander Off Nowhere [2]; What's the Use?; You'll Never Know What Love Is Till I Say I Love You (L: Will D. Cobb; Matthew C. Woodward); Zabelle

Cast: Bessie Clayton; Mabel Fenton; Lew Fields; Tom Lewis; Charles Ross; Amelia Stone;

Valeska Suratt; Harry Tighe; Fay Tincher; Joseph Weber

Notes: [1] Sheet music only. [2] Not in program.

1901 • HIP-HIP-HOORAY (1915)

OPENED: 09/30/1915   Theatre: New York Hippodrome
Revue   Broadway: 425

Composer: Raymond Hubbell
Lyricist: John Golden
Librettist: R.H. Burnside
Producer: Charles Dillingham
Director: R.H. Burnside

Choreographer: Mariette Lorette; **Costumes:** William H. Matthews; Robert McQuinn; Frances Zeibarth; **Lighting Designer:** Joseph Ellsner; **Musical Director:** Raymond Hubbell; **Set Design:** Homer Emens

Songs: Cabaret Dancer, The (C: John Philip Sousa); Chin Chin Open Your Heart and Let Me In (C/L: A. Seymour Brown); Flirting at St. Moritz Ballet (inst.) (C: Jules Einedshofer); Flower Garden Ball, The (C: Jean Schwartz; L: William Jerome); Good Ship Honeymoon, The [1]; Hip-Hip-Hooray; How D'Ye Do Fifth Avenue; Ladder of Roses, The (L: R.H. Burnside); Lamp Post of Old Broadway, The (C: Benjamin Hapgood Burt); Land of Love and Roses, The; March of the States, The (inst.) (C: John Philip Sousa); My Fox Trot Wedding Day (C/L: Benjamin Hapgood Burt); My Land, My Flag (C: Zoel J. Parenteau; L: Marc Connelly); New York Hippodrome March, The (inst.) (C: John Philip Sousa); Open Secret, An; Wedding of Jack and Jill, The

Cast: Arthur Deagon; John Philip Sousa; Belle Storey; Toto; Nat Wills

Notes: Ballet libretto by Leo Bartushek. [1] Sheet music only. [2] Also in CHIN-CHIN.

1902 • HIRED GIRL'S MILLIONS

OPENED: 08/12/1907
Musical   Closed out of town

Librettist: Charles E. Blaney
Producer: Charles E. Blaney
Director: James R. Garey
Musical Director: Jules Friquet

Songs: Any Old Time at All; Bye-Bye My Caroline; Handle Me with Care; I Couldn't Make a Hit with Molly; I'd Rather Two-Step than Waltz; Killarney; Laughing Eyes; Let Me Put My Arms Around You; School Days; They All Look Alike to Mary; Torpedo Till; Tropical Moon; When the Band Plays Yankee Doodle; Where the River Shannon Flows (C/L: James Russell)

Cast: Charles J. Diem; Harry S. Fisher; Flora Bonfanti Russell; James Russell; John Russell

Notes: A New York suburban show.

1903 • HIRED MAN, THE

OPENED: 11/10/1988   Theatre: 47th Street
Musical   Off-Broadway: 33

Composer: Howard Goodall
Lyricist: Melvyn Bragg
Librettist: Melvyn Bragg
Producer: Heritage Project, Inc., The
Director: Brian Aschinger

Source: HIRED MAN, THE (Novel: Melvyn Bragg); **Choreographer:** Rodney Griffin; **Costumes:** Patricia Adshead; **Lighting Designer:** Leon Di Leone; **Musical Director:** Ann Crawford; **Set Design:** Tamara Kinkman

Songs: Crossbridge Dance; Fade Away; Farewell Song; Fill It to the Top; Get Up and Go, Lad; Hear Your Voice; I Wouldn't Be the First; If I Could; Men of Stone; No Choir of Angels; Now for the First Time; Song of the Hired Man; War Song: So Tell Your Children; What a Fool I've Been; What Would You Say to Your Son?; Who Will You Marry Then?; Work Song: It's All Right for You; You Never See the Sun

Cast: Paul Avedisian; Ray Collins; Ray Luetters; Carolyn Popp

1904 • HIS BRIDAL NIGHT

OPENED: 08/16/1916   Theatre: Republic
Play   Broadway: 77

Author: Margaret Mayo; Lawrence Rising
Producer: A.H. Woods
Director: Bertram Harrison

Songs: Beware of Pink Pajamas (C: Jean Schwartz; L: Sam M. Lewis; Joe Young)

Cast: Roszika Dolly; Yancsi Dolly; Jessie Ralph; Lucile Watson; John Westley; Pedro de Cordoba

1905 • HIS EXCELLENCY
OPENED: 10/14/1895   Theatre: Broadway
Musical   Broadway: 88

Composer: F. Osmond Carr
Lyricist: W.S. Gilbert
Librettist: W.S. Gilbert
Producer: Charles Frohman; Al Hayman
Director: John Gunn

Costumes: Percy Anderson; **Set Design:** Ernest Gros; E.G. Unitt

Songs: Come Hither, Every One; Here Are the Warriors All Ablaze; If All Is As You Say; King Who Is Pestered with Cares, A; My Wedded Life; Now All That We've Agreed Upon, O; Now If You Would Atone; Now What Would I Do If You Proved Untrue; Oh My Goodness, Here's the Nobility!; Oh What a Fund of Joy; One Day the Synic of This Town; Quixotic Is His Enterprise; Ring the Bells and Bang the Brasses!; See the Merry Bunting Flying; So This Is How You'd Have Us Sue You; There Once Was a Corporal Bold; When a Gentleman Supposes; When I Bestow My Bosom's Store; With Anger Stern

Cast: William Philip; Julius Steger; Ellaline Terriss

Notes: No songs listed in program.

1906 • HIS EXCELLENCY, THE PRESIDENT
OPENED: 1915
Musical

Composer: J. Homer Tutt; Salem Tutt Whitney
Lyricist: J. Homer Tutt; Salem Tutt Whitney
Librettist: J. Homer Tutt; Salem Tutt Whitney
Producer: J. Homer Tutt; Salem Tutt Whitney

Cast: Babe Brown; Helen Harper; Greenberg Holmes; Emma Jackson; William "Babe" Townsend; Salem Tutt Whitney

Notes: No other information available.

1907 • HIS HEART'S DESIRE
OPENED: 08/1916
Play   Closed out of town

Composer: Theodore Morse
Lyricist: Bartley Costello; Fiske O'Hara
Producer: Augustus Pitou

Songs: Be Sure and Kiss the Blarney Stone; Heart's Desire; How the Fairies Came to Ireland; Mollie Mine; Overture — His Heart's Desire (inst.) (C: Cassius Freeborn)

Cast: Lisle Leigh; Fiske O'Hara; Helen Vallely

Notes: Marshalltown, Iowa program used.

1908 • HIS HIGHNESS THE BEY
OPENED: 11/21/1904   Theatre: La Salle
Musical   Chicago

Composer: Joseph E. Howard
Lyricist: Frank R. Adams; Will M. Hough
Librettist: Frank R. Adams; Will M. Hough
Director: Joseph E. Howard

Songs: Caliph I, The; Coronation; Drink to the Glorious Night; Honolulu-lu; I'm Going to Leave You (L: Joseph E. Howard); In Dear Old Kankakee; In the Orange Blossom Land; Insurgents; Julie Dooley; Kitty and the Owl, The; Land of Nod, The [2]; Lovie; Mermaid and the Rainbow, The (Song of the Mermaid); My Gypsy Maid; Not Because Your Hair Is Curly [1] (C: Bob Adams); Stories of a Summer Night; Sweetheart of Boyhood Days

Cast: Al Shean

Notes: [1] Not in program. [2] Also in THE LAND OF NOD.

1909 • HIS HONOR THE BARBER
OPENED: 05/08/1911   Theatre: Majestic
Musical   Broadway: 16

Composer: James T. Brymn
Lyricist: James Burris; Chris Smith
Librettist: Edwin Hanaford
Producer: Southern Enchantment Co.
Director: S.H. Dudley

Songs: Consolation Lane; Corn Shucking Time; Crybaby Moon; Isles of Love, The; Leave 'Fore Supper Time; Merry Widow Brown; Porto Rico (inst.) (C: Ford T. Dabney); Rainbow Sue; You Needn't Come at All

Cast: James Burris; Mrs. S.H. Dudley; S.H. Dudley; Will Grundy; Elizabeth Hart; James Lightfoot; George McClain; Alberta Ormes; Andrew Tribble; Aida Overton Walker

Notes: No New York program available. One review stated there were 15 songs in this show.

1910 • HIS HONOR THE MAYOR

OPENED: 05/28/1906   Theatre: New York
Musical   Broadway: 104

Composer: Julian Edwards
Lyricist: Charles J. Campbell; Ralph Skinner
Librettist: Charles J. Campbell; Ralph Skinner
Producer: Alfred E. Aarons
Director: J.S. Murray

Musical Director: Daniel Dore

Songs: Call Around on Sunday (C: Alfred E. Aarons); Champagne (C: Alfred E. Aarons; Julian Edwards); Come Take a Skate with Me (C: Gus Edwards); Dainty Milliners, The (C: Alfred E. Aarons); Daisy, the Girl from Illinois; Finale Act I; Flower Song (C: Unknown); From the Lips [1] (C: Unknown); If the Folks Down Home Could See Me Now [1] (C/L: Bob Adams); Ifs [1] (C: Unknown); I'll Travel the Links with You (C: Alfred E. Aarons); In the Starlit Skies; Land You Left Behind, The; Little Girl from Illinois, The; Little Girl Like Me, A (C: Alfred E. Aarons); Mayor of Kankakee, The (Entrance of Todd); Military Willie; Military Willie; Mygar Maid; No Wonder Man Won't Wed [1] (C: Unknown); Opening Chorus; Opening Chorus Act II; She's All My Own (Mary Ann); Sweet Anastasia Brady [2] (C: Jean Schwartz; L: William Jerome); Sweet Tokay; Waltz Me Around Again Willie (C: Ren Shields; L: Will D. Cobb); Where the Wild Vine Clings; You're Drunk, By Gosh, You're Drunk [1] (C: Unknown)

Cast: Harry Kelly; James Murray; Fletcher Norton; Blanche Ring; E.E. Van Rensselaer; Fred Walton; Nella Webb

Notes: Out of town titled THE PINK HUSSARS. [1] Sheet music only. [2] Out of town program only.

1911 • HIS LITTLE WIDOWS

OPENED: 04/30/1917   Theatre: Astor
Musical   Broadway: 72

Composer: William Schroeder
Lyricist: William Cary Duncan; Rida Johnson Young
Librettist: William Cary Duncan; Rida Johnson Young
Producer: G.M. Anderson; L. Lawrence Weber
Director: Frank Stammers

Choreographer: David Bennett; **Orchestrations:** Silvio Hein

Songs: Brides' Lullaby [1]; I Don't Want to Be Loved By a Lot of Little Boys (But By One Little Boy a Lot) [6] (C: James F. Hanley; L: Arthur Jackson); I Need Someone's Love; I Want Them All; If It Should Be You [4]; I'm Crazy About the Way You Dance with Me [1]; I'm Wondering [2]; In Cabaret-Land; It's All in the Family [1]; Johnny Come Follow Me; Kiss, Kiss, Kiss [4]; Little Lady Opportunity [1]; Love Me Best of All; Maybe I Could If I Tried [4]; My Love Is a Secret; Oh, You Girls! [3]; Our Wedding Day [6] (C: James F. Hanley; L: Ballard Macdonald); Poor Sam [4]; Saints of the Latter Day; Salt Lake City [2]; Six Little Love-Birds [1]; Some Little Girl [1]; Teach Me to Love in Mexico [4]; That Creepy Weepy Feeling (L: Rida Johnson Young); That's the Kind of a Wifie to Be [1]; There'll Be a Rainbow in the Sky for You [1]; This Is the Best We Ever Struck; Twinkle, Little Broadway Star [1]; We Are the Modern Musketeers [1]; When the Animals Are Gone [5] (C: Malvin F. Franklin; L: Thomas J. Gray); When You Waltz with Me; Wife for Each Day in the Week, A; You're Falling in Love After All [1]

Cast: Hattie Burks; Frances Cameron; Carter De Haven; Haley Sisters, The; Robert Emmett Keane; Frank Lalor; Flora Parker; Alma Pickard; Julia Ralph; Harry Tighe

Notes: Out of town the show was titled SOME LITTLE GIRL. [1] Songs from Syracuse program of 3/18. [2] Cut after opening. [3] Titled "Oh! You James" in out-of-town program. [4] Sheet music only. [5] Titled "The Animal Rag" out of town. [6] ASCAP/Library of Congress only.

1912 • HIS MAJESTY

OPENED: 03/19/1906   Theatre: Majestic
Musical   Broadway: 24

Composer: Shafter Howard
Lyricist: Shafter Howard

Librettist: Shafter Howard
Producer: Nelson Roberts
Director: Richard Carroll

Choreographer: Hugh Flaherty; **Musical Director:** Clarence Rogerson

Songs: Are You a Single or a Married Man?; Conspirators; Crazyisms; Fairies Chorus; His Majesty; Isabel; Jemima Green; Maid from Boston Town, The; Maid of Arcadie, The; My Own; Opening Chorus; R. Strenuous Brown and Summer Girls; Serenade

Cast: Harry Kelly; Anna Laughlin; Blanche Ring; Van Rensselaer Wheeler

1913 • HIS-MUD-SCOW-PINAFORE
OPENED: 02/21/1879   Theatre: New York Opera
                       House
Musical   Broadway

Composer: Arthur Sullivan
Librettist: Add Ryman

Arrangements: W.S. Mullally

Cast: Billy Birch; George Powers; R.M. Ricardo; Add Ryman

Notes: A burlesque on H.M.S. PINAFORE.

1914 • HISTORY OF THE AMERICAN FILM, A
OPENED: 03/30/1978   Theatre: ANTA
Play   Broadway: 21

Composer: Mel Marvin
Lyricist: Christopher Durang
Author: Christopher Durang
Producer: Richard S. Bright; Judith Gordon
Director: David Chambers

Choreographer: Graciela Daniele; **Costumes:** Marjorie Slaiman; **Lighting Designer:** William Mintzer; **Musical Director:** Clay Fullum; **Orchestrations:** Robert M. Freedman; **Set Design:** Tony Straiges

Songs: Apple Blossom Victory; Euphemism; Isn't It Fun to Be in the Movies; Minstrel Song; Ostende Nobis Tosca; Pretty Pin-Up; Red, the White and

the Blue, The; Search for Wisdom; Shanty Town Romance; They Can't Prohibit Love; We're in a Salad

Cast: Gary Bayer; Bryan Clark; David Garrison; Ben Halley Jr.; Swoosie Kurtz; Joan Pape; April Shawhan; Eric Weitz; Mary Catherine Wright

1915 • HIT PARADE, THE
OPENED: 07/12/1985   Theatre: Manhattan
                       Punch Line
Play   Off-Off-Broadway

Composer: Jim Wann
Lyricist: Jim Wann
Author: Richard Dresser
Producer: Manhattan Punch Line
Director: Don Scardino

Costumes: David C. Woolard; **Set Design:** Daniel Conway

Cast: Pamela Blair; Larry Block; Nada Despotovich; George Gardes; Keith Reddin

Notes: No songs listed in program.

1916 • HIT THE DECK!
OPENED: 04/25/1927   Theatre: Belasco
Musical   Broadway: 352

Composer: Vincent Youmans
Lyricist: Clifford Grey; Leo Robin
Librettist: Herbert Fields
Producer: Lew Fields; Vincent Youmans
Director: Lew Fields; Alexander Leftwich

Source: SHORE LEAVE (Play: Hubert Osborn); **Choreographer:** Seymour Felix; **Costumes:** Mark Mooring; **Musical Director:** Paul Lannin; **Orchestrations:** Stephen Jones; Paul Lannin; **Set Design:** Ward & Harvey

Songs: Armful of You, An [4]; Fancy Me Just Meeting You [6] (L: Bert Lee; R.P. Weston); For Myself Alone [4]; Hallelujah [8]; Harbor of My Heart [2]; If He'll Come Back to Me [2]; Join the Navy; Kiss or Two, A [7] (C: Leo Robin); Loo-Loo; Lucky Bird; Nothing Could Be Sweeter [3]; Opening Act II; Quite the Thing [4]; Shore Leave; Sometimes I'm Happy [5]; Thing to Do, The [4]; Way You Manoeuvre, The [4]; Utopia [10]; What's a Kiss Among Friends? [1]; Why Oh Why [9]

Cast: Edward Allen; Madeline Cameron; Nancy Corrigan; Brian Donlevy; Louise Groody; Charles King; Stella Mayhew; John McCauley; Bobbie Perkins; Franker Woods

Notes: [1] First in TWO LITTLE GIRLS IN BLUE as part of "We're Off to See India," then "I Love You" in WILDFLOWERS and "Wedding Bells Ring On" in GREAT DAY! [2] Added after opening. [3] New lyric from "Why Oh Why." [4] Cut prior to opening. [5] Music used as "Come On and Pet Me" with an Irving Caesar lyric in MARY JANE MCKANE. First used as "Sometimes I'm Happy" in A NIGHT OUT. [6] Added to London production. [7] Not used. [8] Music written in 1918 for Sousa's Navy band. [9] Cut and music given new lyric and titled "Nothing Could Be Sweeter." [10] Cut after three weeks and replaced by "If He'll Come Back to Me."

1917 • HIT THE STRIDE
OPENED: 1958

Composer: Eubie Blake
Lyricist: Flournoy E. Miller

Songs: Cajun Dance, The; Don't Cheat on the Meat; Gal from Baton Rouge, The; Hep Cats Done Gone High Hat; Hit the Stride; Hobble on the Cobbles; If It Pleases You; It's Hard to Love Somebody (When That Somebody Don't Love You); It's Not Wrong to Have Fun; No Good Man (Will Make a Good Good Woman Bad), A; Shack Town; Strange What Love Will Do; There Are Some Things (You Just Can't Tell About); We Gotta Get Hitched Baby; You Can't Cash in On an Alibi; You Got to Git the Gittin' (While the Gittin' Is Good)

Notes: No other information available.

1918 • HIT THE TRAIL
OPENED: 12/02/1954   Theatre: Mark Hellinger
Musical   Broadway: 4

Composer: Frederico Valerio
Lyricist: Elizabeth Miele
Librettist: Frank O'Neill
Producer: Elizabeth Miele
Director: Byrle Cass; Charles W. Christenberry Jr.

Choreographer: Gene Bayliss; **Costumes:** Michi; **Lighting Designer:** Leo Kerz; **Musical Director:**

Arthur Norris; **Orchestrations:** Don Walker; **Set Design:** Leo Kerz; **Vocal Arranger:** Arthur Norris

Songs: Blue Sierras; Dynamic; Gold Cannot Buy; Happy Birthday; It Was Destiny; Just a Wonderful Time; Men Are a Pain in the Neck; Mr. Right; My Fatal Charm; Nevada Hoe Down; New Look Feeling; No! No! No!; On with the Show; Remember the Night; Set Me Free; Somehow I've Always Known; Take Your Time; Tell Me How; Wherever I May Go; Wide Open Spaces

Cast: Irra Petina; Paul Valentine; Robert Wright

Notes: Titled ON WITH THE SHOW out of town.

1919 • HITCHY-KOO (1917)
OPENED: 06/07/1917   Theatre: Cohan and
                            Harris
Revue   Broadway: 220

Composer: E. Ray Goetz
Lyricist: E. Ray Goetz; Glen MacDonough
Librettist: Harry Grattan; Glen MacDonough
Director: Leon Errol; Julian Mitchell

Set Design: Washington Square Players

Songs: Chinese Letter Song (C: Willy White; L: E. Ray Goetz); Dreamy Parisian Coon, The [1]; Driving Home with Angeline [1]; Have You Seen the Ducks [4] (C: Felix Powell; L: E. Ray Goetz; Glen MacDonough); Hitchy-Koo [4] (C: E. Ray Goetz; L: Glen MacDonough); I May Be Gone for a Long, Long Time (C: Albert Von Tilzer; L: Lew Brown); I Wish I Was a Big Sky Rocket [1] (C/L: E. Ray Goetz; Arthur James; Willy White); I'd Like to Be a Monkey in the Zoo (C: Willy White; L: Bert Hanlon); If You Were Here [1] (C/L: E. Ray Goetz; Arthur James; Willy White); Isle of Lost Romance, The; It's Easier to Kiss than Talk [1] (C: Milton Ager; L: E. Ray Goetz); Jim Jam Jems [1]; Knocking the 'K' Out of Kaiser [1]; Lady of the Sea [4]; M-i-s-s-i-s-s-i-p-p-i [3] (C: Harry Tierney; L: Bert Hanlon; Benny Ryan); My Little Bugaboo [1]; Pill Box Revue, The; Ragtime Alphabet [2]; Six Times Six Is Thirty Six (C: William White; L: Bert Hanlon); When I Went to School with You (C: Gus Edwards; L: Will D. Cobb); When You've Picked Your Basket of Peaches (The Girls of Home Sweet Home) [1] (L: E. Ray Goetz)

Cast: Irene Bordoni; Leon Errol; Raymond Hitchcock; William Holbrook; Grace LaRue; George Monroe; Louise Orth; William Rock; Frances White

Notes: [1] Sheet music only. [2] Out-of-town program only. [3] Not in program. Later also interpolated into the London show THE BEAUTY SPOT. [4] ASCAP/Library of Congress only.

1920 • HITCHY-KOO OF 1918

OPENED: 06/06/1918   Theatre: Globe
Revue   Broadway: 68

Composer: E. Ray Goetz
Lyricist: E. Ray Goetz; Glen MacDonough
Librettist: E. Ray Goetz; Glen MacDonough
Producer: Raymond Hitchcock
Director: Leon Errol

Musical Director: Oscar Radin; **Orchestrations:** Maurice DePackh; Frank Saddler; **Set Design:** H. Robert Law

Songs: Clara; Come Dance with Me (C: Harold Orlob; L: Ned Wayburn); Good Bye France [1] (C/L: Irving Berlin); Here Come the Yanks with Their Tanks [2] (C: Harold Orlob; L: Ned Wayburn); Hitchy Koo Girl [1] (C: Percy Wenrich); How Can You Tell? (C: Harold Orlob; L: Ned Wayburn); It Will All End Up with the Right End Up; Jazz-Ma-Tazz [2] (C: Harold Orlob; L: Ned Wayburn); Let's Play Hookie; Lily of Longacre Square, The (C: Raymond Hubbell); Resurrection Rag (C: Raymond Hubbell); San Sebastian's Shores [2] (C: Harry Carroll); Say Hitchy-Koo, That's All [2] (C: Willy White; L: Sidney D. Mitchell); Solitaire Lane [3] (C: Raymond Hubbell; L: Glen MacDonough); Twilight Night [2] (C: Harold Orlob; L: Ned Wayburn); Underneath a Parasol (C: Harold Orlob; L: Ned Wayburn); When the Girls Get Wise; Where Do They Come From? (C: Harold Orlob; L: Fred Herendeen); You-oo Just You (C: George Gershwin; L: Irving Caesar)

Cast: Irene Bordoni; Ray Dooley; Leon Errol; Emma Haig; Raymond Hitchcock; George Austin Moore; Florence O'Denishawn

Notes: E. Ray Goetz not mentioned in program. [1] Out Washington, D.C. 2/9/18. [2] Not in program. [3] Sheet music only.

1921 • HITCHY-KOO OF 1919

OPENED: 10/06/1919   Theatre: Liberty
Revue   Broadway: 56

Composer: Cole Porter
Lyricist: Cole Porter
Librettist: George V. Hobart
Producer: Raymond Hitchcock
Director: Julian Alfred

Orchestrations: Stephen Jones

Songs: Ah Fong Low [2]; Another Sentimental Song [1]; Bring Me Back My Butterfly; China Doll [1]; Hitchy's Garden of Roses; I Introduced; I'm an Anaesthetic Dancer; I've Got Somebody Waiting; My Cozy Little Corner in the Ritz; Oh So Soon [1]; Old-Fashioned Garden; Pagliacci; Peter Piper; Sea Is Calling, The; Since Little Baby Brother Became a Movie Star [1]; Since Ma Got the Craze Espagnole [1]; That Black and White Baby of Mine [1]; Tired of Living Alone [1]; When Black Sallie Sings Pagliacci; When I Had a Uniform On; You and Me [3]

Cast: Joe Cook; Lillian Kemble Cooper; Raymond Hitchcock; Ruth Mitchell; Florence O'Denishawn

Notes: [1] Not used. [2] Not used and also not used in HITCHY-KOO OF 1922. [3] Not same as Porter song of same name in LA REVUE DES AMBASSADEURS.

1922 • HITCHY-KOO OF 1920

OPENED: 10/19/1920   Theatre: New Amsterdam
Musical   Broadway: 71

Composer: Jerome Kern
Lyricist: Anne Caldwell; Glen MacDonough
Librettist: Anne Caldwell; Glen MacDonough
Producer: Raymond Hitchcock
Director: Ned Wayburn

Costumes: O'Kane Conwell; Mme. B. Rasimi; **Musical Director:** Cassius Freeborn; **Orchestrations:** Frank Saddler

Songs: Bring 'Em Back [4]; Buggy Riding; By the Sea [3]; Canajoharie; Chick! Chick! Chick! [5]; Congo Nights [6] (C: Sol Violinsky; L: Rubey Cowan); Costumes for 1950 [1]; Cupid, the Winner; Dance-O-Mania; Ding, Dong It's Kissing Time; (There Are Plenty of) Girls in the Sea [1]; I Am Daguerre; I Want to Marry; Millinery

Mannequin, The; Moon of Love; Old Fashioned
Dances; Old New York; Only for You [1]; Race of
the Year, The [1]; Star of Hitchy-Koo, The;
Sweetie; Treasure Island; We'll Make a Bet;
We've Been Married Today [3]; Won't You All
Fall in Love with Me [2]

Cast: Inez Ford; Raymond Hitchcock; G.P.
Huntley; Grace Moore; Florence O'Denishawn;
Julia Sanderson

Notes: [1] Cut. [2] Out Philadelphia 1/17/21. [3]
Out Boston 10/11/20. [4] Music revised later for
"In Dahomey" from SHOW BOAT. [5] Cut. In
THE NIGHT BOAT. [6] Sheet music only.

1923 • HITCHY-KOO OF 1922

OPENED: 10/10/1922
Revue   Closed out of town

Composer: Cole Porter
Lyricist: Cole Porter
Librettist: Harold Atteridge
Producer: J.J. Shubert; Lee Shubert
Director: J.C. Huffman

Songs: Ah Fong Low [2]; American Punch (It's
the Punches), The [4]; Bandit Band, The [8];
Curio Song (Old King Solly) [7]; Dancing
Shoes [6]; Daughters of Satan [6]; Do You Love
As I Love [9] (C: Lewis E. Gensler; Joseph
Meyer; L: Irving Caesar); Harbor Deep Down in
My Heart, The [7]; In Hitchy's Bouquet; Jungle
Rose [7]; Love Letter Words; Lullaby Lane [9]
(C: Lewis E. Gensler; L: Irving Caesar);
Maryland Scene; My Spanish Shawl [3];
Oh, Mary; Old-Fashioned Waltz, The [7];
Pitter-Patter [7]; Play Me a Tune [5]; Romeo [9]
(C: Lewis E. Gensler; L: Irving Caesar); Scotch
Twins [1]; South Sea Isles [1]; Sponge, The;
Twin Sisters [7]; Under a Pretty Hat [6];
Versailles [6]; When My Caravan Comes Home

Cast: Edythe Baker; Florence Bert; May Boley;
El Brendel; Helen Dahlia; Raymond Hitchcock;
Benny Leonard; Jack Pearl; Jack Squire

Notes: Closed in Philadelphia. [1] May or may not
have been used (incomplete playbill). [2] Not
used in HITCHY-KOO OF 1919. [3] Not used
later in GREENWICH VILLAGE FOLLIES
(1924). Also revised and included as part of
"I Dream of a Girl in a Shawl" in WAKE UP
AND DREAM. [4] Also used in THE DANCING

GIRL (1923). [5] Also used in THE DANCING
GIRL (1923) and in the London Revue ONE
DAM THING AFTER ANOTHER as "Play Us a
Tune." [6] May not be by Porter. [7] Not used. [8]
Earlier version not used in MAYFAIR AND
MONTMARTRE. [9] ASCAP/Library of
Congress only. Listed in 1923. These might have
been added for tour.

1924 • HOBO

OPENED: 04/10/1961   Theatre: Gate
Musical   Off-Broadway: 32

Composer: John Dooley
Lyricist: John Dooley
Librettist: John Dooley
Producer: George E. Burns
Director: Rinaldo Capillupo

Choreographer: Ray James; **Costumes:** Ken
Starrett; **Dance Arranger:** Dan Gordon; **Lighting
Designer:** Richard Nelson; **Set Design:** Sonia
Lowenstein; **Vocal Arranger:** Robert Hammer;
Phil Orlando

Songs: Bleecker Street; Cindy; From the Moment;
I Hate You; Jonah's Wail; Julie; Little Birds;
Nuthin' for Nuthin'; On the Day When the
World Goes Boom; Somewhere in Your Eyes;
Sweetness; Sympathy; Virgin Polka, The; Who
Put Out the Light That Lit the Candle That
Started the Flame Deep Down in My Heart?

Cast: Ron Holgate; Rita Howell; Eleanor La Forge;
Kenneth Lynch Jr.; Elmarie Wendel

1925 • HODGE, PODGE & CO.

OPENED: 10/23/1900   Theatre: Madison Square
Musical   Broadway: 73

Composer: John W. Bratton
Lyricist: Walter Ford
Librettist: George V. Hobart
Producer: Frank McKee
Director: R.A. Roberts

Source: POSSE IM HIMMELSHOF (Musical: Jean
Kren); **Costumes:** Will R. Barnes; **Set Design:**
Arthur Voegtlin

Songs: Away to the Links [1]; Cindy (C/L: Dave
Reed); Dream Days of Seville; 'E Didn't Know
Just W'at to Say; Gay Golf Girl, The [1]; I Love

You Babe, and You Love Me (C/L: McConnell; Smith); I'm a Scion of the House of Highball; Kissing Trust, The [1]; Modest Maidens We; My Charcoal Charmer (C: Gus Edwards; L: Walter Ford); My Sunflower Sue; Picture No Artist Can Paint, A; Since My Linda's in the Syn-de-cate; Soldier of Love Am I, A; Sweet Bells of Spring; Town Folks Will Be Pleased, The; What a Funny Story (C: Herman Perlet); White and Gray Cadets, The; You Never Can Tell What a Kiss Will Do; You're Altogether Model Girls

Cast: Peter F. Dailey; Edward Garvie; Christie MacDonald; William Roderick

Notes: [1] Out of town only.

1926 • HOITY TOITY

OPENED: 09/05/1901   Theatre: Weber and Fields
                      Music Hall
Revue   Broadway: 225

Composer: John Stromberg
Lyricist: Edgar Smith
Librettist: Edgar Smith
Producer: Lew Fields; Joseph Weber
Director: Julian Mitchell

Costumes: Will R. Barnes; **Set Design:** John Young

Songs: As on Moonlit Waves We Ride; Beautiful Monte Carlo [3]; Bill Simmons [1]; Dainty Little Maid; De Pullman Porter's Ball; Down the Line; Friends That Are Good and True [2]; Girl I Left in Boston Town, The [2]; Girly Girly [1]; Gold! Gold! Gold! [3]; I'm an American Billionaire; King Kazoo of Kacaroo; Love a la Mode; Love Me and the World Is Mine [4]; Ma Poppy Belle; Mary Black; Minstrel Parade [2]; Minstrel Show, The; My Japanese Cherry Blossom [3]; O'er Moonlit Waves [2]; Poor Little Fluttering Moths; Pull Away; Shine! Shine! Shine!; Society Queen, The; Take a Ride with Me [1]; Tea! Tea!; Under the Elms at New Haven [3]; When Mr. Shakespeare Comes to Town [5] (C: Jean Schwartz; L: William Jerome); When Two Little Hearts Are One

Cast: Sam Bernard; Bessie Clayton; Lew Fields; Lee Harrison; DeWolf Hopper; John T. Kelly; Bonnie Maginn; Lillian Russell; Fay Templeton; Joseph Weber; Fritz Williams

Notes: [1] Out Baltimore 4/21/02. [2] Out

Wilkes-Barre 9/24/06. [3] Added after opening. [4] Out Baltimore 4/21/02. The famous song of the same name was written in 1906 by Ernest R. Ball and James Reed Jr. [5] Sheet music only.

1927 • HOKEY-POKEY

OPENED: 02/08/1912   Theatre: Broadway
Revue   Broadway: 108

Composer: W.T. Francis; A. Baldwin Sloane
Lyricist: E. Ray Goetz
Librettist: Edgar Smith
Producer: Lew Fields; Joseph Weber
Director: Gus Sohlke

Costumes: Cora MacGeachy; **Lighting Designer:** David Atchison; **Musical Director:** George A. Nichols; **Set Design:** John Young

Songs: Alexander's Bagpipe Band [1] (C/L: Irving Berlin; E. Ray Goetz; A. Baldwin Sloane); Garden of Yesterday, The; If It Wasn't for the Irish and the Jews (C: Jean Schwartz; L: William Jerome); Island of Roses and Love, The (C/L: Neil Moret); La Belle Paree; La Clare de la Lune; Minstrel Parade, The; My Heather Belle [1]; On the Stage; Overture (C: John Stromberg); Rosie; Senorita; Singer and the Song, The

Cast: Frankie Bailey; George Beban; Bessie Clayton; Willie Collier; Lew Fields; John T. Kelly; Ada Lewis; Lillian Russell; Fay Templeton; Joseph Weber

Notes: Medley of Stromberg tunes from Weber and Fields shows opened act one. The second act was the parody BUNTY BULLS AND STRINGS. [1] Part of BUNTY BULLS AND STRINGS.

1928 • HOLD BACK THE DAWN

Musical   Unproduced

Composer: Jerome Kern
Lyricist: Dorothy Fields
Producer: Cheryl Crawford

Songs: April Fooled Me; Azusa; Barrelhouse Beguine; Introduce Me; Never You Mind; New Number Two; Not Now; Novellette; Once There Were Two of Us; What Do I Know About You?

Notes: No other information available.

1929 • HOLD EVERYTHING!

OPENED: 10/10/1928   Theatre: Broadhurst
Musical   Broadway: 413

Composer: Ray Henderson
Lyricist: Lew Brown; B.G. DeSylva
Librettist: B.G. DeSylva; John McGowan
Producer: Alex A. Aarons; Vinton Freedley

Choreographer: Jack Haskell; Sam Rose;
  Costumes: Kiviette; **Musical Director:** Oscar
  Radin; **Set Design:** Henry Dreyfuss

Songs: Don't Hold Everything, Let Everything Go;
  Footwork; For Sweet Charity's Sake; Genealogy;
  Heel Beat [1]; Here's One Who Wouldn't [1];
  Oh, Gosh; Outdoor Man (for My Indoor Sports);
  'S Over but the Shoutin'; To Know You Is to
  Love You; Too Good to Be True; We're Calling
  on Mr. Brooks; We're Waiting on the Weather
  [1]; When I Love, I Love; You're the Cream in
  My Coffee

Cast: Betty Compton; Bert Lahr; Victor Moore;
  Ona Munson; Jack Whiting

Notes: [1] Not used.

1930 • HOLD IT!

OPENED: 05/05/1948   Theatre: National
Musical   Broadway: 46

Composer: Gerald Marks
Lyricist: Sam Lerner
Librettist: Art Arthur; Matt Brooks
Producer: Sammy Lambert
Director: Robert E. Perry

Choreographer: Michael Kidd; **Costumes:** Julia
  Sze; **Dance Arranger:** Irma Jurist; **Musical
  Director:** Clay Warnick; **Orchestrations:** Ted
  Royal; Hans Spialek; **Set Design:** Edward
  Gilbert; **Vocal Arranger:** Clay Warnick

Songs: About Face; Always You; Buck in the Bank;
  Down the Well; Friendly Enemy; Fundamental
  Character; Heaven Sent; Hold It!; It Was So Nice
  Having You; Nevermore; Opening; Roll 'Em;
  You Took Possession of Me

Cast: Red Buttons; Johnny Downs; Jet MacDonald;
  Patricia Wymore

1931 • HOLD ON TO YOUR HATS

OPENED: 09/11/1940   Theatre: Shubert
Musical   Broadway: 158

Composer: Burton Lane
Lyricist: E.Y. Harburg
Librettist: Guy Bolton; Matt Brooks; Eddie Davis
Producer: George Hale; Al Jolson
Director: Edgar MacGregor

Choreographer: Catherine Littlefield; **Costumes:**
  Raoul Pene du Bois; **Lighting Designer:** Feder;
  Musical Director: Al Goodman; **Orchestrations:**
  Hans Spialek; Don Walker; **Set Design:** Raoul
  Pene du Bois; **Vocal Arranger:** Joseph Lilley

Songs: Bedtime on the Prairie [1]; Crispy, Crunch
  Crackers [2]; Don't Let It Get You Down; Down
  on the Dude Ranch; Hold On to Your Hats; Life
  Was Pie for the Pioneer; Looks Like I'm Off O'
  Ya [1]; Old Timer; She Came, She Saw, She Can
  Canned; Swing Your Calico [1]; Then You Were
  Never in Love; There's a **Great** Day Coming
  Manana; Walkin' Along Mindin' My Business;
  Way Out West Where the East Begins; World Is
  in My Arms, The; Would You Be So Kindly

Cast: Jinx Falkenburg; Bert Gordon; Eunice Healey;
  Al Jolson; Gil Lamb; Martha Raye; Jack Whiting

Notes: [1] Cut Detroit 6/30/40. [2] ASCAP/Library
  of Congress only.

1932 • HOLD YOUR HORSES

OPENED: 09/25/1933   Theatre: Winter Garden
Musical   Broadway: 88

Composer: Robert Russell Bennett
Lyricist: Owen Murphy; Robert A. Simon
Librettist: Russel Crouse; Corey Ford
Additional Dialogue: Joe Cook
Producer: Joe Cook; Messrs. Shubert
Director: R.H. Burnside; John Shubert

Choreographer: Robert Alton; Harriet Hoctor;
  Costumes: Russell Patterson; **Musical Director:**
  Gene Salzer; **Orchestrations:** Robert Russell
  Bennett; **Set Design:** Russell Patterson

Songs: Do You?; Galloping Through the Park;
  Good Evening, Mr. Man in the Moon; Happy
  Little Weekend; High Shoes; Hold Your Horses
  (C: Louis Alter; L: Arthur Swanstrom); I Guess

I Love You; I'd Like to Take You Home to Meet My Mother; If I Love Again (C: Ben Oakland; L: J.P. Murray); Old Man Subway; Peanuts and Kisses; Singing to You (C/L: Margot Millham; Ben Oakland; Robert A. Simon); Swapping Sweet Nothings with You

Cast: Dave Chasen; Joe Cook; Inez Courtney; Harriet Hoctor; Ona Munson; Tom Patricola; Jack Powell; Stanley Smith; Frances Upton; Rex Weber

1933 • HOLIDAY

OPENED: 06/09/1956   Theatre: NBC
TV Musical

Music Based On: Johann Strauss
Composer: Mel Pahl; Clay Warnick
Lyricist: Edward Eager
Producer: Max Liebman
Director: Charles S. Dubin; Max Liebman

Source: GRAND TOUR, THE (Play: Elmer Rice);
Musical Director: Charles Sanford

Cast: Rod Alexander; Keith Andes; Kitty Carlisle; Jacques D'Amboise; Tammy Grimes; George S. Irving; Bambi Lynn; Doretta Morrow; Charles Weidman

1934 • HOLIDAY ON ICE

OPENED: 1946
Revue

Composer: Carmen Nappo
Lyricist: Ben Mann
Director: Truly McGee

Costumes: Ann Elliot; **Musical Director:** Ray Cavanaugh

Cast: Milton Blakely

Notes: No other information available.

1935 • HOLKA-POLKA

OPENED: 10/14/1925   Theatre: Lyric
Musical   Broadway: 21

Composer: Will Ortmann
Lyricist: Raymond B. Egan; Gus Kahn
Librettist: Bert Kalmar; Harry Ruby

Producer: Carl Reed
Director: Oscar Eagle

Source: FRUHLING IM HERBST (Play: W. Walzer); **Choreographer:** Busby Berkeley; **Costumes:** Livingston Platt; **Musical Director:** Max Steiner; **Set Design:** Livingston Platt

Songs: Chimes of the Chapel; Fairy Tale; Goodfellow Days; Highway's Call, The; Holka-Polka; Home of My Heart; I Want to Be a Bad Little Boy; In a Little While (L: Raymond B. Egan); Mary to the Market Went; Nobody; Spring in Autumn; This Is My Dance; When Love Is Near

Cast: Orville Harrold; Patti Harrold; George E. Mack; James C. Morton; May Vokes

Notes: Source translated by Derick Wulff. Also titled SPRING IN AUTUMN and NOBODY'S GIRL.

1936 • HOLLY GOLIGHTLY

Notes: *See BREAKFAST AT TIFFANY'S.*

1937 • HOLLYWOOD BE THY NAME

OPENED: 1933
Vaudeville Act

Songs: Hollywood Be Thy Name (C: Harold Spina; L: Frank Loesser; Jacques Press)

Notes: No other information available.

1938 • HOLLYWOOD HILARITIES

Theatre: Florentine Gardens
Revue   Nightclub

Composer: Roy Ingraham
Lyricist: Dave Oppenheim
Producer: Nils Thor Granlund
Director: Dave Gould

Costumes: Jourge; **Musical Director:** Emil Baffa

Songs: California Summer Sports; Classics, The; Hot Music; I Found a Rainbow; Return of Little Neil; Rose of San Antone; What the Red, White and Blue Did for You

Cast: Jayne Crawford; Sugar Geise; Joe Kirk; Jerrie Kruger; Fred Scott

Notes: Los Angeles nightclub show.

1939 • HOLLYWOOD HOLIDAY

OPENED: 02/15/1935
Play   Closed out of town

Composer: J. Fred Coots
Lyricist: Haven Gillespie; Mitchell Parish
Author: Douglas Gilmore; Kay Kenney
Producer: Mayfair Productions
Director: Thomas Mitchell

Set Design: Donald Oenslager

Songs: Dream Shadows; Hollywood Holiday

Cast: Bebe Daniels; Skeets Gallagher; Ben Lyon

Notes: Name later changed to NO MAN'S A HERO.

1940 • HOLLYWOOD HOLLYWOOD!

OPENED: 1984
Revue   Los Angeles

Composer: Lou Vitacco
Lyricist: Lou Vitacco
Librettist: Lou Vitacco
Producer: Masquers, The
Director: Ernest Sanacino

Choreographer: Nanon Tygett; **Costumes:** Diane Allen; James Wilke; **Set Design:** Jack Hazelton

Songs: Bang Your Way to the Top; Better Idea, A; C'est Cheesecake; Coffee Beans; Could I Ever Have It All?; Did You Think You Would Break My Heart?; Getting Out; Here I Am; Hollywood Hollywood!; I Come to You; I Hear the Music When I'm Dancin' with You; I Really Don't Have Time to Be Thinking about Romance; I'm Gonna Be a Movie Star; Letter, The; Little Macho Me; Love Ranger Rides Again, The; Lovers Waltz, The; Schwabs; Sitting at Home Eating Bon Bons and Doing My Nails; Them Bells; Truckin' in Hollywood

Cast: Christopher Holder; Kristina Martin; Christofer Sands; Marleta Warneke; **Pianist:** Lou Vitacco

1941 • HOLLYWOOD ICE REVUE, THE

OPENED: 1954
Revue

Composer: Robert Allen
Lyricist: Al Stillman
Producer: Arthur M. Wirtz
Director: Carl Littlefield

Choreographer: Carl Littlefield; **Costumes:** Grace Houston; **Musical Director:** Paul Van Loan

Songs: Breakin' the Ice

Cast: Barbara Ann Scott; Freddie Trenkler

1942 • HOLLYWOOD MUSIC BOX REVUE (1925) (SPRING EDITION)

OPENED: 1925
Revue   Los Angeles

Composer: Arthur Freed
Lyricist: Arthur Freed
Librettist: Carter De Haven

Songs: Hold Me in Your Arms Again; Quack, Quack; Who's Who with You

Notes: No other information available.

1943 • HOLLYWOOD MUSIC BOX REVUE (1926)

OPENED: 1926
Revue   Los Angeles

Composer: Nacio Herb Brown

Songs: Doll Dance (What a Peculiar Tune), The (inst.)

Cast: Doris Eaton

Notes: No other information available. The above tune is an instrumental.

1944 • HOLLYWOOD MUSIC BOX REVUE (1927) (SPRING EDITION)

OPENED: 02/02/1927
Revue   Los Angeles

Librettist: Fanny Brice; Herbert Fields; Ned Joyce Heaney; Bert Kalmar; Harry Ruby
Producer: Louis Macloon
Director: Lillian Albertson

Choreographer: George Cunningham; **Costumes:** Howard Greer; **Musical Director:** Arthur Kay

Songs: All Alone Monday [3] (C: Harry Ruby; L: Bert Kalmar); Hold Me in Your Arms [4] (C/L: Arthur Freed); Hollywood Relief, A [2] (C: Arthur Freed; L: Leonard Levinson; Robert Lord); I'm a Little Butterfly [5] (C: Edwin Weber; L: Blanche Merrill); Little Bit of Spain in California, A [1] (C/L: Arthur Freed); Loose Ankles [2] (C: Arthur Freed; L: Blanche Merrill); Make 'Em Laugh [5] (C: Edwin Weber; L: Blanche Merrill); Quack, Quack [4] (C: Arthur Freed; L: Blanche Merrill); Result of Miss Brice's Going to Dancing School, The (C: Edwin Weber; L: Blanche Merrill); Rose of Arizona (C: Richard Rodgers; L: Lorenz Hart); She Won't Charleston (C: Harry Ruby; L: Bert Kalmar); Singin' in the Rain [6] (C: Nacio Herb Brown; L: Arthur Freed); Spring in Autumn (C/L: Will Ortmann); We Don't Know Why-But (C: Arthur Freed; L: Robert Lord); Who's Who with You [4] (C/L: Arthur Freed); Window Cleaners [7] (C: Harry Ruby; L: Bert Kalmar); You Smiled at Me (C: Harry Ruby; L: Bert Kalmar)

Cast: Sam Ash; Fanny Brice; Marie Callahan; Ted Doner; Edythe Maye

Notes: [1] Also in ALL FOR YOU. [2] Also in HOLLYWOOD MUSIC BOX REVUE (1927) (FALL EDITION). [3] Also in THE RAMBLERS. [4] Also in HOLLYWOOD MUSIC BOX REVUE (1925) (SPRING EDITION). [5] Not in program. [6] ASCAP/Library of Congress only. [7] Also in THE GREENWICH VILLAGE FOLLIES (1925) and London production of THE FIVE O'CLOCK GIRL.

1945 • HOLLYWOOD MUSIC BOX REVUE (1934)

OPENED: 1934
Revue   Los Angeles

Songs: Panama (C/L: Gerald Dolin; Edward J. Lambert)

Notes: No other information available.

1946 • HOLLYWOOD MUSIC BOX REVUE (1927) (FALL EDITION)

OPENED: 1927
Revue   Los Angeles

Producer: Carter De Haven

Songs: Hollywood Relief, A [1] (C: Arthur Freed; L: Leonard Levinson; Robert Lord); Loose Ankles (C: Arthur Freed; L: Blanche Merrill); Singin' in the Rain (C: Nacio Herb Brown; L: Arthur Freed); We Don't Know When-But (C: Arthur Freed; L: Arthur Lord)

Notes: No other information available. [1] Also in the HOLLYWOOD MUSIC BOX REVUE (1927) (Spring Edition).

1947 • HOLLYWOOD NINE O'CLOCK REVUE, THE

OPENED: 1931
Revue   Los Angeles

Composer: Val Burton; Will Jason
Lyricist: Val Burton; Will Jason
Producer: Eddie Lambert
Director: Eddie Diamond; Eddie Prinz

Songs: Day I Met You, The; When We're Alone [1]

Cast: Eddie Borden; Julian Eltinge; Max Fisher and His Orchestra; Frankie Heath; Al Herman; Eddie Lambert

Notes: Sheet music only. [1] Also known as "Penthouse Serenade," this song was used in many films.

1948 • HOLLYWOOD PINAFORE (OR THE LAD WHO LOVED A SALARY)

OPENED: 05/31/1945   Theatre: Alvin
Musical   Broadway: 53

Composer: Arthur Sullivan
Lyricist: George S. Kaufman
Librettist: George S. Kaufman
Producer: Max Gordon
Director: George S. Kaufman

Source: H.M.S. PINAFORE (Musical: W.S. Gilbert; Arthur Sullivan); **Choreographer:** Douglas

Coudy; Anthony Tudor; **Costumes:** Katherine Kuhn; Mary Percy Schenck; **Musical Director:** George Hirst; **Orchestrations:** Stephen Jones; Hans Spialek; **Set Design:** Jo Mielziner

Cast: Shirley Booth; Annamary Dickey; Viola Essen; William Gaxton; Victor Moore; Gilbert Russell; Mary Wickes

1949 • HOLLYWOOD REVELS OF 1933

OPENED: 1933
Revue   Los Angeles

Composer: Michael Cleary
Lyricist: Dave Oppenheim
Producer: Jacob Amron; Joe Moss
Director: Danny Dare

Songs: Dolly Dimple's Holiday

Cast: Rudy Vallee

Notes: Nightclub show. No other information available.

1950 • HOLLYWOOD REVELS OF 1934

OPENED: 10/02/1933
Revue   Los Angeles

Composer: Michael Cleary
Lyricist: Dave Oppenheim
Producer: Jacob Amron; Joe Moss
Director: Danny Dare

Musical Director: Charlie Davis

Songs: By a River in Spain; Lenox Avenue

Cast: Barbara Blane; Florenz & Alvarez; Pietro Gentile; Girl Friends, The; Jerry Lester; Rudy Vallee; Rita White

Notes: Produced at The Hollywood Restaurant. No program available.

1951 • HOLLYWOOD REVELS OF 1936

OPENED: 1936
Revue   Los Angeles

Composer: Jerry Livingston [1]
Lyricist: Al J. Neiburg; Marty Symes
Director: Danny Dare

Musical Director: Abe Lyman

Songs: Born to Be Bored; International, The; It's a Lot of Idle Gossip; Kisses from My Violin to You (C: Doris Fisher; L: Alfred Bryan); Topic of the Tropics, The; When April Comes Again

Cast: Jo Moss

Notes: Nightclub show. No other information available. [1] Used real name: Jerry Levinson.

1952 • HOLLYWOOD REVELS OF 1937

OPENED: 1937
Revue   Los Angeles

Songs: Struttin' to Sutton Place (C/L: Jacques Krakeur II; Dave Oppenheim)

Notes: Sheet music only.

1953 • HOLLYWOOD REVUE PRODUCTION (1938-39)

OPENED: 1938
Revue   Los Angeles

Composer: Al Jacobs; Jack Palmer
Lyricist: Al Jacobs; Dave Oppenheim; Jack Palmer
Producer: Bobby Sanford
Director: Bobby Sanford

Songs: Flea Hop, The; Let's Go Broadway; Love, I'd Give My Life for You; Oriental Magic; Sockin' the Cymbal; Swingin' the Nursery Rhymes; We Always Get Our Man; Wiggley Walk

Notes: No other information available.

1954 • HOME AGAIN

Notes: *See HOME AGAIN, HOME AGAIN.*

1955 • HOME AGAIN, HOME AGAIN

OPENED: 03/10/1979
Musical   Closed out of town

2

Composer: Cy Coleman
Lyricist: Barbara Fried
Librettist: Russell Baker
Producer: Stephen R. Friedman; Irwin Meyer
Director: Gene Saks

Choreographer: Onna White; **Costumes:** Jane Greenwood; **Dance Arranger:** Cy Coleman; **Lighting Designer:** Neil Peter Jampolis; **Musical Director:** Stanley Lebowsky; **Orchestrations:** Jim Tyler; **Set Design:** Peter Larkin; **Vocal Arranger:** Cy Coleman; Stanley Lebowsky

Songs: All for Love; America Don't Know How Any More; America Is Bathed in Sunlight; Big People; Finale; French; Home Again; How Can You Say You Feel Rich Anymore; I Gotta; I'm Your Guy; Marriage (Wedding) Song; Superland; Tell It to Me Dad; That Happy American Dream; Thomas Jefferson Witherspoon; Traveling Together; Way I See It, The; What'll It Take; When It Comes to Loving; When the Going Gets Tough; Winter Rain; You Can't Say You Feel Rich Anymore

Cast: Ronny Cox; Rex Everhart; Bob Freschi; Mike Kellin; Lisa Kirk; Anita Morris; Teri Ralston; Dick Shawn; Jeannine Taylor

Notes: Originally titled HOME AGAIN. Opened in Stratford, Ontario. Closed 4/14/79 at the Royal Alexandra Theatre in Toronto. The making of this show became the basis for the Musical 13 DAYS TO BROADWAY. Some of the same songs appear in both shows.

1956 • HOME, JAMES (1917)
OPENED: 03/28/1917
Musical

Composer: Robert Lippmann
Lyricist: Herman A. Axelrod; Oscar Hammerstein II
Librettist: Herman A. Axelrod; Oscar Hammerstein II
Producer: Columbia University Players
Director: Kenneth Webb

Songs: Annie McGinnis Pavlova

Cast: Oscar Hammerstein II

Notes: Amateur show.

1957 • HOME, JAMES (1933)
OPENED: 03/10/1933
Musical   Unknown: 2

Lyricist: Arnold Auerbach
Librettist: Herman Wouk
Director: Kenneth Webb

Choreographer: Paul Wyncoop; **Musical Director:** Jerry McGarrahan; **Set Design:** Belmont Corn

Songs: Forgotten Man, The (C: Harold Namuth); I'll Be a Sister to You (C: Jack Phelps); Send Me a Man (C: J. Morrisey); That's What I Like in a Man (C: M. Billig); We'll Snoop It Out (L: Maurice L. Levin); World of Our Own, A (C: Harold Namuth)

Cast: Willis P. Donklin; Alvin J. Gordon; Martin F. Manulis; Rowland Nelson

Notes: Amateur show. Produced at the Waldorf-Astoria by the Columbia University Players.

1958 • HOME MOVIES
OPENED: 05/11/1964   Theatre: Provincetown Playhouse
Musical   Off-Broadway: 72

Composer: Al Carmines
Lyricist: Rosalyn Drexler
Librettist: Rosalyn Drexler
Producer: Orson Bean Productions; Judson Poets' Theatre
Director: Lawrence Kornfeld

Costumes: Judith Berkowitz; **Lighting Designer:** Nicola Cernovich; **Set Design:** Larry Siegel

Songs: Birdies; Boasting Song; Chocolate Turkey; Daisies; Darkness Song; Do Not Bruise the Fruit; Equipment Song; Here They Come Now; I Know You Sell It; I'm Gwine Lie Down; Lower the Boom; Mania, A; My Number Is Eleven; Once You've Seen Everything; Peanut Song; Pents-un-Wreckum; Power Stronger Than Will, A; Pussy Cat Song; Remember When I Hated You?; Seminary Song; Show Me; Stuttering Song; Swoop of the Moopem; Two Falls to a Finish; You Look Like Me

Cast: Sudie Bond; Al Carmines; Gretel Cummings; Fred Herko

1959 • HOME SWEET HOMER

OPENED: 01/04/1976   Theatre: Palace
Musical   Broadway: 1

Composer: Mitch Leigh
Lyricist: Forman Brown; Charles Burr
Librettist: Roland Kibbee; Albert Marre
Producer: John F. Kennedy Center
Director: Albert Marre

Source: ODYSSEY, THE (Poetry: Homer);
Choreographer: Albert Marre; **Costumes:**
Howard Bay; Ray Diffen; **Lighting Designer:**
Howard Bay; **Musical Director:** Ross
Reismueller; **Orchestrations:** Buryl Red; **Set
Design:** Howard Bay

Songs: Ball, The; Contest, The; Departure, The; Did
He Really Think; Future, The; He Sang Songs; He
Will Come Home Again; Home Sweet Homer;
How Could I Dare to Dream; I Never Imagined
Goodbye; I Was Wrong; Island, The [1]; Love Is
the Prize; Nausikaa's Theme [1]; Penelope's
Hand; Prologue [1]; Rose, The; Sailing, The [1];
Show Me the Sun [1]; Sorceress, The; Tales, The;
Three Hundred Days [1]; Tomorrow; Wherever
You Are [1]

Cast: John Aristides; Daniel Brown; Yul Brynner;
Diana Davila; Brian Destazio; Joan Diener; Bill
Mackey; Ian Sullivan; Russ Thacker; Martin
Vidnovic

Notes: Titled ODYSSEY out of town. [1] Not in
program.

1960 • HONEY

OPENED: 1924
Musical

Composer: Porter Grainger; Bob Ricketts; Jo Trent
Lyricist: Porter Grainger; Bob Ricketts; Jo Trent
Librettist: Aubrey L. Lyles; Flournoy E. Miller
Producer: Aubrey L. Lyles; Flournoy E. Miller

Cast: Alonzo Fenderson; Doe Doe Green; Flournoy
E. Miller; Eddie Rector; George Stamper

Notes: No other information available.

1961 • HONEY GIRL

OPENED: 05/03/1920   Theatre: Cohan and
                         Harris
Musical   Broadway: 142

Composer: Albert Von Tilzer
Lyricist: Neville Fleeson
Librettist: Edward Clark
Producer: Sam Harris
Director: Sam Forrest; Bert French

Source: CHECKERS (Play: Henry Blossom);
Musical Director: Eugene Salzer; **Set Design:**
Unitt & Wickes

Songs: All the Girls Look Wonderful to Me;
Anything You Liked; Can I Find a Toreador?;
Close to Your Heart; I Know That This Must Be
Love [3]; I Love to Fox Trot; I'd Place a Bet; I'm
Losing My Heart to Someone; I'm the Fellow;
I'm Trying; In Catalina [1]; (Follow Me) It's a
Very Simple Matter; Myltyl and Tyltyl (The
Bluebird Song); Racing Blues; Rainbow of Love [4];
Reminiscence [2]; Shopping; Small Town Girl;
They're Not Doing That This Season [3]; Tick,
Tick, Tick [4]; What the Fortune Teller Said [2];
Why Worry?; You've Just the Boy for Me

Cast: Edna Bayes; Louise Myers; Lynne Overman

Notes: Also titled WHAT'S THE ODDS. [1] Out
Boston 4/16/21. [2] Out St. Louis 1/9/21. [3] Out
Atlantic City 2/16/20. [4] Out Washington, D.C.
9/14/19.

1962 • HONEYDEW

OPENED: 09/06/1920   Theatre: Casino
Musical   Broadway: 200

Composer: Efrem Zimbalist Sr.
Lyricist: Joseph W. Herbert
Librettist: Joseph W. Herbert
Producer: Joseph Weber
Director: Hassard Short

Source: SCOURGE OF THE SEA, THE [2] (Play:
Joseph W. Herbert); **Choreographer:** Kuy
Kendall; **Costumes:** Ralph Mulligan; **Musical
Director:** Max Hirschfeld; **Orchestrations:** Carl
Kiefert; J. Bodewalt Lampe; James McCabe; **Set
Design:** Hassard Short

Songs: A-Choo [1]; A La Minute; Believe Me,
Beloved; Chinese Phantasy; Cup of Tea, A;
Dance; Drop Me a Line; Entrance of Bridesmaids;
Eyes of the Girl I Love, The; Fast Step Creation,
A; Honeydew Waltz; Hyrcynian Wood, The [1];
It's a Small, Small World; June Bug, The;
Marriage of Convenience, A [1]; Matter Very

Serious, The [1]; Morals of a Sailor-Man, The; Morning Glory; My Husband's Dearest Friend; Oh, How I Long for Someone!; Polka; Slaves of the Demon; Sound of the Sound, The; Spanish Song; Sunshine of Love; There's No Fool Like an Old Fool [1]; Time to Take a Drink; Unrequited Love; When I Led the Amazon Army [1]; Your Second Wife

Cast: Sam Ash; Dorothy Follis; Hal Forde; Evelyn Herbert; Kuy Kendall; Mlle. Marguerite; John Park; Ethelind Terry

Notes: [1] Out of town only. [2] A burlesque.

1963 • HONEYMOON EXPRESS, THE

OPENED: 02/06/1913   Theatre: Winter Garden
Musical   Broadway: 156

Composer: Jean Schwartz
Lyricist: Harold Atteridge
Librettist: Joseph W. Herbert
Producer: Winter Garden Company
Director: Ned Wayburn

Costumes: Melville Ellis

Songs: At Mammy's Fireside [1] (C: Harry Carroll; L: Ballard Macdonald); At the Flower Garden Ball [1]; Bring Back Your Love; Carolina Lou [1]; Cedro (My Italian Romeo) [2] (C: Harry Von Tilzer; L: Andrew B. Sterling); Down Old Harmony Way [1] (C: James V. Monaco; L: Dave Oppenheim); Down Where the Tennessee Flows [1] (C: Bert L. Rule; L: Ray Sherwood); Good Bye Boys [1] (C: Harry Von Tilzer; L: William Jerome; Andrew B. Sterling); Gum Shoe Man [2] (C: Harry Von Tilzer; L: Andrew B. Sterling); I Love Her Oh! Oh! Oh! [1] (C: James V. Monaco; L: Joseph McCarthy; E.P. Moran); I Want a Toy Soldier Man; I Want the Strolling Good; Little Cabaret at Home, The; Lover of Mine [1] (C/L: Clare Kummer); Lucky Boy [2] (C: Harry Von Tilzer; L: Andrew B. Sterling); Moving Man, The (C: Al W. Brown); My Coca-Cola Belle; My Raggydore; My Yellow Jacket Girl; On the Honeymoon Express (On That Spoony, Spoony Honeymoon Express) [1] (C: James Kendis; Frank Stilwell; L: Lou Klein); Oriental Bacchanale, The (inst.) (C: A. Borodin); Pianologue; Ragtime Express; Same One They Picked for Me, The; Since Mrs. McNott Learned to Do the Turkey Trot [2] (L: William Jerome;

Andrew B. Sterling); Sister Susie's Sewing Shirts for Soldiers [1] (C: Herman Darewski; L: R.P. Weston); Song That Stole My Heart Away, The [2] (C: Harry Von Tilzer; L: Andrew B. Sterling); Southern Heart of Mine [1]; Spaniard that Blighted My Life, The [1] (C/L: Billy Merson); Syncopatia Land; Tennis Tournament; That Gal of Mine; That Little German Band [1] (C: Fred Fisher; L: Joe Goodwin; Joseph McCarthy); That's the Life for Me (This Is the Life for Me); There Was a Time [1] (C: Harry Carroll; L: Alfred Bryan); Upon the Hudson Shore (Give Me the Hudson Shore) (C: Al Jolson); What a Fool I'd Be [2] (L: William Jerome); What Will I Tell Her To-night [1] (C/L: Morrissey; Roberts; Whittaker); When Gaby Did the Gaby Glide; When It's Cotton Blossom Time, Sweet Rosalie [2] (C: Harry Von Tilzer; L: Andrew B. Sterling); When the Honeymoon Stops Shining; When You Said Goodbye [2] (C: Harry Von Tilzer; L: Andrew B. Sterling); When You Speak of Love [2] (C: Harry Von Tilzer; L: Andrew B. Sterling); Where Is She Now? [2] (C: Harry Von Tilzer; L: Andrew B. Sterling); While They Were Dancing Around [1] (C: James V. Monaco; L: Joe McCarthy); Who Paid the Rent for Mrs. Rip Van Winkle when Rip Van Winkle Went Away? [1] (C: Fred Fisher; L: Alfred Bryan); Won't You Please Have a Heart [2] (C: Harry Von Tilzer; L: Andrew B. Sterling); You Are the Someone [1]; You Made Me Love You, I Didn't Want to Do It [3] (C: James V. Monaco; L: Joseph McCarthy); You'll Call the Next Love the First

Cast: Fanny Brice; Gaby Deslys; Yancsi Dolly; Doyle & Dixon; Melville Ellis; Harry Fox; Al Jolson; Ada Lewis; Harry Pilcer

Notes: "The Oriental Bacchanale" staged by Theodore Kosloff and costumed by Robert Edmond Jones. [1] Sheet music only. [2] ASCAP/Library of Congress. [3] Sheet music only. In THE PASSING SHOW OF 1913.

1964 • HONEYMOON GIRLS, THE

OPENED: 04/17/1914
Musical   Closed out of town

Composer: James Patterson
Lyricist: Al Hyland
Librettist: Phil Ott
Producer: Phil Ott; Theatrical Operating Co.

Choreographer: Jack Hart; Victor Hyde

Songs: Ba-Be; Chattanooga; Chesapeake Bay; Finale Act I; Grand Opera Up-to-Date; Happy Little Country Girl, A; I Love to Quarrel with You; I Want Someone to Call Me Papa; I'm Eighteen To-Day; Just One Little Kiss; March on September Morn (C/L: Niel Sullivan); On Broadway; Opening Chorus; Opening Chorus Act II

Cast: Billy Inman; Alice Lazar

Notes: No other information available.

1965 • HONEYMOON LANE

OPENED: 09/20/1926   Theatre: Knickerbocker
Musical   Broadway: 353

Composer: James F. Hanley
Lyricist: Eddie Dowling
Librettist: Eddie Dowling
Producer: A.L. Erlanger
Director: Edgar MacGregor

Choreographer: Bobby Connolly; **Costumes:** Ada Peacock; **Musical Director:** Arthur Lange; **Orchestrations:** Arthur Lange

Songs: Chorus Picking Time on Broadway; Dreams for Sale; Gee, But I'd Like to Be Bad; Half a Moon Is Better Than No Moon [1] (L: Eddie Dowling; Herbert Reynolds); Hallowe'en [2]; Head Over Heels in Love; Honeymoon Lane [2] (C/L: Eddie Dowling; James F. Hanley; Billy Moll); Jersey Walk (Shake 'Em Up Kid) (C/L: Henry Creamer; Eddie Dowling; James F. Hanley); Little Old New Hampshire; Little Smile, a Little Sigh, A; Little White House at the End of Honeymooon Lane; Mary Dear! I Miss You Most of All (C/L: Henry Creamer; Eddie Dowling; James F. Hanley); On to Hollywood; Opening Chorus Act II; Opening Number; Ruffian Ballet, The; Stone Bridge at Eight, The; Understudy Dance Specialty, The; Wad-D'ya-Say We Steal Away?

Cast: Eddie Dowling; Johnny Marvin; Pauline Mason; Al Sexton; Kate Smith

Notes: [1] Eddie Dowling not credited by ASCAP. [2] ASCAP/Library of Congress only.

1966 • HONEYMOON TOWN

OPENED: 06/17/1919   Theatre: La Salle
Musical   Chicago

Composer: Byron Gay; Felix Rice
Lyricist: Will M. Hough
Librettist: Will M. Hough
Producer: Boyle Woolfolk
Director: William Royce

Songs: Arbor Day; Cleopatra Had a Little Song; Come On Along to Honeymoon Town (C: Felix Rice); He Paid His Debt to LaFayette, but He Never Settled Up with Me!; In Jail; Now I Lay Me [1]; Poor Mr. Keeley; Snuggle, Snuggle, Snuggle; There's a Rainbow Shining (C: Milton Schwarzwald); There's Everything Waiting for You (C: Byron Gay); Tip Toe (C: Milton Schwarzwald); We Are Not Married to Each Other; Wedding Night; What Was Adam Doing; Wonderful Night with You [1] (C: Byron Gay; L: Will M. Hough)

Cast: Roy Atwell; Helen Bolton; Bernard Granville

Notes: Program of South Bend, June 1919. [1] Sheet music only.

1967 • HONEYMOON TRAIL

OPENED: 03/23/1908   Theatre: La Salle
Musical   Chicago

Composer: Joe Howard
Lyricist: Frank Adams; Will M. Hough
Librettist: Frank Adams; Will M. Hough
Director: Alvin Laughlin

Choreographer: Ned Wayburn

Songs: Golden West, The [1]; Honeymoon Trail; I Don't Want a Million Dollars; I'm Going to Steal the Moon; Nothing to Do but Nothing; One Little Boy Had Money; Opening Chorus; When I Feel Like Loving; Whose Little Girl Are You?; You Can't Be a Friend to Everybody

Cast: Vera Michelena

Notes: [1] Out Kansas City 11/1/08.

1968 • HONEYMOONERS, THE

OPENED: 06/03/1907   Theatre: Aerial Gardens
Musical   Broadway: 72

Composer: George M. Cohan
Lyricist: George M. Cohan
Librettist: George M. Cohan
Producer: Sam H. Harris

Source: RUNNING FOR OFFICE (Musical: George M. Cohan)

Songs: Honey Babe; If I'm Going to Die I'm Goin' to Have Some Fun; I'll Be There in the Public Square; I'm a Popular Man; In a One-Night Stand; Kid Days [1]; Let's Take an Old-Fashioned Walk; Make a Lot of Noise; Mr. Bingham [2]; Musical Comedy Maid, The; Mysterious Maid; Nothing New Beneath the Sun; Popular March; Story of the Wedding March, The

Cast: Leona Anderson; George M. Cohan; Helen Cohan; Jerry Cohan; Gertrude Hoffman; William Keough; James H. Manning; Jack Webster

Notes: A new version of RUNNING FOR OFFICE. [1] Also in RUNNING FOR OFFICE. [2] ASCAP/Library of Congress only.

1969 • HONKY-TONK HIGHWAY
OPENED: 04/27/1995
Musical

Composer: Robert Nassif-Lindsey
Lyricist: Robert Nassif-Lindsey
Librettist: Richard Berg
Additional Dialogue: Robert Nassif-Lindsey
Producer: Goodspeed Opera House
Director: Gabriel Barre

Arrangements: Steve Steiner; **Costumes:** Robert Strong Miller; **Lighting Designer:** Phil Monat; **Musical Director:** Steve Steiner; **Orchestrations:** Steve Steiner; **Set Design:** Charles E. McCarry

Songs: Answer the Call; Baby, I Love Your Biscuits; Chalhatchee; Come Out and Play; Dr. Love; Easier to Sing Than Say; Far Off Lights; Follow Where the Music Goes; Heartbreak Hall of Fame; Honky-Tonk Highway; I Found a Song; I'll Be There; I'm So Happy I Could Cry; Me, Myself and I; Mr. Money; Music in This Mountain; Perfect Stranger

Cast: Kevin Fox; Erin Hill; David M. Lutken; Sean McCourt

Notes: Goodspeed at Chester.

1970 • HONKY TONK NIGHTS
OPENED: 08/07/1986   Theatre: Biltmore
Musical   Broadway: 4

Composer: Michael Valenti
Lyricist: Ralph Allen; David Campbell
Librettist: Ralph Allen; David Campbell
Producer: Edward H. Davis; Allen M. Shore
Director: Ernest O. Flatt

Choreographer: Ernest O. Flatt; **Costumes:** Mardi Philips; **Dance Arranger:** David Krane; **Lighting Designer:** Natasha Katz; **Musical Director:** George Broderick; **Orchestrations:** Jim Tyler; **Set Design:** Robert Cothran; **Vocal Arranger:** George Broderick

Songs: Brothers Vendetto, The; Choosing a Husband's a Delicate Thing; Eggs; Honky Tonk Nights; Honky Tonk Nights Rag (Professor Walker and His Solo Symphony), The; Hot and Bothered; I Took My Time; I've Had It; Lily of the Alley; Little Dark Bird; Man of Many Parts; Promised Land; Reform Song, The; Roll with the Punches; Sampson Beauties, The; Stomp the Blues Away; Tapaholics; Ticket for the Promised Land, A; Withered Irish Rose

Cast: Susan Beaubian; Teresa Burrell; Yolanda Graves; Ira Hawkins; Kyme; Joe Morton; Danny Strayhorn; Reginald Veljohnson

1971 • HOOP-LA!
OPENED: 04/25/1927
Musical   Closed out of town

Composer: Jay Gorney
Lyricist: Howard Dietz; George E. Stoddard
Librettist: Vivian Crosby; Harry Wagstaff Gribble
Producer: William Dolloff; Lee Wainwright
Director: Harry Wagstaff Gribble

Choreographer: Al Fisher; **Musical Director:** Jay Gorney

Songs: Caravan on a Country Road; Election; Happiness; Hoopla; Let's Make Believe; Love Is a Wonderful Thing; Mayor of Tango Town!; Mr. & Mrs. & Company; Open Your Arms; Pollyanna; Spring; That's Happiness; Tongue Tied Tune; Unlucky in Love; What Makes My Baby Blue

Cast: Arthur Campbell; Bernard Granville; Charles Henderson; Mary Hutchinson; Carol Joyce; James Norris; Jane Oaker; Virginia Smith

Notes: Closed in Stamford, Connecticut after one act! Program of Werba's Brooklyn Theatre used.

1972 • HOORAY FOR THE GIRLS

OPENED: 1918   Theatre: 44th Street Roof
                                      Garden
Revue   Broadway: 1

Composer: Madelyn Sheppard
Lyricist: Annelu Burns
Librettist: Helen S. Woodruff
Director: Frank Smithson

Choreographer: Beatrice Byrne; Grace Crosman; Dorothy Norris; **Musical Director:** Silvio Hein

Songs: Army Life, The; Cinema Queen, The; Dinner Gong Jazz, The; Dixie Roses; Dreams; Good-bye, My Sailor Good-bye; Hooray for the Girls; How Do You Do; I Love the Misses; If You But Dreamed; Neat Little Cat, A; Service Star and Hooverize, The; Society; Telephone Jazz, The; Turn My Tears to Smiles; Waiting and the Wedding; When the Moonbeams Shine in Dear Old Alabama; Will You, Won't You?; Your Flag

Cast: Lt. Fairfax Burger; Capt. Anson Clark; Mrs. Donald F. Jenks; Hope Williams

Notes: A Benefit by the NY Committee for Devastated France.

1973 • HOORAY FOR WHAT!

OPENED: 12/01/1937   Theatre: Winter Garden
Musical   Broadway: 200

Composer: Harold Arlen
Lyricist: E.Y. Harburg
Librettist: Russel Crouse; Howard Lindsay
Producer: Messrs. Shubert
Director: Howard Lindsay

Choreographer: Robert Alton; Agnes de Mille; **Costumes:** Raoul Pene du Bois; **Musical Director:** Robert Emmett Dolan; **Orchestrations:** Don Walker; **Set Design:** Vincente Minnelli; **Vocal Arranger:** Hugh Martin; Kay Thompson

Songs: Buds Won't Bud [1]; Down with Love; Fashion Girl, A; God's Country; Hero Ballet; Hooray for What?; I Click the Heel and I Kiss the Hand; In the Shade of the New Apple Tree; I've Gone Romantic on You; Life's a Dance; Moanin' in the Mornin'; Napoleon's a Pastry; That Night of the Embassy Ball; Vive for Geneva

Cast: Ralph Blane; Ruthanna Boris; Briants, The; Leo Chalzel; June Clyde; Harold Cook; Al Gordon's Dogs; Paul Haakon; Sue Hastings' Marionettes; Hugh Martin; Meg Mundy; Detmar Poppen; Five Reillys; Robert Shafer; John Smedberg; Vivian Vance; Jack Whiting; Ed Wynn

Notes: Conceived by E.Y. Harburg. Kay Thompson was fired from the cast during rehearsals. [1] Cut during tryouts and added later to film CAIRO.

1974 • HOORAY! IT'S A GLORIOUS DAY . . . AND ALL THAT

OPENED: 03/09/1966   Theatre: Theatre Four
Musical   Off-Broadway: 15

Composer: Arthur Gordon
Lyricist: Ethel Bieber; Charles Grodin; Maurice Teitlebaum
Librettist: Charles Grodin; Maurice Teitlebaum
Producer: Jeff Britton
Director: Charles Grodin

Choreographer: Sandra Devlin; **Costumes:** Peter Harvey; **Dance Arranger:** Lanny Meyers; **Lighting Designer:** Jules Fisher; **Musical Director:** Peter Fuchs; **Orchestrations:** Gershon Kingsley; **Set Design:** Peter Harvey; **Vocal Arranger:** Peter Fuchs

Songs: Everything Happens for the Best; For Example; Happy; He's a Comic; I Hope He's Not Ashamed of Me; I Wish I Knew; Inspirational Song; It's a Glorious Day; Love Was a Stranger to Me; Nasality; Panic Ballet; Tap Dance; What's a Gang without a Guy Named Muggsy?; You're Gorgeous, You're Fantastic

Cast: Raymond Allen; Laverne Borden; Joan Eastman; Ron Holgate; Daniel Keyes; Mina Kolb

1975 • HOP O' MY THUMB

OPENED: 11/26/1913   Theatre: Manhattan
                                  Opera House
Musical   Broadway: 46

Composer: Manuel Klein
Lyricist: Sydney Rosenfeld
Librettist: Sydney Rosenfeld

Producer: William Brady; F. Ray Comstock; Morris Gest
Director: Ernest D'Auban

Source: HOP O' MY THUMB (Musical: Arthur Collins; Frank Dix; George R. Sims); **Musical Director:** Manuel Klein

Songs: Bird Talk; Come and Watch the Moon with Me; Date Tree, The; Fee, Fi, Fo, Fum; For a Girl Has Her Living to Make; Forest Bird, The; Happy Noble Outlaw Band, The; Here You See Eight Ladies of Quality; Hop, Hop, Hop; Love Me, Love Me, Won't You?; No Damaged Goods; Run Along Mr. Ogre Man; Salute to the King; Take a Little Perfume; Those Days of Long Ago; Those Seven League Boots

Cast: Flavia Arcaro; Ralph Austin; Marie Clifford; Eva Fallon; Viola Gillette; Texas Guinan; Albert Hart; DeWolf Hopper; Walter S. Wills

Notes: Ballet music by J.M. Glover.

1976 • HORATIO
Notes: *See SMILING THE BOY FELL DEAD.*

1977 • HORSEMAN, PASS BY
OPENED: 01/15/1969   Theatre: Fortune
Musical   Off-Broadway: 37

Composer: John Duffy
Lyricist: Rocco Bufano; John Duffy
Producer: John A. McQuiggan
Director: Rocco Bufano

Source: WRITINGS (William Butler Yeats);
Choreographer: Rhoda Levine; **Costumes:** Nancy Potts; **Lighting Designer:** Jennifer Tipton; **Musical Director:** Stanley Walden; **Orchestrations:** Robert Dennis; John Duffy; Stanley Walden; **Set Design:** Dennis Dougherty

Songs: Before the World Was Made; Brown Penny; Consolation; Crazy Jane on the Day of Judgment; Drunken Man's Praise of Sobriety, A; Final Choral Blessing; For Anne Gregory; Girl's Song; Great Purple Butterfly, The; Her Anxiety; Last Confession; Mad as the Mist and Snow; Salley Gardens; Soldier Takes Pride in Saluting His Captain, A; Soulless a Faery Dies; Three Songs to the One Burden; To an Isle in the Water; What Then?

Cast: Barbara Barrie; Will Geer; Laurence Luckinbill; Novella Nelson; Maria Tucci

Notes: The book and lyrics are based on Yeats' writings.

1978 • HOT AND COLD HEROS
OPENED: 05/09/1973   Theatre: Thirteenth St.
Revue   Off-Off-Broadway: 16

Composer: Islish Baldwin; George Bamford; Arnold Borget; Ronnie Britton; Jehan Clements; Tom Hawkins; Johnny Mann; Lance Mulcahy; Robert W. Preston
Lyricist: Islish Baldwin; George Bamford; Arnold Borget; Ronnie Britton; Jehan Clements; Tom Hawkins; Johnny Mann; Lance Mulcahy; Robert W. Preston
Producer: Mama Hare's Tree

Choreographer: Ivan Todd; **Costumes:** Fran Caruso; **Dance Arranger:** Lee Gillespie; Mark Weiner; **Lighting Designer:** Nancy Golladlay; **Musical Director:** Lee Gillespie; Mark Weiner; **Set Design:** R. Thomas Finch; **Vocal Arranger:** Mark Weiner

Songs: And Freedom; Anna Lee; Ballad of Castle Maiden; Don't Tell Me Too Many Lies; Four Eyes; He Is an Animal; Intro; Man from Glad; Mary Alice, Don't Say Shit; Masks; N.E.T. and This Is Remote; Name Dropping; No Dessert; Ode to Willie; Rape; Rock and Roll Critic; Subway

Cast: Jehan Clements; Susan Conderman; Monica Grignon; Helena Heis; Damien Leake; Melanie Michelle; Murray Shactman; Ron Zarro

1979 • HOT-CHA!
OPENED: 03/08/1932   Theatre: Ziegfeld
Musical   Broadway: 118

Composer: Ray Henderson
Lyricist: Lew Brown
Librettist: Lew Brown; Mark Hellinger; Ray Henderson
Producer: Florenz Ziegfeld
Director: Edward Clarke Lilley; Edgar MacGregor

Source: AN OLD SPANISH CUSTOM (Story: Hy Kraft); **Choreographer:** Bobby Connolly;

Costumes: Charles LeMaire; **Musical Director:** Alfred Goodman; **Orchestrations:** Robert Russell Bennett; **Set Design:** Joseph Urban

Songs: Conchita; Fiesta; For You; I Make Up for That in Other Ways; I Want Another Portion of That; It's Great to Be Alive [1]; Jose, Can't You See!; Little Old New York; Matador Song; Opening Chorus; Say (What I Wanna Hear You Say); So This Is Mexico; There I Go Dreaming Again; There's Nothing the Matter with Me; They All Need a Little Hot-Cha [2]; You Can Make My Life a Bed of Roses (Marry Me)

Cast: Iris Adrian; Miriam Battista; Tito Coral; Antonio DeMarco; Renee DeMarco; Jules Epailly; Robert Glecker; Hernandez Brothers, The; Jack Holland; Art Jarrett; June Knight; Bert Lahr; Gypsy Rose Lee; Marjorie Logan; June MacCloy; Lynne Overman; Eleanor Powell; Buddy Rogers; Roy Sedley; Lupe Velez; Marjorie White

Notes: [1] Out Washington, D.C. 4/18/32. [2] Not used.

1980 • HOT CHOCOLATES (1929)
OPENED: 06/20/1929   Theatre: Hudson
Revue   Broadway: 228

Composer: Harry Brooks; Thomas "Fats" Waller
Lyricist: Andy Razaf
Librettist: Eddie Green
Producer: Connie Immerman; George Immerman
Director: Leonard Harper

Choreographer: Danny Dare; **Orchestrations:** Russell Wooding; **Set Design:** P. Dodd Ackerman

Songs: Ain't Misbehavin'; Black and Blue; Can't We Get Together; Dixie Cinderella; Goddess of Rain; Jungle Jamboree (C: Duke Ellington); My Man Is Good for Nothing but Love; Off Time; Redskinland [2]; Say It with Your Feet [2]; Snake Hip Dance (C: Duke Ellington); Song of the Cotton Fields; Sweet Savannah Sue; That Rhythm Man; Waltz Divine [1]

Cast: Jimmie Baskette; Cab Calloway; Baby Cox; Jubilee Singers; Dolly McCormick; Jazzlips Richardson; Margaret Simms; Three Midnight Steppers; Clarence Todd; Edith Wilson

Notes: Harry Brooks wrote the verses while Waller wrote the refrains. [1] Sheet music only. [2] Added for tour.

1981 • HOT CHOCOLATES (1935)
OPENED: 1935   Theatre: Connie's Inn
Revue   Nightclub

Composer: Paul Denniker
Lyricist: Andy Razaf
Producer: Connie Immerman
Director: Teddy Blackmon

Songs: Lovely Liza Lee; Machinery; Only Time You're Out of Luck, The; That Rhythm Parade; What Harlem Is to Me

Cast: Dewey Brown; Alberta Hunter

Notes: Presented at the downtown Connie's Inn.

1982 • HOT CHOCOLATES (1936)
OPENED: 1936
Revue   Nightclub

Composer: Saul Chaplin
Lyricist: Sammy Cahn
Director: Teddy Blackmon

Songs: Blue Notes (C: Saul Chaplin; Nat Gardner); Darkies Have Music in Their Souls (L: Sammy Cahn; Sammy Colton); Do the Truck; Drum Brigade, The; Four-score and Seven Years Ago; I'm Just a Slave to Your Crave; King Louis Is Havin' a Dream (The King of Swing Is Havin' a Dream); Nature and I (C: Saul Chaplin; Nat Gardner); Rhythm Holiday; Rhythm Makes the World Go Round; Shoe Shine Boy; Spirit of the Tom Tom, The; Three Feet Two of Rhythm; What's on Your Mind

Notes: No other information available.

1983 • HOT CHOPS
OPENED: 1923
Musical

Composer: Jo Trent
Lyricist: Jo Trent
Librettist: Jo Trent
Producer: Nat Nazzarro
Director: Frank Montgomery

Songs: Hot Chops; Moanin' and Groanin'

Cast: Buck and Bubbles; George McGlennon; Jean Starr

Notes: No other information available.

1984 • HOT FROM HARLEM
OPENED: 05/13/1941
Revue   Closed out of town

Composer: Porter Grainger
Lyricist: Porter Grainger
Producer: Marty Forkins
Director: Addison Kerry

Costumes: Mahieu; Mme. Morgan; **Musical Director:** Billy Butler; **Orchestrations:** Thomas Whaley; **Set Design:** Stevens Studio; Kaj Velden

Songs: Down By the Old Southern River; Look What Love Done Done; Ol' Man River [1] (C: Jerome Kern; L: Oscar Hammerstein II)

Cast: Jimmie Baskette; Eubie Blake; John Mason; Bill Robinson; Aida Ward; Edith Wilson

Notes: [1] Kern and Hammerstein not credited in program but I can't imagine anyone else writing a song titled "Ol' Man River."

1985 • HOT GROG
OPENED: 10/06/1977   Theatre: Marymount
                         Manhattan
Musical   Off-Broadway: 22

Composer: Bland Simpson; Jim Wann
Lyricist: Bland Simpson; Jim Wann
Librettist: Jim Wann
Producer: Phoenix Theatre
Director: Edward Berkeley

Choreographer: Patricia Birch; **Costumes:** Hilary Rosenfeld; **Lighting Designer:** James Tilton; **Musical Director:** Jeff Waxman; **Set Design:** James Tilton

Songs: Bastards Have the Best Luck [1]; Bound Away; Break Me Out [1]; Catfish [2]; Change in Direction; Chase, The; Come on Down to the Sea; Difference Is Me, The; Drinking Fool; Got a Notion; Hack 'em; Handsome Cabin Boy [2]; Hayti [2]; Head Song, The; Heaven Must Have

Been Smiling; High Summer [1]; Hot Grog; I'm Just A-Wearyin' for You [2]; Make Way [1]; Marooned Messin' [2]; New Oysters [2]; One of Us; Only a Woman [1]; Pirates Life, The; Sea Breeze; Seizure to Roam; Skye Boat Song; Southern Nights [2]; Swordfight, The; Treasure to Burn

Cast: Patrick Hines; Mimi Kennedy; Mary Bracken Phillips

Notes: [1] Cut prior to opening. [2] Not in programs.

1986 • HOT HARLEM
OPENED: 1932   Theatre: Connie's Inn
Revue   Nightclub

Composer: Thomas "Fats" Waller; Spencer Williams
Lyricist: Andy Razaf
Producer: Leonard Harper

Songs: Burmese Babies (C: Unknown); Girl Who Gets Her Man, The (C: Unknown); Shotgun Papa (C: Andy Razaf); Stealin' Apples (C: Thomas "Fats" Waller); Way Down South (C: James P. Johnson)

Cast: Four Mills Brothers; Don Redman Orchestra

Notes: No other information available.

1987 • HOT MIKADO, THE
OPENED: 03/23/1939   Theatre: Broadhurst
Musical   Broadway: 85

Composer: Arthur Sullivan
Lyricist: W.S. Gilbert
Librettist: W.S. Gilbert; Dave Gregory; William Tracy
Producer: Michael Todd
Director: Hassard Short

Choreographer: Truly McGee; **Costumes:** Nat Karson; **Musical Director:** William Parson; **Orchestrations:** Charles L. Cooke; **Set Design:** Nat Karson

Songs: Behold the Lord High Executioner; Braid the Raven Hair; Comes a Train of Little Ladies; Finale Act I; Finale Act II; Flowers That Bloom in the Spring; Here's a How-de-do; I, Living I;

If You Want to Know Who We Are; I'm the Emperor of Japan; I've Got a Little List; Moon and I, The; My Object All Sublime; Our Great Mikado; So Pardon Us; Three Little Maids; Titwillow; Wandering Minstrel, A; Were You Not to Ko-Ko Plighted; Young Man Despair

Cast: Rose Brown; Maurice Ellis; Eddie Green; Rosetta LeNoire; Robert Parrish; Gwendolyn Reyde; Bill Robinson

Notes: Musical numbers are the same as in the original operetta. Lyrics revised by Dave Gregory and William Tracy.

1988 • HOT OLD TIME
OPENED: 1898
Musical   Broadway

Composer: George M. Cohan
Lyricist: George M. Cohan

Songs: Boy without a Sweetheart, A; Her Gentleman Friend; I Guess I'll Have to Telegraph My Baby; Irish Cakewalk; Patriotic Coon

1989 • HOT RHYTHM
OPENED: 08/21/1930   Theatre: Times Square
Revue   Broadway: 68

Composer: Percy Grainger
Lyricist: Donald Heywood
Librettist: Edwin Hurley; Johnny Lee Long; Ballard Macdonald; Dewey "Pigmeat" Markham; Will Morrissey
Producer: Max Rudnick
Director: Will Morrissey

Choreographer: Nat Cash; Midge Miller; Eddie Rector; **Costumes:** Reine; **Musical Director:** Maurice Coffin; **Set Design:** Wertheim Studios

Songs: Alabamy; Believe Me I'm Blue; For the First Time in My Life (C: Irving Actman; L: Jean Herbert; Al Koppell); Hot Rhythm; Hungry for Love; I'll Get Even with You (C/L: Donald Heywood); In the Air; Loving You the Way I Do [1] (C: Eubie Blake; L: Will Morrissey; Jack Scholl); Mama's Gotta Get Her Rent; Penalty of Love, The (C/L: Donald Heywood; L: Heba Jannath); Rector Rhythm; Say the Word That Will Make You Mine; Since You Went Away; Steppin' on It; Tropical Moon; Up in the Sky;

Will You Be Hating Me Tomorrow (C/L: Irving Actman; L: Jean Herbert)

Cast: Mae Barnes; Madeline Belt; Arthur Bryson; Johnny Hudgins; Revella Hughes; Johnny Lee Long; Dewey "Pigmeat" Markham; Hilda Perlino; Eddie Rector; Inez Seeley; Al Vigel; Edith Wilson

Notes: [1] Also in THE FOLIES BERGERE REVIEW.

1990 • HOT SEPTEMBER
OPENED: 09/14/1965
Musical   Closed out of town

Composer: Kenneth Jacobson
Lyricist: Rhoda Roberts
Librettist: Paul Osborn
Producer: Leland Hayward; David Merrick
Director: Joshua Logan

Source: PICNIC (Play: William Inge); **Choreographer:** Danny Daniels; **Costumes:** Theoni V. Aldredge; **Dance Arranger:** Robert Prince; **Lighting Designer:** Jean Rosenthal; **Musical Director:** Milton Rosenstock; **Orchestrations:** Philip J. Lang; **Set Design:** Oliver Smith; **Vocal Arranger:** Milton Rosenstock

Songs: Another Crummy Day; Come On Strong; Frug; Golden Moment; Goodbye Girls; Guy Like Me, A; Hey, Delilah; Hot September Dance; I Blew It; I Got It Made; Live; Rosemary's Soliloquy; Show Me Where the Good Times Are [2]; Somethin' More; Tell Her [1]; Tell Me the Truth; This Town; What Do You Do?; Whistle of a Train; Who Needs It?; You

Cast: Gene Castle; Ronn Forella; Sean Garrison; Richard Granat; Kathryn Hays; Lee Lawson; Marlyn Mason; Lovelady Powell; Patricia Roe; John Stewart; Paula Trueman

Notes: Closed Boston 10/9/65. [1] Not used. [2] Also in SHOW ME WHERE THE GOOD TIMES ARE.

1991 • HOT SPOT
OPENED: 04/19/1963   Theatre: Majestic
Musical   Broadway: 43

Composer: Mary Rodgers
Lyricist: Martin Charnin
Librettist: Willie Gilbert; Jack Weinstock
Producer: Lawrence Carr; Robert Fryer; John Herman

Costumes: Rouben Ter-Arutunian; **Dance Arranger:** Trude Rittman; **Lighting Designer:** John Harvey; **Musical Director:** Milton Rosenstock; **Orchestrations:** Ralph Burns; Luther Henderson; **Set Design:** Rouben Ter-Arutunian; **Vocal Arranger:** John Morris

Songs: Big Meeting Tonight; Don't Laugh (L: Stephen Sondheim); Far Far Better Way, A [1]; From the Red [1]; Gabie; Gallant Girl [1]; He Needs Somebody [2]; Hey, Love (See What You Can Do for Me); I Had Two Dregs; I Think the World of You; Little Trouble, A; Matter of Time, A; Nebraska; Over [1]; Rich, Rich, Rich; Simple People [1]; Smiles; That's Good-That's Bad (L: Stephen Sondheim); This Little Yankee; Welcome Dance; Welcome to Our Country; You Can Always Count on Us [2]

Cast: Joseph Bova; Joseph Campanella; Arny Freeman; Howard Freeman; Judy Holliday; Mary Louise Wilson; Carmen de Lavallade

Notes: Morton Da Costa (director) and Onna White (choreographer) removed their names prior to this show's opening. Herbert Ross came in to direct but wasn't listed in the program. [1] Out, Washington, D.C. 2/11/63. [2] Not in programs.

1992 • HOTEL MOUSE, THE

OPENED: 03/13/1922　Theatre: Shubert
Musical　　　　　　 Broadway: 88

Composer: Armand Vecsey
Lyricist: Clifford Grey
Librettist: Guy Bolton
Producer: J.J. Shubert; Lee Shubert
Director: John Harwood

Source: SOURIS D'HOTEL (Play: Paul Armont; Marcel Gerbidon); **Choreographer:** Max Scheck; **Set Design:** Watson Barratt

Songs: Bad Man Walk [1] (C: Ivan Caryll); Everything I Do Goes Wrong; Exercise [1] (C: Ivan Caryll); Finale; Good Girl in the Country [1] (C: Ivan Caryll); Honesty [1] (C: Ivan Caryll); I'll Dream of You (C: Ivan Caryll); Little Mother (C: Ivan Caryll; Armand Vecsey); Manana [1] (C: Ivan Caryll); Mauricette (C: Ivan Caryll); Nearly True to You (C: Ivan Caryll); One Touch of Loving; Oozey-Woozey; Opening; Patchwork Quilt, A [1] (C: Ivan Caryll); Quintette; Rhyming; Risk a Little Bit [1] (C: Ivan Caryll); Romance (C: Ivan Caryll); Round on the End and High in the Middle (C: Bert Hanlon; L: Alfred Bryan); Santiago [1] (C: Ivan Caryll); Simple Home [1] (C: Ivan Caryll); Tree of Truth [1] (C: Ivan Caryll); Where Lanterns Gleam; Why Do the Girls (C: Ivan Caryll)

Cast: Taylor Holmes; Frances White

Notes: Titled LITTLE MISS RAFFLES out of town. [1] Out of town when show was titled LITTLE MISS RAFFLES and music ascribed to Ivan Caryll.

1993 • HOTEL PASSIONATO

OPENED: 10/22/1965　Theatre: East
　　　　　　　　　　　Seventy-Fourth Street
Musical　　　　　　　Off-Broadway: 11

Composer: Philip Springer
Lyricist: Joan Javits
Librettist: Jerome J. Schwartz
Producer: L. Slade Brown
Director: Michael Ross

Source: HOTEL PARADISO (Play: Georges Feydeau); **Choreographer:** Bradford Craig; **Costumes:** Robert Mackintosh; **Lighting Designer:** Paul Barnes; **Musical Director:** Gershon Kingsley; **Orchestrations:** Gershon Kingsley; **Set Design:** Paul Barnes

Songs: Confrontation, The; Don't!; Good-Good-Good; Hot Water Bottles; Hotel Passionato; Marry Me; Not Getting Any Younger; Perfectly Charming Visit, A; Russian Dance at the Yabacabana; Tea-Tea-Tea; Tomorrow When the World Comes Crashing Down Around Our Ears; We Saw Everybody There; We'll Suffer Together; What a Curious Girl; What a Night!; What Is This Sensation?; You Gay Dog You!

Cast: Lee Cass; Kane Triplets, The; Linda Lavin; Phil Leeds; Marian Mercer; Paul Sand; Jo Anne Worley

1994 • HOTEL TOPSY-TURVY

OPENED: 1898
Musical

Theatre: Herald Square
Broadway

Composer: Lionel Monckton; Victor Roger
Librettist: Edgar Smith; Arthur Sturges
Producer: Edward E. Rice

Source: L'AUBERGE TOHU-BOHU (Musical: Maurice Ordonneau; Victor Roger)

Songs: Gingerbread Doll, The (C/L: Aubrey Boucicault); I Happened to Be There; It's Not the Weather Cock that Changes, It's the Wind (C/L: Aubrey Boucicault)

Cast: Aubrey Boucicault; Frank Doane; Marie Dressler; Eddie Foy Sr.; Ethel Jackson; Henry Norman

Notes: Smith adapted Sturges' English adaptation of the French hit. No songs listed in program.

1995 • HOTTEST COON IN DIXIE

OPENED: 1906
Musical

Composer: George Bryant
Lyricist: Carter; Ferdos
Librettist: Carter; Ferdos
Producer: I.E. Gideon

Songs: All WIse Chickens Follow Me; Allus de Dame in Dixie; I Don't Know Where I'm Going, but I'm on My Way; I Like Your Way; Love Me and the World Is Mine [2]; My Old Kentucky Home [1]; Sweet Mamie

Cast: A.A. Copeland; Thomas Deaker; Josephine Lazzo

Notes: No other information available. Some of these songs may be popular songs of the day. [1] Probably the famous song by Stephen Foster. [2] Probably the famous song by Ernest R. Ball.

1996 • HOUP-LA

Notes: *See HEAD OVER HEELS (1918).*

1997 • HOUSE IN THE WOODS, A

OPENED: 12/09/1986
Musical

Closed out of town

Composer: Marvin Laird
Lyricist: Ellen Weston
Librettist: Ellen Weston
Producer: Sue Frost; Goodspeed Opera House
Director: Michael Leeds

Choreographer: Michael Leeds; William Fleet Lively; **Costumes:** John Carver Sullivan; **Lighting Designer:** Curt Ostermann; **Musical Director:** Lynn Crigler; **Set Design:** Evelyn Sakash

Songs: Best; Big; Don't Let It Be Today; Finding a Place; House in the Woods, A; If We Didn't Get 'Em Back; It's All Gotta Go Through Me; New Place, A; No One Can Take That Away; Nothing's Wrong; This Is War; Three Million Buck-a-roos; Trustee's Decision, The; Trustee's Song; What's Going On; Who Are You Anabel; Ya Gotta Fit, Boy

Cast: Patti Allison; Marsha Bagwell; Eric Kaufman; Michael Piontek

Notes: Goodspeed Opera House — Norma Terris Theatre.

1998 • HOUSE MELODIOUS, THE

OPENED: 1907
Musical

Songs: In a Little Canoe with You (C: Leo Edwards; L: Leo Wood); Kiss Me Once More Goodnight (C: Leo Edwards; L: Leo Wood); My Belle Zabelle (C: Gus Edwards; L: Will D. Cobb); Pocahontas (C: Leo Edwards; L: Alfred Bryan)

Notes: No other information available.

1999 • HOUSE OF BLUE LEAVES

OPENED: 02/10/1971
Play

Theatre: Truck and Warehouse
Off-Broadway: 337

Composer: John Guare
Lyricist: John Guare
Author: John Guare
Producer: Betty Ann Besch; Warren Lyons
Director: Mel Shapiro

Costumes: Jane Greenwood; **Lighting Designer:** John Tedesco; **Set Design:** Karl Eigsti

Songs: Back Together Again; I Love You So I Keep Dreaming; I'm Here with Bells On; Where Is the Devil in Evelyn?

Cast: William Atherton; Frank Converse; Harold Gould; Katherine Helmond; Margaret Linn; Anne Meara

Notes: No songs listed in program. [1] Song title approximate.

2000 • HOUSE OF FLOWERS
OPENED: 12/30/1954　Theatre: Alvin
Musical　Broadway: 165

Composer: Harold Arlen
Lyricist: Harold Arlen; Truman Capote
Librettist: Truman Capote
Producer: Saint-Subber
Director: Peter Brook

Choreographer: Herbert Ross; Costumes: Oliver Messel; Lighting Designer: Jean Rosenthal; Musical Director: Jerry Arlen; Orchestrations: Ted Royal; Set Design: Oliver Messel

Songs: Albertina's Beautiful Hair [2]; Can I Leave Off Wearin' My Shoes; Dark Song [2]; Do Not Be Afraid of Love [2]; Don't Like Goodbyes; Has I Let You Down?; House of Flowers [6]; House of Flowers Waltz (inst.); Husband Cage [5]; I Never Has Seen Snow; Indoor Girl [4] (L: Michael Brown); Jump de Broom [3]; Love's No Stranger to Me [1]; Madame Tango's Particular Tango [3]; Madame Tango's Tango [1]; Mardi Gras; Monday Through Sunday [1]; One Man Ain't Quite Enough; Sleepin' Bee, A; Slide, Boy, Slide; Smellin' of Vanilla (Bamboo Cage) [5]; Somethin' Cold to Drink [3]; Turtle Song; Two Ladies in de Shade of de Banana Tree; Waitin'; Walk to de Grave [3]; What a Man Won't Do for a Woman [1]; What Is a Friend For?; Woman Never Understan' (Wife Never Understan') [3]; Wonders of a Barrel, The [2]

Cast: Pearl Bailey; Miriam Burton; Diahann Carroll; Dino DiLuca; Juanita Hall; Dolores Harper; Geoffrey Holder; Ada Moore; Enid Mosier; Frederick O'Neal; Don Redman; Rawn Spearman; Ray Walston

Notes: [1] Cut from original production. [2] Cut from revival production. [3] Added to revival production. [4] Added after original opening. [5]

Same music. [6] Music revised from "Let's Go Sailor" cut from film STAR SPANGLED RHYTHM and "I Love a New Yorker" from film MY BLUE HEAVEN.

2001 • HOUSE OF LEATHER, THE
OPENED: 03/18/1970　Theatre: Ellen Stewart
Musical　Off-Broadway: 1

Composer: Dale F. Menten
Lyricist: Frederick Gaines; Dale F. Menten
Librettist: Frederick Gaines
Producer: Marshall Naify; William H. Semans; Richard Shapiro
Director: H. Wesley Balk

Costumes: Judith Cooper; James K. Shearon; Lighting Designer: David F. Segal; Musical Director: Dale F. Menten; Set Design: David F. Segal

Songs: Armies of the Right; Children's Song (Recess with Mrs. Grimm); Copper's Creed; Death and Reality; Dixie Prelude (Civil War); Do You Recall the House of Leather?; Epilogue in Suede; God Is Black; Graduates of Mrs. Grimm's Learning; Here I Am; House of Leather Theme; I'd Give to Her the World of Diamonds; Imagine You're Alive; Mrs. Grimm; Now It's Gone, Gone, Gone; Sara Jane; She Lives with Me [1]; Sherman's March to the Sea; Steady Job; Swanee River Overture; There's Love in the Country; Time Marches On

Cast: Jonelle Allen; Barry Bostwick; Peter DeAnda; Norma Jean Wood

Notes: [1] Cut prior to opening.

2002 • HOUSE THAT JACK BUILT, THE (1918)
OPENED: 1918
Musical

Librettist: Edward Childs Carpenter

Notes: Unfinished and unproduced.

2003 • HOUSE THAT JACK BUILT, THE (1920)
Notes: *See MARY.*

2004 • HOUSE THAT JACK BUILT, THE (1929)

OPENED: 11/08/1929   Theatre: Adelphi
Musical   London: 270

Composer: Ivor Novello
Lyricist: Donovan Parsons
Librettist: Douglas Furber; Ronald Jeans
Producer: Jack Hurlbert
Director: Jack Hulbert

Costumes: Guy De Gerald; **Musical Director:**
Sydney Baynes

Songs: At the Circus; Do Your Daily Dozen
(C: Vivian Ellis; L: Douglas Furber); Doh-Doh-
Dohdy-O [2]; Dowager Fairy Queen, The
(L: Douglas Furber); Ever So [2]; Globe Trotters,
The; House We'd Build, The; I Want a Good
Time [2] (L: Desmond Carter); I've Fallen in Love
(C: Vivian Ellis; L: Douglas Furber); Laying the
Foundations (C: Sydney Baynes); Manchester [2]
(L: Douglas Furber); My Heart Is Saying
(C: Vivian Ellis; L: Douglas Furber; Donovan
Parsons); Playing the Game; Put Your Shoulder
to the Wheel (C: Vivian Ellis); She's Such a
Comfort to Me [1] (C: Arthur Schwartz;
L: Douglas Furber; Donovan Parsons); Tear
Drops from Her Eyes Are Pearls; There Must Be
Something on My Mind [2]; Thought Never
Entered My Head, The; Whoopee! [2]
(L: Desmond Carter)

Cast: Helen Burnell; Bobbie Comber; Cicely
Courtneidge; Jack Hurlbert; Ivor McLaren; Irene
Russell

Notes: [1] Later used in WAKE UP AND DREAM.
[2] From Liverpool Empire program 9/3/29.

2005 • HOUSEBOAT ON THE STYX, THE

OPENED: 12/25/1928   Theatre: Liberty
Musical   Broadway: 103

Composer: Monte Carlo; Alma Sanders
Lyricist: Monte Carlo
Librettist: John E. Hazzard; Kenneth Webb
Producer: Ned Jakobs
Director: Oscar Eagle

Source: HOUSEBOAT ON THE STYX, THE (Novel:
John Kendrick Bangs); **Choreographer:** Chester

Hale; Ray Perez; **Costumes:** John Booth; **Set
Design:** Willy Pogany

Songs: Back in the Days of Long Ago; Cleopatra,
We've Found You; Club Song; Dance of the
Apple; Fountain of Youth, The; Hell's Finest;
Houseboat on the Styx; Irate Pirate Am I, An;
Men of Hades; Ode to the Styx; Pirate Dance;
Queen Elizabeth's Tea; Red River; Roll Call in
the Morning, The; Someone Like You; Soul
Mates; You've Got to Know How to Make
Love

Cast: Sam Ash; Pauline Dee; Hal Forde; John
Hazzard; Alice MacKenzie; Bertram Peacock;
Blanche Ring

2006 • HOUSEWIFE! SUPERSTAR!!

OPENED: 10/29/1977   Theatre: Theatre Four
Revue   Off-Broadway: 34

Author: Barry Humphries
Producer: Arthur Cantor; Michael White
Director: Barry Humphries

Costumes: Kenneth Everage [1]; **Lighting
Designer:** Andrea Wilson; **Set Design:** Brian
Thomason

Songs: At Least You Can Say You Have Seen It
(C/L: Barry Humphries)

Cast: Barry Humphries

Notes: [1] Probably a pseudonym.

2007 • HOUSEWIVES' CANTATA, THE

OPENED: 02/17/1980   Theatre: Theatre Four
Musical   Off-Broadway: 24

Composer: Mira J. Spektor
Lyricist: June Siegel
Librettist: Willy Holtzman
Producer: Cheryl Crawford; Eryk Spektor
Director: Rina Elisha

Choreographer: Rina Elisha; **Costumes:** Judy
Dearing; **Lighting Designer:** Marshal S. Spiller;
Musical Director: Richard A. Schacher;
Orchestrations: Musicworks Inc.; **Set Design:**
Raymond C. Recht; **Vocal Arranger:** Richard A.
Schacher; Mira J. Spektor

Songs: Adultery Waltz; Apartment Lament; Daughter's Lullaby; Dirty Dish Rag; Divorce Lament; Early Morning Rain (L: Charline Spektor); Guinevere Among the Grapefruit Peels; Legs; Little Women; M.C.P.; Middle Aged; Mr. Fixer; New Song, A; Sex; Song of the Bourgeois; Song of the Open Road; Surburban Rose; White House Resident

Cast: Patti Karr; William Perley; Forbesy Russell; Sharon Talbot

2008 • HOW BAXTER BUTTED IN
OPENED: 11/13/1905   Theatre: Murray Hill
Play   New York

Composer: Sidney Toler
Lyricist: Sidney Toler
Author: Owen Davis
Producer: Vance & Sullivan

Songs: Billy Baxter's Swing Song; Jack-O-Lantern Boogieman, The; Same Thing

Cast: Della Clarke; Louis Feirce; May Maurice; Sidney Toler

Notes: Songs are not listed in program.

2009 • HOW COME?
OPENED: 04/16/1923   Theatre: Apollo
Musical   Broadway: 40

Composer: Henry Creamer; Ben Harris; Will Vodery
Lyricist: Henry Creamer; Ben Harris
Librettist: Eddie Hunter
Director: Sam H. Grisman

Choreographer: Frank Montgomery; Henry Vodery; **Musical Director:** Will Vodery; **Orchestrations:** Will Vodery

Songs: Bandanna Anna; Certainly Is the Truth; Charleston Cut Out; Charleston Finale; Count Your Money; Dinah; E-Gypsy-Ann; Gingerena; Goodnight Brother Green; I Didn't Grieve Over Daniel; In My Dixie Dreamland Jazz [1]; Keep the Man You've Got; Love Will Bring You Happiness (C/L: Ben Harris); Opening Chorus; Pickaninny Vamp; Pretty Malinda; Sweetheart, Farewell; Syncopated Strain; When I'm Blue

Cast: Alice Brown; Chappy Chappelle; Eddie Hunter; Nina Hunter

Notes: Bessie Smith appeared in this show out of town Philadelphia. [1] Sheet music only.

2010 • HOW DO YOU DO, I LOVE YOU (1965)
OPENED: 1965   Unproduced

Composer: Elmer Bernstein
Lyricist: Carolyn Leigh

Songs: Here's Where the Action Is; How Do You Do I Love You; I'm a Stranger Here Myself; It's Feminine; M.R.S. for Me; Meet My Girl; Pleasure's About to Be Mine, The; Step to the Rear [1]; They Don't Make Them Like That Any More [1]; Think Ginger Rogers; Where You Are [1]; You'll Get Over It [1]

Notes: *See also HOW NOW, DOW JONES.* [1] Later in HOW NOW DOW JONES.

2011 • HOW DO YOU DO, I LOVE YOU (1967)
OPENED: 10/31/1967
Musical   Closed out of town

Composer: David Shire
Lyricist: Richard Maltby Jr.
Librettist: Michael Stewart

Songs: Dance; Her Laughter in My Life; How Do You Do I Love You; Just Across the River [1]; Life Full of Surprises, A; Life Is Too Short; Meet My Girl; Nine to Five; One Step [1]; Pleased with Myself [1]; Still Single; This Is the Day; Whatever You Want Me to Be; When He Marries Me; You've Got a Good Thing Going; Zeroing in on You

Cast: Joey Baio; Suzanne Barry; Carole Cook; Michael Davis; Jay Gerber; Jerry Holmes; Philip Lucas; Phyllis Newman

Notes: [1] In STARTING HERE, STARTING NOW.

2012 • HOW IT WAS DONE IN ODESSA
OPENED: 04/10/1991
Musical

Composer: Alexander Zhurbin
Lyricist: Erik Haagensen
Librettist: Erik Haagensen
Director: Robert Kalfin

Source: SUNSET (Musical: Asar Eppel; Alexander Zhurbin); **Choreographer:** Dania Krupska; **Costumes:** Paul Wonsel; **Dance Arranger:** Henry Aronson; **Lighting Designer:** Gail Cooper-Hecht; **Musical Director:** Henry Aronson; **Orchestrations:** Paul Schwartz; **Set Design:** Paul Wonsel

Songs: At Least; Do It Properly; Father Vs. Sons; Fathers and Sons; Healthiest Man in Odessa, The; How It Was Done in Odessa; I Am the Boss; I Am Your Master; I Wish; Leave It to Me; Little Lady/Little Man; Make It Night; Make Them Pay; On and On; Open the Gate; Recipe for a Husband; Scandal in the Synagogue; Selling the Business; There Are Men; We Love a Wedding; Your Prayers Are Answered

Cast: Mary Ellen Ashley; Jack Dabdoub; Ted Thurston

Notes: Walnut Street Theatre, Philadelphia.

2013 • HOW NEWTON PREPARED
:OPENED: 1916
Musical

Composer: Taylor L. Corwell; J. Homer Tutt; Salem Tutt Whitney; Clarence G. Wilson
Lyricist: J. Homer Tutt; Salem Tutt Whitney
Librettist: J. Homer Tutt; Salem Tutt Whitney
Producer: J. Homer Tutt; Salem Tutt Whitney
Director: J. Homer Tutt; Salem Tutt Whitney

Songs: All I Want Is Plenty of Loving; Dixie Land Is Calling Me; Finale Farewell; Girls Quartette; Grand Old Veterans in the U.S.A.; Help Cometh from Above; If I Could Make the Sun Stand Still; Little Boy, Little Girl; My Swwet Hawaiian Home; Ode to Allah; Old Veterans Jubilee; Opening Chorus; Pasha's Dream, The; Study in Black and White; Sweet Melody Blues; Tar's Farewell, The; Turkey; Turkish Drill; Wedding of the Flower and the Bee, The; Zoo, The

Cast: Helen Clinton; Julian Costello; Alonzo Fenderson; Carrie King; Mattie Lewis; Dave

Liston; J. Homer Tutt; Al Watts; Salem Tutt Whitney

Notes: No other information available.

2014 • HOW NOW, DOW JONES
OPENED: 12/07/1967   Theatre: Lunt-Fontanne
Musical   Broadway: 220

Composer: Elmer Bernstein
Lyricist: Carolyn Leigh
Librettist: Max Shulman
Producer: David Merrick
Director: George Abbott

Choreographer: Gillian Lynne; **Costumes:** Robert Mackintosh; **Dance Arranger:** Peter Howard; **Lighting Designer:** Martin Aronstein; **Musical Director:** Peter Howard; **Orchestrations:** Philip J. Lang; **Set Design:** Oliver Smith; Vocal Arranger: Peter Howard

Songs: A-B-C; Big Trouble; Charlie's Number [3]; Crazy Night Ballet; Credo (Rich Is Better); Don't Let a Good Thing Get Away [1]; Goodbye, Failure, Goodbye (Gawk, Tousle and Shucks); Guess What Charlie [3]; He's Here!; How Now Dow Jones [1]; I Ain't Got It for the One That's Got It for Me [1]; It's Gonna Be You [3]; Little Investigation, A; Live a Little; Music to Their Ears [1]; One of Those Moments (Just for the Moment); Our Little Mid Manhattan Pied a Terre [3]; Panic; Pleasure's About to Be Mine, The [5]; Sea Chanty [1]; Shakespeare Lied (You'll Get Over It) [5]; Status Quo [1]; Step to the Rear [5]; Take Me There [1]; Tangiers [1]; That's Good Enough for Me [5]; That's Music [1]; They Don't Make 'Em Like That Anymore [5]; Touch and Go [2]; Up in Smoke [1]; Walk Away; Wall Street Hoedown [1]; We'll Stand and Cheer [1]; Where You Are [4]

Cast: Charlotte Jones; Marlyn Mason; Anthony Roberts; Hiram Sherman; Sammy Smith; Fran Stevens; Brenda Vaccaro

Notes: Originally titled HOW DO I DO, I LOVE YOU. [1] Cut before opening. [2] Cut after opening. [3] ASCAP/Library of Congress only. [4] Cut before opening. In score of HOW DO YOU DO I LOVE YOU (1965). [5] In score of HOW DO YOU DO I LOVE YOU (1965).

2015 • HOW THE GRINCH STOLE CHRISTMAS
OPENED: 10/18/1966   Theatre: CBS
TV Musical

Composer: Albert Hague
Lyricist: Dr. Seuss
Librettist: Dr. Seuss
Producer: Chuck Jones; Dr. Seuss
Director: Chuck Jones

Musical Director: Eugene Poddany

Songs: Trim Up the Tree; Welcome Christmas;
You're a Mean One, Mr. Grinch

Narrator: Boris Karloff; **Voice:** Thurl Ravenscroft;
June Foray

Notes: An animated musical.

2016 • HOW TO BE A JEWISH MOTHER
OPENED: 12/28/1967   Theatre: Hudson
Musical   Broadway: 21

Composer: Michael Leonard
Lyricist: Herbert Martin
Librettist: Joseph Bologna; Renee Taylor
Producer: Jon-Lee; Seymour Vall
Director: Avery Schreiber

Source: HOW TO BE A JEWISH MOTHER (Novel:
Dan Greenburg); **Choreographer:** Doug Rogers;
Costumes: Michael Travis; **Lighting Designer:**
John J. Moore; **Musical Director:** Julian Stein;
Orchestrations: Julian Stein; **Set Design:** Robert
Randolph

Songs: Child You Are, Man You'll Be; I Don't Want
to Be in Buttons [1]; Once the Man You Laughed
At; Sacrifice [1]; She's a Nice Jewish Girl (She's a
Perfectly Marvelous Girl from the Bronx) [1]; Since
That Time We Met; So Laugh a Little; Wedding
Song, The; What Does a Little Boy Know? [1]

Cast: Godfrey Cambridge; Molly Picon

Notes: [1] Cut prior to opening.

2017 • HOW TO GET RID OF IT
OPENED: 11/17/1974   Theatre: Astor Place
Musical   Off-Broadway: 9

Composer: Mort Shuman
Lyricist: Eric Blau
Librettist: Eric Blau
Producer: 3W Productions
Director: Eric Blau

Source: AMEDEE (Play: Eugene Ionesco);
Costumes: Don Jensen; **Lighting Designer:** Ian
Calderon; **Musical Director:** Wolfgang Knittel;
Set Design: Don Jensen; Vocal Arranger:
Wolfgang Knittel

Songs: Almost Everybody Suffers More Than Us;
Amedee, Amedee, It Isn't Too Late; Are You the
Man Whose Name Is on the Paper; At the End of
a Period of Time; Five to One; Good Morning;
I Am a Vietnam Veteran; I Am Here at the Place
Where Time Began; I'll Put You Through;
Late, Late Show, The; Mind Your Business;
Mushrooms Are Coming in Here, The; Old Man
Says to the Old Woman, The; Suite for a
Growing Corpse; Well, Yes, He's a Friend; What
an Evening; You've Got to Get Rid of It

Cast: Matt Conley; Muriel Costa-Greenspon; Joe
Masiell

2018 • HOW TO STEAL AN ELECTION
OPENED: 10/13/1968   Theatre: Pocket
Revue   Off-Broadway: 89

Composer: Oscar Brand
Lyricist: Oscar Brand
Librettist: William F. Brown
Producer: FPC; Stephen Mellow; Seymour Vall
Director: Robert H. Livingston

Choreographer: Frank Wagner; **Costumes:** Mopsy;
Lighting Designer: Clarke Dunham; **Musical
Director:** Bhen Lanzaroni; **Orchestrations:** Jay
Dryer; Bhen Lanzaroni; **Set Design:** Clarke
Dunham

Songs: Charisma; Clay and Frelinghuysen; Comes
the Right Man; Down Among the Grass Roots;
Get on the Raft with Taft; Get Out the Vote;
Grant; Grover; How to Steal an Election; Law
and Order; Lincoln and Liberty; Lincoln and
Soda; More of the Same; Mr. Might've Been;
Nobody's Listening; Plumed Knight, The; Silent
Cal; Tippecanoe and Tyler Too; Van Buren;
We're Gonna Win

Cast: Dennis Allen; Beverly Ballard; Clifton Davis; Carole Demas; Bill McCutcheon

2019 • HOW TO SUCCEED IN BUSINESS WITHOUT REALLY TRYING

OPENED: 10/14/1961   Theatre: 46th Street
Musical   Broadway: 1417

Composer: Frank Loesser
Lyricist: Frank Loesser
Librettist: Abe Burrows; Willie Gilbert; Jack Weinstock
Producer: Cy Feuer; Ernest Martin
Director: Abe Burrows

Source: HOW TO SUCCEED IN BUSINESS WITHOUT REALLY TRYING (Book: Shepherd Mead); **Choreographer:** Bob Fosse; Hugh Lambert; **Costumes:** Robert Fletcher; **Lighting Designer:** Robert Randolph; **Musical Director:** Elliot Lawrence; **Orchestrations:** Robert Ginzler; **Set Design:** Robert Randolph

Songs: Been a Long Day; Brotherhood of Man [2]; Cinderella, Darling; Coffee Break; Company Way, The; Grand Old Ivy; Happy to Keep His Dinner Warm; How To; I Believe in You; I Worry About You [1]; Love from a Heart of Gold; Organization Man [1]; Paris Original; Rosemary; Secretary Is Not a Toy, A; Status [1]; Yo Ho Ho, The (dance) [2]

Cast: Ruth Kobart; Virginia Martin; Robert Morse; Paul Reed; Charles Nelson Reilly; Bonnie Scott; Sammy Smith; Claudette Sutherland; Rudy Vallee

Notes: [1] Cut prior to opening. [2] Same music.

2020 • HOW'S THE KING

OPENED: 1925
Musical   Closed out of town

Composer: Jay Gorney
Lyricist: Owen Murphy
Librettist: Marc Connelly
Producer: Earl Carroll
Director: Robert Milton

Choreographer: Allan K. Foster; **Costumes:** Harriet Leibman; **Musical Director:** Jay Gorney; **Orchestrations:** Will Vodery

Songs: Ginger; Girl That's Most Chased After, The; Greetings to the King; Gypsy Rose; How's the King; I'll Save All My Evenings for You; It's Not the Principle, It's Just the Money; It's Tough to Be a Flower Girl in Uric; Lady, You Don't Know Me; My Kingdom for a Queen Like You; One Wonderful Night; Prison Glide; Twilight; When the Right Boy Meets the Right Girl (That's the Right Time to Love); Who Do You Think We Are?

Cast: Joe Cook; John Price Jones; J.M. Kerrigan; Virginia O'Brien; Nina Penn; Charles Senna; James Valentine; Janet Winters

Notes: Program of 9/12/25 Philadelphia.

2021 • HOW'VE YOU BEEN?

OPENED: 1925
Musical

Composer: Donald Heywood
Producer: Pollock Productions

Choreographer: George Stamper

Cast: Lottie Brown; Sidney Easton

Notes: No other information available.

2022 • HOWARD CRABTREE'S WHOOP-DEE-DOO!

OPENED: 06/29/1993   Theatre: Actors'
    Playhouse
Revue   Off-Broadway: 258

Composer: David Gallagher
Librettist: Dick Gallagher; Peter Morris; Mark Waldrop
Producer: Charles Catanese; John Glines; Glines, The; Michael Wantuck
Director: Phillip George

Choreographer: David Lowenstein; **Costumes:** Howard Crabtree; **Lighting Designer:** Tracy Dedrickson; **Musical Director:** Fred Barton; **Set Design:** Bill Wood

Songs: As Plain As the Nose on My Face (C: Eric Schorr; L: Peter Morris); Blue Flame (L: Dick Gallagher); Elizabeth (C/L: David Rambo); I Was Born This way (L: Peter Morris); It's a Perfect Day (L: Mark Waldrop); Last One Picked

(L: Mark Waldrop); Less Is More (L: Mark Waldrop); Magic of Me, The (C/L: Jack Feldman; Bruce Sussman); My Turn to Shine (L: Peter Morris); Nancy: The Unauthorized Musical (L: Mark Waldrop); Soldier's Musical, A (L: Peter Morris); Stuck on You (L: Mark Waldrop); Teach It How to Dance (L: Dick Gallagher); Tough to Be a Fairy (L: Mark Waldrop); Whoop-Dee-Doo (L: Peter Morris); You Are My Ideal (L: Peter Morris)

Cast: Howard Crabtree; Keith Cromwell; Tommy Femia; David Lowenstein; Peter Morris; Jay Rogers; Ron Skobel; Richard Stegman; Alan Tulin

2023 • HOWDY MR. ICE! (1948)
OPENED: 06/24/1948   Theatre: Center
Revue   Broadway: 406

Composer: Alan Moran
Lyricist: Albert Stillman
Producer: Sonja Henie; Arthur M. Wirtz
Director: Catherine Littlefield

Choreographer: Catherine Littlefield; **Costumes:** Katherine Kuhn; Billy Livingston; **Dance Arranger:** Paul Van Loan; **Lighting Designer:** Eugene Braun; **Musical Director:** David Mendoza; **Orchestrations:** Paul Van Loan; **Set Design:** Bruno Maine

Songs: Cradle of Jazz; Forty-Eight States; I Only Wish I Knew; In the Pink; Plenty More Fish in the Sea; World's Greatest Show

Cast: Dick Craig; William Douglas; Nola Fairbanks; Fred Martell

Notes: Cast listed are singers not skaters. *See also HOWDY MR. ICE OF 1950.*

2024 • HOWDY MR. ICE OF 1950
OPENED: 05/26/1949   Theatre: Center
Revue   Broadway: 430

Composer: Alan Moran
Lyricist: Albert Stillman
Librettist: Sonja Henie; Arthur M. Wirtz
Director: Catherine Littlefield

Choreographer: Catherine Littlefield; **Costumes:** Grace Houston; Katherine Kuhn; Billy

Livingston; **Dance Arranger:** Paul Van Loan; **Lighting Designer:** Eugene Braun; **Musical Director:** David Mendoza; **Orchestrations:** Paul Van Loan; **Set Design:** Bruno Maine

Songs: Big City; We're the Doormen of New York; You Was

Cast: Dick Craig; Nola Fairbanks

Notes: A revised edition of HOWDY MR. ICE! (1948). Cast are singers not skaters.

2025 • HOYDEN, THE
OPENED: 10/19/1907   Theatre: Knickerbocker
Musical   Broadway: 58

Composer: Robert Hood Bowers
Lyricist: Henry Blossom
Librettist: Cosmo Hamilton
Producer: Charles B. Dillingham
Director: Ben Teal

Source: LA SOEUR (Play: Tristan Bernard); **Costumes:** Dazian; **Musical Director:** Robert Hood Bowers; **Set Design:** Homer Emens

Songs: Every Fellow Wants to Love Me [1] (L: Raymond W. Peck); I'm Growing Fond of You [4] (C/L: John Golden); Likin' Ain't Like Lovin' [4] (C/L: James Reese Europe); Lock Your Heart [1] (L: Raymond W. Peck); Love's Prescription (C: Egbert Van Alstyne; L: Harry Williams); My Father's Wooden Leg [1] (C: Harry Dillon; L: Joseph Cawthorn); Solitary Finish, A [1] (C: John Golden); That's Why I Never Married [1] (C: John Golden; L: Joseph Cawthorn)

Cast: Joseph Cawthorn [2]; Harry Depp; Kathryn Hutchinson; Elsie Janis; Sidney Jarvis [2]; Armand Kaliz [3]; Robert Lett [3]; Mae Murray [2]; Rita Pierson [3]; Samuel Reed; Arthur Stanford

Notes: After opening the show's cast and score were changed. [1] Added after opening. [2] Joined cast after opening. [3] Left cast after opening. [4] Sheet music only.

2026 • HUBBA HUBBA
Musical   Closed out of town

Composer: Gene Casey; Jan Casey
Lyricist: Gene Casey

Librettist: Jan Casey
Producer: Goodspeed Opera House
Director: William Gile

Choreographer: George Bunt; **Costumes:** David Toser; **Dance Arranger:** Lynn Crigler; **Lighting Designer:** Peter M. Ehrhardt; **Musical Director:** Lynn Crigler; **Set Design:** Raymond T. Kurdt

Songs: Agreed, Agreed; American Eagle; Boogie Woogie GI Joe; Come with Me to Rio; Everyday Blues; Fake It; Hubba Hubba; Ixed Mup; Look at Me; Magical Spell; Milkmaid Known As Joan; Please Don't Ration Love; Rosie the Riveter; Victory Garden; While My Baby's Gone

Cast: Mary Jo Catlett; Martin Ross; Hansford Rowe; Janie Sell; Maureen Silliman; B.J. Slater

Notes: Goodspeed Opera House.

2027 • HUCK AND JIM ON THE MISSISSIPPI

OPENED: 11/11/1983
Musical   Closed out of town

Composer: Bruce Pomahac
Lyricist: Joshua Logan
Librettist: Joshua Logan
Producer: Joe Conaway; Florida Atlantic University
Director: Joshua Logan

Source: ADVENTURES OF HUCKLEBERRY FINN, THE (Novel: Mark Twain); **Choreographer:** Robert Simpson; **Conductor:** William Prince; **Costumes:** Beverly Jane Thomas; **Lighting Designer:** Edward Madden; **Musical Director:** Vicki Carter; **Set Design:** Rex Fluty

Songs: Almost Nearly Friend, An; Critters; England; Escape, The; Finale; Gates of Hell, The; Goin' Where the River Goes; Good Mornin' Mornin'; Grangeford Prayer; I'm Old Enough to Know; Jackson Island; Love Like Mine, A; My Kind of Batid; Song of Mourning; Stretchers; Touch of a Woman, The; Vignettes; Widow Douglas' House, The; Widow's Song, The

Cast: Howard Da Silva; Raymond George Forchion; Melissa Hart; Julie Prosser; Alan S. Reynolds; Don Sparks; Carolyn Viglione; Jonathan Ward

Notes: Florida Atlantic University, Boca Raton. Amateur production.

2028 • HUCK FINN
OPENED: 05/07/1954
Musical

Composer: George Herman
Lyricist: George Herman
Librettist: George Herman
Director: Leo Brady

Source: ADVENTURES OF HUCKLEBERRY FINN, THE (Novel: Mark Twain); **Source:** LIFE ON THE MISSISSIPPI (Novel: Mark Twain); Arrangements: Joseph Jenkins; **Choreographer:** Jeri Nagle; **Costumes:** Joseph Lewis; **Set Design:** James D. Waring

Songs: Ain't You Heard?; Arabas 'n' Elephants; Dance-American Impromptu; Duke, the Dauphin, The; Here Busted a Captive Heart; Hi-Diddle-I-Dee; Holiday; If You Were a Tree; Lamentation; Loafin'; Lord and I, The; No Man Better 'n His Pa; Pick a Star; Raid on the Sunday School Picnic, The (dance); Rejuvenation; Saturday Night; Saturday Night in Napoleon (dance); Song of a Summer Night; Susan's Soliloquy; Susquehanna!; Travelin' Show, A; When a Boy Gets Siviled

Cast: Philip Bosco; Mary Harkleroad; Trent Knepper; Ben Rogers; Danny Ruslander; Joseph Shubert; Owen Simon

Notes: Amateur show. Catholic University.

2029 • HUCKLEBERRY FINN (1902)
OPENED: 1902
Musical   Closed out of town

Composer: Frederic Solomon
Lyricist: R.C. McPherson
Librettist: Lee Arthur; Mark Twain
Producer: Klaw & Erlanger

Source: ADVENTURES OF HUCKLEBERRY FINN, THE (Novel: Mark Twain); **Costumes:** F. Richard Anderson; **Musical Director:** John Harding; **Set Design:** Ernest Gros

Songs: Animal's Convention (C: Bob Cole; L: Billy Johnson); Courting; Good Night, Lucindy; Good

Night Weirdy [2] (C: James T. Brymn); I Want to Be a Drummer in the Band (C: Silvio Hein; L: Matthew Woodward); Oh, Isn't It Fine to Be Robbers; Sunflower and the Violet, The; When Little Tommy Sawyer Saw the Circus (C: Ben Jerome; L: Matthew Woodward)

Cast: Marie Bingham; Leonie Darmon; Arthur Dunn; Charles K. French; William Sampson; John C. Slavin; Charles Stanley

Notes: Program of Hartford, Conn. 11/11/02. [1] One source lists the composer as James T. Brymn but not the program consulted. [2] Not in program.

2030 • HUCKLEBERRY FINN (1950)

OPENED: 1950
Musical   Unproduced

Composer: Kurt Weill
Lyricist: Maxwell Anderson
Librettist: Maxwell Anderson

Source: ADVENTURES OF HUCKLEBERRY FINN, THE (Novel: Mark Twain)

Songs: Apple Jack; Catfish Song; Come In, Mornin'; River Chanty; This Time Next Year

Notes: Unfinished musical.

2031 • HULBERT'S FOLLIES

OPENED: 1941
Revue

Songs: My Romance [1] (C: Richard Rodgers; L: Lorenz Hart)

Notes: Show toured England but closed out of London because of lack of suitable theatre space. [1] From JUMBO.

2032 • HULLABALOO

OPENED: 06/09/1932
Revue   Closed out of town

Composer: Ralph Rainger
Lyricist: Paul Gerard Smith
Librettist: Paul Gerard Smith
Producer: Harold Hecht; Paul Gerard Smith
Director: Paul Gerard Smith

Choreographer: Harold Hecht; **Costumes:** Sogata; **Musical Director:** Rudolph Schrager; **Set Design:** Corliss McGee

Songs: Butcher Baker; Color of Her Eyes, The [1] (C: Richard Rodgers; L: Lorenz Hart); Coming Home to Harlem (C/L: Eugene Burton; Leonard Sillman); Hairpin Turn; Lies; Manhattan [2] (C: Richard Rodgers; L: Lorenz Hart); Marihuana; Night Wind; Old Fashioned Theatre; Patent Leather City (dance); Talking to Myself Again; Uniform; When Does the Bus Come By?

Cast: Teddy Hart; Sterling Holloway; June Shafer; June Sillman; Leonard Sillman

Notes: A Hollywood show. [1] Cut from SPRING IS HERE. [2] From THE GARRICK GAIETIES.

2033 • HUMAN COMEDY, THE

OPENED: 12/28/1983   Theatre: Public
Musical   Broadway: 92

Composer: Galt MacDermot
Lyricist: William Dumaresq
Librettist: William Dumaresq
Producer: N.Y. Shakespeare Festival; Joseph Papp; Shubert Organization
Director: Wilford Leach

Source: HUMAN COMEDY, THE (Novel: William Saroyan); **Conductor:** Tania Leon; **Costumes:** Rita Ryack; **Lighting Designer:** James F. Ingalls; **Musical Director:** Galt MacDermot; **Orchestrations:** Galt MacDermot; **Set Design:** Bob Shaw

Songs: Assyrians, The; Beautiful Music; Birds in the Sky, The; Birds in the Trees, The; Cocoanut Cream Pie; Daddy Will Not Come Walking Through the Door; Dear Brother; Diana; Don't Tell Me; Everlasting; Everything Is Changed; Fathers and Mothers (And You and Me); Fourth Telegram, The; Give Me All the Money; Happy Anniversary; Happy Birthday; Hello Doc; Hi Ya Kid; How I Love Your Thingamajig; I Can Carry a Tune; I Said, Oh No; I Think the Kid Will Do; I Wish I Were a Man; I'll Always Love You; I'll Tell You About My Family; I'm Home; In a Little Town in California; I've Known a Lot of Guys; Long Past Sunset; Lot of Men, A; Marcus, My Friend; Mr. Grogan, Wake Up; My Sister Bess; Noses; Orphan I Am; Parting; Remember Always to Give; Somewhere, Someone; We're a

Little Family; What Am I Supposed to Do?; When I Am Lost; World Is Full of Loneliness, The; You're a Little Young for the Job

Cast: Josh Blake; Gordon Connell; Leata Galloway; Stephen Geoffreys; Don Kehr; Joseph Kolinski; Bonnie Koloc; Mary Elizabeth Mastrantonio; Caroline Peyton; Rex Smith

Notes: Moved to the Royale Theater on April 5, 1984 after playing 79 performances at the Public.

2034 • HUMMIN' SAM

OPENED: 04/08/1933   Theatre: New Yorker
Musical   Broadway: 1

Composer: Alexander Hill
Lyricist: Alexander Hill
Librettist: Eileen Nutter
Producer: Allan K. Foster

Source: IN OLD KENTUCKY (Play: Charles T. Dazey); **Choreographer:** Davis & Carey; **Costumes:** Brooks; **Musical Director:** Jimmie Davis; **Orchestrations:** Arthur Knowlton; Edith Watson

Songs: Ain'tcha Glad You Got Music?; Answer My Heart; Change Your Mind About Me; Dancing, and I Mean Dancing; Fifteen Minutes a Day; Harlem Dan; How the First Song Was Born; If I Didn't Have You; I'll Be True, But I'll Be Blue; In the Stretch; Jitters; Jubilee; Little Bit of Quicksilver, A; Pinching Myself; Steppin' Along; Stompin' 'Em Down; They're Off

Cast: Madeline Belt; Flo Brown; Gertrude "Baby" Cox; Louise Lovelle; Miller Brothers, The; Cecil Rivers; Speedy Smith; Robert Underwood; Edith Wilson

2035 • HUMPTY DUMPTY (1904)

OPENED: 11/14/1904   Theatre: New Amsterdam
Musical   Broadway: 132

Composer: J. Rosamond Johnson
Lyricist: Bob Cole; James Weldon Johnson
Librettist: John J. McNally
Producer: Klaw & Erlanger
Director: Herbert Gresham; Ned Wayburn

Source: HUMPTY DUMPTY (Musical: Arthur Collins; J. Hickory Wood); **Choreographer:** Ernest D'Auban

Songs: Chorus of Villagers; Conspirators' Chorus; Cupid Reigns King (C: Frederic Solomon); Down at the Bottom of the Sea; Down in Mulberry Bend; Egg Has Fallen Down, The; Fairyland; Grand Finale (C: J.M. Glover; Frederic Solomon); I Am the King (C: Frederic Solomon); I'm a Very Good Sailor on Land; Man, **Man**, Man (C: Bob Cole; L: James Weldon Johnson); Mary from Tipperary; Mexico (C: Bob Cole); On Lalawana's Shore (L: James Weldon Johnson); Opening Chorus of Cooks (C: Frederic Solomon); Opening Chorus of King's Guards (C: J.M. Glover); Pantomime Bouffe Fantastique (C: Frederic Solomon); Pussy and the Bow-Wow (L: James Weldon Johnson); Sambo and Dinah (C: Bob Cole); We Go to Find the Ring; Will He Ever Smile Again?

Cast: Maude Lillian Berri; Nellie Daly; John McVeigh; Frank Moulan

2036 • HUMPTY DUMPTY (1932)

Notes: *See TAKE A CHANCE.*

2037 • HUNCHBACK OF NOTRE DAME

OPENED: 05/16/1991   Theatre: Charles Ludlam
Musical   Off-Broadway: 54

Composer: Mark Bennett
Lyricist: Everett Quinton
Librettist: Everett Quinton
Producer: Ridiculous Theatrical Co.
Director: Everett Quinton

Source: HUNCHBACK OF NOTRE DAME, THE (Novel: Victor Hugo); **Costumes:** Everett Quinton; **Lighting Designer:** Richard Currie; **Set Design:** Tom Moore

Cast: Eureka; Sophie Maletsky; Gary Mink; Stephen Pell; Hapi Phace; Everett Quinton; Cheryl Reeves

Notes: No songs listed in program.

2038 • HUNDREDS OF HATS

OPENED: 06/13/1995   Theatre: WPA
Revue   Off-Off-Broadway

Composer: Alan Menken
Lyricist: Howard Ashman

Producer: WPA Theater
Director: Michael Mayer

Arrangements: Helen Gregory; **Choreographer:** John Ruocco; **Costumes:** Michael Krass; **Lighting Designer:** Jack Mehler; **Musical Director:** Helen Gregory; **Orchestrations:** Helen Gregory; **Set Design:** Mark Beard

Songs: Aria for a Cow; Babkak, Omar, Aladdin, Kassim [10]; Belle [12]; Cheese Nips [3]; Daughter of God; Daughter of Prospero; Day in the Life of a Fat Kid in Philly; Disneyland [8] (C: Marvin Hamlisch); Firestorm Consuming Indianapolis, A [2]; Growing Boy; Hero; High Adventure [10]; How Quick They Forget [10]; Hundreds of Hats (Straw Boater Rag) [13] (C: Jonathan Sheffer); In Our Hands [9] (C: Marvin Hamlisch); Kiss the Girl [11]; Les Poissons [11]; Little Dental Music, A [6]; Magician's Work, A; Maria's Song; Part of Your World [11]; Poor Unfortunate Souls [11]; Proud of Your Boy [10]; Rhode Island Tango [4]; Sheridan Square; Since You Came to This Town [5]; Skid Row Downtown [7]; Somewhere That's Green [6]; Song for a Hunter College Graduate [13] (C: Jonathan Sheffer); Suddenly Seymour [6]; Thank God for the Volunteer Fire Brigade [5]; Thirty Miles from the Banks of the Ohio [2]; We'll Have Tomorrow [6]; Your Day Begins Tonight

Cast: John Ellison Conlee; Bob Kirsh; Philip Lehl; Amanda Naughton; Nancy Opel

Notes: A revue of previously written Ashman/Menken songs. [1] Part of medley. [2] Part of medley. From GOD BLESS YOU MR. ROSEWATER. [3] From GOD BLESS YOU MR. ROSEWATER. [4] Part of medley. From GOD BLESS YOU MR. ROSEWATER. Lyrics credited to Dennis Green in original program. [5] From GOD BLESS YOU MR. ROSEWATER. Lyrics credited to Dennis Green in original program. [6] From LITTLE SHOP OF HORRORS. [7] Part of medley. From LITTLE SHOP OF HORRORS. [8] From SMILE. [9] Part of medley. From SMILE. [10] From film ALADDIN. [11] From film THE LITTLE MERMAID. [12] Part of medley. From film BEAUTY AND THE BEAST. [13] From DIAMONDS.

2039 • HUNGRY WOMEN OF 1903

OPENED: 12/05/1902
Musical   Closed out of town

Songs: As Long As We're Together (C/L: Pat Jacobs); At the Crossroads of Life (We'll Meet Again) (C: Brook Flinn; L: Dylan Flinn; Steven Higgins); Harvard Beet Song, The (C/L: Eric Abrahamson); Saxophone Baby (C: Susan Goodman; L: Sharon Wolfe); Star of Love (C: Harvey Biern; L: Natalie Biern); Woman Who Rules the Kitchen Is the Woman Who Rules the World, The (C: John Schasny; L: John A. Morse)

Cast: Jeffrey Brown; Ronnie Brown

Notes: No other information available.

2040 • HURDY GURDY GIRL, THE

OPENED: 09/23/1907   Theatre: Wallack
Musical   Broadway: 24

Composer: H.L. Heartz
Lyricist: Richard Carle
Librettist: Richard Carle
Producer: Charles Marks
Director: Richard Carle

Choreographer: Richard Carle; Ad Newberger; **Musical Director:** Alfred Dalby; **Orchestrations:** Robert Hood Bowers; Alfred Dalby; **Set Design:** Olive P. Bernard

Songs: Bluff; Come Little Dearie; Croquet Game, The; Four Little Flirty Girls; Hope On; Hurdy-Gurdy Girl, The; I'm a Mischievous Girl; In Bohemia; Modest Manicure, The; My Busy Day; Sausage King, The; She's the Apple of My Eye; Stories; Style

Cast: May Boley; John E. Hazzard; Maym Kelso; Bertha Mills; John Ransome; Adele Rowland; Annie Yeamans

2041 • HURLY BURLY (1898)

OPENED: 09/08/1898   Theatre: Weber & Fields
                               Broadway Music Hall
Musical   Broadway

Composer: John Stromberg
Librettist: Edgar Smith; Harry B. Smith
Director: Julian Mitchell

Costumes: Will R. Barnes; **Set Design:** John Young

Songs: Clink, Clink; Dinner Party, The [1]; Floral Flirtation, A [2]; Great Cleopatra Comes; Hurly-Burly [2]; I Think I Shall Learn, Don't You?; I'd Like to Be a Gunner in the Navy [2]; I'm All Right [1]; In the Music Hall Bar when the Curtain Is Down; Irish Sidewalk Conversationalists, The [3]; Keep Away from Emmaline; Kiss Me Honey Do; Large Cold Bottle and a Small Hot Bird, A; Little Old New York Is Good Enough for Me; Loidy Wot Is Studyin' for the Stoige, A; Musketeers, The [1]; My Josephine [1]; Oriental Guards [1]; Perhaps You May Not Like It [3]; Popularity [1]; Progressive Poker Game, The; Tell Me Dusky Maiden [2]; There Was a Time When on Broadway; Trelawney [1]; Vegetable Party, The; What, Marry That Gal [1]; Who'll Help Me Spend My Money?; Zaza [2]

Cast: Josephine Allen; Angeles Sisters, The; Nelly Beaumont; Bessie Clayton; Peter F. Dailey; Lew Fields; John T. Kelly; Charles J. Ross; Fay Templeton; David Warfield; Joseph Weber

Notes: Also on this bill was Henry Lee and a song cycle titled "Great Men-Past and Present." [1] From 1899 edition. [2] From 1902 edition. [3] From a different 1899 edition.

2042 • HURLY-BURLY (1953)

OPENED: 08/05/1953
Musical   Closed out of town

Composer: Carl Eugster
Lyricist: Carl Eugster; Harry Haldane
Librettist: Irving Phillips

Notes: No other information available. University of California.

2043 • HURRY, HARRY

OPENED: 10/12/1972   Theatre: Ritz
Musical   Broadway: 2

Composer: Bill Weeden
Lyricist: David Finkle
Librettist: Lee Kalcheim; Jeremiah Morris; Susan Perkis
Producer: Peter Grad
Director: Jeremiah Morris

Choreographer: Gerald Teijelo; **Costumes:** Sara Brook; **Lighting Designer:** Martin Aronstein; **Musical Director:** Arthur Azenzer;

Orchestrations: Lee Norris; **Set Design:** Fred Voelpel

Songs: Africa Speaks; Goodby; He Is My Bag; Hurry, Harry; I'm Gonna; Life; Love Can; Somewhere in the Past; Trip Through My Mind, A; When a Man Cries; You Won't Be Happy

Cast: Louis Criscuolo; Robert Darnell; Donna Liggitt Forbes; Randee Heller; Jack Landron; Phil Leeds; Mary Bracken Phillips; Samuel D. Ratcliffe; Liz Sheridan

2044 • HUSBAND, THE

OPENED: 1909
Musical

Composer: Joe Jordan
Lyricist: Aubrey L. Lyles
Librettist: Aubrey L. Lyles
Producer: J. Ed Green
Director: J. Ed Green

Songs: Dissipation; Friend of the Family; Good Evening, Caroline; Happiness; I've Got Good Common Sense; Lulu; Mine, All Mine; Oh, You Kid!; Running Wild (C/L: James Brymn); Susanna (C/L: Bob Cole; J. Rosamond Johnson); Take Your Time; You Dear

Cast: Charles A. Gilpin; Lottie Grady; Jerry Mills; Jennie Ringgold; Ada Smith; Harrison Stewart

Notes: No other information available.

2045 • HUSHABYE LANE

OPENED: 1932

Songs: Lullaby Lady (C: Frank Black; L: Joe Young)

Notes: No other information available.

2046 • HYSTERICAL BLINDNESS

OPENED: 05/19/1994   Theatre: Playhouse on
                                        VanDam
Musical   Off-Broadway

Composer: Joe Patrick Ward
Lyricist: Joe Patrick Ward
Librettist: Leslie Jordan
Producer: Dana Matthew
Director: Carolyne Barry

Choreographer: Mark Knowles; **Costumes:** Wern-Ying Hwarng; **Lighting Designer:** Phil Monat; **Musical Director:** Joe Patrick Ward; **Set Design:** Charles E. McCarry; Vocal Arranger: Joe Patrick Ward

Songs: Ace's Revelation (Inst.); Come Little Children; God Loves the Baptist; Hymn of Shame, The; I'm Twirling; Just the Way We're Bred; Keep Smilin' Through; Long Long Way to Heaven; Mother, May I Be Forgiven?; Pessimistic Voices; Postlude (Inst.); Prayer for Mama, A; Precious Twins; Prelude (Inst.); Sing, All Ye Women of the Lord; Trashy Effeminate Hoodlum, The; What a Friend We Have in Jesus [1] (C/L: C.C. Converse; George Scriven)

Cast: Matthew Bennett; Mary Bond Davis; Leslie Jordan; David Titus

Notes: [1] Not written for this show.

I

2047 • I AND ALBERT

OPENED: 11/06/1972   Theatre: Piccadilly
Musical   London: 120

Composer: Charles Strouse
Lyricist: Lee Adams
Librettist: Jay Allen
Producer: Lewis M. Allen; Si Litvinoff; Theatre Projects
Director: John Schlesinger

Costumes: Alan Barrett; **Lighting Designer:** Robert Ornbo; **Musical Director:** Gareth Davies; **Set Design:** Luciana Arrighi

Songs: All Bless the Genius of Man; Draw the Blinds; Enough!; Go to It, Old Girl!; Hans; His Royal Highness [1]; I and Albert; It Has All Begun; I've 'Eard the Bloody 'Indoos 'As It Worse; Just You and Me; Leave It Alone; No One to Call Me Victoria; This Gentle Land; This Noble Land; Victoria; Victoria and Albert Waltz, The (inst.); Vivat! Vivat Regina!; When You Speak with a Lady; Widow at Windsor, The

Cast: Lewis Fiander; Polly James; Sven-Bertil Taube; Aubrey Woods

Notes: [1] Music later used for "You Can Never Go Back" from BRING BACK BIRDIE.

2048 • I CAN GET IT FOR YOU WHOLESALE

OPENED: 03/22/1962   Theatre: Shubert
Musical   Broadway: 300

Composer: Harold Rome
Lyricist: Harold Rome
Librettist: Jerome Weidman
Producer: David Merrick
Director: Arthur Laurents

Source: I CAN GET IT FOR YOU WHOLESALE (Novel: Jerome Weidman); **Choreographer:** Herbert Ross; **Costumes:** Theoni V. Aldredge; **Dance Arranger:** Peter Howard; **Lighting Designer:** Will Steven Armstrong; **Musical**

Director: Lehman Engel; **Orchestrations:** Sid Ramin; **Set Design:** Will Steven Armstrong; **Vocal Arranger:** Lehman Engel

Songs: Ballad of the Garment Trade; Eat a Little Something; Family Way, The; Funny Thing Happened (On My Way to Love), A; Gift Today, A (The Bar Mitzvah Song); Grab Them While You Can [1]; Have I Told You Lately?; I'm Not a Well Man; Miss Marmelstein; Momma, Momma; Somebody Else [2]; Sound of Money, The; Too Soon; Way Things Are, The; What Are They Doing to Us Now?; What's in It for Me?; When Gemini Meets Capricorn; Who Knows?

Cast: Marilyn Cooper; Elliott Gould; Jack Kruschen; Harold Lang; Ken Le Roy; Bambi Linn; Sheree North; Lillian Roth; Barbra Streisand

Notes: [1] Cut prior to opening. [2] ASCAP/Library of Congress only.

2049 • I CAN'T KEEP RUNNING IN PLACE

OPENED: 05/14/1981   Theatre: Westside Arts
Musical   Off-Broadway: 187

Composer: Barbara Schottenfeld
Lyricist: Barbara Schottenfeld
Librettist: Barbara Schottenfeld
Producer: Ray Gaspard
Director: Susan Einhorn

Choreographer: Baayork Lee; **Costumes:** Christina Weppner; **Lighting Designer:** Victor En Yu Tan; **Musical Director:** Robert Hirschhorn; **Orchestrations:** Barbara Schottenfeld; **Set Design:** Ursula Belden

Songs: Almosts, Maybes and Perhapses; Don't Say Yes If You Want to Say No; Get the Answer Now [1]; I Can Count on You; I Can't Keep Running in Place; I Live Alone; I'm Glad I'm Here; I'm on My Own; More of Me to Love [1]; Penis Envy; What If We . . .; Where Will I Be Next Wednesday Night?

Cast: Evalyn Baron; Mary Donnet; Joy Franz; Helen Gallagher; Bev Larson; Marcia Rodd; Jennie Ventriss

Notes: [1] Orchestrated by Robert Henderson.

2050 • I DO! I DO!

OPENED: 12/05/1966   Theatre: 46th Street
Musical   Broadway: 560

Composer: Harvey Schmidt
Lyricist: Tom Jones
Librettist: Tom Jones
Producer: David Merrick
Director: Gower Champion

Source: THE FOURPOSTER (Play: Jan de Hartog); **Choreographer:** Gower Champion; **Costumes:** Freddy Wittop; **Lighting Designer:** Jean Rosenthal; **Musical Director:** John Lesko; **Orchestrations:** Philip J. Lang; **Set Design:** Oliver Smith

Songs: All the Dearly Beloved; Echoes of the Past [2]; Father of the Bride, The; Flaming Agnes; Good Night; Honeymoon Is Over, The; I Do! I Do! (1) [1]; I Do! I Do! (2); I Love My Wife; Love Isn't Everything; My Cup Runneth Over; Nobody's Perfect; Roll Up the Ribbons; Someone Needs Me; Something Has Happened; Spring Cleaning [1]; This House; Thousands of Flowers [1]; Together Forever; Well Known Fact, A; What Can I Tell Her? [1]; What Is a Woman; When the Kids Get Married; Where Are the Snows

Cast: Mary Martin; Robert Preston

Notes: [1] Cut prior to opening. [2] Out Washington D.C. 10/66.

2051 • I DREAMT I DWELT IN BLOOMINGDALE'S

OPENED: 02/12/1970   Theatre: Provincetown Playhouse
Musical   Off-Broadway: 5

Composer: Ernest McCarty
Lyricist: Ernest McCarty; Jack Ramer
Librettist: Jack Ramer
Producer: Sam Levine
Director: David Dunham

Choreographer: Bick Goss; **Lighting Designer:** Jim Hardy; **Orchestrations:** Ernest McCary; **Set Design:** Ed Wittstein

Songs: Any Spare Change?; Ballad of Dry Dock Country; Brown Paper Bag; I Dreamt I Dwelt in Bloomingdale's; Makin' Believe; Naomi; Smart; We Didn't Ask to Be Born; Who Will I Be?

Cast: Richard Darrow; Michael De Medico; Liz Otto; Lucy Saroyan

2052 • I FEEL WONDERFUL

OPENED: 10/18/1954   Theatre: Theatre de Lys
Musical   Off-Broadway: 49

Composer: Jerry Herman
Lyricist: Jerry Herman
Librettist: Barry Alan Grael
Producer: Sidney S. Oshrin
Director: Jerry Herman

Choreographer: Frank Wagner; **Costumes:** Romain Johnston; **Musical Director:** Wally Levine; **Set Design:** Romain Johnston

Songs: Dior, Dior; I Feel Wonderful; It's Christmas Today; Jailhouse Blues; Lonesome in New York; My Love Song; Over and Over; Since Eve; This Has Never Been Done Before; When I Love Again

Cast: Nina Dova; Barry Grael; Bob Miller; Tom Mixon; Phyllis Newman

Notes: No program available.

2053 • I HAD A BALL

OPENED: 12/15/1964   Theatre: Martin Beck
Musical   Broadway: 184

Composer: Stan Freeman; Jack Lawrence
Lyricist: Stan Freeman; Jack Lawrence
Librettist: Jerome Chodorov
Producer: Joseph Kipness
Director: Lloyd Richards

Choreographer: Onna White; **Costumes:** Ann Roth; **Dance Arranger:** Luther Henderson; **Lighting Designer:** Will Steven Armstrong; **Musical Director:** Pembroke Davenport; **Orchestrations:** Philip J. Lang; **Set Design:** Will Steven Armstrong; **Vocal Arranger:** Pembroke Davenport

Songs: Addie's At It Again; Affluent Society, The; Almost [1]; Be a Phony [2]; Boys, Boys, Boys; Can It Be Possible?; Coney Island, U.S.A.; Dr. Freud;

Everything I Want; Faith; Fickle Finger of Fate, The; Garside the Great [2]; I Had a Ball; Lament [2]; Like Everyone Else (Soliloquy) [2]; Neighborhood Song, The; Other Half of Me, The; Red-Blooded American Boy; Some Crummy Season [2]; Think Beautiful; True Blue Pals [2]; You Deserve Me

Cast: Buddy Hackett; Richard Kiley; Rosetta LeNoire; Luba Lisa; Karen Morrow; Steve Rowland; Ted Thurston

Notes: [1] Cut after opening. [2] Cut.

2054 • I, JUPITER
Notes: *See OUT OF THIS WORLD.*

2055 • I KNOCK AT THE DOOR
OPENED: 04/12/1976
Musical   Off-Broadway: 4

Composer: Paul Dick
Lyricist: Paul Dick
Librettist: Paul Shyre
Producer: Marc Hamerman
Director: Ron Nash

Costumes: John Reid; **Musical Director:** Sal Sicari

Songs: At the Annual Vice-Regal Ball; Ay, Michael, Oh, Michael; Brook, The; Cock Robin; Irish Ireland, An; Last Shake o' the Bag, The; Little Boy Blue; My Country's Call; My Love Goes Down; Ounce of Cavendish Cut Plug; Prepare Ye Now for the World to Come; Same Way Home; Soliloquy on a Sunny Wedding Morn; There Was a Funny Man; White Bum; Why Are You Weepin' Jenny?

Cast: Susan J. Baum; William Fredericks; Lisa Hall; Kevin Hunter; Richard Ianni; Jonathan Howard Jones; Margo Lacy; Norman Weiler

Notes: Limited engagement.

2056 • I LOVE A LASSIE
OPENED: 05/15/1919
Musical   Closed out of town

Composer: Jerome K. Jerome
Lyricist: Clifton Crawford
Librettist: Clifton Crawford

Producer: Clifton Crawford; White Heather Producing Co.
Director: Frank Stammers

Choreographer: Will H. Smith; **Musical Director:** Augustus Barratt

Songs: Billy; Broadway for Mine; Dancing Through the Ages; Down Lovers' Lane; Hop Scotch; I Used to Go to School with Annie Laurie; I Want to Be a Vampire; Man; Manana Land; Morning After, The; Mother; Off to the Heelands; Scotch Quadrille; Sweetheart o' Mine; Tiddledum; Tourists, The

Cast: Harriet Burt; Clifton Crawford; Julia Kelety; Gill Mack; Jim Miller; Eileen Van Biene

Notes: Shubert Theatre, New Haven, Connecticut.

2057 • I LOVE LYDIA
OPENED: 12/18/1950
Musical   Closed out of town

Composer: Jay Livingston
Lyricist: Ray Evans; Jay Livingston
Librettist: Julius J. Epstein; Philip G. Epstein
Producer: Players Ring, The
Director: Terry Kilburn

Source: RIVALS, THE (Play: Richard Brinsley Sheridan); **Choreographer:** Nelson Barclift; **Musical Director:** Stanley Lebowsky; **Set Design:** Sidney Rushakoff

Songs: Bon Nuit; (My Most) Delectable Dream; Gee It's Gonna Be Wonderful; Give It All You've Got [1]; Give the Little Girl a Great Big Hand; I Love Lydia; I Should Have Quit When I Was Ahead; Lecon le Danse; Let Me Put It This Way; One Last Fling; Order of the Garter; Riviera; Viva la Buck; Viva la Duel; (I Was) Waiting for You; Wondering Who

Cast: Nelson Barclift; King Donovan; Kathleen Freeman; Margot Powers

Notes: [1] Later in OH CAPTAIN!

2058 • I LOVE MY WIFE
OPENED: 04/17/1977   Theatre: Ethel Barrymore
Musical   Broadway: 857

Composer: Cy Coleman
Lyricist: Michael Stewart
Librettist: Michael Stewart
Producer: Joseph Kipness; Terry Allen Kramer; Harry Rigby
Director: Gene Saks

Source: VIÉNS CHEZ-MOI, J'HABITE CHEZ UNE COPINE (Play: Luis Rego); **Choreographer:** Onna White; **Costumes:** Ron Talsky; **Dance Arranger:** Cy Coleman; **Lighting Designer:** Gilbert V. Hemsley Jr.; **Musical Director:** John Miller; **Set Design:** David Mitchell; **Vocal Arranger:** Cy Coleman

Songs: By Threes; Everybody Today Is Turning On; Hey There Good Times; I Love My Wife; Love Revolution; Lovers on Christmas Eve; Married Couple Seeks Married Couple; Monica; Mover's Life, A; Scream; Sexually Free; Someone Wonderful I Missed; We're Still Friends [1]

Cast: Lenny Baker; Ken Bichel; Joanna Gleason; Ilene Graff; Michael Mark; John Miller; James Naughton; Joe Saulter

Notes: There was also a new opening number written for this show when the Smothers Brothers joined the cast. [1] Dropped after opening when Smothers Brothers joined the cast.

2059 • I LOVE YOU
OPENED: 04/28/1919   Theatre: Booth
Play   Broadway: 56

Author: William Le Baron
Producer: G.M. Anderson

Songs: I Love You (C: M.H. Hollins; L: William Le Baron)

Cast: Richard Dix; Gilbert Douglas; Doris Mitchell; Gypsy O'Brien; Dianthia Patterson; Robert Strange; Ruth Terry; John Westley

2060 • I LOVED YOU WEDNESDAY
OPENED: 10/11/1932   Theatre: Sam H. Harris
Play   Broadway: 63

Author: William DuBois; Molly Ricardel
Producer: Crosby Gaige
Director: Worthington Miner

Set Design: Raymond Sovey

Songs: I Loved You Wednesday (C/L: Milton Drake; Walter Kent; Abner Silver)

Cast: Humphrey Bogart; Henry Fonda; Arlene Francis; Frances Fuller; Rose Hobart; Henry O'Neill; Jane Seymour

Notes: No mention of song in program.

2061 • I MARRIED AN ANGEL
OPENED: 05/11/1938   Theatre: Shubert
Musical   Broadway: 338

Composer: Richard Rodgers
Lyricist: Lorenz Hart
Librettist: Lorenz Hart; Richard Rodgers
Producer: Dwight Deere Wiman
Director: Joshua Logan

Source: ANGYALT VETTEM FELESEGUL (Play: Janos Vaszary); **Choreographer:** George Balanchine; **Costumes:** John Hambleton; **Musical Director:** Gene Salzer; **Orchestrations:** Hans Spialek; **Set Design:** Jo Mielziner

Songs: Angel without Wings; At the Roxy Music Hall; Did You Ever Get Stung?; Honeymoon Ballet (inst.); How to Win Friends and Influence People; I Married an Angel; I'll Tell the Man in the Street; I'm Ruined; Men from Milwaukee, The [1]; Modiste, The; Othello (inst.); Spring Is Here; Twinkle in Your Eye, A; Women Are Women [2]

Cast: Audrey Christie; Dennis King; Charles Laskey; Casper Reardon; Vivienne Segal; Walter Slezak; Morton L. Stevens; Charles Walters; Vera Zorina

Notes: [1] Probably not used. [2] Not used.

2062 • I.O.U.
OPENED: 1906
Musical   Closed out of town

Composer: Lee Johnson
Lyricist: William Carlton
Librettist: Judson D. Brusie
Producer: Max M. Dill; C. William Kolb; Francis Lieb; Maud K. Williams

Songs: Bill Poster's Song; Blew, Blew, Blew; Circus Parade; Dainty Flo from Idaho; Dreaming; Labor Day Parade; Little Tin Pail; Moonlight; Motley Assemblage, A; My Maori Maid; New Zealand Maori Dance; Opening Chorus; Ring Master's Song

Cast: Max M. Dill; C. William Kolb

Notes: No other information available. Program of Wilkes- Barre 2/12/06.

2063 • I PICKED A DAISY

Notes: *See ON A CLEAR DAY YOU CAN SEE FOREVER.*

2064 • I REMEMBER MAMA

OPENED: 05/31/1979   Theatre: Majestic
Musical   Broadway: 108

Composer: Richard Rodgers
Lyricist: Martin Charnin
Librettist: Thomas Meehan
Producer: Alexander H. Cohen; Hildy Parks
Director: Cy Feuer

Source: I REMEMBER MAMA (Play: John van Druten); **Source:** MAMA'S BANK ACCOUNT (Story: Kathryn Forbes); **Choreographer:** Danny Daniels; **Costumes:** Theoni V. Aldredge; **Lighting Designer:** Roger Morgan; **Musical Director:** Jay Blackton; **Orchestrations:** Philip J. Lang; **Set Design:** David Mitchell; Vocal Arranger: Jay Blackton

Songs: Day Sven Gundersen Died, The [2]; Don't Laugh at Trina [2]; Easy Come, Easy Go (L: Raymond Jessel); Ev'ry Day (Comes Something Beautiful); Fair Trade; Fam'ly We Will Be, A [4]; How Do You Bring Up Children? [2]; I Don't Know How [5] (L: Raymond Jessel); I Remember Mama; It Is Not the End of the World; It's Going to Be Good to Be Gone; Lars, Lars (L: Raymond Jessel); Little Bit More, A (L: Raymond Jessel); Lullaby; Mama Always Makes It Better [1]; Maybe, Maybe, Maybe [4]; Midsummer Night [4]; Most Disagreeable Man, A (1) [4]; Most Disagreeable Man A, (2); Old City Boy at Heart, A [4]; Such Good Fun (1) [4]; Such Good Fun (2); Time;

Uncle Chris (L: Raymond Jessel); We're Staying Here [3]; What Kind of Man? [2]; When? [2]; Where We Came From [5] (L: Raymond Jessel); Women Without Men [3]; Writer Writes at Night, A; You Could Not Please Me More [6]

Cast: Betty Ann Grove; George Hearn; Carrie Horner; Elizabeth Hubbard; George S. Irving; Myvanwy Jenn; Tara Kennedy; Armin Shimerman; Maureen Silliman; Liv Ullmann; Kristen Vigard; Dolores Wilson; Ian Ziering

Notes: [1] Same music as "Getting Married to a Person" cut from TWO BY TWO. [2] Cut prior to opening. [3] Not used. [4] Cut during tryout. [5] Cut during previews. [6] Previously cut from TWO BY TWO.

2065 • I SENT A LETTER TO MY LOVE

OPENED: 02/08/1995   Theatre: Primary Stages
Musical   Off-Off-Broadway

Composer: Melissa Manchester
Lyricist: Melissa Manchester; Jeffrey Sweet
Librettist: Jeffrey Sweet
Producer: Primary Stages
Director: Pat Birch

Source: I SENT A LETTER TO MY LOVE (Novel: Bernice Rubens); **Arrangements:** Aaron Hagan; Melissa Manchester; **Costumes:** Rodney Munoz; **Lighting Designer:** Kirk Bookman; **Musical Director:** Aaron Hagan; **Set Design:** James Noone

Songs: Across the Lake; Chance of You; Change in the Air; Day I Meet My Friend, The; God Never Closes a Door; Grass Between My Toes; I Never Knew; Lady Seeks Gentleman; Last Night; Pants, Angela; Perfect Timing; Prologue; Rosy Red; Someone in a Chair; Very Truly Yours; What I Am; Your Prince

Cast: Bethe B. Austin; Meagen Fay; John Hickok; Robert Westenberg; Lynne Wintersteller

2066 • I TOLD YOU SO
Notes: See PIGGY.

2067 • I WANT YOU

OPENED: 09/14/1961   Theatre: Maidman
                                    Playhouse
Musical   Off-Broadway: 4

Composer: Joseph Grayhorn; Stefan Kanfer; Jess J.
   Korman
Lyricist: Joseph Grayhorn; Stefan Kanfer; Jess J.
   Korman
Librettist: Stefan Kanfer
Producer: Theodore J. Flicker; Sam W. Gelfman;
   Joseph Grayhorn
Director: Theodore J. Flicker

Choreographer: Rhoda Levine; **Lighting Designer:**
   Jerome Liotta; **Musical Director:** Harold Beebe;
   Set Design: Frieda Evans

Songs: Ain't It Funny; Farewells, The; Hong Kong
   Gong; I Want You; Loyal American; My Daddy
   Was Right; Perfect Man; Remarkable; So Long,
   Yesterday; Street, The; Take Every Opportunity;
   That's What the Public Wants; This Is a Dollar
   Bill; You Devil You

Cast: Al Mancini; Barbara Quaney; Joshua Shelley

2068 • I'D RATHER BE RIGHT

OPENED: 11/02/1937   Theatre: Alvin
Musical   Broadway: 289

Composer: Richard Rodgers
Lyricist: Lorenz Hart
Librettist: Moss Hart; George S. Kaufman
Producer: Sam Harris
Director: George S. Kaufman

Choreographer: Ned McGurn; Charles Weidman;
   Costumes: John Hambleton; Irene Sharaff;
   Musical Director: Harry Levant; **Orchestrations:**
   Hans Spialek; **Set Design:** Donald Oenslager

Songs: Baby Bond for Baby, A; Ev'rybody Loves
   You [2]; Have You Met Miss Jones?; Here He Is;
   His Chances Are Not Worth a Penny (Finaletto) [2];
   Homogeneous Cabinet, A; I'd Rather Be
   Right (1) [4]; I'd Rather Be Right (2); Labor Is the
   Thing; Little Bit of Constitutional Fun, A; No So
   Innocent Fun (Nine Young Girls and Nine Old
   Men) (Nine Young Girls and Nine Old Men) [2];
   Off the Record; Spring in Vienna [1]; Sweet Sixty-
   Five; Take and Take and Take; Treaty, My Sweety
   with You, A [2]; We Just Sing and Dance [2];
   We're Going to Balance the Budget (Tune Up
   Bluebird); What's It All About [3]; World Is My
   Oyster, The [2]

Cast: Florenz Ames; George M. Cohan; Bijou
   Fernandez; Marion Green; Joy Hodges; Taylor
   Holmes; Joseph Macaulay; Austin Marshall;
   Irene McBride; Marie Nash; Margaret Sande;
   Georgie Tapps; Mary Jane Walsh

Notes: [1] Changed to "Spring in Milwaukee" after
   opening. [2] Cut prior to opening. [3] Added
   after opening. [4] Cut prior to opening. Music
   later used as "Now That I Know You" from
   show TWO WEEKS WITH PAY.

2069 • I'LL DIE IF I CAN'T LIVE FOREVER

OPENED: 10/31/1974   Theatre: Improvisation,
                                    The
Revue   Off-Broadway: 81

Composer: William Boswell; Joyce Stoner
Lyricist: Joyce Stoner
Librettist: William Brooke
Producer: Improvisation, The; Stoner Arts, Inc.
Director: Joyce Stoner

Choreographer: Joyce Stoner; **Musical Director:**
   William Boswell; **Set Design:** Irving Milton
   Duke; Vocal Arranger: William Boswell

Songs: A Is For; Being Too Good Has Its Bad
   Points [1]; Computer Love Song, The [1];
   Finale, The; Great White Way, The; How
   Can I Tell You That It's Over? [1]; I Hate
   Football; I Should Have Waited for You [1]; I
   Want a Man Who Can Cook [1]; I'll Die If I
   Can't Live Forever; I'm in Love; I'm in Love
   with Walter Cronkite [1]; I'm So Bored;
   Improvisation, The; It's Great to Be Gay; Joys
   of Manhattan Life; Less Is More and More;
   Let's Have a Rodgers and Hammerstein Affair;
   Murder Isn't Proper [1]; My Life's a Musical
   Comedy; My Place or Yours?; Ode to Electricity;
   Opening Number, The; Roommate Beguine,
   The; Showing a Little Ankle [1]; Take Me!;
   There's Always Someone Who'll Tell You No;
   They Left Me; 24 Hours from This Moment;
   We're Strangers Who Sleep Side By Side; Where
   Would We Be without Perverts?; Who Do We
   Thank!; With Your Help I'll Stand Alone [1];
   Yesterday It Rained [1]

Cast: Don Bradford; Tom Hastings; Gail Johnston; Michael David Laibson; Maureen Maloney; Nancy Reddon

Notes: [1] Cut prior to opening.

2070 • I'LL SAY SHE DOES
OPENED: 1920
Musical   Closed out of town

Composer: B.G. DeSylva
Lyricist: B.G. DeSylva
Librettist: Avery Hopwood
Producer: A.H. Woods
Director: Edward Royce

Musical Director: Pierre de Reeder;
  Orchestrations: Frank Saddler

Songs: Call of the Wild Women, The; Hundred Years from Now, A; It's Naughty-But It's Nice; Morning After, The; On an Island with You; Settling Down; Sunny May Afternoon, A [1]; What the Doctor Ordered; What's Weak About the Weaker Sex; While the City Sleeps; You're All That I Need; You're All That Queed; Zis Lettle Girl

Cast: Juliette Day; Ernest Glendinning; Roland Young

Notes: Program of Stamford, Conn. 5/13/20. [1] Sheet music only.

2071 • I'LL SAY SHE IS
OPENED: 05/19/1924   Theatre: Casino
Musical   Broadway: 313

Composer: Tom Johnstone
Lyricist: Will B. Johnstone
Librettist: Will B. Johnstone
Producer: James P. Beury
Director: Eugene Sanger

Choreographer: Vaughn Godfrey; **Costumes:** Brooks; Mahieu; **Musical Director:** Ted Coleman

Songs: Break Into Your Heart; Cinderella Backwards [1]; Do It; Give Me a Thrill; Glimpses of the Moon; I See Your Face [1]; Marathon Street [1]; Only You; Pretty Girl; Rainy Day; San Toy; Wall Street Blues; When the Shadows Fall; Wonderful Nile, The

Cast: Chico Marx; Groucho Marx; Harpo Marx; Zeppo Marx; Edward Metcalfe; Alice Webb

Notes: [1] Out Boston 9/3/23.

2072 • I'M A FAN
OPENED: 01/25/1972   Theatre: CBS
TV Musical

Composer: Leroy Holmes
Lyricist: Carolyn Leigh
Librettist: Bob Ellison; Carolyn Leigh
Producer: Alexander H. Cohen
Director: Clark Jones

Musical Director: Leroy Holmes

Songs: All the Way Home; At the Hockey Game; Basketball; Brave and the Free, The; Charge; Defense; Dump the Ump; Half Time; I'm a Fan; My Cousin Beauregard; Sport Star of T.V. Today, The; Ten Strokes Under Par; Time Out

Cast: Carol Channing; MacIntyre Dixon; Brandon Maggart; Donna McKechnie; Karen Morrow; Trisha Noble; Dick Van Dyke; Mary Louise Wilson

2073 • I'M GETTING MARRIED
OPENED: 03/16/1967   Theatre: ABC
TV Musical

Composer: Jule Styne
Lyricist: Betty Comden; Adolph Green

Songs: F.F. (Forbidden Fruit) [1]; Getting Married (Living As One) [2]; Love Is Our Umbrella; Roots; Venezia

Cast: Anne Bancroft; Dick Shawn

Notes: Part of the "Stage 67" series. [1] From score of FADE OUT-FADE IN. [2] Not the same as the song of same title from score of SUBWAYS ARE FOR SLEEPING.

2074 • I'M GETTING MY ACT TOGETHER AND TAKING IT ON THE ROAD
OPENED: 06/14/1978   Theatre: Circle in the Square
Musical   Broadway: 1165

Composer: Nancy Ford
Lyricist: Gretchen Cryer
Librettist: Gretchen Cryer
Producer: Joseph Papp
Director: Word Baker

Costumes: Pearl Somner; **Lighting Designer:** Martin Tudor; **Orchestrations:** Scott Berry; Nancy Ford; Bob George; Lee Grayson; Don Scardino; Dean Swenson

Songs: Dear Tom; Feel the Love; Happy Birthday; If Only Things Was Different [1]; In a Simple Way I Love; Lonely Lady (C: Gretchen Cryer); Miss America; Natural High; Old Friend; Put in a Package and Sold; Smile; Strong Woman Number

Cast: Betty Aberlin; Gretchen Cryer; Margot Rose; Don Scardino

Notes: Opened at the Public Theater and moved to Broadway 12/16/78. [1] Added to London production.

2075 • I'M SOLOMON

OPENED: 04/23/1968   Theatre: Mark Hellinger
Musical   Broadway: 7

Composer: Ernest Gold
Lyricist: Anne Croswell
Librettist: Dan Almagor; Anne Croswell
Producer: Zvi Kolitz; Abe Margolies; Solomon Sagall
Director: Michael Benthall

Source: KING SOLOMON AND THE COBBLER (Play: Sammy Gronemann); THE KING AND THE COBBLER (Musical); **Choreographer:** Donald McKayle; **Costumes:** Jane Greenwood; **Dance Arranger:** Dorothea Freitag; **Lighting Designer:** Martin Aronstein; **Musical Director:** Gershon Kingsley; **Orchestrations:** Hershy Kay; **Set Design:** Rouben Ter-Arutunian; Vocal Arranger: Gershon Kingsley

Songs: Citation, The; David and Bathsheba; Hail the Son of David; Have You Ever Been Alone with a King Before? (C: Bill Weeden; L: David Finkle); Have You Heard?; I Am What I Am; In Love with a Fool; In Someone Else's Sandals; Jerusalem [1]; Lord, I Am but a Little Child; Once in 2.7 Years; Preposterous; Put Your Hand on My Hand [1]; Someone Like Me; Something in His Eyes; That Guilty Feeling (C: Bill Weeden; L: David Finkle);

Three Riddles, The (L: Erich Segal); Time to Let Go; With Your Hand in My Hand

Cast: Salome Jens; Carmen Mathews; Garrett Morris; Karen Morrow; Fred Pinkard; Dick Shawn; Barbara Webb

Notes: Originally titled IN SOMEONE ELSE'S SANDALS. [1] Cut prior to opening.

2076 • I'VE HEARD THAT SONG BEFORE

OPENED: 07/14/1995
Revue   21

Composer: Jule Styne
Lyricist: Sammy Cahn; Betty Comden; Adolph Green; E.Y. Harburg; Bob Hilliard; Frank Loesser; Bob Merrill; Leo Robin; Stephen Sondheim
Librettist: Virginia Irwin; Roger Sturtevant
Producer: Island Stage
Director: Virginia Irwin

Arrangements: Don Rickenback; **Costumes:** Judy Cook; **Lighting Designer:** Linda Knox; **Musical Director:** Don Rickenback

Cast: Anita Anderson; Laura Gallagher; John Knox-Johnston; Don Rickenback

Notes: Produced at The Performance Center, Nantucket, Mass. The show consisted mainly of medleys of Styne's work.

2077 • ICE-CAPADES OF 1941

OPENED: 1941
Revue

Composer: Peter De Rose
Lyricist: John Latouche
Director: Russell Markert

Arrangements: Jerry Mayhall; Earl Moss; **Costumes:** Willa Van

Songs: Forever and Ever (C: Jule Styne; L: George Brown; Sol Meyer); Guy with the Polka Dotted Tie, The [1] (C: Jule Styne; L: Sol Meyer); I Hear America Singing (L: Mitchell Parish); Somewhere; Yankee Doodle Polka, The (C: Vernon Duke; L: Mitchell Parish)

Cast: George Byron; Serge Flash; Byron Jackson; Joe Jackson Jr.; Robin Lee; Eric Waite

Notes: [1] ASCAP/Library of Congress only. In film ICE- CAPADES.

2078 • ICE-CAPADES OF 1943
OPENED: 1943
Revue

Producer: Arena Managers Association

Choreographer: Chester Hale; **Costumes:** Freddy Wittop; **Lighting Designer:** Carlton Winkler

Songs: Guy with the Polka Dotted Tie [2] (C: Jule Styne; L: Sol Meyer)

Cast: Vera Hruba[1]; Bobby Specht

Notes: No other information available. [1] Later known as Vera Hruba Ralston. [2] From film ICE CAPADES OF 1941.

2079 • ICE CAPADES (1957)
OPENED: 1957
Revue

Songs: When You Are Seventeen (C: Lew Spence; L: Alan Bergman; Marilyn Bergman)

Notes: No other information available.

2080 • ICE CAPADES (1973)
OPENED: 1973
Revue

Composer: James Harbert; Bill Stafford
Lyricist: James Harbert; Bill Stafford
Director: Robert Turk

Choreographer: George Foster; Robert Turk; **Costumes:** Bill Campbell; **Musical Director:** Gilbert C. Stevens; **Orchestrations:** John Handy; James Harbert; Bill Stafford; Gilbert C. Stevens; **Set Design:** Bill Goodwin

Songs: Ship-a-Hoy (C/L: Billy Barnes); Summer Has Gone (C/L: Jim Harbert)

Cast: Sashi Kuchiki; Jo Jo Starbuck

Notes: 34th Edition.

2081 • ICE CAPADES (1981)
Notes: *See LIGHT UP THE ICE.*

2082 • ICE-CAPADES (LIGHT UP THE ICE)
OPENED: 01/21/1981
Revue

Composer: Don James; Tom Worrall
Lyricist: Don James; Tom Worrall

Notes: No other information available.

2083 • ICE FOLLIES (1957)
OPENED: 1957
Revue

Composer: Larry Morey
Lyricist: Larry Morey
Producer: Oscar Johnson; Eddie Shipstad; Roy Shipstad
Director: Frances Claudet; Stanley D. Kahn; Mary Jane Lewis

Costumes: Renie; **Musical Director:** George Hackett; **Orchestrations:** Foster Cope; Bob Gordon; Greig McRitchie; Dave Strech; Frank Ventre

Songs: Baby, Please Thaw Out; Candy Cane Rock 'n' Roll; Candystick; Fifi; It's a Fine Night for Romance; Lady Likes to Dance, The; Lookin' for a Gentleman

Cast: Frances Dorsey; Richard Dwyer; Mr. Frick; Andra McLaughlin; Florence Rae

2084 • ICE FOLLIES (1973)
OPENED: 1973
Revue

Composer: Dick Friesen; Ray Linn
Lyricist: Dick Friesen; Ray Linn
Producer: Bob Shipstad
Director: Bob Maxson; Helen Maxson

Choreographer: Bob Maxson; Helen Maxson; **Costumes:** Helen Colvig; **Musical Director:** Paul Walberg; **Orchestrations:** Mark Davidson; Gus Donahue; Dick Friesen; Dick Hazard; Mundell Lowe; Greig McRitchie; Lyle Murphy; Don

Specht; Paul Walberg; **Vocal Arranger:** Ray Linn

Songs: Bad News Report; Child Is a Horse's Best Friend, A; Fun Band, The; Gotta Move; Happy Factory; Rhapsody of Sounds and Motion (C/L: Dick Friesen; Ray Linn; Lyle Murphy); Rock 'n Horse; Sour Grape Theme; Spark Plug Blues March

Cast: Susan Berens; Richard Dwyer; Mr. Frick; Ricky Inglesi; Trixi Schuba

2085 • ICE FOLLIES OF 1934
OPENED: 1934
Revue

Composer: Stanley Cowan; Bobby Worth
Lyricist: Stanley Cowan; Bobby Worth
Producer: Shipstads & Johnson
Director: Miss Fanchon

Choreographer: Miss Fanchon; **Costumes:** Helen Rose; **Musical Director:** Ernest Kratzinger; **Orchestrations:** George Hackett; **Vocal Arranger:** Arthur Kay

Songs: In Snowman's Land; Jive; Sunday-Go-to-Meeting; Tuamani; We'll Stick Together

Cast: Betty Atkinson; Mary Barton; Bob Blake; Heinie Brock; George Burnson; Frick and Frack; Paul Gannon; Jane McGowan; Joseph Sullivan

2086 • ICE FOLLIES OF 1941
OPENED: 1940
Revue

Composer: Stanley Cowan; Bobby Worth
Lyricist: Stanley Cowan; Bobby Worth
Producer: Oscar Johnson; Eddie Shipstad; Roy Shipstad
Director: Miss Fanchon

Choreographer: Mary Jane Lewis; **Costumes:** Helen Rose; **Musical Director:** Ernest Kratzinger

Songs: Learn to Skate; Pretty Little Pirate; Waltzing on a Moonbeam

Cast: Evelyn Chandler; Bess Ehrhardt; Frick & Frack; Paul Gannon; Les Hamilton; Papez & Zwack

2087 • ICE FOLLIES OF 1942
OPENED: 1942
Revue

Composer: Stanley Cowan; Bobby Worth
Lyricist: Stanley Cowan; Bobby Worth
Producer: Oscar Johnson; Eddie Shipstad; Roy Shipstad
Director: Miss Fanchon

Choreographer: Mary Jane Lewis; **Costumes:** Helen Rose; **Musical Director:** Ernest Kratzinger

Songs: Be Young Again; Devil in My Angel's Eyes, The; My Heart Flies Blind; Romancing the Mardi Gras; We'll Always Be in Love

Cast: Osborne Colson; Paul Gannon; Valerie & Jenna

2088 • ICE FOLLIES OF 1944
OPENED: 1944
Revue

Composer: Ben Black
Lyricist: Ben Black
Producer: Oscar Johnson; Eddie Shipstad; Roy Shipstad

Costumes: Helen Rose; **Musical Director:** Ernest Kratzinger

Songs: Derby Day; 18th Century Garden (inst.) (C: Eddie Ward); Polka Dot Polka

Cast: Heinie Brock; Frick & Frack; Oscar Johnson; Ruby Maxson; Roy Shipstad

2089 • ICE FOLLIES OF 1949
OPENED: 1949
Revue

Composer: Larry Morey
Lyricist: Larry Morey
Producer: Oscar Johnson; Eddie Shipstad; Roy Shipstad
Director: Frances Claudet; Stanley Kahn; Mary Jane Lewis

Costumes: Helen Rose; **Musical Director:** Walter Rudolph; **Orchestrations:** Foster Cope; George Hackett; Stan Myers; Dave Strech; **Set Design:** Tommy Lawless

Songs: Building Bee, The [1]; Candy Choo-Choo; Candy Soldiers on Parade; Chickady Chay; Circus Day [1]; I Got a Gal in Californy; It's a Good Good Mornin' [1]; Lollypop Polka, The; Me and My Heart Went A-Gadding; Shake 'Em Off [1]; Smooth Sailin'; Song Bird Singing in a Bamboo Tree; Swing Waltz, The (C: Josef Strauss); Tinkle Ting Ting; Upside Down Song, The; Walkin' with Mariah [1]; When It's Young and It's Spring; With a Song in Your Hair

Cast: Bill Cameron; Hazel Franklin; Frick and Frack; Paul Gannon; Hugh Hendrickson; Mae Ross; Betty Schalow; Roy Shipstad

Notes: Songs are from two editions of this show. [1] Sheet music only.

2090 • ICE FOLLIES OF 1950
OPENED: 1950
Revue

Composer: Larry Morey
Lyricist: Larry Morey
Producer: Oscar Johnson; Eddie Shipstad; Roy Shipstad
Director: Frances Claudet; Mary Jane Lewis

Arrangements: Walter J. Rudolph; **Costumes:** Helen Rose; **Musical Director:** Walter J. Rudolph; **Orchestrations:** Foster Cope; George Hackett; Dave Stretch

Songs: At the Widder Sadie Simpkins Buildin' Bee; Blow Your Own Horn; Circus Day; It's a Good Good Morning; Milk Bottle Parade, The; School Bells Ringin' Out; Shake 'Em Off; Walkin' with Mariah

Cast: Bill Cameron; Jeanne Crystall; Frick and Frack; Stanley D. Kahn; Leduc Brothers; Schramm Twins; Marilyn Ruth Take

Notes: No other information available.

2091 • ICE FOLLIES OF 1954
OPENED: 1953
Musical

Composer: Larry Morey
Lyricist: Larry Morey
Producer: Oscar Johnson; Eddie Shipstad; Roy Shipstad

Choreographer: Frances Claudet; Stanley D. Kahn; Mary Jane Lewis; **Costumes:** Helen Rose; **Musical Director:** George Hackett; **Set Design:** Fernando Carrere

Songs: Eat the Bubbles in Your Soup; I Love the Ladies; Make-Believing; Piggy Bank Song, The

Cast: Inga Brita; Richard Dwyer; Paul Gannon; Marlene Jackson

2092 • ICE FOLLIES OF 1967
OPENED: 09/08/1966
Revue

Composer: Dick Friesen
Lyricist: Dick Friesen
Producer: Oscar Johnson; Eddie Shipstad; Roy Shipstad
Director: Bob Shipstad

Arrangements: George Hackett; **Choreographer:** Frances Claudet; **Costumes:** Mary Wills; **Musical Director:** George Hackett; **Orchestrations:** Foster Cope; Dick Friesen; Bob Gordon; George Hackett; Alex Law; Greig McRitchie; Dave Strech; **Vocal Arranger:** Ray Linn Jr.

Songs: Happiness Is Going on a Picnic; Magical Garden of Dreams, The; Mushroom Ride; Rock Garden Rock; Thomas Alva Edison; Wake Up Little Dream Girl

Cast: Dick Cooper; Cathy Freed; Rik McKinnon; Bill Wall; Debbie Williams; Voice: Daws Butler

2093 • ICE FOLLIES OF 1968
OPENED: 09/07/1967
Revue

Composer: Dick Friesen
Lyricist: Dick Friesen
Producer: Oscar Johnson; Eddie Shipstad; Roy Shipstad
Director: Bob Shipstad

Arrangements: George Hackett; **Choreographer:** Frances Claudet; **Costumes:** Helen Colvig; **Musical Director:** George Hackett; **Orchestrations:** Foster Cope; Bob Gordon; Alex Law; Greig McRitchie; Lyle Murphy

Songs: Climb-Out; Co-operation; Debbie's Pastry Order; Gingerbread Train, The; Inky's Pastry

Shop; Jelly Roll Party; Patti-Cake Waltz, The; Stage Door Johnny

Voice: Daws Butler

2094 • ICE FOLLIES OF 1969
OPENED: 1969
Revue

Composer: Dick Friesen
Lyricist: Dick Friesen
Producer: Oscar Johnson; Eddie Shipstad; Roy Shipstad
Director: Bob Shipstad

Arrangements: George Hacket; **Costumes:** Helen Colvig; **Musical Director:** George Hackett; **Orchestrations:** Foster Cope; Greig McRitchie; Dave Strech; **Vocal Arranger:** Ray Linn Jr.

Songs: Commander Robot and the Squiggles; Everything's New in Old New York; Official Looney Gooney Bird Patrol Hand Clapping and Marching Song, The; Tiffany Girl; Welcome to Looneyland; Will Make It to the Moon Tonight

Cast: Dick Cooper; Peggy Fleming; Gene Floyd; Ricky Inglesi; Donald Jackson; Rik McKinnon; Joe Niederhorn

2095 • ICE FOLLIES OF 1971
OPENED: 1971
Revue

Composer: Dick Friesen
Lyricist: Dick Friesen
Producer: Bob Shipstad

Arrangements: Dick Friesen; **Choreographer:** Helen Maxson; **Costumes:** Helen Colvig; **Musical Director:** George Hackett; Paul Walberg; **Orchestrations:** Bob Ballard; Mundell Lowe; Greig McRitchie; Lyle Murphy; **Vocal Arranger:** Ray Linn Jr.

Songs: Honey, Be My Little Honey Bee; New Ice Age, The; Shoo-Fly Crow; Soil, Seed, Sun, and Rain; T.L.C. (Tender Loving Care); Tip Your Hat to a Carrot; Town Meeting

Cast: Lucienne Boyer; Rika Boyer; Dick Cooper; Jay Humphrey; Kathy Kay; Rik McKinnon; Cathy Miller; James Stuart

2096 • ICE FOLLIES OF 1972
OPENED: 1972
Revue

Composer: Dick Friesen; Ray Linn
Lyricist: Dick Friesen; Ray Linn
Producer: Bob Shipstad
Director: Bob Maxson; Helen Maxson

Choreographer: Bob Maxson; Helen Maxson; **Costumes:** Helen Colvig; **Musical Director:** Paul Walberg; **Orchestrations:** Bob Ballard; Mark Davidson; John Friesen; Dick Hazard; Mundell Lowe; Greig McRitchie; Lyle Murphy; Paul Walberg; **Vocal Arranger:** Ray Linn

Songs: Chop Stix; Kiddie Medley; Riddle Song, The; School Days (C/L: Gus Edwards; Dick Friesen; Ray Linn); Through the Eyes of Your Imagination; What Kind of Animal Is That?

Cast: Colin Beatty; Susan Berens; Ricky Inglesi; Bob Leduc

2097 • ICE-TRAVAGANZA
OPENED: 1964
Revue   N.Y. World's Fair

Composer: John Morris
Lyricist: Gerald Freedman; John Morris
Librettist: Gerald Freedman
Producer: Dick Button; Paul Feigay
Director: Dick Button

Choreographer: Dick Button; **Costumes:** Winn Morton; **Lighting Designer:** Will Steven Armstrong; **Musical Director:** John Morris; **Orchestrations:** Ralph Burns; **Set Design:** Will Steven Armstrong

Songs: Come Skate with Me; Everyone Knows; Happy New Year -Every Day; I'm Going to Be a Boy; Inspiration; Now That Winter's Here; Solo for Everyone; There'll Be a Time; We Haven't Begun to Live; Who's That?

Cast: Sandy Culbertson; Jerry Howard; Guy Longpre; Barbara Martin; Don McPherson; Pat Pauley; Fred Randall; Ronnie Robertson; Eric Waite

Notes: New York City Pavilion.

2098 • ICETIME

OPENED: 06/20/1946   Theatre: Center
Revue   Broadway: 405

Composer: John Fortis
Lyricist: John Fortis
Producer: Sonja Henie; Arthur M. Wirtz
Director: Catherine Littlefield

Choreographer: Catherine Littlefield; **Costumes:** Lou Eisele; Billy Livingston; **Dance Arranger:** Paul Van Loan; **Lighting Designer:** Eugene Braun; **Musical Director:** David Mendoza; **Orchestrations:** Paul Van Loan; **Set Design:** Edward Gilbert

Songs: Cuddle Up; Her Dream Man; Loveable You; Mandy; Mary, Mary; Ole King Cole; Song of the Silver Blades

Cast: Denise Brandt; Richard Craig; Jay Martin; Shirley Weber

Notes: Cast listed are singers not skaters.

2099 • ICETIME OF 1947-48

OPENED: 05/28/1947   Theatre: Center
Revue   Broadway: 422

Composer: John Fortis
Lyricist: John Fortis
Producer: Sonja Henie; Arthur M. Wirtz
Director: Catherine Littlefield

Choreographer: Catherine Littlefield; **Costumes:** Katherine Kuhn; **Dance Arranger:** Paul Van Loan; **Lighting Designer:** Eugene Braun; **Musical Director:** David Mendoza; **Orchestrations:** Paul Van Loan; **Set Design:** Edward Gilbert; Bruno Maine

Songs: Breakin' the Ice (C: Paul McGrane; L: Al Stillman)

Cast: Richard Craig; Nola Fairbanks; Joan Hyldorf; Melba Welch

Notes: This was a revised version of the 1946 ICETIME with an additional song.

2100 • ICHABOD

OPENED: 01/12/1977   Theatre: Town Hall
Musical   Off-Broadway: 1

Composer: Tom Tierney
Lyricist: Gene Traylor
Librettist: Gene Traylor
Producer: Interludes
Director: Michael Montel

Source: LEGEND OF SLEEPY HOLLOW, THE (Story: Washington Irving); **Choreographer:** Michel Stuart; Terri White; **Costumes:** James Edward Brady; **Lighting Designer:** Jeffrey Schissler

Songs: Aspirations; Bird of Love, The; Brom Bones; Education; Ghost's Turn, The; Glory of Sleepy Hollow, The; Just a Moment; Katrina Waltz, The; Pleasing Land, A; Protections; Ride, The; Ripening Heart; She Could Do a Lot Worse; Sleepy Little Valley; Tales; Vote for Crane

Cast: Tommy Tune

Notes: A one performance showcase as part of the "Interludes" series.

2101 • IDOL'S EYE, THE

OPENED: 10/25/1897   Theatre: Broadway
Musical   Broadway: 56

Composer: Victor Herbert
Lyricist: Harry B. Smith
Librettist: Harry B. Smith
Producer: Kirke La Shelle
Director: Julian Mitchell

Costumes: Caroline Seidle; **Musical Director:** Frank Palma; **Set Design:** Ernest Albert

Songs: Absent-Minded Maid; Captain Cholly Chumley of the Guards; Cuban Song; Entrance of Brahmins; Fairy Tales; Holding Hands; I Just Dropped In; Lady and the Kick, The; Lancers; Letter Duet; March; Mindin' the Baby; Minding the Baby; Only for Thee; Opening Chorus; Opening Chorus Act II and Dance of the Nautch Girls; Pretty Isabella and Her Umbrella; Sealed Orders; Skirt Dancer, The; Song of the Priestess; Talk About Yo' Luck; Tattooed Man, The; Tom and Jack; Two-Step

Cast: Will Danforth; Frank Daniels; Maurice Darcy; Norma Kopp; Helen Redmond; Alf C. Whelan

2102 • IF I WERE KING

OPENED: 03/25/1923
Musical

Composer: Richard Rodgers
Lyricist: Richard Rodgers
Librettist: Richard Rodgers
Producer: Benjamin School for Girls
Director: Herbert Fields

Musical Director: Richard Rodgers

Songs: Band of the Ne'er Do Wells, The (L: Lorenz Hart); Courtly Etiquette; Daughters of Pleasure; If I Were King [1] (L: Lorenz Hart); March Louis XI (inst.); Minuet Waltz (inst.); Sextette; Waltz (inst.)

Notes: Amateur production. [1] From score of WINKLE TOWN and also in BAD HABITS OF 1925.

2103 • IF THE SHOE FITS

OPENED: 12/05/1946   Theatre: Century
Musical   Broadway: 20

Composer: David Raksin
Lyricist: June Carroll
Librettist: June Carroll; Robert Duke
Producer: Leonard Sillman
Director: Eugene Brydon

Source: CINDERELLA (Fairy Tale); **Choreographer:** Don Liberto; Charles Weidman; **Costumes:** Katherine Kuhn; **Musical Director:** Will Irwin; **Orchestrations:** Robert Russell Bennett; Joe Glover; Walter Paul; Ted Royal; Hans Spialek; **Set Design:** Edward Gilbert

Songs: Am I a Man or a Mouse?; Come and Bring Your Instruments; Every Eve; Have You Seen the Countess Cindy?; I Took Another Look; I Want to Go Back to the Bottom of the Garden; I Wish; If the Shoe Fits; I'm Not Myself Tonight; In the Morning; My Business Man; Night After Night; Prologue; Start the Ball Rollin'; This Is the End of the Story; Three Questions; What's the Younger Generation Coming To?; With a Wave of My Wand

Cast: Joe Besser; Florence Desmond; Edward Dew; Leila Ernst; Barbara Perry; Jack Williams

Notes: Some sources list number of performances as 21.

2104 • IF YOU PLEASE

OPENED: 11/28/1950
Revue   Closed out of town

Composer: Frank Fay
Lyricist: Frank Fay
Librettist: Frank Fay

Choreographer: Marilyn Christine; **Costumes:** Thomas Charles Pratt; **Lighting Designer:** Richard Jackson; **Set Design:** Richard Jackson

Cast: Frank Fay

2105 • ILLUSTRATORS' SHOW, THE

OPENED: 01/22/1936   Theatre: 48th Street
Revue   Broadway: 5

Composer: Irving Actman
Lyricist: Frank Loesser
Librettist: Hy Alexander; Donald Blackwell; Harry Evans; Frank Gabrielson; David Lesan; Max Liebman; Napier Moore; Otto Soglow; Kenneth Webb
Producer: Society of Illustrators; Tom Weatherly
Director: Tom Weatherly

Choreographer: Carl Randall; **Costumes:** Carl Sidney; **Musical Director:** Gene Salzer; **Set Design:** Arne Lundborg

Songs: Bang, the Bell Rang!; Finale (L: Frank Loesser; Carl Randall); Helen Lynd and the Girls (C: Berenece Kazounoff); Hello, Ma (C: Michael H. Cleary; L: Max Lief; Nathaniel Lief); I Like to Go to Strange Places; I Love a Polka So (C: Berenece Kazounoff; L: Carl Randall); I Want to Play with the Girls (C: Edgar Fairchild; L: Milton Pascal); If You Didn't Love Me, Who Else Would; I'm You; I've Walked in the Moonlight [1] (C: Edgar Fairchild; L: Milton Pascal); Just for Tonight (C/L: Charlotte Kent); Let's Talk About the Weather [2] (C/L: Charlotte Kent); Park Avenue's Going to Town (C: Edgar Fairchild; L: Milton Pascal); Waltz Was Born in Vienna, A (C: Earle Crooker; L: Frederick Loewe); Wherefore Art Thou, Juliet (C/L: Charlotte Kent); Wild Trumpets and Crazy Piano (Got a Guy to Forget)

Cast: Gomez; Niela Goodelle; Don Harden; Elizabeth Houston; Helen Lynd; Earl Oxford; Otto Soglow; O.Z. Whitehead; Winona

Notes: [1] Cut prior to opening. [2] Also in EARL CARROLL'S VANITIES OF 1931.

2106 • ILLYA DARLING

OPENED: 04/11/1967   Theatre: Mark Hellinger
Musical   Broadway: 320

Composer: Manos Hadjidakis
Lyricist: Joe Darion
Librettist: Jules Dassin
Producer: Kermit Bloomgarden
Director: Jules Dassin

Choreographer: Onna White; **Costumes:** Theoni V. Aldredge; **Dance Arranger:** Roger Adams; **Lighting Designer:** Jean Rosenthal; **Musical Director:** Karen Gustafson; **Orchestrations:** Ralph Burns; **Set Design:** Oliver Smith; **Vocal Arranger:** Karen Gustafson

Songs: After Love [1]; Bread and Love [2]; Dear Mr. Schubert; Fleet's In [2]; Fugue [2]; Golden Land; Heaven Help the Sailors on a Night Like This; Her Eyes, Her Eyes [2]; I Think She Needs Me; I'll Never Lay Down Any More; Illya Darling; Lesson, The; Love, Love, Love [1]; Maressi [2]; Medea Tango; Never on Sunday [3]; Piraeus, My Love; Po, Po, Po; Take a Little Drink of Ouzo [4]; They Don't Like Me [2]; Ya Chara; Zebekiko (Youao's Dance)

Cast: Orson Bean; Rudy Bond; Despo; Harold Gary; Nikos Kourkoulos; Hal Linden; Joe E. Marks; Melina Mercouri; Titos Vandis

Notes: Stephen Sondheim doctored some of the songs but which they are is unknown. [1] Cut after opening. [2] Cut before opening. [3] From film NEVER ON SUNDAY. [4] Added after opening.

2107 • IN AND OUT (1915)

OPENED: 1915
Musical

Composer: Leon De Costa
Librettist: George Totten Smith

Choreographer: Lew Morton

Songs: Any Old Night; Araby; At the Rag-Time Ball; Bom-Bom Day; Circus Day in Dixie; Close

to My Heart; Every Body Must Love Someone; In Again; Rose of Argentine; Summer Morn; Tell Me Some More; Yale and Harvard Days

Cast: Gus Fay; Hal Skelly

Notes: A burlesque musical. This show probably included popular songs of the day.

2108 • IN AND OUT (1918)

OPENED: 01/22/1918
Musical   Closed out of town

Composer: Joseph E. Howard
Lyricist: Collin Davis
Librettist: Collin Davis
Director: John Nicholson

Choreographer: Allan K. Foster

Songs: Blow the Whistle; Captain; Chasing Butterflies; Dancing the Numbers; El Bruta; Gee Whiz! Those Eyes; Hello, Girlie; Hep, Hep, Hep; Honey, Come Hurry Along; Let Me Build a Little Fence Around Your Heart; Liberty Glide, The; Now That We're Married; Prohibition Blues; Sobs; That Dream-Waltz Melody

Cast: David Adler; Peggy Coudray; Lew Hearn

2109 • IN BAMVILLE

Notes: See CHOCOLATE DANDIES.

2110 • IN CIRCLES

OPENED: 06/25/1968   Theatre: Cherry Lane
Revue   Off-Broadway: 56

Composer: Al Carmines
Lyricist: Gertrude Stein
Librettist: Gertrude Stein
Producer: Samuel J. Friedman; Judson Poets' Theatre; Alexander E. Racolin; Dina Racolin
Director: Lawrence Kornfeld

Lighting Designer: Barry Arnold; **Set Design:** Johnnie Jones; Roland Turner

Cast: Al Carmines; Jacque Lynn Colton; Lee Guilliatt; Julie Kurnitz

Notes: No songs listed in program.

2111 • IN DAHOMEY

OPENED: 02/18/1903 Theatre: New York
Musical Broadway: 53

Composer: Will Marion Cook
Lyricist: Paul Laurence Dunbar
Librettist: J.A. Shipp
Producer: Hurtig & Seamon
Director: J.A. Shipp

Costumes: Pauline Reed

Songs: All Goin' Out an' Nothin' Comin' In [5]
(C: Bert Williams; L: George Walker);
Ambulance [2]; Annie Laurie [2]; Attuck's
March, The [1]; Barber's Society of Philosophical
Research [2]; Broadway in Dahomey (C: Johnson;
L: Alex Rogers); Brown Skin Baby Mine [3];
Caboceer's Choral; Captain Kidd (Spread the
News) [2]; Chin Chin [1]; Chocolate Drops [2];
Czar, The (Czar of Dixie) (C/L: Alex Rogers);
Dahomian Queen [3] (C: F.H. Williams;
L: J. Leubrie Hill); Dance of the Frogs [2];
Dancing Sue [2]; Dat Gal of Mine; Dear Luzon
[1] (C: Tom Lemonier; L: Alex Rogers); Dream of
the Philippines, A [1]; Emancipation Day; Every
Darkey Is a King [2] (C: John H. Cook; L: Paul
Laurence Dunbar; E.P. Moran); Finale Act II;
Florida [2]; Happy Jim [2]; I May Be Crazy But I
Ain't No Fool [1] (C/L: Alex Rogers); I Wan' to
Be a Real Lady (C: Tom Lemonier; L: Alex
Rogers); I Wants to Be a Actor Lady [4] (C: Harry
Von Tilzer; L: Vincent Bryan); I'm a Jonah Man
(C/L: Alex Rogers); Jig [2]; Leader of the Colored
Aristocracy; Me and de Minstrel Band [1]
(C: James Vaughn; L: Alex Rogers); Mollie
Green; My Castle on the Nile [3] (C/L: Bob Cole;
J. Rosamond Johnson); My Dahomian Queen [3];
My Lady Frog [2]; On Broadway and in
Dahomey [1]; Ragtime Drummer [2]; Rich
Coon's Babe, A [6] (C/L: Alex Rogers); Shine [1]
(C: Ford Dabney; L: Lew Brown; Cecil Mack);
Society; Song of the Colonization Society [2];
Swing Along [1]; That's How the Cakewalk's
Done; There's a Land [2]; Un Oncore [1]; When
Sousa Comes to Coontown (C: James Vaughn;
L: Alex Rogers); When the Moon Shines on the
Moonshine [1]; Why Adam Sinned [1]

Cast: William Barker; George Catlin; Fred Douglas;
Pete Hampton; James Hill; Hattie McIntosh;
Walter Richardson; Alexander Rogers;
J.A. Shipp; Aida Overton Walker; George W.
Walker; Bert Williams; Lottie Williams

Notes: No program available. Cook dropped out
of the show after London. He was replaced by
James Vaughn who wrote most of the songs for
the 1904 revival. [1] Added to revival (1904). [2]
Published score only — not in program. [3]
Added to London (1903). [4] Added to revival
(1904) and to London (1903). [5] First in SONS
OF HAM (1899) and interpolated into this score.
[6] Cut prior to opening. Added to London
(1903).

2112 • IN DUTCH

OPENED: 09/22/1924
Musical Closed out of town

Composer: William Daly; Joseph Meyer; Alfred
Newman
Lyricist: Irving Caesar; William Cary Duncan
Librettist: Irving Caesar; William Cary Duncan
Producer: Morris Green; A.L. Jones
Director: Frank Smithson

Choreographer: Jack Connors; **Musical Director:**
Fred Hoff

Songs: Because You're You; Dipping in the
Moonlight (C: Joseph Meyer; L: Irving Caesar);
Do You Love As I Love; Girl Is Nobody, A;
Governor's Lady; Land of Rocky Boo; Love
C.O.D.; Nicest Sort of Feeling; Only in Dreams
(C: William Cary Duncan; Alfred Newman;
L: Irving Caesar); Twilight Serenade (C: William
Daly; Joseph Meyer; L: Irving Caesar); When the
Weekend Comes Round; You Know Me, Al

Cast: Grace Fisher; Edward Gallagher; Maurice
Holland; Robert Holliday; Al Shean; Nancy
Welford

Notes: From a program of 9/22/24 Newark.

2113 • IN ETHIOPIAVILLE

OPENED: 1913
Musical

Composer: Frank Montgomery
Lyricist: Frank Montgomery
Librettist: Frank Montgomery
Producer: Frank Montgomery

Songs: Bless Your Everyloving Little Heart; Crazy
About Some Boy; Dixie; I Wonder Why They

Call Me Snowball; Musical Moon; Oh, Ho, in the Morning; Old Boston Town; On the Mississippi; Our Old Man; Peace Wid the World; Syncopated Boogie Boo; When Will I Plant the Tree

Cast: Ed Lea Coleman; Florence McClain; Frank Montgomery; Emma Morton; Charles Nickerson; Charlie Rose

Notes: No other information available.

2114 • IN GAY COMPANY

OPENED: 10/29/1974   Theatre: Upstairs at New
                   Jimmy's
Revue   Off-Broadway: 13

Composer: Fred Silver
Lyricist: Fred Silver
Librettist: Leo Barkdull
Producer: MCB Company
Director: Sue Lawless

Musical Director: John Franceschina; **Set Design:** Michael J. Hotopp; Paul de Pass

Songs: Beginner's Guide to Cruising; Days of the Dancing Are Gone; Finale; Freddy Liked to Fugue; Handsome Stranger; I Met My Love; If He'd Only Be Gentle; I've Just Been to a Wedding; Lament; Phantom of the Opera; Remembrances; Special Boy, A; True Confession; Two Strangers; Welcome; Where There's Smoke; Your Home Away from Home

Cast: Candice Earley; Rick Gardner; Cola Pinto; Gordon Ramsey; Robert Tananis

Notes: Opened at The Little Hippodrome Dinner Theatre Off-Off- Broadway where it ran for 244 performances. It moved to Upstairs at New Jimmy's on March 28, 1975.

2115 • IN GAY NEW ORLEANS

OPENED: 12/25/1946
Musical   Closed out of town

Composer: Carl Frederickson
Lyricist: Forbes Randolph
Librettist: Forbes Randolph
Producer: Forbes Randolph
Director: Forbes Randolph

Choreographer: Felicia Sorel; **Costumes:** Mary Grant; **Lighting Designer:** Leo Kerz; **Musical**

Director: Ray Kavanaugh; **Orchestrations:** Robert Russell Bennett; **Set Design:** Watson Barratt

Songs: Barcarolle from 'Anthony and Cleopatra'; Belles of Basin Street; Carnival; Charwoman's Song; Concert Waltz; Don't Break the Spell; Don't Pull the Wool Over My Eyes; Forever Spring; Heavens Declare; House on a Cloud; If He Hollers; In a Hundred Years from Now; Is You Happy-Go-Lucky?; Just to Say That I Love You; Lonely Straggler; Love Came By; Madame la Duchesse; Music at Night; New Orleans; New Orleans Saga; Now and Evermore; Sky of Stars; What Kind of Noise Annoys an Oyster?; What Would You Do?; When the Weddin' March Is Ended; Wind from the Bayou

Cast: Maria Bambrelli; Monica Coyero; Helen Raymond; Gilbert Russell

2116 • IN GAY NEW YORK

OPENED: 05/25/1896   Theatre: Casino
Revue   Broadway

Composer: Gustave Kerker
Librettist: Hugh Morton
Producer: Thomas Canary; George W. Lederer
Director: George W. Lederer

Choreographer: Signor Francioli; **Costumes:** Mme. Siedle; **Musical Director:** Gustave Kerker; **Set Design:** D. Frank Dodge

Songs: Yer Baby's a Comin' to Town (C: John T. Kelly)

Cast: La Petite Adelaide; Richard Carle; Virginia Earle; Madge Lessing; Nanette Nixon; John Slavin; Lillian Swain; David Warfield

Notes: No songs listed in program.

2117 • IN GAY PAREE

OPENED: 03/20/1899   Theatre: Casino
Musical   Broadway: 48

Composer: Ludwig Englander
Lyricist: Grant Stewart
Librettist: Clay M. Greene
Producer: George W. Lederer
Director: Ben Teal

Choreographer: Carl Marwig; **Set Design:** Ernest Albert; Walter Burridge; Ernest Gros; John H. Young

Cast: Robert F. Cotton; Harry Davenport; Marie George; Mabel Gilman

Notes: No songs listed in program.

2118 • IN GREATER NEW YORK
Notes: *See MRS. RADLEY BARTON'S BALL.*

2119 • IN HAYTI
OPENED: 08/30/1909   Theatre: Circle
Musical   Broadway: 56

Composer: Jean Schwartz
Lyricist: William Jerome
Librettist: John J. McNally
Producer: Klaw & Erlanger
Director: Al Holbrook

Choreographer: Julian Alfred

Songs: A-L-E; American Monte Carlo, The; Bamboo Lane; Captain Flo; Chicken; Come, Toddle Along; Everybody's Rag Time Crazy; Good Bye, Miss Liberty; I Would Like to Correspond with You; Love Me Just Like Romeo Loved His Juliet [2]; Mister Izzy Always Busy Rosenstein [1]; My Haytian Queen; Revolutionary Man, The

Cast: Alfred Fisher; Thomas Heath; Carl McCullough; John McIntyre; Fletcher Norton; Julian Rose; Adele Rowland; Marion Stanley

Notes: [1] Program reads "Mister Bizzy Rosenstein." [2] Program reads "Romeo and Miss Juliet."

2120 • IN HEIDELBERG
Notes: *See THE STUDENT PRINCE.*

2121 • IN LOVE WITH LOVE
OPENED: 08/06/1923   Theatre: Ritz
Play   Broadway: 122

Author: Vincent Laurence
Producer: William Harris Jr.
Director: Robert Milton

Set Design: Livingston Platt

Songs: In Love with Love (C: Rudolf Friml; L: Dailey Paskman)

Cast: Benton Churchill; Lynn Fontanne; Henry Hull; Wanda Lyon; Ralph Morgan; Maryland Morne; Robert Strange

2122 • IN NEW YORK TOWN
OPENED: 1907
Musical   Closed out of town

Composer: Telford Taylor
Lyricist: Cliff Meech
Producer: Jules Hurtig
Director: Jules Hurtig

Choreographer: Jack Mason; **Costumes:** Madame Katz

Songs: Bathing; Belle of New York [1]; Bit of Nonsense; Espanita [2] (C: Albert Von Tilzer; L: Unknown); Great Big Judge, A; Have You Seen My Henry Brown [2] (C: Albert Von Tilzer; L: Unknown); Hungarian Dance; I Can't Find Another Girl Like You (L: Joe Hollander); I Like to See It [2] (C: Albert Von Tilzer); It's New York Town for Mine [2] (C: Albert Von Tilzer; L: Unknown); My Georgiana [2] (C: Albert Von Tilzer; L: Unknown); My Sweet Sunflower; New York Town for Mine; Notoriety; On the Great White Way; Rose Rosetta; Stein Song [2] (C: Albert Von Tilzer; L: Unknown); When the Moon Looks Down; Won't You Let Me Put My Arms Around You?; You Can Play with My Dolly

Cast: Clara Austin; Jennie Austin; Charles Howard

Notes: Apparently Albert Von Tilzer wrote the score for the show when it toured in 1906. There was no lyricist credited in the program at that time. William Holcomb was credited with the libretto then but by 1907 his name and Von Tilzer's were struck from the program. [1] Also in show out of town when music was credited to Albert Von Tilzer. [2] In show (1906).

2123 • IN NEWPORT
OPENED: 12/26/1904   Theatre: Liberty
Musical   Broadway: 24

Composer: J. Rosamond Johnson
Lyricist: Bob Cole; James Weldon Johnson
Librettist: John J. McNally
Producer: Klaw & Erlanger
Director: Herbert Gresham; Ned Wayburn

Set Design: Ernest Albert; D. Frank Dodge; Richard Marston

Songs: Don't Go To Dangerously Nigh; Hello, Ma Lulu; House That Jack Built, The; How a Monocle Helps the Mind; Mary Was a Manicure; Newport Dip, The; Nobody But You; Peggy Is a New Yorker Now; Rehearsal, The; Roaming Around the Town; Scandal; Stockings; When I Am Chief of Police; Women; Zel, Zel

Cast: Joe Coyne; Peter Dailey; Virginia Earle; Lee Harrison; Fay Templeton

2124 • IN PRAISE OF DEATH

OPENED: 03/11/1978
Musical   Off-Broadway

Composer: Al Carmines
Lyricist: Al Carmines
Director: Dan Wagoner

Songs: Come Drink of the Fountain of Life; I Cannot Live with You (L: Emily Dickinson)

Cast: Emily Adams; John Barrett; Essie Borden; Alice Bosveld; Susan Chasin; Ann Doemland; Karl Garlid; Lee Guilliatt; Richard Leete; Eileen McNutt; Judy Murphy

2125 • IN SOMEONE ELSE'S SANDALS

Notes: *See I'M SOLOMON.*

2126 • IN THE BARRACKS

OPENED: 1912
Musical   Closed out of town

Composer: Robert Hood Bowers
Lyricist: Grant Stewart
Librettist: Cecil B. DeMille
Producer: Jesse Lasky
Director: Cecil B. DeMille

Musical Director: Ernest G. Grooney

Songs: Call to Arms, The; Farewell to the Flag; I Love You Best of All; Love Is the Leaven; Man

of Rank, A; One of My Own Hussars; You'll Have to Do the Turkey Trot (C: Dave Stamper; L: Gene Buck)

Cast: W.H. Clark; John H. Purcell; Frank Rushworth

Notes: From a program of Milwaukee and sheet music. A one-act vaudeville musical. Note Jesse Lasky and Cecil B. DeMille's participation — they would soon make the move to Hollywood.

2127 • IN THE JUNGLES

OPENED: 1911
Musical

Composer: Will Marion Cook; Alex Rogers
Lyricist: Will Marion Cook; Alex Rogers
Librettist: Will A. Cook; Al F. Watts
Director: Jerry Mills

Songs: Baby Rose; Home Sweet Home; Let the Juice Ooze Through; Love Is King; My Dreamland; My Jewel of the Nile; Never Let the Same Bee Sting You Twice; O, Say Wouldn't That Be a Dream; Plant a Watermelon by My Grave; Ragtime Love; Roll a Little Pill for Me

Cast: Will A. Cook; Julius Glenn; Sissieretta Jones; Tillie Seguin; Al F. Watts

Notes: No other information available.

2128 • IN THE LIMELIGHT

Notes: *See THE REVUE OF REVUES.*

2129 • IN THE OLD DAYS AND TODAY

Notes: *See LA REVUE DES AMBASSADEURS.*

2130 • IN THE PINK

OPENED: 1955
Musical   Unproduced

Composer: Harold Rome
Lyricist: Harold Rome
Librettist: Moss Hart

Songs: I Wonder What Happened to Miss O'Brien; My IBM and I

Notes: No other information available.

2131 • IN TOWN

OPENED: 09/06/1897   Theatre: Knickerbocker
Musical   Broadway: 40

Composer: F. Osmond Carr
Lyricist: Adrian Ross
Librettist: Adrian Ross; James T. Tanner
Producer: Charles Frohman; Al Hayman
Director: J.A.E. Malone

Choreographer: Willie Warde

Songs: Ambiguity Girls; Call-Boy's Song; Dreamless Rest; Drinks of the Day; Finale Act I; Friar Larry; Golden Mean, The; Heart That Is Still the Same, A; House of Lords, The; I Am Pining for a Little Bit of Fun; I Shall Not Mind; Maid with a Wink in Her Eye, The; Man About Town, The; Milord Sir Smith; My Propensities Are All the Other Way; Opening Chorus; Petticoat Dance [1] (C: F. Eplet); Romeo and Juliet; Taradiddle; Waltz Refrain, The

Cast: W, Kiyus Bradfield; Laurence Caird; Florence Lloyd; Marjorie Pryor

Notes: No program available. Songs from English vocal score. [1] Added after London opening.

2132 • IN TROUSERS

OPENED: 02/22/1981   Theatre: Playwrights
                                            Horizons
Musical   Off-Broadway: 15

Composer: William Finn
Lyricist: William Finn
Librettist: William Finn
Producer: Second Stage, The
Director: Judith Swift

Choreographer: Sharon Kinney; **Costumes:** Karen D. Miller; **Lighting Designer:** Victor En Yu Tan; **Musical Director:** Michael Starobin; **Orchestrations:** Michael Starobin; **Set Design:** Nancy Winters

Songs: Another Sleepless Night; Breakfast Over Sugar; Goodnight; Helluva Day, A; High School Ladies at Five O'Clock [1]; How America Got Its Name; How Marvin Eats His Breakfast; How the Body Falls Apart [1]; I Am Wearing a Hat; I Can't Sleep; I Feel Him Slipping Away [1]; I Have a Family [1]; I Swear I Won't Ever Again; I'm Breaking Down [2]; Love Me for What I Am; Marvin Takes a Victory Shower; Marvin's Giddy Seizures; Mommy Dear Has Dropped Dead in Her Sleep; My High School Sweetheart; Nausea Before the Game; No Hard Feelings [1]; Packing Up [1]; Rape of Miss Goldberg, The; Rit Tit Tat; Set Those Sails; Three Seconds [1]; Time to Wake Up [1]; Wedding Song [1]; Whizzer Brown; Whizzer Gong Down [1]

Cast: Kate Dezina; Karen Jablons; Alaina Reed; Jay O. Sanders

Notes: [1] Added to 1985 revival. [2] Added to Broadway production of FALSETTOS.

2133 • INACENT BLACK

OPENED: 05/06/1981   Theatre: Biltmore
Play   Broadway: 14

Composer: McFadden; Moore; Whitehead
Lyricist: McFadden; Moore; Whitehead
Author: A. Marcus Hemphill
Producer: Jay J. Cohen; Marjorie Moon; Gloria Hope Sher
Director: Mikell Pinkney

Costumes: Marty Pakledinaz; **Lighting Designer:** Tim Philips; **Musical Director:** Barry Eastmond; **Set Design:** Felix E. Cochren

Songs: He's All That We Need; Somebody Told Me; Stand Together

Cast: Rosanna Carter; Lorey Hayes; Gregory Miller; Barbara Montgomery; Melba Moore; Ronald "Smokey" Stevens; Count Stovall; Bruce Strickland; Joyce Sylvester; Reginald Vel Johnson

Notes: No songs listed in program. Ran in Brooklyn for seven months under title INACENT BLACK AND THE FIVE BROTHERS.

2134 • INNER CITY

OPENED: 12/19/1971   Theatre: Ethel Barrymore
Revue   Broadway: 97

Composer: Helen Miller
Lyricist: Eve Merriam
Producer: Lawrence Kasha; Joseph Kipness; Tom O'Horgan
Director: Tom O'Horgan

Source: INNER CITY MOTHER GOOSE, THE (Book: Eve Merriam); **Costumes:** Joseph G. Aulisi; **Dance Arranger:** Gordon Harrell; **Lighting Designer:** John Dodd; Jane Reisman;

Musical Director: Clay Fullum; **Orchestrations:** Gordon Harrell; **Set Design:** Robin Wagner; **Vocal Arranger:** Helen Miller

Songs: Apartment House; As I Went Over; Boys and Girls Come Out to Play; Brave Old City of New York, The; Christmas Is Coming; City Life; Cow Jumped Over the Moon, The; Dealer, The; Deep in the Night; Diddle Diddle Dumpling; Ding Dong Bell; Fee Fi Fo Fum; Great If, The; Half Alive; Hickety, Pickety; Hooker, The; Hushabye Baby; I Had a Little Teevee; If Wishes Were Horses; I'm Sorry Says the Machine; It's My Belief; Jack Be Nimble; Jeremiah Obadiah; Kindness; Law and Order; Little Jack Horner; Locks; Lucy Locket; Man in the Doorway; Mary, Mary; My Mother Said; Now I Lay Me; Nub of the Nation, The; Numbers; On This Rock; One Man; One Misty, Moisty Morning; One, Two; Pickpocket, The; Poverty Program; Rub a Dub Dub; Shadow of the Sun; Simple Simon; Spirit of Education, The; Starlight, Starbright; Statistics; Street Sermon; Subway Dream; Summer Nights; Taffy; Take-a-Tour, Congressman; There Was a Little Man; This Is the Way We Go to School; Tom, Tom; Twelve Rooftops Leaping; Urban Renewal; Who Killed Nobody; Wino Will; Winter Nights; Wisdom; You'll Find Mice

Cast: Delores Hall; Linda Hopkins; Larry Marshall

2135 • INNOCENT EYES

OPENED: 05/20/1924   Theatre: Winter Garden
Revue   Broadway: 119

Composer: Sigmund Romberg; Jean Schwartz
Lyricist: Harold Atteridge; Tot Seymour
Librettist: Harold Atteridge
Producer: Messrs. Shubert

Choreographer: Seymour Felix; Jack Mason; **Costumes:** Charles Gesman; **Musical Director:** Al Goodman; **Orchestrations:** Al Goodman; **Set Design:** Watson Barratt

Songs: Africa (C: James F. Hanley; L: Henry Creamer); American Jazz [3]; Apache Dance; Bal Tabarin, The [1]; Ballet Dance; Bang Up Time [1]; Behind Milady's Fan; Buck [3]; Chiquette [4] (C: J. Fred Coots; Jean Schwartz; L: McElbert Moore); Damn Clever, These Chinese; Dance of Beauty; Danse de Volstead; Day Dreams; Dear Old Moulin Rouge; En Douce; Fan Number; Few Fast Steppers, A; Fountain of Youth [1]; Franco-American Step, The [1]; Garden of Love

(C: Jean Schwartz; L: Tot Seymour); Hard Hearted Hannah [2] (C: Milton Ager; Robert Bigelow; L: Charles Bates; Jack Yellen); Hula Dance; Hula, Hula, Sailor Man; Hurry Up [1]; I Love a Lark [1]; I Love the Boys [3]; I Loved Her Best of All; Innocent Eyes [4] (C: J. Fred Coots; Jean Schwartz; L: McElbert Moore); Inspiration; La Java [3]; Lesson in Love, A [3]; Let's Have a Good Time; Lolita [3]; Love Is Like a Pinwheel; Maybells [1]; Millennium, The [1]; Musical Shoes [3]; My Rose [4] (C: J. Fred Coots; Jean Schwartz; L: McElbert Moore); Organdie Days (C: Jean Schwartz; L: Tot Seymour); Our Emblem Is the Lily; Peacock Strut; Perfume Waltz; Pianologue; Powder Your Nose [1]; Pretty Ankle [1]; Rin-Tin-Tin [1]; Sextette; Spanish Dance; Spoony Croony Tune; Su L'Boul'vard; Surrounded by the Girls; Take Me [3]; We Are Puritans [3]; Yankee Strut

Cast: Edythe Baker; Ted Doner; Lew Hearn; Marjory Leach; Cecil Lean; Earl Leslie; Cleo Mayfield; Mistinguett; Vanessi; Frances Williams

Notes: The show BAL-TABARIN closed out of town and the costumes and some of the songs found their way into this show. [1] Out Atlantic City. [2] Sheet music only. [3] Out Washington D.C. 1/13/24. [4] From score of BAL-TABARIN.

2136 • INSIDE THE EARTH
Notes: *See A TRIP TO JAPAN.*

2137 • INSIDE U.S.A.

OPENED: 04/30/1948   Theatre: Century
Revue   Broadway: 399

Composer: Arthur Schwartz
Lyricist: Howard Dietz
Librettist: Arnold Auerbach; Moss Hart; Arnold B. Horwitt
Producer: Arthur Schwartz
Director: Robert H. Gordon
Source: INSIDE U.S.A. (Book: John Gunther); **Choreographer:** Helen Tamiris; **Costumes:** Castillo; Eleanor Goldsmith; **Dance Arranger:** Genevieve Pitot; **Musical Director:** Jay Blackton; **Orchestrations:** Robert Russell Bennett; **Set Design:** Lemuel Ayers

Songs: At the Mardi Gras; Atlanta [1]; Better Luck Next Time [2]; Blue Grass; Come O Come (to Pittsburgh); Feller from Indiana [2]; First Prize at the Fair; Forty Winks [2]; Haunted Heart; If We Had a Little More Time [2]; Inside U.S.A.; Leave

My Pulse Alone [2]; Massachusetts Mermaid; My Gal Is Mine Once More; Protect Me [1]; Rhode Island Is Famous for You; School for Waiters [2]; Song to Forget, A [2]; Tiger Lily Ballet (dance); We Won't Take It Back

Cast: Rod Alexander; Valerie Bettis; Thelma Carpenter; Jack Haley; Beatrice Lillie; Louis Nye; Carl Reiner; Herb Shriner; John Tyers

Notes: [1] Cut after opening. [2] Not used.

2138 • INSTANT REPLAY

OPENED: 08/06/1968   Theatre: Downstairs at the Upstairs
Revue   Nightclub

Producer: Rod Warren

Cast: Lily Tomlin

Notes: No other information available.

2139 • INTERNATIONAL CUP, THE

OPENED: 09/03/1910   Theatre: Hippodrome
Musical   Broadway: 333

Composer: Manuel Klein
Lyricist: Manuel Klein
Librettist: R.H. Burnside
Producer: Messrs. Shubert
Director: R.H. Burnside

Costumes: Mme. Ziebarth; **Lighting Designer:** Joseph Eisner; **Musical Director:** Manuel Klein; **Set Design:** Arthur Voegtlin

Songs: Fighting Regiment, The; Hail the Hero of Today; Love Is Like a Rainbow; Loving; Seaside Frolics [1]; Sons of Every Nation Are American Today, The; Take a Trip to the Seaside; Yachting

Cast: W.H. Clark; Albertina Rasch; Bert Wainwright

Notes: Part two of this show was titled THE BALLET OF NIAGARA and part three was titled THE EARTHQUAKE. *See THE BALLET OF NIAGARA.* [1] Sheet music only. May be the song titled "Take a Trip to the Seaside" in the program.

2140 • INTERNATIONAL REVUE, THE (1930)

OPENED: 02/25/1930   Theatre: Majestic
Revue   Broadway: 95

Composer: Jimmy McHugh
Lyricist: Dorothy Fields
Librettist: Nat Dorfman; Lew Leslie
Producer: Lew Leslie
Director: Lew Leslie; Edward Clarke Lilley

Choreographer: Busby Berkeley; Harry Crosley; Chester Hale; **Costumes:** Dolly Tree; **Musical Director:** Harry Levant; **Set Design:** Anthony Street; **Vocal Arranger:** Louise Mann

Songs: Big Papoose Is on the Loose; Boop-Boop-a-Doop [2] (C: Alberta Nichols; L: Mann Holiner); Cinderella Brown; Exactly Like You; Gypsy Love; I Could Go for You [1]; I'm Feelin' Blue 'Cause I've Got Nobody [5]; International Rhythm; I've Got a Bug in My Head [1]; I've Got the Blues [1]; Keys to My Heart; Make Up Your Mind [4]; Margineers, The [4]; On the Sunny Side of the Street; Spain; That's Why We're Dancing; Working Girl, The [3] (L: Max Liebman); World Is Full of Love, The [3] (C: Paul Ballantine; L: Max Liebman)

Cast: Argentinita; Viola Dobos; Anton Dolin; Robert Hobbs; Harry Jans; Gertrude Lawrence; Livia Marracci; Florence Moore; Jack Pearl; Radaelli; Harry Richman; Harold Whalen

Notes: [1] Out Philadelphia 2/3/30. [2] Out Newark 2/10/30. [3] Out Tamamint Lodge, Pocanos, Pennsylvania. [4] Also in CLOWNS IN CLOVER. [5] ASCAP/Library of Congress only.

2141 • INTERNATIONAL REVUE, THE (1933)

OPENED: 1933
Revue

Composer: Sam H. Stept
Lyricist: Bud Green

Songs: Broadway Lady; Crazy Walk; Paradise Waltz

Notes: No other information available.

2142 • INTO THE LIGHT

OPENED: 10/22/1986   Theatre: Neil Simon
Musical   Broadway: 6

Composer: Lee Holdridge
Lyricist: John Forster

Librettist: Jeff Tambornino
Producer: Richard Kughn; Joseph Z. Nederlander; Jerrold Perenchio
Director: Michael Maurer

Choreographer: Mary Jane Houdina; **Costumes:** Karen Roston; **Lighting Designer:** Neil Peter Jampolis; **Musical Director:** Peter Howard; **Orchestrations:** Ira Hearshen; **Set Design:** Neil Peter Jampolis; Hervig Libowitsky

Songs: Be There; Data, The; Fede, Fede; Into the Light; It Can All Be Explained; Let There Be Light; Neat/Not Neat; Rainbow Logic; Rose and I, The; Talk About Time, A; Testing, The; Three of Us, The; To Measure the Darkness; Trading Solos; Wishes

Cast: Susan Bigelow; Danny Gerard; Mitchell Greenberg; Dean Jones; Kathryn McAteer; William Parry; Casper Roos; Gordon Stanley; Lenny Wolpe

2143 • INTO THE WOODS
OPENED: 11/05/1987   Theatre: Martin Beck
Musical   Broadway: 765

Composer: Stephen Sondheim
Lyricist: Stephen Sondheim
Librettist: James Lapine
Producer: M. Anthony Fisher; Jujamcyn Theaters; Heidi Landesman; Rocco Landesman; Frederic H. Mayerson; Rick Steiner
Director: James Lapine

Choreographer: Lar Lubovitch; **Costumes:** Ann Hould-Ward; **Lighting Designer:** Richard Nelson; **Musical Director:** Paul Gemignani; **Orchestrations:** Jonathan Tunick; **Set Design:** Tony Straiges

Songs: Agony; Any Moment; Back to the Palace [2]; Boom, Crunch! [3]; Children Will Listen; Cinderella at the Grave; Every After; First Midnight; Giants in the Sky; Hello, Little Girl; I Guess This Is Goodbye; I Know Things Now; Interesting Questions [2]; Into the Woods; It Takes Two; Lament; Last Midnight; Last Night [2]; Maybe They're Magic; Moments in the Woods; No More; No One Is Alone; On the Steps of the Palace; Our Little World [1]; Ready for the Woods [2]; Second Midnight; So Happy; Stay with Me; Very Nice Prince, A [2]; Your Fault

Cast: Tom Aldredge; Barbara Byrne; Kim Crosby; Maureen Davis; Danielle Ferland; Joy Franz; Joanna Gleason; Philip Hoffman; Jean Kelly; Merle Louise; Edmund Lyndeck; Kay McClelland; Lauren Mitchell; Bernadette Peters; Chuck Wagner; Robert Westenberg; Pamela Winslow; Ben Wright; Chip Zien

Notes: [1] Added to London production. [2] Out San Diego 1/86. [3] Cut during previews in New York.

2144 • INVITATION TO A MARCH
OPENED: 10/29/1960   Theatre: Music Box
Play   Broadway: 113

Author: Arthur Laurents
Producer: Theatre Guild, The
Director: Arthur Laurents

Costumes: Lucinda Ballard; **Incidental Music:** Stephen Sondheim; **Lighting Designer:** Paul Morrison; **Set Design:** William Pitkin

Cast: Jane Fonda; Tom Hatcher; Eileen Heckart; Celeste Holm; James MacArthur; Madeleine Sherwood

2145 • IOLE
OPENED: 12/29/1913   Theatre: Longacre
Musical   Broadway: 24

Composer: William F. Peters
Lyricist: Robert W. Chambers; Ben Teal
Librettist: Robert W. Chambers; Ben Teal
Producer: H.H. Frazee
Director: Ben Teal

Source: IOLE (Novel: Robert W. Chambers); **Musical Director:** John McGhie; **Set Design:** Ernest Albert

Songs: Amo; And That Is All; Back to Nature; Comes an Exquisite Situation; I Wonder Why; If Dreams Come True; Iole; Like a Sherpherdess; None but the Brave Deserves the Fair; Nude Descending a Staircase; Oh Precious Thought; Oh What's the Use?; Take It from Me; Think of That; Time Is Flying; To Rent, to Let; Why Do You Think I Love You So?

Cast: Stewart Baird; Gretchen Eastman; Rexford Kendrick; Hazel Kirke; Frank Lalor

2146 • IONESCOPADE

OPENED: 04/25/1974   Theatre: Theatre Four
Revue   Off-Broadway: 14

Composer: Mildred Kayden
Lyricist: Mildred Kayden
Producer: Roger Ailes; Kermit Bloomgarden
Director: Robert Allan Ackerman

Source: UNKNOWN (Play: Eugene Ionesco);
   Choreographer: Merry Lynn Katis; **Costumes:**
   Patricia Adshead; **Dance Arranger:** Michael
   Gibson; Mildred Kayden; **Lighting Designer:**
   David Sackeroff; **Musical Director:** Ed
   Linderman; **Set Design:** David Sackeroff; **Vocal
   Arranger:** Michael Gibson; Mildred Kayden

Songs: Bobby Watson and Family; Cirque-O-Pade;
   Fire; Flying; In the Cellar; Josette; Knocks;
   Madeleine; Mother Peep; Surprising People; Two
   Robertas, The

Cast: Joseph Abaldo; Gary Beach; Veronica
   Castang; Bob Morrisey

Notes: Songs not listed in program.

2147 • IPI-TOMBI

OPENED: 01/12/1977   Theatre: Harkness
Revue   Broadway: 39

Composer: Bertha Egnos
Lyricist: Gail Lakier
Librettist: Bertha Egnos
Producer: A. Deshe; Topol
Director: Bertha Egnos

Choreographer: Neil McKay; Sheila Wartski;
   Lighting Designer: Timothy Heale; John Wain;
   Set Design: Elizabeth MacLeish

Songs: Arieni (Let's Dance); Baby, Baby;
   Bayakhala (Zulu-The Child); Emdudeni (Street
   Sweepers); Going Home; Gum Boot Dance;
   Hamba Bheklie (Let the Drinks Be Served);
   Ipi-Tombi (Where Are the Girls?); Madiwa-
   Madiwa (Calling for Rain); Mokhibo (The Sotho
   Girls' Dance); Momma Tembu's Wedding;
   Moriva; Nadia (Song of Hope); Ntaba Zenyuka
   (The Mountains Are High); Oo-Le-Le; Orgy the
   Temptress; Phata Phata (Touch, Touch);
   Qhobosha (The Unfaithful One Will Die);
   Sesiyahamba (We Are Going About Our

Labors); Shamanile; Shangaan (A Dance of
Happiness); Shosholaza (A Work Song);
Uthando Luphelile (Love Is Lost, Love Is Gone);
Wishing; Zimbaba

Cast: Betty-Boo Hlela; Count Wellington Judge

2148 • IRENE

OPENED: 11/18/1919   Theatre: Vanderbilt
Musical   Broadway: 675

Composer: Harry Tierney
Lyricist: Joseph McCarthy
Librettist: James Montgomery
Director: Edward Royce

Source: IRENE O'DARE (Play: James
   Montgomery); **Costumes:** Finchley; Lucille;
   Musical Director: Gus Salzer; **Set Design:**
   H. Robert Law

Songs: Alice Blue Gown; Castle of Dreams; Down
   Town East of Broadway [4] (C/L: Noel Gay);
   Family Tree, The; Great Lover Tango, The [1]
   (C: Charles Gaynor; L: Otis Clements); Hobbies;
   Honeymoon Lane [3] (C/L: Joseph Connor);
   If He Only Knew [5] (C/L: Norman Newell;
   Michael Reed); Irene; Irish Girl, An [1]
   (C: Charles Gaynor; L: Otis Clements); Last Part
   of Any Party, The; Lucy [4] (C/L: Noel Gay); Me
   That I Want to Be, The [6] (C/L: Timothy Gray;
   Hugh Martin); Mother Angel Darling [1] (C/L:
   Charles Gaynor); Opening Act I; Opening Act II;
   Opening Chorus Act II Scene 2; 'Paul Jones', The
   (dance); Reminiscence; Riviera Rage (dance), The
   [1] (C: Wally Harper); Skyrocket; Stepping on
   Butterflies (inst.) [1] (C: Wally Harper); Talk of
   the Town, The; There's Something in the Air;
   This Dear Lady [2] (C: Charles Gaynor; L: Otis
   Clements); To Love You; Too Much Bowden [3];
   We're Getting Away with It; World Must Be
   Bigger Than an Avenue, The [1] (C: Wally
   Harper; L: Jack Lloyd); Worthy of You; You've
   Got Me Out on a Limb [3]

Cast: Hobart Cavanaugh; Walter Croft; Edith Day;
   John B. Litel; Gladys Miller; Florence Mills; Eva
   Puck; Walter Regan; Bobby Watson

Notes: [1] Added to the 3/13/73 revival. [2]
   Written for revival but not used. [3] Sheet music
   only. [4] Added to the 1945 London revival. [5]
   Added to 1976 London revival. [6] Written for
   the 3/13/73 revival but not used.

2149 • IRISH EYES

OPENED: 1921

Songs: Kathleen (C: Ted Snyder; L: Harry B. Smith)

Notes: No other information available.

2150 • IRMA LA DOUCE

OPENED: 09/29/1960   Theatre: Plymouth
Musical   Broadway: 527

Composer: Marguerite Monnot
Lyricist: David Heneker; Julian Moore; Monty Norman
Librettist: David Heneker; Julian Moore
Producer: David Merrick
Director: Peter Brook

Source: IRMA LA DOUCE (Musical: Alexandre Breffort; Marguerite Monnot); **Choreographer:** Onna White; **Costumes:** Rolf Gerard; **Dance Arranger:** John Kander; **Lighting Designer:** Joe Davis; **Musical Director:** Stanley Lebowsky; **Orchestrations:** Robert Ginzler; Andre Popp; **Set Design:** Rolf Gerard; **Vocal Arranger:** Stanley Lebowsky; Bert Walker

Songs: Arctic Ballet (Storm Ballet), The; Because [2]; Bravo! [3]; Bridge of Caulaincourt, The; But; Christmas Child; Dis-donc, Dis-donc; Freedom of the Seas, The; From a Prison Cell; Irma La Douce [1]; Le Grisbi Is le Root of le Evil in Man; Our Language of Love; She's Got the Lot; Sons of France; That's a Crime; There Is Only One Paris for That; Valse Milieu [1]; Wreck of a Mec, The

Cast: Stuart Damon; Fred Gwynne; George S. Irving; Zack Matalon; Keith Michell; Clive Revill; Elizabeth Seal; Rudy Tronto

Notes: [1] Same music. [2] From original French production only. [3] Cut.

2151 • IRVIN C. MILLER'S BROWN SKIN MODELS

OPENED: 1955
Revue

Composer: Eubie Blake
Lyricist: Flournoy E. Miller
Producer: Irvin C. Miller

Songs: I'm Just a Simple Girl; Let's Wreck the Joint; Mississippi Honeymoon; Ole Man River Is Lonely Now; She'll Say Bye Bye to You; Strange What Love Will Do; Thrill in Spain; When a Carnation Meets a Red Red Rose

Notes: No other information available.

2152 • IS THERE LIFE AFTER HIGH SCHOOL?

OPENED: 05/03/1982   Theatre: Ethel Barrymore
Musical   Broadway: 12

Composer: Craig Carnelia
Lyricist: Craig Carnelia
Librettist: Jeffrey Kindley
Producer: Clive Davis; Francois De Meuil; Harris Maslansky
Director: Robert Nigro

Source: IS THERE LIFE AFTER HIGH SCHOOL (Book: Jeffrey Kindley); **Choreographer:** Larry Fuller; **Costumes:** Carol Oditz; **Lighting Designer:** Dennis Parichy; **Musical Director:** Bruce Coughlin; **Orchestrations:** Bruce Coughlin; **Set Design:** John Lee Beatty

Songs: Beer; Diary of a Homecoming Queen; For Them; Fran and Janie; High School All Over Again; I'm Glad You Didn't Know Me; Kid Inside, The; Nothing Really Happened; Reunion; School Song, The [1]; Second Thoughts; Shove It [1]; Things I Learned in High School; Thousands of Trumpets

Cast: Raymond Baker; Cynthia Carle; Alma Cuervo; Sandy Faison; Harry Groener; Philip Hoffman; David Paul Kelly; James Widdoes

Notes: [1] Cut prior to Broadway.

2153 • ISABEL'S A JEZEBEL

OPENED: 12/15/1970   Theatre: Duchess
Musical   London: 61

Composer: Galt MacDermot
Lyricist: William Dumaresq
Librettist: William Dumaresq
Producer: James Vermer
Director: Julie Arenal; Michael Wearing

Choreographer: Julie Arenal

Songs: Down By the Ocean; Hah; In Another Life; Isabel's a Jezebel; Love Knows No Season; Mama Don't Want No Baby; Moon Should Be Rising Soon, The; More than Earth; My God When I Think; Nothing; Oh Fish in the Sea; Oh Mummy Darling; On the Sands By the Sea; Saddest Moon, The; Sand; So Ends Our Night; Stanley Irritability; These Are the Things; Use My Name; Weeds in the Wind, The

Cast: Frank Aiello; Helen Chappell; Peter Farrell; Miguel Sergides

2154 • ISLE O' DREAMS

OPENED: 01/27/1913   Theatre: Grand Opera
                                              House
Play   Broadway: 32

Composer: Ernest R. Ball
Author: Rida Johnson Young
Director: Henry Miller

Songs: Calling of the Sea, The (L: George Graff Jr.; Chauncey Olcott); Isle O' Dreams (L: George Graff Jr.; Chauncey Olcott); Kathleen Aroon (L: Chauncey Olcott; Louis Weslyn); Mother Machree [1] (C: Ernest R. Ball; Chauncey Olcott; L: Rida Johnson Young); When Irish Eyes Are Smiling (L: George Graff Jr.; Chauncey Olcott)

Cast: Jenny Lamont; Chauncey Olcott; John Sheehan; M. Tello Webb

Notes: [1] Also in BARRY OF BALLYMORE.

2155 • ISLE OF BONG BONG, THE

OPENED: 03/14/1905   Theatre: La Salle
Musical   Chicago

Composer: Joseph E. Howard
Lyricist: Frank Adams; Will M. Hough
Librettist: Frank Adams; Will M. Hough
Producer: B.C. Whitney
Director: Bartley Cushing; Gus Sohlke

Choreographer: Gus Sohlke

Songs: Ask the Man; Bohemia; Brownies; Diplomacy; Finale; Floating Isle of Bong Bong, The; Heap Love (An Indian Serenade); Hunter's Chorus, The; I Guess I'll Take a Ride; I Like You, Too; If I Were the Man in the Moon; I'm

Lonesome for You; Jail Bird and the Tiger, The; Just Use a Bit of Blarney; Lonesome for You; My Illinois; My Uncle Sam [1]; Nicholini; Oh the Deuce, What's the Use; Old Timer, An; Opening Chorus; Pequita; You're Just the Same to Me [1]

Cast: Florence Holbrook; Joseph E. Howard; Francis Kennedy; Cecil Lean; Al Shean; Olive Vail

Notes: [1] Sheet music only.

2156 • ISLE OF CHAMPAGNE, THE

OPENED: 12/31/1892   Theatre: Manhattan
Musical   Broadway

Composer: William Furst
Librettist: Charles Alfred Byrne; Louis Harrison

Choreographer: Mimert Bibevran; **Musical Director:** Paul Steindorff; **Set Design:** Henry E. Hoyt

Cast: Walter Allen; Elvia Crox; Minnie Landers; Thomas Q. Seabrooke; Frank Soule

Notes: No songs listed in program.

2157 • ISLE OF GOLD, THE

OPENED: 04/26/1897   Theatre: Hammerstein's
                                              Olympia
Musical   Broadway: 8

Composer: Herman Perlet
Lyricist: C.A. Byrne
Librettist: C.A. Byrne
Producer: Oscar Hammerstein I

Cast: J. Aldrich Libby; Madeline Marshall; W.H. Sloan

Notes: No program available.

2158 • ISLE OF LOVE, THE

OPENED: 1910
Musical

Songs: You and I and Cupid (C: Grace LeRoy Kahn; L: Gus Kahn)

Notes: No other information available.

2159 • ISLE OF SPICE, THE

OPENED: 08/23/1904   Theatre: Majestic
Musical   Broadway: 80

Composer: Ben M. Jerome; Paul Schindler
Lyricist: George E. Stoddard
Librettist: Allen Lowe
Producer: B.C. Whitney
Director: Gus Sohlke

Choreographer: Gus Sohlke; **Costumes:** Arlene Falls; Mme. Freisinger; **Musical Director:** Paul Schindler; **Set Design:** W. Franklin Hamilton

Songs: Ambitious Animals, The (C: Paul Schindler); Basket Trio [3]; Ching Ling Foo [3]; Coax Me [2]; Come to My Heart (1) [1] (C: Ben M. Jerome); Come to My Heart (2) [2] (C: Paul Schindler); Dost Thou Know that Fair Land [4]; Face of the Girl You Love, The [3]; Father's Always Talking in His Sleep; Glorious Highball [3]; Goo-Goo Man, The (C: Ben M. Jerome); Hail Bompopka (C: Paul Schindler); How Can You Tell Till You Try (C: Paul Schindler); Japanese Umbrella, A; Kow Tow (C: Paul Schindler); Little Maid of Nicobar (C: Paul Schindler); Maid of My Dreams [4]; Mercenary Mary Ann (C: Ben M. Jerome); Opening Act I (C: Paul Schindler); Opening Act II (C: Ben M. Jerome); Opening Act III (C: Ben M. Jerome); Peggy Brady (C: Paul Schindler); Silly Sailors (C: Paul Schindler); Sporting King of Nicobar, The (C: Paul Schindler); Star of Fate (C: Paul Schindler); Take Me Home [2] (C: Paul Schindler); Uncle Sam's Marines (C: Paul Schindler); Witches, The (C: Paul Schindler; L: A.L. Jansson); You and I (C: Ben M. Jerome)

Cast: Herbert Cawthorne; Alexander Clarke; George Fiske; Gilbert Gregory; Lillian Harvey; Aida Vaughn; Alice Yorke

Notes: [1] Out Buffalo 2/10/??. [2] Out Cedar Rapids 2/08/05. [3] Out Spokane 8/1/?? [4] Out Boston 12/30/12.

2160 • IT HAPPENED IN NORDLAND

OPENED: 12/05/1904   Theatre: Lew Fields
Musical   Broadway: 154

Composer: Victor Herbert
Lyricist: Glen MacDonough

Librettist: Glen MacDonough
Producer: Lew Fields; Fred R. Hamlin; Julian Mitchell
Director: Julian Mitchell

Musical Director: Max Hirschfeld; **Set Design:** John Young

Songs: Absinthe Frappe [4]; Any Old Tree [1] (C/L: Unknown); Bandanna Land; Beatrice Barefacts [5]; Carnival (Al Fresco), The; Commandress-in-Chief; Coon Banshee, The; Dr. Blotz; Dream On; Folly Is Our King [6]; Friends that Are Staunch and True [6]; Goodybe My Love [6]; I Brought Them Home to Mother [2]; If I Were the Governor of Guam; Jack O'Lantern Girl, The; Knot of Blue, The; Little Class of One, A; Long Live the Queen [3]; Man Meant Well, The; Matinee Maid, The; My Catamaran; My Hindoo Man [1] (C/L: Unknown); Nordland; Opening Chorus; Oyaneetah (Seminole Love Song); Saturday Sadies [6]; She's a Very Dear Friend of Mine [6]; Slippery James; Tell It All; Woman in the Case, The

Cast: Marie Cahill; Bessie Clayton; Harry Davenport; Lew Fields; Harry Fisher; Pauline Frederick; Joseph W. Herbert; May Robson; Julius Steger

Notes: Act One of this show was titled THE MUSIC MASTER — a burlesque with book by Joseph W. Herbert and music by Hans Siegfried Linne. [1] Interpolated into score not by Herbert. May be part of THE MUSIC MASTER. [2] Also listed as "I Took Them Home to Mother" in some programs. [3] Sheet music only. [4] Also in ZIEGFELD FOLLIES OF 1924. [5] Also in BABES IN TOYLAND. [6] ASCAP/Library of Congress only.

2161 • IT HAPPENS ON ICE

OPENED: 10/10/1940   Theatre: Center
Revue   Broadway: 180

Composer: Fred E. Ahlert
Lyricist: Al Stillman
Producer: Sonja Henie; Arthur M. Wirtz
Director: Leon Leonidoff; Gene Snyder

Choreographer: Catherine Littlefield; Gene Snyder; **Costumes:** Norman Bel Geddes; **Musical Director:** David Mendoza; Jack Pfeiffer; **Set Design:** Norman Bel Geddes

Songs: Between You and Me and the Lamppost;
Don't Blow That Horn, Gabriel (C: Vernon Duke;
L: Will Hudson); Fast Colors (inst.) (C: Raymond
Scott); Long Ago (C: Vernon Duke); Moon Fell in
the River, The (C: Peter De Rose; L: Mitchell
Parish); Pavanne (inst.) (C: Morton Gould); So
What Goes?; Two of a Kind; What's on the
Penny?

Cast: Dorothy Allan; Joe Cook; June Forrest; Jack
Kilty

Notes: Joe Cook joined the show after opening. *See
also IT HAPPENS ON ICE (SECOND EDITION).*

2162 • IT HAPPENS ON ICE (SECOND EDITION)

OPENED: 07/15/1941   Theatre: Center
Revue   Broadway: 386

Producer: Sonja Henie; Arthur M. Wirtz
Director: Leon Leonidoff; Gene Snyder

Choreographer: Catherine Littlefield; Gene Snyder;
Costumes: Norman Bel Geddes; Willa Van;
Musical Director: David Mendoza; Jack Pfeiffer;
Set Design: Norman Bel Geddes

Songs: As Good As Gold (C: John Gerald; L: David
Gregory); Better Late Than Never (C: John
Gerald; L: David Gregory); Cubana (C/L:
Davenport; Linz); Lonely Lamp, The (C: John
Gerald; L: David Gregory); Tonight We Love
(C: Peter Tchaikowsky; L: Bobby Worth); Waltz
of Memory, The (C: John Burger; L: Pierre
Noman)

Cast: Dorothy Allan; Joe Cook; June Forrest; Jack
Kilty

Notes: Credits are same as IT HAPPENS ON ICE.
These songs replaced some of the earlier ones.

2163 • IT'S A BIRD . . . IT'S A PLANE . . . IT'S SUPERMAN

OPENED: 03/29/1966   Theatre: Alvin
Musical   Broadway: 129

Composer: Charles Strouse
Lyricist: Lee Adams
Librettist: Robert Benton; David Newman
Producer: Ruth Mitchell; Harold Prince
Director: Harold Prince

Source: SUPERMAN (Comic Strip: Joe Shuster;
Jerry Siegel); **Choreographer:** Ernest Flatt;
Costumes: Florence Klotz; **Dance Arranger:**
Betty Walberg; **Lighting Designer:** Robert
Randolph; **Musical Director:** Harold Hastings;
Orchestrations: Eddie Sauter; **Set Design:**
Robert Randolph

Songs: Didja See That [1]; Doing Good; Dot, Dot,
Dot [2]; Everything's Easy When You Know
How; I Never Felt This Way for Anyone Before [1];
I'm Not Finished Yet; I'm Too Young to Die [2];
It's a Great Country [4]; It's a Long, Slow
Climb Going Up but a Short Fast Slide Coming
Down [3]; It's Super Nice; It's Superman;
It's Up to Me [5]; Karabitz! [5]; Later [5];
Meanwhile [1]; Nuts to You [5]; Ooh, Do You
Love You!; Pow! Bam! Zonk!; Revenge; So Long,
Big Guy; Strongest Man in the World, The; Super
Note, The [1]; Superman March, The (inst.) [2];
Thanks to You [5]; We Don't Matter at All; We
Need Him; What I've Always Wanted; Woman
Alone, A [6]; Woman for the Man (Who Has
Everything), The; You've Got Possibilities;
You've Got What I Need

Cast: Jack Cassidy; Don Chastain; Bob Holiday;
Linda Lavin; Patricia Marand; Michael
O'Sullivan

Notes: [1] Cut prior to rehearsals. [2] Cut prior to
opening. [3] Cut prior to opening. Sometimes
titled "It's a Long Slow Climb Going Up but a
Short Quick Slide Coming Down." [4] Written
for 1975 television production. [5] Written for
1992 Goodspeed revival. [6] Cut prior to
opening. Music used for "Auf Wiedersehn" in
DANCE A LITTLE CLOSER.

2164 • IT'S A BRAND NEW WORLD

OPENED: 1976   Theatre: NBC
TV Musical

Composer: Andy Badale; Al Elias; Murray Lemos
Lyricist: Andy Badale; Al Elias; Murray Lemos

Musical Director: Sammy Lowe

Songs: Down Along the Vineyards; Four Would Be
Angels; It Rained 30 and 10; It's a Brand New
World; Jaw Bone of a Donkey; Riddle, The;
Samson's Gonna Be Born; Shem, Ham and
Japheth; They Laughed for 120 Years; 300 Foxes

Cast: Dennis Cooley; Malcolm Dodd; Charmaine Elias; Boni Enten; George Hirsh; Joe Silver

2165 • IT'S A SMALL WORLD
OPENED: 1950
Musical

Composer: Harold Spina
Lyricist: Jack Elliott

Songs: I Got No Talent; It's a Big, Big, Big, Big Day; It's So Nice to Have a Man Around the House; Waitin' at the Station; You Look Like Someone I Used to Know

Notes: No other information available.

2166 • IT'S A WONDERFUL LIFE
Notes: *See A WONDERFUL LIFE.*

2167 • IT'S ABOUT TIME (1942)
OPENED: 03/28/1942   Theatre: Barbizon-Plaza
Revue   Nightclub

Composer: Will Lorin; Al Moss
Lyricist: David Gregory
Producer: Martin Blaine

Choreographer: Helen Tamiris; **Set Design:** William F. Marlatt

Cast: Jimmy Blair; Paul Mann; Helen Tamiris

Notes: No program available.

2168 • IT'S ABOUT TIME (1951)
OPENED: 03/14/1951
Revue   Closed out of town

Librettist: Reginald Beckworth; Charles Gaynor; Hermione Gingold; Ronny Graham; Nina Warner Hook; John Jewett; Alan Melville; Peter Myers; David Rogers; Orford St. John
Producer: George David; Willie Frank
Director: Walter Grisham

Choreographer: Peter Hamilton; **Costumes:** Robert Fletcher; **Lighting Designer:** Miles Morgan; **Set Design:** Robert O'Hearn

Songs: Autumn Day (C: Max Showalter; L: Albert G. Miller); Borgia Orgy (C: Bert Gordon; L: John Jowitt); Coo Coo Jug Jug (C: Jack Pleis; L: Sonny Kane); Devil in My Feet (C: Dean Fuller; L: David Craig); General Effect (C: Arthur Siegel; L: Jeff Bailey); Great American Opera [1] (C/L: Ronny Graham); Herbert (C: George Engel; L: David Rogers); I and the King (C: Marie Gordon; L: Hermione Gingold; David Rogers); It's About Time (C: Arthur Siegel; L: Jeff Bailey); Knock Wood (C: Max Showalter; L: Albert G. Miller); La Loge (C: Charles Zwar; L: Gerald Bryant); Lampoon for Louis (C: Arthur Siegel; L: Jeff Bailey); Mabel (C/L: Charles Gaynor); Masseuse (C/L: Peter Myers); Misty Mountain (C: Albert Hague; L: Ruth Hughes Aarons); Picasso (C: Charles Zwar; L: Alan Melville); Raft, The (C: Arthur Siegel; L: David Rogers); Rainy Day (C: Baldwin Bergerson; L: John Rox); School of Bop (C/L: Ronny Graham); Settee, Stereoscope and You (C: Arthur Siegel; L: Jeff Bailey); Souvenirs (C/L: Norman Hackforth); Step Out and Dance (C: David Baker; L: David Craig); Tapestry Piece (C: Marie Gordon; L: David Rogers); That Wonderful Rhythm (C: Elma Showalter; L: Max Showalter)

Cast: Hermione Gingold; Ronny Graham; Jenny Lou Law; Bill Shirley

Notes: This show opened at the Brattle Theatre, Cambridge, Massachusetts. [1] Later used in NEW FACES OF 1952.

2169 • IT'S ABOUT TIME (1970)
OPENED: 04/18/1970
Revue   Closed out of town

Composer: Jay Chernis
Librettist: Stuart Bishop
Producer: Bucks County Playhouse
Director: Lee R. Yopp

Musical Director: Arthur Frank

Cast: Lorna Dallas; Joshua Hecht; Timothy Jerome

Notes: No program available. Produced at the Bucks County Playhouse.

2170 • IT'S ALL YOURS
Notes: *See STARS IN YOUR EYES.*

2171 • IT'S BETTER WITH A BAND

OPENED: 03/28/1983   Theatre: Sardi's
Revue   Nightclub: 47

Lyricist: David Zippel
Producer: Better Company, The; Roger Alan Gindi
Director: Joseph Leonardo

Costumes: Cinthia Waas; **Lighting Designer:** John Hastings; **Musical Director:** Rob LaRocco; **Set Design:** Michael J. Hotopp; Paul dePass

Songs: Another Mr. Right [2]; Camel Song, The [1] (C: Doug Katsaros); Forget It (C: Rob LaRocco); God's Gift (C: Rob LaRocco); Horsin' Around (C: Jimmy Roberts); I Can't Remember Living without Loving You (C: Wally Harper); I Reach for a Star [2] (C: Jonathan Sheffer); Ingenue, The [3] (C: Wally Harper); It's Better with a Band [3] (C: Wally Harper); Life's Ambition (C: Wally Harper); Loud Is Good (C: Jonathan Sheffer); Lullaby [1] (C: Doug Katsaros); Make Me a Star (C: Pamela Stanley; Bryon Summers); Movie Queen (C: Pamela Stanley; Bryon Summers); Song for Myself, A (C: Pamela Stanley); Time on Our Side (C: Bryon Sommers); What I Like Is You (C: Pamela Stanley); Why Don't We Run Away; You'll Never See Me Run (C: Alan Menken)

Cast: Scott Bakula; Catherine Cox; Nancy LaMott; Jenifer Lewis

Notes: [1] From JUST SO. [2] From GOING HOLLYWOOD. [3] Written for Barbara Cook's nightclub act.

2172 • IT'S ME, SYLVIA

OPENED: 04/13/1981   Theatre: Playhouse
Musical   Off-Broadway: 9

Composer: Galt MacDermot
Lyricist: Sylvia Miles
Librettist: Sylvia Miles
Producer: Steven A. Greenberg
Director: Arthur Sherman

Costumes: Clifford Capone; **Lighting Designer:** Roger Morgan; **Musical Director:** Galt MacDermot; **Set Design:** Eugene Lee

Songs: All I Need is Me (I Need Me Babe); I Believe in Me; I Can't Hide My Grief No More; I Have Born So Much Pain; I'm Desperate for Your Love; I'm Your Space Angel; I've Got to Do What I Want Today; Please Find Me (I Really Need You To See Me Through); River of Change; There's a Room for Me; This Time

Cast: Sylvia Miles

2173 • IT'S SO NICE TO BE CIVILIZED

OPENED: 06/03/1980   Theatre: Martin Beck
Revue   Broadway: 8

Composer: Micki Grant
Lyricist: Micki Grant
Librettist: Micki Grant
Producer: Jay Julien; Larry Kalish; Arnon Milchan
Director: Frank Corsaro

Choreographer: Mabel Robinson; **Costumes:** Ruth Morley; **Dance Arranger:** Carl Maultsby; **Lighting Designer:** Charles E. Hoefler; Ralph Madero; **Musical Director:** Coleridge-Taylor Perkinson; **Orchestrations:** Danny Holgate; Neal Tate; **Set Design:** Charles E. Hoefler; **Vocal Arranger:** Tasha Thomas

Songs: Alice [3]; American Dream, The; Antiquity; Bright Lights; Come Back, Baby [2]; Everybody's Got a Pitch [2]; God Help Us; I Want to Be Your Congressman [2]; It's So Nice to Be Civilized; I've Still Got My Bite; Jub Jub [1]; Keep Your Eye on the Red; Like a Lady; Look at Us; Me and Jesus [1]; Old Things [2]; Out on the Street; Pass a Little Love Around; Step into My World; Subway Rider; Talking to People [2]; Terrible Tuesday [1]; Up Front Behind [2]; Wake-Up Sun; Walkin' the Dog [2]; Welcome Mr. Anderson; When I Rise; Who's Going to Teach the Children?; Why Can't Me and You?; World Keeps Going Round

Cast: Obba Babatunde; Deborah Burrell; Mabel King; Vivian Reed; Larry Stewart; Dan Strayhorn

Notes: Opened at the AMAS Repertory Theatre 2/22/79 where it played 12 performances. Moved to Broadway on 6/3/80 for 8 performances. [1] Cut during previews. [2] In AMAS Rep version only. [3] Cut during previews and also in ALICE.

2174 • IT'S UP TO YOU (1921)

OPENED: 03/28/1921   Theatre: Casino
Musical   Broadway: 24

Composer: John L. McManus; Ray Perkins
Lyricist: Harry Clarke; Edward Paulton
Librettist: Douglas Leavitt; Augustin McHugh
Producer: William Moore Patch
Director: Frank Stammers

Choreographer: David Bennett; **Musical Director:** John L. McManus; **Set Design:** H. Robert Law

Songs: Any Pretty Little Thing; Burglar's Lament (Like Butterflies That FLith from Flower to Flower); Dee Deedle De Dum Dey; Dream Girl; Ev'ry Time I See You, Dear [1] (C: Manuel Klein; L: Edward Paulton); Firefly [1]; Havana; I Want a Bungalow [2]; I Want a Home [1] (C: Manuel Klein; L: Edward Paulton); I Will, I Won't; I'll Always Believe in You [1]; I'll Tell the World; In Our Little Castle in the Air (C/L: John McManus; L: Harry Clarke); Kuckoo Kapers [1]; Love Me (C/L: Ray Perkins); Man Is As Old As He Feels, A [1]; Moontime; Smoke Dreams; Someone to Console Me (C: Manuel Klein); That Oriental Blues; Umty-Gumty-Goo; We Never Thought of That [1]; When I Dance Alone

Cast: Charles King; Ruth Mary Lockwood; Betty Pierce

Notes: A revision of the show HI AND DRI which closed out of town. [1] Cut. [2] Is this the same song as "I Want a Home." Maybe the programs gave the titles wrong.

2175 • IT'S UP TO YOU (1945)

OPENED: 03/31/1945
Play   Off-Broadway: 1

Composer: Earl Robinson
Lyricist: Lewis Allan; Alfred Hayes; Hy Zaret
Author: Arthur Arent
Producer: American Theatre Wing, The; Food Industries, The; Skouras Theatres; U.S. Dept. of Agriculture
Director: Elia Kazan

Costumes: Peggy Clark; **Lighting Designer:** Moe Hack; **Set Design:** Howard Bay

Songs: Get the Point, Mrs. Brown?; It's Up to You; Plain Men in Dirty Overalls (C/L: Woody Guthrie); Porterhouse Lucy; Victory Begins at Home; We Can Take It

Cast: Richard Beckhard; John Berry; Dulcie Cooper; Wendell Corey; James Dobson; Laura Duncan; Woody Guthrie; Lester Lonergan Jr.; George Spaulding; Helen Tamiris; **Pianist:** Irma Jurist

2176 • IT'S UP TO YOU, JOHN HENRY

OPENED: 10/23/1905
Musical   Closed out of town

Source: UP THE LINE, JOHN HENRY (Book: George V. Hobart)

Notes: Grand Opera House.

2177 • IT'S WILDE!

OPENED: 05/25/1980   Theatre: Theater East
Revue   Off-Broadway: 7

Composer: Randy Klein
Lyricist: Burton Wolfe
Librettist: Burton Wolfe
Producer: Stages Theatrical Prod.
Director: Burton Wolfe

Choreographer: Buck Heller; **Costumes:** James Corry; **Dance Arranger:** Randy Klein; **Lighting Designer:** Frances Aronson; **Orchestrations:** Randy Klein; **Set Design:** John Falabella; **Vocal Arranger:** Randy Klein

Songs: All the Flowers Turn to Snow; Exquisite Passions; Get Thee to Bed; Hot Chocolate and Marshmallow; I Need One Man; It's Wilde!; Jailhouse Blues; Love Please Stay; Masses of Masses; Medley; Our Special Love; Poor Teddy Bear; Rape Me; Reach for the Sky; Society Means Propriety; Times Divine; Two Should Be Harmonious; We're Back; What Do I Believe In; You Are My Gold

Cast: Carol Cass; Betsy Jamison; Ross Petty; Allan Stevens; Peter Toran

2178 • ITALIAN STRAW HAT, THE

OPENED: 09/30/1957   Theatre: Fourth St.
Musical   Off-Broadway: 7

Composer: Jacques Ibert

Lyricist: Mitchell Parish
Librettist: Richard G. Mason; Regina Wojak
Producer: David Ross
Director: David Ross

Source: ITALIAN STRAW HAT, THE (Play: Eugene Labiche; Marc- Michel); **Choreographer:** Ellida Geyra; **Musical Director:** Zenon Fishbein; **Set Design:** Richard G. Mason

Songs: Do You Recall?; Gallop; Happy, Happy Day; I Have a Single Track Mind; I Knew a Girl in Barcelona; Is He Nisnardi?; It's Matrimonial Weather; Parade; Tho' I Had Never Meant to Tell You

Cast: Larry Blyden; Gerald Price

Notes: The librettists listed are the translators.

J

2179 • JACINTA OR THE MAID OF MANZARILLO

OPENED: 11/26/1894   Theatre: Fifth Avenue
Musical   Broadway: 16

Composer: Alfred G. Robyn
Librettist: William H. Lepere
Producer: Fred C. Whitney
Director: Max Freeman

Musical Director: Herman Perlet; **Set Design:**
D. Frank Dodge

Cast: Louise Beaudet; Cecile Eissing; Sidmund
Perugini; Edwin Stevens

Notes: No songs listed in program.

2180 • JACK AND JILL

OPENED: 03/22/1923   Theatre: Globe
Musical   Broadway: 92

Composer: Augustus Barratt
Lyricist: Otto Harbach
Librettist: Otto Harbach; Frederic Isham
Producer: Chelsea Productions
Director: John Murray Anderson; John Harwood

Choreographer: Larry Ceballos; **Costumes:** Gilbert
Clark; Howard Greer; Frederick Jones III; Robert
E. Locher; **Musical Director:** Charles Previn;
Orchestrations: Maurice DePackh; Stephen
Jones; **Set Design:** Frederick Jones III

Songs: Antiques; Back to Killarney [1]; Concentrate
(C: Alfred Newman); Dancing in the Dark
(C: Muriel Pollock; L: Oliver Deerin); Fleeting
Honeymoon; Georgie [1]; Girls Grow More
Wonderful Day by Day; Hello! Good-Bye
(C: William Daly); Hoping [2] (C: William Daly;
L: Irving Caesar); How Did They Know I Was
American [1]; I Love America [1]; I Love, Thou
Lovest [1] (C/L: Augustus Barratt; L: John
Murray Anderson); I Want a Pretty Girl [3]
(C: William Daly); Jack and Jill; Keys of Heaven,
The (C/L: Traditional); Keys of My Heart, The [1];

Lace Makers Song [1]; Married Life Blues; My
Cherokee Rose; No Other Eyes (L: John Murray
Anderson; Augustus Barratt); Poor Little Wall
Flower [1] (C: Muriel Pollock; L: Blanche
Merrill); Pretty City Girl (C: William Daly); Snug
As a Bug in a Rug; Toe Tangling Tune [3]
(C: William Daly); Voodoo Man (C: Alfred
Newman); Web of Dreams

Cast: Beth Berri; Brooke Johns; Donald Macdonald;
Georgia O'Ramey; Ann Pennington; Clifton
Webb

Notes: [1] Out Buffalo 12/12/23. [2] Sheet music
only. [3] Not used.

2181 • JACK AND THE BEANSTALK (1896)

OPENED: 11/02/1896   Theatre: Casino
Musical   Broadway: 65

Composer: A. Baldwin Sloane
Librettist: R.A. Barnet
Producer: A.L. Erlanger; Marc Klaw
Director: Ben Teal

Choreographer: Carl Marwig; **Set Design:** Ernest
Albert

Cast: Irene Bentley; Dan Daly; William Dunlay;
Paula Edwardes; Eddie Girard; Madge Lessing

Notes: No songs listed in program.

2182 • JACK AND THE BEANSTALK (1956)

OPENED: 11/12/1956   Theatre: NBC
TV Musical

Composer: Jerry Livingston
Lyricist: Helen Deutsch

Musical Director: Joe Leahy

Songs: Ballad of Jack and the Beanstalk, The; Fee Fi
Fo Fum; He Never Looks My Way; I'll Go Along

with You; Jack and the Giant; Looka Me; March of the Ill-Assorted Guards, The; People Should Listen to Me; Song of the Harp; Sweet World; This Is the One; Twelve Feet Tall; Where Are the White Birds Flying?

Cast: Ray Charles Choir; Billy Gilbert; Joel Grey; Celeste Holm; Peggy King; Cyril Ritchard; Arnold Stang

Notes: Original television musical.

2183 • JACK AND THE BEANSTALK (1967)
OPENED: 02/26/1967   Theatre: NBC
TV Musical

Composer: James Van Heusen
Lyricist: Sammy Cahn
Producer: Gene Kelly
Director: Gene Kelly

Musical Director: Lennie Hayton

Songs: Half Past April, and a Quarter to May; I Sure Hate Love; It's Been Nice; One Starry Moment; Stiffen Up That Upper Lip; Tiny Bit of Faith, A; Woggle-Bird Song, The

Cast: Gene Kelly; Marni Nixon; Bobby Riha

Notes: Originally titled GENE AND JACK AND THE BEANSTALK.

2184 • JACK O'LANTERN
OPENED: 10/16/1917   Theatre: Globe
Musical   Broadway: 265

Composer: Ivan Caryll
Lyricist: R.H. Burnside; Anne Caldwell
Librettist: R.H. Burnside; Anne Caldwell
Producer: Charles Dillingham
Director: R.H. Burnside

Costumes: Percy Anderson; **Set Design:** Ernest Albert; Homer Emens; Joseph Urban

Songs: Along Came Another Little Girl (L: Benjamin Hapgood Burt); And Then I Danced Away [2] (L: Louis Harrison); Candyland (L: Anne Caldwell); Come and Have a Swing with Me (L: Anne Caldwell); Follow the Girls Around (L: Anne Caldwell); Girls I've Met, The

(L: Louis Harrison); Hear the Bell; I'll Take You Back to Italy [1] (C/L: Irving Berlin); Kidnapper, The; Knit, Knit; Oh, Papa; Recruiting Doll, The (L: Louis Harrison); Sweetheart of My Own, A (L: R.H. Burnside; Anne Caldwell); Wait Till the Cows Come Home (L: Anne Caldwell)

Cast: Charles T. Aldrich; Edna Bates; Allene Crater; Helen Falconer; Oscar "Rags" Ragland; Fred Stone; Violet Zell

Notes: [1] Also titled "Sunny Italy." [2] Sheet music only.

2185 • JACK'S HOLIDAY
OPENED: 03/05/1995   Theatre: Playwrights
                                          Horizons
Musical   Off-Broadway

Composer: Randy Courts
Lyricist: Randy Courts; Mark St. Germain
Librettist: Mark St. Germain
Producer: Playwrights Horizons
Director: Susan H. Schulman

Choreographer: Michael Lichtefeld; **Costumes:** Catherine Zuber; Incidental Music: Steve Tyler; **Lighting Designer:** Robert Wierzel; **Musical Director:** Steve Tyler; **Orchestrations:** Douglas Besterman; **Set Design:** Jerome Sirlin; **Vocal Arranger:** Steve Tyler

Songs: Act One Finale; Act Two Finale; All You Want Is Always; Changing Faces; City of Dreams; Don't Think About It; Hands of God, The; If You Will Dream of Me; Letter #4; Letter #1; Letter #3; Letter #2; Line, The; Never Time to Dance; Pandarus' Song; Stage Blood; Tricks of the Trade; What I Almost Said; What Land Is This; You Never Know Who's Behind You

Cast: Judy Blazer; Nicolas Coster; Allen Fitzpatrick; Alix Korey

2186 • JACK'S ROMANCE
OPENED: 11/26/1914
Play   Closed out of town

Composer: Linda Bloodgood
Lyricist: Fiske O'Hara
Author: Augustus Pitou Sr.
Producer: Augustus Pitou Jr.
Director: Augustus Pitou Jr.

Musical Director: Linda Bloodgood

Songs: Colleen Machree; Highwayman, The; You and I

Cast: Fiske O'Hara; Ethel Von Waldren

2187 • JACKPOT

OPENED: 01/13/1944   Theatre: Alvin
Musical   Broadway: 67

Composer: Vernon Duke
Lyricist: Howard Dietz
Librettist: Guy Bolton; Ben Roberts; Sidney Sheldon
Producer: Vinton Freedley
Director: Roy Hargrave

Choreographer: Lauretta Jefferson; Charles Weidman; **Costumes:** Kiviette; **Musical Director:** Max Meth; Clay Warnick; **Orchestrations:** Robert Russell Bennett; Vernon Duke; Ted Royal; Hans Spialek; **Set Design:** Robert Edmond Jones; Raymond Sovey

Songs: Blind Date; Dear Little Cottage [1]; Exhibition Dance (inst.) [1]; First Night [1]; Girl with the Green Eye, The [1]; He's Good for Nothing but Me; Hour Ago, An [1]; I Dearly Adore a Saloon [1]; I Kissed My Girl Goodbye; I Wanna Go Back [1]; It Was Nice Knowing You; I've Got a One Track Mind; Jackpot [1]; Last Long Mile, The; Little Marriage Is a Dangerous Thing, A [1]; Little Streptococcus, The [1]; (I'm in Love with) My Top Sergeant; Nobody Ever Pins Me Up; Piece of a Girl, A; Since the Ballet Came to Shubert Alley [1]; Sugarfoot; There Are Yanks (from the Banks of the Wabash); What Happened?; What's Mine Is Yours

Cast: Benny Baker; Wendell Corey; Nanette Fabray; Betty Garrett; Allan Jones; Jerry Lester; Jacqueline Susann; Mary Wickes

Notes: [1] Not used.

2188 • JACQUES BREL IS ALIVE AND WELL AND LIVING IN PARIS

OPENED: 01/22/1966   Theatre: Village Gate
Revue   Off-Broadway: 1847

Composer: Jacques Brel
Lyricist: Eric Blau; Jacques Brel; Mort Shuman
Producer: 3W Productions
Director: Moni Yakim

Costumes: Ilka Suarez; **Lighting Designer:** James Nisbet Clark; **Musical Director:** Mort Shuman; **Orchestrations:** Wolfgang Knittel; **Set Design:** Henry E. Scott III

Songs: Alone (L: Eric Blau); Amsterdam; Bachelor's Dance (L: Eric Blau); Brussels (C: Jacques Brel; Gerard Jouannest; L: Eric Blau); Bulls, The (C: Jacques Brel; Jean Corti; Gerard Jouannest); Carousel (L: Eric Blau); Desperate Ones, The (C: Gerard Jouannest); Fannette; Funeral Tango (C: Gerard Jouannest); Girls and Dogs; I Loved (C: Gerard Jouannest; L: Francois Rauber); If; If We Only Have Love; Jackie (C: Gerard Joannest); Madeleine (C: Jacques Brel; Jean Corti; Gerard Jouannest; L: Eric Blau); Marathon; Marieke (C: Jacques Brel; Gerard Joannest; L: Eric Blau); Mathilde (C: Gerard Joannest); Middle Class, The; My Death; Next; Old Folks, The (C: Jacques Brel; Jean Corti; Gerard Joannest); Sons Of (C: Gerard Joannest); Statue, The; Timid Frieda; You're Not Alone

Cast: Shawn Elliot; Mort Shuman; Elly Stone; Alice Whitfield

Notes: English lyrics by Blau and Shuman.

2189 • JAKE THE PLUMBER

OPENED: 1927

Composer: Lew Brown
Lyricist: Lew Brown

Songs: For No Reason at All; Songs My Mother Used to Sing to Who, The; Suppose I Came Home at Nine (C: Jack Glogau)

Notes: No other information available.

2190 • JAMAICA

OPENED: 10/31/1957   Theatre: Imperial
Musical   Broadway: 555

Composer: Harold Arlen
Lyricist: E.Y. Harburg
Librettist: E.Y. Harburg; Fred Saidy
Producer: David Merrick
Director: Robert Lewis

Choreographer: Jack Cole; **Costumes:** Miles White; **Dance Arranger:** Peter Matz; **Lighting Designer:** Jean Rosenthal; **Musical Director:** Lehman Engel; **Orchestrations:** Philip J. Lang; **Set Design:** Oliver Smith

Songs: Ain't It de Truth [2]; Beach Ballet; Cocoanut Sweet; For Every Fish There's a Little Bigger Fish; Hooray for the Yankee Dollar (Workin' for the Yankee Dollar); I Don't Think I'll End It All Today; Incompatibility; Leave the Atom Alone; Little Biscuit; Monkey in the Mango Tree; Napoleon; Pity de Sunset; Pretty to Walk With; Push de Button; Savannah; Savannah's Wedding Day; Sweet Wind Blowin' My Way [1]; Take It Slow, Joe; What Did Noah Do (When the Big Wind Came?) [1]; What Good Does It Do?; Whippoorwill [1]

Cast: Ethel Ayler; Ossie Davis; Hugh Dilworth; Adelaide Hall; Lena Horne; Ricardo Montalban; Josephine Premice; Erik Rhodes

Notes: [1] Cut prior to opening. [2] Written for the film CABIN IN THE SKY.

2191 • JANE O'DAY FROM BROADWAY

Notes: *See BROADWAY AND BUTTERMILK.*

2192 • JARDIN DE PARIS

Notes: *See ZIEGFELD FOLLIES OF 1911.*

2193 • JAZZ A LA CARTE

OPENED: 06/02/1922
Musical

Composer: Richard Rodgers
Lyricist: Frank Hunter
Librettist: Dorothy Crowthers; Richard Rodgers
Producer: Institute of Musical Art
Director: Herbert Fields; Richard Rodgers

Musical Director: William Kroll

Songs: Another Mad Scene (C: William Kroll); Another Melody in F (L: Lorenz Hart); Breath of Spring (L: Lorenz Hart); Every Girlie Wants to Be a Sally; Everytime I Think of You (C: Gerald Warburg); Mary, Queen of Scots [1]; Moonlight and You; My Prince of Wales (C: Gerald Warburg); Poster Girl, The; That Pathetique

Melody (L: Sigmund Krumgold); There's Always Room for One More (L: Oscar Hammerstein II); Waiting (C: Gerald Warburg); What Ragtime Did to Business

Notes: [1] Also in POOR LITTLE RITZ GIRL and YOU'D BE SURPRISED.

2194 • JAZZ SINGER, THE

OPENED: 09/14/1925   Theatre: Fulton
Play   Broadway: 315

Author: Samson Raphaelson
Producer: Sam H. Harris; Lewis and Gordon
Director: Albert Lewis

Source: DAY OF ATONEMENT, THE (Story: Samson Raphaelson)

Songs: Home Pals (C: M.K. Jerome; L: Sam M. Lewis; Joseph Young)

Cast: Edward Arnold; Sam Jaffe; George Jessel; Tom Johnstone; Howard Lang; Dorothy Raymond

2195 • JAZZBO BROWN

OPENED: 06/24/1980   Theatre: City Lights
Musical   Off-Broadway: 44

Composer: Stephen H. Lemberg
Lyricist: Stephen H. Lemberg
Librettist: Stephen H. Lemberg
Producer: Barbara Gittler
Director: Louis Johnson

Choreographer: Louis Johnson; **Costumes:** Vel Riberto; Karen Roston; **Dance Arranger:** Zulema Cusseaux; Luther Henderson; **Lighting Designer:** Bill Mintzer; **Musical Director:** Tod Cooper; **Orchestrations:** Luther Henderson; **Set Design:** Harry Lines; **Vocal Arranger:** Luther Henderson

Songs: Best Man, The; Born to Sing; Broadway; Bump Bump Bump; Dancin' Shoes; First Time I Saw You; Funky Bessie; Give Me More; Harlem Follies; He Had the Callin'; I'm Bettin' You; Jazzbo Brown; Million Songs; Precious Patterns; Pride and Freedom; Same Old Tune, The; Take a Bow; When I Die; When You've Loved Your Man

Cast: Chris Calloway; Andre De Shields; Jerry Jarrett

Notes: Additional Music Arrangements by Zulema Cusseaux.

2196 • JEAN SEBERG

OPENED: 11/15/1983   Theatre: National
Musical   London

Composer: Marvin Hamlisch
Lyricist: Christopher Adler
Librettist: Julian Barry

Notes: No other information available.

2197 • JEKYLL AND HYDE (1990 A)

OPENED: 06/25/1990   Theatre: Promenade
Musical   Off-Broadway: 45

Composer: Michael Skloff
Lyricist: David Crane; Marta Kauffman
Librettist: David Crane; Marta Kauffman
Producer: Theatreworks USA
Director: Jay Harnick

Source: STRANGE CASE OF DR. JEKYLL AND MR. HYDE, THE (Novel: Robert Louis Stevenson); **Choreographer:** Helen Butleroff; **Costumes:** Ann-Marie Wright; **Lighting Designer:** Mathew J. Williams; **Musical Director:** Wayne Abravanel; **Set Design:** Vaughn Patterson

Cast: Emily Bear; Frederick Einhorn; Amanda Green; Eric Ruffin; Christopher Scott

Notes: Alley Theatre, Houston. [1] Cut.

2198 • JEKYLL AND HYDE (1990 B)

OPENED: 05/25/1990
Musical

Composer: Frank Wildhorn
Lyricist: Leslie Bricusse
Librettist: Leslie Bricusse
Producer: Fox Theatricals; Jerry Frankel; PACE Theatrical Group
Director: Gregory Boyd

Source: STRANGE CASE OF DR. JEKYLL AND MR. HYDE, THE (Novel: Robert Louis Stevenson); **Choreographer:** Larry Fuller; **Costumes:** Johnathan Bixby; **Lighting Designer:** Howell Binkley; **Musical Director:** Jeremy Roberts; **Orchestrations:** Kim Scharnberg; **Set**

Design: Vince Mountain; **Vocal Arranger:** Jason Howland; Frank Wildhorn

Songs: Alive!; Bitch, Bitch, Bitch [1]; Board of Governors; Bring on the Men; Confrontation; Engagement Party, The [1]; Facade; Girls of the Night, The; His Work — and Nothing More; How Can I Continue On? [1]; I Need to Know [1]; In His Eyes; It's a Dangerous Game; Letting Go [1]; Lisa Carew; Lucy Meets Hyde [1]; Lucy Meets Jekyll [1]; Mass [1]; Murder, Murder!; New Life, A; No One Knows Who I Am [1]; No One Must Ever Know [1]; Once Upon a Dream; Possessed [1]; Prologue [1]; Reflections [1]; Someone Like You; Streak of Madness [1]; Sympathy- Tenderness [1]; Take Me As I Am; This Is the Moment; Transformation; Wedding Reception, The [1]; World Has Gone Insane, The [1]

Cast: Lisa Carew; Robert Cuccioli; Linda Eder; Brad Oscar; Gabriel John Utterson

Notes: Alley Theatre, Houston. [1] Cut.

2199 • JEKYLL AND HYDE (1990 C)

OPENED: 03/14/1990
Musical

Composer: Norman Sachs
Lyricist: Mel Mandel
Librettist: Lenora Thuna
Director: Gregory S. Hurst

Source: STRANGE CASE OF DR. JEKYLL AND MR. HYDE, THE (Novel: Robert Louis Stevenson); **Choreographer:** Lynne Taylor-Corbett; **Costumes:** Barbara Forbes; **Lighting Designer:** Donald Holder; **Musical Director:** Joel Silberman; **Set Design:** Deborah Jasien

Cast: Rebecca Baxter; John Cullum; Terrence Currier; Cady Huffman; Jamie Ross; David Sabin

Notes: George Street Playhouse, New Brunswick, New Jersey. A reworking of AFTER YOU, MR. HYDE. See under that title also.

2200 • JELLY'S LAST JAM

OPENED: 04/26/1992   Theatre: Virginia
Musical   Broadway: 569

Music Based On: Jelly Roll Morton
Lyricist: Susan Birkenhead

Librettist: George C. Wolfe
Producer: Pamela Koslow; Margo Lion
Director: George C. Wolfe

Choreographer: Hope Clarke; Gregory Hines; Ted L. Levy; **Costumes:** Toni-Leslie James; **Lighting Designer:** Jules Fisher; **Music Adaptation:** Luther Henderson; **Musical Director:** Linda Twine; **Orchestrations:** Luther Henderson; **Set Design:** Robin Wagner

Songs: Chicago Stomp, The; Creole Blues (C: Luther Henderson); Creole Way, The (C: Luther Henderson); De Chimney Man; Dr. Jazz (C: Walter Melrose; King Oliver); Get Away, Boy (C: Luther Henderson); Here with You; Hunnie's Rag, The; I'm Here; In My Day; Jelly's Jam; Last Chance Blues, The (C/L: Traditional); Legacy Blues (C: Luther Henderson); Listen Fool; Lonely Boy Blues (C/L: Traditional); Lovin' Is a Lowdown Blues; Michigan Water (C/L: Traditional); Play the Music for Me; Requiem Blues; Short Piano Roll (C: Luther Henderson); Somethin' More; Street Scene (L'Abandonnement) (C: Luther Henderson); That's How You Jazz (C/L: Traditional); That's the Way We Do Things in New York; Too Late, Daddy (C: Luther Henderson); Whole World's Waitin' to Sing Your Song

Cast: Keith David; Mary Bond Davis; Savion Glover; Gregory Hines; Tonya Pinkins

2201 • JENNIE

OPENED: 10/17/1963 Theatre: Majestic
Musical Broadway: 82

Composer: Arthur Schwartz
Lyricist: Howard Dietz
Librettist: Arnold Schulman
Producer: Cheryl Crawford; Richard Halliday
Director: Vincent J. Donehue

Source: LAURETTE (Book: Margaret Courtney); **Choreographer:** Matt Mattox; **Costumes:** Irene Sharaff; **Dance Arranger:** Trude Rittman; **Lighting Designer:** Jean Rosenthal; **Musical Director:** John Lesko; **Orchestrations:** Robert Russell Bennett; Philip J. Lang; **Set Design:** George Jenkins; **Vocal Arranger:** Trude Rittman

Songs: Before I Kiss the World Goodbye [1]; Born Again; Close Your Eyes [2]; Dinner Is Served [2]; Femme Fatale [2]; For Better or Worse; High Is

Better Than Low; I Believe in Takin' a Chance; I Still Look at You That Way; I Think I'm Going to Like It Over Here; It Isn't What You Have [3]; Jennie [2]; Jig, The (dance); Lonely Nights; Mother Who's Really a Mother, A [2]; Night May Be Dark, The; No Hope for the Human Race [2]; O'Conner [2]; On the Other Hand [2]; On the Thomas J. Muldoon [2]; Sauce Diable (dance); See Seattle; Waitin' for the Evening Train; Welcome; When You're Far Away from New York Town; Where You Are

Cast: Robin Bailey; Jack De Lon; Imelda De Martin; Mary Martin; Ethel Shutta; George Wallace

Notes: [1] Written for the unproduced MRS 'ARRIS GOES TO PARIS. [2] Cut or not used. [3] Song title not found on any list.

2202 • JEREMIAH

OPENED: 02/03/1939 Theatre: Guild
Play Broadway: 35

Composer: Chemjo Vinaver
Lyricist: Ruth Langner
Librettist: Cedar Paul; Eden Paul; Stefan Zwroh

Choreographer: Felicia Sorel; **Costumes:** Harry Horner; **Orchestrations:** Chemjo Vinaver; **Set Design:** Harry Horner

Cast: Arthur Byron; Vincent J. Donehue; Cameron Mitchell; Effie Shannon; Kent Smith; Paul Tripp; Cornel Wilde

Notes: Translated by Eden and Cedar Paul. No songs listed in program. Acting version prepared by John Gassner and Worthington Miner.

2203 • JERICHO-JIM CROW

OPENED: 01/05/1964 Theatre: Sanctuary
Musical Off-Broadway: 32

Composer: Traditional
Lyricist: Traditional
Librettist: William Hairston; Langston Hughes
Producer: Greenwich Village Players
Director: Alvin Ailey

Costumes: Ves Harper; **Lighting Designer:** Ves Harper; **Musical Director:** Hugh Porter

Songs: Battle Hymn of the Republic [4] (C: Anonymous; L: Julia Ward Howe); Battle of

Old Jim Crow, The [2]; Better Leave Segregation Alone [2]; Come and Go with Me [2]; Ezekiel Saw the Wheel [2]; Follow the Drinking Gourd (C/L: Paul Campbell); Freedom Land (C/L: Langston Hughes); Go Down, Moses [2]; God's Gonna Cut You Down [2]; How Much Do You Want Me to Bear? [2]; I Been 'Buked and I Been Scorned [2]; I'm on My Way [2]; Is Massa Gwine to Sell Us Tomorrow? [2]; John Brown's Body [3]; Meeting Here Tonight, A [2]; My Mind on Freedom [2]; Oh, Freedom! [2]; Slavery Chain Done Broke at Last [2]; Stay in the Field [2]; Such a Little King (C/L: Langston Hughes); We Shall Overcome [2]; Where Will I Lie Down? [2]

Cast: Joseph Attles; Gilbert Price

Notes: [1] Not in program. [2] Not written for production. [3] Not written for production. Lyrics attributed to Charles S. Hall, Henry Howard Brownell or Thomas Brigham Bishop. The music was attributed to William Steffe (tune is "Glory, Glory, Hallelujah"). [4] Not written for production. Tune is "Glory Glory Hallelujah" which has been attributed to William Steffe.

2204 • JEROME KERN GOES TO HOLLYWOOD

OPENED: 01/23/1986   Theatre: Ritz
Revue   Broadway: 13

Composer: Jerome Kern
Lyricist: Oscar Hammerstein II
Librettist: Dick Vosburgh
Producer: Arthur Cantor; Bonnie Nelson Schwartz
Director: David Kernan

Costumes: Christine Robinson; **Lighting Designer:** Ken Billington; **Musical Director:** Peter Howard; **Set Design:** Colin Pigott

Songs: All the Things You Are; Bill (L: Oscar Hammerstein II; P.G. Wodehouse); Bojangles of Harlem (L: Dorothy Fields); Californ-i-ay (L: E.Y. Harburg); Can I Forget You?; Can't Help Lovin' Dat Man; Daydreaming (L: Gus Kahn); Dearly Beloved (L: Johnny Mercer); Don't Ask Me Not to Sing (L: Otto Harbach); Fine Romance, A (L: Dorothy Fields); Folks Who Live on the Hill, The; Here Comes the Showboat! (C: Maceo Pinkard; L: Billy Rose); I Dream Too Much (L: Dorothy Fields); I Have the Room Above Her; I Still Suits Me; I Won't Dance (L: Dorothy Fields); I'll Be Hard to Handle (L: Bernard

Dougall); I'm Old Fashioned (L: Johnny Mercer); I've Told Every Little Star; I've Told Every Little Star; Just Let Me Look at You (L: Dorothy Fields); Last Time I Saw Paris, The; Let's Begin (L: Otto Harbach); Long Ago and Far Away (L: Ira Gershwin); Look for the Silver Lining (L: B.G. DeSylva); Lovely to Look At (L: Dorothy Fields); Make Believe; Make Way for Tomorrow (L: Ira Gershwin; E.Y. Harburg); Ol' Man River; Pick Yourself Up (L: Dorothy Fields); Remind Me (L: Dorothy Fields); She Didn't Say Yes (L: Otto Harbach); Show Must Go On, The (L: Ira Gershwin); Smoke Gets in Your Eyes (L: Otto Harbach); Song Is You, The; They Didn't Believe Me (L: Herbert Reynolds); Till the Clouds Roll By (L: P.G. Wodehouse); Way You Look Tonight, The (L: Dorothy Fields); Who? (L: Oscar Hammerstein II; Otto Harbach); Why Do I Love You?; Why Was I Born?; Yesterdays (L: Otto Harbach)

Cast: Elaine Delmar; Scott Holmes; Liz Robertson; Elisabeth Welch

Notes: No songs were original to this production.

2205 • JEROME ROBBINS' BROADWAY

OPENED: 02/26/1989   Theatre: Imperial
Revue   Broadway: 634

Librettist: Jason Alexander
Producer: Emanuel Azenberg; Roger Berlind; Byron Goldman; Shubert Organization, The; Suntory International Corp.
Director: Jerome Robbins

Choreographer: Jerome Robbins; **Lighting Designer:** Jennifer Tipton; **Musical Director:** Paul Gemignani; **Orchestrations:** William D. Brohn; Sid Ramin

Songs: Charleston [2] (C: Morton Gould; L: Betty Comden; Adolph Green); Comedy Tonight [3] (C/L: Stephen Sondheim); Dreams Come True [1] (C: Morton Gould; L: Betty Comden; Adolph Green); Fiddler on the Roof selections [4] (C: Jerry Bock; L: Sheldon Harnick); I Still Get Jealous [5] (C: Jule Styne; L: Sammy Cahn); I'm Flying [6] (C: Moose Charlap; L: Carolyn Leigh); Mr. Monotony [7] (C/L: Irving Berlin); New York, New York [8] (C: Leonard Bernstein; L: Betty Comden; Adolph Green); On a Sunday By the Sea [5] (C: Jule Styne; L: Sammy Cahn);

Sailors on Leave (inst.) [8] (C: Leonard Bernstein); Small House of Uncle Thomas, The [9] (C: Richard Rodgers; L: Oscar Hammerstein II); Some Other Time [8] (C: Leonard Bernstein; L: Betty Comden; Adolph Green); Suite of Dances (inst.) [10] (C: Leonard Bernstein); Ya Got Me [8] (C: Leonard Bernstein; L: Betty Comden; Adolph Green); You Gotta Have a Gimmick [11] (C: Jule Styne; L: Stephen Sondheim)

Cast: Jason Alexander; Charlotte D'Amboise; Susann Fletcher; Nancy Hess; Michael Kubala; Robert La Fosse; Michael Lynch; Luis Perez; Faith Prince; Tom Robbins; Debbie Shapiro; Mary Ellen Stuart; Scott Wise

Notes: No original songs in this show. [1] From BILLION DOLLAR BABY. Cut during previews. [2] From BILLION DOLLAR BABY. [3] From A FUNNY THING HAPPENED ON THE WAY TO THE FORUM. [4] From FIDDLER ON THE ROOF. [5] From HIGH BUTTON SHOES. [6] From PETER PAN. [7] Cut from CALL ME MADAM, film EASTER PARADE and MISS LIBERTY. [8] From ON THE TOWN. [9] From THE KING AND I. [10] From WEST SIDE STORY. [11] From GYPSY.

2206 • JERRY

OPENED: 03/18/1914   Theatre: Lyceum
Play   Broadway: 41

Author: Catherine Chisholm Cushing
Producer: Charles Frohman

Songs: Sunset Sue (C/L: Edwin Burch)

Cast: Billie Burke; Gladys Hanson; Lumsden Hare; Alan Pollock

2207 • JERRY FOR SHORT

OPENED: 08/12/1929   Theatre: Waldorf
Play   Broadway: 64

Author: William A. Grew
Producer: Eugene Productions
Director: William A. Grew

Set Design: Eddie Eddy

Songs: Jerry for Short (C/L: Fiske O'Hara)

Cast: Don Ameche; Fiske O'Hara; Patricia Quinn

Notes: No songs listed in program.

2208 • JERRY'S GIRLS

OPENED: 12/18/1985   Theatre: St. James
Revue   Broadway: 139

Composer: Jerry Herman
Lyricist: Jerry Herman
Producer: Zev Bufman; Kenneth-John Productions
Director: Larry Alford

Choreographer: Wayne Cilento; **Costumes:** Florence Klotz; **Dance Arranger:** Mark Hummel; **Lighting Designer:** Tharon Musser; **Musical Director:** Janet Glazener; **Orchestrations:** Christopher Bankey; Joseph Gianono; Jim Tyler; **Set Design:** Hal Tine

Songs: Before the Parade Passes By [1]; Best of Times, The [7]; Bosom Buddies [3]; Have a Nice Day [7]; Hello, Dolly [1]; I Am What I Am [7]; I Don't Want to Know [5]; I Won't Send Roses [4]; If He Walked Into My Life [3]; It Only Takes a Moment [1]; It Takes a Woman [1]; It's Today [12]; Just Go to the Movies [6]; Just Leave Everything to Me [10]; Kiss Her Now [5]; La Cage Aux Folles [7]; Look What Happened to Mabel [4]; Mame [3]; Man in the Moon, The [3]; Milk and Honey [8]; Movies Were Movies [4]; My Type [9]; Nelson [6]; Put on Your Sunday Clothes [1]; Shalom [8]; So Long Dearie [1]; Song on the Sand [7]; Take It All Off; Tap Your Troubles Away [4]; Tea Party, The [5]; That's How Young I Feel [3]; There Is No Tune Like a Show Tune [11]; Time Heals Everything [4]; Two-a-Day [2]; We Need a Little Christmas [3]; Wherever He Ain't [4]

Cast: Kim Crosby; Dorothy Loudon; Joni Masella; Chita Rivera; Leslie Uggams

Notes: Opened 8/17/81 at The Onstage Theatre, Off-Broadway where it ran 101 performances. [1] Written for HELLO, DOLLY! [2] Written for PARADE. [3] Written for MAME. [4] Written for MACK AND MABEL. [5] Written for DEAR WORLD. [6] Written for A DAY IN HOLLYWOOD . . . A NIGHT IN THE UKRAINE. [7] Written for LA CAGE AUX FOLLES. [8] Written for MILK AND HONEY. [9] Written for NIGHTCAP. [10] Written for film HELLO, DOLLY. [11] Written for PARADE. Same music as "It's Today." [12] Written for MAME. Same music as "There Is No Tune Like a Show Tune."

2209 • JERSEY LILY, THE
OPENED: 09/14/1903   Theatre: Victoria
Musical   Broadway: 24

Composer: Reginald De Koven
Lyricist: George V. Hobart
Librettist: George V. Hobart
Producer: George W. Lederer
Director: George W. Lederer

Choreographer: Joseph C. Smith; **Costumes:** Archie Gunn; **Musical Director:** A. DeNovellis

Songs: Aurora [3]; Bedelia [2] (C: Jean Schwartz; L: William Jerome); Cincinnati [1]; Dreaming, Dreaming (The Moon Song); Gingerbread Boy, The; Girl Wanted [1]; Half-Past Kissing Time [3]; Lily's Promenade, The; Lobster and the Lady [1]; My Dear Old New Jersey Home; 'Neath Thy Window, Senorita (C: Max Hoffmann); New Cook, The; Old Glory; On a Chinese Honeymoon (C: Max Hoffmann); Patsy Bolivar; Rosie Lee; She Walks Like This [1]; Some Beautiful Day; Sweetheart Mine; Ump-Pom Man, The; Waltz Reve d'Amour [1]; Welcome the Brides

Cast: William Cameron; Louis Harrison; Gertrude Hoffman; Maude Raymond; Blanche Ring; Billie Taylor; Billy B. Van

Notes: [1] Out of town programs only. [2] Also in WHEN CLAUDIA SMILES and the London show THE ORCHID. [3] Sheet music only.

2210 • JES' LAK WHITE FO'KS
OPENED: 1899   Theatre: Cherry Blossom
Musical   New York

Composer: Will Marion Cook
Lyricist: Paul Laurence Dunbar
Librettist: Paul Laurence Dunbar
Producer: Ernest Hogan

Notes: One-act musical.

2211 • JEST, THE
OPENED: 02/04/1926   Theatre: Plymouth
Play   Broadway: 78

Author: Sem Bonnelli
Producer: Arthur Hopkins
Director: Arthur Hopkins

Set Design: Robert Edmond Jones

Songs: Madrigal of May (C/L: Maurice Nitke)

Cast: Ferdinand Gottschalk; Violet Heming; Maria Ouspenskaya; Basil Sydney

2212 • JESUS CHRIST SUPERSTAR
OPENED: 10/12/1971   Theatre: Mark Hellinger
Musical   Broadway: 711

Composer: Andrew Lloyd Webber
Lyricist: Tim Rice
Producer: MCA; Robert Stigwood
Director: Tom O'Horgan

Costumes: Randy Barcelo; **Lighting Designer:** Jules Fisher; **Musical Director:** Marc Pressel; **Orchestrations:** Andrew Lloyd Webber; **Set Design:** Robin Wagner

Songs: Arrest, The; Could We Start Again, Please; Crucifixion, The; Damned for All Time; Everything's Alright; Gethsemane; Heaven on Their Minds; Hosanna; I Don't Know How to Love Him [1]; John 19:41; Judas' Death; King Herod's Song; Last Supper, The; Peter's Denial; Pilate and Christ; Pilate's Dream; Poor Jerusalem; Simon Zealotes; Strange Thing Mystifying; Superstar; Temple, The; This Jesus Must Die; Trial Before Pilate; What's the Buzz?

Cast: Paul Ainsley; Bob Bingham; Alan Braunstein; Dennis Buckley; Barry Dennen; Yvonne Elliman; Jeff Fenholt; Michael Jason; Phil Jethro; Ben Vereen

Notes: [1] Same music as pop song "Kansas Morning."

2213 • JEWEL OF ASIA, THE
OPENED: 02/16/1903   Theatre: Criterion
Musical   Broadway: 64

Composer: Ludwig Englander
Lyricist: Frederick Ranken; Harry B. Smith
Librettist: Frederick Ranken; Harry B. Smith
Producer: George W. Lederer
Director: George W. Lederer

Musical Director: Max Hirschfeld; **Set Design:** Ernest Albert [1]

Songs: Beggars' Chorus; Better Late Than Never [3]; Blanche Ring's Doll Song [4]; Everybody Wants to See the Baby [4]; I Am the Pasha; I Found a Way (I Lost Another Chance to Be a Hero); I Love You Dolly; Love Is a Game [3]; My Honey Bunch [5]; Off to Turkey; Oh! Thou Art Fair, My Love; Oh, What's the Use?; Pierre; Please Don't Move; Same Old Crowd The [2]; Twelve Pretty Wives from Turkey; Wanted: A Fly (Spider and Fly); We Say We'll Do a Thing; Woman's "No" Means "Yes", A (L: Harry B. Smith)

Cast: Harriet Burt; William Cameron; Clifton Crawford; James T. Powers; Blanche Ring

Notes: [1] Designer of Act II only. [2] There was a popular song "Same Old Crowd" written by Farrell and Morse in 1902. [3] Sheet music only. [4] Sheet music only. Interpolated. [5] Interpolated.

2214 • JIM JAM JEMS
OPENED: 10/04/1920   Theatre: Cort
Musical   Broadway: 105

Composer: James F. Hanley
Lyricist: Harry L. Cort; George E. Stoddard
Librettist: Harry L. Cort; George E. Stoddard
Producer: John Cort
Director: Edgar MacGregor

Choreographer: Robert Marks; **Musical Director:** Gus Salzer

Songs: All in a Short Half Hour [2]; Don't Let Me Catch You Falling in Love; Everybody's Got Somebody but Me (Ev'rybody but Me) (L: Joe Goodwin); From Your Heart to Mine (L: Harry L. Cort; Arthur J. Lamb; George E. Stoddard); I'm Tillie of Longacre Square [2]; I've Always Been Fond of Babies (That's Why I'm in Love with You); Jim Jam Jems; Just a Little Bit Behind the Times; Little Bo Peep; Magic Kiss, The; Poor Little Rich Little Me; Poor Old Florodora Girl (L: Ballard Macdonald); Raggedy Ann; Show Me the Town; Sweet Little Stranger; That Funny Little Movement [2]; They're Making Them Wonderful; When the Right Little Girl Comes Along [1]

Cast: Joe E. Brown; Frank Fay; King Sisters, The; Harry Langdon; Ned Sparks; Ada Mae Weeks

Notes: Titled HELLO, LESTER! on tour after New York. [1] Titled "Right Little Girl" in program. [2] Out 9/6/20.

2215 • JIM-JAM REVUE
OPENED: 1917
Revue

Composer: Unknown
Lyricist: Unknown

Songs: Chin Chin Chow (C: Louis Silvers; L: Edward Madden); I Found the Heart of You (C: Louis Silvers; L: Arthur Freed); Jack O'Lantern Man; Jim-Jam Man; Won't You Take Me Home with You

Notes: No other information available.

2216 • JIMMIE
OPENED: 10/17/1920   Theatre: Apollo
Musical   Broadway: 71

Composer: Herbert Stothart
Lyricist: Oscar Hammerstein II; Otto Harbach
Librettist: Oscar Hammerstein II; Otto Harbach; Frank Mandel
Producer: Arthur Hammerstein
Director: Oscar Eagle

Choreographer: Bert French; **Costumes:** Henri Bendel; **Musical Director:** Herbert Stothart; **Set Design:** Joseph Physioc

Songs: All That I Want; Aria, An; Baby Dreams; Below the Macy-Gimbel Line; Cabaret Girl [1]; Carlotti's; Clothes [1]; Cute Little Two by Four; Dig, Sister, Dig [1]; Do, Re, Mi; Don't Yo' Want to See de Moon?; Fantasie; I Wish I Was a Queen; It Isn't Hard to Do; Jimmie; Just a Smile; Little Plate of Soup, A; Ming Poo [1]; Rickety Crickety [2]; She Alone Could Understand; Some People Make Me Sick; That's As Far As I Can Go [1]; Toodle Oodle Um; Try Me [1]; Tu Carrisimo [1]; Tum-Tiddly-Tum-Tum [1]; Up Is a Long, Long Climb [1]

Cast: Hattie Burks; Harry Delf; Mary Jane; Dee Loretta; Paul Porcasi; Frances White

Notes: [1] Cut prior to opening. [2] Cut prior to opening but reinstated in January at run's end.

2217 • JIMMY

OPENED: 10/23/1969   Theatre: Winter Garden
Musical   Broadway: 84

Composer: Bill Jacob; Patti Jacob
Lyricist: Bill Jacob; Patti Jacob
Librettist: Melville Shavelson
Producer: Jack L. Warner
Director: Joseph Anthony

Source: BEAU JAMES (Book: Gene Fowler);
   Choreographer: Peter Gennaro; **Costumes:**
   W. Robert Lavine; **Dance Arranger:** John
   Berkman; **Lighting Designer:** Peggy Clark;
   Musical Director: Milton Rosenstock;
   Orchestrations: Jack Andrews; **Set Design:**
   Oliver Smith; **Vocal Arranger:** Milton
   Rosenstock

Songs: Charmin' Son-of-a-Bitch, The; Darlin' of
   New York, The; Five Lovely Ladies; I Only
   Wanna Laugh; It's a Nice Place to Visit; Jimmy;
   Life Is a One-Way Street; Little Woman, The; Oh,
   Gee!; One in a Million; Our Jimmy; Riverside
   Drive; Squabble Song, The; That Old Familiar
   Ring; They Never Proved a Thing; Walker Walk,
   The; What's Out There for Me?; Will You Think
   of Me Tomorrow?

Cast: Anita Gillette; Frank Gorshin; William Griffis;
   Stanley Simmonds; Julie Wilson

2218 • JIMMY SHINE

OPENED: 12/05/1968   Theatre: Brooks Atkinson
Play   Broadway: 161

Composer: John Sebastian
Lyricist: John Sebastian
Author: Murray Schisgal
Producer: Zev Bufman; Claire Nichtern
Director: Donald Driver

Costumes: Lewis Brown; **Lighting Designer:**
   Thomas Skelton; **Musical Director:** Irving
   Joseph; **Set Design:** Edward Burbridge

Songs: Future in Fish, A; Original Jimmy Shine,
   An; She's a Lady

Cast: Rose Gregorio; Dustin Hoffman; Cleavon
   Little; Rue McClanahan; Eli Mintz; Pamela
   Payton-Wright; David Sabin

Notes: No songs listed in program.

2219 • JO

OPENED: 02/12/1964   Theatre: Orpheum
Musical   Off-Broadway: 63

Composer: William Dyer
Lyricist: William Dyer; Don Parks
Librettist: William Dyer; Don Parks
Producer: Victoria Crandall
Director: John Bishop

Source: LITTLE WOMEN (Novel: Louisa May
   Alcott); **Choreographer:** Chele Abel; Gerald
   Teijelo; **Costumes:** Evelyn Norton Anderson;
   Lighting Designer: Miller-Moffatt; **Musical
   Director:** Jane Douglass White; **Orchestrations:**
   Robert Page; **Set Design:** Gordon Micunis; **Vocal
   Arranger:** Robert Page

Songs: Afraid to Fall in Love; Castles in the Air;
   Deep in the Bosom of the Family; Friendly Polka;
   Genius Burns; Harmony, Mass.; Hurry Home;
   I Like; If You Can Find a True Love; Let's Be
   Elegant or Die!; Moods; More Than Friends; Nice
   As Any Man Can Be; Taking the Cure; Time Will
   Be; Wedding! A Wedding!, A; What a Long Cold
   Winter!

Cast: Susan Browning; Joy Hodges; Judith
   McCauley; Mimi Randolph; April Shawhan; Don
   Stewart; Karin Wolfe

2220 • JOAN

OPENED: 06/19/1972   Theatre: Circle in the
                                Square
Musical   Off-Broadway: 64

Composer: Al Carmines
Lyricist: Al Carmines
Librettist: Al Carmines
Producer: Seymour Hacker; Paul Libin; Theodore
   Mann
Director: Al Carmines

Choreographer: Gus Solomons Jr.; David Vaughn;
   Costumes: Joan Kilpatrick; Ira Siff; **Lighting
   Designer:** Earl Eidman; **Musical Director:**
   Al Carmines; **Set Design:** Earl Eidman

Songs: Come on Joan; Country of the Mind, A;
   Despair; Faith Is Such a Simple Thing; Go Back;
   I Live a Little; I'm Madame Margaret the
   Therapist; In My Silent Universe; Ira, My Dope
   Fiend; It's So Nice; Look at Me, Joan; Praise the
   Lord; Religious Establishment, The; Rivers of

Roses; Salve Madonna; Spoken Aria; Take Courage, Daughter; They Call Me the Virgin Mary; What I Wonder; Woman I Love, The

Cast: Emily Adams; Essie Borden; Al Carmines; Lee Guillatt; Julie Kurnitz; David McCorkle; Ira Siff

Notes: Opened at the Judson Poet's Theatre in Judson Church in November, 1971 where it played for 10 performances.

2221 • JOAN OF ARKANSAW (1920)

Notes: *See ALWAYS YOU.*

2222 • JOAN OF ARKANSAW (1927)

OPENED: 10/1927
Musical   Closed out of town

Composer: Kenneth Sheridan
Lyricist: Will Carleton
Librettist: Will Carleton
Producer: Metropolitan Stage Prods.
Director: Frank M. Rainger

Musical Director: A.H. Cokayne

Songs: Barcarolle; Beautiful Girl; Danse d'Abandon; Gamboling on the Green; Hark to the Lark; Hello, Hannah; I Wonder Why; In the Summertime; Rainbow Hook and Ladder, The; Rainbows; Say It with Flowers; Venus de Milo; When She Gets Up in the Morning

Cast: Cora Bird; Kathryn Crawford; Flora Bonfanti Russell

2223 • JOE HURTIG'S SOCIAL MAIDS

OPENED: 09/05/1922   Theatre: Columbia
Revue   Broadway

Composer: Hughie Woolford
Lyricist: Andy Razaf
Producer: Joe Hurtig

Songs: My Waltz Divine

Notes: A burlesque revue.

2224 • JOHN & JEN

OPENED: 06/01/1995   Theatre: Lamb's
Musical   Off-Broadway

Composer: Andrew Lippa
Lyricist: Tom Greenwald
Librettist: Tom Greenwald; Andrew Lippa
Producer: Carolyn Rossi Copeland; Lamb's Theater Company
Director: Gabriel Barre

Costumes: D. Polly Kendirck; **Lighting Designer:** Stuart Duke; **Musical Director:** Joel Fram; **Orchestrations:** Jason Robert Brown; **Set Design:** Charles E. McCarry

Songs: At the Game [1]; Bye Room; Christmas; Dear God; Epilogue [1]; Every Goodbye Is Hello; Graduation; Hold Down the Fort; I Gotta Go [1]; I Still Remember [1]; It Took Me a While [1]; It's Not Christmas Yet [1]; Just Like You; Letters [1]; Old Clothes Little League; Out of My Sight; Prologue [1]; Road Ends Here, The; Run and Hide; Smile of Your Dreams; That Was My Way; Think Big; This Is What You Want [1]; Timeline; Tomorrow Is Christmas [1]; Two Little Kids [1]; Vaudeville, The [1]; Welcome to the World; What Can I Do?; What Is Love? [1]; World Is Upside Down, The [1]

Notes: [1] In Goodspeed Opera House production prior to New York only.

2225 • JOHN HENRY

OPENED: 01/10/1940   Theatre: 44th Street
Musical   Broadway: 7

Composer: Jacques Wolfe
Lyricist: Roark Bradford
Librettist: Roark Bradford
Producer: Sam Byrd
Director: Anthony Brown; Charles Friedman

Costumes: John Hambleton; **Musical Director:** Donald Vorhees; **Set Design:** Albert Johnson

Songs: All the People on the Levee; Bad, Bad Stacker Lee; Captain's Song, The; Careless Love; Caught Ole Blue; Coonjine; Got a Head Like a Rock; He Went to the East; High Ballin'; How Come I'm Born Wid a Hook in My Hand; I Don't Care Where They Buried My Body; I Want Jesus to Walk with Me; I'm Born in the Country; I'm Gonna Git Down on My Knees; I'm Singing

About a Man; I've Trampled All Over; Jaybird; John Singing About a Man; Let De Sun Sink Down; Lullaby; No Bottom; Now You Talks Might Big in the Country; Old John Henry; Po' Li'l Frenchie; Ship of Zion; So Stand Back, All You Bullies; Stingaree Song; Sundown in My Soul; Take Me a Drink of Whiskey; Where Did You Get Dem High Heeled Shoes?; Whiffer's Song; Workin' on de Railroad; Ya Gotta Bend Down

Cast: Joe Attles; Minto Cato; Ruby Elzy; Alexander Gray; Robert Harvey; George Jones Jr.; Henrietta Lovelace; Paul Robeson; Joshua White

2226 • JOHN MURRAY ANDERSON'S ALMANAC (1929)

Notes: *See MURRAY ANDERSON'S ALMANAC.*

2227 • JOHN MURRAY ANDERSON'S ALMANAC

OPENED: 12/10/1953   Theatre: Imperial
Revue   Broadway: 227

Composer: Richard Adler; Jerry Ross
Lyricist: Richard Adler; Jerry Ross
Librettist: Sumner Locke Elliot; Herbert Farjeon; Jean Kerr; Arthur Macrae; William K. Wells; Laurie Wylie
Director: John Murray Anderson; Cyril Ritchard

Choreographer: Donald Saddler; **Costumes:** Thomas Becher; **Dance Arranger:** Gerald Alters; **Musical Director:** Buster Davis; **Orchestrations:** Ted Royal; **Set Design:** Raoul Pene du Bois; **Vocal Arranger:** Buster Davis

Songs: Acorn in the Meadow; Anema E Corre [7] (C: Salve d'Esposito; L: Harry Akst; Mann Curtis); Earth and the Sky, The (C/L: John Rox); Fini; Harlequinade; Hold 'Em, Joe (C/L: Harry Belafonte); I Dare to Dream (C: Michael Grace; Carl Tucker; L: Sammy Gallup); If Every Month Were June (C: Henry Sullivan; L: John Murray Anderson); Mark Twain (C/L: Harry Belafonte); Merry Little Minuet [2] (C/L: Sheldon Harnick); My Love Is a Wanderer [3] (C/L: Bart Howard); Nightingale, Bring Me a Rose [1] (C: Henry Sullivan; L: John Murray Anderson); Paisan [5]; Raft Song, The [5] (C: David Baker; L: Hermione Gingold; Sheldon Harnick); Riviera, The [4] (C: Cy Coleman; L: Joseph McCarthy Jr.); Sea Is

All Around Us, The [6] (C: David Baker; L: Sheldon Harnick); Souvenirs [5] (C/L: Norman Hackforth); Summer [5]; Sweet Belinda [5] (C: Richard Addinsell; L: Arthur Macrae); Tin Pan Alley (C: Cy Coleman; L: Joseph McCarthy Jr.); True [5]; When Am I Going to Meet Your Mother?; Which Witch? (C: Charles Zwar; L: Alan Melville); You're So Much a Part of Me

Cast: Orson Bean; Harry Belafonte; Polly Bergen; Carleton Carpenter; Nanci Crompton; Billy De Wolfe; Elaine Dunn; Hermione Gingold; Larry Kert; Celia Lipton; Tina Louise; Kay Medford; Alice Pearce; Monique Van Vooren

Notes: [1] Originally in GREENWICH VILLAGE FOLLIES OF 1922. [2] Originally in TWO'S COMPANY. Also in JOY RIDE. [3] Cut after opening. [4] Cut. [5] Cut out of town prior to New York. [6] Cut out of town prior to New York. Also in SHOESTRING REVUE. [7] Added when Tony Bavaar replaced Belafonte.

2228 • JOHNNY JOHNSON

OPENED: 11/19/1936   Theatre: 44th Street
Musical   Broadway: 68

Composer: Kurt Weill
Lyricist: Paul Green
Librettist: Paul Green
Producer: Group Theatre
Director: Lee Strasberg

Costumes: Paul du Pont; **Musical Director:** Lehman Engel; **Orchestrations:** Kurt Weill; **Set Design:** Donald Oenslager

Songs: Aggie's Sewing Machine Song; Allied High Command, The; Asylum Chorus [3]; Battle, The (inst.); Battle of San Juan Hill, The; Captain Valentine's Tango; Democracy's Call; Epitaph [3]; Farewell, Goodbye [3]; How Sweetly Friendship Binds; Hymn to Peace; In No Man's Land (inst.); In Times of War and Tumults; Interlude After Scene III (inst.); Introduction (inst.); Johnny's Arrest and Homecoming; Johnny's Dream (inst.); Johnny's Song (Listen to My Song) [1]; Johnny's Speech; Laughing Generals (inst.); Minny Belle's Song [3]; Mon Ami, My Friend; Music of the Stricken Redeemer (inst.); O, Heart of Love; Oh, the Rio Grande (Cowboy Song); Over in Europe; Prologue [2]; Psychiatry Song, The; Sergeant's Chant; Song of the Goddess [5]; Song of the Guns; Song of the Wounded Frenchman; Tea Song, The;

Up Chickamauga Hill; We Need a Man [3]; West Pointers, The

Cast: Luther Adler; Roman Bohnen; Phoebe Brand; Grover Burgess; Morris Carnovsky; Lee J. Cobb; Russell Collins; Albert Dekker[4]; John Garfield; Elia Kazan; Gerrit Tony Kraber; Will Lee; Robert Lewis; Sanford Meisner; Paula Miller; Joseph Pevney; Susanna Senior; Art Smith

Notes: [1] Later published as "To Love You and to Lose You" with lyrics by Edward Heyman. [2] Music used as "The Liquor Dealer's Dream" in HAPPY END. [3] Not used. [4] Billed as Albert Von Dekker. [5] Music first used for song "Youkali" with lyrics by Roger Fernay.

2229 • JOHNNY PYE AND THE FOOLKILLER

OPENED: 10/31/1993   Theatre: Lamb's
Musical   Off-Broadway: 49

Composer: Randy Courts
Lyricist: Randy Courts; Mark St. Germain
Librettist: Mark St. Germain
Producer: Lamb's Theater Company
Director: Scott Harris

Source: JOHNNY PYE AND THE FOOLKILLER (Story: Stephen Vincent Benet); **Choreographer:** Janet Watson; **Costumes:** Claudia Stephens; **Lighting Designer:** Kenneth Posner; **Musical Director:** Steven M. Alper; **Orchestrations:** Douglas Besterman; **Set Design:** Peter Harrison

Songs: Another Day; Barbershop, The; Challenge to Love; End of the Road, The; Epilogue (The Answer); Goodbye Johnny; Handle with Care; Land Where There Is No Death, The; Married with Children; Never Felt Better in My Life; Occupations; Shower of Sparks; Time Passes

Cast: Peter Gerety; Conor Gillespie; Ralston Hall; Kaitlin Hopkins; Michael Ingram; Daniel Jenkins; Mark Lotito; Spiro Malas; Tanny McDonald; Heather Lee Soroka

2230 • JOKERS

OPENED: 10/14/1986
Musical   Closed out of town

Composer: Luigi Creatore; Hugo Peretti; George David Weiss

Lyricist: Luigi Creatore; Hugo Peretti; George David Weiss
Librettist: Luigi Creatore; Hugo Peretti; George David Weiss
Producer: Goodspeed Opera House
Director: Martin Charnin

Source: GIN GAME, THE (Play: D.L. Coburn); **Choreographer:** Linda Haberman; **Costumes:** Ann Hould-Ward; **Dance Arranger:** Michael Skloff; **Lighting Designer:** Judy Rasmuson; **Musical Director:** Paul Trueblood; **Orchestrations:** Larry Wilcox; **Set Design:** Leonard John Joy; **Vocal Arranger:** Paul Trueblood

Songs: Gin Game, The; I Can't Believe It; I Was Gonna Be Big; It's a Duck; It's Only a Game; Jokers; Make Believe; Old Is In; One More Time; Pact with the Devil, A; Secrets; Something Tells Me; That Does the Trick for Me; That's a Ridiculous Statement!; Zanzibar

Cast: Sasha Charnin; Nick Corley; Ronny Graham; Kim Hunter; Eddie Korbich

Notes: Norma Terris Theatre, Goodspeed Opera House.

2231 • JOLEY

OPENED: 03/08/1979
Musical   Closed out of town

Composer: Milton De Lugg
Lyricist: Herbert Hartig
Librettist: Herbert Hartig
Producer: Jeff Britton; Bob Funking; Bill Stutler
Director: Jay Harnick

Choreographer: George Bunt; **Costumes:** Carol H. Beule; **Dance Arranger:** Donald Johnston; **Lighting Designer:** Marc B. Weiss; **Musical Director:** Liza Redfield; **Orchestrations:** Walt Levinsky; **Set Design:** David Chapman; **Vocal Arranger:** Donald Johnston

Songs: Dullest Couple in Scarsdale; 'Ello England 'Ello; Finale; Graceful Exit, A; Henrietta; Here We Are Again; I Gotta Perform; Kissing Rock, The; Mama; Melons; Mrs. Ulysses; Oh! You Beautiful Doll [1]; Pardon Me Porter; Pettin' on the Old Porch Swing; Robert E. Lee Cakewalk [2]; Ruby; Song of the Immigrant Mothers; This Time; Times Square; You Ain't Seen Nuthin' Yet

Cast: Jerry Jarrett; Mitchell Jason; Larry Kert; Suzanne Walker

Notes: No program available. [1] May be the popular tune of the same name. [2] May be based on "Waitin' for the Robert E. Lee" by Lewis Muir and L. Wolfe Gilbert.

2232 • JOLLY BACHELORS, THE

OPENED: 01/06/1910   Theatre: Broadway
Musical   Broadway: 84

Composer: Raymond Hubbell
Lyricist: Glen MacDonough
Librettist: Glen MacDonough
Producer: Lew Fields
Director: Ned Wayburn

Costumes: Melville Ellis; **Orchestrations:** Frank Saddler; **Set Design:** Arthur Voegtlin

Songs: Aeroplane Joy Ride, The (The Air Ship Joy Ride); Anything Can Happen in New York [6]; College Education, A [6]; Come Along, Mandy [1] (C/L: Jack Norworth; C: Nora Bayes); Dinny Maginnity [6]; Freshie, O Freshie; Half Moon, The [6]; Has Anybody Here Seen Kelly [2] (C/L: Will Letters; C.W. Murphy; L: William C. McKenna); Hey! Hey! Hey! (C: Burt Peters; L: Marvin Lee); If the Managers Only Thought the Same As Mother [4] (C: Ted Snyder; L: Irving Berlin); I've Lost My Gal [3] (C: Egbert Van Alstyne; L: Harry Williams); Language of Signs; Little Bit of Blarney, A [3]; Little Things [3]; Luncheon Line, The; Maggie Your Roast Is Burning [6]; Mind Reader, The [3]; Moon, Moon, Moon [3]; Music with Meals [6]; My Prince o' Dreams [6]; My Yesterday Shop [6]; Never Try to Be Somebody What You Ain't [6]; Oh, That Beautiful Rag [5] (C: Ted Snyder; L: Irving Berlin); Please, Oh, Please; Red Cross Girl, The; Rosa Rosetta (C: Albert Von Tilzer; L: Earle C. Jones; Jack Norworth); Rounders' Serenade, The [6]; Savannah; Silver Path, The [6]; Single Bird, The; Stop That Rag (Keep on Playing Honey) (C: Ted Snyder; L: Irving Berlin); Sweet Marie, Make a Rag-a-Time Dance with Me [4] (C: Ted Snyder; L: Irving Berlin); Tax the Bachelors; That's What We Do at the Club [6]; Walk This Way [3]; We'uns from Dixie; What Am I Going to Do to Make You Love Me?; Young America (C/L: Jack Norworth; C: Nora Bayes)

Cast: Nora Bayes; Elizabeth Brice; Nat Fields; Stella Mayhew; Jack Norworth; Josie Sadler; Billie Taylor; Gertrude Vanderbilt

Notes: [1] Based on the English song by Tom Mallor, Alfred J. Lawrence and Henry Gifford. [2] McKenna Americanized the lyrics. [3] Out Kansas City 12/04/10. [4] Not in program. [5] Sheet music only. Also in UP AND DOWN BROADWAY. [6] Sheet music only.

2233 • JOLLY MUSKETEER, THE

OPENED: 11/14/1898   Theatre: Broadway
Musical   Broadway: 32

Composer: Julian Edwards
Lyricist: Stanislaus Stange
Librettist: Stanislaus Stange
Producer: Jefferson De Angelis Opera Company
Director: Richard Barker

Set Design: Walter Burridge; Ernest Gros

Songs: Courtship; Dancing Lesson, The; Explanation I Demand, An; Flower Song (Introduction); Friends; I Am More Than Young, I Am Childish; Just to Pass the Time Away; King's Own Musketeers, The; Letter from Papa, The; Love for an Hour; Oh, Happy Day; Revenge Is Sweet; Sweet the Birds Were Singing; That Sweet Oblivion-Drink; There Are Many Kinds of Kisses [1]; This Is Most Exciting; Wicked Man; Willful Woman; Wishing Well, The; Woman, Source of All Our Bliss; Woman, Woman

Cast: Jefferson De Angelis; Maud Hollins; Harry MacDonough; Joseph Smiley; Bertha Waltzinger; Van Rensselaer Wheeler

Notes: [1] Sheet music only.

2234 • JOLLYANNA

OPENED: 08/11/1952
Musical   Closed out of town

Composer: Sammy Fain
Lyricist: E.Y. Harburg
Librettist: E.Y. Harburg; Fred Saidy
Producer: Edwin Lester
Director: Jack Donahue

Source: FLAHOOLEY (Musical: E.Y. Harburg; Fred Saidy); **Choreographer:** Ruthanna Boris; Jack Donahue; **Costumes:** Jay Morley; **Lighting Designer:** Peggy Clark; **Musical Director:** Louis Adrian; **Orchestrations:** Hershy Kay; **Set Design:** Howard Bay

Songs: B.G. Bigelow, Inc [1]; Come Back Little Genie [1]; Fabulous (C: William Friml); Gal Named Cinderella, A; How Lucky Can You Get?; Jollyanna (C: William Friml); Jump, Chillun, Jump [2]; Leave a Message (C: William Friml); Little Bit of Magic [4] (C: Burton Lane); Scheherazade [1]; Springtime Cometh, The [1]; What's Gonna Happen? (C: Burton Lane); World Is Your Balloon, The [1]; You Too Can Be a Puppet [3] (C: William Friml)

Cast: Bil Baird Marionettes; John Beal; Bobby Clark; Martha Errolle; Mitzi Gaynor; Biff McGuire; Beverly Tyler

Notes: Also see FLAHOOLEY. This show opened at the L.A. Civic Light Opera. [1] From FLAHOOLEY. [2] Same song as "Jump, Little Chillun" in FLAHOOLEY. [3] Has same lyric as song in FLAHOOLEY. [4] Written for original FLAHOOLEY but not used when Lane left the project.

2235 • JOLSON

OPENED: 11/08/1978
Musical   Closed out of town

Composer: L. Russell Brown; Irwin Levine
Lyricist: L. Russell Brown; Irwin Levine
Librettist: Leslie Eberhard; David Levy
Director: Bill Guske

Choreographer: Bill Guske; **Dance Arranger:** Ken Collins; **Lighting Designer:** Helen Pond; Herbert Senn; **Musical Director:** Jonathan Anderson; **Orchestrations:** Jimmy Wisner; **Set Design:** Helen Pond; Herbert Senn; **Vocal Arranger:** Jonathan Anderson; Mel Pahl

Songs: Boyola; Falena; Give Me a Good Old Mammy Song; Good Guy Always Gets the Girl, The; I Got a Song in Me; If It Wasn't for You; It's a Great Idea; Jolie's Back in Town; Little Sammy; Nobody Do Me Like My Daddy Do Me; Question, The; Tappin-G-Minor; We're Only Here for a Day; When Ya Get Yourself

Married; Who Needs Love; Why Can't I Be Happy Too?

Cast: Clive Baldwin; Maureen Brennan; Joseph Leon; Sherry Rooney

2236 • JONAH (1966)

OPENED: 02/15/1966   Theatre: American Place
Musical   Off-Broadway: 24

Composer: Meyer Kupferman
Lyricist: Paul Goodman
Librettist: Paul Goodman
Producer: American Place Theatre
Director: Lawrence Kornfeld

Choreographer: Remy Charlip; **Costumes:** Remy Charlip; **Lighting Designer:** Roger Morgan; **Set Design:** Remy Charlip

Songs: Angel's Ballet; Day After Day; Evocation; Forty Days; Hey, What's This?; I Am a Little Worm; I Cried for My Troubles; I'll Carry You an Inch; Jonah's Melodrama; Leviathan; Madrigal; Miserere; My God, Why Hast Thou Forsaken Me?; Paradise Quintet; Puppet Dream; Sailor's Round; Sleep Little Mouse; Suns that Daily Rise, The; There's Nothing New Under the Sun

Cast: Yolande Bavan; Sorrell Booke; John Coe; Earle Hyman; Ruth Jaroslow

2237 • JONAH (1990)

OPENED: 03/20/1990   Theatre: Public
Musical   Off-Broadway: 8

Composer: Elizabeth Swados
Lyricist: Elizabeth Swados
Librettist: Elizabeth Swados
Producer: N.Y. Shakespeare Festival
Director: Elizabeth Swados

Source: JONAH AND THE WHALE (Novel: Robert Nathan); **Choreographer:** Bill Castellino; **Costumes:** Judy Dearing; **Lighting Designer:** Beverly Emmons; **Musical Director:** Michael S. Sottile; **Set Design:** Michael E. Downs

Cast: Jake Ehrenreich; Ann Marie Milazzo; Cathy Porter

Notes: No songs listed in program.

2238 • JONICA

OPENED: 04/07/1930   Theatre: Craig
Musical   Broadway: 40

Composer: Joseph Meyer
Lyricist: William Moll
Librettist: Moss Hart
Producer: William B. Friedlander
Director: William B. Friedlander

Source: HAVE A GOOD TIME, JONICA (Play: Dorothy Heyward); **Choreographer:** Pal'mere Brandeaux; **Musical Director:** Carl C. Gray; **Set Design:** William Hawley

Songs: Apple and the Bough, The; Au Revoir; Beautiful Girls; Gotta Do My Duty [1]; Here in My Heart; I Gave You Me [1]; I Want Someone (C/L: William B. Friedlander); March of the Rice and Old Shoes; Million Good Reasons, A; My Story Ends that Way [1]; Night It Happened, The; One Step Nearer the Moon; Specially Made for You; Tie Your Cares to a Melody; Tonight or Never (L: William B. Friedlander); Wedding Parade, The

Cast: Joyce Barbour; Earle S. Dewey; Madeline Grey; Bert Mathews; Jerry Norris; June O'Dea; Neil Roy; Harry T. Shannon; Irene Swor

Notes: [1] Out Washington, D.C.

2239 • JONIN'

OPENED: 12/17/1985   Theatre: New York Shakespeare Festival
Play   Off-Broadway: 46

Additional Music: Bill Toles
Author: Gerard Brown
Producer: N.Y. Shakespeare Festival; Joseph Papp
Director: Andre Robinson Jr.

Costumes: Karen Perry; **Lighting Designer:** Ric Rogers; **Set Design:** Wynn P. Thomas

Songs: Dreams (Follow Your Dreams) (C: Kenneth Taylor; L: Tonya Wynne); Dreams (C/L: Sheldon Becton); Foreign Eyes (C/L: Ralph Piper Jr.; Michael Raye); Hymn, The (C/L: Noble Lee Lester); Party with Me (C/L: Bill Toles)

Cast: Jerome Preston Bates; Carla Brothers; Gregory Holtz Sr.; Eriq LaSalle; Eric A. Payne; Jaime Perry; Timothy Simonson; John Canada Terrell; Mark Vaughn

Notes: Fraternal lyrics by Jerome Preston Bates.

2240 • JORROCKS

OPENED: 12/22/1966   Theatre: New
Musical   London: 181

Composer: David Heneker
Lyricist: David Heneker
Librettist: Beverly Cross
Producer: Donald Albery
Director: Val May

Source: JORROCKS JAUNTS & JOLLITIES and HANDLEY CROSS, (Novels: R.S. Surtees); **Choreographer:** Irving Davies; **Musical Director:** Grant Hossack; **Set Design:** Disley Jones

Songs: Ask Mr. Jorrocks; Belinda; Cat and the Custard Pot, The; Fresh, Bloomin' Health; Give Me a Pink Coat; Happiest Man Alive, The; Hounds of John Jorrock's, The; I Don't Want to Behave Like a Lady; I Don't Want to Say Goodnight; I Will Recall the Day; Jorrocks; Little Bit Individual, A; Love Your Neighbor; Midsummer Fox; Once He's In; Opening Act I; Opening Act II; Sport of Kings, The; Toasts of the Town; We'd Imagined a Man; When You're In; You Can Depend on Me

Cast: Joss Ackland; Paul Eddington; Cheryl Kennedy; Bernard Lloyd; Richard Stilgoe

2241 • JOSEPH AND MARY

OPENED: 1995
Musical

Composer: Randy Courts; Mark St. Germain
Lyricist: Randy Courts; Mark St. Germain
Director: Patricia Birch

Musical Director: Aaron Hagan

Songs: Annunciation, The; Happy Enough; Herod; Only Human; Prologue of the Magi; Song of the Shepherds, The; Thinking Always Thinking; We Believe; Where is the Angel Now

Cast: Donna Bullock; DeMattis; Kris Kristofferson; Francis Ruivivar; J.K. Simmons; Peter Slutsker

Notes: A reading at the Lamb's Theatre Company.

2242 • JOSEPH AND THE AMAZING TECHNICOLOR DREAMCOAT

OPENED: 11/18/1981   Theatre: Entermedia
Musical   Off-Broadway: 751

Composer: Andrew Lloyd Webber
Lyricist: Tim Rice
Producer: Zev Bufman; Melvyn J. Estrin; Susan R. Rose
Director: Tony Tanner

Choreographer: Tony Tanner; **Costumes:** Judith Dolan; **Lighting Designer:** Barry Arnold; **Musical Director:** David Friedman; **Orchestrations:** Martin Silvestri; Jeremy Stone; **Set Design:** Karl Eigsti

Songs: Any Dream Will Do; Benjamin Calypso; Brothers Came to Egypt, The; Close Every Door; Go, Go, Go, Joseph; Grovel, Grovel; Jacob and Sons; Jacob in Egypt; Joseph All the Time; Joseph's Coat; Joseph's Dream; May I Return to the Beginning; One More Angel in Heaven; Pharoah's Dream Explained; Pharoah's Story; Poor, Poor Joseph; Poor, Poor Pharoah; Potiphar; Song of the King; Stone the Crows; Those Canaan Days; Who's the Thief

Cast: David Ardao; Laurie Beechman; Tom Carder; Bill Hutton; Robert Hyman; Steve McNaughton; Charlie Serrano; Gordon Stanley

Notes: This show opened at the Brooklyn Academy of Music 12/26/76 where it ran 22 performances and again 12/13/77 for 24 performances. It then moved to the Entermedia Theatre Off Broadway. On January 27, 1982 it moved to the Royale Theatre.

2243 • JOURNEY OF SNOW WHITE, THE

OPENED: 05/29/1975   Theatre: Judson Poets'
Musical   Off-Off-Broadway: 10

Composer: Al Carmines
Lyricist: Al Carmines
Librettist: Al Carmines

Choreographer: Katherine Litz; **Costumes:** Michele Edwards; Ira Siff; **Lighting Designer:** Earl Eidman; **Set Design:** Earl Eidman

Songs: Becoming Is a Lot Like Dying; Big Apple; Creatures Go to Sleep in Peace; Darkness Here Is Only Darkness; Dirge; Every Woman Brings Something with Her; Everything Is Only for a Little While; Everytime I Look I See a Stranger; Further Comments; Girl Really Needs a Woman, A; Goodbye; Hi There!; I Am a Handsome Prince; I Am an Absence; I Don't Want to Be a Mirror Anymore; I Hate Being Me; I Have a Charge to Fulfill; I Love Myself in Two; I Remember a Feeling Called Love; I'm Here and You're Here; I'm Snow White — A Human Woman; Image of Our Retina Has Gone, The; Introductions; Kingly Duties; La-La-La-La-La — Love Is Our Epistemology!; Night! Healing Darkness!; Oh Mio Snow White!; On the Checkerboard of Time; Scoobi-doo; Spirits of Banality and Hate!; There Can Be One and There Can Be Two; Wandering, Walking Every Day; We Think You Ought to Stay; When Everything Human Has Failed You; When You Looked at Me for the First Time; Who's This Chick?

Cast: Essie Borden; Semina De Laurentis; Bobby De Russo; Eric Ellenburg; Lee Guilliatt; Dan Held; Julie Kurnitz; Katherine Litz; Michael Petro; Clarke Salonis; Ira Siff; Phyllis Somerville; Margaret Wright

2244 • JOY (0000)

Unproduced

Composer: Harvey Schmidt
Lyricist: Tom Jones

Source: ROMEO AND JULIET (Play: William Shakespeare)

Songs: Follow Along with Me [1]

Notes: [1] Later in PORTFOLIO REVUE.

2245 • JOY (1970)

OPENED: 01/27/1970   Theatre: New
Revue   Off-Broadway: 205

Composer: Oscar Brown Jr.
Lyricist: Oscar Brown Jr.
Librettist: Oscar Brown Jr.
Producer: Sunbar Productions

Lighting Designer: F. Mitchell Dana

Songs: Afro Blue (C/L: Oscar Brown Jr.; Mongo Santamaria); Brother, Where Are You?; Brown Baby; Flowing to the Sea; Funky World; Funny

Feelin' (C/L: Oscar Brown Jr.; Luis Henrique);
If I Only Had (C/L: Charles Aznavour; Oscar
Brown Jr.); Mother Africa's Day (C/L: Oscar
Brown Jr.; Sivuca); Much As I Love You
(C/L: Oscar Brown Jr.; Luis Henrique); New
Generation, A (C/L: Oscar Brown Jr.; Luis
Henrique); Nothing but a Fool (C/L: Oscar
Brown Jr.); Sky and Sea (C/L: Johnny Alf; Oscar
Brown Jr.); Time; Under the Sun; What Is a
Friend? (C/L: Oscar Brown Jr.; Luis Henrique);
Wimmen's Ways

Cast: Oscar Brown Jr.; Jean Pace; Sivuca

Notes: More a concert than a theatre piece.

2246 • JOY RIDE
OPENED: 05/12/1958
Revue   Closed out of town

Librettist: Richard Maury; Lester Pine; Danny
Simon; Neil Simon
Producer: Ray Golden; Huntington Hartford
Director: Ray Golden

Choreographer: Nick Castle; Bob Hamilton;
Costumes: Campbell; **Musical Director:** Milton
Greene; **Orchestrations:** Milton Greene; **Set
Design:** Jay Krause

Songs: Charlie on the M.T.A. (L: Bess Lomax);
Churinga (C/L: Milton Greene); Element of
Doubt [3] (C: Sammy Fain; L: Howard Dietz);
Gruntles (C/L: Ray Golden; Sy Kleinman;
C: Philip Charig); Hey, Chicago (C: Dean Fuller;
L: Marshall Barer); Holiday in Court (C: Jay
Navarre; L: I.A.L. Diamond; Ray Golden); Joy
Ride (C: Ray Golden; L: Paul Francis Webster);
Man's Inhumanity to Man [1] (C: Charles
Strouse; L: Michael Stewart); Merry Little Minuet
[2] (C/L: Sheldon Harnick); My Crazy Sister
Rose (C: Edward Scott; L: Leonard Adelson);
Story of Alice, The (C: Jerry Bock; L: Larry
Holofcener); To Be or Not to Be (C: Philip
Charig; L: Ray Golden; Milton Pascal; Dan
Shapiro); World of Strangers (C: Sammy Fain;
L: Ray Golden; Paul Francis Webster)

Cast: Dorothy Greener; Joel Grey; Will Holt;
Conrad Janis; Pat Nestor; Barbara Nichols

Notes: [1] Also in MEDIUM RARE and SHOE-
STRING REVUE (1955). [2] Also in TWO'S
COMPANY and JOHN MURRAY

ANDERSON'S ALMANAC. [3] Also in
ZIEGFELD FOLLIES OF 1957.

2247 • JOY SHOP, THE
OPENED: 1924

Songs: Levee Lou (C: Joseph E. Howard; L: Charles
K. Harris)

Notes: No other information available.

2248 • JOYFUL NOISE, A
OPENED: 12/15/1966   Theatre: Mark Hellinger
Musical   Broadway: 12

Composer: Oscar Brand; Paul Nassau
Lyricist: Oscar Brand; Paul Nassau
Librettist: Edward Padula
Producer: Sid Bernstein; L. Slade Brown; Edward
Padula
Director: Edward Padula

Source: INSOLENT BREED, THE (Novel: Borden
Deal); **Choreographer:** Michael Bennett;
Costumes: Peter Joseph; **Dance Arranger:** Lee
Holdridge; **Lighting Designer:** Peter Wexler;
Musical Director: Rene Wiegert; **Orchestrations:**
William Stegmeyer; **Set Design:** Peter Wexler

Songs: All My Life [1]; Ballad Maker; Barefoot Gal;
Big Guitar, The; Clog Dance; Dollar Song, A [1];
Fool's Gold; Hymn, The [1]; I Like to Look My
Best; I Love Nashville; I Say Yes; I'm Ready;
Joyful Noise, A; Longtime Travelin'; Lord, You
Sure Know How to Make a Sunday [3]; Love Was;
Nashville U.S.A. [2]; Natural Man [1]; No Talent;
Not Me; Quiet Town [1]; Spring Time of the Year;
Swinging a Dance; To the Top; Until Today; We
Won't Forget to Write; Whither Thou Goest

Cast: Clifford David; Karen Morrow; Leland
Palmer; John Raitt; Swen Swenson; Tommy
Tune; Art Wallace; Susan Watson

Notes: [1] Out Shady Grove Music Fair prior to
N.Y. [2] Changed to "I Love Nashville." [3]
Changed to "Lord, You Sure Know How to
Make a New Day."

2249 • JOYS OF YOUTH
OPENED: 1941
Musical

Composer: Leo Fall
Lyricist: John A. Bassett
Librettist: John A. Bassett

Source: BRUDERLEIN FEIN (Musical: Leo Fall; Julius Wilhelm)

Songs: After This [1] (C: Emil Hilb; L: John A. Bassett); Brother of Mine; Do You Remember the Night in May?; Not Too Fast and Not Too Slowly; Youth Is Gay

Notes: A one-act operetta based on Fall's 1908 work. Whether ever produced is unknown. [1] Music and lyrics original to this production.

2250 • JUBA

OPENED: 02/12/1991   Theatre: AMAS
Musical   Off-Off-Broadway

Composer: Robert Walden
Lyricist: Wendy Lamb
Librettist: Wendy Lamb
Director: Sheldon Epps

Choreographer: Mercedes Ellington; **Costumes:** Daniel Lawson; **Lighting Designer:** Susan White; **Musical Director:** Ted Kociolek; **Set Design:** James Leonard Joy

Songs: Challenge Match; Eighth Wonder, The; Every Step You Take; Five Points; Gift, The; Heartless; Here and Now; Irish Air; It Wouldn't Be Fair; Juba; Kick Up Your Heels; Listen to Me; Long Way, A; My Blue-Eyed Gal; My Yellow Sun; Next Time We Meet; No Irish Need Apply; One Chance; Prologue; Rivals; Take Heart; This Isn't What I Expected; Today Is the Day; You Do

Cast: Steve Boles; James Brennan; Katherine Buffaloe; Lawrence Clayton; Mark Hardy; Ken Prymus; Kevin Ramsey; Terri White

2251 • JUBALAY

Notes: *See A BISTRO CAR ON THE CNR.*

2252 • JUBILEE

OPENED: 10/12/1935   Theatre: Imperial
Musical   Broadway: 169

Composer: Cole Porter
Lyricist: Cole Porter

Librettist: Moss Hart
Producer: Max Gordon; Sam Harris
Director: Hassard Short; Monty Woolley

Choreographer: Albertina Rasch; **Costumes:** Connie DePinna; Irene Sharaff; **Lighting Designer:** Hassard Short; **Musical Director:** Frank Tours; **Orchestrations:** Robert Russell Bennett; **Set Design:** Jo Mielziner

Songs: Beach Scene; Begin the Beguine; Cabinet Music; Entrance of Eric; Ev'rybod-ee Who's Anybod-ee; Gather Ye Autographs While Ye May; Gay Little Wives (Six Little Wives); Good Morning, Miss Standing; Greek Scene [1]; Jubilee Presentation; Judgement of Paris, The; Just One of Those Things [3]; Kling-Kling Bird on the Divi-Divi Tree, The; Me and Marie; Mr. and Mrs. Smith; My Loulou; My Most Intimate Friend; Our Crown; Picture of Me without You, A; Sing "Jubilee" [1]; Sunday Morning Breakfast Time; Swing That Swing; There's Nothing Like Swimming [1]; To Get Away; Waltz Down the Aisle [2]; We're Off to Feathermore; What a Nice Municipal Park; When Love Comes Your Way; When Me, Mowgli, Love; Why Shouldn't I?; Yours [1]

Cast: Margaret Adams; Mary Boland; May Boley; Montgomery Clift; Melville Cooper; Ted Fetter; June Knight; Marc Platt; Charles Walters; Derek Williams

Notes: [1] Cut prior to opening. [2] Cut prior to opening. It was also cut from ANYTHING GOES and an unproduced musical, ONCE UPON A TIME. [3] Not the same song as in THE NEW YORKERS (1930).

2253 • JUDY

OPENED: 02/08/1927   Theatre: Royale
Musical   Broadway: 104

Composer: Charles Rosoff
Lyricist: Leo Robin
Librettist: Mark Swan
Producer: John Henry Mears
Director: John Hayden

Source: JUDY FORGOT (Play: Mark Swan); **Choreographer:** Bobby Connolly; **Costumes:** Hugh Willoughby; **Musical Director:** Sid Riley; **Orchestrations:** Maurice DePackh

Songs: Curfew Shall Not Ring Tonight, The; Hard to Get Along With; Hobohemia; Judy, Who D'Ya Love?; Looking for a Thrill [1]; One Baby; Poor Cinderella; Pretty Little Stranger; Six Little Cinderellas; Start Stompin'; Wear Your Sunday Smile; What a Whale of a Difference a Woman Can Make; When Gentlemen Grew Whiskers and Ladies Grew Old; When the One You Care For

Cast: Dorothy Casey; Elizabeth Mears; George Meeker; Charles Purcell; Queenie Smith

Notes: [1] Cut after opening.

2254 • JUDY FORGOT

OPENED: 10/06/1910   Theatre: Broadway
Musical   Broadway: 44

Composer: Silvio Hein
Lyricist: Avery Hopwood
Librettist: Avery Hopwood
Producer: Daniel V. Arthur
Director: Daniel V. Arthur

Choreographer: Lewis Morton; **Musical Director:** Anton Heindl

Songs: Give Me All the Flowers (Flower Song); Good Morning Judge (C/L: John Golden; C: Silvio Hein; L: Avery Hopwood); I Want a Little Lovin', Sometimes (C/L: Chris Smith); Judy Two-Step, The (inst.); Judy Waltz, The (inst.); My Dream, Dream Man [1]; My Lotus Flower [1]; My Soldier Boy; My Toreador; Quarrel, The; Society Circus, The; Song of the Honeymoon, The (Honeymoon); Star Factory, The; Students' Serenade; Thinky Thanky Thunk; Turkish Love Song; Whoop 'er Up (with a Whoop-La-La) (C: Will Marion Cook; L: Andrew B. Sterling); World Is Full of Women's Eyes, The

Cast: Marie Cahill; Anna Ford; Joseph Santley; Truly Shattuck; Arthur Stanford

Notes: [1] Sheet music only.

2255 • JULIE

OPENED: 1934
Play   Closed out of town

Composer: Hugo Rubens
Lyricist: Jules Loman; Allan Roberts
Author: Frederic Arnold Kummer

Producer: Ivan Cedar
Director: Harry Wagstaff Gribble

Set Design: Stewart Chaney

Songs: Love in My Life, The; Tea Leaves Say Good-Bye, The

Cast: Paula Laurence; George Meader; Lenore Ulric

Notes: Out of town Long Island and Westport. No songs listed in program.

2256 • JULIET
Notes: *See ENTER JULIET.*

2257 • JULIUS CAESAR

OPENED: 11/11/1937   Theatre: Mercury
Play   Broadway: 157

Author: William Shakespeare
Producer: John Houseman; Orson Welles
Director: Orson Welles

Incidental Music: Marc Blitzstein; **Musical Director:** L.I. Epstein; **Set Design:** Samuel Leve

Songs: Orpheus (C: Marc Blitzstein; L: William Shakespeare)

Cast: Francis Carpenter; Joseph Cotten; George Coulouris; Martin Gabel; Joseph Holland; Norman Lloyd; Stefan Schnabel; Hiram Sherman; Orson Welles

2258 • JUMBO

OPENED: 11/16/1935   Theatre: Hippodrome
Musical   Broadway: 221

Composer: Richard Rodgers
Lyricist: Lorenz Hart
Librettist: Ben Hecht; Charles MacArthur
Producer: Billy Rose
Director: George Abbott; John Murray Anderson

Choreographer: Allan K. Foster; **Costumes:** Raoul Pene du Bois; James Reynolds; Wynn; **Musical Director:** Adolph Deutsch; **Orchestrations:** Murray Cutter; Adolph Deutsch; Joseph Nussbaum; Conrad Salinger; Hans Spialek; **Set Design:** Albert Johnson; **Vocal Arranger:** Charles Henderson

Songs: Circus Is on Parade, The; Diavalo; Laugh; Little Girl Blue; Memories of Madison Square Garden; More I See of Other Girls, The (Elephant Song) [2]; Most Beautiful Girl in the World, The; My Romance; Over and Over Again; Song of the Roustabouts, The; There's a Small Hotel [1]; Women

Cast: Big Rosie; Jimmy Durante; Gloria Grafton; Poodles Hanneford; Bob Lawrence; W.J. McCarthy; Ray Miller; Donald Novis; Arthur Sinclair; Paul Whiteman and His Orchestra

Notes: [1] Cut. Added to ON YOUR TOES. [2] Not used.

2259 • JUMP FOR JOY

OPENED: 07/10/1941
Revue   Closed out of town: 101

Composer: Duke Ellington
Lyricist: Paul Francis Webster
Librettist: Hal Fimberg; Langston Hughes; Sid Kuller; Charles Leonard; Richard Weil
Producer: American Revue Theatre; Walter Jurmann
Director: Nick Castle; Sid Kuller; Everett Wile

Choreographer: Nick Castle; **Orchestrations:** Hal Borne; Duke Ellington; William Strayhorn; **Vocal Arranger:** Hal Borne; Eddie Jones

Songs: Bli-Blip (L: Duke Ellington; Sid Kuller); Brown-Skin Gal in the Calico Gown, The; Chocolate Shake; Cindy with the Two Left Feet (C: Hal Borne); Clementine [?] (C/L: Billy Strayhorn); Cymbal Sockin' Sam (C: Mickey Rooney; L: Sidney Miller); Emperor's Bones, The (C: Otis Rene); Flame Indigo; Flamingo [2] (C: Ted Grouya; L: Ed Anderson); Giddybug Gallop, The (inst.) [2]; Hickory Stick (C: Hal Borne); I Got It Bad and That Ain't Good; If Life Were All Peaches and Cream (C: Hal Borne); I've Got a Passport from Georgia (and I'm Going to the U.S.A. [1] (C: Hal Borne; L: Ray Golden; Paul Francis Webster); Jump for Joy (L: Sid Kuller; Paul Francis Webster); Just a-Settin' and a-Rockin' [2] (C: Duke Ellington; Billy Strayhorn; L: Lee Gaines); Just Squeeze Me [3] (L: Lee Gaines; Paul Francis Webster); Nothin' (C: Hal Borne; L: Ray Golden; Sid Kuller); Old-Fashioned Waltz (L: Sid Kuller); Pot, Pan and Skillet; Rocks in My Bed [2] (L: Duke Ellington); Sharp Easter (L: Sid Kuller); Shhhhh! He's on the

Beat! (L: Hal Fimberg; Sid Kuller); Stump Caprice (C: Mercer Ellington); Subtle Slough [2] (L: Duke Ellington); Sun-Tanned Tenth of the Nation (C: Hal Borne; Otis Rene); Take the 'A' Train [2] (C/L: Billy Strayhorn); Two Left Feet [2] (C: Hal Borne)

Cast: Ivy Anderson; Marie Bryant; Dorothy Dandridge; Duke Ellington and His Orchestra; Al Guster; Hi-Hatters, The [5]; Herb Jeffries; Pot, Pan and Skillet; Rockets, The [4]; Wonderful Smith; Paul White

Notes: Opened at the Mayan Theatre, Los Angeles. [1] Cut after opening. [2] Added after opening. [3] Cut from 1958 revival. [4] Consisted of Henry Roberts, Andrew Jackson and John Thomas. [5] Consisted of Clarence Landry, Udell Johnson and Vernod Bradley.

2260 • JUMPERS

OPENED: 04/22/1974   Theatre: Billy Rose
Play   Broadway: 48

Author: Tom Stoppard
Producer: Billy Rose Foundation; Frederick Brisson; John F. Kennedy Center; Roger L. Stevens
Director: Peter Wood

Choreographer: Dennis Nahat; **Costumes:** Willa Kim; Fernando Sanchez; **Lighting Designer:** Gilbert V. Hemsley Jr.; **Orchestrations:** Claus Ogerman; **Set Design:** Josef Svoboda

Songs: Beyond My Reach (C: Claus Ogerman; L: Mort Goode); Forget Yesterday [1] (C: Marc Wilkinson; L: Tom Stoppard)

Cast: Brian Bedford; Jill Clayburgh; Remak Ramsay; Robert Rhys

Notes: [1] London production.

2261 • JUMPING JUPITER

OPENED: 03/06/1911   Theatre: New York
Musical   Broadway: 24

Composer: Karl Hoschna
Lyricist: Richard Carle
Librettist: Richard Carle; Sydney Rosenfeld
Producer: H.H. Frazee; George Lederer
Director: Richard Carle

Musical Director: Hans S. Linne

Songs: Angelo (C: Irving Berlin; L: Ted Snyder); Angle Worm Wriggle [2]; Bill and Coo [2]; Cupid's Cooking School (Fascination); Dearie, Won't You Snuggle Close to Me?; Finale Act II [1] (C: Hans S. Linne); Geography (C: Albert Von Tilzer; L: Junie McCree); Give Me a Good Havana [1]; Honeymooning Honey in Bombay [4] (C/L: Dave Reed Jr.); I Am a Poor Unfortunate [2]; I Like to Have a Flock of Men Around Me (C: Harry Auracher; L: Francis DeWitt); I'm Awfully Afraid of Girls; I'm Crazy to Marry Again [4]; It All Goes Up in Smoke (C: Grace LeRoy Kahn; L: Gus Kahn); It Can't Be Did (C: Irving Berlin; L: Ted Snyder); Kiss Me; Little Girl, I Love You [4]; Little Old Dream Waltz [1] (C: Grace LeRoy Kahn; L: Gus Kahn); Love Me [1]; Mail Man, The; Meet Me Tonight at 9; Miss Helen of Troy [1] (C/L: Richard Carle); Nothing (C/L: James Brockman); Oh Innocent Young Thing [2]; Oh You Chicago, Oh You New York [2]; Only a Man; Pet of the Family; Possum Rag; Rest of the Week She's Mine, The (Caroline) (C: John W. Bratton; L: Charles W. Taylor); Rosa Rosana; Soap Bubble Days [3] (C: Grace LeRoy Kahn; L: Gus Kahn); Songs of Long Ago, The [4]; Teachers [4]; 'Thank You, Kind Sir!' Said She (C: Irving Berlin; L: Ted Snyder); To the Strains of That Wedding March; What Has Become of the English Language [4]; What Would My Poor Wife Say [4]

Cast: Richard Carle; Ina Claire; Jeanne Eagels; Edna Wallace Hopper

Notes: [1] Out of town only, I believe. [2] Out Boston 4/10/11. [3] ASCAP/Library of Congress only. [4] Sheet music only.

2262 • JUNE BRIDE, THE

OPENED: 09/23/1912
Musical   Closed out of town

Composer: Edmund Eysler
Lyricist: E. Ray Goetz
Librettist: Edgar Smith
Producer: Lew Fields; Joe Weber
Director: J.C. Huffman; Gustave Sohlke

Source: JOHANN DER ZWEITE Musical: Edward Eysler; Carl Lindau; Leo Stein); **Musical Director:** August Kleinecke

Songs: All for You; Cling, Clang; Gypsy Dance; In the Good Old Days; Just Like Me; Man, A; Marietta [1]; Marry a Girl in June; My Girl of Dreams; One, Two, Three (Dance with Me); Pension Elite, The; Raven Tresses or Golden Locks; Welcome and Au Revoir; When You Marry; Wonderful, Wonderful Tulip Land

Cast: Arthur Aylesworth; Hazel Kirke; Arthur Lipson; Amelia Stone; Ernest Truex

Notes: Program of Boston. [1] Sheet music only.

2263 • JUNE DAYS

OPENED: 08/06/1925   Theatre: Astor
Musical   Broadway: 48

Composer: J. Fred Coots
Lyricist: Clifford Grey
Librettist: Harry Wagstaff Gribble; Cyrus Wood
Director: J.J. Shubert

Source: CHARM SCHOOL, THE (Play: Alice Duer Miller)

Songs: All I Want Is Love (C: Hal Dyson; L: James Kendis); Anytime, Anywhere, Anyhow (C: Richard Rodgers; L: Lorenz Hart); Busy Evening, A; Charming Women; Girls Dream of One Thing; How Do You Doodle Do?; June Days (C: Stephen Jones; L: Clifford Grey; Cyrus Wood); Lucky; Naughty Little Step; Please, Teacher; Remembering You; Safety in Numbers; Something Wrong with Me; Strike [1]; Take 'em to the Door Blues [1]; Why Is Love?

Cast: Jay C. Flippen; Elizabeth Hines; Miller James; Roy Royston

Notes: [1] ASCAP/Library of Congress only.

2264 • JUNE LOVE

OPENED: 04/25/1921   Theatre: Knickerbocker
Musical   Broadway: 48

Composer: Rudolf Friml
Lyricist: Brian Hooker
Librettist: Otto Harbach; William H. Post
Producer: Sherman Brown
Director: George Vivian

Source: IN SEARCH OF A SINNER (Story: Charlotte Thompson); **Choreographer:** David

Bennett; **Costumes:** Bertha A. Fields; **Musical Director:** Gene Salzer

Songs: Be Careful; Comme Ci, Comme Ca; Dear Love, My Love; Don't Call Them Dearie; Egyptian Dance, The; Flapper and the Vamp, The; Harvest Moon, The; I'm Not in Love with You; June Love; Keep Your Eye on the Ball; Opening Chorus; Runaway Little Girl; Someone Like You; Spider's Web, The; With a Woman You Can Never Tell

Cast: Elsa Adler; W.B. Davidson; Johnny Dooley; Clarence Nordstrom

2265 • JUNE MOON
OPENED: 10/09/1929   Theatre: Broadhurst
Play   Broadway: 272

Composer: George S. Kaufman
Lyricist: George S. Kaufman; Ring Lardner
Librettist: Ring Lardner
Author: George S. Kaufman; Ring Lardner
Producer: Sam H. Harris
Director: George S. Kaufman

Set Design: William Oden-Waller

Songs: June Moon; Montana Moon

Cast: Jean Dixon; Norman Foster; Philip Loeb; Frank Otto; Lee Patrick; Florence D. Rice; Harry Rosenthal; Linda Watkins

2266 • JUNIOR BLACKBIRDS
OPENED: 1926   Theatre: Lafayette
Revue   New York

Composer: Thomas "Fats" Waller
Lyricist: Spencer Williams

Notes: No other information available.

2267 • JUNIOR MISS
OPENED: 12/20/1957   Theatre: CBS
TV Musical

Composer: Burton Lane
Lyricist: Dorothy Fields
Librettist: Will Glickman; Joseph Stein
Producer: Richard Lewine
Director: Ralph Nelson

Source: JUNIOR MISS (Play: Jerome Chodorov; Joseph Fields); **Musical Director:** Norman Luboff

Songs: Happy Heart; Have Feet Will Dance; I'll Buy It; It's Just What I Wanted; Junior Miss; Let's Make It Christmas All Year 'Round; Male Is an Animal, A

Cast: Don Ameche; Joan Bennett; Paul Ford; Diana Linn; Carol Lynley; Susanne Sidney; Jill St. John; David Wayne

2268 • JUNO
OPENED: 03/09/1959   Theatre: Winter Garden
Musical   Broadway: 16

Composer: Marc Blitzstein
Lyricist: Marc Blitzstein
Librettist: Joseph Stein
Producer: Playwrights' Company, The; Oliver Rea; Oliver Smith
Director: Jose Ferrer

Source: JUNO AND THE PAYCOCK (Play: Sean O'Casey); **Choreographer:** Agnes de Mille; **Costumes:** Irene Sharaff; **Lighting Designer:** Peggy Clark; **Musical Director:** Robert Emmett Dolan; **Orchestrations:** Robert Russell Bennett; Marc Blitzstein; Hershy Kay; **Set Design:** Oliver Smith

Songs: Bird Upon the Tree; Daarlin' Man; Dublin Night Ballet; Farewell, Me Butty [1]; For Love; From This Out [1]; His Own Peculiar Charm [1]; Hymn; I Wish It So; Ireland's Eye (dance) [2]; It's Not Irish; Jig (dance); Johnny (dance); Lament [1]; Liffey Waltz, The; Music in the House; My True Heart; Old Sayin's; On a Day Like This; One Kind Word; Quarrel Song [1]; Shillelagh Dance (dance); Slip Jig (dance); Song of the Ma; We Can Be Proud; We're Alive; What Is the Stars?; Where?; You Poor Thing; You're the Girl [1]

Cast: Monte Amundsen; Nancy Andrews; Clarice Blackburn; Shirley Booth; Melvyn Douglas; Beulah Garrick; Earl Hammond; Jack McGowan; Tommy Rall; Jean Stapleton; Glen Tetley; Sada Thompson; Gemze de Lappe

Notes: [1] Cut prior to opening. [2] Cut prior to opening. Lyric cut before song cut.

2269 • JUNON AND AVOS: THE HOPE

OPENED: 01/07/1990   Theatre: City Center
Musical   Broadway: 48

Composer: Alexis Ribnikov
Lyricist: Andrey Voznesensky
Librettist: Andrey Voznesensky
Producer: Pierre Cardin
Director: Mark Zakharov

Choreographer: Vladimir Vassiliev; **Costumes:** Valentina Komolova; **Set Design:** Oleg Sheintsiss

Songs: Avos; Hallelujah to Love; I Will Never See You Again, I Will Never Forget You; The Wild White Rose

Cast: Alexander Abdulov; Philip Casnoff; Nikolai Karachentsev; Yuri Naumkin; Ludmilla Porgina; Yelena Shanina; Vladimir Shiryayev

Notes: A Russian Musical performed in Russian with English narration. Narration written by Susan Silver and Albert Todd. No songs listed in program.

2270 • JUST A MINUTE (1919)

OPENED: 10/29/1919   Theatre: Cort
Musical   Broadway: 40

Composer: Harold Orlob
Lyricist: Harry L. Cort; Harold Orlob; George E. Stoddard
Librettist: Harry L. Cort; Harold Orlob; George E. Stoddard
Producer: John Cort
Director: Robert Marks

Musical Director: Arthur H. Gutman

Songs: Because You're Different; Five Profiteers, The [1]; Girl I Want to Call My Wife, The; Grandfather's Clock; I'll Say I Will; I'm Going to Be Lonesome; Just Imagine; Melody; No Birdie Ever Flew So High; On the Boardwalk [1]; Over and Over Again; Roll Me; Some Other Girl; To Make Them Fall; When You Dance with a Certain Girl [1]; Wonderful Girl

Cast: Wellington Cross; Johnny Hines; Mabel Withee

Notes: [1] Out Pittsburgh 4/19/20.

2271 • JUST A MINUTE (1928)

OPENED: 10/08/1928   Theatre: Ambassador
Musical   Broadway: 80

Composer: Harry Archer
Lyricist: Walter O'Keefe
Librettist: H.C. Greene
Producer: H.C. Greene; Phil Morris
Director: H.C. Greene

Choreographer: Russell Markert; **Musical Director:** Berni Vici; **Orchestrations:** Claude MacArthur; William Moore; **Set Design:** P. Dodd Ackerman

Songs: Anything Your Heart Desires; Break-Me-Down, The; Coming Out of the Garden; Dog-gone; Heigh-Ho Cheerio; I Got a Cookie Jar but No Cookies; I'm Ninety-Eight Pounds of Sweetness; Just a Minute; Pretty, Petite and Sweet; We'll Just Be Two Commuters; You'll Kill 'Em

Cast: Gypsy Byrne; Madeline Grey; Arthur Havel; Morton Havel; Tommy Havel; Harry Holbrook; Helen Lockhart; Helen Patterson; Sam Sidman; Count Berni Vici & His Symphonic Girls; Walker and Thompson; Billie Yarbo

2272 • JUST A NIGHT OUT

OPENED: 02/16/1992   Theatre: Top of the Gate
Musical   Off-Broadway: 65

Librettist: Richard Turner; Susan Turner
Producer: Negro Ensemble Company
Director: Leslie Dockery

Costumes: Gregory Clenn; **Lighting Designer:** Sandra Ross; **Set Design:** Lisa Watson

Cast: Bruce Butler; Deborah Keeling; Zanzele Scott; Chandra Simmons; Messeret Stroman

Notes: Songs by Cole Porter and Comden and Green were used. No original songs were in this musical. No songs listed in program.

2273 • JUST APPLES

OPENED: 03/09/1923
Musical   Closed out of town

Composer: J. Fred Coots
Lyricist: William Cary Duncan
Librettist: William Cary Duncan

Notes: Academy of Music, Brooklyn.

2274 • JUST AROUND THE CORNER (1919)

OPENED: 02/15/1919 Theatre: Longacre
Play Broadway: 13

Author: George V. Hobart; Herbert Hall Winslow
Producer: G.M. Anderson

Songs: Just Around the Corner (C: Egbert Van Alstyne; L: Gus Kahn); On a Little Farm in Normandie (C: Nat Osborne; L: Ballard Macdonald)

Cast: Glenn Anders; Roy Briant; Marie Cahill; Clara Macklin; Wallace Owen

Notes: In Atlantic City program (1918), Miss Cahill's songs were especially written for her by Bert Grant and George Graff Jr. There's no mention of this in the New York program.

2275 • JUST AROUND THE CORNER (1950)

OPENED: 07/31/1950
Musical Closed out of town

Composer: Joe Sherman
Lyricist: Langston Hughes
Additional Lyrics: George Jaffe
Librettist: Bernard Drew; Abby Mann
Producer: Mrs. Walter Hartwig; John Lane
Director: John Kirkpatrick

Choreographer: Fred Kelly; **Costumes:** Lygia Bernard; **Set Design:** Tom Jewett

Songs: Dance; Devil Is Responsible; Falling for You; Gents for Rent; I'm Learning to Live All Alone; It's Hard to Be a Lady All Night Long; Let's Take a Look Into the Future; No Telling; Not Today (Soliloquy); Nothing But a Slight Recession; People Like Us; Push Cart Man; Rise and Meet the Sun Half Way; So Long Herbert; Swing's Gonna Rock Your Bones; Thanks to the Banks; Two of Us; Walk Me Around Through the Village; When I Was Your Age Young Man; Where Can That Someone Be; Wouldn't It Be Nice

Cast: Daisy Atherton; Francis Compton; Belle Flower; Beverly Janis; Fred Kelly; Bob

Kennedy; Avon Long; Mary Ann Niles; Dotty Saulter

Notes: From a program of Ogunquit Playhouse.

2276 • JUST BECAUSE

OPENED: 03/22/1922 Theatre: Earl Carroll
Musical Broadway: 46

Composer: Madelyn Sheppard
Lyricist: Helen S. Woodruff
Librettist: Anna Wynne O'Ryan; Helen S. Woodruff
Director: Oscar Eagle

Choreographer: Bert French; **Costumes:** Anna Spencer; **Musical Director:** Ivan Rudisill; **Set Design:** H. Robert Law

Songs: Associated Press; Busy Bee; Chop Sticks; Daisy Tell Me Truly; Day Dream Bay; Eloping; Here's to the Bride; Hiking to a No Woman's Land; I'll Name My Dolly for You; It's Hard to Be a Lady; Jazzing Toes; Just Because; Line Is Busy, The; Love Me, Love Me Not; Music Scene; Oh Dad; Opening; Orphan's Drill; Our Dollies; Pots and Pans; Rep Up Your Step; Simply Love; Widows Blues

Cast: Olin Howland; Frank Moulan; Queenie Smith; Charles Trowbridge

2277 • JUST FANCY

OPENED: 10/11/1927 Theatre: Casino
Musical Broadway: 79

Composer: Philip Charig; Joseph Meyer
Lyricist: Leo Robin
Librettist: Gertrude Purcell; Joseph Santley
Producer: Joseph Santley
Director: Joseph Santley

Source: JUST SUPPOSE (Play: A.E. Thomas); **Choreographer:** Johnny Ford

Songs: Ain't Love Grand; Coo-Coo; Dressed Up for Your Sunday Beau; Humpty-Dumpty; I'm a Highway Gentleman; Memories; Mi Chiquita; Naughty Boy; Shake, Brother!; Two Loving Arms; You Came Along [1]

Cast: Eric Blore; Raymond Hitchcock; Joseph Santley; Ivy Sawyer; Mrs. Thomas Wiffen

Notes: [1] Later interpolated into London show
LADY MARY.

2278 • JUST FOR LOVE
OPENED: 10/17/1968   Theatre: Provincetown
                                      Playhouse
Musical   Off-Broadway: 6

Composer: Michael Valenti
Lyricist: Michael Valenti
Librettist: Henry Comor; Jill Showell
Producer: Investors Production Co.; Seymour Vall
Director: Henry Comor

Costumes: Sara Brook; **Lighting Designer:** Jack
Blackman; **Musical Director:** George Taros;
Orchestrations: George Taros; **Set Design:** Jack
Blackman

Songs: Bella; Birthday, A [1]; Come Live with Me;
Did Not [1]; Echo [1]; Epitaph [1]; Jenny Kissed
Me [1]; Just for Love; Man Is for Woman Made [1];
Mary Ann [1]; One and Twenty; So We'll Go No
More a- Roving [1]; Two Strings to a Bow; What
Is Love? [1]

Cast: Henry Comor; Jacqueline Mayro; Steve Perry;
Jill Showell

Notes: See also BLOOD RED ROSES. [1] Also in
LOVESONG. Note additional lyric credit in
LOVESONG.

2279 • JUST FOR OPENERS
OPENED: 11/03/1965   Theatre: Upstairs at the
                                      Downstairs
Revue   Nightclub: 395

Librettist: Fannie Flagg; Bill Kaufman; Paul
Koreto; Rod Warren
Producer: Rod Warren
Director: Sandra Devlin

Songs: Adaptations (C: Lee Holdridge; L: Ed
Fearon); America the Beautiful (C: Rod Warren;
L: Michael McWhinney); Anyone Who's Anyone
(C: Bill Weeden; L: David Finkle); 'Dolly' Sisters,
The (C: Ed Kresley; L: Drey Sheppard); Just for
Openers (C/L: Rod Warren); Mr. Know-It-All
(C: William Goldenberg; L: Larry Alexander);
New York without Bob (C/L: Alan Friedman);
Where Did We Go Wrong? (C: Stephen

Lawrence; L: John Meyer); You're a Big Boy Now
(C/L: Rod Warren)

Cast: Betty Aberlin; Richard Blair; Stockton Brigel;
R.G. Brown; Fannie Flagg; Madeline Kahn;
Pianist: Michael Cohen; Edward Morris

2280 • JUST GIRLS
Notes: *See ZIEGFELD MIDNIGHT FROLIC 2nd of
series, September 1915.*

2281 • JUST MARRIED
OPENED: 04/26/1921   Theatre: Comedy
Play   Broadway: 307

Author: Adelaide Matthews; Anne Nichols
Producer: Jules Hurtig; Messrs. Shubert
Director: J.C. Huffman; Clifford Stork

Songs: Just Married (C: Don Kendall; L: Adelaide
Matthews)

Cast: Vivian Martin; Lynne Overman

2282 • JUST ONE OF THE BOYS
OPENED: 03/07/1910
Musical   Closed out of town

Composer: William Schroeder
Lyricist: Rida Johnson Young
Librettist: Rida Johnson Young
Producer: Lee Shubert; Sam S. Shubert
Director: J.C. Huffman

Orchestrations: Oscar Radin

Songs: Deportment; Every Fellow Wants Someone
to Love; Goodbye Girl; Grub Time; Here's to
You; Hubble Bubble; I Am the Herr Professor;
It May Be Good, Good, Good to Be in Love [1]
(C/L: Unknown); Just a Kiss from Someone;
Love Is Like a Rose; One of the Boys; Our Girls;
Please, Please [1] (C: Walter Kollo; L: M.E.
Rourke); True Blue; Wily Gazzoo, The; You're
the Only Girl I Want to Marry

Cast: Lulu Glaser; Jobyna Howland

Notes: From a program of Washington D.C.
3/7/10. [1] Sheet music only.

2283 • JUST SO

OPENED: 12/03/1985   Theatre: Jack Lawrence
Musical   Off-Broadway: 6

Composer: Doug Katsaros
Lyricist: David Zippel
Librettist: Mark St. Germain
Producer: Ivan Bloch; Mary Fisher Productions; New Day Productions; Joanne L. Zippel
Director: Julianne Boyd

Source: JUST SO STORIES (Story: Rudyard Kipling); **Choreographer:** David Storey; **Costumes:** Ann Hould-Ward; **Dance Arranger:** Doug Katsaros; **Lighting Designer:** Craig Miller; **Musical Director:** David Friedman;

Orchestrations: Doug Katsaros; **Set Design:** Atkin Pace; **Vocal Arranger:** Doug Katsaros

Songs: Answer Song, The; Arm in Arm in Harmony; Camel's Blues [1]; Chill Out!; Desert Dessert; Eat, Eat, Eat; Everything Under the Sun; Giraffe's Reprise; Gospel According to the Leopard; I Have Changed; I've Got to Know; Lullaby [1]; My First Mistake; Shadowy Forest of Garandufi Dance; Whole World Revolves Around You, The

Cast: Teresa Burrell; Keith Curran; Andre De Shields; Jason Graae; Tina Johnson; Tom Robbins; Tico Wells

Notes: [1] Also in IT'S BETTER WITH A BAND.

K

2284 • KABOOM! (1974)

OPENED: 05/01/1974   Theatre: Bottom Line
Musical   Nightclub: 1

Composer: Doris Schwerin
Lyricist: Ira Wallach
Librettist: Ira Wallach
Producer: Joseph Rhodes
Director: Don Price

Choreographer: Don Price; **Costumes:** Lohr Wilson; **Lighting Designer:** Timmy Harris; **Musical Director:** Arnold Gross; **Orchestrations:** Eddie Sauter; **Set Design:** Peter Harvey

Songs: Ave Nelson; Busy Lady; Buying and Selling; Existential; God Is Smiling on You; High School Diploma; I'm Gonna Make It; Is It Too Late; Mother Darling; On Her Own; Ritual; Sex, Sex, Sex; Supermarket; Time Was; Velvet's Vest; While They Were Sleeping

Cast: Marjorie Barnes; Jack Blackton; James Donahue; Charles Hudson; Corinne Kason; Bernice Massi; Tom Matthew Tobin

2285 • KA-BOOM (1980)

OPENED: 11/20/1980   Theatre: Carter
Musical   Off-Broadway: 70

Composer: Joe Ercole
Lyricist: Bruce Kluger
Librettist: Bruce Kluger
Producer: Bruce Kluger; Jim Payne
Director: John-Michael Tebelak

Choreographer: Lynne Gannaway; **Costumes:** Erica Hollmann; **Lighting Designer:** Kirk Bookman; **Musical Director:** John Lehman; **Orchestrations:** Joe Ercole; **Set Design:** Ken Holamon; **Vocal Arranger:** John Lehman

Songs: Ballad of Adam and Eve; Believe Us Receive Us; Bump and Grind for God; Few Get Through, A; Gimme a 'G'; Judgement Day; Let Me Believe in Me; Let the Show Go On!; Light Around the Corner, The; Little Bit O' Glitter;

Maybe for Instance; Now We Pray; Oh Lord; Smile; Soft Spot, The; Those ABC's; With a World to Conquer; You Are You

Cast: Terry Barnes; Judith Bro; John Hall; Ken Ward; Fannie Whitehead; Andrea Wright

2286 • KAFOOZELUM

OPENED: 05/21/1905
Musical   Closed out of town

Composer: George Rosey
Lyricist: Allen Lowe
Librettist: Allen Lowe; George Rosey
Producer: Will J. Block
Director: Charles H. Jones

Choreographer: Clayton Kennedy; **Costumes:** Archie Gunn; **Musical Director:** Paul Schindler; **Set Design:** Edouard Biedermann

Songs: Baby Lonesome (C: Paul Schindler); Back to Old Montana; Beauty Brigade, The; Booze Tree, The; Change If to Is; Coming U.S.A.; Entrance of Kafoozelum; Farewell; Hiram Greene (C: C.M. Chapel; Arthur Gillespie); I Don't Want to Be a Sailor (C: Arthur Gillespie); Legend of a Stocking, The; Lulu, Come into the Zoo; Molly Malone; Mr. Fox, I'm Sorry for You; Neat Cafe, A; Picnic for Two, A (C: Albert Von Tilzer; L: Arthur J. Lamb); Shrimp and a Crab, A; Sunny South, The; Tubal Cain (C: Paul Schindler); Voice of Nature, The (C: Paul Schindler); We've Never Seen the Sun or Stars

2287 • KALEIDOSCOPE, THE (1913)

OPENED: 04/30/1913
Musical

Composer: Cole Porter
Lyricist: Cole Porter
Producer: Yale Univ. Dramatic Assn.

Songs: Absinthe; Absinthe Drip; As I Love You; At the Dawn Tea; Beware of the Sophomore;

Chaperons; Duodecimalogue; Flower Maidens; Good-Bye My True Love; In the Land Where My Heart Was Born; Maid of Santiago; Meet Me Beside the River; Member of the Yale Elizabethan Club; Moon Man; My Georgia Gal; Oh, What a Pretty Pair of Lovers; On My Yacht; Rick-Chick-a-Chick; We Are Prom Girls; We're a Group of Nonentities

Cast: Howard T. Cumming; Rufus F. King; Archibald MacLeish; Newbold Noyes; Arnold Whitridge

Notes: Amateur show. First performance at Hotel Taft, New Haven. Second performance at Yale Club of NYC 5/7/13.

2288 • KALEIDOSCOPE (1957)

OPENED: 06/13/1957   Theatre: Provincetown
                                      Playhouse
Revue   Off-Broadway

Composer: Gerald Alters; David Baker; Cherry Balaban; Lesley Davison; William Dyer; Raoul Gonzalez; Marie Gordon; Sheldon Harnick; David Hollister; Robert Kessler; Don Peterson; Kenneth Welch; G. Wood
Lyricist: Sheryn Alexander; Cherry Balaban; Martin Charnin; Lesley Davison; Raoul Gonzalez; Sheldon Harnick; Herbert Hartig; Tom Jones; Don Richards; David Rogers; Kenneth Welch; Cy Wood
Librettist: Lee Adams; Herbert Hartig; Tom Jones; David Panich; Don Parks; Herbert Reich; Michael Stewart
Producer: Jeanellen McKec; Richard D. Stainbrook
Director: Paul Mazursky

Choreographer: Edmund Balin; **Costumes:** Mariana Elliot; **Lighting Designer:** Mariana Elliott; **Set Design:** Lin Emery

Songs: Ladies of Fiction (C: William Dyer; L: Lesley Davison); November in Kenya (C: Bob Kessler; L: Martin Charnin)

Cast: Wisa D'Orso; Mickey Deems; Leonard Drum; Maria Karnilova; Bobo Lewis; Tom Mixon; Kenneth Nelson

Notes: No program available.

2289 • KALEIDOSCOPE (1987)

OPENED: 05/12/1987
Musical   Closed out of town

Composer: Jan Mulaney; Mary Bracken Phillips
Lyricist: Mary Bracken Phillips
Librettist: Mary Bracken Phillips
Producer: Sue Frost; Goodspeed Opera House
Director: Munson Hicks

Choreographer: Terry Rieser; **Costumes:** Mardi Philips; **Lighting Designer:** Judy Rasmuson; **Musical Director:** Jeff Waxman; **Set Design:** Jim Jozwick

Songs: Beautiful Baby; Choices; Father's Day; Game Goes On, The; Greatest Man in the World, The; Hickory Dickory Dock; Is It Anybody's Business; Lovely Child; Nobody's Perfect; Ordinary Day, An; People Like Us; Rational Love Song, A; Trade a Minute; What If

Cast: P.J. Benjamin; Gibby Brand; Louisa Flaningam; Mary Bracken Phillips

Notes: Norma Terris Theatre, East Haddam, CT. Later titled CRADLE SONG.

2290 • KARL MARX PLAY, THE

OPENED: 03/16/1973   Theatre: American Place
Musical   Off-Broadway: 32

Composer: Galt MacDermot
Lyricist: Rochelle Owens
Librettist: Rochelle Owens
Producer: American Place Theatre
Director: Mel Shapiro

Costumes: Linda Fisher; **Lighting Designer:** Roger Morgan; **Set Design:** Karl Eigsti; **Vocal Arranger:** Galt MacDermot

Songs: Baby Johann; Comes the Revolution; Dying Child; Hand of Fate, The; He Eats; Hello, Hello; Holy Mystery; It's Me They Talk About; Jenny Is Like an Angel; Jenny von Westphalen; My Knees Are Weak; O Mistress Mine; Pretty Woman; Red Leather Wrist Watch; So I Give You; Tempting Salome; There Was a Hen; We Doubt You, Papa; White Sheeting; World of Creation; Ya Ta Ta

Cast: Ralph Carter; Leonard Jackson; Randy Kim; Norman Matlock

Notes: No songs listed in program.

2291 • KATIE DID

OPENED: 02/18/1910
Musical   Closed out of town

Composer: Karl Hoschna
Lyricist: William Cary Duncan
Librettist: William Cary Duncan; Frank Smithson
Producer: Joseph M. Gaites

Musical Director: Gus Salzer

Songs: Come Closer (Come a Little Closer); Homeland (Dear Old Homeland); I, John, Take Thee Matilda; In the Swim; Katie Did; My Friend from India; Night Time (C: Felix Arndt; L: Louis Weslyn); Nobody Loves Me; Opening Chorus; Opening Chorus Act II; Out with the Owl; Save Up Your Kisses for a Rainy Day; That's the Way We Do It Out in Kansas; Yellow Robe, The

Cast: La Petite Adelaide; Josie Intropodi; Florence May; Jed Prouty; Louis Simon; May Vokes; Anna Wilkes

Notes: No program available. Played the Colonial Theatre, Chicago 2/18/1910.

2292 • KATINKA

OPENED: 12/23/1915   Theatre: 44th Street
Musical   Broadway: 220

Composer: Rudolf Friml
Lyricist: Otto Harbach
Librettist: Otto Harba
Producer: Arthur Hammerstein
Director: Frank Smithson

Musical Director: John McGhie; Frank Robb

Songs: Allah's Holiday; Bride, The [2]; Charms Are Fairest When They're Hidden [2]; Circassian Dance; Finale Act I; Finale Act II; Finale Act III; Goodnight [1]; I Can Tell By the Way You Dance, Dear; I Think You'd Better Hurry Home [1]; I Want All the World to Know; I Want to Marry a Male Quartette; In a Hurry; In Vienna; Katinka; Mignonette [2]; My Paradise; One Who Will Understand; Opening Chorus; Opening Chorus Act II; Rackety-Coo!; Russian Dance; Russian Wedding March; Skidiskischatch; Stamboul; 'Tis the End, So Farewell [2]; Vienna Girls; Walking Music Store, The; Weekly Wedding, The; Your Photo

Cast: Franklyn Ardell; Samuel Ash; Nina Napier; Adele Rowland

Notes: [1] Not used. [2] In vocal score but not playbill.

2293 • KATJA

OPENED: 10/18/1926   Theatre: 44th Street
Musical   Broadway: 113

Composer: Jean Gilbert
Lyricist: Harry Graham
Librettist: Isabel Leighton; Frederick Lonsdale
Producer: Messrs. Shubert
Director: J.C. Huffman; Lewis Morton

Source: KATJA, DIE TANZERIN Musical: Jean Gilbert; Leopold Jacobson; Rudolph Oesterreicher); **Choreographer:** Max Scheck; **Costumes:** Max Weldy; **Musical Director:** Irving Schloss; **Set Design:** Watson Barratt

Songs: All the World Loves a Lover; Back to My Heart [2] (C: Vernon Duke; L: Percy Greenbank); Balkan Dance; Congratualtions; Cruel Chief; Dance with You; Euranian Anthem; Eyes So Tender; I Feel a Real Bad Lad Tonight [1]; I Fell Head Over Heels in Love; If You Care; In Jail; I've Planned a Rendezvous [1]; Just for a Night (C: Maurie Rubens; L: Clifford Grey); Leander; Love and Duty [1]; Love's in the Air; Night Birds; Oh Woe Is Me-oh [1]; Politics [1]; Tails Up [1]; Through Life We Go Dancing Together [1]; Try a Little Kiss [3] (C: Vernon Duke; L: Percy Greenbank; Arthur Wimperis); When We Are Married [1]

Cast: Lillian Davies; Oscar Figman; Dennis Hoey; Doris Patston; Allan Prior; Jack Sheehan; D. Whitmore

Notes: [1] Cut from previous London production, titled KATJA, THE DANCER, 10/19/25. [2] Added after opening of London production. [3] From London production.

2294 • KAYE BALLARD: WORKING 42ND STREET AT LAST

OPENED: 05/16/1988   Theatre: Kaufman
Revue   Off-Broadway: 29

Producer: Martin R. Kaufman
Director: Barry Kleinbort

Costumes: Grace Costumes; Reuben Panis; Clovis Ruffin; **Lighting Designer:** Jeffrey Schissler; **Set Design:** Jeffrey Schissler

Songs: After Forty (C: Cy Coleman; L: Carolyn Leigh); Burger Beguine (C/L: Leslie Eberhard; David Levy); Country Song (C/L: Suzanne Buhrer); Don't Ask the Lady What the Lady Did Before (C: Cy Coleman; L: Carolyn Leigh); Folk Song (C/L: Gordon Connell); I Gotta Make My Own Music (C: Arthur Siegel; L: Charlotte Kent); I Hate Spring (C/L: Martha Caples; Nancy Hamilton); I Just Found Out [1] (C/L: Fred Silver); I Just Kissed My Nose Goodnight (C/L: Kaye Ballard; Mary McCarty; Buddy Pepper); Irving Berlin Medley (C/L: Irving Berlin); Is That All There Is?; Lizzie Borden (C/L: Michael Brown); Love Is a Simple Thing (C: Arthur Siegel; L: June Carroll); My City (C/L: Charles Strouse); My Son (C/L: Suzanne Buhrer); Old Soft Shoe, The (C/L: Nancy Hamilton; Morgan Lewis); Paramount, Capitol and the Strand (C/L: Norman Martin); Remind Me (C: Jerome Kern; L: Dorothy Fields); Sondheim Song (C/L: Barry Kleinbort); Tale of the Oyster (C/L: Cole Porter); Time You Old Gypsy Man (C: Philip Springer; L: E.Y. Harburg); When? (C/L: Barry Kleinbort); Wizard of Oz Medley [1] (C: Harold Arlen; L: E.Y. Harburg); Yellow Flower (C: Jerome Moross; L: John Latouche); You Can Be a New Yorker Too (C/L: Charles Strouse)

Cast: Kaye Ballard; Miss Faun; Arthur Siegel

Notes: Ben Bagley was Creative Consultant to the show. Accompaniment was by Arthur Siegel and Miss Faun. There was also a "Lady Lyricists" medley. [1] Cut in previews.

2295 • KEAN

OPENED: 11/02/1961   Theatre: Broadway
Musical   Broadway: 92

Composer: George Forrest; Robert Wright
Lyricist: George Forrest; Robert Wright
Producer: Robert Lantz
Director: Jack Cole

Source: KEAN (Play: Jean-Paul Sartre);
Choreographer: Jack Cole; **Costumes:** Ed Wittstein; **Dance Arranger:** Elie Siegmeister; **Lighting Designer:** John Harvey; **Musical Director:** Pembroke Davenport; **Orchestrations:** Philip J. Lang; **Set Design:** Ed Wittstein; **Vocal Arranger:** Pembroke Davenport

Songs: Ado About Kean [2]; Amsterdam [4]; Apology?; Chime In!; Civilized People; Clown of London; Disorder and Genius [2]; Domesticity [3]; Elena [1]; Fog and the Grog, The; Fracas at Old Drury; Inevitable [2]; King of London; Let's Improvise; Man and Shadow; Mayfair Affair; Penny Plain, Twopence Colored; Queue at Drury Lane; Service for Service; Shadow Play [2]; Social Whirl, The [3]; Sweet Danger; Swept Away; To Look Upon My Love; Willow, Willow, Willow

Cast: Roderick Cook; Patricia Cutts; Alfred Drake; Oliver Gray; Christopher Hewett; Arthur Rubin; Lee Venora; Joan Weldon

Notes: [1] Same melody as "Isola" in AT THE GRAND. [2] Cut prior to opening. [3] Cut after opening. [4] Cut prior to opening. Same music as "Toinette" in THE CAREFREE HEART.

2296 • KEEP IT CLEAN

OPENED: 06/24/1929   Theatre: Selwyn
Revue   Broadway: 16

Librettist: Jimmy Duffy; Will Morrissey
Producer: William Duffy; John Hickey Jr.

Choreographer: Russell Markert; **Musical Director:** Jimmie Carr

Songs: All I Need Is Someone Like You (C: Harry Archer; L: Charles Tobias); Broadway Mammy (C/L: Jimmy Duffy; Clarence Gaskill); Doin' the Hot-Cha-Cha (C/L: Lester Lee); Hokum (C/L: Jimmy Duffy; James F. Hanley; Will Morrissey); I See You but What Do You See in Me? (C/L: Lester Lee); Just a Little Blue for You (C/L: James F. Hanley); Let Me Hold You in My Arms (C/L: Clarence Gaskill); Someone to Love (C/L: Harry Archer; Jimmy Duffy; James F. Hanley)

Cast: Midge Miller; Will Morrissey

2297 • KEEP IT IN THE FAMILY

OPENED: 09/27/1967   Theatre: Plymouth
Play   Broadway: 5

Author: Bill Naughton
Producer: David Merrick
Director: Allan Davis

Costumes: Mary McKinley; **Set Design:** Lloyd Burlingame

Songs: Keep It in the Family (C: Cy Coleman; L: Dorothy Fields)

Cast: Karen Black; Sudie Bond; Burt Brinckerhoff; Maureen O'Sullivan

2298 • KEEP KOOL

OPENED: 05/22/1924   Theatre: Morosco
Revue   Broadway: 148

Composer: Jack Frost
Lyricist: Paul Gerard Smith
Librettist: Paul Gerard Smith
Producer: E.K. Nadel
Director: Edgar MacGregor

Choreographer: Earl Lindsay; **Costumes:** Kiviette; **Musical Director:** Oscar Loraine; **Orchestrations:** Albert Chiffarelli; **Set Design:** H. Robert Law

Songs: Broadway Battle Cry, The; Dandelion Time; Dawn Will Come; Fairy Tales; How You Gonna Keep Kool?; In They Go, Out They Come; Irish Sheik, The; My Calicoquette; Nellie Kelly; Out Where the Pavement Ends; Painted Rose; Ring in the Joys; Shalimar; Shall I Sing It Now

Cast: Hazel Dawn; Johnny Dooley; Lon Hascall; Charles King

Notes: **Art Director:** Walter Harvey.

2299 • KEEP MOVING (1916)

OPENED: 08/27/1916
Musical   Closed out of town

Composer: Harry Von Tilzer
Lyricist: Aaron Hoffman

Choreographer: Lester Templeton

Songs: As We Pass By; Coney Island; Dangerous Girl; Don't Forget Me; Everybody Has a Tip; French Flip Flop; Honolulu Blues; My Yiddish Colleen; Opening Carnival Scene; Opening Chorus; Sweet Babette (She Always Did the Minuet) (L: E.P. Moran; Andrew B. Sterling); Two Key Rag; You're Just Made to Order for Me

Cast: Charles Raymond

Notes: Played in Chicago on 8/27/16 and Philadelphia on 11/14/16. Newspaper clippings refer to 30 songs.

2300 • KEEP MOVING (1934)

OPENED: 08/23/1924   Theatre: Forrest
Revue   Broadway: 21

Composer: Max Rich
Lyricist: Jack Scholl
Librettist: Newman Levy; George Rosener; Jack Scholl
Producer: White Horse Tavern Prod.
Director: George Rosener

Choreographer: Harry Losee; **Costumes:** Robert Stevenson; **Musical Director:** J. Dell Lampe; **Set Design:** Clark Robinson

Songs: Command to Love (C: Henry Sullivan); Hot-Cha Chaquita; Isn't It a Funny Thing?; Lovely, Lovely Day (C: Max Rich; Billy Taylor); Midtown; Now Is the Time; Play Is the Bunk, The; Superstition; Wake Up, Sleepy Moon

Cast: Joan Abbott; Dan Carthay; Clyde Hager; Tom Howard; Harriet Hutchins; Ernest Lambert; Woods Miller; Nayan Pearce; Kay Picture; William Redford; Singer Midgets, The; Billy Taylor

2301 • KEEP OFF THE GRASS

OPENED: 05/23/1940   Theatre: Broadhurst
Musical   Broadway: 44

Composer: Jimmy McHugh
Lyricist: Al Dubin
Librettist: Melvin Frank; S. Jay Kaufman; Parke Levy; Mort Lewis; Alan Lipscott; Norman Panama
Producer: Messrs. Shubert
Director: Edward Duryea Dowling

Songs: Cabby's Serenade, The; Clear Out of This World; Crazy As a Loon; Fugitive from Esquire, A (L: Howard Dietz); Horse with the Hansom Behind, The [1] (C/L: Irving Berlin); I'll Applaud You with My Feet; Latin Tune, a Manhattan Moon and You, A; Look Out for My Heart; Old Jitterbug; Old Park Bench, The (L: Howard Dietz); Raffles (C: Vernon Duke); Rhett, Scarlett, Ashley; This Is Spring; This Is Winter; Three Little Topical Debutantes [1]; Toscanini,

Stokowski and Me [1]; Two in a Taxi (L: Howard Dietz)

Cast: Larry Adler; Ray Bolger; Ilka Chase; Jimmy Durante; Jane Froman; Virginia O'Brien

Notes: [1] Out Boston prior.

2302 • KEEP SHUFFLIN'
OPENED: 02/27/1928   Theatre: Daly's
Musical   Broadway: 104

Librettist: Aubrey L. Lyles; Flournoy E. Miller
Producer: Con Conrad
Director: Con Conrad

Choreographer: Clarence Robinson; **Costumes:** Mahieu; **Musical Director:** James P. Johnson; **Orchestrations:** Will Vodery; **Set Design:** Karle O. Amend

Songs: Brothers [5]; Bugle Blues [5]; Charlie, My Back Door Man [2] (C: Clarence Todd; L: Henry Creamer); Choc'late Bar (C: Thomas "Fats" Waller; L: Andy Razaf); Deep Blue Sea [5]; Don't Wake 'Em Up [5]; Dusky Love (C: Will Vodery; L: Henry Creamer); Everybody's Happy in Jimtown (C: Thomas "Fats" Waller; L: Andy Razaf); Exhortation (C: Con Conrad; L: Henry Creamer); Give Me the Sunshine (C: James P. Johnson; L: Con Conrad; Henry Creamer); Got Myself Another Jockey Now [1] (C: Thomas "Fats" Waller; L: Andy Razaf); Harlem Rose (C: Con Conrad; L: Gladys Rodgers); Holiday in Jimtown [5]; How Jazz Was Born (C: Thomas "Fats" Waller; L: Andy Razaf); Keep Shufflin' (C: Thomas "Fats" Waller; L: Andy Razaf); Labor Day Parade (C: Clarence Todd; L: Andy Razaf); Leg It (C: Clarence Todd; L: Con Conrad; Henry Creamer); Let's Go to Town [5]; My Old Banjo [5]; On the Levee (C: James P. Johnson; L: Henry Creamer); Opening Chorus (C: Will Vodery; L: Henry Creamer); Pining (C: Clarence Todd; L: Con Conrad; Henry Creamer); Pretty Soft, Pretty Soft [5]; 'Sippi (C: James P. Johnson; L: Con Conrad; Henry Creamer); Skiddle-de-Scow [1] (C: James P. Johnson; L: Perry Bradford); Teasing Mama (Teasing Baby) [3] (C: James P. Johnson; L: Henry Creamer); 'Twas a Kiss in the Moonlight [1] (C: Stephen Jones; L: Con Conrad; Henry Creamer); Washboard Ballet (inst.) (C: Thomas "Fats" Waller); Where Jazz was Born [5];

Whoopem Up [5]; Willow Tree [1] (C: Thomas "Fats" Waller; L: Andy Razaf); You May Be a Whale in Georgia [5]

Cast: George Battles; Honey Brown; Josephine Hall; Byron James; James P. Johnson[4]; Evelyn Keyes; Aubrey L. Lyles; Flournoy E. Miller; Jerry Mills; Clarence Robinson; Maude Russell; Jabbo Smith[4]; Jean Starr; John Vigal; Thomas "Fats" Waller[4]

Notes: [1] Sheet music only. [2] Conrad also sometimes credited as co-lyricist but not in most sources. [3] Added after opening. [4] In orchestra. [5] Added after opening. In program of 9/3/28.

2303 • KEEPING UP WITH THE JONESES
OPENED: 1920
Musical   Off-Broadway

Composer: Edward Hutchinson
Librettist: James P. Mulgrew
Director: Thomas J. Grady

Source: KEEPING UP WITH THE JONESES (Comic Strip: Pop Momand); **Musical Director:** Ken Arnold

Songs: Best in the World; Couldn't Happen Now; Dancing Devil Dolls, The; Havana Bound; Heart Ache; Hold Me; I'll Be Your Carmen; Love's Sweet Mystery; No One But You; Sing Home Sweet Home for Me; Telephone Song; What a Day It Would Be

Cast: Marshal Arnold; Beatrice Harlon; James K. Wesley

Notes: No New York program available. Opened 9/6/20 Harrisburg.

2304 • KELLY
OPENED: 02/06/1965   Theatre: Broadhurst
Musical   Broadway: 1

Composer: Moose Charlap
Lyricist: Eddie Lawrence
Librettist: Eddie Lawrence
Producer: Joseph E. Levine; Daniel Melnick; David Susskind
Director: Herbert Ross

Choreographer: Herbert Ross; **Costumes:** Freddy Wittop; **Dance Arranger:** Betty Walberg; **Lighting Designer:** Tharon Musser; **Musical Director:** Sam Matlovsky; **Orchestrations:** Hershy Kay; **Set Design:** Oliver Smith

Songs: Augie Masters [2]; Ballad to a Brute; Big Time [2]; Blackouts [2]; Don't Come Near Me [2]; Everyone Here Loves Kelly; He'll Get It [1]; Heavyweight Champ of the World; Home Again [1]; I'm Gonna Walk Right Up to Her; Insurance [2]; It Kinda Makes You Wonder [2]; Life Can Be Beautiful; Me and the Elements; Moment Ago, A; (I'll) Never Go There Anymore; Ode to the Bridge; Simple Ain't Easy; Six Blocks from the Bridge; That Old Time Crowd; This Is a Tough Neighborhood; Times That Linger, The; Tried Jumpin' You Once [2]; We Got a Deal [1]

Cast: Wilfred Brambell; Don Francks; Anita Gillette; Leon Janney; Eileen Rodgers; Mickey Shaughnessy; Jesse White

Notes: [1] Cut prior to opening. [2] Not used.

2305 • KEYSTONE

OPENED: 01/13/1981
Musical   Closed out of town

Composer: Lance Mulcahy
Lyricist: John McKellar
Librettist: John McKellar
Producer: McCarter Theatre Company
Director: Nagle Jackson

Costumes: Desmond Heeley; **Lighting Designer:** F. Mitchell Dana; **Musical Director:** Rick Jensen; **Set Design:** Desmond Heeley

Songs: Come On Mabel; Falling Through Life; Get a Personality; Hey, Mister Conductor; Hollywood Baby; I Gotta Have Music; Keystone Strut; Laughter Ain't There Anymore; Mabel What's-Her-Name; One Chance; Remember the Good Times; Shadows; Slapstick and Laughter; Toons; Two; Two-Dollar Ring; Washing My Memories Away; What Am I Gonna Do

Cast: Tommy Breslin; Keith Curran; Randy Graff; Mark Martino; John Sloman; Douglas Walker

2306 • KICKS AND CO.

OPENED: 10/11/1961
Musical   Closed out of town

Composer: Oscar Brown Jr.
Lyricist: Oscar Brown Jr.
Librettist: Oscar Brown Jr.
Producer: Burt Charles D'Lugoff; Robert B. Nemiroff
Director: Lorraine Hansberry

Choreographer: Donald McKayle; Walker Vicks; **Costumes:** Edith Lutyens Bel Geddes; **Lighting Designer:** Jack Blackman; **Musical Director:** Jack Lee; **Orchestrations:** Alonzo Levister; **Set Design:** Jack Blackman; **Vocal Arranger:** Jack Lee

Songs: Beautiful Girl; Call of the City; Comb Is Hot, The; Doin' the Freedom Ride; Hazel's Ballet; Hazel's Hips; Hooray for Friday; I'll Get You Killed; Like a Newborn Child; Lucky Guy; Most Folks Are Dopes; Mr. Kicks; Opportunity, Please Knock; Prologue; Turn the Other Cheek; Virtue Is Its Own Reward; What's in It for Me?; While I Am Still Young; World Full of Grey

Cast: Lynne Forrester; Al Freeman Jr.; Burgess Meredith; Nichelle Nichols; Vi Velasco

Notes: Closed 10/14/1961.

2307 • KICKS: THE SHOWGIRL MUSICAL

OPENED: 1984
Musical   Unproduced

Composer: Alan Menken
Lyricist: Tom Eyen
Librettist: Tom Eyen
Director: Tom Eyen

Choreographer: Christopher Chadman; **Costumes:** William Ivey Long; **Set Design:** Robin Wagner

Songs: I Want to Be a Rockette; You Are the Only One

Notes: Two workshops but not produced.

2308 • KID BOOTS

OPENED: 12/13/1923   Theatre: Earl Carroll
Musical   Broadway: 479

Composer: Harry Tierney
Lyricist: Joseph McCarthy
Librettist: Otto Harbach; William Anthony McGuire

2312 • KING AND I, THE

Producer: Florenz Ziegfeld
Director: Edward Royce

Orchestrations: Frank Barry

Songs: Birdie, A [1]; Cake-Eaters' Ball, The; Day at the Club, A; Down Round the 19th Hole [1]; Dumber They Come the Better I Like 'Em, The [3] (C/L: Fred E. Ahlert; Eddie Cantor; Harry DeCosta); Fountain of Youth, The [2]; Got to Have More; He's the Hottest Man in Town [4] (C: Jay Gorney; L: Owen Murphy); If You Do What You Do [4] (C: J. Russel Robinson; L: Eddie Cantor; Roy Turk); If Your Heart's in the Game; I'm in My Glory; In the Swim; Intruder Dance, The [1]; It's Just that Feeling for Home [3] (C: Fred E. Ahlert; L: Sam M. Lewis; Joe Young); Keep Your Eye on the Ball; Let Me Introduce You to My Rosie [3] (C/L: Lew Brown; Eddie Cantor; Henry W. Santly); Let's Do and Say We Didn't; Mah Jong [1]; Old Lake Trail, The; On with the Game; Play-Fair Man!, A; Polly Put the Kettle On [2]; Same Old Way, The; Skipping the Skips [1]; Social Observer, The [2]; Some One Loves You After All; That's All There Is [1]; When the Cocoanuts Call; Why Don't You Say So? [2]; Win for Me

Cast: Beth Berri; Eddie Cantor; Harland Dixon; Mary Eaton; George Olsen; Ethelind Terry

Notes: [1] Out Washington D.C. 12/17/23. [2] Sheet music only. [3] Not in programs. [4] ASCAP/Library of Congress only.

2309 • KIKI

OPENED: 11/29/1921   Theatre: Belasco
Play   Broadway: 580

Composer: Zoel Parenteau
Lyricist: Schuyler Greene
Author: David Belasco
Producer: David Belasco
Director: David Belasco

Source: KIKI (Play: Andre Picard); **Choreographer:** Walter Brooks; **Set Design:** Ernest Gros

Songs: Kiki; Some Day I'll Find You [1]

Cast: Max Figman; Sam B. Hardy; Thomas Mitchell; Pauline Moore; Sidney Toler; Lenore Ulric

Notes: [1] Not in program.

2310 • KILKENNY

OPENED: 02/14/1916
Play   Closed out of town

Author: Augustus Pitou Sr.
Producer: Augustus Pitou Jr.
Director: Augustus Pitou Sr.

Songs: Countrary Mary Clary; Dear Mother Mine; Girl O' My Heart; Ireland Is Ireland to Me (C: Ernest R. Ball; L: J. Keirn Brennan; Fiske O'Hara); When It's Moonlight in Mayo

Cast: Adelaide Matthews; William T. Morgan; Anne Nichols; Fiske O'Hara; Marie Quinn; J.P. Sullivan

2311 • KILL THAT STORY

OPENED: 08/29/1934   Theatre: Booth
Play   Broadway: 117

Composer: Billy Rose
Lyricist: Paul Francis Webster
Author: Philip Dunning; Harry Madden
Producer: Abbott-Dunning Inc.
Director: George Abbott

Set Design: Stewart Chaney

Songs: Two Cigarettes in the Dark (C: Lew Pollack; L: Paul Francis Webster)

Cast: James Bell; Matt Briggs; William Foran; Gloria Grafton; William Shea

Notes: No songs listed in program.

2312 • KING AND I, THE

OPENED: 03/29/1951   Theatre: St. James
Musical   Broadway: 1246

Composer: Richard Rodgers
Lyricist: Oscar Hammerstein II
Librettist: Oscar Hammerstein II
Producer: Oscar Hammerstein II; Richard Rodgers
Director: John van Druten

Source: ANNA AND THE KING OF SIAM (Book: Margaret Landon); **Choreographer:** Jerome Robbins; **Costumes:** Irene Sharaff; **Dance Arranger:** Trude Rittman; **Lighting Designer:** Jo Mielziner; **Musical Director:** Frederick Dvonch; **Orchestrations:** Robert Russell Bennett; **Set Design:** Jo Mielziner

Songs: Anna and Son Klin [1]; Getting to Know You [2]; Hello, Young Lovers; I Have Dreamed; I Whistle a Happy Tune; March of the Royal Siamese Children (inst.); My Lord and Master; Now You Leave [1]; Puzzlement, A; Royal Bangkok Academy, The; Shall I Tell You What I Think of You?; Shall We Dance?; Small House of Uncle Thomas Ballet, The; Something Wonderful; Song of the King; Waiting [1]; We Kiss in a Shadow; Western People Funny; Who Would Refuse? [1]; Why? Why? Why? [1]

Cast: Yul Brynner; Larry Douglas; Sandy Kennedy; Gertrude Lawrence; Baayork Lee; Doretta Morrow; Dorothy Sarnoff; Johnny Stewart

Notes: [1] Cut prior to opening. [2] Music originally used "Suddenly Lucky" cut song from SOUTH PACIFIC.

2313 • KING AND MRS. CANDLE, THE

OPENED: 08/22/1955   Theatre: NBC
TV Show

Composer: Moose Charlap
Lyricist: Chuck Sweeney
Librettist: Sumner Locke Elliott
Producer: Fred Coe
Director: Arthur Penn

Choreographer: Tony Charmoli; **Costumes:** Guy Kent; **Musical Director:** Harry Sosnik; **Set Design:** Paul Barnes

Songs: What Is the Secret of Your Success; Young Ideas

Cast: Philippa Bevans; Theodore Bikel; Joan Greenwood; Richard Haydn; Irene Manning; Cyril Ritchard

Notes: Producers' Showcase. No song list available.

2314 • KING CASEY

OPENED: 11/18/1907
Musical   Closed out of town
Librettist: Aaron Hoffman

Songs: Deutschland; My Dixie Girl; 'Neath the Old Cherry Tree; Prairie Mary; Uncle Sam Land

Cast: Dan Coleman; Johnny Ray; Ford Sterling

Notes: No program available.

2315 • KING DODO

OPENED: 05/12/1902   Theatre: Daly's
Musical   Broadway: 64

Composer: Gustav Luders
Lyricist: Frank Pixley
Librettist: Frank Pixley
Producer: Daniel Frohman; Henry Savage
Director: Charles H. Jones

Set Design: Walter Burridge

Songs: Cat's Quartet, The; Claim Thou Thine Own; Diana [2]; Eminent Doctor Fizz, The; For Love I Live Alone; I Adore Thee; I'll Do or Die; I'll Shut My Eyes; Jolly Old Potentate, A; Lad Who Leads, The; Look in the Book and See; Mother Goose [1] (C/L: Unknown); Old Father Time; Pound the Drum [2]; Tale of a Bumblebee, The; They Gave Me a Medal for That; Troubadours; True Barbaric Soldier, A; Two Hearts Made One; Zamona [1] (C/L: Unknown)

Cast: Arthur Deagon; Raymond Hitchcock; Eugene O'Rourke; Gertrude Quinlan

Notes: [1] Interpolated. [2] Sheet music only.

2316 • KING HIGHBALL

OPENED: 09/06/1902   Theatre: New York
Musical   Broadway: 33

Composer: Frederick Bowers
Lyricist: Charles Horwitz
Librettist: Charles Horwitz
Producer: Edward E. Rice

Songs: Girl from Mars, The

Cast: George H. Carr; Marie Dressler; Will H. Sloan; Charles Sturges; Grace Walton

Notes: No other songs listed in program.

2317 • KING OF CADONIA, THE

OPENED: 01/10/1910   Theatre: Daly's
Musical   Broadway: 16

Composer: Sidney Jones
Lyricist: Adrian Ross
Librettist: Frederick Lonsdale
Producer: Lee Shubert; Sam S. Shubert
Director: Joseph Herbert

Costumes: Melville Ellis; **Musical Director:** Hugo Bryk; **Set Design:** Arthur Voegtlin

Songs: As Happy As a King [4]; Barber, The; Barcarolle [4]; Blue Bulgarian Band (C: Jerome Kern; L: M.E. Rourke); Catamarang [1] (C: Jerome Kern; L: Percival Knight); Change Partners [4]; Come Along, Pretty Girl [2] (C: Jerome Kern; L: M.E. Rourke); Coo-oo, Coo-oo [3] (C: Jerome Kern; L: Maurice Stonehill); Disguises (C: Frederick Rosse; L: Arthur Wimperis); Do Not Hesitate to Shoot; Every Girl I Meet (C: Jerome Kern; L: Percival Knight); Finale Act I; Hail to the King; In the Swim [4] (C: Frederick Rosse); It Is Time for the King to Behold the Fair Princess [4]; It's a Bomb; Lady of the Castle in the Air, The [4]; Lena, Lena (C: Jerome Kern; L: M.E. Rourke); Love and Duty [4]; Man I Marry, The [4]; Mother and Father (C: Jerome Kern; L: M.E. Rourke); Not a Little Bit Like You [4] (L: Adrian Ross; Arthur Wimperis); Opening Chorus; Opening Chorus Act II; Overrated [4]; Portrait, The; Reasons of State [4]; Situations [4] (L: Arthur Wimperis); Sparrow and Hippopotamus (C: Jerome Kern; L: Adrian Ross); There's a King in the Land To-day [4]; Things That I Know I Could Do [4] (C: Frederick Rosse); Time for the King; When a Fellow Loves a Girl; Wind of Love, The [4]; Woman and the Man, The [4]; You're Not the Only Cinder in the Grate

Cast: Marguerite Clark; William Danforth; Roger Dempster; William Norris; Clara Palmer; Mabel Weeks

Notes: [1] Music later used as title song of SALLY. [2] Also in THE GIRL AND THE DRUMMER. [3] The lyric is ascribed in some sources to Paul West. West may have written a diffrerent song titled "Oo-oo." [4] In London vocal score only.

2318 • KING OF HEARTS

OPENED: 10/22/1978   Theatre: Minskoff
Musical   Broadway: 48

Composer: Peter Link
Lyricist: Jacob Brackman
Librettist: Joseph Stein

Producer: Patty Grubman; Joseph Kipness
Director: Ron Field

Source: KING OF HEARTS (Film: Maurice Bessy; Daniel Boulanger; Philippe de Broca); **Choreographer:** Ron Field; **Costumes:** Patricia Zipprodt; **Dance Arranger:** Dorothea Freitag; **Lighting Designer:** Pat Collins; **Musical Director:** Karen Gustafson; **Orchestrations:** Bill Brohn; **Set Design:** Santo Loquasto

Songs: Any Old Girl [2]; Battle, The; Brand New Day, A; Close Upon the Hour; Day in Our Life, A [2]; Deja Vu; Down at Madeleines [2]; Femme Fatale [1]; Going Home Tomorrow; Hey, Look at Me, Mrs. Draba; I'm on My Own [2]; King of Hearts; Le Grand Cirque de Provence; March, March, March; Nothing, Only Love; Now We Need to Cry [2]; Only Time Is Now, The [2]; Promenade; Ready or Not [2]; Say Mama [2]; Somewhere Is Here; Stain on the Name, A; Take a Look at Me Now [1]; Truce, The [1]; Turn Around; What a Wretched Way to Run St. Anne's [2]; With My Friends [2]; World Is a Jungle, The [2]

Cast: Scott Allen; Pamela Blair; Bob Gunton; Rex David Hays; Millicent Martin; Michael McCarty; Gary Morgan; Neva Rae Powers; Gerrianne Raphael; Donald Scardino; Gordon J. Weiss

Notes: [1] Cut prior to opening. [2] Not in program.

2319 • KING OF SCHNORRERS, THE (1970)

OPENED: 1970
Musical   Closed out of town

Composer: Bernard Herrmann
Lyricist: Diane Lampert

Source: KING OF SCHNORRERS, THE (Novel: Israel Zangwill); **Musical Director:** Lynn Crigler

Songs: Before I Was Born; If I Had You for a Father; It Is Writ; La-De-Da; Long Live He; Long Way to Jerusalem; Mind Your Own Heart; More Than Music; Swain and Swain; Tree Without Sun, A; What the Butler Sang; Wind Bloweth, The

Cast: Jay Garner; Lou Gilbert; Raul Julia; Joe Ponazecki; Peggy Pope

Notes: Produced at the Goodspeed Opera House.

2320 • KING OF SCHNORRERS (1979)

OPENED: 10/04/1979   Theatre: Harold Clurman
Musical   Off-Broadway: 117

Composer: Judd Woldin
Lyricist: Judd Woldin
Librettist: Judd Woldin
Producer: Eric Krebs; Sam Landis
Director: Grover Dale

Source: KING OF SCHNORRERS, THE (Novel: Israel Zangwill); **Choreographer:** Grover Dale; **Conductor:** Robert Billig; **Costumes:** Patricia Adshead; **Lighting Designer:** Richard Nelson; **Musical Director:** Hank Ross; **Set Design:** Adrianne Lobel; **Vocal Arranger:** Norman L. Berman

Songs: Chutzpah (L: Amy Seidman; Judd Woldin); Dead; Each of Us; Fine Art of Schnorring, The; Guided By Love; Hail to the King [1]; I Have Not Lived in Vain; I'm Only a Woman; It's a Living [1] (L: Susan Birkenhead); It's Better to Give [2]; It's Over (L: Herb Martin); Just for Me [2]; Man Is Not Meant to Reason, A [1] (L: Susan Birkenhead; Judd Woldin); Murder; Petticoat Lane [2]; Sephardic Lullaby; Tell Me (L: Susan Birkenhead); Try Me [1]; What Do You Do

Cast: Lloyd Battista; Philip Casnoff; Ed Dixon; Rick McElhinay; Sophie Schwab

Notes: Originally titled PETTICOAT LANE (and titled that again after New York run). Titled TATTEDEMALION when revived Off-Broadway 10/27/85. See under that name also. [1] Cut after opening. [2] Added after opening.

2321 • KING OF THE SCHNORRERS, THE (1971)

OPENED: 1971   Theatre: Gallery
Musical   Los Angeles

Composer: Gary Koroll
Lyricist: Evelyn Rudie
Librettist: Ted Roter
Director: Edward Ludlum

Source: KING OF SCHNORRERS (Story: Israel Zangwill); **Choreographer:** Evelyn Rudie; **Costumes:** Lottie Zelby; **Musical Director:** Evelyn Rudie

Cast: Neva Davis; Ben Frank; Ruth Marcus; Ted Roter

Notes: No songs listed in program.

2322 • KING OF THE WHOLE DAMN WORLD!

OPENED: 04/12/1964   Theatre: Jan Hus
                              Playhouse
Musical   Off-Broadway: 43

Composer: Robert Larimer
Lyricist: Robert Larimer
Librettist: George Panetta
Producer: Norman Forman
Director: Jack Ragotzy

Source: COMIC STRIP (Play: George Panetta); **Choreographer:** Zachary Solov; **Costumes:** Rachel Mehr; **Dance Arranger:** Gershon Kingsley; **Lighting Designer:** William Ritman; **Musical Director:** Dobbs Franks; **Set Design:** Jack H. Cornwell

Songs: Don't Tear Up the Horse Slips; Far Rockaway; Grasshopper Song; How Do They Ever Grow Up?; Iggie's Nightmare; King of the World; Little Dog Blue; Night Gondolfi Got Married, The; Poor Little Boy; Riddle of You, The; There's Gotta Be a Villain; We March You Off in Style; What to Do?; What's a Mama For?; Who's Perfect?; Who's Perfect for You?

Cast: Sheldon Golomb; Alan Howard; Floria Mari; Tom Pedi

2323 • KINGDOM FOR A COW, A

OPENED: 06/28/1935   Theatre: Savoy
Musical   London

Composer: Kurt Weill
Lyricist: Reginald Arkell; Desmond Carter
Librettist: Reginald Arkell; Desmond Carter

Source: DIE KUBBANDEL (Musical: Robert Vanbery)

Songs: As Long As I Love; Two Hearts [1]

Notes: Played two weeks. [1] Same music as "Le Roi D'Aquitaine" from MARIE GALANTE.

2324 • KING'S CARNIVAL, THE
OPENED: 05/13/1901   Theatre: New York
Musical   Broadway: 80

Composer: A. Baldwin Sloane
Lyricist: George V. Hobart; Sydney Rosenfeld
Librettist: George V. Hobart; Sydney Rosenfeld
Producer: Sydney Rosenfeld
Director: Frank Smithson

Costumes: Caroline Seidle; **Set Design:** St. John Lewis

Songs: And the Band Began to Play; If I Had a Little Boy to Love Me; My Evaline (C/L: Mae Anwerda Sloane); My Sailor Boy; Ragtime Will Be My Finish

Cast: Harry Bulger; Emma Carus; Marie Dressler; Mayme Gehrue; Louis Harrison; Charles Prince; Adele Richie; Amelia Summerville

Notes: Preceded by A DEVIL'S DREAM, a ballet. There was also a vaudeville section.

2325 • KINGS OF KOONDOM
OPENED: 08/1898   Theatre: Koster and Bial's
                           Music Hall
Musical   Broadway

Composer: Bob Cole
Lyricist: Billy Johnson

Notes: No other information available.

2326 • KISMET (1895)
OPENED: 08/12/1895   Theatre: Herald Square
Play   Broadway

Composer: Gustave Kerker
Author: Richard F. Carroll
Producer: Harry Askin
Director: Max Freeman

Set Design: Frank E. Gates; Edward A. Morange; John Thompson

Cast: Aubrey Boucicault; Harry Davenport; Mabel Irvine; Lizzie Macnichol

Notes: No songs listed in program.

2327 • KISMET (1953)
OPENED: 12/03/1953   Theatre: Ziegfeld
Musical   Broadway: 583

Music Based On: Alexander Borodin
Composer: George Forrest; Robert Wright
Lyricist: George Forrest; Robert Wright
Librettist: Luther Davis; Charles Lederer
Producer: Charles Lederer; Edwin Lester
Director: Albert Marre

Source: KISMET (Play: Edward Knoblock); **Choreographer:** Jack Cole; **Costumes:** Lemuel Ayers; **Lighting Designer:** Peggy Clark; **Musical Director:** Louis Adrian; **Orchestrations:** Arthur Kay; **Set Design:** Lemuel Ayers; **Vocal Arranger:** Arthur Kay

Songs: Ababu (dance); And This Is My Beloved; Baubles, Bangles and Beads; Bazaar of the Caravans; Bored [2]; Fate; Gesticulate; He's in Love!; My Magic Lamp [4]; Night of My Nights; Not Since Nineveh; Oasis of Delightful Imagining, The [1]; Olive Tree, The; Rahadlakum [5] (C: George Forrest; Robert Wright); Rhymes Have I; Samaris Dance (dance); Sands of Time [3]; Stranger in Paradise; Was I Wazir?; Zubbediya

Cast: Henry Calvin; Joan Diener; Alfred Drake; Richard Kiley; Doretta Morrow

Notes: *See also TIMBUKTU!* [1] Cut prior to Broadway. [2] Written for show and not used. Added to film and subsequent revivals. [3] Does not appear in original Broadway programs but was in show. [4] Cut and then used in TIMBUKTU! [5] Tune originally written for Copacabana nightclub. Originally titled "I'm Going Moroccan for Johnny." Only song not based on Borodin music.

2328 • KISS BURGLAR, THE
OPENED: 05/09/1918   Theatre: Cohan
Musical   Broadway: 100

Composer: Raymond Hubbell
Lyricist: Glen MacDonough
Librettist: Glen MacDonough
Producer: William P. Orr
Director: Edgar MacGregor; Julian Mitchell

Musical Director: Leo Merriman; **Set Design:** Clifford Pember

Songs: Because You Do Not Know; Girl I Can't Forget, The; He Loves Me, He Loves Me Not; I Want to Learn to Dance; Little Black Sheep, The; Little Class of One, A; Mantelpiece Tragedy,

The; One Day; Rose, The; Shimmering, Glimmering Nile, The; Since I Met Wonderful You; Solitaire Land [1]; Temperament [2]; Your Kiss Is Champagne

Cast: Fay Bainter; Armand Kaliz; Janet Velie

Notes: [1] Sheet music only. [2] Out Atlantic City 5/18/18.

2329 • KISS FOR CINDERELLA, A
OPENED: 12/25/1916 Theatre: Empire
Play Broadway: 152

Author: James M. Barrie
Producer: Charles Frohman

Orchestrations: Paul Tietjens

Songs: Kiss for Cinderella, A (C: Paul Tietjens)

Cast: Maude Adams; Angela Ogden; Morton Selten

2330 • KISS ME
OPENED: 07/21/1927 Theatre: Lyric
Musical Broadway: 28

Composer: Winthrop Cortelyou
Lyricist: Derick Wulff
Librettist: Max Simon; Derick Wulff
Producer: Edward Elsner; J.J. Levinson
Director: Edward Elsner ·

Choreographer: M. Senia Gluck; **Costumes:** Mahieu; **Musical Director:** Alfred Newman; **Set Design:** Robert Stevenson; August Vimnera

Songs: Always Another Girl; Arab Maid with Midnight Eyes; Dance of the Green Eyes; Dodo; I Have Something Nice for You; If You'll Always Say Yes; Kiss Me!; Opening Ensemble; Pool of Love; Rose of Iran; Sleeping; Sleeping Beauty's Dream; Two Is Company; Welcome Home; You in Your Room, I in Mine

Cast: Desiree Ellinger; Joseph Macaulay; Fred Santley

2331 • KISS ME, KATE
OPENED: 12/30/1948 Theatre: New Century
Musical Broadway: 1077

Composer: Cole Porter
Lyricist: Cole Porter
Librettist: Bella Spewack; Sam Spewack
Producer: Lemuel Ayers; Saint-Subber
Director: John C. Wilson

Choreographer: Hanya Holm; **Costumes:** Lemuel Ayers; **Dance Arranger:** Genevieve Pitot; **Musical Director:** Pembroke Davenport; **Orchestrations:** Robert Russell Bennett; **Set Design:** Lemuel Ayers; **Vocal Arranger:** Pembroke Davenport

Songs: Always True to You in My Fashion; Another Op'nin, Another Show; Bianca; Brush Up Your Shakespeare; I Am Ashamed That Women Are So Simple; I Hate Men; I Sing of Love; If Ever Married I'm [1]; I'm Afraid, Sweetheart, I Love You [1]; It Was Great Fun the First Time [1]; I've Come to Wive It Wealthily in Padua; Kiss Me, Kate; So in Love; Tom, Dick or Harry; Too Darn Hot; We Open in Venice; We Shall Never Be Younger [2]; Were Thine That Special Face; What Does Your Servant Dream About [1]; Where Is the Life That Late I Led?; Why Can't You Behave; Woman's Career, A [1]; Wunderbar

Cast: Harry Clarke; Jack Diamond; Alfred Drake; Lorenzo Fuller; Annabelle Hill; Lisa Kirk; Harold Lang; Patricia Morison

Notes: [1] Cut prior to opening. [2] Cut prior to opening. Release has same music as "No Lover" in OUT OF THIS WORLD.

2332 • KISS NOW
OPENED: 04/20/1971 Theatre: Martinique
Musical Off-Broadway: 3

Composer: William S. Fischer
Lyricist: Maxine Klein
Librettist: Maxine Klein
Producer: William Formead; John Ramsey; Milan Stitt
Director: Maxine Klein

Choreographer: Sandra Caprin; **Costumes:** Nancy Adzima; **Lighting Designer:** Richard Devin; **Musical Director:** Herbert Kaplan; **Orchestrations:** Bill Brohn; **Set Design:** Richard Devin; **Vocal Arranger:** Herbert Kaplan

Songs: Death Dance; French Thing Tango; June Taylor, The; Kabuki Rock; Kiss Now; No Touch

Mine; Rodeo; Strawberry Day; This City Is a Kisser; Too Tired to Love; Touch Kiss; Travelin' Man; Try the Sky

Cast: Lloyd Bremseth; Sandra Caprin; Nancy Denning; Lyle Pearsons

2333 • KISS OF THE SPIDER WOMAN

OPENED: 05/03/1993   Theatre: Broadhurst
Musical   Broadway: 906

Composer: John Kander
Lyricist: Fred Ebb
Librettist: Terrence McNally
Producer: Livent (U.S.) Inc.
Director: Harold Prince

Source: KISS OF THE SPIDER WOMAN (Novel: Manuel Puig); **Choreographer:** Rob Marshall; Vincent Paterson; **Costumes:** Florence Klotz; **Dance Arranger:** David Krane; **Lighting Designer:** Howell Binkley; **Orchestrations:** Michael Gibson; **Set Design:** Jerome Sirlin

Songs: Anything for Him; Bluebloods; Come; Cookies [2]; Day After That, The; Dear One; Don't Even Think About It [1]; Dressing Them Up; Every Day [2]; Gabriel's Letter; Gimme Love; Good Clean Fight [2]; Good Times; Her Name Is Aurora; I Do Miracles; I Don't Know [2]; I Draw the Line; Kiss of the Spider Woman; Letter from a Friend [2]; Mama, It's Me; Man Overboard [2]; Maria [1]; Morphine Tango; My First Woman; Never You [2]; Only in the Movies; Over the Wall; Russian Movie; She's a Woman; Visit, A; Where You Are; You Could Never Shame Me

Cast: Kirsti Carnahan; Brent Carver; Anthony Crivello; Philip Hernandez; Herndon Lackey; Merle Louise; Michael McCormick; Chita Rivera

Notes: [1] Out Toronto 6/14/92. [2] Out Purchase, NY. 1991.

2334 • KISS WALTZ, THE

OPENED: 09/18/1911   Theatre: Casino
Musical   Broadway: 88

Composer: Carl M. Ziehrer
Lyricist: Matthew Woodward
Librettist: Edgar Smith

Producer: Lee Shubert; Sam S. Shubert
Director: J.C. Huffman

Source: LIEBESWALZER (Musical: Robert Bodanzky; Alfred Grunbaum; Carl M. Ziehrer); **Choreographer:** Gus Sohlke; William J. Wilson; **Costumes:** Melville Ellis; **Musical Director:** Frank Tours

Songs: Belle of Vienne!, The (C: Leslie Stuart); Do As You Please [3] (C/L: Harry Gifford; Alfred S. Lawrence; Tom Mellor; L: Martin Brown); Elevation (What I Seen I Done) (C: Louis A. Hirsch); Entrance Lisa; Fan Me with a Movement Slow (C: Jerome Kern); Finale Act I; Fishing [1]; Happy Married Life, A [2]; Help, I Implore [1]; I Feel a Bump Inside [2]; It Might Have Been Worse [2]; Jealousy [1]; Kiss Waltz, The; Laughing Song; Love Is Like a Little Rubber Band (Hoop Song) (C: Jerome Kern); Love Is Making a Sport of Me [1]; Love's Charming Art (The Dove Duet) (C: Jerome Kern); My Girl Takes Another Beau [2]; Nella's Entrance; O'er the Blue Waters; Oh Grand Riviera [1]; Oh! You Girls!; Opening Chorus; Opening Chorus Act II; Ta-Ta, Little Girl (C: Jerome Kern); Temperament; There's a Resting Place for Every Girl (Sun Chair Song) (C: Jerome Kern); Waltz Lesson, The (That's the Waltz for Me) [2]; Woe Betide [1]

Cast: Winifred Browne; Harry MacDonough Jr.; Adele Rowland

Notes: [1] Out Boston 5/22/11. [2] Sheet music only. [3] American version by Martin Brown.

2335 • KISSING GIRL, THE

OPENED: 10/25/1909
Musical   Chicago

Composer: Harry Von Tilzer
Lyricist: Vincent Bryan
Librettist: Stanislaus Stange
Director: Stanislaus Stange

Choreographer: Charles Jones; **Musical Director:** Leo Merriman

Songs: Come Little Girl and Dance with Me; Good Old German Beer; Hair of the Dog that Bit You, The; Hunter's Holiday; Little Band of Gold, A; Love Is Like a Rose; Major General Pumpernickel; My Soldier Boy; (On the B, on the Bou) On the

Boulevard; Schuetzen Corps, The; Waltzing; When You Kiss the One You Love

Cast: Mort Lorenz; Joseph Miron; John Park; Amelia Stone; Olive Vail

2336 • KISSING TIME

OPENED: 10/11/1920   Theatre: Lyric
Musical   Broadway: 65

Composer: Ivan Caryll
Lyricist: Irving Caesar; Clifford Grey; Philander Johnson
Librettist: George V. Hobart
Producer: Empire Producing Company
Director: Edward Royce

Source: MIMI (Musical: Edward Paulton; Adolf Philipp); **Musical Director:** Max Steiner; **Orchestrations:** Ivan Caryll; Claude MacArthur

Songs: Absolute Don of a Juan; Absolutely Certain; As Long As the World Goes Round (Tra-La-La); Bill and Coo (L: George V. Hobart); Custom-Made Maids; It's the Nicest Sort of Feeling (Ting-a-ling-a- ling) (C: William Daly; L: Irving Caesar); Keep a Fox Trot for Me; Kikerikee; Kissimee; Kissing Time; Let's Go What Do You Say? Let's Go! [1]; Love's Telephone; Mimi; Mimi Jazz; Oui Oui Marie (Wee Wee Marie) [2] (C: Fred Fisher; L: Alfred Bryan); Temporary Wives

Cast: Paul Frawley; Frank Norris; Mabel Taliaferro

Notes: Caryll wrote another musical titled KISSING TIME — for the London stage. It was titled THE GIRL BEHIND THE GUN when on Broadway. [1] Out Boston 8/30/20. [2] This song was registered by ASCAP in 1918. It might have been written for a different KISSING TIME.

2337 • KITCHEN MECHANIC'S REVUE

OPENED: 1930   Theatre: Small's Paradise
Revue   Nightclub

Composer: James P. Johnson
Lyricist: Andy Razaf
Director: Addison Carey; Charles Davis

Songs: Bantu Baby; Elevator Papa — Switchboard Mama; Go Harlem; Good for Nothin'; Kitchen Mechanic's Parade; Mammy Land; On the Level with You; Porter's Love Song to a Chambermaid, A; Sambo's Syncopated Russian Dance; Shake Your Duster; Slippery Hips; Swanee Fashion Plate; Ya Gotta Be Versatile

Cast: Harriet Calloway; Myra Johnson; Charles Johnson Orchestra

Notes: No program available.

2338 • KITCHEN OPERA

OPENED: 1947
Opera   Unproduced

Composer: James P. Johnson
Lyricist: Flournoy E. Miller

Songs: Accusation; At Home with My Range; Butler and the Cook Desire; Butler and the Handy Man; Chauffeur; Finale Love; Handy Man; Lindy Lou; Love; Mandy's Blessing; Solution; Spring Cleaning; Where Is the Handy Man

Notes: No other information available.

2339 • KITTIWAKE ISLAND

OPENED: 10/12/1960   Theatre: Martinique
Musical   Off-Broadway: 7

Composer: Alec Wilder
Lyricist: Arnold Sundgaard
Librettist: Arnold Sundgaard
Producer: Joseph Beruh; Lawrence Carra
Director: Lawrence Carra

Choreographer: Peter Hamilton; **Costumes:** Al Lehman; **Lighting Designer:** George Corrin; **Musical Director:** Joseph Stecko; **Orchestrations:** Jack Martin; **Set Design:** Romain Johnston

Songs: Bard, The; Can This Be a Toe Print?; Don't Give Up the Hunt, Dr. Puffin; Good Morning, Dr. Puffin; Hail, the Mythic Smew; I Delight in the Sight of My Lydia; I'd Gladly Walk to Alaska; If Love's Like a Lark; It Doesn't Look Deserted; It's So Easy to Say; Kittiwake Island; Never Try Too Hard; Nothing Is Working Quite Right; Oceanography and Old Astronomy; Robinson Crusoe; Smew Song, The; So Raise the Banner High; Under a Tree; Were This to Prove a Feather in My Heart; When a Robin Leaves Chicago; When One Deems a Lady Sweet

Cast: Lainie Kazan; Joe Lautner; Don Liberto; Kathleen Murray; G. Wood; Caroline Worth

2340 • KITTY DARLIN'

OPENED: 11/07/1917   Theatre: Casino
Musical   Broadway: 14

Composer: Rudolf Friml
Lyricist: P.G. Wodehouse
Librettist: Guy Bolton; P.G. Wodehouse
Producer: F. Ray Comstock; William Elliot; Morris Gest
Director: Edward Royce

Source: SWEET KITTY BELLAIRS (Play: David Belasco); Musical Director: William P. Axt

Songs: Am I To Blame?; Blarney Stone, The; Dawn of Love, The; Dear Bath; Dear Curracloe [1]; Dear Old Dublin; Health to Noah; I'd Do the Same; Just We Two; Kitty Darlin' (L: Otto Harbach); Land Where Dreams Come True, The [1]; Maid and the Valet, The; Mother of the Regiment, The [1]; Peggy's Leg; Spread the News; Swing Song; Sword of My Father, The; Tick, Tick, Tick [2]; Vanity [2]; When She Gives Him a Shamrock Bloom (L: Otto Harbach); You'll See

Cast: George Callahan; Glenn Hall; Jackson Hines; Alice Nielsen; H. Jess Smith; Frank Westerton

Notes: [1] Sheet music only. [2] Cut prior to opening.

2341 • KITTY GREY

OPENED: 01/25/1909   Theatre: New Amsterdam
Musical   Broadway: 48

Composer: Lionel Monckton; Howard Talbot
Lyricist: J.W. Piggot
Librettist: J.W. Piggot
Producer: Charles Frohman
Director: Austen Hurgon

Source: LES FETARDS (Play: J.W. Pigott); Musical Director: W.T. Francis

Songs: Belle of the Stage; Eulalie [1] (C: Jerome Kern; L: M.E. Rourke); Gentleman's Gentleman, A; Have You Got Another Girl Like Mary; If the Girl Wants You (Never Mind the Color of Her Eyes) (C: Jerome Kern; L: M.E. Rourke); Incognito; Just Good Friends (C: Jerome Kern;

L: M.E. Rourke); King Hal's Gals; Kitty's Not Built That Way; Look Aloft [2]; M'lle Pirouette; Mr. Soldier (C: Harold Lonsdale; L: Ralph Roberts); Ode, The; Strolling in the Gloaming (C/L: Hal Gaze); Sweet Kitty; Tract, The; Walking Home with Angeline [3] (C: Rundback; L: George Totten Smith); Welcome to His Majesty

Cast: G.P. Huntley; Percival Knight; Julia Sanderson; Valli Valli

Notes: [1] Sheet music only. [2] Out Waterbury, Conn. 10/14/??. [3] London only.

2342 • KITTY'S KISSES

OPENED: 05/06/1926   Theatre: Playhouse
Musical   Broadway: 170

Composer: Con Conrad
Lyricist: Gus Kahn
Librettist: Philip Bartholomae; Otto Harbach
Producer: William A. Brady
Director: John Cromwell

Source: LITTLE MISS BROWN (Play: Philip Bartholomae); Choreographer: Bobby Connolly; Costumes: Milgrim; Musical Director: John McManus; Orchestrations: Maurice DePackh; Set Design: Livingston Platt

Songs: Bounce Me; Choo Choo Love; Crystal Ball; Early in the Morning; I Don't Want Him; I Love to Dance; I'm a Little Too Old to Dance [1]; I'm in Love (L: Otto Harbach; Gus Kahn); Kitty's Kisses; Mr. and Mrs. (L: Con Conrad; Gus Kahn); Needles; Promise Your Kisses; Steppin' on the Blues (C: Con Conrad; Walter Donaldson; L: Otto Harbach); Thinkin' of You; Two Fellows and a Girl; Walkin' the Track; Whenever I Dream

Cast: John Boles; Dorothy Dilley; Nick Long Jr.

Notes: [1] Out Newark 4/26/26.

2343 • KNICKERBOCKER GIRL, THE

OPENED: 06/15/1900   Theatre: Herald Square
Musical   Broadway: 14

Composer: Alfred E. Aarons; W.H. Sloan
Lyricist: George Totten Smith
Librettist: George Totten Smith

Cast: Nellie Beaumont; Grace Belmont; Ada Bernard; Alice Clifford; Sydney Deane; Josephine Hall; Charles Judels; Harry Kelly

Notes: No songs listed in program.

2344 • KNICKERBOCKER HOLIDAY

OPENED: 10/19/1938   Theatre: Ethel Barrymore
Musical   Broadway: 168

Composer: Kurt Weill
Lyricist: Maxwell Anderson
Librettist: Maxwell Anderson
Producer: Playwrights' Company, The
Director: Joshua Logan

Source: KNICKERBOCKER HISTORY OF NEW YORK (Book: Washington Irving); **Choreographer:** Edwin Denby; Carl Randall; **Costumes:** Frank Bevan; **Musical Director:** Maurice Abravanel [4]; **Orchestrations:** Kurt Weill; **Set Design:** Jo Mielziner

Songs: All Hail the Political Honeymoon; Another Law; Bachelor Song, The [1]; Ballad of the Robbers; Brom's Compaint [3]; Clickety-Clack; Clump! Clump! Swish! [1]; Consequence Is Awful, The [3]; Dance of the Aborigines; Dirge for a Soldier; Entry of the Council [3]; History of New York, A; How Can You Tell an American?; How Far Will You Go with Me [3]; Hush Hush; I Do Business in My Hat [1]; I'll Sing of a Golden Age [3]; It Never Was You [2]; It's a Law [1]; May and January; No Ve Vouldn't Gonto Do It; Old Pete Is in the City [3]; One Indispensable Man, The; One Touch of Alchemy; Our Ancient Liberties; Romance and Musketeer; Scars, The (1) [3]; Scars, The (2); Scrubbing Song [5]; September Song; Sitting in Gaol; There's Nowhere to Go but Up; To War!; We Are Cut in Twain; We Want to Make the Laws [3]; Will You Remember Me?; Young People Think about Love

Cast: Howard Freeman; Walter Huston; Richard Kollmar; Jeanne Madden; Ray Middleton; Clarence Nordstrom; Francis Pierlot; Robert Rounseville; Mark Smith; George Watts

Notes: [1] Out Boston 9/27/38. [2] Music same as "You Cannot Buy Me Love" in DAVY CROCKETT. [3] Cut. [4] Used name Maurice d'Abravanel. [5] ASCAP/Library of Congress only.

2345 • KNICKERBOCKERS, THE

OPENED: 06/03/1893   Theatre: Garden
Musical   Broadway

Composer: Reginald De Koven
Lyricist: Harry B. Smith
Librettist: Harry B. Smith
Producer: Bostonians
Director: John Nash

Costumes: Mme. Siedle; **Musical Director:** Samuel L. Studley

Songs: Chorus and Entrance of the Governor; Country Dance and Chorus of Fiddlers; Finale Act III; Good Old Dame, The (Song of the Cuckoo Clock); Hans Rap; Hasten Time; Here's a Song for the Flag; I Have a Pipe; I Have a Swain in the Army; If There Is a Lad; If You and I Should Meet; Maiden Vexed, A (Spinning Song); Only in Dreams; Opening Scene and Chorus; Overworked Trumpeter, An; Puritan Damsel, A; Sing Your Merriest Lays; Sleep You Pretty Creatures; Song of the Flint and Steel; Twelve Hours a Day; Upon Our Little Farm; War to the Knife

Cast: Henry Clay Barnabee; Eugene Cowles; Fatimah Diard; Edwin H. Hoff; W.H. Macdonald

Notes: No songs listed in program.

2346 • KNIFE, THE

OPENED: 03/10/1987   Theatre: Public
Musical   Off-Broadway: 32

Composer: Nick Bicat
Lyricist: Tim Rose Price
Librettist: David Hare

Songs: Ache in Acorn; Africa; Agnus Dei; At Least There Are Parties; Between the Sheets; Blow Slow Kisses; Gay Rap, The; Hello Jeremy; Hello Peter We're Going Out; Knife, The; Macumba; Men's Eyes; Miserere; Open Sea, The; Shadows Dance Behind You; Shape I'm In, The; Someone Who Touches Me; To Be at Sea; What Would You Do in My Place?; What You Mean to Me; When I Was a Man; You're Not Unique

Cast: Ronn Carroll; Louisa Flaningam; Kevin Gray; Mary Elizabeth Mastrantonio; Cass Morgan; Mary Gordon Murray; William Parry; Mandy

Patinkin; Hansford Rowe; Mary Testa; Michael Willson

2347 • KNIGHT FOR A DAY, A

OPENED: 12/16/1907   Theatre: Wallack
Musical   Broadway: 176

Composer: Raymond Hubbell
Lyricist: Robert B. Smith
Librettist: Robert B. Smith
Producer: B.C. Whitney
Director: Gus Sohlke

Costumes: Arlene Falls; **Musical Director:** Paul Schindler; **Set Design:** D. Frank Dodge

Songs: Corsica; Garden of Dreams (C/L: Clare Kummer); Girl of the Great Divide, The [1]; Hurroo, Hurray and Hurrah for That [2]; I'd Like Another Situation Just Like That; I'm a Lawyer [1]; I'm Afraid to Go Home in the Dark [4]; Life Is a See-Saw [2]; Little Girl in Blue, The; Marceline's Meat Sauce; Mrs. Oho [1]; My Very Own (C/L: Clare Kummer); Situation [1]; Sweet Girl Graduate, The; Two Little Kittens [1]; What Fools We Mortals Be; Whistle When You Walk Out [1]; You Never Told Me That Before We Married [3]

Cast: Percy Bronson; Sallie Fisher; John Slavin; May Vokes

Notes: This was a reworking of MAM'SELLE SALLIE. [1] Sheet music only. [2] Used in MAM'SELLE SALLIE. [3] Cut 2/26/08 Kansas City. [4] There was a popular song titled "I'm Afraid to Come Home in the Dark," written by Egbert Van Alstyne and Harry Williams in 1907. This might be that song.

2348 • KNIGHTS OF SONG

OPENED: 10/17/1938   Theatre: 51st Street
Play   Broadway: 16

Composer: Arthur Sullivan
Lyricist: W.S. Gilbert
Librettist: Laurence Schwab
Author: Glendon Allvine
Director: Oscar Hammerstein II

Source: UNKNOWN (Story: Glendon Allvine; Adele Gutman Nathan); **Costumes:** Kate Drain Lawson; **Set Design:** Raymond Sovey

Songs: Act II Finale [1]; Bow Bow [11]; Bright Blue Sea [1]; Finale, Act I [6]; Finale, Act II [4]; Flowers That Bloom in the Spring, The [6]; For I Am Blithe [9]; Happy with Winged Feet [5] (L: Julian Sturgis); I Am a Judge [7]; I Was a Pale Young Curate Then [2]; Merry Young Heart [2]; None Shall Part Us [5] (L: Julian Sturgis); Now Give Three Cheers [1]; Oh, Is There Not One Maiden Breast [4]; Onward, Christian Soldiers; Opening Chorus [4]; Policeman's Song [4]; Poor Wandering One [4]; Ring the Merry Bells [1]; Screw May Twist, The [8]; Sir Joseph's Barge is Seen [1]; Take a Pair of Sparkling Eyes [10]; Three Little Maids from School [6]; When I, Good Friends [3]; When I Was a Lad [1]

Cast: Nigel Bruce; Natalie Hall; John Moore; Monty Woolley

Notes: Used songs from Gilbert and Sullivan operettas and the Sullivan/Sturgis opera IVANHOE. [1] From H.M.S. PINAFORE. [2] From THE SORCERER. [3] From TRIAL BY JURY. [4] From PIRATES OF PENZANCE. [5] From IVANHOE. [6] From THE MIKADO. [7] From TRIAL BY JURY. [8] From YEOMAN OF THE GUARD. [9] From PATIENCE. [10] From THE GONDOLIERS. [11] From IOLANTHE.

2349 • KNOCKERS OF 1919

OPENED: 1919
Revue

Composer: Edward Golden; Frank "Rags" Murphy
Lyricist: Edward Golden; Frank "Rags" Murphy
Librettist: Edward Golden; Frank "Rags" Murphy

Songs: All the World Wants Ragtime; Bell Boys Brigade; Blue Bird; Broadway Belles; Coontown Bank; Good Night; Honey, Come and Shimmie with Me; I'm Coming Back to You; Sweeter Than Sugar; Sweetie; They're All Sweeties (C: Harry Von Tilzer; L: Andrew B. Sterling); When the Band Plays Killarney; When the Sun Goes Down in Chinatown; You Cannot Roll Ze Eyes No More

2350 • KOREANS, THE

OPENED: 05/03/1898   Theatre: Herald Square
Musical   Broadway: 7

Composer: Lucius Hosmer
Librettist: Emerson Cooke

Cast: Richard F. Carroll; Samuel Edwards; Alice Holbrook; Gertrude Reynolds

Notes: No program available. Known as THE WALKING DELEGATE out of town prior to New York.

2351 • KOSHER KITTY KELLY

OPENED: 06/15/1925   Theatre: Times Square
Musical   Broadway: 166

Composer: Leon De Costa
Lyricist: Leon De Costa
Librettist: Leon De Costa
Producer: Arch Productions
Director: A.H. Van Buren

Choreographer: Ralph Riggs; **Musical Director:** Fred Schwartz; **Orchestrations:** Hilding Anderson; **Set Design:** H. Robert Law

Songs: Dancing Toes; I Want to Dance with You; I'll Cuddle Up to You; Kosher Kitty Kelly; What's in Store for You; Where We Can Be in Love; Why Should a Little Girl Be Lonely?

Cast: Beatrice Allen; Basil Loughrane; Fred Santley; Helen Shipman

Notes: Reopened 10/21/25 at Daly's 63rd St. Theatre after 105 performances at The Times Square.

2352 • KOSHER WIDOW, THE

OPENED: 10/31/1959   Theatre: Anderson
Musical   Off-Broadway: 87

Composer: Sholom Secunda
Lyricist: Sholom Secunda
Librettist: Louis Freeman; Jacob Kalich
Director: Jacob Kalich

Choreographer: Henrietta Jacobson; **Set Design:** Henrietta Jacobson

Songs: Actress, An; All Long Island Gossips; Belles of Belle Harbor, The; Good Luck; I Need You; Israel Shall Live; They've Gotcha on the Hutska; To Health; What's Destined to Be

Cast: Bruce Adler; Julius Adler; Henrietta Jacobson; Irving Jacobson; Jacob Kalich; Molly Picon; Mae Schoenfeld

Notes: No songs listed in program.

2353 • KRONBERG: 1582
Notes: *See ROCKABYE HAMLET.*

2354 • KUNI-LEML

OPENED: 10/09/1984   Theatre: Audrey Wood
Musical   Off-Broadway: 298

Composer: Raphael Crystal
Librettist: Richard Engquist; Nahma Sandrow
Producer: Jarick Prods. Ltd.; Jewish Repertory Theater
Director: Ran Avni

Choreographer: Haila Strauss; **Costumes:** Karen Hummel; **Lighting Designer:** Dan Kinsely; **Musical Director:** Raphael Crystal; **Orchestrations:** Raphael Crystal; **Set Design:** Joel Fontaine

Songs: Be Fruitful and Multiply; Boy Is Perfect, The; Carolina's Lament; Celebrate; Cuckoo; Do Horses Talk to Horses?; Little Learning, A; Lovesongs and Lullabies; Matchmaker's Daughter, The; Meeting of the Minds, A; Nothing Counts but Love; Purim Song; What's My Name; World Is Getting Better, The

Cast: Susan Friedman; Adam Heller; Barbara McCulloh; Steve Sterner; Gene Varrone; Scott Wentworth; Stuart Zagnit; Mark Zeller

2355 • KWAMINA

OPENED: 10/23/1961   Theatre: 54th St.
Musical   Broadway: 32

Composer: Richard Adler
Lyricist: Richard Adler
Librettist: Robert Alan Arthur
Producer: Alfred DeLiagre Jr.
Director: Robert Lewis

Choreographer: Agnes de Mille; **Costumes:** Motley; **Dance Arranger:** John Morris; **Lighting Designer:** Will Steven Armstrong; **Musical Director:** Colin Romoff; **Orchestrations:** Irwin Kostal; Sid Ramin; **Set Design:** Will Steven Armstrong

Songs: Another Time, Another Place; Cocoa Bean Song, The; Did You Hear That?; Fetish (dance);

Happy Is the Cricket [1]; I'm Seeing Rainbows [1]; Mammy Traders; Man Can Have No Choice, A; Naji's Nuptial Dance; Nothing More to Look Forward To; One Wife; Ordinary People; Seven Sheep, Four Red Shirts and a Bottle of Gin; Something Big; Sun Is Beginning to Crow, The; Welcome Home; What Happened to Me

Tonight?; What's Wrong with Me?; You're As English As

Cast: Ethel Ayler; Terry Carter; Robert Guillaume; Sally Ann Howes; Rex Ingram; Brock Peters

Notes: [1] Cut prior to New York.

L

2356 • L'CHAIM TO LIFE

OPENED: 11/05/1986   Theatre: Town Hall
Revue   Broadway: 42

Producer: International Artistic Prods., Inc.; Ralph Mercardo

Songs: Alleh Villn (C/L: Ben Zion Witler); Bei Mir Bistu Shayn (C: Sholom Secunda; L: Jackie Jacob); C'est Si Bon (C: Henri Betti; L: Andre Hornez); Chiribin (C/L: Traditional); Dance, Milonga, Dance! (inst.) (C: Eber Lobato); Du Iz Mein Hartz (C: Eber Lobato; L: Neil Steinberg); Dus Yiddishe Leid (C/L: Sholom Secunda); Far Mir Alayn (C/L: Max Perlman); Ich Vel Dir Kayn Mol Nisht Fabeytn (C/L: Ben Zion Witler); Kinder Yurn (C/L: Mordechai Gebirtig); La Vie en Rose (C: Louiguy; L: Edith Piaf); Lomir Trachtn Nor Fin Haynt (C/L: Ben Zion Witler); Mayn Ruchele (C/L: Ben Zion Witler); My Way (C/L: Paul Anka); Naches Fin Kinder (C/L: Traditional); Papirosn (C/L: Herman Yablokoff); Rivkele (C/L: Ben Zion Witler); Roumania, Roumania (C/L: Aaron Lebedeff); Shabbos (C/L: Ben Bonus); Shayn Vi Di Levune (C: Joseph Rumshinsky; L: Chaim Tauber); Sholom Aleichem (C/L: Leybele Schwartz); Tanguera (inst.) (C: Mariano Mores); This Is the Show (C/L: Eber Lobato); Valentine (C: Henri Christine; L: Albert Willemote); Yiddish (C/L: Ben Zion Witler)

Cast: Mina Bern; Gerri-Ann Frank; Michael Fritzke; Jackie Jacob; Eric Kaufman; Leon Liebgold; Mary Ann Marek; Ari Roussimoff

2357 • LA BELLE

OPENED: 08/13/1962
Musical   Closed out of town

Music Based On: Jacques Offenbach
Composer: William Roy
Lyricist: Marshall Barer
Librettist: Brenden Gill; Bill Hoffman
Producer: Albert Marre; Gerard Oestreicher
Director: Albert Marre

Source: LA BELLE HELENE (Opera: Jacques Offenbach); **Choreographer:** Todd Bolender; **Costumes:** Robert Fletcher; **Dance Arranger:** Genevieve Pitot; **Lighting Designer:** Ed Wittstein; **Musical Director:** Pembroke Davenport; **Orchestrations:** Philip J. Lang; **Set Design:** Ed Wittstein; **Vocal Arranger:** Pembroke Davenport

Songs: Canard, The; Go to the Mountains; Golden Crowns of Greece, The; How Will I Know?; I Give Up; I'll Fall in Love Again; I'm Called the King; It Isn't the Way You Play the Game; Night Music; No One Is Perfect; No Sad Songs for Me; Oh! What a Ball!; Peaceful Place, A; Play Nice; There Is No Such Thing as Love; This Is the Night; Transformation; Vengeance (Ballet)

Cast: Howard Da Silva; Joan Diener; Bob McClure; George Segal; Menasha Skulnik

Notes: No program available.

2358 • LA BELLE PAREE

OPENED: 03/20/1911   Theatre: Winter Garden
Musical   Broadway: 104

Composer: Frank Tours
Lyricist: Edward Madden
Librettist: Edgar Smith
Producer: Messrs. Shubert
Director: J.C. Huffman; William J. Wilson

Choreographer: William J. Wilson; **Costumes:** Melville Ellis; **Musical Director:** Oscar Radin; **Set Design:** Arthur Voegtlin

Songs: Bosphorus; Dat Lovin' Touch [3] (C: Leo Bennett; L: Sam M. Lewis); De Goblin's Glide (C: Jerome Kern; L: Frederick Day); Duel, The; Edinboro Wriggle, The [4] (C: Jerome Kern; L: M.E. Rourke); I'm the Human Brush (That Paints the Crimson of Paree) [4] (C: Jerome Kern); Look Me Over Dearie [2] (C: Jerome Kern); Monte Carlo Moon; Opening Chorus; Paris Is a Paradise for Coons (C: Jerome Kern); Pretty Little Leader of the Band, The [3]; Pretty

Milliners, The; Russian Dance; Sing Trovatore (C: Jerome Kern); Susan Brown from a Country Town; Teasing; That Deviling Tune (Rag) (C: Billie Taylor); That Lovin' Traumerei [3] (C/L: Aubrey Stauffer; musicbased on Robert Schumann); That's All Right for McGilligan [2] (C: Jerome Kern; L: M.E. Rourke); What Kind of a Place Is This?; Widows; You're Just a Perfect Peach Beyond My Reach [1]

Cast: Edgar Atchinson-Ely; Barney Bernard; Arthur Cunningham; Mlle. Dazie; Harry Fisher; Kitty Gordon; Mitzi Hajos; Dorothy Jardon; Al Jolson; Stella Mayhew; Paul Nicholson; Grace Studdiford

Notes: Included a one-act Chinese fantasy opera titled BOW SING. [1] Not used. [2] Added after opening. [3] Sheet music only. [4] Some sources attribute this song to Kern, Frank Tours and Edward Madden.

2359 • LA BOHEME

OPENED: 11/29/1984   Theatre: New York
                      Shakespeare Festival
Opera   Off-Broadway: 38

Composer: Giacomo Puccini
Lyricist: David Spencer
Librettist: David Spencer
Producer: N.Y. Shakespeare Festival; Joseph Papp
Director: Wilford Leach

Source: LA BOHEME (Opera: Giuseppe Giacosa; Luigi Illica; Giacomo Puccini); Source: SCENES DE LA VIE DE BOHEME (Novel: Henri Murger); Conductor: William Elliott; Costumes: Jane Greenwood; Lighting Designer: Paul Gallo; Orchestrations: Michael Starobin; Set Design: Bob Shaw

Cast: David Carroll; Patti Cohenour; Keith David; Merwin Goldsmith; Howard McGillin; Cass Morgan; Gary Morris; Caroline Peyton; Linda Ronstadt

Notes: No songs listed in program. Carroll and Morris alternated the same role. Cohenour, Ronstadt and Peyton alternated the same role.

2360 LA CAGE AUX FOLLES

OPENED: 08/21/1983   Theatre: Palace
Musical   Broadway: 1761

Composer: Jerry Herman
Lyricist: Jerry Herman
Librettist: Harvey Fierstein
Producer: Barry Brown; Allan Carr; Kenneth D. Greenblatt; Fritz Holt; Marvin A. Krauss; Stewart F. Lane; James M. Nederlander; Martin Richards
Director: Arthur Laurents

Source: LA CAGE AUX FOLLES (Play: Jean Poiret); Choreographer: Scott Salmon; Costumes: Theoni V. Aldredge; Dance Arranger: Gordon Harrell; Lighting Designer: Jules Fisher; Musical Director: Donald Pippin; Orchestrations: Jim Tyler; Set Design: David Mitchell; Vocal Arranger: Donald Pippin

Songs: Best of Times, The; Cocktail Counterpoint [5]; Have a Nice Day [6]; I Am What I Am [3], La Cage aux Folles; Little More Mascara, A [2]; Look Over There; Masculinity; Promenade, The; Song on the Sand; We Are What We Are [3]; Where Did We Go Wrong? [1]; With Anne on My Arm [4]; With You on My Arm [4]

Cast: Gene Barry; Walter Charles; Jay Garner; George Hearn; Brian Kelly; Merle Louise; Elizabeth Parrish; Leslie Stevens; William Thomas Jr.; John Weiner

Notes: [1] Cut prior to opening. [2] Same music as "Beautiful" from MADAME APHRODITE. [3] Same music. [4] Same music. [5] Uses some of the same music as "Have a Nice Day." [6] Cut prior to opening. Uses some of the same music as "Counterpoint."

2361 • LA FALOTE

OPENED: 03/01/1897   Theatre: Casino
Musical   Broadway: 16

Composer: Louis Varney
Lyricist: J. Cheever Goodwin
Librettist: J. Cheever Goodwin
Director: J.C. Duff

Cast: Paula Edwards; W.J. LeMoyne; Georgia Powers; Guy Standing

Notes: No songs listed in program.

2362 • LA GROSSE VALISE

OPENED: 12/14/1965   Theatre: 54th St.
Revue   Broadway: 7

Composer: Gerard Calvi
Lyricist: Harold Rome
Librettist: Robert Dhery
Producer: Joseph Kipness; Arthur Lesser
Director: Robert Dhery

Choreographer: Colette Brosset; **Costumes:** Jacques Dupont; **Lighting Designer:** John Gleason; **Musical Director:** Lehman Engel; **Orchestrations:** Gerard Calvi; **Set Design:** Jacques Dupont

Songs: Big One, A; C'est Defendu; Delilah Done Me Wrong (The No Haircut Song); For You; Hamburg Waltz; Happy Song; Hawaii; La Grosse Valise; La Java; Sandwich for Two; Slippy Sloppy Shoes; Spanish Dance; Xanadu (Les Elephants Roses) (La Marijuana)

Cast: France Arnell; Ronald Fraser; John Maxim; Victor Spinetti; Brigitte Valadin

2363 • LA-LA-LUCILLE

OPENED: 05/26/1919   Theatre: Henry Miller's
Musical   Broadway: 104

Composer: George Gershwin
Lyricist: B.G. DeSylva; Arthur Jackson
Librettist: Fred Jackson
Producer: Alex A. Aarons; George B. Seitz
Director: Herbert Gresham

Choreographer: Julian Alfred; **Musical Director:** Charles Previn; **Set Design:** H. Robert Law

Songs: All the While [1] (C: Constance Uhl); Best of Everything, The [5]; From Now On; Golden Days [1] (C/L: Nat Goldstein); Hotel Life [1]; In My Home Town [1]; It Sort of Makes a Fellow Stop and Think [1]; It's Great to Be in Love; It's Hard to Tell [2]; Kindly Pay Us [1]; Love of a Wife, The [3]; Money, Money, Money!; My Dream of Love Is You [1]; My Fannie [1]; Nobody but You [2]; Oo, How I Love to Be Loved by You [4] (L: Lou Paley); Opening Chorus; Our Little Kitchenette [3]; Reputation [1]; Some Sunny Day [1] (C/L: Irving Berlin); Somehow It Seldom Comes True; Tee-Oodle- Um-Bum-Bo; Ten Commandments of Love, The; There's More to the Kiss than the X X X (L: Irving Caesar); Un Peu D'Amour [1]; When You Live in a Furnished Flat; Yodel O [1] (C: Bryan Foy)

Cast: Helen Clark; Stanley Forde; Clarence Harvey; John E. Hazzard; Janet Velie

Notes: Extra lyrics by George Baldwin but not identified in program. Out of town produced by Oliver Morosco. [1] Cut prior to opening. [2] Added after opening. [3] Not used. [4] Also in ED WYNN CARNIVAL. [5] Later in the 1923 London show STOP FLIRTING.

2364 • LA PLUME DE MA TANTE

OPENED: 11/11/1958   Theatre: Royale
Revue   Broadway: 835

Composer: Gerard Calvi
Lyricist: Gerard Calvi; Robert Dhery
Librettist: Robert Dhery
Producer: Joseph Kipness; David Merrick
Director: Robert Dhery; Alec Shanks

English Lyrics: Ross Parker; **Choreographer:** Colette Brosset; **Costumes:** Marcel Vertes; **Lighting Designer:** Charles Elson; **Musical Director:** Gershon Kingsley; **Orchestrations:** Gerard Calvi; **Set Design:** Erte

Songs: Acrobatie; Administration; Ballet Classique; Ballet Moderne; Billet Doux; Courting Time; Femmes Fatales; Frere Jacques; Hommage Musical; Husbands Beware!; In a Small Cafe; In an Indian Temple; In the Tuileries Gardens; La Corrada; Le Bal Chez Madame de Mortemouille; Les Finale de Paris; Light Soprano; Men at Work; Mobile Squad; On the Beach; 'Precision'; Queen of the Striptease; Rider to the Sea; Song of the Swing; Speakerine; Take-Off; This Other Eden; 'Trapped'; Ventriloquist, The

Cast: Pamela Austin; Colette Brosset; Roger Caccia; Robert Dhery; Jean Lafevre; Jacques Legras; Pierre Olaf; Nicole Parent; Ross Parker; Henri Pennec

Notes: These are sketches as well as songs. English lyrics by Ross Parker. Digmont, Lilla De Nobile, Alec Shanks, Jacques Esterel, and Henri Pennec created additional designs.

2365 • LA POUPEE

OPENED: 10/21/1897   Theatre: Lyric
Musical   Broadway: 46

Composer: Edmond Audran
Librettist: Arthur Sturges
Producer: Oscar Hammerstein I

Source: LA POUPEE (Musical: Edmond Audran; Maurice Ordonneau)

Cast: G.W. Anson; Trixie Friganza; Ferris Hartman; Anna Held

Notes: No songs listed in program.

2366 • LA REVUE DES AMBASSADEURS

OPENED: 05/10/1928   Theatre: Ambassadeurs
                                            Cafe
Revue   Paris

Composer: Cole Porter
Lyricist: Cole Porter
Producer: Edmond Sayag
Director: Bobby Connolly

French Lyrics: Rene Pujol

Songs: Almiro; Alpine Rose; Baby, Let's Dance; Blue Hours [2]; Boulevard Break; Fish; Fountain of Youth; Gershwin Specialty Introduction [3]; Hans; In a Moorish Garden; Keep Moving; Looking at You [4]; Lost Liberty Blues, The; Military Maids; Old-Fashioned Girl (Boy), An; Omnibus [1]; Pilot Me; You and Me

Cast: Morton Downey; Frances Gershwin; Muriel Harrison; Evelyn Hoey; Basil Howes; Mary Leigh; Pearson Brothers, The; Kathryn Ray; Eleanor Shaler; Three Eddies, The; Carter Wardell; Fred Waring's Orchestra; Buster West; John West

Notes: The program titled this show TROISIEME AMBASSADEURS — SHOW OF 1928. A book of lyrics was titled IN THE OLD DAYS AND TODAY. [1] Revised into "Do You Want to See Paris?" in FIFTY MILLION FRENCHMEN. [2] Cut from PARIS. [3] This short number by Porter served as an introduction to a medley of Gershwin songs. [4] Cut. Later in WAKE UP AND DREAM.

2367 • LA RONDE DES HEURES

OPENED: 1932

Songs: I Wouldn't Care (C: P. Read; L: Leo Robin)

Notes: No other information available.

2368 • LA STRADA

OPENED: 12/14/1969   Theatre: Lunt-Fontanne
Musical   Broadway: 1

Composer: Lionel Bart
Lyricist: Lionel Bart
Librettist: Charles Peck Jr.
Producer: Canyon Productions; Charles Peck Jr.
Director: Alan Schneider

Source: LA STRADA (Film: Federico Fellini); **Choreographer:** Alvin Ailey; **Costumes:** Nancy Potts; **Dance Arranger:** Peter Howard; **Lighting Designer:** Martin Aronstein; **Musical Director:** Hal Hastings; **Orchestrations:** Eddie Sauter; **Set Design:** Ming Cho Lee

Songs: All My Worldly Belongings [1]; Belonging; Encounters (dance) [5]; End of the Road, The (C: Elliot Lawrence; L: Martin Charnin); Everything Needs a Something (C: Elliot Lawrence; L: Martin Charnin); Great Zampano, The; He Who Laughs Last [1]; Hullo and Goodbye [1]; I Can't Wait (C: Elliot Lawrence; L: Martin Charnin); I Don't Like You (C: Elliot Lawrence; L: Martin Charnin); If Her Mother Only Knew [6]; Introduction [1]; La-La-La-La (C: Elliot Lawrence; L: Martin Charnin); Living in Dreamland (Tan-Tan-Ta-Ra! Farewell) [1]; My Turn to Fall [1]; Nothing [1]; Only More! (C: Elliot Lawrence; L: Martin Charnin); Road, The (inst.) (C: Elliot Lawrence); Seashell Game [1]; Something Special [3]; Sooner or Later (C: Elliot Lawrence; L: Martin Charnin); Starfish, Seagull, Pebble (C: Elliot Lawrence; L: Martin Charnin); Tan-Tan-Ta-Ra! Farewell [1]; There's a Circus in Town; To Be a Performer [1]; Trouble with Marriage, The (C: Elliot Lawrence; L: Martin Charnin); Wedding Dance (inst.) [4]; What's Going On Inside? (C: Elliot Lawrence; L: Martin Charnin); What's Left (C: Elliot Lawrence; L: Martin Charnin); Where Will We Be Tomorrow (C: Elliot Lawrence; L: Martin Charnin); With a Man [2] (C: Elliot Lawrence; L: Martin Charnin); With All These Worldly Possesions [1]; You're Musical (C: Elliot Lawrence; L: Martin Charnin)

Cast: John Coe; Peggy Cooper; Anne Hegira; Larry Kert; Lucille Patton; Stephen Pearlman; Bernadette Peters

Notes: [1] Cut prior to New York. [2] Program error titles this song "What a Man." [3] Cut prior to New York. Music used as part of "Encounters." [4] Same music as "If Her Mother Only Knew." [5]

Contains themes by Bart and Lawrence including "Seashell Game," "Everything Needs Something" and "Something Special." [6] Cut prior to New York. Same music as "Wedding Dance."

2369 • LA TICKERO
Notes: *See FRIARS FROLIC.*

2370 • LA VIVANDIERE
OPENED: 1893
Musical

Composer: Victor Herbert
Librettist: Francis Neilson

Cast: Lillian Russell

Notes: Closed out of town.

2371 • LACE PETTICOAT, THE
OPENED: 01/04/1927   Theatre: Forrest
Musical   Broadway: 15

Composer: Carle Carlton; Emil Gerstenberger
Lyricist: Howard Johnson
Librettist: Stewart St. Clair
Producer: Carle Carlton
Director: Carle Carlton

Choreographer: J.J. Hughes; **Musical Director:** Leon Rosebrook; **Set Design:** Carle Carlton

Songs: Boy in the Blue Uniform; Creole Crawl; Dear, Dear Departed; Engagement Ring (C: Emil Gerstenberger); Girl That I Adore, The [1] (C: Emil Gerstenberger; L: Carle Carlton); Have You Forgotten?; Heart Is Free, The; Hoppin' the Buck [1]; Little Lace Petticoat (L: Carle Carlton); One Word from You [1]; Opening Chorus; Playthings of Love [1] (C: Emil Gerstenberger); Renita Reinette; Rose Aria, The; Skeleton Ghost; Southwind Is Calling; Watch the Birdies

Cast: Luis Alberni; Vivian Hart; Stella Mayhew; Elcie Peck; Dick Powell

Notes: [1] Out 12/13/1926.

2372 • LADIES AND GENTLEMEN, JEROME KERN
OPENED: 06/10/1985   Theatre: Harold Clurman
Revue   Off-Broadway: 22

Composer: Jerome Kern
Lyricist: Oscar Hammerstein II
Producer: West Dobson
Director: William E. Hunt

Choreographer: Valerie Pettiford; **Costumes:** David P. Pearson; **Lighting Designer:** Dan Kotlowitz; **Musical Director:** Hank Levy; **Set Design:** James Wolk

Songs: All the Things You Are [11]; All Through the Day [19] (L: E.Y. Harburg); Can't Help Lovin' Dat Man [6]; Can't Help Singing [17] (L: E.Y. Harburg); Don't Ever Leave Me [7]; Fine Romance, A [13] (L: Dorothy Fields); Folks Who Live on the Hill, The [14]; Go Little Boat [4] (L: Anne Caldwell); How'd You Like to Spoon with Me? [1] (L: Edward Laska); I Won't Dance [12] (L: Dorothy Fields); In Love in Vain [19] (L: Leo Robin); I've Told Every Little Star [9]; Last Time I Saw Paris, The [16]; Let's Begin [10] (L: Otto Harbach); Life Upon the Wicked Stage [6]; Long Ago and Far Away [17] (L: Ira Gershwin); Lovely to Look At [12] (L: Dorothy Fields); Night Was Made for Love, The [8] (L: Otto Harbach); Ol' Man River [6]; Pick Yourself Up [13] (L: Dorothy Fields); Remind Me [15] (L: Dorothy Fields); She Didn't Say Yes [8] (L: Otto Harbach); Smoke Gets In Your Eyes [10] (L: Otto Harbach); Sunny [5] (L: Oscar Hammerstein II; Otto Harbach); Sure Thing [17] (L: Ira Gershwin); They Didn't Believe Me [2] (L: Herbert Reynolds); Till the Clouds Roll By [3] (L: P.G. Wodehouse); Way You Look Tonight, The [13] (L: Dorothy Fields); Who? [5] (L: Oscar Hammerstein II; Otto Harbach); Why Was I Born [7]; Yesterdays [10] (L: Otto Harbach); You Couldn't Be Cuter [20] (L: Dorothy Fields)

Cast: Michael Howell Deane; Louise Edeken; Milton B. Grayson Jr.; Delores Hall; Michele Pigliavento; John Scherer; Toba Sherwood; Frank Torren

Notes: [1] From THE EARL AND THE GIRL. [2] From THE GIRL FROM UTAH. [3] From OH, BOY. [4] From MISS 1917. [5] From SUNNY. [6] From SHOW BOAT. [7] From SWEET ADELINE. [8] From THE CAT AND THE FIDDLE. [9] From MUSIC IN THE AIR. [10] From ROBERTA. [11] From VERY WARM FOR MAY. [12] From the film ROBERTA. [13] From the film SWING TIME. [14] From the film HIGH, WIDE AND HANDSOME. [15] From the film ONE NIGHT IN THE TROPICS. [16] From the film LADY BE GOOD. [17] From the film COVER GIRL. [18] From the film CAN'T HELP SINGING. [19] From the film CENTENNIAL SUMMER. [20] From the film JOY OF LIVING.

2373 • LADIES FIRST

OPENED: 10/24/1918   Theatre: Broadhurst
Musical   Broadway: 164

Composer: A. Baldwin Sloane
Lyricist: Harry B. Smith
Librettist: Harry B. Smith
Producer: Nora Bayes; Frank Smithson
Director: Frank Smithson

Musical Director: Oscar Radin; **Set Design:** Dodge & Castle

Songs: All My Life (C: Harry Akst; Nora Bayes; L: Irving Fisher); Caroline [2]; Crowd of Girls; Drink Out the Old Drink [2]; Goodbye America (C/L: James O'Keefe); Happy Days; Here Comes the Bride [2]; I'll Tell the World [2] (C/L: Seymour B. Simons; L: Nora Bayes); Just Like a Gypsy [2] (C/L: Seymour B. Simons; L: Nora Bayes); Just the Two of Us [2] (C/L: Seymour B. Simons); M-A-Y-B-E [2] (C: Harry Ruby; L: Edgar Leslie); Me and You (C: Harry Akst; Nora Bayes; L: Irving Fisher); Older They Are the Harder They Fall, The [2]; On to Victory; Prohibition Blues [2]; Real American Folk Song Is a Rag, The (C: George Gershwin; L: Ira Gershwin); Some Wonderful Sort of Someone [3] (C: George Gershwin; L: Schuyler Greene); Spanish (C/L: Harry Clarke); Tea Party, The; Tell Me [2]; Waiting for This [3] (C: Harry Akst; Nora Bayes; L: Irving Fisher); What a Girl Can Do [1] (C: Harry Ruby; L: Bert Kalmar); What Could Be Fairer Than That [2]; What Men Can Do [2]; What Will We Do on a Saturday Night when the Town Goes Dry [2]; When I Build a Home (C: Harry Akst; Nora Bayes; L: Irving Fisher); Without You (C: Nora Bayes; L: Irving Fisher); Zing Boom Bah [4]

Cast: Nora Bayes; Lou Cooper; Irving Fisher; Stanley Forde; William Kent; Florence Morrison; Clarence Nordstrom; Charles Olcott

Notes: Titled LOOK WHO'S HERE out of town. Program of 11/13/1919 Toledo and 4/21/19 New York used. Gershwin songs not listed in either program. [1] Kalmar and Ruby not credited in Broadway program. [2] Out of town program only. [3] Not in any program. [4] ASCAP/Library of Congress only.

2374 • LADIES' PARADISE, THE

OPENED: 09/16/1901   Theatre: Metropolitan
                                    Opera House
Musical   Broadway: 24

Composer: Ivan Caryll
Lyricist: Richard Carle; George Dance
Librettist: George Dance
Producer: Alfred E. Aarons
Director: William Parry

Choreographer: M. Albertieri

Cast: Richard Carle; Alexander Clark; Josephine Hall; John Hyams; La Torjada; Templar Saxe; Queenie Vassar

Notes: No songs listed in program. Later revised and revived as MY ANTOINETTE. Templar Saxe is credited with one song.

2375 • LADY AUDLEY'S SECRET

OPENED: 10/03/1972   Theatre: Eastside
                                    Playhouse
Musical   Off-Broadway: 8

Composer: George Goehring
Lyricist: John Kuntz
Librettist: Douglas Seale
Producer: Arnold H. Levy; Haila Stoddard
Director: Douglas Seale

Source: LADY AUDLEY'S SECRET (Novel: Mary Elizabeth Braddon); **Choreographer:** George Bunt; **Costumes:** Alicia Finkel; **Lighting Designer:** Lawrence Metzler; **Musical Director:** John Cina; **Set Design:** Alicia Finkel; **Vocal Arranger:** John Cina

Songs: Audley Family Honour, The; Civilized; Comes a Time; Dead Men Tell No Tales; English Country Life, The; Firemen's Quartet; Forgive Her, Forgive Her; How? What? Why?; I Knows What I Knows; I Wait for Him [1]; La-de-da-da; Mother's Wish Is a Daughter's Duty, A; Old Maid, An; Pas de Deux; Repose; That Lady in Eng-a-land; Winter Rose, The

Cast: Rick Atwell; Donna Curtis; June Gable; Russell Nype; Douglas Seale; Danny Sewell

Notes: [1] Out Washington, D.C. prior to New York.

2376 • LADY, BE GOOD!

OPENED: 12/01/1924   Theatre: Liberty
Musical   Broadway: 330

Composer: George Gershwin
Lyricist: Ira Gershwin
Librettist: Guy Bolton; Fred Thompson
Producer: Alex A. Aarons; Vinton Freedley
Director: Felix Edward

Choreographer: Sammy Lee; **Costumes:** Iverson & Henneage; Jenkins; Kiviette; **Musical Director:** Paul Lannin; **Orchestrations:** Stephen Jones; **Set Design:** Norman Bel Geddes

Songs: Bad, Bad Men, The [7]; Buy a Little Button from Us [2] (L: Desmond Carter); Carnival Time; End of a String, The; Evening Star [1]; Fascinating Rhythm; Finale Act I; Half of It, Dearie, Blues, The; Hang on to Me; I'd Rather Charleston [2] (C: Desmond Carter); Insufficient Sweetie [3] (C/L: Cliff Edwards; Wells); Juanita; Laddie Daddy [1]; Leave It to Love; Linger in the Lobby; Little Jazz Bird; Little Theatre [1]; Man I Love [5]; Oh Lady, Be Good!; Rainy Afternoon Girls [4]; Robinson Hotel, The; Seeing Dickie Home [7]; Singin' Pete [1]; So Am I; Something About Love [2] (L: Lou Paley); Swiss Miss (L: Ira Gershwin; Arthur Jackson); We're Here Because; Weather Man [4]; Will You Remember Me? [1]; Wonderful Party, A [6]

Cast: Adele Astaire; Fred Astaire; Walter Catlett; Alan Edwards; Cliff Edwards; Kathlene Martyn; **Pianist:** Victor Arden; Phil Ohman

Notes: [1] Not used. [2] Added to London production 4/14/26. [3] Added after opening. [4] Cut after opening. [5] Not used. Also cut from STRIKE UP THE BAND (1927) and ROSALIE. [6] Titled "Oh, What a Lovely Party" in London program. [7] Cut prior to opening.

2377 • LADY BILLY

OPENED: 12/14/1920   Theatre: Liberty
Musical   Broadway: 188

Composer: Harold A. Levey
Lyricist: Zelda Sears
Librettist: Zelda Sears
Producer: Henry W. Savage
Director: John McKee

Choreographer: Julian Alfred; **Set Design:** Arnold A. Kraushaar

Songs: Come to Arcady; Futurist Rag, The; Goodbye, Goodbye; Greenwich Village; His Pipe; Historic Huzzies; If; Just Plant a Kiss; Legend, The; Love Comes Like a Butterfly; That's All He Wants; Tune They Play, The [1]; Vision, A (The Girl I Can't Forget) [2]; Worm's Revenge, The

Cast: Sydney Greenstreet; Boyd Marshall; Mitzi

Notes: [1] Also listed in some programs as "The Tune They Plug." [2] Sheet music only.

2378 • LADY BUTTERFLY

OPENED: 01/22/1923   Theatre: Globe
Musical   Broadway: 128

Composer: Werner Janssen
Lyricist: Clifford Grey
Librettist: Clifford Grey
Producer: Oliver Morosco
Director: Ned Wayburn

Source: UNKNOWN (Play: James T. Powers; Mark Swan); **Costumes:** Shirley Barker; **Lighting Designer:** Ned Wayburn; **Musical Director:** Harry James; **Orchestrations:** Stephen Jones; Oscar Radin; **Set Design:** Ned Wayburn

Songs: Bad Man Walk, The; Beautiful Love; Booze of Auld Lang Syne, The; By the Garden Wall; Chase, The; Doll's House; Don't Tell the Old Home Town; Girls I Have Met; Kiss Time; Lady Butterfly; Man Overboard!; My Cottage in Sunshine Lane; Sailors Sail Away; Waltz Time; When the Wedding Bells Ring Out; Wonderful You

Cast: Florenz Ames; Marjorie Gateson; Allen Kearns

2379 • LADY COMES ACROSS, THE

OPENED: 01/09/1942   Theatre: 44th Street
Musical   Broadway: 3

Composer: Vernon Duke
Lyricist: John Latouche
Librettist: Dawn Powell; Fred Thompson
Producer: George Hale
Director: Romney Brent

Choreographer: George Balanchine; **Costumes:** Stewart Chaney; **Musical Director:** Jacques Rabiroff; **Orchestrations:** Domenico Savino; **Set Design:** Stewart Chaney; **Vocal Arranger:** Charles L. Cooke; Domenico Savino

Songs: Coney Island Ballet; Daybreak; Eenie, Meenie, Minee, Mo; February (C/L: Lester Lee; Jerry Seelen; Danny Shapiro); Hit the Ramp; I'd Like to Talk About the Weather [1]; I'm Feeling Lucky Today; Kaltenborn Blues [3] (C/L: Lester Lee; Jerry Seelen; Danny Shapiro); Lady; Mistreated Gypsy [3] (C/L: Lester Lee; Danny Shapiro); Modes Made in Manhattan; Prairie Belle [1]; Queen of the Opera, The; Summer Is A-Comin' In [2]; Tango [1]; This Is Where I Came In; Three Rousing Cheers; Upsala [1]; What Every Young Man Should Know [1]; You Can't Get the Merchandise (C/L: Lester Lee; Danny Shapiro); You Took Me By Surprise

Cast: Mischa Auer; Gower Champion; Ronald Graham; Joe E. Lewis; Wynn Murray; Marc Platt; Evelyn Wyckoff

Notes: Production under the supervision of Morrie Ryskind. Assistance by Edgar MacGregor and Charles Walters. [1] Out New Haven 1/41. [2] Later in THE LITTLEST REVUE. [3] Out Boston 12/17/41.

2380 • LADY DO

OPENED: 04/18/1927   Theatre: Liberty
Musical   Broadway: 56

Composer: Abel Baer
Lyricist: Sam M. Lewis; Joe Young
Librettist: Albert Cowles; Jack McClellan
Producer: Frank L. Teller
Director: Edgar MacGregor

Choreographer: Busby Berkeley; **Costumes:** Ellis Porter; **Musical Director:** Louis Gress; **Orchestrations:** Frank Barry; **Set Design:** Kennel & Entwhistle

Songs: (I May Feel) Blah! But Not Too Blue; Buddy Rose; Dreamy Montmartre; In My Castle in Sorrento; In the Long Run (You'll Run After Me); Jiggle Your Feet; Keep Your Eye on the Ball [1]; Lady Do; Little Miss Small Town; Live Today; O Sole Mi-Whose Soul Are You?; On Double Fifth Avenue; Paris Taught Me 'Zis; Snap Into It; This Is My Wedding Day; You Can't Eye a Shy Baby

Cast: Lew Hearn; Karyl Norman; Frances Upton; Nancy Welford

Notes: Titled BUDDY ROSE out of town. [1] Out Washington, D.C. 4/3/27.

2381 • LADY FAIR
Notes: *See THE DESERT SONG.*

2382 • LADY FINGERS
OPENED: 01/31/1929   Theatre: Vanderbilt
Musical   Broadway: 132

Composer: Joseph Meyer
Lyricist: Edward Eliscu
Librettist: Eddie Buzzell
Producer: Lyle D. Andrews
Director: Edgar MacGregor

Source: EASY COME, EASY GO (Play: Owen Davis); **Choreographer:** Sammy Lee; **Costumes:** Kiviette; **Musical Director:** Roy Webb; **Orchestrations:** Hans Spialek; Roy Webb; **Set Design:** Ward & Harvey

Songs: All Aboard; Follow Master; Ga-Ga; I Kiss Your Hand Madame (C: Ralph Erwin; L: Sam M. Lewis; Joe Young); I Love You More Today Than Yesterday [4] (C: Richard Rodgers; L: Lorenz Hart); I Want You All to Myself; Let Me Weep on Your Shoulder [2]; Life of a Nurse, The; My Wedding; Open Book, An; Shah! Raise the Dust!; Sing [1] (C: Richard Rodgers; L: Lorenz Hart); Slow Down [3]; Something to Live For; There's Something in That [4]; Turn to Me [2]; You're Perfect [3]

Cast: Louise Brown; John Price Jones; Dorothy McCarthy; Margaret McCarthy; Marjorie White

Notes: [1] Originally in BETSY 1926. [2] Not in program. [3] Sheet music only. [4] Cut after opening.

2383 • LADY FROM LANES, THE
OPENED: 08/19/1907   Theatre: Lyric
Musical   Broadway: 47

Composer: Gustave Kerker
Lyricist: George Broadhurst
Librettist: George Broadhurst
Producer: George Broadhurst; Currie
Director: Thomas Wise

Choreographer: Lewis Hooper

Songs: Correspondence School, The; Dear Old England [1]; I Met My Love in a Restaurant; I Never Do It Now; It Takes a Woman to Catch a Man; Ladies Day; Opening Chorus; Rock-Rock-Rock Let Me Rock in My Old Rocking Chair (C/L: George Spink); Roller Skates for Mine [1]; Story Book Days; Sweetest Words That E'er Were Said, The; Take a Maid; That Really Was a Lovely Place for Me; Woman, Lovely Woman; You, Just You

Cast: Percy Bronson; Robert Peyton Carter; Ida Hawley; Walter Percival; Truly Shattuck; Thomas Wise

Notes: [1] Sheet music only.

2384 • LADY IN ERMINE, THE
OPENED: 10/02/1922   Theatre: Ambassador
Musical   Broadway: 238

Composer: Jean Gilbert; Al Goodman
Lyricist: Harry Graham; Cyrus Wood [2]
Librettist: Frederick Lonsdale; Cyrus Wood
Producer: Messrs. Shubert
Director: Charles Sinclair

Source: DIE FRAU IM HERMELIN (Musical: Jean Gilbert; Rudolf Schanzer; Ernst Welisch); **Choreographer:** Allan K. Foster; Jack Mason; **Musical Director:** Oscar Bradley; **Set Design:** Watson Barratt

Songs: Catch a Butterfly; Childhood Days; Dove Song, The [1]; Espanole; Farewell to Adrian (C: Al Goodman; Sigmund Romberg; L: Cyrus Wood); Follow You All Over the World (C: Al Goodman; L: Cyrus Wood); How Fiercely You Dance; I Love You So (C: Al Goodman; Sigmund Romberg; L: Cyrus Wood); Lady in Ermine (C: Al Goodman; L: Cyrus Wood); Land O' Mine (C: Al Goodman; L: Cyrus Wood); Little Boy; Marianna (C: Jean Gilbert; L: Harry Graham); Men Grow Older; Play with Fire (C: Al Goodman; Sigmund Romberg; L: Cyrus Wood); Silhouette Duet; When Hearts Are Young (In Springtime) (C: Al Goodman; Sigmund Romberg; L: Cyrus Wood); Woman's No, A (C: Al Goodman; Sigmund Romberg; L: Cyrus Wood)

Notes: [1] Out Newark 10/8/23. [2] Wood wrote the Romberg and Goodman lyrics.

2385 • LADY IN RED, THE
OPENED: 05/12/1919   Theatre: Lyric
Musical   Broadway: 48

Composer: Richard Winterberg
Lyricist: Anne Caldwell
Librettist: Anne Caldwell
Producer: Herndon Corp, The
Director: Robert Milton; Frank Smithson

Costumes: Will R. Barnes; **Musical Director:** Frank Tours

Songs: Beautiful Lady in Red; Chinese Dragon Blues [3] (C: Walter Donaldson; L: Irving Caesar); Columbia; Cupid's Alphabet (C: Worton David; L: George Arthurs); Down by the Kongaloo; Eyes of the Girl You Love, The; Family Faces; Garibaldi Band [3]; Gypsy Dance; I Can't Forget Your Eyes [3]; I Want Somebody [3]; I Want to Be Like Cleo [3]; I'd Rather Dance Here than Hereafter; Just Like Eva; Little Bit of Scotch, A [3] (C: P.H. Christine); Made by Dirks; Mr. Love Will Catch You Yet (C: Jean Gilbert); My Own California; Opening Chorus; Play Me That Tune (Ya-Da-De-Dum-Dum) [3] (C: Walter Donaldson; L: Irving Caesar); Pretty Little Girls Like You; Reconciliation [1]; Ships That Pass in the Night; Some Wonderful Sort of Someone; Something About Love [3] (C: George Gershwin; L: Lou Paley); Take Her to Pigeon Walk; Tumble El Toro [1]; Visions of the Fireside; Waltz of My Heart's Desire; Where's the Girl for Me [2] (C: Jerome Kern; L: Harry B. Smith)

Cast: Ward DeWolf; Glenn Hall; Ann Herndon; Donald Macdonald; Will Phillips; Adele Rowland; Valli Valli; Gertrude Vanderbilt

Notes: [1] Out Atlantic City 9/28/19. [2] Originally in 90 IN THE SHADE. [3] Added to show when brought back to Broadway.

2386 • LADY IN THE DARK
OPENED: 01/23/1941   Theatre: Alvin
Musical   Broadway: 467

Composer: Kurt Weill
Lyricist: Ira Gershwin
Librettist: Moss Hart
Producer: Sam H. Harris
Director: Hassard Short

Choreographer: Albertina Rasch; **Costumes:** Hattie Carnegie; Irene Sharaff; **Lighting Designer:** Hassard Short; **Musical Director:** Maurice Abravanel; **Orchestrations:** Kurt Weill; **Set Design:** Harry Horner; **Vocal Arranger:** Kurt Weill

Songs: Bats About You [3]; Best Years of His Life, The; Boss Is Bringing Home a Bride, The [1]; Dance of the Tumblers (inst.); Girl of the Moment; Greatest Show on Earth, The; Hollywood Party (Party Parlando) [1]; Home in San Fernando Valley [1]; Huxley; It Looks Like Liza; It's Never Too Late to Mendelssohn [3]; Mapleton High Chorale; Minstrel Dream [1]; My Ship; No Matter Under What Star You're Born [4]; Oh, Fabulous One in Your Ivory Tower; One Life to Live; Party Parlando [1]; Princess of Pure Delight, The; Saga of Jenny, The; Song of the Zodiac [2]; Tchaikowsky (and Other Russians); This Is New; Trial Combined with Circus, A [1]; Unforgettable [1]; Unspoken Law, The [1]; What a Lovely Day for a Wedding; Woman at the Altar, The; You Are Unforgettable [1]

Cast: Macdonald Carey; Margaret Dale; Danny Kaye; Gertrude Lawrence; Bert Lytell; Victor Mature; Natalie Schafer; Evelyn Wykoff

Notes: [1] Not used. [2] Not used. Music later used for "Madame Zuzu" in LOVE LIFE. This song was adapted into "You Have to Do What You Do Do" from THE FIREBRAND OF FLORENCE. [3] Cut prior to opening. [4] Not used. Song later adapted into "You Have to Do What You Do Do" in THE FIREBRAND OF FLORENCE.

2387 • LADY KITTY, INC.

OPENED: 02/16/1920
Musical   Closed out of town

Composer: Paul Lannin
Lyricist: Melville Alexander; Irving Caesar
Librettist: Edward A. Paulton
Producer: Melville Alexander
Director: Clifford Brooke

Choreographer: David Bennett; **Musical Director:** Orville Mayhood

Songs: Any Place Is Home Sweet Home with You; Be Aesthetic; Breath of a Rose; Great, Great Lover, The; I Always Give the Wrong Impression [1] (L: Irving Caesar); Language of Love, The; Mexico; Moonbeams [1]; Once in a Lifetime; One Little Girl; Perfume of Paradise, The (C: Alfred Solman); Row, Row; Say It Once Again; Star of Love, The; To Like to Love One Girl [1]; To Live, to Love Again [2]; You Can Dance Your Way Into Her Heart

Cast: Kitty Gordon; Marguerite Lamare; Donald Macdonald; Fay Marke; John Merkyl

Notes: Opened Ford's Theatre Baltimore. [1] Sheet music only. [2] ASCAP/Library of Congress only.

2388 • LADY LILY

OPENED: 11/28/1978
Musical   Closed out of town

Composer: Hank Beebe
Lyricist: Hank Beebe
Librettist: Marge Greene
Producer: Tarrytown Music Hall
Director: Marge Greene

Choreographer: Diane Coupe-Frankel; **Dance Arranger:** Frank Still; **Lighting Designer:** Howard Becknell; **Musical Director:** Frank Still; **Orchestrations:** Frank Still; **Set Design:** Jeffrey Glave; **Vocal Arranger:** Frank Still

Songs: But I Was There; Dare I; 'Enery the Eighth I Am (C/L: Traditional); Got a Match; Hold Back (C: Frank Still; L: Michael Lindon); Home Again; I'm Here (C/L: Tessie O'Shea); It All Belongs to Me (C/L: Tessie O'Shea); It's Men Like You (C/L: Tessie O'Shea); I've Got a Song to Sing; Lily of Laguna (C/L: Leslie Stuart); Oh, Charles; Song and Dance; We Mind Our Own Business

Cast: Richard Hayes; Tessie O'Shea

2389 • LADY LUCK

OPENED: 04/27/1928   Theatre: Carlton
Revue   London: 324

Composer: H.B. Hedley; Jack Strachey
Lyricist: Stanley Carter
Librettist: Shephard Firth
Producer: Felix Edwardes

Choreographer: Max Rivers; **Set Design:** Joseph Harker; Phil Harker

Songs: Blue Pipes of Pan; Happy; If I Were You [1] (C: Richard Rodgers; L: Lorenz Hart); If You Think of Speculating; I've Learnt a Lot; Oriental Atmosphere; Poor but Honest Working Girl, A; Sex Appeal (L: Greatrex Newman); Sing [1] (C: Richard Rodgers; L: Lorenz Hart); Six Little Lonely Hearts; Syncopated City; Turn Your Thoughts and Faces

Cast: Laddie Cliff; Leslie Henson; Phyllis Monkman; Cyril Ritchard

Notes: [1] Originally in BETSY.

2390 • LADY LUXURY

OPENED: 12/25/1914   Theatre: Casino
Musical   Broadway: 35

Composer: William Schroeder
Lyricist: Rida Johnson Young
Librettist: Rida Johnson Young
Director: J.H. Benrimo

Choreographer: Charles S. Morgan Jr.; **Musical Director:** Arthur Kautzenbach

Songs: Birthday Ensemble; Dance Climatique; Don't You Really Think I'll Do?; Dream On, My Princess; Hi There, Buddy; I'll Take You All; Kiss Me Once More; Lady Luxury; Longing for You; Opening Chorus; Pick-A-Pickaninny; Poster Dance; Tango Glide; That Rag-Tag Dance; Those Awful Tattle-Tales; When I Sing in Grand Opera; Whistle When You Want Me; Written in the Book of Destiny

Cast: Frank Andrews; Ina Claire; Harry Conor; Forrest Huff

2391 • LADY MADCAP

Notes: *See MY LADY'S MAID OR LADY MADCAP.*

2392 • LADY MARY

OPENED: 02/23/1928   Theatre: Daly's
Musical   London: 181

Composer: Albert Sirmay
Lyricist: Harry Graham; Leo Robin
Librettist: Frederick Lonsdale; John Hastings Turner
Director: John Harwood

Choreographer: Jack Hulbert; **Costumes:** Morris Angel; Idare & Cie; Laddie, Ltd.; Irene Segalla; **Musical Director:** Charles Prentice; **Set Design:** Joseph Harker; Phil Harker

Songs: Bulldog Breed, The; Calling Me Home (C: Phil Charig; Joseph Mayer; Albert Sirmay); Go Where You Go (C: Phil Charig; Albert Sirmay); If You're a Friend of Mine [1] (C: Jerome Kern; L: Graham John); I've Got a Feeling for Somebody (C: Phil Charig; Albert Sirmay); One You Care For, The (C: Charles Rosoff; Albert Sirmay); What About Me?; Why Should I Feel Lonely (C: Phil Charig; Joseph Meyer; Albert Sirmay); You Came Along (C: Phil Charig; Joseph Meyer); You Can't Have My Sugar for Tea [2] (C/L: Harry Graham; Bert Kalmar; Harry Ruby)

Cast: Vera Bryer; Paul Cavanagh; Richard Dolman; George Grossmith; Lester Matthews; Herbert Mundin

Notes: [1] Same melody as "In Love with Love" from STEPPING STONES and "Die Susse Pariserin" from DIE BALLKONIGIN. [2] ASCAP/Library of Congress only.

2393 • LADY OF MEXICO

OPENED: 10/19/1962   Theatre: Blackfriars'
Musical   Off-Broadway: 56

Composer: Rev. Joseph Roff
Lyricist: Sister Mary Francis P.C.
Librettist: Sister Mary Francis P.C.
Director: Walter Cool

Choreographer: Leonard A. Temme; **Costumes:** Alice Merrigal; **Lighting Designer:** A. Edward Klein; **Musical Director:** Paul Meyer; **Set Design:** A. Edward Klein

Cast: James Branch; Alfred Coda

Notes: No songs listed in program.

2394 • LADY OF THE SLIPPER, THE

OPENED: 10/28/1912   Theatre: Globe
Musical   Broadway: 232

Composer: Victor Herbert
Lyricist: James O'Dea
Librettist: Anne Caldwell; Lawrence McCarthy

Producer: Charles B. Dillingham
Director: R.H. Burnside

Costumes: Wilhelm; **Musical Director:** William MacQuinn; **Set Design:** Homer Emens

Songs: All Hallowe'en; And They Lived Happily Ever Afterward; Bagdad (L: Anne Caldwell); Bal Masque; Ballet Suite, The (inst.); Ballet-Youth; Cinderella's Dream; Drums of All Nations; Entrance of Cinderella; Fairy Music [1]; Finale Ultimo; Fond of the Ladies; Games of Hallowe'en; Garden Party, The; Harlequinade (inst.); Introducing the Lady of the Slipper; Jack O'Lantern Love [1]; Just Love Me All the Time [1]; Just You and I in Dreamland [1]; Lady of the Slipper, The; Little Girl at Home (L: Anne Caldwell); Love Me Like a Real, Real Man; Meow! Meow! Meow!; My Russian Girlski; Opening Chorus; Princess of Far-Away; Punch Bowl Glide (inst.); Put Your Best Foot Forward Little Girl; Ride to the Castle, The (inst.); Them Was Our Childhood Days; Witches Ballet (inst.)

Cast: Vernon Castle; Elsie Janis; Dave Montgomery; James Reaney; Lillian Rice; Fred Stone; Florence Williams; Peggy Wood; Gladys Zell

Notes: [1] ASCAP/Library of Congress only.

2395 • LADY PASSING FAIR, A

OPENED: 01/03/1947
Play   Closed out of town

Author: Harry Wagstaff Gribble
Producer: Henri Leiser
Director: Harry Wagstaff Gribble

Costumes: Henrietta Harra; **Set Design:** Frederick Fox

Songs: Sensemaya (C: Heitor Villa-Lobos; L: Nicolas Guillen)

Cast: Frederick O'Neal; Hilda Simms

2396 • LADY PRECIOUS STREAM

OPENED: 01/27/1936   Theatre: Booth
Play   Broadway: 104

Author: S.I. Hsiung
Producer: Morris Gest
Director: S.I. Hsiung

Costumes: Mei Lan-Fang; Lucille Samuels; **Set Design:** Watson Barratt

Songs: Lady Precious Stream (C: Edgar Fairchild; L: Milton Pascal)

Cast: Helen Chandler; Clarence Derwent; Bramwell Fletcher; Delmar Pappen; Molly Pearson; Natalie Schafer

2397 • LADY SAYS YES, A

OPENED: 01/10/1945   Theatre: Broadhurst
Musical   Broadway: 87

Composer: Arthur Gershwin; Fred Spielman
Lyricist: Stanley Adams
Librettist: Clayton Ashley
Producer: J.J. Shubert

Choreographer: Natalie Kamarova; Boots McKenna; **Costumes:** Lou Eisele; **Lighting Designer:** William Thomas; **Musical Director:** Ving Merlin; **Orchestrations:** Frank Denning; Ralph Lane; Ving Merlin; Irving Riskin; Paul Shelley; **Set Design:** Watson Barratt

Songs: Brooklyn U.S.A. (C/L: Will Morrissey); Chinese Ballet (C: George Kamaroff); Don't Wake Them Up Too Soon; Hop, a Skip, a Jump, a Look, A; I Don't Care What They Say about Me; I Wonder Why You Wander; I'm Setting My Cap for a Throne [1]; It's the Girl Everytime, It's the Girl; Leave Us Let Things Alone Like They Was (C: Harold Cohen; L: Bud Burtson); Lesson in Terpsichore, A [1]; Pillow for His Royal Head, A; Take My Heart with You; Venice Sings to One and All [2]; Viva Vitamins; Without a Caress; You're More than a Name and Address; You're the Lord of Any Manor [1]

Cast: Jack Albertson; Christine Ayers; Carole Landis; Sue Ryan; Jacqueline Susann

Notes: [1] Cut after opening. [2] Added after opening.

2398 • LADY SLAVEY, THE

OPENED: 02/03/1896   Theatre: Casino
Musical   Broadway: 128

Composer: Gustave Kerker
Librettist: George Dance; George W. Lederer
Director: George Dance; George W. Lederer

Costumes: Mme. Siedle; **Musical Director:** Gustave Kerker; **Set Design:** D. Frank Dodge

Cast: La Petite Adelaide; Richard Carle; Dan Daly; Charles Danby; Marie Dressler; Virginia Earle; Walter Jones

Notes: No songs listed in program.

2399 • LADY TEAZLE

OPENED: 12/24/1904   Theatre: Casino
Musical   Broadway: 57

Composer: A. Baldwin Sloane
Lyricist: John Kendrick Bangs
Librettist: John Kendrick Bangs; Roderic C. Penfield
Producer: Messrs. Shubert
Director: R.H. Burnside

Source: SCHOOL FOR SCANDAL, THE (Play: Richard Brinsley Sheridan); **Musical Director:** Augustus Barratt

Songs: Auction Song, The [1]; Charity; Consciousness of Innocence, The; Dainty Little Milliner, The; Dance, The [1]; Dear Old London Town; Gay Divorcee, The; Here's to a Bashful Girl of Fifteen; Hypocrite, The; In Dear Old Grandma's Days [1]; Love By Proxy; Macaronis We; Power of the Press, The; Roger De Coverly; Scandal Club, The; Smart Set, The; Tittle-Tattle; Were I Happily Married; Wherefore and the Why, The; Would You; You Mustn't Do That in High Society; You've Lied to Me

Cast: William Carleton; Stanley Hawkins; Lillian Russell; Elsa Ryan; Van Rensselaer Wheeler

Notes: [1] Out Boston 3/4/5.

2400 • LAFFING ROOM ONLY

OPENED: 12/23/1944   Theatre: Winter Garden
Revue   Broadway: 232

Composer: Burton Lane
Lyricist: Burton Lane
Librettist: Eugene Conrad; Chic Johnson; Ole Olsen
Producer: Chic Johnson; Ole Olsen; Messrs. Shubert
Director: John Murray Anderson; Edward Cline

Choreographer: Robert Alton; **Costumes:** Billy Livingston; **Musical Director:** John McManus; **Set Design:** Stewart Chaney

Songs: Doolittle Hop, The [2]; Feudin' and Fightin' [1] (L: Burton Lane; Frank Loesser); Go Down to Boston Harbor; Got That Good Time Feelin'; Gotta Get Joy (L: Al Dubin); Hellzapoppin Polka, The; Hooray for Anywhere; Mother Mississippi; Steps of the Capitol, The; Stop That Dancing; Sunny California; This Is As Far As I Go; Two on an Island; You Excite Me [3]

Cast: Betty Garrett; Chic Johnson; Frank Libuse; Mata & Hari; Jean Moorehead; Ole Olsen; Fred Waring Glee Club

Notes: [1] Titled "Fussin', Feudin' & Fightin'" in program. Loesser actually wrote the lyrics for this song, not Al Dubin as is usually credited. [2] Out Washington D.C. 6/3/46. [3] Out Boston prior to opening.

2401 • LAMBS ANNUAL DINNER, GAMBOL AND BALL, THE

OPENED: 12/06/1941
Revue   New York

Director: Arnold Johnson

Musical Director: Robert Shaw; Fred Waring

Songs: Lambshine Pudding (Madrigal) (C: Stanley Miller; L: Alan Jay Lerner); Sawbuck, a Fin or a Dime, A (C: John McManus; L: Bruce Balfour Evans); Unknown [1] (C: Arnold Johnson; L: Earle Crooker)

Cast: Ray Bolger; Danny Kaye; Marty May; Gil Stratton Jr.; Fred Waring's Pennsylvanians

Notes: A benefit at the Waldorf-Astoria, the night before Pearl Harbor. There was also a mini-musical HERE WE ARE AGAIN in this show. See under that name for those credits. [1] Part of an act performed by Gil Stratton, Jr.

2402 • LAMBS ANNUAL GAMBOL, THE

OPENED: 12/03/1938
Revue

Librettist: Marc Connelly; David Friedman; Frederick Howard; George S. Kaufman

Songs: Debonairs, The (C: Unknown; L: Edwin Gale); Low Down, The (C: Percy Wenrich; L: Harry Clarke)

Cast: Bobby Clark; Hal Forde; William Gaxton; Benny Goodman; Paul Haakon; Victor Moore; Fred Waring & His Pennsylvanians; Jack Whiting

Notes: Waldorf-Astoria Hotel.

2403 • LAMBS ANNUAL PUBLIC SPRING GAMBOL, THE

OPENED: 04/26/1925   Theatre: Metropolitan
                     Opera House
Revue   New York

Director: R.H. Burnside; Carl Randall

Musical Director: Hugo Riesenfeld

Songs: Advertising Blues (C: Percy Wenrich; L: Roger Gray)

Cast: Fred Astaire; Lionel Barrymore; Eddie Cantor; Walter Catlett; Joseph Cawthorn; Bobby Clark; Criterion Theatre Orchestra; Harland Dixon; Cliff Edwards; John Emerson; Leon Errol; W.C. Fields; James Gleason; DeWolf Hopper; Al Jolson; Paul McCullough; Carl Randall; Rialto Theatre Orchestra; Rivoli Theatre Orchestra; Will Rogers; Pat Rooney; Hal Skelly; John Philip Sousa; Ernest Truex; Louis Wolheim

Notes: The evening included mini-musicals titled BIRDS OF THE EVENING, THE DASHING BELLES OF YESTERDAY AND THE DUMBBELLES OF TODAY and another titled A NIGHT IN OLD PARIS. See under those names for each show. There was also a one-act version of Gilbert and Sullivan's TRIAL BY JURY as well as a dancing exhibition titled DANCING FOOLS.

2404 • LAMBS FROLIC

OPENED: 1904
Revue

Songs: Lambs in Toyland (C: Victor Herbert; L: Grant Stewart)

Notes: Produced at the Lambs Club. No other information available.

2405 • LAMBS SPRING GAMBOL, THE

OPENED: 04/25/1936
Revue

Musical Director: August Kleinecke

Songs: Riverside Sailors (C: Percy Wenrich; L: Harry Clarke)

Cast: Richard Crooks; Cliff Edwards; Eddie Garr; Fred Waring & His Pennsylvanians

Notes: Waldorf-Astoria Hotel. This revue also featured a "Musical Fantasy" A WALTZ WAS BORN IN VIENNA. See under that title for its credits.

2406 • LAMBS WINTER GAMBOL, THE

OPENED: 12/05/1936
Revue

Musical Director: August Kleinecke

Songs: Beautiful Dolls (C/L: Fred Hillebrand); Hamlets of the Ages (C/L: Fred Hillebrand)

Cast: Roy Atwell; Edgar Bergen; Paul Draper; Rudy Vallee; Paul Whiteman

Notes: Waldorf-Astoria Hotel. This show contained a one-act "Musical Fantasy" titled ONE APRIL DAY. *See under that name for that show's credits.* [1] This is a "Musical Fantasy" that comprised several songs which were not listed in the program.

2407 • LAND OF JOY, THE

OPENED: 10/31/1917   Theatre: Park
Revue   Broadway: 86

Composer: Joaquin Valverde
Lyricist: Ruth Boyd Ober
Librettist: Montague Glass; Ruth Boyd Ober; C.A. de Lima
Producer: Velasco Brothers
Director: Eulogio Velasco

Source: UNKNOWN (Musical: J.F. Elizondo; Eulogio Velasco); **Musical Director:** Julian Beneboch

Songs: Ay! Que Rico; Basilica [1]; Garrotin Sarrano; Garrotin Song and Dance; Holy Week; Jerezanos; Latirana; Maja de Goya; Maja Moderna; Marshosito; Off to Spain; Oh My Darling; Pepe Hillo; Serafina; Serenade; Torrito, Torerazo; Wedding Song, A; Zingara Dance

Cast: Irving Brooks; Nanette Flack; Matt Hanley; George Lydercker; Maria Marco; Jesus Navarro; Ruth Boyd Ober

Notes: [1] Out of town program only.

2408 • LAND OF NOD, THE

OPENED: 04/01/1907   Theatre: New York
Musical   Broadway: 17

Composer: Joseph E. Howard
Lyricist: Frank Adams; Will M. Hough
Librettist: Frank Adams; George V. Hobart[8]; Will M. Hough
Producer: F.C. Whitney

Songs: April Fool Ditty [1]; Belle of Bald Head Row, The; Blame the Weather Man [1]; Bonnie Briar Bush [1]; Burglar's Serenade [4]; Cock-a-doodle-doo [1]; Come On, Let's Two Step [1]; Dear Heart [9]; Devil's Serenade, The [2]; Girl You Dream About, The [9]; Heart to Let, A [4] (L: Joseph E. Howard); How Was I to Know [1]; If You Grow Tired Little Girl [1]; In the Shade of My Bungalow [2]; It's Great to Be an Actor [1]; Jealousy; Jingles and Jokes [3]; Just a Paper Doll [4]; Land of Nod, The [5]; Love Contagious [1]; Merry Old King [1]; My Cinderella; Nightmare and Goblin March, The [3]; Nonsense [1]; Once More to Dream [1]; Same Old Moon, The; Smarty [6]; Wedding of the Chafing Dish and the Alcohol Lamp, The [2]; When You Grow Tired Just Let Me Know [4] (L: Addison Burkhardt); You Can't Keep a Good Man Down [7]

Cast: Mabel Barrison; Carrie DeMar; Joseph E. Howard; William Norris; Knox Wilson

Notes: Interpolated numbers by Joseph Hart. Second half of bill was THE SONG BIRDS with music by Victor Herbert and lyrics by George V. Hobart. [1] Out Cedar Rapids, 1906. [2] Out Newport 5/5/08. [3] Out Toledo 3/22/06. [4]

Sheet music only. [5] Out Newport 5/5/08. Also in HIS HIGHNESS THE BEY. [6] Out Newport 5/5/08. There was a popular song of the same name written by M.F. Carey in 1900. [7] Out Cedar Rapids 1906. There was a popular song of the same name with music by Albert Von Tilzer and lyrics by Jack Norworth written in 1908. [8] Hobart adapted Adams and Hough's libretto. [9] ASCAP/Library of Congress only.

2409 • LAND OF SMILES, THE
Notes: *See YOURS IS MY HEART.*

2410 • LAND OF THE BIRDS
Notes: *See SPORTING DAYS.*

2411 • LARK, THE

OPENED: 11/17/1955   Theatre: Longacre
Play   Broadway: 229

Composer: Leonard Bernstein
Lyricist: Leonard Bernstein
Author: Jean Anouilh
Adaptation: Lillian Hellman
Producer: Kermit Bloomgarden
Director: Joseph Anthony

Costumes: Alvin Colt; Incidental Music: Leonard Bernstein; **Lighting Designer:** Jo Mielziner; **Set Design:** Jo Mielziner

Songs: Benedictus; Court Song; Gloria; Prelude; Requiem; Sanctus; Soldier's Song; Spring Song

Cast: Theodore Bikel; Ward Costello; Roger De Koven; Julie Harris; Michael Higgins; Boris Karloff; Christopher Plummer; Ralph Roberts; Joseph Wiseman

2412 • LASSIE

OPENED: 04/06/1920   Theatre: Nora Bayes
Musical   Broadway: 159

Composer: Hugo Felix
Lyricist: Catherine Chisholm Cushing
Librettist: Catherine Chisholm Cushing
Producer: Lassie Company
Director: Edward Royce

Source: KITTY MCKAY (Play: Catherine Chisholm Cushing); **Musical Director:** Erno Rapee

Songs: Boo-Hoo; Echo; Fairy Whispers; Flirting; Kitty of Juniper Green; Lady Bird; Lassie; Lovely Corals; O' Barrin'-o'-the-Door; Piper o' Dundee; Skeletons; Teacup and a Spoon, A; Under the Jessamine

Cast: Dorothy Dickson; Carl Hyson; Tessa Kosta

2413 • LAST FRONTIER, THE

OPENED: 06/08/1936
Revue

Composer: Dana Suesse
Lyricist: Irving Kahal; Billy Rose
Producer: Billy Rose
Director: Verne Elliott; Edward Clarke Lilley

Choreographer: Alexander Oumansky; **Costumes:** Raoul Pene du Bois; **Lighting Designer:** Carlton Winkler; **Musical Director:** Emile Hollander; **Set Design:** Albert Johnson

Songs: Another Mile; Home on the Range [2]; I Want to Be in Texas for the Round-Up in the Spring [1]; Memories of Buffalo Bill (L: Billy Rose)

Narrator: Irving O'Hay; **Cast:** Chief Iron Shell; Mamie Francis; George Keyes; Mitzy Lucas; Don McLaughlin; Gene McLaughlin; Tommy Shelton

Notes: Produced at the Fort Worth Frontier Centennial along with CASA MANANA and BILLY ROSE'S SHOW OF SHOWS. The show closed either 11/30/36 or 12/1/36. [1] May have been replaced by "The Last Round Up." [2] Probably added after opening. [3] Not listed in program. May have been added after opening.

2414 • LAST LEAF, THE

Notes: *See O. HENRY DUET.*

2415 • LAST MINSTREL SHOW, THE

OPENED: 03/20/1978
Musical   Closed out of town

Librettist: Joe Taylor Ford
Producer: Ken Marsolais
Director: Donald McKayle

Costumes: Robert Mackintosh; **Lighting Designer:** Ian Calderon; **Musical Director:** Howard Roberts; **Orchestrations:** Howard Roberts; **Set Design:** Edward Burbridge

Songs: Always Left Them Laughing (C/L: George M. Cohan); At the Garbage Gentlemen's Ball; Camptown Races (C/L: Stephen Foster); Can't You Hear Me Callin', Caroline (C: Caro Roma; L: William H. Gardner); Darktown Is Out Tonight; Dixie (C/L: Dan Emmett); Do Lord [1]; Down Where the Watermelon Grows [1]; Gee, I'm Glad I'm from Dixie [1]; Georgia Camp Meeting, A; Good News; Happy Days in Dixieland [1] (C: Kerry Mills); I Don't Mind Walkin' in the Rain [1]; I'll Lend You Anything [1]; Minstrel's Prayer [1]; My Old Kentucky Home (C/L: Stephen Foster); Oh Dem Golden Slippers (C/L: James A. Bland); Pickaninny's Paradise [1]; Polly Wolly Doodle [1] (C/L: Traditional); Sally's Blues; She's Gettin' Mo' Like the White Folks Every Day; Shine, Shine, Shine [1] (C: Cecil Mack; L: Ford Dabney); Strut Miss Lizzie; Swanee; Tain't No Sin; There'll Be a Hot Time in the Old Town Tonight (C: Theodore M. Metz; L: Joe Hayden); Turkey in the Straw (C/L: Traditional); Wait Till the Sun Shines Nellie (C: Harry Von Tilzer; L: Andrew B. Sterling); Waitin' for the Robert E. Lee (C: Lewis F. Muir; L: L. Wolfe Gilbert); What He'd Done for Me; When the Bell in the Lighthouse Rings Ding Dong (C: Alfred Solman; L: Arthur J. Lamb)

Cast: Ralston Hill; Gregory Hines; Eugene Jackson; Della Reese; Dick Vance; Ned Wright

Notes: Traditional and turn-of-the-century minstrel songs used. Closed 4/30/78. Many of these song titles are not correct but I left them as in program. [1] From 1978 production only.

2416 • LAST MUSICAL COMEDY, THE

OPENED: 02/12/1988   Theatre: Riverwest
Musical   Off-Off-Broadway

Composer: Arthur Siegel
Lyricist: Tony Lang
Librettist: Tony Lang
Producer: CHS Productions
Director: Pamela Hunt

Arrangements: Bob McDowell; **Choreographer:** Pamela Hunt; **Costumes:** Robert de Mora;

Lighting Designer: Matt Ehlert; **Musical Director:** Bob McDowell; **Set Design:** Alan Kimmel

Songs: Last Dream Ballet, The; Last Eleven O'Clock Number, The; Last Finale, The; Last Hate Duet, The; Last Home Town Song, The; Last Jazz Specialty, The; Last Love Duet, The; Last Opening, The; Last Overture, The; Last Production Number, The; Last Seduction Song, The; Last Soft Shoe, The; Last Soliloquy, The; Last Soubrette Song, The; Last Tap Dance, The; Last Torch Song, The; Last Waltz, The

Cast: Jonathan Ball; Beth Blatt; Suzanne Dawson; Michael DeVries; Donna English; Mark Esposito; Eddie Korbich; Laura Streets

2417 • LAST RESORTS, THE
OPENED: 1956
Musical   Unproduced

Composer: Stephen Sondheim
Lyricist: Stephen Sondheim
Librettist: Jean Kerr
Producer: Robert E. Griffith; Harold Prince

Songs: I Wouldn't Change a Thing; I've Known You All My Life; On the River; Pour Le Sport

2418 • LAST SWEET DAYS OF ISAAC, THE
OPENED: 01/26/1970   Theatre: Eastside Playhouse
Musical   Off-Broadway: 485

Composer: Nancy Ford
Lyricist: Gretchen Cryer
Librettist: Gretchen Cryer
Producer: Haila Stoddard; Duane Wilder; Mark Wright
Director: Word Baker

Costumes: Caley Summers; **Lighting Designer:** David F. Segal; **Musical Director:** Clay Fullum; **Orchestrations:** Clay Fullum; **Set Design:** Ed Wittstein

Songs: Herein Lies the Seeds of Revolution [1]; I Can't Live in Solitary [1]; I Want to Walk to San Francisco; Last Sweet Days of Isaac, The; Love You Came to Me; My Most Important Moments Go By; Somebody Died Today [1]; Touching Your

Hand Is Like Touching Your Mind; Transparent Crystal Moment, A; Yes, I Know That I'm Alive

Cast: C. David Colson; Austin Pendleton; Fredricka Weber

Notes: [1] Added after opening.

2419 • LAST WALTZ, THE
OPENED: 05/10/1921   Theatre: Century
Musical   Broadway: 185

Composer: Oscar Straus
Lyricist: Harold Atteridge; Edward Delaney Dunn
Librettist: Harold Atteridge; Edward Delaney Dunn
Producer: J.J. Shubert; Lee Shubert
Director: J.C. Huffman; Frank Smithson

Choreographer: Allan K. Foster; Jack Mason; **Musical Director:** Louis Kroll; **Set Design:** Watson Barratt

Songs: Baby in Love, A (C: Ralph Benatzky; Al Goodman; L: Harold Atteridge); Bring Him My Love Thoughts; Charming Ladies; Hail to Our General; Just for a While [1] (C/L: Anderson; Geiger); Ladies' Choice; Last Waltz, The (L: Edward Delaney Dunn); Live for Today (C: Al Goodman; A. Werau; L: Harold Atteridge); Love the Minstrel [1] (L: Ackel); My Heart Is Waking; Next Dance with You, The (C: Al Goodman; L: Louis Friedman); Now Fades My Golden Love Dream (L: Edward Delaney Dunn); Oo-La-La; Reminiscence; Roses Out of Reach; Whip Hand, The

Cast: James Barton; Ted Lorraine; Eleanor Painter; Gladys Walton; Walter Woolf

Notes: [1] In London production only.

2420 • LATE NITE COMIC
OPENED: 10/15/1987   Theatre: Ritz
Musical   Broadway: 4

Composer: Brian Gari
Lyricist: Brian Gari
Librettist: Allan Knee
Producer: Rory Rosegarten

Choreographer: Dennis Dennehy; **Costumes:** Gail Cooper-Hecht; **Dance Arranger:** James Raitt;

Lighting Designer: Ken Billington; **Musical Director:** Gregory J. Dlugos; **Orchestrations:** Larry Hochman; **Set Design:** Clarke Dunham; **Vocal Arranger:** James Raitt

Songs: Best in the Business, The; Clara's Dancing School; Dance; Gabrielle; Having Someone; It Had to Happen Sometime; It's Such a Different World; Late Nite Comic; Relax with Me, Baby; Stand-Up; Think Big; This Lady Isn't Right for Me; When I Am Movin'

Cast: Robert LuPone; Teresa Tracy

2421 • LAUGH A LIFETIME
OPENED: 10/22/1978   Theatre: Norman Thomas
Revue   Off-Broadway: 20

Composer: Sol Berezowsky; Hanoch Cohen; I. Lustig
Lyricist: J. Bratt; J. Tunkeler
Librettist: I. Heyblum; Ephaim Kishon; M. Nudelman; A. Shulman
Producer: Lively and Yiddish Co., The
Director: Shimon Dzigan

Musical Director: William Gunther

Songs: Cave of the Patriachs; Face to Face Meeting, A; Fortunate Father, A; Hitch-Hiker, The; How to Prevent a Nuclear Explosion; In the Theatre Mirror; Let's Make Up; Star? No a Bomb, A; Tel-Aviv Construction Worker; There Were Times

Cast: Mina Bern; Ben Bonus; Shimon Dzigan; Herschel Fox; Shoshana Ron

2422 • LAUGH A LITTLE, CRY A LITTLE
OPENED: 06/06/1974
Revue   Closed out of town

Composer: Gary William Friedman
Lyricist: Arnold Horwitt
Librettist: Arnold Horwitt

Source: JOYS OF YIDDISH, THE (Book: Leo Rosten); **Musical Director:** Peter Howard

Songs: Citizen of the United States; East Side Glide; Golden Land; I Just Fell in Love; Mama the Balabusta; Morris Brodkin Loves Me; Nice

to Know; Piano in the Parlor; Sabbath Song; Someday My Grandson; Village of Chelm; We'll See; What a Language; When You're an Alright-nick; Wonderful Man, A; Your Darling Daughter

Cast: Boris Aplon; Gary Beach; Marilyn Chris; Jerry Jarrett; Jan Peerce; Lee Wallace

Notes: Playhouse on the Mall, Paramus, New Jersey.

2423 • LAUGH PARADE, THE
OPENED: 11/02/1931   Theatre: Imperial
Revue   Broadway: 243

Composer: Harry Warren
Lyricist: Mort Dixon; Joe Young
Librettist: Ed Preble; Ed Wynn
Producer: Ed Wynn
Director: Ed Wynn

Choreographer: Albertina Rasch; **Costumes:** Weld; **Lighting Designer:** Clark Robinson; **Musical Director:** John McManus; **Orchestrations:** Robert Russell Bennett; Hans Spialek; **Set Design:** David S. Gaither; Weld

Songs: Excuse of Song and Dance; Got to Go to Town [1]; I Wish I Could Laugh at Love; Laugh Parade, The; Love Me Forever; Ohh! That Kiss; Punch and Judy Man; Torch Song, The; You're My Everything

Cast: Jeanne Aubert; Ed Cheney; Lawrence Gray; Eunice Healey; Jack Powell; Bartlett Simmons; Ed Wynn

Notes: [1] With new lyric as "Gettin' Out of Town" in 42ND STREET.

2424 • LAUGHING HUSBAND, THE
OPENED: 02/02/1914   Theatre: Knickerbocker
Musical   Broadway: 48

Composer: Edmund Eysler
Lyricist: Arthur Wimperis
Librettist: Arthur Wimperis
Producer: Charles Frohman
Director: Edward Royce

Source: DER LACHENDE EBEMANN (Musical: Julius Brammer; Edmund Eysler; Alfred Grunwald)

Songs: Away from Thee; Bought and Paid For [2] (C: Jerome Kern; L: Harry B. Smith); Forbidden Fruit; Go to Paris or Vienna; Heart Will Fall, A; Husband in Love with His Wife, A; In Beautiful Italiano; Just a Little Gossip; Little Miss Understood; Lizette; Love Is Like a Violin (C: Jerome Kern; L: Harry B. Smith); Marital Malignity; Silken Screen; Since Grandpa Learned to Tango; Take a Step with Me [1] (C: Jerome Kern; L: Harry B. Smith); Tango Edward; Telephone Duet; Wine Song; You're Here and I'm Here [3] (C: Jerome Kern; L: Harry B. Smith)

Cast: Roy Atwell; Frances Demarest; Josie Intropodi; William Norris; Fred Walton

Notes: [1] Cut out of town. Same music as "Rosalie" in THE SPRING CHICKEN. [2] Music later used as "I've Looked for Trouble" from SUNNY and "You Will — Won't You" from CRISS-CROSS. [3] Also used in THE MARRIAGE MARKET.

2425 • LAVENDER LADY, THE

Musical

Lyricist: Otto Harbach
Librettist: Otto Harbach

Notes: Unproduced.

2426 • LE BELLYBUTTON

OPENED: 04/02/1976   Theatre: Diplomat
                                        Cabaret
Revue   Off-Broadway: 28

Composer: Scott Mansfield
Lyricist: Scott Mansfield
Librettist: Johnathan Copley; Scott Mansfield; Joel Scott
Producer: Jolandrea Music Inc.
Director: Scott Mansfield

Choreographer: Katherine Hull; Louise Quick; **Costumes:** David Chapman; **Lighting Designer:** David Chapman; **Musical Director:** Ken Werner; **Orchestrations:** Ken Werner; **Set Design:** David Chapman

Songs: Apache; Bi Sexual Blues; Come Back Home Baby; Dance with Me; Disco; Disco Baby; Gotta Get Back to You; I Never Let Anyone Beat Me but You; Jenny; Let Me Make Love to You; Love Child; Marilyn's Theme; Morning Light; Night Lady; S & M Polka, The; She; Sucker's Soliloquy, A

Cast: Marilyn Chambers; Alan Scott

2427 • LEADER OF THE PACK

OPENED: 04/08/1985   Theatre: Ambassador
Revue   Broadway: 120

Composer: Jeff Barry; Ellie Greenwich; Phil Spector
Lyricist: Jeff Barry; Ellie Greenwich; Phil Spector
Librettist: Anne Beatts
Producer: Pack, The
Director: Michael Peters

Choreographer: Michael Peters; **Costumes:** Robert de Mora; **Dance Arranger:** Timothy Graphenreed; **Lighting Designer:** Pamela Cooper; **Musical Director:** Jimmy Vivino; **Set Design:** Tony Walton; **Vocal Arranger:** Marc Shaiman

Songs: A . . . My Name Is Ellie (C/L: Ellie Greenwich); And Then He Kissed Me; Baby I Love You; Be My Baby; Chapel of Love; Christmas — Baby Please Come Home; Da Doo Ron Ron; Do Wah Diddy (C/L: Jeff Barry; Ellie Greenwich); Hanky Panky (C/L: Jeff Barry; Ellie Greenwich); I Can Hear Music; I Want to Love Him So Bad; Jivette Boogie Beat (C/L: Ellie Greenwich); Keep It Confidential (C/L: Ellen Foley; Ellie Greenwich; Jeff Kent); Leader of the Pack (C/L: Jeff Barry; Ellie Greenwich; George "Shadow" Morton); Look of Love (C/L: Jeff Barry; Ellie Greenwich); Maybe I Know (C/L: Jeff Barry; Ellie Greenwich); Maybe I Know (C/L: Jeff Barry; Ellie Greenwich); Not Too Young (To Get Married); River Deep, Mountain High; Rock of Rages (C/L: Ellie Greenwich; Jeff Kent); Today I Met the Boy I'm Gonna Marry (C/L: Ellie Greenwich; Tony Powers; Phil Spector); Wait 'Til My Bobby Gets Home; We're Gonna Make It (After All) (C/L: Ellie Greenwich); What a Guy; Why Do Lovers Break Each Others' Hearts (C/L: Ellie Greenwich; Tony Powers; Phil Spector)

Cast: Dennis Bailey; Shirley Black-Brown; Patrick Cassidy; Pattie Darcy; Annie Golden; Ellie Greenwich; Jasmine Guy; Darlene Love; Dinah Manoff; Keith McDaniel; Peter Neptune; Zora Rasmussen; Gina Taylor; Barbara Yeager

2428 • LEATHER PATCH, THE

OPENED: 02/15/1886
Musical   Broadway

Composer: Dave Braham
Librettist: Edward Harrigan
Director: M.W. Hanley

Musical Director: Simon Hassler

Songs: Baxter Avenue; Denny Grady's Hack; It Showered Again; Love, Put on Your Bridal Veil

Cast: Harry Fisher; Edward Harrigan; Joseph Sparks; Annie Yeamans

Notes: Program of Philadelphia — not dated.

2429 • LEAVE IT TO BEAVER IS DEAD

OPENED: 03/29/1979   Theatre: Public
Musical   Off-Broadway: 15

Composer: Larry David; Des McAnuff
Lyricist: Des McAnuff
Librettist: Des McAnuff
Producer: N.Y. Shakespeare Festival; Joseph Papp
Director: Des McAnuff

Costumes: Jennifer von Mayrhauser; **Lighting Designer:** Victor En Yu Tan; **Musical Director:** Larry Davis; **Set Design:** Heidi Landesman

Cast: Maury Chaykin; Mandy Patinkin; Saul Rubinek; Brent Spiner; Dianne Wiest

Notes: No songs listed in program.

2430 • LEAVE IT TO JANE

OPENED: 08/28/1917   Theatre: Longacre
Musical   Broadway: 167

Composer: Jerome Kern
Lyricist: P.G. Wodehouse
Librettist: Guy Bolton; P.G. Wodehouse
Producer: F. Ray Comstock; Morris Gest
Director: Edward Royce

Source: COLLEGE WIDOW, THE (Play: George Ade); **Choreographer:** David Bennett; **Musical Director:** John McGhie; **Orchestrations:** Frank Saddler

Songs: Atwater College Songs (Good Old Atwater); Cleopatterer; Crickets Are Calling, The [2]; Days of Chivalry, The; Finale Act I; Finale Act II; Football Song (Opening Act II); I'm Going to Find a Girl Someday [3]; I'm So Happy; It's a Great Big Land [7]; I've Had My Share [5]; I've Never Found a Girl Like You [4]; I've Played for You [4]; Just You Watch My Step; Leave It to Jane; Peach of a Life, A; Poor Prune [4]; Sir Galahad; Siren's Song, The; Sun Shines Brighter, The [1]; There It Is Again [6]; Wait Till To-morrow; What I'm Longing to Say; When the Orchestra's Playing Your Favorite Waltz; Why? [4]

Cast: Jane Carroll; Arlene Chase; Edith Hallor; Oscar Shaw

Notes: [1] Titled "I'm So Happy" out of town. [2] Same main theme as "Whistling Dan" in 90 IN THE SHADE. [3] Same tune as "Little Billie" from GLORIA'S ROMANCE. [4] Cut. [5] Cut on the road. [6] Titled "When the Orchestra's Playing Your Favorite Waltz" out of town and titled "When the Orchestra's Playing Your Favorite Dance" in OH, BOY! tryout. [7] Sheet music only.

2431 • LEAVE IT TO ME (1926)

Notes: *See SWEETHEART TIME.*

2432 • LEAVE IT TO ME! (1938)

OPENED: 11/09/1938   Theatre: Imperial
Musical   Broadway: 291

Composer: Cole Porter
Lyricist: Cole Porter
Librettist: Bella Spewack; Samuel Spewack
Producer: Vinton Freedley
Director: Samuel Spewack

Source: CLEAR ALL WIRES (Play: Bella Spewack; Samuel Spewack); **Choreographer:** Robert Alton; **Costumes:** Raoul Pene du Bois; **Musical Director:** Max Meth; **Orchestrations:** Don Walker; **Set Design:** Albert Johnson

Songs: As Long As It's Not about Love [1]; Comrade Alonzo; Far Away; From Now On; From the U.S.A. to the U.S.S.R.; Get Out of Town; How Do You Spell Ambassador?; I Want to Go Home; I'm Taking the Steppes to Russia; Information Please [1]; Just Another Page in Your Diary [4]; Most Gentlemen Don't Like Love [2]; My Heart Belongs to Daddy; Recall Goodhue [3];

Thank You [3]; There's a Fan [1]; Tomorrow; Vite, Vite, Vite; We Drink to You J.H. Brody; When All's Said and Done; When the Hen Stops Laying [1]; Why Can't I Forget You? [1]; Wild Wedding Bells [1]

Cast: April; Walter Armin; Alexander Asro; William Gaxton; Adele Jergens; Joseph Kallini; Gene Kelly; George E. Mack; Mary Martin; Victor Moore; Kay Picture; Edward H. Robins; Tamara; George Tobias; Sophie Tucker

Notes: Originally titled CLEAR ALL WIRES (same as source title). [1] Not used. [2] Written for unproduced show GREEK TO YOU. [3] May have been cut before opening. [4] Not used. Later in TWO WEEKS WITH PAY.

2433 • LEAVES OF GRASS

OPENED: 09/12/1971   Theatre: Theatre Four
Revue   Off-Broadway: 49

Composer: Stan Harte Jr.
Lyricist: Walt Whitman
Librettist: Stan Harte Jr.
Producer: New Era Productions
Director: Stan Harte Jr.

Source: LEAVES OF GRASS (Poetry: Walt Whitman); **Choreographer:** Bert Michaels; **Musical Director:** Karen Gustafson; **Orchestrations:** Bill Brohn; **Set Design:** David Chapman

Songs: As Adam; Come Said My Soul; Dirge for Two Veterans; Do You Suppose Enough; Excelsior; Give Me; Goodbye, My Fancy; How Solemn; I Hear America Singing; In the Prison; Oh, Captain! My Captain!; Pioneers; Song of Myself; Song of the Open Road; Tears; Thanks in Old Age; There Is That in Me; Twenty- Eight Men; Twenty Years; Unseen Buds; Who Makes Much of a Miracle?; Woman Waits for Me, A

Cast: Yolande Bavan; Lynn Berg; Scott Jarvis; Joe Masiell

2434 • LEFT OVER, THE

Notes: *See LOLLIPOP.*

2435 • LEGEND

OPENED: 05/13/1976   Theatre: Ethel Barrymore
Play   Broadway: 5

Composer: Dan Goggin
Author: Samuel Taylor
Producer: John F. Kennedy Center; Gladys Rackmil
Director: Robert Drivas

Costumes: Florence Klotz; **Lighting Designer:** Thomas Skelton; **Set Design:** Santo Loquasto

Songs: Legend (C/L: Ronee Blakely)

Cast: F. Murray Abraham; Elizabeth Ashley; Stephen Clarke; Sebastian Stuart

2436 • LEGENDS IN CONCERT

OPENED: 05/10/1989   Theatre: Academy
Revue   Off-Broadway: 22

Producer: John Stuart
Director: John Stuart

Choreographer: Inez Mourning; **Costumes:** Betty Lurenz; **Lighting Designer:** Dennis Condon; **Musical Director:** Kerry McCoy

Cast: Clive Baldwin; Eddie Carroll; Katie LaBourdette; George Trullinger; Daryl Wagner

Notes: A collection of performances by impersonators. Subjects included: Jack Benny, Buddy Holly, Liberace, Al Jolson, Marilyn Monroe, John Lennon, Judy Garland, Nat King Cole, Elvis Presley. No original songs in this show. No songs listed in program.

2437 • LEGS DIAMOND

OPENED: 12/26/1988   Theatre: Mark Hellinger
Musical   Broadway: 64

Composer: Peter Allen
Lyricist: Peter Allen
Librettist: Harvey Fierstein; Charles Suppon
Producer: Entertainment Group, The; James M. Nederlander; Arthur Rubin; George M. Steinbrenner III
Director: Robert Allan Ackerman

Source: RISE AND FALL OF LEGS DIAMOND, THE (Film); **Choreographer:** Alan Johnson; **Costumes:** Willa Kim; **Dance Arranger:** Mark Hummel; **Lighting Designer:** Jules Fisher; **Musical Director:** Eric Stern; **Orchestrations:** Michael Starobin; **Set Design:** David Mitchell; **Vocal Arranger:** Eric Stern

Songs: Ain't I Something? [1]; All I Wanted Was the Dream; Applause; Charge It to A.R.; Come Save Me [1]; Cut of the Cards; Gangland Chase; I Was Made for Champagne; Knockers; Man Nobody Could Love, The; Music Went Out of My Life, The; Now You See Me, Now You Don't; Only an Older Woman; Only Steal from Thieves; Say It Isn't So; Speakeasy; Speakeasy Christmas; Sure Thing Baby; Taxi Dancer's Tango; To Overcome Passion and Acquire Perfection [1]; Tropicabana Rhumba; When I Dream My Dream [1]; When I Get My Name in Lights

Cast: Peter Allen; Jim Fyfe; Christian Kauffmann; Raymond Serra; Joe Silver; Julie Wilson

Notes: [1] Cut prior to opening.

2438 • LEMMINGS

Notes: *See NATIONAL LAMPOON LEMMINGS.*

2439 LEND AN EAR

OPENED: 12/16/1948   Theatre: National
Revue   Broadway: 460

Composer: Charles Gaynor
Lyricist: Charles Gaynor
Librettist: Charles Gaynor; Will Glickman; Joseph Stein
Producer: William Eythe; Franklin Gelbert; William R. Katzell
Director: Hal Gerson

Choreographer: Gower Champion; **Costumes:** Raoul Pene du Bois; **Lighting Designer:** Raoul Pene du Bois; **Musical Director:** George Bauer; **Orchestrations:** Clare Grundman; **Set Design:** Raoul Pene du Bois; **Vocal Arranger:** Dorothea Freitag

Songs: After Hours; Ballade; Doin' the Old Yahoo Step [2]; Everybody's Got a Guy but I [4]; Friday Dancing Class; Give Your Heart a Chance to Sing; Hot and Cold [4]; I Must Find Out About Love [4]; I'll Be True to You [1]; I'm Not in Love; I'm on the Lookout; In Our Teeny Little Weeny Nest [2]; It's Spring [4]; Join Us in a Cup of Tea [2]; Little Game of Tennis [1]; Mabel [4]; Molly O'Reilly; Neurotic You and Psychopathic Me; No More Swing [4]; Old McGinty Place, The [3]; Once Is Not Enough [4]; Romantically Inclined [3]; Rough Stuff [4];

Something in My Eye [4]; Three Little Queens of the Silver Screen; When Someone You Love Loves You; Where Is the She for Me? [1]; Who Hit Me?; Who Knows [4]

Cast: Yvonne Adair; Carol Channing; William Eythe; George Hall; Gloria Hamilton; Beverly Hosier; Jenny Lou Law; Arthur Maxwell; Tommy Morton; Gene Nelson; Bob Scheerer; **Pianist:** George Bauer; Dorothea Freitag

Notes: [1] Part of the GLADIOLA GIRL segment. [2] Part of the GLADIOLA GIRL segment. Also in SHOW GIRL (1961). [3] Out Las Palmas prior to New York. [4] Out Cohasset.

2440 • LENNON

OPENED: 10/05/1982   Theatre: Entermedia
Play   Off-Broadway: 25

Author: Bob Eaton
Producer: Sid Bernstein; Stanley Bernstein; Abe Margolies; Dennis Paget
Director: Bob Eaton

Costumes: Deborah Shaw; **Lighting Designer:** Dennis Parichy; **Set Design:** Peter David Gould

Cast: Gusti Bogok; Katherine Borowitz; Vincent Irizarry; John Jellison; David Patrick Kelly; Robert LuPone; Greg Martyn; Bill Sadler

Notes: No original songs in this show.

2441 • LENNY AND THE HEARTBREAKERS

OPENED: 12/22/1983   Theatre: New York
                      Shakespeare Festival
Musical   Off-Broadway: 20

Composer: Scott Killian; Kim D. Sherman
Lyricist: Scott Killian; Kenneth Robins; Kim D. Sherman
Librettist: Kenneth Robins
Producer: N.Y. Shakespeare Festival
Director: Murray Louis; Alwin Nikolais

Choreographer: Murray Louis; Alwin Nikolais; **Costumes:** Lindsay W. Davis; **Lighting Designer:** Peter Kolezke; Alwin Nikolais; **Musical Director:** James McElwaine; **Orchestrations:** Robert Kilgore; Scott Killian;

James McElwaine; Kim D. Sherman; **Set Design:** Alwin Nikolais; Nancy Winters

Notes: No songs listed in program.

2442 • LES MISERABLES
OPENED: 03/12/1987   Theatre: Broadway
Musical   Broadway

Composer: Claude-Michel Schonberg
Lyricist: Herbert Kretzmer
Librettist: Alain Boublil; Claude-Michel Schonberg
Producer: Cameron Mackintosh
Director: John Caird; Trevor Nunn

Source: LES MISERABLES (Novel: Victor Hugo);
  Costumes: Andreane Neofitou; **Lighting
  Designer:** David Hersey; **Musical Director:**
  Robert Billig; **Set Design:** John Napier

Songs: At the End of the Day; Beggars at the Feast; Bring Him Home; Castle on a Cloud; Come to Me; Do You Hear the People Sing?; Dog Eats Dog; Drink with Me to Days Gone By; Empty Chairs at Empty Tables; Heart Full of Love, A; I Dreamed a Dream; In My Life; Little Fall of Rain, A; Look Down; Lovely Ladies; Master of the House; On My Own; One Day More; Prologue; Red and Black; Soliloquy; Stars; Thernadier Waltz; Turning; Wedding Chorale; Who Am I?

Cast: Leo Burmester; Jennifer Butt; Anthony Crivello; Ann Crumb; Braden Danner; Susan Goodman; Randy Graff; Judy Kuhn; Marcus Lovett; Michael Maguire; Terrence Mann; John Norman; Frances Ruffelle; Colm Wilkinson

Notes: Still running. Original French libretto and songs by Alain Boublil and Jean-Marc Natel. Additional material by James Fenton.

2443 • LES POUPEES DE PARIS
OPENED: 04/22/1964
Revue   N.Y. World's Fair

Composer: Jimmy Van Heusen
Lyricist: Sammy Cahn
Producer: Marty Krofft; Sid Krofft
Director: Marty Krofft; Sid Krofft

Costumes: Bill Campbell; Edward Wassall; **Dance
  Arranger:** Joe Reisman; **Lighting Designer:**
  Michael Shere; **Musical Director:** Joe Reisman;

Orchestrations: Joe Reisman; Wayne Robinson;
  Set Design: Nicky Nadeau; Edward Wassall;
  Vocal Arranger: Joe Reisman

Songs: Bonsoir; Circus, the Circus, The; Don't Say Paris, Say Paree; I Can't Wait to Take You Home to Mother; It's a Living; Kook Spooks; Les Poupees de Paris; Let's Be Frank, Mr. Frankenstein; Love Is a Bore; On the Wings of Romance; Sadie Fats; You Can't Make It Anywhere

Notes: A puppet show presented at the New York World's Fair. Included the taped voices of Milton Berle, Edie Adams, Pearl Bailey, Cyd Charisse and Phil Silvers.

2444 • LET 'EM EAT CAKE
OPENED: 10/21/1933   Theatre: Imperial
Musical   Broadway: 89

Composer: George Gershwin
Lyricist: Ira Gershwin
Librettist: George S. Kaufman; Morrie Ryskind
Producer: Sam H. Harris
Director: George S. Kaufman

Choreographer: Ned McGurn; Eugene Van Grona;
  Costumes: John Booth; Kiviette; **Musical
  Director:** William Daly; **Orchestrations:** Edward
  Powell; **Set Design:** Albert Johnson

Songs: All the Mothers of the Nation; Blue, Blue, Blue; Climb Up the Social Ladder (The New Blue D.A.R.); Cloistered from the Noisy City (The Union League); Comes the Revolution; Double Dummy Drill, The (inst.); Down with Everything That's Up; Fashion Show; First Lady and First Gent [1]; General's Gone to a Party, The; Hanging Throttlebottom in the Morning; Hell of a Hole, A; I Know a Foul Ball; It Isn't What You Do; League of Nations Finale; Let 'Em Eat Cake; Let 'Em Eat Caviar; Mine; Nine Supreme Ball Players; No Better Way to Start a Case; No Comprenez, No Capish, No Versteh!; On and On and On; Oyez, Oyez, Oyez [1]; Play Ball!; Shirts by Millions; That's What He Did; There's Something We're Worried About; Throttle Throttlebottom; Tweedledee for President; Union Square; Up and At 'Em!, on to Vict'ry; What More Can a General Do? (I've Brushed My Teeth); What's the Proleteriat?; Who's the Greatest?; Whole Truth, The; Why Speak of Money? [2]; Yes, He's a Bachelor

Cast: Florenz Ames; Dudley Clements; Consuelo Flowerton; William Gaxton; Philip Loeb; George E. Mack; Victor Moore; Lois Moran; Ralph Riggs; Edward H. Robins; Gracie Worth

Notes: LET 'EM EAT CAKE is a sequel to OF THEE I SING. [1] Not used. [2] Cut prior to opening.

2445 • LET 'EM ROT

Notes: *See WELCOME TO THE CLUB.*

2446 • LET 'ER GO LETTY

OPENED: 1921
Musical   Closed out of town

Composer: James F. Hanley
Lyricist: Ballard Macdonald
Librettist: George E. Stoddard
Producer: Oliver Morosco
Director: Julian Alfred; Julia McKee

Musical Director: Harry James; **Vocal Arranger:** Alfred Dalby

Songs: Bermuda; Coo-ee-doo (C: James F. Hanley; Werner Janssen; L: Leo Wood); Flirting (C: Werner Janssen; L: Bernard Grossman); Hoodoo Blues (C: Werner Janssen; L: Bernard Grossman); I Love to Dance (C: Werner Janssen; L: Irving Bibo; Leo Wood); I'm Glad I Met You (C: Werner Janssen; L: Irving Bibo; Leo Wood); Lend Us a Daddy (L: Gene Buck); Let 'Er Go Letty (C: Werner Janssen; L: Bernard Grossman); Little Souvenir, A; Longing for You (C: Werner Janssen; L: Irving Bibo; Leo Wood); My Little Sea Shell; Opening Chorus; Pantomime (inst.); Pas Seul (inst.); Silly Thoughts; We Gotta Find a New Kentucky Home [1]; What a Position for Me; Wonderful Time Was Had By All; You and Me

Cast: Charlotte Greenwood; A.J. Herbert; Jane King; Mary King; Stuart Wilson

Notes: Progam of 12/26/21 New Haven. [1] Titled "I've Gotta Find a New Kentucky Home" in program.

2447 • LET FREEDOM SING

OPENED: 10/05/1942   Theatre: Longacre
Revue   Broadway: 8

Composer: Harold Rome
Lyricist: Harold Rome
Librettist: Sam Locke
Producer: Youth Theatre
Director: Joseph C. Pevney

Choreographer: Dan Eckley; **Conductor:** David Mordecai; **Costumes:** Paul du Pont; **Musical Director:** Lou Cooper; **Orchestrations:** Morton Gould; Philip J. Lang; **Set Design:** Herbert Andrews

Songs: Be Calm; Flowers in Bloom (C: Jack Gerald; L: David Gregory); Fraught [2] (C/L: Marc Blitzstein); Give a Viva!; Grandpa Guerrilla (C: Walter Kent; L: Hy Zaret); History Eight to the Bar; House I Live In, The (C: Earl Robinson; L: Lewis Allan); I Did It for Defense; It's Fun to Be Free; Johnny Is a Hoarder; Lady Is a WAAC, The; Little Miss Victory Jones; Little Things We Like, The (C: Lou Cooper; L: Roslyn Harvey); Mittel-Europa [1] (C: Jay Gorney; L: Edward Eliscu; Henry Myers); Of the People Stomp [3]; Ring Up the Curtain; We Have a Date (C: Lou Cooper; L: Roslyn Harvey)

Cast: Joan Dexter; Betty Garrett; Berni Gould; Mitzi Green; Phil Leeds; Lee Sullivan

Notes: [1] Also in THEY CAN'T GET YOU DOWN. [2] Also in NO FOR AN ANSWER. [3] From THE LITTLE DOG LAUGHED.

2448 • LET GEORGE DO IT

OPENED: 04/22/1912   Theatre: West End
Musical   New York

Composer: Nat D. Ayer
Lyricist: Paul West
Librettist: Aaron Hoffman
Producer: Leffler-Bratton Co.
Director: Al Holbrook

Source: LET GEORGE DO IT (Comic Strip: George McManus); **Musical Director:** Eugene Salzer

Songs: Band Came Back, The (L: A. Seymour Brown); Confidences; Don't You Ever Think About Me, Dearie?; Dramatic Ring, The; Gee, How I Hate You; Gum Shoe Man, The; Helene's Hat; I'd Rather Go to Jail; In a Bungalow for Two; Night Time's the Right Time to Spoon with the Girl You Love (C: George W. Meyer; L: Joe Goodwin); Spoony Words; Subway Squeeze,

The; Telegraph Girl; Two Lips Are Waiting in Tulip Town; Waltz Me to the Altar, Walter; We've Painted All the Morning

Cast: Iva Irby; Rusell Lennon; George P. Murphy; Abbott Worthley; Minthorne Worthley

2449 • LET IT RIDE!

OPENED: 10/12/1961   Theatre: Eugene O'Neill
Musical   Broadway: 68

Composer: Jay Livingston
Lyricist: Ray Evans; Jay Livingston
Librettist: Abram S. Ginnes
Producer: Joel Spector
Director: Stanley Prager

Source: THREE MEN ON A HORSE (Play: George Abbott; John Cecil Holm); **Choreographer:** Onna White; **Costumes:** Guy Kent; **Dance Arranger:** Billy Goldenberg; **Lighting Designer:** Jean Eckart; William Eckart; **Musical Director:** Jay Blackton; **Orchestrations:** Raymond Jaimes; **Set Design:** Jean Eckart; William Eckart; **Vocal Arranger:** Jerry Packer

Songs: Best Undressed Girl in Town [1]; Broads Ain't People; Everything Beautiful; Happy Birthday, Erwin; He Needs You; Hey Jimmy, Joe, John, Jack; His Own Little Island; Honest Work [1]; I Wouldn't Have Had To; If Flutterby Wins; I'll Learn Ya; Just an Honest Mistake; Let It Ride; Love Is the Greatest [2]; Love, Let Me Know; Nicest Thing, The; Run, Run, Run; Sweet Man [2]; There's Something About a Horse; Trust Me [2]; Who's Doing What to Erwin?

Cast: Larry Alpert; Harold Gary; George Gobel; Stanley Grover; Sam Levene; Barbara Nichols; Paula Stewart; Ted Thurston

Notes: [1] Cut prior to opening. [2] Not in program.

2450 • LET ME HEAR THE MELODY

OPENED: 03/09/1951
Play   Closed out of town

Author: S.N. Behrman
Producer: Harold Clurman; Walter Fried
Director: Burgess Meredith

Lighting Designer: Ben Edwards

Songs: High-Ho, At Last [1] (C: George Gershwin; L: Ira Gershwin); Prelude (inst.) (C: George Gershwin)

Cast: J. Edward Bromberg; Morris Carnovsky; Melvyn Douglas; Mike Kellin; Cloris Leachman; Anthony Quinn

Notes: [1] Cut from the film SHALL WE DANCE.

2451 • LET MY PEOPLE COME

OPENED: 01/08/1974   Theatre: Morosco
Revue   Broadway: 1273

Composer: Earl Wilson Jr.
Lyricist: Earl Wilson Jr.
Librettist: Phil Oesterman
Director: Phil Oesterman

Choreographer: Ian Naylor; **Dance Arranger:** Billy Cunningham; **Lighting Designer:** Centaur Productions; **Musical Director:** Billy Cunningham; **Vocal Arranger:** Billy Cunningham

Songs: Ad, The; And She Loved Me; Choir Practice; Come In My Mouth; Cunnilingus Champion of Co. C, The; Dirty Words; Doesn't Anybody Love Anymore; Fellatio 101; Give It to Me; Giving Life; I Believe My Body; I'm Gay; Let My People Come; Linda, Georgina, Marilyn and Me; Mirror; Opening Number; Poontang; Show Business Nobody Knows, The; Take Me Home with You; Whatever Turns You On

Cast: Christine Andersen; Lorraine Davidson; Alan Evans; Lola Howse; Joe Jones; James Moore; Ian Naylor; Larry Paulette; Peachena

Notes: Opened at the Village Gate where it ran for 1167 performances. It moved to the Morosco on July 22, 1976 where it ran for an additional 106 performances.

2452 • LET'S CELEBRATE

OPENED: 1972
TV Musical   Unproduced

Composer: Elliott Lawrence
Lyricist: Betty Comden; Adolph Green

Songs: Columbus' Blues; Don't Touch Him; Flirtatious Frascita; Make Way for the Law; My

Friend; Nicole You Is My Woman Now; Successame Street; They Handed Me You; We Are the Royal Canadian Mounties; Wealthiest Girl in the Country

2453 • LET'S FACE IT!

OPENED: 10/29/1941   Theatre: Imperial
Musical   Broadway: 547

Composer: Cole Porter
Lyricist: Cole Porter
Librettist: Dorothy Fields; Herbert Fields
Producer: Vinton Freedley
Director: Edgar MacGregor

Choreographer: Charles Walters; **Costumes:** John Harkrider; **Musical Director:** Max Meth; **Orchestrations:** Ted Royal; Hans Spialek; Don Walker; **Set Design:** Harry Horner; **Vocal Arranger:** Edna Fox; Carley Mills; Lyn Murray

Songs: Ace in the Hole; Baby Games; Cuttin' the Persian Rug; Ev'rything I Love; Fairy Tale, A (C/L: Sylvia Fine; Max Liebman); Farming; Get Yourself a Girl [2]; I Hate You, Darling; I've Got Some Unfinished Business with You; Jerry, My Soldier Boy; Lady Needs a Rest, A; Let's Face It; Let's Not Talk About Love; Little Rhumba Numba, A; Make a Date with a Great Psychoanalyst [1]; Melody in Four F (C/L: Sylvia Fine; Max Liebman); Milk, Milk, Milk; Pets [1]; Revenge [1]; Rub Your Lamp; Up to His Old Tricks Again [1]; What Are Little Husbands Made Of? [1]; You Can't Beat My Bill [1]; You Irritate Me So

Cast: Eve Arden; Benny Baker; Nanette Fabray; Danny Kaye; Edith Meiser; Sunnie O'Dea; Vivian Vance; Mary Jane Walsh; Frances Williams; Jack Williams

Notes: [1] Not used. [2] Most of song cut from score.

2454 • LET'S GET MARRIED

OPENED: 09/21/1914   Theatre: Morosco
Musical   Broadway

Composer: Josephine Ihmsen; William Lorraine
Librettist: William H. Clifford; Miles Overholt
Producer: Walter Lawrence

Costumes: Mme. Keeler; **Musical Director:** William Lorraine

Songs: Acushla (C/L: Josephine Ihmsen); Cinderella and Prince Charming; Come Fly with Me (C/L: Josephine Ihmsen); Family Cycle Car (C/L: Josephine Ihmsen); Game of Make Believe; Go to the Movies; How Dot Man Played the Flute; Kiss and Make Up (C/L: Josephine Ihmsen); Laughing Song; Little Ford Rambled Right Along (C/L: Foster; Gay); Love's Longing; Model Maid, A (C/L: Josephine Ihmsen); Personality; Won't You Keep Me Company (C/L: Josephine Ihmsen)

Cast: Frances Cameron; Walter Lawrence; Ursula March; Willie Pollard

2455 • LET'S GO (0000)

Revue

Composer: Edgar A. Vinal
Lyricist: Edgar A. Vinal
Librettist: Harry Sedley
Producer: John M. Sheesley
Director: Harry Sedley

Choreographer: Edgar I. Schooley; **Costumes:** Hilaire Mahieu; **Lighting Designer:** Harry Noodles; **Musical Director:** Edgar A. Vinal; **Set Design:** Millard France

Songs: Grande Ensemble; Happy, Laughing Girls!; Hello, Friends; I've Got to Get a Drink; Just You; Opening Chorus; Powder Puff (C/L: Sidney King); Pretty Little Rainbow; Ragtime Marriage; Taking Ways; Two Wise Cops; When Butterfly Does the Shimmy; Wonderful Girls

Cast: Harry Clarke; Dell Evans; Elizabeth Fox; William H. Malone

Notes: No other information avaiable.

2456 • LET'S GO (1918)

OPENED: 03/09/1918
Revue   Broadway: 25

Librettist: George Abbott; Frederick Wallace

Songs: Have You Seen the Ducks Go By; I'm Only a Poor Little Kid; Land of Yesteryear, The (C/L: E. Ray Goetz); Newspaper Girl, The (C/L: E. Ray Goetz)

Cast: Bobby Edwards; Beatrice Herford; William Rock; Frances White

Notes: No other information available. This was a vaudeville revue. No other credits appear in programs. The librettists above are authors of one of the sketches.

2457 • LET'S GO (1927)
OPENED: 1927
Revue

Composer: Ruby Cowan
Lyricist: Ruby Cowan
Director: Fred Clark

Choreographer: Fred Clark; **Musical Director:** Hughie Morton; **Set Design:** Karle O. Amend

Songs: Blue Zulu; Dancing Mad; Ding Dong Bell; Girl in the Moon, The; I'll Be Waiting for You; Modern Eve, The; No Foolin'; Rainy Days; Tickle Me; Wait for the Big Gate of Lover's Lane; What a World This Would Be

Notes: Burlesque Musical.

2458 • LET'S GO (1940)
OPENED: 1940 — Theatre: International Theatre-Restaurant
Revue — Nightclub

Composer: Nicholas Brodszky
Lyricist: D. Bernard Simon
Director: Nat Karson; Gene Snyder

Choreographer: Gene Snyder; **Costumes:** Nat Karson; Incidental Music: Nicholas Brodszky; **Musical Director:** Brooks Steele; **Set Design:** Nat Karson

Songs: Arms; Ballroom for Two (C/L: James Shelton); Cold Hands-Warm Heart; Every Thing Happens to Me; History Repeats Itself (C/L: Pembroke Davenport); I Could Go Places with You; I'll Wait (C/L: Pembroke Davenport); Musical Chairs (C/L: Pembroke Davenport); Out of a Dream; Reverie in Rhythm; This Modern Age (C/L: Pembroke Davenport); This Time No Bananas (C/L: Pembroke Davenport); Turn of the Year; Yours with a Song (C/L: Pembroke Davenport)

Cast: Betty Bruce; Carol Bruce; Walter Cassel; Sergio De Karlo; Debonaires, The

2459 • LET'S HAVE FUN
OPENED: 10/22/1935
Radio Musical

Composer: Richard Rodgers
Lyricist: Lorenz Hart

Songs: I'll Take a Little of You on Toast; Please Make Me Be Good; You've Got That

Cast: Romney Brent; Helen Morgan; Ken Murray; Freddie Rich and His Orchestra

2460 • LET'S PLAY FAIR
OPENED: 01/18/1938 — Theatre: Casa Manana
Revue — Nightclub

Composer: Ned Lehac; Dana Suesse
Lyricist: Ted Fetter; Billy Rose
Producer: Billy Rose
Director: John Murray Anderson

Choreographer: Robert Alton; Lauretta Jefferson; **Costumes:** Thomas Becher; Raoul Pene du Bois; **Lighting Designer:** John Murray Anderson; **Set Design:** Raoul Pene du Bois

Songs: Butterfly Love (C: Joe Burke; L: Edgar Leslie); Crystal Temple, The; Give Them Girls; Handlebar Moustache, The; New York on Parade; Oriental Yogi; Perfume Counter on the Rue de la Paix, A (At a Perfume Counter) (C: Joe Burke; L: Edgar Leslie); Throw a Little Party

Cast: Stan Cavanaugh; Morton Downey; Jane Frazee; Abe Lyman and His Californians; Tom Patricola; Sally Rand; Doctor Rockwell; Oscar Shaw

2461 • LETTY PEPPER
OPENED: 04/10/1922 — Theatre: Vanderbilt
Musical — Broadway: 32

Composer: Werner Janssen
Lyricist: Irving Bibo; Leo Wood
Librettist: George V. Hobart; Oliver Morosco
Producer: Oliver Morosco
Director: George V. Hobart

Choreographer: Julian Alfred; **Musical Director:** Harry James; **Orchestrations:** Frank Barry

Songs: Blue Bird Blues; Coo-Ee-Doo (C: James F. Hanley; Werner Janssen; L: Leo Wood); Dope Song; Every Little Miss; From the Bottom to the Top; Greenbaum [1]; I Love to Dance; Lavender and Lace; Long, Lean, Lanky, Letty Pepper; Paul Poirot Number; Ray of Sunshine; Sittin' Pretty; What Could Be Sweeter [1]; Yes, Yes; You Teach Me (C: James F. Hanley; L: Ballard Macdonald)

Cast: Master Gabriel; Charlotte Greenwood; Josie Intropodi

Notes: [1] Out Philadelphia 3/13/22.

2462 • LEW LESLIE'S BLACKBIRDS (1926)

OPENED: 09/11/1926   Theatre: London Pavilion
Revue   London: 279

Composer: George W. Meyer
Lyricist: George W. Meyer
Producer: Charles Cochran; Lew Leslie

Musical Director: Shrimp Jones

Songs: Arabella's Wedding Day; Bambalina Maid; Be Happy; Butcher, the Baker, the Candlestick Maker, The; Don't Cry When He's Gone; He Only Comes to See Me Once in a While (but Oh That Once in a While) [1] (C: Arthur Johnston; George W. Meyer; L: Grant Clarke; Roy Turk); Home Again; Hotten Trot, The; I'm a Little Blackbird Looking for a Bluebird [1] (C: Arthur Johnston; George W. Meyer; L: Grant Clarke; Roy Turk); In Darkest Russia; Jazz Time Came from the South [1] (C: Arthur Johnston; George W. Meyer; L: Grant Clarke; Roy Turk); Jungle Nights in Dixie Land (Jungle Town Has Moved to Dixieland) [1] (C: Arthur Johnston; George W. Meyer; L: Grant Clarke; Roy Turk); Levee Gang; Mammie's Day in Dixie Land; Mandy Make Up Your Mind [1] (C: Arthur Johnston; George W. Meyer; L: Grant Clarke; Roy Turk); Shufflin' Home; Silver Rose; Smilin' Joe [2]; Three Pullman Porters; Waika Kiki Blues

Cast: Johnny Hudgins; Florence Mills; Aida Ward; Edith Wilson

Notes: From a London program of 9/20/26. [1] Also in DIXIE TO BROADWAY. [2] Not in program. Only in ASCAP list.

2463 • LEW LESLIE'S INTERNATIONAL REVUE

Notes: *See THE INTERNATIONAL REVUE.*

2464 • LIAR, THE

OPENED: 05/18/1950   Theatre: Broadhurst
Musical   Broadway: 12

Composer: John Mundy
Lyricist: Edward Eager
Librettist: Alfred Drake; Edward Eager
Producer: Thomas Hammond; Dorothy Willard
Director: Alfred Drake

Source: LIAR, THE (Play: Carlo Goldoni);
Choreographer: Hanya Holm; **Costumes:** Motley; **Musical Director:** Lehman Engel; **Orchestrations:** Lehman Engel; Ben Ludlow Jr.; **Set Design:** Donald Oenslager

Songs: Call of Spring, The [2]; Che Mai T'Ho Fall' Amor [2] (C/L: Traditional); Cleonice [1]; Columbina's Song [2]; Coreggio Ben Mio [2] (C/L: Traditional); Drinking Song [2] (C/L: Traditional); Funeral March; Funeral March [2]; Jewel of a Duel, A; Lack-a-Day; Ladies' Opinion, The; Liar's Song, The; March of the Guards; Michelemma [2] (C/L: Traditional); Nightingale Song, A [2]; Out of Sight, Out of Mind; Plot to Catch a Man In, A; Serenade [2] (C: Jacques Offenbach; L: Unknown); Spring; Stomachs and Stomachs; Stop Holding Me Back; Supper Trio; Truth; 'Twill Never Be the Same; Un Mazzo di Fiori [2] (C/L: Traditional); Vermicelli Minestrone [2]; We'll Make a Plot [2]; What's in a Name?; Witty Invention [2]; Woman's Work (C: Lehman Engel); You've Stolen My Heart

Cast: Martin Balsam; Russell Collins; Melville Cooper; William Eythe; Paula Laurence; Walter Matthau; Barbara Moser; Robert Penn; Joshua Shelley

Notes: [1] Out Philadelphia 4/24/50. [2] Out Cleveland Playhouse 11/13/51.

2465 • LIBERTY BELLES, THE

OPENED: 09/30/1901   Theatre: Madison Square
Musical   Broadway: 104

Composer: John W. Bratton
Lyricist: Harry B. Smith

Librettist: Harry B. Smith
Producer: Klaw & Erlanger
Director: Herbert Gresham

Costumes: F. Richard Anderson; **Musical Director:** Aime Lauchaume; **Set Design:** Ernest Albert

Songs: Beautiful Fairy Tales [1] (C: Harry Von Tilzer); Billet-Doux, A [1] (C: John W. Bratton; Harry Von Tilzer); Dancing Girl, A; De Trop (C/L: Clifton Crawford); Ethiopian Essence, An (C: Aime Lauchaume); Finale (C: Alex A. Aarons; Aime Lauchaume); Finale Act III (C: Aime Lauchaume); Follow the Man that Leads the Band [1] (C: Aime Lauchaume); Gunner in the Navy, A (C: William Accooe); In Florida (C: Louis F. Gottschalk); Instrumental Man, The [1] (C: Harry Linton; L: John Gilroy); Jack O'Lantern (C: Mae Anwerda Sloane); Just to Know What's Going On in New York Town [1] (C: Harry Linton; L: John Gilroy); Lesson Book Song (C: Aime Lauchaume); Lesson with a Fan, A [1]; Little Child Like Me, A (C: A. Baldwin Sloane); My Filipino Pet [2] (C: A. Baldwin Sloane); My Gal! My Gal! [3] (C: Victor Herbert); My Gal! My Sal! [4] (C: Albert Rezlit); Oh, What a Dream (C: Harry Von Tilzer); Quaker Maids, The [1] (C: Aime Lauchaume); Shopping Chorus (C: A. Baldwin Sloane); Spring Hat (C: A. Baldwin Sloane); Starlight (C/L: Clifton Crawford); Supper Chorus (C: Aime Lauchaume); To Marry a Millionaire; Way that Walker Walked Away, The (C: H.T. MacConnell); Yankee Tar, A (C: Louis F. Gottschalk)

Cast: Harry Davenport; Lotta Faust; Harry Gilfoil; Violet Jewell; John Slavin

Notes: [1] Out Elizabeth N.J. 09/10/03. [2] Out Elizabeth N.J. 09/10/03. Some sources credit Aime Lachaume with the music. [3] Some sources credit A. Baldwin Sloane with the music. Herbert's ASCAP card doesn't mention this song. [4] ASCAP/Library of Congress only.

2466 • LICKPENNY LOVER, A

Notes: *See O. HENRY DUET.*

2467 • LIDO LADY

OPENED: 12/10/1926   Theatre: Gaiety
Musical   London: 259

Composer: Richard Rodgers
Lyricist: Lorenz Hart

Librettist: Ronald Jeans
Producer: Jack Hulbert; Paul Murray
Director: Jack Hulbert

Source: ORIGINAL LIBRETTO (Musical: Guy Bolton; Bert Kalmar; Harry Ruby); **Costumes:** Guy De Gerald; Hoban et Jeanne; **Musical Director:** Sydney Baynes

Songs: Atlantic Blues [2]; Beauty of Another Day, The; But Not Today (C: Con Conrad; L: Jean Boyer; Vincent Scott); Camera Shoot [6]; Cheri-Beri; Cup of Tea, A (Lido Lady, Opening); Dancer, The; Do You Really Mean to Go? (Finale Act II); Ever-Ready Freddie [3]; Exercise [3]; Good Old Harry (Finale Act I); Here In My Arms [5]; I Must Be Going; I Want a Man [3]; It All Depends on You [4] (C: Ray Henderson; L: Lew Brown; B.G. DeSylva); Lido Lady; Morning Is Midnight [3]; My Heart Is Sheba Bound; Tiny Flat Near Soho Square, A [1]; Try Again Tomorrow; Two to Eleven [3]; What's the Use; You're on the Lido Now

Cast: Phyl Arnold; Cicely Courtneidge; Phyllis Dare; Dave Fitzgibbon; Harold French; Eddie Garr; Laurence Green; April Harmon; Jack Hulbert; Muriel Montrose

Notes: [1] Same music as "A Little House in Soho" in SHE'S MY BABY. [2] Same music as "Blue Ocean Blues" in PRESENT ARMS. [3] Cut prior to opening. [4] According to ASCAP written for or added to BIG BOY. Added to GEORGE WHITE'S SCANDALS (1926) after opening. [5] In DEAREST ENEMY. [6] Cut prior to opening. Slightly revised in SHE'S MY BABY.

2468 • LIE OF THE MIND, A

OPENED: 12/05/1985   Theatre: Promenade
Play   Off-Broadway: 186

Author: Sam Shepard
Producer: Lewis Allen; Stephen Graham
Director: Sam Shepard

Costumes: Rita Ryack; **Lighting Designer:** Anne E. Militello; **Set Design:** Andy Stacklin

Cast: James Gammon; Harvey Keitel; Geraldine Page; Will Patton; Amanda Plummer; Aidan Quinn; Red Clay Ramblers, The; Ann Wedgworth; Karen Young

Notes: This show contained traditional songs as well as numbers by Stephen Foster, Jack Herrick and Tommy Thompson, Lefty Frizzell, and Mike Craver.

2469 • LIEBER AUGUSTIN

OPENED: 09/03/1913 Theatre: Casino
Musical Broadway: 37

Composer: Leo Fall
Lyricist: Edgar Smith
Librettist: Edgar Smith

Source: DER LIEBER AUGUSTIN (Musical: Rudolf Bernauer; Leo Fall; Ernst Welisch)

Songs: Anna, What's Wrong with You?; Lieber Augustin; Look in Her Eyes [2] (C: Jerome Kern; L: M.E. Rourke); Take Your Time [1] (L: Harry Beswick)

Cast: May DeSousa; Roszika Dolly; DeWolf Hopper; George MacFarlane

Notes: Titled MISS CAPRICE on tour. Produced in London with different authors as PRINCESS CAPRICE. [1] Sheet music only. [2] Later used as "Look In His Eyes" in HAVE A HEART.

2470 • LIES AND LEGENDS: THE MUSICAL STORIES OF HARRY CHAPIN

OPENED: 04/24/1985 Theatre: Village Gate
Revue Off-Broadway: 79

Composer: Harry Chapin
Lyricist: Harry Chapin
Producer: Jason Brett; Lewis Friedman; Ken Kragen; Albert Nocciolino; Stuart Oken; Ken Yates
Director: Sam Weisman

Choreographer: Tracy Friedman; **Conductor:** Karl Jurman; **Costumes:** Marsha Kowal; **Dance Arranger:** Stephen Chapin; Tom Chapin; **Lighting Designer:** Vicki Baral; Gerry Hariton; **Musical Director:** Stephen Chapin; **Orchestrations:** Tom Chapin; **Set Design:** Vicki Baral; Gerry Hariton; **Vocal Arranger:** Stephen Chapin; Tom Chapin

Songs: Bananas; Better Place to Be; Cat's in the Cradle (C/L: Harry Chapin; Sandy Chapin); Circle; Corey's Coming; Dance Band on the Titanic; Dogtown; Dreams Go By; Get on with It; Halfway to Heaven; Mail Order Annie; Mr. Tanner; Old College Avenue; Old Job Man; Rock, The; Salt and Pepper; Shooting Star; Sniper; Story of a Life; Tangle Up Puppet (C/L: Harry Chapin; Sandy Chapin); Taxi; W*O*L*D; You Are the Only Song

Cast: Joanna Glushak; John Herrera; Terri Klausner; Ron Orbach; Martin Vidnovic

2471 • LIEUTENANT GUS

OPENED: 1916 Theatre: 44th Street
Musical Broadway

Lyricist: Edgar A. Smith; Matt Woodward
Librettist: Edgar Smith; Matt Woodward

Source: WENN ZWEI SICH LIEBEN

Notes: No program available.

2472 • LIEUTENANT, THE

OPENED: 03/09/1975 Theatre: Lyceum
Musical Broadway: 9

Composer: Gene Curty; Nitra Scharfman; Chuck Strand
Lyricist: Gene Curty; Nitra Scharfman; Chuck Strand
Librettist: Gene Curty; Nitra Scharfman; Chuck Strand
Producer: Spofford J. Beadle; Joseph S. Kutrzeba
Director: William Martin

Choreographer: Dennis Dennehy; **Costumes:** Frank J. Boros; Chuck Strand; **Dance Arranger:** Gus Montero; **Lighting Designer:** Ian Calderon; **Musical Director:** Chuck Strand; **Set Design:** Frank J. Boros; **Vocal Arranger:** Gus Montero; Chuck Strand

Songs: At 0700 Tomorrow; Conscience of a Nation, The; Damned No Matter How He Turned; Eulogy; Final Report; Finale; He Wants to Put the Army in Jail; I Don't Want to Go Over to Vietnam; I Will Make Things Happen; I'm Going Home; Indictment, The; Is This Any Way to Fight a War? [1]; Join the Army, Kill; Let's Believe in the Captain; Look for the Men with Potential; Massacre; On Trial for My Life; Something's Gone Wrong; Star of This War, The; There's No Other Solution; Twenty-Eight; Verdict, The; We've Chosen You, Lieutenant

Cast: Jim Litten; Eddie Mekka; Burt Rodriguez; Jo Speros; Tom Tofel

Notes: [1] Cut prior to opening.

2473 • LIFE, THE
Musical   Unproduced

Composer: Cy Coleman
Lyricist: Ira Gasman
Librettist: Cy Coleman; Ira Gasman; David Newman

Songs: I Start Sneezing; It's My Body

2474 • LIFE AND ADVENTURES OF NICHOLAS NICKLEBY, THE
OPENED: 10/04/1981   Theatre: Plymouth
Play   Broadway: 49

Composer: Stephen Oliver
Lyricist: Stephen Oliver
Author: David Edgar
Producer: Elizabeth I. McCann; Nelle Nugent; Shubert Organization
Director: Trevor Nunn

Source: LIFE AND ADVENTURES OF NICHOLAS NICKLEBY, THE (Novel: Charles Dickens); **Costumes:** John Napier; **Lighting Designer:** Beverly Emmons; David Hersey; **Musical Director:** Alan Gout; Donald Johnston; **Set Design:** Dermot Hayes; Neil Peter Jampolis; John Napier

Songs: At the Opera; Christmas Carol; Journey to Portsmouth; Mrs. Grudden's Goodbye; Patriotic Song; Wedding Anthem

Cast: Suzanne Bertish; Janet Dale; Priscilla Morgan; Edward Petherbridge; Roger Rees; Emily Richard; David Trelfall; John Woodvine

Notes: Since this show was performed over two evenings the number of performances is for both parts.

2475 • LIFE BEGINS AT 8:40
OPENED: 08/27/1934   Theatre: Winter Garden
Revue   Broadway: 238

Composer: Harold Arlen
Lyricist: Ira Gershwin; E.Y. Harburg
Librettist: Alan Baxter; David Freedman; Frank Gabrielson; Ira Gershwin; E.Y. Harburg; H.I. Phillips; Henry Clapp Smith

Choreographer: Robert Alton; Charles Weidman; **Costumes:** Kiviette; Pauline Lawrence; Billy Livingston; Raoul Pene du Bois; James Reynolds; Irene Sharaff; Wynn; **Musical Director:** Al Goodman; **Orchestrations:** Robert Russell Bennett; Hans Spialek; Don Walker; **Set Design:** Albert Johnson

Songs: Album Song [2]; All the Elks and Masons; C'est La Vie; Fun to Be Fooled; I Couldn't Hold My Man; I Knew Him When [1]; I'm a Collector of Moonbeams [1]; I'm Not Myself; It Was Long Ago; It Was Never Like This [2]; Let's Take a Walk Around the Block; Life Begins (At Exactly 8:40 or Thereabouts); Life Begins at City Hall (Beautifying the City); My Paramount-Publix-Roxy Rose; Quartet Erotica; Shoein' the Mare; Spring Fever; Things!; Weekend Cruise, A (Will You Love Me Monday Morning as You Did on Friday Night?) [1]; What Can You Say in a Love Song? (That Hasn't Been Said Before?); You're a Builder-Upper

Cast: Ray Bolger; Brian Donlevy; Dixie Dunbar; Luella Gear; Josephine Huston; Esther Junger; Bert Lahr; James MacColl; Adrienne Matzanauer; Emmett Oldfield; Earl Oxford; Bartlett Simmons; Walter Dare Wahl; Robert Wildhack; Frances Williams

Notes: [1] Cut prior to opening. [2] ASCAP/Library of Congress only.

2476 • LIFE IS LIKE THAT
OPENED: 12/23/1930   Theatre: Little
Play   Broadway: 32

Composer: Jack Hyman; Clifford Lang
Lyricist: Jack Hyman; Clifford Lang
Author: Jo Milward
Producer: Curtis W. Emery
Director: Paul Martin

Set Design: Philip Gelb

Songs: Weary Soul (C: Hazel Chisholm; L: Helen Kaminsky)

Cast: Mary Morris; Edward Pawley; Peggy
Shannon; Helen Shipman

Notes: Songs not listed in program.

2477 • LIFE IS NOT A DORIS DAY MOVIE

OPENED: 06/08/1982   Theatre: Top of the Gate
Revue   Off-Broadway: 47

Composer: Stephen Graziano
Lyricist: Boyd Graham
Librettist: Boyd Graham
Producer: Stephen O. Reid
Director: Norman Rene

Choreographer: Marcia Milgrom Dodge;
  Costumes: Walter Hicklin; **Lighting Designer:**
  Debra J. Kletter; **Musical Director:** Jim Cantin;
  Orchestrations: Elliot Weiss; **Set Design:** Mike
  Boak

Songs: Cavalcade of Curtain Calls; Don't Cry for
  Me; Fashion Show, The; Geographically
  Undesirable; I'm So Fat; Influenza; It's a Doris
  Day Morning; Junk Food Boogie; Lament; Last
  Chance Revue, The; Last Chance Series; Last
  Thing That I Want to Do Is Fall in Love, The;
  Little Girl-Big Voice; Man Who Isn't, A; Not
  Mister Right; Oh Oh Could It Be That I'm an Oh
  No Tango, The; Oh, William Morris; Pause for
  Prayer; Public Service Message; Report on Status;
  Right Image, The; Singer Who Moves Well;
  Super Wasp; Think of Me; Tribute; Waiting for
  the Bus of Life; Whoa Boy; You'll Be Sorry

Cast: Boyd Graham; Neva Small; Mary Testa

2478 • LIFE OF A MAN, THE

OPENED: 10/1972   Theatre: Judson Poets'
Musical   Off-Off-Broadway

Composer: Al Carmines
Lyricist: Al Carmines
Librettist: Al Carmines

Choreographer: Dan Wagoner; **Costumes:** Ira Siff;
  Lighting Designer: Earl Eidman

Songs: American Business; Bedsheets; Charity;
  Chew Your Bitter Nails; Coca-Cola Girl; Do You
  Ever?; Einstein; Father's Song; Freud; Gordita Es

Bonita; He's a Peculiar Guy; If You're a Woman;
I'll Still Be Here; I'm an Upper East Side
Neurotic; I'm Just a Toy; Just a Piece of Ass;
Lullabye; Marx; Mommy We Love You; Now
You've Been to the Big Time; Oh Man; One Kind
of Man; Sally; Sickness; Song of the Pregnant
Women; Take Courage Heart; Thinking of You;
Tragedy Waltz; Welcome to Broadway; When
Love Comes Finaletto; Womb Chant; Your Life

Cast: Reathel Bean; Jacque Lynn Colton; Julie
  Kurnitz

2479 • LIFE OF THE PARTY

OPENED: 10/08/1942
Musical   Closed out of town

Composer: Frederick Loewe
Lyricist: Earle Crooker
Librettist: Alan Jay Lerner
Producer: Henry Duffy
Director: Russell Fillmore

Choreographer: Theodore Adolphus; **Musical
  Director:** Ray Kavanaugh; **Orchestrations:**
  Robert Russell Bennett; Ted Royal; Hans Spialek;
  Vocal Arranger: Ted Scott **Songs:** Alone in a
  Crowd; El Rancho; Hand Me Down, The; Hot
  Gavotte; I'll Tell the World; Let's Waltz and
  Whistle; Life of the Party; No Olive in My
  Martini, Please (L: Raymond Knight); One Robin
  Doesn't Make a Spring [1]; Opening; Somehow;
  Sunny Day; Wearin' the Grin; West Is Best, The

Cast: Marty Allen; Dudley Clements; Charles
  Collins; Margaret Dumont; Louise Kirtland;
  Arthur Laurents; Charlie Ruggles; Dorothy Stone

Notes: Based on songs from SALUTE TO SPRING.
  Lerner revised some of these lyrics. [1] Also in
  SALUTE TO SPRING.

2480 • LIFTING THE CUP
Notes: See MID SUMMER NIGHTS FANCIES.

2481 • LIFTING THE LID
OPENED: 06/05/1905   Theatre: New Amsterdam
Musical   Broadway: 112

Composer: Jean Schwartz
Lyricist: William Jerome

Librettist: John J. McNally
Producer: Klaw & Erlanger
Director: Herbert Gresham; Ned Wayburn

Costumes: F. Richard Anderson; **Musical Director:** Frederic Solomon

Songs: Albany; Baa, Baa, Black Sheep (C: William C. Polla; L: James O'Dea); Borneo [1]; Cocktail and a Cherry, A [1] (C/L: Kenneth S. Clark); Come and Take a Walk with Me [2]; Conversational Song [1]; Coonland (C/L: Kenneth Clark); Dear Old Dixieland [2]; Home with the Milk in the Morning; How to Get in Central Park; I Love You [1]; Jerome the Bogie Man; Life on the Stage (inst.) (C: Victor Herbert); Line It Out, Mr. Maginnity; Making Eyes (C: Harry Von Tilzer); Moonlight Buggy Ride, A [1]; Mrs. Maloney; My First Smoke [1]; My Syndi-Kate (Cindy Kate) [1]; Nobody but You [1]; Oh, Marie!; Over Sunday (C: William C. Polla; L: James O'Dea); Reminds Me of Home Sweet Home (C/L: Frank Bryan); Rosy [1] (C/L: J.B. Mullen); Sombrero (C: William C. Polla; L: James O'Dea); Texas Dan; There's Nothing Doing in the Old, Old Town; Turn Over [1]; What Has the Night Time to Do with the Girl [2]; What You Want and What I Get (C/L: R.A. Brown)

Cast: A. Seymour Brown; Corrine; Virginia Earle; Louis Harrison; Maude Lambert; Eddie Leonard; Stella Mayhew; Julius Tannen; Fay Templeton

Notes: Part One was titled LIFTING THE LID. Part Two was the movie THE AUTOMOBILE CHASE by Georges Melies and Part Three was THE WHOLE DAMN FAMILY. [1] In THE WHOLE DAMN FAMILY. [2] Sheet music only.

2482 • LIGHT UP THE ICE

OPENED: 1981
Revue

Composer: Don James; Tom Worrall
Lyricist: Don James; Tom Worrall
Producer: Robert Turk
Director: Robert Turk

Choreographer: Shirley Costello; George Foster; Robert Turk; **Costumes:** David Doucette; Paul Lopez; **Orchestrations:** Don James; Tom Worrall; **Set Design:** W.J. Evans

Songs: Alice in Wonderland Ball (C: Jay Thompson; L: Tom Worrall)

Notes: An Ice Capades revue.

2483 • LIGHTER SIDE, THE

OPENED: 04/14/1955
Revue   Closed out of town

Composer: Gloria Siegle
Lyricist: Rose Harte; Rosalie Hazin
Librettist: Herbert Farjeon; Charles Gaynor; Hermione Gingold; Ronald Jeans; Arthur Macrae; Eric Maschwitz; Virginia Sale
Producer: Frederick Burleigh

Choreographer: Jere McMahon; **Costumes:** Elizabeth Birbari; Ruth Points; **Lighting Designer:** Paul Landry; **Musical Director:** Dennis Wiley; **Set Design:** Chandler Potter

Songs: Cultural Sunday (C: Unknown; L: Ed Collins; Peg Harig); Feel Free (C/L: Mitzi Cottle); Finaletto [1] (C/L: Charles Gaynor); Hey Dreamboat! (inst.) (C: Frank McNulty); If Love Ever Comes My Way; I'll Be True to You [1] (C/L: Charles Gaynor); Join Us in a Cup of Tea [1] (C/L: Charles Gaynor); Little Game of Tennis, A [1] (C/L: Charles Gaynor); Look What's Happened to Me (C: Frank McNulty; L: Bert Pollock); Loving You Is My Career (C/L: Charles Gaynor); Old Yahoo Step, The [1]; On the Lighter Side (C: Frank McNulty; L: Bert Pollock); Spring Returns (C: Dennis Wiley; L: Jere McMahon); Teeny Little Nest [1] (C/L: Charles Gaynor); That Ivy League Look; Where Is the She for Me [1] (C/L: Charles Gaynor)

Cast: Donna Jean Henry; Robert Parks; Renee Rogoff; Gloria Siegle

Notes: Program of Playhouse, Pittsburgh. [1] Part of THE GLADIOLA GIRL — a mini-musical also in SHOW GIRL.

2484 • LI'L ABNER

OPENED: 11/15/1956   Theatre: St. James
Musical   Broadway: 693

Composer: Gene DePaul
Lyricist: Johnny Mercer
Librettist: Melvin Frank; Norman Panama

Producer: Melvin Frank; Michael Kidd; Norman Panama
Director: Michael Kidd

Source: LI'L ABNER (Comic Strip: Al Capp); **Choreographer:** Michael Kidd; **Costumes:** Alvin Colt; **Dance Arranger:** Genevieve Pitot; **Lighting Designer:** Jean Eckart; William Eckart; **Musical Director:** Lehman Engel; **Orchestrations:** Philip J. Lang; **Set Design:** Jean Eckart; William Eckart

Songs: Country's in the Very Best of Hands, The; If I Had My Druthers; I'm Past My Prime; In Society (dance) (High Society); It's a Nuisance Having You Around [1]; It's a Typical Day; Jubilation T. Cornpone; Love in a Home, Matrimonial Stomp, The; Namely You; Oh, Happy Day; Otherwise [2]; Progress Is the Root of All Evil; Put 'Em Back; Rag Offen the Bush, Sadie Hawkins Ballet (inst.); There's Room Enough for Us; There's Somethin' Might Peculiar Goin' On [3]; Unnecessary Town; Way to a Man's Heart, The [1]; Wedding Song, The [3]; What's Good for General Bullmoose (Is Good for the U.S.A.)

Cast: Edith Adams; Carmen Alvarez; Marc Breaux; Grover Dale; Stubby Kaye; Ralph Linn; Tony Mordente; Peter Palmer; Charlotte Rae; George Reeder; Stanley Simmonds; Howard St. John; Deedee Wood

Notes: [1] Cut prior to opening. [2] Out Washington D.C. 9/17/56. Added to film version. [3] ASCAP/Library of Congress only.

2485 • LI'L MOSE

OPENED: 04/20/1908
Musical   Closed out of town

Composer: A. Baldwin Sloane
Lyricist: Owen Davis; George Totten Smith
Librettist: Owen Davis; George Totten Smith
Producer: Nixon & Zimmerman
Director: Ned Wayburn

Musical Director: Cassius Freeborn

Songs: American Girl, The [1]; Andy You Are de Candy [1]; Bambino; Good By Mr. Ragtime; I Know the Kind of a Girl for You (L: Charles D. Brown); I Want Someone to Love Me (L: Charles D. Brown); If; It's Love That Makes the World Go 'Round (L: Charles D. Brown); It's Tough to Love a Girl Who Doesn't Love You (C/L: Electric Comedy Four); Maid of My Dreams [1]; My Dusky Dago Boy (L: Charles H. Brown); My Roly Poly Oly Tulip Maid [1]; Nursey Won't You Go A-Fishing; On the Bluff [1]; One O' Clock; Songs That Mother Sang, The (Lullaby) [1]; Yiddish Cowboy, The

Cast: Martin Healy; Bert Kalmar; Charlotte Lesley; Janet Priest

Notes: Atlantic City. Sheet music credits the libretto to Fred G. Nixon-Nirdlinger and Charles H. Brown. Lyrics from those songs are credited to Charles H. Brown. Note different credits from Playbill. [1] From sheets crediting Charles H. Brown with lyrics, though individual sheets could not be found.

2486 • LILAC DOMINO, THE

OPENED: 10/28/1914   Theatre: 44th Street
Musical   Broadway: 109

Composer: Charles Cuvillier
Lyricist: Robert B. Smith
Librettist: Harry B. Smith
Producer: Henry B. Harris Estate
Director: Sydney Ellison

Source: DER LILA DOMINO (Musical: Charles Cuvillier; Bela Jenbach; Emmerich Von Gatti); **Musical Director:** Anselm Goetzl

Songs: Ah! Ah! Ah!; Corrandoli Song [1]; Cupid Keeps the Love Light Burning; Film Music (inst.); Finale Act I; Finale Act II; I Call You Back to Me (C: Ellen Tuckfield; L: Wilfred Douthitt); It's a Good World After All; King Carnival; Ladies Day; Let the Music Play; Lilac Domino; Opening Chorus; Opening Chorus Act II; Song of the Chimes (Bim Bam); Still We Smile; Sunny Riviera Bay, The [1] (C: Malvin M. Franklin; L: L. Wolfe Gilbert); Tarantella (inst.); Tell Me Lilac Domino; True Love Will Find a Way; What Every Woman Knows (Frocks and Frills); What Is Done You Can Never Undo; Where Love Is Waiting; Won't Someone Find Me a Sweetheart? [1]

Cast: George Curzon; Rose Detling; Wilfred Douthitt[2]; James Harrod; John E. Hazzard; Jeanne Maubourg; Robert O'Connor; Eleanor Painter

Notes: Lyrics reworked by SJ Adair Fitzgerald for subsequent London production. [1] Out Wilmington 1/8/16. [2] Later changed name to Louis Graveure.

2487 • LILIOM

OPENED: 04/20/1921   Theatre: Garrick
Play   Broadway: 316

Author: Ferenc Molnar
Producer: Theatre Guild, The
Director: Frank Reicher

Costumes: Lee Simonson; **Orchestrations:** Deems Taylor; **Set Design:** Lee Simonson

Songs: Damn Police (Thieves March) (C: Deems Taylor; L: Benjamin Glazer)

Cast: Eva Le Gallienne; Joseph Schildkraut

Notes: English text by Benjamin Glazer.

2488 • LINDA

OPENED: 05/02/1993   Theatre: Charles Ludlam
Musical   Off-Broadway: 42

Composer: Mark Bennett
Lyricist: Mark Bennett; Everett Quinton
Librettist: Everett Quinton
Director: David Ganon

Costumes: Toni Nanette Thompson; **Lighting Designer:** Richard Currie; **Set Design:** T. Greenfield

Songs: If God Had Call Waiting

Cast: Eureka; Lisa Herbold; Grant Neale; Everett Quinton; Bobby Reed; Chris Tanner

Notes: No songs listed in program.

2489 • LINGER LONGER LETTY

OPENED: 11/20/1919   Theatre: Fulton
Musical   Broadway: 69

Composer: Al Goodman
Lyricist: Bernard Grossman
Librettist: Anne Nichols
Producer: Oliver Morosco
Director: Frank McCormick

Choreographer: Frank Smith

Songs: Climbing the Ladder of Love; Denishawn [1]; Did You, My Boy, Did You?; Jazz Town Jazz [1]; Let's Pretend; Linger Longer, Letty; Love; Maid to Order Maid [1] (C: Vincent Youmans); Movements; My Little Highland Highball [1]; Oh By Jingo! (Oh By Gee You're the Only Girl for Me) (C: Albert Von Tilzer; L: Lew Brown); Parisienne Mechanical Marvels; Slow Town Is Jazz Town Now; Spanish Dance [1]; Ssh! Ssh! Ssh!; Strawberry Festival [1]; Ten to One; Twentieth Century Lullaby, A; What's the Matter with Letty? [1]

Cast: Oscar Figman; Charlotte Greenwood; Arthur Hartley; Eleanor Henry; Olin Howard

Notes: [1] Out Stamford 10/24/19.

2490 • LISTEN DEARIE

OPENED: 12/27/1926
Musical   Closed out of town

Composer: Charles Gilpin
Lyricist: Charles Gilpin
Librettist: Harold Atteridge; Gertrude Purcell
Producer: Messrs. Shubert
Director: Lawrence Marston

Choreographer: Raymond B. Perez

Songs: Be Be Beatrice; Every Shade of Blue; For You a Rose; Get Your Man; Good-Bye Bill; Here Come the Rah Rah Boys; Hi-Ho; In a Little Canoe; Just a Kiss from You; Loose Ankles; Loveable You; Nancy Lee; Never Been the Petted Party; Night Club Nights; Nothing to Do but Dance; Petting Party Baby; Ship Concert; Songs Tell You What to Do; Spanish Melody; Sweet Sweetheart of Mine; Sweetest Little Girl; There Must Be One; Wasting Time; Yo Ho

Cast: Fred Hildebrand; Vera Michelena; Ann Milburn; Eddie Pardo; Jane Taylor

Notes: Program Atlantic City 12/27/26 used. Also a 1927 program used.

2491 • LISTEN LESTER

OPENED: 12/23/1918   Theatre: Knickerbocker
Musical   Broadway: 272

Composer: Harold Orlob
Lyricist: Harry L. Cort; George E. Stoddard
Librettist: Harry L. Cort; George E. Stoddard
Producer: John Cort
Director: Robert Marks

Musical Director: Gus Salzer

Songs: B Valse [1]; Feather Your Nest; For a Girl Like You; I Was a Very Good Baby (in the Daytime); I Wonder If It's You; I'd Love To; See Her First; Show a Little Something New; Sweet Stuff; Two Is Company; Waiting for You; When the Shadows Fall; When Things Come Your Way; Who Was the Last Girl (You Called By Her First Name)?

Cast: Johnny Dooley; Eddie Garvie; Ada Lewis; Mary Milburn; Gertrude Vanderbilt; Clifton Webb; Ada Mae Weeks

Notes: [1] Out 4/16/20 Wilkes-Barre.

2492 • LISTEN TO ME

OPENED: 1922
Musical   Closed out of town

Composer: Charles George
Lyricist: Charles George
Librettist: Charles George
Producer: Le Comte & Fisher
Director: Charles George

Costumes: Charles George; **Set Design:** Charles George

Songs: Devilish Blues, The; Doctor Cupid; Letters; Listen to Me; Oh! You Kewpie Kandy Doll; Our Bungalow in Winter Time; Where's the Girl for Me

Cast: Barbara Bronell; Grace Forbes; Charles Gates; Virginia O'Brien; Ross Robertson

Notes: Partially complete program of Scranton 12/27/22 used.

2493 • LITTLE BIT OF EVERYTHING, A

OPENED: 06/06/1904   Theatre: Aerial Gardens
Revue   Broadway: 120

Music Based On: Jacques Offenbach
Librettist: John J. McNally

Producer: Klaw & Erlanger
Director: Herbert Gresham; Ned Wayburn

Set Design: Richard Marston

Songs: Blue Eyed Sue [1] (C/L: James Reese Europe); Como le Gusta Me? (C: J. Rosamond Johnson; L: Bob Cole); Della and Ella (C: Gus Edwards; L: Robert B. Smith); Evolution of Rag Time, The (C: J. Rosamond Johnson; L: Bob Cole); Fishing (C: J. Rosamond Johnson; L: Bob Cole); Good-By, Little Girl Good-By (C/L: Gus Edwards); Hiss, Hiss, Hiss (C: J. Fred Helf; L: Will Heelan); I Hate to Wake Up (C/L: Frederic Solomon); I Love to Hear a Yankee Doodle Tune (C/L: George M. Cohan); Just a Little Ever-Loving Girl (C: Mullen; L: Bryan); Little Bit of Blarney, A (C: J. Fred Helf; L: Will Heelan); Oh, Joy (C: Mullen; L: Bryan); Pas Seul (C/L: Frederic Solomon); Pretty Little Squaw from Utah, The (C: J. Rosamond Johnson; L: Bob Coile); Salt of the Sea (C/L: Arthur Penn); Stroll in the Moonlight (C/L: Harding; Kennedy); You Won't Do Any Business If You Haven't Got a Band (C/L: George M. Cohan)

Cast: Peter F. Dailey; Gus Edwards; Susie Fisher; Leila McIntyre; Neil McNeil; George Schiller; Joseph Sparks; Fay Templeton

Notes: [1] Also in MOTHER GOOSE. Sheet music only.

2494 • LITTLE BLUE DEVIL, THE

OPENED: 11/03/1919   Theatre: Central
Musical   Broadway: 75

Composer: Harry Carroll
Lyricist: Harold Atteridge
Librettist: Harold Atteridge
Producer: Joe Weber
Director: Oscar Eagle

Source: BLUE MOUSE, THE (Play: Clyde Fitch); **Choreographer:** Bert French; **Musical Director:** Eugene Salzer

Songs: All the Comforts of Home [1]; Are You Stepping Out Tonight [2]; Auction Rag; Butler's Fox-Trot, The; Cuckoo Town; Dancing Shoes; Hello, Everybody; I'm So Sympathetic; Just a Kiss; Office Blues, The; Omar Khayyam; Owl and the Turtle Doves, The [1]; Peter Pan; Red Riding Hood [1]; Secret Service Club, The;

Shimmy-Shaking Love; Stroller in Dreamland, A;
You Little Blue Devil

Cast: Eddie Cox; Bernard Granville; Lillian
Lorraine; Edward Martindel; Jack McGowan;
Marion Mosby; W.H. Powers

Notes: Fitch's Play was based on Horst and Engel's
DIE BLAUE MAUS. [1] Not in programs. [2]
ASCAP/Library of Congress only.

2495 • LITTLE BOY BLUE (1911)

OPENED: 11/27/1911   Theatre: Lyric
Musical   Broadway: 176

Composer: Henry Bereny
Lyricist: Grant Stewart
Librettist: Edward Paulton; A.E. Thomas
Producer: Henry W. Savage
Director: Frank Smithson

Source: LORD PICCOLO (Musical: Henry Bereny;
Carl Lindau; Rudolf Schanzer); **Choreographer:**
Jack Mason; **Musical Director:** Arthur Weld

Songs: Aeroplane Duet; Angus Gordon Donald
Douglas Ewart John McKee (C/L: Edward A.
Paulton); Boy in Blue (L: Edward A. Paulton);
Crystal Ball, The; Daisy's Entrance Song
(L: Caroline Wells); Detective (C: Arthur Weld;
L: Edward Paulton); Finale Act I; Flirt
(L: William Kirk; Edward Madden); Gathering of
the Clans; In the Heart of the Golden Wine; It
Seems Somehow, They Want Me Now; King of
the Boulevards (C: Paul Rubens; L: Edward A.
Paulton; A.E. Thomas); Kiss Me, Dearest, Kiss
Me Do (L: Edward A. Paulton); Love Never Dies
(L: Edward A. Paulton); Oliver (L: Edward A.
Paulton); Opening Chorus; Opening Chorus Act
II; Sandy McDougal (C/L: Edward A. Paulton);
Two Cockatoos (C/L: Edward A. Paulton);
When the Mists of the Night (C: Arthur Weld);
You're Very Like Your Sister, Dear (L: Edward
A. Paulton)

Cast: Gertrude Bryan; Otis Harlan; Maude Odell;
Katheryn Stevenson

Notes: Additional lyrics not credited in program.
[1] Sheet music only.

2496 • LITTLE BOY BLUE (1950)

OPENED: 09/11/1950   Theatre: El Capitan
Musical   Los Angeles

Composer: Max Showalter
Lyricist: Albert G. Miller
Librettist: Albert G. Miller
Producer: Mike Sloane; Paula Stone
Director: George Murphy

Choreographer: Louis Da Pron; **Costumes:** Odette
Myrtil; **Musical Director:** Leon Leonardi;
Orchestrations: Ruby Raskin; **Set Design:** Rita
Glover

Songs: All American Boy, The; Bang, Bang, Bang,
You're Dead; Bartender's Song, The; How Do
You Do?; I Can't Believe My Arms; Keep Your
Distance; Knock on Wood; Lovely Autumn Day,
A; March of the Beaver Patrol; Molly By Golly;
New Kind of Blues, A; Three Hundred Letters a
Day; We Love Thee, Krispy Krackles; We've
Travelled Far; Who in the Name of Pete Is
R.M.B.?; Wolf Dance; Wouldja Like It If —?;
Year from Today, A

Cast: Margaret Hamilton; Johnny Kirby; Mary Ann
Niles; Carol Richards; Craig Stevens

Notes: Hollywood show.

2497 • LITTLE CAFE, THE

OPENED: 11/10/1913   Theatre: New Amsterdam
Musical   Broadway: 144

Composer: Ivan Caryll
Lyricist: C.M.S. McLellan
Librettist: C.M.S. McLellan[1]
Producer: Klaw & Erlanger
Director: Herbert Gresham

Source: LE PETIT CAFE (Play: Tristan Bernard);
Choreographer: Julian Mitchell

Songs: Best Queen of All; Do You Call That
Dancing?; I Wonder Whom I'll Marry; I'm
A-Hunting Jaguar; Just Because It's You; My
Pretty Little Family; Serve the Caviar; So I Smile;
They Found Me; This Gay Paree; Thy Mouth Is a
Rose; You Little Cafe, Good Day

Cast: Hazel Dawn; Harry Depp; Marjorie Gateson;
Fred Graham; Joseph Monehan; Harry Neville;
John E. Young

Notes: [1] McLellan also used the pseudonym
Hugh Morton.

2498 • LITTLE CHERUB, THE
OPENED: 08/06/1906   Theatre: Criterion
Musical   Broadway: 155

Composer: Ivan Caryll
Lyricist: Owen Hall
Librettist: Owen Hall
Producer: Charles Frohman
Director: Ben Teal

Songs: As a Friend; Cupid's Rifle Range (C: Frank Tours); Dear Little Girls; Doggie in Our Yard, The (C/L: Marie Doro); Experience; Girl You Take Out to Supper, The; I Haven't Told Him; I Should So Love to Be a Boy (C: Frank Tours; L: C.H. Bovill); It's the Girls [2]; Jest Her Way (C: G. Aitken); Little Willie Brown (C/L: Charles Collins); Love's Last Word; Meet Me at Twilight (C: Jerome Kern; L: Clifford Harris); Message of the Eyes, The [2] (C: Ernest R. Ball; L: Michael Resnick); My Irish Rosie (C: Jean Schwartz; L: William Jerome); My Wife Will Be My Lady; Oh, How I Love My Teacher; Olympian Octet; Pierrot and Pierrette; Plain Rustic Ride ('Neath the Silv'ry Moon) [1] (C/L: Jerome Kern; C: Jackson Gouraud); Popular Songs (C/L: Clare Kummer); Supper Girl, The (L: George Grossmith); Under the Linden Tree [1] (C: Jerome Kern; L: M.E. Rourke); When You Mention It Don't Mention That I Mentioned It to You [2] (C: Seymour Furth; L: Edward P. Moran); Won't You Waltz?

Cast: Jane Blakeley; John Mayon; Hattie Williams; Winona Winter; Tom Wise

Notes: [1] Cut after opening. [2] Sheet music only.

2499 • LITTLE CHRISTOPHER
Notes: See LITTLE CHRISTOPHER COLUMBUS.

2500 • LITTLE CHRISTOPHER COLUMBUS
OPENED: 10/15/1894   Theatre: Garden
Musical   Broadway: 208

Composer: Ivan Caryll
Lyricist: Cecil Raleigh; George R. Sims
Librettist: Cecil Raleigh; George R. Sims
Producer: Edward E. Rice
Director: Edward E. Rice; Thomas Terriss; George Walton

Musical Director: Gustave Kerker; **Set Design:** Henry Heinman; Richard Marston; Frank Rafter; Hugh Logan Reid

Songs: All Hail! All Hail! [1]; Captain Bold, The (C: Gustave Kerker); Chorus of Foreigners [1]; Columbus Was a Famous Man; Dancing Lesson, The [1]; Fates, Fates, Fates (C: Gustave Kerker); For I'm O'Hoolegan (C: Gustave Kerker); Hail to the Bey (C: Gustave Kerker); Here in Cadiz; I Love, I Adore Her (C: Gustave Kerker); If in Your Dreams [1]; In an Unconventional Way; India Rubber Shoe, The [1]; Land of Love, The [1]; Law of Barataria, The (C: Gustave Kerker); Lazily, Drowsily; Moonlight Fancies (inst.) (C: Harry MacDonough); Nummy Num Num [1]; Oh, Honey, My Honey; Oh, Yes! Oh, Yes!; On to Chicago (C: Gustave Kerker); Policemen's Chorus, The (C: Gustave Kerker); Rumpty Tumpty [1]; Sisters Giggle, The; Turkish and German [1]; We Are Gay Young American Tars (C: Gustave Kerker); We Pay No Attention to That [1]; Yo, Ho! Yo, Ho! (C: Gustave Kerker)

Cast: Grace Belasco; Helen Bertram; Charles A. Bigelow; Edwin Chapman; Alexander Clarke; Harry MacDonough; Edgar Temple

Notes: Numbers attributed to Kerker are those not in the English vocal score. Kerker's lyricist is unknown. [1] From London vocal score.

2501 • LITTLE COMEDY, THE
Notes: See ROMANCE, ROMANCE.

2502 • LITTLE CORPORAL, THE
OPENED: 09/19/1898   Theatre: Broadway
Musical   Broadway: 68

Composer: Ludwig Englander
Lyricist: Harry B. Smith
Librettist: Harry B. Smith
Producer: Ariel Barney
Director: Richard Barker

Costumes: Percy Anderson; **Musical Director:** John McGhie; **Set Design:** Richard Marston

Songs: Cobbler's Ghost, The; Old War Horse, The; Song of a Veteran, The

Cast: Maud Lillian Barri; Allene Crater; Ambrose Daly; Lulu Glaser; A.M. Holbrook; Denis O'Sullivan; Francis Wilson

Notes: No songs listed in program.

2503 • LITTLE COTTAGE
Musical

Composer: Walter L. Rosemont
Lyricist: Darl MacBoyle
Producer: George Choos

Songs: Shake Your Little Shoulder

Notes: No other information available.

2504 • LITTLE DOG LAUGHED, THE
OPENED: 08/13/1940
Musical   Closed out of town

Composer: Harold Rome
Lyricist: Harold Rome
Librettist: Joseph Schrank
Producer: Eddie Dowling
Director: Eddie Dowling

Choreographer: Chester Hale; **Costumes:** Nicolas De Molas; **Musical Director:** Lehman Engel; **Set Design:** Jo Mielziner; **Vocal Arranger:** Lehman Engel

Songs: Beware the Dragon; Bunch of Cows, A; Court Dance; Dragon Dance; Easy Does It; Fairy Tales Are All Untrue; Friend of Mine, A; Hail Number One; Happily Ever After; Hero, A; I Have a Song; I Want Romance; I'll Be a Hero Too!; I'm a King; I'm Cynical; Of the People Stomp; Red Heads; Some Things a Man Must Have; You're You [1]; You're Your Highness

Cast: Marjorie Bell; Paul Draper; Augustin Duncan; Tess Gardella; Philip Loeb; Mili Monti; Dennie Moore; Eric Roberts; Joseph Vitale

Notes: Garden Pier Theater, Atlantic City. [1] ASCAP/Library of Congress only.

2505 • LITTLE DOLLY DIMPLES
OPENED: 1908
Musical   Closed out of town

Composer: C. Herbert Kerr

Songs: Dolly Dimples; Girl That I'd Call Mine, The; Good Bye, Jennie Jones; Good Bye, Old Home; I Am So Shy; Maid from Gay Paree; My Alsatian Maid; Naughty Kid Song; No One Dreams About Me; Opening Chorus; Take a Stroll

Cast: Grace Carmeron

Notes: From Kansas City program of 4/13/08. No other information available. Also called DOLLY DIMPLES.

2506 • LITTLE DUCHESS, THE
OPENED: 10/14/1901   Theatre: Casino
Musical   Broadway: 136

Composer: Reginald De Koven
Lyricist: Harry B. Smith
Librettist: Harry B. Smith
Producer: Florenz Ziegfeld
Director: George Marion

Musical Director: Herman Perlet; **Set Design:** Ernest Albert

Songs: Chloe; Dago and Monk, The; Darling [1]; Dip in the Ocean, A; Fencing Girl, The; Finale (C: Herman Perlet); Flirtation on the Beach; L'Amoureuse; Maiden with the Dreamy Eyes [1] (C: J. Rosamond Johnson; L: Bob Cole; James Weldon Johnson); Make Allowance for Love; Man with the Tamborine, The; Mandy [1]; Menagerie Song; Mollie Shannon; Only Girl, The; Opening Chorus; Ostend; Pretty Betsy Brown; Pretty Molly Shannon (C: Walter Woolf; L: Gus Ryan); Sadie (C/L: Leo LeBrunn); Silas; Since Sister Nell Heard Paderewski Play [1]; Swimming Master, The; Those Great Big Eyes (C/L: Leo LeBrunn); Violets (C: Silvio Hein; L: Ellen Wright); Wading We Go; What'd Yo' Do Wid de Letter, Mr. Johnson?; When You Are Near; You Come and Float Me

Cast: Sydney Barraclough; Charles A. Bigelow; Joseph W. Herbert; Willie Howard; George Marion; Joe Welch; Bessie Wynn

Notes: [1] Out Baltimore 10/27/02.

2507 • LITTLE DUKE, THE
OPENED: 08/04/1884   Theatre: Casino
Musical   Broadway

Composer: Charles Lecocq
Librettist: Max Freeman
Director: Max Freeman

Source: LE PETIT DUC (Musical: Ludovic Halevy; Charles Lecocq; Henri Meilhac); **Costumes:** Siedle; **Musical Director:** Paul Steindorff; **Set Design:** Henry E. Hoyt

Cast: Joseph Herbert; Al Holbrook; Richie Ling; Lillian Russell; Frederic Solomon

Notes: No songs listed in program.

2508 • LITTLE DUTCH GIRL, A (1901)

OPENED: 1901
Musical   Closed out of town

Composer: Melville E. Stone Jr.
Lyricist: John A. Carpenter
Librettist: John A. Carpenter

Songs: Dream Song; I'll Be Waiting for Your Coming; In Gay Bohemia; Thou Wilt Surely Know

Notes: No other information available.

2509 • LITTLE DUTCH GIRL, A (1920)

OPENED: 1920   Theatre: Lyric
Musical   London

Composer: Emmerich Kalman
Lyricist: Harry Graham
Librettist: Harry Graham; Seymour Hicks
Producer: Seymour Hicks

Source: DAS HOLLANDWEIBECHEN (Musical: Bela Jenbach; Emmerich Kalman; Leo Stein); **Costumes:** Lucille; **Musical Director:** Jacques Heuvel; Willie Warde

Songs: Bridal Hour, The; By the Silver Sea; Dance Till Break of Day [1]; Dreamland Lover, The; Finale Act II; Hail! Royal Bride; In the Spring; It's a Wonderful Land!; Little Dutch Girls; Love in a Cottage; Opening Chorus Act II (C: St. John Brougham); Opening Chorus Act III (C: St. John Brougham); Prince of My Maiden Fancies; This Day Our Dear Princess We Loyally Greet; Tired; Waltz; Women Always Get Their Way

Cast: Lauri DeFrece; Cecily Debenham; Jack Hulbert; Martin Iredale; Maggie Tayte

Notes: [1] From English vocal score only.

2510 • LITTLE FOXES, THE

OPENED: 02/15/1939   Theatre: National
Play   Broadway: 410

Author: Lillian Hellman
Producer: Herman Shumlin
Director: Herman Shumlin

Costumes: Aline Bernstein; **Set Design:** Howard Bay

Songs: Never Feel Too Weary to Pray (C/L: Meredith Willson)

Cast: Tallulah Bankhead; Patricia Collinge; Frank Conroy; Dan Duryea; Abbie Mitchell; Carl Benton Reid

2511 • LITTLE GREEN ISLE

OPENED: 08/28/1953
Musical   Closed out of town

Composer: Norman Meranus
Lyricist: Norman Meranus
Librettist: Charles Jule
Director: Dan Wargo

Choreographer: William Hidlay; **Musical Director:** Louise Sparks; **Set Design:** Joe Gerson

Songs: At a Time Like This; Betting Song, The; Did You Know; For Publicity's Sake; It's Traditional; Let Me Take You Away from All This; Little Green Isle; Lonely Women; Love Doesn't Ask Any Questions; March of the Dejected; Melancholy; Shan Shan-O' Han; Twin Soliloquies; Welcome Song; What This Country Needs

Cast: Jeanne Beauvais; Jim Coco; William Hidlay; Gloria Michaels; Jim Mills

Notes: Opened at the Millville Playhouse, Pennsylvania.

2512 • LITTLE HALF BREED, THE

OPENED: 1915
Musical

Composer: Joseph E. Howard

Songs: Beneath Those Sunny Skies (L: Frank R. Adams; Will M. Hough); I'm Proud I'm Irish (L: Jerry Breen)

Notes: No other information available.

2513 • LITTLE HAM

OPENED: 08/31/1987
Musical   Closed out of town

Composer: Judd Woldin
Lyricist: Richard Engquist; Judd Woldin
Librettist: Daniel Owens

Source: LITTLE HAM (Play: Langston Hughes);
Choreographer: John Parks; **Costumes:** Bernard Johnson; **Dance Arranger:** Luther Henderson; **Lighting Designer:** Shirley Prendergast; **Musical Director:** Leonard Oxley; **Orchestrations:** Luther Henderson; **Vocal Arranger:** Luther Henderson

Songs: All in the Point of View; Angels; Big Idea; Dance Contests, The; Get Yourself Some Lovin'; Helluva Big Job; Hot Stuff; I'm Cuttin' Out: Goodbye; It Don't Add Up; Mojo; Noi; Numbers (Gonna Hit Today); Room for Improvement; Say Hello to Your Feet; Wastin' Time

Cast: Billie Allen; Obba Babatunde

Notes: Westport Country Playhouse, CN

2514 • LITTLE HANS ANDERSEN

OPENED: 12/23/1903   Theatre: Adelphi
Musical   London: 23

Composer: Walter Slaughter
Librettist: Basil Hood

Choreographer: E.W. Royce Jr.; **Musical Director:** Hamish MacCunn; **Set Design:** W. Harford

Cast: Alec Fraser; Roy Lorraine; Louie Pounds; Olive Rae

Notes: No songs listed in program.

2515 • LITTLE HOST, THE

OPENED: 12/26/1898   Theatre: Herald Square
Musical   Broadway: 24

Composer: Thomas Chilvers; W.T. Francis
Librettist: Edgar Smith; Louis de Lange
Producer: Nat Roth
Director: Max Frieman

Choreographer: John C. Slavin; **Set Design:** Walter Burridge; Frank Gates

Cast: Della Fox; Alice Johnson; Frank Kelly; John C. Slavin

Notes: No songs listed in program.

2516 • LITTLE JESSIE JAMES

OPENED: 08/15/1923   Theatre: Longacre
Musical   Broadway: 385

Composer: Harry Archer
Lyricist: Harlan Thompson
Librettist: Harlan Thompson
Producer: L. Lawrence Weber
Director: Walter Brooks

Costumes: Mabel E. Johnston; **Set Design:** P. Dodd Ackerman

Songs: Bluebird, The; Come On; Concerted Number; Dance, Tenderfoot, Dance [1]; From Broadway to Main Street; Gotta Have a Man Around the House [3]; How Did It Happen to Me? [3]; I Just Want to Make Friends [3]; I Love You [3]; I'm Me and You're You [1]; Isn't That Always the Way [2]; Knocking Bookworms, The; Little Jack Horner; Little Jesse James; My Home Town in Kansas; Quiet Afternoon; Rainy Afternoon [3]; Such Is Life in a Love Song; Suppose I Had Never Met You; Talk It Over [2]; Teach Me to Dance [3]; What Could Be Sweeter [2]; Who's to Blame?; Wonderful [3]

Cast: Nan Halperin; Miriam Hopkins; Allen Kearns; Frances Upton; Jay Velie

Notes: *See also HEELS TOGETHER.* [1] Out St. Paul 9/4/26. [2] Out Long Branch, N.J. 7/10/23. [3] Complete score for later revival (with additional lyrics by Gladys Shelley). These songs were also used for the reworking titled HEELS TOGETHER. [4] Only from revival which closed out of town in 1953.

2517 • LITTLE JOHNNY JONES

OPENED: 11/07/1904   Theatre: Liberty
Musical   Broadway: 52

Composer: George M. Cohan
Lyricist: George M. Cohan
Librettist: George M. Cohan
Producer: Sam Harris
Director: George M. Cohan

Musical Director: E.T. Howe; **Orchestrations:** Charles J. Gebest; **Set Design:** John Young

Songs: Always Leave Them Laughing When You Say Good-Bye [2]; Captain of a Ten-Day Boat; Cecil in London Town, The; George Washington, Jr.; Girl I Know, A; Girls of the U.S.A.; Give My Regards to Broadway; Good-Bye Flo; Good Old California; If Mr. Boston Lawson Has His Way [1], I'm Mighty Glad I'm Living and That's All; Irish American; Life's a Funny Proposition After All; Little Johnny Jones; Mam'selle Fauchette; March of the Frisco Chinks; Nesting in a New York Tree (Nesting Time in New York Town); Nothing New Beneath the Sun; Off to the Derby; 'Op in My 'Ansom; Sailors of the St. Hurrah; So Long, Sing Song; They're All My Friends; Under a Blanket in a Folding Bed [3]; Yankee Doodle Boy

Cast: Donald Brian; George M. Cohan; Helen Cohan; Jerry Cohan; Ethel Levey; Tom Lewis, Sam J. Ryan; Truly Shattuck

Notes: [1] Sheet music only. [2] Not used in RUN-NING FOR OFFICE. [3] ASCAP/Library of Congress.

2518 • LITTLE JOKER, THE
OPENED: 01/27/1901
Musical   Closed out of town

Composer: James O'Dea
Lyricist: Anne Caldwell
Librettist: Herbert Hall Winslow
Producer: Richard F. Carroll

Songs: Crazy Over You; If I Were Only Taller; I'm Growing; Just a Little Widow; Little Joker, The; Looking for a Man; May I?; Through All Eternity (C/L: Max Witt); Why I Love You

Cast: Arthur Dunn; Marie Glazier; Henry Leone; Jean Salisbury

Notes: Program of Cedar Rapids.

2519 • LITTLE KANGAROO, THE
OPENED: 1922
Musical   Closed out of town

Composer: Werner Janssen
Lyricist: James T. Powers
Librettist: James T. Powers; Mark Swan
Producer: Oliver Morosco
Director: Ned Wayburn

Choreographer: Ned Wayburn; **Costumes:** Shirley Barker; **Musical Director:** Leon Rosebrook; **Orchestrations:** Oscar Radin; **Set Design:** Ned Wayburn

Songs: Aristocratic Servants; Come Down to Me Love (L: Clifford Grey); Everything Is Coming Rosie's Way; Hello, Lizzie; Her First Kiss; Hugh! Hugh!; I Want to Live; It's Hopper; Kangaroo Ragout, The; Kiss of Yore, The; Kissland; Lady Butterfly; Little Kangaroo, The; Looking for Another Job; Love Song to Order, A; Mariner's Tale, The; Miss Venus; Poor Dear Mabel; Rest Rest; We Are Starting Off for England; When You're Away from Me; Your Heart Is Palpitating

Cast: Marjorie Gateson; Allen Kearns; Patricia O'Hearn; James T. Powers; George Trabert

Notes: From a program of New Haven 11/30/22.

2520 • LITTLE KILN CLUB, THE
OPENED: 1911
Musical

Composer: Bob Bailey
Librettist: Jesse A. Shipp
Producer: Sam Croker Jr.

Cast: Allie Gillian; Charles Gilpin; Billy Harper; Fanny Wise

Notes: No other information available.

2521 • LITTLE LIKE MAGIC, A
OPENED: 10/26/1986   Theatre: Lyceum
Revue   Broadway: 49

Producer: Famous People Players
Director: Diane Lynn Dupuy

Lighting Designer: Ken Billington

Songs: Little Like Magic, A (C/L: Victor Davies)

Cast: Darlene Arsenault; Michelle Busby; Sandra Ciccone; Charlene Clarke; Benny D'Onofrio; Annastasia Danyliw; Any Fitzpatrick; Kim

Hansen; Greg Kozak; Debbie Lim; Renato Marulli; Debbie Rossen; Mary Thompson; Neil Thompson; Lenny Turner

Notes: There were other prerecorded songs in this show, for example, Barbra Streisand's recording of "Don't Rain on My Parade." The one song listed above is the only written for this production.

2522 • LITTLE MARY SUNSHINE

OPENED: 11/18/1959   Theatre: Orpheum
Musical   Off-Broadway: 1143

Composer: Rick Besoyan
Lyricist: Rick Besoyan
Librettist: Rick Besoyan
Producer: Cynthia Baer; Howard Barker; Robert Chambers
Director: Rick Besoyan; Ray Harrison

Choreographer: Ray Harrison; **Costumes:** Howard Barker; **Dance Arranger:** Jack Holmes; **Lighting Designer:** Jim Gore; **Musical Director:** Glenn Osser; **Orchestrations:** Arnold Goland; **Set Design:** Howard Barker; **Vocal Arranger:** Jack Holmes

Songs: Colorado Love Call; Coo Coo; Do You Ever Dream of Vienna?; Every Little Nothing; Forest Rangers, The; How Do You Do?; In Izzenschnooken on the Lovely Essenzook Zee; Little Mary Sunshine; Look for a Sky of Blue; Mata Hari; Me, a Big Heap Indian; Naughty, Naughty Nancy; Once in a Blue Moon; Playing Croquet; Say 'Uncle'; 'Shell' Game, A (dance); Such a Merry Party; Swinging; Tell a Handsome Stranger; What Has Happened?; You're the Fairest Flower

Cast: John Aniston; Eileen Brennan; William Graham; Ray James; John McMartin; Elizabeth Parrish; Mario Siletti; Elmarie Wendel

2523 • LITTLE ME

OPENED: 11/17/1962   Theatre: Lunt-Fontanne
Musical   Broadway: 257

Composer: Cy Coleman
Lyricist: Carolyn Leigh
Librettist: Neil Simon
Producer: Cy Feuer; Ernest Martin
Director: Cy Feuer; Bob Fosse

Source: LITTLE ME (Novel: Patrick Dennis); **Choreographer:** Bob Fosse; **Costumes:** Robert Fletcher; **Dance Arranger:** Fred Werner; **Lighting Designer:** Robert Randolph; **Musical Director:** Charles Sanford; **Orchestrations:** Ralph Burns; **Set Design:** Robert Randolph; **Vocal Arranger:** Clay Warnick

Songs: Be a Mother [2]; Be a Performer! [4]; Birthday Party (Rich Kids Rag); Boom-Boom (Le Grand Boom-Boom); Deep Down Inside; Dimples; Doing Time [2]; Don't Ask a Lady [1]; Gift of a Second Chance, The [3]; Here's to Us; I Love You (As Much As I Am Able); I Wanna Be Yours [1]; I've Got Your Number; Lafayette [3]; Little Me; Mama's Little Girl [3]; Other Side of the Tracks, The; Poor Little Hollywood Star; Prince's Farewell (Goodbye), The; Real Live Girl; Smart People Stay Single [3]; Thanks! Don't Mention It [2]; Truth, The; Vitabelle [2]

Cast: John Anania; Nancy Andrews; Sid Caesar; Gretchen Cryer; Mickey Deems; Joey Faye; Eddie Gasper; Marc Jordan; Mort Marshall; Virginia Martin; Adnia Rice; John Sharpe; Michael Smuin; Swen Swenson; Peter Turgeon

Notes: [1] Added for revival. [2] Not used. [3] Cut prior to opening. [4] Originally written as part of a demo for the job of writing GYPSY.

2524 • LITTLE MICHUS, THE

OPENED: 01/31/1907   Theatre: Garden
Musical   Broadway: 29

Composer: Andre Messager
Lyricist: Percy Greenbank
Librettist: Henry Hamilton
Director: J.A.E. Malone

Source: LES P'TITES MICHU (Musical: Georges Duval; Andre Messager; Albert Vanloo); **Choreographer:** Willie Warde; **Musical Director:** Augustus Barratt; Howard Talbot; **Set Design:** Walter Hann; Joseph Harker

Songs: I Would Like to Be a Grand Lady; It's No Use Crying for the Moon!; Little Sister; Miss Nobody from No-Where; My Heart's a Weatherglass; My Old Home; Regiment of Frocks and Frills, The; Song of the Regiment, The; This Little Girl and That

Cast: Flavia Arcaro; Amy Augard; Ethel Dudley;

George Fortesque; George Graves; May Griffiths; Alice Judson; Lotta Parker; William C. Weedon

Notes: No songs listed in program.

2525 • LITTLE MILLIONAIRE, THE
OPENED: 09/25/1911   Theatre: Cohan
Musical   Broadway: 192

Composer: George M. Cohan
Lyricist: George M. Cohan
Librettist: George M. Cohan
Producer: George M. Cohan; Sam H. Harris
Director: George M. Cohan

Choreographer: James Gorman

Songs: Any Place the Old Flag Flies; Barnum Had the Right Idea; Characteristic Waltz; Come with Me to My Bungalow (Cohan's Bungalow Song); Dancing Wedding, The; Down in My Heart [1] (C/L: Irving Berlin); Drill of the Seventh; Little Millionaire, The; Musical Moon, The; New Yorkers; Oh, You Wonderful Girl; We Do the Dirty Work

Cast: George M. Cohan; Helen Cohan; Jerry Cohan; Donald Crisp; Tom Lewis; George Parsons

Notes: [1] Sheet music only.

2526 • LITTLE MISS BLUEBEARD
OPENED: 08/28/1923   Theatre: Lyceum
Play   Broadway: 175

Lyricist: E. Ray Goetz
Author: Avery Hopwood
Producer: Charles Frohman
Director: W.H. Gilmore

Source: A KISASSONYI FERJE (Play: Gabriel Dregely)

Songs: Gondola and the Girl, The (C: Paul Rubens); I Won't Say I Will, but I Won't Say I Won't (C: George Gershwin; L: B.G. DeSylva; Ira Gershwin [1]); So This Is Love (C: E. Ray Goetz); Who'll Buy My Violets? (C: Jose Padilla)

Cast: Eric Blore; Irene Bordoni; Stanley Logan; Bruce McRae; Jeannette Sherwin

Notes: Percy Graham was also credited as a song writer but the songs were not identified in the program. [1] Ira Gershwin used the pseudonym Arthur Francis.

2527 • LITTLE MISS CHARITY
OPENED: 09/02/1920   Theatre: Belmont
Musical   Broadway: 76

Composer: S.R. Henry; M. Savin
Lyricist: Edward Clark
Librettist: Edward Clark
Producer: Richard G. Herndon
Director: Alfred Hickman; C.A. de Lima

Source: UNKNOWN (Story: Edgar S. Franklin); **Choreographer:** Sammy Lee; **Musical Director:** Gus Salzer; **Orchestrations:** Arthur Lange; M. Savin; **Set Design:** P. Dodd Ackerman

Songs: Angel Town; Crinoline Girl; Dance Me Around; Eyes of Youth; Finale Act I; I Think So, Too; Little Miss Charity; Poor Workingman; Revenge; Step Inside; That Certain Something; When Love Comes to Your Heart; Woman's Touch, A

Cast: Juanita Fletcher; Marjorie Gateson; Frank Moulan; Frederick Raymond Jr.

2528 • LITTLE MISS FIX-IT
OPENED: 04/03/1911   Theatre: Globe
Musical   Broadway: 56

Composer: Nora Bayes; Jack Norworth
Lyricist: Jack Norworth
Librettist: William J. Hurlbut; Harry B. Smith
Producer: Mark A. Luescher; Louis F. Werba
Director: Gustave von Seyffertitz

Musical Director: Ivan Rudisill

Songs: Excuse Me Mr. Moon [4] (C: J. Rosamond Johnson; L: James Weldon Johnson); For Months and Months; Have You Ever Loved Any Other Girl? [4] (C: J. Rosamond Johnson; L: James Weldon Johnson); If You'll Be My Eve I'll Build an Eden for You (C: J. Rosamond Johnson; L: James Weldon Johnson); I've a Garden in Sweden [5] (C/L: Nora Bayes; Dan Lipton; C.W. Murphy; Jack Norworth; Hugh Owens); Little Miss Fix It; Mister Moon Man, Turn Off Your Light; No More Staying Out Late [1] (C/L: Nora

Bayes; Bert Lee; Jack Norworth); Opening March; Parlor Games [3]; Please Go Find My Billy Boy; Strawberries; Tantalizing Ida; There Is a Happy Land (Tale of Woe) (C: Jerome Kern; L: Jack Norworth); Turkey Trot (inst.) [2] (C: Jerome Kern; Dave Stamper)

Cast: Nora Bayes; William Danforth; Grace Field; Jack Norworth; Frank Shannon; Pauline de Lorme

Notes: [1] American version of this song by Norworth and Bayes. [2] Kern not credited in all sources. He's not credited on sheet music. [3] ASCAP/Library of Congress only. [4] Sheet music only. [5] Bayes and Norworth Americanized the English song (or they simply added their names to the credits).

2529 • LITTLE MISS MODESTY
OPENED: 1901
Musical   Unproduced

Composer: Walter Slaughter
Lyricist: Richard Carle

Notes: No other information available.

2530 • LITTLE MISS RAFFLES
Notes: *See THE HOTEL MOUSE.*

2531 • LITTLE MISS SPRINGTIME
Notes: *See MISS SPRINGTIME.*

2532 • LITTLE MISSUS, THE
OPENED: 04/23/1917
Musical   Closed out of town

Composer: Paul Eisler
Lyricist: A.E. Thomas
Librettist: A.E. Thomas
Producer: H.L. Gillespie
Director: George Marion

Musical Director: John McGhie; **Set Design:** Henry Ives Cobb Jr.

Songs: Bubbling; Gossip; I Miss You So; It's a Way the Old Thing Has; Love Leads On; Lover's Quarrel; Off with the Old; Purity League, The; Stockings; You Must Walk Like This

Cast: Roy Atwell; Frank Bradley; Alice Hills; Christie MacDonald; George Leon Moore

Notes: From program of 4/23/17 Washington D.C.

2533 • LITTLE NELLIE KELLY
OPENED: 11/13/1922   Theatre: Liberty
Musical   Broadway: 276

Composer: George M. Cohan
Lyricist: George M. Cohan
Librettist: George M. Cohan
Producer: George M. Cohan
Director: George M. Cohan

Musical Director: Charles J. Gebest

Songs: All in the Wearing; (They're) All My Boys; Busy Bees of DeVere's, The; Dancing Detective, The; Dancing My Worries Away; Finale Act I; Finale Act II; Girls of DeVere's; Great New York Police, The; Mystery Play, The; Name of Kelly, The; Nellie Kelly I Love You; Nellie's Entrance [1]; Over the Phone (Telephone Song); Something's Got to Be Done; Until My Luck Comes Rolling Along; Voice in My Heart, The; When You Do the Hinky Dee; You Remind Me of My Mother

Cast: Georgia Caine; Arthur Deagon; Barrett Greenwood; Elizabeth Hines; Charles King; Marjorie Lane

Notes: [1] Vocal score only.

2534 • LITTLE NEMO
OPENED: 10/20/1908   Theatre: New Amsterdam
Musical   Broadway: 111

Composer: Victor Herbert
Lyricist: Harry B. Smith
Librettist: Harry B. Smith
Producer: Klaw & Erlanger
Director: Herbert Gresham

Source: LITTLE NEMO IN SLUMBERLAND (Comic Strip: Windsor McKay); **Costumes:** F. Richard Anderson; **Musical Director:** Max Hirschfeld; **Set Design:** Ernest Albert; John Young

Songs: Away We'll Float [2]; Barbecue, The; Blow Upon Your Bugles; Cannibal Barbecue [2]; Cannibal Island, The [2]; Central Park Scene (inst.); Chime of the Liberty Bell; Cupid Is the Postman; Different Kinds of Weather; Entrance of the School Children [4]; Give Us a Fleet; Happy Land of Once-Upon- a-Time; Hen and the Weather Vane, The; I Guess I Talk Too Much; I Want to Be a Naughty Little Girl [2]; I Wouldn't Take a Case Like That; If I Could Teach My Teddy Bear to Dance; In Happy Slumberland; Is My Face on Straight; It's the Irish [1]; March of the Valentines (inst.); May Day March (inst.); Nemo's Dream of Fourth of July (inst.); Newspaper Song (Read the Papers Every Day); Oh What Fools We Mortals Be; Olympian Dance, The; Opening Chorus; Remember the Old Continentals; Review of Athletes [4]; Slumberland; Sunbeams, Snowflakes, Raindrops; There's Nothing the Matter with You; They Were Irish [3]; Valentines (inst.); Weather Factory in Cloudland [2]; Will-O-the-Wisp; Won't You Be My Playmate?; Won't You Be My Valentine?

Cast: Joseph Cawthorn; Master Gabriel; Harry Kelly; Florence Tempest; Billy B. Van

Notes: [1] Out Boston 2/1/09. [2] Not in programs. In vocal selection only. [3] ASCAP/Library of Congress only. [4] Not in programs or vocal selection.

2535 • LITTLE NIGHT MUSIC, A (1963)

OPENED: 1963
Musical   Unproduced

Composer: Hugh Martin
Lyricist: Marshall Barer

Songs: Did I Just Fall in Love; Dirty Face; Face, The; Here Come the Dreamers; Inspiration; Little Night Music, A; Morning Star; Obbligato; On Such a Night As This; Someone to Talk To; Technique; There Go the Dreamers; "Up" Number, The; Wasn't It Romantic? [1]; Write About What You Know; You're About to Be Beautiful; You're As Young As You Feel

Notes: This musical was to star Jeanette MacDonald and Liza Minnelli. [1] A counterpoint to "Isn't It Romantic" by Rodgers and Hart.

2536 • LITTLE NIGHT MUSIC, A (1973)

OPENED: 02/25/1973   Theatre: Shubert
Musical   Broadway: 601

Composer: Stephen Sondheim
Lyricist: Stephen Sondheim
Librettist: Hugh Wheeler
Producer: Ruth Mitchell; Harold Prince
Director: Harold Prince

Source: SMILES OF A SUMMER NIGHT (Film: Ingmar Bergman); **Choreographer:** Patricia Birch; **Costumes:** Florence Klotz; **Lighting Designer:** Tharon Musser; **Musical Director:** Harold Hastings; **Orchestrations:** Jonathan Tunick; **Set Design:** Boris Aronson

Songs: Bang! [1]; Every Day a Little Death; Glamorous Life, The (1) [3]; Glamorous Life, The (2); In Praise of Women; It Would Have Been Wonderful; Later; Liaisons; Miller's Son, The; My Husband, the Pig [2]; Night Waltz (1) [1]; Night Waltz (2); Not Quite Night [1]; Now (1) [1]; Now (2); Perpetual Anticipation; Remember?; Send in the Clowns; Silly People [1]; Soon; Sun Won't Set, The; Two Fairy Tales [1]; Weekend in the Country, A; You Must Meet My Wife

Cast: George Lee Andrews; D'Jamin Bartlett; Len Cariou; Despo; Patricia Elliott; Beth Fowler; Hermione Gingold; Laurence Guittard; Glynis Johns; Judy Kahan; Mark Lambert; Barbara Lang; Victoria Mallory; Sherry Mathis; Teri Ralston; Gene Varrone

Notes: [1] Cut. [2] Cut. Middle section became "Every Day a Little Death." [3] Cut. Later used in film version.

2537 • LITTLE OLD NEW YORK

OPENED: 09/08/1920   Theatre: Plymouth
Musical   Broadway: 311

Author: Rida Johnson Young
Producer: Sam Harris
Director: Sam Forrest

Songs: Do You Hear Me Calling? (C: William Schroeder; L: Rida Johnson Young)

Cast: Ernest Glendinning; Donald Meek; Genevieve Tobin

Notes: The music was based on "an old air arranged by William Schroeder."

2538 • LITTLE PARISIENNE, THE

OPENED: 1913
Musical

Composer: Felix Albini
Lyricist: Harold Atteridge
Librettist: Harold Atteridge; Joseph W. Herbert
Producer: Winter Garden Company
Director: Joseph W. Herbert

Source: MADAME TROUBADOUR (Musical: Felix Albini; Bela Jenbach; Richard Pohl); **Musical Director:** Daniel Dore

Songs: Ancient Minstrel, The; Came from Germany [1]; Ding Dong; Don't Be Rash; From the Meadow's Fairest Flower; Gaby Glide, The (C: Louis A. Hirsch; L: Harry Pilcer); High Society; I Can't Keep My Eyes from Looking at You [1]; I Have Courted in Vain; I'd Like to Borrow a Kiss (C: Al W. Brown); Oh How That Taxi Got on My Nerves; Take Me Back to Town; Vous Etes Jolie; World-Wide Romeo, A (C: Al W. Brown)

Cast: Gaby Deslys; Harry Pilcer

Notes: Program of New York 11/24/13 used — but not Broadway. Program of Chicago 3/2/14 also used. This was a touring version of the Broadway show MADAME TROUBADOUR with new book and lyrics. *See MADAME TROUBADOUR.* [1] Added after opening.

2539 • LITTLE PRINCE AND THE AVIATOR, THE

OPENED: 1982   Theatre: Alvin
Musical   Broadway

Composer: John Barry
Lyricist: Don Black
Librettist: Hugh Wheeler
Producer: Little Prince Productions; A. Joseph Tandet
Director: Jerry Adler

Source: LE PETIT PRINCE (Book: Antoine de Saint-Exupery); **Choreographer:** Billy Wilson; **Costumes:** Christa Scholtz; **Dance Arranger:** Grant Sturiale; **Lighting Designer:** Roger

Morgan; **Musical Director:** David Friedman; **Orchestrations:** Don Walker; **Set Design:** Eugene Lee; **Vocal Arranger:** David Friedman

Songs: Day Will Never Be the Same, A; First Impressions; Grain of Sand; I Don't Regret a Thing; I Like My Misfortunes to Be Taken Seriously; I Pity the Poor Poor Parisians; It Was You; I've Got You to Thank for All This; Little Prince [1]; Made for Each Other; Making Every Minute Count; More Than Just a Pretty Flower; Par Avion; Playground of the Planets; Power Comes, Power Goes; Stars Will Be Laughing; Sunset Song; Volcano Song, The; Watch Out for the Baobabs; We Couldn't We Mustn't We Won't; Wind, Sand & Stars

Cast: Janet Eilber; Chip Garnett; Ellen Greene; David Purdham; Anthony Rapp; Michael York

Notes: Closed 1/17/83 in previews. [1] Music later used as the main theme of the film THE GOLDEN SEAL.

2540 • LITTLE RACKETEER, A

OPENED: 01/18/1932   Theatre: 44th Street
Musical   Broadway: 48

Composer: Henry Sullivan[1]
Lyricist: Edward Eliscu
Librettist: Harry Clarke; R. Wilde
Producer: Messrs. Shubert
Director: William Caryl

Source: UNKNOWN (Play: F. Kalbuss; R. Wilde); **Choreographer:** Jack Donahue; Albertina Rasch; **Costumes:** Alison McLellan Hunter; Ernest Schrapps; **Musical Director:** Maurie Rubens; **Set Design:** Watson Barratt

Songs: Ballyhoo (C: Dimitri Tiomkin); Blow, Gabriel; Brazilian Suite (C: Dimitri Tiomkin); Danger If I Love You; Dou, Dou [2]; Here's to Night [2]; I Have a Run in My Stocking [2]; I'll Ballyhoo You [3] (C: Dimitri Tiomkin); Inside Looking Out [3]; Mr. Moon (C: Lee Wainer; L: Lupin Fein; Moe Jaffe); Night Club Nights; Rio de Janeiro (C: Dimitri Tiomkin); Southern Belles Ballet (C: Dimitri Tiomkin); Spring Tra La (C: Lee Wainer; L: Lupin Fein; Moe Jaffe); Starry Sky (C: Dimitri Tiomkin); Thanks to You (C: Berenece Kazounoff; L: Earle Crooker); Throwing a Party; What Great Big Eyes You Have; When That Band Plays; Whiling My Time

Away [2]; You and I Could Be Just Like That; You've Got to Sell Yourself

Cast: Jeanette Bradley; John Garrick; Hamtree Hamilton; Grace Hayes; William Kent; Barbara Newberry; Carl Randall; Queenie Smith; Lorraine Weimar; Betty Wonder; Tommy Wonder

Notes: Henry Sullivan and Louis Alter were credited with the music when this show was out-of-town. Haskell Brown may be a pseudonym for those composers. [1] Program credited music to Haskell Brown, probably a pseudonym for Sullivan, who is credited by ASCAP and out-of-town programs. [2] Cut after opening. [3] Not used.

2541 • LITTLE RASCALS, THE (1986)

OPENED: 1986
Musical   Unproduced

Composer: David Bishop; Carl Earl Weaver
Lyricist: Carl Earl Weaver
Librettist: Ken Bloom; Carl Earl Weaver

Source: LITTLE RASCALS, THE (Film)

Songs: Darlin' Darla; Everybody Who's Anybody; Flora Dora Girls; Goodbye Little Rascals; He's My B-B-B-Baby; Hello, Broadway, Hello; I Believe in You; Let's Do It for Granny; Our Gang; Remembering; Rollerskating Granny; Skeleton Dance; Spanky's Clubhouse Show; Tale of Bro' Crow, The; Villain's Credo Tango, The; We'll Still Be Friends; Why Does It Always Happen to Me?

2542 • LITTLE RASCALS, THE (1987)

OPENED: 10/07/1987
Musical   Closed out of town

Composer: Joe Raposo
Lyricist: Joe Raposo
Librettist: Michael Loman
Producer: Goodspeed Opera House
Director: Robert Nigro

Source: LITTLE RASCALS, THE (Film);
    Choreographer: Marcia Milgrom Dodge;
    Costumes: Franne Lee; **Dance Arranger:** Gordon

Harrell; **Lighting Designer:** Craig Miller; **Musical Director:** Lynn Crigler; **Set Design:** James Leonard Joy

Songs: American Way, The; Another Summer; Chase, The; Club, The; Everything; Fourth of July; Good Way to Be Bad, A; If Love Never Comes; Just Kids; Last Man on Earth; Lazy Summer Days; Love or Money; Not Much of a Dog; Prologue; Rascals; Seven Lucky Ways; Waldo's Song; Where Did I Go Wrong; Whoosh, Bang

Cast: Eugene J. Anthony; Ronn Carroll; Erick Devine; Dule Hill; Ken Jennings; Betsy Joslyn

Notes: Goodspeed Opera House.

2543 • LITTLE RED RIDING HOOD

OPENED: 01/08/1900   Theatre: Casino
Musical   Broadway: 24

Composer: Charles Denee; Frederick J. Eustis; E.E. Rice
Lyricist: Harrison Ward
Librettist: George T. Richardson
Producer: Edward Rose
Director: Dan Mason

Musical Director: George Lowell Tracy; **Set Design:** Albert Operti; Frank Rafter; John Thompson

Songs: Art of Making Love, The; Bogie Man; Come Blow Your Horn; Legend of the Stork, The; Little Boy Blue; Love Is an Infant; Nellie the Manicure; Pickaninny's Lullaby, The; Pussy's in the Well; Soldier Bold, The; Sunshine Girl, The

Cast: William Burress; Gertie Carlisle; Snitz Edwards; Ethel Jackson; Madge Lessing; Dan Mason; Joseph Reynolds

Notes: Boston program only.

2544 • LITTLE SHOP OF HORRORS

OPENED: 07/27/1982   Theatre: Orpheum
Musical   Off-Broadway: 2209

Composer: Alan Menken
Lyricist: Howard Ashman

Librettist: Howard Ashman
Producer: David Geffen; Cameron Mackintosh; Shubert Organization; WPA Theatre
Director: Howard Ashman

Source: LITTLE SHOP OF HORRORS (Film: Roger Corman); **Choreographer:** Edie Cowan; **Costumes:** Sally Lesser; **Lighting Designer:** Craig Evans; **Musical Director:** Robert Billig; **Orchestrations:** Robby Merkin; **Set Design:** Edward T. Gianfrancesco; **Vocal Arranger:** Robert Billig

Songs: Call Back in the Morning; Closed for Renovations; Dentist!; Don't It Go to Show Ya Never Know; Finale (Don't Feed the Plants); Git It!; Grow for Me; I Found a Hobby [1]; Little Dental Music, A [1]; Meek Shall Inherit, The; Mushnik and Son; Now (It's Just the Gas); Prologue (Little Shop of Horrors); Skid Row (Downtown); Somewhere That's Green; Suddenly, Seymour; Suppertime; We'll Have Tomorrow [1]

Cast: Hy Anzell; Marlene Danielle; Sheila Kay Davis; Ellen Greene; Franc Luz; Martin P. Robinson; Ron Taylor; Jennifer Leigh Warren; Lee Wilkof

Notes: [1] Not used.

2545 • LITTLE SHOW, THE
OPENED: 04/30/1929   Theatre: Music Box
Revue   Broadway: 321

Composer: Arthur Schwartz
Lyricist: Howard Dietz
Librettist: Howard Dietz
Producer: William A. Brady; Tom Weatherly; Dwight Deere Wiman
Director: Alexander Leftwich; Dwight Deere Wiman

Choreographer: Danny Dare; **Costumes:** Ruth Brenner; **Musical Director:** Gus Salzer; **Set Design:** Jo Mielziner

Songs: Can't We Be Friends (C: Kay Swift; L: Paul James); Caught in the Rain (C: Henry Sullivan); Get Up on a New Routine; Hammacher Schlemmer, I Love You; Hut in Hoboken (C/L: Herman Hupfeld); I Guess I'll Have to Change My Plan [1]; I've Made a Habit of You; Little Old New York; Man About Town; Moanin' Low

(C: Ralph Rainger); Or What Have You? (C: Morris Hamilton; L: Grace Henry); Six Little Sinners (C: Frank Grey; L: Earle Crooker); Song of the Riveter (L: Lew Levenson); Stick to Your Dancing, Mabel (C/L: Charlotte Kent); Theme Song, The; Tiller Girls at Home Sketch, The (inst.); What Every Little Girl Should Know (L: Henry Myers); Work Alive (C: Frank Grey; L: Earle Crooker)

Cast: Fred Allen; Romney Brent; Peggy Conklin; Bettina Hall; Libby Holman; Clifton Webb; **Pianist:** Adam Carroll; Ralph Rainger

Notes: [1] Music first used for camp song "I Love to Lie Awake in Bed" with lyric by Lorenz Hart.

2546 • LITTLE SIMPLICITY
OPENED: 11/04/1918   Theatre: Astor
Musical   Broadway: 112

Composer: Augustus Barratt
Lyricist: Rida Johnson Young
Librettist: Rida Johnson Young
Producer: Messrs. Shubert
Director: Edward P. Temple

Choreographer: Jack Mason; **Costumes:** S. Zalud; **Musical Director:** Augustus Barratt; **Set Design:** Watson Barratt

Songs: Boom a Rang; Can You Hear Me Calling [1]; Days of Youth; Dot and Carry One; First Love; Follow the Boys; Hush! Hush!; I Cannot Leave You; It's Worth While Waiting for Someone Worth While; Just a Little Sunshine; Learning to Love; March; Maybe You'll Look Good to Me; Military Fox Trot Tune, A; My Caravan; My Lulu; National Air's Medley; Ooh! La! La! [1]; Please Buy My Flowers; Reminiscence, A; Same Old Way; Verb to Love, A [1]; Voice Calling Me, A; Women; You Don't Know

Cast: Walter Catlett; Carl Gantvoort; Marjorie Gateson; Mabel Withee

Notes: Titled MISS "I DON'T KNOW" out of town. [1] Out Stamford 9/14/18.

2547 • LITTLE TOMMY TUCKER
OPENED: 11/19/1930   Theatre: Daly's
Musical   London: 83

Composer: Vivian Ellis
Lyricist: Desmond Carter
Librettist: Desmond Carter; Caswell Garth; Bert Lee; R.P. Weston
Producer: Herbert Clayton
Director: William Mollison

Choreographer: Ralph Reader; **Costumes:** Flora Godard; **Set Design:** F.L. Lyndhurst

Songs: Aladdin; Follow the Girl; Glad; I Have No Words [1] (C: Arthur Schwartz); Let's Be Sentimental; Lift Your Skirt (A Little Bit Higher); Out of the Blue (C: Vivian Ellis; Arthur Schwartz); Practice on Me; Take It from Me

Cast: Binnie Barnes; Melville Cooper; Rita Page; Ivy Tresmand; Jane Welsh

Notes: [1] Same music as "Something to Remember You By" in THREE'S A CROWD.

2548 • LITTLE TROOPER, THE
OPENED: 08/30/1894   Theatre: Casino
Musical   Broadway: 68

Composer: William Furst
Librettist: Clay M. Greene
Producer: Nat Roth
Director: Richard Barker

Set Design: Ernest Gros

Cast: Paul Arthur; Eva Davenport; Jefferson De Angelis; Della Fox; Ed Knight; Alf C. Whelan; Hattie Williams

Notes: No songs listed in program.

2549 • LITTLE WHOPPER, THE
OPENED: 10/13/1919   Theatre: Casino
Musical   Broadway: 224

Composer: Rudolf Friml
Lyricist: Bide Dudley; Otto Harbach
Librettist: Otto Harbach
Producer: Abraham Levy
Director: Oscar Eagle

Choreographer: Bert French

Songs: Bye-Bye My Little Wife [1] (L: Otto Harbach); Good Morning All; I Have a Date; If You Go I'll

Die (L: Otto Harbach); I'm Lonely When I'm Alone (C: Otto Harbach); It Can't Be Wrong; It's Great to Be Married (L: Otto Harbach); I've Got to Leave You; Kiss, The (L: Unknown); Let It Be Soon (L: Otto Harbach); Oh! What a Little Whopper (L: Otto Harbach); Oh, You Major Scales (L: Otto Harbach); 'Round the Corner (L: Otto Harbach); Snap Your Fingers (L: Otto Harbach); Sweet Dreams (L: Otto Harbach); There's Only One Thing to Do (L: Otto Harbach); Twinkle Little Star (L: Otto Harbach); We'll Build a Cute Little Nest (L: Otto Harbach); You'll Dream and I'll Dream — Then Wake to Find Your Dreams Come True [2] (L: Unknown)

Cast: Nellie Graham-Dent; Sydney Grant; Vivienne Segal; David Torrence

Notes: [1] Not used. [2] ASCAP/Library of Congress only.

2550 • LITTLE WOMEN
OPENED: 10/16/1958   Theatre: CBS
TV Musical

Composer: Richard Adler
Lyricist: Richard Adler
Librettist: Wilson Lehr
Producer: Albert Selden
Director: William Corrigan

Source: LITTLE WOMEN (Novel: Louisa May Alcott); **Musical Director:** Hal Hastings; **Orchestrations:** Don Walker

Songs: Dance, Why Not?; Four of Us, The; How Do You Write a Book?; I Don't Want to Be a Fly; Letter (My Little Women), The; Live I Mean; Man of the Family; Party Shoes

Cast: Zina Bethune; Jeannie Carson; Bill Hayes; Florence Henderson; Margaret O'Brien; Rise Stevens; Roland Winters

2551 • LITTLE WORLD, HELLO!
OPENED: 1966
Musical

Composer: Dick Manning
Lyricist: Dick Manning
Librettist: Lee Cooley
Producer: Jack Beekman; John C. Cohan
Director: Lee Cooley

Source: LITTLE WORLD, HELLO! (Book: Jimmy Savo); **Choreographer:** Matt Mattox; **Costumes:** Audre; **Lighting Designer:** Phil Hymes; **Musical Director:** Richard Hayman; **Orchestrations:** Jim Tyler; **Set Design:** Peter Dohanos; **Vocal Arranger:** Richard Hayman

Songs: Above! Above!; Benediction, The; Choose! Choose! Choose!; Don't Put Me 'On'; Got to Get Away from Here; Hey Gimme, Jimmy; If I Could Buy a Dream; Just To Know That He's Around; Little Witch, The [1]; Little World, Hello; Loneliness; Meraviglioso!; My First Love; Nino and Dino and Gino; Now, She Is Rich [1]; O, Salty Sea; On the Via Veneto; Stupidina; Veranda's Toe; Very Fortunate Man, A; Wait Till After the Wedding

Cast: Pinky Lee

Notes: Never got into rehearsal. [1] Same music.

2552 • LITTLE YENNIE YENSEN
OPENED: 09/30/1907
Musical   Closed out of town

Composer: J. Ward Kett
Lyricist: J. Ward Kett
Librettist: J. Ward Kett
Producer: Stuart & Kent

Arrangements: Will Rossiter

Songs: Bohemia; Foolish; In the Silent Deep; My Irish Rosie; Robinson Crusoe's Isle; Senora; When the Moon Plays Peek-a-Boo; Why Must We Part?; Wish Me Good Luck on My Journey; You've Got to Be American to Feel That Way

Cast: Louis Chevalier; Florence Hart; J. Ward Kett; Lucille Reynolds

Notes: Cedar Rapids. Rossiter may be the compser of the songs, the program is unclear.

2553 • LITTLEST ANGEL, THE
OPENED: 12/06/1969   Theatre: NBC
TV Musical

Composer: Lan O'Kun
Lyricist: Lan O'Kun
Librettist: Patricia Gray; Lan O'Kun
Producer: Burr Smidt
Director: Joe Layton

Source: LITTLEST ANGEL, THE (Story: Charles Tazwell); **Musical Director:** John Morris

Songs: Heavenly Ever After, The; I Bring You Good Tidings; I Have Saved; Master of All I Survey, The; May It Bring Him Pleasure; Once Upon Another Time; What Do You Do; Where Am I; Where Is Blue; You Can Fly; You're Not Real

Cast: Cab Calloway; James Coco; Fred Gwynne; Corinna Manetto; E.G. Marshall; Tony Randall; George Rose; Connie Stevens; Johnnie Whitaker

2554 • LITTLEST REVUE, THE
OPENED: 05/22/1956   Theatre: Phoenix
Revue   Off-Broadway: 32

Composer: Vernon Duke
Lyricist: Ogden Nash
Librettist: George Baxt; Billy Friedberg; Nat Hiken; Allan Mannings; Bud McCreery; Michael Stewart; Bob Van Scoyk; Eudora Welty
Producer: Phoenix Theatre
Director: Paul Lammers

Choreographer: Charles Weidman; **Costumes:** Alvin Colt; **Lighting Designer:** Klaus Holm; **Musical Director:** Will Irwin; **Orchestrations:** Joe Glover; Tommy Goodman; John Strauss; **Set Design:** Klaus Holm

Songs: Ballad of the Shape of Things (C/L: Sheldon Harnick); Born Too Late; Fly Now, Pay Later; Good Little Girls [1] (L: Sammy Cahn); I Lost the Rhythm (C/L: Charles Strouse); I'm Glad I'm not a Man; Little Love, a Little Money, A [4]; Littlest Revue, The (C: John Strauss; L: Kenward Elmslie; John Latouche); Love Is Still in Town; Madly in Love; Nothing Ever Happens [5]; Power of Negative Thinking, The (C/L: Bud McCreery); Second Avenue and 12th Street Rag; Spring Doth Let Her Colours Fly (C: Charles Strouse; L: Lee Adams); Summer Is A-Comin' In [2] (L: John Latouche); Third Avenue El [3] (C/L: Michael Brown); You're Far from Wonderful

Cast: Beverley Bozeman; Joel Grey; Tammy Grimes; Dorothy Jarnac; George Marcy; Tommy Morton; Charlotte Rae; Larry Storch

Notes: Conceived and cast assembled by Ben Bagley. [1] Cut from TWO'S COMPANY. Written for film APRIL IN PARIS (film) and not used. [2] Originally in THE LADY COMES

ACROSS. [3] Originally in FOUR BELOW and later in DEMI DOZEN. [4] From HE AND SHE. [5] Not used. From HE AND SHE.

2555 • LIVIN' DOLLS
OPENED: 03/09/1982   Theatre: Manhattan
                      Theatre Club
Musical   Off-Broadway: 40

Composer: Marc Shaiman; Scott Wittman
Lyricist: Marc Shaiman; Scott Wittman
Librettist: Marc Shaiman; Scott Wittman
Producer: Manhattan Theater Club
Director: Richard Maltby Jr.

Choreographer: Richard Maltby Jr.; Scott Wittman; **Costumes:** Timothy Dunleavy; **Lighting Designer:** Pat Collins; **Musical Director:** Marc Shaiman; **Set Design:** John Lee Beatty; **Vocal Arranger:** Marc Shaiman

Songs: Down in the Sand; G.I. Joe; Girls; Lifesaver; Livin' Doll, A; Lost in Space (C: Bobby Siems); Love Come A-Callin'; No Questions Asked; Nobody's Valentine; Poindexter's Lament; 'Round About Midnight; Something Special; There's a Girl Waiting for Our Wave; Wipeout at Panic Point (C: Bobby Siems)

Cast: Lisa Embs; Linda Hart; Kim Milford; Zora Rasmussen; James Rich; Deborah Van Valkenburgh; Tom Wiggin

2556 • LIVIN' THE LIFE
OPENED: 04/27/1957   Theatre: Phoenix
Musical   Off-Broadway: 25

Composer: Jacques Urbont
Lyricist: Bruce Geller
Librettist: Bruce Geller; Dale Wasserman
Producer: Phoenix Theatre
Director: David Alexander

Source: ADVENTURES OF HUCKLEBERRY FINN, THE (Novel: Mark Twain); **Choreographer:** John Butler; **Costumes:** Alvin Colt; **Dance Arranger:** Genevieve Pitot; **Lighting Designer:** Klaus Holm; **Musical Director:** Anton Coppola; **Orchestrations:** Joe Glover; Hershy Kay; **Set Design:** Jean Eckart; William Eckart

Songs: Ain't It a Shame; All of 'Em Say; Don't Tell Me; Jim's Lament; Late Love; Livin' the Life;

MacDougal's Cave; Mock Battle; Nightmare Ballet; Probably in Love; River Ballad; Someone; Steamboat; Sunday Promenade; Supersational Day; Take Kids; Whiskey Bug

Cast: Patsy Bruder; Lee Charles; Timmy Everett; Alice Ghostley; Richard Ide; James Mitchell; Edward Villella

2557 • LIZA (1922)
OPENED: 11/27/1922   Theatre: Daly's
Musical   Broadway: 172

Composer: Maceo Pinkard
Lyricist: Maceo Pinkard; Nat Vincent
Librettist: Irvin C. Miller
Producer: Al Davis
Director: Walter Brooks

Costumes: Mme. Gilman; **Musical Director:** Tim Brymn

Songs: Charleston Dancy, The; Dandy; Don't Be Blue; Essence; Forget Your Troubles; I'm Gwine to Talk [1]; I'm the Sheriff; Just a Barber Shop Chord; Liza; Love Me; My Creole Girl; My Old Man; On the Moonlit Swanee; Planning; Pleasure; Runnin' Wild Blues; Tag Day; That Brownskin Flapper

Cast: Thaddius Drayton; Snippy Mason; Irvin C. Miller; Gertrude Saunders; Margaret Simms

Notes: [1] Added after opening.

2558 • LIZA (1974)
OPENED: 01/06/1974   Theatre: Winter Garden
Musical   Broadway: 23

Composer: John Kander
Lyricist: Fred Ebb
Producer: Ron Delsener; Shubert Organization
Director: Bob Fosse

Choreographer: Bob Fosse; Ron Lewis; **Lighting Designer:** Jules Fisher; **Musical Director:** Jack French

Songs: And I in My Chair (C: Charles Aznavour; David Newburger); Anywhere You Are [2]; Circle, The (C: Edith Piaf); Exactly Like Me; I Believe You [1]; I'm One of the Smart Ones [2]; Liza with a 'Z'; Ring Them Bells

Cast: Liza Minnelli

Notes: These songs were previously performed by Miss Minnelli and others. I only listed the songs written for Miss Minnelli, not the standards or songs from previous shows. No songs listed in program. [1] Cut from FLORA, THE RED MENACE. [2] From GOLDEN GATE.

2559 • LO
OPENED: 08/29/1909
Musical   Closed out of town

Composer: A. Baldwin Sloane
Lyricist: Franklin P. Adams
Librettist: O. Henry

Songs: Caramba; Dear Yankee Maid; In Yucatan; It's the Little Things That Count; Let Us Sing; Little Old Main Street for Mine; Love Is All That Matters; Never Forget Your Parents; Sailor's Number; Snapshots; Statue Song; Tammany on Parade; While Strolling Through the Forest; You May Always Be My Sweetheart

Cast: Annette Hall; Juliette Lange; Robert Wilson; John E. Young

Notes: Note that O. Henry wrote the book to this show.

2560 • LO AND BEHOLD
OPENED: 1949
Revue   Closed out of town

Composer: Brown Furlow
Lyricist: Brown Furlow
Librettist: William Happ; Eudora Welty
Producer: Robert Daggett; Red Barn Theatre
Director: Paul Lammers

Choreographer: Anna Walker; **Set Design:** William Harp

Songs: Suddenly

Notes: Program Westboro 08/30/49.

2561 • LOAD OF COAL
OPENED: 1929   Theatre: Connie's Inn
Revue   Nightclub

Composer: Thomas "Fats" Waller
Lyricist: Andy Razaf
Producer: Leonard Harper

Songs: Honeysuckle Rose; My Fate Is in Your Hands; Zonky

Cast: Louis Armstrong; Dewey Brown; "Chink" Collins; Dudley Dickerson; Maude Russell; "Red" Simmons; Jean Starr

Notes: No program available. The three songs listed were the only ones written for this show. The remainder of the score were songs from HOT CHOCOLATES.

2562 • LOAD OF KOAL
Notes: *See LOAD OF COAL.*

2563 • LOCK UP YOUR DAUGHTERS
OPENED: 04/27/1960
Musical   Closed out of town

Composer: Laurie Johnson
Lyricist: Lionel Bart
Librettist: Bernard Miles
Producer: Douglas Crawford
Director: Alfred Drake

Source: RAPE UPON RAPE (Play: Henry Fielding); **Choreographer:** Rhoda Levine; **Costumes:** Sean Kenny; **Lighting Designer:** Lloyd Burlingame; Sean Kenny; **Musical Director:** Max Goberman; **Set Design:** Lloyd Burlingame

Songs: All's Well; Constant's Entrance [1]; Gentle Art of Seduction, The [2]; If I'd Known You; I'll Be There; Is This the Happy Ending?; It Must Be True; Kind Fate; Lock Up Your Daughters; Lovely Lover; Mister Jones; On the Side; Proper Man, A; Red Wine and a Wench; Sunny Sunday Morning; There's a Plot Afoot; 'Tis Plain to See; When Does the Ravishing Begin?

Cast: Nancy Dussault; Elizabeth Hubbard; George S. Irving; John Michael King; Jamie Ross

Notes: Closed out of town in Boston 05/07/60. [1] In London version prior to America. [2] Added after opening of London production.

2564 • LOLA (1922)

OPENED: 1922
Musical   Closed out of town

Composer: James F. Hanley
Lyricist: Ballard Macdonald
Librettist: George E. Stoddard
Producer: Leslie Morosco
Director: John McKee

Songs: At the End of the Road; Close Your Eyes
   (C: Werner Janssen; L: Francis DeWitt); Lola
   Waltz (Close in Your Arms) (L: Darl MacBoyle);
   My Little Sea Shell Told Me So

Cast: Helen Shipman

Notes: No program available.

2565 • LOLA (1982)

OPENED: 03/24/1982   Theatre: York
Musical   Off-Off-Broadway

Composer: Claibe Richardson
Lyricist: Kenward Elmslie
Librettist: Kenward Elmslie
Producer: York Theatre Company
Director: John Going

Choreographer: David Holdgrive; **Costumes:**
   William Schroder; **Lighting Designer:** David
   Gotwald; **Musical Director:** David Bishop;
   Orchestrations: Bruce Pomahac; **Set Design:**
   James Morgan; **Vocal Arranger:** Bruce
   Pomahac

Songs: Abandoned; Another Soiree; Beauty
   Secrets; Dansa de la Arana; Do What You Do;
   Down Under; Healing Chant, The (1); Healing
   Chant, The (2); Hooked!; I Lay Alone All Winter;
   Little Old Lady in Black; Lola in Bavaria;
   Lolaland; Many Happy Returns; Mirrors and
   Shadows; My Lola; New Life, A; Oranges from
   Seville; Palace of Pleasure, The; Pledge, The;
   Princess of Herzogovinia, The; Rise Up!; Shuffle
   the Cards; Spanish Mazurka; Staring; Staying In;
   Uncrowned Queen of Californiay; Whip Dance,
   The; Whores Behind the Doors, The; Winter
   Comes in Summer

Cast: Gretchen Albrecht; Leigh Beery; Jack
   Dabdoub; Robert Stillman; Jane White

2566 • LOLA FROM BERLIN

OPENED: 09/16/1907   Theatre: Liberty
Musical   Broadway: 35

Composer: Jean Schwartz
Lyricist: William Jerome
Librettist: John J. McNally
Producer: Klaw & Erlanger
Director: Al Holbrook

Songs: Altdeutscher Leibersreim; Beneath the
   Moon; I Think of You the Whole Year Round;
   I'd Sooner Be a Has Been Than a Never Was at
   All; Just Home from College; Madchenlied; Poor
   Little Foolish Man; Signs; There's Not Another
   Girlie in the World Like You; Unter Den Linden,
   in Germany

Cast: Lulu Glaser; Ralph Herz; Gladys Zell

2567 • LOLA IN LOVE

OPENED: 1922
Musical   Closed out of town

Composer: Hugo Hirsch
Lyricist: Irving Caesar
Librettist: Irving Caesar
Producer: F.C. Coppicus
Director: Herman Beyer

Source: DIE TOLLE LOLA (Musical: Hugo Hirsch);
   Choreographer: Julian Mitchell; **Costumes:**
   Charles LeMaire; **Musical Director:** Anton
   Heindl

Songs: Devil's in Your Toes, The; Fox Trot; Gave
   Me One Day; I Mean No-One-Else-but-You;
   If Wives Were Put on Sale; I'll Always Need
   Someone Like You; Lola; Lola Cornero from the
   Trocadero; Perfect Model for Your Arms, A;
   Russian Love; We'll Greet Each Tomorrow
   Together; Weaker Is the Stronger After All, The;
   Your Eyes Shall Speak to Me

Cast: Arthur Albro; Carl Dietz; Florence Earle; Hal
   Forde; Eddie Garvie; Fay Marbe

Notes: Program of Scranton 12/25/22.

2568 • LOLITA, MY LOVE

OPENED: 02/15/1971
Musical   Closed out of town

Composer: John Barry
Lyricist: Alan Jay Lerner
Librettist: Alan Jay Lerner
Producer: Norman Twain
Director: Noel Willman

Source: LOLITA (Novel: Vladimir Nabokov);
Choreographer: Dan Siretta; **Costumes:** Jose
Varona; **Dance Arranger:** John Morris; **Lighting
Designer:** Jules Fisher; **Musical Director:**
Herbert Grossman; **Orchestrations:** Eddie
Sauter; **Set Design:** Ming Cho Lee; **Vocal
Arranger:** Herbert Grossman

Songs: All You Can Do Is Tell Me You Love Me; At
the Bed-D-Bye Motel; Beardsley School for Girls;
Buckin' for Beardsley; Charlotte's Letter; Dante,
Petrarch and Poe; Farewell, Little Dream, Good-
bye; Going, Going, Gone; Have You Got What
You Came With?; How Far Is It to the Next
Town?; I Always Believe Me; I Found You at
Last; If It Ain't Fun; In the Broken Promise Land
of Fifteen; It's a Bad, Bad World; Lolita; March
Out of My Life; Mother Needs a Boyfriend; Same
Old Song, The; Saturday; Sur Les Quais; Tell Me,
Tell Me

Cast: Leonard Frey; Dorothy Loudon; John Neville;
Denise Nickerson; John Witham

Notes: Closed 3/27/71 Boston after playing
Philadelphia.

2569 • LOLLIPOP

OPENED: 01/21/1924   Theatre: Knickerbocker
Musical   Broadway: 145

Composer: Vincent Youmans
Lyricist: Zelda Sears
Librettist: Zelda Sears
Producer: Henry W. Savage
Director: Ira Hards

Choreographer: Bert French; Mary Read; John Tiller;
Costumes: Finchley; **Musical Director:** Russell
Tarbox; **Orchestrations:** Robert Russell Bennett;
Set Design: William Castle; Sheldon K. Viele

Songs: All She Did Was This [2]; Ballet Modern; Bo
Koo; Come On, Let's Go [1]; Deep in My Heart;
Going Rowing; Hand-Me-Down Blues, The [2];
Honey-Bun; It Must Be Love [4]; Louis XIII
Gavotte; Love in a Cottage; Novelty Dance;

Opening Act I; Opening Act II; Opening Act III;
Orphan Girl (An Orphan Is the Girl for Me);
Take a Little One Step [3]; Tie a String Around
Your Finger; Time and a Half for Overtime;
When Greek Meets Greek [1]; When We Are
Married

Cast: Adora Andrews; Leonard Ceeley; Gloria
Dawn; Nick Long Jr.; Harry Puck; Zelda Sears;
Gus Shy; Mark Smith; Virginia Smith; Florenz
Tamara; Florence Webber; Ada Mae Weeks

Notes: Titled THE LEFT OVER out of town. [1]
Cut in rehearsals. [2] Cut in tryout. [3] Added to
score of revival of NO, NO, NANETTE. [4] Cut
in tryout. Music used for "Kissing" in A NIGHT
OUT.

2570 • LONDON CALLING

OPENED: 09/04/1923   Theatre: Duke of York's
Revue   London: 316

Composer: Noel Coward
Lyricist: Noel Coward
Librettist: Noel Coward; Ronald Jeans
Producer: Violet Melnotte
Director: Herbert Mason

Choreographer: David Bennett; **Costumes:**
Edward Molyneux; **Musical Director:** Philip
Braham; **Set Design:** Laverdet; Marc-Henri

Songs: I Don't Know (C: Philip Braham; L: Ronald
Jeans); Limehouse Night, A (C: Philip Braham;
L: Peggy Connor); Little Baggie Maggy; March
with Me [1] (C: Ivor Novello; L: Douglas Furber);
My Spanish Love; Parisian Pierrot; Russian
Blues; Shake Your Feet (C: Dave Stamper;
L: Gene Buck); Temperamental Honeymoon;
There's Life in the Old Girl Yet; What Love
Means; When We Were Girls; You Were Meant
for Me [1] (C: Eubie Blake; L: Noble Sissle)

Cast: Joyce Barbour; Noel Coward; Maisie Gay;
Teddie Gerard; Gertrude Lawrence

Notes: [1] Also in ANDRE CHARLOT'S REVUE
OF 1924 and also CHARLOT REVUE OF 1926.

2571 • LONDON FOLLIES

OPENED: 03/06/1922
Revue   Closed out of town

Composer: Frederic Chappelle; Herman Darewski
Lyricist: Albert de Courville
Librettist: Wal Pink; Albert de Courville
Producer: Albert de Courville

Songs: All Pull Together; Fair India; Love Spans the World; Off We Go; Old World Melody, An; Rag from Home, The; Rainbow of Flowers, The; Whirling

Cast: Connie Browning; Isabelle Dorothy; Harry Tate; Dean Tribune

Notes: Mason Opera House, Los Angeles.

2572 • LONDONERS, THE

OPENED: 03/27/1972   Theatre: Theatre Royal
                                          Stratford East
Musical   London

Composer: Lionel Bart
Additional Music: Michael Carr
Lyricist: Lionel Bart
Librettist: Stephen Lewis
Producer Theatre Workshop
Director: Joan Littlewood

Source: SPARROWS CAN'T SING (Novel: Stephen Lewis); **Costumes:** Willie Burt; **Set Design:** Guy Hodgkinson; Mark Pritchard

Cast: Lionel Bart [1]; Griffith Davies; Nicholas Denney; Ron Hackett; Ray Hoskins; Yootha Joyce

Notes: [1] Appeared using the name "Walter Plinge."

2573 • LONE STAR, THE

OPENED: 1987
Musical

Composer: Mark Janas
Lyricist: Mark Janas
Author: Paul Green
Director: Denton Yockey

Costumes: Nelson Fields; **Lighting Designer:** Carol Glawson; **Musical Director:** Mark Janas; **Orchestrations:** Alan Campbell; Robert Mitchell; **Set Design:** Richard Cromwell; Matthew Grant; Michael Massee

Songs: Alamo Widows' Lament; Gone to Texas; Liberty; Little Girls; Mexico Querido; Migration Song; Paloma Blanca; Sadie's Song; Sound the Call; Will You Come to the Bow'r

Cast: Jack Dabdoub; Ann Forgy; Jerry Rago; Carroll Van Cleave; Denton Yockey

Notes: A historical pagent produced at the Mary Moody Northen Amphitheatre, Galveston, Texas.

2574 • LONELY ROMEO, A

OPENED: 06/10/1919   Theatre: Shubert
Musical   Broadway: 87

Composer: Malvin F. Franklin
Lyricist: Robert B. Smith
Librettist: Lew Fields; Harry B. Smith
Producer: Messrs. Shubert
Director: W.H. Post

Choreographer: Jack Mason; **Costumes:** Cora MacGeachy; **Musical Director:** Robert Hood Bowers; **Orchestrations:** Charles Grant[2]; **Set Design:** P. Dodd Ackerman

Songs: Any Old Place with You [1] (C: Richard Rodgers; L: Lorenz Hart); Candy Eating Scene; Candy Jag; Cute an' Cunnin' (inst.) (L: Robert Hood Bowers); Don't Do Anything Till You Hear from Me; Flirtation Fantasies; I Guess I'm More Like Mother Than Like Father [1] (C: Richard A. Whiting; L: Raymond B. Egan); I Want a Lonely Romeo; Influenza Blues, Jolly Me (C: Robert Hood Bowers); Leave It to Your Milliner (C: Robert Hood Bowers); Let's Go! (C: Robert Hood Bowers); One I Love, Two I Love (C: Robert Hood Bowers); Opening Act II; Opening Act III (Singing and Dancing School) (inst.); Opening of Hat Shop (C: Robert Hood Bowers); Save a Little Daylight for Me (C: Robert Hood Bowers); Slumber Music; Sweets to the Sweet; Underneath a Big Umbrella; Wait for Me (C: Robert Hood Bowers); Will O' the Wisp (C: Malvin M. Franklin; Otis Spencer); You Never Can Tell (C: Robert Hood Bowers)

Cast: Frances Cameron; Herbert Fields; Lew Fields; Alan Hale

Notes: [1] Added after opening. [2] Orchestrated Irene Franklin's number.

2575 • LONESOME LASSES
OPENED: 01/18/1915   Theatre: Colonial
Musical

Lyricist: Will M. Hough

Notes: No other information available.

2576 • LONESOME TOWN
OPENED: 01/20/1908   Theatre: New Circle
Musical   Broadway: 88

Composer: J.A. Raynes
Lyricist: Judson D. Brusie
Librettist: Judson D. Brusie
Producer: Max M. Dill; C. William Kolb
Director: Max M. Dill; C. William Kolb

Songs: Big Chief Smoke; California Sunrise; Game of Golf, The; Gee! But This Is a Lonesome Town (C/L: Billy Gaston); I'm Running After Nancy; Just Someone (C/L: Will R. Anderson); Lanky Yankee Boys in Blue, The (C: Theodore Morse; L: Edward Madden); Mission Bells; My Cigarette Maid; Old Barn Dance, The; There's a Big Cry Baby in the Moon; When the Moon Plays Peek-a-boo; Whistle When You're Lonely; Women's Eyes

Cast: Max M. Dill; C. William Kolb; Maude Lambert; Georgia O'Ramey

2577 • LONG LEGGED LETTY
Notes: *See PRETTY MRS. SMITH.*

2578 • LONG WAY TO BOSTON, A
OPENED: 09/1979
Musical   Closed out of town

Composer: Michael Siegal
Lyricist: Susan Birkenhead
Librettist: Michael Loman
Producer: Goodspeed Opera House
Director: Craig Anderson

Source: SEE HOW SHE RUNS (Television Program: Marvin A. Gluck; Lucille Kallen); **Choreographer:** Donald Saddler; **Costumes:** David Toser; **Dance Arranger:** Michael Abene; Russell Warner; **Lighting Designer:** Peter M. Ehrhardt; **Musical Director:** Lynn Crigler; **Orchestrations:** Michael Abene; **Set Design:** John Lee Beatty

Songs: Aw C'mon Evie; How Are You Feeling?; I'd Do It Again; It's How You Deal with It; Long Way to Boston, A; Lookin' Out for Mame After Dark; Marathon; Margaret; September in Boston; Street Moves; Warm Up; What About Me?; Where Is She When We Need Her?; Your Own Two Feet; Zamboanga

Cast: George Ball; Shelley Bruce; Leonard John Crofoot; Nancy Dussault; Robyn Finn; Rita Gardner; Dee Hoty; Daniel Keyes; Alex Molina; Lenny Wolpe

Notes: Goodspeed Opera House.

2579 • LOOK AT THE FIFTIES, A
OPENED: 02/1973
Musical   Closed out of town

Composer: Al Carmines
Lyricist: Al Carmines
Librettist: Al Carmines
Producer: Arena Stage; Zelda Fichandler
Director: Lawrence Kornfeld

Choreographer: Dan Wagoner; **Costumes:** Marjorie Slaiman; **Lighting Designer:** William Mintzer; **Musical Director:** Susan Romann; **Orchestrations:** Al Carmines; **Set Design:** Robert U. Taylor; **Vocal Arranger:** Al Carmines

Songs: Benediction; Daffodils and Mud; Dinner Is Served; Dissatisfied Women; Eisenhower-Grandfather Hero to the World; Hallelujah Basketball; Heroes; How Did Freud Know?; Innocence; It Ain't Nice Not to Play on Your Own Turf; It's Teen Time; Locker Room, The; Lullaby; Montgomery Moon; Montgomery School Song; Peculiar That Way; Plunger, The; Scooby Do; Win for Us, Guys; Winning Is Half the Fun; Without Rules

Cast: Essie Borden; Semina De Laurentis; Boni Enten; Louisa Flaningam; Edmund Gaynes; Lee Guilliatt; Julie Kurnitz; Rick Podell; Ira Siff

Notes: Program Arena Stage Washington D.C.

2580 • LOOK AT US
OPENED: 06/05/1962   Theatre: Actors'
                                    Playhouse
Revue   Off-Off-Broadway

Producer: Leo Brody; Fred Martin
Director: Michael Wright

Choreographer: Michael Wright; **Dance Arranger:** Lorenzo Fuller; **Musical Director:** Lorenzo Fuller; **Vocal Arranger:** Lorenzo Fuller

Songs: Black Silence (C: Sano Marco); Bored (C: Constance Conrad); Caryl Ann (C: Frank Wille); Each Night Is a New Day (C: Lorenzo Fuller); Helping Hand and a Willing Heart, A (C/L: Alan Greene; Ray Passman); It's Great to Hate Yourself (C: Lorenzo Fuller); It's the Hat That Makes the Lady (C: Constance Conrad); Make Believe World (C: Frank Wille); Most People (C: Frank Wille); Odalie (C: Raoul Gonzalez); One Woman Man (C: Johnny Myers); Rich Enough to Be Rude (C: Lorenzo Fuller); Slow Rockin' Blues (C: Terry Morin); Sound of Laughter, The (C: Jimmy Glitter); Whatever Happened to Spring (C: Benny Wagman)

Cast: Ray Ramirez; Cathi Romano; Rich Samuelson; Bettye Voohees

Notes: Lyricists not identified in program.

2581 • LOOK HOMEWARD ANGEL

Notes: *See ANGEL.*

2582 • LOOK MA, I'M DANCIN'!

OPENED: 01/29/1948   Theatre: Adelphi
Musical   Broadway: 188

Composer: Hugh Martin
Lyricist: Hugh Martin
Librettist: Jerome Lawrence; Robert E. Lee
Producer: George Abbott
Director: George Abbott; Jerome Robbins

Choreographer: Jerome Robbins; **Costumes:** John Pratt; **Dance Arranger:** Trude Rittman; **Musical Director:** Pembroke Davenport; **Orchestrations:** Don Walker; **Set Design:** Oliver Smith; **Vocal Arranger:** Hugh Martin

Songs: Gotta Dance; Horrible, Horrible Love! [1]; If You'll Be Mine; I'm Not So Bright; I'm the First Girl in the Second Row in the Third Scene of the Fourth Number; I'm Tired of Texas; Jazz; Let's Do a Ballet [1]; Little Boy Blues, The; Look Ma, I'm Dancin'! [3]; Lost in This Town [3]; Lullaby

[3]; Mademoiselle Marie (Mlle. Scandale Ballet) (inst.) (C: Trude Rittman); New Look, The; Pajama Dance; Shauny O'Shay; Tiny Room; Toast, The [3]; Two of Us, The; Way It Might Have Been, The [3]

Cast: Virginia Gorski[2]; Robert Harris; Harold Lang; Don Liberto; Alice Pearce; Tommy Rall; Nancy Walker; Loren Welch

Notes: [1] Out Boston 1/5/48. [2] Later changed name to Virginia Gibson. [3] ASCAP/Library of Congress only.

2583 • LOOK TO THE LILIES

OPENED: 03/29/1970   Theatre: Lunt-Fontanne
Musical   Broadway: 25

Composer: Jule Styne
Lyricist: Sammy Cahn
Librettist: Leonard Spigelgass
Producer: Max J. Brown; Edgar Lansbury; Richard Lewine; Ralph Nelson
Director: Joshua Logan

Source: LILIES OF THE FIELD (Novel: William E. Barrett); **Choreographer:** Joyce Trisler; **Costumes:** Carrie F. Robbins; **Lighting Designer:** Jo Mielziner; **Musical Director:** Milton Rosenstock; **Orchestrations:** Larry Wilcox; **Set Design:** Jo Mielziner; **Vocal Arranger:** Buster Davis

Songs: Casamagordo; Chant; Does It Really Matter?; Dont Talk About God; First Class Number One Bum; Follow the Lamb; Gott Is Gut; Himmlisher Vater; Homer's Pitch; I Admire You Very Much, Mr. Schmidt [1]; I Am What I Am [1]; I, Yes Me, That's Who [3]; I'd Sure Like to Give It a Shot; Kick the Door [2]; Look to the Lilies; Meet My Seester; Nicest Time to Say Goodnight, The [1]; On That Day of Days [2]; One Little Brick at a Time; Prayer; Some Kind of Man; Them and They; There Comes a Time; To Do a Little Good; When I Was Young; Why Can't He See?; You're a Rock [1]

Cast: Carmen Alvarez; Linda Andrews; Shirley Booth; Virginia Craig; Taina Elg; Al Freeman Jr.; Patti Karr

Notes: [1] Cut prior to opening. [2] Cut prior to opening. Same music. [3] Music later used for "Am I to Wish Her Love" from RED SHOES.

2584 • LOOK WHERE I'M AT!

OPENED: 03/05/1971   Theatre: Theatre Four
Musical   Off-Broadway: 1

Composer: Jordan Ramin
Lyricist: Frank H. Stanton
Librettist: Gib Dennigan; James Leasor; Murray Semos
Producer: Jean Marie Lee
Director: Wakefield Poole

Source: RAIN IN THE DOORWAY (Novel: Thorne Smith); **Choreographer:** Wakefield Poole; Conductor: Mack Shlefer; **Costumes:** Rosemary Heyer; **Dance Arranger:** Wally Harper; **Lighting Designer:** Robert Guerra; **Musical Director:** Jack Lee; **Orchestrations:** Wally Harper; **Set Design:** Robert Guerra; **Vocal Arranger:** Sid Ramin

Songs: Animals; Change of Scene; Company of Men; Euphoria; Little Sparrow; Look Where I'm At!; Me I Want to Be, The; Money Isn't Everything, But . . .; Never, Never Leave Me; Partners; Party Scene; What a Day for a Wonderful Day; What Are You Running from, Mister?; Who Does She Think She Is?

Cast: Arthur Bartow; Ron Husmann; Mary Bracken Phillips; Martin Ross; Sherri Spillane

2585 • LOOK WHO'S HERE (1912)

Notes: *See THE RED PETTICOAT.*

2586 • LOOK WHO'S HERE (1918)

Notes: *See LADIES FIRST.*

2587 • LOOK WHO'S HERE (1920)

OPENED: 03/02/1920   Theatre: 44th Street
Musical   Broadway: 87

Composer: Silvio Hein
Lyricist: Edward Paulton
Librettist: Frank Mandel
Producer: Spiegel's Productions
Director: Edward T. Emery

Choreographer: Edward Hutchinson; **Costumes:** Mahieu; **Musical Director:** William Howard; **Set Design:** H. Robert Law

Songs: Bell Hop Blues (C/L: Frank Goodman; Al Piantadosi); (I'll Make) Bubbles; Finale Act I; Give Me a Cozy Corner; I Cannot Understand; I Know and You Know (L: Cecil Lean; Edward Paulton); I Wonder What She's Thinking of Now; If I Had Only Met You, Dear; I'll Make Bubbles; Look Who's Here; Love; Love, Love, Love; Love Never Changes (L: Cecil Lean; Edward Paulton); Me and You [1] (C: Harry Akst; Nora Bayes; L: Irving Fisher); My Heart's a Roomy Hotel [1]; My Night in Venice; Opening Ensemble; Since My Wife Got Fat (L: Cecil Lean); Some Wonderful Sort of Someone [1] (C: George Gershwin; L: Schuyler Greene); There's a Romeo for Every Girl I Know [2] (C: Sam H. Stept; L: Bud Green; Cecil Lean); Tia-Da-Tia-Da-Dee [1] (C: Sam H. Stept; L: Bud Green); Turk Has the Right Idea, The (L: Cecil Lean; Edward Paulton)

Cast: Louise Kelley; Cecil Lean; Georgie Mack; Cleo Mayfield; Dave Quixano; Madge Rush

Notes: [1] Sheet music only. [2] ASCAP/Library of Congress.

2588 • LORD DON'T PLAY FAVORITES, THE

OPENED: 09/17/1956   Theatre: NBC
TV Musical

Composer: Hal Stanley
Lyricist: Irving Taylor

Musical Director: Hal Mooney

Songs: For Better or Worse; Good Book, The; I Never Saw a Better Day; Rain, Rain; Things I Never Had, The

Cast: Louis Armstrong; Kay Starr

Notes: Original television musical.

2589 • LORD NELSON

Musical   Unproduced

Composer: Jerry Bock
Lyricist: Sheldon Harnick

Notes: No song list available.

2590 • LORELEI

OPENED: 01/27/1974   Theatre: Palace
Musical   Broadway: 320

Composer: Jule Styne
Lyricist: Betty Comden; Adolph Green
Librettist: Gail Parent; Kenny Solms
Producer: Shelly Gross; Lee Guber
Director: Robert Moore

Choreographer: Ernest Flatt; **Costumes:** Ray Aghayan; Alvin Colt; Bob Mackie; **Dance Arranger:** Jay Thompson; **Lighting Designer:** John Gleason; **Musical Director:** Milton Rosenstock; **Orchestrations:** Philip J. Lang; Don Walker; **Set Design:** John Conklin; **Vocal Arranger:** Buster Davis; Hugh Martin

Songs: American Dollars [3]; Button Up with Esmond [4] (L: Leo Robin); Bye, Bye, Baby [4] (L: Leo Robin); Coquette [4] (L: Leo Robin); Diamonds Are a Girl's Best Friend [4] (L: Leo Robin); Diet Song [3]; Girl Like I, A [1]; High Time [4] (L: Leo Robin); Homesick [4] (L: Leo Robin); I Love What I'm Doing [4] (L: Leo Robin); I Won't Let You Get Away; It's Delightful Down in Chile [4] (L: Leo Robin); Keeping Cool with Coolidge [4] (L: Leo Robin); Let's Live in Sin [1]; Little Rock [4] (L: Leo Robin); Looking Back; Lorelei [1]; Mamie Is Mimi [4] (L: Leo Robin); Men; Miss Lorelei Lee [1]; Paris [2]; That's What Friends Are For [3]; Waiting [3]

Cast: Jean Bruno; Carol Channing; Robert Fitch; Jack Fletcher; Dody Goodman; Tamara Long; Brandon Maggart; Peter Palmer; Lee Roy Reams; Ian Tucker

Notes: *See GENTLEMEN PREFER BLONDES*, of which this is a reworking. [1] Cut prior to Broadway. [2] Cut prior to Broadway. Same music as "Sunshine" from GENTLEMEN PREFER BLONDES. [3] Not in program. [4] From GENTLEMEN PREFER BLONDES.

2591 • LOST IN THE STARS

OPENED: 10/30/1949   Theatre: Music Box
Musical   Broadway: 281

Composer: Kurt Weill
Lyricist: Maxwell Anderson
Librettist: Maxwell Anderson
Producer: Playwrights' Company, The
Director: Rouben Mamoulian

Source: CRY, THE BELOVED COUNTRY (Novel: Alan Paton); **Costumes:** Anna Hill Johnstone; **Dance Arranger:** Kurt Weill; **Musical Director:** Maurice Levine; **Orchestrations:** Kurt Weill; **Set Design:** George Jenkins; **Vocal Arranger:** Kurt Weill

Songs: Big Mole [3]; Bird of Passage, A; Cry, the Beloved Country; Fear!; Four O'Clock [1]; Gold! [1]; Hills of Ixopo, The; Little Gray House, The [4]; Little Tin God, The [2]; Lost in the Stars [3]; Murder in Parkwold; O Tixo, Tixo, Help Me; Search, The; Shadowy Glass, The [2]; Soliloquy [2]; Stay Well [3]; Thousands of Miles; Train to Johannesburg; Trouble Man [3]; Who'll Buy?; Wild Justice, The

Cast: Leslie Banks; Herbert Coleman; Todd Duncan; Inez Matthews; Julian Mayfield; Frank Roane

Notes: [1] Cut prior to New York. [2] Cut prior to New York. Same music as "Little Gray House." First written for the unproduced ULYSSES AFRICANUS. [3] First written for the unproduced ULYSSES AFRICANUS. [4] Same music as "The Little Tin God."

2592 • LOST, STRAYED OR STOLEN

OPENED: 09/16/1896   Theatre: Fifth Avenue
Musical   Broadway: 77

Composer: Woolson Morse
Librettist: J. Cheever Goodwin
Director: Ben Teal

Choreographer: Rose Beckel; **Set Design:** Walter Burridge

Cast: Georgia Caine; John Gilroy; Louis Harrison; Joseph Herbert; Emma Janvier

Notes: No songs listed in program. Also known as A DAY IN PARIS.

2593 • LOU HOLTZ' MERRY-GO-ROUND

OPENED: 1951
Revue

Composer: Sam Coslow
Lyricist: Sam Coslow

Songs: Three Little Hollywood Wolves; To Be or Not to Be in Love

Notes: No other information available.
Information from ASCAP/Library of Congress.

2594 • LOUIE THE 14TH

OPENED: 03/03/1925   Theatre: Cosmopolitan
Musical   Broadway: 319

Composer: Sigmund Romberg
Lyricist: Arthur Wimperis
Librettist: Arthur Wimperis
Producer: Florenz Ziegfeld
Director: Edward Royce

Source: LUDWIG XIV (Play: Paul Frank; Julius Wilhelm); **Musical Director:** Gus Salzer; **Orchestrations:** Emil Gerstenberger

Songs: Celebration of St. Joan the Good; Crossword Puzzle [1]; Don't Let Anybody Vamp Your Man [1]; Edelweiss (L: Clifford Grey); Follow the Rajah; Give a Little, Get a Little Kiss [1] (L: Irving Caesar); Homeland; I'm Harold, I'm Harold; Little Blue Pig, The; Little Peach; Love Is a Lie; Major Domo, The; Market Day; Moon Flower; My First Love Letter [1] (L: Irving Caesar); Pep; Regimental Band; Rin-Tin-Tin; Schoe Plattler Tanz; Sweetheart of Mine [1]; Taking a Wife; True Hearts; Vamp Your Man; Wayside Flower

Cast: Leon Errol; Harry Fender; Frederick Graham; Evelyn Law; Ethel Shutta

Notes: [1] Sheet music only.

2595 • LOUISIANA LADY

OPENED: 03/03/1925   Theatre: Century
Musical   Broadway: 319

Composer: Monte Carlo; Alma Sanders
Lyricist: Monte Carlo; Alma Sanders
Librettist: Eugene Berton; Isaac Green Jr.
Producer: Hall Shelton
Director: Edgar MacGregor

Source: CREOLES (Play: Kenneth Perkins; Samuel Shipman); **Choreographer:** Felicia Sorel; **Costumes:** Frank Thompson; **Lighting Designer:** Leo Kerz; **Musical Director:** Hilding Anderson; **Orchestrations:** Robert Russell Bennett; Hans Spialek; **Set Design:** Watson Barratt; **Vocal Arranger:** Hilding Anderson

Songs: Beware of Lips That Say "Cherie"; Cuckoo-Cheena, The; Gold, Women and Laughter; I Want to Live-I Want to Love; It's Mardi Gras; Just a Bit Native; Louisiana's Holiday; Mammy's Little Baby; Men About Town; Night Was All to Blame, The; No, No, Mamselle; No One Cares for Dreams; That's Why I Want to Go Home; When You Are Close to Me

Cast: George Baxter; Edith Fellows; Charles Judels; Monica Moore

2596 • LOUISIANA LOU

OPENED: 09/03/1911   Theatre: La Salle
Musical   Chicago

Composer: Ben M. Jerome
Lyricist: Addison Burkhardt; Frederick Donaghey
Librettist: Addison Burkhardt; Frederick Donaghey
Director: Frank Smithson

Songs: How Much Am I Bid; I Think You Think to Much about Too Many; If Love Is Madness; It's Not for Me; Joys and the Glooms, The; Jumping Jack; Louisiana Lou; My Rose of the Ghetto; Puritan Prance, The; When Paddy Goes A-Courtin'; Wouldn't That Tickle You

Cast: Alexander Carr; Bernard Granville; Sophie Tucker

Notes: No other information available.

2597 • LOUISIANA PURCHASE

OPENED: 05/28/1940   Theatre: Imperial
Musical   Broadway: 444

Composer: Irving Berlin
Lyricist: Irving Berlin
Librettist: Morrie Ryskind
Producer: B.G. DeSylva
Director: Edgar MacGregor

Source: ORIGINAL STORY (Story: B.G. DeSylva); **Choreographer:** George Balanchine; Carl Randall; **Costumes:** Tom Lee; **Musical Director:** Robert Emmett Dolan; **Orchestrations:** Robert Russell Bennett; N. Lang Van Cleve; **Set Design:** Tom Lee; **Vocal Arranger:** Ralph Blane; Hugh Martin

Songs: Apologia [1]; Dance with Me (Tonight at the Mardi Gras) [3]; Fools Fall in Love; I'd Like to Be Shot from a Cannon with You [1]; It'll Come to You [1]; It's a Lovely Day Tomorrow; Latins Know How; Lord Done Fixed Up My Soul, The; Louisiana Purchase; Old Man's Darling, Young Man's Slave; Opening Act II; Outside of That I Love You; Sex Marches On; What Chance Have I with Love; Wild About You [2]; You Can't Brush Me Off; You're Lonely and I'm Lonely

Cast: Ralph Blane [3]; Irene Bordoni; Carol Bruce; Georgia Carroll; William Gaxton; Charles Laskey; Nick Long Jr.; Hugh Martin [3]; Victor Moore; Nicodemus; Ralph Riggs; Jo Jean Rogers [3]; Phyllis Rogers [3]; Vera Zorina

Notes: [1] Cut prior to opening. [2] Cut prior to opening. Written as an independent song in 1934 and revived for this show. [3] Members of The Martins singing group.

2598 • LOVE

OPENED: 04/15/1984   Theatre: Audrey Wood
Musical   Off-Broadway: 17

Composer: Howard Marren
Lyricist: Susan Birkenhead
Librettist: Jeffrey Sweet
Producer: Joy Klein; Maggie Minskoff; Haila Stoddard
Director: Larry Fuller

Source: LUV (Play: Murray Schisgal); **Costumes:** Kevin Rupnik; **Dance Arranger:** Uel Wade; **Lighting Designer:** Ruth Roberts; **Musical Director:** Uel Wade; **Orchestrations:** Jack Gale; Robby Merkin; **Set Design:** Kevin Rupnik; **Vocal Arranger:** Uel Wade

Songs: Carnival Ride; Chart, The; Do I Love Him?; Harry's Resolution; I Believe in Marriage; If Harry Weren't Here; Lady; Love; My Brown Paper Bag; Paradise; Polyarts U.; Sincerely, Harold Berlin; Somebody; What a Life!; Yes, Yes, I Love You

Cast: Judy Kaye; Nathan Lane; Stephen Vinovich

Notes: Originally titled A LUV MUSICAL.

2599 • LOVE AND LET LOVE

OPENED: 01/03/1968   Theatre: Sheridan Square
    Playhouse
Musical   Off-Broadway: 14

Composer: Stanley Jay Gelber
Lyricist: Don Christopher; John Lollos
Librettist: John Lollos
Producer: Love and Let Love Company
Director: John Lollos

Source: TWELFTH NIGHT (Play: William Shakespeare); **Choreographer:** Rhoda Levine; **Costumes:** Yves; **Lighting Designer:** Fred Allison; **Musical Director:** Daniel Paget; **Orchestrations:** Arthur Rubinstein; **Set Design:** Barbara Miller

Songs: Dancing Rogue, The; Epistle of Love; How Do I Know You're Not Mad, Sir?; I Found My Twin; I Like It; I Will Have Him; If She Could Only Feel the Same; I'll Smile; I've Got a Pain; Love Lesson; Man Is Made for Woman; She Called Me Fellow; Some Are Born Great; They'll Say I've Been Dreaming; This Is His First Love [1]; Will He Ever Know?; Write Him a Challenge

Cast: John Cunningham; Michael Hawkins; Michael O'Sullivan; Marcia Rodd; Virginia Vestoff

Notes: [1] Not in programs.

2600 • LOVE AND POLITICS

OPENED: 04/03/1911
Musical   Chicago

Composer: Joseph E. Howard
Lyricist: Collin Davis
Director: Ned Wayburn

Songs: Frisco Frizz; Hello Hello; Just a Little Smile (L: Joseph E. Howard); Just for You; Lindy Come Along (L: Joseph E. Howard); Love's a Dreamy Tune; Mary Ann

Notes: No program available. A rewrite of THE DISTRICT LEADER. *See that show for more information.*

2601 • LOVE BIRDS

OPENED: 03/15/1921   Theatre: Apollo
Musical   Broadway: 103

Composer: Sigmund Romberg
Lyricist: Ballard Macdonald
Librettist: Edgar Allen Woolf
Producer: Sigmund Romberg; Max Wilner
Director: Julian Alfred; Edgar MacGregor; Frank Smithson

Costumes: Mme. Gilman; Lighting Designer: P. Dodd Ackerman; Musical Director: J. Frank Cork; Set Design: P. Dodd Ackerman

Songs: Can Macy Do without Me?; Carnival Night; Fat-Fat-Fatima; Girl Like Grandma; I Love to Go Swimmin' with Wimmin'; In Bokhara, Miss O'Hara; Introducing the Futurity Debutante Chorus (L: Edgar Allen Woolf); Is It Hard to Guess?; Laugh and Grow Fat [1]; Let's Pretend; Little Dream that Lost Its Way, A; Love Will Always Find a Way; Mind Your Own Business [1]; Murrayisms; Opening Chorus; Opening Chorus Act II; Persian Fantasy (Persiana) (L: Clarence Marks; Jack Stern); Prevalent Condition of the Mind, The [1]; Rooneyisms; Trousseau Incomplete, The; Two Little Love Birds; When the Cat's Away

Cast: Marion Bent; Tom Dingle; Elizabeth Hines; Vincent Lopez; Elizabeth Murray; Pat Rooney

Notes: [1] Out Washington, D.C. 1/2/24.

2602 • LOVE CALL, THE

OPENED: 10/24/1927   Theatre: Majestic
Musical   Broadway: 81

Composer: Sigmund Romberg
Lyricist: Harry B. Smith
Librettist: Edward Locke
Producer: Messrs. Shubert
Director: J.C. Huffman; Lew Morton

Source: ARIZONA (Play: Augustus Thomas); Choreographer: Ed Hutchinson; Musical Director: Max Steiner; Set Design: Watson Barratt

Songs: Bonita; Eyes That Love; Fiesta; Fortune Teller's Song; Good Pals; Hear the Trumpet Call; I Am Captured; I Live, I Die for You; If That's What You Want; Lark, The; Opening Number; Poker Game; Ranger's Song, The; Spanish Love; 'Tis Love; Tony, Tony, Tony; When I Take You All to London; You Appeal to Me

Cast: John Barker; Berna Deane; June Egbert; Joseph Macaulay; Lora Sonderson

Notes: Titled BONITA while out of town. Titled MY GOLDEN WEST in sheet music.

2603 • LOVE CURE, THE

OPENED: 09/01/1909   Theatre: New Amsterdam
Musical   Broadway: 35

Composer: Edmund Eysler
Lyricist: Oliver Herford
Librettist: Oliver Herford
Producer: Henry W. Savage

Source: KUENSLER-BLUT (Musical: Edmund Eysler; Carl Lindau; Leo Stein); Lighting Designer: Joseph Wilson; Musical Director: Augustus Barratt

Songs: Because I Love Her [1]; Chicks [2]; Cupid's March; Finale Act I; Flirtation; Forget Me Not; Gather Ye Rosebuds; He Comes, He Is Alone! [3]; How Fair the World; I Am an Actor, All the Rage (Matinee Idol); I Am an Indian; I Wonder What the Audience Would Say; Just a Play; Life By Love Unlighted [1]; Love and Wine (Drinking Song); Oh Be Jolly; Oh, Pray Make No Mistake in Me [3]; Peek-a-Boo!; Pretty Part for Me to Play, A; Roses Are Sweetest [2]; There Once Was a Butterfly [3]; Toast, A; When Skies Are Bright

Cast: Lina Abarbanell; Eva Fallon; Charles J. Ross

Notes: [1] Sheet music only. [2] Out N.Y.C. 1/30/10. [3] Vocal score only.

2604 • LOVE DOCTOR, THE

Notes: See THE CAREFREE HEART.

2605 • LOVE DREAMS

OPENED: 10/10/1921   Theatre: Times Square
Musical   Broadway: 40

Composer: Werner Janssen
Lyricist: Oliver Morosco
Librettist: Anne Nichols
Producer: Oliver Morosco
Director: John McKee; Oliver Morosco

Musical Director: Mario Agnolucci

Songs: Any Time Is Love Time; Entre Nous; Here and There and Everywhere; Knights of the Table [1]; Lonesome Boy; Love Dreams; My Dream of Love Is You [1]; Oriental Dance; Pity Me; Reputation; Toddle Top Whirl, The; Two's Company, Three's a Crowd; Where Smoke Rings Go [1]; World Owes You This My Dear, The

Cast: Amelia Allen; Maude Eburne; Orrin Johnson; Vera Michelena; Harry K. Morton; Tom Powers

Notes: [1] Out Philadelphia 9/10/21.

2606 • LOVE FLOWER, THE
OPENED: 1920

Songs: Love Flower, The (C: Louis Silvers; L: Irving Caesar; B.G. DeSylva)

Notes: No other information available.

2607 • LOVE FOR LOVE
OPENED: 11/11/1974   Theatre: Helen Hayes
Musical   Broadway: 24

Composer: Paul Gemignani
Lyricist: Hugh Wheeler
Author: William Congreve
Producer: Phoenix Theatre
Director: Harold Prince

Costumes: Franne Lee; **Lighting Designer:** Ken Billington; **Set Design:** Douglas Higgins

Cast: Glenn Close; David Dukes; George Ede; Joel Fabiani; Peter Friedman; Marybeth Hurt; Charles Kimbrough; John McMartin; Charlotte Moore; Ellen Tovatt

Notes: Limited engagement. No songs in program.

2608 • LOVE FROM JUDY
OPENED: 09/25/1952   Theatre: Saville
Musical   London: 594

Composer: Hugh Martin
Lyricist: Timothy Gray[2]; Hugh Martin
Librettist: Eric Maschwitz
Director: Charles Hickman

Source: DADDY LONG LEGS (Novel: Jean Webster); **Choreographer:** Pauline Grant; **Lighting Designer:** Berkeley Sutcliffe; **Musical Director:** Philip Martell; **Orchestrations:** Phil Green; **Set Design:** Berkeley Sutcliffe

Songs: Ballet (inst.) (C: Phil Green); Daddy Long-Legs; Dumb-Dumb-Dumb; Get a Horse for Your Horseless Carriage [3]; Go and Get Your Old Banjo; Goin' Back to School; Here We Are; I Ain't Gonna Marry; I Never Dream When I'm Asleep [1]; It's Better Rich; It's Great to Be an Orphan; Kind to Animals; Love from Judy; Mardi Gras; My True Love; Skipping Rope Hornpipe; Touch of Voodoo, A; What Do I See in You?

Cast: Johnny Brandon; Jean Carson; Barbara Decks; Adelaide Hall; Moiya Kelly; Pixie Murphy; June Whitfield

Notes: [1] Jerome Lawrence suggested the title to this number. [2] Used the name Jack Gray. [3] Cut out of town.

2609 • LOVE IN A MIST
Notes: *See ONE TOUCH OF VENUS.*

2610 • LOVE IN THE SNOW
OPENED: 03/15/1946
Musical   Closed out of town

Composer: Ralph Benatzky
Lyricist: Rowland Leigh
Librettist: Rowland Leigh
Producer: Messrs. Shubert
Director: John Baird

Source: HERZEN IM SCHNEE (Musical: Ralph Benatzky; H. Gilbert; Robert Gilbert; Armin Robinson); **Choreographer:** Myra Kinch; **Costumes:** Jac-Lewis; **Musical Director:** Pierre de Reeder; **Orchestrations:** David Mendelsohn; **Set Design:** Lawrence L. Goldwasser

Songs: Collette; Farewell Letter; First Love; Half Way Chalet; Interlude; Love in the Snow; Make Up Your Mind; Once in a Lifetime; Party Dress; Portrait for Posterity; Queen of Sheba; Savoire Faire; Serenade; Twilight; When We're Together

Cast: Nancy Donovan; Le Roi Operti

2611 • LOVE IS A BALL!
OPENED: 09/27/1965
Revue   Closed out of town

Composer: Dave Brubeck; Stan Kenton; John
 Lewis; Henry Mancini; Franz Waxman
Lyricist: Jules Feiffer; J. Marks; James Thurber
Additional Lyrics: J. Marks
Librettist: Jules Feiffer; J. Marks; James Thurber
Producer: Robert T. Gaus
Director: J. Marks

Arrangements: Jerry Cournoyer; Stan Kenton;
 Lennie Niehaus; Bill Popp; **Choreographer:**
 J. Marks; **Costumes:** James Croshaw; **Lighting
 Designer:** J. Marks; **Musical Director:** Bob
 Ayres; **Set Design:** Jean Cocteau; Peter Girolami

Songs: Balled of Lovers; Blues, The; Blues in the
 Night [5] (C: Harold Arlen; L: Johnny Mercer);
 Boogie; Boston Beguine, The [4] (C/L: Sheldon
 Harnick); Courtly Lovers; Dialogue of the Clown;
 Elegant Lovers; First Love; Four Seasons, The;
 Goddesses of Love; Hello, Young Lovers [3]
 (C: Richard Rodgers; L: Oscar Hammerstein II);
 If Ever I Would Leave You [2] (C: Alan Jay Lerner;
 L: Frederick Loewe); I've Been Waiting for Your
 Phone Call; Johnny Come Lately [1] (C: Claibe
 Richardson; L: Seymour Zogott); Love for Sale [6]
 (C/L: Cole Porter); Love Is a Ball!; Naked Love;
 Oom-Pah-Pah; Orpheus; Thurber Set, The

Cast: Ingrid Anderson; Raymond Evans; Alice
 Ghostley; J. Marks; Diana Russell; Sandra Shea;
 Sandra Viera

Notes: No program available. Souvenir program
 and Theatre World do not credit songs. [1] From
 DIME A DOZEN. [2] From CAMELOT. [3] From
 THE KING AND I. [4] From NEW FACES OF
 1952. [5] From BLUES IN THE NIGHT. [6] From
 THE NEW YORKERS.

2612 • LOVE IS ALL
Notes: *See THROUGH THE YEARS.*

2613 • LOVE LAUGHS
OPENED: 05/20/1919   Theatre: Bijou
Musical   Broadway: 31

Author: George D. Parker
Producer: Edwin E. Kohn
Director: John Harwood

Set Design: Mabel Buell

Songs: Love Laughs (C/L: Leon De Costa)

Cast: Katherine Alexander; Jessie Glendinning;
 Harold Hendee

2614 • LOVE LETTER, THE
OPENED: 10/04/1921   Theatre: Globe
Musical   Broadway: 31

Composer: Victor Jacobi
Lyricist: William Le Baron
Librettist: William Le Baron
Producer: Charles B. Dillingham
Director: Edward Royce

Source: PHANTOM RIVAL, THE (Play: Ferenc
 Molnar); **Choreographer:** Edward Royce

Songs: Any Girl; Canzonetta; First Love; I'll Return
 for You; I'll Say I Love You; My Heart Beats to
 You; Only Girl, The; Rainbow; Scandal Town;
 To the Girl You Dance With; Upside Down; We
 Were in Love; You Are Free; You're Mine

Cast: Adele Astaire; Fred Astaire; Alice Brady;
 Marjorie Gateson; Katherine Stewart; John
 Charles Thomas

2615 • LOVE LIFE
OPENED: 10/07/1948   Theatre: 46th Street
Musical   Broadway: 252

Composer: Kurt Weill
Lyricist: Alan Jay Lerner
Librettist: Alan Jay Lerner
Producer: Cheryl Crawford
Director: Elia Kazan

Choreographer: Michael Kidd; **Costumes:** Lucinda
 Ballard; **Dance Arranger:** Kurt Weill; **Lighting
 Designer:** Peggy Clark; **Musical Director:** Joseph
 Littau; **Orchestrations:** Kurt Weill; **Set Design:**
 Boris Aronson; **Vocal Arranger:** Kurt Weill

Songs: Baby [4]; Can't We Have a Rally? [3]; Cop's
 Lament [3]; Cop's Serenade [3]; Csardas [3];
 Economics; Green-Up Time; Here I'll Stay; Ho,
 Billy, O!; Home of Our Own, A [3]; I Remember
 It Well [5]; I'm Your Man; Is It Him or Is It Me?
 [2]; Locker Room, The [1]; Love Song; Madame
 Zuzu [6]; Minstrel Parade; Mother's Getting

Nervous; Mr. Right; Mr. Right and Mrs. Dream [3]; My Kind of Night; My Name Is Samuel Cooper; Progress; Punch and Judy Divorce (Ballet); Reality! [3]; Susan's Dream [1]; Taking No Chances; There's Nothing Left for Daddy (But the Rhumba) [3]; This Is the Life; Viva the Women! [2]; We're Selling Sunshine [3]; We're Taking Over Now [3]; What More Do I Want? [2]; Where Do I Belong? [3]; Who Is Samuel Cooper?; Women's Club Blues; You Understand Me So [1]

Cast: Cheryl Archer; Lyle Bettger; Nanette Fabray; Holly Harris; Jay Marshall; Ray Middleton; Johnny Steward; Evans Thornton

Notes: Original title — OCEAN SONG. Lerner's working title — A DISH FOR THE GODS. [1] Out Boston 9/7/48. [2] Cut after opening. [3] Cut. [4] Cut. Same music as "A Little Swing for Swinging" not used in STREET SCENE. [5] Different song from that in GIGI although lyric and concept is very similar. [6] Music was the "Zodiac Song" from ONE TOUCH OF VENUS.

2616 • LOVE! LOVE! LOVE!

OPENED: 06/15/1977 Theatre: Astor Place
Revue Off-Off-Broadway: 25

Composer: Johnny Brandon
Lyricist: Johnny Brandon
Librettist: Johnny Brandon
Producer: Robert E. Richardson
Director: Buck Heller

Choreographer: Buck Heller; **Costumes:** Don Jensen; **Lighting Designer:** Jeff Davis; **Musical Director:** Clark McClellan; **Set Design:** Don Jensen; **Vocal Arranger:** Clark McClellan

Songs: Age Is a State of Mind; Battle of Chicago, The; Come On In; Consenting Adults; Empty Space; Find Someone to Love; Great-All-American-Power- Driven-Engine; I Am You; Law and Order; Look All Around You; Love! Love! Love!; Lovin'; Middle-Class-Liberal-Blues; Mother's Day; Preacher Man; Reach Out; Searching for Love; Searching for Yesterdays; Somewhere Along the Road; Streets of Bed-Stuy, The; What Did We Do Wrong?; What Is There to Say?; Where Did the Dreams Go

Cast: Michael Calkins; Mel Johnson Jr.; Pat Lundy; Neva Rae Powers; Glory Van Scott

2617 • LOVE MATCH

OPENED: 11/03/1968
Musical Closed out of town

Composer: David Shire
Lyricist: Richard Maltby Jr.
Librettist: Christian Hamilton
Producer: Center Theatre Group
Director: Danny Daniels

Choreographer: Danny Daniels; **Costumes:** Ray Diffen; **Dance Arranger:** David Shire; **Lighting Designer:** Jules Fisher; **Musical Director:** Theodore Saidenberg; **Orchestrations:** Hershy Kay; **Set Design:** Robin Wagner; **Vocal Arranger:** David Shire

Songs: As Plain as Daylight; Beautiful; Coronation Parade; Grand Diversion, The; I Don't Believe It; I Hear Bells [1]; I May Want to Remember Today [1]; I Won't Sleep a Wink Tonight; Little Part of Me That's Mine, The; Meaningful Life, A; Mine; Never Again; Packing Song; Play It Again; Presentation of Albert; These Two Hands; Today Is the First Day of the Rest of My Life [1]; Woman Looking for Love, A; World and You; World of Love, A

Cast: Michael Allinson; Laurence Guittard; Bill Hinnant; Hal Linden; Patricia Ripley; Rex Robbins; Patricia Routledge

Notes: Closed Los Angeles 01/04/69. [1] Used later in STARTING HERE, STARTING NOW.

2618 • LOVE ME, LOVE MY CHILDREN

OPENED: 11/03/1971 Theatre: Mercer-O'Casey
Musical Off-Broadway: 187

Composer: Robert Swerdlow
Lyricist: Robert Swerdlow
Librettist: Robert Swerdlow
Producer: Edward F. Kook; Joel W. Schenker
Director: Paul Aaron

Choreographer: Elizabeth Swerdlow; **Costumes:** Patricia Quinn Stuart; **Lighting Designer:** Dahl Delu; **Musical Director:** Michael Alterman; **Orchestrations:** Michael Alterman; **Set Design:** Jo Mielziner; **Vocal Arranger:** Robert De Cormier

Songs: Critics; Deca Dance; Do the Least You Can; Don't Be a Miracle; Don't Twist Her Mind; Don't

Twist My Mind; Face to Face; Fat City; Ginger-bread Girl; Journey Home; Leave the World Behind; Let Me Down; Love Me, Love My Children; North American Shmear; Plot and Counterplot; Reflections; Running Down the Sun; See; Walking in the World; You're Dreaming

Cast: Don Atkinson; Salome Bey; Ed Evanko; Patsy Rahn; Chapman Roberts; Rose Mary Taylor

2619 • LOVE MILL, THE
OPENED: 02/07/1918   Theatre: 48th Street
Musical   Broadway: 52

Composer: Alfred Francis
Lyricist: Earl Carroll
Librettist: Earl Carroll
Producer: Andreas Dippel
Director: Mack Whiting

Source: UNKNOWN (Unknown: Envel; Heinrich Stobitzer); **Musical Director:** Louis Kroll

Songs: Ask Dad-He Knows [1]; Down the Bridle Path of Love; Every Flower Has a Melody; Follow Mama's Advice; I Am a Hundred Years Ahead of All the Rest [1]; I Love Him for He Loved the Love That I Loved; I May Look Strong but I'm Far from Healthy; In the State of Matrimony; It's Really Very Singular [1]; It's the Women; Love Mill, The; Przeaprodensky; Q.T.U.C.I.M.4.U. (Cutey, You See I Am for You) [2]; Seasick Buccaneer, A; Watch the Things You Eat; We Must Hooverize; When You Feel a Little Longing; Where Those Cotton Blossoms Grow; Why Can't It All Be a Dream?

Cast: Grace Fisher; Victor Morley; Clarence Nordstrom; Harry Tighe

Notes: [1] Out of town 2/19/17. [2] Titled "A.2.Z.I.M.4.U."

2620 • LOVE O' MIKE
OPENED: 01/15/1917   Theatre: Shubert
Musical   Broadway: 192

Composer: Jerome Kern
Lyricist: Harry B. Smith
Librettist: Sydney Smith; Augustus Thomas Jr.
Producer: Elisabeth Marbury; Messrs. Shubert
Director: Benrimo

Musical Director: Frank Tours; **Orchestrations:** Frank Saddler

Songs: Baby Vampire, The; Dance Through Life with Me [2]; Don't Tempt Me; Drift with Me; Hoot Man; How Was I to Know?; I Am Human After All [2]; I Wonder Why; It Can't Be Done [2]; It Wasn't My Fault [1] (L: Herbert Reynolds); Life's a Dance; Look in the Book [3]; Lulu; Moo Cow; Simple Little Tune, A [4]; Take the Eyes of Mabel [2]; Tell Me Why the World [2]; We'll See; Who Cares? [2]

Cast: Luella Gear; Lawrence Grossmith; George Hassell; Allison McBain; Clifton Webb; Peggy Wood

Notes: Titled GIRLS WILL BE GIRLS out of town. [1] Same tune as "It Isn't Your Fault" cut from 90 IN THE SHADE with lyrics by Herbert Reynolds. [2] Cut prior to opening. [3] Also titled "It's in the Book." Same music as "Paris Is a Paradise for Coons" from LA BELLE PAREE. [4] Program lists song title as "A Lonesome Little Tune."

2621 • LOVE SCHOOL, THE
Musical   Closed out of town

Notes: No other information available.

2622 • LOVE SONG, THE
OPENED: 01/13/1925   Theatre: Century
Musical   Broadway: 167

Music Based On: Jacques Offenbach
Lyricist: Harry B. Smith
Librettist: Harry B. Smith
Producer: Messrs. Shubert
Director: Fred G. Latham

Source: OFFENBACH (Musical: Jeno Farago; Mihaly Nador); **Choreographer:** Alexis Kosloff; Max Scheck; **Costumes:** Rene Hubert; E.R. Schrapps; **Musical Director:** Al Goodman; **Set Design:** Watson Barratt

Songs: All Aboard for Paris; Barcarolle [2]; Entrance of the Emperor and the Empress; Fair Land of Dreaming; Farmer's Life, A; Finale Act II; Follow the Flag We Love; He Writes a Song; Home from Algeria; Is It Love? [1]; Love Is Not for a Day; Love Will Find You Some Day

(C: Edward Kunneke); Military Men I Love [2]; Only a Dream; Opening Act II; Remember Me (Love Song); Take a Walk with Me; Tell Me Not That You Are Forgetting; Vintage Chorus; Violets; When My Violin Is Calling; Yes or No; Your Country Needs You [1]

Cast: Dorothy Francis; Evelyn Herbert; Harry K. Morton; Odette Myrtil; Allan Prior

Notes: Based on the life and music of Offenbach. Kunneke adapted Offenbach's melodies. The one song by Kunneke is not based on an Offenbach melody. Review claims there were 26 songs in show. [1] Not in program. [2] ASCAP/Library of Congress only.

2623 • LOVE WAGER, THE

OPENED: 1912
Musical   Closed out of town

Composer: Charles Hambitzer
Lyricist: William Cary Duncan
Librettist: Edith Ellis
Producer: Joseph M. Gaites
Director: Edward Temple

Source: SEVEN SISTERS (Play: Robert Jones); **Musical Director:** Louis Stoll

Songs: Cradle Song and Aria; Cupid's Ladder; Dark Eyes; Four-Leaved Clover, The; From Out the Convent Walls; I'm Very Glad to Meet You; In Housekeeping I Am a Martinet; Love Wager, The; Mazurka; My Love Is a Flower; Pierrot and Pierrette; Puppy Love; We Bachelor Blades (A Bachelor's Song); We're Always Glad to See You, But You'd Better Call Again [1]; Wedding Chorus

Cast: George Anderson; Frederick Howard; Fritzi Scheff

Notes: Program of Toledo 12/25/12 used. [1] Not in program.

2624 • LOVE WATCHES

OPENED: 08/29/1908   Theatre: Lyceum
Play   Broadway: 172

Author: Gladys Unger
Producer: Charles Frohman
Director: William Seymour

Source: UNKNOWN (Play: G. Caillavet; R. DeFlers); **Set Design:** Ernest Gros

Songs: Good Night Dear (C/L: Will R. Anderson); Love Watches (inst.) (C/L: Walter Pulitzer)

Cast: Billie Burke; Louise Drew; Cyril Keightley; Ernest Lawford; Kate Meek; Maude Odell

Notes: [1] Interpolated.

2625 • LOVELAND

Notes: *See THE GEEZER OF GEEK.*

2626 • LOVELY LADIES, KIND GENTLEMEN (1970)

OPENED: 12/28/1970   Theatre: Majestic
Musical   Broadway: 16

Composer: Stan Freeman; Franklin Underwood
Lyricist: Stan Freeman; Franklin Underwood
Librettist: John Patrick
Producer: Herman Levin
Director: Lawrence Kasha

Source: TEAHOUSE OF THE AUGUST MOON (Play: John Patrick); **Source:** TEAHOUSE OF THE AUGUST MOON, THE (Novel: Vern J. Sneider); **Choreographer:** Marc Breaux; **Costumes:** Freddy Wittop; **Dance Arranger:** Al Mello; **Lighting Designer:** Thomas Skelton; **Musical Director:** Theodore Saidenberg; **Orchestrations:** Philip J. Lang; **Set Design:** Oliver Smith

Songs: All That Has Happened [1]; Batata [1]; Call Me Back; Chaya; Find Your Own Cricket; Garden Guaracha; Geisha; If It's Good Enough for Lady Astor; I'll Grow a Garden for You [1]; Lovely Ladies, Kind Gentlemen; Miracle [1]; One More for the Last One; One Side of the World; Right Hand Man; Simple Word; Suddenly Now [1]; This Time; Very Simple [2]; Very, Very Lucky Lady [1]; With a Snap of My Finger; You Say-They Say; You've Broken a Fine Woman's Heart

Cast: David Burns; Eleanor A. Calbes; Ron Husmann; Kenneth Nelson; Remak Ramsay; David Steele; Lou Wills

Notes: [1] Cut prior to opening. [2] Not in program.

2627 • LOVELY LADIES, KIND GENTLEMEN (UNPRODUCED)

OPENED: 1970
Musical   Unproduced

Composer: Walter Marks
Lyricist: Walter Marks

Songs: August Moon, The; Find Your Own Cricket; Just This Once; Plan B; Problem, Solution, Conclusion; Teahouse, The; We Got Optimism

Notes: Written as an audition for LOVELY LADIES, KIND GENTLEMEN but not chosen.

2628 • LOVELY LADY

OPENED: 12/29/1927   Theatre: Sam H. Harris
Musical   Broadway: 164

Composer: Harold Levey; Dave Stamper
Lyricist: Cyrus Wood
Librettist: Gladys Unger; Cyrus Wood
Producer: Messrs. Shubert
Director: J.C. Huffman

Choreographer: David Bennett; Chester Hale; **Costumes:** Charles LeMaire; E.R. Schrapps; **Musical Director:** Harold Levey; **Set Design:** Watson Barratt

Songs: At the Barbecue (L: Harry A. Steinberg; Edward Ward); Bad Luck, I'll Laugh at You; Boy Friends; Breakfast in Bed; Dance Espagnol [2]; Decoys; Hey, Hey [2]; I Want a Good Time [2]; If France [2]; If I Could Love a Girl Like You; Just Say the Word [2]; Lingerie; Lost Step, The; Lovely Lady (L: Harry A. Steinberg; Eddie Ward); Make Believe You're Happy; One Step to Heaven [1]; Opening Chorus

Cast: Ruth Gordon; William Holden; Edna Leedom; Doris Patston; Guy Robertson; Jack Sheehan

Notes: Titled AIN'T LOVE GRAND out of town. [1] Out Chicago 12/25/28. [2] Out 3/4/27.

2629 • LOVELY ME

OPENED: 12/25/1946   Theatre: Adelphi
Play   Broadway: 37

Composer: Arthur Siegel
Lyricist: Jeff Bailey
Author: Beatrice Cole; Jacqueline Susann
Producer: David Lowe
Director: Jessie Royce Landis

Costumes: Eleanor Goldsmith; **Lighting Designer:** Donald Oenslager; **Set Design:** Donald Oenslager

Songs: Life Can Be Beautiful; Lovely Me

Cast: Mischa Auer; Luba Malina; Millard Mitchell; Arthur Siegel

Notes: Originally titled THE TEMPORARY MRS. SMITH.

2630 • LOVERS

OPENED: 01/27/1975   Theatre: Players
Musical   Off-Broadway: 118

Composer: Steve Sterner
Lyricist: Peter del Valle
Librettist: Peter del Valle
Producer: Michael Brown; Phillip Graham-Geraci
Director: Peter del Valle

Costumes: Reve Richards; **Lighting Designer:** Paul Sullivan; **Set Design:** Eugene Hide

Songs: Argument; Belt and Leather; Don't Betray His Love; Hymn; I Don't Want to Watch TV; Look at Him; Lovers; Make It; Role-Playing; Somebody, Somebody Hold Me; Somehow I'm Taller; There Is Always You; Trucks, The; Twenty Years; Where Do I Go from Here?; You Came to Me as a Young Man

Cast: Reathel Bean; Michael Cascone; John Ingle; Martin Rivera; Robert Sevra; Gary Sneed

2631 • LOVERS AND LUNATICS

OPENED: 1906
Musical   Closed out of town

Librettist: Walter Coleman Parker
Director: Charles Sinclair

Songs: Automobiling; Carolina; Dainty House-maids We; Four Lunatics, The; Georgianna Dunn; He's Ma Romeo; I'se Juliet; Lover's Quarrel, The; My Old Boy; Off to the Hunt;

Parody Man, The; Prince of Borneo; Roll On Silver Moon; Sly Old Fox; True Blue; Would You Do It?; You're the Kind of a Girl I Like

Cast: Wilbur Mack; Joe Morris

Notes: Wilkes-Barre program 09/20/06.

2632 • LOVE'S LOTTERY

OPENED: 10/03/1904   Theatre: Broadway
Musical   Broadway: 50

Composer: Julian Edwards
Lyricist: Stanislaus Stange
Librettist: Stanislaus Stange
Producer: F.C. Whitney
Director: Max Freeman

Musical Director: William E. MacQuinn

Songs: Behold Our Lady Great; Blarney of Killarney, The; Cupid's a Lad; Entrance of Twiller; Follow the Flag; Glimpse of Eden, A; Hoax and Coax; Holiday Joys; Honeymoon, The; If We Part; Kind Fortune Smiles Today; Love Forgotten; My First True Love; She Is the Right Girl, Right for Your Money, O! [1]; Song of the Tub; Sounds We Love to Hear, The; Spanish Grandee, A [1]; Sweet Thoughts of Home; Temptation, The; Village Recruits, The; What Art Thou?; You'll Find Nothing Better Than Beer [1]

Cast: Wallace Brownlow; Louise Gunning; Madame Schumann-Heink; John Slavin

Notes: [1] Sheet music only.

2633 • LOVESONG

OPENED: 10/05/1976   Theatre: Top of the Gate
Musical   Off-Broadway: 24

Composer: Michael Valenti
Lyricist: Michael Valenti
Producer: Wayne Starr

Choreographer: John Montgomery; **Costumes:** Joan Mayo; **Lighting Designer:** Martin Friedman; **Musical Director:** David Krane; **Orchestrations:** Michael Valenti; **Set Design:** Jack Logan; **Vocal Arranger:** Michael Valenti

Songs: April Child (L: Kenneth Pressman); Bid Me Love [2] (L: Henry Comor; Robert Herrick); Birthday, A [3] (L: Henry Comor; Christina Rossetti); Blood Red Roses (L: John Lewin); Did Not [2] (L: Henry Comor; Thomas Moore); Echo [1] (L: Anonymous); Epitaph, An [3] (L: Henry Comor; Richard Crashaw); Fair Dissenter Lass, The (L: John Lewin); I Remember [2] (L: Henry Comor; Thomas Hood); In Youth [2] (L: Henry Comor; Dorothy Parker); Indian Summer (L: Unknown); Jenny Kiss'd Me [3] (L: Henry Comor; Leigh Hunt); Just Suppose (L: Edwin Dulchin); Let the Toast Pass [2] (L: Henry Comor; Richard Brinsley Sheridan); Man Is for Woman Made (A Rondelay) [2] (L: Henry Comor; Peter Anthony Motteaux); Many a Fairer Face (L: Unknown); Mary Ann (L: Anonymous); Open All Night [2] (L: James Agee; Henry Comor); So We'll Go No More A-Roving [3] (L: Lord Bryon; Henry Comor); Song [2] (L: Henry Comor; Thomas Lodge); Sophia (L: Edwin Dulchin); To My Dear and Loving Husband (If Ever Two Were One) [2] (L: Anne Bradstreet; Henry Comor); Unhappy Bella (L: Anonymous); What Is a Woman Like? (L: Anonymous); What Is Love [2] (L: Henry Comor; Sir Walter Raleigh); When I Was One and Twenty [2] (L: Henry Comor; A.E. Houseman); When We're Married (L: Elsa Rael); Young Was I (L: Anonymous)

Cast: Melanie Chartoff; Sigrid Heath; Ty McConnell; Jess Richards

Notes: [1] Also in JUST FOR LOVE. [2] Lyrics adapted from early American and British literature. [3] Also in JUST FOR LOVE. Lyrics adapted from early American and British literature.

2634 • LOW AND BEHOLD

Notes: *See NEW FACES OF 1934.*

2635 • LOWER BIRTH THIRTEEN

OPENED: 10/16/1910   Theatre: Whitney Opera
                                              House
Musical   Chicago

Composer: Joseph E. Howard
Lyricist: Collin Davis; Arthur Gillsepie
Librettist: Collin Davis; Arthur Gillsepie

Songs: Dearie, You and I; I'll Take You Home Tomorrow If You'll Take Me Home Tonight; In a Bungalow; Just Keep A-Dreaming; Scare Crow

Maidie; When Nancy Brown Kissed Hirem Green Good Bye

Notes: No other information available.

2636 • LUANA

OPENED: 09/17/1930   Theatre: Hammerstein
Musical   Broadway: 21

Composer: Rudolf Friml
Lyricist: J. Keirn Brennan
Librettist: Howard Emmett Rogers
Producer: Arthur Hammerstein
Director: Howard Emmett Rogers

Source: BIRD OF PARADISE, THE (Play: Richard Walton Tully); **Choreographer:** Earl Lindsay; **Costumes:** Charles LeMaire; **Musical Director:** Ivan Rudisill; **Orchestrations:** Joseph Meyer; **Set Design:** Cirker & Robbins

Songs: Aloha; By Welawela; Drums of Kane; Glad I Have a Boy [1]; Hawaii's Shore; Hawaiian Moon; Hoku Loa; I'm Nuts on You [1]; In the Clouds; In Your Cradle of Love [2]; Jimsy [2]; Love, I Give You My All [1]; Luana; Magic Spell of Love, The; My Bird of Paradise; My Hills of Home [2]; Shore Leave; Son of the Sun, A; There Are No Tomorrows [2]; Wanapoo Bay; What a Lot of Loving [2]; Where You Lead; World of Melody, A [2]; Yankyula

Cast: Ruth Altman; Lillian Bond; Doris Carson; Robert Chisholm; Harry Jans; Joseph Macaulay; Donald Novis; Sally Rand; Marguerita Sylva; Harold Whelan

Notes: [1] Out London 11/21/32. [2] Out Philadelphia 8/25/30.

2637 • LUCKEE GIRL

OPENED: 09/15/1928   Theatre: Casino
Musical   Broadway: 81

Composer: Maurie Rubens; Maurice Yvain
Lyricist: Max Lief; Nathaniel Lief
Librettist: Gertrude Purcell
Producer: Messrs. Shubert
Director: Lew Morton

Source: UN BON GARCON (Play: Andre Barde; Maurice Yvain); **Choreographer:** Harry Puck;

Costumes: Ernest Schrapps; **Musical Director:** Earl Busby; **Set Design:** Watson Barratt

Songs: Bad Girl; Chiffon; Come On and Let's Make Whoopee (C: Werner Janssen; L: Mann Holiner); Facts of Life; Flat in Montmartre, A (C/L: Lew Pollack; Maurice Yvain); Friends and Lovers; Good Old Egg, A; Hold Your Man; I Hate You; I Love You So; If You'd Be Happy, Don't Fall in Love; I'll Take You to the Country; Laugh the Clouds Away [1] (C: Billy House); Magic Melody; Slow Down [1] (C: Billy House); When I'm in Paree; Wild About Music

Cast: Irene Dunne; Irving Fisher; Frank Lalor; Harry Puck

Notes: [1] Out Washington D.C. 9/8/29.

2638 • LUCKY

OPENED: 03/23/1927   Theatre: New Amsterdam
Musical   Broadway: 71

Composer: Harry Ruby
Lyricist: Otto Harbach; Bert Kalmar
Librettist: Otto Harbach
Producer: Charles Dillingham
Director: Hassard Short

Choreographer: David Bennett; Albertina Rasch; **Costumes:** James Reynolds; **Musical Director:** Gus Salzer; **Orchestrations:** Robert Russell Bennett; **Set Design:** James Reynolds

Songs: Cingalese Village (Cingalese Girls) (C: Jerome Kern; L: Bert Kalmar; Harry Ruby); Cocoanut Dance (inst.) [3]; Dancing the Devil Away (C: Jerome Kern; L: Bert Kalmar; Harry Ruby); Entrance of Lucky [4]; Lucky (C: Jerome Kern; L: Bert Kalmar; Harry Ruby); Pearl of Broadway (C: Jerome Kern; L: Bert Kalmar; Harry Ruby); Pearl of Ceylon Ballet, The (inst.); Pearl of Ceylon, The (1) [1]; Same Old Moon, The; Spring Is Here [4]; That Little Something [2] (C: Jerome Kern; L: Bert Kalmar; Harry Ruby); Treasure Hunt, The (inst.) [3]; When the Bo-Tree Blossoms Again (C: Jerome Kern; L: Bert Kalmar; Harry Ruby); Without Thinking of You [4]

Cast: Walter Catlett; Mary Eaton; Richard "Skeets" Gallagher; Ruby Keeler; Joseph Santley; Paul Whiteman

Notes: [1] Song cut in Philadelphia and music retained as ballet. [2] Added to post Broadway tour of CRISS-CROSS. [3] Composed by either Kern or Ruby. [4] Composer and lyricist not known.

2639 • LUCKY BREAK, A
OPENED: 08/11/1925   Theatre: Cort
Play   Broadway: 23

Author: Zelda Sears
Producer: American Producing Company

Cast: Ursula Ellsworth; Louise Galloway; George Macfarlane; Lucille Sears

Notes: This play reputedly contained five songs.

2640 • LUCKY DAY (1932)
OPENED: 02/01/1932
Revue   Closed out of town

Composer: Leon Rene; Otis Rene
Lyricist: Ben Ellison
Librettist: Edmund Joseph; Nat Perrin
Producer: Harold Morehouse; Rodney Pantages; Arthur Silber
Director: Earl Dancer; LeRoy Prinz

Choreographer: Harold Hecht; **Costumes:** John Clayton Poole; **Musical Director:** Hal Findlay

Songs: Cleo from the Congo; Come Seven; Get Out of My Way; Good Morning Sunshine; High, Wide and Handsome; I Got Religion; If You'll Just Come Back to Me; Never Had a Dream; No More; Shuffle Yo' Black Feet; Sinful Music; Singing Sweet Melodies; When the Jiggs Do the Juba; When You See Miss Load of Coal

Cast: Eddie Anderson; Edna Barr; Broomfeld & Greeley; Hallelujah Quartette; Alex Lovejoy; Ludwig, the Wonder Horse; Leon Rene's Lucky Day Band; Alma Travers; Mildred Washington

Notes: Program of the Mayan Theatre, Los Angeles.

2641 • LUCKY DAY (1950)
OPENED: 04/28/1950
Musical

Composer: Edward Cashman
Lyricist: Leo Brady

Librettist: Leo Brady
Director: Rev. Gilbert V. Hartke

Choreographer: Barbara Cole; **Costumes:** Cynthia Ketterer; **Set Design:** James D. Waring

Songs: Boy Meets Girl; Everything's Like a Picnic; I'm in Love with a Girl Named Dora May; It Takes a Lot of Trouble to Be Bad; It's Nice to Have Some Money; Keep the Conversation Going; Lucky Day; Meet My Sister; My Affair; Off to the Races; Sing Me No Love Songs; What a Break; What's a Barber Shop Quartet; You Gotta Depend on Luck

Cast: Virginia Bradley; Louis Camuti Jr.; Jill Leahy; Rickie Rudel; Meredith Schoonover

Notes: Amateur show. Catholic University.

2642 • LUCKY DOG, A
OPENED: 1907
Musical   Closed out of town

Composer: George A. Nichols
Librettist: Mark Swan
Producer: E.D. Stair

Choreographer: Jack Mason; **Musical Director:** George A. Nichols

Songs: All for You; Beautiful Bed; By the Pyramids; Cinderella; I Would Do Anything in the World for You; Just Like Jane; Mandy; Mexico; Morning Cy; Ruben's Holiday; Sad Affair, A; Trio; Willing to Learn

Cast: Peter Griffin; Chas. W. Udell; Nat M. Wills

Notes: Kansas City program 11/24/07 and Cedar Rapids program of 3/15/07.

2643 • LUCKY GUY
Musical   Closed out of town

Composer: Willard Beckham
Lyricist: Willard Beckham
Librettist: Willard Beckham
Producer: Bailey and Schwartz Prods.; Plaza Theatre; Victor I. Rosenberg
Director: Gerald Gutierrez

Choreographer: Peter Gennaro; **Costumes:** Ann Hould-Ward; **Dance Arranger:** Michael Kosarin;

Lighting Designer: Marilyn Rennagel; **Musical Director:** Randy Booth; **Orchestrations:** Steven Margoshes; **Set Design:** Jean Eckart; William Eckart

Songs: Big Al; Blue Jean Blues; Chicky; Do What You Can Do; Find Him and Bring Him Home; Folks Makin' Money; I Wonder Why; Lucky Guy; My Old Friend; Needle in a Haystack; Osage County Line; Outta Your Mind; Queen of Country Music; Trailer Park Romance; Yo' a Little Lady

Cast: Beth Fowler; Terry Kirwin; Kurt Knudson; Faith Prince; Susan Terry; Scott Waara

Notes: Program of The Plaza Theatre, Dallas.

2644 • LUCKY HOODOO
Musical

Composer: Billy B. Van
Lyricist: Billy B. Van

Songs: Everybody Two-Step; Golden Dreams; Just a Little Quaker Girl; Loving Moon

Notes: No other information available.

2645 • LUCKY SAMBO
OPENED: 06/06/1925   Theatre: Colonial
Musical   Broadway: 9

Composer: Porter Grainger; Freddie Johnson
Lyricist: Porter Grainger; Freddie Johnson
Librettist: Porter Grainger; Freddie Johnson
Producer: Harlem Productions
Director: Leigh Whipper

Choreographer: Freddie Johnson; **Costumes:** A.E. Mathison; **Musical Director:** Fred Tunstall

Songs: Alexander's Ragtime Wedding Day; Always on the Job; Anybody's Man Will Be My Man; Aunt Jemima (I'm Comin' Home); Charley from That Charleston Dancin' School; Coal Oil; Dandy Dan; Don't Forget Bandanna Days; Dreary, Dreary, Rainy Days; Happy; Havin' a Wonderful Time; If You Can't Bring It, You've Got to Send It; June; Keep A-Diggin'; Legomania; Love Me While You're Gone; Midnight Cabaret; Not So Long Ago; Porterology; Runnin'; Singing Nurses; Stop; Strolling; Take Him to Jail

Cast: Porter Grainger; Monette Moore; Tim Moore

2646 • LUCKY STIFF
OPENED: 04/25/1988   Theatre: Playwrights Horizons
Musical   Off-Broadway: 15

Composer: Stephen Flaherty
Lyricist: Lynn Ahrens
Librettist: Lynn Ahrens
Director: Thommie Walsh

Source: MAN WHO BROKE THE BANK AT MONTE CARLO, THE (Play: Michael Butterworth); **Costumes:** Michael Krass; **Lighting Designer:** Beverly Emmons; **Musical Director:** Jeffrey Saver; **Orchestrations:** Michael Abbott; **Set Design:** Bob Shaw

Songs: Confession #2; Day Around Town Dance, A; Dogs Versus You; Fancy Meeting You Here; Good To Be Alive; Him, Them, It, Her; Lucky; Monte Carlo; Mr. Witherspoon's Friday Night; Nice; Phone Call, The; Rita's Confession; Something Funny's Going On; Speaking French; Times Like This; Woman in My Bathroom, A

Cast: Ron Faber; Patty Holley; Barbara Rosenblat; Stephen Stout; Mary Testa; Stuart Zagnit

2647 • LUDLOW LADD
Musical

Composer: Gerald J. Markoe
Lyricist: Michael Colby
Librettist: Michael Colby

Notes: No other information available.

2648 • LULLABY AND GOODNIGHT
OPENED: 02/07/1982   Theatre: Public
Musical   Off-Broadway: 33

Composer: Elizabeth Swados
Lyricist: Elizabeth Swados
Librettist: Elizabeth Swados
Producer: N.Y. Shakespeare Festival; Joseph Papp
Director: Elizabeth Swados

Choreographer: Ara Fitzgerald; **Costumes:** Hilary Rosenfeld; **Lighting Designer:** Marcia Madeira; **Set Design:** David Jenkins

Songs: Blond Haired Little Girl; Deprogramming Song; Don't You Ever Give It All Away;

Gentleman of Leisure; Getting From Day to Day; I Am Sick of Love; In the Life; Keep Working; Ladies Look at Yourselves; Let the Day Perish When I Was Born; Lies, Lies, Lies; Love Loves the Difficult Things; Man That Is Born of a Woman; Moth and the Flame, The; Nightmare Was Me, The; Now You Are One of the Family; Port Authority; Prologue; Revenge Song; Sub-Babylon; Sweet Words; Turn Her Out; When a Pimp Meets a Whore; When Any Woman Makes a Running Issue Out of Her Flesh; Why We Do It; Wife Beating Song; You Gave Me Love; You're My Favorite Lullabye

Cast: Frances Asher; Gail Boggs; Bruce Hubbard; Larry Marshall; Rudy Roberson; Jossie de Guzman

2649 • LULU'S HUSBANDS
OPENED: 04/14/1910 Theatre: Maxine Elliott's
Play   Broadway: 42

Author: Thompson Buchanan
Producer: Messrs. Shubert
Director: J.C. Huffman

Musical Director: D.S. Samuels

Songs: Little One [1] (C/L: Joseph E. Howard)

Cast: Mabel Barrison; Harry Conor; Sophie Tucker

Notes: [1] Song not in program. Sheet music only.

2650 • LUMPKIN
Musical   Closed out of town

Composer: Jill Williams
Lyricist: Jill Williams
Librettist: William Glover
Director: William Glover

Source: SHE STOOPS TO CONQUER (Play: Oliver Goldsmith); **Choreographer:** Gene Castle; **Costumes:** Ivy Trent; **Musical Director:** Jill Williams

Songs: Charity Begins at Home; Compliments; Damn You, Tony Lumpkin!; Epilogue; Five Minutes; I Wish You Success; If It Was Up to Me; My Son Charles; Nectar, Sweet Nectar; Olde Books; Robbed; She Stoops to Conquer; Stout

Cast: William Glover; Carol Kristy; Beth Peters; Jeff Redford

Notes: Program of The Shakespeare Society of America at the Globe Theatre, Los Angeles.

2651 • LUNCH
OPENED: 06/28/1994
Musical   Closed out of town

Composer: Steve Dorff
Lyricist: John Bettis
Librettist: Rick Hawkins
Producer: Charles Gray; John Kimball; North Shore Music Theater; Pitts. Civic Light Opera
Director: Glenn Casale

Arrangements: Ron Abel; Steve Dorff; Larry Herbstritt; **Choreographer:** Sharon Halley; **Costumes:** Lindsay Davis; **Dance Arranger:** Sand Lawn; **Lighting Designer:** Stuart Duke; **Musical Director:** Brian W. Tidwell; **Orchestrations:** Bruce Coughlin; **Set Design:** Russell Metheny

Songs: He'll Never Know; I Never Danced with You; I'm No Angel; Lunch; Man Like Me, A; Offerings du Jour; One Blink of an Eye; One Step at a Time; Perfectly Alone; Requiem for a Lightweight; Skyline; Time Stands Still; What If?; Why Fall at All?

Cast: Kirsten Benton; Marilyn Cooper; Stanley Grover; Heather Lee; Barney Martin; Andrew Hill Newman; Teri Ralston

2652 • LUNCH HOUR FOLLIES
Notes: *See LUNCHTIME FOLLIES.*

2653 • LUNCHTIME FOLLIES
OPENED: 1943
Revue

Composer: Marc Blitzstein; Jerome Kern; Henry Nemo
Lyricist: Ira Gershwin
Librettist: Maxwell Anderson; Laura Benet; Norman Corwin; Joseph Fields; Ham Fisher; Moss Hart; Lillian Hellman; Nat Hiken; Langston Hughes; George S. Kaufman; Groucho Marx; Zero Mostel; S.J. Perelman; Billy Rose; Stephen Vincent
Producer: American Theatre Wing, The; Kurt Weill

Choreographer: Lil Liandre

Songs: Ballad of Sloppy Joe, The (C/L: Harold Rome); Buddy on the Nightshift (C: Kurt Wcill; L: Oscar Hammerstein II); Dear Joe (C/L: Harold Rome); Gee, But It's Cold in Russia (C/L: Unknown); Hayfoot, Strawfoot (C/L: Unknown); He Got His (C/L: Unknown); Jeremiah (C/L: Bob Musel; Henry Nemo); Lady's on the Job (on Time), The (C/L: Harold Rome); Men Behind the Man Behind the Gun (C/L: Harold Rome); On That Old Production Line (C/L: Harold Rome); On Time (C/L: Harold Rome); Put Another Nail in Hitler's Coffin (C/L: Unknown); Quiet Girl, A (C/L: Marc Blitzstein); Schickelgruber (C: Kurt Weill; L: Howard Dietz); Song of the Free, The (C: Kurt Weill; L: Archibald MacLeish); Story of an Inventory (C: Kurt Weill; L: Lewis Allan); That's My Pop (C/L: Harold Rome); Victory Symphony, Eight to the Bar (C/L: Harold Rome)

Cast: Jack Albertson; Anita Alvarez; Milton Berle; Shirley Booth; David Burns; Howard Da Silva; Joey Faye; Jay C. Flippen; Arlene Frances; Anne Francine; Betty Garrett; Will Geer; Georgia Gibbs; Sam Jaffe; Rosetta LeNoire; Fredric March; Zero Mostel; Sunnie O'Dea; Alan Reed; Vivienne Segal; Helen Tamiris; Benay Venuta

Notes: Sometimes referred to as LUNCH HOUR FOLLIES. Head of production committee: Kurt Weill. General Manager: Kermit Bloomgarden. Billed as an entertainment for war plants. Several editions during World War II.

2654 • LUST

OPENED: 1995   Theatre: John Houseman
Musical   Off-Broadway

Composer: Heather Brothers, The
Lyricist: Heather Brothers, The
Librettist: Heather Brothers, The
Producer: Eric Krebs; Anne Strickland Squadron; Frederic B. Voget
Director: Bob Carlton

Source: COUNTRY WIFE, THE (Play: William Wycherley); **Choreographer:** Barry Finkel; **Costumes:** Rodney Ford; **Lighting Designer:** F. Mitchell Dana; **Musical Director:** John Johnson; **Set Design:** Rodney Ford

Songs: Art of Deceiving, The; Captain's Jig, The; China; Come Tomorrow; Dear Sir; Husbands Beware; I Live for Love; Ladies of Quality; Lust; Master Class, The; Ode to the One I Love; One of You; Pox on Love and on Wenching, A; Serve the Dog Right; Somewhere Out There; Vengeance; Wait and See; What a Handsome Little Fellow; Why Did You Have to Come Into My Life

Cast: Janet Aldrich; Jennifer Lee Andrews; David Barron; Barry Finkel; Lee Golden; Suzanne Ishee; Denis Lawson; Robert McCormick; Judith Moore; Jennifer Piech; Dan Schiff; A.J. Vincent

2655 • LUTE SONG

OPENED: 02/06/1946   Theatre: Plymouth
Musical   Broadway: 142

Composer: Raymond Scott
Lyricist: Bernard Hanighen
Librettist: Sidney Howard; Will Irwin
Producer: Michael Myerberg
Director: John Houseman

Source: PI-PA-KI (Play); **Choreographer:** Yeichi Nimura; **Costumes:** Robert Edmond Jones; **Lighting Designer:** Robert Edmond Jones; **Musical Director:** Eugene Kusmiak; **Orchestrations:** Raymond Scott; **Set Design:** Robert Edmond Jones

Songs: Beggar's Music; Bitter Harvest; Chinese Market Place; Dirge Song; Eunuch Scene; Genie's Music; Imperial March; Lion Dance; Lute Song, The; Marriage Music; Monkey See, Monkey Do; Mountain High, Valley Low; North Road; Phoenix Dance; Vision Song; Where You Are; Willow Tree

Cast: Yul Brynner; Nancy Davis[1]; Clarence Derwent; Mildred Dunnock; Mary Martin; Mickey Morris; Rex O'Malley

Notes: [1] Later went on to become Mrs. Ronald Reagan.

2656 • LUV MUSICAL, A

Notes: *See LOVE.*

2657 • LYLE (1970)

OPENED: 03/20/1970   Theatre: McAlpin Rooftop
Musical   Off-Broadway: 4

Composer: Janet Gari
Lyricist: Toby Garson

Librettist: Chuck Horner
Producer: Marilyn Cantor Baker
Director: Marvin Gordon

Source: HOUSE ON EAST 88TH STREET (Novel: Bernard Weber); **Costumes:** Winn Morton; **Lighting Designer:** Jack Blackman; **Musical Director:** Robert Estey; **Set Design:** Jack Blackman; **Vocal Arranger:** Robert Estey

Songs: Along Came Lyle [1]; Alternate Parking; Always Leave 'Em Wanting More; Crocodiles Cry; Everybody Wants to be Remembered; Generation Gap; Happy Place Is in My Heart, A [1]; How Did I Lose a Friend? [1]; I Belong; I Can't Believe It's Real; It's Great to Be an Animal in America [1]; Look at Me; Loretta; Lyle; Lyle's Turn; Me, Me, Me; Movin' Day [1]; On the Road; Sea's Too Salty for Me, The [1]; Suddenly You're a Stranger; Things Were Much Better in the Past; To Keep Up My Spirits [1]; Try to Make the Best of It; We Belong; We'll Have a Birthday Party for You [1]

Cast: Richard Bonelle; Joey Faye; Steve Harmon; Ann Vivian

Notes: [1] Not in programs.

2658 • LYLE (1987)

OPENED: 1987 Theatre: Egg, The
Musical

Composer: Charles Strouse
Lyricist: Charles Strouse
Librettist: Charles Strouse
Director: Barbara Siman

Source: HOUSE ON EAST 88TH STREET, THE (Novel: Bernard Weber); **Choreographer:** Barbara Siman; **Costumes:** Judanna Lynn; **Lighting Designer:** Ann G. Wrightson; **Musical

Director: Louis St. Louis; **Set Design:** Duke Durfee

Songs: Call Your Police; Crocodile, a Crocodile, A; Don't Leave Me Now; Has Anyone Seen My Crocodile; Homeless; I Know; I've Got to Keep Busy; Let Them See a Star; Look on the Bright Side; Love Power; Lyle and Valenti; Mailman's Song; Me Oh Me Oh Man Do I Miss Milwaukee; Moving Into a New House; Nobody Loves You Like I Do; There's No Hotel Like the Algonquin

Cast: Richard Barrows; Jason Brown; John Thomas McGuire III; Jeanne Vigialante

Notes: Opened at ESIPA in Albany, New York.

2659 • LYSISTRATA

OPENED: 11/13/1972 Theatre: Brooks Atkinson
Play Broadway: 8

Composer: Peter Link
Lyricist: Peter Link
Author: Aristophanes
Translator: Michael Cacoyannis
Producer: David Black; David Seltzer
Director: Michael Cacoyannis

Costumes: Willa Kim; **Lighting Designer:** Jules Fisher; **Musical Director:** Henry "Bootsie" Norman; **Set Design:** Robin Wagner

Songs: Are We Strong?; As I Choose; Cavalry Captain, A; Eels Are a Girl's Best Friend; Kalimera; Let Me Tell You a Little Story; Lysistrata; Many the Beasts; Oh! What a Siege That Was; On, On, On; To Touch the Sky; Woman's Hands, A; You Out There

Cast: Emory Bass; Mary Jo Catlett; Gordon Connell; Jane Connell; Jack Fletcher; Patti Karr; Priscilla Lopez; Melina Mercouri

M

2660 • MACK AND MABEL

OPENED: 10/06/1974   Theatre: Majestic
Musical   Broadway: 66

Composer: Jerry Herman
Lyricist: Jerry Herman
Librettist: Michael Stewart
Producer: David Merrick
Director: Gower Champion

Choreographer: Gower Champion; **Costumes:** Patricia Zipprodt; Incidental Music: John Morris; **Lighting Designer:** Tharon Musser; **Musical Director:** Donald Pippin; **Orchestrations:** Philip J. Lang; **Set Design:** Robin Wagner; **Vocal Arranger:** Donald Pippin

Songs: Big Time; Call in the Cops [3]; Hit 'Em on the Head [1]; Hundreds of Girls; I Promise You a Happy Ending; I Wanna Make the World Laugh; I Won't Send Roses; Look What Happened to Mabel; Movies Were Movies; My Heart Leaps Up; Tap Your Troubles Away; Time Heals Everything; Today I'm Gonna Think About Me [2]; When Mabel Comes in the Room; Wherever He Ain't

Cast: Roger Bigelow; Jerry Dodge; Robert Fitch; Lisa Kirk; Bert Michaels; James Mitchell; Bernadette Peters; Robert Preston; Marie Santell; Stanley Simmonds

Notes: [1] Out Washington D.C. 9/74. [2] Not used. [3] Not used. Same music as "Get Off My Lawn" in PARADE (1960).

2661 • MACKEY OF APPALACHIA

OPENED: 10/06/1965   Theatre: Blackfriar's Guild
Musical   Off-Broadway: 48

Composer: Walter Cool
Lyricist: Walter Cool
Librettist: Walter Cool
Producer: Blackfriars' Guild
Director: Walter Cool

Choreographer: Robert Charles; **Costumes:** Alice Merrigal; **Lighting Designer:** Allen Edward Klein; **Set Design:** Allen Edward Klein

Songs: Blue and Troubled; Everybody Loves a Tree; Go Up to the Mountain; Gotta Pay; How We Would Like Our Man; I Wonder Why; It's Sad to Be Lonesome; Judging Song; Lonely Voice; Love Me Too; Love Will Come Your Way; Mackey of Appalachia; My Little Girl; My Love, My Love; Only a Day Dream; Slatey Fork; There Goes My Gal; There's Got to Be Love; Things Ain't As Nice; We Are Friends; We Got Troubles; We're Having a Party; You're Too Smart

Cast: Francis Beck; James Bormann; Virginia Ellen Haynes; Michael Murray; Christopher Smith

2662 • MACUSHLA

OPENED: 02/05/1912   Theatre: Grand Opera
                                         House
Play   Broadway

Composer: Ernest R. Ball
Lyricist: J. Keirn Brennan
Author: Rida Johnson Young
Producer: Augustus Pitou
Director: William Henry Miller

Incidental Music: Frederic Knight Logan

Songs: Girl I'll Call My Sweetheart Must Look Like You, The (C/L: Chauncey Olcott; Dan J. Sullivan); Good-Bye My Emerald Land (C/L: Frederic Knight Logan; Chauncey Olcott); I'll Miss You, Old Ireland; Ireland, You're the Motherland [2] (C: Arthur R. Grant; L: Thomas Meehan); Macushla (C: Dermont MacMurrough; L: Josephine V. Rowe); Macushla Asthore; My Land (C: Ernest R. Ball; Chauncey Olcott; L: Bartley Costello); Pulse of My Heart; She's Irish [2] (C: James Rule; L: Alex Sullivan); That's How the Shannon Flows; 'Tis an Irish Girl I Love and She's Just Like You [1] (L: J. Keirn Brennan; Al Dubin); Who Knows? [2] (L: Paul Laurence

Dunbar); With the Twinkle in Her Eye (L: Chauncey Olcott; Louis Weslyn); Word from an Irishman's Tongue, The [2] (C: Arthur R. Grant; L: Thomas Meehan)

Cast: Robert V. Ferguson; Gail Kane; Jennie Lamont; Chauncey Olcott; E.H. Reardon; Charles Wellesley

Notes: Also titled PULSE OF MY HEART. [1] Dubin's lyric added for 1920 version. [2] From the production starring Barry McCormack and were copyrighted in 1919.

2663 • MAD SHOW, THE
OPENED: 01/09/1966   Theatre: New
Revue   Off-Broadway: 871

Composer: Mary Rodgers
Lyricist: Marshall Barer
Librettist: Stan Hart; Larry Siegel
Producer: Ivor David Balding
Director: Steven Vinaver

Costumes: Peter Harvey; **Lighting Designer:** V.C. Fuqua; **Musical Director:** Sam Pottle; **Set Design:** Peter Harvey

Songs: Boy From..., The (L: Stephen Sondheim [1]); Ecch; Gift of Maggie, The; Hate Song (L: Steven Vinaver); Hey, Sweet Mamma [2] (L: Steven Vinaver); Looking for Someone; Misery Is; Opening [2]; Real Thing, The; Snappy Answers [3]; Well It Ain't (L: Stan Hart; Larry Siegel); You Never Can Tell (L: Steven Vinaver)

Cast: MacIntyre Dixon; Linda Lavin; Richard Libertini; Paul Sand; Jo Anne Worley

Notes: [1] Used pseudonym Estaban Rio Nido. [2] Cut prior to opening. [3] Cut after opening.

2664 • MADAME APHRODITE
OPENED: 12/29/1961   Theatre: Orpheum
Musical   Off-Broadway: 13

Composer: Jerry Herman
Lyricist: Jerry Herman
Librettist: Tad Mosel
Producer: Cynthia Baer; Howard Barker; Robert Chambers
Director: Robert Turoff

Costumes: Patricia Zipprodt; **Lighting Designer:** Lee Watson; **Musical Director:** Peg Foster; **Set Design:** David Ballou

Songs: Afferdytie; And a Drop of Lavender Oil; Beat the World; Beautiful [1]; Girls Who Sit and Wait, The [2]; Gotta Be a Dream [6]; I Don't Mind; Miss Euclid Avenue; Only Love [3]; Sales Reproach; Take a Good Look Around; Theme [5]; There Comes a Time; Turkish Corner [5]; You I Like [4]

Cast: Nancy Andrews; Rod Colbin; Cherry Davis; Jack Drummond; June Hyer; Mona Paulee

Notes: [1] Same music as "A Little More Mascara" in LA CAGE AUX FOLLES. [2] Some of the same music as "And I Was Beautiful" from DEAR WORLD. [3] Same music as release of "It's Today" from MAME. The other part of "It's Today" is from "There's Is No Tune Like a Show Tune (Show Tune in 2/4)" from PARADE and also NIGHTCAP. [4] Not the same song as in THE GRAND TOUR. [5] Cut. [6] Cut. Same music as "Love Is Only Love" cut from MAME and in film HELLO, DOLLY!

2665 • MADAME MOSELLE
OPENED: 05/23/1914   Theatre: Shubert
Musical   Broadway: 9

Composer: Ludwig Englander
Lyricist: Edward A. Paulton
Librettist: Edward A. Paulton
Director: George W. Lederer

Choreographer: Allan K. Foster; **Costumes:** Samuel Zalud; **Musical Director:** August Kleinecke

Songs: Back Out While the Backing Is Good; By Tumna's Rolling Waters; Ding, Dong; Everybody Knows Madame Moselle; Good Bye Little Girl; If I Should Lose My Only Girl (C/L: William P. Chase); I'll Be There; In Constantinople; Is That All?; Model, The; Rosie from Palermo; Students of Art Are We; Tell Me the French Word for Squeeze Me; What Are We Going to Do About It?

Cast: Ralph Herz; Josie Intropodi; Ernest Lambert; William Pruette; Olga Roller

2666 • MADAME POMPADOUR

OPENED: 11/11/1924   Theatre: Martin Beck
Musical   Broadway: 80

Composer: Leo Fall
Lyricist: Clare Kummer
Librettist: Clare Kummer
Producer: Martin Beck; Charles Dillingham
Director: R.H. Burnside

Source: MADAME POMPADOUR (Musical: Leo Fall; Rudolf Schanzer; Ernst Welisch); **Choreographer:** Julian Alfred; **Costumes:** Wilhelm; **Lighting Designer:** George Schaaf; **Musical Director:** Oscar Radin; **Set Design:** Willy Pogany

Songs: By the Light of the Moon; Carnival Time; Entrance of the King; I'll Be Your Soldier; Inspiration; Madame Pompadour; Magic Moments; Oh! Joseph; Oh Pom-Pom-Pom-Pompadour!; One, Two and One, Two, Three; Reminiscence; Serenade; Tell Me what Your Eyes Were Made For

Cast: Wilda Bennett; Louis Harrison; Frederick Lewis; John Quinlan

2667 • MADAME SHERRY

OPENED: 08/30/1910   Theatre: New Amsterdam
Musical   Broadway: 231

Composer: Karl Hoschna
Lyricist: Otto Harbach
Librettist: Otto Harbach
Producer: H.H. Frazee; George Lederer; A.H. Woods
Director: George Lederer

Musical: Hugo Felix; Maurice Ordonneau); **Costumes:** Mme. Francis; Kate Keeler; **Musical Director:** Hans S. Linne; **Set Design:** Ernest Albert

Songs: Aesthetic Dancing; Athletic Prancing; Birth of Passion, The; Butterfly, The (Birth of the Butterfly); Dance of Danger, The; Dublin Rag, The (C: Phil Schwartz; L: Harold Atteridge); Dunerwetter; Every Little Movement; I Want to Play House with You; I'll Build for You a Little Nest; I'm All Right; I'm Looking for a Financier [2]; Intermezzo, The; Kiss You Gave, The; Loading Up the Mandy Lee [1] (C: Henry I. Marshall; L: Stanley Murphy); Looney Mooney Man [2];

Love Dance, The; Mad Madrid, The; Mr. Johnson, Good Night; Off for a Sail; Other Fellow, The; Out with the Owl [2]; Put Your Arms Around Me Honey (C: Albert Von Tilzer; L: Junie McCree); Seduction, The (C: Hugo Felix); She Shook Him in Chicago; Smile She Means for You, The; Terzetto Buffo (C: Hugo Felix); Theophilus; Uncle Says I Mustn't, So I Won't; We Are Only Poor Weak Mortals; Won't Someone Take Me Home?; You Can't Argue

Cast: Lina Abarbanell; Frances Demarest; Jack Gardner; Ralph Herz; Elizabeth Murray

Notes: Music of original by Hugo Felix. [1] Not in programs. [2] Not used.

2668 • MADAME TROUBADOUR

OPENED: 10/10/1910   Theatre: Lyric
Musical   Broadway: 80

Composer: Felix Albini
Lyricist: Joseph W. Herbert
Librettist: Joseph W. Herbert
Producer: Messrs. Shubert
Director: Joseph W. Herbert

Source: MADAME TROUBADOR (Musical: Felix Albini; Bela Jenbach; Richard Pohl); **Musical Director:** Oscar Radin

Songs: Chimes Number; Don't Be Rash; Introduction; Oh How That Taxi Got on My Nerves; Please, Please; Tra-la-la, Etcetera; Trou-Trou-Ba-Ba-Troubadour; Yesterday and Today

Cast: Edgar Atchinson-Ely; Georgia Caine; Grace LaRue; Anna Wheaton; Van Rensselaer Wheeler

Notes: *See also THE LITTLE PARISIENNE.*

2669 • MADCAP, THE

OPENED: 01/31/1928   Theatre: Royale
Musical   Broadway: 103

Composer: Maurie Rubens
Lyricist: Clifford Grey
Librettist: Gertrude Purcell; Gladys Unger
Producer: Messrs. Shubert
Director: Frank Smithson

Source: CHIBI (Play: Regis Gignoux; Jacques Thery); **Choreographer:** Carl Hemmer

Songs: Birdies; Buy Your Way; Honey, Be My Honey Bee (C: J. Fred Coots; Maurie Rubens); Honeymooning Blues; I Want to Tell a Story; Knife, The [2]; Me, the Moonlight and Me; My Best Pal; Odle-De-O Do, 'I Do'; Old Enough to Marry; Sheik with New Ideas, A [2]; Something to Tell (C: J. Fred Coots; Maurie Rubens); Step to Paris Blues [1]; Stop! Go! (C: J. Fred Coots; Maurie Rubens); What Has Made the Movies?; Why Can't It Happen to Me?

Cast: Sydney Greenstreet; Ethel Intropodi; Mitzi; Harry Puck; Charley Sylber; Arthur Treacher

Notes: [1] Sheet music only. [2] Out Washington, D.C. 4/23/27.

2670 • MADCAP DUCHESS, THE

OPENED: 11/11/1913   Theatre: Globe
Musical   Broadway: 71

Composer: Victor Herbert
Lyricist: Justin Huntley McCarthy; David Stevens
Librettist: Justin Huntley McCarthy; David Stevens
Producer: H.H. Frazee
Director: Fred G. Latham

Source: SERAPHICA (Novel: Justin Huntley McCarthy); **Choreographer:** Gilbert Clayton; **Costumes:** W.H. Matthews; **Musical Director:** Max Hirschfeld; **Orchestrations:** Victor Herbert

Songs: Aurora Blushing Rosily; Babette of Beaujolais; Canzonetta [2]; Companions, I Have Summoned You; Deuce Young Man!, The; Do You Know?; Far Up the Hill; Goddess of Mine (Star of Love) [1]; Love and I Are Playing; Love and I Are Playing [2]; Love Is a Story That's Old; Now Is the South Wind Blowing; Oh, Up! It's Up!; Sun Is Aslant, The; Sweehearts Waltzes [2]; That Is Art; Three Favorite Airs [2]; To Paris!; Tweedledum and Tweedledee; Winged Love

Cast: Glenn Hall; Harry MacDonough; Ann Swinburne; Peggy Wood

Notes: [1] Title changed to "Star of Love" after opening. [2] ASCAP/Library of Congress.

2671 • MADCAP PRINCESS, A

OPENED: 09/05/1904   Theatre: Knickerbocker
Musical   Broadway: 48

Composer: Ludwig Englander
Lyricist: Harry B. Smith
Librettist: Harry B. Smith
Producer: Charles Dillingham
Director: Edward P. Temple

Source: WHEN KNIGHTHOOD WAS IN FLOWER (Novel: Charles Major); **Musical Director:** A. DeNovellis; **Set Design:** Emens & Unitt

Songs: A-L-E-X-A-N-D-R-I-A (C: Alfred Solman; L: John B. Lowitz); Cavalier Song; Come, Fill Up a Brimming Flagon; If I Marry the King of France; If You Were Mine Alone; I'm Bluff King Hal; Kings of the Sea, The; Let a Good Ship Be Made Ready; Letter Chansonette; Lonesome Little Maid (C: Alfred Solman; L: Benjamin Hapgood Burt); Madcap Princess, A; Maids of Honor to the Princess; May Day Is Hey Day; May Day Processional; Ontario (C: Alfred Solman; L: John B. Lowitz); Rings of the Sea; Sir! You Wear a Sword; That Beautiful Isle of the Sea; Thrice Noble Is He; Woman Rules the King

Cast: Lulu Glaser; Elizabeth Murray; William Pruette; Bertram Wallis

Notes: No songs listed in program.

2672 • MADE IN HARLEM

OPENED: 06/1918   Theatre: Lincoln
Revue   New York

Songs: Harlem Blues [1] (C/L: Perry Bradford)

Cast: Mamie Smith

Notes: No other information avaiable on this Harlem show. [1] Later titled "Crazy Blues."

2673 • MADELEINE, OR THE MAGIC KISS

OPENED: 02/25/1895   Theatre: Bijou
Musical   Broadway: 80

Composer: Julian Edwards
Lyricist: Stanislaus Stange
Librettist: Julian Edwards; Stanislaus Stange
Producer: Camille D'Arville
Director: Max Freeman

Musical Director: Julian Edwards

Songs: Baron's 100th Birthday, The; Betrothal, The; Bridal Song, The [1]; Dickie and the Birdie [1]; Doctor and the Scribe, The [1]; Festival of Roses, The; Heart Foolish Heart [1]; I Love You So [1]; I Would Have Told Thee Long Ago [1]; Legend Fulfilled, The; Legend of Grimm, The; Madeleine's First Kiss; Marriage, The; Mary Had a Little Lamb [1]; Second Kiss, The; Sequel to the Legend, The; Serenade [1]; Song of the Husbands [1]; Third Kiss, The; 'Tis Sad to Love in Vain [1]; 'Twas but a Dream [1]

Cast: George C. Boniface Jr.; Aubrey Boucicault; Camille D'Arville; Marie Dressler; Hilda Hollins; Maud Hollins; J.K. Murray; Henry A. Stanley

Notes: [1] Sheet music only.

2674 • MADEMOISELLE COLOMBE

OPENED: 12/09/1987   Theatre: Theatre Off Park
Musical   Off-Broadway: 28

Composer: Michael Valenti
Lyricist: Edwin Dulchin
Librettist: Edwin Dulchin; Albert Harris; Michael Valenti
Director: Albert Harris

Source: MADEMOISELLE COLOMBE (Play: Jean Anouilh; Louis J. Kronenberger); **Choreographer:** William Fleet Lively; **Costumes:** Lindsay Davis; Donald Holder; **Musical Director:** Rod Derefinko; **Orchestrations:** Greg Smith; **Set Design:** Philipp Jung

Songs: After Rehearsal; And If I Told You That I Wanted You; Color Red, The; Flower Shop; Folies Bergeres; From This Day; Georgie and I; Left, Right, Left; Moon Dear; More Than One Man in Her Life; Only So Much I Can Give; Perfect; She's an Actress; This Bright Morning; Two Against the World; What's the Mail?; Why Did It Have to Be You; Years from Now; Yes Alexandra, No Alexandra

Cast: Victoria Brasser; Keith Buterbaugh; Georgia Creighton; David Cryer; Dick Decareau; Tom Galantich; Tammy Grimes; Joaquin Romaguera; Michael Tartel

2675 • MADGE SMITH, ATTORNEY

OPENED: 12/10/1900   Theatre: Bijou
Musical   Broadway: 38

Composer: Francis Bryant; Ernest Hogan; Theodore Northrup; Dave Reed Jr.; A. Baldwin Sloane
Lyricist: Francis Bryant; Ernest Hogan; Theodore Northrup; James O'Dea; Dave Reed Jr.
Librettist: Ramsey Morris
Director: Louis Harrison

Musical Director: Watty Hydes; **Set Design:** Lewis & MacCoughtry

Songs: Bull-Frog Ben; Dance on Friday Night; Give Me Back My Liza; I Ain't Gonna Work No More; I'm Gwine to Marry Angeline; I've Got Troubles of My Own; I've Laid Him on the Shelf; Oui! Oui! Mademoiselle; Turkey and the Turk, The (C/L: Francis Bryant); When I'm By Her Side; Why Don't the Band Play?

Cast: George A. Beane; May Irwin; Ignacio Martinetti; Carrie Radcliffe; Joseph M. Sparks; Bert Thayer

Notes: The songs were not credited to specific composers or lyricists.

2676 • MADISON AVENUE

OPENED: 12/29/1992   Theatre: Lone Star
Musical   Off-Broadway: 48

Composer: Gary Cherpakov; Robert Moehl
Lyricist: Gary Cherpakov; Paul Streitz
Librettist: Paul Streitz
Director: David C. Wright

Arrangements: Robert Marks; **Choreographer:** David C. Wright; **Costumes:** Brenda Burton; **Lighting Designer:** Chris O'Leary; **Musical Director:** Joel Maisano; **Set Design:** Chris O'Leary; **Vocal Arranger:** Robert Marks

Songs: All a Matter of Strategy; Client Service; It's Not a Commerical, It's Art; L.A. Freeway; Leonardo's Lemonade (Lennie's Lemonade) (Leonard's Lemonade); Look, The; Madison Avenue; Office Romance; Residuals; Something for Me; Squeeze, Squeeze, Squeeze; Thirty Seconds; Typical American Consumer; Upper

East Side Blues; Woman at Home, A; Women on the Move

Cast: Jordan Church; Randi Cooper; Donald Fish; Bill Goodman; Michelle McDermott; Tony Rossi; Nicole Sislian; Sarah Laine Terrell

2677 • MADWOMAN OF CENTRAL PARK WEST, THE

OPENED: 06/13/1979 Theatre: 22 Steps
Revue Broadway: 86

Librettist: Arthur Laurents; Phyllis Newman
Producer: Fritz Holt; Gladys Rackmil
Director: Arthur Laurents

Costumes: Theoni V. Aldredge; **Lighting Designer:** Ken Billington; **Musical Director:** Herbert Kaplan; **Orchestrations:** John Clifton; **Set Design:** Philipp Jung

Songs: (It's Not Easy) Bein' Green [7] (C/L: Joe Raposo); Better (C/L: Ed Kleban); Cheerleader (C: John Kander; L: Fred Ebb); Come in from the Rain [8] (C: Melissa Manchester; L: Carole Bayer Sager); Copacabana [4] (C/L: Jack Feldman; Barry Manilow; Bruce Sussman); Don't Laugh [3] (C: Mary Rodgers; L: Stephen Sondheim); Don't Wish (C: Peter Allen; L: Carole Bayer Sager); It Was Just One of Those Things [9] (C/L: Cole Porter); List Song (C: John Clifton; L: Phyllis Newman); Married I Can Always Get [11] (C/L: Gordon Jenkins); My Mother Was a Fortune Teller (C: John Clifton; L: Phyllis Newman); My New Friends (C/L: Leonard Bernstein); No One's Toy [10] (C/L: Joe Raposo); Some People [5] (C: Jule Styne; L: Stephen Sondheim); Tiny Feet (The Princess of the Disco Rio Bamba) [8] (C: Herb Kaplan; L: Arthur Laurents; Phyllis Newman); Up, Up, Up (C: Leonard Bernstein; L: Betty Comden; Adolph Green); Wait Till You See Her [6] (C: Richard Rodgers; L: Lorenz Hart); What Makes Me Love Him [2] (C: Sheldon Harnick; L: Jerry Bock); You And I Are Changing Too [8] (C/L: Unknown)

Cast: Phyllis Newman

Notes: First produced under the title MY MOTHER WAS A FORTUNE TELLER at the Hudson Guild Theatre where it opened on April 26, 1978 and played 24 performances. The show moved to Broadway under its new title and ran 86 performances. There was also a medley of "woman" songs arranged by Glen Roven. Cut prior to Broadway was a Carmen Miranda medley and a fragment of "Puffy Daddy Blues." [1] Cut prior to Broadway opening. [2] From THE APPLE TREE. [3] From HOT SPOT. [4] Not written for show. [5] From GYPSY. Cut prior to Broadway opening. [6] From BY JUPITER. Cut prior to Broadway opening. [7] From TV show SESAME STREET. Cut prior to Broadway opening. [8] Not written for show. Cut prior to Broadway opening. [9] Written for JUBILEE. Cut prior to Broadway opening. [10] From the film RAGGEDY ANN AND ANDY. [11] From written for the score of MANHATTAN TOWER.

2678 • MADWOMAN OF CHAILLOT, THE

Musical Unproduced

Composer: Claibe Richardson
Lyricist: Kenward Elmslie
Producer: Richard Barr; Clinton Wilder

Source: MADWOMAN OF CHAILLOT, THE (Play: Jean Anouilh)

Songs: Richest Man in the World, The

Cast: Lotte Lenya

Notes: Written in the 1960's. No song list available.

2679 • MAGDALENA

OPENED: 09/20/1948 Theatre: Ziegfeld
Musical Broadway: 88

Composer: Heitor Villa-Lobos
Lyricist: George Forrest; Robert Wright
Librettist: Frederick Hazlett Brennan; Homer Curran
Producer: Homer Curran; L.A. Civic Light Opera
Director: Jules Dassin

Choreographer: Jack Cole; **Costumes:** Irene Sharaff; **Lighting Designer:** Howard Bay; **Musical Director:** Arthur Kay; **Set Design:** Howard Bay

Songs: Bon Soir, Paris; Broken Bus, The; Broken Pianolita, The [1]; Children, The; Chivor Dance (dance); Civilized People, The; Come to Colombia; Emerald, The; Food for Thought; Forbidden Orchard, The; Freedom!; Greeting [1]; Lost; Magdelena; My Bus and I; Omen Bird (Teru, Teru), The; Peteca!; Piece de Resistance; Plan It by the Planets; River Song; Seed of God, The; Singing Tree, The; Travel, Travel, Travel; Vals de Espana; Women Weaving

Cast: Hugo Haas; Matt Mattox; Irra Petina; John Raitt; Dorothy Sarnoff

Notes: [1] Cut after opening.

2680 • MAGGIE

OPENED: 02/18/1953   Theatre: National
Musical   Broadway: 5

Composer: William Roy
Lyricist: William Roy
Librettist: Hugh Thomas
Producer: John Fearnley; Franklin Gilbert
Director: Michael Gordon

Source: WHAT EVERY WOMAN KNOWS (Play: James Barrie); **Choreographer:** June Graham; **Costumes:** Raoul Pene du Bois; **Dance Arranger:** Dean Fuller; **Lighting Designer:** Peggy Clark; **Musical Director:** Maurice Levine; **Orchestrations:** Don Walker; **Set Design:** Raoul Pene du Bois

Songs: Any Afternoon about Five; Charm; Fun in the Country; He's the Man; I Never Laughed in My Life; It's Only Thirty Years; Long and Weary Wait; My Mind's on You [1]; New Me, The; People in Love; Practical; Smile for Me; Thimbleful; Train with the Cushioned Seats, The; What Every Woman Knows; You Become Me

Cast: Keith Andes; James Broderick; Bramwell Fletcher; Celia Lipton; Frank Maxwell; Odette Myrtil; Betty Paul; Marc Platt

Notes: [1] Sheet music only.

2681 • MAGGIE FLYNN

OPENED: 10/23/1968   Theatre: ANTA
Musical   Broadway: 81

Composer: Luigi Creatore; Hugo Peretti; George David Weiss

Lyricist: Luigi Creatore; Hugo Peretti; George David Weiss
Librettist: Luigi Creatore; Hugo Peretti; George David Weiss
Producer: John Bowab
Director: Morton Da Costa

Choreographer: Brian MacDonald; **Costumes:** W. Robert LaVine; **Dance Arranger:** Trude Rittman; **Lighting Designer:** Tharon Musser; **Musical Director:** John Lesko; **Orchestrations:** Philip J. Lang; **Set Design:** Jean Eckart; William Eckart; **Vocal Arranger:** John Lesko

Songs: Don't You Think It's Very Nice?; Fill, Fill, Fill Our Little Basket [2]; Game of War, The; Homeless Children [2]; How About a Ball?; I Won't Let It Happen Again; I Wouldn't Have You Any Other Way; It Works! [2]; Learn How to Laugh; Let's Drink to That [2]; Look Around Your Little World; Maggie Flynn; Mr. Clown; Pitter, Patter; Riot, The (dance); Thank You Song, The; They're Never Gonna Make Me Fight; Walkin' My Dog on Christopher Street [1]; What Does He Think? [1]; Why Can't I Walk Away?

Cast: Jack Cassidy; Shirley Jones; Robert Kaye; Stanley Simmonds

Notes: [1] Not in program. [2] Added to Equity Library Theatre revival.

2682 • MAGGIE MAY

OPENED: 09/22/1964   Theatre: Adelphi
Musical   London: 501

Composer: Lionel Bart
Lyricist: Lionel Bart
Librettist: Alun Owen
Producer: Tom Arnold; Bernard Delfont
Director: Ted Kotchoff

Choreographer: Paddy Stone; **Costumes:** Leslie Hurry; **Musical Director:** Marcus Dods; **Set Design:** Sean Kenny

Songs: Away from Home; Ballad of the Liver Bird; Carryin' On; Casey; Dey Don't Do Dat T'day; I Love a Man; I Told You So; I'm Me; It's Yourself; Land of Promises, The; Leave Her, Johnny, Leave Her; Lullaby; Maggie, Maggie May; Right of Way; Shine You Shine; Stroll On; There's Only One Union; We Don't

All Wear D'Same Size Boots; World's a Lovely Place, The

Cast: Malcolm Collingham; Marie Conmee; Margo Cunningham; Janet Gail; Kenneth Haigh; Charlotte Howard; Margaret Howe; Barry Humphries; Andrew Keir; Julia McKenzie; Vernon Rees; Rachel Roberts; Stephen Taylor; Janet Webb

2683 • MAGIC KNIGHT, THE
Notes: *See DREAM CITY.*

2684 • MAGIC MELODY, THE
OPENED: 11/11/1919   Theatre: Shubert
Musical   Broadway: 143

Composer: Sigmund Romberg
Lyricist: Frederic Arnold Kummer
Librettist: J. Clifford Brooke; Frederic Arnold Kummer
Producer: Sigmund Romberg; Max Wilner
Director: J. Clifford Brooke; J.C. Huffman

Choreographer: Allan K. Foster; **Costumes:** Willy Pogany; **Musical Director:** Charles Previn; **Orchestrations:** Oscar Radin; **Set Design:** Willy Pogany

Songs: Come and Dance with Me; Dance; Dance Eccentric [1]; Dance Orientale [1]; Dance Vampire; Down on the Nile; Dream Girl, Give Back My Dream to Me; Finale Act I; Gianina; Honeymoon Land [1] (C: E. Hussar; Sigmund Romberg; L: Alex Gerber); I Am the Pasha; Lips, Lips, Lips; Little Church Around the Corner, The (L: Alex Gerber); Love Makes the World Go 'Round; Melody of Dance (L: Alex Gerber); Night of Love; Once Upon a Time (The Magic Melody); Opening Act I; Opening Chorus Act II; There Are No Lips So Sweet As Yours [1]; Three Trees, The [2] (C/L: Tom McNaughton); Two's Company, Three's a Crowd; We Are the Fixers; We Take It Just Take It from You (L: Alex Gerber); When You're in Right with the Right Little Girl [2]; You Know and I Know [1] (L: Alex Gerber)

Cast: Flavia Acaro; Fay Marbe; Aileen Poe; Charles Purcell

Notes: [1] Sheet music only. [2] Out Boston 3/15/20.

2685 • MAGIC NUTCRACKER, THE
OPENED: 1961
Musical

Composer: Sol Kaplan
Lyricist: Edward Eliscu

Songs: Pillow Magic; Puffed Up Proud; When I'm Dancing; Your Hand in Mine

Notes: No other information available.

2686 • MAGIC RING, THE
OPENED: 10/01/1923   Theatre: Liberty
Musical   Broadway: 96

Composer: Harold Levey
Lyricist: Zelda Sears
Librettist: Zelda Sears
Producer: Henry W. Savage
Director: Ira Hards

Choreographer: David Bennett; **Costumes:** Adrian; **Lighting Designer:** Joseph Wilson; **Musical Director:** Harold Levey; **Set Design:** Adrian

Songs: Abdullah's Farewell; Broken Hearts; Chant; Deep in Someone's Heart; Education; Famous Falls; Finale Act II; Gate of Dreams, The [1]; Hand Organ, The [1]; Imaginative Opera; Keepsakes; Love Song, The; Malaiya; Play the Game and Smile [1]; Poor Relations [1]; Self-Expression [1]; When I Walk with Minnie [1]; When the Organ Plays

Cast: Sydney Greenstreet; Jeanette MacDonald; Joseph Macaulay; Mitzi

Notes: Originally titled MINNIE AND ME. [1] Sheet music only under title MINNIE AND ME.

2687 • MAGIC SHOW, THE
OPENED: 05/28/1974   Theatre: Cort
Musical   Broadway: 1859

Composer: Stephen Schwartz
Lyricist: Stephen Schwartz
Librettist: Bob Randall
Producer: Joseph Beruh; Edgar Lansbury; Ivan Reitman
Director: Grover Dale

Choreographer: Grover Dale; **Costumes:** Randy Barcelo; **Dance Arranger:** David Spangler; **Lighting Designer:** Richard Nelson; **Musical Director:** Stephen Reinhardt; **Set Design:** David Chapman

Songs: Before Your Very Eyes; Bit of Villainy, A; Charmin's Lament; Goldfarb Variations, The; Lion Tamer; Solid Silver Platform Shoes; Style; Sweet, Sweet, Sweet; Two's Company; Up to His Old Tricks; West End Avenue

Cast: Doug Henning; Robert LuPone; Annie McGreevey; Anita Morris; David Ogden Stiers

2688 • MAGNIFICENT CHRISTMAS SPECTACULAR, THE (1979)

OPENED: 1979   Theatre: Radio City Music Hall

Revue   Broadway

Songs: Sing a Little Song of Christmas (C: Don Pippin; L: Carolyn Leigh)

Notes: No other information available.

2689 • MAGNIFICENT CHRISTMAS SPECTACULAR, THE (1985)

OPENED: 11/15/1985   Theatre: Radio City Music Hall

Revue   Broadway: 120

Producer: Robert F. Jani
Director: Robert F. Jani

Choreographer: Violet Holmes; Linda Lemac; Marilyn Magness; **Costumes:** Frank Spencer; **Lighting Designer:** Ken Billington; **Musical Director:** Bo Ayers; **Orchestrations:** Elman Anderson; Robert M. Freedman; Michael Gibson; Don Harper; Arthur Harris; Bob Krogstad; Philip J. Lang; **Set Design:** Charles Lisanby

Songs: Christmas in New York (C: Stanley Lebowsky; L: Billy Butt); My First Real Christmas (C: Don Pippin; L: Nan Mason); They Can't Start Christmas Without Us (C: Stanley Lebowsky; L: Fred Tobias); T'was the Night Before Christmas (C/L: Tom Bahler)

Cast: Ann-Marie Blake; Bradley Latham; Stacy Latham; Edward Prostak; Rockettes, The; Thomas Ruisinger

Notes: There were also several traditional Christmas songs used.

2690 • MAGNOLIA

OPENED: 1926
Musical

Composer: C. Luckeyth Roberts; Alex Rogers
Lyricist: Alex Rogers
Librettist: Alex Rogers

Choreographer: Charley Davis

Cast: Paul Bass; Percy Colston; Lionel Monagas; Hilda Rogers; Dink Stewart

Notes: No other information available.

2691 • MAGNOLIA LADY, THE

OPENED: 11/25/1924   Theatre: Shubert
Musical   Broadway: 49

Composer: Harold A. Levey
Lyricist: Anne Caldwell
Librettist: Anne Caldwell
Producer: Henry Miller
Director: Hassard Short

Source: COME OUT OF THE KITCHEN (Play: Alice Duer Miller; A.E. Thomas); **Choreographer:** Julian Alfred; Chester Hale; **Costumes:** Charles LeMaire; W.H. Matthews; **Musical Director:** Harold A. Levey; **Orchestrations:** Robert Russell Bennett; **Set Design:** William Castle

Songs: A la Gastronome; Djinn of Algazam [1]; French Lesson, The; I Will Be Good; Liza Jane; Magic Hour, The; Moon Man; My Heart's in the Sunny South; Old Fashioned Irish Stew [1]; Old Red Gate, The; On the Washington Train; Phantoms of the Ballroom; Thank You Kindly Sir [1]; Three Little Girls; Tiger Lily Lou; When the Bell Goes Ting-A-Ling-Ling; When Whiteman Starts to Play

Cast: Ruth Chatterton; Ralph Forbes; Skeets Gallagher; Muriel Stryker; Minor Watson

Notes: [1] Out Washington D.C. 11/9/24.

2692 • MAHALIA

OPENED: 05/31/1978
Musical   Off-Broadway: 14

Composer: John Lewis
Lyricist: Don Evans
Librettist: Don Evans
Producer: Carousel Group, Inc.; Lucy Productions Corp.
Director: Oz Scott

Source: JUST MAHALIA BABY (Unknown: Laurraine Goreau); **Choreographer:** Mabel Robinson; **Costumes:** Beverly Parks; **Lighting Designer:** Victor En Yu Tan; **Musical Director:** Luther Henderson; **Set Design:** Richard Williams; **Vocal Arranger:** Brenda Fountain Saunders

Songs: Chi-Town Strut; Don't You Start Me Talking; Home Folks Theme; I'd Always Be There; Negotiation; One More Chance; Strait and Narrow; Time to Think of Yourself; Wedding

Cast: Nat Adderley; Loretta Devine; Esther Marrow; Chuck Patterson

Notes: Based on the life of Mahalia Jackson. Only original songs listed.

2693 • MAID AND MULE

OPENED: 1906
Musical

Composer: Sam Rice
Lyricist: Sam Rice

Songs: Hee Haw

Notes: No other information available.

2694 • MAID AND THE MILLIONAIRE, THE

OPENED: 06/22/1907   Theatre: Madison Square
                                    Garden Roof
Musical   Broadway: 72

Composer: Frederic Chapin
Lyricist: Frederic Chapin
Librettist: Frederic Chapin
Producer: Mortimer M. Theise

Cast: Charles Burke; John C. Hart; Lily Hart; Henry Linkey; Fred Wyckoff

Notes: No other information available.

2695 • MAID AND THE MUMMY, THE

OPENED: 07/25/1904   Theatre: New York
Musical   Broadway: 42

Composer: Robert Hood Bowers
Lyricist: Richard Carle
Librettist: Richard Carle
Producer: Richard Carle
Director: Richard Carle

Choreographer: Adolph Newberger; **Costumes:** Archie Gunn; **Musical Director:** Robert Hood Bowers; **Set Design:** D. Frank Dodge

Songs: Dame Rumor [4]; Finale Act I; Flo; I Fell in Love with Polly (C: Richard Carle); I'm So Dizzy (C: Richard Carle); It's Great to Be Crazy; Letters [2]; Lion and the Lamb, The [4]; Maggie Got Another Situation [3]; My Egyptian Queen; My Gasoline Automobile; No Doubt You'd Like to Cuddle Up to Baby [4]; Opening Chorus; Opening Chorus Act II; Opening Chorus Act III; Peculiar Julia (C: Richard Carle); Poster Specialty [1]; Sad Experience; Sales Lady, The; Whenever I Visit the Town [1]

Cast: May Boley; Richard Carle; Violet Dale; Edward Garvie; Fred Lennox; Edgar Norton; Janet Priest; Adele Rowland; John Slavin; Annie Yeamans

Notes: [1] Out 7/10/04 Chicago. [2] Also in MARY'S LAMB. [3] Sheet music only. [4] Vocal score only.

2696 • MAID IN AMERICA

OPENED: 02/18/1915   Theatre: Winter Garden
Revue   Broadway: 108

Composer: Harry Carroll; Sigmund Romberg
Lyricist: Harold Atteridge
Librettist: Harold Atteridge
Producer: Winter Garden Company
Director: J.C. Huffman

Choreographer: Jack Mason; **Costumes:** Melville Ellis; **Musical Director:** Oscar Radin; **Set Design:** H. Robert Law

Songs: Ain't That Always the Way [2]; At the Fox Trot Ball [1]; Blarney Castle Walk [3]; Castles in the Air; Dancing Around the U.S.A. (C: Harry Carroll; George L. Cobb; L: Jack Yellen); Diana (C: Sigmund Romberg); Dr. Baltimore M.D. [5] (C: Otto Motzan; L: Schuyler Greene); Everyone's Moving Up Town (Everyone's Moving Up on Broadway); Garden of Paradise (C: Sigmund Romberg); Girlie from the Cabaret, The (C: Sigmund Romberg); Ha, Ha, Ha; Have a Restaurant of Your Own; Here's a Bale of Cotton for You (C: Harry Carroll); If You Ever Come Down to Virginia There'll Be Nothing too Good for You [4] (C: Albert Gumble; L: A. Seymour Brown); I'm Looking for Someone's Heart (C: Sigmund Romberg); I'm 'Lord Knows Who' [2]; It Is All for You (C: Sigmund Romberg); I've Been Floating Down the Old Green River [3] (C: Joe Cooper; L: Bert Kalmar); Let's Bungalow [2]; Made in the U.S.A. (C: Harry Carroll); Manhattan Mad (C: Sigmund Romberg); Marc Antony [2] (C: Sigmund Romberg); Mr. Tosti Goodbye [2]; Oh, Those Days (C: Sigmund Romberg); Olympian Glide, The; (It Is All for You) Only for You [3] (C: Sigmund Romberg); Ragtime Dinner Order, The [2]; Rathskeller Trio, The [2]; Sister Susie's Started Syncopation (C: Sigmund Romberg); Stolen Melody, The (C: Nora Bayes; L: Phil Schwartz); Suzi Ann [1]; There Was a Time (C: Harry Carroll); There's a Little Bit of Everything on Broadway (C/L: Leo Edwards); Times Square Arguments, The; Typical Opening Chorus, The; When Grandma Was a Girl; Where My Caravan Rests [2]; (If You Want a Little Doggie) Whistle and I'll Come to You [4] (C: Leo Edwards; L: Blanche Merrill); You Can't Get Away from Tipperary [1]

Cast: Nora Bayes; Lew Brice; Harry Carroll; Mlle. Dazie; Yancsi Dolly; Hal Forde; Harry Fox; Joe Jackson; Blossom Seeley; Yvette

Notes: [1] Out Wilmington 1/26/16. [2] Out Buffalo 2/1/15. [3] Not in program. [4] Sheet music only. [5] ASCAP/Library of Congress.

2697 • MAID MARIAN

OPENED: 01/27/1902   Theatre: Garden
Musical   Broadway: 64

Composer: Reginald De Koven
Lyricist: Harry B. Smith
Librettist: Harry B. Smith
Producer: Bostonians, The
Director: Herbert Gresham

Musical Director: Samuel L. Studley

Songs: Annabel Was Fairest; Callarer's Toast, The; Can I Forget; Cobbler and the Flies, The; Crusaders March, The; Dew Lies on the Heather, The; Entrance of Sheriff; Farewell to the Forest; Finale Act I; Finale Act II; Finale Act III; Forester's Song, The; Ho for the Greenwood; If You Were I and I Were You; If You Were I and I Were You; Love May Come and Love May Go; Madrigal; Magpie, The; Mistletoe Bough, The; Monk and the Magpie, The; Never in the Wide, Wide World; Opening Chorus; Opening Chorus Act II; Popular Tune, A; Saracen Patrol, The; Sherrif's Song; Snake Charmer's Song; Song of the Crusader; Song of the Falcon; Tell Me Again, Sweetheart; True Love Is Not for a Day; Under the Mistletoe Bough

Cast: Henry Clay Barnabee; Josephine Bartlett; George B. Frothingham; W.H. MacDonald; Albert Parr; Adele Rafter; Grace Van Studdiford

Notes: No songs listed in program.

2698 • MAID OF THE MOUNTAINS, THE

OPENED: 09/11/1918   Theatre: Casino
Musical   Broadway: 37

Composer: Harold Fraser-Simpson
Lyricist: Harry Graham
Librettist: Frederick Lonsdale
Producer: F. Ray Comstock; William Elliott; Morris Gest
Director: J.A.E. Malone

Source: UNKNOWN (Play: Frederick Lonsdale); **Choreographer:** Bert French; **Costumes:** Dazian; Schneider & Anderson; **Musical Director:** John McGhee; **Set Design:** Unitt & Wickes

Songs: Anyone Else but You [2]; Bachelor Gay, A (C: James W. Tate; L: Clifford Harris; Arthur Valentine); Dirty Work; Dividing the Spoils; Farewell; For Many a Year; Friends Have to Part; Friendship and Love [1]; Good People Gather Round; Governor of the State; Husbands and Wives; I Don't Care; I Understood; If Love Is There [2]; Live for Today; Love Will Find a Way; My Life Is Love (C: James W. Tate; L: Clifford Harris; Arthur Valentine); New Moon [3] (C: Merlin Morgan; L: Unknown); Over There and Over Here; Paradise for Two, A (C: James

W. Tate; L: Clifford Harris; Arthur Valentine);
Save Us; Through Curs May Quail; Waiting for
You (C: Gitz Rice; L: Marc Connelly); We're
Gathered Here; When Each Day; When You're in
Love (C: James W. Tate; L: Clifford Harris;
Arthur Valentine)

Cast: William Courtenay; William Danforth;
Sidonie Espero; Gertrude Hamilton; John Steel

Notes: No program available. The source was an
unproduced play. This show played 1,352
performances in London. [1] Listed in vocal
selection as a "Supplemental Number." It was
added after the London opening. [2] Cut prior to
London opening. [3] Added after London
opening.

2699 • MAID TO LOVE
Notes: *See THE RIGHT GIRL.*

2700 • MAIDEN VOYAGE
OPENED: 1926
Musical   Closed out of town

Composer: Carey Morgan
Lyricist: Arthur Swanstrom
Librettist: Paul Gerard Smith
Producer: Ned Wayburn
Director: Ned Wayburn

Songs: Honeymoon Cruise, A; Hot Patootie Land;
I Am Angling for You; I Want You; Just One
More Waltz with You; Oui! Oui!; Pango Moon;
Persian Skies; Pompadour; Rain! Rain! Rain!;
Whole World's Doing It Now Charleston

2701 • MAIDS OF ATHENS
OPENED: 02/19/1914   Theatre: New Amsterdam
Musical   Broadway: 22

Composer: Franz Lehar
Lyricist: Carolyn Wells
Librettist: Carolyn Wells
Director: George Marion

Source: DIE IDEALE GATTIN (Musical: Franz
Lehar; Victor Leon; Leo Stein); **Musical Director:**
John McGhie

Songs: Ah, Yes, I Am in Love; Bid Me Forget;
Brigand's Chorus, The; Clever Detective, The
(C: Charles J. Anditzer); Finale Act I; Finale Act

III; Finale-Prologue; Girl He Couldn't Kiss, The;
Heavenly Ladies; Life Is Lonely; Nurse, Nurse,
Nurse; One or Another (C: Oscar Haase); Our
Glorious Stripes and Stars (C/L: Frederick
Norton); Waltz, You Siren of Melody; When the
Heart Is Young

Cast: Bert Gilbert; Leila Hughes; Albert Pellaton;
W.S. Percy

2702 • MAIL
OPENED: 04/14/1988   Theatre: Music Box
Musical   Broadway: 36

Composer: Michael Rupert
Lyricist: Jerry Colker
Librettist: Jerry Colker
Producer: ANTA; Susan Dietz; Michael Frazier;
Kennedy Center, The; Stephen Wells
Director: Andrew Cadiff

Choreographer: Grover Dale; **Costumes:** William
Ivey Long; **Dance Arranger:** Tom Fay; **Lighting
Designer:** Richard Nelson; **Musical Director:**
Tom Fay; **Orchestrations:** Michael Gibson; **Set
Design:** Vicki Baral; Gerry Hariton

Songs: Ambivalent Rag; Blank Piece of Paper, A;
Cookin' with Steam (C: Brian Mitchell; Michael
Rupert; L: Jerry Colker); Crazy World;
Disconnected; Don't Count on It; Family Ties;
Friends for Life; Gone So Long; Helplessness at
Midnight; Hit the Ground Running; It's Getting
Harder to Love You; It's Just a Question of
Technique; It's None of My Business; It's Your
Life; Junk Mail; Monolithic Madness; One Lost
Weekend; One Step at a Time; Pages of My
Diary; Publish Your Book; Sweepstakes;
Twenty-Nine Years Ago; We're Gonna Turn Off
Your Juice; What Have You Been Doing for the
Past Ten Years; Where Are You/Where Am I?;
World Set on Fire By a Black and a Jew, The; You
Better Get Outta Town

Cast: Antonia Ellis; Mara Getz; Robert Mandan;
Brian Mitchell; Michael Rupert

2703 • MAIN STREET
Musical   Unproduced

Composer: Michael Kessler
Lyricist: Michael Kessler; Greer Sucke
Librettist: Greer Sucke

Source: OUR TOWN (Play: Thornton Wilder)

Songs: Can You Hear the Morning? (L: Greer Sucke); Five More Hours (L: Michael Kessler); Hey, Star; Homework (L: Michael Kessler); Joe Crowell (L: Greer Sucke); May 7th, 1901 (L: Greer Sucke); Quiet Road to Sundown (L: Greer Sucke)

Cast: Richard Chrisman; Ellen Fitzhugh; Larry French; Joseph Kolinski; Jeanne Lehman; Lenny Wolpe

Notes: Information from program of a reading.

2704 • MAJESTIC KID, THE

OPENED: 12/01/1988   Theatre: St. Peter's
                                        Church
Play   Off-Broadway: 54

Composer: Jan Scarbrough
Lyricist: Mark Medoff; Jan Scarbrough
Author: Mark Medoff
Producer: Golden Glow Unlimited, Ltd.
Director: Derek Wolshonak

Costumes: Debra Stein; Lighting Designer: Scott Pinkney; Set Design: Lewis Folden

Cast: Eliza Berry; Michael Cullen; Juliette Kurth; Rande Mele; Kay Wallbye; Alex Wipf; Stuart Zagnit

Notes: No songs listed in program.

2705 • MAKE A WISH

OPENED: 04/18/1951   Theatre: Winter Garden
Musical   Broadway: 102

Composer: Hugh Martin
Lyricist: Hugh Martin
Librettist: Preston Sturges
Producer: Alexander H. Cohen; Harry Rigby; Jule Styne
Director: John C. Wilson

Source: GOOD FAIRY, THE (A JO TUNDER) (Play: Ferenc Molnar); Choreographer: Gower Champion; Costumes: Raoul Pene du Bois; Dance Arranger: Richard Pribor; Musical Director: Milton Rosenstock; Orchestrations: Philip J. Lang; Allan Small; Set Design: Raoul Pene du Bois; Vocal Arranger: Hugh Martin

Songs: Dirty Pitchers, Dirty Books [4]; Hello, Hello, Hello; I Lost You [4]; I Only Meant [4]; I Wanna Be Good 'n' Bad; I'll Never Make a Frenchman Out of You (L: Timothy Gray); Janette [1]; Kip [4]; Make a Wish (L: Timothy Gray); One I Need, The; Over and Over; Paris, France; Patisserie, The [3]; Rainbow's End [4]; Sale, The (ballet); She's Not in a Class with You [6]; Students Ball (We're Havin' a Ball); Suits Me Fine [5]; Take Me Back to Texas with You [2] (L: Timothy Gray); That Face!; There's Music in the Metro [4]; Time Step, The; Toast, The [4]; Tonight You Are in Paree; Tour Must Go On, The; Vive the USA [1]; Weather's in Your Eyes, The [4]; What I Was Warned About; When Does This Feeling Go Away?; Who Am I [4]; Who Gives a Sou; You're Lovely Love [4]

Cast: Melville Cooper; Stephen Douglass; Nanette Fabray; Helen Gallagher; Harold Lang; Phil Leeds

Notes: Vocal direction: Buster Davis. [1] Out New Haven 3/12/51. [2] Title and concept by Leo Robin. [3] Cut prior to opening. [4] Not used. [5] Music based on theme written for "Grandma Moses Suite." [6] Dropped after final dress rehearsal prior to opening.

2706 • MAKE IT SNAPPY

OPENED: 04/13/1922   Theatre: Winter Garden
Musical   Broadway: 96

Composer: Jean Schwartz
Lyricist: Harold Atteridge
Librettist: Harold Atteridge
Producer: Winter Garden Company
Director: J.C. Huffman

Choreographer: Allan K. Foster; Costumes: Cora MacGeachy; Musical Director: Louis Gress; Orchestrations: J. Dell Lampe; Set Design: Watson Barratt

Songs: Blossom Time (L: Alfred Bryan); Bouquet of Girls; Butterfly on the Wheel; Cheeky Kiki (C/L: William B. Friedlander); Desert Rose; Doing the Eddie Cantor [2]; Don't Don't Stop Loving Me Now [4] (C: James F. Hanley; L: Joe Goodwin; Murray Roth); Flapper, The; Gay Butterfly (on the Wheel); Good-Bye Main Street; He Was the Only Man I Ever Loved (C/L: William B. Friedlander); Hootch Rhythm (L: Alfred Bryan); Humoresquimos; I Learned About Women from Her [1]; I Love Her-She Loves Me [2] (C/L:

Irving Caesar; L: Eddie Cantor); I'll Be in My Dixie Home Again Tomorrow [2] (C: J. Russel Robinson; L: Roy Turk); I'm Hungry for Beautiful Girls [4] (C: Fred Fisher; L: Wilbur Held; Billy Rose); I'm Wild About Wild Men [2] (L: Alfred Bryan); Jazza Painted Jazza Ma Renos [2] (L: Alfred Bryan); Lamplight Land; Little Rover (Don't Forget to Come Back Home) [2] (C: Walter Donaldson; L: Gus Kahn); (Tell Me What's the Matter) Loveable Eyes; Lovin' Sam the Sheik of Alabam' [3] (C: Milton Ager; L: Jack Yellen); My Beautiful Fragonard Girl (L: Alfred Bryan); My Castilian Girl; My Vision in Vermillion [2] (L: Alfred Bryan); My Yiddishe Mammy [2] (C: Jean Schwartz; L: Eddie Cantor; Alex Gerber); Seven or Eleven, My Dixie Pair o' Dice [3] (C: Walter Donaldson; L: Lew Brown); Sheik of Araby, The (C: Ted Snyder; L: Harry B. Smith; Francis Wheeler); Sophie [2] (C/L: Abner Silver); To Make Them Beautiful Ladies; Tomorrow [2] (C/L: J. Russel Robinson); Waikiki, I Hear You Calling Me [4] (C: Harry Ruby; L: Bert Kalmar); Wedding Ring Don't Mean a Thing When You're Married, The [4] (C/L: Eddie Cantor; Fred Fisher); When the Wedding Chimes Are Ringing; Where the Bamboo Babies Grow [2] (C: Walter Donaldson; L: Lew Brown); Won't You Buy a Flower?

Cast: Eddie Cantor; Georgie Hale; Nan Halperin; Lew Hearn; J. Harold Murray; Tot Qualters

Notes: [1] Lyrics based on Rudyard Kipling poem. [2] Sheet music only. [3] Not in program. [4] ASCAP/Library of Congress only.

2707 • MAKE MINE MANHATTAN

OPENED: 01/15/1948   Theatre: Broadhurst
Revue   Broadway: 429

Composer: Richard Lewine
Lyricist: Arnold B. Horwitt
Librettist: Arnold B. Horwitt
Producer: Joseph Hyman
Director: Max Liebman; Hassard Short

Choreographer: Lee Sherman; **Costumes:** Morton Haack; **Lighting Designer:** Hassard Short; **Musical Director:** Jerry Arlen; Charles Sanford; **Orchestrations:** Ted Royal; **Set Design:** Frederick Fox

Songs: Anything Can Happen in New York; Gentleman Friend; Glad to Be Back; Good Old

Days, The (L: Ted Fetter; Arnold B. Horwitt); I Don't Know Her Name; I Fell in Love with You; Movie House in Manhattan; My Brudder and Me; Night Out, A; Noises in the Street (L: Peter Barry; David Greggory; Arnold B. Horwitt); Phil the Fiddler; Ringalevio; Saturday Night in Central Park; Schrafft's; Subway Song; Take It Back, We're Through [1]; Talk to Me

Cast: Sheila Bond; David Burns; Sid Caesar; Danny Daniels; Nelle Fisher; Bob Fosse; Kyle MacDonnell; Joshua Shelley; Max Showalter

Notes: [1] Cut prior to opening.

2708 • MAKE YOURSELF AT HOME

OPENED: 10/09/1917
Revue   Broadway: 32

Producer: Arthur Hammerstein

Songs: Make Yourself at Home (C: Silvio Hein; L: Oscar Hammerstein II)

Notes: No other information available.

2709 • MAKING MARY (1931)

OPENED: 03/01/1931
Musical   Closed out of town

Composer: Harold Lewis
Lyricist: Harold Orlob
Librettist: Grace Johnson; Harold Orlob
Producer: Gordon-Lennox
Director: Edward Clarke Lilley

Choreographer: John Boyle; **Costumes:** Goggie; **Set Design:** Robert Adams Reamer

Cast: Will Ahern; Audrey Christie; William Frawley; June Mantell; Lou Parker

Notes: Program of Washington, D.C. used. No songs listed in program.

2710 • MAMA'S BABY BOY

OPENED: 05/25/1912   Theatre: Broadway
Musical   Broadway: 9

Composer: Will H. Becker; Hans Linne
Lyricist: Will H. Becker; Junie McCree

Librettist: Junie McCree
Producer: George W. Lederer

Source: MRS. BLACK IS BACK (Play: George V. Hobart); **Choreographer:** Julian Alfred; **Musical Director:** Hans Linne

Songs: Back from Thirty-Six to Twenty-Nine; Capital H; Cecelia; Demonstration Number; Every Coon; Finale Act I; Finale Act II; Finale Act III; Hysterical Tune; If the Man in the Moon Would Only Speak; Kitchen Cabaret, The; Lonegan; Opening Chorus Act I; Opening Chorus Act II; Opening Chorus Act II; Opening Chorus Act III; Quartette; Time Has Changed So Many Customs in the Last Decade; White Lies, Black Lies; White Man's Hope, The

Cast: Lew Dockstader; Albert Hart; Al Jolson; Anna Laughlin; Junie McCree; Grace Tyson

Notes: No program available.

2711 • MAMA'S PAPA
OPENED: 02/01/1905
Musical   Closed out of town

Composer: A. Baldwin Sloane
Lyricist: Joseph Hart
Librettist: Joseph Hart
Producer: William A. Brady

Songs: Fate of the Sailor, The; Fighting for U.S.A.; Four O'Clock on Broadway; Jane, Jane, Jane; Jess and Jamie; Misfit Family, The; My Blushing Rose; My Filipino Belle; On the Choo Choo Cars; Puff, Puff, Puff; Rowing, Rowing; Song of Plays; Two Sides to a Story; What Did the Woggle Bug Say?

Cast: Maurice Darcy; Carrie DeMar; Ferral Desmond; Joseph Hart

Notes: Grand Opera House, Salem Mass.

2712 • MAMBA'S DAUGHTERS
OPENED: 01/03/1939   Theatre: Empire
Play   Broadway: 162

Author: Dorothy Heyward; DuBose Heyward
Producer: Guthrie McClintic
Director: Guthrie McClintic

Source: MAMBA'S DAUGHTERS (Novel: DuBose Heyward); **Orchestrations:** Hans Spialek; **Set Design:** Perry Watkins; **Vocal Arranger:** Reginald Beane

Songs: Lonesome Walls (C: Jerome Kern; L: DuBose Heyward)

Cast: Willie Bryant; Alberta Hunter; J. Rosamond Johnson; Canada Lee; Fredi Washington; Ethel Waters

2713 • MAME
OPENED: 05/24/1966   Theatre: Winter Garden
Musical   Broadway: 1508

Composer: Jerry Herman
Lyricist: Jerry Herman
Librettist: Jerome Lawrence; Robert E. Lee
Producer: Lawrence Carr; Robert Fryer; Joseph P. Harris
Director: Gene Saks

Source: AUNTIE MAME (Play: Jerome Lawrence; Robert E. Lee); **Source:** AUNTIE MAME (Novel: Patrick Dennis); **Choreographer:** Onna White; **Costumes:** Robert Mackintosh; **Dance Arranger:** Roger Adams; **Lighting Designer:** Tharon Musser; **Musical Director:** Donald Pippin; **Orchestrations:** Philip J. Lang; **Set Design:** Jean Eckart; William Eckart; **Vocal Arranger:** Don Pippin

Songs: Bosom Buddies; Camouflage [1]; Fox Hunt, The; Fred Astaire [1]; Gooch's Song; If He Walked Into My Life; It's Today [4]; Letter, The [3]; Love Is Only Love [2]; Mame [3]; Man in the Moon, The; My Best Girl; Open a New Window; St. Bridget; Sterling Silver Boy [1]; That's How Young I Feel; We Need a Little Christmas

Cast: Beatrice Arthur; George Coe; Jane Connell; Jerry Lanning; Angela Lansbury; Frankie Michaels; Sab Shimono; Willard Waterman

Notes: [1] Cut prior to opening. [2] Cut prior to opening. Put in movie version of HELLO, DOLLY! [3] Same music. [4] Melody combines parts of "There Is No Tune Like a Show Tune (Show Tune in 2/4)" from NIGHTCAP and PARADE and "Only Love" from MADAME APHRODITE.

2714 • MAM'SELLE 'AWKINS
OPENED: 02/26/1900   Theatre: Victoria
Musical   Broadway: 35

Composer: Herman Perlet
Lyricist: Richard Carle
Librettist: Richard Carle
Producer: Alfred E. Aarons

Songs: Don't Believe a Tale Like That; Everybody Wondered Why He Knew (C: Howard Talbot); I'm Sorry Dat I Left My Happy Home (C/L: Irving Jones); Our Land of Dreams; Tin Gee-Gee, The [1]

Cast: Nellie Beaumont; Rose Beaumont; George Boniface Jr.; Richard Carle; Maude Creighton; Josephine Hall; Marguerita Sylva; Lawrence Wheat

Notes: No songs listed in program. [1] Sheet music only.

2715 • MAM'SELLE NAPOLEON
OPENED: 12/08/1903   Theatre: Knickerbocker
Musical   Broadway: 43

Composer: Gustav Luders
Lyricist: Joseph W. Herbert
Librettist: Joseph W. Herbert
Producer: Florenz Ziegfeld
Director: Joseph W. Herbert

Musical Director: Herman Perlet; **Set Design:** Ernest Albert

Songs: A la Mode Girl, The; All Hail, Guignol!; Art Cannot Improve the Rose; Art of Stimulation, The; Brava! Brava!; Brave Soldier Boy, The; Cockatoo and the Chimpanzee, The; Dearie (L: Rida Johnson Young); Everything Finds Its Way to Paris; For We Turn the Bull's Eye On; Glory of France, The; Hit Enormous; I'll Love You Then as Now; Language of Love, The; Le Lion et La Souris (The Lion and the Mouse); Le Rigodon; Life's No Blooming Airy Bubble; Long Live Folly; Love's Dream Is O'er [1]; My Heart Will Be True to You (Too-Whoo); Nymphs and the Satyr; On to Paris; Opening Chorus; Opening Chorus Act II; Opening Chorus Act III; Out with the Boys!; Prithee Gentle Echo [1]; Romance of the Laundry [1]; She's the Same Old Girl; Silas; Soft Zephyr; Song of the Grenadier; Stage and

Fashion Hand in Hand, The; Then As Now; You Will Need Them at Home Some Day [1]

Cast: Edna Goodrich; Anna Held; Joseph W. Herbert; Dan MacAvoy; Bessie McCoy; Nellie McCoy; Fletcher Norton

Notes: No N.Y. program available. Program used from Chicago 5/25/04. Dan McAvoy replaced Frank Moulan on the second night. [1] Sheet music only.

2716 • MAM'SELLE SALLIE
OPENED: 11/26/1906   Theatre: Grand Opera House
Musical   Broadway: 24

Composer: Raymond Hubbell
Lyricist: Harry B. Smith
Librettist: Harry B. Smith
Producer: John C. Fisher
Director: Charles H. Jones

Songs: And I Laughed; Day Dreams; Every Little Object Has a History; Farewell Prosperity [1] (C: Lester Keith; L: John Kemble); Her Portrait; Home, Sweet Home; Hurroo, Hurray and Hurrah for That [2]; I'm a Lawyer; It's Not the World, It's You [1]; La Danse Parisienne [1]; Life Is a See-Saw [2]; Mam'selle Sallie; Million, A; Parisienne; Sweet Girl Graduate, The; Thessaly; When My Ship Comes In; Whistle When You Walk Out [2]; You Never Told Me That Before We Married

Cast: Katie Barry; Wm. P. Carleton Jr.; Agnes Findlay; George E. Mack; Florence Quinn; John Slavin

Notes: This show was later rewritten and titled A KNIGHT FOR A DAY. [1] Sheet music only. [2] Later used in A KNIGHT FOR A DAY.

2717 • MAM'ZELLE CHAMPAGNE
OPENED: 06/25/1906   Theatre: Madison Square Garden Roof
Revue   Broadway: 60

Composer: Cassius Freeborn
Lyricist: Edgar Allen Woolf
Librettist: Edgar Allen Woolf
Producer: Henry Pincus
Director: Lionel Lawrence

Songs: Could I Fascinate You; Finale Act I; Finale Act II; Frog, The; Glorianna; I Could Love a Million Girls; I'm in Search of a Novelty; Land of Golden Dreams; Life; Lover's Lane; Moonlight, You and I; Never Again; Opening Chorus Act II; Peter Pan; Somewhere; Statue of Liberty; Tale of the Tadpole; That's Atmosphere; There Was a Maid

Cast: Viola De Costa; Maud Earl; Edwin Fowler; Harry Short

Notes: No songs listed in program. It was during the opening night performance of this show that Harry Thaw killed architect Stanford White. Originally mounted as a Columbia varsity show — moved to open the Madison Square Garden Roof. The show's opening night was a failure but after White was murdered the show became a hit and seats at the table at which White sat went at a premium.

2718 • MAN AND WIFE

Musical   Unproduced

Composer: Harold Rome
Lyricist: Harold Rome

Notes: No song list available.

2719 • MAN BETTER MAN

OPENED: 04/02/1969   Theatre: St. Marks
                          Playhouse
Play   Off-Broadway: 32

Composer: Coleridge-Taylor Perkinson
Lyricist: Errol Hill
Author: Errol Hill
Producer: Negro Ensemble Company, The
Director: Douglas Turner Ward

Choreographer: Percival Borde; **Costumes:** Bernard Johnson; **Lighting Designer:** Buddy Butler; **Set Design:** Edward Burbridge

Songs: Beautiful Heaven; Briscoe, the Hero; Colie Gone; Girl in the Coffee; I Love Petite Belle; Man Better Man; Me Alone; One Day, One Day, Congotay; One, Two, Three; Petite Belle Lily; Procession; Thousand, Thousand; Tiny, the Champion; War and Rebellion

Cast: Arthur French; Esther Rolle; Hattie Winston; Aston Young

2720 • MAN FROM BALTIMORE, THE

OPENED: 1934
Musical

Composer: Wen Talbert
Lyricist: Alonzo Govern
Librettist: John Raines
Producer: Joe Hurtig
Director: Joe Hurtig

Choreographer: Lew Crawford; John Dancey

Cast: Alfred "Slick" Chester; Archie Cross; Baby Joyce; Hattie King; Lionel Monagas; Trixie Smith; Percy Verwayen

Notes: No other information available.

2721 • MAN FROM 'BAM, THE

OPENED: 1906
Musical   Chicago

Composer: Joe Jordan; Will H. Vodery
Librettist: Aubrey L. Lyles; Flournoy E. Miller
Producer: Pekin Stock Company
Director: Charles S. Sager

Songs: Alabama Cadets, The; Feather Your Nest; I'd Like to Steal You; I'm Just from 'Bam; Man from 'Bam, The; Strolling

Cast: L.D. Henderson; Charles Sager; Andrew Tribble; Joe Weatherly

Notes: No other information available.

2722 • MAN FROM CHINA, THE

OPENED: 05/02/1904   Theatre: Majestic
Musical   Broadway: 41

Composer: John W. Bratton
Lyricist: Paul West
Librettist: Paul West
Producer: Melville B. Raymond
Director: John P. Slocum

Choreographer: Barney Fagan; **Costumes:** A. Wilbur Crane; **Musical Director:** Gus Salzer; **Set Design:** Ernest Albert

Songs: Amorous Esquimeaux, The; Bashful Moon, The; Be a Spy for Love's Sake; Chorus of

Welcome; Clorinda; Columbine (The Timid Humming Bird); Finale Act I; Finale Act II; For Glory and for Love; For I Am a Married Man; Frightened Fawn, The; Hail, Gracious Owner of This Spot; How I Thought I Looked; Human Band, The; In a Pagoda [1]; Just Another Silly Day; Life Is Too Short to be Wasting Your Time; Make Believe; My Black Cloud; One Nice Little Million; Opening Chorus; Peach King, The; (What Would You Do Without) Reggy; There Are Fifty-Seven Ways to Catch a Man; Ting, Tang, Kee (If You Understood Chinese)

Cast: Edgar Atchinson-Ely; Charles A. Bigelow; Stella Mayhew; Billie Taylor

Notes: [1] Played in between the acts.

2723 • MAN FROM COOK'S, THE

OPENED: 03/25/1912   Theatre: New Amsterdam
Musical   Broadway: 32

Composer: Raymond Hubbell
Lyricist: Henry Blossom
Librettist: Henry Blossom
Producer: Klaw & Erlanger
Director: Ben Teal

Source: UN VOYAGE COOK (Musical: Maurice Ordonneau); **Costumes:** F. Richard Anderson; **Musical Director:** Anton Heindl; **Orchestrations:** Frank Saddler; **Set Design:** Walter Burridge; Ernest Gros

Songs: All for You; Doctor's, Doctor's; Everything Is All Right [1]; Just As You Are; L'Amour [2]; Little Pot of Tea, A; Little Tin Soldier; Little World for Two; My Girl of Chance; Off to Italy [1]; Opening Chorus; Opening Chorus Act II; Perhaps [1]; We Can't Do without Men; Why Is a Girl? Do You Know?; Woman's Work Is Never Done, A [1]; You and I

Cast: Flavia Arcaro; Walter Percival; Fred Walton

Notes: [1] Out Boston 2/26/12. [2] Cut.

2724 • MAN FROM NOW, THE

OPENED: 09/03/1906   Theatre: New Amsterdam
Musical   Broadway: 28

Composer: Manuel Klein
Lyricist: Charles Kendrick Bangs

Librettist: Vincent Bryan
Producer: Henry W. Savage
Director: George Marion

Costumes: Archie Gunn; **Musical Director:** John McGhie; **Set Design:** Walter Burridge

Songs: Astronomy; Call Around Some Other Day [2]; Coaxing (C: Bernard Rolt); College Chums (C: Gertrude Hoffman); Come Along My Boys; Dainty Music Maid, The (L: Manuel Klein); Daisy Chain; Dora [1] (L: Manuel Klein); Finale Act I (L: Manuel Klein); Girls Just Girls (L: Isabel deWitt Kaplan); I Want to Go Home Now; I Will Love You Forever, My Dear (L: Manuel Klein); I'm the College President [1]; In Pity Spare Them; Irrisistible Tune, The (L: Manuel Klein); Liquid Air; Liquid Air Police (L: Manuel Klein); Lunch Is Ready; Mary Ann; My Gasoline Maid; Oh, It's Rah, Rah, Rah; Only Way to Love, The (Love's Lesson) (L: Manuel Klein); Opening Chorus; Opening Chorus Act II; Pull [2]; Scientific Classes (C: Harry Von Tilzer); That's Why We're Here [2]; There Isn't Anything That Can't Be Cured (C: Harry Bulger); We Are the Laddies (Entrance of College Students); What's the Matter with Our Team (C: Harry Von Tilzer); Wireless Telephone, The

Cast: Grace Cameron; William Cameron; Marguerite Clark; DeWolf Hopper; W.L. Romaine

Notes: [1] Out Boston 7/23/06. In vocal score. [2] Vocal score only.

2725 • MAN IN THE MOON, THE (1899)

OPENED: 1899   Theatre: New York
Musical   Broadway

Composer: Reginald De Koven; Ludwig Englander; Gustave Kerker
Producer: George W. Lederer
Director: George W. Lederer

Choreographer: Carl Marwig; **Set Design:** Ernest Albert; D. Frank Dodge; Henry E. Hoyt; St. John Lewis

Cast: Sam Bernard; Marie Dressler; John E. Henshaw; Walter Jones; Christie MacDonald

Notes: No songs listed in program.

2726 • MAN IN THE MOON (1963)
OPENED: 11/22/1963   Theatre: Biltmore
Musical   Broadway: 7

Composer: Jerry Bock
Lyricist: Sheldon Harnick
Librettist: Arthur Burns
Producer: Arthur Cantor; Joseph Harris
Director: Gerald Freedman

Orchestrations: Alvy West

Songs: Ain't You Never Been Afraid?; Itch to Be
Rich; Look Where I Am; Segue to Story; Worlds
Apart; You Treacherous Men

Puppeteer: Bil Baird; Cora Baird; Bob Brown; Franz
Fazakas; Michael King; Frank Sullivan

Notes: MAN IN THE MOON was the first act of
the bill. The second act featured puppets from
around the world.

2727 • MAN OF LA MANCHA
OPENED: 11/22/1965   Theatre: ANTA
                      Washington Square
Musical   Broadway: 2329

Composer: Mitch Leigh
Lyricist: Joe Darion
Librettist: Dale Wasserman
Producer: Hal James; Albert W. Selden
Director: Albert Marre

Source: DON QUIXOTE (Novel: Miguel de
Cervantes); **Choreographer:** Jack Cole;
Costumes: Howard Bay; Patton Campbell;
Dance Arranger: Music Makers, Inc.; **Lighting
Designer:** Howard Bay; **Musical Director:** Neil
Warner; **Orchestrations:** Music Maker, Inc.; **Set
Design:** Howard Bay; **Vocal Arranger:** Music
Maker, Inc.

Songs: Abduction, The; Aldonza; Barber's Song,
The; Don't Talk to Me of Love [1]; Dubbing
(Knight of the Woeful Countenance), The;
Dulcinea; Golden Helmet; I Really Like Him; I'm
Only Thinking of Him; Impossible Dream (The
Quest), The; It's All the Same; Little Bird, Little
Bird; Little Gossip, A; Man of La Mancha (I, Don
Quixote); Mask of Evil [1]; Psalm; To Each His
Dulcinea (To Every Man His Dream); What Do
You Want of Me?

Cast: Gino Conforti; Jon Cypher; Joan Diener;
Irving Jacobson; Richard Kiley; Eleanor Knapp;
Ray Middleton; Robert Rounseville; Mimi
Turque

Notes: Moved to the Martin Beck Theatre. [1] Out
Goodspeed 8/9/1965.

2728 • MAN ON THE MOON
OPENED: 01/29/1975   Theatre: Little
Musical   Broadway: 5

Composer: John Phillips
Lyricist: John Phillips
Librettist: John Phillips
Producer: Richard Turley; Andy Warhol
Director: Paul Morrissey

Costumes: Marsia Trinder; **Lighting Designer:**
Jules Fisher; **Musical Director:** Karen Gustafson;
Set Design: John J. Moore; **Vocal Arranger:**
Michael Gibson; Jim Tyler

Songs: American Man on the Moon; Boys from the
South; Canis Minor Bolero Waltz; Champagne
and Kisses; Convent; Everybody Needs Someone
to Hold Them Tight [1]; Family of Man; Far Far
Away [1]; Girls; Hang By Your Heels in a Cave [1];
Love Is Coming Back; Midnight Deadline
Blastoff; Mission Control; My Name Is Can;
Penthouse of Your Mind; Place in Space;
Prologue; Speed of Light; Star Stepping Stranger;
Starburst; Stepping to the Stars; Sunny Moon;
Though I'm a Little Angel; Truth Cannot Be
Treason; We're Banking on You Now [1];
Welcome to the Moon; Yesterday I Left the Earth

Cast: Eric Lang; Monique Van Vooren; Genevieve
Waite

Notes: [1] Cut.

2729 • MAN WHO CAME TO DINNER, THE
OPENED: 10/16/1939   Theatre: Music Box
Play   Broadway: 739

Author: Moss Hart; George S. Kaufman
Producer: Sam H. Harris
Director: George S. Kaufman

Set Design: Donald Oenslager

Songs: What Am I to Do (C/L: Cole Porter)

Cast: Joseph Allen Jr.; David Burns; Virginia Hammond; Claudia Morgan; Rex O'Malley; Le Roi Operti; Philip Truex; Mary Wickes; Monty Woolley

2730 • MAN WHO OWNS BROADWAY, THE

OPENED: 10/11/1909   Theatre: New York
Musical   Broadway: 128

Composer: George M. Cohan
Lyricist: George M. Cohan
Librettist: George M. Cohan
Producer: George M. Cohan; Sam H. Harris
Director: George M. Cohan

Source: POPULARITY (Play: George M. Cohan)

Songs: Everybody Sometimes Must Love Someone [1]; I'll Go the Route for You; I'm All O.K. with K&E; I'm in Love with One of the Stars; In the Waldorf Halls; I've Always Been a Good Old Sport; Love Will Make or Break a Man; Man Who Owns Broadway, The; March of the King's Amazons; My Daughter Is Wed to a Friend of Mine; Nice Little Plot for a Play; On a Hundred Different Ships; Secrets of the Household; Something About a Uniform; When a Servant Learns a Secret; Why They Made Him King; You'd Think You Were in Paris

Cast: Stanley Forde; Raymond Hitchcock; George Lydecker; Thomas Shields; Scott Welsh; Flora Zabelle

Notes: [1] Out 2/9/14 Springfield, Mass. [2] ASCAP/Library of Congress.

2731 • MAN WITH A LOAD OF MISCHIEF

OPENED: 11/06/1966   Theatre: Jan Hus Playhouse
Musical   Off-Broadway: 240

Composer: John Clifton
Lyricist: John Clifton; Ben Tarver
Librettist: Ben Tarver
Producer: Donald H. Goldman
Director: Tom Gruenewald

Source: MAN WITH A LOAD OF MISCHIEF (Play: Ashley Dukes); **Choreographer:** Noel Schwartz; **Costumes:** Volavkova; **Lighting Designer:** Joan Larkey; **Musical Director:** Sande Campbell; **Set Design:** Joan Larkey

Songs: Any Other Way; Come to the Masquerade; Dinner Minuet (dance); Entrance Polonaise (dance); Forget!; Friend Like You, A; Goodbye, My Sweet; Hulla-Baloo-Balay; Little Rag Doll; Lover Lost; Make Way for My Lady; Man with a Load of Mischief; Once You've Had a Little Taste; Rescue, The; Romance!; Wayside Inn; What Style!; Wonder, A; You'd Be Amazed

Cast: Alice Cannon; Lesslie Nicol; Tom Noel; Reid Shelton; Raymond Thorne; Virginia Vestoff

2732 • MAN WITH THREE WIVES, THE

OPENED: 01/23/1913   Theatre: Weber & Fields Music Hall
Musical   Broadway: 52

Composer: Franz Lehar
Lyricist: Harold Atteridge; Paul M. Potter
Librettist: Agnes Morgan; Paul M. Potter
Producer: Messrs. Shubert
Director: J.C. Huffman; William J. Wilson

Source: DER MANN MIT DEN DREI FRAUEN (Musical: Julius Bauer; Franz Lehar); **Costumes:** Melville Ellis; **Musical Director:** Oscar Radin

Songs: All in a Little Dance; Cupid's Soldiers; Hello, Hello (C: Al W. Brown; L: Harold Atteridge); Kisses That I Have Missed; Kranko Waltz; Love's Fairy Tales; Love's Flower Is Always Blooming [1]; Lullaby; Man Is Faithful till He's Caught; Opening Chorus; Paris, Oh Festive Land; Rose of Yesterday; Tale of the Jealous Cat (C: Al W. Brown; L: Harold Atteridge); Tempo di Gavotte; Temporary Widow, The; There's Always a Girl Who Is Waiting; To London; Tootsie- Wootsie; Vale of Dreaming, The; Vengeance; We Are Free; When You're Traveling; Women of Temperament

Cast: Sydney Grant; Charlotte Greenwood; Cecil Lean; Cleo Mayfield; Alice Yorke

Notes: [1] Not in programs.

2733 • MANDARIN, THE
OPENED: 11/02/1896   Theatre: Herald Square
Musical   Broadway: 40

Composer: Reginald De Koven
Librettist: Harry B. Smith
Director: Richard Barker

Choreographer: Samuel Marion; **Costumes:** Mme. Siedle; **Set Design:** Frederick Dangerfield

Songs: Dresden China Love Affair, A; Her Faults; Japanese Elopement, A

Cast: George C. Boniface Jr.; Henry Norman; Adele Ritchie; Joseph Sheehan

Notes: No songs listed in program.

2734 • MANHATTAN MARY
OPENED: 09/26/1927   Theatre: Apollo
Musical   Broadway: 264

Composer: Ray Henderson
Lyricist: Lew Brown; B.G. DeSylva
Librettist: William K. Wells; George White
Producer: George White
Director: George White

Costumes: Erte; **Musical Director:** Maurice DePackh; **Set Design:** William Oden-Waller

Songs: Broadway (The Heart of the World); Dawn; Five-Step, The; Hudson Duster; I'd Like You to Love Me [1]; It Won't Be Long Now; Just a Cozy Hideaway [1]; Manhattan Mary; Memories; My Blue Bird's Home Again; Nothing but Love; Pedestrian Song

Cast: Harland Dixon; Paul Frawley; Lou Holtz; Ona Munson; George White; Ed Wynn

Notes: [1] Not used.

2735 • MANHATTAN MOVES
OPENED: 01/24/1993   Theatre: American Place
Revue   Off-Broadway: 45

Producer: Virginia L. Dean; M&M American Dance Theatre; David H. Peipers
Director: Michael Kessler

Arrangements: Jon Gordon; **Choreographer:** Michael Kessler; **Costumes:** Geff Rhian; **Lighting Designer:** Randy Becker

Songs: Manhattan Moves (C/L: Michael Kessler)

Cast: Adrienne Armstrong; Kevin Gaudin; Andre George; El Tahra Ibrahim; Melinda Jackson; Michael Kessler; Barry Wizoreck

Notes: An all-dancing revue to a recorded score. Only one original song.

2736 • MANHATTAN MUSIC HALL REVUE
OPENED: 1934
Revue

Composer: Donald Heywood
Lyricist: Abe Tuvim

Songs: Dancing My Dinner Down; Plodding Along; Spring Is Blue; Zaru Zaru Zee

Notes: No other information available. Sheet music only.

2737 • MANHATTAN SHOWBOAT
OPENED: 06/30/1980   Theatre: Radio City Music
                              Hall
Revue   Broadway: 191

Composer: Donald Pippin
Lyricist: Sammy Cahn
Librettist: Stan Hart
Producer: Robert F. Jani; Radio City Music Hall
Director: Frank Wagner

Choreographer: Violet Holmes; Linda Lemac; Howard Parker; Debra Pigliavento; **Costumes:** Michael Casey; Frank Spencer; **Lighting Designer:** David F. Segal; **Musical Director:** Donald Pippin; **Orchestrations:** Elman Anderson; Michael Gibson; Arthur Harris; Philip J. Lang; **Set Design:** Robert Guerra

Songs: Alike, Alike; It's Spring; Manhattan Showboat; My Big Moment; Right Here (C/L: Nan Mason); There Are No Girls Quite Like Showgirls; You're at the Music Hall

Cast: Karen Anders; Louis Carry; Buddy Crutchfield; Lou Ann Csaszar; Tony Moore;

Thomas Ruisinger; Laurie Stephenson; Frank Wagner; Steven Williford

2738 • MANHATTAN VANITIES
Notes: *See BELMONT VARIETIES.*

2739 • MANHATTERS, THE
OPENED: 08/03/1927   Theatre: Selwyn
Revue   Broadway: 77

Composer: Alfred Nathan Jr.
Lyricist: George S. Oppenheimer
Librettist: Alene Erlanger; George S. Oppenheimer
Producer: Manhatters Company
Director: David Bennett; Elizabeth B. Grimball

Choreographer: David Bennett; Costumes: Henry Dreyfuss; Musical Director: Fred Hoff; Set Design: Henry Dreyfuss; Sophie Rosebach

Songs: Close Your Eyes; Down on the Delta; Every Animal Has Its Mate; James the Chauffer; Little Kleptomaniac, The; Love's Old Sweet Song; Mammy; Nigger Heaven Blues; Not a Song at Twilight; Too Bad

Cast: Sally Bates; Ben Bernie; Raymond Knight; Mary Marsh; Eleanor Shaler; Aida Ward

2740 • MANICURE GIRL, THE
OPENED: 06/29/1914
Musical   Closed out of town

Composer: Herbert Stothart
Lyricist: Joseph E. Howard
Librettist: Theodore Stempfel Jr.

Notes: Suburban Garden, St. Louis. Referred to in some sources as THE MANICURE SHOP.

2741 • MANICURE SHOP, THE
Notes: *See THE MANICURE GIRL.*

2742 • MANY HAPPY RETURNS (1969)
OPENED: 01/16/1969
Musical   Closed out of town

Composer: Ray Golden
Lyricist: Ray Golden

Librettist: Ray Golden; Jack Marlowe
Producer: Frank Sennes
Director: Danny Dayton

Choreographer: Earl Barton; Costumes: Betty Kreisel; Lighting Designer: Randy Wood; Musical Director: Carleton Hayes; Orchestrations: Luchi DeJesus; Set Design: Harvey Warren

Songs: And Then I Saw Him; Another Girl and Boy Thing; Believe in Me, Baby; Everybody Wants to Be in Show Business; Finaletto; Give the Public What It Wants; Go for Broke; Longest Running Unproduced Production; Many Happy Returns; Us-ness of We, The; What This Country Needs

Cast: Victor Buono; John Carroll; Pat Carroll; Paul Gilbert; Linda Michele; John Raitt; Tucker Smith

Notes: From a program of the Desert Inn, Las Vegas.

2743 • MANY HAPPY RETURNS (1974)
OPENED: 1974

Songs: Many Happy Returns (C: Arthur Schwartz; L: Howard Dietz)

Notes: No other information available. Information from ASCAP/Library of Congress.

2744 • MARAT/SADE
Notes: *See THE PERSECUTION AND ASSISSINATION OF MARAT AS PERFORMED BY THE INMATES OF THE ASYLUM OF CHARENTON UNDER THE DIRECTION OF THE MARQUIS DE SADE.*

2745 • MARCELLE
OPENED: 10/01/1908   Theatre: Broadway
Musical   Broadway: 68

Composer: Gustav Luders
Lyricist: Frank Pixley
Librettist: Frank Pixley
Producer: Lee Shubert; Sam S. Shubert
Director: Frank Smithson

Musical Director: Clarence Rogerson

Songs: Baron's Entrance; Cupid-Sly Little Rascal; Drink and Be Jolly To Day; Far, Far Away (Memories, Fond and True); Finale Act II; Foam Crested Beer, The [1]; Forget It; Girl's First Love, A; Good Evening (A Dream of the Dance); It's Not the Proper Thing; Kalamazoo; Lesson in Love, A (Kiss Song); Love the Magician; Memories Fond and True (Far Away) [1]; Message of the Red, Red Rose, The; My Little Lamb; My Own Paree; Oh Gee-Poor-Me Never No More [1] (C: Thomas S. Allen; L: Jess Dandy); Once in a While; Opening Chorus Act II; Schwindle Corps, The; Soldier Boy, The; Something's Always Going Wrong; To Live and Die a Soldier Bold (Battle Song); Volunteers, The; Watchmen's Chorus; Welcome, Otto, Welcome Home

Cast: Herbert Cawthorne; Jess Dandy; Louise Gunning; Lawrence Wheat

Notes: [1] Sheet music only.

2746 • MARCH OF THE FALSETTOS

OPENED: 04/01/1981   Theatre: Playwrights Horizons
Musical   Off-Broadway: 310

Composer: William Finn
Lyricist: William Finn
Librettist: William Finn
Producer: Playwrights Horizons
Director: James Lapine

Costumes: Maureen Connor; **Lighting Designer:** Frances Aronson; **Musical Director:** Michael Lee Stockler; **Orchestrations:** Michael Starobin; **Set Design:** Douglas Stein

Songs: Chess Game, The; Everyone Tells Jason to See a Psychiatrist; Father to Son; Four Jews in a Room Bitching; Games I Play, The; I Never Wanted to Love You; Jason's Therapy; Love Is Blind; Making a Home; March of the Falsettos; Marvin at the Psychiatrist; Marvin Hits Trina; My Father's a Homo; Please Come to My House; This Had Better Come to a Stop; Thrill of First Love, The; Tight-knit Family, A; Trina's Song

Cast: Stephen Bogardus; Alison Fraser; James Kushner; Michael Rupert; Chip Zien

Notes: Original title was THE PETTINESS OF MISOGYNY. That was changed to FOUR JEWS

IN A ROOM BITCHING. That was changed too. The show moved to the Chelsea Westside Arts Theatre on October 12, 1981 where it played 200 of the above performances.

2747 • MARCHING BY

OPENED: 03/03/1932   Theatre: Chanin's 46th St.
Musical   Broadway: 32

Composer: Jean Gilbert; Harry Revel
Lyricist: Mack Gordon
Librettist: Harry Clarke; Harry B. Smith
Producer: Messrs. Shubert
Director: J.C. Huffman

Source: HOTEL STADT-LEMBERG (Opera: Ernst Neubach); **Choreographer:** Allan K. Foster; **Costumes:** Ernest Schrapps; **Musical Director:** George Hirst; **Set Design:** Watson Barratt

Songs: All's Fair in Love and War (C: John Gilbert; L: Harry B. Smith); Finery; For You [1]; Forward March into My Arms; Here We Are in Love (C: Jean Gilbert; L: Harry B. Smith); I Love You, My Darling (C: Jean Gilbert; L: Edward Eliscu; George Hirst); It Might Have Been You (C: Gus Arnheim; Neil Moret; L: George Waggoner); I've Gotta Keep My Eye on You (C: Harry Revel); Leave It to Love [1]; Let Fate Decide (C: Maurie Rubens; L: Harry B. Smith); Light Up; Marching By (C: Gus Edwards; L: Harry Clarke; Guy Robertson); On Through the Night; To the Victor Belongs the Spoils [1]; We're on Our Way to Hell; You Burn Me Up When You Turn Me Down [1] (C: Jean Gilbert; L: Harry B. Smith)

Cast: Donald Burr; Victor Casmore; Leonard Ceeley; Kathleen Edwardes; Arthur Geary; Philip Lord; Hugh Miller; Ethel Norris; Guy Robertson; Desiree Tabor; Solly Ward

Notes: First titled ARMS AND THE MAID. [1] Out Newark 11/23/31.

2748 • MARCHING WITH JOHNNY

OPENED: 01/22/1943
Revue   Closed out of town

Composer: Jay Gorney
Lyricist: Edward Eliscu; Edward Myers
Librettist: Edward Eliscu; Jay Gorney; Edward Myers

Producer: National CIO War Prods.
Director: Robert H. Gordon; Philip Loeb

Choreographer: Dan Eckley; Charles Weidman;
Costumes: Rose Bogdanoff; **Lighting Designer:**
Howard Bay; **Musical Director:** Pembroke
Davenport; **Orchestrations:** Charles L. Cooke;
Set Design: Howard Bay; **Vocal Arranger:**
Pembroke Davenport

Songs: Crispus Attucks (C: Phil Moore; L: Edward
Eliscu; Robert Meltzer); Damn the Torpedoes
(Full Speed Ahead) [2]; Early Monday Morning;
Four Freedoms, The [2]; Four Rivers, The; He
Was All Right Here (He'll Be All Right There)
[2]; Let's Go Out and Ring Doorbells; Lincoln
and Juarez [3]; Love in a Changing World;
Mamma, It's Saturday Night; Marching with
Johnny; Mr. Roosevelt and Mr. Churchill; That
Mittel-Europa Europe Man [1]; You and Your
Broken Heart, You're Good for My Morale [2]

Cast: Beatrice Kay; Rosetta LeNoire; Mervyn
Nelson

Notes: Additional songs and sketches by Leonard
Keller, William Copeland, Searle Kramer and
Stella Bloch but not credited in program. Later
titled THE NEW MEET THE PEOPLE. [1] Also
in THEY CAN'T LET YOU DOWN. [2]
ASCAP/Library of Congress only. [3] Also
referred to as "Juarez and Lincoln."

2749 • MARCUS SHOW OF 1920

OPENED: 1921
Revue   Closed out of town

Composer: Charles Abbate
Lyricist: Charles Abbate
Producer: A.B. Marcus
Director: Charles A. Lellon

Choreographer: Raymond Midgley

Songs: Anybody Want a Baby; Classy Clothes;
Dainty Lingerie; Dance of the Nile; Dixie,
I Love You; Goodbye Bachelor Days; Listen to
the Band; Oh, Baby, Glide; Salvation Army
Girl; Smile with Me; Sun Worshippers; Under
the Sea

Cast: Billy Dale; Mike Sacks

Notes: Washington D.C. program 4/10/21.

2750 • MARDI GRAS

OPENED: 06/26/1965   Theatre: Jones Beach
                                       Marine
Musical   New York: 68

Composer: John Jacob Loeb; Carmen Lombardo
Lyricist: John Jacob Loeb; Carmen Lombardo
Librettist: Sig Herzig
Producer: Guy Lombardo
Director: June Taylor

Choreographer: June Taylor; **Costumes:** Winn
Morton; **Dance Arranger:** Milt Sherman;
Lighting Designer: George Jenkins; **Musical
Director:** Mitchell Ayres; **Orchestrations:** Philip
J. Lang; **Set Design:** George Jenkins; **Vocal
Arranger:** Mitchell Ayers

Songs: Come Along Down; Down with Whiskey;
I'd Know That Smile; Kind of a Girl; Ladies of
the Ballet; Mardi Gras Waltz, The; Mumbo
Jumbo; Pirate's Lament; Pirate's Polka; Someone
I Could Love; We're Gonna See the Voodoo
Queen; We're Wanted; When I Take My Lady;
When My Man Sails Home

Cast: David Atkinson; Juanita Hall; Ruth Kobart;
Phil Leeds; Ralph Purdom; Karen Shepard

Notes: No program available.

2751 • MARIANNE

OPENED: 01/10/1944
Musical   Closed out of town

Composer: Abraham Ellstein
Lyricist: Beatrice Metzl; Lothar Metzl
Librettist: Sylvia Regan; Kenneth White
Producer: Marion Gering; B.P. Schulberg
Director: Marion Gering

Choreographer: Helen Tamiris; **Costumes:** Kenn
Barr; **Musical Director:** Abraham Ellstein;
Orchestrations: Abraham Ellstein; **Set Design:**
Frederick Fox

Songs: Always Goodbye (L: Robert B. Sour); Black
Horsemen, The; Crepe Suzette; Germ in the
German, The (L: Robert B. Sour); Kind of a Man
(L: Robert B. Sour); Marianne; My Heart Is Like a
Bird (L: Robert B. Sour); No More; Out of the
Dark (L: Robert B. Sour); Pom Pom on Your Hat,
The (L: Robert B. Sour); Vive Pichon; What Do
I Have to Do (L: Robert B. Sour)

Cast: Jean Darling; Virginia MacWatters; Ernest Truex; Mary Jane Walsh; Jerry Wayne

2752 • MARIE DRESSLER'S ALL STAR GAMBOLS

Notes: *See ALL STAR GAMBOLS.*

2753 • MARIE GALANTE

OPENED: 12/22/1934
Musical

Composer: Kurt Weill
Lyricist: Jacques Deval
Librettist: Jacques Deval
Producer: Leon Volterra
Director: Andre Lefour

Source: MARIE GALANTE (Novel: Jacques Deval)

Songs: J'Attends Un Navire; Le Grand Lustucru; Le Roi D'Aquitaine [2]; Le Train du Ciel; Les Filles de Bordeaux [1]; Marche de L'Armee Panemeenne (Panamanian Army March) (inst.); Scene Au Dancing (inst.); Tango [3]

Cast: Alcover; Joe Alex; Florelle; Inkijinoff; Serge Nadoud

Notes: Produced at the Theatre de Paris, Paris. No program available. [1] Music same as "In Der Jugend Gold'nem Schimmer (In Youth's Golden Glimmer)" from HAPPY END and "The Trouble with Women" from ONE TOUCH OF VENUS. [2] Same music as "Two Hearts" from A KINGDOM FOR A COW. [3] Later published as "Youkali" with a new lyric by Roger Fernay.

2754 • MARILYN: AN AMERICAN FABLE

OPENED: 12/04/1983   Theatre: Minskoff
Musical   Broadway: 16

Composer: Beth Lawrence; Norman Thalheimer
Lyricist: Beth Lawrence; Norman Thalheimer
Librettist: Patricia Michaels
Producer: Renee Blau; Arnold Bruck; Malcolm Cooke; June Curtis; Joseph DioGuardi; James Kabler; Tom Kaye; William May; Jerome Minskoff; Dolores Quinton; John Ricciardelli; Leo Rosenthal; Harper Sibley
Director: Kenny Ortega

Choreographer: Kenny Ortega; **Costumes:** Joseph G. Aulisi; **Dance Arranger:** Donald Johnston; Ronald Melrose; **Lighting Designer:** Marcia Madeira; **Musical Director:** Steven Margoshes; **Orchestrations:** Bill Brohn; Donald Johnston; Steven Margoshes; **Set Design:** Tom H. John; **Vocal Arranger:** Steven Margoshes

Songs: All Roads Lead to Hollywood; Best of Me, The; Can't Keep My Heart from Racing [1] (C/L: Beth Lawrence); Church Doors; Close the Door Norma [1] (C/L: Beth Lawrence); Cold Hard Cash (C: Wally Harper; L: David Zippel); Cultural Pursuits (C/L: Doug Frank); Don't Hang Up the Telephone (C/L: Jeanne Napoli; Gary Portnoy); Finally; Golden Dream, The; Gossip (C/L: Doug Frank; Komack); I'll Send You Roses [1]; I'm a Fan; In Disguise [1] (C/L: Doug Frank); It's a Premiere Night; Jimmy Jimmy (C/L: Doug Frank; Jeanne Napoli); Miss Bubbles (C/L: Doug Frank; Jeanne Napoli; Gary Portnoy); Money Men and More [1] (C/L: Doug Frank; Jeanne Napoli); My Heart's an Open Door; Run Between the Raindrops (C/L: Jeanne Napoli; Gary Portnoy); She's the One [1] (C/L: Unknown); Shootin' [1]; Single Dream, A (C/L: Doug Frank; Jeanne Napoli); Special Man, A [1] (C/L: Doug Frank; Jeanne Napoli); Stairway Leading Nowhere [1] (C/L: Doug Frank; Jeanne Napoli); Swing Shift (Miss Parachute); Uh-Huh [1]; We Are the Ones; We'll Help You Through the Night (C/L: Dawson; Jeanne Napoli; Turner); When You Run the Show; You Are So Beyond (C/L: Doug Frank; Jeanne Napoli); You Cheated Me [1] (C/L: Unknown)

Cast: Scott Bakula; Peggie Blue; Kristi Coombs; George Dvorsky; Willy Falk; Will Gerard; Mitchell Greenberg; James Haskins; Michael Kubala; Lise Lang; Alyson Reed

Notes: [1] Cut prior to opening.

2755 • MARINKA

OPENED: 07/18/1941   Theatre: Winter Garden
Musical   Broadway: 165

Composer: Emmerich Kalman
Lyricist: Karl Farkas; George Marion
Librettist: Karl Farkas; George Marion
Director: Karl Farkas; George Marion; Hassard Short

Choreographer: Albertina Rasch; **Costumes:** Mary Grant; **Set Design:** Howard Bay

Songs: Cab Song; Czardas [1]; If I Never Waltz Again; My Prince Came Riding; Old Man Danube; One Last Love Song; Paletas [1]; Sigh by Night; Treat a Woman Like a Drum; Turn on the Charm

Cast: Ethel Levey; Joan Roberts; Harry Stockwell

Notes: Also known as SONG OF VIENNA. [1] Out Washington D.C. 6/11/45.

2756 • MARJOLAINE
OPENED: 01/24/1922   Theatre: Broadhurst
Musical   Broadway: 136

Composer: Hugo Felix
Lyricist: Brian Hooker
Librettist: Catherine Chisholm Cushing
Producer: Russell Janney
Director: Oscar Eagle

Source: POMANDER WALK (Play: Louis N. Parker); **Choreographer:** Bert French; **Costumes:** W.H. Matthews; **Musical Director:** Milan Roder; **Set Design:** Joseph Wickes

Songs: Cuddle Up Together (My Old Brown Coat); Don't-Don't- Don't; Dream Melody; Ducks and Geese; Fishing [1]; I Want You; If He Should Come; In the Park; Marjolaine; Music Box; Oh Dr. Sternroyd; Punch and Judy; River of Dreams; Song of a Sailor; Stars of Your Eyes; Syringa Tree; Woman-Woman; Wonderland

Cast: Irving Beebe; Mary Hay; Lennox Pawle; Peggy Wood

Notes: [1] Out Providence 1/2/22.

2757 • MARJORIE
OPENED: 08/11/1924   Theatre: Shubert
Musical   Broadway: 144

Composer: Sigmund Romberg; Herbert Stothart
Lyricist: Harold Atteridge
Librettist: Clifford Grey; Fred Thompson
Producer: Richard W. Krakeur; Rufus LeMaire
Director: W.H. Gilmore

Choreographer: David Bennett; **Musical Director:** John L. McManus; **Set Design:** Watson Barratt

Songs: Brindle's Farm (C: Philip Calkin); Finale (C: Sigmund Romberg); Forty-Second Street Man [1] (C: Sigmund Romberg; L: Irving Caesar; Clifford Grey); Go Away Girls Go Away (C: Herbert Stothart); Good Things and Bad Things (C: Sigmund Romberg); Happy Endings (C: Herbert Stothart); Hollywood [1]; Leading Man (C: Stephen Jones); Listening to the Radio (C: Sigmund Romberg); Marjorie [1]; Monastery [1] (C: Stephen Jones); My Twilight Rose (C: Sigmund Romberg; L: Clifford Grey); Nature (C: Herbert Stothart); Popularity (C: Stephen Jones); Shuffle Your Troubles Away (C: James F. Hanley; L: Henry Creamer); Song of Love (C: Sigmund Romberg); Super-Sheik (C: Sigmund Romberg); What Do You Say? (C: Herbert Stothart); Yesterday [1]

Cast: Skeets Gallagher; Elizabeth Hines; Ethel Shutta; Jack Squires

Notes: Music also credited to Philip Culkin but not identified. [1] Sheet music only.

2758 • MARJORIE MORNINGSTAR
Musical

Songs: Marjorie Morningstar (C: Charles Strouse; L: Lee Adams)

Notes: This show was never finished.

2759 • MARLOWE
OPENED: 10/12/1981   Theatre: Rialto
Musical   Broadway: 48

Composer: Jimmy Horowitz
Lyricist: Jimmy Horowitz; Leo Rost
Librettist: Leo Rost
Producer: John Arrnunziato; Tony Conforti
Director: Don Price

Choreographer: Don Price; **Costumes:** Natalie Walker; **Lighting Designer:** Mitch Acker; Rick Belzer; **Musical Director:** Kenny Landrum; **Orchestrations:** Jimmy Horowitz; **Set Design:** Cary Chalmers; **Vocal Arranger:** Jimmy Horowitz; Patrick Jude

Songs: Act II Prologue; Because I'm a Woman; Can't Leave Now; Christopher; Emelia; Ends Justify the Means, The; Funeral Dirge, The; Higher Than High; I'm Coming 'Round to Your Point of View; Live for the Moment; Madrigal Blues, The; Prologue; Rocking the Boat; So Do I (Ode to Virginity); Two Lovers

Cast: Lennie Del Duca Jr.; Debra Greenfield; Steve Hall; Patrick Jude; Lisa Mordente; Raymond Serra

2760 • MARRIAGE A LA CARTE

OPENED: 01/02/1911   Theatre: Casino
Musical   Broadway: 64

Composer: Ivan Caryll
Lyricist: C.M.S. McLellan
Librettist: C.M.S. McLellan
Producer: Liebler & Company
Director: Austen Hurgon

Songs: Captain Dinklepop; Cassie's Not a Bit Like Mother; Did You Ever, Etc.; Finale Act I; Finale Act II; Finale Act III; For I'm Just I; No Doubt I Ought to Try; Of All Her Sex a Paragon; Oh, Rosalie; Opening Chorus Act III; Silly Cock-a-Doodle-Doo; Smile, Smile, Smile!; Such a Bore; Take Him Away to the Mountains; Thrifty Little Mabel; Toddle Go the Girls; Walking on a Wire; What's the Use of Going to Bed; When Zim Zim Got the Cymbals; You, You

Cast: Norman A. Blume; Harry Conor; C. Morton Horne; Harold Vizard

2761 • MARRIAGE MARKET, THE

OPENED: 09/22/1913   Theatre: Knickerbocker
Musical   Broadway: 80

Composer: Victor Jacobi
Lyricist: Arthur Anderson; Adrian Ross
Librettist: Gladys Unger
Producer: Charles Frohman
Director: Edward Royce

Source: LEANYVASAR (Musical: Max Brody; Victor Jacobi; Ferenc Martos); **Musical Director:** Harold Vicars

Songs: American Courtship; Boys (C: Edwin Burch; L: M.E. Rourke); By the Country Stile (C/L: Jerome Kern); Come Nestle in My Arms; Complements; Futurist Whirl, The (C: Edwin Burch; L: M.E. Rourke); Golden Day of Love, The (L: Adrian Ross); Hand in Hand; Honeymoon; I Don't Believe in Fairies Now (C/L: Paul Rubens); I'm Looking for an Irish Husband [1] (C: Jerome Kern; L: M.E. Rourke); I'm Not a Silly Billy (C/L: Paul Rubens); It Might Be an Oomps Sight Worse; June Is in the Air; Little Bit of Silk, A [1] (C: Jerome Kern; L: M.E. Rourke); Love and You; Love of Mine; Marriage Market, The; Mendocino Stroll, The (C/L: Donald Brian); Middy, The; Naval Manoeuvres; Never Count Your Chicks before They're Hatched; Oh How Near and Yet So Far; One I Love, The (L: Adrian Ross); Over the Hills in Monterey; I've Got Money in the Bank (C: Jerome Kern; L: M.E. Rourke); Very Little Time for Loving Nowadays (C: Pedro de Zulueta); You're Here and I'm Here [2] (C: Jerome Kern; L: Harry B. Smith)

Cast: Frank Adair; Donald Brian; Venita Fitzhugh; Percival Knight; George J. Meech; Cissie Sewell

Notes: No New York program available. Program of 1/26/14 Washington. Anderson may have "Americanized" the London lyrics by Ross. Therefore the lyric credits on sheet music to Ross alone may reflect the London billing although the sheet was issued in the United States. [1] Cut after opening. [2] Added to tour after Broadway. Originally in THE LAUGHING HUSBAND.

2762 • MARRIED BY WIRELESS

OPENED: 1918
Musical

Librettist: William K. Pollard
Producer: William K. Pollard

Songs: Au Revoir, but Not Goodbye; Give Me All of You; Hello, Aloha, Hello; Love Light in Your Eyes; Married Via Wireless; Some Sunday Morning; Submarine Attack; Sweetest Little Girl in Tennessee

Cast: Tom Gordon; Henry Hainert; May Pollard; Queenie Williams

Notes: Vaudiville Musical — Chicago. These songs are probably popular songs of the day.

2763 • MARRY IN HASTE

OPENED: 08/05/1918
Play   Closed out of town

Composer: George H. Gartlan
Lyricist: Anne Nichols; Fiske O'Hara
Author: Anne Nichols
Producer: Augustus Pitou

Musical Director: Karl F. Kelsey

Songs: I'm Falling in Love with You Dear; Kind of Girl I; My Little Irish Girl (C/L: Cyril Morton Home); Peggy McVey; There's a Charm of Dear Old Ireland in Your Eyes (L: George H. Gartlan)

Cast: Patricia Clary; J.E. Miller; Fiske O'Hara

Notes: Program of Stamford Connecticut.

2764 • MARRY ME A LITTLE

OPENED: 03/12/1981   Theatre: Actors'
                                          Playhouse
Musical   Off-Broadway: 96

Composer: Stephen Sondheim
Lyricist: Stephen Sondheim
Producer: William B. Young; Diane de Mailly
Director: Norman Rene

Choreographer: Don Johansson; **Costumes:** Oleksa; **Lighting Designer:** Debra J. Kletter; **Musical Director:** E. Martin Perry; **Set Design:** Jane Thurn

Songs: All Things Bright and Beautiful [3]; Bang! [1]; Can That Boy Fox Trot [3]; Class [11]; Girls of Summer, The [4]; Happily Ever After [6]; I Do Like You [12]; It Wasn't Meant to Happen [3]; Little White House [9]; Marry Me a Little [6]; Moment with You, A [2]; Pour Le Sport [7]; Saturday Night [2]; Silly People [1]; So Many People [2]; That Old Piano Roll [10]; There Won't Be Trumpets [8]; Two Fairy Tales [1]; Uptown, Downtown [3]; Who Could Be Blue? [9]; Your Eyes Are Blue [5]

Cast: Suzanne Henry; Craig Lucas

Notes: Consisted of songs written for other shows. [1] Cut from A LITTLE NIGHT MUSIC. [2] From unproduced show SATURDAY NIGHT. [3] Cut from FOLLIES. [4] From incidental music written for play by N. Richard Nash THE GIRLS OF SUMMER. [5] Cut from A FUNNY THING HAPPEND ON THE WAY TO THE FORUM. [6] Cut from COMPANY. [7] From THE LAST RESORTS. [8] Cut from ANYONE CAN

WHISTLE. [9] Cut prior to opening. Cut from FOLLIES. [10] Added to London production. Cut from FOLLIES. [11] Added to London production. From unproduced show SATURDAY NIGHT. [12] Added to London production. Cut from A FUNNY THING HAPPENED ON THE WAY TO THE FORUM.

2765 • MARRYING MARY

OPENED: 08/27/1906   Theatre: Daly's
Musical   Broadway: 43

Composer: Silvio Hein
Lyricist: Benjamin Hapgood Burt
Librettist: Edwin Milton Royle
Producer: Daniel V. Arthur
Director: Edwin Milton Royle

Musical Director: Silvio Hein

Songs: Coo Coo (The Fable of the Dove) [1]; Do, Re, Mi, Fa, Sol, La, Si, Do [1] (C: Benjamin Hapggod Burt; L: William Cahill); Dummy Love Song [4] (C/L: Marie Cahill); Gwendolyn; He's a Cousin of Mine (C: Silvio Hein; Chris Smith; L: Cecil Mack [2]); Hottentot Love Song, A [3] (C: Bob Cole; L: J. Rosamond Johnson); I Love the Last One Best of All; I Want to Wed a Soldier Boy [1]; Is There Anyone Here By the Name of Smith?; Mr. Cupid; Noah Knew a Thing or Two; No-body Knows the Answer [1]; Old Reliable Jokes; Three Men in a Boat

Cast: Roy Atwell; Marie Cahill; William Courtleigh; Eugene Cowles; Virginia Staunton

Notes: [1] Out 4/26/07 Wilkes Barre. [2] Cecil Mack is a pseudonym for R.C. McPherson. [3] Credited to Burt and Hein on sheet music. [4] Sheet music only.

2766 • MARTIN GUERRE

OPENED: 01/22/1993
Musical   Closed out of town

Composer: Roger Ames
Lyricist: Laura Harrington
Librettist: Laura Harrington
Director: Mark Lamos

Choreographer: Liza Gennaro; **Costumes:** Jess Goldstein; **Lighting Designer:** Jennifer Tipton; **Musical Director:** Sue Anderson;

Orchestrations: William Harper; **Set Design:** Michael Yeargan

Songs: Adulteress; All Alone; Bear, The; By the Grace of the Land; Distant Lands; Girl Becomes a Woman, A; Girl Is Gone, The; I Had a Son; Land, The; Magic and Charms; Not Alone; Outsider; Scythe and the Sickle, The; Starry Night; Trail, The; Truth and Lies; Waiting Is Over, The; We Will Survive; Wedding, The; Wedding Night, The; White Moon; Who Is This Man?; You Have Touched Me

Cast: Patrick Cassidy; Walter Charles; Beth Fowler; Malcolm Gets; Cris Groenendaal; Judy Kuhn; Peter Samuel

Notes: Hartford Stage Company.

2767 • MARY

OPENED: 10/18/1920   Theatre: Knickerbocker
Musical   Broadway: 220

Composer: Louis A. Hirsch
Lyricist: Otto Harbach
Librettist: Otto Harbach; Frank Mandel
Producer: George M. Cohan
Director: Sam Forrest; Julian Mitchell

Musical Director: Charles J. Gebest

Songs: Anything You Want to Do, Dear; Deeper; Don't Fall Until You've Seen Them All; Down on the Old Kansas Farm (That Farm Out in Kansas); Every Time I Meet a Lady; Flirtation Dance; It's a Widow for Mine [1]; Love Nest, The; Mary; Money, Money, Money; That Might Have Satisfied Grandma; Tom-Tom-Toddle; Waiting; We'll Have a Wonderful Party; When a Woman Exits Laughing

Cast: Jack McGowan; Janet Velie

Notes: Titled THE HOUSE THAT JACK BUILT out of town. [1] Out Washington D.C. 3/29/20.

2768 • MARY JANE MCKANE

OPENED: 12/25/1923   Imperial
Musical   Broadway: 151

Composer: Herbert Stothart; Vincent Youmans
Lyricist: William Cary Duncan; Oscar Hammerstein II

Librettist: William Cary Duncan; Oscar Hammerstein II
Producer: Arthur Hammerstein
Director: Alonzo Price

Choreographer: Sammy Lee; **Costumes:** Charles LeMaire; **Musical Director:** Herbert Stothart; **Set Design:** Frank Gates; E.A. Morange

Songs: All for Charity [5] (L: Oscar Hammerstein II); Come on and Pet Me [1] (C: Vincent Youmans); Down where the Mortgages Grow; Flannel Petticoat Gal, The [4] (C: Vincent Youmans); Give a Girl a Chance [5]; Just Look Around [2]; Laugh It Off; Lovely Lady [5]; Mary Jane McKane; My Boy and I [3] (C: Vincent Youmans); Not in Business Hours; Plain Jane [5]; Rumble of the Subway, The (Subway Chant); Speed; Stick to Your Knitting (C: Herbert Stothart); Thistledown (C: Herbert Stothart); Time-Clock Slaves; Toodle-oo (C: Vincent Youmans); You're Never Too Old [2]

Cast: Eva Clark; Laura DeCardi; Mary Hay; Elizabeth Keene; Margaret Keene; Kitty Kelly; Stanley Rodges; Hal Skelly; Dallas Welford

Notes: Originally titled PLAIN JANE. [1] In scores of A NIGHT OUT (1925) and HIT THE DECK as "Sometimes I'm Happy" with new lyric by Irving Caesar and Clifford Grey. Cut before opening. [2] Added after opening. [3] Became title song of NO, NO, NANETTE with a new lyric by Otto Harbach. [4] Was also in HAMMERSTEIN'S NINE O'CLOCK REVUE. [5] ASCAP/Library of Congress only.

2769 • MARY POPPINS

Musical

Songs: Sun Is Blue, The (C/L: Stephen Sondheim)

Notes: Unfinished. No other information available.

2770 • MARY'S LAMB

OPENED: 05/25/1908   Theatre: New York
Musical   Broadway: 16

Composer: Richard Carle
Lyricist: Richard Carle
Librettist: Richard Carle
Producer: Richard Carle
Director: James Darling

Source: MME. MANGDOLIN (Play); **Musical Director:** Frank Darling

Songs: Betsy's the Belle of the Bathers, The; Finale Act I; I Idolize Ida; If Number 1 Met Number 2; Jamais D'La Vie; Letters [3] (C: Robert Hood Bowers); Love Is Elusive [2] (C: H.L. Heartz); Marching [3]; Modest Little Model, The; My Madagascar Maid; Never Borrow Trouble; Nursie [1]; We're Hollandaise

Cast: Richard Carle; Elita Proctor Otis; John Park

Notes: [1] Out 09/24/13. [2] Also in THE TENDERFOOT. [3] Also in THE MAID AND THE MUMMY. [4] Also in THE SPRING CHICKEN.

2771 • MA'S NEW HUSBAND
OPENED: 10/20/1907
Musical   Closed out of town

Composer: George Fletcher
Lyricist: George Fletcher
Librettist: David Edwin
Producer: Scott & Raynor

Musical Director: Clad Nef

Songs: All the World Loves a Lover; Finale Act III; Great Professor, The; I'd Like to Have a Sweetheart; Jokes; Just a Plain American Girl; Just Arrived from New York; Kiss, A; Let Well Enough Alone; Little Stick of Candy and a Jumping Jack, A; Opening Song; Put Your Loving Arms Around Me; Quiet Little Game, A; Talk Sunshine

Cast: Flora Dorsett; Burt M. Jack; Maud Phelps; Frank Pierlot

Notes: Program of Cedar Rapids.

2772 • MASK AND GOWN
OPENED: 09/10/1957   Theatre: John Golden
Revue   Broadway: 39

Librettist: Sidney Carroll; Ronny Graham
Producer: Bryant Haliday; Leonard Sillman
Director: Leonard Sillman

Choreographer: Jim Russell; **Dance Arranger:** Dorothea Freitag; **Lighting Designer:** Lee

Watson; **Musical Director:** Dorothea Freitag; **Vocal Arranger:** Dorothea Freitag

Songs: Bolero (inst.) (C: Dorothea Freitag); Circus Is Over, The (C: Arthur Siegel; L: June Carroll); Don't Give Up the Ship [2] (C: Harry Warren; L: Al Dubin); Hesitation Waltz (inst.) [1] (C: Emile Waldteufel); House of Blue Lights (C/L: Ronny Graham); How Did He Look? [1] (C/L: Gladys Shelley; Abner Silver); I Cover the Waterfront [4] (C: Johnny Green; L: Edward Heyman); I'll Be Seeing You [6] (C: Sammy Fain; L: Irving Kahal); Make Friends (inst.) (C: Arthur Siegel); New Sounds (C/L: Ronny Graham); Remind Me [3] (C: Jerome Kern; L: Dorothy Fields); Shangri La (C/L: Ronny Graham); Speedy Gonzales (C/L: Ronny Graham); Ten Cents a Dance [7] (C: Richard Rodgers; L: Lorenz Hart); You Better Go Now [5] (C/L: Irvin Graham; Bickley Reichner)

Cast: T.C. Jones; Rod Strong

Notes: [1] Not written for this production. [2] From film SHIPMATES FOREVER. [3] From film ONE NIGHT IN THE TROPICS. [4] From film I COVER THE WATERFRONT. [5] From NEW FACES OF 1936. [6] From RIGHT THIS WAY. [7] From SIMPLE SIMON.

2773 • MASKED MODEL, THE (1916)
Notes: *See MOLLY O'.*

2774 • MASKED MODEL, THE (1917)
OPENED: 04/17/1917
Musical   Closed out of town

Composer: Harold Orlob
Lyricist: Fred Herendeen
Librettist: Harry B. Smith; Robert B. Smith
Producer: John Cort

Songs: Caravan Land; Chat-Chat-Chatter; F-A-S-H-I-O-N; It's a Wonderful World; It's the Clothes that Make the Man; Road to the Girl You Love, The; Two Clocks, The; We Should Care; When Two Hearts Beat in Time; Where Do They Come From

Notes: No program available. Opened in Johnstown, Pa. *See also MOLLY O'.*

2775 • MASS
OPENED: 06/28/1972

Composer: Leonard Bernstein
Lyricist: Leonard Bernstein; Stephen Schwartz
Producer: Sol Hurok; John F. Kennedy Center
Director: Gordon Davidson

Source: LITURGY OF THE ROMAN MASS
  Choreographer: Alvin Ailey; **Costumes:** Frank
  Thompson; **Lighting Designer:** Gilbert V.
  Hemsley Jr.; **Musical Director:** Maurice Peress;
  Set Design: Oliver Smith

Songs: Agnus Dei (L: Liturgy of the Roman Mass);
  Alleluia (L: Liturgy of the Roman Mass);
  Almighty Father (L: Liturgy of the Roman Mass);
  Confiteor (L: Liturgy of the Roman Mass);
  Dominus Vobiscum (L: Liturgy of the Roman
  Mass); Easy; Epiphany (L: Liturgy of the Roman
  Mass); Gloria in Excelsis (L: Liturgy of the
  Roman Mass); Gloria Tibi (L: Liturgy of the
  Roman Mass); God Said [1]; Half the World
  (L: Leonard Bernstein; Stephen Schwartz; Paul
  Simon); Hurry; I Believe in God; I Don't Know;
  I Go On; In Nomine Patris (L: Liturgy of the
  Roman Mass); Kyrie Eleison [1] (L: Liturgy of
  the Roman Mass); Non Credo; Our Father...
  (L: Liturgy of the Roman Mass); Prefatory
  Prayers (L: Liturgy of the Roman Mass); Sanctus
  (L: Liturgy of the Roman Mass); Secret Songs;
  Simple Song, A; Thank You; Things Get Broken;
  Word of the Lord, The; World Without End

Cast: Alvin Ailey American Dance Th.; Berkshire
  Boys' Choir; Jacqueline Britt; David Cryer; Judith
  Jamison; Larry Marshall; Hector Mercado; Mary
  Bracken Phillips; Marion Ramsey; Norman
  Scribner Choir; Neva Small; Louis St. Louis; Alan
  Titus

Notes: Commissioned for the opening of the John
  F. Kennedy Center for the Performing Arts in
  Washington, D.C. on September 5, 1971. This
  production played the Metropolitan Opera
  House. [1] Melody from THE EXCEPTION
  AND THE RULE.

2776 • MASS MURDER IN THE BALCONY OF THE OLD RITZ-RIALTO, A
OPENED: 11/14/1975   Theatre: Elysian
                       Playhouse
Musical   Off-Broadway: 20

Composer: Bill Vitale
Lyricist: Bill Vitale
Librettist: Ed Kuczewski
Producer: Fantasy Factory, The
Director: Bill Vitale

Choreographer: Teddy Kern; Martin Rivera;
  Costumes: Reve Richards; **Dance Arranger:**
  Leon Odenz; **Lighting Designer:** Rick Claflin;
  Musical Director: Leon Odenz; **Orchestrations:**
  James Fradrich; Leon Odenz; **Set Design:**
  Virginia Dancy; Elmon Webb; **Vocal Arranger:**
  Leon Odenz

Songs: Anybody Wanna Buy a Little Love; Comic,
  The; Dope; Dope Double Time; Dope Rag; 42nd
  Street; Homely Woman; I Got Rhythm Too; Let's
  All Go to the Lobby; Musical Chairs; Old Days,
  The; Pictures and an Exhibition; Pink Lady;
  Popcorn and Piss; Savin' Souls; Shadow Song;
  Slumming; Sung-Fu; Time to Go Home; Vernon;
  When You're Shot in the Movies

Cast: Ed Kuczewski; Prima Stephen

2777 • MATA HARI
OPENED: 11/18/1967
Musical   Closed out of town

Composer: Edward Thomas
Lyricist: Martin Charnin
Librettist: Jerome Coopersmith
Producer: David Merrick
Director: Vincente Minnelli

Choreographer: Jack Cole; **Costumes:** Irene
  Sharaff; **Dance Arranger:** Roger Adams;
  Lighting Designer: Jo Mielziner; **Musical
  Director:** Colin Romoff; **Orchestrations:** Robert
  Russell Bennett; **Set Design:** Jo Mielziner; **Vocal
  Arranger:** Colin Romoff

Songs: Arrest Ballet, The (inst.); Choice Is Yours,
  The [2]; Everyone Has Something to Hide [2];
  Hello, Yank! [2]; How Young You Were
  Tonight [2]; I Don't See Him Very Much
  Anymore [2]; I'm Saving Myself for a Soldier [2];
  In Madrid; Interrogation Ballet (inst.); Is This
  Fact? [2]; Maman [2]; Mata Hari in Spain [3];
  Mata Hari's Dance at the Salon [4]; No More
  than a Moment [2]; Not Now, Not Here [2];
  Sextette [4]; There Is No You; There Will Be
  Love Again; This Is Not a Very Nice War [3];
  You Have No Idea

Cast: Blythe Danner; Mark Dempsey; Marisa Mell; Pernell Roberts; Martha Schlamme

Notes: Closed 12/9/67 National Theatre, Washington D.C. Rewritten as BALLAD FOR A FIRING SQUAD. *See BALLAD FOR A FIRING SQUAD.* [1] Not in program. [2] Also later included in BALLAD FOR A FIRING SQUAD. [3] Cut. From script of 8/67 when title was TONIGHT — MATA HARI. [4] Also later included in BALLAD FOR A FIRING SQUAD. Cut. From scirpt of 8/67 when title was TONIGHT — MATA HARI.

2778 • MATER

OPENED: 09/23/1908   Theatre: Savoy
Play   Broadway: 27

Author: Percy MacKaye
Producer: Henry Miller
Director: Frank Brownlee

Songs: Mater's Song (C/L: Unknown)

Cast: Isabel Irving; Hazel MacKaye; Charles A. Stevenson

2779 • MATILDA

OPENED: 12/31/1906   Theatre: Lincoln Square
Musical   Broadway: 17

Composer: George H. Gartlan
Lyricist: Everett Ruskay
Librettist: I.N. Morris
Producer: Walter N. Lawrence
Director: George Foster Platt

Musical Director: John J. Braham

Songs: Affinity; I Wonder If the Thing's Worthwhile; Innocent Debutante, The; It's Nice to Be a Girl; Love Me in the Winter; Mermaids; Roll On; What Is Life-What Is Love?; Who's Your Gen'man Frien'?; Wow-Yip-Po

Cast: Maude Fulton; Charles Lane; Amy Ricard

2780 • MATINEE GIRL, THE (1926)

OPENED: 02/01/1926   Theatre: Forrest
Musical   Broadway: 25

Composer: Frank H. Grey
Lyricist: Bide Dudley; McElbert Moore

Librettist: Bide Dudley; McElbert Moore
Producer: Edward Rosenbaum
Director: Oscar Grey

Choreographer: S. Lee Rose; **Musical Director:** Frank H. Grey; **Set Design:** Joseph Physioc

Songs: At the Matinee; Biggest Thing in My Life, The; Do I Dear?, I Do (C/L: McElbert Moore); Havanola Roll; His Spanish Guitar; Holding Hands; Joy Ride (C: Frank Grey; McElbert Moore); Jumping Jack; Like-a-Me, Like-a-You (C: Frank Grey; L: McElbert Moore); Little Bit of Spanish, A; Mash Notes (C: Frank Grey; McElbert Moore); Never Say Diet [1]; One You Love, The; Only One (C: Frank Grey; L: McElbert Moore); Raisin and You [1]; Waiting All the Time for You; What Difference Does It Make (C: Constance Shepard); When My Ship Comes In

Cast: James Hamilton; Jack Squire; Olga Steck

Notes: [1] Out Wilkes-Barre 12/25/25.

2781 • MATINEE GIRLS (1914)

OPENED: 1914
Musical

Composer: Gus Edwards
Lyricist: Gus Edwards
Producer: Gus Edwards

Songs: I'm Going to Let the Whole World Know I Love You

Cast: Gus Edwards

Notes: No other information available.

2782 • MATINEE IDOL, A

OPENED: 04/28/1910   Theatre: Daly's
Musical   Broadway: 68

Composer: Silvio Hein
Lyricist: A. Seymour Brown; E. Ray Goetz
Librettist: Armand Barnard
Producer: Daniel V. Arthur

Songs: Hypnotic Waltz, The (Hyp-Hyp-Hypnotism) (inst.) [1]; I Will Always Love You, Dear; I'm Looking for a Husband [1]; Little Lady in the Moon; Loving Ways; Nonsense; That Dancing Big Banshee; Won't You Let Me Build a

Nest for You (The Robin and the Wren); Won't You Write Your Autograph in My Album (L: E. Ray Goetz); Yankee Romeo (L: E. Ray Goetz)

Cast: Louise Dresser; DeWolf Hopper; Georgie Mack; Joseph Santley

Notes: No program available. [1] Sheet music only.

2783 • MATINEE KIDS, THE
OPENED: 03/10/1981   Theatre: BTA
Musical   Off-Broadway: 15

Composer: Brian Lasser
Lyricist: Garry Bormet; Gary Gardner; Brian Lasser
Librettist: Garry Bormet; Gary Gardner
Producer: Fisher Theatre Foundation
Director: Garry Bormet; Brian Lasser

Choreographer: Carol Marik; **Costumes:** Bruce H. Brumage; **Lighting Designer:** Peter Anderson; **Musical Director:** Laurence J. Esposito; **Orchestrations:** Don Jones; **Set Design:** Nancy Winters

Songs: Alborada; Couple of Years from Now, A; Date, The; Favorite Son; First to Walk Away; Footprints; Hello Tom; Hi!; Hold Me; Just to Look at Him; Lucky Baby; Lucky Love; Matinee

Cast: Scott Baker; Liz Callaway; Michael Corbett; Colleen Dodson; Will Jeffries; Karen Mason

2784 • MATTER OF OPINION, A
OPENED: 09/30/1980   Theatre: Players
Musical   Off-Broadway: 8

Composer: Harold Danko; John Jacobson
Lyricist: Mary Elizabeth Hauer
Librettist: Mary Elizabeth Hauer
Producer: Miracle Expressions, Inc.
Director: Shari Upbin

Choreographer: Shari Upbin; **Costumes:** John Arnone; **Dance Arranger:** Dan Palkowsky; **Lighting Designer:** Joanna Schielke; **Musical Director:** John Jacobson; **Set Design:** John Arnone; **Vocal Arranger:** Dan Palkowsky

Songs: ABC to XYZ; Almost Working; Average Man, The; Determination; Free Time; Gotta

Pretend; Hobo's Song; Hooray for the Judge; Humanity; I Am Here; If the Sun Didn't Shine Each Day; Just the Facts; Matter of Opinion; Mrs. Finished Lament; No Thank You from a Mocking Sun; Not Every Day Can Be a Day of Shine; Opening; Sandman, The; Shopping Bag Lady; Wanderer, The

Cast: David Anchel; Andy Bey; Janet Bliss; Ralph Braun; Vickie Chappell; Leigh Finner; Kate Klugman; Seymour Penzner; Suzanne Smartt; Charles Randolph Wright

2785 • MATTER OF TIME, A
OPENED: 04/27/1975   Theatre: Playhouse
Musical   Off-Broadway: 1

Composer: Philip F. Margo
Lyricist: Philip F. Margo
Librettist: Russell Leib; Hap Schlein
Producer: Jeff Britton
Director: Tod Jackson

Choreographer: Tod Jackson; **Dance Arranger:** Arnold Gross; **Lighting Designer:** Martin Aronstein; **Musical Director:** Arnold Gross; **Orchestrations:** Eliot Gilman; **Set Design:** David Guthrie; **Vocal Arranger:** Arnold Gross

Songs: Devil in Your Eyes, The; Don't Let Me Bother You; I Am the Next; I Can Count on Me [1]; I Can Give You Music; If This Were My World; I'm Not Just Another Mother [1]; It Will Be My Day; It's Not Easy Being Next; Matter of Time, A; Me God, Please God; Oh, What a Wonderful Plan; Oh, World; Purgatory U; Ritual, The; Sex Is a Spectator Sport; Snake; This Is Your Year 1976; This Moment; Time Is a Travellin' Show; Welcome to Hell; Winner

Cast: David-James Carroll; Carol Estey; Joe Masiell; Leland Schwantes; Glory Van Scott

Notes: [1] Cut prior to New York opening.

2786 • MAY WINE
OPENED: 12/05/1935   Theatre: St. James
Musical   Broadway: 212

Composer: Sigmund Romberg
Lyricist: Oscar Hammerstein II
Librettist: Frank Mandel

Producer: Laurence Schwab
Director: Jose Ruben

Source: HAPPY ALIENIST, THE (Novel: Wallace Smith); **Costumes:** Kay Morrison; **Musical Director:** Robert Emmett Dolan; **Orchestrations:** Robert Russell Bennett; Don Walker; **Set Design:** Raymond Sovey

Songs: Always Be a Gentleman; Chanson on the Prater, A; Dance, My Darlings; Doll Fantasy, A; Finale Act I; I Built a Dream One Day; Interlude in a Barber Shop [1]; Just Once Around the Clock; Somebody Ought to Be Told; Something the Air of May; Something New Is in My Heart; You Wait and Wait and Wait

Cast: Leo G. Carroll; Jack Cole; Robert C. Fischer; Walter Woolf King; Earle MacVeigh; Nancy McCord; Walter Slezak

Notes: [1] ASCAP/Library of Congress only.

2787 • MAYBE I'M DOING IT WRONG

OPENED: 03/14/1982   Theatre: Astor Place
Musical   Off-Broadway: 33

Composer: Randy Newman
Lyricist: Randy Newman
Librettist: Joan Micklin Silver
Producer: Raphael Silver
Director: Joan Micklin Silver

Choreographer: Eric Elice; **Costumes:** Hilary Rosenfeld; **Lighting Designer:** Fred Buchholz; **Musical Director:** Michael S. Roth; **Set Design:** Heidi Landesman; **Vocal Arranger:** Michael S. Roth

Songs: Birmingham; Caroline; Davy the Fat Boy; Dayton Ohio 1903; Debutante's Ball, The; God's Song (That Why I Love Mankind); I'll Be Home; It's Money That I Love; Jolly Coppers on Parade; Love Story; Marie; Maybe I'm Doing It Wrong; My Old Kentucky Home; Old Man; Political Science; Rider in the Rain; Rollin'; Sail Away; Short People; Simon Smith and the Amazing Dancing Bear; Tickle Me; Yellow Man; You Can Leave Your Hat On

Cast: Mark Linn-Baker; Patti Perkins; Deborah Rush; Treat Williams

Notes: Consisted of previously written songs.

2788 • MAYFAIR AND MONTMARTRE

OPENED: 03/09/1922   Theatre: New Oxford
Revue   London: 77

Composer: Cole Porter
Lyricist: Cole Porter
Librettist: John Hastings Turner
Producer: Charles Cochran; Oxford Ltd, The
Director: Edward Dolly

Choreographer: Edward Dolly; **Costumes:** Robert E. Locker; James Reynolds; **Musical Director:** J.B. Hastings; **Set Design:** Robert E. Lochner; James Reynolds

Songs: Bandit Band, The [1]; Blue Boy Blues, The; Cocktail Time; Olga (Come Back to the Volga); Sponge, The [1]; Wond'ring Night and Day [2]

Cast: Joyce Barbour; A.W. Baskcomb; Albert Bruno; Alice Delysia; Teddy Edlin; George Hassell; Edna May; Nellie Taylor; Lady Tree

Notes: [1] Not used. Later in HITCHY-KOO of 1922. [2] Not used.

2789 • MAYFLOWERS

OPENED: 11/24/1925   Theatre: Forrest
Musical   Broadway: 81

Composer: Edward Kunneke
Lyricist: Clifford Grey
Librettist: Clifford Grey
Producer: Messrs. Shubert
Director: Joseph Santley; William J. Wilson

Source: NOT SO LONG AGO (Play: Arthur Richman); **Choreographer:** Earl Lindsay; **Costumes:** Marion Frazee; Harriet Liebman; **Musical Director:** J. Frank Cork; **Set Design:** Watson Barratt

Songs: Down on a Country Farm; Finale Act I; Foolish Wives; Good Night Ladies; Grecian Bend, The; How Do You Do? How Do You Do?; Lancers, The; Mayflower I Love You (C: J. Fred Coots; Maurie Rubens; Pat Thayer; L: Clifford Grey; Donovan Parsons); Oh! Sam (C: J. Fred Coots; Maurie Rubens); Opening Act II; Play Me a New Tune (C: J. Fred Coots; Maurie Rubens); Put Your Troubles in a Candy Box (C: J. Fred Coots); Regiment Loves the Girls, The; Road to Dreams, The (C: J. Fred Coots; Maurie Rubens; Pat Thayer; L: Clifford Grey; Donovan Parsons); Seven Days; Take a Little Stroll with Me (C: J. Fred Coots; Maurie Rubens); Wedding Rehearsal, The; Whoa, Emma!; Woman

Cast: Joseph Santley; Ivy Sawyer; Robert Woolsey

Notes: Additional numbers credited to Frank Tours but not identified.

2790 • MAYOR

OPENED: 05/13/1985   Theatre: Top of the Gate
Musical   Off-Broadway: 185

Composer: Charles Strouse
Lyricist: Charles Strouse
Librettist: Warren Leight
Producer: Mary Lea Johnson; Jerry Kravat; Martin Richards
Director: Jeffrey B. Moss

Choreographer: Barbara Siman; **Costumes:** Randy Barcelo; **Dance Arranger:** Michael Kosarin; **Lighting Designer:** Richard Winkler; **Musical Director:** Michael Kosarin; **Orchestrations:** Christopher Bankey; **Set Design:** Randy Barcelo; **Vocal Arranger:** Michael Kosarin

Songs: Ballad (1); Ballad (2) (L: Warren Leight); Good Times; Hootspa; How'm I Doin'?; I Want to Be the Mayor; Isn't It Time for the People; Last 'I Love New York' Song, The; March of the Yuppies; Mayor; My City; New York [1]; Oh, I Want to Be the Mayor [1]; We Are One; What You See Is What You Get; You Can Be a New Yorker Too!; You're Not the Mayor

Cast: Douglas Bernstein; Marion J. Caffey; Keith Curran; Nancy Giles; Ken Jennings; Ilene Kristen; Kathryn McAteer; Lenny Wolpe

Notes: [1] ASCAP/Library of Congress only.

2791 • MAYOR OF NEWTOWN, THE (1909)

OPENED: 1909
Musical

Composer: J. Homer Tutt; Salem Tutt Whitney
Lyricist: J. Homer Tutt; Salem Tutt Whitney
Librettist: J. Homer Tutt; Salem Tutt Whitney
Producer: Salem Tutt Whitney

Cast: Will Dixon; Frank Jenkins; Ethel Marshall; Russell Smith; Al Stauder; J. Homer Tutt; George Warden; Salem Tutt Whitney

Notes: No other information available.

2792 • MAYOR OF NEWTOWN, THE (1912)

OPENED: 1912
Musical

Composer: T.L. Corwell; J. Homer Tutt; Henry Watterston
Lyricist: J. Homer Tutt; Salem Tutt Whitney
Librettist: J. Homer Tutt; Salem Tutt Whitney
Producer: Salem Tutt Whitney

Songs: Good Night, Marie; Here I Is and Here I Stay; Hot Tamale Sam; I Could Learn to Love a Boy Like You; I'm the Mayor of Newtown; Neat Ned Nuff Sed; Tell Me Rose; You, Babe, Only You

Cast: Ethel Marshall; Alfred Strauder; Edward Tolliver; J. Homer Tutt; Leigh Whipper; Salem Tutt Whitney

Notes: No other information available.
A reworking of the 1909 show with additional credits.

2793 • MAYOR OF TOKIO, THE

OPENED: 12/04/1905   Theatre: New York
Musical   Broadway: 50

Composer: William Frederick Peters
Lyricist: Richard Carle
Librettist: Richard Carle
Producer: Richard Carle

Choreographer: Ad Newberger

Songs: Bridal Song; Cheer Up Everybody; Comic Opera Capsule, A; Conspirators Are We; Cruising Home; Danse Blanche et Noir; Entrance of Kow Tow (L: Robert I. Beecher); Entrance of Princes (L: Robert I. Beecher); Festival of Mourning (L: Robert I. Beecher; James R.

Montague); Finale, Act I; Foolishness (L: Arthur Gillespie); I Like You [2] (L: Campbell; Richard Carle; Skinner); I Wouldn't Do That, Would You? (L: Arthur Gillespie); Is Marriage a Failure?; Josie from Joliet; Kidder's Reception; Mayor of Tokio, The; Pity My Pitiful Plight; Silver Sea of Love, The [1]; Tale of a Monkey [1]; They Kiss (L: M.E. Rourke); Toast to the Moon (Round Red Moon) (L: James Montague); Tokio; Welcome Oloto; When the Ocean Breezes Blow (L: Arthur Gillespie)

Cast: May Boley; Richard Carle; Emma Janvier; William Rock; Adele Rowland

Notes: [1] Sheet music only. [2] New version of lyrics by Richard Carle.

2794 • MAYTIME

OPENED: 08/16/1917   Theatre: Shubert
Musical   Broadway: 492

Composer: Sigmund Romberg
Lyricist: Rida Johnson Young
Librettist: Rida Johnson Young
Producer: Messrs. Shubert
Director: Edward P. Temple

Source: WIE EINST IM MAI (Musical: Rudolf Bernauer; Willy Bredschneider; Walter Kollo; Rudolf Schanzer); **Choreographer:** Allan K. Foster; **Costumes:** Homer Conant; **Musical Director:** Frank Tours; **Set Design:** Homer Conant

Songs: Dancing Will Keep You Young (L: Cyrus Wood); Everything Has Been Done [1]; Go Away, Girls (L: Cyrus Wood); Gypsy Song; In Our Little Home Sweet Home; It's a Windy Day at the Battery; Jump Jim Crow; Just What I Wanted [1]; Odd Lots, Job Lots (Opening Chorus Act III); Only One Girl for Me; Opening Chorus Act I; P.T. Barnum [1]; Reminiscence; Road to Paradise, The; Selling Gowns (L: Cyrus Wood; Rida Johnson Young); Spanish Dance [2]; Will You Remember (Sweetheart); You Matthew Dear [1]

Cast: William Norris; Charles Purcell; Peggy Wood

Notes: Cyrus Wood credited with book and lyrics out of town. [1] Out Stamford 8/7/17. [2] Sheet music only.

2795 • MCFADDEN'S FLATS

OPENED: 02/28/1907
Play   Closed out of town

Author: Glen McDonough; E.W. Townsend

Musical Director: M.L. Lake

Songs: Bull Frog and the Coon; If the Man in the Moon Were a Coon; Is Everybody Happy; Next Horse I Ride On, The; Oh, What a Night to Spoon; Old Black Crow, The; Tale of a Stroll; Tell the Band to Play an Irish Tune; When I Get Back to Boston Town

Cast: Lillian Beach; Edna Dorman; John Price; James Purvis

Notes: Program of Wilkes-Barre. The songs were almost certainly all popular songs of the day.

2796 • ME AND BESSIE

OPENED: 10/22/1975   Theatre: Ambassador
Revue   Broadway: 453

Librettist: Will Holt
Producer: Lee Apostoleris; Center Theatre Group
Director:

Choreographer: Lester Wilson; **Costumes:** Pete Menefee; **Lighting Designer:** Tharon Musser; **Musical Director:** Howlett Smith; **Set Design:** Donald Harris

Songs: After You've Gone (C: Turner Layton; L: Henry Creamer); Do Your Duty; Empty Bed Blues; Fare Thee Well; Gimme a Pigfoot; God Shall Wipe All the Tears Away; Good Man Is Hard to Find, A (C/L: Eddie Green); Hot Time in the Old Town Tonight (C: Theodore Metz; L: Joe Hayden); I Feel Good; Jazzbo Brown; Kitchen Man; Mama Don't 'Low; Man's Alright, The; Moan You Moaners; New Orleans Hop Scotch Blues; Nobody Knows You When You're Down and Out; Preach Them Blues; Put It Right Here; Romance in the Dark; Tain't Nobody's Bizness If I Do; Trombone Cholly; Trouble; You've Been a Good Old Wagon but You've Done Broke Down (C/L: Ben Harney)

Cast: Gerri Dean; Linda Hopkins; Lester Wilson

Notes: Moved to the Edison Theatre 12/3/75. No songs written for this show.

2797 • ME AND JULIET

OPENED: 05/28/1953   Theatre: Majestic
Musical   Broadway: 358

Composer: Richard Rodgers
Lyricist: Oscar Hammerstein II
Librettist: Oscar Hammerstein II
Producer: Oscar Hammerstein II; Richard Rodgers
Director: George Abbott

Choreographer: Robert Alton; **Costumes:** Irene Sharaff; **Dance Arranger:** Roger Adams; **Lighting Designer:** Jo Mielziner; **Musical Director:** Salvatore Dell'Isola; **Orchestrations:** Don Walker; **Set Design:** Jo Mielziner; **Vocal Arranger:** Don Walker

Songs: Baby You Love, The [1]; Big Black Giant, The; I'm Your Girl; Intermission Talk; It Feels Good; It's Me; Julius Baum [1]; Keep It Gay; Marriage Type Love; Me and Juliet; Me, Who Am I [1]; Meat and Potatoes [1]; No Other Love [2]; Opening; Opening Second Act; That's the Way It Happens; Very Special Day, A; Wake Up Little Theatre [1]; We Deserve Each Other; You Never Had It So Good [1]

Cast: Isabel Bigley; Barbara Carroll; Mark Dawson; Bob Fortier; Bill Hayes; George S. Irving; Jackie Kelk; Michael King; Ralph Linn; Arthur Maxwell; Joan McCracken; Buzz Miller; Helena Scott; Ray Walston

Notes: [1] Dropped. [2] Same music as "Beneath the Southern Cross" written for TV show VICTORY AT SEA.

2798 • ME AND MY GIRL

OPENED: 08/10/1986   Theatre: Marquis
Musical   Broadway: 1420

Composer: Noel Gay
Lyricist: Douglas Furber; L. Arthur Rose
Librettist: Stephen Fry; Douglas Furber; Mike Ockrent; L. Arthur Rose
Producer: Richard Armitage; Terry Allen Kramer; James M. Nederlander; Stage Promotions Ltd. & Co.
Director: Mike Ockrent

Choreographer: Gillian Gregory; Conductor: Thomas Helm; **Costumes:** Ann Curtis; **Dance Arranger:** Chris Walker; **Lighting Designer:** Chris Ellis; Roger Morgan; **Musical Director:** Stanley Lebowsky; **Orchestrations:** Chris Walker; **Set Design:** Martin Johns

Songs: English Gentleman, An (Domestic Discussion, A) [3]; Family Solicitor, The [1]; Hold My Hand [4] (L: Maurice Elwin; Noel Gay; Harry Graham); I Would If I Could [1]; If Only You Had Cared for Me [5]; Lambeth Walk, The [1]; Laugh and the World Laughs with You [2]; Leaning on a Lamppost (L: Noel Gay); Love Makes the World Go Round (L: Noel Gay); Me and My Girl [1]; Once You Lose Your Heart; Opening Number [3]; Preparation Fugue; Raspberries [2]; Song of Hareford (L: Noel Gay); Sun Has Got Its Hat On, The (L: Ralph Butler); Take It on the Chin [1] (L: Douglas Furber); That's That [2]; Thinking of No-One but Me [1]; Weekend at Hareford, A

Cast: Jane Connell; Eric Hutson; George S. Irving; Timothy Jerome; Justine Johnston; Elizabeth Larner; Leo Leyden; Robert Lindsay; Maryann Plunkett; Jane Summerhays; Nick Ullett

Notes: [1] From original London production (1937). [2] Cut prior to original London opening. [3] From original London production but not in Broadway or London revival. [4] Originally title song of HOLD MY HAND. [5] Cut from London revival.

2799 • ME FOR YOU

Notes: *See HEADS UP!*

2800 • ME, HIM, AND I (1905)

OPENED: 03/13/1905
Musical   Chicago

Composer: Max Hoffmann
Lyricist: Vincent Bryan
Librettist: Willard Holcomb
Director: Jules Hurtig

Choreographer: Gertrude Hoffman; **Orchestrations:** William Shaffer

Songs: Aber Nit; All Aboard; Floating Down the Old Green River [1]; Football Girls, The; Football Song [1]; Good Night, Evangeline; Good Ship Whip-poor-will [1]; Harry, Harry; Henry Dinkenspiel; In Dear Old Fatherland; Jelly Roll [1]; Me, Him and I; Midnight Mooch [1]; My Bonita Conchita; My Seminole [1]; My Yukon Belle; Old Fashioned Melody [1]; Over the

Moonlit Sea; Professor and His Pupils, The; Sailing; Self-Made Man, The; Songs of Nations; Worst Woman on the Stage, The [1]

Cast: George Richel; Harry Watson

Notes: Program from Cedar Rapids. Opened at the Great Northern Theatre, Chicago. [1] From program of Wilmington 11/22/15.

2801 • ME NOBODY KNOWS, THE

OPENED: 05/18/1971 Theatre: Orpheum
Revue Off-Broadway: 587

Composer: Gary William Friedman
Lyricist: Will Holt
Producer: Jeff Britton
Director: Robert H. Livingston

Source: ME NOBODY KNOWS, THE (Book); **Choreographer:** Patricia Birch; **Costumes:** Patricia Quinn Stuart; **Dance Arranger:** Gary William Friedman; **Lighting Designer:** Clarke Dunham; **Musical Director:** Edward Strauss; **Orchestrations:** Gary William Friedman; **Set Design:** Clarke Dunham; **Vocal Arranger:** Gary William Friedman

Songs: Black; Dream Babies; Flying Milk and Runaway Plates; Fugue for Four Girls; Horse, The; How I Feel; I Love What the Girls Have; If I Had a Million Dollars; Jail Life Walk; Let Me Come In; Light Sings; Me Nobody Knows, The [1]; Numbers; Rejoice; Robert, Alvin, Wendall and Jo Jo; Something Beautiful; Sounds; Take Hold the Crutch; This World; Tree, The; War Babies; What Happens to Life

Cast: Northern J. Calloway; Irene Cara; Hattie Winston

Notes: The run of this show was interrupted by the Actors' Equity strike. It reopened at the Helen Hayes Theatre on Broadway on 12/18/71. The libretto is based on works by children of ages 7-18 which were written for teacher Stephen M. Joseph. These works by inner city children were collected into a book of the same name. [1] Added to television version.

2802 • MECCA

OPENED: 10/04/1920 Theatre: Century
Musical Broadway: 130

Composer: Percy E. Fletcher
Lyricist: Oscar Asche
Librettist: Oscar Asche
Producer: F. Ray Comstock; Morris Gest
Director: E. Lyall Swete

Choreographer: Percy Anderson; **Costumes:** Leon Bakst; Alice O'Neil; **Musical Director:** Frank Tours; **Set Design:** Joseph Harker; Phil Harker

Songs: Allah Guard Thee; Bacchanale; Chinese Interlude; Dance Poem; Fool There Was, A; From Bagdad We Come; Gates of Cairo, The; Hast Thou Been to Mecca?; In the Harem; In the Palace Gardens; Intermezzo; Kin of Nur Al-Din, The; Love in My Breast [1]; Me Welly Poor Old Chinaman; My King of Love; Pilgrim's Prayer, The; Procession and Ballet; Sharazad's Theme; Slave Market, The; When Love Knocked Upon the Door

Cast: Lionel Braham; Orville R. Caldwell; Herbert Grimwood; Gladys Hanson; John Nicholson; Hannah Toback

Notes: [1] Lyric adapted from Sir Richard Burton.

2803 • MEDAL AND THE MAID, THE

OPENED: 01/11/1904 Theatre: Broadway
Musical Broadway: 49

Composer: Sidney Jones
Lyricist: Charles H. Taylor
Librettist: Owen Hall
Producer: John C. Fisher; Thomas W. Ryley
Director: Cyril Scott

Choreographer: Tom Terriss; **Musical Director:** Arthur Weld; **Set Design:** Moses & Hamilton

Songs: Any Sort of Girl; Brigand Chief; Consequences; Frills Upon Their Petticoats; Hide and Seek; If Girls Had Wings; I'm Going to Be a Marquis; In My Curriculum; In Zanzibar (C: Gus Edwards; L: Will D. Cobb); Katie and Her Kodak; Man Behind, The; My Love I Dare Not Tell Thee (C/L: Stenhammer); Opening Chorus; Polo; Prize for That, A; Publicity; Rain or Shine; Well-Bred Girl, A; Who'll Buy My Flowers

Cast: W.T. Carleton; Emma Carus; Ignacio Martinetti; James T. Powers; Cyril Scott

2804 • MEDIUM RARE

OPENED: 07/06/1960
Revue   Chicago

Librettist: Herbert Hartig; Bud McCreery
Producer: Robert Weiner
Director: Bill Penn

Dance Arranger: Dorothea Freitag; **Musical Director:** Joseph Richter; **Set Design:** Ritholz Associates; **Vocal Arranger:** Bud McCreery; Joseph Richter; Marty Rubenstein

Songs: Arts, The [6] (C: Charles Strouse; L: Lee Adams); Career Malice (C/L: Jay Thompson); Circus Sort of Day (C/L: Jay Thompson); Downtown (C: Charles Strouse; L: Lee Adams); Garbage [1] (C/L: Sheldon Harnick); Guess Who Was There [3] (C/L: Bud McCreery); Isms [5] (C: David Baker; L: Sheldon Harnick); Love Song (C: Charles Strouse; L: Lee Adams); Man's Inhumanity to Man [2] (C: Charles Strouse; L: Michael Stewart); Medea in Disneyland [1] (C: Lloyd Norlin; L: Sheldon Harnick); Mink, Mink, Mink [1] (C/L: Bud McCreery); Street Songs (C: Charles Strouse; L: Lee Adams); Summer Is [4] (C: Jerry Bock; L: Sheldon Harnick); Tempo of the Times (C: Cy Coleman; L: Carolyn Leigh); Who Do We Thank (C: Charles Strouse; L: Lee Adams)

Cast: Jean Arnold; Bobo Lewis; Anne Meara; Jerry Stiller

Notes: [1] Also in SHOESTRING REVUE (1955). [2] Also in JOY RIDE and SHOESTRING REVUE. [3] Also in DEMI-DOZEN. [4] From THE BODY BEAUTIFUL. [5] Also in VINTAGE '60. [6] Also in SHOESTRING REVUE '57.

2805 • MEET ME IN ST. LOUIS

OPENED: 11/02/1989   Theatre: Gershwin
Musical   Broadway: 253

Composer: Ralph Blane; Hugh Martin
Lyricist: Ralph Blane; Hugh Martin
Librettist: Hugh Wheeler
Producer: Brickhill-Burke Prods.; EPI Productions; Christopher Seabrooke
Director: Louis Burke

Source: KENSINGTON STORIES, THE (Story: Sally Benson); **Source:** MEET ME IN ST. LOUIS (Film: Irving Brecher; Fred F. Finklehoffe);

Choreographer: Joan Brickhill; **Costumes:** Keith Anderson; **Dance Arranger:** James Raitt; **Lighting Designer:** Ken Billington; **Musical Director:** Bruce Pomahac; **Orchestrations:** Michael Gibson; **Set Design:** Keith Anderson; **Vocal Arranger:** Hugh Martin; Bruce Pomahac

Songs: Almost [5]; Ball, The; Banjos [6]; Be Anything But a Girl [2]; Boy Next Door, The [1]; Day in New York, A; Diamonds in the Starlight [7]; Ghosties and Ghoulies and Things That Go Bump in the Night; Have Yourself a Merry Little Christmas [1]; How Do I Look? [5]; How to Behave Like a Lady (How to Dress Like a Lady) (How to Faint Like a Lady) [5]; I Happen to Love You [8]; Ice [2]; If I Had an Igloo [5]; Meet Me in St. Louis [1] (C/L: Kerry Mills; Andrew B. Sterling); Paging Mr. Sousa; Raving Beauty [4]; Skip to My Lou [3] (C/L: Ralph Blane; Hugh Martin; Traditional); Touch of the Irish, A; Trolley Song, The [1]; Under the Bamboo Tree [1] (C: J. Rosamond Johnson; L: Bob Cole); Wasn't It Fun; What's-His-Name [5]; Would You Let Me [5]; You Are for Loving [4]

Cast: Betty Garrett; Rachael Graham; George Hearn; Donna Kane; Juliet Lambert; Charlotte Moore; Milo O'Shea; Michael O'Steen; Courtney Peldon; Gordon Stanley; Jason Workman

Notes: [1] From movie version. [2] From TV Musical HANS BRINKER. [3] From movie version. Martin and Blane's arrangement of this favorite was originally recorded in 1941 by The Martins (Hugh Martin, Jo Jean Rogers, Phyllis Rogers and Ralph Blane). [4] From revival of BEST FOOT FORWARD. [5] In 1960 Municipal Opera, St. Louis production only. [6] Written but not used in an MGM film. [7] From 1960 Municipal Opera, St. Louis production. [8] From TV Musical HANS BRINKER. Refrain included in "The Boy Next Door" in this production.

2806 • MEET MISS APRIL

OPENED: 1947
Musical   Unproduced

Composer: Jerome Kern
Lyricist: Otto Harbach

Songs: Born in April; Glory of the Corps; Gonna Go Along with Lincoln; Headin' for a Weddin' in the Sky; I Heard a Bugle Blowing; Illinois; In the Shadows; Let's Dance Till the Dawn; Let's

Dream Together; Psychology; Soldier Like You, A; Song of the Napkin Rings; When They Call the Roll at West Point

Notes: Written by Harbach after Kern's death (11/11/45) using Kern trunk melodies.

2807 • MEET MISS JONES
OPENED: 1947
Musical   New York

Composer: James P. Johnson
Lyricist: Flournoy E. Miller
Librettist: Flournoy E. Miller
Producer: Walter Brooks
Director: Walter Brooks

Songs: Don't Lose Your Head (And Lose Your Gal); I've Got to Be Lovely for Harry; You're My Rose

Notes: No other information available. Produced at the Experimental Theatre on 125th Street.

2808 • MEET MY SISTER
OPENED: 12/30/1930   Theatre: Shubert
Musical   Broadway: 165

Composer: Ralph Benatzky
Lyricist: Ralph Benatzky
Librettist: Harry Wagstaff Gribble
Producer: Messrs. Shubert
Director: William Mollison

Source: MA SOEUR ET MOI (Play: Georges Berr; Louis Verneuil); **Source:** MEINE SCHWESTER UND ICH (Musical: Ralph Benatzky; Robert Blum); **Choreographer:** John Pierce; **Musical Director:** Irving Schloss; **Set Design:** Watson Barratt

Songs: Always in My Heart; Birds in the Spring; Devil May Care, The; Do Something Different [1] (C: Harry Revel; L: Mack Gordon); Five Thousand Francs; Friendship; I Gotta Have My Moments; I Like You (C: Harry Revel; L: Mack Gordon); I Stumbled Over You and Fell in Love [1] (C: Harry Revel; L: Mack Gordon); If You Want to Be Successful in the Cinema [1] (C: Harry Revel; L: Mack Gordon); It's Money-It's Fame-It's Love; I've Fallen Out of Love [1] (C: Harry Revel; L: Mack Gordon); Lonely Little Extras [2] (C: Harry Revel; L: Mack Gordon); Look and Love Is Here; Love Is Faded

Away; Radziwill; She Is My Ideal; Tell Me What Can This Be; There Will Be a Girl (There Will Be a Boy) [1] (C: Harry Warren; L: Mack Gordon)

Cast: Boyd Davis; George Grossmith; Bettina Hall; Kay McKay; Olive Olsen; Walter Slezak; Harry Welsh

Notes: [1] ASCAP/Library of Congress only. These songs were registered in 1931. They might have been written for a tour? [2] ASCAP/Library of Congress only. These songs were registered in 1931. They might have been written for a tour? Also not used in the score of SMILING FACES.

2809 • MEET THE PEOPLE
OPENED: 12/25/1940   Theatre: Mansfield
Revue   Broadway: 160

Composer: Jay Gorney
Lyricist: Henry Myers
Librettist: Ben Barzman; Sol Barzman; Henry Blankfort; Danny Dare; Edward Eliscu; Ray Golden; Milt Gross; Sid Kuller; Bert Lawrence; Mortimer Offner; Mike Quin; Arthur Ross
Producer: Hollywood Alliance
Director: Danny Dare; Mortimer Offner

Costumes: Kate Drain Lawson; Gerda Vanderneers; **Dance Arranger:** Art Wilson; **Lighting Designer:** Roy Holmes; **Musical Director:** Archie Bleyer; **Orchestrations:** George Bassman; Archie Bleyer; Charles Miller; David Raksin; **Set Design:** Fred Stover

Songs: American Plan; Bill of Rights, The (Congress Shall Make No Law); (It Seems There Was a) Fellow and a Girl, A (L: Edward Eliscu); Fellow and a Girl, A [1]; Hurdi Gurdi Verdi (C: Giuseppe Verdi); In Chi-chi-castinango; It's the Same Old South, The (L: Edward Eliscu); Legend of the Sleeping Beauty, The (Scene) (C: George Bassman); Let's Steal a Tune from Offenbach; Meet the People; No Lookin' Back (L: Edward Eliscu; Henry Myers); Senate in Session; Stars Remain, The; Union Label (L: Edward Eliscu; Henry Myers); Voulez Vous, May I Have the Next Waltz, Mrs. Yiffnif [1]; We Have Sandwiches [1]

Cast: Jack Albertson; Marion Colby; Nanette Fabray; Jack Gilford; Robert Nash; Peggy Ryan; Doodles Weaver; Jack Williams

Notes: Revue editor: Edward Eliscu. [1]
ASCAP/Library of Congress only.

2810 • MEET THE PEOPLE OF 1955

OPENED: 1955
Revue

Composer: Jay Gorney
Lyricist: Edward Eliscu

Songs: Are You Now; Honey Trust Me; That Mittle-Europa Mine (L: Edward Eliscu; Henry Myers); Whatever Goes Swoop Lilting Lofting (L: Edward Eliscu; Henry Myers)

Notes: No other information available.

2811 • MEGILLAH OF ITZAK MANGER, THE

OPENED: 10/09/1968   Theatre: John Golden
Musical   Broadway: 78

Composer: Dov Seltzer
Lyricist: Joe Darion
Librettist: Joe Darion
Producer: Zvi Kolitz; Alice Pearce; Solomon Sagall
Director: Shmuel Bunin

Lighting Designer: Eldon Elder; **Musical Director:** Dov Seltzer; **Orchestrations:** Dov Seltzer; **Set Design:** Shlomo Vitkin

Songs: Cause Uncle Mord'che Is So Smart; Chiribim; Drinking Song, Um Pa Pa Pa; Fastrigossa's Lament; Fly Little Bird; From Stopchut to Kolomay; Gevald Aria, The; Lechaim; Mother's Tears, A; Revolutionary Song; S'a Mechaye; Song of the Golden Peacock; Song of the Walnut Tree; Tailor's Drinking Song, The; Theme of the Megillah; Vashti's Farewell

Cast: Mike Burstein; Pesach Burstein; Ariel Furman; Zisha Gold; Lillian Lux; Susan Walters

2812 • MELODIOUS MENU, THE

OPENED: 08/01/1901
Revue

Songs: Ma Angelina (C: Jerome Kern)

Cast: Robert L. Davis; Jerome Kern

Notes: Amateur class show.

2813 • MELODY

OPENED: 02/14/1933   Theatre: Casino
Musical   Broadway: 80

Composer: Sigmund Romberg
Lyricist: Irving Caesar
Librettist: Edward Childs Carpenter
Producer: George White
Director: George White

Choreographer: Bobby Connolly; **Costumes:** Charles LeMaire; **Musical Director:** Alfred Goodman; **Set Design:** Joseph Urban

Songs: C'est Paree; Fashion Parade; Finale Act I; Give Me a Roll on a Drum; Good Friends Surround Me; I Am the Singer, You Are the Song; I'd Write a Song; In My Garden; Melody; Musical Interlude; Never Had an Education; On to Africa; Opening Chorus; Our Little Lady Upstairs; Pompadour; Rendezvous; Tea Number; Tonight May Never Come Again; Vision Scene; Whole World Loves, The; You Never Need Latin or Greek

Cast: Jeanne Aubert; Milton Douglas; Vivian Fay; Consuelo Flowerton; Evelyn Herbert; George Houston; Ina Ray Hutton; Barry Hyams; Louise Kirtland; Gypsy Rose Lee; Everett Marshall; Victor Morley; Mildred Parisette; Hal Skelly; Venita Varden; Walter Woolf

2814 • MELODY MAN, THE

OPENED: 05/13/1924   Theatre: Ritz
Play   Broadway: 61

Composer: Herbert Richard Lorenz [1]
Lyricist: Herbert Richard Lorenz [1]
Author: Herbert Richard Lorenz [1]
Producer: Lew Fields
Director: Alexander Leftwich; Lawrence Marston

Songs: I'd Like to Poison Ivy; Moonlight Mama

Cast: Jerry Devine; Lew Fields; Jules Jordan; Louise Kelley; Fredric March; Eva Puck; Eleanor Rowe; Sammy White

Notes: [1] Pseudonym for Herbert Fields, Richard Rodgers and Lorenz Hart.

2815 • MELODY OF LOVE

OPENED: 05/27/1954
Musical   New York

Composer: Lehman Engel
Librettist: Lewis Allen

Notes: Columbia University show.

2816 • MELTING OF MOLLY, THE
OPENED: 12/30/1918   Theatre: Broadhurst
Musical   Broadway: 88

Composer: Sigmund Romberg
Lyricist: Cyrus Wood
Librettist: Marie Thompson Davies; Edgar Smith
Producer: J.J. Shubert; Lee Shubert
Director: Oscar Eagle

Source: MELTING OF MOLLY, THE (Novel: Marie Thompson Davies); **Choreographer:** Allan K. Foster; **Musical Director:** Victor Baravalle; **Set Design:** Watson Barratt

Songs: Bills; Bread and Jam (C: Burton Green; L: Irene Franklin); Bridesmaids; Dancing School; Darling; Dear Old Gown; Eat and the World Eats with You [1]; Floating Down a Moonlight Stream; Grandma Dear Grandma [1]; I Want My Husband When I Wed; Jazz All Your Troubles Away (L: Augustus Barratt); Jazz-How I Love It; Lodger; Oh Doctor, Doctor; Opening Chorus; Reminiscence; Rolling Exercise; Wedding By Proxy; You Remember Me; You Win

Cast: Ted Lorraine; Gertrude Purcell; Gladys Walton

Notes: [1] Sheet music only.

2817 • MEMPHIS BOUND!
OPENED: 05/24/1945   Theatre: Broadway
Musical   Broadway: 36

Music Based On: W.S. Gilbert
Composer: Don Walker
Lyricist: Clay Warnick
Librettist: Albert Barker; Sally Benson
Producer: John Wilberg
Director: Robert Ross

Source: H.M.S. PINAFORE (Musical: W.S. Gilbert; Arthur Sullivan); **Choreographer:** Al White Jr.; **Costumes:** Lucinda Ballard; **Musical Director:** Charles Sanford; **Orchestrations:** Ted Royal; Don Walker; **Set Design:** George Jenkins; **Vocal Arranger:** Clay Warnick; Rene de Knight

Songs: Big Old River (C: Don Walker); Farewell My Own; Gilbert and Sullivan Blues, The; Growing Pains (C: Don Walker); Nightingale, the Moon and I, The; Old Love and Brand New Love (C: Don Walker); Stand Around the Bend (C: Don Walker)

Cast: Ada Brown; Thelma Carpenter; Billy Daniels; Delta Rhythm Boys; Timothy Grace; Sheila Guys; Ida James; Avon Long; Ann Robinson; Bill Robinson; William C. Smith; Edith Wilson; Frank Wilson

Notes: Production supervised by Vinton Freedley. The songs were based on Gilbert's melodies from H.M.S. PINAFORE excepting the numbers credited individually to Don Walker.

2818 • MERCENARY MARY
OPENED: 04/13/1925   Theatre: Longacre
Musical   Broadway: 136

Composer: Con Conrad; William B. Friedlander
Lyricist: Con Conrad; William B. Friedlander
Librettist: William B. Friedlander; Isabel Leighton
Producer: L. Lawrence Weber
Director: William B. Friedlander

Source: WHAT'S YOUR WIFE DOING? (Play: Emil Nyitray; Herbert Hall Winslow); **Choreographer:** William Seabury; **Orchestrations:** Louis Katzman

Songs: Beautiful Baby; Charleston Mad; Cherchez la Femme (Get Your Woman); Come on Along; Everything's Going to Be All Right; Honey I'm in Love with You; I Want to Be a Chaste Woman; I'm a Little Bit Fonder of You than of Myself [2] (C/L: Irving Caesar); Just You and I and the Baby; Mercenary Mary; Over a Garden Wall; That's When a Fellow Needs a Friend [2]; They Still Look Good to Me; Tomorrow [1]

Cast: Ambassadors, The; Winnie Baldwin; Madeleine Fairbanks; Sam Hearn; Allen Kearns

Notes: Irving Caesar may have made uncredited contributions to the score. [1] Melody based on Chopin's 12th Nocturne. [2] Added to London version.

2819 • MERELY MARY ANN
OPENED: 12/28/1903   Theatre: Garden
Play   Broadway: 148

Author: Israel Zangwill
Producer: Liebler & Company
Director: Charles Cartwright

Set Design: Frank Gates; E.A. Morange

Songs: Kiss Me Good-Night Dear (C/L: Malcolm Williams); Mariana of the Moated Grange (C: Cecile Hartig; L: Alfred Lord Tennyson)

Cast: Laura Hope Crews; Eleanor Robson

2820 • MERLIN

OPENED: 02/13/1983   Theatre: Mark Hellinger
Musical   Broadway: 199

Composer: Elmer Bernstein
Lyricist: Don Black
Librettist: Richard Levinson; William Link
Producer: Columbia Pictures Stage Pr.; Marvin A. Krauss; James M. Nederlander; Ivan Reitman
Director: Ivan Reitman

Choreographer: Christopher Chadman; Billy Wilson; **Costumes:** Theoni V. Aldredge; **Dance Arranger:** Mark Hummel; **Lighting Designer:** Tharon Musser; **Musical Director:** David Spear; **Orchestrations:** Larry Wilcox; **Set Design:** Robin Wagner; **Vocal Arranger:** David Spear

Songs: Anything for a Quiet Life [1]; Beyond My Wildest Dreams; Elements, The; Fergus' Dilemma; He Who Knows the Way; I Can Make It Happen; It's About Magic; It's About Power [1]; Nobody Will Remember Him; Put a Little Magic in Your Life; Satan Rules; Something About Palaces [1]; Something More; These Are Not the Merriest of Days [1]; We Haven't Fought a Battle in Years

Cast: George Lee Andrews; Alan Brasington; Doug Henning; Nathan Lane; Edmund Lyndeck; Michelle Nicastro; Chita Rivera; Christian Slater; Rebecca Wright

Notes: [1] Cut prior to opening.

2821 • MERRILY WE ROLL ALONG (1934)

OPENED: 09/29/1934   Theatre: Music Box
Play   Broadway: 155

Author: Moss Hart; George S. Kaufman
Producer: Sam H. Harris
Director: George S. Kaufman

Costumes: John Hambleton; **Set Design:** Jo Mielziner

Songs: Merrily We Roll Along (C/L: Unknown)

Cast: Walter Abel; Jessie Royce Landis; Cecilia Loftus; Kenneth McKenna; Grant Mills

2822 • MERRILY WE ROLL ALONG (1981)

OPENED: 11/16/1981   Theatre: Alvin
Musical   Broadway: 16

Composer: Stephen Sondheim
Lyricist: Stephen Sondheim
Librettist: George Furth
Producer: Robert Fryer; Lord Grade; Harold Prince; Martin Starger
Director: Harold Prince

Source: MERRILY WE ROLL ALONG (Play: Moss Hart; George S. Kaufman); **Choreographer:** Larry Fuller; **Costumes:** Judith Dolan; **Dance Arranger:** Tom Fay; Arnold Gross; **Lighting Designer:** David Hersey; **Musical Director:** Paul Gemignani; **Orchestrations:** Jonathan Tunick; **Set Design:** Eugene Lee

Songs: Blob, The; Bobby and Jackie and Jack; Darling! [1]; Franklin Shepard, Inc.; Good Thing Going; Growing Up [2]; Hills of Tomorrow, The; Honey [1]; It's a Hit!; Like It Was; Merrily We Roll Along; Not a Day Goes By; Now You Know; Old Friends; Opening Doors; Our Time; Rich and Happy; Thank You for Coming [1]; That Frank [2]

Cast: Jason Alexander; Terry Finn; Sally Klein; Ann Morrison; Lonny Price; Jim Walton

Notes: [1] Cut prior to opening. [2] Added to 1985 revival.

2823 • MERRY CHRISTMAS

OPENED: 1959

Composer: Jay Gorney
Lyricist: Henry Myers

Songs: Kris Kringle Rides Again; Postman's March (Hurray for the Postman)

Notes: No other information available.

2824 • MERRY COUNTESS, THE (1895)

OPENED: 11/02/1895　Theatre: Garrick
Musical　Broadway: 10

Composer: Johann Brandl
Lyricist: Thomas Frost
Librettist: Charles Klein
Director: Eugene Presbury

Source: NINICHE (Play: Maurice Hennequin; Albert Millaud); **Costumes:** Mme. Siedle; **Set Design:** John H. Young

Cast: Dan Daly; Charles Dickson; Marie Jansen; Edwin Stevens

Notes: No songs listed in program.

2825 • MERRY COUNTESS, THE (1912)

OPENED: 08/20/1912　Theatre: Casino
Musical　Broadway: 135

Music Based On: Johann Strauss
Composer: Leslie Stuart
Lyricist: Arthur Anderson
Librettist: Gladys Unger
Producer: Messrs. Shubert
Director: Charles A. Maynard

Source: DIE FLEDERMAUS (Opera: Johann Strauss); **Choreographer:** Emile Agoust; **Costumes:** Melville Ellis; **Musical Director:** Oscar Radin

Songs: Jail Birds, The (C: Melville Ellis; L: Martin G. Brown); Just that You Are You [1]; Letter Song; Must We Say Goodbye? (C: Arthur Gutman; L: Joseph H. McKeon); Serenade

Cast: Roszika Dolly; Yancsi Dolly; Maurice Farkoa; Forrest Huff; Fritzi Vonn Busing

Notes: Music based on score of DIE FLEDERMAUS. Production supervised by Melville Ellis. [1] Music based on "The Blue Danube."

2826 • MERRY-GO-ROUND, THE (1908)

OPENED: 04/25/1908　Theatre: Circle
Musical　Broadway: 97

Composer: Gus Edwards
Lyricist: Paul West
Librettist: Edgar Smith
Producer: Circle Production Co.
Director: George Marion

Choreographer: Joe C. Smith

Songs: Betty, the One Best Bet; Cafe Girl (I Met Her at the Metropole, but I Lost Her at Jacks); Captain of the Mineola Guards, The; Have You Seen My Baby; I Won't Be Home to Dinner; In Bohemia with You; My Brudda Sylvest [1] (C: Fred Fisher; L: Jesse Lasky); My Little Tailor Maid; Orchids of the Opera; Stupid Mr. Cupid [1] (C: Theodore Morse; L: Edward Madden); There's Not a Girl, In All This World That Won't Have Me; Two Horse Fellow in a One Horse Town; Won't You Come Under My Merry Widow Hat

Cast: Louise Carter; Mabel Hite; Dorothy Jardon; Ignacio Martinetti; James J. Morton; Bobby North; Rita Perkins; Melville Stewart

Notes: [1] Sheet music only.

2827 • MERRY-GO-ROUND (1927)

OPENED: 05/31/1927　Theatre: Klaw
Musical　Broadway: 135

Composer: Jay Gorney; Henry Souvaine
Lyricist: Howard Dietz; Morrie Ryskind
Librettist: Howard Dietz; Morrie Ryskind
Producer: Richard Herndon
Director: Allan Dinehart

Choreographer: Walt Kuhn; Raymond Midgley; **Musical Director:** Gene Salzer; **Set Design:** P. Dodd Ackerman

Songs: Carnival [1]; Gabriel Is Blowing His Horn; Happy Days; Hogan's Alley (C: Jay Gorney); If Love Should Come to Me; In the Bathroom Tra La [3]; I've Got a 'Yes' Girl; Let's Be Happy Now [1]; Mockowitz, Gogeloch, Babblekroit and Svonk (The Lawyer Song); New York Town (Is Wearing Its Bandannas on Broadway); Park Avenue [1]; Sea Chanty [1]; Sentimental Silly;

Something Tells Me; Spring Is in the Air [3] (L: Howard Dietz); Tampa; They Come, They Come [3]; Usher [2] (C: Manning Sherwin; L: Edward Eliscu); What D'Ya Say [1]

Cast: Don Barclay; Marie Cahill; Willie Collier; Frances Gershwin; Etienne Giradot; Libby Holman; Philip Loeb; Leonard Sillman

Notes: [1] May be sketch not song. [2] Added after opening. [3] ASCAP/Library of Congress only.

2828 • MERRY GRAFTERS, THE
Musical   Chicago

Notes: No other information available. Harold Orlob had some numbers interpolated into this score.

2829 • MERRY MALONES, THE
OPENED: 09/26/1927   Theatre: Erlanger
Musical   Broadway: 216

Composer: George M. Cohan
Lyricist: George M. Cohan
Librettist: George M. Cohan
Producer: George M. Cohan
Director: Sam Forrest; Edward Royce

Choreographer: Jack Mason; **Costumes:** E.J. Heuett; Mabel Johnston; Cora MacGeachy; **Musical Director:** Charles J. Gebest; **Orchestrations:** Mike Lake; **Set Design:** Joseph Wickes

Songs: Behind the Mask; Blue Skies, Gray Skies; Busy Little Center, A; Charming; Easter Sunday Parade; Feeling in Your Heart, A; Flirtation Waltz; Gip-Gip; God's Good to the Irish; Honor of the Family, The; Like a Little Ladylike Lady Like You; Like a Wandering Minstrel; Molly Malone; Night of Masquerade, A; Our Own Way of Going Along; Roses Understand; Son of a Billionaire; Talk About a Busy Little Housewife; To Heaven on the Bronx Express; Twentieth Century Love [1]; We've Got Him; We've Had a Grand Old Time; Yankee Father in a Yankee Home, The [1]

Cast: George M. Cohan; Alan Edwards; Polly Walker

Notes: [1] ASCAP/Library of Congress only.

2830 • MERRY MARTYR
OPENED: 1913
Musical   Closed out of town

Composer: Hugo Riesenfeld
Lyricist: Glen MacDonough
Librettist: Glen MacDonough
Producer: Klaw & Erlanger
Director: Herbert Gresham

Source: NARRENTANZ (Play: Leo Birinski); **Choreographer:** Julian Mitchell; **Costumes:** Schneider & Anderson; **Musical Director:** Hugo Riesenfeld; **Set Design:** Unitt & Wickes

Songs: Alcalde Mayor; Bolero; Dance; Dance Drama; Habanera; Heart Dance, The; King Carnival; Love Is a Bubble; Say to Him; Sevillian Serenade; Song of the Barricade; Sunlight of My Heart; Telepathic Eye, The; Tette-a-Tette at 8; Tokay! (Hungarian Song); Unlearnable Lesson, The

Cast: Maclyn Arbuckle; Tessa Kosta

Notes: Programs Philadelphia 9/29/13 and Boston 1913.

2831 • MERRY MARY
OPENED: 04/16/1911
Musical   Chicago

Cast: Sophie Tucker

Notes: No other information available.

2832 • MERRY MARY BROWN
OPENED: 1919
Musical   Closed out of town

Composer: Al Goodman
Lyricist: Bernard Grossman
Librettist: Elmer Harris; Oliver Morosco
Producer: Oliver Morosco

Cast: Charles Judels; Vera Michelena

Notes: Program Stamford 11/11/19.

2833 • MERRY, MERRY
OPENED: 09/24/1925   Theatre: Vanderbilt
Musical   Broadway: 197

Composer: Harry Archer
Lyricist: Harlan Thompson
Librettist: Harlan Thompson
Producer: Lyle D. Andrews
Director: Harlan Thompson

Choreographer: Harry Puck; Set Design: P. Dodd Ackerman

Songs: Bubbling Over with Joy [1] (C: Henry Waller; L: Bert Lee; R.P. Weston); But I Do Say So [1] (C: Henry Waller; L: Bert Lee; R.P. Weston); Every Little Note; Glad Feet [1] (C: Joseph Tunbridge; L: Jack Waller); I Was Blue; It Must Be Love; Little Girl; My Own; Oh Wasn't It Lovely?; Poor Pierrot; Spanish Mick, The; Step, Step Sisters; We Were a Wow; What a Life; Wonderful You (C: Joseph Tunbridge; L: Jack Waller); You're the One

Cast: William Frawley; Harry Puck; Marie Saxon

Notes: [1] Not in program.

2834 • MERRY WHIRL, THE
OPENED: 05/30/1910   Theatre: New York
Musical   Broadway: 24

Composer: Leo Edwards
Lyricist: Ed Ray
Librettist: Don Roth
Producer: Gordon-North Amus. Rev. Co.
Director: Julian Alfred

Choreographer: Julian Alfred

Songs: Havana Bay [1]; I Love a Yankee Doodle Girl [1]; I'll Be There with You [1]; I'll Do As Much for You [1]; La Belle Francaise [1]; Lima Bean [1]; Man with the Money, The [1]; Million Dollar Ball [2]; Model of Fashion Am I, A; Opening Chorus Part One; Paris Push, The; Play, Play, Play [1]; Ragtime Soldier Man [2]; Ring the Wedding Bells; Strike Up a Bagpipe Tune; Under the Wisteria [2]; When I Waltz with You; When I'm Alone, I'm Lonesome [1]

Cast: Mildred Elaine; Frank F. Moore; James C. Morton; Rita Redmond

Notes: [1] From part of show titled THE MAGIC RING. [2] Sheet music only.

2835 • MERRY WIDOW AND THE DEVIL, THE
OPENED: 01/02/1908   Theatre: Weber's Music
                                           Hall
Musical   Broadway: 156

Composer: Franz Lehar
Lyricist: George V. Hobart
Librettist: George V. Hobart
Producer: Joseph Weber
Director: Julian Mitchell

Musical Director: Hugo Frey; Set Design: John Young

Songs: Bonny, My Highland Lassie; Gee, Ain't I Glad I'm Single; Girls; Girls at Maxims, The; I'm the Original Devil; In Farsovia; She's My Daisy [1]; Waltz; Yip-I-Adee-I-Ay! (C: John H. Flynn; L: Will D. Cobb)

Cast: Bessie Clayton; Peter F. Dailey; Blanche Deyo; Lillian Fitzgerald; Lulu Glaser; Albert Hart; Walter Jones; Blanche Ring; Charles J. Ross; Max Sheck; Joseph Weber; Gladys Zell

Notes: [1] A Harry Lauder song interpolated in this show.

2836 • MERRY WIDOW, THE (1907)
OPENED: 10/21/1907   Theatre: New Amsterdam
Musical   Broadway: 416

Composer: Franz Lehar
Lyricist: Adrian Ross
Librettist: Basil Hood
Producer: Henry W. Savage
Director: George Marion

Source: DIE LUSTIGE WITWE (Musical: Franz Lehar; Victor Leon; Leo Stein); Costumes: Percy Anderson; Mme. Hermann; Mme. Zimmerman; Musical Director: Louis F. Gottschalk; Set Design: Walter Burridge

Songs: Butterflies (Dance); Cavalier, The; Dutiful Wife, A; Finale Act I: Ladies Choice/O, Come Away; Finale Act II: I Am Free So Tra La La La La La (My Marriage Will Be One Arranged); Finale Act III; Girls at Maxim's (Girls, Girls, Girls), The; I Love You So (The Merry Widow Waltz); In Marsovia; Love in My Heart; Maxim's; Oh, Say No More; Opening Act III: The Girls at Maxim's/ Ritantou Ritantirelle [2]; Opening Chorus; Vilia; Women

Cast: Donald Brian; Frances Cameron; Lois Ewell; R.E. Graham; Ethel Jackson; Blanche Rice; William C. Weedon; Ralph Whiting; Walter C. Wilson

Notes: [1] Sometimes credited to Edward Morton. [2] Lyric rewritten by Robert Gilbert for 1943 revival.

2837 • MERRY WIDOW, THE (1955)

OPENED: 04/09/1955   Theatre: NBC
TV Musical

Composer: Franz Lehar
Lyricist: Carolyn Leigh
Librettist: William Friedberg; Will Glickman; Neil Simon
Producer: Max Liebman

Source: DIE LUSTIGE WITWE (Musical: Franz Lehar; Victor Leon; Leo Stein)

Songs: At Maxims; Come to the Pavillion; Fidelity; Girls, Girls, Girls; Legend of Villa; No One Thanks the Go-Between; Something So Delightful; Sympathy (C: Oscar Strauss); We Are Here to Sing a Chorus; When You Dance (For the Love of the Dance); You'll Love Me in Paris

Cast: Rod Alexander; Helena Bliss; John Conte; Edward Everett Horton; Anne Jeffreys; Beatrice Kraft; Bambi Linn; Jack Russell; Brian Sullivan

2838 • MERRY WIDOW, THE (1964)

OPENED: 08/17/1964
Musical   New York: 40

Composer: Franz Lehar
Lyricist: Forman Brown
Librettist: Milton Lazarus
Producer: Music Theatre of Lincoln Center
Director: Edward Greenberg

Source: DIE LUSTIGE WITWE (Musical: Franz Lehar; Victor Leon; Leo Stein); **Choreographer:** Zachary Solov; **Costumes:** Rene Hubert; **Musical Director:** Franz Allers; **Set Design:** Rouben Ter-Arutunian

Songs: Finale Act I; Finale Act II; Finale Act III; Girls at Maxims; I Love You So (The Merry Widow Waltz); Marsovian Dance (inst.); Maxim's; Respectable Wife, A; Riding on a Carousel; Romance; Vilia; When in France; Who Knows the Way to My Heart?; Women

Cast: Sig Arno; Mischa Auer; Dixie Carter; Robert Goss; Joseph Leon; Patrice Munsel; Frank Poretta; George Quick; Wood Romoff; Joan Weldon; Bob Wright

Notes: Produced at the State Theatre, Lincoln Center.

2839 • MERRY WIDOW, THE (1978)

OPENED: 1978
Musical   New York

Composer: Franz Lehar
Lyricist: Sheldon Harnick

Musical Director: Julius Rudel

Songs: Act One Finale; Act Three Finale; Act Two Finale; Anna's Entrance; Dances and Vilia; Do Listen, Please; Ev'ry Woman; Grisette Song; Hela! See the Horseman Come; Just As a Rosebud Blossoms; Oh, Fatherland (Maxim's); Strings Are Sighing; Tres Parisien (L: Unknown)

Cast: Vincent Angeli; James Billings; Harlan Foss; Glenys Fowles; Thomas Jamerson; Alan Kays; Henry Price; Beverly Sills; David Rae Smith; Alan Titus

Notes: New York City Opera.

2840 • MERRY WIDOWER, THE

OPENED: 1907
Musical

Composer: Bernard Adler
Lyricist: Victor H. Smalley
Librettist: Victor H. Smalley

Songs: Dat Lovin' Rag

Cast: Lottie Grady; Jerry Mills

Notes: No other information available on this burlesque which featured an all-black cast.

2841 • MERRY WIVES SWING IT!, THE

OPENED: 06/14/1940   Theatre: El Capitan
Musical   Los Angeles

Lyricist: George Houston; Dr. Hugo Strelitzer

Librettist: Donald Alden; George Houston; Dr. Hugo Strelitzer

Source: MERRY WIVES OF WINDSOR, THE (Opera: Nicolai; William Shakespeare); **Source:** MERRY WIVES OF WINDSOR, THE (Opera: Nicolai); **Arrangements:** Lothar Perl; **Musical Director:** Dr. Hugo Strelitzer; **Set Design:** Ernest Glover

Songs: We Win in Love (C/L: Ann Ronell)

Cast: George Burnson; Virginia Card; John Ellis; Gueneth Omeron; Johnny Silver; Maurice Winthrop

2842 • MERRY WORLD, THE (1895)
OPENED: 06/08/1895   Theatre: Casino
Musical   Broadway: 32

Composer: Nicholas Biddle
Librettist: Edgar Smith
Producer: Thomas Canary; George W. Lederer

Songs: I Went to Paris with Papa [1]

Cast: La Petite Adelaide; Dan Daly; Charles Dickson; Louis Granat; May Howard; Marie Laurens; Nanette Nixon; David Warfield

Notes: No songs listed in program. [1] Interpolated.

2843 • MERRY WORLD, THE (1926)
OPENED: 06/08/1926   Theatre: Imperial
Revue   Broadway: 87

Composer: Herman Hupfeld; Sammy Timberg
Lyricist: Clifford Grey
Producer: Messrs. Shubert
Director: J.C. Huffman; Charles Judels

Choreographer: Larry Ceballos; **Costumes:** E.R. Schrapps; Max Weldy; **Musical Director:** Al Radin; **Set Design:** Watson Barratt

Songs: Beauty Adorned (C: J. Fred Coots; Maurie Rubens); Come Over to Deauville (C/L: Herman Hupfeld); Dancing Jim (C: Marc Anthony; L: Donovan Parsons); Don't Fall in Love with Me (C/L: Herman Hupfeld); Enchanted; Fall of the Leaves, The (C: J. Fred Coots; Maurie Rubens); Girofle-Girofla; Golden Gates of Happiness (C: J. Fred Coots); Heroes of Yesterday; I Fell

Head Over Heels in Love (C: Pat Thayer; L: Donovan Parsons); Jabberwocky; Love's Call (C: J. Fred Coots; Maurie Rubens); Military Charleston; Silk Stockings; Sunday (C: J. Fred Coots); Tallahassee; Versailles; Whispering Trees (C: J. Fred Coots; Maurie Rubens; L: Herbert Reynolds); White Rose, Red Rose

Cast: Alexander Gray; Elna Gudrun; Grace Hayes

Notes: The show was retitled PASSIONS OF 1926. It toured as THE PASSING SHOW OF 1926.

2844 • MESSENGER BOY, THE
OPENED: 09/16/1901   Theatre: Daly's
Musical   Broadway: 128

Composer: Lionel Monckton
Lyricist: Adrian Ross
Librettist: Alfred Murray; James T. Tanner
Producer: Nixon & Zimmerman
Director: Herbert Gresham

Costumes: F. Richard Anderson; **Musical Director:** Louis F. Gottschalk; **Set Design:** Joseph Harker; T.E. Ryan

Songs: Ask Papa (C: Ivan Caryll; L: Percy Greenbank); Ask the Advice of the Captain [2] (L: Percy Greenbank); Aspirations; Boys of London Town, The [2]; Bradshaw's Guide (C: Ivan Caryll); Can't You Take My Word?; Captain Pott (They Are All After Pott); Cooee, Ma Girlee! [2] (C: A.D. Cammeyer; J.M. Capel); Dervish Dance (inst.); Dialect Soubrette, The [1]; Finale Act I (C: Ivan Caryll); Finale Act II; Grand Chorus [2] (C: Ivan Caryll); Has Anybody Seen My Cat?; Hooker Pasha [2]; It's Got to Be Done [2] (L: Percy Greenbank); Little Bit Furter On, A [2]; Maisie (L: Leslie Mayne); Mary, Mary, Quite Contrary [2] (C: Ivan Caryll); Merry Marriage Market of the East [2]; Messenger Boy, The (L: Percy Greenbank); Mummies (C: Ivan Caryll); Off to Cairo (C: Ivan Caryll); Pansy [1]; Perfectly Peaceful Person, A (C/L: Paul A. Rubens); Sheltered from the Noonday Glare (L: Percy Greenbank); Tarantella (inst.) (C: Ivan Caryll); Tittle-Tattle [2] (C: Ivan Caryll; L: Percy Greenbank); To Our Charity Bazaar (C: Ivan Caryll); To the Paris Exposition; Up the Nile [2] (C: Ivan Caryll; L: Percy Greenbank); Volunteers, The; Wash, Wash, Wash! (In the Wash) (C: Lionel Monckton); What Would Society Say? [2] (L: Percy Greenbank); Your Own [1]

Cast: Georgia Caine; Jobyna Howland; John Park; James T. Powers; May Robson; Flora Zabelle

Notes: [1] Out 4/26/02 Boston. [2] In vocal score only.

2845 • MESSIN' 'ROUND
OPENED: 04/22/1929 Theatre: Hudson
Revue Broadway: 33

Composer: James P. Johnson
Lyricist: Percy Bradford
Producer: Louis Isquith
Director: Louis Isquith

Choreographer: Eddie Rector; **Musical Director:** James P. Johnson; **Set Design:** Louis Wortheim

Songs: Circus Days; Get Away from My Window; Harlem Town; I Don't Love Nobody; I Need You; Messin' Around; Mississippi Moan; Put Your Mind Right on It; Roust-abouts; Shout On!; Skiddle-de-Scow; Sorry; Your Love I Crave

Cast: Cora La Redd; Bamboo McCarver

2846 • METRO
OPENED: 04/16/1992 Theatre: Minskoff
Musical Broadway: 13

Lyricist: Agata Miklaszewska; Maryna Miklaszewska; Mary Bracken Phillips
Librettist: Janusz Jozefowicz; Agata Miklaszewska; Maryna Miklaszewska; Mary Bracken Phillips
Director: Janusz Jozefowicz

Arrangements: Janusz Stoklosa; **Choreographer:** Janusz Jozefowicz; **Costumes:** Marie Anne Chiment; Juliet Polcsa; **Lighting Designer:** Ken Billington; **Musical Director:** Janusz Stoklosa; **Set Design:** Janusz Sosnowski; **Vocal Arranger:** Janusz Stoklosa

Songs: Benjamin Franklin, in God We Trust; Bluezwis; But Not Me; Dreams Don't Die; Love Duet; Love Duet II; Metro; My Fairy Tale; Pieniadze; Tower of Babel; Uciekali; Waiting; Windows

Cast: Mariusz Czajka; Edyta Gorniak; Katarzyna Groniec; Robert Janowski; Janusz Jozefowicz; Violetta Klimczewska; Iwona Runowska

Notes: A Polish Musical with English book by Mary Bracken Phillips and Janusz Jozfowicz and English lyrics by Mary Bracken Phillips.

2847 • MEXICAN HAYRIDE
OPENED: 01/28/1944 Theatre: Winter Garden
Musical Broadway: 479

Composer: Cole Porter
Lyricist: Cole Porter
Librettist: Dorothy Fields; Herbert Fields
Producer: Michael Todd
Director: John Kennedy; Hassard Short

Choreographer: Paul Haakon; George Jenkins; **Costumes:** Mary Grant; **Lighting Designer:** Hassard Short; **Musical Director:** Harry Levant; **Orchestrations:** Robert Russell Bennett

Songs: Abracadabra; Carlotta; Count Your Blessings; Entrance of Montana; Girls; Good-Will Movement, The; He Certainly Kills the Women [1]; Here's a Cheer for Dear Old Ciro's [1]; Hereafter [1]; Humble Hollywood Executive, A [1]; I Love You; I'm Afraid I Love You [1]; I'm So Glahd to Meet You [1]; It Must be Fun to Be You [1]; It's a Big Night [1]; It's Just Like the Good Old Days [1]; It's Just Yours [1]; Octet [1]; Put a Sack Over Their Heads [1]; Sight-Seeing Tour, A [1]; Sing to Me Guitar; Tequila [1]; That's What You Mean to Me [1]; There Must Be Someone for Me; We're Off for a Hayride in Mexico [1]; What a Crazy Way to Spend Sunday

Cast: Bobby Clark; Wilbur Evans; George Givot; Paul Haakon; June Havoc; Luba Malina; Corinna Mura

Notes: [1] Not used.

2848 • MEXICANA
OPENED: 01/29/1906 Theatre: 46th Street
Musical Broadway: 82

Composer: Raymond Hubbell
Lyricist: Robert B. Smith
Librettist: Clara Driscoll; Robert B. Smith
Producer: Lee Shubert; Sam S. Shubert
Director: R.H. Burnside

Musical Director: Herman Perlet

Songs: Bolero, The; Entrance of Johnny Rocks;

Fickle Weather Vane, The; Graft; Hark to the Voice of Your Lover; How Do You Account for That?; I Am the Wizard of Wall Street; I Heard So Much About You; I Was Just Supposing; Lorelei, The; Major Margery; My Double the Man Who Looks Like Me [1]; Opening Chorus; Take Care-Senor; United We Stand; We've Got a Lot to Learn; Where E'er I Go [1]

Cast: Blanche Deyo; Joseph W. Herbert; Christie MacDonald; Edward Martindel; Caro Roma; Thomas Q. Seabrooke

Notes: [1] Sheet music only.

2849 • MIAMI BILTMORE WATER REVUE

Revue

Songs: You're Thrilling (C/L: Walter DeVivo)

Notes: No other information available.

2850 • MICHAEL TODD'S PEEP SHOW

OPENED: 06/28/1950   Theatre: Winter Garden
Revue   Broadway: 278

Librettist: Bobby Clark; H.I. Phillips; William Roos; William K. Wells
Producer: Michael Todd
Director: Bobby Clark; Hassard Short

Choreographer: James Starbuck; **Costumes:** Irene Sharaff; **Dance Arranger:** Mel Pahl; **Lighting Designer:** Hassard Short; **Musical Director:** Clay Warnick; **Orchestrations:** Ken Hopkins; Irwin Kostal; **Set Design:** Howard Bay; **Vocal Arranger:** Mel Pahl

Songs: Blue Night (C/L: Bhumibol [1]; B. Chakraband; N. Tong Yai); Desire [2] (C/L: Raymond Scott); Falling Rain-Dream of You [2] (C/L: Bhumibol [1]; B. Chakraband; N. Tong Yai); Francie (C: Jule Styne; L: Bob Hilliard); Gimme the Shimmy (C/L: Harold Rome); Got what It Takes (C: Sammy Stept; L: Dan Shapiro); I Hate a Parade (C/L: Harold Rome); I've Got a Pocketful of Dreams (C/L: Harold Rome); Love at Sundown (C/L: Bhumibol [1]; B. Chakraband; N. Tong Yai); Model Hasn't Changed, The (C/L: Harold Rome); Seems Like Yesterday [2]

(C: Sammy Stept; L: Dan Shapiro); Song without Words [2] (C/L: Bhumibol [1]; B. Chakraband; N. Tong Yai); Stay with the Happy People (C: Jule Styne; L: Bob Hilliard); Violins from Nowhere (C: Sammy Fain; L: Herb Magidson); You've Never Been Loved (C: Sammy Stept; L: Dan Shapiro)

Cast: Lily Christine; Dick "Gabby" Dana; Clifford Guest; Spike Hamilton; Peanuts Mann; Red Marshall; Peiro Brothers, The; Lina Romay; Bozo Snyder

Notes: [1] King of Thailand. [2] Not in programs.

2851 • MID SUMMER NIGHT'S FANCIES

OPENED: 06/22/1903   Theatre: Crystal Gardens
Musical   Broadway: 30

Composer: Ben M. Jerome
Lyricist: John Gilroy; Matthew C. Woodward
Librettist: John Gilroy; Matthew C. Woodward
Producer: George Lederer
Director: George Lederer

Musical Director: Max Hoffmann

Songs: Bee, Be My Honey Bee [1] (L: Nicholas Biddle); Ella [1] (L: Nicholas Biddle); Flirtation [1] (L: Nicholas Biddle); Hinky Dee [2]; Ida Bell; If You Ever want a Favor Mention Me; Kiyomori; Marriage of the Daffodil and Daisy, The [1] (L: Nicholas Biddle); Mozart Lincoln; My Japanese Baby; New York Forever [1] (L: Nicholas Biddle); Omi Omai; Oshi Dori; Silvery Moon, Keep on a Shining [1] (L: Nicholas Biddle); Watch Me Tonight in the Torchlight Parade; Whoa San; Will Lipton Lift the Cup [1] (L: Nicholas Biddle); Yo Ho, My Lads, Heave Ho [1] (L: Nicholas Biddle)

Cast: Emma Carus; Trixie Friganza; Junie McCree; Pat Rooney

Notes: The first act was titled THE DARLING OF THE GALLERY GODS, the second act was titled LIFTING THE CUP and had lyrics by Nicholas Biddle. THE DRESS PARADE was also part of this show. [1] From LIFTING THE CUP. [2] There was a popular song "Hinkey-Dee" by Harry Morris written in 1902. This might be that song.

2852 • MIDDLE OF NOWHERE, THE

OPENED: 11/20/1988   Theatre: Astor Place
Musical   Off-Broadway: 24

Composer: Randy Newman
Lyricist: Randy Newman
Producer: Frank Basile; Lewis Friedman; Tom O. Meyerhoff; Albert Nocciolino
Director: Tracy Friedman

Choreographer: Tracy Friedman; **Costumes:** Juliet Polcsa; Loren Sherman; **Dance Arranger:** Robby Merkin; **Lighting Designer:** Phil Monat; **Musical Director:** Jonny Bowden; **Orchestrations:** Robby Merkin; **Set Design:** Loren Sherman; **Vocal Arranger:** Robby Merkin

Songs: Baltimore; Davy the Fat Boy; I Think It's Going to Rain Today; I'm Different; It's Money That I Love; Lonely at the Top; Louisiana 1927; Lover's Prayer; Marie; Maybe I'm Doing It Wrong; Mr. President; Old Kentucky Home; Old Man; Political Science; Rednecks; Sail Away; Short People; Sigmund Freud's Impersonation; Simon Smith; Song for the Dead; They Just Got Married; Tickle Me; Yellow Man; You Can Leave Your Hat On

Cast: Michael Arkin; Diana Castle; Vondie Curtis-Hall; Tony Hoylen; Roger Robinson

Notes: No original songs in this musical.

2853 • MIDNIGHT ELOPERS, THE

OPENED: 1919
Musical   Closed out of town

Lyricist: Ed Hanford; Charles Robinson
Librettist: Ed Hanford; Charles Robinson
Producer: Charles Robinson
Director: Charles Robinson

Choreographer: Robert Marks; **Costumes:** Ruth Lamb

Songs: Banshee Man; Bolo, Bolo Man; Come Back to Erin; Do What Your Mother Did; Girl from Childs, The; He's Got a Bungalow; Ireland Must Be Heaven; Jackies; Man Behind the Hammer and Saw, The; Oh, How She Could Yacki, Hacki, Wicki, Wacki, Woo; On an Island Surrounded by Girls; Opening Chorus; Two Key Rag, The; We Can't Get Along without Money; Welcome,

Honey, to Your Old Plantation Home; When the Sun Goes Down in Romany; When Uncle Sammy Leads the Band

Cast: Harry S. LeVan; Mabel Lee; Fred Lehr; Willie Mack; Charles Robinson

Notes: Chicago program 1/27/19. Included popular songs of the day.

2854 • MIDNIGHT GIRL, THE

OPENED: 02/23/1914   Theatre: 44th Street
Musical   Broadway: 104

Composer: Adolf Philipp[1]
Lyricist: Edward A. Paulton; Adolf Philipp
Librettist: Edward A. Paulton; Adolf Philipp
Producer: Messrs. Shubert
Director: Ben Teal

Source: DIE MITTERNACHTSMADEL [4] (Musical: Adolf Philipp); **Choreographer:** Jack Mason; **Costumes:** Melville Ellis; **Musical Director:** Herbert Kerr

Songs: Burglars; Certain Something About You, A; Come Back to the Old Cabaret; Decorations; Dolly; Eyes Right! Here's a Girlie [1]; Good Night, Love; Honeymoon Hall; Love and Victory; Midnight Cabaret, The; Midnight Girl, The; Oh, Gustave!; Oh You John [2]; On the Lovely Lagoon [2]; Path to Honeymoon Land, The; Please Don't Cry [1]; Red, White & Blue, The [1] (C: Louis A. Hirsch; L: George Arthurs); She's Different Now [1]; Since I Am Your Auntie to Be [1]; Song of the Little Mouse, The [1]; Ten O'Clock; There Was Something About Her; We Will Ramble, You & I, Dear [1]; When the Band Begins to Play; You & I [1]

Cast: Zoe Barnett; Harry Delf; Eva Fallon; Marie Flynn; George MacFarlane; Margaret Romaine

Notes: This show was originally produced in German at Philipp's 57th Street theatre before being remounted in English on Broadway. Sigmund Romberg had his first theatre song presented in this show. I couldn't identify its title. [1] Sheet music only. [2] In Romberg biography only. [3] The music was credited to Jean Briquet, which was almost certainly a pseudonym for Philipp. [4] The source was credited to Paul Herve, probably a made-up person standing in for Philipp.

2855 • MIDNIGHT JOLLIES, THE

OPENED: 11/18/1922
Revue   New York

Director: Hassard Short

Songs: Follow the Star [1] (C: Victor Herbert; L: Grant Stewart); Women of Equity (C: Henry Hodley; L: Joseph W. Herbert)

Cast: Ethel Barrymore; Jack Donahue; Carl Randall; Savoy & Brennan; Vivienne Segal; Queenie Smith; Laurette Taylor

Notes: A benefit for Actors' Equity presented at the Hotel Astor. The cast list is incomplete. [1] Not written for this benefit. The Equity logo was a star.

2856 • MIDNIGHT ROUNDERS OF 1920, THE

OPENED: 07/12/1920   Theatre: Century
                        Promenade
Revue   Broadway: 120

Composer: Jean Schwartz
Lyricist: Alfred Bryan
Librettist: Howard Emmett Rogers
Producer: Messrs. Shubert
Director: Lew Morton

Choreographer: Jack Mason; **Costumes:** Homer Conant; **Musical Director:** Louis Gress; Oscar Radin; **Set Design:** Homer Conant

Songs: At the Piano; Beautiful Shoulders; Beauty Is Like a Rose; By the O-Hi-O (O-My-O) [2] (C: Abe Olman; L: Jack Yellen); Century Promenade, The; Chanson (C: Leo Edwards; L: Howard E. Rogers); Clock Song; Grieving for You [2] (C/L: Joe Gibson; Joe Ribaud; C: Joe Gold); Heartbreakers; I Never Knew (I Could Love Anybody Like I'm Loving You) [2] (C/L: Roy K. Marsh; Tom Pitts; L: Raymond B. Egan); Je Ne Comprends Pas; Josephine [2]; La Veda; Mansion of Roses, The; Mouth Full of Kisses, A [3]; My Lady of the Cameo; My Vision Girl [1] (C: Eubie Blake; L: Noble Sissle); Now I Lay Me Down to Sleep [2] (C: George W. Meyer; L: Sidney D. Mitchell); O You Heavenly Body; Palesteena [2] (C/L: Con Conrad; J. Russel Robinson); Rag Doll, The; Rattle Rattle; Shimmy Nods from Chaminade; Swing, The; Three Little Marys; Whisper in My Ear; Who Cares (C: Leo Edwards;

L: Howard E. Rogers); Wild Romantic Blues; William Tell It to Me (William Tell Me); You're Like a Red, Red Rose [2] (C: Leo Edwards; L: Howard E. Rogers)

Cast: Lew Hearn; Harry Kelly; Madelon La Varre; Ted Lorraine; Vivian Oakland; Tot Qualters; Gladys Walton; Walter Woolf

Notes: THE MIDNIGHT ROUNDERS was the late night (11:30) version of THE CENTURY REVUE (8:30). Both were performed at the Century Promenade atop the Century Theatre. [1] Not in program. [2] Sheet music only. [3] Also used out of town in the SHUBERT GAIETIES OF 1919.

2857 • MIDNIGHT ROUNDERS OF 1921, THE

OPENED: 02/07/1921   Theatre: Century
                        Promenade
Revue   Broadway: 49

Composer: Jean Schwartz
Lyricist: Lew Pollack
Librettist: Harold Atteridge
Producer: J.J. Shubert; Lee Shubert
Director: Jack Mason

Songs: Angels (We Call Them Mother Down Here) (C: Harry Ruby; L: Bert Kalmar); Ballet of the Pyramids (inst.); Beautiful Girls Are Like Opium; Blue Blondes; Century Toddle; Dapper Dan (C: Albert Von Tilzer; L: Lew Brown); Gold Fish; He Talks with His Fingers; I Want My Mammy [2] (C: Louis Breau; L: George B. Wehner); I'd Love to Be in Ireland the Day They Set Old Ireland Free (C: William Polla; L: Charles Tobias); If You Knew (C: James Blyler; Con Conrad; L: Sidney Clare; Harry Tobias); Keep Them in a Golden Cage; La Vie Parisienne; Ma (C: Con Conrad; L: Sidney Clare); Mama! Mama! Papa's Got a Lot of Lovin' (All Saved Up for You) (C/L: Cliff Friend; Irving Hup); My Sunny Tennessee (C: Harry Ruby; L: Bert Kalmar; Herman Ruby); Oh! Mabel Behave [1] (C/L: Cliff Friend; Irving Hup); Passionettes; Perfume and Passion; Picket Fence; Sand Witches; Scandinavia (Sing Dose Song and Make Dose Music) (C: Ray Perkins); Snap a Wishbone with Me; Spirit of Java; Sprinkle Me with Diamonds; Take a Chance with Me; Why Do I Care for You? [1] (C: Albert Hay Malotte; L: Jack Yellen); Wimmin (I Got to Have 'Em That's All) (C/L: Eddie

Cantor; Fred Fisher); Would You Like to Sleep Upon My Pillow; You Tickle Me (C: Lew Pollack; L: Sidney Clare)

Cast: Eddie Cantor; Bessie Clifford; Arthur Donnelly; Jane Green; La Petite Marguerite; J. Harold Murray; Tot Qualters; Gladys Walton

Notes: This information from a program of 2/5/21. [1] ASCAP/Library of Congress only. [2] Sheet music only.

2858 • MIDNIGHT SONS, THE

OPENED: 05/22/1909   Theatre: Broadway
Musical   Broadway: 257

Composer: Raymond Hubbell
Lyricist: Glen MacDonough
Librettist: Glen MacDonough
Producer: Lew Fields
Director: Ned Wayburn

Costumes: Melville Ellis; **Musical Director:** August Kleinecke; **Orchestrations:** Frank Saddler; **Set Design:** Arthur Voegtlin

Songs: Amina (C/L: Paul Lincke); Amina Queen of the Night or the Arab's Dream [4] (C: Paul Lincke; L: Ballard Macdonald); Billiken Man, The; Call Me Bill; Carmen the Second; Cinderella at the Shoe Store; Columbine's Courtship; Cynical Owl, The; Eily Riley; Goo-Goo Land [4] (C: C.W. Murphy; L: Fred W. Leigh); Harlequin Hoops, The; High! High! High! [1]; Human Pin-Wheel, The; I've Got Rings on My Fingers or Mumbo-Jumbo-Jijjiboo-J. O'Shay [5] (C: Maurice Scott; L: F.J. Barnes; R.P. Weston); Kelly's Gone to Kingdom Come [2]; Lithograph Land; Little Mary Gardeners, The; Mlle. DeLeon [2]; My Fire-Fly Lady; My Sist' Tetrazin' [3] (C: Anatol Friedland; L: Edward J. Madden); Parasol Dance; Soubrette's Secret, The; True Blue; Twinkling Toes [2]; Yankee Honeymoon; Yip-I-Addy-I-Ay! (C: John H. Flynn; L: Will D. Cobb)

Cast: Vernon Castle; Lotta Faust; Harry Fisher; Taylor Holmes; George Monroe; Gladys Moore; Blanche Ring; Fritz Williams

Notes: [1] Also as "Hi!, Hi!, Hi" in some programs. [2] Out of town. [3] "With due credit to Mascagni." [4] Sheet music only. [5] Also in THE YANKEE GIRL.

2859 • MIDSUMMER NIGHT'S DREAM, A

OPENED: 06/20/1958
Play

Composer: Marc Blitzstein
Author: William Shakespeare
Producer: American Shakespeare Festival; John Houseman
Director: Jack Landau

Choreographer: George Balanchine; Incidental Music: Marc Blitzstein

Songs: Court Song (L: Anonymous); Lullaby (The Spotted Snakes with Double Tongues) (L: William Shakespeare); Sweet Is the Rose (L: Amoretti)

Cast: Barbara Barrie; Morris Carnovsky; John Colicos; Will Geer; June Havoc; Ellis Rabb; Hiram Sherman; Richard Waring

Notes: Presented at the American Shakespeare Festival, Stratford, Connecticut. No program available.

2860 • MIGHTY MAN IS HE, A

OPENED: 1955
Musical

Songs: Rag Me That Mendlessohn March (C/L: Stephen Sondheim)

Notes: No other information available.

2861 • MIKADO, INC.

OPENED: 05/16/1990
Musical   Closed out of town

Music Based On: Arthur Sullivan
Composer: Glen Kelly
Lyricist: Albert Evans
Librettist: Jane Waterhouse
Director: Robert Johanson

Source: MIKADO, THE (Musical: W.S. Gilbert; Arthur Sullivan); **Choreographer:** Robert Johanson; **Costumes:** Lindsay W. Davis; **Lighting Designer:** Phil Monat; **Musical Director:** Tom Helm; **Set Design:** Michael Anania

Songs: Contract, The; Floppy Disk, The; Here's a Little Clue; How Do You Spot a Geishanette?; I Am the Boss; I Knew It; If Love Is Love; If You Want to Know Who We Are; Jersey Heart; Manager of Personnel, The; Micro-Chip Jingle; Mikado Anthem; Once in a Glade; Robot Will Never Say No, A; Samurai Stomp, The; Teahouse of the Sliding Screens, The; Three Little Temps; Till the Blossoms Fall; Titipu; Wand'ring Man Am I, A; What Turns You On; Yum-Yum's Vision

Cast: Ako; Marsha Bagwell; Thomas Ikeda; Jason Ma; Philip William McKinley; Michael Mulhern; James Rocco

Notes: Paper Mill Playhouse, Millburn, New Jersey.

2862 • MIKE
Notes: *See AIN'T BROADWAY GRAND.*

2863 • MILITARY MAID, THE
OPENED: 10/05/1900　Theatre: Savoy
Musical　　　　　　　Broadway: 8

Composer: Alfred E. Aarons
Lyricist: George V. Hobart
Librettist: George V. Hobart
Producer: Alfred E. Aarons

Songs: Madagascar Guards, The; Sister Mary Has the Measles; Tin Gee-Gee, The [1]

Cast: Sallie Berg; Henry Bergman; Taylor Granville; Josephine Hall; David Torrence

Notes: [1] Interpolated.

2864 • MILK AND HONEY
OPENED: 10/10/1961　Theatre: Martin Beck
Musical　　　　　　　Broadway: 543

Composer: Jerry Herman
Lyricist: Jerry Herman
Librettist: Don Appell
Producer: Gerard Oestreicher
Director: Albert Marre

Choreographer: Donald Saddler; **Costumes:** Miles White; **Dance Arranger:** Genevieve Pitot; **Lighting Designer:** Howard Bay; **Musical**

Director: Max Goberman; **Orchestrations:** Hershy Kay; Eddie Sauter; **Set Design:** Howard Bay

Songs: As Simple As That; Chin Up, Ladies; Give Me a Word [1]; Hymn to Hymie; I Will Follow You; Independence Day Hora; Let's Not Waste a Moment; Like a Young Man; Milk and Honey; Shalom; Shepherd's Song; That Was Yesterday; There's No Reason in the World; Wedding, The

Cast: Juki Arkin; Mimi Benzell; Thelma Pelish; Molly Picon; Tommy Rall; Robert Weede

Notes: [1] Out New Haven 8/26/61.

2865 • MILLION DOLLARS, A
OPENED: 09/27/1900　Theatre: New York
Musical　　　　　　　Broadway: 28

Composer: A. Baldwin Sloane
Lyricist: George V. Hobart
Librettist: Louis Harrison; George V. Hobart
Director: Frank Smithson

Choreographer: Carl Marwig; **Musical Director:** Jose Vandenberg

Songs: March of the Allies; Sixteen to One (Gold and Silver Ballet)

Cast: Ignacio Martinetti; Joseph Ott; Charles H. Prince; Pat Rooney; Nat Wills

Notes: No other songs listed in program.

2866 • MILLIONAIRE IN TROUBLE, A
OPENED: 01/16/1980　Theatre: Town Hall
Musical　　　　　　　Off-Broadway: 55

Composer: Alexander Lustig
Lyricist: Yankele Alperin
Librettist: Moshe Tamir
Producer: Shalom Musical Comedy Theatre
Director: Yankele Alperin

Choreographer: Felix Fibich; **Musical Director:** Renee Solomon

Songs: Drunkenness; Happy Life, A; Hard to Be a Pauper; How Do You Do; Longing; Many Trades; Mazel Tov; Mother Son; Promises and Love

Cast: Yakov Bodo; Diane Cypkin; Chaim Levin; Solo Moise; Raquel Yossiffon

2867 • MIMI

OPENED: 03/13/1920
Musical   Closed out of town

Composer: Adolf Philipp; Frank E. Tours
Lyricist: Edward Paulton
Librettist: Edward Paulton; Adolf Philipp

Cast: Chapine

2868 • MIMIC AND THE MAID, THE

OPENED: 01/11/1907   Theatre: Bijou
Musical   Broadway: 2

Composer: A. Baldwin Sloane
Lyricist: Allen Lowe
Librettist: Allen Lowe
Producer: Herman Oppenheimer Co.
Director: Tom Collins

Cast: Hattie Palmer; Dorothy Russell; Harry B. Watson; Gus Weinberg

Notes: No program available.

2869 • MIMIC WORLD, THE (1908)

OPENED: 07/09/1908   Theatre: Casino
Revue   Broadway: 92

Composer: Seymour Furth; Ben Jerome
Lyricist: Addison Burkhardt; Edward Madden
Librettist: Edgar Smith
Producer: Lew Fields; Lee Shubert; Sam S. Shubert
Director: J.C. Huffman

Choreographer: Ned Wayburn; **Set Design:** H. Robert Law; Arthur Voegtlin

Songs: All Days Are Gay Days in Paris [1]; All the Stars and Stripes Belong to Me; Ambassador's March; Any Old Nag (C: Seymour Furth; L: Addison Burkhardt); Chip Along; Eyes, Eyes, Eyes [1]; Girls, Girls, Girls [1]; I Want to Be a Bachelor [1]; I'm His Loving Wife [1]; I'm No Stingy Romeo; In Monte Carlo Town (C: Ben M. Jerome; L: Edward Madden); Love's Roulette [1]; Mademoiselle; Making Eyes; Mary Carey; Miss Hook of Holland; My Lady Wine; My Little

Blarney Stone [1]; On a Pullman Honeymoon [1]; Phoebe Snow; Polly of the Circus [1]; Rag Man, Music Man [2] (C: Louis A. Hirsch); Recipe of Love, The [1]; Salome Dance (C: Melville Ellis); Since I Sang E Flat [1]; Suffragettes [1]; Two Hearts Beat as One; What's the Use? [1]; When a Woman Has Her Way [1]; When Johnny Comes Marching Home from College Again (C: Louis A. Hirsch); When Tetrazzini Sings High F; Woman, Lovely Woman; Yankee Prince Waltz; You're the One for Me [1]; Your Lips Say No, but Your Eyes Say Yes (C: Ben M. Jerome; L: Edward Madden)

Cast: Roy Atwell; Irene Bentley; William Bonelli; Vernon Castle; Lotta Faust; Charles King; Dave Lewis; George Monroe; Grace Tyson

Notes: [1] Out Atlantic City 6/15/08. [2] Also called "The Ragtime Minstrel Man."

2870 • MIMIC WORLD OF 1921, THE

OPENED: 08/15/1921   Theatre: Century Roof
Revue   Broadway: 27

Composer: Owen Murphy; Lew Pollack; Jean Schwartz
Lyricist: Harold Atteridge; James Hussey
Producer: Messrs. Shubert
Director: Allan K. Foster

Musical Director: Al Goodman; **Set Design:** Watson Barratt

Songs: Any Night on Old Broadway [1] (C: Jean Schwartz; L: Harold Atteridge); Baby Vampire (L: Harold Atteridge; James Hussey; Owen Murphy); Bridget McShane; Broadway Pirates; Chicago (C: Lew Pollack; L: Sidney Clare); Daddy Buy Me a Bow Wow; Daisy Days; Fine Feathers; Gay Brazilian; Jazzanova; Knee Dance; Ma Temme; Mason Dixon Blues; Midnight Rounders; Mighty Like a Rosenbloom; Moth and the Flame; My Screen Maid; Old Fashioned Sweetheart; Posty and a Maid, A; Rose of the Rotisserie; Shakespeare's Garden of Love; Sidewalk; Star of Love; Tennis Terpsichorean; Waiter's Dance; Watermelon Time; Weep No More, My Mammy (C: Lew Pollack; L: Sidney Clare); When the Statues Come to Life

Cast: El Brendel; Cliff Edwards; Ann Toddings; Mae West

Notes: Titled THE WHIRL OF THE TOWN out of town. *See also TATTLE TALES,* an earlier version of this show. [1] ASCAP also credits Otto Motzan, Sigmund Romberg and Harold Atteridge with this song.

2871 • 'MIND THE PAINT' GIRL, THE

OPENED: 09/09/1912   Theatre: Lyceum
Play   Broadway: 136

Author: Arthur Wing Pinero
Producer: Charles Frohman
Director: Dion G. Boucicault

Songs: If You Would Only Love Me (C: Jerome Kern; L: John Crook); Mind the Paint (C: Jerome Kern; L: Arthur Wing Pinero); Our Honeymoon [1] (C/L: Emily Smith)

Cast: Billie Burke; Jeanne Eagels; H.E. Herbert; Jeannette Lowrie; William Raymond

Notes: [1] Sheet music only.

2872 • MING TOY

OPENED: 1929
Musical   Unproduced

Composer: George Gershwin
Lyricist: Ira Gershwin
Librettist: William Anthony McGuire
Producer: Florenz Ziegfeld

Source: EAST IS WEST (Play: John B. Hymer; Samuel Shipman)

Songs: Awake, Children, Awake; China Girl; East Is West; Embraceable You [1]; I Speak English Now; In the Mandarin's Orchid Garden; Lady of the Moon [3]; Sing-Song Girl; Under the Cinnamon Tree; We Are Visitors Here; Yellow Blues [2]

Cast: Bobbe Arnst; Oscar Shaw; Ed Wynn

Notes: [1] Later in GIRL CRAZY. [2] The music was later published as "Impromptu in Two Keys." [3] Music later used for "I Just Looked at You" which was not used in SHOW GIRL and also used for "Blah, Blah, Blah" in the film DELICIOUS.

2873 • MINNIE AND ME

Notes: *See THE MAGIC RING.*

2874 • MINNIE'S BOYS

OPENED: 03/26/1970   Theatre: Imperial
Musical   Broadway: 76

Composer: Larry Grossman
Lyricist: Hal Hackady
Librettist: Arthur Marx; Robert Marx
Producer: Max Brown; Byron Goldman; Arthur Whitelaw
Director: Stanley Prager

Choreographer: Marc Breaux; **Costumes:** Donald Brooks; **Dance Arranger:** Marvin Hamlisch; Peter Howard; **Lighting Designer:** Jules Fisher; **Musical Director:** John Berkman; **Orchestrations:** Ralph Burns; **Set Design:** Peter Wexler; **Vocal Arranger:** John Berkman

Songs: Act, The; Be Happy; Empty [1]; Five Growing Boys; Four Nightingales; If You Wind Me Up; I'll Say She Is [1]; Mama, a Rainbow; Minnie's Boys; More Precious Far; Rich Is; Smell of Christmas, The; Stagedoor Johnny [1]; They Give Me Love [1]; Underneath It All; Where Was I When They Passed Out Luck; You Don't Have to Do It for Me; You Remind Me of You; You're Getting Younger Every Day [1]

Cast: Jacqueline Britt; Daniel Fortus; Alvin Kupperman; Julie Kurnitz; Robert LuPone; Irwin Pearl; Gary Raucher; Casper Roos; Richard B. Shull; Lewis J. Stadlen; Shelley Winters

Notes: [1] Cut prior to opening.

2875 • MINSTREL OF CLARE

OPENED: 1896
Play

Composer: Chauncey Olcott
Lyricist: Chauncey Olcott

Songs: Love Remains the Same; Olcott's Home Song

Cast: Chauncey Olcott

Notes: No other information available. Sheet music only.

2876 • MIS-GUIDED TOUR

OPENED: 10/12/1959   Theatre: Downtown
Revue   Off-Broadway: 56

Composer: Shirley Botwin; Margaret Foster; James Allen Reid; Blair Weille; Jane White
Lyricist: James Allen Reid
Librettist: James Allen Reid
Producer: Robert D. Feldstein; James Allen Reid
Director: James Allen Reid

Choreographer: Charles Nicoll; **Musical Director:** Margaret Foster

Songs: Alice Again; Alice Alone; Alice Back Home; Alice in Italy; Alice in Spain; Am I Late?; Another Bumper Crop; At Least We Can Say; Better Safe Than Sorry; Copenhagen, Denmark; Desert Incident; Djibuti; Family Plan, The; First Ones There; Go! Go! Go!; High Seas, The; I Am; Le Folly Bergere; Lower Deck Diplomacy; Maiden's Voyage; Nomad; Now Isn't That Lovely?; Port of Debarkation; Second Deck Diplomacy; Shandu Misboo Ganash; Take a Chance on Me; Take a Ride!; Transplant; Try, Try Again; Two Bags; We Is Wonderful; Who Are You?

Cast: Leo Bloom; Jane Judge

Notes: Songs and sketches listed. Composers are not credited by song titles.

2877 • MISANTHROPE, THE

OPENED: 10/04/1977   Theatre: Public
Musical   Off-Broadway: 62

Composer: Jobriath Boone
Lyricist: Jobriath Boone
Librettist: Richard Wilbur
Producer: N.Y. Shakespeare Festival; Joseph Papp
Director: Bill Gile

Source: MISANTHROPE, THE (Play: Moliere); **Choreographer:** Rachel Lampert; **Costumes:** Carrie F. Robbins; **Lighting Designer:** Arden Fingerhut; **Musical Director:** Allan Shawn; **Orchestrations:** Bill Brohn; Robert Rodgers; **Set Design:** Bill Stabile

Songs: Altogether Too Outrageous; Art of Pleasing Me, The; Be Witness to My Madness; Double; He Loves to Make a Fuss; How Dare You?; I Confess; I Love You More; Lovers Manage; Madame; Other Day I Went to an Affair; Paris;

Second Best; Sonnet; Substitute; Symphonie; Things Are Most Mysterious; Waltz; We Women; Where in the World

Cast: Seth Allen; John Bottoms; Helen Gallagher; Paul Hecht; John McMartin; Joshua Mostel; Deborah Rush; Virginia Vestoff

Notes: Additional songs are credited to Margaret Pine and Arthur Bienstock. However, these songs are not identified in the program.

2878 • MISS BLUE EYES

OPENED: 10/03/1918
Musical   Closed out of town

Composer: Silvio Hein
Lyricist: George V. Hobart
Librettist: George V. Hobart

Source: WHAT'S YOUR HUSBAND DOING? (Play: George V. Hobart)

Notes: Apollo Theatre, Atlantic City.

2879 • MISS BO-PEEP

Musical   Closed out of town

Composer: Max S. Witt
Lyricist: Earle C. Jones

Songs: Dandelion Coon; Girlie of All the Year; It's Very Hard to Be a Boy; My Mississippi Missus Misses Me; Won't Your Momma Let You Come Out and Play

Cast: Melville Raymond

Notes: Information from sheet music. No other information available.

2880 • MISS BOB WHITE

OPENED: 1901
Musical   Closed out of town

Composer: Willard Spencer
Lyricist: Willard Spencer
Producer: Nixon & Zimmerman
Director: A.M. Holbrook; Willard Spencer

Songs: Bee Song; By Chance We're Both Willy's; Churning Song; Curiosity; Cute Little Quaker

Maids Are We; Egg Song; English Sparrow Told Me So, An; Ha, Ha, Ha! Millionaires!; Hunger Song; Hunting Chorus; If I Possessed Aladdin's Lamp; If You Would Be a Jackie; I'll Be True, I Love You; May We Come A'Wooing; Milk-maids' Chorus; My Eyes Speak Love; Mystery of Love; One Only-Al Dame, The; Society; Swing Song; There Once Was a King; Threshing Song; Tramp Has Ups and Downs, A; Watermelon, The; Why?

Notes: Credits from program of Ithica 3/26/04. The songs come from the 1901 vocal selection.

2881 • MISS CALICO

OPENED: 1926
Musical

Composer: Donald Heywood
Lyricist: Earl Dancer
Librettist: Earl Dancer
Producer: Earl Dancer
Director: Earl Dancer

Songs: Black Bottom; Down Home Stomp; I'm Coming Virginia (L: Will Marion Cook; Donald Heywood); I'm Satisified; Sweet Mama, Lulu Belle

Cast: Alec Lovejoy; Lionel Monagas; Marshall Rogers; Ethel Waters

Notes: No other information available. There were many specialty numbers, for example, Ethel Waters sang in a spot titled "Some Songs That You Have Heard in Your Home," which didn't identify specific songs.

2882 • MISS CAMILLE

OPENED: 04/14/1907   Theatre: Lambs' Club
Musical   Broadway

Composer: Victor Herbert
Librettist: George V. Hobart

Songs: I Want to Be a Gambling Man; My Toast to You; Spanish Serenade, The

Notes: A one-act musical at the Lambs' Club.

2883 • MISS CAPRICE

Notes: *See LIEBER AUGUSTIN.*

2884 • MISS DAISY

OPENED: 09/09/1914   Theatre: Shubert
Musical   Broadway: 29

Composer: Silvio Hein
Lyricist: Philip Bartholomae
Librettist: Philip Bartholomae
Producer: Philip Bartholomae
Director: J.C. Huffman

Choreographer: Jack Mason; Costumes: Orange; Musical Director: August Kleinecke; Set Design: Frank Gates; E.A. Morange

Songs: Cheer Up; Cherries Are Ripe; Dreams! Oh Dreams!; Gentle Moon; I Adore the American Girl; I Love You, Dear, I Love but You; If You Propose to Propose; Interruptions; Kissing; Little Girl, What Have You Done to Me?; Love Is the Same the Whole World Over [1]; Melodrama; My Little Queen Bee; Pierrot's Ball; Race of Life, The; Rose of Yesternight [1]; Shadows; Tea Leaves; Weave From Your Loom; Won't You Dance?; You Can't Stop Me from Thinking; You Were Made for Love; Youth

Cast: John Boyle; Allen Kearns; Charles Murray; Mae Murray; Anna Wheaton

Notes: Titled THE MODEL MAID out of town prior to Broadway. Titled AT THE BALL out of town after Broadway. [1] In show when titled THE MODEL MAID.

2885 • MISS DOLLY DOLLARS

OPENED: 09/04/1905   Theatre: Knickerbocker
Musical   Broadway: 72

Composer: Victor Herbert
Lyricist: Harry B. Smith
Librettist: Harry B. Smith
Producer: Charles B. Dillingham
Director: A.M. Holbrook

Costumes: Mme. Seidle; Musical Director: A. DeNovellis; Orchestrations: Victor Herbert

Songs: American Heiress, An; American Music ('Tis Better Than Old Parsifal to Me); Barney McGuire [1]; Dolly Dollars; Educated Fool, An (It Keeps Me Guessing All the Time); Entrance of Dolly; Entrance of Dorothy; Entrance of the Friendly Rival's Club; Finale Act I; Finale Act III; It's All in the Book You Know (Ollendorf Duet);

Just Get Out and Walk; Life's a Masquerade;
Moth and the Moon, The; My Fair Unknown; My
Word! (It Surely Was a Treat); No One Will Steal
Him [1]; Opening Chorus; Opening Chorus Act
II; Queen of the Ring; Self-Made Family (She's a
Lady with Money), The; Walks; Waltz Me
Around Again Willie [1] (C: Ren Shields; L: Will
D. Cobb); Woman Is Only a Woman but a Good
Cigar Is a Smoke (Puff, Puff, Puff), A

Cast: Carter De Haven; Elsie Ferguson; Lulu
Glaser; Ralph Herz; Melville Stewart

Notes: [1] Sheet music only.

2886 • MISS DUDELSACK

OPENED: 10/16/1911
Musical   Closed out of town

Composer: Rudolph Nelson
Lyricist: Grant Stewart
Librettist: Grant Stewart
Producer: Mark A. Luescher; Louis F. Werba
Director: A.M. Holbrook

Source: MISS DUDELSACK (Musical: Fritz
Grunbaum; Rudolph Nelson; Heinz Reichert);
Musical Director: Max Hirschfeld

Songs: Cat's Away, The; Chess Duet; Finale Act I;
Ghost, The; I Am Yours, You Are Mine; It's
Raining; Just a Little, Little Kiss; Mac, Mac, Macs,
The; Oh You, You Darling!; Pluck Not the Rose;
Ride, Red Captain, Ride!; See Ourselves As
Others See Us (L: Joseph W. Herbert); They Call
Me a Dudelsack; Three Words; Wealth, Beauty
and Power; You're Annoying Me

Cast: Arthur Clough; Lulu Glaser; Matthew
Hanley; Joseph W. Herbert; Thomas Richard;
David Torrence

Notes: Boston Theatre.

2887 • MISS EMILY ADAM

OPENED: 03/29/1960   Theatre: Theatre Marquee
Musical   Off-Broadway: 21

Composer: Sol Berkowitz
Lyricist: James Lipton
Librettist: James Lipton
Producer: Paul E. Davis; Winthrop Palmer; Stanley
G. Weiss
Director: Paul E. Davis

Source: ROSEMARY AND THE PLANET (Story:
Winthrop Palmer); **Choreographer:** Alex
Palermo; **Costumes:** Gene Barth; **Lighting
Designer:** Paul Saitta; **Musical Director:** Liza
Redfield; **Orchestrations:** David Hollister; **Set
Design:** Joseph Weishar

Songs: According to Plotnik; All Aboard; At the
Ball; Dear Old Friend; Fun; Home; I'm Your
Valentine; It's Positively You; Love Is; Name:
Emily Adams; Obedian March; Oh, the Shame;
Once Upon a Time; Storm Ballet; Talk to Me;
Ultivac

Cast: Cherry Davis; Francis Dux; Robert Fitch;
Richard Latessa; Betty Low

2888 • MISS HAPPINESS

OPENED: 1926
Musical   Closed out of town

Composer: Jay Gorney
Lyricist: George E. Stoddard
Librettist: Jay Gorney; George E. Stoddard
Producer: C.C. Wanamaker
Director: Frank McCormack

Choreographer: Ralph Reader; **Musical Director:**
Jay Gorney

Songs: Blue Print Blues; Danse Diversement;
Dictation; Feeding the Chickens; Follow the
Crowd; Here Comes the Bride; I Want to Be a
Liberty Belle; Independance; Lady, You Don't
Know Me; Let's Make Believe; Long Is a
Wonderful Thing; Mr. and Mrs. and Company;
Nice Small Town Girls; Oh, How that Baby
Could Baby Me; Open Your Arms (And Close
Your Eyes); That's Happiness; When Knott's Not
Tying Knots

Cast: May Boley; William Gaxton; Peggy Hope;
Charles Williams; Mabel Withee

Notes: From a program of Poli's Theatre
Washington D.C. 12/05/26.

2889 • MISS HOOK OF HOLLAND

OPENED: 12/31/1907   Theatre: Criterion
Musical   Broadway: 119

Composer: Paul Rubens
Lyricist: Paul Rubens

Librettist: Austen Hurgon; Paul Rubens
Producer: Charles Frohman
Director: T. Reynold

Costumes: Dazian; **Set Design:** Unitt & Wickes

Songs: Amsterdam; Bottles; Cream of the Sky; Fly Away Kite; Flying Dutchman; Have You Been to Arndyk? [3]; House that Hook Built, The; I Want to Be Your Wife; Knitting Sextet; Little Bit of Cheese, A; Little Liqueurs [1]; Little Miss Wooden Shoes; Miss Hook; Pink Petty from Peter, A; Sleepy Canal, The; Soldiers of the Netherlands; Tra-La-La; Violincello, The [2]; Water Never Did That [4] (C: Egbert Van Alstyne; L: Harry Williams)

Cast: Georgia Caine, Christie MacDonald; Florence Nash; Tom Wise

Notes: [1] Originally in London version but dropped after opening. [2] Added after opening in London version. [3] Added to later London productions. [4] ASCAP/Library of Congress only.

2890 • MISS 'I DON'T KNOW'
Notes: *See LITTLE SIMPLICITY.*

2891 • MISS INFORMATION
OPENED: 10/05/1915   Theatre: Cohan
Musical   Broadway: 47

Composer: Jerome Kern
Lyricist: Elsie Janis
Librettist: Paul Dickey; Charles W. Goddard
Producer: Charles Dillingham
Director: Robert Milton

Songs: Banks of Wye, The (C: Frank Tours; L: Fred E. Weatherly); Constant Lover (C: Herman Finck; L: Arthur Wimperis); Little Love, A (But Not for Me) [1]; Mix-up Rag, The; On the Sands of Wah-ki-ki [2] (C: Henry Kailimai; Jerome Kern); Pianologue; Some Sort of Somebody [1]; Two Big Eyes (C: Cole Porter; L: John Golden)

Cast: Irene Bordoni; Melville Ellis; Annie Esmond; Howard Estabrook; Maurice Farkoa; Elsie Janis

Notes: [1] Later in VERY GOOD EDDIE. [2] Later in VERY GOOD EDDIE. Verse by Jerome Kern, chorus by Henry Kailimai.

2892 • MISS INNOCENCE
OPENED: 11/30/1908   Theatre: New York
Musical   Broadway: 176

Composer: Ludwig Englander
Lyricist: Harry B. Smith
Librettist: Harry B. Smith
Producer: Florenz Ziegfeld
Director: Julian Mitchell

Songs: Afraid to Go Home at All; Am I a Wife, Widow or Maid?; By the Light of the Silvery Moon [1] (C: Gus Edwards; L: Edward Madden); I Have Lost My Little Brown Bear [3] (C/L: Bob Cole; C: J. Rosamond Johnson); I Want to Be Naughty Too [6]; I Wonder What's the Matter with My Eyes (C: Egbert Van Alstyne; L: Harry Williams); I'm Crazy when the Band Begins to Play (C: Jean Schwartz; L: William Jerome); I'm Learning Something Every Day (C/L: Nora Bayes; Jack Norworth); I'm Not That Kind of Girl [1] (C: Nat D. Ayer; L: A. Seymour Brown); Marie, Marie; My Cousin Caruso [2] (C: Gus Edwards; L: Edward Madden); My Pony Boy [4] (C: Charlie O'Donnell; L: Bobby Heath); My Post Card Girl [7] (C: Louis A. Hirsch; L: Addison Burkhardt); Nicer Girl than You, A [1] (C/L: J.W. Stern); Oh! That Yankiana Rag (C: Melville Gideon; L: E. Ray Goetz); Opening Chorus; Perfectly Terrible, Dear; Pierrot Patrole and Dance; Please Tell Me What They Mean; Railroad Number; See, What You've Done to Me [6] (C/L: Benjamin Hapgood Burt); Shine On Harvest Moon [5] (C/L: Nora Bayes; Jack Norworth); Spanish Dance; Students' Chorus; Three Weeks with You; We Two in an Aeroplane; What Kind of a Wife to Choose (C/L: Gus Edwards)

Cast: Charles A. Bigelow; Lawrence D'Orsay; Anna Held; Emma Janvier; Lillian Lorraine; Florence Walton; Gladys Zell

Notes: [1] Out of town only. [2] Also in ZIEGFELD FOLLIES OF 1909. [3] Published as "I've Lost My Teddy Bear." [4] Not in programs. [5] Also in ZIEGFELD FOLLIES OF 1908. [6] Sheet music only. [7] Matt Woodward also credited with lyrics in some programs.

2893 • MISS JACK
OPENED: 09/04/1911   Theatre: Herald Square
Musical   Broadway: 16

Composer: William F. Peters
Lyricist: Mark Swan
Librettist: Mark Swan
Producer: Ben Sangor
Director: Lewis Morton

Choreographer: Bothwell Browne; **Costumes:** Bothwell Browne; **Set Design:** H. Robert Law

Songs: Deacon Pettigue; English Language, The; Fencing Girl, The; Good-Bye, Little Girl; If You Could Fancy Me; Opening Chorus; Serpent of the Nile, The; Skylark, The; Slumbertown; That's Peculiar Isn't It? Very; There Really Isn't Any More to Tell; This Is No Place for a Good Little Girl; Visions of Love

Cast: Bothwell Browne; Hazel Cox; Olive Ulrich; Ernest F. Young

2894 • MISS LIBERTY

OPENED: 07/15/1949   Theatre: Imperial
Musical   Broadway: 308

Composer: Irving Berlin
Lyricist: Irving Berlin
Librettist: Robert E. Sherwood
Producer: Irving Berlin; Moss Hart; Robert E. Sherwood
Director: Moss Hart

Choreographer: Jerome Robbins; **Costumes:** Motley; **Lighting Designer:** Oliver Smith; **Musical Director:** Jay Blackton; **Orchestrations:** Don Walker; **Set Design:** Oliver Smith

Songs: Business for a Good Girl Is Bad [1]; Extra, Extra!; Falling Out of Love Can Be Fun; Follow the Leader Jig; Give Me Your Tired, Your Poor (L: Emma Lazarus); Homework; Honorable Profession of the Fourth Estate, The [1]; I'd Like My Picture Took; Just One Way to Say I Love You; Let's Take an Old-Fashioned Walk; Little Fish in a Big Pond, A; Me an' My Bundle; Miss Liberty; Most Expensive Statue in the World, The; Mr. Monotony [2]; Only for Americans; Paris Wakes Up and Smiles; Policeman's Ball, The; Pulitzer Prize, The [1]; Sing a Song of Sing Sing [1]; Train, The; What Do I Have to Do to Get My Picture in the Paper? [1]; You Can Have Him

Cast: Eddie Albert; Herbert Berghof; Philip Bourneuf; Charles Dingle; Ethel Griffies; Maria

Karnilova; Mary McCarty; Allyn McLerie; Tommy Rall

Notes: [1] Cut prior to opening. [2] Cut prior to opening. Originally cut from film EASTER PARADE.

2895 • MISS MANHATTAN (1897)

OPENED: 03/30/1897   Theatre: Wallack's
Musical   Broadway: 40

Composer: Herman Perlet; F. Puehringer
Librettist: George V. Hobart

Cast: William Cameron; Adele Francis; Maude Le Roy; Budd Ross; John Young

Notes: No program available.

2896 • MISS MANHATTAN (1926)

OPENED: 08/09/1926
Musical   Closed out of town

Composer: Paul Fairfax Fuller
Lyricist: Paul Fairfax Fuller
Librettist: Paul Fairfax Fuller
Director: Walter Kenny

Choreographer: Frank Marion; **Musical Director:** Paul Fuller

Songs: Change Your Mind; Charley Does the Charleston; Come On — Dance; Every Day Will Be a Happy Day; Gorgeous; Hayseed; Maudlin Maiden; Passers Bye; Roseanne; So's Your Old Lady; Variety; Wedding Bells; When I'm Sad

Cast: Ada Howard; Preston Lewis; Garry Owen; Sylvia Stoll

Notes: Program of Asbury Park, New Jersey.

2897 • MISS MILLIONS

OPENED: 12/09/1919   Theatre: Punch and Judy
Musical   Broadway: 47

Composer: Raymond Hubbell
Lyricist: R.H. Burnside
Librettist: R.H. Burnside

Songs: Brazil; Cutest Little House; Dancing Lesson; Don't Say Goodbye; Dreams [1]; Everything

Comes to Those Who Wait; Farmer's Daughters; Hiram; Hustle and Bustle; I Know That I'm in Love with You; I Want to Marry; If You'll Just Wait a Little While; Letter Song-Goodbye; Makes No Difference Now; Mary; My Advice; Opening Chorus; Opening Chorus Act III; Scandal; Toast Song; Way Down in Jersey

Cast: Vinton Freedley; Valli Valli

Notes: [1] Sheet music only.

2898 • MISS MOFFAT

OPENED: 10/07/1974
Musical   Closed out of town

Composer: Albert Hague
Lyricist: Emlyn Williams
Librettist: Joshua Logan; Emlyn Williams
Producer: L. Slade Brown; Eugene V. Wolsk
Director: Joshua Logan

Source: CORN IS GREEN, THE (Play: Emlyn Williams); **Choreographer:** Donald Saddler; **Costumes:** Robert Mackintosh; **Dance Arranger:** Albert Hague; Robert Rogers; **Lighting Designer:** Jo Mielziner; **Musical Director:** Jay Blackton; **Orchestrations:** Robert M. Freedman; **Set Design:** Jo Mielziner; **Vocal Arranger:** Albert Hague

Songs: Debt I Owe, The; Go, Go, Morgan; Here in the South; I Can Talk Now; I Shall Experience It Again; If I Weren't Me; Peekaboo, Jehovah; Pray for the Snow; There's More to a Man than His Head; Time's A Flyin'; Tomorrow; What Could Be Fairer Than That?; Wonderful Game, A; Words Unspoken, The; You Don't Need a Nailfile in a Cornfield

Cast: Nell Carter; Bette Davis; Giancarlo Esposito; Anne Francine; Dody Goodman; Lee Goodman; Dorian Harewood; Avon Long; Marion Ramsey; Gil Robbins; David Sabin

Notes: Closed Philadelphia 10/17/74.

2899 • MISS MOLLY MAY

OPENED: 1909
Musical   Closed out of town

Composer: Julian Edwards
Producer: Alfred E. Aarons

2900 • MISS 1917

OPENED: 11/05/1917   Theatre: Century
Revue   Broadway: 40

Composer: Jerome Kern
Lyricist: P.G. Wodehouse
Librettist: Guy Bolton; P.G. Wodehouse
Producer: Charles B. Dillingham; Florenz Ziegfeld
Director: Ned Wayburn

Choreographer: Adolph Bolm; **Costumes:** Paul Chaflin; Dazian; Faibsey; Lady Duff Gordon; Cora MacGeachy; Elspeth Phelps; Willy Pogany; Max Weldy; **Musical Director:** Robert Hood Bowers; **Set Design:** Joseph Urban

Songs: Beauty Doctor, The (C: Victor Herbert); Dancing Courtship, A (C: Unknown); Dancing M.D., A; Falling Leaves Ballet (inst.) (C: Victor Herbert); Go Little Boat [1]; Good-Bye Broadway (C: Unknown); Honor System, The; I'm the Old Man in the Moon, The; Irish Jig (The Singing Blacksmith of Curriclough) (inst.) (C: Victor Herbert); Land Where the Good Songs Go, The [2]; Mosquito Song, The (inst.) (C: Victor Herbert); Palm Beach Girl, The; (Papa Would Persist in Picking) Peaches; Picture I Want to See, The [3]; Society Farmerettes, The (C: Victor Herbert); Tell Me All Your Troubles, Cutie; Toy Clog Dance (inst.); We Want to Laugh; We're Crooks; Who's Zoo in Girl Land; You're the Little Girl I've Looked So Long For [1]

Cast: Elizabeth Brice; Irene Castle; Marion Davies; Lew Fields; Harry Kelly; Cecil Lean; Cleo Mayfield; Bessie McCoy; Ann Pennington; Savoy & Brennan; Joe Schenck; Vivienne Segal; Lilyan Tashman; Gus Van; George White

Notes: Irish jig arranged by Herbert from tune by his grandfather. George Gershwin was the rehearsal pianist. [1] Not in programs. [2] From OH, BOY! [3] Also used in OH LADY! LADY!!

2901 • MISS NOBODY FROM STARLAND

OPENED: 01/31/1910   Theatre: Princess
Musical   Chicago

Composer: Joseph E. Howard
Lyricist: Frank R. Adams; Will M. Hough
Librettist: Howard Johnstone Mitchell

Songs: Dear Little Ghost of Your Smile, The; Every Girl I Love Is Someone's Wife; I'd Rather Love What I Can't Have (C/L: Harold Orlob); If You Won't Marry Me, Then I'll Marry You; I'll Be Your Honey When It's Moonlight; It Must Be Great to Be a General but I'd Rather Lead the Band (C/L: Paul Rubens); Kiss Me; Let Me Be Your Last Sweetheart (C/L: Harold Orlob)

Cast: Ralph Herz; Bessie Wynn

Notes: No program available.

2902 • MISS POCAHONTAS

OPENED: 10/28/1907   Theatre: Lyric
Musical   Broadway: 16

Composer: Dan Sullivan
Lyricist: R.M. Baker
Librettist: R.M. Baker; R.A. Barnet
Producer: Boston Cadet Corps; R.L. Griffen

Songs: Dance of the Woodland Sprites (inst.); Drama, The; Ghost Dance, The (inst.); Hail! Hail! Big Chief John!; Huskin' Bee, The; In a Dory (C: Carl Wilmore; L: Harry H. Luther); In a Jewelled Grotto; In the Motor Car; John Smith; Katie Carney, Stop Your Blarney! (L: Dan Sullivan); Mama, Do Not Leave Your Pappoose; Mickey O'Toole; Name a Day, Love!; Night Shift, The; Opening Chorus; Play the Star-Spangled Banner; Then I Became the Manager; Tip for Little Girls, A; Twang of My Trusty Bow (C: Carl Wilmore; L: Harry H. Luther); Whispering Shade; Won't You Say: "Yes" to Me?

Cast: Lester Allen; Blanche Deyo; Marie Dupuis; George Fox; Walter Jones; Violet Zell

Notes: No New York program available.

2903 • MISS PRINCESS

OPENED: 12/23/1912   Theatre: Park
Musical   Broadway: 16

Composer: Tom Johnstone
Lyricist: Will Johnstone
Librettist: Frank Mandel

Songs: Ay-Oomps; Come, My Sweetheart; Galloping Cavalree, The; Give Me Love, Love, Love; Humpty Dumpty; I Want to Be the Last to Kiss You; It Might Have Been; Little Red Book and a Five Cent Bag, A; Temperamental Dances; Queen Thou Art; We All Agree on a Pretty Girl; When I Propose; Wireless Way, The

Cast: Lina Abarbanell; Robert Warwick

Notes: No program available. Songs from sheet music only.

2904 • MISS PRINNT

OPENED: 12/25/1900   Theatre: Victoria
Musical   Broadway: 28

Composer: John Golden
Lyricist: John Golden
Librettist: George V. Hobart
Producer: Joseph Immerman

Musical Director: William MacQuinn

Cast: Marie Dressler; Jobyna Howland; Dave Lewis; Kitty Nugent; Charlotte Walker

Notes: No songs listed in program. Act III titled THE VILLAGE BEAUTY and had book and lyrics by J. Clarence Harvey.

2905 • MISS SAIGON

OPENED: 04/11/1991   Theatre: Broadway
Musical   Broadway

Composer: Claude-Michel Schonberg
Lyricist: Alain Boublil; Richard Maltby Jr.
Librettist: Alain Boublil; Richard Maltby Jr.; Claude-Michel Schonberg
Producer: Cameron Mackintosh
Director: Nicholas Hytner

Choreographer: Bob Avian; **Costumes:** Suzy Benzinger; Andreane Neofitou; **Lighting Designer:** David Hersey; **Orchestrations:** William D. Brohn; **Set Design:** John Napier

Songs: American Dream, The; Back in Town; Bui-Doi; Ceremony, The; Confrontation, The; Guilt Inside Your Head, The; Heat Is on in Saigon, The; Her or Me [2]; I Still Believe; I'd Give My Life for You; If You Want to Die in Bed; Last Night of the World, The; Little God of My Heart; Morning of the Dragon, The; Movie in My Mind, The; Now That I've Seen Her [1]; Please; Room 317; Sun and Moon; Telephone, The; What a Waste; Why God Why?; You Will Not Touch Him

Cast: Brian R. Baldomero; Hinton Battle; Barry K. Bernal; Liz Callaway; Kam Cheng; Willy Falk; JoAnn M. Hunter; Jonathan Pryce; Lea Salonga

Notes: Kim Cheng played for Lea Salonga on matinees. Still running as of this time. [1] New lyric for "Her or Me." [2] Cut. Music used for "Now That I've Seen Her."

2906 • MISS SIMPLICITY
OPENED: 02/10/1902   Theatre: Casino
Musical   Broadway: 56

Composer: H.L. Heartz
Lyricist: R.A. Barnet
Librettist: R.A. Barnet
Producer: Kirke La Shelle
Director: Ned Wayburn

Songs: And You Were Shy Eighteen; Babette (C: Benjamin Hapgood Burt; L: Paul West); But He Said It So Politely; Charity; Chestnutty Language of Lovers, The [1]; Don't Forget You're Talking to a Lady (C: William Spink; L: Henry Blossom); Don't Mind Me (C: Clifton Crawford); Girlie with the Baby Stare, The (C/L: William H. Penn); Good Little Sunday School Boy, The; Interrogative Child (Mrs. Wimple's Party), The; King's Own, The; Love Me Little, Love Me Long; Love Me Sweetheart in Sweet Song [1]; Me and You [1] (C: Clifton Crawford); Oh What a Delight to Be Dancing; Phoebe; Rosalie (C: E.W. Corliss); Roses Begin with R, Love; Some Do! Some Don't!; Stand Back; Sweet Ecstasy; Ways to Catch a Man [1]; When Will My Dreams Come True, Love [1]; With All Proprietee; Without a Chaperon [1]; You'd Better Take It Back

Cast: Grace Belmont; Allene Crater; William Danforth; Frank Daniels; Harry Holliday; Helen Lord; Lawrence Wheat

Notes: [1] Vocal score only.

2907 • MISS SPRINGTIME
OPENED: 09/25/1916   Theatre: New Amsterdam
Musical   Broadway: 224

Composer: Emmerich Kalman
Lyricist: Herbert Reynolds; P.G. Wodehouse
Librettist: Guy Bolton
Producer: Klaw & Erlanger
Director: Herbert Gresham

Source: ZSUZSI KISASSZONY (Musical: Miska Brody; Emmerich Kalman; Ferenc Martos); **Choreographer:** Julian Mitchell; **Costumes:** F. Richard Anderson; Alice O'Neil; **Lighting**

Designer: Ben Beerwald; **Musical Director:** Charles Previn; **Set Design:** Joseph Urban

Songs: All Full of Talk (C: Jerome Kern; L: P.G. Wodehouse); Dance Eccentrique (dance); Dance of Isis, The (dance); Finale Act I; Finale Act II; Finale Act III; In the Garden of Romance (L: Herbert Reynolds); Life Is a Game of Bluff (L: Herbert Reynolds); Little Bid for Sympathy, A (L: Herbert Reynolds); Little Country Mouse, A (L: Herbert Reynolds); Love Calls Us, Dear [2]; Love Monopoly, The (L: Herbert Reynolds); My Castle in the Air (C: Jerome Kern; L: P.G. Wodehouse); Old Fashioned Drama, The; Once Upon a Time [1]; Opening Act II; Rosemary [2]; Saturday Night (A Very Good Girl on Sunday) (C: Jerome Kern; L: P.G. Wodehouse); Some One (C: Jerome Kern; L: Herbert Reynolds); Sunrise; That's All Charming [2]; These Are the Words [1] (L: Herbert Reynolds); This Is the Existence [1]; Throw Me a Rose (L: Herbert Reynolds; P.G. Wodehouse)

Cast: Elsie Alder; John E. Hazzard; George MacFarlane; Georgia O'Ramey; Jed Prouty

Notes: Titled LITTLE MISS SPRINGTIME out of town prior to New York. [1] Sheet music only. [2] Out Philadelphia prior to New York.

2908 • MISS TRUTH
OPENED: 06/05/1979   Theatre: Apollo
Musical   Off-Broadway: 16

Composer: Thom Bridwell; Louis Johnson; Glory Van Scott
Lyricist: Glory Van Scott
Librettist: Glory Van Scott
Producer: Apollo Theatre
Director: Louis Johnson

Choreographer: Louis Johnson; **Costumes:** Alice E. Carter; Judy Dearing; **Dance Arranger:** Thom Bridwell; Louis Johnson; **Lighting Designer:** Gary Harris; **Musical Director:** Thom Bridwell; **Set Design:** Louis Johnson; **Vocal Arranger:** Thom Bridwell; Louis Johnson

Songs: Children Are for Loving; Disco; Do Your Thing Miss Truth; Freedom Diet; I Sing the Rainbow; Lift Every Voice and Sing [1] (C: J. Rosamond Johnson; L: James Weldon Johnson); Miss Truth; My Religion; Self-Made Woman; Shame; This Is a Very Special Day

Cast: Loretta Devine; Christopher Pierre; Herbert Lee Rawlings Jr.; Glory Van Scott; Charles LaVont Williams

Notes: Additional music and arrangements by Louis Johnson. [1] This was a popular song written in 1909.

2909 • MISS UNDERGROUND
OPENED: 1943
Musical   Unproduced

Composer: Emmerich Kalman
Lyricist: Lorenz Hart
Librettist: Paul Gallico

Choreographer: George Balanchine

Songs: Alexander's Blitztime Band; Bad Little Apple and the Wise Old Tree, The; Do I Love You?; France Is Free; Get Your Man; It Happened in the Dark; Jean's Magic Song; Lucio's Victorian Family; Messieurs, Mesdames; Mother, Look, I'm an Acrobat; New York Number; One Who Yells the Loudest Is the Captain, The; Otto and the Elephants; Otto's German/English Song; Otto's Patter Song; Vendor's Song; You Crazy Little Thing (Fall in Love) [1]

Notes: [1] Music later used in MARINKA.

2910 • MISTRESS OF THE INN, THE
OPENED: 1957
Musical   Closed out of town

Composer: Don Walker
Lyricist: Ira Wallach
Librettist: Ira Wallach
Director: Ezra Stone

Source: MISTRESS OF THE INN (Play: Carlo Goldoni); **Choreographer:** Ralph Linn; **Lighting Designer:** David Hale Hand; **Musical Director:** Bruce Prince-Joseph; **Set Design:** W. Broderick Hackett

Songs: Alone in a World of Men; Cavalier's Waltz; I Am Who I Am; I'm All Right; Mad; Masculine Man, A; Mirandolina's Dander; Monkey in My Mind, The; Never Let Your Dander Down; O, Shed Not Blood; Restless Rover; Simpatico; Something Indescribable;

Sweet Mistress of My Heart; Tan-Tivy; To Love with a Lovely Life

Cast: Beatrice Arthur; John Call; Jack Cassidy; Lester Ferguson; Louise Hoff; Millicent Martin; Gene Saks

Notes: From a program of the Bucks County Playhouse, New Hope, Pennsylvania.

2911 • MITZI
Notes: *See WHITE LIGHTS.*

2912 • MIX UP AT RENO, A
Musical

Composer: Otto Herman
Lyricist: William K. Wells
Librettist: James E. Cooper; Tom McRae

Songs: Beautiful Roses; Broadway Love; Cupid; Daddy Won't You Buy Him for Me; Meet Me in Panama; My Bonny Heeland Lassie; My Crooning Melody; Yankee Girl

Notes: A burlesque musical.

2913 • MIXED DOUBLES
OPENED: 10/19/1966   Theatre: Upstairs at the Downstairs
Revue   Nightclub: 428
Librettist: John Boni; Marshall Brickman; Sid Davis
Producer: Edward Morris; Rod Warren
Director: Robert Audy

Choreographer: Robert Audy; **Dance Arranger:** Michael Cohen; **Lighting Designer:** Richard Mensoff; **Orchestrations:** Michael Cohen; **Vocal Arranger:** Michael Cohen

Songs: And a Messenger Appeared (C/L: Gene Bissell); Best Wishes (C: Stephen Lawrence; L: John Meyer); Bobby the K (C/L: Richard Robinson); Bon Voyeur (C/L: James Rusk); Brief Encounter (C: Bill Kaufman; L: Paul Koreto); Britannia Rules (C: Jerry Powell; L: Rod Warren); Das Chicago Song [1] (C: Michael Cohen; L: Tony Geiss); Fat Song, The (C/L: James Rusk); Friendly Liberal Neighborhood (C/L: June Reizner); Holden and Phoebe (C: Michael Cohen; L: Michael McWhinney); Mixed Doubles

(C: Johann Sebastian Bach; L: Rod Warren);
Mixed Marriages (C: Bill Weeden; L: David
Finkle); New York Is a Festival of Fun (C/L:
Gene Bissell); Questions (C: Ed Kresley; L: Drey
Sheppard); Ronald Reagan (C: Ed Kresley;
L: Drey Sheppard); Sartor Sartoris (C/L: Franklin
Underwood); Spoleto (C: Jerry Powell;
L: Michael McWhinney); Walter Kerr (C/L: Rod
Warren; L: Michael McWhinney)

Cast: Judy Graubart; Madeline Kahn; Larry Moss;
Robert Rovin; Janie Sell; Gary Sneed; **Pianist:**
Michael Cohen

Notes: [1] Also in NEW FACES OF 1968.

2914 • MLLE. MISCHIEF
OPENED: 09/28/1908   Theatre: Lyric
Musical   Broadway: 96

Composer: Carl M. Ziehrer
Lyricist: Sydney Rosenfeld
Librettist: Sydney Rosenfeld
Producer: Lee Shubert; Sam S. Shubert
Director: J.C. Huffman

Source: EIN TOLLES MADEL (Musical: Kurt
Kraatz; Wilhelm Sterk; Heinrich Stobitzer; Carl
M. Ziehrer); **Choreographer:** Ned Wayburn

Songs: And Other Things; Army Corps, The; Ev'ry
Hour Brings Its Flower; I'm Looking for My
Sweetheart [1]; Joy Duet, The; Ladies Beware; Le
Coeur de Ninon; Lonesome [1]; My Own Vienna;
Opening Chorus; She Knew a Thing or Two;
Single Day, A; Sweetheart; To the Regiment
We'll Go; Verily, Merrily

Cast: Elizabeth Brice; W.T. Carleton; Alexander
Clark; Lulu Glaser; Ethel Intropodi; Josie
Intropodi

Notes: [1] Out of town.

2915 • MLLE. MODISTE
OPENED: 12/25/1905   Theatre: Knickerbocker
Musical   Broadway: 202

Composer: Victor Herbert
Lyricist: Henry Blossom
Librettist: Henry Blossom
Producer: Charles Dillingham
Director: A.M. Holbrook; Fred G. Latham

Musical Director: John Lund; **Orchestrations:**
Victor Herbert; **Set Design:** Homer Emens

Songs: Ah, But in Dreams [2]; Ballet (inst.) [2];
Bazaar Opening Chorus [2]; Charity Bazaar,
The; Chorus of Footmen (Servants' Chorus)
(Charge of the Footmen); Dear Little Girl Who
Is Good, The; Furs and Feathers, Buckles and
Bows (Opening Chorus); Hats Make the
Woman; I Should Think That You Could
Guess; I Want What I Want When I Want It;
If I Were on the Stage (Kiss Me Again); I'm
Always Misunderstood; In Dreams So Fair [1];
Keokuk Culture Club, The; Love Me, Love
My Dog; Mascot of the Troop, The (Mascot of
the Moon); Nightingale and the Star, The;
Time and the Place and the Girl, The; When
the Cat's Away the Mice Will Play; Ze English
Language

Cast: Claude Gillingwater; Walter Percival;
William Pruette; Fritzi Scheff; Mack Sennett

Notes: [1] Sheet music only. [2] ASCAP/Library of
Congress only.

2916 • MLLE. ROSITA
Notes: See THE DUCHESS.

2917 • MOCKING BIRD, THE
OPENED: 11/10/1902   Theatre: Bijou
Musical   Broadway: 64

Composer: A. Baldwin Sloane
Lyricist: Sydney Rosenfeld
Librettist: Sydney Rosenfeld
Producer: Messrs. Sire
Director: R.H. Burnside

Costumes: Will R. Barnes; **Musical Director:** Max
Knauer

Songs: Carried Off; Entrance of Immigrants; Flash
of the Skipper's Eye, A [1]; France, Glorious
France; From a Different Point of View [1];
Gossipers, The; Governor's Song, The; If You
Couldn't Change Your Mind; In Silence; Just a
Kiss; King of France, The [1]; Lion and the
Mouse, The; Moon Song, The; One I Love the
Other I Abhor [1]; Point of View, The; Rigadoon,
The; Ship Ahoy (Opening Chorus); Sly Musette;
Stale World and a Pale World, A; What's the
Matter with the Moon Tonight?

Cast: Edgar Atchinson-Ely; Mabelle Gilman; Walter Shannon; Grace Walton

Notes: [1] Sheet music only. [2] Vocal score only.

2918 • MOD DONNA
OPENED: 04/24/1970   Theatre: Public
Musical   Off-Broadway: 48

Composer: Susan Hulsman Bingham
Lyricist: Myrna Lamb
Librettist: Myrna Lamb
Producer: N.Y. Shakespeare Festival; Joseph Papp
Director: Joseph Papp

Choreographer: Ze-eva Cohen; **Costumes:** Milo Morrow; **Lighting Designer:** Martin Aronstein; **Musical Director:** Dorothea Freitag; Liza Redfield; **Orchestrations:** Liza Redfield

Songs: All the Way Down; Astrociggy; Beautiful Man; Charlie's Plant; Creon; Deal, The; Earth Dance; Earthworms; First Act Crisis; Food Is Love; Hollow; Incantation; Jeff's Plaints; Liberia; Morning After, The; Now!; Panassociative; Sacrifice; Second Act Beginning; Second Honeymoon, The; Seduction Second Degree; Special Bulletin; Take a Knife; Trapped; Trinity; We Are the Whores; Worker and the Shirker, The

Cast: Larry Bryggman; Peter Haig; Sharon Laughlin; April Shawhan

2919 • MODEL GIRL, THE
OPENED: 01/26/1915
Musical   Closed out of town

Composer: Raymond Hubbell
Lyricist: Anne Caldwell
Librettist: Anne Caldwell
Producer: L.C. Wiswell
Director: Frank Smithson

Source: MODEL GIRL, A (Play: Anne Caldwell); **Costumes:** Will R. Barnes; **Musical Director:** August Kleinecke; **Orchestrations:** Frank Saddler

Songs: Bye and Bye; Dathydill; Dreams; Gay Young Students; How Would You Like to Have Me for a Model?; I Like 'Em All; In an Oriental Garden; Into the Dream (Act I Finale); Jolly Good Uncle; Keep Me from Falling Asleep; Love, Honor and Obey; Murmuring Water; Pause

Oriental; Pierrot and Pierrette; Poor Little Model Girl; Sentimental Turk; Sweet Shirren; With Silver Splendor; Won't You Come Over

Cast: Annette Kellerman; Edwin Wilson

Notes: Atlantic City. Sometimes titled THE MODEL MAID.

2920 • MODEL MAID, THE (1914)
Notes: See MISS DAISY.

2921 • MODEL MAID, THE (1915)

Composer: Raymond Hubbell
Lyricist: Anne Caldwell
Librettist: Anne Caldwell

Cast: Annette Kellerman

Notes: See THE MODEL GIRL.

2922 • MODERN EVE, A
OPENED: 05/03/1915   Theatre: Casino
Musical   Broadway: 56

Composer: Jean Gilbert; Victor Hollander
Lyricist: Will M. Hough
Librettist: Benjamin Hapgood Burt
Director: Julian Alfred

Source: DIE MODERNE EVA (Musical: Georg Okonkowski; A. Schoenfield); **Costumes:** William H. Matthews; **Musical Director:** Ben M. Jerome

Songs: Every Day Is Christmas When You're Married [1] (C: Victor Hollander); Excuse Me? Certainly! (C: Victor Hollander; L: Charles Brown); Game I've Been Teaching You, The (Same Old Love) [3] (C: Victor Hollander); Good-bye Everybody (C: Jean Gilbert); Hello Sweetheart [2] (C: Victor Hollander); I'd Love to Dance Through Life with You [1] (C: Jerome Kern; L: Harry B. Smith); I'll Introduce You to My Father [3] (C: Victor Hollander); Is the Girl You Marry Still the Girl You Love (C: Victor Hollander); I've Just Been Waiting for You (C: Jerome Kern; L: Harry B. Smith); Keep Moving (C: Otto Motzan; L: Benjamin Hapgood Burt; Stanley Murphy); Love in Transit (I'm Leaving Home Papa) [2] (C: Victor Hollander);

Quiet Evening at Home, A (C: Ben Jerome); Rita, My Marguerita [2] (C: Victor Hollander); Song of the Sirens, The; Star of Mine (Aeroplane Song) [3] (C: Victor Hollander); That's the Lesson I'm Teaching to You; When Love Comes Stealing In; When the Madame Goes Away (C: Ben Jerome); Won't You Smile?; You're Such a Lonesome Moon Tonight [1] (C: Jean Gilbert)

Cast: Alexander Clark; Ernest Glendinning; Leila Hughes; Georgia Drew Mendum; William Norris

Notes: [1] Not in program. [2] Out Toledo 12/32/12. [3] Sheet music only.

2923 • MODEST SUZANNE

OPENED: 01/01/1912   Theatre: Liberty
Musical   Broadway: 24

Composer: Jean Gilbert
Lyricist: Harry B. Smith; Robert B. Smith
Librettist: Harry B. Smith; Robert B. Smith
Producer: A.H. Woods
Director: George Marion

Source: DIE KEUSCHE SUSANNE (Musical: Jean Gilbert; Georg Okonkowski; Alfred Schonfeld); **Costumes:** Mme. Francis, **Musical Director:** Louis F. Gottschalk

Songs: All the World Loves a Lover; Confidence; Ensemble; Father and Son; Finale Act I; Finale Act II; Finale Act III; I Would Like to See the Peaches (C: Jean Schwartz; L: Harry B. Ralph); Model Married Pair; Opening Chorus Act II; Paris; Return, The; Suzanne, Suzanne; Tangolango Tap (C: Jean Schwartz; L: Grant Clarke); Virtue Is Its Own Reward

Cast: Sallie Fisher; Ernest Torrence; Lawrence Wheat

2924 • MODESTE'S SHOP, THE

Notes: *See A GLIMPSE OF THE GREAT WHITE WAY.*

2925 • MOLLY

OPENED: 11/01/1973   Theatre: Alvin
Musical   Broadway: 68

Composer: Jerry Livingston
Lyricist: Leonard Adelson; Mack David

Librettist: Leonard Adelson; Louis Garfinkle; Murray Schisgal
Producer: Complex IV; George Daley; Don Kaufman; Don Saxon
Director: Alan Arkin

Source: GOLDBERGS, THE (Television Program: Gertrude Berg); **Choreographer:** Grover Dale; **Costumes:** Carrie F. Robbins; **Dance Arranger:** Arnold Gross; **Lighting Designer:** Jules Fisher; **Musical Director:** Jerry Goldberg; **Orchestrations:** Eddie Sauter; **Set Design:** Marsha Louis Eck; **Vocal Arranger:** Jerry Goldberg

Songs: Appointments (L: Leonard Adelson); Before Your Very Eyes [3] (L: Leonard Adelson); Cahoots (L: Mack David); Class of Summer '32 [3] (L: Leonard Adelson); Go In the Best of Health (L: Leonard Adelson); Have You Heard? (L: Unknown); High Class Ladies and Elegant Gentlemen (L: Mack David); I Had a Night [1] L: Leonard Adelson); I See a Man (C/L: Norman L. Martin); I Want to Share It with You (L: Mack David); I Was There (L: Mack David); If Everyone Got What They Wanted (L: Mack David); In the Afternoon of Our Years (Afternoon of Your Years) [1] (L: Leonard Adelson); In Your Eyes (L: Mack David); It Pays to Have Friends [3] (L: Leonard Adelson); I've Got a Molly (L: Leonard Adelson); Kinder, The [3] (L: Leonard Adelson); Lobby of the Roxy, The [3] (L: Leonard Adelson); Mandarin Palace on the Grand Concourse, The (L: Mack David); Maybe I Ought to Stay [3] (L: Leonard Adelson); Molly [3] (L: Leonard Adelson); Mothers [3] (L: Leonard Adelson); Neighbors Song, The [3] (L: Leonard Adelson); Nothing's All Good and Nothing's All Bad [1] (L: Unknown); Oak Leaf Memorial Park (L: Leonard Adelson); Oh There You Are [3] (L: Leonard Adelson); Opening; Peter Rabbit [3] (L: Leonard Adelson); Piece of the Rainbow, A [4] (C/L: Norman L. Martin); Simon's Song [3] (L: Leonard Adelson); So I'll Tell Him (L: Mack David); Sullivan's Got a Job (L: Leonard Adelson); Sunshiny California [3] (L: Leonard Adelson); There's a New Deal on the Way (L: Mack David); There's Gold on the Trees (L: Mack David); Tomorrow Is Only a Moment [1] (L: Unknown); Tremont Avenue Cruisewear Fashion Show, The (L: Leonard Adelson); What Else Is There to Do (L: Leonard Adelson); When You Have a Son [1] (L: Unknown); Yoohoo [3] (L: Leonard Adelson); You Remember [3] (L: Leonard Adelson)

Cast: Kay Ballard [2]; Connie Day; Daniel Fortus; Justine Johnston; Ruth Manning; Eli Mintz; Lisa Rochelle; Hazel Weber Steck; Swen Swenson; Lee Wallace

Notes: [1] Cut prior to New York. [2] A numerologist told Ms. Ballard that there were too many letters in her name so she dropped the "e" from Kaye for this production. [3] ASCAP/Library of Congress only. [4] Credited to Mack David by ASCAP but I believe the above credit is correct.

2926 • MOLLY AND I

OPENED: 08/31/1915   Theatre: La Salle
Musical   Chicago

Composer: Louis A. Hirsch
Lyricist: Frank R. Adams
Librettist: Frank R. Adams

Source: MOLLY AND I (Play: Frank R. Adams)

Cast: Lina Abarbanell

2927 • MOLLY DARLING (1922)

OPENED: 09/01/1922   Theatre: Liberty
Musical   Broadway: 101

Composer: Tom Johnstone
Lyricist: Phil Cook
Librettist: William Cary Duncan; Otto Harbach
Producer: Moore & Megley
Director: Walter Wilson

Choreographer: Julian Mitchell; **Musical Director:** Milton E. Schwarzwald; **Orchestrations:** Maurice DePackh; **Set Design:** Herbert Ward

Songs: Afterthought, An; Contrary Mary; Dear Little Gad- About; Don't Tag Along; Educated Whisk Broom, An [1]; Making Them Beautiful [2]; Mellow Moon; Melody Dreams; Molly Darling; My Kiki Girl [2]; Some Little Someone [2]; Some One; Spirit of the Radio; Stepping Some; Stop, Look, Listen [2]; Sweet Nothings [2]; Syncopate; Syncopated Whisk Brooms, The; There's an Eve in Ev'ry Garden; (They Love It) When All Your Castles Come Tumbling Down (C: Milton Schwarzwald; L: Ira Gershwin [3])

Cast: Jack Donahue; Hal Forde; Mary Milburn

Notes: [1] Out Washington, D.C. 3/18/23. [2] Out Cleveland 4/24/22. [3] Used pseudonym Arthur Francis.

2928 • MOLLY DARLING (1962)

OPENED: 1962
Musical   Closed out of town

Composer: Tommy Wolf
Lyricist: Fran Landesman
Librettist: Jay Landesman; Martin Quigley
Producer: John Kennedy
Director: James Vincent Russo

Choreographer: Ted Cappy; Marc Hertsens; **Costumes:** Bill Hargate; **Orchestrations:** Seth Greiner; Carl Hohengarten; Ben Pearlmutter; **Set Design:** Paul C. McGuire

Songs: Apples on the Lilac Tree; Ballad of Phoebe Cousins; Bill of Fare; Chandelier Waltz, The; Choosing a Husband's a Delicate Thing; Dorris, the Moon, and the Dart, The; Green As Grass; Heart that Broke Was Mine, The; I Want to Be First to the Moon; I Will Make My Way Alone; If She Were Only Mine; It's Not My Dish of Tea; I've Got My Eyes on Tomorrow; Let's Listen to the Ladies; Man for You, The; Money Talks; Progress Will Ruin Us Yet; Repent St. Louis; There's a Blip Where There Should Have Been a Bleep; There's Nothing Fair About It; Twentieth Century Is Almost Here, The; We've Got a Little Dirty Work to Do; Who Needs the Vote?

Cast: Camila Ashland; Helen Gallagher; Edmund Lyndeck; Edwin Steffe; Kelley Stephens; Richard Tone; Nolan Van Way

Notes: From a program of St. Louis Municipal Opera.

2929 • MOLLY MAY

OPENED: 04/08/1910   Theatre: Hackett
Musical   Broadway: 27

Composer: Julian Edwards
Lyricist: Walter Browne
Librettist: Walter Browne
Producer: Byron Chandler
Director: Edward Temple

Cast: Eva Fallon; Sydney Grant; Grace LaRue; James E. Sullivan

Notes: No program available.

2930 • MOLLY ME OWN

Musical

Composer: Bryan Lee
Lyricist: Eileen Lee

Songs: Molly, Me Own; O'Brien Is Tryin' to Learn to Talk Hawaiian; 'Twas Only an Irishman's Dream

Notes: Sheet music only. No other information available.

2931 • MOLLY O'

OPENED: 05/17/1916   Theatre: Cort
Musical   Broadway: 45

Composer: Carl Woess
Lyricist: Harry B. Smith; Robert B. Smith
Librettist: Harry B. Smith; Robert B. Smith
Producer: John Cort
Director: George Marion

Source: UNKNOWN (Story: Giovanni Boccaccio);
Orchestrations: Clarence West; **Set Design:**
H. Robert Law

Songs: Aesop Was a Very Moral Man; Anna of Havana; Champagne and Laughter; Isn't That Like a Man!; Little Women; Love Is an Art; Marionettes; Marry Me and See; One Way of Doing It; Opening Chorus; Right Girl, The; Voice of Love, The; When Fortune Smiles; Your Last Love Is Your First [1]

Cast: Grace Field; Elizabeth Hines; Josie Intropodi; Tom Lewis; Donald Macdonald; John E. Young

Notes: Titled THE MASKED MODEL out of town prior to Broadway. While out of town it also featured Texas Guinan, Thomas Coskey and Katherine Galloway. [1] Out 2/17/16 Washington, D.C.

2932 • MOMS

OPENED: 08/04/1987   Theatre: Astor Place
Musical   Off-Broadway: 152

Composer: Grenoldo Frazier
Lyricist: Grenoldo Frazier

Librettist: Ben Caldwell
Producer: Moms Company
Director: Walter Dallas

Costumes: Judy Dearing; **Lighting Designer:**
Robert Wierzel; **Set Design:** Rosario Provenza

Cast: Carol Dennis; Grenoldo Frazier; Clarice Taylor

2933 • MONA AND LISA

OPENED: 1969
Musical

Composer: Jay Gorney
Lyricist: Henry Myers

Songs: Are You Smiling?; Could Be; Darling, I Am Growing Young; Fine Art of Treachery, The; I Love My Machine Gun; Lady Lizzie of Milan; Madrigal; Welcome to Milan; When I Enter Paree

Notes: No other information available.

2934 • MONARCH AND THE MAID

Musical   Closed out of town

Composer: Dan Sullivan
Lyricist: D.K. Stevens
Librettist: Matthew Ott
Producer: Ott & Wallin

Songs: Advice to the Lovelorn (C: Phil Ott; L: Dan Sullivan); American Invasion, The; Angus, Are You There?; Down in Honeymoon Alley; Gaby Waltz, The; I'd Like to Have a Girl Like You, Like Me; Moonbeams, The; My Sunday Girl (L: Matthew Ott; Dan Sullivan); On the Road that Leads to You; Palmy Days; Right Across from Brooklyn (Oh, Yes, New York); Saucy Moon (L: Dan Sullivan); Verb to Love (I Love You), The; Wild Flowers

2935 • MONEY

OPENED: 07/12/1963   Theatre: Upstairs at the Downstairs
Revue   Off-Broadway

Composer: Sam Pottle
Lyricist: David Axlerod; Tom Whedon
Librettist: David Axlerod; Tom Whedon
Producer: Upstairs at the Downstairs
Director: Ronny Graham

Costumes: Mr. Williams; **Dance Arranger:** Sam Pottle; **Lighting Designer:** George Curley; **Musical Director:** Sam Pottle; **Set Design:** Peter Harvey; **Vocal Arranger:** Sam Pottle

Songs: Beautiful Day; Commitment; Cuyahoga [1]; Domus Sur Pampas [1]; Give a Cheer; How Can I Tell?; I Hate the Avant Garde [1]; Man with a Problem, A; Philanthropist's Progress, The; San Fernando; She Just Walked In; Who Wants to Work?

Cast: George Coe; Barbara Quaney; David Rounds; Jon Stone

Notes: [1] Out Cleveland 3/7/63.

2936 • MONKS OF MALABAR, THE

OPENED: 09/14/1900   Theatre: Knickerbocker
Musical   Broadway: 39

Composer: Ludwig Englander
Lyricist: J. Cheever Goodwin
Librettist: J. Cheever Goodwin
Director: Al Holbrook

Costumes: Dazian; **Musical Director:** Enrico Morreale; **Set Design:** Henry E. Hoyt

Songs: Article 213; Dear Little French Grisette, The; Ebb and Flow; Ere I Wed You; Go on and Marry!; Ha! Ha! Ha! Ha! Ha! Ha!; Hail the Groom and Hail the Bride; Here! Here!; Here We Are Sir; I Love My Love; In Gay Paree; Joseph, James and John; Monks of Malabar, The; No More Weighted Down By Sorrow; Singing and Dancing; Then, If I Understand Aright; Where He Goes We Go Too; With Glad Acclaim; With Keen Anticipation; You Know That I Adore You

Cast: Madge Lessing; Clara Palmer; Van Rensselaer Wheeler; Francis Wilson

Notes: No songs listed in program.

2937 • MONSIEUR BEAUCAIRE

OPENED: 12/11/1919   Theatre: New Amsterdam
Musical   Broadway: 143

Composer: Andre Messager
Lyricist: Adrian Ross
Librettist: Frederick Lonsdale
Producer: Gilbert Miller

Source: MONSIEUR BEAUCAIRE (Story: Booth Tarkington); **Costumes:** Percy Anderson

Songs: Beaux and Belles of Bath, The; Come with Welcome; English Maids; Finale Act I; Finale Act II; Finale Act III; Going to the Ball; Gold and Blue and White; Have You Heard (Opening Act III); Honour and Love; Honours of War, The; I Do Not Know; Lightly, Lightly; Little More, A; No Offence; Pastoral Fete; Philomel; Red Rose; Rose Minuet; Say No More; Son of France, A; That's a Woman's Way; Under the Moon; Voyageur's Song; Way for the Ambassador; We Are Not Speaking Now; What Are Names?; When I Was King of Bath; Who Is This?

Cast: John Clarke; Robert Cunningham; Marion Green; Robert Parker; Lennox Pawle; Yvan Servais; Blanche Tomlin

2938 • MONTE CARLO

OPENED: 03/21/1898   Theatre: Herald Square
Musical   Broadway: 48

Composer: Howard Talbot
Lyricist: Harry Greenbank
Librettist: Sidney Carlton
Producer: Edward E. Rice
Director: Frank Smithson

Choreographer: H. Marchetti; **Costumes:** Will R. Barnes; **Musical Director:** Herman Perlet; **Set Design:** Frank Rafter

Songs: Act I Finale (C: Herman Perlet; L: Edgar Smith); Act II Grand Finale — The New York Herald Topical Song (C/L: Unknown); Along the Way Where Lovers Go; At the 'Alls (C: Herman Perlet; L: Joseph W. Herbert); Barcelona Girls; Billiard and Baccarat Ballet (inst.) (C: Edward E. Rice); Dancing Dean, The; Ditto Ditto; General Boomerang; Here at Monte Carlo; Here's a Chance for Visitors; Hi Boys, Ho Boys; How Can Harry Marry; I Only Know I Love Thee; If I Only Knew the Way; In the Mediaeval Ages; Ladies' Maid, The; Land of Heart's Desire; Melodramatic Captain, The; Ready, Steady Sailor Man, The (C: Herman Perlet; L: Albert Bigelow Paine); Sailor Ballet, The (inst.) (C: Edward E. Rice); Sisters Galatine; Sparrow and the Bullfinch, The; Summer Girl, The; Use of French, Red Is the Wine, The; Very Careful, If You Please; Waiting for Me; We're an Able Bodied Crew

Cast: Marie Cahill; Augustus Cramer; Thomas F. Kearns; Nell McNeil; Josie Sadler; Frank Smithson; Marguerita Sylva; Helene Tuesart; Jennie Winston; Sidney de Gray

2939 • MONTE CRISTO, JR.

OPENED: 02/12/1919   Theatre: Winter Garden
Musical   Broadway: 254

Composer: Sigmund Romberg; Jean Schwartz
Lyricist: Harold Atteridge
Librettist: Harold Atteridge
Producer: J.J. Shubert; Lee Shubert
Director: J.C. Huffman

Choreographer: Allan K. Foster; Costumes: Kiviette; S. Zalud; Set Design: Watson Barratt; P. Strahlendorff

Songs: Are You Steppin' Out Tonight; Carnival Time; Come Back to Me [1]; Empire Days; Fast Steppers; Festive Nights; Fiji; Flutter on By, My Broadway Butterfly; Girl in Every Port; Hoop-Ti- Do [1]; I Always Think I'm Up in Heaven when I'm Down in Dixieland [1] (C: Maurice Abrahams; L: Sam M. Lewis; Joe Young); Indoor Sports; Jazz Marimba (Jazzamarimba Dance); Jewel Ballet; Just My Type (They're All My Type); Marseilles; Military Glide, The; Monte Cristo; My Lady's Dress; Nanette and Rin Tin Tin; Sahara (Now We're As Dry As You) (C: Jean Schwartz; L: Alfred Bryan); Sentimental Knights; Sugar Baby; Sweetheart Special (On the Lovey-Dove Line), The [1]; There's a World of Beauty in You [1] (C: Maurice Abrahams; L: Sam M. Lewis; Joe Young); Toy Dance; Vampire Dance; Who Played Poker with Pocahontas when John Smith Went Away? (C: Fred E. Ahlert; L: Sam M. Lewis; Joe Young); Women and Light (C/L: Earl Carroll)

Cast: Adelaide and Hughes; Sam Ash; Ralph Herz; Tom Lewis; Charles Purcell; Chic Sale

Notes: [1] Sheet music only. [2] Sheet music only. Music credits Romberg, Schwartz and Atteridge.

2940 • MONTH OF SUNDAYS, A (1951)

OPENED: 12/25/1951
Musical   Closed out of town

Composer: Albert Selden
Lyricist: Ted Fetter; Burt Shevelove
Librettist: Burt Shevelove
Producer: Carly Wharton
Director: Burt Shevelove

Source: EXCURSION (Play: Ted Wolfson); Choreographer: Anna Sokolow; Costumes: Kenn Barr; Lighting Designer: Jo Mielziner; Musical Director: Lehman Engel; Orchestrations: Ted Royal; Set Design: Jo Mielziner; Vocal Arranger: Lehman Engel

Songs: Away, Away, Away; Get Married Shirley [1]; Good Old Times, The; Having a Ball; I Feel Fine; I'm in Trouble; Looking for a Bluebird; Lullaby; Other Girls; Semi- Tropical Isle, A; So Right; Sunday; Think Beautiful Thoughts; Time for a Quickie; What's Gonna Be; You Have to Have Love

Cast: Richard Kiley; Gene Lockhart; Estelle Loring; Eddie Phillips; Nancy Walker

Notes: Opened in Boston. Closed Philadelphia 1/26/52. [1] Also in SMALL WONDER and WALK TALL.

2941 • MONTH OF SUNDAYS, A (1968)

OPENED: 09/16/1968   Theatre: Theatre de Lys
Musical   Off-Broadway: 8

Composer: Maury Laws
Lyricist: Jules Bass
Librettist: Romeo Muller
Producer: Jules Bass; Arthur Rankin Jr.
Director: Stone Widney

Source: GREAT GIT-AWAY, THE (Play: Romeo Muller); Costumes: Sara Brook; Lighting Designer: Joan Larkey; Musical Director: Irv Dweir; Orchestrations: Irv Dweir; Set Design: Robert T. Williams

Songs: Communicate; Elbow Room; Flower, I Don't Need You Anymore; How Far Can You Follow; I Won't Worry; It's Out of My Hands; Month of Sundays [1]; My First Girl; Part of the Crowd; Summer Love; Way Things Are [1]; We Know Where We've Been; Wedding, The; Who Knows Better Than I; Words Will Pay My Way; You Can Wait Too Long [1]

Cast: Patti Karr; John Bennett Perry; Dan Resin; Gil Robbins; Martha Schlamme

Notes: [1] Not in programs.

2942 • MOOCHIN' ALONG
OPENED: 12/07/1925   Theatre: Lafayette
Musical   New York

Composer: James P. Johnson
Lyricist: Cecil Mack
Librettist: Jesse A. Shipp
Producer: Billy Mitchell

Choreographer: Hartwell Cook; Roscoe Simmons Jr.

Songs: Everybody's Doin' the Charleston Now (C/L: James P. Johnson; Cecil Mack; Elmore White); Mistah Jim; You for Me

Cast: Ollie Burgoyne; Edgar Connors; Billy Cumby; Inez Dennis; Alonzo Fenderson

Notes: No program available.

2943 • MOON MADNESS
OPENED: 09/30/1929   Theatre: Figueroa
                                       Playhouse
Musical   Los Angeles

Composer: Sol Cohen
Librettist: Alice Barney; William Cary Duncan

Notes: No other information available.

2944 • MOON MAIDEN, THE
OPENED: 1924
Musical   Closed out of town

Composer: Charles Berton
Lyricist: George E. Stoddard
Librettist: George E. Stoddard
Director: Lester Brown

Choreographer: Walter Willis; **Musical Director:** Charles Berton

Songs: Away with Them; Childhood Days; Cupid Holds the Key; Financial Status; Forever; Foxy Little Bee; Here's a Lucky Find; Hope On, Dear Heart; In Love Am I; Japanese Flirtation Dance; Just for You; Lucky Boy; Maiden Fair; Marriage; Moon Maiden, The; Pansy and the Poppy; Pretty Little Flowers, How I Envy You; Say You'll Be My Own, Dear; She Is Fast Asleep; Thus You May Detect; We're Never Too Particular; With Weary Limbs

Cast: Robert Millikin; Mabel Wilbur

Notes: *See also CHINA ROSE.*

2945 • MOON OVER MIAMI
OPENED: 02/14/1989
Play   Closed out of town

Composer: John Guare
Lyricist: John Guare
Author: John Guare
Director: Andrei Belgrader

Arrangements: Lawrence Yurman; **Choreographer:** Wesley Fata; **Costumes:** Candice Donnelly; **Incidental Music:** Lawrence Yurman; **Lighting Designer:** Scott Zielinski; **Musical Director:** Lawrence Yurman; **Set Design:** Judy Gallen

Songs: Missed the Toilet Last Night [1]; Moon Over Miami; Osvaldo's Song (C: Galt MacDermot)

Cast: Julie Hagerty; Susan Kellermann; Oliver Platt; Tony Shalhoub; Lewis J. Stadlen; Sam Stoneburner; Stanley Tucci

Notes: Produced at the Yale Repertory Theatre. No songs listed in program. [1] Originally set to the tune of "Don't Get Around Much Anymore." It was changed.

2946 • MOON OVER MULBERRY STREET
OPENED: 09/04/1935   Theatre: Lyceum
Play   Broadway: 140

Author: Nicholas Consentino
Producer: Paul De Maria; Standish O'Neill
Director: William Muir

Set Design: Louis Kennel

Songs: Moon Over Mulberry Street (C: Harry Tierney; L: Raymond B. Egan)

Cast: Olga Druce; Betty Kashman; Gladys Shelley; Cornel Wilde

2947 • MOON RISES, THE
OPENED: 04/23/1934
Musical   Closed out of town

Composer: Franz Lehar
Lyricist: Kay Kenney
Librettist: Kay Kenney
Producer: Lawrence Shubert Lawrence
Director: Frank W. Shea

Source: ZIGEUNERLIEBE (Musical: Robert Bodanzky; Franz Lehar; A.M. Willner); **Choreographer:** Chester Hale; **Costumes:** Ernest Schrapps; **Musical Director:** Pierre de Reeder; **Set Design:** Watson Barratt

Songs: Best Game; Bridegroom Trio; Broken; Czardas; Exquisite Moments; Finale Act I; Finaletto; Grand Parade; I Don't Know How You Do It; If You Dare; In Love with You; Kissing; Ladies! Ladies!; Little Maiden; Melody of Love; Opening Act II; Tell the Blushing Bridegroom; Wild Bird, The; Wild Rose; Wine, Wine, Wine; Zingara

Cast: Joseph Macaulay; Ethelind Terry

Notes: The music of this show was from GYPSY LOVE. Additional numbers were by Yenesc Rabonovic but not credited.

2948 • MOONCALF
OPENED: 1949
Musical   Closed out of town

Composer: Lehman Engel
Lyricist: John Latouche
Librettist: Lewis Allan; Alexander King; Joanna Roos
Producer: Jeff Bailey; Thomas Hammond
Director: Mary Hunter

Source: BIBLICAL STORY OF JOSEPH (Book); **Choreographer:** Hanya Holm; **Costumes:** Ladislas Czettel; **Set Design:** Boris Aronson

Notes: Had a tryout in Cleveland. No other information available.

2949 • MOONEY SHAPIRO SONGBOOK, THE
OPENED: 05/03/1981   Theatre: Morosco
Revue   Broadway: 1

Composer: Monty Norman
Lyricist: Julian More
Librettist: Julian More; Monty Norman
Producer: Stuart Ostrow
Director: Jonathan Lynn

Choreographer: George Faison; **Costumes:** Franne Lee; **Dance Arranger:** Timothy Graphenreed; **Lighting Designer:** Tharon Musser; **Musical Director:** Elman Anderson; **Set Design:** Saul Radomsky; **Vocal Arranger:** Ray Cook

Songs: April in Wisconsin; Bring Back Tomorrow; Bumpity-Bump; Climbin'; Don't Play That Lovesong Anymore; East River Rhasody; Girl in the Window, The; Golden Oldie [1]; Happy Hickory; I Accuse; I Found Love; I'm Gonna Take Her Home to Momma; It's Only a Show; Je Vous Aime Milady; Les Halles; Lovely Sunday Mornin'; Meg; Messages I; Messages II; Mister Destiny; Nazi Party Pooper; Nostalgia; Olympics '36; Pokenhatchit Public Protest Committee, The; Pretty Face; Rusty's Dream Ballet; Songbook; Storm in My Heart, A; Talking Picture Show; Victory; When a Brother Is a Mother to His Sister; Your Time Is Different to Mine

Cast: Gary Beach; Jeff Goldblum; Timothy Jerome; Judy Kaye; Annie McGreevey

Notes: [1] This song had a different melody in the prior British version.

2950 • MOONLIGHT
OPENED: 01/30/1924   Theatre: Longacre
Musical   Broadway: 174

Composer: Con Conrad
Lyricist: William B. Friedlander
Librettist: William Le Baron
Producer: L. Lawrence Weber
Director: William B. Friedlander

Choreographer: Larry Ceballos; **Costumes:** Mabel Johnston; **Lighting Designer:** Lohmuller and Phillips; **Musical Director:** Hilding Anderson

Songs: Aren't We All?; Ballet (inst.) [1] (C: William B. Friedlander); Daffydill, The; Dancing; Don't Put Me Out of Your Heart (C: William B. Friedlander); Fair Weather Friends; Forever; Hold Me (C: William B. Friedlander); Honeymoon Blues; How Can a Lady Be Certain?; How Do I Know He Loves Me?; I Cannot Live

Without Love [1] (L: William B. Friedlander);
I Love Them All; If I Were of the Hoi Polloi; In a
Bungalow; Old Man in the Moon [1] (C: William
B. Friedlander); On Such a Night; One Note;
Passing of the Night, The; Say It Again; Tell Me
Am I Shooting at the Moon; Turn on the Popular
Moon

Cast: Maxine Brown; Ernest Glendinning; Allyn
King

Notes: [1] Out Newark 1/19/25.

2951 • MOONSHINE
OPENED: 10/30/1905   Theatre: Liberty
Musical   Broadway: 53

Composer: Silvio Hein
Lyricist: George V. Hobart; Edwin Milton Royle
Librettist: George V. Hobart; Edwin Milton Royle
Producer: Daniel V. Arthur
Director: Frederick Parry

Choreographer: Gertrude Hoffman; **Musical
Director:** Silvio Hein

Songs: All She Could Say Was 'Oui'; Conjure Man,
The (C: Bob Cole; L: James Weldon Johnson);
Don't Be What You Ain't; Finale Act I; Finale Act
II (L: George V. Hobart); Foolish (L: George V.
Hobart); Friendship; How Happy Could This
Chappie Be (L: George V. Hobart); Hundred
Years from Now, A (L: George V. Hobart; Edwin
Milton Royle); I Like You Very Much (L: George
V. Hobart); I Want to Go Back to the Boulevard
(L: George V. Hobart); I'm a' Looking for My Ten
(L: George V. Hobart); In My Submarine
(L: George V. Hobart); In Our Set (L: George V.
Hobart); Mister Bonaparte (L: Benjamin
Hapgood Burt); Musical Gypsy, The; Opening
Chorus; Robinson Crusoe's Isle (C/L: Benjamin
Hapgood Burt); They Never Do That in Our Set

Cast: Roy Atwell; George Beban; Marie Cahill;
Clara Palmer

Notes: [1] Sheet music only.

2952 • MORALS OF MARCUS, THE
OPENED: 11/18/1907   Theatre: Criterion
Play   Broadway: 44

Author: W.J. Locke
Producer: Charles Frohman

Musical Director: Harry G. Mullaly; **Set Design:**
Ernest Gros

Songs: Eastern Moon (C: Jerome Kern; L: M.E.
Rourke); I Met My Love in a Restaurant
(C: Gustave Kerker); I'm Head and Heels in Love
with You (C: M.H. Rosenfeld); Sizilietta (C: F.V.
Blon); Tipperary Twinkle, The (C: Charles Bendix)

Cast: Marie Doro; Beatrice Forbes-Robinson;
C. Aubrey Smith

2953 • MORE THAN YOU DESERVE
OPENED: 11/21/1973   Theatre: Public
Musical   Off-Broadway: 63

Composer: Jim Steinman
Lyricist: Jim Steinman; Michael Weller
Librettist: Michael Weller
Producer: N.Y. Shakespeare Festival; Joseph Papp
Director: Kim Friedman

Choreographer: Scott Salmon; **Costumes:** Lowell
Detweiler; **Dance Arranger:** Steve Margoshes;
Lighting Designer: Martin Aronstein; **Musical
Director:** Steve Margoshes; **Set Design:** Miguel
Romero; **Vocal Arranger:** Steve Margoshes

Songs: Come with Me...We Know Love; Could She
Be the One; Give Me the Simple Life; Go, Go, Go
Guerrillas; If Only; Mama You Better Watch Out
for Daughter; Midnight Lullabye; More Than
You Deserve; O, What a War; Song of the City of
Hope; Song of the Golden Egg; To Feel So
Needed; What Became of the People We Were?;
Where Did It Go?

Cast: Seth Allen; Stephen Collins; Kimberly Farr;
Fred Gwynne; Marybeth Hurt; Graham Jarvis;
Terry Kiser; Larry Marshall; Meat Loaf; Justin
Ross

2954 • MORNING
OPENED: 11/28/1968   Theatre: Henry Miller's
Play   Broadway: 52

Composer: John Hall
Lyricist: Israel Horovitz

Author: Israel Horovitz
Director: Theodore Morse

Costumes: Michael Annals; **Lighting Designer:** Martin Aronstein; **Set Design:** Michael Annals

Songs: Tillich's Nightmare; Uncle Martin; White Like Me

Cast: Sorrell Booke; John Heffernan; Robert Klein; Charlotte Rae; Jane Marla Robbins

Notes: Three one act plays under the name MORNING, NOON and NIGHT. Only MORNING had songs. NOON is by Terrence McNally and NIGHT is by Leonard Melfi.

2955 • MORNING AFTER, THE

OPENED: 12/16/1927   Theatre: Hollywood Playhouse
Musical   Closed out of town

Lyricist: Oliver Morosco
Librettist: Oliver Morosco
Producer: Oliver Morosco

Notes: No other information available.

2956 • MORNING, NOON AND NIGHT (1908)

OPENED: 10/05/1908   Theatre: Yorkville
Musical   New York

Composer: Jean Schwartz
Lyricist: William Jerome
Librettist: Joseph W. Herbert

Notes: No other information available.

2957 • MORNING, NOON AND NIGHT (1968)

Notes: *See MORNING.*

2958 • MORNING SUN

OPENED: 10/06/1963   Theatre: Phoenix
Musical   Off-Broadway: 9

Composer: Paul Klein
Lyricist: Fred Ebb
Librettist: Fred Ebb
Producer: T. Edward Hambleton; Martin Tahse
Director: Daniel Petrie

Source: UNKNOWN (Story: Mary Deasy); **Choreographer:** Donald Saddler; **Costumes:** Patricia Zipprodt; **Lighting Designer:** Martin Aronstein; Eldon Elder; **Musical Director:** John Strauss; **Orchestrations:** Fred Karlin; **Set Design:** Eldon Elder; **Vocal Arranger:** Fred Karlin

Songs: All the Pretty Little Horses; Follow Him; For Once in My Life; Good As Anybody; I Seen It with My Own Eyes; It's a Lie; Missouri Mule; Morning Sun; Mr. Chigger; My Sister-in-Law; New Boy in Town; Pebble Waltz; Seventeen Summers; Square Dance; Tell Me Goodbye; Thad's Journey; That's Right!; This Heat; Why?

Cast: Sammy Bayes; Sol Berkowitz; Bert Convy; Carole Demas; Danny Lockin; Will Mackenzie; Patricia Neway

2959 • MOROCCO BOUND

Musical   Closed out of town

Producer: A.H. Chamberlyn

Songs: My Maid from Hindoostan (C: Byrd Dougherty; L: William H. Penn); Smiles, Smiles, Smiles (C: Byrd Dougherty; L: William H. Penn)

Cast: William Herman West

Notes: Originally produced in America at the Park Theatre, Boston.

2960 • MORRIS GEST'S MIDNIGHT WHIRL

OPENED: 12/27/1919   Theatre: Century Grove
Revue   Broadway: 110

Composer: George Gershwin
Lyricist: B.G. DeSylva; John Henry Mears
Librettist: B.G. DeSylva; John Henry Mears
Producer: Morris Gest
Director: David Bennett; Julian Mitchell

Musical Director: Frank Tours; **Set Design:** Joseph Urban

Songs: Baby Dolls [1]; Depends on Beautiful Clothes; Doughnuts; I'll Show You a Wonderful World; League of Nations, The; Let Cutie Cut Your Cuticle [1]; Limehouse Nights [1]; Peggy (C: Neil Moret; L: Harry Williams); Poppyland [1]

Cast: Bessie McCoy Davis; Dorothy Dixon; Bernard Granville; Carl Hyson; Rath Brothers, The; Helen Shipman

Notes: Performed in rooftop theatre above the Century Theatre. Music credited to Harry Tierney and no Mears lyrics credited when the show was out of town. Some songs (see footnotes) were also in THE BROADWAY WHIRL. In that show they were credited to Tierney although the program also credited Gershwin with some unidentified songs. [1] Also in THE BROADWAY WHIRL. See Notes section.

2961 • MOST HAPPY FELLA, THE

OPENED: 05/03/1956   Theatre: Imperial
Musical   Broadway: 676

Composer: Frank Loesser
Lyricist: Frank Loesser
Librettist: Frank Loesser
Producer: Kermit Bloomgarden; Lynn Loesser
Director: Joseph Anthony

Source: THEY KNEW WHAT THEY WANTED (Play: Sidney Howard); **Choreographer:** Dania Krupska; **Costumes:** Motley; **Lighting Designer:** Jo Mielziner; **Musical Director:** Herbert Greene; **Orchestrations:** Don Walker; **Set Design:** Jo Mielziner

Songs: Abbondanza; Aren't You Glad?; Benvenuta; Big 'D'; Cold and Dead; Cowboy Hoedown; Don't Cry; Eyes Like a Stranger [1]; Fresno Beauties; Goodbye, Darlin'; Happy to Make Your Acquaintance; House and Garden [2]; How Beautiful the Days; I Don't Know (The Letter); I Don't Like This Dame; I Know How It Is; I Like Everybody; I Love Him; I Made a Fist!; I'll Buy Everybody a Beer [4]; Joey, Joey, Joey; Like a Woman Loves a Man; Long Time Ago, A; Love and Kindness; Mama, Mama; Maybe He's Some Kinda of Crazy; Most Happy Fella, The; My Heart Is So Full of You; No Home, No Job; Nobody's Ever Gonna Love You; Old People; Ooh, My Feet; Please Let Me Tell You; Plenty Bambini; Rosabella; Seven Million Crumbs; She Gonna Come Home with Me; Somebody, Somewhere; Song of a Summer Night; Soon You Gonna Leave Me, Joe; Special Delivery! (I Seen Her at the Station); Sposalizio; Standin' on the Corner; Tell Tony and Rosabella Good-bye for Me; Tony's Thoughts; Wanting to Be Wanted [3]; Warm All Over; Young People

Cast: Zina Bethune; Helon Blount; Lee Cass; Rico Froehlich; Susan Johnson; Keith Kaldenberg; Shorty Long; Art Lund; Mona Paulee; Jo Sullivan; Robert Weede

Notes: [1] Cut prior to opening. Part of the music is used in "Greenwillow Christmas" from GREENWILLOW. Added to 1980 revival. [2] Cut prior to opening. Put into revival then cut although the number does appear on the TV tape. [3] Cut prior to opening. [4] ASCAP/Library of Congress only.

2962 • MOTHER EARTH

OPENED: 10/19/1972   Theatre: Belasco
Revue   Broadway: 12

Composer: Toni Shearer
Lyricist: Ron Thronson
Librettist: Ron Thronson
Producer: Roger Ailes
Director: Ray Golden

Choreographer: Lynne Morris; **Costumes:** Mary McKinley; **Lighting Designer:** Paul Sullivan; **Musical Director:** Sande Campbell; **Set Design:** Alan Kimmel

Songs: Chemicals [1]; Corn on the Macabre (C/L: Roger Ailes; Ray Golden; Ron Thronson); Ecology Waltz, The (L: Ray Golden); Good Morning World; Happy Mother's Day; Mater Terra; Mother Earth; Ozymandias; Pills; Plow It All Under; Rent a Robot; Room to Be Free; Sail on Sweet Universe; Save the World for Children; Taking the Easy Way Out; Talons of Time; Tiger! Tiger!; Time of Our Life, The; Too Many Old Ideas; What Color Is the Sky? [1]; Who Cares If the World Is Round? [1]; Xanadu

Cast: Gail Boggs; Frank T. Coombs; Kimberly Farr; Kelly Garrett; Will Jacobs; Carol Kristy; Laura Michaels; John Bennett Perry; Rick Podell; Charlie J. Rodriguez

Notes: [1] Cut prior to opening

2963 • MOTHER GOOSE (1899)

OPENED: 05/01/1899   Theatre: 14th St.
Musical   Broadway: 10

Composer: Frederick Eustis; Frederick Gagel
Librettist: Edgar Smith; Louis de Lange

Producer: Junius Howe
Director: Max Freeman

Cast: Kitty Mitchell; Olive Redpath; Hubert Wilke

Notes: No program available.

2964 • MOTHER GOOSE (1903)
OPENED: 12/02/1903   Theatre: New Amsterdam
Musical   Broadway: 105

Lyricist: George V. Hobart
Librettist: John J. McNally
Producer: Klaw & Erlanger
Director: Herbert Gresham; Ned Wayburn

Source: MOTHER GOOSE (Musical: Arthur Collins; J. Hickory Wood); **Choreographer:** Ernest D'Auban; **Set Design:** R. Caney; Henry Emden; C. Formilli; R.C. McCleary; Bruce Smith

Songs: Always Leave 'Em Laughing (When You Say Good-Bye) (C/L: George M. Cohan); Blue Eyed Sue [1] (C/L: James Reese Europe); Chorus of Snobs (C: Frederic Solomon); Chorus of Villagers and Policemen (C: Frederic Solomon); Everybody's Happy When the Sun Shines [2] (C/L: George M. Cohan); Everybody's Loved by Someone (C: Frederic Solomon); Evolution of Ragtime (C: J. Rosamond Johnson; L: Bob Cole); Girls Will Be Girls and Boys Will Be Boys (C: Frederic Solomon); He's Ravin', Let Him Rave [3] (C/L: George M. Cohan); Hey There! Hey There! [2] (C/L: George M. Cohan); I Don't Want to be a Lady (C/L: J.M. Glover); I Want to Hear a Yankee Doodle Tune [2] (C/L: George M. Cohan); I'll Run in from Troy [3] (C/L: George M. Cohan); Laughing Water (C: Frederick W. Hager; L: George Totten Smith); On the Go (C: Frederic Solomon); Our Goose Has a Mint in Her Little Insides (C: Frederic Solomon); Pansy Faces (C/L: William H. Penn); Rafferty (C/L: Clifton Crawford); Rose of the Riviera, The (C: Bernard Rolt); Rube Song (C/L: George M. Cohan); Social Eclat (C/L: Clifton Crawford); Still in the Old Front Line (C/L: Matthew Woodward); Stories Adam Told to Eve, The (C: Jean Schwartz; L: William Jerome); Sweeter Den a Sugar Cane (C/L: Billy Johnson); Time to Love, The (C: Frederic Solomon); Under the Mistletoe Bough (C: J. Fred Helf; L: Will Heelan); We Marched Away (C: Frederic Solomon); When I Do the Highland Fling (C: J. Fred Helf; L: Will Heelan)

Cast: Harry Bulger; Joseph Cawthorn; Clifton Crawford; Leila McIntyre; Pat Rooney

Notes: [1] Not in programs. Also in A LITTLE BIT OF EVERYTHING. [2] Sheet music only. [3] ASCAP/Library of Congress only.

2965 • MOTHER'S KISSES, A
OPENED: 09/23/1968
Musical   Closed out of town

Composer: Richard Adler
Lyricist: Richard Adler
Librettist: Bruce Jay Friedman
Producer: Richard Horner; Lawrence Kasha; Lester Osterman
Director: Gene Saks

Source: MOTHER'S KISSES, A (Novel: Bruce Jay Friedman); **Choreographer:** Onna White; **Costumes:** Alvin Colt; **Dance Arranger:** Colin Romoff; **Lighting Designer:** Tharon Musser; **Musical Director:** Colin Romoff; **Orchestrations:** Jack Andrews; **Set Design:** Jean Eckart; William Eckart; **Vocal Arranger:** Colin Romoff

Songs: Course in Your Mother, A; Fellas Kiss Their Dads; I Have a Terrible Secret; I Told Them We Were Lovers; Left by the Wayside; Look at Those Faces; Meg's New York; People of Passionate Nature; There Goes My Life; They Won't Regret It; Wait, Baby, Wait; We've Got Meg; When You Gonna Learn (To Put Your Money on This Baby); Where Did the Summer Go; With a Little Help from Your Mother

Cast: Beatrice Arthur; Carl Ballantine; Rudy Bond; Bill Callaway; Cindi Howard; Ruth Jaroslow; Kate Wilkinson

Notes: Dance music: Roger Adams. Closed 10/19/68 Baltimore.

2966 • MOTOR GIRL, THE
OPENED: 06/15/1909   Theatre: Lyric
Musical   Broadway: 95

Composer: Julian Edwards
Lyricist: Charles J. Campbell; Ralph Skinner
Librettist: Charles J. Campbell; Ralph Skinner
Director: Frank Smithson

Musical Director: Ben M. Jerome

Songs: All the World Loves a Lover; Belle of the Dairy Lunch, The; Coffee and Cheese (L: Charles J. Campbell); Finale Act I; Finale Act II; Finesse; Friend of Mine Gave This to Me, A; Honor of Altenstein, The (L: Charles J. Campbell); I'm Old Enough to Do a Little Thinking (L: Charles J. Campbell); I'm the Motor Girl; In Philadelphia (L: Charles J. Campbell); Just Like This (L: Charles J. Campbell); Just Suppose You Loved Me; Opening Chorus; Out in the Barnyard; Prosit (L: Charles J. Campbell); Trot-I-Ty Trot (L: Charles J. Campbell); What Can a Fellow Do? (L: Charles J. Campbell); When I Was Twenty-One (L: Charles J. Campbell); When I'm a Duchess (L: Charles J. Campbell); Wilhelmina

Cast: Elizabeth Brice; Martin Brown; Georgia Caine; Bessie Franklin; Ted Lorraine; George Marjoroni; Adelaide Sharp

Notes: *See also TWO MEN AND A GIRL, an earlier version of this show.*

2967 • MOUNTAIN MAN, THE
OPENED: 12/12/1921   Theatre: Maxine Elliott's
Play   Broadway: 163

Author: Clare Kummer
Producer: Charles L. Wagner
Director: Edward Elsner; Clare Kummer

Set Design: Robert Edmond Jones

Songs: Cut Down the Tree (C/L: Clare Kummer); Through All the World (C/L: Clare Kummer)

Cast: Sidney Blackmer; Lawrence Eddinger; Marjorie Kummer; Chester Morris

2968 • MOVIE BUFF, THE
OPENED: 03/14/1977   Theatre: Actors'
                                    Playhouse
Musical   Off-Broadway: 18

Composer: John Raniello; Hiram Taylor
Lyricist: John Raniello; Hiram Taylor
Producer: Free Space Ltd.
Director: Jim Payne; Hiram Taylor

Source: MOVIE BUFF (Novel: Hiram Taylor);
Choreographer: Jack Dyville; **Costumes:** Carol Wenz; **Dance Arranger:** Donald G. Jones;

Lighting Designer: Jo Mayer; **Musical Director:** Donald G. Jones; **Set Design:** Jimmy Cuomo; **Vocal Arranger:** Donald G. Jones

Songs: All-Talking, All-Singing, All-Dancing; Coming Attractions; May I Dance with You?; Movie Cowboy, The; Movie Stars; Movietown; Something to Believe In; Song of Yesterday; Tell a Little Lie or Two; Tomorrow; Where Is the Man [1]; You Are Something Very Special

Cast: Deborah Carlson; Nora Cole; Keith Curran; Nancy Rich; Jim Richards; Charlie Scatamacchia; Mary Travizo; Mark Waldrop

Notes: [1] Cut after opening.

2969 • MOVIE STAR
OPENED: 1982
Musical   Closed out of town

Composer: Billy Barnes
Lyricist: Billy Barnes
Librettist: Ray Aghayan; Billy Barnes; Bob Mackie
Producer: Ray Aghayan; Bob Mackie
Director: Ray Aghayan

Choreographer: Alton Ruff; **Costumes:** Bob Mackie; **Dance Arranger:** Steven Smith; **Lighting Designer:** Jerry Grollner; **Musical Director:** Bob Rozario; **Orchestrations:** Bob Rozario; **Set Design:** Jef Billings; **Vocal Arranger:** Earl Brown

Songs: Blondes; Blondes Intro; Busby Berkeley Girl; Chaplin Walked Here; Close-Up; Columbia Pictures; Does Anybody Here Love Me?; Elizabeth Vanities, The; Esther, Sonja and Carmen; Everybody Wants to Be a Movie Star; Faces; Fan Intro; Flash in the Pan; Fred; Gun Moll; I'm a Fan; I'm the Only One; Join the Movies; Madcap, the Vamp and the Sweet Young Thing, The; MGM; Movie Star; Movies Ruined My Life, The; San Simeon; Some Kind'a Woman; Three Dog Knights; 20th Century Fox; Warner Brothers

Cast: Gale Baker; Eileen Barnett; Christopher Callan; Larry Cedar; Daniel Fortus; Katie LaBourdette; Brad Maule; Leigh Scarritt; Kathryn Skatula; Jordan Suffin

Notes: Played in Hollywood.

2970 • MOWGLI

OPENED: 09/26/1985
Musical   Closed out of town

Composer: Kirk Nurock
Lyricist: C.J. Ellis
Librettist: Tom O'Horgan
Producer: American Musical Theatre Festival
Director: Tom O'Horgan

Source: JUNGLE BOOK, THE (Novel: Rudyard Kipling); **Arrangements:** Kirk Nurock; **Costumes:** Alice Farley; Annie Hickman; Stacy Morse; Joan Peters; **Lighting Designer:** John McLain; **Set Design:** Bill Stabile; **Vocal Arranger:** Kirk Nurock

Songs: Another Road, Another Destiny; Bandar-Logs, The; Better Off Dead; Burning Flower; Conflict at Council Rock; Darkness Fades; His End Is Near; How Fear Came; I Was Born Where You Were Born; Kaa's Rescue; Law of the Jungle; Long Overdue; Nightsong in the Jungle; Patterns; Place to Hide, A; Praise; Raksha's Lullabye; Rann's Message; Rope Song; Shere Khan Sniffs Out Mowgli Blues, The; Shere Khan's Dream of the Dance of Death; Thunder Drumming; Truth Is Spoken with Your Eyes, The; We Are of One Blood; Who Is This?

Cast: Bertilla Baker; Edwin Battle; Ray Contreras; Andrew Hammond; Michael Leslie; Steve Schocket

Notes: Closed in Philadelphia.

2971 • MR. AMBASSADOR

OPENED: 1949
Musical   Unproduced

Notes: This show was to be produced at the L.A. Civic Light Opera and was to star Ezio Pinza. However, Rodgers and Hammerstein bought out Pinza's contract for $25,000 and starred him in SOUTH PACIFIC. No other information available.

2972 • MR. BATTLING BUTTLER

OPENED: 10/08/1923   Theatre: Selwyn
Musical   Broadway: 288

Composer: Walter L. Rosemont
Lyricist: Ballard Macdonald
Librettist: Ballard Macdonald

Producer: George Choos
Director: Guy Bragdon

Source: BATTLING BUTLER (Musical: Stanley Brightman; Douglas Furber; Quentin Melford); **Choreographer:** Bebe Barri; David Bennett; **Costumes:** Kiviette; **Dance Arranger:** Walter L. Rosemont; **Musical Director:** Paul Yartin; **Set Design:** William E. Castle; **Vocal Arranger:** Walter L. Rosemont

Songs: Apples, Bananas and You; As We Leave the Years Behind (C: Joseph Meyer); Dancing Honeymoon (C/L: Philip Braham); If Every Day Was Sunday (C: A. Dorian Otvos); In the Spring (C: A. Dorian Otvos); Musical Calisthenics; Musical Opening; Tinkle Tune (C: Louis Breau; A. Dorian Otvos); Two Little Pals; Will You Marry Me?; You're So Sweet (C: Joseph Meyer)

Cast: Francis Halliday; William Kent; Irving Mills; Charles Ruggles; Marie Saxon; Jack Squire

Notes: The show was also titled THE DANCING HONEYMOON out of town.

2973 • MR. BLARNEY FROM IRELAND

Play   Closed out of town

Author: Charles E. Blaney

Songs: If You'll Be Good, Like My Own Mother Dear (C/L: Fiske O'Hara); One Little Baby; Rollicking Blarney O; Sunbeam of My Heart (C/L: Fiske O'Hara)

Cast: Fiske O'Hara

Notes: No other information available.

2974 • MR. BLUEBEARD

OPENED: 01/21/1903   Theatre: Knickerbocker
Revue   Broadway: 134

Composer: Frederic Solomon
Lyricist: J. Cheever Goodwin
Librettist: John J. McNally
Producer: Klaw & Erlanger
Director: Herbert Gresham; Ned Wayburn

Source: MR. BLUEBEARD (Musical: Arthur Collins; J. Hickory Wood); **Choreographer:**

Ernest D'Auban; **Costumes:** Comelli; **Set Design:** Ernest Albert; H. Emden; Hicks and Brooks; R.C. McCleary; Bruce Smith

Songs: Algerian Slave Song and Chorus; Beer that Made Milwaukee Famous, The (C: Dan McAvoy); Billy Grey, U.S.A., O.K. (C: Gus Edwards; L: Will D. Cobb); Come Buy Our Luscious Fruit; Daylight Is Dawning; Grand Processional March (inst.) [1]; Hamlet Was a Melancholy Dane (C: Jean Schwartz; L: William Jerome); He's Gone; I'll Set My True Love Free [1]; I'm a Poor Unhappy Maid (C: Jean Schwartz; L: William Jerome); I'm as Good as I Ought to Be; Julie (C: Jean Schwartz; L: William Jerome); Let Us Be Jolly as Long as We Can; Let Us Swear It By the Pale Moonlight (C: Matt C. Woodward; L: William Jerome); Marriage Is Sublime (C: Theodore Morse; L: Alfred Bryan); Most Unpopular Potentate, A; Nautch Girls' Dance [1]; Old Woman Who Lived in a Shoe, The (C: Theodore Morse; L: Alfred Bryan); Oriental Slaves Are We; Pony Ballet (inst.) (C: Jean Schwartz); Poor Unfortunate Sister Anne; Raving [1] (C: Theodore F. Morse; L: Vincent Bryan); Read the Answers in the Stars (C: Nat Vincent; L: Alfred Bryan); Songbird of Melody Lane (C: Gus Edwards; L: Alfred Bryan); Stories Adam Told to Eve [1] (C: Jean Schwartz; L: William Jerome); Then Away We Go; There's Nothing Like the Life We Sailors Lead; We Come from Dalmatia; Welcome Fatima; When the Cat's Away the Mice Will Play [1]; When the Colored Band Comes Marching Down the Street (C: J. Rosamond Johnson; L: Bob Cole); Yankee Tourist Girl, The (C: Matt C. Woodward; L: Ben Jerome)

Cast: Herbert Cawthorne; William Danforth; Bessie DeVoie; Eddie Foy Sr.; Bonnie Maginn; Dan McAvoy; Flora Parker

Notes: Also by C. Herbert Kerr. [1] Sheet music only. [2] Also known as "In the Pale Moonlight."

2975 • MR. BROADWAY
OPENED: 05/11/1957   Theatre: NBC
TV Musical

Composer: George M. Cohan
Lyricist: George M. Cohan
Librettist: Spewack, Bella; Spewack, Samuel
Producer: Sidney Lumet
Director: Sidney Lumet

Musical Director: George Bassman

Songs: Give My Regards to Broadway; Harrigan; Mary; Yankee Doodle Dandy; You're a Grand Old Flag

Narrator: Garry Moore; **Cast:** Gloria De Haven; James Dunn; Eddie Foy Jr.; Arny Freeman; June Havoc; Henry Lascoe; Mickey Rooney; Roberta Sherwood

Notes: No song list available.

2976 • MR. CINDERS
OPENED: 11/02/1929   Theatre: Adelphi
Musical   London

Composer: Vivian Ellis; Richard Myers
Lyricist: Clifford Gray; Greatrex Newman
Additonal Lyrics: Leo Robin
Librettist: Clifford Gray; Greatrex Newman
Producer: Julian Wylie
Director: George D. Parker

Choreographer: Charles Brooks; Fred A. Leslie; Max Rivers; **Musical Director:** Arthur E. Godfrey

Songs: At the Ball (C: Vivian Ellis; L: Greatrex Newman); Blue Blood (C: Richard Myers; L: Clifford Grey; Leo Robin); Every Little Moment (C: Vivian Ellis; L: Greatrex Newman); Honeymoon for Four, A (C: Vivian Ellis; L: Greatrex Newman); I Could Get Used to You [3]; I Want the World to Know (C: Richard Meyer; L: Leo Robin); I've Got You (C: Vivian Ellis; L: Greatrex Newman); Jill; Le Cygne; Oh, What You Can Do to Me [3]; On the Amazon (C: Vivian Ellis; L: Greatrex Newman); On with the Dance (C: Vivian Ellis); One Man Girl [2] (C: Richard Myers; L: Clifford Grey; Leo Robin); Paradise Bound [3]; Please, Mr. Cinders [1] (C/L: Vivian Ellis; L: Greatrex Newman); Seventeenth Century Rag, The (18th Century Drag) (C/L: Vivian Ellis; L: Clifford Grey; Greatrex Newman); She's My Lovely [4] (C/L: Vivian Ellis); Spread a Little Happiness (C: Vivian Ellis); Tennis (C: Richard Myers; L: Clifford Grey; Greatrex Newman; Leo Robin); True to Two [2] (C: Richard Myers; L: Clifford Gray; Leo Robin); Where's Jim? [3]

Cast: Binnie Hale; Basil Howes; Bobby Howes; Henry Kemp; Ruth Maitland; Jack Melford; Reita Nugent; Edith Savile

Notes: [1] Written for 1983 revival. [2] From BUBBLING OVER with additional lyrics by Clifford Grey. [3] Cut prior to opening. [4] Added to 1983 revival. Originally in HIDE AND SEEK.

2977 • MR. GILBERT, MR. SULLIVAN, AND MR. GREEN

Musical   Closed out of town

Composer: Arthur Sullivan
Lyricist: W.S. Gilbert
Librettist: Martyn Green; Frank Wilson
Director: Martyn Green

Choreographer: Robert Haddad; **Lighting Designer:** Jock Stockwell; **Musical Director:** Anthony Makas; **Set Design:** Jock Stockwell

Songs: All Hail, Great Judge [1]; Hail Poetry [4]; Hark the Hour [1]; Hours Creep on Apace, The [3]; I Have a Song [10]; I Once Was a Very Abandoned Person [9]; I Rejoice That It's Decided [2]; If You Give Me Your Attention [7]; If You Want a Receipt [5]; List and Learn [11]; None Shall Part Us [6]; O, Weary Wives [10]; Oh, Better Far to Live [4]; Oh, I Love the Jolly Rattle [7]; Sparkling Eyes [11]; Sprites of Earth and Air [2]; There Lived a King [11]; Tit Willow [8]; We're Soldiers of the Queen [5]; Were I Thy Bride [10]; Were You Not to Ko Ko Plighted [8]; When Britain Really Ruled [6]; When First My Old, Old Love [1]; When I, Good Friends [1]; When I Was a Lad [3]; When I Went to the Bar [6]; With Cat Like Tread [4]; Would You Know the Kind of Maid [7]

Narrator: Robert Sonderskov; **Cast:** William Diard; Martyn Green; Karol Kostka; Maxine Makas; Ora McBride

Notes: [1] From TRIAL BY JURY. [2] From THE SORCERER. [3] From H.M.S. PINAFORE. [4] From PIRATES OF PENZANCE. [5] From PATIENCE. [6] From IOLANTHE. [7] From PRINCESS IDA. [8] From THE MIKADO. [9] From RUDDIGORE. [10] From YEOMAN OF THE GUARD. [11] From THE GONDOLIERS.

2978 • MR. HAMLET OF BROADWAY

OPENED: 12/23/1908   Theatre: Casino
Musical   Broadway: 54

Composer: Ben M. Jerome
Lyricist: Edward Madden
Librettist: Edgar Smith
Producer: Lee Shubert; Sam S. Shubert
Director: Ned Wayburn

Musical Director: Ben M. Jerome; **Set Design:** Arthur Voegtlin

Songs: Bah [1]; Beautiful Eyes [2] (C: Ted Snyder; L: Carter De Haven; George Whiting); Dancing Is Delightful; De Ebony Spook; Down Where the Watermelon Grows [1] (C: George "Honey Boy" Evans; L: Ren Shields); Dusky Salome, The; Everything Depends on Money; Goodbye, Molly Brown; Hornpipe Rag, The; I Want to Join the Army; In a Summer Hotel; In the Golden Dawn; Man Who Built the Summer Hotel, The [1]; Mr. Hamlet of Broadway [3]; Nimble Symbaline [3]; None of Them's Got Anything on Me; Poor Little Girl Like Me, A; Regimental Review; Sunshine Lane [1] (C: Byrd Dougherty; L: Ned Wayburn); Tell Us What's the Row?; That's As Far As You Can Go; Under the Honeymoon; Waltz Me Away with You Dearie [3]; We've Been Taken In; When I Get Home [1]; When I Was a Kid Like You; When We Made the Gallant Charge Up Bunker Hill; Won't You Harmonize with Me?

Cast: Mabel Baker; Eddie Foy Sr.; Daphne Pollard; Oscar "Rags" Ragland; Maude Raymond

Notes: [1] Out of town only. [2] Not in program. [3] Sheet music only.

2979 • MR. LODE OF KOAL

OPENED: 11/01/1909   Theatre: Majestic
Musical   Broadway: 40

Composer: J. Rosamond Johnson; Bert Williams
Lyricist: Alex Rogers; J.A. Shipp
Librettist: Alex Rogers; J.A. Shipp
Producer: F. Ray Comstock

Musical Director: James J. Vaughn

Songs: Believe Me; Bygone Days in Dixie; Can Song; Chink-Chink, Chink-Chink, Chinyman; Christening, The [1]; Fate of the Veiled Mugs; Harbor of Lost Dreams, The; Hodge Podge; In Far Off Mandalay (C/L: Al Johns); Lament; Mum's the Word, Mr. Moon (C/L: J. Leubrie Hill); My Old Man; Start, The; That's a Plenty [1]

Cast: Ada Banks; Tom Brown; Lottie Grady; J. Leubrie Hill; Hattie McIntosh; Alex Rogers; Bert Williams

Notes: [1] Not in programs.

2980 • MR. MAGOO'S CHRISTMAS CAROL

OPENED: 1962
TV Musical

Composer: Jule Styne
Lyricist: Bob Merrill

Source: CHRISTMAS CAROL, A (Story: Charles Dickens)

Songs: Alone in the World; It's Great to Be Back on Broadway; Lord's Bright Blessing, The; Ringle, Ringle; We're Despicable (Plunderer's March)

Voice: Jim Backus; Jack Cassidy

Notes: No other information available.

2981 • MR. MONEYPENNY

OPENED: 02/16/1928   Theatre: Liberty
Play   Broadway: 62

Composer: Albert Gumble
Lyricist: Albert Gumble
Author: Channing Pollock
Producer: Richard Boleslavsky
Director: Richard Boleslavsky

Costumes: Omar Kiam; **Lighting Designer:** Robert Edmond Jones; **Musical Director:** Mussina Wachtel; **Set Design:** Robert Edmond Jones

Songs: Buy, Baby; Nora

Cast: Evan Heflin; Donald Meek; Lyons Wickland; Margaret Wycherly

Notes: The show also used "The music theme from HIT THE DECK."

2982 • MR. PICKWICK

OPENED: 01/19/1903   Theatre: Herald Square
Musical   Broadway: 32

Composer: Manuel Klein
Lyricist: Grant Stewart
Librettist: Charles Klein
Producer: DeWolf Hopper
Director: George Marion

Source: PICKWICK PAPERS, THE (Novel: Charles Dickens); **Musical Director:** Manuel Klein

Songs: Acting; Boys Will Be Boys; Coach Arrival; Finale Act II; Forest Air, The; Golden Rules; Gratitude; I'll Have the Law, I'll Have My Right; Lay of the Merry Ha! Ha!, The; Love; On the Side; Opening Chorus; Opening Chorus Act II; Pickwick Club, The; Pickwick's Horse Brigade (C: George A. Spink); Potato Song, The; Speak Low (L: Hermann Klein); Story of the Rainbow, The; Three Little Piggies; To Ascertain the Knowledge; What's the Latest News from Town?; What's the Matter?; You Never Can Tell How It's Going to Turn Out

Cast: Digby Bell; Marguerite Clark; Louise Gunning; DeWolf Hopper

2983 • MR. PRESIDENT

OPENED: 10/20/1962   Theatre: St. James
Musical   Broadway: 265

Composer Irving Berlin
Lyricist: Irving Berlin
Librettist: Russel Crouse; Howard Lindsay
Producer: Leland Hayward
Director: Joshua Logan

Choreographer: Peter Gennaro; **Costumes:** Theoni V. Aldredge; **Dance Arranger:** Jack Elliott; **Lighting Designer:** Jo Mielziner; **Musical Director:** Jay Blackton; **Orchestrations:** Philip J. Lang; **Set Design:** Jo Mielziner; **Vocal Arranger:** Jay Blackton

Songs: Don't Be Afraid of Romance; Empty Pockets Filled with Love; First Lady, The; Glad to Be Home [1]; I'm Gonna Get Him [2]; In Our Hide-Away; Is He the Only Man in the World? [4]; It Gets Lonely in the White House; I've Got to Be Around; Laugh It Up; Let's Go Back to the Waltz; Meat and Potatoes; Mr. President [3]; Once Every Four Years [3]; Only Dance I Know (Song for Belly Dancer), The; Opening; Pigtails and Freckles; Poor Joe [3]; Secret Service, The; They Love Me; This Is a Great Country; Washington Twist, The; You Need a Hobby

Cast: David Brooks; Wisa D'Orso; Nanette Fabray; Anita Gillette; Stanley Grover; Jack Haskell; Robert Ryan

Notes: [1] Previously titled "I Keep Running Away from You" as a 1957 pop song. [2] Written in 1956 with a different lyric. [3] Cut prior to New York. [4] A rewrite of the 1954 song "Is She the Only Girl in the World" and a reworking of "Where Is the Song of Songs for Me," a song written in 1929 for the Lupe Velez movie LADY OF THE PAVEMENTS.

2984 • MR. RAGTIME

OPENED: 1914
Musical

Composer: Will Dorsey
Lyricist: Irvin C. Miller
Librettist: Irvin C. Miller
Producer: Kid Brown; Irvin C. Miller

Songs: All Aboard for Dixie Land; Bleeding Heart; Carmina; Croony Melody; Every Road; Finale Act II; Flippity Flop; Hello Little Miss U.S.A.; Hesitation Waltz; I'm Going to Exit; Long Lost Blues; Ragtime Chimes; When You Sang the Rosary to Me

Cast: Kid Brown; Currie Caisons; Tillie Cross; Eva Harris; Ethel James; Eleanor Johnson; Irvin C. Miller

Notes: No information available.

2985 • MR. STRAUSS GOES TO BOSTON

OPENED: 09/06/1945   Theatre: Century
Musical   Broadway: 12

Composer: Robert Stolz
Lyricist: Robert Sour
Librettist: Alfred Gruenwald; Geza Herczeg; Leonard I. Levinson
Producer: Felix Brentano
Director: Felix Brentano

Choreographer: George Balanchine; **Costumes:** Walter Florell; **Musical Director:** Robert Stolz; **Orchestrations:** George Lessner; **Set Design:** Stewart Chaney

Songs: Can Anyone See?; Down with Sin; For the Sake of Art; Going Back Home; Grand and Glorious Fourth, The; Into the Night; Laughing Waltz [1]; Midnight Waltz [2] (C: George Lessner; Robert Stolz;); Mr. Strauss Goes to Boston; What's a Girl Supposed to Do?; Who Knows?; You Never Know What Comes Next

Cast: Ralph Dumke; Harold Lang; Virginia MacWatters; Ruth Matteson

Notes: Levinson translated the German libretto which was written for this production. [1] Adaptation of Johann Stauss melody. [2] Adaptation of Johann Strauss melody by Stolz and Lessner.

2986 • MR. WIX OF WICKHAM

OPENED: 09/19/1904   Theatre: Bijou
Musical   Broadway: 41

Composer: Jerome Kern
Lyricist: Jerome Kern
Librettist: Herbert Darnley; John H. Wagner
Producer: Edward E. Rice
Director: Tom Ricketts

Costumes: Madame Ripley; **Musical Director:** Whitney Bennington; **Set Design:** Frank Rafter; Theodore Reisig

Songs: Angling By a Babbling Brook; Because I Am a Duke (L: John H. Wagner); Bluff (L: John H. Wagner); Cupid's Garden (C: Max C. Eugene [2]); Dancing Kangaroo, The; Finale Act I (C: Herbert Darnley); Finale Act II; From Saturday to Monday (L: John H. Wagner); Googy-oo (C: Edward E. Rice, L: John H. Wagner); Handle to My Name, A (C: Herbert Darnley); Her First Can Can (L: John H. Wanger); Important Man, The; Love Is King [1]; Military Maids; New York Way [1]; Not Like Other Girls (C: Andros Hawley); One Thing Different (C: Herbert Darnley; Jerome Kern); Opening Chorus (C: George Everard); Opening Chorus Act II (C: Herbert Darnley); Raindrops (C: George Everard); Rub a Dub; Sergeant Wix (C: Herbert Darnley); Susan; Volunteers (C: George Everard); Waiting for You (L: John H. Wagner); When You're in Love with Somebody [3] (C: Lester Keiffer; L: John Kemble)

Cast: Henry Corson Clarke; Sydney De Grey; Julian Eltinge; Thelma Fair; Laura Guerite; Frank

Lalor; David Lythgow; Milt Pollock; Alice Maude Poole; Fred Waters; Arthur Wooley

Notes: If a lyricist is unidentifed then composer probably wrote lyrics also. [1] Out of town 9/12/04. [2] Pen name for music publisher Max Dreyfus. [3] Sheet music only.

2987 • MR. WONDERFUL

OPENED: 03/22/1956   Theatre: Broadway
Musical   Broadway: 383

Composer: Jerry Bock; Larry Holofcener; George David Weiss
Lyricist: Jerry Bock; Larry Holofcener; George David Weiss
Librettist: Will Glickman; Joseph Stein
Producer: George Gilbert; Lester Osterman; Jule Styne
Director: Jack Donahue

Choreographer: Jack Donahue; **Costumes:** Robert Mackintosh; **Lighting Designer:** Peggy Clark; **Musical Director:** Morton Stevens; **Orchestrations:** Ted Royal; Morton Stevens; **Set Design:** Oliver Smith

Songs: Big Time [1]; Charlie Welch; Ethel, Baby; I'm Available; I've Been Too Busy; Jacques D'Iraq; Miami; Mr. Wonderful; Sing You Sinners [2] (C: W. Franke Harling; L: Sam Coslow); 1617 Broadway; Talk to Him; There; Too Close for Comfort; Without You I'm Nothing

Cast: Jack Carter; Sammy Davis Jr.; Sammy Davis Sr.; Olga James; Hal Loman; Pat Marshall; Will Mastin; Chita Rivera

Notes: Music and vocal supervision of Oscar Kosarin. [1] Added after opening. [2] Not written for show.

2988 • MR. WOOLWORTH HAD A NOTION

OPENED: 06/16/1965   Theatre: Biltmore Hotel Ballroom
Revue   New York: 1

Composer: Michael Brown
Lyricist: Michael Brown
Librettist: Michael Brown
Producer: Donahue Sales Corporation; F.W. Woolworth Company
Director: Michael Brown

Choreographer: Alex Palermo; **Lighting Designer:** Claire Carter; **Musical Director:** Norman Paris; **Set Design:** John Byrne

Songs: I Love the Rain; Opening Day at the Five-and-Ten; She's a Big Girl Now; Shopping at a Woolworth Store; We'd Just Die; What a Notion; When In Rome; Woolworth Country; Woolworth Manager's Work Song, The

Cast: John Baylis; Joy Franz; Ellen Martin; Barbara Strouse

Notes: Industrial show.

2989 • MRS. ARRIS GOES TO PARIS

Musical

Composer: Arthur Schwartz
Lyricist: Howard Dietz

Source: MRS. ARRIS GOES TO PARIS (Novel: Paul Gallico)

Songs: Sewing Circle on the Seine, The

Notes: I don't believe this show was completed though a demo was produced.

2990 • MRS. BLACK IS BACK

OPENED: 11/07/1904   Theatre: Bijou
Play   Broadway: 71

Author: George V. Hobart

Musical Director: George A. Nichols

Songs: Albany or Dat's de Only Town Looks Good to Me (C: Hughie Cannon; L: May Irwin); Bible Stories (C: Al Johns; L: John Lee Clarke); Bygone Days Are Best (C/L: Will Marion Cook); Dinner Bells (C/L: Harry Brown); Dreaming (C: May Irwin; L: John E. Hazzard); Guess, Guess, Guess (C: John W. Bratton; L: Paul West); I Love to Two Step with My Man (C/L: Hughie Cannon); I'm Worried to Death About That (C/L: May Irwin); In the Shadow of the Pyramids (C: Ernest R. Ball; L: R.C. McPherson); Keep Away from Broadway (C: Al Johns; L: C. Noel Douglas); Mum's the Word (C: Gus Edwards; L: Will D. Cobb); Nothing but Talk (C/L: Harry Brown); 'Tain't No Use in Lovin' That Way [1] (C/L: May

Irwin); Tennessee, That's the Place for Me
(C: Jean Schwartz; L: Harry Williams)

Cast: Edgar Atchinson-Ely; May Irwin; Nick Long
Jr.; John G. Sparks

Notes: [1] Sheet music only.

2991 • MRS. DELANY OF NEWPORT

OPENED: 11/03/1903
Play

Composer: Jean Schwartz
Lyricist: William Jerome
Author: William Jerome
Producer: James Hyde

Source: ENGLISH DAISY, AN (Musical: Seymour
Hicks; Walter Slaughter)

Songs: Barney (A Song Full of Blarney) (C/L: Ed
Rogers); Bedelia

Cast: John F. Clark; Ellmore Sisters

Notes: No other information available.

2992 • MRS. FARMER'S DAUGHTER

OPENED: 07/20/1983
Musical   Closed out of town

Composer: Jack Eric Williams
Lyricist: Jack Eric Williams
Librettist: Tom O'Horgan; Joseph Stockdale; Jack
Eric Williams
Producer: PepsiCo Summerfare '83
Director: Tom O'Horgan

Choreographer: Ted Rotante; **Conductor:** Marc
Irwin; **Costumes:** Randy Barcelo; **Lighting
Designer:** John McLain; **Musical Director:** Jack
Eric Williams; **Set Design:** Bill Stabile

Songs: Bad Girl of West Seattle, The; Barnyard
Blues; Bird Americana; Board Meeting; Boy
Needs Love, A; Christmas in Laurel Canyon;
Episodes, The; Especially in the Dark; Frances
Discovers Nietzsche; Full Moon, The; Garbo Bit,
The; God's Peculiar Care; Gospel According to
Lillian; Hairdresser Sequence; Hollywood Rag;
If You Could Love Me; In Flagrante Delicto;

Inventory; Jacob's Ladder; Jazztown Features;
Jesus Sweetest Name I Know; Kingdom of Love,
The; Knocking in Vain; Last Resort, The; Life as
Rumor; Lord's Prayer, The; Manhattan; Maybe
Now a Little House; Mental Hygiene; Mother-
love; Nothing's Left but Hollywood; Of When
Stars Fall Down; Old Prayer, An; Police Trouble;
Rib of Adam; She Showed Me; Slow Dancing; St.
Agnes Eve; Stub Me Out I'm a Cigarette; That
Feels Good; There Are B-Girls All Over Heaven;
Thrill Is Gone, The; Time of Your Life, The;
Tomorrow; Too Bad; "Vive Le Demimonde"

Cast: Stephen Berger; Don Chastain; Rhonda
Coullet; Mary Dale; Brian Hurley; William Kiehl;
Raymond Patterson

2993 • MRS. MCTHING

OPENED: 10/12/1984
Musical   Closed out of town

Composer: Jack Urbont
Lyricist: Michael Colby
Librettist: Michael Colby
Producer: Gerald A. Davis; Goodspeed Opera
House; Warren Pincus
Director: Edward Stone

Source: MRS. MCTHING (Play: Mary Chase);
Arrangements: Jacques Urbont; **Choreographer:**
Dennis Dennehy; **Costumes:** Susan Hirschfeld;
Dance Arranger: John McKinney; **Lighting
Designer:** Jason Kantrowitz; **Musical Director:**
Barry Koron; **Set Design:** Mark Morton

Songs: Change, The; Chef's Complaint; Crazy;
Doin' All I've Dreamed Of; Fantasy; Finale;
Golden Days; Hat Attack, The; Heist, The; How
Do You Make Magic?; Know You; Larue's Blues;
Loveliest Child in the World, The; Mrs. McThing;
Poopsie Woopsie; Shantyland Pool Hall Lunch-
room Crowd, The; Slumming; Soon We'll Be
Home; What's a Witch?; What's the Big To-do?;
Who Is the Phony?; Witches' Sabbath, The; Ya've
Got What It Takes

Cast: G. Brandon Allen; Gibby Brand; Deborah
Dotson; Jeanne Lehman

Notes: Goodspeed at Chester.

2994 • MRS. PATTERSON

OPENED: 12/01/1954   Theatre: National
Play   Broadway: 102

Composer: James Shelton
Lyricist: James Shelton
Author: Greer Johnson; Charles Sebree
Producer: Leonard Sillman
Director: Guthrie McClintic

Costumes: Raoul Pene du Bois; **Musical Director:** Abba Bogin; **Orchestrations:** George Stravo; **Set Design:** Raoul Pene du Bois

Songs: Be Good, Be Good, Be Good; I Wish I Was a Bumble Bee (L: Greer Johnson; Charles Sebree); If I Was a Boy; Mrs. Patterson; My Daddy Is a Dandy; Tea in Chicago

Cast: Ruth Attaway; Terry Carter; Helen Dowdy; Estelle Helmsley; Eartha Kitt; Avon Long; Enid Markey

2995 • MRS. RADLEY BARTON'S BALL OR IN GREATER NEW YORK

OPENED: 03/26/1897   Theatre: Lyric
Musical   Broadway: 48

Composer: Oscar Hammerstein I
Lyricist: Oscar Hammerstein I
Librettist: Oscar Hammerstein I
Producer: Oscar Hammerstein I

Cast: William Bach; George W. Monroe; Alice Rose

Notes: After the first performance, the title of this Musical was changed to IN GREATER NEW YORK. No program available.

2996 • MRS. WILSON, THAT'S ALL

OPENED: 11/05/1906   Theatre: Bijou
Play   Broadway: 51

Author: George V. Hobart
Producer: May Irwin

Musical Director: John C. Sorg

Songs: Bonnie Sue Sunshine [1]; Come to the Land of Bohemia [4] (C: Ted Snyder; L: Ren Shields); Dan (C: May Irwin; L: Earle C. Jones); Honora Doolin (C: Ted Snyder; L: Bowman Brothers); Kitty (C: Silvio Hein; L: George V. Hobart); Lady (Bless Your Heart I Loves You Lady) (L: Margaret Crosse); Matrimony (C/L: J.P.

McKenna); Moonshine (C: Silvio Hein; L: George V. Hobart); Moses Andrew Jackson, Goodbye (C: Ted Snyder; L: Ren Shields); Never Raise a Razor 'Less You Want to Raise a Row [1] (C: John B. Lowitz; L: John E. Hazzard); No Wedding Bells for Me [1] (C: Seymour Furth; L: Will Heelan; Edward P. Moran); Save a Little Money for a Rainy Day [3] (C: Ted Snyder; L: Ren Shields)

Cast: Lillian Dix; Maude Forrest; John E. Hazzard; May Irwin; C. Russell Sage; Mary K. Taylor

Notes: On November 19th the title was changed to MRS. WILSON-ANDREWS. [1] Sheet music only. [2] Also in THE ORCHID. [3] Sheet music credits Maxwell Silver with music. [4] Music credited to George Evans on sheet music.

2997 • MRS. WILSON-ANDREWS
Notes: *See MRS. WILSON, THAT'S ALL.*

2998 • MS. PRES
OPENED: 1979
Musical   Unproduced

Composer: Arthur Siegel
Lyricist: Diane David Harris

Songs: Crossover; Dirty Words; Doin' the Ethnic Reach; I'm Forty; Man to Man; Maybe the World Has a Chance; Mugging Sequence; Old Ways Are the Best Ways; Responsible; She Doesn't Have a Chance; Should I? (My Land); This Is a Man I Could Love; We're the People; (Am I a) Woman; Woman Was Meant to Be Woman; You Gotta Please All the People; You Have to Choose Sides

2999 • MUCH ADO ABOUT LOVE
Notes: *See THE FIREBRAND OF FLORENCE.*

3000 • MUCH ADO ABOUT NOTHING
OPENED: 08/19/1972   Theatre: Winter Garden
Play   Broadway: 136

Composer: Peter Link
Lyricist: Peter Link
Author: William Shakespeare
Producer: N.Y. Shakespeare Festival; Joseph Papp
Director: A.J. Antoon

Choreographer: Donald Saddler; **Costumes:** Theoni V. Aldredge; **Lighting Designer:** Martin Aronstein; **Musical Director:** Peter Phillips; **Set Design:** Ming Cho Lee

Songs: Ballad for a Summer Evening; Goodbye Fred; Hogwash; Jimmie; Light of Love; Marcella; Meet You 'Hind the Barn

Cast: Frederick Coffin; Lindsay Crouse; Marshall Efron; Arny Freeman; Mark Hammer; Barnard Hughes; Will Mackenzie; Leland Schwantes; April Shawhan; Sam Waterston; Douglass Watson; Kathleen Widdoes

Notes: Opened at the Delecorte Theatre, Central Park for 20 performances. Moved to Broadway on 11/11/72 for an additonal 116 performances.

3001 • MULE BONE

OPENED: 02/14/1991   Theatre: Vivian Beaumont
Play   Broadway: 67

Composer: Taj Mahal
Lyricist: Langston Hughes
Author: Langston Hughes; Zora Neale Hurston
Producer: Lincoln Center Theater
Director: Michael Schultz

Choreographer: Dianne McIntyre; **Costumes:** Lewis Brown; **Lighting Designer:** Allen Lee Hughes; **Set Design:** Edward Burbridge

Songs: Bound No'th Blues; But I Rode Some; Crossing; Finale (inst.); Graveyard Mule (L: George Houston Bass); Hey Hey Blues; Intermission Blues, The (inst.); Jubilee (inst.); Me and the Mule; Shake That Thing (C/L: "Poppa" Charlie Jackson); Song for a Banjo Dance

Cast: Akosua Busia; Robert Earl Jones; Joy Lee; Theresa Merritt; Eric Ware; Vanessa Williams; Samuel E. Wright

Notes: Prologue and epilogue by George Houston Bass. Songs not listed in program. Titles from CD.

3002 • MURDER AT THE VANITIES

OPENED: 09/12/1933   Theatre: New Amsterdam
Musical   Broadway: 298

Composer: Richard Myers
Lyricist: Edward Heyman
Librettist: Earl Carroll; Rufus King
Producer: Earl Carroll
Director: Earl Carroll; Burk Symon

Choreographer: Chester Hale; Ned McGurn; **Costumes:** Brymer; **Lighting Designer:** Stuart C. Whitman; **Musical Director:** Ray Kavanaugh; **Orchestrations:** Edward Powell; Hans Spialek; **Set Design:** Max Teuber

Songs: Dust in Your Eyes (C/L: Irving Newman; Lionel Newman); Me for You Forever; Savage Serenade (C/L: Herman Hupfeld); Sweet Madness (C: Victor Young; L: Ned Washington); Virgins Wrapped in Cellophane (C: John Jacob Loeb; L: Paul Francis Webster); We're Going to Be Dramatic; Weep No More, My Baby (C: Johnny Green); Who Committed the Murder?; You Love Me (C/L: Herman Hupfeld)

Cast: Jean Adair; Olga Baclanova; Hope Carol; Paul Gerrits; Lisa Gilbert; Billy House; Bela Lugosi; Woods Miller; Pauline Moore; Gay Orlova; Naomi Ray; James Rennie; Una Vallon; Beryl Wallace

3003 • MURDER IN THE OLD RED BARN

OPENED: 02/01/1936   Theatre: American Music Hall
Play   Off-Broadway: 251

Composer: Richard Lewine
Lyricist: John Latouche
Author: John Latouche
Producer: Jerrold Krimsky; John Krimsky

Songs: Don't Turn Us Out of Your House; Not on Your Tintype

Cast: Harry Meehan; Margaret Walker

3004 • MURDER ON BROADWAY

OPENED: 03/18/1991
Musical

Composer: James Campodonico
Lyricist: James Campodonico
Librettist: Bryan D. Leys
Director: Mark S. Kerko

Arrangements: Eric Barnes; **Choreographer:** SuSu Sparkman; **Costumes:** Cory Chenault; **Lighting Designer:** Ed Stone; **Musical Director:** Eric Barnes; **Orchestrations:** Eric Barnes; **Set Design:** Michael DuMouchel; **Vocal Arranger:** Seth Rudetsky

Songs: After Your Lover Has Gone; Big Town; Blackbird Knows; Bye Bye Osiris; Debutante Who Wanted a Ph.D., The; I Can't Say No to You; It Requires a Man; It Wasn't Me; Killer on the Loose; Maracas Make Me Nervous; Nothin' to No One; Perfect; Purgatory; Second Banana; Superior Soap Jingle, The; This Gumshoe's Gonna Stick Around; Tough Guy; We Have a Lot in Common

Cast: Valerie De Pena; Stanton Garr; SuSu Sparkman

Notes: Show Boat Dinner Theatre, St. Petersburg, Fla.

3005 • MURRAY ANDERSON'S ALMANAC (1929)

OPENED: 08/04/1929   Theatre: Erlanger
Revue   Broadway: 69

Librettist: John Murray Anderson; Peter Arno; Noel Coward; Rube Goldberg; Ronald Jeans; John McGowan; Harry Ruskin; Wynn
Producer: John Murray Anderson
Director: John Murray Anderson; Harry Ruskin

Choreographer: William Holbrook; **Costumes:** Peter Arno; Jacques Darcy; Charles LeMaire; Robert E. Locker; Wynn; **Musical Director:** Gene Salzer; **Set Design:** Clark Robinson

Songs: Almanac Covers, The (C: Henry Sullivan; L: Edward Eliscu); Builders of Dreams (C: Henry Sullivan; L: John Murray Anderson); Educate Your Feet (C: Milton Ager; L: Jack Yellen); Getting Into the Talkies (C/L: Neville Fleeson); I Can't Remember the Words (C: Milton Ager; Henry Cabot Lodge; L: Jack Yellen); I May Be Wrong (But I Think You're Wonderful) (C: Henry Sullivan; L: Harry Ruskin); In the Village By the Sea (C/L: Unknown); Metropolis (scene) (C: Henry Sullivan); New Yorker, The (C: Milton Ager; L: Jack Yellen); Nightingale Song, The (C: Milton Ager; L: Jack Yellen); Page Nine (C: Henry Sullivan; L: Jack Yellen); Polka Dot, The (C: Henry Sullivan; L: Clifford Orr); Same Old Moon (C: Henry Sullivan; L: John Murray Anderson;

Clifford Orr); Schrafft's University (C: Henry Sullivan; L: Edward Eliscu); Tiller, Foster, Hoffman, Hale and Albertina Rasch (C: Henry Sullivan; L: Henry Myers); Tinkle! Tinkle! (C: Milton Ager; L: Jack Yellen); Wait for the Happy Ending (C: Milton Ager; L: Jack Yellen); Young King, The (scene) (C: Henry Sullivan)

Cast: Roy Atwell; Trixie Friganza; Fred Keating; Charles Royal; Jimmy Savo; Eleanor Shaler; Helen Thompson

3006 • MUSIC BOX REVUE

OPENED: 09/22/1921   Theatre: Music Box
Revue   Broadway: 440

Composer: Irving Berlin
Lyricist: Irving Berlin
Librettist: Willie Collier; T.J. Gray; George V. Hobart; Frances Nordstrom
Director: Willie Collier; Hassard Short

Choreographer: Bert French; I. Tarasoff; **Costumes:** Cora MacGeachy; Ralph Mulligan; Alice O'Neil; **Lighting Designer:** John Brunton; **Musical Director:** Anton Heindl; Frank Tours; **Orchestrations:** Harry Akst; Alfred Dalby; Maurice DePackh; Charles Grant; Stephen Jones; Oscar Radin; Frank Tours; **Set Design:** Clark Robinson

Songs: At the Court Around the Corner [1]; Behind the Fan; Dancing the Seasons Away; Everybody Step; I'm a Dumb-Bell; In a Cozy Kitchenette Apartment; Legend of the Pearls, The; My Ben Ali Haggin Girl; My Little Book of Poetry; Play Without a Bedroom, A; Say It with Music; Schoolhouse Blues, The; Tell It with a Melody [2]; They Call It Dancing

Cast: Wilda Bennett; Irving Berlin; Sam Bernard; Brox Sisters, The; Hugh Cameron; Willie Collier; Paul Frawley; Emma Haig; Chester Hale; Richard Keene; Florence Moore; Joseph Santley; Ivy Sawyer; Ethelind Terry

Notes: [1] Sheet music only. [2] Written for London version.

3007 • MUSIC BOX REVUE (SECOND EDITION)

OPENED: 10/23/1922   Theatre: Music Box
Revue   Broadway: 330

Composer: Irving Berlin
Lyricist: Irving Berlin
Librettist: Walter Catlett; George V. Hobart; Frances Nordstrom; Paul Gerard Smith
Producer: Sam H. Harris
Director: Hassard Short

Choreographer: William Seabury; Stowitts; **Costumes:** Gilbert Adrian; Ralph Mulligan; **Lighting Designer:** Charles E. Rush; **Musical Director:** Frank Tours; Will Vodery; **Orchestrations:** Harry Akst; Alfred Dalby; Charles Grant; Arthur Gutman; Stephen Jones; Frank Tours; Will Vodery; Roy Webb; **Set Design:** Clark Robinson

Songs: Bring on the Pepper; Crinoline Days; Dance Your Troubles Away; Dancing Honeymoon [1]; I'm Looking for a Daddy Long Legs; Lady of the Evening; Little Red Lacquer Cage, The [1]; Mont Martre [1]; My Diamond Horseshoe of Girls; Pack Up Your Sins and Go to the Devil; Porcelain Maid; Take a Little Wife; Three Cheers for the Red, White and Blue; Too Many Boys; Will She Come from the East (North, West, or South)?

Cast: Clark & McCullough; Fairbanks Twins, The; William Gaxton; Charlotte Greenwood; Grace LaRue; Ruth Page; John Steel

Notes: [1] Sheet music only.

3008 • MUSIC BOX REVUE (THIRD EDITION)

OPENED: 09/22/1923   Theatre: Music Box
Revue   Broadway: 277

Composer: Irving Berlin
Lyricist: Irving Berlin
Producer: Sam H. Harris
Director: Hassard Short

Choreographer: Sammy Lee; Alexander Oumansky; **Costumes:** Adrian; Charles LeMaire; Ralph Mulligan; **Lighting Designer:** Charles E. Rush; **Musical Director:** Frank Tours; **Orchestrations:** Maurice DePackh; Charles Grant; Stephen Jones; Frank Tours; **Set Design:** Clark Robinson; **Vocal Arranger:** Arthur Johnstone

Songs: Climbing Up the Scale; Learn to Do the Strut; Little Butterfly; Maid of Mesh; One Girl; Orange Grove in California, An; Tell Me a

Bedtime Story; Too Many Sweethearts [2]; Waltz of Long Ago, The; What'll I Do [3]; When You Walked Out Somebody Else Walked Right In [2]; Yes! We Have No Bananas (Parody) [1] (C: Irving Conn; L: Frank Silver); Your Hat and My Hat

Cast: Phil Baker; Robert Benchley; Brox Sisters, The; Florence Moore; Grace Moore; Florence O'Denishawn; Joseph Santley; Ivy Sawyer; John Steel; Frank Tinney; Solly Ward

Notes: [1] Berlin turned "Yes! We Have No Bananas" into parody of arias from AIDA, LUCIA, RIGOLETTO, TALES OF HOFFMAN, TROVATORE and the MESSIAH. [2] Cut. Also in THE COCOANUTS. [3] May have been added after opening.

3009 • MUSIC BOX REVUE (FOURTH EDITION)

OPENED: 12/01/1924   Theatre: Music Box
Revue   Broadway: 184

Composer: Irving Berlin
Lyricist: Irving Berlin
Librettist: Bert Kalmar; Harry Ruby
Producer: Sam H. Harris
Director: John Murray Anderson; Sam H. Harris

Choreographer: Carl Randall; Madame Serova; **Costumes:** Mabel Johnston; Max Ree; Roy Requa; James Reynolds; **Lighting Designer:** Frank Schneider; **Musical Director:** Frank Tours; **Orchestrations:** Maurice DePackh; Stephen Jones; Frank Tours; **Set Design:** James Reynolds; Clark Robinson; **Vocal Arranger:** Arthur Johnson

Songs: Alice in Wonderland (Come Along with Alice) [4]; All Alone [2]; Bandana Ball; Call of the South, The [1]; Couple of Senseless Censors, A; Don't Send Me Back to Petrograd; Don't Wait Too Long [3]; Happy New Year Blues, The [3]; I Want to Be a Ballet Dancer; In the Shade of a Sheltering Tree; Listening; Moving Picture Baby (C/L: Leo Edwards; Blanche Merrill); Polly of Hollywood [5] (C: James F. Hanley; L: B.G. DeSylva); Rock-A-Bye Baby; Sixteen, Sweet Sixteen; Tell Her in the Springtime; Tokio Blues; Unlucky in Love; Where Is My Little Old New York?; Who; Wildcats

Cast: Fanny Brice; Brox Sisters, The; Clark & McCullough; Claire Luce; Grace Moore; Carl Randall; Oscar Shaw; Tamara

Notes: [1] Grace Moore sang this in countermelody to Stephen Foster's "Old Folks at Home." [2] Interpolated into show after being introduced on a radio show that also introduced "What'll I Do?" Put into London show THE PUNCH BOWL. [3] Sheet music only. [4] Not same song as in THE CENTURY GIRL. [5] Probably written in 1925, this song was either added after opening or added to the tour.

3010 • MUSIC-HALL SIDELIGHTS

OPENED: 10/26/1978
Revue   Off-Broadway: 19

Composer: John McKinney
Lyricist: Jack Heifner
Librettist: Jack Heifner
Producer: Lion Theatre Company
Director: Garland Wright

Source: L'ENVERS DU MUSIC HALL (Story: Colette); **Choreographer:** Randolyn Zinn; **Costumes:** David James; **Lighting Designer:** Frances Aronson; **Set Design:** John Arnone

Cast: Kathy Bates; James McLure

Notes: No songs listed in program.

3011 • MUSIC HATH CHARMS

OPENED: 12/29/1934   Theatre: Majestic
Musical   Broadway: 25

Composer: Rudolf Friml
Lyricist: Rowland Leigh; John Shubert
Librettist: Rowland Leigh; George Roesner; John Shubert
Producer: Messrs. Shubert
Director: George Rosener

Choreographer: Alex Yakovieff; **Costumes:** Ernest Schrapps; **Musical Director:** Al Goodman; **Set Design:** Watson Barratt

Songs: Annina [1]; Carnival Ballet; Cavaliers; Comedy Dance [1]; Court Dance [1]; Dance Characteurtique; Dance of Times; Danse Modern [1]; Everything Changes but Love [1]; Exquisite Moment; Frutti Di Mare; Gavotte [1]; Gondolier Song; I Cannot Be Faithful [1]; It Happened; It's Three O'Clock; It's You I Want to Love Tonight; Ladies, Beware; Let Me Be Free; Longing [1]; Love Is Only What You Make It; Lovey-Dovey; Maria (Annina); Midnight Flirtation; Minuet; Music Hath Charms (My Heart Is Yours); My Palace of Dreams; One Tender Smile [1]; Polka [1]; Processional; Romance; Scandal Number; Smile, a Kiss, A; Sweet Fool; Tarentella [1]

Cast: Robert Lee Allen; Constance Carpenter; Cyril Chadwick; John Clarke; Elizabeth Crandell; Truman Gaige; Paul Haakon; Natalie Hall; Robert Halliday; Harry Mestayer; Billy Rey; Andrew Tombes; Nina Whitney; Gracie Worth

Notes: Titled ANNINA out of town. [1] Out Washington, D.C. 3/26/34.

3012 • MUSIC IN MAY

OPENED: 04/01/1929   Theatre: Casino
Musical   Broadway: 80

Composer: Maurie Rubens
Lyricist: J. Keirn Brennan
Librettist: Fanny Todd Mitchell
Producer: Messrs. Shubert
Director: Stanley Logan; Lew Morton

Source: UNKNOWN (Musical: Emil Berte; Kurt Breuer; Heinz Merley); **Choreographer:** Chester Hale; **Set Design:** Watson Barratt

Songs: Every Month Is May [1] (C: Emil Berte); For the Papa; Glory of Spring, The; High, High, High; I Found a Friend; I'd Like to Love Them All (C: Maurie Rubens; Phil Svigals); I'm in Love (C: Emil Berte; Maurie Rubens); Lips that Laugh at Love; No Other Love; Open and Shut Idea; Open Your Window; Sweetheart of Our Student Corps; There's Love in the Heart I Hold; Unto Your Heart (C: Emil Berte)

Cast: Greek Evans; Gertrude Lang; Bartlett Simmons; Solly Ward

Notes: [1] Not in program.

3013 • MUSIC IN MY HEART

OPENED: 10/02/1947   Theatre: Adelphi
Musical   Broadway: 124

Music Based On: Peter Illitch Tchaikowsky
Composer: Franz Steininger
Lyricist: Forman Brown
Librettist: Patsy Ruth Miller
Producer: Henry Duffy
Director: Hassard Short

Choreographer: Ruth Page; **Costumes:** Alvin Colt; **Lighting Designer:** Hassard Short; **Musical Director:** Franz Steininger; **Set Design:** Alvin Colt

Songs: Am I Enchanted?; Balalaika Serenade, The; Ballerina's Story, The; Beauty and the Beast; Dance Arabe; Flower Waltz; Gossip; Love Is a Game for Soldiers; Love Is the Sovereign of My Heart; Love Song; Natuscha; No! No! No!; Once Upon a Time; Song of the Claque; Song of the Troika; Stolen Kisses; Three's a Crowd; Trepak; Unrequited Love or the Storm; While There's a Song to Sing

Cast: Robert Carroll; Dorothy Etheridge; Charles Fredericks; Jan Murray; Vivienne Segal; James Starbuck; Olga Suarez; Martha Wright

Notes: Music adapted from Tchaikovsky. Later revived as THE LADY FROM PARIS (10/26/50) — closed in Philadelphia.

3014 • MUSIC IN THE AIR

OPENED: 11/08/1932   Theatre: Alvin
Musical   Broadway: 342

Composer: Jerome Kern
Lyricist: Oscar Hammerstein II
Librettist: Oscar Hammerstein II
Producer: A.C. Blumenthal; Peggy Fears
Director: Oscar Hammerstein II

Costumes: John Harkrider; Howard Shoup; **Musical Director:** Victor Baravalle; **Orchestrations:** Robert Russell Bennett; **Set Design:** Joseph Urban

Songs: And Love Was Born; At Stony Brook [4]; Episode of the Swing [5]; Hold Your Head Up High (Opening Hymn); I Am So Eager; I'm Alone; I'm Coming Home (Letter Song); In Egern on the Tegern See; Interlude [5]; I've Told Ev'ry Little Star; Melodies of May [3]; Night Flies By [2]; One More Dance [1]; Prayer (Our Journey May Be Long); Scena (Tingle Tangle) [5]; Song Is You, The; Terzetto [5]; There's a Hill Beyond a Hill; We Belong Together; When the Spring Is in the Air

Cast: Tullio Carminati; Katherine Carrington; Natalie Hall; Nicholas Joy; Marjorie Main; Al Shean; Walter Slezak

Notes: [1] Same music as "Night Flies By." [2] Same music as "One More Dance." [3] Based on Beethoven's Piano Sonata No. 3 in C opus 2. [4] Not in programs. [5] ASCAP/Library of Congress only.

3015 • MUSIC IS

OPENED: 12/20/1976   Theatre: St. James
Musical   Broadway: 8

Composer: Richard Adler
Lyricist: Will Holt
Librettist: George Abbott
Producer: Richard Adler; Roger Berlind; Edward R. Downs Jr.
Director: George Abbott

Source: TWELFTH NIGHT (Musical: William Shakespeare); **Choreographer:** Patricia Birch; **Costumes:** Lewis D. Rampino; **Dance Arranger:** William Cox; **Lighting Designer:** H.R. Poindexter; **Musical Director:** Paul Gemignani; **Orchestrations:** Hershy Kay; **Set Design:** Eldon Elder; **Vocal Arranger:** William Cox

Songs: Big Bottom Betty; Blindman's Bluff; Dance for Six; Duel, The; Hate to Say Goodbye to You; I Am It; Lady's Choice; Music Is; No Matter Where; Please Be Human; Should I Speak of Loving You; Sing Hi; Sudden Lilac; Tennis Song; Time Is Ripe for Loving, The; Twenty One Chateaux; What You Will; When First I Saw My Lady's Face

Cast: Daniel Ben-Zali; Catherine Cox; Christopher Hewett; David Holliday; Marc Jordan; Sherry Mathis; David Sabin; Laura Waterbury

3016 • MUSIC MAN, THE

OPENED: 12/19/1957   Theatre: Majestic
Musical   Broadway: 1375

Composer: Meredith Willson
Lyricist: Meredith Willson
Librettist: Meredith Willson
Producer: Kermit Bloomgarden; Frank Productions; Herbert Greene
Director: Morton Da Costa

Source: UNTITLED (Story: Franklin Lacey; Meredith Willson); **Choreographer:** Onna White; **Costumes:** Raoul Pene du Bois; **Dance Arranger:** Laurence Rosenthal; **Lighting Designer:**

Howard Bay; **Musical Director:** Herbert Greene; **Orchestrations:** Don Walker; **Set Design:** Howard Bay; **Vocal Arranger:** Herbert Greene

Songs: Amarillys at the Piano [7]; Blessings [7]; Chicago [7]; Fireworks [2]; Gary, Indiana; Goodnight My Someone [1]; I Found a Horseshoe [2]; If You Don't Mind My Saying So; Iowa Stubborn; It's You; Lida Rose; Marian the Librarian; My White Knight [6]; Piano Lesson; Pick-a-Little, Talk-a-Little; Rasmussin's Law [2]; Rock Island [8]; Sadder-but-Wiser Girl, The; Seventy Six Trombones [1]; Shipoopi; Sincere; Till There Was You [5]; (I've Already Started In) To Try to Figure Out a Way to Go to Work to Try to Get You [3]; Tomorrow [4]; Wells Fargo Wagon, The; Will I Ever Tell You; Ya Got Trouble; You Don't Have to Kiss Me Goodnight [2]

Cast: Buffalo Bills, The; David Burns; Barbara Cook; Eddie Hodges; Pert Kelton; Robert Preston; Helen Raymond; Paul Reed; Iggie Wolfington

Notes: [1] These two songs share the same melody line. [2] Cut. [3] Cut. Used in THE UNSINKABLE MOLLY BROWN. [4] Cut and also cut from THE UNSINKABLE MOLLY BROWN. [5] Original title when a previously written popular song "Till I Met You." [6] Rumor has it (from a semi-reliable source) that Frank Loesser wrote much of this song. In fact, the section that Loesser supposedly wrote is not in the film. [7] ASCAP/Library of Congress only. [8] Originally titled "Rock Island Rock."

3017 • MUSIC MASTER, THE

Notes: One act Musical in IT HAPPENED IN NORDLAND. *See IT HAPPENED IN NORDLAND.*

3018 • MUSIC! MUSIC!

OPENED: 04/11/1974   Theatre: City Center
Revue   Broadway: 37

Librettist: Alan Jay Lerner
Producer: Alvin Bojar; City Center, The
Director: Martin Charnin

Choreographer: Tony Stevens; **Costumes:** Theoni V. Aldredge; **Dance Arranger:** Wally Harper; **Lighting Designer:** Martin Aronstein; **Musical**

Director: John Lesko; **Orchestrations:** Al Cohn; William Elton; Elliot Lawrence; **Set Design:** David Chapman; **Vocal Arranger:** John Lesko

Songs: Abraham, Martin and John (C/L: Dick Holler); Basin Street Blues (C: Spencer Williams); Bess, You Is My Woman Now (C: George Gershwin; L: Ira Gershwin; DuBose Heyward); Bill (C: Jerome Kern; L: Oscar Hammerstein II; P.G. Wodehouse); Brother Can You Spare a Dime? (C: Jay Gorney; L: E.Y. Harburg); Call Me Mister (C/L: Harold Rome); Composers' Song, The [1] (L: Alan Jay Lerner); "Fiddler on the Roof medley" (C: Jerry Bock; L: Sheldon Harnick); "Gershwin Medley" (C: George Gershwin; L: Ira Gershwin); Girl Friend, The (C: Richard Rodgers; L: Lorenz Hart); Great Day (C: Vincent Youmans; L: Edward Eliscu; Billy Rose); "Hello, Dolly! medley" (C/L: Jerry Herman); Hinky Dinky Parlay Voo (C: Julian Dash; Jimmy McHugh; L: Al Dubin; Irving Mills); Hooray for Hollywood (C: Richard A. Whiting; L: E.Y. Harburg); How Ya Gonna Keep 'Em Down on the Farm? (C: Walter Donaldson; L: Sam M. Lewis; Joe Young); I Believe in Music (C/L: Mac Davis); I Didn't Raise My Boy to Be a Soldier (C: Al Piantadosi; L: Alfred Bryan); I Loves You Porgy (C: George Gershwin; L: Ira Gershwin; DuBose Heyward); I'll See You Again (C/L: Noel Coward); In the Mood (C: Joe Garland; L: Andy Razaf); Look for the Silver Lining (C: Jerome Kern; L: B.G. DeSylva); Lucky Lindy (C: Abel Baer; L: L. Wolfe Gilbert); Lullaby of Broadway (C: Harry Warren; L: Al Dubin); Mamam (C: Edward Thomas; L: Martin Charnin); Manhattan (C: Richard Rodgers; L: Lorenz Hart); Merry Widow Waltz, The (C: Franz Lehar); "My Fair Lady medley" (C: Frederick Loewe; L: Alan Jay Lerner); "Oklahoma medley" (C: Richard Rodgers; L: Oscar Hammerstein II); Over There (C/L: George M. Cohan); Stormy Weather (C: Harold Arlen; L: Ted Koehler); Stout Hearted Men (C: Sigmund Romberg; L: Oscar Hammerstein II); There Are Such Things (C: George W. Meyer; L: Stanley Adams; Abel Baer); "West Side Story medley" (C: Leonard Bernstein; L: Stephen Sondheim); When the Saints Go Marching In (C/L: Traditional); White Cliffs of Dover, The (C: Walter Kent; L: Nat Burton); Yankee Doodle Dandy (C/L: George M. Cohan); Yes Sir, That's My Baby (C: Walter Donaldson; L: Gus Kahn)

Cast: Robert Guillaume; Larry Kert; Will Mackenzie; Donna McKechnie; Karen Morrow;

Gail Nelson; Gene Nelson; Ted Pritchard; Arnold Soboloff; Russ Thacker

Notes: Consisted of American music from 1895 to the present. No original songs. [1] No music for this poem.

3019 • MUSICAL CHAIRS
OPENED: 05/18/1980   Theatre: Rialto
Musical   Broadway: 15

Composer: Tom Savage
Lyricist: Tom Savage
Librettist: Barry Berg; Ken Donnelly; Tom Savage
Producer: Lesley Savage; Bert Stratford
Director: Rudy Tronto

Choreographer: Rudy Tronto; **Costumes:** Michael J. Cesario; **Dance Arranger:** Ada Janik; Dick Leib; **Lighting Designer:** Peggy Clark; **Musical Director:** Barry H. Gordon; **Orchestrations:** Ada Janik; Dick Leib; **Set Design:** Ernest Allen Smith; **Vocal Arranger:** Ada Janik; Dick Leib

Songs: Better Than Broadway; Every Time the Music Starts; Hit the Ladies; If I Could Be Beautiful; Musical Chairs; My Time; Other People; Suddenly Love; There You Are Sally; Tonight's the Night; What I Could Have Done Tonight; Who's Who

Cast: Tom Breslin; Edward Earle; Randall Easterbrook; Joy Franz; Ron Holgate; Patti Karr; Grace Keagy; Brandon Maggart; Lee Meredith; Jess Richards

3020 • MUSICAL JUBILEE, A
OPENED: 11/13/1975   Theatre: St. James
Revue   Broadway: 92

Librettist: Max Wilk
Producer: Jonathan Conrow; Theatre Guild, The
Director: Morton Da Costa

Choreographer: Robert Tucker; **Costumes:** Donald Brooks; **Dance Arranger:** Trude Rittman; **Lighting Designer:** Thomas Skelton; **Musical Director:** John Lesko; **Orchestrations:** Elman Anderson; Hershy Kay; Philip J. Lang; **Set Design:** Herbert Senn

Songs: Ain't Misbehavin' (C: Harry Brooks; Thomas "Fats" Waller; L: Andy Razaf); And Her Mother Came Too (C: Ivor Novello; L: Dion Titheradge); At the Moving Picture Ball (C: Joseph Santley; L: Howard Johnson); Battle Hymn of the Republic (C: William Steffe; L: Julia Ward Howe); Best Things in Life Are Free, The (C: Ray Henderson; L: Lew Brown; B.G. DeSylva); Bonnie Blue Flag (C: Henry Macarthy; L: Annie Chambers-Ketchum); Der Shimmy (C: Emmerich Kalman); Fascinating Rhythm (C: George Gershwin; L: Ira Gershwin); Find Me a Primitive Man (C/L: Cole Porter); Gilbert the Filbert (C: Herman Finck; L: Arthur Wimperis); Great Day (C: Vincent Youmans; L: Edward Eliscu; Billy Rose); Gypsy Love (C: Franz Lehar); Hallelujah (C: Vincent Youmans; L: Clifford Grey; Leo Robin); Happy Days (C: Johann Strauss; L: Howard Dietz); Hold On Abraham (C/L: William B. Bradbury); How Jazz Was Born (C: Thomas "Fats" Waller; L: Henry Creamer; Andy Razaf); I Didn't Raise My Boy to Be a Soldier (C: Al Piantadosi; L: Alfred Bryan); I Guess I'll Have to Change My Plan (C: Arthur Schwartz; L: Howard Dietz); I Wanna Be Loved by You (C: Harry Ruby; Herbert Stothart; L: Bert Kalmar); If You Knew Susie (C: Joseph Meyer; L: B.G. DeSylva); I'm in Love with Vienna (C: Johann Strauss); I'm Just Wild About Harry (C: Eubie Blake; L: Noble Sissle); It's a Long, Long Way to Tipperary (C/L: Jack Judge; Harry Williams); I've Got Something (C: Franz Lehar; L: Harry B. Smith; Robert B. Smith); I've Told Every Little Star (C: Jerome Kern; L: Oscar Hammerstein II); Liza (C: George Gershwin; L: Ira Gershwin; Gus Kahn); Lorena (C: J.P. Webster; L: Rev. H.D.L. Webster); Love Me or Leave Me (C: Walter Donaldson; L: Gus Kahn); Lucky Day (C: Ray Henderson; L: Lew Brown; B.G. DeSylva); Lullaby of Broadway (C: Harry Warren; L: Al Dubin); Mademoiselle from Armentieres (C/L: Howard Ross); Me and My Shadow (C: Dave Dreyer; Al Jolson; L: Billy Rose); Miss Annabelle Lee (C: Lew Pollack; Harry Richman; L: Sidney Clare); Moonstruck (C: Ivan Caryll; Lionel Monckton; L: James T. Tanner); Oh, the Women (C: Franz Lehar); Over There (C/L: George M. Cohan); Poor Little Rich Girl (C/L: Noel Coward); 'S Wonderful (C: George Gershwin; L: Ira Gershwin); Serenade (C: Sigmund Romberg; L: Dorothy Donnelly); Skip to My Lou (C/L: Traditional); Something Seems Tingle Ingleing (C: Rudolf Friml; L: Otto Harbach); Sometimes I'm Happy (C: Vincent Youmans; L: Irving Caesar); Song Is You, The (C: Jerome Kern; L: Oscar Hammerstein II); Song of the Vagabonds (C: Rudolf Friml; L: Brian Hooker); Sophisticated Lady (C: Duke Ellington;

L: Irving Mills; Mitchell Parish); Sweet Betsy from Pike (C/L: Traditional); They Didn't Believe Me (C: Jerome Kern; L: Herbert Reynolds); Totem Tom Tom (C: Rudolf Friml; L: Oscar Hammerstein II; Otto Harbach); We're Blase (C: Ord Hamilton; L: Bruce Sievier); Wein, Wein, You're Calling Me (C: Sieczynski); Where or When (C: Richard Rodgers; L: Lorenz Hart); Whoa-Haw (C/L: Traditional); Why Was I Born? (C: Jerome Kern; L: Oscar Hammerstein II); Yankee Doodle Tune; You Are Love (C: Jerome Kern; L: Oscar Hammerstein II); You Go to My Head (C: J. Fred Coots; L: Haven Gillespie)

Cast: Igors Gavon; Lillian Gish; Tammy Grimes; Larry Kert; Patrice Munsel; John Raitt; Cyril Ritchard; Leland Schwantes; Dick Shawn

Notes: Musical Supervision: Lehman Engel. Traditional and popular songs used in this show. No original songs.

3021 • MUTT AND JEFF (1913)
OPENED: 1913
Musical   Closed out of town

Composer: Howard Webster
Lyricist: E.S.S. Hutchinson
Librettist: Bud Fisher; Frank Tannehill Jr.
Producer: Gus Hill
Director: Frank Tannehill Jr.

Source: MUTT AND JEFF (Comic Strip: Bud Fisher)

Songs: For Instance; I Love You; I Was Never Meant for You; I'm a Trout; Just a Little Smile; Moonlight; Pretty Boy; Racing; Spanish Moon; Sweet Land of Dreams; Tale of the Mermaid; When I Dream of You

Notes: Program of 2/23/13.

3022 • MUTT AND JEFF (1922)
OPENED: 1922
Musical

Composer: Leroy Brown; Richard Carroll; Joseph Conoly; T.A. Hammel; Frank Montgomery; Phil Worde
Lyricist: Leroy Brown; Richard Carroll; Joseph Conoly; T.A. Hammel; Frank Montgomery; Phil Worde

Producer: Joseph Conoly; Gus Hill
Director: Richard F. Carroll

Musical Director: Frank Montgomery; Phil Worde;
Orchestrations: Robert W. Ricketts

Songs: Cabaret Entertainers, The; Carolina Sue; Chiquita; Echoes of Jazzland; Good Night Number; Hello, Belmont Park; How Long; Jefferson Jazz Band; Jockey Jamboree, The; My Cavalier; No One Like You; Poor Little Me; Pretty Melody; Shimmy Wedding, The; Sport of Kings, The; Tale of the Mermaid, The; Two Handsome Men; Widow Kiddo; WIld About Rose

Cast: Leroy Brown; Marguerite Lee; Joe Russell; Lillian Russell; Henry Sapara; Ben Williams

Notes: No other information available.

3023 • MUTT AND JEFF AT THE RACES
Musical   Closed out of town

Notes: No program available.

3024 • MUTT AND JEFF DIVORCED
OPENED: 1917
Musical   Closed out of town

Composer: W.C. Henderson
Lyricist: Frank Dumont
Librettist: Gus Gill
Director: Frank Tannehill Jr.

Source: MUTT AND JEFF (Comic Strip: Bud Fisher); **Choreographer:** Ed Hutchinson

Songs: Be Joyful To-day; Can't You Hear Me Calling?; Ciribiribi; Don't Forget Me; Girls!; I Love a Piano; Ideal Girl; I'll Cling to You; Mississippi; Moonbeams; My Wonderful Love for Thee; Oh, La! La!; Scarecrow Dance, The; South Sea Isle; Votes for Women; We Are Nuts

Cast: Rose Kessner; Earl Redding; Katie Rooney; Jerry Sullivan

Notes: Chicago Playbill. Note songs that appear to be interpolations of popular songs of the day.

3025 • MUTT AND JEFF IN CHINATOWN

OPENED: 1920
Musical   Closed out of town

Composer: Harry Collins
Lyricist: Unknown
Librettist: E.J. Carpenter
Director: Richard Carroll

Source: MUTT AND JEFF (Comic Strip: Ham Fisher); **Choreographer:** Bert Angles

Songs: Answer That; Bells and Bells; Dixie; Echoes of Swannee; Frances Dances with Me [1]; Gypsy Rose; Hunting; John Chinamen; Mutt and Jeff in Chinatown; New York Town; Old Town Hall, The; Only One; Study in Black; Theirs; Wee Bit of Scotch, A

Cast: Billy Browning; Madelyn Fisher; Danny McCormack; Miss Minter; Blanche Newcombe; Miss Pickford; Josephine Sabel; Evelyn Vartanian

Notes: No indication of lyricist. Some of these songs appear to be interpolations of popular songs. Notes from 11/1/20 program-Harrisburg, Pa. Miss Pickford and Miss Minter were listed in the chorus. This could be Lotte Pickford and Mary Miles Minter. [1] Might be the popular song "When Frances Dances with Me."

3026 • MUTT AND JEFF IN COLLEGE

OPENED: 1915
Musical   Closed out of town

Composer: Edward Hutchinson
Lyricist: E.S. Hutchinson
Librettist: Junie McCree
Producer: Gus Hill
Director: George Gorman

Source: MUTT AND JEFF (Comic Strip: Bud Fisher); **Choreographer:** Edward Hutchinson; **Musical Director:** Charles K. Hicks

Songs: Charlie Chaplin; College Days; Everyone's a Good American; Everything's Fair When You're in Love; Geography; I Love Them All; I Want to the World to Know I Love You; I'm the Sheriff; It's a Queer Old World; That's What the Little Girl Said; Tinker Tom; When a Maiden Comes to School

Cast: Harry Bartlett; Don Burroughs; Danny McCormack; Gertrude Rudd

Notes: Notes from 9/11/15 program from Wilmington.

3027 • MUTT AND JEFF IN MEXICO

Musical   Closed out of town

Notes: No program available.

3028 • MUTT AND JEFF'S WEDDING

OPENED: 1917
Musical   Closed out of town

Composer: W.H. Smith
Librettist: Frank Dumont
Producer: Gus Hill
Director: Frank Tannehill Jr.

Source: MUTT AND JEFF (Comic Strip: Bud Fisher)

Songs: Be Joyful Today; Bridal Chorus; Building a Bridge to Ireland; Chin-Chin; Don't Forget Me; Health, Wealth and the Girl You Love; Hinkey Dee; I See Everything Beautiful; Isle of Man, The; Laughing Song; Oh, La La; Romany; Some Little Bug Will Get You; Somewhere a Voice Is Calling; Sunshine of Virginia; Swannee River; When I Was Twenty-One; Yaddie Caddie

Cast: Rita Abbott; Gus Alexander; Harry B. Kay; Alden McClaskie; Minnie Palmer; Robert H. Wilson

Notes: Songs of the day are present, I believe — many specialty numbers. No lyricist credited. Program Brooklyn 1/15/17.

3029 • MY ANTOINETTE

OPENED: 1901
Musical   Closed out of town

Composer: Alfred E. Aarons

Notes: A revised version of THE LADIES' PARADISE. See that show also.

3030 • MY AUNT FROM UTAH

OPENED: 1917
Musical   Closed out of town

Composer: Theodore Morse
Lyricist: Howard Johnson
Librettist: Charles Horowitz
Producer: Gus Hill

Cast: Donald Archer; Whitlock Davis; Kate Elinore; Josephine Sabel; Marjorie Sweet; Waldo Whipple

Notes: No songs listed in program. Program 2/3/17.

3031 • MY BEST GIRL

OPENED: 09/12/1912   Theatre: Park
Musical   Broadway: 68

Composer: Augustus Barratt; Clifton Crawford
Lyricist: Clifton Crawford; Rennold Wolf
Librettist: Channing Pollock
Director: Sydney Ellison

Musical Director: Augustus Barratt

Songs: Back to Broadway [3]; Catamaran; Come Take a Dance with Me; Follow Me Around [1] (C/L: Irving Berlin); Howdy-Do; I Can't Do Without the Men; I Do Like Your Eyes (C/L: Clifton Crawford); I Love My Art [2]; If the Morning After Were the Night Before; I'm Smiling at de Moon Dat Smiles at You (L: Channing Pollock; Rennold Wolf); Language of Lover's Smiles, The [2]; Love and the Automobile; Missionary Maids; Mr. Schnoodle; My Best Girl (C/L: Clifton Crawford); Opening Chorus; Regular Army Man; Soft Shoes; That Syncopated Bogie Boo, The [1] (C: George Meyer; L: Sam M. Lewis); Treasure of a Girl, A; When the Henry Clay Comes Steaming into Mobile Bay [1] (C: Jean Schwartz; L: Grant Clarke; William Jerome)

Cast: Clifton Crawford; James O'Neill; Vivien Rogers; Rita Stanwood

Notes: [1] Added after opening. [2] Cut after opening. [3] Out Boston 11/25/12.

3032 • MY BOY FRIEND

OPENED: 12/01/1924
Musical   Closed out of town

Composer: Con Conrad
Lyricist: Harold Christy
Librettist: Jack Lait
Producer: Messrs. Shubert
Director: Frank Smithson

Source: GUS THE BUS (Comic Strip: Jack Lait)

Songs: All Alone in a Crowd; Dancin' on a Dime; Dreamy Araby [1]; Evelyn; Once in a While [1]

Notes: Also known as GUS THE BUS. Parsons Theater, Hartford. [1] May not be from score. May have been a pop song the same year.

3033 • MY CINDERELLA GIRL

OPENED: 1911
Musical   Closed out of town

Composer: William Frederick Peters
Lyricist: Robert N. Baker; Richard Walton Tully
Producer: A.G. Delamater; William Norris
Director: William Norris

Musical Director: Gus Sohlke

Songs: Captain Mutt of the Lemonade Brigade; Get Me Right; I'd Rather Be a Friend of Yours Than Someone Else's Dear; Put the Ball Over the Pan, McCann; Sewash Today; Will All My Dreams Come True; Won't You Let Me Creep Into Your Heart

Cast: Florence Tanner; Frank Woods

Notes: Program Wilkes-Barre 4/8/11.

3034 • MY CUP RUNNETH OVER

OPENED: 06/08/1978   Theatre: Circle Repertory
Play   Off-Broadway: 15

Composer: Henry Krieger
Lyricist: Robert Patrick
Author: Robert Patrick
Producer: Circle Repertory Theatre
Director: Marilyn Baum

Costumes: Menkes; **Lighting Designer:** Gary Seltzer; **Set Design:** Linda Hacker

Notes: No songs listed in program.

3035 • MY DARLIN' AIDA

OPENED: 10/27/1952   Theatre: Winter Garden
Musical   Broadway: 89

Music Based On: Giuseppe Verdi
Composer: Hans Spialek
Lyricist: Charles Friedman
Librettist: Charles Friedman
Producer: Robert L. Joseph
Director: Charles Friedman

Source: AIDA (Opera: Giuseppe Verdi);
  Choreographer: Hanya Holm; **Costumes:**
  Lemuel Ayers; **Lighting Designer:** Hassard
  Short; **Musical Director:** Franz Allers;
  Orchestrations: Hans Spialek; **Set Design:**
  Lemuel Ayers

Songs: Alone; Away; Dance; Gotta Live Free;
  Homecoming; I Don't Want You; I Want to Pray;
  Jamboree; King Called Cotton; Knights of the
  White Cross; Land of Mine; Letter Duet; Love Is
  Trouble; March On for Tennessee; Master and
  Slave; Me and Lee; My Darlin' Aida; Oh, Sky,
  Goodbye; Sing! South! Sing!; Soldier's March;
  Spiritual Ballet; There'll Have to Be Changes
  Made; Three Stones to Stand On; Trail, The;
  When You Grow Up; Why Ain't We Free?; You
  Are My Darlin' Bride; You're False

Cast: Howard Jarratt; Elaine Malbin; William
  Olvis; Dorothy Sarnoff; Kenneth Schon; William
  Wilderman

Notes: Music adapted by Hans Spialek.

3036 • MY DEAR PUBLIC

OPENED: 09/09/1943   Theatre: 46th Street
Revue   Broadway: 44

Librettist: Irving Caesar; Charles Gottesfeld
Producer: Irving Caesar
Director: Edgar MacGregor

Choreographer: Felicia Sorel; **Costumes:** Lucinda
  Ballard; **Musical Director:** Harry Levant;
  Orchestrations: Ted Royal; Hans Spialek; **Set
  Design:** Albert Johnson; **Vocal Arranger:** Clay
  Warnick

Songs: Baroness Bazooka [1] (C/L: Revuers, The [3]);
  Breakfast with Hazel [1]; Buy a Song; Feet on
  the Sidewalk (Head in the Sky) (C: Gerald
  Marks; L: Sam Lerner); Honeymoon of Pancho

Pincus, The [1]; I Love to Sing the Words (While
We're Dancing) (C: Gerald Marks; L: Irving
Caesar; Sam Lerner); If You Want to Make a Deal
with Russia; Last Will and Testament; Laugh It
Off [1] (L: Lothar Metzl; Werner Michel); Little
Gamins; Love Is Such a Cheat (C: Irma
Hollander; Gerald Marks; L: Irving Caesar);
Lulu; May All Our Children Have Rhythm; My
Dear Public; My Spies Tell Me (You Love
Nobody But Me) (C: Gerald Marks; L: Irving
Caesar; Sam Lerner); Now That I'm Free [1]
(C/L: Irving Caesar; Irma Hollander; Sammy
Lerner); Our Private Love Song (C: Sammy
Lerner; L: Irving Caesar); Pipes of Pan
Americana (C: Gerald Marks; L: Irving Caesar);
Rain on the Sea (C: Gerald Marks; L: Irving
Caesar; Sam Lerner); Rhumba Jake; There Ain't
No Color Line Around the Rainbow (C: Gerald
Marks; L: Irving Caesar; Sam Lerner); This Is Our
Private Love Song [4] (C: Gerald Marks; L: Irving
Caesar; Sammy Lerner); Variety [1]; We Had a
Show [1] (C/L: Revuers, The [3])

Cast: Eric Brotherson; David Burns; Nanette
  Fabray; Willie Howard; Ethel Shutta; Georgie
  Tapps; Jesse White

Notes: [1] Cut New Haven prior to opening. [2]
  Cut Boston prior to New York. [3] The Revuers
  were Betty Comden, Adolph Green, Judy
  Holliday, Alvin Hammer and John Frank. [4]
  ASCAP/Library of Congress only. Different
  song than "Our Private Love Song?"

3037 • MY FAIR LADY (1925)
Notes: *See TELL ME MORE!*

3038 • MY FAIR LADY (1956)

OPENED: 03/15/1956   Theatre: Mark Hellinger
Musical   Broadway: 2717

Composer: Frederick Loewe
Lyricist: Alan Jay Lerner
Librettist: Alan Jay Lerner
Producer: Herman Levin
Director: Moss Hart

Source: PYGMALION (Play: George Bernard
  Shaw); **Choreographer:** Hanya Holm; **Costumes:**
  Cecil Beaton; **Dance Arranger:** Trude Rittman;
  Lighting Designer: Feder; **Musical Director:**
  Franz Allers; **Orchestrations:** Robert Russell
  Bennett; Philip J. Lang; **Set Design:** Oliver Smith

Songs: Ascot Gavotte; Decorating Eliza [1]; Embassy Waltz (dance); Get Me to the Church on Time; Hymn to Him, A; I Could Have Danced All Night; I'm an Ordinary Man; I've Grown Accustomed to Her Face; Just You Wait; Oh Come to the Ball [1]; On the Street Where You Live; Rain in Spain, The; Say a Prayer for Me Tonight [2]; Show Me; Why Can't the English?; With a Little Bit of Luck; Without You; Wouldn't It Be Loverly?; You Did It

Cast: Julie Andrews; Philippa Bevans; Robert Coote; Gordon Dilworth; Rex Harrison; Stanley Holloway; John Michael King; Rod McLennan; Cathleen Nesbitt; Reid Shelton

Notes: [1] Cut prior to Broadway. [2] Cut prior to Broadway. Added to film GIGI.

3039 • MY FAVORITE YEAR

OPENED: 12/10/1992   Theatre: Vivian
                                          Beaumont
Musical   Broadway: 37

Composer: Stephen Flaherty
Lyricist: Lynn Ahrens
Librettist: Joseph Dougherty
Producer: Lincoln Center Theater
Director: Ron Lagomarsino

Source: MY FAVORITE YEAR (Film); **Choreographer:** Thommie Walsh; **Costumes:** Patricia Zipprodt; **Dance Arranger:** Wally Harper; **Lighting Designer:** Jules Fisher; **Musical Director:** Ted Sperling; **Orchestrations:** Michael Starobin; **Set Design:** Thomas Lynch

Songs: Clarence Duffy [1]; Comedy Cavalcade Theme Song [1]; Exits; Funny: The Duck Joke; Gospel According to King, The; If the World Were Like the Movies; Larger Than Life; Lights Come Up, The; Manhattan; Maxford House; Monday [1]; Musketeer Sketch, The; Musketeer Sketch Finale, The; Musketeer Sketch Rehearsal, The; My Favorite Year; Naked in the Bethesda Fountain; Pop! Fizz! Happy! [1]; Professional Showbizness Comedy; Rookie in the Ring; Shut Up and Dance; Twenty Million People; Waldorf Suite; Welcome to Brooklyn

Cast: Tim Curry; Lainie Kazan; Tom Mardirosian; Andrea Martin; Josh Mostel; Evan Pappas; Ethan Phillips; Lannyl Stephens

Notes: [1] Cut prior to opening.

3040 • MY FRIEND FROM KENTUCKY (1909)

OPENED: 1909
Musical

Composer: Taylor L. Corwell; J. Homer Tutt; Salem Tutt Whitney
Lyricist: J. Homer Tutt; Salem Tutt Whitney
Librettist: J. Homer Tutt; Salem Tutt Whitney
Producer: J. Homer Tutt; Salem Tutt Whitney

Songs: Come Out, Dear Louise; Dat's Sufficiency; For Honor; Hymn by the Royal Roosters; Man That Rules the Town, The; My Spanish Maid; Pride of Company B; Reminiscing of Dixie; Smile On, Sue; Strutting Sam; Way Back in Dixie Land; Where I Long to Be

Cast: Sam Gardner; Frank Jackson; J. Homer Tutt; Salem Tutt Whitney

Notes: No other information available.

3041 • MY FRIEND FROM KENTUCKY (1913)

OPENED: 1913
Musical

Composer: J. Leubrie Hill
Lyricist: J. Leubrie Hill
Librettist: J. Leubrie Hill
Producer: J. Leubrie Hill

Songs: At the Ball, That's All [1]; Dear Old Dixie; Gay Manhattan Rag; Goodby, Dixieland; Goodtime While I Can; Grand Finale; Happy Time; Has Anybody Seen Jim Jackson?; Lou, My Lou; Man of the Hour, The; My Friend from Kentucky; Night Time Is the Right Time [1]; No Place Like Dixieland; Ragtime Dance (inst.); Rock Me in the Cradle of the Deep [1]; Take Me Away to Jail; That's the Kind of Man I Want; Waiting All Day Long; Waiting at the Depot; What's the Matter with Jasper Green?; You

Cast: Daisy Brown; Sam Gaines; J. Leubrie Hill; Adel Johnson; Edna Morton; Anna Packey

Notes: No other information available. [1] Later in the ZIEGFELD FOLLIES.

3042 • MY GIRL

OPENED: 11/24/1924   Theatre: Vanderbilt
Musical   Broadway: 201

Composer: Harry Archer
Lyricist: Harlan Thompson
Librettist: Harlan Thompson
Producer: Lyle D. Andrews
Director: Walter Brooks

Musical Director: Ernest Cutting; **Set Design:**
P. Dodd Ackerman

Songs: Before the Dawn; Desert Isle; Fellow Like
Me Likes a Girl Like You, A; Fifteen Minutes a
Day; In My Heart [1]; It Never Will Get You a
Thing; Little Place of Your Own, A; Love Sick;
Rainbow of Jazz; Solo on the Drum, A; There
Was a Time They Say; You and I; You Women!

Cast: Russell Mack; Harry Puck; Jane Taylor;
Frances Upton

Notes: [1] Out 11/11/24 Worcester, Mass.

3043 • MY GOLDEN GIRL

OPENED: 02/02/1920   Theatre: Nora Bayes
Musical   Broadway: 105

Composer: Victor Herbert
Lyricist: Frederic Arnold Kummer
Librettist: Frederic Arnold Kummer
Producer: Harry Wardell
Director: J. Clifford Brooke

Choreographer: Julian Alfred; **Musical Director:**
Philip James

Songs: Change Partners; Darby and Joan;
Hobbies [1]; I Want You; I'd Like a Honeymoon
with You; If We Had Met Before; In Venice;
Jaggy-Jazz, The; Little Nest for Two, A; My
Golden Girl; Name the Day; Oh Day in June! [2];
Ragtime Terpsichore; Shooting Star; Song
without (Many) Words, A; Think It Over;
Variety [1]; What Shall We Do If the Moon
Goes Out [1]

Cast: Marie Carroll; Victor Morley; Edna May
Oliver; Ned Sparks

Notes: [1] Out Stamford 12/19/20. [2] In program
but apparently not in show.

3044 • MY GOLDEN WEST

Notes: *See THE LOVE CALL.*

3045 • MY HOME TOWN GIRL

OPENED: 1917
Musical   Closed out of town

Composer: Louis A. Hirsch
Lyricist: Frank Stammers
Librettist: Frank Stammers
Producer: Perry J. Kelly
Director: Frank Stammers

Costumes: Madam Keeler; **Musical Director:**
William Lorraine

Songs: All Alone; Boy of Mine, I Wait for You;
Bride Shop; Fortune Telling Man, The; Games
of Childhood; Hello, Dorothy May; Hello
Dorothy May (There She Goes); I'll Take
You to Your Home Town; I'm Over Here All
Alone; Love Me in the Morning Early; Madame
Marie; My Cigarette; My Home Town; Ode to
Victrola; Perfume of Love; Rag Dance; Ray
Dance (inst.); Show Me 'Round the Town;
Spooky Girl; Take a Little Kiss; There's Always
a Way; Thousands of Girlies (The Reason of
Love); Till You Belong to Me; To-night at Ten;
When I Found You

Cast: John Hyams; Leila McIntyre; Roy Purviance;
Doris Vernon

Notes: Program Toledo 1/9/17.

3046 • MY L.A.

OPENED: 1951
Revue   Closed out of town

Composer: Sammy Fain
Lyricist: Paul Francis Webster
Librettist: Larry Gelbart; William Manhoff;
Laurence Marks
Producer: 764 Californians; Harold Maresch;
William Trenk
Director: William Trenk

Choreographer: Trudi Schoop; **Musical Director:**
Pembroke Davenport; **Orchestrations:** Al
Harris; Frank Marks; Al Woodbury; **Set Design:**
Harry Horner; **Vocal Arranger:** Pembroke
Davenport

Songs: Bit Player Polka; Civic Improvement; Farmers Market Hoe Down; Heaven Help You (When You Fall in Love); In the Red; Native Son; On the Seventh Day He Rested; Our Little Gray Home (in the Red); Something for the Books; That's My L.A.; Trouble with Women Is Men, The; Twist My Arm; You Haven't Lived Until You Die in L.A.

3047 • MY LADY
OPENED: 02/11/1901   Theatre: Victoria
Musical   Broadway: 93

Composer: Edward W. Corliss; Clifton Crawford; H.L. Heartz; Robert G. Morse; D.K. Stevens
Lyricist: R.A. Barnet
Librettist: R.A. Barnet
Producer: A.H. Chamberlyn

Source: THREE MUSKETEERS, THE (Novel: Alexandre Dumas); **Musical Director:** Paul Schindler; **Set Design:** William Gill

Songs: Simple Little Sister Mary Green (C/L: Clifton Crawford)

Cast: Nick Adams; Gilbert Gregory; Charles Simpson; Gus Yorke

Notes: No songs listed in program.

3048 • MY LADY FRIENDS
OPENED: 12/03/1919   Theatre: Comedy
Play   Broadway: 214

Librettist: Frank Mandel; Emil Nyitray
Producer: H.H. Frazee
Director: William Collier; H.H. Frazee

Source: UNKNOWN (Novel: May Edington); **Costumes:** Mme. Louis Cerlian; **Set Design:** Dodge & Castle

Songs: I Want to Spread a Little Sunshine (C/L: Clifton Crawford)

Cast: Clifton Crawford; Robert Fiske; Edith King; Frank Morgan; Paula Shay; June Walker

3049 • MY LADY MOLLY
OPENED: 01/05/1904   Theatre: Daly's
Musical   Broadway: 15

Composer: Sidney Jones
Lyricist: George H. Jessop
Librettist: George H. Jessop
Producer: Charles Frohman
Director: Gilbert Laye

Musical Director: W.P. Brown

Songs: At My Lady's Feet; Ballinasloe; Barn Dance; Don't Whistle So Loud; Hurray for the Field [1]; I Mean to Be a Good Girl Now [1]; Lancers; Merry Medieval Maid (L: Percy Greenbank); My Lady Molly Waltz; Oh! I'll Greet Him; Once Too Often; Opeless Ze State of Me [1]; Seaside Sultan, The; Soft and Low; There's a Little Maid I Know (L: Percy Greenbank); To You Sir Miles [1]

Cast: Richard Carroll; Sydney Deane; Adele Ritchie; Vesta Tilley; David Torrence

Notes: Additional lyrics also credited to C.H. Taylor but not identified in program. [1] London version only.

3050 • MY LADY PEGGY GOES TO TOWN
OPENED: 05/04/1903   Theatre: Daly's
Play   Broadway: 24

Author: Eugene W. Bresbey; Frances Aymar Mathews
Producer: Cecil Spooner

Cast: Walter Hale; Edward Locke; Cecil Spooner; Frank Stanton

3051 • MY LADY'S GLOVE
OPENED: 06/18/1917   Theatre: Lyric
Musical   Broadway: 16

Composer: Sigmund Romberg; Oscar Straus
Lyricist: Edward A. Paulton
Librettist: Edward A. Paulton; Edgar Smith
Producer: Messrs. Shubert
Director: J.C. Huffman

Source: DIE SCHONE SCHWEDIN (Musical: Julius Brammer; Alfred Grunwald; Robert Winterberg); **Choreographer:** Allan K. Foster; **Costumes:** Mme. Kahn; **Musical Director:** Gaetano Merola

Songs: Amorous Rose (C: Oscar Straus); An-ti-ci-pa-tion; Bridal March [1] (C: Oscar

Straus); Charity Bazaar, The [1] (C: Oscar Straus); Daughter of the Regiment [1] (C: Sigmund Romberg); Do Buy Some Candy, Sir; Don't Go Away (C: Sigmund Romberg); Foolish Little Maiden I (C: Sigmund Romberg); I Have a Heart [1] (C: Oscar Straus); I Mean to Be Married as Soon as I Can (C: Oscar Straus); I'll Hate to Leave the Boys; I'm a Rough Man [3] (C: Sigmund Romberg); I'm Madly in Love with a Dream Girl; It's Possible [3] (C: Oscar Straus); I've Been Looking for You [1] (C: Oscar Straus); Keep Repeating It (C: Sigmund Romberg); King of My Heart [1] (C: Oscar Straus); L-O-V-E [1] (C: Oscar Straus); Look Before You Leap (C: Sigmund Romberg); Love Is an Intrusion [1] (C: Sigmund Romberg); Love Is for Youth (Prudence Has Fled) (C: Oscar Straus); Love They Assure Us Is Blind [2] (C: Oscar Straus); No More Girls for Me; Officers of the 125th [1] (C: Sigmund Romberg); Oh, Beautiful Star (Falling Star) [1] (C: Oscar Straus); Secrecy (C: Oscar Straus); Since Today Our Colonel's Mating (C: Oscar Straus); Star, The [1] (C: Oscar Straus); They Laugh and March Away [1] (C: Oscar Straus); Who Are You Beautiful Unknown? [3] (C: Oscar Straus); With Drum and Fife [2] (C: Oscar Straus); Woman's Said to Be the Fickle Sex (C: Sigmund Romberg; Oscar Straus)

Cast: Charles McNaughton; Charles Purcell; Vivienne Segal

Notes: Title THE BEAUTIFUL UNKNOWN out of town where Straus was the principal composer and Paulton was credited with the book. Also Edward P. Temple was the director. [1] Out Philadelphia 3/17. [2] Sheet music only under the title THE BEAUTIFUL UNKNOWN. [3] Out New Haven 1/17.

3052 • MY LADY'S MAID OR LADY MADCAP

OPENED: 09/20/1906   Theatre: Casino
Musical   Broadway: 44

Composer: Paul Rubens
Lyricist: Percy Greenbank; Paul Rubens
Librettist: R.H. Burnside; Edward A. Paulton
Producer: Lee Shubert; Sam S. Shubert
Director: R.H. Burnside

Source: LADY MADCAP (Musical: N. Newnham Davis; Paul Rubens); **Costumes:** Caroline Seidle; **Musical Director:** Clarence West

Songs: All I Want Is You (C: Jerome Kern; L: Paul West); I'd Like to Call You Mine; Don't You Care (C: Harold Orlob; L: Joseph E. Miller); Entrance of Yeomanry; Hard to Understand the Ladies; I Love You in Velvet; It's Lovely When Your Love Loves You (C/L: E. Ray Goetz); I've No Patience with a Soldier; Mum's the Word; My Lady's Maid; Opening Chorus; Primrose; Soldier of My Own, A; They Handed Me a Lemon [1] (C: J. Fred Helf); Way We Have in the Army, A

Cast: Joseph Coyne; Madge Crichton; Della Mason

Notes: [1] Sheet music only.

3053 • MY LITTLE FRIEND

OPENED: 05/19/1913   Theatre: New Amsterdam
Musical   Broadway: 24

Composer: Oscar Straus
Lyricist: Harry B. Smith; Robert B. Smith
Librettist: Harry B. Smith; Robert B. Smith
Producer: Whitney Opera Company
Director: Herbert Gresham

Source: DER KLEINE FREUNDIN (Musical: Leo Stein; Oscar Straus; A.M. Wilner); **Choreographer:** Joseph C. Smith; **Musical Director:** A. DeNovellis

Songs: Love the World Over Is Much the Same; My Little Friend; No Journey's Too Far for a Lover; When I Was Young

Cast: Louis Harrison; Leila Hughes; William Pruette; Fred Walton

Notes: Program did not list songs.

3054 • MY MAGNOLIA

OPENED: 07/12/1926   Theatre: Mansfield
Musical   Broadway: 4

Composer: C. Luckeyth Roberts
Lyricist: Alex Rogers
Librettist: Eddie Hunter
Producer: Walter Campbell
Director: C. Luckeyth Roberts; Alex Rogers

Songs: At Your Service; Baby Mine; Baby Wants; Gallopin' Dominoes; Gee Chee; Hard Times; Headin' South; Laugh Your Blues Away; Merry Christmas; My Magnolia; Oof Dah Man, The;

Our Child; Parade of the Christmas Dinner; Pay Day; Shake Your Duster; Spend It; Struttin' Time; Sundown Serenade; Sweet Popopper

Cast: Paul Bass; Eddie Hunter; Hilda Rogers

3055 • MY MAN GODFREY
OPENED: 1985
Musical   Unproduced

Composer: Gerard Kenny
Lyricist: Alan Jay Lerner

Source: MY MAN GODFREY (Novel: Eric Hatch)

Songs: Dancin' My Blues Away; Garbage; Happy Thanksgiving; It Was You Again; I've Been Married; Miss Hilary Bacon of Beacon Hill; Some People

3056 • MY MARYLAND
OPENED: 09/12/1927   Theatre: Jolson
Musical   Broadway: 312

Composer: Sigmund Romberg
Lyricist: Dorothy Donnelly
Librettist: Dorothy Donnelly
Producer: Messrs. Shubert
Director: J.C. Huffman

Source: BARBARA FRITCHIE (Play: Clyde Fitch); **Choreographer:** Jack Mason; **Set Design:** Watson Barratt

Songs: Bonnie Blue Flag, The; Boys in Gray; Country Dance; Hail Stonewall Jackson; Intermezzo [1]; June Night; Ker-choo!; Mexico; Mocking Bird, The; Mother; Mr. Cupid; Old John Barleycorn; Same Silver Moon, The; Schottische; Something Old, Something New; Song of Victory; Strawberry Jam; Strolling with the One I Love the Best; Won't You Marry Me?; Your Land and My Land

Cast: James Ellis; Evelyn Herbert; Fuller Mellish; Nathaniel Wagner

Notes: [1] Sheet music only.

3057 • MY MIDNIGHT SWEETHEART
OPENED: 1919
Musical

Composer: Joseph E. Howard; I.B. Kornblum
Lyricist: Zeke Meyers

Songs: All I Want from You Is You; Alone with You; Apologize; Eyes of the Girl I Love; I Will Wait; Modern Butterfly; My Midnight Sweetheart; Oh How He Could Plink-A-Plunk; Save It for Me; Shy Little, My Little Girl; Suppose; Sweet Sylvia; Syncopated Wedding; Town Called Might-Have- Been

Notes: No other information available.

3058 • MY MOTHER WAS A FORTUNE TELLER
Notes: *See THE MADWOMAN OF CENTRAL PARK WEST.*

3059 • MY OLD FRIENDS
OPENED: 01/12/1979   Theatre: Orpheum
Musical   Off-Broadway: 154

Composer: Mel Mandel; Norman Sachs
Lyricist: Mel Mandel; Norman Sachs
Librettist: Mel Mandel; Norman Sachs
Producer: Larry Abrams
Director: Philip Rose

Choreographer: Bob Tucker; **Costumes:** George Drew; **Lighting Designer:** Leon Munier; **Set Design:** Leon Munier

Songs: Battle at Eagle Rock (inst.); For Two Minutes; I Bought a Bicycle [1]; I Work with Wood; Little Starch Left, A; Mambo '52; My Old Friends; Oh, My Rose; Only Place for Me, The; Our Time Together [1]; Thank God I'm Not Old; What We Need Around Here; You've Got to Keep Building

Cast: Leslie Barrett; Grace Carney; Sylvia Davis; Brenda Gardner; Norberto Kerner; Fred Morsell; Maxine Sullivan; Allen Swift; Peter Walker; Robert Weil

Notes: [1] From AFTER YOU, MR. HYDE.

3060 • MY ONE AND ONLY
OPENED: 05/01/1983   Theatre: St. James
Musical   Broadway: 767

Composer: George Gershwin
Lyricist: Ira Gershwin

Librettist: Timothy S. Mayer; Peter Stone
Producer: Kenneth-Mark Productions; Francine LeFrak; Paramount Theatre Prods.
Director: Tommy Tune

Choreographer: Tommy Tune; Thommie Walsh; **Costumes:** Rita Ryack; **Dance Arranger:** Wally Harper; Peter Larson; **Lighting Designer:** Marcia Madeira; **Musical Director:** Jack Lee; **Orchestrations:** Michael Gibson; **Set Design:** Adrianne Lobel

Songs: Blah, Blah, Blah; Boy Wanted; Funny Face; He Loves and She Loves; High Hat; How Long Has This Been Going On?; I Can't Be Bothered Now; In the Swim; Just Another Rumba; Kickin' the Clouds Away (L: B.G. DeSylva; Ira Gershwin); My One and Only; Nice Work If You Can Get It; 'S Wonderful; Soon; Strike Up the Band; Sweet and Low-Down; What Are We Here For

Cast: Roscoe Lee Browne; Charles "Honi" Coles; Denny Dillon; Bruce McGill; Tommy Tune; Twiggy

Notes: No original songs.

3061 • MY PEARL MAIDEN

OPENED: 1911
Musical

Songs: As the Years Roll On (C: Melville T. Gideon; L: Edgar Selden)

Notes: No other information available.

3062 • MY PEOPLE

OPENED: 1917
Musical

Composer: C. Luckeyth Roberts
Lyricist: J. Homer Tutt; Salem Tutt Whitney
Librettist: J. Homer Tutt; Salem Tutt Whitney
Producer: J. Homer Tutt; Salem Tutt Whitney

Cast: T.L. Corwell; B. Hillman; J. Homer Tutt; Salem Tutt Whitney

Notes: No other information available.

3063 • MY PRINCESS

OPENED: 10/06/1927   Theatre: Shubert
Musical   Broadway: 20

Composer: Sigmund Romberg
Lyricist: Dorothy Donnelly
Librettist: Dorothy Donnelly
Producer: Alfred E. Aarons
Director: Sam Forrest; J.C. Huffman

Source: UNKNOWN (Play: Edward Sheldon); **Choreographer:** David Bennett; Albertina Rasch; **Costumes:** Charles LeMaire; **Musical Director:** Charles A. Prince; **Set Design:** P. Dodd Ackerman

Songs: Dear Girls, Goodbye; Etiquette Quintette [1]; Eviva; Follow the Sun to the South; Gigolo; Glorioius Chase, The; Help the Drive [1]; Here's How; Hunting Dance, The; I Wonder Why; Kiss the Bride [1]; Moulin Rouge Girls, The; My Mimosa [1]; My Passion Flower; Nobody Rings the Telephone [1]; Opening Act II; Opening Act III; Our Bridal Night; Prince Charming [1]; Springtime on the Avenue [1]; Steppe Sisters, The; Wedding Ensemble; When I Was a Girl Like You

Cast: Luis Alberni; Leonard Creeley; Hope Hampton; Donald Meek

Notes: [1] Out New Haven 8/29/27.

3064 • MY ROMANCE

OPENED: 10/29/1948   Theatre: Shubert
Musical   Broadway: 95

Composer: Sigmund Romberg
Lyricist: Rowland Leigh
Librettist: Rowland Leigh
Producer: Messrs. Shubert
Director: Rowland Leigh

Source: ROMANCE (Play: Edward Sheldon); **Choreographer:** Frederic N. Kelly; **Costumes:** Lou Eisele; **Musical Director:** Roland Fiore; **Orchestrations:** Don Walker; **Set Design:** Watson Barratt

Songs: Aria; Bella Donna; Come Farballe; Debutante; Desire; 1898; Ensemble Song [3]; Entre Nous [2]; Everytime I Dance the Polka [2]; Finale Act II; First Bouquet [2]; Food for Thought [2]; From Now Onward; If Only; In Love with Romance; Laugh at Life [2]; Little Emmaline; Love and Laughter; Love Is New [3]; Magic Moment [2]; Millefleurs; No One's Heart [2]; Paradise Stolen; Polka [1]; Prayer; Romance [2]; Romance with Music [2]; Souvenir; Vision, The [2]; Waltz Interlude; Why [3]; Written in Your Hand; You're Near and Yet So Far [2]

Cast: Lawrence Brooks; Hazel Dawn Jr.; Rex Evans; Luella Gear; Hildegarde Halliday; Anne Jeffreys

Notes: In Chicago the music was credited to Denes Agay and Philip Redowski. [1] Sheet music only. [2] Out Chicago 4/19/48. [3] ASCAP/Library of Congress only.

3065 • MY SWEETHEART

OPENED: 1908
Musical   Closed out of town

Composer: Alfred G. Robyn
Lyricist: Thomas Railey; R.A. Roberts
Producer: R.A. Roberts

Songs: Come, Come, Come; Heart That's Free, A; If You Are Looking for a Sweetheart; I'm Head and Heels in Love with You; It Takes a Drum to Make a Band; My Boardwalk Girl; My Tina Dear; New Coon, A; Opening Chorus; Teeter-Totter

Cast: Helen Byron; Charles Winninger

Notes: From 9/27/08 program Kansas City.

3066 • MY THREE ANGELS

OPENED: 12/02/1985
Musical   Closed out of town

Composer: David Warrack
Lyricist: David Warrack
Librettist: David Warrack
Producer: Warrack Prods.
Director: Heinar Piller

Source: MY THREE ANGELS (Play: Bella Spewack; Sam Spewack); **Choreographer:** Ken Walsh; **Costumes:** Rita Brown; **Lighting Designer:** Stephen Ross; **Musical Director:** Stephen Woodjetts; **Set Design:** Lawrence Schaffer

Songs: Be Young, Young Man; Christmas Eve; Christmas Is Over; He's Dead; Honest Man, An; If Only Someone Like You; It Doesn't Seem a Lot Like Christmas; It's So Clear; Missa Solemnis; Old Book Cooker, The; St. Anthony; Was I Blind; We Got Caught; Where Does One Begin?; You've Been Bitten

Cast: Douglas Chamberlain; Cynthia Dale; Sharon Dyer; Sharon Flett; Eric House; Gerry Salsberg; Tony Van Bridge

Notes: Closed in Toronto, Canada at the Bluma Appel Theatre, St. Lawrence Center.

3067 • MY WIFE AND I

OPENED: 10/10/1966   Theatre: Theatre Four
Musical   Off-Broadway: 14

Composer: Bill Mahoney
Lyricist: Bill Mahoney
Librettist: Bill Mahoney
Producer: Katydid Productions
Director: Tom Ross Prather

Choreographer: Darwin Knight; **Lighting Designer:** Robert Green; **Musical Director:** James Reed Lawlor; **Orchestrations:** James Reed Lawlor; **Set Design:** Robert Green

Songs: Baltimore; Busy, Busy Day; Confusion; Dad Got Girls; Family Tree; I Really Love You; I'll Come By; I'll Try to Smile; It's Pouring; I've Got a Problem; My Wife and I; Pay, Pay, Pay; Please God; Principle of the Thing, The; They've Got to Complain; Why Grow Old?

Cast: Helon Blount; Carol-Leigh Jensen; Ron Leath; Ed Penn

3068 • MY WIFE'S FAMILY

OPENED: 11/05/1906
Play   Closed out of town

Author: Harry Linton; Hal Stephens

Costumes: Arlene Falls

Songs: Accidents Will Happen; Be Sure and See Them All; Ding a Long Dong; Everyone Is in Slumberland but You and Me; Father Wants the Cradle Back; Good Evening, Friends; It Will Keep You Guessing; Life Is Such a Funny Proposition; Merrily, Mary Lee; My Wife's Family; Pair of Trousers, A; Who Said He Couldn't Dance?

Cast: Edward De Noyer; Gladys George; Giles Harrington; Minnie St. Claire

Notes: Program of Wilkes-Barre. Songwriters not identified. These may be interpolated songs —

for example Cohan's "Life's a Funny Proposition After All" was written in 1904 and this show as a song titled "Life Is Such a Funny Proposition."

3069 • MYSTERY MOON

OPENED: 06/23/1930   Theatre: Royale
Musical   Broadway: 1

Composer: Alma Sanders
Lyricist: Monte Carlo
Librettist: Fred Herendeen
Producer: James M. Graf; Paul M. Trebitsch
Director: Victor Morley

Choreographer: Bunny Weldon; **Costumes:** Brooks; **Musical Director:** Ernie Valle; **Orchestrations:** Hilding Anderson, Maurice DePackh; **Set Design:** Theatrical Art Studios

Songs: Clean Out the Corner; If You and I Incorporate; It's All O.K.; Mechanical Man; Milkmaids from Broadway; Mystery Moon; One Night in the Rain; Pepper and Salt; What Could I Do, but Fall in Love with You; You Always Talk of Friendship

Cast: Arthur Campbell; Pauline Dee; Juliana; Kitty Kelly; Charles Lawrence; Nat Nazzarro Jr.; Frances Shelley; Jane Taylor

3070 • MYSTERY OF EDWIN DROOD, THE

OPENED: 12/02/1985   Theatre: Imperial
Musical   Broadway: 608

Composer: Rupert Holmes
Lyricist: Rupert Holmes
Librettist: Rupert Holmes
Producer: Joseph Papp
Director: Wilford Leach

Source: MYSTERY OF EDWIN DROOD, THE (Novel: Charles Dickens); **Choreographer:** Graciela Daniele; **Costumes:** Lindsay W. Davis; **Lighting Designer:** Paul Gallo; **Musical Director:** Michael Starobin; **Orchestrations:** Rupert Holmes; **Set Design:** Bob Shaw

Songs: Both Sides of the Coin; British Subject, A [1]; Ceylon; Don't Quit While You're Ahead; Evensong [1]; Garden Path to Hell, The; I Wouldn't Say No [1]; Jasper's Vision; Man Could Go Quite Mad, A; Moonfall; Name of Love, The; No Good Can Come from Bad; Off to the Races; Perfect Strangers; Sapsea's Song [1]; Setting Up the Score; There You Are; There'll Be England Again [1]; Two Kinsmen; Wages of Sin, The

Cast: Betty Buckley; Patti Cohenour; Jerome Dempsey; Joe Grifasi; John Herrera; Judy Kuhn; Cleo Laine; Rob Marshall; George N. Martin; Howard McGillin; Donna Murphy; George Rose; Jana Schneider

Notes: [1] Only in Central Park engagement prior to Broadway.

N

3071 • NAKED TRUTH, THE
OPENED: 06/1908   Theatre: Fifth Avenue
Musical   Broadway

Librettist: Edward Paulton

Notes: A one-act musical. No other information available.

3072 • NANCY
OPENED: 05/16/1926
Musical   Closed out of town

Composer: Jean Schwartz
Lyricist: William H. Clifford
Librettist: William H. Clifford
Producer: Thomas Wilkes
Director: Dickson Morgan

Songs: And the Moonlight's Calling You; Just a Bunch of Wild Flowers; Loving You; Nancy; Rum-Dum-Dum-Dum

Cast: Nancy Carroll; Nancy Welford

Notes: Mission Theatre, Long Beach. Moved to The Playhouse (Los Angeles) 5/24/26.

3073 • NANCY BROWN
OPENED: 02/16/1903   Theatre: Bijou
Musical   Broadway: 104

Composer: Henry Hadley
Lyricist: Frederick Ranken
Librettist: Frederick Ranken
Producer: Daniel V. Arthur
Director: Frank Smithson

Set Design: Gates & Morange

Songs: American, Oh Girls?; Congo Love Song [3] (C: J. Rosamond Johnson; L: Bob Cole; James Weldon Johnson); Cupid's Ramble; Glow Worm and the Moth, The (C: Max S. Witt; L: Frederick Ranken); I Could Be Happy with Either One [1] (C: Silvio Hein; L: Will A. Heelan); I Jot It Down (Stenographers Song) [2]; I'm Glad I'm Not Methusalem (C/L: Eugene Ellsworth); In Gay Ballyhoo [1]; It's a Most Disagreeable Thing to Do; It's Wasn't a Real One (C: Sayer; L: Jeff T. Branen); June [1]; Just for Me (An Awful Bore) [2]; Katydid, the Cricket and the Frog, The (C: James Weldon Johnson; L: Bob Cole); Little Birdie Told Me, The; Melancholy Marshmallow, The (C: Louis G. Munz; L: Aaron S. Hoffman); Military Band, The; Navajo [1] (C: Egbert Van Alstyne; L: Harry H. Williams); Octette to Bacchus [1]; Red, White and Blue Girl; Royal Crocodile, The (C: Theodore F. Morse; L: Edward Madden); Save It for Me! [2] (C: Bob Cole; L: J. Rosamond Johnson); Soldier Is the Idol of the Nation, The [1]; Strange, Odd, Queer; Two Eyes (C: James Weldon Johnson; L: J. Rosamond Johnson); What's Sauce for the Goose Is Sauce for the Gander [2] (C/L: Anna Marble); Wise Old Owl, A [1] (C: Theodore F. Morse; L: Edward Madden); You Can't Fool All the People All the Time

Cast: George Beban; Marie Cahill; Albert Parr; Edward Stevens

Notes: Kurt Ganzl in his excellent "The Encyclopedia of the Musical Theatre" states that Cole and Johnson interpolated eight songs into this show. [1] Out Ithica, New York 11/21/03. [2] Sheet music only. [3] Bob Cole not credited in sheet music.

3074 • NANTUCKET
OPENED: 1950
Musical   Unproduced

Composer: Vernon Duke
Lyricist: Harold Rome

Songs: Alone (the Whaling Widows); Diddle-daddle; I Knew You Well; Je T'Aime — I Love You; Love Is Like an Elephant; Made in Nantucket; My Heart Decided; Nothing Is Too Good; Pincus et Cie; Song of Our Love (C: Vernon Duke; Harold Rome); There You Are Again; They Never Told Me; Unlucky Pierre;

Whaler's Life, A; Whaler's Return, The; When It's Love; When the Devil Played the Fiddle; You After All These Years

3075 • NASH AT NINE
OPENED: 05/17/1973 Theatre: Helen Hayes
Revue Broadway: 21

Composer: Milton Rosenstock
Lyricist: Ogden Nash
Librettist: Lee Schecter; Barbara Schwei
Director: Martin Charnin

Costumes: Theoni V. Aldredge; **Lighting Designer:** Martin Aronstein; **Musical Director:** Karen Gustafson; **Orchestrations:** John Morris; **Set Design:** David Chapman

Cast: Steve Elmore; Bill Gerber; E.G. Marshall; Richie Schechtman; Virginia Vestoff

Notes: No songs listed in program.

3076 • NATIONAL LAMPOON'S CLASS OF '86
OPENED: 05/22/1986 Theatre: Village Gate
  Downstairs
Revue Off-Broadway: 53

Librettist: John Belushi; Chevy Chase; Stephen Collins; Lance Contrucci; Christopher Guest; Dave Hanson; Andrew Simmons; Matty Simmons; Michael Simmons; Larry Sloman
Producer: Michael Simmons; Jonathan Weiss
Director: Jerry Adler

Choreographer: Nora Brennan; **Costumes:** Nancy Konrardy; **Lighting Designer:** Robert Strohmeier; **Set Design:** Daniel Proett

Songs: Apartheid Lover (C/L: Michael Sansonia; Robert Bond; Paul Guzzone; Stuart Ziff; Jan Kirschner; Brian Brucker O'Connor); Cocaine (C/L: Jim Mentel; Larry Sloman); Don't Drop the Bomb (C/L: Richard Levinson; Will Etra); I've Got It (C/L: Michael Garin); My Bod Is for God (C/L: Jeff Mandel; Phil Proctor); President's Dream, The (C/L: Michael Sansonia); They Lost the Revolution (C/L: Richard Levinson; Michael Sansonia); Ticket, The (C/L: Michael Sansonia); Yuppie Love (C/L: Richard Levinson; Will Etra)

Cast: Rodger Bumpass; Cast, The; Veanne Cox; Annie Golden; John Michael Higgins; Tommy Koenig; Brian Brucker O'Connor

3077 • NATIONAL LAMPOON'S LEMMINGS
OPENED: 01/25/1973 Theatre: Village Gate
Revue Off-Broadway: 350

Composer: Paul Jacobs
Lyricist: John Boni; Sean Kelly; Doug Kenney; P.J. O'Rourke
Librettist: David Axelrod; Cast, The; Tony Hendra; Sean Kelly
Producer: Tony Hendra
Director: Tony Hendra

Lighting Designer: Beverly Emmons; **Musical Director:** Paul Jacobs; **Orchestrations:** Christopher Guest; Tony Hendra; **Vocal Arranger:** Christopher Guest; Tony Hendra

Songs: Colorado (C: Christopher Guest; L: Tony Hendra; Sean Kelly); Highway Toes (C: Christopher Guest; L: Sean Kelly); Lemmings Lament (C: Paul Jacobs; L: Sean Kelly); Lonely at the Bottom (C: Paul Jacobs; L: Sean Kelly); Megadeath (C: Paul Jacobs; L: Sean Kelly); Papa Was a Running Dog Lackey of the Bourgeoisie (C: Paul Jacobs; L: Tony Hendra); Pizza Man (C: Chrisopher Guest; L: Tony Hendra; Sean Kelly); Positively Wall Street (C: Christopher Guest; Paul Jacobs; L: Sean Kelly)

Cast: John Belushi; Chevy Chase; Garry Goodrow; Christopher Guest; Paul Jacobs; Mary-Jennifer Mitchell; Alice Playten

Notes: No songs listed in program.

3078 • NATJA
OPENED: 02/16/1925 Theatre: Knickerbocker
Musical Broadway: 32

Music Based On: Peter Illitch Tchaikowsky
Composer: Karl Hajos
Lyricist: Harry B. Smith
Librettist: Harry B. Smith
Producer: B.C. Whitney; F.C. Whitney
Director: Edgar MacGregor

Costumes: Mme. Freisinger; **Musical Director:** Max Hirschfeld

Songs: Comrade, You Have a Chance Here; Entrance and Song of Czardas; Entrance of Czarinia; Eyes That Haunt Me; Finale Act III; Honor and Glory; Love Calls Me (I Hear Love Call Me); March On; Moonlight and Lace; Music of Moonlight and Love [1]; Opening; Opening Chorus Act II; Reminiscence; Reveille; Shall I Tell Him?; Star of Glory, The; There Is a Garden in Loveland; Ups and Downs; You'll Have to Guess

Cast: Alexander Clark; Madeline Collins; Mary Mellish; George Reimherr

Notes: [1] ASCAP/Library of Congress only.

3079 • NAUGHTY CINDERELLA

OPENED: 11/09/1925   Theatre: Lyceum
Play   Broadway: 125

Author: Avery Hopwood
Producer: Charles Frohman; E. Ray Goetz
Director: W.H. Gilmore

Source: POUCHE (Play: Henri Falk; Rene Peter)

Songs: Do I Love You? (C/L: E. Ray Goetz; Henri Christine); I Love the Moon [1] (C: Paul Rubens; L: E. Ray Goetz); J'ai Deux Amants (C: Andre Messager; L: Sacha Guitry); Mia Luna (C: Giacomo Puccini [2]; L: E. Ray Goetz); She Was So Blue, He Was So Lonely [1] (C/L: Irving Berlin); That Means Nothing to Me (C/L: A.L. Keith; Lee Sterling)

Cast: Irene Bordoni; Orlando Daly; Evelyn Gosnell; Henry Kendall; Nat Pendleton

Notes: [1] Out Washington D.C. 9/28/25. [2] Not Giacomo Puccini.

3080 • NAUGHTY GIRL

Musical   Unproduced

Composer: Christopher Seppe
Lyricist: Scott Hayes; Christopher Seppe
Librettist: Scott Hayes
Director: Bill Gile

Lighting Designer: Scott Scheidt; Richard Weick; **Musical Director:** Jan Rosenberg

Songs: All of It All; Debutantes; Do You?; Doomed; Double Step Drag, The; Naughty Girl; Nobody Else but You; Now That I Know; One-I-Want-Doesn't-Want-Me Blues, The; Pretty Babies; Race Sequence; Riding on a High Horse; Waiting in the Wings

Cast: George Lee Andrews; June Gable; Christopher Seppe; Richard B. Shull

Notes: Program of a reading at the THEATRE OFF PARK, NY.

3081 • NAUGHTY MARIETTA

OPENED: 11/07/1910   Theatre: New York
Musical   Broadway: 136

Composer: Victor Herbert
Lyricist: Rida Johnson Young
Librettist: Rida Johnson Young
Producer: Oscar Hammerstein I
Director: Jacques Coini

Choreographer: Pauline Verhoeven; **Costumes:** Will R. Barnes; **Musical Director:** Gaetano Merola; **Orchestrations:** Victor Herbert; **Set Design:** Julius Dowe; Theodore Reisig

Songs: Act I Finale; Ah! Sweet Mystery of Life (Dream Melody); All I Crave Is More of Life; Come, Come, Come/Convent Maids; Dance of the Marionettes; Gambling; Governor's Entrance [1]; If I Were Anybody Else but Me; I'm Falling in Love with Someone; Intermezzo; It Never, Never Can Be Love; Italian Street Song; It's Pretty Soft for Simon; Live for Today; Loves of New Orleans; Mr. Voodoo [1]; Mysterious Melody; Naughty Marietta; 'Neath the Southern Moon; New Orleans Jeunesse Doree; Opening of the Ball; Prelude to Live for Today; Song from the Fountain; Sweet By and By; Taisez-Vous; Tramp! Tramp! Tramp!; We've Hunted the Wolf in the Forest [2]; You Marry a Marionette

Cast: Harry Cooper; Orville Harrold; Edward Martindel; Emma Trentini

Notes: [1] Cut prior to opening. [2] ASCAP/Library of Congress only.

3082 • NAUGHTY-NAUGHT '00

OPENED: 01/23/1937   Theatre: American Music
                      Hall
Musical   Off-Broadway: 173

Composer: Richard Lewine
Lyricist: Ted Fetter
Librettist: John Van Antwerp[2]
Producer: Jerrold Krimsky; John Krimsky
Director: Morgan Lewis

Costumes: Eaves; **Musical Director:** Howard Johnson; **Set Design:** Eugene Dunkel

Songs: Coney by the Sea; Goodbye Girls, Hello Yale; Just Like a Woman [1]; Love Makes the World Go Round; Mother Isn't Getting Any Younger [1]; Naughty-Naught; Pull the Boat for Eli; What's Good About Good Morning [1]; When We're in Love [1]; Zim Zam Zee

Cast: Alexander Clark; Barbara Hunter; Leslie Litomy; Harry Meehan; Eleanor Phelps; Bartlett Robinson

Notes: [1] Added to 1946 revival. [2] Pseudonym for Jerrold Krimsky.

3083 • NAUGHTY PRINCESS, THE
OPENED: 09/25/1917   Theatre: Palace
Musical

Composer: William B. Friedlander
Librettist: Will M. Hough

Notes: No other information available.

3084 • NAUGHTY RIQUETTE
OPENED: 09/13/1926   Theatre: Cosmopolitan
Musical   Broadway: 88

Composer: Oscar Straus
Lyricist: Harry B. Smith
Librettist: Harry B. Smith
Producer: Messrs. Shubert
Director: Fred G. Latham

Source: RIQUETTE (Musical: Rudolf Schanzer; Oscar Straus; Ernst Welisch); **Choreographer:** Seymour Felix; **Set Design:** Watson Barratt

Songs: Alcazar; Brother of Mine [2]; He May Say 'Yes' Today [1]; I May (C: Kendall Burgess; Maurie Rubens); In Armenia; Letter of Farewell, A [1]; Make Believe You're Mine; Me; Naughty Riquette (C: Kendall Burgess; Maurie Rubens); Opening Ensemble; Plant Roses in Memory's Garden [1]; Somehow I'd Rather Be Good;

Someone (C: Alfred Goodman; Maurie Rubens); Two Are Company; Wait a Bit [1]; What Great Men Cannot Do (C: R.P. Weston; L: Bert Lee); You've Got to Be an Acrobat [1]

Cast: Alexander Gray; Stanley Lupino; Audrey Maple; Mitzi

Notes: [1] Out Baltimore 12/14/25. [2] ASCAP/Library of Congress only.

3085 • NEARLY A HERO
OPENED: 02/24/1908   Theatre: Casino
Musical   Broadway: 116

Composer: Seymour Furth
Lyricist: Edward B. Claypoole; Will Heelan
Librettist: Harry B. Smith
Producer: Lee Shubert; Sam S. Shubert
Director: J.C. Huffman; George Marion

Choreographer: William Rock; **Set Design:** Arthur Voegtlin

Songs: After Office Hours; Bridge; Don't You Ever Tell I Told You; Drawing Lesson, The; I Don't Want to Marry You (L: Edward B. Claypoole); I Get a Lonesome Feeling [1] (C/L: Mignon Ziegfeld); I Want a Steam Yacht; I Was a Hero (C: Egbert Van Alstyne; L: Harry Williams); I Wish I Was a Hero Too [2] (C: Egbert Van Alstyne; L: Harry Williams); I'm So Particular; Mary My Hearther Queen [1] (C: Louis A. Hirsch; L: John B. Lowitz); My Sahara Girl (L: Edward B. Claypoole); Not Really; Queen of Belle Parce, The; Singer Sang a Song, A; Stitch, Stitch; Walking Tour, The; Waltz and Two-Step; When the Band Plays 'Home Sweet Home' (L: Seymour Furth)

Cast: Sam Bernard; Elizabeth Brice; Ethel Levey; Edgar Norton; Zelda Sears

Notes: [1] Sheet music only. [2] ASCAP/Library of Congress only.

3086 • NED WAYBURN'S GAMBOLS
OPENED: 01/15/1929   Theatre: Knickerbocker
Revue   Broadway: 31

Composer: Walter G. Samuels
Lyricist: Morrie Ryskind

Librettist: Emmet Crozier; Roger Gray; George Haight Jr.; Lew Hearn; Morrie Ryskind; Gus Weinberg
Producer: Ned Wayburn
Director: Ned Wayburn

Set Design: Ted Weidhaus

Songs: Church Around the Corner, The; Crescent Moon; Gypsy Days (C: Arthur Schwartz); I Bring My Boys Along (L: Clifford Gray); In the Days Gone By; Indian Prayer; Little Dream That's Coming True [1]; March Gypsys; Mothers O' Men; Palm Beach Walk, The; Ride 'Em Cowboys (C: Arthur Schwartz; L: Clifford Grey); Savannah Stomp; Ship of Love [1]; Sun Will Shine, The (C: Arthur Schwartz); Sweet Old Fashioned Waltz; There Ain't No Sweet Man That's Worth the Salt [1] (C/L: Fred Fisher); What Is the Good? (C: Lew Kessler; L: Clifford Grey)

Cast: Lew Hearn; William Holbrook; Libby Holman; Charles Irwin; Fuzzy Knight

Notes: [1] Not in programs.

3087 • NED WAYBURN'S TOWN TOPICS
OPENED: 09/23/1915   Theatre: Century
Revue   Broadway: 68

Composer: Harold Orlob
Lyricist: Thomas J. Gray; Robert B. Smith
Librettist: Thomas Gray; Harry B. Smith; Robert B. Smith
Producer: Ned Wayburn
Director: Benrimo; Ned Wayburn

Choreographer: Allan K. Foster; **Costumes:** Cora MacGeachy; **Musical Director:** Hilding Anderson; **Orchestrations:** Frank Saddler

Songs: All Full of Ginger (L: Thomas J. Gray); Barcarole; Brazilian Nut; Cotton-Blossom Serenade (L: Thomas Gray); Dance of Bewilderment; Dance of Joy; Heap Big Suffragette; I Want Someone Who's Lonesome; I Wonder Who She Spoons with Now; Idol of Eyes, The (L: Robert B. Smith); I'll Get You Yet Cigarette (L: Thomas J. Gray); I'll Keep the Roses Blooming for You; In Time of Peace Prepare for War (L: Robert B. Smith); It's the Gown that Makes the Girl; Keystone Glide, The (L: Thomas J. Gray);

Marionettes (L: Frank M. Stammers); Melody of the Century (L: Thomas J. Gray); Midsummer Waltz; Old Are Getting Younger Every Day, The (L: Robert B. Smith); Old-Fashioned Groom and an Up-To-Date Bride, An (L: Robert B. Smith); Oskaloosa Pets, The (L: Robert B. Smith); Paprica; Plaza and Astor, The [1] (L: Robert B. Smith); Put It Over (L: Robert B. Smith); Red Fox Trot, The; Riff-Raff-Rafferty (L: Robert B. Smith); Subway Love; Take It from Me (L: Robert B. Smith); Town Topics; Wake Up! It's Cake-Walk Day (L: Thomas J. Gray); Walking on the Lake; What a Beautiful Baby You Are; What You Are and What You Want to Be; You Have Got the Style (L: Thomas J. Gray)

Cast: Adelaide and Hughes; Wellington Cross; Trixie Friganza; Lew Hearn; Bert Leslie; Vera Michelena; Will Rogers; Blossom Seeley; Clifton Webb

Notes: The lyricists did not collaborate. They are credited where known. [1] In vocal score only.

3088 • NEFERTITI
OPENED: 09/20/1977
Musical   Closed out of town

Composer: David Spangler
Lyricist: Christopher Gore
Librettist: Christopher Gore
Producer: Sherwin M. Goldman
Director: Jack O'Brien

Choreographer: Daniel Lewis; **Conductor:** Robert Billig; **Costumes:** Sam Kirkpatrick; **Dance Arranger:** Wally Harper; **Lighting Designer:** Gilbert V. Hemsley Jr.; **Musical Director:** John DeMain; **Orchestrations:** Robert M. Freedman; **Set Design:** Sam Kirkpatrick

Songs: Another Free Translation; Beautiful Has Come; Breakfast at Thebes; Brothers; Diary of a Dying Princess, The; Dinner at Thebes; Egypt Is Egypt Again; Everything Is Possible; Father; Forevermore; Free Translation, A; It Happens Very Softly; Lama Su Apapi; Legions; Legions of the Night; Light Will Shine; New World, The; Nothing Ever Dies; Pardon Me a Minute; Penmut's Apology; Please Continue; Soldier; Someone Was Here; Take Off the Sandal; Tiy's Song: Fear Is a Faraway Country; Under the Sun; Welcome to the Army (Brotherhood of Light); Whatever Happened to Me

Cast: Marilyn Cooper; Robert LuPone; Andrea
Marcovicci; Michael Nouri; Jane White

Notes: Closed in Chicago 10/27/77.

3089 • NEGRO NUANCES

OPENED: 1924
Revue

Composer: Will Marion Cook; James P. Johnson
Lyricist: Will Marion Cook
Librettist: Aubrey L. Lyles; Flournoy E. Miller;
Abbie Mitchell
Producer: Will Marion Cook

Musical Director: James P. Johnson

Cast: Louis Douglass; Lucille Handy; Aubrey L.
Lyles; Flournoy E. Miller; Abbie Mitchell

Notes: No other information available.

3090 • NELL GO IN

OPENED: 10/31/1900   Theatre: New York
Musical   Broadway

Composer: A. Baldwin Sloane
Lyricist: George V. Hobart
Librettist: George V. Hobart

Notes: A one-act musical.

3091 • NELLIE BLY

OPENED: 01/21/1946   Theatre: Adelphi
Musical   Broadway: 16

Composer: James Van Heusen
Lyricist: Johnny Burke
Producer: Eddie Cantor; Nat Karson
Director: Nat Karson

Choreographer: Edward Caton; Lee Sherman;
Musical Director: Charles Drury;
Orchestrations: Elliot Jacoby; Ted Royal, **Set
Design:** Nat Karson

Songs: Aladdin's Daughter; All Around the World;
Can Can [2]; Choral Russe; Divertissement [1];
Fogarty and Mandolin Girls [2]; Fogarty and
Nellie Bly Parade [2]; Fogarty the Great;
Harmony; Hong Kong to Hoboken [1]; How

About a Date?; I Did It for the Missus [1]; It's a
Gentlemen's World [2]; It's Your Life [3]; I've
Got to Get Somewhere with You [1]; Just My
Luck; Less Than Eighty Days [1]; L'Exposition
Universalle; May the Best Man Win; Minute
Maid [3]; Nellie Bly; No News Today; Only for
Men [2]; Promenade [2]; Sky High; Start
Dancing; That's Class; There's Nothing Like
Travel; Very Silly Story, A [1]; Wake Up Song, A
[3]; When a Fellow Gets to Thinking [1]; Why Do
I Like You? [3]; You May Not Love Me; You
Never Saw That Before

Cast: William Gaxton; Joy Hodges; Marilyn
Maxwell; Victor Moore; Benay Venuta;
Puppeteer: Bil Baird; Cora Baird

Notes: [1] Out 10/12/45. [2] Cut. [3]
ASCAP/Library of Congress only.

3092 • NELLY NEIL

OPENED: 01/10/1907   Theatre: Aldwych
Musical   London: 107

Composer: Ivan Caryll
Lyricist: C.M.S. McLellan
Librettist: C.M.S. McLellan
Producer: Charles Frohman
Director: Sydney Ellison

Costumes: Percy Anderson; **Musical Director:**
W.T. Francis; **Set Design:** Hugo Baruch; W.
Helmsley; Walter Johnstone

Songs: Back, Back, Back to the Land!; Boo! Boo!
Boo-oo!; Butterfly, The; Cigarette Song, A;
Dainty Tizzle Twins, The; Girls, Be Girls for
Ever; Good Morning, Nelly Neil!; I'm Sorry, I'm
Sure, To Intrude; Just Something Pretty; Little
Smith Minor; Military Touch, The; Millennium,
The; Now, Now, Now; Oh, My Heart Has
Awakened Again; Oh, What Does Mr. Baedeker
Say; Our Teacher Says "Be Mild, My Child";
Poor Bobby!; Riding in the Choo-Choos; Such a
Bore; Take the Road; There's a Man in a
Motor-Car; Try My Way; We Presume You Have
Come for the Succulent Plum; What's the Use of
Going to Bed?

Cast: Joseph Coyne; E. Dagnall; Kitty Gordon;
Langford Kirby; Edna May

Notes: No program available.

3093 • NEPTUNE'S DAUGHTER

OPENED: 11/28/1906   Theatre: Hippodrome
Revue   Broadway: 288

Composer: Manuel Klein
Lyricist: Manuel Klein; Edward P. Temple
Librettist: Manuel Klein; Edward P. Temple
Director: Edward P. Temple

Choreographer: Vincenzo Romeo; **Costumes:**
Mme. Castel-Bert; Alfredo Edel; Frances
Ziebarth; **Set Design:** Arthur Voegtlin

Cast: Sam Baker; Edwin A. Clarke; W.H. Clarke; J.
Parker Coombs; Harry Dale; Rose La Harte;
Marceline; Vincent Romeo Jr.; John G. Sparks;
Margaret Townsend

Notes: The first part of this bill was PIONEER
DAYS. *See also under that title.* The second part
of this bill was CIRCUS EVENTS. The famous
Hippodrome water effect in which the female
chorus disappeared into the Hippodrome "lake"
first was presented in this production. It was
invented by H.L. Bowdoin.

3094 • NERVOUS SET, THE

OPENED: 05/12/1959   Theatre: Henry Miller's
Musical   Broadway: 23

Composer: Tommy Wolf
Lyricist: Fran Landesman
Librettist: Theodore J. Flicker; Jay Landesman
Producer: Robert Lantz
Director: Theodore J. Flicker

Source: NERVOUS SET, THE (Novel: Jay
Landesman); **Costumes:** Theoni V. Aldredge;
Lighting Designer: Paul Morrison; **Musical
Director:** Tommy Wolf; **Set Design:** Paul
Morrison; **Vocal Arranger:** Tommy Wolf

Songs: Apples in the Lilac Tree [1]; Ballad of the
Sad Young Men; Country Gentleman, A; Fun
Life; How Do You Like Your Love?; If I Could
Put You in a Song [1]; It's Nice Weather for
Ducks [1]; I've Got a Lot to Learn About Life;
Laugh, I Thought I'd Die; Man, We're Beat; Max
the Millionaire; New York (New York Con-
fidential); Night People; Night Remembers [1];
Party Song; Pas de Deux (Choreography)
(dance); Pitch for Pot [1]; Rejection [1]; Season in
the Sun [1]; Spring Can Really Hang You Up the
Most [1]; Stars Have Blown My Way; Tell Me

Lies [1]; Travel the Road of Love; What's to Lose;
You Can't Go Home Again [1]

Cast: Thomas Aldredge; Del Close; Larry Hagman;
Richard Hayes; Gerald Hiken; Tani Seitz

Notes: [1] Not used.

3095 • NEVER GO THERE ANYMORE

Notes: *See KELLY.*

3096 • NEVER HOMES, THE

OPENED: 10/05/1911   Theatre: Broadway
Musical   Broadway: 92

Composer: Raymond Hubbell
Lyricist: E. Ray Goetz
Librettist: Glen MacDonough
Producer: Lew Fields
Director: J.C. Huffman; Ned Wayburn; William J.
Wilson

Orchestrations: Hilding Anderson

Songs: Baseball Girl, The; Fire Belles; Fire Ladies'
Ball, The; First Love Days (C: A. Baldwin
Sloane); Good Morning Judge; Here We Are
Scrubbing; I'm All for You; In the Shadows
(C: Herman Finck); Just a Little Bit of Lingerie;
Kiss Burglar, The (C: A. Baldwin Sloane); Post
Card Beau, A; Take Me Along with You Dearie
(C: A. Baldwin Sloane); That Spooky Tune
(C: A. Baldwin Sloane); There's a Girl in Havana
[1] (C/L: Irving Berlin; E. Ray Goetz); Tonight's
the Night (C: A. Baldwin Sloane)

Cast: Bessie Clifford; Jess Dandy; Helen Hayes;
George Monroe; Joseph Santley

Notes: [1] Although credited to Sloane and Goetz,
it was actually written by Berlin.

3097 • NEVER TOO LATE

OPENED: 11/27/1962   Theatre: Playhouse
Play   Broadway: 1007

Author: Sumner Arthur Long
Producer: Daniel Hollywood; Elliot Martin
Director: George Abbott

Costumes: Florence Klotz; Incidental Music: John
Kander; **Lighting Designer:** Jean Eckart;

William Eckart; **Set Design:** Jean Eckart; William Eckart

Songs: Never Too Late Cha-Cha-Cha (C: Jerry Bock; L: Sheldon Harnick)

Cast: John Alexander; Orson Bean; Paul Ford; House Jameson; Maureen O'Sullivan

3098 • NEW ALADDIN, THE
OPENED: 09/1906   Theatre: Gaiety
Musical   London: 203

Composer: Ivan Caryll
Lyricist: Adrian Ross
Librettist: W H Risque; James T Tanner
Producer: George Edwardes

Choreographer: Harry Grattan; **Costumes:** Wilhelm; **Musical Director:** Ivan Caryll; **Set Design:** Hawes Craven; Joseph Harker; Phil Harker

Songs: Cadi, The (C: Frank E. Tours; L: Percy Greenbank); Dougal (C/L: Gerald Grafton); Down Where the Vegetables Grow (C: Lionel Monckton; L: Leslie Mayne; Adrian Ross); Dream of You, The; English Language, The; Finale Act I; Finale Act II; Gallic Cock, The (C: Frank E. Tours; L: W.H. Risque); Grandmamma (C: Lionel Monckton); I Don't Want Much (L: Percy Greenbank); I Want to Be a Mortal (C: Frank E. Tours; L: Percy Greenbank); I'm Lally (C: Frank E. Tours); In London; Lamp, The; Miniature Girl, The (C: Lionel Monckton; L: Percy Greenbank); No-Hat Brigade, The (C: Ivan Caryll; Lionel Monckton; L: George Grossmith Jr.); Oh, Pan! (L: W.H. Risque); Old Companions (L: George Grossmith Jr.); On the Strand; Opening Chorus Scene 2 (C: Frank E. Tours; L: Percy Greenbank); Please Don't Go (L: Percy Greenbank); Rub the Lamp (L: George Grossmith Jr.); Rubbing Our Eyes in Surprise (Opening Chorus Act II) (C: Lionel Monckton; L: Percy Greenbank); Smart Set, The (L: George Grossmith Jr.); Sur La Plage (L: George Grossmith Jr.); Three Big Hands (L: George Grossmith Jr.); We're Taking a Trip (L: W.H. Risque); Who Would Be a Boy (C: Frank E. Tours; L: W.H. Risque)

Cast: Adrienne Augarde; Gaby Deslys; Connie Ediss; George Grossmith Jr.; Gertie Millar; Robert Nainby; Edmund Payne

Notes: Reopened in a revised version on 11/24/06. The run above is for both versions. No program available.

3099 • NEW AMERICANA
Notes: *See AMERICANA (1932).*

3100 • NEW AQUACADE REVUE, THE
OPENED: 1940
Revue   N.Y. World's Fair

Composer: James Van Heusen
Lyricist: Joseph McCarthy; Billy Rose
Librettist: Billy Rose
Director: John Murray Anderson

Choreographer: Gae Foster; **Costumes:** Raoul Pene du Bois; **Lighting Designer:** John Murray Anderson; **Musical Director:** Vincent Lopez; **Orchestrations:** Hawley Ades; **Set Design:** Raoul Pene du Bois; **Vocal Arranger:** Roy Ringwald

Songs: Eleanor, I Adore You; Le Can Can; There's a New Gang on the Way; When the Spirit Moves Me; You Think of Everything

Cast: Buster Crabbe; Eleanor Holm; Everett Marshall; Fred Waring Glee Club

Notes: *Also see AQUACADE REVUE and BILLY ROSE'S AQUACADE REVUE.*

3101 • NEW CHARLOT SHOW, THE
Notes: *See EARL CARROL'S VANITIES FEATURING THE NEW CHARLOT SHOW.*

3102 • NEW DICTATOR, THE
Notes: *See THE GIRL FROM HOME.*

3103 • NEW FACES (1934)
OPENED: 03/15/1934   Theatre: Fulton
Revue   Broadway: 148

Librettist: John Goodwin; William Griffith; Nancy Hamilton; Newman Levy; Mindret Lord; Viola Brothers Shore; Beth Wendall
Producer: Charles Dillingham
Director: Elsie Janis

Costumes: Sergei Soudeikine; **Musical Director:** Gus Salzer; **Orchestrations:** Hans Spialek; **Set Design:** Sergei Soudeikine

Songs: Byrd Influence, The (C: Warburton Guilbert; L: Nancy Hamilton; June Sillman); 'Cause You Won't Play House (C: Morgan Lewis; L: Nancy Hamilton; E.Y. Harburg); Emperor Jones (C: Donald Honrath; L: George Grande; June Sillman); Frustration (C: Morgan Lewis); Gangster Influence, The (C: Warburton Guilbert; L: Viola Brothers Shore; June Sillman); Gloom Heaven (C: Walter Feldkamp; L: Harold Goldman); Gutter Song, The (C/L: James Shelton); Harlequinade (C: Donald Honrath); He Loves Me (C: Cliff Allen; L: Nancy Hamilton); It's High Time I Got the Low Down on You [1] (C: Joseph Meyer; L: Edward Heyman); Lamplight (C/L: James Shelton); Look at Me Please (C/L: James Shelton); Love Is a Dancer [1] (C: Muriel Pollock; L: Jean Southern); Modern Madrigal (C: Warburton Guilbert; L: Viola Brothers Shore; June Sillman); Music in My Heart (C: Warburton Guilbert; L: June Sillman); My Last Affair (C/L: Haven Johnson); My Love Is Young [1] (C: Robert Graham; L: Bickley Reichner); New Faces (C: Martha Caples; L: Nancy Hamilton); On the Other Hand (C: Martha Caples; L: Nancy Hamilton); People of Taste (C: Martha Caples; L: Nancy Hamilton); Service with a Smile (C: Warburton Guilbert; L: Viola Brothers Shore); So Low (C: Donald Honrath; L: Nancy Hamilton; June Sillman); Something You Lack (C: Warburton Guilbert; L: Nancy Hamilton; June Sillman); Spring Song (C: Warburton Guilbert; L: Nancy Hamilton; Viola Brothers Shore); Sweet Rhythm (C/L: George Hickman); Tonight's the Night [1] (C: Alex Fogarty; L: June Sillman); Village Gossip, The (C: Sandra Corona; L: J.J. Robins); Visitors Ashore (C: Warburton Guilbert; L: Nancy Hamilton; Everett Marcy); You Better Go Now [1] (C: Robert Graham; L: Bickley Reichner); You're My Relaxation (C: Charles Schwab; L: Robert Sour); Your Face Is So Familiar [1] (C: Alex Fogarty; L: Edwin Gilbert)

Cast: Cliff Allen; Imogene Coca; Frances Dewey; Henry Fonda; Hildegarde Halliday; Nancy Hamilton; Alan Handley; Dolores Hart; Billie Haywood; Dorothy Kennedy-Fox; Louise Teddy Lynch; Helen O'Hara; Gordon Orme; Melvin Parks; Gus Schirmer; James Shelton; Edith Sheridan; Leonard Sillman; Roger Stearns; Mildred Todd; Charles Walters; O.Z. Whitehead

Notes: This was a revised version of LOW AND BEHOLD. [1] Sheet music only. Also in NEW FACES OF 1936.

3104 • NEW FACES OF 1936

OPENED: 05/19/1936   Theatre: Vanderbilt
Revue   Broadway: 192

Librettist: Joseph Alger; Homer Fickett; Edwin Gilbert; Irvin Graham; Mort Lewis; Mindret Lord; Everett Marcy; Edwin Meiss; Leonard Sillman
Producer: Leonard Sillman
Director: Anton Bundsmann; Leonard Sillman

Choreographer: Ned McGurn; **Costumes:** Stewart Chaney; **Lighting Designer:** Feder; **Musical Director:** Ray Kavanaugh; **Orchestrations:** David Raksin; Hans Spialek; **Set Design:** Stewart Chaney

Songs: Chi-Chi [2] (C: Irvin Graham; L: June Sillman); Do-Nuts [1] (C: Reverand Hines Rubel [3]; L: June Sillman); Give Me a Song I Can Whistle (C: Alex Fogarty; L: June Sillman); I Was a Gyp in Egypt (C: Bud Harris; L: Lawrence Harris); Introduction (C: Martha Caples; L: Nancy Hamilton); It's High Time I Got the Low-Down [5] (C: Joseph Meyer; L: Edward Heyman); Lottie of the Literati (C: Alex Fogarty; L: Edwin Gilbert); Love Is a Dancer [4] (C: Muriel Pollock; L: Jean Sothern); My Love Is Young (C: Irvin Graham; L: Bickley Reichner); New Faces (C: Alex Fogarty; L: Edwin Gilbert); Off to the Deacon (C: Robert Sour; L: June Sillman); Slap My Face (C: Alex Fogarty; L: Edwin Gilbert); There Is a Santa Claus (C: Irvin Graham; L: Bickley Reichner); Tonight's the Night (C: Alex Fogarty; L: June Sillman); Too Too Too [1] (C: Irvin Graham; L: Everett Marcy); Two Queens (C: Harold Duncan); You'd Better Go Now [4] (C: Irvin Graham; L: Bickley Reichner); Your Face Is So Familiar (C: Alex Fogarty; L: Edwin Gilbert)

Cast: Cliff Allen; Robert Bard; Jack Blair; June Blair; Ralph Blane; George Byron; Imogene Coca; Helen Craig; Rose Dexter; Billie Haywood; Bobby Johnson; Stretch Johnson; Van Johnson; Winnie Johnson; Marion Martin; Kathryn Mayfield; Nancy Noland; Marsha Norman; Melvin Parks; Marion Pearce; Gerry Probst; Gloria Rondell; Tom Rutherford; Jack Smart; Karl Swenson

Notes: [1] Added after opening. [2] Originally titled "We Shriek of Chic." [3] A pseudonym of Hal Raynor. [4] Also in NEW FACES. [5] Written for NEW FACES OF 1934 but not used.

3105 • NEW FACES OF 1943

OPENED: 12/22/1942   Theatre: Ritz
Revue   Broadway: 94

Librettist: June Carroll; John Lund; J.B. Rosenberg
Producer: June Sillman
Director: Lawrence Hurdle

Choreographer: Charles Weidman; John Wray; **Costumes:** Edward Gilbert; **Lighting Designer:** Carlton Winkler; **Musical Director:** Lee Wainer; **Set Design:** Edward Gilbert

Songs: Animals Are Nice (C: Lee Wainer; L: J.B. Rosenberg); Back to Bundling (C: Lee Wainer; L: Dorothy Sachs); Hey, Gal! (C: Will Irwin; L: June Carroll); Land of Rockefellera (C: Lee Wainer; L: June Carroll); Love, Are You Raising Your Head? (C: Lee Wainer; L: June Carroll); Opening (C: Lee Wainer; L: John Lund); Radio City, I Love You (C: Lee Wainer; L: June Carroll); Richard Crudnut's Charm School (C: Lee Wainer; L: June Carroll; John Lund); Shoes (C: Will Irwin; L: June Carroll); Ten Percenters (C: Lee Wainer); We'll Swing It Through (C: Lee Wainer; L: John Lund); Well, Well! (C: Lee Wainer; L: June Carroll); Yes, Sir, I've Made a Date (C: Lee Wainer; L: J.B. Rosenberg)

Cast: Tony Farrar; John Lund; Mervyn Nelson; Alice Pearce; Leonard Sillman

3106 • NEW FACES OF 1948

OPENED: 1948   Theatre: Persian Room
Revue   Nightclub

Notes: No program available.

3107 • NEW FACES OF 1952

OPENED: 05/16/1952   Theatre: Royale
Musical   Broadway: 365

Composer: Arthur Siegel
Lyricist: June Carroll
Librettist: Mel Brooks; John Cleveland; Luther Davis; Peter DeVries; Ronny Graham; Sheldon Harnick; Paul Lynde; Alan Melville; Roger Price

Producer: Leonard Sillman
Director: John Murray Anderson; John Beal

Choreographer: Richard Barstow; **Costumes:** Thomas Becher; **Musical Director:** Anton Coppola; **Orchestrations:** Ted Royal; **Set Design:** Raoul Pene du Bois

Songs: Bal Petit Bal (C/L: Francis Lemarque); Bard and the Beard, The (L: June Carroll; Sheldon Harnick); Boston Beguine (C/L: Sheldon Harnick); Convention Bound (C/L: Ronny Graham); Don't Fall Asleep (C/L: Ronny Graham); Guess Who I Saw Today? (C/L: Murray Grand; L: Elisse Boyd); Hark the Extra Marital Lark (C/L: Ronny Graham; L: Peter DeVries); He Takes Me Off His Income Tax; I'm in Love with Miss Logan (C/L: Ronny Graham); Lizzie Borden [2] (C/L: Michael Brown); Love Is a Simple Thing; Lucky Pierre (C/L: Ronny Graham); Monotonous; Nanty Puts Her Hair Up (L: Herbert Farjeon); Penny Candy; Raining Memories (C/L: Ronny Graham); Restoration Piece (L: Alan Melville); Scotch on the Rocks [1] (C/L: Ronny Graham); Take Off the Mask (C/L: Ronny Graham); Time for Tea; Waltzing in Venice with You (C/L: Ronny Graham); Young and Fresh and Willing [1] (C/L: Ronny Graham)

Cast: June Carroll; Robert Clary; Alice Ghostley; Ronny Graham; Patricia Hammerlee; Eartha Kitt; Carol Lawrence; Paul Lynde; Virginia de Luce

Notes: [1] Out Philadelphia 4/28/52. [2] Also in CURTAIN UP.

3108 • NEW FACES OF 1956

OPENED: 06/14/1956   Theatre: Ethel Barrymore
Revue   Broadway: 220

Composer: Arthur Siegel
Lyricist: June Carroll
Librettist: Louis Botto; Sidney Carroll; Paul Lynde; Richard Maury
Producer: John Roberts; Leonard Sillman
Director: Paul Lynde

Choreographer: David Thimar; **Costumes:** Thomas Becher; **Lighting Designer:** Peggy Clark; **Musical Director:** Jay Blackton; **Orchestrations:** Joe Glover; Ted Royal; Albert Sendry; **Set Design:** Peter Larkin

Songs: And He Flipped (C/L: John Rox); April in Fairbanks (C/L: Murray Grand); Boy Most Likely to Succeed; Broken Kimono, The (C: Robert Stringer; L: Richard Maury); Change of Heart, A [1] (C/L: John Rox); Doll's House, A; Don't Wait Till It's Too Late to See Paris; Girls 'n' Girls 'n' Girls (C/L: Irvin Graham); Greatest Invention, The (C/L: Sid Silvers; C: Harold Karr; L: Matt Dubey); Hurry (C/L: Murray Grand; L: Elisse Boyd); I Could Love Him (C/L: Paul Nassau); Isn't She Lovely? (C: Dean Fuller; L: Marshall Barer); La Ronde (C: Dean Fuller; L: Marshall Barer); Mustapha Abdullah Abu Ben Al Raajid (C: Dean Fuller; L: Marshall Barer); One Perfect Moment (C: Dean Fuller; L: Marshall Barer; Leslie Julian-Jones); Rouge (C/L: Michael Brown); Scratch My Back (C: Dean Fuller; L: Marshall Barer); She's Got Everything (C: Dean Fuller; L: Marshall Barer); Talent (C/L: Paul Nassau); Tell Her; This Is Quite a Perfect Night (C: Dean Fuller; L: Marshall Barer); Washingtons Are Doin' Okay (C/L: Michael Brown); What Does That Dream Mean? (C: Harold Karr; L: Matt Dubey); White Witch of Jamaica, The

Cast: Jane Connell; Tiger Haynes; T.C. Jones; Virginia Martin; Bill McCutcheon; John Reardon; Bob Shaver; Maggie Smith; Inga Swenson

Notes: [1] Cut prior to opening.

3109 • NEW FACES (1957)

OPENED: 1957   Theatre: Cocoanut Grove
Revue   Nightclub

Notes: This show was presented in Miami. No other information available.

3110 • NEW FACES OF 1962

OPENED: 02/01/1962   Theatre: Alvin
Revue   Broadway: 28

Librettist: R.G. Brown; Joey Carter; Ronny Graham; Paul Lynde; Richard Maury; Jean Shepherd
Producer: Carroll Masterson; Harris Masterson
Director: Richard Maury; Leonard Sillman

Choreographer: James Moor; **Costumes:** Thomas Becher; **Dance Arranger:** Jack Holmes; **Lighting Designer:** Martin Reiss; **Musical Director:** Abba Bogin; **Orchestrations:** Joy Bower; Mark Bucci; Sy Oliver; Ted Royal; David Terry; **Set Design:** Martin Reiss

Songs: A.B.C.'s (C: Mark Bucci; L: David Rogers); Althea [1] (C/L: Elisse Boyd); Ballad of a Bus [1] (C/L: Jack Holmes); Collective Beauty (C: William Roy; L: Michael McWhinney); Do You Wonder What Became of Romanoff? [1] (C/L: Unknown); Freedomland (C/L: Jack Holmes); Girls in Their Summer Dresses [1] (C/L: Unknown); Happiness (C: Marie Gordon; L: David Rogers); I Want You to Be the One First to Know [2] (C: Arthur Siegel; L: June Carroll); I Was Beautiful [1] (C/L: Murray Grand); In the Morning (C/L: Ronny Graham); It Depends on How You Look at Things (C: Arthur Siegel; L: June Carroll); Johnny Mishuga (C/L: Mark Bucci; L: David Rogers); Launching, The (C: John Kander; L: David Rogers); Love Is Good for You (C: Arthur Siegel; L: June Carroll); Moment of Truth, A (C/L: Jack Holmes); Moral Rearmament (C/L: Jack Holmes); Opening (C/L: Ronny Graham); Other One, The (C: Arthur Siegel; L: June Carroll); Over the River and Into the Woods (C/L: Jack Holmes); Pi in the Sky (C/L: Mark Bucci); Togetherness (C/L: Mavor Moore); Untalented Relative, The (C: Arthur Siegel; L: Joey Carter; Richard Maury); Wall Street Reel (C: Arthur Siegel; L: Jim Fuerst); Wanna Make a Bet? [1] (C/L: Unknown)

Cast: R.G. Brown; Joey Carter; Travis Hudson; Marian Mercer

Notes: [1] Cut before opening. [2] Later in SEVEN COMES ELEVEN (SECOND EDITION).

3111 • NEW FACES OF 1966

OPENED: 1966
Revue   Closed out of town

Librettist: David Axelrod; Peter DeVries; Ronny Graham; Bill Majeski; Richard Maltby Jr.; Michael McWhinney; Gail Parent; Sam Pottle; David Shire; Treva Silverman; Kenny Solms
Director: Ronny Graham; Leonard Sillman

Arrangements: Robert Rogers; **Choreographer:** Ronny Graham; James Moore; **Lighting Designer:** Ting Barrow; **Musical Director:** Robert Rogers; **Set Design:** Richard Shoemaker

Songs: Believe It or Not Tango [1] (C/L: David Axelrod; Sam Pottle); By the Sea (C/L: Clark Gesner); Go Slow Saturday (C/L: Michael McWhinney; Jerry Powell); Hungry [1] (C/L:

Murray Grand); Opening (C/L: Ronny Graham); Sade [2] (C/L: Ronny Graham; C: Clint Ballard; L: Hal Hackady); Show Your Love (C/L: Ronny Graham); Sortie a La Guerre (C/L: Ronny Graham); Where Is Me (C: Arthur Siegel; L: June Carroll); You're the One I'm For [1] (C/L: Clark Gesner)

Cast: Suzanne Astor; Rodd Barry; Marilyn Child; Dottie Frank; Ronny Graham; Kevin Lloyd; Brandon Maggart; Marian Mercer; George Ormiston; Morgan Paull; Rod Perry; Nancie Philips; Brooke Winsten

Notes: Goodspeed Opera House production. [1] Later in NEW FACES OF 1968. [2] Additional music and lyrics by Ronny Graham.

3112 • NEW FACES OF 1968
OPENED: 05/02/1968   Theatre: Booth
Revue   Broadway: 32

Lyricist: Norman Kline
Librettist: David Axelrod; William F. Brown; Peter DeVries; Ronny Graham; Robert Klein; Gail Parent; Jack Sharkey; Kenny Solms
Producer: Jack Rollins
Director: Leonard Sillman; Frank Wagner

Choreographer: Frank Wagner; **Costumes:** Winn Morton; **Lighting Designer:** Paul Sullivan; **Musical Director:** Ted Simons; **Orchestrations:** Lanny Meyers; **Set Design:** Winn Morton

Songs: By the Sea (C/L: Clark Gesner); Cymbals and Tambourines (C/L: Arthur Siegel); Das Chicago Song [2] (C: Michael Cohen; L: Tony Geiss); Die Zusammenfugung (C: Sam Pottle; L: David Axelrod); Evil (C/L: Sydney Shaw); Girl in the Mirror, The (C: Fred Hellerman; L: Fran Minkoff); Girl of the Minute, The [3] (C: David Shire; L: Richard Maltby Jr.); Hullabaloo at Thebes (C/L: Ronny Graham); Hungry (C/L: Murray Grand); Love in a New Tempo (C/L: Ronny Graham); Luncheon Ballad (C: Jerry Powell; L: Michael McWhinney); Missed America (C/L: Gail Parent; Kenny Solms); New Waltz, A (C: Fred Hellerman; L: Fran Minkoff); #X9RL220 (C: Jerry Powell; L: Michael McWhinney); Peanut Butter Affair [4] (C/L: Clark Gesner); Philosophy (C: Carl Friberg; L: Hal Hackady); Prisms (C: Carl Friberg; L: Hal Hackady); Right About Here (C/L: Arthur Siegel); Something Big (C: Sam Pottle; L: David Axelrod); Tango (C: Sam Pottle;

L: David Axelrod); Toyland (C/L: Gene P. Bissell); Where Is Me? (C: Arthur Siegel; L: June Carroll); Where Is the Waltz [1] (C: Alonzo Levister; L: Paul Nassau); You Are (C/L: Clark Gesner); You're the One I'm For (C/L: Clark Gesner)

Cast: Suzanne Astor; Rod Barry; Gloria Bleezarde; Elaine Giftos; Madeline Kahn; Robert Klein; Brandon Maggart; Rod Perry

Notes: [1] In WET PAINT. [2] In MIXED DOUBLES. [3] In STARTING HERE STARTING NOW. [4] Cut prior to opening.

3113 • NEW GIRL IN TOWN
OPENED: 05/14/1957   Theatre: 46th Street
Musical   Broadway: 431

Composer: Bob Merrill
Lyricist: Bob Merrill
Librettist: George Abbott
Producer: Frederick Brisson; Robert E. Griffith; Harold Prince
Director: George Abbott

Source: ANNA CHRISTIE (Play: Eugene O'Neill); **Choreographer:** Bob Fosse; **Costumes:** Rouben Ter-Arutunian; **Dance Arranger:** Roger Adams; **Lighting Designer:** Rouben Ter-Arutunian; **Musical Director:** Hal Hastings; **Orchestrations:** Robert Russell Bennett; Philip J. Lang; **Set Design:** Rouben Ter-Arutunian

Songs: Anna Lilla; At the Check Apron Ball; Chess and Checkers; Did You Close Your Eyes?; Elegance [2]; Flings; Here We Are Again [1]; If That Was Love; It's Good to Be Alive; Look at 'Er; On the Farm; Pay As You Go [1]; Red Light Ballet, The (inst.); Roll Yer Socks Up; Sunshine Girl; There Ain't No Flies on Me; Ven I Valse; Yer My Friend, Aintcha?

Cast: Del Anderson; Lulu Bates; H.F. Green; Eddie Phillips; Cameron Prud'homme; Michael Quinn; Thelma Ritter; Gwen Verdon; George Wallace

Notes: [1] Out New Haven 4/6/57. [2] Cut. Later put into HELLO, DOLLY!

3114 • NEW GIRL, A
Notes: *See SHE'S A GOOD FELLOW*

3115 • NEW GRAND TERRACE REVUE

Notes: *See GRAND TERRACE REVUE.*

3116 • NEW MEET THE PEOPLE, THE

Notes: *See MARCHING WITH JOHNNY.*

3117 • NEW MOON, THE

OPENED: 09/19/1928   Theatre: Imperial
Musical   Broadway: 519

Composer: Sigmund Romberg
Lyricist: Oscar Hammerstein II
Librettist: Oscar Hammerstein II; Frank Mandel;
  Laurence Schwab
Producer: Frank Mandel; Laurence Schwab
Director: Oscar Hammerstein II; Frank Mandel;
  Laurence Schwab

Choreographer: Bobby Connolly; **Costumes:**
  Charles LeMaire; **Musical Director:** Al
  Goodman; **Orchestrations:** Emil Gerstenberger;
  Al Goodman; Hans Spialek; **Set Design:** Donald
  Oenslager

Songs: Call of Home, The [2]; Chanty, A; Dainty
  Wisp of Thistledown; Fair Rosita; Fancy Me Just
  Meeting You [3] (C: R.P. Weston; L: Bert Lee);
  Finale; First Man I Kiss, The [1]; Funny Little
  Sailor Men; Girl on the Prow, The; Gorgeous
  Alexander; Hot and Cold [1]; I Love You [2]; I'm
  Just a Sentimental Fool [1]; Interrupted Love
  Song, An; La-La-La-La [2]; Liar [1]; Love Is Quite
  a Simple Thing; Love That Lasts, A [1]; Lover,
  Come Back to Me; Marianne; 'Neath a New
  Moon [2]; Never for You; One Day [2]; One Kiss
  (Is Waiting for One Man); One Kiss Is Waiting
  for One Man [1]; Paree [2]; Softly, As in A
  Morning Sunrise; Stouthearted Men (Liberty
  Song); Tango [4] (L: Oscar Hammerstein II;
  Frank Mandel; Laurence Schwab); Tavern Song
  (Red Wine); Trial, The (Ladies of the Jury); Try
  Her Out at Dances; Voice in the Dark, A [2];
  Wanting You; When I Close My Eyes [2];
  Women, Women, Women [2]

Cast: Olga Albani; Marie Callahan; Max Figman;
  Robert Halliday; Evelyn Herbert; Esther
  Howard; Edward Nell Jr.; William O'Neal; Pacie
  Ripple; Gus Shy

Notes: [1] Cut prior to opening. [2] Cut after
  opening. [3] Added for London production. [4]
  ASCAP/Library of Congress only.

3118 • NEW ORLEANS

Notes: *See SUNNY RIVER.*

3119 • NEW PINS AND NEEDLES

Notes: *See PINS AND NEEDLES 1937.*

3120 • NEW PLANTATION REVUE

OPENED: 1925   Theatre: Plantation Cafe
Revue   Nightclub

Composer: Harry Akst
Lyricist: Sam M. Lewis; Joe Young

Songs: Dinah; Hot-Foot'n; We're Gonna Have Fun

Notes: No other information available.

3121 • NEW PRIORITIES OF 1943

OPENED: 09/15/1942   Theatre: 46th Street
Revue   Broadway: 54

Composer: Lester Lee; Jerry Seelen
Lyricist: Lester Lee; Jerry Seelen
Producer: Clifford C. Fischer
Director: Jean Le Seyeux

Choreographer: Truly McGee; **Musical Director:**
  Lou Forman

Cast: Tom Adair; Aeromaniacs, The; Bricklayers,
  The; Carol Bruce; Harry Richman; Bert Wheeler;
  Henny Youngman

3122 • NEW SONG BIRDS, THE

OPENED: 1914   Theatre: Palace
Revue

Composer: Victor Herbert
Lyricist: George V. Hobart

Songs: Battle of B Flat, The; Hammershine;
  Mazuma

Cast: Stella Barre; William Burress

Notes: A vaudeville show.

3123 • NEW WORLD!, A

OPENED: 05/09/1977   Theatre: New Dramatists
Revue   Off-Broadway: 4

Composer: Albert Hague
Lyricist: Marian Winters
Librettist: Marian Winters
Director: Marian Winters

Lighting Designer: Ned Hallick

Cast: Barbara Andres; Stanley Grover

Notes: A reading at New Dramatists. No program available.

3124 • NEW YORK COLORING BOOK

OPENED: 04/22/1963
Revue   Nightclub: 84

Composer: Jerry Powell
Lyricist: Michael McWhinney
Producer: Jan Wallman
Director: Bill Penn

Choreographer: Bill Miller

Songs: Beyond the Binge I Want to Get Off; Big Walk, The; Bunny's Lament, The; Cafe Society; Coloring Book; Everything for Roz; Family Affair, A; Gal Who Took the Minutes, The; Low Fidelity; My Friends, the Celebrities; No Sign of the Times; Old Miss; On My Own; Rocky on the Rocks; S-E-X; Silent Spring; Souvenirs; Spoleto; Time and Time Again; When Will They Finish New York?; Will My Real Love Please Stand Up

Cast: Gloria Bleezarde; Barbara Gilbert; Ronnie Hall; Ronny Whyte

3125 • NEW YORK ROCK

OPENED: 03/30/1994   Theatre: WPA
Musical   Off-Off-Broadway

Composer: Yoko Ono
Lyricist: Yoko Ono
Librettist: Yoko Ono
Director: Phillip Oesterman

Arrangements: Jason Robert Brown;
  Choreographer: Kenneth Tosti; **Costumes:** Terry
Leong; **Lighting Designer:** Craig Evans; **Musical Director:** Jason Robert Brown; **Orchestrations:** Jason Robert Brown; **Set Design:** Terry Leong

Songs: Don't Be Scared; Even When You're Far Away; Give Me Something; Good-bye to Sadness; Growing Pain; Hell in Paradise; I Felt Like Smashing My Face in a Clear Glass Window; I Want My Love to Rest Tonight; If Only; I'll Always Be with You; It Happened; Light on the Other Side; Lonliness; Midsummer New York; Never Say Good-bye; No, No, No; Now or Never; O'Sanity; Peter the Dealer; Sleepless Night; Speck of Dust; Story of an Oak Tree; Tomorrow May Never Come; Toy Boat; Warzone; We're All Water; What a Bastard the World Is; Where Do We Go from Here; Yes, I'm Your Angel

Cast: Sean Dooley; Jan Horvath; Pat McRoberts; Lynnette Perry

Notes: No songs written for this production.

3126 • NEW YORK SUMMER, A

OPENED: 06/01/1979   Theatre: Radio City Music
                       Hall
Revue   Broadway: 203

Composer: Tom Bahler; Mark Vieha
Lyricist: Tom Bahler; Mark Vieha
Librettist: Stanley Hart
Producer: Robert F. Jani; Radio City Music Hall
Director: Robert F. Jani

Choreographer: Dru Davis; Violet Holmes; Louis Johnson; Linda Lemac; Howard Parker; **Costumes:** Frank Spencer; **Lighting Designer:** Billy B. Walker; **Musical Director:** Donald Pippin; **Orchestrations:** Elman Anderson; Bill Byers; Jack Eskew; Mitch Farber; Allen Faust; Michael Gibson; Quincy Jones; Jay Kennedy; Philip J. Lang; John Mandel; Peter Matz; Glenn Osser; Larry Wilcox; Ray Wright; **Set Design:** John William Keck

Songs: Avenue, Fifth Avenue; I Thank Heaven (C: Tom Bahler; Quincy Jones; L: Mark Vieha); New York at Night; New York Lullaby; New York Summer, A

Cast: Karen Anders; Tim Cassidy; Anthony Falco; John Hallow; John J. Martin; Christina Saffran

3127 • NEW YORK WORLD'S FAIR (1939-1940)

OPENED: 1939

N.Y. World's Fair

Songs: Dawn of a New Day (C: George Gershwin; L: Ira Gershwin)

Notes: Official theme song for Fair.

3128 • NEW YORK WORLD'S FAIR (1964-65)

OPENED: 04/22/1964

N.Y. World's Fair

Songs: Fair Is Fair (C/L: Richard Rodgers)

Notes: Official theme song for Fair.

3129 • NEW YORKERS, THE (1901)

OPENED: 10/07/1901   Theatre: Herald Square
Musical   Broadway: 64

Composer: Ludwig Englander
Lyricist: George V. Hobart
Librettist: Glen MacDonough
Producer: George W. Lederer
Director: George W. Lederer

Costumes: Mme. Seidle; **Set Design:** Ernest Albert; D. Frank Dodge

Songs: And the Band Began to Play; Dat's All, Ragtime Girl (C/L: Will Marion Cook); Gossip Song; Honolulu Lulu (C: Emil Bierman; L: George Totten Smith); If I Should Say Goodbye; 'Is Old Man's 'At Won't Fit 'Im; Keb, Sir, Want a Keb? (C: Arthur Weld); Kodak Girl; Octette; Oh, Fudge (C: Paul Schindler; L: George Sidney); Opening Chorus (C: Arthur Weld); Russia the Fatherland; Strolling in Society; Take Me Back to Herald Square; Three Women to Every Man; When You Sail for Paris in the Spring (C: Jack Gouraud)

Cast: William Cameron; Marguerite Clark; Dan Daly; Virginia Earle; Anna Laughlin

3130 • NEW YORKERS, THE (1927)

OPENED: 03/10/1927   Theatre: Edyth Totten
Revue   Broadway: 52

Composer: Arthur Schwartz
Lyricist: Henry Myers
Librettist: Jo Swerling
Director: Milton Bender

Costumes: Margaret Daye; **Musical Director:** Alex Magnes; **Set Design:** Connors & Bennett; Mischa Solotaroff

Songs: Burn 'Em Up (C: Edgar Fairchild); Floating Through the Air; He Who Gets Slapped; Here Comes the Prince of Wales; How to Welcome Home Your Hubby [1] (C: Charles M. Schwab); I Can't Get Into the Quota; Indian Chant; 99% Pure; Nothing Left but Dreams (C: Edgar Fairchild); Old Fashioned Ballet (C: Edgar Fairchild); Pretty Little So-and-So (C: Edgar Fairchild); Romany; Self- Expression; Side-Street Off Broadway, A (C: Edgar Fairchild); Slow River (C: Charles M. Schwab); Song of Love, A; Triangle (C: Charles M. Schwab); Words and Music (C: Charles M. Schwab)

Cast: Chester Clute; Florence Faun; Lilyan Lauren; Rima Swan; Tamara[2]

Notes: [1] Sheet music only. [2] Billed as Tamara Drasin.

3131 • NEW YORKERS, THE (1930)

OPENED: 12/08/1930   Theatre: Broadway
Musical   Broadway: 158

Composer: Cole Porter
Lyricist: Cole Porter
Librettist: Herbert Fields
Producer: E. Ray Goetz
Director: E. Ray Goetz; Monty Woolley

Source: UNKNOWN (Story: Peter Arno); **Choreographer:** Georgie Hale; **Costumes:** Peter Arno; Charles LeMaire; **Musical Director:** Al Goodman; **Orchestrations:** Hans Spialek; **Set Design:** Dale Stetson

Songs: But He Never Says He Loves Me [6]; Data! (C/L: Jimmy Durante); Drinking Song (C: Fred Waring; L: Charles Henderson); Extra Man, The [5]; Flit Drill, The [1] (C: Fred Waring; L: Charles Henderson); Go Into Your Dance; Hot Patata, The (C/L: Jimmy Durante); I Happen to Like New York [3]; I'm Getting Myself Ready for You; It Only Happens in Dreams [1]; Just One of Those Things [2]; Let's Fly Away; Love for Sale;

Mona and Her Kitties [1]; Money (C/L: Jimmy Durante); My Louisa [4]; Poor Are Rich, The [1]; Say It with Gin; Sing Sing for Sing Sing; Take Me Back to Manhattan; Venice; We've Been Spending the Summer with Our Families [1]; Where Can One Go to Powder Her Nose? [1]; Where Have You Been; Why Talk About Sex [1]; Wood (C/L: Jimmy Durante); You're Too Far Away [1]; You've Got to Be Hard Boiled [1]

Cast: Iris Adrian; Marie Cahill; Richard Carle; Lou Clayton; Kathryn Crawford; Jimmy Durante; Ralph Glover; Paul Huber; Eddie Jackson; Charles King; Barrie Oliver; Ann Pennington; Oscar "Rags" Ragland; Fred Waring & His Pennsylvanians; Frances Williams; Hope Williams; Tammany Young

Notes: [1] Cut prior to opening. [2] Not used. Not the well known song from JUBILEE with the same name. [3] Added after opening. [4] Not used. Also not used in NYMPH ERRANT and WAKE UP AND DREAM. [5] Not used. Also unused in 9:15 REVUE and WAKE UP AND DREAM. [6] Cut prior to opening. Rewritten as "The Physician" in NYMPH ERRANT.

3132 • NEW ZIEGFELD FOLLIES OF 1936-1937

Notes: *See ZIEGFELD FOLLIES OF 1936.*

3133 • NEWCOMERS, THE

OPENED: 08/08/1923   Theatre: Ambassador
Musical   Broadway: 20

Composer: Will Morrissey
Lyricist: Will Morrissey
Librettist: Joe Burrows; Will Morrissey
Producer: Will Morrissey
Director: Will Morrissey

Choreographer: Paisley Noon

Songs: California Sunshine; Covered Wagon Days; Mother, Me and the Flag [1]; Sun and Rain; Take This Little Rosebud; Ultra Peacock Strut, The; Washington Square Long Ago; When I Think of You

Cast: Al Fields; Frank Gaby; Mason & Shaw; Grace Masters; Florence Stone; **Pianist:** Irving Fisher

Notes: Titled THE NEWLYWEDS out of town. [1] Sheet music only.

3134 • NEWLYWEDS AND THEIR BABY, THE

OPENED: 03/22/1909   Theatre: Majestic
Musical   Broadway: 40

Composer: Nat D. Ayer; John W. Bratton
Lyricist: A. Seymour Brown
Librettist: Aaron Hoffman; Paul West
Producer: Leffler-Bratton Co.
Director: Frank Smithson

Source: NEWLYWEDS, THE (Comic Strip: George McManus); **Choreographer:** Chris Maxwell

Songs: Baby's Gone; Bon-Bon-Buddy the Chocolate Man [7]; Boogie-Boo, The; Bubble and the Butterfly, The [2]; Bye and Bye [1]; Cake Walk Ball [3]; Can't You See I Love You?; Clorinda [2]; Come On Over Here [3]; Darkie's Serenade; Down Red Rose Lane [1]; Every Baby Is a Sweet Bouquet; Father Keeps on Doing It [2]; For He's the One, the Only Baby [2]; Girls Who Go Upon the Stage; Great Big Blue Eyed Baby [1]; Honey Moon Land; Honeymoon Bells [3]; I Love You Oh! Oh! Oh! [1]; I'm Crazy Over You; I'm Glad I'm Single [2]; King of Baby Land, The [6]; Latest Creation in Girls, The [2]; Love Time; Lullabyland; Mammy's Jubilee [1]; Mamzelle Fifi; Meet Me in Rose Time, Rosie [4]; Minstrels on Parade [1]; Mr. Jiggers [5] (C: John W. Bratton; L: Paul West); My Switzer Bride (C: Frank Stratton; L: Paul West); Napoleon; Natural History Class, The [2]; Nonsensical Nonsense [3]; Operatic Solution, An; Santa Rosa Rose; Sleepyland; Supper Out of Doors; Take Me to That Tango Tea [1]; Teddy the Jungle Boogie Man [5] (C/L: Kenneth S. Clark); That Chop Stick Rag [1]; Velvet Foot [3]; Wilhelm Der Grosser [3]

Cast: Flavia Arcaro; William Clifton; Fletcher Norton

Notes: [1] Out 11/30/13. [2] Out 12/30/08. [3] Out 12/12/15. [4] Out 3/22/09. [5] Sheet music only. [6] Out Wilmington 11/01/15 where the lyrics were also credited to Paul West. [7] Out 3/22/09. There was also a 1907 song "Bon Bon Buddy the Chocolate Drop" by Will Marion Cook and Alex Rogers.

3135 • NEWLYWEDS, THE

Notes: *See THE NEWCOMERS.*

3136 • NEWS, THE
OPENED: 11/07/1985   Theatre: Helen Hayes
Musical   Broadway: 4

Composer: Paul Schierhorn
Lyricist: Paul Schierhorn
Librettist: R. Vincent Park; David Rotenberg; Paul Schierhorn
Producer: Zev Bufman; Kathleen Lindsey; Nicholas Neubauer; R. Vincent Park
Director: David Rotenberg

Choreographer: Wesley Fata; **Conductor:** John Rinehimer; **Costumes:** Richard Hornung; **Dance Arranger:** John Rinehimer; Paul Schierhorn; **Lighting Designer:** Norman Coates; **Orchestrations:** John Rinehimer; **Set Design:** Jane Musky; **Vocal Arranger:** John Rinehimer; Paul Schierhorn

Songs: Acts of God (Births, Deaths and the Weather); Beautiful People; Classifieds/Personals; Contest, The; Dad; Dear Editor; Dear Felicia; Editorial; Front Page Expose; Horoscope; Hot Flashes; I Am the News; Mirror, Mirror; Open Letter; Ordinary, Extraordinary Day; Pyramid Land; She's on File; Shooting Stars; Super Singo; Talk to Me; They Write the News; Violent Crime; What in the World; What's the Angle; Wonderman

Cast: Cheryl Alexander; Frank Baier; Jeff Conaway; Anthony Crivello; Patrick Jude; Lisa Michaelis

3137 • NIC-NAX OF 1926
OPENED: 08/02/1926   Theatre: Cort
Revue   Broadway: 13

Composer: Werner Janssen; Gitz Rice
Lyricist: Paul Porter
Librettist: Roger Gray; Matt Kennedy; Paul Porter
Producer: Knick Knacks Inc.
Director: Paul Porter

Choreographer: Jack Conners; **Musical Director:** August Kleinecke; **Set Design:** John Dwyer

Songs: Broads of Broadway; Burma Moon; Eight Little Nobodies; Everything Is High Yellow Now; For a Girl Like You (L: Joe Goodwin); I Have Forgotten You Almost (L: Anna Fitziu); Love Pirates; Oh Daddy! (C: Gitz Rice); Rangoon Wedding; Sesquicentennial; When the Sun Kissed the Rose Goodnight; Without the One You Love (C: Werner Janssen)

Cast: Nat Nazzarro Jr.; Gitz Rice; Ralph Riggs; Frederick Santley; Katherine Witchie

Notes: No program available.

3138 • NICE GOIN'
OPENED: 09/1939
Musical   Closed out of town

Composer: Ralph Rainger
Lyricist: Leo Robin
Librettist: Laurence Schwab
Producer: Laurence Schwab
Director: Arthur Sircom

Source: SAILOR BEWARE (Play: Kenyon Nicholson; Charles Robinson); **Choreographer:** Al White Jr.; **Costumes:** Billy Livingston; **Musical Director:** Don Walker; **Set Design:** Harry Horner; **Vocal Arranger:** Don Walker

Songs: Blow Me Down; I Should've Stood in Bed; I Was Afraid of That; I've Gone Off the Deep End; Nice Goin'; Stick to Your Arithmetic; Wind at My Window, The

Cast: Carol Bruce; Vicki Cummings; Lee Dixon; Tom Ewell; Pert Kelton; Mary Martin; Bert Wheeler

3139 • NICE GOINGS ON
OPENED: 09/13/1933   Theatre: Strand
Musical   London: 221

Composer: Arthur Schwartz
Lyricist: Frank Eyton
Librettist: Douglas Furber
Producer: Leslie Henson; F. Firth Shephard
Director: Leslie Henson

Choreographer: Buddy Bradley; **Costumes:** Morris Angel & Co.; Barbosa; Jill Casson; Norman Hartnell; Charles Judd; L & H Nathan; Victor Stiebel; **Musical Director:** Arthur Rule; **Orchestrations:** Percival Mackey; **Set Design:** Joseph Harker; Phil Harker

Songs: I Know the Kind of Girl (A Girl Like You) (L: Douglas Furber); Life-Saver's Song, The; Nice Goings On; Place in the Sun; Sweet One [1]

(L: Arthur Schwartz); Twixt the Devil and the Deep Blue Sea; We've Got to Get On; What a Young Girl Ought to Know; Whatever You Do; With You Here and Me Here; You're an Old Smoothie [2] (C: Nacio Herb Brown; Richard A. Whiting; L: B.G. DeSylva)

Cast: Marjorie Brooks; Robertson Hare; Leslie Henson; Zelma O'Neal

Notes: [1] Sheet music only. [2] From TAKE A CHANCE.

3140 • NICE TO SEE YOU

OPENED: 1953   Theatre: Versailles
Revue   Nightclub

Lyricist: Irving Caesar; Jack Yellen

Songs: Nice to See You (C: Belle Fenstock); Pain in the Heart (C: Louis Cobey)

Cast: Irwin Corey

Notes: No other information available. Information from ASCAP records. Charles Strouse also wrote for this show. George White was also involved in this show.

3141 • NICHOLAS NICKLEBY

Notes: *See THE LIFE AND ADVENTURES OF NICHOLAS NICKLEBY.*

3142 • NICK & NORA

OPENED: 12/08/1991   Theatre: Marquis
Musical   Broadway: 9

Composer: Charles Strouse
Lyricist: Richard Maltby Jr.
Librettist: Arthur Laurents
Producer: Terry Allen Kramer; Elizabeth Ireland McCann; Charlene Nederlander; James M. Nederlander; Daryl Roth
Director: Arthur Laurents

Source: CHARACTERS (Dashiell Hammett); **Source:** THIN MAN, THE (Film: Frances Goodrich; Albert Hackett); **Choreographer:** Tina Paul

Songs: As Long As You're Happy; Beyond Words [1]; Boom Chicka Boom; Busy Night at Lorraine's, A; Class; Detectiveland; Everybody Wants to Do a musical; Is There Anything Better Than Dancing?; Let's Go Home; Look Who's Alone Now; Married Life [2]; May the Best Man Win; Men; Not Me; Now You See Me Now You Don't [3]; People Get Hurt; Swell

Cast: Christine Baranski; Barry Bostwick; Jeff Brooks; Joanna Gleason; Michael Lombard; Debra Monk; Kathy Morath; Kip Niven; Faith Prince; Remak Ramsay; Riley; Chris Sarandon; Thom Sesma

Notes: [1] ASCAP/Library of Congress. [2] Cut before opening. Same music as "Let's Go Home." [3] Cut before opening.

3143 • NICKLEBY AND ME
Musical   Unproduced

Composer: Arthur Schwartz
Lyricist: Arthur Schwartz

Source: NICHOLAS NICKLEBY (Novel: Charles Dickens)

Notes: Written by Schwartz during the 70's and 80's.

3144 • NIFTIES OF 1923

OPENED: 09/25/1923   Theatre: Fulton
Revue   Broadway: 47

Librettist: Sam Bernard; William Collier
Producer: Charles B. Dillingham
Director: R.H. Burnside; William Collier

Choreographer: William Holbrook; **Costumes:** Gilbert Adrian; Cesar Girio; Kiviette; Cora MacGeachy; **Musical Director:** Victor Baravalle; **Set Design:** Ernest Gros; Herbert Ward

Songs: Are You Here Maggie Mooney Are You Here? (C: Worton David; L: C.W. Murphy); At Half Past Seven (C: George Gershwin; L: B.G. DeSylva); Calico Days [2] (C/L: Eubie Blake; Ray Perkins; Noble Sissle); Fabric of Dreams (C: Raymond Hubbell; L: B.G. DeSylva; Ira

Gershwin [4]); Grinding Out a Revue [1] (C: Harry Ruby; L: Bert Kalmar); If You Will Marry Us We'll Stroll Beneath the Babbling Brook [3] (C: Harry Ruby; L: Bert Kalmar); Little Brown Jug [3] (C/L: Frank Crumit); Nashville Nightingale (C: George Gershwin; L: Irving Caesar); Old Gray Owl, The [3] (C/L: Unknown); Old- Time Tune, An [3] (C: Gus Van; L: Joe Schenck); Opening Chorus (C: Harry Ruby; L: Bert Kalmar); Sweet Alice [3] (C/L: Unknown); That Bran' New Gal O' Mine [3] (C: Harry Akst; Gus Van; L: Benny Davis; Joe Schenck); When I Have Become a Social Butterfly [1] (C: Harry Ruby; L: Bert Kalmar); When It's Snowing in Hawaii (C/L: Frank Crumit); Where Are the Old Pals of Yesterday [3] (C: Gus Van; L: Joe Schenck)

Cast: Helen Broderick; Frank Crumit; Hazel Dawn; Ray Dooley; Joe Schenck; Gus Van

Notes: [1] Out Buffalo 9/10/23. [2] Credited to Perkins only on sheet music. [3] Sheet music only. [4] Used pseudonym Arthur Francis.

3145 NIGHT AT THE COPA, A

OPENED: 1946   Theatre: Copacabana
Revue   Nightclub

Songs: For Those in Love (C: Ted Murry; L: Benny Davis)

Notes: No other information available. Information from ASCAP/Library of Congress.

3146 • NIGHT BOAT, THE

OPENED: 02/02/1920   Theatre: Liberty
Musical   Broadway: 318

Composer: Jerome Kern
Lyricist: Anne Caldwell
Librettist: Anne Caldwell
Producer: Charles B. Dillingham
Director: Fred G. Latham

Source: LE CONTROLLEUR DES WAGON-LITS (Play: Alexandre Bisson); **Choreographer:** Ned Wayburn; **Costumes:** O'Kane Conwell; **Musical Director:** Victor Baravalle; **Orchestrations:** Frank Saddler

Songs: Bob White [2]; Catskills, Hello; Chick! Chick! Chick! [3]; Don't You Want to Take Me?;

Girls Are Like a Rainbow; Girls in the Sea [3]; Good Night Boat (L: Anne Caldwell; Frank Craven); Heart for Sale, A; I Love the Lassies (I Love Them All); I'd Like a Lighthouse [1]; Jazz [2]; Jug Band and Dance; Laundry Duet; Left All Alone Again Blues; Lorelei, The [4]; Maid's Sextette; Rip Van Winkle and His Little Men [3]; She's Spanish [2]; Some Fine Day; Whose Baby Are You?

Cast: Louise Groody; John E. Hazzard; Ada Lewis; Hal Skelly; Ernest Torrence

Notes: [1] Same tune as "Honeymoon Land" in TOOT TOOT. [2] Out Baltimore prior to opening. [3] Cut. [4] Cut during rehearsals and put into SALLY.

3147 • NIGHT IN OLD PARIS, A

OPENED: 04/26/1925
Musical

Composer: Henry Hadley
Librettist: Frederick Truesdell
Director: Frank McCormack; Hassard Short

Source: UNKNOWN (Play: Glen MacDonough); **Musical Director:** Henry Hadley

Cast: Charles Hart; John Willard

Notes: A one-act musical. Part of THE LAMBS ANNUAL PUBLIC SPRING GAMBOL. *See under that name for further information.* No songs listed in program.

3148 • NIGHT IN PARIS, A

OPENED: 01/05/1926   Theatre: Casino de Paris
Revue   Broadway: 335

Librettist: Harold Atteridge
Producer: Messrs. Shubert
Director: J.C. Huffman

Choreographer: George Dobbs; Gertrude Hoffman; **Costumes:** Ernest Schrapps; **Set Design:** Watson Barratt

Songs: Amy (C: Roy Webb; L: F. Coulon); Black Mask (Temptation), The (C: J.J. Shubert Jr.; L: Clifford Grey; McElbert Moore); Bobbed Haired Baby (C: J. Fred Coots; Maurie Rubens; L: McElbert Moore); Fascinating Lady [2]

(C: J. Fred Coots; Maurie Rubens; L: McElbert Moore); In Chinatown in Frisco (C: Maurice Yvain; L: Clifford Grey; McElbert Moore); Louisiana (C: J. Fred Coots; Maurie Rubens; L: McElbert Moore); Newport Glide, The [2] (C: J. Fred Coots; Maurie Rubens; L: Clifford Grey); Nile, The (C/L: Xaver Leroux); Powder Puff (C: J. Fred Coots; Maurie Rubens; L: Clifford Grey; McElbert Moore); Voodoo of the Zulu Isle (C: J. Fred Coots; Maurie Rubens; L: Clifford Grey; McElbert Moore); Why Should We Be Wasting Time [1] (C: J. Fred Coots; Al Goodman; Maurie Rubens; L: Eddie Conrad; McElbert Moore)

Cast: Ray Bolger; Yvonne George; Gertrude Hoffman Girls, The; Jack Osterman; Jack Pearl; Norma Terris

Notes: [1] Sheet music only. [2] ASCAP/Library of Congress only.

3149 • NIGHT IN SPAIN, A

OPENED: 05/03/1927   Theatre: Century
Revue   Broadway: 174

Composer: Jean Schwartz
Lyricist: Alfred Bryan
Librettist: Harold Atteridge
Producer: Messrs. Shubert
Director: Charles Judels

Choreographer: Gertrude Hoffman; Ralph Reader; **Costumes:** Ernest Schrapps; **Musical Director:** Max Hoffmann; **Set Design:** Watson Barratt

Songs: Argentine; Bambazoola; Curfew Walk, The; De Dum Dum; Did You Mean It? [1] (C/L: Phil Baker; C: Abe Lyman; L: Sid Silvers); Four Walls [1] (C: Dave Dreyer; L: Al Jolson; Billy Rose); Golden Gate [1] (C: Dave Dreyer; Joseph Meyer; L: Al Jolson; Billy Rose); Hot, Hot Honey; International Vamp; Love and Kisses [1] (C/L: Phil Baker; L: Sid Silvers); Million Eyes, A; My Rose of Spain; Nocturne, The; Nothin' [1] (C/L: Lou Handman; Roy Turk); Promenade the Esplanade; Rainy Day Pal [1] (C/L: Phil Baker; L: Sid Silvers); Room for Two [1]; Simple Spanish Maid; Sky Girl, The; Spanish Shawl, A; Under the Clover Moon [1] (C/L: Ted Healy)

Cast: Phil Baker; Ted Healy; Helba Huara; Helen Kane; Sid Silvers; Aileen Stanley; Norma Terris

Notes: [1] Sheet music only.

3150 • NIGHT IN VENICE, A (1929)

OPENED: 05/21/1929   Theatre: Shubert
Revue   Broadway: 175

Composer: Lee David; Maurie Rubens
Lyricist: J. Keirn Brennan; Moe Jaffe
Librettist: J. Keirn Brennan; Moe Jaffe
Producer: Messrs. Shubert
Director: Thomas A. Hart; Lew Morton

Source: EIN NACHT IN VENEDIG (Musical: Richard Genee; Johann Strauss; F. Zell); **Choreographer:** Busby Berkeley; Chester Hale; **Costumes:** Barbier; Erte; Ernest Schrapps; **Set Design:** Watson Barratt

Songs: Cellini's Plate; Dance Venitian; Fans; I'm for You, You're for Me (C: Lee David; L: J. Keirn Brennan); "It" in Italy, The; Legend of Leda, The; Lesson in French; Little Old Dreamy New York (Any Side Street of New York); Loose Ankles (C/L: Clay Boland; C: Maurie Rubens; L: Moe Jaffe); One Girl, The [1] (C: Vincent Youmans; L: Oscar Hammerstein II); One Night of Love (C: Maurie Rubens; L: J. Keirn Brennan); Sliding Down a Silver Cloud (C: Lee David; L: J. Keirn Brennan); Slow Motion; Stork Don't Come Around Anymore, The (C/L: Betty Morse Laidlaw); Strolling on the Lido (Lido Shores) (C: Lee David; Maurie Rubens; L: J. Keirn Brennan; Moe Jaffe); Tondelayo; With the Ile de France on the Horizon

Cast: Allen K. Foster Girls; Chester Hale Girls; Ted Healy; Anne Seymour

Notes: No program available. [1] Originally in RAINBOW. [2] Not in program.

3151 • NIGHT IN VENICE, A (1952)

OPENED: 06/1952   Theatre: Jones Beach
                            Marine
Musical   New York

Composer: Johann Strauss
Lyricist: Ruth Martin; Thomas Martin
Producer: Michael Todd

Source: EINE NACHT IN VENEDIG (Musical: Richard Genee; Johann Strauss; F. Zell); **Musical Director:** Thomas Martin

Songs: Ballet; Bells of St. Marks; Birthday Serenade; Don't Speak of Love to Me; Fireworks Gallop; Gondola Duet; Gondola Song; I Can't Find My

Wife; Loveable Fellow, A; Ni-nana Duet; Now That We Are Alone; Now the Day Is Done; Pigeons of San Marco, The; Quintet; Spaghetti Song; Tarantella; We Always Got Our Man; Women Are Here to Stay

Cast: Nola Fairbanks; Thomas Tibbet Hayward; Laurel Hurley; David Kurlan; Guen Omeron; Jack Russell; Kenneth Schon; Norwood Smith; Enzo Stuarti

3152 • NIGHT OF LOVE, A
OPENED: 01/07/1941   Theatre: Jolson
Musical   Broadway: 7

Composer: Robert Stolz
Lyricist: Rowland Leigh
Librettist: Rowland Leigh
Producer: Messrs. Shubert
Director: Barrie O'Daniels

Source: TONIGHT OR NEVER (Play: Lila Hatvany); **Costumes:** Ernest Schrapps; **Musical Director:** Joseph Littau; **Orchestrations:** George Lessner; **Set Design:** Watson Barratt

Songs: Chiquitin Trio; I'm Thinking of Love; Loosen Up; My Loved One; One Man I Need, The; Serenade for You; Streamlined Pompadour; Tonight or Never; Without You

Cast: Helen Gleason; John Lodge; Marguerite Namara

3153 • NIGHT OF STARS
OPENED: 09/20/1934
Revue

Songs: Night of Stars (C/L: George M. Cohan)

Cast: Fred E. Ahlert; Louis Alter; Harold Arlen; Harry Armstrong; Jack Benny; Milton Berle; Irving Berlin; Donald Brian; Lew Brown; Burns and Allen; Cab Calloway; George M. Cohan; Eddie Dowling; Eddie Duchin; Gus Edwards; Stuart Erwin; Dorothy Fields; Michel Fokine; George Gershwin; George Givot; Al Goodman; John Green; Phil Harris; Mark Hellinger; Ray Henderson; Lou Holtz; Bob Hope; Herman Hupfeld; J. Rosamond Johnson; Jerome Kern; Frances Langford; Mana Lucca; Jimmy McHugh; Mills Brothers; Mae Murray; Jack Pearl; Jan Peerce; Molly Picon; Harry Richman; Blanche Ring; Bill Robinson; Richard Rodgers; Sigmund Romberg; Rose Marie; Julia

Sanderson; Jimmy Savo; Arthur Schwartz; Jean Schwartz; Vivienne Segal; George Sidney; Kate Smith; Louis Sobol; Leopold Stokowski; Dana Suesse; Ed Sullivan; Tamara; James Thornton; Arthur Tracy; Rudy Vallee; Harry Von Tilzer; Fred Waring; Percy Wenrich; Paul Whiteman; Walter Winchell; Ed Wynn; Yacht Club Boys

Notes: A benefit for the United Jewish Appeal on behalf of German Jews. Presented at Yankee Stadium! This is an incomplete list of participants.

3154 • NIGHT OF THE FOURTH, THE
OPENED: 01/21/1901   Theatre: Victoria
Musical   Broadway: 14

Composer: Max Hoffmann
Lyricist: J. Sherrie Mathews
Librettist: George Ade

Musical Director: Max Hoffmann; **Vocal Arranger:** George Wiseman

Songs: Bal Masque, The; Cord on the Hat, The; Fiddle and I; Finale Act III; I've Hardly Known You Long Enough; Love Me Lize; M-O-N-E-Y Spells Money; Opening Chorus Act II; Stars of the Vaudeville; Stepsons of the Revolution; Violets; Walk; When Shakespeare Comes to Town; Whirlwind Dance

Cast: Harry Bulger; Joseph Coyne; Thomas Daly; Tony Hart Jr.; Walter Jones; Blanche Sherwood; Bessie Tannehill

Notes: No New York program available. Ade not credited in New York program.

3155 • NIGHT ON A ROOF GARDEN

Composer: Ed Hutchinson
Lyricist: Lee Barth; Ruby Lusby

Songs: I Was Never Meant for You

Notes: Sheet music only. No other information available.

3156 • NIGHT OUT, A (1920)
OPENED: 09/18/1920   Theatre: Winter Garden
Musical   London: 309

Composer: Cole Porter
Lyricist: Clifford Grey
Librettist: Arthur Miller; George Grossmith Jr.
Producer: Tom Reynolds
Director: Sydney Ellison

Source: L'HOTEL DU LIBRE EXCHANGE (Play: Maurice Desvallieres; Georges Feydeau; **Choreographer:** Espinosa; **Costumes:** Comelli; **Musical Director:** Willie Redstone)

Songs: Look Around; Our Hotel; Why Didn't We Meet Before

Cast: Stanley Holloway; Leslie Henson; Austin Melford; Phyllis Monkman

Notes: No program available.

3157 NIGHT OUT, A (1925)

OPENED: 09/07/1925
Musical   Closed out of town

Composer: Vincent Youmans
Lyricist: Irving Caesar; Clifford Grey
Librettist: George Grossmith; Arthur Miller
Producer: Alex A. Aarons
Director: Tom Reynolds

Source: NIGHT OUT, A (Musical: George Grossmith; Arthur Miller; Willie Redstone); **Choreographer:** Max Scheck; **Costumes:** Charles LeMaire; **Musical Director:** Charles Previn; **Orchestrations:** Paul Lannin; Hans Spialek; **Set Design:** August Vimnera

Songs: Bolshevik Love; Carnival; Daughters [1]; Happy Family, A; Hotel Never Tell; I Want a Yes Man [3] (L: Irving Caesar; Ira Gershwin; Clifford Grey); It's a Long Day at Our Hotel; I've Got a Day Off Today; Kissing [4]; Like a Bird on the Wing; Opening Act II; Opening Ensemble; Police, The; Queens [3]; Rag Picker's Dance, The; Really, Would You Believe It? [2]; So This Is Kissing; Sometimes I'm Happy [5]; Waiting for Something

Cast: Zelda Edwards; Robert Greig; Norman Griffen; Frederick Lord; Gwen Mannering; Toots Pounds; Ralph Roberts; Edward Scott; Philip Simmons

Notes: [1] Cut during rehearsal. Later used as "It's Every Girl's Ambition," which was cut from MARY JANE MCKANE and later put in THROUGH THE YEARS. [2] Music later used in "The Way You Manoeuvre" in HIT THE DECK. [3] Cut during rehearsal. [4] Same music

as "It Must Be Love" cut from LOLLIPOP score back when it was titled THE LEFT OVER. [5] Same music as "Come On and Pet Me" in MARY JANE MCKANE. Later put into HIT THE DECK.

3158 • NIGHT OWLS, THE

OPENED: 1919
Musical   New York

Composer: Joe Wilton
Lyricist: Joe Wilton
Librettist: Joe Wilton
Producer: Joe Wilton
Director: Joe Wilton

Choreographer: Joe Wilton

Songs: Alexander's Back from France; Bally Hoo Bay; Blues; Eyes; He's an American; If It Comes from Dixieland; Impromptu Review; Jerry; She's for Me; Wild Women; Women in Room Thirteen; You Didn't Want Me

Cast: George Douglas; Jessie Hiatt; Danny Murphy; Kitty Van; Joe Wilton

Notes: A burlesque musical. Program New York 1919.

3159 • NIGHT THAT MADE AMERICA FAMOUS, THE

OPENED: 02/26/1975   Theatre: Ethel Barrymore
Musical   Broadway: 75

Composer: Harry Chapin
Lyricist: Harry Chapin
Producer: Joseph Beruh; Edgar Lansbury; Shubert Organization
Director: Gene Frankel

Choreographer: Doug Rogers; **Costumes:** Randy Barcelo; **Dance Arranger:** John Morris; **Lighting Designer:** Imero Fiorentino; **Musical Director:** Stephen Chapin; **Set Design:** Kert Lundell

Songs: As I Grow Older; Battleground Bummer; Beginning of the End; Better Place to Be; Cat's in the Cradle; Changing of the Guard; Cockeyed John, Give Me a Dream; Give Me a Cause; Give Me a Road; Give Me a Wall; Great Divide; I'm a Wonderfully Wicked Woman; It's My Day; Love Can't; Maxie; Mr. Tanner; Night That Made America Famous, The; Peace Teachers; Pigeon Run; Prologue; Six String Orchestra; Sniper; Stoopid; Sunday Morning Sunshine; Taxi; Too

Much World; Welfare Rag; When I Look Up; When Maudey Wants a Man

Cast: Harry Chapin; Stephen Chapin; Tom Chapin; Mercedes Ellington; Kelly Garrett; Delores Hall; Gilbert Price; Ernie Pysher; Bill Starr; Lynne Thigpen

3160 • NIGHT THE ANIMALS TALKED, THE

OPENED: 1971
TV Musical

Composer: Jule Styne
Lyricist: Sammy Cahn

Songs: Greatest Miracle of All, The; It's Great to Communicate; Let's Not Behave Like People; Parable; Place Like This, A

Notes: No other information available.

3161 • NIGHTCAP

OPENED: 05/18/1958   Theatre: Showplace
Revue   Nightclub: 400

Composer: Jerry Herman
Lyricist: Jerry Herman
Producer: Jim Paul Eilers
Director: Jerry Herman

Choreographer: Phyllis Newman; **Costumes:** Nilo; **Lighting Designer:** Bud Nicholes; **Set Design:** Hal Jacobs

Songs: As for the Future; Confession to a Park Avenue Mother [1]; Finale; I Wish I Could Say; I'll Dance; In the Sack; Jolly Theatrical Season, A [1]; My Type; Naughty Forty-Second Street; Nice Running in to You; Number 1 on Your Hit Parade; Opening; Producer Didn't Hire Me, The; Showtune in 2/4 [2]; That Revue; Washington Square; Why Don't They Believe Me; Wrong Kind of Man; Your Good Morning [1]

Cast: Rita Gardner; Bobo Lewis; Kenneth Nelson; Charles Nelson Reilly

Notes: [1] Also in PARADE. [2] Also in PARADE as "There Is No Tune Like a Show Tune." Later music used as "It's Today" in MAME.

3162 • NIGHTCLUB CANTATA

OPENED: 01/09/1977   Theatre: Top of the Gate
Revue   Off-Broadway: 145

Composer: Elizabeth Swados
Lyricist: Elizabeth Swados
Producer: Charles Hollerith Jr.; Rosita Sarnoff
Director: Elizabeth Swados

Costumes: Kate Carmel; **Lighting Designer:** Cheryl Thacker; **Set Design:** Patricia Woodbridge

Songs: Adolescents; Applicant, The; Are You with Me?; Ballad of the Sad Cafe, The; Bestiario; Bird Chorus; Bird Lament; Dance, The; Dibarti; In Dreams Begin Responsibilities; Indecision; Isabella; On Living; Pastrami Brothers; Raga; Things I Didn't Know I Loved; To the Harbormaster; Ventriloquist and Dummy; Waiting; Waking This Morning

Cast: Karen Evans; Rocky Greenberg; Paul Kandel; JoAnna Peled; Shelley Plimpton; David Schechter; Elizabeth Swados; Mark Zagaeski

3163 • NIGHTINGALE, THE (1927)

OPENED: 01/03/1927   Theatre: Jolson
Musical   Broadway: 96

Composer: Armand Vecsey
Lyricist: P.G. Wodehouse
Librettist: Guy Bolton; P.G. Wodehouse
Producer: Messrs. Shubert
Director: Lewis Morton

Songs: Another One Gone Wrong; Breakfast in Bed; Fairyland; Finale Act I; He Doesn't Know; Homeland; Josephine (L: Clifford Grey); Love Like Yours Is Rare Indeed; May Moon; Once in September (L: Clifford Grey); Opening Chorus; Rabbit Song; Santa Claus; Two Little Ships

Cast: Stanley Lupino; Eleanor Painter; Tom Wise

3164 • NIGHTINGALE (1982)

OPENED: 03/12/1982   Theatre: First All
                     Children's
Musical   Off-Broadway

Composer: Charles Strouse
Lyricist: Charles Strouse
Librettist: Charles Strouse

Producer: First All Children's Th.
Director: Meridee Stein

Source: EMPEROR AND THE NIGHTINGALE, THE (Story: Hans Christian Andersen); **Choreographer:** Linda Reiff; **Costumes:** Christine Andrews; **Lighting Designer:** Victor En Yu Tan; **Musical Director:** Wayne Green; **Set Design:** Oliver Smith

Songs: Charming; Death Duet; Emperor Is a Man, The; I Was Lost; Mechanical Bird, The; Never Speak Directly to an Emperor; Nightingale, The; Perfect Harmony; Please Don't Make Me Hear That Song Again; Rivers Cannot Flow Upwards; Singer Must Be Free, A; Take Us to the Forest; We Are China; Who Are Those People?; Why Am I So Happy?

Cast: John Shuck

Notes: No songs listed in program of this opera.

3165 • NIGHTMARE!!

OPENED: 12/14/1977   Theatre: New
Playwrights'
Musical   Washington

Composer: Tim Grundmann
Lyricist: Tim Grundmann
Librettist: Tim Grundmann
Producer: Harry M. Bagdasian; Ken Bloom; New Playwrights' Theatre
Director: Ken Bloom

Choreographer: Anne Reynolds Day; **Costumes:** Mary Kay MacGregor; **Lighting Designer:** Tomm Tomlinson; **Musical Director:** Tim Grundmann; **Orchestrations:** Tim Grundmann; **Set Design:** Russell Metheny; **Vocal Arranger:** Tim Grundmann

Songs: Arrivederci My Little Iron; Bingo Blast; Don't Get Your Hopes Up; Girl with Talent, A; Gypsy Madness; Just Like That; Lucky By Lucky Girl; Maybe Monday I'll Conquer; Okey-Doke; Spaghetti Jamboree; Three Square Meals a Day; Tough Cookie; Where Is My Handsome Knight?; Why?; Why Did Daddy Tell Me Those Lies?; Why Don't We Save Our Love for Marriage?

Cast: Debra Cerruti; Gus Hathaway; A. David Johnson; Chris Kauffmann; Barbara Rappaport; Tanis Roach; Jan Frederick Shiffman

3166 • NIGHTS OF GLADNESS

OPENED: 1940   Theatre: Diamond
Horseshoe
Revue   Nightclub

Producer: Billy Rose
Director: John Murray Anderson

Choreographer: Gene Kelly; **Costumes:** Raoul Pene du Bois; **Orchestrations:** Don McGrane; **Set Design:** Raoul Pene du Bois

Songs: Old Army Game, The (C: Sammy Fain; L: Billy Rose)

Cast: Harold Dixon; Julian Eltinge; Gilda Gray; Eddie Leonard; Blanche Ring; Pat Rooney; Wini Shaw; Noble Sissle and His Orchestra

Notes: Only original song listed. Others were not identified in program.

3167 • NIGHTSONG

OPENED: 11/01/1977   Theatre: Village Gate
Revue   Off-Broadway: 35

Composer: Ron Eliran
Lyricist: Ron Eliran
Producer: Irwin Steiner
Director: Dan Early

Costumes: Margot Miller; Ron Whitehead; **Lighting Designer:** Jo Mayer; **Musical Director:** Jaroslav Jakubovic; **Set Design:** Harry Silverglat

Songs: All in the Name of Love; Butterfly Child; Come Elijah, Come; Come with Me [1]; Dusty Roads; Grain of Sand; Have a Little Fun [1]; I Believe [1]; I Hear a Song [1]; It Was Worth It [1]; Lady Vagabond; Looking at Us; Moments by the Sea; Music in the City; My Land [1]; Nightsong; Sweet Fantasy; Who Am I?; Young Days [1]

Cast: Ron Eliran; Joy Kohner; Holly T. Lipton; Dian Sorel

Notes: [1] Also in DON'T STEP ON MY OLIVE BRANCH.

3168 • NIKKI

OPENED: 09/29/1931   Theatre: Longacre
Musical   Broadway: 40

Composer: Philip Charig
Lyricist: James Dyrenforth
Librettist: John Monk Saunders
Producer: Harrison Hall
Director: William B. Friedlander

Source: LAST FLIGHT, THE (Film: John Monk Saunders); **Source:** NIKKI AND HER WAR BIRDS (Story: John Monk Saunders); **Source:** SINGLE LADY, A (Play: John Monk Saunders); **Choreographer:** Pal'mere Brandeaux; **Musical Director:** Jules Lenzberg; **Orchestrations:** Louis Katzman; **Set Design:** P. Dodd Ackerman; Karle O. Amend

Songs: Ghost of Little Egypt, The; My Heart Is Calling; Now I Know; On Account of I Love You; Screwy Little Tune; Taking Off; Wonder Why

Cast: Rudolfo Badloni; John Brooke; Frank Chapman; Adele Dixon; Cary Grant; Louis Jean Heydt; Douglass Montgomery; Bobby Tremaine; Nathaniel Wagner; Fay Wray

3169 • NIMROD AND THE TOWER OF BABEL

OPENED: 1989   Theatre: Neil Simon
Musical   Broadway

Composer: Tom O'Horgan
Librettist: John Walker
Producer: Chester Fox; Adela Holzer
Director: Tom O'Horgan

Choreographer: Wesley Fata; **Costumes:** Randy Barcelo; **Lighting Designer:** John McLain; **Musical Director:** Gordon Lowry Harrell; **Orchestrations:** Kenneth Bichel; **Set Design:** Bill Stabile

Cast: Cheryl Alexander; Tom Desrocher; J.P. Dougherty; Elena Ferrante; Michael Leslie; Raymond Patterson; Maggi-Meg Reed; Ric Ryder

Notes: This show was to be performed in repertory with SENATOR JOE. That show closed in previews. See under that name for those credits. This was advertised as an opera and so there were no songs listed in the program.

3170 • NINA ROSA

OPENED: 09/20/1930   Theatre: Majestic
Musical   Broadway: 129

Composer: Sigmund Romberg
Lyricist: Irving Caesar
Librettist: Otto Harbach
Producer: Messrs. Shubert
Director: J.C. Huffman; J.J. Shubert

Costumes: Orry Kelly; **Musical Director:** Max Meth; **Orchestrations:** Hans Spialek; **Set Design:** Watson Barratt

Songs: Adored One [1]; Arrival of Guests; Caballero [2]; Charming Senoritas [2]; Entrance of Dancers [2]; Gaucho Love Song, A; Gaucho March; I'm a Daughter of Peru; Kiss I Must Refuse You, A; Latigo; My First Love, My Last Love (L: Irving Caesar; Otto Harbach); My Idea of a Wife (My Idea of a Man) [1]; Nina Rosa; One Step [3]; Opening; Pablo; Pay Day; Payador; Perusing in Peru [2]; Pizarro Was a Very Narrow Man; Secret of My Life, The; Serenade of Love Tango; There Can Only Be One for Me; Valse Duet [3] (L: Irving Caesar; Otto Harbach); With the Dawn; Your Rose [1]; Your Smiles, Your Tears

Cast: Armida; Don Barclay; Victor Casmore; Zachary Caully; Leonard Ceeley; Clay Clement; Frank Horn; Stanley Jessup; Kalil- Ogly; George Kirk; Marion Marchante; Guy Robertson; Jack Sheehan; Ethelind Terry; Yo-Hay-Tong

Notes: [1] Sheet music only. [2] In British vocal score. [3] ASCAP only.

3171 • NINE

OPENED: 05/09/1982   Theatre: 46th Street
Musical   Broadway: 729

Composer: Maury Yeston
Lyricist: Maury Yeston
Librettist: Mario Fratti; Arthur Kopit
Producer: Roger S. Berlind; Kenneth D. Greenblatt; Harvey J. Klaris; Francine LeFrak; James M. Nederlander; Michel Stuart
Director: Tommy Tune

Source: 8 1/2 (Film: Federico Fellini; Ennio Flaiano; Tullio Pinelli); **Choreographer:** Tommy Tune; **Costumes:** William Ivey Long; **Lighting Designer:** Marcia Madeira; **Musical Director:** Wally Harper; **Orchestrations:** Jonathan Tunick; **Set Design:** Lawrence Miller; **Vocal Arranger:** Maury Yeston

Songs: Be Italian; Be On Your Own; Bells of St. Sebastian, The; Call from the Vatican, A; Coda di Guido; Duet; Folies Bergeres; Germans at the Spa, The; Getting Tall; Grand Canal, The; Guido's Song; I Can't Make This Movie; Long Ago; Man Like You, A; My Husband Makes Movies; Nine; Not Since Chaplin; Now's the Moment [1]; Only with You; Overture Delle Donne [2]; Simple; Spa Music; Ti Voglio Bene; Unusual Way; Waltz from Nine (inst.)

Cast: Karen Akers; Shelly Burch; Taina Elg; Cameron Johann; Raul Julia; Liliane Montevecchi; Anita Morris; Camille Saviola

Notes: [1] Added to tour. [2] A sung overture.

3172 • NINE-FIFTEEN REVUE

OPENED: 02/11/1930　Theatre: George M. Cohan
Revue　Broadway: 7

Librettist: Eddie Cantor; John Emerson; H.W. Hanemann; Geoffrey Kerr; Ring Lardner; Anita Loos; A. Dorian Otvos; Robert Ruskin; Paul Gerard Smith; Ruth Wilcox
Producer: Ruth Selwyn
Director: Alexander Leftwich

Choreographer: Busby Berkeley; Leon Leonidoff; **Costumes:** Kiviette; **Musical Director:** Donald Vorhees; **Set Design:** Clark Robinson

Songs: Ankle Up the Altar [2] (C: Richard Myers; L: Edward Eliscu); Boudoir Dolls (C: Ned Lehac; L: Edward Eliscu); Breakfast Dance (C: Ralph Rainger; L: Edward Eliscu); Bring Him Back Here [2] (C: Harold Arlen; L: Ted Koehler); Chimney Pots [2] (C: Kay Swift; L: Paul James); Couldn't We Be Like That? [2] (C: Kenneth Smith; L: Edward Hayman); Extra Man, The [2] (C/L: Cole Porter); Fashion Parade (inst.) [2] (C: Rudolf Friml); Gee It's So Good, It's Too Bad (C: Harold Arlen; L: Ted Koehler); Get Happy (C: Harold Arlen; L: Ted Koehler); Gotta Find a Way to Do It (C: Roger Wolfe Kahn; L: Paul James); How Would a City Girl Know? (C: Kay Swift; L: Paul James); I Actually Am [2] (C: Roger Wolfe Kahn; L: Irving Caesar); I Give Myself Away [2] (C: Jacques Fray; L: Edward Eliscu); I Like the Looks of You [2] (C: Tom Ford; L: Harry Revel); Knockin' on Wood (C: Richard Myers; L: Edward Eliscu); One Way Street [2] (C: Richard Myers; L: Edward Eliscu); Purty Little Thing, A

(C: Philip Broughton; L: Will B. Johnstone); Ta Ta, Ol' Bean (C: Manning Sherwin; L: Edward Eliscu); They Sing, They Dance, They Talk [2] (C: Richard Rodgers; L: Lorenz Hart); Toddlin' Along (C: George Gershwin; L: Ira Gershwin); Two Gat Gertie [2] (C/L: Herman Hupfeld); Up Among the Chimney Pots (C: Kay Swift; L: Paul James); Winter and Spring (C: Rudolf Friml; L: Edward Eliscu); Wonders with You [2] (C: Richard Rodgers; L: Lorenz Hart); World of Dreams (C: Victor Herbert; L: Edward Eliscu); You Wanted Me, I Wanted You (C: Harold Arlen; L: Ted Koehler); You Will Never Know (C: Vincent Youmans; L: Paul James)

Cast: Nan Blackstone; Lynn Dore; Ruth Etting; Helen Gray; Fred Keating; Paul Kelly; Charles Lawrence; Carmen Mathews; Harry McNaughton; Margaret Merle; Joe Michon; Pete Michon; Mary Murray; Oscar "Rags" Ragland; Frances Shelley

Notes: [1] ASCAP/Library of Congress only. [2] Out New Haven 1/21/30.

3173 • NINE O'CLOCK REVUE, THE (1931)

OPENED: 07/27/1931
Revue　Los Angeles

Composer: Val Burton; Will Jason
Lyricist: Val Burton; Will Jason
Librettist: Harry Sauber
Producer: Comedian's Guild
Director: Eddie Diamond; Eddie Prinz; Harry Sauber

Choreographer: Eddie Diamond; Eddie Prinz; **Costumes:** Bernard Hassert; **Musical Director:** Max Fisher; **Set Design:** Ralph Goodacre

Songs: Cherry Blossom Time; Day I Met You, The; Gotta New Song; Here Comes the Big Brass Band; Hi Low Downs, The; Hum Da Di Di; Neptune's Son; Never Mind Ma'mselle; Penthouse Serenade (When We're Alone); Sing a Song of Sixpence; Tale of Woe, A (L: Eddie Lambert); Tight; Trail of No's, A

Cast: Eddie Borden; Julian Eltinge; Frankie Heath; Al Herman; Eddie Lambert

Notes: A Hollywood production.

3174 • NINE O'CLOCK REVUE, THE (1933)

OPENED: 1933
Revue   Los Angeles

Songs: I'm Just a Jungle Jidjolo

Cast: Virginia Kami; Carla Laemmle; Eddie Lambert; John T. Murray; Doris Whitney

Notes: A Hollywood production. No program available.

3175 • 1940'S RADIO HOUR, THE

OPENED: 10/07/1979   Theatre: St. James
Revue   Broadway: 105

Librettist: Walton Jones
Producer: Roger Berlind; Ira Bernstein; Joseph P. Harris; Jujamcyn Productions
Director: Walton Jones

Choreographer: Thommie Walsh; **Costumes:** William Ivey Long; **Lighting Designer:** Tharon Musser; **Musical Director:** Stanley Lebowsky; **Orchestrations:** Gary S. Fagin; **Set Design:** David Gropman; **Vocal Arranger:** Paul Schierhorn

Songs: Ain't She Sweet (C: Milton Ager; L: Jack Yellen); All the Things You Are [1] (C: Jerome Kern; L: Oscar Hammerstein II); At Last (C: Harry Warren; L: Mack Gordon); Blue Moon (C: Richard Rodgers; L: Lorenz Hart); Blues in the Night (C: Harold Arlen; L: Johnny Mercer); Boogie Woogie Bugle Boy; Chattanooga Choo Choo (C: Harry Warren; L: Mack Gordon); Chiquita Banana (C/L: Len Mackenzie; Garth Montgomery; William Wirges); Daddy; For Me and My Gal [1] (C: George W. Meyer; L: E. Ray Goetz; Edgar Leslie); Have Yourself a Merry Little Christmas (C/L: Ralph Blane; Hugh Martin); How About You (C: Burton Lane; L: Ralph Freed); I Got It Bad and That Ain't Good (C: Duke Ellington; L: Paul Francis Webster); I'll Be Around [1] (C/L: Alec Wilder); I'll Never Smile Again (C/L: Ruth Lowe); Jingle Bells (C/L: J.S. Pierpont); Lady Is a Tramp, The [1] (C: Richard Rodgers; L: Lorenz Hart); Little Brown Jug (C/L: J.E. Winner); My Funny Valentine [1] (C: Richard Rodgers; L: Lorenz Hart); Our Love Is Here to Stay (C: George Gershwin; L: Ira Gershwin); Prelude to a Kiss [1]; Rose of the Rio Grande (C: Ross Gorman; Harry Warren; L: Edgar Leslie); Strike Up the Band (C: George Gershwin; L: Ira Gershwin); That Old Black Magic (C: Harold Arlen; L: Johnny Mercer); Top Hat, White Tie and Tails [1] (C/L: Irving Berlin); You Go to My Head [1] (C: J. Fred Coots; L: Haven Gillespie); You're Driving Me Crazy (C/L: Walter Donaldson)

Cast: Dee Dee Bridgewater; Arny Freeman; Stephen James; Stanley Lebowsky; Josef Sommer; Crissy Wilzak

Notes: No original songs in this show. [1] Cut prior to New York opening.

3176 • 1999

OPENED: 11/15/1897   Theatre: Casino
Musical   Broadway

Composer: Edouard Holst
Librettist: Herman Lee Ensign
Director: Gerald Coventry

Costumes: Mme. Siedle; **Set Design:** Joseph Physioc

Cast: Hugh Chilvers; Warwick Ganor; Emma Janvier; Clara Alene Jewell; Bertha Waltinger

Notes: No songs listed in program.

3177 • 90 IN THE SHADE

OPENED: 01/25/1915   Theatre: Knickerbocker
Musical   Broadway: 40

Composer: Jerome Kern
Lyricist: Harry B. Smith
Librettist: Guy Bolton
Producer: Daniel V. Arthur
Director: Robert Milton

Choreographer: Julian Alfred; **Musical Director:** John McGhie

Songs: Can't You See I Mean You [6] (L: Herbert Reynolds); Courtship Dance; Foolishness; Human Nature; It Isn't Your Fault [3] (L: M.E. Rourke); I've Been About a Bit; Jolly Good Fellow (L: Clare Kummer); Lonely in Town (C/L: Clare Kummer); My Lady's Dress; My Mindanao Chocolate Soldier (C: P.H. Christine; L: Clare Kummer); Package of Seeds [2] (L: Herbert Reynolds; P.G. Wodehouse); Peter Pan; Regular Guy, A; Rich Man, Poor Man (L: Clare Kummer); Triangle, The [4] (L: Guy

Bolton); Where's the Girl for Me? [5]; Whistling Dan [1]; Wonderful Days (L: Clare Kummer

Cast: Marie Cahill; Richard Carle; Otis Harlan; Victor Morley; Pedro de Cordoba

Notes: [1] Music used as title song of LEAVE IT TO JANE. [2] Used later in OH, BOY! [3] Added after opening. Later used in LOVE O' MIKE. Also used with a Harry B. Smith lyric in the London show HIGH JINKS. [4] Later used in VERY GOOD EDDIE. [5] Later used in THE LADY IN RED. [6] Not in programs.

3178 • NITE CLUB CONFIDENTIAL

OPENED: 05/14/1984   Theatre: Ballroom
Revue   Off-Broadway: 156

Composer: Dennis Deal; Albert Evans
Lyricist: Dennis Deal; Albert Evans
Librettist: Dennis Deal
Producer: CHS Productions; Greentrack Entertainment
Director: Dennis Deal

Choreographer: Dennis Deal; **Costumes:** Stephen Rotondaro; **Lighting Designer:** Richard Latta; **Orchestrations:** Dennis Deal; Albert Evans; **Set Design:** Christopher Cole; **Vocal Arranger:** Dennis Deal; Albert Evans

Songs: Black Slacks [1] (C/L: Joseph Bennett; Jimmy Denton); Bonjour; Canarsie Diner, The; Cloudburst [1] (C/L: Jimmy Harris; Jon Hendricks; Leroy Kirkland); Commont Allez-Vous [1] (C/L: Murray Grand); Crazy New Words; Dead End Street; Dorothy's Opener; Dressed to Kill; Ev'rybody's Boppin' [1] (C/L: Jon Hendricks); French with Tears [2] (C/L: Harold Rome); Goody, Goody [1] (C: Matt Malneck; L: Johnny Mercer); I Thought About You [1] (C: Jimmy Van Heusen; L: Johnny Mercer); Long Goodbye, The; Love Isn't Born It's Made [3] (C: Arthur Schwartz; L: Frank Loesser); Nite Club; Nothing Can Replace a Man [4] (C: Sammy Fain; L: Dan Shapiro); Other One (Darling), The [5] (C: Arthur Siegel; L: June Carroll); Put the Blame on Mamie; Saturday's Child [6] (C: Baldwin Bergersen; L: Phyllis McGinley); Something's Gotta Give [7] (C/L: Johnny Mercer); That Old Black Magic [8] (C: Harold Arlen; L: Johnny Mercer); Yodelin' Dixieland [1] (C/L: Fred Rauch; Wally Schmied)

Cast: Stephen Berger; Fay De Witt; Steve Gideon; Denise Nolin; Tom Spiroff

Notes: [1] Not written for show. [2] Not written for show. From ALIVE AND KICKING. [3] Not written for show. From film THANK YOUR LUCKY STARS. [4] Not written for show. From ANKLES AWEIGH. [5] Not written for show. From NEW FACES OF 1962. [6] Not written for show. From SMALL WONDER. [7] Not written for show. From film DADDY LONGLEGS. [8] Not written for show. From STAR SPANGLED RHYTHM.

3179 • NO FOOLIN'

OPENED: 06/24/1926   Theatre: Globe
Revue   Broadway: 108

Composer: James F. Hanley
Lyricist: Gene Buck
Librettist: Gene Buck; Irving Caesar; James F. Hanley; J.P. McEvoy
Producer: Florenz Ziegfeld
Director: Walter Wilson

Choreographer: John Boyle; **Costumes:** John Harkrider; **Musical Director:** Alfred Goodman; **Orchestrations:** Emil Gestenberger; Charles Grant; Walter Haenschen; Steve Jones; Will Vodery; **Set Design:** Joseph Urban; John Wenger

Songs: Don't Do the Charleston; Every Little Thing You Do; Florida, the Moon and You (C: Rudolf Friml); Gentlemen Prefer Blondes (C: Rudolf Friml; L: Irving Caesar); Honey, Be Mine; How Could Little Red Riding Hood (C/L: A.P. Randolph); I Want a Girl to Call My Own (C: Rudolf Friml); Little Marie (L: Gene Buck; James F. Hanley; Billy Rose); Nize Baby [1] (L: Ballard Macdonald); No Foolin'; Only Thing Green About the Girl of Today Is the Green Upon Her Hat, The [2] (C: Rudolf Friml); Poor Little Marie (L: Irving Caesar); That's As Far As It Goes [2] (C: Rudolf Friml); Wasn't It Nice? (C: Rudolf Friml; L: Irving Caesar); We're Cleaning Up Broadway (C: Rudolf Friml; L: Irving Caesar); When I Hear an Old Fashioned Waltz [2] (C: Rudolf Friml); When the Shaker Plays a Cocktail Tune [1]

Cast: Bugs Baer; James Barton; Ray Dooley; Peggy Fears; Irving Fisher; Charles King; Claire Booth Luce; Moran & Mack; Greta Nissen; Polly Walker

Notes: When trying out previous to New York the show was titled ZIEGFELD'S PALM BEACH NIGHTS, ZIEGFELD'S PALM BEACH GIRL and ZIEGFELD'S AMERICAN REVUE OF 1926. It was titled ZIEGFELD FOLLIES OF 1926 on the road following Broadway. It was also titled ZIEGFELD'S AMERICAN REVUE OF 1926 after opening. [1] Sheet music only. [2] ASCAP/Library of Congress only.

3180 • NO FOR AN ANSWER

OPENED: 01/05/1941   Theatre: Mecca Temple
Musical   Broadway: 3

Composer: Marc Blitzstein
Lyricist: Marc Blitzstein
Librettist: Marc Blitzstein
Director: William E. Watts

Set Design: Howard Bay

Songs: Dimples; Francie; Fraught; Gina; In the Clear; Litt'ry and Artistic Scene, 1930, The [1]; Make the Heart Be Stone; Mike; Nick; No for an Answer; Outside Agitator [1]; Penny Candy; Purest Kind of a Guy; Secret Singing; Song of the Bat, The; Take the Book

Cast: Carol Channing; Bert Conway; Curt Conway; Olive Deering; Lloyd Gough; Norma Green; Elaine Perry; Charles Polacheck; Martin Ritt; Coby Ruskin; Alfred Ryder; Robert Simon; Hester Sondergaard; Martin Wolfson

Notes: No program available. [1] Cut.

3181 • NO-FRILLS REVUE, THE

OPENED: 11/25/1987   Theatre: Cherry Lane
Revue   Off-Broadway: 207

Librettist: Michael Abbott; Douglas Bernstein; Martin Charnin; Ronny Graham; Denis Markell; Thomas Meehan; Sarah Weeks
Producer: Beam One, Ltd.; David H. Peipers; Del Tenney
Director: Martin Charnin

Choreographer: Frank Ventura; **Costumes:** Perry Ellis; **Lighting Designer:** Clarke W. Thornton; **Musical Director:** David Gaines; **Orchestrations:** Steven M. Alper; **Set Design:** Evelyn Sakash

Songs: Being with Me (C: Brian Lasser; L: Michael Leeds); Brand New Hammer, A (C/L: Sally Fay; David Finkle; Bill Weeden); Come On, Midnight [2] (C: Harold Arlen; L: Martin Charnin); I Know Where the Bodies Are Buried (C/L: Martin Charnin); It Hasn't Been Easy (C/L: Sally Fay; David Finkle; Bill Weeden); My Reunion Prayer (C/L: Sally Fay; David Finkle; Bill Weeden); Nine Supreme Chords, The (C: Steven M. Alper; L: Martin Charnin); No-Frills Revue, The (C/L: Martin Charnin); Privacy (C/L: Craig Carnelia); Someone's Got to Do It (C/L: Michael Abbott; Martin Charnin; Sarah Weeks); Stools [1] (C/L: Martin Charnin); Tippy-Tappy (C: Marvin Hamlisch; L: Martin Charnin); We Have to Sing This Song (C/L: Douglas Bernstein; Denis Markell)

Cast: Adinah Alexander; Sasha Charnin; Clare Fields; Stephani Hardy; Sarah Knapp; Andre Montgomery; Lynn Paynter; Justin Ross; Bob Stillman

Notes: [1] From UPSTAIRS AT O'NEALS. [2] Written for SOFTLY.

3182 • NO MAN CAN TAME ME

OPENED: 02/01/1959   Theatre: CBS
TV Musical

Composer: Ray Evans; Jay Livingston
Lyricist: Ray Evans; Jay Livingston

Songs: How Can I Be Alone Again; I Heard; One Hand Tied Behind My Back

Cast: Eddie Foy Jr.; Gisele MacKenzie; John Raitt

3183 • NO MAN'S A HERO

Notes: *See HOLLYWOOD HOLIDAY.*

3184 • NO! NO! NANETTE!

OPENED: 09/16/1925   Theatre: Globe
Musical   Broadway: 329

Composer: Vincent Youmans
Lyricist: Irving Caesar
Librettist: Otto Harbach; Frank Mandel
Producer: H.H. Frazee
Director: H.H. Frazee

Source: MY LADY FRIENDS (Play: Frank Mandel; Emil Nyitray); **Choreographer:** Sammy Lee; **Musical Director:** Nicholas Kempner; **Set Design:** P. Dodd Ackerman

Songs: Boy Next Door, The [2] (L: Schuyler Greene; Otto Harbach); Call of the Sea, The (L: Otto Harbach); Chase of the Fox, The [2]; Fight Over Me (L: Otto Harbach); Flappers Are We (Opening Chorus); Hello, Hello, Telephone Girlie (L: Otto Harbach); I Don't Want a Girlie [2] (L: B.G. DeSylva); I Want to Be Happy; I'm Waiting for You (L: Otto Harbach); It's the Cook Who Saves the Day [1] (L: Unknown); I've Confessed to the Breeze I Love You (L: Otto Harbach); Lilies of the Field [2]; My Doctor [3] (L: Otto Harbach); No, No, Nanette [5] (L: Otto Harbach); Pay Day Pauline (L: Otto Harbach); Peach on the Beach (L: Otto Harbach); Perfect Gentleman, A [1]; Santa Claus [2] (L: Otto Harbach); Take a Little One Step [4] (L: Zelda Sears); Tea for Two; Too Many Rings Around Rosie; We're All of Us Excited (Finale Act II); When You're Sad [6]; Who's the Who (Where Has My Hubby Gone Blues); You Can Dance with Any Girl at All

Cast: Jack Barker; Wellington Cross; Elinor Dawn; Louise Groody; Mary Lawlor; Beatrice Lee; Georgia O'Ramey; Edna Whistler; Josephine Whittell; Charles Winninger

Notes: Where lyricist is unknown the lyricist was probably not Irving Caesar. [1] Cut in rehearsals. [2] Cut prior to opening. [3] Cut after NY opening. [4] Added to London production. From LOLLIPOP. [5] Music first as "My Boy and I" in MARY JANE MCKANE. ASCAP lists lyricists as Harbach, Caesar and Frank Mandel. [6] In London version. [7] Sheet music only.

3185 • NO OTHER GIRL

OPENED: 08/13/1924   Theatre: Morosco
Musical   Broadway: 56

Composer: Harry Ruby
Lyricist: Bert Kalmar
Librettist: Aaron Hoffman
Producer: Morris Green; A.L. Jones
Director: John Meehan

Choreographer: Larry Ceballos; **Costumes:** Erle Frank; **Musical Director:** Alfred Newman; **Set Design:** Livingston Platt

Songs: After the Curfew Rings; Best in the Trade, The; Day Dreams; Doing the Town; Honduras; I Know That I Love You; I Would Rather Dance a Waltz; In the Corner of My Mind; It's the Dancer You Love Who Makes You Love to Dance; Keep the Party Going; Look Out for Us, Broadway; Molly; No Other Girl; Pleasant Greeting, A; You Flew Away from the Nest

Cast: Eddie Buzzell; Doris Eaton; Helen Ford; Aileen Meehan; John Sheehan; William Sully

3186 • NO SHOESTRINGS

OPENED: 09/16/1963   Theatre: Upstairs at the
                                      Downstairs
Revue   Off-Broadway: 66

Composer: John Pritchard
Lyricist: Peter Myers
Librettist: Woody Allen; Dee Caruso; Herb Hartig
Producer: Sam Pottle; Upstairs at the Downstairs
Director: Ben Bagley

Choreographer: Robert Haddad; **Costumes:** Dick Granger; **Lighting Designer:** George Curley; **Musical Director:** Dorothea Freitag; **Set Design:** William Ritman; **Vocal Arranger:** Dorothea Freitag

Songs: Ballad of Beauregard Green [8] (C: Ronnie Cass); Billy Sol Estes [1] (C/L: Louis Botto); Cinema I and Cinema II [1] (C/L: Michael McWhinney); Dark Lady of the Senates; Don't Let Me Down [1] (C: Ronnie Cass); Fun and Games [7] (C/L: Bud McCreery); Good Book and Lyrics [4] (C: Ronnie Cass); Heavenly Bodies [7] (C: Arthur Siegel; L: Michael McWhinney); Hoffa Love Is Better Than None [7] (C: Arthur Siegel; L: Michael McWhinney); It's a Great Little World [9] (C: Ronnie Cass); It's Time to Say Goodnight [5] (C: John Pritchard; L: Francis Essex); I've Been True to Myself [7] (C: Richard Chodosh; L: Barry Alan Grael); Lac des Scenes [5] (C/L: Ronnie Cass); Little Girl Blue (C: Arthur Siegel; L: Michael McWhinney); Lollipop Lane [7] (C/L: Bud McCreery); Mr. Henderson [3] (C: Ronnie Cass); Pawn for Wernher Von Braun, A [7] (C/L: Larry Grossman); 1600 Pennsylvania Avenue [7] (C/L: Rod Warren); Story of Alice [1] (C/L: Larry Holofcener); Suburban Lullaby [7] (C: Richard Wernick; L: Barry Alan Grael); That Isn't Done [7] (C: Stephen Lawrence; L: Treva Silverman); Thing that Johnny Did!, The [7] (C: Arthur Siegel; L: Michael McWhinney); This Year of Disgrace [7] (C: Ronnie Cass); Two Mrs. Browns, The [6] (C: Richard Addinsell; L: Arthur Macrae); Vagabond Student [2] (C: Ronnie Cass)

Cast: Danny Carroll; Jane Connell; Barry Dennam; Bill McCutcheon; Patti Regan; June Squibb; **Pianist:** Dorothea Freitag

Notes: [1] Cut after opening. [2] Cut after opening. Originally in FOR AMUSEMENT ONLY in London. [3] Cut after opening. Originally in FOR ADULTS ONLY in London. [4] Cut after opening. Originally in INTIMACY AT 8:30 in London. This song is a satire on THE MUSIC MAN. [5] Originally in LORD CHAMBERLAIN REGRETS in London. [6] Cut after opening. Originally in LIVING FOR PLEASURE in London. [7] Added after opening. [8] Cut after opening. Originally in LORD CHAMBERLAIN REGRETS in London. [9] Added after opening. Originally in LORD CHAMBERLAIN REGRETS in London.

3187 • NO STRINGS

OPENED: 03/15/1962　Theatre: 54th St.
Musical　　　　　　　　Broadway: 580

Composer: Richard Rodgers
Lyricist: Richard Rodgers
Librettist: Samuel Taylor
Producer: Richard Rodgers
Director: Joe Layton

Choreographer: Joe Layton; **Costumes:** Donald Brooks; Fred Voelpel; **Dance Arranger:** Peter Matz; **Lighting Designer:** David Hays; **Musical Director:** Peter Matz; **Orchestrations:** Ralph Burns; **Set Design:** David Hays

Songs: Be My Host; Eager Beaver; How Sad; La La La; Loads of Love; Look No Further; Love Makes the World Go; Maine; Man Who Has Everything, The; No Strings; Nobody Told Me; Orthodox Fool, An; Sweetest Sounds, The; Yankee, Go Home [1]; You Don't Tell Me

Cast: Noelle Adam; Diahann Carroll; Don Chastain; Alvin Epstein; Mitchell Gregg; Ann Hodges; Richard Kiley; Bernice Massi; Polly Rowles

Notes: [1] Cut prior to opening.

3188 • NO TIME FOR SERGEANTS

OPENED: 10/20/1955　Theatre: Alvin
Play　　　　　　　　　Broadway: 796

Author: Ira Levin
Producer: Maurice Evans; Emmett Rogers
Director: Morton Da Costa

Source: NO TIME FOR SERGEANTS (Novel: Mac Hyman); **Costumes:** Noel Taylor; **Lighting Designer:** Peggy Clark; **Set Design:** Peter Larkin

Songs: No Time for Sergeants (C/L: McRae; Rutherford)

Cast: Rex Everhart; Andy Griffith; Earle Hyman; Don Knotts; Myron McCormick; Roddy McDowall

3189 • NO. 13 WASHINGTON SQUARE

OPENED: 08/23/1915　Theatre: Park
Play　　　　　　　　　Broadway: 56

Author: Leroy Scott
Director: William Collier

Songs: Buzzin the Bee (C/L: Jack Wells)

Cast: May Irwin; John Junior; Ffoliott Paget

3190 • NO. 33 WASHINGTON SQUARE

Notes: *See NO. 13 WASHINGTON SQUARE.*

3191 • NOAH'S ARK

OPENED: 1907

Composer: Clare Kummer
Lyricist: Clare Kummer

Songs: Arab of Ararat; Avalon; Down By the Sea; Fade Away; Mary Come Down; My Castle in the Air; My Very Own; Noah's Ark; Rosebud; There's a Lot of Things That Noah Never Knew (C: E. Ray Goetz; L: Vincent Bryan); Where Do You Buy Your Chapeau; Wilderness; You're the Girl I'm Looking For

Notes: No other information available.

3192 • NOBLE ROGUE, A

OPENED: 07/19/1929　Theatre: Gansevoort
Musical　　　　　　　　Broadway: 9

Composer: Kenyon Scott
Lyricist: Kenyon Scott
Librettist: Kenyon Scott
Director: Paul Gilmore; Adrian S. Perrin

Choreographer: J.R. O'Neil; Adrian S. Perrin

Songs: Spirit of Jasmine; When a Girl's in Love; Wonderful Dream; Zina

Cast: Nanette Flack; Robert Rhodes; Marguerite Zender

Notes: No program available.

3193 • NOBODY HOME
OPENED: 04/20/1915   Theatre: Princess
Musical   Broadway: 135

Composer: Jerome Kern
Librettist: Guy Bolton
Producer: F. Ray Comstock; Elisabeth Marbury
Director: Benrimo

Source: MR. POPPLE (OF IPPLETON) (Musical: Joseph W. Herbert); **Choreographer:** David Bennett; **Musical Director:** Max Hirschfeld; **Orchestrations:** Frank Saddler; **Set Design:** Elsie De Wolfe

Songs: Another Little Girl (L: Herbert Reynolds); Any Old Night Is a Wonderful Night [7] (C: Jerome Kern; Otto Motzan; L: Schuyler Greene; Harry B. Smith); At that San Francisco Fair [4] (C: Ford Dabney; James Reese Europe; Jerome Kern; L: Schuyler Greene); Bed, Wonderful Bed [6] (C: Dan Lipton; C.W. Murphy; L: Lawrence Grossmith); Chaplin Walk, The (C: Jerome Kern; Otto Motzan; L: Schuyler Greene); Cupid at the Plaza [2]; In Arcady (L: Herbert Reynolds); Keep Moving [3]; Magic Melody, The (L: Schuyler Greene); Military Dance (inst.); Nobody Home Cakewalk (inst.) (C: Otto Motzan); That Peculiar Tune [8] (C: Jerome Kern; Otto Motzan; L: Schuyler Greene; Herbert Reynolds); Wedding Bells Are Calling Me [5] (L: Harry B. Smith); Why Take a Sandwich to a Banquet (You Don't Take a Sandwich to a Banquet) (C: Worton David; L: J.P. Long); You Know and I Know (and We Both Understand) [1] (L: Schuyler Greene)

Cast: Alice Dovey; Lawrence Grossmith; George Lydecker; Maude Odell; Adele Rowland

Notes: [1] Originally in A GIRL OF TODAY. [2] Cut after opening. [3] Out Brooklyn 11/22/15. [4] Kern composed chorus only. [5] Added after opening. Later in VERY GOOD EDDIE. [6] Titled "Bed, Beautiful Bed" in sheet music. [7] Later interpolated into British show TONIGHT'S THE NIGHT! [8] Cut.

3194 • NOBODY'S GIRL
Notes: *See HOLKA POLKA.*

3195 • NOBODY'S PERFECT
OPENED: 06/1974
Musical   Closed out of town

Composer: Alec Wilder
Lyricist: Ethan Ayer
Librettist: Arnold Sundgaard
Producer: Williamstown Theatre Festival
Director: Nikos Psacharopoulos

Source: IMPORTANCE OF BEING ERNEST, THE (Play: Oscar Wilde); **Costumes:** Linda Fisher; **Lighting Designer:** Richard Devin; **Musical Director:** Herbert Kaplan; **Orchestrations:** Dennis Allan; James-Mark; Herbert Kaplan; **Set Design:** John Conklin

Songs: At Last; Cecily; Ernest Beware; Girl Brought Up with the Utmost Care, A; Guardians of the Nation; How Wonderful Blue Your Eyes; I Worship the Lily; In This Delicious World; Jack in the Country; Miss Fairfax Ever Since I Met You; Most Important Thing, The; On the Day I Lost My Novel; Pray Don't Talk about the Weather; Well, to Speak with Perfect Candor

Cast: Emery Battis; John Cunningham; Clifford David; June Gable; Marian Mercer; Elizabeth Parrish; Henrietta Valor

3196 • NOEL COWARD'S SWEET POTATO
OPENED: 09/29/1968   Theatre: Ethel Barrymore
Musical   Broadway: 44

Composer: Noel Coward
Lyricist: Noel Coward
Librettist: Roderick Cook
Producer: Robert L. Steele
Director: Lee Theodore

Choreographer: Lee Theodore; **Costumes:** David Toser; **Dance Arranger:** Fred Werner; **Lighting Designer:** Peter Hunt; **Musical Director:** Charles Schneider; **Set Design:** Helen Pond; Herbert Senn; **Vocal Arranger:** Charles Schneider

Songs: Alice; Bar on the Piccola Marina, A; Consecutive Fifths; Dance Little Lady; Don't Put Your Daughter on the Stage Mrs. Worthington; I Like America; If Love Were All; Karate [1]; Let's Do It (C: Cole Porter); Mad About the Boy; Mad Dogs and Englishmen; Matelot; Men About Town; Room with a View, A; Sunset in Samolo; Teach Me a Dance Like Grandma; Three White Feathers; Why Does Love Get in the Way?; World Weary

Cast: George Grizzard; Dorothy Loudon; Robert LuPone; Arthur Mitchell; Carole Shelley

Notes: No songs were written for this production. [1] Cut after opening.

3197 • NON PASQUALE

OPENED: 08/09/1983   Theatre: Delacorte
Musical   Off-Broadway: 32

Music Based On: Gaetano Donizetti
Composer: William Elliott
Lyricist: Anthony Giles; Nancy Heikin
Librettist: Anthony Giles; Nancy Heikin
Producer: N.Y. Shakespeare Festival

Source: DON PASQUALE (Opera: Gaetano Donizetti; Giovanni Ruffini)

Songs: Ah, Sweet Revenge; Always; Duchess Song, The; Fight to the Death; Finale (Bravo, Bravo); From the Convent; Holy and Innocent; House of Don Pasquale, The; If Only; Just Like a Young Man; La Morale; Love Must Be Delicate; Lullaby; Oh, What a Wedding; Pazzo; Permission; Poor Don Pasquale; Recitativo; Serenade; She's a Virgin; Si, Signora; Softly, Softly in the Garden; Subito (Nearer to the Lord); Tell Me You Love Me; That Is Normal; We Must Talk; We Need a Few More Servants; Wedding Ceremony, The; What on Earth Is Going on Tango, The

Cast: Joe Grifasi; Ron Leibman; Priscilla Lopez; Joe Masiell; Maureen Sadusk

3198 • NORMAL HEART, THE

OPENED: 04/21/1985   Theatre: New York
                                          Shakespeare Festival
Play   Off-Broadway: 294

Author: Larry Kramer
Producer: N.Y. Shakespeare Festival; Joseph Papp
Director: Michael Lindsay-Hogg

Costumes: Bill Walker; **Lighting Designer:** Natasha Katz; **Set Design:** Eugene Lee; Keith Raywood

Songs: We're Living in Wartime (C/L: Michael Callen)

Cast: Philip Richard Allen; David Allen Brooks; Brad Davis; William DeAcutis; Robert Dorfman; Lawrence Lott; D.W. Moffett; Michael Santoro; Concetta Tomei

3199 • NORMANDY WEDDING, A

OPENED: 02/21/1898   Theatre: Herald Square
Musical   Broadway: 32

Composer: William Furst
Lyricist: Fred C. Whitney
Librettist: Charles Wilson Byrne; J. Cheever Goodwin
Producer: Fred C. Whitney
Director: A.M. Holbrook

Source: LA GARDEUSE D'OIES (Musical)

Cast: Mabel Bouton; Richard Carroll; Dorothy Morton; William Norris

Notes: No songs listed in program.

3200 • NORTH AIN'T SOUTH

OPENED: 1923
Musical

Composer: Donald Heywood
Librettist: J.A. Shipp; J. Homer Tutt; Salem Tutt Whitney
Producer: J. Homer Tutt; Salem Tutt Whitney

Choreographer: Frank Montgomery

Songs: Keep-A-Stepping Along; On Parade; Pickaninny All Dressed Up; Po' Little Lamb; Shake a Leg; What Kind of a Woman Does a Man Expect?

Cast: Mae Kemp; George McClennon; Jesse A. Shipp; J. Homer Tutt; Salem Tutt Whitney

Notes: No other information available.

3201 • NORTH ATLANTIC

OPENED: 01/16/1977   Theatre: Gene Frankel
                                  Theatre Workshop
Musical   Off-Off-Broadway

Composer: James Fradrich
Lyricist: Michael Colby
Librettist: Michael Colby; James Fradrich

Musical Director: Bill Brohn

Songs: Ballet; Before I Fall; Deep in My Mind; Duo Thoughts; Erase Him; Happier Side; I Held a Hope; North Atlantic; Now Is Here; Raising an Igloo; Reindeer Moss; Sign Song; Sleigh with the Cream Colored Team; Solo Thoughts; Something Special; There's a Rainbow at the End; Where the Hell Is Annie?; Who'd Have Guessed It?; Ya Won't Complain

Cast: Susan Bigelow; Rick Emery; Julie Kurnitz; Alvin Lum

Notes: No program available.

3202 • NOT TONIGHT, BENVENUTO!

OPENED: 06/05/1979   Theatre: Carter
Musical   Off-Broadway: 2

Composer: Virgil Engeran
Lyricist: Virgil Engeran
Librettist: Virgil Engeran
Producer: Virgil Engeran; Jim Payne
Director: Jim Payne

Choreographer: Robin Reseen; **Costumes:** Sherri Buchs; **Dance Arranger:** Larry Hochman; **Lighting Designer:** Jessie Ira Berger; **Musical Director:** Steven Freeman; **Set Design:** James Morgan; Peter A. Schue; **Vocal Arranger:** Larry Hochman

Songs: Can't Make Love Without You; Diana; Funeral Procession; Gona Get Right Some Day; How Do You Do?; Lullaby; Now I Lay Me Down to Sleep; Poppin'; Search for Diana (C: Larry Hochman); This Is Our World; Together;

Wedding Ball; Who Can Control the Human Heart; Why Do I Love Bennie?

Cast: Ada Berry; Daniel Fortier; Christopher Hensel; Roger Noonan; Gene Stilwell; Paula Ward; Ron Wyche

3203 • NOT TONIGHT JOSEPHINE

Musical

Composer: Seymour Furth
Lyricist: Edward Hutchinson
Librettist: Mlle. Flovie; Frank Kennedy; Ben Linn
Producer: Edward Hutchinson
Director: Edwin T. Emery

Songs: Absolutely Nothing Tonight; Fifty Years Ago; Hello, Goodby; It Can't Keep Raining All the Time; I've a Parasol for You Dear; Kiss You Never Get, The; Lingerie; Love Comes without a Call; Love Dreams; Mexican Bean; Whispering Whispers

Notes: No program available.

3204 • NOT WHILE I'M EATING

OPENED: 12/19/1961   Theatre: Madison Avenue
                                  Playhouse
Revue   Off-Broadway: 2

Composer: Arthur Siegel
Lyricist: Arthur Sherman
Librettist: Herbert Hartig; Arthur Sherman
Producer: David Silberman
Director: Warren Enters

Choreographer: Tom Panko; **Costumes:** Stanley Simmons; **Dance Arranger:** Milton Greene; **Lighting Designer:** Richard Nelson; **Musical Director:** Milton Greene; **Set Design:** Charles A. Brandon; **Vocal Arranger:** Milton Greene

Songs: Bring Back the Good Old Days; Gold Rush in the Sky; Golden Eagle; How Jolly Our Folly; I Want; I've Got a Man on the Moon; Letter of the Law [1]; Moment, a Minute, A; My Heart's a Marionette; Not While I'm Eating; Take the Picture First!; Trial By Jury [2]; What Did You Put in That Look?; What Good Are You?; Wonderful Underworld [1]

Cast: Wisa D'Orso; Buzz Halliday; Judd Jones

Notes: [1] Not in program. [2] Production number featuring many songs.

3205 • NOT YET BUT SOON
OPENED: 1907
Musical

Composer: Egbert Van Alstyne
Lyricist: Harry Williams

Choreographer: Joseph C. Smith

Songs: Campmeetin' Time; I Like You Too; I'm the Leading Lady; I'm Wise; Larry; Mary Wise; My Irish Girl; Nurse Girls and Doctors; O Come My Love; San Antonio; Some Day When Dreams Come True (C/L: Phil Staats); Things That Happen Every Day; Way Down on the Farm; Wedding of the Blue and Grey; Wonderland

Cast: Lucy Daly; Alice Kelly; Fred Wyckoff

Notes: No other information available.

3206 • NOTHING BUT GIRLS
Notes: *See ZIEGFELD MIDNIGHT FROLIC (1st Edition).*

3207 • NOTHING BUT LOVE
OPENED: 10/14/1919   Theatre: Lyric
Musical   Broadway: 39

Composer: Harold Orlob
Lyricist: Frank Stammers
Librettist: Frank Stammers
Producer: Maddock & Hart
Director: Frank Stammers

Choreographer: David Bennett; **Musical Director:** Fred Hoff; **Set Design:** John Dudley

Songs: Ask the Stars; At the Shore; Beware; Dawn; I'll Remember You; It's Not What You Say; Moonbeams; Some Other Time; Stop Waltz, The; When I Walk Out with You; Wonderful Man

Cast: Donald Meek; Clarence Nordstrom; Ruby Norton; Marion Sunshine; Andrew Tombes; Robert Woolsey

3208 • NOTRE DAME
OPENED: 06/25/1991
Musical

Composer: Callum McLeod
Lyricist: Paul Leigh
Librettist: Mark Bramble

Source: NOTRE DAME DE PARIS (Book: Victor Hugo)

Notes: Old Fire Station, Oxford.

3209 • NOW IS THE TIME FOR ALL GOOD MEN
OPENED: 09/26/1967   Theatre: Theatre de Lys
Musical   Off-Broadway: 111

Composer: Nancy Ford
Lyricist: Gretchen Cryer
Librettist: Gretchen Cryer
Producer: David Cryer; Albert Poland
Director: Word Baker

Costumes: Jeanne Button; **Lighting Designer:** Carol Rubenstein; **Musical Director:** Stephen Lawrence; **Set Design:** Holly Haas; **Vocal Arranger:** Nancy Ford; Stephen Lawrence

Songs: All Alone; Campfire Songs; Down Through History; Halloween Hayride; He Could Show Me; It Was Good Enough for Grandpa; Katy Did; Keep 'Em Busy; Keep 'Em Quiet; My Holiday; On My Own; Quittin' Time; Rain Your Love on Me; See Everything New; Simple Life, A; Star of the Monument, A; Stuck-Up; Tea in the Rain; There's Going to Be a Wedding; Washed Away; We Shall Meet in the Great Hereafter; What's a Guy Like You Doin' in a Place Like This?; What's in the Air

Cast: David Cryer; Judy Frank; Anne Kaye; Sally Niven; David Sabin; Steve Skiles; Art Wallace

3210 • NOWHERE TO GO BUT UP
OPENED: 11/10/1962   Theatre: Winter Garden
Musical   Broadway: 9

Composer: Sol Berkowitz
Lyricist: James Lipton
Librettist: James Lipton
Producer: Kermit Bloomgarden; Herbert Greene; Steven H. Scheuer
Director: Sidney Lumet

Choreographer: Ron Field; **Costumes:** Robert Fletcher; **Lighting Designer:** Tharon Musser;

Musical Director: Herbert Greene;
Orchestrations: Robert Ginzler; **Set Design:**
Peter Larkin; **Vocal Arranger:** Herbert Greene

Songs: Ain't It a Joy [1]; Ain't You Ashamed?;
Baby, Baby; Couple of Clowns, A [1]; Dear Mom;
Follow the Leader Septet; Gimmie, Gimmie,
Gimmie [1]; Here I Am [1]; I Love You for That;
Live a Little; Nowhere to Go but Up; Odds and
Ends of Love, The; Out of Sight, Out of Mind;
Take Me Back; We Makin' Cash with Sour Mash:
No Rickie Tickie No Licq-ie Rag, The [2]; When a
Fella Needs a Friend; Yes, Mr. Baiello

Cast: Martin Balsam; Tom Bosley; Frank
Campanella; Bert Convy; Bruce Gordon; Phil
Leeds; Dorothy Loudon; Mary Ann Mobley

Notes: [1] Out Philadelphia 10/22/62. [2] Titled
"The Way We Makin' Dough You So and So: No
Rickie-Tickie No Washie-Rag" out of town

3211 • NUNSENSE

OPENED: 12/12/1985   Theatre: Cherry Lane
Musical   Off-Broadway

Composer: Dan Goggin
Lyricist: Dan Goggin
Librettist: Dan Goggin
Producer: Nunsense Theatrical Co.
Director: Dan Goggin

Choreographer: Felton Smith; **Lighting Designer:**
Susan A. White; **Musical Director:** Michael Rice;
Set Design: Barry Axtell

Songs: Benedicite; Biggest Ain't the Best, The;
Difficult Transition, A; Drive In, The; Gloria in
Excelsis Deo; Growing Up Catholic; Holier Than
Thou; Home Movie, A; I Could've Gone to
Nashville; I Just Want to Be a Star; Just a Coupla
Sisters; Lilacs Bring Back Memories; Nunsense Is
Habit-Forming; Playing Second Fiddle; So You
Want to Be a Nun; Soup's On (The Dying Nun
Ballet); Turn Up the Spotlight; We've Got to
Clean Out the Freezer

Cast: Christine Anderson; Vicki Belmonte; Semina
De Laurentis; Marilyn Farina; Suzi Winson

3212 • NUTCRACKER JIVE

OPENED: 1943
Musical   Unproduced

Music Based On: Peter Illitch Tchaikowsky
Composer: Herbert Kingsley
Lyricist: John Latouche

Notes: This show, which was written, was to be
produced at Christmas as a puppet show for
adults. In fact, one big scene was a puppet
stripping! Unfortunately, at his death,
Latouche's family destroyed his papers, leaving
no record of this show's score.

3213 • NUTS AND WINE

OPENED: 01/04/1914
Revue   London: 7

Composer: Melville Gideon; Frank E. Tours
Lyricist: C.H. Bovill; Guy Jones; P.G. Wodehouse
Librettist: C.H. Bovill; P.G. Wodehouse
Producer: Oscar Barrett Jr.
Director: Julian Alfred

Cast: Babette; Phyllis Bedella; Maidie Hope; R.G.
Knowles; Albert Le Fre; Violet Lloyd; Dorothy
Monkman; Eric Thorne

Notes: No other information available.

3214 • NYMPH ERRANT

OPENED: 10/06/1933   Theatre: Adelphi
Musical   London: 154

Composer: Cole Porter
Lyricist: Cole Porter
Librettist: Romney Brent
Producer: Charles B. Cochran
Director: Romney Brent

Choreographer: Agnes de Mille; **Costumes:** Doris
Zinkeisen; **Musical Director:** Hyman
Greenbaum; **Orchestrations:** Robert Russell
Bennett; **Set Design:** Doris Zinkeisen

Songs: Back to Nature with You; Casanova;
Cocotte, The; Experiment; French Colonial
Exposition Scene [2]; Georgia Sand; Greek
Dance; Harem Dance; How Could We Be
Wrong?; It's Bad for Me; My Louisa [1];
Neauville-Sur-Mer; Nymph Errant; Physician,
The [3]; Plumbing; Ruins; Si Vous Aimez Les
Poitrines; Solomon; Sweet Nudity [2]; They're
Always Entertaining; Tiller Routine; When
Love Comes Your Way [5]; You're Too Far
Away (I Look at You) [4]

Cast: David Burns; Betty Hare; Gertrude Lawrence; Queenie Leonard; Moya Nugent; Ralph Roberts; Austin Trevor; Elisabeth Welch

Notes: [1] Not used. Also not used in THE NEW YORKERS (1930) and WAKE UP AND DREAM. [2] Not used. [3] Cut from THE NEW YORKERS (1930) as "But He Never Said He Loved Me." [4] Cut. Also not used in THE NEW YORKERS (1930). [5] Not used. Later put into JUBILEE.

3218 • O'BRIEN GIRL, THE

O

3215 • O MARRY ME!

OPENED: 10/27/1961   Theatre: Gate
Musical   Off-Broadway: 21

Composer: Robert Kessler
Lyricist: Lola Pergament
Librettist: Lola Pergament
Producer: Lily Turner
Director: Michael Howard

Source: SHE STOOPS TO CONQUER (Play: Oliver Goldsmith); **Costumes:** Sonia Lowenstein; **Dance Arranger:** Sam Morgenstern; **Lighting Designer:** Helen Pond; Herbert Senn; **Musical Director:** Lowell Farr; **Orchestrations:** Sam Morgenstern; **Set Design:** Helen Pond; Herbert Senn; **Vocal Arranger:** Sam Morgenstern

Songs: Ale House Song; Be a Lover; Betrayed; Braggart Song, The; Fashions; I Love Everything That's Old; Kind of Man, The; Let's All Be Exactly and Precisely What We Are; Meeting, The; Morality; Motherly Love; O Marry Me!; Perish the Baubles; Proper Due; Say Yes, Look No; Time and Tide

Cast: Chevi Colton; Leonard Drum; Muriel Greenspon; Joe Silver; Elly Stone; Ted Van Griethuysen

3216 • O MISTRESS MINE

OPENED: 12/03/1936   Theatre: St. James
Play   London

Author: Ben Travers
Producer: William Mollison
Director: William Mollison

Songs: Good-Bye, Little Dream, Good-Bye [1] (C/L: Cole Porter)

Cast: Pierre Fresnay; Yvonne Printemps

Notes: No program available. [1] Cut from RED, HOT AND BLUE!

3217 • O SAY CAN YOU SEE!

OPENED: 10/08/1962   Theatre: Provincetown
                                          Playhouse
Musical   Off-Broadway: 32

Composer: Jack Holmes
Lyricist: Bill Conklin; Bob Miller
Librettist: Bill Conklin; Bob Miller
Producer: Greenville Company, The
Director: Cynthia Baer

Choreographer: Ray Harrison; **Costumes:** June K. Stevens; **Dance Arranger:** Lanny Meyers; **Lighting Designer:** Jules Fisher; **Musical Director:** Jack Holmes; **Orchestrations:** Lanny Meyers; **Set Design:** Jack H. Cornwell; **Vocal Arranger:** Lanny Meyers

Songs: Buy Bonds, Buster, Buy Bonds [1]; Canteen Serenade [1]; Chico-Chico Chico-Layo Tico-Tico Pay Pa Payo Bueno Vista de Banana By-the-Sea [1]; Dogface Jive; Doughnuts for Defense [1]; Dreamboat from Dreamland [1]; Flim Flam Flooey [1]; Freedom Choo Choo Is Leaving Today, The [1]; Hat Crossover [2]; Just the Way You Are; Master Race Polka, The [2]; My G.I. Joey [1]; Now and Then; O Say Can You See! [1]; Pearl [2]; So Long for Now [2]; Someone a Lot Like You; Take Me Back to Texas; Tan 'n' Hot; These Are Worth Fighting For [1]; Us Two [1]; Veronica Takes Over; When the Bluebirds Fly All Over the World [1]; Woogie Boogie, The

Cast: Nicholas Coster; Paul B. Price; Marcia Rodd; Joel Warfield; Elmarie Wendel

Notes: BUY BONDS BUSTER was a rewrite of this show. [1] Also in BUY BONDS BUSTER. [2] Written for BUY BONDS BUSTER.

3218 • O'BRIEN GIRL, THE

OPENED: 10/03/1921   Theatre: Liberty
Musical   Broadway: 164

Composer: Louis A. Hirsch
Lyricist: Otto Harbach

Librettist: Otto Harbach; Frank Mandel
Producer: George M. Cohan
Director: Julian Mitchell

Costumes: Alice O'Neil; **Musical Director:** Charles J. Gebest; **Set Design:** Unitt & Wickes

Songs: Conversation Step, The; Curiosity; Entrance of Dancers; Give, Give; Happy Family [3]; I Wonder How I Ever Passed You By; I'll Treat You Just Like a Sister; I'm So Excited; Indian Prance; Last Dance, The [1]; Learn to Smile; Murder; My Little Canoe; Partners; That O'Brien Girl; There Can't Be Any Harm in Saying Goodbye [2]; To Keep You in Your Seats; Un Sourire [4]

Cast: Georgia Caine; Elizabeth Hines; Truman Stanley; Ada Mae Weeks

Notes: [1] Sheet music only. [2] Out Atlantic City 4/25/21. [3] Out Washington, D.C. 3/12/22. [4] Not used.

3219 • O'FLYNN, THE
OPENED: 12/27/1934   Theatre: Broadway
Musical   Broadway: 11

Composer: Franklin Hauser
Librettist: Brian Hooker; Russell Janney
Producer: Russell Janney
Director: Robert Milton

Source: UNKNOWN (Play: Justin Huntley McCarthy); **Choreographer:** Louis Chalif; **Costumes:** James Reynolds; **Musical Director:** Giuseppe Bamboschek; **Set Design:** James Reynolds

Songs: Child of Erin (L: Russell Janney); Lovely Lady (L: Russell Janney); Man I Love Is Here, The (L: Brian Hooker); Song of My Heart (L: Brian Hooker)

Cast: William Balfour; Colin Campbell; H. Cooper-Cliffe; Frank Fenton; George Houston; Lucy Monroe; Walter Munroe; Will Philbrick

3220 • O'NEILL OF DERRY
OPENED: 11/25/1907   Theatre: Liberty
Play   Broadway: 33

Composer: Chauncey Olcott
Lyricist: Chauncey Olcott

Author: Theodore Burt Sayre
Producer: Augustus Pitou

Musical Director: Gus Salzer; **Set Design:** Homer Emens; Unitt & Wickes

Songs: Bowl of Roses, A; Every Star Falls in Love with Its Mate (C/L: Charles E. Casey; Chauncey Olcott); Michael McGinnity (C/L: Melville Ellis; Chauncey Olcott); One Little, Sweet Little Girl (C/L: Chauncey Olcott; Daniel J. Sullivan); Rose of Old Derry, A (C/L: J.J. Dillon; William G. Kopp; Chauncey Olcott)

Cast: Arthur Jarrett; Daniel Jarrett; George A. Lessey; Chauncey Olcott; Leonard Shepherd

3221 • O. HENRY DUET
OPENED: 04/21/1980
Musical

Composer: Eric Stern
Lyricist: Erik Haagensen
Librettist: Erik Haagensen; Eric Stern
Director: Ira Weitzman

Source: LAST LEAF, THE (Story: O. Henry); **Source:** LICKPENNY LOVER, A (Story: O. Henry); **Musical Director:** Eric Stern

Songs: Anything Can Happen [1]; Don't You Think [2]; I Like Him [2]; I'll Be Here [2]; Old Friend [2]; On the Other Side of the Counter [1]; One of the Crowd [1]; Poetry [2]; Take What Comes [2]; To the Ends of the Earth [1]; Two Rooms [2]; While I'm Waiting [2]; Why? [2]; Wonder What He's Like [2]; World's Largest Department Store, The [1]

Cast: George S. Irving; Kathy Morath; Jan Neuberger

Notes: A reading of two one-act musicals: A LICKPENNY LOVER and THE LAST LEAF. [1] From A LICKPENNY LOVER. [2] From THE LAST LEAF.

3222 • ODDS AND ENDS OF 1917
OPENED: 11/19/1917   Theatre: Bijou
Revue   Broadway: 112

Composer: James Byrnes
Lyricist: Bide Dudley; Jack Norworth [2]
Librettist: Bide Dudley; Jack Norworth [2]

Producer: Jack Norworth; Shannon
Director: Julian Alfred

Costumes: Kiviette; **Musical Director:** James Byrnes

Songs: Bravo, Antonio!; Dear Old Bronx; Do You Want Us to Lose?; Dove Dance, The (inst.) (C: Jack Norworth); Fancy You Fancying Me [1] (C/L: Nora Bayes; Jack Norworth); Further It Is from Tipperary, The; Give Me an Old-Fashioned Girlie; Hector; My Lady's Clothes; North of 53; Sister Susie Glide; There's a Lovely Crop of Girls This Year (C: Jack Norworth; L: R.P. Weston); Vampire Maid, The; Voice with a Smile Wins, The; We've Got to Put Up with It; When He's Away [3] (C: Jack Norworth; L: R.P. Weston); When I Wave My Flag (C: Jack Norworth; L: R.P. Weston); Where Did You Get Those Irish Eyes?; Would You Like to Make a Fuss Over Me?

Cast: Paul Frawley; Laura Hamilton; Lillian Lorraine; Jack Norworth; Harry Watson Jr.

Notes: Interpolated songs by Weston and Lee but not credited in program. Probably titled OH LA LA out of town. [1] Ascribed on sheet music to Weston and Lee unless this is a different song with the same name as the one in the show. [2] Norworth used the pseudonym John Godfrey. [3] From OH LA LA.

3223 • ODYSSEY

Notes: *See HOME SWEET HOMER.*

3224 • OF MICE AND MEN

OPENED: 12/04/1958   Theatre: Provincetown
                                    Playhouse
Musical   Broadway: 37

Composer: Alfred Brooks
Lyricist: Ira J. Bilowit
Librettist: Ira J. Bilowit
Producer: Ira J. Bilowit; Unicorn Productions
Director: Jerome Eskow

Source: OF MICE AND MEN (Play: John Steinbeck); **Choreographer:** Zoya Leporaka; **Costumes:** Charles A. Brandon; **Lighting Designer:** Charles A. Brandon; **Musical Director:** Samuel Matlovsky; **Orchestrations:** Samuel Matlovsky; **Set Design:** Charles A. Brandon

Songs: Buckin' Barley; Candy's Lament; Curley's Wife; Dudin' Up; Guy, a Guy, a Guy, A; Is There Some Place for Me?; Just Someone to Talk To; Lemme Tell Ya; Never Do A Bad Thing; Nice Fella; Nice House We Got Here; No Ketchup; Strangely; Wanta, Hope to Feel at Home; We Got a Future; Why Try Hard to Be Good?

Cast: Byrne Gwin; John F. Hamilton; Art Lund; Les Penn; Jo Sullivan

3225 • OF THEE I SING

OPENED: 12/26/1931   Theatre: Music Box
Musical   Broadway: 446

Composer: George Gershwin
Lyricist: Ira Gershwin
Librettist: George S. Kaufman; Morrie Ryskind
Producer: Sam H. Harris
Director: George S. Kaufman

Choreographer: George Hale; **Costumes:** Charles LeMaire; **Musical Director:** Charles Previn; **Orchestrations:** Robert Russell Bennett; William Daly; **Set Design:** Jo Mielziner

Songs: As the Chairman of the Committee; Because, Because; Call Me Whate'er You Will [1]; Dimple on My Knee, The; Entrance of Supreme Court Judges; Entrance of the French Ambassador; Entrance of Wintergreen and Mary [1]; Garcon, S'il Vous Plait; Hello, Good Morning; How Beautiful; I Was the Most Beautiful Blossom; Illegitimate Daughter, The; I'm About to Be a Mother (Who Could Ask for Anything More?); Impeachment Proceeding; Jilted; Kiss for Cinderella, A; Love Is Sweeping the Country; Never Was There a Girl So Fair; Of Thee I Sing (Baby); On That Matter, No One Budges; Opportunity Has Beckoned [1]; Posterity Is Just Around the Corner; Senatorial Roll Call, The; Some Girls Can Bake a Pie; Strike the Loud-Resounding Zither [1]; Trumpeter, Blow Your Golden Horn; We'll Impeach Him; While We're Waiting for the Baby [1]; Who Cares?; Who Is the Lucky Girl to Be?; Wintergreen for President; You'll Pardon Me If I Reveal [1]; Zwei Hertzen [2]

Cast: Florenz Ames; Grace Brinkley; Dudley Clements; William Gaxton; George E. Mack; Sam Mann; Harold Moffatt; Victor Moore; Lois Moran; George Murphy; James O'Dea; Ralph Riggs; Edward H. Robins

Notes: [1] Not used. [2] Cut prior to opening.

3226 • OF V WE SING

OPENED: 02/11/1942   Theatre: Concert
Revue   Broadway: 76

Librettist: Al Geto; Sam Locke; Mel Tolkin
Producer: American Youth Theatre; Alexander H. Cohen
Director: Perry Bruskin

Choreographer: Susanne Remos; **Musical Director:** Lou Cooper

Songs: Brooklyn Cantata (C: George Kleinsinger; L: Mike Stratton); Don't Sing Solo (C: George Kleinsinger; L: Roslyn Harvey); Freedom Road (C: Toby Sacher; L: Lewis Allan); Gertie the Stool Pigeon's Daughter (C: Ned Lehac; L: Joe Darion); Juke Box (C: Alex North; L: Alfred Hayes); Of V We Sing (C: Lou Cooper; L: Arthur Zipser); Priorities (C: Lou Cooper; L: Roslyn Harvey); Queen Esther (C: George Kleinsinger; L: Beatrice Goldsmith); Sisters Under the Skin (C: Baldwin Bergersen; L: Sylvia Marks); Take a Poem (C: George Kleinsinger; L: Norman Corwin); We Have a Date (C: Lou Cooper; L: Roslyn Harvey); You Can't Fool the People (C: George Kleinsinger; L: Alfred Hayes); You've Got to Appease with a Strip Tease (C: Toby Sacher; L: Lewis Allan)

Cast: Perry Bruskin; Curt Conway; Betty Garrett; Phil Leeds; Daniel Nagrin

3227 • OFF-KEY

OPENED: 04/07/1995
Musical

Composer: Richard Adler
Lyricist: Richard Adler; Bill C. Davis
Librettist: Bill C. Davis
Director: Marcia Milgrom Dodge

Choreographer: Marcia Milgrom Dodge; **Costumes:** Gail Brassard; **Lighting Designer:** Christopher Akerlind; **Musical Director:** Darren R. Cohen; **Set Design:** Narelle Sissons

Songs: After; Citizens' Assault; Come Tomorrow; Dear Dad; Do You Wear Glasses?; Don't Cry Anymore; How Long Is from Now On?; I Ask Myself; I Did It; I Don't Wanna Work; I Made the Day Shorter; I See All of It; I'll Find Her There; Law Is, The; Listen with Your Heart; Look!; Matthew; Never Saw Myself; Pillow Song, The; Please Not Me; Ronald Liebowitz, My Hero; Shadow; Weather Song, The; When the Bus Stops; Why Should She Be Happy?; With This Lock; Work Song, The; You Knew What I Needed

Cast: Mana Allen; Christy Baron; Reathel Bean; M. Eliot Beisner; Paul Binotto; Derek Gentry; Michael Greenwood; Frank Raiter; Marcell Rosenblatt; Christopher Sieber; Lannyl Stephens; Robert Vargas

Notes: Produced at the George Street Theatre, New Brunswick, NJ.

3228 • OFF THE EARTH

OPENED: 01/21/1895   Theatre: Harlem Opera House
Musical   New York: 8

Composer: Fred J. Eustis
Lyricist: John D. Gilbert
Librettist: John D. Gilbert
Director: Gerald Coventry

Arrangements: Fred J. Eustis; **Choreographer:** Harry Barnes; **Costumes:** Wilhelm; **Lighting Designer:** Peter Armstrong; **Musical Director:** Fred J. Eustis; **Set Design:** Frank E. Gates; E.A. Morange

Songs: And Still His Whiskers Grew

Cast: Eddie Foy Sr.; Lillian Hawthorne; Sadie McDonald; Louise Montagne; H.W. Trednick

Notes: No songs listed in program.

3229 • OFFICE BOY, THE

OPENED: 11/02/1903   Theatre: Victoria
Musical   Broadway: 66

Composer: Ludwig Englander
Lyricist: Harry B. Smith
Librettist: Harry B. Smith
Producer: Charles B. Dillingham
Director: Al Holbrook

Source: LE JOCKEY MALGRE LUI (Musical); **Musical Director:** Watty Hydes

Songs: After Business Hours; Because I Love You So; Bohemia; Embassy Burglarious, An (The Burglars); Finale Act I; Finale Act II; I Never Had to Work (C/L: Benjamin Hapgood Burt); I Thought Wrong [1] (C/L: R.G. Knowles; Richard Morton); If I Were the Bride of a Soldier; I'm on the Water Wagon Now (C: John W. Bratton; L: Paul West); Jockey Song, The; Maiden's Heart, A; Opening Chorus Act II; Opening Number; Plain Mamie O'Hooley; Proper Way to Kiss, The; Signs; Song of the Drum and Fife; Summer Proposals; Trials of a Simple Maid, The; When the Band Plays Ragtime [1]; Will You Be My Hero, Noble Sir?

Cast: Frank Daniels; Louise Gunning; Walter C. Kelly; James C. Reaney; Eva Tanguay; Sidney Toler; Lawrence Wheat

Notes: [1] Out Baltimore 2/22/04.

3230 • OH, BOY!

OPENED: 02/20/1917   Theatre: Princess
Musical   Broadway: 463

Composer: Jerome Kern
Lyricist: P.G. Wodehouse
Librettist: Guy Bolton; P.G. Wodehouse
Producer: F. Ray Comstock; William Elliot
Director: Robert Milton; Edward Royce

Costumes: Faibsey; **Musical Director:** Max Hirschfeld; **Orchestrations:** Frank Saddler; **Set Design:** D.M. Aiken

Songs: Ain't It a Grand and Glorious Feeling [2]; Bachelor, The [2]; Be a Little Sunbeam [2]; Finale Act I; Finale Act II; First Day of May, The; Flubby Dub the Cave Man; Koo-La-Loo; Land Where the Good Songs Go, The [4]; Let's Make a Night of It; Little Bit of Ribbon, A; Nesting Time in Flatbush (L: Jerome Kern; P.G. Wodehouse); Oh, Daddy, Please; Old-Fashioned Wife, An (L: Guy Bolton; P.G. Wodehouse); Package of Seeds, A [1] (L: Herbert Reynolds; P.G. Wodehouse); Pal Like You, A [6]; Rolled Into One; 'Till the Clouds Roll By (L: Guy Bolton; Jerome Kern; P.G. Wodehouse); When the Orchestra's Playing Your Favorite Dance [3]; Why Can't They Hand It to Me? [2]; Words Are Not Needed [5]; You Never Knew About Me (L: Guy Bolton; P.G. Wodehouse)

Cast: Marie Carroll; Marion Davies; Hal Forde;

Justine Johnstone; Frank McGinn; Edna May Oliver; Tom Powers; Anna Wheaton

Notes: Titled OH, JOY! in London. [1] From 90 IN THE SHADE. [2] Cut prior to opening. [3] Cut prior to opening. Titled "When the Orchestra's Playing Your Favorite Waltz" during the tryouts of this show and LEAVE IT TO JANE. It was titled "There It Is Again" when performed in LEAVE IT TO JANE. [4] Cut prior to opening. In MISS 1917. [5] Originally titled "Every Day." [6] Originally titled "We're Going to Be Pals."

3231 • OH, BROTHER!

OPENED: 11/10/1981   Theatre: ANTA
Musical   Broadway: 3

Composer: Michael Valenti
Lyricist: Donald Driver
Librettist: Donald Driver
Producer: Zev Bufman; John F. Kennedy Center
Director: Donald Driver

Source: COMEDY OF ERRORS, THE (Play: William Shakespeare); **Choreographer:** Donald Driver; **Costumes:** Ann Emonts; **Dance Arranger:** Marvin Laird; **Lighting Designer:** Richard Nelson; **Musical Director:** Marvin Laird; **Orchestrations:** Jim Tyler; **Set Design:** Michael J. Hotopp; Paul dePass; **Vocal Arranger:** Marvin Laird

Songs: Chase, The; Everybody Calls Me By My Name; How Do You Want Me?; I to the World; It's a Man's World [1]; Loud and Funny Song, A; Man, A; O.P.E.C. Maiden; Oh Brother; Revolution [1]; Tell Sweet Saroyana; That's Him; We Love an Old Story; What Do I Tell People This Time

Cast: Bruce Adler; David-James Carroll; Harry Groener; Judy Kaye; Larry Marshall; Mary Elizabeth Mastrantonio; Joe Morton; Alyson Reed; Richard B. Shull; Alan Weeks

Notes: [1] Out Washington, D.C. 9/28/81.

3232 • OH, BY JINGO

OPENED: 1920
Revue   Closed out of town

Lyricist: Lew Rose
Librettist: Lew Rose

Producer: George LaTour
Director: Lew Rose

Cast: Lew Rose

Notes: Program from Harrisburg 9/3/20. This show contained popular songs of the day.

3233 • OH! CALCUTTA!

OPENED: 01/17/1969   Theatre: Eden
Revue   Broadway: 5959

Composer: Open Window, The [1]
Lyricist: Open Window, The [1]
Librettist: Samuel Beckett; Robert Benton; Jules Feiffer; Dan Greenburg; John Lennon; Jacques Levy; Leonard Melfi; David Newman; Sam Shepard; Clovis Trouille; Kenneth Tynan; Sherman Yellen

Choreographer: Margo Sappington; **Costumes:** Fred Voelpel; **Lighting Designer:** David F. Segal; **Set Design:** James Tilton

Songs: Ballerina; Clarence and Mildred; Don't Have a Song to Sing; Exchanges of Information; Freeze Music; Green Pants; I Like the Look; I Want It; I'm an Actor; Jack and Jill; Much Too Soon; Oh! Calcutta!; Sincere Replies; Suite for Five Letters; Taking Off the Robe

Cast: Mark Dempsey; Boni Enten; Bill Macy; Margo Sappington

Notes: This show moved to the Belasco on 1/25/71. [1] Consists of Peter Schickele, Robert Dennis and Stanley Walden.

3234 • OH CAPTAIN!

OPENED: 02/04/1958   Theatre: Alvin
Musical   Broadway: 192

Composer: Jay Livingston
Lyricist: Ray Evans; Jay Livingston
Librettist: Jose Ferrer; Al Morgan
Producer: Howard Merrill; Theatre Corp. of America
Director: Jose Ferrer

Source: CAPTAIN'S PARADISE, THE (Film: Alec Coppel); **Choreographer:** James Starbuck; **Costumes:** Miles White; **Dance Arranger:** Jay Blackton; **Lighting Designer:** Jo Mielziner;

Musical Director: Jay Blackton; **Orchestrations:** Walter Eiger; Robert Ginzler; Joe Glover; Ray Jaimes; Oscar Kosarin; Philip J. Lang; Sy Oliver; Cornel Tannassy; **Set Design:** Jo Mielziner; **Vocal Arranger:** Jay Blackton

Songs: All the Time [5]; Anywhere but Here [2]; Captain Henry St. James; Double Standard; Femininity; Frenchman's Paree, The [2]; Give It All You Got [3]; Hey, Madame; It's Never Quite the Same; I've Been There and I'm Back; Jubi-lie, Jubi-lo [2]; Keep It Simple; Life Does a Man a Favor (When It Gives Him Simple Joys); Love Is Hell; Morning Music of Montmartre, The; Surprise; Three Paradises [1]; Very Proper Town, A; We're Not Children; You Don't Know Him; You're So Right for Me [4]

Cast: Alexandra Danilova; Jack Eddleman; Susan Johnson; Abbe Lane; Jacquelyn McKeever; Edward Platt; Tony Randall; Paul Valentine

Notes: Originally titled CAPTAIN'S PARADISE. [1] Same melody as "All the Time." [2] Cut. [3] Previously in I LOVE LYDIA. [4] Written for TV musical SATINS AND SPURS. [5] First a commercial recording by Johnny Mathis it was slightly changed and put into the score. Same melody as "Three Paradises."

3235 • OH COWARD!

OPENED: 10/04/1972   Theatre: New
Revue   Off-Broadway: 294

Composer: Noel Coward
Lyricist: Noel Coward
Producer: Wroderick Productions
Director: Roderick Cook

Musical Director: Rene Wiegert; **Orchestrations:** Nicholas Deutsch; Herbert Helbig; **Set Design:** Helen Pond; Herbert Senn; **Vocal Arranger:** Rene Wiegert

Songs: Alice [1]; Aunt Jessie; Bar on the Piccolo Marina, A; Bright Young People; Chase Me Charlie; Critic, The; Dance Little Lady; Elderly Actress, The; End of the News, The; Gertie; Has Anybody Seen Our Ship?; I Am No Good at Love; If Love Were All; I'll Follow My Secret Heart; I'll See You Again; Island of Bolamazoo; Let's Do It (C: Cole Porter); Let's Say Goodbye; London Pastoral; London Pride; Loving; Mad About the Boy; Mad Dogs and Englishmen;

Marvelous Party, A; Men About Town; Mrs. Worthington; Nina; Passenger's Always Right, The; Play Orchestra Play; Poor Little Rich Girl; Question of Lighting, A; Room with a View; Sail Away; Saturday Night at the Rose and Crown; Sex Talk; Someday I'll Find You; Something to Do with Spring; Star, The; Stately Homes of England; This Is a Changing World; Three White Feathers; Too Early or Too Late; Uncle Harry; We Were Dancing; What Happened to Him [1]; What Ho Mrs. Brisket!; Where Are the Songs We Sung?; Why Do the Wrong People Travel?; World Weary; You Were There; Ziegeuner

Cast: Barbara Cason; Roderick Cook; Jamie Ross

Notes: No songs written for this production. Some of the song titles may be poems or recitations. [1] Cut after opening.

3236 • OH, ERNEST!

OPENED: 05/09/1927   Theatre: Royale
Musical   Broadway: 56

Composer: Robert Hood Bowers
Lyricist: Francis DeWitt
Librettist: Francis DeWitt
Producer: P.T. Rossiter
Director: William J. Wilson

Source: IMPORTANCE OF BEING ERNEST, THE (Play: Oscar Wilde); **Choreographer:** Ralph Riggs; **Musical Director:** Robert Hood Bowers

Songs: Ancestry [2]; Cecily [2]; Cupid's College; Dastardly Attack on W. Epigram [2]; Didoes [2]; Don't Scold; Feeling Wonderful [1]; Give Me Someone; It's All Right with Me; Just a Little Stranger; Let's Pretend [1]; Mama [1]; Never Trouble Trouble [2]; On the Beach; Over the Garden Wall; Pollyanna; Rose in Bloom [2]; Shake a Little Shoe [1]; Taken by Surprise [1]; Tangles [2]; Tea [1]; There's a Muddle [2]; There's Trouble [1]; True to Two [1]; What Can a Girl Do [1]

Cast: Dorothy Dilley; Hal Forde; Marjorie Gateson; Vivian Marlowe; Harry McNaughton

Notes: [1] Added after opening. [2] Cut after opening.

3237 • OH, I SAY!

OPENED: 10/30/1913   Theatre: Casino
Musical   Broadway: 68

Composer: Jerome Kern
Lyricist: Harry B. Smith
Librettist: Sidney Blow; Douglas Hoare
Producer: Messrs. Shubert
Director: J.C. Huffman

Source: UNE NUIT DE NOCES (Play: Barre; Keroul); **Choreographer:** Julian Alfred; **Costumes:** Melville Ellis; **Musical Director:** Alfred Bendell; **Orchestrations:** Frank Saddler

Songs: Alone at Last [1]; Each Pearl a Thought; Good Bye Everybody (C: Jean Gilbert); Have an Old Waltz with Me; I Can't Forget Your Eyes [2]; I Know and She Knows; Katy-Did; Old Clarinet, The; Sidonie; Well, This Is Jolly; Wifie of Your Own, A; Woman's Heart, A

Cast: Wellington Cross; Joseph W. Herbert; Walter Jones; Nellie King; Clara Palmer; Alice Yorke

Notes: On the road prior to Broadway titled THEIR WEDDING NIGHT. [1] Not the same song as the one with the same title from VERY GOOD EDDIE. Revised as "In Love" in BLUE EYES. [2] Music later used as "Sunshine" in SUNNY and also "In Araby with You" from CRISS-CROSS.

3238 • OH JOHNNY (1927)

OPENED: 1928
Musical

Composer: Stanley Royce
Lyricist: J. Keirn Brennan

Songs: Alomo; Along the Road to Love; Boy, a Girl and the Moon, A; Honeymoon Hop; Longest Way 'Round Is the Sweetest Way Home, The; My Pipe of Peace; Sunshine of Your Song, The; Tree-Top of Love; Wrapped Up in a Blanket; You Know and I Know the Way

Notes: No other information available.

3239 • OH, JOHNNY (1982)

OPENED: 01/10/1982   Theatre: Players
Musical   Off-Broadway: 1

Composer: Gary Cherpakov
Lyricist: Paul Streitz
Librettist: Paul Streitz
Producer: Paul Streitz
Director: Alan Weeks

Choreographer: Alan Weeks; **Costumes:** Gene Galvin; **Dance Arranger:** Robert Marks; **Lighting Designer:** Toni Goldin; **Musical Director:** Robert Marks; **Set Design:** Jim Chesnutt; **Vocal Arranger:** Robert Marks

Songs: Ancient Oriental Custom (L: Gary Gherpakov); Boogie Bug (L: Gary Cherpakov); Boost the Morale; Business As Usual (L: Gary Cherpakov); Can't Can't (L: Gary Cherpakov); Cowboy's Burning Desire; Dance Around the World with Me; I Love a Man with a Uniform On Polka (L: Gary Cherpakov); I'd Love to Be in Love with You; Johnny Is the Man for Me; Mission, The; Oh, Johnny (L: Gary Cherpakov); Soldier Boy; Song of the Orient; Ten Thousand Feet in the Air; Why Am I Afraid to Love (L: Gary Cherpakov); Win the War for Lili

Cast: Michael Crouch; Nazig Edwards; Mark Frawley; Christine Toy; Janet Wong

3240 • OH, JOY! (1917)
Notes: *See OH, BOY!*

3241 • OH JOY! (1922)
OPENED: 1922

Composer: J. Homer Tutt; Salem Tutt Whitney
Lyricist: J. Homer Tutt; Salem Tutt Whitney
Librettist: J. Homer Tutt; Salem Tutt Whitney
Producer: Louis T. Rogers

Songs: Bamboo Isle (C: Ray Henderson; Eddie Kamnetz; L: Billy Bernard; Cliff Hall); Georgia Rose; Valley of the Nile; What's the Use?

Cast: Julian Costello; Andrew Tribble; J. Homer Tutt; Ethel Waters; Salem Tutt Whitney

Notes: No other information available.

3242 • OH, JUSTINE!
Notes: *See OVER THE TOP.*

3243 • OH, KAY!
OPENED: 11/08/1926   Theatre: Imperial
Musical   Broadway: 257

Composer: George Gershwin
Lyricist: Ira Gershwin

Librettist: Guy Bolton; P.G. Wodehouse
Producer: Alex A. Aarons; Vinton Freedley
Director: John Harwood

Choreographer: Sammy Lee; **Costumes:** Brooks; Hattie Carnegie; **Musical Director:** William Daly; **Orchestrations:** William Daly; **Set Design:** John Wenter

Songs: Ain't It Romantic [9]; Ask Me Again [10]; Bride and Groom; Bring on the Ding Dong Dell [1]; Clap Yo' Hands [7] (L: Howard Dietz; Ira Gershwin); Dear Little Girl (I Hope You've Missed Me); Do, Do, Do; Don't Ask! [5]; Fidgety Feet; Finale Act I; Finaletto Act II Scene 1; Guess Who [6]; Heaven on Earth (L: Howard Dietz; Ira Gershwin); Home [3] (L: P.G. Wodehouse); Maybe; Moon Is on the Sea, The [8]; Oh, Kay! (L: Howard Dietz; Ira Gershwin); Pophams, The [2] (L: P.G. Wodehouse); Show Me the Town [8]; Someone to Watch Over Me; Stepping with Baby [8]; Twenties Are Here to Stay, The [2] (L: P.G. Wodehouse); What's the Use? [8]; When Our Ship Comes Sailing In [8] (L: Howard Dietz; Ira Gershwin); Woman's Touch, The; You'll Still Be There [4] (L: P.G. Wodehouse)

Cast: Constance Carpenter; Betty Compton; Harland Dixon; Fairbanks Twins, The; Gertrude Lawrence; Victor Moore; Oscar Shaw; Gerald Oliver Smith; Pianist: Victor Arden; Phil Ohman

Notes: Originally titled CHEERIO. [1] Cut prior to opening. Revised as "Ring-a-Ding-a-Ding — Dong Dell in STRIKE UP THE BAND (1930). [2] Originally in PRIMROSE. Interpolated with new Wodehouse lyrics into the 1960 revival. [3] Originally music used for "Don't Ask". Interpolated with new Wodehouse lyric into the 1960 revival. [4] Originally music used for "Dear Little Girl." Interpolated with new Wodehouse lyric into the 1960 revival. [5] Same music as "Guess Who." [6] Same music as "Don't Ask." Not used. [7] Dietz made uncredited contributions to this song according to a conversation with the author. [8] Cut during rehearsals. [9] Cut prior to opening. [10] From 1920's or early 30's, not for this production. Interpolated into the 1990 revival.

3244 • OH LA LA
Notes: *See ODDS AND ENDS OF 1917.*

3245 • OH, LADY! LADY!!

OPENED: 02/01/1918   Theatre: Princess
Musical   Broadway: 219

Composer: Jerome Kern
Lyricist: P.G. Wodehouse
Librettist: Guy Bolton; P.G. Wodehouse
Producer: F. Ray Comstock; William Elliot; Morris Gest
Director: Robert Milton; Edward Royce

Costumes: Harry Collins; **Musical Director:** Max Hirschfeld; **Orchestrations:** Frank Saddler; **Set Design:** Clifford Pember

Songs: Before I Met You; Bill [1]; Dear Old Prison Days [3]; Do It Now [2]; Do Look at Him [2]; Finale Act II; Finaletto Act I; Greenwich Village [4]; I'm to Be Married Today; It's a Hard, Hard, World (for a Man); Moon Song; Not Yet [5]; Oh, Lady! Lady!; Opening Chorus Act One (Wedding Day) [2]; Our Little Nest; Picture I Want to See, The [6]; Sun Starts to Shine Again, The; Waiting Around the Corner [7]; Wheatless Days; When the Ships Come Home [8]; You Found Me and I Found You

Cast: Carl Randall; Vivienne Segal; Janet Velie

Notes: [1] Cut. Added to SHOW BOAT. Same music used for song of same name in ZIP GOES A MILLION. [2] In vocal score only. [3] Sheet music only. [4] Same music as "A Little Thing Like a Kiss" from A DOLL GIRL. [5] Same music as "You're the Only Girl He Loves" from A POLISH WEDDING. [6] Also in MISS 1917. [7] Sometimes titled "Some Little Girl." [8] Listed in program as "Little Ships Come Sailing Home."

3246 • OH, LOOK!

OPENED: 03/17/1918   Theatre: Vanderbilt
Musical   Broadway: 68

Composer: Harry Carroll
Lyricist: Joseph McCarthy
Librettist: James Montgomery; Edward Royce
Producer: Harry Carroll; William Sheer
Director: Robert Milton

Source: READY MONEY (Play: James Montgomery); **Choreographer:** David Bennett; **Musical Director:** Oscar Radin

Songs: Back in the Quaint Little School in Caroline [4]; Changeable Girls; Dolly Twinkle, The [3] (L: Joseph McCarthy; Edward Royce); Far Apart, You're Still in My Heart [4]; Good Little Things We Do, The [4]; I Know; I Think You're Absolutely Wonderful (What Do You Think of Me); I Want to Marry [3]; I'm Always Chasing Rainbows [1]; I'm Just a Good Man; It's a Long Way to Tiffany's; Kiss for Cinderella, A; My Isle of Golden Dreams [5] (C: Walter Blaufuss; L: Gus Kahn); Oh, Look! [3]; Old Fashioned Girl, An [3]; Opening Chorus; Sunkissed Land; Tell Me Why [2] (C: Vincent Rose; L: Richard Coburn); These Colors Will Not Run; Typical Topical Tunes; Vamp a Little Lady (The Vamp) [2] (C/L: Byron Gay); We Will Love and Love Alone [4]; When I Marry [4]; When I Think of the Sweethearts That I Might Have Had [3]; Wherever There's Music and Beautiful Girls

Cast: Harry Fox; Clarence Nordstrom; George Sidney; Genevieve Tobin

Notes: [1] Music based on Chopin's "Fantasie Impromptu in C Sharp Minor." [2] Out Wilkes-Barre 3/26/?? [3] Added Washington, D.C. 3/16/19. [4] Cut Stamford 2/22/18. [5] Out Wilkes-Barre 3/26/?? In HELLO ALEXANDER.

3247 • OH MAMA! (0000)

Notes: *See GIRL O' MINE.*

3248 • OH! MAMA (1925)

OPENED: 08/19/1925   Theatre: Playhouse
Play   Broadway: 70

Composer: Arthur Johnston
Author: Wilton Lackaye
Producer: William A. Brady
Director: John Cromwell

Source: UNKNOWN (Play: Louis Verneuil); **Set Design:** Livingston Platt

Songs: Just One Kiss (L: Cyrus Ruby); Oh, Mama (L: Herman Ruby); Parfum du Passe (C: Edward Mayson; L: Verna Roovray)

Cast: Alice Brady; Ralph Locke

3249 • OH ME, OH MY, OH YOUMANS

OPENED: 01/14/1981   Theatre: Wonderhorse
Revue   Off-Broadway: 20

Composer: Vincent Youmans
Librettist: Darwin Knight; Tom Taylor
Producer: New World Theatre; Jane Stanton
Director: Darwin Knight

Costumes: Andrew B. Marlay; **Lighting Designer:** Eric Cornwell; **Musical Director:** Sand Lawn; **Set Design:** Bob Phillips; **Vocal Arranger:** Sand Lawn

Songs: Bambalina [2] (L: Oscar Hammerstein II; Otto Harbach); Bird on the Wing [5] (L: Irving Caesar; Clifford Grey); Carioca, The [15] (L: Edward Eliscu; Gus Kahn); Come On and Pet Me [3] (L: William Cary Duncan; Oscar Hammerstein II); Deep in My Heart [4] (L: Zelda Sears); Dolly [1] (L: Ira Gershwin); Drums in My Heart [13] (L: Edward Heyman); Flannel Petticoat Gal, The [3] (L: William Cary Duncan; Oscar Hammerstein II); Flying Down to Rio [15] (L: Edward Eliscu; Gus Kahn); Great Day [11] (L: Edward Eliscu; Billy Rose); Hallelujah! [8] (L: Clifford Grey; Leo Robin); Happy Because I'm in Love [11] (L: Edward Eliscu; Billy Rose); I Know That You Know [7] (L: Anne Caldwell); I Want a Yes-Man [5] (L: Irving Caesar; Clifford Grey); I Want to Be Happy [6] (L: Irving Caesar); Iloveyouiloveyouiloveyou [2] (L: Oscar Hammerstein II; Otto Harbach); I've Confessed to the Breeze [6] (L: Otto Harbach); Keepin' Myself for You [9] (L: Sidney Clare); Kinda Like You [13] (L: Edward Heyman); More Than You Know [11] (L: Edward Eliscu; Billy Rose); Music Makes Me [15] (L: Edward Eliscu; Gus Kahn); My Lover [14] (L: B.G. DeSylva); No, No, Nanette [6] (L: Otto Harbach); Oh Me! Oh My! [1] (L: Ira Gershwin); Orchids in the Moonlight [15] (L: Edward Eliscu; Gus Kahn); Rise and Shine [14] (L: B.G. DeSylva); Should I Be Sweet? [14] (L: B.G. DeSylva); So This Is Kissing [5] (L: Irving Caesar; Clifford Grey); Sometimes I'm Happy [8] (L: Clifford Grey; Leo Robin); Tea for Two [6] (L: Irving Caesar); Through the Years [13] (L: Edward Heyman); Tie a String Around Your Finger [4] (L: Zelda Sears); Time on My Hands [12] (L: Harold Adamson; Mack Gordon); Too Many Rings Around Rosie [6] (L: Irving Caesar); Toodle-oo [3] (L: William Cary Duncan; Oscar Hammerstein II); Where Has My Hubby Gone Blues [6] (L: Irving Caesar); Who Am I [10] (L: Gus Kahn); Who's Who Are You? [1] (L: Ira Gershwin); Why Oh Why? [8] (L: Clifford Grey; Leo Robin); Wildflower [2] (L: Oscar Hammerstein II; Otto Harbach); Without a Song [11] (L: Edward Eliscu; Billy Rose); You Can Always Find Another Partner [2] (L: Oscar Hammerstein II; Otto Harbach); You Can Dance with Any Girl [6] (L: Irving Caesar); You Started Something When You Came Along [1] (L: Ira Gershwin)

Cast: Jo Ann Cunningham; Todd Taylor; Sally Woodson; Ronald Young

Notes: No songs written for this show. [1] From TWO LITTLE GIRLS IN BLUE. [2] From WILDFLOWER. [3] From MARY JANE MCKANE. [4] From LOLLIPOP. [5] From A NIGHT OUT. [6] From NO! NO! NANETTE! [7] From OH, PLEASE. [8] From HIT THE DECK. [9] From film version of HIT THE DECK. [10] Cut from RAINBOW. [11] From GREAT DAY. [12] From SMILES. [13] From THROUGH THE YEARS. [14] From TAKE A CHANCE. [15] From film FLYING DOWN TO RIO.

3250 • OH, MY DEAR!

OPENED: 11/27/1918   Theatre: Princess
Musical   Broadway: 189

Composer: Louis A. Hirsch
Lyricist: P.G. Wodehouse
Librettist: Guy Bolton; P.G. Wodehouse
Producer: F. Ray Comstock; William Elliot
Director: Robert Milton; Edward Royce

Set Design: Robert Milton

Songs: Ask Dad; Finale Act I; Finale Act II; Finaletto Act II Scene I; Go Little Boat [2] (C: Jerome Kern); I Love a Musical Comedy Show (C: Jean Schwartz); I Shall Be All Right Now; I Wonder Whether I've Loved You All My Life; If They Ever Parted Me from You; If You Only Know the Way; I'll Ask No More; Isn't It Wonderful?; It Makes a Fellow Sort of Stop and Think; Land Where Journeys End, The [1]; Now and Then But Not All the Time (C: Jean Schwartz); Oh, My Dear; Our City of Dreams; Phoebe Snow; Sas'parilla [1] (C: Jean Schwartz); Shall Be All Right Now; Try Again; Women and Song [1] (C: Jean Schwartz); You Never Know

Cast: Roy Atwell; Joseph Santley; Ivy Sawyer

Notes: Titled ASK DAD out of town. [1] Sheet music only. [2] Published also as "Boat Song" with Hirsch credited!

3251 • OH! OH! DELPHINE
OPENED: 09/30/1912   Theatre: Knickerbocker
Musical   Broadway: 248

Composer: Ivan Caryll
Lyricist: C.M.S. McLellan
Librettist: C.M.S. McLellan
Producer: Klaw & Erlanger
Director: Herbert Gresham

Source: VILLA PRIMROSE (Play: Georges Berr; Marcel Guillemaud); **Choreographer:** Julian Mitchell; **Musical Director:** Frederic Solomon

Songs: Allaballa Goo-Goo; Can We Forget?; Everything's at Home Except Your Wife; Finale Act I; Hush! Hush! Hush!; If the Col'nel Wasn't Coming (Opening Chorus); Maxim Girl, The; Oh, Gifted Master Sleep! (Opening Chorus Act II); Oh! Oh! Delphine; Oh! The Difference; Pavlova (Opening Chorus Act III); Please Turn Your Backs; Poor Bouchette; Posing for Venus; Quarrel, The; Then All Come Along; Toodles Is the Elephant's Name; Venus Waltz, The; Why Shouldn't You Tell Me That?

Cast: Octavia Broske; Frank Doane; Grace Edmond; Dorothy Langdon; Frank McIntyre

3252 • OH! OH! NURSE
OPENED: 12/07/1925   Theatre: Cosmopolitan
Musical   Broadway: 32

Composer: Alma Sanders
Lyricist: Monte Carlo
Librettist: George E. Stoddard
Producer: Clarke Ross
Director: Walter Brooks

Musical Director: Hilding Anderson; **Set Design:** Walter Schaffner

Songs: Butter and Egg Baby; Cleopatra; Goodnight My Lady Love; I'll Give the World to You; Is It Any Wonder?; Keep a Kiss for Me; Love Will

Keep Us Young; Newlywed Express; No Hearts for Sale; No, I Won't; Opening; Pierre; Shooting Stars; Show a Little Pep; Under My Umbrella; Way Out in Rainbowland; Who Bites the Holes in Schweitzer Cheese?; You May Have Planted Many a Lily

Cast: Don Barclay; May Boley; Rebekah Cauble; James Doyle; John Price Jones; Ignacio Martinetti; Gertrude Vanderbilt

3253 • OH! PAT
Musical

Composer: Sigmund Romberg

Notes: Abandoned before rehearsals. Planned for actor Pat Rooney.

3254 • OH, PLEASE!
OPENED: 12/17/1926   Theatre: Fulton
Musical   Broadway: 79

Composer: Vincent Youmans
Lyricist: Anne Caldwell; Otto Harbach
Librettist: Anne Caldwell; Otto Harbach
Producer: Charles Dillingham
Director: Hassard Short

Source: LA PRESIDENTE (Play: Maurice Hennequin; Pierre Veber); **Choreographer:** David Bennett; **Costumes:** James Reynolds; **Musical Director:** Gus Salzer; **Orchestrations:** Hans Spialek; **Set Design:** James Reynolds

Songs: Floating Along [1]; Girls of the Old Brigade, The [3] (C/L: Unknown); Greyhound [1]; Homely, But Clean; I Can't Be Happy [1]; I Can't Make My Husband Behave; I Know That You Know; I'd Steal a Star; I'm Waiting for a Wonderful Girl; Like She Loves Me; Lily of the Valley [1]; Love and Kisses 'n' Everything [2]; Love Me [3] (C/L: Unknown); Moments [1]; Nicodemus; Opening Act II; She Was a Wonderful Queen [1]; Snappy Show in Town; Week-End in July, A [1]; When Daddy Goes A-Hunting [1]

Cast: Helen Broderick; Gertrude Clemens; Pearl Hight; Blanche Latell; Beatrice Lillie; Cynthia MacVae; Gertrude McDonald; Charles Purcell; Josephine Sabel; Charles Winninger

Notes: [1] Cut prior to opening. [2] Cut after NY opening. [3] Interpolated, not by Youmans.

3255 • OH SAY CAN YOU SING

OPENED: 12/11/1936   Theatre: Great Northern
Revue   Chicago

Composer: Phil Charig
Lyricist: Ray Golden; Sid Kuller
Librettist: Ray Golden; Sid Kuller
Producer: George Kondolf
Director: Hedley Gordon Graham

Songs: Night After Night

Cast: Virginia Crane; Grace Graff; Kurt Graff; Charlie Herbert; Grace Herbert; Buddy Rich; Dan Seymour; Joe Whitehead

Notes: A WPA Federal Theatre show. No other information available.

3256 • OH! SO HAPPY

OPENED: 07/19/1917
Musical   Closed out of town

Composer: Harry B. Olsen
Lyricist: Roland Oliver
Librettist: Charles Dickson; Roland Oliver
Producer: Ralph Herz
Director: Benrimo

Costumes: Lucille; **Musical Director:** Harry B. Olsen; **Set Design:** Peltz & Carson

Songs: Constancy; Eenie, Weenie, Lovey Dovey; Flattery; Good Night Paul; I LIke You; I've Given My Heart to You, Dear; Lovey Dovey; Nothing Seems Right; Oh! the World Is All Wrong; On Monday Wear a Blue One; Pity Me; Poor Mary Anne O'Shea (C: Art Aarseth; L: George C. Mack); Purity; Sailing on the Henry Clay; Serenade; Sleep My Darling; You Have a Straight and Shapely Back

Cast: Frank Lalor

Notes: Closed in Chicago.

3257 • OH! UNCLE

Notes: *See OH, WHAT A GIRL!*

3258 • OH, WHAT A GIRL!

OPENED: 07/28/1919   Theatre: Shubert
Musical   Broadway: 68

Composer: Charles Jule; Jacques Presburg
Lyricist: Edward Clark; Edgar Smith
Librettist: Edward Clark; Edgar Smith
Producer: J.J. Shubert; Lee Shubert
Director: Edward Clark

Musical Director: Louis Silvers; **Orchestrations:** Jacques Presburg; **Set Design:** Watson Barratt

Songs: At the Wheel of an Auto [4] (L: Edgar Smith); Birds of a Feather [1]; Breeze in the Trees; Chirp Along [4] (L: Edgar Smith); Could You Teach Me?; Dainty Little Girl Like You; Fine Guy, A [4] (L: Edgar Smith); Get Him Up; Gimme [3]; Hard to Be a Lady [4] (L: Edgar Smith); Here We Are Dance [4] (L: Edgar Smith); I Hate a Fly [4] (L: Edgar Smith); I Want to Dance My Way In [1]; I'd Like to Give a Nice Sweet Kiss [4] (L: Edgar Smith); I'm a Shy Little Innocent Thing [4] (L: Edgar Smith); In the House [1]; It Isn't the Moonlight [4] (L: Edgar Smith); Life on a Farm [4] (L: Edgar Smith); Madelon [4] (L: Edgar Smith); Movies, The [4] (L: Edgar Smith); Musical Poker Game; Oh That Shimmy!; Oh, Uncle [4] (L: Edgar Smith); Oh, What a Girl!; Once in a Blue Moon [1]; One Little Girl [3]; Pot Pourri; Prince Charming; Purity [4] (L: Edgar Smith); Specialty [4] (L: Edgar Smith); Such a Baby; Sweetheart [4] (L: Edgar Smith); Travesty Opera [3]; Yip Yip [4] (L: Edgar Smith); You'd Be Surprised [2] (C/L: Irving Berlin)

Cast: Sam Ash; Frank Fay; Harry Kelly; Hazel Kirke

Notes: Out of town titled THE WRONG NUMBER and OH! UNCLE. Edgar Smith was credited with the book and lyrics when out of town. [1] Out New York City 10/10/21. [2] Added after opening. Also in SHUBERT GAIETIES OF 1919 and ZIEGFELD FOLLIES OF 1919. [3] From show when titled THE WRONG NUMBER. [4] Cut. From show when titled THE WRONG NUMBER.

3259 • OH, WHAT A LOVELY WAR

OPENED: 12/30/1964   Theatre: Broadhurst
Revue   Broadway: 125

Librettist: Joan Littlewood
Producer: David Merrick
Director: Joan Littlewood

Choreographer: Bob Stevenson; **Costumes:** Una Collins; **Dance Arranger:** Alfred Ralston; **Lighting Designer:** John Bury; **Musical Director:** Shepard Coleman; **Set Design:** John Bury; **Vocal Arranger:** Alfred Ralston

Songs: Are We Downhearted? No; Belgium Put the Kibosh on the Kaiser (C/L: Ellerton); Bells of Hell, The; Christmas Day in the Cookhouse; Far, Far from Wipers; Forward, Joe Soap's Army [3] (C: Arthur Sullivan; L: Sabine Baring-Gould); Fred Karno's Army; Gassed Last Night; Goodbye — ee (C: R.P. Weston; L: Bert Lee); Hitchy Koo (C: Maurice Abrahams; Lewis F. Muir; L: L. Wolfe Gilbert); Hold Your Hand Out Naughty Boy; Hush Here Comes a Whizzbang; I Don't Want to Be a Soldier [6] (C: Herman Finck); I Want to Go Home; I Wore a Tunic [2] (C: Percy Wenrich; L: Jack Mahoney); If the Sergeant Steals Your Rum; If You Want the Old Battalion; I'll Make a Man of You [1] (C/L: Herman Finck); It's a Long Way to Tipperary (C/L: Jack Judge; Harry H. Williams); Kaiser Bill; Keep the Home Fires Burning (C: Ivor Novello; L: Lena Guilbert Ford); La Chanson de Craonne; Oh What a Lovely War (Oh It's a Lovely War) (C/L: Long; Scott); Old Soldiers Never Die; Pack Up Your Troubles (C: Felix Powell; L: George Asaf); Roses of Picardy (C: Haydn Wood; L: Frederick E. Weatherly); Row Row Row (C: James V. Monaco; L: William Jerome); Silent Night (Heilige Nacht) (C: Franz Gruber; L: Joseph Mohr); Sister Susie's Sewing Shirts (C: Hermann E. Darewski; L: R.P. Weston); There's a Long, Long Trail (C: Zo Elliott; L: Stoddard King); They Didn't Believe Me [4] (C: Jerome Kern; L: Cole Porter); They Were Only Playing Leapfrog; Wash Me in the Water; We Don't Want to Lose You (Your King and Country Want You) (C/L: Paul Rubens); When This Lousy War Is Over [5] (C: Henry Tucker; L: Charles Carroll Sawyer)

Cast: Fanny Carby; Murray Melvin; Brian Murphy; Reid Shelton; Victor Spinetti; Bob Stevenson; Barbara Windsor

Notes: No songs written for this show. Many of these songs were parodies of more famous songs. Composers and lyricists listed for parodies are the authors of the original songs.

[1] From British show THE PASSING SHOW. [2] A parody of "When You Wore a Tulip." [3] A parody of "Onward Christian Soldiers." [4] A parody of "They Didn't Believe Me." M.E. Rourke is the original lyricist. Porter wrote the parody. [5] A parody of "Weeping, Sad and Lonely" also known as "When This Cruel War Is Over." [6] A parody of "I'll Make a Man of You," which was also in this show.

3260 • OH YOU
Notes: *See THE FLORIDA GIRL.*

3261 • OIL CITY SYMPHONY
OPENED: 11/05/1987   Theatre: Circle in the Square Downtown
Revue   Off-Broadway: 626

Composer: Mark Hardwick; Debra Monk
Lyricist: Mike Craver
Librettist: Mike Craver; Mark Hardwick; Debra Monk; Mary Murfitt
Director: Larry Forde

Lighting Designer: Natasha Katz; **Set Design:** Jeffrey Schissler

Songs: Baby, It's Cold Outside [1] (C/L: Frank Loesser); Beaver Ball at the Bug Club; Beehive Polka (C/L: Debra Monk; C: Mike Craver; Mark Hardwick); Bus Ride (C: Mark Hardwick; Debra Monk; L: Mike Craver); Coaxing the Ivories (inst.) [5] (C: Zez Confrey); Count Your Blessings [2] (C/L: E.O. Excell; Rev. Johnson Oatman); Czardus [2] (C/L: Traditional); Dizzy Fingers (inst.) [2] (C: Zez Confrey); End of the World, The [2] (C: Arthur Kent; L: Sylvia Dee); Exodus Song, The (inst.) [3] (C: Ernest Gold; L: Pat Boone); Getting to Know You (inst.) [4] (C: Richard Rodgers; L: Oscar Hammerstein II); In a Gadda de Vida (inst.) [2] (C/L: Doug Ingle); In the Sweet Bye and Bye [2] (C/L: Traditional); Iris (C/L: Mark Craver); My Old Kentucky Rock and Roll Home; Ohio Afternoon; Patriotic Fantasy (inst.) [2] (C: John Philip Sousa); Stars and Stripes (inst.) [2] (C: John Philip Sousa)

Cast: Mike Craver; Mark Hardwick; Debra Monk; Mary Murfitt

Notes: There were additional numbers added which were not listed in program. [1] Not written for show. From film NEPTUNE'S DAUGHTER. [2] Not written for show. [3] Not written for show. From film EXODUS. [4] Not used. Not written for show. From THE KING & I. [5] Not written for show. Real title is "Coaxing the Piano."

3262 • OK, USA!
OPENED: 1945
Revue

Composer: Frank Loesser
Lyricist: Frank Loesser

Songs: I Was Down Texas Way; My Chicago; Tall Pines, The; Tonight in San Francisco; Trip Round the U.S.A., A; When He Comes Home [1] (C/L: Frank Loesser); You're OK, U.S.A.!

Notes: Army revue. No other information available. Music and lyrics may not all be by Loesser. [1] Also in ABOUT FACE!

3263 • OKLAHOMA!
OPENED: 03/31/1943   Theatre: St. James
Musical   Broadway: 2248

Composer: Richard Rodgers
Lyricist: Oscar Hammerstein II
Librettist: Oscar Hammerstein II
Producer: Theatre Guild, The
Director: Rouben Mamoulian

Source: GREEN GROW THE LILACS (Play: Lynn Riggs); **Choreographer:** Agnes de Mille; **Costumes:** Miles White; **Musical Director:** Jay Blackton [3]; **Orchestrations:** Robert Russell Bennett; **Set Design:** Lemuel Ayers

Songs: All er Nothin'; Boys and Girls Like You and Me [1]; Farmer and the Cowman, The; I Cain't Say No; It's a Scandal! It's an Outrage!; Kansas City; Laurey Makes Up Her Mind Ballet (inst.); Lonely Room; Many a New Day; Oh, What a Beautiful Mornin'; Oklahoma; Out of My Dreams; People Will Say We're in Love; Pore Jud Is Daid; Surrey with the Fringe on Top, The; When I Go Out Walkin' with My Baby [2]; Why Oh Why [2]

Cast: Joseph Buloff; Howard Da Silva; Lee Dixon; Alfred Drake; Betty Garde; Celeste Holm; George S. Irving; Barry Kelley; Bambi Lynn;

Owen Martin; Joan McCracken; Marc Platt; Ralph Riggs; Joan Roberts; Katherine Sergava

Notes: Performance total includes 44 special Armed Services matinees. Titled AWAY WE GO! out of town. [1] Cut. Also cut from films TAKE ME OUT TO THE BALLGAME and MEET ME IN ST. LOUIS. [2] Cut prior to opening. [3] Billed as Jacob Schwartzdorf.

3264 • OLD BUCKS AND NEW WINGS
OPENED: 11/05/1962   Theatre: Mayfair
Revue   Off-Broadway: 8

Composer: Eddie Stuart
Lyricist: Harvey Lasker
Librettist: Harvey Lasker
Producer: Harvey Lasker
Director: Harvey Lasker

Choreographer: Buster Burnell; **Musical Director:** Gerald Alfonso; **Orchestrations:** Gerald Alfonso

Songs: Get the News; It Could Be Calais; Keith's, Pantages and Loews; Let's Bring Back Show Business; Our Business Is News; So, So, Sophie; Stand Up and Cheer; Sweet Memories; That Day Will Come; That Was Your Life; You Made It Possible, Dear

Cast: Charles Dale; Tom Patricola Jr.; Carol Perea; Mickie Rogers; Joe Smith; Al Tucker; Gus Van; Rex Weber; Flip Wilson

3265 • OLD DUTCH
OPENED: 11/22/1909   Theatre: Herald
                                      Square
Musical   Broadway: 88

Composer: Victor Herbert
Lyricist: George V. Hobart
Librettist: Edgar Smith
Producer: Lew Fields; Lee Shubert; Sam S. Shubert
Director: Ned Wayburn

Costumes: Melville Ellis; **Musical Director:** Louis F. Gottschalk

Songs: Algy; Barn Dance [1]; Dance Fantastique; Drink to the Health of This Great Man; Entrance of Lew Fields with Children [1]; Fantastic Dance [1]; Honor the Brave; I Love Ze Parisienne;

I Want a Man to Love Me; If You Ever Want a Favor Mention Me [1]; Mrs. Grundy; My Gypsy Sweetheart; Pourquoi [1]; Pretending; Rich Man, Poor Man (Beggar Man, Thief); Russian Duo and Dance; Sweet Wireless Whispers [1]; That Is Love; U Dearie

Cast: John Bunny; Vernon Castle; Alice Dovey; Lew Fields; Helen Hayes; Charles Judels; Ada Lewis

Notes: Based on a German farce. [1] ASCAP/Library of Congress only.

3266 • OLD LAVENDER
OPENED: 09/03/1877   Theatre: Park
Musical   Broadway

Composer: Dave Braham
Lyricist: Edward Harrigan
Librettist: Edward Harrigan

Songs: Extra! Extra!; Get Up Jack, John Sit Down; Jolly Old Owl, The; Love, Love, Sweetest Love; Please to Put That Down; Poverty's Tears Ebb and Flow; When the Clock in the Tower Strikes Twelve

Cast: Edward Harrigan

Notes: No other information available.

3267 • OLD LIMERICK TOWN
OPENED: 09/14/1902
Play   Closed out of town

Composer: Chauncey Olcott
Lyricist: Chauncey Olcott
Author: Augustus Pitou
Producer: Augustus Pitou
Director: Augustus Pitou

Songs: Every Little Dog Must Have His Day; Limerick Girls; Noreen Mavourneen; Voice of the Violet, The

Cast: Miriam Nesbitt; Chauncey Olcott; Blanche Sweet; Alice Taylor; Edwin Tilton

Notes: Closed in Chicago.

3268 • OLD TOWN, THE
OPENED: 01/10/1910   Theatre: Globe
Musical   Broadway: 171

Composer: Gustav Luders
Lyricist: George Ade
Librettist: George Ade
Producer: Charles Dillingham
Director: Ben Teal

Costumes: Will R. Barnes; Wilhelm; **Musical Director:** Charles Zimmerman; **Set Design:** Homer Emens

Songs: Electric Signs [1]; Good Bye Christina Swenson; He Was a Cowboy (C: Egbert Van Alstyne; L: Harry Williams); Keep Your Whip in Your Hand [1]; Kissing Time [1] (C: Henry E. Pether; L: T.F. Robson); Little Flat in a Great Big Town, A [1] (C: Egbert Van Alstyne; L: Harry Williams); Man Who Will Not Love Back, The [1]; Minnesota [1] (C/L: Unknown); Modern Japanese, The; My Japanese; Noo-vo Riche, The [1]; Popular Song, A (C: Alfred G. Robyn; L: Thomas Railey); Queen of the One Ring Show [1]; Travel, Travel, Travel, Little Star (C: Arthur Pryor; L: Vincent Bryan); Weak Little Women (Suffragette) [1]; What Man Dare Say? (My Truant Heart) [1]; When I Would Think of You; Yearning, Burning [1]

Cast: Dave Montgomery; Fred Stone; Peggy Wood

Notes: [1] Sheet music only.

3269 • OLDEST TRICK IN THE WORLD, THE
Notes: *See DOUBLE ENTRY.*

3270 • OLE OLSON
OPENED: 04/19/1908
Play   Closed out of town

Composer: Harry S. Brummel
Lyricist: Harry S. Brummel
Producer: William Gray
Director: William Gray

Musical Director: Ralph Gray

Songs: Memories of My Swedish Home; Strawberries; Swagger Swedish Swell

Cast: Harry S. Brummel; Lizzie Conway; Chas. T. Hart; G.G. Wright

Notes: Program of Cedar Rapids.

3271 • OLIVER!

OPENED: 01/06/1963　Theatre: Imperial
Musical　Broadway: 774

Composer: Lionel Bart
Lyricist: Lionel Bart
Librettist: Lionel Bart
Producer: Donald Albery; David Merrick
Director: Peter Coe

Source: OLIVER TWIST (Novel: Charles Dickens); **Costumes:** Sean Kenny; **Lighting Designer:** John Wyckham; **Musical Director:** Donald Pippin; **Orchestrations:** Eric Rogers; **Set Design:** Sean Kenny

Songs: As Long As He Needs Me; Be Back Soon; Boy for Sale; Consider Yourself; Food, Glorious Food; I Shall Scream; I'd Do Anything; It's a Fine Life; My Name; Oliver!; Oom-Pah-Pah; Reviewing the Situation; That's Your Funeral; Where Is Love?; Who Will Buy; You've Got to Pick a Pocket or Two

Cast: Georgia Brown; Dortha Duckworth; Willoughby Goddard; Barry Humphries; Hope Jackman; David Jones; Ruth Maynard; Alice Playten; Bruce Prochnik; Clive Revill; Danny Sewell

3272 • OLYMPUS ON MY MIND

OPENED: 07/15/1986　Theatre: Lamb's
Musical　Off-Broadway: 207

Composer: Grant Sturiale
Lyricist: Barry Harman
Librettist: Barry Harman
Producer: Harve Brosten; Mainstage Productions
Director: Barry Harman

Source: AMPHITRYON (Play: Heinrich Von Kleist); **Choreographer:** Pamela Sousa; **Costumes:** Steven Jones; **Lighting Designer:** Fabian Yeager; **Set Design:** Christopher Stapleton

Songs: At Liberty in Thebes; Back So Soon?; Back to the Play; Don't Bring Her Flowers; Final Sequence; Generals' Pandemonium; Gods on Tap, The; Heaven on Earth; I Know My Wife; It Was Me; Jupiter Slept Here; Olympus Is a Lonely Town; Star Is Born, A; Surprise!; Wait 'Til It Dawns; Welcome to Greece; Wonderful

Cast: Jason Graae; Peggy Hewett; Lewis J. Stadlen; Martin Vidnovic; Emily Zacharias

3273 • OLYMPUS 7-0000

OPENED: 09/28/1966　Theatre: ABC
TV Musical

Composer: Richard Adler
Lyricist: Richard Adler
Librettist: Jerome Chodorov
Producer: Richard Adler; Willard Levitas
Director: Stanley Prager; Gordon Rigsby

Choreographer: Hugh Lambert; **Costumes:** Robert Fletcher; **Musical Director:** Philip Della Penna; **Orchestrations:** Ralph Burns; **Set Design:** John Ward

Songs: Better Things to Do; For You; I Get Around; I've Got Feelings; Olympus 7-000; Three of Us, The; We're Gonna Win; What I Mean

Cast: Larry Blyden; Eddie Foy Jr.; Lou Jacobi; New York Football Jets, The; Phyllis Newman; Donald O'Connor

3274 • ON A CLEAR DAY YOU CAN SEE FOREVER

OPENED: 10/17/1965　Theatre: Mark Hellinger
Musical　Broadway: 280

Composer: Burton Lane
Lyricist: Alan Jay Lerner
Librettist: Alan Jay Lerner
Producer: Alan Jay Lerner
Director: Robert Lewis

Choreographer: Herbert Ross; **Costumes:** Donald Brooks; Freddy Wittop; **Dance Arranger:** Betty Walberg; **Lighting Designer:** Feder; **Musical Director:** Theodore Saidenberg; **Orchestrations:** Robert Russell Bennett; **Set Design:** Oliver Smith; **Vocal Arranger:** Trude Rittman

Songs: Come Back to Me (2); Come Back to Me (1) [9] (C: Richard Rodgers); Dolly's Seduction [8]; Domestic Champagne Waltz, The [2]; Don't Tamper with My Sister; Go to Sleep [4]; Gout, The (The Spasms) (dance); Hellrakers', The (dance); Hurry! It's Lovely Up Here!; I'll Not Marry [3]; Marriage a La Mode [1]; Melinda [7]; Mom [8]; Normal Thing to Do, The [8]; On a Clear Day You Can See Forever; On the S.S.

Bernard Cohn; Ring Out the Bells; She Wasn't You; Solicitor's Song [5]; Someone in April [11]; Tosy and Cosh; Wait 'Til We're Sixty-Five; What Did I Have That I Don't Have; When I Come Around Again [6]; When I'm Being Born Again; Who Is There Among Us Who Knows [10] (C: Richard Rodgers); Yankee Doodle [3]

Cast: Rae Allen; John Cullum; William Daniels; Clifford David; Barbara Harris; Michael Lewis; Gerry Matthews; Titos Vandis; Byron Webster

Notes: Titled I PICKED A DAISY when Richard Rodgers was the composer. [1] Added for national tour. [2] Cut. [3] Out Seattle 11/80. [4] Out Seattle 11/80. From film version. [5] Added for national tour. Included music from "Ring Out the Bells." [6] Added for national tour. Rewritten version of "When I'm Being Born Again." [7] Music written for unproduced Israeli musical. [8] Out Boston 9/13/65. [9] Cut. Written before Lane replaced Rodgers when the show was titled I PICKED A DAISY. The lyric was later set to music by Lane. [10] Cut. Written before Lane replaced Rodgers. The lyrics was later set to music by Lane for the film version. The Lane version was cut from the film though recorded. [11] Cut. Used in CARMELINA.

3275 • ON THE FLIP SIDE

OPENED: 12/07/1966   Theatre: ABC
TV Musical

Composer: Burt Bacharach
Lyricist: Hal David
Librettist: Robert Emmett
Producer: Richard Lewine
Director: Joe Layton

Arrangements: Peter Matz; **Choreographer:** Joe Layton; **Musical Director:** Peter Matz

Songs: Fender Mender; It Doesn't Matter Anymore; Juanita's Place; Juanita's Place Montage; Take a Broken Heart; They Don't Give Medals (To Yesterday's Heroes); They're Gonna Love It; Try to See It My Way

Cast: Rick Nelson; Joanie Sommers; Donna Jean Young

Notes: Part of Stage 67 series.

3276 • ON THE LOCK-IN

OPENED: 04/27/1977   Theatre: Public
Musical   Off-Broadway: 47

Composer: David Langston Smyrl
Lyricist: David Langston Smyrl
Librettist: David Langston Smyrl
Producer: N.Y. Shakespeare Festival; Joseph Papp
Director: Robert Macbeth

Costumes: Grace Williams; **Lighting Designer:** Victor En Yu Tan; **Musical Director:** George Stubbs; **Orchestrations:** Paul Griffin; **Set Design:** Karl Eigsti; **Vocal Arranger:** Paul Griffin

Songs: Alone; Born to Lose; Circumstances; Dry Mouth with No Water; 42nd Street Blues; Marlene; Peace Will Come; Sister Paradise; Talkin' Blues; Whatever It Happens to Be

Cast: Manuel Santiago; David Langston Smyrl; Alan Weeks

Notes: Previewed from 4/14/77.

3277 • ON THE SWING SHIFT

OPENED: 05/20/1983   Theatre: Manhattan
                                 Theatre Club
Revue   Off-Broadway: 37

Composer: Michael Dansicker
Lyricist: Sarah Schlesinger
Producer: Manhattan Theater Club

Choreographer: Janie Sell; **Costumes:** Jess Goldstein; **Dance Arranger:** Michael Dansicker; **Lighting Designer:** Arden Fingerhut; **Musical Director:** Janet Glazener; **Set Design:** Tony Straiges; **Vocal Arranger:** Michael Dansicker

Songs: Bond Sequence; Chorale; Evening; I'm Someone Now; Killing Time; Morning; Night on the Town; Row 10 Aisle 6 Bench 114; Something to Do Tonight; There's a War Going On; We Got a Job to Do; When Tomorrow Comes

Cast: Kay Cole; Ann-Ngaire Martin; Valerie Perri

3278 • ON THE TOWN

OPENED: 12/28/1944   Theatre: Adelphi
Musical   Broadway: 462

Composer: Leonard Bernstein
Lyricist: Betty Comden; Adolph Green
Librettist: Betty Comden; Adolph Green
Producer: Paul Feigay; Oliver Smith
Director: George Abbott

Choreographer: Jerome Robbins; **Costumes:** Alvin Colt; **Lighting Designer:** Sam Amdrus; **Musical Director:** Max Goberman; **Orchestrations:** Leonard Bernstein; Elliot Jacoby; Hershy Kay; Ted Royal; Don Walker; **Set Design:** Oliver Smith

Songs: Ain't Got No Tears Left [2]; Another Love [1] (L: Leonard Bernstein; Betty Comden; Adolph Green); Carnegie Hall Pavanne (inst.); Carried Away; Come Up to My Place; Do-Do-Re-Do; Dream with Me [3]; Gabey's Comin' [4]; Got to Be Bad to Be Good [1]; I Can Cook Too (L: Leonard Bernstein; Betty Comden; Adolph Green); I Feel Like I'm Not Out of Bed Yet (Sleep in Your Baby's Arms); I Understand; I'm Afraid It's Love [1]; I'm Blue; Imaginary Coney Island Ballet (dance); Intermission's Great, The [1]; Lonely Me [1]; Lonely Town; Lucky to Be Me; Miss Turnstiles (dance); New York, New York; Nicest Time of the Year [1]; Pitkin's Song [1]; Real Coney Island, The (dance); Say When [1]; So Long, Baby; Some Other Time; Times Square Dance (dance); Ya Got Me

Cast: Cris Alexander; John Battles; Betty Comden; Adolph Green; Ray Harrison; Sono Osato; Alice Pearce; Nancy Walker

Notes: [1] Cut from show prior to opening. [2] Cut from show prior to opening. Music used in Bernstein's "Second Symphony" ("Age of Anxiety"). [3] Cut from show prior to opening. Also cut from PETER PAN. [4] Cut but music used in "Lonely Town Pas de Deux."

3279 • ON THE TWENTIETH CENTURY

OPENED: 02/19/1978   Theatre: St. James
Musical   Broadway: 460

Composer: Cy Coleman
Lyricist: Betty Comden; Adolph Green
Librettist: Betty Comden; Adolph Green
Producer: Producers Circle 2, The
Director: Harold Prince

Source: TWENTIETH CENTURY (Play: Ben Hecht; Charles MacArthur; Bruce Milholland); **Choreographer:** Larry Fuller; **Costumes:** Florence Klotz; **Lighting Designer:** Ken Billington; **Musical Director:** Paul Gemignani; **Orchestrations:** Hershy Kay; **Set Design:** Robin Wagner

Songs: Babbette; Five Zeros; Grand Central Station [1]; I Have Written a Play; I Rise Again; Indian Maiden's Lament, The; I've Got It All; Legacy, The; Life Is Like a Train (Entr'acte); Lily Garland [3]; Lily, Oscar; Lucky Lily [1]; Max Jacobs; Mine; Never; On the 20th Century; Our Private World; Repent; Saddle Up the Horse; She's a Nut; Sign, Lily, Sign; Stranded Again; This Is the Day [2]; Together; Veronique

Cast: George Lee Andrews; Tom Batten; Willi Burke; Imogene Coca; George Coe; John Cullum; Keith Davis; Dean Dittman; Quitman Fludd III; Madeline Kahn; Judy Kaye; Kevin Kline; Sal Mistretta; Stanley Simmonds; Rufus Smith; Ray Stephens; Joseph Wise

Notes: Judy Kaye replaced Kahn early in the run. [1] Cut prior to opening. [2] Cut prior to opening. Used as underscoring. [3] Part of song remains in the score.

3280 • ON TIME

Revue   Closed out of town

Composer: Charles Burr
Lyricist: Charles Burr
Adaptation: Howard Da Silva; Alfred Drake; Felix Leon
Producer: Hal James
Director: Howard Da Silva

Choreographer: Grover Dale; **Costumes:** Michael Hotopp; **Lighting Designer:** Laura Mae Jackson; **Musical Director:** Pembroke Davenport; **Orchestrations:** Luther Henderson; William Stegmeyer; Cornel Tannassy; **Set Design:** Michael Hotopp

Songs: All Glory to the Young; Ceremonial Beheading; Clown Song, The (L: William Shakespeare); Harmony; Hero Sandwiches; I Met My Love; I Wanted to Do Something Dirty; I Was a Hollywood Baby; If I Had a Hammer; If I Had a Hammer; Into a Green and Smiling Age;

I've Conquered My Fears of Younger Boys; I've Spent All My Life Preserving Things; Madrigal (C: Arthur Sullivan; L: W.S. Gilbert); Man They Meant, The; Other People's Waltzes; She Stopped It; We Lived Our Lives in the Gap; Who Knew My Father; Why Should the Young Men Fight

Cast: Alfred Drake; Nancy Dussault; Keith Jochim; Marian Winters

Notes: Goodspeed Opera House. [1] From RUDDIGORE.

3281 • ON WITH THE SHOW (1927)

OPENED: 1927
Revue

Notes: No other information available.

3282 • ON WITH THE SHOW (1954)

Notes: *See HIT THE TRAIL.*

3283 • ON YOUR TOES

OPENED: 04/11/1936   Theatre: Imperial
Musical   Broadway: 318

Composer: Richard Rodgers
Lyricist: Lorenz Hart
Librettist: George Abbott; Lorenz Hart; Richard Rodgers
Producer: Dwight Deere Wiman
Director: George Abbott; Worthington Miner

Choreographer: George Balanchine; Costumes: Irene Sharaff; Musical Director: Gene Salzer; Orchestrations: Hans Spialek; Set Design: Jo Mielziner

Songs: Glad to Be Unhappy; Heart Is Quicker Than the Eye, The; It's Got to Be Love; La Princess Zenobia Ballet (inst.); On Your Toes; Quiet Night; Slaughter on Tenth Avenue (ballet); There's a Small Hotel; Three B's, The (Questions and Answers); Too Good for the Average Man; Two-a-Day for Keith (Twice a Night)

Cast: Ray Bolger; Doris Carson; Luella Gear; Tamara Geva; Ethel Hampton; Dave Jones; Tyrone Kearney; David Morris; Monty Woolley

3284 • ON YOUR WAY

OPENED: 1915
Musical

Composer: Roy S. Webb
Lyricist: Kenneth S. Webb
Librettist: Kenneth S. Webb
Producer: Columbia University Players
Director: Kenneth S. Webb

Musical Director: Roy S. Webb

Cast: Oscar Hammerstein II

Notes: Amateur show.

3285 • ONCE ON THIS ISLAND

OPENED: 10/18/1990   Theatre: Booth
Musical   Broadway: 469

Composer: Stephen Flaherty
Lyricist: Lynn Ahrens
Librettist: Lynn Ahrens
Producer: Capital Cities/ABC Inc.; Shubert Organization, The; Suntory International Corp.; James Walsh
Director: Graciela Daniele

Source: MY LOVE, MY LOVE (Novel: Rosa Guy); Choreographer: Graciela Daniele; Costumes: Judy Dearing; Lighting Designer: Allen Lee Hughes; Musical Director: Steve Marzullo; Orchestrations: Michael Starobin; Set Design: Loy Arcenas

Songs: And the Gods Heard Her Prayer; Ball, The; Come Down from the Tree [1]; Forever Yours; Human Heart, The; Mama Will Provide; One Small Girl; Part of Us, A; Pray; Rain; Sad Tale of the Beauxhommes, The; Some Girls; Sons Say; Ti Monte; Waiting for Life; We Dance; Why We Tell the Story

Cast: Jerry Dixon; Andrea Freirson; Sheila Gibbs; La Chanze; Kecia Lewis-Evans; Afi McClendon; Gerry McIntyre; Milton Craig Nealy; Nikki Rene; Eric Riley; Ellis E. Williams

Notes: Opened originally at Playwrights Horizons on 05/06/1990. [1] Cut during previews Off-Broadway.

3286 • ONCE OVER LIGHTLY

OPENED: 1955   Theatre: Barbizon
                                            Playhouse
Revue   Off-Broadway

Librettist: Mel Brooks; Ira Wallach
Producer: Cuadro Productions
Director: Stanley Prager

Choreographer: Lee Theodore; **Dance Arranger:** Peter Matz; **Musical Director:** Peter Matz; **Set Design:** Warwick Brown; **Vocal Arranger:** Peter Matz

Songs: Benedictine (C: Murray Grand; L: Ira Wallach); Bop-A- Bye (C: Ralph Strain; L: Marshall Barer); Here Beside Me (C: Alec Wilder; L: William Engvick); I Got Lucky (C/L: Dean Fuller; L: Marshall Barer); I'll Dance You (C: Dean Fuller; L: Marshall Barer); It's Silk, Feel It (C: Dean Fuller; L: Marshall Barer); Melvin (C: Dean Fuller; L: Marshall Barer); Opening (C: Dean Fuller; L: Marshall Barer); Osteopathy Rag, The (C: Alec Wilder; L: William Engvick); Peter Pan (C: Samuel Matlovsky)

Cast: June Ericson; Jack Gilford; George Mills; Zero Mostel; Sono Osato; Victor Reilley; Joe Sargent; Lee Theodore; Royce Wallace; Patricia Wilkes

3287 • ONCE UPON A CHRISTMAS TREE

OPENED: 12/09/1959   Theatre: NBC
TV Musical

Composer: Robert Allen; Al Stillman
Lyricist: Robert Allen; Al Stillman
Librettist: A.J. Russell
Producer: Jack Philbin
Director: Kirk Browning

Source: THIRTEENTH ORPHAN, THE (Story: Paul Gallico); **Musical Director:** Kenyon Hopkins

Cast: Patty Duke; Margaret Hamilton; Pat Henning; Claude Rains; Ronnie Robertson; Charlie Ruggles; Kate Smith

Notes: No song list available.

3288 • ONCE UPON A MATTRESS

OPENED: 04/11/1959   Theatre: Alvin
Musical   Broadway: 460

Composer: Mary Rodgers
Lyricist: Marshall Barer
Librettist: Marshall Barer; Dean Fuller; Jay Thompson
Producer: Jean Eckart; William Eckart; T. Edward Hambleton; Norris Houghton
Director: George Abbott

Choreographer: Joe Layton; **Costumes:** Jean Eckart; William Eckart; **Dance Arranger:** Roger Adams; **Lighting Designer:** Tharon Musser; **Musical Director:** Hal Hastings; **Orchestrations:** Arthur Beck; Hershy Kay; **Set Design:** Jean Eckart; William Eckart

Songs: Happily Ever After; In a Little While; Lullaby; Man to Man Talk; Many Moons Ago; Minstrel, the Jester and I, The; Normandy; Opening for a Princess, An; Quiet; Sensitivity; Shy; Song of Love; Spanish Panic (dance); Swamps of Home, The; Under a Spell [1]; Very Soft Shoes; Yesterday I Loved You

Cast: Joe Bova; Carol Burnett; Allen Case; Jack Gilford; Matt Mattox; Harry Snow; Robert Weil; Jane White

Notes: Opened at the Phoenix Theatre on above date. After 216 performances it moved to Broadway for an additional 244 performances. This show moved from the Alvin to the Winter Garden, then to the Cort and finally closed at the St. James. [1] Written for 1964 TV version.

3289 • ONCE UPON A TIME

Notes: *See EVER YOURS.*

3290 • ONE APRIL DAY

OPENED: 12/05/1936
Musical

Composer: Frederick Loewe
Lyricist: Earle Crooker; Charles Locke
Librettist: Alexander Clark; Arthur Pierson
Director: Hal Forde

Choreographer: Charles Mosconi

Pianist: Hans Fredhoven; Frederick Loewe

Notes: A one-act "Musical Fantasy" that was part of THE LAMBS WINTER GAMBOL at the

Waldorf-Astoria Hotel. There were no songs idenitfied as part of this mini-musical. *See THE LAMBS WINTER GAMBOL* for additional credits.

3291 • ONE DAM THING AFTER ANOTHER

OPENED: 05/19/1927   Theatre: London Pavilion
Revue   London: 237

Composer: Richard Rodgers
Lyricist: Lorenz Hart
Librettist: Ronald Jeans
Producer: Charles B. Cochran
Director: Frank Collins

Choreographer: Max Rivers; **Costumes:** Kitty Shannon; Doris Zinkeisen; **Musical Director:** J.B. Hastings; **Orchestrations:** Robert Russell Bennett; **Set Design:** Marc Henri

Songs: Election, The; Gigolo [5]; I Need Some Cooling Off [6]; Idles of the King [5]; Ladies and Gentlemen, We're Here Again (Opening Act II); Make Hey! Hey! Hey! (While the Moon Shines); My Heart Stood Still [2]; My Lucky Star [6]; One Dam Thing After Another; Paris Is Really Divine [4]; Play Us a Tune [1] (C/L: Cole Porter); Pretty Little Lady [7]; Shuffle [3]

Cast: Edythe Baker; Douglas Byng; Melville Cooper; Sheilah Grahame; Sonnie Hale; Lance Lister; Jessie Matthews; Max Wall; **Pianist:** Leslie Hutchinson

Notes: No program available. [1] In HITCHY- KOO OF 1922 and THE DANCING GIRL as "Play Me a Tune." [2] Also in A CONNECTICUT YANKEE. [3] Also in BETSY. [4] Also in PEGGY-ANN. [5] Also in THE GARRICK GAIETIES (1926). [6] Also in SHE'S MY BABY. [7] Cut prior to opening.

3292 • ONE FOR THE MONEY

OPENED: 02/04/1939   Theatre: Booth
Revue   Broadway: 132

Composer: Morgan Lewis
Lyricist: Nancy Hamilton
Librettist: Nancy Hamilton
Producer: Robert F. Cutler; Stanley Gilkey; Gertrude Macy
Director: John Murray Anderson; Edward Clarke Lilley

Choreographer: Robert Alton; **Costumes:** Raoul Pene du Bois; **Musical Director:** Ray Kavanaugh; **Orchestrations:** Hans Spialek; **Set Design:** Raoul Pene du Bois

Songs: I Hate Spring [1] (C: Martha Caples); I Only Know; Kiss Me and We'll Both Go Home; Little Bit Delighted with the Weather, A; Once Upon a Time; Rhapsody; Send a Boy; Teeter Totter Tessie; Yoo-Hoo Blues, The

Cast: William Archibald; Maxine Barrat; Philip Bourneuf; Frances Comstock; Alfred Drake; Brenda Forbes; Nadine Gae; Nancy Hamilton; Gene Kelly; George Lloyd; Don Loper; Ruth Matteson; Grace McDonald; Nell O'Day; Robert Smith; Keenan Wynn

Notes: [1] Added after opening.

3293 • ONE GIRL IN A MILLION

OPENED: 09/06/1914   Theatre: La Salle
Musical   Chicago

Composer: Ted Snyder
Lyricist: Bert Kalmar; Edgar Leslie
Librettist: Addison Burkhardt; Charles Collins

Songs: Moonlight on the Rhine

Notes: No other information available.

3294 • 110 IN THE SHADE

OPENED: 10/24/1963   Theatre: Broadhurst
Musical   Broadway: 330

Composer: Harvey Schmidt
Lyricist: Tom Jones
Librettist: N. Richard Nash
Producer: David Merrick
Director: Joseph Anthony

Choreographer: Agnes de Mille; **Costumes:** Motley; **Dance Arranger:** William Goldenberg; **Lighting Designer:** John Harvey; **Musical Director:** Donald Pippin; **Orchestrations:** Hershy Kay; **Set Design:** Oliver Smith; **Vocal Arranger:** Robert De Cormier

Songs: Another Hot Day [5]; Cinderella; Come On Along [4]; Dance Hall Saturday Night [1]; Evening Star [3]; Everything Beautiful Happens at Night; Fliberty Jibits [1]; Hungry Men; I Can Dance [1]; I Live By Myself (and I Like It) [1]; Is It Really Me?; Little Red Hat; Lizzie's Coming Home; Love, Don't Turn Away; Man and a

Woman, A; Melisande; Old Maid; 110 in the Shade [2]; Overhead [4]; Poker Polka; Pretty Is [1]; Rain Song, The; Raunchy; Shooting Star [4]; Simple Little Things; Sweet River [1]; Too Many People Alone [7]; Whole Hot or Nothin' [1]; Why Can't They Leave Me Alone [6]; Wonderful Music; You're Not Foolin' Me

Cast: Don Crabtree; Gretchen Cryer; Jerry Dodge; Stephen Douglass; Will Geer; Robert Horton; Vernon Lusby; Steve Roland; Inga Swenson; Scooter Teague; Lesley Ann Warren

Notes: [1] Cut prior to New York. [2] Added for London production. [3] Cut prior to New York. Same music as "Another Hot Day." [4] Added to 1992 City Opera revival. [5] Same music as "Evening Star." [6] Added to 1992 City Opera revival. Same music as "Too Many People Alone." [7] Cut prior to New York. Same music as "Why Can't They Leave Me Alone."

3295 • ONE KISS

OPENED: 11/27/1923   Theatre: Fulton
Musical   Broadway: 95

Composer: Maurice Yvain
Lyricist: Clare Kummer
Librettist: Clare Kummer
Producer: Charles Dillingham
Director: Fred G. Latham

Source: TA BOUCHE (Play: Yves Mirande; Alfred Willmetz); **Choreographer:** Julian Alfred

Songs: Don't Ever Be a Poor Relation; Gentlemen; In My Day; Little Bit of Lace, A; Little Love, A; London Town; One Kiss; There Are Some Things We Can Never Forget; Up There; When We Are Married; Your Lips

Cast: Louise Groody; John E. Hazzard; John Price Jones; Oscar Shaw

3296 • ONE MINUTE PLEASE

OPENED: 12/29/1917
Musical

Composer: Richard Rodgers
Lyricist: Ralph G. Engelsman; Richard Rodgers
Librettist: Ralph G. Engelsman
Producer: Akron Club
Director: Milton G. Bender

Songs: At the Movies (C: Milton G. Bender); Auto Show Girl (L: David Dyrenforth); He Stole the Heart of a Vamp; I'm a Vampire; Lest We Forget; My Camera Man; They've Got Nothing on Us 'Over There'; When They Rub Noses in Alaska; Whispers

Notes: Amateur production.

3297 • ONE MO' TIME

OPENED: 10/22/1979   Theatre: Village Gate
Musical   Off-Broadway: 1372

Producer: Art D'Lugoff; Burt D'Lugoff; Shari Upbin; Jerry Wexler
Director: Vernel Bagneris

Costumes: Jo Ann Clevenger; **Lighting Designer:** Joanna Schielke; **Orchestrations:** Lars Edegran; Orange Kellin; **Set Design:** Elwin Charles Terrel II

Songs: After You've Gone (C: Turner Layton; L: Henry Creamer); Black Bottom (C: Ray Henderson; L: Lew Brown; B.G. DeSylva); C.C. Rider (C/L: Arrant; Ma Rainey); Cake Walkin' Babies from Home (C/L: Chris Smith; Henry Todd; Clarence Williams); Darktown Strutters' Ball, The (C/L: Shelton Brooks); Don't Turn Your Back on Me (C: Clarence Williams; L: Andy Razaf); Down in Honky Tonk Town (C/L: Charles McCarron; Chris Smith); Everybody Loves My Baby (C/L: Jack Palmer; Spencer Williams); Get on Out of Here (C/L: Wilson); Hindustan (C/L: Oliver G. Wallace; Harold Weeks); Hot Time in the Old Town, A (C/L: Theodore A. Matz); I've Got What It Takes (C/L: Hezekiah Henkins; Clarence Williams); Jenny's Ball (C/L: Reed); Kiss Me Sweet (C/L: Steve J. Lewis; A.J. Piron); Kitchen Man (C: Alex Belledna; L: Andy Razaf); Love (C/L: Jabbo Smith); Muddy Water (C: Peter De Rose; Harry Richman; L: Jo Trent); Muskrat Ramble (inst.) (C: Kid Ory); My Man Blues (C/L: Bessie Smith); New Orleans Hop Scop Blues (C/L: George W. Thomas); Papa Do Da Da (C/L: Clarence Todd; Clarence Williams; Spencer Williams); Right Key but the Wrong Key Hole, The (C/L: Eddie Green; Clarence Williams); Shake That Thing (C/L: Charlie Jackson); (I Got a Woman Crazy for Me) She's Funny That Way (C/L: Neil Moret; Richard A. Whiting); Tiger Rag (C: Original Dixieland Jazz Band; L: Harry DeCosta); Wait 'til You See My Baby do the Charleston (C/L: Rosseau Simmons;

Clarence Todd; Clarence Williams); What It Takes to Bring You Back (C/L: Spencer Williams); Yes, Yes (C/L: Jabbo Smith)

Cast: Vernel Bagneris; Topsy Chapman; Thais Clark; John Stell; Sylvia "Kuumba" Williams

Notes: No songs written for this show.

3298 • ONE NIGHT AND GONE
Musical

Composer: Harry Von Tilzer
Librettist: J.A. Fraser
Director: George Marion

Choreographer: Wilhelm Shaffer

Songs: All Aboard for Gay Paree; Any Old Place I Can Hang My Hat Is Home, Sweet Home for Me [1]; Haughtiest Naughtiest Girls, The; Life in a Harem; My Lady Hottentot; Sing Hey, For a Gallant Baroque; Sparkling Wine; Where Are You Going, My Pretty Maid?; Whoa Bill; Ze American Millionaire Barcarolle

Notes: A burlesque musical. [1] Probably the pop song by Jean Schwartz and William Jerome.

3299 • ONE NIGHT STAND
OPENED: 1980   Theatre: Nederlander
Musical   Broadway

Composer: Jule Styne
Lyricist: Herb Gardner
Librettist: Herb Gardner
Producer: Joan Cullman; Joseph Kipness; James M. Nederlander; Lester Osterman; Alfred Taubman
Director: John Dexter

Choreographer: Peter Gennaro; **Costumes:** Patricia Zipprodt; **Dance Arranger:** Marvin Laird; **Lighting Designer:** Andy Phillips; **Musical Director:** Eric Stern; **Orchestrations:** Philip J. Lang; **Set Design:** Robin Wagner

Songs: Don't Kick My Dreams Around [2]; Everybody Loves Me [3]; For You [3]; Gettin' Some [1]; Go Out Big; Here Comes Never; I Am Writing a Love Song for You; Let Me Hear You Love Me (Everbody Love Me); Little Travelin' Music Please, A; Long Way from Home; 'Now' Dance, The (inst.); Some Day Soon [4]; Some-

body Stole My Kazoo; There Was a Time [4]; Too Old to Be So Young; We Used to Talk Once [2]

Cast: Catherine Cox; Charles Kimbrough; Brandon Maggart; John Mineo; Kate Mostel; Terri Treas; Jack Weston

Notes: Closed October 25, 1980 after 8 previews. [1] Same music as "Ugly, Ugly Gal" cut from HALLELUJAH, BABY! [2] Cut prior to previews. [3] ASCAP/Library of Congress only. [4] Music later used in SERAFINA.

3300 • ONE OF THE BOYS
OPENED: 05/24/1915   Theatre: Palace
Musical   Broadway

Composer: Silvio Hein
Lyricist: Philip Bartholomae
Librettist: Philip Bartholomae

Notes: Vaudeville musical.

3301 • ONE TOUCH OF VENUS
OPENED: 10/07/1943   Theatre: Imperial
Musical   Broadway: 567

Composer: Kurt Weill
Lyricist: Ogden Nash
Librettist: Ogden Nash; S.J. Perelman
Producer: Cheryl Crawford; John Wildberg
Director: Elia Kazan

Source: TINTED VENUS, THE (Story: F. Anstey); **Choreographer:** Agnes de Mille; **Costumes:** Kermit Love; Mainbocher; Paul du Pont; **Dance Arranger:** Kurt Weill; **Musical Director:** Maurice Abravanel; **Orchestrations:** Kurt Weill; **Set Design:** Howard Bay; **Vocal Arranger:** Kurt Weill

Songs: Bacchanale (Ballet) [1]; Catch Hatch; Dr. Crippen; Foolish Heart [4]; Forty Minutes for Lunch (Ballet); Fresh Air and Exercise [1]; How Much I Love You; I'm a Stranger Here Myself; It Must Be Ernie [1]; Jersey Plunk, The [1]; Love in a Mist [1]; New Art Is True Art; One Touch of Venus; Same Time, Same Place [1]; Speak Low; That's Him; Too Soon [1]; Trouble with Women, The [3]; Venus in Ozone Heights (Ballet); Venus Was a Modest Goddess [1]; Very, Very [2]; Vive La Difference [1]; Way Out West in Jersey; West Wind; Who Am I [1]; Who Dealt? [1]; Wooden Wedding; You'll Find It on the Bill [1]

3302 • ONE WONDERFUL NIGHT

Cast: Kenny Baker; John Boles; Teddy Hart; Paula Laurence; Mary Martin; Sono Osato

Notes: Originally titled LOVE IN A MIST. [1] Cut prior to opening. [2] Chorus from music of DER KUHHANDEL. [3] Music originally used as a companion piece to "Les Filles de Bordeaux" in MARIE GALANTE. [4] Music later used for "(Don't Look Now) My Heart Is Showing" from film version with new lyrics by Ann Ronell.

3302 • ONE WONDERFUL NIGHT

OPENED: 1983
Musical   Unproduced

Composer: Dennis Buck; Timothy Gray
Lyricist: Timothy Gray
Librettist: Timothy Gray
Director: Christopher Hewett

Source: SHE STOOPS TO CONQUER (Play: Oliver Goldsmith); **Choreographer:** Paddy Stone; **Costumes:** Leo Meyer; **Lighting Designer:** Marilyn Rennagel; **Set Design:** Leo Meyer

Notes: No other information available.

3303 • ONIONS

OPENED: 1899   Theatre: Weber & Fields' Music Hall

Musical   Broadway

Composer: John Stromberg
Lyricist: Edgar Smith
Librettist: Edgar Smith
Producer: Lew Fields; Joseph Weber

Cast: Lew Fields; Joseph Weber

Notes: A one-act burlesque.

3304 • ONLY GIRL, THE

OPENED: 11/02/1914   Theatre: 39th St.
Musical   Broadway: 240

Composer: Victor Herbert
Lyricist: Henry Blossom
Librettist: Henry Blossom
Producer: Joseph Weber
Director: Fred G. Latham

Source: OUR WIVES (Play: Helen Kraft; Frank Mandel); **Choreographer:** Joseph C. Smith; **Musical Director:** Robert Hood Bowers; **Orchestrations:** Victor Herbert

Songs: Antoinette; Be Happy Boys Tonight; Compact, The; Connubial Bliss; Equal Rights; Here's How; Here's to Health, Here's to Wealth (Here Is Health) [1]; Here's to the Land We Love, Boys!; Hesitation [1]; Husbands! Husbands! Husbands! [1]; I Love Not One but All [1]; More I See of Others the Better I Love You, The; Only Girl, The [1]; Personality; Tell It All Over Again; Valse Hesitation [1]; When You're Away; When Your Ankle Wears the Ball and Chain (L: Harry B. Smith); Why Should We Stay Home and Sew [1]; You Have to Have a Party to Make a Hit; You're the One Girl for Me

Cast: Wilda Bennett; Thurston Hall; Louise Kelley; Jed Prouty; Adele Rowland; Ernest Torrence

Notes: Source based on JUGENDFREUNDE. [1] ASCAP/Library of Congress only.

3305 • ONWARD VICTORIA

OPENED: 12/14/1980   Theatre: Martin Beck
Musical   Broadway: 1

Composer: Keith Herrmann
Lyricist: Charlotte Anker; Irene Rosenberg
Librettist: Charlotte Anker; Irene Rosenberg
Producer: John N. Hart Jr.
Director: Julianne Boyd

Choreographer: Michael Shawn; **Costumes:** Theoni V. Aldredge; **Dance Arranger:** Donald Johnston; **Lighting Designer:** Richard Nelson; **Musical Director:** Larry Blank; **Orchestrations:** Michael Gibson; **Set Design:** William Ritman; **Vocal Arranger:** Larry Blank; Keith Herrmann

Songs: Age of Brass, The; Another Life; Beecher's Defense; Beecher's Processional; Changes; Curiosity; Everyday I Do a Little Something for the Lord; I Depend on You; In New York the Only Sin Is Being Timid [1]; It's Easy for Her; Love and Joy; Magnetic Healing; Read It in the Weekly; Respectable; Taste of Forever, A; Unescorted Women; Valentine for Beecher, A; Victoria's Banner; Woman Like Beth, A [1]; You Cannot Drown the Dreamer

Cast: Beth Austin; Jill Eikenberry; Gordon Stanley; Ted Thurston; Laura Waterbury; Carrie Wilder; Lenny Wolpe; Michael Zaslow

Notes: [1] Cut prior to opening.

3306 • OPAL

OPENED: 02/18/1995
Musical

Composer: Robert Nassif Lindsey
Lyricist: Robert Nassif Lindsey
Librettist: Robert Nassif Lindsey
Producer: George Street Playhouse
Director: Lynne Taylor-Corbett

Choreographer: Lynne Taylor-Corbett; **Costumes:** Ann Hould Ward; **Lighting Designer:** Tom Sturge; **Musical Director:** James Stenborg; **Orchestrations:** Douglas Besterman; **Set Design:** Michael R. Smith

Songs: Angel Mother, Angel Father; Everybody's Looking for Love; Little Lamb; Night of Shooting Stars; Opal; Prologue; Sears and Roebuck Wedding Band; Someone; They Will Send Ye a Sign; To Conquer the Land; What Mighta Been; Why Do I See Good

Cast: Mana Allen; Jackie Angelescu; Christopher Chew; Hal Davis; Deb G. Girdler

Notes: George Street Playhouse, New Brunswick, New Jersey.

3307 • OPEN YOUR EYES

OPENED: 1929
Musical   Closed out of town

Composer: Vernon Duke
Lyricist: Collie Knox
Librettist: Fred Jackson
Director: John Harwood

Songs: Happily Ever After; Jack and Jill; Open Your Eyes; Such a Funny Feeling; Too, Too Divine [1]; You'd Do for Me-I'd Do for You

Cast: Marie Burke; Geoffrey Gwyther; Ella Logan

Notes: Closed in Edinburgh, Scotland before London. No program available. [1] With same title but new lyric in THE GARRICK GAIETIES (Third Edition).

3308 • OPERA BALL, THE

OPENED: 02/12/1912   Theatre: Liberty
Musical   Broadway: 32

Composer: Richard Heuberger
Lyricist: Clare Kummer; Sydney Rosenfeld
Librettist: Clare Kummer; Sydney Rosenfeld
Producer: Daniel V. Arthur

Source: DER OPERNBALL (Musical: Victor Leon; H. Von Waldberg); **Costumes:** Max & Mahieu; **Musical Director:** Josiah Zuro

Songs: Cupid, Mind Your Business [3]; Folly; I Want a Little Loving Sometimes (C/L: Chris Smith); Kiss and Be Friends; Lady with the Twinkling Feet [3]; Let Us Find a Cosey Little Nook (Let Us Find a Charming Rendezvous); Letter Trio; Listen to Me; Marie- Louise [1] (C: Jerome Kern); Never Again; Nurses Are We [2] (C: Jerome Kern; L: Sydney Rosenfeld); Opening Chorus Act II; Paris Is a Spot So Fair; Quarrel Trio; Sergeant Philip of the Dancers [2] (C: Jerome Kern; L: Sydney Rosenfeld); Tho' Delight, Dany and Night [3]; We Have Only One Life to Live; What Are We Coming To?

Cast: Marie Cahill; Viola Cain; Harry Conor; George Lydecker; Frank Tierney

Notes: Kern is credited in the vocal scores but not playbills. See footnotes. [1] Not in playbills. Probably by Kern. [2] Not in playbills. [3] Sheet music only.

3309 • OPERATION SIDEWINDER

OPENED: 03/12/1970   Theatre: Lincoln Center
Play   Broadway: 52

Author: Sam Shepard
Producer: Repertory Theatre of Lincoln Center
Director: Michael A. Schultz

Costumes: Willa Kim; **Lighting Designer:** John Gleason; **Set Design:** Douglas W. Schmidt

Songs: Alien Song (C/L: Sam Shepard); Bad Karma (C/L: Antonia; Peter Stampfel); C.I.A. Man (C/L: Antonia; Tuli Kupferberg; Peter

Stampfel); Catch Me (C/L: Sam Shepard); Do It Girl (C/L: Antonia; Peter Stampfel); Don't Leave Me Dangling in the Dust (C/L: Robin Remaily); Euphoria (C/L: Robin Remaily); Float Me Down Your Pipeline (C/L: Antonia); Generalonely (C/L: Steve Weber); Hathor (C/L: Peter Stampfel); I Disremember Quite Well (C/L: Antonia); Synergy (C/L: Antonia; Peter Stampfel)

Cast: Roberts Blossom; Philip Bosco; Catherine Burns; Barbara Eda-Young; Joseph Mascolo; Garrett Morris; Robert Phalen; Paul Sparer

3310 • OPTIMISTS, THE

OPENED: 01/30/1928   Theatre: Casino de Paris
Musical   Broadway: 24

Composer: Melville Gideon
Lyricist: Clifford Grey; Austin Melford; Greatrex Newman
Librettist: Clifford Grey; Austin Melford; Greatrex Newman
Producer: Melville Gideon

Choreographer: Jack Haskell; **Musical Director:** Harold Stern; **Set Design:** Watson Barratt

Songs: Amapu (L: Edward Knoblock); Bow-Wow; Dreamy Days; I Made Them Step; I Promise I'll Be Practically True to You (L: Clifford Grey); If I Gave You a Rose (L: Granville English); Little Laquer Lady (L: Clifford Seyler); London Town; Rolling Stones; Spare a Little Love; Three Little School-Girls; To the Races; We All Play the Grand Piano

Cast: Luella Gear; Melville Gideon; George Hassell; Eleanor Powell; Bobby Watson

3311 • OPTIONS

OPENED: 07/11/1985   Theatre: Circle Repertory
Musical   Off-Broadway: 2

Composer: Jeffrey Silverman
Lyricist: Walter Willison
Librettist: Walter Willison
Producer: Marck Adrian Fedor; Jeffrey Betancourt Prods.
Director: Michael Shawn

Costumes: Dona Granata; **Lighting Designer:** Tom Hennes; **Set Design:** Ron Placzek

Cast: Julie Budd; Jo Anna Rush; Jeffrey Silverman; Walter Willison

3312 • ORANGE BLOSSOMS

OPENED: 09/19/1922   Theatre: Fulton
Musical   Broadway: 95

Composer: Victor Herbert
Lyricist: B.G. DeSylva
Librettist: Fred De Gresac
Producer: Edward Royce
Director: Edward Royce

Source: LA PASSERELLE (Play: Fred De Gresac; Francois de Croisset); **Costumes:** Paul Poiret; **Musical Director:** Gus Salzer; **Orchestrations:** Victor Herbert; **Set Design:** Norman Bel Geddes

Songs: Because I Love You So; Dream of Orange Blossoms, A; Every Girl Is Like a Weather Glass [1]; Finale Act II; Finale Act III; How Can I Win You Now?; I Can't Argue with You; In Hennequeville; I've Missed You; J. J. Flynn; Just Like That; Kiss in the Dark, A; Legend of the Glowworm; Let's Not Get Married; Lonely Nest, The; Moonshine (inst.); Mosquito Ballet (inst.); New York Is the Same Old Place; On the Riviera; Opening Chorus; Orange Blossoms; Quite and Nifty and Effective Detective Am I [2]; Then Comes the Dawning; This Time It's Love; Way Out West in Jersey; Why Do We Love Them? [1]

Cast: Frank Curran; Edith Day; Hal Skelly; Queenie Smith; Jack Whiting

Notes: [1] Out Boston 12/18/22. [2] ASCAP/Library of Congress only.

3313 • ORCHID, THE

OPENED: 04/08/1907   Theatre: Herald Square
Musical   Broadway: 178

Composer: Lionel Monckton
Lyricist: Adrian Ross
Librettist: Joseph W. Herbert; James T. Tanner
Producer: Lee Shubert; Sam S. Shubert
Director: Frank Smithson

Choreographer: William Rock

Songs: A-Lack-A-Day [3] (L: Percy Greenbank); Advertisements [3]; And They Say He Went to College (C: Seymour Furth; L: Edward P.

Moran); Bedelia [5] (C: Jean Schwartz; L: George Grossmith Jr.; William Jerome); Carnival Is Nearly Ended [3]; Come Along with Me; Come Around on Our Veranda (C/L: Jerome Kern; Paul West); Dance of the Orchid (C: Hugo Frey); Debutantes, The [3]; Emperor of Sahara, The [3] (C: Ivan Caryll); Fancies [3] (L: Percy Greenbank); Fancy Dress; Finale Act I (C: Ivan Caryll); From Far Peru (C: Ivan Caryll); He Goes to Church on Sunday (C: E. Ray Goetz; L: Vincent Bryan); Horticultural College, The (C: Ivan Caryll); I Do All the Dirty Work [3] (L: Percy Greenbank); I Do, I Do, I Do! (C/L: Dave Reed Jr.); I Don't Want the Dark (L: Percy Greenbank; Leslie Mayne); I Must Propose to You (C/L: Paul Rubens); I'm Well Known [4] (C/L: Jerome Kern); La Promenade Anglais; Ladies in Society; Lady Secretary, The; Little Blanche Marie; Little Chimney Sweep; Little Mary [2] (L: Leslie Mayne); Liza Ann (A Yorkshire Idyll) [3] (L: Leslie Mayne); Mulberry Street (C/L: Junie McCree); No Wedding Bells for Me [2] (C: Seymour Furth; L: Will Heelan; Edward P. Moran); Off to the Ball [3] (C: Ivan Caryll); Oh, Mr. Registrar! (L: Percy Greenbank); Our Marriage Lines [3] (C: Ivan Caryll); Pas de Trois (inst.) [3]; Perfect Lady, A (C: Hugo Frey; L: Harold Atteridge); Prizes [3]; Pushful [3]; Recipe, The [1] (C/L: Jerome Kern; Paul West); Rose-a-Rubie [3] (C/L: Bernard Rolt); Unemployed, The [3] (C: Ivan Caryll; L: George Grossmith Jr.); Up and Down, Over the Town (Opening Chorus Act II) (L: Percy Greenbank); Waltzing [3] (C: Ivan Caryll); We Are Going to the Ball All in White [3]

Cast: Melville Ellis; Eddie Foy Sr.; Irene Franklin; Trixie Friganza; Maude Fulton; Joseph W. Herbert; William Rock; Amelia Stone; Grace Studdiford

Notes: Pianologue numbers by Jerome Kern. [1] Originally in THE RICH MR. HOGGENHEIMER. [2] Also in MRS. WILSON ANDREWS. [3] In London version only. [4] Sheet music only. [5] In London version only. Lyric revised by Grossmith.

3314 • ORCHIDS PREFERRED

OPENED: 05/11/1937   Theatre: Imperial
Musical   Broadway: 7

Composer: Dave Stamper
Lyricist: Fred Herendeen

Librettist: Fred Herendeen
Producer: Charles H. Abramson
Director: Alexander Leftwich

Choreographer: Robert Sanford; **Costumes:** Jenkins; **Musical Director:** Louis Gress; **Orchestrations:** Paul Sprosty; **Set Design:** Frederick Fox

Songs: Boy, Girl, Moon; Dying Swan, The; Echo of a Song, The; Eddy-Mac; I'm Leaving the Bad Girls for Good; Man About Town; Million Dollars, A; Minsky; My Lady's Hand; Paying Off; Selling a Song; Strictly Confidential; Sub-Debs' First Fling; Three Little Pigs [1]; Three R's, The (C/L: Morry Olsen; Henry Russell); What Are You Going to Do About Love?

Cast: Leslie Austin; Vicki Cummings; John Donaldson; Eddie Foy Jr.; Hilda Knight; Cela Krebs; Frances Thress; Benay Venuta; Jack Whitredge

Notes: [1] Sheet music only.

3315 • ORGANIZER, THE

OPENED: 1940   Theatre: Carnegie Hall
Musical   New York: 1

Composer: James P. Johnson
Lyricist: Langston Hughes
Librettist: Langston Hughes
Producer: Labor Stage; Ladies Garment Workers Union

Songs: Hungry Blues

Notes: Songs lost. No program available of this "Blues Opera."

3316 • ORIGINAL COHEN, THE

OPENED: 12/16/1907
Musical

Librettist: J. Edwin Owen
Producer: Rowland & Clifford Amusement Company

Cast: Gus Arthur

Notes: No program available. A New York suburban show.

3317 • ORIGINALITIES

Songs: Little Home for Two (Somewhere that Little Home Is Waiting) (C/L: B.C. Hilliam)

Cast: James Kilpatrick

Notes: No other information available. Information from sheet music.

3318 • ORPHAN'S REVENGE, THE
OPENED: 02/20/1982
Musical   Closed out of town

Composer: Suzanne Buhrer; Gene Casey
Lyricist: Suzanne Buhrer; Gene Casey
Librettist: Suzanne Buhrer; Gene Casey
Producer: Catalina Prod. Group Ltd.; Ford's Theatre Society
Director: Allen Hunt

Choreographer: Jay Smith; **Costumes:** Madeline Ann Graneto; **Lighting Designer:** Neil Peter Jampolis; **Musical Director:** Michael Howe; **Orchestrations:** Gene Casey; **Set Design:** A. Clark Duncan

Songs: 8:14 to Nooma City, The; Good Times; Happiest Day of Your Life; If I Became His Bride; It's Nice to Be Nasty; Look for the Sunshine; Nightingale's Song, The; Nothing As Sweet As a Sweetheart; Painted, Tainted Doll; Poor Me, Oh My; Repent! Repent!; Resist; Time for You; Vengeance of Valdez; With Alice

Cast: Suzanne Buhrer; J. Dan Curry; Gay Hagen; Lon Huber; Jeremy Mayer; Lindy Nisbet; Deborah Nishimura; Roxann Parker; James Reeder; Peter Shawn

Notes: Asst. Stage Manager: Lu Anne Origer.

3319 • OUI MADAME
OPENED: 03/22/1920
Musical   Closed out of town

Composer: Victor Herbert
Lyricist: Robert B. Smith
Librettist: G.M. Wright [3]
Producer: Alex A. Aarons; Alfred E. Aarons
Director: Herbert Gresham

Choreographer: Julian Alfred; **Musical Director:** Max Steiner

Songs: At Last; Every Hour Away from You Is Sixty Minutes Lost; Girl Who Can Love, A; Girl Who Keeps You Waiting, The; He Wanted to Go and He Went; If I Saw Much of You; If That's Not Love What Do You Call It?; I'll Be There [1]; My Day Has Come (L: Irving Caesar); Night Time, The [4]; (Oui) Oui Madame; Over the Garden Wall; Play Me Something I Can Dance To; Such a Happy Family; Table D'Hote Cabaret, The; When I Find My Romeo [1]; When You and I Were Tadpoles; When You Know Me Better; Where Were You?; Wooing of the Violin, The

Cast: Glenn Anders; Vinton Freedley; Harry Kelly; Dorothy Maynard; Georgia O'Ramey

Notes: Titled SOME COLONEL out of town Stamford 10/1/20 after tryout as OUI MADAME. G.M. Wright is Mrs. Robert B. Smith. [1] Out Stamford 10/1/20. [2] Also cut from THE GIRL IN THE SPOTLIGHT. [3] Mrs. Robert B. Smith. [4] Out Stamford 10/1/20. Also cut from THE GIRL IN THE SPOTLIGHT.

3320 • OUR HEARTS WERE YOUNG AND GAY
Musical   Unproduced

Composer: Arthur Siegel
Lyricist: June Carroll

Source: OUR HEARTS WERE YOUNG AND GAY (Novel: Emily Kimborough)

Songs: Anticipation Is Much More Fun, The; Before You Love [1]; Cornelia-Emily Letters (Opening); Gertrude Stein's Song; Ladies of My Day, The; On Our Own; Our Hearts Were Young and Gay; Silver Screen, The; There'll Be 29 for Dinner; This Is Right Where It Happened; Throw Your Cares Overboard; What Is the Matter with Me?; Yesterday Is Today Is Tomorrow; You'll Always Remember the First Time

Notes: [1] Also in score of unproduced show SERENA.

3321 • OUR LAN'
OPENED: 04/18/1947   Theatre: Henry Street
Play   Broadway: 53

Author: Theodore Ward
Producer: Eddie Dowling; Louis J. Singer
Director: Eddie Dowling

Choreographer: Joshua Lee; **Lighting Designer:** Ralph Alswang; **Set Design:** Ralph Alswang

Songs: Cotton Song (C: Joshua Lee; L: Theodore Ward); Hoe, Boy, Hoe (C: Joshua Lee; L: Theodore Ward)

Cast: Valerie Black; Julie Haydon; Theresa Merritt; Muriel Smith; William Veasey

Notes: Opened Off-Broadway then moved on 9/17 to the Royale Theatre where it played 41 performances.

3322 • OUR MISS GIBBS

OPENED: 08/29/1910   Theatre: Knickerbocker
Musical   Broadway: 64

Composer: Ivan Caryll; Lionel Monckton
Lyricist: Percy Greenbank
Librettist: James T. Tanner
Producer: Charles Frohman
Director: Thomas Reynolds

Source: OUR MISS GIBBS (Musical: Ivan Caryll; George Edwardes [3]; Lionel Monckton; James T. Tanner); **Musical Director:** W.T. Francis

Songs: Baby Nurse [2] (C: Lionel Monckton; L: Percy Greenbank); Bedtime at the Zoo (C: Lionel Monckton; L: Percy Greenbank; Leslie Mayne); Bertie the Bounder (C: Clarke; L: George Grossmith); Betty's Advice (C: Jerome Kern; L: Frederick Day); Bridesmaids' Sextette (Chorus of Bridesmaids) (C: Lionel Monckton; L: Percy Greenbank); Come Tiny Goldfish to Me (C: Harry Marlowe; L: Jerome Kern); Correct (C: Lionel Monckton; L: Adrian Ross); Country Cousins [1] (C: Lionel Monckton; L: Adrian Ross); Dougal (C/L: Unknown); Eight Little Girls (C: Jerome Kern; L: M.E. Rourke); English Gentleman, An (C: Lionel Monckton; L: Percy Greenbank); Hats (C: Ivan Caryll; L: Percy Greenbank; Adrian Ross); Hughie [2] (C: Ivan Caryll; L: Adrian Ross); I Don't Want You to Be a Sister to Me (C: Jerome Kern; L: Frederick Day); I Love MacIntosh (C: Harold Lonsdale; L: George Arthur); In Yorkshire [1] (C/L: Lionel Monckton; L: Ralph Roberts); Little Change, A (C/L: Unknown); March of the Foreign Commissioners (C: Unknown); Mary (C: Lionel Monckton; L: Adrian Ross); Moon-Fairies (C: Ivan Caryll; L: Adrian Ross); Moonstruck

(C/L: Lionel Monckton); My Yorkshire Lassie [2] (C: Ivan Caryll; L: Percy Greenbank); Not That Sort of Person (C: Lionel Monckton; L: George Grossmith); Opening Chorus and Entrance of Irish Girls (C: Lionel Monckton; L: Percy Greenbank); Our Farm (C/L: Lionel Monckton); Romance (C: Ivan Caryll; L: Adrian Ross); We Will Be Quick and Do Our Shopping (Opening Chorus) (C: Ivan Caryll; L: Adrian Ross); White City, The [2] (C: Ivan Caryll; L: Percy Greenbank); Will You Sing This Glee with Me? (C: George Arthurs; L: Worton David); Yip-I-Addy-I-Ay [2] (C: John Flynn; L: Will D. Cobb; George Grossmith); Yorkshire (C: Lionel Monckton; L: Ralph Roberts); You Come and Stay with Me (C: Ivan Caryll; L: Adrian Ross)

Cast: Jean Aylwin; Pauline Chase; Ernest Lambert; Bert Leslie; Gertrude Vanderbilt

Notes: [1] In London version only. [2] Not in programs. [3] Used psudonym Cryptos.

3323 • OUR NELL

OPENED: 12/04/1922   Theatre: Nora Bayes
Musical   Broadway: 40

Composer: William Daly; George Gershwin
Lyricist: Brian Hooker
Librettist: Brian Hooker; A.E. Thomas
Producer: Hayseed Productions [1]
Director: W.H. Gilmore; Edgar MacGregor

Choreographer: Julian Mitchell; **Musical Director:** Charles Stieger

Songs: By and By (C: George Gershwin); Cooney Country Fair, The (C: George Gershwin); Custody of the Child, The [3] (C: George Gershwin); Gol-Durn!; Innocent Ingenue Baby (L: Clifford Grey; Brian Hooker); Little Villages; Madrigal (C: George Gershwin); Names I Love to Hear; Oh, You Lady!; Old New England Home [2]; Walking Home with Angeline (C: George Gershwin); We Go to Church on Sunday (C: George Gershwin)

Cast: Jimmie Barry; Mrs. Jimmy Barry; Eva Clark; Thomas Conkey; Emma Haig; Olin Howland; Frank Mayne; John Merkyl

Notes: Originally titled THE HAYSEED. [1] Ed Davidow and Rufus LeMaire. [2] Sheet music only. [3] Not used.

3324 • OUR TOWN
OPENED: 09/19/1955   Theatre: NBC
TV Musical

Composer: James Van Heusen
Lyricist: Sammy Cahn
Librettist: David Shaw
Producer: Fred Coe
Director: Delbert Mann

Source: OUR TOWN (Play: Thornton Wilder);
   Musical Director: Nelson Riddle

Songs: Grovers Corner; Impatient Years, The;
   Impatient Years, The; Look to Your Heart; Love
   and Marriage; Our Town; Perfect Married Life,
   A; Wasn't It a Wonderful Wedding

Cast: Sylvia Field; Paul Hartman; Paul Newman;
   Nelson Riddle; Eva Marie Saint; Frank Sinatra;
   Ernest Truex

Notes: Original television musical.

3325 • OUT O' LUCK
OPENED: 1925
Revue

Composer: Cole Porter
Lyricist: Cole Porter
Librettist: Tom Cushing
Producer: Yale Univ. Dramatic Assn.
Director: Monty Woolley

Songs: Butterflies; Madamazelle; Opera Star

Cast: John Hoysradt; Henry C. Potter; Theodore S.
   Ryan; Roger V. Stearns; Edward R. Wardewell

Notes: Amateur show. Also produced in 1926.

3326 • OUT OF THIS WORLD
OPENED: 12/21/1950   Theatre: New Century
Musical   Broadway: 157

Composer: Cole Porter
Lyricist: Cole Porter
Librettist: Reginald Lawrence; Dwight Taylor
Producer: Lemuel Ayers; Saint-Subber
Director: Agnes de Mille

Choreographer: Hanya Holm; **Costumes:** Lemuel
   Ayers; **Musical Director:** Pembroke Davenport;

Orchestrations: Robert Russell Bennett; **Set
Design:** Lemuel Ayers

Songs: Away from It All [3]; Cherry Pies Ought to
   Be You; Climb Up the Mountain; From This
   Moment On [2]; Hail, Hail, Hail; Hark to the Song
   of the Night; Hush, Hush, Hush [3]; I Am Loved;
   I Got Beauty; I Jupiter, I Rex; I Sleep Easier Now;
   Maiden Fair; Midsummer Night [3]; No Lover [4];
   Nobody's Chasing Me; Oh, It Must Be Fun [3];
   Prologue; They Couldn't Compare to You; To Hell
   with Everyone but Us [3]; Tonight I Love You
   More [3]; Use Your Imagination; We're on the
   Road to Athens [3]; What Do You Think About
   Men?; Where, Oh Where?; Why Do You Want to
   Hurt Me So? [3]; You Don't Remind Me [3]

Cast: Barbara Ashley; David Burns; Janet Collins;
   William Eythe; Priscilla Gillette; Charlotte
   Greenwood; Ray Harrison; George Jongeyans[1];
   William Redfield

Notes: Comden and Green wrote a new book for
   this show when it was in trouble out of town.
   Although they retained the Porter songs they
   discarded the Amphytrion story substituting a
   plot with a baseball background! That script was
   rejected since the producers were only interested
   in a book with Greek gods. [1] Later known as
   George Gaynes. [2] Cut. In film KISS ME KATE.
   [3] Not used. [4] Release music same as "We Shall
   Never Be Younger" cut from KISS ME KATE.

3327 • OUT ON BROADWAY
OPENED: 1913
Musical

Composer: Gus Edwards
Lyricist: Jean Havez
Producer: Gus Edwards

Songs: If You'll Let Me Be Your Husband, I'll Let
   You Be My Wife; Little Miss Killarney; Miss Bell
   of the Telephone; My Idea of a Girl; When the
   Whole World Has Gone Back on You (L: Edward
   Madden)

Cast: William J. Ward

Notes: No other information available.

3328 • OUT THERE
OPENED: 03/27/1917   Theatre: Globe
Play   Broadway: 80

Producer: Klaw & Erlanger; George C. Tyler
Director: J. Hartley Manners

Songs: I Want to Go Home (C/L: Gitz Rice)

Cast: Frank Kemble Cooper; Lynn Fontanne; Laurette Taylor

3329 • OUT TO LUNCH
OPENED: 07/07/1978   Theatre: New Playwrights'
Musical   Washington

Composer: Tim Grundmann
Lyricist: Tim Grundmann
Librettist: Tim Grundmann
Producer: Harry M. Bagdasian; Ken Bloom; New Playwrights' Theatre

Choreographer: Anne Reynolds Day; **Costumes:** Richard Dwight McGee; **Dance Arranger:** Tim Grundmann; **Lighting Designer:** Tomm Tomlinson; **Musical Director:** Tim Grundmann; **Orchestrations:** Tim Grundmann; **Set Design:** Kit Grover; **Vocal Arranger:** Tim Grundmann

Songs: Back in Circulation; I Found Youse; It's Nice to Know; Life of a Buckaroo; Out to Lunch; Pixie's Holiday; Poor Grandma; Squash the Blues Away; Wonderful World

Cast: John Healey Jr.; A. David Johnson; Stuart Lerch; John A. Morse; Barbara Rappaport; Tanis Roach; Jan Frederick Shiffman; Dana Vance

Notes: New Playwrights' Theatre, Washington, D.C.

3330 • OVER HERE!
OPENED: 03/06/1974   Theatre: Shubert
Musical   Broadway: 341

Composer: Richard M. Sherman; Robert B. Sherman
Lyricist: Richard M. Sherman; Robert B. Sherman
Librettist: Will Holt
Producer: Maxine Fox; Kenneth Waissman
Director: Tom Moore

Choreographer: Patricia Birch; **Costumes:** Carrie F. Robbins; **Dance Arranger:** Louis St. Louis; **Lighting Designer:** John Gleason; **Musical Director:** Joseph Klein; **Orchestrations:** Michael Gibson; Jim Tyler; **Set Design:** Douglas W. Schmidt; **Vocal Arranger:** Louis St. Louis

Songs: Beat Begins, The (Overture); Big Beat, The [1]; Buy a Victory Bond; Charlie's Place; Don't Shoot the Hooey to Me, Louie; Dream Drumming; Good-Time Girl, The (V.D. Polka); Grass Grows Green (in No Man's Land), The; Hey Yvette!; My Dream for Tomorrow; No Goodbyes; Over Here! [1]; Since You're Not Around; Soft Music; Wait for Me Marlene; Wartime Wedding; We Got It [1]; Where Did the Good Times Go?

Cast: Maxene Andrews; Patty Andrews; MacIntyre Dixon; John Driver; Marilu Henner; John Mineo; Ann Reinking; Janie Sell; April Shawhan; John Travolta; Douglass Watson; Treat Williams; Samuel E. Wright

Notes: [1] Had creative contribution by Walter Wechsler.

3331 • OVER TEXAS
Notes: *See FIRST LADY SUITE.*

3332 • OVER THE RIVER
OPENED: 01/08/1912   Theatre: Globe
Musical   Broadway: 120

Composer: John Golden
Lyricist: John Golden
Librettist: George V. Hobart; H.A. du Souchet
Producer: Charles Dillingham; Florenz Ziegfeld

Musical Director: DeWitt Coolman

Songs: Bees Ain't to Blame [1]; Broadway Cabaret, The (C: Charles N. Grant; L: E.J. Griffin); Chop Stick Rag, The (C: Jean Schwartz; L: Edward Clark); Coontown Quartet; Day We Celebrate Edna May, The; For de Lawd's Sake, Play a Waltz (C/L: Elsie Janis); I Ain't to Blame for Lovin' You [3] (C: John Golden; Silvio Hein); I Want Him Saved; Injun Love [2] (C: Egbert Van Alstyne; L: Harry Williams); Lock-Step, Two-Step Slide; Mexico; Montezuma [4] (C: Charles Eggett; L: Earl Carroll); My Irish Senorita; New York Isn't Such a Bad Old Town (C: Jean Schwartz; L: William Jerome); Our Hero; Prisoners' Patrol [1]; Raggety Man, The (C: Egbert Van Alstyne; L: Harry Williams); Ring-A-Ting-A-Ling on the Telephone (C: Jean Schwartz; L: William Jerome); River of Faces, The [1]; Save the Men [1]; When There's No Light at All

Cast: Mae Busch; Eddie Foy Sr.; Lillian Lorraine; Peggy Wood

Notes: One of the Mexican songs was written by Earl Carroll. [1] Out Philadelphia 12/11/11. [2] ASCAP/Library of Congress only. [3] Sheet music only. [4] "As successfully introduced by Jeanette Methvin of the Methvin Sisters Singing the Highest Not Ever Reached by the Human Voice."

3333 • OVER THE TOP
OPENED: 11/28/1917   Theatre: 44th Street
Revue   Broadway: 78

Composer: Sigmund Romberg; Herman Timberg
Lyricist: Harold Atteridge; Philip Bartholomae
Librettist: Philip Bartholomae
Producer: J.J. Shubert; Lee Shubert
Director: J.C. Huffman

Costumes: Homer Conant; **Musical Director:** Louis Silvers

Songs: Algerian Girl; Frocks and Frills; Galatea! (L: Philip Bartholomae); Girl for Me, The; Golden Pheasant, The (L: Matthew C. Woodward); Greenwich Village Belle; Justine Johnstone Rag, The (C: Frank Carter; Sigmund Romberg; Herman Timberg; L: Charles Manning); My Rainbow Girl; Posterland; That Airship of Mine; Where Is the Language to Tell?

Cast: Adele Astaire; Fred Astaire; T. Roy Barnes; Mary Eaton; Justine Johnstone; Joe Laurie; Ted Lorraine; Vivian Oakland

Notes: Titled OH, JUSTINE! on tour after Broadway.

3334 • OVERSEAS REVUE
Notes: *See TOOT SWEET.*

3335 • OVERTONS, THE
OPENED: 02/06/1945   Theatre: Booth
Play   Broadway: 175

Author: Vincent Lawrence
Producer: Paul Czinner
Director: Elisabeth Bergner

Costumes: Hattie Carnegie; **Set Design:** Edward Gilbert

Songs: Two Hearts in Danger (C: Jerome Gottler; L: Archie Gottler)

Cast: Judith Evelyn; Walter N. Greaza; June Knight; Jack Whiting

3336 • OY IS DAS A LEBEN!
OPENED: 10/12/1942   Theatre: Molly Picon
Musical   Off-Broadway: 139

Composer: Molly Picon
Librettist: Jacob Kalich
Producer: Edwin A. Relkin
Director: Jacob Kalich

Choreographer: David Lubritzky; **Set Design:** Harry Gordon Bennett

Cast: Boris Auerbach; Izidor Casher; Jennie Casher; Jacob Kalich; Molly Picon

Notes: No songs listed in program.

3337 • OYSTERMAN, THE
OPENED: 1908
Musical   Closed out of town

Composer: Ernest Hogan; Will H. Vodery
Lyricist: Henry Creamer
Librettist: Aubrey L. Lyles; Flournoy E. Miller
Producer: Hurtig & Seamon
Director: Ernest Hogan

Costumes: Will R. Barnes; **Musical Director:** Will H. Vodery

Songs: All Hail the King; Contribution Box; Dogalo; Enough; Fish Chorus; I Just Can't Keep My Eyes Off You; Meet Me at the Barber Shop; Mermaids' Chorus [1]; Mina; No You Didn't, Yes I Did [1]; Oysterman, The; Roll On, Mighty Wave; Suannee River [1]; To Blazassus; To-morrow; When Buffalo Bill and His Wild West Show First Came to Baltimore; White Wash; Yankee Doodle Coon

Cast: Charles Foster; Ernest Hogan; Harry Reed

Notes: Information from New York Dramatic Mirror and program. Played Subway Circuit in New York. May have begun in 1907. [1] Not in program.

P

3338 • P.S. I LOVE YOU

OPENED: 11/19/1964   Theatre: Henry Miller's
Play   Broadway: 12

Author: Lawrence Roman
Producer: Helen Bonfils; Morton Gottlieb
Director: Henry Kaplan

Source: L'AMOUR QUI NE FINIT PAS (Play:
Andre Roussin); **Costumes:** Theoni V. Aldredge;
Raoul Pene du Bois; **Lighting Designer:** Jules
Fisher; **Set Design:** Raoul Pene du Bois

Songs: Days of the Waltz [1] (C/L: Jacques Brel;
L: Will Holt)

Cast: Lynn Carlysle; Warren Lyons; Geraldine
Page; Gilles Pelletier

Notes: [1] Same music as "Carousel" from
JACQUES BREL IS ALIVE AND WELL AND
LIVING IN PARIS.

3339 • PACIFIC 1860

OPENED: 12/19/1946   Theatre: Theatre Royal,
                                        Drury Lane
Musical   London: 129

Composer: Noel Coward
Lyricist: Noel Coward
Librettist: Noel Coward
Director: Noel Coward

Costumes: Gladys E. Calthrop; **Musical Director:**
Mantovani; **Set Design:** Gladys E. Calthrop

Songs: Birthday Toast; Bright Was the Day; Come
Back to the Island; Dear Madame Salvador
(Letter Song); Family Grace; Fumfumbolo;
Gipsy Melody; His Excellency Regrets; I Never
Knew; I Saw No Shadow; I Wish I Wasn't Quite
Such a Big Girl; If I Were a Man; Invitation to
the Waltz; Make Way for Their Excellencies;
Mother's Lament; My Horse Has Cast a Shoe;
One Two Three; Party's Going with a Swing;
Pretty Little Bridesmaids; Samoan Song (Ka
Tahua); This Is a Changing World; This Is a

Night for Lovers; This Is the Night; Uncle Harry;
Wedding Toast

Cast: Sylvia Cecil; Peter Evans; Tudor Evans; Betty
Hare; Denis Martin; Mary Martin; Moya Nugent;
Graham Payn

3340 • PACIFIC OVERTURES

OPENED: 01/11/1976   Theatre: Winter Garden
Musical   Broadway: 193

Composer: Stephen Sondheim
Lyricist: Stephen Sondheim
Librettist: John Weidman
Producer: Harold Prince
Director: Harold Prince

Choreographer: Patricia Birch; **Costumes:** Florence
Klotz; **Dance Arranger:** Daniel Troob; **Lighting
Designer:** Tharon Musser; **Musical Director:**
Paul Gemignani; **Orchestrations:** Jonathan
Tunick; **Set Design:** Boris Aronson

Songs: Advantages of Floating in the Middle of
the Sea, The; Bowler Hat, A; Chrysanthemum
Tea (1) [1]; Chrysanthemum Tea (2); Four Black
Dragons [3]; Lion Dance; Next; Please Hello;
Poems; Prayers [2]; Pretty Lady; Someone in a
Tree; There Is No Other Way; We Float [1];
Welcome to Kanagawa

Cast: James Dybas; Timm Fujii; Alvin Ing; Patrick
Kinser-Lau; Mako; Freddy Mao; Soon-Teck Oh;
Isao Sato; Yuki Shimoda; Sab Shimono; Mark
Hsu Syers; Conrad Yama

Notes: [1] Cut prior to opening. [2] Cut prior to
opening. Sections used in "Chrysanthemum Tea
(2)." [3] Working title is "Alarms."

3341 • PACK UP YOUR TROUBLES

OPENED: 1918
Play   Closed out of town

Composer: Arthur Guy Empery
Lyricist: Arthur Guy Empery
Author: George C. Hazelton

Songs: Liberty Statue; We Are Looking at You; Your Lips Are No-Man's-Land but Mine

Cast: Arthur Guy Empery; Rose Stahl

Notes: Program of Washington, D.C. 6/17/18.

3342 • PADLOCKS OF 1927
OPENED: 07/05/1927   Theatre: Shubert
Revue   Broadway: 95

Composer: Lee David; Jesse Greer; Henry Tobias
Lyricist: Ballard Macdonald; Billy Rose
Librettist: Ballard Macdonald; Paul Gerard Smith
Producer: C. William Morganstern; Anton F. Scibila
Director: William J. Wilson

Choreographer: John Boyle; **Costumes:** Orry Kelly; Mahieu; Robert Stevenson; **Musical Director:** Carlton Kelsey; **Orchestrations:** Joseph Nussbaum

Songs: College Days [1] (C: Unknown); Here I Am (C: Unknown); Hoppin' the Buck (C: Unknown); Hot Heels (C: Lee David; L: Ballard Macdonald; Billy Rose); I Haven't Got You [2] (C: Unknown); If I Had a Lover (C: Henry Tobias; L: Ballard Macdonald; Billy Rose); It's Tough to Be a Hostess (C: Unknown); Let's Make Whoopie (C: Unknown); Opened Up Again (C: Unknown); Rhinestones (C: Unknown); Say It with a Red Red Rose [2] (C: Jesse Greer; L: Billy Rose); String Along with Texas (C: Unknown); Summertime (C: Unknown); Tap, Tap, The (C: Jesse Greer; L: Ballard Macdonald; Billy Rose); Texas (C: Unknown); That Stupid Melody (C: Unknown); Tom-Tom (C: Unknown); Vo-De-O-Do-Do [2] (C: Unknown)

Cast: Jay C. Flippen; Texas Guinan; Frances Healy; George Raft; Lillian Roth; Helen Shipman

Notes: [1] Added after opening. [2] Cut Newark 5/3/27.

3343 • PADLOCKS OF 1929
OPENED: 1929
Revue

Composer: George David Weiss
Lyricist: Mack Gordon

Songs: For You Baby; Wake Up Your Feet; When I Dream

Notes: No other information available.

3344 • PAGE MISS VENUS
Musical   Closed out of town

Composer: Leon De Costa
Lyricist: Leon De Costa
Librettist: Lewis Allen Browne; Adelaide French
Producer: Leon De Costa
Director: Earl Lindsay

Choreographer: Earl Lindsay

Songs: Anytime; Fees and Dues; Fireside Dreams; Little Coronas, The; Lost Paradise, The; Love Makes the World Go 'Round; Page Miss Venus; Polka Dot; Tell Us the Story of Love; Won't You Be My Little Kewpie

Cast: Roland Bottomley; Marie Flynn; Janet Velie

3345 • PAGE MR. CUPID
OPENED: 05/17/1920
Musical   Closed out of town

Composer: Jean Schwartz
Lyricist: Blanche Merrill
Librettist: Owen Davis
Producer: Messrs. Shubert

Songs: I Can't Do This and I Can't Do That; Little Wigwam for Two, A; Love Is an Old-Fashioned Feeling; My Little Dancing Heart; Page Mr. Cupid; Purpose in Life; There Is Life in the Old Boy Yet; Why Didn't I Meet You Long Ago

Cast: Marjorie Gateson; Robert Pitkin; Charles Vernon

Notes: Crescent Theatre, Brooklyn.

3346 • PAGEANT
OPENED: 05/02/1991   Theatre: Blue Angel
Musical   Off-Broadway: 462

Composer: Albert Evans
Lyricist: Frank Kelly; Bill Russell
Librettist: Frank Kelly; Bill Russell

Producer: Jonathan Scharer
Director: Robert Longbottom

Arrangements: James Raitt; **Choreographer:** Robert Longbottom; Tony Parise; **Costumes:** Gregg Barnes; **Lighting Designer:** Timothy Hunter; **Musical Director:** James Raitt; **Orchestrations:** James Raitt; **Set Design:** Daniel Ettinger

Songs: Girl Power; Good Bye; It's Gotta Be Venus; Miss Glamouresse; Natural Born Females; Something Extra

Cast: Randl Ash; J.T. Cromwell; David Drake; Russell Garrett; Joe Joyce; John Salvatore; Dick Scanlan

3347 • PAINT YOUR WAGON

OPENED: 11/12/1951   Theatre: Shubert
Musical   Broadway: 289

Composer: Frederick Loewe
Lyricist: Alan Jay Lerner
Librettist: Alan Jay Lerner
Producer: Cheryl Crawford
Director: Daniel Mann

Choreographer: Agnes de Mille; **Costumes:** Motley; **Lighting Designer:** Peggy Clark; **Musical Director:** Franz Allers; **Orchestrations:** Ted Royal; **Set Design:** Oliver Smith; **Vocal Arranger:** Trude Rittman

Songs: All for Him; Another Autumn; Carino Mio; Hand Me Down That Can o' Beans; How Can I Wait?; I Still See Eliza; I Talk to the Trees; I'm on My Way; In Between; Lonely Men (inst.); Movin'; Rope Dance (inst.); Rumson; Sh! [1]; Strike!; Take the Wheels Off the Wagon [2]; There's a Coach Comin' In; They Call the Wind Maria; Trio; Wand'rin Star; What's Goin' On Here?; Whoop-Ti-Ay

Cast: James Barton; Tony Bavaar; Robert Penn; Olga San Juan; Rufus Smith; Dave Thomas

Notes: [1] Cut. [2] Added out of town 10/24/52.

3348 • PAINTING THE TOWN

OPENED: 01/02/1907
Musical   Closed out of town

Composer: Herman Perlet
Lyricist: Herman Perlet
Librettist: W.F. Carrol
Producer: Chas. H. Yale

Choreographer: Aurelio Coccia

Songs: All Aboard; At the Seaside [1]; Bohemia Is the Life for Me; Dainty Little Maid, The [1]; Dressing Room Echoes; Drink Up; Emigrants, The; Fatima the Fair [1]; Fifteen Minutes; Grand Operatic Finale Act II; Great Ram-Jam, The [1]; He's a Jolly Good Fellow; Hoolah Goolah Stone; List to the Pleading; Night Bird Is Calling, The; One Night Stands, The; Painting the Town; Ram Jam; Salaam Salaam [1]; Tail of a Kite, The [1]; Waiters, The [1]; Walking Family, The; When There Isn't a Girl About [1]

Cast: M.T. Bohannon; Will Halliday; Mazie King; John F. Leonard

Notes: Program of Cedar Rapids. [1] Out 11/27/07 Cedar Rapids.

3349 • PAIR O' FOOLS

OPENED: 01/25/1926
Musical   Closed out of town

Composer: Arthur Freed
Lyricist: Arthur Freed
Librettist: John Emerson; Anita Loos
Director: George Cunningham

Source: WHOLE TOWN'S TALKING, THE (Play: Grant Mitchell)

Songs: Hello, Hello, Sandy; Honky Tonk Toodle; In a Taxi Cab; Isn't It Strange; Tell Me That You Love Me

Cast: Charles Cunningham; Max M. Dill; Doris Duncan; C. William Kolb

3350 • PAIR OF PINKS, A

OPENED: 1905
Musical   Closed out of town

Composer: Fred Schwartz
Lyricist: Harry Vokes; Will West

Songs: Flirting with the Bus; For Our Country, Our U.S.A.; Good-Bye Sweet Marie; Hiram Green; It's

Best Not to Say too Much About It; Josephine; Just for a Day; La-da-diddle-de-dum; My Merry Oldsmobile [1]; My Mocking Bird; Oh, Gee, It's Great to Be Great; Two Little Girls Loved One Little Boy

Cast: Harry Vokes; Margaret Daly Vokes; Will West

Notes: Program of Wilkes-Barre, PA. 10/23/05. Some of these songs may be popular songs of the period. [1] "In My Merry Oldsmobile" by Vincent Bryan and Gus Edwards was written in 1905.

3351 • PAJAMA GAME, THE

OPENED: 05/13/1954   Theatre: St. James
Musical   Broadway: 1061

Composer: Richard Adler; Jerry Ross
Lyricist: Richard Adler; Jerry Ross
Librettist: George Abbott; Richard Bissell
Producer Frederick Brisson; Robert E. Griffith; Harold Prince
Director: George Abbott; Jerome Robbins

Source: 7 1/2 CENTS (Novel: Richard Bissell); **Choreographer:** Bob Fosse; **Costumes:** Lemuel Ayers; **Musical Director:** Hal Hastings; **Orchestrations:** Don Walker; **Set Design:** Lemuel Ayers

Songs: All You Need Is a Fife and Drum [3]; Her Is; Hernando's Hideaway; Hey There; I Never Dreamed [3]; If You Win, You Lose [4] (C/L: Richard Adler); I'll Never Be Jealous Again; I'm Not at All in Love; Liebchen, Liebchen [3]; New Town Is a Blue Town, A; Once a Year Day; Pajama Game, The; Racing with the Clock; 71/2 Cents; Sleep-Tite; Small Talk; Steam Heat; There Once Was a Man; Think of the Time I Save; Watch Your Heart [2] (C/L: Richard Adler); World Around Us, The [1]

Cast: Marion Colby; Ralph Dunn; Eddie Foy Jr.; Peter Gennaro; Carol Haney; Buzz Miller; Janis Paige; Thelma Pelish; Stanley Prager; John Raitt; Reta Shaw; Jack Waldron

Notes: [1] Cut after opening. [2] Added to 1973 revival. [3] Not used. [4] Added to 1986 Leicester, England production.

3352 • PAJAMA LADY, THE

OPENED: 10/06/1930
Musical   Closed out of town

Composer: Philip Charig; Richard Myers
Lyricist: Johnny Mercer; Robert B. Smith
Librettist: George Lederer; Harry B. Smith
Producer: George Lederer
Director: George Lederer

Choreographer: Albertina Rasch; **Musical Director:** Alex Sater; **Set Design:** Nicholas Yellenti

Songs: All at Sea; Down Through the Ages (L: Johnny Mercer); In the Interval Between Dusk and Dawn; Legend of the Sea; Let's Suppose (L: Robert B. Smith); My Better Half; No One Could Love You More Than I Do; One Two Three (L: Johnny Mercer); Study in Color; Three Guesses (L: Johnny Mercer); You Never Can Tell

Cast: Lester Allen; John Barker; Dick Keene; Barbara Newberry

Notes: The music was a collaboration, the lyrics were not. Program of Washington, D.C.

3353 • PAL JOEY

OPENED: 12/25/1940   Theatre: Ethel Barrymore
Musical   Broadway: 374

Composer: Richard Rodgers
Lyricist: Lorenz Hart
Librettist: George Abbott; John O'Hara
Producer: George Abbott
Director: George Abbott

Source: Pal Joey stories in the "New Yorker Magazine" (Story: John O'Hara); **Choreographer:** Robert Alton; **Costumes:** John Koenig; **Lighting Designer:** Jo Mielziner; **Musical Director:** Harry Levant; **Orchestrations:** Hans Spialek; **Set Design:** Jo Mielziner

Songs: Bewitched, Bothered and Bewildered; Chicago (A Great Big Town); Den of Iniquity; Do It the Hard Way; Flower Garden of My Heart, The; Happy Hunting Horn; I Could Write a Book; I'm Talking to My Pal [1]; Joey Looks into the Future Ballet (inst.); Love Is My Friend [2]; Pal Joey (What Do I Care for a Dame?); Plant You Now, Dig You Later; Take Him; That Terrific Rainbow; What Is a Man? [3]; You Mustn't Kick It Around; Zip

Cast: Jean Casto; Stanley Donen; Jack Durant; Leila Ernst; Jane Fraser; June Havoc; Van Johnson; Gene Kelly; Robert J. Mulligan; Vivienne Segal

Notes: Abbott wrote the libretto and got the scenes approved by O'Hara. [1] Cut before opening. [2] Changed after opening to "What Is a Man?" [3] Same music as "Love Is My Friend." This number may not have been used.

3354 • PALLADIUM FROLICS

OPENED: 1936   Theatre: London
                              Palladium
Revue   London

Composer: Harry Carroll
Lyricist: Mitchell Parish

Songs: Beat of the Feet in the Street, The; Love Is a Ripple on the Water; Put Down an Empty Blues (C: Lou Leaman); Wotch-Ma- Callit, The

Notes: No program available.

3355 • PALM BEACH

Musical   Unproduced

Composer: Charles Strouse
Lyricist: Charles Strouse

Source: THIEVES CARNIVAL (Play: Jean Anouilh)

Songs: All I Want Is Not to Want; Ashley; Fight Duet, The; I Don't Love You Anymore; I Don't Want to Grow Old; I Want to Sleep with You Now; I'm Here; Looking for Daddy; Love Can Get You Crazy; Palm Beach; She!; She's Gonna Love Me!; She's Not Made for You; Start of an Affair, The; Welcome to Washington; You're Working for Me Now

Notes: Written for Robert Morse. This list of songs may include some new songs since Strouse is currently working on the score again.

3356 • PAN-AMERICAN CASINO REVUE

OPENED: 1937
Revue   Nightclub

Composer: Sammy Fain
Lyricist: Irving Kahal
Producer: George Preston Marshall

Songs: Don't You Know or Don't You Care; El Gaucho; Pin a Bluebonnet on Your New Bonnet; Texatina

Notes: No other information available.

3357 • PAN HANDLE PETE

OPENED: 09/19/1907
Musical   Closed out of town

Composer: Samuel Lehman
Lyricist: David Kemper; Joseph Lasha
Librettist: Willard Holcomb
Producer: Abe Levy

Source: UNKNOWN (Comic Strip: George McManus); **Musical Director:** Oscar Goodfriend

Songs: California Belle; Columbia; Every Body Hands Me a Lemon; Finale Act I; Finale Act II; Finale Act III; German Specialty; Going on the War Path; I Got Another One; I'd Like to Call You Mine; I'm a Natural Born Hoodoo; Jennie Jones; Luna, Opening Chorus; Opening Chorus Act II; Pleasant Day; Two Hearts Beat as One; We're the Handy Dandy Cops

Cast: Charlotte Hart; Alma McGill; Will Philbrick; William Trainor; Frank Walsh

Notes: Program of Cedar Rapids.

3358 • PANAMA

OPENED: 1908
Musical   Chicago

Composer: James T. Brymn; H. Lawrence Freeman
Librettist: Marion A. Brooks; Charles A. Hunter
Producer: J. Ed Green
Director: J. Ed Green

Songs: Awful; Happy Sam Chow; I'd Like to Run Away with You; Julius Caesar Johnson; Put It Right in My Hand; Summertime, The; Things Ain't Just Right; What I Know I Knows

Cast: Abbie Mitchell; Harrison Stewart

Notes: No other information available.

3359 • PANAMA HATTIE

OPENED: 10/30/1940   Theatre: 46th Street
Musical   Broadway: 501

Composer: Cole Porter
Lyricist: Cole Porter
Librettist: B.G. DeSylva

Producer: B.G. DeSylva; Herbert Fields
Director: Edgar MacGregor

Choreographer: Robert Alton; **Costumes:** Raoul Pene du Bois; **Musical Director:** Gene Salzer; **Orchestrations:** Robert Russell Bennett; Hans Spialek; Don Walker; **Set Design:** Raoul Pene du Bois; **Vocal Arranger:** Lyn Murray

Songs: All I've Got to Get Now Is My Man; Americans All Drink Coffee [1]; Fresh As a Daisy; God Bless the Women; Here's to Panama Hattie [1]; I'm Throwing a Ball Tonight; I've Still Got My Health; Join It Right Away; Let's Be Buddies; Make It Another Old-Fashioned, Please; My Mother Would Love You; Stroll on the Plaza Sant'ana, A; They Ain't Done Right by Our Nell; Visit Panama; We Detest a Fiesta; Welcome to Jerry; Who Would Have Dreamed?; You Said It

Cast: Phyllis Brooks; Joan Carroll; Larry Docket[2]; James Dunn; Pat Harrington; Betty Hutton; Frank Hyers; Ethel Merman; Oscar "Rags" Ragland; Arthur Treacher

Notes: [1] Not used. [2] Larry Douglas.

3360 • PANJANDRUM
OPENED: 05/01/1893   Theatre: Broadway
Musical   Broadway

Composer: Woolson Morse
Librettist: J. Cheever Goodwin
Director: H.A. Cripps

Costumes: Alfred Thompson; **Musical Director:** J.S. Hiller; **Set Design:** Ernest M. Gros

Cast: Della Fox; DeWolf Hopper; Edmund Stanley

Notes: No songs listed in program.

3361 • PANSY
OPENED: 05/14/1929   Theatre: Belmont
Musical   Broadway: 3

Composer: Maceo Pinkard
Lyricist: Maceo Pinkard
Librettist: Alex Belledna
Producer: Maceo Pinkard
Director: Frank Rye

Choreographer: Nat Cash

Songs: Bouquet of Fond Memories, A; Breakin' th' Rhythm; Campus Walk; Gettin' Together; I'd Be Happy; If the Blues Don't Get You; It's Commencement Day; Pansy; Shake a Leg; Stranger Interlude, A

Cast: Al Fresco; Ralph Harris; Pearl McCormick; Bessie Smith; Elizabeth Taylor

3362 • PAPA'S DARLING
OPENED: 11/02/1914   Theatre: New Amsterdam
Musical   Broadway: 40

Composer: Ivan Caryll
Lyricist: Harry B. Smith
Librettist: Harry B. Smith
Producer: Klaw & Erlanger

Source: LE FILS SURNATURAL (Play: Maurice Vaucaire; Grenet d'Ancourt)

Songs: Dolores; Edelweiss; Land of the Midnight Sun, The; Oh, This Love!; Sparkling Moselle, The; Where Shall We Go for Our Honeymoon; Who Cares!

Cast: Alice Dovey; Dorothy Jardon; Frank Lalor; Fred Walton

Notes: Program does not list songs. Song titles from sheet music.

3363 • PAPA'S WIFE
OPENED: 11/13/1899   Theatre: Manhattan
Musical   Broadway

Composer: Reginald De Koven
Lyricist: Harry B. Smith
Librettist: Harry B. Smith

Source: UNKNOWN (Play: Paul Bilhaud; Maurice Hennequin)

Songs: Inconsistency

Cast: Henry Bergman; Charles A. Bigelow; Eva Davenport; Agnes Findlay; Anna Held; George Marion; Henry Woodruff

3364 • PAPER MOON
OPENED: 09/08/1993
Musical   Closed out of town

Composer: Larry Grossman
Lyricist: Ellen Fitzhugh
Librettist: Martin Casella
Director: Matt Casella

Source: ADDIE PREY (Novel: Joe David Brown); PAPER MOON (Film: Alvin Sargent); **Costumes:** Jeffrey Kurland; **Lighting Designer:** Pat Collins; **Musical Director:** Steve Marzullo; **Set Design:** Martin Anania; **Vocal Arranger:** Steve Marzullo

Songs: Alabama Family; Doin' Business; Entrepreneur (L: Carol Hall); Ev'rybody Says So; Girls Like Us; I Do What I Can (With What I Get); Miss Addie Loggins (L: Carol Hall); Parners; Place Where You Belong, A; Pretty Like Your Mama; Put Your Hand on the Radio; Someday, Baby; Startin' from Sweet; Take Her Where She's Goin' (L: Carol Hall); Turns Out (L: Carol Hall); Wido' Waltz, The

Cast: Gregory Harrison; Roxie Lucas; Keith Perry; Norrice Raymaker; Mary Stout

Notes: Paper Mill Playhouse, Milburn, NJ.

3365 • PARADE (1935)

OPENED: 05/20/1935   Theatre: Guild
Revue   Broadway: 40

Composer: Jerome Moross
Lyricist: Paul Peters; George Sklar
Librettist: Alan Baxter; Michael Blankfort; Turner Bullock; Kyle Crichton; Frank Gabrielson; Harold Johnsrud; David Lesan; Paul Peters; George Sklar
Producer: Theatre Guild, The
Director: Philip Loeb

Choreographer: Robert Alton; **Costumes:** Billy Livingston; Constance Ripley; Irene Sharaff; **Musical Director:** Max Meth; **Orchestrations:** Robert Russell Bennett; Jerome Moross; David Raksin; Conrad Salinger; **Set Design:** Lee Simonson

Songs: Bon Voyage (L: Kyle Crichton); Boys in Blue; Decadence (C: Will Irwin); Fear in My Heart; I'm an International Orphan; I'm Telling You, Louie; Join Our Ranks; Life Could Be So Beautiful; Marry the Family (L: Michael Blankfort); My Feet Are Firmly Planted on the Ground (L: Emanuel Eisenberg); On Parade; Selling Sex (L: Kyle Crichton); Send for the Militia (C/L: Marc Blitzstein); Smart Set (C: Will Irwin); You Ain't So Hot

Cast: Edgar Allen; Avis Andrews; Eve Arden; Charles D. Brown; Evelyn Dall; Dorothy Fox; Leon Janney; Esther Junger; David Lawrence; David Lesan; Vera Marsh; Melton Moore; Earl Oxford; Ralph Riggs; Jimmy Savo; Ezra Stone; Jean Travers; Charles Walters

3366 • PARADE (1960)

OPENED: 01/20/1960   Theatre: Players
Revue   Off-Broadway: 95

Composer: Jerry Herman
Lyricist: Jerry Herman
Producer: Lawrence Kasha
Director: Jerry Herman

Choreographer: Richard Tone; **Costumes:** Nilo; **Set Design:** Gary Smith

Songs: Another Candle; Antique Man, The; Audition, The; Bless This House (Save the Village); Confession to a Park Avenue Mother (I'm in Love with a West Side Girl) [4]; Get Off My Lawn [3]; Jolly Theatrical Season [4]; Just Plain Folks; Maria in Spats; Naughty Forty-Second Street; Next Time I Love, The; Nice Running Into You [2]; Paris, I'm Prepared; Peace [2]; Skip the Opening Number [2]; There Is No Tune Like a Show Tune [1]; Two a Day, The; Your Good Morning [4]; Your Hand in Mine

Cast: Dody Goodman; Lester James; Tia Karin; Charles Nelson Reilly; Richard Tone

Notes: [1] Rewritten as "It's Today" in MAME. Same song as "Show Tune in 2/4 Time" in NIGHTCAP. [2] Added to West Coast version. [3] Music later used as cut song "Call in the Cops" in MACK AND MABEL. [4] From NIGHTCAP.

3367 • PARADERS, THE

OPENED: 12/21/1902   Theatre: La Salle
Musical   Chicago

Composer: Joseph E. Howard
Lyricist: Raymond W. Peck
Librettist: Raymond W. Peck

Notes: No other information available.

3368 • PARADISE!

OPENED: 09/28/1985   Theatre: Playwrights
                                    Horizons
Musical   Off-Broadway: 14

Composer: Robert Forrest
Lyricist: George C. Wolfe
Librettist: George C. Wolfe
Producer: Playwrights Horizons
Director: Theodore Pappas

Choreographer: Theodore Pappas; **Costumes:**
David C. Woolard; **Lighting Designer:** Frances
Aronson; **Musical Director:** David Loud;
Orchestrations: John McKinney; **Set Design:**
James Noone

Songs: Atlanta; Dear Diary; Doom Is Due at Dawn;
Inside; Last Paradise, The; Mama Will Be
Waiting with the Dawn; On Mahaneyheya;
Rubber Plant Song, The; Something's Gonna
Happen Really Strange Tonight; Take Me Away;
This Could Be the End; This Is Not the End; This
Must Be the End; Uncle Dan Song, The; We're
Needed Here; Welcome to Paradise; With the
Dawn; You've Got to Let Go

Cast: Danielle Ferland; Tommy Hollis; Jerry
Lanning; Janice Lynde; Charlaine Woodard; Ben
Wright

3369 • PARADISE ALLEY

OPENED: 03/03/1924   Theatre: Casino
Musical   Broadway: 64

Composer: Harry Archer; Carle Carlton; A. Dorian
Otvos
Lyricist: Howard Johnson
Librettist: Charles W. Bell; Edward Clark
Producer: Carle Carlton
Director: Carle Carlton

Choreographer: Jack Mason; **Musical Director:**
Anton Heindl; **Set Design:** P. Dodd Ackerman

Songs: Alley Pantomime Dance [1]; Always Look
for a Rainbow [1] (C: Carle Carlton); Any Old
Alley Is Paradise Alley (C: Harry Archer; Carle
Carlton); As Long As They Keep On Making
Them (C: Howard E. Johnson); Bonnie [1]
(C: Harry Archer); Boxing Bout According to
F. Sharp, A [1]; Come Down to Argentine [1]
(C: Harry Archer); Doing the Light Fantastic Alley
Style [1]; First Nighters, The (C: A. Dorian Otvos);
Friendship Leads Us to Love (C: A. Dorian
Otvos); Garden Ballet; Happiness; If We Could
Live on Promises (C: Harry Archer); I'm Only
Human, That's All [1] (C: Harry Archer); In the
Musical Comedy Shows (C: Howard E. Johnson);
In This Automatical World [1] (C: Harry Archer);
One Moment of Paradise [1]; Promises; Put on the
Ritz (C: Irving Bibo); Reporters; Rolland from
Holland (C: Howard E. Johnson); Success; Tell Me
Truly [2] (C: Carle Carlton); That's Why They Call
Us Johns; Those Beautiful Chimes [2] (C: Harry
Archer); We're Looking for the Bobbed Hair
Bandit (C: Howard E. Johnson); What the Future
Holds for Me (C: Harry Archer); What You Could
Be If You Had Me [3]; When I Make the Grade
with O'Grady (C: Harry Archer); Where Have the
Old Timers Gone; Your Way or My Way
(C: Harry Archer)

Cast: George Bickel; Ida May Chadwick; Hallie
Manning; Evelyn Martin; William Renaud;
Helen Shipman; Dorothy Walters

Notes: [1] Out Philadelphia 9/25/22. [2] Sheet
music only. [3] Titled "If I Had You and You
Had Me" in program.

3370 • PARADISE GARDENS EAST

OPENED: 03/10/1969   Theatre: Fortune
Play   Off-Broadway: 16

Composer: Mildred Kayden
Lyricist: Frank Gagliano
Author: Frank Gagliano
Producer: Doris Kuller; Simon L. Saltzman
Director: Neil Israel

Costumes: John David Ridge; **Lighting Designer:**
David F. Segal; **Musical Director:** Wolfgang
Knittel; **Set Design:** David F. Segal

Songs: Beat of the City, The; Black and Blue
Pumps; Bodoni Country; Gussy and the
Beautiful People; Harmony; I'll Bet You're a Cat
Girl; Incinerator Hour, The; Look at My Sister;
That's RIght, Mr. Syph

Cast: Lenny Baker; Raul Julia; Terry Kiser; Lynn
Milgrim

Notes: One-act play in FRANK GAGLIANO'S
CITY SCENE. Part two is CONERICO WAS
HERE TO STAY and has no music.

3371 • PARADISE ISLAND

OPENED: 06/22/1961   Theatre: Jones Beach
                               Marine
Musical   Broadway: 75

Composer: Carmen Lombardo
Lyricist: John Jacob Loeb
Librettist: John Jacob Loeb; Carmen Lombardo; Francis Swann
Producer: Carmen Lombardo
Director: Francis Swann

Choreographer: June Taylor; **Costumes:** Winn Morton; **Dance Arranger:** Milt Sherman; **Lighting Designer:** Peggy Clark; **Musical Director:** Pembroke Davenport; **Orchestrations:** Joe Glover; **Set Design:** George Jenkins; **Vocal Arranger:** Pembroke Davenport

Songs: Beyond the Clouds; Ceremonial Chant; Ceremonial March; Coconut Wireless, The; Happy Hukilau, A; I'll Just Pretend; It's a Great Day for Hawaii; Luau Chant; Menehune, The; Miss Emily Fleetwood; My World and Your World; Never Any Time to Play; No One Ever Leaves Our Island [1]; Now the Time Has Come; Once Upon a Time; Paradise Island; We're in a Race; What Could Be More Romantic; With a Yo Ho Heave Ho

Cast: William Gaxton; Elaine Malbin; Ralph Purdom; Arthur Treacher; Jack Washburn

Notes: [1] Added to next year's revival.

3372 • PARADISE OF MAHOMET, THE

OPENED: 01/17/1911   Theatre: Herald Square
Musical   Broadway: 23

Composer: Robert Planquette
Lyricist: Harry B. Smith
Librettist: Harry B. Smith; Robert B. Smith
Producer: Daniel V. Arthur

Source: LE PARADIS DE MAHOMET (Musical: Henri Blondeau; Robert Planquette); **Choreographer:** Lew Morton; **Musical Director:** Silvio Hein

Songs: Can You Forget [1]; Forgive and Forget; Gypsy Song; I Can't Get Enough; I Have Found Them All; I've Got to Give Her Her Own Way; Joys of Love, The; Life Oriental; Look Out! Look Out! Look Out!; Ma Belle; My Idea of Paradise;

My Wedding Day; Opening; There's Something About You That Appeals to Me (C: John Golden; Silvio Hein; L: Frank Craven); Those Eyes; When His Eyes Look into Mine; When Orient Roses Bloom; When the Cat Comes Back; Y.M.D.; You're So Different from the Rest

Cast: Harry MacDonald; Maude Odell; Karl Stall; Grace Van Studdiford

Notes: [1] Sheet music only.

3373 • PARADISE PARADE OF 1935

OPENED: 1935
Revue

Composer: Sam H. Stept
Lyricist: Ned Washington

Songs: Bells of Monterey; Prayin' in Rhythm; That's What I Get for Wearing My Heart on My Sleeve

Notes: No other information available.

3374 • PARADISE PARADE

OPENED: 1936
Revue

Composer: Ben Oakland
Lyricist: Milton Drake

Songs: Avenue of Trees; From the Circle to the Square; Hand in Hand in Heaven; Tambourine Jamboree; We're Off to a Wonderful Start (L: Milton Drake; Ralph Freed)

Notes: No other information available.

3375 • PARADISE RESTAURANT AND REVUE

OPENED: 1938
Revue   Nightclub

Composer: Harry Tobias
Lyricist: Dave Oppenheim
Librettist: Nicholas Blair
Director: Marjery Fielding

Songs: Swingin' with the Wind; Things They Do in Hollywood, The; You Walked Out of the Picture (C: Little Jack Little; Henry Tobias)

Notes: No other information available.

3376 • PARADISE REVUE

OPENED: 1933
Revue

Songs: I've Got to Pass Your House to Get to My House (C/L: Lew Brown)

Notes: No other information available.

3377 • PARAMOUR

OPENED: 1995
Musical

Composer: Howard Marren
Lyricist: Joe Masteroff
Librettist: Joe Masteroff
Director: Gabriel Barre

Source: WALTZ OF THE TOREADORS, THE (Play: Jean Anouilh); **Musical Director:** Sue Anderson

Cast: George Lee Andrews; Danielle Ferland; Judy Kaye; Jennifer Naimo; Amanda Naughton; Timothy Nolen

Notes: Presented as a reading by the National Music Theater Conference. No songs listed in program.

3378 • PARANOIA

OPENED: 04/24/1914
Musical

Composer: Cole Porter
Lyricist: Cole Porter
Librettist: Cole Porter; T. Lawrason Riggs
Producer: Yale Univ. Dramatic Assn.
Director: Monty Woolley

Songs: Down in a Dungeon Deep; Down Lovers' Lane; Dresden China Soldiers; Flower Song [3]; Funny Little Tracks in the Snow; Hail to Cyril; I Want to Row on the Crew; Idyll [2]; Innocent, Innocent Maids; I've a Shooting Box in Scotland [1]; Naughty, Naughty; Oh, What a Lovely Princess; Paranoia; Prep School Widow, The; Slow Sinks the Sun; What Love Is; Won't You Come Crusading with Me [4]

Cast: Rufus F. King; Archibald MacLeish; Newbold Noyes

Notes: Originally titled BELLE OF THE BALKANS. Performed at the Hotel Taft, New Haven. Amateur show. [1] Later in SEE AMERICA FIRST. [2] Later in SEE AMERICA FIRST rewritten as "Love Came and Crowned Me." [3] In SEE AMERICA FIRST as "The Language of Flowers." [4] In SEE AMERICA FIRST as "Damsel, Damsel."

3379 • PARDON MY ENGLISH

OPENED: 01/20/1933   Theatre: Majestic
Musical   Broadway: 43

Composer: George Gershwin
Lyricist: Ira Gershwin
Librettist: Herbert Fields
Producer: Alex A. Aarons; Vinton Freedley
Director: Vinton Freedley; John McGowan

Choreographer: George Hale; **Costumes:** Robert Stevenson; **Musical Director:** Earl Busby; **Orchestrations:** Robert Russell Bennett; William Daly; Adolph Deutsch, **Set Design:** John Wenger

Songs: Dancing in the Streets; Dresden Northwest Mounted, The; Fatherland, Mother of the Band (Drink, Drink, Drink) [3]; Finaletto Act II Scene 4; Freud and Jung and Adler [3]; Hail, the Happy Couple [2]; He's Not Himself; He's Oversexed! [1]; In Three-Quarter Time; Isn't It a Pity?; I've Got to Be There; Lorelei, The; Luckiest Man in the World; My Cousin in Milwaukee; No Tickee, No Washee [1]; Opening, Act II [3]; Pardon My English; Poor Michael! Poor Golo!; So What?; Together at Last [3]; Tonight; Two Waltzes in C; Watch Your Head [1]; What Sort of Wedding Is This?; Where You Go, I Go

Cast: George Givot; Cliff Hall; Josephine Huston; Barbara Newberry; Jack Pearl; Carl Randall; Lyda Roberti; Eleanor Shaler; Harry T. Shannon; Gerald Oliver Smith

Notes: [1] Not used. [2] Refrain music from "Watch Your Head" and later used for "Comes the Revolution" in LET 'EM EAT CAKE. [3] Cut prior to opening.

3380 • PARDON OUR ANTENNA

OPENED: 10/16/1954
Revue   Closed out of town

Composer: Michael Simpson; Nora Simpson
Lyricist: Michael Simpson; Nora Simpson

Librettist: Eugene Conrad
Producer: Broadway Productions
Director: David Thimar

Costumes: Harry Bosen; Paul Brune; **Musical Director:** Jack Cavan; **Set Design:** Manuel Avilla

Cast: Chic Johnson; Sid Krofft; Ole Olsen

Notes: No songs listed in program.

3381 • PARDON OUR FRENCH
OPENED: 10/05/1950   Theatre: Broadway
Revue   Broadway: 100

Composer: Victor Young
Additional Music: Jack Mosser
Lyricist: Edward Heyman
Librettist: Chic Johnson; Ole Olsen
Producer: Chic Johnson; Ole Olsen

Choreographer: Ernst Matray; Maria Matray;
   Costumes: Jack Mosser; **Musical Director:** Harry
   Sukman; **Orchestrations:** Fran Frey; Ruby
   Raskin; Al Woodbury; **Set Design:** Albert
   Johnson; **Vocal Arranger:** Fran Frey; Ruby
   Raskin; Al Woodbury

Songs: Bella Signora [2]; Dolly from the Folies
   Bergere (C: Harry Sukman; L: Chic Johnson;
   Ole Olsen); Face in the Crowd, A [1]; Flower
   Song, The [1]; Half of Me [2]; I Ought to Know
   More About You [1]; I'm Gonna Make a Fool
   Out of April [1]; It's Love (C: Armour; L: John
   Edwards); Pardon Our French (C: Harry
   Sukman; L: Chic Johnson; Ole Olsen);
   Poker-Polka, The [1]; Sweetheart Semicolon [2];
   There's No Man Like a Snowman [1]; Until
   Tonight [2]; Venezia and Her Three Lovers
   (ballet) [1]

Cast: Denise Darcel; Fay De Witt; Chic Johnson;
   Marty May; Ole Olsen; Bill Shirley; Helene
   Stanley

Notes: *See also A LA CARTE (1949), an earlier
   incarnation of this show.* [1] Previously in A LA
   CARTE (1949). [2] ASCAP/Library of Congress
   only. Previously in A LA CARTE (1949).

3382 • PARIS
OPENED: 10/08/1928   Theatre: Music Box
Musical   Broadway: 194

Composer: Cole Porter
Lyricist: Cole Porter
Librettist: Martin Brown
Producer: E. Ray Goetz; Gilbert Miller
Director: W.H. Gilmore

Songs: An' Furthermore (C: Harry Warren; L: Bud
   Green); Bad Girl in Paree [3]; Blue Hours [3];
   Dizzy Baby [1]; Don't Look at Me That Way;
   Heaven Hop [2]; Land of Going to Be, The (C/L:
   E. Ray Goetz; C: Walter Kollo); (Let's Do It) Let's
   Fall in Love; Let's Misbehave [1]; Noah's Ark
   (C/L: Miller; C: Kenneth Burton; L: William
   Craig); Paris (C: Louis Alter; L: E. Ray Goetz);
   Practice in Love (C/L: Miller; C: Kenneth Burton;
   L: William Craig); Quelque-Chose [4]; (Oh You)
   Sweet Whatch-May-Call-It (C: Fred Ahlert; L:
   Roy Turk); Two Little Babes in the Wood [2];
   Vivienne; When I Found You [3]; Which? [1];
   Wob-a-ly Walk (C: Harry Warren; L: Bud Green)

Cast: Irving Aaronson's Commanders; Irene
   Bordoni; Louise Closser Hale

Notes: [1] Cut prior to opening. [2] From THE
   GREENWICH VILLAGE FOLLIES (1924).
   [3] Not used. Later in LA REVUE DES
   AMBASSADEURS. [4] Cut prior to opening. Not
   used in THE GREENWICH VILLAGE FOLLIES
   1924. [5] Later in WAKE UP AND DREAM.

3383 • PARIS AFTER DARK
Musical   Unproduced

Composer: Vernon Duke
Lyricist: Leonard Adelson; Dusky Negulesco

Songs: Everybody Loves Everybody; I Haven't a
   Bean in My Jeans; It's Been Pleasant, Pleasant;
   Jenny, Jenny (Save Your Dreams); Language of
   Love, The; Lonely in Paris; Paris After Dark

3384 • PARIS BY NIGHT
OPENED: 07/02/1904   Theatre: Madison Square
                     Garden Roof
Musical   Broadway: 50

Composer: Alfred Solman
Lyricist: Henry Marshall
Librettist: Henry Marshall
Producer: Weber & Rush
Director: Sol Fields

Musical Director: Robert W. Edwards

Songs: Belle of the Boulevard [1]; Bit of Foolishness, A [1]; Black Bogie Man, The [1]; Boulevardiers, The (C: Henry Marshall); Cherry Hill [1]; Dear Old Broadway (C: Henry Marshall); Girl with the Changeable Eyes, The; I Love You Lady Deed I Do (C/L: Joseph Nathan); In Gay Paree (C: Robert W. Edwards); In Sweet Loveland; Lulu [1]; Mandie; Milady [1]; My Sweet Crow [1]; Study in Pink [1]; That Horrid Mosquito; Turn Those Eyes Away; Waltz, Waltz, Waltz (C: Bloodgood; L: John E. Hazzard)

Cast: Hugh Cameron; Fleurette DeMar; Cassius Freeborn; Madge Lawrence; Edgar Temple; Ben Welch; Maud Wynne

Notes: When out of town the music was credited to Robert W. Edwards and the book to Moran and Hellan. The lyrics were uncredited. Will R. Barnes was credited for the costumes. [1] Out Wilkes-Barre 9/28/05.

3385 • PARIS IN SPRING

OPENED: 02/26/1931   Theatre: Hollywood
                                           Playhouse
                                           Los Angeles

Composer: Emmerich Kalman
Lyricist: Johnny Mercer

Songs: Don't Ask Too Much of Love; Moon Shines Down, The; Until We Kiss

Cast: Perry Askam; Eddie Lambert

Notes: No other information available.

3386 • PARIS '90

OPENED: 03/04/1952   Theatre: Booth
Revue   Broadway: 87

Composer: Kay Swift
Lyricist: Kay Swift
Librettist: Cornelia Otis Skinner
Producer: Alden S. Blodget
Director: Alden S. Blodget

Costumes: Helene Pons; **Lighting Designer:** Donald Oenslager; **Musical Director:** Nathaniel Shilkret; **Orchestrations:** Robert Russell Bennett; **Set Design:** Donald Oenslager

Songs: Calliope; Can-Can; From a Window on the Seine; Fughetta; House Where I Was Born, The; La Goulue; Lament; Lend Me a Bob Till Monday; Madame Arthur (C/L: Yvette Guilbert; L: Kay Swift); Moonlight on Notre Dame; Saint Lazare (C: Aristide Bruant); Turn My Little Millwheel (C: Paul Delmet); Waltz I Heard in a Dream, The

Cast: Cornelia Otis Skinner

3387 • PARISIAN MODEL, THE

OPENED: 11/27/1906   Theatre: Broadway
Musical   Broadway: 179

Composer: Max Hoffmann
Lyricist: Harry B. Smith
Librettist: Harry B. Smith
Producer: Florenz Ziegfeld
Director: Julian Mitchell

Costumes: Caroline Seidle; **Lighting Designer:** Louis Lamont

Songs: American Girl in Paris, The (L: Vincent Bryan; Harry B. Smith); Artists and Models; Bells (L: Max Hoffmann); Gibson Girl, The; Gown for Each Hour of the Day, A; I Am the Man They Talk So Much About [5]; I Just Can't Make My Eyes Behave [4] (C: Gus Edwards; L: Will D. Cobb; Harry B. Smith); I Love You Ma Cherie (C/L: Paul Rubens); I Want You Ma' Honey; I'd Like to See a Little More of You (C: Gus Edwards; L: Will D. Cobb); I'm the Man In Washington (C: Gertrude Hoffman; L: Vincent Bryan; Harry B. Smith); It's Delightful to Be Married [1] (C: Vincent Scotto; L: Anna Held); La Mattchiche; Lesson in Kissing, A (Kiss, Kiss, Kiss) (C: Gertrude Hoffman); Mr. Monkey [2] (C: Gus Edwards; L: Will D. Cobb); Paris Carnival; Parisian Model, A [5]; San Francisco Bay (L: Vincent Bryan); Story That Never Grows Old, The [5] (C: Seymour Furth; L: E.P. Moran); Trying on Dresses; When Uncle Sammy Sings the Marseillaise [5] (C: Herman Avery Wade; L: Earle C. Jones); When We're Married [3] (C: P.H. Christine); Whistling Yankee Girl, The; Will You Be My Teddy Bear (L: Vincent Bryan); You're All the World to Me [5] (L: Addison Burkhardt)

Cast: Charles A. Bigelow; Anna Held; Gertrude Hoffman; Truly Shattuck

Notes: [1] Music credited to A.V. Scotto and Christine on early sheet music. [2] Out Baltimore 10/15/06. [3] Out Baltimore 10/15/06.

May be same song as "It's Delightful to Be Married." [4] Not credited to Smith on sheet music, only in program. [5] Sheet music only.

3388 • PARISIANA
OPENED: 02/09/1928   Theatre: Edyth Totten
Revue   Broadway: 28

Composer: Vincent Valentini
Lyricist: Vincent Valentini
Librettist: Vincent Valentini
Producer: Associated Artists, Inc.
Director: Vincent Valentini

Songs: Ghost of Old Black Joe, The; Golliwog; In a Gondola with You; Keep It Under Your Hat; Keep on Dancing; Paree Has the Fever Now; Paris Green; Parisiana Roses; Peepin' Tommy; Since Nora Brought Her Angora Around; They're Hot Now Up in Iceland; Unfortunate Rose; What's Become of the Bowery?; Who Wouldn't

Cast: Carol Lynne; Olive May; Beth Miller; Thomas Sisters

3389 • PARK
OPENED: 04/22/1970   Theatre: John Golden
Musical   Broadway: 5

Composer: Lance Mulcahy
Lyricist: Paul Cherry
Librettist: Paul Cherry
Producer: Edward Padula
Director: John Stix

Choreographer: Lee Theodore; **Costumes:** Peter Harvey; **Lighting Designer:** Martin Aronstein; **Musical Director:** Oscar Kosarin; **Orchestrations:** Oscar Kosarin; **Set Design:** Peter Harvey

Songs: All the Little Things in the World Are Waiting; Bein' a Kid; Compromise; Elizabeth; He Talks to Me; Hello Is the Way Things Begin; I Can See; I Want It Just to Happen; I'd Marry You Again; Jamie; One Man; Park; Tomorrow Will Be the Same; We Live for Another Day [1]

Cast: David Brooks; Joan Hackett; Don Scardino; Julie Wilson

Notes: [1] Cut prior to opening.

3390 • PARK AVENUE
OPENED: 11/04/1946   Theatre: Shubert
Musical   Broadway: 72

Composer: Arthur Schwartz
Lyricist: Ira Gershwin
Librettist: Nunnally Johnson; George S. Kaufman
Producer: Max Gordon
Director: George S. Kaufman

Source: Park Avenue Stories in the "New Yorker" (Story: Nunnally Johnson); **Choreographer:** Helen Tamiris; **Costumes:** Tina Leser; **Dance Arranger:** Clay Warnick; **Lighting Designer:** Donald Oenslager; **Musical Director:** Charles Sanford; **Orchestrations:** Don Walker; **Set Design:** Donald Oenslager; **Vocal Arranger:** Clay Warnick

Songs: Dew Was on the Rose, The; Dinner Song [1]; Don't Be a Woman If You Can; Echo (dance); For the Life of Me; Future Mrs. Coleman, The [1]; Good-Bye to All That; Heavenly Day [1]; Hope for the Best; In the Courtroom (dance); Land of Opportunitee, The; My Son-In-Law; Remind Me Not to Leave the Town [1]; Stay As We Are [2]; Sweet Nevada (waltz version); Sweet Nevada (western version); There's No Holding Me (If I Can Keep on Holding You); There's Nothing Like Marriage for People; Tomorrow Is the Time

Cast: Robert Chisholm; Leonora Corbett; Martha Errolle; Arthur Margetson; Ray McDonald; David Wayne; Mary Wickes

Notes: [1] Not used. [2] Cut prior to New York.

3391 • PARK THEATER REVUE
Theatre: Park
Revue   Broadway

Composer: Martin Broones

Notes: No other information available.

3392 • PARLOR MATCH, A
OPENED: 09/21/1896   Theatre: Herald Square
Musical   Broadway: 48

Librettist: Charles Hoyt
Producer: Florenz Ziegfeld

Source: BOOK AGENT, THE (Play: Charles Hoyt); **Source:** PARLOR MATCH, A (Play: Charles Hoyt)

Songs: Ah, There; Come and Play with Me; Dear Golden Days; Diamond King, The; I Love Not but You; Parlor Match, A; Somebody; Spanish Fantasie; Spanish Sweetheart; Your Baby Is Comin' to Town

Cast: Charles Evans; Anna Held; Bill Hoey

Notes: A musical version of the hit play that opened at Tony Pastor's Opera House on 9/22/1884. This musical introduced Anna Held to Broadway. The original non-musical version played over 2,500 performances on Broadway and around the country with Evans and Hoey. No songwriter credits.

3393 • PARTNERS
Notes: *See DOUBLE FEATURE.*

3394 • PASSING SHOW, THE (1894)
OPENED: 05/12/1894   Theatre: Casino
Musical   Broadway: 145

Composer: Ludwig Englander
Librettist: Sydney Rosenfeld

Notes: No other information available. After 121 performances, the show reopened 10/29/1894 for 24 performances.

3395 • PASSING SHOW OF 1912, THE
OPENED: 07/22/1912   Theatre: Winter Garden
Revue   Broadway: 136

Composer: Earl Carroll; Louis A. Hirsch
Lyricist: Harold Atteridge
Librettist: Harold Atteridge
Producer: Winter Garden Company
Director: Ned Wayburn

Choreographer: Theodore Kosloff[2]; Ned Wayburn; **Musical Director:** Samuel Lehman; **Orchestrations:** Oscar Radin; Frank Saddler

Songs: All the World Is Madly Prancing; Always Together; Bacchanal Rag, The; Cohen's Yiddisha Band (C: Harry M. Piani; L: Ballard Macdonald); Fearless Waltz, The; Foolishness [1]; Girlish Laughter; Handy Andy; Haunting Melody [1]; Ida; In 2010; It's All Over Now; Kangaroo Hop, The; Metropolitan Squak-tette, The; Modern Love; Mr. Pagliacci [1]; My Reuben Girlie; Oh! You Dream (C/L: Earl Carroll); Philadelphia Drag, The (C/L: Harold Orlob); Pirates and Quaker Girl;

Policeman's Lot Is a Happy One, A; Ragtime Jockey Man (C/L: Irving Berlin); Rum, Tum, Fidele [1]; Spark of Life Dance, The; There You Have New York Town; We've Been to Europe; Wedding Glide, The (C/L: Louis A. Hirsch); When Was There Ever a Night Like This (C/L: Louis A. Hirsch); You Never Could Tell We Were Married

Cast: Adelaide and Hughes; Harry Fox; Trixie Friganza; Sydney Grant; Charlotte Greenwood; Ernest Hare; Eugene Howard; Willie Howard; Jobyna Howland; Anna Wheaton

Notes: Kosloff choreographed the ballet. [1] Out Cincinnati 4/6/13. [2] Choreographed ballet.

3396 • PASSING SHOW OF 1913, THE
OPENED: 07/24/1913   Theatre: Winter Garden
Revue   Broadway: 116

Composer: Albert W. Brown; Jean Schwartz
Lyricist: Harold Atteridge
Librettist: Harold Atteridge
Producer: Winter Garden Company
Director: Ned Wayburn

Costumes: Melville Ellis

Songs: Baltimo' [1] (C/L: Andy Razaf); Butterfly [1] (C: Jean Schwartz); Do You Take This Woman for Your Lawful Wife (I Do, I Do) (C: Harry Von Tilzer; L: Andrew B. Sterling); Foolish Cinderella Girl; Golden Stairs of Love, The (C: Jean Schwartz); Irish Romeo [4] (C: Al W. Brown); Love Me While the Loving Is Good [4] (C: Harry Von Tilzer; L: Stanley Murphy); Melodrama Known as Married Life (C: Al W. Brown); My Irish Romeo (C: Al W. Brown); Passing Show Cakewalk; Pauline (C: Al W. Brown); Ragging the Nursery Rhymes [1] (C: Al W. Brown); Red Bandanna Rag, The (C: Arthur Lange; L: Jeff T. Branen); Romance Land (C: Al W. Brown); Strong Heart [1] (C: Al W. Brown); That Good Old Fashioned Cake Walk [1] (C: Al W. Brown; Jean Schwartz); When I Want to Settle Down [4] (C: Jean Schwartz); Whistling Cowboy Joe [1] (C: Al W. Brown); Winter Garden Girl (C/L: Bobby Jones); You Made Me Love You I Didn't Want to Do It [3] (C: James V. Monaco; L: Joseph McCarthy)

Cast: May Boley; Lew Brice; Sadie Burt; Bessie Clayton; Herbert Corthell; Wellington Cross; Anne Dancrey; Carter De Haven; Sydney Grant; Charlotte Greenwood; Laura Hamilton; Charles

King; Mollie King; John Charles Thomas; George Whiting

Notes: No program available. [1] Not listed in program. [2] Some sources list additional music to Al W. Brown. [3] Sheet music also claims the song was used in THE HONEYMOON EXPRESS. [4] Sheet music only.

3397 • PASSING SHOW OF 1914, THE (NEW YORK)

OPENED: 06/10/1914   Theatre: Winter Garden
Revue   Broadway: 133

Composer: Sigmund Romberg
Lyricist: Harold Atteridge
Librettist: Harold Atteridge
Producer: Winter Garden Company
Director: J.C. Huffman

Choreographer: Jack Mason; **Costumes:** Melville Ellis; **Dance Arranger:** Melville Ellis; **Lighting Designer:** Nick Kronyack; **Musical Director:** Oscar Radin

Songs: Brazilian Max-Cheese [1] (C: Ernesto Nazareth; L: Muriel Window); California; Crinoline Girl, The [1]; Divertissement [1]; Don't Hesitate with Me; Dreams of the Past; Eagle Rock, The (C: Harry Carroll); Eugenic Girls; Gilbert the Filbert [2] (C: Herman Finck; L: Arthur Wimperis); Girl of To-Day, The; Good Old Levee Days (C: Harry Carroll); Grape Dance, The; Impressions [1]; Kitty MacKay (C: Harry Carroll); Maude Adams of the Screen, The; Midnight Girl at the Midnight Cabaret, The; Moving Picture Glide, The (C: Harry Carroll); Omar Khayyam; On a Modern Wedding Day; Out in Frisco Town (C: Harry Carroll); Sari Dance, The; Sloping Path, The; Tennessee, I Hear You Calling Me [1] (C: Jeff Godfrey; L: Harold Robe); That Bohemian Rag (C: Gus Edwards; Louis Silvers; L: Lou Havez); Way Down East [1]; Working for the Pictures; You Can't Go Wrong with Us; You're Just a Little Better (Than the One I Thought Was Best) (C: Harry Carroll)

Cast: Lew Brice; Jose Collins; Frances Demarest; Bernard Granville; Marilyn Miller; George Monroe; Nat Nazzarro Jr

Notes: [1] Sheet music only. [2] Sheet music only. Also in THE PASSING SHOW in London and THE GIRL FROM UTAH.

3398 • PASSING SHOW, THE (1914) (LONDON)

OPENED: 04/20/1914
Revue   London

Composer: Herman Finck
Lyricist: Arthur Wimperis
Librettist: Arthur Wimperis
Producer: Alfred Butt

Songs: Gilbert the Filbert [2]; I'll Make a Man of One of You; You're Here and I'm Here [1] (C: Jerome Kern; L: Harry B. Smith)

Cast: Basil Hallam; Elsie Janis

Notes: No program available. [1] Originally in THE LAUGHING HUSBAND. [2] Also in THE PASSING SHOW OF 1914 and THE GIRL FROM UTAH.

3399 • PASSING SHOW OF 1915, THE

OPENED: 05/29/1915   Theatre: Winter Garden
Revue   Broadway: 145

Composer: Leo Edwards; J. Leubrie Hill; William F. Peters
Lyricist: Harold Atteridge
Librettist: Harold Atteridge
Producer: Winter Garden Company
Director: J.C. Huffman

Choreographer: Theodore Kosloff; Jack Mason; **Costumes:** Mrs. J.J. Shubert; **Musical Director:** Oscar Radin

Songs: (You'd Better See) America First (C: Phil Schwartz); Any Old Time with You (C: Leo Edwards); Bill Simmons [6] (C/L: J. Leubrie Hill); Billy Shakespeare (The Shakespearian Rag) [5] (C: Leo Edwards); Broadway Sam (C: Leo Edwards; L: Blanche Merrill); Daddy Longlegs [6] (C: Leo Edwards); First Love (Is the Best Love of All) (C: Leo Edwards); Fishing [1] (C: Leo Edwards); Flower of My Heart, My Rose (C: Leo Edwards); Gamble on Me! (C: Leo Edwards); Hello Hawaii [2] (C: Jean Schwartz; L: Bert Kalmar; Edgar Leslie); I Don't Like the Sea (C: William F. Peters); Isle d'Amour; My Brother Bill; My Hula Maid (C: Leo Edwards); My Trilby Maid (C/L: Bobby Jones; Will Morrissey); Panama-Pacific Drag (C: Leo Edwards); Peasant Girl, The [4] (C: Leo Edwards); Primrose Way,

The (C: Leo Edwards); Ragtime Overture of Grand Operas [6] (C: Leo Edwards); Rosey Posey [6] (C: J. Leubrie Hill); Rosie Rosenblott [2]; Seven Ages, The [6] (C: Leo Edwards); Shopping (C: W.H. Peters); Silk Stockings (I Will Follow Her) (C: William F. Peters); Sing Me to Sleep with an Old- Fashioned Melody [3]; Small Town Girlie (Every Small Town Girlie Has a Big Town Way) (C: Leo Edwards); Spanish Fandango, The; Springtime in the Country; Summer Sports; Take Me to the Midnight Cakewalk Ball (C/L: Maurice Abrahams; Eddie Cox; Arthur Jackson); There's Something Missing in the Movies; Trombone Man (My Trombone Man) (C: J. Leubrie Hill); Vale of Dreams [6] (C: Leo Edwards)

Cast: John Boles; Frances Demarest; Ernest Hare; Eugene Howard; Willie Howard; Marilyn Miller; George Monroe; John T. Murray; Daphne Pollard; John Charles Thomas

Notes: [1] Sheet music only. [2] Out 5/15/16 (?). [3] Out Toledo 1/2/16. [4] Cut after opening. [5] Cut after opening. *See also ZIEGFELD FOLLIES OF 1912* for "That Shakespearian Rag." [6] Not in programs.

3400 • PASSING SHOW OF 1916, THE

OPENED: 06/22/1916   Theatre: Winter Garden
Revue   Broadway: 140

Composer: Otto Motzan; Sigmund Romberg
Lyricist: Harold Atteridge
Librettist: Harold Atteridge
Producer: Winter Garden Company
Director: J.C. Huffman

Choreographer: Allan K. Foster; **Costumes:** Faibsey; **Musical Director:** Oscar Radin

Songs: Any Night on Broadway; Around the Town; Broadway School Days; Faces [1] (C/L: Unknown); How to Make a Pretty Face [1] (C/L: Unknown); Let Cupid In (C: Otto Motzan); Little Usher, A [1] (C/L: Unknown); Making of a Girl, The (C: George Gershwin; Sigmund Romberg); My Runaway Girl (C: George Gershwin; L: Murray Roth); Nothing's Good Enough for a Good Little Girl [1] (C/L: Unknown); Play My Melody; Pretty Baby (C: Tony Jackson; Egbert Van Alstyne; L: Gus Kahn); Ragging the Apache (C: Sigmund Romberg; L: Otto Motzan); Ragtime Calisthenics; Romeo and Juliet (C: Otto

Motzan; Sigmund Romberg); Roosevelt, Bryan and Hughes [1] (C/L: Unknown); Roosevelt, Wilson and Hughes; So This Is Paris! (C: Harry Tierney); Sweet and Pretty (C: Otto Motzan); That's Called Walking the Dog (C: Otto Motzan); What's the Matter with You? (C/L: Clifton Crawford); Wine, Woman and Song; Your Auto Ought to Get Girls [1] (C/L: Unknown); Yours Sincerely U.S.A. [1] (C/L: Unknown)

Cast: Jack Boyle; Frances Demarest; Stella Hoban; James Hussey; Florence Moore; Will Philbrick; Herman Timberg; Fred Walton; Ed Wynn

Notes: [1] Out Jefferson Theatre 4/8/17.

3401 • PASSING SHOW OF 1917, THE

OPENED: 04/26/1917   Theatre: Winter Garden
Revue   Broadway: 196

Composer: Otto Motzan; Sigmund Romberg
Lyricist: Harold Atteridge
Librettist: Harold Atteridge
Producer: Winter Garden Company
Director: J.C. Huffman

Choreographer: Allan K. Foster; **Musical Director:** Oscar Radin

Songs: America's Fighting Back; Awkward Age, The; Chorus Girl, The; (I'll Be a) College Boy's Dear (C: Sigmund Romberg); Dancing Family; Faster and Faster; Father Knickerbocker Fox Trot (C: Sigmund Romberg); Girl Who Drinks Champagne, The; Golden West, The; Good-Bye Broadway, Hello France [1] (C: Billy Baskette; L: Benny Davis; C. Francis Reisner); It's a Long Way to Berlin, but We'll Get There [1] (C: Leon Flatow; L: Arthur Fields); Language of the Fan, The (C: Sigmund Romberg); (I've a) Little Bit of Scotch (in Me), A (C: Sigmund Romberg); Meet Me at the Station Dearie (C: Ted Snyder; L: Sam M. Lewis; Joe Young); My Bedouin Girl (C: Sigmund Romberg); My Yokohoma Girl (C: Harry Tierney; L: Unknown); Orgy; Passing Show, The; Pierrot; Ready Made Sandwich, The; Ring Out the Liberty Bell (C: Sigmund Romberg); Ruth St. Denis; Same Old Song; Table for Two, A (C: Ray Perkins); Telephone Girl, The; That Peach-A-Reeno, Phil-I-Peeno Dance; Under the Willow Tree (C: Sigmund Romberg); Won't You Be My Daddy (C: Sigmund Romberg);

Won't You Write to Me (Won't You Send a Letter to Me) (C: Sigmund Romberg)

Cast: Franklyn Battie; Zeke Colvan; Jefferson De Angelis; Johnny Dooley; Irene Franklin; Burton Green; DeWolf Hopper; Tom Lewis; Marie Nordstrom; Yvette Rugel

Notes: Motzan is not credited on sheet music, just Romberg. [1] Sheet music only.

3402 • PASSING SHOW OF 1918, THE

OPENED: 07/25/1918   Theatre: Winter Garden
Revue   Broadway: 124

Composer: Sigmund Romberg; Jean Schwartz
Lyricist: Harold Atteridge
Librettist: Harold Atteridge
Producer: Messrs. Shubert
Director: J.C. Huffman

Choreographer: Jack Mason; **Set Design:** Watson Barratt

Songs: At the Jazz Town Novelty Ball [1] (C: Lew Pollack; L: Nat Vincent); Bring on the Girls; Dress, Dress, Dress; Duchess of Devonshire, The [1]; Duchess of the Long Ago, The; Galli Curci Rag; Go West Young Girl (C: Russell Tarbox); I (Really) Can't Make My Feet Behave (C: Sigmund Romberg; L: Jean Schwartz); I'm Forever Blowing Bubbles [2] (C/L: John William Kellette; Jean Kenbrovin); Little Devil [1]; Meet Me in Bubble Land [1] (C: Isham Jones; L: Joe Manne; Caspar Nathan); My Baby Talking Girl (My Baby Talk Lady); My Holiday Girls (C: Augustus Barratt); Oh You Vampire Girls (C: Sigmund Romberg; Jean Schwartz); On the Level You're a Little Devil, but I'll Soon Make an Angel of You [1] (C: Jean Schwartz; L: Joe Young); Serenade; Smiles [3] (C: Lee S. Roberts; L: J. Will Callahan); Squab Farm, The; Tell Me [1] (C: Max Kortlander; L: J. Will Callahan); Trombone Jazz [1] (C: Jean Schwartz); Won't You Buy a War Stamp (War Stamps) (C: Ray Perkins)

Cast: Adele Astaire; Fred Astaire; Lou Clayton; Frank Fay; George Hassell; Eugene Howard; Willie Howard; Nita Naldi; Jessie Reed; Charles Ruggles; Sam White

Notes: [1] Sheet music only. [2] Not in programs. [3] Added after opening.

3403 • PASSING SHOW OF 1919, THE

OPENED: 10/23/1919   Theatre: Winter Garden
Revue   Broadway: 280

Composer: Sigmund Romberg; Jean Schwartz
Lyricist: Harold Atteridge
Librettist: Harold Atteridge
Producer: J.J. Shubert; Lee Shubert
Director: J.C. Huffman

Choreographer: Allan K. Foster; **Musical Director:** Oscar Radin; **Orchestrations:** J. Bodewalt Lampe; James C. McCabe; Oscar Radin; Frank Tours; **Set Design:** Watson Barratt

Songs: A la Hockey; America's Popular Tune; Dreamy Florence; Good-Bye; In a Love Boat with You; In Salem; It's Always Summertime at the Winter Garden (C: Jean Schwartz; L: Alfred Bryan); King's Favorite, The; Kiss Burglar; Lovable Moon (C: Jean Schwartz); Mischief in Your Eyes; Miss Unruly; Molly Malone; Neapolitan Jazz; Orient (C: Jean Schwartz; L: Alfred Bryan); Plate Dance; Road to Destiny, The (C: Jean Schwartz); Seven Ages of Women; Shimmy a La Egyptian; Sing Song Girl (C: Sigmund Romberg); Solomon (C: Jean Schwartz; L: Alfred Bryan); Tumble Inn (C: Jean Schwartz); Water Lily; Wine Ballet

Cast: Avon Comedy Four; James Barton; Reginald Denny; Lon Hascall; Dick Raft; George Raft; Blanche Ring; Charles Winninger; Walter Woolf

Notes: No mention of Romberg in programs!

3404 • PASSING SHOW OF 1921, THE

OPENED: 12/29/1920   Theatre: Winter Garden
Revue   Broadway: 191

Composer: Lew Pollack; Jean Schwartz
Lyricist: Harold Atteridge
Librettist: Harold Atteridge
Producer: J.J. Shubert; Lee Shubert
Director: J.C. Huffman

Costumes: Cora MacGeachy; **Incidental Music:** Al Goodman; **Set Design:** William Weaver

Songs: Allah Jazz [2] (C: Unknown); Beautiful Faces (C: Lew Pollack); Beautiful Girls Are Like Opium; Becky from Babylon (C/L: Abner Silver); Bit of

Opera, A (C: Unknown); Blonde Blues [4] (C: Unknown); Broadway in Sahara (C: Unknown); Charm School, The (C: Jean Schwartz; L: Alfred Bryan); Dancing Blues, The (C: Lew Pollack); Dream Fantasies (C: Unknown); Fire Cracker [2]; Hawaiian Skies (C: Fred Rose; L: Ernie Erdman); Hay-Long [5] (C: Sammy Fain; L: Eugene Howard; Willie Howard); Hello Miss Knickerbocker (C: Unknown); I'm Oriental (C: Lew Pollack); In Little Old New York (C: Jean Schwartz); Let's Have a Rattling Good Time (C: Jean Schwartz; L: Alfred Bryan); Mecca [2] (C: Unknown); Modern Crusaders [2] (C: Unknown); My Lady of the Lamp (C: Jean Schwartz); My Wife (C: Unknown); Parisienne Passionettes [2] (C: Unknown); Rubaiyats from the Rubaiyat (C: Unknown); Shakespeare's Garden of Love [2] (C: Unknown); Silks and Satins (C: Unknown); Smiling Sam (C: Unknown); Snap a Wishbone with Me (C: Lew Pollack; Jean Schwartz; L: Alfred Bryan); Sprinkle Me with Diamonds [2] (C: Unknown); Sweetest Melody (C: Unknown); Ta Voo [3] (C: Jean Schwartz); Tip Top Toreador (C: Unknown); Underneath Hawaiian Skies [6] (C: Ernie Erdman; L: Fred Rose); When Shall We Meet Again [1] (C: Richard A. Whiting; L: Raymond B. Egan); When There's No One to Love (C: Jean Schwartz); You Hoo [1] (C: Al Jolson; L: B.G. DeSylva); You May Be a Bad Man (C: Unknown)

Cast: Janet Adair; Marie Dressler; J. Harold Murray; Harry Watson

Notes: [1] Out Washington, D.C. 2/5/21. [2] Out New Haven 12/21/20. [3] Also titled "Ta Woo." [4] Out New Haven 12/21/20 also in THE PASSING SHOW OF 1920. [5] ASCAP/Library of Congress only. [6] Sheet music only.

3405 • PASSING SHOW OF 1922, THE

OPENED: 09/20/1922   Theatre: Winter Garden
Revue   Broadway: 95

Composer: Al Goodman
Lyricist: Harold Atteridge
Librettist: Harold Atteridge; Jack Stanley
Producer: J.J. Shubert; Lee Shubert
Director: J.C. Huffman

Choreographer: Allan K. Foster; **Musical Director:** Alfred Goodman; **Set Design:** Watson Barratt; Rollo Wayne

Songs: American Jazz; Ballet of Siam, A; Camp's Daily Dozen; Carolina in the Morning (C: Walter Donaldson; L: Gus Kahn); Cinema Girl [2]; Circus Days; Daughter of Satan [2]; Days of Pharaoh [3]; Do You, Don't You, Will You, Won't You [1] (C/L: Howard Brothers; George A. Little; Larry Schaetzlein); Eleanor; Eugene O'Neill's Hairy Ape; First, Last and Always [3]; Humming a Tune [2]; I Came! I Saw! I Fell!; I Love Me (I'm Wild About Myself) [1] (C: Edwin J. Weber; L: Jack Hines; Will Mahoney); In Italy; Love of Long Ago; Melody Land [2]; My Coal Black Mammy; My Diamond Girls; Orphans of the Storm; Passing Show, The; Poor J'en-Ai-Marie; Prince of Wales; Radiance; Study in Black and White, A; Underneath a Pretty Hat [2]; Underneath the Palms

Cast: Janet Adair; Mlle. Alcorn; Fred Allen; Sam Ash; George Hazzell; Eugene Howard; Willie Howard; Nat Nazzarro Jr.; Ethel Shutta

Notes: [1] Sheet music only [2] Out Atlantic City 9/4/22. [3] Out Toledo 12/9/33. [4] Not in programs.

3406 • PASSING SHOW OF 1923, THE

OPENED: 06/14/1923   Theatre: Winter Garden
Revue   Broadway: 118

Composer: Sigmund Romberg; Jean Schwartz
Lyricist: Harold Atteridge
Librettist: Harold Atteridge
Producer: J.J. Shubert; Lee Shubert
Director: J.C. Huffman

Choreographer: Allan K. Foster; **Costumes:** Paul Arlington; **Musical Director:** Alfred Goodman; **Set Design:** Watson Barratt

Songs: Aux Armes; Ball Begins, The (C: Sigmund Romberg); Beautiful and Damned; Birds of Plumage; Go Into Your Dance; Golfing Blues (C: Jean Schwartz); Jackie Coogan (C: Jean Schwartz); Jewel Song, The; Kissable Lips (C: Jean Schwartz); Life of a Rose, The (Rose of the Morning) [1] (C: Sigmund Romberg; L: Cyrus Wood); Lovelit Eyes [2] (C: Sigmund Romberg); Manita Wanna Eat, Wanna Eat [3] (C: Al Sherman; L: Sam Coslow); Mirror Mine (C: Jay Gorney); My Dutch Lady (C: Jean Schwartz); My Gaby Doll; My Little Lotus Flower (C: Sigmund Romberg; L: Cyrus Wood); My Rainbow;

Prologue; Royal Wedding; Step on It; Your Other Side

Cast: Phil Baker; Roy Cummings; George Hassell; George Jessel; Alex Morrison; Nat Nazzarro Jr.; Helen Shipman; Walter Woolf

Notes: [1] Out Newark 4/7/24. [2] Sheet music only. [3] ASCAP/Library of Congress only.

3407 • PASSING SHOW OF 1924, THE

OPENED: 09/03/1924   Theatre: Winter Garden
Revue   Broadway: 106

Composer: Sigmund Romberg; Jean Schwartz
Lyricist: Harold Atteridge
Librettist: Harold Atteridge
Producer: .J. Shubert; Lee Shubert
Director: J.C. Huffman

Choreographer: Seymour Felix; Kotchetovsky; Max Scheck; **Costumes:** Charles LeMaire; Ernest Schrapps; **Musical Director:** Al Goodman; **Orchestrations:** Emil Gerstenberger; **Set Design:** Watson Barratt

Songs: Beaded Bag, The [1] (L: Alex Gerber); Day Will Come, The [2] (C/L: Ed East; Ted Lewis); Dublinola; Everybody Dance; Flappers; Gold, Silver and Green; Holidays; In Every Dancing Show [1]; John Held, Jr. [1]; Joy and Gloom; Mooching Along (L: Alex Gerber); Nothing Naughtie in a Nightie; Society Blues; Study in Porcelain, A; When Knighthood Was in Flower

Cast: James Barton; Olga Cook; George Hassell; Lula McConnell; Harry McNaughton; Allan Prior; Jack Rose

Notes: [1] Out of town program. [2] Sheet music only.

3408 • PASSING SHOW OF 1926, THE

Notes: *See THE MERRY WORLD (1926).*

3409 • PASSING SHOW OF 1932, THE

OPENED: 09/05/1932
Revue   Closed out of town

Composer: Michael Cleary; Will Irwin; Samuel Pokrass; Serge Walter
Lyricist: Herman Hupfeld; Charles Kenny; Max Lief; Nathaniel Lief; Harry Ruskin; Frank Sullivan
Producer: Messrs. Shubert
Director: Zeke Colvan

Choreographer: Dan Carthe; Gertrude Hoffman; **Costumes:** Ernest Schrapps, **Musical Director:** Tom Jones; **Set Design:** Rollo Wayne

Songs: Afraid of You; Better or Worse; Bring 'Em Back Alive; Cokey Joe; Columnists; Dancing in the Sky; Egyptian Eyes; Horse- Car Days; I Want to Go Home; Ice-Box; Lackadaisical; Music in the Sky; Nude Ranch; Paintings for Sale; Rio Rhapsody; Season's Ended, The; Sing a Little Song (C/L: Herman Hupfeld); Slave Market; Spring Ballet (inst.); Stars and Pool; Thanks to You; Unfinished Symphony; Walking with You; Wedding; Wonderful

Cast: Lester Allen; Joe Besser; Shemp Howard; George Marshall; Jack McCauley; Florence Moore; Gertrude Niesen; Jack Osterman; Eddie Shubert

3410 • PASSING SHOW OF 1945, THE

OPENED: 11/09/1945
Revue   Closed out of town

Composer: Irving Actman; Eugene Burton; Will Morrissey; Dana Slawson
Lyricist: Eugene Burton; Will Morrissey; Dana Slawson; Ross Thomas
Producer: Messrs. Shubert
Director: Russell Mack

Choreographer: Carl Randall; **Costumes:** Mlle. Kamarova; **Musical Director:** Alfred Evans; **Set Design:** Watson Barratt

Songs: Along the South American Coastline; Avenue of Americas, The; Back in the Kitchen Again; Come On Over and Dance; Could You Use a New Friend?; How Long Will It Be?; Living in a Brand New Day; Passing Show; Skyhook; Song Is Born, A; Then There's Romance; White Rhapsody; You're My Kind of Ugly

Cast: Willie Howard; Al Kelly; Sue Lyon; Bobby Morris; Rowena Rowland

3411 • PASSION

OPENED: 05/09/1994   Theatre: Plymouth
Musical   Broadway: 280

Composer: Stephen Sondheim
Lyricist: Stephen Sondheim
Librettist: James Lapine
Producer: Roger Berlind; Capital Cities/ABC;
  Scott Rudin; Shubert Organization, The
Director: James Lapine

Source: FOSCA (Novel: I.U. Tarchetti); PASSIONE
  DI AMORE (Film: Ettore Scola); **Costumes:** Jane
  Greenwood; **Lighting Designer:** Beverly
  Emmons; **Musical Director:** Paul Gemignani;
  Orchestrations: Jonathan Tunick; **Set Design:**
  Adrianne Lobel

Songs: Farewell Letter; First Letter; Flashback;
  Forty Days; Fourth Letter; Garden Sequence;
  Happiness; I Read; I Wish I Could Forget You;
  Is This What You Call Love?; Loving You; No
  One Has Ever Loved Me; Second Letter;
  Soldiers' Gossip; Sunrise Letter; Third Letter;
  Transition 1; Transition 2; Transition 3;
  Transition 4; Transition 5; Trio

Cast: Tom Aldredge; Gibby Brand; George
  Dvorsky; Gregg Edelman; Colleen Fitzpatrick;
  Cris Groenendaal; Juliet Lambert; Frank
  Lombardi; Marin Mazzie; Donna Murphy;
  Marcus Olson; William Parry; Matthew
  Poretta; Francis Ruivivar; Jere Shea; John
  Leslie Wolfe

Notes: This was to be one act of a two one-act
  musicals evening. The second show, titled
  MUSCLES, apparently only had one song
  written for it, an opening number. No songs
  listed in program — song titles from recording.

3412 • PASSION FLOWER, THE

OPENED: 01/13/1920   Theatre: Greenwich
                        Village
Play   Off-Broadway: 144

Author: Jacinto Benavente; John Garrett Underhill

Songs: Passion Flower, The (C/L: Irving Berlin)

Cast: Nance O'Neil

Notes: No program available.

3413 • PASSIONELLA

Notes: *See THE APPLE TREE for the Bock and
  Harnick version. See THE WORLD OF JULES
  FEIFFER for the Sondheim version.*

3414 • PASSIONS OF 1926

Notes: *See THE MERRY WORLD.*

3415 • PATRICIA

OPENED: 1949
Musical   Closed out of town

Composer: George Grandee
Lyricist: J. Keirn Brennan
Librettist: Barry Connors
Producer: Henry Duffy
Director: Russell Fillmore

Source: THE PATSY (Play: Barry Connors);
  Musical Director: Robert Nurok

Songs: Desert of Dreams; Exquisite; Hot Dog,
  Mustard and You; Nuggets; Penguins; Roll Pony,
  Roll; So Long-No Longer; To Know You Is to
  Like You

Cast: Charles Collins; Earl Covert; Catherine Doucet;
  Russell Fillmore; Kathryn Mayfield; Dorothy Stone

3416 • PATSY

OPENED: 03/08/1926
Musical   Closed out of town

Cast: Lou Holtz

Notes: Played the Mason Theatre, Los Angeles.
  No other information available.

3417 • PATSY IN POLITICS

OPENED: 09/02/1907
Musical   Closed out of town

Composer: Seymour Furth
Lyricist: Carl Hand
Librettist: Joe Doe

Songs: Back to Old Broadway; Much Obliged to You

Cast: Florence Brooks; Mabel Reed; Billy B. Van

Notes: No program available.

3418 • PEACE

OPENED: 11/01/1968   Theatre: Astor Place
Musical   Off-Broadway: 224

Composer: Al Carmines
Lyricist: Al Carmines
Librettist: Tim Reynolds
Director: Lawrence Kornfeld

Source: PEACE (Play: Aristophanes);
  Choreographer: Arlene Rothlein; **Costumes:**
Nancy Christofferson; **Lighting Designer:** Roger
Morgan; **Musical Director:** Al Carmines

Songs: All the Dark Is Changed to Sunshine;
America the Beautiful; Don't Do It Mr. Hermes;
Gods Have Gone Away, The; I Just Can't Help
It; I Want to See Peace Again; Just Let Me Get
My Hands on Peace; Just Sit Around; Muse,
Darling; My Name's Abundance; Oh Daddy
Dear; Oh God; Peace Anthem; Plumbing; Poor
Mortals; Summer's Nice; Things Starting to
Grow Again; Through Excessive Concern; Trio;
Up in Heaven; You've Got Yourself a Bunch of
Women

Cast: Reathel Bean; Essie Borden; Julie Kurnitz;
George McGrath; David Vaughan; Margaret
Wright; **Pianist:** Al Carmines

Notes: Opened at the Judson Memorial Church.
Moved 1/27/69 to the Astor Place where it
played 192 performances. No songs listed in
program.

3419 • PEACE PIRATES, THE

OPENED: 1916
Musical

Composer: Ray Perkins
Lyricist: Herman J. Mankiewicz
Librettist: Herman J. Mankiewicz
Producer: Columbia University Players
Director: Kenneth S. Webb

Songs: Sandman, The (C: Roy Webb; L: Lorenz
Hart)

Cast: Oscar Hammerstein II; Lorenz Hart

Notes: Amateur show. Interpolated scene from
Oscar Hammerstein II.

3420 • PEACHES

OPENED: 1923
Musical   Closed out of town

Composer: Max Steiner
Lyricist: Harry B. Smith; Robert B. Smith

Songs: Every Heart Has a Dream; I Wish I Could
Believe You; Insignificant Me; Listen Mr. Verdi;
Passes By; Ring for Rosy

Notes: No program available.

3421 • PEACOCK ALLEY

OPENED: 1921

Producer: Robert Z. Leonard

Songs: Peacock Alley (C/L: Louis Silvers)

Cast: Mae Murray

Notes: No other information available.

3422 • PEARL AND THE PUMPKIN, THE

OPENED: 08/21/1905   Theatre: Broadway
Musical   Broadway: 72

Composer: John W. Bratton
Lyricist: Paul West
Librettist: W.W. Denslow; Paul West
Producer: Klaw & Erlanger
Director: Herbert Gresham; Ned Wayburn

Musical Director: A.M. Langstaff; **Set Design:**
W.W. Denslow

Songs: Canny Canner, The; Come My True Love [2];
Daughter of Annie Rooney, The; Fairies'
Meeting, The; Fol-De-Iddledy-Ido; Hail to Our
Queen; Hang Together (We'll Hang Together);
Honeymoon Hall; Innocent Games of Childhood,
The [1]; It Is the English; Jack O'Lantern Joe; Lily
White; My Baby Elephant; My Combination Girl;
My Party; On a Desert Island with the One You
Love [1]; Opening Chorus; Phantom Ship, The;
Pirates Are We; Sitting on the Starboard Tack;
Stars Are Shining; String of Pearls, A; Submarine
Fire Bridgade, The (Fighters of Flame Are We);
When the Moon Is in the Sky (Shadow Song);
Who Makes the Finest Ginger Bread?

3423 • PEARL MAIDEN, THE

Cast: Gertie Carlisle; Taylor Granville; Harry MacDonough; Carroll McComas; Thomas Whiffen

Notes: W.W. Denslow was the illustrator of the Wizard of Oz books. [1] Sheet music only. [2] Titled "Come My Dear Love" in program. Sheet music title used.

3423 • PEARL MAIDEN, THE

OPENED: 01/22/1912   Theatre: New York
Musical   Broadway: 24

Composer: Harry Auracher
Lyricist: Earle C. Anthony; Arthur F. Kales
Librettist: Earle C. Anthony; Arthur F. Kales
Director: Al Holbrook

Choreographer: James Gorman

Songs: Cloudland [2]; Coral Isle; Cruise of the Boozemobile, The; Davy Jones; Entrance of Girls [1]; Finale; I Am Lonely for You (Story of the Pearl); If One Little Girl Loves Me; King of a South Sea Isle; Look at the Package They Handed to Me; My Old Brass Band; Nothing So Soft Ever Happened to Me [2]; Our Morals Are Most Refined; Pearl Maiden, The; Salvation [2]; Taboo; Take Us 'Round the Island; That Typical, Topical, Tropical Tune; You Can Never Tell Until You Try

Cast: Jefferson De Angelis; Daisy Leon; Jerry McAuliffe; Charles Prince; Flora Zabelle

Notes: [1] Out Philadelphia 2/12/12. [2] Sheet music only.

3424 • PEASANT GIRL, THE

OPENED: 03/02/1915   Theatre: 44th Street
Musical   Broadway: 111

Composer: Oscar Nedbal
Lyricist: Harold Atteridge; Herbert Reynolds
Librettist: Edgar Smith
Producer: Messrs. Shubert
Director: J.H. Benrimo; J.C. Huffman

Choreographer: Jack Mason; **Costumes:** Melville Ellis

Songs: Advice to the Young; After the Rain-Sunshine (C: Rudolf Friml); And Dreams Come True (C: Rudolf Friml); Best Waltz of All, The [1]; Childhood Lesson; Danse Poetic (C: Rudolf Friml); Flame of Love, The (C: Rudolf Friml; L: Harold Atteridge); Game of Cards, A; Gypsy Dance; Harvest Days (C: Unknown); Heart of a Rose [2] (C: Rudolf Friml); Knock-Knock Nobody Home [3] (C: Rudolf Friml; L: Herbert Reynolds); Love Is Like a Butterfly (C: Rudolf Friml; L: Herbert Reynolds); Love Is the Reason; Love, Love Alone; Love's Awakening (C: Rudolf Friml; Oscar Nedbal); March Song [1] (C: Oscar Nedbal); Native Women; Not Dancing This Evening; On to Conquer; One and Only; Peasant Girl [1] (C: Rudolf Friml); Prosperity; That Little Lamb Was Me (Mary's Li'l Lamb) (C/L: Clifton Crawford); Wanda; When One You Love (C: Rudolf Friml; L: Harold Atteridge)

Cast: Clifton Crawford; Ernest Hare; John Charles Thomas; Emma Trentini

Notes: Titled THE BALLET GIRL in Albany when first opened out of town. [1] Out Wilmington 10/27/15. [2] Also in BROADWAY NIGHTS. [3] ASCAP/Library of Congress only.

3425 • PECK O' PICKLES

OPENED: 1912
Musical

Composer: Percy Wenrich
Lyricist: Jack Mahoney
Librettist: Frank M. Stammers
Producer: Max Dill; Clarence Kolb
Director: George Mooser

Songs: Ante-Bellum Days; I'll Build a Bungalow for Two; I'm an Honorary Member of the G.A.R.; Jack O'Lantern Moon (L: Julian Eltinge); Walpole Band, The; Waltzing Wedding Night

Cast: Max M. Dill; William Kolb

3426 • PEEK-A-BOO!

Musical   Closed out of town

Composer: Michael Zelenko
Lyricist: Michael Zelenko
Librettist: Jean Bedini
Director: Larry Ceballos

Songs: . . . ing Down the Amazon; . . . Lady's Boudoir; . . . of Harmony; . . . Song; Arrival of

Robert E. Lee; . . . Baby Blue; . . . Circus Comes to Town; Dixie Jubilee; Our Health Farm; Rube Wedding; Vanities; Village Band, The; Wedding Medley; When the Preacher Makes You Mine

Cast: Bobby Clark; Joe Cook; Paul McCullough

Notes: The program used was in bad condition so complete song titles were unavailable.

3427 • PEG (1967)

OPENED: 08/01/1967
Musical   Closed out of town

Composer: Johnny Brandon
Lyricist: Johnny Brandon
Librettist: Robert Emmett; Mike Sawyer
Producer: Shelly Gross; Lee Guber
Director: Christopher Hewett

Source: PEG O' MY HEART (Play: J. Hartley Manners); **Choreographer:** Katherine Dunham; **Costumes:** Sara Brook; **Dance Arranger:** Leslie Harnley; **Lighting Designer:** Lester Tapper; **Musical Director:** Ted Saidenberg; **Orchestrations:** Philip J. Lang; **Set Design:** Designers Circle; **Vocal Arranger:** Ted Saidenberg

Songs: All Alone; Education of Peg Ballet, The; Heavens to Betsy; It Took a Long Time; Keep that Beat; Look at Me; Madam of the Manor; Nothing Like a Friend; Right Kind of People, The; Ruined; She Touches My Heart; Sing Me Sunshine; This Is What I Give to You; What'll It Be; Where Do I Stand; Where Is Away; You Can Do It

Cast: Emory Bass; Igors Gavon; Eartha Kitt; Lawrence Weber

3428 • PEG (1983)

OPENED: 12/14/1983   Theatre: Lunt-Fontanne
Revue   Broadway: 5

Composer: Paul Horner
Lyricist: Peggy Lee
Librettist: Peggy Lee
Producer: Zev Bufman; Irv Cowan; Marge Cowan; Georgia Frontiere
Director: Robert Drivas

Costumes: Florence Klotz; **Lighting Designer:** Thomas Skelton; **Musical Director:** Larry Fallon; **Orchestrations:** Dominic Frontiere; Bill Holman;

Gordon Jenkins; Philip J. Lang; Johnny Mandel; Billy May; Leon Pendarvis; Don Sebesky; Larry Wilcox; Torrie Zito; **Set Design:** Tom H. John; **Vocal Arranger:** Ray Charles

Songs: Angels on Your Pillow; Big Spender [1] (C: Cy Coleman; L: Dorothy Fields); Daddy Was a Railroad Man; Fever [2] (C/L: Eddie Cooley; Johnny Davenport; L: Peggy Lee); Flowers and Flowers; Goody Goody [2] (C: Matt Malneck; L: Johnny Mercer); He'll Make Me Believe That He's Mine; I Don't Know Enough about You [2] (C: Dave Barbour); I Love Being Here with You [2] (C/L: Peggy Lee); I'm a Woman [2] (C/L: Jerry Leiber; Mike Stoller); Is That All There Is? [2] (C/L: Jerry Leiber; Mike Stoller); It's a Good Day [2] (C: Dave Barbour); Lover [3] (C: Richard Rodgers; L: Lorenz Hart); Mama; Manana [2] (C: Dave Barbour); No More Rainbows; One Beating a Day (C: Peggy Lee); Other Part of Me, The; Sometimes You're Up; Soul; Stay Away from Louisville Lou [2] (C: Milton Ager; L: Jack Yellen); That Old Piano; That's How I Learned to Sing the Blues; There Is More; What Did Dey Do to My Goil?; Why Don't You Do Right? [2] (C/L: Joe McCoy)

Cast: Peggy Lee

Notes: The non-Horner/Lee songs were not written for this production. [1] Not written for this show. From SWEET CHARITY. [2] Not written for this show. [3] Not written for this show. From film LOVE ME TONIGHT.

3429 • PEG (1984)

OPENED: 04/12/1984   Theatre: Phoenix
Musical   London: 146

Composer: David Heneker
Lyricist: David Heneker
Librettist: Robin Miller
Producer: Louis Busch Hager
Director: Ian Judge

Source: PEG O' MY HEART (Play: J. Hartley Manners); **Choreographer:** Sheila Falconer; **Costumes:** Peter Rice; **Lighting Designer:** Simon Tapping; **Musical Director:** Kevin Amos; **Orchestrations:** Larry Wilcox; **Set Design:** Peter Rice

Songs: Brent's Credo [1]; Come Away with Me; Ethel's Waltz; Fishing Fleet, The; Flat Broke [1];

Genuine Hall-Marked Alpha-Plus Little Brick, A;
How Would You Like Me?; I Want to Dance;
Manhattan Hometown; Matter of Minutes, A;
Peg and Jerry; Peg o' My Heart [2] (C: Fred
Fisher; L: Alfred Bryan); Pretty Dresses; Steamers
Go By, The; That's My Father; There's a Devil in
Me; Three of a Kind; When a Woman Has to
Choose; Who Needs 'Em? [1]

Cast: Edward Duke; John Hewer; David McAlister;
Patricia Michael; Ann Morrison; Sian Phillips;
Martin Smith; Julia Sutton

Notes: [1] Cut out of town, Guilford, England. [2]
Written for original play (1912).

3430 • PEG O' MINE
OPENED: 1927

Songs: For a Little While (C: Will Ortmann;
L: Desmond Carter; Raymond B. Egan; Gus
Kahn)

Notes: PEG O' MY HEART was first produced in
1926. No other information available on this
show.

3431 • PEG-O-MY-DREAMS
OPENED: 05/05/1924   Theatre: Jolson
Musical   Broadway: 32

Composer: Hugo Felix
Lyricist: Anne Caldwell
Librettist: J. Hartley Manners
Producer: Richard Herndon
Director: J. Hartley Manners

Source: PEG O' MY HEART (Play: J. Hartley
Manners); **Choreographer:** Chester Hale;
Costumes: Charles LeMaire; **Musical Director:**
Gus Salzer; **Set Design:** Clark Robinson

Songs: All Alone; Dainty Nosegay, A; Door Mats;
Finale Act I; Gap in the Hedge, The; Haven't We
Met Before?; Her Bright Shawl; Hunt Ball
Rehearsal; L'Heure Bleu Ballet; Lily Bell Polka;
Love Is Like a Firefly; Love's Young Dream;
Moscow Belles; Peg O' My Dreams; Right-O;
Rose in the Snow; Shy Little Irish Smile; There's
a Rainbow Waiting for You

Cast: Oscar Figman; Chester Hale; G.P. Huntley;
Suzanne Keener; Roy Royston

3432 • PEG O' MY HEART
OPENED: 12/20/1912   Theatre: Cort
Play   Broadway: 603

Author: J. Hartley Manners
Producer: Oliver Morosco
Director: J. Hartley Manners

Songs: Peg o' My Heart [1] (C: Fred Fisher;
L: Alfred Bryan); Valse Mauve 1912 (inst.)
(C: Rudolf Johanis)

Cast: Peter Bassett; Reginald Mason; Emile
Melville; Christine Norman; H. Reeves-Smith;
Laurette Taylor

Notes: [1] Written in 1913.

3433 • PEGGY (1911)
OPENED: 12/07/1911   Theatre: Casino
Musical   Broadway: 36

Composer: Leslie Stuart
Lyricist: C.H. Bovill
Librettist: George Grossmith Jr.
Producer: Thomas W. Ryley
Director: Ned Wayburn

Source: L'AMORCAGE (Play: Guerin; Xanroff)

Songs: Be a Lady All the Time; Come to Friville;
Danse Fascination (inst.); Fete, The; Go Away,
Little Girl — Go Back to School; I Beg Your
Pardon; Juliet and Romeo; Ladies, Beware
(When the Lights Are Low) (L: C.H. Bovill;
Leslie Stuart); Lass with the Lasso, The; New
Hotel, the New Hotel, The (Opening Chorus);
Off We Go, the Festive Four of Us; Oh, Friville,
Friville, frivolous and Gay (Opening Act II); Oh,
Uncle Monty, Uncle Monty! (Finale Act II);
Peggy; Pierrot and Pierrette; Three Little
Pebbles; Tomorrow's My Big Day; Uncle Monty;
Whistle and the Girls Come Round; Who Is That
Person Over There? (Finale Act I); With My
Well-Trimmed Moustache; You're the One Man
I'm Looking For

Cast: Gertrude Bryan; Tom Dingle; Otis Harlan;
Maude Odell; John W. Ransome; Florence
Walton; Alva York

Notes: No program available. Songs from British
vocal score.

3434 • PEGGY (1921)

OPENED: 1921
Musical   Closed out of town

Composer: Lou Dymond
Lyricist: Fred Caryll
Librettist: Fred Caryll
Producer: Mack Hilliard; Savoy Producing
  Cooperative
Director: Neil Twomey

Choreographer: Allan K. Foster; **Musical Director:**
  Lou Dymond; **Set Design:** Joseph Physioc

Songs: Dream Boat; Eight Little Daughters;
  Fantasy; In the Morning; Kiss Trot; On Fifth
  Avenue; Opening Chorus; Peggy O' Mine;
  Saturday Evening Post; Specialty Dance; Tony;
  Wall Street Zoo; Wonderful Hindoo

Cast: Virginia Eastman; "Skeets" Gallagher; Russell
  Mack; James C. Morton; Lenora Novasio;
  Virginia O'Brien

Notes: Program Atlantic City 1/6/21.

3435 • PEGGY (1926)

Notes: *See PEGGY-ANN.*

3436 • PEGGY-ANN

OPENED: 12/27/1926   Theatre: Vanderbilt
Musical   Broadway: 354

Composer: Richard Rodgers
Lyricist: Lorenz Hart
Librettist: Herbert Fields
Producer: Lyle D. Andrews; Lew Fields
Director: Robert Milton

Source: TILLIE'S NIGHTMARE (Musical:
  A. Baldwin Sloane; Edgar Smith);
  Choreographer: Seymour Felix; **Costumes:** Mark
  Mooring; **Musical Director:** Roy Webb;
  Orchestrations: Roy Webb; **Set Design:** Clark
  Robinson

Songs: Charming, Charming (Store Opening);
  Chuck It!; Come and Tell Me [2]; Give This Little
  Girl a Hand (Give That Little Girl a Hand);
  Havana (Havana Opening); Hello!; Howdy,
  London [4]; Howdy to Broadway; I'm So Humble
  (Inferiority Complex) [1]; In His Arms [1]; Little
  Birdie Told Me So, A; Maybe It's Me [3]; Paris Is

Really Divine [1]; Peggy (Oh You Peggy) (The
  Race) [5]; Pipes of Pansy, The [6]; Trampin'
  Along [2]; Tree in the Park, A; We Pirates from
  Weehawken; Wedding Procession (Finale Act I);
  Where's That Rainbow?

Cast: Lester Cole; Helen Ford; Lulu McConnell;
  Edith Meiser; Harold Mellish; Fuller Mellish Jr.;
  Betty Starbuck

Notes: Titled PEGGY out of town prior to New
  York. [1] Cut after opening. [2] Cut prior to
  opening. [3] Also in FIFTH AVENUE FOLLIES.
  [4] Same song as "Howdy to Broadway" but
  changed for London production. [5] Possibly
  added after opening. [6] Not used in this show,
  DEAREST ENEMY, THE GIRL FRIEND or
  SHE'S MY BABY.

3437 • PEGGY FROM PARIS

OPENED: 09/10/1903   Theatre: Wallack
Musical   Broadway: 85

Composer: William Lorraine; J.A. Raynes
Lyricist: George Ade
Librettist: George Ade
Producer: Henry W. Savage
Director: George Marion; Frank Tannerhill Jr

Set Design: Walter Burridge; Edward LaMoss

Songs: Art (C: William Lorraine); Autograph
  Gals' Song; Chappies Song; Come to the Club
  To-night (C: William Lorraine); Dear Old Farm
  (C: William Lorraine); Finale Act I; Finale Act I
  Scene 1; Gay Fleurette (C: William Lorraine);
  Girl who Comes from the West, The (C: William
  Lorraine); Happy Happy Illinois (C: William
  Lorraine); Henny (C: William Lorraine);
  Hifalutin' Music (C: William Lorraine); I Left
  My Heart in Dixie; I Like You Lil, for Fair;
  Imported Yes We Are; Janitor, The (King
  Janitoro) (C: William Lorraine); Lunita
  (C: William Lorraine); My Emmaleen; Old
  Fashioned Songs; Paree, I Love but Thee;
  Regular Limited Train, The; Sweet Married Life!
  (C: William Lorraine); We Are the Principals;
  We're True to the College Days (C: William
  Lorraine; L: William D. Nesbit); Welcome
  Chorus; When He's Not Near (C: William
  Lorraine); When This You See [1]

Cast: Georgia Caine; Arthur Deagon; Helen Hale;
  John Park; Josie Sadler

Notes: Out of town additional music was credited to John J. Braham. Vocal score only credits Loraine with music! [1] Out Trenton 3/25/05.

3438 • PENNY BY PENNY
Notes: *See A CHRISTMAS CAROL.*

3439 • PENNY FRIEND, THE
OPENED: 12/26/1966   Theatre: Stage 73
Musical   Off-Broadway: 32

Composer: William Roy
Lyricist: William Roy
Librettist: William Roy
Producer: Thomas Hammond
Director: Benno D. Frank

Source: KISS FOR CINDERELLA, A (Play: James M. Barrie); **Choreographer:** Lou Kristofer; **Lighting Designer:** Robert L. Steele; **Set Design:** Ben Shecter

Songs: Diagnostician, The; Feet; Grand Parade, The; Great Unknown, The; How Doth the Apple Butterfly; I Am Going to Dance; Mrs. Bodie; Penny Friend, The; She Makes You Think of Home; Time We Were Dancing; Utterly Delicious; Very Full and Productive Day, A; Who Am I, Who Are You, Who Are We?; Won't You Come to the Party; World Today, The

Cast: Georgia Creighton; Bill Drew; Charlotte Fairchild; Bernadette Peters; Jamie Ross; Michael Wager

3440 • PEOPLE IS THE THING THE WORLD IS FULLEST OF
OPENED: 2/20/1967   Theatre: Bil Baird
Musical   Off-Broadway

Songs: Cachita (inst.) (C: Rafael Hernandez); Conformity (C: Bil Baird; Alvy West); Dance of Scheherezade (inst.) (C: Bil Baird; Alvy West); Opera (C/L: Unknown); People (C: Buster Davis; L: Divers Hands); Population Explosion (L: Divers Hands); Social Notes (C/L: Divers Hands); Vivian Beaumont Song (C: Divers Hands)

Notes: No program available.

3441 • PEPPER MILL
OPENED: 01/05/1937   Theatre: Chanin
                              Auditorium
Musical   Off-Broadway: 6

Composer: Magnus Henning
Lyricist: John Latouche; Erika Mann
Librettist: W.H. Auden; Erika Mann; Klaus Mann; Erich Muhsam; Ernst Toller
Adaptation: Edwin Denby; John Latouche
Producer: Columbia Concerts Corp.; F.C. Coppicus
Director: Theodore Giehse

Musical Director: Magnus Henning; **Set Design:** Anton Refregier

Songs: Children's Song (L: Erika Mann); Cold (L: Erika Mann); Demagogue (C: Aaron Copland; L: W.H. Auden; Ernst Toller); Doctor's Orders; Especially for Mr. Winterbottom; Famous People of the Week (L: Edwin Denby; Erika Mann; Klaus Mann); Gangster of the Puppet Show, The; Little Revolutionary, The (C: Werner Kruse; L: John Latouche; Erich Muhsam); Lorelei, The (L: John Latouche; Klaus Mann); Ski Teacher, The (C: Peter Kreuder; L: Erika Mann; Klaus Mann); Spies (C: Herbert Murril; L: W.H. Auden; Ernst Toller); Stupidity Talks; Yodeler, The

Cast: Therese Giehse; Lotte Goslar; John Latouche; Wallace Rooney; Sybille Schloss

3442 • PERFECT
OPENED: 1936
Musical

Composer: Francis K. Shuman
Lyricist: Jules Loman; Allan Roberts

Songs: Are You Thrilling; Beating the Groom Bay; Boy Meets Girl; Give Me a Martial Air; I'm Clay in Your Hands; Wiggly-Woggly-Walk, The; With a Dollar in Your Pocket; You're a Standout

Notes: No other information available.

3443 • PERFECT FOOL, THE
OPENED: 11/07/1921   Theatre: George M.
                              Cohan
Musical   Broadway: 275

Composer: Ed Wynn
Lyricist: Ed Wynn
Librettist: Ed Wynn
Producer: B.C. Whitney
Director: Julian Mitchell

Costumes: Ada Fields; Cora MacGeachy; Albertine Randall Wheelan; **Lighting Designer:** Tony Greshoff; **Musical Director:** Antonio Bafunno

Songs: Daisy [1]; Days of Romance; Doll House, A (L: Lou Davis; Harry Richman); Girls Pretty Girls; My Garden of Perfumes; My Log-Cabin Home (C: George Gershwin; L: Irving Caesar; B.G. DeSylva); No One Else But that Girl of Mine (C: George Gershwin; L: Irving Caesar); Old Home Week; She Loves Me, She Loves Me Not; Sweetheart, Answer You (C: Rolf Piquel; L. James Brennan; Al Wilson); Typewriter Song, The; Visions That Pass in the Night

Cast: Guy Robertson; Janet Velie; Ed Wynn

Notes: No New York program available. Brooklyn 4/23/23 program used. [1] Sheet music only.

3444 • PERFECTLY FRANK

OPENED: 11/30/1980   Theatre: Helen Hayes
Revue   Broadway: 16

Composer: Frank Loesser
Lyricist: Frank Loesser
Librettist: Kenny Solms
Producer: Fred Levinson; Gladys Rackmil
Director: Fritz Holt

Choreographer: Tony Stevens; **Costumes:** John Falabella; **Dance Arranger:** Ronald Melrose; **Lighting Designer:** Ken Billington; **Musical Director:** Yolanda Segovia; **Orchestrations:** Bill Byers; **Set Design:** John Falabella

Songs: Adelaide's Lament [17]; Anywhere I Wander [19]; Baby, It's Cold Outside [20]; Big D [22]; Blame It on the Danube [32] (C: Harry Akst); Boys in the Back Room, The [6] (C: Frederick Hollander); Brotherhood of Man [15]; Bubbles in the Wine (C: Lawrence Welk); Bushel and a Peck, A [17]; Can't Get Out of This Mood [24] (C: Jimmy McHugh); Can't Stop Talking [29]; Dachshund in a Dusenberg, A [30]; Dancing on a Dime [34] (C: Burton Lane); Dolores [25] (C: Louis Alter); Duck, The; Fugue for Tinhorns [17]; Guys and Dolls [17]; Happy to

Keep His Dinner Warm [15]; Happy to Make You Acquantance [28]; Heart and Soul (C: Hoagy Carmichael); Hoop-Dee-Doo (C: Milton De Lugg); How'dja Like to Love Me [21] (C: Burton Lane); I Believe in You [15]; I Don't Know (The Letter) [22]; I Don't Want to Walk Without You [9] (C: Jule Styne); I Hear Music [2] (C: Burton Lane); I Like Everybody [22]; I Wish I Didn't Love You So [11]; If I Were a Bell [17]; Inchworm, The [27]; I've Never Been in Love Before [17]; (I Got Spurs That) Jingle Jangle Jingle (C: Joseph J. Lilley); Joey, Joey, Joey [28]; Junk Man (C: Joseph Meyer); Kiss the Boys Goodbye [3] (C: Victor Schertzinger); Lady's in Love with You, The [8] (C: Burton Lane); Like a Woman Loves a Man [22]; Luck Be a Lady [17]; Make a Miracle [16]; Marry the Man Today [17]; Mexican Magic [33] (C: Harry Revel); Moon of Manakoora, The [5] (C: Alfred Newman); More I Cannot Wish You [17]; Murder, He Says [7] (C: Jimmy McHugh); My Darling, My Darling [16]; My Heart Is So Full of You [22]; My Time of Day [17]; Never Will I Marry [23]; New Ashmolean Marching Society and Students Conservatory Band, The [16]; No Two People [19]; (Where Are You) Now That I Need You [12]; On a Slow Boat to China; Once in Love with Amy [16]; One Little WAC [31] (C: Eddie Dunstedter); Ooh, My Feet [22]; Praise the Lord and Pass the Ammunition; Rosabella [22]; Roseanna [10]; Rumble, Rumble, Rumble [11]; Sand in My Shoes [3] (C: Victor Schertzinger); Sing a Tropical Song [7] (C: Jimmy McHugh); Sit Down You're Rockin' the Boat [17]; Small Fry [26] (C: Hoagy Carmichael); Snug As a Bug in a Rug [4] (C: Matty Malneck); Some Like It Hot [8] (C: Remo Biondi; Gene Krupa); Somebody Somewhere [22]; Sposalizio [22]; Spring Will Be a Little Late this Year [14]; Standing on the Corner [22]; Take Back Your Mink [17]; They're Either Too Young or Too Old [13] (C: Arthur Schwartz); Three Cornered Tune [1]; Two Sleepy People [18] (C: Hoagy Carmichael); Warm All Over [22]; What Are You Doing New Year's Eve; What Do You Do in the Infantry; Why Do They Call a Private a Private? [30] (C: Peter Lind Hayes); Wonderful Copenhagen [27]

Cast: Andra Akers; Wayne Cilento; Jill Cook; Don Correia; David Holliday; David Ruprecht; Virginia Sandifur; Debbie Shapiro; Jo Sullivan; Jim Walton

Notes: No original songs in this production. Most of these songs were in medleys. [1] Cut from GUYS AND DOLLS. [2] From the film

DANCING ON A DIME. [3] From the film KISS THE BOYS GOODBYE. [4] From the film THE GRACIE ALLEN MURDER CASE. [5] From the film THE HURRICANE. [6] From the film DESTRY RIDES AGAIN. [7] From the film HAPPY GO LUCKY. [8] From the film SOME LIKE IT HOT. [9] From the film SWEATER GIRL. [10] From the film ROSEANNA MCCOY. [11] From the film PERILS OF PAULINE. [12] From the film RED, HOT AND BLUE. [13] From the film THANK YOUR LUCKY STARS. [14] From the film CHRISTMAS HOLIDAY. [15] From HOW TO SUCCEED IN BUSINESS WITHOUT REALLY TRYING. [16] From WHERE'S CHARLEY? [17] From GUYS AND DOLLS. [18] From the film THANKS FOR THE MEMORY. [19] From the film HANS CHRISTIAN ANDERSEN. [20] From the film NEPTUNE'S DAUGHTER. [21] From the film COLLEGE SWING. [22] From THE MOST HAPPY FELLA. [23] From GREENWILLOW. [24] From the film SEVEN DAYS LEAVE. [25] From the film LAS VEGAS NIGHTS. [26] From the film SING YOU SINNERS. [27] Cut out of town. From the film HANS CHRISTIAN ANDERSEN. [28] Cut out of town. From THE MOST HAPPY FELLA. [29] Cut out of town. From the film LET'S DANCE. [30] Cut out of town. [31] Cut out of town. From ABOUT FACE! [32] Cut out of town. From the film FIGHT FOR YOUR LADY. [33] Cut out of town. From the film MOON OVER BURMA. [34] Cut out of town. From the film DANCING ON A DIME.

3445 • PERSECUTION AND ASSASSINATION OF JEAN-PAUL MARAT AS PERFORMED BY THE INMATES OF THE ASYLUM OF CHARENTON UNDER THE DIRECTION OF THE MARQUIS DE SADE, THE

OPENED: 12/27/1965   Theatre: Martin Beck
Play   Broadway: 145

Composer: Richard Peaslee
Lyricist: Peter Weiss
Author: Peter Weiss
Adaptation: Adrian Mitchell
Translator: Geoffrey Skelton
Producer: David Merrick
Director: Peter Brook

Choreographer: Malcolm Goddard; **Costumes:** Gunilla Plamstierna-Weiss; **Lighting Designer:** David Read; **Set Design:** Sally Jacobs

Songs: Copulation Round; Corday Waltz; Fifteen Glorious Years; Finale; Homage to Marat; Marat We're Poor; Marat's Nightmare; Old Song, The; One Day It Will Come to Pass; People's Reaction; Poor Marat in Your Bathtub Seat; Poor Old Marat; Royal Anthem; Song and Mime of Corday's Arrival in Paris; Those Fat Monkeys; Tumbrel Song, The

Cast: Glenda Jackson; Patrick Magee; Ian Richardson

3446 • PERSIAN GARDEN, A

OPENED: 1912
Musical   Closed out of town

Composer: Anatole Friedland
Lyricist: Edgar Allen Woolf
Librettist: Edgar Allen Woolf
Director: Edgar Allen Woolf

Songs: Girl on the Persian Rug, The; Little Persian Rug, The; Who Sent Those Persian Plums

Cast: Bessie Cottrell; John Linn; Helen May

Notes: Program Milwaukee 12/9/12. A one-act vaudeville musical.

3447 • PERSONALITIES, THE

OPENED: 06/1950
Revue   Nightclub

Composer: Billy Barnes
Lyricist: Billy Barnes

Cast: Billy Barnes

Notes: Presented at the Chi-Chi, Palm Springs, California.

3448 • PERSONALS

OPENED: 11/24/1985   Theatre: Minetta Lane
Revue   Off-Broadway: 265

Lyricist: David Crane; Seth Friedman; Marta Kauffman
Librettist: David Crane; Seth Friedman; Marta Kauffman

Producer: John-Edward Hill; Arthur MacKenzie; Jon D. Silverman
Director: Paul Lazarus

Choreographer: D.J. Giagni; **Costumes:** Ann Hould-Ward; **Lighting Designer:** Richard Nelson; **Musical Director:** Michael Skloff; **Orchestrations:** Steven Oirich; **Set Design:** Loren Sherman; **Vocal Arranger:** Michael Skloff

Songs: After School Special (C: William Dreskin); Guy I Love, The (C: William Dreskin); I Could Always Go to You (C: Alan Menken); I Think You Should Know (C: Joel Phillip Friedman; Seth Friedman); I'd Rather Dance Alone (C: Alan Menken); Imagine My Surprise (C: William Dreskin); Little Happiness, A (C: Joel Phillip Friedman; Seth Friedman); Mama's Boys (C: Joel Phillip Friedman; Seth Friedman); Michael (C: William Dreskin); Moving in With Linda (C: Stephen Schwartz); Mr. Potato Head [1] (C: William Dreskin); Night Alone, A (C: Michael Skloff); Nothing to Do with Love (C: Stephen Schwartz); Or More [1] (C: William Dreskin); Picking Up the Pieces (C: Joel Phillip Friedman; Seth Friedman); Second Grade (C: Michael Skloff); Some Things Don't End (C: Stephen Schwartz)

Cast: Jason Alexander; Laura Dean; Dee Hoty; Jeff Keller; Nancy Opel; Trey Wilson

Notes: [1] Cut.

3449 • PETER AND THE WOLF
OPENED: 12/06/1974   Theatre: Bil Baird
Musical   Off-Broadway: 77

Music Based On: Serge Prokofiev
Composer: Paul Weston
Lyricist: Ogden Nash
Librettist: A.J. Russell
Producer: American Puppet Arts Council; Bil Baird
Director: Paul Leaf

Lighting Designer: Carl Harms; **Musical Director:** Alvy West; **Set Design:** Bil Baird; **Vocal Arranger:** Alvy West

Voice: George S. Irving; William Tost; **Puppeteer:** Peter Baird; Rebecca Bondor; Mary Case; Tim Dobbins; Olga Felgemacher; Steve Hansen; Bill Tost; Steve Wilderman

Notes: Assistant to Paul Weston was Sheldon Harnick (who was credited as colyricist for TV version). *See also ART CARNEY MEETS PETER AND THE WOLF.*

3450 • PETER PAN (1905)
OPENED: 11/06/1905   Theatre: Empire
Play   Broadway: 223

Composer: James Crook
Lyricist: James M. Barrie
Author: James M. Barrie

Set Design: Ernest Gros

Songs: God Save the King [1] (C/L: Henry Carey; C: D. Thomas Bull); Golden Slumbers (L: Thomas Dekker); I Wish I Had a Darling House; John Anderson, My Jo John [1] (C: Traditional; L: Robert Burns); Lagoon Scene; Lass of Richmond Hill [1] (C: James Hook; L: Leonard McNally); Mermaid's Tail, The; Rule Britannia [1] (C: Thomas Arne; L: David Mallet; James Thompson); Sally in the Alley [1] (C/L: Henry Carey; L: James M. Barrie); Shadow March, The [1] (C: James M. Barrie; L: Robert Louis Stevenson); Song of the Pirates (Avast Belay!), The; Watch on the Rhine [1] (C/L: Carl Wilhelm); Won't You Have a Little Feather? [2] (C: Jerome Kern; L: Paul West)

Cast: Maude Adams; Margaret Gordon; Ernest Lawford; Thomas McGrath; Martha McGraw; Mildred Morris; Walter Robinson; Charles H. Weston; Jane Wren

Notes: [1] Not written for show. [2] Added to tour in 1907.

3451 • PETER PAN (1924)
OPENED: 11/06/1924   Theatre: Knickerbocker
Play   Broadway: 120

Composer: Jerome Kern
Author: James M. Barrie
Producer: Charles Dillingham
Director: Basil Dean

Songs: Sweetest Thing in Life [1] (L: B.G. DeSylva); Won't You Have a Little Feather (L: Paul West)

Cast: Leslie Banks; Anne Delafield; Charles Eaton; Jack Grattan; Dorothy Hope; Marilyn Miller; Tandy; Jane Wren

Notes: [1] Same music as "When Three Is Company" in THE DOLL GIRL and "Just Because You're You" in ZIEGFELD FOLLIES OF 1917.

3452 • PETER PAN (1950)

OPENED: 04/24/1950   Theatre: Imperial
Musical   Broadway: 321

Composer: Leonard Bernstein
Lyricist: Leonard Bernstein
Librettist: James M. Barrie
Producer: Peter Lawrence; Roger L. Stevens
Director: John Burrell

Source: PETER PAN (Play: James M. Barrie);
Costumes: Motley; **Dance Arranger:** Trude Rittman; **Lighting Designer:** Ralph Alswang; **Musical Director:** Ben Steinberg; **Orchestrations:** Hershy Kay; **Set Design:** Ralph Alswang; **Vocal Arranger:** Trude Rittman

Songs: Captain Hook's Soliloquy [1]; Dream with Me [1] (L: Leonard Bernstein; Betty Comden; Adolph Green); Hallapalooza [2]; My House; Never Land; Peter, Peter; Pirate Song, The; Plank, The; Who Am I?

Cast: Jean Arthur; Marcia Henderson; Peg Hillias; Boris Karloff; Joe E. Marks; Nehemiah Persoff; Norman Shelly

Notes: [1] Cut from show prior to opening. [2] Cut from show prior to opening. Later titled "Lallapalooza" and cut from WONDERFUL TOWN.

3453 • PETER PAN (1954)

OPENED: 10/20/1954   Theatre: Winter Garden
Musical   Broadway: 154

Composer: Moose Charlap
Lyricist: Carolyn Leigh
Librettist: James M. Barrie
Producer: Richard Halliday; Edwin Lester
Director: Jerome Robbins

Source: PETER PAN (Play: James M. Barrie);
Choreographer: Jerome Robbins; **Costumes:** Motley; **Dance Arranger:** Trude Rittman; **Incidental Music:** Elmer Bernstein; Trude Rittman; **Lighting Designer:** Peggy Clark; **Musical Director:** Louis Adrian; **Orchestrations:** Albert Sendry; **Set Design:** Peter Larkin

Songs: Another Princely Scheme (Tarantella); Be Our Mother [1]; Be Our Parents [5]; Beware of the Boy with His Mind Made Up [7]; Big Battle, The [5]; Captain Hook's Waltz (C: Jule Styne; L: Betty Comden; Adolph Green); Capturing the Boys and Wendy [5]; Death of Tinker Bell [5]; Distant Melody (C: Jule Styne; L: Betty Comden; Adoph Green); Dressing Up [5]; Echo Song [7]; First Impression [6]; Happily Ever After [4] (C: Jule Styne; L: Betty Comden; Adolph Green); Happy Is the Boy [2]; Hook's Entrance Song [7]; Hook's Hook [3] (C: Jule Styne; L: Tom Adair); Hook's Tarantella [7] (C: Trude Rittman); I Won't Grow Up; I'm Flying; I'm Hook [2] (L: Roger Adams); Indians; Indians Are About [5]; Introduction to Neverland [5]; It's What You Believe In [2]; I've Gotta Crow; Mysterious Lady (C: Jule Styne; L: Betty Comden; Adolph Green); Never Land [2]; Never Never Land (C: Jule Styne; L: Betty Comden; Adoph Green); Now It's Hook or Me [5]; Old Gavotte, The [1] (C: Morgan Lewis; L: Nancy Hamilton); Parade, The [2]; Pirate Song; Poisoning Peter's Medicine [5]; Pow Wow, The [2]; Pow-Wow Polka, The (dance) (C: Jule Styne); Princely Scheme (Hook's Tango), A (C: Trude Rittman; L: Carolyn Leigh); Remember Me [5]; Saturday Night Polka [1]; Soliloquy and Song [5]; Storm, The [5]; Tag [2] (C: Jule Styne; L: Betty Comden; Adolph Green); Tender Shepherd; This Time It's Hook or Me [7]; Today I Went Adventuring [5]; Ugg-a-Wugg (C: Jule Styne; L: Betty Comden; Adolph Green); Wendy (C: Jule Styne; L: Betty Comden; Adolph Green); When I Went Home [2]; Who Are You [5]; Whole Long Year from Today, A [7]; Wild Indians [7]; Youth, Joy and Freedom [3] (C: Jule Styne; L: Tom Adair)

Cast: Margalo Gilmore; Heller Halliday; Robert Harrington; Sondra Lee; Joe E. Marks; Mary Martin; Kathy Nolan; Cyril Ritchard; Norman Shelly; Joseph Stafford; Joan Tewkesbury

Notes: [1] Out L.A. Civic Light Opera production tryout. [2] Not in programs. [3] Added to touring production 1973. [4] Cut from 1979 revival. [5] Only in first draft. [6] Not used. [7] ASCAP/Library of Congress.

3454 • PETER PAN (1976)

OPENED: 12/12/1976   Theatre: NBC
TV Musical

Composer: Leslie Bricusse; Anthony Newley

Lyricist: Leslie Bricusse; Anthony Newley
Librettist: Andrew Birkin; Jack Burns
Producer: Dwight Hemion; Gary Smith
Director: Dwight Hemion

Source: PETER PAN (Play: James M. Barrie);
Conductor: Jack Parnell; **Musical Director:** Ian
Fraser

Songs: By Hook or By Crook; Fly!; Growing Up;
Happiness Hill; I'm Better with You Than
without You; Little Jesus/Little Light; Mothers;
Never Never Land; Once Upon a Bedtime; Once
Upon a Time; Peter Pan; Pretending; Rotter's
Hall of Fame, The; Song Called Love, A; They
Don't Make 'Em Like That Anymore

Narrator: Sir John Gielgud; **Cast:** Mia Farrow; Jill
Gascoine; Danny Kaye; Paula Kelly; Virginia
McKenna; Briony McRoberts; Ian Sharrock;
Adam Stafford

Notes: No song list available.

3455 • PETER PENNY UNDER THE DREAM TREE

OPENED: 1939
Musical

Composer: F.D. Ballard; James F. Hanley
Lyricist: F.D. Ballard; James F. Hanley

Songs: Under the Dream Tree; War Song

Notes: No other information available.

3456 • PETRIFIED PRINCE, THE

OPENED: 12/18/1994   Theatre: Public
Musical   Off-Broadway

Composer: Michael John LaChiusa
Lyricist: Michael John LaChiusa
Librettist: Edward Gallardo
Producer: N.Y. Shakespeare Festival
Director: Harold Prince

Source: UNKNOWN (Screenplay: Ingmar
Bergman); **Arrangements:** Jason Robert Brown;
Choreographer: Rob Marshall; **Costumes:** Judith
Dolan; **Lighting Designer:** Howell Binkley;
Musical Director: Jason Robert Brown;
Orchestrations: Jonathan Tunick; **Set Design:**
James Youmans

Songs: Abbe's Appearance; Addio, Bambino;
Animal Song, The; Dormez-Vous; Easy Life, The;
Fernando's Suicide; His Family Tree; I Would
Like to Say; Look Closer, Love; Move;
Napoleon's Nightmare; Never Can Tell; One
Little Taste; Pointy's Lament; Samson's
Epiphany; Samson's Thoughts; Stay; There Are
Happy Endings; What the Prince Is Saying;
Without Me; Woman in Search of Happiness, A

Cast: Loni Ackerman; Gabriel Barre; Alan
Braunstein; Candy Buckley; Ralph Byers;
Marilyn Cooper; Wendy Edmead; Alexander
Gaberman; Timothy Jerome; Mal Z. Lawrence;
Darren Lee; Daisy Prince; Jane White

3457 • PETTICOAT FEVER

OPENED: 03/04/1935   Theatre: Ritz
Play   Broadway: 137

Composer: Frederick Loewe
Lyricist: Irene Alexander
Author: Mark Reed
Producer: Richard Aldrich; Alfred DeLiagre Jr.
Director: Albert Bannister

Set Design: Robert Barnhart

Songs: Love Tiptoed Through My Heart;
Something to Remember [1] (C: Karl Vacek;
L: Billy Hill)

Cast: Dennis King; Oscar Shaw

Notes: [1] Sheet music only.

3458 • PETTICOAT LANE
Notes: See KING OF THE SCHNORRERS.

3459 • PETTINESS OF MYSOGYNY, THE
Notes: See MARCH OF THE FALSETTOS.

3460 • PFC MARY BROWN

OPENED: 1944
Revue

Composer: Unknown
Lyricist: Unknown

Songs: Come On Honey; First Class Private Mary
Brown [1] (C/L: Frank Loesser); Lonely M.P.;

Lost in a Cloud of Blue; New Style Bonnet; Something New; Twenty Five Words or Less; WAC Hymn, The (C/L: Frank Loesser)

Cast: Arnold Auerbach

Notes: No program available of this Army Show. Music and lyrics "Mostly by Frank Loesser" but not credited in script. [1] From ABOUT FACE!

3461 • PHANTOM OF THE COUNTRY PALACE, THE

OPENED: 06/22/1994
Musical   Closed out of town

Composer: Michael Duff
Lyricist: Cheri Coons
Librettist: Sean Grennan; Kathy Santen
Director: Joe Leonardo

Choreographer: Mark S. Hoebee; **Costumes:** Nancy Missimi; **Lighting Designer:** Diane Ferry Williams; **Musical Director:** Patti Garwood; **Orchestrations:** David Siegel; **Set Design:** Thomas M. Ryan

Songs: Antonio's Telegram; Calling Me Home; Country Music Is My Home; Did You Want to Hear a Country Tune?; Does Your Daddy Know You Like to Kiss the Cowboys?; For Better, For Worse; Ghost Town; God Save Our Glorious Queen; Hog-Butcher's Daughter; If I Could Hold You; La Forza del Vino et Morte; Maybe When You're Older; Missin' Men; Mort's Telegram; Night of Terror; Open Door, An; Someone Is Calling Me Home; Train of Adolescence; Two Roads Meet

Cast: Evans Colton; Don Forston; Jamie Dawn Gangi; Carlton Miller; Christopher Wals; Gene Weygandt

Notes: Marriott's Lincolnshire Theatre, Chicago.

3462 • PHANTOM OF THE OPERA, THE (1984)

OPENED: 1984   Theatre: Theatre Royal
                                    Stratford East
Musical   London

Lyricist: Ken Hill
Librettist: Ken Hill

Source: PHANTOM OF THE OPERA, THE (Novel: Gaston Leroux)

Notes: Played the Theatre Royal, Stratford East in London in 1984. It then opened at the St. Louis Repertory Theatre in 1986. It also played an extended tour of the United States. Music based on previously written compositions. No original songs in this show.

3463 • PHANTOM OF THE OPERA, THE (1986)

OPENED: 04/19/1986
Musical   Closed out of town

Composer: David Bishop
Lyricist: Kathleen Masterson
Librettist: Kathleen Masterson
Director: Peter H. Clough

Source: PHANTOM OF THE OPERA, THE (Novel: Gaston Leroux); **Costumes:** Lloyd K. Waiwaiole; **Lighting Designer:** Dale F. Jordon; **Musical Director:** Hank Levy; **Set Design:** Dale F. Jordon

Songs: Call, The; Christina's Room; Cro-Ack; Dreams of 1897; Everything Serves Its Purpose; Explorers and Angels; Faust Finale; Finding the Door; Gabrielle's Dream; In Another Life; It Happens When I See You; It's a Ghost!; Journey Underground; Lesson Five; Lesson One; Little More Champagne, A; Masked Ball; Mirages; On the Music; Ordinary Life; Second Journey, The; Singing Lessons; Siren's Song; Violin in the Graveyard

Cast: John Barone; Al DeCristo; Joseph Kolinski; Yvette de Botton

Notes: Capital Repertory Co., Albany, N.Y.

3464 • PHANTOM OF THE OPERA, THE (1988)

OPENED: 01/26/1988   Theatre: Majestic
Musical   Broadway

Composer: Andrew Lloyd Webber
Lyricist: Charles Hart; Richard Stilgoe
Librettist: Andrew Lloyd Webber; Richard Stilgoe
Producer: Cameron Mackintosh; Really Useful Company, The
Director: Harold Prince

Source: PHANTOM OF THE OPERA, THE (Novel: Gaston Leroux); **Choreographer:** Gillian Lynne; **Lighting Designer:** Andrew Bridge; **Musical Director:** David Caddick; **Orchestrations:** David

Cullen; Andrew Lloyd Webber; **Set Design:** Maria Bjornson

Songs: All I Ask of You; Angel of Music; Bravo, Bravo; Down Once More; I Remember; Little Lotte; Magical Lasso; Masquerade; Music of the Night, The; Notes; Phantom of the Opera, The (L: Mike Batt; Charles Hart; Richard Stilgoe); Point of No Return, The; Poor Fool, He Makes Me Laugh; Prima Donna; Raoul, I've Been There; Stranger Than You Dreamt It; Think of Me; Track Down This Murderer; Twisted Every Way; Wandering Child; Why Have You Brought Me Here; Why So Silent; Wishing You Were Somehow Here Again

Cast: George Lee Andrews; Steve Barton; Sarah Brightman; Patti Cohenour; Michael Crawford; Cris Groenendaal; Jan Horvath; Judy Kaye; Rebecca Luker; Leila Martin; Nicholas Wyman

Notes: Still running at time of publication.

3465 • PHANTOM OF THE OPERA, THE (1991)
OPENED: 1991
Musical

Composer: Maury Yeston
Lyricist: Maury Yeston
Librettist: Arthur Kopit

Source: PHANTOM OF THE OPERA, THE (Novel: Gaston Leroux)

Songs: As You Would Love Paree; Christine's Obligato; Dressing for the Night; Home; Melodie de Paris; Music Lessons, The; My Mother Bore Me; My True Love; Paree Is a Lark; Paris Is a Tomb; Phantom Fugue; Sing; This Place Is Mine; Where in the World; Who Could Ever Have Dreamed Up You; Without Your Music; You Are Music; You Are My Own

Notes: Though written before the Lloyd Webber version this was produced after.

3466 • PHI PHI (1921)
OPENED: 10/1921
Musical   Closed out of town

Composer: Henri Christine
Lyricist: E. Ray Goetz

Librettist: Henry Wagstaff Gribble; Glen MacDonough
Director: W.H. Gilmore

Source: PHI PHI (Musical: Henri Christine; Fabien Sollar; Albert Willemetz)

Songs: Ballet-Pantomime (C: Arthur H. Gutman); Chant, Dance and Prayer to Venus; Chorus of Models; Finale; Grecian Skies; Hubby, the Wifey, the Sweetie and the Vamp, The; I Don't Know How You Do It; If You Can't Be Good, Be Careful; In Athens; In May and June; Just a Tiny Cup of Tea; Love Lives in Dreams; Opening Chorus; Passing Centuries, The; Personality; Princess Charming; Two Little Bits of Greece; When They're Petite; Where Are the Days; Why Is Love

Cast: Irving Beebe; Helen Broderick; Frank Doane; Frank Lalor; Maude Odell; Frances White; Robert Woolsey

Notes: Program of the Globe Theatre, Atlantic City.

3467 • PHI-PHI (1922)
OPENED: 08/16/1922   Theatre: London Pavilion
Revue   London

Composer: Henri Christine
Lyricist: Clifford Grey
Librettist: Fred Thompson
Producer: Charles B. Cochran
Director: Edward Dolly

Choreographer: Edward Dolly; Dolly Sisters; **Costumes:** Edward Dulac; **Musical Director:** I.A. de Orellana; **Set Design:** Edward Dulac

Songs: Ragtime Pipes of Pan [1] (C/L: Cole Porter)

Cast: Vera Freeman; Jay Laurier; Evalyn Laye; Stanley Lupino; Alice O'Day; Arthur Roberts; Arthur Treacher; Clifton Webb; Walter Williams

Notes: No program available. [1] Later in THE GREENWICH VILLAGE FOLLIES (1924) as "Syncopated Pipes of Pan."

3468 • PHILADELPHIA STORY, THE
OPENED: 11/14/1980   Theatre: Lincoln Center
Play   Broadway: 60

Composer: Claibe Richardson
Lyricist: Claibe Richardson
Author: Philip Barry
Producer: Lincoln Center Theater
Director: Ellis Rabb

Costumes: Nancy Potts; **Lighting Designer:** John Gleason; **Set Design:** John Conklin

Songs: It's You Again; Peppersauce Woman

Cast: Robert Burr; Blythe Danner; George Ede; Michael Gross; Edward Herrman; Meg Mundy; Count Stovall; Douglass Watson; Frank Watson; Mary Louise Wilson

3469 • PHILEMON
OPENED: 01/03/1975   Theatre: Portfolio
Musical   Off-Broadway: 12

Composer: Harvey Schmidt
Lyricist: Tom Jones
Librettist: Tom Jones
Producer: Portfolio Productions
Director: Harvey Schmidt [1]

Choreographer: Janet Kerr; **Costumes:** Charles Blackburn; **Musical Director:** Ken Collins

Songs: Antioch Prison; Come with Me; Don't Kiki Me; Greatest of These, The; He's Coming; How Free I Feel; I Believe in Music [2]; I Love His Face; I Love Order; I'd Do Almost Anything to Get Out of Here and Go Home; My Secret Dream; Name: Cockian; Nightmare, The; Oh How Easy to Be Scornful; Sometimes; Streets of Antioch Stink, The; Within this Empty Space

Cast: Charles Blackburn; Michael Glenn-Smith; Virginia Gregory; Dick Latessa; Leila Martin; Howard Ross; Kathrin King Segal

Notes: [1] Used pseudonym Lester Collins. [2] Cut prior to opening.

3470 • PHILPOENA
Notes: *See HIGGLEDY PIGGLEDY.*

3471 • PHINNEY'S RAINBOW
OPENED: 1948
Musical

Composer: Stephen Sondheim
Lyricist: Stephen Sondheim
Librettist: Josiah T.S. Horton; Stephen Sondheim
Producer: Cap and Bells, Inc.
Director: David C. Bryant

Songs: How Do I Know?; Phinney's Rainbow; Still Got My Heart

Notes: A college show produced at the Adams Memorial Theatre, Williamstown, Mass. No program available.

3472 • PHOEBE OF QUALITY STREET
OPENED: 05/09/1921   Theatre: Shubert
Play   Broadway: 16

Composer: Walter Kollo
Lyricist: Edward Delaney Dunn
Author: Edward Delaney Dunn
Producer: J.J. Shubert; Lee Shubert
Director: W.H. Gilmore

Source: QUALITY STREET (Play: James M. Barrie); **Choreographer:** Max Scheck; **Musical Director:** Max Steiner

Songs: Autumn Sun; Dawn Turns to Morning; Dream of Joy; Gavotte; I Want to Be Merry (L: Mrs. Edward Delaney Dunn); Is It Safe to Depend on the Irish; Let's Make Up (L: Mrs. Edward Delaney Dunn); Little Wallflowers; Opening Act I; O'Toole; Patty Dear, Oh, Stop Your Teasin' [1]; Waltzing Is Passing from Land to Land; You'll Find the Rainbow (L: Mrs. Edward Delaney Dunn)

Cast: Shaun Glenville; Jessamine Newcomb; Warren Proctor; Dorothy Ward

Notes: [1] Sheet music only.

3473 • PHOENIX '55
OPENED: 04/23/1955   Theatre: Phoenix
Revue   Off-Broadway: 97

Composer: David Baker
Lyricist: David Craig
Librettist: Ira Wallach
Producer: Phoenix Theatre
Director: Marc Daniels

Choreographer: Boris Runanin; **Costumes:** Alvin Colt; **Dance Arranger:** John Morris; **Lighting Designer:** Klaus Holm; **Musical Director:** Buster Davis; **Orchestrations:** Ralph Burns; Clare Grundman; **Set Design:** Eldon Elder

Songs: All Around the World; Charade of the Marionettes; Down to the Sea; Funny Heart, A; It Says Here; Just Him; Never Wait for Love; Suburban Retreat; This Tuxedo Is Mine!; Tomorrow Is Here

Cast: Harvey Lembeck; Marge Redmond; Joshua Shelley; Nancy Walker; Gemze de Lappe

3474 • PHOTO FINISH

OPENED: 03/08/1968   Theatre: Upstairs at the Downstairs
Revue   Nightclub

Cast: Lily Tomlin

Notes: No other information available.

3475 • PHOTO SHOP, THE

OPENED: 1910
Musical

Composer: Karl Hoschna
Lyricist: Otto Harbach

Songs: French You Hear on Broadway; I Want You in the Picture; Queen of Manhattan Island

Notes: No other information available.

3476 • PIANO BAR

OPENED: 06/08/1978   Theatre: Westside
Musical   Off-Broadway: 133

Composer: Rob Fremont
Lyricist: Doris Willens
Librettist: Rob Fremont; Doris Willens
Producer: Lantern Productions
Director: Albert Takazauckas

Choreographer: Nora Peterson; **Costumes:** Michael Massee; **Lighting Designer:** Gary Porto; **Musical Director:** Joel Silberman; **Set Design:** Michael Massee; **Vocal Arranger:** Philip J. Lang

Songs: Believe Me; Closing; Congratulations; Dinner at the Mirklines; Everywhere I Go; Greenspons; Intro; It's Coming Back to Me;

Meanwhile Back in Yonkers; Moms and Dads; New York Cliche; Nobody's Perfect; One Two Three; Personals; Pigeon-Hole Time; Scenes from Some Marriages; Sweet Sue's; Tango; Today; Tomorrow Night; Walt's Truth

Cast: Kelly Bishop; Karen DeVito; Steve Elmore; Jim McMahon; Richard Ryder; Joel Silberman

3477 • PICCADILLY

Notes: *See BUSKER ALLEY.*

3478 • PICCADILLY TO BROADWAY

OPENED: 09/27/1920
Revue   Closed out of town

Composer: George Gershwin
Lyricist: Ira Gershwin[3]; E. Ray Goetz; Glen MacDonough
Producer: E. Ray Goetz
Director: Julian Alfred; George Marion

Songs: Baby Blues [1] (L: E. Ray Goetz); Bambino [6] (C: Vincent Youmans); Gondolier [6] (C: Vincent Youmans); (Now That We're) Mr. and Mrs. [4] (C: Vincent Youmans); On the Brim of Her Old Fashioned Bonnet [1] (L: E. Ray Goetz); Piccadilly's Not a Bit Like Broadway [6] (C: Vincent Youmans); Pick Yo' Partner! (Get Ready for the Raggy Blues) [6] (C: Vincent Youmans); Somehow I Knew [6] (C: Vincent Youmans); Something Peculiar [5]; Who's Who with You? [2] (C: Vincent Youmans)

Cast: Helen Broderick; Johnny Dooley; Clifton Webb; Anna Wheaton

Notes: No program available. Titled HERE AND THERE and VOGUES AND VANITIES at one time or another. [1] Later in SNAPSHOTS OF 1921. [2] Later in TWO LITTLE GIRLS IN BLUE. [3] Used pseudonym Arthur Francis. [4] Later cut from TWO LITTLE GIRLS IN BLUE. [5] Not used. Later also not used in LADY, BE GOOD! and GIRL CRAZY. [6] Not used.

3479 • PICK A NUMBER XV

Revue   Nightclub

Librettist: William F. Brown; Robert Elliot; Tony Geiss; Ted James
Director: Julius Monk

Arrangements: Robert Colston; Frederick Silver;
Choreographer: Frank Wagner; **Musical
Director:** Robert Colston; Frederick Silver

Songs: Almost a Love Song (C/L: Clark Gesner);
Coney Island (C: Fred Silver; L: Nelson
Garringer); Good Old Days, The (C: Bill Weeden;
L: David Finkle); Happiness Is a Bird (C/L: Claibe
Richardson); Love, Here I Am (C/L: Walter
Marks); McNamara's Band (C: Shamus O'Connor;
L: Howard Liebling); New Menace, The (C/L:
June Reizner); New York Is a Summer Festival [1]
(C: Harvey Schmidt; L: Tom Jones); On the
Weekend (C: Stanley Lebowsky; L: Fred Tobias);
Pick a Number XV (C: Stanley Lebowsky;
L: William F. Brown); Plaza's Going Native, The
(C: Stanley Lebowsky; L: Fred Tobias); Pop Song
(C/L: Lesley Davison); Saga of Killer Joe, The
(C: Fred Silver; L: Nelson Garringer); Signs of the
Season (C/L: June Reizner); Societies Magnificat:
An Oratorio (C/L: Clark Gesner)

Cast: Leigh Berry; Bill Hinnant; Nancy Parell; Rex
Robbins; Liz Sheridan; John Svar; Elizabeth
Wilson

Notes: [1] From DEMI DOZEN.

3480 • PICKINGS FROM PUCK
OPENED: 02/09/1908
Musical   Closed out of town

Producer: Barney Dubinsky; M.M. Dubinsky

Songs: College Life; Good Bye Sweet Old
Manhattan Isle; Hinkee Dee; I'm Married Now; In
Monkey Land; It's Great to Be a Soldier Man;
Manhattan Isle; Rag Time Lil; Save a Little Money
for a Rainy Day; Sister; Some Day when Dreams
Come True; Sweethearts in Every Town; That's
Gratitude; When the Moon Plays Peek-a-Boo with
You; Won't You Be My Teddy Bear

Cast: Helen Brown; Bertha M. Bunson; Barney
Dubinsky; M.M. Dubinsky; Jeanne Eagels; Chas.
Jordan; E.P. Mille

Notes: No credits but producers and actors in this
program!

3481 • PICKWICK (1927)
OPENED: 09/05/1927   Theatre: Empire
Play   Broadway: 72

Author: Cosmo Hamilton; C. Reilly
Producer: Frank C. Reilly
Director: Campbell Gullan

Source: PICKWICK PAPERS, THE (Novel: Charles
Dickens)

Songs: Cupid's Dart (C/L: Bernard Hamblin)

Cast: Ralph Bunker; John Cumberland; Olga
Katzan; Charles McNaughton; Hugh Miller;
Harry Plimmer; Katherine Stewart; Elaine
Temple; MacKenzie Ward; Bruce Winston

3482 • PICKWICK (1965)
OPENED: 10/04/1965   Theatre: 46th Street
Musical   Broadway: 56

Composer: Cyril Ornadel
Lyricist: Leslie Bricusse
Librettist: Wolf Mankowitz
Producer: Bernard Delfont; David Merrick
Director: Peter Coe

Source: PICKWICK PAPERS, THE (Novel:
Charles Dickens); **Choreographer:** Gillian
Lynne; **Costumes:** Roger Furse; Peter Rice;
Lighting Designer: Jules Fisher; **Musical
Director:** Ian Fraser; **Orchestrations:** Eric
Rogers; **Set Design:** Sean Kenny; **Vocal
Arranger:** Ian Fraser

Songs: Bit of Character, A; British Justice; Business
Is Booming [2]; Damages; Debtors Lament [2];
Do As You Would Be Done By [2]; Fizkin and
Pickwick; Gentleman's Gentleman, A; Good Old
Pickwick [1]; Hell of an Election, A [2]; I Like the
Company of Men; If I Ruled the World; I'll
Never Be Lonely Again (C/L: Leslie Bricusse);
Learn a Little Something [2]; Look Into Your
Heart [1]; More of Everything [2]; Pickwickians,
The; Talk; That's the Law; That's the Trouble
with Women [1]; That's What I'd Like for
Christmas; There's Something About You; Very;
You Never Met a Feller Like Me (I Never Met a
Feller Like Me)

Cast: Nancy Barrett; Peter Bull; John Call; Helena
Carroll; Roy Castle; Michael Logan; Julian
Orchard; Charlotte Rae; Harry Secombe

Notes: [1] Only in London production prior to
New York. [2] Out San Francisco 4/65.

3483 • PIECEFUL PALACE, THE

Notes: *See BELLE STARR.*

3484 • PIECES OF EIGHT (1959)

OPENED: 09/17/1959   Theatre: Upstairs at the
                      Downstairs
Revue   Off-Broadway

Librettist: Jerry Goldman; Abe Goldsmith; Dave Axelrod; Bruce Hart; Bill Dana
Producer: Julius Monk
Director: Buddy Schwab

Songs: And Then I Wrote (C: William Roy; L: David Davenport); Appian Way, The (C/L: Bud McCreery; L: Ronny Graham); Ardent Admirer (C/L: John Meyer); Clandestine [2] (C: Bob Kessler; L: Martin Charnin); Election Spectacular (C/L: Bud McCreery); Everybody Wants to Be Loved [3] (C/L: Bart Howard); Farewell (C/L: William Roy); Happiness Is a Bird (C/L: Claibe Richardson); Holy Man and the New Yorker [1] (C: Harvey Schmidt; L: Tom Jones); M'Lady Chatterley (C: William Roy; L: Bruce Williamson); Miss Williams (C/L: Elisse Boyd); Name of Our Own, A (C: Alan Friedman; L: Dennis Marks); Night the Hurricane Struck, The (C/L: Bud McCreery); Oriental [2] (C: Bob Kessler; L: Martin Charnin); Pieces of Eight (C/L: Bud McCreery); Radio City Music Hall (C/L: Rod Warren); Season's Greetings (C/L: Rod Warren); Steel Guitars and Barking Seals (C/L: Bud McCreery)

Cast: Ceil Cabot; Del Close; Gordon Connell; Jane Connell; Gerry Matthews; Estelle Parsons; **Pianist:** Carl Norman; William Roy

Notes: [1] Originally in DEMI DOZEN. [2] Originally in FALLOUT. [3] Added after opening.

3485 • PIECES OF EIGHT (1985)

OPENED: 11/27/1985
Musical   Closed out of town

Composer: Jule Styne
Lyricist: Susan Birkenhead
Librettist: Mark Bramble; Michael Stewart
Producer: Citadel Theatre; Edmonton Jounal
Director: Joe Layton

Source: TREASURE ISLAND (Novel: Robert Louis Stevenson); **Choreographer:** Joe Layton; **Musical**

Director: Eric Stern; **Orchestrations:** Lucio Agostini; **Set Design:** Neil Peter Jampolis

Songs: Apples; Beyond My Wildest Dreams; Bit of Home, A; Drill [1] (L: Carolyn Leigh; Ron Miller); Drum in My Heart — Gun in My Hand [1] (L: Carolyn Leigh; Ron Miller); Find the Map [1] (L: Carolyn Leigh; Ron Miller); I'd Do It All Over Again [1] (L: Carolyn Leigh; Ron Miller); If You Were My Son; I've Got a Secret [1] (L: Carolyn Leigh; Ron Miller); Keep Me Close to You; Luxury Lane; Man Who Was My Boy, The [1] (L: Carolyn Leigh; Ron Miller); Me & Thee [1] (L: Carolyn Leigh; Ron Miller); Mountains of Gold; My Last Strike; My Part of Somewhere [1] (L: Carolyn Leigh; Ron Miller); My Treasure Island; One Leg Is Better Than Two; Rainbows End (L: Susan Birkenhead); Rum [1] (L: Carolyn Leigh; Ron Miller); Sailor Talk; Sea, The (2); Sea, The (1) [1] (L: Carolyn Leigh; Ron Miller); Secret; Six Bells; That's the Time to Go [1] (L: Carolyn Leigh; Ron Miller); There Are No Heroes; To Become a Man [1] (L: Carolyn Leigh; Ron Miller); Whatever Became of Jenny?

Cast: George Lee Andrews; Graeme Campbell; George Hearn; Jonathan Ross

Notes: Closed Citadel Theatre, Edmonton, Canada. No program available. This show had two scores, the first with lyrics by Carolyn Leigh and Ron Miller and the second by Susan Birkenhead and Mark Bramble. [1] Not used. From first score.

3486 • PIED PIPER, THE

OPENED: 12/03/1908   Theatre: Majestic
Musical   Broadway: 52

Composer: Manuel Klein
Lyricist: R.H. Burnside
Librettist: R.H. Burnside; Austin Strong
Producer: Lee Shubert; Sam S. Shubert
Director: R.H. Burnside

Songs: Adam and Eve; Dresden China Plate, The; I Should Like to Know the Reason; I'm Looking for a Sweetheart and I Think You'll Do; It All Depends; It Really Was a Very Pretty Story; It's Going to Be a Very Busy Day; It's the Little Things That Count in Life; Love Is a Curious Feeling; Nursery Rhymes; Official Adviser and Reminder, The [1]; Sentimental Sarah; We Tell Him Just What to Do; What Do You Think of

That?; Whose Little Girl Are You?; Woman's a Wonderful Thing

Cast: Grace Cameron; William Cameron; Marguerite Clark; DeWolf Hopper; W.L. Romaine

Notes: [1] Sheet music only.

3487 • PIED PIPER OF HAMLIN, THE

OPENED: 11/26/1957   Theatre: NBC
TV Musical

Composer: Edvard Grieg
Lyricist: Hal Stanley; Irving Taylor

Musical Director: Pete King

Songs: Exodus of Children; Feats of Piper; Flim Flam Floo; Fool's Gold; How Can I Tell You; Morning Song (inst.); Mother's Lament; Prestige; Rat Exodus (inst.); Return of the Children (inst.); Welcome Home; Work Song

Cast: Van Johnson

3488 • PIFF! PAFF!! POUF!!!

OPENED: 04/02/1904   Theatre: Casino
Musical   Broadway: 264

Composer: Jean Schwartz
Lyricist: William Jerome
Librettist: Stanislaus Stange
Producer: F.C. Whitney
Director: Gerard Coventry

Choreographer: Gus Sohlke; **Costumes:** Caroline Seidle; **Musical Director:** John Sebastian Hiller; **Orchestrations:** Frank Saddler; **Set Design:** Homer Emens; Edward G. Unitt

Songs: Barney Donohue [1]; Cordelia Malone; Dear Old Manhattan Isle; For You; Forte with Your Trumpets and Your Drums (L: Stanislaus Stange); Ghost That Never Walked, The; Good-night My Own Love (L: William Jerome; Stanislaus Stange); I Don't Want Any Wurzburger; I'm So Happy; Love-Love-Love; Lutie; M.a.c.a.r.o.n.i.; March of the Flags; Melancholy Sunbeam and the Rose, The; My Unkissed Man (L: Stanislaus Stange); Opening Chorus Act II (L: Stanislaus Stange); Pixies Entrance (L: Stanislaus Stange); Radium Dance

(inst.); Since Dolly Dimple's Made a Hit (Dolly Dimples); Under the Goo-Goo Tree (L: Stanislaus Stange); Under the Shade of Our Lovely Umbrellas (L: William Jerome; Stanislaus Stange); We Really Ought to Be Married

Cast: Grace Cameron; Alice Fisher; Eddie Foy Sr.; John Hyams; Mack Sennett

Notes: [1] Sheet music only.

3489 • PIGGY

OPENED: 01/11/1927   Theatre: Royale
Musical   Broadway: 79

Composer: Cliff Friend
Lyricist: Lew Brown
Librettist: Alfred Jackson; Daniel Kussell
Producer: William B. Friedlander
Director: William B. Friedlander

Choreographer: John Boyle; **Costumes:** Hugh Willoughby; **Musical Director:** Louis Gress; **Set Design:** John Wenger

Songs: All Decked Out; America [1]; Didn't It?; Ding, Dong Dell (Spells I Love You); Do It for Charity; Emigrants' Song; Follow Through; How D'Ye Do; I Need a Little Bit, You Need a Little Bit (A Little Bit of Love); I Wanna Go Voom Voom; It Just Had to Happen; It's Easy to Say Hello (But So Hard to Say Goodbye); It's Heaven to Me [1]; Just the Same; Keep Your Eye on the Girl [1]; Let's Stroll Along and Sing a Song of Love; Little Change of Atmosphere, A [1]; Music of a Little Rippling Stream, The; Oh, Baby! (I Know That You Wouldn't but Gosh How I Wish That You Would) [1]; One of Those Windows; Red Head Blues [1]; So This Is Venice [1]; When [1]

Cast: Sam Bernard; Brooke Johns; Wanda Lyon; Harry McNaughton

Notes: Titled THAT'S MY BABY out of town. Name changed to I TOLD YOU SO after opening. [1] Out Brooklyn 12/27/26.

3490 • PILGRIM'S PROGRESS

OPENED: 03/20/1962   Theatre: Gate
Musical   Off-Broadway: 8

Composer: Edwin Greenberg
Lyricist: Edwin Greenberg

Librettist: Edwin Greenberg
Producer: Vincent Tourag
Director: Ted Vermont

Choreographer: Graeme Carlton; Conductor: Bob Hess; Costumes: Edward Myers; Lighting Designer: Domingo Rodriguez; Musical Director: Russ Case; Orchestrations: Russ Case; Set Design: Domingo Rodriguez

Songs: A + B = C; Ballad of Bedford Gaol; Blackest of Tresses; Capital of the World; Girls Who Sell Orangeade, The; Giza-on-the-Nile; Husband of Mine; I'm Feeling Better All the Time; My Daughter, My Angel; Prisoner's Lullaby; Sing Out in the Streets; Take My Hand in Friendship; Tomorrow Waltz, The; Voice of God, The; What Do They Care?

Cast: Francis Bernard; Michael Davis; Delmar Roos

3491 • PIMPERNEL!

OPENED: 01/06/1964   Theatre: Gramercy Arts
Musical   Off-Broadway: 3

Composer: Mimi Stone
Lyricist: William Kaye
Librettist: William Kaye
Producer: Gerard Krone; Dorothy Olim
Director: Malcolm Black

Source: SCARLET PIMPERNEL, THE (Novel: Baroness Orczy); Choreographer: Sandra Devlin; Costumes: Sonia Lowenstein; Lighting Designer: Lloyd Burlingame; Musical Director: Robert Rogers; Orchestrations: Julian Stein; Set Design: Lloyd Burlingame

Songs: A La Pimpernel; As If I Weren't There; Dangerous Game; Everything's Just Divine; I'm Seeing Things; Le Bon Mot; Le Croissant; Liberty, Equality, Fraternity; Love of Long Ago; Nose Ahead; Sing, Jacques, Sing; This Is England; Touch of Paris; What a Day for Me; Woman, A

Cast: John Canemaker; John Cunningham; David Daniels; Jeanne Devine; William Larsen; Dick Latessa; Leila Martin

3492 • PINK HUSSARS, THE

Notes: *See HIS HONOR THE MAYOR.*

3493 • PINK JUNGLE, THE

OPENED: 10/14/1959
Musical   Closed out of town

Composer: Vernon Duke
Lyricist: Vernon Duke
Librettist: Leslie Stevens
Producer: Paul Gregory
Director: Joseph Anthony

Choreographer: Matt Mattox; Costumes: Jean Louis; Lighting Designer: Donald Oenslager; Musical Director: Sherman Frank; Orchestrations: Albert Sendry; Set Design: Donald Oenslager; Vocal Arranger: John Lattimer

Songs: All the Luck in the World; Blow the Man Down; Brian; Chic Talk; Don't You Ever Cross Me Path; Free As the Air; Funeral Music (inst.); Ghost Music (inst.); Harvey's Theme (inst.); Hundred Women in One, A; It's Tough to Be a Man; It's Tough to Be a Working Girl; Just Like Children; Love for Sure; M-10; M-11; My Sky without a Star; Nobody but Tess; One Hundred Women in One; Paris in New York; Persian Room-Ba; Pink Jungle, The; Plaza Music; Prelude; Same Old Love; Tess Mambo; There Was I [1]; Together in Central Park; Where Do You Go When You Arrive?; Where Do You Go When You're on Top?

Cast: Leif Erickson; Maggie Hayes; Agnes Moorehead; Ginger Rogers

Notes: No songs listed in program. [1] Titled "There I Was" by ASCAP.

3494 • PINK LADY, THE

OPENED: 03/13/1911   Theatre: New Amsterdam
Musical   Broadway: 312

Composer: Ivan Caryll
Lyricist: C.M.S. McLellan
Librettist: C.M.S. McLellan
Producer: Klaw & Erlanger
Director: Herbert Gresham

Source: LE SATYR (Play: Georges Berr; Marcel Guillemaud); Choreographer: Julian Mitchell; Costumes: F. Richard Anderson; Musical Director: Arthur Weld; Set Design: Ernest Albert

Songs: Again a Cry (Finale Act II) [1]; Bring Along the Camera; By the Saskatchewan; Donny Didn't, Donny Did; Duel, The; Flow River Flow (Finale Act III [1]; Game I Hunt I Never Miss, The (Finale Act I) [1]; Gently (L: George Grossmith); Here's a Lady (Opening Chorus); Hide and Seek [1]; I Like It; I'm Single for Six Weeks More (I'm Going to Be Married in June); In a French Girl's Heart [1]; Intriguers, The; Kiss Waltz, The; Love Is Divine [1]; My Beautiful Lady; Oh Fortunate Man Who Has Taste and Gold (Opening Act II) [1]; Parisian Two-Step, The; Right to Love, The [1]; When Love Goes A-Straying

Cast: Hazel Dawn; Alice Dovey; Frank Lalor; Florence Walton; John E. Young

Notes: [1] In London vocal score only.

3495 • PINOCCHIO (1938)

OPENED: 12/23/1938   Theatre: Ritz
Musical   Broadway: 197

Composer: Armando Loredo; Eddison Von Ottenfeld
Lyricist: Armando Loredo; Eddison Von Ottenfeld
Librettist: Yasha Frank
Producer: WPA
Director: Yasha Frank

Source: PINOCCHIO (Story: Carlo Collodi);
   Choreographer: Alexandra Mamlet; **Costumes:**
   James Cochrane; **Dance Arranger:** I.L. Epstein;
   Lighting Designer: Feder; **Musical Director:**
   Aaron Pressman; **Set Design:** Perry Watkins;
   Vocal Arranger: I.L. Epstein

Songs: Cat and Fox Song; Lullaby; Pinocchio; Song of the Jolly Coachman

Cast: Georgiana Brand; Allen Frank; Edward Lalor; Sam M. Lewis; Edwin Michaels; Vito Scotti

Notes: *See also PINOCCHIO (1957).*

3496 • PINOCCHIO (1957)

OPENED: 10/13/1957   Theatre: NBC
TV Musical

Composer: Alec Wilder
Lyricist: William Engvick
Librettist: Yasha Frank
Producer: Herbert M. Moss
Director: Paul Bogart

Source: PINOCCHIO (Story: Carlo Collodi);
   Choreographer: Hanya Holm; **Musical Director:**
   Glenn Osser

Songs: Birthday Song, The; Fox's Pitch, The; Happy News; Jolly Coachman, The; Listen to Your Heart; Lullabye; Pinocchio's Song

Cast: Fran Allison; Jerry Colonna; Martyn Green; Stubby Kaye; Sondra Lee; Matt Mattox; Mickey Rooney; Walter Slezak

3497 • PINOCCHIO (1968)

OPENED: 12/08/1968
TV Musical

Composer: Walter Marks
Lyricist: Walter Marks
Librettist: Ernest Kinoy
Producer: Richard Lewine
Director: Sid Smith

Source: PINOCCHIO (Story: Carlo Collodi)

Cast: Pierre Epstein; Jack Fletcher; Anita Gillette; Burl Ives; Mort Marshall; Peter Noone; Charlotte Rae; Ned Wertimer

Notes: No song list available.

3498 • PINOCCHIO (1973)

OPENED: 12/15/1973
Musical   Off-Broadway: 134

Composer: Mary Rodgers
Lyricist: Sheldon Harnick
Librettist: Jerome Coopersmith
Producer: American Puppet Arts Coun.; Bil Baird
Director: Lee Theodore

Source: PINOCCHIO (Story: Carlo Collodi);
   Lighting Designer: Peggy Clark; **Musical**
   Director: Alvy West; **Set Design:** Howard
   Mandel; **Vocal Arranger:** Alvy West

Songs: Fish Scales; Hey, Sweet Columbine; I'm Off to School; Little Wooden Boy; Money Tree; Nose with a Mind of It's Own, A; Out in the Cold

Cast: Jonathan E. Freeman; Robert Gorman; Sean Malley; John O'Malley; **Voice:** Margery Gray; Marcia Rodd; Bill Tost; Byron Whiting; **Puppeteer:** Peter Baird; Olga Felgemacher

Notes: Puppeteers and voices credited in cast list. Presented as one part of bill along with BIL BAIRD'S VARIETY.

3499 • PINOCCHIO (1976)
OPENED: 03/27/1976   Theatre: CBS
TV Musical

Composer: Billy Barnes
Lyricist: Billy Barnes
Librettist: Herbert Baker
Producer: Bernard Rothman; Jack Wohl
Director: Ron Field; Sid Smith

Source: PINOCCHIO (Story: Carlo Collodi);
Musical Director: Eddie Karam

Cast: Don Correia; Sandy Duncan; Danny Kaye; Clive Revill; Liz Torres; Flip Wilson

Notes: No song list available.

3500 • PINS AND NEEDLES (1922)
OPENED: 02/01/1922   Theatre: Shubert
Musical   Broadway: 46

Composer: Frederic Chappelle
Lyricist: Irving Caesar; Rupert Hazel
Librettist: Wal Pink; Edgar Wallace; Albert de Courville
Producer: Albert de Courville
Director: Julian Mitchell; Albert de Courville

Songs: Ah! Ah! Ah! (C: James F. Hanley; L: Ballard Macdonald); All Pull Together; Gypsy Warned Me, The; Hollow of My Hand; Jungle Bungalow (I'll Build a Home in the Jungle) (C: James F. Hanley; L: Ballard Macdonald); Little Tin Soldier and the Little Rag Doll, The (L: Darl MacBoyle); Love Spans the World; Melancholy Blues; Off We Go; Piccadilly Walk, The (C: Edward Horan; L: Ira Gershwin [1]; Arthur Riscoe); Slow Movies; South Sea Sweethearts (C: Maurice Yvain); Souvenirs [2]; Sunny Sunbeam (C: James F. Hanley; L: Joe Goodwin; Ballard Macdonald); Syncopated Minuet, The; Vanity Box, The; Varsity Bug, The

Cast: Maisie Gay; Edith Kelly Gould; Teddy Knox; Jimmy Norvo; Harry Pilcer

Notes: No program available. [1] Used pseudonym Arthur Francis. [2] Sheet music only.

3501 • PINS AND NEEDLES (1937)
OPENED: 11/27/1937   Theatre: Labor Stage
Revue   Off-Broadway: 1108

Composer: Harold Rome
Lyricist: Harold Rome
Librettist: Arthur Arent; Marc Blitzstein; Emanuel Eisenberg; Charles Friedman; David Gregory
Producer: Labor Stage, Inc.
Director: Charles Friedman

Choreographer: Gluck Sandor; Benjamin Zemach;
Set Design: Sointu Syrjala

Songs: Back to Work [1]; Brittania Waives the Rules [1] (C: Berenece Kazounoff; L: Arnold B. Horwitt; John Latouche); Chain Store Daisy; Cream of Mush Song [2]; Doin' the Reactionary; Economics; First Impressions (L: Charles Friedman; Harold Rome); Four Little Angels of Peace; General Unveiled (inst.) [3]; Harmony Boys, The [1]; I'm Just Nuts About You [2]; It's Better with a Union Man (Bertha the Sewing Machine Girl) [1]; I've Got the Nerve to Be in Love [1]; Just an Ordinary Guy [4]; Lorelei on the Rocks (C: Berenece Kazounoff; L: John Latouche); Men Awake; Mene, Mene, Tekel [1]; Nobody Makes a Pass at Me; Not Cricket to Picket; Oh, Give Me the Good Old Days [1]; One Big Union for Two; Papa Don't Love Mama Any More [3]; Papa Lewis, Mama Green [1]; Public Enemy No. 1; Red Mikado [1]; Room for One [2]; Sing Me a Song with Social Significance; Sitting on Your Status Quo [1]; Song of the Ads (The Pluto Boys, We're the Ads); Stay Out, Sammy [1]; Sunday in the Park; We Sing America [1]; We'd Rather Be Right (L: Arthur Kramer); We've Just Begun (L: Charles Friedman; Harold Rome); What Good Is Love?; What This Party Needs (L: Arthur Kramer; Harold Rome); When I Grow Up (The G-Man Song) [1]; Yanks Aren't Coming! The

Cast: Al Eben; Hy Goldstein; Nettie Harary; Lynne Jaffee; Al Levy; Murray Modick; Ruth Rubinstein; Paul Seymour; Millie Weitz

Notes: After opening, in May 1938 Robert H. Gordon credited as director and Adele Jerome for choreography. By April 1939 the choreography was credited to Felicia Sorel. By November 1939 all sketches were by Joseph Schrank. [1] Added after opening. [2] Sheet music only. [3] ASCAP/Library of Congress only. [4] ASCAP/Library of Congress only. In SING OUT THE NEWS.

3502 • PINS AND NEEDLES 1939

Notes: *See PINS AND NEEDLES (1937).*

3503 • PINS AND NEEDLES (1940)

Notes: *See PINS AND NEEDLES (1937).*

3504 • PIONEER DAYS

OPENED: 11/28/1906   Theatre: Hippodrome
Revue   Broadway: 288

Composer: Manuel Klein
Lyricist: Manuel Klein
Librettist: Carroll Fleming
Producer: M.C. Anderson; Messrs. Shubert
Director: Edward P. Temple

Set Design: Arthur Voegtlin

Songs: Hymn to the Sun; Indian War Song; Lucia My Italian Maid [1]; Red Sky

Cast: W.H. Clark; J.P. Coombs; George Holland; John G. Sparks

Notes: NEPTUNE'S DAUGHTER was the third part of the bill. See under that name also. The second part of the show was CIRCUS EVENTS. [1] Later in London show THE GAY GORDONS.

3505 • PIPE DREAM

OPENED: 11/30/1955   Theatre: Shubert
Musical   Broadway: 246

Composer: Richard Rodgers
Lyricist: Oscar Hammerstein II
Librettist: Oscar Hammerstein II
Producer: Oscar Hammerstein II; Richard Rodgers
Director: Harold Clurman

Source: SWEET THURSDAY (Novel: John Steinbeck); **Choreographer:** Boris Runanin; **Costumes:** Alvin Colt; **Dance Arranger:** John Morris; **Lighting Designer:** Jo Mielziner; **Musical Director:** Salvatore Dell'Isola; **Orchestrations:** Robert Russell Bennett, **Set Design:** Jo Mielziner

Songs: All at Once You Love Her; All Kinds of People; Bums' Opera; Ev'rybody's Got a Home but Me; Happiest House on the Block, The; How Long?; I Am a Witch [1]; I Have Loved and I've Learned [1]; Lopsided Bus, A; Man I Used to Be, The; Next Time It Happens, The; Party Gets Going, The [1]; Party That We're Gonna Have Tomorrow Night, The; Sitting on the Back Porch [2]; Suzy Is a Good Thing; Sweet Thursday; Thinkin'; Tide Pool, The; Will You Marry Me?

Cast: Annabelle Gold; Jayne Heller; William Johnson; Patti Karkalits; Mike Kellin; Ruth Kobart; Jerry LaZarre; Jackie McElroy; Mildred Slavin; Temple Texas; Helen Traubel; Louise Troy; Judy Tyler; G.D. Wallace

Notes: [1] Cut. [2] ASCAP/Library of Congress only.

3506 • PIPPIN

OPENED: 10/23/1972   Theatre: Imperial
Musical   Broadway: 1944

Composer: Stephen Schwartz
Lyricist: Stephen Schwartz
Librettist: Bob Fosse [1]; Roger O. Hirson
Producer: Stuart Ostrow
Director: Bob Fosse

Choreographer: Bob Fosse; **Costumes:** Patricia Zipprodt; **Dance Arranger:** John Berkman; **Lighting Designer:** Jules Fisher; **Musical Director:** Stanley Lebowsky; **Orchestrations:** Ralph Burns; **Set Design:** Tony Walton

Songs: Corner of the Sky; Extraordinary; Glory; Good Time Ladies Rag [2]; I Guess I'll Miss the Man; Just Between the Two of Us [2]; Kind of Woman; Love Song; Magic to Do; Morning Glow; No Time at All; On the Right Track; Simple Joys; Spread a Little Sunshine; War Is a Science; We're Only Marking Time [2]; Welcome Home with You [2]

Cast: Eric Berry; Christopher Chadman; Jill Clayburgh; Gene Foote; Roger Hamilton; Richard Korthaze; John Mineo; Leland Palmer; John Rubinstein; Irene Ryan; Ben Vereen

Notes: *See also PIPPIN, PIPPIN,* an earlier version of this show. [1] Uncredited. [2] Cut prior to opening.

3507 • PIPPIN, PIPPIN

OPENED: 05/01/1967
Musical

Composer: Stephen Schwartz [1]
Lyricist: Stephen Schwartz
Librettist: Ron Strauss

Conductor: David Gerwig

Songs: Begging Milady's Pardon; Come with Me;
Easy to Be Happy; Father Said; Goodbye,
Yesterday; I Don't Owe You a Thing; Kyrie; My
Son; Next King, The; Pippin, Pippin; Preparations;
Run Into Your Arms; Simple Dance, A; Soliloquy;
Somebody Loves You; They Will Listen to You;
To Be a King; Victorious; While You Were Away

Cast: Bob Calvert; Bob Rastelli; Rebecca Smith;
David Sheridan Spangler

Notes: Amateur show presented at
Carnegie-Mellon University's Scotch 'n' Soda
Theatre. *See also PIPPIN*, a later version of this
show. [1] Used name Lawrence Stephens.

3508 • PITTER PATTER

OPENED: 09/28/1920   Theatre: Longacre
Musical   Broadway: 111

Composer: William B. Friedlander
Lyricist: Will M. Hough
Librettist: Will M. Hough
Producer: William B. Friedlander

Source: CAUGHT IN THE RAIN (Play William
Collier; Grant Stewart); **Choreographer:** David
Bennett; **Musical Director:** Ivan Rudisill

Songs: Bagdad on the Subway (L: William B.
Friedlander); Everything Will Be All Right [1];
I Saved a Waltz for You (L: Will M. Hough); I'm
a Bachelor; Little Bit of Love, A [1]; Love Me
Tonight; Man a Maid, A [1]; Meet Your True
Love Half Way; Painted Women [1]; Pitter Patter
(L: Will M. Hough); Send for Me; Since You
Came Into My Life; Somebody's Waiting for Me;
Take a Raisin [1]; They're Jazzing It Up in
Havana; Wedding Blues; You Never Can Tell
(L: William B. Friedlander)

Cast: Helen Bolton; James Cagney; John Price
Jones; Mildred Keats; William Kent; Jack Squires

Notes: [1] Out of town only.

3509 • PLAIN AND FANCY

OPENED: 01/27/1955   Theatre: Mark Hellinger
Musical   Broadway: 461

Composer: Albert Hague
Lyricist: Arnold B. Horwitt
Librettist: Will Glickman; Joseph Stein
Producer: James W. Gardiner; Richard Kollmar
Director: Morton Da Costa

Choreographer: Helen Tamiris; **Costumes:** Raoul
Pene du Bois; **Lighting Designer:** Peggy Clark;
Musical Director: Franz Allers; **Orchestrations:**
Philip J. Lang; **Set Design:** Raoul Pene du Bois;
Vocal Arranger: Crane Calder

Songs: Carnival Ballet; City Mouse, Country
Mouse; Follow Your Heart; How Do You Raise
a Barn?; I'll Show Him!; It Wonders Me; It's a
Helluva Way to Run a Love Affair; Lantern
Dance; Plain We Live; Plenty of Pennsylvania;
Shunning, The; Take Your Time and Take Your
Pick; This Is All Very New to Me; Why Not
Katie?; You Can't Miss It; Young and Foolish

Cast: Nancy Andrews; Shirl Conway; Barbara
Cook; David Daniels; Richard Derr; Gloria
Marlowe; Daniel Nagrin; Douglas Fletcher
Rodgers; Stefan Schnabel; Sammy Smith

3510 • PLAIN JANE (1923)

Notes: *See MARY JANE MCKANE.*

3511 • PLAIN JANE (1924)

OPENED: 05/12/1924   Theatre: New Amsterdam
Musical   Broadway: 168

Composer: Tom Johnstone
Lyricist: Phil Cook
Librettist: Phil Cook; McElbert Moore
Producer: Plain Jane Incorporated
Director: Walter Brooks

Costumes: Evlyn McHorter; **Musical Director:** Ira
Jacobs; **Set Design:** Mabel Buell

Songs: Along the Road to Love; Beneath the Stars;
Come on Feet, Let's Go; Don't Take Your
Troubles to Bed (C: Phil Cook; Tom Johnstone);

Hand in Hand; I Love a Fight; If Flowers Could Speak (C: Phil Cook; Tom Johnstone); Plain Jane; Playhouse Planned for You, A; Proverbs; Puttin' on the Ritz; Tricks of the Trade; What's New?; When the Whistle Blows; When Your Heart's in the Ring; Winning the Prize

Cast: Jay Gould; Dan Healy; Joe Laurie Jr.; Lorraine Manville; Charles McNaughton

3512 • PLANTATION DAYS

OPENED: 1922 Theatre: Lafayette
Revue New York

Composer: Eubie Blake
Lyricist: Noble Sissle
Producer: O'Neil & Greenwald

Musical Director: James P. Johnson

Songs: Bandana Days [1]; Gypsy Blues [1]; I'm Crazy for That Kind of Love [1]; Ukulele Blues (C: James P. Johnson; L: Merton Bories)

Cast: Dave and Tressie; Eddie Dean; Harper and Blanks; Smith and DeForrest

Notes: No program available. This show moved to London and became part of THE RAINBOW. [1] From SHUFFLE ALONG.

3513 • PLANTATION REVUE (1922)

OPENED: 06/1922 Theatre: 48th Street
Revue Broadway

Composer: J. Russel Robinson
Lyricist: Roy Turk
Producer: Lew Leslie

Musical Director: Will Vodery

Songs: Bugle Call Blues; Gypsy Blues; Hawaiian Night in Dixieland; I Want to Be Vamped in Georgia; Mandy; Minstrels on Parade; Old Black Joe; Robert E. Lee; Southern Hobby; Southland [1]; Swanee River; Sweet Man o' Mine

Cast: Shelton Brooks; Lew Keene; Florence Mills; U.S. Thompson; Edith Wilson

Notes: No program available. [1] ASCAP/LIbrary of Congress only.

3514 • PLANTATION REVUE (1923)

OPENED: 1923 Theatre: Winter Garden
Roof
Revue Broadway

Producer: Lew Leslie

Songs: He Wasn't Born in Araby (C: Edgar Dowell; L: Andy Razaf)

Notes: No other information available.

3515 • PLATINUM

OPENED: 11/12/1978 Theatre: Mark Hellinger
Musical Broadway: 33

Composer: Gary William Friedman
Lyricist: Will Holt
Librettist: Will Holt; Bruce Vilanch
Producer: Barry M. Brown; Fritz Holt; Gladys Rackmil
Director: Joe Layton

Choreographer: Joe Layton; **Costumes:** Bob Mackie; **Dance Arranger:** Fred Thaler; **Lighting Designer:** John Gleason; **Musical Director:** Fred Thaler; **Orchestrations:** Jimmie Haskell; Fred Thaler; **Set Design:** David Hays; **Vocal Arranger:** Gary William Friedman; Jimmie Haskell; Fred Thaler

Songs: Back with a Beat; Bug on the Windshield of Life [2]; Destiny; Disco Destiny; Funky [2]; Gonna Get Hot [1]; How Do You Like It? [2]; I Am the Light; I Like You; Moments [2]; Movie Star Mansion; 1945; Nothing But; Old Times, Good Times; Platinum Dreams; Retreat [2]; Ride, Baby, Ride; Rock Is My Way of Life [2]; Standing in Need of Your Love [2]; Sunset; Too Many Mirrors; Trials and Tribulations; True Music [2]; Waltz [2]

Cast: Richard Cox; Damita Jo Freeman; Lisa Mordente; Alexis Smith; Avery Sommers

Notes: First titled SUNSET. Later revised and produced Off- Broadway as SUNSET. See under that title. [1] Out Washington, D.C. 10/78. [2] Cut prior to opening.

3516 • PLAY IT AGAIN, SAM

OPENED: 02/12/1969 Theatre: Broadhurst
Play Broadway: 453

Author: Woody Allen
Producer: David Merrick
Director: Joseph Hardy

Costumes: Ann Roth; **Lighting Designer:** Martin Aronstein; **Set Design:** William Ritman

Songs: Play It Again, Sam (C: Hal Hackady; L: Larry Grossman)

Cast: Woody Allen; Diane Keaton; Jerry Lacy; Anthony Roberts; Sheila Sullivan

3517 • PLAY ME A COUNTRY SONG

OPENED: 06/27/1982   Theatre: Virginia
Musical   Broadway: 1

Composer: John R. Briggs; Harry Manfredi
Lyricist: John R. Briggs; Harry Manfredi
Librettist: Jay Broad
Director: Jerry Adler

Choreographer: Margo Sappington; **Costumes:** Carol Oditz; **Lighting Designer:** Marc B. Weiss; **Musical Director:** Phil Hall; **Set Design:** David Chapman; **Vocal Arranger:** Phil Hall

Songs: All of My Dreams; Big City; Coffee, Beer and Whiskey; Eighteen-Wheelin' Baby; If You Don't Mind; Jerome's Song; Just Thought I'd Call; Ladies' Lament; My Sweet Woman; Only a Fool; Play Me a Country Song; Playing for Position; Rodeo Dreams; Rodeo Rider; Sail Away; Sing-A-Long; Waitin' Tables; Why Does a Woman Leave Her Man; You Came Along; You Can't Get Ahead; You Have to Get It Out to Get Away

Cast: Ronn Carroll; Mary Jo Catlett; Stephen Crain; Louisa Flaningam; Reed Jones; Mary Gordon Murray; Candice Tovar

3518 • PLAY'S THE THING, THE

Composer: Richard Rodgers
Lyricist: Lorenz Hart

Songs: Italy; Ladies and Gentlemen, Good Evening; Music and the Emotions

Notes: An unfinished musical probably written in the late 1920's.

3519 • PLAYING THE PONIES (1907)

OPENED: 12/23/1907
Musical   Closed out of town

Composer: Theodore Morse
Lyricist: Edward Madden
Librettist: Aaron Hoffman
Producer: B.E. Forrester
Director: Frank Smithson

Costumes: Mme. Freisinger; **Musical Director:** Al Smyth; **Set Design:** Frank Gates; E.A. Morange

Songs: Cosy Little Cottage By the Sea, A; Cupid's Wedding Bells; Family Tree, The; I Could Give My Heart to You; I Would Like to Flirt with You; I'd Rather Be a Lobster Than a Wise Guy; Love, Love, Love; Moon Beams; Opening Chorus Act II; When I Count Three; Wind Yourself Around Me, Dearie

Cast: Nick Adams; Georgie Mack; Gus Yorke

Notes: *See also PLAYING THE PONIES* (1908). From program of Pittsburgh 3/16/08 and New York City 12/23/07.

3520 • PLAYING THE PONIES (1908)

OPENED: 1908
Musical   Closed out of town

Composer: J.A. Raynes
Librettist: Aaron Hoffman
Producer: Max Dill; C. William Kolb
Director: Charles Sinclair

Songs: Dreamland; Easy Money; Opening Chorus; Opening Chorus Act II; Paraguay; Queen of the Boulevards; Something Seems to Say You Love Me; Summer Girls; Telephone Me Dearie

Cast: Max Dill; C. William Kolb; Charles Sinclair

Notes: From program 11/9/08. *See also PLAYING THE PONIES* (1907).

3521 • PLEASE!

OPENED: 11/16/1933
Revue   London: 108

Producer: Andre Charlot

Songs: Baby's Best Friend, A [1] (C: Richard Rodgers; L: Lorenz Hart); Rhythm [2] (C: Richard Rodgers; L: Lorenz Hart)

Cast: Lupino Lane; Beatrice Lillie

Notes: [1] Originally in SHE'S MY BABY. [2] Revised and put into THE SHOW IS ON (1936) and in the London production HAPPY RETURNS (1938).

3522 • PLEASE DON'T CRY AND SAY NO

OPENED: 12/06/1972   Theatre: Circle in the Square
Play   Off-Broadway: 15

Composer: Dorothy A. Dinroe
Author: Townsend Brewster
Producer: Primavera Productions; Sally Sears
Director: Philip Taylor

Costumes: Jon Haggins; **Lighting Designer:** Hal Tine; **Set Design:** Hal Tine

Songs: Bossa Nova, The; Conscience Is a Coward; Man Who Plays the Alto Flute, The; Rain of Summer, The; She Needs a Good Cry

Cast: Tyrone Browne; David Downing; Vanessa K. Gilder; Janet League

Notes: This entry is three one-act plays with music. THE BROWN OVERCOAT by Victor Sejour and THE BOTANY LESSON by Joaquim Maria and Machado de Assis complete the bill.

3523 • PLEASURE BOUND

OPENED: 02/18/1929   Theatre: Majestic
Revue   Broadway: 136

Composer: Muriel Pollock
Lyricist: Harold Atteridge; Max Lief; Nathaniel Lief
Librettist: Harold Atteridge
Producer: Messrs. Shubert
Director: Lew Morton

Choreographer: Busby Berkeley; John Boyle; **Costumes:** Ernest Schrapps; **Musical Director:** Harold Stern; **Orchestrations:** Archie Bleyer; Emil Gerstenberger; **Set Design:** Watson Barratt

Songs: Cross Word Puzzles; Glory of Spring; Just Suppose (C: Phil Baker; Maurie Rubens; L: Moe Jaffe; Sid Silvers); Mannikin Dolls (C: Phil Baker; Maurie Rubens); My Melody Man [1] (C: Peter De Rose; L: Henry Clare; Charles Tobias); Park Avenue Strut (C: Phil Baker; Maurie Rubens; L: Harold Atteridge; Moe Jaffe); Spanish Fado; Things That Were Made for Love, The [1] (C: Peter De Rose; L: Irving Kahal; Charles Tobias); We Love to Go to Work; We'll Get Along; Why Do You Tease Me?

Cast: Phil Baker; Sam Lee; Jack Pearl; Al Shaw; Aileen Stanley

Notes: Out of town titled WELL, WELL, WELL. See also under that title. [1] Not in program.

3524 • PLEASURE DOME

OPENED: 12/13/1956
Musical

Composer: Dean Fuller
Lyricist: Marshall Barer
Librettist: Coleman Jacoby; Arnold Rosen; Ira Wallach
Producer: Jack Segasture
Director: David Thimar

Choreographer: Alex Romero; **Costumes:** Moyen; **Musical Director:** Buster Davis; **Orchestrations:** Ralph Burns; **Set Design:** Leo Kurz; **Vocal Arranger:** Buster Davis

Cast: Kaye Ballard; Jimmie Komack; Josephine Premice

Notes: Closed in rehearsals.

3525 • PLEASURE SEEKERS, THE

OPENED: 11/03/1913   Theatre: Winter Garden
Revue   Broadway: 72

Composer: E. Ray Goetz
Lyricist: E. Ray Goetz
Librettist: Edgar Smith
Producer: Lew Fields
Director: William J. Wilson

Costumes: Cora MacGeachy; William Henry Matthews; **Musical Director:** Oscar Radin

Songs: Alpine Girl, The (C: Bert Grant); At That Bully Wooly Wild West Show (C: Maurice Abrahams; L: Grant Clarke; Edgar Leslie); At the Picture Show [1]; Don't Blame It All on Broadway (C: Bert Grant; L: Henry Williams; Joe Young); Ensemble; Faust Up to Date; Follow the Midnight Girl (C: E. Ray Goetz; Bert Grant); Give Me Something in a Uniform of Blue; He'd Have to Get Under, Get Out and Get Under (To Fix His Automobile) (C: Maurice Abrahams; L: Grant Clarke; Edgar Leslie); In the Shade of the Lemon Tree [1]; Interlude; I've Got a Little Chalet in the Valley (C: E. Ray Goetz; Bert Grant); Levi Is a Grand Old Name; Love Me to a Viennese Melody; My Averne Rose (C: Bert Grant); Opening Chorus; Serpentine Dance, The; Sit Down, You're Rockin' the Boat (Stop Rocking the Boat) [2] (C: Jean Schwartz; L: Grant Clarke; William Jerome); Switzerland; There's a Lot of Pretty Little Things in Paris; They're on Their Honeymoon; Une Nuit Paris

Cast: Harry Cooper; Dorothy Jardon; William Montgomery; Florence Moore; Bobby North; Max Rogers

Notes: [1] Sheet music only. [2] Some sources list the lyricists as Jerome and Harry Williams. Goetz's ASCAP sheet lists him as the composer.

3526 • PLEASURES AND PALACES

OPENED: 02/11/1965
Musical   Closed out of town

Composer: Frank Loesser
Lyricist: Frank Loesser
Librettist: Frank Loesser; Sam Spewack
Producer: Frank Productions; Allen Whitehead
Director: Bob Fosse

Source: ONCE THERE WAS A RUSSIAN (Play Sam Spewack); **Choreographer:** Bob Fosse; **Costumes:** Freddy Wittop; **Lighting Designer:** Robert Randolph; **Musical Director:** Fred Werner; **Orchestrations:** Philip J. Lang; **Set Design:** Robert Randolph

Songs: Ah, To Be Home Again; Barabanchik; Far, Far, Far Away; Hail Majesty (1); Hail Majesty (2); Hoorah for Jones; Horse Finale [2]; I Hear Bells; In Your Eyes [1]; My Lover Is a Scoundrel; Neither the Time Nor the Place; Pleasures and Palaces; Propaganda; Salute; Sins of Sura, The;

Tears of Joy; Thunder and Bells [2]; Thunder and Lightning; To Marry; To Your Health; Truly Loved [1]; Turkish Delight (dance); What Is Life?

Cast: John Anania; Eric Brotherson; Michael Davis; Eddie Gasper; Hy Hazell; Leon Janney; Alfred Marks; Mort Marshall; John McMartin; Phyllis Newman; Stan Page; Leland Palmer; Woody Romoff; Barbara Sharma; Sammy Smith

Notes: [1] Later in show HANS ANDERSEN. [2] ASCAP/Library of Congress only.

3527 • PLOT AGAINST THE CHASE MANHATTAN BANK, THE

OPENED: 11/26/1963   Theatre: Theater East
Revue   Off-Broadway: 15

Composer: Richard R. Wolf
Lyricist: Frank Spiering Jr.
Librettist: David Dozer; Lawrence B. Eisenberg; Betty Freedman; Carl Larsen; Ernest Leogrande
Producer: Eaton Associates
Director: Tom Gruenwald

Choreographer: Bick Goss; Karen Kristen; **Costumes:** Sylvia Kalegi; **Musical Director:** Joe Bousard; **Set Design:** Robert T. Williams

Songs: Almost Real; Closing, The; He She We; Hour Is Ripe, The; Josephine; Let the Play Begin; Only Fool; Only Two Allowed; Our Little Family; Pamplona; Reach Out and Touch Her; Seal, The; There's Nothing Left to Give Away; Thoughts By a River; Three Horsemen of the Metropolis, The

Cast: Renee Gorsey; Brian Watson

3528 • POLICY KINGS, THE

OPENED: 12/30/1938   Theatre: Nora Bayes
Musical   Broadway: 3

Composer: James P. Johnson
Lyricist: Louis Douglass
Librettist: Michael Ashwood
Producer: Michael Ashwood
Director: Louis Douglass

Arrangements: Ken Macomber; **Choreographer:** Jimmy Payne

Songs: Court House Sequence; Deed I Do Do Blues; Dewey Blues, The; Harlem Number Man; Harlem Woogie; Havin' a Blues; I'm Gonna Hit the Numbers Today; News News; Prologue; Radium Numbers (inst.) [1]; To Do What We Like; Walking My Baby Back Home; We Like to Play Numbers; You, You, You! [2]

Cast: Irene Cort; Billy Cumby; Willor Guilford; Frankie Jaxson; Ray Sneed Jr.

Notes: Program credits direction to Winston Douglass. Sheet music as in book. [1] Not in show. [2] May also be titled "Nobody Jes You You."

3529 • POLISH WEDDING, A

OPENED: 08/31/1912
Musical   Closed out of town

Composer: Jean Gilbert
Lyricist: George V. Hobart
Librettist: George V. Hobart
Producer: George M. Cohan; Sam Harris

Source: POLNISCHE WIRTSCHAFT (Musical: Jean Gilbert; Kurt Kraatz; Georg Okonkowski; Alfred Schonfeld)

Songs: Bygone Days (C/L: Jerome Kern); He Must Be Nice to Mother (C: Jerome Kern); I Want to Be the One to Show Her That (C: Jerome Kern); Let Us Build a Little Nest [2] (C/L: Jerome Kern; L: George V. Hobart); You're the Only Girl He Loves [1] (C: Jerome Kern)

Cast: William Burress; Ann Pennington; Lincoln Plumer; Genevieve Tobin; Valli Valli

Notes: Closed in Syracuse, NY. [1] Music revised as "Not Yet" in OH, LADY! LADY! [2] Cut from HEAD OVER HEELS (1918)

3530 • POLITICAL PARTY, A

OPENED: 09/26/1963   Theatre: 41st St.
Musical   Off-Broadway: 14

Librettist: Jean Anne; C.D.B. Bryan
Producer: Arch Lustberg
Director: Arch Lustberg

Costumes: Jean Anne; **Musical Director:** Daniel Ruslander

Songs: Ballad of Federal City, The (C: Bob Vigoda; L: Jean Anne); Church of Birch, The (C: Bob Vigoda; L: Jean Anne); Cocktail Party Types (C: Tony Mataresse; L: Jean Anne); Cuba Si, Yanqui No (C: Bob Vigoda; L: Jean Anne); Culture Twist, The (C: Sidney Schwartz; L: Gwen Gibson Schwartz); Father, Dear Father, Stop Testing (C/L: Shirley Grossman); Filibuster (C: Tony Mataresse; L: Jean Anne); Hootenanny with Peter, Paul, Irving (C: Bob Vigoda; L: Jean Anne); Ins and the Outs, The (C: Bob Vigoda; L: Jean Anne); Medicare Rock, The (C/L: Shirley Grossman); Minorities Is No Damn Good (C/L: Shirley Grossman); Mississippi (C/L: Shirley Grossman); Pennsylvania 1600 (C: Sidney Schwartz; L: Gwen Gibson Schwartz); Red Visitors, The (C/L: Shirley Grossman; C: Bob Vigoda); Rilly Great Shew, A (C: Herschel Horowitz; L: Pierce Rollins); Rocky Road to the White House, The (C/L: Shirley Grossman); Thy Neighbor and Thy Shelter (C/L: Shirley Grossman); Under Secretary (C/L: Shirley Grossman); V.I.P's: Very Influential Politicos (C: Bob Vigoda; L: Jean Anne); Washington Is Your Home (C: Kurt Moss; L: Daniel Ruslander); Where Is the News? (C: Herschel Horowitz; L: Pierce Rollins)

Cast: Jean Anne; Bill Holter; Arch Lustberg; Daniel Ruslander

3531 • POLITICIANS, THE

OPENED: 1909
Musical   Closed out of town

Librettist: Aaron Hoffman
Producer: Max Dill; C. William Kolb
Director: Frank Stammers

Songs: Autograph Girls; Election Day; Honey, Won't You Please Come Down?; Katie Strauss; March; Old Barn Dance, The; Overland Mail, The; Rock, Rock; Shadowgraph Chase; Thinking; Time to Kiss a Girl, The

Cast: Max Dill; C. William Kolb

Notes: Composer and lyricist not credited in program.

3532 • POLLY

OPENED: 01/08/1929   Theatre: Lyric
Musical   Broadway: 15

Composer: Philip Charig
Lyricist: Irving Caesar
Librettist: Guy Bolton; Isabel Leighton; George Middleton
Producer: Arthur Hammerstein
Director: John Harwood

Source: POLLY WITH A PAST (Play David Belasco); Choreographer: Jack Haskell; Musical Director: Herbert Stothart; Set Design: Joseph Urban

Songs: Abadaba Club, The; Be the Secret of My Life; Comme Ci, Comme Ca; Heel and Toe; Life Is Love; Little Bo-Peep; Lots of Time for Sue; Love Come Back to Me; Nobody Wants Me; On with the Dance; Polly; Sing a Song in the Rain (C: Harry Rosenthal; L: Irving Caesar; Douglas Furber); Sweet Liar (C: Herbert Stothart); There's Something Spanish in Your Eyes (C: Cliff Friend); What Can Be Sweeter; When a Fellow Meets a Flapper on Broadway

Cast: Fred Allen; Inez Courtney; Lucy Monroe; Harry K. Morton; Alonzo Price; Leonard Sillman

3533 • POLLY OF HOLLYWOOD
OPENED: 02/21/1927   Theatre: George M. Cohan
Musical   Broadway: 24

Composer: Edmund Joseph; Will Morrissey
Lyricist: Edmund Joseph; Will Morrissey
Librettist: Edmund Joseph; Will Morrissey
Producer: Harry L. Cort
Director: Will Morrissey

Choreographer: Walter Brooks; Costumes: Paul Aimes; Musical Director: Gus Salzer

Songs: Company Manners; Midnight Daddy; New Kind of Rhythm; Polly of Hollywood; Texas Stomp; Wanting You

Cast: John Agee; Hugh Hubert; Midgie Miller; Marguerite Zender

Notes: No program available.

3534 • POLLY OF THE CIRCUS
OPENED: 10/20/1924
Musical   Closed out of town

Composer: Hugo Felix
Lyricist: Margaret Mayo
Librettist: Margaret Mayo

Source: POLLY OF THE CIRCUS (Play Margaret Mayo)

Notes: Closed San Francisco. No other information available.

3535 • POLLY PREFERRED
OPENED: 01/11/1923   Theatre: Little
Play   Broadway: 202

Author: Guy Bolton
Producer: F. Ray Comstock; Morris Gest
Director: Winchell Smith

Set Design: P. Dodd Ackerman

Songs: Red Moon (C: Henri De Martini; Max Kortlander; L: Lew Brown; John Traver)

Cast: David Burns; Genevieve Tobin

3536 • POLONAISE
OPENED: 10/06/1945   Theatre: Alvin
Musical   Broadway: 113

Music Based On: Frederic Chopin
Composer: Bronislau Kaper
Lyricist: John Latouche
Librettist: Gottfried Reinhardt; Anthony Veiller
Producer: Harry Bloomfield
Director: Stella Adler

Choreographer: David Lichine; Costumes: Mary Grant; Musical Director: Ignace Strasfogel; Orchestrations: Don Walker; Set Design: Howard Bay; Vocal Arranger: Irving Landow

Songs: Au Revoir, Soldier (C: Bronislau Kaper); Autumn Songs; Battle Ballet (inst.); Exchange for Lovers; Hay, Hay, Hay (C: Bronislau Kaper); I Wonder As I Wander; Imperial Conference, An; Just for Tonight; Laughing Bells; Mazurka; Meadowlark; Moonlight Soliloquy; Next Time I Care, The (C: Bronislau Kaper); Now I Know Your Face by Heart; O Heart of My Country; Polonaise; Stranger (C: Bronislau Kaper); Tecla's Mood; Wait for Tomorrow

Cast: Curt Bois; Marta Eggerth; Rose Inghram; Jan Kiepura; James MacColl; Walter Munroe; Tania Riabouchinska

Notes: Music based on Frederic Chopin unless credited solely to Kaper.

3537 • POM-POM

OPENED: 02/28/1916   Theatre: Cohan
Musical   Broadway: 128

Composer: Hugo Felix
Lyricist: Anne Caldwell
Librettist: Anne Caldwell
Producer: Henry W. Savage
Director: George Marion

Source: CSIBESZKIRALY (Musical: Akos Buttkay; Lajos Szell); **Musical Director:** Max Bendix; **Set Design:** Joseph Urban

Songs: Behind the Scenes; Circus in the Moon, The; Come and Cuddle Me; Evelyn; Grand Army of Crooks; I'm Unlucky (C: Jean Schwartz; L: William Jerome); In the Dark; Kiss Me; Mister Love; Mon Desir; Only One Hour; Opening Chorus; Opening Chorus Act II; Pom-Pom; She's Gone; Ships in the Night; You Shall Not Go; Zim-Zim

Cast: George Brugger; Eric Campbell; Rita Dane; Edith Day; Mitzi Hajos; Carl Judd; Sydney Mather; Tom McNaughton

3538 • POOR LITTLE RITZ GIRL

OPENED: 07/27/1920   Theatre: Central
Musical   Broadway: 93

Composer: Richard Rodgers
Lyricist: Lorenz Hart
Librettist: George Campbell; Lew Fields
Producer: Lew Fields
Director: Ned Wayburn

Choreographer: David Bennett; **Costumes:** Marie Cook; Cora MacGeachy; Anna Spencer; **Lighting Designer:** Ned Wayburn; **Musical Director:** Charles Previn; **Set Design:** H. Robert Law

Songs: All You Need to Be a Star; Bombay Bombashay, The [5] (C: Ray Perkins; L: Alex Gerber); Boomerang, The [8]; Call the Doc [4]; Daisy and the Lark, The; Gown Is Mightier Than the Sword, The [4]; I Love to Say Hello to the Girls (I Hate to Say Goodbye) (C: Sigmund Romberg; L: Alex Gerber); I Surrender [4]; In the Land of Yesterday (C: Sigmund Romberg;

L: Alex Gerber); Lady Raffles-Behave [4]; Let Me Drink in Your Eyes [7]; Lord Only Knows, The [4]; Love Will Call [6]; Love's Intense in Tents [2]; Mary Queen of Scots [9] (L: Herbert Fields); Midnight Girl, The (One Midnight Supper at Home) [4]; My Violin (C: Sigmund Romberg; L: Alex Gerber); Nothing New Beneath the Sun [3] (C/L: Unknown); Phantom Waltz, The (dance) (inst.) (C: Sigmund Romberg); Poor Little Ritz Girl (1) [4]; Poor Little Ritz Girl (2) (C: Sigmund Romberg; L: Alex Gerber); Pretty Ming Toy (C: Sigmund Romberg; L: Alex Gerber); Souvenir [4]; What Happened Nobody Knows; When I Found You (C: Sigmund Romberg; L: Alex Gerber); Will You Forgive Me? [4]; You Can't Fool Your Dreams [1]

Cast: Eleanor Griffith; Lulu McConnell; Aileen Poe; Charles Purcell; Andrew Tombes; Florence Webber

Notes: Out of town the book was credited to Henry B. Stillman and William J. O'Neil. Out of town the entire score was by Rodgers and Hart. Romberg and Gerber were brought in to supplement the score. [1] Same music as "Don't Love Me Like Othello" from FLY WITH ME. [2] Same music as "Peek in Pekin" in FLY WITH ME. [3] Out Washington, D.C. prior to Broadway. [4] Cut prior to Broadway. [5] Sheet music credits Perkins. Program credits Romberg. [6] Same music as "Dreaming True" in FLY WITH ME and SAY IT WITH JAZZ. [7] Cut prior to Broadway. Also in YOU'LL NEVER KNOW. [8] Cut prior to Broadway. Also in YOU'D BE SURPRISED. [9] Cut prior to Broadway. Also in YOU'D BE SURPRISED and in JAZZ A LA CARTE.

3539 • POP

OPENED: 04/03/1974   Theatre: Players
Musical   Off-Broadway: 1

Composer: Donna Cribari; Larry Schiff
Lyricist: Chuck Knull; Larry Schiff
Librettist: Chuck Knull; Larry Schiff
Producer: Brad Gromelski; William Murphy III
Director: Allen R. Belknap

Source: KING LEAR (Play William Shakespeare); **Choreographer:** Ron Spencer; **Costumes:** Pat Gorman; **Dance Arranger:** Donna Cribari; **Lighting Designer:** Hallam B. Derx; **Musical Director:** Donna Cribari; **Set Design:** Pat Gorman; **Vocal Arranger:** Donna Cribari

Songs: Cindelia; Dad; Friends (L: Ron Spencer); Guess What from Guess Who? (L: Chuck Knull; Larry Schiff; Ron Spencer); Hail Hio; Her Song (L: Ron Spencer); Here I Go Bananas! (L: Ron Spencer); Heroes; Hollow Faces; Locker of Love (L: Ron Spencer); Love Is . . . (L: Ron Spencer); No One Listens; Revolution Now; See the Light; We Shall Release You; Wedding Song, The

Cast: Stephan Dunne; Dennis Ferden; Anna Gianiotis; T. Galen Girvin; Lois Greco; Lyman Jones; Frank Juliano; Frank W. Kopyc; Karen Magid; Bill Nightingale

3540 • POPPY

OPENED: 09/13/1923   Theatre: Apollo
Musical   Broadway: 346

Composer: Stephen Jones; Arthur Samuels
Lyricist: Dorothy Donnelly
Librettist: Howard Dietz; Dorothy Donnelly
Producer: Philip Goodman
Director: Dorothy Donnelly

Choreographer: Julian Alfred; **Costumes:** Charles LeMaire

Songs: Alibi Baby (C: Arthur Samuels; L: Howard Dietz); Dancing Lesson, The (C: John Egan); Fortune Telling; Girl I've Never Met, The; Hang Your Sorrows in the Sun (C: John Egan); Kadoola, Kadoola; On Our Honeymoon; Poppy Dear; Someone Will Make You Smile (Vienna Dreams) [1] (C: Rudolf Sieczynski; L: Irving Caesar); Stepping Around; Two Make a Home; Whaddaye Do Sundays, Whaddaye Do Mondays, Mary? (C: Stephen Jones; L: Irving Caesar); When Men Are Alone; When You Are in My Arms [1] (C: Nicholas Kempner)

Cast: Alan Edwards; W.C. Fields; Luella Gear; Madge Kennedy; Robert Woolsey

Notes: [1] Sheet music only.

3541 • PORGY AND BESS

OPENED: 10/10/1935   Theatre: Alvin
Musical   Broadway: 124

Composer: George Gershwin
Lyricist: Ira Gershwin; DuBose Heyward
Librettist: DuBose Heyward
Producer: Theatre Guild, The
Director: Rouben Mamoulian

Source: PORGY (Play Dorothy Heyward; DuBose Heyward); **Musical Director:** Alexander Smallens; **Orchestrations:** George Gershwin; **Set Design:** Sergei Soudeikine; **Vocal Arranger:** Eva Jessye

Songs: Bess, You Is My Woman Now; Buzzard Song, The [1] (L: DuBose Heyward); Clara, Don't You Be Downhearted (L: DuBose Heyward); Crap Game Fugue (L: DuBose Heyward); Gone, Gone, Gone! (L: DuBose Heyward); Good Mornin' Brother [1] (L: DuBose Heyward); I Ain't Got No Shame [1]; I Got Plenty o' Nuthin'; I Hate Your Struttin' Style [1] (L: DuBose Heyward); I Loves You, Porgy; I'm on My Way (L: DuBose Heyward); It Ain't Necessarily So (L: Ira Gershwin); It Take a Long Pull to Get There (L: DuBose Heyward); Jasbo Brown [1]; Leavin' fo' de Promis' Lan' (L: DuBose Heyward); Lonely Boy [1] (L: DuBose Heyward); My Man's Gone Now (L: DuBose Heyward); Oh, Bess, Oh Where's My Bess? (L: Ira Gershwin); Oh, De Lawd Shake De Heaven (L: DuBose Heyward); Oh I Can't Sit Down (L: Ira Gershwin); Overflow (L: DuBose Heyward); Red-Headed Woman, A (L: Ira Gershwin); Six Prayers, The (Oh, Heav'nly Father) (L: Ira Gershwin; DuBose Heyward); Street Cries (L: DuBose Heyward); Summertime (L: DuBose Heyward); Sure to Go to Heaven [1] (L: DuBose Heyward); There's a Boat dat's Leavin' Soon for New York (L: Ira Gershwin); They Pass By Singing (L: DuBose Heyward); Time and Time Again (Oh, Doctor Jesus) (L: DuBose Heyward); What You Want Wid Bess? (L: DuBose Heyward); Woman Is a Sometime Thing, A (L: DuBose Heyward); Woman to Lady (L: DuBose Heyward)

Cast: Anne Brown; John Bubbles; Ford Buck; Warren Coleman; Helen Dowdy; Todd Duncan; Ruby Elzy; Georgette Harvey; J. Rosamond Johnson; Edward Matthews; Abbie Mitchell; Musa Williams

Notes: [1] Cut prior to Broadway.

3542 • PORTFOLIO REVUE

OPENED: 12/06/1974   Theatre: Portfolio
Revue   Off-Broadway: 12

Composer: Harvey Schmidt
Lyricist: Tom Jones
Producer: Drew Katzman; Portfolio Studios; John Schak

Choreographer: Janet Kerr; **Costumes:** Charles Blackburn

Songs: At the Music Hall [14]; Autumn Afternoon, The [14]; Boulloux Girls, The [13]; Celebration [12]; Dance Hall Saturday Night [9]; Earthly Paradise [13]; Everyone Looks Lonely [2]; Femme Du Monde [13]; Fifty Million Years Ago [12]; Flaming Agnes [11]; Fliberty Jibits [9]; Follow Along with Me [1]; Freshman Song, A [6]; Gonna Be Another Hot Day [9]; Growing Older [14]; His Love [14]; Holy Man and the New Yorker, The [8]; Honeymoon Is Over, The [11]; I Can Dance [9]; I Do! I Do! Waltz [10]; I Know Loneliness Quite Well [2]; Isn't That a Wonderful Way to Die? [3]; Love Is Not a Sentiment [14]; Melisande [9]; Mister Off-Broadway [8]; My Cup Runneth Over [11]; Not My Problem [12]; Now I'm Back in New York City [2]; Seasonal Sonata, A [8]; Simple Little Things [9]; Thank Them for Your Love [5]; Try to Remember [7]; Wandrin' Child [4]; Wassail [5]; Well Known Fact, A [11]

Cast: David Cryer; Tom Jones; Jeanne Lucas; Harvey Schmidt; Kathrin King Segal; **Pianist:** Harvey Schmidt

Notes: Limited engagement. [1] From unproduced Musical version of ROMEO AND JULIET titled JOY. [2] From TV production NEW YORK SCRAPBOOK. [3] From THE BONE ROOM, a work in progress. [4] From the film score BAD COMPANY with lyrics added for this show. [5] Cut prior to New York. Popular song. [6] Cut prior to New York. The songwriters' first college song. [7] From JOY and later THE FANTASTICKS. [8] From DEMI DOZEN. [9] From 110 IN THE SHADE. [10] Written for unproduced TV version of I DO! I DO! [11] From I DO! I DO! [12] From CELEBRATION. [13] From COLETTE. [14] Cut prior to New York. From COLETTE.

3543 • PORTOFINO

OPENED: 02/21/1958 Theatre: Adelphi
Musical Broadway: 3

Lyricist: Richard Ney
Librettist: Richard Ney
Director: Karl Genus

Choreographer: Ray Harrison; Charles Weidman; **Costumes:** Michael Travis; **Lighting Designer:**

Lee Watson; **Musical Director:** Will Irwin; **Orchestrations:** Philip J. Lang, **Set Design:** Wolfgang Roth; **Vocal Arranger:** Joseph Moore

Songs: Bacchanale; Beware of Love [1] (C: Louis Bellson); Come Along (C: Will Irwin; L: Sheldon Harnick); Come to Portofino [1] (C: Louis Bellson); Dance of the Whirling Wimpus (inst.); Dream for Angela, A (C: Louis Bellson); Drink the Wine [1] (C: Will Irwin); Festa (dance); Grand Prix of Portofino, The (C: Will Irwin); Guido's Tango (inst.); Here I Come (C: Louis Bellson; Will Irwin; L: Sheldon Harnick); I Don't Care [1] (C: Will Irwin); I'm in League with the Devil (C: Will Irwin); Isn't It Wonderful? (C: Louis Bellson); It Might Be Love (C: Louis Bellson); Kitty Car Ballet; Little Boy Blue [1] (C: Louis Bellson); Madrigal, The [1] (C: Richard Ney); Morning Prayer (C: Will Irwin); New Dreams for Old (C: Louis Bellson); No Wedding Bells for Me (C: Will Irwin); Padre's Theme, The [1] (C: Louis Bellson); Portofino (C: Louis Bellson); Prologue (C: Will Irwin; L: Sheldon Harnick); Red Collar Job (C: Louis Bellson; Will Irwin; L: Sheldon Harnick); That's Love (C: Richard Ney); Too Little Time for Love (1) [1] (C: Louis Bellson); Too Little Time for Love (2) (C: Will Irwin); Under a Spell (C: Louis Bellson; Richard Ney; L: Sheldon Harnick); Why Not for Marriage (C: Louis Bellson); You'll Never Make Heaven That Way [1] (C: Will Irwin)

Cast: Jan Chaney; Helen Gallagher; Georges Guetary; Robert Strauss

Notes: [1] Cut prior to opening.

3544 • PORTRAIT OF JENNIE

OPENED: 1984
Musical

Composer: Howard Marren
Lyricist: Enid Futterman
Librettist: Enid Futterman; Dennis Rosa
Producer: New Federal Theatre
Director: Dennis Rosa

Source: PORTRAIT OF JENNIE (Story: Robert Nathan); **Choreographer:** Dennis Rosa; **Costumes:** Charles Schoonmaker; **Lighting Designer:** Jeff Davis; **Musical Director:** Uel Wade; **Orchestrations:** William D. Brohn; **Set Design:** Michael H. Yeargan; **Vocal Arranger:** Uel Wade

Songs: Alhambra Nights; Epilogue; Green Place, A; Hammerstein's Music Hall; I Love You; My City; Paris; Portrait of Jennie; Prologue; Remember Today; Secrets; Time Stands Still in Truro; Where I Come From; Winter of the Mind; Wish

Cast: Jean Barker; Brent Barrett; John Bedford-Lloyd; Donna Bullock; Karen Lynn Dale; Paul Milikin; Maggie O'Connell; Brian Phipps; Stratton Walling; David Wohl

Notes: Showcase production.

3545 • POSSUM HUNT CLUB REVUE, THE

OPENED: 1910
Revue   Closed out of town

Composer: Edward V. Cupero
Lyricist: Vincent Bryan
Librettist: Vincent Bryan
Producer: Lew Dockstader
Director: Lew Dockstader

Musical Director: Edward V. Cupero

Songs: Espanola Prance; I Will Love You Always; Just for Auld Lang Syne; My Love Is Greater than the World; Oh You Bear Cut Rag; Patrick J. O'Hara; Sweet Sixteen; Wanderer, The; When a Boy from New Hampshire Loves a Girl from Tennessee

Cast: Lew Dockstader; Carroll Johnson; Eddie Mazier

Notes: Program of Kansas City 10/16/10.

3546 • POST DEPRESSION GAIETIES, THE

OPENED: 02/24/1935
Revue   Broadway: 1

Producer: Marc Connelly

Songs: What Are You Doing in Here? (C: Richard Rodgers; L: Lorenz Hart)

Notes: Benefit of the Authors League Fund and Stage Relief Fund.

3547 • POT OF GOLD, THE

OPENED: 11/26/1912
Musical

Composer: Cole Porter
Lyricist: Cole Porter
Librettist: Almet F. Jenks Jr.; Cole Porter
Director: Almet F. Jenks Jr.

Songs: At the Rainbow; Bellboys; Exercise; Ha, Ha, They Must Sail for Siberia; I Love You So; I Want to Be Married (to a Delta Kappa Epsilon Man); I Wonder Where My Girl Is Now; If I Were a Football Man [1]; It's Awfully Hard when Mother's Not Along; Loie and Chlodo; Longing for Dear Old Broadway; My Houseboat on the Thames; My Salvation Army Queen; Scandal; She Was a Fair Young Mermaid; Since We've Met; So Let Us Hail; That Rainbow Rag [1]; We Are So Aesthetic; What a Charming Afternoon; What an Awful Hullabaloo; When I Used to Lead the Ballet

Cast: Cole Porter

Notes: Fall initiation play at Delta Kappa Epsilon and Hotel Taft, New Haven 12/4/12. Amateur show. [1] Not used.

3548 • POTHOLES

OPENED: 10/09/1979   Theatre: Cherry Lane
Revue   Off-Broadway: 15

Composer: Ted Simons
Lyricist: Elinor Guggenheimer
Librettist: Elinor Guggenheimer
Producer: Rodger Hess
Director: Sue Lawless

Choreographer: Wayne Cilento; **Costumes:** Ann Emonts; **Lighting Designer:** Robby Monk; **Musical Director:** Steven Oirich; **Set Design:** Kenneth Foy

Songs: Back in the Street; Can You Type?; Dog Walker; Fast Food; Finale; Giant; Just Sit Back; Looking for Someone; Lost New York; Mad About; Madison Avenue; Network; Politicians' Song; Ropin' Dogies; Sound and Light; St. Patrick's Day Parade; Starved; Suddenly She Was There; Tickets' Song; Typical New Yorkers; Welcome; Yoga and Yoghurt

Cast: Jill Cook; Brandon Maggart; Carol Morley;

Cynthia Parva; Lee Roy Reams; Joe Romagnoli; J. Keith Ryan; Samuel E. Wright

3549 • POUND IN YOUR POCKET, A

OPENED: 1957
Musical   Nightclub

Composer: Charles Strouse
Lyricist: Lee Adams

Songs: Best Ain't Good Enough, The; Duet; Ethics Waltz, The; Few Small Tasks, A; It's a Topsy Turvy World; Lovely Party; Pound in Your Pocket, A; Simple Girl, A; Sleeping Dreams, Waking Dreams; Someone Who Cares; When I Plot a Plan

Notes: Presented at the Royal Poinciana, Palm Beach, Florida.

3550 • POUSSE-CAFE, OR THE WORST BORN (1897)

OPENED: 12/02/1897   Theatre: Weber & Fields
                       Broadway Music Hall
Musical   Broadway

Composer: John Stromberg
Librettist: Edgar Smith; Louis de Lange

Notes: No program available.

3551 • POUSSE-CAFE (1966)

OPENED: 03/18/1966   Theatre: 46th Street
Musical   Broadway: 3

Composer: Duke Ellington
Lyricist: Marshall Barer
Librettist: Jerome Weidman
Producer: Guy de la Passardiere
Director: Jose Quintero

Source: PROFESSOR UNRATH (Novel: Heinrich Mann); **Choreographer:** Valerie Bettis; **Costumes:** Albert Wolsky; Patricia Zipprodt; **Lighting Designer:** V.C. Fuqua; **Musical Director:** Sherman Frank; **Orchestrations:** Larry Wilcox; **Set Design:** Will Steven Armstrong

Songs: Amazing [3]; Be a Man [1]; C'est Comme Ca; Colonel's Lady [3]; Do Me a Favor [3]; Easy to Take; Eleventh Commandment, The (C: Michael Leonard; L: Herbert Martin); Fleugel Street Rag [1]; Follow Me Up the Stairs; Forever [3]; Good Old Days, The; Goodbye, Charlie (L: Marshall Barer; Fred Tobias); Here You Are [3]; If I Knew Now [1]; If You Knew Now (What I Knew Then) [1]; Je Ne Ai Rien [3]; Let's; My Heart Is a Stranger [1]; Natchez Trace [3]; Old World Charm; Rules and Regulations; Settle for Less [1]; Someone to Care For; Spacious and Gracious [3]; Spider and the Fly, The (1) [1]; Spider and the Fly, The (2) (C: Michael Leonard; L: Herbert Martin); Sugar City [3]; Swivel, The [1]; Take Love Easy [2] (L: John Latouche); Thank You, Ma'am; These Are the Good Old Days [3]; Up Your Ante [1]; Wedding, The

Cast: Theodore Bikel; Charles Durning; Travis Hudson; Ellis Larkins; Lilo; Robert Rovin; Jeff Siggins; Richard Tone

Notes: [1] Cut prior to opening. [2] Not in programs. From BEGGAR'S HOLIDAY. [3] ASCAP/Library of Congress only.

3552 • POWDER PUFF REVUE

Revue

Composer: Edward F. Breier; Edward A. Weinstein
Lyricist: Edward F. Breier; Edward A. Weinstein

Songs: Blue Diamonds; I Found the Sweetest Rose That Grows in Dixie; Just a Little Sunshine Makes a Rainbow; Take Me

Notes: No other information available.

3553 • PRAIRIE

OPENED: 1983
Musical   Unproduced

Composer: Lucy Simon
Lyricist: Jacques Levy
Librettist: Jacques Levy

Source: LITTLE HOUSE ON THE PRAIRIE SERIES (Book: Laura Ingalls Wilder)

Notes: No other information available.

3554 • PRAY BY BLECHT, A

Notes: *See THE EXCEPTION AND THE RULE.*

3555 • PREPPIES

OPENED: 08/18/1983   Theatre: Promenade
Musical   Off-Broadway: 52

Composer: Judy Hart Angelo; Gary Portnoy
Lyricist: Judy Hart Angelo; Gary Portnoy
Librettist: Carlos Davis; David Taylor
Producer: Carlos Davis; Anthony Fingleton
Director: Tony Tanner

Choreographer: Tony Tanner; **Costumes:** Patricia McGourty; **Lighting Designer:** Richard Winkler; **Musical Director:** Jeff Lodin; **Orchestrations:** Peter Larson; **Set Design:** David Jenkins; **Vocal Arranger:** Jeff Lodin

Songs: Bells; Bring on the Loot; Chance of a Lifetime, The; Fairy Tales; Finale; Gonna Run; Moving On; No Big Deal; One Night; One Step Away; Parents' Farewell, The; People Like Us; Summertime; We've Got Each Other; Worlds Apart

Cast: Susan Dow; Beth Fowler; Tom Hafner; Michael Ingram; Peter Larson; Tudi Roche; Bob Walton

3556 • PRESENT ARMS

OPENED: 04/26/1928   Theatre: Mansfield
Musical   Broadway: 147

Composer: Richard Rodgers
Lyricist: Lorenz Hart
Librettist: Herbert Fields
Producer: Lew Fields
Director: Alexander Leftwich

Choreographer: Busby Berkeley; **Costumes:** Milgrim; **Musical Director:** Roy Webb; **Set Design:** Ward & Harvey

Songs: Blue Ocean Blues [1]; Crazy Elbows; Do I Hear You Saying 'I Love You'?; Down by the Sea (Whoopie); Hawaii (Coralline); I Love You More Than Yesterday [2]; I'm a Fool, Little One; Is It the Uniform?; Kiss for Cinderella, A; Kohala Welcome; Nuts, He Travels with Us Nuts; Tell It to the Marines (A Bunch o' Nuts); This Rescue Is a Calamity (Finaletto, Act II, Scene 3); What Price Love [3]; You Took Advantage of Me

Cast: Joyce Barbour; Busby Berkeley; Demaris Dore; Charles King; Flora Le Breton; Fuller Mellish Jr.; Franker Woods

Notes: [1] Same music as "Atlantic Blues" in LIDO LADY. [2] Cut prior to opening. In LADY FINGERS. [3] Cut prior to opening.

3557 • PRESENT TENSE, THE

OPENED: 11/04/1977   Theatre: Park Royal
Revue   Off-Broadway: 23

Librettist: Ralph Buckley; Cast, The; Stephen Rosenfeld; Haila Strauss; Jeffrey Sweet
Producer: Roger Ailes; John Fishback
Director: Stephen Rosenfeld

Costumes: Paul dePass; **Lighting Designer:** John Fishback; **Musical Director:** Skip Kennon; **Set Design:** Paul de Pass

Songs: Carter Song, The (C/L: Allen Cohen); Cautiously Optimistic (C/L: Alan Menken); Come to Cuba (C/L: Don Siegal); Love Me or Leave Me (C/L: Don Siegal); Man on a Subway (C/L: Bob Joseph; Don Siegal); Margaret (C/L: Alan Menken; Muriel Robinson); Possum Pie (C/L: Lee S. Wilkof); Sklip, Dat, Doobee (C/L: Don Siegal); Song for a Crowded Cabaret (C/L: Jeffrey Sweet); Yankee Man (C/L: Alan Menken)

Cast: Barbara Brummel; Chris Carroll; Jim Cyrus; Lianne Kressin; Michael Nobel; Lee Wilkof

3558 • PRESIDENT, THE

OPENED: 1960
TV Musical

Composer: Jerry Livingston
Lyricist: Leonard Adelson

Songs: All Men; Andy Jackson; Back to Normal; Brother Against Brother; Bunker Hill to Yorktown; Dwight D. Eisenhower; Father of Our Country, The; Go Get 'Em Harry; Honest Abe; It's Only Or-ee-vwor (Au Revoir); People's Choice, The; President, The; Remember the Alamo; Rough Riders; Saga of the Presidents, The; Tippecanoe and Tyler Too; U.S. Grant; War of 1812; We Have Nothing to Fear

Notes: No other information available.

3559 • PRESIDENT'S DAUGHTER, THE

OPENED: 11/03/1970   Theatre: Billy Rose
Musical   Broadway: 72

Composer: Murray Rumshinsky
Lyricist: Jacob Jacobs
Librettist: H. Kalmanov
Producer: Jacob Jacobs
Director: Jacob Jacobs

Choreographer: Henrietta Jacobson; **Musical Director:** Murray Rumshinsky; **Set Design:** Barry Arnold

Songs: Everything Is Possible in Life; I Have What You Want!; If Only I Could Be a Kid Again; Lesson in Yiddish, A; Love at Golden Years; Old Man Shouldn't Be Born, An; President's Daughter, The; Stiochket; We Two; Welcome, Mr. Golden!; What More Do I Need?; What Would You Do?; Without a Mother; Women's Liberation

Cast: Diana Goldberg; George Guidall; Jacob Jacobs; Jack Rechzeit; Chayele Rosenthal

3560 • PRESS AGENT, THE

OPENED: 11/27/1905   Theatre: Lew Fields
Musical   Broadway: 40

Composer: William Lorraine
Lyricist: John P. Wilson
Librettist: Mark Swan; John P. Wilson
Producer: Lee Shubert; Sam S. Shubert

Songs: Float Me Charlie (C: Jean Schwartz; L: William Jerome)

Cast: Kate Condon; Peter F. Dailey; Theodore Friebus; Frank Lalor

Notes: No program available.

3561 • PRETTY FACES

OPENED: 10/21/1990   Theatre: Actors Outlet
Musical   Off-Broadway: 49

Composer: Robert W. Cabell
Lyricist: Robert W. Cabell
Librettist: Robert W. Cabell
Producer: Tommy De Maio
Director: Gene Foote

Arrangements: Arnie Gross; **Choreographer:** Gene Foote; **Costumes:** George Bergeron; **Lighting Designer:** Clifton Taylor; **Musical Director:** Jim Mironchik; **Set Design:** Peter Rogness

Songs: Are You the One; Daddy Doesn't Care; 42-32-42; Furs, Fortune, Fame, Glamor; Global Glamor Girls; Heartbreaker; How Do You Like Your Men; Interviews; Moment Is Mine, This; On with the Show; Pretty Faces; Purple Hearted Soldiers; Sleep Walkers Lament; Solo for the Telephone; Song for Jesus; Taking Chances; Tears and Tears Ago; Too Plump for Prom Night; Waiting for the Curtain; What Is Missing in My Life; What's Missing in My Life; Woman That I Am

Cast: Lynn Halvertson; Liz Leisek; Ron Meier; Michael Winther

3562 • PRETTY MRS. SMITH

OPENED: 09/21/1914   Theatre: Casino
Musical   Broadway: 48

Composer: Henry James; Alfred G. Robyn
Lyricist: Earl Carroll
Librettist: Elmer Harris; Oliver Morosco
Producer: Oliver Morosco
Director: T. Daniel Frawley

Set Design: Robert Brunton; Homer Emens; Kellam

Songs: Back to Old Broadway [1] (C: Henry James); Bensonhurst Gavotte, The (C: Alfred G. Robyn); Dawn in Florida (C: Henry James); Dreaming [1] (C: Earl Carroll; L: Archibald Joyce); Drucilla (C: Alfred G. Robyn); How D'Ye Do [1] (C: Henry James); Let Bygones Be Bygones (C: Alfred G. Robyn); Long, Lean, Lanky Letty (C/L: Sidney Grant); Love Has Come to Live in Our House (C: Henry James); Lovely Woman [1] (C: Henry James); Make Love to Me [1] (L: Henry James); Mrs. Sippi You're a Grand Old Belle (C: Ashlyn; L: Billy Gould); My Dream of Dreams (C: Alfred G. Robyn); On the Mississippi [1] (C: Henry James); One Little Wink [1] (L: Henry James); Plain Ol' Name of Smith, The (C: Alfred G. Robyn); Pretty Mrs. Smith (C: Henry James)

Cast: James Gleason; Sydney Grant; Charlotte Greenwood; Charles Purcell; Fritzi Scheff

Notes: Titled LONG LEGGED LETTY on tour after New York. [1] Out Boston 4/20/14.

3563 • PRETTY PENNY

OPENED: 06/20/1949
Revue   Closed out of town

Composer: Harold Rome
Lyricist: Harold Rome
Librettist: Jerome Chodorov
Producer: Leonard Field
Director: George S. Kaufman

Choreographer: Michael Kidd

Songs: Cry, Baby, Cry [1]; French with Tears [1]; Pocketful of Dreams [2]; You Never Know What Hit You (When It's Love) [3]

Cast: David Burns; Peter Gennaro; Michael Kidd; Lenore Lonergan; Carl Reiner; Onna White

Notes: Produced at Bucks County Playhouse, New Hope, PA. [1] Also in ALIVE AND KICKING. [2] Also in MICHAEL TODD'S PEEP SHOW. [3] Also in THAT'S THE TICKET and BLESS YOU ALL.

3564 • PRETTYBELLE

OPENED: 02/01/1971
Musical   Closed out of town

Composer: Jule Styne
Lyricist: Bob Merrill
Librettist: Bob Merrill
Producer: Alexander H. Cohen
Director: Gower Champion

Source: PRETTYBELLE (Novel: Jean Arnold); **Costumes:** Ann Roth; **Lighting Designer:** Nananne Porcher; **Musical Director:** Peter Howard; **Orchestrations:** Ralph Burns; Jack Cortner; Elliot Lawrence; **Set Design:** Oliver Smith

Songs: Adirondacks [2]; Back from the Great Beyond; Friggin New Orleans Interlude (inst.) [2]; Funeral Exit (inst.) [2]; Give Me a Share in America; God's Garden; Goodbye Chickasaw County [2]; How Could I Know What Was Goin' On?; I Met a Man; I Never Did Imagine; I'm Doin' Okay in My Own Way; I'm in a Tree; In the Japanese Gardens; Individual Thing, An [1]; Japanese Procession (inst.) [2]; John Sweet Ballet, The (dance); Just Don't Take It Away [2]; Manic Depressives (Don't Do Rewrites); Mother's Blues [2]; New Orleans Poon; No-Tell Motel, The; Piciyumi Gazette; Policemen's Hymn; Prettybelle; Rape and Resurrection [2]; Shine Your Lantern [2]; Some Beer, Some Bowlin' [2]; Tasy Freeze [2]; To a Small Degree; When I'm

Drunk I'm Beautiful; You Ain't Hurtin' Your Ole Lady None; You Never Looked Better

Cast: Chad Block; Jon Cypher; Mark Dawson; Igors Gavon; Angela Lansbury; Renee Lippen; Peter Lombard; Bert Michaels; Joe Morton; Howard Porter; Charlotte Rae

Notes: [1] Cut from FUNNY GIRL. [2] ASCAP/Library of Congress only.

3565 • PRETZELS
OPENED: 12/16/1974   Theatre: Theatre Four
Revue   Off-Broadway: 120

Composer: John Forster
Lyricist: John Forster
Librettist: Jane Curtin; Fred Grandy; Judy Kahan
Producer: Walter Boxer; Burry Fredrik; Phoenix Theatre
Director: Patricia Carmichael

Choreographer: Francis Patrelle; **Costumes:** Clifford Capone; **Lighting Designer:** Ken Billington; **Set Design:** Stuart Wurtzel

Songs: Classical Music; Cockroach Song, The; Jane's Song; Monologue; Pretzels; Reunion, The; Sing and Dance; Take Me Back

Cast: Jane Curtin; Timothy Jerome; Judy Kahan

3566 • PRIMA DONNA, THE (1901)
OPENED: 04/17/1901   Theatre: Herald Square
Musical   Broadway: 36

Composer: Aime Lauchaume
Lyricist: Harry B. Smith
Librettist: Harry B. Smith
Producer: A.H. Chamberlyn

Songs: Honeysuckle and the Bee, The (C/L: Fitz; Penn)

Cast: Mabel Barrison; Charles B. Bowers; William Cameron; W.P. Carleton; Herbert Cawthorne; Lulu Glaser

Notes: No other songs listed in program.

3567 • PRIMA DONNA, THE (1908)
OPENED: 11/30/1908   Theatre: Knickerbocker
Musical   Broadway: 72

Composer: Victor Herbert
Lyricist: Henry Blossom
Librettist: Henry Blossom
Producer: Charles Dillingham
Director: Fred G. Latham

Musical Director: John Lund

Songs: Dream Love ('Twas Only Dreaming); Espagnola; Everybody Else's Girl Looks Better to Me Than Mine; Game of Love, The; Here's to My Comrades and You; If I Were on the Stage; If You Were I and I Were You; I'll Be Married to the Music of a Military Band; Jolly Cuirassier; La, La; Love Light; Man and a Maid, A; Monarch and a Maid, A; O! Mia Speranza (L: Signor Ciucicini); Oh! Oh! Oh!; One You're Looking For; Soldier's Life Is Never Long; Soldier's Love; Something Always Happens When It Shouldn't; There's Only One Rose in the Garden of Love (Opening Chorus); Think of Me; 'Twas Different Years Ago; Twenty Years Ago!; What Is Love; When Girls Command the Army; Where the Fairest Flowers Blooming; You'd Be Surprised

Cast: St. Clair Bayfield; William J. Harcourt; William Raymond; Fritzi Scheff

Notes: No songs listed in program.

3568 • PRIME TIME PROPHET

OPENED: 06/10/1993   Theatre: Players
Musical   Off-Broadway: 54

Composer: Kevin Connors
Lyricist: Kevin Connors
Librettist: Randy Buck
Producer: Prophet Company, The
Director: Kevin Connors

Costumes: David Robinson; **Lighting Designer:** John Michael Deegan; **Musical Director:** David Wolfson; **Set Design:** Don Jensen; **Vocal Arranger:** David Wolfson

Songs: Armageddon; Award, The; Devil to Pay, The; Diva Supreme; Expect a Miracle; Heavenly Party; Homesick for Hell; Hot Shot; How Does She Do It?; Leap of Faith; Necessarily Evil; Saved!; So Help Me God; Step Into the Light; Tina Seeks Solace; Tina's Final Hour; Tips from Tina

Cast: Janet Aldrich; David Brand; Beth Glover; Jonathan Hadley; Marcus Maurice

3569 • PRIMROSE

OPENED: 09/11/1924   Theatre: Winter Garden
Musical   London: 255

Composer: George Gershwin
Lyricist: Desmond Carter
Librettist: Guy Bolton; George Grossmith
Producer: George Grossmith; J.A.E. Malone
Director: Charles A. Maynard

Choreographer: Laddie Cliff; Carl Hyson; **Musical Director:** John Ansell

Songs: Ballet Music; Beau Brummel; Berkeley Square and Kew; Boy Wanted [4] (L: Desmond Carter; Ira Gershwin); Can We Do Anything? (L: Desmond Carter; Ira Gershwin); Countryside (This Is the Life for a Man), The; Four Little Sirens [5] (L: Ira Gershwin); I Make Hay While the Moon Shines; Isn't It Terrible What They Did to Mary Queen of Scots; Isn't It Wonderful (L: Desmond Carter; Ira Gershwin); It Is the Fourteenth of July; Leaving Town While We May; Live Wire, The [1]; Mophams, The; Naughty Baby (L: Desmond Carter; Ira Gershwin); Pep! Zip! and Punch! [1]; Roses of France; Some Far-Away Someone [2] (L: B.G. DeSylva; Ira Gershwin); That New-Fangled Mother of Mine; 'Till I Meet Someone Like You; Wait a Bit, Susie [3] (L: Desmond Carter; Ira Gershwin); When Toby Is Out of Town

Cast: Percy Heming; Leslie Henson; Margery Hicklin; Claude Hulbert; Vera Lennox; Heather Thatcher

Notes: [1] Cut. [2] Same music as "At Half-Past Seven" from NIFTIES OF 1923. [3] Same music as "Beautiful Gypsy" cut from ROSALIE (1928). [4] Revised from song written by the Gershwins for A DANGEROUS MAID. [5] Revised from song "The Sirens" written by the Gershwins for A DANGEROUS MAID.

3570 • PRINCE ANANIAS

OPENED: 11/20/1894   Theatre: Broadway
Musical   Broadway: 55

Composer: Victor Herbert
Librettist: Francis Neilson
Director: Jerome Sykes

Choreographer: Signor Romeo; **Costumes:** Mme.

Siedle; **Musical Director:** S.L. Studley; **Set Design:** Ernest Albert

Songs: Ah! Cupid, Meddlesome Boy!; Ah! He's a Prince; Ah! List to Me; Amaryllis; Hamlet of Fancy, The; His Highness; I Am No Queen; It Needs No Poet; Love Is Spring; Love Ne'er Came Night; March; Polka; Regal Sadness Sits on Me; Schottische; Two- Step; Waltz; Who Might You Do?

Cast: Henry Clay Barnabee; Eugene Cowles; Jessie Bartlett Davis; George Frothingham; Caroline Hamilton; Peter Lang; W.H. McDonald; Joseph Sheehan

Notes: No songs listed in program.

3571 • PRINCE AND THE PAUPER, THE

OPENED: 10/12/1963   Theatre: Judson Hall
Musical   Off-Broadway: 158

Composer: George Fischoff
Lyricist: Verna Tomasson
Librettist: Verna Tomasson
Producer: Joseph Blinhorn
Director: David Shanstrom

Source: PRINCE AND THE PAUPER, THE (Novel: Mark Twain); **Choreographer:** Bick Goss; **Costumes:** Norman Womack; **Set Design:** Norman Womack

Songs: Coronation Song; Do This, Do That; Ev'rybody Needs Somebody to Love; Garbage Court Round; In a Story Book; I've Been a-Bragging; King Foo-Foo the First; Oh, Pity the Man; Prince Is Mad, The; Tree and the Sun, The; Why Don't We Switch?; With a Sword in My Buckle

Cast: Carol Blodget; Joe Bousard; John Davidson; Flora Elkins; Joan Shepard

3572 • PRINCE AND THE PEASANTS

Musical   Chicago

Notes: No other information available. Harold Orlob had some songs interpolated into this score.

3573 • PRINCE CHU CHANG

OPENED: 10/06/1930
Musical   Closed out of town

Composer: Franz Lehar
Lyricist: Harry B. Smith
Librettist: Henry Clarke; Edgar Smith
Producer: Messrs. Shubert
Director: Lew Morton

Source: DAS LAND DES LACHELNS (Musical: Ludwig Herzer; Franz Lehar; Fritz Lohner-Beda); **Choreographer:** Pal'mere Brandeaux; **Costumes:** William Weaver; **Musical Director:** Leonard Hornsey; **Set Design:** Watson Barratt

Songs: Acrobatic Dance; Bacchus; Bestowal of the Yellow Jacket; Ceremonial to the Wedding; Chinese Love Song, A; Complements; Cup of Tea, A; Entrance of Lisa; Finale; Hot China; I Enter the Shrine; In My Country Oriental; King of Old; Let Us Part Good Friends; Love Has Come to Me at Last; Love's the Same, the Same Old Game; Mi Mi, Tu Li; My Almond Eyes of Eastern Skies; Opening; Pretty Little You, Homely Little Me; Sword Dance; We Are Alone; When Love Has Gone; Wreath of Fragrant Orange Blossoms, A; Yours Is My Heart Alone

Cast: Gladys Baxter; Marice Christie; Clifford Newdahl

Notes: Opened at the Shubert Theatre, Newark.

3574 • PRINCE HUMBUG

OPENED: 08/31/1908
Musical   Closed out of town

Composer: Karl Hoschna
Librettist: Mark Swan
Producer: Samuel E. Rork

Cast: Frank Lalor

Notes: This show played Springfield, Mass. on 8/31/08. No program available.

3575 • PRINCE OF BOHEMIA, THE

OPENED: 01/13/1910   Theatre: Hackett
Musical   Broadway: 20

Composer: A. Baldwin Sloane
Lyricist: E. Ray Goetz
Librettist: J. Hartley Manners
Producer: Lew Fields
Director: Ned Wayburn

Songs: Correspondence [1]; Cupid's Wireless Telegraph; Dollars and Debutantes; Gentle River [1]; Go 'Way Mistah Moon [1] (C/L: Andrew Mack); Goodbye Sweetheart [1]; If You'll Only Say You'll Be a Friend of Mine; Just a Little Bit of Blarney; Love Sign (C: A. Baldwin Sloane; L: E. Ray Goetz); Prince of Bohemia [1]; Sentimental Tommy; Shannon Belles; Voices from Home (C: Andrew Mack); Yankee Bohemia

Cast: W.T. Carleton; Harold Crane; Christie MacDonald; Andrew Mack

Notes: No program available. [1] Out of town only.

3576 • PRINCE OF CENTRAL PARK

OPENED: 11/09/1989   Theatre: Belasco
Musical   Broadway: 4

Composer: Don Sebesky
Lyricist: Gloria Nissenson
Producer: Abe Hirschfeld; Jan McArt
Director: Tony Tanner

Source: PRINCE OF CENTRAL PARK (Novel: Evan H. Rhodes); **Choreographer:** Tony Tanner; **Costumes:** Michael Botari; Ronald Case; **Dance Arranger:** Henry Aronson; **Lighting Designer:** Norman Coates; **Musical Director:** Joel Silberman; **Set Design:** Michael Botari; Ronald Case; **Vocal Arranger:** Joel Silberman

Songs: All I've Got Is Me; Fight Sequence [1]; Follow the Leader; Good Evening; Hang Tough [1]; Harbor Haven Heaven on the Sound [1]; Here and Now [1]; Here's When I Belong; I Fly By Night; I Love Central Park [1]; I Miss Him (Her) [1]; It Feels Like a Party [1]; Margie's Lament [1]; New Leaf (New Life, New Me); Night Pulse [1]; Once Upon My Life [1]; One of a Kind; Out on a Limb [1]; Prince of Central Park, The; Red; Run for Your Life [1]; They Don't Give You Life at Sixteen; We Were Dancing; When You Choose to Love Somebody [1]; You Gotta Fight Harder [1]; Zap!

Cast: Richard H. Blake; Chris Callen; Anthony Galde; Sean Grant; Jason Ma; Jo Anne Worley

Notes: [1] Cut.

3577 • PRINCE OF GRAND STREET, THE

OPENED: 03/07/1978
Musical   Closed out of town

Composer: Bob Merrill
Lyricist: Bob Merrill
Librettist: Bob Merrill
Producer: Shubert Organization; Roger L. Stevens; Robert Whitehead
Director: Gene Saks

Choreographer: Lee Theodore; **Costumes:** Jane Greenwood; **Dance Arranger:** David Baker; **Lighting Designer:** Tom Skelton; **Musical Director:** Colin Romoff; **Orchestrations:** Michael Gibson; **Set Design:** David Mitchell; **Vocal Arranger:** Colin Romoff

Songs: Do I Make You Happy?; Fifty Cents; Grand Street Presentation, A; Grand Street Tivoli Presentation, A; I Know What It Is to Be Alone; I'm a Girl with Too Much Heart; I'm a Star; Look at Me; My Potential; Place in the World, A; Prince of Grand Street, The; Sew a Button [1]; Stay with Me; What Do I Do Now?; Where Does Love Go?; Youngest Person I Know, The

Cast: Darlene Anders; Bob Carroll; Werner Klemperer; Sam Levene; David Margulies; Bernice Massi; Richard Muenz; Addison Powell; Robert Preston; Neva Small; Sammy Smith

Notes: Closed in Boston 4/15/78. [1] Later cut from HANNAH . . . 1939.

3578 • PRINCE OF PILSEN, THE

OPENED: 03/17/1903   Theatre: Broadway
Musical   Broadway: 143

Composer: Gustav Luders
Lyricist: Frank Pixley
Librettist: Frank Pixley
Producer: Henry W. Savage
Director: George Marion

Costumes: Will R. Barnes; **Musical Director:** Gustav Luders

Songs: American Girl, The (Song of the Cities); Artie; Back to the Boulevards; Biff! Bang!; Didn't Know Exactly What to Do; Entrance; Fall In!; Field and Forest, The; Finale Act I; Finale Act II; Flower Fete (Our Floral Queen); Hail to Our Noble Guest; Heidelberg (Stein Song); How Far a Girl Should Go [1]; Imagination; Keep It Dark; Message of the Violet; Modern Pirate, The; Opening Chorus; Opening Chorus Act II; Pictures in the Smoke; Season at the Shore, A; Something Should Be Done [1]; Tale of the Sea Shell, The; Walk, Mister, Walk; We Know It's Wrong to Flirt; We've Had a Stormy Trip; When You at Last Are Mine [1]; White Lies [1]; Widow, The

Cast: Lillian Coleman; Arthur Donaldson; Edgar Norton; John Ransome

Notes: [1] Cut after opening.

3579 • PRINCE OF TONIGHT, THE

OPENED: 03/09/1909   Theatre: Princess
Musical   Chicago

Composer: Joe Howard
Lyricist: Frank Adams; Will M. Hough
Librettist: Frank Adams; Will M. Hough

Songs: Best Thing a Waiter Does Is Wait, The [1]; Can It Be Love [1]; Everything That Father Did Was Right [3]; Follow the Rainbow's Trail; Girls That Can Never Be Mine, The [3]; Her Eyes Are Blue for Dear Old Yale; I Can't Be True So Far Away; I Don't Want to Marry Your Family; I Fell in Love on Monday; I Wonder Who's Kissing Her Now [6] (C: Harold Orlob); It Is a Dear Old World After All [4]; Mean Moon Man [1] (C/L: Omar Hebert); My Lady Nicotine [2]; Tonight Will Never Come Again; Transformation Lullaby; When Love Is Waiting 'Round the Corner; You Won't Know Anybody There [5]

Cast: Alice Dovey; Sallie Fisher; Henry Woodruff

Notes: [1] Out Toledo 1/9/1916. [2] Out St. Louis 10/29/11. [3] Sheet music only. [4] Sometimes listed as "You're a Dear Old World After All." [5] ASCAP/Library of Congress only. [6] Howard bought the melody from Orlob who was not credited on early sheets. Orlob later sued and won the right to credit and royalties.

3580 • PRINCESS APRIL

OPENED: 12/01/1924   Theatre: Ambassador
Musical   Broadway: 24

Composer: Monte Carlo; Alma Sanders
Lyricist: Monte Carlo; Alma Sanders
Librettist: Lewis Allen Browne; William Cary Duncan
Producer: Barry Townly
Director: Oscar Eagle

Source: UNKNOWN (Story: Frank R. Adams); **Choreographer:** Raymond Midgley; **Costumes:** D. Gilman; William Weaver; **Musical Director:** Louis Kroll; **Orchestrations:** Louis Kroll; William Redfield; **Set Design:** William Weaver

Songs: Champagne; Come on Kittens [2]; Daddy's Sweetheart [1]; Dreamy Eyes; Dumbbells May Be Foolish; Etiquette [1]; Irish Rose for Me, An [1]; Love Clock, The; Mary, Get Up [1]; One-Piece Blues; Page a Man for Me; Princess April [2]; Scandal; Society; String 'Em Along; Sweatheart of Mine; Syncojassologists [1]; Tantalizing April; We're All in the Swim; When Knights Were Bold

Cast: Harry Allen; May Boley; Harry Clarke; Stanley Forde; Tessa Kosta; Nathaniel Wagner

Notes: [1] Out 10/5/24. [2] Out Albany 1/10/??.

3581 • PRINCESS BEGGAR

OPENED: 01/07/1907   Theatre: Casino
Musical   Broadway: 40

Composer: Alfred G. Robyn
Lyricist: Edward A. Paulton
Librettist: Edward A. Paulton
Director: Frank Smithson

Set Design: Ernest Albert; E.G. Unitt

Songs: Beautiful Maidens Are We; Bells of Long Ago, The; Chimes of Long Ago; Daddy; Dear Little Daisy; Echo (C: Leo Friedman; L: Edward Montague); Elaine (Girl of My Heart); Entrance of the King; Entrance of the Queen; Finale Act I; Finale Act II; Giddy, Gay Lothario, The; Guess; I Want It All; I'm a Hermit; It's All the Same to Me; Opening Chorus; Opening Chorus Act II; Rook and the Robin, The; When It's Raining; Woodcutters, The; Wouldn't You Like to Learn to Love Me?; You're the Only One for Me

Cast: Paula Edwardes; Stanley Forde; Eddie Garvie; Harry MacDonough

Notes: No program available. Songs from vocal score.

3582 • PRINCESS BONNIE

OPENED: 09/02/1895   Theatre: Broadway
Musical   Broadway: 40

Composer: Willard Spencer
Lyricist: Willard Spencer
Librettist: Willard Spencer
Director: Richard Barker

Set Design: Ernest M. Gros

Cast: Will M. Armstrong; Hilda Clark; Jenny Dickerson; Fred Lennox; George O'Donnell

Notes: No songs listed in program.

3583 • PRINCESS CHARMING (1926)

OPENED: 10/21/1926   Theatre: Palace
Musical   London: 362

Composer: Albert Szirmay
Lyricist: Arthur Wimperis
Librettist: Arthur Wimperis; Laurie Wylie
Producer: William Mollison

Source: ALEXANDRA (Musical: Ferenc Marton; Albert Szirmay); **Choreographer:** Kelland Espinosa; **Costumes:** Percy Anderson; Gordon Conway; **Set Design:** F.L. Lyndhurst

Songs: Babying You (C: Harry Ruby; L: Bert Kalmar)

Cast: W.H. Berry; Bernard Clifton; Alice Delysia; Peter Gawthorne; George Grossmith; Winnie Melville; Eileen Redcott

Notes: No program available. Additional numbers by Russell Bennett and Jack Waller.

3584 • PRINCESS CHARMING (1930)

OPENED: 10/13/1930   Theatre: Imperial
Musical   Broadway: 56

Composer: Arthur Schwartz; Albert Sirmay
Lyricist: Arthur Swanstrom
Librettist: Jack Donahue
Producer: Bobby Connolly; Arthur Swanstrom
Director: Bobby Connolly; Edward Clarke Lilley

Source: PRINCESS CHARMING (Musical: Ferenc Marton; Arthur Wimperis; Laurie Wylie); **Choreographer:** Albertina Rasch; **Costumes:** Charles LeMaire; **Musical Director:** Al Goodman; **Set Design:** Joseph Urban

Songs: First Sunbeam; Here Is a Sword; I Love Love (C: Robert Emmett Dolan; L: Walter O'Keefe); I Must Be One of Those Roses [1]; I'll Be There [2]; I'll Never Leave You; I'm Designed for Love; Just a Friend of Mine; Never Mind How [1]; One for All; Opening; Opening Act II; Palace of Dreams; Panic's On, The; Reception of the Court; Take a Letter to the King; Trailing a Shooting Star; Wings in the Morning; You

Cast: Jeanne Aubert; Douglas Dumbrille; Roy Gordon; Portia Grafton; George Grossmith; Robert Halliday; Evelyn Herbert; Paul Huber; Dorothea James; Duke McHale; Victor Moore; Howard St. John

Notes: [1] Sheet music only. [2] ASCAP/Library of Congress only.

3585 • PRINCESS CHIC, THE

OPENED: 02/17/1900   Theatre: Casino
Musical   Broadway: 22

Composer: Julian Edwards
Lyricist: Kirke La Shelle
Librettist: Kirke La Shelle
Director: Julian Mitchell

Choreographer: Julian Mitchell; **Costumes:** C.F. Seidle; **Lighting Designer:** Joseph Menchen; **Musical Director:** William E. MacQuinn; **Set Design:** E. Castel-Bert

Songs: Cavaliers; Charger Good, A; Come Love, Go Love; Days of Magic, The; Entrance of Duke; Envoy's Duty, An; Fair Burgandy; Fighting Man, A; Finale Act I; Finale Act II; Finale Act III; Foolish Swallow, The; Hold I Command (Septette); How Are We to Know; Love and War; Love Came to Me One Day; Love Light in Your Eyes, The; Opening Chorus; Opening Chorus Act II; Opening Chorus Act III; Princesses Men at

Arms Are We; She's but a Woman, He's but a Man; Soldier of Fortune, A; Story Book, The; War Is a Beautiful Jade; Weak As a Woman; Wood Nymph and the River God, The

Cast: Winfield Blake; Melville Collins; Christie MacDonald; J.C. Miron; Edgar Temple

Notes: No N.Y. program available. Songs from vocal score.

3586 • PRINCESS FLAVIA
OPENED: 11/02/1925   Theatre: Century
Musical   Broadway: 152

Composer: Sigmund Romberg
Lyricist: Harry B. Smith
Librettist: Harry B. Smith
Producer: J.C. Huffman; J.J. Shubert; Lee Shubert
Director: J.C. Huffman

Source: PRISONER OF ZENDA, THE (Novel: Anthony Hope); **Source:** PRISONER OF ZENDA, THE (Play Anthony Hope); **Choreographer:** Max Scheck; **Musical Director:** Alfred Goodman; **Set Design:** Watson Barratt

Songs: Alone on Life's Highway; By This Token; Chorus of Soldiers; Convent Bells Are Ringing; Coronation Song; Dance with Me; I Dare Not Love You; I Love Them All; In Ruritania; Intermezzo; Kermesse Dance; Marionettes; Martin Luther Drinking Song; Oh, Comrades; Only One; Twilight Voices; What Do I Care; Yes or No?

Cast: Douglas Dumbrille; Helen Frederic; Evelyn Herbert; Henry Welchman

3587 • PRINCESS JIMMY
OPENED: 1985
Musical   Unproduced

Composer: Barry Kleinbort
Lyricist: Barry Kleinbort; Joseph Weiss
Librettist: Barry Kleinbort; Joseph Weiss

Songs: Blessing Your Counts; Celebration Dance (Serfs Up); Chanson de Paree (The "Oo-La-La, Ca C'est Paree" Song) [1]; Confessional (Dear Abbe); Doin' the Dishes; I Wanna Be Gay (And Have a Good Time); Joustin' Time (I Found You); Oh, What a Knight! (The Best Knight of

My Life); Princess Jimmy Sure Has Big Balls; Queen McButterfly's Lament; Shopping Is Torture (Even Off the Rack); Tale of the Calamari [2]; Tale of the Scungilli [2]; Time to Change My Earl; Welcome to Kafeteria; You're Underrated

Cast: Betty Grey; Scott Martin

Notes: [1] Cut. [2] Same song.

3588 • PRINCESS OF KENSINGTON, A
OPENED: 08/31/1903   Theatre: Broadway
Musical   Broadway: 41

Composer: Edward German
Lyricist: Basil Hood
Librettist: Basil Hood
Producer: John C. Fisher
Director: Cyril Scott

Songs: At the Seaside; By a Piccadilly Cab Stand; Fairies, Fairies, Come Forth; From Where the Scotch Mountains; German Prince May Wed Me Since, A; High and Dry Let Her Lie; If All the Stars Were Mine [1]; If Love in a Cottage Be All that They Tell; If We Pass Beyond the Portals; If You Will Spare the Time; It's a Pressing Invitation That I Bring; Now Here's to the 'Prentices; Oh, What Is a Woman's Duty?; See a Rainbow Arch; Seven O'Clock in the Morning; Seven O'Clock in the Evening; Sprig of Rosemarie, A; Till the Day of My Majority; Twin Butterflies That Fitfully Fall; We're Butchers and Bakers and Candlestick Makers; We're Four Jolly Sailor Men; Who That Knows How I Love You, Love; Yarns

Cast: Pauline Frederick; Fred Huntley; James T. Powers

Notes: [1] Out Newark 11/00/03.

3589 • PRINCESS OF RAGTIME
OPENED: 1914   Theatre: Palace
Musical   Broadway

Composer: Walter Donovan
Lyricist: Arthur Fields

Songs: Aba Daba Honeymoon

Cast: Wilbur Mack; Ruth Roye

Notes: Ruth Roye was the "Princess of Ragtime." This vaudeville musical played 14 weeks and introduced the famous song above. No other information available.

3590 • PRINCESS PAT, THE

OPENED: 09/29/1915 Theatre: Cort
Musical Broadway: 158

Composer: Victor Herbert
Lyricist: Henry Blossom
Librettist: Henry Blossom
Producer: John Cort
Director: Fred G. Latham

Choreographer: Bena Hoffman; **Musical Director:** Gustave Salzer; **Orchestrations:** Victor Herbert

Songs: All for You; Allies; Arrival of the Princess Pat; Ballet Suite [3]; Estellita; Finale Act I; Finale Act II [3]; Finale Ultimo [3]; Flirting [1]; For Better or for Worse; I Need Affection; I Wish I Was an Island in an Ocean of Girls; I'd Like to Be a Quitter, but I Find It Hard to Quit; I'd Like to Have You Around; In a Little World for Two; In Day Dreams [2]; Love Is the Best of All; Make Him Guess; Melodrama [4]; Neapolitan Love Song (Sweet One How My Heart Is Yearning) (T'Amo); Opening Chorus Act II; Opening Chorus Act III; Opening Music; Pat [1]; Shoes of Husband No. 1 Are Worn by Number Two, The; There's a Message of Love in Your Eyes [3]; Two Laughing Irish Eyes; When a Girl's About to Marry

Cast: Alexander Clark; Eva Fallon; Sam Hardy; Doris Kenyon; Eleanor Paintor; Ralph Riggs; Al Shean

Notes: [1] Out Philadelphia 9/14/16. Same music as "In Day Dreams." [2] Cut. Same music as "Flirting." [3] Not in programs. [4] ASCAP/Library of Congress.

3591 • PRINCESS SLIPS AWAY, THE

OPENED: 1935
Musical

Composer: Geoffrey O'Hara
Lyricist: Harry B. Smith

Songs: Comrades; Face Lifting; Hail and Reign; I Do It All By Proxy; I Hate to Love You So; In Monticello's Kingdom Grand; Marriage Is a Game of Blind Man's Bluff; Model Happy Fair, A; On to Victory; Try Out My Song; We Work Away; We're All in the Bread Line Together; We're the Statesmen Great; What's the Use; World of Dreamland, The; You Can't Keep Me Away from You; You're Married Under False Pretenses

Notes: No other information available.

3592 • PRINCESS TRA-LA-LA

Musical

Composer: Leo Ascher
Lyricist: Matthew Woodward

Songs: Fate Is Such a Mystic Puzzle; If I Only a Laugh Could Hear; If You Please; Little Crinolira; Love Is the Springtime of Life; My Heart; Oh, Father Don't Sell; Oh, the Music Is Sublime; On the Blue Danube's Bank; Papers! Papers!; Pure Gold Is My Security; Star That Warms My Heart, The; Swallow and the Lark, The; There Goes the Princess Tra-La-La; When in Vienna a Waltz Is Played; When the Plumber Goes A'Plumbing

Notes: No other information available.

3593 • PRINCESS VIRTUE

OPENED: 05/04/1921 Theatre: Central
Musical Broadway: 16

Composer: Gitz Rice
Lyricist: B.C. Hilliam
Librettist: L.A. Browne; B.C. Hilliam
Producer: Gerald Bacon
Director: Leon Errol

Songs: Dear Sweet Eyes; Life Is All Sunshine with You; Little Red Riding Hood; Princess Virtue; Smoke Rings; When I Met Love

Cast: Bradford Kirksbride; Tessa Kosta; Frank Moulan

Notes: No program available.

3594 • PRIORITIES OF 1942

OPENED: 03/12/1942 Theatre: 46th Street
Revue Broadway: 353

Composer: Charles Barnes; Marjery Fielding
Lyricist: Charles Barnes; Marjery Fielding
Producer: Clifford C. Fischer

Choreographer: Marjery Fielding; **Musical Director:** Lou Forman

Songs: I Danced With a Major; Vaudeville Is Back

Cast: Phil Baker; Paul Draper; Lou Holtz; Willie Howard; Hazel Scott; Gene Sheldon

Notes: Vaudeville show.

3595 • PRISONER OF ZENDA, THE
OPENED: 03/23/1924
Musical

Composer: Richard Rodgers
Lyricist: Herbert Fields
Producer: Benjamin School for Girls
Director: Herbert Fields

Source: PRISONER OF ZENDA, THE (Novel: Anthony Hope); **Musical Director:** Richard Rodgers

Songs: Farewell to Rudolph; Make Way; My King Can Do No Wrong; Oh Dear!; Song of Russia; This Is a Situation; When Men Are in Love; Without Love; Worst of Friends, The

Cast: Dorothy Fields

Notes: Amateur production.

3596 • PRIVATE AFFAIR, A
OPENED: 05/14/1936   Theatre: Masque
Play   Broadway: 28

Author: Gaston Valcourt
Producer: Albert Bannister
Director: Albert Bannister

Costumes: Mary Walls

Songs: Scene Changes, The (C/L: Billy Hill)

Cast: Florence Britton; Betty Linley; Helen Raymond; Oscar Shaw

3597 • PRIVATE LIVES
OPENED: 01/27/1931   Theatre: Times Square
Play   Broadway: 248

Producer: Charles B. Cochran; Noel Coward
Director: Noel Coward

Set Design: G.E. Calthrop

Songs: Someday I'll Find You (C/L: Noel Coward)

Cast: Noel Coward; Jill Esmond; Gertrude Lawrence; Laurence Olivier; Therese Quadri

3598 • PRIVATES ON PARADE
OPENED: 08/23/1989   Theatre: Christian C. Yegan
Musical   Off-Broadway: 64

Composer: Denis King
Lyricist: Peter Nichols
Author: Peter Nichols
Producer: Roundabout Theater Company
Director: Larry Carpenter

Choreographer: Daniel Pelzig; **Costumes:** Lindsay W. Davis; **Lighting Designer:** Marcia Madeira; **Musical Director:** Philip Campanella; **Set Design:** Loren Sherman

Songs: Better Far Than Sitting This Life Out [2]; Black Velvet [1] (C: Traditional); Could You Please Inform Us; Danke Schoen; Latin American Way, The; Les Girls; Little Things We Used to Do, The; Movie to End Them All, The [2]; Prince of Peace, The; Privates on Parade; S.A.D.U.S.E.A.; Sunnyside Lane; Western Approaches Ballet (inst.)

Cast: Ross Bickell; Donald Burton; John Curry; Jim Dale; Jim Fyfe; Edward Hibbert; Gregory Jbara; Simon Jones; Stephen Lee; Tom Matsusaka; Donna Murphy

Notes: [1] Music is "Greensleeves." [2] Not used.

3599 • PRODIGAL SISTER, THE
OPENED: 11/25/1974   Theatre: Theatre de Lys
Musical   Off-Broadway: 42

Composer: Micki Grant
Lyricist: J.E. Franklin; Micki Grant
Librettist: J.E. Franklin
Producer: Woodie King Jr.
Director: Shauneille Perry

Choreographer: Rod Rodgers; **Costumes:** Judy Dearing; **Musical Director:** Neal Tate; **Set Design:** C. Richard Mills

Songs: Ain't Marryin' Nobody; Big City Dance; Celebration; Employment Office Dance; First Born; Flirtation Dance; Hot Pants Dance; I Been Up in Hell; If You Know What's Good for You; Look at Me; Prodigal Has Returned, The; Remember; Remember Caesar; Sister Love; Slip Away; Superwoman; Talk, Talk, Talk; Thank You Lord; Woman Child

Cast: Ethel Beatty; Esther Brown; Frank Carey; Frances Salisbury

3600 • PROFESSIONALLY SPEAKING

OPENED: 05/22/1986   Theatre: St. Peter's Church
Revue   Off-Broadway: 37

Composer: Frederic Block; Ernst Muller; Peter Winkler
Lyricist: Frederic Block; Ernst Muller; Peter Winkler
Producer: Frederic Block; Irving Welzer
Director: Tony Tanner

Costumes: P. Chelsea Harriman; **Lighting Designer:** Barry Arnold; **Musical Director:** Bruce W. Coyle; **Set Design:** Robert Alan Harper

Songs: Best Part-Time Job in Town, The; Doctor's Out Today, The; Doctor's Prayer, A; Emmy-Lou, Lafayette and the Football Team; Equitable Distribution Waltz; First Let's Kill All the Lawyers; Gastrointestinal Rag; Guadalajara; I Hate It; I Professionisti; Lawyer's Out Today, The; Lawyerman; Malpractice; Mathematical Quartet; Over the Hill; Patient's Lament; Portia's Plan; Remember There Was Me; Sibling Rivalry; Stupidly in Love; Tamara, Queen of the Nile; Teacher's Out Today, The; Three Doctor's Wives; What Price Have I Paid?; Who the Hell Do These Wise Guys Think They Are?

Cast: David Ardao; Dennis Bailey; Meg Bussert; Hal Davis; Kathy Morath; Marilyn Pasekoff

3601 • PROM QUEENS UNCHAINED

OPENED: 06/30/1991   Theatre: Village Gate
Musical   Off-Broadway: 57

Composer: Keith Herrmann
Lyricist: Larry Goodsight
Librettist: Stephen Witkin
Producer: PQU Productions, Inc.
Director: Karen Azenberg

Choreographer: Karen Azenberg; **Costumes:** Robert Strong Miller; **Dance Arranger:** Keith Herrmann; Stuart Malina; **Lighting Designer:** Nancy Collings; **Musical Director:** Stuart Malina; **Set Design:** Bob Phillips; **Vocal Arranger:** Keith Herrmann; Stuart Malina

Songs: Corsage; Down the Hall; Dustbane: The Ballad of Minka; Eat the Lunch; Give Your Love; Going All the Way; Most Likely; Perfect Family, The; Seeing Red; Sherry's Theme; Squeeze Me in the Rain; That Special Night; Venulia, The

Cast: Becky Adams; Don Crosby; Ron Kurowski; Susan Levine; Gary Mendelson; Mark Traxler

3602 • PROMENADE

OPENED: 06/04/1969   Theatre: Promenade
Musical   Off-Broadway: 259

Composer: Al Carmines
Lyricist: Maria Irene Fornes
Librettist: Maria Irene Fornes
Producer: Joseph Beruh; Edgar Lansbury
Director: Lawrence Kornfeld

Conductor: Susan Romann; **Costumes:** Willa Kim; **Lighting Designer:** Jules Fisher; **Musical Director:** Al Carmines; **Orchestrations:** Eddie Sauter; **Set Design:** Rouben Ter-Arutunian

Songs: All Is Well in the City; Apres Vous I; Bliss; Capricious and Fickle; Chicken Is He; Cigarette Song, The; Clothes Make the Man, The; Crown Me; Czardas; Dig, Dig, Dig; Don't Eat It; Finger Song, The; Flower, A; Four; I Saw a Man; Isn't That Clear?; Laughing Song, The; Listen, I Feel; Little Fool; Madeline; Moment Has Passed, The; Mother's Love, A; Mr. Phelps; Passing of Time, The; Poor Man, A; Promenade Theme; Rosita Rodriguez; Serenade; Spring Beauties; Thank You; Two Little Angels; Unrequited Love; Why Not?

Cast: Shannon Bolin; Pierre Epstein; George S. Irving; Madeline Kahn; Ty McConnell; Alice Playten; Gilbert Price

3603 • PROMISES, PROMISES

OPENED: 12/01/1968   Theatre: Shubert
Musical   Broadway: 1281

Composer: Burt Bacharach
Lyricist: Hal David
Librettist: Neil Simon
Producer: David Merrick
Director: Robert Moore

Source: APARTMENT, THE (Film: I.A.L. Diamond; Billy Wilder); **Choreographer:** Michael Bennett; **Costumes:** Donald Brooks; **Dance Arranger:** Harold Wheeler; **Lighting Designer:** Martin Aronstein; **Musical Director:** Harold Wheeler; **Orchestrations:** Jonathan Tunick; **Set Design:** Robin Wagner

Songs: Christmas Day; Fact Can Be a Beautiful Thing, A; Grapes of Roth (dance); Half As Big As Life; Hot Food [3]; I'll Never Fall in Love Again; In the Right Kind of Light [3]; Knowing When to Leave; Let's Pretend We're Grown Up [2]; Loyal, Resourceful and Cooperative [1]; Our Little Secret; Phone Calls [3]; Promises, Promises; She Likes Basketball; Tick Tock Goes the Clock [3]; Turkey Lurkey Time; Upstairs; Wanting Things; What Am I Doing Here [3]; Where Can You Take a Girl?; Whoever You Are (I Love You); Wouldn't That Be a Stroke of Luck [1]; You'll Think of Someone; Young Pretty Girl Like You, A

Cast: Carole Bishop; Graciela Daniele; Robert Fitch; A. Larry Haines; Ken Howard; Baayork Lee; Donna McKechnie; Marian Mercer; Jill O'Hara; Jerry Orbach; Paul Reed; Margo Sappington; Michael Shawn; Norman Shelly; Millie Slavin; Edward Winter

Notes: [1] Out 11/68 Washington, D.C. [2] Not in programs. [3] Not used.

3604 • PROPS

OPENED: 1914

Cast: Nellie Beaumont; Rose Beaumont; Jack McIntyre; Billy B. Van

Notes: A 1914 vaudeville musical. No other information available.

3605 • PROVINCETOWN FOLLIES

OPENED: 11/03/1935   Theatre: Provincetown Playhouse

Revue   Off-Broadway: 63

Composer: Dave Stamper
Lyricist: Frederick Herendeen
Librettist: George K. Arthur; Frederick Herendeen; Gwynn Langdon; Barrie Oliver
Producer: Greenwich Musical Guild
Director: Lee Morrison

Choreographer: Mary Read; **Set Design:** John Plumer Ludlum

Songs: Gal with a Past; Got Myself a New Love; Nantucket, The (C: Louis Levine; L: Trevor Jones); New Words for an Old Love Song; Poor Porgy (C: Sylvan Green); Rain Over Manhattan (C/L: Arthur Jones); Red Sails in the Sunset (C: Hugh Williams; L: James Kennedy); Restless River (C/L: Mary Schaffer); River Man (C/L: Unknown); Spanish Shawl, A (C/L: Unknown)

Cast: Marie Alverez; Phyllis Austen; Eileen Graves; Billy Green; Wood Hawkins; Beatrice Kay; Barrie Oliver; Cyril Smith

Notes: No N.Y. program available.

3606 • PSYCHO BEACH PARTY

OPENED: 07/20/1987   Theatre: Players
Musical   Off-Broadway: 344

Author: Charles Busch
Producer: Gerald A. Davis; Kenneth Elliott; Theater-in-Limbo
Director: Kenneth Elliott

Incidental Music: Tom Kochan

Songs: Chicklet (C: Tom Kochan; L: Kenneth Elliott)

Cast: Michael Belanger; Ralph Buckley; Charles Busch; Robert Carey; Andy Halliday; Judith Hansen; Arnie Kolodner; Mike Leitheed; Becky London; Theresa Marlowe; Meghan Robinson

3607 • PULSE OF MY HEART

Notes: *See MACUSHLA.*

3608 • PUMP BOYS AND DINETTES

OPENED: 07/10/1981   Theatre: Princess
Musical   Broadway: 685

Composer: Jim Wann
Lyricist: Jim Wann
Producer: Dodger Productions, Inc.; Louis Busch Hager; Marilyn Strauss; Kate Studley; Warner Theatre Productions; Max Weitzenhoffer
Director: Doug Johnson

Costumes: Patricia McGourty; **Lighting Designer:** Fred Buchholz; **Set Design:** Doug Johnson; Christopher Nowak

Songs: Be Good or Be Gone; Best Man, The; Catfish [1] (C/L: B. Simpson; Jim Wann); Caution: Men Cooking (C/L: John Foley; Debra Monk; Cass Morgan; Jim Wann); Closing Time; Drinkin' Shoes (C/L: Mark Hardwick; Debra Monk; Cass Morgan); Farmer Tan; Fisherman's Prayer; Highway 57; Mamaw; Menu Song (C/L: Debra Monk; Cass Morgan); Mona; No Holds Barred (C/L: Cass Morgan; Jim Wann); Pump Boys; Serve Yourself; Sisters (C/L: Cass Morgan); T.N.D.P.W.A.M.; Takin' My Time [1] (C/L: Spider John Koerner; L: John Foley); Taking It Slow (C/L: John Foley; Mark Hardwick; John Scimmel; Jim Wann); Tips (C/L: Debra Monk; Cass Morgan); Vacation; Who Will the Next Fool Be [1] (C/L: Charlie Rich)

Cast: John Foley; Mark Hardwick; Debra Monk; Cass Morgan; John Schimmel; Jim Wann

Notes: Played 132 performances off-Broadway prior to move to Broadway on 2/4/82. [1] Out prior to Broadway.

3609 • PUNCH, JUDY & CO.
OPENED: 06/01/1903   Theatre: Paradise Roof Garden
Revue   Broadway: 72

Composer: Oscar Hammerstein I
Lyricist: Oscar Hammerstein I
Librettist: Oscar Hammerstein I
Producer: Oscar Hammerstein I

Songs: Girl in Blue, The; If I Again Would Be a Baby; There's But One New York

Cast: Gertrude Hoffman; Josie Sabel

3610 • PURLIE
OPENED: 03/15/1970   Theatre: Broadway
Musical   Broadway: 688

Composer: Gary Geld
Lyricist: Peter Udell
Librettist: Ossie Davis; Philip Rose; Peter Udell
Producer: Philip Rose
Director: Philip Rose

Source: PURLIE VICTORIOUS (Play Ossie Davis); **Choreographer:** Louis Johnson; **Costumes:** Ann Roth; **Dance Arranger:** Luther Henderson; **Lighting Designer:** Thomas Skelton; **Musical Director:** Joyce Brown; **Orchestrations:** Luther Henderson; Garry Sherman; **Set Design:** Ben Edwards; **Vocal Arranger:** Luther Henderson; Garry Sherman

Songs: Big Fish, Little Fish; Charlie's Songs; Down Home; Easy Goin' Man [1]; First Thing Monday Mornin'; Great White Father; Harder They Fall, The; He Can Do It; I Got Love; New Fangled Preacher Man; Purlie; Skinnin' a Cat; Walk Him Up the Stairs; World Is Comin' to a Start, The

Cast: C. David Colson; George Faison; John Heffernan; Sherman Hemsley; Linda Hopkins; Cleavon Little; Helen Martin; Melba Moore; Novella Nelson; Michael Peters; Ted Ross

Notes: [1] Cut prior to opening.

3611 • PURPLE COW, THE

Composer: Edwin I. Helms
Lyricist: Gelett Burgess
Librettist: Carolyn Wells
Director: Oscar Eagle

Choreographer: Jack Haskell

Songs: Any Man Is Easy (If You Just Know How); Magical Isle; Only One; What You Don't Know Won't Hurt You

Notes: No other information available.

3612 • PURPLE DUST
OPENED: 1965
Musical   Closed out of town

Composer: Mitch Leigh
Lyricist: Sean O'Casey
Librettist: Sean O'Casey
Producer: Albert W. Selden

Source: PURPLE DUST (Play Sean O'Casey); **Choreographer:** Edward Roll; **Costumes:** Patton

Campbell; **Lighting Designer:** Howard Bay; **Musical Director:** Neil Warner; **Set Design:** Howard Bay

Songs: Bosky Countrie (Sic), The; Canon's Song; Come from the Dyin'; For to Tie Up My Shoe; Heights of a Pillow, The; How I Grieve; I Saw from the Beach

Cast: Gino Conforti; Jon Cypher; Al DeSio; Joan Diener; Arlene Golonka; Irving Jacobson; Richard Kiley; Monty Landis; Ray Middleton; Shev Rodgers; Robert Rounseville; Harry Theyard; Mimi Turque

Notes: Goodspeed Opera House.

3613 • PURPLE ROAD, THE

OPENED: 04/07/1913   Theatre: Liberty
Musical   Broadway: 136

Composer: William Frederick Peters; Heinrich Reinhardt
Lyricist: Fred De Gresac; William Cary Duncan
Librettist: Fred De Gresac; William Cary Duncan
Producer: Joseph M. Gaites
Director: George Marion; Edward P. Temple

Source: NAPOLEON UND DIE FRAUEN (Musical: Heinrich Reinhardt); **Musical Director:** Gustave Salzer; **Set Design:** P. Dodd Ackerman; Walter H. Harvey

Songs: Austrian Patrol (inst.) (C: William Frederick Peters); Break-Neck Quadrille, The (inst.) (C: William Frederick Peters); Dear Little Pages [1] (C: William Frederick Peters; L: William Cary Duncan); Diplomacy (C: William Frederick Peters; L: William Cary Duncan); Feed Me with Love (C: Heinrich Reinhardt); Finale Act II (C: William Frederick Peters); He Is Gone; Holding Hands [2]; I Am All Alone (C: Heinrich Reinhardt); I Am Simply Irresistible (C: William Frederick Peters); Love Spell, The; Maiden of Caprice, The [2]; March of the Bridegrooms (C: William Frederick Peters); Mysterious Kiss, The (C: William Frederick Peters); Pretty Little Chichis [3] (C: William Frederick Peters); Song of the Reapers, The (C: William Frederick Peters); To Make a Hit in Par-ee (C: William Frederick Peters); Valley of Beautiful Dreams, The (C: William Frederick Peters); When Someone Marries Me (C: William Frederick Peters)

Cast: Janet Beecher; Eva Fallon; Edward Martindel; Elita Proctor Otis; Valli Valli; Clifton Webb

Notes: [1] Titled "Five Little Pages" in sheet music. [2] Sheet music only. [3] Titled "Wicked Little Chichis" in sheet music.

3614 • PUT AND TAKE

OPENED: 08/23/1921   Theatre: Town Hall
Revue   Broadway: 32

Composer: Spencer Williams
Lyricist: Spencer Williams
Librettist: Irvin C. Miller
Producer: Jack Goldberg; Irvin C. Miller
Director: Irvin C. Miller

Musical Director: Tim Brymn

Songs: Beedle 'Em Boo; Broadway Down in Dixieland (C/L: Bernie Barber); Chocolate Brown; Creole Gal; Dog; Georgia Rose (C: Harry Rosenthal; L: Jimmy Flynn; Alex Sullivan); I Can't Forget the Dear Old Folks at Home [1]; June Love; Lincoln Stroll; Meanest Man in the World, The [1]; Old Time Blues; Put and Take; Separation Blues; Snap 'Em Blues; Stop, Rest Awhile (C: Tim Brymn; L: L. Wolfe Gilbert); Wedding Bells; Wedding Day in Georgia; Yodel

Cast: Cora Green; Hamtree Harrington

Notes: Additional music by Tim Brymn and Perry Bradford but not credited in program. [1] Sheet music only.

3615 • PUT IT IN WRITING

OPENED: 05/13/1963   Theatre: Theatre de Lys
Revue   Off-Broadway: 24

Producer: Arthur Cantor; Lucille Lortel
Director: Bill Penn

Choreographer: Joyce Trisler; **Costumes:** Andre; **Dance Arranger:** Gershon Kingsley; **Lighting Designer:** Gene Tunezi; **Musical Director:** Gordon Connell; **Set Design:** Peter Harvey; **Vocal Arranger:** Gershon Kingsley

Songs: Arty (C: James Wise; L: David Bimonte); Ayes of Texas, The (C: Norman L. Martin;

L: Fred Ebb); Case of the Hum- drum Killer, The (C/L: Jay Thompson); Cut Movie Songs (C/L: Fred Ebb); Daisy (C/L: G. Wood); Emmy Lou (C: Norman L. Martin; L: Fred Ebb); Give 'Em a Kiss (C/L: G. Wood); I Hope You're Happy (C: Norman L. Martin; L: Fred Ebb); Literary Cocktail Party (C/L: Bud McCreery); People's Choice, The (C: Norman L. Martin; L: Fred Ebb); Put It in Writing (C: Alan Kohan); Stock Report (C: Norman L. Martin; L: Fred Ebb); Top of the List (C/L: Jay Thompson); Triology (C/L: Bud McCreery); Walking Down the Road (C/L: William Angelos; Alan Kohan); What Kind of Life Is That? (C: Norman L. Martin; L: Fred Ebb); What's Cooking? (C: Norman L. Martin; L: Fred Ebb); Youngest President, The (C: Robert Kessler; L: Martin Charnin)

Cast: Jane Connell; Buzz Halliday; Brandon Maggart; Barbara Mitchell

3616 • PUTTING IT TOGETHER

Notes: *See SONDHEIM — PUTTING IT TOGETHER.*

3617 • PUZZLES OF 1925

OPENED: 02/02/1925   Theatre: Fulton
Revue   Broadway: 104

Librettist: Elsie Janis
Producer: Charles B. Dillingham

Choreographer: Julian Alfred; **Costumes:** Mabel E. Johnston; James Reynolds; **Musical Director:** Raymond Hubbell

Songs: Doo-Dab, The (C: Harry Ruby; L: Bert Kalmar); Give the Little Kids a Chance (C: Raymond Hubbell); Je Vous Aime (C/L: Arthur L. Beiner); Just a Flower from an Old Bouquet (C: Lucien Denni; L: Gwynne Genni); Lady Osteopath, The (C/L: Blanche Merrill); Old Established Firm (C/L: Blanche Merrill); Titania (C: Leo Daniderff; L: Bertal-Maubon; E. Ronn); Tra-la-la-la (C/L: Elsie Janis; Vincent Scotto); Undecided Blues, The (C/L: Elsie Janis); We Beg to Announce (C/L: Elsie Janis); We're Jumping Into Something (C/L: Blanche Merrill); When the Cat's Away (C/L: Blanche Merrill)

Cast: Helen Broderick; Jimmy Hussey; Walter Pidgeon; Cyril Ritchard; Phil Saxe

Q

3618 • QUAKER GIRL, THE

OPENED: 10/23/1911   Theatre: Park
Musical   Broadway: 240

Composer: Lionel Monckton
Lyricist: Adrian Ross
Librettist: James T. Tanner
Producer: Henry B. Harris
Director: J.A.E. Malone

Costumes: Lucille; Maison Blum **Musical Director:** Augustus Barratt **Set Design:** H. Robert Law

Songs: Ah, Oui! [2] (L: Lionel Monckton); Bad Boy and a Good Girl, A (L: Percy Greenbank); Barbizon [2]; Champagne [2]; Come to the Ball; Couleur de Rose [2] (L: Percy Greenbank); Dancing Lesson, A; Finale Act I; Finale Act II; Finale Act III; First Dance, The; I Want to Tell You Something [1] (C/L: Clifton Crawford); In This Abode of Madame la Mode (Opening Chorus Act II) (L: Percy Greenbank); Jarge, We've Such a Tale to Tell (Opening Chorus); Just a Little Word Unspoken [5] (C/L: Augustus Barratt); Just as Father Used to Do (L: Percy Greenbank); Keep Away from a Married Man (I'm a Married Man) (C/L: Clifton Crawford); (I Wore a) Little Grey Bonnet [2]; Mr. Jeremiah Esqiure [2] (L: Percy Greenbank); O, Time, Time! [2] (L: Percy Greenbank); On Revient de Chantilly; Or Thereabouts (C: Hugo Felix); Petticoats for Women [4]; Quaker Girl, A; Quakers' Meeting; Runaway Match, A; Take a Little Shine to Me [5] (C: Hilding Anderson; L: Collin Davis); Take a Step [3]; Thee Loves Me and I Love Thee [2]; Tip-toe; Tony from America (L: Lionel Monckton); Wilderness and Thou, A [2]; Wonderful

Cast: Ina Claire; Clifton Crawford; Lawrence Eddinger; Percival Knight; Olga Petrova

Notes: [1] Titled "Something to Tell" in program. [2] In London program. [3] Added after London opening. [4] London vocal score only. [5] Sheet music only.

3619 • QUARTER FOR THE LADIES ROOM, A

OPENED: 11/12/1972   Theatre: Village Gate
Revue   Off-Broadway: 1

Composer: John Clifton
Lyricist: Ruth Batchelor
Producer: Philip R Productions
Director: Darwin Knight

Costumes: Miles White **Lighting Designer:** Lee Watson **Musical Director:** Karen Gustafson **Set Design:** David Ballou **Vocal Arranger:** Bill Brohn

Songs: Baby Dolls; Butterfly's Lament; Epitaph (C: Arthur Siegel); Feel at Home (C: Arthur Siegel); First Quarter; Gemini; Incest and Apples; Incomplete (C: Arthur Siegel); Kind of Guy, The (C: Arthur Siegel); Last Quarter; Married Man; My Hero's Grenades (C: Arthur Siegel); My Man; Princess, The; Talk About the Men (C: Arthur Siegel); Talk to Me; Turn Around (C: Arthur Siegel); Whatshisname; When the Time Comes (C: Arthur Siegel); When Will the Music Be Gone; Why Don't I Leave Him (C: Arthur Siegel); Woman Power (C: Arthur Siegel)

Cast: Helon Blount; Paula Cinko; Norma Donaldson; Judy MacMurdo; Benay Venuta

3620 • QUEEN ANNA

Notes: *See HER LITTLE HIGHNESS*.

3621 • QUEEN ANNE

Musical

Composer: Reginald De Koven
Director: Frank Rainger

Cast: Mitzi Hajos; Wallace McCutcheon

Notes: A vaudeville musical. No other information available.

3622 • QUEEN HIGH!

OPENED: 09/05/1926   Theatre: Ambassador
Musical   Broadway: 367

Composer: Lewis E. Gensler
Lyricist: B.G. DeSylva
Librettist: B.G. DeSylva; Laurence Schwab
Director: Edgar MacGregor

Source: PAIR OF SIXES, A (Play: Edward Peple)
  Choreographer: Sammy Lee **Costumes:** Jeanne
  Laurence **Musical Director:** Ivan Rudisill
  Orchestrations: Robert Russell Bennett **Set
  Design:** Willy Pogany

Songs: Beautiful Baby (C: James F. Hanley); Cross
  Your Heart; Don't Forget (Your Auntie)
  (C: James F. Hanley); Everything Will Happen
  for the Best; Gentlemen Prefer Blondes; Get in
  Touch with Me [4]; It Pays to Advertise; My
  Lady [2] (C: Ben Jerome; L: Frank Crumit); Oh,
  What a Lovely Day [5]; One Never Knows [4];
  One Smile from Polly [4]; Opening; Sez You? Sez
  I!; Springtime; Surplus Women [1] (C/L: Bernard
  Green); Weaker Sex, The; Who? You!; Who'll
  Mend a Broken Heart?; You Must Come Over
  Blues [3]; You'll Never Know

Cast: Luella Gear; Helen Harrington; Mary Lawlor;
  Frank McIntyre; Clarence Nordstrom; June
  O'Dea; Charles Ruggles

Notes: [1] Out London. [2] Out Montreal 7/16/28.
  [3] Out Washington, D.C. 2/10/29. [4] Out
  Providence 4/5/26. [5] ASCAP/Library of
  Congress only.

3623 • QUEEN O' HEARTS

OPENED: 10/10/1922   Theatre: Cohan
Musical   Broadway: 40

Composer: Lewis E. Gensler
Lyricist: Oscar Hammerstein II
Librettist: Oscar Hammerstein II; Frank Mandel
Producer: Max Spiegel
Director: Ira Hards

Choreographer: David Bennett **Costumes:** Cora
  MacGeachy **Musical Director:** Gene Salzer **Set
  Design:** Herbert Ward

Songs: Dear Little Girlie (C: Dudley Wilkinson;
  L: Nora Bayes); Ding Dong Ding [1] (C: Lewis E.
  Gensler); Dreaming Alone (C: Dudley

Wilkinson); Every Silver Lining [1]; Just a
  Touch [1]; Long Time Ago, A (L: Morrie Ryskind);
  Marriage C.O.D.; My Busy Day; My Highbrow
  Fling; Sizing Up the Girls; Some Fine Day [1];
  Stop, Look and Kiss 'Em [1]; System; That's That
  (C: Dudley Wilkinson; L: Nora Bayes; Harry
  Richman); Tom-Tom (C: Lewis E. Gensler);
  Topics of the Day (C/L: Cliff Friend; Harry
  Richman); When You're Only Seventeen [1];
  Why Do You Keep Us Guessing? [1]; You Need
  Someone (C: Lewis E. Gensler)

Cast: Nora Bayes; Max Hoffmann Jr.; Florence
  Morrison; Lorin Raker; Harry Richman; Eva
  Taylor; Norma Terris; Arthur Uttry; Dudley
  Wilkinson; Franker Woods

Notes: Additional lyrics credited to Sidney D.
  Mitchell but not identified in programs.
  Additional music credited to Dudley Wilkinson
  with some songs identified. [1] Cut.

3624 • QUEEN OF BASIN STREET

OPENED: 1982

Unproduced

Composer: Maury Yeston
Lyricist: Maury Yeston
Librettist: Jay Presson Allen
Director: Mike Nichols

Source: LA CAGE AUX FOLLES (Play Jean Poiret)
  Choreographer: Tommy Tune

Notes: This was a version of the film LA CAGE
  AUX FOLLES that was rejected by producer
  Allan Carr who then hired Jerry Herman.

3625 • QUEEN OF BRILLIANTS

OPENED: 11/07/1894   Theatre: Abbey's
Musical   Broadway: 29

Composer: Edward Jakobowski
Librettist: H.J.W. Dam

Source: DES BRILLANTEN-KONIGIN (Musical:
  Isadore Fuchs; Edward Jakobowski; Theodore
  Taub) **Set Design:** Hawes Craven; Joseph
  Harker; W. Perkins

Cast: Digby Bell; Laura Jones Bell; Suzanne
  Leonard [1]; Lillian Russell; Owen Westford;
  Robert Witke

Notes: No songs listed in program. [1] Lillian Russell's sister and Owen Westford's wife.

3626 • QUEEN OF THE MOULIN ROUGE, THE

OPENED: 12/07/1908   Theatre: Circle
Musical   Broadway: 160

Composer: John T. Hall
Lyricist: Vincent Bryan
Librettist: Paul Potter
Producer: Thomas W. Ryley
Director: Frank Smithson

Choreographer: Joseph C. Smith **Costumes:** Will R. Barnes **Orchestrations:** Charles Zimmerman

Songs: Clock Song; Drill of the Coquette Corps; Drink the Wine [1]; Drinking Trio; Drummed Out; Hip-Hip-Hip [3]; In Orcania; I've Waited Long for Thee; Kicking Polka, The; L'Amour de L'Apache [3]; Little Old New York; Love Is King [5]; Love's Dream Is O'er; Love's Mystery [1]; Marching Home in the Rain [4]; Nipper, The [1]; Nobody New [2]; Opening Chorus; Painting Paris; Parisian Two-Step [5]; Physical Society, The; Pleasure Brigade, The; Poppa's Popular Boy; Pyjama Song [2]; Quarrel, The; Quat-Z Arts; Shy Little Violet Blue; Sweet Rosa Pompetta; Take That Off, Too; Telegraph Me; Tonight's the Night [5]; Underworld, The (Apache Dance) (inst.) [5]; When I'm Alone with You; Won't You Take Me There? [1]

Cast: Francis X. Bushman [6], Carter De Haven, Flora Parker

Notes: [1] Out Wilkes-Barre 8/29/10. [2] Out of town in 1909. [3] Out Philadelphia. [4] Out Buffalo 4/1/10. [5] Added after opening. [6] Billed as Frank X. Bushman.

3627 • QUEEN OF THE MOVIES, THE

OPENED: 01/12/1914   Theatre: Globe
Musical   Broadway: 104

Composer: Jean Gilbert
Lyricist: Glen MacDonough; Edward Paulton
Librettist: Glen MacDonough; Edward Paulton
Director: Herbert Gresham

Source: DIE KINO KOENIGIN (Musical: Julius Freund; Georg Okonkowski) **Choreographer:** Julian Mitchell **Musical Director:** Hugo Riesenfeld

Songs: As You Rest in His Arms [2]; Carmencita Shea [2] (C/L: John H. Dunsmore); Cutie; Follow the Crowd (C/L: Irving Berlin); Forgive and Forget; Girls Run Along; Oh, Cecelia; Pardon Me If I Stutter; We Laugh, We Love, We Live [2]; When the Moon Slyly Winks in the Night; Whistle (C: Leslie Stuart); Who Is to Know?; You're Here and I'm Here [1] (C: Jerome Kern; L: Harry B. Smith)

Cast: Alice Dovey; Frank Moulan; Valli Valli

Notes: [1] Originally in THE LAUGHING HUSBAND. [2] Sheet music only.

3628 • QUEENIE PIE

OPENED: 10/09/1986
Musical   Closed out of town

Composer: Duke Ellington
Lyricist: Duke Ellington; George David Weiss
Librettist: George C. Wolfe
Producer: American Music Theatre Festival
Director: Garth Fagan

Choreographer: Garth Fagan **Conductor:** Constantine Kitsopoulos **Costumes:** Eduardo Sicangco **Dance Arranger:** Maurice Peress **Lighting Designer:** Ken Billington **Musical Director:** Maurice Peress **Orchestrations:** Barrie Lee Hall Jr.; Maurice Peress **Set Design:** Romare Bearden; David Mitchell **Vocal Arranger:** Maurice Peress

Songs: All Hail the Queen; Blues for Two Young Women, A; Cafe Au Lait; Creole Love Call; Discovery of Queenie Pie on the Beach; Earthquake; Epilogue; Finale; Finale Act I; Hairdo Hop, The; Harlem Scat; Hawk, The; Hey, I Don't Need Nobody Now; Island Update 1; Island Update 2; It's Time for Something New; My Father's Island; Oh Gee; Queenie Pie; Rhumbop; Smile As You Go By; Soliloquy; Stix; Style; There; Truly a Queen; Two Cat Scat Fight; Woman; Won't You Come Into My Boudoir

Cast: Teresa Burrell; Patty Holley; Larry Marshall; Wendell Pierce; Ken Prymus; Lillias White

Notes: Program of John F. Kennedy Center for the Performing Arts, Washington, D.C. This show was originally commisioned from Ellington by the WNET Opera Program. It was never produced.

3629 • QUICK CHANGE

OPENED: 10/30/1980   Theatre: Bijou
Revue   Off-Broadway: 4

Composer: Roy M. Rogosin
Lyricist: Bruce Belland
Librettist: Bruce Belland; Michael McGiveney; Roy M. Rogosin
Director: Roy M. Rogosin

Costumes: Mary Wills **Set Design:** Chris Flower; John Shipley

Cast: McGiveney

Notes: No songs listed in program.

3630 • QUILLOW AND THE GIANT

OPENED: 1961
TV Musical

Composer: Wade Barnes; Ralph Blane
Lyricist: Wade Barnes; Ralph Blane
Librettist: Wade Barnes; Ralph Blane
Additional Dialogue: Biff McGuire

Source: QUILLOW AND THE GIANT (Story: James Thurber)

Songs: Chimneys Are Black, The; Far Off Village; Full Moon Street; Hardest Thing in the World to Do, The; How Many Stars Are There in the Sky?; Hunder Runs Off to the Sea (inst.); I Believe in Me; I Hunder; It's a Serious Situation!; Offering Ballet (inst.); Quillow Plants the Blue Men; Roll Call; There's No Such Word As "Can't"; Wind Quillow Up (inst.); Would You Let Me; You Are for Loving

Cast: Ronnie Barker; Jeannie Carson; Biff McGuire; Cardew Robinson

Notes: Produced for the BBC.

3631 • QUILTERS

OPENED: 09/25/1984   Theatre: Jack Lawrence
Musical   Broadway: 24

Composer: Barbara Damashek
Lyricist: Barbara Damashek
Librettist: Barbara Damashek; Molly Newman
Producer: American Theatre and Academy; Denver Theatre Center; John F. Kennedy Center; Brockman Seawell
Director: Barbara Damashek

Source: QUILTERS: WOMEN AND DOMESTIC ART, THE (Book: Norma Bradley Allen; Patricia Cooper) **Costumes:** Elizabeth Palmer **Lighting Designer:** Allen Lee Hughes **Set Design:** Ursula Belden

Songs: Are You Washed in the Blood of the Lamb (C/L: E.A. Hoffman); Butterfly, The; Cornelia; Dandelion (L: Clara J. Denton); Every Log in My House; Everything Has a Time; Green, Green, Green; Hands Around; Hoedown (C/L: Traditional); Land Where We'll Never Grow Old (C/L: J.C. Moore); Little Babes That Sleep All Night (L: Almon C. Varney); Lord Don't Rain Down Manna, The; Needle's Eye, The (L: Barbara Damashek; Traditional); Pieces of Lives; Quiltin' and Dreamin'; Rocky Road; Thread the Needle; Who Will Count the Stitches?; Windmill Song, The

Cast: Evalyn Baron; Marjorie Berman; Alma Cuervo; Lynn Lobban; Rosemary McNamara; Jennifer Parsons; Lenka Peterson

3632 • QUO VASS IS!

OPENED: 09/06/1900   Theatre: Weber and Fields
                              Music Hall
Musical   Broadway

Composer: John Stromberg
Lyricist: Edgar Smith
Librettist: Edgar Smith
Producer: Lew Fields; Joseph Weber

Cast: Lew Fields; Joseph Weber

Notes: A one-act burlesque of QUO VADIS. No program available.

R

3633 • R.J.
Notes: *See RAINBOW JONES.*

3634 • R.S.V.P.
OPENED: 11/09/1926
Revue   London

Composer: Harold Fraser-Simpson
Lyricist: A.A. Milne
Producer: Archibald de Bear

Songs: Sentimental Me [1] (C: Richard Rodgers;
L: Lorenz Hart)

Cast: Joyce Barbour; Mimi Crawford; Cyril
Ritchard; J.H. Roberts

Notes: No program available. [1] Originally in
GARRICK GAIETIES (1925).

3635 • RACE TO URGA, THE
Notes: *See THE EXCEPTION AND THE RULE.*

3636 • RACHAEL LILY ROSENBLOOM AND DON'T YOU EVER FORGET IT
OPENED: 11/26/1973   Theatre: Broadhurst
Musical   Broadway

Composer: Paul Jabara
Lyricist: Paul Jabara
Librettist: Tom Eyen; Paul Jabara
Producer: Ahmet Ertegun; Robert Stigwood
Director: Tom Eyen

Choreographer: Tony Stevens; **Costumes:** Joseph
G. Aulisi; **Dance Arranger:** Bill Cunningham;
Lighting Designer: Jules Fisher; **Set Design:**
Robin Wagner

Songs: Academy Awards Theme; Broadway I Love
You; Broadway Rhythm; Change in Raquel; Cobra
Woman; Dear Miss Streisand; Delivery Boys'
Lament; East Brooklyn Blues; Get Your Show
Rolling; Gorgeous Lily; Hollywood! Hollywood!;
Hollywood Is Dying; Me and My Perch (L: David
Debin; Paul Jabara); Never Lose Your Sense of
Humor (C/L: Paul Jabara; Greg Mathieson; Donna
Summer); Ochos Rios (L: Paul Issa; Paul Jabara);
One Man; Overdose; Party Sickness; Raquel Gives
the Dish; Raymond's Song; Rona, Mona and Me;
Seduction Samba; Silver Diamond Rhinestone
Glasses; Take Me Savage; Things (L: Paul Issa;
Paul Jabara); We'll Be There (L: Paul Issa; Paul
Jabara); Working for Stella

Cast: Carole Bishop; Kenneth Carr; Andre De
Shields; Ellen Greene; Paul Jabara; Anita Morris;
Marion Ramsey; Jozella Reed; Jane Robertson;
Thomas Walsh

Notes: Choreographic supervision: Grover Dale.
Closed in previews, which began 11/26 and
ended 12/1/73.

3637 • RADIO CITY CHRISTMAS SPECTACULAR
OPENED: 11/13/1992   Theatre: Radio City Music
                         Hall
Revue   Broadway: 179

Producer: Robert F. Jani
Director: Scott Salmon

Choreographer: Violet Holmes; Linda Lemac; Scott
Salmon; Marianne Selbert; **Costumes:** Jose
Lengson; Pete Menefee; Frank Spencer; **Dance
Arranger:** Mark Hummel; Marvin Laird;
Lighting Designer: Ken Billington; **Musical
Director:** Don Pippin; **Set Design:** Charles
Lisanby

Songs: Christmas in New York (C: Stanley
Lebowsky; L: Billy Butt); Sing a Little Song of
Christmas (C: Don Pippin; L: Carolyn Leigh);
What Do You Want for Christmas (C: Larry
Grossman; L: Hal Hackady)

Cast: Charles Edward Hall; Arte Phillips;
Rockettes, The; Scott Spahr

Notes: There were also traditional songs used in this annual production. Only original songs listed here.

3638 • RADIO CITY MUSIC HALL CHRISTMAS 1977

OPENED: 11/03/1977   Theatre: Radio City Music Hall

Revue

Producer: Radio City Music Hall

Choreographer: Violet Holmes; **Musical Director:** Will Irwin; **Orchestrations:** Don Smith; Jim Timmens; **Vocal Arranger:** Will Irwin; Don Smith

Songs: It's That Time of the Year (C/L: Will Irwin)

3639 • RADIO CITY MUSIC HALL OPENING

OPENED: 12/27/1932   Theatre: Radio City Music Hall

Revue

Composer: Jimmy McHugh
Lyricist: Dorothy Fields
Producer: Samuel "Roxy" Rothafel

Choreographer: Russell Markert; **Musical Director:** Erno Rapee; **Orchestrations:** Maurice Baron; Otto Cesana; Desdit D'Antalffy; Ferde Grofe; Earle Most; **Set Design:** Robert Edmond Jones

Songs: Happy Times; Hey Young Fella!; Journey's End; Mad Moments (C: Harry Revel; L: Mack Gordon); Radio City Overture (C: Ferde Grofe; L: Irving Caesar); Riding High (C: Harry Revel; L: Mack Gordon); With a Feather in Your Cap

Cast: Joan Abbott; Berry Brothers; Ray Bolger; Patricia Bowman; Otto Fassell; Dorothy Fields; Lew Fields; Coe Glade; Martha Graham and Her Dance Group; DeWolf Hopper; Arnoldo Linti; Jimmy McHugh; Jan Peerce [1]; Dr. Rockwell; Titta Ruffo; Vera Schwarz; Tuskegee Institute Choir; Joe Weber

Notes: [1] Billed as John Pierce.

3640 • RADIO CITY MUSIC HALL PRODUCTION

OPENED: 1936
Revue

Songs: King of Swing (C: George Gershwin; L: Al Stillman)

Notes: No other information available.

3641 • RADIO GALS

OPENED: 1995
Musical

Composer: Mike Craver; Mark Hardwick
Lyricist: Mike Craver; Mark Hardwick
Librettist: Mike Craver; Mark Hardwick
Director: Alan Bailey

Costumes: Dawna Oak; **Lighting Designer:** Kevin Mahan; **Musical Director:** Steven Smith; **Set Design:** Gary Wissman

Songs: Aviatrix Love Song; Buster, He's a Hot Dog Now; Dear Mr. Gershwin; Edna, the Elephant Girl; Fairies in My Mother's Flower Garden; Fireside, a Pipe and a Pet, A; Gal's Got to Do What a Gal's Got to Do; Horehound Compound; Kittens in the Snow; Old Gals; Queenie, Take Me Home with You; Royal Radio; Sign Off; Sunrise Melody; Tranquil Boxwood, The; Weather Song; Wedding of the Flowers; When It's Sweetpea Time in Georgia; Whispering Pines; Why Did You Make Me Love You?; Wicky Wacky Hula Hula Honka Wonka Honolulu Hawaiian Honey of Mine, The

Cast: Eileen Barnett; Klea Blackhurst; Mike Craver; Helen Geller; Emily Mikesell; Mark Nadler; Lenny Wolpe

Notes: Produced at the Pasadena Playhouse, CA.

3642 • RAGGED ROBIN

OPENED: 1921
Play   Closed out of town

Author: Rita Olcott; Rida Johnson Young
Producer: Augustus Pitou

Songs: Click of Her Little Brogans, The (C: Ernest R. Ball; L: J. Keirn Brennan); Eyes That Come from Ireland (C: Chauncey Olcott; L: Richard Le Gallienne); I Used to Believe in Fairies (C/L: George Spink); If You'll Remember Me (C: Ernest R. Ball; L: George Graff Jr.); Laugh with a Tear in It, A (Laugh and the World Will Laugh with You, Weep and You'll Weep Alone) (C/L: Manuel Klein; Chauncey Olcott); Sweet Girl of My Dreams (C/L: Chauncey Olcott; Daniel J. Sullivan)

Cast: Chauncey Olcott

Notes: No other information available.

3643 • RAGGEDY ANN

OPENED: 10/16/1986   Theatre: Nederlander
Musical   Broadway: 5

Composer: Joe Raposo
Lyricist: William Gibson
Librettist: William Gibson
Producer: Donald K. Donald; Empire State Institute; John F. Kennedy Center; Jon Silverman Assoc. Ltd.
Director: Patricia Birch

Choreographer: Patricia Birch; **Conductor:** Ross Allen; **Costumes:** Carrie Robbins; **Dance Arranger:** Louis St. Louis; **Lighting Designer:** Marc B. Weiss; **Musical Director:** Ross Allen; Roy Rogosin; **Orchestrations:** Stan Applebaum; **Set Design:** Vicki Baral; Gerry Hariton

Songs: Blue; Carry On; Delighted; Diagnosis; Gingham and Yarn; Gone; Heavenly Chorus, A; I Come Riding; Light, The; Little Music, A; Make Believe; Rag Dolly; Shooting Star, The; So Beautiful; Something in the Air; Somewhere; Wedding, The; Welcome to L.A.; What Did I Lose; Why Not; You'll Love It

Cast: Ivy Austin; Leo Burmester; Carolyn Marble; Bob Morrisey; Lisa Rieffel; Scott Schafer; Michelan Sisti

3644 • RAGS

OPENED: 08/21/1986   Theatre: Mark Hellinger
Musical   Broadway: 4

Composer: Charles Strouse
Lyricist: Stephen Schwartz
Librettist: Joseph Stein

Producer: Lee Guber; Martin Heinfling; Marvin A. Krauss
Director: Gene Saks

Choreographer: Ron Field; **Costumes:** Florence Klotz; **Lighting Designer:** Jules Fisher; **Musical Director:** Eric Stern; **Orchestrations:** Michael Starobin; **Set Design:** Beni Montresor

Songs: Big Tim; Blame It on the Summer Night; Brand New World; Bread and Freedom; Cheer Up Hamlet [2]; Cherry Street Cafe, The; Children of the Wind; Dancing with the Fools; Democratic Club Dance; Easy for You; For My Mary [1]; Greenhorns; Hard to Be a Prince; I Remember; In America; It's Gonna Belong to Me [2]; Kaddish; Nothing Will Hurt Us Again [2]; Now That Papa's Back [2]; On the Fourth Day of July; Open Your Eyes [2]; Penny a Tune; Rags; Sound of Love, The; Three Sunny Rooms; Uptown; Wanting; What's Wrong with That?; Yankee Boy

Cast: Evalyn Baron; Josh Blake; Michael Davis; Rex Everhart; Larry Kert; Judy Kuhn; Dick Latessa; Mordecai Lawner; Marcia Lewis; Terrence Mann; Lonny Price; Bonnie Schon; Teresa Stratas

Notes: [1] Same music as "Sentimental" from unproduced film musical THE BORROWERS. [2] Cut.

3645 • RAH-RAH-DAZE

Producer: Fred Waring

Songs: I'm in the Mood; So Beats My Heart for You (C/L: Pat Ballard; Charles Henderson; Tom Waring); What's the Use of Lovin' (If I Can't Have You)

Cast: Fred Waring & His Pennsylvanians

Notes: No other information available.

3646 • RAIDERS, THE
Notes: *See A YANKEE CIRCUS ON MARS.*

3647 • RAILROADS ON PARADE
OPENED: 04/30/1939
Revue   N.Y. World's Fair

Composer: Kurt Weill
Librettist: Edward Hungerford
Producer: Edward Hungerford
Director: Charles Alan

Choreographer: Bill Matons; **Costumes:** Harry Horner; Helene Pons; **Musical Director:** Isaac Van Grove; **Set Design:** Harry Horner

Songs: Mile After Mile [1] (L: Charles Alan; Buddy Bernier); Wheels Through the Night (L: Charles Alan)

Cast: Don DeFore; Mary Drayton; Wallace Walter Folmer; Michael Kidd; Robert Rounseville; Ted Shawn Dancers; Bernice Tyler

Notes: [1] Not in show. Based on music Weill wrote for "This Train Is Bound for Glory."

3648 • RAIN OR SHINE

OPENED: 02/09/1928   Theatre: George M.
                                          Cohan
Musical   Broadway: 360

Composer: Milton Ager
Lyricist: Jack Yellen
Librettist: James Gleason; Maurice Marks
Producer: Morris Green; A.L. Jones
Director: Alexander Leftwich

Songs: Add a Little Wiggle; Breakfast with You; Circus Days; Falling Star; Feelin' Good (C: Owen Murphy); Forever and Ever; Glad Tidings; Hey, Rube; Oh, Baby! (C/L: Owen Murphy); Pierrot and Pierrette; Rain or Shine; Roustabouts' Song (We Follow the Trail) C: Milton Ager; Owen Murphy); So Would I; Who's Gonna Get You?

Cast: Joe Cook; Tom Howard; Warren Hull; Joe Lyons; Nancy Welford

3649 • RAINBOW, THE (1923)

OPENED: 04/03/1923   Theatre: Empire
Musical   London: 113

Composer: George Gershwin
Lyricist: Clifford Grey
Librettist: Noel Scott; Edgar Wallace; Albert de Courville
Producer: Albert de Courville
Director: Allan K. Foster

Musical Director: Kennedy Russell

Songs: All Over Town [1]; Any Little Tune; Beneath the Eastern Moon; Blue Baby; Give Me My Mammy [1]; Good Night, My Dear; In the Rain; Innocent Lonesome Baby (C: William Daly; George Gershwin; L: Clifford Grey; Brian Hooker); Midnight Blues; Moonlight in Versailles; Oh! Nina; Strut Lady with Me; Sunday in London Town [1]; Sweetheart (I'm So Glad That I Met You)

Cast: Grace Hayes; Fred A. Leslie; Lola Raine; Earl Rickard; Stephanie Stephens

Notes: [1] Not used.

3650 • RAINBOW (1928)

OPENED: 11/21/1928   Theatre: Gallo
Musical   Broadway: 29

Composer: Vincent Youmans
Lyricist: Oscar Hammerstein II
Librettist: Oscar Hammerstein II; Laurence Stallings
Producer: Philip Goodman
Director: Oscar Hammerstein II

Choreographer: Busby Berkeley; **Costumes:** Charles LeMaire; **Musical Director:** Max Steiner; **Orchestrations:** Paul Lannin; Oscar Radin; Max Steiner; **Set Design:** Frank Gates; E.A. Morange

Songs: Bride Was Dressed in White, The; Coming Through the Rye [2]; Diamond in the Rough [1]; Faded Rose, A [2]; Forty-Niner and His Clementine [2]; Get a Horse, Get a Mule [2]; Hay! Straw!; How to Win a Man [2]; I Like You As You Are; I Look for Love [2]; I Want a Man; Let Me Give All My Love to Thee; My Mother Told Me Not to Trust a Soldier; On the Golden Trail; One Girl, The; Primping [2]; Soliloquy; Sunrise [2]; Virginia [3]; Who Am I That You Should Care for Me? [2] (L: Gus Kahn); Who Wants to Love Spanish Ladies?

Cast: Louise Brown; Harland Dixon; Brian Donlevy; Libby Holman; Helen Lynd; Allan Price; Charlie Ruggles

Notes: [1] Same music as "When We Are Married" in LOLLIPOP. [2] Cut prior to opening. [3] Same music as "The Road to Home" in THROUGH

THE YEARS, "If I Told You" in WILDFLOWER and "Sweet as Sugar Cane" in GREAT DAY.

3651 • RAINBOW (1972)

OPENED: 12/18/1972   Theatre: Orpheum
Musical   Off-Broadway: 48

Composer: James Rado
Lyricist: James Rado
Librettist: James Rado; Ted Rado
Producer: James Rado; Ted Rado
Director: Joe Donovan

Choreographer: Joe Donovan; **Costumes:** Nancy Potts; **Dance Arranger:** Steve Margoshes; **Lighting Designer:** James Tilton; **Musical Director:** Steve Margoshes; **Set Design:** James Tilton; **Vocal Arranger:** Steve Margoshes

Songs: Bathroom; Be Not Afraid; Cacophony; Deep in the Dark; Fruits and Vegetables; Garden for Two, A; Give Your Heart to Jesus; Globligated; Groovy Green Man Groovy; Guinea Pig; Heliopolis; How Dreamlike; I Am a Cloud; I Am Not Free; I Don't Hope for Great Things; I Want to Make You Cry; Joke a Cola; Love Me, Love Me, Dorothy Lamour, La Sarong; Mama Loves You; Man, The; Moosh, Moosh; My Lungs; O.K. Goodbye; Obedience; Oh I Am a Fork; Oh, Oh, Oh; People Stink; Questions Questions; Somewhere Under the Rainbow; Song to Sing; Star Song; Starry Old Night; Stars and Bars; Tangled Tangents; Ten Days Ago; We Are the Clouds; Welcome Banana; What Can I Do for You; Who Are We; World Is Round, The; You Got to Be Clever; You Live in Flowers

Cast: Kay Cole; Gregory V. Karliss; Meat Loaf; Janet Powell; Marie Santell

3652 • RAINBOW GIRL, THE

OPENED: 04/01/1918   Theatre: New Amsterdam
Musical   Broadway: 160

Composer: Louis A. Hirsch
Lyricist: Rennold Wolf
Librettist: Rennold Wolf
Producer: Klaw & Erlanger
Director: Herbert Gresham; Julian Mitchell

Source: NEW LADY BANTOK, THE (Play Jerome K. Jerome); **Costumes:** Marie Cook; Alice O'Neil; **Lighting Designer:** Tony Greshoff; **Musical Director:** Max Steiner; **Set Design:** Joseph Urban

Songs: Alimony Blues; Beautiful Lady Tell Me; I Don't Know How to Pick the Proper Girl [1]; I Wonder; I'll Think of You; In a Month or Two; Just You Alone; Let's Go Down to the Shop; Love's Ever New; Many a Time [1]; Mister Drummer Man; My Love Is for Thee; My Rainbow Girl; Nurse Me [1]; Rainbow Girl; Soon We'll Be Seen Upon the Screen; We Fear You Will Not Do, Lady Wetherell; Wedding Ceremony, The; Won't Someone Marry Me?; You're the Finest of Them All

Cast: William Clifton; Harry Delf; Ethel Delmar; Sydney Greenstreet; Claire Grenville; Laura Hamilton; Frederic Solomon; Billy B. Van

Notes: [1] Out Washington, D.C. 2/17/18.

3653 • RAINBOW JONES

OPENED: 02/13/1974   Theatre: Music Box
Musical   Broadway: 1

Composer: Jill Williams
Lyricist: Jill Williams
Librettist: Jill Williams
Producer: Rubykate Inc.
Director: Gene Persson

Choreographer: Sammy Bayes; **Costumes:** James Berton Harris; **Lighting Designer:** Spencer Mosse; **Musical Director:** Danny Holgate; **Orchestrations:** Danny Holgate; **Set Design:** Richard Ferrer

Songs: Alone at Last, Alone; Bad Breath; Do Unto Others; Free and Easy; Her Name Is Leona; I'd Like to Know You Better; It's So Nice; Ju, Ju, Jupiter; Just Listen to Me; Little Bit of Me in You, A; One Big Happy Family; Only Man for the Job, The; Our Just Portion; Wait a Little While; We All Need Love; Who Needs the Love of a Woman

Cast: Peter Kastner; Daniel Keyes; Peggy Hagen Lamprey; Ruby Persson; Gil Robbins; Andy Rohrer

Notes: Titled R.J. out of town prior to Broadway.

3654 • RAINBOW RAPE TRICK, THE

OPENED: 04/13/1975   Theatre: Bert Wheeler
Musical   Off-Broadway: 4

Composer: Ann K. Lipson
Lyricist: Ann K. Lipson; Greg Reardon
Librettist: Greg Reardon
Producer: Hyperion Productions
Director: Robert Davison

Choreographer: Robin Rassen; **Costumes:** Mary Ann Tolka, **Lighting Designer:** Chaim Gitter; **Musical Director:** Elliot Ames; **Set Design:** Francis Pezza

Songs: Act Like a Villager; Crush on You; Democracy Is Lunacy; Divorce of Course; Empty World of Power; Free; Itch to Be a Witch; Little Blue Star; Love Me, Baby!; Most Confused Prince; Northchester; Stay with Me; Three Fierce Men; Tis of Thee; Zip Community

Cast: Jean Greer; Jeremy Stockwell; Joseph Tripolino

3655 • RAINBOW ROSE
OPENED: 03/16/1926   Theatre: Forrest
Musical   Broadway: 55

Composer: Harold Levey; Owen Murphy
Lyricist: Owen Murphy
Librettist: Walter De Leon; Owen Murphy
Producer: George MacFarlane
Director: Walter Wilson

Source: LUCKY BREAK, A (Play Zelda Sears); **Choreographer:** Ray Perez

Songs: Dreams; First, Last, and Only; Going Over the Bumps; If You Were Someone Else; Jealous; Let's Run Away and Get Married; Rainbow (L: Zelda Sears); Something Tells Me I'm in Love; Steppin' Baby; We Want Our Breakfast; When the Hurdy Gurdy Plays; You're All the World to Me

Cast: Louise Galloway; Jack Squire; Margaret Walker; Jack Whiting

3656 • RAISIN
OPENED: 10/18/1973   Theatre: 46th Street
Musical   Broadway: 847

Composer: Judd Woldin
Lyricist: Robert Brittan
Librettist: Robert Nemiroff; Charlotte Zaltzberg
Producer: Robert Nemiroff
Director: Donald McKayle

Source: RAISIN IN THE SUN, A (Play Lorraine Hansberry); **Arrangements:** Dorothea Freitag; **Choreographer:** Donald McKayle; **Costumes:** Bernard Johnson; **Dance Arranger:** Judd Woldin; **Lighting Designer:** William Mintzer; **Musical Director:** Howard A. Roberts; **Orchestrations:** Al Cohn; Robert M. Freedman; **Set Design:** Robert U. Taylor; **Vocal Arranger:** Joyce Brown; Howard A. Roberts

Songs: African Dance; Alaiyo; Booze; He Came Down This Morning; It's a Deal; Man Say; Measure the Valleys; Not Anymore; Prologue; Runnin' to Meet the Man; Same Old Color Scheme; Sidewalk Tree; Sweet Time; Whole Lotta Sunlight, A; Whose Little Angry Man; You Done Right

Cast: Deborah Allen; Virginia Capers; Ralph Carter; Ernestine Jackson; Robert Jackson; Joe Morton; Ted Ross

3657 • RAISIN' CAIN
OPENED: 07/09/1923   Theatre: Lafayette
Revue   New York

Composer: James P. Johnson
Producer: Nat Nazzarro

Choreographer: Frank Montgomery

Songs: Barber Shop Harmony; Call a Cop; Come Out; Fattening Frogs for Snakes; Happenings; Harmony; Hot Chops; Jungle Jump; Laughing Clarinet; Let's Go; Mammy's Black Baby; Oh, Foot; Raisin' Cain; Senegambian Moon; Sentimental Oriental Blues; Tropical Chant; When My Man Comes Home

Cast: Buck & Bubbles; Emory Hutchins; Coressa Madison; Jean Starr

Notes: A Harlem revue. No other information available.

3658 • RAMBLER ROSE
OPENED: 09/10/1917   Theatre: Empire
Musical   Broadway: 72

Composer: Victor Jacobi
Lyricist: Harry B. Smith
Librettist: Harry B. Smith
Producer: Charles Frohman
Director: W.H. Bentley

Musical Director: Harold Vicars; **Set Design:** Homer Emens

Songs: Bundle of Nerves; But Not for You; Cinderella Song; Dream! Dream!; Finale Act I; Finale Act II; Gypsy Song (Come to Gypsy Land); I Know You; I Might Say 'Yes' To You; Just a Little Love; Land of the Midnight Sun, The; Lead Me Out Upon the Ballroom Floor; Now Won't That Be Nice; One Look, One Word; Opening Chorus; Opening Chorus Act II; Opening Chorus Act III; Poor Little Rich Girl's Dog (C/L: Irving Berlin); Queen of Laughter, The; Rambler Rose; Reminiscence; Smile a Little Smile for Me; What I'll Do for You; Whenever I Think of You (C: Charles N. Grant; L: Schuyler Greene)

Cast: Stewart Baird; W.H. Bentley; Joseph Cawthorn; George E. Mack; Ada Meade; Julia Sanderson; Walter Smith

3659 • RAMBLERS, THE

OPENED: 09/20/1926   Theatre: Lyric
Musical   Broadway: 291

Composer: Harry Ruby
Lyricist: Bert Kalmar
Librettist: Guy Bolton; Bert Kalmar; Harry Ruby
Producer: Philip Goodman
Director: John Harwood

Choreographer: Sammy Lee; **Costumes:** Charles LeMaire; **Musical Director:** Alfred Newman; **Set Design:** Raymond Sovey

Songs: All Alone Monday [2]; Any Little Tune; California Skies; Just One Kiss; Like You Do; Movie Ball, The; Oh! How We Love our Alma Mater [1]; We Won't Charleston; Whistle [1]; You Smiled at Me

Cast: Bobby Clark; Paul McCullough; Georgia O'Ramey; Marie Saxon; Jack Whiting

Notes: Previously titled THE FLY-BY-KNIGHTS. [1] Not in program. [2] Also in HOLLYWOOD MUSIC BOX REVUE (1927) (SPRING EDITION).

3660 • RANG-TANG

OPENED: 07/12/1927   Theatre: Royale
Musical   Broadway: 119

Composer: Ford Dabney
Lyricist: Jo Trent
Librettist: Kaj Gynt
Director: Charles Davis; Aubrey L. Lyles; Flournoy Miller

Songs: Brown; Come to Africa; Everybody Shout; Harlem; Jungle Rose; Monkey Land; Rang-Tang; Sambo's Banjo; Sammy and Topsy; Some Day; Summer Nights; Sweet Evening Breeze; Tramps of the Desert

Cast: Mae Barnes; Zaidee Jackson; Aubrey L. Lyles; Lavinia Mack; Flournoy Miller; James Strange; Lillian Westmoreland

3661 • RAP MASTER RONNIE

OPENED: 10/03/1984   Theatre: Top of the Gate
Revue   Off-Broadway: 49

Composer: Elizabeth Swados
Lyricist: Garry Trudeau
Additional Lyrics: Elizabeth Swados
Producer: Rosita Sarnoff
Director: Caymichael Patten

Choreographer: Ronni Stewart; **Costumes:** David Woolard; **Lighting Designer:** Anne Militello; **Musical Director:** John Richard Lewis; **Set Design:** Neil Peter Jampolis; **Vocal Arranger:** John Richard Lewis

Songs: Assistant Undersecretary of State for Human Rights, The; Cheese; Class of 1984, The; Empire Strikes First, The; Facts; Majority, The; New Years in Beirut, 1983; Nine to Twelve; O, Granada; One More Study; Rap Master Ronnie; Round Up, The; Self Made Man; Something for Nothing (with appreciation to Mayfair Music Hall); Take That Smile Off Your Face; Thinking the Unthinkable; You're Not Ready

Cast: Reathel Bean; Catherine Cox; Ernestine Jackson; Mel Johnson Jr.; Richard Ryder

3662 • RAYMOND HITCHCOCK'S PINWHEEL

OPENED: 06/15/1922   Theatre: Earl Carroll
Revue   Broadway: 35

Producer: Richard G. Herndon

Choreographer: Michio Ito; **Costumes:** Lillian Greenfield; William Troy

Songs: My Lady of the Fan (C/L: Earl Carroll); Oh Say, Oh Sue! (C: Joseph Meyer; L: Irving Caesar); Silver Stars (C/L: Percy Wenrich)

Cast: Eva Clark; Frank Fay; Raymond Hitchcock

3663 • RAZZLE DAZZLE (1916)

OPENED: 06/19/1916
Revue   London: 408

Composer: Herman Darewski; Maurice Klein
Lyricist: Ballard Macdonald; Wal Pink; Albert de Courville
Librettist: Basil Macdonald Hastings; Wal Pink; Albert de Courville
Producer: Albert de Courville
Director: William J. Wilson

Costumes: Comelli; Lucille

Songs: Did You Send Me these Beautiful Flowers?; England Remember; I Like You; Ice Cream Girl, The; I'll Build a House for You; I'll Shoot My Way; Land's End to John O'Groats; Life in the Old Girl Yet; Maid-o-the-Mist; Menu Dance, The; Only a Rose in the Strand; Opening Chorus; Pony Trot, The; Same Sweet Baby, The; Scotland for Ever!; Ten Little Bridesmaids; Turnip Time

Cast: Alex Fraser; Shirley Kellogg

3664 • RAZZLE DAZZLE (1951)

OPENED: 02/19/1951   Theatre: Arena
Revue   Off-Broadway: 8

Lyricist: Michael Stewart
Librettist: Michael Stewart
Producer: David Heilweil; Derrick Lynn-Thomas
Director: Edward Reveaux

Choreographer: Nelle Fisher; **Dance Arranger:** James Reed Lawlor; **Musical Director:** James Reed Lawlor; **Set Design:** William Riva; **Vocal Arranger:** Herbert Schutz

Songs: Catch Me If You Can (C: Shelley Mowell); Frivolity Frolics (C: Leo Schumer); Haven't We Met Before? (C: Irma Jurist); Light Fantastic, The (C: James Reed Lawlor); N.Y.C. (C: Leo Schumer); Sign Here (C: Leo Schumer); Someone (C: Shelley Mowell); Then I'm Yours (C: Leo Schumer); Two Hearts in Gypsy Time (C: Shelley Mowell); Wages of Sin, The (C: James Reed Lawlor);

What's a Show (C: Shelley Mowell); You're Only Young Once or Twice (C: Bernice Kroll)

Cast: Dorothy Greener; Bob Herget; Jane White

3665 • REAL GIRL

OPENED: 1911
Musical   Closed out of town

Composer: Irving Berlin
Lyricist: Irving Berlin
Producer: Bonita Amusement Co.

Songs: Cuddle Up; One O'Clock in the Morning; That Mysterious Rag (C: Irving Berlin; L: Ted Snyder); When You're in Town

Cast: Bonita; Lew Hearn

Notes: No program available.

3666 • REAL LIFE FUNNIES

OPENED: 02/11/1981   Theatre: Manhattan Theatre Club
Revue   Off-Broadway: 35

Composer: Alan Menken
Lyricist: Alan Menken
Librettist: Howard Ashman
Producer: Manhattan Theater Club
Director: Alan Menken

Source: REAL LIFE FUNNIES (Comic Strip: Stan Mack); **Choreographer:** Douglas Norwick; **Lighting Designer:** Frances Aronson; **Musical Director:** Larry Hochman; **Vocal Arranger:** Larry Hochman

Songs: Ah Men; Divorce Has Brought Us Together; Every Thursday Night; I Love Your Brains; Is It Art?; Lifted; People Collecting Things; Pleasantly Plump; Real Life Funnies; Someday; Someone to Come Home with Me Tonight; Way of My Father, The

Cast: Pamela Blair; Gibby Brand; Merwin Goldsmith; Janie Sell; Dale Soules; Chip Zien

3667 • REAL LIFE STORY OF JOHNNY DE FACTO, THE

OPENED: 11/08/1989
Musical   Closed out of town

Composer: Douglas Post
Lyricist: Douglas Post
Librettist: Douglas Post
Producer: Goodspeed Opera House
Director: Andre Ernotte

Arrangements: Joseph Baker; **Costumes:** Roslyn Brunner; **Lighting Designer:** Phil Monat; **Musical Director:** Alkiviades "Alki" Steriopoulos; **Set Design:** William Barclay

Songs: Critical List; Day and Age; End of the Line; Everything I Do Is News; Hearts to Be Young; History of a Rock Star, The; If This Is Paradise; Kill Johnny One Note Dead; Laughing Americans; Long Before I Die; Money and Insanity; Mother of Exiles; No Light in Your Eyes; Real Life; Resurrection; Undaunted

Notes: Goodspeed Opera House.

3668 REALLY ROSIE

OPENED: 09/30/1980   Theatre: Chelsea Theatre
                                         Center
Musical   Off-Broadway: 274

Composer: Carole King
Lyricist: Maurice Sendak
Librettist: Maurice Sendak
Producer: John H.P. Davis; Sheldon Riss
Director: Patricia Birch

Source: SIGN ON ROSIE'S DOOR, THE (Novel: Maurice Sendak); **Choreographer:** Patricia Birch; **Costumes:** Maurice Sendak; **Dance Arranger:** Joel Silberman; **Musical Director:** Joel Silberman; **Set Design:** Maurice Sendak; **Vocal Arranger:** Joel Silberman

Songs: Alligators All Around; Avenue F; Awful Truth, The; Chicken Soup with Rice; One Was Johnny; Pierre; Really Rosie; Screaming and Yelling; Simple Humble Neighborhood; Such Sufferin' [1]; Very Far Away

Cast: B.J. Barie; Jermaine Campbell; Tisha Campbell; Bibi Humes; Matthew Kolmes; Joe LaBenz IV; April Lerman; Wade Raley

Notes: [1] Cut prior to opening.

3669 • REBBITZEN FROM ISRAEL, THE

OPENED: 10/10/1972   Theatre: Mayfair
Musical   Off-Broadway: 168

Composer: Lili Amber
Lyricist: Lili Amber
Librettist: Pesach Burstein
Producer: Moishe Baruch
Director: Pesach Burstein

Source: REBBITZEN FROM ISRAEL, THE (Play L. Freiman); **Choreographer:** Yona Aloni; **Musical Director:** Elliot Finkel; **Set Design:** Peter Achilles

Songs: I Should Live So; I Wish It Was Over; I'm in Love; Ladies Should Be Beautiful; Love Is International; Oy Der Pesach Pesach; Tel-Aviv; Traditional Seder; Where Were You?; Yehi Rutzoin; Yeverechecha

Cast: Gene Barrett; Pesach Burstein; David Carey; Rina Ellis; Lillian Lux; Janece Martel; Bernard Sauer

3670 • REBECCA, THE RABBI'S DAUGHTER

OPENED: 11/04/1979   Theatre: Town Hall
Musical   Off-Broadway: 84

Composer: Abraham Ellstein
Additional Music: Alexander Lustig
Lyricist: Abraham Ellstein
Librettist: William Siegel
Producer: Shalom Musical Comedy Theatre
Director: Michael Greenstein

Choreographer: Felix Fibich; **Musical Director:** Renee Solomon; **Set Design:** Adina Reich

Songs: Charleston; Chassene; Couplet; Everyone Has a Right to Love; Forget Me Not; Hollywood; How Good It Is; I Want to Be a Bride; My Dreams; Once It Was Different; Potpourri; Prologue; Rivkele Dem Rebns; When a Jew Sings; You Are My Solace

Cast: Yankele Alperin; Mary Soreanu

3671 • RED BLUE-GRASS WESTERN FLYER SHOW, THE

OPENED: 08/16/1977
Musical   Closed out of town

Composer: Clint Ballard Jr.
Lyricist: Conn Fleming
Librettist: Conn Fleming

Producer: Goodspeed Opera House
Director: John Cullum

Choreographer: Dan Siretta; **Costumes:** David Toser; **Dance Arranger:** Russell Warner; **Lighting Designer:** Peter M. Ehrhardt; **Musical Director:** Lynn Crigler; **Orchestrations:** Clint Ballard Jr.; **Set Design:** John Lee Beatty; **Vocal Arranger:** Clint Ballard Jr.

Songs: As We Go Along; Blue-Grass Dreamers; Don't Change the Way You Love Me; Gate in the Road, The; Hattie's Time; I Don't Know How to Be My Daddy's Father; I Wanna Be a Country Music Singer; I'll Never Sing a Song; Letter, The; Listenin' to the Grand Ol' Opry; Old Folks at Home, The; Opening; Sally Bright Self-Risin' Flour Song, The; Very Young Man, A; When the Record Player's On

Cast: Barbara Coggin; Candy Darling; Robert Donley; Ralph Drischell; Victoria Goggin; Bob Gunton; David Keith; Barbara Lea

3672 • RED CANARY, THE

OPENED: 04/13/1914   Theatre: Lyric
Musical   Broadway: 16

Composer: Harold Orlob
Lyricist: Alex Johnstone; William Le Baron
Librettist: Will Johnstone
Producer: Mackay Production Co.
Director: Ben Teal

Songs: Call of Love, The; Globe-Trotter, The; Poor Rose; Something New

Cast: T. Roy Barnes; Leila Hughes; Adele Rowland

3673 • RED FEATHER

OPENED: 11/09/1903   Theatre: Lyric
Musical   Broadway: 60

Composer: Reginald De Koven
Lyricist: Charles Emerson Cook
Librettist: Charles Klein
Producer: Florenz Ziegfeld
Director: Max Figman; Joseph W. Herbert

Musical Director: Louis F. Gottschalk

Songs: Arrest Him; Bird Song; Carissima (C/L: Arthur A. Penn); Choral Prelude; Conspirators, The; Entrance of Hilda; Finale Act II; Garden of Dreams, The; Humorous Ghost, The; If I Only Had a Mustache Like the Kaiser; Lessons in Verse; Little Milliner, The; Madrigal, A; Merry Cavalier, The; Mo Ticht-tit!; Opening Chorus; Opening Chorus Act III; Our Cabinet; Prince of Good Fellows, The; Red Feather; Rose and the Breeze, The; Song of the Guard; Tale of the Highborn Rooster, The; There's a Little Street in Heaven They Call Broadway (C: A. Baldwin Sloane; L: James T. Waldon); To Call Thee Mine; Tragedy of the Hats; Wanda

Cast: Olive Celeste; Elsie De Bere; Thomas Q. Seabrooke; Grace Van Studdiford

Notes: [1] Sheet music only.

3674 • RED, HOT AND BLUE!

OPENED: 10/29/1936   Theatre: Alvin
Musical   Broadway: 181

Composer: Cole Porter
Lyricist: Cole Porter
Librettist: Russel Crouse; Howard Lindsay
Producer: Vinton Freedley
Director: Howard Lindsay

Choreographer: George Hale; **Costumes:** Constance Ripley; **Musical Director:** Frank E. Tours; **Orchestrations:** Robert Russell Bennett; **Set Design:** Donald Oenslager

Songs: At Ye Olde Coffee Shoppe in Cheyenne; Bertie and Gertie [2]; Carry On; Down in the Depths; Five Hundred Million; Good Bye, Little Dream, Goodbye [3]; Hymn to Hymen; It's a Great Life; It's Delovely [1]; Little Skipper from Heaven Above, A; Lonely Star [2]; Ours; Ozarks Are Callin' Me Home, The; Perennial Debutantes; Red, Hot and Blue; Ridin' High; That's the News I'm Waiting to Hear [2]; We're About to Start Big Rehearsin'; What a Great Pair We'll Be; When Your Troubles Have Started [2]; Where? [2]; Who, but You [4]; You're a Bad Influence on Me; You've Got Something

Cast: Thurston Crane; Jimmy Durante; Grace Hartman; Paul Hartman; Bob Hope; Ethel Merman; Forrest Orr; Vivian Vance; Dorothy Vernon; Polly Walters

Notes: [1] In THE FLEET'S LIT UP (1938) London. [2] Not used or cut. [3] Not used. Also not used in BORN TO DANCE (film). Used in OH, MISTRESS MINE in London in 1936.

3675 • RED MILL, THE
OPENED: 09/24/1906   Theatre: Knickerbocker
Musical   Broadway: 274

Composer: Victor Herbert
Lyricist: Henry Blossom
Librettist: Henry Blossom
Producer: Charles Dillingham
Director: Fred G. Latham

Costumes: Wilhelm; **Musical Director:** Max Hirschfeld; **Orchestrations:** Victor Herbert; **Set Design:** Homer Emens; Gates & Morange

Songs: Accident!, An; Beautiful Isle of Dreams; Because You're You; By the Side of the Mill; Enough of Work [3]; Every Day Is Ladies' Day with Me; Go While the Goin' Is Good; Gooda-Bye John [1] (C: Egbert Van Alstyne; L: Harry Williams); Gossip's Chorus; I Want You to Marry Me; If You Love but Me [4]; I'll Ring the Bell [2]; I'm Always Doing Something I Don't Want to Do; In the Isle of Our Dreams; Legend of the Mill, The; Love but You; Mignonette; Moonbeams; Streets of New York (In Old New York), The; Teach Them What to Say [4]; Wedding Bells (Wedding Chorus); When You're Pretty and the World Is Fair; Whistle It; Widow Has Ways, A; You Never Can Tell About a Woman

Cast: Edward Begley; Allene Crater; Augusta Greenleaf; Ethel Johnson; Dave Montgomery; Joseph M. Ratliff; Fred Stone

Notes: [1] In THE BELLE OF AVENUE A. [2] Not in program. [3] Cut. [4] ASCAP/Library of Congress only.

3676 • RED MOON, THE
OPENED: 05/03/1909   Theatre: Majestic
Musical   Broadway: 32

Composer: J. Rosamond Johnson
Lyricist: Bob Cole
Librettist: Bob Cole
Producer: A.L. Wilbur

Songs: Ada, My Sweet Potater (C: Bob Cole; James Reese Europe; L: Chas. A. Hunter); Ain't Had No Lovin' in a Long Time; As Long As the World Goes Round; Big Red Shawl, The; Bleeding Moon; I Ain't Had No Lovin' in a Long Time (C: James Reese Europe); I've Just Lost My Teddy Bear (C: Bob Cole; J. Rosamond Johnson); Life Is a Game of Checkers; Love Me Baby Mine; On the Road to Monterey; Pathway of Love, The; Picaninny Days (C: James Reese Europe); Pliney, Come Out in the Moonlight (C: James Reese Europe); Red Moon (C: James Reese Europe); Sambo (C: James Reese Europe); Same Old Silv'ry Moon Is Shining, The

Cast: Bob Cole; Lottie Gee; Henry Grant; J. Rosamond Johnson; Sam Lucas; Elizabeth Williams

Notes: No program available.

3677 • RED PEPPER (1922)
OPENED: 05/29/1922   Theatre: Shubert
Musical   Broadway: 24

Composer: Albert Gumble; Owen Murphy
Lyricist: Owen Murphy
Librettist: Emily Young
Producer: Messrs. Shubert
Director: Frank Smithson

Choreographer: Allan K. Foster; **Musical Director:** Vernon Bestor; **Orchestrations:** J. Dell Lampe

Songs: Boys, Boys, Boys; Bugaboo; Butterfly; Chickens; Dreamy Hollow [3]; Game of Love; Ginger; Havanola Jazz [3]; Hiawatha's Melody of Love; In the Starlight; It Must Be You; Land of Sky Blue Waters [1]; Lasso Queen; Levee Land; Look Before You Leap [3]; Mississippi Cradle; Opening Chorus; Senora; Southland [2]; Strong for Girls; Strut Your Stuff; Waters of Minnetonka [2]; Wedding Bells; Wedding Day

Cast: Mabel Elaine; Barrett Greenwood; Heath; James McIntyre; Dan Quinlan; Ferne Rogers; Ada Summerville

Notes: [1] Out Seattle 5/27/23. [2] Out Toledo 12/16/22. [3] Out Baltimore 11/28/21.

3678 • RED PEPPERS (1936)
OPENED: 11/24/1936   Theatre: National
Play   Broadway: 113

Composer: Noel Coward
Lyricist: Noel Coward
Author: Noel Coward

Producer: John C. Wilson
Director: Noel Coward

Musical Director: John McManus; **Set Design:** G.E. Calthrop

Songs: Has Anybody Seen Our Ship?; Men About Town

Cast: Joyce Carey; Noel Coward; Gertrude Lawrence; Moya Nugent; Edward Underdown; Alan Webb

Notes: Part of TONIGHT AT 8:30. TONIGHT AT 8:30 ran 113 performances. RED PEPPERS was performed in repertory and appeared only two or three times per week.

3679 • RED PETTICOAT, THE

OPENED: 11/13/1912   Theatre: Daly's
Musical   Broadway: 61

Composer: Jerome Kern
Lyricist: Paul West
Librettist: Rida Johnson Young
Producer: Messrs. Shubert
Director: Joseph W. Herbert

Source: NEXT (Play Rida Johnson Young); **Musical Director:** Clarence West; **Orchestrations:** Frank Saddler

Songs: Correspondence School, The; Dance, Dance, Dance; I Wonder; Joy of That Kiss, The [2]; Little Golden Maid; My Peaches and Cream; Oh, You Beautiful Spring (L: M.E. Rourke); Oo-oo-oo; Opening Act II [1]; Prisoner of Love, A; Ragtime Restaurant, The; Since the Days of Grandmama; Sing, Sing, You Tetrazzini [2]; Vigilantes, The [1]; Walk, Walk, Walk; Waltz Time Girl, The; Where Did the Bird Hear That? [2]

Cast: Grace Field; Francis Kennedy; Helen Lowell; Charles MacDonald; Donald Macdonald; Gertrude Millington; William Pruette

Notes: Titled LOOK WHO'S HERE when out of town prior to Broadway. [1] Out of town only. [2] Not used.

3680 • RED ROBE, THE

OPENED: 12/25/1928   Theatre: Shubert
Musical   Broadway: 167

Composer: Jean Gilbert
Lyricist: Harry B. Smith
Librettist: Harry B. Smith
Producer: Messrs. Shubert
Director: J.C. Huffman

Source: UNDER THE RED ROBE (Novel: Stanley Weyman); **Choreographer:** Chester Hale; Raymond Midgley; **Costumes:** Ernest Schrapps; **Musical Director:** Oscar Radin; **Set Design:** Watson Barratt

Songs: Believe in Me (C: Arthur Schwartz); Home o' Mine; I Plead, Dear Heart; If I Could Forget (In Dreamland Fancies) [1]; I'll Love Them All to Death; I've Got It (C: Alberta Nichols; L: Mann Holiner); Joy or Strife; King of the Sword (C: Maurie Rubens; Robert Stolz; L: J. Keirn Brennan); Lady Luck; Land of Provence; Laugh at Life (C: Maurie Rubens; L: Edward Delaney Dunn); Mine for Aye; Oh, How the Girls Adore Me; Only a Smile; Roll of the Drums; Soldier of Fortune, A; Thrill of a Kiss, The; When the Banners Lead; Where Love Grows; Wings of Romance; You and I Are Passersby

Cast: S. Herbert Bragiotti; Violet Carlson; Helen Gilliland; Manila Powers; Jose Ruben; Walter Woolf

Notes: [1] ASCAP/Library of Congress only.

3681 • RED ROSE, THE

OPENED: 06/22/1911   Theatre: Globe
Musical   Broadway: 76

Composer: Robert Hood Bowers
Lyricist: Harry B. Smith; Robert B. Smith
Librettist: Harry B. Smith; Robert B. Smith
Producer: Lee Harrison
Director: R.H. Burnside

Choreographer: Jack Mason; **Costumes:** Valeska Suratt; **Musical Director:** Louis F. Gottschalk; **Set Design:** Valeska Suratt

Songs: Buy Buy Baby (L: Harry B. Smith); Come Along, Ma Cherie (L: Robert B. Smith); Confetti March (inst.); Dance Duet (L: Robert B. Smith); Hammock Song (Then You Swing, Swing, Swing) (L: Robert B. Smith); I'd Like to Go on a Honeymoon with You (L: Harry B. Smith); If You Can't Sing, Dance (L: Robert B. Smith); I'm All Thine (L: Harry B. Smith); Land of the Free, The

(L: Robert B. Smith); Love and Beauty; Men! Men! Men! (L: Harry B. Smith); Mysterious Moon [1] (C: Nat D. Ayer; L: A. Seymour Brown); Oh, You Beautiful Doll (C: Nat D. Ayer; L: A. Seymour Brown); Old Ballet Days, The; Opening Chorus (L: Robert B. Smith); Opening Chorus Act II (L: Harry B. Smith); Posing Scene (L: Robert B. Smith); Queen of Vanity Fair, The (L: Harry B. Smith); Rosy Morn, The; Spanish Song (L: Harry B. Smith); Students' Glide (Turkey Wing) (inst.); Wedding Bells; You Can Go As Far As You Like with Me (L: Harry B. Smith)

Cast: Flavia Arcaro; Zoe Barnett; Alexander Clark; John E. Hazzard; Ernest Lambert; Wallace McCutcheon; Valeska Suratt

Notes: Only out of town program available. Songs from vocal score. [1] From sheet music.

3682 • RED SHOES, THE

OPENED: 12/16/1993   Theatre: Gershwin
Musical   Broadway: 5

Composer: Jule Styne
Lyricist: Bob Merrill [5]
Librettist: Marsha Norman
Producer: MCA/Universal; James M. Nederlander; Martin Starger
Director: Stanley Donen

Source: RED SHOES, THE (Film: Michael Powell; Emeric Pressburger); **Arrangements:** Donald Pippin; **Choreographer:** Lar Lubovitch; **Costumes:** Catherine Zuber; **Dance Arranger:** Gordon Harrell; **Lighting Designer:** Ken Billington; **Musical Director:** Donald Pippin; **Orchestrations:** William D. Brohn; Sid Ramin; **Set Design:** Heidi Landesman

Songs: Alone in the Light; Am I to Wish Her Love [1]; Audition, The; Be Somewhere; Come Home [6]; Corps de Ballet; Do Svedanya (L: Bob Merrill; Marsha Norman); Home Again [7] (L: Marsha Norman); I'll Never Know [2] (L: Marsha Norman); Impresario; It's a Fairy Tale; It's Always Like the First Time [2] (L: Marsha Norman); Miss Page; One and One Are Two [2] (L: Marsha Norman); Rag, The; Red Shoes, The [2] (L: Marsha Norman); Red Shoes Ballet (dance) [3]; Top of the Sky; When It Happens to You (1) [4]; When It Happens to You (2) [2] (L: Marsha Norman); When You Dance for a King

Cast: Steve Barton; Leslie Browne; Pamela Burrell; George De La Pena; Scott Fowler; Laurie Gamache; Lydia Gaston; Charles Goff; Margaret Illmann; Tad Ingram; Robert Jansen; Jeff Lander; Hugh Panaro; John Marshall Sharp; Jamie-Chandler Torns; Amy Wilder; Daniel Wright

Notes: Bob Merrill used the pseudonym Paul Stryker. Practically none of Marsha Norman's lyrics remained. Amy Wilder played Margaret Illmann's role at certain performances. Roger Rees was replaced during previews. This was Jule Styne's last-score for the theatre. [1] Same music as "I, Yes Me, That's Who" in LOOK TO THE LILIES. [2] Cut prior to opening. [3] Main theme is "Scherzo" from GENTLEMEN PREFER BLONDES. Also contains music from "Sunshine" from GENTLEMEN PREFER BLONDES. [4] Same music as "The World Is Beautiful Today" from HAZEL FLAGG. [5] Bob Merrill used the pseudonym Paul Stryker. When Jule Styne first reported to work at Republic Studios it was suggested he change his name (perhaps to avoid confusion with MCA head Jules Stein). Republic suggested Styne use the name Paul Stryker. [6] Same music as "The World Is Beautiful Today" from HAZEL FLAGG. [7] Not used. Same music as "The World Is Beautiful Today" from HAZEL FLAGG.

3683 • RED, WHITE AND BLUE

OPENED: 10/07/1950
Revue   Chicago

Composer: Vi Bradley
Lyricist: Barry Trivers
Librettist: Ed Haldeman; Henry Taylor; Barry Trivers
Producer: American Legion
Director: Owen Crump; LeRoy Prinz

Choreographer: Cliff Ferre; Paul Haakon; **Costumes:** Howard Shoup; **Lighting Designer:** James McCamm; **Musical Director:** David Rose; **Orchestrations:** Frank Perkins; **Set Design:** James McCamm; **Vocal Arranger:** Frank Perkins

Songs: All American Rainbow (C: Victor Young; L: Bob Hilliard); Are You My Darlin' (C: M.K. Jerome; L: Jack Scholl); Away from Home (C: David Rose; L: Jack Elliott); Changing of the Guards; For the Right Guy (C/L: Hal Borne); Forty-Eight States (L: Vi Bradley); Get Away from It All; Heads Up; I Hear America Singing (C/L: George Forrest; Robert Wright); I'm from the Middle West (C: Al Rinker; L: Floyd Huddleston); Keep Alookin' Straight Ahead (C: David Rose; L: Sammy Cahn); Love Life of a Sailor (C/L: George Forrest; Robert Wright); Main Street Ballet (inst.) (C: David Rose); Mask Waltz, The (C: David Rose; L: Leo Robin); Monday You Love Me; My Kind of People (C: Al Rinker; L: Floyd Huddleston); Strollin' Along (C: Al Rinker; L: Floyd Huddleston); Sweet Spirit of '76 (inst.) (C: David Rose); Symphony for Today (inst.) (C: David Rose); There'll Be a Beautiful Tomorrow (C: Al Rinker; L: Floyd Huddleston); Three Foolish Monkeys (C: M.K. Jerome; L: Jack Scholl)

Cast: Bob Carroll; Paul Haakon; Gail Sherwood; Larry Storch; Bobby Van

Notes: No program available. May have also played the Paramount Theatre in Los Angeles with George Jessel in the cast.

3684 • RED, WHITE AND MADDOX

OPENED: 01/26/1969   Theatre: Cort
Musical   Broadway: 41

Composer: Don Tucker
Lyricist: Don Tucker
Librettist: Jay Broad; Don Tucker
Producer: Edward Padula; Theatre Atlanta
Director: Jay Broad; Don Tucker

Costumes: David Chapman; **Lighting Designer:** Richard Casler; **Set Design:** David Chapman

Songs: Ballad of a Redneck; Billy Joe Ju; City Life; First Campaign Song; General's Song, The; Givers and Getters; God Is an American; Hip-Hooray for Washington; Hoe Down; Impeachment Waltz, The; Jubilee Joe; Little Mary Sue; Phooey; Red, White and Maddox Kazoo March; Second Campaign Song; Song of the Malcontents; What America Means to Me

Cast: Georgia Allen; Fran Brill; Clarence Felder; Jay Garner; Ted Martin; Arlene Nadel

3685 • RED WIDOW, THE

OPENED: 11/05/1911   Theatre: Astor
Musical   Broadway: 128

Composer: Charles J. Gebest
Lyricist: Channing Pollock; Rennold Wolf
Librettist: Channing Pollack; Rennold Wolf
Producer: George M. Cohan; Sam H. Harris
Director: Fred G. Latham

Source: MY OFFICIAL WIFE (Story: Archibald Clavering Gunther); **Choreographer:** James Gorman; **Musical Director:** Charles J. Gebest

Songs: Avenue of Palms, The; Come Dance with Me [1] (C/L: Billy Gaston; George White); I Love Love (I Love You Dear); I Shall Never Look at a Pretty Girl Again; I'm a Wonderful Man in Yonkers (L: William Jerome); In Society It's Always Dress Parade; Just for You; Never Mind Singing Just Dance, My Dear; Nihilists, The; Off to Russia; Opening Chorus; Patrons of the Play; Soldiers of the Czar; We Can Do Without the Men [1] (C: Raymond Hubbell; L: Henry Blossom); We Will Go, Go to Go-Go; When Woman Is the Question; White Fete, The (inst.); You Can't Pay the Landlord with Love

Cast: Raymond Hitchcock; Gertrude Vanderbilt

Notes: [1] Sheet music only.

3686 • REDEMPTION (THE LIVING CORPSE)

OPENED: 10/03/1918   Theatre: Plymouth
Play   Broadway: 204

Composer: Maurice Nitke
Lyricist: Arthur Hopkins
Author: Leo Tolstoy
Director: Arthur Hopkins

Costumes: Fanin Mindell; **Musical Director:** Maurice Nitke; **Set Design:** Robert Edmond Jones

Songs: Masha's Song (L: August Post); No More at Evening (L: Alexander Ivanoff)

Cast: John Barrymore; Gladys Fairbanks; Thomas Mitchell; Helen Westley

3687 • REDHEAD

OPENED: 02/05/1959   Theatre: 46th Street
Musical   Broadway: 452

Composer: Albert Hague
Lyricist: Dorothy Fields

Librettist: Dorothy Fields; Herbert Fields; David
Shaw; Sidney Sheldon
Producer: Lawrence Carr; Robert Fryer
Director: Bob Fosse

Choreographer: Bob Fosse; **Costumes:** Rouben Ter-
Arutunian; **Dance Arranger:** Roger Adams;
Lighting Designer: Jean Rosenthal; **Musical
Director:** Jay Blackton; **Orchestrations:** Robert
Russell Bennett; Philip J. Lang; **Vocal Arranger:**
Jay Blackton

Songs: Behave Yourself; Chase (dance); Dream
Dance; Erbie Fitch's Twitch; I'll Try; I'm Back in
Circulation; It Doesn't Take a Minute [2]; Just for
Once; Look Who's in Love; Merely Marvelous;
My Gal's a Mule [3]; My Girl Is Just Enough
Woman for Me [1]; Pick-Pocket Tango (dance);
Right Finger of My Left Hand, The; She's Not
Enough Woman for Me [1]; Simpson Sisters, The;
Two Faces in the Dark; Uncle Sam Rag, The; We
Loves Ya, Jimey

Cast: Richard Kiley; Cynthia Latham; William
LeMassena; Buzz Miller; Doris Rich; Leonard
Stone; Gwen Verdon

Notes: [1] Same music. [2] Cut. [3] ASCAP/Library
of Congress only.

3688 • REEL AMERICAN HERO, A
OPENED: 03/25/1981   Theatre: New Rialto
Musical   Broadway

Composer: Gordon Kent; Stephanie Peters
Lyricist: Gerald Paul Hillman; Stephanie Peters
Librettist: Judy GeBauer; Burt Vinocur
Producer: Gerald Paul Hillman
Director: Nancy Tribush Hillman

Choreographer: George Bunt; **Costumes:** Carol
Wenz; **Dance Arranger:** Roger Neil; **Lighting
Designer:** Harry Silverglat Darrow; Giles Hogya;
Musical Director: Roger Neil; **Orchestrations:**
Gordon Kent; **Set Design:** Harry Silverglat
Darrow; **Vocal Arranger:** Gordon Kent

Songs: Ballad of '39; Chan Ballet; Dance with Me;
Fly Eagle Fly; Fred and Ginger [1]; Garter Song;
Gunfighter, The; Here's a Love Song; Hero Time;
I Want to Be a Somebody; I'll Be Waitin'; Lili Is a
Lady with a Suitcase Up Her Sleeve; Little Horse
Sense [1]; Monster Medley; Movie Game of Make
Believe, The; My Sergeant Doesn't Look Like Big

John Wayne; Ratta Tat Tat; Silver Vision [1];
Snow White My Daughter; Student Arch Duke,
The [1]; Sugar Daddy Blues; Tempus Fugit;
What's Gone Wrong; World of Black and White,
The [1]; You Mustn't Eat People

Cast: Hillary Bailey; Vidya Kaur; Peter Newman;
Jess Richards; Roxanna White

Notes: Closed March 29, 1981 after five previews.
Originally titled THE WORLD OF BLACK AND
WHTE. [1] Cut prior to previews.

3689 • REGATTA GIRL, THE
OPENED: 03/14/1900   Theatre: Koster and Bial's
                       Music Hall
Musical   Broadway

Composer: Harry McLellan
Lyricist: Clay M. Greene
Librettist: Clay M. Greene

Source: UNKNOWN (Play Charles Bradley; J.
Cheever Goodwin)

Notes: No program available.

3690 • REGGAE
OPENED: 04/27/1980   Theatre: Biltmore
Musical   Broadway: 21

Librettist: Stafford Harrison; Kendrew Lascelles;
Melvin Van Peebles
Producer: Michael Butler; Eric Nazhad
Director: Gui Andrisano; Glenda Dickerson

Choreographer: Mike Malone; **Costumes:** Raoul
Pene du Bois; **Lighting Designer:** Beverly
Emmons; **Musical Director:** Michael Kamen; **Set
Design:** Edward Burbridge

Songs: Banana, Banana, Banana (C/L: Michael
Kamen; Ras Karbi); Chase the Devil (C/L: Max
Romeo); Ethiopian Pageant (C/L: Michael
Kamen); Everything That Touches You (C/L:
Michael Kamen); Farmer (C/L: Max Romeo);
Flowers [1] (C/L: Michael Kamen); Gotta Take a
Chance (C/L: Michael Kamen; Max Romeo); Hey
Man (C/L: Ras Karbi; C: Michael Kaman;
L: Michael Kamen); I and I (C/L: Kendrew
Lascelles; Max Romeo); Jamaica Is Waiting (C/L:
Michael Kamen; Ras Karbi; Max Romeo); Market
[1] (C/L: Michael Kamen; Ras Karbi); Mash 'Em

Up (C/L: Michael Kamen; Ras Karbi; Kendrew Lascelles; Jackie Mittoo); Mash Ethiopia (C/L: Michael Kamen; C: Ras Karbi; Kendrew Lascelles; Jackie Mittoo); Mrs. Brown (C/L: Max Romeo; L: Stafford Harrison); No Sinners in Jah Yard (C/L: Ras Karbi; Max Romeo); Now I See It (C/L: Randy Bishop; Kendrew Lascelles); Promised Land (C/L: Ras Karbi); Rasta Roll Call (C/L: Ras Karbi); Rastafari (C/L: Michael Kamen); Reggae Music Got Soul (C/L: Jackie Mittoo); Rise Tafari (C/L: Ras Karbi); Rise Up Jah- Jah Children (C/L: Ras Karbi); Roots of the Tree (C/L: Ras Karbi; Kendrew Lascelles); Silly Simon [1] (C/L: Randy Bishop); Star of Zion (C/L: Michael Kamen); Talkin' About Reggae (C/L: Stafford Harrison; Michael Kamen; Kendrew Lascelles; Jackie Mittoo); Vision [1] (C/L: Ras Karbi)

Cast: Obba Babatunde; Calvin Lockhart; Sheryl Lee Ralph; Fran Salisbury; Philip Michael Thomas

Notes: [1] Cut prior to opening.

3691 • REGINA
OPENED: 10/31/1949　　Theatre: 46th Street
Opera　　Broadway: 56

Composer: Marc Blitzstein
Lyricist: Marc Blitzstein
Librettist: Marc Blitzstein
Producer: Cheryl Crawford; Clinton Wilder
Director: Robert Lewis

Source: LITTLE FOXES, THE (Play Lillian Hellman); **Choreographer:** Anna Sokolow; **Costumes:** Aline Bernstein; **Lighting Designer:** Charles Elson; **Musical Director:** Maurice Abravanel; **Orchestrations:** Marc Blitzstein; **Set Design:** Horace Armistead

Songs: Away!; Best Things of All, The; Big Rich; Blues; Chinkypin; Deedle Doodle; Finale (Certainly Lord); Gallantry [1]; Galop; Greedy Girl; Greetings; Horace's Entrance; I Don't Know; I'm Sick of You (Horace's Last); Lionet; Make a Quiet Day; Music, Music, Music; Prologue; Regina's Aria; Sing Hubbard; Small Talk (Marshall); Summer Day (Two Old Drybones) [1]; Things (Regina's Waltz); Transition (Bonds); Veranda, The (inst.); What Will It Be?

Cast: Priscilla Gillette; Brenda Lewis; Russell Nype; Jane Pickens; William Warfield; William Wilderman

Notes: No songs listed in program.　[1] Same music.

3692 • REGULAR GIRL, A
OPENED: 09/18/1916
Musical　　Closed out of town

Composer: Winthrop Cortelyou; Charles Hambitzer
Librettist: Otto Drayton; William Cary Duncan

Notes: Rochester, N.Y.

3693 • REJUVENATION OF AUNT MARY, THE
OPENED: 11/12/1907　　Theatre: Garden
Play　　Broadway: 56

Author: Anne Waner
Producer: L.S. Sire

Songs: Hindoo Honey (C: Herman Avery Wade; L: Earle C. Jones)

Cast: David Proctor; May Robson; Nina Saville; Jack Storey

3694 • RELUCTANT LADY
OPENED: 07/1947　　Theatre: Cain Park
Musical　　Cleveland

Composer: Albert Hague
Lyricist: Maurice Valency
Librettist: Maurice Valency

Notes: No information available.

3695 • RETURN TO THE FORBIDDEN PLANET
OPENED: 10/13/1991　　Theatre: Variety Arts
Musical　　Off-Broadway: 245

Librettist: Bob Carlton
Producer: Andre Ptaszynski; Don Taffner
Director: Bob Carlton

Source: FORBIDDEN PLANET (Film); **Costumes:** Sally I. Lesser; **Lighting Designer:** Richard Nelson; **Musical Director:** Kate Edgar; **Set Design:** Rodney Ford

Songs: Born to Be Wild (C/L: Mars Bonfire); Don't Let Me Be Misunderstood (C/L: Bennie

Benjamin; Gloria Caldwell; Sol Marcus); Gloria (C/L: Van Morrison); Go Now (C/L: Larry Banks; Milton Bennett); Good Golly Miss Molly (C/L: Robert Blackwell; John Marascalco); Good Vibrations (C/L: Mike Love; Brian Wilson); Great Balls of Fire (C/L: Otis Blackwell; Jack Hammer); I Can't Turn You Loose (C/L: Otis Redding); I Heard It Through the Grapevine (C/L: Barrett Strong; Norman Whitfield); I'm Gonna Change the World (C/L: Eric Burdon); It's a Man's World (C/L: James Brown; Betty Newsome); It's His Kiss (The Shoop Shoop Song) (C/L: Rudy Clark); Mister Spaceman (C/L: Roger McGuinn); Monster Mash (C/L: Leonard Capizzi; Bobby Pickett); Oh, Pretty Woman (C/L: Billy Dees; Roy Orbison); Only the Lonely (C/L: Joe Melson; Roy Orbison); Robot Man (C/L: Sylvia Dee; George Goehring); Shake, Rattle and Roll (C/L: Charles Calhoun); Shakin' All Over (C/L: Johnny Kidd); She's Not There (C/L: Rod Argent); Tell Her (C/L: Bert Berns); Telstar (C/L: Joe Meek); Who's Sorry Now (C: Harry Ruby; L: Bert Kalmar; Ted Snyder); Why Must I Be a Teenager in Love? (C/L: Doc Pomus; Mort Shuman); Wipeout (C/L: Robert Berryhill; Patrick Connolly; James Fuller; Robert Wilson); Young Girl (C/L: Jerry Fuller)

Cast: Gabriel Barre; Julie Cruise; Robert McCormick; Steve Steiner; Louis Tucci

Notes: No songs written for this show.

3696 • REUBEN, REUBEN
OPENED: 10/10/1955
Musical   Closed out of town

Composer: Marc Blitzstein
Lyricist: Marc Blitzstein
Librettist: Marc Blitzstein
Producer: Cheryl Crawford
Director: Robert Lewis

Choreographer: Hanya Holm; **Costumes:** Jean Eckart; William Eckart; **Orchestrations:** Marc Blitzstein; Hershy Kay; Bill Stegmeyer; **Set Design:** Jean Eckart; William Eckart; **Vocal Arranger:** Abba Bogin

Songs: Be with Me; Cop's Lament; Have Yourself a Night; Hills of Amalfi, The; It's in the Cards; Love at the First Word; Miracle Song; Moment of Love; Monday Morning Blues; Mother of the Bridegroom; Musky and Whiskey; Mystery of

the Flesh; Never Get Lost; Reuben Talks; Rose Song; San Gennaro; Shave and a Haircut; Sleep; Song of the Arrow; Spot, The; Such a Little While; Tell It to Bart; Thank You; There Goes My Love; Upstairsy; We Gotta Pack; With a Woman to Be [1]; Yeth, Yeth

Cast: Eddie Albert; Kaye Ballard; Allen Case; Anita Darian; Crandall Diehl; Dean Dittman; Timmy Everett; Rico Froehlich; Edmund Gaynes; George Gaynes; Evelyn Lear; Sondra Lee; Enzo Stuarti; Charles Welch; G. Wood

Notes: [1] Later added to opera SACCO AND VANZETTI.

3697 • REUNION
OPENED: 05/12/1978   Theatre: Cubiculo
Musical   Off-Off-Broadway: 12

Composer: Ron Roullier
Lyricist: Melvin H. Freedman; Robert Kornfeld
Librettist: Melvin H. Freedman; Robert Kornfeld
Producer: Sally E. Parry
Director: Jeffrey K. Neill

Choreographer: Jeffrey K. Neill; **Costumes:** Chas W. Roeder; **Lighting Designer:** Christopher Peabody; **Set Design:** Dale Engle

Songs: All My Yesterdays; Childhood; Give Me Love; Golden Days; Got to Sing Me a Song; Great Wind, The; I'm All It Takes to Make You Happy; I'm Gonna Make It; Reunion; That Moment Is Now; Today; World I'll Make for Me, A; Young Dreams

Cast: Lou Corato; Howard Hagan; Geraldine Hanning; Eleanor Reissa; David Schall; Brian Watson; Beverly Wideman

Notes: Additional songs by Carly Simon and Lucy Simon but not credited in program.

3698 • REUNION IN NEW YORK
OPENED: 02/21/1940   Theatre: Little
Revue   Broadway: 89

Composer: Werner Michel
Lyricist: Lothar Metzl; Werner Michel
Producer: American Viennese Group
Director: Herbert Berghof; Ezra Stone

943

Choreographer: Lotte Goslar; **Costumes:** Lester Polakov; **Set Design:** Harry Horner

Songs: At the Rail; Blitz; Carmen; Character in Search of a Character, A (C: Berenece Kazounoff; L: David Greggory); Dachau (C: Andre Singer; L: Milton Hindus; Jura Soyfer); I'm Going Crazy with Strauss (L: Peter Barry; Werner Michel); Keep Laughing; Only Time of Day, The (C: Andre Singer; L: Richard Holden; Lothar Metezl); Oratorium Salzburgiensis (C: Andre Singer); Party with Our Memories, A; Shooting Gallery (C: Andre Singer); Stars in Your Eyes (C/L: Fritz Kreisler); Where Is My Homeland (C: Nelly Franck; L: Werner Michel; Auguste Spectorsky)

Cast: Klaus Brill; Lotte Goslar; Fred Lorenz

3699 • REVENGE WITH MUSIC

OPENED: 11/28/1934   Theatre: New Amsterdam
Musical   Broadway: 158

Composer: Arthur Schwartz
Lyricist: Howard Dietz
Librettist: Howard Dietz
Producer: Harold B. Franklin; Arch Selwyn
Director: Marc Connelly; Howard Dietz; Theodore Komisarjevsky; Worthington Miner

Source: THREE-CORNERED HAT, THE (Novel: Pedro de Alarcon); **Choreographer:** Michael Mordkin; **Costumes:** Constance Ripley; **Musical Director:** Victor Baravalle; **Orchestrations:** Robert Russell Bennett; **Set Design:** Albert Johnson

Songs: Flamenco; If There Is Someone Lovelier Than You; I'm Part of You [1]; In the Middle of the Night; In the Noonday Sun; Maria; My Father Said; Never Marry a Dancer; Once-in-a-While; That Fellow Manuelo; Think It Over; Wand'ring Heart; When You Love Only One; You and the Night and the Music [2]

Cast: Marcus Blechman; Andre Charise; Ilka Chase; Libby Holman; George Kirk; Margaret Lee; Joseph Macaulay; Georges Metaxa; Rex O'Malley; Detmar Poppen; Ivy Scott; Charles Winninger

Notes: [1] Cut. [2] Same music as "To-Night" from film THE QUEEN.

3700 • REVUE DE LUXE

Notes: *See ALL ABOARD (1918).*

3701 • REVUE OF REVUES, THE

OPENED: 09/27/1911   Theatre: Winter Garden
Revue   Broadway: 55

Composer: Melville Gideon; Louis A. Hirsch
Lyricist: Harold Atteridge; Leo Donnelly; Jean Havez
Librettist: Leo Donnelly; Jean Havez; Edgar Smith
Producer: Winter Garden Company
Director: Lewis Morton

Choreographer: Gus Sohlke; William J. Wilson; **Costumes:** Melville Ellis; **Musical Director:** Silvio Hein

Songs: Boardwalk Crawl, The (C: Louis A. Hirsch); Carmen Girl, The; College Boys; Girls and French Chauffeurs; Minstrel Band, The; On the Congo; Oriental Eyes; (I Met You In) Pittsburgh, Pa. (C: Louis A. Hirsch); Shooting Show; Sombrero Land; Sousa's Marches, The; Toni Caponi (C: Louis A. Hirsch); Tra-La-Li; Twenty Years Ago; Visit Looney Park

Cast: Lydia Berry; Gaby Deslys; Ernest Hare; Dorothy Jardon; Harry Jolson; Maude Raymond; Frank Tinney

Notes: Show within the show titled IN THE LIMELIGHT.

3702 • REX

OPENED: 04/25/1976   Theatre: Lunt-Fontanne
Musical   Broadway: 49

Composer: Richard Rodgers
Lyricist: Sheldon Harnick
Librettist: Sherman Yellen
Producer: Richard Adler; Roger Berlind
Director: Harold Prince; Edwin Sherin

Choreographer: Dania Krupska; **Costumes:** John Conklin; **Dance Arranger:** David Baker; **Lighting Designer:** Jennifer Tipton; **Musical Director:** Jay Blackton; **Orchestrations:** Irwin Kostal; **Set Design:** John Conklin

Songs: As Once I Loved You; At the Field of Cloth of Gold; Away from You; Basse Dance; Chase, The; Christmas at Hampton Court; Come to

Court [2]; Dear Jane [1]; Don't Come to Court [2]; Elizabeth; Eternal Stars [2]; From Afar [3]; I Brought You a Gift [1]; I'll Miss You [1]; In Time; Let Me Have a Son [2]; Masque, The; Morris Dance and Sword Dance; My Daughter [2]; No Song More Pleasing; Pears of Anjou, The [1]; Rex [1]; So Much You Loved Me [4]; Te Deum; Tell Me [5]; There Are Kings [2]; To Please My King [1]; Wee Golden Warrior, The; Where Is My Son?; Why?; Would I Not Love You [1]

Cast: Tom Aldredge; Barbara Andres; Glenn Close; Martha Danielle; Ed Evanko; Penny Fuller; Merwin Goldsmith; William Griffis; Michael John; Stephen D. Newman; Charles Rule; April Shawhan; Lillian Shelby; Gerald R. Teijelo; Nicol Williamson

Notes: [1] Cut prior to opening. [2] Not used. [3] Same music as "So Much You Loved Me." [4] Cut prior to opening. Same music as "From Afar." [5] Cut prior to opening. Used as incidental music.

3703 • RHAPSODY

OPENED: 11/22/1944 Theatre: Century
Musical Broadway: 13

Composer: Fritz Kreisler
Lyricist: Robert Russell Bennett; Blevins Davis; John Latouche
Librettist: Leonard Louis Levinson; Arnold Sundgaard
Producer: Blevins Davis; Lorraine Manville Dresselhuys
Director: David Lechine

Source: UNKNOWN (Story: A.N. Nagler); **Costumes:** Frank Bevan; **Dance Arranger:** Robert Russell Bennett; **Lighting Designer:** Stanley McCandless; **Musical Director:** Fritz Mahler; **Orchestrations:** Robert Russell Bennett; **Set Design:** Oliver Smith; **Vocal Arranger:** Robert Russell Bennett

Songs: Because You're Mine; Caprice Viennois; Chinese Porcelain Ballet (dance); Dandy's Polka; Happy Ending; Heart, The; Heaven Bless Our Home; May Wine Polka; Midnight Ballet (dance); My Rhapsody; Presentation; Rosemarin; Roulette Game, The; Scherzo; Song of Defiance; Take Love; They're All the Same; To Horse; When Men Are Free; World Is Young Again, The

Cast: Annamary Dickey; Eddie Mayehoff; George Young

Notes: No program available. The music was previously written for Kreisler's operetta SISSY.

3704 • RHAPSODY IN BLACK (1931)

OPENED: 05/04/1931 Theatre: Sam H. Harris
Revue Broadway: 80

Composer: Alberta Nichols
Lyricist: Mann Holiner
Producer: Blackbirds Productions; Lew Leslie
Director: Lew Leslie

Musical Director: Pike Davis

Songs: Dance Hall Hostess; Eccentricity; Eli Eli (C: Traditional); Harlem Moon; Harlem Rhumbola [3] (C: Jimmy McHugh; L: Dorothy Fields); I'm Feelin' Blue [2] (C: Jimmy McHugh; L: Dorothy Fields); March of the Toys (inst.) [4] (C: Victor Herbert); Rhapsody in Blue (inst.) (C: George Gershwin); St. Louis Blues [6] (C/L: W.C. Handy); Till the Real Thing Comes Along [5]; Washtub Rubsudy; What's Keeping My Prince Charming; You Can't Stop Me from Loving You [1]

Cast: Avis Andrews; Berry Brothers, The; Robert Ecton; Cecil Mack Choir; Blue McAllister; Al Moore; Eddie Rector; Eloise Uggams; Valaida; Geneva Washington; Ethel Waters

Notes: [1] Originally in CORNED BEEF AND ROSES. [2] Cut from INTERNATIONAL REVUE. [3] Out Detroit 2/28/32. [4] Originally in BABES IN TOYLAND. [5] The popular song of the same name by Alberta Nichols, Mann Holiner, L.E. Freeman, Saul Chaplin and Sammy Cahn was written in 1936. [6] Interpolated.

3705 • RHAPSODY IN BLACK (1941)

OPENED: 01/20/1941
Revue Closed out of town

Composer: Louis Haber
Lyricist: Edgar Leslie; Dorothy Sacks
Librettist: Nat Dorfman; Lew Leslie; Cecil Mack
Producer: Rhapsody in Black, Inc.
Director: Lew Leslie

Vocal Arranger: Cecil Mack

Songs: America, I Love You (C: Archie Gottler; L: Edgar Leslie); Babylon Is Falling; Barbershop Opera; Dixie Isn't Dixie Any More [2] (C: Rube Bloom; L: Johnny Mercer); Don't Advertise Your Man; Jericho; Just Walking Through Mocking Bird Lane; Refugees on Parade; Rhapsody in Black; Rhapsody in Blue (inst.) [1] (C: George Gershwin); Swing Struck [3] (C: Louis Haber; L: Dorothy Sacks); Thursday [3] (C: Louis Haber; L: Dorothy Sacks)

Cast: Honi Coles; Cecil Mack Choir; Tim Moore; Edith Wilson

Notes: Only songs written for this show listed. [1] From earlier edition. [2] Also in LEW LESLIE'S BLACKBIRDS OF 1936. [3] Also in BLACKBIRDS OF 1939.

3706 • RHYTH-MANIA

Notes: *See RHYTHMANIA.*

3707 • RHYTHM FOR SALE

OPENED: 1934   Theatre: Grand Terrace Cafe

Revue   Chicago

Composer: Paul Denniker
Lyricist: Andy Razaf
Producer: Leonard Harper

Songs: If You Can't Get Five Take Two (C/L: Joe Davis; Paul Denniker; Andy Razaf); No More Thrills; Show Me Your Qualifications

Cast: Carroll Dickerson Orchestra; Avon Long; Alma Smith

Notes: No program available.

3708 • RHYTHM RANCH

OPENED: 11/01/1989
Musical

Composer: Fred Stark
Lyricist: Hal Hackady
Librettist: Hal Hackady
Director: Philip William McKinley

Choreographer: Susan Stroman; **Costumes:** Lindsay W. Davis; **Dance Arranger:** Glen Kelly;

Lighting Designer: Jeff Davis; **Musical Director:** Phil Hall; **Set Design:** Michael Anania

Cast: Christopher Durham; Liz Larsen; Nora Mae Lyng; Jason Opsahl; Billy Padgett; Bill Rowley; Ruth Williamson

Notes: Millburn, NJ. — Paper Mill Playhouse.

3709 • RHYTHMANIA

OPENED: 03/1931   Theatre: Cotton Club
Revue   Nightclub

Composer: Harold Arlen
Lyricist: Ted Koehler
Producer: Dan Healy
Director: Dan Healy

Songs: Bandana Babies [8] (C: Jimmy McHugh; L: Dorothy Fields); Between the Devil and the Deep Blue Sea [9]; Breakfast Dance; Creole Love Call (inst.) [1] (C: Duke Ellington); Dinah [5] (C: Harry Akst; L: Sam M. Lewis; Joe Young); Get Up, Get Out, Get Under the Sun; Go Back Where You Stayed Last Night [1] (C/L: Sidney Easton; Ethel Waters); Harlem Holiday [1]; I Love a Parade [9]; If Dreams Come True [1] (C/L: Unknown); Kickin' the Gong Around [9]; Mooche, The (inst.) [4] (C: Duke Ellington); 'Neath the Pale Cuban Moon; Oh, Lady, Be Good! [7] (C: George Gershwin; L: Ira Gershwin); Papa-De-Da-Da [3] (C/L: Clarence Todd; Clarence Williams; Spencer Williams); Satan Leads the Band; Shake That Thing [6] (C/L: Papa Charlie Jackson); Trickeration; White Heat [2] (C: Arthur Schwartz; L: Howard Dietz); Without Rhythm

Cast: Roy Atkins; Berry Brothers, The; Cab Calloway and His Orchestra; Leitha Hill; Mae Johnson; Cora La Redd; Paul Meers; Clarence Robinson; Bernice Short; Swan & Lee; Elma Turner; Elmer Turner; Aida Ward; Henri Wessels

Notes: Sometimes titled RHYTH-MANIA. Calloway left the cast and was replaced by Ellington and his orchestra. [1] Added after opening. [2] Added after opening. From THE BAND WAGON. [3] Added after opening. From BLACKBIRDS OF 1930. [4] Added after opening. From COTTON CLUB REVUE (1928). [5] Added after opening. From PLANTATION REVUE. [6] Added after opening. From AFRICANA. [7] Added after opening. From LADY, BE GOOD!

[8] Added after opening. From BLACKBIRDS OF 1928. [9] Cut after opening.

3710 • RICH MR. HOGGENHEIMER, THE

OPENED: 10/22/1906   Theatre: Casino
Musical   Broadway: 187

Composer: Ludwig Englander
Lyricist: Harry B. Smith
Librettist: Harry B. Smith
Producer: Charles Frohman
Director: Ben Teal

Songs: Any Old Time at All (C: Jean Schwartz; L: William Jerome); Au Revoir My Little Hyacinth (C: Herman Darewski; L: A.E. Sidney Davis); Bag-pipe Serenade (C/L: Jerome Kern); Be Demure; Blue, Blue [1] (C: Jerome Kern; L: Paul West); Cupid's Auctioneer; Don't You Want a Paper Dearie (C: Jerome Kern; L: Paul West); Five O'Clock Tea; For Charity's Sake; Homesick Yankee or You're Thinking of Home Sweet Home, The (C/L: Kenneth S. Clark); Homeward Bound; How'd You Like to Spoon with Me? [3] (C: Jerome Kern; L: Edward Laska); I've a Little Favor (C: Jerome Kern; L: M.E. Rourke); Little Old America for Me [1]; My Hungarian Girl [1] (C: Jerome Kern; L: Paul West); Poker Love (Card Duet) (C/L: Jerome Kern; L: Paul West); Recipe, A [2] (C/L: Jerome Kern; L: Paul West); This World Is a Toy Shop

Cast: Percy Ames; Sam Bernard; Georgia Caine

Notes: [1] Sheet music only. Also in THE EARL AND THE GIRL. [2] Added for tour. Also in THE ORCHID. [3] Published under this show's name. It might have been interpolated into some productions.

3711 • RIDE THE WINDS

OPENED: 04/16/1974   Theatre: Bijou
Musical   Broadway: 3

Composer: John Driver
Lyricist: John Driver
Librettist: John Driver
Producer: Bill Tchakirides; Berta Walker
Director: Lee D. Sankowich

Choreographer: Jay Norman; **Costumes:** Samuel C. Ball; **Lighting Designer:** Jeff Davis; **Musical Director:** Robert Brandzel; **Orchestrations:** Robert Brandzel; **Set Design:** Samuel C. Ball; **Vocal Arranger:** Robert Brandzel

Songs: Are You a Man; Breathing the Air; Emperor Me, The; Every Days; Flower Song; Gentle Buffoon, The; Loving You; Pleasures; Remember That Day; Ride the Winds; Run, Musashi, Run; Someday I'll Walk; Tengu; That Touch; Those Who Speak; You're Loving Me

Cast: Ernesto Gonzalez; Irving Lee; Alexander Orfaly; Elaine Petricoff; Sab Shimono; Chip Zien

3712 • RIGHT GIRL, THE

OPENED: 03/15/1921   Theatre: Times Square
Musical   Broadway: 98

Composer: Percy Wenrich
Lyricist: Raymond W. Peck
Librettist: Raymond W. Peck
Producer: Virgil Randolph
Director: Walter Wilson

Choreographer: David Bennett; **Costumes:** Bert French; **Musical Director:** J. Albert Browne; **Orchestrations:** Arthur Lange

Songs: Aladdin; Call of Love [1]; Cocktail Hour; Finale Act II; Girl in Your Arms, A; Girls All Around Me; Harmony; Look for the Girl; Look Into My Eyes [2]; Love's Little Journey; Love's Romantic Sea [3]; Lovingly Yours; Old Flames; Oriental Serenade; Right Girl, The; Rocking Chair Fleet; There's an Old Flame Burning; Things I Learned in Dear Old Jersey; Waltz; We Were Made to Love; You Can Trust Me [2]; You'll Get Nothing from Me

Cast: Tom Lewis; Helen Montrose; Charles Purcell; Robert Woolsey

Notes: Titled MAID TO LOVE out of town. [1] Cut after opening. [2] Out 9/6/20 Buffalo. [3] Sheet music only.

3713 • RIGHT THIS WAY

OPENED: 01/04/1938   Theatre: 46th Street
Musical   Broadway: 15

Composer: Sammy Fain
Lyricist: Irving Kahal
Librettist: Parke Levy; Alan Lipscott; Marianne Brown Waters
Producer: Alice Alexander
Director: Bertrand Robinson

Songs: Don't Listen to Your Heart (C: Bradford Greene; L: Marianne Brown Waters); Doughnuts and Coffee; He Can Dance; I Can Dream, Can't I?; I Love the Way We Fell in Love; I'll Be Seeing You; It's Great to Be Home Again; Love Design (C: Bradford Greene; L: Marianne Brown Waters); Right This Way [1] (C: Bradford Greene; L: Marianne Brown Waters); Soapbox Sillies (C: Bradford Greene; L: Marianne Brown Waters); Tip Your Hat (C: Bradford Greene; L: Marianne Brown Waters); You Click with Me (C: Bradford Greene; L: Marianne Brown Waters)

Cast: April; Henry Arthur; Joe E. Lewis; Leona Powers; Blanche Ring; Guy Robertson; Tamara; Thelma White; Jack Williams

Notes: [1] Sheet music only.

3714 • RIGHT UP YOUR ALLEY
Musical   Harvard University

Composer: Irwin Carson
Lyricist: Steve Kaplan
Librettist: Brian McGunigle; Steve Shea
Producer: Robert L. DeNormandie
Director: Billy Wilson

Arrangements: Michael Tschudin; **Costumes:** Barbara Matheson; **Musical Director:** Jay Gorney; **Set Design:** Fran Mahard

Songs: As Wonderful As I; Boys Will Be Boys (C: Michael Tschudin); Career Girls; Class with a Capital K; Dauntless; Heart of Gold [1] (C: Irwin Carson; Michael Tschudin); Lady Be Dainty (C: Michael Tschudin); Life Goes On; Miss America Teen (C: Michael Tschudin); Over the Top; Please Mr. President; Right Up Your Alley (C: Michael Tschudin); Wanderlust; Your Momma Is Your Number One Friend

Cast: Stu Beck; George Denny; Ed Kovachy; Billy Mason; Tom Oliphant; Genaro Payan; Dean Stolber; Bill Weld[2]

Notes: Amateur show. The 118th production of Harvard's HASTY PUDDING THEATRICALS. [1] Introduction music by Tschudin, chorus by Carson. [2] Governor of Massachusetts at time of writing.

3715 • RINGLING BROTHERS-BARNUM AND BAILEY CIRCUS (1952)
OPENED: 1952

Composer: John Ringling North
Lyricist: E. Ray Goetz
Producer: John Ringling North
Director: Richard Barstow; Pat Valdo

Choreographer: Edith Barstow; **Set Design:** Miles White

Songs: New Orleans Mardi Gras and You, The; Someday Today Will Be the Good Old Times

3716 • RINGLING BROTHERS-BARNUM AND BAILEY CIRCUS (1954)
OPENED: 1953

Composer: John Ringling North
Lyricist: E. Ray Goetz

Songs: Dreamland; Fiesta; Rocket to the Moon; U.N.

3717 • RINGS OF SMOKE
OPENED: 1920
Musical

Composer: Cliff Hess; Joseph Santley
Lyricist: Cliff Hess
Producer: Carleton Hoagland
Director: Pat Rooney; Edgar Allen Woolf

Songs: Daughter of Rosie O'Grady (C: Walter Donaldson; L: Monte Brice); I'm Rosie O'Grady Herself (L: Edgar Allen Woolf); In Barcelona; Jazzy Scene (C/L: Eddie Conrad); Leetle Bit Too Much, A; Rings of Smoke (C: Eddie Conrad; L: Edgar Allen Woolf); Smokey-Mokey Elf, The (C: Cliff Hess; L: Edgar Allen Woolf); Stop Your Teasin'; Waiting

Cast: Marion Bent; Vincent Lopez and His Orchestra; Pat Rooney

Notes: A vaudeville musical.

3718 • RINK, THE

OPENED: 03/09/1984   Theatre: Martin Beck
Musical   Broadway: 204

Composer: John Kander
Lyricist: Fred Ebb
Librettist: Terrence McNally
Producer: Roger Berlind; Joan Cullman; Jonathan Farkas; Jules Fisher; Kenneth-John Productions; Milbro Productions
Director: A.J. Antoon

Choreographer: Graciela Daniele; **Costumes:** Theoni V. Aldredge; **Dance Arranger:** Tom Fay; **Lighting Designer:** Marc B. Weiss; **Musical Director:** Paul Gemignani; **Orchestrations:** Michael Gibson; **Set Design:** Peter Larkin

Songs: After All These Years; All the Children in a Row; Angel's Rink and Social Center; Apple Doesn't Fall, The; Blue Crystal; Chief Cook and Bottle Washer; Colored Lights; Don't Ask Me; Leche Bella [1]; Marry Me; Mirror Ball [1]; Mrs. A; Murphy's Law [1]; Not Enough Magic; Only in the Movies [3]; Postcards [1]; Rink, The; So It's Over Then [1]; Under the Roller Coaster; Wallflower; We Can Make It; What Happened to the Old Days?; When the Antonellis Were Here [1]; Wine and Peaches [1]; Yesterday [2]; You Kept Me in Touch with Mama [1]

Cast: Jason Alexander; Ronn Carroll; Scott Ellis; Kim Hauser; Scott Holmes; Mel Johnson Jr.; Frank Mastrocola; Liza Minnelli; Chita Rivera

Notes: [1] Cut prior to opening. [2] Cut prior to opening. From GOLDEN GATE, a show written for George Abbott as a demo to illustrate the team's talents for the job of writing for FLORA, THE RED MENACE. In GOLDEN GATE the song was titled "Yesterday Is Yesterday." [3] Cut prior to opening. Used later in KISS OF THE SPIDER WOMAN.

3719 • RIO RITA

OPENED: 02/02/1927   Theatre: Ziegfeld
Musical   Broadway: 494

Composer: Harry Tierney
Lyricist: Joseph McCarthy
Librettist: Guy Bolton; Fred Thompson

Producer: Florenz Ziegfeld
Director: John Harwood

Choreographer: Sammy Lee; Albertina Rasch; **Costumes:** John Harkrider; **Musical Director:** Oscar Bradley; **Orchestrations:** Frank Barry; **Set Design:** Joseph Urban

Songs: Are You There?; Best Little Lover in Town, The; Charro Dance, The; Come Take a Trip [2]; Eight Little Gringitos; Following the Sun Around; I Can Speak Espagnol; I'd Rather Have a Memory of You [1] (C/L: Geoffrey Gwyther); If You're in Love, You'll Waltz; Jingle Dance, The; Jumping Bean, The; Kinkajou, The; Moonlight Ballet; Moonshine; Opening Dance; Out on the Loose; Pirates (Yo Ho and a Bottle of Rum), The; Rangers' Song, The; Rio Rita; River Song; Siesta Time; Spanish Shawl, The; Sweethearts; Tambourine Dance, The; Wedding Scene [2]

Cast: Walter Catlett; Ada May; J. Harold Murray; Pedro Rubin; Vincent Serrano; Ethelind Terry; Bert Wheeler; Robert Woolsey

Notes: [1] Added to London version. [2] In London vocal score only.

3720 • RIP VAN WINKLE

OPENED: 07/13/1953
Musical   Closed out of town

Composer: Edwin McArthur
Lyricist: Morton Da Costa
Librettist: Morton Da Costa

Source: RIP VAN WINKLE (Story: Washington Irving)

Notes: Muny Opera, St. Louis.

3721 • RIPPLES

OPENED: 02/11/1930   Theatre: New Amsterdam
Musical   Broadway: 55

Composer: Oscar Levant; Albert Sirmay
Lyricist: Irving Caesar; Graham John
Librettist: William Anthony McGuire
Producer: Charles B. Dillingham
Director: William Anthony McGuire

Choreographer: William Holbrook; Mary Read; **Costumes:** Charles LeMaire; **Musical Director:** Gus Salzer; **Set Design:** Joseph Urban

Songs: Anything Can Happen Any Day (C: Jerome Kern; L: Graham John); Babykins (C: Oscar Levant); Barefoot Girl; Cane Dance, The; Gentlemen of the Press; Girl Is Nobody, A; Girls of Long Ago; Hunting Days; I Take After Rip; I'm a Little Bit Fonder of You [1] (C/L: Irving Caesar); I'm Afraid (C: Albert Sirmay); Is It Love? (C: Oscar Levant; L: Irving Caesar); Opening; Sunrise Dance, The; Talk with My Heel and Your Toe (C: Oscar Levant; L: Irving Caesar); There's Nothing Wrong in a Kiss (C: Oscar Levant); We Never Sleep; You Never Can Tell About Love (C: J. Fred Coots; L: Benny Davis)

Cast: Charles Collins; Eddie Foy Jr.; Kathryn Hereford; Janet Martin; Dorothy Stone; Fred Stone; Mrs. Fred Stone; Paula Stone; Andrew Tombes

Notes: [1] Originally in MERCENARY MARY.

3722 • RISE OF DAVID LEVINSKY, THE

OPENED: 01/12/1987   Theatre: John Houseman
Musical   Off-Broadway: 31

Composer: Bobby Paul
Lyricist: Isaiah Sheffer
Librettist: Isaiah Sheffer
Producer: Eric Krebs
Director: Sue Lawless

Source: RISE OF DAVID LEVINSKY, THE (Novel: Abraham Cahan); **Costumes:** Mimi Maxmen; **Lighting Designer:** Phil Monat; **Musical Director:** Lanny Meyers; **Set Design:** Kenneth Foy

Songs: Be Flexible; Bittersweet; Boarder, The; Credit Face; Five Hundred Garments; Five Hundred Pages; Garment Trade, The; Grand Street; Hard Times; In America; Just . . . Like . . . Me; Little Did I Know; Little Did We Know; Married Man, A; Sharp; Some Incredible Guy; Survival of the Fittest; Transformation, The; Two of a Kind; View from the Top, A; Who Is This Man?

Cast: Bruce Adler; Avi Hoffman; Larry Kert; Larry Raiken; Eleanor Reissa; David Vosburgh; Lynne Wintersteller

3723 • RISE OF ROSIE O'REILLY, THE

OPENED: 12/25/1923   Theatre: Liberty
Musical   Broadway: 97

Composer: George M. Cohan
Lyricist: George M. Cohan
Librettist: George M. Cohan
Director: John Meehan

Choreographer: Julian Mitchell; **Costumes:** Ada Fields; Cora MacGeachy; **Musical Director:** George A. Nichols; **Orchestrations:** M.L. Lake; **Set Design:** Joseph Wickes

Songs: All Night Long; Arrival of Society, The; Arrival of the Plot, The; At Madame Regay's; Born and Bred in Brooklyn, Over the Bridge; Gathering; I Never Met a Girl Like You; In the Slums of the Town; Italian Whirlwind, The; Just Act Natural; Keep A- Countin' Eight; Let's You and I Just Say Good-Bye; Love Dreams; Marathon Step, The; My Gang; Nothing Like a Darned Good Cry; On a Holiday; Plot Again, The; Poor Old World; Ring to the Name of Rosie, The; Servants' Frolic Dance, The; Something's Happened to Rosie; Stage Society; Two Girls from the Chorus; Water Front Pastime Dance; When June Comes Along with a Song; Whip Dance, The

Cast: Ruby Keeler[1]; Mary Lawlor; Jack McGowan; Virginia O'Brien; Bobby Watson

Notes: [1] A 14-year-old chorus girl.

3724 • RIVER, THE

OPENED: 01/13/1988   Theatre: Promenade
Musical   Off-Broadway: 41

Composer: Peter Link
Lyricist: Peter Link
Producer: William P. Suter; Donald V. Thompson
Director: Michael Shawn

Choreographer: Michael Shawn; **Costumes:** David Dille; **Lighting Designer:** Phil Monat; **Musical Director:** Ronald P. Metcalf; **Set Design:** William Barclay; **Vocal Arranger:** Danny Madden

Songs: Burnin' Up; Carnival; Circle; Didn't It Rain; Don't It Feel Good; Genesis; Lead Me to the Water; Love Runs Deeper Than Pride; One Drop Alone; Over the Edge; Put the Fire Out;

Revelation; River, The; River's in Me, The; Run River Run; Sea, The; Still Small Voice, A; Stream, The; Take Me Up; This Is All I Ask; Wallowing in the Mire; Wanderin' in the Wilderness; Waterfall, The

Cast: Jenny Burton; Carol Dennis; Valerie K. Eley; Lawrence Hamilton; Stephanie Renee James; Danny Madden; Ray Stephens

3725 • RIVERWIND

OPENED: 12/11/1962   Theatre: Actors'
                                      Playhouse
Musical   Off-Broadway: 443

Composer: John Jennings
Lyricist: John Jennings
Librettist: Joseph Benjamin
Producer: Bushe Company
Director: Adrian Hall

Choreographer: Ronnie Fields; **Costumes:** Robert Soule; **Dance Arranger:** Abba Bogin; **Lighting Designer:** Jules Fisher; **Musical Director:** Joseph Stecko; **Set Design:** Robert Soule; **Vocal Arranger:** Abba Bogin

Songs: Almost, But Not Quite; American Family Plan; I Cannot Tell Her So; I Love Your Laughing Face; I Want a Surprise; I'd Forgotten How Beautiful She Could Be; Pardon Me While I Dance; Riverwind; Sew the Buttons On; Wishing Song; Woman Must Never Grow Old, A; Woman Must Think of These Things, A

Cast: Helon Blount; Lawrence Brooks; Martin J. Cassidy; Brooks Morton; Dawn Nickerson; Elizabeth Parrish; Lovelady Powell

3726 • RIVIERA FOLLIES OF 1937

OPENED: 1937
Revue   Nightclub

Composer: Fred E. Ahlert
Lyricist: Joe Young
Producer: Ben Marden

Songs: I'm Happy Darling, Dancing with You; Image of You, The; It's the Smile That Gets 'Em; Whippoorwill in a Willow Tree, A; You'll Get a Cold in Your Toes

Notes: No other information available.

3727 • RIVIERA GIRL, THE

OPENED: 09/24/1917   Theatre: New Amsterdam
Musical   Broadway: 78

Composer: Emmerich Kalman
Lyricist: P.G. Wodehouse
Librettist: Guy Bolton; P.G. Wodehouse
Producer: Klaw & Erlanger
Director: Herbert Gresham

Source: DIE CSARDASFURSTIN (Musical: Bela Jensbach; Emmerich Kalman; Leo Stein); **Choreographer:** Julian Mitchell; **Costumes:** Alice O'Neil; **Lighting Designer:** Ben Beerwald; **Musical Director:** Charles Previn; **Set Design:** Joseph Urban

Songs: (A Little) Bungalow in Quogue (C: Jerome Kern); Fall of Man, The; Finale Act I; Finale Act II; Finale Act III; Gypsy Bring Your Fiddle; Half a Married Man; Just a Voice to Call Me Dear; Life's a Tale; Lilt of a Gypsy Strain, The; Man, Man, Man; Opening Act III; Opening Chorus Act II; Opening Song and Chorus Act I; Sometimes I Feel Just Like Grandma; There'll Never Be Another Girl Like Daisy; Why Don't You Hand It to Me?; Will You Forget?

Cast: Wilda Bennett; Juliette Day; Sam Hardy; Gene Lockhart

3728 • RIVIERA REVUE

OPENED: 1935
Revue   Nightclub

Songs: I Want to Report a Fire (C/L: Edward Heyman; Muriel Pollock; Ned Wever)

Notes: No other information available.

3729 • ROAD TO MANDALAY, THE

OPENED: 03/01/1916   Theatre: Park
Musical   Broadway: 21

Composer: Oreste Vessella
Lyricist: William McKenna
Librettist: William H. Post
Director: William J. Wilson

Musical Director: A. DeNovellis

Songs: Arrival of the Boom; Back to Paris; Bright Day Dawning; Father's Whiskers; Firefly; Heart of My Heart; Imagination; Looking for a Girl My Size; Moonlight Gavotte; Ocean of Dreams; Oriental Dance; Road to Mandelay (L: Jack Appleton); Sail Away; See America First; Shadows; Till You Try; Tourists; Waltz; You'll Find the Party Isn't There

Cast: Herbert Corthell; Gretchen Eastman; Hazel Kirke; Leola Lucey; Frank Pollock; Stanley Ridges

3730 • ROAD TO YESTERDAY, THE

OPENED: 12/31/1906   Theatre: Park
Play   Broadway: 216

Composer: Melville Ellis
Author: Beulah Marie Dix; Evelyn Greenleaf Sutherland
Producer: Lee Shubert; Sam S. Shubert
Director: J.C. Huffman

Musical Director: John Hickey

Songs: Busy Bee; Gavotte; Louis XIV; Nell Gwynne; Pan Americana; Road to Yesterday, The

Cast: Robert Dempster; Minnie Dupree; Helen Ware; White Whittlesey

3731 • ROAR OF THE GREASEPAINT-THE SMELL OF THE CROWD, THE

OPENED: 05/16/1965   Theatre: Shubert
Musical   Broadway: 231

Composer: Leslie Bricusse; Anthony Newley
Lyricist: Leslie Bricusse; Anthony Newley
Librettist: Leslie Bricusse; Anthony Newley
Producer: David Merrick
Director: Anthony Newley

Choreographer: Gillian Lynne; **Costumes:** Freddy Wittop; **Dance Arranger:** Peter Howard; **Lighting Designer:** Sean Kenny; **Musical Director:** Herbert Grossman; **Orchestrations:** Philip J. Lang; **Set Design:** Sean Kenny; **Vocal Arranger:** Peter Howard

Songs: Beautiful Land, The; Feeling Good; Funny Funeral, A; It Isn't Enough; Joker, The; Look at

That Face; My First Love Song; My Way; Nothing Can Stop Me Now; Put 'Im in the Box [2]; Put It in the Book; Sweet Beginning; That's What It Is to Be Young; Things to Remember; This Dream; What a Man!; Where Would You Be Without Me?; Who Can I Turn To (When Nobody Needs Me); With All Due Respect [1]; Wonderful Day Like Today, A

Cast: Joyce Jillson; Anthony Newley; Gilbert Price; Cyril Ritchard; Sally Smith

Notes: [1] Added after opening. [2] Cut during previews.

3732 • ROB ROY

OPENED: 10/21/1894   Theatre: Herald Square
Musical   Broadway: 168

Composer: Reginald De Koven
Lyricist: Harry B. Smith
Librettist: Harry B. Smith
Producer: Fred C. Whitney
Director: Max Freeman

Costumes: Will R. Barnes; **Musical Director:** Antonio DeNovellis; **Set Design:** D. Frank Dodge; Henry E. Hoyt; Joseph Physioc

Songs: Ah! Yon Is No Song of Triumph; Chansonette; Come, Lairds of the Highlands; Dearest Heart of My Heart; Entrance Song; Finale Act I; Grenadier's Song; In Spain; Jolly Miller, The; Lay of the Cavalier; Love Land; Merry Miller, The; My Hairt Is in the Highlands; My Home Is Where the Heather Blooms; My True Love Is a Shepherdess; Opening Act I; Prince Rupert's Cavaliers; Rob Roy and Janet Duet; Rob Roy's Song; Rustic Song; Song of the Balladmongers; Song of the Turnkey; Thou Dear Heart; Town Crier's Song; Turnkey's Song; We Come!; White and the Red!, The

Cast: Barron Berthald; Julia Corden; Joseph Herbert; Lizzie Macnichol; William Pruette

Notes: No songs listed in program. Songs listed here from vocal score.

3733 • ROBBER BRIDEGROOM, THE

OPENED: 10/09/1976   Theatre: Biltmore
Musical   Broadway: 145

Composer: Robert Waldman
Lyricist: Alfred Uhry
Librettist: Alfred Uhry
Producer: Margot Harley; John Houseman;
Michael B. Kapon
Director: Gerald Freedman

Source: ROBBER BRIDEGROOM, THE (Novel:
Eudora Welty); **Choreographer:** Donald Saddler;
Costumes: Jeanne Button; **Dance Arranger:**
Robert Waldman; **Lighting Designer:** David F.
Segal; **Set Design:** Douglas W. Schmidt; **Vocal
Arranger:** Robert Waldman

Songs: Deeper in the Woods; Goodbye Salome;
Love Stolen; Nothin' Up; Once Upon the
Natchez Trace; Poor Tied Up Darlin'; Pricklepear
Bloom, The; Real Mike Fink [1]; Riches;
Rosamund's Dream; Sleepy Man; Steal with
Style; Two Heads; Where Oh Where

Cast: Barry Bostwick; Rhonda Coullet; Barbara
Lang; Mary Lou Rosato; Stephen Vinovich

Notes: [1] Cut prior to Broadway opening.

3734 • ROBERT AND ELIZABETH
OPENED: 11/03/1982
Musical   Closed out of town

Composer: Ron Grainer
Lyricist: Ronald Miller
Librettist: Ronald Miller
Producer: Angelo Del Rossi
Director: Robert Johanson

Source: BARRETTS OF WIMPOLE STREET, THE
(Play Rudolf Besier); **Choreographer:** Robert
Johanson; **Costumes:** Guy Geoly; **Lighting
Designer:** Nananne Porcher; **Musical Director:**
Jim Coleman; **Set Design:** Paul Wonsek; **Vocal
Arranger:** Jim Coleman

Songs: Escape Me Never; Family Moulton-Barrett,
The; Frustration; Girls That Boys Dream About,
The; Hate Me Please; I Know Now; I Said Love;
I'm the Master Here; In a Simple Way; Long Ago
I Loved You [2]; Love and Duty; Moon in My
Pocket, The; Pass the Eau de Cologne; Real
Thing, The; Soliloquy; Under a Spell; Want to Be
Well [1]; What the World Calls Love [1]; What's
Natural; Wimpole Street Song, The (Here on the
Corner of Wimpole Street); Woman and Man;
World Outside, The; You Only to Love Me

Cast: Leigh Beery; Mark Jacoby; Ron Randell

Notes: Paper Mill Playhouse production. [1] Not
in program. [2] Cut prior to London opening.

3735 • ROBERTA
OPENED: 11/18/1933   Theatre: New Amsterdam
Musical   Broadway: 294

Composer: Jerome Kern
Lyricist: Otto Harbach
Librettist: Otto Harbach
Producer: Max Gordon
Director: Hassard Short

Source: GOWNS BY ROBERTA (Novel: Alice Duer
Miller); **Choreographer:** Jose Limon; John
Lonergan; **Costumes:** Kiviette; **Musical Director:**
Victor Baravalle; **Orchestrations:** Robert Russell
Bennett; **Set Design:** Clark Robinson

Songs: Alpha, Beta, Pi; Armful of Trouble [3];
Clementina [3]; Don't Ask Me Not to Sing [1];
Hot Spot; I'll Be Hard to Handle (L: Bernard
Dougall); Let's Begin; Scene and Pas de Seul;
Sewing Department Dance (inst.); (When Your
Heart's on Fire) Smoke Gets in Your Eyes [4];
Something's Got to Happen; Touch of Your
Hand, The; Yesterdays; You Inspire a Mad
Desire [3]; You're Devastating [2]

Cast: Roberta Beatty; California Collegians, The;
Helen Gray; Sydney Greenstreet; William Hain;
Bob Hope; Ray Middleton; George Murphy;
Nayan Pearce; Lyda Roberti; Fay Templeton

Notes: The California Collegians included Fred
MacMurray. During tryouts titled GOWNS BY
ROBERTA. [1] From THE CAT AND THE
FIDDLE. [2] Same music as "Do I Do Wrong"
from BLUE EYES. [3] Out Philadelphia
10/21/33. [4] Music written as tap dance music
in SHOW BOAT but not used. Then it was to be
used as a theme for an NBC radio series that was
not produced.

3736 • ROBIN HOOD
OPENED: 09/28/1891   Theatre: Standard
Musical   Broadway

Composer: Reginald De Koven
Lyricist: Harry B. Smith
Librettist: Harry B. Smith

Songs: All Is Fair in Love and War; All Nature Is at Peace and Rest (Forest Song); Armorer's Song, The; As Life Is Short, Let Life Be Gay; Auctioneer's Song [1]; Bells of St. Swithin's, The; Brown October Ale; Churning, Churning; Come Dream, So Bright; Come the Bowmen in Lincoln Green; Finale Act I; Get Black Crow; Halo-Halo-Halo; Happy Day! Happy Day! (Country Dance); Heart, My Heart! [1]; Hey for the Merry Greenwood; I Am the Sheriff of Nottingham; I Come As a Cavalier; In Sherwood Forest; It Takes Nine Tailors to Make a Man; Legend of the Chimes, The; Let Us Put Him in the Stocks (Finale Act II); Maiden's Thought, A [3]; Milkmaid's Song; 'Neath the Greenwood Tree; Now Let Each Bonny Bridegroom Take His Bonny Bride (Finale Act III); O, Promise Me [2] (L: Clement Scott); O, See the Lambkins Play; Oh, Cheerily Soundeth the Huntsman's Horn; Oh, See the Lambkins Play!; Robin Hood's Entrance; Roundelay; Serenade; Sweetheart, My Own Sweetheart; Tailor and the Crow, The; There Will Come a Time When Thou and I, Love, Shall Be One, and Never Shall Part; Though It Was Within This Hour We Met; Time Will Come, A [3]; Tinker's Song; 'Tis the Morning of the Fair (Opening Chorus); Troubadour Sang to His Love, A; When a Maiden Weds; When a Peer Makes Love to a Damsel Fair; When Life Seems Made of Pains and Pangs

Cast: Henry Clay Barnabee; Agnes Brown; Kate Condon; George Frothingham; Joseph Ratliff

Notes: No program available. Songs from several productions and vocal score. [1] Added for London production which was titled MAID MARIAN. [2] Added for London production and subsequently added to Broadway. [3] Added after opening.

3737 • ROBINSON CRUSOE, JR.

OPENED: 02/17/1916   Theatre: Winter Garden
Musical   Broadway: 139

Composer: James F. Hanley; Sigmund Romberg
Lyricist: Harold Atteridge
Librettist: Harold Atteridge; Edgar Smith
Producer: Winter Garden Company
Director: J.C. Huffman

Choreographer: Allan K. Foster; **Costumes:** Aloys Bohner; Faibsey; **Orchestrations:** Oscar Radin; Frank Saddler; **Set Design:** P. Dodd Ackerman; H. Robert Law; John Young

Songs: Bring Along Your Lovin' Ways [2]; (Go Ahead and) Dance a Little More (C: James F. Hanley); Don't Be a Sailor (C: Sigmund Romberg); Down Where the Suwannee River Flows [3] (C: Albert Von Tilzer; L: Charles S. Alberte; Charles McCarron); Fast Steppers [2]; (You'll Have To) Gallop Some (C: Sigmund Romberg); Happy Hottentots (C: Sigmund Romberg); Hunter's Fox Trot Ball; Minstrel Days (C: Phil Schwartz); My Pirate Lady (C: Sigmund Romberg); My Voodoo Maiden (C: Sigmund Romberg); Now He's Got a Beautiful Girl [2] (C: Grant Clarke; L: Edgar Leslie; Ted Snyder); Pretty Little Mayflower Girl [2] (C: James F. Hanley); Robinson Crusoe (C: Sigmund Romberg; L: James F. Hanley); Sailor's Fling; Simple Life (C: Sigmund Romberg); Spanish Ballet [2]; Spinning a Yarn (C/L: John Golden); Strolling Eyes [2] (C: James F. Hanley); Tillie Tit Willow [2] (C: Phil Schwartz); War Babies [2] (C: James F. Hanley; L: Ballard Macdonald; Edward Madden); When You're Starring in the Movies (C: Sigmund Romberg); Where Did Robinson Crusoe Go with Friday on Saturday Night (C: George W. Meyer; L: Sam M. Lewis; Joe Young); Where the Black Eyed Susan Grows [1] (C: Richard A. Whiting; L: Dave Radford); While They Were Dancing Around [2] (C: James V. Monaco; L: Joseph McCarthy); Yacki Hula Hicki Doola [1] (C: Pete Wendling; L: E. Ray Goetz; Joe Young); You're a Dangerous Girl [2] (C: James V. Monaco; L: Grant Clarke)

Cast: Lawrence D'Orsay; Kitty Doner; Al Jolson; Barry Lupino; Helen Shipman

Notes: [1] Out prior to opening. [2] Sheet music only. [3] The popular song "Down Where the Swanee River Flows" by Charles S. Alberte and Charles McCarron was written in 1916.

3738 • ROCK AND FULTON ACT

OPENED: 1912

Composer: Frederic Chapin
Lyricist: Orville L. Mayhood

Songs: Dope; Now I'm Satisfied; Oh, You Men; Pierrot et Pierette; You're Just the Girlie

Cast: Maude Fulton; Jack Leonard; William Rock

Notes: From vaudeville program of 3/29/12.

3739 • ROCK AND ROLL! THE FIRST 5,000 YEARS

OPENED: 10/24/1982   Theatre: St. James
Revue   Broadway: 9

Producer: Dick Clark Inc.; Fred Disipio; Annie Fargue; Jules Fisher
Director: Joe Layton

Choreographer: Joe Layton; **Costumes:** Franne Lee; **Dance Arranger:** John Simon; **Lighting Designer:** Jules Fisher; **Musical Director:** Andrew Dorfman; **Orchestrations:** John Simon; **Set Design:** Mark Ravitz; **Vocal Arranger:** John Simon

Songs: American Pie (C/L: Don McLean); Benny and the Jets (C/L: Elton John; Bernie Taupin); Blowin' in the Wind (C/L: Bob Dylan); Blueberry Hill (C: Vincent Rose; L: Al Lewis; Larry Stock); Boogie Woogie Bugle Boy (C: Hughie Prince; L: Don Raye); Both Sides Now (C/L: Joni Mitchell); Concrete Shoes (C/L: Chosei Funahara Power; Rod Swenson); Cry Baby (C/L: Norman Meade; Burt Russell); Da Doo Ron Ron (C/L: Jeff Barry; Ellie Greenwich; Phil Spector); Everybody Is a Star (C/L: Sylvester Stewart); Everybody's Talking (C/L: Fred Neil); Good Vibrations (C/L: Mike Love; Brian Wilson); Great Balls of Fire (C/L: Otis Blackwell; Jack Hammer); Hard Day's Night, A (C/L: John Lennon; Paul McCartney); Heartbreak Hotel (C/L: Max Boren Axton; Tommy Durden); Here Comes the Sun; Higher and Higher (C/L: Gary Jackson; Renard Miner; Carl Smith); Hound Dog (C/L: Jerry Leiber; Mike Stoller); I Feel Like I'm Gonna Die Rag (C/L: Joe McDonald), I Feel the Earth Move (C/L: Carole King); I Got You Babe (C/L: Sonny Bono); I Will Survive (C/L: Dino Fekaris; Frederick J. Perren); I'll Be There (C/L: Hal Davis; Berry Gordy; Willie Hutch; Bob West); Imagine (C/L: John Lennon); Jocko Homo (C/L: Mark Mothersbaugh); Johnny B. Goode (C/L: Chuck Berry); Joy to the World (C/L: Hoyt Axton); Land of a Thousand Dances (C/L: Antoine "Fats" Domino; Chris Kenner); Like a Rolling Stone (C/L: Bob Dylan); Love Is a Many Splendored Thing (C: Sammy Fain; L: Paul Francis Webster); Love Me Tender (C/L: Vera Matson); Love to Love You Baby (C/L: Pete Bellote; Georgio Morder; Donna Summer); Message in a Bottle (C/L: Sting Summer); Mrs. Robinson (C/L: Paul Simon); My Generation (C/L: Peter Townshend); Night They Drove Old Dixie Down, The (C/L: J. Robbie Robertson); Nothing from Nothing (C/L: Bruce Fisher; Billy Preston); On the Run (inst.) (C: David Gilmour; Roger Waters; Rick Wright); Our Lips Are Sealed (C/L: Terry Hall; Jane Weidlin); People Got to Be Free (C/L: Edward Brigate; Felix Cavaliere); Proud Mary (C/L: John C. Fogarty); Respect (C/L: Otis Redding); Rock & Roll All Night (C/L: Gene Simmons; Paul Stanley); Rock and Roll Music (C/L: Chuck Berry); Rock Around the Clock (C/L: Jimmy DeKnight; Max Freedman); Satisfaction (C/L: Mick Jagger; Keith Richards); Say It Loud I'm Black and Proud (C/L: James Brown); School's Out (C/L: Michael Bruce; Alice Cooper); Sh-Boom (Life Could Be a Dream) (C/L: James Edwards; Carl Feaster; James Keyes; Floyd F. McRae); Space Oddity (C/L: David Bowie); Star Spangled Banner (C: Traditional; L: Francis Scott Key); Stayin' Alive (C/L: Barry Gibb; Maurice Gibb; Robin Gibb); Summer in the City (C/L: Steve Boone; John Sebastian; Mark Sebastian); Sunshine of Your Love, The (C/L: Peter Brown; Jack Bruce; Eric Clapton); Take a Walk on the Wild Side (C/L: Lou Reed); Tubular Bells (inst.) (C: Mike Oldfield); Tutti Frutti (C/L: Richard Peneman); Twist, The (C/L: Hank Ballard); Wake Up Little Susie (C/L: Boudleaux Bryant; Felice Bryant); When Will I Be Loved (C/L: Phil Everly); White Rabbit (C/L: Grace Slick); Whiter Shade of Pale (C/L: Gary Brooker; Keith Reid); Whole Lotta Love (C/L: John Baldwin; John Bonham; John Patrick Page); Why Do Fools Fall in Love (C/L: Frankie Lymon); Will You Still Love Me Tomorrow (C/L: Gerry Goffin; Carole King); You Keep Me Hanging On (C/L: Lamont Dozier; Brian Holland; Eddie Holland); You've Got a Friend (C/L: Carole King)

Cast: Lon Hoyt; Jenifer Lewis; Michael Pace; Raymond Patterson; Marion Ramsey; Russell Velazquez; Carl Earl Weaver; Lillias White

Notes: No original songs in this show.

3740 • ROCK-A-BYE BABY

OPENED: 05/22/1918   Theatre: Astor
Musical   Broadway: 85

Composer: Jerome Kern
Lyricist: Herbert Reynolds
Librettist: Margaret Mayo; Edgar Allen Woolf
Producer: Arch Selwyn; Edgar Selwyn
Director: Edward Royce

Source: BABY MINE (Play Margaret Mayo); **Choreographer:** Robert Marks; **Costumes:** Lucille; **Musical Director:** Frank Tours; **Set Design:** Joseph Physioc

Songs: According to Dr. Holt; Bella Mia; Big Spring Drive, The; Cretonne [3]; Hurry Now; I Believed All They Said; I Can Trust Myself with a Lot of Girls; I Never Thought; Just One Kiss [3]; Kettle Is Singing (The Kettle Song), A; Little Tune Go Away; Motoring Along the Old Post Road; My Boy [3]; My Own Light Infantry (Nursery Fanfare) [2]; Not You [3]; One, Two, Three; Rock-a-Bye Baby Dear (Lullaby); Signorina Adelina [3]; Stitching, Stitching; There's No Better Use for Time than Kissing [1]; Think of Where You Might Be Instead of Where You Are [3]

Cast: Dorothy Dickson; Louise Dresser; Carl Hyson; Arthur Lipson; Frank Morgan

Notes: [1] Adapted from "Two Heads Are Better than One" from COUSIN LUCY. [2] Also published as "Nursery Fanfare." [3] Cut prior to opening.

3741 • ROCKABYE HAMLET

OPENED: 02/17/1976   Theatre: Minskoff
Musical   Broadway: 7

Composer: Cliff Jones
Lyricist: Cliff Jones
Librettist: Cliff Jones
Producer: Joseph Kipness; Lester Osterman
Director: Gower Champion

Source: HAMLET (Play William Shakespeare); **Choreographer:** Gower Champion; **Costumes:** Joseph G. Aulisi; **Dance Arranger:** Doug Katsaros; **Lighting Designer:** Jules Fisher; **Musical Director:** Gordon Lowry Harrell; **Set Design:** Kurt Lundell; **Vocal Arranger:** Gordon Lowry Harrell

Songs: All By Yourself; All My Life; Denmark Is Still; Didn't She Do It for Love; Don't Unmask Your Beauty to the Moon; Gentle Lover; Get Thee to a Nunnery [1]; Have I Got a Girl for You; He Got It in the Ear; Hello-Hello; Hey!; I Cannot Turn to Love [1]; If My Morning Begins; If Not to You; It Is Done; Laertes Coercion; Last Blues, The; Mad Waltz, The [1]; Mama [1]; Midnight- Hot Blood; Midnight Mass; Off Her Rocker and Roll [1]; Pass the Biscuits; Rockabye Hamlet; Rosencrantz and

Guildenstern Boogie; Set It Right; Shall We Dance; Sing Alone; Somebody Wrote the Wrong Words to My Song [1]; Something's Rotten in Denmark; Swordfight; That It Should Come to This; Tis Pity, Tis True; Twist Her Mind; Wart Song, The; Wedding, The; Where Is the Reason; Why Did He Have to Die?; With a Pick and a Shovel [1]; Your Daddy's Gone Away

Cast: Christopher Chadman; Beverly D'Angelo; Rory Dodd; Leata Galloway; Judy Gibson; Winston De Witt Hemsley; Irving Lee; Larry Marshall; Meat Loaf; Kim Milford; Alan Weeks; Randal Wilson

Notes: [1] Not in programs.

3742 • ROCKY HORROR SHOW, THE

OPENED: 03/10/1975   Theatre: Belasco
Musical   Broadway: 32

Composer: Richard O'Brien
Lyricist: Richard O'Brien
Librettist: Richard O'Brien
Producer: Lou Adler
Director: Jim Sharman

Costumes: Sue Blane; **Dance Arranger:** Richard Hartley; **Lighting Designer:** Chipmonck; **Musical Director:** D'Vaughn Pershing; **Set Design:** Brian Thomson; **Vocal Arranger:** Richard Hartley

Songs: Charles Atlas Song; Eddie's Teddy; Finale; I'm Going Home [1]; It Was Great When It All Began; Once in a While; Over at the Frankenstein Place; Planet Shmanet Janet; Science Fiction; Super Heroes; Sweet Transvestite; Sword of Damocles, The; Time Warp; Touch a Touch Me; Wedding Song; What Ever Happened to Saturday Night

Cast: Tim Curry; Jamie Donnelly; Boni Enten; Abigale Haness; Graham Jarvis; Meat Loaf; Kim Milford; Bill Miller; Ritz O'Brien

Notes: [1] Not in program.

3743 • RODGERS AND HART

OPENED: 05/13/1975   Theatre: Helen Hayes
Revue   Broadway: 111

Composer: Richard Rodgers
Lyricist: Lorenz Hart

Producer: Richard Horner; Lester Osterman
Director: Burt Shevelove

Choreographer: Donald Saddler; **Costumes:** Stanley Simmons; **Dance Arranger:** Buster Davis; **Lighting Designer:** Ken Billington; **Musical Director:** Buster Davis; **Orchestrations:** Robert Russell Bennett; Bill Brohn; Luther Henderson; Jim Tyler; **Set Design:** David Jenkins; **Vocal Arranger:** Luther Henderson

Cast: Barbara Andres; Jimmy Brennan; Wayne Bryan; David-James Carroll; Jamie Donnelly; Tovah Feldshuh; Mary Sue Finnerty; Laurence Guittard; Stephen Lehew; Jim Litten; Virginia Sandifur; Rebecca York

Notes: There were over 100 Rodgers and Hart songs in this revue. Some were just a few bars long while others were complete. None were written for this show.

3744 • ROGERS BROTHERS IN CENTRAL PARK, THE

OPENED: 09/17/1900   Theatre: Hammerstein's
                                       Victoria
Musical   Broadway: 72

Composer: Maurice Levi
Lyricist: J. Cheever Goodwin
Librettist: John J. McNally
Producer: Klaw & Erlanger
Director: Ben Teal

Musical Director: Maurice Levi

Songs: Bottle and a Bird, A; Brave Hussar, The; Darktown Barbeque; Duchess of Central Park, The; If Cabby Told Half what He Knows; In Central Park; Is It Yes or Is It No?; Lina, Mah Lady; Matrimonial Agent, The; Run, Brudder Possum, Run; Sally; Up on the Roof; When Reuben Comes to Town

Cast: Della Fox; Lee Harrison; Eugene O'Rourke; Gus Rogers; Max Rogers

Notes: There was an interpolated song by Cole and Johnson but unidentified in program.

3745 • ROGERS BROTHERS IN HARVARD, THE

OPENED: 09/01/1902   Theatre: Knickerbocker
Musical   Broadway: 63

Composer: Maurice Levi
Lyricist: Ed Gardenier; J. Cheever Goodwin
Librettist: John J. McNally
Producer: Klaw & Erlanger
Director: Ben Teal

Costumes: F. Richard Anderson; **Set Design:** Ernest Gros

Songs: Ain't It Tough to Be So Absent-Minded [1] (C: Ben M. Jerome; L: Matt C. Woodward); College Girls (L: J. Cheever Goodwin); Dear Old College Days (L: J. Cheever Goodwin); Drama of Love (L: Vincent Bryan); I'm a Lady (L: Ed Gardenier); I'm Getting Quite American You Know (L: J. Cheever Goodwin); Linda, Look Out De Windah (L: Ed Gardenier); Ma Starlight Queen (L: Ed Gardenier); Mary the Wary (L: Ed Gardenier); Pretty Peggy (L: Unknown); 'Round the Town (L: J. Cheever Goodwin); Sporting Girls (L: J. Cheever Goodwin); Troubles of the Reuben and the Maid (L: J. Cheever Goodwin); Upper Broadway After Dark (L: Ed Gardenier)

Cast: James Cherry; Pauline Frederick; Lee Harrison; Gus Rogers; Max Rogers; Pat Rooney; Hattie Williams

Notes: [1] Sheet music only.

3746 • ROGERS BROTHERS IN IRELAND, THE

OPENED: 09/04/1905   Theatre: Liberty
Musical   Broadway: 106

Composer: Max Hoffmann
Lyricist: George V. Hobart
Librettist: John J. McNally
Director: Herbert Gresham; Ned Wayburn

Songs: Alice O'Grady [1]; Blarney Stone, The [1]; Hannah Dooley [2]; I Simply Can't Resist You [1] (L: Addison Burkhardt); Irish Girl I Love, The [2]; Killarney; Maids of Killarney; Mary Cary [1] (L: Addison Burkhardt); My Irish Maid (L: George V. Hobart; Max Hoffmann); Shamrock of Ireland, The; So Different; St. Patrick's Day; Tourists, The; When I Rode on the Choo Choo Cars

Cast: Corrine; Ethel Intropodi; Josie Intropodi; Gus Rogers; Max Rogers

Notes: [1] Out Cedar Rapids 11/21/06. [2] Sheet music only.

3747 • ROGERS BROTHERS IN LONDON, THE

OPENED: 09/07/1903   Theatre: Knickerbocker
Musical   Broadway: 64

Composer: Melville Ellis; Max Hoffmann
Lyricist: Ed Gardenier; George V. Hobart
Librettist: John J. McNally
Producer: Klaw & Erlanger
Director: Herbert Gresham; Ned Wayburn

Songs: American Beauty, The (C: Max Hoffmann; L: Unknown); By the Sycamore Tree (C: Max Hoffmann; L: George V. Hobart); Coster's 'Oliday, The (C: Max Hoffmann; L: George V. Hobart); Going Home (C: Max Hoffmann; L: Unknown); In Gay New York (C: Max Hoffmann; L: Ed Gardenier); It's Awfully Hard to Shop (C: Melville Ellis; L: George V. Hobart); King Edward's Subjects (C: Max Hoffmann; L: George V. Hobart); Mr. Breezy (C: Melville Ellis; L: Ed Gardenier); On a Starlight Night (C: Melville Ellis; L: Ed Gardenier); Queen of the Bungaloo (C: Unknown; L: Ed Gardenier); Say You'll Be a Friend of Mine (C: Moss; L: Bryan); Shopping (C: Max Hoffmann; L: Ed Gardenier)

Cast: George Austin-Moore; Lillian Coleman; Melville Ellis; Lee Harrison; Gus Rogers; Max Rogers

3748 • ROGERS BROTHERS IN PANAMA, THE

OPENED: 09/02/1907   Theatre: Broadway
Musical   Broadway: 71

Composer: Max Hoffmann
Lyricist: Edward Madden
Librettist: Aaron Hoffman; Sylvester Maguire
Producer: Gus Rogers; Max Rogers
Director: Ben Teal

Choreographer: Pat Rooney

Songs: Adorable Toreador, The; In Panama; Laugh and the World Laughs Too; My Cigarette; 'Neath the Old Palm Tree [1] (L: Ed Gardenier); (I Could Learn to Love You When You) Smile! Smile! Smile!; Sunrise at the Zoo; Under the Jungle Moon; Way Down in Colon Town

Cast: Lottie Greenwood; George Lydecker; Gus Rogers; Max Rogers; Marion Stanley

Notes: Complete program not available. [1] Sheet music only.

3749 • ROGERS BROTHERS IN PARIS, THE

OPENED: 09/05/1905   Theatre: New Amsterdam
Musical   Broadway: 72

Composer: Max Hoffmann
Lyricist: George V. Hobart
Librettist: John J. McNally
Producer: Klaw & Erlanger
Director: Herbert Gresham; Ned Wayburn

Songs: American Minstrels in Paris, The; Belle of the Silvery Nile; By the Old Oak Tree; By the Silvery Nile [1] (L: Ed Gardenier); Kindness; McNabb (Who Drives the Cab) (L: Ed Gardenier); Pretty Polly; Quarreling Coachmen; Society (L: Ed Gardenier); Soldier Boy; Student's Ball, The; Village Maid, The (C/L: Max Hoffmann); Yankee Land

Cast: Josephine Cohan; George Austin Moore; Fred Niblo; Gus Rogers; Max Rogers

Notes: [1] Sheet music only.

3750 • ROGERS BROTHERS IN WALL STREET, THE

OPENED: 09/18/1899   Theatre: Victoria
Musical   Broadway: 108

Librettist: John J. McNally

Cast: Georgia Caine; Louise Gunning; Lee Harrison; Ada Lewis; Maude Raymond; Gus Rogers; Max Rogers; Ross Snow; John G. Sparks; David Warfield

Notes: No program available.

3751 • ROGERS BROTHERS IN WASHINGTON, THE

OPENED: 09/02/1901   Theatre: Knickerbocker
Musical   Broadway: 49

Composer: Maurice Levi
Lyricist: Harry B. Smith
Librettist: John J. McNally
Producer: Klaw & Erlanger
Director: Ben Teal

Set Design: Ernest Gros

Songs: At the Pan-American; Diplomacy; Electric Light Cadets, The; Englishman's Idea of Ragtime, An; Game of Love, The; Get Next to the Man with a Pull; Girl of Greater New York, The; In the Swim; Ma Ebony Belle; My Bunco Queen; 1776 to 1901; Watermelon Party; Wedding of the Reuben and the Maid, The

Cast: Nora Bayes; James Cherry; Gus Rogers; Max Rogers; Pat Rooney; Charles A. Weinberg; Hattie Williams

3752 • ROLLER DERBY! THE MUSICAL

OPENED: 09/11/1985
Musical   Closed out of town

Composer: John Brandon
Lyricist: John Brandon
Librettist: Barry Arnold; Michael Maurer
Producer: Jerry Seltzer; Hal Silen
Director: Michael Maurer

Arrangements: Jeffrey Waxman; **Choreographer:** John Henry; **Costumes:** Christina Haatainen; **Lighting Designer:** Neil Peter Jampolis; **Musical Director:** Jeffrey Waxman; **Set Design:** Gene Aingell; Ron Pratt

Songs: Being Bad; Dirty; 55 Cities in 62 Days; Guys Like You; Match Race, The; Me and the Bombers; My Very Best New Friend; New Girl on the Town; Nobody's Lookin' Out for Me But Me; Out to Set the World on Fire; She Could Have Been My Girl; Since When; Team Spirit; This Is Where I Belong; Training Rap, The; Waikiki; We Gotta; What About Me?; Wheels

Cast: Kelly Britt; Zoe Connor; Norwood Smith; Deborah Van Valkenburgh; Virginia Watson

Notes: San Francisco production.

3753 • ROLLICKING GIRL, THE

OPENED: 05/01/1905   Theatre: Herald Square
Musical   Broadway: 192

Composer: W.T. Francis
Lyricist: Sydney Rosenfeld
Librettist: Sydney Rosenfeld

Producer: Charles Frohman
Director: Ben Teal

Costumes: Alfredo Edel; **Lighting Designer:** William Remlinger; **Musical Director:** Gus Salzer; **Set Design:** Ernest Gros

Songs: As We Swing Sweetheart (L: Vernon Roy); Bored (C: A. Baldwin Sloane; L: Frederick Ranken); Contented Caterpillar, The; Coonjine (inst.); Finale Act I; Finale Act III; Friends That Are Good and True (C: Julius Steger; L: Edward Eysler); Girl from My Own Town, The (C: Ernest R. Ball; John W. Bratton; L: Noel Douglas); Girl I Left in Boston Town, The (C: Ernest R. Ball; L: John W. Bratton; Charles Noel Douglas); Indians Along Broadway (C/L: Benjamin Hapgood Burt); Life of Love, The [1]; Midnight, Midnigh, Hour of True Love's Vow; Miranda (C/L: Clare Kummer); My Cabin Door (C: Tom Lemonier; L: Grant Stewart); My Little Sunbeam Sue (L: Dave Reed Jr.); My Native Land (Opening Act II); Nita (C: W. Aletter; L: Vernon Roy); Old Time Song and Dance (L: Vernon Roy); Opening Chorus; Opening Chorus Act III; Tricks (C: John W. Bratton; L: Paul West); When Love Begins; Won't You Be My Lovey Dovey (C: Seymour Furth; L: E.P. Moran)

Cast: Aimee Angeles; Sam Bernard; Joseph Coyne; Harry Fairleigh; George Howard; Hattie Williams

Notes: [1] Sheet music only.

3754 • ROLY BOLY EYES

OPENED: 09/25/1919   Theatre: Knickerbocker
Musical   Broadway: 100

Composer: Eddy Brown; Louis Gruenberg
Lyricist: Edgar Allen Woolf
Librettist: Edgar Allen Woolf
Producer: John Cort
Director: Will H. Smith

Songs: Ain't She Sweet?; All Washed Up; Biddle-De-Boo; Blushing, Gushing Widow, The; Bungalow for Two, A; Harvester's Song; I Want a Man; Ida, Sweet As Apple Cider (C: Eddie Munson; L: Eddie Leonard); Just a Girl, Just a Boy; Matron's Good Night Sleep, A; Minstrel Serenade; Old Fashioned Flowers; Spring; That

Minstrel Man; When Dancing's a Profession; When They Do the Dippy Doodlums; Where Is She?; Your Voice I Hear

Cast: May Boley; Eddie Leonard; Kate Pullman; Queenie Smith

3755 • ROLY POLY

OPENED: 11/21/1912   Theatre: Broadway
Musical   Broadway: 60

Composer: A. Baldwin Sloane
Lyricist: E. Ray Goetz
Librettist: Edgar Smith
Director: Gus Sohlke

Costumes: Cora MacGeachy; **Musical Director:** DeWitt Coolman

Songs: At Gay Raatenbad; Dear Old Heidelberg; Die Neue Art; I Cannot Drink the Old Drinks; I'm a Lonesome Romeo; In My Birch Bark Canoe (With Emmy Lou); Pinkerton Detective Moon (C/L: Nora Bayes; Jack Norworth); Prima Donnas, The; Regimental Roly Poly Girl, The; Steinland; Way Down in C-U-B-A [2] (C: Nora Bayes; Antonio Torroella Chijo; L: Jack Norworth); When I'm Waltzing [1]; When It's Apple Blossom Time in Normandy (C/L: Harry Gifford; Tom Mellor; Huntley Trevor); Zingaras, The

Cast: Nora Bayes; Bessie Clayton; Frank Daniels; Marie Dressler; Lew Fields; Hazel Kirke; Jack Norworth; Joe Weber

Notes: Part of this evening was a burlesque on WITHIN THE LAW titled WITHOUT THE LAW. [1] ASCAP/Library of Congress only. [2] Sheet music credits the song to score of THE SUN DODGERS also.

3756 • ROMANCE IN CANDLELIGHT

OPENED: 09/15/1955   Theatre: Piccadilly
Musical   London: 53

Composer: Sam Coslow
Lyricist: Sam Coslow
Librettist: Eric Maschwitz
Producer: Emile Littler
Director: Richard Bird

Source: BY CANDLELIGHT (BEI KERZENLICHT) (Play Carl Farkas; Siegfried Geyer); **Choreographer:** Phyllis Blackston; **Costumes:** Doris Zinkeisen; **Musical Director:** Alexander Faris; **Set Design:** Doris Zinkeisen

Songs: Board of Directors of Continental Steel, The; Bonjour Finis; Fromage; I Just Dropped in to Say Goodbye; Lady Was Made to Be Loved, The; Live a Little, Love a Little; My Heart Says Yes; Oh La La Boom Boom; Quarrelling Song (You're a Cad, You're a Bounder); Romance in Candlelight (L: Emile Littler; Eric Maschwitz); Toujours L'Amour on the Cote D'Azur; You Have a Way with You

Cast: Patricia Burke; Charles Clay; Richard Curnock; Roger Dann; Jacques Pils

3757 • ROMANCE IN HARD TIMES

OPENED: 12/28/1989   Theatre: Public
Musical   Off-Broadway: 6

Composer: William Finn
Lyricist: William Finn
Librettist: William Finn
Producer: N.Y. Shakespeare Festival

Songs: All Fall Down; Blame It on These Times; Charity Quartet; Eleanor Roosevelt: A Discussion of Soap; Feeling Rich; Gaggle of Celebrities, A; Good Times Are Here, The; Goodbye; Harvey; Harvey Promised to Change the World; Hennie Soup; Hold My Baby Back; How Could You Do This to Someone Who Robbed for You? (Prison Music); I Don't Want to Feel What I Feel; I Never Said I Didn't Love You; I'll Get You Out of My Life; Out of Here; Places I Fainted from Hunger; Prosperity Song, The; Standing in Line; Supreme Court Saved from Fire, The; That's Enough for Me; That's Enough for Me Duet; Thinking About You; Time Passes; You Can't Let Romance Die; You Got Me Grinding My Teeth

Cast: Stacey Lynn Brass; Lawrence Clayton; Victor Trent Cook; Cleavant Derricks; J.P. Dougherty; Peggy Hewett; Alix Korey; Michael Mandell; Amanda Naughton; Lillias White

Notes: *See also AMERICA KICKS UP ITS HEELS*, an earlier version of this show.

3758 • ROMANCE OF A HINDO PRINCESS

Notes: *See A SOCIETY CIRCUS.*

3759 • ROMANCE OF ATHLONE, A

OPENED: 03/18/1901　　Theatre: 14th St.
Play　　　　　　　　　Broadway: 16

Composer: Chauncey Olcott
Lyricist: Chauncey Olcott
Author: Augustus Pitou
Director: Augustus Pitou

Songs: Irish Swell, The; Many Years Ago; My Wild Irish Rose; Olcott's Lullaby; We'll Drown It in the Bowl

Cast: Dustin Farnum; Grace Freeman; Daniel Gilfether; Luke Martin; Chauncey Olcott; Olive White

3760 • ROMANCE, ROMANCE

OPENED: 05/01/1988　　Theatre: Helen Hayes
Musical　　　　　　　　Broadway: 297

Composer: Keith Herrmann
Lyricist: Barry Harman
Librettist: Barry Harman
Producer: Harve Brosten; Jay S. Bulmash; Dasha Epstein
Director: Barry Harman

Source: LITTLE COMEDY, THE (Story: Arthur Schnitzler); **Source:** PAIN DE MENAGE (Play Jules Renard); **Choreographer:** Pamela Sousa; **Costumes:** Steven Jones; **Dance Arranger:** Keith Herrmann; Kathy Sommer; **Lighting Designer:** Craig Miller; **Musical Director:** Kathy Sommer; **Orchestrations:** Michael Starobin; **Set Design:** Steven Rubin; **Vocal Arranger:** Keith Herrmann; Kathy Sommer

Songs: Goodbye, Emil [1]; Great News [1]; Happy, Happy, Happy [1]; How Did I End Up Here? [2]; I'll Always Remember the Song [1]; It's Not Too Late [3]; Let's Not Talk About It [2]; Little Comedy, The [1]; Moonlight Passing Through a Window [2]; My Love for Her [2]; Night It Had to End, The [1]; Now [2]; Oh, What a Performance! [1]; Plans A & B [2]; Romance!;

Romance!; Romantic Notions [2]; Rustic Country Inn, A [1]; Small Craft Warnings [2]; So Glad I Married Her [2]; Summer Share [2]; Think of the Odds [2]; Women of Vienna [1]; Words He Doesn't Say [2]; Yes, It's Love [1]

Cast: Scott Bakula; Alison Fraser; Deborah Graham; Robert Hoshour

Notes: This show consisted of two one-act Musicals — THE LITTLE COMEDY and SUMMER SHARE. This Helen Hayes theatre was formerly the Little Theatre and was named after the actress after the previous Helen Hayes Theatre was demolished. [1] From THE LITTLE COMEDY. [2] From SUMMER SHARE. [3] In both one-act musicals.

3761 • ROMANOFF AND JULIET

OPENED: 10/10/1957　　Theatre: Plymouth
Play　　　　　　　　　Broadway: 389

Composer: Anthony Hopkins; Peter Ustinov
Lyricist: Anthony Hopkins; Peter Ustinov
Author: Peter Ustinov
Producer: David Merrick
Director: George S. Kaufman

Costumes: Helene Pons; **Incidental Music:** Harold Rome; **Set Design:** Denis Malcles

Songs: Lullaby (C/L: Harold Rome)

Cast: Elizabeth Allen; Fred Clark; Jack Gilford; Henry Lascoe; Phil Leeds; Natalie Schafer; Peter Ustinov

Notes: No songs listed in program.

3762 • ROMANY LOVE

OPENED: 1925
Musical

Songs: Show Me How to Make Love (C: Harry Rosenthal; L: Irving Caesar)

Notes: No other information available.

3763 • RONDELAY

OPENED: 11/05/1969　　Theatre: Hudson West
Musical　　　　　　　　Off-Broadway: 11

Composer: Hal Jordan
Lyricist: Jerry Douglas
Librettist: Jerry Douglas
Producer: Rick Hobard
Director: William Francisco

Source: LA RONDE (Play Arthur Schnitzler); **Choreographer:** Jacques D'Amboise; **Costumes:** Raoul Pene du Bois; **Lighting Designer:** Neil Peter Jampolis; **Musical Director:** Karen Gustafson; **Orchestrations:** Philip J. Lang; **Set Design:** Raoul Pene du Bois; **Vocal Arranger:** Karen Gustafson

Songs: Afterward; Angel Face; Answer, The; Auf Wiedersehen; Back to Nature; Before Breakfast; Castle in India, A; Champagne; Closer; Days of My Youth, The; Dessert; Easy; Failure; First Kiss, The; Give and Take; Gusto; Happy Ending; Honor; I'll Show You the World Tonight; I've Got a Surprise for You; Lovers of the Lamplight; Masquerade; Not So Young Love; One Hundred Virgins; Opera Star; Reflections; Reidhof's; Rondelay; Saint Genesius; She Deserves Me; Success; Tonight You Dance with Me; What You Are; When Lovers Fall in Love

Cast: Carole Demas; Gwyda DonHowe; Barbara Lang; Terence Monk

3764 • ROSA

OPENED: 05/10/1978   Theatre: St. Clement's
Musical   Off-Off-Broadway: 12

Composer: Baldwin Bergersen
Lyricist: William Archibald
Librettist: William Archibald
Producer: Wendell Minick
Director: Patricia Carmichael

Source: ROSA (Play Brenda Forbes); **Choreographer:** Roger Preston-Smith; **Costumes:** Danny Morgan; **Dance Arranger:** Robert Goldstone; **Lighting Designer:** Curt Ostermann; **Musical Director:** Robert Colston; **Set Design:** Daniel Thomas Field; **Vocal Arranger:** Robert Goldstone

Songs: Be Kind to the Young; Before It's Too Late; Dear Friend; Fame; Fish Soup Song; From the Bottom of the Sea; Herb Song, The; I Am Royal; Let Us Charm Each Other; Oh, How We Love You, Mrs. Cornwall; Peace Celebration; Per-

fection; Place of My Own, A; Rosa; Time Goes Faster; Where's My Love A'Wanderin'

Cast: John Deyle; Jill Harwood; Ted Houck; Nancy Lipner; Everett McGill; Donald C. Moore; Marnie Mosiman; Elizabeth Torgerson; Steve Vinovich; Victoria Wyndham

3765 • ROSALIE (1906)

OPENED: 1906
Musical   Closed out of town

Composer: Willard Spencer
Lyricist: Willard Spencer
Librettist: Willard Spencer
Producer: Nixon & Zimmerman

Musical Director: Max Winne

Songs: Chinese Song, The; Fairies Rule the World; Farewell Love; I Love You to Distraction; I Represent the Evening Blow; I'm the Bravest of the Brave; It's Better to Have Loved and Lost Than Never to Have Loved at All; Just a Little Chinaman; Lover's Quarrels; Message from the Sea, A; Rosalie; True Love; We're Regular Army Soldiers; When Hearts Are Broken; You Are All the World to Me; Ze Patent Love Perfume

Cast: Cora Tracy

Notes: This was probably a tour of a show that opened in Philadelphia on 4/23/06. Program of Wilkes-Barre 9/29/06.

3766 • ROSALIE (1928)

OPENED: 01/10/1928   Theatre: New Amsterdam
Musical   Broadway: 327

Composer: George Gershwin
Lyricist: Ira Gershwin
Librettist: Guy Bolton; William Anthony McGuire
Producer: Florenz Ziegfeld
Director: William Anthony McGuire

Choreographer: Seymour Felix; **Musical Director:** Oscar Bradley

Songs: Abdication (C: Sigmund Romberg; L: P.G. Wodehouse); At the Ex-King's Club; Beautiful Gypsy [6]; Cadet Song [3] (C: Unknown); Enjoy Today [3]; Entrance of the Hussars (C: Sigmund

Romberg; L: P.G. Wodehouse); Ev'rybody Knows I Love Somebody [4]; Finale Act I (C: Sigmund Romberg); Follow the Drum [2]; Glad Tidings [3]; Here They Are (C: Sigmund Romberg; L: P.G. Wodehouse); How Long Has This Been Going On? [1]; Hussar March [8] (C: Sigmund Romberg; L: Ira Gershwin; P.G. Wodehouse); I Forget What I Started to Say [12]; King Can Do No Wrong, The [11] (C: Sigmund Romberg; L: Ira Gershwin; P.G. Wodehouse); Kingdom of Dreams (C: Sigmund Romberg; L: P.G. Wodehouse); Let Me Be a Friend to You (The Kind of Friend); Man I Love, The [5]; Merry- Andrew (inst.); New York Serenade; Now That the Dance Is Over [3] (C: Unknown); Oh Gee! Oh Joy! (L: Ira Gershwin; P.G. Wodehouse); Rosalie [3]; Say So! [9] (L: Ira Gershwin; P.G. Wodehouse); Setting Up Exercise (C: Sigmund Romberg; L: P.G. Wodehouse); Show Me the Town [7]; True to Them All [3]; Under the Furlough Moon [3] (C: Sigmund Romberg); West Point Bugle (C: Sigmund Romberg; L: P.G. Wodehouse); West Point March (C: Sigmund Romberg; L: P.G. Wodehouse); West Point Song (C: Sigmund Romberg; L: P.G. Wodehouse); What Could I Do? [10]; When Cadets Parade [13]; When the Right One Comes Along [3]; Why Must We Always Be Dreaming? (C: Sigmund Romberg; L: P.G. Wodehouse); Yankee Doodle Rhythm [3]; You Know How It Is [3]

Cast: Bobbe Arnst; Margaret Dale; Jack Donahue; Gladys Glad; Oliver McLennan; Marilyn Miller; Frank Morgan

Notes: [1] Dropped from FUNNY FACE. [2] Added after opening. [3] Not used. [4] Added after opening. Same music as "Dance Alone with You" dropped from FUNNY FACE. [5] Not used. Later in LADY, BE GOOD. Also in STRIKE UP THE BAND (1927). [6] Cut prior to opening. Same music as "Wait a Bit, Susie" in PRIMROSE. [7] Written for but not used in OH, KAY! [8] Lyrics to verse by Wodehouse and chorus by Gershwin. [9] Music previously used for "When the Right One Comes Along" which was not used in FUNNY FACE. [10] Not used if actually intended for this show. Same music as "Oh Gee! Oh Joy!" [11] An early version had lyrics by Wodehouse alone. [12] Cut prior to opening. [13] Not used. Music originally set to a Clifford Grey lyric titled "When the Mites Go By" for FLYING ISLAND. [14] Not used. Written for STRIKE UP THE BAND (1927).

3767 • ROSALINDA

OPENED: 10/28/1942   Theatre: 44th Street
Musical   Broadway: 521

Music Based On: Johann Strauss
Composer: Erich Wolfgang Korngold
Lyricist: Paul Kerby
Librettist: John Meehan Jr.; Gottfried Reinhardt; Max Reinhardt
Producer: New Opera Company, The; Lodewick Vroom
Director: Felix Brentano

Source: DIE FLEDERMAUS (Opera: Johann Strauss); **Choreographer:** George Balanchine; **Costumes:** Ladislas Czettel; **Lighting Designer:** Jean Rosenthal; **Musical Director:** Erich Wolfgang Korngold; **Set Design:** Oliver Smith

Cast: Gene Barry; Paul Best; Oscar Karweis; Jose Limon; Virginia MacWatters; Ernest McChesney; Dorothy Sarnoff; Louis Sorin; Everett West; Shelley Winters [1]

Notes: [1] Billed as Shelley Winter.

3768 • ROSE BRIAR

OPENED: 12/25/1922   Theatre: Empire
Play   Broadway: 89

Lyricist: Booth Tarkington
Author: Booth Tarkington
Producer: Charles Dillingham; Florenz Ziegfeld

Choreographer: Ned Wayburn; **Costumes:** Ben Ali Haggin; **Set Design:** Joseph Urban

Songs: Give Me That Rose (C: Donald McGibeney); Love and the Moon (C: Jerome Kern); Rose Briar (C: Jerome Kern)

Cast: Billie Burke; Frank Conroy; Allan Dinehart; Richie Ling; Florence O'Denishawn

3769 • ROSE DE FRANCE

OPENED: 10/23/1933   Theatre: Theatre de Chatelet
Musical   Paris

Composer: Sigmund Romberg
Lyricist: Albert Willemetz
Librettist: Mouezy-Eon
Producer: Maurice Lehmann

Songs: Baron de Ragotin; Chant des Galleriens; Frivolette; Il est de Beaux Reves [1]; Je Vous Aimerai dans L'Ombre [1]; Ma Belle Petronilla; Pour Faire le Tournedos; Pour Se Faire Adorer; Pour Vivre Aupres Vous; Quand les Soldats Vont au Pas; Rose de France; Sur la Mer Immense

Cast: Monique Best

Notes: [1] Not used.

3770 • ROSE GIRL, THE
OPENED: 02/11/1920   Theatre: Ambassador
Musical   Broadway: 99

Composer: Anselm Goetzl
Lyricist: William Cary Duncan
Librettist: William Cary Duncan
Producer: Anselm Goetzl
Director: Hassard Short

Choreographer: Max Scheck; **Costumes:** Ralph Mulligan; **Musical Director:** Max Steiner; **Set Design:** William Weaver

Songs: All the World Loves a Winner [1]; Beauty's Candy Shop; Dear Little Rose Girl; Down Where the Mortgages Grow [2]; Flirtation Quartette; Ghosts [2]; Girl You Never Have Kissed, The [1]; I Am a One Girl Boy [2]; I Love the Love That's New [1]; If You Keep Them Wondering [1]; Lingerie; Love That's New, The [2]; Ma! [1] (C: Sidney Clare; L: Con Conrad); Magnetism [2]; May and September; My Old New Jersey Home (C: Nat Vincent; L: Ballard Macdonald); Nice Little Girl on the Side, A [2]; Perfume Number [2]; Proteges, The; Rose Girl Blues, The; Rose Girl Waltz; Something New [1]; Spanish Senorita, The; That One Sweet Hour with You; That's Me; There Comes a Some Day; When Our Sundays Are Blue; When That Somebody Comes; Wondrous Midnight Eyes

Cast: May Boley; Charles Purcell; Mabel Withee

Notes: [1] Sheet music only. [2] Out Harrisburg 9/2/70.

3771 • ROSE MAID, THE
OPENED: 04/22/1912   Theatre: Globe
Musical   Broadway: 176

Composer: Bruno Granichstaedten
Lyricist: Robert B. Smith

Librettist: Raymond W. Peck; Harry B. Smith
Producer: Werba & Luescher
Director: George Marion

Source: BUB ODER MADEL? (Musical: Adolf Altmann; Felix Dormann; Bruno Granichstaedten); **Musical Director:** Robert Hood Bowers

Songs: American Heiress, The; Course of True Love, The; Dance Into His Heart [1]; Finale Act I; Finale Act III; Girls from Yankee Land (C: Robert Hood Bowers; L: Raymond W. Peck); Happy Family, The; Heiresses, The (C: Robert Hood Bowers; L: Raymond W. Peck); I Live for You Alone; Jolly Good Fellow [1]; Liberty Hall; Lost a Heart; Love Is the Same Old Game (C: Robert Hood Bowers; L: Raymond W. Peck); Mighty Dollar Greets You, The [1]; Money Talks; Moon, Lovely Moon!; Now His Choice We See; One Waltz-Only One Waltz; Opening Chorus; Opening Chorus Act II (C: Robert Hood Bowers; L: Raymond W. Peck); Riders of Every Nation; Roses Bloom for Lovers; Soldier of Bohemia, A (C: Robert Hood Bowers; L: Raymond W. Peck); Stork, Stork [1]; Sweethearts, Wives and Good Fellows; Telephone Song; When Two Little Hearts Beat Together; Yankee Millionairess, A (C: Robert Hood Bowers; L: Raymond W. Peck)

Cast: Edith Decker; J.H. Duffrey; Ed Gallagher; Al Shean

Notes: [1] Out Boston 2/26/12. [2] ASCAP/Library of Congress only.

3772 • ROSE-MARIE
OPENED: 09/02/1924   Theatre: Imperial
Musical   Broadway: 581

Composer: Rudolf Friml
Lyricist: Oscar Hammerstein II; Otto Harbach
Librettist: Oscar Hammerstein II; Otto Harbach
Producer: Arthur Hammerstein
Director: Paul Dickey

Choreographer: David Bennett; **Costumes:** Charles LeMaire; **Musical Director:** Herbert Stothart; **Orchestrations:** Robert Russell Bennett; **Set Design:** Frank Gates; E.A. Morange

Songs: Bridal Finale (Bridal Procession) (C: Herbert Stothart); Door of Her Dreams; Eccentric Dance

(C: Herbert Stothart); Finale Act I (C: Rudolf
Friml; Herbert Stothart); Finale Ultimo; Hard-
Boiled Herman (C: Herbert Stothart); I Love Him;
Indian Love Call; Lak Jeem; Mam'selle [1]
(L: Forman Brown); Minuet of the Minute, The
(C: Herbert Stothart); Mounties, The (C: Rudolf
Friml; Herbert Stothart); One Man Woman
(C: Herbert Stothart); Only a Kiss (C: Herbert
Stothart); Pretty Things; Rose-Marie; Totem
Tom-Tom (C: Rudolf Friml; Herbert Stothart);
Vive La Canadienne (C: Herbert Stothart); Waltz
Song [1] (L: Forman Brown); Whenever Night
Falls (1) [1] (L: Forman Brown); Whenever Night
Falls (2) [1] (L: Otto Harbach); Why Shouldn't
We? (C: Herbert Stothart)

Cast: Eduardo Ciannelli; Arthur Deagon; Mary
Ellis; Frank Greene; William Kent; Dennis King;
Arthur Ludwig; Dorothy Mackaye; Pearl Regay

Notes: [1] Written for 1950 revival.

3773 • ROSE OF ALGERIA, THE

OPENED: 09/20/1909   Theatre: Herald Square
Musical   Broadway: 40

Composer: Victor Herbert
Lyricist: Glen MacDonough
Librettist: Glen MacDonough
Producer: Lew Fields
Director: Ned Wayburn

Source: ALGERIA (Musical: Victor Herbert; Glen
MacDonough); **Musical Director:** John McGhie;
Orchestrations: Victor Herbert; **Set Design:**
Ernest Albert

Songs: Ask Her While the Band Is Playing [1]
(L: Vincent Bryan); Bayaderes [2]; Bohemia
Good-Bye [1]; Boule Miche [1]; Foolish
Gardener, The [1]; Go Happy Bride [2]; Great
White Easiest Way, The [1]; He Was a Soldier,
Too [2]; I'll Dream of Thee [2] (L: Vincent
Bryan); In Jail [1]; I've Been Decorated [1]; Lady
Sleeps, The; Letters from Home; Little Birds of
Paradise [1]; Love Is Like a Cigarette [1]; Mardi
Gras, The; Only One of Anything [1]; Rose of the
World (My Life I Love Thee) [1]; Same Old Two,
The [1]; Thanksgiving Day [2] (L: Vincent
Bryan); Twilight in Barakeesh [1]; You'll Feel
Better Then [1]

Cast: Eugene Cowles; Lillian Herlein; Anna
Wheaton

Notes: This was a rewrite of ALGERIA. See that
entry. [1] Originally in ALGERIA. [2]
ASCAP/Library of Congress only.

3774 • ROSE OF ALHAMBRA, THE

OPENED: 02/04/1907   Theatre: Majestic
Musical   Broadway: 26

Composer: Lucius Hosmer
Lyricist: Charles Emerson Cook
Librettist: Charles Emerson Cook
Director: Charles Emerson Cook

Set Design: Homer Emens; Frank E. Gates; E.A.
Morange; Edward G. Unitt

Songs: All the King's Horses and Men; Castles in
Spain; Entrance Song; Falcon, The; Give Him a
Welcome Quite Spanish; Lay of the Lute, The;
Long Live the King!; Love's Eternal Song;
Manana; Nightingale and the Rose, The; Oh,
Won't You Shed a Little Tear for Me?; Pilgrim of
Love, The; Serenade; Song of the Millers; Splash!
Dash! Bang!; Vagrant Stream, The [1]

Cast: Agnes Cain Brown; George Eaton Collins;
Eddie Heron

Notes: [1] Out Trenton 2/24/06.

3775 • ROSE OF CHINA, THE

OPENED: 11/25/1919   Theatre: Lyric
Musical   Broadway: 47

Composer: Armand Vecsey
Lyricist: P.G. Wodehouse
Librettist: Guy Bolton
Producer: F. Ray Comstock; Morris Gest
Director: Robert Milton; Julian Mitchell

Musical Director: William P. Axt; **Set Design:**
Joseph Urban

Songs: Broken Blossoms; Bunny Dear; College
Spirit; Down on the Banks of Subway; Finale Act
I; Finale Act II; Finale Act III; Hymn to the Sun;
It's Wonderful; Legend of the Tea Tree, The;
Little Bride; My China Rose; Our Chinese
Bungalow; Proposals; Romeo and Juliet; Spirit of
the Drum, The; Sunrise Intermezzo; What! What!
What!; When You Are in China; Yale; Yesterday

Cast: Cecil Cunningham; Frank McIntyre; Jane
Richardson; Oscar Shaw

3776 ROSE OF PANAMA

OPENED: 01/22/1912   Theatre: Daly's
Musical   Broadway: 24

Composer: Heinrich Berte
Lyricist: Sydney Rosenfeld
Librettist: Sydney Rosenfeld; John L. Shine
Producer: John Cort
Director: Frank Smithso

Source: KREOLENBLUT (Musical: Heinrich Berte; Ignaz Schnitzer; Emmerich Von Gatti)

Cast: Fay Bainter; Chapine; Forrest Huff; Mortimer Weldon

Notes: No program available.

3777 • ROSE OF PERSIA

OPENED: 09/06/1900   Theatre: Daly's
Musical   Broadway: 25

Composer: Arthur Sullivan
Librettist: Basil Hood

Songs: As We Lie in Langour Lazy; Finale Act I; From Morning Prayer the Sultan; Golden Key, The; Hassan, the Sultan with His Court Approaches; I Care Not If the Cup I Hold; If a Sudden Stroke of Fate; If You Ask Me to Advise You; If You or I Should Tell the Truth; I'm Abu-el-Hassan; I'm the Sultan's Vigilant Vizier; In My Heart of Hearts I've Always Known; It Has Reached Me a Lady Named Hubbard; It's a Busy Day; Laughing Low, on Tip-Toe; Let a Satirist Enumerate a Catalogue of Crimes; Mystical Maidens Are We; 'Neath My Lattice; Our Tale Is Told; Something in the City; Suppose-I Say, Suppose; There Once Was a Small Street Arab; Tramps and Scamps; We Have Come to Invade; What Does It Mean?; What Is Love?; What Will Become of Me?; When Islam First Arose; Where Am I?

Cast: Sidney Bracey; Herbert Clayton; John Le Hay; Hettice Lund; Ruth Vincent

Notes: No program available. Songs from London version.

3778 • ROSE OF STAMBOUL, THE

OPENED: 03/07/1922   Theatre: Century
Musical   Broadway: 111

Composer: Leo Fall; Sigmund Romberg
Lyricist: Harold Atteridge
Librettist: Harold Atteridge
Producer: J.J. Shubert; Lee Shubert
Director: J.C. Huffman

Choreographer: Allan K. Foster; **Musical Director:** Alfred Goodman; **Set Design:** Watson Barratt

Songs: Ballet Oriental; Blue Book of Girls, A; Ladies from the Cultured West, The; Love Test, The; Lovey Dove (C: Sigmund Romberg); Mazuma (C: Sigmund Romberg); My Heart Is Calling (C: Sigmund Romberg); Rose of Stamboul (C: Leo Fall); Time, Only Time Deary (C: Sigmund Romberg); Ting-A-Ling (C: Leo Fall; Sigmund Romberg); Waltz-Duet; Waltz It Should Be, A (C: Leo Fall; Sigmund Romberg); Waltz Song; Wedding March, The; Why Do They Die at the End of Classical Dance?; With Papers Duly Signed

Cast: James Barton; Marion Greene; Tessa Kosta

3779 • ROSY RAPTURE, THE PRIDE OF THE BEAUTY CHORUS

OPENED: 03/22/1915   Theatre: Duke of York's
Musical   London

Composer: John Crook; Herman Darewski; Jerome Kern
Author: James M. Barrie
Producer: Charles Frohman

Songs: Best Sort of Mother, Best Sort of Child [1] (C: Jerome Kern; L: F.W. Mark)

Cast: Gaby Deslys; Helen Hayes; Jack Norworth; Leon Quartermaine

Notes: No other information available. [1] Same music as "The Same Sort of Girl" from THE GIRL FROM UTAH.

3780 • ROTHSCHILDS, THE

OPENED: 10/19/1970   Theatre: Lunt-Fontanne
Musical   Broadway: 505

Composer: Jerry Bock
Lyricist: Sheldon Harnick
Librettist: Sherman Yellen
Producer: Hillard Elkins; Lester Osterman
Director: Michael Kidd

Source: ROTHSCHILDS, THE (Book: Frederic Morton); **Choreographer:** Michael Kidd; **Costumes:** John Bury; **Dance Arranger:** Clay Fullum; **Lighting Designer:** Richard Pilbrow; **Musical Director:** Milton Greene; **Orchestrations:** Don Walker; **Set Design:** John Bury; **Vocal Arranger:** Milton Greene

Songs: Allons; Bonds; Damn [4]; Everything; French Auction, The [4]; Give England Strength; Have You Ever Seen a Prettier Little Congress?; He Tossed a Coin; I Will Bow [2]; I'm in Love! I'm in Love!; In My Own Lifetime; Jew Do Your Duty [3]; Just a Map [1]; Mayer's Fine Coins [3]; Momma, Come Stay with Me [1]; Money [3]; My Cousin Christian [2]; My Hannah [1]; One Room; Pleasure and Privilege; Rothschild and Sons; Royal Hessian Auction [2]; Sons; Stability; They Say; This Amazing London Town; Troubled Lullaby [1]; William's Fine Troops [3]

Cast: Robby Benson; Jill Clayburgh; Keene Curtis; Paul Hecht; Hal Linden; Leila Martin; David Rounds; Chris Sarandon

Notes: [1] Cut in rehearsal. [2] Out Detroit 8/14/70. [3] Out Philadelphia prior to New York. [4] Not used.

3781 • ROUMANIAN WEDDING, THE

OPENED: 10/25/1981
Musical   Off-Broadway

Composer: Peretz Sandler
Lyricist: Peretz Sandler
Librettist: Moshe Schorr
Producer: Raymond Ariel; David Carey
Director: Michael Greenstein

Choreographer: Felix Fibich; **Costumes:** Renee Gladstein; **Orchestrations:** Renee Solomon; **Set Design:** Adina Reich

Songs: Bleinelech Tzvey; Chassene Habn Iz Doch Zeyer Git; Dvoyreh; Dvoyreh Fan Rumeynie; Geendikt Iz Der Tog; Gvald Ich Vil Es; Huliet Huliet Kinderlech; Ich Bin Gerecht; Ich Lib Dich; Kinder Yohrn; Mach Es Motkeh Noch Amol; Mayn Rochele; Mit Zaltz un Fefer; Roumeynische Libe; Wedding Dance

Cast: Yankele Alperin; Reizl Bozyk; David Carey; David Ellen; Leon Liebgold; Mary Soreanu

Notes: The score was adapted by Yankele Alperin and Mordechay Gebirtig.

3782 • ROUND 'N' ROUND IN RHYTHM

Theatre: Ubangi Club
Revue   Nightclub

Composer: Alex Hill; Andy Razaf
Lyricist: Alex Hill; Andy Razaf
Producer: Leonard Harper

Songs: Beautiful Legs (C: Thomas "Fats" Waller); Hot Jello (C: Unknown); My Joe Louis of Love (C: Paul Denniker); On Robinson Crusoe Isle (C: Paul Denniker); Small Mama — Big Mama (C: Unknown); Stealin' My Thunder (C: Andy Razaf); Struggles (C: Unknown); Sunflower Sue (C: Unknown); Switch It Miss Mitchell (C: Unknown); Tippin' Out Tonight (C: Unknown); Wastin' Our Talents (C: Unknown); When That Dixie Sun Goes Down (C: Unknown)

Cast: Gladys Bentley; Teddy Hill Orchestra; Avon Long; Mabel Scott

Notes: Produced in the 1930's. No program available.

3783 • ROUND THE TOWN

OPENED: 05/21/1924   Theatre: Century Roof
Revue   Broadway: 13

Librettist: Marc Connelly; George S. Kaufman; Herman J. Mankiewicz
Producer: S. Jay Kaufman; Herman J. Mankiewicz
Director: Herman J. Mankiewicz

Choreographer: Lew Leslie

Songs: Chiquita (C/L: Walter Donaldson); I Wonder Why the Glow-Worm Winks His Eye [2] (C: Herbert Stothart; L: Oscar Hammerstein II); If One of Us Was You Dear (C: Jay Velie; L: George S. Kaufman); It's Good for You to Exercise Your Mind (C: Arthur H. Samuels; L: Dorothy Parker); Liza Jane (C: Alfred Nathan Jr.; L: Ned Wever); Romeo, Juliet, Johnny and Jane [1] (C: Victor Herbert; L: Dorothy Parker); Save a Kiss for Rainy Weather [3] (C: Will Ortmann; Richard A. Whiting; L: Raymond B. Egan); Wallflower (C: Alfred Nathan Jr.; L: Ned Wever)

Cast: Heywood Broun; Irene Delroy; Harry Fox; Jack Haley; Julius Tennen; Janet Velie; Jay Velie

Notes: [1] Out-of-town program only. [2] Also in HAMMERSTEIN'S 9 O'CLOCK REVUE. [3] Titled "Save a Kiss for a Rainy Day" in program.

3784 • ROUNDERS, THE

OPENED: 07/12/1899   Theatre: Casino
Musical   Broadway: 97

Composer: Ludwig Englander
Lyricist: Harry B. Smith
Librettist: Harry B. Smith
Producer: George W. Lederer
Director: Max Freeman

Source: LES FETARDS (Musical: Maurice Hennequin; Antony Mars; Victor Roger)

Songs: American Heiresses; De Stories Uncle Remus Tells; Entrance of Maginnis Pasha; Entrance of the Duke de Baccarat; Finale Act II; Here We Gather Every Summer (Opening Chorus); In Philadelphia; Life Is a Toyshop; Object Matrimony; Oh Where Is Dancer; Only a Hundred Girls; Opening Chorus Act II; Philadelphia Maid, The; Rounders Song, The; Same Old Story, Nothing New; She Didn't Understand; We're Adding Local Color; When You Know These Men

Cast: Joseph Cawthorne; Dan Daly; Harry Davenport; Max Freeman; Marie George; Mabel Gilman; Phyllis Rankin; Thomas Q. Seabrooke; Frederick Urban

3785 • ROXANNE

Notes: *See THE WHITE PLUME. See also CYRANO DE BERGERAC.*

3786 • ROYAL CHEF, THE

OPENED: 09/01/1904   Theatre: Lyric
Musical   Broadway: 17

Composer: Ben M. Jerome
Lyricist: George E. Stoddard; Charles A. Taylor
Librettist: Charles A. Taylor
Producer: La Salle Theatre Co.
Director: Frank Smithson

Musical Director: Ben M. Jerome

Songs: Admirable Admiral, An; All Through the Love of You; As Befits My Rank and Station; Away to the Mountains; Hail the Rajah; In the Morning; It's a Way That They Have in Chicago; Let Me Go Back; Maiden and the Kissing Bug, The; Napanee [1]; Oh Glorious Sun; Old Mother Goose; O'Reilly; Tale of the Tailless Frog, The; We Are a Band of Gentlemen; What Color Eyes Do You Love Best?; What's the Matter with My Man in the Moon; When Old Glory Floats from Everywhere; Would You If You Were I?

Cast: Joseph Allen; Dave Lewis; John Park; Amelia Stone

Notes: No New York program available. Songs as of 9/18/04 Chicago. [1] Sheet music only.

3787 • ROYAL FAMILY, THE

OPENED: 12/30/1975   Theatre: Helen Hayes
Play   Broadway: 232

Composer: Claibe Richardson
Lyricist: Claibe Richardson
Author: Edna Ferber; George S. Kaufman
Producer: Barry Brown; Richmond Crinkley; Burry Fredrik; Fritz Holt; Sally Spears; Roger L. Stevens
Director: Ellis Rabb

Costumes: Ann Roth; **Lighting Designer:** John Gleason; **Set Design:** Oliver Smith

Songs: Julie [1]; Julie's Tango (inst.); Look Out I'm Falling in Love; While We're Waltzing

Cast: Rosemary Harris; Eva Le Gallienne; Rosetta LeNoire; Sam Levene; Joseph Maher; Ellis Rabb; Mary Louise Wilson

Notes: [1] Out Princeton prior to New York.

3788 • ROYAL FLUSH

OPENED: 12/31/1964
Musical   Closed out of town

Composer: Jay Thompson
Lyricist: Jay Thompson
Librettist: Robert Schlitt; Jay Thompson
Producer: L. Slade Brown
Director: June Havoc

Source: GREEN BIRD, THE (Novel: Nina Savo); **Choreographer:** Ralph Beaumont; **Costumes:**

Raoul Pene du Bois; **Dance Arranger:** Hal Schaefer; **Lighting Designer:** Jules Fisher; **Musical Director:** Skip Redwine; **Orchestrations:** Larry Wilcox; **Set Design:** Raoul Pene du Bois

Songs: Being Quiet with You; Bye Bye; Caveat Emptor; Edge of the World, The; For God, Home, Mother and Country; It Could Be Worse; Just Reach Out and Touch Me; Lotus Blossom; Magic Time; No Happy Ending; Oh What an Island; Right, Right, Right; Road to Hell, The; She's Sweet; Think Up!; Try a Little ; You'll Be Something

Cast: Kaye Ballard; Jane Connell; Al De Sio; Mickey Deems; Louis Edmonds; Charlotte Jones; Kenneth Nelson; Jill O'Hara; Beverly Todd; Jodi Williams

Notes: Closed 1/23/65. The original director/choreographer was Jack Cole, who was replaced by Martyn Green, who was also replaced.

3789 • ROYAL PALM REVUE (FIFTH EDITION)

OPENED: 1940   Theatre: Royal Palm
Revue   Nightclub

Songs: Love Song of Renaldo (C: Sammy Fain; L: Irving Kahal)

Notes: No other information available.

3790 • ROYAL ROGUE, A

OPENED: 12/24/1900   Theatre: Broadway
Musical   Broadway: 30

Composer: William T. Francis
Lyricist: Grant Stewart
Librettist: Charles Klein
Producer: Jefferson De Angelis
Director: R.H. Burnside

Costumes: Caroline Seidle; **Musical Director:** William T. Francis; **Set Design:** D. Frank Dodge

Songs: Daughters of a Minister, The

Cast: Eva Davenport; Jefferson De Angelis; Josephine Hall

Notes: No New York program available.

3791 • ROYAL VAGABOND, THE

OPENED: 02/17/1919   Theatre: Cohan and Harris
Musical   Broadway: 208

Composer: George M. Cohan; Anselm Goetzl
Lyricist: William Cary Duncan
Librettist: William Cary Duncan; Stephen Ivor-Szinngey
Producer: George M. Cohan; Sam H. Harris
Director: Sam Forrest; Julian Mitchell

Costumes: Alice O'Neil

Songs: Charming (C: Harry Tierney; L: Joseph McCarthy); Coronation Rehearsal (inst.) (C: Anselm Goetzl); Democracy (C: Anselm Goetzl; L: William Cary Duncan); Finale Act I (C: Anselm Goetzl; L: William Cary Duncan); Good-Bye Bargravia (C/L: George M. Cohan); Here Come the Soldiers (C/L: George M. Cohan); I Want Someone to Love Me [1] (C/L: Unknown); If the World Were Upside Down [1] (C/L: Unknown); I'm Looking for Hubby Dear [1] (C/L: Unknown); In a Kingdom of Our Own (C/L: George M. Cohan); Love of Mine (C: Anselm Goetzl; L: William Cary Duncan); Messenger Number and Dance (C: Anselm Goetzl; L: George M. Cohan); Nice Little Girl on the Side, A [1] (C/L: Unknown); Opening Act II (C: Anselm Goetzl; L: George M. Cohan); Opera, Comic Opera (C/L: George M. Cohan); Royalty (C: Anselm Goetzl; L: George M. Cohan); Test of Love, The (C/L: Unknown); That Revolutionary Rag (C/L: Irving Berlin); Thistledown Girl [1] (C/L: Unknown); Wee Bit of Lace, A (C: Harry Tierney; L: George M. Cohan); What You Don't Know Won't Hurt You (C: Anselm Goetzl; L: William Cary Duncan); When the Cherry Blossoms Fall (Love Is Love) (C: Anselm Goetzl; L: William Cary Duncan)

Cast: Dorothy Dickson; Carl Hyson; Tessa Kosta; Fred Santley; Gladys Zell

Notes: [1] Out Washington, D.C. 1/5/19.

3792 • ROZA

OPENED: 10/01/1987   Theatre: Royale
Musical   Broadway: 12

Composer: Gilbert Becaud
Lyricist: Julian More
Librettist: Julian More

Producer: Sam Crothers; Mary Lea Johnson; Producers Circle Co.; Marty Richards; Shubert Organization, The
Director: Harold Prince

Source: LA VIE DEVANT SOI (Novel: Romain Gary); **Choreographer:** Patricia Birch; **Costumes:** Florence Klotz; **Dance Arranger:** Louis St. Louis; **Lighting Designer:** Ken Billington; **Musical Director:** Louis St. Louis; **Orchestrations:** Michael Gibson; **Set Design:** Alexander Okun; **Vocal Arranger:** Louis St. Louis

Songs: Bravo Bravo; Don't Make Me Laugh; Got the Lady Dressed; Hamil's Birthday; Happiness; House in Algiers; Is Me; Life Is Ahead of Me; Live a Little; Lola's Ceremony; Max's Visit; Merci; Moon Like a Silver Window; Sweet Seventeen; Yusef's Visit

Cast: Yamil Borges; Georgia Brown; Al DeCristo; Bob Gunton; Ira Hawkins; Marcia Lewis; Michele Mais

3793 • RUDOLPH AND FROSTY

OPENED: 12/1975   Theatre: ABC
TV Musical

Composer: Johnny Marks
Lyricist: Johnny Marks

Songs: Chicken Today and Feathers Tomorrow; Christmas in July; Don't Let the Parade Pass You By; Everything I've Always Wanted; Frosty the Snowman (C: Jack Rollins; L: Steve Nelson); Holly Jolly Christmas, A [1]; I Heard the Bells on Christmas Day (C/L: Traditional); I See Rainbows; No Bed of Roses; Now and Then; Rockin' Around the Christmas Tree (C/L: Dub Allbritton; Brenda Lee); Rudolph the Red-Nosed Reindeer; We're a Couple of Misfits

Voice: Red Buttons; Ethel Merman; Mickey Rooney; Shelly Winters

Notes: [1] From RUDOLPH THE RED-NOSED REINDEER (TV Musical).

3794 • RUDOLPH THE RED-NOSED REINDEER

OPENED: 12/1964   Theatre: NBC
TV Musical

Composer: Johnny Marks
Lyricist: Johnny Marks

Songs: Holly Jolly Christmas, A; I Heard the Bells on Christmas Day; Jingle Jingle Jingle; Merry Merry Christmas, A; Most Wonderful Day of the Year, The; Night Before Christmas Song, The; Rockin' Around the Christmas Tree; Rudolph the Red-Nosed Reindeer; Silver and Gold; There's Always Tomorrow; We Are Santa's Elves; We're a Couple of Misfits; When Santa Claus Gets Your Letter

Cast: Burl Ives

Notes: This animated special ran for 19 years — the longest running special in TV history.

3795 • RUDOLPH'S SHINY NEW YEAR

OPENED: 12/1975
TV Musical

Composer: Johnny Marks
Lyricist: Johnny Marks

Songs: 4th of July Parade, The; Have a Happy; Have a Little Faith in Me; It's Raining Sunshine; Moving Finger Writes, The; Rudolph the Red-Nosed Reindeer; Turn Back the Years; What a Wonderful World

Voice: Red Skelton

3796 • RUFUS LEMAIRE'S AFFAIRS

OPENED: 03/28/1927   Theatre: Majestic
Revue   Broadway: 56

Composer: Martin Broones
Lyricist: Ballard Macdonald
Librettist: Jack Lait; Ballard Macdonald; Andy Rice; Edgar Allen Woolf
Producer: Rufus LeMaire
Director: William Halligan

Choreographer: Bobby Connolly; **Costumes:** Charles LeMaire; **Dance Arranger:** John L. McManus; **Musical Director:** John L. McManus; **Orchestrations:** John L. McManus; **Vocal Arranger:** John L. McManus

Songs: Boulevard Street [1]; Bring Back Those

Minstrel Days; Dancing By Moonlight; Golden Girl [1]; Hosanna [1]; I Can't Get Over a Girl Like You (L: Harry Ruskin); Jungly Tune [1]; Land of Broken Dreams; Lily [1] (C: Harry Warren; L: Martin Broones; Ballard Macdonald); Love Baby [1] (C: Jesse Greer; L: Billy Rose); Love May Not Hide [1]; Mexico; Nagasaki's Butterfly [1] (C: Dave Stamper; L: Billy Rose); Remember Cameo [1]; Rose of the Studios [1]; Scandalizing Fashion [1]; Since Henry Ford Apologized to Me [1] (C: Dave Stamper; L: Billy Rose); Underneath the Wabash Moon [1] (C: Dave Stamper; L: Billy Rose); Wah-Wah; Wandering in Dreamland; When I Think about the Girls I Fell For [1]; When the Eenie Meenies Do the Minie Mo [1]; Where the Morning Glories Twine; You'll Find a Beautiful Face Behind a Love Song [1]; You'll Find the End of the Rainbow in Your Own Back Yard [1] (C: Unknown; L: Billy Rose); You'll Learn How, Bye and Bye [1]

Cast: Bobbe Arnst; Peggy Fears; Charlotte Greenwood; John Price Jones; Ted Lewis; Sophie Tucker

Notes: [1] Sheet music only.

3797 • RUFUS RASTUS

OPENED: 1906
Musical

Composer: Ernest Hogan; Joe Jordan; Tom Lemonier
Lyricist: Frank Williams
Librettist: William D. Hall
Producer: J. Ed Green

Songs: Consolation; Hornet and Bee; Isle of Repose, The; Maude; My Mobile Mandy; Old Kentucky Home

Cast: J.F. Fores; J. Ed Green; J. Leubrie Hill; Anna Cook Pankey

Notes: No other information available.

3798 • RUGANTINO

OPENED: 02/06/1964   Theatre: Mark Hellinger
Musical   Broadway: 28

Composer: Armando Trovaioli
Lyricist: Edward Eager; Pietro Garinei; Sandro Giovannini

Librettist: Festa Campanile; Alfred Drake; Massimo Franciosa; Pietro Garinei; Sandro Giovannini
Producer: Alexander H. Cohen; Jack Hylton
Director: Pietro Garinei; Sandro Giovannini

Choreographer: Dania Krupska; **Costumes:** Guilio Coltellacci; **Lighting Designer:** Vannio Vanni; **Musical Director:** Anton Coppola; **Set Design:** Giulio Coltellacci

Songs: Boy and Man (E L'omo Mio); Ciumachella (Ciumachella de Trastevere); Dance of the Candle Killers; Game of Morra, The (La Morra); Headsman and I, The; House Is Not the Same Without a Woman, A (E Bello Ave 'Na Donna Dentro Casa); I'm Happy (Tira e Campa); It's Quick and Easy ('No Botta E Via); Just Look! (Anvedi Si Che Paciocca); Just Stay Alive (Sempre Boia E); Lantern Night; Nothing to Do (Ballaia De Rugantino); Passatella; Roma (Roma Nun Fa La Stupida Stasera); Rugantino in the Stocks (La Berlina); Saltarello, The (La Saltarello); San Pasquale; Tirrallallera (Tirollallero)

Cast: Aldo Fabrizi; Lando Fiorini; Nino Manfredi; Bice Valori; Ornelia Vanoni

3799 • RUGGLES OF RED GAP (1915)

OPENED: 12/25/1915   Theatre: Fulton
Musical   Broadway: 33

Composer: Sigmund Romberg
Lyricist: Harold Atteridge
Librettist: Harrison Rhodes
Producer: Messrs. Shubert

Songs: Chin-Chin; Eight Bells; Everybody Hum with Me; Lustspiel; Marconigram; Memories; Military Maid; Sing Me a Song of Love; Tulips and Pansies; When the Colored Regiment Goes Off to War

Cast: Louise Closser Hale; George Hassell; Ralph Herz; Jobyna Howland

3800 • RUGGLES OF RED GAP (1957)

OPENED: 02/03/1957   Theatre: NBC
TV Musical

Composer: Jule Styne
Lyricist: Leo Robin
Librettist: David Shaw
Producer: Charles Friedman
Director: Clark Jones

Source: RUGGLES OF RED GAP (Story: Harry Leon Wilson); **Musical Director:** Buddy Bregman

Songs: Finale; I Don't Want to Be a Gentleman; I Have You to Thank; I'm in Pursuit of Happiness [1]; It's a Glorious Fourth; It's Terribly, Horribly, Frightfully Nice; Kickapoo Kick, The; Oh, Those Americans; Ride on a Rainbow, A [2]; Way to a Family's Heart, The; Welcome Home; When You Dance in Paris, France

Cast: Imogene Coca; Joan Holloway; Peter Lawford; Hal Linden; Paul Lynde; Jane Powell; Michael Redgrave; David Wayne

Notes: Original TV musical. [1] Same music as "You'll Never Get Away from Me" used in GYPSY. [2] Added to 1995 revival of GENTLEMEN PREFER BLONDES.

3801 • RUMPLE

OPENED: 11/06/1957   Theatre: Alvin
Musical   Broadway: 45

Composer: Ernest G. Schweikert
Lyricist: Frank Reardon
Librettist: Irving Phillips
Producer: Mike Sloane; Paula Stone
Director: Jack Donahue

Choreographer: Bob Hamilton; **Costumes:** Alvin Colt; **Dance Arranger:** Robert Atwood; **Lighting Designer:** George Jenkins; **Musical Director:** Frederick Dvonch; **Orchestrations:** Ted Royal; **Set Design:** George Jenkins

Songs: All Dressed Up; Coax Me; First Time I Spoke of You, The; General Consensus of Opinion [1]; Gentlemen of the Press; How Do You Say Goodbye?; In Times Like These; It's You for Me; Oblivia; Peculiar State of Affairs; Red Letter Day; To Adjust Is a Must; Wish

Cast: Jerome Cowan; Stephen Douglass; Eddie Foy Jr.; Gretchen Wyler

Notes: [1] Out Boston 10/5/57.

3802 • RUMPLESTILTSKIN

OPENED: 05/23/1973   Theatre: Town Hall
Musical   Off-Off-Broadway: 4

Composer: Philip Fleishman; Joan Shepard
Lyricist: Evan Thompson
Librettist: Joan Shepard
Producer: Performing Arts Repertory Theatre; Town Hall
Director: Evan Thompson

Costumes: Jennie Cleaver; **Musical Director:** John Clifton; **Set Design:** John Nelson

Songs: Down By the Mill; Guess My Name; Killer-Diller Miller; Love Match, A; Never; Straw into Gold; Traveling Troubador; What Will You Give Me?; Woman in the Palace, A

Cast: David Burrow; Joan Shepard; Bill Steele; Nancy Temple; Evan Thompson; Chester Thornhill

Notes: Limited engagement.

3803 • RUNAWAY GIRL, A

OPENED: 08/25/1898   Theatre: Daly's
Musical   Broadway: 212

Composer: Ivan Caryll; Lionel Monckton
Lyricist: Harry Greenbank; Aubrey Hopwood
Librettist: Seymour Hicks; Harry Nichols
Producer: Augustin Daly
Director: Augustin Daly

Songs: Beautiful Venice; Boy Guessed Right, The (C/L: Lionel Monckton); Convent Bell, The; Finale Act II; Follow the Man from Cook's (C: Lionel Monckton); No One in the World Like You (C: Alfred D. Cammeyer); Not the Sort of Girl I Care About (C: Lionel Monckton); Opening Chorus; Opening Chorus Act I Scene 2; Opening Chorus Act II; Over the Sea! (C: Lionel Monckton); Pickaninnies, The; Sea-Girt Land of My Home; Singing Girl, The; Sly Cigarette, The (C: Lionel Monckton); Society (C: Lionel Monckton); Soldiers in the Park (C: Lionel Monckton); To Venice; We've Left Barcelona Society; Welcome to the Water Fete; When the Little Pigs Begin to Fly (C: Lionel Monckton; L: Leslie Mayne); You Know

Cast: Virginia Carle; Wilfred Clarke; Cyril Scott; Yvette Violette

Notes: No program available. Songs listed from London vocal score.

3804 RUNAWAY SLAVE

OPENED: 1911
Musical

Songs: If Dreams Are True; Stop, Stop, Stop; That Was Me; There Is No Place Like the Old Folks After All

Cast: Edna Campbell; Edwards and Edwards; Lee and Lee

Notes: No other information available.

3805 • RUNAWAYS, THE (1903)

OPENED: 05/11/1903   Theatre: Casino
Musical   Broadway: 167

Composer: Raymond Hubbell
Lyricist: Addison Burkhardt
Librettist: Addison Burkhardt
Producer: Nixon & Zimmerman; Sam S. Shubert
Director: Gerard Coventry

Choreographer: Sam Marion; **Costumes:** Caroline Seidle; **Musical Director:** Arthur Weld

Songs: Entrance of General Hard Tack; For Thee I'm Sighing; Forever and a Day; Hiawatha; Hints on Love; How to Write a Comic Opera; I Am the Royal Chancellor; I Would Be Your Romeo; If I Were a Bright Little Star; I'm Going Home to Dixie Land; In a General Sort of Way; In Swell Society; Kiss for Each Day in the Week, A; Land I Love, The; Love Is an Ailment; Maiden and the Jay, The (C: William Gould); Miss Susanna from Urbana; My Radiant Fire Fly; Our Cause Is the Cause; Pretty Maid Adelaide; Queen of the Track; Strolling; Suburban Day, The (Suburban Summer Girl, The); Teach Us the Subtle Art of Kissing; To the Island; Tra La, La, La, La, La; Way Down South; Widows Song, The; Yet I'm the Same Little Girl

Cast: Alexander Clark; Dorothy Dorr; Edna Goodrich; Van Rensselaer Wheeler

Notes: Titled CHOW CHOW out of town Chicago.

3806 • RUNAWAYS (1978)

OPENED: 03/09/1978   Theatre: Public
Revue   Off-Broadway: 276

Composer: Elizabeth Swados
Lyricist: Elizabeth Swados
Librettist: Elizabeth Swados
Producer: N.Y. Shakespeare Festival; Joseph Papp
Director: Elizabeth Swados

Costumes: Hilary Rosenfeld; **Lighting Designer:** Jennifer Tipton; **Set Design:** Woods Mackintosh; Douglas W. Schmidt

Songs: Appendectomy; Appendectomy II; Basketball Song, The; Christmas Puppies; Clothes; Current Events; Enterprise; Every Now and Then; Find Me a Hero; Footstep; I Had to Go; I Went Back Home; I Will Not Tell a Soul; In the Sleeping Line; Lazar's Heroes; Let Me Be a Kid; Lonesome of the Road; Lullaby for Luis; Lullaby from Baby to Baby; Minnesota Strip; Mr. Graffiti; Once Upon a Time; Out on the Street; Parent/Kid Dance; Problem After Problem; Revenge Song; Scrynatchkieloosaw; Senoras de la Noche; Sometimes; Song of a Child Prostitute; Spoons; This Is What I Do When I'm Angry; To the Dead of Family Wars; Tra Gog Vo In Dien Whole; Undiscovered Son, The; Untrue Pigeon, The; We Are Not Strangers; We Have to Die?; Where Are Those People Who Did 'Hair'?; Where Do People Go; You Don't Understand; You Have No Heart [1]

Cast: Bernie Allison; Trini Alvarado; Mark Anthony Butler; Ray Contreras; Karen Evans; Jonathan Fieg; Carlo Imperato; Diane Lane; Jon Matthews; Evan Miranda; Nan-Lynn Nelson; Randy Ruiz; David Schechter; Jossie de Guzman

Notes: Moved to the Plymouth Theatre, Broadway 5/13/78 for an additional 199 performances. [1] Cut during Off-Broadway run.

3807 • RUNNIN' DE TOWN

OPENED: 1930
Musical

Composer: James C. Johnson
Lyricist: James C. Johnson
Librettist: Leigh Whipper

Cast: Susan Brown; Sam Cross; Ollie Perkins; Muriel Rahn; Leigh Whipper; Marie Young

Notes: No other information available.

3808 • **RUNNIN' WILD**

OPENED: 10/29/1923   Theatre: Colonial
Musical   Broadway: 167

Composer: James P. Johnson
Lyricist: Cecil Mack [4]
Librettist: Aubrey L. Lyles; Flournoy Miller
Producer: George White

Choreographer: Lyda Webb

Songs: Banjo Land [1]; Charleston; Easy Goin'
Man [3] (C: Turner Layton; L: Darl MacBoyle);
Ghost Recitative; Gingerbrown; Heart Breakin'
Joe [3] (C: Porter Grainger; L: Jo Trent); Jazz
Your Troubles Away; Juba Dance; Keep
Moving; Log Cabin Days; Love Bug;
Old-Fashioned Love; Open Your Heart;
Opening Chorus; Pay Day on Levee; Red Cap
Cappers; Roustabouts; Set 'em Sadie [2]; Sheik
of Alabam' Wed a Brown Skin Vamp, The [1];
Slow and Easy Goin' Man [1]; Snowtime; Song
Birds Quartette; Sun Kist Rose [1]; Swannee
River; Watching the Clock [3] (C: Porter
Grainger; L: Jo Trent)

Cast: Adelaide Hall; Revella Hughes; Aubrey L.
Lyles; Cecil Mack [4]; Flournoy Miller; George
Stamper; Elisabeth Welch

Notes: [1] Out Bronx 1/19/25. [2] Added after
opening. [3] Not in programs. [4] A pseudonym
for R.C. McPherson.

3809 • **RUNNING FOR OFFICE**

OPENED: 04/27/1903   Theatre: 14th St.
Musical   Broadway: 48

Composer: George M. Cohan
Lyricist: George M. Cohan
Librettist: George M. Cohan
Producer: Fred Niblo
Director: George M. Cohan; James Gorman

Musical Director: Charles J. Gebest;
  Orchestrations: Charles J. Gebest

Songs: Always Leave Them Laughing (When You
Say Goodbye) [2]; Elopement, The; Flirtation on
the Beach; Football Boys and Girls, The;
Homeless Girl in Harlem, The [4]; I Want to Go
to Paree, Papa; If I Were Only Mr. Morgan; I'll Be

There in a Public Square; In a One-Night Stand;
Johnny, Get Off the Corner; Kid Days [3];
Reubens on Parade, The; Root for Riley; Sweet
Popularity; Then I'd Be Satisfied with Life [1];
They Are Hypnotized

Cast: George M. Cohan; Helen Cohan; Jerry Cohan;
Josie Cohan; Ethel Levey

Notes: Later reworked as THE HONEY-
MOONERS. [1] Sheet music only. [2] Out
Wilkes-Barre 11/27/05. Later in LITTLE
JOHNNY JONES. [3] Also in THE HONEY-
MOONERS. [4] ASCAP/Library of Congress.

3810 • **RUSSELL PATTERSON'S SKETCH BOOK**

OPENED: 02/06/1960   Theatre: Maidman
Musical   Off-Broadway: 3

Composer: Ruth Cleary Patterson
Librettist: Rube Goldberg; Irwin Hasen; Leo
Kramer; Otto Soglow
Producer: Hudson Faussett; Russell Patterson
Director: Hudson Faussett

Choreographer: Nelle Fisher; **Costumes:** William
Ritman; **Lighting Designer:** William Ritman;
Musical Director: Ruth Cleary Patterson; **Set
Design:** William Ritman

Songs: Dancing to the Rhythm of the Raindrops
(L: Gladys Shelley); I Want to Take 'Em Off for
Norman Rockwell (L: Les Kramer); La Calinda
(L: Gladys Shelley); Let's Not Get Married
(L: George Blake; Les Kramer); May in
Manhattan (L: Tom Romano); My First Love
(L: Fred Heider); Singing Wheels (L: Fred
Heider); Sweet Charity (L: Les Kramer); That's
What I Got Not Listening to My Mother
(L: Floria Vestoff); That's Why I'm Here Tonight
(L: Les Kramer); We Know What You Want and
We Got It (L: Floria Vestoff); When the Wings of
the Wind Take Me Home (L: Les Kramer);
Wonderful Way of Life, A (L: Les Karmer; Floria
Vestoff)

Cast: Jerry Bergen; Phyllis Ford; Anita Gillette;
Ralph Lowe

3811 • **RUTHLESS!**

OPENED: 05/06/1992   Theatre: Players
Musical   Off-Broadway: 302

Composer: Marvin Laird
Lyricist: Joel Paley
Librettist: Joel Paley
Producer: Musical Theater Works
Director: Joel Paley

Costumes: Gail Cooper-Hecht; **Lighting Designer:** Kenneth Posner; **Musical Director:** Marvin Laird; **Set Design:** James Noone

Songs: Angel Mom; Born to Entertain; Eave's Song; I Hate Musicals; Kisses and Hugs; Lippy Song, The; Look at Me; Ruthless!; Talent; Third Grade; Tina, My Daughter; Tina's Mother; To Play This Part; Where Tina Gets It From

Cast: Joanne Baum; Laura Bundy; Donna English; Denise Lor; Susan Mansur; Joel Vig

S

3812 • SADIE LOVE

OPENED: 11/29/1915   Theatre: Gaiety
Play   Broadway: 80

Composer: Earl Carroll
Lyricist: Earl Carroll
Author: Avery Hopwood
Producer: Oliver Morosco
Director: Robert Milton

Cast: Betty Callish; Marjorie Rambeau; Franklyn Underwood; Pedro de Cordoba

Notes: No song listed in program.

3813 • SADIE THOMPSON

OPENED: 11/16/1944   Theatre: Alvin
Musical   Broadway: 60

Composer: Vernon Duke
Lyricist: Howard Dietz
Librettist: Howard Dietz; Rouben Mamoulian
Producer: A.P. Waxman
Director: Rouben Mamoulian

Choreographer: Edward Caton; **Costumes:** Motley; **Musical Director:** Charles Sanford; **Orchestrations:** Charles Cooke; Vernon Duke; Walter Eiger; Joe Glover; John Klein; Irving Landau; Julian Work; **Set Design:** Boris Aronson; **Vocal Arranger:** Vernon Duke

Songs: Any Woman Who Is Willing Will Do [1]; Barrel of Beads; Below the Equator; (You'll Be) Born All Over Again; Dance to the Sun God; Dancing Lesson; Dancing Politely [1]; Deep Down Inside You [1]; Devil in You Is Strong, The [2]; Fisherman's Wharf; Fool That I Was [2]; From the Cradle to the Grave [2]; Garden in the Sky; Happy Again; Heathen; Hurdy Gurdy [1]; I Lived in a House with a Piano; If You Can't Get the Love You Want; Join the Marines [1]; Jungle Dance; Key to the Gates, The [1]; Life's a Funny Present from Someone; Love I Long For, The; Men's Dance [2]; Mountains of Nebraska Ballet, The; My Handsome; Poor As a Church Mouse; Sailing at Midnight; Siren of the Tropics; Trio;

Weeping Sky, The [1]; When You Live on an Island; Where the Sun God Walks [2]; You U.S.A. [1]; You're Dreamlike [3]

Cast: Ralph Dumke; Lansing Hatfield; June Havoc

Notes: The play RAIN was based on a short story "Miss Sadie Thompson" by W. Somerset Maugham. Ethel Merman left this show during rehearsals. [1] Out Philadelphia 10/30/44. [2] Not used. [3] Not used. Also not used in ZIEGFELD FOLLIES OF 1943.

3814 • SAFARI 300

OPENED: 07/12/1972   Theatre: Mayfair
Revue   Off-Broadway: 29

Librettist: Tony Preston
Producer: Richie Havens
Director: Hugh Gittens

Choreographer: Larl Becham; **Costumes:** Lee Lynn; **Lighting Designer:** David Adams; **Musical Director:** Scat Wilson; **Set Design:** Bob Olsen

Songs: Adunde; Akiwawa; Baron Samedi; Black Rape; Cakewalk; Cotton Club Revue; Doin' It by the Book; Dombaye; Get It Together; Goin' to Chicago; Hallucinations; It's Rainin'; Johnny Too Bad; Little Black Baby; Man and His Message, The; My Children Searching; 1950's Singing Group; 1960's Twist; O Negros Bahianos; Oratorio; Prayer; Return to Africa; Rock 1975; Royal Court Dance; Sage; Singing Drums; Size Places; Slave Auction; Song of Sorrow; Song of Troubles; Soon I'll Be Done; This Little Light; Voodoo; Waiting Song; What Have We Done; World Keeps Turnin'; Younger Men Grow Older

Cast: Ernest Andrews; Larl Becham; Joyce Griffen; Holly Hamilton; Onike Lee; Fredi Orange; Andre Robinson; Tad Truesdale; Grenna Whitaker; Dorian Williams

Notes: Music and lyrics not credited in program.

3815 • SAIL AWAY

OPENED: 10/03/1961   Theatre: Broadhurst
Musical   Broadway: 167

Composer: Noel Coward
Lyricist: Noel Coward
Librettist: Noel Coward
Producer: Bonard Productions
Director: Noel Coward

Choreographer: Joe Layton; **Costumes:** Helene
Pons; Oliver Smith; **Dance Arranger:** Peter Matz;
Lighting Designer: Peggy Clark; **Musical
Director:** Peter Matz; **Orchestrations:** Irwin
Kostal; **Set Design:** Oliver Smith; **Vocal
Arranger:** Fred Werner

Songs: Beatnik Love Affair; Bronxville Darby
and Joan [5]; Come to Me; Customer's Always
Right [4]; Don't Turn Away from Love; Go Slow,
Johnny; I Am No Good at Love [6]; Later Than
Spring; Little One's ABC, The; Passenger's
Always Right, The [4]; Sail Away [3]; Somethin'
You Gotta Find Out Yourself [1]; Something
Very Strange; This Is a Changing World [2]; This
Is a Night for Lovers [2]; Useful Phrases; When
You Want Me; Where Shall I Find Him?; Why
Do the Wrong People Travel?; You're a Long,
Long Way from America

Cast: Charles Braswell; Grover Dale; Margalo
Gilmore; Patricia Hardy; Alice Pearce; Keith
Prentice; James Pritchett; Dan Siretta; Elaine
Stritch; Richard Woods

Notes: [1] Cut. [2] Cut. From PACIFIC 1860,
London. [3] Originally in ACE OF CLUBS,
London. [4] Same music. [5] Cut. Added to
London version. [6] Cut Boston prior to opening.

3816 • SAILOR'S DELIGHT

OPENED: 11/22/1954
Play   Closed out of town

Author: Peter Blackmore
Producer: Huntington Hartford; Richard Skinner
Director: Arthur Sircom

Costumes: Gene Coffin; **Lighting Designer:** Paul
Bertelsen; **Set Design:** Paul Bertelsen

Songs: I Wouldn't Know (C: Richard Myers;
L: Jack Lawrence)

Cast: Philippa Bevans; Eva Gabor; Paul McGrath

3817 • SAINTS

OPENED: 06/30/1976
Musical   Off-Off-Broadway: 10

Composer: William Penn
Lyricist: Merle Kessler
Librettist: Merle Kessler
Producer: Steve Kimball
Director: Edward Berkeley

Source: SAINTS (Novel: Merle Kessler);
Choreographer: Nora Peterson; **Musical
Director:** Bob Goldstone

Songs: Bastard for the Lord; Death Comes Like a
Thief; I Am the Sign; I Believe in Survival; I Can't
Walk on Water; In the Sweet By and By; It's
Hard I Know; Ladies Come from Baltimore, The;
Let It Fall; Mama Lazarus; Night Is a Weapon;
O My Soul; Old Rabbit Hole, The; Remember
Love; See the River Flow; Stand By Me; Sweet
Jesus, Blessed Savior; This Darkness; What Will
Daddy Say; Years Are Burning, The

Cast: Dennis Bailey; Jill Eikenberry; Dean
Pitchford; Marti Rolph

3818 • SALAD DAYS

OPENED: 11/10/1958   Theatre: Barbizon-Plaza
Musical   Off-Broadway: 80

Composer: Julian Slade
Lyricist: Dorothy Reynolds; Julian Slade
Librettist: Dorothy Reynolds; Julian Slade
Producer: Nicholas Benton; Stanley Flink
Director: Barry Morse

Choreographer: Alan Lund; Blanche Lund;
Costumes: Clare Jeffrey; **Musical Director:**
Gordon Kushner; **Orchestrations:** John Fenwick;
Gordon Kushner; Bruce Snell; **Set Design:**
Murray Laufer

Songs: Cleopatra; Don's Chorus (The Things That
Are Done By a Don), The; Find Yourself Some-
thing to Do; Hush-Hush; I Sit in the Sun; It's Easy
to Sing; Let's Take a Stroll through London [1];
Oh, Look at Me!; Out of Breath; Sand in My Eyes;
Saucer Song, The; Time of My Life, The; We
Don't Understand Our Children; We Said We
Wouldn't Look Back; We're Looking for a Piano

Cast: Helen Burns; Eric Christmas; Richard Easton; Barbara Franklin; Tom Kneebone

Notes: [1] Though in U.S. production, this song was cut from the original London version.

3819 • SALLY

OPENED: 12/21/1920   Theatre: New Amsterdam
Musical   Broadway: 570

Composer: Jerome Kern
Lyricist: Clifford Grey; P.G. Wodehouse
Librettist: Guy Bolton
Producer: Florenz Ziegfeld
Director: Edward Royce

Source: LITTLE THING, THE [5] (Musical: P.G. Wodehouse); **Choreographer:** Edward Royce; **Costumes:** Alice O'Neil; **Musical Director:** Gus Salzer; **Set Design:** Joseph Urban

Songs: At the Play [2]; Butterfly Ballet (inst.) (C: Victor Herbert); Joan of Arc (You Can't Keep a Good Girl Down) (L: P.G. Wodehouse); Little Church Around the Corner (L: P.G. Wodehouse); Look for the Silver Lining [3] (L: B.G. DeSylva); Lorelei, The [4] (L: Anne Caldwell); Nervous Wrecks [2]; (It's) The Night Time [2]; On with the Dance; Opening Ensemble; Sally [1]; Schnitza Komisski, The; Social Game, The; This Little Girl; Way Down East; Whip-Poor-Will [3] (L: B.G. DeSylva); Wild Rose, The

Cast: Jack Barker; Walter Catlett; Leon Errol; Irving Fisher; Mary Hay; Marilyn Miller; Stanley Ridges; Betty Williams

Notes: [1] Same music as "Catamarang" from KING OF CADONIA. [2] Out Baltimore prior to opening. [3] Cut from ZIP GOES A MILLION. [4] Cut from THE NIGHT BOAT. [5] An unproduced musical.

3820 • SALLY IN OUR ALLEY

OPENED: 08/29/1902   Theatre: Broadway
Musical   Broadway: 67

Composer: Ludwig Englander
Lyricist: George V. Hobart
Librettist: George V. Hobart
Producer: George W. Lederer
Director: George W. Lederer

Costumes: C.F. Siedle; **Set Design:** D. Frank Dodge; Edward G. Unitt

Songs: Bill, the Bill Poster; Come Take a Stroll with Me; Ellen, Ellen; Girlie with the Baby Stare, The (C: William H. Penn; L: Ernest Hanegan); I Want to Be a Soldier Lady; Microbes in a Kiss, The; My Matilda (C: William F. Peters; L: Henry Blossom); My Queen of Ping Pong; Nora Ryan; Ping Pong, Ping; Sally (C/L: Will E. Haines; Harry Leon; Leo Towers); Sally in Our Alley (C/L: Henry Carey); Sport, Joke and Two Spot; Under the Bamboo Tree (C: J. Rosamond Johnson; L: Bob Cole); When I Am Yours Dear; When It's All Goin' Out and Nothin' Comin' In [1] (C/L: James Weldon Johnson; George Walker; Bert Williams); When the Troupe Comes Back to Town (C: Harry Von Tilzer; L: George Totten Smith); Whistling Bill; You Are My Fiancee

Cast: Marie Cahill; Georgia Caine; Harry Farleigh; Joseph W. Herbert; Georgia Kelly; Dan McAvoy

Notes: Program did not list any Englander/Hobart songs, only interpolations. [1] Johnson credited on sheet music as "Words Revised By."

3821 • SALLY, IRENE AND MARY

OPENED: 09/04/1922   Theatre: Casino
Musical   Broadway: 318

Composer: J. Fred Coots
Lyricist: Raymond Klages
Librettist: Eddie Dowling; Cyrus Wood
Producer: Messrs. Shubert
Director: Frank Smithson

Choreographer: Allan K. Foster; **Musical Director:** Claude MacArthur

Songs: After the Clouds Roll By [1]; Clouds Roll By Dance; Do You Remember?; Electricity; How I Missed You, Mary; I Wonder Why; Jimmie [2]; Kid Days; Old Fashioned Gown [1]; Opportunity; Our Home, Sweet Home; Pals; Peacock Alley; Right Boy Comes Along; Something in Here; Stage Door Johnnies; Time Will Tell; Until You Say Yes; We Are Waiting; Wedding Time; When a Regular Girl Loves a Regular Boy [1]

Cast: Jean Brown; Eddie Dowling; Kitty Flynn; Edna Moon

Notes: Previous to this show there were the Broadway hits SALLY by Kern, IRENE by Tierney and MARY by Hirsch. Note also that some of the song titles in this show are reminiscent of songs in the previous shows. [1] Out Asbury Park 8/21/22. [2] Sheet music only.

3822 • SALUTA

OPENED: 08/28/1934 Theatre: Imperial
Musical Broadway: 40

Composer: Frank D'Armond
Lyricist: Will Morrissey
Librettist: Eugene Conrad; Maurice Marks; Will Morrissey
Producer: Arthur Lipper[2]
Director: Frank Melin; Edwin Saulpaugh

Choreographer: Boots McKenna; **Costumes:** John N. Booth Jr.; **Musical Director:** John McManus; **Set Design:** Hugh Willoughby

Songs: Author, The [1]; Ballo Moderno; Black Horse Tavern; Great Dictator and Me, The; Help the Seamen; I'll Produce for You; Italia [1]; I've Got the Right to Moan [1]; Just Say the Word (L: Milton Berle); La Vita; Mi! Mi!; Night; Simple Love Song [1]; Tarantella Rhythm; There's a Chill in the Air; Walking the Deck; We Incorporated (L: Milton Berle; Maurice Sigler); You Have My Heart

Cast: Ann Barrie; Milton Berle; Chaz Chase; Dudley Clements; William Hargrave; Edward J. Lambert; Maxcellas, The; Felicia Sorel; Demetrios Vilan; Milton Watson; Thelma White

Notes: [1] Out Atlantic City 8/13/34. [2] Used pseudonym R.A. Reppil.

3823 • SALUTE TO SPRING

OPENED: 07/12/1937
Musical Closed out of town

Composer: Frederick Loewe
Lyricist: Earle Crooker
Librettist: Earle Crooker
Director: Zeke Colvan

Choreographer: Theodore Adolphus; Al White Jr.; **Musical Director:** George Hirst; **Set Design:** Raymond Sovey

Songs: Another Lovely April Day; Extraordinary; High Pressure; Hurdy-Gurdy; Law Is Law; Life Is Tough; Love Is Love; One Robin Doesn't Make a Spring [2]; Rhumba; Salute to Spring; Somehow; Time Off for Love; Very Charming Spot, A; Waltz Was Born in Vienna, A [1]

Cast: Annamary Dickey; Gus Howard; Earle MacVeigh; Lew Parker; Helen Raymond; Guy Robertson

Notes: St. Louis program used. *See LIFE OF THE PARTY.* [1] From THE ILLUSTRATOR'S SHOW. [2] Later in LIFE OF THE PARTY.

3824 • SALVATION

OPENED: 09/24/1969 Theatre: Jan Hus
Playhouse
Musical Off-Broadway: 239

Composer: C.C. Courtney; Peter Link
Lyricist: C.C. Courtney; Peter Link
Librettist: C.C. Courtney; Peter Link
Producer: David Black
Director: Paul Aaron

Choreographer: Katheryn Posin; **Musical Director:** John Bauman; **Orchestrations:** Kirk Nurock; **Set Design:** Joan Larkey

Songs: Back to Genesis; Ballin'; Daedalus; Deuteronomy XVII Verse 2; Footloose Youth and Fancy Free; For Ever; Gina; Honest Confession Is Good for the Soul; If You Let Me Make Love to You Then Why Can't I Touch You; In Between; Let the Moment Slip By; Let's Get Lost in Now; Lost in the Catacombs [1]; 1001; Salvation; Schwartz; There Ain't No Flies on Jesus; Tomorrow Is the First Day of the Rest of My Life

Cast: Yolande Bavan; C.C. Courtney; Marta Heflin; Peter Link; Joe Morton; Anne Rachael; Chapman Roberts

Notes: [1] Cut prior to opening.

3825 • SAMBO

OPENED: 12/12/1969 Theatre: Public
Musical Off-Broadway: 37

Composer: Ron Steward; Neal Tate
Lyricist: Ron Steward

Librettist: Ron Steward
Producer: N.Y. Shakespeare Festival; Joseph Papp
Director: Gerald Freedman

Choreographer: Tommy Jonsen; **Costumes:** Milo Morrow; **Lighting Designer:** Martin Aronstein; **Musical Director:** Neal Tate; **Set Design:** Marjorie Kellogg; Ming Cho Lee

Songs: Aries; Ask and You Shall Receive; Astrology; Baddest Mammyjammy; Be Black; Black Man; Boy Blue; Come On Home; Do You Care Too Much?; Eternal Virgin, The; Get an Education; Hey Boy; I Am Child; I Could Dig You; Let's Go Down; Mama Always Said; Peace Love and Good Damn; Piscean, The; Pretty Flower; Sambo Was a Bad Boy; Sing a Song of Sambo; Son of Africa; Untogether Cinderella; Young Enough to Dream

Cast: Gerri Dean; Janice Lynn Montgomery; Ron Steward; Hattie Winston

3826 • SAMBO GIRL

Notes: *See THE BLONDE IN BLACK.*

3827 • SAMPLES

OPENED: 1915
Revue   London

Librettist: Harry Grattan
Producer: Andre Charlot

Choreographer: George Shurley; **Costumes:** Gerald Davis; Janine; **Set Design:** Laverdet; Marc-Henri; George de Feure

Songs: Broken Doll, A (C: James W. Tate; L: Clifford Harris); Clarinet and the Coronet (C: Melville Gideon; L: Harold Atteridge); Dancing Jubilee, The (C: Nat D. Ayer); Dresses (C: Robert Gattinguer); How Things Have Changed (C: Ernest R. Ball; L: Earl Carroll); I Work Eight Hours, Sleep Eight Hours, That Leaves Eight Hours for Love (C: Ted Snyder; L: Bert Kalmar; Edgar Leslie); I'm a Lonesome Melody (C: George W. Meyer; L: Joe Young); Moana Loa (dance) (C: Melville Gideon); My Bird of Paradise (C/L: Irving Berlin); One on the Drum (C: Nat D. Ayer; L: Unknown); Peter (C: Melville Gideon; Elsie Muntz; L: Dan Lipton); Providing (C: Alfred Bryan; L: Herman Paley); Song with a Chorus, A (C: Edward Jones;

L: Unknown); When I Leave the World Behind (C/L: Irving Berlin); Winter Nights (C: Jean Schwartz; L: Grant Clarke)

Notes: No other information available.

3828 • SAN TOY, OR THE EMPEROR'S OWN

OPENED: 10/01/1900   Theatre: Daly's
Musical   Broadway: 65

Composer: Sidney Jones
Lyricist: Harry Greenbank; Adrian Ross
Librettist: Edward Morton
Producer: Augustin Daly Musical Co.
Director: Edwin Price; B.D. Stevens

Choreographer: Willie Warde; **Musical Director:** John J. Braham

Songs: A.B.C.; All I Want Is a Little Bit of Fun [2] (C: Lionel Monckton); Back to London [1]; Butterfly, The [1]; By Our Majesty's Monarch Command; Catchy Coo [3] (C/L: Herbert Shelley); Chinese Soje Man (C: Lionel Monckton); Emperor's Own, The; Entrance of English Visitors [1]; Finale Act II [1]; I Mean to Introduce It into China; I'm So Fond of a Little Bit of Fun; It's Nice to Be a Boy Sometimes (C: Lionel Monckton); Lady's Maid (C: Lionel Monckton); Little China Maid, The; (Love Has Come from) Lotus Land; Make It Snappy [4] (C/L: Patrick Barrow); Mandarin, The; Moon, The; Mousetrap, The [3] (C: Paul Rubens); One in the World, The [1]; Pas Seul (inst.) [1]; Petals of the Plum Tree, The [1]; Plenty Little Chinee; Posey from Over the Sea, A [1]; Pretty Little Chinee [3]; Private Tommy Atkins (C/L: L.S. Potter); Pynka Pong; Rhoda and Her Pagoda (C: Lionel Monckton); Samee Gamee; Six Little Wives; Somebody [3]; We Have Come to See; We'll Keep the Feast in Pynka Pong; We're the Cream of Courtly Creatures; When He Goey La-di-da [3] (C: Paul Rubens); When You Are Wed to Me; Whole Story, The [1]

Cast: Marie Celeste; Wilfred Clarke; George K. Fortesque; James T. Powers; Melville Stewart; Flora Zabelle

Notes: [1] From London vocal score only. [2] In London production only. [3] Added after London opening. [4] In London revival (1902).

3829 • SANCHO PANZA

OPENED: 11/26/1923   Theatre: Hudson
Musical   Broadway: 40

Composer: Hugo Felix
Lyricist: Hugo Felix
Librettist: Melchoir Lengyil
Producer: Russell Janney
Director: Richard Boleslavsky

Source: DON QUIXOTE (Novel: Miguel de Cervantes); **Costumes:** James Reynolds; **Musical Director:** Rupert Graves; **Set Design:** James Reynolds

Cast: Robert Robson; Otis Skinner

Notes: No songs listed in program.

3830 • SANCOCHO

OPENED: 03/28/1979   Theatre: Public
Musical   Off-Broadway: 7

Composer: Jimmy Justice; Ramiro Ramirez
Lyricist: Jimmy Justice; Ramiro Ramirez
Librettist: Ramiro Ramirez
Producer: N.Y. Shakespeare Festival; Joseph Papp
Director: Miguel Godreau

Choreographer: Miguel Godreau; **Costumes:** Frank J. Boros; **Lighting Designer:** Nananne Porcher; **Musical Director:** Jimmy Justice; **Set Design:** Frank J. Boros

Songs: Arrival, The; Ay Mi Do; Chair Dance, The; Danza and Danzon; First Jam Session, The; Get Off on Somebody Else; Give Me the Love; Going Out, The; I Don't Want to Hear No But, But, But; Las Siete Potencias and Despoho; Love Duet, The; My Country 'Tis of Thee; Purification, The; Rhythm of the Line, The; Sancocho; Second Jam Session, The; Slave Scene, The; Touch Me; You Can't Beat the System

Cast: Ka-Ron Brown; Hector Jaime Mercado; Dan Strayhorn

Notes: No songs listed in program.

3831 • SANDHOG

OPENED: 11/29/1954   Theatre: Phoenix
Musical   Off-Broadway: 48

Composer: Earl Robinson
Lyricist: Waldo Salt
Librettist: Earl Robinson; Waldo Salt
Producer: Phoenix Theatre; Rachel Productions
Director: Howard Da Silva

Source: ST. COLUMBA AND THE RIVER (Story: Theodore Dreiser); **Choreographer:** Sophie Maslow; **Costumes:** Toni Ward; **Lighting Designer:** Howard Bay; **Musical Director:** Ben Steinberg; **Orchestrations:** Hershy Kay; **Set Design:** Howard Bay

Songs: By the Glenside; Come and Be Married; Come Down; Fugue on a Hot Afternoon in a Small Flat; Good Old Days; Greathead Shield; Hey Joe; High Air; Johnny O; Johnny's Cursing Song; Katie O'Sullivan; Ma, Ma, Where's My Dad?; Oh, Oh, Oh, O'Sullivan; Ring Iron; Sandhog Song; Sing Sorrow; Some Said They Were Crazy; Song of the Bends; Stand Back; Sweat Song; T-W-I-N-S; 28 Men; Waiting for the Men; Work Song; You Want to Mourn

Cast: Leon Bibb; David Brooks; Jack Cassidy; Eliot Feld; Alice Ghostley; Michael Kermoyan; Betty Oakes

3832 • SANDS HOTEL COPA ROOM SHOW

OPENED: 1958   Theatre: Copa Room
Revue   Nightclub

Composer: James Van Heusen
Lyricist: Sammy Cahn

Songs: Here Comes Another Song About Texas (Pass the Cotton, Pass the Cotton); Sands Hotel Song

Notes: Las Vegas show. No other information available.

3833 • SANTA CLAUS IS COMIN' TO TOWN

OPENED: 12/13/1970   Theatre: ABC
TV Musical

Composer: Maury Laws
Lyricist: Jules Bass

Songs: Be Prepared to Pay; First Toymaker to the King; My World Is Beginning Today; Put One

Foot in Front of the Other; Santa Claus Is Comin' to Town (C: J. Fred Coots; L: Haven Gillespie); What Better Way to Tell You

Voices: Fred Astaire; Paul Frees; Mickey Rooney; Keenan Wynn

3834 • SANTA MARIA
OPENED: 09/24/1896   Theatre: Olympia
Musical   Broadway: 100

Composer: Oscar Hammerstein I
Lyricist: Oscar Hammerstein I
Librettist: Oscar Hammerstein I
Producer: Oscar Hammerstein I

Cast: Edna May; James T. Powers; Julius Steger; Camille d'Arville

Notes: No program available.

3835 • SAP OF LIFE, THE
OPENED: 10/02/1961   Theatre: One Sheridan
                                        Square
Musical   Off-Broadway: 49

Composer: William Francisco; David Shire
Lyricist: Richard Maltby Jr.
Producer: Quartet Productions
Director: William Francisco

Costumes: John Conklin; **Dance Arranger:** David Shire; Julian Stein; **Lighting Designer:** Peter Hunt; **Musical Director:** Ted Simons; **Orchestrations:** David Shire; Julian Stein; **Set Design:** John Conklin; **Vocal Arranger:** David Shire; Julian Stein

Songs: Charmed Life; Children Have It Easy; Family; Farewell; Fill Up Your Life with Sunshine; Good Morning; Hero's Love, A; Love of Your Life, The; Mind Over Matter; New Life Coming, A; Saturday Morning; She Loves Me Not; Time and Time Again; Watching the Big Parade Go By [2]; Word Is Love, The [3]

Cast: Jack Bittner; Jerry Dodge; Kenneth Nelson; Dina Paisner

Notes: [1] Cut prior to opening. [2] Later in STARTING HERE, STARTING NOW. [3] Cut prior to opening. Later in STARTING HERE, STARTING NOW.

3836 • SARAFINA!
OPENED: 01/28/1988   Theatre: Cort
Musical   Broadway: 597

Composer: Mbongeni Ngema
Librettist: Mbongeni Ngema
Producer: Lincoln Center Theater
Director: Mbongeni Ngema

Conductor: Ndaba Mhlongo; **Costumes:** Sarah Roberts; **Dance Arranger:** Hugh Masekela; Mbongeni Ngema; **Lighting Designer:** Mannie Manim; **Set Design:** Sarah Roberts; **Vocal Arranger:** Hugh Masekela; Mbongeni Ngema

Songs: Africa Burning in the Sun (C/L: Hugh Masekela); Afunani Amaphoyisa eSoweto? (What Is That Army Doing in Soweto?); Bring Back Nelson Mandela (C/L: Hugh Masekela); Excuse Me Baby, Please If You Don't Mind Baby, Thank You (C/L: Hugh Masekela); Freedom Is Coming Tomorrow; Give Us Power; Isizwe (The Nation Is Dying); Kilimanjaro; Lord's Prayer, The (C/L: Traditional); Mama; Meeting Tonight (C/L: Hugh Masekela); Niyayibona Lento Engiyibonayo (Do You See What I See?) (C/L: Traditional); Nkosi Sikeleli'Afrika (C/L: Traditional); Olayithi (It's All Right); Sarafina (C/L: Hugh Masekela); Sechaba (C/L: Hugh Masekela); Stimela Sasezola; Talking About Love (C/L: Hugh Masekela; Mbongeni Ngema); Uyamemeza Ungoma; We Are Guerrillas (C/L: Traditional); We Will Fight for Our Land; Wololo! (C/L: Traditional); Yes! Mistress It's a Pity (C/L: Hugh Masekela; Mbongeni Ngema); Zbuyile Emasisweni (It's Finally Happening)

Cast: Khumbuzle Diamini; Ntomb'khona Diamini; Leleti Khumalo; Mhlathi Khuzwayo; Nhlanhla Ngema; Thandekile Nhlanhla

Notes: Moved from Lincoln Center.

3837 • SARATOGA
OPENED: 12/07/1959   Theatre: Winter Garden
Musical   Broadway: 80

Composer: Harold Arlen
Lyricist: Johnny Mercer
Librettist: Morton Da Costa
Producer: Robert Fryer
Director: Morton Da Costa

Source: SARATOGA TRUNK (Novel: Edna Ferber); **Choreographer:** Ralph Beaumont; **Costumes:** Cecil Beaton; **Dance Arranger:** Genevieve Pitot; **Lighting Designer:** Jean Rosenthal; **Musical Director:** Jerry Arlen; **Orchestrations:** Philip J. Lang; **Set Design:** Cecil Beaton; **Vocal Arranger:** Herbert Greene

Songs: Al Fresco [1]; Bon Appetit [1]; Countin' Our Chickens; Cure, The; Dog Eat Dog; Gamblers, The (dance); Game of Poker, A; Gettin' a Man (C: Johnny Mercer); Goose Never Be a Peacock; Have You Heard? (Gossip Song); Here Goes Nothing [3]; I'll Be Respectable; I'm Headed for Big Things [1]; Lessons in Love [1]; Love Held Lightly; Man in My Life, The; Men Who Run the Country, The (C: Johnny Mercer); One Step, Two Step; Parks of Paris, The [2]; Petticoat High; Polka, The (dance); Promenade (Street Cries); Railroad Fight (dance); Reading the News [1]; Saratoga; Why Fight This? (C: Johnny Mercer); Work Songs [2]; You for Me [1]; You or No One [4]

Cast: Carol Brice; Warde Donovan; Truman Gaige; Richard Graham; Howard Keel; Edith King; Carol Lawrence; James Millhollin; Odette Myrtil; Augie Rios; Tun Tun

Notes: [1] Cut prior to opening. [2] Cut prior to opening. Music used as incidental scoring. [3] Cut. Same music as "You or No One." [4] Same music as "Here Goes Nothing."

3838 • SARAVA

OPENED: 02/23/1979   Theatre: Mark Hellinger
Musical   Broadway: 140

Composer: Mitch Leigh
Lyricist: N. Richard Nash
Librettist: N. Richard Nash
Producer: Eugene V. Wolsk
Director: Rick Atwell

Source: DONA FLOR AND HER TWO HUSBANDS (Novel: Jorge Amado); **Choreographer:** Rick Atwell; **Costumes:** Santo Loquasto; **Dance Arranger:** Dom Salvador; **Lighting Designer:** David F. Segal; **Musical Director:** David Friedman; **Orchestrations:** Daniel Troob; **Set Design:** Santo Loquasto; **Vocal Arranger:** David Friedman

Songs: Hosanna; I'm Looking for a Man; Makulele; Muito Bom; Nothing's Missing; Play

the Queen; Remember; Sarava; Simple Man, A; Single Life, A; Take Love [1]; Vadinho Is Gone; Viva a Vida; We're Love [1]; Which Way Do I Go?; You Do

Cast: P.J. Benjamin; Tovah Feldshuh; Michael Ingram

Notes: [1] Cut before opening.

339 • SARI

OPENED: 01/13/1914   Theatre: Liberty
Musical   Broadway: 151

Composer: Emmerich Kalman
Lyricist: C.C.S. Cushing; E.P. Heath
Librettist: C.C.S. Cushing; E.P. Heath
Producer: Henry W. Savage
Director: George Marion

Source: DER ZIGEUNERPRIMAS (Musical: Fritz Grunbaum; Emmerich Kalman; Julius Wilhelm); **Costumes:** Albertine Randall Wheelan

Songs: Contest, The; Follow Me; Ha-Za-Za; Long Live the King (Vive le Roi); Love Has Wings; Love's Own Sweet Song; Marry Me; My Faithful Stradivari; Paris? (Oh My! Yes Dear); Pick a Husband; Simple Little Village Maid; Softly Through the Summer Night; Stop It, Stop It; There's No Place Like Home with You; Time, Oh Time You Tyrant King; Triumphant Youth; With Lowered Head

Cast: Harry Davenport; Mitzi Hajos; Van Rensselaer Wheeler

3840 • SATCHMO: AMERICA'S MUSICAL LEGEND

OPENED: 07/14/1987
Musical   Closed out of town

Composer: Jerry Bilik
Lyricist: Jerry Bilik
Librettist: Jerry Bilik
Producer: Kenneth Feld
Director: Jerry Bilik

Choreographer: Maurice Hines; **Costumes:** Judy Dearing; **Dance Arranger:** William Pruyn; **Lighting Designer:** Thomas Skelton; **Set Design:** Edward Burbridge; **Vocal Arranger:** William Pruyn

Songs: After You've Gone [1] (C: Turner Layton; L: Henry Creamer); All for You, Louis (C/L: Unknown); Back Home Again in Indiana [1] (C: James F. Hanley; L: Ballard Macdonald); Bamboula; Basin Street Blues [1] (C/L: Spencer Williams); By the Waters of Minnetonka [1] (C: Thurlow Lieurance; L: J.M. Cavanass); Callin' the Children Home; Chicago Jazz; Daisy's Blues; Dippermouth Blues [1] (C/L: Louis Armstrong; King Oliver); Do You Know What It Means to Miss New Orleans [1] (C: Louis Alter; L: Edgar Leslie); Heebie Jeebies [1] (C/L: Boyd Atkins); Hello, Dolly [2] (C/L: Jerry Herman); Home, Sweet Home [1] (C/L: Traditional); Hoodlums and Whores; I'll Be Glad When You're Dead You Rascal You [1] (C/L: Sam Theard); Jeepers Creepers [1] (C: Harry Warren; L: Johnny Mercer); Love, It's Not Easy; Mack the Knife [3] (C: Kurt Weill; L: Marc Blitzstein; Bertolt Brecht); New Year's in New Orleans; Red Beans and Rice; Royal Garden Blues (inst.) [1] (C/L: Clarence Williams; Spencer Williams); St. Louis Blues [1] (C/L: W.C. Handy); Struttin' with Some Barbecue (inst.) [1] (C: Louis Armstrong); This Train Is Bound for Glory [1] (C/L: Woody Guthrie; Traditional); Trading Fours; Trading Fours — Prelude; Trumpet Rag (inst.); When It's Sleepy Time Down South [1] (C/L: Clarence Muse; Leon Rene; Otis Rene); When the Saints Go Marching In [1] (C/L: Traditional)

Cast: Matilda A. Haywood; James Rowan; Byron Stripling

Notes: [1] Not written for this show. [2] Not written for this show. From HELLO, DOLLY! [3] Not written for this show. Written for THE THREEPENNY OPERA.

3841 • SATINS AND SPURS

OPENED: 09/12/1954   Theatre: NBC
TV Musical

Composer: Ray Evans; Jay Livingston
Lyricist: Ray Evans; Jay Livingston
Librettist: William Friedberg; Max Liebman
Producer: Max Liebman
Director: Max Liebman

Arrangements: Irwin Kostal; Nelson Riddle; **Choreographer:** Charles O'Curran; **Costumes:** Paul duPont; **Lighting Designer:** Jim Gibbings; **Musical Director:** Charles Sanford; **Set Design:** Frederick Fox

Songs: Back Home; Chihuahua Choo-Choo; I've Had Enough; Little Rock Roll; Nobody Cares; Satins and Spurs; Sexy Saddle; Whoop-Diddy-Ay; Wildcat Smathers; You're So Right for Me [2]

Cast: Genevieve; Betty Hutton; Kevin McCarthy[1]; Mary Ellen Moylan; Neva Patterson; Guy Raymond; Josh Wheeler

Notes: Original television musical. [1] Dubbed by Earl Wrightson. [2] Later in OH CAPTAIN!

3842 • SATIRES OF 1920

OPENED: 1920
Revue   Closed out of town

Composer: Fanchon & Marco
Lyricist: Fanchon & Marco
Librettist: Jean C. Havez
Producer: Fanchon & Marco

Costumes: Miss Fanchon; **Musical Director:** Reuben Wolff

Songs: Ain't We Got Fun (C: Richard A. Whiting; L: Raymond B. Egan; Gus Kahn); Big-Hearted Ned; Bragging Song; Breaking Into the Movies; For No Reason Whatsoever; I Dun-No-Wat, The [1]; I Want to Meet You Some Day in California [1]; Little Nell; Lo! Hear the Gentle Lark; Love a Gypsy Knows, The [1]; My Sweetie's Smile [1]; (They Call Me) Pollyanna [1]; Pretty Dance Is Like a Violin, A [1]; Use Your Own Judgment; What the Critics Said

Cast: Eva Clark; Daisy De Witte; Fanchon & Marco; Lucille Harmon; John Sheehan; Arthur West; Al Wohlman

Notes: No other information available. [1] Also in SUNKIST.

3843 • SATURDAY NIGHT (1954)

OPENED: 1954
Musical   Unproduced

Composer: Stephen Sondheim
Lyricist: Stephen Sondheim
Librettist: Julius J. Epstein

Source: FRONT PORCH IN FLATBUSH (Play Julius J. Epstein; Philip G. Epstein)

Songs: All for You; Class; Delighted, I'm Sure; Exhibit "A"; I Remember That; In the Movies; Isn't It?; It's That Kind of a Neighborhood; Love's a Bond; Moment with You, A; One Wonderful Day; Saturday Night; So Many People; What More Do I Need?

3844 • SATURDAY NIGHT (1977)
OPENED: 1977   Theatre: CBS
TV Show

Composer: Mitch Leigh
Lyricist: Sammy Cahn

Songs: Blair Rose; Bremen Town Musician, The; Day of Day; Don't Tell Me I'm Flying; Happily Married Wolf, A; I Love a Fat Man; I Made a Deal; If the Shoe Fits; I'm Rotten I'm Rotten; Life Can Be a Fairy Tale; Life Is Not a Fairy Tale; Me and Him; My Name Is Rumpelstiltskin; Name Song, The; Once Upon a Time Is Always; Only Way to Go Is Up, The; Saturday Night (C: Jule Styne); Schlaf Mein Kind; Spin-Off Blues, The (C: Jule Styne); Sweets for Sweet

Notes: A television special.

3845 • SAY, DARLING
OPENED: 04/03/1958   Theatre: ANTA
Musical   Broadway: 332

Composer: Jule Styne
Lyricist: Betty Comden; Adolph Green
Librettist: Marian Bissell; Richard Bissell; Abe Burrows
Producer: Peter Howard; Lester Osterman; Jule Styne
Director: Abe Burrows

Choreographer: Matt Mattox; **Costumes:** Alvin Colt; **Lighting Designer:** Peggy Clark; **Set Design:** Oliver Smith

Songs: And a Host of Others Too Numerous to Mention [1]; Carnival Song, The; Chief of Love; Dance Only with Me; Husking Bee, The; It's Doom; It's the Second Time You Meet that Matters; Let the Lower Lights Be Burning; My Little Yellow Dress [1]; Say, Darling [2]; Something's Always Happening on the River; Try to Love Me Just As I Am

Cast: Vivian Blaine; Jerome Cowan; Johnny

Desmond; Constance Ford; Walter Klavan; Matt Mattox; Horace McMahon; Robert Morse; David Wayne; **Pianist:** Colin Romoff

Notes: [1] Cut prior to opening. [2] Music from "Some Other Time" from STEP LIVELY.

3846 • SAY HELLO TO HARVEY!
OPENED: 09/14/1981
Musical   Closed out of town

Composer: Leslie Bricusse
Lyricist: Leslie Bricusse
Librettist: Leslie Bricusse
Producer: Michael McAloney; David Mirvish; Edwin Mirvish
Director: Mel Shapiro

Source: HARVEY (Play Mary Chase); **Choreographer:** Donald Saddler; **Costumes:** Olga Dimitrov; **Dance Arranger:** Ian Fraser; **Lighting Designer:** Neil Peter Jampolis; **Musical Director:** Milton Rosenstock; **Orchestrations:** Bill Byers; **Set Design:** Neil Peter Jampolis; **Vocal Arranger:** Ian Fraser

Songs: Be Glad; Bring It to the Bar; Do Your Own Thing; Dr. Chumley; Elwood P. Dowd; Human Beings; I'd Rather Look at You; Lousy Life, A [1]; One Last Fling; Perfect Person, The; Say Hello to Harvey; Smalltown, U.S.A.; Sue; That Brother of Mine; We Like the Very Same Things; Wednesday Forum, The

Cast: Tommy Breslin; Sidney Miller; Donald O'Connor; Patricia Routledge; Joe Silver

Notes: [1] Later used in SHERLOCK HOLMES.

3847 • SAY IT WITH JAZZ
OPENED: 06/01/1921
Musical

Composer: Richard Rodgers
Lyricist: Lorenz Hart
Librettist: Dorothy Crowthers; Frank Hunter; Maurice Lieberman
Producer: Institute of Musical Art

Songs: Chorus Girl Blues [3]; Don't Love Me Like Othello [1]; Dreaming True; Hindoo Moon (C: William Kroll); Hymn to the Moon (L: Frank Hunter); If I Knew (C: Gerald Warburg); Just a

Little Lie; Just Remember Coq d'Or (L: Lorenz Hart; Frank Hunter); Moon and You, The [2]; Oh, Harold (L: Lorenz Hart; Frank Hunter); See This Golden Rooster (L: Lorenz Hart; Frank Hunter); Something Like Me [4]; Weaknesses [2] (L: Oscar Hammerstein II); Working for the Institute [5] (L: Lorenz Hart; Frank Hunter); Your Lullaby [4]

Notes: Amateur show. The Hart/Hunter songs may have lyrics by Hunter alone. [1] Previously in FLY WITH ME and YOU'D BE SURPRISED. [2] Previously in FLY WITH ME. [3] Also in SAY MAMA and YOU'LL NEVER KNOW. [4] Also in YOU'LL NEVER KNOW. [5] May have same music as "Working for the Government" in FLY WITH ME.

3848 • SAY MAMA

OPENED: 02/12/1921
Musical

Composer: Richard Rodgers
Lyricist: Lorenz Hart
Producer: Akron Club
Director: Herbert Fields

Songs: Chorus Girl Blues [2]; First Love; I Surrender!; Jack and Jill; Over the Lowlands [1]; Poor Little Model; Priscilla [1]; Show Him the Way; Under the Mistletoe; Wake Up; Watch Yourself [3]; When the Crime Wave Rolls [1]

Cast: Dorothy Fields

Notes: Amateur show. [1] ASCAP/Library of Congress only. [2] Also in SAY IT WITH JAZZ and YOU'LL NEVER KNOW. [3] Also in YOU'LL NEVER KNOW.

3849 • SAY WHEN (1928)

OPENED: 06/26/1928   Theatre: Morosco
Musical   Broadway: 15

Composer: Jesse Greer
Lyricist: Raymond Klages; Max Lief; Nathaniel Lief
Librettist: Calvin Brown
Producer: Elisabeth Marbury; Carl Reed
Director: Bertram Harrison

Choreographer: Max Scheck; **Musical Director:** Ernest Cutting; **Set Design:** Livingston Platt

Songs: Cheerio (L: James J. Walker); Give Me a Night (C/L: W. Frank Harling); How About It? (L: Raymond Klages); In My Love Boat (C: Ray Perkins; L: Max Lief; Nathaniel Lief); Little White Lies (1) (C: Arthur Sheekman; L: Helen Wallace); Little White Lies (2) [1] (C: Kay Swift; L: Paul James); Love Boat [1] (C: Daisy de Segouzac [2]); My One Girl (C: W. Frank Harling); No Room in My Heart (C: Ray Perkins; L: Max Lief; Nathaniel Lief); One Step to Heaven (L: Raymond Klages); Opening Chorus (C: Daisy de Segouzac [2]; L: Max Lief; Nathaniel Lief); Paris [1] (C/L: Irma Hopper); Say When (C: Jesse Greer; L: Raymond Klages); When the Lights Turn Green [1] (C: Kay Swift; L: Paul James); Who's the Boy (C: Ray Perkins; L: Max Lief; Nathaniel Lief)

Cast: Dorothy Fitzgibbon; Bartlett Simmons; Alison Skipworth

Notes: [1] Added 7/11/28. [2] Also referred to as Daisy Segovia.

3850 • SAY WHEN (1934)

OPENED: 11/08/1934   Theatre: Imperial
Musical   Broadway: 76

Composer: Ray Henderson
Lyricist: Ted Koehler
Librettist: Jack McGowan
Producer: Ray Henderson; Jack McGowan
Director: Bertram Harrison

Choreographer: Russell Markert; **Costumes:** Charles LeMaire; **Musical Director:** Max Meth; **Orchestrations:** Robert Russell Bennett; Conrad Salinger; **Set Design:** Clark Robinson

Songs: Bridesmaids Ballet; Declaration Day; Don't Tell Me It's Bad; Isn't It June?; It Must Have Been the Night; Let's Take Advantage of Now; Put Your Heart in a Song; Say When; So Long for Ever So Long; Sunday Morning; Torch Parade; When Love Comes Swinging Along

Cast: Charles Collins; Lillian Emerson; Taylor Holmes; Bob Hope; Nick Long Jr.; Dennie Moore; Harry Richman; Prince Michael Romanoff; Linda Watkins; Cora Witherspoon

3851 • SAYONARA

OPENED: 09/16/1987
Musical   Closed out of town

Composer: George Fischoff
Lyricist: Hy Gilbert
Librettist: William Luce
Producer: Angelo Del Rossi; Paper Mill Playhouse
Director: Robert Johanson

Source: SAYONARA (Novel: James A. Michener);
  Choreographer: Susan Stroman; **Costumes:**
  David Toser; **Musical Director:** Ted Kociolek;
  Set Design: Michael Anania

Notes: Paper Mill Playhouse, Millburn, N.J.

3852 • SCANDAL
OPENED: 1984
Musical   Unproduced

Composer: Jimmy Webb
Lyricist: Jimmy Webb
Librettist: Treva Silverman
Director: Michael Bennett

Cast: Victor Garber; Swoosie Kurtz; David Rasche;
  Fisher Stevens; Treat Williams

Notes: Workshopped but not produced.

3853 • SCAPIN
OPENED: 01/20/1993   Theatre: CSC
Musical   Off-Off-Broadway

Composer: Rusty McGee
Lyricist: Rusty McGee
Librettist: Andrei Belgrader; Shelley Berc
Producer: CSC Repertory
Director: Andrei Belgrader

Source: SCAPIN (Play: Moliere); **Costumes:**
  Elizabeth Hope Clancy; Candice Donnolly;
  Lighting Designer: Stephen Strawbridge; **Set
  Design:** Anita Stewart

Songs: Act One Finale; Another Girl; Gypsy Song,
  The; Heir to My Fortune, The; Money and
  Family; Monsieur; Scapin; Vile Thing; Way I Got,
  The; What? What? What?

Cast: Alexander Draper; Walker Jones; Michael
  McCormick; Mary Testa; Stanley Tucci; Sarah
  McCord Williams

3854 • SCARLETT
Notes: *See GONE WITH THE WIND.*

3855 • SCHOOL DAYS
OPENED: 09/14/1908   Theatre: Circle
Revue   Broadway: 32

Composer: Gus Edwards
Lyricist: Vincent Bryan; Ed Gardenier
Librettist: Aaron Hoffman
Producer: Gus Edwards
Director: Ned Wayburn

Songs: Arithmetic; Calendar of Love, The (L: Ed
  Gardenier); Campbell Soup Kids (L: Ed
  Gardenier); Childhood's Happiest Moments;
  Fighting Kid, The (L: Ed Gardenier); Geography;
  Get on the Merry-Go-Round (L: Ed Gardenier);
  Going to Fight the Indians; Hurdy Gurdy Man,
  The (L: Will D. Cobb); If I Only Said My Name
  Was Flannigan; I'll Be Your Jujube; It Takes the
  Cop to Cop the Girls (L: Vincent Bryan); Katie
  Gray; Lady Love; Little Snowflake; Little Tittle
  Tattle Tale (L: Ed Gardenier); May-be It's a Bear
  (L: Vincent Bryan); Moon Bird; My Old Lady;
  On the Old See Saw [1] (L: Ed Gardenier); Paper
  Hat Brigade, The (L: Vincent Bryan); School
  Days (When We Were a Couple of Kids) [1]
  (L: Will D. Cobb); School Mates (L: Ed
  Gardenier); Squeeze Me Tight; Sunbonnet Sue
  [2] (L: Will D. Cobb); Teddy Bird, The
  (L: Edward A. Paulton); We're Going to Fight
  the Indians [1] (L: Vincent Bryan); When I'm an
  American Citizen; You Have Me; You're Just the
  Boy for Me (L: Ed Gardenier)

Cast: John Hines; Gregory Kelly; Joe Keno; Janet
  Priest; Herman Timberg

Notes: No New York program available. Songs
  listed from sheet music and program of 1/9/10.
  [1] Not in program. [2] Also in SUNBONNET
  SUE.

3856 • SCHOOL GIRL, THE (1895)
OPENED: 12/30/1895   Theatre: Bijou
Musical   Broadway: 8

Composer: Albert Maurice
Librettist: George Manchester

Choreographer: Carl Marwig; **Set Design:** D.
  Frank Dodge; Arthur Voegtlin

Songs: American Girls; Belinda on the Telephone;
  Call 'Round Again; Daughters of the Guard; Days
  of Romance; English Girl, An; Florrie

(C: Paul Rubens); Honeymoon Girl, A; I Love You All the Time; If Ma Says No; In Black and White (C: John W. Bratton; L: Paul West); It's a Good World for All (C: Gus Edwards; L: Vincent Bryan); Jolly Little Japs (C: Paul Rubens); Lancers, The; Little Girl You'll Do; Lonesome (C: Albert Von Tilzer; L: Joseph Rosey); My Cosy Corner Girl; My Little Canoe; Needle in a Haystack; Old English Cake Walk, The (C: Paul Rubens); One of the Boys (C: Howard Talbot); Real Town Lady (L: Paul Rubens); Simpler; Sweet Sans-oo (C: W.T. Francis); When I Was a Girl

Cast: William Gill; Lucia Hartford; Minnie Palmer; William E. Wilson

Notes: No songs in program. Songs from programs of Boston 1905, Montauk 1/05 and New York 9/12/04 (Rubens' songs).

3857 • SCHOOL GIRL, THE (1904)
OPENED: 09/01/1904   Theatre: Daly's
Musical   Broadway: 120

Composer: Leslie Stuart
Lyricist: Charles H. Taylor
Librettist: Henry Hamilton; Paul Potter
Producer: Charles Frohman
Director: J.A.E. Malone

Musical Director: William T. Francis; **Set Design:** Ernest Gros

Songs: American Girls (Chickoo We're Only Just Sixteen); Belinda on the Telephone [4] (L: Paul A. Rubens); Call 'Round Again (L: Leslie Stuart); Clytie [6]; Daughters of the Guard, The (L: Leslie Stuart); Finale Act I (L: Leslie Stuart; Charles H. Taylor); Florrie (C/L: Paul Rubens); Honeymoon Girl, A; If Ma Says No; In Black and White (C: John W. Bratton; L: Paul West); It's a Good World After All [3] (C: Gus Edwards; L: Vincent Bryan); Jolly Little Japs; Just the Tale By Night and Day [6] (L: Leslie Stuart; Charles H. Taylor); La Rosiere [6] (L: Adrian Ross); Lancers, The [1]; Little Girl You'll Do [7] (C: Alfred Solman; L: Benjamin Hapgood Burt); Lonesome [1] (C: Albert Von Tilzer; L: Joseph Rosey); Looking for a Needle in a Haystack [5]; My Cosey Corner Girl [2] (C: John W. Bratton; L: Charles Noel Douglas); My Little Canoe (L: Leslie Stuart); Now They've Got Into the London Way [6] (C: Maurice Scott; L: Edgar Bateman); Oh Woman in Days of Romance; Old English Cake Walk (C/L: Paul Rubens); One

Girl Too Many [6]; One of the Boys (C: Howard Talbot); Opening Chorus; Opening Chorus Act I Scene 2; Opening Chorus Act II; Real Town Lady (C/L: Paul Rubens); She May Not Be That Sort of Girl (A Legend of the Laundry) [6] (L: Leslie Stuart); She's an English Girl (L: Adrian Ross; Leslie Stuart); Simpler; Sweet San-oo [1] (C/L: W.T. Francis); There's Nothing Like a Wife [6]; We Want to Be Simpler [6]; When I Was a Girl Like You

Cast: Mildred Baker; Clara Braithwaite; George Grossmith; Edna May

Notes: [1] Out Baltimore 4/3/05. [2] Original tune "In a Cosy Corner." [3] Out Boston 1/16/05. [4] Titled in London "Belinda on the Link." [5] "Melody of the refrain suggested by an old Norwegian tune." [6] In London only. [7] Sheet music only.

3858 • SCRAMBLED FEET
OPENED: 06/11/1979   Theatre: Village Gate
Revue   Off-Broadway: 831

Composer: John Driver; Jeffrey Haddow
Lyricist: John Driver; Jeffrey Haddow
Librettist: John Driver; Jeffrey Haddow
Producer: James Adams Vaccaro; Jimmy Wisner
Director: John Driver

Costumes: Kenneth M. Yount; **Lighting Designer:** Robert F. Strohmeier; **Musical Director:** Jimmy Wisner; **Orchestrations:** Jimmy Wisner; **Set Design:** Ernest Allen Smith; **Vocal Arranger:** Roger Neil; Jimmy Wisner

Songs: Advice to Producers; Agent; Answering Machine; Composer Tango; Could Have Been; Going to the Theatre; Good Connections; Guru; Happy Family; Have You Ever Been on Stage?; Haven't We Met?; Huns/British Improv/EDT; Love in the Wings; Makin' the Rounds; More Than Love; No Small Roles; Olympics; Only One Dance; P.T. Playwrighting Kit; Party Doll; Sham Dancing; Stanislaw; Theatre Party Ladies

Cast: Evalyn Baron; John Driver; Jeffrey Haddow; Hermione; Roger Neil

Notes: Songs and sketches listed.

3859 • SCROOGE
Notes: *See COMIN' UPTOWN.*

3860 • SEA LEGS

OPENED: 05/18/1937   Theatre: Mansfield
Musical   Broadway: 15

Composer: Michael H. Cleary
Lyricist: Arthur Swanstrom
Librettist: Arthur Swanstrom
Producer: Albert Bannister; J. Edmund Byrne
Director: Bertram Harrison

Source: CAT CAME BACK, THE (Play Avery Hopwood; Lawrence E. Johnson; Beula King); **Choreographer:** Johnny Mattison; **Costumes:** Brooks; Jay-Thorpe; **Musical Director:** J. Frank Cork; **Orchestrations:** Joseph Jordan; **Set Design:** Mabel Buell

Songs: Catalina; Chasing Henry; Dark Stranger, A; Infatuation; Looks Like Love Is Here to Stay; Off on a Weekend Cruise; Opposite Sex, The; Ten O'Clock Town; Touched in the Head; Wake Me Up a Star

Cast: Rosco Ates; Charles Collins; Deedee; Charles King; Patricia Knight; Kathryn Mayfield; Rosie Moran; Mary Sargent; Dorothy Stone; Ben Yost's Catalina Eight

3861 • SECOND LITTLE SHOW, THE

OPENED: 09/02/1930   Theatre: Royale
Revue   Broadway: 63

Composer: Arthur Schwartz
Lyricist: Howard Dietz
Librettist: Donald Blackwell; Norman Clark; James Coghlan; Marc Connelly; Bert Hanlon; William Miles
Producer: William A. Brady Jr.; Tom Weatherly; Dwight Deere Wiman
Director: Dwight Deere Wiman; Monty Wooley

Choreographer: Dave Gould; **Costumes:** Helene Pons; Raymond Sovey; **Musical Director:** Gus Salzer; **Set Design:** Jo Mielziner

Songs: Foolish Face; Good Clean Sport; I Like Your Face; I Started on a Shoestring; Lucky Seven; My Heart Begins to Thump! Thump! (C: Morgan Lewis; L: Ted Fetter); My Intuition; New New York; Practising Up on You (C: Phil Charig); Sing Something Simple (C/L: Herman Hupfeld); Swing Your Tails; Tired of Love (C: Del Cleaveland; L: Ted Fetter); What a Case I've Got

on You; You're the Sunrise

Cast: Fay Brady; Yukona Cameron; Jay C. Flippen; Gloria Grafton; Helen Gray; Davey Jones; Arline Judge; Joey Ray; Tashamira; Ruth Tester; Al Trahan; Ned Wever

3862 • SECRET GARDEN, THE

OPENED: 04/25/1991   Theatre: St. James
Musical   Broadway: 706

Composer: Lucy Simon
Lyricist: Marsha Norman
Librettist: Marsha Norman
Producer: Dodger Productions; Jujamcyn Theaters; Heidi Landesman; Frederic H. Mayerson; Rick Steiner; TV ASAHI; Elizabeth Williams
Director: Susan H. Schulman

Source: SECRET GARDEN, THE (Novel: Frances Hodgson Burnett); **Choreographer:** Michael Lichtefeld; **Costumes:** Theoni V. Aldredge; **Dance Arranger:** Jeanine Levenson; **Lighting Designer:** Tharon Musser; **Musical Director:** Michael Kosarin; **Orchestrations:** William D. Brohn; **Set Design:** Heidi Landesman; **Vocal Arranger:** Michael Kosarin

Songs: Bit of Earth, A; Clusters of Crocus [1]; Come Spirit, Come Charm; Come to My Garden; Disappear; Final Storm; Fine White Horse, A; Girl I Mean to Be, The; Girl in the Valley, A; Hold On; House Upon the Hill, The; How Could I Ever Know; I Heard Someone Crying; It's a Maze; Letter Song; Lily's Eyes; Opening Dream; Quartet; Race You to the Top of the Morning; Round-Shouldered Man; Show Me the Key; Storm I; Storm II; There's a Girl; Where in the World; Wick; Winter's on the Wind

Cast: Daisy Eagan; Alison Fraser; Rebecca Judd; Rebecca Luker; John Cameron Mitchell; Mandy Patinkin; Tom Toner; Robert Westenberg

Notes: [1] Cut.

3863 • SECRET LIFE OF WALTER MITTY, THE

OPENED: 10/26/1964   Theatre: Players
Musical   Off-Broadway: 96

Composer: Leon Carr
Lyricist: Earl Shuman

Librettist: Joe Manchester
Producer: Joe Manchester
Director: Mervyn Nelson

Source: SECRET LIFE OF WALTER MITTY, THE (Story: James Thurber); **Choreographer:** Robert Arlen; **Costumes:** Al Lehman; **Dance Arranger:** Ray Ellis; **Lighting Designer:** Lloyd Burlingame; **Musical Director:** Joe Stecko; **Set Design:** Lloyd Burlingame; **Vocal Arranger:** Ray Ellis

Songs: Aggie; Confidence; Don't Forget; Drip, Drop, Tapoketa; Fan the Flame; Hello, I Love You, Goodbye; Lonely Ones; Marriage Is for Old Folks; Now That I Am Forty; Secret Life, The; She's Talking Out; Two Little Pussycats; Walking with Peninnah; Walter Mitty March, The; Willa; You're Not

Cast: Cathryn Damon; Marc London; Christopher Norris; Eugene Roche; Charles Rydell; Lorraine Serabian; Rudy Tronto

3864 • SEDUCTION OF A LADY, THE

OPENED: 05/11/1984
Musical

Composer: Richard Wargo
Lyricist: Richard Wargo
Librettist: Richard Wargo
Producer: Music Theater Workshop
Director: Dorothy Danner

Source: GOOD DOCTOR, THE (Play: Neil Simon); **Costumes:** Karen Gerson; **Lighting Designer:** Jeffrey Schissler; **Musical Director:** Evans Haile; **Set Design:** James Morgan

Songs: Cadenza; Epilogue; Irena's Aria; Prologue/Overture; Romanza; Scene; Scene and Aria; Scherzo; Theme and Variations; Toccata; Waltz and Polka

Cast: David Barron; Stephen Costing; Sharon Daniels

Notes: This was a workshop production on a double bill with the songs from BLANCO.

3865 • SEE AMERICA FIRST

OPENED: 03/28/1916   Theatre: Maxine Elliott's
Musical   Broadway: 15

Composer: Cole Porter
Lyricist: Cole Porter
Librettist: Cole Porter; T. Lawrason Riggs
Producer: Elisabeth Marbury
Director: Benrimo

Choreographer: Edward Hutchinson; Theodore Kosloff; **Costumes:** Homer Conant; Melville Ellis; **Musical Director:** Clarence West; **Set Design:** Frank Gates; E.A. Morange

Songs: Badmen; Beautiful, Primitive Indian Girls; Bichloride of Mercury [1]; Buy Her a Box at the Opera; Damsel, Damsel (Prithee Come Crusading with Me) [4]; Dawn Music (inst.); Dinner [1]; Ever and Ever Yours; Fascinating Females; Finale (Hail the Female Relative); Finale Act II; Greetings Gentlemen; Hail, Ye Indian Maidens; Hold-Up Ensemble; If in Spite of Our Attempts [7]; Indian Girls Chant; Indian Maiden's Chorus [7]; I've Got a Shooting Box in Scotland [4]; I've Got an Awful Lot to Learn; Lady Fair, Lady Fair [1]; Lady I've Vowed to Wed, The; Language of Flowers, The [4]; Lima; Love Came and Crowned Me [5]; Mirror, Mirror; Oh, Bright, Fair Dream [1]; Pity Me Please [1]; Revelation Ensemble [1]; See America First; Serenade [1]; Slow Sinks the Sun [8]; Social Coach of All the Fashionable Future Debutantes, The [1]; Something's Got to Be Done; Step We Grandly [1]; Strolling Quite Fancy Free [1]; Sweet Simplicity [1]; To Follow Ever Fancy; Wake, Love, Wake [1]; When a Body's in Love [1]; When I Used to Lead the Ballet [2]; Will You Love Me When My Flivver Is a Wreck? [3]; Woodland Dance; Younger Sons of Peers [6]

Cast: Felix Adler; Dorothie Bigelow; Jeanne Cartier; Sam Edwards; John Goldsworthy; Clara Palmer; Clifton Webb

Notes: [1] Not used. [2] Originally in THE POT OF GOLD. [3] Probably not by Porter. [4] Originally written for PARANOIA. [5] Unused. Rewritten from PARANOIA. [6] May not have been used. [7] May be same song. [8] Not used. Originally written for PARANOIA.

3866 • SEE YOU LATER

OPENED: 04/15/1918
Musical   Closed out of town

Composer: William F. Peters; Jean Schwartz
Lyricist: Guy Bolton; P.G. Wodehouse

Librettist: P.G. Wodehouse
Producer: A.H. Woods
Director: Robert Milton

Source: GIRL FROM RECTOR'S (Play: Paul Potter); **Source:** LOUTE (Play: Pierre Veber); **Choreographer:** Julian Alfred; **Costumes:** Harry Collins; **Musical Director:** Eugene Salzer

Songs: Any Time Is Dancing Time (C: Jean Schwartz); Finale Act I; Finale Act II; Finale Act III; Finest Thing in the Country, The; Honeymoon Island; I Never Knew! (C: Jean Schwartz); If You Could Read My Mind; I'm Going to Settle Down; In Our Little Paradise [1]; Isn't It Wonderful! [1] (C: Jean Schwartz); It Doesn't Matter [1] (C: Jean Schwartz); Keep Out of the Moon; Love's a Very Funny Thing [1] (L: Guy Bolton; P.G. Wodehouse); Nerves; No One Ever Loved Like Me; Opening Cantata Act II; Opening Number; Our Little Desert Island; Rally Around; Run Away; See You Later Girls! [1]; See You Later Shimmy [1] (C: William Daly; Jean Schwartz); That Old Church Bell; Train That Leaves for Town, The [1]; Young Man [1]

Cast: Betty Alden; Herbert Corthell; Marie Flynn; Charlotte Granville; Mabel McCane; John Daly Murphy; Isabel O'Madigan; Jed Prouty; Tot Qualters; Charles Ruggles; Ernest Torrence

Notes: [1] Sheet music only.

3867 • SEEING NEW YORK

OPENED: 06/05/1906   Theatre: New York Roof
                                          Garden
Musical   Broadway: 75

Composer: A. Baldwin Sloane
Lyricist: Clifton Crawford; Joseph Hart
Librettist: Clifton Crawford; Joseph Hart
Producer: William Brady; Joseph Hart

Songs: Astor Hotel, The; At the Party; Different Girls on Broadway; General Bingham's Brigade; Howdy-Do?; I'm Not Particular; Mimette Doll, The; Misfit Family, The; Miss Daisy's Gown; My Blushing Rosie; Shady Side of Broadway, The; Tell the Band to Play an Irish Tune

Cast: Clifton Crawford; Carrie DeMar; Fleurette DeMar

3868 • SEE-SAW (1919)

OPENED: 09/23/1919   Theatre: Cohan
Musical   Broadway: 89

Composer: Louis A. Hirsch
Lyricist: Earl Derr Biggers
Librettist: Earl Derr Biggers
Producer: Henry W. Savage
Director: John McKee

Choreographer: Julian Alfred; **Lighting Designer:** Joseph P. Wilson; **Musical Director:** Max Steiner; **Set Design:** Frank Gates; E.A. Morange

Songs: Good-Bye! Hello!; Happiest Moment I've Ever Known, The; I Just Want Jazz; I'll Take Care of Him; Join the Navy?; Peep-Peep; See-Saw; Senorita-Senorita; This Is the Life; When Two Hearts Discover; When You Come Near I Feel All of a Ooh!; When You Dance; Whistle and I'll Wait for You [1]; World Full of Girls, A; You'll Have to Find Out

Cast: Frank Carter; Elizabeth Hines; Dorothea McKaye; Guy Robertson

Notes: [1] Out Stamford 7/30/19.

3869 • SEESAW (1973)

OPENED: 03/18/1973   Theatre: Uris
Musical   Broadway: 296

Composer: Cy Coleman
Lyricist: Dorothy Fields
Librettist: Michael Bennett
Producer: Lawrence Kasha; Joseph Kipness; James M. Nederlander; Lorin E. Price; George M. Steinbrenner III
Director: Michael Bennett

Source: TWO FOR THE SEESAW (Play: William Gibson); **Choreographer:** Michael Bennett; Grover Dale; **Costumes:** Ann Roth; **Dance Arranger:** Cy Coleman; **Lighting Designer:** Jules Fisher; **Musical Director:** Don Pippin; **Orchestrations:** Larry Fallon; **Set Design:** Robin Wagner; **Vocal Arranger:** Don Pippin

Songs: Big Fat Heart [1]; Chapter 54, Number 1909; Concert, The (dance); Did You Ever Look at You [1]; He's Good for Me; Hospitality [1]; If There Were More People Like You [3]; I'm in a Highly Emotional State [1]; I'm Way Ahead; In Tune; It's Not Where You Start; Megatron (dance) [1]; My

City; Nobody Does It Like Me; Party's on Me, The [2]; Pick Up the Pieces [1]; Poor Everybody Else [4]; Ride Out the Storm; Salt [5]; Seesaw (1) [1]; Seesaw (2); Spanglish; Tutu and Tights [1]; Visitors [5]; We've Got It; Welcome to Holiday Inn; You're a Lovable Lunatic

Cast: Giancarlo Esposito; Ken Howard; Baayork Lee; Michele Lee; Anita Morris; Cecilia Norfleet; Tommy Tune

Notes: [1] Cut prior to opening. [2] Added for tour. [3] Cut prior to opening. Written for unfinished musical based on the life of Eleanor Roosevelt (ELEANOR). [4] Cut from SWEET CHARITY. [5] ASCAP/Library of Congress only.

3870 • SELL YOUR PAPERS
Musical

Songs: Blackout! Hold Me Tight (C: Clay Boland; L: Bickley Reichner)

Notes: No other information available.

3871 • SELLING OF THE PRESIDENT, THE
OPENED: 03/22/1972　Theatre: Shubert
Musical　　　　　　　Broadway: 5

Composer: Bob James
Lyricist: Jack O'Brien
Librettist: Stuart Hample; Jack O'Brien
Producer: John Flaxman
Director: Robert H. Livingston

Source: SELLING OF THE PRESIDENT, THE (Book: Joe McGinness); **Choreographer:** Ethel Martin; **Costumes:** Nancy Potts; **Lighting Designer:** Thomas Skelton; **Musical Director:** Harold Hastings; **Orchestrations:** Jonathan Tunick; **Set Design:** Tom H. John

Songs: America; Captain Terror; Come-on-a-good Life; He's a Man; If You Like People; I've Got to Trust You; Little Moon; Mason Cares; On the Winning Side; Passacaglia, A; Something Holy; Stars of Glory; Sunset; Take My Hand; Termanix; We're Gonna Live It Together

Cast: Johnny Alson; Barbara Barrie; Pi Douglass; Suellen Estey; Robert Fitzsimmons; John Glover;

Richard Goode; Delores Hall; Pat Hingle; Karen Morrow; Pamela Myers

3872 • SEMINARY GIRLS, THE
Musical　　　　　　　Closed out of town

Notes: No other information available. Harold Orlob had some songs interpolated into this score.

3873 • SENATOR JOE
OPENED: 01/05/1989　Theatre: Neil Simon
Musical　　　　　　　Broadway

Composer: Tom O'Horgan
Lyricist: Perry Arthur Kroeger
Librettist: Perry Arthur Kroeger
Producer: Chester Fox; Adela Holzer
Director: Tom O'Horgan

Choreographer: Wesley Fata; **Costumes:** Randy Barcelo; **Lighting Designer:** John McLain; **Musical Director:** Gordon Lowry Harrell; **Orchestrations:** Jimmy Vivino, **Set Design:** Bill Stabile

Songs: Aftermath; Almighty American; America; Army, The; Black and Blue; Book Burning; Boozin' & Barfin'; Briefcase, The; Charisma; Cocktail Party; Cold War; Communism; Dealing in Wheeling; Dirt Between My Fingers; 50's, The; Flashback; Haunted Television; Have You No Shame; Hearings, The; Hysteria; I Knew a Man; Ism #1; Jeannie; Joe's Liver; Jungle of Lies; Make Up; Mamie and Bess Bicker; Microfilm; Personal President; Pussyfootin'; Rape of Liberty; Ron and Bobby; See It Now; Slow As the Moon; Take a Professor; Telephone, The; Three First Ladies; Time Heals All Wounds; Twenty Years of Treason; Was There Love; Weakest Point, The; Wedding, The; What He Needs I Got; What's My Lie; What's Up for You; Where the War Left Us

Cast: J.P. Dougherty; Kristen Gray; Jeff Johnson; Michael Rapposelli; Ric Ryder

Notes: Closed during previews. This show was to be performed in repertory with the opera NIMROD AND THE TOWER OF BABEL. See under that name for those credits.

3874 • SEND ME NO FLOWERS
OPENED: 12/05/1960　Theatre: Brooks Atkinson
Play　　　　　　　　　Broadway: 40

Author: Norman Barasch; Carroll Moore
Producer: Courtney Burr; Edward Spector Prod. Inc.
Director: James Dyas

Lighting Designer: Frederick Fox; **Set Design:** Frederick Fox

Songs: Send Me No Flowers (C: Will Lorin; L: George David Weiss)

Cast: Helen-Jean Arthur; Heywood Hale Broun; Frank Merlin; Michael Miguel O'Brien; Nancy Olson; Joe Ponazecki; David Wayne

3875 • SENOR DISCRETION
OPENED: 1969
Musical

Composer: Frank Loesser
Lyricist: Frank Loesser
Librettist: Frank Loesser; Budd Schulberg; Anthony Stimac

Source: SENOR DISCRETION HIMSELF (Story: Budd Schulberg)

Songs: Companeros; Heaven Smiles on Tepancingo; I Cannot Let You Go; I Got to Have a Somebody; I Love Him; Mexico City; Padre, I Have Sinned; Pan Pan Pan; Pancito, She Would Call Me; Papa, Come Home; Paseo, The; To See Her; Wisdom of the Heart, The; World Peace; You Understand Me

Notes: Unproduced.

3876 • SENSATIONS
OPENED: 10/25/1970   Theatre: Theatre Four
Musical   Off-Broadway: 16

Composer: Wally Harper
Lyricist: Paul Zakrzewski
Librettist: Paul Zakrzewski
Producer: John Bowab; Charles Celian
Director: Jerry Dodge

Source: ROMEO AND JULIET (Play: William Shakespeare); **Costumes:** Jeanne Button; **Lighting Designer:** Beverly Emmons; **Musical Director:** Jack Lee; **Orchestrations:** Bill Brohn; **Set Design:** Jean Eckart; William Eckart

Songs: And Then They Dream of Love [1]; Beginning, The; Cannot Wait; Friar's Tune; Good Little Boy [1]; I'll Stay, I'll Go; In Nomine Dei; Kill, The; Lonely Children; Lying Here; Middle Class Revolution; Morning Sun; No Place for Me; Now That We're Married [1]; Oh, My Age; Outracing Light; Power; Queen Mab; Sensations; Sounds; Suddenly I'm Real [1]; Up and Down; War Is Good Business; What Kind of Parents

Cast: Paulette Attie; Arthur Bartow; Judy Gibson; Ron Martin; Joe Masiell; John Savage; Bruce Scott

Notes: [1] Not in program.

3877 • SEPTEMBER MORN
OPENED: 12/1913   Theatre: La Salle
Musical   Chicago

Composer: Aubrey Stauffer
Lyricist: Arthur Gillespie
Librettist: Arthur Gillespie
Director: Frank Tannehill Jr.

Choreographer: Virgil Bennett; **Musical Director:** Elmer B. Chapman

Songs: Beautiful Dreams I'm Dreaming; Bit of Harmony, A; Dixie Doodle (You're the Land for Me); Everybody's Tango Crazy; I Lost My Girl on Broadway; In Berlin; In Paree; Maxixe, The; My Autumn Leaf Girl; My Cornfield Queen; Oh! You; Opening Chorus; Opening Chorus Act II; So I've Been Told (C: Omar Hebert); Spare Rib from the Butcher Shop of Life, A; Sun-Shade Girl, The; That Dance of Mine (C: Omar Hebert); They Call It Dixie Land; When a Little Boy Loves a Little Girl; Where Is the Pleasure in Wine and Song-If the Woman Is Not There

Cast: Dorothy Earle; Leslie Julian Jones; Clarence Nordstrom; Maude Potter

3878 • SEPTEMBER EVENING
Musical   Unproduced

Composer: Paul Piercely-Jones
Lyricist: Amy Day Mozart

Notes: No other information available.

3879 • SERAFINA
OPENED: 1970
Musical   Unproduced

Composer: Jule Styne
Lyricist: Leslie Bricusse

Source: ROSE TATTOO, THE (Play Tennessee Williams)

Songs: Go Easy with Mama; Go Easy with Rosa; Lady of the Year; Long Time Dead, A; Look at Me with Love; Me and You; New Orleans; Rosario; Sarafina; Things a Girl Should Be, The; Time Goes By; Time of the Roses, The; Una a Dieci; White Flags; Who Needs You

3880 • SERENA
Musical   Unproduced

Composer: Arthur Siegel
Lyricist: June Carroll
Librettist: S.N. Behrman; Lehman Engel
Producer: Leonard Sillman

Source: SERENA BLANDISH (Play S.N. Behrman)

Songs: Before You Love [1]; Every Day Is a Challenge Sweet; Gaiety of the Gaiety, The; I Don't Have the Time; I Don't Really Mind; I Have to Get Used to Being in Love; If I Were 80 Years Younger; I'll Fascinate You; I'm on My Way; Lovely Little Diamond; My Little Book of Poetry; Once Upon No Particular Time (Opening); Patrick Would Be Proud of Me Now; Peacock and I, The; Serena; Settle Down; Somebody Thinks I'm Wonderful; There's Another Woman in Your Mind; You Must Keep a Little Actress in Your Life

Notes: [1] Also in score of unproduced show OUR HEARTS WERE YOUNG AND GAY.

3881 • SERENADE, THE
OPENED: 03/16/1897   Theatre: Knickerbocker
Musical   Broadway: 79

Composer: Victor Herbert
Lyricist: Harry B. Smith
Librettist: Harry B. Smith

Musical Director: Samuel L. Studley

Songs: All for Thee [1]; Angelus, The; Charity [1]; Cupid and I; Don Jose of Sevilla; Dreaming, Dreaming; Entrance of the Duke (Hola-ho, Hola-ho!); For I'm a Jolly Postillion; Fra Francisco's Flirtation [1]; Funny Side of That, The (Although a Duke of High Degree); Gaze on This Face So Noble; Here Merrily Ride the Bandit Tribe (When Day's Honest Work Is Done); I Envy the Bird; I Love Thee, I Adore Thee (Serenade); I'm Sure Tis She; In Attitudes Alert! [1]; In Fair Andalusia; In Our Quiet Cloister [1]; March [1]; Monk and the Maid, The; Monk's Chorus Act II; Opening Chorus; Opening Chorus Act II; Peering Left and Peering Right (For We Are the Duke's Bodyguard); Singing Lesson, The; Song of the Carbine, The; Who Can This Be (Entrance of Duke and Dolores); Woman, Lovely Woman

Cast: Henry Clay Barnabee; Harry Brown; Eugene Cowles; Jessie Bartlett Davis; George Frothingham; W.H. McDonald; Alice Neilson

Notes: No songs listed in program. Song list from 1930 revival at the Jolson Theatre and vocal selection. "Based on an interlude by Goldoni." [1] Titles from revival that can't be traced to original vocal score.

3882 • SERGEANT BRUE
OPENED: 04/25/1905   Theatre: Knickerbocker
Musical   Broadway: 152

Composer: Liza Lehman
Lyricist: Owen Hall
Librettist: Owen Hall
Producer: Charles B. Dillingham
Director: Herbert Gresham

Source: SERGEANT BRUE (Musical: J. Hickory Wood); **Musical Director:** Watty Hydes

Songs: All in the Line of Duty [3] (C: John W. Bratton; L: Paul West); Cup of Tea, A; Dearie (C/L: Clare Kummer); Every Saturday Afternoon (C: Clare Kummer; L: James O'Dea); Hail to the Magistrate; Hail to the Piccadilly Hero; Half a Dozen Little Bits of Lace [2] (C: James W. Tate; L: Clifford Harris); Hey! Ho! [2] (C: Liza Lehmann; L: J. Hickory Wood); I Was Born on a Friday; I'm a Sergeant of Police; Lancers; Let Me Sing (C/L: Frank Leo); Line of Duty; My Irish Molly-O (C: Jean Schwartz; L: William Jerome); My Lady Busy [2] (C: Liza Lehmann; L: J. Hickory

Wood); Never Mind the Weather [2] (C: Liza Lehmann; L: T. Heffernan); Nora, My Irish Rose [1] (C: Anne Caldwell; L: James O'Dea); Oh, Help!; Old Man Shea (C/L: Benjamin Hapgood Burt); On the Rialto [3] (C/L: Clare Kummer); Our Emporium; Put Me in My Little Cell; Saturday After Two [1] (C/L: D.K. Stevens); Sergeant Brue; Skating [2] (C: John W. Bratton; L: Paul West); Thine Eyes Are Like Twin Stars [3] (C/L: Frederick Rosse); We Have Dined; Welcome, Mr. Brue; Young Man in a Shop; Zoological Party

Cast: Frank Daniels; Sallie Fisher; Harry MacDonough; Walter Percival; Blanche Ring; Lawrence Wheat

Notes: [1] Out of town program only. [2] From London sheet music. [3] Sheet music only.

3883 • SERGEANT KITTY
OPENED: 01/18/1904　Theatre: Daly's
Musical　　　　　　　Broadway: 55

Composer: A. Baldwin Sloane
Lyricist: R.H. Burnside
Librettist: R.H. Burnside
Producer: George White
Director: R.H. Burnside

Songs: Girl He Left Behnid Him, The; Just Take Things As They Come; Love; Love Laughs at Locksmiths; Ninon's Father Doesn't Seem to Mind; Oh, Kitty; Oh, Star of Hope; One I Love the Best Gave that to Me; To the Guard House; True Love Lives but in Our Dreams; War; We Are a Gallant Regiment; Wedding Ensemble; What Is a Poor Girl to Do; You Never Know What's Going to Happen Next

Cast: Grace Belmont; Harry Braham; Virginia Earle; Sylvain Langlois; George E. Mack; Junie McCree; Albert Parr; Harry Stone

Notes: No program available. Songs listed from sheet music.

3884 • SERIOUS MONEY
OPENED: 02/09/1988　Theatre: Royale
Play　　　　　　　　Broadway: 45

Author: Caryl Churchill
Producer: Joseph Papp
Director: Max Stafford-Clark

Costumes: Peter Hartwell; **Lighting Designer:** Rick Fisher; **Set Design:** Peter Hartwell

Songs: Freedom (C: Chas Jankel; L: Ian Drury); Futures (C: Micky Gallagher; L: Ian Drury)

Cast: Alec Baldwin; Melinda Mullins; Kate Nelligan; John Pankow; Michael Wincott

Played 30 performances at the New York Shakespeare Festival beginning on 12/3/87. Played an additional 15 performances on Broadway.

3885 • SET TO MUSIC
OPENED: 01/18/1939　Theatre: Music Box
Revue　　　　　　　Broadway: 129

Composer: Noel Coward
Lyricist: Noel Coward
Librettist: Noel Coward
Producer: John C. Wilson
Director: Noel Coward

Costumes: G.E. Calthrop; **Musical Director:** John McManus; **Orchestrations:** Hans Spialek; **Set Design:** G.E. Calthrop

Songs: Children of the Ritz [2]; I Went to a Marvelous Party; I'm So Weary of It All; Mad about the Boy [2]; Midnight Matinee; Never Again; Party's Over Now, The [2]; Stately Homes of England, The [1]; Three Little Debutantes [2]; Three White Feathers

Cast: Maidie Andrews; Kenneth Carten; Laura Duncan; Hugh French; Richard Haydn; Gladys Henson; Beatrice Lillie; Angus Menzies; Moya Nugent; Eva Ortega; Antony Pelissier; Penelope Dudley Ward

Notes: This was the American edition of WORDS AND MUSIC. [1] Originally in OPERETTE. [2] Originally in WORDS AND MUSIC.

3886 • SETS AND COSTUMES
Notes: *See 13 DAYS TO BROADWAY.*

3887 • SEVEN AGES, THE
OPENED: 10/14/1889　Theatre: Standard
Musical　　　　　　　Broadway

Composer: Edward E. Rice
Librettist: Henry E. Dixey; William Gill
Producer: Edward E. Rice
Director: Henry E. Dixey

Costumes: Alfred Thompson; **Musical Director:** John J. Braham; **Set Design:** Alfred Thompson

Songs: Chorus of Perambulator Girls; Court Office Song; During Life; Emigrants Chorus; Grand March; Hail to the Judge; Here's My Ticket; Hush Little Girl Don't Cry; I'm a Harem Scarum Boy; In Fashion's Ring; Judges Comic Opera, The; Military Song; Off We Go; Reason Why, The; Saved By the One She Loves; Skipping Rope Chorus; Understand Don't You See, Don't You Know; Welcome the Bridegroom; When We Chance to Meet; With Caution Tread

Cast: Henry E. Dixey; George W. Howard; Marie Williams

3888 • SEVEN BRIDES FOR SEVEN BROTHERS

OPENED: 07/08/1982   Theatre: Alvin
Musical   Broadway: 5

Composer: Joel Hirschhorn
Lyricist: Joel Hirschhorn; Al Kasha
Librettist: Al Kasha; David S. Landay
Producer: Al Kasha; David S. Landay
Director: Al Kasha

Source: SEVEN BRIDES FOR SEVEN BROTHERS (Film: Francis Goodrich; Albert Hackett; Dorothy Kinsley); **Source:** SOBBIN' WOMEN, THE (Story: Stephen Vincent Benet); **Choreographer:** Jerry Jackson; **Costumes:** Robert Randolph; **Dance Arranger:** Robert Webb; **Lighting Designer:** Tom Skelton; **Musical Director:** Richard Parrinello; **Orchestrations:** Irwin Kostal; **Set Design:** Robert Randolph

Songs: Bless Your Beautiful Hide [3] (C: Gene DePaul; L: Johnny Mercer); Get a Wife [2]; Glad That You Were Born; Goin' Courting [3] (C: Gene DePaul; L: Johnny Mercer); I Married Seven Brothers [2]; If I Was a Different Man [1]; I'm Jumpin' In [1]; It's Up to Us [2]; June Bride [4] (C: Gene DePaul; L: Johnny Mercer); Lonesome Polecat [4] (C: Gene DePaul; L: Johnny Mercer); Love Never Goes Away; One Man; Sobbin' Women [3] (C: Gene DePaul; L: Johnny Mercer);

Social Dance (inst.) [3] (C: Gene DePaul); Spring Dance; Spring, Spring, Spring [4] (C: Gene DePaul; L: Johnny Mercer); Townsfolk's Lament, The; We Gotta Make It Through the Winter; Wedding Dance (inst.) [3] (C: Gene DePaul); When They Grow Up [2]; When You're in Love [4] (C: Gene DePaul; L: Johnny Mercer); Woman Ought to Know Her Place, A; Woman's Work [1]; Wonderful, Wonderful Day [3] (C: Gene DePaul; L: Johnny Mercer)

Cast: Debby Boone; David-James Carroll; Nancy Fox; Craig Peralta; Lara Teeter

Notes: [1] Not in programs. [2] Cut out of town. [3] From film score. [4] Cut prior to New York. From film score.

3889 • SEVEN COME ELEVEN (FIRST EDITION)

OPENED: 10/11/1961   Theatre: Upstairs at the Downstairs
Revue   Nightclub

Producer: Carl Norman

Choreographer: Frank Wagner; **Costumes:** Donald Inglett; **Musical Director:** William Roy; **Vocal Arranger:** William Roy

Songs: Alma What's the Matter (C/L: Lesley Davison); Captain of the Pinafores (C/L: Rod Warren); Christmas Long Ago (C: Ralph Strain; L: Marshall Barer); Forbidden Tropics (C/L: G. Wood); I Flew to Havana Last Wednesday (C/L: Michael Brown); I Found Him [1] (C: Jack Urbont; L: Bruce Geller); Jackie Look, The (C/L: Lesley Davison); John Birch Society (C/L: Michael Brown); New York Has a New Hotel (C/L: Michael Brown); Poet Aster Is Cornered, The (C: John Kesner; L: Martin Charnin); School Daze (C/L: Michael Brown); Seven Come Eleven (C/L: William Roy); Sick (C: William Roy; L: Maxwell Seigal); Stock on the Rocks (C/L: Jacques Urbont); Suddenly Last Tuesday (C/L: William F. Brown); This Is New York (C/L: Jack Holmes)

Cast: Philip Bruns; Ceil Cabot; Rex Robbins; Steve Roland; Donna Sanders; Mary Louise Wilson; **Pianist:** William Roy

Notes: No program available. [1] From ALL IN LOVE.

3890 • SEVEN COME ELEVEN (SECOND EDITION)

OPENED: 08/1963   Theatre: Upstairs at the Downstairs
Revue   Nightclub

Producer: Arthur Siegel; Upstairs at the Downstairs
Director: Ben Bagley; Jonathan Lucas

Choreographer: Jonathan Lucas; **Musical Director:** Arthur Siegel; **Vocal Arranger:** Arthur Siegel

Songs: After Burton, Who? (C: Arthur Siegel; L: Louis Botto); Auf Wiedersehen (C/L: Stan Daniels; Ray Jessel); Ave Maria (C/L: Jack Johnson); Before and After (C/L: Jack Holmes); Bring Out the Beast in Me (C/L: Lance Mulcahy); How to Succeed in Business without Really Trying (C: Arthur Siegel; L: Louis Botto); Open Bright (C/L: John Meyer); Simple Tune, A (C/L: Jack Holmes); Story of Alice, The (C: Jerry Bock; L: Larry Holofcener); This Is New York [2] (C/L: Jack Holmes); Time for Another Affair (C: Thomas Wagner; L: Paul Rosner); Tune to Take Away (C: Ronald Cass; L: Peter Myers); We Miss Ike (C: Ronald Cass; L: Peter Myers); We Want You to Be the First Ones to Know [1] (C: Arthur Siegel; L: June Carroll)

Cast: Sudie Bond; Hal Buckley; Ralph Roberts; Cy Young; Myra de Groot

Notes: "Bring Out the Beast in Me" was credited incorrectly in the program. [1] Also in NEW FACES OF 1962. [2] Also in first edition of this show.

3891 • SEVEN HOURS IN NEW YORK

Musical

Composer: Will Morrissey
Lyricist: Hal Burton

Songs: Come Take a Trip in My Automobile; I Can't See You at All; I'd Like to Make a Date with You; Mermaid and Merman, The; Oriental Rag, The; Ragtime Base Ball; Seven Hours in New York; Sleepy Time

Notes: No other information available.

3892 • SEVEN LITTLE WIDOWS, THE

Musical

Lyricist: Rida Johnson Young
Librettist: Rida Johnson Young

Notes: Unproduced.

3893 • SEVEN LIVELY ARTS

OPENED: 12/07/1944   Theatre: Ziegfeld
Revue   Broadway: 182

Composer: Cole Porter
Lyricist: Cole Porter
Librettist: Moss Hart; Ben Hecht; George S. Kaufman; Robert Pirosh; Joseph Schrank; Charles Sherman
Producer: Billy Rose
Director: Jack Donahue; Philip Loeb; Hassard Short

Songs: Band Started Swinging a Song, The; Big Parade, The; Big Town; Cafe Society Still Carries On [1]; Dainty Quainty Me [1]; Dancin' to a Jungle Drum (Let's End the Beguine); Drink; Ev'rytime We Say Goodbye; Frahngee-Pahnee; Hence It Don't Make Sense; I Wrote a Play [1]; If I Hadn't a Husband [2]; Is It the Girl? (Or Is It the Gown); Only Another Boy and Girl; Pretty Little Missus Bell [1]; When I Was a Little Cuckoo; Where Do We Go from Here? [1]; Wow-ooh-wolf!; Yours for a Song [1]

Cast: Paula Bane; Anton Dolin; Helen Gallagher; Benny Goodman; Dolores Gray; Bert Lahr; Beatrice Lillie; Alicia Markova; Jere McMahon; Red Norvo; Mary Roche; William Tabbert; Teddy Wilson; Billie Worth; Nan Wynn

Notes: [1] Not used. [2] Not used. Music later used in AROUND THE WORLD as "Should I Tell You I Love You?"

3894 • SEVEN YEAR ITCH, THE

OPENED: 11/20/1952   Theatre: Fulton
Play   Broadway: 1141

Author: George Axelrod
Producer: Courtney Burr; Elliott Nugent
Director: John Gerstad

Costumes: Clare Potter; **Lighting Designer:** Frederick Fox; **Musical Director:** Gleb Yellin; **Set Design:** Frederick Fox

Songs: Girl without a Name, The (C/L: Dana Suesse; L: Scott Olson)

Cast: Vanessa Brown; Robert Emhardt; Tom Ewell; George Keane; Neva Patterson

3895 • SEVENTEEN
OPENED: 06/21/1951   Theatre: Broadhurst
Musical   Broadway: 180

Composer: Walter Kent
Lyricist: Kim Gannon
Librettist: Sally Benson
Producer: Milton Berle; Bernie Foyer; Sammy Lambert
Director: Hassard Short; Richard Whorf

Source: SEVENTEEN (Novel: Booth Tarkington); **Choreographer:** Dania Krupska; **Costumes:** David Ffolkes; **Musical Director:** Joseph Littau; **Orchestrations:** Ted Royal; **Set Design:** Stewart Chaney; **Vocal Arranger:** Crane Calder

Songs: After All, It's Spring; Headache and a Heartache, A; Hoosier Way; How Do You Do, Miss Pratt; I Could Get Married Today; If We Could Only Stop the Old Town Clock; Ode to Lola; Ooh, Ooh, Ooh, What You Do to Me; Reciprocity; Summertime Is Summertime; Things Are Gonna Hum This Summer; This Was Just Another Day; Weatherbee's Drug Store

Cast: Frank Albertson; Anne Crowley; Doris Dalton; Dick Kallman; Kenneth Nelson

3896 • 1776 (1884)
OPENED: 02/26/1884   Theatre: Thalia
Musical   New York

Composer: Ludwig Englander
Lyricist: Leo Goldmark
Librettist: Leo Goldmark

Cast: Marie Geistinger; Hans Junker

Notes: A German language production. No program available.

3897 • 1776 (1969)
OPENED: 03/16/1969   Theatre: 46th Street
Musical   Broadway: 1217

Composer: Sherman Edwards
Lyricist: Sherman Edwards
Librettist: Peter Stone
Producer: Stuart Ostrow
Director: Peter Hunt

Choreographer: Onna White; **Costumes:** Patricia Zipprodt; **Dance Arranger:** Peter Howard; **Lighting Designer:** Jo Mielziner; **Musical Director:** Peter Howard; **Orchestrations:** Eddie Sauter; **Set Design:** Jo Mielziner; **Vocal Arranger:** Elise Bretton

Songs: But Mr. Adams; Cool, Cool, Considerate Men; Egg, The; He Plays the Violin; Is Anybody There?; Lees of Old Virginia, The; Molasses to Rum; Momma Look Sharp; Piddle, Twiddle and Resolve; Sit Down, John; Till Then; Yours, Yours, Yours

Cast: Emory Bass; Betty Buckley; Howard Da Silva; William Daniels; Clifford David; David Ford; Paul Hecht; Ronald Holgate; Ken Howard; Edmund Lyndeck; Roy Poole; Virginia Vestoff

3898 • SEVENTH HEART, THE
OPENED: 05/02/1927   Theatre: Mayfair
Play   Broadway: 16

Composer: Arthur Brander
Lyricist: Arthur Brander
Author: Sarah Ellis Hyman
Producer: Lionel Productions
Director: Edward Elsner

Set Design: R.N. Robbins

Songs: Cinema Blues; For I'm in Love; I Wonder If Love Is a Dream; When My Eyes Meet Yours

Cast: Sylvia Beecher; Ralph Dunn; Aileen Poe

3899 • SEVENTH HEAVEN
OPENED: 05/26/1955   Theatre: ANTA
Musical   Broadway: 44

Composer: Victor Young
Lyricist: Stella Unger
Librettist: Victor Wolfson
Producer: William Bacher; Gant Gaither
Director: John C. Wilson

Source: SEVENTH HEAVEN (Play Austin Strong);
Choreographer: Peter Gennaro; **Costumes:**
Marcel Vertes; **Lighting Designer:** Feder;
Musical Director: Max Meth; **Orchestrations:**
David Terry; **Set Design:** Marcel Vertes

Songs: Blessings [1]; C'est la Vie; Camille, Colette,
Fifi; Chico's Reverie; Glove Dance; Happy Little
Crook; If It's a Dream; Love at My Door; Love,
Love, Love; Love Sneaks Up on You; Man with a
Dream; 'Miss You' Kiss, A; Remarkable Fellow;
Sun at My Window; Where Is That Someone for
Me?; White and Gold Ballet

Cast: Beatrice Arthur; Robert Clary; Gloria De
Haven; Patricia Hammerlee; Kurt Kasznar;
Ricardo Montalban; Gerrianne Raphael; Chita
Rivera

Notes: [1] Cut before opening.

3900 • 70, GIRLS, 70
OPENED: 04/15/1971   Theatre: Broadhurst
Musical   Broadway: 36

Composer: John Kander
Lyricist: Fred Ebb
Librettist: Fred Ebb; Norman L. Martin; Joe
Masteroff
Producer: Arthur Whitelaw
Director: Paul Aaron; Stanley Prager

Source: BREATH OF SPRING (Play Peter Coke);
Choreographer: Onna White; **Costumes:** Jane
Greenwood; **Lighting Designer:** Robert
Randolph; **Musical Director:** Oscar Kosarin;
Orchestrations: Don Walker; **Set Design:** Robert
Randolph; **Vocal Arranger:** Oscar Kosarin

Songs: Believe; Boom Ditty Boom; Broadway, My
Street; Caper, The; Coffee in a Cardboard Cup;
Do We?; Elephant Song, The; Folk Song [1]; Go
Visit; Hit It, Lorraine; Home; Old Folks; One,
Two, Three [1]; See the Light; 70, Girls, 70; Well
Laid Plans [2]; Yes; You and I, Love

Cast: Tommy Breslin; Hans Conreid; Joey Faye;
Dorothea Freitag; Lillian Hayman; Henrietta
Jacobson; Gil Lamb; Lucie Lancaster; Mildred
Natwick; Lillian Roth; Jay Velie

Notes: [1] Cut prior to opening. [2] Added for
London

3901 • SEX TIPS FOR MODERN GIRLS
OPENED: 12/19/1986   Theatre: Susan Bloch
Revue   Off-Broadway: 198

Composer: John Sereda
Lyricist: John Sereda
Librettist: Edward Astley; Susan Astley; Kim
Seary; Hilary Strang; Peter Eliot Weiss; Christine
Willes
Producer: Raymond L. Gaspard; Ray Waves
Prods.
Director: Susan Astley

Costumes: Pearl Bellesen; **Lighting Designer:**
Llewellyn Harrison; **Musical Director:** John
Sereda; **Set Design:** Pearl Bellesen

Songs: Baby, Baby; Easy for Them to Say; Go for It;
More and More; Motherload; Oh! K-Y Chorale
(or, Beyond the Labia Majora); Ordinary
Women; Penis Envoy (L: Gary Fisher; John
Sereda); Up to My Tits in Water (C/L: Kim
Seary; Adrian Smith); Victim of Normality; Who
Will Be There

Cast: Edward Astley; Kim Seary; Hilary Strang;
Christine Willes

3902 • SEXTET
OPENED: 03/03/1974   Theatre: Bijou
Musical   Broadway: 9

Composer: Lawrence Hurwit
Lyricist: Lee Goldsmith
Librettist: Lee Goldsmith; Harvey Perr
Producer: Balemar Productions; Lawrence E. Sokol
Director: Jered Barclay

Choreographer: Jered Barclay; **Costumes:** Zoe
Brown; **Lighting Designer:** Marc B. Weiss;
Musical Director: David Frank; **Orchestrations:**
David Frank; **Set Design:** Peter Harvey

Songs: Going-Staying; Hi; How Does It Start?;
I Love You All the Time; I Wonder; It'd Be Nice;
Keep on Dancing; Nervous; Roseland; Someone
to Love; Spunk; Visiting Rights; What the Hell
Am I Doing Here?; Women and Men

Cast: Dixie Carter; Harvey Evans; Jerry Lanning;
John Newton; Mary Small; Robert Spencer

3903 • SGT. PEPPER'S LONELY HEARTS CLUB BAND ON THE ROAD

OPENED: 11/17/1974   Theatre: Beacon
Musical   Off-Broadway: 66

Composer: John Lennon
Lyricist: John Lennon; Paul McCartney
Librettist: Paul McCartney; Tom O'Horgan; Robin Wagner
Producer: Brian Avnet; Robert Stigwood
Director: Tom O'Horgan

Source: SGT. PEPPER'S LONELY HEARTS CLUB BAND (Record Album: John Lennon; Paul McCartney); **Costumes:** Randy Barcelo; **Lighting Designer:** Jules Fisher; **Musical Director:** Gordon Lowry Harrell; **Set Design:** Robin Wagner; **Vocal Arranger:** Gordon Lowry Harrell

Songs: Because; Being for the Benefit of Mr. Kite; Carry That Weight; Come Together; Day in the Life, A; Fixing a Hole; Get Back; Getting Better; Golden Slumbers; Good Morning, Good Morning; Her Majesty; I Want You; Long and Winding Road, The; Lovely Rita; Lucy in the Sky with Diamonds; Maxwell's Silver Hammer; Mean Mr. Mustard; Nowhere Man; Oh! Darling; Polythene Pam; Sgt. Pepper's Lonely Hearts Club Band; She Came in Through the Bathroom Window; She's Leaving Home; Strawberry Fields Forever; Sun Queen; When I'm 64; With a Little Help from My Friends; You Never Give Me Your Money

Cast: Kay Cole; B.G. Gibson; David Patrick Kelly; Ted Neeley; Allan Nicholls; William Parry; Alaina Reed; Walter Rivera

Notes: No original songs in this show.

3904 • SHADES OF HADES

OPENED: 1922
Musical

Composer: Dave Payton
Lyricist: Dave Payton
Librettist: Tim Owsley
Producer: J. Samuel Stanfield
Director: Julia Rector

Songs: Caroline; Holiday in Hades Today; Nashville Blues, The

Cast: Laura Bowman; B.B. Joyner; Sidney Kirkpatrick; Tim Owsley

Notes: No other information available. Songs from 1923 program.

3905 • SHADES OF HARLEM

OPENED: 08/21/1984   Theatre: Village Gate Downstairs
Musical   Off-Broadway: 258

Composer: Frank Owens
Lyricist: Jeree Palmer; Ty Stephens
Producer: Tom Conforti; Jerry Saperstein
Director: Mical Whitaker

Choreographer: Ty Stephens; **Costumes:** Sharon Alexander; **Dance Arranger:** Frank Owens; **Lighting Designer:** Robert Strohmeier; **Musical Director:** Frank Owens; **Set Design:** Linda Lombardi; **Vocal Arranger:** Frank Owens

Songs: At a Georgia Camp Meetin' [1] (C/L: Kerry Mills); Black Coffee [1] (C: Sonny Burke; L: Paul Francis Webster); Body and Soul [2] (C: John Green; L: Howard Dietz; Frank Eyton; Edward Heyman; Robert Sour); Diga Diga Doo [3] (C: Jimmy McHugh; L: Dorothy Fields); God Bless the Child [1] (C/L: Arthur Herzog Jr.; Billie Holliday); Harlem (C: Jeree Palmer; L: Branice McKenzie; Ty Stephens); Harlem Hop (L: Frank Owens; Ty Stephens); I Got It Bad and That Ain't Good [1] (C: Duke Ellington; L: Paul Francis Webster); I Got Rhythm [4] (C: George Gershwin; L: Ira Gershwin); I Love Harlem; If You Wanna Keep Your Man (C/L: Branice McKenzie); I'm Just Simply Full of Jazz [1] (C: Eubie Blake; L: Noble Sissle); It Don't Mean a Thing [1] (C/L: Duke Ellington); Jitterbug (inst.), The; My Man [1] (C: Maurice Yvain; L: Jacques Charles; Channing Pollock; Albert Willemetz); On the Sunny Side of the Street [1] (C: Jimmy McHugh; L: Dorothy Fields); Perdido [1] (C: Juan Tizol; L: Ervin Drake; Hans Lengsfelder); Right Key, Wrong Keyhole [1] (C/L: Unknown); Satin Doll [1] (C: Duke Ellington; Billy Strayhorn; L: Johnny Mercer); Shades of Harlem; Stowaway (C/L: Ty Stephens); Sweet Georgia Brown [1] (C/L: Ben Bernie; Kenneth Casey; Maceo Pinkard); Take the 'A' Train [1] (C/L: Billy Strayhorn); That Ol' Black Magic [5] (C: Harold Arlen; L: Johnny Mercer)

Cast: Branice McKenzie; Jeree Palmer; Ty Stephens

Notes: [1] Not written for this show. [2] Not written for this show. In THREE'S A CROWD. [3] Not written for this show. In BLACKBIRDS OF 1928. [4] Not written for this show. In GIRL CRAZY. [5] Not written for this show. From film STAR SPANGLED RHYTHM.

3906 • SHADOW PLAY

OPENED: 11/24/1936   Theatre: National
Musical   Broadway: 113

Composer: Noel Coward
Lyricist: Noel Coward
Author: Noel Coward
Producer: John C. Wilson
Director: Noel Coward

Musical Director: John McManus; **Set Design:** G.E. Calthrop

Songs: Play, Orchestra, Play!; Then; You Were There

Cast: Joyce Carey; Noel Coward; Gertrude Lawrence; Moya Nugent; Edward Underdown; Alan Webb

Notes: Part of TONIGHT AT 8:30. SHADOW PLAY was a one-act in repertory with other Coward works. The run of 113 performances reflects the run of TONIGHT AT 8:30 of which SHADOW PLAY only ran maybe a third of the time.

3907 • SHADY LADY

OPENED: 07/05/1933   Theatre: Shubert
Musical   Broadway: 30

Composer: Sam H. Stept
Lyricist: Bud Green
Librettist: Irving Caesar; Estelle Morando
Producer: Henry Meyer
Director: Theodore Hammerstein

Choreographer: Jack Donahue; **Costumes:** Brooks; Billy Livingston; **Musical Director:** Max Hoffmann; **Orchestrations:** Charles Cooke; Henry Redfield; **Set Design:** Tom Adrian Cracraft

Songs: Any Way the Wind Blows (L: Cliff Friend; Bud Green); Everything but My Man (C: Serge Walter; L: Charles Kenny); Farewell, Time to Go [1] (C: Jesse Greer; L: Stanley Adams); Get Hot Foot; Hiya Sucker (C: Jesse Greer; L: Stanley Adams); I'll Betcha That I'll Getcha (C: Jesse Greer; L: Stanley Adams); I'm Takin' a Chance on You; Isn't It Remarkable (C: Jesse Greer; L: Stanley Adams); Isn't It Swell to Dream (C: Jesse Greer; Sam H. Stept; L: Stanley Adams; Bud Green); Live, Laugh and Love; One Heart; Swingy Little Thingy; Where, Oh Where Can I Find Love? (C: Jesse Greer; L: Stanley Adams); You're Not the One (C: Jesse Greer; L: Stanley Adams); Your Type Is Coming Back

Cast: Lester Allen; Audrey Christie; Jack Donahue; Max Hoffmann Jr.; Helen Kane; Louise Kirtland; Charles Purcell; Helen Raymond

Notes: [1] Program credits composer as Sam H. Stept. Sheet music lists Jesse Greer.

3908 • SHAKESPEARE AND THE INDIANS

OPENED: 05/27/1983
Musical   Closed out of town

Composer: Allan Jay Friedman
Lyricist: Rita Briggs; Rob Preston
Librettist: Dale Wasserman
Producer: PepsiCo Summerfare '83
Director: Dennis Rosa

Choreographer: Dennis Rosa; **Conductor:** Patrick Brady; **Costumes:** Ruth Morley; **Lighting Designer:** John McLain; **Musical Director:** William D. Brohn; **Set Design:** Christina Weppner

Songs: Ain't That Langwidge Though; Ample Fronts; Be a Mountain Man; Countin' Cobblestones; Don't Be Afraid of the Dark; Elisha's Vision; Foofaraw; Grace; How Do You Know; Indian Talk; Muddling Through; Nobody Said; Part of the Plan; Part of the Plan Finale; Players' Plaint; Stages; War Ritual; We Wanna Be His Paw; We'll Give Him a Home; Where I Belong; Who Is This Woman

Cast: David Berman; Meg Bussert; Ned Coulter; Timothy Jecko; Ken Land; Jerry Scurlock; Rino Thunder

3909 • SHAKESPEARE'S CABARET

OPENED: 02/01/1980   Theatre: Bijou
Revue   Broadway: 94

Composer: Lance Mulcahy
Lyrics Based On: William Shakespeare
Producer: Arthur Shafman
Director: John Driver

Choreographer: Lynne Taylor-Corbett; **Costumes:** Frank J. Boros; **Lighting Designer:** Marc B. Weiss; **Musical Director:** Don Jones; **Orchestrations:** Don Jones; **Set Design:** Frank J. Boros; **Vocal Arranger:** Don Jones

Songs: All That Glitters [5]; Celebration [1] (L: Christopher Marlowe); Come Away Death [10]; Come Live with Me and Be My Love [1] (L: Christopher Marlowe); Come Unto These Yellow Sands [18]; Crabbed Age and Youth [3]; Epitaph for Marina [20]; Fathers that Wear Rags [11]; Fear No More the Heat of the Sun [21]; Grave Digger's Song, The [16]; Have More Than Thou Showest [11]; How Should I Your True Love Know? [17]; I Am St. Jacques' Pilgrim [2]; If Music and Sweet Poetry Agree [3]; If Music Be the Food of Love [9]; Immortal Gods [15]; Lawn As White As Driven Snow [12]; Let the Canakin Clink [14]; Music with Her Silver Sound [8]; Now [4]; Orpheus with His Lute [7]; Phoenix and the Turtle, The; Pyramus Arise [2]; Rosalynde [6]; Shakespeare's Epitaph; Shall I Compare Thee to a Summer's Day [19]; Shepherd's Song [2]; Tell Me Where Is Fancy Bred? [5]; Tomorrow Is St. Valentine's Day [16]; Venus and Adonis Suite; What Thou See'st When Thou Doest Awake [4]; Why Should This a Desert Be? [6]; Will You Buy Any Tape? [13]; Willow Song, The [14]

Cast: Alan Brasington; Catherine Cox; Pauletta Pearson; Patti Perkins; Larry Riley; Michael Rupert

Notes: Played 40 performances Off-Broadway at the Colonades Theatre Lab then was remounted on Broadway on 1/21/81. [1] By Christopher Marlowe as quoted by Shakespeare in TWELFTH NIGHT. [2] Cut prior to move to Broadway. [3] From THE PASSIONATE PILGRIM. [4] From A MIDSUMMER NIGHT'S DREAM. [5] From THE MERCHANT OF VENICE. [6] From AS YOU LIKE IT. [7] From HENRY VIII. [8] From ROMEO AND JULIET. [9] From TWELFTH NIGHT. [10] Cut prior to move to Broadway. From TWELFTH NIGHT. [11] From KING LEAR. [12] From THE WINTER'S TALE. [13] Cut prior to move to Broadway. From THE WINTER'S TALE. [14] From OTHELLO. [15] From TIMON OF ATHENS. [16] From

HAMLET. [17] Cut prior to Broadway. From HAMLET. [18] From THE TEMPEST. [19] From SONNET 18. [20] From PERICLES. [21] From CYMBELINE.

3910 • SHAMEEN DHU

OPENED: 02/02/1914   Theatre: Grand Opera
House
Play   Broadway: 32

Composer: Cassius Freeborn
Author: Rida Johnson Young
Director: Henry Miller

Musical Director: Cassius Freeborn

Songs: Bubbie; Dream Girl O' Mine [1] (L: Chauncey Olcott); I Never Met Before a Girl Like You [1] (C: Cassius Freeborn; Chauncey Olcott; L: George Graff Jr.); In Those Good Old Days of Fairies [2] (C: Cassius Freeborn; Chauncey Olcott; L: George Graff Jr.); Le Reflection; L'Evasion; My Little Dudeen [1] (C: Ernest R. Ball; L: George Graff Jr.); Shameen; Shameen Dhu (C/L: Chauncey Olcott); Too-ra-loo-ra-loo-ra That's an Irish Lullaby [1] (C/L: James Royce Shannon); Vis-a-vis

Cast: Maurice Drew; Beth Franklyn; Arthur Maitland; Constance Molineaux; Chauncey Olcott; Robert Watt

Notes: [1] Sheet music only. [2] ASCAP/Library of Congress only.

3911 • SHAMROCK

Musical

Composer: Cliff Hess
Lyricist: Joseph Santley
Librettist: Edgar Allen Woolf
Director: Pat Rooney; Edgar Allen Woolf

Songs: Anastasia Reilly; I Want a Girl Like Mother Was; Irish Moon; Shamrock; Two Best Girls I Love, The

Cast: Marion Bent; Pat Rooney

Notes: No other information available.

3912 • SHAMUS O'BRIEN

OPENED: 01/05/1897   Theatre: Broadway
Musical   Broadway: 56

Composer: C. Villiers Stanford
Librettist: George H. Jessop

Choreographer: Edward Murphy; Carr Shaw

Songs: Glengall; My Heart Is in Thrall; Ochone, When I Used to Be Young; Song of the Banshee, The; Where Is the Man?

Cast: Denie O'Sullivan; Annie Roberts; Donald Roberts

Notes: No songs listed in program. Songs from sheet music.

3913 • SHANGRI-LA

OPENED: 06/13/1956   Theatre: Winter Garden
Musical   Broadway: 21

Composer: Harry Warren
Lyricist: Jerome Lawrence; Robert E. Lee
Additional Lyrics: Sheldon Harnick
Librettist: James Hilton; Jerome Lawrence; Robert E. Lee
Producer: Lawrence Carr; Robert Fryer
Director: Albert Marre

Source: LOST HORIZON (Novel: James Hilton);
Choreographer: Donald Saddler; **Costumes:** Irene Sharaff; **Dance Arranger:** Genevieve Pitot; **Musical Director:** Lehman Engel; **Orchestrations:** Philip J. Lang, **Set Design:** Peter Larkin, **Vocal Arranger:** Lehman Engel

Songs: Beetle Race, The; Chant of the Dead Pilot [3]; Dance of Moderate Chastity (dance); Dance of Time (dance); Dance of Welcome (dance); Every Night [1]; Every Time You Dance with Me; I'm Just a Little Bit Confused; In the Hollow of His Hand [1]; It's Fun to Be in London [2]; Listen to the Sound of My Love [4]; Long Ago [2]; Lost Horizon; Love Is What I Never Knew; Man I Never Met, The (L: James Hilton; Jerome Lawrence; Robert E. Lee); Man in the Dark [2] (L: James Hilton; Jerome Lawrence; Robert E. Lee); Men Are Only Boys Grown Tall [1] (L: James Hilton; Jerome Lawrence; Robert E. Lee); Moderation [1]; No Night to Fear [2] (L: James Hilton; Jerome Lawrence; Robert E. Lee); Nothing Much to Do [2]; Om Mani Padme Hum; Remember Him [2] (L: James Hilton; Jerome Lawrence; Robert E. Lee); Requiem; Second Time in Love; Shangri-La; Somewhere; Talkin' with Your Feet; Walk Sweet; We've

Decided to Stay; What Do You Do [1] (L: James Hilton; Jerome Lawrence; Robert E. Lee); What Every Old Girl Should Know; When We Are Born Again [2]; World Outside, The

Cast: Jack Cassidy; Alice Ghostley; Martyn Green; Joan Holloway; Dennis King; Berry Kroeger; Harold Lang; Carol Lawrence; Shirley Yamaguchi

Notes: [1] Cut Boston 4/30/56. [2] Not used. [3] Added to television version. [4] ASCAP/Library of Congress only.

3914 • SHAPE OF THINGS, THE

OPENED: 07/26/1947
Revue   Closed out of town

Composer: James Shelton
Lyricist: James Shelton
Librettist: George Hall; Sally Humason; James Shelton; Leslie Stevens; Irving Wexler
Producer: Francis I. Curtis
Director: Lew Kesler

Choreographer: William Skipper; **Set Design:** Frederick Stover

Songs: As We Told You [1]; Come Home and Get Cozy with Me [1] (C/L: Carley Mills); Finale; Gertrude, You and Me (C/L: Carley Mills); Harem, The; I'm the Girl; Is It You or the Cocktail?; Life of the Party (C: Richard Lewine; L: Ted Fetter); Mama at the Bat; Mama, What's Love (C: Clay Boland; L: Eddie De Lange); Once; Opening Number; Susie's Back in Town; That's Love; This Is Heaven

Cast: Elna Anderson; Eleanor Bagley; George Hall; Ray Long; Bibi Osterwald; Elaine Stritch; **Pianist:** Bud Gregg; Randy Kraft

Notes: Program of John Drew Theatre, East Hampton, NY. [1] Also in ALMOST CRAZY but with Lew Kesler credited with music.

3915 • SHARLEE

OPENED: 11/22/1923   Theatre: Daly's
Musical   Broadway: 36

Composer: C. Luckeyth Roberts
Lyricist: Alex Rogers
Librettist: Harry L. Cort; George E. Stoddard

Producer: John Cort
Director: Charles Sinclair

Musical Director: Hilding Anderson

Songs: Broadway Rose; Doing the Ritz; Ensemble Entrance; Heart Beats; Honeymoon Row; Leaping Leopards; Little Drops of Water; Love Is the Bunk; Love To-day; Loving Is a Habit; My Caveman-My Venus; My Sunshine; Opening Ensemble; Princess Nicotine; Sharlee; Toodle-Oo

Cast: Juliette Day; Sydney Grant

3916 • SHE HAD TO SAY YES

OPENED: 12/30/1940
Musical   Closed out of town

Composer: Sammy Fain
Lyricist: Al Dubin
Librettist: Bob Henley; Richard Pinkham
Producer: Dennis King
Director: William Miles

Choreographer: Charles Walters; **Costumes:** Stewart Chaney; **Musical Director:** Jacques Rabiroff; **Orchestrations:** Van Cleve; **Set Design:** Stewart Chaney

Songs: Between Romances; Concerto in E-Flat Major; Customer's Always Right, The; Girl Who Works in the Laundry, The; How Is Your Technique?; Man Who Came to Win 'Er; Meet the Elite; Merrily on My Way; My DeeTees; My Most Embarrasing Moment; Never Take No for an Answer; Our Memoirs; Serenade to a Chambermaid; Spend Your Vacation on Broadway; Stranger in the Mirror; You for Me

Cast: Dennis King; Paula Stone; Charles Walters; Marcy Wescott

Notes: Opened in Philadelphia. After this show folded the set was used in THE LADY COMES ACROSS.

3917 • SHE KNOWS BETTER NOW

OPENED: 01/15/1912
Play   Closed out of town

Author: Agnes Crimmins
Producer: Eisfeldt and Anhalt
Director: William Collier

Songs: I'm Going Back to Dixie (C/L: Irving Berlin; Ted Snyder); Ragtime Mocking Bird, The (C/L: Irving Berlin)

Cast: Arthur Byron; May Irwin

Notes: Closed at Plymouth Theatre, Chicago.

3918 • SHE LOVES ME

OPENED: 04/23/1963   Theatre: Eugene O'Neill
Musical   Broadway: 302

Composer: Jerry Bock
Lyricist: Sheldon Harnick
Librettist: Joe Masteroff
Producer: Lawrence Kasha; Philip C. McKenna; Harold Prince
Director: Harold Prince

Source: PARFUMERIE (Play Miklos Nikolaus Laszlo); **Choreographer:** Carol Haney; **Costumes:** Patricia Zipprodt; **Lighting Designer:** Jean Eckart; William Eckart; **Musical Director:** Harold Hastings; **Orchestrations:** Don Walker; **Set Design:** Jean Eckart; William Eckart

Songs: Christmas Eve [1]; Days Gone By; Dear Friend; Good Morning, Good Day; Goodbye, George; Grand Knowing You; Heads I Win [2]; Hello Love [1]; I Don't Know His Name; I Resolve; Ice Cream; Ilona; Letters [2]; Merry Christmas Bells [1]; My Drug Store [1]; No More Candy; Perspective; Romantic Atmosphere, A; Seasonal Pleasure [1]; She Loves Me; Sounds While Selling; Tango Tragique; Tell Me I Look Nice [1]; Thank You, Madam; Three Letters; Tonight at Eight; Trip to the Library, A; Try Me; Twelve Days to Christmas; Where's My Shoe?; Will He Like Me?

Cast: Barbara Baxley; Jack Cassidy; Gino Conforti; Barbara Cook; Al De Sio; Ludwig Donath; Nathaniel Frey; Daniel Massey; Peg Murray; Wood Romoff; Ralph Williams

Notes: [1] Not used. [2] Added to London version.

3919 • SHE LOVES ME NOT

OPENED: 11/20/1933   Theatre: 46th Street
Play   Broadway: 367

Composer: Arthur Schwartz
Lyricist: Edward Heyman

Author: Howard Lindsay
Producer: Tom Weatherly; Dwight Deere Wiman
Director: Howard Lindsay

Source: UNKNOWN (Novel: Edward Hope);
  Choreographer: Andy Anderson; **Set Design:**
  Raymond Sovey

Songs: After All, You're All I'm After; She Loves
  Me Not

Cast: Burgess Meredith; Polly Walters

3920 • SHE SHALL HAVE MUSIC
OPENED: 01/22/1959   Theatre: Theatre Marquee
Musical   Off-Broadway: 54

Composer: Dede Meyer
Lyricist: Dede Meyer
Librettist: Stuart Bishop
Producer: Stuart Bishop; Dede Meyer; Edwin West
Director: Louis MacMillan

Source: COUNTRY WIFE, THE (Play William
  Wycherly); **Choreographer:** Tao Strong; **Lighting
  Designer:** Bernic Joy; **Musical Director:** Julian
  Stein; **Set Design:** Helen Pond; Herbert Senn

Songs: Basic; Blind Man's Buff; Feign a Faint,
  Ladies [1]; Here's What a Mistress Ought to Be;
  I Live to Love; I Love to Flirt with the Ladies [1];
  If I Am to Marry You; Maude, the Bawd; Moi;
  No True Love; One Sweet Moment; Scarlet
  Trimmings; She Shall Have Music; Someday,
  Maybe; Theatre Quadrille; Twelve O'Clock Song;
  Who Are You?; Who Needs It?; Wonder Where
  My Heart Is

Cast: Laurence Chelsi; Cherry Davis; Skedge
  Miller; Betty Oakes; Barbara Pavell; Honey
  Sanders; Lawrence Weber

Notes: [1] Cut prior to opening.

3921 • SHE TOOK A CHANCE
OPENED: 06/1918
Musical   Closed out of town

Composer: Uda Waldrop
Lyricist: Henry Blossom
Librettist: Henry Blossom
Producer: Klaw & Erlanger
Director: Edgar MacGregor

Source: FULL HOUSE, A (Play Fred Jackson);
  Choreographer: Julian Mitchell; **Musical
  Director:** Alfred Goodman; **Set Design:** Clifford
  Pember

Songs: Always Wear a Smile; Anytime New York
  Goes Dry; Beautiful Bouquet; Bubbles; Every
  Time I Look at You; Fainting Ensemble [1];
  Happiness; Hundred Years from Now, A; I Don't
  Know Nothin'; I Love to Look Again; Just to
  Make the World a Little Brighter; Logic; Love
  Has Come to Me [1]; No One Would Steal You
  from Me; Policeology; Souvenirs;
  Spooky-ookum; Susie from Sioux City; There's
  No Time Like Now Time; There's Something
  About You; Throwing the Bull; When Your Love
  Is Away

Cast: Alfred Gerrard; Wanda Lyon; Mary Milburn;
  Ray Raymond

Notes: Program of 11/10/18 Washington D.C. and
  one of Boston used. Later with a new score
  became THE VELVET LADY. See that entry. [1]
  Sheet music only.

3922 • SHE WALKED HOME
Musical

Composer: Don Hunt
Lyricist: Don Hunt
Producer: Anne Nichols

Songs: I Do; I Got a Lucy Break; Rosette; You're
  My Temptation

Notes: No other information available.

3923 • SHE'S A GOOD FELLOW
OPENED: 05/05/1919   Theatre: Globe
Musical   Broadway: 120

Composer: Jerome Kern
Lyricist: Anne Caldwell
Librettist: Anne Caldwell
Producer: Charles Dillingham
Director: Fred G. Latham

Costumes: Gladys Monkhouse; **Musical Director:**
  William Daly; **Orchestrations:** Frank Saddler

Songs: Bullfrog Patrol; Bumble Bee, The; Faith,
  Hope and Charity; First Rose of Summer, The [4];

Ginger Town [3]; Happy Wedding Day, A; Home Sweet Home [5]; I Believe in Signs [3]; I Want My Little Gob; I've Been Waiting for You All the Time [2]; Jubilo [1] (L: Anne Caldwell; Henry Clay Work); Just a Little Line; Little Pip, A [3]; Navy Foxtrot Man, The; Oh, You Beautiful Person!; Over the Hills; Semiramis [3]; Snip, Snip, Snip; Some Party; Teacher Teacher; Wine Women and Song [3]

Cast: Duncan Sisters, The; Olin Howland; Ann Orr; Joseph Santley; Ivy Sawyer

Notes: Titled A NEW GIRL prior to Broadway. [1] Found on "Kingdom Comin'" by Henry Clay Work. [2] A rewrite of "Oh Promise Me You'll Write Him Today" from THE CANARY. [3] Cut out of town prior to New York. [4] Quotes "Last Rose of Summer" and Kern's "Where's the Girl for Me." [5] From sheet music for A NEW GIRL.

3924 • SHE'S MY BABY

OPENED: 01/03/1928   Theatre: Globe
Musical   Broadway: 71

Composer: Richard Rodgers
Lyricist: Lorenz Hart
Librettist: Guy Bolton; Bert Kalmar; Harry Ruby
Producer: Charles B. Dillingham
Director: Edward Royce

Choreographer: Mary Read; **Costumes:** Francillion; Raymond Sovey; **Musical Director:** Gene Salzer; **Set Design:** Raymond Sovey

Songs: Baby's Best Friend, A [1]; Camera Shoot [8]; Here She Comes (Musical Entrance — Tilly) (All Set! Let's Go); How Was I to Know? [6]; I Need Some Cooling Off [12]; If I Were You [7]; Little House in Soho, A [5]; March with Me [4] (C: Ivor Novello; L: Douglas Furber); Morning Is Midnight [11]; My Lucky Star [9]; Pipes of Pansy, The [3]; Smart People [4]; Swallows, The; This Goes Up (Smile) (Keep Your Eye on Me); Try Again Tomorrow [8]; Wasn't It Great? (It's All Over Now) [2]; When I Go on the Stage; When I Saw Him Last (Finale Act I); Where Can the Baby Be?; Whoopsie [2]; You're What I Need [10]

Cast: Joan Clement; Frank Doane; Irene Dunne; Pearl Eaton; William Frawley; Beatrice Lillie; Nick Long Jr.; William McCarthy; Phyllis Rae; Clifton Webb; Jack Whiting

Notes: [1] Same music as "Lullaby" from CHARLOT'S MASQUERADE. [2] Cut after opening. [3] Not used in this show, DEAREST ENEMY, THE GIRL FRIEND and PEGGY-ANN. [4] Added after opening. [5] Same music, and mostly the same lyric, as "A Tiny Flat Near Soho Square" from LIDO LADY. [6] Cut prior to opening. Same music as "Why Do You Suppose?" from HEADS UP. [7] Cut prior to opening then added after the show opened. Also in BETSY and the London show LADY LUCK. [8] Not used in LIDO LADY. [9] Also in ONE DAM THING AFTER ANOTHER. [10] Cut from A CONNECTICUT YANKEE. [11] Cut prior to opening. Also not used in LIDO LADY. [12] Also in ONE DAM THING AFTER ANOTHER.

3925 • SHEBA

OPENED: 07/24/1974
Musical   Closed out of town

Composer: Clint Ballard Jr.
Lyricist: Lee Goldsmith
Librettist: Lee Goldsmith
Producer: Sidney Eden
Director: William Francisco

Source: COME BACK, LITTLE SHEBA (Play: William Inge); **Choreographer:** William Francisco; Gus Giordano; **Costumes:** Jody Kessler; **Lighting Designer:** Michael S. Hooker; **Musical Director:** Glen Clugston; **Orchestrations:** Ralph Burns; **Set Design:** James E. Maronek; **Vocal Arranger:** Glen Clugston

Songs: Busy Day; Contented Man; Dream Girl; Everything's All Right [1]; Going to Make It Better All the Time; It Doesn't Have to Be That Way; Lola Delaney; Lola's Theme (Lola Pretty Lola); Lola-Marie (She Isn't Lola); My Own Place; Plain, Old Room; Pretty Girl; Sweet Ukulele [2]; What Do I Do Now, Mom?

Cast: Kay Ballard; Kimberly Farr; Gary Sandy; George D. Wallace

Notes: [1] Lead-in to "Dream Girl" but not listed in program. [2] Written for an earlier show.

3926 • SHEIK OF AVENUE B, THE

OPENED: 11/22/1992   Theatre: Town Hall
Revue   Broadway: 54

Librettist: Isaiah Sheffer
Producer: Alan Glist; Kathi Glist; Mazel Musicals; Lawrence Topall
Director: Dan Siretta

Arrangements: Lanny Meyers; **Choreographer:** Dan Siretta; **Costumes:** Deirdre Burke; **Lighting Designer:** Robert Bessoir; **Musical Director:** Lanny Meyers; **Set Design:** Bruce Goodrich

Songs: Abe and Me and the Baby (C: Harry Von Tilzer; L: Fanny Brice; Lew Brown); Beckie, Stay in Your Own Back Yard [2] (C/L: Norman; Young; L: Lanny Meyers); Change Your Immigrant Ways [2] (C/L: Unknown; L: Isaiah Sheffer); Cohen Owes Me $97 (C/L: Irving Berlin); Doin' the Neighborhood Rag (C/L: Harry Von Tilzer; L: Lanny Meyers; Isaiah Sheffer); East Side Moon (C: Sam M. Lewis; Leo Meyer; L: Isaiah Sheffer); Ish-Ga-Bibble (I Should Worry) (C/L: Sam M. Lewis; Leo W. Meyer; L: Lanny Meyers; Isaiah Sheffer); Jake the Ball Player (C/L: Irving Berlin); Matinee Girl (C/L: Unknown); My Yiddisha Colleen (C: Edward Madden; L: Leo Edwards); Nathan, Nathan, What Are You Waitin' For? (C/L: Unknown); Nice Baby (C/L: Mac Ruthchild; Leonard Whitcup); Rabbi's Daughter, A (C/L: Charles K. Harris); Rosenthal Ain't Rosenthal No More (C/L: Robert A. Simon); Rosie Rosenblatt, Stop the Turkey Trot! (C/L: Unknown); Sam, You Made the Pants Too Long (C/L: Fred Whitehouse; L: Milton Berle); Serenade Me Sadie with a Ragtime Tune (C: Joe Young; L: Bert Grant); Sheik of Avenue B, The (C: Harry Ruby; L: Bert Kalmar); Since Henry Ford Apologized to Me (C/L: Billy Rose); That's an Egg Cream! [2] (C/L: Lanny Meyers; Isaiah Sheffer); Whose Izzy Is He? (C/L: Lew Brown; Bud Green; Murray Sturm; L: Lanny Meyers); Yiddisha Charleston (C: Fred Fisher; L: Billy Rose); Yiddisha Luck and Irisha Love (Kelly and Rosenbaum, That's Mazel-Toff) (C/L: Alfred Bryan; Fred Fisher); Yiddisha Nightingale (C/L: Irving Berlin)

Cast: Amanda Green; Paul Harman; Mark Nadler; Jack Plotnick; Judy Premus; Michele Ragusa; Larry Raiken; Virginia Sandifur

Notes: [1] A parody of "Lord, You Made the Night Too Long" by Sam M. Lewis and Victor Young. [2] Written for this show.

3927 • SHELTER

OPENED: 02/06/1973   Theatre: John Golden
Musical   Broadway: 31

Composer: Nancy Ford
Lyricist: Gretchen Cryer
Librettist: Gretchen Cryer
Producer: Richard Fields; Peter Flood
Director: Austin Pendleton

Choreographer: Sammy Bayes; **Costumes:** Tony Walton; **Lighting Designer:** Richard Pilbrow; **Musical Director:** Kirk Nurock; **Orchestrations:** Thomas Pierson; **Set Design:** Tony Walton; **Vocal Arranger:** Kirk Nurock

Songs: Changing; Don't Tell Me It's Forever; Going Home with My Children; Her's a Fool; I Bring Him Seashells; It's Hard to Care; Mary Margaret's House in the Country; She's My Girl; Sleep, My Baby, Sleep; Sunrise; Too Many Women in My Life [1]; Welcome to a New World; Woke Up Today; Woman on the Run

Cast: Susan Browning; Charles Collins; Terry Kiser; Philip Kraus; Joanna Merlin; Marcia Rodd; Britt Swanson; Tony Wells

Notes: [1] Cut prior to New York opening.

3928 • SHENANDOAH

OPENED: 01/07/1975   Theatre: Alvin
Musical   Broadway: 1050

Composer: Gary Geld
Lyricist: Peter Udell
Librettist: James Lee Barrett; Philip Rose; Peter Udell
Producer: Philip Rose; Gloria Sher; Louis K. Sher

Source: SHENANDOAH (Film: James Lee Barrett); **Choreographer:** Robert Tucker; **Costumes:** Winn Morton; Pearl Somner; **Dance Arranger:** Russell Warner; **Lighting Designer:** Thomas Skelton; **Musical Director:** Lynn Crigler; **Orchestrations:** Don Walker; **Set Design:** C. Murawski

Songs: Freedom; If I Were You [1]; It's a Boy; I've Heard It All Before; Meditation; Next to Lovin' I Like Fightin'; Only Home I Know, The; Over the Hill; Papa's Gonna Make It Alright; Pass the Cross to Me; Pickers Are Comin', The; Raise the Flag of Dixie; Violets and Silverbells; We Make a Beautiful Pair; Why Am I Me

Cast: Ted Agress; John Cullum; Chip Ford; Joel Higgins; Craig Lucas; Penelope Milford; Casper Roos; David Russell; Jordan Suffin; Donna Theodore

Notes: Originally titled SHENANDOAH, THE ONLY HOME I KNOW. [1] Cut prior to opening.

3929 • SHENANDOAH, THE ONLY HOME I KNOW

Notes: *See SHENANDOAH.*

3930 • SHERLOCK HOLMES AND THE CASE OF THE MISSING SANTA CLAUS

OPENED: 1985
Musical   Unproduced

Composer: Charles Strouse
Lyricist: Don Black
Librettist: Simon Brett; David Wood

Notes: No song list available.

3931 • SHERRY!

OPENED: 03/28/1967   Theatre: Alvin
Musical   Broadway: 65

Composer: Laurence Rosenthal
Lyricist: James Lipton
Librettist: James Lipton
Producer: Frank Ford; Shelly Gross; Lee Guber
Director: Joe Layton

Source: MAN WHO CAME TO DINNER, THE (Play: Moss Hart; George S. Kaufman); **Choreographer:** Joe Layton; **Costumes:** Robert Mackintosh; **Dance Arranger:** John Morris; **Lighting Designer:** Robert Randolph; **Musical Director:** Jay Blackton; **Orchestrations:** Larry Wilcox; **Set Design:** Robert Randolph; **Vocal Arranger:** Jay Blackton

Songs: Alas, Lorraine; Au Revoir; Christmas Eve; Cream of Mush; Crockfield [1]; Fred Astaire Affair, The; Harriet Sedley; Harriet's Pavan (dance); How Can You Kiss Those Times Good Bye; I Always Stay at the Ritz [1]; Imagine That; In the Very Next Moment; Listen, Cosette; Maggie's Date; Marry the Girl Myself; Maybe It's Time for Me; Meet Mesalia (dance); Proposal Duet; Putty in Your Hands; Sherry; Turn on the Radio; Why Does the Whole Damn World Adore Me?; With This Ring

Cast: Elizabeth Allen; Donald Burr; Jon Cypher; Janet Fox; Dolores Gray; Eddie Lawrence; Mary Loane; Clive Revill; Byron Webster

Notes: [1] Out Boston 1/18/67.

3932 • SHIM SHAM

OPENED: 01/03/1983
Musical   Closed out of town

Composer: Johnny Brandon
Lyricist: Johnny Brandon
Librettist: Eric Blau
Director: Gregory S. Hurst

Arrangements: Timothy Graphenreed; **Choreographer:** Bick Goss; Henry LeTang; **Costumes:** Bernard Johnson; **Lighting Designer:** Sid Bennett; **Musical Director:** Thomas Bridwell; **Orchestrations:** Timothy Graphenreed; **Set Design:** David Potts

Cast: Hinton Battle

Notes: Pennsylvania Stage Company, Allentown, PA.

3933 • SHIM SHAM REVUE

Revue

Composer: J.C. Lewis Jr.
Lyricist: J.C. Lewis Jr.
Librettist: Benny Baker; Sid Walker
Producer: Moe Morton
Director: Dave Gould

Songs: I Do, I Do, I Do; Keep Moving; Sweetness of It All, The (C: Charley Kisco); Without That Man

Notes: No other information available.

3934 • SHINBONE ALLEY

OPENED: 04/13/1957   Theatre: Broadway
Musical   Broadway: 49

Composer: George Kleinsinger
Lyricist: Joe Darion
Librettist: Mel Brooks; Joe Darion
Producer: Peter Lawrence

Source: ARCHY AND MEHITABEL (Story: Don Marquis); **Choreographer:** Rod Alexander; **Costumes:** Motley; **Lighting Designer:** Tharon Musser; **Musical Director:** Maurice Levine; **Orchestrations:** George Kleinsinger; **Set Design:** Eldon Elder

Songs: Be a Pussycat; Big Bill; Come to Mee-ow;
Dog and Cat Ballet; Flotsam and Jetsam; I Gotta
Be; Lady Bug Song, The; Lightning Bug Song,
The; Lullaby, The; Moth Song, The; Pretty Kitty;
Queer Little Insect; Quiet Street; Romeo and
Juliet; Shinbone Alley; Suicide Song; Toujours
Gai; True Romance; Vacant Lot Ballet; Way
Down Blues; What Do We Care?; What the Hell;
Woman Wouldn't Be a Woman, A

Cast: Eddie Bracken; Jacques D'Amboise; George S.
Irving; Eartha Kitt; Erik Rhodes

3935 • SHINE IT ON

Notes: *See THE ACT.*

3936 • SHIRLEY MACLAINE ON BROADWAY

OPENED: 04/19/1984   Theatre: Palace
Revue   Broadway: 47

Composer: Marvin Hamlisch
Lyricist: Christopher Adler
Producer: Guber & Gross Productions;
Nederlander Organization
Director: Alan Johnson

Choreographer: Alan Johnson; **Costumes:** Pete
Mennefee; **Lighting Designer:** Ken Billington;
Musical Director: Jack French

Songs: Cockeyed Optimist [1] (C: Richard Rodgers;
L: Oscar Hammerstein II); Imagine [1] (C/L:
John Lennon); In the Movies; Life Is Just a Bowl
of Cherries [3] (C: Ray Henderson); Nobody
Does It Like Me [2] (C: Cy Coleman; L: Buz
Kohan); Now

Cast: Jamilah Lucas; Shirley MacLaine; Mark
Reina; Larry Vickers; Antoinette Yuskis

Notes: Additional material by Larry Grossman.
There was also a Harold Arlen medley. [1] Not
written for this production. [2] Originally written
for SEESAW with new lyrics added for this
production. [3] Originally written for GEORGE
WHITE'S SCANDALS with new lyrics written
for this production.

3937 • SHLEMIEL THE FIRST

OPENED: 05/13/1994
Musical

Composer: Hankus Netsky
Additional Music: Zalmen Mlotek
Lyricist: Arnold Weinstein
Librettist: Robert Brustein
Director: David Gordon

Source: SHLEMIEL THE FIRST (Play: Isaac
Bashevis Singer); **Choreographer:** David
Gordon; **Costumes:** Catherine Zuber; **Lighting
Designer:** Peter Kaczorowski; **Musical Director:**
Zalmen Mlotek; **Orchestrations:** Hankus Netsky;
Set Design: Robert Israel

Songs: Beadle with a Dreydl; Can This Be Hell?;
Geography Song (Rumania, Rumania); He's
Going to Die; Matters of the Heart; Meshugah;
Mrs. Shlemiel's Lament; My One and Only
Shlemiel; Rascal's Song; Screen Song, The; Twos;
Wake Up Song; We're Talking Chelm; Wisdom;
Yetta's Blintzes

Cast: Remo Airaldi; Larry Block; Scott
Cunningham; Benjamin Evett; Rosalie Gerut;
Charles Levin; Vontress Mitchell; Marilyn Sokol

Notes: From program of American Repertory
Theatre, Boston prior to Serious Fun festival at
Lincoln Center.

3938 • SHOEMAKER AND THE PEDDLER, THE

OPENED: 10/14/1960   Theatre: East 74th Street
Musical   Off-Broadway: 43

Composer: Frank Fields
Lyricist: Armand Aulicino
Librettist: Armand Aulicino
Producer: Jullis Productions
Director: Lee Nemetz

Choreographer: Sophie Maslow; **Costumes:** David
Ballou; **Lighting Designer:** Lee Watson; **Musical
Director:** Richard Cumming; **Orchestrations:**
Frank Fields; **Set Design:** David Ballou

Songs: Ah, Hum, Oh, Hum; Childhood Lullaby;
Fish Song; Goodbye, My City; Guilty!; Headlines;
Is This the Way?; Letter, The; Mio Fratello;
Naughty Bird Tarantella; Nightmare Quartet, The;
Remember, Remember; Robbery, The; Sometimes
I Wonder; Vedi la Vita; Wide-Awake Morning

Cast: James Basotina; Anita Darian; Jose Duval;
Elinor Miller

3939 • SHOEMAKER'S HOLIDAY

OPENED: 03/02/1967   Theatre: Mercury
Musical   Off-Broadway: 6

Composer: Mel Marvin
Lyricist: Ted Berger
Librettist: Ted Berger
Producer: Ken Costigan; R. Robert Lussier
Director: Ken Costigan

Source: SHOEMAKER'S HOLIDAY, THE (Play: Thomas Dekker); **Choreographer:** Robert Conley; **Musical Director:** Elman Anderson; **Orchestrations:** Elman Anderson; **Set Design:** Whitney Blausen

Songs: Cold's the Wind; Down a Down Down Derry; Everythin' Is Tinglin'; Gather Ye Rose Buds; My Lovely Lad; Poor Man at Parting, A; Recipe for Husbandry, The; Ribbons I Will Give Thee; Shaking of the Sheets, The; Trowl the Bowl; What a Life; What Do We Care If It Rains; When a Maid Wears Purple Stockings; Where Is the Knight for Me?; Who Gives a Hey; Wonder of the Kingdom; Would That I

Cast: Penny Gaston; Tom Lacy; Sue Lawless; Gary Oakes; Tom Urich

3940 • SHOESTRING '57

OPENED: 11/05/1956   Theatre: Barbizon-Plaza
Revue   Off-Broadway: 110

Producer: Ben Bagley; Edwin H. Morris
Director: Ben Bagley; Paul Lammers

Choreographer: Danny Daniels; **Costumes:** Jeanne Partington; **Musical Director:** Dorothea Freitag; **Orchestrations:** Dorothea Freitag; **Set Design:** William Riva

Songs: Always One Day More (Death of a Ballad) (C: Philip Springer; L: Carolyn Leigh); Arts, The [2] (C: Charles Strouse; L: Lee Adams); At Twenty-Two (C: Harvey Schmidt; L: Tom Jones); Best Loved Girls (C: David Baker; L: Sheldon Harnick); Can You See a Girl Like Me in the Role? (C: William Howe; L: Max Showalter); Don't Say You Like Tchaikowsky (C: Claibe Richardson; L: Paul Rosner); Doop-De-Doop (C/L: Harvey Schmidt); Family Trouble (C: Leopold Antelme; L: Anthony Chalmers); For Critics Only (C: Shelley Mowell; L: Michael Stewart); Gonna Be Rich (C/L: G. Wood); I Just

Slipped Away from My Wedding (C/L: Bud McCreery); In the Dark of an Arkansas Moon [3] (C: Phil Springer; L: Carolyn Leigh); It Was My Father's Fashion [1] (C: Moose Charlap; L: Norman Gimbel); Lament on Fifth Avenue (C: Claibe Richardson; L: Paul Rosner); Love Is a Feeling (C: Moose Charlap; L: Norman Gimbel); On a Shoestring (C/L: G. Wood); Paradiddle (C/L: Sol Berkowitz); Queen of Spain (C: Harvey Schmidt; L: Tom Jones); Renoir, Degas and Toulouse (C/L: Bud McCreery); Reverie in Blue [3] (C: Phil Springer; L: Carolyn Leigh); Rochelle Hudson Tango, The (C: Claibe Richardson; L: Paul Rosner); Saroyan [1] (C: Philip Springer; L: E.Y. Harburg); Stitch in Time (ballet) (C: Moose Charlap); Sweet Belinda (C: Richard Addinsell; L: Arthur Macrae); Tea Chanty (C/L: Harvey Schmidt); What's a Show? (C: Shelley Mowell; L: Michael Stewart)

Cast: Fay De Witt; Dody Goodman; Dorothy Greener; Paul Mazursky; Bud McCreery

Notes: [1] Cut prior to opening. [2] Also in MEDIUM RARE. [3] ASCAP/Library of Congress only.

3941 • SHOESTRING REVUE (1955)

OPENED: 02/28/1955   Theatre: President
Revue   Off-Broadway: 96

Librettist: Sheldon Harnick; Richard Maury; Michael Stewart
Producer: Ben Bagley
Director: Ben Bagley; Christopher Hewett

Choreographer: Dania Krupska; **Lighting Designer:** Carter Morningstar; **Musical Director:** Charles Strouse; **Set Design:** Carter Morningstar; **Vocal Arranger:** Charles Strouse

Songs: Entire History of the World in Two Minutes and Thirty-Two Seconds (C: Charles Strouse; L: Michael Stewart); Fresh and Young (C/L: Ronny Graham); Garbage (C/L: Sheldon Harnick); Inevitably Me (C/L: Ken Welch); Kings and Queens (C: Arthur Siegel; L: June Carroll); Laddie (C/L: Jim Mahoney); Man's Inhumanity [1] (C: Charles Strouse; L: Lee Adams); Medea in Disneyland (C: Lloyd Norlin; L: Sheldon Harnick); Million Windows and I, A (C: Alec Wilder; L: Norman Gimbel); Mink, Mink, Mink [2] (C/L: Bud McCreery); New to

Me (C: Ken Welch; L: Bud McCreery); Nobody's Doin' It (C/L: Bud McCreery); Paducah (C/L: Bud McCreery); Sea Is All Around Us, The (C: David Baker; L: Sheldon Harnick); Someone Is Sending Me Flowers (C: David Baker; L: Sheldon Harnick); Things Are Going Well Today (C: Arthur Siegel; L: June Carroll); Three Loves (C: Charles Strouse; L: Michael Stewart); Wabash 4-7473 (C: G. Wood; L: Kirby)

Cast: Beatrice Arthur; Dody Goodman; Dorothy Greener; Arte Johnson; Mel Larned; Chita Rivera

Notes: [1] Also in JOY RIDE and MEDIUM RARE. [2] Also in MEDIUM RARE.

3942 • SHOESTRING REVUE IN FORT WORTH
OPENED: 09/1958
Revue

Producer: Ben Bagley

Songs: Arts, The [1] (C: Charles Strouse; L: Lee Adams); Game of Dance [2] (C: Sol Berkowitz; L: Don Mayer); Night the Hurricane Hit, The (C/L: Bud McCreery); Red Hot Mama (C: Shelley Mowell; L: Michael Stewart); Renoir, Degas & Toulouse Lautrec [1] (C/L: Bud McCreery); Sweet Belinda (C/L: Jerry Herman); Tranquilizers (C/L: Bud McCreery)

Cast: Fay De Witt; Dorothy Greener; Bill McCutcheon; G. Wood

Notes: No program available. Played the Casa Manana. [1] From SHOESTRING '57. [2] From THE LITTLEST REVUE.

3943 • SHO-GUN, THE
OPENED: 10/10/1904   Theatre: Wallack
Musical   Broadway: 125

Composer: Gustav Luders
Lyricist: George Ade
Librettist: George Ade
Producer: Henry W. Savage
Director: George Marion

Musical Director: John McGhie; **Set Design:** Walter Burridge

Songs: Chorus of Mourners; Chorus of Soldiers; Crime Is Merely a Disease; Entrance of Flai-Hai; Entrance of Hanki-Pank; Entrance of Widows; Flutter Little Bird; Games We Used to Play, The; Go Where Fate Will Lead [2]; Hi-Ko, Hi-Ko; I Am "Yours Truly"; I'll Live for You [2]; Irrepressible Yank, The; Jackie, The; Keep Your Eye on the Girl Just Out [2]; Life All Free from Care, A; Little Moozoo-May; Love, You Must Be Blind; Man She'll Never Meet, The; Opening Chorus; Opening Chorus Act II; Schemes [1]; She's Just a Little Different from the Others That I Know; Sho-Gun of Kachoo, The; Teach the Young Idea How to Shoot; This Is How I Do; Wedding Ceremony, The; Wisteria, My Bride; Your Honeymoon Will Last

Cast: Georgia Caine; Charles Evans; Christie MacDonald; Edward Martindel; David Torrence

Notes: [1] Out Trenton 8/31/05. [2] Sheet music only.

3944 • SHOGUN: THE MUSICAL
OPENED: 11/20/1990   Theatre: Marquis
Musical   Broadway: 72

Composer: Paul Chihara
Lyricist: John Driver
Librettist: John Driver
Producer: James Clavell; Joseph Harris; Haruki Kadokawa
Director: Michael Smuin

Source: SHOGUN (Novel: James Clavell); **Choreographer:** Michael Smuin; **Costumes:** Patricia Zipprodt; **Lighting Designer:** Natasha Katz; **Musical Director:** Edward G. Robinson; **Orchestrations:** David Cullen; Steven Margoshes; **Set Design:** Loren Sherman

Songs: Absolution; Assassination; Born to Be Together; Cha-No-Yu; Death Walk; Escape; Fireflies; He Let Me Live; Honto; How Nice to See You; Impossible Eyes; Island, An; Karma; Mad Rum Below; Night of Screams; Ninja Raid; No Man; No Word for Love; One Candle; Pillowing; Poetry Competition; Resolutions; Royal Blood; Rum Below; Sail Home; Shogun; This Is Samurai; Trio; Winter Battle

Cast: June Angela; Philip Casnoff; Eric Chan; JoAnn M. Hunter; Leslie Ishii; Jason Ma; Francis Ruivivar; Jenny Woo

3945 • SHOO-FLY REGIMENT, THE

OPENED: 08/06/1907   Theatre: Bijou
Musical   Broadway: 15

Composer: J. Rosamond Johnson
Lyricist: James Weldon Johnson
Librettist: Bob Cole

Songs: De Bode o' Edicashun; Down in the Philippines [2]; Floating Down the Nile; Ghost of Deacon Brown, The; I Think an Awful Lot of You; If Adam Hadn't Seen the Apple Tree (C/L: Bob Cole); I'll Always Love Old Dixie; Just How Much I Love You [2]; Lemons [1]; Li'l Gal (L: Bob Cole; James Weldon Johnson); Little Choo Choo Gee-Gee, The [2]; My Sweeheart's a Soldier in the Army [1]; Old Flag Never Touched the Ground, The [2]; On the Gay Luneta (C: James Reese Europe; L: Bob Cole); Run, Brudder Rabbit, Run!; Southland [2]; That Small Still Voice [1]; There's Always Something Wrong [1] (L: Bob Cole); We've Been to Boston Town; Who Do You Love? (L: Bob Cole)

Cast: Herbert Amos; Bob Cole; Frank De Lyons; Mollie Dill; Nettie Glenn; J. Rosamond Johnson; Arthur Ray; Arthur Talbot

Notes: [1] Sheet music only. [2] Out Wilkes-Barre 2/16/07.

3946 • SHOOT THE WORKS

OPENED: 07/21/1931   Theatre: George M.
                                       Cohan
Musical   Broadway: 87

Composer: Michael H. Cleary
Lyricist: Max Lief; Nathaniel Lief
Librettist: Peter Arno; Heywood Broun; Sig Herzig; Nunnally Johnson; Milton Lazarus; Dorothy Parker; H.I. Phillips; E.B. White
Producer: Heywood Broun; Milton Raison
Director: Theodore Hammerstein

Choreographer: Johnny Boyle; **Costumes:** Kiviette; Charles LeMaire; **Lighting Designer:** Henry Dreyfuss; **Musical Director:** Harry Archer; **Orchestrations:** Frank Barry; King Ross; **Set Design:** Henry Dreyfuss

Songs: Back in Circulation Again; (Just) Begging for Love (C/L: Irving Berlin); Chirp, Chirp [2] (C: Philip Charig; Joseph Mayer; L: Ira

Gershwin); Das Lied Ist Aus (C: Robert Stolz; L: Walter Reisch; A. Robinson); Do What You Like (C: Philip Charig; L: Leo Robin); First Lady of the Land, The; Hot Moonlight (C: Jay Gorney; L: E.Y. Harburg); How's Your Uncle? (C: Jimmy McHugh; L: Dorothy Fields); I Want to Chisel in on Your Heart; I'm Just a Doorstep Baby; It's in the Stars; Muchacha (C: Vernon Duke; Jay Gorney; L: E.Y. Harburg); My Heart's a Banjo (C: Jay Gorney; L: E.Y. Harburg); Out in the Open Air [1] (C/L: Ann Ronell); Pie in the Sky; Shoulders (C/L: Herbert Goode; Alexander Williams); Taken for a Ride

Cast: Johnny Boyle; Lee Brody; Heywood Broun; Imogene Coca; Frances Dewey; Bobby Gillette; Al Gold; Taylor Gordon; Jack Hazzard; Julie Johnson; George Murphy; Frances Nevins; William O'Neal

Notes: Heywood Broun organized this show to give out-of-work actors work. [1] Program credits Muriel Pollack as composer. [2] Also in THAT'S A GOOD GIRL.

3947 • SHOOTIN' STAR

OPENED: 04/04/1946
Musical   Closed out of town

Composer: Sol Kaplan
Lyricist: Bob Russell
Librettist: Walter Hart; Louis Jacobs; Halsted Welles
Producer: Joseph Kipness; Max Liebman
Director: Halsted Welles

Choreographer: Lester Horton; **Costumes:** Kenn Barr; **Musical Director:** Pembroke Davenport; **Orchestrations:** Hershy Kay; **Set Design:** Frederick Fox

Songs: Billy's Fight with Chuck; Chin-Che; Footloose; Friendly Country; He'll Make Some Girl a Wonderful Husband; Hip- di-di-o-tee; I'm Payin' You; It's a Cold, Cruel World; Kid Stuff; Mighty Big Dream; Music to a Dancing Bird; No Ross Dixon; Nothin'; Opening (After Saga 1); Party Dance (dance); Saga of Billy the Kid; Sometime Tomorrow; What Do I Have to Do?

Cast: Andrew Andrews; David Brooks; Howard Da Silva; Nelle Fisher; Ray Harrison; Doretta Morrow; Bernice Parks; Herbert Ross; Art Smith

3948 • SHOP GIRL, THE
OPENED: 10/28/1895   Theatre: Palmer's
Musical   Broadway: 72

Composer: Ivan Caryll; Lionel Monckton
Lyricist: Adrian Ross
Librettist: H.J. Dam
Producer: Charles Frohman; Al Hayman
Director: A.E. Dodson

Costumes: Wilhelm; **Musical Director:** Barter
   Johns; **Set Design:** Ernest Gros

Cast: Connie Ediss; George Grossmith Jr.; Seymour
   Hicks; Walter McEwen; W.H. Rawlins

Notes: No songs listed in program.

3949 • SHOW BOAT
OPENED: 12/27/1927   Theatre: Ziegfeld
Musical   Broadway: 575

Composer: Jerome Kern
Lyricist: Oscar Hammerstein II
Librettist: Oscar Hammerstein II
Producer: Florenz Ziegfeld
Director: Zeke Colvan; Oscar Hammerstein II

Source: SHOW BOAT (Novel: Edna Ferber);
   Choreographer: Sammy Lee; **Costumes:** John
   Harkrider; **Musical Director:** Victor Baravalle;
   Orchestrations: Robert Russell Bennett; **Set
   Design:** Joseph Urban; **Vocal Arranger:** Will
   Vodery

Songs: After the Ball (C/L: Charles K. Harris);
   At the Fair; Be Happy, Too; Bill [6] (L: Oscar
   Hammerstein II; P.G. Wodehouse); Bully Song [2]
   (C/L: Traditional); C'mon Folks (Queenie's
   Ballyhoo); Can't Help Lovin' Dat Man; Captain
   Andy's Entrance and Ballyhoo; (Be Happy, Too)
   Cheer Up [2]; Cheer Up [2]; Coal Black Lady [2]
   (C/L: Traditional); Cotton Blossom; Creole Love
   Song, The [1]; Dance Away the Night [4]; Dandies
   on Parade (The Sports of Gay Chicago); Finale Act
   I (Wedding); Goodbye, My Lady Love (C/L: Joe
   Howard); Happy the Day; Hello Ma Baby [2]
   (C/L: Joe Howard); Hey, Feller!; I Might Fall Back
   on You [9]; I Would Like to Play a Lover's Part [2];
   In Dahomey [7]; It's Getting Hotter in the North [2];
   Life Upon the Wicked Stage; Make Believe; Me
   and My Boss [5]; Mis'ry's Comin' 'Round [2]; My
   Girl [2]; Nobody Else but Me [3]; Ol' Man River;
   Out There in an Orchard [1]; Pack of Cards, A [1];

Pantry Scene [1]; 'Till Good Luck Comes My Way;
   Trocadero Opening: Happy New Year [1]; Villain
   Dance (inst.); Waterfront Saloon Scene [1];
   Where's the Mate for Me?; While We Tell them
   About It All (Opening Act II) [2]; Why Do I Love
   You?; Yes Ma'am (You're from the Show Boat) [1];
   You Are Love

Cast: Jules Bledsoe; Tess Gardella; Francis X.
   Mahoney; Howard Marsh; Helen Morgan; Edna
   May Oliver; Eva Puck; Norma Terris; Sammy
   White; Charles Winninger

Notes: [1] Cut during rehearsal. [2] Cut prior to
   opening. [3] Written for 1946 revival. [4] Written
   for London production. [5] Cut before London
   production. [6] Written for OH, LADY! LADY!
   Music also used for "Bill" with B.G. De Sylva
   lyric in ZIP GOES A MILLION. [7] Same music
   as "Bring 'Em Back" from HITCHY-KOO OF
   1920. [8] Cut prior to opening. Music used for "
   I Might Fall Back on You." [9] Music same as for
   cut song "Be Happy, Too."

3950 • SHOW BOAT REVUE OF 1933
OPENED: 1933
Revue

Composer: Frank Perkins
Lyricist: Mitchell Parish
Producer: Bobby Sanford

Songs: Bulls and Bears; I've Got My Man Where I
   Want Him; Rock-a-Bye River; Wait'll My Ship
   Comes In; You Excite Me

Notes: No other information available.

3951 • SHOW GIRL OR THE MAGIC CAP, THE
OPENED: 05/05/1902   Theatre: Wallack
Musical   Broadway: 64

Composer: Edward W. Corliss; H.L. Heartz
Lyricist: D.K. Stevens
Librettist: R.A. Barnet
Producer: Edward E. Rice
Director: Will Carlton

Choreographer: Joseph C. Smith; **Costumes:** Will
   R. Barnes; **Lighting Designer:** Joseph Menchen;
   Set Design: D. Frank Dodge

Songs: Adeline (C: E.W. Corliss); Advice (C: H.L. Heartz); As the Prince Waked the Princess (C: H.L. Heartz); Be My Little Apple Dumplin' Do (C: John W. Bratton; L: Walter Ford); By-and-By (C: W.T. Francis); Champagne and Terrapin, Vision Divine! (C: H.L. Heartz); Come Down Mister Man in the Moon [2]; Cuddle [1]; Dolly Dimple Song; Don't Want to Be a Lady [3]; Family Ghost, The (C: H.L. Heartz); Fate, The (C: Edward W. Corliss); Garden of Love [1]; Glow-Worm, The [1]; He Loves the Flag [1]; Idaho [3]; I'm a Simple Author-Manager (C: H.L. Heartz); I'm Crazy Over You [1]; I'm Crazy to Go on the Stage [2]; I'm Props [3]; I'm the Manager [3]; In Gay Japan (C: M.W. Daniels); In Spotless Town (C: William Jerome; L: Jean Schwartz); In Zanzibar [2]; Invocation to Pie (C: M.W. Daniels); Jolly Life Is the Sailors, A [1]; Julie [3]; Katrina (C: Edward W. Corliss); Let Her Drown [3]; Lily and the Dew, The; Love Is Just the Same (C: H.L. Heartz); Love of Long Ago [3]; Lover's Lane (C: H.L. Heartz); My Java Lady [1]; Nellie Kellie [2]; Oh Shrine of Psyche (C: H.L. Heartz); One That He Loves Best (C: Edward W. Corliss); Property Boy, The [1]; Psyche (C: Edward W. Corliss); Quiet Cafe, The [1]; Reggie's Family Tree (C: H.L. Heartz); Rose and a Lily, A (C: Edward W. Corliss); Seminole [2]; Sometime-Perhaps (C: L.S. Thompson); Stupid Mr. Cupid [4]; That's the Way of a Sailor (C: H.L. Heartz); That's Where She Sits All Day; Tippecanoe [2]; Walked Right In [3]; We Are Trying to Support Our Only Mother (C: M.W. Daniels); When You Smile at Me [1]; Where Jasmine Flowers Are Twining (C: Edward W. Corliss); Would You Leave Your Happy Home for Me? [3]

Cast: Rose Barnett; Paula Edwardes; Clarence Harvey; Stanley Hawkins; Frank Lalor; Alonzo Price; Frances Wilson

Notes: Titled THE CAP OF FORTUNE out of town. [1] Out of town 7/20/??. [2] Sheet music only. [3] Out 3/7/07. [4] Out of town 7/20/?? There was a popular song of the same name written in 1908 by Edward Madden and Theodore Morse.

3952 • SHOW GIRL, THE (1906)

OPENED: 12/04/1906
Musical   Closed out of town

Songs: Champagne and Terrapin; Could You But Read My Heart; Don't Want to Be a Lady; He's My Pal; Idaho; I'm Props; I'm the Manager; Jule; Let Her Down; Man in the Moon; One That He Loves Best; Psyche; Sailor Song; Toreador Song; Waiting at the Church; Wooden Shoe Dance

Cast: Kathryn Florence; Grace Neil; Hilda Thomas

Notes: Cedar Rapids program.

3953 • SHOW GIRL (1929)

OPENED: 07/02/1929   Theatre: Ziegfeld
Musical   Broadway: 111

Composer: George Gershwin
Lyricist: Ira Gershwin; Gus Kahn
Librettist: William Anthony McGuire
Producer: Florenz Ziegfeld
Director: Zeke Colvan

Source: SHOW GIRL (Novel: J.P. McAvoy); **Choreographer:** Bobby Connolly; Albertina Rasch; **Costumes:** John Harkrider; **Musical Director:** William Daly; **Set Design:** Joseph Urban

Songs: Adored One [3]; American in Paris Blues Ballet, An (inst.); At Mrs. Simpkin's Finishing School [3]; Because They All Love You [4] (C: J. Little; L: T. Malie); Black and White; Broadway My Street (C: Jimmy Durante; L: Sidney Skolsky); Bye Bye for Baby [5] (C: Joseph Meyer; L: Irving Caesar); Casanova, Romeo, and Don Juan [3]; Do What You Do!; Feeling Sentimental [9]; Finaletto Act I Scene 1; Follow the Minstrel Band [1]; Happy Birthday; Harlem Serenade; Home Blues [8]; Home Lovin' Gal [3]; Home Lovin' Man [3]; How Could I Forget; I Can Do without Broadway (C/L: Jimmy Durante); I Just Looked at You [10]; I Must Be Home By Twelve O'Clock; I'm Just a Bundle of Sunshine [3]; I'm Out for No Good Reason Tonight [3]; Jimmy the Well Dressed Man (C/L: Jimmy Durante); Liza (All the Clouds'll Roll Away); Lolita, My Love [1]; Magnolia Finale [7]; Minstrel Show [3]; Mississippi Day [2] (C: Vincent Youmans; L: J. Russel Robinson); My Sunday Fella; One Man; So Are You!; So I Ups to Him (C/L: Jimmy Durante); Somebody Stole My Heart Away [3]; Someone's Always Calling a Rehearsal [3]; Spain [1]; Stage Door Scene [3]; Tonight's the Night [11]; Who Will Be with You When I'm Far Away [4] (C/L: W.H. Farrell)

Cast: Lou Clayton; Jimmy Durante; Duke Ellington and His Orchestra; Eddie Foy Jr.; Harriet Hoctor; Eddie Jackson; Ruby Keeler; Nick Lucas; Joseph Macaulay; Frank McHugh; Barbara Newberry

Notes: [1] Cut after opening. [2] Added after opening. [3] Not used. [4] Not in programs. [5] ASCAP only. [7] May have been cut prior to opening. [8] Music for the refrain used as part of AN AMERICAN IN PARIS. [9] Cut prior to opening. [10] Not used. Music of refrain first intended for "Lady of the Moon" from the unproduced MING TOY. Music later used for "Blah, Blah, Blah" in film DELICIOUS. [11] Not used. Later put into CRAZY FOR YOU.

3954 • SHOW GIRL (1961)
OPENED: 01/12/1961   Theatre: Eugene O'Neill
Revue   Broadway: 100

Composer: Charles Gaynor
Lyricist: Charles Gaynor
Librettist: Ernest Chambers; Charles Gaynor
Producer: James A. Doolittle; Charles Lowe; Oliver Smith
Director: Charles Gaynor

Choreographer: Richard D'Arcy; **Costumes:** Orry Kelly; Miles White; **Lighting Designer:** Peggy Clark; **Musical Director:** Robert Hunter; **Orchestrations:** Clare Grundman; Robert Hunter; **Set Design:** Oliver Smith

Songs: Calypso Pete; Girl in the Show, The; Girl Who Lives in Montparnasse, The; In Our Teeny Little Weeny Little Nest for Two [1]; Join Us in a Cup of Tea [1]; Love Is Sickness; Mambo-Java (C/L: Noel Guyves); My Kind of Love; S Eureka Presents (sketch); Somewhere There's a Little Bluebird [2]; Story of Marie, The; Switchblade Bess; This Is a Darned Fine Funeral; Yahoo Step, The [1]; You Haven't Lived Until You've Played the Palace

Cast: Carol Channing; Les Quat' Jeudis; Jules Munshin

Notes: [1] Also in LEND AN EAR. [2] Not in program.

3955 • SHOW IS ON, THE
OPENED: 12/25/1936   Theatre: Winter Garden
Revue   Broadway: 236

Librettist: David Freedman; Moss Hart
Producer: Messrs. Shubert
Director: Edward Clarke Lilley; Vincente Minnelli

Choreographer: Robert Alton; **Costumes:** Vincente Minnelli; **Musical Director:** Gordon Jenkins; **Orchestrations:** Gordon Jenkins; **Set Design:** Vincente Minnelli

Songs: Al Fleagle Arrangement, An [1] (C: Richard Rodgers; L: Lorenz Hart); Buy Yourself a Balloon (C/L: Herman Hupfeld); By Strauss (C: George Gershwin; L: Ira Gershwin); Cake Walk [1] (C: Will Irwin; L: Norman Zeno); Casanova (C: Vernon Duke; L: Ted Fetter); Epilogue (C: Vernon Duke; L: Ted Fetter); It's Easy to Love [1] (C: Hoagy Carmichael; L: Ted Fetter); Josephine Waters (C: Arthur Schwartz; L: Ira Gershwin); Little Old Lady (C: Hoagy Carmichael; L: Stanley Adams); Long As You've Got Your Health (C: Will Irwin; L: E.Y. Harburg; Norman Zeno); Now (C: Vernon Duke; L: Ted Fetter); Parade Night (C: Will Irwin; L: Norman Zeno); Prologue Shakespearean Opening [3] (C: Arthur Schwartz; L: Howard Dietz); Rhythm (C: Richard Rodgers; L: Lorenz Hart); Show Is On, The (C: Hoagy Carmichael; L: Ted Fetter); Song of the Woodman (C: Harold Arlen; L: E.Y. Harburg); Sway Brittania [1] (C: Vernon Duke; L: Ted Fetter); Tap-Tap-Tapnotized [1] (C: Felix Bernard; L: Ted Fetter); Tragedian Ballet (inst.) [1] (C: Vladimir Dukelsky [2]); Twinkle, Twinkle [1] (C: Will Irwin; L: Norman Zeno); Ventriloquist [1] (C: Will Irwin; L: Norman Zeno); What Has He Got? (C: Vernon Duke; L: Ted Fetter); Woof (C: Will Irwin; L: Norman Zeno)

Cast: Vera Allen; Gracie Barrie; Roy Campbell's Continentals; Reginald Gardiner; Paul Haakon; Bert Lahr; Beatrice Lillie; Mitzi Mayfair; Jack McCauley; Ralph Riggs; Robert Shafer; Evelyn Thawl; Charles Walters

Notes: [1] Cut Philadelphia prior to New York. [2] Vladimir Dukelsky is Vernon Duke. [3] Also in AT EASE.

3956 • SHOW ME WHERE THE GOOD TIMES ARE
OPENED: 03/05/1970   Theatre: Edison
Musical   Off-Broadway: 29

Composer: Kenneth Jacobson
Lyricist: Rhoda Roberts

Librettist: Lee Thuna
Producer: Barbara Lee Horn; Lorin E. Price
Director: Morton Da Costa

Source: IMAGINARY INVALID, THE (Play: Moliere); **Choreographer:** Bob Herget; **Costumes:** Gloria Gresham; **Lighting Designer:** Neil Peter Jampolis; **Musical Director:** Karen Gustafson; **Orchestrations:** Philip J. Lang; **Set Design:** Tom H. John; **Vocal Arranger:** Karen Gustafson

Songs: Cafe Royale Rag; Follow Your Heart; He's Wonderful; How Do I Feel?; I'm Not Getting Any Younger; Look Up; Look Who's Throwing a Party; One Big Happy Family; Show Me Where the Good Times Are [1]; Staying Alive; Test, The; When Tomorrow Comes; Who'd Believe; You're My Happiness

Cast: Michael Berkson; Cathryn Damon; Denny Martin Flinn; Christopher Hewett; Gloria Le Roy; Neva Small; Arnold Soboloff

Notes: [1] Originally in HOT SEPTEMBER.

3957 • SHOW OF SHOWS
Notes: *See BILLY ROSE'S SHOW OF SHOWS.*

3958 • SHOW OF WONDERS, THE
OPENED: 10/26/1916   Theatre: Broadway
Revue   Broadway: 209

Composer: Otto Motzan; Sigmund Romberg; Herman Timberg
Lyricist: Harold Atteridge
Librettist: Harold Atteridge
Producer: Winter Garden Company
Director: J.C. Huffman

Choreographer: Allan K. Foster; **Costumes:** Homer Conant; **Musical Director:** Oscar Radin

Songs: Aladdin (C: Sigmund Romberg); Angels; Back to Nature; Bis Bolo [1]; Bit of Opera, A [3]; Bring Your Kisses to Me (C: Sigmund Romberg); Burmese Ballet, A; Dancing Around the Town [2]; Diabolo (C: Herman Timberg); Down Virginia Way [2]; Fashion Waltz [2]; Get a Girlie (C: Herman Timberg); Ghosts of the Ukulele, The [3]; Girl on the Square; Girls Prepare (C: Sigmund Romberg); Hicky Do; I Want a Girl Like You [2]; Italian Ballet Miniature [1];

Louisiana (C/L: Harry Tierney); Love Is Like a Bubble (C: Sigmund Romberg); Mendelssohn and Liszt; My Yiddishe Butterfly [3] (C: Joseph A. Burke; L: Al Dubin); Naughty, Naughty, Naughty (C: Nat Vincent; L: Joe Goodwin; William Tracey); Pajama Girlies (C: Otto Motzan); Photograph of You [2]; Roll Your Hoop [2]; Slavlova; Study in Black and White, A [1]; Wedding Bells (C: Otto Motzan); Wedding By the Sea; When Pavlova Starts Buck and Winging; Winter Garden Hop; Zoo Step, The (C: Clarence Wilson; L: J. Homer Tutt)

Cast: Lou Clayton; Ernest Hare; Eugene Howard; Willie Howard; Walter C. Kelly; Tom Lewis; McIntyre & Heath; Marilyn Miller; George Monroe; John T. Murray; Sam White

Notes: [1] Sheet music only. [2] Out New Haven 10/17/16. [3] Out Philadelphia 12/31/17.

3959 • SHOWBUSINESS
Notes: *See SHOW GIRL (1961).*

3960 • SHOWING OFF
OPENED: 05/18/1989   Theatre: Steve McGraw's
Revue   Off-Broadway: 172

Composer: Douglas Bernstein; Denis Markell
Lyricist: Douglas Bernstein; Denis Markell
Librettist: Douglas Bernstein; Denis Markell
Producer: Jennifer Manocherian; Suzanne J. Schwartz
Director: Michael Leeds

Choreographer: Michael Leeds; **Costumes:** Jeanne Button; **Lighting Designer:** Josh Starbuck; **Musical Director:** Stephen Flaherty; **Set Design:** Penny Holpit; Joseph Varga

Songs: How Things Change; I Don't Get It; Joshua Noveck; Michele; Ninas; Old Fashioned Song; Raffi: The Concert Movie; Rental Cruelty; S.I.P.; 72nd Street; Showing Off; Take de Picture; They're Yours

Cast: Douglas Bernstein; Veanne Cox; Jason Graae; Donna Murphy

3961 • SHUBERT ALLEY
OPENED: 1983
Musical   Unproduced

Composer: Jule Styne
Lyricist: Susan Birkenhead
Librettist: Dale Wasserman

Notes: I'm not sure if any songs were actually written for this show.

3962 • SHUBERT GAIETIES OF 1919

OPENED: 07/17/1919   Theatre: 44th Street
Revue   Broadway: 87

Composer: Jean Schwartz
Lyricist: Alfred Bryan
Librettist: Edgar Smith
Producer: J.J. Shubert; Lee Shubert
Director: J.C. Huffman

Choreographer: Allan K. Foster; Kuy Kendall

Songs: Baby Vampire Land; Beale Street Blues (C/L: W.C. Handy); Chanson Apache [1]; Cherry Blossom Lane; Cosy Corner; Freedom of the C's; He Does Me So Much Good; He Went in Like a Lion and Came Out Like a Lamb (C: Harry Von Tilzer; L: Andrew B. Sterling); Heart-Breakers; I've Made Up My Mind to Mind a Maid Made Up Like You; Jazz Babies Ball (C: Maceo Pinkard; L: Charles Bayha); Lamp of Love; Let Us Keep the Shimmie; Little Bull, A; Military Decoration Dance; Mouth Full of Kisses, A [2]; My Beautiful Tiger Girl; Oh, How She Can Dance; On My Private Telephone; Peachie [1]; Please Don't Take Away the Girls; Rainbow Ball; Roller Skating Waltz [1]; Sweeties (C: Harry Von Tilzer; L: Andrew B. Sterling); This Is the Day [1]; Valparaiso; What Are We Going to Do? [1]; You'd Be Surprised [3] (C/L: Irving Berlin); You'll See the Day (C/L: Ted Fiorito; Bud Green; Charlie Pierce)

Cast: Irving Fisher; Gilda Gray; George Jessel; Henry Lewis; Ted Lorraine; Gladys Walton; Ed Wynn

Notes: [1] Out of town only. [2] Out of town only. Later in THE MIDNIGHT ROUNDERS OF 1920. [3] Interpolated after opening. Also in OH, WHAT A GIRL and ZIEGFELD FOLLIES OF 1919.

3963 • SHUFFLE ALONG

OPENED: 05/23/1921   Theatre: 63rd Street
Musical   Broadway: 504

Composer: Eubie Blake
Lyricist: Noble Sissle
Librettist: Aubrey L. Lyles; Flournoy Miller
Producer: Nikko Producing Company
Director: Walter Brooks

Choreographer: Charles Davis; Lawrence Deas; **Musical Director:** Eubie Blake; **Orchestrations:** Will Vodery

Songs: African Dip; Ain't Cha Coming Back, Mary Ann to Maryland [2]; Baltimore Buzz; Bandana Days; Daddy Won't You Please Come Home; Election Day; Everything Reminds Me of You; Good Night Angeline [2] (C: Eubie Blake; James Reese Europe); Gypsy Blues [1]; He May Be Your Man (But He Comes to See Me Once in a While) [7] (C/L: Lemuel Fowler); I Am Craving for That Kind of Love (Kiss Me); If You've Never Been Vamped By a Brown Skin (You've Never Been Vamped at All); I'm Just Simply Full of Jazz; I'm Just Wild About Harry [3]; In Honeysuckle Time (When Emmaline Said She'd Be Mine); Jimtown's Fisticuffs; Kentucky Sue [4]; Liza Quit Vamping Me [4]; Love Will Find a Way; Low Down Blues [2]; My Vision Girl [6]; Old Black Joe and Uncle Tom (Old Black Joe and Uncle Tom); On Patrol in No Man's Land [2] (C: Eubie Blake; James Reese Europe); Oriental Blues; Pickaninny Shoes [5]; Shuffle Along; Sing Me to Sleep Dear Mammy (with a Hushabye Pickaninny Tune); Syncopation Stenos

Cast: Eubie Blake; Lottie Gee; Aubrey L. Lyles; Roger Matthews; Flournoy E. Miller; Gertrude Saunders; Noble Sissle

Notes: [1] "With Apologies to Victor Herbert." [2] Interpolated from vaudeville. [3] Same lyric as pop song "My Loving Baby." [4] Cut. [5] Sheet music only. [6] Originally in MIDNIGHT ROUNDERS. Added after opening. [7] Added after opening.

3964 • SHUFFLE ALONG OF 1930

OPENED: 04/1930
Revue   Closed out of town

Lyricist: Noble Sissle

Songs: Porter's Love Song to a Chambermaid, A [1] (C: James P. Johnson)

Notes: Closed after performances in Brooklyn. There were no original songs in this show. Songs

were collected from KEEP SHUFFLIN' and
KITCHEN MECHANIC'S REVUE. [1] From
KITCHEN MECHANIC'S REVUE.

3965 • SHUFFLE ALONG OF 1933

OPENED: 12/26/1932   Theatre: Mansfield
Revue   Broadway: 17

Composer: Eubie Blake
Lyricist: Noble Sissle
Librettist: Flournoy E. Miller
Producer: Mawin Productions
Director: Walter Brooks

Choreographer: Davis & Carey; **Costumes:** Robert
Stevenson; **Musical Director:** Eubie Blake;
Orchestrations: Will Vodery; **Set Design:** Karle
O. Amend

Songs: Arabian Moon [1]; Bandana Ways; Breakin'
'Em In; Chickens Come Home to Roost; Dusting
Around; Falling in Love; Glory; Harlem Moon;
Here 'Tis; If It's Any News to You; In the Land of
Sunny Sunflowers; Joshua Fit de Battle; Keep
Your Chin Up [1]; Labor Day Parade; Lonesome
Man [1]; Reminiscing Saturday Afternoon; Sing
and Dance Your Troubles Away; Sore Foot
Blues; Sugar Babe; Waiting for the Whistle to
Blow [1]; We're a Couple of Salesmen; You Don't
Look for Love; You've Got to Have Koo Wah

Cast: Lavada Carter; Four Flash Devils; George
McClennon; Flournoy E. Miller; Taps Miller;
Mantan Moreland; Noble Sissle; Edith Wilson

Notes: [1] Cut prior to opening.

3966 • SHUFFLE ALONG OF 1952

OPENED: 05/08/1952   Theatre: Broadway
Revue   Broadway: 4

Composer: Eubie Blake
Lyricist: Noble Sissle
Librettist: Flournoy Miller; Paul Gerard Smith
Producer: Irving Gaumont; Grace Rosenfeld
Director: George Hale; Paul Gerard Smith

Choreographer: Henry LeTang; Aleigh Peterson;
Costumes: Waldo Angelo; **Orchestrations:**
Charles L. Cooke; **Set Design:** Albert Johnson;
Vocal Arranger: Claude Garreau

Songs: Alone with Love [2]; Bitten By Love
(C: Joseph Meyer; L: Floyd Huddleston);
Bongo-Boola; City Called Heaven; Falling
(C: Joseph Meyer; L: Floyd Huddleston); Farewell
with Love; Give It Love (C: Joseph Meyer;
L: Floyd Huddleston); Here 'Tis [1] (C: Joseph
Meyer; L: Floyd Huddleston); It's the Gown That
Makes the Gal That Makes the Guy (L: Joan Javits;
Noble Sissle); Jive Drill; My Day (C: Joseph Meyer;
L: Floyd Huddleston); Rhythm of America;
Swanee Moon; You Can't Overdo a Good Thing
(C: Joseph Meyer; L: Floyd Huddleston)

Cast: Eubie Blake; Thelma Carpenter; Avon Long;
Flournoy Miller; Noble Sissle

Notes: [1] Not in program. [2] Not used.

3967 • SIDE BY SIDE BY SONDHEIM

OPENED: 04/18/1977   Theatre: Music Box
Revue   Broadway: 390

Composer: Stephen Sondheim
Lyricist: Stephen Sondheim
Librettist: Ned Sherrin
Producer: Harold Prince
Director: Ned Sherrin

Choreographer: Bob Howe; **Costumes:** Florence
Klotz; **Lighting Designer:** Ken Billington;
Musical Director: Ray Cook; **Set Design:** Peter
Docherty

Songs: Ah, Paris! [1]; Another Hundred People [2];
Anyone Can Whistle [3]; Barcelona [2]; Beautiful
Girls [1]; Boy From . . ., The [4] (C: Mary
Rodgers); Boy Like That, A [5] (C: Leonard
Bernstein); Broadway Baby [1]; Buddy's Blues [1];
Can That Boy Fox Trot [1]; Comedy Tonight [6];
Company [2]; Could I Leave You [1]; Everybody
Says Don't [3]; Getting Married Today [2]; I Have
a Love [5] (C: Leonard Bernstein); I Never Do
Anything Twice [7]; I Remember [8]; If Momma
Was Married [9] (C: Jule Styne); I'm Still Here [1];
Little Things You Do Together, The [2]; Losing
My Mind [1]; Love Is in the Air [6]; Marry Me a
Little [2]; Pretty Lady [10]; Send in the Clowns [11];
Side By Side By Side [2]; Two of Us, The [13];
We're Gonna Be All Right [12] (C: Richard
Rodgers); You Could Drive a Person Crazy [2];
You Gotta Have a Gimmick [9] (C: Jule Styne);
You Must Meet My Wife [11]

Cast: David Kernan; Millicent Martin; Julia
McKenzie; Ned Sherrin

Notes: No songs written for this show. There is also an arrangement of brief pieces of songs titled "Conversation Piece." Other companies internationally and nationally have added or subtracted various songs. [1] From FOLLIES. [2] From COMPANY. [3] From ANYONE CAN WHISTLE. [4] From THE MAD SHOW. [5] From WEST SIDE STORY. [6] From A FUNNY THING HAPPENED ON THE WAY TO THE FORUM. [7] From film THE SEVEN PERCENT SOLUTION. [8] From television Musical EVENING PRIMROSE. [9] From GYPSY. [10] From PACIFIC OVERTURES. [11] From A LITTLE NIGHT MUSIC. [12] From DO I HEAR A WALTZ? [13] Added for Chicago production. Written for, but not used by, Kukla, Fran and Ollie.

3968 • SIDEWALKS OF NEW YORK

OPENED: 10/03/1927   Theatre: Knickerbocker
Musical   Broadway: 112

Composer: James F. Hanley
Lyricist: Eddie Dowling
Librettist: Eddie Dowling
Producer: Charles B. Dillingham
Director: Edgar MacGregor

Choreographer: Earl Lindsay; **Costumes:** Maybelle Manning; Robert Stevenson

Songs: Confirmation; Goldfish Glide; Headin' for Harlem; Just a Little Smile from You; Little Bum; Move Over [1]; Nothing Can Ever Happen in New York; Oh, for the Life of a Cowboy; Play-Ground in the Sky; Sidewalks of New York (C: C.B. Lawlor; L: J.W. Blake); Springtime of Long Ago; Table for Two [1]; Way Down Town; We're the Girls You Can't Forget; Wherever You Are; Younger Set, The

Cast: Charles Dale; Ray Dooley; Eddie Dowling; Barney Fagan; Bob Hope; Ruby Keeler; Fiske O'Hara; Josephine Sabel; Joe Smith; Jim Thornton

Notes: [1] ASCAP/Library of Congress.

3969 • SIGN OF THE ROSE, THE

OPENED: 1923
Play

Songs: Sign of the Rose, The (C: Leo Edwards; L: Lew Brown)

Notes: This play was originally produced on Broadway on 10/11/11.

3970 • SIGNS ALONG THE CYNIC ROUTE

OPENED: 12/14/1961   Theatre: Actors' Playhouse
Revue   Off-Broadway: 93

Composer: Will Holt
Lyricist: Will Holt
Librettist: Will Holt; Dolly Jonah
Producer: Precarious Productions
Director: Walt Witcover

Lighting Designer: Gene Tunezi; **Musical Director:** Don Evans

Songs: Bertha; Blondes Song, The; Carnival; Croquet; Discussion; Four More Shopping Days; I Know You; Kulturny; Last; Marriage Counsel; Modern Housing; News Item; Princeton Pastorale; Rise and Fall of the City of Movieville, The; Second Glances; Second Thoughts; Seconds; Signs; Social Director's Song, The; Summer Stock; Terre Haute; Till the Birds Sing; Tin Can Incantation; Weekend; Welcome

Cast: Robert Barand; Will Holt; Dolly Jonah

Notes: Songs and sketches listed.

3971 • SILAS GREEN FROM NEW ORLEANS

Notes: See FUNNY MONEY.

3972 • SILK STOCKINGS

OPENED: 02/24/1955   Theatre: Imperial
Musical   Broadway: 477

Composer: Cole Porter
Lyricist: Cole Porter
Librettist: Abe Burrows; George S. Kaufman; Leueen MacGrath
Producer: Cy Feuer; Ernest Martin
Director: Cy Feuer

Source: NINOTCHKA (Film: Charles Brackett; Walter Reisch; Billy Wilder); **Choreographer:** Eugene Loring; **Costumes:** Lucinda Ballard; Robert Mackintosh; **Dance Arranger:** Tommy Goodman; **Lighting Designer:** Jo Mielziner; **Musical Director:** Anton Coppola;

Orchestrations: Don Walker; **Set Design:** Jo Mielziner; **Vocal Arranger:** Herbert Greene

Songs: All of You; Art [1]; As On Through the Seasons We Sail [3]; Bebe of Gay Paree [1]; Give Me the Land [1]; Hail Bibinski; If Ever We Get Out of Jail [2]; I'm the Queen Thamar [1]; It's a Chemical Reaction, That's All; Josephine; Keep Your Chin Up [1]; Let's Make It a Night [1]; Paris Loves Lovers; Perfume of Love, The [1]; Red Blues, The; Satin and Silk; Siberia; Silk Stockings; Stereophonic Sound; There's a Hollywood That's Good [1]; Too Bad; Under the Dress [1]; What a Ball [1]; Why Should I Trust You? [1]; Without Love

Cast: Don Ameche; Leon Belasco; Henry Lascoe; Hildegarde Neff; Julie Newmar; David Opatoshu; George Tobias; Gretchen Wyler

Notes: [1] Not used. [2] Not used. Same music as "As on Through the Seasons We Sail." [3] Same music as "If Ever We Get Out of Jail."

3973 • SILKS AND SATINS

OPENED: 07/15/1920   Theatre: George M. Cohan

Musical   Broadway: 60

Composer: Leon Rosebrook
Lyricist: Louis Weslyn
Librettist: Thomas Duggan
Producer: William Rock

Choreographer: Earl Lindsay; **Costumes:** Kiviette; **Musical Director:** Leon Rosebrook; **Orchestrations:** Alfred Dalby; Leon Rosebrook

Songs: Alibi Blues (C/L: Arthur Swanstrom); Annie Laurie; Around the Town; Chili Bean (C: Albert Von Tilzer; L: Lew Brown); He Went In Like a Lion (C/L: Jules Von Tilzer); I Want to Be Somebody's Baby (C: Jesse Greer; L: Ed Smalle); I Wish That I'd Been Born in Borneo [2] (C: Walter Donaldson; L: Grant Clarke); I'm Glad to Be Back Again; I've Got a Sentry (C: Oliver G. Wallace; L: Arthur Freed); I've Shaken Everything I've Got; Life Was Worth While; Midsummer Maiden; My Rose of Memory; Nanking Blues; Signora [1]; Step Along with Me; Sunday's Child; That Colored Jassboray (C: Oliver G. Wallace; L: Arthur Freed); Tommy Atkins; Was Mrs. MacBeth Really Sleeping When She Took That Famous Walk? [1]

Cast: William Demarest; Thomas Duggan; Jay Regan; William Rock; Aileen Stanley

Notes: [1] Out Atlantic City 7/5/20. [2] ASCAP only. Not in program.

3974 • SILVER FOX, THE

OPENED: 09/05/1921   Theatre: Maxine Elliott's
Play   Broadway: 112

Composer: Jack Snyder
Lyricist: Jack Snyder
Author: Cosmo Hamilton
Producer: Lee Shubert
Director: William Faversham

Source: UNKNOWN (Play: Franz Herczeq); **Costumes:** Joseph; **Set Design:** Watson Barratt

Songs: Comedy Version for Frankie

Cast: Violet Kemble Cooper; William Faversham; William Fox; Lawrence Grossmith; Ian Keith; Vivienne Osborne

3975 • SILVER SCREEN, THE

OPENED: 1941   Theatre: Diamond Horseshoe
Revue   Nightclub

Composer: Dana Suesse
Lyricist: Billy Rose
Producer: Billy Rose
Director: John Murray Anderson

Choreographer: Marjery Fielding; **Costumes:** Raoul Pene du Bois; **Lighting Designer:** John Murray Anderson; **Musical Director:** Noble Sissle; **Set Design:** Raoul Pene du Bois

Songs: Colossal, Tremendous, Terrific; Glamour Girl

Cast: Carlyle Blackwell; Georges Fontana; Gilda Gray; Joseph E. Howard; Charles King; Lila Lee; Della Lind; June Mann; Mae Murray; Nita Naldi; Noble Sissle's Orchestra

Notes: There were also unlisted popular songs in this show.

3976 • SILVER SLIPPER, THE

OPENED: 10/27/1902   Theatre: Broadway
Musical   Broadway: 160

Composer: Leslie Stuart
Lyricist: W.H. Risque
Librettist: Clay M. Greene
Producer: John C. Fisher
Director: John C. Fisher

Source: SILVER SLIPPER, THE (Musical: Owen Hall; W.H. Risque; Leslie Stuart); **Musical Director:** Arthur Weld

Songs: Although I Am a Soldier I Prefer a Private Life; Baby with the Dimple and the Smile, The; Because I Love You Dear; Class [4] (L: Charles H. Taylor); Come Little Girl, and Tell Me Truly (L: Leslie Stuart); Detrimental Man, The; Downcast Eye, The [1] (C: Jerome Kern; L: Edgar Smith); Duet (C: Arthur Weld); Finale Act I (L: Leslie Stuart); Four and Twenty Little Men; Fun on a Motor; Girl You Love, The [2]; Glimpse-Impse-Impse, A; Go Home with Nursey, Do [4] (C: Landon Ronald); Good Behaviour [4] (L: George Rollit); Hunt the Slipper [4] (L: Leslie Stuart); I'd Be Satisfied with Life; If I Were a Girl Instead (L: Leslie Stuart); Invocation of Venus (L: Leslie Stuart); My Celia [3] (C/L: Jerome Kern); Opening Chorus Act II; Our College Gowns [4]; Ping Pong Duet (C: Ivan Caryll; L: Percy Greenbank); Riding [4] (C: Landon Ronald); She Didn't Know Enough About the Game [2] (L: George Rollit); Soldiers of the Army [2]; Tessie You Are the Only, Only, Only (C/L: Will R. Anderson); That's the Way [4]; To-night's the Night; Tup'ny Show, The [4]; Two Eyes Of Blue (L: Charles H. Taylor); Valse Lente (C: Arthur Weld); We'll Just Let It Go Like That [4]; When No One Knows [4]; You and Me [2]

Cast: Sam Bernard; Edna Wallace Hopper; Josie Sadler; Cyril Scott

Notes: [1] Added for tour 1904. [2] Out Boston 9/14/03. [3] Added for tour 1904. Though lyrics are credited to John Golden, Kern wrote the lyric. [4] In London only.

3977 • SILVER STAR, THE

OPENED: 11/01/1909   Theatre: New Amsterdam
Musical   Broadway: 80

Composer: Robert Hood Bowers
Lyricist: Harry B. Smith
Librettist: Harry B. Smith
Producer: Klaw & Erlanger
Director: Herbert Gresham

Choreographer: Julian Mitchell; **Costumes:** F. Richard Anderson; **Musical Director:** Robert Hood Bowers; C.J.M. Glaser; **Set Design:** Ernest Albert

Songs: Ballet (inst.) (C: C.J.M. Glaser); Boat Race Chorus; Carnival; Christmas Dances (inst.) (C: C.J.M. Glaser); Cooney-Spooney Dance, The (That Spooney Dance) (C: Jean Schwartz; L: William Jerome); Dancing the Cotillion (C: Raymond Hubbell); Franco-American Ragtime (C: Jean Schwartz; L: William Jerome); I Can't Resist Your Smile [1] (C: Albert Gumble); If Only I Were Santa Claus; (You Can Have Your "Oh, You Kids" but) It's a Loving Wife for Mine (C/L: Herbert Ingraham); Let Georgie Do It (C: Al Piantadosi; L: Edgar Leslie); Silver Star, The (C: Albert Gumble); Sleigh Bells May Be Wedding Bells; Springtime Ballet (C: C.J.M. Glaser); They're Not Doing That This Season (C: Albert Gumble); To Bring Up a Girl (C: Karl Hoschna)

Cast: George Bickel; Nellie McCoy; Harry Watson II

Notes: [1] Sheet music only.

3978 • SILVER SWAN, THE

OPENED: 11/27/1929   Theatre: Martin Beck
Musical   Broadway: 21

Composer: H. Maurice Jacquet
Lyricist: William S. Brady
Librettist: William S. Brady; Alonzo Price
Producer: Herman & Gantvoort
Director: Alonzo Price

Choreographer: LeRoy Prinz; **Costumes:** John Booth; William H. Matthews; **Musical Director:** Augustus Barratt

Songs: A la Viennese; Autumn Flowers [2]; Brave Deserve the Fair, The; Cigarette; Four O'Clock Girls [2]; Graceful and Fair; I Like the Military Man; I Love You, I Adore You; Lonely Road, The [1]; Love Is Mystery [1]; Love Letters; Lucy at Cards [2]; Merry-Go-Round; Only Game That I Would Play, The; Serenade; Shoe-Clap-Platter; Till I Met You (L: William S. Brady; Alonzo Price); Trial Song, The [1]

Cast: Lina Abarbanell; Vivian Hart; Alice McKenzie; Edward Well Jr.

Notes: [1] Out Pittsburgh 11/4/29. [2] Out Brooklyn 3/18/29.

3979 • SIMPLE MOLLY

OPENED: 1908
Musical   Chicago

Composer: Henri Wise
Lyricist: Henri Wise
Producer: Robert Motts; Pekin Stock Company

Songs: Poor Little Maid; Summer Time; Sweet Mollie-O; Taffy Finally [1]

Cast: Lottie Grady; Lew Lammar; Katie Milton; Tim Owsley; Augusta Stevens; Henri Wise

Notes: One-act musical. No other information available. [1] May have meant "Taffy Finale" as this was the last number in the show.

3980 • SIMPLE SIMON

OPENED: 02/18/1930   Theatre: Ziegfeld
Musical   Broadway: 135

Composer: Richard Rodgers
Lyricist: Lorenz Hart
Librettist: Guy Bolton; Ed Wynn
Producer: Florenz Ziegfeld
Director: Zeke Colvan

Choreographer: Seymour Felix; **Musical Director:** Oscar Bradley; **Set Design:** Joseph Urban

Songs: Bluebeard's Beard (inst.) [2]; Come On, Men (FInaletto Act I Scene 5) [11]; Come Out of the Nursery (and Dance) [7]; Coney Island (Opening Act I); Cottage in the Country (That's the Thing), A (C/L: Walter Donaldson); Dancing on the Ceiling [5]; Don't Tell Your Folks; Dull and Gay (The Gay and the Dull); Happy Days and Lonely Nights [1] (C: Fred Fisher; L: Billy Rose); He Was Too Good to Me [7]; Hunting Ballet (dance); Hunting the Fox; I Can Do Wonders with You [10]; I Still Believe in You [3]; I Want That Man [9]; I'm Yours [2] (C: Johnny Green; L: E.Y. Harburg); Kissing Forest Ballet (dance); Love Me or Leave Me [8] (C: Walter Donaldson; L: Gus Kahn); Magic Music; Oh So Lovely [12]; On with the Dance (inst.); Peter Pan [2]; Prayers of Tears and Laughter [7]; Rags and Tatters; Say When-Stand Up-Drink Down [7]; Send for Me [4]; Simple Simon Instep [12]; Sing Glory Hallelujah [12];

Sweetenheart; Ten Cents a Dance; Trojan Horse, The (inst.) [6]

Cast: Will Ahern; Bobbe Arnst; Hugh Cameron; Alan Edwards; Ruth Etting; Hazel Forbes; Harriet Hoctor; Doree Leslie; Lennox Pawle; Jack Squires; Paul Stanton; Helen Walsh; Ed Wynn

Notes: [1] Added after opening. [2] Added for tour. [3] Cut after opening. Same music as "Singing a Love Song" from CHEE-CHEE. [4] Same music as "I Must Love You" from CHEE-CHEE. [5] Cut before opening. Later in movie EVERGREEN. [6] Cut after opening. [7] Cut before opening. [8] Added after opening. Also in WHOOPEE. [9] Added after opening. Then cut. [10] Cut after opening. Not used in HEADS UP! [11] Not in programs but probably in show. [12] Not used.

3981 • SIMPLE SIMON SIMPLE

OPENED: 1907
Musical   Closed out of town

Lyricist: Charles H. Brown; Otis F. Wood
Director: Lewis Morton

Songs: Bachelor Girls (C: MacArthur); Bargain Day (C: Bendix); Bull Frog and the Coon, The (C: Armstrong); College Days (C: Bendix; MacArthur); Coy Young Maid, A (C: MacArthur); Dear Old Pals (C: MacArthur); Finale (C: Bendix; Curti); Holding Hands (C: Von Tilzer); La Tiddle De Um (C: Unknown); Love Me and the World Is Mine [1] (C: Ernest R. Ball; L: Dave Reed); Ma Southern Oriole (C: Koenig); Nursery Rhyme Dances (C: Bendix); Pickaninny Mose (C: Bond); Sand Man, The (C: MacArthur; Varley); Shine, Shine, Shine (C: MacArthur); Venetia (C: Von Tilzer); Yankee Doodle Up-To-Date (C: Unknown)

Cast: Drury Rector; William C. Whelp

Notes: From program of Wilkes-Barre 1/4/07. [1] Also cut from BUSTER BROWN.

3982 • SIMPLEX MARRIAGE PARLORS

OPENED: 04/24/1916   Theatre: New
Musical   New York

Composer: Al Reeves
Lyricist: Al Reeves

Librettist: Al Reeves
Director: Al Reeves

Songs: Araby; Discovering Talent; Don't Forget Your Old Pal, Al; I've Got Everybody's Number; Joe Simon; Lamp Post in New York Town; Old Plantation Ball; We Want a Mighty Navy; When It's Moonlight on the Mississippi

Cast: Maude Rockwell; Arthur Thornton

Notes: A vaudeville musical.

3983 • SIMPLY HEAVENLY
OPENED: 05/21/1957   Theatre: Playhouse
Musical   Broadway: 62

Composer: David Martin
Lyricist: Langston Hughes
Librettist: Langston Hughes
Producer: Vincent Cerow; Abel Euklewitz
Director: Joshua Shelley

Lighting Designer: Raymond Sovey; **Musical Director:** Sticks Evans; **Orchestrations:** David Martin; **Set Design:** Raymond Sovey

Songs: Broken String Blues; Did You Ever Hear the Blues?; I'm a Good Old Girl; I'm Gonna Be John Henry; Let Me Take You for a Ride; Let's Ball Awhile; Look for the Morning Star; Love Is Simply Heavenly; Men in My Life, The; When I'm in a Quiet Mood

Cast: John Bowie; Anna English; Brownie McGhee; Claudia McNeil; Melvin Stuart

Notes: Number of performances does not include original Off- Broadway run. Moved to Broadway on 8/20/57.

3984 • SIN OF PAT MULDOON, THE
OPENED: 03/13/1957   Theatre: Cort
Play   Broadway: 5

Author: John McLiam
Producer: Richard Adler; Roger L. Stevens
Director: Jack Garfein

Costumes: Anna Hill Johnstone; **Lighting Designer:** Paul Morrison; **Set Design:** Mordecai Goralik

Songs: Sin of Pat Muldoon, The (C/L: Richard Adler)

Cast: James Barton; Patricia Bosworth; Katherine Squire; Elaine Stritch

3985 • SINBAD
OPENED: 02/14/1918   Theatre: Winter Garden
Musical   Broadway: 164

Composer: Sigmund Romberg
Lyricist: Harold Atteridge
Librettist: Harold Atteridge
Producer: J.J. Shubert; Lee Shubert
Director: J.C. Huffman

Choreographer: Jack Mason; **Costumes:** Homer Conant; Cora MacGeachy; S. Zalud; **Musical Director:** Alfred Goodman; **Set Design:** Watson Barratt

Songs: Alexander's Band Is Back in Dixieland (C: Albert Gumble; L: Jack Yellen); Avalon [1] (C: Vincent Rose; L: Al Jolson); Bagdad [2] (C: Al Jolson; Sigmund Romberg); Beauty and the Beast; Bedalumbo, The (C: Al Jolson); By the Honeysuckle Vine (C: Al Jolson; L: B.G. DeSylva); Chloe [1] (C: Al Jolson; L: B.G. DeSylva); Cleopatra (C: Harry Tierney; L: Alfred Bryan); Darktown Dancing School (C: Albert Gumble; L: Jack Yellen); Dixie Rose [1] (C: George Gershwin; L: Irving Caesar; B.G. DeSylva); Fox Trot (C: Al Jolson; Sigmund Romberg); Hello Central, Give Me No Man's Land (C: Jean Schwartz; L: Sam M. Lewis; Joe Young); How'd You Like to Be My Daddy [4] (C: Ted Snyder; L: Sam M. Lewis; Joe Young); I Gave Her That (C: Al Jolson; L: B.G. DeSylva); I Hail from Cairo; I Love the Heart of Dixie (C: Al Jolson; Jean Schwartz; L: Alfred Bryan); I Wonder Why She Kept on Saying Si-Si- Si-Si Senor! (C: Ted Snyder; L: Sam M. Lewis; Joe Young); I'll Say She Does (C/L: B.G. DeSylva; Al Jolson; Gus Kahn); I'll Sing You a Song about Dear Old Dixie Land (C: Turner Layton; L: Henry Creamer); I'll Tell the World (C: B.G. DeSylva); Isle of Youth; It's Wonderful (C: B.G. DeSylva); I've Got the Blue Ridge Blues [4] (C: Charles L. Cooke; Richard A. Whiting; L: Charles A. Mason); Little Bit of Every Nationality, A; Love Ahoy!; My Mammy (C: Walter Donaldson; L: Sam M. Lewis; Joe Young); 'N Everything (C/L: B.G. DeSylva; Al Jolson; Gus Kahn); Night in the Orient, A; On

Cupid's Green; On the Road to Calais (C: Al Jolson; L: Alfred Bryan); Our Ancestors; Rag Lad of Bagdad, The (C: Al Jolson; Sigmund Romberg); Raz-Ma-Taz (C: Al Jolson); Rock-a-Bye Your Baby with a Dixie Melody (C: Jean Schwartz; L: Sam M. Lewis; Joe Young); Swanee [3] (C: George Gershwin; L: Irving Caesar); Tell That to the Marines (C: Al Jolson; Jean Schwartz); There's a Lump of Sugar Down in Dixie (C: Albert Gumble; L: Alfred Bryan; Jack Yellen); They Can't Fool Me [1] (C: Al Jolson; L: B.G. DeSylva); Thousand and One Arabian Nights, A; Where Do They Get Those Guys? (C: Albert Gumble; L: Alfred Bryan; Jack Yellen); Why Do They All Take the Night Boat to Albany (C: Jean Schwartz; L: Sam M. Lewis; Joe Young); Why Do You Think You're Fooling with That Million Dollar Talk [4] (C: Ted Snyder; L: Sam M. Lewis; Joe Young); Worst Is Yet to Come, The [4] (C: Bert Grant; L: Sam M. Lewis; Joe Young); You Ain't Heard Nothin' Yet [1] (C: Al Jolson; L: B.G. DeSylva; Gus Kahn)

Cast: Edgar Atchinson-Ely; Lawrence D'Orsay; Kitty Doner; Forrest Huff; Al Jolson

Notes: All songs not by Romberg interpolated by Jolson either on Broadway or on tour. [1] Not in programs. [2] Sheet music credit solely to Jolson. [3] Added 12/19. [4] ASCAP/Library of Congress only.

3986 • SING FOR YOUR SUPPER

OPENED: 04/24/1939   Theatre: Adelphi
Revue   Broadway: 60

Composer: Lee Wainer
Lyricist: Robert Sour
Librettist: Turner Bullock; Charlotte Kent; David Lesan; Jack Murray
Producer: WPA Theatre
Director: Robert H. Gordon; H. Gordon Graham; Harold Hecht

Songs: At Long Last; Ballad for Americans (Ballad of Uncle Sam) (C: Earl Robinson; L: John Latouche); Bonnie Banks; Dirge; Her Pop's a Cop (C: Ned Lehac; L: Phil Conwit; Irving Crane); How Can We Swing It?; Imagine My Finding You Here (C: Ned Lehac); Leaning on a Shovel (L: John Latouche); Legitimate (L: John Latouche); Lucky; Oh Boy, Can We Deduct; Opening Night; Papa's Got a Job (C: Ned Lehac; L: Harold Rome; Robert Sour); Perspiration

(L: John Latouche); Story of a Horn, The; Young Man with a Horn

Cast: Bidda Blakely; Virginia Bolen; Carl Chapin; Gordon Clarke; Peggy Coudray; Genora English; Edward Fuller; Paula Laurence; James Mordecai; Coby Ruskin; Sonny Tufts; Hansford Wilson

3987 • SING HALLELUJAH!

OPENED: 11/03/1987   Theatre: Village Gate
           Downstairs
Revue   Off-Broadway: 72

Composer: Traditional
Lyricist: Traditional
Producer: Art D'Lugoff; Burt D'Lugoff; Gerald Wexler Presents Inc.; Lipper Productions
Director: Worth Gardner

Costumes: Rebecca Senske; **Lighting Designer:** Kirk Bookman; **Musical Director:** Donald Lawrence; **Set Design:** Joseph P. Tilford

Songs: Anyway You Bless; Bright Side Somewhere; Can't Nobody Do Me Like Jesus (C/L: Andre Crouch); Couldn't Hear Nobody Pray; Didn't It Rain; Everybody Ought to Know (C/L: Walter Hawkins); Good News; Hollywood Scene (C/L: Andre Crouch); I'm Just Holdin' On (C/L: Dorothy Love Coates); New World (C/L: Michael Terry); No Ways Tired; Oh Happy Day; Oh Mary Don't You Weep; Question Is, The (C/L: Marvin Winans); Right Now (C/L: Andre Crouch); Runnin' for Jesus; Safe in His Arms; Shut de Do'; Sing Hallelujah! (C/L: Donald Lawrence); We Can't Go on This Way (C/L: Richard Smallwood)

Cast: Curtis Blake; Rose Clyburn; Patricia Ann Everson; Ann Nesby; Clarence Snow

3988 • SING MUSE!

OPENED: 12/06/1961   Theatre: Van Dam
Musical   Off-Broadway: 39

Composer: Joe Raposo
Lyricist: Erich Segal
Librettist: Erich Segal
Producer: Robert D. Feldstein
Director: Bill Penn

Costumes: Hal George; **Lighting Designer:** Boyd Dumrose; **Musical Director:** Jerry Goldberg;

Orchestrations: Joe Raposo; **Set Design:** Boyd Dumrose

Songs: Business Is Bad; Day in Sec-Moxena Mambo [1]; Fame!; Helen Quit Your Yellin'; I Am a Travelling Poet; I'm to Blame; In Our Little Salon; No Champagne; O Pallas Athene; Out to Launch; Please Let Me Read; Sing Muse; Tonight's the Fight; Way, The; We'll Find a Way; Wrath of Achilles, The; You're in Love; Your Name May Be Paris

Cast: Paul Michael; Karen Morrow; Ralph Santley; Bob Spencer

Notes: [1] Not in program.

3989 • SING OUT, SWEET LAND!
OPENED: 12/27/1944   Theatre: International
Revue   Broadway: 102

Librettist: Walter Kerr
Director: Walter Kerr; Leon Leonidoff

Choreographer: Doris Humphrey; Charles Weidman; **Costumes:** Lucinda Ballard; **Musical Director:** Elie Siegmeister; **Orchestrations:** Elie Siegmeister; **Set Design:** Albert Johnson; **Vocal Arranger:** Arthur Lessac

Songs: As I Was Going Along (C: Elie Siegmeister; L: Edward Eager); At Sundown (C/L: Walter Donaldson); Basement Blues; Bicycle Built for Two (C/L: Harry Dacre); Big Rock Candy Mountain; Blue-Tail Fly (C/L: Dan Emmett); Camptown Races (C/L: Stephen Foster); Captain Jinks (C: T. Maclagan; L: William Horace Lingard); Casey Jones (C: Eddie Newton; L: T. Lawrence Seibert); Devil and the Farmer's Wife, The; Didn't My Lord Deliver Daniel?; Foggy, Foggy, Dew; Frankie and Johnny; Funny Bunny Hug [1] (C/L: Dave Ringle; William Tracey; Ray Walker); Hallelujah, I'm a Bum (C: Richard Rodgers; L: Lorenz Hart); Hammer Ring; Hardly Think I Will; Heaven Will Protect the Working Girl (C: A. Baldwin Sloane; L: Edgar Smith); Hey Mr. Bossman; I Got Rhythm (C: George Gershwin; L: Ira Gershwin); I Have Been a Good Boy; Little Mohee; Louisiana Gals; Marching Down This Road; More Than These (C: John Mundy; L: Edward Eager); My Blue Heaven (C: Walter Donaldson; L: George Whiting); Oh, Susannah (C/L: Stephen Foster); Polly Wolly Doodle; Roving Gambler, The; Sea Chanty; Some of These Men; Springfield Mountain; Trouble, Trouble; Wanderin'; Watermelon Cry; Way Down the Ohio; When I Was Single; Where (C: John Mundy; L: Edward Eager); While Strolling Through the Park One Day (C/L: Robert A. King); Who Is the Man?; Yes Sir, That's My Baby (C: Walter Donaldson; L: Gus Kahn); You Better Mind

Cast: Philip Coolidge; Alfred Drake; Burl Ives; Alma Kaye; Bibi Osterwald

Notes: [1] Sheet music only.

3990 • SING OUT THE NEWS
OPENED: 09/24/1938   Theatre: Music Box
Revue   Broadway: 105

Composer: Harold Rome
Lyricist: Harold Rome
Librettist: Charles Friedman; Harold Rome
Producer: Max Gordon; Moss Hart; George S. Kaufman
Director: Charles Friedman

Choreographer: Dave Gould; Ned McGurn; Charles Walters; **Costumes:** John Hambleton; **Musical Director:** Max Meth; **Orchestrations:** Hans Spialek; **Set Design:** Jo Mielziner

Songs: Entre-Nous; Franklin D. Roosevelt Jones [3]; How Long Can Love Keep Laughing?; Just an Ordinary Guy [2]; My Heart Is Unemployed; One of These Fine Days; Peace and the Diplomat Ballet (C: Will Irwin); Plaza 6-9423; Rhumba on the Right [1]; We've Got the Song; Yip Ahoy (Adrift on the Lo-one Prairie!)

Cast: June Allyson; Joey Faye; Dorothy Fox; Will Geer; Richard Huey; Rex Ingram; Christina Lind; Leslie Litomy; Philip Loeb; Michael Loring; Ginger Manners; Hazel Scott; Hiram Sherman; Benjamin Wailes; Mary Jane Walsh

Notes: [1] Out Philadelphia 8/29/38. [2] ASCAP also lists this song under PINS AND NEEDLES. [3] Also known as "F.D.R. Jones."

3991 • SING, MAHALIA, SING
OPENED: 03/26/1985
Musical   Closed out of town

Composer: Wayne Davis; George Faison; Richard Smallwood

Lyricist: Wayne Davis; George Faison; Richard Smallwood
Librettist: George Faison
Producer: Edgewood Productions, Inc.
Director: George Faison

Choreographer: George Faison; **Costumes:** Nancy Potts; **Lighting Designer:** Thomas Skelton; **Set Design:** Tom McPhillips

Cast: Lynette Hawkins; Jennifer Holliday; Glen Jones; Esther Marrow; Richard Smallwood Singers, The

3992 • SINGIN' IN THE RAIN

OPENED: 07/02/1985   Theatre: Gershwin
Musical   Broadway: 367

Composer: Nacio Herb Brown
Lyricist: Arthur Freed
Librettist: Betty Comden; Adolph Green
Producer: Cindy Pritzker, Inc.; Lois F. Rosenfeld; Maurice Rosenfield
Director: Twyla Tharp

Source: SINGIN' IN THE RAIN (Film: Betty Comden; Adolph Green); **Choreographer:** Twyla Tharp; **Costumes:** Ann Roth; **Dance Arranger:** Stanley Lebowsky; **Lighting Designer:** Jennifer Tipton; **Musical Director:** Robert Billig; **Orchestrations:** Larry Wilcox; **Set Design:** Santo Loquasto; **Vocal Arranger:** Stanley Lebowsky

Songs: Beautiful Girl; Blue Prelude (C: Al Bishop; L: Gordon Jenkins); Broadway Rhythm; Fit As a Fiddle; Good Mornin'; Hub Bub; I've Got a Feelin' You're Foolin'; Love Is Where You Find It (L: Gus Kahn); Make 'Em Laugh; Moses Supposes (C: Roger Edens; L: Betty Comden; Adolph Green); Singin' in the Rain; Takin' Miss Mary to the Ball; Temptation; Wedding of the Painted Doll; Would You?; You Are My Lucky Star; You Stepped Out of a Dream (L: Gus Kahn)

Cast: Don Correia; Mary D'Arcy; Richard Fancy; Melinda Gilb; Faye Grant; Robert Radford; Hansford Rowe; Peter Slutsker

Notes: No songs written for this production.

3993 • SINGIN' THE BLUES

OPENED: 09/16/1931   Theatre: Liberty
Play   Broadway: 46

Composer: Jimmy McHugh
Lyricist: Dorothy Fields
Author: John McGowan
Producer: Alex A. Aarons; Vinton Freedley
Director: Bertram Harrison

Choreographer: Sammy Lee; **Costumes:** Kiviette; **Musical Director:** Eubie Blake; **Orchestrations:** Robert Russell Bennett; **Set Design:** Donald Oenslager

Songs: Crazy Street (C: Burton Lane; L: Harold Adamson); It's the Darndest Thing; Singin' the Blues

Cast: Eubie Blake and His Orchestra; Ashley Cooper; Mantan Moreland; John Sims; Fredi Washington; Frank Wilson

3994 • SINGING GIRL, THE

OPENED: 10/23/1899   Theatre: Casino
Musical   Broadway: 80

Composer: Victor Herbert
Lyricist: Harry B. Smith
Librettist: Stanislaus Stange
Producer: Alice Nielsen Opera Company
Director: Julian Mitchell

Musical Director: Paul Steindorff; **Set Design:** Joseph Physioc

Songs: Allow Me to Inform You; Alpine Horn, The (Tyrolean Song); By My Mien (Greta's Waltz); Chink, Chink, Don't Talk to Me of Marriage; Do You Follow Me?; Don't Talk to Me of Marriage; Entrance of Duke Rodolph; Here's an End to Vaciliation; If Only You Were Mine; Lanciers; Love Is Merest Folly; Love Is Tyrant; Mazurka; Opening Chorus Act II; Our Native Land; Singing Girl, The; Siren of the Ballet, The; So I Bid You Beware; Song of the Danube, The; To Be a Little Singing Girl; Wedding Music; Well Beloved, The; Wonderful Magician, The (Love, the Marvelous Magician)

Cast: May Boley; Joseph Cawthorn; Eugene Cowles; Joseph W. Herbert; Louis Kelso; Richie Ling; Alice Nielsen; John C. Slavin

3995 • SINGING RABBI, THE

OPENED: 09/10/1931   Theatre: Selwyn
Musical   Broadway: 4

Composer: Joseph Rumshinsky
Lyricist: L. Wolfe Gilbert
Librettist: Boris Thomashefsky; Harry Thomashefsky
Producer: Harry Thomashefsky
Director: William E. Morris

Choreographer: Florenz Ames; **Musical Director:** Harry Lubin; **Set Design:** Orestes Raineri

Songs: Hear O Israel; I'm Wide Awake When I Dream [1] (C: Harry Lubin); Only Your Heart Can Tell [1] (C: Harry Lubin); Sholom Aleichem; Vision of the Future, A; Yonkele and Rifkelel [1] (C: Harry Lubin)

Cast: Florenz Ames; Sam Ash; Flora Le Breton; Philip Ryder; Boris Thomashefsky; Regina Zuckerberg

Notes: [1] ASCAP/Library of Congress only.

3996 • SIREN, THE
OPENED: 08/21/1911   Theatre: Knickerbocker
Musical   Broadway: 136

Composer: Leo Fall
Lyricist: Harry B. Smith
Librettist: Harry B. Smith
Producer: Charles Frohman
Director: Thomas Reynolds

Source: DIE SIRENE (Musical: Leo Fall; Leo Stein; A.M. Wilner); **Musical Director:** Harold Vicars; **Set Design:** Homer Emens

Songs: Ancestors Bold; Beware of the Sirens; Blind Man's Buff [4]; Bold Barons of the Rhine [8]; Confidential Source [6] (C: Jerome Kern); Cupid the Conqueror [6]; Donkey and the Hay, The; Farming Life-Country Life [4]; Follow Me 'Round (C: Leo Fall; L: Jerome Kern; Adrian Ross); Good-Bye, Little Girls, Good-Bye (C/L: Donald Brian); Hm! She Is the One Girl; I Always Come Back to You [3]; I Want to Sing in Opera [1] (C/L: Jerome Kern; C: Worton David; L: George Arthurs); Ladies! Ladies! [4] (C: Egbert Van Alstyne; L: Herbert Thomson); Little Girls Beware; Love Makes the World Go 'Round [4]; Love Me to That Beautiful Tune [3] (C: Nat D. Ayer; L: Harry Williams); Maid from Montbijou (In the Valley of Montbijou) (C: Jerome Kern; L: M.E. Rourke); Music Caresssing of Violins (Waltz Caprice); My Heart I Cannot Give You

(C: Jerome Kern; L: Matthew Woodward); Oh Do Step the Two-Step (C: Howard Talbot); On the Farm; Polka Is Good Fun, The; Postillion, The [4]; Siren's Honeymoon, The [5] (C/L: Donald Brian); Sirens So Fair [7]; Song of the Sirens [7]; Wallflow'r Sweet; You're Just a Perfect Peach Beyond My Reach [2] (C: Jerome Kern)

Cast: Donald Brian; Frank Moulan; Julia Sanderson

Notes: [1] Kern probably made minor contributions. [2] Probably not used. [3] Out Witchita 4/9/13. [4] Sheet music only. [5] In Witchita 4/9/13 songs titled "Beware of the Sirens" and "Sirens So Fair" were listed. Sheet music includes a song titled "Song of the Sirens." They may all be this song. [6] Cut after opening. [7] ASCAP/Library of Congress. [8] Vocal score only.

3997 • SIROCCO
OPENED: 08/13/1976
Revue

Composer: Tim Grundmann
Lyricist: Tim Grundmann
Librettist: Ken Bloom; Company, The; Tim Grundmann
Producer: Ken Bloom; New Playwrights' Theatre
Director: Ken Bloom

Choreographer: Susan Groberg; **Costumes:** Henry Shaffer; **Dance Arranger:** Tim Grundmann; **Lighting Designer:** Ken Bloom; **Musical Director:** Tim Grundmann; **Orchestrations:** Tim Grundmann; **Set Design:** Ken Bloom; **Vocal Arranger:** Tim Grundmann

Songs: Holiday for Nuns; It's Time for an Improvisation; Nikita Marlena; Nuts about Nuns; Punting on the Thames; Taxi to Dreamland; That's Amusement; When You Plow Through the Fields; You're You

Cast: A. David Johnson; Dawn Leland; Hunt Meadows; Tanis Roach; Jan Frederick Shiffman

3998 • SIS HOPKINS
OPENED: 1903
Play   Closed out of town

Author: Carroll Fleming; Edward Kidder
Producer: J.R. Stirling

Songs: Baby on the Shore [1] (C/L: John Keefe); Come Birdie Come [3]; Commencement Day Ode [1] (C: George Nichols; L: Carroll Fleming); Down the Road [4]; Girl My Heart Beats For, The [2]; Haying Chorus [1] (C: George Nichols; L: Carroll Fleming); I Love You, 'Deed I Do' [3]; I'm Not a Bit Like Other Girls [1] (C: George Nichols; L: Carroll Fleming); I'm Thinking About You Honey All the While [4]; It's Up to Me [3]; Lovers' Springtime [4]; Mem'rys of Childhood Day [1] (C/L: Rose Melville); My Dearest Pal Is Albert, Prince of Wales [1] (C: George Nichols; L: Carroll Fleming); My Rose [2]; Not a Bit Like Other Girls [2] (C/L: Frank Minzey); Playing Golf [1] (C: George Nichols; L: Carroll Fleming); Put Me in My Little Bed [4]; Silver Moon [4]; Sisseretta [2]; Tell Me, Do You Love Me As of Old? [1] (C: George Nichols; L: Carroll Fleming); Thinking of Our Childhood Days [4]; Wilhelmina [3]

Cast: Rose Melville

Notes: [1] From an undated program at the Lyceum Theatre. [2] Sheet music only. [3] Out Elizabeth N.J. 2/26/03. [4] Out Brooklyn 1904.

3999 • SISTER MARY

OPENED: 10/27/1899 Theatre: Bijou
Musical Broadway: 120

Librettist: Glen MacDonough
Producer: May Irwin

Musical Director: Watty Hydes

Songs: Cake-Walk, The (C/L: Cissie Loftus); Creole Love Song and Dance, A; He Certainly Has a Soft Spot for Me (C/L: Herbert Cawthorne); I Don't Care to Be Yo' Lady Fren' No Mo' (C: Will D. Cobb; L: Gus Edwards); Louisiana Lize (C: Billy Johnson; L: Bob Cole); Mary Was a Housemaid; Midnight Serenade, The (C/L: Cissie Loftus); My Bed Is Like a Little Boat (C: Cissie Loftus; L: Robert Louis Stevenson); Not the Proper Way to Treat a Lady [1] (C: Ivan Caryll; Lionel Monckton; L: Harry Greenbank; Adrian Ross); Why Don't My Baby Write? (C: Billy Johnson; L: Bob Cole)

Cast: George A. Beane; Melville Ellis; Herbert Gresham; May Irwin; Joseph M. Sparks; Queenie Vassar

Notes: All songs not credited in program. [1] From THE CIRCUS GIRL. [2] Lyrics based on poetry by Robert Louis Stevenson.

4000 • SITTIN' PRETTY (1921)

OPENED: 1924
Musical

Composer: J. Fred Coots
Lyricist: McElbert Moore

Songs: Cognac; Comforts of Home Sweet Home; French Fling; Knitting Song; Love's Crystal; Sittin' Pretty; Smoke Dreams IThe Cigarette Song)

Notes: No other information available. Song titles from ASCAP.

4001 • SITTING PRETTY (1924)

OPENED: 04/08/1924 Theatre: Fulton
Musical Broadway: 95

Composer: Jerome Kern
Lyricist: P.G. Wodehouse
Librettist: Guy Bolton
Director: Julian Alfred; Fred G. Latham

Costumes: Charles LeMaire; Alice O'Neil; **Musical Director:** Max Steiner; **Orchestrations:** Robert Russell Bennett; **Set Design:** P. Dodd Ackerman

Songs: All the World Is Dancing Mad [4]; All You Need Is a Girl; Ancient Days [4]; Bongo on the Congo; Charity Class, The; Coaching [2]; Dancing Time [1]; Days Gone By; Dear Old Fashioned Prison of Mine (Tulip Time in Sing Sing); Enchanted Train; Finale Act II; Finaletto Act I; Grab a Girl [1]; I'm Looking All Over for You [1]; Is This Not a Lovely Spot? [3]; Just Wait [2]; Ladies Are Present [2]; Mr. and Mrs. Rover; On a Desert Island with You; Polka Dot, The; Roses Are Nodding [2]; Shadow of the Moon; Shufflin' Sam; Sitting Pretty (L: Jerome Kern; P.G. Wodehouse); There Isn't One Girl; Worries; Year from Today, A; You Alone Would Do [2]

Cast: Gertrude Bryan; Rudolph Cameron; Dwight Frye; Frank McIntyre; Queenie Smith

Notes: [1] Out Newark 3/25/25. [2] Out Detroit prior to New York. [3] Same music as "The

Pergola Patrol" from THE CABARET GIRL. [4] Not in programs.

4002 • SIX
OPENED: 04/12/1971   Theatre: Cricket
Musical   Off-Broadway: 8

Composer: Charles Strouse
Lyricist: Charles Strouse
Librettist: Charles Strouse
Producer: L. Slade Brown
Director: Peter Coe

Choreographer: Denny Martin Flinn; **Musical Director:** Wally Harper; **Set Design:** Richard Nelson

Songs: Beginning, The, Coming Attractions; Critic, The; Dream, The; Garden, The; Invisible Man, The; Love Song; Sissiphus [1]; Six; Trip; What If [1]; What Is There to Sing About?

Cast: Johanna Albrecht; Leigh Beery; Alvin Ing; Gail Nelson; Gilbert Price; Hal Watters

Notes: [1] ASCAP/Library of Congress only.

4003 • $600 AND A MULE
OPENED: 08/28/1973
Musical   Closed out of town

Composer: Arthur Smalls Jr.
Lyricist: Lester Wilson
Librettist: Lester Wilson
Producer: Michael Moriarty
Director: Lester Wilson

Choreographer: Lester Wilson; **Costumes:** Andrea Lilly; **Lighting Designer:** Ken Billington; **Musical Director:** Phil Moore; **Orchestrations:** Luther Henderson; Phil Moore; **Set Design:** Terry Gates

Songs: Angels; Bessie Smith; Brother; Can My Son Be President?; Fanga; Flesh for Sale; Games; Good Morning, Mr. Sun; Josephine; Lighted Candles; Proving Ground; Sniff Me, Snort Me, Steal Away; Subway (Funky R.T.D.); Swinging Uptown; Toe, Head, Tap, Tap; Touch Me

Cast: Gary Chapman; Winston De Witt Hemsley; Michael Peters; Arthur Smalls Jr.; Lester Wilson

Notes: Closed in L.A.

4004 • 1600 PENNSYLVANIA AVENUE
OPENED: 05/04/1976   Theatre: Mark Hellinger
Musical   Broadway: 7

Composer: Leonard Bernstein
Lyricist: Alan Jay Lerner
Librettist: Alan Jay Lerner
Producer: Roger L. Stevens; Robert Whitehead
Director: George Faison; Gilbert Moses

Choreographer: George Faison; **Costumes:** Whitney Blausen; Dona Granata; **Lighting Designer:** Tharon Musser; **Musical Director:** Roland Gagnon; **Orchestrations:** Hershy Kay; Sid Ramin; **Set Design:** Kurt Lundell

Songs: American Dreaming (1) [10]; American Dreaming (2) [12] (L: Erik Haagensen; Alan Jay Lerner); Another Kind of Man [12] (L: Erik Haagensen; Alan Jay Lerner); Auctions; Bright and Black; Can You Love [12] (L: Erik Haagensen; Alan Jay Lerner); Duet for One (The First Lady of the Land); Forty Acres and a Mule; Grand Old Party, The [5]; Honor of Your Presence, The; I Love My Wife; I Love This Land [3]; If I Was a Dove; It's My Country [12] (L: Erik Haagensen; Alan Jay Lerner); Little White Lie, The; Lud's Birthday Party [12] (L: Erik Haagensen; Alan Jay Lerner); Lud's Wedding (1); Lud's Wedding (2) [12] (L: Erik Haagensen; Alan Jay Lerner); Mark of a Man, The; Me [11]; Middle C [4]; Nation that Wasn't There, The [1]; On Ten Square Miles by the Potomac River; Philadelphia [1]; Pity the Poor; Prelude [2]; President Jefferson Sunday Luncheon Party March, The [7]; Proud [8]; Red, White and Blues, The; Rehearse! [9]; Robber-Baron Minstrel Parade, The; Seena (1); Seena (2) [12] (L: Erik Haagensen; Alan Jay Lerner); Sonatina (1); Sonatina (2) [12] (L: Erik Haagensen; Alan Jay Lerner); Take Care of This House; That House/This Time [6]; They've Done It [12] (L: Erik Haagensen; Alan Jay Lerner); They've Started [12] (L: Erik Haagensen; Alan Jay Lerner); Uncle Tom [1]; We Must Have a Ball; Welcome Home Miz Adams

Cast: Ken Howard; Richard Muenz; Gilbert Price; Howard Ross; Patricia Routledge; Reid Shelton; Emily Yancy

Notes: Kurt Lundell redesigned Tony Walton's original set designs when Walton left the show. The costume designs were Walton's assistants on the show. [1] Cut prior to opening. [2] Cut prior to opening. Same music as "Middle C." [3] Cut prior to opening. Same music as "Proud." [4] Same music as "Prelude." Music later used in SONGFEST. [5] Cut prior to opening. Music used in "Slava! (A Political Overture)." [6] Cut prior to opening. Music used in A QUIET PLACE. [7] Cut dance music later used in "Divertimento." [8] Same music as "I Love This Land." [9] Music used in "Slava! (A Political Overture)." [10] Cut prior to opening. Section retained became "Proud." [11] Cut prior to opening. [12] Written for 1/27/95 reading at Theatre 603.

4005 • SIXTH FINGER IN A FIVE FINGER GLOVE, THE

OPENED: 10/08/1956   Theatre: Longacre
Play   Broadway: 2

Author: Scott Michel
Producer: Gertrude Caplin; Thelma Finger
Director: John Holden

Lighting Designer: Paul Morrison; **Set Design:** Paul Morrison

Songs: Sixth Finger Tune (inst.) (C: Charles Strouse)

Cast: Conrad Bain; Frank Campanella; Salome Jens; Jimmie Komack

4006 • SKATING VANITIES

Revue   Closed out of town

Composer: Vic Mizzy
Lyricist: Irving Taylor
Producer: Harold Steinman
Director: Gae Foster

Choreographer: Gae Foster; **Costumes:** Joan Personette; **Dance Arranger:** Hal Beckett; **Musical Director:** Jay Freeman; **Orchestrations:** Hal Beckett; **Vocal Arranger:** Hal Beckett

Songs: Here We Go Again (C: Frank Ventry); We'll Keep 'Em Rolling; Wheels of Progress; You're Invited to Attend a Dream

Cast: Otto Easen; Ben Klassen; Bobby May

Notes: No other information available.

4007 • SKI-HI

OPENED: 06/02/1908   Theatre: Madison Square
                                    Garden Roof
Musical   Broadway: 25

Composer: Charles Alphin
Lyricist: Charles Alphin
Librettist: Charles Alphin
Producer: N.I.M. and A. Co.
Director: Robert A. Marks

Songs: Dance of Sing Ling Foo; Girl Worth the While; My Tokio Queen; Pretty Little Japanese Lady

Cast: Lottie Kendall; Tom Kendall; George Powers; Harry Short

4008 • SKIN OF OUR TEETH, THE

OPENED: 1964
Musical   Unproduced

Composer: Leonard Bernstein
Lyricist: Betty Comden; Adolph Green
Librettist: Betty Comden; Adolph Green

Source: SKIN OF OUR TEETH, THE (Play: Thornton Wilder)

Songs: Here Comes the Sun; Spring Will Come Again

Notes: These songs were included in BY BERNSTEIN. The music for both was used in the CHICHESTER PSALMS.

4009 • SKIRTS

OPENED: 01/25/1944   Theatre: Cambridge
Revue   London

Composer: Harold Rome
Lyricist: Harold Rome
Producer: U.S. 8th Air Force
Director: Arthur G. Brest

Choreographer: Wendy Toye

Songs: Jumping to the Juke Box [1]; Little Brown Suit My Uncle Bought Me, The [1]; My Pin-Up Girl [1]; Skirts (C/L: Frank Loesser)

Notes: No program available. [1] From STARS AND GRIPES.

4010 • SKY HIGH (1925)

OPENED: 03/02/1925   Theatre: Shubert
Musical   Broadway: 217

Composer: Robert Stolz
Lyricist: Harold Atteridge
Librettist: Harold Atteridge; Harry Graham
Producer: Messrs. Shubert
Director: Fred G. Latham; Alexander Leftwich

Source: DER TANZ INS GLUCK (Musical: Robert Bodanzky; Bruno Hardt-Warden; Robert Stolz); **Source:** WHIRLED INTO HAPPINESS (Musical: Harry Graham); **Choreographer:** Seymour Felix; **Musical Director:** Carlton Kelsey; **Set Design:** Watson Barratt

Songs: Barbering Wop of Seville, The (C: Carlton Kelsey; Maurie Rubens; L: Clifford Grey); Best Song of All, The (C: Carlton Kelsey; Maurie Rubens; L: Clifford Grey); Find a Good Time (C: Carlton Kelsey; Maurie Rubens; L: Clifford Grey); Give Your Heart in June-Time (C: Victor Herbert; L: Harold Atteridge; Clifford Grey); Gossiping (C/L: Unknown); Hello, the Little Birds Have Flown; Intermezzo; Keep on Croonin' a Tune [2] (C: Sammy Fain; Jimmy McHugh; L: Irving Weill); Lancashire Lassies [1]; Let It Rain (C/L: Hal Dyson; James Kendis); Letter Song, The; London Johnnies (C/L: Unknown); Man o' My Dreams (C: Al Goodman; L: Clifford Grey); New Moon [1] (C/L: Unknown); Once in a While; Opening Act II (C: Carlton Kelsey; Maurie Rubens; L: Clifford Grey); Opening Chorus Act III; Oxford Days (C: Al Goodman; L: Clifford Grey); Robinson Crusoe's Island [1] (C/L: Unknown); Sky High; Somewhere in Lovers' Land; There's Life in the Old Dog Yet; Trim Them All but the One You Love (C: Carlton Kelsey; Maurie Rubens; L: Clifford Grey); We Make the Show; Whirled Into Happiness; Why Are They Following Me? (C: Carlton Kelsey; Maurie Rubens; L: Clifford Grey)

Cast: Florenz Ames; Joyce Barbour; Willie Howard; Dorothy McNulty; Ann Milburn; Mercer Templeton; Vannessi

Notes: [1] Out Brooklyn 2/9/25. [2] ASCAP/Library of Congress.

4011 • SKY HIGH (1979)

OPENED: 06/28/1979   Theatre: Players
Musical   Off-Broadway: 38

Composer: Ann Harris
Lyricist: Ann Harris
Librettist: Brian O'Hara
Producer: Hibiscus Productions
Director: Brian O'Hara

Choreographer: Jayne Anne Harris; Lulu Belle Harris; **Costumes:** Angel Jack; **Dance Arranger:** Frederic Harris; **Lighting Designer:** Johnny Dodd; **Set Design:** Angel Jack; **Vocal Arranger:** Frederic Harris

Songs: Au Revoir; Behold the Coming of the Sun; Birdie Follies; Broadway New York; Champagne Song; Clown Song; Devil Man; Do It Yourself; Fly Away; Giddyup; Gut Rocks; Hot as Hades; I'm Betting on You; I'm Lazy; I'm Mother Nature of You All; Kitty Kat Song; Let's Go to the Dogs; Miss America; One Cell; Opium Song; Queen Cobra; Rainbow; Ringmaster Song; Sheik Song; She'll Get the Business in the End; Singing Mermaids; South American Way; Toast of the Town; Walk Thru That Golden Gate; When He Calls Half-Hour

Cast: Jayne Anne Harris; Lulu Belle Harris; Angel Jack; Tom Matthews; Brian O'Hara

4012 • SKYLARK, A

OPENED: 04/04/1910   Theatre: New York
Musical   Broadway: 24

Composer: Frank Dossert
Lyricist: William Harris Jr.
Librettist: William Harris Jr.
Producer: Henry B. Harris
Director: Ben Teal

Choreographer: David Bennett; **Costumes:** William H. Matthews; **Musical Director:** Theodore Bendix; **Set Design:** H. Robert Law

Songs: And I Believe Him; Anytime at All [1] (C: Joel P. Corin; L: Felix F. Feist); Broadway Lament; Chicken and the Frog, The; Diana (The Lady of the Moon) [1]; Gallus Old Goddess of

Greece, The; Goodbye Yankee Doodle; I Just Can't Wait; I'm Looking for a Little Girl Who's Looking for a Man; In Praise of the Jolly Tar; In the Garden; Just Because I'm Me [1]; March of the Dos; Oh, Mr. Jupiter; Oh, We Know; Opening Chorus; Princess of Dreams [1]; Style, Style, Style; Tuck Me in a Taxi Cab [1]; Wedding Bells [1]; When Love Is There; When the Bloom Is on the Bottle

Cast: May DeSousa; John Slavin; Gertrude Vanderbilt

Notes: [1] Sheet music only.

4013 • SKYSCRAPER

OPENED: 11/13/1965   Theatre: Lunt-Fontanne
Musical   Broadway: 248

Composer: Jimmy Van Heusen
Lyricist: Sammy Cahn
Librettist: Peter Stone
Producer: Cy Feuer; Ernest Martin
Director: Cy Feuer

Source: DREAM GIRL (Play Elmer Rice);
Choreographer: Michael Kidd; **Costumes:**
Theoni V. Aldredge; **Dance Arranger:** Marvin
Laird; **Lighting Designer:** Robert Randolph;
Musical Director: John Lesko; **Orchestrations:**
Fred Werner; **Set Design:** Robert Randolph

Songs: And Your Mother Said [1]; Are You Asking Me to Forget? [1]; Don't Worry, Don't Worry (I Don't Worry); Everybody Has the Right to Be Wrong; Gaiety, The (Delicatessen) (A Way of Life); Haute Couture; I'll Only Miss Her When I Think of Her; Is That Good? [1]; It . . . That . . . [1]; Just the Crust; Local 403 (The Socially Conscious Civic Minded Iron Workers Union); More Than One Way; Mother Shouldn't Have Daughters [1]; Occasional Flight of Fancy, An; Opposites; Run for Your Life; Spare That Building; Stuck for an Answer [1]; Wrong!

Cast: Rex Everhart; Julie Harris; Peter L. Marshall; Dick O'Neill; Charles Nelson Reilly

Notes: [1] Not used.

4014 • SLEEPING BEAUTY AND THE BEAST, THE

OPENED: 11/04/1901   Theatre: Broadway
Musical   Broadway: 241

Composer: J.M. Glover; Frederic Solomon
Lyricist: J. Cheever Goodwin
Librettist: J. Cheever Goodwin; John J. McNally
Producer: Klaw & Erlanger
Director: Marshall Moore

Source: SLEEPING BEAUTY AND THE BEAST (Musical: Arthur Collins; J. Hickory Wood); **Set Design:** Julian Hicks; R.C. McCleary

Songs: B'Gosh!; Bang, Bang, Bang; By Love Undying Crowned; Clock on the Mantel, The [3]; Come Out Dinah on the Green (C: J. Rosamond Johnson; L: Bob Cole); Cure or Kill; Day Dreams; Dear Sing Sing [2] (C: Jean Schwartz; L: William Jerome); Dolly Dimple [2] (C: Jean Schwartz; L: William Jerome); Drowsily, Dreamily; Fairies We; Flora I Am Your Adorer (L: Vincent Bryan); Hygiene; I'm Sixteen Years Old Today; It's a Dream That Never Comes True; Let Them Go; Multi-Millionaires; My Princess Zulu Lulu (C/L: Dave Reed Jr.); Nursery Rhymes (C: Jean Schwartz; L: William Jerome); On to Glory [2]; Onward; Owl and the Moon, The [1] (C: J. Rosamond Johnson; L: Bob Cole; James Weldon Johnson); Pansy of the Dell; Princess We Adore, The; Rip Van Winkle Was a Lucky Man [4] (C: Jean Schwartz; L: William Jerome); Royal Pair Are Off Today, The; Spirits of the Midnight Bell [3]; Take Her Away; Take Thy Way to Earth; Tell Me Dusky Maiden (C: J. Rosamond Johnson; L: Bob Cole; James Weldon Johnson); Time to Love, The [2]; Viva la Liberte; Was Ever a Daintier Infant Seen?; Years Ago

Cast: R. Caney; H. Emsden; Bruce Smith

Notes: [1] Listed in program as "The Moon and the Owl" and published as "Nobody's Lookin' but the Owl and the Moon." [2] Out Manhattan Beach 8/7/03. [3] Out Wilkes-Barre 10/8/06. [4] Also in London show THE CHERRY GIRL.

4015 • SLEEPY HOLLOW

OPENED: 06/03/1948   Theatre: St. James
Musical   Broadway: 12

Composer: George Lessner
Lyricist: Miriam Battista; Russell Maloney
Librettist: Miriam Battista; Russell Maloney
Producer: Lorraine Lesker
Director: John O'Shaughnessy

Source: LEGEND OF SLEEPY HOLLOW, THE (Story: Washington Irving); **Choreographer:**

Anna Sokolow; **Costumes:** David Ffolkes; **Lighting Designer:** Jo Mielziner; **Musical Director:** Irving Actman; **Orchestrations:** George Lessner; Ted Royal; Hans Spialek; **Set Design:** Jo Mielziner; **Vocal Arranger:** Elie Siegmeister

Songs: Alone [1]; Ask Me Again [1]; Englishman's Head, The; Good Night; Gray Goose, The; Headless Horseman Ballet; Here and Now; Hereabouts [1]; I Still Have Plenty to Learn; Ichabod; If; I'm Lost (L: Ruth Hughes Aarons); In the Hay [1]; Musical Lesson, A; My Lucky Lover; Never Let Her Go; Pedro; Poor Man (L: Ruth Hughes Aarons; Miriam Battista; Russell Maloney); There's History to Be Made (L: Ruth Hughes Aarons); Things that Lovers Say, The; Time Stands Still; Why Was I Born on a Farm? (L: Ruth Hughes Aarons); You've Got that Kind of Face (L: Ruth Hughes Aarons)

Cast: Gil Lamb; Mary McCarthy; James Starbuck; Betty Jane Watson

Notes: [1] Out Philadelphia 5/10/48.

4016 • SLICE OF SATURDAY NIGHT, A

OPENED: 03/1995
Musical   Closed out of town

Composer: Heather Brothers, The
Lyricist: Heather Brothers, The
Librettist: Heather Brothers, The
Producer: Jeffrey Finn Productions
Director: Lea Heather

Lighting Designer: Shelly Sabel; **Musical Director:** Keith Hayman

Songs: Baby I Love You; Boy of My Dreams, The; Club A Go-Go; Don't Touch Me; Eric's Gonna Keep Doing; Eric's Hokey Cokey; Heartbreaker; I Fancy You; If You Wanna Have Fun; It Wouldn't Be a Saturday Night Without a Fight; King, The; Last Saturday Night; Lies; Long Walk Back, The; Love on Our Side; Oh So Bad; PE; Please Don't Tell Me; Romance; Saturday Chat; Sentimental Eyes; Seventeen; Slice of Saturday Night, A; Twiggy; Waiting; Wham Bam; What Do I Do Now?; What Do You Do?; Who'd Be Seventeen?; You're Oh So

Cast: Luther Creek; Nick Hasomeris; Jasmine Stocken; Paul Woodson

Notes: Charles Playhouse, Boston.

4017 • SLIM PRINCESS, THE

OPENED: 01/02/1911   Theatre: Globe
Musical   Broadway: 104

Composer: Leslie Stuart
Lyricist: Henry Blossom
Librettist: Henry Blossom
Producer: Charles Dillingham
Director: Austen Hurgon

Source: SLIM PRINCESS, THE (Story: George Ade); **Choreographer:** Jack Mason; **Costumes:** Percy Anderson; **Musical Director:** William MacQuinn

Songs: Bless Your Ever Loving Little Heart (C: Henry I. Marshall; L: Stanley Murphy); Certain Sort of Father, A; Do You Belong to Anyone Particular?; Finale Act II (C: Victor Herbert); For I Love Only You (C: Herman Darewski; L: Elsie Janis); I Like 'Em Plump; I'm Glad My Home Is in the States; Land of the Free, The; Let Me Live and Stay in Dixieland (C/L: Elizabeth Brice; Charles King); Little Pot of Tea, A; Love's Lesson; My Yankee Doodle Girl (C: John Golden; Victor Herbert); Nursery Rhymes; Oh What a Chance to Take; Queen of My Dreams; We Will Gladly Live in a Bungalow

Cast: Elizabeth Brice; Joseph Cawthorn; Elsie Janis; Charles King; Wallace McCutcheon; Queenie Vassar

Notes: No songs listed in program.

4018 • SMALL WONDER

OPENED: 09/15/1948   Theatre: Coronet
Revue   Broadway: 134

Composer: Albert Selden
Lyricist: Burt Shevelove[3]
Librettist: George Axelrod; Louis Laun; Charles Spalding; Max Wilk
Producer: George Nichols III
Director: Burt Shevelove

Choreographer: Gower Champion; **Costumes:** John Derro; **Lighting Designer:** Ralph Alswang; **Musical Director:** William Parson; **Orchestrations:** Ted Royal; **Set Design:** Ralph Alswang; **Vocal Arranger:** Herbert Greene

Songs: Badaroma; Ballad for Billionaires; Commuters' Song, The (C: Baldwin Bergersen; L: Phyllis McGinley); Count Your Blessings (C: Baldwin Bergersen; L: Phyllis McGinley); Flaming Youth; From A to Z; Get Married Shirley [2]; I Like a Man Around the House [1] (C: Baldwin Bergersen; L: Phyllis McGinley); Just an Ordinary Guy (L: Phyllis McGinley; Burt Shevelove); No Time (C: Baldwin Bergersen; L: Phyllis McGinley); Nobody Told Me (C: Baldwin Bergersen; L: Phyllis McGinley); Pistachio (C/L: Mark Lawrence); Saturday's Child (C: Baldwin Bergersen; L: Phyllis McGinley); Show Off (L: Albert Selden); Some Sweet Day [1] (C: Irma Jurist; L: Millard Lampell); Things [1] (C: Irma Jurist); When I Fall in Love (L: Albert Selden); William McKinley High

Cast: Jack Cassidy; Chandler Cowles; Joan Diener; Tom Ewell; Kate Friedlich; Hayes Gordon; Mort Marshall; Mary McCarty; Alice Pearce; Tommy Rall

Notes: [1] Cut prior to opening. [2] Cut prior to opening. Also in A MONTH OF SUNDAYS (1951) and WALK TALL. [3] Used the pseudonym Billings Brown.

4019 • SMILE (1985)

OPENED: 1985
Musical   Unproduced

Composer: Marvin Hamlisch
Lyricist: Carolyn Leigh
Librettist: Jack Heifner
Producer: Zev Bufman; Howard Feuer; Lawrence Gordon; Richard Kagan; Jeremy Ritzer; Sidney Shlenker
Director: Graciela Daniele

Choreographer: Graciela Daniele; **Costumes:** Patricia Zipprodt; **Dance Arranger:** Thomas Fay; **Lighting Designer:** Jules Fisher; **Set Design:** Douglas W. Schmidt; **Vocal Arranger:** Buster Davis

Songs: After High School; Any Moment Now; Awards; Classical Music; Fraternal Fiesta; Heat Is On; Here's Lookin' at You; Interviews; It Goes Like This; Lie a Little; Made in the U.S.A.; Next Year Gonna Be Pink; Night Life in Santa Rosa; Nothing but the Best; Rehearsal; 6 O'Clock News; Smile [1]; Talent; Those Royal Princesses;

Vet; Walking in the Sunshine; Wizard of Magic Town; Y.A.M. Survival Manual, The

Cast: Trini Alvarado; Frederick Coffin; Grover Dale; Steve Elmore; Maureen McGovern; Michael O'Hare; Saundra Santiago

Notes: Carolyn Leigh died before the score could be finished. Her lyrics were discarded and Howard Ashman ended up writing the show with Marvin Hamlisch. The credits listed are those for the workshop production. [1] Same music as title song of 1987 version.

4020 • SMILE (1987)

OPENED: 01/03/1987   Theatre: Lunt-Fontanne
Musical   Broadway: 48

Composer: Marvin Hamlisch
Lyricist: Howard Ashman
Librettist: Howard Ashman
Producer: Lawrence Gordon; Richard M. Kagan; Sidney L. Shlenker
Director: Howard Ashman

Source: SMILE (Film: Jerry Belson); **Choreographer:** Mary Kyte; **Costumes:** William Ivey Long; **Lighting Designer:** Paul Gallo; **Musical Director:** Paul Gemignani; **Orchestrations:** Bill Byers; Dick Hazard; Sid Ramin; Torrie Zito; **Set Design:** Douglas W. Schmidt; **Vocal Arranger:** Buster Davis

Songs: Bob's Song [1]; Disneyland; Dressing Room Scene; In Our Hands; Letters [1]; Nerves; Orientation; Postcard #1; Pretty As a Picture; Shine; Smile; Until Tomorrow Night; Very Best Week of Our Lives, The [1]; Young and American

Cast: Jodi Benson; Anne Marie Bobby; Veanne Cox; Jeff McCarthy; Michael O'Gorman; Dick Patterson; Marsha Waterbury; Jeffrey Wilkins; Ruth Williamson; K.C. Wilson; Richard Woods

Notes: [1] Written for revised rental version after show closed.

4021 • SMILE AT ME

OPENED: 08/23/1935   Theatre: Fulton
Revue   Broadway: 27

Composer: Gerald Dolin
Lyricist: Edward J. Lambert

Librettist: Edward J. Lambert
Producer: Harold Berg
Director: Frank S. Merlin

Choreographer: Paul Florenz; **Costumes:** Dorothy Van Winkle; **Musical Director:** Gerald Dolin; **Set Design:** Karle O. Amend

Songs: Calcutta; Caribbeana; Doin' the Truck; Fiesta in Madrid, The; Goona Goona; Here and There; I Love to Flutter; I'm Dreaming While We're Dancing; Is This the End?; Smile at Me (C: Edward J. Lambert); There's a Broadway Up in Heaven [1]; Tired of the South; You're a Magician

Cast: Avis Andrews; Eddie Bruce; Ruth Edell; Gene Fontaine; Edward J. Lambert; Dorothy Morrison; Jack Osterman; Hal Thompson; Jesse Wolk

Notes: [1] Not in program.

4022 • SMILE, SMILE, SMILE
OPENED: 04/04/1973   Theatre: Eastside
                                        Playhouse
Musical   Off-Broadway: 7

Composer: Luigi Creatore; Hugo Peretti; George David Weiss
Lyricist: Luigi Creatore; Hugo Peretti; George David Weiss
Librettist: Robert Russell
Producer: Stuart Duncan
Director: Robert Simpson

Costumes: Patricia McGourty; **Dance Arranger:** Bob Tartaglia; **Lighting Designer:** Barry Arnold; **Orchestrations:** Jack Andrews; **Set Design:** Philip Gilliam

Songs: Adios; Breakin' the Spell; Buttercup; Friends; Garland of Roses; God Bless the Fig Tree; Good Old-Fashioned Revolutionary, A; Haven't I Seen You Somewhere Before?; I'm the Cockalorum; It's All for the Good of the People; Love Is a Fragile Thing; Love Is a Pain; Magnetic; Open Your Heart; Paradise; Smile, Smile, Smile; To Find True Love

Cast: Gary Beach; Casey Craig; Suellen Estey; Diane Findlay; Donna Liggitt Forbes; William Pierson; Marilyn Saunders; Rudy Tronto; Chip Zien

Notes: This is a revised version of COMEDY. See that entry.

4023 • SMILES
OPENED: 11/18/1930   Theatre: Ziegfeld
Musical   Broadway: 63

Composer: Vincent Youmans
Lyricist: Harold Adamson; Clifford Grey
Librettist: William Anthony McGuire
Producer: Florenz Ziegfeld
Director: William Anthony McGuire

Choreographer: Ned Wayburn; **Costumes:** John Harkrider; **Musical Director:** Frank Tours; **Orchestrations:** Paul Lannin; **Set Design:** Joseph Urban

Songs: Anyway, We've Had Fun [3] (L: Ring Lardner); Be Good to Me (L: Ring Lardner); Blue Bowery [8] (L: Harold Adamson); Carry On Keep Smiling [7] (L: Ring Lardner); Clever, These Chinese; Dancing Wedding; Down Where the East River Flows [5]; Here's a Day to Be Happy; Hotcha Ma Chotch [1]; If I Were You, Love (L: Ring Lardner); I'm Glad I Waited; Keep Smiling and Carry On [3] (C/L: Walter Donaldson); La Marseillaise (C/L: Rouget De Lisle); Madelon [5]; More Than Ever [5] (L: Harold Adamson); Rally 'Round Me [2] (L: Ring Lardner); Say Young Man of Manhattan; Smile [5]; Something to Sing About; Time on My Hands, You in My Arms [6] (L: Harold Adamson; Mack Gordon); What Can I Say? [4] (L: Ring Lardner); Why Ain't I Home? [3] (L: Ring Lardner); You're Driving Me Crazy [3] (C/L: Walter Donaldson)

Cast: Arline Aber; Charline Aber; Larry Adler; Adele Astaire; Fred Astaire; Virginia Bruce; Georgia Caine; Clare Dodd; Eddie Foy Jr.; Paul Gregory; Kathryn Hereford; Bob Hope; Tom Howard; Marilyn Miller; Edward Raquello; Adrian Rosley; Harry Tighe

Notes: [1] Cut after opening. [2] Cut after opening. May be same song as "Carry On Keep Smiling." [3] Added after opening. [4] Music rewritten with new lyrics as "Time on My Hands" but still kept in show. [5] Cut before opening. [6] Same music as "What Can I Say?" [7] Added after opening. Then cut to make room for "Keep Smiling and Carry On." May be same song as "Rally 'Round Me." [8] Same music as "My Lover" from TAKE A CHANCE.

4024 • SMILIN' THROUGH
Notes: *See THROUGH THE YEARS.*

4025 • SMILING FACES
OPENED: 08/30/1932   Theatre: Shubert
Musical   Broadway: 33

Composer: Harry Revel
Lyricist: Mack Gordon
Librettist: Harry Clarke
Producer: Messrs. Shubert
Director: R.H. Burnside

Choreographer: Merriel Abbott; **Costumes:** Ernest Schrapps; **Set Design:** Watson Barratt

Songs: Bootblack Blues [1]; Bread and Kisses [1]; Can't Get Rid of Me; Cane Dance [1]; Do Say You Do [1] (C: Harry Revel; L: Harold Adamson; Mack Gordon); Do Something Different [1]; Falling Out of Love; I Like You [2]; I Stumbled Over You; If You Want to Be Successful in the Cinema [1]; In a Little Stucco in the Sticks; In Havana; It's Just an Old Spanish Custom; I've Fallen Out of Love; Landlord at My Door!; Lonely Little Extras [3]; Poor Little, Shy Little, Demure Little Me; Quick Henry, the Flit!; Shakin' the Shakespeare; Smart Set; Something to Think About [1]; Sport a Sport; Sweet Little Stranger; Thank You, You're Welcome, Don't Mention It; There Will Be a Girl (There Will Be a Boy); Think of My Reputation

Cast: Charles Collins; Hope Emerson; Eddie Garvie; Doris Patston; Roy Royston; Dorothy Stone; Fred Stone

Notes: [1] Out Washington D.C. 2/8/32. [2] ASCAP/Library of Congress only. [3] ASCAP/Library of Congress only. Not used in the score of MEET MY SISTER.

4026 • SMILING ISLAND, THE
OPENED: 12/15/1904
Musical   Closed out of town

Composer: Kenneth S. Clark; J. Sebastian Hiller; Albert von Tilzer
Lyricist: George V. Hobart

Notes: Casino Theatre, Philadelphia.

4027 • SMILING THROUGH
OPENED: 02/02/1994   Theatre: Theatre Four
Musical   Off-Broadway: 14

Librettist: Ivan Menchell
Producer: Lois Teich
Director: Patricia Birch

Arrangements: Tom Fay; **Choreographer:** Patricia Birch; **Costumes:** Frank Krenz; **Lighting Designer:** Craig Miller; **Musical Director:** Tom Fay; **Set Design:** James Morgan

Songs: All Our Tomorrows (C/L: Jimmy Kennedy); Dancing with My Shadow (C/L: Harry Woods); Deepest Shelter in Town, The (C/L: Leslie Julian Jones); Don't Dilly Dally on the Way (C/L: Charles Collins; Fred W. Leigh; Dick Manning); I'm Gonna Get Lit Up (C/L: Hubert Gregg); Nightingale Sang in Berkeley Square, A (C: Manning Sherwin; L: Eric Maschwitz); No One Believes (C: Noel Gay; L: Desmond Carter); Nobody Loves a Fairy (C/L: Arthur LeClerq); Underneath the Arches (C/L: Reg Connelly; Bud Flanagan); We'll Meet Again (C/L: Hughie Charles; Ross Parker); White Cliffs of Dover, The (C: Walter Kent; L: Nat Burton); Wish Me Luck (C: Harry Parr-Davies; L: Phil Park)

Cast: Vicki Stuart

Notes: No original songs in this show. Later revived and titled WE'LL MEET AGAIN.

4028 • SMILING, THE BOY FELL DEAD
OPENED: 04/19/1961   Theatre: Cherry Lane
Musical   Off-Broadway: 22

Composer: David Baker
Lyricist: Sheldon Harnick
Librettist: Ira Wallach
Producer: George Kogel; Theodore Mann
Director: Theodore Mann [1]

Conductor: Jack Easton; **Costumes:** Theoni V. Aldredge; **Lighting Designer:** David Hays; **Musical Director:** Julian Stein; **Set Design:** Helen Pond; Herbert Senn; **Vocal Arranger:** Julian Stein

Songs: ABC's of Success, The; Daydreams; Dear Old Dad; Gatsby Bridge March, The;

Heredity-Environment; If I Felt Any Younger Today; I've Got a Wonderful Future; Let's Evolve; Me and Dorothea; More Than Ever Now; Small Town; Sons of Greentree; Temperance Polka; Two by Two; Wonderful Machine, The; World to Win, A

Cast: Ted Beniades; Claiborne Cary; Gino Conforti; Justine Johnstone; Louise Larabee; Phil Leeds; Joseph Macaulay; Danny Meehan; Warren Wade

Notes: Titled HORATIO out of town Dallas 3/8/54. [1] Uncredited. Billed as "Production supervised by."

4029 • SMITH

OPENED: 05/19/1973   Theatre: Eden
Musical   Off-Broadway: 18

Composer: Dean Fuller
Lyricist: Matt Dubey
Librettist: Matt Dubey; Dean Fuller; Tony Hendra
Producer: Jordan Hott
Director: Neal Kenyon

Choreographer: Michael Shawn; **Costumes:** Winn Morton; **Dance Arranger:** John Berkman; **Lighting Designer:** Martin Aronstein; **Musical Director:** Richard Parrinello; **Orchestrations:** Jonathan Tunick; **Set Design:** Fred Voelpel; **Vocal Arranger:** Dean Fuller

Songs: Balinasia; Boy Meets Girl; G'bye; How Beautiful It Was; Island Ritual; It Must Be Love; Melody; Miss Hazelton [1]; Onh-Honh-Honh!; People Don't Do That; Police Song; Song of the Frog; There's a Big Job Waiting for You; To the Ends of the Earth; You Need a Song; You're in New York Now

Cast: Mort Marshall; Carol Morley; Don Murray; Virginia Sandifur; Ted Thurston; David Vosburgh

Notes: [1] Not used.

4030 • SMOKE ON THE MOUNTAIN

OPENED: 05/12/1990   Theatre: Lamb's
Musical   Off-Broadway: 452

Librettist: Connie Ray
Producer: Lamb's Theater Company
Director: Alan Bailey

Arrangements: Mike Craver; Mark Hardwick; **Costumes:** Pamela Scofield; **Lighting Designer:** Don Ehman; **Musical Director:** Mike Craver; John Foley; **Set Design:** Peter Harrison

Songs: Christian Cowboy (C/L: Cindy Walker); Filling Station, The (C/L: April Ann Nye); I Wouldn't Take Nothing for My Journey Now (C/L: Jimmy Davis; Charles Goodman); I'll Fly Away (C/L: Albert E. Brumley); I'll Live a Million Years (C/L: Lee Roy Abernathy); I'll Never Die (I'll Just Change My Address) (C/L: J. Preston Martinez); I'll Walk Every Step of the Way (C/L: Mike Craver; Mark Hardwick); I'm Taking a Flight (C/L: Kathryn Boyington); I'm Using My Bible for a Roadmap (C/L: Don Reno; Charles Schroeder); Jesus Is Mine (C/L: Virginia Cook; Wally Fowler); No Tears in Heaven (C/L: Robert S. Arnold); Smoke on the Mountain (C/L: Alan Bailey); Wonderful Time Up There (C/L: Lee Roy Abernathy)

Cast: Reathel Bean; Kevin Chamberlin; Linda Kerns; Dan Manning; Robert Olsen; Jane Potter; Connie Ray

4031 • SMOKEY JOE'S CAFE

OPENED: 03/02/1995   Theatre: Virginia
Revue   Broadway

Composer: Jerry Leiber; Mike Stoller
Lyricist: Jerry Leiber; Mike Stoller
Producer: Steven Baruch; Richard Frankel; Jujamcyn Theaters; Frederic H. Mayerson; Rick Steiner; Thomas Viertel
Director: Jerry Zaks

Arrangements: Louis St. Louis; **Choreographer:** Joey McKneely; **Costumes:** William Ivey Long; **Lighting Designer:** Timothy Hunter; **Musical Director:** Louis St. Louis; **Orchestrations:** Steve Margoshes; **Set Design:** Heidi Landesman

Songs: Charlie Brown; D.W. Washburn; Dance with Me; Don Juan; Falling; Fools Fall in Love; Hound Dog; I Keep Forgettin'; I (Who Have Nothing); I'm a Woman; Jailhouse Rock; Kansas City; Keep On Rollin'; Little Egypt; Love Me/Don't; Love Potion #9; Loving You; Neighborhood; On Broadway; Pearl's a Singer; Poison Ivy; Ruby Baby; Saved; Searchin'; Shoppin' for Clothes; Smokey Joe's Cafe; Some Cats Know; Spanish Harlem (C/L: Jerry Leiber; Phil Spector); Stand By Me; Stay a While; Teach

Me How to Shimmy; That Is Rock and Roll; There Goes My Baby; Treat Me Nice; Trouble; Yakety Yak; You're the Boss; Young Blood

Cast: Ken Ard; Adrian Bailey; Brenda Braxton; Victor Trent Cook; B.J. Crosby; Pattie Darcy Jones; DeLee Lively; Frederick B. Owens; Michael Park

Notes: No songs written for this production. Still running as of publication.

4032 • SMUGGLERS OF BADAYEZ, THE

OPENED: 1899
Musical   Closed out of town

Composer: Giack Minkowski
Lyricist: Frederick Ranken
Librettist: Frederick Ranken
Producer: Bostonians

Songs: All Hail the Bride; All Pleasures in Life; Come, Come; Don Brandeiro, We Await You; Female Chorus of Muleteers; Finale Act I; Finale Act II; Finale Act III; From Barcelona I Come; Happy is the Summer's Day; Health, a Health in Ruby Wine, A; Hermit, The; I Am a Noble Grandee, Ha! Ha!; If but One Spark of Pity; In Sunny Spain; It's Very Clear; Love Is a Mixture; Lullaby; O'er Our Love Forever Blessing; Opening Chorus Act II; Opening Chorus Act III; Sing Hey! For a Smuggler Bold; Soldier's Life Is One of Strife, A; When I Was but a Little Lad; Wine of Malaga, The; With Fear I Tremble

Notes: No other information available.

4033 • SNAPSHOTS OF 1921

OPENED: 06/02/1921   Theatre: Selwyn
Revue   Broadway: 44

Producer: Lew Fields; Arch Selwyn; Edgar Selwyn
Director: Leon Errol

Songs: Baby Blues (C: George Gershwin; L: E. Ray Goetz); Baby Dollie Walk (C/L: Con Conrad); Bamboula, The (El Relicario) (C: Jose Padilla; L: E. Ray Goetz); Beautiful Feathers Make Beautiful Birds (C: George W. Meyer; L: E. Ray Goetz); Dab-Derro [1] (C: Malvin F. Franklin; L: Frances Nordstrom); Every Girlie Wants to Be a Sally (C: Malvin F. Franklin; L: Alex Gerber); Futuristic Melody (C: George Gershwin;

L: E. Ray Goetz); Memories (C: Harry Ruby; L: Bert Kalmar); Moonlight [2] (C/L: Con Conrad); Mother, Dixie, the Flag and You (C: George Meyer; L: E. Ray Goetz); On the Brim of Her Old-Fashioned Bonnet (C: George Gershwin; L: E. Ray Goetz); Rendezvous (C: Leopold Godowsky; L: Sidney D. Mitchell); Saturday [3] (C: Harry Brooks; L: Sidney D. Mitchell); Sky High Bungalow (C: George W. Meyer; L: E. Ray Goetz); Yokohama Lullaby (C: James V. Monaco; L: Grant Clarke)

Cast: Delyle Alda; Nora Bayes; Alan Edwards; Lew Fields; Gilda Gray; DeWolf Hopper; Ernest Lambert; Lulu McConnell

Notes: [1] Titled "Bebura" and lyrics credited to Alex Gerber out of town. [2] Out Stamford 5/27/21. [3] ASCAP/Library of Congress only.

4034 • SNOOPY!!!

OPENED: 12/20/1982   Theatre: Lamb's
Musical   Off-Broadway: 152

Composer: Larry Grossman
Lyricist: Hal Hackady
Librettist: Michael L. Grace; Warren Lockhart; Arthur Whitelaw
Producer: Gene Persson
Director: Arthur Whitelaw

Source: PEANUTS (Comic Strip: Charles M. Schulz); **Choreographer:** Marc Breaux; **Costumes:** David Graden; **Lighting Designer:** Ken Billington; **Musical Director:** Ronald Melrose; **Orchestrations:** Ronald Melrose; **Set Design:** David Graden

Songs: Big Bow-Wow, The; Bows; Clouds; Daisy Hill; Dime a Dozen; Don't Be Anything Less Than Everything You Can Be; Edgar Allan Poe; Friend [1]; I Know Now; It Was a Dark and Stormy Night (The Great Writer); Just One Person; Mother's Day; Poor Sweet Baby; Sit Up! Lie Down! Roll Over! Play Dead!; Snoopy's Song; Vigil; Where Did That Little Dog Go?; Wishy-Washy [1]; Woodstock's Theme; World According to Snoopy, The

Cast: Cathy Cahn; Kay Cole; Stephen Fenning; David Garrison; Deborah Graham; Terry Kerwin; Vicki Lewis

Notes: [1] Out Boston 11/3/82.

4035 • SNOW WHITE AND THE SEVEN DWARFS

OPENED: 10/18/1979   Theatre: Radio City Music Hall

Musical   Broadway: 103

Composer: Jay Blackton
Lyricist: Joe Cook
Librettist: Joe Cook
Producer: Robert F. Jani; Radio City Music Hall
Director: Frank Wagner

Source: SNOW WHITE AND THE SEVEN DWARFS (Film: Dorothy Ann Blank; Frank Churchill; Richard Creedon; Merrill De Maris; Otto Englander; Earl Hurd; Larry Morey; Dick Rickard; Ted Sears; Webb Smith);
Choreographer: Frank Wagner; **Costumes:** Frank Spencer; Joe Stephen, **Lighting Designer:** Ken Billington; **Musical Director:** Don Smith; **Orchestrations:** Philip J. Lang; **Set Design:** John William Keck

Songs: Bluddle-Uddle-Um-Dum (The Washing Song) [1] (C: Frank Churchill; L: Larry Morey); Dwarf's Yodel Song (The Silly Song) [1] (C: Frank Churchill; L: Larry Morey); Heigh-Ho [1] (C: Frank Churchill; L: Larry Morey); Here's the Happy Ending; I'm Wishing [1] (C: Frank Churchill; L: Larry Morey); One Song [1] (C: Frank Churchill; L: Larry Morey); Queen's Presentation; Someday My Prince Will Come [1] (C: Frank Churchill; L: Larry Morey); Welcome to the Kingdom; Whistle While You Work [1] (C: Frank Churchill; L: Larry Morey); Will I Ever See Her Again; With a Smile and a Song [1] (C: Frank Churchill; L: Larry Morey)

Cast: Yolande Bavan; Richard Browne; Anne Francine; Mary Jo Salerno

Notes: Executive Musical Director: Donald Pippin. [1] From film score.

4036 • SNOWMAN, THE

Notes: *See THE GIRLS OF HOLLAND.*

4037 • SO LONG, LETTY

OPENED: 10/23/1916   Theatre: Shubert

Musical   Broadway: 96

Composer: Earl Carroll
Lyricist: Earl Carroll

Librettist: Elmer Harris; Oliver Morosco
Producer: Oliver Morosco
Director: Oliver Morosco

Choreographer: Julian Alfred; **Musical Director:** Harry James

Songs: After You've Gone [1] (C: Henry Creamer; L: Turner Layton); All the Comforts of Home; Blame It All on the Girls [7]; Busiest Week, The [5]; Butterflies [6]; By the Blue Summer Sea [2]; Cab-arabian Nights; Castles in Spain [2]; Dances All Turned Around [4]; Do You Believe Me [7]; Escamillo [2]; Here Come the Married Men; I Showed That I Know Something When I Fell in Love with You [5]; If I Could Read the Kisses Others Printed on Your Lips; If the Good Die Young (You'll Live to Be a Hundred!); I'm Going to Follow the Boys [1]; I've Got Enough to Marry You [4]; I've Got the Nicest Little Home in Dixie [5]; I've Got the Sweetest Girl in Maryland (C/L: Walter Donaldson); Kentucky Jubilee [4]; Let's Not Have a Kissless Day [7]; Letter Trio; Maryland [7]; Mr. Patrick Henry Must Have Been a Married Man; Old Masters' Fox Trot [6]; On a Beautiful Beach; Pass Around the Apples Once Again; Play Me a Ukulele; Same Old Thing Turned Around, The; So Long Letty; Summertime Moon [3]; That Rushin' Rag; There's a Lonely Girl in Honolulu [4]; There's a Rainbow in America; To Hear Your Voice [8]; When They Start to Yodel Ragtime Songs in Tennessee [7]; When You Hear Jackson Moan on His Saxophone; Whiffle Walk, The [8] (C: David M. Minton Jr.; L: Edwin H. Knopf); You Used to Be Good to Me [8]; You're Welcome Back to California [3]

Cast: May Boley; Cameron Sisters, The; Walter Catlett; Sydney Grant; Charlotte Greenwood

Notes: [1] Out N.Y. 5/20/18. [2] Out Chicago 4/16/16. [3] Out Los Angeles 8/1/15. [4] Out Oakland 10/10/15. [5] Out Wilkes-Barre 10/1/17. [6] Out Lyric Theatre 4/16/17. [7] Out Washington, D.C. 3/4/18. [8] Sheet music only.

4038 • SO LONG, 174TH STREET

OPENED: 04/27/1976   Theatre: Harkness

Musical   Broadway: 16

Composer: Stan Daniels
Lyricist: Stan Daniels
Librettist: Joseph Stein

Producer: Frederick Brisson
Director: Burt Shevelove

Source: ENTER LAUGHING (Play Joseph Stein);
Source: ENTER LAUGHING (Novel: Carl
Reiner); **Choreographer:** Alan Johnson;
Costumes: Stanley Simmons; **Dance Arranger:**
Wally Harper; **Lighting Designer:** Richard
Nelson; **Musical Director:** John Lesko;
Orchestrations: Luther Henderson; **Set Design:**
James Riley

Songs: Being with You; Bolero on Rye; Boy Oh
Boy; Butler's Song, The; David Kolowitz, the
Actor; Do What You Want to Do [1]; Hot-Cha
Cha [1]; If You Want to Break Your Father's
Heart [1]; It's Like; Men; My Son the Druggist [1];
Say the Words; So Long, 174th Street;
Undressing Girls with My Eyes; Whoever You
Are; You [1]; You Touched Her

Cast: Loni Ackerman; Lee Goodman; George S.
Irving; Mitchell Jason; Barbara Lang; Robert
Morse; Lawrence John Moss; Gene Varrone

Notes: [1] Cut prior to opening.

4039 • SO PROUDLY WE HAIL
OPENED: 1938
Musical

Lyricist: David Lannon
Librettist: Nathaniel Benchley; John McDougal
Graham; Benjamin Welles II
Producer: Hasty Pudding Club
Director: Edward Clarke Lilley

Choreographer: William Holbrook

Songs: Came the Dawn; Chance to Dream (C/L:
Alan Jay Lerner); Look Before You Leap;
Rainbow in the Sky (C: Benjamin Welles II);
Something New for a Change; Story Book Land

Cast: Charles Dillingham; Vinton Freedley Jr.; Alan
Jay Lerner; Marvin Scaife

Notes: Songs also composed by Stanley Miller but
individual composers are not credited in the
program. One performance at the Waldorf
Astoria.

4040 • SO THIS IS PARIS
Notes: *See HELLO, PARIS (1930).*

4041 • SO WHAT!
OPENED: 04/28/1955
Revue   Yale University

Composer: Alan Dundes; Aubrey Goodman;
Lyricist: Aubrey Goodman; Richard Heller;
Anthony Howarth
Librettist: Aubrey Goodman; Richard Heller;
Robin Jones; John Owen
Producer: Yale University Dramatic Association
Director: Leo S. Lavendero; John Owen

Songs: Boo-Hoo Blues, The; Burt and I; Crazy
Pops; Give Me a Sock with Your Shoes; Griselda,
the Inn Keeper's Daughter; Happy Feet; I Won't
Play Games with You Anymore; It's Spring I
Guess; Ivan Valensky; Let's Get Drunk; Let's Hit
the Road; Melissa's Refrain; My Kind of Guy;
New Haven; Rat Killing; Some Time Ago;
Wonder of the Age

Cast: Bill Hinnant; Tony Noto; Sam Pottle; Brandon
Stoddard; **Pianist:** Sam Pottle; Ron Singer

Notes: An amateur musical.

4042 • SOCIAL MAIDS
Notes: *See JOE HURTIG'S SOCIAL MAIDS.*

4043 • SOCIAL REGISTER, THE
OPENED: 11/09/1931   Theatre: Fulton
Play   Broadway: 97

Author: John Emerson; Anita Loos
Producer: Erlanger Productions
Director: John Emerson; Anita Loos

Choreographer: Billy Pierce; **Set Design:** William
Oden- Waller

Songs: Key to My Heart, The (C: Louis Alter; L: Ira
Gershwin)

Cast: Sidney Blackmer; Betty Garde; Cesar Romero;
Lenore Ulric

4044 • SOCIAL WHIRL, THE
OPENED: 04/09/1906   Theatre: Casino
Musical   Broadway: 195

Composer: Gustave Kerker
Lyricist: Joseph W. Herbert

Librettist: Charles Doty; Joseph W. Herbert
Producer: Lee Shubert; Sam S. Shubert
Director: R.H. Burnside

Songs: As She Played on the Cal-li-o-pay! [1]; Bill Simmons (I've Got to Dance Till the Band Gits Through) (C/L: George A. Spink); Finale Act I; Just Kids; Just the One I'm Looking For (C/L: E. Ray Goetz); Love Among the Freaks; Manicure Song (Profession of a Manicure, The); Old Man Manhattan (C: Anne Caldwell; L: James O'Dea); Opening Chorus; Opening Chorus Act II; Racing Scene; Rainy Day!; Run Away, Naughty Man (L: Hugh Morton); Tally Ho!!! (We'll Blow the Jolly Horn); Vi, Vi!

Cast: Frederic Bond; Elizabeth Brice; Joseph Coyne; Blanche Deyo; Mabel Fenton; Ada Lewis; Maude Raymond; Adele Richie; Charles J. Ross

Notes: [1] In vocal score only.

4045 • SOCIETY BUDS, THE
OPENED: 1914

Composer: Irving Berlin
Lyricist: Irving Berlin
Producer: Jesse L. Lasky

Songs: Furnishing a House for Two; That's My Idea of Paradise

Cast: Henry Bergman; Gladys Clark

Notes: Vaudeville act.

4046 • SOCIETY CIRCUS, A
OPENED: 12/13/1905   Theatre: Hippodrome
Musical   Broadway: 596

Composer: Manuel Klein
Lyricist: Manuel Klein; Sydney Rosenfeld
Librettist: Sydney Rosenfeld
Producer: Elmer S. Dundy; Frederick W. Thompson
Director: Edward P. Temple

Choreographer: Vincenzo Romeo; **Costumes:** Alfredo Edel; Archie Gunn; **Set Design:** Arthur Voegtlin

Songs: Appearance of Lady Volumnia with Court; Arrival of Gypsies; Breaking Camp; But It Ain't; Conspiracy, The; Entrance of Major Domo and His Shadow; Everybody Must Be Happy; Exit of Lady Volumnia; Formation of Camp; Good, Kind, Jolly Man, The (L: Manuel Klein); Gypsy Wedding Ceremony and Festivities; In Bright Array; Laughing School, The (L: Sydney Rosenfeld); Let the Circus Now Appear; Moon Dear (L: Manuel Klein); Morning in the Gypsy Camp; Song of the Flowers (ballet) (C: Gustav Luders); Tainted Gold (C: Sydney Rosenfeld); They Have Carried the Bridegroom Off; Two Little Doves [1] (L: Manuel Klein)

Cast: Francis J. Boyle; Edwin A. Clark; Rita Dean; Felix Haney; Rose La Harte; Marceline; Olive North; Silvers Oakley; Leila Romer

Notes: [1] Sheet music only.

4047 • SOCIETY OF ILLUSTRATORS SHOW 1955
OPENED: 1955
Revue

Librettist: Rube Goldberg; Howard Munce; F.E. Smith; S.B. Valentine
Producer: Stuart Campbell; Society of Illustrators
Director: Ben Bagley

Choreographer: Mary Ann Niles; **Costumes:** Grace Brown; Frances Dormont; **Lighting Designer:** Ken Demick; Robert Jacobus; **Set Design:** Stevan Dohanos; Bob Geissmann; Charles Heilemann; Homer Hill; Robert J. Lee; Ervine Metzl; Carl Setterberg; George Shealy

Songs: Bright and Early (C: Ken Welch; L: Bud McCreery); Damn Connecticut Yankees (C/L: Arnold Copeland); I Just Slipped Away from My Wedding (C/L: Bud McCreery); Juvenile Deliquency (C: J.D. Cushing; L: F.E. Smith); Mink, Mink, Mink (C/L: Bud McCreery); Sing, Sing, Sing (C/L: Earl Brent)

Cast: Stu Campbell; Marilyn Cantor; Dody Goodman; Mary Ann Niles

4048 • SOFTLY
OPENED: 1967
Musical   Unproduced

Composer: Harold Arlen
Lyricist: Martin Charnin

Librettist: Santha Rama Rau
Director: Hanya Holm

Choreographer: Hanya Holm

Songs: Baby San; Been a Hell of an Evening; Brush Off, The; Come On, Midnight; Don't Say 'Love'-I've Been There and Back; Fish Go Higher than Tigers; Happy Any Day; Hello (Herro); I Could Be Good for You; I Will; Momma Know Best; More You See of It, The; My Lady Fair; Once I Wore Ribbons Here; Pacific; Spring Has Me Out on a Limb; Suddenly the Sunrise; Temples; This Ol' World; We Were Always to Be Married; Why Do You Make Me Like You; Yellow Rain; You Are Tomorrow; You're Never Fully Dressed without a Smile [1]

Cast: Jason Robards

Notes: Was to open at the Colonial Theatre, Boston on 9/5/67. [1] Not the same song as in ANNIE.

4049 • SOME COLONEL
Notes: *See OUI MADAME.*

4050 • SOME DAY
OPENED: 10/06/1925
Musical   Closed out of town

Composer: Albert Von Tilzer
Lyricist: Neville Fleeson
Librettist: Frances Nordstrom
Producer: Mrs. Henry B. Harris
Director: A.H. Van Buren

Choreographer: Jack Haskell

Songs: Gypsy Saraband; I'm the New Clerk; It's Love; There's a Woman at the Bottom of It All; Virginia Town

Cast: Robert Alton; Inez Courtney; Gloria Foy; Charles King; Lotta Linthicum; Marion Saki; Al Sexton; Gus Shy

Notes: No program available. This is from a newspaper clipping from Brooklyn.

4051 • SOME LIKE IT HOT
Notes: *See SUGAR.*

4052 • SOME LITTLE GIRL
Notes: *See HIS LITTLE WIDOWS.*

4053 • SOME NIGHT
OPENED: 09/23/1918   Theatre: Harris
Musical   Broadway: 24

Composer: Harry Delf
Lyricist: Harry Delf
Librettist: Harry Delf
Producer: Joseph Klaw
Director: Julian Mitchell; W.H. Post

Musical Director: Hilding Anderson

Songs: All Alone; Alone in a Great Big World; Can't You See?; Everything Is Going Higher; Forethought!; I'll Be Waiting for You [4]; I'll Keep You Here All Night [1]; Look Before You Leap; Once Upon a Time; Painting My Picture of You; Send Me a Girl; Snap of the Whip, The [2]; Some Night; Something That Money Can't Buy; Somewhere! [3]; We Ain't Got No Luck [1]; When We Are Married; With the Boy I Love

Cast: Roma June; James C. Marlowe; Forrest Winant

Notes: [1] Out Boston 8/26/18. [2] Out Providence 9/22/19. [3] Titled "Somehow, Somewhere" out of town. [4] Titled "By My Window (I'll Be Waiting for You)" out of town.

4054 • SOME PARTY
OPENED: 04/15/1922   Theatre: Jolson 59th Street
Revue   Broadway: 17

Composer: Silvio Hein; Raymond Hubbell
Lyricist: R.H. Burnside
Librettist: R.H. Burnside
Producer: DeWolf Hopper
Director: R.H. Burnside

Musical Director: Anton Heindl

Songs: Bells of the Sea (C: Alfred Solman); Burning to Sing (sketch) (C: Gustave Kerker); In Rose Time (C: Mary Earl); In Yama Yama Land (C: Turner Layton; L: Henry Creamer); Keep on Building Castles in the Air (C: Percy Wenrich); Minstrel Days (C: Percy Wenrich); Rustic Ann (C: Percy Wenrich)

Cast: Sam Ash; Jefferson De Angelis; Lew Dockstader; DeWolf Hopper; Jed Prouty

4055 • SOME SWEET DAY

OPENED: 08/06/1992
Musical   Closed out of town

Composer: Sy Kahn
Lyricist: Sy Kahn
Librettist: Don Jones; Mac Pirkle
Producer: Goodspeed Opera House
Director: Mac Pirkle

Arrangements: Dennis West; Costumes: Charlotte M. Yetman; Lighting Designer: Stuart Duke; Musical Director: Dennis West; Set Design: Brian Laczko; Vocal Arranger: Allen Moore; Stan Tucker

Songs: Beside Me; Didn't It Rain; Don't It Sometimes; Field By Field; Freedom and Rain; Here in My Hands; High Cotton; King of the Delta, Queen of the River; Life That You Own, A; My Old Times; Stones in the Furrow; Threads of Life; We Go On

Cast: Lehman Beneby; Gregory Butler; Susan Dawn Carson; Catherine Cox; Scott K. Ivey; Shona Tucker; Wade Williams

Notes: Goodspeed Opera House.

4056 • SOMEBODY'S SWEETHEART

OPENED: 12/23/1918   Theatre: Central
Musical   Broadway: 224

Composer: Anthony Bafunno
Lyricist: Alonzo Price
Librettist: Alonzo Price
Producer: Arthur Hammerstein
Director: Alonzo Price

Costumes: Homer Conant; Musical Director: Rupert Graves

Songs: Follow Me; Girl of My Heart; Gypsy Melodies; In the Old Fashioned Way (C: Herbert Stothart; L: Arthur Hammerstein); Is It Your Smile?; It Gets Them All (C: Herbert Stothart; L: Arthur Hammerstein); On Wings of Doubt; Serenade; Somebody's Sweetheart; Spain (C: Herbert Stothart; L: Arthur Hammerstein);

Sultana; Then I'll Marry You; Twinkle; Viva la Toreador; What Shall We Sing?

Cast: Eva Fallon; William Kent; Walter Scanlon

4057 • SOMETHING COOL

OPENED: 02/1957   Theatre: Cabaret Concert
Revue   Los Angeles

Composer: Billy Barnes
Lyricist: Billy Barnes

Notes: No other information available.

4058 • SOMETHING FOR THE BOYS

OPENED: 01/07/1943   Theatre: Alvin
Musical   Broadway: 422

Composer: Cole Porter
Lyricist: Cole Porter
Librettist: Dorothy Fields; Herbert Fields
Producer: Michael Todd
Director: Herbert Fields; Hassard Short

Choreographer: Jack Cole; Lew Kessler; Costumes: Billy Livingston; Lighting Designer: Hassard Short; Musical Director: William Parson; Orchestrations: Robert Russell Bennett; Ted Royal; Hans Spialek; Don Walker; Set Design: Howard Bay; Vocal Arranger: William Parson

Songs: Announcement of Inheritance; By the Mississinewah; Could It Be You?; He's a Right Guy; Hey Good Lookin'; I'm in Love with a Soldier Boy; Leader of a Big-Time Band, The; Oh, How I Could Go for You [1]; Riddle Diddle Me This [1]; See That You're Born in Texas; So Long, San Antonio [1]; Something for the Boys; Texas Will Make You a Man [1]; There's a Happy Land in the Sky; Washington, D.C. [1]; Well, I Just Wouldn't Know [1]; When My Baby Goes to Town; When We're Home on the Range; Wouldn't It Be Crazy [1]

Cast: Betty Bruce; Betty Garrett; Allen Jenkins; Bill Johnson; Paula Laurence; Ethel Merman; Jed Prouty

Notes: [1] Not used.

4059 • SOMETHING GAY

OPENED: 04/29/1935   Theatre: Morosco
Play   Broadway: 72

Author: Adelaide Heilbron
Producer: Messrs. Shubert
Director: Thomas Mitchell

Set Design: Donald Oenslager

Songs: You Are So Lovely and I Am So Lonely (C: Richard Rodgers; L: Lorenz Hart)

Cast: Percy Ames; Tallulah Bankhead; Walter Pidgeon

4060 • SOMETHING MORE!

OPENED: 11/10/1964   Theatre: Eugene O'Neill
Musical   Broadway: 15

Composer: Sammy Fain
Lyricist: Alan Bergman; Marilyn Bergman
Librettist: Nate Monaster
Producer: Lester Osterman
Director: Jule Styne

Source: PORTOFINO P.T.A. (Novel: Gerald Green); **Choreographer:** Bob Herget; **Costumes:** Alvin Colt; **Dance Arranger:** Robert Prince; **Lighting Designer:** Robert Randolph; **Musical Director:** Oscar Kosarin; **Orchestrations:** Ralph Burns; **Set Design:** Robert Randolph; **Vocal Arranger:** Buster Davis

Songs: Ballad for a Pencil [3]; Better All the Time; Bravo, Bravo, Novelisto; Church of My Choice; Come Sta; Don't Make a Move; Grazie Per Niente; I Can See It All Now [4]; I Feel Like New Year's Eve (C: Jule Styne); Il Lago de Innamoratti (dance) (C: Robert Prince); In No Time at All; It's Good for a Woman's Morale [1]; I've Got Nothin' to Do; Jaded, Degraded Am I (C: Jule Styne); Life Is Too Short; Master of the Greatest Art of All, The; Mineola (C: Jule Styne); No Questions (C: Jule Styne); Ode to a Key; One Long Last Look; Party Talk; Portofino [1]; Something More; Straw That Broke the Camel's Back, The; That Faraway Look [3]; Wanna Trade [4]; What Would Happen? [1]; Who Fills the Bill (C: Jule Styne); You Gotta Take All the Fruit [2]; You'll Be the Prettiest Girl at the Party (C: Jule Styne)

Cast: Barbara Cook; Joan Copeland; Ronny Graham; Arthur Hill; Michael Kermoyan; Hal Linden; Peg Murray; Neva Small

Notes: [1] Cut prior to opening. [2] Cut prior to opening. Later used in the film MYRA

BRECKENRIDGE. [3] Out Philadelphia 9/64. [4] Not used.

4061 • SOMETHING TO DO — A SALUTE TO THE AMERICAN WORKER

OPENED: 09/1976

Composer: Morton Gould
Lyricist: Carolyn Leigh

Musical Director: Robert De Cormier

Songs: I'm a Genius Too; It Got to Be a Habit; It's a Living; Peaceful Warriors; Red Tape Blues; Secretary Bird; So Long Lily; Something to Do; Throckmorton's Permanent Pleasure; Twobly's Thingamajig; With These Hands

Cast: Pearl Bailey

Notes: A Bi-Centennial production produced on Labor Day 1976 at the Kennedy Center in Washington. This is a cantata.

4062 • SOMETHING'S AFOOT

OPENED: 05/27/1976   Theatre: Lyceum
Musical   Broadway: 61

Composer: Robert Gerlach; James McDonald; David Vos
Additional Music: Ed Linderman
Lyricist: Robert Gerlach; James McDonald; David Vos
Librettist: Robert Gerlach; James McDonald; David Vos
Producer: Emanuel Azenberg; Dasha Epstein; John Mason Kirby
Director: Tony Tanner

Choreographer: Tony Tanner; **Costumes:** Clifford Capone; Walter Watson; **Lighting Designer:** Richard Winkler; **Musical Director:** Buster Davis; **Orchestrations:** Peter Larson; **Set Design:** Richard Seger

Songs: Be Courageous [1]; Carry On, Chums [1]; Dinghy; I Don't Know Why I Trust You But I Do; I Owe It All; I Resign [1]; I'd Like to Get Close to You [1]; Je Cousse [1]; Legal Heir; Let's Reminisce [1]; Man with the Ginger Mustache, The; Marvelous Weekend, A; New Day; Problematical Solution [1]; Something's Afoot; Suspicious; You Fell Out of the Sky

Cast: Gary Beach; Willard Beckham; Gary Gage; Barbara Heuman; Marc Jordan; Tessie O'Shea; Jack Schmidt; Liz Sheridan; Neva Small; Sel Vitella

Notes: [1] Cut prior to opening.

4063 • SOMETIME

OPENED: 10/04/1918   Theatre: Shubert
Musical   Broadway: 283

Composer: Rudolf Friml
Lyricist: Rida Johnson Young
Librettist: Rida Johnson Young
Producer: Arthur Hammerstein
Director: Oscar Eagle

Choreographer: Allan K. Foster; **Musical Director:** Herbert Stothart

Songs: Any Kind of Man; Argentine Tango (inst.); Baby Doll; Beautiful Night; Constantina Number [2]; Dancing Spanish [1]; Dearie [1]; Just Like This [1]; Keep on Smiling; No One but You [4]; Oh! Argentine (L: Ed Wynn); Picking Peaches; Prunes [1]; Rottenest Job; Smiles [3]; So Near and Yet So Far [1]; Some Time; Spanish Maid (Nina Espagnola); Tune You Can't Forget, The; What Do You Have to Do?

Cast: Frances Cameron; Charles De Haven; Francine Larrimore; Beatrice Summers; Mae West; Ed Wynn

Notes: [1] Out Atlantic City 8/28/18. [2] Out Parkersburg, W. Va. 1919. [3] ASCAP/Library of Congress only. [4] Sheet music only.

4064 • SOMEWHERE ELSE

OPENED: 01/20/1913   Theatre: Broadway
Musical   Broadway: 9

Composer: Gustav Luders
Lyricist: Avery Hopwood
Librettist: Avery Hopwood
Producer: Henry W. Savage
Director: Frank Smithson

Choreographer: David Marion; **Costumes:** Hy Mayer; **Lighting Designer:** Joseph Wilson

Songs: As Birds Greet Morning Skies; B-a-b-e-e; Boy Scouts, The; Can You Do This?; Cupid's

Entrance; Dance d'Amour; Dingle Dangle; Father; For You Dear Heart; Forget Me Not; How Do You Do; I Just Want Somebody to Love Me [1]; If I Kissed You [1]; It's Distinctly Nice [1]; Lay of an Egg, The [1]; Look Out for the Strange Young Man [1]; Love at First Sight; Man, His Pipe and His Dog, A [1]; Moving Pictures [1]; Opening Number; Queen's Entrance; Somebody's Eyes; Song of the Rosebuds [1]; Twinkle, Twinkle Little Star; Wake Up Little Hepzibah; Well Fellows, I Guess We're Here

Cast: Taylor Holmes; Elene Leska; Will Philbrick

Notes: [1] Sheet music only.

4065 • SON OF FOUR BELOW, THE

OPENED: 09/27/1956
Revue   Nightclub

Producer: Stan Keen; Julius Monk

Cast: Ceil Cabot; June Ericson; Jack Fletcher; Gerry Matthews; **Pianist:** Murray Grand

Notes: No other information available.

4066 • SON-DAUGHTER, THE

OPENED: 11/19/1919   Theatre: Hudson
Play   Broadway: 223

Composer: Anselm Goetzl
Author: David Belasco; George Scarborough
Producer: David Belasco
Director: David Belasco

Costumes: Albertine Randall Wheelan; **Set Design:** Ernest Gros

Songs: In the Bamboo Tree (L: David Belasco; George Scarsborough); Who Comes in My Garden (L: David Belasco)

Cast: Frederic Burt; Thomas Findlay; Edmond Love; Lenore Ulric

4067 • SONDHEIM — PUTTING IT TOGETHER

OPENED: 04/01/1993   Theatre: City Center
Revue   Off-Broadway: 59

Composer: Stephen Sondheim
Lyricist: Stephen Sondheim

Producer: Manhattan Theater Club
Director: Julia McKenzie

Arrangements: Chris Walker; **Choreographer:** Bob Avian; **Costumes:** Theoni V. Aldredge; **Lighting Designer:** Tharon Musser; **Musical Director:** Scott Frankel; **Set Design:** Robin Wagner

Songs: Ah, but Underneath . . . ! [1]; Back in Business [2]; Bang! [3]; Being Alive [4]; Could I Leave You? [5]; Country House [1]; Every Day a Little Death [3]; Everybody Ought to Have a Maid [6]; Getting Married Today [4]; Gun Song [7]; Have I Got a Girl for You [4]; Hello Little Girl [8]; I Could Drive a Person Crazy [4]; I'm Calm [6]; Impossible [6]; Invocation and Instructions [9]; Like It Was [10]; Live Alone and Like It [2]; Lovely [6]; Marry Me a Little [4]; Merrily We Roll Along [10]; Miller's Son, The [8]; My Husband the Pig [3]; Night Waltzes [3]; Now [3]; Old Friends [4]; Pretty Women [11]; Putting It Together [12]; Rich and Happy [10]; Sooner or Later [2]; Sorry-Grateful [4]; Sweet Polly Plunkett [13]

Cast: Julie Andrews; Stephen Collins; Christopher Durang; Michael Rupert; Rachel York

Notes: No songs written for this production. [1] From the London version of FOLLIES. [2] From the film DICK TRACY. [3] From A LITTLE NIGHT MUSIC. [4] From COMPANY. [5] From FOLLIES. [6] From A FUNNY THING HAPPENED ON THE WAY TO THE FORUM. [7] From ASSASSINS. [8] From INTO THE WOODS. [9] From THE FROGS. [10] From MERRILY WE ROLL ALONG. [11] From PACIFIC OVERTURES. [12] From SUNDAY IN THE PARK WITH GEORGE. [13] From SWEENEY TODD.

4068 • SONG & DANCE

OPENED: 09/18/1985   Theatre: Royale
Musical   Broadway: 474

Composer: Andrew Lloyd Webber
Lyricist: Don Black
Additional Lyrics: Richard Maltby Jr.
Producer: F.W.M. Producing Group; Cameron Mackintosh; Shubert Organization
Director: Richard Maltby Jr.

Choreographer: Peter Martins; **Costumes:** Willa Kim; **Lighting Designer:** Jules Fisher; **Musical**

Director: John Mauceri; **Orchestrations:** David Cullen; Andrew Lloyd Webber; **Set Design:** Robin Wagner

Songs: Capped Teeth and Caesar Salad; Come Back with the Same Look in Your Eyes; English Girls; First Letter Home; I Love New York; I'm Very You, You're Very Me [1]; Let Me Finish; Married Man; Nothing Like You've Ever Known [1]; Second Letter Home; So Much to Do in New York; Take That Look Off Your Face; Tell Me on a Sunday; Third Letter Home; Unexpected Song; What Have I Done?; You Made Me Think You Were in Love

Cast: Gregg Burge; Charlotte D'Amboise; Bernadette Peters; Scott Wise; Christopher d'Amboise

Notes: *See also TELL ME ON A SUNDAY* which became one of this show's acts. [1] Cut.

4069 • SONG AND FUN

Notes: No other information available.

4070 • SONG BIRDS, THE (1907)

OPENED: 04/01/1907   Theatre: New York
Musical   Broadway: 17

Composer: Victor Herbert
Lyricist: George V. Hobart

Songs: Mazuma (The Plaint of the Prima Donna); Yankee Land

Notes: This was the second half of THE LAND OF NOD. Individual songs were not listed for this operatic skit. The skit was first performed on May 13, 1906 at the Lambs Club. It was repeated on May 18, 1906 at a benefit by the Lambs Club as part of their Ladies' Gambol at the Broadway Theatre. The benefit raised money for victims of the San Francisco earthquake. *See also THE LAND OF NOD.*

4071 • SONG BIRDS (1918)

OPENED: 1918

Songs: Gee Whiz! Those Eyes [1] (C: Joseph E. Howard; L: Collin Davis)

Notes: No other information available. [1] Also in IN AND OUT.

4072 • SONG FOR A SATURDAY

Notes: *See BAR MITZVAH BOY.*

4073 • SONG FOR CYRANO, A

OPENED: 09/04/1972
Musical   Closed out of town

Composer: George Forrest; Robert Wright
Lyricist: George Forrest; Robert Wright
Librettist Jose Ferrer

Source: CYRANO DE BERGERAC (Play: Edmond Rostand)

Songs: All Paris; Bit of a Ballad, A; Gazette, The; I Love You No More Than . . .; Letter, The; Melancholy Melody; Moment in the Dark; My Love Does No Know; My Nose; My Plume (My Life); Now and Always Yours; On the Moon; One Friend; Other You, The; Phoebus Apollo; Prelude; Second to None; Sleep, Sleep, Sleep; Song of Cyrano; Take Care of Him; What Is a Kiss?

Cast: Jose Ferrer

Notes: Produced at the Pocono Playhouse, Pennsylvania.

4074 • SONG OF JACOB ZULU, THE

OPENED: 03/24/1993   Theatre: Plymouth
Play   Broadway: 53

Composer: Ladysmith Black Mambazo
Lyricist: Ladysmith Black Mambazo; Tug Yourgrau
Author: Tug Yourgrau
Producer: Randall Arney; Stephen Eich; K. Todd Freeman; Bette Cerf Hill; Susan Liederman; Albert Poland; Steppenwolf Theatre Co.
Director: Eric Simonson

Costumes: Erin Quigley; **Lighting Designer:** Robert Christen; **Set Design:** Kevin Rigdon

Cast: Gerry Becker; Pat Bowie; Robert Breuler; David Connelly; Ladysmith Black Mambazo; Zakes Mokae

Notes: No songs listed in program.

4075 • SONG OF NORWAY

OPENED: 08/21/1944   Theatre: Imperial
Musical   Broadway: 860

Music Based On: Edvard Grieg
Composer: George Forrest; Robert Wright
Lyricist: George Forrest; Robert Wright
Librettist: Milton Lazarus
Producer: Edwin Lester
Director: Charles K. Freeman

Source: UNKNOWN (Play: Homer Curran); **Choreographer:** George Balanchine; **Musical Director:** Arthur Kay; **Orchestrations:** Arthur Kay; **Set Design:** Lemuel Ayers; **Vocal Arranger:** Arthur Kay

Songs: At Christmastime; Bon Vivant; Chocolate Pas de Trois; Down Your Tea; Freddy and His Fiddle; Hill of Dreams; Hymn of Betrothal; I Love You; Legend, The; March of the Trollgers; Midsummer's Eve; Nordraak's Farewell; Now; Song of Norway, The; Strange Music; Tree Loves; Waltz Eternal

Cast: Sig Arno; Helena Bliss; Lawrence Brooks; Dudley Clements; Alexandra Danilova; Frederic Franklin; Walter Kingsford; Irra Petina; Ivy Scott; Robert Shafer; Maria Tallchief

4076 • SONG OF SINGAPORE

OPENED: 05/23/1991   Theatre: Song of
                               Singapore
Musical   Off-Broadway: 459

Composer: Erik Frandsen; Michael Garin; Robert Hipkens; Paula Lockheart
Lyricist: Erik Frandsen; Michael Garin; Robert Hipkens; Paula Lockheart
Librettist: Erik Frandsen; Michael Garin; Robert Hipkens; Allan Katz; Paula Lockheart
Producer: Steven Baruch; Richard Frankel; Thomas Viertel
Director: A.J. Antoon

Costumes: Frank Krenz; **Lighting Designer:** Peter Kaczorowski; **Orchestrations:** John Carlini; **Set Design:** John Lee Beatty; **Vocal Arranger:** Yaron Gershovsky

Songs: Fly Away Rose; Foolish Geese; Harbour of Love; I Can't Remember; I Miss My Home in Harlem; I Remember; I Want to Get Offa This Island; Inexpensive Tango; Necrology; Never

Pay Musicians What They're Worth; Rose of Rangoon, The; Serve It Up; Shake, Shake, Shake; Song of Singapore; Sunrise; We're Rich; You Gotta Do What You Gotta Do

Cast: Art Baron; Cathy Foy; Erik Frandsen; Michael Garin; Jon Gordon; Robert Hipkens; Oliver Jackson Jr.; Francis Kane; Earl C. May; Donna Murphy

4077 • SONG OF THE FLAME

OPENED: 12/30/1925   Theatre: 44th Street
Musical   Broadway: 214

Composer: George Gershwin; Herbert Stothart
Lyricist: Oscar Hammerstein II; Otto Harbach
Librettist: Oscar Hammerstein II; Otto Harbach
Producer: Arthur Hammerstein
Director: Frank Reicher

Choreographer: Jack Haskell; **Costumes:** Mark Mooring; **Musical Director:** Herbert Stothart; **Orchestrations:** Robert Russell Bennett; **Set Design:** Joseph Urban

Songs: Cossack Love Song, The (Don't Forget Me); Far Away; Finaletto; First Blossom, The (ballet); Going Home on New Year's Morning; Great Big Bear (C: Herbert Stothart); I Want Two Husbands [2] (C: Herbert Stothart); Midnight Bells [2] (C: George Gershwin); Protest; Signal, The (C: George Gershwin); Song of the Flame; Tartar (C: Herbert Stothart); Vodka (Don't Give Me Vodka); Wander Away (C: Herbert Stothart); Women's Work Is Never Done (C: George Gershwin); You and You and Me [1] (C: Herbert Stothart); You Are You [1]

Cast: Phebe Brune; Hugh Cameron; Greek Evans; Bernard Gorcey; Tessa Kosta; Dorothy Mackaye; Guy Robertson; Ula Sharon; Leonard St. Leo

Notes: [1] Cut before N.Y. opening. [2] Cut after opening.

4078 • SONG OF VIENNA

Notes: *See MARINKA.*

4079 • SONG REVUE OF 1921

OPENED: 1921
Revue

Composer: Gus Edwards
Lyricist: Will D. Cobb

Songs: Every Mother's Lullaby; I Must Be Loved By Someone (and That Someone Must Be You); I Want You Morning, Noon and Night; Lend Me a Kiss Until To-morrow; Letters That Lighten Broadway; Little Partner of Mine; Lucky Day That I Found You, The; Mediterrania; When Old New York Was Young

Notes: No other information available.

4080 • SONG ROMANCE, A

OPENED: 1919
Musical

Composer: Armand Kaliz
Lyricist: Edgar Allen Woolf

Cast: Armand Kaliz; Amelia Stone

Notes: A vaudeville show from Phildelphia program. No other information available.

4081 • SONGBOOK

Notes: *See THE MOONEY SHAPIRO SONGBOOK.*

4082 • SONGS OF PARADISE

OPENED: 01/23/1989   Theatre: Public
Musical   Off-Broadway: 168

Composer: Rosalie Gerut
Lyricist: Itsik Manger
Librettist: Rena Berkowicz Borow; Miriam Hoffman
Producer: Joseph Papp Yiddish Theater
Director: Avi Hoffman

Source: POEMS (Poetry: Itsik Manger); **Arrangements:** Bevan Manson; **Choreographer:** Eleanor Reissa; **Lighting Designer:** Anne Militello; **Musical Director:** James Mironchik; **Set Design:** Steven Perry

Songs: Avrum and Sore's Duet; Di Demerung (The Twilight); Farewell Song, The; Hoger and the Turks; Hoger's Lament; Khave and the Apple Tree; Odem and Khave Duet; Shir Hamaylesn (Song of Blessings); Sore's Lullaby; Yankev and Rokhl Duet; Yosef's Tango

Cast: Adrienne Cooper; Rosalie Gerut; Avi Hoffman; David Kener; Eleanor Reissa

Notes: A Musical in Yiddish. After 136 performances this show moved to the Astor Place Theatre on 11/13/89 for 32 performances. The number of performances reflects both runs.

4083 • SONGWRITER, THE

OPENED: 08/13/1928   Theatre: 48th Street
Play   Broadway: 54

Author: Crane Wilbur
Producer: Alexander Yokel
Director: Alexander Leftwich

Set Design: William Oden-Waller

Songs: Sing Me a Song of the South (C: Georgie Price; L: Abner Silver); You Are My Heaven (C: Georgie Price; L: Herb Magidson); You're Gone (C/L: Unknown)

Cast: Mayo Methot; Jennie Moscowitz; Georgie Price

Notes: Phil Baker and Sid Silvers also credited with music in program.

4084 • SONNY

Notes: *See SONNY BOY.*

4085 • SONNY BOY

OPENED: 08/16/1921   Theatre: Cort
Musical   Broadway: 31

Composer: Raymond Hubbell
Lyricist: George V. Hobart
Librettist: George V. Hobart
Producer: Selwyns, The
Director: George V. Hobart

Choreographer: Carl Randall; **Musical Director:** Mario Agnolucci; **Orchestrations:** Maurice DePackh; **Set Design:** Clifford F. Pember

Songs: Dream; I Wonder If You Could Be Happy with Anyone Else but Me [1]; I'm in Love Dear; My Dear Old Chum; Peaches; Sonny

Cast: Ernest Glendinning; Carl Randall; Mabel Withee

Notes: Known as SONNY out of town. [1] Out Stamford 7/20/21.

4086 • SONS O' FUN

OPENED: 12/01/1941   Theatre: Winter Garden
Revue   Broadway: 742

Composer: Sammy Fain
Lyricist: Jack Yellen
Librettist: Hal Block; Chic Johnson; Ole Olsen
Producer: Messrs. Shubert
Director: Edward Duryea Dowling

Choreographer: Robert Alton; **Costumes:** Raoul Pene du Bois; **Dance Arranger:** Domenico Savino; **Lighting Designer:** Edward Duryea Dowling; **Musical Director:** Harold Stern; **Orchestrations:** Charles L. Cooke; Domenico Savino; **Set Design:** Raoul Pene du Bois; **Vocal Arranger:** Pembroke Davenport

Songs: Happy in Love; Hi, Ho the Hoe-Down Way (L: Irving Kahal); I'm Dancing with the Mamas with the Moolah [1]; It's a Mighty Fine Country We Have Here (dance) (C: Will Irwin); It's a Mighty Fine Country We Have Here; It's a New Kind of Thing; Joke's on Us, The (C: Will Irwin); Let's Say Goodnight with a Dance; Manuelo (L: Irving Kahal); Manuelo (dance) (C: Will Irwin); Oh Auntie [1]; Thank You, South America; Thank You, South America (dance) (C: Will Irwin)

Cast: Joe Besser; Chic Johnson; Ella Logan; Carmen Miranda; Ole Olsen

Notes: Additional music and lyrics credited to Jay Livingston and Ray Evans according to program but not identified. The team wrote two songs for the film version of HELLZAPOPPIN the same year. Maybe those songs were interpolated into this score. [1] ASCAP/Library of Congress only.

4087 • SONS O' GUNS

OPENED: 11/26/1929   Theatre: Imperial
Musical   Broadway: 297

Composer: J. Fred Coots
Lyricist: Benny Davis; Arthur Swanstrom
Librettist: Jack Donahue; Fred Thompson
Producer: Bobby Connolly; Arthur Swanstrom
Director: Bobby Connolly

Choreographer: Albertina Rasch

Songs: Can-Canola, The; Cross Your Fingers; I'm That Way Over You; It's You I Love; Let's Merge; May I Say I Love You?; Over Here; Red Hot and Blue Rhythm; Sentimental Melody; There's a Rainbow on the Way; We'll Be There; When Two Hearts Are True Hearts [1]; Why; Younger Set, The

Cast: Lily Damita; Jack Donahue; William Frawley

Notes: No program available. [1] ASCAP/Library of Congress only.

4088 • SONS OF HAM
OPENED: 1900
Musical

Composer: Will Marion Cook
Lyricist: Alex Rogers
Librettist: Jesse A. Shipp; George Walker; Bert Williams
Producer: George Walker; Bert Williams

Songs: Beyond the Gates of Paradise; Leader of the Ball, The; My Castle on the Nile; Phrenologist Coon, The; Zulu Babe

Cast: Lloyd Gibbs; Hattie McIntosh; J.A. Shipp; Lottie Thompson; Aida Overton Walker; George Walker; Bert Williams

Notes: No other information available.

4089 • SOON
OPENED: 01/12/1971   Theatre: Ritz
Musical   Broadway: 3

Composer: Scott Fagan; Joseph Martinez Kookoolis
Lyricist: Scott Fagan
Librettist: Martin Duberman
Producer: Sagittarius Productions; Bruce W. Stark
Director: Gerald Freedman

Choreographer: Fred Benjamin; **Costumes:** David Chapman; **Lighting Designer:** Jules Fisher; **Musical Director:** Louis St. Louis; **Orchestrations:** Jon Huston; Howard Wyeth; **Set Design:** Kert Lundell; **Vocal Arranger:** Jacqueline Penn; Louis St. Louis

Songs: Annie's Thing; Child of Sympathy; Country Store Living; Doing the High; Everybody's Running; Faces, Names and Places; Frustration; Glad to Know Ya; Henry Is Where It's At; I See the Light/Gentle Sighs; In Your Hands; It Won't Be Long; Let the World Begin Again; Marketing, Marketing; Molecules; Music, Music; On the Charts; One More Time; Rita Cheeta; Roll Out the Morning; So Much That I Know; Soon; Straight; Sweet Henry Loves You; To Touch the Sky; Wait; What's Gonna Happen to Me?

Cast: Peter Allen; Barry Bostwick; Pendleton Brown; Nell Carter; Leata Galloway; Richard Gere; Marta Heflin; Marion Ramsey; Larry Spinelli

4090 • SOPHIE
OPENED: 04/15/1963   Theatre: Winter Garden
Musical   Broadway: 8

Composer: Steve Allen
Lyricist: Steve Allen
Librettist: Phillip Pruneau
Producer: Len Bedsow; Hal Grossman
Director: Jack Sydow

Choreographer: Donald Saddler; **Costumes:** Fred Voelpel; **Dance Arranger:** Genevieve Pitot; **Lighting Designer:** Robert Randolph; **Musical Director:** Liza Redfield; **Orchestrations:** Sid Ramin; **Set Design:** Robert Randolph; **Vocal Arranger:** Liza Redfield

Songs: Don't Look Back; Fast Cars and Fightin' Women; Fight for the Man [1]; Hold On to Your Hats; I Love You Today; I Want the Kind of a Fella; I'd Know It; I'll Show Them All; I've Got 'Em Standing In Line; Mr. Henry Jones; Patsy; Queen of the Burlesque Wheel; Ragtime; Red Hot Mama; Sailors of the Sea; Sophie in New York; Sunshine Face; They Led Me to Believe [1]; They've Got a Lot to Learn; Waltz; When I'm in Love; When You Carry Your Own Suitcase; Who Are We Kidding; With You; You've Got to Be a Lady

Cast: Berta Gersten; Rosetta Le Noire; Phil Leeds; Art Lund; Eddie Roll; Libi Staiger

Notes: [1] Cut prior to opening.

4091 • SOPHISTICATED LADIES
OPENED: 03/01/1981   Theatre: Lunt-Fontanne
Revue   Broadway: 767

Composer: Duke Ellington
Lyricist: Duke Ellington
Producer: Roger Berlind; Manheim Fox; Sondra Gilman; Burton L. Litwin; Louise Westergaard
Director: Michael Smuin

Choreographer: Henry LeTang; Donald McKayle; Michael Smuin; **Costumes:** Willa Kim; **Dance Arranger:** Lloyd Mayers; **Lighting Designer:** Jennifer Tipton; **Musical Director:** Mercer Ellington; **Orchestrations:** Al Cohn; **Set Design:** Tony Walton; **Vocal Arranger:** Malcolm Dodds; Lloyd Mayers

Songs: Bli-Blip [1] (L: Sid Kuller); Caravan (C: Duke Ellington; L: Irving Mills; Juan Tizol); Cotton Tail; Dancers in Love (inst.); Diminuendo in Blue (inst.); Do Nothing 'Til You Hear from Me (L: Bob Russell); Don't Get Around Much Anymore (L: Bob Russell); Drop Me Off in Harlem (L: Nick Kenny); Duke's Place (L: Bill Katz; Bob Thiele); Echoes of Harlem (inst.); Fat and Forte (C/L: Skeets Tolbert); I Iey Rube (inst.); Hit Me with a Hot Note and Watch Me Bounce (L: Don George); I Got It Bad and That Ain't Good (L: Paul Francis Webster); I Let a Song Go Out of My Heart (L: Irving Mills; Henry Nemo; John Redmond); I Love You Madly; I'm Beginning to See the Light (C/L: Duke Ellington; Don George; Johnnie Hodges; Harry James); I'm Checkin' Out Goombye (C/L: Duke Ellington; Billy Strayhorn); I'm Just a Lucky So-and-So (L: Mack David); Imagine My Frustration (C/L: Duke Ellington; Billy Strayhorn; Gerald Wilson); In a Sentimental Mood (L: Manny Kurtz; Irving Mills); It Don't Mean a Thing (L: Irving Mills); I've Got to Be a Rug Cutter; Just Squeeze Me (L: Lee Gaines); Kinda Dukish (inst.); Ko-Ko; Mooche, The (inst.) (C: Duke Ellington; Irving Mills); Mood Indigo (C/L: Barney Bigard; Duke Ellington; Irving Mills); Music Is a Woman (L: John Guare); Old Man Blues (C/L: Duke Ellington; Irving Mills); Perdido (C/L: Ervin Drake; Hans Lengsfelder; Juan Tizol); Rockin' in Rhythm (C: Harry Carney; Duke Ellington; Irving Mills); Satin Doll (L: Johnny Mercer; Billy Strayhorn); Solitude (L: Eddie De Lange; Irving Mills); Something to Live For (C/L: Duke Ellington; Billy Strayhorn); Sophisticated Lady (L: Irving Mills; Mitchell Parish); Take the "A" Train (C/L: Billy Strayhorn)

Cast: Adrian Bailey; Priscilla Baskerville; Hinton Battle; P.J. Benjamin; Gregg Burge; Mercedes Ellington; Gregory Hines; Phyllis Hyman; Judith Jamison; Terri Klausner

Notes: No songs written for this production. [1] From JUMP FOR JOY.

4092 • SORORITY DAYS
OPENED: 01/16/1913
Musical   Closed out of town

Composer: Hamilton Coleman
Lyricist: Hamilton Coleman
Librettist: Hamilton Coleman
Director: Hamilton Coleman

Set Design: Eugene Cox

Songs: Ghost of Sorority Days; Guess We've Fallen in Love; Kiss Me Honey; Little Girl; My Mississippi Miss

Cast: Gertrude Decker; Christine Durfus; Evelyn Harkins; Roso Laird; Emil Rousseau; Eddie Winslow

Notes: A one-act vaudeville musical. Milwaukee program.

4093 • SORRY, CHARLIE, YOUR TIME IS UP
OPENED: 02/24/1964
Musical   Unknown: 20

Composer: Ronald Lowden
Lyricist: Stephen de Baum
Librettist: Stephen de Baum
Producer: Chet Cooper
Director: Carl Leswing

Arrangements: Lee Holdridge; **Choreographer:** Walter Keenan; **Costumes:** Waas & Son; **Musical Director:** William Lessig; **Set Design:** Stephen Goff

Songs: Bachelor's Lament; Hey, Little Star (C: Bobby Troup); I Left My Heart in Bala Cynwyd; I Like What I See; It's the Little Things That Irritate the Most (C: John Schupf); Lo, Swings the Pendulum; Love and Devotion; Plaza, the Barclay and the Old Waldorf, The; Praises Be to David Ogilvy; Sorry Charlie Your Time Is Up; Stately Homes of England, The; Thanks Just the Same; Three Cheers (C: Stephen de Baum); Tiny Tours (C/L: Ferris; Robert Gardner; Howard Jaffe; Kernan; Stanwood); When I Happen By; Where Am I? (C: Bobby Troup); Ziegfeld, Where Are You Now?; Zip Code I Love You

Cast: Wharton Donaldson; Paul Mahoney; David du Pont

Notes: Amateur show. Mask & Wig Club, University of Pennsylvania.

4094 • SOUL KISS, THE
OPENED: 01/28/1908   Theatre: New York
Musical   Broadway: 122

Composer: Maurice Levi
Lyricist: Harry B. Smith
Librettist: Harry B. Smith
Producer: Florenz Ziegfeld
Director: Herbert Gresham; Julian Mitchell

Songs: Any Old Place in the World with You; Awake Dearest One [2]; Cutie Come and Tie My Tie [2]; Dances of the Tabarin, The; Dollar Sign, The (C: Fleta Ian Brown; L: Jessie Villars); Genee Waltzes (inst.); Happy Days (inst.); Home Again [1]; How I Love Flowers [1]; Hunting Chorus [1]; I Wonder Where They'll Go; I'm Glad to Get Back to New York; I'm the Human Night Key of New York; Jag, a Drone and a Tank of Air, A [1]; Language of Love [1]; Latin Quarter, The [1]; Lauder Melodies [1]; Let the Soul Kiss Be Mine Today [2]; Let's Pretend; Little Mary Waited for the Pie [5] (L: Arthur J. Lamb); Meet Me at the Masquerade (C: Paul Lincke); Meet Me at the Station [4]; Meet Me at the Tabarin; My Affinity; My Diabalo Beau (C/L: Kenneth S. Clark); Queen of My Dreams [1]; Quiet Sunday in 1920, A; Rah! Rah! Rah! (Those College Yells) (C: C.M. Chapel; L: Cecil Lean); Since My Mariutch Learned the Merry Widow Waltz [3] (C/L: Bert Fitzgibbon); Song of Songs, The [1]; Soul Kiss, The (Just for You from Above) (L: Lewis Gates); Sunshine Is Bright [1]; Take Me Back to Old Broadway [5]; Temptations [1]; That Wasn't All (C: Louis A. Hirsch; L: Addison Burkhardt; Matt Woodward); There Were Actors Then; They Cannot Smoke with Me [5]; This Is No Place for Me [3] (C: Seymour Furth; L: Will Heelan; Edward P. Moran); Under the "Bargain Tree" [5]; Very Well Then [1]; When Swallows Return in the Spring; Will o' the Wisp [1]; Yankee Son of a Gun [1]; Yiddish Wedding Jubilee [1]

Cast: Adeline Genee; Lee Harrison; Ralph Herz; Florence Holbrook; Cecil Lean; Florence Walton

Notes: [1] Out Washington, D.C. 01/21/18. [2] Out Wilkes-Barre 9/3/10. [3] Sheet music only. [4]

Out Washington, D.C. 01/21/18. May be the 1917 popular song of the same name by Ted Snyder, Sam M. Lewis and Joe Young. [5] Vocal score only.

4095 • SOUND OF MUSIC, THE
OPENED: 11/16/1959   Theatre: Lunt-Fontanne
Musical   Broadway: 1443

Composer: Richard Rodgers
Lyricist: Richard Rodgers
Librettist: Russel Crouse; Howard Lindsay
Producer: Richard Halliday; Oscar Hammerstein II; Leland Hayward; Richard Rodgers
Director: Vincent J. Donehue

Source: TRAPP FAMILY SINGERS, THE (Book: Maria Augusta Trapp); **Choreographer:** Joe Layton; **Costumes:** Lucinda Ballard; Mainbocher; **Lighting Designer:** Jean Rosenthal; **Musical Director:** Frederick Dvonch; **Orchestrations:** Robert Russell Bennett; **Set Design:** Oliver Smith; **Vocal Arranger:** Trude Rittman

Songs: Climb Ev'ry Mountain; Do-Re-Mi; Edelweiss; How Can Love Survive?; Laendler (dance) [1]; Lonely Goatherd, The [1]; Maria; My Favorite Things; No Way to Stop It; Ordinary Couple, An; Preludium; Processional (inst.); Sixteen Going on Seventeen; So Long, Farewell; Sound of Music, The

Cast: Theodore Bikel; Brian Davies; Kathy Dunn; Stefan Gierasch; Joey Heatherton; Kurt Kasznar; Marion Marlowe; Mary Martin; Patricia Neway; Lauri Peters; William Snowden; Joseph Stewart

Notes: [1] Same music.

4096 • SOUTH PACIFIC
OPENED: 04/07/1949   Theatre: Majestic
Musical   Broadway: 1925

Composer: Richard Rodgers
Lyricist: Oscar Hammerstein II
Librettist: Oscar Hammerstein II
Producer: Oscar Hammerstein II; Leland Hayward; Joshua Logan; Richard Rodgers
Director: Joshua Logan

Source: TALES OF THE SOUTH PACIFIC (Novel: James A. Michener); **Choreographer:** Joshua Logan; **Costumes:** Motley; **Musical Director:**

Salvatore Dell'Isola; **Orchestrations:** Robert Russell Bennett; **Set Design:** Jo Mielziner

Songs: Bali Ha'i; Bloody Mary; Cockeyed Optimist, A; Dites- moi; Happy Talk; Honey Bun; I'm Gonna Wash That Man Right Outa My Hair; Loneliness of Evening [1]; My Girl Back Home [3]; Now Is the Time [2]; Some Enchanted Evening; Suddenly Lucky [6]; There Is Nothin' Like a Dame; This Nearly Was Mine; Twin Soliloquies (Wonder How It Feels); Will My Love Come Home to Me [5]; Wonderful Guy, A; You've Got to Be Carefully Taught; Younger Than Springtime [4]

Cast: Michael DeLeon; Noel DeLeon; Sandra Deel; Dickinson Eastham; Alan Gilbert; Juanita Hall; Jim Hawthorne; Barbara Luna; Mary Martin; Myron McCormick; Biff McGuire; Henry Michel; Ezio Pinza; Archie Savage; Richard Silvera; Henry Slate; Betta St. John; William Tabbert

Notes: [1] Cut. Used in TV production of CINDERELLA. Same music as "Will My Love Come Home to Me." [2] Cut. [3] Cut. Later used in film version. [4] Music same as "My Wife" from ALLEGRO. [5] Cut. Same music as "Loneliness of Evening." [6] Cut. Same music as "Getting to Know You" from THE KING AND I.

4097 • SOUTH SIDE RHYTHM
Notes: See CHICAGO RHYTHM.

4098 • SOUTHERNERS, THE
OPENED: 05/23/1904   Theatre: New York
Musical   Broadway: 36

Composer: Will Marion Cook; Will Mercer
Lyricist: Richard Grant; Will Mercer
Librettist: Richard Grant
Producer: George W. Lederer
Director: George W. Lederer

Choreographer: Joseph C. Smith; **Costumes:** Mme. Siedle; **Musical Director:** A. DeNovellis; **Set Design:** D. Frank Dodge

Songs: Amorous Star (C/L: Marie Sutherland); It's Allus de Same in Dixie; Mongst the Magnolias; When the Sunflower Turns to the Sun

Cast: William Gould; Albert Hart; Eddie Leonard; Junie McCree

Notes: No songs listed in program.

4099 • SOUTHPAW, THE
OPENED: 1969
Musical   Unproduced

Composer: Harold Rome
Lyricist: Harold Rome

Songs: As I Was Remarking; Henry; Lonely Stranger; Love That Game; Mary Pistologlione; Rosie; You Get in My Way

Notes: No other information available.

4100 • SPEAK EASY
OPENED: 09/26/1927   Theatre: Mansfield
Play   Broadway: 57

Author: Edward Knoblock; George Rosener
Producer: William B. Friedlander
Director: William B. Friedlander

Songs: Forever and a Day (C: John Philip Sousa; L: Irving Bibo)

Cast: Leo G. Carroll; Dorothy Hall; Beatrice Lee; Ann Shoemaker

4101 • SPEAK, LUCINDA!
Notes: See THE CAREFREE HEART.

4102 • SPEED GETS THE POPPYS
OPENED: 07/25/1972   Theatre: Mercer-Brecht
Musical   Off-Broadway: 7

Composer: Lorenzo Fuller
Lyricist: Lorenzo Fuller; Lila Levant
Librettist: Lila Levant
Producer: Daffodil Productions
Director: Charles Abbott

Choreographer: Charles Abbott; **Costumes:** Milton Duke; **Dance Arranger:** Robert Estey; **Lighting Designer:** Milton Duke; **Musical Director:** Robert Estey; **Set Design:** Milton Duke; **Vocal Arranger:** Robert Estey

Songs: Caught; Good Triumphs Over Evil; I'll Bring the Roses; Instant Magic; Living Next Door to the Sun; My Moustache Is Twitchin';

Old-Fashioned Chase, An; Speed Won't Get Me; Take It from a Pal; Try, Try Again; What Is a Melodrama?; What Real True Friends Are For; Whatever Happened to Tomorrow?

Cast: Robert Browning; Raymond Cerabone; Robin Field; Randi Kallan; Anita Keal; Joanna Myers; Edward Penn

4103 • SPHINX, THE

OPENED: 07/08/1895   Theatre: Casino
Musical   Broadway: 40

Composer: Lewis S. Thompson
Librettist: William Maynadier Browne
Producer: Harry Askin
Director: William Seymour

Set Design: Charles W. Whitham

Cast: Tallmadge Baldwin; Laura Joyce Bell; Christie MacDonald; Edwin Stevens

Notes: No program available.

4104 • SPICE OF 1922

OPENED: 07/06/1922   Theatre: Winter Garden
Revue   Broadway: 85

Composer: James F. Hanley
Lyricist: Jack Stanley
Librettist: Jack Lait
Producer: Armand Kaliz
Director: Allan K. Foster

Costumes: Ernest Schrapps; **Musical Director:** Alfred Goodman; **Set Design:** Herbert Ward

Songs: Angel Child (C: Abner Silver; L: Benny Davis; George E. Price); Burglar Inn (C: Seymour Furth; L: Ed Moran); Clothes and the Flapper (C/L: Unknown); Dreams for Sale (L: Herbert Reynolds); Egyptian Melange (L: James F. Hanley; Jack Stanley); Garden of Eden (L: Armand Kaliz); Girl from the Golden West, A (C: J. Fred Coots; L: McElbert Moore); I Had My Pitcher Tooken (C/L: Unknown); I'm in Love with You (C: Kenneth Keith; L: Armand Kaliz); In My Little Red Book (C: J. Fred Coots; L: McElbert Moore); Lilies of the Field (C: J. Fred Coots; L: Jack Lait); Little Side Street in Paree, A; Llamala (C: William J. Lewis; L: Guy Nankwill); My Dixie [1] (C: Maceo Pinkard; L: Sidney D. Mitchell); My

Lady Silhouette (C/L: Owen Murphy); Old Fashioned Cake Walk; Opening Chorus (C: J. Fred Coots; L: McElbert Moore); Society (C: J. Fred Coots; L: McElbert Moore); Swanee Sway, The; Two Little Wooden Shoes; Wail of a Debutante (C/L: Unknown); Way Down Yonder in New Orleans (C: Turner Layton; L: Henry Creamer); Yankee Doodle Blues (C: George Gershwin; L: Irving Caesar; B.G. DeSylva)

Cast: Flavia Arcaro; Nan Halperin; Sam Hearn; Armand Kaliz; Georgie Price; Valeska Suratt

Notes: [1] ASCAP/Library of Congress.

4105 • SPIDER, THE

OPENED: 03/22/1927   Theatre: Chanin's 46th St.
Play   Broadway: 100

Author: Lowell Brentano; Fulton Oursler
Producer: Sam Harris; Albert Lewis
Director: Albert Lewis

Set Design: William Oden-Waller

Songs: Kiss Before the Dawn, The (C/L: Ray Perkins)

Cast: Germaine Giroux; Eleanor Griffith; John Halliday; Roy Hargrave; Paul Harvey; Donald MacKenzie; William E. Morris

4106 • SPINNING TALE, A

OPENED: 02/20/1990   Theatre: Playhouse 91
Musical   Off-Broadway: 92

Composer: C.E. Kenneny
Lyricist: A. Kenneny; C.E. Kenneny
Librettist: A. Kenneny; C.E. Kenneny
Producer: Mariner James Pezza
Director: C.E. Kenneny; Jack Ross

Source: RUMPLESTILTSKIN (Fairy Tale: Brothers Grimm); **Choreographer:** Sally O'Shea; **Costumes:** Dandora Associates; **Lighting Designer:** Kevin Connaughton; **Orchestrations:** C.E. Kenneny; **Set Design:** Mariner James Pezza

Songs: Ah, Sweet Youth!; Another Life; Gold, Gold; Hello Stranger!; I Have a Little Secret; Last Elf Aria, The; Locked and Secluded; Never Met a Man I Didn't Like; Precious to Me; Remember the Time; Shadow, The; Spin! Spin! Spin!; Straw

Into Gold; Together As One; Trust Me Tango;
Under the Spell; What's in a Name?; You Get
What You Give

4107 • SPITTIN' IMAGE
OPENED: 04/01/1994
Musical

Composer: Stephen A. Weiner
Lyricist: Laura Szabo-Cohen
Librettist: Karin Kasdin
Director: Peter J. Loewy

Source: TAPS FOR PRIVATE TUSSIE (Novel: Jesse
Stuart); **Choreographer:** Dan Siretta; **Costumes:**
Jose M. Rivera; **Lighting Designer:** Mathew J.
Williams; **Musical Director:** Larry N. Rothweiler
Jr.; **Orchestrations:** Steve Cohen; **Set Design:**
Perry Arthur Kroeger

Songs: Big White House; Bury Him Here;
Children's Taunt; Come On Dance; Come On In;
Different; Divine Decree, A; Gravy Train; Knock,
Knock; My Fine Golden Boy; Spittin' Image;
Takin' Care; Telegram, The; Waltzing Tonight
Together; When You Hold Your Husband's Hand

Cast: Leonard Drum; Joe Glopen; Ramzi Khalaf;
Eden Riegel

Notes: Metuchen, New Jersey.

4108 • SPLIT DECISION
Revue   Chicago

Composer: Arthur Siegel
Lyricist: Diane Harris

Songs: All My Life I Lost It for Him; Charge!;
Enough!; Everybody's Doing It; Everything That
Goes Around Comes Around; I'm Forty; I'm
Taking Timothy; It's So Frightening Out There;
No- Fault Waltz, The; Once Upon a Time;
Suddenly There Was You; That's the Way It Is;
This Is a Man I Could Love; We; We Get the Fee;
You Brought Me Through It; You Think It's Easy?

4109 • SPOKESONG, OR THE COMMON WHEEL
OPENED: 03/15/1979   Theatre: Circle in the
                       Square
Play   Broadway: 77

Composer: Jimmy Kennedy
Lyricist: Stewart Parker
Author: Stewart Parker
Producer: Circle in the Square; Long Wharf
Theatre
Director: Kenneth Frankel

Costumes: Bill Walker; **Lighting Designer:** John
McLain; **Musical Director:** Thomas Fay; **Set
Design:** Marjorie Kellogg

Songs: Anthem Song of the Common Wheel, The;
Army Song, The; Cocktail Song Energy; Cowboy
Song; Daisy Bell (C/L: Harry Dacre); Parlor
Songs; Song of the Spokesong (Spokesong);
Spinning Song

Cast: John Horton; John Lithgow; Joseph Maher;
Josef Sommer; Maria Tucci; Virginia Vestoff

Notes: No songs listed in program.

4110 • SPOOK SCANDALS
OPENED: 12/08/1944   Theatre: President
Revue   Off-Broadway: 2

Composer: Sergio De Karlo
Lyricist: Sergio De Karlo
Librettist: Arthur Gondra; Al Henderson; Jerry
Sylvon
Producer: Jerry Sylvon; Michael Todd Midnight
Players
Director: Jerry Sylvon

Choreographer: Paul Haakon; Marta Nita; Raul
Reyes

Songs: Ming Ting Hai; Night of Nights; Nightly
My Love; No One but You; Secret of Love, The
(L: Don Anes; Bob Randolph); Since We Met in
Paris; We're So Happy

Cast: Paul Haakon; Dean Miles

4111 • SPOON RIVER ANTHOLOGY
OPENED: 09/29/1963   Theatre: Booth
Revue   Broadway: 111

Composer: Naomi Caryl Hirschhorn
Lyricist: Charles Aidman
Librettist: Charles Aidman
Producer: Joseph Cates

Source: SPOON RIVER ANTHOLOGY (Book: Edgar Lee Masters); **Lighting Designer:** Jules Fisher

Songs: Freedom; He's Gone Away (C/L: Traditional); I Am, I Am; Illinois; In the Night; Spoon River; Times Are Getting Hard; Water Is Wide, The (C/L: Traditional)

Cast: Charles Aidman; Robert Elston; Betty Garrett; Naomi Caryl Hirschhorn; Hal Lynch; Joyce Van Patten

Notes: Titled EDGAR LEE MASTERS' SPOON RIVER ANTHOLOGY when it first opened.

4112 • SPOONY SAM
OPENED: 1911
Musical

Producer: William M. Benbow

Songs: All That I Ask Is Love; In the Land Harmony; Tell Her No, That's All

Cast: William M. Benbow; Mose Graham; Rebecca Kinzy

Notes: No other information available.

4113 • SPORTING DAYS
OPENED: 09/05/1908   Theatre: Hippodrome
Musical   Broadway: 448

Composer: Manuel Klein
Lyricist: Manuel Klein
Librettist: R.H. Burnside
Producer: G.M. Anderson; R.H. Burnside; J.J. Shubert; Lee Shubert
Director: R.H. Burnside

Costumes: Alfredo Edel; **Musical Director:** Manuel Klein; **Set Design:** Arthur Voegtlin

Songs: Dear Motherland (Victory) [1]; Good Old Cambria; Love Is King [1]; Opening Chorus [1]; Racing Game, The; Rowing; Toast to the King of War, A [1]; What a Sense of Beauty Glorious [1]; When the Circus Comes to Town; Whole Year Round, The

Cast: G. Bonfiglio; Harry Dale; George Holland; Lesley Leigh; Marceline; Ella Smith; Margaret Townsend; Marie Tyler; Ester Zanini

Notes: Followed by THE LAND OF BIRDS BALLET and BATTLE IN THE SKIES. [1] In BATTLE IN THE SKIES.

4114 • SPOTLIGHT
OPENED: 01/08/1978
Musical   Closed out of town

Composer: Jerry Bresler
Lyricist: Lyn Duddy
Librettist: Richard Seff
Producer: Sheldon R. Lubliner
Director: David Black

Choreographer: Tony Stevens; **Costumes:** Robert Mackintosh; **Dance Arranger:** Wally Harper; **Lighting Designer:** Roger Morgan; **Musical Director:** Jack Lee; **Orchestrations:** Will Schaefer; **Set Design:** Robert Randolph; **Vocal Arranger:** Jack Lee

Songs: Didn't You Used to Be Him?; Everything; Hole in the Wall; No Regrets; Notice Me; Round and Round; Spotlight; Stranger in the Glass, The; Such a Business; Tricks of the Trade; What Am I Bio; Where Is Everybody; You Are You; You Need Someone

Cast: Gene Barry; D'Jamin Bartlett; David-James Carroll; Marc Jordan; Lenora Nemetz; Polly Rowles; Debbie Shapiro

4115 • SPRING CHICKEN, THE
OPENED: 10/08/1906   Theatre: Daly's
Musical   Broadway: 66

Composer: Ivan Caryll
Lyricist: Adrian Ross
Librettist: Richard Carle
Producer: Richard Carle

Source: COQUIN DE PRINTEMPS (Play: Duval; Jaime); **Source:** SPRING CHICKEN, THE (Musical: Ivan Caryll; Percy Greenbank; George Grossmith; Lionel Monckton; Adrian Ross); **Choreographer:** Ad Newberger; **Musical Director:** Frank Palma

Songs: Alice Sat By the Fire [6] (C: Lionel Monckton; L: Leslie Mayne); All the Girls Love Me (C: Richard Carle; L: M.E. Rourke); Baby and Nursie [3] (C: Robert Hood Bowers; L: Richard Carle); Baron Papouche; Beautiful Spring, The (L: George Grossmith Jr.); British Tourist, The [6] (L: Percy Greenbank); Coquin de Printemps! (L: George

Grossmith Jr.); Cordial Understanding, The [6]
(C: Lionel Monckton; L: Leslie Mayne); Delights of
London [6] (C: Lionel Monckton); Finale Act I [6]
(L: Percy Greenbank); Gwendoline of Grosvenor
Square [6] (C: Jerome Kern; L: George Grossmith
Jr.); I Don't Know, But I Guess [1] (C: Lionel
Monckton); I Made Them Jump [6]; In Rotterdam
(C: Lionel Monckton; L: Percy Greenbank; Leslie
Mayne); In Seville (C: Richard Carle; L: M.E.
Rourke); I've Come Along to Paris (C: Lionel
Monckton; L: Leslie Mayne); Lemon in the Garden
of Love, A [4] (C: Richard Carle; L: M.E. Rourke);
Lucky Little Lucy [6] (C: Lionel Monckton; L:
Leslie Mayne); Marching [5] (C/L: Richard Carle);
Modiste, A [6] (L: George Grossmith Jr.); Moon of
May, The [6] (C: Lionel Monckton); National
Theatre, The [6] (L: George Grossmith); Nice New
Parasol, The [6] (L: Lionel Monckton); Not So Very
Old [6] (L: George Grossmith Jr.); Oh, So Gently [6]
(L: George Grossmith Jr.); Old Noblesse, The [6]
(C: Lionel Monckton; L: George Grossmith Jr.);
Opening Chorus (If We Live in the Land We
Love) [6] (L: George Grossmith Jr.); Opening
Chorus Act II [6] (C: Lionel Monckton; L: Percy
Greenbank); Regent Street [6] (L: George
Grossmith Jr.); Rosalie [2] (C: Jerome Kern; L:
George Grossmith Jr.); Sunday Afternoon [6] (C:
Jerome Kern; L: George Grossmith Jr.); Swallows [6]
(C: Lionel Monckton; L: Percy Greenbank);
Tres Bien, Monsieur [6] (L: George Grossmith Jr.);
Under and Over Forty [6] (C: Lionel Monckton);
Very First Time, The [6] (C: Lionel Monckton); Vice
Versa [6] (L: Percy Greenbank); Vive la Boheme!
(The Latin Quarter) [6]; Waiting for a Certain Girl
(C: Milton W. Lusk; L: Richard Carle)

Cast: Emma Janvier; Bessie McCoy; Victor Morley;
Adele Rowland

Notes: [1] Out New York 10/14/07. [2]
Interpolated after opening. Music later used for
"Take a Step with Me" from THE LAUGHING
HUSBAND. [3] Titled "No Doubt You'd Like to
Cuddle Up to Baby" in sheet music. [4] Also in
THE AMERICAN WAY. [5] Also in MARY'S
LAMB. [6] In London version only.

4116 • SPRING IN AUTUMN
Notes: *See HOLKA-POLKA.*

4117 • SPRING IN BRAZIL
OPENED: 10/01/1945
Musical   Closed out of town

Composer: George Forrest; Robert Wright
Lyricist: George Forrest; Robert Wright
Librettist: Philip Rapp
Producer: Messrs. Shubert
Director: John Murray Anderson; Philip Rapp

Choreographer: Marjery Fielding; Esther Junger;
Costumes: Mary Schenck; Ted Shore; **Dance
Arranger:** Arthur Kay; **Musical Director:** Toni
Morelli; **Orchestrations:** Arthur Kay; **Set Design:**
Howard Bay; **Vocal Arranger:** Arthur Kay

Songs: Bean of the Coffee, The; Carnival in Rio;
Chi-ni-qui- chi; Frenetica; Great God Boogie, The;
Hymn to Jongo; I Envy You Rio; I'm Gonna Miss
Him So; Little Ol' Boy; New Worlds; Noe Noe;
Our Day; Rough, Rugged and Robust; Samba at
Daybreak; Spring in Brazil; Star Isn't Born, A

Cast: Talley Beatty; Milton Berle; Jack Cassidy;
Joseph Macaulay; Bernice Parks; Rose Marie

Notes: Closed at the Great Northern Theatre,
Chicago.

4118 • SPRING IS HERE
OPENED: 03/11/1929   Theatre: Alvin
Musical   Broadway: 104

Composer: Richard Rodgers
Lyricist: Lorenz Hart
Librettist: Owen Davis
Producer: Alex A. Aarons; Vic Arden; Vinton
Freedley; Phil Ohman
Director: Alexander Leftwich

Source: SHOTGUN WEDDING (Play: Owen
Davis); **Choreographer:** Bobby Connolly;
Costumes: Kiviette; **Musical Director:** Alfred
Newman; **Set Design:** John Wenger

Songs: Baby's Awake Now; Color of Her Eyes,
The [1]; Lady Luck Is Grinning [2]; Oh, Look
(Finale Act I); Red Hot Trumpet; Rich Man! Poor
Man!; Spring Is Here in Person [3]; There's Magic
in a Cup of Tea (Cup of Tea, A) [1]; This Is Not
Long Island (Opening Act II); We're Gonna Raise
Hell (Finaletto Scene 1); What a Girl!; Why Can't
I?; With a Song in My Heart; Word in Edgeways,
A [1]; You Never Say Yes; Yours Sincerely

Cast: Joyce Barbour; Inez Courtney; John Hundley;
Glenn Hunter; Dick Keene; Charles Ruggles; Gil
Squires; Lillian Taiz; Thelma White

Notes: [1] Cut prior to opening. [2] Cut prior to opening. Might have been written for LADY LUCK. [3] Not the same song as "Spring Is Here" in I MARRIED AN ANGEL.

4119 • SPRING MAID, THE

OPENED: 12/26/1910   Theatre: Liberty
Musical   Broadway: 192

Composer: Heinrich Reinhardt
Lyricist: Harry B. Smith; Robert B. Smith
Librettist: Harry B. Smith; Robert B. Smith
Producer: Mark A. Luescher; Louis F. Werba
Director: George Marion

Source: DIE SPRUDELFEE (Musical: Heinrich Reinhardt; Julius Wilhelm; A.M. Willner); **Musical Director:** Max Bendix

Songs: Carlsbad Legend, The; Cure, The; Dance with Me; Day Dreams [2] (C: Robert Hood Bowers; Heinrich Reinhardt); Day Dreams, Visions of Bliss; Duet; Finale Act I; Finale Act II; Finale of Operetta (C: Robert Hood Bowers; Heinrich Reinhardt); Fountain Fay, The (L: Robert B. Smith); Fountain Fay Protective Institution, The; How I Love a Pretty Face; Interrupted Allegory; Introduction; Introduction Act II; Loving Cup, The (C: Robert Hood Bowers); Next May Be the Right, The; On the Track; Take Me Dear (C: Robert Hood Bowers); Three Trees [1]; Two Little Love Bees

Cast: William Burress; Christie MacDonald; Tom MacNaughton; Lawrence Rea; Joseph H. Smith

Notes: [1] ASCAP/Library of Congress only. [2] Verse melody by Bowers, chorus melody by Reinhardt.

4120 • SPRINGTIME IN MAYO

OPENED: 01/17/1921
Play   Closed out of town

Composer: George H. Gartlan
Lyricist: Anna Nichols Duffy; Fiske O'Hara
Author: Anna Nichols Duffy
Producer: Augustus Pitou

Songs: Bit o' the Brogue, A; Don't You Love the Dream of Dear Old Ireland?; Lilac Tree, The; Springtime in Mayo; Top o' the Morning

Cast: Nan Bernard; Patricia Clary; Fiske O'Hara; W.T. Sheehan

Notes: Buffalo program used.

4121 • SPRINGTIME OF YOUTH

OPENED: 10/26/1922   Theatre: Broadhurst
Musical   Broadway: 68

Composer: Sigmund Romberg
Lyricist: Cyrus Wood
Librettist: Cyrus Wood; Matthew C. Woodward
Producer: Messrs. Shubert
Director: J.C. Huffman

Source: STERNE, DIE WIEDER LEUCHTAT (Musical: Rudolf Bernauer; Walter Kollo; Rudolf Schanzer); **Choreographer:** Allan K. Foster; **Orchestrations:** Emil Gerstenberger; **Set Design:** Watson Barratt; Rollo Wayne

Songs: Best of Good Friends (C: Walter Kollo); But in Brazil (C: Sigmund Romberg); Chorus of Welcome (C: Walter Kollo); I Knew 'Twould Be So (C: Walter Kollo); Just Like a Doll (C: Sigmund Romberg); Love Finds a Way (C: Sigmund Romberg); Love While You May (C: Sigmund Romberg); Opening Act II (C: Walter Kollo); Our Busy Needles Fly (C: Sigmund Romberg); Pretty Polly (C: Sigmund Romberg); Sailor's Bride, A (C: Sigmund Romberg); Si, Si, Senorita (C: Sigmund Romberg); Somewhere in Love's Garden (C: Sigmund Romberg); Starlight of Hope (C: Sigmund Romberg); There May Bloom a Rose for Me (C: Sigmund Romberg; L: Harry B. Smith); Won't You Take Me to Paris (C: Sigmund Romberg); Youth in Spring (C: Sigmund Romberg)

Cast: Grace Hamilton; George MacFarlane; J. Harold Murray; Olga Steck

4122 • SQUAW MAN'S GIRL OF THE GOLDEN WEST, THE

Notes: *See HIGGLEDY PIGGLEDY.*

4123 • ST. LOUIS WOMAN

OPENED: 03/30/1946   Theatre: Martin Beck
Musical   Broadway: 113

Composer: Harold Arlen
Lyricist: Johnny Mercer

Librettist: Arna Bontemps; Countee Cullen
Producer: Edward Gross
Director: Rouben Mamoulian

Source: GOD SENDS SUNDAY (Novel: Arna Botemps); **Choreographer:** Charles Walters; **Costumes:** Lemuel Ayers; **Musical Director:** Leon Leonardi; **Orchestrations:** Walter Paul; Ted Royal; Menotti Salta; Allan Small; **Set Design:** Lemuel Ayers; **Vocal Arranger:** Leon Leonardi

Songs: Any Place I Hang My Hat Is Home; Cakewalk Your Lady; Chinquapin Bush; Come On, Li'l Augie; Come Rain or Come Shine; High, Low, Jack and the Game [1]; I Feel My Luck Comin' Down; I Had Myself a True Love; I Wonder What Became of Me? [2]; Least That's My Opinion; Leavin' Time; Legalize My Name; Li'l Augie Is a Natural Man; Lim'ricks [1]; Lullaby; Man's Gotta Fight, A [1]; Racin' Form; Ridin' on the Moon; Sleep Peaceful, Mr. Used-to-Be; Somethin' You Gotta Find Out for Yourself [1]; Sow the Seed and Reap the Harvest [1]; Talkin' Glory [1]; We Shall Meet to Part, No Never; Woman's Prerogative, A

Cast: Pearl Bailey; Juanita Hall; June Hawkins; Ruby Hill; Rex Ingram; Fayard Nicholas; Harold Nicholas; Robert Pope

Notes: [1] Not used. [2] Cut after opening.

4124 • STAG MOVIE

OPENED: 01/03/1971   Theatre: Gate
Musical   Off-Broadway: 88

Composer: Jacques Urbont
Lyricist: David Newburger
Librettist: David Newburger
Producer: Robert L. Steele
Director: Bernard Barrow

Choreographer: Doug Rogers; **Costumes:** David Toser; **Dance Arranger:** Jacques Urbont; **Lighting Designer:** David Chapman; **Musical Director:** Jacques Urbont; **Set Design:** David Chapman; **Vocal Arranger:** Jacques Urbont

Songs: Bows; Get in Line; Get Your Rocks Off Rock; Grocery Boy; I Want More Out of Life Than This; It's So Good; Looking at the Sun; Splendor in the Grass; Stag Movie; Try a Trio; We Came Together

Cast: Adrienne Barbeau; Tod Miller; Brad Sullivan; Stan Wiest

4125 • STAG PARTY, OR A HERO IN SPITE OF HIMSELF, A

OPENED: 12/17/1895   Theatre: Garden
Musical   Broadway: 16

Composer: Herman Perlet
Librettist: Bill Nye; Paul Potter
Producer: A.M. Palmer
Director: Richard Barker

Set Design: Richard Marston

Cast: Grace Belasco; Charles A. Burke; Leo Ditrichstein; Marie Dressler; Louis Harrison; Geraldine McCann; Mabel Montgomery; John Slavin

Notes: No songs listed in program.

4126 • STAGE DOOR CHARLIE
Notes: *See BUSKER ALLEY.*

4127 • STAGGERLEE

OPENED: 03/18/1987   Theatre: Second Avenue
Musical   Off-Broadway: 118

Composer: Allen Toussaint
Lyricist: Vernel Bagneris; Allen Toussaint
Additional Lyrics: Vernel Bagneris
Producer: Encore A Partnership; Ruth Mieszkuc; Program Devlopment Co.; John H. Williams
Director: Vernel Bagneris

Choreographer: Pepsi Bethel; **Conductor:** Allen Toussaint; **Costumes:** JoAnn Clevenger; **Lighting Designer:** Allen Lee Hughes; **Set Design:** Akira Yoshimura

Songs: Big Chief; Devil's Disguise; Discontented Blues; Evil Bumble Bee [1]; Going Down Slowly; Happy Time (inst.); I Cried a Tear [1]; Iko Iko; It's Mardi Gras Time [1]; Knocking Myself Out; Let's Live It Up; Lighting Me a Candle; Look Up [1]; Lover of Love; Mardi Gras Time; Mean Old Man's World, A [1]; My Blue Heaven [1]; Night People; One Monkey Don't Stop No Show; Pimp Like That, A; Ruler of My Heart; Saved By Grace; Staggerlee; Victims of the Darkness; We're Gonna Do It Good; What Am I Living For? [1]; With You in Mind; You Knew I Was No Good

Cast: Juanita Brooks; Ruth Brown; Marva Hicks; Kevin Ramsey; Reginald Veljohnson; Adam Wade

Notes: [1] Cut prior to New York.

4128 • STAIRWAY IDEA
Revue

Producer: Fanchon & Marco
Director: Marco

Songs: Stairway of Dreams (C: Adrian Mack; L: Gene Stone)

Notes: A Fanchon and Marco show. No other information available.

4129 • STANDUP SHAKESPEARE
OPENED: 04/04/1987   Theatre: Theater 890
Revue   Off-Broadway: 2

Composer: Ray Leslee
Lyricist: William Shakespeare
Producer: Shubert Organization, The
Director: Mike Nichols

Costumes: Cynthia O'Neal; **Lighting Designer:** Michael Bogard; **Musical Director:** Ray Leslee; **Set Design:** John Arnone; **Vocal Arranger:** Thomas Young

Cast: Taborah Johnson; Kenneth Welsh; Thomas Young

4130 • STAR AND GARTER (1900)
OPENED: 11/26/1900   Theatre: Victoria
Revue   Broadway: 29

Composer: John W. Bratton
Lyricist: Walter Ford
Librettist: John J. McNally
Producer: Frank McKee
Director: Ben Teal

Choreographer: Ned Wayburn; **Costumes:** F. Richard Anderson; **Lighting Designer:** Peter King; **Set Design:** Joseph Physioc

Songs: After the Show; Auto-Mo-Biling (C/L: Matthew Woodward); Dickie the King of the Dudes (C: Arthur Trevelyan); Every Inch a Lady (C: Herman Perlet; L: Matthew Woodward); Give Me Back My Liza (C/L: Dave Reed Jr.); I Wouldn't Mind a Job Like That; My Hannah Lady (L: William Jerome); My Lady Bug; Opening Chorus; 3:33 in the Morning (C/L: Dave Reed Jr.); When Sousa Leads the Band (C: Frederick V. Bowers; L: William Jerome)

Cast: Agoust Family, The; Marie Cahill; Joseph Coyne; Otis Harlan; John G. Sparks

4131 • STAR AND GARTER (1942)
OPENED: 06/24/1942   Theatre: Music Box
Revue   Broadway: 605

Producer: Michael Todd
Director: Hassard Short

Choreographer: Albertina Rasch; Al White Jr.; **Costumes:** Irene Sharaff; **Lighting Designer:** Hassard Short; **Musical Director:** Raymond Sinatra; **Orchestrations:** Lionel Rand; Raymond Sinatra; **Set Design:** Harry Horner; **Vocal Arranger:** Raymond Sinatra

Songs: Blues in the Night [1] (C: Harold Arlen; L: Johnny Mercer); Brazilian Nuts (C: Dorival Caymmi; L: Al Stillman); Bunny, Bunny, Bunny (C/L: Harold Rome); Clap Your Hands (C/L: Unknown); For a Quarter (C: Lester Lee; L: Jerry Seelen); Girl on the Police Gazette, The [2] (C/L: Irving Berlin); Harem, The (C/L: Jerome Brainin; Irving Gordon; Allan Roberts); I Don't Get It (C: Doris Tauber; L: Sis Wilner); Les Sylphides avec La Bumpe (C/L: Jerome Brainin; Irving Gordon; Allan Roberts); Robert the Roue [3] (C: Jimmy McHugh; L: Al Dubin); Star and Garter Girls (C: Lester Lee; L: Jerry Seelen); Turkish Oomph (C: Lester Lee; L: Jerry Seelen)

Cast: Bobby Clark; Pat Harrington; Marjorie Knapp; Professor Lamberti; Gypsy Rose Lee

Notes: [1] From film BLUES IN THE NIGHT. [2] From film ON THE AVENUE. [3] From THE STREETS OF PARIS.

4132 • STAR DUST
OPENED: 1931
Musical   Unproduced

Composer: Cole Porter
Lyricist: Cole Porter

Songs: Auf Wiedersehen [5] (L: Unknown); But He Never Says He Loves Me [2]; I Get a Kick Out of You [4]; I Still Love the Red, White and Blue [3]; I Worship You [1]; I've Got You on My Mind [3]; Mister and Mrs. Fitch [3]; Mysteriously [6]; Pick Me Up and Lay Me Down

Notes: [1] Later used in FIFTY MILLION FRENCHMEN. [2] Not used. Also not used in THE NEW YORKERS (1930). Music used for "The Physician" in NYMPH ERRANT. [3] Later in GAY DIVORCE. [4] Later in ANYTHING GOES. [5] Same music as "The Old-Fashioned Waltz" from HITCHY-KOO OF 1922. [6] Same music as "I'm Yours" in YOU NEVER KNOW.

4133 • STAR GAZER, THE

OPENED: 11/26/1917   Theatre: Plymouth
Musical   Broadway: 8

Composer: Franz Lehar
Lyricist: Matthew C. Woodward
Librettist: Cosmo Hamilton
Producer: J.J. Shubert; Lee Shubert
Director: Edward P. Temple

Musical Director: Gaetano Merola

Songs: As a Butterfly Sips the Roses; Bachelor's Button, A; But You Alone; Butterfly; Drink Some Tea; If a Bachelor in Love Should Fall; If You Only Knew; My Heart Is Like a Bird in May; Rhyming for a Dance; Star Gazer; Twinkle, Twinkle; We Loved and We Lost, Goodbye; When You Are Mine All Mine; While All Are Asleep; Won't You Come Up to the Table?; You My Sweetheart Will Have to Be; You, You, You!

Cast: Elizabeth Goodhall; Jennetta Mathven; John T. Murray; John Charles Thomas

4134 • STAR TIME

Composer: William Roy
Lyricist: Roderick Cook

Notes: No other information available.

4135 • STAR WARS

OPENED: 1995
Musical   Unproduced

Composer: Charles Strouse
Lyricist: Lee Adams

Source: STAR WARS (Film: George Lucas)

Songs: Hans' the Man; My Star

4136 • STARCROSSED THE TRIAL OF GALILEO

OPENED: 11/03/1994
Musical

Composer: Jeanine Tesori
Lyricist: Alexa Junge; Keith Levenson
Librettist: Alexa Junge; Keith Levenson
Producer: Goodspeed Opera House
Director: Martin Charnin

Choreographer: Daniel Pelzig; **Costumes:** Gail Brassard; **Lighting Designer:** Ken Billington; **Musical Director:** Michael O'Flaherty; **Set Design:** Kenneth Foy

Songs: Blue Flame; He Works at Night; How Bright the Sky; I Think I'd Better Go; I'll Break the Chain; Little Tea, A; Mass, The; Only God I See; Perfect Place, A; Remember to Forget; Simple; Still the Same Sky; There's a Brilliant Age; Trial, The; You'll Remember Love

Cast: Ellyn Arons; Ed Dixon; Phillip Officer; Elizabeth Richmond; Cordell Stahl; Tom Treadwell

Notes: Goodspeed at Chester. Previously titled GALILEO.

4137 • STARDUST

OPENED: 02/19/1987   Theatre: Biltmore
Revue   Broadway: 102

Lyricist: Mitchell Parish
Producer: William H. Kessler Jr.; Burton L. Litwin; Martin Rein; Howard Rose; Louise Westergaard
Director: Albert Harris

Choreographer: Henry LeTang; Patrice Soriero; **Costumes:** Mardi Philips; **Lighting Designer:** Ken Billington; **Musical Director:** James Raitt; **Orchestrations:** James Raitt; **Set Design:** David Jenkins; **Vocal Arranger:** James Raitt

Songs: Belle of the Ball (C: Leroy Anderson); Carolina Rolling Stone (C: Harry D. Squires;

Eleanor Young); Ciao, Ciao, Bambino (C: Domenic Modugno); Deep Purple (C: Peter De Rose); Dixie After Dark (C: Irving Mills; Ben Oakland); Does Your Heart Beat for Me? (C: Arnold Johnson; Russ Morgan); Don't Be That Way (C: Benny Goodman; Edgar Sampson); Evenin' (C: Harry White); Forgotten Dreams (C: Leroy Anderson); Hands Across the Table (C: Jean Delettre); Happy Cigarettes (C: James Raitt; L: Peter Jablonski); I Would If I Could but I Can't (C: Bing Crosby; Alan Grey); It Happens to the Best of Friends (C: Rube Bloom); Midnight at the Onyx (C: Will Hudson); Moonlight Serenade (C: Glenn Miller); Nel Blue di Pinto di Blue (Volare) (C: Domenic Modugno; L: Migliani; Mitchell Parish); Organ Grinder's Swing (C: Will Hudson; Irving Mills); Riverboat Shuffle (C: Hoagy Carmichael; Irving Mills; Dick Voynow); Ruby (C: Heinz Roemheld); Scat Song, The (C: Cab Calloway; Frank Perkins); Sentimental Gentleman from Georgia (C: Frank Perkins); Sidewalks of Cuba (C: Irving Mills; Ben Oakland); Sleigh Ride (C: Leroy Anderson); Sophisticated Lady (C: Duke Ellington; Irving Mills); Sophisticated Swing (C: Will Hudson); Stairway to the Stars (C: Matt Malneck; Frank Signorelli); Star Dust (C: Hoagy Carmichael); Stars Fell on Alabama (C: Frank Perkins); Sweet Lorraine (C: Cliff Burwell); Syncopated Clock, The (C: Leroy Anderson); Take Me in Your Arms (C: Fred Markush); Tell Me Why (C: Michael Edwards; Sigmund Spaeth); Wealthy, Shmelthy, as Long as You're Healthy (C: Sammy Fain); You're So Indiff'rent (C: Sammy Fain); Your Cavalcade of Hits (C: James Raitt; L: Jay Jeffries)

Cast: Michele Bautier; Maureen Brennan; Kim Criswell; Andre De Shields; Jason Graae; Jim Walton

Notes: This revue of the songs of Mitchell Parish was originally produced Off-Off-Broadway at the Theater Off Park.

4138 • STARLIGHT EXPRESS

OPENED: 03/17/1987   Theatre: Gershwin
Musical   Broadway: 761

Composer: Andrew Lloyd Webber
Lyricist: Richard Stilgoe
Producer: Lord Grade; Martin Starger
Director: Trevor Nunn

Choreographer: Arlene Phillips; **Costumes:** John Napier; **Lighting Designer:** David Hersey;

Musical Director: Paul Bogaev; David Caddick; **Orchestrations:** David Cullen; Andrew Lloyd Webber; **Set Design:** John Napier

Songs: AC/DC; Belle; Call Me Rusty [2]; CB [2]; Chase; Crazy [4]; Engine of Love [1] (L: Peter Reeves; Richard Stilgoe); Final Selection; First Final; Freight; He Whistled at Me [2]; I Am the Starlight; Laughing Stock; Light at the End of the Tunnel; Lotta Locomotion, A; Make Up My Heart; Next Time You Fall in Love [4] (L: Don Black); One Rock & Roll Too Many; Only You; Poppa's Blues; Pumping Iron; Race One; Rap, The [4]; Right Place, Right Time; Rolling Stock; Silver Dollar; Starlight Express; There's Me; U.N.C.O.U.P.L.E.D.; Wide Smile, High Style, That's Me [3]

Cast: Braden Danner; Ronald Garza; Sean Grant; Jane Krakowski; Frank Mastrocola; Andrea McArdle; Greg Mowry; Robert Torti; Angel Vargas; Melanie Vaughan

Notes: [1] A revision of "Call Me Rusty." [2] In original London production. [3] A revision of "CB." [4] In 1995 Las Vegas production.

4139 • STARMITES

OPENED: 04/27/1989   Theatre: Criterion Center Stage Right
Musical   Off-Broadway: 60

Composer: Barry Keating
Lyricist: Barry Keating
Librettist: Barry Keating; Stuart Ross
Producer: Mary Keil; Hinks Shimberg; Steven Warnick
Director: Larry Carpenter

Choreographer: Michele Asaf; **Costumes:** Susan Hirschfeld; **Dance Arranger:** Henry Aronson; **Lighting Designer:** Jason Kantrowitz; **Musical Director:** Henry Aronson; **Orchestrations:** James McElwaine; **Set Design:** Lowell Detweiler; **Vocal Arranger:** Dianne Adams

Songs: Afraid of the Dark; Attack of the Banshees; Beauty Within; Bizabara's Wedding; Burning Desire [1]; Comic Book Hero [1]; Cruelty Stomp, The; Cuisine! [1]; Dance of Pleasures and Pulchritude [1]; Dance of Spousal Arousal, The; Garden of Evil [1]; Hard to Be Diva; Immolation; It Wasn't a Dream [1]; Little Hero; Love Duet; Lullaby [1]; Milady; Power of Love, The [1]; Processional [1]; Reach Right Down; Sacrifice, The [1]; Shak Graa's Tirade [1]; Starmites;

Superhero Girl; Trink's Narration; Woe and Misery [1]

Cast: Gabriel Barre; Bennett Cale; Liz Larson; Sharon McNight

Notes: [1] In off-off-Broadway production 10/23/80.

4140 • STARRING NORMA DESMOND

Notes: *See SWANSON ON SUNSET.*

4141 • STARS AND GRIPES

OPENED: 07/13/1943
Revue

Composer: Harold Rome
Lyricist: Harold Rome
Librettist: Martin Gabel; Ace Goodrich
Producer: U.S. Army
Director: Glenn Jordan

Choreographer: Ace Goodrich; **Musical Director:** Murray Karpilovsky; **Orchestrations:** Charles Mackenberg

Songs: Army Service Forces, The; Blow It Out Your Barracks Bag (C/L: Ace Goodrich); Hup! Tup! Thrup! Four! (Jack the Sleepy Jeep); I Wanna Bivouac with a WAC (C/L: Ace Goodrich); Jumping to the Jukebox [1]; Little Brown Suit My Uncle Bought Me, The [1]; Love Sometimes Has to Wait; Mess Call, The; My Pin-Up Girl [1]; Passing the Buck; Remington Rainger (C/L: Ace Goodrich); Women in Uniform, The

Cast: Martin Gable; Ace Goodrich; Ziggy Lane; Dave Sugarman

Notes: An Army show that toured bases. [1] Put in London revue SKIRTS which was produced by the U.S. Air Force.

4142 • STARS IN YOUR EYES

OPENED: 02/09/1939   Theatre: Majestic
Musical   Broadway: 127

Composer: Arthur Schwartz
Lyricist: Dorothy Fields
Librettist: J.P. McEvoy
Producer: Dwight Deere Wiman
Director: Joshua Logan

Choreographer: Carl Randall; **Costumes:** John Hambleton; **Musical Director:** Alfred Goodman; **Orchestrations:** Alfred Goodman; Hans Spialek; Don Walker; **Set Design:** Jo Mielziner; **Vocal Arranger:** Ralph Blane; Hugh Martin

Songs: All the Time; As of Today; He's Goin' Home; I'll Pay the Check; It's All Yours; Just a Little Bit More; Lady Needs a Change, The; Never a Dull Moment; Okay for Sound; One Brief Moment; Places, Everybody; Self Made Man; Terribly Attractive; This Is It

Cast: Alicia Alonzo; Richard Carlson; Walter Cassel; Davis Cunningham; Dan Dailey; Jimmy Durante; Ted Gary; Paul Godkin; Edward Kane; Maria Karnilova[1]; Nora Kaye; Ethel Merman; David Morris; Mildred Natwick; Jerome Robbins; Robert Ross; Robert Shanley; Roger Stearns; Clinton Sundberg; Tamara Toumanova; Mary Wickes; Nancy Wiman

Notes: [1] Billed as Maria Karniloff.

4143 • STARS ON ICE

OPENED: 07/02/1942   Theatre: Center
Revue   Broadway: 827

Composer: Paul McGrane
Lyricist: Al Stillman
Producer: Sonja Henie; Arthur M. Wirtz
Director: May Judels; Catherine Littlefield

Choreographer: Catherine Littlefield; **Costumes:** Lucinda Ballard; **Lighting Designer:** Eugene Braun; **Musical Director:** David Mendoza; **Orchestrations:** Paul Van Loan; **Set Design:** Bruno Maine

Songs: Big Broad Smile; Cavalier Cat, The; Gin Rummy; I Love You; Juke Box Saturday Night; Like a Leaf Falling in the Breeze; Little Jack Frost; Stars on Ice; You're Awfully Smart

Cast: Vivienne Allen; Skippy Baxter; Four Bruises, The; Jack Kilty; Carol Lynne; Guy Owen; Mary Jane Yeo

4144 • STARS ON MY SHOULDERS

OPENED: 1948
Revue

Songs: What Can You Do with a General (C/L: Irving Berlin)

Notes: No other information available.

4145 • STARTING HERE, STARTING NOW

OPENED: 06/19/1977   Theatre: Barbarann
Revue   Off-Broadway: 120

Composer: David Shire
Lyricist: Richard Maltby Jr.
Producer: Steve Abrams; Scott Mansfield; Mary Jo Slater
Director: Richard Maltby Jr.

Choreographer: Ethel Martin; **Costumes:** Stanley Simmons; **Lighting Designer:** Joan Liepman; **Musical Director:** Robert W. Preston

Songs: Autumn [6]; Barbara; Beautiful (1) [2]; Beautiful (2) [8]; Crossword Puzzle [5]; I Don't Believe It [8]; I Don't Remember Christmas; I Hear Bells [2]; I Think I May Want to Remember Today [2]; I'm a Girl You Should Know; Just Across the River [4]; Little Bit Off, A; New Life Coming, A [10]; One Step [4]; Pleased with Myself [4]; Song of Me [7]; Starting Here, Starting Now; Today Is the First Day of the Rest of My Life [2]; Travel [7]; Watching the Big Parade Go By [1]; We Can Talk to Each Other [3]; We Have to Give You More [9]; What About Today (L: David Shire); Word Is Love, The [1]

Cast: Loni Ackerman; George Lee Andrews; Margery Cohen

Notes: [1] From THE SAP OF LIFE. [2] From LOVE MATCH. [3] From GIRL OF THE MINUTE. [4] From HOW DO YOU DO, I LOVE YOU. [5] From GRAHAM CRACKERS. [6] From CYRANO. [7] From THE RIVER. [8] From LOVE MATCH but rewritten for this production. [9] Cut after opening. [10] Based on "A Charmed Life" from THE SAP OF LIFE.

4146 • STATE FAIR

OPENED: 1995
Musical

Composer: Richard Rodgers
Lyricist: Oscar Hammerstein II
Librettist: Tom Briggs; Louis Mattioli

Producer: Theatre Guild, The
Director: James Hammerstein; Randy Skinner

Choreographer: Randy Skinner; **Costumes:** Michael Bottari; Ronald Case; **Dance Arranger:** Scot Woolley; **Lighting Designer:** Natasha Katz; **Musical Director:** Kay Cameron; **Orchestrations:** Bruce Pomahac; **Set Design:** James Leonard Joy; **Vocal Arranger:** Kay Cameron

Songs: All I Owe Ioway [1]; Boys and Girls Like You and Me [2]; Isn't It Kinda Fun? [1]; It Might As Well Be Spring [1]; It's a Grand Night for Singing [1]; Man I Used to Be, The [3]; More Than Just a Friend [4] (L: Richard Rodgers); Next Time It Happens, The [3]; Our State Fair [1]; So Far [5]; That's for Me [1]; That's the Way It Happens [6]; When I Go Out Walkin' with My Baby [2]; You Never Had It So Good [6]

Cast: Kathryn Crosby; John Davidson; Andrea McArdle; Donna McKechnie; Scott Wise; Ben Wright

Notes: Not opened in New York as of publication. Program from Des Moines — 8/12/95. [1] From film score. [2] Cut from OKLAHOMA! [3] From PIPE DREAM. [4] From 1962 film version of STATE FAIR. [5] From ALLEGRO. [6] From ME AND JULIET.

4147 • STEEL

OPENED: 04/14/1991
Musical

Composer: Galt MacDermot
Lyricist: Derek Walcott
Librettist: Derek Walcott
Producer: American Repertory Theatre
Director: Robert Scanlan; Derek Walcott

Choreographer: Mary Barnett; **Costumes:** Catherine Zuber; **Lighting Designer:** Richard Riddell; **Musical Director:** Galt MacDermot; **Set Design:** Richard Montgomery

Songs: Back to You; By Peaceful Streams; Chaguanas; Champion; Circles; Dark Chords and Somber Notes; Face the Music; Gentle As Dew; Gospel News; Growler's Last Will and Testament; Hill, The Hill, The; How Long Ago; I Send a Suit to the Tailor; I'm Sitting Down in a Ricefield; In a Backyard in Belmont; Just Like the Movies; Limbo; Mai Mai; Melody Rises, A;

Morning, Morning, Morning; Names; Neighbor, Neighbor; No, Joe; Oh-Ree-Oh; One-Step Two-Step; Run Something; Simple Raga; Someone You Thought You Could Trust; Streets of Steel; Tableland; This Is My Hill; Three Kings; Universal Language; Were You There?; Who Walked Across the Water; You Want to Be an Idler; Zora, Zora, Come Dance

Cast: Byrd Mansur; Larry Marshall; Norman Matlock; Leon Morenzic

Notes: Cambridge, Massachusetts.

4148 • STEP THIS WAY

OPENED: 05/29/1916   Theatre: Shubert
Musical   Broadway: 88

Composer: Bert Grant
Lyricist: E. Ray Goetz
Librettist: Edgar Smith
Director: Frank McCormack

Choreographer: Jack Mason

Songs: Bit of Ribbon, a Bit of Love, A; By the Sad Luana Shore [3] (C: E. Ray Goetz); Egypt [1]; I Wonder Why; If I Knock the 'L' Out of Kelly (It Would Still Be Kelly to Me) (L: Sam M. Lewis; Joe Young); In Florida Among the Palms [1] (C/L: Irving Berlin); I've Got a Sweet Tooth Bothering Me (C/L: Irving Berlin); Just We Two; Little Bandbox Girl; Live for Today; Love Me at Twilight (C: Bert Grant; L: William Jerome; Joe Young); My Ninette; Old Home Town; Other Side, The; Step This Way [2] (C/L: Irving Berlin); They All Look Good to Me; Tripping, Tripping; When the Sun Goes Down in Romany (C: Bert Grant; L: Sam M. Lewis; Joe Young); When We Are Married; When We Were Twenty-One; When You Drop Off at Cairo, Illinois (C: Cliff Hess; L: E. Ray Goetz); Wonderful Girl; You Ought to Go to Paris

Cast: Lew Brice; Gladys Clark; Lew Fields; Alice Fisher; John Charles Thomas; Ernest Torrence

Notes: Program of Washington, D.C. 12/31/17 used as basis with additional sources. No New York program available. This was a revised version of THE GIRL BEHIND THE COUNTER. [1] Sheet music only. Also in ZIEGFELD FOLLIES OF 1916. [2] May not be by Berlin. [3] ASCAP/Library of Congress only.

4149 • STEPHEN FOSTER STORY, THE

OPENED: 1973
Musical

Composer: Stephen Foster
Lyricist: Stephen Foster
Director: Horace L. Kelly

Arrangements: Isaac Van Grove; **Choreographer:** Scot Ray; **Costumes:** Anne S. Arnold; **Lighting Designer:** Edward M. Carty Jr.; **Musical Director:** William C. Cathon

Songs: Ah, May the Red Rose Live Alway; Away Down Souf; Beautiful Dreamer; Beautiful Shore, The; Camptown Races; Comrades Fill No Glass for Me; Don't Bet Your Money on de Shanghai; Down on the River; Gentle Annie; Glendy Burk; Hour for Thee and Me, The; If Only You Had a Moustache; Jeannie with the Light Brown Hair; Katy Bill; Louisiana Belle; Merry Little Birds Are We; My Old Kentucky Home; Nelly Bly; Oh! Leonard!; Oh, Susanna; Oh, Why Am I So Happy?; Old Brudder Gum; Old Dog Trey; Old Folks at Home; Open the Lattice, Love; Ring, Ring de Banjo; Some Folks Do; There's No Such Girl As Mine; Why No One to Love?; Wilt Thou Be Gone, Love?

Cast: David Brown; Gary Holcombe; Daune Mahy; Nancy Owen

Notes: Produced at My Old Kentucky Home State Park in Bardstown, KY. as an annual summer show. All songs by Stephen Foster, obviously not written for this production.

4150 • STEPPING STONES, THE

OPENED: 01/16/1923   Theatre: Globe
Musical   Broadway: 241

Composer: Jerome Kern
Lyricist: Anne Caldwell
Librettist: R.H. Burnside; Anne Caldwell
Producer: Charles Dillingham
Director: R.H. Burnside

Musical Director: Victor Baravalle; **Orchestrations:** Robert Russell Bennett

Songs: Babbling Babette; Because You Love the Singer; Cane Dance (inst.); Dear Little Peter Pan; Dolls [2]; Growing Man, The [2]; I Saw the Roses and Remembered You [1] (L: Herbert Reynolds); In Love with Love [3]; Little Angel Cake; Little Gypsy Lady [2]; (Everybody Calls Me) Little Red Riding Hood; Magician Does His Stuff, The [2]; Mystic Hussars, The; National Dish, The [2]; Nursery Clock, The (inst.); Once in a Blue Moon; Our Lovely Rose; Palace Dance (inst); Pie; Prelude to Puppet Scene (inst.); Raggedy Ann; Skeleton Janitor, The; Stepping Stones; When I Went to School [2]; White Cavaliers, The [2]; Wonderful Dad; Wood Nymphs, The

Cast: Evelyn Herbert; Roy Hoyer; Bert Jordan; John Lambert; Oscar Ragland; Tony Sarg's Marionettes; Allene Stone; Dorothy Stone; Fred Stone; Tiller Sunshine Girls; Lilyan White; Ruth White; Jack Whiting

Notes: [1] Cut during rehearsals. [2] Out New Haven 10/16/23. [3] Same music as "Die Susse Pariserin" from DIE BALLKONIGIN and "If You're a Friend of Mine" in LADY MARY.

4151 • STICKS AND BONES

OPENED: 11/07/1971   Theatre: Public
Play   Off-Broadway: 366

Producer: N.Y. Shakespeare Festival; Joseph Papp
Director: Jeff Bleckner

Costumes: Theoni V. Aldredge; **Lighting Designer:** Ian Calderon; **Set Design:** Santo Loquasto

Songs: Baby When I Find You (C: Galt MacDermot; L: David Rabe)

Cast: Tom Aldredge; Cliff DeYoung; David Rabe; Drew Snyder; Elizabeth Wilson

Notes: Transferred to Broadway's John Golden on 3/1/72 for 244 performances.

4152 • STICKS AND STONES (1939)

OPENED: 08/14/1939
Revue   Los Angeles: 1

Librettist: Edward Eliscu; Harold Goldman; Kathleen Goldman; Arthur Kober; Hy Kraft; Allen Rivkin; William C. White
Producer: Motion Pictures Artists Co.
Director: Garson Kanin; John Murray

Costumes: Gladys Carroll; **Musical Director:** John Green

Songs: Broken Guitar, A (C: Jay Gorney; L: E.Y. Harburg); California (C: John Green; L: Edward Eliscu); Hitler und Goering und Goebbels und Schacht (C: Jay Gorney; L: E.Y. Harburg); I Sits Down (C: John Green; L: Hy Kraft); It Can't Happen Here (C/L: John Murray); It's a Noel Coward Custom (C/L: Lee Brody); Red Blues (L: Lee Brody); Send for the Militia (C/L: Marc Blitzstein); Swing Left, Sweet Chariot (C: Ray Henderson; L: Dorothy Fields); (T' Me Baby) You're News (C: John Green; L: Ira Gershwin; E.Y. Harburg)

Cast: Jack Albertson; Eve Arden; Milton Berle; Edith Evans; John Garfield; Bert Lahr; Ray Mayer

4153 • STICKS AND STONES (1957)

OPENED: 06/30/1957
Revue   Closed out of town

Librettist: George Bauer; Dee Caruso; Herbert Farjeon; Hermione Gingold; Murray Grand; Nina Warner Hook; Lucille Kallen; Constance Kelly; Walter Leigh; Charles Manna; Dennis Waldock
Producer: Ron Rawson
Director: John Fearnley

Choreographer: John Heawood; **Costumes:** Paul Morrison; **Dance Arranger:** George Bauer; **Lighting Designer:** Elliot Krancer; **Musical Director:** George Bauer; **Set Design:** Hal Shafer; **Vocal Arranger:** George Bauer

Songs: Black Widow (C/L: Peter Cadby); Borgia Orgy (C/L: John Jowitt); Cloudy Morning (C: Joseph McCarthy; L: Marvin Fisher); Come By Sunday (C/L: Murray Grand); Daisy Goes Out with Bert (C: Walter Leigh; L: Herbert Farjeon); Finale Tune (C/L: Leslie Julian Jones); Hats (C/L: George Bauer); I Came Here to Dance (C: Alan Jeffreys; L: Tommy Garlock); I Want More (C/L: Alan Jeffreys); Ill Met (dance) (C: George Bauer); Jewel Song (C/L: Murray Grand); Let Me Run to You (C/L: Allistair Thompson); Man Upon My Mind (C: George Bauer; L: Charles Gaynor); Moonlight on the Ganges (C: Sherman Miles; L: Chester Wallace); Mother's Day (C/L: Portia Nelson); My Faces of 1958 (C: Murray Grand;

L: Hermione Gingold); Nobody Ever Asked Me (C/L: Buster Davis); Office Hours (C/L: Irving Berlin); People Were Nice (C: Buster Davis; L: Mark Lawrence); Play Street (C: Walter Leigh); Queen of Song (C/L: Jack Strachey); Sign of the Times (C: David Baker; L: Ira Wallach); Southern Discomfort (C/L: Louise Hoff); Sticks and Stones (C: David Baker; L: David Craig); Well Met (dance) (C: George Bauer); Which Witch? (C: Charles Zwar; L: Alan Melville); Woman's Day, A (C/L: Peter Cadby)

Cast: Jack Fletcher; Hermione Gingold; Charles Manna; Marti Stevens

Notes: Closed 8/25/57 — Cincinnati.

4154 • STILL DANCING

OPENED: 09/11/1925   Theatre: London Pavillion
Revue   London: 114

Librettist: John Bull; Marc Henry
Producer: Charles B. Cochran
Director: Ernest Thesiger

Choreographer: Leonide Massine; Max Rivers; **Costumes:** Geza Farago; William Nicholson; Max Weldy; Doris Zinkeisen; **Musical Director:** J.B. Hastings; **Set Design:** Geza Farago; William Nicholson; Doris Zinkeisen

Songs: First Up Is the Best Dressed, The (C: Ivor Novello; L: Arthur Wimperis); Georgie (C/L: Chateau Albertino); I'm Tired of Everything but You (C/L: Isham Jones); Lady of the Moon [1] (C: Eubie Blake; L: Noble Sissle); Poppy (C: Melville Ellis; L: Arthur Wimperis); Pyjama Jazz (C: Marc Anthony; L: Arthur Wimperis); Rake, The (Ballet) (C: Roger Quilter); Remember (C/L: Irving Berlin); South Sea Blues (C: Marc Anthony; L: Arthur Wimperis); Still Dancing (C/L: Philip Braham); That Means Nothing to Me (C: Worton David; L: Godfrey)

Cast: Hermione Baddeley; Nigel Bruce; Douglas Byng; Alice Delysia; Pat Kendall; Leonide Massine; Ernest Thesiger

Notes: [1] Not in program.

4155 • STINGIEST MAN IN TOWN, THE

OPENED: 12/23/1956   Theatre: NBC
TV Musical

Composer: Fred Spielman
Lyricist: Janice Torre
Producer: Joel Spector
Director: Dan Petrie

Source: CHRISTMAS CAROL, A (Story: Charles Dickens); **Choreographer:** John Heawood; **Costumes:** Motley; **Musical Director:** Tutti Camarata; **Set Design:** Kim Swados

Songs: Birthday Party of the King; Christmas Carol, A; Christmas Spirit, The; Concerto Inferno (inst.); Golden Dreams; Humbug; I Wear a Chain; It Might Have Been; Mankind Should Be My Business; Old Fashioned Christmas, An; One Little Boy; Spirit Theme; Stingiest Man in Town, The; Yes, There Is a Santa Claus

Cast: Philippa Bevans; Jack Bittner; Vic Damone; Johnny Desmond; Four Lads, The; Martyn Green; Betty Madigan; Patrice Munsel; Basil Rathbone; Robert Weede; Robert Wright

Notes: Original television musical.

4156 • STOCK IN TRADE

OPENED: 07/10/1953
Revue

Producer: Bud McCreery; Julius Monk
Director: Julius Monk

Cast: Jack Fletcher; Bibi Osterwald; Alice Pearce; **Pianist:** Edward C. Redding

Notes: Performed in Bermuda. No other information available.

4157 • STONES OF JEHOSHAPHAT, THE

OPENED: 12/17/1963   Theatre: Rodale
Musical   Off-Broadway: 6

Composer: Dede Meyer
Lyricist: Dede Meyer
Librettist: J.J. Rodale
Producer: J.J. Rodale
Director: John Glines

Choreographer: Eleanor Chapin; **Costumes:** Freida Evans; **Set Design:** Chuck Eisler

Songs: Beauteous Is the Bride; I Could Go with the Wind; Jehoshaphat Makes Up His Mind; Jester's

Tale, The; Long Live the Greedy; Look Through the Moongate; Man Who Speaks for Himself, A; Psalm of Jehoshaphat, The; Riblah's Lament; Song of the Witch; Stones of Jehoshaphat, The; Talk with One's Conscience, A; Wedding Celebration, The

Cast: Ernie Adano; R.D. Blitz; John Clifton; Rochelle Marek; Robert Morea; Prima Stefanni

4158 • STOP! LOOK! LISTEN!

OPENED: 12/25/1915   Theatre: Globe
Musical   Broadway: 105

Composer: Irving Berlin
Lyricist: Irving Berlin
Librettist: Harry B. Smith
Producer: Charles Dillingham
Director: R.H. Burnside

Costumes: Robert McQuinn; **Musical Director:** Robert Hood Bowers; **Orchestrations:** Frank Saddler; **Set Design:** Robert McQuinn

Songs: And Father Wanted Me to Learn a Trade; Blow Your Horn; England Every Time for Me [1]; Everything in America Is Ragtime; Girl on the Magazine Cover, The; I Love a Piano; I Love to Dance; I'll Be Coming Home with a Skate On (Skating Song); Law Must Be Obeyed, The; Oozums; Opening Chorus; Pair of Ordinary Coons, A; Ragtime Melodrama; Sailor Song [2]; Stop! Look! Listen!; Take Off a Little Bit; Teach Me How to Love; That Hula-Hula; Until I Fell in Love with You [2]; When I Get Back to the U.S.A.; When I'm Out with You; Why Don't They Give Us a Chance

Cast: Marion Davies; Gaby Deslys; Doyle & Dixon; Harry Fox; Frank Lalor; Harry Pilcer; Joseph Santley; Blossom Seeley; Marion Sunshine; Florence Tempest

Notes: Titled FOLLOW THE CROWD in London. [1] Written for London version. [2] Sheet music only.

4159 • STOP PRESS

OPENED: 02/21/1935   Theatre: Adelphi
Revue   London

Composer: Irving Berlin
Lyricist: Irving Berlin

Producer: Hassard Short
Director: Clifford Wheatley

Songs: Beggar's Dream [1] (C: Arthur Schwartz; L: Howard Dietz); Confession [1] (C: Arthur Schwartz; L: Howard Dietz); Easter Parade; How Can I Hold You Close Enough (C: Johnny Green; L: E.Y. Harburg; Edward Heyman); How's Chances?; Lonely Heart; You and the Night and the Music [2] (C: Arthur Schwartz; L: Howard Dietz)

Cast: Eve Becke; Charles Collins; Dorothy Dickson; Robert Helpmann; Phyllis Monkman; Margaret Sande; Edwin Styles

Notes: No program available. The British version of AS THOUSANDS CHEER. [1] From THE BAND WAGON. [2] From REVENGE WITH MUSIC.

4160 • STOP THE WORLD - I WANT TO GET OFF

OPENED: 10/03/1962   Theatre: Shubert
Musical   Broadway: 556

Composer: Leslie Bricusse; Anthony Newley
Lyricist: Leslie Bricusse; Anthony Newley
Librettist: Leslie Bricusse; Anthony Newley
Producer: David Merrick
Director: Anthony Newley

Choreographer: John Broome; Virginia Mason; **Costumes:** Kiki Byrne; **Lighting Designer:** Sean Kenny; **Musical Director:** Milton Rosenstock; **Orchestrations:** Ian Fraser; Gordon Langford; David Lindup; Burt Rhodes; **Set Design:** Sean Kenny

Songs: A.B.C. Song, The; All American [3]; Family Fugue; Glorious Russian [3]; Gonna Build a Mountain; I Want to Be Rich; Life Is a Woman [1]; Lumbered; Meilinki Meilchick; Mumbo Jumbo; Nag! Nag! Nag!; Once in a Lifetime; Someone Nice Like You; Special Announcement, A; Typically English [3]; Typische Deutsche [3]; Welcome to Sludgepool [2]; Welcome to Sunvale [2]; What Kind of Fool Am I?

Cast: Jennifer Baker; Susan Baker; Anthony Newley; Anna Quayle

Notes: [1] Added to revival. [2] Same music. [3] Same music.

4161 • STORKS, THE

OPENED: 05/18/1902 Theatre: Dearborn
Musical   Chicago

Composer: Fredric Chapin
Lyricist: Guy F. Steeley
Librettist: Richard Carle; Guy F. Steeley
Director: W.W. Tillotson

Songs: Fisher and the Mermaid, The [2]; Flirtie Little Gertie (C/L: Richard Carle); He Disappeared [1] (C/L: Richard Carle); It's All Such a Horrible Bore [1]; It's Up with the Cup and Down with the Ale; Merry Mystic Man (I Did It), The [1]; Mystic Sorcerers; Noble Ladies [1]; Picnic Song, The; Rosebud Queen; Sad Is the Whippoorwill; Soldiers to the King [1]; Song of the Night; Sorrow Is Mine; Sweet Penelope; Terrible Puppy Dog [1]; That Was the Last That I Remembered; That's How Calisthenics Go [1]; Tootsie Wootsie; We Are Strolling Peddlers [1]; What! Marry?; When the Cuckoo Met the Pussy Cat [1]

Cast: Richard Carle; Myra Davis; May DeSousa; Ada Deaves; Josie Intropodi; Francis Lieb; William Rock; Edmund Stanley; Jessie Stanley; Gus Weinberg; Alma Youlin

Notes: Program of 2/18/03 used. [1] Sheet music only. [2] Out Boston 2/18/03.

4162 • STORYVILLE

OPENED: 01/27/1979
Musical   Closed out of town

Composer: Mildred Kayden
Lyricist: Mildred Kayden
Librettist: Ed Bullins
Producer: Ford's Theatre Society; Frankie Hewitt
Director: Arthur Faria

Choreographer: Arthur Faria; **Costumes:** Carol Oditz; **Dance Arranger:** Luther Henderson; **Lighting Designer:** Neil Peter Jampolis; **Orchestrations:** Luther Henderson; **Set Design:** John Lee Beatty; **Vocal Arranger:** Luther Henderson

Songs: Animal Stomp; Back o' Town; Best Is Yet to Be, The; Blue Book; Everybody's Got Something; Fat Tuesday Parade; Feel That Jazz; Makin' It; Mamma Taught Me; Prove It; Rollin' Up the River; So Beautiful; What's for Real

Cast: Edye Byrde; Ira Hawkins

4163 • STOVEPIPE HAT

OPENED: 1944
Musical   Closed out of town

Composer: Harold Spina
Lyricist: Harold Spina
Librettist: Harold Spina
Producer: Dan Seymour
Director: Harold Spina

Choreographer: June Morris; **Musical Director:** Ray Henderson; **Set Design:** Charles T. Morrison Jr.

Songs: Aches, Pains an' Strains; Battle Was Over, It Was Quiet Now, The; Great Man Says, The [1] (L: Edward Heyman); He Lost; He Walks Across the Sky (L: Edward Heyman); Honest Abe (L: Walter F. Hannan; Harold Spina); How Do I Grow a Rose?; I Know a Man; Illinois Republican, An (L: Walter F. Hannan; Harold Spina); It Looks Like More People Were Agin' Him; It Would Be No Holiday; Let's Walk Home the Long Way 'Round (L: Edward Heyman); Lincoln Soliloquy (L: Walter F. Hannan; Harold Spina); Loo-Low; Love Was Young As an April Leaf (L: Walter F. Hannan; Harold Spina); Lovely Lady [1] (L: Edward Heyman); Mother's Prayer, A (L: Edward Heyman); Seven Miles; Softly My Heart Is Singing [1] (L: Edward Heyman); Spiked Fist of War, The; Sweethcart's Cotillion, The; There Were a Lot o' People for 'Im; There's Trouble Brewin'; Until Eternity; Yes I Know It Was Long Ago (L: Walter F. Hannan; Harold Spina)

Cast: Tex Ritter

Notes: No program available. [1] ASCAP/Library of Congress only.

4164 • STRANGE ADVENTURES OF JACK AND THE BEANSTALK, THE

Notes: *See JACK AND THE BEANSTALK (1896).*

4165 • STRANGER IN NEW YORK

OPENED: 09/13/1897 Theatre: Garrick
Play   Broadway: 64

Composer: Richard Stahl
Lyricist: Charles H. Hoyt
Author: Charles H. Hoyt
Producer: Charles H. Hoyt; Frank McKee
Director: Charles H. Hoyt

Costumes: Dazian; **Set Design:** Arthur Voegtlin

Songs: Baron's Star Act, The; Broadway Beauty Show, The; Choir Boy, The; Father, Won't You Speak to Sister Mary? (C: A. Baldwin Sloane); Gayest Old Sport, The; Hattie; I've Got Him Dead; Languid Man, The; Lou and Sue; Love's Serenade; March Song; Once Excess Baggage; Pattison Valse Song; They're Always Taking Me for Someone Else; Walker's Dancing School (C: A. Baldwin Sloane)

Cast: Nellie Butler; Harry Conor; Harry Gilfoil; Sadie Martinot; Amelia Stone; Lloyd Wilson

Notes: No songs listed in program. Songs from programs of 9/17/1898 and 12/25/1898.

4166 • STRAW HAT REVUE, THE

OPENED: 09/29/1939   Theatre: Ambassador
Revue   Broadway: 75

Composer: Sylvia Fine
Lyricist: Sylvia Fine
Librettist: Max Liebman
Producer: Harry Kaufman; Messrs. Shubert
Director: Max Liebman

Choreographer: Jerome Andrews; **Musical Director:** Edward A. Hunt; **Set Design:** Edward Gilbert

Songs: Anatole of Paris; Crashing Through; Four Young People (C/L: James Shelton); Great Chandler, The; Our Town (C/L: James Shelton); Swingaroo Trio, The

Cast: Jerome Andrews; Leon Barte; Dorothy Bird; Ruthanna Boris; Lee Brody; Robert Burton; Imogene Coca; Alfred Drake; Bronson Dudley; Otto Hari; Albia Kavan; Danny Kaye; Meta Mata; Jerome Robbins; James Shelton

4167 • STRAWS IN THE WIND

OPENED: 02/21/1975   Theatre: American Place
Revue   Off-Broadway: 33

Composer: Cy Coleman
Lyricist: Betty Comden; Adolph Green
Librettist: Donald Bartholomae; Marshall Brickman; Lanny Meyers; Peter Stone
Producer: American Place Theatre
Director: Phyllis Newman

Costumes: Ruth Morley; **Lighting Designer:** Roger Morgan; **Musical Director:** Lanny Meyers; **Set Design:** Peter Harvey

Songs: Finale; Goin' Home; In Which to Marry Me (C: Galt MacDermot; L: Ira Gasman); It's Not Such a Brave New World, Mr. Huxley (C: Galt MacDermot; L: Ira Gasman); Lost Word; Noah (C/L: Stephen Schwartz); Opening; Simplified Language; You'll Have Your Moment (C/L: Billy Nichols)

Cast: Tovah Feldshuh; Carol Jean Lewis; Brandon Maggart; Josh Mostel; George Pentecost

4168 • STREET JESUS

OPENED: 11/16/1974   Theatre: People's
                      Performing Company
Musical   Off-Off-Broadway: 52

Composer: Peter Copani; Chris Staudt
Lyricist: Peter Copani
Librettist: Peter Copani
Producer: Peoples Performing Company
Director: Peter Copani

Choreographer: John Werkheiser; **Costumes:** Gary Langley; **Lighting Designer:** Gary Langley; **Musical Director:** Ed Vogel; **Set Design:** Gary Langley

Songs: Bad But Good; Better Day, A; Corruption; Dance; Down on Me; Flame of Life; For the Good Times; Friends; God's in the People; Good News, The; Hail, Hail; If Jesus Walked the Earth Today; In the Name of Love; L'America Ha Fato per Te [1]; Love Is Beautiful; Make Them Hate; Manufacture and Sell; One of Us; Riot; Special Man; Strawberries, Pickles and Ice Cream; Street Jesus; Today Will Be; Wait and See; Who Can Say

Cast: Larry Campbell; Robin Cantor; Regina Cashone; Aixa Clemente; Joe Garrambone; Michael D. Knowles; Angel Martin; Vernon Spencer; Anita Tamaino; Meri Weiner

Notes: [1] Also in FIRE OF FLOWERS.

4169 • STREET SCENE

OPENED: 01/09/1947   Theatre: Adelphi
Musical   Broadway: 148

Composer: Kurt Weill
Lyricist: Langston Hughes
Librettist: Elmer Rice
Producer: Playwrights' Company, The; Dwight Deere Wiman
Director: Charles Friedman

Choreographer: Anna Sokolow; **Costumes:** Lucinda Ballard; **Dance Arranger:** Kurt Weill; **Lighting Designer:** Jo Mielziner; **Musical Director:** Maurice Abravanel; **Orchestrations:** Kurt Weill; **Set Design:** Jo Mielziner; **Vocal Arranger:** Kurt Weill

Songs: Ain't It Awful the Heat (L: Langston Hughes; Elmer Rice); Boy Like You, A; Buon Giorno, Signore [1]; Catch Me If You Can; Children's Game (L: Langston Hughes; Elmer Rice); Colombo [1]; Don't Forget the Lilac Bush (L: Langston Hughes; Elmer Rice); Farewell Duet; Fat, Fat, the Water Rat; Get a Load of That (L: Langston Hughes; Elmer Rice); Gossip; Great Big Sky, The [1]; Hail to the School; Hot-Dog Waltz [1]; I Got a Marble and a Star; I Live for That Day [1]; I Loved Her Too (L: Langston Hughes; Elmer Rice); Ice Cream; Italy in Technicolor [1]; It's the Irish [1]; Kids in School, The [1]; Let Things Be Like They Always Was; Little Swing for Swinging, A [1]; Lonely House; Lullaby (Sleep Baby Dear) (L: Elmer Rice); Moon-Faced, Starry Eyed; Morning; Nation of Nations, A [1]; Remember That I Care; Rose's Goodbye to Easter [1]; Somehow I Never Could Believe; Street Light Is My Moonlight; That's Where Our Horoscopes Lie (She's a Gemini Girl) [1]; There'll Be Trouble (L: Langston Hughes; Elmer Rice); We'll Go Away Together; What Good Would the Moon Be?; When a Woman Has a Baby (L: Langston Hughes; Elmer Rice); Woman Who Lived Up There, The (L: Langston Hughes; Elmer Rice); Wouldn't You Like to Be on Broadway? (L: Langston Hughes; Elmer Rice); Wrapped in a Ribbon (and Tied in a Bow) (L: Langston Hughes; Elmer Rice)

Cast: Sheila Bond; Danny Daniels; Hope Emerson; Peter Griffith; Anne Jeffreys; Irving Kaufman; Polyna Stoska; Brian Sullivan

Notes: [1] Cut prior to opening.

4170 • STREET SINGER, THE

OPENED: 09/17/1929   Theatre: Shubert
Musical   Broadway: 189

Composer: Jean Gilbert; Nicholas Kempner; Sammy Timberg
Lyricist: Graham John
Librettist: Edgar Smith; Cyrus Wood
Producer: Busby Berkeley
Director: Busby Berkeley

Choreographer: Busby Berkeley; **Costumes:** Barbier; **Musical Director:** Pierre de Reeder; **Set Design:** Watson Barratt

Songs: From Now On (C: Richard Myers; L: Edward Eliscu); Girl That I'll Adore, The; I May Be Wrong; Jumping Jimminy (C: Nicholas Kempner); Knocking on Wood; My Little Piano Man; Oh, Theobold, Oh, Elmer; Opening; Opening Act II; So Beats My Heart for You [1] (C/L: Pat Ballard; Charles Henderson; Tom Waring); Statues; When Everything Is Hunky-Dory; You Might Have Known I Loved You [2]; You Never Can Tell; You've Made Me Happy Today! (C: Nicholas Kempner)

Cast: Nell Kelly; Nick Long Jr.; Harry K. Morton; Guy Robertson; Cesar Romero; Queenie Smith; Andrew Tombes

Notes: [1] Out Detroit 10/26/30. [2] Sheet music only.

4171 • STREETHEAT

OPENED: 01/27/1985   Theatre: 54th Street Theater Cabaret
Revue   Broadway: 20

Producer: Bert Stratford
Director: Rick Atwell

Choreographer: Rick Atwell; **Costumes:** Franne Lee; **Dance Arranger:** James Gregory; Frank Owens; **Lighting Designer:** John McLain; **Orchestrations:** James Gregory; Frank Owens; **Set Design:** Franne Lee

Songs: Danger Men Working (C/L: James Curiale; Bob Garrett); Full Circle (C/L: Charles Mortimer; Laura Taylor); Hold On (C/L: Chris Darway); I Want a Real Man (C/L: Geoff Bradford); I'm a Wow (C/L: Ron Abel; Bob Garrett); King

Becomes a Clown, The (C/L: Laura Taylor); Lucky Louie (C/L: Rick Atwell; Perry Arthur Kroeger; Frank Owens); Nirvana (C/L: James Gregory; Perry Arthur Kroeger); Picasso's Theme (inst.) (C: Frank Owens); Power (C/L: Dave Mortiz; Vinnie Rich); Power Lies Within, The (C/L: Rick Atwell; James Gregory; Joe Hudson); Sacrifice Your Body (C/L: Rick Atwell; James Gregory; Charles Mortimer); To Dance Is To Fly (C/L: Kyra Kaptzan); Today I Found Me (C/L: Laura Taylor); Uptown Dreamer's Express (C/L: Rick Atwell; James Gregory); We Paint Life (C/L: Rick Atwell; Perry Arthur Kroeger)

Cast: Michael DeLorenzo; James Arthur Johnson; Vicki Lewis; Ron Lee Savin; Glenn Scarpelli; Tico Wells

4172 • STREETS OF GOLD, THE

OPENED: 11/25/1977
Musical   Off-Broadway: 12

Composer: Ted Simmons
Lyricist: Marvin Gordon
Librettist: Marvin Gordon
Producer: Ballet Concepts; Workmen's Circle, The
Director: Scott Redman

Choreographer: Tony Masullo; **Costumes:** A. Christina Giannini; **Lighting Designer:** Clarke Thornton; **Musical Director:** Harrison Fisher; **Set Design:** Michael Molly

Songs: Another Cold Day; Another Sad Penny; Buy My Passamentaries; Coney Island; Dreidel; Greenhorn; Hester Street; Hottest Knishe; Kravitz to Snyder to Smith; Look Around You; Old Ways; Pogrom Ballet; Sabbath Blessing; Streets of Gold; Tammany; This Time; Troubles of My Own; Why Can't I

Cast: Annie Abbott; Dorothy Chansky; Paul Corman; Nancy Diaz; Susan Jacks; Tom Lantzy; Shifee Lovitt; Donald Mark; Jared Matesky; Gregory Salata; Stuart Silver

4173 • STREETS OF NEW YORK, THE

OPENED: 10/29/1963   Theatre: Maidman
Musical   Off-Broadway: 318

Composer: Richard B. Chodosh
Lyricist: Barry Alan Grael

Librettist: Barry Alan Grael
Producer: Gene Dingenary; Jane Gilliland
Director: Joseph Hardy

Source: STREETS OF NEW YORK, THE (Play Dion Boucicault); **Choreographer:** Neal Kenyon; **Costumes:** W. Thomas Seitz; **Lighting Designer:** Howard Becknell; **Musical Director:** Jack Holmes; **Set Design:** Howard Becknell; **Vocal Arranger:** Jack Holmes

Songs: Aren't You Warm?; Arms for the Love of Me; California; Christmas Carol; Close Your Eyes; First Act Finale; He'll Come to Me Crawling; I May Blush from Anger [1]; If I May; Laugh After Laugh; Love Wins Again; Prologue; Tourist Madrigal; Where Can the Rich and Poor Be Friends

Cast: Ian Brown; David Cryer; Barry Alan Grael; Margot Hand; Ralston Hill; Gail Johnston; Barbara Williams

Notes: [1] Cut.

4174 • STREETS OF PARIS, THE

OPENED: 06/19/1939   Theatre: Broadhurst
Revue   Broadway: 274

Composer: Jimmy McHugh
Lyricist: Al Dubin
Librettist: Lee Brody; Edward Duryea Dowling; Frank Eyton; S. Jay Kaufman; James Laver; Tom McKnight; Charles Sherman
Producer: Chic Johnson; Ole Olsen; Messrs. Shubert
Director: Edward Duryea Dowling

Choreographer: Robert Alton; **Costumes:** Irene Sharaff; **Musical Director:** John McManus; **Orchestrations:** Hans Spialek; **Set Design:** Lawrence L. Goldwasser; **Vocal Arranger:** Hugh Martin

Songs: Danger in the Dark; Doin' the Chamberlain; French Have a Word for It, The (C/L: Harold Rome); History Is Made at Night (C/L: Harold Rome); Is It Possible?; Reading, Writing and a Little Bit of Rhythm; Rendezvous Time in Paree; Robert the Roue (from Reading, Pa.) [1]; South American Way; Streets of Paris, The; Thanks for the Francs; Three Little Maids; We Can Live on Love (We Haven't Got a Pot to Cook In)

Cast: Bud Abbott; Yvonne Bouvier; Billy Branch; Gower Champion; Bobby Clark; Lou Costello; Ben Dova; Luella Gear; Gloria Gilbert; Hylton Sisters, The; Margaret Irving; Della Lind; Hugh Martin; Jack McCauley; Carmen Miranda; Jeanne Readinger; Jo Readinger; Jean Sablon; Jeanne Tyler; Ramon Vinay

Notes: [1] Later in STAR AND GARTER.

4175 • STREETSONGS

OPENED: 10/14/1980   Theatre: Roundabout
Revue   Off-Broadway: 16

Librettist: Geraldine Fitzgerald
Producer: Roundabout Theater Company
Director: Richard Maltby Jr.

Costumes: Bill Walker; **Lighting Designer:** Robert F. Strohmeier; **Musical Director:** Stanley Wietrzychowski; **Orchestrations:** Philip Campanella; Stanley Wietrzychowski

Cast: Geraldine Fitzgerald

Notes: No original songs.

4176 • STRIDER

OPENED: 05/31/1979   Theatre: Chelsea Theatre
                              Center
Play   Off-Broadway: 615

Composer: M. Rozovsky; S. Vetkin
Additional Music: Norman L. Berman
Lyricist: Uri Riashentsev
English Lyrics: Steve Brown
Author: Mark Rozovsky
Producer: Miriam Bienstock; Chelsea Theatre Center; Lita Starr; Arthur Whitelaw
Director: Lynne Gannaway; Robert Kalfin

Source: UNKNOWN (Story: Leo Tolstoy); **Costumes:** Andrew B. Marlay; **Lighting Designer:** Robby Monk; **Musical Director:** Norman L. Berman; **Orchestrations:** Norman L. Berman; **Set Design:** Wolfgang Roth; **Vocal Arranger:** Norman L. Berman

Cast: Pamela Burrell; Roger De Koven; Gordon Gould; Gerald Hiken; Ronnie Newman

Notes: After 401 performances, moved to Broadway's Helen Hayes Theatre on 11/14/79 for another 214 performances.

4177 • STRIKE ME PINK

OPENED: 03/04/1933   Theatre: Majestic
Revue   Broadway: 122

Composer: Ray Henderson
Lyricist: Lew Brown
Librettist: Lew Brown; Mack Gordon; Ray Henderson; Jack McGowan
Producer: Lew Brown; Waxey Gordon; Ray Henderson
Director: Lew Brown; Ray Henderson; Jack McGowan

Choreographer: Seymour Felix; **Costumes:** Kiviette; Charles LeMaire; **Musical Director:** Alfred Goodman; **Set Design:** Henry Dreyfuss

Songs: Forward March [3]; Hollywood, Park Avenue and Broadway [2]; Home to Harlem; I Hate to Think That You'll Grow Old Baby; If I Feel This Way Tomorrow (Then It's Love) [4]; It's Great to Be Alive [1]; Let's Call It a Day; Love and Rhythm; Old Mother Nature [3]; On Any Street [2]; Ooh, I'm Thinking; Restless; Steins [3]; Strike Me Pink; Theatre Marquis [3]; Torch Songs [3]

Cast: Roy Atwell; Gracie Barrie; Dorothy Dare; Johnny Downs; Jimmy Durante; Alex Fisher; Eddie Garr; Ruth Harrison; Hal LeRoy; Carolyn Nolte; Lupe Velez; Will Vodery Singers; George Dewey Washington; Milton Watson; Hope Williams

Notes: [1] Originally in HOT-CHA! [2] Not in program. [3] Out 10/17/32 when titled FORWARD MARCH. [4] Not used. Lyric used in its 1936 STRIKE ME PINK film.

4178 • STRIKE UP THE BAND (1927)

OPENED: 08/29/1927
Musical   Closed out of town

Composer: George Gershwin
Lyricist: Ira Gershwin
Librettist: George S. Kaufman
Producer: Edgar Selwyn
Director: R.H. Burnside

Choreographer: John Boyle; **Musical Director:** William Daly

Songs: Come-Look-at-the-War Choral Society [4]; Finaletto, Act I; Fletcher's American Cheese

Choral Society [2]; Girl I Love, The; Homeward Bound; Hoping That Some Day You'd Care [3]; How About a Man? [2]; Jim, Consider What You Are Doing!; Man I Love, The [1]; Meadow Serenade; Military Dancing Drill; Nursie, Nursie [5]; Oh, This Is Such a Lovely War; Patriotic Rally; 17 and 21 (Seventeen and Twenty-One); Strike Up the Band! [2]; Typical Self-Made American [2]; Unofficial Spokesman, The [2]; War That Ended War, The; Yankee Doodle Rhythm

Cast: Herbert Corthell; Morton Downey; Vivian Hart; Max Hoffmann Jr.; Edna May Oliver; Roger Pryor; Jimmy Savo

Notes: Tryouts: Long Branch, N.J. 8/29/27 and Philadelphia 9/5/27. The show was revised in 1930. *See also STRIKE UP THE BAND* (1930). [1] Cut from both ROSALIE and LADY, BE GOOD! [2] Later in revised version of this show as "Fletcher's American Chocolate Choral Society." [3] Music of verse later used for the verse of "Soon" in the 1930 revision. [4] Probably not used. [5] Cut during rehearsals.

4179 • STRIKE UP THE BAND (1930)

OPENED: 01/14/1930   Theatre: Times Square
Musical   Broadway: 191

Composer: George Gershwin
Lyricist: Ira Gershwin
Librettist: Morrie Ryskind
Producer: Edgar Selwyn
Director: Alexander Leftwich

Source: STRIKE UP THE BAND (Musical: George Gershwin; Ira Gershwin; George S. Kaufman); **Choreographer:** George Hale; **Costumes:** Charles LeMaire; **Musical Director:** Hilding Anderson; **Set Design:** Raymond Sovey

Songs: Finaletto Act II, Scene 1 [2]; First There Was a Fletcher; Fletcher's American Chocolate Choral Society [5]; Hangin' Around with You; He Knows Milk [8]; How About a Boy? [10]; I Mean to Say; I Want to Be a War Bride [1]; If I Became the President; In the Rattle of the Battle; I've Got a Crush on You [3]; Mademoiselle in New Rochelle; Man of High Degree, A (Entrance of Colonel Homes) [4]; Military Dancing Drill [9]; Official Resume; Ring-a-Ding-a-Ding Dong Dell [11]; Soldier's March (Unofficial March of

General Holmes); Soon [6]; Strike Up the Band [4]; Thanks to You [2]; There Was Never Such a Charming War [12]; This Could Go on for Years [7]; Three Cheers for the Union! [7]; Typical Self-Made American, A [4]; Unofficial Spokesman, The [4]

Cast: Doris Carson; Bobby Clark; Dudley Clements; Helen Gilligan; Jerry Goff; Katherine Hamill; Paul McCullough; Red Nichols Orchestra; Blanche Ring; Gordon Smith

Notes: Revision of 1927 version of this show. *See also STRIKE UP THE BAND* (1927). [1] Deleted after opening. [2] Not used. [3] Also in TREASURE GIRL. [4] From previous version. [5] From previous version where it was titled "Fletcher's American Cheese Choral Society." [6] Music of verse is from verse of "Hoping that Someday You'd Care" from earlier version. The refrain is from the earlier version's "Finaletto Act I." [7] These songs together made up the "Patriotic Rally" from previous version. [8] Basically the same as "Finaletto Act I" from previous version. [9] With a new verse, same as in previous version. [10] Not the same song as "How About a Man" from previous version. [11] Earlier version not used in OH, KAY! [12] Not used. Lyric adapted from prior version's "Oh, This Is Such a Lovely War."

4180 • STRIP FOR ACTION

OPENED: 03/17/1956
Musical   Closed out of town

Composer: Jimmy McHugh
Lyricist: Harold Adamson
Librettist: Eli Basse; Paul Streger
Producer: Igor Cassini; Howard Hoyt
Director: Don Hershey

Source: STRIP FOR ACTION (Play: Russel Crouse; Howard Lindsay); **Choreographer:** James Starbuck; **Costumes:** Miles White; **Dance Arranger:** Roger Adams; **Lighting Designer:** Gene Braun; **Musical Director:** Buster Davis; **Orchestrations:** Ralph Burns; **Set Design:** Stewart Chaney

Songs: Chaps from Annapolis; Dame Crazy; Don't Join the Navy to See the World; Finishing School [1]; Good Old Days of Burlesque; Gotta Have a Man, Sometime; I Just Found Out about Love; I Just Want to Be a Song and Dance Man;

Kickin' Up a Storm; Love Me As Though There Was No Tomorrow; My Papa from Panama; Rock and Roll Bump; Strip for Action; Too Young to Go Steady; Welcome to Union City

Cast: Yvonne Adair; Lily Christine; Jerome Courtland; Joey Faye; Jessica James; Jack Whiting

Notes: [1] Not used.

4181 • STROLLERS, THE

OPENED: 06/24/1901   Theatre: Knickerbocker
Musical   Broadway: 70

Composer: Ludwig Englander
Lyricist: Harry B. Smith
Librettist: Harry B. Smith
Producer: George W. Lederer
Director: A.M. Holbrook

Source: DIE LANDSTREICHER (Play: Ludwig Englander; L. Krenn; Carl Lindau); **Costumes:** Caroline Siedle; **Musical Director:** Ludwig Englander; **Set Design:** Ernest Albert

Songs: Alone on My Honeymoon (C: Sager; L: Jeff T. Branen); Automobile Ensemble; Bold Hussars, The; Capital Punishment; English Coon Song, An; Finale Act I; Finale Act II; Good-Bye Little Girl, Good-Bye (C: Gus Edwards; L: Will D. Cobb); Gossip Chorus; I'm Tired (C: Jean Schwartz; L: William Jerome); Lady Bird (C: Evans Lloyd; L: Jeff T. Branen); Lesson in Flirtation, A; Opening Ensemble; Opening Ensemble Act II; Song of Loretta; Song of the Strollers; When the Orchestra Plays

Cast: Irene Bentley; Edwin Foy; Marie George; Harry Gilfoil; Francis Wilson

Notes: No songs listed in program. Songs listed from vocal score and sheet music. Best Plays lists the directors as Nixon & Zimmerman.

4182 • STRUT MISS LIZZY

OPENED: 06/03/1922   Theatre: National Winter Garden
Revue   Broadway: 96

Composer: Turner Layton
Lyricist: Henry Creamer
Librettist: Henry Creamer

Musical Director: Joe Jordan

Songs: Argentina; Bernice (C: Joe Jordan); Beware of the Chickens; Breakin' a Leg; Buzz Mirandy; Crooning; Dear Old Southland; Ebony Rag (C: Joe Jordan); Four Fo' Me; Hoola from Coney Isle; I'm Nobody's Girl; In Yama; Jazz Blues; Lonesome Longing Blues; Mandy; On a South Sea Isle; Some Sunny Day; Sweet Angeline; Way Down Yonder in New Orleans; When You Look in the Eyes of a Mule; Wyoming Lullaby

Cast: Alice Brown; Henry Creamer; Cora Green; Hamtree Harrington; Turner Layton; Grace Rector

4183 • STRUT YOUR STUFF

OPENED: 1920
Musical

Composer: Dave Payton
Lyricist: "Babe" Townsend
Librettist: "Babe" Townsend
Producer: Aaron Gates
Director: Dave Payton

Songs: Dancing Is the Work of the Evil One; Darktime Dancing School; Hold Me; Honey Child; I Want to Shimmy; Louisiana Blues; Summer Time; Wedding Blues, The

Cast: Billy Brown; Billy Gulfport; Gertrude Saunders; Margaret Ward Thomas

Notes: No other information available.

4184 • STRUTTIN' SAM FROM ALABAM'

OPENED: 1927
Musical

Composer: Charles Alpin
Lyricist: Charles Alpin
Librettist: Charles Alpin
Producer: Arthur Hockwald

Songs: Chin Chin Chinaman; Clever People, These Chinese; Dancing on the Old Plantation; Don't Think Because My Name Is Cleopatra; Girl I Left in Zanzibar, The; Guide Me Mystic Moon to Dixieland; I'd Rather Be a Street Sweeper; I'm a Samoan Maid; I'm the King; My Queen of Poppyland; On Our Carolina Honeymoon;

Samoan Dancing Girl, The; Struttin' Sam Is Coming Back to Dixie

Cast: Tom Harris; Margaret Jackson; Amy Loften; Mal Patton; Edward Tolliver; Mildred Washington

Notes: No other information available.

4185 • STUBBORN CINDERELLA, A

OPENED: 01/25/1909   Theatre: Broadway
Musical   Broadway: 88

Composer: Joseph E. Howard
Lyricist: Frank Adams; Will M. Hough
Librettist: Frank Adams; Will M. Hough
Producer: Mort H. Singer
Director: George Marion

Musical Director: Arthur Pell

Songs: Don't Be Anybody's Moon but Mine; Don't Be Cross with Me; Don't Teach Me to Swim Alone; Dream Minute (Finale Act II); Finale Act I; Hurrah for the Bars and Stripes [1]; If They'd Only Left Poor Adam's Rib Alone; I'm in Love with All the Girls I Know; I've Lost My Heart but I Don't Care; Land of the Sky, The (Adios Senorita) [3]; Landslide, The [3]; Love Me Just Because; My Land of Nod [2]; None but the Brave Deserve the Fair; Opening Chorus; There's Something Wrong with My Smile [1]; What's the Use; When You First Kiss the Last Girl You Love

Cast: John Barrymore; Alice Dovey; Sallie Fisher; James Marlowe; Louise Mink; Charles Prince

Notes: [1] Sheet music only. [2] Out of town. [3] Out Wilkes- Barre 4/22/11.

4186 • STUDENT GYPSY OR THE PRINCE OF LIEDERKRANTZ, THE

OPENED: 09/30/1963   Theatre: 54th St.
Musical   Broadway: 16

Composer: Rick Besoyan
Lyricist: Rick Besoyan
Librettist: Rick Besoyan
Producer: Sandy Farber
Director: Rick Besoyan

Choreographer: Ray Harrison; **Costumes:** Raoul Pene du Bois; **Dance Arranger:** Arnold Goland; **Lighting Designer:** Paul Morrison; **Musical Director:** Shepard Coleman; **Orchestrations:** Arnold Goland; **Set Design:** Raoul Pene du Bois; **Vocal Arranger:** Arnold Goland

Songs: Drinking Song, The; Greetings; Grenadiers' Marching Song, The; Gypsy Dance, A; Gypsy Life, The; Gypsy of Love; It's a Wonderful Day to Do Nothing; Kiss Me; Merry May; My Love Is Yours; Our Love Has Flown Away; Romance; Seventh Heaven Waltz; Singspielia; Somewhere; There's Life in the Old Folks Yet; Ting-a- ling Dearie; Very Much in Love; Walk-on; Welcome Home; Whistle Works, A; Woman Is a Woman Is a Woman, A; You're a Man

Cast: Donald Babcock; Shannon Bolin; Eileen Brennan; Dom De Luise; Don Stewart; Allen Swift

4187 • STUDENT KING, THE

OPENED: 12/25/1906   Theatre: Garden
Musical   Broadway: 40

Composer: Reginald De Koven
Lyricist: Frederick Ranken; Stanislaus Stange
Librettist: Frederick Ranken; Stanislaus Stange
Producer: Henry W. Savage
Director: George Marion

Costumes: A. Comelli; **Musical Director:** Arthur Weld

Songs: Carnival Scene [3]; Columbine and Harlequin [3]; Czardas; Election Ensemble; Entrance of Ilsa [3]; Entrance of the King [3]; Finale Act I; Finale Act II; Finale Act III; Gay Lieutenant, The [2]; Give Me Thy Heart, Love; His Majesty Advances; I Play On My Old Bassoon; I Took Them All; In Bohemia; Jolly Miller, The; Kneipe, The; Nudel, Nudel, Nup, Nup! [3]; Opening Chorus; Opposites Are We; Pray Pretty Maid; Pretty Tyrolese, The [3]; Queen of Carnival [3]; Same Old Game!, The; So We Drink; Student King, A; Such Is Love (How to Woo); Tarantella; To Arms; Tyrolean Maid; Would You Like a Little Girl Like Me

Cast: Lina Abarbanell; Flavia Arcaro; Eva Fallon; Raymond Hitchcock; Thomas C. Leary; Willliam C. Weedon; Gustave von Seyffertitz

Notes: [1] Sheet music only. [2] Out Boston 10/22/06. [3] Vocal score only.

4188 • STUDENT PRINCE, THE

OPENED: 12/02/1924   Theatre: Jolson
Musical   Broadway: 608

Composer: Sigmund Romberg
Lyricist: Dorothy Donnelly
Librettist: Dorothy Donnelly
Producer: Messrs. Shubert
Director: J.C. Huffman

Source: OLD HEIDELBERG (Play: Rudolf Bleichman); **Choreographer:** Max Scheck; **Costumes:** Max Weldy; **Musical Director:** Oscar Bradley; **Orchestrations:** Emil Gerstenberger; **Set Design:** Watson Barratt

Songs: Birds Are Winging [1]; By Our Bearing So Sedate; Carnival of Springtime [1]; Come, Answer to Our Call [1]; Come Boys; Come Sir, Will You Join Our Noble Saxton Corps [1]; Deep in My Heart, Dear; Drinking Song; Farewell, Dear; Farmer Jacob; Flag That Flies, The [1]; Garlands Bright; Gavotte; Golden Days; I'm Coming at Your Call [1]; In the Park [1]; Just We Two; Magic of Springtime, The [1]; May I Come to See You, Dear, Tonight? [2]; Oh, Tell Me If with Your Heart [2]; Serenade; Sing a Little Song; Students' Life; Thoughts Will Come to Me [1]; To the Inn We're Marching; Waltz Ensemble; We're Off to Paris; Welcome to Prince; What Memories; You're in Heidelberg

Cast: Roberta Beatty; Violet Carlson; George Hassell; Howard Marsh; Ilse Marvenga

Notes: [1] Not in program. [2] ASCAP/Library of Congress only.

4189 • STUDIO GIRL, THE

OPENED: 1927
Musical

Composer: Will Ortmann
Lyricist: J. Keirn Brennan

Songs: Because I Love You; Moonlight and Love and All; There's No One As Sweet As Trilby; Way Down in Barbizon

Notes: No other information available.

4190 • SUBWAYS ARE FOR SLEEPING

OPENED: 12/27/1961   Theatre: St. James
Musical   Broadway: 205

Composer: Jule Styne
Lyricist: Betty Comden; Adolph Green
Librettist: Betty Comden; Adolph Green
Producer: David Merrick
Director: Michael Kidd

Source: SUBWAYS ARE FOR SLEEPING (Novel: Edmund G. Love); **Choreographer:** Michael Kidd; **Costumes:** Freddy Wittop; **Dance Arranger:** Peter Howard; **Lighting Designer:** Will Steven Armstrong; **Musical Director:** Milton Rosenstock; **Orchestrations:** Philip J. Lang; **Set Design:** Will Steven Armstrong

Songs: Be a Santa; Comes Once in a Lifetime; Getting Married [3]; Girls Like Me; Hey Fellas Let's Talk [1]; How Can You Describe a Face? [2]; I Just Can't Wait; I Said It and I'm Glad [2]; I Walk a Little Dog [1]; I Was a Shoo-In; I'm Just Taking My Time; Man of Vision, A [1]; Man with a Plan, A [1]; Now I Have Someone [1]; Ride Through the Night; Station Rush (dance), Strange Duet (When You Help a Friend Out) [5]; Subway Directions; Subway Incident (dance); Subways Are for Sleeping; Swing Your Projects; What Is This Feeling in the Air [4]; Who Knows What Might Have Been?

Cast: Orson Bean; Michael Bennett; Sydney Chaplin; Gordon Connell; Bob Gorman; Grayson Hall; Valerie Harper; Carol Lawrence; Phyllis Newman; Gene Varrone; Cy Young

Notes: [1] Cut prior to opening. [2] Cut after opening. [3] Cut prior to opening. Not the same song as the title song of the TV musical GETTING MARRIED. [4] Originally music used as title tune from film MELODY RANCH. [5] Music later used as "Putney on the Thames" from DARLING OF THE DAY.

4191 • SUDDEN SPRING, A

OPENED: 09/04/1956
Play   Closed out of town

Composer: Irving Actman
Lyricist: Ruth Hughes Aarons
Author: Halsted Welles
Director: Lawrence Carra

Orchestrations: Norman Paris

Songs: Ban Joe; Love Me; Move Along; No Song; No Where; One Song; Pink Lemonade; Seven Songs; So I Didn't Marry Him; Soliloquy; Such a Sudden Spring; When You Touch Me

Cast: Wolfe Barzell; Reginald Beane; Mickey Calin; Grace Genteel; Ernest Graves; Celeste Holm; Cavada Humphrey; Phyllis Newman; Frank Overton

Notes: Program from Melody Circus, Detroit, Michigan. Script adapted by Elihu Winer.

4192 • SUDDENLY THE MUSIC STARTS

OPENED: 05/03/1979   Theatre: AMAS
Revue   Off-Broadway: 12

Composer: Johnny Brandon
Lyricist: Johnny Brandon
Librettist: Johnny Brandon
Producer: AMAS Repertory Theatre
Director: Henry LeTang; Lucia Victor

Choreographer: Henry LeTang; **Costumes:** Virginia Johnson; **Dance Arranger:** Danny Holgate; **Lighting Designer:** Paul Sullivan; **Musical Director:** Neal Tate; **Set Design:** Patrick Mann; **Vocal Arranger:** Carl Maultsby; Neal Tate

Songs: Boogie Woogie Ball; Dance! Dance! Dance!; Dancing Dan; Everybody's Doing the Disco; Faces in a Crowd; Funky People; Goodnight; Guides Stuff; I'll Scratch Your Back; It's My Turn Now; Kansas City Blues; Manhattan Lullaby; My Home Town; One Day at a Time; Remember Someone; Strolling Down Broadway; Suddenly the Music Starts; Super Bad; Syncopatin'; Talk Your Feelings; Whole Lotta Real Good Feeling; You; Your Love Is My Love

Cast: Mary Louise

4193 • SUDS

OPENED: 09/25/1988   Theatre: Criterion Center
Musical   Off-Broadway: 81

Composer: Jeff Barry; Ellie Greenwich
Lyricist: Jeff Barry; Ellie Greenwich
Librettist: Melinda Gilb; Steve Gunderson; Bryan Scott

Producer: David Langworthy; Norma Langworthy; Richard Redlin; Will Robertson; Bryan Scott
Director: Will Robertson

Choreographer: Javier Velasco; **Costumes:** Gregg Barnes; **Lighting Designer:** Kent Dorsey; **Musical Director:** William Doyle; **Set Design:** Alan Okazaki; **Vocal Arranger:** Steve Gunderson

Songs: (There's) Always Something There to Remind Me (C: Burt Bacharach; L: Hal David); Anyone Who Had a Heart (C: Burt Bacharach; L: Hal David); Are You Lonesome Tonight (C: Roy Turk; L: Lou Handman); Baby It's You (C: Burt Bacharach; L: Hal David); Be My Baby; Big Man (C/L: B. Belland; G. Larson); Birthday Party (C/L: J. Madera; D. White); Chapel of Love (C/L: Jeff Barry; Ellie Greenwich; Phil Spector); Cindy's Birthday (C/L: J. Hoover; H. Wynn); Color My World (C/L: Tony Hatch; Jackie Trent); Dedicated to the One I Love (C/L: R. Bass; L. Palling); Do Wah Diddy; Do You Want to Know a Secret (C/L: John Lennon; Paul McCartney); Don't Make Me Over (C: Burt Bacharach; L: Hal David); Easier Said Than Done (C/L: L. Huff; W. Linton); End of the World, The (C/L: Sandra Dee; A. Kert); Happy Birthday Sweet Sixteen (C/L: Neil Sedaka); Help Me Girl (C/L: S. English; L. Weiss); How Can I Be Sure (C/L: E. Brigati; F. Cavaliere); I Don't Wanna Be a Loser (C/L: M. Barkan; R. Raleigh); I Got You (I Feel Good) (C/L: James Brown); I Know a Place (C/L: Tony Hatch); I Say a Little Prayer (C: Burt Bacharach; L: Hal David); I Will Follow Him (C/L: Arthur Altman; Norman Gimbel; F. Pourcel); It's My Party (C/L: J. Gluck; W. Gold; S. Gottlieb; H. Wiener); Johnny Angel (C/L: Lyn Duddy; Lee Pockriss); Letter, The (C/L: W. Thompson); Little Bit of Soup, A (C/L: Bob Russell); (The) Loco-Motion (C/L: Gerry Goffin; Carole King); Lollipops and Roses (C/L: Tony Velona); Look of Love, The; Mystery Date (C/L: J. Harvey); Our Day Will Come (C: M. Garson; L: Bob Hilliard); Please Mr. Postman (C/L: R. Bateman; F. Gorman; Brian Holland); Reach Out in the Darkness (C/L: J. Post); Respect (C/L: Otis Redding); Round Every Corner (C/L: Tony Hatch); Secret Agent Man (C/L: J. Rivers); Shout (C/L: B. Isley; O. Isley; R. Isley); Tell Him (C/L: Bob Russell); These Boots Are Made for Walking (C/L: Lee Hazelwood); Today I Met the Boy I'm Gonna Marry (C/L: Ellie Greenwich; T. Powers; Phil Spector); Town Without Pity (C: Dimitri Tiomkin; L: Ned Washington); Walk on By (C: Burt Bacharach; L: Hal David); We Can Work It Out (C/L: John Lennon; Paul McCartney); Where the Boys Are (C/L: H. Greenfield; Neil Sedaka); Wishing and Hoping (C: Burt Bacharach; L: Hal David); Wonderful Wonderful (C/L: S. Edwards; Ben Raleigh); You Can't Hurry Love (C/L: Lamont Dozier; Brian Holland; Eddie Holland); You Don't Have to Say You Love Me (C/L: S.N. Bell; Pino Donaggio; V. Pallavicini); You Don't Own Me (C/L: J. Madera; B. White)

Cast: Melinda Gilb; Steve Gunderson; Susan Mosher; Christine Sevec

Notes: No original songs in this show.

4194 • SUE, DEAR

OPENED: 07/02/1922   Theatre: Times Square
Musical   Broadway: 97

Composer: Frank H. Grey
Lyricist: Bide Dudley
Librettist: Bide Dudley; Joseph W. Herbert; C.S. Mactayne
Producer: Bide Dudley
Director: Joseph W. Herbert

Choreographer: Jack Mason; **Musical Director:** Frank H. Grey

Songs: Bet on the Jockey [1]; By Radiophone [1]; Da, Da, Daddy Dear [2]; Dance Me Darling Dance Me; Foolishment; Hiram Skinner's Comb; Key to Lorayne [1]; Love Ship, The [1]; Lover's Lane with You; Love's Corporation; Men, Men, Men [1]; My Little Full-Blown Rose; Opening Number; Opening of Act II; Pidgie Widgie; Riverside Drive; Smile and Forget; Tell Us, Handsome Man [1]; That Samson and Delilah Melody

Cast: Bradford Kirkbride; Bobby O'Neil; Olga Steck

Notes: [1] Out Stamford 4/28/22. [2] Added after opening.

4195 • SUFFRAGETTE PITCHER, THE

Musical

Composer: Raymond Walker
Lyricist: Thomas J. Gray
Librettist: Thomas J. Gray

Costumes: Mme. Francis; **Musical Director:** George A. Nichols

Cast: Rube Marquard; Blossom Seeley

Notes: A vaudeville sketch with songs.

4196 • SUGAR

OPENED: 04/09/1972   Theatre: Majestic
Musical   Broadway: 505

Composer: Jule Styne
Lyricist: Bob Merrill
Librettist: Peter Stone
Producer: David Merrick
Director: Gower Champion

Source: SOME LIKE IT HOT (Film: I.A.L. Diamond; Billy Wilder); **Choreographer:** Gower Champion; **Costumes:** Alvin Colt; **Dance Arranger:** John Berkman; **Lighting Designer:** Martin Aronstein; **Musical Director:** Elliot Lawrence; **Orchestrations:** Philip J. Lang; **Set Design:** Robin Wagner; **Vocal Arranger:** Elliot Lawrence

Songs: All You Gotta Do Is Tell Me [1]; Beautiful Through and Through; Beauty That Drives Men Mad, The; Daphne [2] (C: Bob Merrill); Don't Be Afraid [2]; Girls in the Band [6]; Givers and Takers [2]; Hey, Why Not!; I'm Naive [8]; It's Always Love; Jerry's Ecstasy [1]; Kooka-Rooki Bongo [1]; Magic Nights; Maple Leaf Rag [7] (C: Scott Joplin; Jule Styne; L: Bob Russell); Massacre, The [1]; My Nice Ways [9]; (My) Nice Ways [1]; November Song; Penniless Bums; People in My Life, The [5]; See You Around [3]; Spats-s-s Palazzo [1]; Speakeasy, The [1]; Sugar (Doin' It for Sugar); (With the) Sun on My Face; Sun on My Face [2]; Tear the Town Apart (dance); These Eyes Have Seen Too Much [2]; Three Hot Tamales, The [2]; We Could Be Close; We Wish We Could Turn Back the Clock [1]; What Do You Give to a Man Who's Had Everything?; When You Meet a Man in Chicago [4]; Windy City Marmelade [4]

Cast: Pamela Blair; Arthur Faria; Denny Martin Flinn; Igors Gavon; Elaine Joyce; John Mineo; Robert Morse; Cyril Ritchard; Tony Roberts; Sheila Smith; Pamela Sousa

Notes: Titled SOME LIKE IT HOT subsequently in London. [1] Out Washington, D.C. 1/17/72. [2]

Cut. [3] Added after Broadway for West Coast production. [4] Same music. [5] Out Washington, D.C. 1/17/72 then added again for West Coast production. Music based on "Look at You, Look at Me" from film SIS HOPKINS. [6] Out Washington, D.C. 1/17/72 then added again for West Coast production. [7] Added to London production. A previously written pop song. [8] From TV musical THE DANGEROUS CHRISTMAS OF RED RIDING HOOD. Added to London production which was titled SOME LIKE IT HOT. [9] ASCAP/Library of Congress only.

4197 • SUGAR BABIES

OPENED: 10/09/1979   Theatre: Mark Hellinger
Revue   Broadway: 1208

Composer: Jimmy McHugh
Lyricist: Dorothy Fields
Librettist: Ralph G. Allen
Producer: Terry Allen Kramer; Harry Rigby
Director: Rudy Tronto

Choreographer: Ernest Flatt; **Costumes:** Raoul Pene du Bois; **Dance Arranger:** Arnold Gross; **Lighting Designer:** Gilbert V. Hemsley Jr.; **Musical Director:** Glen Roven; **Orchestrations:** Dick Hyman; **Set Design:** Raoul Pene du Bois; **Vocal Arranger:** Arthur Malvin

Songs: City Song [3] (C/L: Mickey Rooney); Cuban Love Song (C: Jimmy McHugh; Herbert Stothart); Don't Blame Me; Down at the Gaiety Burlesque (C/L: Arthur Malvin); Every Day Another Tune (C/L: Arthur Malvin); Exactly Like You; Goin' Back to New Orleans (C/L: Arthur Malvin); Good Old Burlesque Show, A (L: Arthur Malvin); Good Old Mammy Song, A [5] (C/L: L. Russell Brown; Irwin Levine); I Can't Give You Anything but Love [4]; I Feel a Song Comin' On; I Just Want to Be a Song and Dance Man [1] (L: Harold Adamson); I Want a Girl (C: Harry Von Tilzer; L: William Dillon); I'm in the Mood for Love [5]; I'm Keeping Myself Available for You (L: Arthur Malvin); I'm Shooting High [4] (L: Ted Koehler); I'm the Last of the Red Hot Mamas [5] (C: Milton Ager; L: Jack Yellen); Immigration Rose [2] (L: Irwin Dash; Eugene West); In Louisiana (L: Arthur Malvin); Instructional Rag, The [1] (C/L: Arthur Malvin); Let Me Be Your Sugar Baby (C/L: Arthur Malvin); Mr. Banjo Man (C/L: Arthur Malvin); On the Sunny Side of the Street [4]; Papa Don't Go Out Tonight [5] (C: Milton Ager;

L: Jack Yellen); Sally (L: Arthur Malvin); Some of These Days [5] (C/L: Shelton Brooks); Song of the Auctioneer [1] (C/L: Leroy Van Dyke); Sugar Baby Bounce, The [2] (C/L: Ray Evans; Jay Livingston); Warm and Willing (L: Ray Evans; Jay Livingston); When You and I Were Young, Maggie Blues [4] (L: Jack Frost); Wouldn't You Like to Taste My Pear? [1] (L: Arthur Malvin); You Can't Blame Your Uncle Sammy (C: Irwin Dash; Jimmy McHugh; L: Al Dubin)

Cast: Tom Boyd; Jack Fletcher; Ann Jillian; Peter Leeds; Jimmy Mathews; Ann Miller; Mickey Rooney; Scot Stewart; Sid Stone

Notes: Libretto based on old burlesque routines. [1] Cut prior to Broadway. [2] Cut after opening. [3] Added after Broadway run. [4] Part of a McHugh medley. [5] Added to national tour.

4198 • SUGAR HILL (1931)

OPENED: 12/25/1931   Theatre: Forrest
Musical   Broadway: 11

Composer: James P. Johnson
Lyricist: Jo Trent
Librettist: Charles Tazewell
Producer: Moveing Day Company

Costumes: Mahieu; **Lighting Designer:** Detric; **Set Design:** Theodore Kahn

Songs: Boston; Fooling Around with Love; Hanging Around Yo' Door; Hot Harlem; Hot Rhythm; I Love You, Honey; Keep 'Em Guessin' [1]; Movin' Day; My Sweet Hunk O' Trash [1]; Noisy Neighbors; Peace, Sister, Peace [1]; Rumbola; Something's Going to Happen to You; What Have I Done?; You Can't Lose a Broken Heart [1]

Cast: Chappy Chappelle; Ina Duncan; Carrie Huff; Broadway Jones; Aubrey L. Lyles; Flournoy Miller

Notes: [1] Not in program.

4199 • SUGAR HILL (1949)

OPENED: 1949   Theatre: Las Palmas
Musical   Los Angeles

Composer: James P. Johnson
Lyricist: Flournoy E. Miller
Librettist: Flournoy E. Miller

Producer: Alvin B. Baranov; Paul P. Schreibman
Director: Charles O'Curran

Musical Director: Dudley Brooks; **Set Design:** Les Marzoff

Songs: Apple Jack; Bad Bill Jones; Busy Body; Caught; Chivaree; Don't Lose Your Head, Then Lose Your Girl; Faraway Love; I Don't Want Any Labor in My Job; I've Got to Be Lovely for Harry; Keep 'Em Guessing; Love Don't Need a Referee; Lovin' Ain't My Aim; Mr. Dumbbell and Mr. Tough; My Sweet Hunk of Trash; Peace, Sister, Peace; Sender; Sepia Fashion Plate; Smilin' Through My Tears; That Was Then; Until You Are Caught; We're Going to Blitz the Blitz; What Kind of Tune Did Nero Play; You Can't Lose a Broken Heart; You're My Rose

4200 • SUITE SIXTEEN
OPENED: 1919
Musical

Composer: Silvio Hein
Lyricist: Edward Paulton
Librettist: Parker Hord; Edward Paulton
Producer: F.C. Whitney

Songs: Beauty Dance (inst.); First Step, The; Good Bye; I Dare You; I Want Some Love; I'd Like to Plant a Smile; If I Were You; Joy Out of Life; Pond of Girlies; Quaker Song; Reason Why, The; Suspicion; Teach Me; Wiggle Waggle

Notes: No other information available.

4201 • SULTAN OF SULU, THE
OPENED: 12/29/1902   Theatre: Wallack
Musical   Broadway: 192

Composer: Alfred G. Walthall
Lyricist: George Ade
Librettist: George Ade
Producer: Henry W. Savage
Director: Charles Jones

Choreographer: James F. MacDonald; **Costumes:** Will R. Barnes; John T. McCutcheon; **Musical Director:** Alexander Spencer; **Set Design:** Walter Burridge

Songs: Allah! Strike for Thee [2]; Always Late; Candidates' March [1]; Carmena; Chorus of

Greeting; Dangle Him Lightly [3]; Dawning Day, The; Delia; Engaged in a Sort of Way; Entrance [3]; Entrance of Colonel Budd [3]; Entrance of Sultan [3]; Finale Act I [3]; Finale Act II [3]; Finale Act III [3]; Foolish Wedding Bells; Hike!; I Don't Know What to Do [3]; If I But Knew; Imperial Guards' March; In Our Little School [2]; In the U.S.A. [1]; Ki Ram's Wedding March [1] (C: George L. Brun); Loudly We Shout [2]; (Come Back to) Manistee; My Sulu Lulu Lou (C: Nat D. Mann); Oh, What a Bump!; Old Jay Bird, The; Palm Branches Waving; Peachy Teacher, The; Queer Little Ostrich, The; R-E-M-O-R-S-E; Rosabella Clancy; Salute; Schoolma'm's Song [2]; Since I First Met You; Slumber On; Smiling Isle; Some Sweet Day [2] (C: Lee Orean Smith; L: Walter A. Lawrence); Song of Yesterday, A [1]; Tell Me Shooting Star (Money! Money! Money!) [3]; Three Cheers for Education [2]; Till the Volunteers Return; We Are Engaged [2]

Cast: Maude Lillian Berri; Frank Moulan; Gertrude Quinlan; Templar Saxe

Notes: Marches by Charles H. Jones. [1] Out Ithaca, NY 12/16/03. [2] Out Trenton 08/19/05. [3] Vocal score only.

4202 • SUMMER SHARE
Notes: *See ROMANCE, ROMANCE.*

4203 • SUMMER WIDOWERS, THE
OPENED: 06/04/1910   Theatre: Broadway
Musical   Broadway: 140

Composer: A. Baldwin Sloane
Lyricist: Glen MacDonough
Librettist: Glen MacDonough
Producer: Lew Fields
Director: Ned Wayburn

Choreographer: Ned Wayburn; **Orchestrations:** Frank Saddler; **Set Design:** Arthur Voegtlin

Songs: Calcium Moon, The; Come Take a Dip in the Sea with Me; Flying High; Gee But I'd Like to Furnish a Flat for You, Dear; Happy Days [2]; I Knew Her When (C: Burton Green); I Never Know How to Behave When I'm with Girls, Girls, Girls [1]; Lady-Ushers Ball, The; Mandalay [2]; Miss Dennett (C: Burton Green);

Muscovite; Oh, You Summertime Romeo!;
On the Boardwalk; Red Head (C: Burton Green;
L: Irene Franklin); Sahara Twins, The; There's No
Place Like Home Boys When Your Wife Has
Gone Away; Those Were the Happy Days; We'll
Go to the Minstrel Show; We're Looking for
Something in Peaches

Cast: Vernon Castle; Alice Dovey; Lew Fields;
Irene Franklin; Burton Green; Helen Hayes; Ada
Lewis; Willis P. Sweatnam; Fritz Williams

Notes: [1] Out of town only. [2] Sheet music only.

4204 • SUMMER WIVES

OPENED: 04/13/1936   Theatre: Mansfield
Play   Broadway: 8

Composer: Sam Morrison
Lyricist: Dolph Singer
Author: Mark Linder
Producer: Jack Linder; D.S. Wolfson
Director: Ira Hards

Set Design: Mabel A. Buell

Songs: Chatterbox, The; I Wrote a Song for You
(L: By Dunham [1]; Dolph Singer);
Lowen-Green Country Club, I Love You;
Mickey; My Love Carries On; Play Me an Old
Time Two-Step; Us on a Bus (C: Vee Lawnhurst;
L: Tot Seymour)

Cast: Charles Dale; Joe Smith

Notes: [1] Billed as William Dunham.

4205 • SUN ALWAYS SHINES FOR THE COOL, THE

OPENED: 09/27/1979   Theatre: 78th Street
                                      Theatre Lab
Play   Off-Broadway: 16

Composer: Galt MacDermot
Author: Miguel Pinero
Producer: BMC Productions
Director: Jaime Sanchez

Choreographer: Julie Arenal; **Costumes:** Ticia
Blackburn; Carrie Robbins; **Lighting Designer:**
Ruth Roberts; **Set Design:** David Potts

Cast: Ramon Franco; Chino Melso; Bruce Waite

4206 • SUN DODGERS, THE

OPENED: 11/30/1912   Theatre: Broadway
Musical   Broadway: 29

Composer: A. Baldwin Sloane
Lyricist: E. Ray Goetz
Librettist: Edgar Smith
Producer: Lew Fields
Director: Ned Wayburn

Musical Director: August Kleinecke;
  Orchestrations: Hilding Anderson; William
Redfield

Songs: At the Automat; At the Picture Show (C/L:
Irving Berlin; E. Ray Goetz); Dixie Love; Down
in the Old Rathskeller; Every Flower Has a
Melody; Garden of Flowers; Ginger; Good
Morning; Hiram's Band [1] (C/L: Irving Berlin;
E. Ray Goetz; A. Baldwin Sloane); How Can They
Tell I'm Irish [1]; I Never Would Do It in Society;
I'm Crazy 'Bout Somebody [1] (C: Dave Stamper;
L: Gene Buck); In My Birch Bark Canoe [1]; Little
Girl Who Couldn't Care [3]; Marry a Sunshine
Girl; Night Brigade, The; Night the Old Cow
Died, The [1]; Pinkerton Detective Moon [1]
(C/L: Jack Norworth; C: Nora Bayes); Rag Me
Around; She Believes in Brooklyn Tonight [1];
Song of the Cocktail; Take Me to the Chicken
Ball [1] (C: O.E. Story; L: Bobby Jones); Two
Heads Are Better Than One; Way Down in
C-U-B-A [4] (C: Nora Bayes; Antonio Torroella
Chijo; L: Jack Norworth); What Happened to
Mary; When It's Apple Blossom Time in
Normandy [1] (C/L: Harry Gifford; Tom Mellor;
Huntley Trevor); When You Said How Do You
Do; You're My Baby [2]

Cast: Nan Brennan; Harry Clarke; Harold Crane;
George Monroe; Bessie Wynn

Notes: [1] Sheet music only. [2] The popular song
of the same name by Nat D. Ayer and A.
Seymour Brown was written in 1912. [3]
ASCAP/Library of Congress only. [4] Sheet
music only. Also in ROLY POLY.

4207 • SUN NEVER SETS, THE

OPENED: 06/09/1938   Theatre: Theatre Royal,
                                      Drury Lane
Play   London: 35

Composer: Kenneth Leslie-Smith
Lyricist: Desmond Carter

Author: Guy Bolton; Pat Wallace
Producer: Theatre Royal Drury Lane
Director: Basil Dean

Source: SANDERS OF THE RIVER (Story: Edgar Wallace); **Choreographer:** Bertha Slosberg; Lydia Sokolov; **Costumes:** Laurence Irving; **Set Design:** Laurence Irving

Songs: Dreams; My Love Is Like the River; River God (C/L: Cole Porter); Sun Never Sets, The [1] (C/L: Vivian Ellis)

Cast: Leslie Banks; Edna Best; Todd Duncan; Charles Farrell; Stewart Granger; Adelaide Hall; Henry Oscar; Mackenzie Ward

Notes: [1] Not in program.

4208 • SUN SHOWERS

OPENED: 02/05/1923   Theatre: Astor
Musical   Broadway: 48

Composer: Harry Delf
Lyricist: Harry Delf
Librettist: Harry Delf
Producer: Lew Cantor
Director: Frederick Stanhope

Choreographer: Larry Ceballos; Seymour Felix; **Costumes:** Mabel Johnston; **Musical Director:** Fred Fleming

Songs: Clip the Coupons; Each Little Jack; Every One Is Beautiful in Someone's Eyes; He Loves Me; How Do You Doodle?; If the Old Folks Could See Us Now; I'm the Greenwich Village Chambermaid; In the Morning; It Always Happens for the Best [1]; Joy of Living, The; My Little Jail-Bird [1]; Oh, Professor!; On a Moonlight Night; Speak Without Compunction; Sun Showers; With You Beside Me [1]; Worth Waiting For; Yours Truly

Cast: Harry Delf; Tom Dingle; Allyn King; Douglas Stevenson

Notes: [1] Out Stamford 12/25/22. [2] Sheet music only.

4209 • SUNBONNET SUE

OPENED: 1923
Musical   Closed out of town

Composer: Gus Edwards
Lyricist: Robert B. Smith; Margaret Wright
Librettist: Robert B. Smith; Margaret Wright
Director: Alonzo Price

Choreographer: Max Scheck

Songs: Art of Fascination, The; Dancing Around the Course; Demonstrate; Down Where the Bluebells Grow; I'm Going to Meet Minnie Tonight (L: Howard E. Johnson); Kid Is Clever, The; Ladies and Babies a la Mode; Little Boy Blue Jeans (L: Robert B. Smith); Love Is a Garden of Roses (L: Robert B. Smith); 'Member When (L: Robert B. Smith); Oh, For the Life of a Bootlegger's Wife; Oui, Oui, Madame; School Days Are Over; She's the Same Old Sunbonnet Sue (L: Robert B. Smith); Shimmy on Your Own Side; Sunbonnet Sue [1] (L: Will D. Cobb); They Always Blame the Caddy

Cast: Olga Cook; Chester Fredericks; Fred Hildebrand; Helen Lynd

Notes: [1] Also in SCHOOL DAYS.

4210 • SUNDAY IN THE PARK WITH GEORGE

OPENED: 05/02/1984   Theatre: Booth
Musical   Broadway: 604

Composer: Stephen Sondheim
Lyricist: Stephen Sondheim
Librettist: James Lapine
Producer: Emanuel Azenberg; Playwrights Horizons; Shubert Organization
Director: James Lapine

Costumes: Anne Hould-Ward; Patricia Zipprodt; **Lighting Designer:** Richard Nelson; **Musical Director:** Paul Gemignani; **Orchestrations:** Michael Starobin; **Set Design:** Tony Straiges

Songs: Beautiful; Children and Art; Chromolume #7; Color and Light; Day Off, The [2]; Everybody Loves Louis; Finishing the Hat; Gossip; It's Hot Up Here; Lesson #8; Move On; No Life; One on the Left, The [3]; Putting It Together; Soldiers and Girls [1]; Sunday; Sunday in the Park with George; We Do Not Belong Together; Yoo-Hoo! [3]

Cast: Barbara Byrne; Mary D'Arcy; Cris Groenendaal; Dana Ivey; Charles Kimbrough;

Nancy Opel; Mandy Patinkin; Bernadette Peters; Melanie Vaughan; Robert Westenberg

Notes: [1] In the middle of "The Day Off." [2] Same music as "Pour Le Sport" from THE LAST RESORTS. [3] Cut prior to opening.

4211 • SUNKIST
OPENED: 05/23/1921   Theatre: Globe
Revue   Broadway: 27

Composer: Fanchon & Marco
Lyricist: Fanchon & Marco
Librettist: Fanchon & Marco
Producer: Fanchon & Marco
Director: Fanchon & Marco

Musical Director: Reuben Wolff

Songs: Bragging Song; Breaking Into the Movies [1]; I Dunno What, The [1]; I Want to Meet You Some Day in California [1]; Lo Hear the Gentle Lark [1]; Love a Gypsy Knows, The [1]; My Sweetie's Smile [1]; Pretty Dance Is Like a Violin, A [1]; They Call Me Pollyanna [1]; Use Your Own Judgment [1]

Cast: Eva Clark; Fanchon & Marco; Donald Kerr; Muriel Stryker

Notes: [1] Previously used in SATIRES OF 1920.

4212 • SUNNY
OPENED: 09/23/1925   Theatre: New Amsterdam
Musical   Broadway: 517

Composer: Jerome Kern
Lyricist: Oscar Hammerstein II; Otto Harbach
Librettist: Oscar Hammerstein II; Otto Harbach
Producer: Charles Dillingham
Director: Hassard Short

Choreographer: Fred Astaire; David Bennett; Alexis Kosloff; Julian Mitchell; John Tiller; **Costumes:** James Reynolds; **Musical Director:** Gus Salzer; **Orchestrations:** Robert Russell Bennett; **Set Design:** James Reynolds

Songs: All These People I Have Wronged [6]; Chase, The; Dream a Dream [1]; D'Ye Love Me?; Ev'ry Guest Is in the Room [6]; Fox Has Left His Lair, The [2]; Hartman Ballet (inst.) [7]; Heaven's Gift to the Girls [1]; Here We Are Together Again

(Opening Act I); Hunt Dance, The (inst.); I Might Grow Fond of You [2] (L: Desmond Carter); I'm Moving Away [6] (C/L: Irving Caesar; Cliff Edwards); It Won't Mean a Thing [5]; I've Looked for Trouble [3] (L: Desmond Carter); Just a Little Thing Called Rhythm (C: Eddie Ward; L: Chick Endor); Let's Say Goodnight 'Til It's Morning; Magnolia in the Woods (C/L: Pert Kelton); Paddlin' Madelin' Home (C/L: Harry Woods); Pas D'Equestrienne (inst.) [7]; So's Your Old Man; Strolling, or What Have You?; Sunny; Sunshine [4]; To Think He Remembered Me [1]; Tonsils [1]; Two Little Bluebirds; Two Little Losses [1]; Under the Sky [1]; We're Gymnastic; Wedding Knell, The; When We Get Our Divorce; Who?

Cast: Charles Angelo; Joseph Cawthorn; Jack Donahue; Cliff Edwards; Dorothy Francis; Paul Frawley; Helene Gardner; Mary Hay; Esther Howard; Pert Kelton; Marilyn Miller; Clifton Webb

Notes: [1] Out Philadelphia 9/9/25. [2] Added for London version. [3] Added for London version. Same music as "Bought and Paid For" from THE LAUGHING HUSBAND and "You Will-Won't You" from CRISS-CROSS. [4] Same music as "I Can't Forget Your Eyes" from OH, I SAY! and "In Araby with You" from CRISS-CROSS. [5] Out Philadelphia 9/9/25 and later added for London version. [6] ASCAP/Library of Congress only. [7] Not in program.

4213 • SUNNY DAYS
OPENED: 02/08/1928   Theatre: Imperial
Musical   Broadway: 101

Composer: Jean Schwartz
Lyricist: William Cary Duncan; Clifford Grey
Librettist: William Cary Duncan; Clifford Grey
Producer: Hassard Short
Director: Hassard Short

Source: LE MONSIEUR DE CINQ HEURES (Play: Maurice Hennequin; Pierre Veber); **Choreographer:** Ralph Reader; **Musical Director:** Leon Rosebrook; **Set Design:** Watson Barratt

Songs: Belle, a Beau and a Boutonniere, A; Ginette; Hang Your Hat on the Moon; I'll Be Smiling; One Sunny Day; Orange Blossoms; Really and Truly; 'Sno Use Talking I've Got to Be Good; So Do I; Trample Your Troubles

Cast: Jeanette MacDonald; Frank McIntyre; Lynne Overman; Carl Randall; Billy B. Van

Notes: Additional numbers by Eleanor Dunsmuir uncredited in program.

4214 • SUNNY RIVER
OPENED: 12/04/1941   Theatre: St. James
Musical   Broadway: 36

Composer: Sigmund Romberg
Lyricist: Oscar Hammerstein II
Librettist: Oscar Hammerstein II
Producer: Max Gordon
Director: John Murray Anderson; Oscar Hammerstein II

Choreographer: Carl Randall; Costumes: Irene Sharaff; Lighting Designer: Al Alloy; Musical Director: Jay Blackton [2]; Orchestrations: Don Walker; Set Design: Stewart Chaney

Songs: Along the Winding Road; Bow-Legged Sal; Bundling; Butterflies and the Bees, The; Call It a Dream; Can You Sing?; Duello, The; Eleven Levee Street [1]; Finale Ultimo; Finaletto Act I; Finaletto Act II; It Can Happen to Anyone; Let Me Live Today; Lordy [1]; Making Conversation; My Girl and I; She Got Him; Sunny River; Symphonic Pantomime (inst.); Time Is Standing Still

Cast: Muriel Angelus; Helen Claire; Vicki Cummings [3]; Gordon Dilworth; Tom Ewell; Bob Lawrence; Ethel Levey; William O'Neal; Joan Roberts

Notes: Out of town titled NEW ORLEANS. [1] Cut. [2] Billed as Jacob Schwartzdorf. [3] Billed as Vicki Charles.

4215 • SUNNY SIDE OF BROADWAY, THE
Musical

Composer: Boyle Woolfolk
Lyricist: Boyle Woolfolk
Librettist: Charles A. Murray; Eugene Walter

Songs: Butterfly Life, The; Circus Queen, The; Good Old College Days; I'd Rather Be a Billy Goat; Meet Me at the Stage Door, Johnnie; Most Every Town Has a Broadway; Oh Mr. Moon

You're Full Tonight; Sahara Sarah; That Nifty Song Show

Notes: No other information available.

4216 • SUNSET
OPENED: 11/07/1983   Theatre: Village Gate
Musical   Off-Broadway

Composer: Gary William Friedman
Lyricist: Will Holt
Librettist: Will Holt
Producer: Diane de Mailly
Director: Andre Ernotte

Source: PLATINUM (Musical: Gary William Friedman; Will Holt); Choreographer: Buzz Miller; Costumes: Patricia Zipprodt; Lighting Designer: Robert Jared; Musical Director: Donald York; Orchestrations: Gary William Friedman; Set Design: Kate Edmunds; Vocal Arranger: Gary William Friedman

Cast: Ronee Blakely; Tammy Grimes; Walt Hunter; Kim Milford

Notes: *See also PLATINUM*, which was an earlier production of this musical. In fact, PLATINUM was originally titled SUNSET. No songs listed in program. Closed after one preview before announced opening date.

4217 • SUNSET BOULEVARD
OPENED: 11/17/1994   Theatre: Minskoff
Musical   Broadway

Composer: Andrew Lloyd Webber
Lyricist: Don Black; Christopher Hampton
Librettist: Don Black; Christopher Hampton
Producer: Really Useful Company, The
Director: Trevor Nunn

Source: SUNSET BOULEVARD (Film: Charles Brackett; D.M. Marksman Jr.; Billy Wilder); Choreographer: Bob Avian; Conductor: Paul Bogaev; Costumes: Anthony Powell; Lighting Designer: Andrew Bridge; Musical Director: David Caddick; Orchestrations: David Cullen; Andrew Lloyd Webber; Set Design: John Napier

Songs: As If We Never Said Goodbye; Eternal Youth Is Worth a Little Suffering [1]; Every Movie's a Circus; Girl Meets Boy; Greatest Star of All, The; Lady's Paying, The [1]; Let's Have Lunch; New Ways to Dream; Perfect Year, The; Prologue; Salome; Sunset Boulevard; Surrender; This Time Next Year; Too Much in Love to Care; With One Look

Cast: Sandra Allen; Darrin Baker; Bryan Batt; Lada Boder; Alan Campbell; Susan Dawn Carson; Glenn Close; Matthew Dickens; George Hearn; Alan Oppenheimer; Alice Ripley; Vincent Tumeo

Notes: Still playing as of publication. [1] Same music.

4218 • SUNSHINE

OPENED: 1920
Musical   Closed out of town

Composer: Alexander Johnstone
Lyricist: William Cary Duncan
Librettist: William Cary Duncan
Producer: Alexander Johnstone
Director: Edward Elsner

Choreographer: Robert Marks; **Musical Director:** Charles Weinberg; **Set Design:** William Oden-Waller

Songs: Dashing Matador [1]; Farewell to Love; Here's to Love [2]; Hispanola Crawl; Home Again; I Like to Look Around a Little; Idol of the Ring, The; Land of Make-Believe; Love Is Like This Little Wheel of Mine; Loving a la Spain [1]; Marbella Maid [1]; Minnowillen [1]; Pussyfoot Detective, The; Something Nice in Lingerie; Treat 'Em Rough; What Are We Going to Do?; What's the Idea [1]

Cast: Caroline Andrews; Richard Carle; Milton Dawson; Ethel Johnson; Harry Luckstone

Notes: Program from Wilkes-Barre 1/16/20 used. [1] Sheet music only. [2] London production only.

4219 • SUNSHINE GIRL, THE

OPENED: 02/03/1913   Theatre: Knickerbocker
Musical   Broadway: 160

Composer: Paul Rubens
Lyricist: Paul Rubens; Arthur Wimperis
Librettist: Cecil Raleigh; Paul Rubens
Producer: Charles Frohman
Director: J.A.E. Malone

Musical Director: Augustus Barratt; **Set Design:** Ernest Albert; Homer Emens

Songs: Argentine, The (L: Paul Rubens; Arthur Wimperis); Brighton [1]; Butler, The; Chorus of Welcome; Finale Act I; Finale Act II; Get a Move On!; Goodbye to Flirtation; Here's to Love (L: Arthur Wimperis); Honeymoon Lane [3] (C: Jerome Kern; L: M.E. Rourke); In Your Defence; I've Been to America; I've Been to the Durbar [1]; Josephine; Kitchen Range, The (L: Paul Rubens); Ladies (L: Arthur Wimperis); Lazy [1]; Little Girl, Mind How You Go! (L: Paul Rubens); Love [2]; Men of Business [2] (L: Paul Rubens); Miss Blush!; Nuts; Opening Chorus (When You Want a Cake of Soap); Opening Chorus Act II; Other Chap, The [2]; Take Me For — [1] (L: Paul A. Rubens); Tiny Touch, A; What Did the Butler See? [1]; When the Ladies Have Their Way [2]; Who's the Boss?; You and I; You Can't Play Every Instrument in the Band (C: John Golden; L: Joseph Cawthorn)

Cast: Irene Castle; Vernon Castle; Joseph Cawthorn; Tom Lewis; Julia Sanderson

Notes: [1] In London program only. [2] In English vocal score only. [3] Also used in the London revue NOT LIKELY.

4220 • SUNSHINE TRAIN, THE

OPENED: 06/15/1972   Theatre: Abbey
Musical   Off-Broadway: 280

Producer: Jay Sessa
Director: William E. Hunt

Lighting Designer: Philip Gilliam; **Musical Director:** Louis Hancock; Nealy; **Set Design:** Philip Gilliam

Cast: Larry Coleman; Dottie Coley; Barbara Davis; Gladys Freeman; Peggie Henry; Ron Horton; Joe Ireland; Mary Johnson; Ernest McCarroll; Carl Murray

4221 • SUPERMAN

Notes: See IT'S A BIRD . . . IT'S A PLANE... IT'S SUPERMAN.

4222 • SUPPER CLUB, THE

OPENED: 12/23/1901   Theatre: Winter Garden
Musical   Broadway: 40

Composer: Sydney Rosenfeld
Lyricist: Sydney Rosenfeld
Librettist: Sydney Rosenfeld
Producer: Sire Bros.

Cast: Alex Clarke; Ada Lewis; Junie McCree; John W. Ransome; Josie Sadler; Thomas Q. Seabrooke; Bessie Wynn

Notes: No songs listed in program. Bob Cole and Billy Johnson interpolated songs into this show.

4223 • SURE CURE, A

OPENED: 09/26/1898   Theatre: Star
Musical   Broadway: 8

Librettist: Harry Doel Parker

Cast: Anne Caldwell; Eva Tanguay; Charles Wayne

Notes: No program available.

4224 • SURPRISE

Notes: *See FLIM-FLAM.*

4225 • SUSANNA AND THE ELDERS

Notes: *See BALLET BALLADS.*

4226 • SUZANNE

OPENED: 01/25/1926
Musical   Closed out of town

Composer: Harold Orlob
Lyricist: William Cary Duncan
Librettist: William Cary Duncan
Producer: John Cort
Director: James Durkin

Source: LIKE A KING (Story: John Hunter Booth); **Choreographer:** Julian Mitchell; **Musical Director:** Karl Hajos; **Orchestrations:** Karl Hajos

Songs: Blue Bird; Broadway Lights; Cave Girl; Finale Act I; Finale Act II; If the Telephone Could Tell; Little One; Loving Time; Maybe I Will; Oh, Henry; Only Boy; Opening; Opening Act II; Phil's Entrance; Suzanne; Suzanne's Entrance; What Do You Do When I'm Gone?; When a Rolls Rolls In

Cast: Phyllis Cleveland; Frank Lalor; Nick Long Jr.

Notes: Later reworked as TALK ABOUT GIRLS. See also under that title.

4227 • SUZETTE

OPENED: 11/24/1921   Theatre: Princess
Musical   Broadway: 4

Composer: Arthur H. Gutman
Lyricist: Roy Dixon
Librettist: Roy Dixon
Producer: Suzette Producing Company
Director: Charles D. Pitt

Choreographer: Larry Ceballos; **Musical Director:** Arthur H. Gutman; **Orchestrations:** Arthur H. Gutman; Keifert –

Songs: Bagdad; Dreams of Tomorrow; Forest Legend, A; Gypsy Rose; Honey-Love-Moon; Modern Diplomat, A; No No!; Oh, Waiter; Opening Act I; Opening Act II; Saturday Evening Post; Suzette; Sweetheart

Cast: Marie Astroba; John Cherry; Frank Lalor; James R. Marshall

4228 • SUZI

OPENED: 11/03/1914   Theatre: Casino
Musical   Broadway: 55

Composer: Aladar Renyi
Lyricist: Otto Harbach
Librettist: Otto Harbach
Producer: Lew Fields
Director: George Marion

Source: A KIS GROF (Musical: Ferenc Martos; Aladar Renyi)

Songs: Angling; Best Toast of All, The (Kiss Her and Look in Her Eyes) (C: Franz Lehar); Brave Hussar, The; Heaven Measured You for Me; I'll Love You Marina [1]; I'll Not Let Love Disparage Marriage [1]; It Thrills! It Thrills!; Life Is a Garden; Marina; Match Makers, The; Ocean, the Ocean, The; Oh Fascinating Night; Secrets [1]; Teenie-Eenie-Weenie (C: Paul Lincke); Tick-a-Tock (Suzi I'm Ticking Love Taps) (C: Max Perschk); 'Twas in a Garden; Venus and I Are Pals; Venus Calls and I'll Obey [1]

Cast: Jose Collins; Lew Hearn; Tom MacNaughton

Notes: [1] Not used.

4229 • SVENGALI

OPENED: 04/03/1991
Musical   Closed out of town

Composer: Frank Wildhorn
Lyricist: John Bettis; Gregory Boyd; Frank
  Wildhorn
Librettist: Gregory Boyd
Director: Gregory Boyd

Source: TRILBY (Novel: Gerald du Maurier);
  Costumes: Jane Suttell; **Lighting Designer:**
  Howard Binkley; **Musical Director:** Douglas
  Besterman; **Orchestrations:** Jeremy Roberts; **Set**
  Design: Jerome Sirlin; **Vocal Arranger:** Douglas
  Besterman

Songs: If He Never Said Hello; I'll Never Be the
  One He Wants Me to Be

Cast: Linda Eder; Gerald Hiken; Philip Hoffman;
  Marty Simpson; Chuck Wagner

Notes: Alley Theatre, Houston. No song list
  available.

4230 • SVENGALI AND THE
BLONDE

OPENED: 07/30/1955   Theatre: NBC
TV Musical

Composer Charles Gaynor; Alan Handley
Lyricist: Charles Gaynor; Alan Handley
Producer: Alan Handley
Director: Alan Handley

Source: TRILBY (Novel: George du Maurier)

Cast: Russell Arms; Ethel Barrymore; Carol
  Channing; Nancy Kulp; Mitzi McColl; Franklin
  Pangborn; Basil Rathbone

Notes: No song list available.

4231 • SWANEE RIVER HOME

OPENED: 1923
Musical

Composer: Benton Overstreet
Librettist: Sandy Burns
Producer: Sandy Burns
Director: Inez Dennis

Cast: Sandy Burns; Inez Davis; Helen Dolly; Sam
  Russell

Notes: No other information available.

4232 • SWANSON ON SUNSET

OPENED: 12/07/1994
Musical   Los Angeles

Composer: Richard Stapley
Lyricist: Dickson Hughes
Librettist: Dickson Hughes
Producer: Swanset Productions
Director: Luke Yankee

Lighting Designer: Richard Moore; **Set Design:**
  Richard Moore

Songs: Dance; Doors Are Closed, The; Hand It to
  the Glands; I'm a Native; Map Sellers; Maybe
  There's an Angle; On with the New; Silent
  Music, The; Stay Close; Talk, Talk, Talk; Those
  Wonderful People Out There in the Dark;
  Untitled Love Story; What's the Answer? It's
  Love!; When You're Above the Crowd

Cast: Laurie Franks; Dickson Hughes; Richard
  Leibell

Notes: A workshop at the Hollywood Roosevelt
  Cinegrill. This show was originally devised in
  1955 by Gloria Swanson as a Musical version of
  her film SUNSET BOULEVARD. The show was
  to be titled STARRING NORMA DESMOND.
  This new show presents songs from the original
  along with a dramatization of the trials of
  trying to mount the original production. This
  list of songs is from STARRING NORMA
  DESMOND.

4233 • SWEENEY TODD, THE
DEMON BARBER OF
FLEET STREET

OPENED: 03/01/1979   Theatre: Uris
Musical   Broadway: 557

Composer: Stephen Sondheim
Lyricist: Stephen Sondheim
Librettist: Hugh Wheeler
Producer: Richard Barr; Robert Fryer; Mary Lea
  Johnson; Martin Richards; Charles Woodward
Director: Harold Prince

Source: SWEENEY TODD (Play: Christopher Bond); **Choreographer:** Larry Fuller; **Costumes:** Franne Lee; **Lighting Designer:** Ken Billington; **Musical Director:** Paul Gemignani; **Orchestrations:** Jonathan Tunick; **Set Design:** Eugene Lee

Songs: Ah, Miss; Ballad of Sweeney Todd, The; Barber and His Wife, The; By the Sea; City on Fire!; Contest, The; Deedle, Deedle Dumpling [2]; Epiphany; Final Sequence; God, That's Good!; Green Finch and Linnet Bird; Johanna (1); Johanna (2); Johanna (3) [1]; Kiss Me; Ladies in Their Sensitivities; Letter, The; Little Priest, A; My Friends; No Place Like London; Not While I'm Around; Parlor Songs; Pirelli's Miracle Elixir; Poor Thing; Pretty Women; Quartet; Wait; Wigmaker's Sequence; Worst Pies in London, The

Cast: Len Cariou; Victor Garber; Cris Groenendaal; Ken Jennings; Betsy Joslyn; Angela Lansbury; Merle Louise; Edmund Lyndeck; Robert Ousley; Sarah Rice; Joaquin Romaguera; Jack Eric Williams

Notes: [1] Cut during previews. [2] Cut. Later added to London production.

4234 • SWEET ADELINE

OPENED: 09/03/1929   Theatre: Hammerstein's
Musical   Broadway: 233

Composer: Jerome Kern
Lyricist: Oscar Hammerstein II
Librettist: Oscar Hammerstein II
Producer: Arthur Hammerstein
Director: Reginald Hammerstein

Choreographer: Danny Dare; **Costumes:** Charles LeMaire; **Musical Director:** Gus Salzer; **Orchestrations:** Robert Russell Bennett; **Set Design:** Frank Gates; E.A. Morange

Songs: Don't Ever Leave Me; Fin de Siecle; Finaletto; First Mate Martin; Here Am I; I'm Dreaming; Indestructible Kate (C: Jerry Jarnagin; L: Irene Franklin); I've Got a New Idea [2]; Mollie O'Donahue [4]; My Husband's First Wife (L: Irene Franklin); Naughty Boy; Oriental Moon [1]; Out of the Blue; Play Us a Polka Dot; Some Girl Is on Your Mind; Spring Is Here; Sun About to Rise, The; Take Me for a Honeymoon Ride [3]; 'Twas Not So Long Ago; Why Was I Born?; Winter in Central Park

Cast: Helen Ault; Caryl Bergman; Charles Butterworth; Violet Carlson; Robert C. Fischer; Irene Franklin; Max Hoffmann Jr.; Helen Morgan; Gus Salzer; John D. Seymour

Notes: [1] Titled "Oriental Dreams" in FUN AT THE FAYRE and THE CABARET GIRL, both in London. [2] Cut prior to opening. [3] Titled "Take Me for a Bicycle Ride" out of town. [4] Same music as "All You Need Is a Girl" in SITTING PRETTY.

4235 • SWEET AND LOW

OPENED: 11/17/1930   Theatre: 46th Street
Revue   Broadway: 184

Librettist: David Freedman
Producer: Billy Rose
Director: Alexander Leftwich

Choreographer: Busby Berkeley; Danny Dare; **Costumes:** James Reynolds; **Musical Director:** Bill Daly; **Set Design:** Jo Mielziner

Songs: Boo Hoo Hoo, Ha Ha Ha! (I'm Between a Laugh and a Cry) [1] (C: Harry Warren; L: Edgar Leslie); Cheerful Little Earful [8] (C: Harry Warren; L: Ira Gershwin, Billy Rose); Cover a Clover with Kisses [1] (C: Harry Warren; L: Mort Dixon); Dancing with Tears in Their Eyes (C: Will Irwin; L: Mort Dixon; Billy Rose); East St. Louis Toodle-oo (inst.) (C: Duke Ellington; Bubber Miley); For I'm in Love Again (C: Mischa Spoliansky; L: Mort Dixon; Billy Rose); He's Not Worth Your Tears [1] (C: Harry Warren; L: Mort Dixon; Billy Rose); I Knew Him Before He Was Spanish (C: Dana Suesse; L: Ballard Macdonald; Billy Rose); I Wonder Who's Keeping Him Now [1] (C: Louis Alter; L: Charlotte Kent; Billy Rose); Ma Mere [4] (C: Harry Warren; L: Irving Caesar; Al Jolson); Mistaken in Love [5] (C: Lew Pollack; L: Mort Dixon); Mr. Jessel (C/L: Charlotte Kent); Outside Looking In (C: Harry Archer; L: Edward Eliscu); Overnight (C: Louis Alter; L: Charlotte Kent; Billy Rose); Revival Day (C: Will Irwin; L: Malcolm McComb); River and Me, The [1] (C: Harry Warren; L: Al Dubin); Sky City [3] (C: Richard Rodgers; L: Lorenz Hart); (You) Sweet So-and-So [7] (C: Philip Charig; Joseph Meyer; L: Ira Gershwin); Ten Minutes in Bed (C: Ned Lehac; L: Allen Boretz); What Good Is the Lane, If You Can't Have the Girl of Your Dreams [1] (C: Harry Warren; L: Joe Young); When a Pansy Was a Flower (C: Will Irwin;

L: Malcolm McComb; Billy Rose); Would You Like to Take a Walk? (Sump'n Good'll Come from That) [2] (C: Harry Warren; L: Mort Dixon; Billy Rose)

Cast: James Barton; Fanny Brice; George Jessel; Bubber Miley; Borrah Minevitch; Jerry Norris; Hal Thompson; Arthur Treacher; Paula Trueman; Hannah Williams

Notes: This was a revised version of CORNED BEEF AND ROSES. It was further revised as BILLY ROSE'S CRAZY QUILT. [1] Not in program. [2] Also in BILLY ROSE'S CRAZY QUILT. [3] Cut in Philadelphia prior to New York. Also cut from HEADS UP. [4] Not in program. Also in THE WONDER BAR. [5] Not used. [6] Not in program. Some sources credit this song's lyrics to Mort Dixon. [7] With additional Douglas Furber lyrics used in THAT'S A GOOD GIRL. [8] Out of town Philadelphia this song was credited to Ned Lehac, Billy Rose and Allen Boretz. Either a different song or a mistake in the program.

4236 • SWEET ANNE PAGE

OPENED: 12/03/1900   Theatre: Manhattan
Musical   Broadway: 29

Composer: W.H. Neidlinger
Lyricist: Edgar Smith
Librettist: Louis de Lange
Producer: Lulu Glaser and Company
Director: Max Freeman

Costumes: F. Richard Anderson; **Musical Director:** Albert Krause; **Set Design:** D. Frank Dodge

Cast: Alexander Clark; Arthur Donaldson; Lulu Glaser; Josie Intropodi

Notes: No program available.

4237 • SWEET BYE AND BYE

OPENED: 10/10/1946
Musical   Closed out of town

Composer: Vernon Duke
Lyricist: Ogden Nash
Librettist: Al Hirschfeld; S.J. Perelman
Producer: Nat Karson
Director: Curt Conway; Nat Karson

Choreographer: Fred Kelly; **Musical Director:** Charles Blackman; **Set Design:** Boris Aronson; **Vocal Arranger:** Vernon Duke

Songs: Breakfast in Bed [2]; Crispy and Crunchy; Diana; Eskimo Bacchante; Factory Ballet (dance) [2]; Good Deed for Today; Ham That I Am; Hymn [3]; I Says to Him; It's Good; Just Like a Man [1]; Let's Be Young; Low and Lazy; My Broker Told Me So; Old Fashioned Tune; Roundabout [1]; Sea-Gull and the Ea-gull [2]; Singing Commercial [3]; Sweet Bye and Bye; Texas, Brooklyn and Love; We Love Us; Where Is Bundy?; Yes, Yes

Cast: Dolores Gray; Walter O'Keefe; Erik Rhodes; Gene Sheldon

Notes: [1] Later in TWO'S COMPANY. [2] Not in program. [3] ASCAP/Library of Congress only.

4238 • SWEET CHARITY

OPENED: 01/29/1966   Theatre: Palace
Musical   Broadway: 608

Composer: Cy Coleman
Lyricist: Dorothy Fields
Librettist: Neil Simon
Producer: Lawrence Carr; Robert Fryer; Joseph P. Harris
Director: Bob Fosse

Source: NIGHTS OF CABIRIA (Film: Federico Fellini; Ennio Flaiano; Tullio Pinelli); **Choreographer:** Bob Fosse; **Costumes:** Irene Sharaff; **Dance Arranger:** Fred Werner; **Lighting Designer:** Robert Randolph; **Musical Director:** Fred Werner; **Orchestrations:** Ralph Burns; **Set Design:** Robert Randolph

Songs: Baby, Dream Your Dream; Big Spender; Charity's Soliloquy; Charity's Theme (dance); Did You Ever Look at You [1]; Free Thought in Action Class Song [1]; Gimme a Raincheck [1]; Good Impression [1]; I Can't Let You Down [1]; I Love to Cry at Weddings; If My Friends Could See Me Now; I'll Take Any Man [1]; I'm a Brass Band; I'm the Bravest Individual; I'm the Greatest Individual [5]; I'm Way Ahead [1]; I've Tried Everything [1]; Keep It in the Family [1]; Pink Taffeta Sample, Size 10 [1]; Poor Everybody Else [4]; Rhythm of Life, The; Rich Man's Frug (dance); Sweet Charity; There's Gotta Be Something Better Than This; Too Many

Tomorrows; When Did You Know? [3]; Where Am I Going?; You Can't Lose 'Em All [1]; You Should See Yourself; You Wanna Bet [2]

Cast: Ruth Buzzi; Helen Gallagher; James Luisi; John McMartin; Thelma Oliver; Harold Pierson; Barbara Sharma; Arnold Soboloff; Gwen Verdon; John Wheeler

Notes: [1] Cut prior to opening. [2] Cut prior to opening. Same music as "Sweet Charity." [3] Cut prior to opening. Same music as "Love Makes Such Fools of Us All" in BARNUM. [4] Cut prior to opening. Put into SEESAW. [5] Written for 1986 revival with same lyric as "I'm the Bravest Individual" but with new music.

4239 • SWEET INNISCARRA
OPENED: 04/26/1897
Play   Broadway

Composer: Chauncey Olcott
Lyricist: Chauncey Olcott
Author: Augustus Pitou
Director: Augustus Pitou

Costumes: H.A. Ogden; **Incidental Music:** Dave Braham; **Musical Director:** Lloyd Bowron

Songs: Fly Song, The (Olcott's Fly Song); Kate O'Donoghue; Old Fashioned Mother, The; Only to Love Her (C/L: Charles Santley); Sweet Inniscarra

Cast: Georgia Busby; Daniel Gilfether; Chauncey Olcott

4240 • SWEET LADY
OPENED: 1926
Musical   Closed out of town

Composer: Thomas Ball; Delos Owen
Lyricist: Bud Green
Librettist: Jack McGowan; Delos Owen
Producer: Thomas Ball
Director: William Caryl

Choreographer: Busby Berkeley

Songs: Be Naughty; Forever; Hot Water; I Adore You (C: Rene Mercier; L: Henri Bataille; Sam Coslow; Ballard Macdonald; Charles Pothier); I Don't Want to Go Home; I'm Through with the

Blues; Just Want You; Mauve Decade; On a Side Street; Opening Number; Sex Appeal; Statues; Sweet Lady; To Make You Love Me; Will You Promise

Cast: Inez Courtney; Marie Nordstrom; Harry Puck; Gus Shy; Jane Taylor

Notes: Programs of Syracuse 12/3/26 and Washington, D.C. 1/31/27 used. Ball was sole composer credited in Washington.

4241 • SWEET LITTLE DEVIL
OPENED: 01/21/1924   Theatre: Astor
Musical   Broadway: 120

Composer: George Gershwin
Lyricist: B.G. DeSylva
Librettist: Frank Mandel; Laurence Schwab
Producer: Laurence Schwab
Director: Sammy Lee; Edgar MacGregor

Musical Director: Ivan Rudisill

Songs: Be the Life of the Crowd [1]; Hey! Hey! Let 'Er Go!; Hooray for the U.S.A.!; Jijibo, The; Just Supposing; Mah-Jongg [2]; Matrimonial Handicap, The; (You're Mighty Lucky) My Little Ducky [1]; Pepita [1]; Quite a Party; Same Old Story, The; Someone Who Believes in You; Strike, Strike, Strike; Sweet Little Devil [1]; System; Under a One-Man Top; Virginia (Don't Go too Far)

Cast: Franklyn Ardell; Irving Beebe; Constance Binney; Marjorie Gateson; Ruth Warren; William Wayne

Notes: [1] Not used. [2] Not used. Also in GEORGE WHITE'S SCANDALS (1924).

4242 • SWEET MARIE
OPENED: 10/10/1901   Theatre: Hammerstein's
                               Victoria
Musical   Broadway: 28

Composer: R. Jackson
Lyricist: W. Brown
Librettist: W. Brown
Producer: Oscar Hammerstein I

Songs: Cecilia and Amelia (C/L: Oscar Hammerstein I)

Cast: Eleanor Falk; Master Gabriel; Albert LaMar; Louis Montgomery; James Russell; John Russell; Rhys Thomas; Countess Olga Von Hatzfeldt

Notes: Jackson and Brown may actually be Oscar Hammerstein I since the only song listed in the program is credited to Hammerstein.

4243 • SWEET MIANI

OPENED: 09/25/1962   Theatre: Players
Musical   Off-Broadway: 22

Composer: Ed Tyler
Lyricist: Ed Tyler
Librettist: Stuart Bishop
Producer: Edmund Brophy; Donal Currie
Director: Louis MacMillan

Choreographer: Edward Earle; Costumes: Andre; Dance Arranger: Edward Earle; Lighting Designer: Norman Finkelstein; Musical Director: Robert Lenn; Set Design: Stuart Slade

Songs: Black Pearls; Canticle to the Wind; Code of the Licensed Pilot; Far Away Island; Forever and Always; Going Native; Homesick in Our Hearts; Honey to Love, A; Just Sit Back and Relax; Legend of the Islands; Maluan Moon; Miani; Middle of the Sea; Not Tabu; Ritual of Ruku; Sailing; Silvery Days; Turoola; Warm Breezes at Twilight

Cast: Virgil Curry; Isabelle Farrell; Victor Pierantozzi; Sheila Smith

4244 • SWEET MISTRESS

OPENED: 09/08/1976
Musical   Closed out of town

Composer: David Spangler
Lyricist: Susan Dias
Additional Lyrics: David Spangler; Ira Wallach
Librettist: Ira Wallach
Director: Charles Maryan

Source: MISTRESS OF THE INN (Play Carlo Goldoni); Choreographer: William Van Keyser; Costumes: Sigrid Insull; Lighting Designer: Don Coleman; Musical Director: John Lesko; Set Design: Bennet Averyt

Songs: Cavalier's Lament, The; Everything You Are; Here in the Inn; I'd Love to Hate Her; I'll Go On; Just Another Guest; Mazzini and Mankind; None

of My Dreams; Since We Met; Sweet Mistress; Think of It; We Give Her Up; You're the First

Cast: Mike Dantuono; Ronald Drake; Gwyllum Evans; Rita Gardner; Lynn Ann Leveridge; George F. Maguire; Robert Sevra

Notes: From a program of the Barter Theatre, Abingdon, Virginia.

4245 • SWEET REBEL

Notes: See DEAREST ENEMY.

4246 • SWEET WILL

OPENED: 01/05/1986   Theatre: New Silver
                                              Lining
Revue   Off-Broadway: 9

Composer: Lance Mulcahy
Lyricist: William Shakespeare
Producer: David K. Drummond
Director: John Olon

Choreographer: Dennis Dennehy; Lighting Designer: John Michael Deegan; Musical Director: Michael Ward

Notes: Sequel to SHAKESPEARE'S CABARET (1981). Lyrics are from the sonnets as well as LOVE'S LABOR'S LOST, TWELFTH NIGHT, MUCH ADO ABOUT NOTHING, AS YOU LIKE IT and A MIDSUMMER NIGHT'S DREAM.

4247 • SWEETEST GIRL IN PARIS, THE

OPENED: 08/29/1910   Theatre: La Salle
Musical   Chicago

Composer: Joseph E. Howard
Lyricist: Collin Davis
Librettist: Addison Burkhardt

Costumes: William Henry Matthews; Set Design: Ernest Albert

Songs: American Millionaire, An; Bombashay (L: Addison Burkhardt); Boys! Boys! Boys!; Buyers, The; Don't Forget the Number [1] (L: Addison Burkhardt); Honest Injun!-I Love You!; I Love 'Em All from A to Z (L: Addison Burkhardt); I Want a Man (L: Addison Burkhardt); Iddle-Iddle-Iddle-E; Lady Wine [2]

(L: Unknown); Mary! Mary!; Nothing Too Good for You, Dear (L: Bock); O! Weather-Man! (L: Addison Burkhardt); Paris Today; Sweetest Girl in Paris, The; That Tantalizing Nod [2] (L: Unknown); That's How Imitations Look to Me

Cast: Trixie Friganza; Edgar Murray; Alice Yorke

Notes: [1] Also in THE GODDESS OF LIBERTY. [2] ASCAP/Library of Congress only.

4248 • SWEETHEART SHOP, THE
OPENED: 08/31/1920   Theatre: Knickerbocker
Musical   Broadway: 55

Composer: Hugo Felix
Lyricist: Anne Caldwell
Librettist: Anne Caldwell
Producer: Edgar MacGregor; William Moore Patch
Director: Edgar MacGregor

Choreographer: Julian Alfred; **Lighting Designer:** Tony Greshoff; **Musical Director:** Hilding Anderson; **Set Design:** Herbert Moore

Songs: As We Go Out Walking; Didn't You?; Dresden China Belle, The; Glow of the Cigarette, The; I Want to Be a Blooming Bride; I'd Like to Teach you the ABC of Love; Is There Any Little Thing I Can Do for You?; June Bells; Life Is a Carousel; Long Road of Love, The [3]; My Caravan; My Merry Go Round; Oh, Mr. Postman; Plum Blossom; She's Artistic; Sweetheart Shop, The; Sweetheart Shop Wedding, A; Syringa Tree, The [1]; This and That and the Other [1]; Waiting for the Sun to Come Out (C: George Gershwin; L: Ira Gershwin [2])

Cast: Helen Ford; Dan Healy; William K. Morton

Notes: [1] Out 1/19/20. [2] Used the pseudonym Arthur Francis. [3] Sheet music only.

4249 • SWEETHEART TIME
OPENED: 01/19/1926   Theatre: Imperial
Musical   Broadway: 145

Composer: Walter Donaldson
Lyricist: Ballard Macdonald
Librettist: Harry B. Smith
Producer: James La Penner; Edward A. Miller
Director: William Collier

Source: NEVER SAY DIE (Play: William Collier; W.H. Post); **Choreographer:** Larry Ceballos; **Costumes:** Charles LeMaire; **Musical Director:** Don Juielle; **Orchestrations:** Stephen Jones; Hans Spialek; Maurice DePackh; **Set Design:** Karle O. Amend

Songs: Actions Speak Louder Than Words [1]; At the Party (C: Harry Ruby; L: Bert Kalmar); At the Prom [1]; Cocktail Melody; Girl in Your Arms, A (C: Jay Gorney; L: Irving Caesar); How Different Things Would Be [1]; I Don't Like Them Too [1]; I Know That You Love Me [3] (C: Harry Ruby; L: Bert Kalmar); In Sweetheart Time [2] (C: J. Fred Coots; L: Henry Meyer); Little Song in My Heart, The [1]; Marian; One Way Street; Opening Chorus (C: Joseph Mayer; L: Harry B. Smith); Rue de la Paix; So Near Yet So Far [1]; Step on It (C: Joseph Meyer; L: Irving Caesar); Sweetheart Time (C: Joseph Meyer; L: Irving Caesar); Tahiti Sweetie [1]; There's Something About Sympathy [2] (C: J. Fred Coots; L: Henry Myers); Time for Love [2] (C: J. Fred Coots; L: Henry Myers); Two By Two [2] (C: Joseph Meyer; L: Irving Caesar); Who Loves You As I Do [2] (C: Joseph Meyer; L: Irving Caesar); Who's Who?

Cast: Eddie Buzzell; Irene Dunne; Fred Leslie; Dorothy McNulty; Mary Milburn; Marion Saki; Al Sexton

Notes: Originally titled LEAVE IT TO ME. [1] Not used. [2] ASCAP only. [3] In program as "I Know That I Love You."

4250 • SWEETHEARTS (1913)
OPENED: 09/08/1913   Theatre: New Amsterdam
Musical   Broadway: 136

Composer: Victor Herbert
Lyricist: Robert B. Smith
Librettist: Harry B. Smith; Fred De Gresac [2]
Producer: Werba & Luescher
Director: Fred G. Latham

Choreographer: Charles S. Morgan Jr.; **Costumes:** William Adler; Max & Mahieu; **Musical Director:** John McGhie; **Orchestrations:** Victor Herbert; **Set Design:** Castle; D. Frank Dodge

Songs: Angelus, The; Cricket on the Hearth; Dance Eccentrique (dance); Entrance of Sylvia [3]; Every Lover Must Meet His Fate [3]; Finale Act I; For Every Lover; Game of Love; Hail, Franz of

Zilania (L: Harry B. Smith; Fred De Gresac);
I Don't Know How I Do It but I Do (L: Harry B.
Smith); I Might Be Your Once-In-a-While; In
the Convent They Never Taught Me That; Iron!
Iron! Iron! (Opening Chorus); Ivy and the Oak,
The [1]; Jeannette and Her Little Wooden Shoes
(Sabot Dance) (Clip Clop Clop) (Wooden Shoes
Dance); Land of My Own Romance; Monks'
Quartette, The; Mother Goose; On Parade;
Opening Chorus; Pilgrims of Love; Pretty As a
Picture; Smiles; Sweethearts (If You Ask Where
Love Is Found); Talk About This-Talk About
That [1]; There Is Magic in a Smile; Waiting for
the Bride; Welcoming the Bride [3]; What She
Wanted and What She Got [1] (L: Harry B.
Smith)

Cast: Ethel Dufre Houston; Christie MacDonald;
Tom MacNaughton

Notes: [1] Cut prior to opening. [2] De Gresac is a
pseudonym for Mme. Victor Mauel, the wife of a
famous French opera baritone. [3]
ASCAP/Library of Congress.

4251 • SWEETHEARTS (1988)

OPENED: 12/07/1988   Theatre: Actors'
                                    Playhouse
Revue   Off-Broadway: 54

Producer: Will You Remember Prods.

Arrangements: Don Chan; **Conductor:** David
Wolfson; **Costumes:** Josie Garner; **Lighting
Designer:** Paul Lindsay Butler

Songs: Beyond the Blue Horizon; Ciribiribin;
Cuban Love Song; Farewell to Dreams; Giannina
Mia; Italian Street Song; Marsovia; My Own
United States; Naughty Marietta selections; New
Moon selections; Rogue Song, The; Rose-Marie
selections; San Francisco; Shenandoah;
Sweethearts; While My Lady Sleeps; Will You
Remember

Cast: Walter Adkins; Antoinette Mille

Notes: No original songs in this production. A
tribute to Jeanette MacDonald and Nelson Eddy.

4252 • SWING

OPENED: 12/25/1980
Musical   Closed out of town

Composer: Robert Waldman
Lyricist: Alfred Uhry
Librettist: Conn Fleming
Producer: Edgar M. Bronfman; Stuart Ostrow
Director: Stuart Ostrow

Choreographer: Kenneth Rinker; **Costumes:**
Patricia Zipprodt; **Dance Arranger:** Peter
Howard; **Lighting Designer:** Richard Pilbrow;
Musical Director: Peter Howard;
Orchestrations: Eddie Sauter; **Set Design:** Robin
Wagner; **Vocal Arranger:** Elise Bretton

Songs: All Clear; Doowah Diddy Blues, The;
Dream Time; Duet; Girl Can Go Wacky, A; Good
from Any Angle; Home; If You Can't Trot, Don't
Get Hot; Love Jitters, The; Marilyn; Michigan
Bound; Miliaria Rubra; One Hundred Percent
Cockeyed; Piece of Cake, A; Real Thing, The;
Saroot; Swing

Cast: Roy Brocksmith; Janet Eilber; Robert LuPone;
Pat Lysinger; Adam Redfield; Debbie Shapiro;
Mary Catherine Wright

Notes: Closed Washington D.C. 3/29/81.

4253 • SWING IT

OPENED: 07/22/1937   Theatre: Adelphi
Musical   Broadway: 60

Composer: Eubie Blake
Lyricist: Cecil Mack; J. Milton Reddie
Librettist: Cecil Mack [1]
Producer: Frank Merlin; WPA Variety Theatre
Director: Cecil Mack [1]; Jack Mason

Choreographer: Benny Johnson; Miriam Schiller;
Costumes: Alexander Jones; **Musical Director:**
Lorenzo Caldwell; **Orchestrations:** Lorenzo
Caldwell; **Set Design:** Walter Walden

Songs: Ain't We Got Love; Blue Classique (inst.);
By the Sweat of Your Brow; Captain, Mate and
Crew; Green and Blue; Huggin' and Muggin';
It's the Youth in Me (L: J. Milton Reddie); Old
Time Swing; Rhythm Is a Racket; Shine (C: Ford
Dabney; L: Lew Brown; Cecil Mack); Sons and
Daughters of the Sea; Susan Belle, The; What Do
I Want with Love?

Cast: George Booker; James Boxwill; Marion
Brantley; Genora English; Frances Everett;
Edward Frye; James Mordecai; Olena Williams

Notes: [1] Cecil Mack is a pseudonym for R.C. MacPherson.

4254 • SWING MIKADO, THE

OPENED: 03/01/1939   Theatre: New Yorker
Musical   Broadway: 86

Composer: Arthur Sullivan
Lyricist: W.S. Gilbert
Librettist: W.S. Gilbert
Producer: Chicago Federal Theatre
Director: Harry Minturn

Choreographer: Hazel Davis; Sammy Dyer; **Costumes:** John Pratt; **Musical Director:** Edward Wurtzebach; **Orchestrations:** Charles Levy; **Set Design:** Clive Rickabaugh

Cast: Gladys Boucree; Maurice Cooper; Edward Fraction; William Franklin; Herman Greene; Mabel Walker

Notes: Musical numbers are the same as in the original operetta.

4255 • SWINGIN' ON A STAR

OPENED: 04/05/1995
Musical

Composer: James Van Heusen
Lyricist: Johnny Burke
Librettist: Michael Leeds
Producer: Goodspeed Opera House
Director: Michael Leeds

Arrangements: Ron Drotos; **Choreographer:** Kathleen Marshall; **Costumes:** Judy Dearing; **Dance Arranger:** Peter Howard; **Lighting Designer:** Richard Nelson; **Musical Director:** Barry Levitt; **Orchestrations:** Brian Besterman; Barry Levitt; **Set Design:** James Youmans; **Vocal Arranger:** Barry Levitt

Songs: Ain't It a Shame (C: James V. Monaco); Annie Doesn't Live Here Anymore [2] (C: James V. Monaco; L: Johnny Burke; Joe Young); Apple for the Teacher, An [3] (C: Arthur Johnston); Chicago Style [4]; Doctor Rhythm [5] (C: James V. Monaco); His Rocking Horse Ran Away [6]; Irresistible (C: Harold Spina); One, Two, Button Your Shoe [7] (C: Arthur Johnston); Pennies from Heaven [7] (C: Arthur Johnston); Personality [8]; Polka Dots and Moonbeams; Scatterbrain [1]

(C: Beane; Keene; Frankie Masters); Swinging on a Star [9]; Thank Your Lucky Stars and Stripes [10]; There's Always the Blues (C: Joe Bushkin); What Does It Take to Make You Take to Me?; What's New [11] (C: Bob Haggart); When Stanislaus Got Married [6]; Whoopsie Daisy Day (C: Johnny Burke); You're Not the Only Oyster in the Stew (C: Harold Spina)

Cast: Terry Burrell; Lewis Cleale; Kathy Fitzgerald; Eugene Fleming; Alvaleta Guess; Lori Hart; Michael McGrath

Notes: Goodspeed Opera House. Set to open on Broadway after press time. [1] From the film SCATTERBRAIN. [2] From the film GEORGE WHITE'S SCANDALS OF 1934. [3] From the film THE STAR MAKER. [4] From the film THE ROAD TO BALI. [5] From the film DOCTOR RHYTHM. [6] From the film AND THE ANGELS SING. [7] From the film PENNIES FROM HEAVEN. [8] From the film ROAD TO UTOPIA. [9] From the film DUFFY'S TAVERN. [10] From the film PLAYMATES. [11] From the film DIVE BOMBER.

4256 • SWINGIN' THE DREAM

OPENED: 11/29/1939   Theatre: Center
Musical   Broadway: 13

Composer: Jimmy Van Heusen
Lyricist: Eddie De Lange
Librettist: Erik Charell; Gilbert Seldes
Producer: Erik Charell; Jean Rodney
Director: Erik Charell; Philip Loeb

Source: MIDSUMMER NIGHT'S DREAM, A (Play: William Shakespeare); **Choreographer:** Herbert White; Agnes de Mille; **Costumes:** Herbert Andrews; **Musical Director:** Don Vorhees; **Orchestrations:** Ardon Cornwall; Fletcher Henderson; Herb Quigley; Phil Wall; **Set Design:** Herbert Andrews; Walter Jagermann; **Vocal Arranger:** Lyn Murray

Songs: Darn That Dream; Doing the Saboo; Flying Home [1]; Jumpin' at the Woodside; Love's a Riddle (C: Alec Wilder; L: Eddie De Lange; Jimmy Van Heusen); Moonland; Opera, Pyramus, and Thisbe, The; Peace, Brother!; Pick a Rib; Spring Song [2] (C: Benny Goodman; Jimmy Van Heusen; Music Based On: Felix Mendelssohn); Swingin' a Dream; There's Gotta Be a Wedding

Cast: Louis Armstrong; Bill Bailey; Troy Brown; Warren Coleman; Thomas Coley; Boyd Crawford; Dorothy Dandridge; Etta Dandridge; Vivian Dandridge; Deep River Boys; Ruth Ford; Bud Freeman's Summa Cum Laude; Benny Goodman; Benny Goodman Sextette; Juan Hernandez; Joseph Holland; George LeSoir; Eleanor Lynn; Jackie "Moms" Mabley; Dorothy McGuire; Butterfly McQueen; Nicodemus; Oscar Polk; Muriel Rahn; Rhythmettes, The; Maxine Sullivan; Gerald de la Fontaine

Notes: [1] Added to 1941 version. [2] Adapted from Mendelssohn's "Spring Song."

4257 • SWITZERLAND SAM

OPENED: 1917
Musical

Songs: Oh-Oh-Lady (C: Ted Snyder; L: Sam M. Lewis; Joe Young)

Notes: No other information available.

4258 • SYBIL

OPENED: 01/10/1916   Theatre: Liberty
Musical   Broadway: 168

Composer: Victor Jacobi
Lyricist: Harry Graham; Harry B. Smith
Librettist: Harry Graham; Harry B. Smith
Producer: Charles Frohman
Director: Fred G. Latham

Source: SZIBILL (Musical: Miksa Brody; Victor Jacobi; Ferenc Martos); **Choreographer:** Jack Mason; Julian Mitchell; **Musical Director:** Harold Vicars; **Set Design:** Homer Emens

Songs: All Hearts with a Keen Curiosity Burn (Opening Chorus) (L: Harry Graham); At a Grand Hotel; Colonel of the Crimson Hussars, The; Cup of Tea, The; Finale Act I; Finale Act II; Following the Drum; Girls You Are Such Wonderful Things (L: Harry B. Smith); Good

Advice (L: Harry B. Smith); I Can Dance with Everybody but My Wife (C/L: John Golden; L: Joseph Cawthorn); I Like the Boys (L: Harry B. Smith); Keep Cool; Letter Duet (My Dearest Paul); Lift Your Eyes to Mine; Love May Be a Mystery [1] (L: Harry Graham); Opening Chorus Act II; Opening Chorus Act III; Orphans from the Convent School (Chorus of Orphans); Politenss Pays; That Wonderful 'One' Girl (C/L: Harold Vicars); Two Can Play That Game (C: Harry B. Smith); Way to Do It, The; When Cupid Calls (The Rat-Tat-Tat-Song) (L: Harry B. Smith); With Money You Can't Go Wrong

Cast: Stewart Baird; Donald Brian; Joseph Cawthorn; Maisie Gay; George E. Mack; Julia Sanderson

Notes: [1] Graham not credited alone in vocal score.

4259 • SYMPHONY IN BROWN

OPENED: 1942   Theatre: Trocadero
Revue   Nightclub

Songs: Life Could Be a Cakewalk with You (C: Harold Arlen; L: Ted Koehler)

Notes: No other information available.

4260 • SYN-CYR-ITIES OF 1952

OPENED: 1952
Revue   Closed out of town

Composer: Jerry Bock; Sula Levitch; Lee Pockriss
Lyricist: Eddie Dean; Bernie Hern; Larry Holofcener; Bob Kobin; Lee Sherman

Costumes: Jac Venza

Songs: Bon Soir (C/L: Bernie Bennett); Sherlock Holmes (C: Lee Pockriss; L: Bob Kobin)

Cast: Lily St. Cyr